AN

ARABIC-ENGLISH LEXICON

AN

ARABIC-ENGLISH LEXICON

BY

EDWARD WILLIAM LANE

IN EIGHT PARTS

PART 5 ع - ض

القاموس

AN

ARABIC-ENGLISH LEXICON,

DERIVED FROM THE BEST AND THE MOST COPIOUS EASTERN SOURCES;

COMPRISING A VERY LARGE COLLECTION
OF WORDS AND SIGNIFICATIONS OMITTED IN THE ḲÁMOOS,
WITH SUPPLEMENTS TO ITS ABRIDGED AND DEFECTIVE EXPLANATIONS,
AMPLE GRAMMATICAL AND CRITICAL COMMENTS,
AND EXAMPLES IN PROSE AND VERSE:

COMPOSED BY MEANS OF THE MUNIFICENCE OF THE MOST NOBLE
ALGERNON,
DUKE OF NORTHUMBERLAND, K.G.,
ETC. ETC. ETC.,

AND THE BOUNTY OF
THE BRITISH GOVERNMENT:

BY EDWARD WILLIAM LANE,
CORRESPONDENT OF THE INSTITUTE OF FRANCE, ETC.

IN TWO BOOKS:

THE FIRST CONTAINING ALL THE CLASSICAL WORDS AND SIGNIFICATIONS COMMONLY KNOWN
TO THE LEARNED AMONG THE ARABS:
THE SECOND, THOSE THAT ARE OF RARE OCCURRENCE AND NOT COMMONLY KNOWN.

BOOK I.—PART 5.

ض — ع

KALPAZ

ISBN: 978-93-5128-814-5(Set)
ISBN: 978-93-5128-827-5(PB)

First Published in 1874
Indian Reprint in 2017

Published by

Kalpaz Publications
C-30, Satyawati Nagar,
Delhi – 110052
E-mail: kalpaz@hotmail.com
Website: kalpazpublications.com
Ph.: +91-9212142040

Cataloging in Publication Data—DK

Courtesy: D.K. Agencies (P) Ltd. <docinfo@dkagencies.com>

Lane, Edward William, 1801-1876, **author.**

Madd al-qa˜mu˜s = An Arabic-English lexicon : derived from the best and the most copious eastern sources, comprising a very large collection of words and significations omitted in the Kamoos, with supplements to its abridged and defective explanations, ample grammatical and critical comments, and examples in prose and verse : composed by means of the munificence of the most noble algernon, Duke of Northumberland, K. G., etc. etc. etc., and the bounty of the British Government / by Edward William Lane.

volumes cm

English and Arabic.

Parts 6-8 edited with a memoir by Stanley Lane Poole.

"First published in 1863"—Title page verso.

"In two books: the first containing all the words and significations commonly known to the learned among the Arabs : the second, those that are of rare occurrence and not communly known."
ISBN 9789351288145 (set :

1. Arabic language—Dictionaries—English. 2. English language—Dictionaries—Arabic. I. Lane-Poole, Stanley, 1854-1931, editor. II. Title. III. Title: Arabic-English lexicon.

PJ6640.L36 2017 DDC 492.7321 23

EDITOR'S PREFACE.

SINCE the Fifth Part of this work was published, the hand that wrote it has become still. After thirty-four years of labour at the Lexicon, Mr. Lane died, on the tenth of August, 1876.

It was his special wish that the work which had occupied so large a part of his life should be completed by me, and that wish absolves me from the charge of presumption to which I might otherwise be exposed. To complete it as it has been begun is indeed beyond the power of any living Orientalist: but I hope that, so far as knowledge of my Uncle's methods of work and jealous love for his memory may avail, I may not prove altogether unworthy of the great trust he reposed in me.

Informed of my purpose, Her Grace the Dowager Duchess of Northumberland immediately offered to continue to the work that generous support which she had given during my Uncle's life.

A careful examination of the manuscripts and notes which my Uncle had accumulated convinced me that there was more to be done than I had at first supposed. I found articles in three different stages: some consisting only of Mr. Lane's own notes, without any reference to the original authorities; others written, but needing to be collated with one or two manuscripts acquired later; and some completely written and ready for the press. The difference is explained by the fact that Mr. Lane was of necessity obliged to write in the order of the Ṣiḥáḥ, and that as the printers gradually approached him he finished those articles which were likely to be speedily wanted: for he began to print when he had written rather more than half the work. The notes of his own were simply the results of his long experience in the language, and were to be interwoven with the translations from the original authorities when the articles came to be written.

At the time of his death my Uncle was engaged on the article قد. Up to this point every article is ready for the printers. Of the rest the majority are written, but some need collation.

In these circumstances I think it best to publish in Part VI. only to the end of the letter ف. A part of the following letter is not completed, and to fill the lacunae would delay the publication of the volume. The present Part therefore contains only غ and ف. Up to p. 2386 the proofs were corrected by Mr. Lane; after that, by myself. The next Part, which I shall bring out so soon as is compatible with sound work and careful printing, will contain ق, ك, ل, م; and the last, ن, ه, و, ى. After the publication of Part VIII., I shall begin to prepare Book II., comprising the rare words and ἅπαξ λεγόμενα, which Mr. Lane estimated as two Parts, or one thick Part.

The appearance of this Part has been delayed by the difficulties presented in the composition of the Memoir which is prefixed. I have had to tell the story of a life spent, partly on account of ill health, but mainly for the sake of work, in seclusion! Few men knew Mr. Lane personally in his later years, and as time went on and the improbability of his living to finish his work became more and more apparent, his unwillingness to see anyone beyond his family circle and a few special friends became stronger than ever. Thus I have had no assistance from the recollections of friends. Nor have I derived the smallest help from letters. Mr. Lane had a deeply-rooted objection to the publication of letters meant only for private friends, and he took care to have all his own letters from Egypt destroyed; whilst after his return to England he hardly ever wrote one except on questions of scholarship which he was asked to decide.

Thus the only materials I have had for the foundation of the Memoir have been (1) the MS. of the "Description of Egypt," which contains a certain amount of personal incident; (2) certain note-books kept by Mr. Lane during his first and second visits to Egypt; (3) his published works; (4) his sister's journal, kept during the third visit to Egypt, and certain passages in her "Englishwoman in Egypt." I should add that Mrs. Lane, my Grandmother Mrs. Poole, and my Uncle Reginald Stuart Poole, have aided me greatly with their recollections. For the last ten years I can of course write from my own intimate relations with my Great-Uncle.

The diary of Mr. Lane's second visit to Egypt I have thought it well to reproduce almost *in extenso.* As the daily jotting-down of what he called his "idle moments" it reveals something of himself, and as the record of the changes which nearly ten years had brought about in the country it will be acceptable to students of the history of Europeanizing in Egypt.

STANLEY LANE POOLE.

July, 1877.

POSTSCRIPT

The present Part completes the publication of the MS. materials which Mr. Lane left for the continuation of his Lexicon. The incompleteness of these materials has already been explained in the Preface to Part V. My original intention was to compile the missing articles from Mr. Lane's MS. copy of the Táj-el-'Aroos, with the addition of such notes as he had himself prepared during the progress of the work. This intention, however, was modified when the publication of the Táj-el-'Aroos at Booláḳ deprived Mr. Lane's MS. copy of its peculiar importance. The text can now be consulted by any scholar for himself, and to offer a bare translation of it, in a Lexicon intended mainly for the use of scholars, would be superfluous. The great value of Mr. Lane's work lies not so much in his translations from standard works of Arabic lexicography, as in the comments and explanations which he was able to add from his own profound knowledge of the language and its literature. Any scholar can translate the Táj-el-'Aroos: but none could have elucidated the obscurities of the native lexicographers with the precision and illumination which characterize Mr. Lane's commentary. The translation from the Táj-el-'Aroos has therefore been abandoned, and the Supplement appended to the present Part, instead of containing all the articles omitted from Parts V.—VIII., includes only such *notes* as Mr. Lane had made from time to time with a view to the eventual writing of these articles. These notes are not to be accepted as the final decision of their writer, far less as finished or even approximately complete articles. They have not enjoyed the benefit of his revision, and many of them are clearly the record of contemporary speech, which he would doubtless have excluded from a Lexicon of the classical language. Nevertheless, Mr. Lane's habitual accuracy and caution are sufficient guarantees that these notes were not made without careful deliberation. They contain many significations which are not to be found in the ordinary dictionaries; and the numerous cross-references, which I have verified, will prove of service, and to some extent supply the want of more complete explanations, especially for the commonest meanings of words. The notes refer chiefly to the less common meanings, and those most familiar to the student will often be found missing.

With regard to the "Book II." which Mr. Lane contemplated, and which was to contain rare words and explanations, I am obliged to admit that the materials are wanting. Some few articles are partly prepared, but are not sufficient to warrant any prospect of this part of the work being completed. It is the less needed since the publication of the late Professor Dozy's valuable *Supplément*.

Fifty years have passed since Mr. Lane undertook to write this Lexicon, and thirty since the first Part appeared. If there has been considerable delay in the production of the recent Parts, I must plead that the collation, revision, and verification of about two thousand columns of this work represent no little labour; and this duty has had to be done in the midst of other and no less pressing occupations.

S. LANE-POOLE.

1*st January*, 1893.

EDWARD WILLIAM LANE.

1801—1825.

The life of a great scholar should not be suffered to pass away into forgetfulness. The Arabs have indeed a proverb, 'He who has left works behind him dies not': but although so long as there are students of the life and the literature of the East, the memory of Lane cannot die, the personality of the great Orientalist is rigidly excluded from his writings; they reveal almost nothing of himself. If to stimulate the endeavours of others by the example of a chief of their kind, to encourage fainter hearts by telling them of the strength and devotion of a master, be one of the ends of biography, this brief and inadequate memoir of perhaps the truest and most earnest student this century has seen will not be deemed superfluous. As the record of half a hundred years of ceaseless labour, crowned with a perfection of scholarship to which even Germany avowedly yields the palm of undisputed supremacy, the life of Lane must needs be written.

Edward William Lane was born at Hereford on September 17th, 1801. He was the third son of the Rev. Theophilus Lane, LL.D., a Prebendary of Hereford; and his mother was Sophia Gardiner, a niece of Gainsborough the Painter. At first his education was conducted by his father, after whose sudden death in 1814 he was placed successively at the grammar-schools of Bath and Hereford, where he distinguished himself by his unusual power of application and by an almost equal mastery of classics and mathematics. The latter formed his principal study, for his mind was bent upon taking a degree at Cambridge, and then entering the Church. This desire to devote himself to a religious profession may have had its origin in the training of his mother, under whose influence his education was completed. Mrs. Lane was a woman of no ordinary mould. Gifted with high intellectual powers, which she had spared no pains to cultivate, she possessed a strength and beauty of character that won not only admiration but affection from all who were privileged to know her. It is easy to understand how great and how good must have been the influence of such a mother upon Edward Lane. He was wont to say that he owed his success in life to her teaching, and the saying, characteristic in its modesty, was doubtless partly true. His success was the result as much of character as of intellect.

The Cambridge project was never carried out. Lane indeed visited the university, but did not enter his name on the books of any college. A few days' experience of university life as it was in the first quarter of this century was sufficient to show him that in living in such society as he was then introduced to, and in conforming to its ways, he would be sacrificing what was to him dearer than all academic distinctions. That his mathematical training had been thorough is shown by the fact that immediately after giving up the idea of Cambridge, Lane procured a copy of the honour papers of the year and discovered that he could without difficulty solve every problem save one; and, as he has often told me, going to bed weary with puzzling out this single stumbling-block, he successfully overcame it in his sleep and, suddenly waking up, lit his candle in the middle of the night and wrote out the answer without hesitation.

The plan of Cambridge, and with it the Church, being given up, and his later training being too exclusively mathematical for him to think of Oxford, Lane joined his elder brother Richard (afterwards renowned for his skill in lithography, which was recognized by the Royal Academy in the election to an associateship) in London, where he spent some time in engraving. Although this profession was also shortly abandoned, the years devoted to it were not thrown away. The taste for art which he had inherited with the Gainsborough blood and which his mother, who had spent a great part of her girlhood in her uncle's studio, spared no endeavour to foster, aided by the mechanical training of the graver, was afterwards turned to admirable results in Egypt. Side by side with his engraving, however, was the growing passion for Eastern things. Lane could not by his nature be idle for a moment, and the hours unfilled by his art were given up to hard reading. To such an extent was this zeal for study carried, that he began to grudge the time necessary for food and exercise. The result of inattention to the ordinary rules of health was a state of weakness that could offer but a faint resistance to the attack of typhus fever which now assailed him. With difficulty escaping with his life, he found his health unequal to the sedentary habits of the engraver. A man who was so weak, partly from the exhaustion of chronic bronchitis, and partly from the effects of the fever, that he sometimes could not walk along a street without clinging for support, was not fit to bend over copper-plate all day. He therefore determined to adopt some other way of life.

As early as 1822, Eastern studies had more than merely attracted Lane's interest. A manuscript grammar of colloquial Arabic in his handwriting bears this date: and he must have been studying some time before he could attempt a grammar of Arabic, even though it is only an abridgement of other works. From this year or earlier dates that severe devotion to the language and character of the Arabs which for more than half a century filled every moment of his studious life.

It was this taste for Oriental matters, seconded by his weak health, which could ill withstand a northern winter, that determined Lane to visit Egypt. Another motive may have been the hope of a post in the service of the British Government, which, he was informed by those who were qualified to speak, he stood a good chance of obtaining if he made himself well acquainted with Easterns at home. Whatever the motives, in 1825 Lane left England for the first of his three visits to the land of the Pharaohs.

1825—1828.

THE FIRST VISIT TO EGYPT.

The "Description of Egypt."

On Monday the 18th July 1825 Lane embarked on board the brig "Findlay," 212 tons, bound for Alexandria, and on the 24th he lost sight of the coast of England. The voyage, which occupied two months, was not altogether uneventful. On the 2nd September the "Findlay" nearly foundered in a hurricane off Tunis. The master seems to have been an incapable person, and no one else of the crew understood navigation. The night was starless; the sea ran so high that the heavy storm-compass in the binnacle could not traverse and was unshipped at every lurch; and, driven along between a lee shore and a dangerous reef, without compass, and the main topmast carried away, the ship seemed doomed to destruction. It was at this critical moment that the captain entreated Lane to take the helm. Fortunately navigation had formed part of his mathematical studies: but he was little more than a boy and this was his first voyage; he might well have shrunk from the responsibility. But he went at once to the wheel, where he had to be lashed, or he had been washed overboard by the seas that swept momently over the deck. He had noticed the bearings of the lightning, and by the flashes he steered. At last the moon rose, and by her light the wreck was cleared away and steering was less hazardous. As day dawned the wind abated, and Lane was able to bring the ship safely into Malta harbour on the morning of the 4th. Here she remained six days for repair; and meanwhile the crew mutinied, seemingly not without reason; and Lane was aroused one morning with a shot through his pillow. He had come prepared for dangers in Egypt, and these accidents by the way did not discompose him. On Monday the 19th September the shores of the Delta came in sight: first the ruined tower of Aboo-Seer rose above the horizon; then "a tall distant sail," which proved to be the Great Pillar of Alexandria; then high hills of rubbish, crowned with forts; and at last the ships in the Old Harbour. The "Findlay" was ordered to enter the New Harbour, and there cast anchor in the midst of a shoal of Rosetta boats.

Although it was late in the afternoon and little could be seen before dark, Lane was too impatient to wait for the next day. He landed filled with profound emotion, feeling, he writes, like an Eastern bridegroom about to lift the veil of his as yet unseen bride. For his was not the case of an ordinary traveller. "I was not visiting Egypt merely for my amusement; to examine its pyramids and temples and grottoes, and after satisfying my curiosity to quit it for other scenes and other pleasures: but I was about to throw myself entirely among strangers, among a people of whom I had heard the most contradictory accounts; I was to adopt their language, their customs, and their dress; and in order to make as much progress as possible in the study of their literature, it was my intention to associate almost exclusively with the Muslim inhabitants."

The first sight that met his eye was singularly impressive. It was the time of afternoon prayers, and the chant of the Muëddin had just ceased as they landed. Muslims were performing the ablutions at the sea, or, this done, were praying on the beach, with that solemn gravity and with those picturesque and striking attitudes which command the respect of all standers-by. Lane always felt a strong veneration for a Muslim at his prayers, and it was a singularly auspicious moment for an enthusiastic Englishman to set foot on the Egyptian soil. As he walked on, till he reached one of the principal streets, his delight and wonder grew at every step. The peculiar appearance of the narrow street and its shops, the crowded passengers of every nation bordering on the Mediterranean, the variety of costume and countenance, the "bearded visage of the Turk, the Moor, and the Egyptian,—the noble and hardy look of the sunburnt Bedawee enveloped in his ample woollen sheet or hooded cloak,—the mean and ragged clothing of many of the lower orders, contrasted with the gaudy splendour or graceful habit of some of their superiors,—the lounging soldier with his pipe and pistols and yataghán,—the blind beggar,—the dirty naked child, and the veiled female," afforded a picture beyond even what his dreams of the land of the Arabian Nights had conjured up. It is true the shady side of the scene was somewhat forcibly disclosed a few paces further on, by a brawl, a murder, and a decapitation, all occurring in the space of a few minutes before the eyes of the young traveller. And as he examined Alexandria at leisure, he began to feel disappointed with it, and to long for Cairo. Notwithstanding the characteristic sights that first greeted him, the city was not Eastern enough, and he would have found his stay there wearisome but for the kindness and hospitality of Mr. Salt, the British Consul-General, who received him like an old friend, although they were strangers to each other, and gave him a room in his country-house near the Báb-es-Sidr. Lane found a "delightful retreat" in Mr. Salt's garden, and plenty of entertainment in the company that visited the Consul. One of these friends, M. Linant, the indefatigable cartographer of Egypt, proposed that Lane should join his party to Cairo, an offer which, as a stranger and as yet unprovided with a servant, he gladly accepted.

On the 28th September the Reyyis and crew chanted the Fát'hah, the beautiful prayer which opens the Ḳur-án, and M. Linant and his party, accompanied by Lane, set sail on the Maḥmoodeeyeh canal for the "El-Ḳáhirah the Guarded." The voyage was in no wise remarkable. Lane made his usual careful notes of every thing he saw, from the saráb to the creaking of the sáḳiyehs and the croaking of the frogs. He described each village or town he passed, and observed the ways of the people working on shore or bathing in the Nile; and watched the simple habits of the boatmen, when the boat was made fast and their day's work was over, grouped round the fire on the bank, smoking and singing, and blowing their terrible double-pipes and making night hideous with their national drums; and then contentedly spreading their mats, and, despising pillow and covering, falling happily asleep. On the 2nd October Lane had his first distant and hazy view of the Pyramids, and about five o'clock the boat was moored at Booláḳ, the port of Cairo, and the Reyyis thanked God for their safe arrival—"El-ḥamdu li-lláh bi-s-selámeh."

They rode at once to the city to tell the Vice-Consul of their arrival, that rooms might be made ready for them in Mr. Salt's house. The first view of Cairo delighted Lane even more than he had expected, and here at least, where all was thoroughly Eastern and on a grand scale, no after disappointment could be expected. When he saw the numberless minarets towering above the wilderness of flat-roofed houses, and in turn crowned by the citadel, with the yellow ridge of El-Moḳaṭṭam in the background, Lane took heart again and rejoiced in the prospect of his future home. The next day he took up his quarters at the Consulate, abandoned his English dress and adopted the Turkish costume, and set out to look for a house. He soon found one near the Báb-el-Ḥadeed, belonging to 'Osmán, a Scotsman in the employ of the British Consul, who proved a very useful neighbour and a faithful friend. The furniture, after the usual native pattern, always a simple affair in the East, was quickly procured and the house was soon ready for his reception.

These matters took up the first five days in Cairo: but on the 8th October, every thing being in a fair way to completion at the house, a small party of Europeans, with Lane among them, made an excursion to the Pyramids. It was only a flying visit, to take the edge off his ardent curiosity, for he meant to go again and make careful drawings and measurements. He explored the Great Pyramid, and then in the night climbed to its summit and enjoyed a sight such as one hardly sees twice in a lifetime. The cold wind sweeping up the sides, with a sound like the roar of a distant cataract, echoed the weird feeling of the place and the time, with which the vaguely vast outline of the Second Pyramid, faintly discernable, and the wild figures of the Bedawee guides were in full harmony. Then the moon rose and lighted up the eastern side of the nearer pyramid with a magic effect. Two hours more and the sun had revealed the plain of Egypt, and Lane had been already amply rewarded for the dangers and trouble of his journey from England by one of the most wonderful views in the world.

After two months spent in Cairo, in the study of the people and their language, and in seeing the thousand beautiful things that the most picturesque of cities could then show, Lane again visited the Pyramids, this time for a fortnight, armed with stores and necessaries for living, and with materials for drawing and surveying, above all the camera lucida, with which all his drawings were made.

He took up his abode in a tomb of an unusually luxurious kind. It had three holes for windows, and was altogether about eight feet wide by twice as long, with a partition wall in the middle. Before the door was the usual accumulation of bones and rags, and even whole bodies of mummies: but the contemplation of these details gave Lane no unpleasant sensations; he merely observed that the skulls were extraordinarily thick. Into this cheerful habitation the baggage was carried, and though at first the interior looked "rather gloomy," when "the floor was swept, and a mat, rug, and mattress spread in the inner apartment, a candle lighted, as well as my pipe, and my arms hung about upon wooden pegs driven into crevices in the wall,"—the paintings had been effaced long before,—"I looked around me with complacency, and felt perfectly satisfied." He was waited on by his two servants, an Egyptian and a Nubian, whom he had brought from Cairo, and at the door were two Arabs hired from the neighbouring village to guard against passing Bedawees. All day long he was engaged in drawing and describing and making plans; and then in the evening he would come out on the terrace in front of the tomb, and sit in the shade of the rock (at Christmastide), drinking his coffee and smoking his long chibook, and "enjoying the mild air and the delightful view over the plain towards the capital."

"In this tomb I took up my abode for a fortnight, and never did I spend a more happy time, though provided with fewer articles of luxury than I might easily and reasonably have procured. My appearance corresponded with my mode of living; for on account of my being exposed to considerable changes of atmospheric temperature in passing in and out of the Great Pyramid, I assumed the Ḥirám (or woollen sheet) of the Bedawee, which is a most convenient dress under such circumstances; a part or the whole being thrown about the person according to the different degrees of warmth which he may require. I also began to accustom myself to lay aside my shoes on many occasions, for the sake of greater facility in climbing and descending the steep and smooth passages of the pyramid, and would advise others to do the same. Once or twice my feet were slightly lacerated; but after two or three days they were proof against the sharpest stones. From the neighbouring villages I procured all that I wanted in the way of food; as eggs, milk, butter, fowls, and camels' flesh; but bread was not to be obtained anywhere nearer than the town of El-Geezeh, without employing a person to make it. One family, consisting of a little old man named 'Alee, his wife (who was not half his equal in years), and a little daughter, occupied a neighbouring grotto, guarding some antiquities deposited there by Caviglia. Besides these I had no nearer neighbours than the inhabitants of a village about a mile distant." The solitude, however, was broken two days after his arrival by the appearance of a young Bedawee, who frankly confessed he had deserted from the Páshà's army and could not enter the villages, and claimed Lane's hospitality, which was of course immediately granted. The young fellow used to amuse his host in the evening, while he smoked his pipe, by telling the famous stories from the romance of Aboo-Zeyd, all the while exciting the indignation of the Egyptian servant by his contempt for the Felláheen. He stayed till Lane left, and when the latter asked him where he would find protection now, he replied with characteristic reliance upon providence, "Who brought *you* here?"

After a fortnight in his tomb at the Pyramids of El-Geezeh, spent in making drawings and plans of the pyramids and the surrounding tombs, Lane returned to Cairo on New Year's Eve. Here for two months and a half he devoted himself to the study of the "Mother of the World" and her inhabitants. Already possessed of an accurate knowledge of the modern Arabic language; being conformed to the customs of the people in all such external matters as dress and manners and outward habit of life; and being of that calm and self-possessed nature absolutely necessary to one who would be intimate with Easterns, and moreover of a cast of countenance resembling so closely that of a pure Arab family of Mekkeh that an Egyptian, though repeatedly assured of the mistake, persisted in his belief that the reputed Ingleezee was a member of that family; Lane was able, as scarcely one other European has been, to mix among the people of Cairo as one of themselves, and to acquire not only the refinements of their idiomatic speech and the minute details of their etiquette, but also a perfect insight into their habits of mind and ways of thought. The Spirit of the East is a sealed book to ninety-nine out of every hundred orientalists. To Lane it was transparent. He knew the inner manners of the Egyptian's mind as well as those of his outer life. And this was the result of the many years he lived among the people of Cairo, of which these few months in 1826 were the beginning.

His life at this time, however, was not wholly spent among Easterns. There was still a European side. He was one of the brilliant group of discoverers who were then in Egypt: and young as he was he was received among them with cordial welcome and unfeigned appreciation. Within the charmed circle to which Lane was now admitted were men such as Wilkinson and James Burton (afterwards Haliburton), the hieroglyphic scholars; Linant and Bonomi; the travellers Humphreys, Hay, and Fox-Strangways; the accomplished Major Felix, and his distinguished friend Lord Prudhoe, of whose noble appreciation of Lane's work much will presently be said. With such friends and in such a city as Cairo, the life of the young orientalist must have been enviable.

But the time had now come for the first Nile-voyage. The journey from Alexandria to Cairo had not damped the enthusiastic longing with which Lane looked forward to the upper country—Thebes and Philae and Denderah. He determined to ascend to the Second Cataract, a limit further than most travellers then ventured and beyond which travelling was almost impossible. In March 1826 he hired a boat, for twenty-five dollars a month, manned by a crew of eight men, who were to find their own provisions, and on the 15th he embarked, set his cabin in order and sailed.

Lane's plan was, in the up-voyage to see in a cursory manner everything that could be seen, and in the down-voyage to make the notes and drawings from which he intended to construct his "Description of Egypt." In the up-voyage we see him sailing from one place of interest to another, with as little delay as possible; spending the whole day in walking to some ruin at a distance from the bank, and so the next day, and every day, so long as there was anything worth visiting on shore. As a sightseer in Egypt Lane was indefatigable. He would walk on the hot plain, with the thermometer at 112° in the shade, till his feet were blistered, and he had to throw himself on his back to relieve them from the burning of the sand. When there was nothing to take him on shore, he would smoke his pipe on deck, and watch the people in the villages as he passed, or rest his eyes on the long lines of palms and dom and nabḳ trees that fringe the bank. Sometimes a compulsory variety was made by the wind dropping, when the boatmen would turn out and drag the tow-rope. Or the boat was kept for days in an uninteresting place by a wind against which towing was vain labour. A sandstorm would now and then cause an unpleasant diversion, and not only keep Lane in his cabin, but follow him there and fill every crevice. It was quite another matter, though, with the sand-pillar; which was the work of an 'Efreet, who stirred up the dust in his flight, and, being an 'Efreet, might be amenable to persuasion. Lane encountered one of these pillars of sand in one of his walks, and following the instructions of his guide he accosted the 'Efreet with the cry of "Ḥadeed" ("iron"), and the sprite passed at a respectful distance. The modern life of Egypt claimed the traveller's attention no less than the ancient. He visited the tombs of the Sheykh El-Harcedee and the Sheykh 'Abd-el-Ḳádir El-Geelánee, and went through the usual ceremonies with a precision in which no Muslim could find a fault; he received the calls of the various dignitaries on the way with the utmost courtesy, although he was obliged to decline the presents of Abyssinian girls and nargeelehs which they were fond of offering; and he seldom missed an opportunity of strolling through an Arab town, or watching an encampment of Bedawees, and learning something more of the ways of the people.

At Denderah, near the end of April, Lane met James Burton, and together they suffered from the Khamáseen winds, and found they could make no drawings nor leave their boats. On the 6th of May the great Propylæum of Thebes came in view; on the 15th at Philae, they found Linant, who had left Cairo a couple of days earlier. After going on to Aboo-Simbel, and then to the Second Cataract, Lane turned his boat and prepared to descend the Nile. Lane seems to have spent his time during the whole of this return voyage in drawing and measuring and describing, often sitting under an almost vertical sun, his thermometer occasionally bursting at 150°, and with no other protection from the scorching heat than a single ṭarboosh. At Philae he again found Linant, waiting for the rising of the river to pass the Cataract, and during the eight days they spent together there Strangways made his appearance, went to Wádee Ḥalfeh, and then came back to them; and in company with him Lane continued his way down the river. Seventy-three days (July 30 to October 11, 1826) were spent at Thebes, where he met Hay, in making a minute survey of the tombs and temples. Here he lived in three different houses. The first was Yáni's house, among the tombs on the western side; then he moved to a ruined part of the first propylæum of El-Ḳarnak; and for fifteen days he lived in one of the Tombs of the Kings, for the sake of its comparative coolness. In the former abodes the thermometer ranged from 90° to 108° in the shade; but in the Tombs of the Kings it did not rise above 87°.

Coming back to Cairo, Lane went among the people as before, busy in preparing his account of their manners and customs, and his description of their city. After several months thus spent, he again started for the Nile, again ascended to the Second Cataract, and stayed forty-one days (November 1 to December 12, 1827) at Thebes, completing his survey of the temples. And, having accomplished the great object of his travels, having prepared a complete description of Egypt and Lower Nubia, the country and the monuments and the people, he came back to Cairo in the beginning of 1828, and after a short stay at the capital, and a final visit in the spring to the Pyramids of El-Geezeh and Saḳḳarah, in company with Hay, he returned to England in the autumn of the year.

These three years of the first visit to Egypt had not been years of idleness. Lane was not the typical traveller, who travels for amusement, and perhaps writes a book to record his sensations for the gratification of an admiring public. Lane's object was a far different one. He travelled, so to say, to map the country. And his was a propitious time. Egypt had but recently been opened up to explorers, and no one had yet fully taken stock of her treasures. Hamilton, indeed, and Niebuhr had broken the ground with their books; but no systematic account of the country, its natural characteristics, its people, and its monuments, had yet been attempted. Successfully to perform such a work demanded long and unceasing labour and considerable abilities. Lane never shrank from toil of any kind, and he possessed just those natural gifts which were needed by one who should do this work. Lord Brougham once said, "I wonder if that man knows what his *forte* is?—Description:" and Brougham was right. Very few men have possessed in an equal degree the power of minutely describing a scene or a monument, so that the pencil might almost restore it without a fault after the lapse of years. This power is eminently shown in the "Description of Egypt." Every temple or tomb, every village, every natural feature of the country, is described in a manner that permits no improving. The objects stand before you as you read, and this not by the use of imaginative language, but by the plain simple description. Lane had a vehement hatred of "fine writing," and often expressed his dislike to those authors who are credited with the habit of sacrificing the truth of their statements to the fall of the sentence. He always maintained that the first thing was to find the right word to express your meaning, and then to let the sentence fall as it pleased. It is possible that in his earliest work he carried this principle a little too far; and in his most finished production, the notes to "The Thousand and One Nights," considerable care may be detected in the composition. But in every thing he wrote, the prominent characteristic was perfect clearness, and nowhere is this more conspicuous than in the "Description of Egypt." But further, to prevent the scant possibility of mistaking the words, the work was illustrated by 101 sepia drawings, made with the camera lucida, (the invention of his friend Dr. Wollaston,) and therefore as exact as photography could make them, and far more pleasing to the eye. Those whose function it is to criticise artistic productions have unanimously expressed their admiration of these drawings. And though Lane would always say that the credit belonged to his instrument and not to himself, it is easy to see that they are the work of a fine pencil-hand, and could not have been done by any one who chose to look through a camera lucida. Altogether, both in drawings and descriptions, the book is unique of its kind.

It has never been published. And the reason is easily seen in the expense of reproducing the drawings. Lane himself was never a rich man, and could not have issued the book at his own expense, and no publisher was found sufficiently enterprising to risk the first outlay. An eminent firm, indeed, accepted the work with enthusiasm, but subsequently retracted from its engagement in consequence of the paralysis of trade which accompanied the excitement of the Reform agitation. It is needless, however, to refer to affairs that happened nearly fifty years ago, although they were a cause of much annoyance and disappointment to the author of the "Description of Egypt"; who naturally was ill-disposed to see the work of several years wasted, and who could not forget the high praises that had been passed upon the book and the drawings by all who were competent to form an opinion. There can be no doubt in the mind of any one who has studied the manuscript and the drawings, that travellers in Egypt have sustained in this work a loss which has not yet been filled up, and is not likely to be, unless the "Description of Egypt" should yet be published.

We have seen Lane in a phase of his life distinct from all the remainder. The years 1825—28 are the only time in which he could be called a traveller. Even then the traveller bent on the enjoyment of the wonders of a new land is swallowed up in the student intent on understanding the monuments of a marvellous antiquity. But after this first visit all traces of the traveller disappear, and the serious laborious student becomes everything. Once again in after years did Lane ascend the Nile as far as Thebes, and live the old life in his tomb; but it was to avoid the Plague, and his visit there was still devoted to study. Henceforward we shall see, not the enterprising and often daring explorer, climbing flat-faced cliffs, swinging down a mummy-pit, crawling in the low passages of tombs and pyramids, but a scholar at his desk, a learned man honoured in learned circles, the highest authority on matters Arabian to whom England or Europe could appeal.

THE SECOND VISIT TO EGYPT (1833—5.)

For some time after his return to England, Lane was occupied in working his Egyptian notes and diaries into the form that the manuscript of the "Description of Egypt" now wears. It has already been said that the negotiations with the publishers for the production of the book fell to the ground. But before this happened, Lane had separated from the body of the work his account of the modern inhabitants of Egypt, which it was thought would appear to greater advantage and be more widely read as a distinct book. This part of the "Description" was shown to Lord Brougham, who at once recognised its high merit, and recommended it to the Society for the Diffusion of Useful Knowledge, of which he was a Member of Committee. It was in consequence of the acceptance of the work by the Society that Lane determined to visit Egypt again, in order to enlarge and perfect his account of the people. This is an instance of that thoroughness which is shown in every work of his. Whatever came to his hand to do, he did it with all his might. He would never condescend to anything approaching slovenly work; and thought little of crossing the Mediterranean and staying two years at Cairo in order to bring nearer to perfection a sketch of the manners and customs of the inhabitants of Egypt, which to an ordinary writer would have seemed to stand in need of no revision. Without hesitation he went over the whole ground again, verified each statement, and added much that had been omitted from the earlier and more concise work. During the two years he spent in the Egyptian metropolis, scarcely a day passed without his going out among his Muslim friends and accustoming himself more completely to their manners, or witnessing the various public festivals of the year. Every day's experience was carefully recorded in a little library of note-books, all written in his singularly clear and neat hand, except where here and there an Egyptian friend has scribbled his own statement in Arabic. One of these note-books appears to have been kept for recording the more important scenes that Lane witnessed, and is fortunately dated, so as to form an intermittent diary. As this is this is the only journal he ever kept, to my knowledge, except a brief account of his first Nile-voyage, it is here reproduced. Besides the necessary suppression of a few passages relating to family matters, certain long passages have been omitted, since they occur verbatim in Lane's published works. It is not often that the pages of a diary can be transferred to a finished book like "The Modern Egyptians" without even verbal alteration. But it was the same with everything Lane wrote. If he was asked a question by letter, his answer was always fit for publication, both in style and in accuracy of matter.

London, 25th Oct., 1833.—Engaged my passage to Alexandria on board the merchant brig Rapid, Capt. Phillips, 162 tons, for 30 guineas, to be found with all necessary stores, poultry, &c.—6th Nov. Embarked at St. Katharine's Dock.—7th. Sailed.—25th. Passed Gibraltar.—5th Dec. Passed Malta.—13th (1st of Shaabán, 1249). Arrived at Alexandria.

It had rained almost incessantly, and very heavily, during the three nights previous to our arrival at Alexandria; and the streets were consequently in a most filthy state. The general appearance of the people was also far more miserable than when I was here before. The muddy state of the streets doubtless confined most well-dressed persons to their houses; but it is rather to the severe oppression of late years, and to repeated conscriptions, which have deprived many parents of the support they received from the labour of their sons, that I attribute the difference which I remarked in the general aspect of the population of this place. A few days before my arrival, some persons from Constantinople had brought the plague there. They were put into quarantine; and the disease had thus been confined within the Lazarette, which was surrounded by a cordon of soldiers. There had been 87 cases, and 23 deaths.—I dined and slept at Mr. Harris's country-house, which is in an angle of the garden in which the house that

Mr. Salt resided in is situated, where I stayed during my first visit to Alexandria. A part of this garden is converted into a burial-place for the English. Mr. Salt is buried there.—Alexandria is rapidly increasing towards the site of the old city: several large and handsome buildings have lately been erected in that quarter.

14th. Removed my luggage from the brig to a boat on the Maḥmoodeeyeh; and in the afternoon set sail for the Nile. Paid 45 piasters for the voyage to the Nile.—15th. Arrived before sunrise at the Foom, or the mouth of the canal, where it communicates with the Nile. A bridge with gates has lately been constructed across the mouth, to retain the water in the canal during the season of low Nile.—I here had to engage another boat, on the Nile. Bargained for 80 piasters for the voyage to Maṣr (or Cairo). Proceeded to Fooweh; but could not continue our voyage in consequence of a violent contrary wind. The air was very thick; and I could hardly fancy myself in Egypt. The river still very turbid. There were many boats here conveying Turkish pilgrims on their way to join the Egyptian Caravan to Mekkeh. Fooweh seems to be falling to utter ruin and to be inhabited by the most squalid miserable people I ever beheld. I am told that I shall remark the same at all the villages we have to pass; and the reason is this:—all the best-looking young men have been picked for the army or navy, and their wives and lovers have mostly followed them; but being parted from them on their arrival at the metropolis have there betaken themselves to prostitution; and Maṣr now absolutely swarms with prostitutes. Thus the villages have been half desolated; and seem to be peopled in general with the most wretched, ugly, old, and haggard paupers. I see scarcely one good-looking young woman among a hundred; or scarcely one where I used to see a score; and almost all are in rags.—16th. In the afternoon, though the wind was still very high and from the S.W., we proceeded. Stopped for the night under the west bank, a little below Shubra Kheet. Several heavy showers of rain fell, accompanied with violent gusts of wind, which obliged many boats, loaded with Turkish pilgrims, to stop at the same part. From a boat next above ours, during a shower of rain, there poured forth a number of these pilgrims, each with his ewer in his hand, to perform the ablution preparatory to prayer; and some of them aged and decrepit. While meditating on their zeal and the hardships which awaited them and admiring their grave and venerable aspect, I was surprised to see six of them, and among these some of the most aged, run to a táboot (a kind of water-wheel used for irrigation), and, with shouts such as their children would have used on a similar occasion, amuse themselves by exerting what little strength they had to perform, all the six together, the work of one cow; and turn, which they could only do very slowly, the stiff and creaking wheel. A few minutes after, they performed their devotions, all of them together, with the utmost solemnity and decorum, ranged in ranks, four abreast, under the partial shelter of some durah about 12 feet high: one acted as Imám, in the first rank; and having previously chanted the *adán*, recited the prayers, chanting the *farḍ*-prayers in a high key and loud voice.—To-day I began to feel the effect which is often produced by first drinking the water of the Nile, and by the cool air of the night; my cabin being only furnished with blinds, like those of an English carriage, to the windows, I was much exposed to the night-air.—17th. Advanced to Shubra Kheet. The weather being boisterous and rainy, and my reiyis determined to proceed, I made a new agreement with him; to pay 20 piasters a day, and to stop when and where I desired. Accordingly I remained the rest of this day, and the following night, at Shubra Kheet.—18th. Of the prudence of the new arrangement which I had made for my boat I received a strong proof in information brought me to-day that a boat which I had first hired at the Foom, about the same size and on the same terms as that in which I now am, but afterwards left for the latter boat in consequence of an order that vessels there should take their departure according to the order in which they lay, had been capsized in the night: the crew and passengers were saved; but remained shivering in their wet clothes for many hours; no village being near. Had this been my case, in my present indisposed state, I should probably have lost my life; or, if not, my books &c. would have been lost or spoiled. My informant thanked God for my preservation; and I most heartily joined him. —19th. Proceeded to Sháboor: the wind still very violent and contrary: on the 20th, to Nádir; 21st, to Záwiyet Razeem, by the tow-rope; having scarcely a breath of wind.—22nd. Calm. Proceeded, by towing, to Wardán.—23rd and 24th. As the wind was violent and contrary during the greater part of each of these days, my reiyis absented himself from the boat. I punish him by deducting two days' pay.—25th. Arrived within five miles of Boolák.

26th. Arrived at Boolák about noon. Sent for a janisary from the Consulate to pass my luggage at the custom-house, and rode up to my old friend 'Osmán, who had made preparations for my reception in a house belonging to him and next to that in which he resides. This house I have engaged for the period of my intended stay in Maṣr. It is situated in the most healthy part of the town, near the N.W. angle; and to me, who have suffered from ophthalmia, it is a desirable residence, as it has glass windows. I have no doubt that ophthalmia in this country is generally the effect of suppressed perspiration, which is most commonly induced by the night-air (the windows of almost all the houses in Maṣr and the other towns being merely of wooden lattice-work); and that it is aggravated by the habit of keeping the head too warm, and the feet too cool.

The aspect of Maṣr, as seen in the approach from the port, has been much improved since the period of my last visit by the removal of many of the mounds of rubbish which rose along that side, and by most of the space which these unsightly objects occupied being converted into gardens. A short time ago, European travellers, if habited in the Turkish or Egyptian dress, were not allowed to enter the gates of Maṣr without a passport (called *teskereh*), which was shown to the guard. This custom is now dispensed with. It was adopted in order to ascertain the number of the population; and to insure that no one of the natives might be unknown, and so escape paying the firdeh or poll-tax. In the interior of the metropolis I observe more ruined houses than when I was last here; and in the appearance of the lower orders, more wretchedness. No change has taken place in the style of the costume of the natives; but the military officers, and the Turks in the employ of the Báshà, have adopted the Nizámee dress, which was becoming common among them before I last quitted Maṣr. The head-dress (being merely a ṭarboosh, without the muslin or Kishmeeree shawl wound round it) has lost its elegance; and the whole dress is less becoming and graceful than the Memlook costume which it has superseded; though it is more convenient for walking and any active exertion. Formerly, a grandee of Maṣr, with his retinue of twenty or more well-mounted men, clad in habits of various and brilliant hues, and with splendid accoutrements, the saddles covered with embroidered velvet and plates of gilt and embossed silver, and the bridles, headstalls, and other trappings ornamented in a similar manner and with rows of gold coins suspended to them, presented a strikingly picturesque and pompous spectacle. Sights of this description are no longer witnessed in the Egyptian metropolis. Even the Báshà, when he occasionally rides through the streets, is followed by only three or four attendants, and is not more distinguished by the habits than by the number of his retinue. As dark colours, and particularly black, are now fashionable among the Turks, and their dresses are generally embroidered with silk, instead of gold lace, there is much less contrast and variety observable in the costumes of the passengers in the crowded streets; but at present there is a little more variety and bustle than is usual, from the number of Turkish pilgrims resting here on their way to Mekkeh.

My old acquaintance the sheykh Aḥmad (or *seyd* Aḥmad, for he is a *shereef*) called on me as soon as he had heard of my arrival. He has resumed his old habit of visiting me almost every day; both for the sake of getting his dinner or supper, or at least tobacco and coffee, and to profit in his trade of bookseller. I wish I could make a portrait which would do justice to his singular physiognomy. For many years he has been nearly blind: one of his eyes is quite closed: the other is ornamented on particular occasions, as the two great festivals, &c., with a border of kohl; though he is a shocking sloven at all times. He tells me that he has taken a second wife, and a second house for her; but that he is as poor as ever; and that my usual yearly present of a dress will be very acceptable.* He has a talent for intrigue and cheating, which he exercises on every opportunity; being lax in morals, and rather so in his religious tenets. Notwithstanding these defects, and sometimes in consequence of his having the latter defect, I find him very useful. Much of the information that I have obtained respecting the manners and customs of his countrymen has been derived from him, or through his assistance; as he scruples not to be communicative to me on subjects respecting which a bigoted Muslim would be silent. He has just brought me a *muṣḥaf* (or copy of the Ḳur-án), which he wishes me to purchase; but he thinks it necessary, as he did on former similar occasions, to offer some excuse for his doing so. He remarks that by my following or conforming with many of the ceremonies of the Muslims I tacitly profess myself to be one of them; and it is incumbent on him to regard me in the most favourable light. "You give me," says he, "the salutation of 'Peace be on you!' and it would be impious in me, and directly forbidden by my religion, to pronounce you an unbeliever; for He whose name be exalted hath said in the Excellent Book,—'Say not unto him who greeteth thee with peace, Thou art not a believer' (ch. iv., v. 96)—therefore," he adds, "it is no sin in me to put into your hands the noble Ḳur-án: but there are some of your countrymen who will take it in unclean hands, and even put it under them and sit upon it! I beg God's forgiveness for talking of such a thing: far be it from you to do so: you, praise be to God, know and observe the command 'None shall touch it but those who are clean.'" (ch. lvi., v. 78: these words are often stamped upon the cover.) He once sold a mushaf on my application to a countryman of mine, who, being disturbed just as the bargain was concluded by some person entering the room, hastily put the sacred book on the deewán and under a part of his dress, to conceal it: the bookseller was much scandalized by this action; thinking that my friend was sitting upon the book, and doing so to show his contempt of it. There was only one thing that I had much difficulty in persuading him to do, during my former visit to this country; which was to go with me to the mosque of the Ḥasaneyn, the burial-place of the head of the Prophet's grandson, El-Ḥoseyn, and the most sacred of the mosques of Maṣr. On passing with him before one of the entrances of this building, one afternoon in Ramaḍán, when it was crowded with Turks, and many of the principal people of the metropolis were among the congregation, I thought it a good opportunity to see it to the greatest advantage, and asked my companion to go in with me. He positively refused, in the fear of my being discovered to be an Englishman, which might so rouse the fanatic anger of some of the Turks there as to expose me to some act of violence. I therefore entered alone. He remained at the door; following me with his eye only (or his only eye), and wondering at my audacity; but as soon as he saw me acquit myself in the usual manner, by walking round the bronze screen which surrounds the monument over the spot where the martyr's head is buried and then going through the regular attitudes of prayer, he came in and said his prayers by my side.—The principal subjects of the conversations which my other Maṣree acquaintances have held with me since my return to their country have been the oppression which they suffer under the present government, the monopolies of the Báshà, and the consequent dulness of trade and dearness of provisions, &c. The sheykh Aḥmad is less querulous: he praises the Báshà for including booksellers among persons of literary and religious professions, from whom no firdeh is exacted. He and another bookseller, who is his superior, are agents for the sale of the books printed at the Báshà's press, at Booláḳ. They have a shop in the principal street of the city (nearly opposite the entrance to Khán El-Khaleelee), which will be a convenient place for me to repair to on the occasions of public processions.

Friday, 10th of January.—Last day (29th) of Shaabán.—In the afternoon of this day I went to the booksellers' shop to see the procession of the *Leylet er-Rooyeh*, or Night of the Observation of the new moon of Ramaḍán, the month of abstinence. Soon after the *'aṣr*, the shops were mostly shut, and the *masṭabahs* occupied by spectators, old and young. The foremost persons in the procession, a company of Niẓám infantry, passed the place where I was sitting (within ten minutes' walk of the Ḳádee's house, whither they were destined) about an hour and a quarter before sunset. The whole procession consisted of nothing more than several companies of Niẓám troops, each company preceded and followed by bearers of mesh'als, to light them on their return, together with small parties of members of those trades which furnish the metropolis with provisions: a group of millers following one party of soldiers; a group of bakers, another: after all of whom came the Moḥtesib, with attendants. The soldiers were accompanied by drummers and fifers, and one band. The members of trades who took part in the procession, with several fakeers, shouted as they passed along—"*O! Eṣ-ṣaláh! Eṣ-ṣaláh! Ṣalloo 'ala-n-Nebee! 'aleyhi-s-selám!*" (O! Blessing! Blessing! Bless ye the Prophet! On him be peace!). After every two or three companies there was an interval of many minutes: so that about an hour elapsed before the procession had passed the place where I sat. After waiting some time at the Ḳádee's, the information that the new moon had been seen was brought there; and the

* Here follows the story of Sheykh Aḥmad's mother, told in the preface to *The Modern Egyptians*, p. xviii. (5th Ed.)

soldiers and other persons who had formed the procession thither divided themselves into several companies, and perambulated different quarters of the town; shouting *Ya' ummata kheyri-l-ana'm! Siya'm! Siya'm!* (O followers of the best of the creation! Fasting! Fasting!). The mosques were all illuminated within; and lamps hung at their entrances, and upon the galleries of the mád'nehs. —When the moon is not seen, the people are informed by the cry of *Ghadà min shahri Shaaba'n! Fitár! Fitár!* (To-morrow is of the month of Shaabán! No fasting! No fasting!).—The people seem as merry to-night as they usually do when released from the miseries of the day's fast.*

11th of January.—1st of Ramadán.—Instead of seeing, as at other times, most of the passengers in the streets with the pipe in the hand, we now see them empty-handed, or carrying a stick or cane; but some of the Christians are not afraid, as they used to be, of smoking in their shops during this month. The streets in the morning have a dull appearance, many of the shops being shut; but in the afternoon they are as much crowded as usual, and all the shops are open. A similar difference is also observable in the manners and temper of the people during the day-time and at night: while fasting, they are generally speaking very morose: in the evening, after breakfast, they are unusually affable and cheerful. As Ramadán now falls in the winter, the fast is comparatively easy; the days being short, and the weather cool: therefore thirst is not felt so severely. The period from the commencement of the fast (the *imsák*), which is at this season within two hours of sunrise, to the time when it ends, or sunset, is now (in the beginning of the month) 12 hours and 12 minutes: at the end of the month it will be 12 hours and 47 minutes. Servants who are fasting (as mine, and most others, are), if they have to bring a pipe to a person who is not keeping the fast, will not draw the smoke as usual at other times, but put a live coal upon the tobacco, and blow upon it, or wave the pipe through the air; and then present it. I take my principal meal now at sunset, in order that it may serve as a breakfast to any friend who may call on me in the evening, at or before that time. Towards evening, and for some time after sunset, the beggars in the streets are now more than usually importunate and clamorous. I often hear the cries of *Fatooree 'aleyk ya' Rabb!* (My breakfast must be thy gift, O Lord!)—*Ana deyf Allah wa-n-Nebee* (I am the guest of God and the Prophet!)—and the following, which exhibits a union (not uncommon in similar cries) of the literary and popular dialects of Arabic—*Men fattar sa'im luh agrun da'im* (Who gives breakfast to a faster will have an enduring recompense). The coffee-shops are now much frequented by persons of the lower orders; many of whom prefer to break their fast with a cup of coffee and a pipe. Parties assemble at these shops a little before sunset, and wait there to hear the evening call to prayer, which announces the termination of the day's fast. Some of the coffee-shops offer the attraction of a reciter of tales, or poetical romances, during the nights of Ramadán. It is also a custom among some of the 'Ulama of Masr to have a Zikr performed in their houses, by a numerous company of fakeers, every night during this month.† My almost daily visiter, the sheykh Ahmad, the bookseller, tells me that he cannot spend much time with me this month; as he sleeps half the day, and breakfasts, and takes part in a Zikr, every evening, at the house of the late sheykh El-'Aroosee, who was one of the four great sheykhs of Masr, presiding over the Hanafeeyeh, of whom he was also the muftee.—As I was sitting at the booksellers' shop to-day, the Básha, Mohammad 'Alee, rode by, on his way to say the afternoon prayers in the mosque of the Hasaneyn, followed by only four attendants; the first of whom bore his seggádeh (or prayer-carpet), in an embroidered kerchief, on his lap. The Báshà was very plainly dressed, with a white turban. I should not have known him, had I not been informed that it was he; for he appears much older than when I was last in Egypt; though he looks remarkably well. He saluted the people right and left as he passed along: all rising to him.—It is the general fashion of the principal Turks in Masr, and of many of their countrymen, to repair to the mosque of the Hasaneyn in the afternoon during Ramadán, to pray and lounge; and on these occasions, a number of Turkish tradesmen (called Tohafgeeyeh, or Tohafjeeyeh) expose for sale, in the court of the meyda-ah (or tank for ablution) of this mosque, a variety of articles of taste and luxury suited to the wants of their countrymen; such as porcelain, glass, gold, silver, brass, and copper wares; cutlery; mouth-pieces of pipes and pipe-sticks; and many other commodities, chiefly from Constantinople, or other places in Europe. The interior of the Hasaneyn during the afternoon in Ramadán is one of the most interesting sights in Masr; but from the circumstances which render it so, and particularly from its being the most sacred of all the mosques in Masr, none but a Muslim can enter and witness the scene which it presents, unless accompanied by an officer of the government, without imminent risk of being discovered, violently turned out, insulted with scurrilous language, and perhaps beaten or spit upon. I only once ventured into this mosque on such an occasion; and then was careful to perform all the usual ceremonies. Many persons go to the mosque of the Hasaneyn to offer up their petitions for particular blessings, in the belief that the sanctity of the place will ensure the success of their prayers.

A man was beheaded to-day, for stealing several pipes and drinking-cups, belonging to the Báshà, in the Citadel.

Feb. 9th.—Last day (30th) of Ramadán.—Ramadán has passed away with scarcely any incident to relieve its dulness, excepting the usual merry-making of the lower orders of the people at night in the coffee-shops, where smoking tobacco or hemp, playing at some kind of game, or listening to a story-teller, were their ordinary amusements. I have not observed funerals to be more numerous than usual during the latter part of the month, as is the case when Ramadán falls in the warmer seasons; but the people have not seemed less out of humour with the fast. Weariness and moroseness are the predominant effects of the observance of Ramadán; and if people are seen at this time more than usually occupied in mumbling portions of the Kur-án, I think their motive is rather to pass away the time than anything else. I am told that many more persons break the fast now than did when I was last here. Even the Kádee told an acquaintance of mine, a few days ago, that it was his custom only to keep the first two and last two days of the fast. By the poor, in general, it is still rigidly kept; and, by them, most severely felt, as they can seldom relax from their ordinary labours. There is now living in this city an old man who fasts every day in the year, from day-break to sunset, excepting on the occasions of the two 'Eeds (or festivals), when it is unlawful for the Muslim to fast. At night he eats very sparingly. He keeps a shop in the shoe-market called Kasabat Rudwán, where he is generally seen occupied in re-

* Cp. *Mod. Eg.* p. 472.

† Cp. *Mod. Eg.* pp. 474—6

citing the Ḳur-án and handling his beads. It is said that there are several other persons here who fast in the same austere manner.—The weather during the month which is just expiring has been of an unusual kind: several very heavy showers of rain have fallen; and the streets have seldom been dry more than two or three days together.

In the afternoon of this day (at the hour of the *'aṣr*) the guns of the Citadel announced the termination of the period of the fast: the new moon having been seen. The fast is, however, kept till sunset. In the evening, the guns fired again. With sunset, the *'Eed* commences. The people are all rejoicing: swings and whirligigs are erected in many parts of the town, and in its environs; and several story-tellers and reciters of poetry have collected audiences in various places.

10th.—First day of the *'Eed.*—At day-break, all the mosques were crowded with worshippers, to perform the prayers of the 'Eed; and now, every minute, friends are seen in the streets congratulating, embracing, and kissing, each other. Many of the people (all who can afford) are seen in complete new suits of clothes: others, with a new 'eree, or ṭarboosh and turban, or, at least, a new pair of red or yellow shoes. Most of the shops are shut, excepting those where eatables are sold. The people are mostly occupied in visits of congratulation; or repairing, particularly the women, to the tombs of their relatives. Donkeys laden with palm-branches, for the visiters of the tombs, obstruct the streets in many places. The guns of the Citadel are fired at noon and in the afternoon (at the *'aṣr*) on each of the three days of the 'Eed.

12th.—Last day of the 'Eed.—This day I accompanied my neighbour 'Osmán to visit the tomb of the sheykh Ibraheem (Burckhardt), in the cemetery of Báb en-Naṣr, on the north of the city, to see that the monument was in good repair, and to pay to the memory of the lamented traveller that tribute of respect which is customary on the occasion of the 'Eed. The principal part of the burial-ground, directly opposite the Báb en-Naṣr, was occupied by dense crowds of persons who had collected there for their amusement, and presented a most singular scene. Vast numbers of tents were erected; some, for the reception of idlers; but most, for the visiters of the tombs; many of whom, conspicuous by their palm-branches, were, like ourselves, making their way with much difficulty through the multitude. A woman who had fallen down here on the first day of the 'Eed was trodden to death. Being mounted on donkeys, we got on better than some others; but our palm-branch, borne before us, and showing our pious intention, had not the effect of inducing any one to move out of our way. A large space was occupied by swings and whirligigs, all in rapid motion, and loaded with boys and girls: the principal objects of attraction to persons of maturer age were conjurors, musicians, dancing-girls, and dancing-men. Having passed through the most crowded part of the cemetery, we soon arrived at the tomb of the sheykh Ibraheem. It is a plain and humble monument of the usual oblong form, constructed of the common, coarse, calcareous stone of the neighbouring mountain-range of Muḳattam, with a stela of the same stone, roughly cut, and without any inscription, at the head and foot. Numerous faḳeers resort to the cemeteries during the three days of the 'Eed, to perform, for the remuneration of a piaster or two, the service usual on those occasions when visiters arrive; consisting of the recital of, at least, one of the longer chapters of the Ḳur-án, and afterwards of the Fát'ḥah, which latter the visiters recite with him. One of them was employed to perform this service by my friend. He did it very rapidly, and without much reverence, seated at the foot of the tomb. This being finished, and the palm-branch broken in pieces and laid on the tomb, a fee was given to the guardian of the tombs, and we returned.—'Osmán performed the pilgrimage in company with the sheykh Ibraheem. He presented me a few days ago with the certificate of Ibraheem's pilgrimage. It is a paper of the size of a small quarto leaf: the greater part occupied by a representation of the temple of Mekkeh, drawn with ink, and ornamented with red, yellow, and green, and with silver leaf: beneath which picture is written the document of which the following is a copy.—"Praise be to God, who hath made the pilgrimage to be rightly accomplished, and the intention rewarded, and sin forgiven. To proceed.—The respected ḥágg Ibraheem hath performed the pilgrimage, according to the divine ordinances, and accomplished all the incumbent ordinances of the Prophet, completely and perfectly. And God is the best of witnesses. The halt was on the 9th day of the month of El-Ḥeggeh, in the year 1229."

15th.—Witnessed the procession of the Kisweh, which I have described in one of my note-books.*

17th.—The Magician 'Abd El-Ḳádir came to me. His performances unsuccessful.

18th.—A man was beheaded yesterday; and another to-day. One was for entering a house to rob, and for attempting to murder the owner. He locked the latter in one of the rooms, and then proceeded to rifle the house. On descending, he saw the owner at a window, calling for assistance; and fired a pistol at him.—The crime of the other, who was a Turk, a ḳowwás of the Báshà, was robbing and murdering a Turkish pilgrim. He arrested the pilgrim on the canal of Alexandria, under pretence of his being required to answer some charge preferred against him before Moḥarram Bey, the Governor of Alexandria. After conducting him some little distance towards Alexandria, he murdered him, and threw his body into the pit of a sáḳiyeh. The companions of the unfortunate man, some days after, being surprised at hearing no tidings of him, applied to Moḥarram Bey; and finding that he knew nothing of the circumstance, searched for and apprehended the murderer.—Robberies have become very frequent here of late: crime, as might be expected, increasing with the oppression and misery of the people.—News arrived to-day of a number of Aḥmad Báshà's horses having been stolen, by a party of Bedawees, from the Feiyoom, where they had been sent for the clover season.

20th.—The Magician came again, in the evening. His performances I have described in one of my note-books.†

27th.—Went to the Ḥasaneyn, to see the Kisweh, the Burḳo', &c., previously to their being packed up and dispatched with the caravan to Mekkeh. The sewing of the Kisweh was not quite completed: several men and women were at work upon it in the great hall, or portico. I asked for, and obtained, for a trifling present, a piece of the Kisweh, a span in length, and nearly the same in breadth. In sewing the several breadths together, it is necessary to cut off some small strips; and these are sold, or given, to persons who apply for them; being considered as amulets. In the saloon of the tomb, I found several pious visiters; and, among them, a poor man, standing before the bronze screen which surrounds the monument, and praying aloud,

* Cp. *Mod. Eg.* p. 480. † Cp. *Mod. Eg.* pp. 268, ff.

with uplifted hands, for food; saying—"Bread, O Lord! I pray for bread: I do not ask for dates: I only pray for bread."—After I had recited the Fát'ḥah, according to custom, at the shrine of Ḥoseyn, I went to a small apartment adjoining the mosque, in which were placed the Burḳo', the covering for the Maḳám Seydna Ibraheem, the covering of the Maḥmal (which were partly unfolded for me to see), the Ḥegáb (or Muṣḥaf), of the Maḥmal, and the embroidered green silk bag in which is kept the key of the Ḳaạbeh. As soon as I had gratified my curiosity by inspecting these sacred objects, and again recited the Fát'ḥah, by desire of the persons who showed them to me, and who did the same, I was overwhelmed with applications for presents by about a dozen ministers and inferior servants of the mosque. Three or four piasters satisfied them; or at least silenced them.—On my way to the Ḥasaneyn, I passed through the great mosque El-Azhar. I was obliged to send my servant by another way because he was carrying my pipe, which could not with propriety be taken into the mosque, though several persons were carrying about bread and other eatables in the great court and in the place of prayer, for sale to the mugáwireen (or students) and the other numerous frequenters of this great temple and university. The weather being not warm, the court was crowded with groups of students and idlers, lounging or basking in the sun; and part of it was occupied by schoolmasters with their young pupils. The interior of this mosque always presents a very interesting scene, at least to me, from its being the principal centre of attraction to the votaries of religion, of literature, and of other sciences, throughout the Muslim world. The college has just been disgraced by one of its members having been convicted of a robbery; and this morning several of the learned community, having heard that eight men were just about to be hanged, were in a state of alarm lest their guilty associate should be one of that number. A brother of this culprit was pointed out to me, conversing, with apparent apathy, with another person, who, turning to me, asked me if I knew of any case on record of a member of the 'Ulamà being hanged.—Shortly after I had quitted the Ḥasaneyn, the eight men above-mentioned were hanged; each in a different part of the town. The member of the college was not among them. In crossing the principal street of the city, I saw one of them, hanging at the window of a sebeel, or public fountain. He was a soldier. His crime was robbery and murder. Another of the eight was hanged for a similar crime. He entered the house of a rich Jewess, ostensibly for the purpose of taking away the dust; murdered her, by cutting off her head; put her remains into a large zeer (or water-jar), and having thrown some dust in the mouth of the jar, carried it away; but it was broken at the bottom, and some blood dripping from it attracted the notice of passengers in the street, and caused his apprehension. Some jewels which had belonged to the murdered woman were found upon his person.

3rd of March.—22nd of Showwál.—Saw the procession of the Maḥmal. It differed from the last which I saw, seven years ago (in 1827), in being attended with less pomp. First, about two hours and a half after sunrise, a small field-piece (for firing the signals for departure after the halts) was drawn along. This was followed by a company of Balṭageeyeh (or Pioneers), and the Báshà's guards, with their band at their head. Then came a train of several camels with large stuffed saddles, upon the forepart of which were fixed two small flags, slanting forwards, and a small plume of ostrich-feathers upon the top of a small stick placed upright. These camels were dyed red, with ḥennà; and had housings ornamented with small shells (cowries): some were decorated with palm-branches, fixed upright upon the saddle: some had a large bell hung on each side; and some bore a pair of the large kettle-drums called nakáḳeer, with the man who beat them. The *takht'rawa'n* of the Emeer El-Ḥágg (or Chief of the Pilgrims) followed next, borne by two camels. Then came numerous groups of darweeshes, with the banners of their several orders (flags, poles, nets, &c.): some of them repeating the name of God, and nodding their heads; and some beating, with a leather strap, a small kettle-drum, which they held in the left hand. Among these groups were two swordsmen, who repeatedly engaged each other in a mock combat; two wrestlers, naked to the waist, and smeared with oil; and the fantastical figure described in my account of the procession of the Kisweh,* mounted on a horse, and clad in sheep-skins, with a high skin cap, and a false beard. The darweeshes were followed by the Mahmal; which has but a poor appearance this year; the covering being old, and its embroidery tarnished. The people crowded to touch it with their hands, or with the end of a shawl; several persons unwinding their turbans, and women at the windows taking off their head-veils, for this purpose. I had been freely allowed to examine and handle it when it was deposited in the mosque of the Ḥasaneyn. The half-naked sheykh whom I have mentioned in my account of the procession of the Kisweh, and in that of the former procession of the Maḥmal, followed the sacred banner, as usual, mounted on a camel, and rolling his head. Some soldiers, with the Emeer el-Ḥágg and other officers who accompany the caravan, closed the procession. In less than an hour, the whole procession had passed the place where I sat.

Many of the shop-keepers in the principal sooks (or bázárs) are painting their shops in a rude kind of European style, decorating the shutters, &c., with flowers and other ornamental devices, painted on a light blue ground. The appearance of these streets may now be compared to that of an old Oriental garment, remarkable for the peculiarity of its form and work, patched over with pieces of European printed calico. I am sorry to observe that Maṣr is not only falling to decay, but that it is rapidly losing that uniform and unique style of architecture which has so long characterized it. Most of the new houses of the grandees and even of persons of moderate wealth, are built in the style of Constantinople; with shelving roofs and glass windows.—One of my friends here remarked to me that the painting the shops blue was a sign of some heavy calamity being about to befal the city: blue (but really of a very *dark* shade) being the colour of mourning. Another observed that these shops resembled the person who recommended their decoration (the Báshà); being fair without, but mean and dirty within.

There has been much talk here for some weeks past (ever since my arrival) of a project which the Báshà is about to put in execution, and which was at first said to be nothing less than the obstruction of the river by a dam to be thrown across it a few miles below the metropolis, in order to throw the whole tide of the river into the canals, and so to irrigate Lower Egypt more effectually: but latterly the real intention of the Báshà has become better known. The two branches of the Nile which enclose the Delta are to flow under two bridges, to be constructed

* Cp. *Mod. Eg.* pp. 481, ff.

a little below the point where the river divides, each in the neck of a peninsula formed by a bend of the river; across which neck or isthmus a new bed for the water is to be made as soon as the bridge is completed; after which the old bed surrounding the peninsula is to be filled up. These two bridges are to be connected with each other, and with Es-Suweys (or Suez) on the one side and Alexandria on the other, by a rail-road. The difficulty of the undertaking is immense; for these bridges are to withstand the tremendous tide of the inundation, and occasionally to be closed by flood-gates, so as to increase the height of the river above sufficiently to cause it to fill all the small canals by which the Delta and the adjacent provinces are irrigated. A similar undertaking was projected by Bonaparte, when here.

18th April.—9th Zu-l-Ḥeggeh.—This is the Day of the Pilgrimage; that is to say, of the six-hours' journey from Mekkeh to Mount 'Arafát, which gives to each person who performs it the title of Pilgrim, and without the performance of which he would not obtain that title even if he had journeyed to Mekkeh from the most remote part of the Muslim world. The halt upon Mount 'Arafát happening this year on a Friday, the Sabbath of the Muslims, has made several of my friends express great regret that they have been unable to perform the pilgrimage under such a propitious circumstance.

19th.—The 'Eed el-Kebeer.—Nothing unusual to remark upon.

May 25th.—We were somewhat alarmed to-day, about an hour after noon, by a shock of an earthquake. I was three times, with less than a moment's intervention, rather violently shaken on my seat; and several long cracks were opened in the walls of the house in which I am living. I have heard of no house having been thrown down or much injured by it. It is supposed to have shown its greatest violence (that is, to have originated) in Syria.

June 7th.—During the week which is now closing all classes of courtesans, including the *ghawázee* (or public dancing-girls), have been suppressed in the metropolis and its neighbourhood. This measure has been talked of, as about to be put in execution, for some months past. The courtesans had become extremely numerous, and were scattered in every quarter of the town; some of them living in houses almost fit to be the residences of grandees; and acquiring considerable wealth.

July 29th.—Went to the Pyramids of El-Geezeh. Stayed in "Caviglia's Tomb."

30th.—We again experienced a shock of an earthquake, more violent than the former, at about half-past nine P.M. Heard of no injury done.

Aug. 2nd.—Returned from the Pyramids.

5th.—The dam of the Canal of Maṣr cut. I have given an account of this in another note-book.*

12th.—Last night, Seleem Bey, a general in the Báshà's service, hired a large party of fiḳees, to perform a recital of the Ḳur-án, in his house in this city; and then went up into his ḥareem, and strangled his wife. He had written to Ibraheem Báshà, accusing this woman (who was the daughter of a Turk in high office) of incontinence; and asking his permission to punish her. He received for answer, that he might do as he pleased. He then sent Ibraheem Báshà's letter to Moḥammad 'Alee, asking the same permission of the latter; and received the same answer. The case presents a sufficient proof of Moḥammad 'Alee's ideas of justice and humanity. Had he wished to indulge his creature with permission to exercise the utmost severity of the law, he could only have said—"If you can produce four witnesses against your wife, or if you can swear that you have witnessed her crime by the oath ordained in cases of this kind, and she will not take the same oath that the accusation is false, let her be stoned to death."

Sept. 17th.—My 33rd birth-day. I have completed, as far as I can see, my notes on the manners and customs of the Muslims of Egypt. I have only to look over them; and to ask a few questions respecting the Copts.*

Oct. 27th.—I generally pay a visit to the shop of the Báshà's booksellers on the mornings of Monday and Thursday, when auction-markets are held in the street where the shop is situated, and in the neighbouring bázár of Khán El-Khaleelee (the chief Turkish bázár) which occasion the street above-mentioned to be much crowded, and to present an amusing scene: but I am often more amused with the persons who frequent the shop where I take my seat. When I went there to-day, I found there an old man who had been possessed of large property in land; but had been deprived of it by the Báshà, and been compelled to become a member of the university, the great mosque El-Azhar. This man, the Ḥágg . . . ., is a celebrated character. He rendered great assistance, both by his wealth and by active service, to Moḥammad 'Alee, in his contest with his predecessor, Khursheed Báshà, when the latter was besieged in the Citadel. The greater part of his property was confiscated by the man he had thus served, through fear of his influence. He thus shared the fate of most of those who had rendered eminent services to Moḥammad 'Alee; but he contrived to hide much of his wealth; and has since employed friends to trade with it privately on his account, so that he has still a large income; but the third part of his receipts he always gives to the poor. The elder of the two booksellers was relating his having just purchased a house. There lived next-door to him, he said, a fiḳee, a member of the Azhar, and of some repute; to whom 14 ḳeeráṭs (or 24th parts) of the house in which he (the fiḳee) lodged belonged: the other 10 ḳeeráṭs of this house belonged to a tailor. The bookseller's house was entered, from the roof, and plundered, three times, of wheat, butter, &c. The fiḳee was accused by the bookseller of having committed these thefts; and confessed that he had; urging, in palliation, that he had only taken his food. The bookseller caused him to be imprisoned in the Citadel; and, after he had been confined there many days, offered to procure his liberation if he would sell him the above-mentioned share of his house. This was done; it was sold for six and a half purses. The bookseller then wanted to procure the tailor's share; and proposed to him to repair or separate or sell: for the house was in a ruined state. The tailor, refusing to do either, was summoned to the Ḳádee's court, and compelled to sell his share; for which he demanded five purses. Having received this sum of money, he met, on his way home, a friend, whom he told what he had done. "You fool"—said his friend—"you might have asked ten purses, and it would have been given." The tailor threw down the purse in the middle of the street; kicked off his shoes; and for several minutes continued slapping his face, and crying out, like a woman,—"O my sorrow!"

* Cp. *Mod. Eg.* pp. 493—8.

* Here follows an account of the nine days' festival which took place on the marriage of the sister of Aḥmad Báshà; cp. Mrs. Poole's ***Englishwoman in Egypt***, vol. iii. pp. 61—77.

He then snatched up the purse, and ran home with it, crying in the same manner all the way; and leaving his friend to follow him with his shoes.—Soon after the bookseller had told this story, there joined us a Persian darweesh, whom I had often met there before, and a fat, merry-looking, red-faced man, loaded with ragged clothing, showing the edge of a curly head of hair below his turban, and carrying a long staff. Everybody at the shop, excepting myself, kissed his hand: he offered me his hand, and, after taking it, I kissed my own, and he did the same. I was informed that he was a celebrated saint. He took snuff; smoked from my pipe; and had a constant smile upon his countenance; though he seldom spoke: almost the only words he uttered were a warm commendation of an answer which I gave to the Persian: on his (the Persian's) asking me why I had not already departed from Maṣr as I had intended, I said that the servant of God was passive and not elective; and this sentiment, though common, seemed much to please the welee: he repeated it with emphasis. —There next joined us a man of a very respectable and intelligent appearance, applying for a copy of the sheykh Rifá'ah's visit to France, lately printed at Boolák. Asking what were the general contents of this book, a person present answered him, that the author relates his voyage from Alexandria to Marseilles; how he got drunk on board the ship, and was tied to the mast, and flogged; that he ate pork in the land of infidelity and obstinacy, and that it is a most excellent meat; how he was delighted with the French girls, and how superior they are in charms to the women of Egypt; and, having qualified himself, in every accomplishment, for an eminent place in Hell, returned to his native country. This was an ironical quizz on the sheykh Rifá'ah for his strict conscientious adherence to the precepts of El-Islám during his voyage and his residence in France. The applicant for this book had a cataract in each of his eyes. I advised him to seek relief from the French surgeon Clot Bey; but he said that he was afraid to go to the hospital; for he had heard that many patients there were killed and boiled, to make skeletons: he afterwards, however, on my assuring him that his fears were groundless, promised to go.—While I was talking with him, there began to pass by the shop a long funeral-train, consisting of numerous fikees, and many of the 'Ulamà. On my asking whose funeral it was, I was answered, "The sheykh El-Menzeláwee," sheykh of the Saadeeyeh darweeshes. I was surprised; having seen him a few days before in apparently good health. Presently I saw him walking in the procession. I asked again; and was answered as before. "Why," said I, "praise be to God, the sheykh is walking with you, in good health:" I was then told that the deceased was his wife. Some Saadeeyeh in the procession were performing a zikr as they passed along; repeating "Allah!" When the bier came in view, I heard the women who followed raising their *zagha'reet*, or cries of joy, instead of lamenting. The deceased was a famous saint. She was the sister of the late sheykh of the Saadeeyeh; and it is believed that her husband, the present sheykh, derived his miraculous powers from her. It is said that she prophesied yesterday the exact hour of her death this day. The women began to lament when the corpse left the house; and, as usual when this is done at the funeral of a saint, the bearers declared that they could not move it: as soon as the lamentations were changed to the cries of joy, the bearers pretended to find their work quite easy.*

Nov. 6th.—To-day, as I was sitting at the booksellers' shop, a reputed welee, whom I have often seen, came and seated himself by me, and began, in a series of abrupt sentences, to relate to me various matters respecting me, past, present, and to come. His name is the sheykh 'Alee el-Leysee. He is a poor man, supported by alms: tall and thin and very dark; about thirty years of age; and wears nothing, at present, but a blue shirt and a girdle, and a padded red cap. "O Efendee!" he said, "thou hast been very anxious for some days. There is a grain of anxiety remaining in thee yet. Do not fear. There is a letter coming to thee by sea, that will bring thee good news. [He then told Lane that all his family were well except one, who was then suffering from an intermittent fever, which was proved afterwards to be true.] . . . . . . I wanted to ask thee for something to-day; but I feared: I feared greatly. Thou must be invested with wiláyeh" (i. e. be made a welee): "the welees love thee; and the Prophet loves thee. Thou must go to the sheykh Mustafà El-Munádee, and the sheykh El-Baháee!" (These are two very celebrated welees). "Thou must be a welee." He then took my right hand, in the manner which is practised on giving the covenant which admits a person a darweesh, and repeated the Fát'ḥah; after which he added, "I have admitted thee my darweesh." Having told me of several circumstances relating to me, some of which he had doubtless learned of persons acquainted with me, and which I could not deny, and some which time only will prove true or false, he ventured at a further prophecy and hazardous guessing; and certainly his guessing was wonderful; for he informed me of matters relating to my family which were perfectly true, matters of an unusual nature, with singular minuteness and truth; making no mistake as far as I yet know. He then added—"To night, please God, thou shalt see the Prophet (Moḥammad) in thy sleep, and El-Khiḍr, and the seyd El-Bedawee. This is Regeb; and I wanted to ask of thee—but I feared—I wanted to ask of thee four piasters, to buy meat and bread and oil and radishes. Regeb! Regeb! I have great offices to do for thee to-night." Less than a shilling for all that he promised was little enough. I gave it him for the trouble he had taken; and he muttered many abrupt prayers for me.*—It is just a year, to-day, since I embarked in London for this country.

7th.—I saw, in my sleep, neither Moḥammad nor El-Khiḍr nor the seyd El-Bedawee; unless, like Nebuchadnezzar, I cannot remember my dreams. The welee, therefore, I fear, is a cheat.

11th.—The Turkish pilgrims are beginning to arrive, in considerable numbers.—Four men were beheaded to-day, for repeated robberies and murders.

18th.—Went to the Moolid of the Seyyideh Zeyneb; which I have described in note-book no. 3.†

20th.—About a hundred boys, from about 11 to 14 years of age, were conducted by my house this evening, to be enlisted. The mothers of many of them followed, screaming, and with their heads, faces, breasts, and the fore part of their clothing, plastered with mud.

22nd.—The government has given orders, which are being put in execution, to pull down the maṣṭabahs and the saḳeefehs, or coverings, of matting, in almost all the sooḳs, or báзárs, and most of the thoroughfare streets. The former are not to be rebuilt in the more narrow and more frequented streets, and in

* Cp. notes to the *Thousand and One Nights*, 2nd ed., ii., p. 64.

* Cp. *Thousand and One Nights*, i., p. 212. † Cp. *Mod. Eg.* pp. 467,8.

most other parts are only to be made about two spans wide. The saḳeefehs are not to be replaced unless constructed of wood. The reason for pulling down or altering the masṭabahs is to afford more room for the passengers, and particularly for the Báshà's carriages, and for carts which are to be employed to remove dust and rubbish. The appearance of the city is rapidly changing, and losing its Arabian aspect.

24th.—The sheykh 'Alee told me to-day that I should not yet set out on my voyage home. In the evening news arrived of the plague having broken out in Alexandria, which prevents my going as I had intended by a ship now loading. I was packing to leave Maṣr. I fear I shall be detained here until next spring or summer.

28th.—Witnessed the festival of the Meạrág, described in note-book no 3.*

1st December.—The shopkeepers are decorating (as they call it) their shops; and most of the larger private houses, and many others, in the thoroughfare streets, are undergoing the same operation, by order of the government, in honour (it is said) of Ibraheem Báshà, who is soon expected in Maṣr, from Syria. Most of the shops and houses are daubed with red and white, in broad, horizontal stripes; which, being very ill done in general, must be called in truth the reverse of decoration. Others are daubed in a more fanciful and more rude style, with lines, spots, &c., of red upon a white ground; and some, with grotesque representations of men, beasts, trees, boats, &c., such as very young children in our country would amuse themselves by drawing.

26th.—I have been in Cairo just a year. I begin now to write out the fair copy of my work on the Modern Egyptians. The plague continues at Alexandria.

4th January, 1835.—The plague has spread beyond Alexandria, and to-day a Maltese, from Alexandria, died here, in the Frank quarter, of this disease. I prepare immediately to go to Thebes, to be secure from the plague, as it is expected now to spread in Cairo. Mr. Fresnel is to accompany me.

5th.—Engaged a large boat to take us to Thebes, for four hundred piasters.

8th.—Embarked for Thebes, in the afternoon. Proceeded to Maṣr el-'Ateeḳah.

9th.—Contrary wind. Remained at Maṣr el-'Ateeḳah.

10th.—Fine wind. Passed Riḳḳah in the evening.

11th.—High N. wind. Arrived at Benee Suweyf at noon. Here some fakeers, thinking us Turkish pilgrims, came and recited the Ḳur-án, for alms, by our boat. Proceeded.

12th.—Passed El-Minyeh after sunset.

13th.—Stopped before the grottoes of Benee Ḥasan at night. Early next morning landed to walk to the Speos Artemidos, which I had not hitherto seen. Took with me one of my servants (Khaleefeh, a young man), a Copt whom we had taken as a passenger to Thebes ('Abd el-Mellák), and two boatmen; one of these two boatmen was a very fine man, the other an old, fat, inactive fellow. Put my pistols in Khaleefeh's girdle; and myself carried nothing but my sword. A little above the grottoes above-mentioned is a ruined and deserted village by the river. About a mile further is another ruined village partly inhabited; and about the same distance beyond this is a third village, wholly inhabited, with palm-trees. We passed the first and second villages. A little beyond the latter we turn towards the mountains, and find a wide ravine or valley, in the right or southern side of which are several grottoes along the lower part of the rock. As we approached this ravine, several groups of people came out from the second village, with nebboots; and some with guns and pistols: two groups, about a dozen altogether, followed us: we saw that we were in danger, but it was too late to retreat. The men came to us. Some went back; others came; and soon there came another group from the third village, with a man in a clean blue gown, meláyeh, and white turban: these sat a while at the entrance of the ravine, while we were within, with the other men, who spoke civilly to us, but looked exceedingly treacherous and savage. A boy who accompanied them whispered to my servant and the younger boatman to keep close to me; for that the men with him had come to take them for soldiers. As it was now impossible to escape, I began to examine the line of grottoes, and prepared to make a drawing; merely that they might not be deceived by my dress, and take me for a Turk; as Europeans are more protected now in Egypt.—Soon after I had begun to make a sketch of this excavation, for the purpose before mentioned, the party that was at the entrance of the ravine came to us; and while my back was turned, they seized my servant and the younger boatman: the pistols were snatched from the servant and discharged and carried away and one of them broken, and the two prisoners were hurried off, while two men held me to prevent my drawing my sword, which, as they truly enough said, would have been the cause of my being immediately killed. As soon as the men who had taken my servant and boatman had proceeded a few hundred yards towards the principal village, the others left me with my two remaining attendants. As quickly as I could, I gathered together my instruments, and then pursued the party who had taken my two men. On my approaching them, three of them turned back (one of these, the chief, with the white turban, &c.), and desired me to return. I said I should follow them to the village, and there liberate the prisoners. Upon this, they attacked with their long staves; and I received from the chief a blow on my chest, which obliged me to retreat, or I should without doubt have been killed. A boy who was with them followed me; brought back my pistols; kissed them twice, and, kneeling on the ground, presented them to me. The flints were taken out. My servant and the boatman, as I learned afterwards, were taken before the governor of the district that same day. A woman followed my servant, with feigned lamentations, crying, "Why do you say you are not my son? Is not that decorated house the house of your father? and are not those palm-trees your father's palm-trees? and have not you eaten the red dates?" This was to make the governor think that he was a young man of the village, and not stolen: for a number of men had been required from the village for soldiers; and the people of the village had been employing themselves in taking passengers instead. They took five others that same day; and one of these, who attempted to escape, they shot, in the presence of my servant.—I returned to my boat, with the intention of applying immediately to the governor (*ma-moor*) of the district. We were informed that he was at the village of Sáḳiyet Moosà, a few miles higher up the river, on the opposite (or western) bank. On arriving there, we found that he was at the opposite village of Esh-sheykh Timáee. The wind was so violent that we could not cross over with safety until the evening. We then landed there, about an hour after sunset. Accompanied by Mr. Fresnel, I went to his house. He was sitting with a

* Cp. *Mod. Eg.* pp. 468—70.

number of attendants, in an open-fronted room (a maḳ'ad) facing a court, and, after the day's fasting (it being Ramaḍán), was amusing himself by listening to the chanting of a public reciter of poetry. We entered with an abrupt and consequential manner, necessary to be assumed on such an occasion; and the governor rose to us, returned us the Muslim salutation, and gave up his own place to me; for I, having to make the complaint, was foremost. He handed me the snake of his sheesheh; and coffee was brought. I then made my complaint, with an air of assumed pride, shewed our firmáns, which nobody present could read, and demanded the restoration of my servant and boatman, and the punishment of the men who had assaulted me; particularly of him who had struck me. The ma-moor did not confess that the servant and boatman had been brought to him that day at Benee Ḥasan, which was the case; but promised that they should be restored, and that he would soften the feet of the men who had assaulted me. — On the following morning the servant was brought and given up to me; but the persons who brought him declared to the ma-moor that the boatman had made his escape, and that the men who had assaulted me had fled. So that I failed in my object of punishing them and gained but half what I wished. I found afterwards that the man who struck me was the sheykh of Benee Ḥasan: had I known this before, I could have insisted upon his being punished; as they could not have had the impudence to say that the sheykh would run away from his superior officer.

14th.—Having obtained the liberation of my servant, proceeded to Mellowee. Remained there the following day.—15th. Proceeded to Gebel El-Ḳuseyr. — 17th. Becalmed under Gebel El-Ḳuseyr. Towed a little. — 18th. Passed Menfeloot after sunset.—19th. Arrived at Asyoot at 1 P.M. Proceeded in the evening.—20th. Passed Aboo Teeg at 1 P.M.—21st. Passed Akhmeem in the afternoon.—22nd. Arrived at Girga. This town is much ruined since I was last here: it has suffered much from the river. Proceeded about noon. Made but little way. Saw a crocodile.—23rd. Calm. Thermometer 73°. Proceeded by towing. Approaching the neighbourhood of Farshoot, saw nine crocodiles together, and shortly after, nineteen more.—24th. Arrived at Hoo at sunset.—25th. To Dishneh.—26th. Saw nine crocodiles on two sand-banks opposite Dendara. Arrived at Ḳinè at night.—27th. Passed Ḳuft at night.—28th. Saw about forty vultures (most of them rakhams, but many nisrs) on a sand-bank, in the morning, near the skeleton of a crocodile: afterwards, many pelicans and cranes. Proceeded a little way by towing, and afterwards by sail.—29th. Last day of Ramaḍán. Arrived at El-Ḳurneh about 1 P.M.

It was our intention to take up our quarters in a tomb which had been converted into a convenient dwelling by Mr. Wilkinson and Mr. Hay. We found Mr. Gosset occupying one apartment of it: I have taken possession of another apartment, separated from the former by a low wall with a door; and Mr. Fresnel has settled in a tomb just below, which was occupied by Bonomi and other artists in the employ of Mr. Hay. Our abode is in the Hill of the Sheykh, overlooking the whole plain of Thebes. A man named 'Owad has the charge of it; and Mr. Gosset and I pay him each 15 piasters a month for his services.

April 3rd.—The Báshà has paid a visit to this part of Egypt; went as far as Isna; and has just passed us on his way down. It is said that he came to inspect the state of the agriculture and to inquire into the conduct of the local governors; which he has not done. He has caused the villages of Erment to be destroyed; and the sheep &c. of all the inhabitants and of strangers who had sent their cattle &c. thither for pasture to be confiscated; because many of the peasants of these villages could not be made to pay their taxes.

17th.—Good Friday.—A man of this place died to-day of the plague, taken by wearing the clothes of a Nubian boatman, who was landed here five days ago, ill of this disease, and placed under the sycamore at the landing-place to die; where he did die very soon after. The man of this place who died to-day was a relation of my guard; whom, as he has had intercourse with the family of the dead man, and, I am told, attended the funeral, I am obliged to dismiss for a time. Put ourselves in strict quarantine. M. Mimaut, the French Consul-General, who is staying at Luxor, put a stop next day to all communication between this side of the river and the opposite; but is to send us meat &c. every two days.

20th.—Another man of this place, a relation of the one abovementioned, and father of Mr. Gosset's guard and water-carrier, died of the plague to-day, taken by wearing the clothes of the Nubian boatman.

May 9th.—No more deaths by plague having occurred here, we gave up our quarantine this day; having confined ourselves three weeks. The plague is said to be very severe in Alexandria; and becoming so in the metropolis.

June 25th.—The plague is said to have almost ceased in the metropolis and Alexandria in the beginning of this month. The French Consul has received intelligence that 75,000 persons have died by it in Maṣr; and that 6000 houses are completely desolated by this disease, and closed. We sent yesterday to Ḳinè, for a boat to convey us to Maṣr,—and Mr. Gosset left yesterday.

Our messengers came back from Ḳinè without having procured a boat; finding the demands for boat-hire very high, on account of the number of pilgrims on their return from the Ḥegáz. We sent again; and procured a large dahabeeyeh to convey us to Maṣr, for 650 piasters; of which I am to pay half.

30th.—Our boat arrived last night. We embarked to-day, and commenced our voyage at about 1 P.M.—1st July. Arrived early at Ḳinè. Went to the remains of Dendara: found the first little temple destroyed; a great portion of the portal before the great temple, and part of the great temple itself, the upper part of the middle of the east side. In and about the temple were many felláḥeen, hiding themselves, in the fear of being taken to work in making a new canal, or of being pressed for the army. Two or three cases of cholera had occurred at Ḳinè: I heard of three deaths by this disease here: it is said to be also in the Ḥegáz. Continued our voyage in the afternoon.—3rd. Arrived at Girga in the forenoon.—4th. Passed Akhmeem, at night.—5th. Stayed most part of the day at Gezeeret Shenduweel.—6th. Stopped at Tahta.—7th. To Aboo Teeg.—8th. Arrived at Asyoot, at 10 A.M.—9th. Arrived at Menfeloot, at 9 A.M. Proceeded at noon. Menfeloot has lately been much ruined by the inundations, towards the river.—10th. Passed Tell el-'Amár'neh at sunset.—11th. Passed El-Minyeh after sunset.—12th. To Aboo Girga.—13th. Passed Benee Suweyf, at night.—14th. Saw the Pyramids of Dahshoor in the evening.—15th. Arrived at Maṣr el-'Ateekah, at 8 A.M.: landed, and took up my abode in my former house.

A few deaths by cholera have happened in the metropolis and its neighbourhood. Some persons say that the plague has not yet quite ceased here. It has destroyed a third, or more, of the population of the city; about 80,000 persons; chiefly young persons, between 10 and 25 years of age; and most of these females. It has also been particularly fatal to Franks and other foreigners. 6000 houses here have been desolated by it; and are closed. In riding through the whole length of the metropolis, from south to north, I saw so few people in the streets compared with the number I used formerly to see, and so few shops open, that I should have thought that more than half the inhabitants had been destroyed. This is partly to be accounted for by the fact of many persons having fled to the country to escape the plague.—Last Friday, a number of persons spread a report that many of the victims of the plague had been buried alive (in trance), and numerous women, children, and others, went out to one of the great burial-grounds to disinter their relations and friends, taking with them bread, water-melons, &c., for them. Several tombs were opened. Some ignorant people even believed that the general resurrection was to take place on that day. The plague is still in Alexandria; but slight; two or three cases a day.

16th.—To-day, being Thursday, when lamentations are renewed for persons not long dead, I was awoke early from my sleep by wailings in several houses around me. A few persons still die of the plague here. These cases are of persons attacked by the disease some days ago; a week or more. No new cases are heard of.

20th.—Exaggerated reports are spread respecting the cholera here. It makes but little progress: the deaths not ten a day. The plague is very severely raging at Dimyát.

The journal ends with two stories of the Plague noted on August 1st and 2nd. Shortly after this Lane returned to England, carrying with him the manuscript of certainly the most perfect picture of a people's life that has ever been written, his "Account of the Manners and Customs of the Modern Egyptians."

1835—1842.

"The Modern Egyptians."

"The Thousand and One Nights."—"Selections from the Ḳur-án."

THE first thing that occupied Lane's attention on his return to England was naturally to put the final touches to his book and to see it through the press. What with the ordinary delays of printers, and the time needed for the preparation of the wood-cuts, which he drew with his own hand on the blocks, the work was not published till December, 1836, by Mr. Charles Knight, who had bought the first edition from the Society for the Diffusion of Useful Knowledge.

Those who had advised the Society in the matter had no cause for disappointment in the success of the book. The first edition, in two volumes, was wholly bought up by the booksellers within a fortnight of its publication. The second, the Society's, was to be much cheaper, and was therefore held back until the market was entirely cleared of the first. In 1837, however, it was brought out and stereotyped, with a first impression of four thousand copies, which were speedily disposed of. Two thousand five hundred copies in addition were struck off from the plates, and continued to be sold long after other and better editions had been issued. A third and revised edition, also in two volumes, was published by Mr. Knight in 1842. In 1846 the book was added to the series of "Knight's Weekly Volumes." Five thousand copies were printed, and half this large issue was sold by 1847. In 1860 my father, E. Stanley Poole, edited the work again, in a single volume, for Mr. Murray, with some important additions; and from this, which must be regarded as the standard edition, a reprint in two small volumes was produced by Mr. Murray in 1871, and is now almost exhausted. Altogether, nearly seventeen thousand copies of the "Modern Egyptians" have been sold, a sufficient evidence of its popularity in England. If it is added, that a German translation was almost immediately produced, with the author's sanction, and that editions have been published in America, some idea will be formed of the European and trans-Atlantic repute of the book.

The reviewers, who do not always echo the popular sentiment, were in this case singularly unanimous in their praise. A feeble but well-meant critique in the "Quarterly Review" could find no fault except with Lane's way of spelling Oriental names, which the reviewer travestied and then pronounced pedantic: the substance of the book met with his unqualified admiration. So it was with, I think, all the criticisms that appeared on the work. It was universally pronounced to be a masterpiece of faithful description.

Oriental scholars, it need hardly be said, received it with acclamation. The distinguished Arabist, Fresnel, after a long residence in Egypt, wrote to Lane from Cairo in 1837: "I have read with a great deal of interest some of your chapters on the Modern Egyptians and felt immensely indebted to you for making me acquainted with so many things of which I should have remained eternally ignorant, had it not been for your *Thesaurus*." The following extract from my father's preface to the fifth edition explains very clearly in what the value of the work lies. If they are the words of a near kinsman, they are also those of an accomplished Arabic scholar and one who had lived long in Egypt.

"Of the Modern Egyptians, as the work of an Uncle and Master, it would be difficult for me to speak, were its merits less known and recognised than they are. At once the most remarkable description of a people ever written, and one that cannot now be re-written, it will always live in the literature of England. With a thorough knowledge of the people and of their language, singular power of description, and minute accuracy, Mr. Lane wrote his account of the "Modern Egyptians," when they could, for the last time, be described. Twenty-five years of steam-communication with Egypt have more altered its inhabitants than had the preceding five centuries. They then retained the habits and manners of their remote ancestors: they now are yearly straying from old paths into the new ways of European civilization. Scholars will ever regard it as most fortunate that Mr. Lane seized his opportunity, and described so remarkable a people while yet they were unchanged.

"A residence of seven years in Egypt, principally in Cairo, while it enabled me to become familiar with the people, did not afford me any new fact that might be added to this work: and a distinguished English as well as Biblical scholar, the Author of 'Sinai and Palestine,' not long ago remarked to me, 'The Modern Egyptians is the most provoking book I ever read: whenever I thought I had discovered, in Cairo, something that must surely have been omitted, I invariably found my new fact already recorded.' I may add that a well-known German Orientalist [Dr. Sprenger] has lately visited Cairo with the express intention of correcting Mr. Lane's descriptions, and confessed that his search after mistakes was altogether vain."*

After the "Modern Egyptians" had been published, and his time was once more his own, Lane employed himself in that favourite amusement of learned men, attending the meetings of societies. Those bodies, however, had more life in them forty years ago than now, and their proceedings had not yet approached that debatable border line between learning and futility which has now been successfully crossed. The Asiatic Society, which still produces some good work, was then under the inspiriting influence of the Earl of Munster, and the Oriental Text Committee and the Translation Fund were bringing out that long series of works of which many are still most valuable, although some have deservedly died the death. At the meetings of these societies Lane was a prominent figure. Lord Munster regarded him as his right hand and would have his advice on everything connected with the work of the Committee and the Asiatic Society; and any problem in Arabic literature, any inscription that defied Prof. Shakespear and the other Orientalists of the Society, was referred to Lane and generally decided on the spot. But he was not a man to remain long contented with a sort of learned kettledrum-tea existence. He was wishing to be at work again; and the opportunity came very quickly. In the "Modern Egyptians" he had referred to the "The Thousand and One Nights," or "Arabian Nights" as they are commonly called, as forming a faithful picture of Arab life: and the remark had drawn more attention to the work than when it was merely regarded as a collection of amusing and questionably moral tales to be given to children with due caution. Lane was asked to translate them afresh. In his prospectus he showed that the ordinary English version was taken from Galland's French translation, which abounds in perhaps every fault which the most ingenious editor could devise for the destruction of a hated author. It is thoroughly inaccurate in point of scholarship; it misunderstands the simplest Arab customs and turns them into customs of India or Persia; it puts the whole into a European dress which destroys the oriental glamour of the original; and it mixes with the true Arabian Nights others which do not belong to the collection at all. Our English versions, based upon this, only magnified each vice and extinguished the few merits the work possessed in the French.

---

* E. Stanley Poole, Editor's Preface to 5th [Standard] Ed. *Modern Egyptians.*

In these circumstances there could be no question that a new translation was necessary; and there was no man better able to translate a work illustrative of Arab life than the author of "The Manners and Customs of the Modern Egyptians." Cairo in Lane's time was still emphatically the Arab city. It had become the sovereign centre of Arab culture when the City of Peace was given up to the Tatar barbarians and Baghdad was no longer the home of the Khaleefehs. Under the Memlook Sultáns, Cairo, and with it Arab art, attained the acme of its splendour; and the kings who left behind them those wonderful monuments of their power and culture in the Mosques of El-Ḳáhirah left also an established order of life, stereotyped habits of mind, and a ceremonious etiquette, which three centuries of Turkish rule had not yet effaced when Lane first visited Egypt. The manners, the dwellings, and the dress; the traditions and superstitions, the ideas about things in heaven above or in the earth beneath, of the actors in "The Thousand and One Nights" were those of the people of Cairo under the Memlook Sultáns: and Lane was fortunate enough to have seen them before the tide of European innovation had begun to sweep over the picturesque scene.*

Lane resolved to make his translation of "The Thousand and One Nights" a cyclopædia of Arab manners and customs. He added to each chapter a vast number of notes, which are in fact monographs on the various details of Arabian life. Never did he write better or bring together more happily the results of his wide oriental reading and of his long Eastern experience than in these Notes. The translation itself is distinguished by its singular accuracy and by the marvellous way in which the oriental tone and colour is retained. The measured and finished language Lane chose for his version is eminently fitted to represent the rhythmical tongue of the Arabs: and one cannot take up the book without being mysteriously carried into the eastern dream-land; where we converse gravely with wezeers and learned sheykhs, or join the drinking-bout of a godless sultán; uncork 'Efreets and seal them up again in their bottles with the seal of Suleymán, on whom be peace; follow Hároon-er-Rasheed and Jaạfar in their nightly excursions; or die for love of a beautiful wrist that has dropped us a kerchief from the latticed meshrebeeyeh of the hareem. Those who would know what the Arabs were at their best time, what were their virtues and what their vices, may see them and live with them in Lane's "Thousand and One Nights."

The book came out in monthly parts in the years 1838 to 1840. It was illustrated profusely by W. Harvey, who succeeded in some slight degree in catching the oriental spirit of the tales; though his work is decidedly the least excellent part of the book. After the first edition, in three volumes, 1840, two others were produced in which the publishers sought to popularize the translation by restoring the old ignorant spelling of the heroes' names. All recognized the value of Lane's work, but they still had a prejudice in favour of their old acquaintances Sinbad and Giaffer, and could not immediately get used to the new comers Es-Sindibád and Jaạfar. Moreover they missed Aladdin, who even under his reformed name 'Alá-ed-deen was not to be found in Lane at all. To obviate these objections, the publishers produced an emasculated edition reviving all the old mistakes and adding the inauthentic tales. Lane, however, immediately made a strong protest and the edition was withdrawn from circulation. In 1859 my father brought out the second and standard edition of the work, and

---

* I do not wish this to be taken as a defence of oriental abuses. There always comes a time when picturesque rottenness must give way to enlightened ugliness. But surely it is possible to reform the Turkish misgovernment of Egypt without pulling down the mosques and the beautiful palaces of Memlook Beys which are still to be found in old corners of Cairo. Is it really a matter of necessity for a reforming Turk to wear a tightly-buttoned frock-coat? But Easterns seem to be able to copy only those peculiarities of Europeans which rightly make us a laughing stock to the judicious savage.

this has since been several times reprinted; a new issue having been required this year. Although from the size and cost of the book,—a cost due mainly to the illustrations, which (as Lane himself thought) might well be dispensed with,—it cannot in its present form entirely drive out the miserable versions that preceded it, and that still live in the nursery: yet it is on all hands acknowledged to be the only translation that students of the East can refer to without fear of being misled. Every oriental scholar knows that the Notes are an essential part of his library.

After this translation was finished, Lane, since he could not be idle, arranged a volume of "Selections from the Ḳur-án," with an introduction, notes, and an interwoven commentary. The book did not appear till 1843, when its author was in Egypt and unable to correct the proofs. Consequently it is defaced by considerable typographical errors, and its publication in that state was a continual source of annoyance to Lane. The notion was an excellent one. He wished to collect together all the important doctrinal parts of the Ḳur-án, in order to show what the religion of Moḥammad really was according to the Prophet's own words: and he omitted all those passages which weary or disgust the student, and render the Ḳur-an an impossible book for general reading. The result is a small volume which gives the ordinary reader a very fair notion of the contents of the Ḳur-án and of the circumstances of its origin. In this latter part of the subject there is, however, room for that addition and improvement which thirty years of continued progress in oriental research could not fail to make needful: and such alteration will be made in the new edition which is presently to be published.

The "Selections" were but a *παρεργον*. Lane was already embarked in the great work of his life, a work to which he devoted thirty-four years of unintermitting labour.

1842—1849.

THE THIRD VISIT TO EGYPT.

LANE had seemingly exhausted modern Egypt. He had described the country, drawn a minute picture of the people's life, and translated their favourite romances. But there remained before him a still greater work, one indeed not bounded to any one country but concerning the whole Mohammadan world, and yet, like his other works, having its roots in Egypt. It was no longer a popular book that he was engaged upon: it appealed only to the narrow circles of the learned. But it is the work by which his name will ever be remembered, and by which England may claim the palm of Oriental scholarship, even above Germany, the home of Eastern study in Europe.

It was impossible for Lane to acquire his intimate knowledge of Arabic without perceiving the lamentable deficiencies of the materials for its study then existing in European languages. Especially weak were the dictionaries: for Grammar could boast the magnificent works of De Sacy and Lumsden; whereas in the dictionaries of Golius and Freytag, if there were signs of learning and industry, there was also a dearth of material and a want of scholarship to interpret it, still more a lack of knowledge of Eastern minds, which resulted in statements calculated as much to mislead as to instruct the student. So long as the young Orientalists of Europe were reared upon the meagre food thus afforded to them, the standard of scholarship would be low and the number of students limited. Lane was well aware that it was not necessary to submit to this state of things from a want of the means of reforming it. On the contrary he knew that in Cairo there existed the richest materials the Arabic lexicographer could desire; and he determined himself to work the quarry and to produce a thesaurus of the language, drawn from original sources, which should once and for all supersede the imperfect productions of Golius and Freytag and bring the labours and learning of the Arab lexicographers within the reach of European students.

The field into which Lane was about to throw all his energy was a peculiar one. The materials for composing such a work as he contemplated were singularly perfect. For the exceptional history of the Mohammadan Arabs had produced a nation of grammarians and lexicologists. The rapid spread of the tide of Muslim conquest had threatened the corruption and even the extinction of the language of the Ḳur-án; other tongues were beginning to intermix with the pure Arab idiom; and it was foreseen that, were the process suffered to continue undisturbed, the sacred book of the Muslims would soon become unintelligible to the great body of the Faithful.

"Such being the case, it became a matter of the highest importance to the Arabs to preserve the knowledge of that speech which had thus become obsolescent, and to draw a distinct line between the classical and post-classical language. For the former language was that of the Ḳur-án and of the traditions of Moḥammad, the sources of their religious, moral, civil, criminal, and political code, and they possessed in that language, preserved by oral tradition,—for the art of writing in Arabia had been almost exclusively confined to the Christians and Jews, — a large collection of poetry consisting of odes and shorter pieces, which they esteemed almost as much for its intrinsic merits as for its value in illustrating their law. Hence the vast collection of lexicons and lexicological works composed by Arabs and by Muslims naturalized among the Arabs; which compositions, but for the rapid corruption of the language, would never have been undertaken.

In the aggregate of these works, with all the strictness that is observed in legal proceedings, ... the utmost care and research have been employed to embody everything that could be preserved or recovered of the classical language, the result being a collection of such authority, such exactness and such copiousness as we do not find to have been approached in the case of any other language after its corruption or decay." *

The earlier lexicographers and commentators constitute the authorities from whom all later writers have gathered their facts. They speak either of their own authority or they cite a statement—a word or a signification—illustrated often by a proverb and more frequently by a couplet, for all of which they produce what may be called a pedigree, so rigidly do they seek to exclude chance of error. "Most of the contents of the best Arabic Lexicons was committed to writing, or to the memory of students, in the latter half of the second century of the Flight, or in the former half of the next century . . . . From these and similar works, either immediately or through the medium of others in which they are cited, and from oral tradition, and, as long as it could be done with confidence, by collecting information from the Arabs of the desert, were composed all the best lexicons and commentaries on the classical poets, &c." † The information these lexicons impart is conveyed after the strict rules of the science of lexicology. Probably no original authorities are so thoroughly original as the works written in accordance with its rules. The writer of such a dictionary frequently says,—"I have heard an Arab of such a tribe say so-and-so," in support of a word or phrase. If he quotes from contemporaries, or from what constituted *his* original authorities, he always gives the source whence he gets his information. He is scrupulous not to assign undue weight to a weak authority. An authority was weak either because he lived after the classical age, or because he belonged to a tribe who spoke a corrupt dialect; or he might, if otherwise qualified, be known to be careless or otherwise inaccurate. The chronological limit of classicality was easily fixed. The period of classical Arabic does not extend much beyond the end of the first century of the Flight, except in the case of isolated tribes or rarely gifted men; but such are always quoted with caution. They were post-Moḥammadan. Even poets (and poetry is the mainstay of the Arab) born during the Prophet's lifetime were of equivocal authority. The unquestioned Arab—he who spoke the pure and undefiled tongue—was either a contemporary of Moḥammad's (i. e. born before but living during his time), or he altogether preceded him and belonged to the "Times of Ignorance." The purest of the recognized tribes were generally considered to be those who dwelt between the lowlands of the coast tracts and the inhabitants of the mountains, or as Aboo-Zeyd somewhat vaguely expresses it, "the higher of the lower and the lower of the higher."‡

Thus the great Arabic dictionaries were gradually compiled. To enumerate them or to attempt to distinguish their several merits is beyond my present object.§ It is enough to say that rather more than a hundred years ago a learned dweller in Cairo, the Seyyid Murtaḍà, collected in a great lexicon, which he called the Táj-el-'Aroos, all that he deemed important in the works of his predecessors. He took for his text a celebrated dictionary, the Ḳámoos of El-Feyroozábádee, and wrote his own vast thesaurus in the form of a commentary upon it, interweaving the results of all the great authorities (especially the Lisán-el 'Arab) and adding from his own wide learning much that is valuable. The Táj-el-'Aroos is, in fact, a

---

* *Preface* to *Lexicon*, viii. † *Preface*, xi., xii.

‡ Cp. an excellent review of Lane's *Lexicon*, Part I., in "The Times" of March 26, 1864, written by a known hand.

§ A full account of them is given in the *Preface* to *Lexicon*, Part I.

combination of all the leading lexicons, and as such, and being compiled with great care and accuracy, is unquestionably the chief and best of native Arabic dictionaries.

During his former residence in Egypt Lane had become aware of the existence of copies, or portions of copies, of this Thesaurus in Cairo; and the thought had come to him that herein lay the opportunity for constructing an Arabic Lexicon of a fullness and accuracy never yet dreamt of. To compose a work in English from the Táj-el-'Aroos would be, he saw, to provide the scholars of Europe with an authority once and for ever, from which there could be no appeal. But to attempt such a work would require another residence in Cairo, tedious and expensive transcribing of the Táj, long years of toil, and the wearisome labour of proof-sheets. And when done, who could be found to venture to publish so vast a work, involving peculiar printing at ruinous cost?

The days of patronage were over: authors no longer waited in the vestibules of great men with odes and dedications. But the spirit that prompted the finest patronage still existed. There were those among the noblemen of England who were ready to devote their wealth to the cause of culture and learning, and who were emulous of promoting a great work that could not advance without their help. In his first visit to Egypt Lane had met Lord Prudhoe and from that time something closer than mere acquaintance had sprung up between them. Few could know Lane without seeking to be his friend: and his worth was not that of an uncut diamond; the courtesy and grace of his manners were conspicuous. Lord Prudhoe found a delight in his society which did not vanish when they returned to England. He would constantly come to the house in Kensington, bringing some choice tobacco—the only luxury Lane indulged in—and there he would sit in the study, talking over old Eastern scenes they had witnessed together, and discussing the work then going on, "The Arabian Nights," and Lane's plans of future study and writing. It was during these frequent meetings in London that the idea of the Lexicon was talked over. Lord Prudhoe entered zealously into the project; offered to provide Lane with the means of collecting the materials in Cairo, and eventually took upon himself the main expense of the production of the work. To understand in any degree the generosity and public spirit evinced in this, it must be remembered that it was no ordinary book, costing a few hundred pounds, that was thus to be produced. It involved the employment for thirteen years of a learned scholar in Cairo, to transcribe the manuscript of the Táj-el-'Aroos; it required peculiar type to be designed and cast; it demanded skilled compositors of special acquirements; and finally, it was not a work of ordinary size, but one of eight large quarto volumes with three columns in the page, reaching when completed probably to four thousand pages. To give more precise details of the expense of the work would be an impertinence to the princely generosity that took no count of the cost. From first to last the Lexicon was the care of Lord Prudhoe. In 1847 he succeeded his brother as fourth Duke of Northumberland, but the serious addition to his duties caused by this and by his acceptance of a place in the Cabinet brought about no change in his interest in Lane's work. He would come almost yearly to Worthing to see my Uncle and learn from himself how "the great book" went on. Of the many who regretted His Grace's death in 1864, few lamented it more deeply than Lane. It was the severing of a long friendship, and a friendship which the generosity of the Duke, instead of destroying, as is the manner with the meaner sort of men, had cemented. But the bright example of the Duke created its own reflection. That support which for nearly a quarter of a century, "with a kindness and delicacy not to be surpassed," he had accorded to Lane's great undertaking was at once and at her own express wish* continued by his widow, Eleanor, Dowager Duchess of Northumberland; and to Her Grace's munificence it still owes its further publication.

* On the death of Duke Algernon, his successor, formerly Lord Beverley, expressed a strong wish to continue the support of the work; and his son, the present Duke, has shown an equal interest in it.

The financial difficulties of the work being now overcome, Lane resolved on an instant departure for Egypt. His two previous visits had been solitary: but now he went surrounded by his family,—his wife, a Greek lady whom he had married in England in 1840, and his sister, Mrs. Poole, with her two sons, to whom he ever bore himself as a father,—just as he did twenty-five years later to two nephews of the next generation. A great sorrow had lately come upon them in the death of Lane's mother. In old age her intellect was as bright, her character as firm and tender, as they had ever been. To her sons and daughter she was as an angel from heaven. Over her youngest son, though he had lived among strange peoples and passed through dangers by sea and by land and was now a man on whom the eyes of the learned waited, this gentle woman still exercised that supreme influence which had inspired him when a boy with the noble principles and pure aspirations of the Higher Life; and to the last he rendered her the same love and obedience he had given as a child. It was this sore trouble that decided Mrs. Poole, who had lived in late years always with her mother, on accompanying her brother to Egypt, and from this time to his death she never left him for more than a few days at a time, unless summoned by the illness of her own sons.

In June 1842 the little party of five returned to London from Hastings, whither they had removed in the autumn of the preceding year; and on July 1st they sailed for Alexandria in the Peninsula and Oriental Company's Steamship "Tagus," in itself an agreeable contrast to the small sailing vessels in which Lane had hitherto travelled, but still more pleasant in consequence of the special instructions of the Directors of the Company as to the comfort of their distinguished passenger. On July 19th they reached Alexandria, whence after a day or two they sailed up the Maḥmoodeeyeh for Cairo. At first the whole party, but especially the two boys, then only twelve and ten years old, were so ill that it became doubtful whether a return to England were not the only remedy. The seasoning sickness, however, passed away, and on arriving at Booláḳ on July 27th Lane began again to look for a house, taking up quarters meanwhile at the General Consul's residence, which Col. Barnet (like Mr. Salt on a former occasion) had courteously placed at his service. It was not till three weeks later that a suitable house could be found, and from the one they then entered, in the Darb-el-Gemel, their servants, and therefore themselves, were driven, after a determined resistance of two months, by a series of extraordinary sounds and sights, which the Muslim servants attributed to the haunting of the place by a Saint and an 'Efreet, and which have not yet received a satisfactory explanation.* Being at length fairly expelled, like many people before and after them, they took refuge (in January 1843) in a house in the Hárat es-Saḳḳá-een, where they remained till the beginning of 1845, when they once more removed, to the Ḳawádees, where they lived till their return to England in 1849.

It was a pleasant little society they entered into, for the seven years of their stay in Cairo: but it was too changing for strong friendships. There were it is true some kindly people always living in Cairo: such as the English Missionary, Mr. Lieder, and his good-natured wife; the English physician Dr. Abbott, to whose friendly services Lane owed much, and not least the Consul Mr. Walne. And for a long time Fulgence Fresnel was in Cairo and constantly with his fellow Orientalist, for whom he felt the affection of a brother. Mr. James Wild, too, the greatest authority on Arab art, was a very welcome addition to the little circle of friends, and it was perhaps partly his long association with Lane that opened his eyes to the beauty of Arab, as distinguished from Moresque, architecture. And the latter part

* For an account of the really curious phenomena exhibited in this house see Mrs. Poole's *Englishwoman in Egypt*, i. pp. 70—78, 109—204; ii. pp. 1—2.

of their stay was brightened by the accession of two special friends,—Sir James Outram, the Bayard of India, who was never tired of coming to the house in the Ḳawádees; and the Hon. Charles Murray (now the Rt. Hon. Sir Charles Murray, K.C.B.), who had succeeded Col. Barnet as Consul-General, and who from the moment of his arrival exerted himself in every way to shield Lane from the importunate visits of passing travellers and to find amusement for my father and uncle, to whom he showed unvarying kindness. Among the Alexandrians, too, who constantly visited Cairo, Lane had found good friends, especially in the late Mr. A. C. Harris, Mr. Alexander Tod and his wife, and Mr. and Mrs Batho.

But with these exceptions the society around them was ever on the ebb and flow, as the season for visiting Egypt went and came again. Of the many travellers who came to see the country, or passed through it on the way to India, not a few had introductions to Lane, and the acquaintance once made was not likely to be dropped so long as they remained in Cairo and the Friday receptions at Lane's house continued. This day, the Sabbath of the Muslims, was set aside for receiving the calls of his Muslim and other friends, and his wife and sister used to see the Europeans who came, in the Hareem rooms; so that on this day there was always a double reception. On different Fridays many of the most distinguished Orientalists of Europe and learned Easterns might be found in Lane's study—Lepsius, Wilkinson, Dieterici, D'Abbadie, Fresnel, Pruner, and others; with Sheykh Moḥammad Eiyád, the Sheykh Rifá'ah, Ḥággee Ḥasan El-Burralee, the poet, and other literati of Cairo, who delighted to converse with the Englishman who had more than once decided the moot-points of the Ulamà of the Azhar; whilst the less exclusively Oriental friends, and the few ladies who visited Cairo, such as Harriet Martineau, would betake themselves to the other side of the house, where Mrs. Lane and Mrs. Poole were "at home."

Except on Fridays Lane denied himself to everybody, unless unusual circumstances made the interruption a necessity. On Sundays he never allowed himself, however much pressed for time, to continue his week-day work; nor did he like Sunday visitors. On all other days he devoted himself uncompromisingly to the preparation of his Lexicon. From an early breakfast to near midnight he was always at his desk, the long hours of work being broken only by a few minutes for meals—he allowed himself no more—and a scanty half-hour of exercise, spent in walking up and down a room or on the terrace on the roof. For six months together he did not cross the threshold of his house; and during all the seven years he only once left Cairo, and that was to take his wife and sister for a three days' visit to the Pyramids. At first he used to devote a short time every day to the classical education of his nephews, but even this was taken off his hands after a time by the kindness of the Rev. G. S. Cautley and the ready counsel of Mr. Charles Murray. But Lane continued to direct their studies, and it was by his advice that the elder devoted himself to the subject of modern Egypt and thus became a distinguished Arabic scholar, whilst the younger turned his attention to the ancient monuments, and, twice ascending the Nile and annotating Lane's earliest work, laid the foundations of his reputation as an Egyptologist.

The Lexicon was indeed begun in earnest. The first thing to be done was the transcription of the Táj-el-'Aroos, and for this purpose Lane before leaving England had already consulted Fresnel, who was then living in Cairo, and who, after careful investigation, recommended the Sheykh Ibráheem Ed-Dásooḳee for the work. The copyist must be able to do more than merely write the Arabic character, it need scarcely be said; he must understand the original as a scholar, and he must hold such a position among the learned of Cairo that he can be trusted with the manuscripts from the Mosques.

Such a man was the Sheykh Ed-Dásoo̱kee; ill-tempered and avaricious, but still the right man for the work. Lane at first hoped to obtain the loan of at least large portions of the manuscript from the Mosque of Moḥammad Bey. The Páshà himself, Moḥammad 'Alee, was anxious to further the work by any means in his power, and the Prime Minister, Arteen Bey, called upon Lane with the view of discovering in what manner the Government could assist him. But the loan of manuscripts from the Mosques was a request beyond the power even of Moḥammad 'Alee to grant; and Lane had to submit to the tedious process of borrowing through his Sheykh a few pages at a time, which were copied and then exchanged for a few more. Thus the transcription went on; and much of Lane's time was occupied in collating it with the original and in reading and annotating it in the company of the Sheykh Ed-Dásoo̱kee. But meanwhile there were other materials to be collected. It is true the main basis of the coming work was to be the Táj-el-'Aroos: but this was founded upon many other lexicons, and Lane determined so far as might be possible to verify its quotations and to take nothing at second-hand which could be obtained from the original source. Hence it was a matter of great consequence to gather together any manuscripts that could be bought in Cairo. Fresnel gave him three most valuable manuscripts, Mr. Lieder another; and by a careful watch on the book-market, by means of his old ally Sheykh Aḥmad, he was fortunate enough to accumulate more than a dozen of the most renowned lexicons; and thus he was able to test the accuracy of the Táj-el-'Aroos, and to add greatly to the perfection and authoritativeness of his own work.

After a preliminary study of Arabic lexicology,—a science complicated by technical terms of varying meaning,—and so soon as a portion of the Táj-el-'Aroos was transcribed, Lane began to compose his own Lexicon from the Táj and from the other dictionaries he had collected. Thus from year to year the work went slowly on; collating, collecting, composing filled each day, each month, each year. At length the materials were gathered, the Táj was transcribed up to a sufficiently advanced point, and Lane felt he need stay no longer in Egypt. So leaving Mr. Lieder to keep the Sheykh to his work of copying,—which, now it is finished, fills 24 large volumes,—Lane and his family bade farewell to the friends who had risen around them, and reaching Alexandria on the 5th October, 1849, sailed on the 16th for England, where they arrived on the 29th.

Such is the brief account of Lane's third visit to Egypt, and the beginning of the Lexicon. It was a time of unremitting exhausting labour: but it was a happy time. Lane had his wife and sister with him, and his home was brightened by two young faces, full of the excitement and delight of their new and marvellous surroundings. A cloud had fallen upon them, indeed, in 1844, when they heard of the death of the eldest brother, Theophilus Lane; and some days of deep anxiety had befallen Lane when both wife and sister lay dangerously ill with cholera and typhus fever. But on the whole the seven years had been years of happiness. His sister had gained for herself a place in literature by her "Englishwoman in Egypt," his two nephews had each marked out for himself a career as an Orientalist; he himself had accomplished his purpose and gathered together the materials and begun the composition of the great work of his life.

1849—1876.

The Arabic Lexicon.

Lane returned to Europe in 1849 the acknowledged chief of Arabic scholars. As the author of "The Modern Egyptians" his fame as the authority upon Egypt had been established; and his translation of the Arabian Nights had gained him the well-earned repute of accurate scholarship. But when it became known on what work he was now engaged and when specimens had shown how thoroughly that work would be done, all who had a care for learning were eager to offer their homage. As early as 1839 the Egyptian Society had enrolled him among their honorary members. In 1846 the German Oriental Society elected him a corresponding member, and in 1871 raised him to their highest rank, that of Ehren-Mitglied; and the example of Germany was followed, at a distance, by England, in the elections to the Honorary Membership of the Royal Society of Literature (1858) and of the Royal Asiatic Society (1866). In 1864 a vacancy occurred in the Académie des Inscriptions et Belles-Lettres of the Institut de France, by the promotion of De Witte, and Lane was unanimously elected a Correspondent in his place; and in 1875, on the occasion of its Tercentenary Festival, the University of Leyden accorded to him the degree of Honorary Doctor of Literature (Philosophiae Theoreticae Magister, Litterarum Humaniorum Doctor)—the only University degree he ever accepted, though not the only one offered to him. Those singular decorations, chiefly of military origin, which learned men are sometimes pleased to receive from their Sovereign, were by Lane decidedly though respectfully declined.

It was not, however, only in the matter of diplomas that a strong interest was shown in the great work my Uncle was preparing. So soon as the immense cost of the production was known, and before Lord Prudhoe had taken upon himself the expense of printing it, efforts were made, though not by the author, to obtain for it the support it needed. The Chevalier Bunsen exerted himself in a most friendly manner to gain the help of the English Universities: but it need hardly be said in vain. On the other hand, Germany was anxious to obtain the distinction of supporting it. At the instance of Bunsen, Lepsius, and Abeken, seconded by many others, it was agreed to offer to publish the Lexicon at the joint expense of the Prussian Government and the Berlin Academy of Sciences; and in 1846 Prof Dieterici was sent by the King of Prussia to Cairo to consult Lane's wishes. There were, however, conditions named to which Lane "could not willingly accede"; and moreover the arrangements for publishing in England were, by the zealous exertions of his brother Richard, nearly completed. In 1848 Lord John Russell, then Premier, made the first of a series of annual grants from the Fund for Special Service, which Lord Aberdeen continued in 1853; and in 1863 the grant was changed into an annual Pension on the Civil List.

On his return to England Lane soon settled down into his old routine of work. The composition went slowly on, and the manuscript of the Táj-el-'Aroos was gradually completed and sent over. At last, when he had been twenty years at the work Lane felt he might begin printing. In 1863 the First Part appeared, and in two years' time the Second followed. The Third was published in 1867, and the Fourth was printed in 1870, but the whole edition of one thousand copies was unfortunately burnt before it reached the publisher, with the exception of a single copy, and the entire Part had to be printed again, and therefore did not appear till 1872. After the necessary two years' interval Part V. was published in 1874. The Sixth Part was half-printed (as far as p. 2386) when its author died; and it has taken me a year to finish it (1877). Two Parts remain to be published, besides the Second Book, which may be estimated at one or perhaps two Parts more.

The publication of the Lexicon more than confirmed the high expectations that had been formed of it. As Jules Mohl well said, each article is a perfect monograph recording all that can be recorded on the subject. Each statement is followed by initials indicating the authorities from which it was derived, except where Lane has interwoven, within brackets, his own remarks and criticisms. Thus the work is, in point of authoritativeness, as sufficient for the student as if he possessed all the original manuscripts from which it is compiled. And whereas in the native writers method is unknown and meaning follows meaning in no settled sequence, Lane has succeeded in arranging each article in logical order, distinguishing between primary and secondary meanings, and making the various significations of each root a connected whole, instead of a chaotic congeries of inexplicable contradictions. The value of the manner as well as of the matter was instantly recognized by the Orientalists of Europe. There was no question of rivalry: all and each were agreed absolutely to submit to an authority which they saw to be above dispute. The greatest Arabist of Germany used to send Lane from time to time monographs of his own inscribed with the words "Unserem Grossmeister" and the like; and his homage is but an example of the reverence felt by all for the "Schatzmeister der arabischen Sprache."

But this universal appreciation of his work did not induce Lane to slacken for a moment the severe tension of his monotonous toil. He never rested on his laurels for a single day. He felt that it was a work demanding more than one lifetime, and he determined to leave as little undone as he could. After a year at Hastings he moved to the milder climate of Worthing, and during the twenty-five years he lived there he left the place but once, going to Brighton to see his old friend Outram; and nothing but severe illness could compel him to take a day's rest.

These years at Worthing were a time of constant unvarying labour,—"Of toil unsever'd from tranquillity, Of labour that in lasting fruit outgrows Far noisier schemes, accomplished in repose, Too great for haste, too high for rivalry." My Uncle would go to his desk after an early breakfast and work for three or four hours in the morning. An early dinner then made a necessary interruption, but afterwards he would begin again without a moment's delay, and continue writing till about four o'clock, when if the weather were fine and he in fair health he would walk with some of his family for an hour or so. Then he would come back to tea, and from six to ten would again bury himself in manuscripts, when a simple supper would end the day. At first his afternoon walk extended to three or four miles; but as his strength waned he gradually shortened the distance, till in his last year he could only saunter gently up and down some shady road for half-an-hour, and even then found himself exhausted. So too he was at last induced by the entreaties of his family to close his books at nine o'clock instead of ten; but even then he accomplished eight hours of study in the day. Nothing was allowed to interfere with these hours of work. Visitors who asked for him were strictly denied, and it was only by calling on his wife or sister that it was possible to see him, and then only if he was at a point in his composition where interruption would not entail a serious delay. Yet these rare moments were sufficient to win for him the lasting affection of a small circle of friends, who were never weary of offering him every attention in their power, and far from taking amiss his rigid seclusion endeavoured in all ways to shield him from the intrusion of strangers. He never called anywhere; but sometimes he would take his afternoon stroll in the gardens of Warwick House, where the bright society of his kindly hostesses was a delightful relief after his arduous hours of study.

One day in the week Lane closed his books. His early training had led him to regard Sunday as a day to be set apart for the things of religion, and his long sojourn in the East had in no wise weakened this feeling. In Egypt he had frequently attended the prayers at the Mosques and there comported himself in all outward appearance as a Muslim: but this was only because without thus conforming to the ways of the people he could never have acquired that knowledge of their character which he afterwards turned to so great an account. To the last he preserved the simple earnest faith of his childhood. His acquaintance with the original languages of the Old and New Testament and his insight into Semitic modes of thought had certainly modified his views on some of the minor points, but in the essential doctrines of Evangelical Christianity his belief never changed. But his religion was not a mere matter of intellectual adhesion to a given series of dogmas: he carried it into his every-day life. The forms of grace at meals, to most people purely ceremonious, were to him realities, and he never began his day's work without uttering the Arab dedication *Bismi-lláh*—"In the name of God." No one who came within the reach of his influence, however great the disagreement in opinion, could fail to be impressed with the earnestness of Lane's convictions; and few talked with him without going away better men than they came. His high and pure soul shone in his countenance, in his manner, in his every word. In his presence a profane or impure speech was an impossibility: yet no one was ever more gentle with that frailty for which the world has no pity. He was a Christian Gentleman, of a fashion of life that is passing away.

Sunday was to Lane a day of religion rather than a day of rest. In the morning or afternoon he would, if he were well enough, attend the office of the Church of England. The remainder of the day he spent chiefly in Biblical study, for which as a Hebrew scholar he possessed a critical knowledge that most of our divines might have envied. But it was not as a philological amusement that he pursued his researches. To him the Bible was the guide of his life; and he used his every endeavour to understand each doubtful passage, to emend each ignorant rendering, to interpret by the light of Semitic thought those dark sayings which the Aryan translators comprehended not, and not least to discover the harmony of Scripture and science. Thus his Sundays were not a time of thorough rest, such as the severe character of his week-day work required them to be. His Biblical reading often tried him more than a day's work at the Lexicon, and the parallel lines of ordinary print weakened eyes accustomed to the flexuous writing of Arabic manuscripts.

So the years wore on. Day followed day, and year year, without seeing any change in the monotony of Lane's life. Manuscript was written, proofs came and went, volumes were published, with unvarying regularity. The Lexicon was Lane's one occupation. The review and the essay, the offspring of the idle hours of learned men, had no attraction to a man who could not boast an idle moment. The only contributions he ever sent to a journal were two essays that appeared in the "Zeitschrift der deutschen morgenländischen Gesellschaft."* With these exceptions Lane never allowed any literary pursuit to divert him from his work. Even the revision of new editions of his earlier works demanded more time than he would spare, and he therefore left it to his nephews.

In 1867 Lane experienced one of the great sorrows of his life. He had seen both his sister's sons well advanced in their several careers: but he was destined to lose the one whom he had regarded as his own successor, the continuer of his life-work and the heir to his fame. My father's early death struck a heavy blow at Lane's love and hope. It was as the loss of an eldest son. Twenty-seven years before, he had taken to his home his sister and her sons; and now, with the same unselfish readiness, he opened his door to the three children whom my father's death had left orphans. From this time my Uncle's house was home and he was a second father to me. It was no slight sacrifice to admit three children to his quiet life: but he never let us know that it was a sacrifice at all. I can never forget the patience with which he suffered all our childish waywardness, the zealous sympathy with which he entered into our plans and pleasures, his fatherly counsel and help in our boy troubles, his loving anxiety in sickness. The few moments that he could spare from his work, which he might well have devoted to his own recreation, were given to us. He delighted to lead us to the studies he had loved himself, and would bring from the stores of his memory that scientific knowledge which had formed the favourite pursuit of his boyhood. And when I had chosen for myself the same field of study to which he had devoted his life, he gave me daily that help and advice which no one could give so well; read and revised everything I wrote; and at length, when his health was failing, gave me a last proof of his trust by confiding to me the completion of his own work.

The life of the great Orientalist was drawing to its close. Frequent attacks of low fever, added to the exhaustion of chronic bronchitis, had seriously weakened a frame already enfeebled by excessive study. I seldom left my Uncle for a few weeks without the dread that I should never see him again. It was a marvel how that delicate man battled against illness after illness, never yielding to the desire of the weary body for rest, but unflinchingly persevering with the great task he had set before him. His own knowledge of his constitution, acquired by long residence in places where medical help was not to be had, served him in good stead; and his life was ever shielded by the devoted care of his wife and sister, and the friendly attention of Dr. Henry Collet, who for many years afforded my Uncle the great advantage of his constant advice; a service of love which was continued after Dr. Collet's death, with the seal of long affection, by his son, Mr. A. H. Collet.

But the time came when there was no longer strength to withstand the approach of death. At the beginning of August, 1876, my Uncle was suffering from a cold, which presently showed signs of a serious nature. He went on with his work till Saturday the 5th; and then a decided change came over him. The weakness increased to such a degree on Sunday that he allowed me to support him about the house, though never before would he accept even the help of an arm. That evening we induced him to go early to his bed; and he never again rose from it. Two days passed in anxious watching. Everything

* The first of these is entitled "Ueber die Lexicographie der arabischen Sprache," and appeared in Bd. III. SS. 90—108 (1849). It is in the form of a letter to Prof. Lepsius, and treats of the principal Arabic Lexicons, and gives specimens of Lane's own work. The other article was "Ueber die Aussprache der arabischen Vocale und die Betonung der arabischen Wörter," an excellent treatise on the pronunciation of the Arabic Vowels and on the accent (Bd. IV. SS. 171—186, 1850).

that love could prompt, or the affection and skill of the doctor could suggest, was done. On Wednesday evening he seemed better: it was but the last effort. Early on Thursday morning the brave loyal spirit fought its last battle, and the mind that had endured the strain of fifty years of ceaseless toil, and yet had never known decay, at last found rest.

So ended the Scholar's life. It was begun, continued, and ended, without hope of reward. For fame he cared little; money, beyond what sufficed for his modest wants, he desired not. Pure love of knowledge was the motive of his work, and to learning, unsoiled with baser aims, he dedicated a long and studious life, rich in fruits. To the world Lane must be the ideal scholar. With us who knew him his memory will live in the sweeter thought of the noble and pure heart that wrapped us in its love.

ض

The fifteenth letter of the alphabet: called ضَادٌ: it is one of the letters termed مَجْهُورَة [or vocal, i. e. pronounced with the voice, and not with the breath only]; (TA;) and of the letters termed شَجْرِيَّة, ('Eyn, Mgh, TA,) from الشَّجْرُ, which is the place of the opening of the mouth: ('Eyn, Mgh, TA on the letter ج:) its place of utterance is from the extremity of the tongue [extended so as to reach] to the part next to the [lateral teeth called] أَضْرَاس; and it is more usually pronounced from the left side than from the right: the vulgar [sometimes] pronounce it as ظَآء, making its place of utterance to be between the extremity of the tongue and the central incisors, which pronunciation is peculiar to a dialect, as mentioned by Fr on the authority of El-Fadl: he says [also] that some of the Arabs substitute it for ظَآء, saying ضَهْر for ظَهْر; but that the doing thus, though allowable in speech, is not allowable in the reciting of the Book of God, which follows the rule, or usage, of the Prophet: (Mṣb in art. ضو:) or its place of utterance is from the foremost part of the edge of the tongue and the part next to the اضراس; and it has no sister [or analogue] accord. to Sb; but accord. to the 'Eyn, it is a sister of ذ and ث, and these three letters are termed لِثَوِيَّة [or gingival], because proceeding from the gum; the substitution of any of these, however, for another of them, vitiates prayers: (Mgh:) it is of the class termed الحُرُوفُ المُسْتَعْلِيَةُ: (L in art. ضود:) and is a letter peculiar to the Arabs, (L and Ḳ in that art.,) accord. to the general and correct opinion; (TA in that art.;) [whence the saying of Mohammad, أَنَا أَفْصَحُ مَنْ نَطَقَ بِالضَّادِ *I am the most chaste in speech of those who have pronounced the letter ḍád;* i. e., of the Arabs, agreeably with another saying, ascribed to him, mentioned voce بَيْدَ;] or it is a letter rarely occurring in the language of any other people. (L in that art.) — It is always a radical letter; and is [said to be] not substituted for another letter; (L in art. ضود;) [but it is so substituted in some cases of إِدْغَام, as, for instance, for the ل of the article ال, and in يَضَّرَّعُ for يَتَضَرَّعُ, and the like; and] it is sometimes substituted for ص, as in مَضَّ الرُّمَّانَةَ for مَصَّهَا, as Ibn-Oṣfoor says, and Ks mentions مَنَاض for مَنَاص; (TA;) and also for ل, as Ibn-Málik says in the Tes-heel, an instance of which is رَجُلٌ جَضْدٌ for جَلْدٌ, mentioned by J; (MF, TA;) and sometimes it is changed into ل, as in the instance of اِلْطَجَعَ for اِضْطَجَعَ. (Ṣ and L &c. in art. ضجع.) — [As a numeral, it denotes *Eight hundred.*]

ضأ

ضُؤْضُؤٌ: see the next paragraph but one, in two places. — Also The *bird called* أَخْيَل [q. v.]: (O, Ḳ:) so says ISd: but IDrd doubts its correctness. (TA.)

ضِئْضَأٌ: see the next paragraph.

ضِئْضِئٌ (Ṣ, O, Ḳ) and ▼ ضِئْضِىءٌ and ▼ ضُؤْضُؤٌ and ▼ ضُؤْضُوءٌ (O, Ḳ) and accord. to ISd ▼ ضِئْضَأٌ, which is of an extr. measure, (TA,) *Origin, root, race,* or *stock;* syn. أَصْلٌ: (Ṣ, O, Ḳ:) and the *place in which a thing originates;* syn. مَعْدِنٌ: (Ḳ:) hence, in a خُطْبَة of Aboo-Ṭálib, الحَمْدُ لِلّٰهِ الَّذِى جَعَلَنَا مِنْ ذُرِّيَّةِ إِبْرَاهِيمَ وَزَرْعِ إِسْمَاعِيلَ وَضِئْضِئِ مَعَدٍّ وَعُنْصُرِ مُضَرَ i. e. [*Praise be to God, who made us to be of the offspring of Abraham and of the seed of Ishmael and*] *of the stock of Ma'add* [*and of the race of Muḍar*]: and يَخْرُجُ مِنْ ضِئْضِئِ هٰذَا, occurring in a trad., i. e. *There shall spring from the stock,* or *race, of this;* or, as some relate it, it is [صِئْصِئِ,] with the unpointed ص, which means the same: and you say ضِئْضِئُ صِدْقٍ and ▼ ضُؤْضُؤُ صِدْقٍ [*An excellent origin* or *race*]: (TA:) [see an ex. voce بُؤْبُؤٌ, in art. بأ: and see also ضِنْءٌ:] or ضِئْضِئٌ &c. signify *multitude,* and *abundance, of offspring* or *breed;* (Ḳ, TA;) whence the ضِئْضِئ of sheep. (TA.)

ضَأْضَآءٌ, [in the CḲ الضَّأْضَأُ is erroneously put for الضَّأْضَآءُ,] as also ▼ ضَوْضَآءٌ (O, Ḳ, TA) and ضَوْضَى, (CḲ,) [which belong to art. ضو and the last of which is mentioned in the K in art. ضوض,] The *voices, cries,* or *shouts, of men,* (AA, O, Ḳ, TA,) *in war,* or *fight.* (O, Ḳ, TA.)

ضَوْضَآءٌ: see the next preceding paragraph.

ضُؤْضُوءٌ: } see ضِئْضِئٌ.
ضِئْضِىءٌ: }

مُضَوْضِئٌ or مُضَوْضٍ, (accord. to different copies of the Ḳ,) the former app. the original of the latter, [which is mentioned in the Ḳ in art. ضوض, but in the CḲ there written مُضَوْضِى,] (TA,) applied to a man, *Crying out, shouting* or *clamouring.* (Ḳ.)

ضأبل

ضِئْبِلٌ, and ضِئْبَلٌ, (Ṣ, M, O, Ḳ,) like زِئْبِرٌ and زِئْبَرٌ, (Ṣ, O, Ḳ,) the latter mentioned by IJ, (M,) but the former the more usual, (Ṣ, M,) *Calamity,* or *misfortune:* (Ṣ, M, O, Ḳ:) [it is said that] زِئْبَرٌ and ضِئْبَلٌ are the only instances of the measure فِعْلَلٌ: (Ḳ:) but accord. to Th, there is no word of this measure in the language; therefore, if these two have been heard, they are extr., unless, as Ibn-Keysán says, the ء be augmentative [and there is no reason for supposing it to be so as there is no known unaugmented word from the root ضبل]: (Ṣ, O:) صِئْبَلٌ, however, with ص, has been mentioned in the Ḳ, as having the same meaning, and is said to be of the dial. of Ḍabbeh, but not so well known as ضئبل, with ض; and IB mentions نِئْدَلٌ, meaning [likewise the same, or] "incubus," or "nightmare:" [but one of these four instances may be excepted; for] it is said in the Ḳ [in art. زأبر] that زِئْبَرٌ may be incorrect. (TA.)

ضأز

1. ضَأَزَ, aor. ـَ, inf. n. ضَأْزٌ and ضَأَزٌ, *He deviated from the right course;* or *acted unjustly, wrongfully, injuriously,* or *tyrannically;* (Ḳ;) like ضَازَ, aor. يَضِيزُ and يَضُوزُ. (TA.) — ضَأَزَهُ حَقَّهُ, (Ḳ,) aor. ـَ, inf. n. ضَأْزٌ and ضَأَزٌ, (TA,) [but the latter is probably a mistake for ضَأْزٌ,] *He deprived him,* or *defrauded him, of a part,* or *the whole, of his right,* or *due:* (Ḳ:) *he refused it to him;* or *withheld it from him:* (TA:) like ضَازَهُ إِيَّاهُ, aor. يَضِيزُهُ (Ṣ* and Ḳ* and TA in art. ضيز) and يَضُوزُهُ. (Ḳ* and TA in art. ضوز.)

ضَأْزَى: } see what here follows.
ضُؤْزَى: }

قِسْمَةٌ ضِيزَى, and ▼ ضُؤْزَى, and ▼ ضَأْزَى, (Ḳ,) the first mentioned by AZ (Ṣ in art. ضيز) and IAar, (TA,) and the second by Fr (Ṣ ubi suprà) and IAar, (TA,) and the third by Fr, (Ṣ ubi suprà,) *A defective,* (Ḳ,) or *an unjust,* (TA,) *division:* (Ḳ, TA:) as also ضِوزَى (IAạr, Ḳ) and ضُوزَى. (IAạr, TA.)

ضأل

1. ضَؤُلَ, [aor. ـُ,] (Ṣ, M, O, Mṣb, Ḳ,) inf. n. ضَآلَةٌ (Ṣ, M, O, Mṣb) and ضُؤُولَةٌ; (Mṣb;) and ▼ تَضَآءَلَ; (M, Mṣb, Ḳ;) *He, or it,* [accord. to the Ṣ and O app. said of a man or of a man's body, and accord. to the Mṣb said of a thing,] *was, or became, small in body,* or *small, and lean:* (Ṣ, O, Mṣb:) or *small, slender,* or *thin, and despicable, abject,* or *ignominious:* and also [simply] *lean,* or *spare:* (M, Ḳ:) and in like manner ▼ اِضْطَأَلَ: (M:) [or *lean,* or *spare, and weak:* or *weak, small, and slender,* or *thin:* (see the part. n., ضَئِيلٌ:)] or ضُؤُولَةٌ signifies the *being lean,* or *emaciated;* and *base, abject,* or *despicable.* (TA.) Accord. to AZ, (Ṣ, O, TA,) ضَؤُلَ, said of a man, (TA,) or ضَؤُلَ رَأْيُهُ, (Ṣ, O,) signifies *He was,* or *became, small,* or *little,* [*in estimation,*] *and weak in judgment.* (Ṣ, O, TA.)

3. ضَاءَلَ شَخْصَهُ, (M, TA,) [in the O, and in copies of the Ḳ, ضَآءَلَ, but the former is the right,] *He made his person small,* (M, O,* Ḳ, TA,) *in order that he might not appear.* (TA.) Zuheyr says,

• فَبَيْنَا نَذُودُ الوَحْشَ جَآءَ غُلَامُنَا •
• يَدِبُّ وَيُخْفِى شَخْصَهُ وَيُضَائِلُهْ •

[*And while we were driving the wild animals, our young man came, creeping, and hiding his person, and making it small*]. (M, TA.)

6. تَضَآءَلَ: see 1. In a verse of Aboo-Khirāsh, تَضَالَ لَهَا جِسْمِى [meaning *My body became lean, or spare, by reason of it,*] occurs for تَضَآءَلَ: or, as AA relates it, he said تَضَآءَلَّ لَهَا, with idghám. (M.) — Also *He became small,* or *thin; he shrank,* or *became contracted;* (O,* TA, and Ḥam* pp. 653 and 658;) by reason of abasement, (TA,) or from fear: (Ḥam p. 658:) *he hid his person, sitting, and shrank,* or *became contracted.* (M, Ḳ, TA.) And *It* (a thing) *shrank, became contracted,* or *drew itself together.* (TA.) AḤn has used it [in this sense] in relation to a herb, or leguminous plant. (M, TA.)

8. اِضْطَأَلَ: see 1.

ضُؤَلَةٌ, (Ṣ, O, TA,) like تُؤَدَةٌ, (O, TA,) in the copies of the Ḳ ضُؤْلَةٌ, but the former is the right, (TA,) an epithet applied to a man, (Ṣ, O,) *Lean,* or *spare:* (Ṣ:) or *weak,* (Ḳ, TA,) *lean,* or *spare, and despicable, abject,* or *ignominious.* (TA.) [See also ضَئِيلٌ.]

هُوَ عَلَيْهِ ضُؤْلَانٌ, (M, Ḳ, TA,) with ḍamm, (TA,) [in the CḲ, erroneously, ضَوْلَانٌ,] *He,* or *it, is a burden upon him;* syn. كَلٌّ. (M, Ḳ, TA.) — And حَسَبُهُ عَلَيْهِ ضُؤْلَانٌ *His grounds of pretension to respect,* or *honour, are a cause of reproach to him.* (M, TA.)

ضَئِيلٌ (also pronounced [by some] ضِئِيلٌ, like شِعِيرٌ [for شَعِيرٌ, q. v.], Ḥam p. 129) *Small in body, and lean;* (Mṣb;) or so ضَئِيلُ الجِسْمِ, applied to a man: (Ṣ, O:) or *small, slender,* or *thin, and despicable, abject,* or *ignominious:* and also [simply] *lean,* or *spare:* and so ▼ مُضْطَئِلٌ, (M, Ḳ,) in both senses: (Ḳ:) or *lean,* or *spare, and weak:* (TA:) or *weak, small, and slender,* or *thin:* (Lth, TA:) and ▼ مُتَضَائِلٌ [likewise] signifies *thin,* or *slender;* applied to a man; syn. شَخْتٌ: (Ṣ, O, TA:) the pl. of ضَئِيلٌ is ضُؤَلَآءُ and ضِئَالٌ (M, Ḳ, TA) and ضَئِيلُونَ: (TA:) and the fem. is ضَئِيلَةٌ. (M, TA.)

ضَئِيلَةٌ fem. of ضَئِيلٌ. (M, TA.) — Also [as a subst.] *A slender serpent:* (Ṣ, O, Ḳ:) or *a serpent resembling the viper.* (M.) — And The لَهَاة [or *uvula*]. (Th, M, Ḳ.)

مُضْطَئِلٌ: see ضَئِيلٌ.

مُتَضَائِلٌ: see ضَئِيلٌ. — It is also applied as an epithet to the weaving of a coat of mail [app. as signifying *Delicate,* or *fine;* or *small,* or *contracted, in the rings*]. (TA.)

ضأن

1. ضَأَنْتُ الضَّأْنَ *I set apart the sheep* [from the goats]. (Az, TA, and Ḳ in art. معز.) One says, اِضْأَنْ ضَأْنَكَ وَٱمْعَزْ مَعْزَكَ *Set apart thy sheep from the goats, and set apart thy goats from the sheep.* (Az, TA.)

4. اضْأَنَ, (Ṣ, M, Ḳ,) said of a man, (Ṣ,) or of a party of men, (M,) *His,* or *their,* ضَأْن [or *sheep*] *became numerous.* (Ṣ, M, Ḳ.)

ضَأْنٌ (Ṣ, M, Mṣb, Ḳ) and ▼ ضَأَنٌ (Ṣ, M, Ḳ) and ▼ ضَئِينٌ, (Ṣ, M, Mṣb, Ḳ,) which is also pronounced ▼ ضِئِينٌ, with kesr to the first letter because of the kesr following, agreeably with a general rule applying to a word [of the measure فَعِيلٌ] having any faucial letter [for its second radical], and ▼ ضِينٌ and ▼ ضَيْنٌ, which are mentioned by IAạr, without ء, and therefore extr., (M,) [*Sheep;*] *such as have wool, of what are termed* غَنَم; one of which is called ▼ ضَائِنٌ; (Mṣb;) [i. e.] they are pls., (Ṣ, Ḳ,) or [rather] quasi-pl. ns., (M,) of ▼ ضَائِنٌ, (Ṣ, M, Ḳ,) which signifies *one that has wool,* (M,) or the *opposite of* مَاعِز, (Ṣ, Ḳ,) *of what are termed* غَنَم: (M, Ḳ:) ضَأْنٌ is of the fem. gender; (IAmb, Mṣb;) and has for its pl. أَضْؤُنٌ [properly a pl. of pauc.] (IAmb, M, Mṣb) and آضُنٌ, which occurs in poetry, and is formed by transposition from أَضْؤُنٌ: (M:) the fem. of ▼ ضَائِنٌ is ضَائِنَةٌ; (Ṣ, M, Mṣb, Ḳ;) the pl. of which is ضَوَائِنُ. (Ṣ, M, Ḳ.) — ضَأْنٌ also signifies *A certain species of* [*the lizards called*] ضِبَاب [pl. of ضَبٌّ]; opposed to the مَاعِز. (TA.) And *A certain species of jerboas, also called* شُفَارِىّ; (T voce تَدْمُرِىّ, q. v.; and TA in art. شفر;) *differing from the* مَاعِز thereof. (T and TA in art. دمر.)

ضَأَنٌ: see the next preceding paragraph.

ضَأْنٌ and ضِينٌ: see ضَأْنٌ.

ضَأْنَةٌ *A* [*ring for the nose of a camel, such as is termed*] خِزَامَة, *when made of sinew.* (Sh, Ḳ.) [But see ضَانَةٌ, in art. ضون.]

ضَأْنِىٌّ is an extr., distorted, rel. n. [from ضَأْنٌ]. (M.) You say مِعْزَى ضَأْنِيَّةٌ *Goats that keep to the* ضَأْن [or *sheep*]. (M.) And سِقَآءٌ ضَأْنِىٌّ *A wide,* (M,) or *large,* (Ḳ,) *skin, of the hides of a sheep,* (M, Ḳ,) *in which* [*milk such as is termed*] رَائِب *is churned.* (Ḳ.)

ضَئِينٌ and ضِئِينٌ: see ضَأْنٌ.

ضَائِنٌ: see ضَأْنٌ, in three places. — It is also used as an epithet: one says كَبْشٌ ضَائِنٌ [app. meaning *A ram:* كَبْش alone having several meanings]. (M.) — And it signifies also ‡ *Weak:* (Ḳ, TA:) [opposed to مَاعِز:] or a *soft* man, as though he were a ewe: (M, TA:) or one *who ceases not to be goodly in body while a scanty eater:* (M, Ḳ:*) or *soft and flaccid in the belly.* (M, Ḳ.*) — And † *Such as is white and broad,* of sands. (Ḳ, TA.)

ضب

1. ضَبَّ, aor. ـِ, (Ḳ,) inf. n. ضَبٌّ, (Ṣ, Ḳ,) *He,* or *it, clave to the ground:* (Ṣ,* Ḳ:) [like ضَبَأَ:] this is the primary signification. (Ṣ.) — And, aor. and inf. n. as above, *It flowed:* (Ḳ, TA:) like بَضَّ: or *it flowed gently,* or *scantily;* as blood when it does not drop, or issue in drops, so as to require the repetition of the ablution for prayer: (TA:) or it is only said of blood and of saliva: (Ḳ:) or, aor. as above, inf. n. ضَبِيبٌ, said of water and of blood, *it flowed.* (Ṣ.) And ضَبَّتْ شَفَتُهُ, aor. as above, inf. n. ضَبٌّ and ضُبُوبٌ, *His lip flowed with blood,* from a tumour &c. (TA. [See also another meaning in what follows.]) And ضَبَّتْ لِثَتُهُ دَمًا *His gum flowed with blood:* (Ṣ:) or ضَبَّتْ بِالدَّمِ: and in like manner, تَرَكْتُ لِثَتَهُ يَدَهُ [*his hand* or *arm*]: (A:) and تَضِبُّ مِنَ الدَّمِ, inf. n. ضَبِيبٌ, *I left his gum flowing with blood.* (TA.) ضَبَّتْ لِثَتُهُ, aor. as above, inf. n. ضَبٌّ, means *His gum watered,* or *flowed with saliva.* (TA.) And one says, جَآءَ فُلَانٌ تَضِبُّ لِثَاتُهُ ‡ [*Such a one came with his gums watering*] (Ṣ, A*) لِكَذَا وَكَذَا [*for such and such things*], (A,) when the person spoken of is vehemently eager, or greedy, for a thing, (Ṣ, A,) or when he is affected with very inordinate desire to eat, or with vehement lust, or carnal desire, or with vehement eagerness, or greediness, for the accomplishment of an object of want. (L, TA.) Bishr Ibn-Abee-Kházim says,

• وَبَنِى تَمِيمٍ قَدْ لَقِينَا مِنْهُمُ •
• خَيْلًا تَضِبُّ لِثَاتُهَا لِلْمَغْنَمِ •

† [*And the sons of Temeem, we have found, of them, horsemen whose gums water for spoil*]: in

which تَضِبُّ is said by AO to be formed by transposition from تَبِضُّ. (Ṣ.) [See another ex. in a verse cited voce أَزْمَلُ.] Another poet says,

أَبَيْنَا أَبَيْنَا أَنْ تَضِبَّ لِثَاتُكُمْ
عَلَى خُرَّدٍ مِثْلِ الظِّبَآءِ وَجَامِلِ

† [*We disallow, we disallow, that your gums should water for virgins, or bashful virgins, like gazelles, and for camels*]. (TA.) One says also, ضَبَّ فَمُهُ, aor. as above, inf. n. ضَبٌّ, meaning *His mouth watered, or flowed with saliva*: (TA:) and يَضِبُّ فُوهُ ‡ [*His mouth waters*] is said of him who is vehemently eager, or greedy, for a thing. (A, TA.) — ضَبَّتِ الدَّابَّةُ, aor. as above, inf. n. ضُبُوبٌ, means *The beast staled while running*. (TA.) — See also 4, in five places. — ضَبَّ said of a boy, or male child, *He became a youth, or young man; he attained to the state termed* شَبَاب. (TA.) — ضَبِبَتِ الشَّفَةُ, aor. as above, (Mṣb, Ḳ,) inf. n. ضَبٌّ and ضُبُوبٌ, (Ḳ,) *The lip became affected with the disease termed* ضَبّ. (Mṣb, Ḳ. [See also another meaning in what precedes.]) — ضَبِبَ, (Ṣ, Ḳ,) sec. pers. ضَبِبْتَ, (TA,) aor. ـَ, inf. n. ضَبَبٌ, said of a camel, *He became affected with the disease termed* ضَبّ (Ṣ, Ḳ) *in his* فِرْسِن [i. e. *in his foot, or the extremity of his foot*]. (Ṣ.) — ضَبِبَ البَلَدُ, (ISk, Ṣ,) or ضَبِبَتِ الأَرْضُ, aor. ـَ; and ضَبُبَتْ; (Ḳ;) [instances of reduplicative verbs preserving their original forms;] and ▼ أَضَبَّ, (Ṣ,) or أَضَبَّتْ; (Mṣb, Ḳ;) *The country, or land, abounded with* [*the lizards called*] ضِبَاب, pl. of ضَبّ. (Ṣ, Mṣb, Ḳ.) — ضَبَّ النَّاقَةَ, aor. ـُ, (Ṣ, O,) inf. n. ضَبٌّ, (O, Ḳ,) *He milked the camel with five fingers* [i. e. *with his thumb and four fingers together*]: (Ṣ, O:) or *with the whole hand:* (Ḳ: or this mode of milking is termed ضَفّ: TA:) or *by putting his thumb upon the teat and turning the fingers over the thumb and the teat together:* (Fr, Ṣ, O, Ḳ: this is done when the teat is long: when it is of middling length, the mode termed بَزْم is adopted, with the joint of the fore finger and the extremity of the thumb: and when it is short, the mode termed فَطْر, with the extremity of the fore finger and the thumb: TA:) or *by taking the two teats together in the hand:* (Ḳ: [or this mode of milking is termed ضَفّ:] and the *milking with a hard squeezing* is termed ▼ ضَبَّة: TA:) or *by contracting the hand upon the udder, and putting the thumb in, or upon,* (فِى,) *the middle of the palm.* (L, TA.) — [ضَبَّ and ▼ ضَبَّبَ, each probably followed by عَلَى, seem to signify sometimes *It covered* a thing, *and became intermixed* with it: the inf. ns. الضبيب (which I think to be a mistranscription for الضَّبُّ) and التضبيب are expl. in the TA as signifying "the covering a thing, and the entering of one part, or portion, of it into another:" see two explanations of each of these verbs, followed by عَلَى, voce أَضَبَّ.]

2: see above, last sentence: — and see 4, in two places. — ضَبَّبَ عَلَى الضَّبِّ *He moved about his hand at the mouth of the hole of the* [*lizard called*] ضَبّ, *in order that it might come forth tail-foremost, and he might lay hold upon its tail.* (TA. [See also مُضَبِّبٌ.]) — ضَبَّبَ البَابَ, (Ṣ, Mṣb, Ḳ,* TA,) and الخَشَبَ, (TA,) ‡ *He put* [or *affixed*] *a* ضَبَّة [q. v.] *upon the door,* (Ṣ, Mṣb, Ḳ,* TA,) and *upon the wood.* (TA.) And ضَبَّبَ الإِنَآءَ † *He made a* ضَبَّة *for the vessel.* (Mṣb.) And ضَبَّبَ أَسْنَانَهُ بِالفِضَّةِ † *He clamped his teeth* (شَدَّهَا) *with silver.* (Mgh.) — [تَضْبِيبٌ also signifies The *putting the numeral* ٢ or ٣ &c. *over each of two words, to indicate that the latter of those words is connected with, or refers to, the former of them.*] — ضَبَّبَ الصَّبِىَّ *He fed the child with* ضَبِيبَة [q. v.]. (Ṣ, Ḳ.)

4. اضبّ عَلَى شَىْءٍ *He kept, or clave, to a thing, and did not quit it:* (TA:) and اضبّ فُلَانًا *He kept, or clave, to such a one, and did not quit him:* (Ḳ:) and اضبّ عَلَيْهِ *He retained him, detained him, or held him in custody:* (AZ, Ḳ, TA:) and اضبّ مَا فِى يَدَيْهِ *He grasped, or kept hold of, that which was in his hands;* like أَضْبَأَ and أَضْبَى. (TA in art. ضبأ.) And the first of these phrases, (TA,) inf. n. إِضْبَابٌ; (Ḳ, TA;) as also ▼ ضَبَّ, [aor. ـُ,] (TA,) inf. n. ضَبٌّ; (Ḳ, TA;) and ▼ ضَبَّبَ, (TA,) inf. n. تَضْبِيبٌ; (Ḳ, TA;) signifies اِحْتَوَى عَلَيْهِ [i. e. *He grasped it; got, or gained, possession of it; took it, got it, or held it, within his grasp, or in his possession:* or *it comprised, comprehended, or contained, it*]: (Ḳ, TA:) and ▼ ضَبَّ عَلَى شَىْءٍ, inf. n. ضَبٌّ, *He took, seized, or grasped, a thing with the hand:* (TA; but only the inf. n. in this case is there mentioned:) and ▼ ضَبَّبَ عَلَى شَىْءٍ, inf. n. تَضْبِيبٌ, *He took, seized, or grasped, a thing violently, or firmly, lest it should escape from his hand.* (ISh, O, TA. [See also 1, last sentence.]) — [It is said that] اضبّ عَلَيْهِ also signifies *He was at the point of getting possession of it,* namely, a thing (O, Ḳ) that he sought, or desired. (Ḳ.) [But it seems from a passage in the TA, in which is an evident mistranscription, that this is a mistake, originated by Lth, for أَضْبَى.] — اضبّ السِّقَآءُ *The skin shed, or poured forth, its water, from a seam, or suture,* (خُرْزَة,) *therein,* (Ḳ, TA,) or *from a cut.* (TA.) [And اضبّ app. signifies *He had a bleeding of the gums:* for] مَا زَالَ مضبًّا [app. ▼ مُضِبًّا] occurs in a trad. said of one whose gums bled [incessantly] when he spoke. (TA.) — اضبّ فِى الغَارَةِ *He arose, and made a hostile incursion:* (TA:) or اضبّ, alone, *he made a hostile incursion.* (Ḳ.) And اضبّ القَوْمُ *The people, or party, rose, or rose and hastened and went forth, all together, to do a thing.* (O, Ḳ.) — اضبّوا لِفُلَانٍ *They dispersed themselves to seek such a one:* and اضبّ القَوْمُ فِى بُغْيَتِهِمْ *The people, or party, dispersed themselves in search of their stray beast.* (T, TA.) And اضبّ النَّعَمُ *The camels, or cattle, approached, or came, in a scattered state.* (Ḳ.) — اضبّوا عَلَيْهِ *They multiplied against him.* (Ṣ, O.) — اضبّت الأَرْضُ *The land became abundant in its plants, or herbage.* (Ḳ. [But the only meaning of this phrase commonly known is one which will be found indicated below.]) Accord. to Ibn-Buzurj, (TA,) one says, اضبّت الأَرْضُ بِالنَّبَاتِ, meaning *The land put forth all its plants, or herbage.* (O, TA.) And اضبّ الشَّعَرُ *The hair became abundant, or much.* (Ḳ.) — أَضْبَبْتُهُ *I made it to flow;* namely, water, and blood. (Ṣ.) And اضبّ لِثَتَهُ *He made his gum to flow* [with blood]. (Ṣ, O.) — And اضبّ *He spoke;* (AZ, Ṣ, O, Ḳ;) as though meaning *he made speech to issue:* (Ṣ, O: [in both of which it is implied that it is app. from what here next precedes:]) or *he spoke uninterruptedly:* (TA:) or *he talked loudly;* as also ▼ ضَبَّ [aor. ـِ]: (AA, TA in art. هضب: [but it will be seen in what follows that both of these verbs have also a contr. meaning:]) and *he called out, or cried out,* (Ḳ, TA,) *and raised a clamour, or confused noise.* (TA.) And اضبّ القَوْمُ *The people, or party, spoke, one to another:* (TA:) or *spoke; and entered, or launched forth, into discourse, or were profuse therein:* (AHát, TA:) or *spoke all together.* (Ḥar p. 543.) And اضبّ مَا فِى نَفْسِهِ *He uttered, or expressed, what was in his mind.* (Aṣ, TA. [See also the same phrase with عَلَى after the verb in what follows.]) — Also, (TA,) inf. n. إِضْبَابٌ; (Ḳ, TA;) and ▼ ضَبَّ, (TA,) [aor. ـُ,] inf. n. ضَبٌّ; (Ḳ, TA;) *He was silent.* (Ḳ, TA. [Thus both of these verbs have two contr. meanings.]) And اضبّ القَوْمُ *The people or party, were silent, and abstained from talking.* (AHát, TA.) And اضبّ عَلَى الشَّىْءِ, and ▼ ضَبَّ; and اضبّ بِهِ; *He was silent respecting the thing* [*and concealed it*]: like أَضْبَأَ. (TA.) And اضبّ عَلَى مَا فِى نَفْسِهِ *He was silent respecting that which was in his mind:* (Aṣ, Ṣ, Ḳ:) like أَضْبَأَ. (Ṣ.) And اضبّ عَلَى غِلٍّ فِى قَلْبِهِ *He concealed rancour, malevolence, malice, or spite, in his heart.* (Ṣ, O.) And اضبّ الشَّىْءَ *He hid, or concealed, the thing.* (Ḳ,* TA.) — اضبّ الغَيْمُ *The clouds covered* [*the earth*]. (TA.) — And اضبّ said of a day, (Ṣ, O, Mṣb, Ḳ,) and اضبّت said of the sky, (A, TA,) *It became cloudy, or misty, with* ضَبَاب [q. v.]. (Ṣ, O, Mṣb, Ḳ, TA.) — اضبّ البَلَدُ and اضبّت الأَرْضُ: see 1, latter half.

5. تضبّب † *He* (a child) *became fat, and his armpits became chapped, or cracked,* (اِنْفَتَقَتْ,) [*in the creases,*] *and his neck became short:* (Ṣ:) or ‡ *he* (a child) *began to grow fat:* (A, TA:) and accord. to AḤn, it is said in this sense of a camel as well as of a human being. (TA.)

10. خُذْ مَا آسْتَضَبَّ *Take thou what is easily attainable; what offers itself without difficulty.* (AA, TA in art. نضب.)

R. Q. 1. ضَبْضَبَ *He bore rancour, malevolence, malice, or spite; or hid enmity, and violent hatred, in his heart.* (O, TA.)

ضَبٌّ [*A species of lizard;* termed *lacerta caudiverbera,* from its habit of striking with its tail; (see حَرْشٌ;) Forskål (Descr. Animalium,

p. 13,) terms it *lacerta Aegyptia*; referring to Hasselquist, p. 302; and adds the following description: "femora teretia sine verrucis: cauda verticillata non longa: squamæ patentes, subconicæ, mucronatæ: corpus nudum, rugosum:"] *a certain reptile, or small creeping thing,* (Ṣ, TA,) *of those termed* حَشَرَات, (TA,) *well known;* (Ḳ, TA;) *resembling the* وَرَل [*q. v., but not so long*]: (TA:) or *resembling the* حِرْذَون [q. v.]; *of which there are two species, one of the size of the* حرذون, *and one larger:* (Mṣb:) accord. to 'Abd-El-Ḳáhir, *of the size of a little young crocodile; having a tail like the tail of the latter: it assumes various colours when exposed to the sun, like as does the chameleon; lives seven hundred years; drinks not water, being satisfied with the air; voids one drop of urine in every forty days; its teeth consist of one curved piece; when it has quitted its hole it knows it not; and it lays eggs, like a bird:* so say IKh and Dmr and others: AM says, the وَرَل is of a lank make, with a long tail; the latter resembling that of a serpent; and the length of some exceeds two cubits; but *the tail of the* ضبّ *is jointed, and its utmost length is a span:* the Arabs deem the ورل a foul and filthy thing, and do not eat it; but *they are eager to hunt and eat the* ضبّ: *this animal has a rough tail, serrated with jags resembling vertebræ; its colour inclines to a blackish dusty hue; and when it becomes fat, its breast becomes yellow; it eats nothing but* [*the locusts called*] جَنَادِب, *and young locusts before their wings have grown* (دَبًا), *and herbage, not venomous or noxious reptiles;* whereas the ورل eats scorpions and serpents and chameleons and beetles: *its flesh is an antidote against poisons, and women grow fat upon it:* (L, TA:) *it is the longest, of the animals, in retaining the remains of life:* (O:) [see also مُطْبِخ:] the fem. is with ة: (Ṣ, O, Mṣb, Ḳ:) and the pl. [of pauc.] is أَضُبٌّ and [of mult.] ضِبَابٌ (Ṣ, O, Mgh, Mṣb, Ḳ) and ضُبَّانٌ, (Ḳ,) which last Lḥ particularizes as used to denote a great number, but ISd sees no reason for this distinction, (TA,) and [quasi-pl. n.] ↓ مَضَبَّةٌ, (O, Ḳ,) like as مَشْيَخَةٌ is of شَيْخ, (O,) this last on the authority of Aṣ, as heard by him from more than one of the Arabs. (TA.) Hence one says رَجُلٌ خَبٌّ ضَبٌّ ‡ [*A very deceitful* or *mischievous, and*] *an abominable, guileful, ireful man:* (TA:) or *a very deceitful* or *mischievous* or *wicked, and guileful man:* (Ṣ:) likened to the [lizard called] ضَبّ on account of his guilefulness: and in like manner, اِمْرَأَةٌ خَبَّةٌ ضَبَّةٌ. (A, TA.) And أَخْدَعُ مِنَ الضَّبِّ *More guileful than the* ضَبّ: (A, TA:) a prov. (TA.) And أَعَقُّ مِنْ ضَبٍّ [*More undutiful to kindred than a* ضَبّ]; because the ضبّ often eats its حُسُول [or young ones when they have just come forth from the eggs]: another prov.: (Ṣ:) أَبُو حِسْلٍ is a surname of the ضبّ. (TA.) One says also أَطْوَلُ ذَمَآءً مِنَ الضَّبِّ, another prov. [expl. in art. ذمى]. (O.) And أَحْيَرُ مِنْ ضَبٍّ, which is likewise a prov. [expl. in art. حير]. (Ḥar p. 166.) And أَتُعَلِّمُنِى بِضَبٍّ أَنَا حَرَشْتُهُ, another prov. [expl. in art. حرش]. (TA.) And لَا أَفْعَلُهُ حَتَّى يَحِنَّ الضَّبُّ فِى إِثْرِ الإِبِلِ الصَّادِرَةِ [*I will not do it until the* ضبّ *utters a yearning cry at the heels of the camels returning from water*]: and لَا أَفْعَلُهُ حَتَّى يَرِدَ الضَّبُّ [*I will not do it until the* ضبّ *comes to water:* i. e. I will never do it:] because the ضبّ does not drink water. (Ṣ, O.) كَفُّ الضَّبِّ [means *The paw of the* ضبّ]: to this the Arabs liken the hand of the niggard when he fails to give: (TA:) and it is also applied by way of comparison to ‡ *a niggard* himself: and to denote ‡ *shortness and littleness.* (A, TA.) — [Hence also,] ‡ *Rancour, malevolence, malice,* or *spite,* (Ṣ, A, O, Mṣb, Ḳ, TA,) *latent in the heart;* (A, TA;) like the [lizard called] ضبّ hiding itself in the furthest extremity of its hole: (A:) and *anger, wrath,* or *rage:* (Ḳ:) or *rancour,* &c., or *vehement rancour,* &c., *and enmity:* (TA:) and ↓ ضِبٌّ signifies the same: (Ḳ:) the pl. is ضِبَابٌ, and [app. ضِبَبٌ also, for] the phrase كُلٌّ مِنْهُمَا حَامِلُ ضِبَبٍ لِصَاحِبِهِ [*Each of them a bearer of latent rancours* &c. *towards his fellow*] occurs in a trad. (TA.) ═ Also *A certain disease in the lip,* (Ṣ, O, Mṣb, Ḳ,) *in consequence of which it flows with blood,* (Ṣ, O, Mṣb,) or *swells, and becomes hard,* or *dry and hard, and flows with blood.* (TA.) — And *A tumour in the breast of a camel.* (O, Ḳ.) — And *A tumour* (Ṣ, O, Ḳ) *in the* خُفّ, (so in copies of the Ḳ [i. e. *foot*], in the TA انف [which is, I doubt not, a mistranscription],) or *in the* فِرْسِن, [which means the same, or the *extremity of the foot,*] (Ṣ, O,) *of the camel.* (Ṣ, O, Ḳ.) — And *A disease in the elbow of a camel;* (Ḳ, TA;) *said to be its cutting into his skin* [*by rubbing against it*]; *or its being distorted, and falling against his side, so as to gall it.* (TA.) — And *A chapping,* or *cracking,* (اِنْفِتَاق,) [*in the crease*] *of the armpit* [of a child, or of a camel], *and abundance of flesh:* (Ṣ, O, TA:) El-'Adebbes El-Kinánee gives the same explanation, and says that this is what is also termed ضَاغِطٌ. (TA. [See 5.]) ═ Also The طَلْع [i. e. the *spadix,* or the *spathe,*] of the palm-tree: pl. ضِبَابٌ: (Ṣ, O:) or ↓ ضَبَّةٌ signifies, (Ḳ, TA,) and so ضَبٌّ, (TA,) [but the latter seems to be a coll. gen. n., and the former its n. un.,] *a* طَلْعَة [meaning *spathe of a palm-tree*] *before it cleaves open* (Ḳ, TA) *from* [*around*] *the* غُرَيض [or *spadix*]. (TA.)

ضِبٌّ: see the next preceding paragraph, latter half.

ضَبَّةٌ [an inf. n. un. of ضَبَّ: as such signifying] *A single bleeding* of the gum [&c.]. (Ḥam pp. 28 and 274.) — See also 1, last sentence but one. ═ Also *A single* [*lizard of the species termed*] ضَبّ [q. v.]. (Ṣ, O, Mṣb, Ḳ.) — And The *skin of a* [*lizard of the species termed*] ضَبّ, *tanned for clarified butter* (Ḳ, TA) *to be put into it.* (TA.) — And ‡ *A broad piece of iron with which a door* (or *wood,* TA) *is clamped* or *strengthened* (يُضَبَّبُ): (Ṣ, Mgh, O, Ḳ, TA:) or *a piece of iron* or *brass* or *the like, with which a vessel is repaired:* (Mṣb:) [a word still used in these senses; commonly applied to *a flat piece of iron* or *the like, which is nailed across a crack in a wooden vessel or a similar thing:* and *a band of metal which is affixed around a cracked vessel:* (see an ex. voce عَضَبَ:) also to *a kind of wooden lock,* figured and described in the Introduction to my work on the Modern Egyptians:] what is first described above is so called because it is broad, like the reptile so termed; and also كَتِيفَةٌ, because it is broad, like a كَتِف [or shoulder-blade]: (AM, TA:) pl. ضَبَّاتٌ (A, Mṣb, TA) and ضِبَابٌ. (A, TA.) The ضَبَّة of a knife is The جُزْأَة [thereof; app. meaning *a ferrule,* or *similar thing, affixed around the handle, next the blade,* like the band of metal thus called which is affixed around a cracked vessel (as mentioned above); though جُزْأَة generally means the "handle" itself]: thus called because it strengthens, or binds, the handle (تَشُدُّ النِّصَابَ). (A, TA.) — See also ضَبّ, last sentence. — And see ضَبِيب.

مَضَبَّةٌ: see أَرْضٌ ضَبِبَةٌ.

ضَبَابٌ [*Mist;* i. e.] *moisture* (نَدًى), (A, Mgh, Mṣb, Ḳ,) *like clouds,* (A, Ḳ,) or *like dust, covering the earth in the early mornings:* (Mgh, Mṣb, TA:) or *thin clouds, like smoke:* (A, Ḳ:) or *thin clouds;* so called because they cover the horizon: n. un. with ة: (TA:) or pl. of ضَبَابَةٌ, [but it is rather a coll. gen. n., and ضَبَابَةٌ is its n. of un.,] (Ṣ, Mgh, O,) and this latter signifies *a cloud that covers the earth, resembling smoke:* (Ṣ, O:) or *a vapour rising from the earth in a rainy,* or *cloudy, day, like a canopy, preventing vision by its darkness.* (TA.)

ضَبُوبٌ A beast *that stales while running.* (Ḳ.) — And A ewe, or she-goat, *having a narrow orifice to the teat,* (O, Ḳ,) *whose milk will not come forth but with difficulty.* (O.)

ضَبِيبٌ The *point,* or *edge,* (syn. حَدّ, [in an. ex. in the O, the former is meant by it,]) of a sword; (O, Ḳ;) and so ↓ ضَبَّةٌ. (El-Khaṭṭábee, TA.)

ضَبِيبَةٌ *Clarified butter, and rob* (رُبّ), *which are put into a skin* (عُكَّة), *for a child, that he may be fed with it.* (Ṣ, Ḳ.)

بَنَاتُ ضُبَيْبَةَ [app. بنات ضبيبة; the latter word, dim. of ضَبَّة;] *A species* [or *variety*] *of the* [*lizards called*] ضِبَاب [pl. of ضَبّ]. (Ḥam p. 61.)

ضِبْضِبٌ *Fat,* as an epithet; (Ḳ;) and so [without ة] applied to a woman: (TA:) and ↓ ضُبَاضِبٌ, applied to a man, *short and fat.* (Ṣ, O.) And *Very foul* or *obscene, and bold* or *daring;* as also ↓ ضُبَاضِبٌ: (Ḳ:) the latter thus expl. by IDrd: (O:) the former applied to a man, and with ة applied to a woman, accord. to AZ, *bold,* or *daring, in deed:* (O, TA:) and *proud;* or *bold,* or *daring, in wickedness:* and with ة, a woman *bold,* or *daring; who glories over her neighbours.* (TA.)

ضُبَاضِبٌ: see the next preceding paragraph, in two places. Also, applied to a man, *Strong;*

(IDrd, O, Ḳ;) and so بُضَابِضٌ: (IDrd, O:) or *short, and very foul* or *obscene*: or *hard*, or *hardy, and strong*: (Ḳ:) and sometimes applied as an epithet to a camel. (TA.)

أَضَبُّ, fem. ضَبَّآءُ, A camel *affected with the disease termed* ضَبّ (Ṣ, Ḳ) *in the* خُفّ (Ḳ) or *in the* فِرْسِن. (Ṣ.) [See ضَبّ.]

مُضِبٌّ: see 4, in the former half. — أَرْضٌ مُضِبَّةٌ: see the next paragraph.

مَضَبَّةٌ *A piece of land abounding with* [*the lizards called*] ضِبَاب [pl. of ضَبّ]: pl. مَضَابُّ: you say, وَقَعْنَا فِى مَضَابَّ [*We found ourselves in pieces of land abounding with* ضِبَاب]. (Ṣ, O.) And أَرْضٌ مَضَبَّةٌ, (Ḳ,) or ↓ مُضِبَّةٌ, (Ṣ, IAth, Mgh, Mṣb,) and ↓ ضَبِبَةٌ, (Ṣ, Ḳ,) the last being one of those [reduplicative] words that preserve the original form, (Ṣ,) *A land abounding with* ضِبَاب. (Ṣ, IAth, Mgh, Mṣb, Ḳ.) — See also ضَبّ, [of which it is a quasi-pl. n.,] in the former half of the paragraph.

مُضَبِّبٌ *A hunter of the* [*lizard called*] ضَبّ, *who pours water into its hole, in order that it may come forth and he may take it*: (Ṣ, O:) or *one who seeks to catch the* ضَبّ *by moving about his hand at its hole in order that it may come forth tail-foremost and he may lay hold upon its tail.* (Ḳ.)

ضبأ

1. ضَبَأَ, (Aṣ, Ṣ, Ḳ,) aor. ـَ, inf. n. ضَبْءٌ and ضُبُوْءٌ, (Ḳ,) *He* (a man, TA) *clave to the ground,* (Aṣ, Ṣ, Ḳ, TA, [like ضَبَّ,]) or *to a tree*: (TA:) or ضَبَأَ بِالأَرْضِ, aor. and inf. n. as above, *he clave to the ground, and hid,* or *concealed, himself*: and in like manner one says of a wolf, meaning *he clave to the ground*; or *he hid,* or *concealed, himself in a covert of trees,* or *in a hollow in the ground, to deceive,* or *circumvent*: (M:) and ضَبَأَ alone, *he hid,* or *concealed, himself*; (M, Ḳ;) as also ↓ اضطبأ: (Ḳ:) and the former, *he concealed himself* (Ḳ, TA) *in a covert of trees,* or *in a hollow in the ground,* (TA,) *to deceive,* or *circumvent,* (Ḳ, TA,) *the game,* or *prey*: (TA:) you say, ضَبَأْتُ فِى الأَرْضِ, inf. n. as above, *I hid,* or *concealed, myself in the land,* or *country.* (AZ, Ṣ. [See also ضَنَأَ.]) — ضَبَأْتُ إِلَيْهِ *I had recourse,* or *betook myself, to him,* or *it, for refuge, protection,* or *covert.* (Ṣ, O, Ḳ.*) — And ضَبَأَ, alone, *He came forth from a place unexpectedly, and ascended* [*upon an eminence*], (O, Ḳ, TA,) *to look.* (TA.) — ضَبَأَ مِنْهُ *He was abashed at,* or *shy of,* or *he shrank from, him,* or *it*; (M, Ḳ, TA;) as also ↓ اضطبأ. (TA. [See also اضطنأ.]) — ضَبَأْتُ بِهِ الأَرْضَ *I made him to cleave to the ground.* (Aṣ, Ṣ, O, Ḳ.*)

4. اضبأ مَا فِى نَفْسِهِ *He concealed what was in his mind*: (Ḳ,* TA:) or اضبأ القَوْمُ عَلَى مَا فِى أَنْفُسِهِمْ *the people,* or *party, concealed what was in their minds.* (M.) And اضبأ عَلَى الشَّىْءِ *He was silent respecting the thing,* (Ṣ, M, O, Ḳ,) *and concealed it.* (Ṣ, O.) And اضبأ عَلَى الدَّاهِيَةِ i. q. أَضَبَّ [i. e. *He was silent respecting the calamity*]. (Ṣ, O, Ḳ.) — And اضبأ عَلَى مَا فِى يَدَيْهِ, (M, TA,) or, accord. to Lḥ, اضبأ مَا فِى يَدَيْهِ, like أَضْبَى and أَضَبَّ, (TA,) *He grasped,* or *kept hold of, that which was in his hands.* (Lḥ, M, TA.)

8. اضطبأ: see 1, in two places.

ضَبِىْءٌ *Cleaving to the ground,* (M, Ḳ, TA,) or *to a tree*; applied to a man. (TA.)

ضَابِئٌ [act. part. n. of 1, *Cleaving to the ground*: &c.:] expl. by El-Harbee as meaning *a sportsman concealing himself.* (TA.) — Also *Ashes*; (M, Ḳ;) because they cleave to the ground. (TA.)

ضَابِئَةٌ: see the last paragraph.

مَضْبَأٌ *A place where one conceals himself,* (Ṣ, TA,) *in a covert of trees,* or *in a hollow in the ground, to deceive,* or *circumvent, the game,* or *prey*: pl. مَضَابِئُ. (TA.)

مَضْبُوْءٌ بِهِ *Made to cleave to the ground.* (Aṣ, Ṣ.)

مُضَابِئٌ, (O,) or مُضَابِئَةٌ, (Ḳ, [and so in the O in an instance mentioned in what here follows, in the next sentence,]) and ↓ ضَابِئَةٌ, (TA, as from the Ḳ, but not in the CḲ nor in my MS. copy of the Ḳ,) *A* [*large sack such as is called*] غِرَارَة *that oppresses by its weight, and conceals, him who carries it* (O, Ḳ, TA) *beneath it.* (O, TA.) — The second of these words is also applied in a poem recited by [its author] Aboo-Hizám El-'Oklee, to ISk, to the said poem, which is one abounding with hemzehs [and difficult to pronounce]. (O,* TA.)

ضبث

1. ضَبَثَ بِهِ, (Ṣ, Ḳ,) aor. ـِ, (Ḳ,) inf. n. ضَبْثٌ, (Ṣ,) *He grasped, seized,* or *laid hold upon, him,* or *it, with his hand*; as also ↓ اضطبث: (Ṣ, Ḳ:) or, accord. to an explanation of the inf. n. by Ibn-Es-Seed, *he did so with the utmost vehemence,* or *strength*: (TA:) or *he grasped, seized,* or *laid hold upon, and took, him,* or *it*: (Sh, TA:) or ضَبَثَ عَلَيْهِ has the first of these meanings; (A, L;) as also ضَبَّثَهُ: (A:) and ضَبَثَ بِهِ signifies *he seized him violently,* or *laid violent hands upon him.* (A, TA.) — Also, i. e. ضَبَثَ بِهِ, aor. and inf. n. as above, *He applied his hand to it,* namely, a thing that he was making, or doing, *diligently, earnestly,* or *with painstaking.* (TA.) — And ضَبَثَهُ *He beat, struck,* or *smote, him,* namely, a man. (Ḳ.) — And *He felt, for the purpose of testing, him,* or *it,* with his hand. (TA.) One says, of a she-camel, تُضْبَثُ, meaning *She is felt with the hand,* when one doubts of her fatness. (Ṣ, A, Ḳ.)

8. اضطبث بِهِ: see the preceding paragraph.

ضَبِثٌ: see شَبِثٌ: — and see also ضُبَاثٌ.

ضَبْثَةٌ *A grasp,* or *seizure.* (O, TA.) [See also أَضْبَاثٌ.] — And ضَبْثَةُ الأَسَدِ, (Ḳ,) or الضَّبْثَةُ, (A, TA,) is the name of *A certain brand, upon a camel,* (A, Ḳ, TA,) *in the form of a ring with some lines before and behind*: (A, TA:) *it is on the side of the thigh.* (TA.)

ضُبَثَةٌ: see شُبْثَةٌ.

ضُبَاثٌ *The nails of the lion.* (Ḳ,* TA.) [See also مَضَابِثُ.] — And الضُّبَاثُ, (O, Ḳ, TA, in the CḲ الضَّبَاثُ, but it is) like غُرَاب, (TA,) [is a name of] *The lion*; as also ↓ الضَّبِثُ, ↓ الضُّبُوثُ, and ↓ المُضْبِثُ, and ↓ المُضْطَبِثُ. (O, Ḳ.)

نَاقَةٌ ضَبُوثٌ ‡ *A she-camel of which one doubts whether she be fat, and which one therefore feels with the hand*: (Ṣ, A, Ḳ:) and so نَاقَةٌ ضَغُوثٌ. (Ṣ and Ḳ in art. ضغث.) — الضُّبُوثُ: see ضُبَاثٌ.

ضُبَاثِىٌّ *Strong in the grasp*; applied to a man; and in like manner to a lion. (O.) And ضُبَاثِيَّةٌ, (O, Ḳ, TA,) with damm, and with teshdeed to the ى, (TA, [in the CḲ without teshdeed,]) *A fore arm* (ذِرَاع) *big, broad, and strong.* (O, Ḳ.)

ضَابِثٌ [act. part. n. of ضَبَثَ]. One says, لَيْثٌ بِأَقْرَانِهِ ضَابِثٌ وَبِأَرْوَاحِهِمْ عَابِثٌ ‡ [*A man like a lion, seizing violently his adversaries, and making sport with their souls*]. (A, TA.)

أَضْبَاثٌ [as though pl. of ضَبْثَةٌ, q. v.,] *Grasps*; syn. قَبَضَات. (Ṣ, Ḳ: but in copies of the Ḳ قُبُضَات.) So in the following words of a trad.: لَا يَدْعُونِى وَالخَطَايَا بَيْنَ أَضْبَاثِهِمْ [i. e. *They shall not invoke Me when sins are in their grasps*]; (Ṣ,* TA;) meaning, while they are still bearing the burden of their sins, not desisting therefrom: said by revelation to David: but it is also related otherwise, with ن [i. e. أَضْبَانِهِمْ]. (TA.)

مُضْبِثٌ: see مَضَابِثُ: — and ضُبَاثٌ.

مَضْبُوثٌ A camel *marked with the brand mentioned above,* voce ضَبْثَةٌ. (A, Ḳ.)

مَضَابِثُ The *nails,* or *claws,* (Ṣ, A, Ḳ,) of the lion: (Ṣ, A:) a pl. having no sing., or its sing. is مضبث [i. e. ↓ مُضْبِثٌ]. (TA.) [See also ضُبَاثٌ.]

المُضْطَبِثُ: see ضُبَاثٌ.

ضبح

1. ضَبَحَتِ الخَيْلُ, (AO, Ṣ, O, Ḳ,* [in the Ḳ ضَبَحَ,]) aor. ـَ, (Ḳ,) inf. n. ضَبْحٌ (AO, Ṣ, Ḳ) and ضُبَاحٌ, (Ḳ,) i. q. نَحَمَتْ, i. e. [*The horses breathed pantingly,* or *hard, with a sound from the chest*; or] *made the breathing to be heard when running*: (Ṣ, O:) [or *breathed laboriously, when fatigued*; and in like manner one says of camels; for] ضَبْحٌ signifies the *breathing* of horses and of camels *when fatigued*: (Suh, TA:) or *caused a sound to be heard from their mouths, different from neighing, and from the sound termed* حَمْحَمَة, (Ḳ, TA,) in their running: (TA:) [or it signifies also *the horses neighed*; for it is said that] الضُّبَاحُ is

also *syn. with* الصُّهَيلُ : (TA:) or, [but probably only with the former of the two inf. ns. mentioned above,] *ran a pace less quick than that which is termed* تَقْرِيب : (Ḳ, TA:) or *i. q.* ضَبَعَتْ, (AO, Ṣ, O, TA,) which means *they stretched forth their arms,* (AO, TA,) *going along,* (AO, Ṣ,* O, TA,) or *running:* (AO, TA:) accord. to I'Ab, one does not say ضَبَحَتْ دَابَّةٌ except in speaking of a dog or a horse: [he app. means that this verb is used thus only as denoting the uttering of a sound, or a manner of breathing:] some of the lexicologists say that those who use it in relation to a camel make ضَبَحَ to have the meaning of ضَبَعَ. (TA.) — ضَبَحَ, (L, TA,) inf. n. ضُبَاحٌ, (Ṣ, A, O, L, Ḳ, TA,) as meaning *He,* or *it, uttered a cry,* or *sound,* is also said of the fox, (Ṣ,* A,* O,* L, Ḳ,* TA,) and of the hare, and of the serpent called أَسْوَد, and of the owl, and of what is termed الصَّدَا [which see, for it is variously explained]: (L, TA:) and is also expl. as meaning نَبَحَ [*he barked,* &c.]. (TA.) — And ضَبَحَتِ القَوْسُ, aor. as above, inf. n. ضَبْحٌ, † *The bow* [*twanged,* or] *made a sound.* (TA.) — And ضَبَحَ is also used as meaning ‡ *He cried out, and entered into an altercation* for a person who had given him money. (IḲt, O,* TA, from a trad.) = ضَبَحَتْهُ النَّارُ, (Ṣ, O, Ḳ, TA,) and الشَّمْسُ, aor. ـَ, inf. n. ضَبْحٌ, (TA,) *The fire,* and *the sun, altered it:* (TA:) or *altered its colour:* (T, TA:) or *altered it, but not in a great degree;* (Ṣ, O, Ḳ, TA;) namely, a thing, (Ḳ, TA,) such as a stick, and an arrow, and flesh-meat, &c. (TA.) And ضَبَحَهُ بِالنَّارِ, aor. ـَ, inf. n. ضَبْحٌ, *He altered it in colour by fire;* namely, an arrow: and *he burned it in a portion of its upper parts;* namely, a stick, and flesh-meat, &c. (L, TA.) And ضَبْحٌ is expl. by AḤn as meaning The act of *roasting, broiling,* or *frying.* (TA.)

3. مُضَابَحَةٌ The act of *mutual reviling,* or *vilifying,* and *encountering,* (Ḳ, TA,) and *contending,* or *striving, to repel.* (TA.)

6. تضابح [*It sent forth a sound*]. (Ḥam p. 615 [q. v.: it is there said to be from الضَّبْح meaning الصَّوْت].)

7. انضبح *It became altered,* (Ḳ, TA,) or *altered in colour,* (TA,) *but not in a great degree,* by fire, (Ḳ, TA,) and by the sun. (TA.) And انضبح لَوْنُهُ *His,* or *its, colour became altered a little towards blackness.* (Ṣ, TA.)

ضُبْحٌ, (so in three copies of the Ṣ, and in the O,) or ↓ ضِبْحٌ, with kesr, (so accord. to the Ḳ,) *Ashes:* (Ṣ, O, Ḳ:) so called because of the alteration of their colour. (TA.)

ضِبْحٌ : see what next precedes.

ضَبْحَةٌ *A cry of a fox* [&c.: an inf. n. un.]. (TA.)

قَوْسٌ ضَبْحَآءُ *A bow upon which fire has taken effect* (Ḳ, TA) *so as to alter its colour:* (TA:) like ضَهْبَآءُ. (TA in art. ضهب. [See also what next follows.])

ضَبِيحٌ An arrow *altered in colour* [by fire]; as also ↓ مَضْبُوحٌ. (TA. [See an ex. of the latter in a verse of Ṭarafeh cited voce مُجْمِدٌ: and see also what here next precedes.]) It is also applied, (Ṣ, O,) in the same sense, (O,) to roasted flesh-meat. (Ṣ, O.) [And Freytag explains it as meaning, in the Deewan of Jereer, "Cutis nigra, usta vulneribus."]

ضَابِحٌ A man *raising his voice in reading* or *reciting:* pl. ضَوَابِحُ, which is anomalous, like فَوَارِسُ [pl. of فَارِسٌ]. (TA.) — And خَيْلٌ ضَوَابِحُ *Horses stretching forth their arms in their going along:* (A:) or *running vehemently;* like ضَوَابِعُ. (TA in art. ضبع.)

مَضْبُوحٌ : see ضَبِيحٌ. — Also The *stone that is in the* [*kind of ground called*] حَرَّة [q. v.]: because of its blackness. (TA.) And مَضْبُوحَةٌ *Stones from which one strikes fire,* (Ṣ, O, Ḳ,) *appearing as though burnt.* (Ṣ, O.)

مَضَابِحُ [a pl. of which the sing. is most probably مِضْبَحٌ] *Frying-pans.* (AḤn, TA.)

ضبر

1. ضَبَرَ, (Ṣ, A, Mṣb, Ḳ,) aor. ـِ, inf. n. ضَبْرٌ (A, Mṣb, Ḳ) and ضَبَرَانٌ, (Ḳ,) *He* (a horse, Ṣ, Mṣb, Ḳ, and a person having his legs shackled, Ḳ, in running, TA, or a horse having his legs shackled, A) *leaped with his legs put together;* (Ṣ, M, A, Mṣb, Ḳ;) and so too, accord. to Zj, ↓ اضبر, said of a horse: (O:) or *he ran:* (TA:) or ضَبْرٌ signifies a horse's *leaping, and alighting with his fore legs put together.* (Aṣ, TA.) — Also, (Ṣ, A, Ḳ,) aor. as above, (Ṣ,) inf. n. ضَبْرٌ, (Ṣ, Ḳ,) *He made* books, or writings, *into a bundle:* (Ṣ, A, Ḳ:) and ↓ ضبّر, (A, TA,) inf. n. تَضْبِيرٌ, (Ḳ,) signifies the same: (A:) or *he collected together* (Ḳ, TA) books, or writings, (A, TA,) &c. (TA.) And the former verb, *He collected together an army for war.* (Ṣ, TA.) And ضَبَرَ عَلَيْهِ الصَّخْرَ, (Ṣ, A, Ḳ,*) aor. as above, (Ṣ, TA,) and so the inf. n., (Ḳ, TA,) *He piled up the rocks,* or *great masses of stone,* (Ṣ, Ḳ,) *upon him,* or *it.* (Ṣ.) — ضَبْرٌ also signifies The act of *binding,* or *tying, firmly, fast,* or *strongly.* (IAạr, TA.) — And [hence, app., as inf. n. of ضُبِرَ,] (TA), and so تَضْبِيرٌ [as inf. n. of ↓ ضُبِّرَ], (Ḳ, TA,) The *being very compact and strong in the bones, and compact and full in flesh.* (Ḳ, TA.) [See مَضْبُورٌ.])

2: see the preceding paragraph, in two places.

4: see 1, first sentence.

ضَبْرٌ an inf. n. used as an epithet: see مَضْبُورٌ. = Also † *A company of men engaged in a warring,* or *warring and plundering, expedition,* (Ṣ, O, Ḳ, TA,) *on foot.* (TA.) And *Footmen* [app. meaning *foot-soldiers*]; syn. رَجَّالَةٌ [quasi-pl. n. of رَاجِلٌ]. (TA.) — Also [The *musculus,* or *testudo; a machine made of*] *skin covering wood,* (Lth, O, Ḳ,) *within which are men,* (Ḳ,) *and which is brought near to fortresses, for the purpose of fighting,* (Lth, O, Ḳ,) i. e. *for fighting the people thereof:* (Lth, O:) pl. ضُبُورٌ, (Lth, O, Ḳ,) which means *what are termed* دَبَّابَاتٌ: (Lth, A, O: [see دَبَّابَةٌ:]) [or it is a coll. gen. n.; for it is said that] one such thing is called ضَبْرَةٌ. (TA.) = Also [The *species of nut called*] the *wild* جَوْز (جَوْزُ البَرِّ), which is *a hard sort of* جوز, not the wild pomegranate, for this is called the مَظّ: (Ṣ, O:) or the *tree of what is called* جَوْزُ البَرِّ; as also ↓ ضِبْرٌ: (Ḳ:) or, accord. to [AḤn] Ed-Deenawaree, each of these words, the latter being a dial. var. of the former, is applied to the *tree of a sort of* جَوْز *found in the mountains of the Saráh* (السَّرَاة), *which blossoms, but does not organize and compact any fruit* (لَا يَعْقِدُ); and the n. un. is ↓ ضِبْرَةٌ [and ضَبْرَةٌ]: he says also that the ضبر was described to him by an Arab of the desert, of Saráh, as *a great tree, as big as the great walnut-tree, having round leaves, as big as the hand, and very numerous.* (O.) And the ضَبْر is [also] *What is called* جَوْزُ بَوَّا [i. e. *the nutmeg*]: (Ḳ:) IAạr says that it is *what the people of the towns and villages call* جَوْزُ بَوَّا. (O.) = And *i. q.* فَقْرٌ [*Poverty,* &c.]. (IAạr, TA.)

ضِبْرٌ The *armpit:* (O, Ḳ, TA:) and so ضِبْنٌ: thus says Ibn-El-Faraj. (TA.)

ضَبِرٌ; and its n. un., with ة: see ضَبْرٌ.

ضِبِرٌّ, applied to a horse, (Ṣ, O, Ḳ,) and to a lion, (O,) and to a man, (TA,) *That leaps much:* (Ṣ, O, Ḳ:) and so طِمِرٌّ. (O.) — See also ضَبُورٌ.

ضِبَارٌ and ضُبَارٌ *Books,* or *writings:* [each a pl.] without a singular. (Ḳ.) [See also إِضْبَارَةٌ.]

ضَبُورٌ *A lion;* as also ↓ ضِبِرٌّ, and ↓ مُضَبَّرٌ: (Ḳ:) or *a lion that leaps much to the animals upon which he preys.* (O.)

ضَبِيرٌ *Hard, firm,* or *strong;* syn. شَدِيدٌ; (Ibn-'Abbád, O, Ḳ;) and so ↓ ضُنْبُرٌ. (TA.) — And (hence, TA) The *penis.* (Ibn-'Abbád, O, Ḳ.)

ذُو ضَبَارَةٍ, (Ṣ, O, Ḳ,) or ذُو ضَبَارَةٍ فِى خَلْقِهِ, (TA,) A man *having firmness of make:* (Ṣ, O:) or *having compactness and firmness of make:* (Ḳ:) and so ↓ ضُبَارِمٌ and ↓ ضُبَارِمَةٌ applied to a lion; (Ḳ in this art.;) the م in these being augmentative, accord. to Kh; (TA;) or the former of them, thus applied, *strong in make;* (Ṣ in art. ضبرم;) or the former of them signifies *a lion,* (ISk, Ḳ and TA in that art.,) as also ضُبَارِكٌ, (ISk, TA ibid.,) and so the latter of them; (Ḳ ibid.;) and the former of them, applied to a man, *courageous;* (ISk, TA ibid.;) or each, (Ḳ ibid.,) or the latter of them, (TA ibid.,) thus applied, *bold against the enemies.* (Ḳ and TA ibid.)

ضِبَارَةٌ and ضُبَارَةٌ: see إِضْبَارَةٌ, in four places. — ضَبَائِرُ is pl. of the former [or of each]: (Mgh, Mṣb:) and, as though pl. of the former, signifies *Companies of men in a state of dispersion.* (TA.)

أُمُّ ضَبَّارٍ i. q. الحَرَّة, q. v. (T in art. امر.)

ضُبَّارٌ *A sort of tree resembling very nearly that of the* بَلُّوط, [i. e. *the oak,*] (AḤn, O, Ḳ,) *the wood of which is good as fuel, like that of the* مَغْ: *its fresh firewood, when kindled, sends forth a sound like that of* مَخَارِيق [pl. of مِخْرَاقٌ, q. v.]; *and therefore they use it to do so at the thickets wherein are lions, which flee in consequence:* (AḤn, O:) the n. un. is with ة. (AḤn, O, Ḳ.)

ضُبَارِمٌ and ضُبَارِمَةٌ: see ضُبَارَةٌ.

ضُنْبُرٌ: see ضَبِيرٌ.

إِضْبَارَةٌ *A bundle* (حُزْمَةٌ, Lth, Mgh, Mṣb, Ḳ, or إِضْمَامَةٌ [q. v.], Ṣ, O) of books or writings; (Lth, Ṣ, Mgh, O, Mṣb, Ḳ;) as also أَضْبَارَةٌ, (Ḳ,) and ▼ ضِبَارَةٌ: (Lth, Mgh, Mṣb:) or of arrows: (Lth:) and ▼ ضِبَارَةٌ signifies *a bundle* [absolutely]; as also ▼ ضُبَارَةٌ: (O, Ḳ:) Lth alone explains ضِبَارَةٌ as applied to a bundle of books or writings; others saying إِضْبَارَةٌ: the pl. of إِضْبَارَةٌ is أَضَابِيرُ; (Ṣ, Mgh, O, Mṣb, Ḳ;) and that of ▼ ضِبَارَةٌ is ضَبَائِرُ. (Mgh, O, Mṣb.)

مُضْبَرٌ: see the following paragraph in three places:— and see also ضُبُورٌ.

مُضْبُورٌ A camel *very compact and strong in the bones, and compact and full in flesh;* as also ▼ مُضْبَرٌ: (Ḳ:) or both signify *compact in make, and smooth:* (Lth,* TA:) and ▼ مُضْبَرُ الخَلْقِ a horse *firm in make:* and ▼ مُضْبَرَةُ الخَلْقِ the same applied to a she-camel: (Ṣ:) and ▼ ضَبْرٌ a horse *compact in make;* an inf. n. used as an epithet. (Mṣb.)

Quasi ضبرم

ضُبَارِمٌ and ضُبَارِمَةٌ: see art. ضبر.

ضبط

1. ضَبَطَهُ, (Lth, IDrd, Ṣ, Mṣb, Ḳ,) aor. ـِ, (Mṣb, MṢ, PṢ,) or ـُ, (TA, TḲ,) inf. n. ضَبْطٌ (IDrd, Mṣb, Ḳ) and ضَبَاطَةٌ, (Ḳ,) *He kept it, preserved it, guarded it, maintained it,* or *took care of it,* (Lth, Ṣ, Mṣb, Ḳ,) namely, a thing, (Lth, Ṣ,) *with prudence, precaution,* or *good judgment,* (Lth, Ṣ, Ḳ,) or *effectually:* (Mṣb:) and hence, † *he managed its affairs* (namely, the affairs of a country &c.,) *thoroughly, soundly, not imperfectly:* (Mṣb:) [*he managed it;* namely, an affair, and his soul or self, his disposition or temper, &c.:] *he kept to it inseparably,* or *constantly;* namely, anything: (Lth:) *he took it,* or *held it,* or *retained it, strongly, vehemently,* or *firmly:* (IDrd:) and ضَبَطَ عَلَيْهِ [has this last signification, likewise; or signifies simply *he detained it,* or *withheld it,* or *restrained it,* or *the like;*] i. q. حَبَسَهُ, namely a thing. (TA.) — فُلَانٌ لَا يَضْبِطُ عَمَلَهُ [or لَا يَضْبُطُهُ] ‡ *Such a one does not,* or *will not, act vigorously in his work,* or *employment,* which is committed to him; syn. لَا يَقُومُ بِهِ. (TA.) And ضَبَطَ أَمْرَهُ [*He managed his affair thoroughly,* or *well*]. (A in art. بد, &c.) [And ضَبَطَ alone, *He* (a camel) *was strong to work* or *labour:* and *he* (a man and a camel) *was strong,* or *powerful.* (See the act. part. n.)] — هُوَ لَا يَضْبِطُ قِرَآءَتَهُ [or لَا يَضْبُطُهَا] ‡ *He does not,* or *will not, perform well* [or *accurately*] *his reading,* or *reciting.* (TA.) — ضَبَطَ لَفْظًا, or كَلِمَةً, † *He fixed the pronunciation of a word;* by adding the syllabical signs, which mode is termed ضَبْطٌ بِالشَّكْلِ, and بِالحَرَكَاتِ, and بِالقَلَمِ; or by stating it to be similar in form, or measure, to another word which is too well known to admit of doubt, which mode is termed ضَبْطٌ بِمِثَالٍ; or by adding the measure, which mode is termed ضَبْطٌ بِوَزْنٍ.] — ضَبَطَ also signifies † *He registered,* or *recorded,* [a name, or] a matter of science, [or any other thing,] in a book or the like; syn. قَيَّدَ; (L in art. قيد;) i. q. أَحْصَى; (Jel in xxxvi. 11, and Bḍ and Jel in lxxviii. 29;) and كَتَبَ. (Bḍ in lxxviii. 29.) — ضَبَطَهُ وَجَعٌ ‡ *A pain seized him.* (TA.) — ضُبِطَتِ الأَرْضُ ‡ *The land was rained upon.* (IAạr, Ḳ, TA.) [See also مَضْبُوطٌ.] ═ ضَبِطَ, aor. ـَ, (Ṣ, Mṣb,) inf. n. ضَبَطٌ, (Mṣb,) *He was,* or *became, ambidextrous; he worked with each of his hands.* (Ṣ, Mṣb.) IDrd knew not this verb. (TA.)

5. تضبّطهُ *He took it with detention and force.* (Ḳ, TA.) — تَضَبَّطَتِ الضَّأْنُ *The sheep obtained somewhat of herbage:* or *hastened,* or *were quick, in pasturing, and became strong* (Ḳ, TA) *and fat.* (TA.) The Arabs say, إِذَا تَضَبَّطَتِ الضَّأْنُ شَبِعَتِ الإِبِلُ [*When the sheep obtain somewhat of herbage,* or *hasten,* &c., *the camels become satiated with food*]: for the former are called the smaller camels, because they eat more than goats; and when the former become satiated with food, men [and camels] live [in plenty], by reason of the abundance of the herbage. (IAạr.)

ضَبْطٌ inf. n. of 1. — [It is often used as signifying † *Exactness; correctness; honesty; and faithfulness:* and particularly in an author or a relater.]

الضُّبَيْطَةُ *A certain game of the Arabs;* (Ḳ, TA;) also called المَسَّةُ and الطُّرَيْدَةُ. (TA. [See the last of these words.])

رَجُلٌ ضَبَّاطٌ لِلْأُمُورِ † *A man having much care, prudence,* or *precaution,* [or *good judgment,*] *with respect to* [*the management of*] *affairs;* (TA;) [*a man who manages affairs with much care,* &c.]

ضَبَنْطَى: see the next paragraph.

ضَابِطٌ [*Keeping, preserving, guarding, maintaining,* or *taking care of,* a thing, *with prudence, precaution,* or *good judgment,* or *effectually:* (see 1:) and hence,] † one *who manages his affairs with prudence, precaution,* or *good judgment;* or *soundly, taking the sure course therein, and exercising caution,* or *care, that they may not become beyond his power of management:* (Ṣ, TA:) [*keeping to* anything *inseparably,* or *constantly:* (see, again, 1:)] *taking, holding,* or *retaining,* a thing *strongly, vehemently,* or *firmly;* applied to a man; as also ▼ ضَبَنْطَى: (IDrd:) or the latter of these, (Ṣ,) which is like حَبَنْطَى, (Ḳ, [in some copies of the Ḳ erroneously written without tenween,]) the ن being augmentative, to render the word quasi-coordinate to سَفَرْجَلٌ; (Ṣ;) or both; applied to a man and to a camel; (Ḳ;) *strong,* or *powerful:* (Ṣ, Ḳ:) or [a man] *great in might,* or *valour, and power, and body:* (T, TA:) and the former, a camel *strong to work* or *labour:* and in like manner, applied to a man, ضَابِطٌ لِلْأُمُورِ ‡ *the strong* [*and resolute* or *firm-minded*] *in the performance* or *management of affairs.* (TA.) See also أَضْبَطُ. — [It often signifies † *Exact; correct;* or *accurate;* (like مُحَقِّقٌ, with which it is said to be syn. in Ḥar p. 254;) and *honest;* and *faithful:* and particularly as applied to an author or a relater.] ═ As a conventional term, ضَابِطٌ, (Mṣb in art. قعد,) or ▼ ضَابِطَةٌ, pl. ضَوَابِطُ, (TA,) is *syn. with* قَاعِدَةٌ, (Mṣb, TA,) signifying † *A universal,* or *general, rule,* or *canon:* (Mṣb:) or *a* ضابط is *one that comprises subdivisions of one class only;* whereas a قاعدة comprises [sometimes] subdivisions of various classes. (Kull, p. 290.)

ضَابِطَةٌ *A place in land,* or *in the ground, to which the rain-water flows, and which retains it;* syn. مُسَّاكَةٌ. (TA.) ═ See also ضَابِطٌ, last sentence.

أَضْبَطُ [*More, and most, strong,* or *firm, of hold*]. It is said in a prov., أَضْبَطُ مِنْ ذَرَّةٍ [*More strong,* or *firm, of hold than a little ant*]: because it drags along a thing several times larger than itself, and sometimes both fall from a high place, and the ant does not let go the thing. (Ḳ.) And أَضْبَطُ مِنْ عَائِشَةَ بْنِ عَثْمٍ; (Ḳ;) so accord. to Ḥamzeh and Abu-n-Nedà; but accord. to El-Mundhiree, عَابِسَةَ; (Ṣgh;) [*More strong,* or *firm, of hold than 'Áisheh the son of 'Athm;* or *than 'Ábiseh;*] because he laid hold of the tail of a young she-camel, and pulled her by it out of a well into which she had fallen. (Ḳ.) And أَضْبَطُ مِنَ الأَعْمَى [*More strong,* or *firm, of hold than the blind*]. (TA.) — *Ambidextrous; who works with each of his hands;* (Ṣ, Mgh, Mṣb;) i. q. أَعْسَرُ يَسَرٌ; (Mgh, Mṣb;) *who works with his left hand like as he works with his right;* an explanation given by the Prophet; as also that next following; (AO, TA;) *who works with both his hands:* (AO, Ḳ:) fem. ضَبْطَآءُ. (Ṣ.) — الأَضْبَطُ *The lion;* (Ḳ;) who makes use of his left paw like as he makes use of his right; but some say that he is so called because he seizes his prey vehemently, and it hardly, or never, escapes from him; (TA;) as also ▼ الضَّابِطُ. (Ḳ.) ضَبْطَآءُ is also applied as an epithet to a lioness; and to a she-camel. (TA.)

مَضْبُوطٌ [pass. part. n. of ضَبَطَ in all its senses. — In the present day often used as signifying *Well-regulated; exact; correct; honest;* and *faithful.*] Applied to a book, or writing, ‡ *Having its defects, faults,* or *imperfections, rectified.* (TA.) [Applied to a word, † *Having its pronunciation fixed,* by any of the means described above in one of the explanations of the verb.] — بَلَدٌ مَضْبُوطٌ بِالمَطَرِ ‡ *A country covered by the rain:*

so in the A: in the O, أَرْضٌ مَضْبُوطَةٌ ‡ *land rained upon in common*, or *throughout its whole extent.* (TA.) [See also 1, near the end of the paragraph.]

ضبع

1. ضَبَعَهُ, aor. َ, (Ṣ, Ḳ,) inf. n. ضَبْعٌ, (TḲ,) *He* (a man, Ṣ) *stretched forth towards him* (another man, Ṣ) *his upper arm* (ضَبْعَهُ), *for the purpose of striking.* (Ṣ, Ḳ.) A poet says,

وَلَا صُلْحَ حَتَّى تَضْبَعُونَا وَنَضْبَعَا

i. e. [*And there shall be no peace*] *until ye stretch forth towards us your upper arms* with the swords *and we stretch forth our upper arms* towards you: or, accord. to AA, *until ye stretch forth* [*towards us*] *your upper arms for the making of peace and the joining of hands* [*and we do the same*]. (Ṣ.) And one says, ضَبَعَ يَدَهُ إِلَيْهِ بِالسَّيْفِ, meaning *He stretched forth his arm towards him with the sword.* (Ḳ.) And ضَبَعَ عَلَى فُلَانٍ, (Ṣ,* Ḳ,) inf. n. as above, (TA,) *He stretched forth his upper arms for the purpose of uttering an imprecation against such a one:* (Ṣ,* Ḳ, TA:) and hence, ضَبْعٌ is metaphorically used to signify ‡ the act of *supplicating* or *imprecating;* because the person supplicating or imprecating raises his hands and stretches forth his upper arms: and ضِبَاعٌ, also, [app. an inf. n. of ↓ ضَابَعَ,] signifies the *raising the hands*, or *arms, in supplication* or *imprecation.* (TA.) And ضَبَعَتِ الخَيْلُ, and الإِبِلُ, (Ṣ, Mṣb, Ḳ,) aor. َ, (Ṣ, Mṣb,) inf. n. ضَبْعٌ (Ṣ, Ḳ) and ضُبُوعٌ and ضَبَعَانٌ, (Ḳ,) *The horses,* and *the camels, stretched forth their arms* (أَضْبَاعَهَا, Ṣ, Mṣb, Ḳ, i. e. أَعْضَادَهَا, Ṣ, Mṣb) *in their going along;* (Ṣ, Mṣb, Ḳ;) as also ↓ ضَبَّعَت, inf. n. تَضْبِيعٌ: (Ṣ, Ḳ:) in [a copy of] the A expl. as meaning مَدَّتْ أَعْنَاقَهَا [*stretched forth their necks;* but this is probably a mistranscription, for مدّت أَعْضَادَهَا]: (TA:) ضَبَعَت said of horses is like ضَبَحَت, (Ḳ, TA,) which is a dial. var.: (TA:) and ضَبَعَت said of a she-camel, inf. n. ضَبْعٌ, signifies the same as ↓ ضَبَّعَت, as also ↓ أَضْبَعَت, on the authority of IḲṭṭ: (TA:) [or,] accord. to Aṣ, ضَبْعٌ signifies the *lifting,* (Ṣ,) or *bending,* (TA,) *of the hoof,* (Ṣ, TA,) by a horse, and the *lifting of the foot,* by a camel, (TA,) *towards the arm:* (Ṣ, TA:) or it signifies the *running a pace above that which is termed* تَقْرِيب: (O, Ḳ:) or ضَبَعَ said of a camel signifies *he hastened,* or *was quick,* (Ḳ, TA,) *in pace,* or *going:* (TA:) or *he went along shaking his arms.* (Ḳ.) ضَبَعَهُ also signifies *He* (a camel) *took him* (another camel) *by his arms, and threw him down.* (L in art. عضد, and TA in the present art.) — ضَبَعُوا لِلصُّلْحِ, (Ḳ, TA,) and لِلْمُصَافَحَةِ; (TA;) or ضَبَعُوا إِلَى الصُّلْحِ; and ضَبِعُوا, inf. n. ضَبَعٌ; (Eṭ-Ṭoosee, TA;) *They inclined to peace,* (Eṭ-Ṭoosee, Ḳ, TA,) and *the joining of hands; they desired peace,* &c. (TA.) — ضَبَعُوا لَنَا الطَّرِيقَ, (Ṣ, Ḳ,) or مِنَ الطَّرِيقِ, inf. n. ضَبْعٌ, (TA,) *They gave us a share of the road:* (Ṣ, Ḳ:) so says ISk: (Ṣ:) and in like manner one says, ذَرَعُوا لَنَا طَرِيقًا. (TA.) And ضَبَعُوا الشَّىْءَ, (Ḳ, TA,) or مِنَ الشَّىْءِ, (TA,) *They gave a share of the thing* (Ḳ, TA) *to every one.* (TA.) — And ضَبَعَ, (Ḳ,) inf. n. ضَبْعٌ, (TA,) *He* (a man) *acted wrongfully, unjustly, injuriously,* or *tyrannically:* (Ḳ:) on the authority of Aboo-Sa'eed. (TA.) — ضَبِعَت, aor. َ, inf. n. ضَبَعٌ (Ṣ, Ḳ) and ضَبَعَةٌ; (Ṣ,* Ḳ; [this latter is said in the TA, on the authority of IAạr, to have been used by an Arab of the desert in relation to a woman; and is, accord. to the Ṣ, app., a simple subst.;]) and ↓ أَضْبَعَت, (Ṣ, Ḳ,) and ↓ استضبعت; (Ḳ;) *She* (a camel) *desired* (Ṣ, Ḳ) *vehemently* (Ṣ) *the stallion.* (Ṣ, Ḳ.)

2: see above, in two places. — ضَبَّعَ فُلَانًا *He intervened between him and the object at which he desired to shoot* or *cast.* (Ibn-'Abbád, O, Ḳ.) — And ضَبَّعَ, inf. n. تَضْبِيعٌ, *He was,* or *became, cowardly,* or *weak-hearted:* (Lth, Ḳ:) thus say the vulgar; derived by them from الضَّبُعُ, because this beast becomes still when one comes in upon it, and then it goes forth. (Lth, TA.)

3. ضَابَعْنَاهُمْ بِالسُّيُوفِ *We stretched forth our arms towards them with the swords, they stretching theirs forth towards us* [*therewith*]: so in the "Nawádir" of AA. (TA.) — See also 1, in the former half. — [The inf. n.] مُضَابَعَةٌ also signifies The *joining of hands;* syn. مُصَافَحَةٌ. (TA.)

4: see 1, near the middle of the paragraph: — and also the last sentence of the same.

8. الِاضْطِبَاعُ, which the circuiter round the House [of God, i. e. the Kaabeh,] is commanded to perform, (Ṣ,) or in the case of the مُحْرِم, (Ḳ,) is *The putting the* [*garment called*] رِدَآء *under one's right armpit, and turning back the extremity thereof over his left* [*shoulder*], *exposing to view his right shoulder* [*and arm*] *and covering the left;* (Ṣ, Ḳ, TA;) *like the man that desires to labour at a thing and prepares himself for doing so;* (TA;) thus termed because of exposing to view one of the two upper arms: (Ṣ, Ḳ:) or *the putting one's garment* (Mgh, Mṣb) *under his right arm,* (Mgh,) or *under his right armpit,* (Mṣb,) *and throwing* [*a portion of*] *it upon his left shoulder:* (Mgh, Mṣb:) or *the taking the* إِزَار, or *the* بُرْد, *and putting the middle of it under one's right armpit, and throwing the extremity thereof upon his left shoulder, over his breast and his back:* (IAth, TA:) التَّأَبُّطُ and التَّوَشُّحُ likewise signify the same: so says Az: (Mṣb:) and so says Aṣ of the former: (Ṣ:) and it is also written الِاطِّبَاعُ. (Thus in the TA in explanation of التَّأَبُّط.) You say, اِضْطَبَعَ بِثَوْبِهِ [*He attired himself with his garment in the manner described above*]. (Mgh, Mṣb.) And اضطبع الشَّىْءَ *He put the thing under his upper arms.* (TA. [But accord. to the Mgh, the verb is trans., correctly, only by means of بِ.])

10. see 1, last sentence.

ضَبْعٌ The عَضُد [i. e. *upper arm* of a human being, and *arm* of a quadruped], (Ṣ, Mgh, O, Mṣb, Ḳ,) *altogether:* (Ḳ:) or the *middle thereof,* (Lth, Mgh, O, Ḳ,) *with its flesh:* (O, Ḳ:) and the *inner side thereof:* (Mgh:) or (so in some copies of the Ḳ, but in others "and,") the *armpit:* or the *portion, of the upper part of the* عَضُد, *that is between the armpit and the half of the former:* (Ḳ:) it is of man and of other than man: (TA:) pl. أَضْبَاعٌ. (Ṣ, Mṣb, Ḳ.) One says, أَبَدَ ضَبْعَيْهِ, [expl. in art. بد,] speaking of a man praying. (O, TA.) And أَخَذْتُ بِضَبْعَىْ فُلَانٍ فَلَمْ أُفَارِقْهُ and مَدَدْتُ بِضَبْعَيْهِ, meaning *I seized the middle of the upper arms of such a one* [*and did not relinquish him*]. (Lth, O, TA.) And جَذَبَهُ بِضَبْعَيْهِ ‡ *He raised him,* or *set him up, and rendered his name famous:* and in like manner, أَخَذَ بِضَبْعَيْهِ, and مَدَّ بِضَبْعَيْهِ. (TA.) — Also *Any* [*hill such as is termed*] أَكَمَة *that is black and somewhat oblong.* (IAạr, Ḳ.) — ذَهَبَ بِهِ ضَبْعًا نَبْعًا means بَاطِلًا [i. e., app., *He took it away with a false pretence;* or *in play,* or *sport*]; (Ibn-'Abbád, O, Ḳ, TA;) namely, a thing; (O, TA;) نَبْعًا being an imitative sequent. (TA.) — See also ضَبُعٌ. — And see what here next follows.

ضَبْع ↓ فلان كُنَّا فِى ضُبْعِ فُلَانٍ (Ṣ, O, Ḳ) and ضِبْع ↓ فلان (Ḳ) *We were in the protection,* or *quarter,* (كَنَف, and نَاحِيَة,) *of such a one.* (Ṣ, O, Ḳ: but in the Ḳ, هُوَ is put in the place of كُنَّا.)

كُنَّا فِى ضُبْعِ فُلَانٍ: see what next precedes.

ضَبُعٌ (Ṣ, Mgh, O, Mṣb, Ḳ) and ↓ ضَبْعٌ, (Mṣb, Ḳ,) the former of the dial. of Ḳeys and the latter of the dial. of Temeem, (Mṣb,) [The *female hyena;* or the *hyena, male* and *female;*] *a certain animal of prey,* (سَبُع, [but see what follows,]) (Ḳ,) *well known,* (Ṣ, O,) the *worst,* or *most abominable, of* سِبَاع, (Mgh,) *resembling the wolf, except that, when it runs, it is as though it were lame, wherefore it is called* العَرْجَآءُ: it flees from him who holds in his hand a colocynth: [and they assert that] the dogs bark not at him who retains with him its teeth: if its skin is bound upon the belly of her that is pregnant, she casts not her young: if seed is measured in a measure covered with its skin, the seed-produce is secure from the banes thereof: and the application of its gall-bladder as a collyrium sharpens the sight: (Ḳ:) it is not reckoned among the hostile animals to which the appellation of سَبُع is applied, wherefore the Sunneh allows that its flesh may be eaten, and requires that a compensation be made for it [by the sacrifice of a ram] if it be smitten [and killed] in the sacred territory by a person in the state of iḥrám: (TA voce سَبُع:) the word is of the fem. gender, (Ṣ,* Mgh,* O,* Mṣb, Ḳ,*) and is [said to be] applied peculiarly to the *female;* (Mṣb;) the *male* being called ↓ ضِبْعَانٌ, (Ṣ, Mgh, O, Mṣb, Ḳ,) of which the pl. is ضَبَاعِينُ; (Ṣ, O, Mṣb, Ḳ;) but AḤát disapproved this pl.; (O;) and the female is called [also] ↓ ضِبْعَانَةٌ, of which the pl. is ضِبْعَانَاتٌ; (Ṣ, O, Ḳ;) or ضِبْعَانَةٌ has not been heard applied to the female, but ضَبُعٌ only, and it seems that J has mentioned ضِبْعَانَةٌ as applied to the female from his having supposed ضِبْعَانَاتٌ to be pl. of ضِبْعَانَةٌ, whereas it is pl. of ضِبْعَانٌ, being like جِمَالَاتٌ and رِجَالَاتٌ: (IB in a marginal note in one of my copies of the Ṣ:) but some say that ضَبُعٌ or ضَبْعٌ is applied to the *male;* and the *female* is termed ضَبْعَةٌ, thus with a quiescent letter: (Mṣb:) or, accord. to Ibn-'Abbád, the *female* is termed ضَبُعَةٌ, and its pl. [or rather the coll. gen. n.] is ضَبُعٌ; (O, Ḳ;) or ضَبُعَةٌ is not allowable: (Ṣ, Ḳ:) the pl. of ضَبُعٌ or ضَبْعٌ is أَضْبُعٌ, (Ḳ,) a pl. of pauc., (TA,) and ضِبَاعٌ, (Ḳ,) or the former is pl. of ضَبْعٌ, (Mṣb,) and the latter is pl. of ضَبُعٌ, (Mgh, Mṣb,) and is of the *male* and of the *female,* (Ṣ, Ḳ,) and ضُبُعٌ, (Ḳ,) as though this were pl. of ضِبَاعٌ, (AAF, TA,) and ضُبْعٌ [a contraction of ضُبُعٌ] (Ḳ) and ضُبُعَاتٌ and ضُبُوعَةٌ (TA [in which it is indicated that this last is pl. of ضَبُعٌ]) and [quasi-pl. n.] ↑ مَضْبَعَةٌ. (O, Ḳ.) One says ↑ ضِبْعَانٌ أَمْدَرُ, [in the CḲ, erroneously, ضُبْعَانٌ,] meaning, [*A male hyena*] *inflated in the sides, big in the belly:* or, accord. to some, *whose sides are defiled with earth, or dust.* (Ṣ.) And سَيْلٌ جَارُّ الضَّبُعِ *A torrent that draws forth the* ضبع *from its den;* (O, Ḳ; in the CḲ, جارُّ الضَّبْعِ;) hence meaning † *a torrent produced by vehement rain.* (TA.) And دُلْجَةُ الضَّبُعِ [*The night-journeying of the hyena*]; because the ضَبُع goes round about until midnight. (O, Ḳ.) And مَا يَخْفَى ذٰلِكَ عَلَى الضَّبُعِ [*That is not unapparent to the hyena*]: because the ضَبُع is deemed stupid. (TA.) أَحْمَقُ مِنَ الضَّبُعِ [*More stupid than the hyena*] is a prov. (Meyd.) And أَكَلَتْهُمُ الضَّبُعُ ‡ [*The hyena devoured them*] is said of such as are held in mean estimation. (TA.) [But this may be otherwise rendered, as will be seen from what follows.] The saying of a poet,

تَفَرَّقَتْ غَنَمِى يَوْمًا فَقُلْتُ لَهَا •
يَا رَبِّ سَلِّطْ عَلَيْهَا الذِّئْبَ وَالضَّبُعَا •

[*My sheep, or goats, dispersed themselves, one day, and I said in relation to them, O my Lord, set upon them the wolf and the hyena*], is said to mean an imprecation, that the wolf might kill the living of them, and the hyena devour the dead of them: or, as some say, it means that the speaker prayed for their safety; because, when both fall upon the sheep, or goats, each of them is diverted from the sheep, or goats, by the other; and thus means the saying, اَللّٰهُمَّ ضَبُعًا وَذِئْبًا [*O God, send a hyena and a wolf*]: but the more probable meaning of the poet is an imprecation, the consequence of his anger and fatigue; and the word سَلِّطْ imports a notification of this meaning. (IB, TA.) — [The pl.] الضِّبَاعُ is applied to † *Numerous stars below* بَنَاتُ نَعْشٍ: (O, Ḳ:) or [*the stars* β, γ, δ, *and* μ, *of Bootes;* i. e.] *the star upon the head, and that upon* [*each of*] *the shoulders, and that upon the club, of* العَوَّآء: and the name of أَوْلَادُ الضِّبَاعِ is given to [*The stars* ϑ, ι, κ, *and* λ, app. *with some other faint stars around these, of Bootes;* i. e.] *the stars upon the left hand and fore arm, and what surround the hand, of the faint stars, of* العَوَّآء. (Ḳzw.) — الضَّبُعُ also signifies ‡ *The year of drought* or *sterility* or *dearth;* (Ṣ, IAth, O, Mṣb, Ḳ, TA;) *that is destructive; severe:* of the fem. gender. (TA.) So in a verse cited in art. اما [voce أَمَّا, and again, with a variation, voce إِمَّا]. (Ṣ, O. [But it is here said in the TA that الضَّبُعُ in this instance means the animal of prey thus called.]) [Hence also,] it is related in a trad. of Aboo-Dharr, that a man said, يَا رَسُولَ ٱللّٰهِ أَكَلَتْنَا الضَّبُعُ ‡ [*O Apostle of God, the year of drought has consumed us*]: and he prayed for them. (TA.) [See also two other exs. voce ذِئْبٌ.] — Also ‡ *Hunger.* (Ibn-'Abbád, O, TA.) — And † *Evil,* or *mischief.* (TA.) El-'Okeyleeyeh said, "When a man whose evil, or mischief, we feared removed from us, we used to light a fire behind him:" and being asked "Why?" she said, لِيَتَحَوَّلَ ضَبُعُهُ مَعَهُ, i. e. † *In order that his evil,* or *mischief, might go away with him.* (IAạr, TA.)

ضَبِعَةٌ A she-camel *desiring* [*vehemently* (see 1, last sentence,)] *the stallion;* (Lth, Ḳ;) as also ↑ مِضْبَاعَةٌ: (L, TA:) pl., accord. to the copies of the Ḳ, ضِبَاعٌ and ضَبَاعَى; but in the L, ضِبَاعَى and ضَبَاعَى: (TA:) and sometimes it is used in relation to women. (Ḳ.)

ضِبْعَانٌ; and its fem., with ة: see ضَبُعٌ, in three places.

ضَابِعٌ A she-camel *stretching forth her arms* (أَعْضَادَهَا, Ṣ, Ḳ, i. e. أَضْبَاعَهَا, Ṣ) *in going along:* (Ṣ, Ḳ:) or *lifting her foot towards her arm in going along:* so accord. to an explanation by Aṣ of the former of the two following pls.: (TA:) the pl. is ضَوَابِعُ (Lth, Aṣ, TA) and ضُبَّعٌ. (TA.) And A horse *that runs vehemently;* (O, Ḳ, TA;) like ضَابِحٌ, of which the pl. is ضَوَابِحُ: (TA:) or *that runs much:* (Lth, O, TA:) or *that bends his hoof towards his arm:* (TA:) or *that inclines towards* (lit. *follows*) *one of his sides, and bends his neck.* (Ibn-'Abbád, O, Ḳ.)

أَضْبَعُ *i. q.* أَعْضَبُ [q. v.]; formed from the latter by transposition. (TA.)

مَضْبَعَةٌ The *portion of flesh that is beneath the armpit, in the fore part.* (O, Ḳ.) — See also ضَبُعٌ [of which it is a quasi-pl. n.].

مِضْبَاعَةٌ: see ضَبِعَةٌ.

مُضْبِعَةٌ A she-camel *whose breast is prominent and whose arms recede.* (Ibn-'Abbád, O, Ḳ.)

حِمَارٌ مَضْبُوعٌ *An ass devoured by the* ضَبُع [or *hyena*]: (O, Ḳ:) or [*an ass which may the hyena devour,* for] accord. to some it means an imprecation that the ضبع may devour him. (TA.)

ضبن

1. ضَبَنَهُ, aor. ِ, inf. n. ضَبْنٌ, *He put him,* or *it,* (i. e. a man, or another thing,) *above his* ضِبْن [q. v.]. (TA.) [See also what next follows.]

4. اضبنهُ *He put it in his* ضِبْن, (Ṣ, Ḳ, TA,) or *on his* ضِبْن; (TA;) or *he took it beneath his* ضِبْن, i. e. *his* حِضْن [or *the part between his armpit and flank*]: (A'Obeyd, TA:) and ↑ اضطبنهُ signifies the same. (Ṣ, Ḳ, TA.) — And *He straitened him,* or *it,* (Ḳ, TA,) *by putting him,* or *it, beneath his side.* (TA.)

8. اضطبنهُ: see 4. — Also *He took him,* or *it, with his hand, and raised him,* or *it, to a little above his navel.* (TA.)

ضِبْنٌ The *part between the armpit and the* كَشْح [or *flank*]; (Ṣ, Ḳ, TA;) or the حِضْن [which generally means as above]; (A'Obeyd, TA;) [or] the *part, of the side, between the armpit and the* حِضْن [which is here evidently used as syn. with كَشْح]: (Ṣ:) or the *armpit* [itself]: so says Ibn-El-Faraj: like ضِبْرٌ: (TA in art ضبر:) or the *armpit and the part next to it:* or the *uppermost part of the side:* or the *part beneath the* كَشْح [or *flank*] *and beneath the armpit:* or the *part between the* خَاصِرَة [or *flank*] *and the head* [or *crest*] *of the hip.* (TA.) — [Hence,] † *A side of a road:* one says, أَخَذَ فِى ضِبْنٍ مِنَ الطَّرِيقِ † *He took a side of the road:* pl. أَضْبَانٌ. (TA.) — And هُوَ فِى ضِبْنِ فُلَانٍ means † *He is in the quarter,* or *protection, of such a one;* as also ↑ فِى ضِبْنَتِهِ. (TA.) — [The pl.] أَضْبَانٌ signifies also ‡ The *narrow places* (مَضَايِق) of the جَمَل [an evident mistranscription for جَبَل i. e. mountain]. (TA.) — And † *Places abounding with beasts of prey:* (Ḳ, TA:) sing. ضِبْنٌ. (TA.) — And الضِّبْنُ signifies † *That* [*place, or ground,*] *which renders people impotent,* or *helpless, to dig it.* (Ḳ.)

ضَبَنٌ *Deficiency,* or *a falling short.* (Ḳ, TA.)

مَكَانٌ ضَبِنٌ *A narrow place.* (Ṣ.)

ضَبْنَةٌ and ضُبْنَةٌ: see what next follows.

ضِبْنَةٌ and ↑ ضَبِنَةٌ (Ṣ, Ḳ) and ↑ ضَبْنَةٌ and ↑ ضُبْنَةٌ (Ḳ) The *household,* or *family,* (Ṣ, Ḳ, TA,) of a man, (Ṣ,) and [his] *relations,* or *servants,* or *other dependents:* (TA:) or the *cattle, and household,* or *family, that are under one's authority, and which he minds,* or *to which he attends, and the maintenance whereof is incumbent on him.* (IAth, TA.) And *A travelling-companion,* or *travelling-companions, in whom is no profit,* or *advantage,* (Ḳ, TA,) *being only such as he who travels with him,* or *them, has the burden of supporting.* (TA.) — See also ضِبْنٌ.

ضَبِنَةٌ: see the next preceding paragraph.

ضبانة [app. ضِبَانَةٌ, like بِطَانَةٌ, which is one of its syns.,] A man's *particular,* or *special, intimates, friends,* or *associates,* and his *aiders,* or *assistants, and kinsfolk.* (TA.)

ضبنط

ضَبَنْطَى : see art. ضبط. It is mentioned in the Ḳ and by Ṣgh both here and in art. ضبط.

ضبو or ضبى

1. ضَبَتْهُ النَّارُ, (Ṣ, M, Ḳ,) and الشَّمْسُ, (M,) aor. ـُ, [or ـِ,] inf. n. ضَبْوٌ, (Ṣ, Ḳ,) or ضَبْىٌ, (M,) or both, (IḲṭṭ, TA,) *The fire,* (Ṣ, M, Ḳ,) and *the sun,* (M,) *altered* [*in colour*], and *roasted, broiled,* or *fried, him,* or *it*: (Ṣ, Ḳ:) or *burned,* or *scorched, him,* or *it.* (M.) —— ضَبَا إِلَيْهِ *He had recourse,* or *betook himself, to him,* or *it, for refuge, protection,* or *covert*: (Ḳ:) a dial. var. of ضَبَأَ. (TA.)

4. اضبى *i. q.* أَمْسَكَ: (M, Ḳ:) so in the phrase, اضبى الرَّجُلُ عَلَى مَا فِى يَدَيْهِ [*The man grasped,* or *kept hold of, that which was in his hands*]: a dial. var. of أَضْبَأَ: (Lḥ, M:) like أَضَبَّ. (TA in art. ضبأ.) — And اضبى عَلَيْهِ *He was,* or *became, at the point of gaining possession of it*; (Ks, T, Ṣ, Ḳ;) namely, a thing. (Ks, Ṣ.) — And *He concealed it, and was silent respecting it.* (IḲṭṭ, TA. [App. a dial. var. of أَضْبَأَ.]) —— And *i. q.* رَفَعَ [*He raised*; &c.]: so in the Ḳ: but in the Tekmileh وَقَعَ [*he,* or *it, fell*; &c.]. (TA.) —— And *i. q.* أَضْوَى [but in what sense is not shown]. (Ḳ.) —— اضبى بِهِمِ السَّفَرُ *The journey failed of fulfilling its promise to them in respect of what they hoped to obtain in it, of gain, and profit,* or *advantage.* (El-Hejeree, M, Ḳ.*)

ضَابٍ *Ashes.* (Ṣ, Ḳ.)

مَضْبَاةٌ, (M, and thus in a copy of the Ṣ,) or مِضْبَاةٌ, (thus in a copy of the Ṣ, [and Freytag states it to be thus accord. to IDrd, but accord. to the Ṣ to be مَضْبَاوَةٌ, which is evidently a mistake,]) or مُضْبَاةٌ, with ḍamm, (Ḳ, and said in the TA to be thus written in copies of the Ṣ,) *A cake of bread baked in hot ashes*: (Ṣ, M, Ḳ:) thus called by some of the people of El-Yemen: but [ISd says, respecting مَضْبَاةٌ as thus expl.,] I know not how this is unless the thing be named by the name of the place. (M.)

مَضَابٍ [a pl. of which the sing. is most probably مِضْبًى] *Frying-pans*: like مَضَابِحُ. (AḤn, TA in art. ضبح.)

ضج

1. ضَجَّ, aor. ـِ, inf. n. ضَجِيجٌ (L, Mṣb, TA) and ضَجٌّ and ضَجَاجٌ and ضُجَاجٌ, the last on the authority of Lḥ, (L, TA,) [and the last but one is said in one place in the L and TA to be a subst. from ضَاجَّهُ,] *He cried out,* or *vociferated*: (L:) or *he cried out,* or *vociferated, calling for aid,* or *succour*: (AA:) or *he cried out,* or *vociferated, and raised a clamour,* or *confused cries* or *shouts* or *noises, being frightened at a thing*: (Mṣb:) or ضَجِيجٌ signifies the *crying out,* or *vociferating, on the occasion of some disagreeable occurrence, and in difficulty,* or *distress, and inability to bear what has befallen one,* or *impatience*: (Kitáb el-Ghareebeyn:) or ↓ أَضَجُّوا, inf. n. إِضْجَاجٌ, signifies *they cried out,* or *vociferated, and raised a clamour,* or *confused cries* or *shouts* or *noises*: and ضَجُّوا, aor. ـِ, inf. n. ضَجِيجٌ, [as meaning *they did so*] *when unable to bear a thing that had befallen them,* or *impatient, and overcome,* (A'Obeyd, Ṣ, Ḳ, TA,) *and frightened.* (TA.) And one says also, ضَجَّ الْبَعِيرُ, (A, L,) inf. n. ضَجِيجٌ, (L,) [*The camel uttered a cry,* i. e. *grumbled,*] مِنَ الْحِمْلِ [*in consequence of the load*]. (A. [See 1 in art. رغو.]) And إِنْ ضَجَّ فَزِدْهُ وِقْرًا [*If he grumble, add to him a load*]: a prov. (A.) The poet El-Ḳanánee uses the phrase فَضَجْضَجَتْ for فَضَجَّتْ ضَجَّةً; and it is cited by Sb as an ex. of the incorporation of ت into ض. (O.)

2. ضَجَّجَ, inf. n. تَضْجِيجٌ, *He went away*: or *he inclined,* or *declined.* (O, Ḳ.) —— And *He poisoned* a bird, or a beast of prey. (O, Ḳ.)

3. ضَاجَّهُ, (Ṣ, O,) inf. n. مُضَاجَّةٌ (Ṣ, O, Ḳ) and ضِجَاجٌ, (Ṣ, Ḳ,) *He acted with him in an evil manner; treated him with enmity,* or *hostility*; (Ṣ, O, Ḳ, TA;) and *contended in altercation with him.* (Ṣ,* O,* Ḳ,* TA.)

4: see 1. —— [Reiske, as mentioned by Freytag, explains اضجّ also as a trans. verb, meaning "*Fatigavit, molestia affecit.*"]

ضَجَّةٌ, a subst., signifying *A crying out,* or *vociferating*: (L:) or *a clamour,* or *confusion of cries* or *shouts* or *noises,* of a people or party. (Ṣ, Mṣb.)

ضَجَاجٌ a subst. from ضَاجَّهُ; [as such signifying *Evil,* or *inimical, conduct*; and *contention*:] (Ṣ, L, TA:) [and] *compulsion.* (Ḳ, TA.) — [Also] an inf. n. of 1, sometimes used as an epithet, [meaning *That cries out,* or *vociferates,* &c.,] applied to a man: pl. ضُجُجٌ. (L.) [Freytag explains it, from the Deewán of Jereer, as meaning "*Vanus, nefas.*"] —— Also *i. q.* عَاجٌ [as meaning *A kind of bracelet*]; (T, O, Ḳ, TA;) which is *like the* سِوَار *of a woman.* (O, TA.) — And *A kind of bead* (خَرَزَة), (O, Ḳ, TA,) *used by women in their attracting* [*of men*]. (TA.) — See also the next paragraph.

ضِجَاجٌ *A certain gum which is eaten* (O, Ḳ, TA) *in its moist state: when it has become dry, it is pounded, then formed into lumps, and made potent with potash, and one washes with it the garment,* or *piece of cloth, which it cleanses like soap.* (O, TA.) And *The fruit of a certain plant*; or *a gum*; *with which women wash their heads*: written by IDrd with fet-ḥ [i. e. ↓ ضَجَاجٌ], but by AḤn with kesr. (TA.) — And (as AḤn says in one place, O, TA) *Any tree with which birds,* or *beasts of prey, are poisoned.* (O, Ḳ, TA.)

ضَجُوجٌ A she-camel *that cries out when being milked, and is impatient.* (Ṣ, O, Ḳ.)

أَضَجُّ, ضَجَاجٌ أَضَجُّ, and, by poetic license أَضْجَجُ, [meaning *Very evil* or *inimical conduct* &c.,] is a phrase like شِعْرٌ شَاعِرٌ. (TA.)

ضجر

1. ضَجِرَ, aor. ـَ, (Ṣ, A, Mgh, Mṣb, Ḳ,) inf. n. ضَجَرٌ; (Ṣ, Mgh, Mṣb;) and ↓ تضجّر; (A, Mgh, Mṣb, Ḳ;) *He was vexed,* or *disquieted by grief*: (Ṣ:) or, followed by مِنْهُ, (A, Mgh, Mṣb, Ḳ,) and by بِهِ, (A, Ḳ,) *he was vexed,* or *disquieted by grief, at it,* or *by reason of it, and by distress of mind, and complained*: (Mgh:) or *he was grieved at it,* or *by reason of it,* (A, Mṣb,) *and distressed in mind,* (A,) or *vexed,* or *disquieted,* (Mṣb,) *and complained*: (A, Mṣb:) or *he was disgusted* (تَبَرَّمَ, A, Ḳ) *at it,* or *by it, and was vexed,* or *disquieted,* (Ḳ,) *by grief.* (TA.) — And ضَجِرَ *He* (a camel) *cried,* or *grumbled, much*: (Ṣ:) and ضَجِرَتْ *she* (a camel) *cried,* or *grumbled,* (A, Ḳ,) *much,* (A,) *on being milked,* (A, Ḳ,) *being distressed thereby.* (A.) In a verse, (of El-Akhṭal, TA,) ضَجِرَ is contracted into ضَجْرَ; like as فَخِذٌ, among nouns, is contracted [into فَخْذٌ]. (Ṣ, TA.)

4. اضجرهُ *He caused him to be vexed,* or *disquieted by grief* (Ṣ, Mgh) *and by distress of mind, and to complain*: (Mgh:) or *he caused him to grieve,* (مِنْهُ *at it,* or *by reason of it,*) *and to be vexed,* or *disquieted, and to complain*: (Mṣb:) or *he caused him to be disgusted, and vexed,* or *disquieted,* (Ḳ,) *by grief.* (TA.)

5: see 1, first sentence.

ضَجْرٌ: see the next paragraph.

ضَجِرٌ A man *vexed,* or *disquieted by grief*: (Ṣ:) or *grieved,* (A, Mṣb,) *and distressed in mind,* (A,) or *vexed,* or *disquieted,* (Mṣb,) *and complaining*: (A, Mṣb:) or *disgusted,* (مُتَبَرِّمٌ, A, Ḳ,) *and vexed,* or *disquieted,* (Ḳ,) *by grief*: (TA:) and ↓ مُتَضَجِّرٌ signifies the same: (A:) and so, but in an intensive manner, ↓ ضُجَرَةٌ: (TA:) and ↓ ضَجُورٌ is also an epithet [in this last, intensive, sense,] applied to a man: (Ṣ, Mṣb:) accord. to Aboo-Bekr, ضَجِرٌ, signifying *straitened,* or *distressed, in mind,* is from the same word in the sense here next following. (TA.) — A *narrow* place; (Aboo-Bekr, Ḳ;) as also ↓ ضَجْرٌ. (Ḳ.)

ضَجْرَةٌ *Grief, and distress of mind, with complaint*: (A:) or *disgust* (تَبَرُّمٌ, A, Ḳ) *and vexation,* or *disquietude,* (Ḳ,) *arising from grief.* (TA.) [SM supposes Z to have said that it is syn. with مُتَضَجِّرٌ: but this is a mistake.] —— Also *A certain small bird*: (AḤát, O, Ḳ:*) as though [so called because], by reason of its disquietude, not remaining in one place. (TA.)

ضُجَرَةٌ: see ضَجِرٌ.

ضَجُورٌ: see ضَجِرٌ. — Also A she-camel *that cries,* or *grumbles,* (A, Ḳ,) *much,* (A,) *on being milked,* (A, Ḳ,) *being distressed thereby.* (A.) — It is said in a prov., applied to a niggard from whom property is obtained by degrees, notwithstanding his niggardliness, إِنَّ الضَّجُورَ قَدْ تُحْلَبُ [*Verily the she-camel that grumbles* (or *that grumbles much*) *on being milked is sometimes milked*]. (A'Obeyd.)

مُضْجِرٌ act. part. n. of 4: pl. مَضَاجِيرُ and مَضَاجِرُ. (Ṣ, Ḳ.)

مُتَضَجِّرٌ: see ضَجِرٌ.

ضجع

1. ضَجَعَ, aor. ـَ, inf. n. ضَجْعٌ and ضُجُوعٌ, [*He lay upon his side*; or] *he laid his side upon the ground*; [and simply *he lay*; and *he slept*;] as also ↓ اِضْطَجَعَ, (Ṣ, Mṣb, Ḳ, TA,) which is also expl. as syn. with نَامَ, [which has the second and third of the meanings mentioned above,] and with اِسْتَلْقَى, [which has the third of those meanings,] (TA,) the ط being substituted for the ت of اِضْتَجَعَ, (Lth, Ṣ, Mṣb,) and ↓ اِضَّجَعَ, (Ṣ, Mṣb, Ḳ,) and ↓ اِلْطَجَعَ, (Ṣ, L, Ḳ, in the CḲ [erroneously] اِلَّجَعَ,) the ض in اضطجع being changed into ل, which is the letter nearest in sound thereto, because the combination of two such letters as ض and ط is disliked, (Ṣ, L,) the same change occurring in اِلْطِرَادٌ for اِضْطِرَادٌ, (Az, TA,) though this change is anomalous; (L;) and ↓ أَضْجَعَ likewise signifies the same as ضَجَعَ; (Mṣb;) [and] so does ↓ انضجع, (Ḳ, TA,) as quasi-pass. of the trans. verb اضجع. (TA.) — [And accord. to Freytag, it occurs in the Deewán of the Hudhalees as signifying *He declined from the way.*] — ضَجَعَ النَّجْمُ means ‡ [*The star, or asterism,* or *the Pleiades,*] *inclined to setting*; as also ↓ ضَجَّعَ, (Ḳ, TA,) inf. n. تَضْجِيعٌ. (TA.) And ضَجَعَتِ الشَّمْسُ is a dial. var. of ↓ ضَجَّعَت, (TA,) which means ‡ *The sun approached the setting*; (Ṣ, Ḳ, TA;) like ضَرَّعَت. (Ṣ, TA.) — ضَجَعَ فِى أَمْرِهِ ‡ *He was,* or *became, weak in his affair*; as also ↓ اضجع; and so ضَجِعَ, like فَرِحَ [in measure], on the authority of IḲṭṭ. (TA. [See also 2, and 5, and 6.]) And ضَجِعَ فِى رَأْيِهِ [not a mistranscription for ضَجَعَ, as is shown by its part. n., q. v.,] ‡ *He was,* or *became, weak in his judgment,* or *opinion.* (TA.)

2: see above, in two places. — ضَجَّعَ فِى الأَمْرِ, (Mgh, Ḳ,) inf. n. تَضْجِيعٌ, (Ṣ,) ‡ *He fell short of doing what was requisite,* or *due, in the affair*; (Ṣ, Mgh, Ḳ, TA;) and *was,* or *became, weak therein.* (Mgh.) [See also ضَجَعَ فِى أَمْرِهِ, and see 5, and 6.] — Hence, التَّضْجِيعُ فِى النِّيَّةِ † *The wavering,* or *vacillating, in intention, and not making it to take effect.* (Mgh.)

3. ضاجعهُ, (Ṣ, TA,) inf. n. مُضَاجَعَةٌ, *He lay upon his side,* or simply *he lay,* or *slept, with him.* (TA.) And ضَاجَعَهَا, (Mṣb, TA,) inf. n. as above, (Mṣb,) *He lay,* or *slept, with her,* (Mṣb, TA,) namely, his girl, or young woman, (TA,) *in,* or *on, one bed,* (Mṣb,) or *in one innermost garment.* (TA.) — And hence, ضاجعهُ الهَمُّ ‡ *Anxiety clave to him.* (TA.)

4. أَضْجَعْتُهُ, (Ṣ, Mṣb, Ḳ,) inf. n. إِضْجَاعٌ, (TA,) *I laid him upon his side*; (Ṣ,* Mṣb;) *I laid his side upon the ground.* (Ḳ.) — And ‡ *I lowered it,* or *depressed it,* namely, a thing. (Ḳ, TA.) — اضجع الرُّمْحُ الطَّعْنَ ‡ [app. *The spear made the thrusting to be in a downward direction*]. (TA.) — اضجع جُوَالِقَهُ † *He emptied his sack, it being full.* (O, Ḳ.) — الإِضْجَاعُ in relation to the vowel-sounds is ‡ like الإِمَالَةُ and الخَفْضُ. (Ḳ, TA. [See arts. ميل and خفض.]) — See also 1, in two places.

5. تضجّع فِى الأَمْرِ ‡ *He held back in the affair,* (Ṣ, Ḳ, TA,) *and did not undertake it.* (Ṣ, TA.) [See also 1, and 2, and 6.] — And تَضَجَّعَ السَّحَابُ ‡ *The clouds continued raining* (أَرَبَّ) *in the place.* (Ṣ, Ḳ, TA.)

6. تضاجع عَنْ أَمْرِ كَذَا وَكَذَا ‡ *He feigned himself unmindful,* or *heedless, of such and such an affair.* (Z, TA.) [See also 1, and 2, and 5.]

7: see 1, first sentence.

8. اِضْطَجَعَ, and its vars. اِضَّجَعَ and اِلْطَجَعَ: see 1, first sentence. — الإِضْطِجَاعُ فِى السُّجُودِ is ‡ *The not drawing up the body from the ground in prostration* [in prayer]; (Mgh, TA;) *the contracting oneself, and making the breast to cleave to the ground, therein.* (Ḳ, TA.) [See also its part. n., below.]

ضَجْعٌ [The *species of glasswort,* or *kali, called*] غَاسُول, *for* [*washing*] *clothes*: n. un. with ة: (Ḳ:) accord. to IDrd, the *gum of a certain plant,* or *a certain plant* [*itself*], *with which clothes are washed*: (O:) of the dial. of El-Yemen: (TA:) and, (O, Ḳ,) accord. to Ed-Deenawaree, (O,) i. e. AḤn, (TA,) *a certain plant,* (Ḳ,) *resembling small cucumbers,* (O, Ḳ, TA,) [or] *in shape like asparagus,* (TA,) *but thicker* (O, Ḳ, TA) *in a great degree,* (O, TA,) *four-sided in the stalks,* (O, Ḳ, TA,) *and having in it an acidity* (O, TA,) *and a bitterness* (مَرَارَة O) or *a taste between sweet and sour* (مَزَازَة TA): *it is crushed* (يُشْدَخُ O) or *cut into slices* (يشرح TA) *and its juice is expressed into milk such as is termed* رَائِب [q. v.], *which in consequence becomes pleasant,* (O, Ḳ, TA,) *and somewhat biting to the tongue; and its leaves are put into sour milk, like as is done with the leaves of the mustard*: (O, TA:) *it is good as an aphrodisiac.* (O, Ḳ, TA.)

ضَجْعٌ † *Inclination*: (O, Ḳ:) so in the phrase ضَجْعُ فُلَانٍ إِلَى فُلَانٍ † [*The inclination of such a one is towards such a one*], (O,) or إِلَىَّ [*towards me*]. (Ḳ.)

ضَجْعَةٌ *A single act of lying, upon the side* or *otherwise,* or *of sleeping*: (IAth, O,* TA:) *a sleep.* (Ḳ, TA.) — And ‡ *Weakness* in judgment; (O, Ḳ, TA;) as also ↓ ضُجْعَةٌ. (Ḳ.) One says, فِى رَأْيِهِ ضَجْعَةٌ ‡ *In his judgment is weakness.* (O, TA.) — And ‡ *Ease; repose; freedom from trouble* or *inconvenience, and toil* or *fatigue*; as also ↓ ضُجْعَةٌ. (TA.)

ضُجَعَةٌ *One whom people often lay upon his side* [or *throw down*]. (Ḳ, TA.) — [And app., *One who lays others on the side,* or *prostrates them*; as is implied by what here follows.] — † *A disease*: (Ḳ, TA:) because it lays the man upon his bed. (TA.) — See also ضُجْعَةٌ, in two places. — And see ضُجَعَةٌ.

ضِجْعَةٌ *A mode,* or *manner, of lying upon the side* [or *in any posture*], (Ṣ, O, Mṣb, Ḳ,) or *of sleeping.* (TA.) — And † *Sluggishness, laziness,* or *indolence.* (Ḳ, TA.) — Also, for ذَاتُ ضِجْعَةٍ, † *A bed.* (JM. [See also مَضْجَعٌ.]) It is said in a trad. that the ضِجْعَة of the Apostle of God was of skins, (IAth, JM, TA,) stuffed with fibres of the palm-tree: (IAth, TA:) meaning his *bed.* (JM.)

ضُجْعَةٌ a gen. n. (O, Ḳ) in the sense of اِضْطِجَاعٌ [i. e. The act of *lying upon the side,* or *in any manner*; and of *sleeping*]. (O.)

ضُجَعَةٌ, (Ṣ, O, Ḳ,) and, accord. to the Ḳ, ↓ ضُجْعَةٌ, but this [as an epithet] has the meaning first assigned to it above, (TA,) and ↓ ضِجْعِيَّةٌ and ↓ ضُجْعِيَّةٌ and ↓ ضُجْعِىٌّ and ↓ ضِجْعِىٌّ, (O, Ḳ,) the last two [in the CḲ, erroneously, ضُجْعَى, but] like قُعْدِىٌّ and قِعْدِىٌّ, (O,) and ↓ ضَاجِعٌ, (Ḳ,) [or this last is a simple part. n.,] ‡ A man *who lies upon his side* [or *in any manner,* or *sleeps,*] *much,* or *often*: (Ṣ, O, Ḳ, TA:) *sluggish, lazy,* or *indolent*: (Ṣ and O in explanation of the first, and Ḳ in explanation of all:) or *who keeps to the house* or *tent*; *seldom,* or *never, going forth*; *nor rising and speeding to do a generous deed*: or *impotent and stationary*: (Ḳ, TA:) [or,] accord. to IB, ↓ ضَاجِعٌ and ↓ ضُجْعِىٌّ and ↓ ضِجْعِىٌّ signify one *who is content with his poverty, and betakes himself to his house* or *tent.* (TA.)

ضُجْعِىٌّ and ضِجْعِىٌّ: see each in two places in the next preceding paragraph.

ضُجْعِيَّةٌ and ضِجْعِيَّةٌ: see ضُجَعَةٌ.

ضَجُوعٌ A water-skin (قِرْبَةٌ) *that makes the drawer of water to lean by reason of its heaviness.* (Ibn-'Abbád, O, Ḳ.) — A *wide* دَلْوٌ [or leathern bucket]; (Ibn-'Abbád, O, Ḳ;) as also ↓ ضَاجِعَةٌ. (Ibn-'Abbád, O.) — ‡ A cloud (سَحَابَةٌ) *slow by reason of the abundance of its water.* (IDrd, O, Ḳ, TA.) — A well (بِئْرٌ) *hollowed in the sides, the water having eaten its interior.* (AA, O, Ḳ.*) — A she-camel *that pastures aside.* (A'Obeyd, O, Ḳ.) — A wife *contrarious to the husband.* (Ibn-'Abbád, O, Ḳ. [See also أَضْجَعُ.]) — And ‡ A man *weak in judgment*; (IDrd, O, Ḳ;) as also ↓ مَضْجُوعٌ. (Ḳ.)

ضَجِيعٌ [*A bedfellow*]. ضَجِيعُكَ means *He who lies,* or *sleeps, with thee*; (Ṣ, O, Mṣb;) i. q. ↓ مُضَاجِعُكَ; (Ḳ;) which latter is likewise applied to a female; as also ضَجِيعَةٌ: and you say,

هُوَ ضَجِيعُهَا meaning *He is he who lies*, or *sleeps*, *with her in one innermost garment*; and هِىَ ضَجِيعَتُهُ *She is she who so lies*, or *sleeps*, *with him*. (TA.) And [hence] one says, بِئْسَ الضَّجِيعُ الجُوعُ ‡ [*Very evil is the bedfellow, hunger*]. (TA.)

ضَاجِعٌ *Lying upon his side* [or *in any manner*; and *sleeping*; see its verb]; (Ṣ, Mṣb, Ḳ;) as also ▼ مُضْطَجِعٌ (TA) and ▼ مُضْجِعٌ. (Mṣb.) See also ضُجَعَةٌ, in two places. — ‡ *Stupid, foolish*, or *unsound in intellect*: (IAạr, O, Ḳ, TA:) because of his impotence, and his cleaving to his place. (TA.) — دَلْوٌ ضَاجِعَةٌ *A leathern bucket that is full*, (IAạr, ISk, O, Ḳ,) *so that it leans in rising from the well by reason of its heaviness*. (ISk, O, Ḳ.) See also ضَجُوعٌ. — And ضَاجِعٌ ‡ A star *inclining to setting*: pl. ضَوَاجِعُ: (O, Ḳ, TA:) [or] الضَّوَاجِعُ signifies [or signifies also] *the fixed stars*. (Ḥam p. 364.) — And ‡ *Inclining* as in the saying أَرَاكَ ضَاجِعًا إِلَى فُلَانٍ ‡ [*I see thee inclining towards such a one*]. (O, TA.) — And † *A place of bending of a valley*: pl. ضَوَاجِعُ. (O, Ḳ.) — Also, applied to a beast, † *Worthless; in which is no good*. (TA.) [But] — غَنَمٌ ضَاجِعَةٌ means *Numerous sheep* or *goats*; as also ▼ ضَجْعَآءُ. (Fr, Ṣ, O, Ḳ.) — And إِبِلٌ ضَوَاجِعُ and ضَاجِعَةٌ † *Camels keeping to the plants called* حَمْض; *remaining among them*. (TA.)

ضَاجِعَةٌ as a subst. i. q. مَصَبُّ وَادٍ; (AA, T, O, Ḳ, TA; [app. meaning The *place where the water flows into it, of a valley*; for] Az adds, in the T, as though it were a رَحَبَة, [see رَحَبَةُ الوَادِى in art. رحب,] then, afterwards, it takes a straight direction, and becomes a valley (وَادٍ): pl. ضَوَاجِعُ. (TA.) — ضَوَاجِعُ [which is likewise pl. of ضَاجِعٌ] also signifies [*Hills such as are called*] هِضَاب [pl. of هَضْبَةٌ]; (Ṣ, O, Ḳ;) and is said to have no sing. [in this sense]: occurring in a verse of En-Nábighah Edh-Dhubyánee: (Ṣ:) but ISk says that, in this instance, it is the name of a certain place. (O.)

أَضْجَعُ الثَّنَايَا ‡ *Having the central incisors inclining*; (O, Ḳ, TA;) applied to a man: (O:) pl. ضُجْعٌ. (TA.) — And أَضْجَعُ signifies also *Contrarious to his wife*. (O, Ḳ. [See also ضَجُوعٌ.]) — For a meaning of its fem., ضَجْعَآءُ, see ضَاجِعٌ, last sentence but one.

مَضْجَعٌ *A place in which*, or *on which, one lies upon his side* [or *in any manner*, or *sleeps*]; (O, Mṣb, Ḳ;) as also ▼ مُضْطَجَعٌ: (O, Ḳ:) [*a bed*; and *the like*:] pl. مَضَاجِعُ: (Mṣb, TA:) which means sometimes *places of sleep*, or *of passing the night*: (Bḍ in iv. 38:) and *beds*; or *other things spread upon the ground to lie upon*. (Jel ibid., and Bḍ in xxxii. 16.) — [Hence] the pl. is used as meaning † *Wives*, or *women*: so in the saying, هُوَ طَيِّبُ المَضَاجِعِ i. e. † *He has well-born wives* or *women*; like كَرِيمُ المَفَارِشِ. (TA.) — And مَضَاجِعُ الغَيْثِ means ‡ *The places of falling of rain*. (O, Ḳ, TA.) One says, بَاتَتِ الرِّيَاضُ مَضَاجِعَ لِلْغَيْثِ ‡ [*The meadows were during the night places of the falling of rain*]. (A, TA.)

مُضْجِعٌ: see ضَاجِعٌ, first sentence.

مَضْجُوعٌ: see ضَجُوعٌ, last sentence.

مُضَاجِعٌ: see ضَجِيعٌ.

مُضْطَجَعٌ: see مَضْجَعٌ. — It is also used as an inf. n. (Ḥar p. 664.)

مُضْطَجِعٌ: see ضَاجِعٌ, first sentence. — [It is said that] صَلَّى مُضْطَجِعًا means ‡ *He prayed lying upon his right side*, [or app., *inclining towards that side*,] *facing the kibleh*. (TA. [But see 8.])

ضجم

1. ضَجِمَ, (MA, Ḳ,) aor. ـَ, (Ḳ,) inf. n. ضَجَمٌ, (MA, Ḳ,*) *It was*, or *became, distorted*, or *crooked*; said of the mouth; (MA, Ḳ;) and in like manner one says of the side of the mouth; and of the lip; and of the chin; and of the neck: (Ḳ:) and likewise, ‡ of a well: and ‡ of a wound. (Ḳ, TA.) [See ضَجَمٌ below.]

6. تضاجم [*He was*, or *became, distorted*, or *crooked, in the mouth*: (see its part. n., below:) and so, accord. to Golius, ▼ اضجم and ▼ اضجامّ. — And] ‡ i. q. اِخْتَلَفَ: (Ṣ, Ḳ, TA:) so in the saying, تَضَاجَمَ الأَمْرُ بَيْنَهُمْ ‡ [*The affair*, or *case, was*, or *became, complicated, intricate*, or *confused, so as to be a subject of disagreement*, or *difference, between them*]. (Ṣ, TA.) And hence the saying, الأَسْمَآءُ تَضَاجَمُ [for تَتَضَاجَمُ] i. e. تَخْتَلِفُ [meaning ‡ *Names are dissimilar, diverse*, or *various*]. (TA.)

9 and 11: see the next preceding paragraph.

ضَجَمٌ inf. n. of ضَجِمَ [q. v.]: (MA, Ḳ:*) [as a simple subst.,] *Distortion*, or *crookedness*, (Ṣ, Ḳ,) [in an absolute sense; and particularly,] in the mouth; and in the side of the mouth; and in the lip; and in the chin; and in the neck: (Ḳ:) and in the nose; (Lth, TA;) its *inclining towards one side* (Lth, Ṣ, TA) *of the face*: (Ṣ, TA:) and in one of the shoulders: (Ṣ, TA:) and, accord. to the M, in the bill [for خط in the TA (an obvious mistranscription) I read خَطْم] of the male ostrich: and sometimes in the mouth together with the nose: (TA:) and in like manner ‡ in a well: and ‡ in a wound. (Ḳ, TA.)

ضُجْمَةٌ *A certain small creeping thing* (دُوَيْبَّةٌ) *of foul odour*, (Ḳ, TA,) *that stings*, or *bites*. (TA.)

أَضْجَمُ *Having the quality termed* ضَجَمٌ, expl. above: (Ḳ:) [or, particularly,] *having the nose inclining towards one side of the face*: (Ṣ:) [fem. ضَجْمَآءُ: and pl. ضُجْمٌ.] And [hence] قَلِيبٌ أَضْجَمُ † *A well having a crookedness in the wall that surrounds its interior*: or *that is not dug in a straight*, or *an even, direction*: pl. قُلُبٌ ضُجْمٌ. (TA.) El-'Ajjáj has applied the phrase قُلُبٌ ضُجْمٌ to ‡ *Wide wounds*; as likened to the wells thus termed. (TA.) — And [the pl.] ضُجْمٌ signifies also † *Men who eat much*. (IAạr, TA.)

مُتَضَاجِمٌ *Distorted*, or *crooked, in the mouth*, (Ṣ, Ḳ.)

ضح

R. Q. 1. ضَحْضَحَ, [inf. n. ضَحْضَحَةٌ, which see below,] said of the سَرَاب [or mirage], *It was*, or *became, in a state of commotion*; or *moved to and fro*; as also ▼ تَضَحْضَحَ. (Ṣ, Ḳ.) — And, (Ḳ, TA,) said of an affair, (TA,) *It was*, or *became, manifest, evident*, or *apparent*. (Ḳ,* TA.)

R. Q. 2: see the preceding paragraph.

ضِحٌّ *The sun*: (Ṣ, O, Ḳ:) and (Ḳ) the *light of the sun*, (Lth, A, O, Ḳ,) *when it has possession of the ground*: (Lth, O, TA:) or the *light of the sun upon the surface of the ground*; *sunshine*; *contr. of* ظِلّ: (AHeyth, T, O, TA:) accord. to AHeyth, originally وِضْحٌ, the و being rejected and a ح added to the radical ح; but correctly, it is originally ضِحْىٌ, from ضحيت الشمس [app. a mistranscription for ضَحِيتُ لِلشَّمْسِ]: (TA; as from the T:) also *land*, or *ground, that lies open and exposed* (Ḳ, TA) *to the sun*: (TA:) and *what is shone upon*, or *smitten, by the sun*: (Ḳ, TA:) it has no pl. in any of these senses. (El-Fihree, TA.) It is said in a trad., لَا يَقْعُدَنَّ أَحَدُكُمْ بَيْنَ الضِّحِّ وَالظِّلِّ فَإِنَّهُ مَقْعَدُ الشَّيْطَانِ (Ṣ, A) ‡ [*None of you shall sit between the sunshine and the shade, for it is the sitting-place of the devil*]; meaning half of him in the sun and half of him in the shade. (TA.) And one says, جَآءَ فُلَانٌ بِالضِّحِّ وَالرِّيحِ ‡ *Such a one came with*, or *brought, that upon which the sun had risen, and that upon which the wind had blown*; (Ṣ, Ḳ, TA;) meaning, *abundance*, or *much*; (Ṣ, A;) or *much property*, or *many cattle*: (TA:) [F asserts that] one should not say بِالضِّيحِ, (Ḳ,) i. e. بِالضِّيحِ وَالرِّيحِ: (TA:) this the vulgar say, but [J affirms that] it is nought: (Ṣ:) several, however, assert that الضِّيح is correct: (MF:) [and the author of the Ḳ, who disallows it in this art., authorizes it in art. ضيح, q. v.:] Kr, also, is related to have said that الضِّحُّ signifies "the sun" and "its light;" and is said to signify "what is exposed to the sun:" and a poet says,

وَالشَّمْسُ فِى اللُّجَّةِ ذَاتِ الضِّحِّ •

[*And the sun in the abyss of sunlight*]: Aboo-Mis-ḥal, moreover, mentions, in his "Nawádir," the saying, أُسْتُعْمِلَ فُلَانٌ عَلَى الضِّحِّ وَالرِّيحِ [meaning † *Such a one was employed as manager of much property*]. (TA.) مَاتَ عَنِ الضِّحِّ وَالرِّيحِ, occurring in a trad., is rendered agreeably with the explanation of the saying in a trad. mentioned above, and means ‡ *He died leaving much property*. (TA.) And it is said of the Prophet, in a trad., يَكُونُ فِى الضِّحِّ وَالرِّيحِ *He will be exposed to the heat of the sun and the blowing of the winds*; meaning, accord. to Hr, † *he will be attended by*, or *in the midst of, numerous horsemen and military forces*. (TA.)

ضَحْضَاحٌ : see ضَحْضَحَةٌ : — and ضَحْضَحٌ.

٧ ضُحْضُحٌ : see what next follows.

ضَحْضَحَةٌ and ▼ ضَحْضَحٌ and ▼ ضُحْضُحٌ The *running* of the سَرَاب [or mirage, along the surface of the ground, *like water*: see R. Q. 1]. (Ḳ.)

ضَحْضَاحٌ *Shallow* water; (Ṣ, A, TA;) and hence metaphorically applied in a trad. to ‡ *a shallow part* of hell-fire: (TA:) or water *little in quantity*; as also ▼ ضَحْضَحٌ : or water *reaching to the ankles*: or *reaching to the middle of the shin*: or *in which there is no being drowned*: (Ḳ:) or water *little in quantity, in a pool left by a torrent, &c.* (TA.) — And *Many*, or *much*; in the dial. of Hudheyl; (AA, O, Ḳ;) not known to others: (TA: [see also ضَحْل :]) accord. to Aṣ, it is applied to sheep or goats, and to camels, as meaning *many*, or *numerous*: and also as meaning *scattered*, or *dispersed, over the surface of the land, but, notwithstanding, few*. (TA.)

ضحك

1. ضَحِكَ, (Ṣ, MA, O, Mṣb, Ḳ, &c.,) and some say ضِحِكَ, with kesr to the ض, (TA, as from the Ḳ, [but not in the CḲ nor in my MS. copy of the Ḳ,]) to agree with the vowel of the ح because the latter is a faucial letter, and this is a correct dial. var. of which similar instances are mentioned, and ضَحْكَ also is said to be a well known dial. var. of ضَحِكَ, (TA,) aor. ـَ, (Ṣ, O,) inf. n. ضَحِكٌ and ضِحْكٌ (Ṣ, MA, O, Mṣb, Ḳ, KL) and ضَحْكٌ, (Ṣ, MA, O, Ḳ, KL,) the first of which is the superior form, (IDrd, O,) [the second and third being contractions thereof,] and ضِحِكٌ, (Ṣ, O, Ḳ, KL,) and if you said ضِحْكٌ it would be agreeable with analogy, (Az, TA,) *He laughed*; (MA, KL, PṢ, TḲ;) *contr. of* بَكَى: (TḲ:) [see also 6:] الضَّحِكُ is well known, as meaning *the expanding of the face, and displaying of the teeth, by reason of happiness, joy*, or *gladness*; and التَّبَسُّمُ is the beginning thereof: thus in the Towsheeḥ and other works: (MF, TA:) and in like manner in the Mufradát [of Er-Rághib]; in which it is added that it is also used as meaning simply *the being happy, joyful*, or *glad*: and sometimes as meaning simply *the wondering* [at a thing]; and this is the meaning intended by him who says that it is peculiar to man: (TA:) [i. e.] ضَحِكَ, said of a man, signifies also *he wondered*; syn. عَجِبَ ; (O, Ḳ, TA;) with مِنْ preposed to the object of wonder: (TA:) or *he was frightened*; or *he feared*. (Ḳ, TA.) You say, ضَحِكَ مِنْهُ and بِهِ, both meaning the same, (Ṣ, O, Mṣb,) i. e. *He laughed at him; derided him*; or *ridiculed him*: or *he wondered at him*. (Mṣb.) And ضَحِكَ إِلَيْهِ [*He behaved laughingly*, or *cheerfully, towards him*]. (IDrd and Ḳ in art. بش. [See بَشَّ لَهُ.]) — Said of an ape, *He uttered a cry* or *cries*: (Ḳ:) or one says of the ape when he utters a cry or cries, يَضْحَكُ, (Ṣ, TA,) meaning *he displays his teeth*, or *grins*. (TA.) — And ضَحِكَ السَّحَابُ ‡ *The clouds lightened*. (Ṣ, O, Ḳ, TA.) Hence the usage of the verb in a trad. cited voce تَحَدَّثَ. (O, TA.) — And ضَحِكَ الغَدِيرُ i. e. ‡ [*The pool of water left by a torrent*] *glistened by reason of its fulness*. (TA.) — [And ضَحِكَ ثَغْرُهُ † *His front teeth*, or *his teeth, glistened* by reason of his laughing; meaning *he laughed so as to show his front teeth*, or *his teeth*.] — And ضَحِكَ الزَّهْرُ ‡ *The flowers* [*looked gay*, or] *were as though they were laughing*. (TA.) And ضَحِكَتِ الأَرْضُ ‡ *The earth*, or *land, put forth its plants*, or *herbage, and its flowers*. (TA.) And ضَحِكَتِ الرِّيَاضُ عَنِ الأَزْهَارِ ‡ *The meadows*, or *gardens, displayed the flowers*. (TA.) — And ضَحِكَتِ النَّخْلَةُ ‡ *The palm-tree put forth* [or *disclosed*] *its* ضَحِك ; as also ▼ أَضْحَكَتْ ; (TA;) [i. e.] *the spathe of the palm-tree*, (Skr, O, TA,) *that covered the* طَلْع [or *spadix*], (O,) *burst open*. (Skr, O, TA.) And ضَحِكَ الطَّلْعُ ‡ *The* طلع [here app. meaning the *spathe of the palm-tree*] *split*, or *clave, open*; and so تَبَسَّمَ. (TA.) — And, as some assert, (ISd, TA,) ضَحِكَتْ signifies also ‡ *She menstruated*; said of a hare; (ISd, Z, O, Mṣb, TA;) accord. to some, from the ضَحَّاك [meaning the interior] of the طَلْعَة [of the palm-tree] when it bursts open; (ISd, TA;) and hence, (Ḳ, TA,) said also in this sense of a woman, (O, Mṣb, Ḳ, TA,) accord. to Mujáhid, (O, TA,) and some others, (TA,) in the Ḳur xi. 74, (O, Ḳ, TA,) where some read فَضَحَكَتْ, which is said to be a well-known dial. var.; (TA;) and likewise, accord. to some, said in this sense of the hyena, (O, TA,) when she sees blood, or as IAạr says, when she eats the flesh of men and drinks their blood: (TA:) [it is commonly asserted by the Arabs that] the hare menstruates like women: (Ḳzw:) but with respect to this meaning as assigned to the verb in the Ḳur xi. 74, Fr says that he had not heard it from any person deserving of confidence; (O, TA;*) and Zj says that it is nought: both say that the meaning there is, *she laughed by reason of happiness*: (TA:) and some say that there is an inversion in this case, what is meant being فَبَشَّرْنَاهَا بِإِسْحٰقَ فَضَحِكَتْ : (Fr, O, TA:) or the meaning is, *she wondered*; so says I'Ab; and so Er-Rághib, who adds that it is confirmed by her saying, "shall I bring forth a child when I am an old woman, and this my husband is an old man? verily this is indeed a wonderful thing:" and that حَاضَتْ which is inserted by some of the expositors after فَضَحِكَتْ is not an explanation of this expression, as some of them have imagined it to be, but is the mention of [a fact which was] a sign that the announcement was not that of an event improbable: or the meaning is, *she was frightened*; so says Fr.: (TA:) and with respect to the meaning of this verb when said of the hyena, mentioned above, it is rejected by AḤát and others: (TA:) IDrd says, on the authority of AḤát, respecting the following verse of Taäbbaṭa-Sharrà,

تَضْحَكُ الضَّبْعُ لِقَتْلَى هُذَيْلٍ
وَتَرَى الذِّئْبَ لَهَا يَسْتَهِلُّ

that the meaning is † *The hyena displays her teeth*, or *grins, on account of the slain* [*of Hudheyl*], when she sees them, like as they say of the ass when he plucks out the [plant called] صِلِّيَانَة ; (O, TA;) or, as others say, † *the hyena snarls, displaying her teeth; and sees the wolf raising his voice in calling* the [other] wolves *to them*, i. e. to the slain: (O, TA:*) Abu-l-'Abbás says that the meaning is, † *the hyena displays her teeth*, because the wolf contends with her over the slain: and some say that the poet means, † *the hyena rejoices because of the slain*. (TA.) — One says also, ضَحِكَتِ السَّمُرَةُ, meaning † *The* سمرة [or *gum-acacia-tree*] *flowed with its gum*: from ضحكت meaning "she menstruated." (Bḍ in xi. 74.)

3. مُضَاحَكَةٌ [inf. n. of ضاحكه] signifies [The *contending*, or *vying, in laughing, with another*; or the *laughing with another*; or] the *laughing together*. (KL.) — [Hence,] one says, النَّوْرُ يُضَاحِكُ الشَّمْسَ † [*The flowers vie in brightness with the sun*]. (TA.) — And إِنَّ رَأْيَكَ لَيُضَاحِكُ المُشْكِلَاتِ ‡ [*Verily thy judgment makes sport with ambiguities*]; said to him to whom confused and dubious things are apparent and known. (TA.)

4. اضحكهُ, (Ṣ, O, Ḳ,) inf. n. إِضْحَاكٌ, (KL,) said of God, (Ṣ, O,) or of a man, (Ḳ,) *He made him*, or *caused him, to laugh*. (Ṣ,* O,* Ḳ,* KL, PṢ.) — [Hence,] اضحك الضَّبُعَ, said of blood, (TA,) or of the sword, (O, TA,) † [*It made the hyena to display her teeth*; or *to snarl, displaying her teeth*: or *to rejoice*: (see 1, latter part:) but explained as meaning] ‡ *it made the hyena to menstruate*. (TA.) — And اضحك الحَوْضَ ‡ *He filled the watering-trough so that it overflowed*: (O, TA:) its glistening being likened to laughing. (TA.) — See also 1, near the middle of the paragraph.

5: see the next paragraph.

6. تضاحك and ▼ تضحّك [are both mentioned in the Ḳ and TA as though *syn. with each other and with* ضَحِكَ : and accord. to the KL, the former signifies *He laughed*: but accord. to the TḲ, the latter signifies *he manifested laughing*: or] the former is *syn. with* ▼ استضحك [app. as meaning *he affected to laugh*, or *laughing*: or, more exactly, agreeably with analogy, like the contr. تَبَاكَى and اِسْتَبْكَى, the former signifies thus; and the latter, *he desired to laugh*]. (Ṣ.) — And you say also, هُمْ يَتَضَاحَكُونَ [meaning *They laugh together, one with another*]. (Ḳ.)

10: see the next preceding paragraph.

ضَحْكٌ [originally an inf. n., a contraction of ضَحِكٌ,] The *appearance*, or *appearing, of the central incisors* [or *of the front teeth*] *by reason of happiness, joy*, or *gladness*. (TA.) — And hence, (TA,) *Wonder*. (Ḳ, TA.) — [As an epithet,] A man *whose teeth are white*. (Aṣ, O, TA.) — [And as a subst., properly so termed,]

White front teeth. (Aṣ, O, Ḳ.) — And † Honey: (Ḳ:) or white honey; (Ibn-Es-Seed, TA;) likened to the front teeth because of its intense whiteness: (AA, O, TA:) or honey in its comb; syn. شُهْدٌ. (Ḳ.) — And, (O, Ḳ,) some say, (O,) † Fresh butter. (O, Ḳ.) — And † Snow. (O, Ḳ.) — And † Blossoms, or flowers, or white blossoms or flowers; syn. نَوْرٌ: (O, and so in copies of the Ḳ:) or light; syn. نُورٌ. (So in a copy of the Ḳ.) — And † The طَلْع [or spadix] of the palm-tree when its envelope bursts open from it; (Ṣ,* O,* Ḳ;) in the dial. of Belḥárith Ibn-Kaab: (O:) accord. to Th, what is in the interior of the طَلْعَة [here meaning spathe of the palm-tree]: as AA says, the وَلِيعَة, or وَلِيع, [thus differently written in two different places in the TA,] of the طَلْع [or spathe of the palm-tree], which is eaten; as also ▼ ضُحَّاكٌ. (TA.) — And † The middle of a road; (Ḳ, TA;) and so, accord. to the Ḳ, ▼ ضُحَّاكٌ; but, correctly, this should have been there mentioned as syn. with ضَحْكٌ in the sense next preceding. (TA.)

ضَحْكَةٌ A single act of ضَحِك [or laughing; i. e. a laugh]. (Ṣ, O.) — [The pl.] ضَحَكَاتٌ signifies ‡ The best of everything: and ضَحَكَاتُ القُلُوبِ, the best of possessions, or wealth, and of children: so says Aboo-Sa'eed. (TA.)

ضُحْكَةٌ A thing, (Lth, TA,) or a man, (Ṣ, O, TA,) that is laughed at, or ridiculed; i.e. يُضْحَكُ مِنْهُ: (Ṣ, O, Ḳ, TA:) an epithet importing more discommendation than ضُحَكَةٌ. (Ḳ.) — See also مَضْحَكٌ.

ضُحَكَةٌ, (Ṣ, O, Mṣb, Ḳ,) an epithet importing discommendation, (Ḳ,) and ▼ ضُحُكَّةٌ, (Ibn-'Abbád, O, Ḳ,) and ▼ ضَحَّاكٌ, (Mṣb, Ḳ,) an epithet importing commendation, (TA, [but the contr. is implied, or rather plainly indicated, in the Ḳ,]) and ▼ ضَحُوكٌ, (Ḳ,) and ▼ مِضْحَاكٌ, (Ṣ, O, Ḳ,) which last is [also] applied to a woman, (Ṣ, O,) One who laughs much (كَثِيرُ الضَّحِكِ). (Ṣ, O, Mṣb, Ḳ.)

ضُحُكَّةٌ: see the next preceding paragraph.

ضَحُوكٌ: see ضُحَكَةٌ. — [Also] A man cheerful in countenance. (O.) — And † A wide road: (Ṣ, O:) or ‡ a distinct, an apparent, or a conspicuous, road; as also ▼ ضَحَّاكٌ: pl. of the former (in this sense, TA) ضُحُكٌ. (Ḳ, TA.)

ضَحَّاكٌ: see ضُحَكَةٌ: — and see ضَحْكٌ, last two sentences: — and ضَحُوكٌ.

ضَاحِكٌ Laughing; [&c.;] (KL;) act. part. n. of ضَحِكَ. (Mṣb, Ḳ.) — Also applied to clouds (سَحَاب), meaning ‡ Appearing, or extending sideways, in the horizon, and lightening. (Ṣ, O, TA.) — [And to the tooth (السِّنّ, used as a gen. n.): thus in the phrase ضَاحِكَ السِّنِّ, meaning † Laughingly, so as to display the teeth.] — See also ضَاحِكَةٌ. — Also, [or perhaps حَجَرٌ ضَاحِكٌ,] ‡ Very white stone appearing in a mountain (IDrd, O, Ḳ, TA) of any colour, as though laughing. (IDrd, O, TA.) — One says also رَأْىٌ ضَاحِكٌ, meaning ‡ Judgment that is plain, or perspicuous, (TA,) not confused or dubious. (O, TA.) — And, [using ضاحك as a gen. n.,] ‡ مَا أَكْثَرَ ضَاحِكَ نَخْلِكُمْ [How numerous are the bursting spathes of your palm-trees!]. (TA.) — [And an instance of ضَاحِكٌ applied to a woman, without ة, meaning † Menstruating, is cited by Bḍ, in xi. 74.]

ضَاحِكَةٌ, (Ṣ, O, Ḳ,) or ▼ ضَاحِكٌ, (Mṣb,) or both, (Mgh,) ‡ The tooth next behind the نَاب [or canine tooth]; (Mgh, Mṣb;) [i. e. the anterior bicuspid;] any one of the four teeth that are between the أَنْيَاب and the أَضْرَاس: (Ṣ, O, Ḳ:) or any one of the teeth that are in front of the أَضْرَاس that appear on the occasion of laughing: (Ḳ:) pl. ضَوَاحِكُ. (Ṣ, Mgh, O, Mṣb, Ḳ.) أَوْضَحُوا بِضَاحِكَةٍ, (O, TA,) a phrase occurring in a trad., (O,) means † They smiled. (TA.)

أُضْحُوكَةٌ [A laughable thing;] a thing at which one laughs: (O, Ḳ, TA:) and ▼ مَضْحَكَةٌ signifies [in like manner a cause of laughter;] a thing at which one laughs, or which one ridicules: pl. of the former أَضَاحِيكُ. (TA.) [See also مُضْحِكَاتٌ.]

[مَضْحَكٌ lit. A place of laughing: the front teeth; because they appear in laughing; like مَبْسِمٌ: pl. مَضَاحِكُ.] One says, بَدَتْ مَضَاحِكُهُ and ▼ ضُحْكَتُهُ and [in like manner] مَبَاسِمُهُ † [His front teeth appeared, by his laughing]. (TA.)

مَضْحَكَةٌ: see أُضْحُوكَةٌ.

مُضْحِكَاتٌ [pl. of مُضْحِكَةٌ] i. q. نَوَادِرُ [as meaning Extraordinary things or sayings, particularly such as cause laughter: see also أُضْحُوكَةٌ]. (TA.)

مِضْحَاكٌ: see ضُحَكَةٌ.

ضحل

1. ضَحَلَ, (O, Ḳ,) aor. ـَ, (Ḳ,) said of water, It was, or became, shallow, (O, Ḳ, TA,) and little in quantity. (TA.) And said of a pool of water left by a torrent, Its water became little in quantity. (Ḳ.)

4. مَا أَضْحَلَ خَيْرَكَ means مَا أَقَلَّهُ [i. e. † How little, or scanty, is thy goodness, or bounty, or beneficence!]. (TA.)

Q. Q. 4. اِضْمَحَلَّ, (Ṣ, O, Ḳ,) mentioned in the K in a separate art., its author, and some others, holding the م to be radical, but most of the leading authorities on inflection hold it, with J [and Ṣgh and Fei], to be augmentative; (TA;) and اِمْضَحَلَّ, (Ṣ, O, Mṣb, Ḳ,) of the dial. of the Kilábees, mentioned by AZ, formed by transposition of the م; (Ṣ, O, TA;) and اِضْمَحَنَّ, (Ḳ,) formed by substitution, mentioned by Yaạḳoob; (TA;) It (a thing, Ṣ, O) went away; (Ṣ, O, Mṣb, Ḳ;) and came to nought. (Mṣb.) — And said of clouds (سَحَاب), They became removed, or cleared off. (Ṣ, O, Mṣb, Ḳ.) — And i. q. اِنْحَلَّ [It became untied, or undone, &c.]. (Ḳ.)

ضَحْلٌ A small quantity of water, (Ṣ, M, O, Ḳ,) upon the ground, (M, Ḳ,) shallow, (M,) not deep; (Ḳ;) i. q. ضَحْضَاحٌ; (Ṣ, O;) or the latter has a more general meaning, applying to little or much: (TA:) accord. to some, such that the bottom of it appears: (MF, TA:) or a small quantity of water in a source, or fountain, and in a well, and in a hot spring, and the like; or in a pool left by a torrent, and the like: or water little in quantity; or near in place: (TA:) pl. [of pauc.] أَضْحَالٌ and [of mult.] ضُحُولٌ and ضِحَالٌ. (Ḳ.) — Hence, (Ṣ, O,) أَتَانُ الضَّحْلِ (Ṣ, O, Ḳ) i. e. A mass of rock of which part is covered by the water and part is protruding; (O;) expl. [more fully and variously] in art. اتن; (Ḳ;) so called because the water does not cover it by reason of its paucity. (Ṣ, O.) — [Hence also,] one says, إِنَّ خَيْرَكَ لَضَحْلٌ i. e. [† Verily thy goodness, or bounty, or beneficence, is] little. (TA.)

غَدِيرٌ ضَاحِلٌ A pool, left by a torrent, the water of which has become shallow and has then gone away. (Sh, TA.)

مَضْحَلٌ The place of a ضَحْل: (M, TA:) or a place in which is little water: (O, K:) the mirage (سَرَاب) is likened thereto: (TA:) pl. مَضَاحِلُ; (O, TA;) to which Ru-beh, (O,) or El-'Ajjáj, (TA,) likens clouds. (O,* TA.)

ضحو and ضحى

1. ضَحَا الطَّرِيقُ, (Ṣ, Ḳ,) aor. يَضْحُو, (Ṣ,) inf. n. ضَحْوٌ, (Ṣ, and so in the CḲ,) or ضُحُوٌّ, (so in other copies of the Ḳ and in the TA,) like عُلُوٌّ, thus accord. to ISd and IḲṭṭ, (TA,) and ضُحِىٌّ, (TA as from the Ḳ, [but not in the CḲ nor in my MS. copy of the Ḳ,]) The road appeared, or became apparent, (Ṣ, Ḳ,) to a person: so says AZ: (Ṣ:) [and so, app., signifies ضَحِىَ, aor. يَضْحَى; for] Aṣ says, يُسْتَحَبُّ مِنَ الفَرَسِ أَنْ يَضْحَى عِجَانُهُ i. e. [It is approved as a quality of the horse] that his عجان [q. v., a word variously expl.,] appear. (Ṣ, TA.) — ضَحِيَتِ اللَّيْلَةُ The night was, or became, cloudless. (TA.) — ضَحِىَ الفَرَسُ The horse was, or became, white. (TA.) — ضَحَا ظِلُّهُ ‡ He died: (Ḳ, TA:) it [properly] means his shade, or shadow, became sun: and when a man's shade, or shadow, becomes sun, he himself becomes nought. (IAmb, TA.) — And ضَحَا and ضَحِىَ, aor. of each يَضْحَى, inf. n. ضَحْوٌ, (Ḳ, TA,) or, accord. to the M, ضُحُوٌّ, (TA,) and ضُحِىٌّ, He, or it, was smitten by the sun; or the sun came, or fell, upon him, or it: (Ḳ, TA:) or ضَحِىَ, aor. يَضْحَى, inf. n. ضُحُوٌّ; and ضَحَا, aor. يَضْحُو, inf. n. ضَحْوٌ and ضُحًا, he, or it, was smitten by the heat of the sun. (Ḥam p. 625.) Hence, in the Ḳur [xx. 117], لَا تَظْمَأُ فِيهَا وَلَا تَضْحَى [Thou shalt not thirst therein nor shalt thou be smitten by the sun]; i. e., thou shalt be preserved from the heat of the sun. (TA.) — And ضَحَا, inf. n. ضَحْوٌ and ضُحُوٌّ

and ضُحِّىَ, *He went forth to the sunshine;* (K;) as also ↓ استضحى لِلشَّمْسِ; (TA;) [and app. ↓ تضحّى also; see Har p. 296, where, for النزول, in النزول للشمس as an explanation of التَّضَحِّى, I think we should read البُرُوزُ:] or ضَحِيتُ لِلشَّمْسِ, inf. n. ضَحَآءٌ; and ضَحَيْتُ also; aor. of each أَضْحَى; *I went forth to the sunshine.* (S.) أَضْحِ [the imperative of ↓ أَضْحَى] occurs in a trad., accord. to the relaters thereof: but As says that it is [correctly] اِضْحَ, with kesr to the ا and fet-h to the ح; from ضَحِيتُ; being a command to go forth to the sunshine. (S.) — And ضَحِىَ, (S, K,) inf. n. ضَحًى [or ضَحًا], *He* (a man, S) *sweated.* (S, K.)

2. ضَحَّيْنَاهُمْ is like صَبَّحْنَاهُمْ [i. e. it signifies *We came to them in the time of the morning called* الضُّحَى]: (TA:) and ↓ ضاحاهُ, (K, TA,) inf. n. مُضَاحَاةٌ, is similar to غَادَاهُ and رَاوَحَهُ, meaning, (TA,) *He came to him in the time called* الضُّحَى. (K, TA.) — ضحّى الغَنَمَ *He pastured the sheep,* or *goats, in the time called* الضُّحَى; (S, K, TA;) and in like manner, الإِبِلَ *the camels.* (TA.) And ضَحَّيْتُ الإِبِلَ عَنِ الوِرْدِ *I pastured the camels with the* [*morning-pasture called*] ↓ ضَحَآء, *so that they might come to the water having satisfied themselves with food:* and in like manner, عَشَّيْتُهَا عَنْهُ "I pastured them with the [evening-pasture called] عَشَآء," &c. (A, TA.) — [Hence,] ضَحَّيْتُهُ, inf. n. تَضْحِيَةٌ, *I fed him in the time called* الضُّحَى: (K, TA:) or *I fed him with the* [*morning-meal called*] غَدَآء, *at any time* [*of the morning*]; but more commonly known as meaning, *in the time called* الضُّحَى: and the verb primarily relates to camels [and sheep or goats]: or ضحّى قَوْمَهُ means *he fed his people,* or *party, with the* [*morning-meal called*] غَدَآء; or *he invited them* [*thereto,* i. e.] *to his* ضَحَآء. (TA.) — IAth says, when the Arabs, in their journeying, or migrating, passed by a piece of land in which was herbage, one of them said, أَلَا ضَحُّوا رُوَيْدًا, meaning [*Now*] *be ye gentle with the camels* حَتَّى تَتَضَحَّى ↓ i. e. *in order that we may obtain of this herbage;* then التَّضْحِيَةُ was applied to mean *the being gentle in order that the camels may reach the place of alighting* [app. *in the morning*] *having satisfied themselves with food:* and then ↓ تَضَحَّى was said of anyone as meaning *he ate in the time called* [الضُّحَى or] الضَّحَآء. (TA.) One says, ضَحَّيْتُ عَنِ الشَّىْءِ † *I was gentle,* or *I acted gently, with the thing.* (S.) And ضحّى عَنِ الأَمْرِ ‡ *He acted gently,* or *deliberately, in the affair:* and so عَشَّى عَنْهُ. (A, TA.) And ضَحِّ رُوَيْدًا, (S, A, TA,) a prov., (A, TA,) meaning ‡ *Hasten thou not;* (S, TA;) from تَضْحِيَةُ الإِبِلِ عَنِ الوِرْدِ: [see the third sentence of this paragraph:] or meaning *be thou patient a little while:* (TA:) or the meaning is, *slaughter thou,* or *sacrifice thou,* [*deliberately, leisurely,* or] *without haste:* (Meyd:) [for] — ضحّى, inf. n. تَضْحِيَةٌ, signifies [also] *He slaughtered,* or *sacrificed, the* [*victim termed*] أُضْحِيَّة, *in the time called* الضُّحَى: and hence, by reason of frequency of usage, *he did so in any time of what are termed* أَيَّامُ التَّشْرِيقِ: (Msb:) and ضحّى بِشَاةٍ, (S, Mgh, Msb, K,) or بِكَبْشٍ أَوْ غَيْرِهِ, (Mgh,) *he slaughtered,* or *sacrificed, a sheep* or *goat,* (S, Msb, K,) or *a ram or other* [victim], (Mgh,) *in the time called* الضُّحَى (Mgh, K) *of the day called* يَوْمُ الأَضْحَى; and afterwards said of him who has done so [*at any time, even*] *in the last part of the* [*said*] *day.* (Mgh.) — See also 4. — And see 5.

3. ضاحت البِلَادُ *The countries,* or *lands, became exposed to the sun, and their herbage consequently dried up.* (TA.) — ضاحاهُ: see 2, first sentence.

4. اضحى *He* (a man, TA) *entered upon the time of morning called* الضُّحَى, (K,* TA,) or *the time called* الضَّحْوَة, (TA,) [or *the time called* الضَّحَآء, for] you say, أَقَمْتُ بِالمَكَانِ حَتَّى أَضْحَيْتُ, from الضَّحَآء [and therefore meaning *I remained in the place until I entered upon the time called* الضَّحَآء], like as you say أَصْبَحْتُ from الصَّبَاحُ. (S, TA.) Hence the saying of 'Omar, أَضْحُوا بِصَلَاةِ الضُّحَى, (S,) or بِصَلَاةِ الضُّحَى, (TA,) i. e. *Perform ye the prayer of the time called* الضحى *at its* [*proper*] *time:* do not delay it until the time called الضَّحَآء has become advanced: (TA:) or do not perform that prayer when the time called الضُّحَى has become advanced. (S.) — And you say, اضحى فُلَانٌ يَفْعَلُ كَذَا, (S, M, K,) like as you say ظَلَّ يفعل كذا; (S;) meaning *Such a one became occupied,* or *engaged, in the time called* الضُّحَى *in doing such a thing:* (M, K, TA:) or *did such a thing in the first part of the day,* (IKtt, TA.) — [This phrase often means also *Such a one became occupied,* or *engaged, in doing such a thing; betook, set,* or *applied, himself to doing such a thing; set about,* or *commenced, doing such a thing;* or *began to do such a thing;* like أَصْبَحَ and ظَلَّ &c. And, like these verbs, اضحى followed by an aor., or by a part. n. in the accus. case, often requires to be rendered simply *He,* or *it, became:* see an ex. in a verse cited voce دَلِفٌ.] — اضحى also signifies *He performed the supererogatory act of prayer* (النَّافِلَة) *in the time called* الضُّحَى. (TA.) — See also 1, last sentence but one. — One says also, اضحى عَنِ الأَمْرِ, meaning ‡ *He withdrew himself far from the affair.* (TA. [See also another meaning of this phrase in what follows.]) And القَطَا يُضْحِى عَنِ المَآءِ ‡ *The birds called* قطا *go far from water.* (TA.) — اضحى الشَّىْءَ *He made apparent, showed,* or *revealed, the thing.* (K, TA.) And ↓ ضحّى عَنِ الأَمْرِ *He made the affair,* or *case, apparent,* or *manifest:* and [so اضحى عنه, for] one says, أَضْحِ لِى عَنْ أَمْرِكَ, with fet-h to the ء, meaning *Make manifest to me thy affair,* or *case:* so in the M. (TA.) — لَا أَضْحَى اللّٰهُ لَنَا ظِلَّكَ is a deprecatory phrase [lit. *May God not cause thy shadow to become sun to us:* meaning † *may God not deprive us of thee by death:* (see ضَحَا ظِلُّهُ:) or it may be similar in meaning to the phrase here following]. (TA.) لَا تُضْحِنَا عَنْ ظِلِّكَ [lit. *Make us not to go forth into the sun from thy shadow*] means † *withdraw not from us the shadow of thy compassion:* the verb being made trans. by means of عن because the phrase implies the meaning of لَا تُخْرِجْنَا مِنْهُ: and ظلّ being here used metaphorically. (Har p. 4.)

5. تَضَحَّى: see 1, latter half. — And see 2, in two places. It [generally] means *He ate in the time of morning called* الضُّحَى: (K:) or *he ate the* [*morning-meal called*] غَدَآء; syn. تَغَدَّى: (S, TA:) and ↓ ضحّى also has the former [or the latter] meaning. (ISd, TA.)

10: see 1, latter half.

ضَحْوٌ: see the next paragraph.

ضُحًى, also written ضُحًا, held by some to be of the measure فُعَلٌ, and by others to be [originally ضُحْوَى i. e.] of the measure فُعْلَى, of the former measure accord. to Mbr, and of the latter accord. to Th, (MF, TA,) [The *early part of the forenoon, after sunrise:* accord. to some, *when the sun is yet low:* accord. to others, *when the sun is somewhat high:*] i. q. ↓ ضَحْوَةٌ, accord. to most authorities: (MF, TA, and so in one place in the K:) or this latter signifies the *period* of the day *after sunrise:* (S:) or this signifies the *advanced state of the day* اِرْتِفَاعُ النَّهَارِ [which is said by the doctors of the law in the present day to mean *when the sun has risen the measure of a* رُمْح, q. v., or *more*]); as also ↓ ضَحْوٌ and ↓ ضَحِيَّةٌ: (K:) and the ضُحَى is *after the* ضَحْوَة (S, K) *a little,* (K,) *when the sun shines brightly:* (S:) or *from sunrise to the time when the day is advanced and very white:* thus in the M: (TA:) or it is the *spreading of the sun* [*upon the earth*], and the *extending of the day:* and the *time* [*thereof*] is thus named: (Er-Rághib, TA:) or ضُحًى is pl. of ↓ ضَحْوَةٌ, like as قُرًى is of قَرْيَةٌ; and its sing. is like ↓ ضَحَآءٌ, which means the *extending of the day,* and is of the masc. gender, as though a name of the *time* [*thereof*]: then ضُحًى became used as a sing., and the *time* was thus called: (Msb:) it is fem. and masc.: (S, K:*) he who makes it fem. holds it to be pl. of ↓ ضَحْوَةٌ; and he who makes it masc. holds it to be [a sing.] noun of the measure فُعَلٌ, like صُرَدٌ and نُغَرٌ: (S:) its dim. is ↓ ضُحَىٌّ, without ة; (Fr, Msb, K;) for they disapproved the affixing the ة lest it should be confounded with the dim. of ضَحْوَةٌ. (Fr, Msb.) Using it as an adv. noun, you say, لَقِيتُهُ ضُحًى, when you mean [*I met him*] *in the* ضحى *of this day;* without tenween. (S, TA.) See also ضَحْوَةٌ. [See also De Sacy's Chrest. Ar., sec. ed., i. 162—167, respecting the prayer that is performed in the time thus called,

i. e. the prayer termed صَلَاةُ الضُّحَى, mentioned above, voce أَضْحَى.] — Also The *sun*: (M, Mṣb, Ḳ:) because of its appearing in the time thus called. (M, TA.) One says, اِرْتَفَعَتِ الضُّحَى, meaning *The sun became high*. (Mṣb.) — And ضُحَى الشَّمْسِ *The light of the sun*: thus is expl. xci. 1 of the Ḳur. (TA.) — مَا لِكَلَامِهِ ضُحًى means † *His speech*, or *language, has no perspicuity*: thus in the M and Ḳ: but in the A, أَنْشَدَنِى شِعْرًا لَيْسَ فِيهِ حَلَاوَةٌ وَلَا ضَحَآءٌ † i. e. [*He recited to me poetry*] *in which was no* [*sweetness nor*] *plainness of meaning*. (TA.)

ضَحْوَةٌ: see the next preceding paragraph, in three places. You say, أَتَيْتُكَ ضَحْوَةً, meaning [*I came to thee*] *in a* [*time called*] † ضُحًى [or rather ضَحْوَة], (Ḳ,* TA,) with tenween, unless you mean *of this day* [in which case you say ضَحْوَةَ, without tenween, like as you say in the latter case ضُحَى]. (TA.)

ضَحْيَا and ضَحْيَآءُ fems. of أَضْحَى [q. v.].

ضَحْيَانٌ, which should by rule be ضَحْوَانٌ, Anything *exposing itself*, or *being exposed, to the sun*. (IJ, TA.) قُلَّةٌ ضَحْيَانَةٌ means [*A mountain-top*] *exposed to the sun*: (Ṣ, Ḳ:) occurring in a saying of Taabbaṭa-sharrà. (Ṣ.) And عَصًا ضَحْيَانَةٌ *A staff*, or *stick, growing in the sun so as to be matured thereby, and extremely hard*. (TA.) — See also أَضْحَى. — Also A man *who eats in the time called* الضُّحَى: fem. with ة. (Ḳ.)

ضَحَآءٌ, with medd, (Ṣ, Hr, Mṣb, TA,) and fet-ḥ, (Hr, Mṣb, TA, [erroneously written in copies of the Ḳ with ḍamm,]) The *period* [*of the forenoon*] *next after that called* الضُّحَى; i. e. *when the day is at the highest*: (Ṣ:) or the *period near midday*: (Ḳ:) or the *period of the day when the sun has risen to the fourth part of the sky*: (TA:) see also ضُحًى, in two places. — And hence, The [*morning-meal called*] غَدَآء; because it is eaten in the time thus called. (Ṣ, TA.) [And also applied to *Pasture eaten in that time*:] see 2, third sentence.

ضُحَيٌّ dim. of ضُحًى, q. v. (Fr, Mṣb, Ḳ.)

ضَحِيَّةٌ: see ضُحًى: — and see also أُضْحِيَّةٌ.

ضَاحٍ [part. n. of 1, *Appearing*, &c.] — You say مَكَانٌ ضَاحٍ *An outer, exterior*, or *exposed, place*: (Ṣ:) and أَرْضٌ ضَاحِيَةٌ *Land not surrounded by a wall*. (TA in art. حوط.) [And particularly *A place exposed to the sun*.] — [Hence,] مَفَازَةٌ ضَاحِيَةُ الظِّلِّ [*A desert*, or *waterless desert*,] *having no shade* or *shadow*; and ضَاحِيَةُ الظِّلَالِ [*having no shades* or *shadows*]. (TA.) And شَجَرَةٌ ضَاحِيَةٌ بِالظِّلِّ [if not a mistake for ضَاحِيَةُ الظِّلِّ] *A tree having no shade*. (Ḥar p. 4.) — And بَدَا بِضَاحِي رَأْسِهِ [*He appeared with*, or *he showed*,] *the side of his head*. (TA.) [See also the next paragraph.]

ضَاحِيَةٌ *An outer, exterior*, or *exposed, side* or *region* or *tract* of anything: [pl. ضَوَاحٍ: whence] one says, هُمْ يَنْزِلُونَ الضَّوَاحِىَ [*They alight*, or *abide, in the exterior tracts*]. (Ṣ.) [Hence also,] ضَوَاحِى الرُّومِ *The exterior districts of the Greeks*. (Ḳ.) And الضَّاحِيَةُ مِنَ البَعْلِ *What are in the open country, of the palm-trees that imbibe with their roots, without being watered*: opposed to الضَّامِنَةُ مِنَ النَّخْلِ: (AO, Ṣ in this art. and in art. ضمن, q. v.:) and الضَّوَاحِى مِنَ النَّخْلِ *what are outside of the town-wall, of the palm-trees*: thus used, الضواحى is an epithet in which the quality of a subst. is predominant. (TA.) And ضَوَاحِى قُرَيْشٍ *Those* [*of Ḳureysh*] *who abide outside of Mekkeh*. (TA.) And هُوَ مِنْ أَهْلِ الضَّاحِيَةِ *He is of the people of the desert*. (TA.) الضَّوَاحِى also signifies *The parts*, of a man, *that stand out*, or *are exposed*, (Ḳ, TA,) *to the sun*, (TA,) *such as the shoulder-blades*, and *the shoulders*: (Ḳ, TA:) pl. of ضَاحِيَةٌ. (TA.) And *The sides* of a watering-trough. (Ḳ.) And *The heavens*. (Ṣ, Ḳ.) — [Hence also,] فَعَلَهُ ضَاحِيَةً *He did it openly*. (Ṣ, A, Ḳ.) — ضَاحِيَةُ المَالِ means *The cattle*, (Ḳ,) or *sheep* or *goats*, (TA,) *that drink in the time of morning called* ضُحًى. (Ḳ, TA.)

أَضْحَى, applied to a horse, *i. q.* أَشْهَبُ [*Of a colour in which whiteness predominates over blackness*; &c.]: fem. ضَحْيَآءُ: (Ṣ, Ḳ:) or الضَّحْيَآءُ was, (Ḳ,) or was also, (Ṣ, and so afterwards in the Ḳ,) the name of a certain mare, belonging to 'Amr Ibn-'Ámir (Ṣ, Ḳ) Ibn-Rabee'ah. (Ṣ.) — And لَيْلَةٌ ضَحْيَآءُ, (Ṣ, Ḳ,) and ضَحْيَا with the short ا, both mentioned by ISd, (TA,) and † إِضْحِيَانَةٌ, (Ṣ, Ḳ,) and † إِضْحِيَّةٌ accord. to the Ḳ, but [SM says] I have not found any mention of this last, [meaning except in the Ḳ,] and probably the right word is † إِضْحِيَانٌ, as in the books of strange words together with إِضْحِيَانَةٌ, and accord. to the "Irtishàf eḍ-Ḍarab" of AḤei one says [also] † أَضْحِيَانٌ with fet-ḥ, (TA,) *A bright night*, (Ṣ, Ḳ, TA,) *in which are no clouds*: (Ṣ, TA:) and in like manner, † يَوْمٌ إِضْحِيَانٌ, in the Ḳ, erroneously, ضَحْيَآءُ, *a bright day, in which are no clouds*, as in the M; or *bright with the brightness of the* ضُحًى, accord. to Er-Rághib; or [simply] *bright*, and so † ضَحْيَانٌ, which is likewise applied in this sense to a moon, as also † إِضْحِيَانٌ, and to a lamp, or its lighted wick. (TA.) — And اِمْرَأَةٌ ضَحْيَآءُ *A woman whose hair of her* عَانَة *will not grow forth*; (Ḳ, TA;) as though her عانة, being bare of hair, had no shade upon it. (TA.) = مَا أَدْرِى أَىُّ الضَّحْيَآءِ هُوَ is a saying mentioned by Az in art. طحى as meaning *I know not what one of mankind*, or *of the people, he is*. (TA.) = أَضْحًى [a coll. gen. n., of which the n. un. is أَضْحَاةٌ]: see أُضْحِيَّةٌ. Hence, يَوْمُ الأَضْحَى [*The day of the victims*; which is the tenth of Dhu-l-Ḥijjeh]; (Ṣ, Mgh, Ḳ,* TA;) so says Yaạkoob; (TA;) or عِيدُ الأَضْحَى [*the festival of the victims*]: (Mṣb:) and by الأَضْحَى when it is made masc. is meant that day. (Fr, Ṣ, Mṣb.)

إِضْحِيَةٌ: see the next preceding paragraph.

إِضْحِيَانٌ and أَضْحِيَانٌ, and the former with ة: see أَضْحَى, in five places. — الإِضْحِيَانُ is also the name of *A certain plant*, (Ḳ, TA,) *resembling the* أُقْحُوَان [or *chamomile*] *in appearance*. (TA.)

أُضْحِيَّةٌ, (Aṣ, Ṣ, Mgh, Mṣb, Ḳ,) of the measure أُفْعُولَةٌ [as though originally أُضْحُويَةٌ], (Mṣb,) and إِضْحِيَّةٌ, (Aṣ, Ṣ, Mṣb, Ḳ,) pl. [of each] أَضَاحِىُّ; and † ضَحِيَّةٌ, of which the pl. is ضَحَايَا; and أَضْحَاةٌ, of which the pl. is † أَضْحًى, (Aṣ, Ṣ, Mgh, Mṣb, Ḳ, [in copies of the Ḳ and in my copy of the Mgh written أَضْحَى, but it is properly speaking a coll. gen. n. of which أَضْحَاةٌ is the n. un., and is therefore with tenween,]) like أَرْطَاةٌ and أَرْطًى; (Aṣ, Ṣ, Mgh, Mṣb;*) *A sheep* or *goat* (Ṣ, Ḳ, KL) &c. [i. e. meaning also *a camel* and *a bull* or *cow*] (KL) *that is slaughtered*, or *sacrificed*, (Ṣ, Ḳ, KL,) *in the time called* الضُّحَى, (Ḳ,) *on the day called* يَوْمُ الأَضْحَى [*the day of the victims*, which is the tenth of Dhu-l-Ḥijjeh]. (Ṣ, Ḳ,* KL.)

أَرْضٌ مَضْحَاةٌ *A land from which the sun is hardly*, or *never, absent*; (Ḳ, TA;) i. e. *an exposed land*. (TA.)

مُضَحٍّ and † مُتَضَحٍّ and † مُسْتَضْحٍ A man *entering upon the time of morning called* الضُّحَى. (Ḳ,* TA.)

مُتَضَحٍّ: } see what next precedes.
مُسْتَضْحٍ: }

ضخم

1. ضَخُمَ, [aor. ـُ,] (Ṣ, Mṣb, Ḳ,) inf. n. ضِخَمٌ, (Ṣ, Mṣb, TA,) accord. to the copies of the Ḳ ضَخْمٌ, but this is wrong, (TA,) and ضَخَامَةٌ, (Ṣ, Mṣb, Ḳ,) *It*, or *he, was*, or *became, large, big, bulky*, (Ṣ,* Mṣb, Ḳ,) or *thick*: (Ṣ:) or *large in body, portly*, or *corpulent, and fleshy*. (Ḳ.)

4. اضخم لَهُ (Ibn-'Abbád and Ḳ* voce أَدْلَفَ) [*i. q.* أَغْلَظَ لَهُ] † *He spoke to him in a rough, harsh, coarse, rude, uncivil*, or *ungentle, manner*. (TḲ in art. دلف.)

ضَخْمٌ (Ṣ, Mṣb, Ḳ) and † ضَخَمٌ (Ḳ) and † ضُخَامٌ (Ṣ, Ḳ) and † أُضْخُمٌ, (Ḳ,) which last is also with teshdeed of the final letter, (Ṣ, Ḳ,) i. e. † أُضْخُمٌّ, in poetry, (Ṣ, TA,) for there is no word [properly] of the measure أُفْعُلٌ, and IJ mentions † إِضْخَمٌ [evidently in the same sense,] like إِرْدَبٌّ [in measure], (TA,) *Large, big, bulky*, (Ṣ,* Mṣb, Ḳ,) or *thick*; (Ṣ;) applied to a thing (Mṣb, Ḳ) of any kind: (Ḳ:) or *large in body, portly*, or *corpulent, and fleshy*: (Ḳ:) pl. ضِخَامٌ; (Ṣ, Mṣb;) like سِهَامٌ pl. of سَهْمٌ: (Mṣb:) fem. ضَخْمَةٌ, (Ṣ, Mṣb,) applied to a woman; (Mṣb;) pl. ضَخْمَاتٌ, with the خ quiescent, (Ṣ, Mṣb,) because it is an epithet. (Ṣ.)

See also مُضْخَمٌ. —— It was said to a man, إِنَّ لَكَ لَضَخْمًا [app. meaning "Verily thou hast wealth"]; and he replied, أَجَلْ خَيْرٌ ضَخْمٌ العُنُقِ [app., ‡ *Yea, large wealth*]; which is tropical. (TA.) And one says, لَهُ سُودَدٌ ضَخْمٌ † [*He has great lordship or dignity*], and شَرَفٌ ضَخْمٌ [*great nobility*], and شَأْنٌ ضَخْمٌ [*great importance* or *rank*]. (TA.) —— ضَخْمٌ applied to a road means ‡ *Wide.* (Ḳ, TA.) —— And applied to water, ‡ *Heavy.* (Ḳ, TA.)

ضُخَمٌ: see the next preceding paragraph.

ضَخْمَةٌ, applied to a woman, ‡ *Very wide,* or *wide and fat,* (عَرِيضَةٌ أَرِيضَةٌ,) *and soft,* or *tender.* (Ḳ, TA.)

ضُخَامٌ: see ضَخْمٌ.

أَضْخَمُ: see ضَخْمٌ. —— One says [also], هٰذَا أَضْخَمُ مِنْهُ [*This is larger, bigger,* &c., *than it,* or *he*]. (Ṣ.)

ضَخَمٌّ and إِضْخَمٌّ: see ضَخْمٌ.

أُضْخُومَةٌ *A woman's* عُظَّامَة [or *thing resembling a pillow*], (Ṣ, Ḳ, TA,) *with which she makes herself* [*to appear*] *large behind her waist* [or *posteriors*]. (TA.)

مِضْخَمٌ, as an epithet applied to a chief, or lord, ‡ *Noble, and portly,* or *corpulent;* (Ḳ, TA;) as also ▼ ضَخْمٌ. (TA.) —— And, applied to a man, (TA,) ‡ *Vehement in dashing himself against another;* and *in striking,* or *beating.* (Ḳ, TA.)

ضد

1. ضَدَّهُ, (AZ, Ḳ,) first pers. ضَدَدْتُهُ, [aor. ـُ,] inf. n. ضَدٌّ, *He overcame him:* (AZ, L:) and also, (AZ, L,) or ضَدَّهُ فِي الخُصُومَةِ, (Ḳ,) *He overcame him in litigation, altercation,* or *contention.* (AZ, L, Ḳ.) —— And ضَدَّهُ عَنْهُ *He averted him; turned him,* or *sent him, away,* or *back;* or *caused him to return,* or *go back,* or *revert; from it:* (L, Ḳ:) i. e., a thing, or an affair: (L:) and *prevented,* or *hindered, him from doing it;* (Ḳ;) *by gentle means:* (L, Ḳ;) as also صَدَّهُ: heard by Aboo-Turáb from Záïdeh. (L.) ═ ضَدَّ القِرْبَةَ, (Ṣ, Ḳ,) aor. ـُ, (Ṣ,) inf. n. ضَدٌّ, (AA, Ṣ,) *He filled the water-skin.* (Ṣ, Ḳ.)

3. ضَادَّهُ, (inf. n. مُضَادَّةٌ, Mṣb,) *He,* or *it, was,* or *became, contrary, opposed,* or *repugnant, to him,* or *it;* (AHeyth, Ṣ,* L, Ḳ;) said with respect to two men when one desires what is long, and the other, what is short; or one, darkness, and the other, light; or one, to pursue one course, and the other, to pursue another: (AHeyth, L:) or *he,* or *it, was,* or *became, separated from him,* or *it, by contrariety, opposition,* or *repugnance:* (Mṣb:) [or, accord. to the explanation of مُتَضَادَّانِ in the Mṣb, *it was,* or *became inconsistent with it.*]

4. اضدّ *He* (a man, Ṣ) *was,* or *became, angry.* (Ṣ, Ḳ.) It is not, as some assert it to be, a quasi-pass. [of ضَدَّهُ], like as أَكَبَّ is of كَبَّهُ. (TA.)

6. [تضادّا *They two were,* or *became, contrary, opposed,* or *repugnant, each to the other:* or, accord. to the explanation of مُتَضَادَّانِ in the Mṣb, *they two were,* or *became, inconsistent, each with the other.*]

ضِدٌّ (Ṣ, L, Mṣb, Ḳ) and ▼ ضَدِيدٌ (Ṣ, L, Ḳ) and ▼ ضَدِيدَةٌ (Th, M) The *contrary,* or *opposite,* (AA, IAạr, Ṣ,* M, Mṣb, Ḳ,) of a thing: (AA, Mṣb:) or ضِدُّ شَىْءٍ signifies *that which is repugnant to a thing, so that it would overcome it;* as black is to white, and death to life: (Lth, L:) [or, accord. to the explanation of مُتَضَادَّانِ in the Mṣb, *that which is inconsistent with a thing:*] pl. of the first أَضْدَادٌ. (Ṣ, Mṣb, &c.) One says also, هُوَ ضِدُّكَ and ▼ ضَدِيدُكَ *He is contrary,* or *opposed,* or *repugnant, to thee;* as when thou desirest what is long, and he, what is short; or thou, darkness, and he, light; or thou, to pursue one course, and he, to pursue another. (AHeyth, L.) And ضِدٌّ is sometimes a pl., (Ḳ,) or sometimes denotes a collective body; (Akh, Ṣ, L;) as in the phrase يَكُونُونَ عَلَيْهِمْ ضِدًّا, (Ṣ, L, Ḳ,) in the Ḳur [xix. 85], (Ṣ, L,) meaning *They shall be adversaries,* or *enemies, to them:* ('Ikrimeh, Jel:) or *helpers against them.* (Fr, Jel.) One says also, القَوْمُ عَلَىَّ ضِدٌّ وَاحِدٌ, meaning *The people are assembled together against me in contention,* or *altercation, with me.* (L.) —— ضِدٌّ in lexicology signifies *A kind of* مُشْتَرَك [or *homonym*]; being *a word that has two contrary meanings;* as جَوْنٌ, which means both "black" and "white;" and جَلَلٌ, which means both "great" and "small:" pl. as above. (Mz, 26th نوع.) [ضِدٌّ is itself a word of this kind, as is shown by what here follows.] —— Also, (AA, Th, Ṣ, L, Mṣb, Ḳ,) and ▼ ضَدِيدٌ, (Ṣ, L, Ḳ,) The *like,* or *equal,* (AA, Th, Ṣ, L, Mṣb, Ḳ,) of a thing. (AA, Mṣb.) Thus they have two contrary meanings. (Ḳ.) One says, لَا ضِدَّ لَهُ and لَا ضَدِيدَ ▼ لَهُ *There is no like,* or *equal, to him,* or *it.* (Ṣ, L.) And لَقِىَ القَوْمُ أَضْدَادَهُمْ *The people,* or *party, found,* or *met, their equals,* or *fellows.* (L.)

ضَدَدٌ: see ضَادٌّ.

ضَدِيدٌ: see ضِدٌّ, in four places.

ضَدِيدَةٌ: see ضِدٌّ, first sentence.

ضَادٌّ, or ▼ ضَادِدٌ and ▼ ضَدَدٌ *One who fills vessels for people when they seek,* or *demand, water:* pl. ضُدَدٌ, [which is anomalous,] on the authority of AA. (L.)

ضَادِدٌ: see what next precedes.

هُمَا مُتَضَادَّانِ *They two are contrary, opposed,* or *repugnant, each to the other:* (Ṣ,* L, Ḳ:) or *they two are inconsistent;* or *such as cannot be,* or *exist, together;* as night and day. (Mṣb.)

ضر

1. ضَرَّهُ, (Ṣ, A, Mṣb, Ḳ,) and ضَرَّ بِهِ, (Ḳ,) aor. ـُ, (Mṣb,) inf. n. ضَرٌّ; (Ṣ, Mṣb, Ḳ;) and ▼ ضارّه, [which see also below,] (Ṣ, A, Mṣb, Ḳ,) inf. n. مُضَارَّةٌ (Mṣb, Ḳ) and ضِرَارٌ; (A, Mṣb, Ḳ;) and ▼ اضرّه, (Ḳ,) or ▼ اضرّ بِهِ, (Mṣb,) or both, inf. n. إِضْرَارٌ; (TA;) *He,* or *it, harmed, injured, hurt, marred, mischiefed,* or *damaged, him,* or *it; contr. of* نَفَعَهُ; (Ṣ, A, Ḳ;) *did to him,* or *it, an act that was evil,* or *disliked,* or *hated.* (Mṣb.) —— ضَرَّهُ إِلَيْهِ: see 8. —— لَا يَضُرُّكَ عَلَيْهِ جَمَلٌ ‡ *No camel will be more sufficient for thee than he;* syn. لَا يَزِيدُكَ: and لَا يَضُرُّكَ عَلَيْهِ رَجُلٌ ‡ [*No man will be more sufficient for thee than he;* or] *thou wilt not find a man who will be more sufficient for thee than he;* i. e. لَا تَجِدُ رَجُلًا يَزِيدُكَ عَلَى مَا عِنْدَ هٰذَا مَا يَضُرُّكَ عَلَى الرَّجُلِ مِنَ الكِفَايَةِ: (ISk, Ṣ:) and الضَّبُّ صَيْدٌ ‡ *No animal that is hunted is more sufficient for thee than the* ضَبّ; and so مَا يَضُرُّكَ: and مَا تَضُرُّكَ عَلَيْهَا جَارِيَةٌ ‡ *No girl,* or *young woman, is more sufficient for thee than she;* syn. مَا تَزِيدُكَ: (A:) and مَا يَضُرُّكَ عَلَيْهِ شَيْئًا ‡ *He,* or *it, is not at all more sufficient for thee than he,* or *it;* syn. مَا يَزِيدُكَ. (IAạr, TA.) ═ ضَرَّ, (sec. pers. app. ضَرِرْتَ, and aor. يَضَرُّ) inf. n. ضَرَارَةٌ, † *He was,* or *became, blind:* part. n. ضَرِيرٌ [q. v.]. (MA.)

3. ضارّه, inf. n. مُضَارَّةٌ and ضِرَارٌ, *He harmed him, injured him,* or *hurt him, in return,* or *in requital:* whence the saying in a trad., لَا ضَرَرَ وَلَا ضِرَارَ فِى الإِسْلَامِ *There shall be no harming, injuring,* or *hurting,* of one man by another, *in the first instance, nor in return,* or *requital, in El-Islám:* (Mgh, TA:*) ضِرَارٌ is *syn. with* مُضَارَّةٌ: (Ṣ:) or, accord. to some, it is *syn. with* ضَرَرٌ; and in the phrase in a trad. mentioned above, is added as a corroborative. (TA.) See also 1. مُضَارَّةٌ in the case of a testament is the not executing it; or the violating it in part; or the bequeathing to any unfit person or persons; and the like; contrary to the سُنَّة. (TA.) —— *He disagreed with,* or *differed from, him; dissented from him; was contrary, opposed,* or *repugnant, to him;* or *he acted contrarily, contrariously, adversely,* or *in opposition, to him;* syn. خَالَفَهُ. (Ḳ.) And hence, accord. to some, the saying in a trad., (O, Ḳ,) relating to the seeing God on the day of resurrection, (O,) لَا تُضَارُّونَ فِى رُؤْيَتِهِ, (O, Ḳ,) i. e. *Ye will not differ, one from another, nor dispute together, respecting* the truth of *the seeing Him;* (Zj, O,* TA;) because of his manifest appearance: (Zj, TA:) or the meaning is, لَا تَضَامُّونَ, (Ṣ, Ḳ,) and thus some relate it, (TA,) meaning *ye will not draw yourselves together,* (Ḳ, TA,) and *straiten one another;* one saying to another "Show me Him," like as people do in looking at the new moon, but each will by himself have the sight of Him: (TA:) or, as some say, it is ▼ لَا تَضَارُّونَ [originally تَتَضَارُّونَ], meaning لَا تَضَامُّونَ, [which is the same in signification as لَا تُضَامُّونَ], i. e. with fet-ḥ to the ت: (TA, and so in one of my

copies of the Ṣ:) and some say, لَا تُضَارُونَ, from الضَّيْر; (Mgh, TA;) [i. e. *ye will not be hurt;*] meaning *ye will not hurt one another:* (M in art. ضير:) and some, لَا تُضَامُونَ, from الضَّيْم. (Mgh, TA.) — See also 4; and the phrase تَزَوَّجَ عَلَى ضِرٍّ, voce مُضَارَّة.

4. اضرّهُ and اضرّ بهِ: see 1, first sentence. — اضرّهُ عَلَى الأَمْرِ *He compelled him against his will to do the thing.* (Ṣgh, Ḳ.) [See also 8.] — اضرّ, intrans., ‡ *It* (anything) *approached so near as to harm, injure, or hurt;* (TA;) or *so near as to straiten, or incommode.* (L.) You say, اضرّ بهِ, meaning ‡ *It approached very near to him, so as to annoy him:* (TA, from a trad.:) or ‡ *he drew very near to him:* (Ṣ, A:) or ‡ *he clave, or stuck, to him.* (A.) And اضرّ بالطَّرِيقِ ‡ *He approached the road, but was not upon it.* (TA.) And بَنُو فُلَانٍ يُضِرُّونَ بِالطَّرِيقِ ‡ *The sons of such a one are on the travelled track.* (A.) And اضرّ السَّيْلُ مِنَ الحَائِطِ † *The torrent drew near to the wall:* and السَّحَابُ إِلَى الأَرْضِ *the clouds to the earth.* (Ḳ.) — اضرّ عَلَيْهِ ‡ *He importuned him; plied him; plied him hard; pressed him; pressed him hard; was urgent with him; persecuted him,* or *harassed him.* (A.) — اضرّ الفَرَسُ عَلَى فَأْسِ اللِّجَامِ ‡ *The horse champed the* فأس [q. v.] *of the bit;* (A'Obeyd, Ṣ, A;) and so اضرّ. (Ṣ.) — اضرّ فُلَانٌ عَلَى السَّيْرِ الشَّدِيدِ † *Such a one bore patiently hard journeying.* (TA.) — Also, (Mṣb,) inf. n. إِضْرَارٌ, (Ṣ,) *He took to himself a wife while having another wife:* (Aṣ, Ṣ, Mṣb, TA:) [and so, app., ▼ضارّ: (see ضِرٌّ:)] or *he gave* [a woman] *in marriage to a man having at the time another wife.* (TA.) — اضرّ يَعْدُو (Ṣ, Ḳ,* TA) signifies *He hastened* (Ṣ, Ḳ, TA) *somewhat in running,* accord. to A'Obeyd; (Ṣ, TA;) but Eṭ-Ṭoosee says that this is a mistake, and that it is correctly اصرّ. (TA.)

5. تضرّر *He was* [*harmed, injured,* or *hurt;* or] *afflicted, grieved,* or *sick:* and *he experienced straitness, pressure,* or *inconvenience.* (KL.)

6. لَا تَضَارُّونَ [originally تَتَضَارُّونَ]: see 3.

8. اضطرّهُ إِلَى كَذَا *It,* (a thing, or an affair, TA,) or *he,* [a man, or God,] *necessitated, constrained, compelled, forced,* or *drove, him to have recourse to,* or *to do, such a thing;* or *impelled,* or *drove, him, against his will, to it,* or *to do it;* (Mṣb, Ḳ;) *so that he had no means of avoiding it;* as also ▼ضَرَّهُ إِلَيْهِ: (Mṣb:) *it made him to want,* or *be in need of, such a thing:* (Ḳ, TA:) from ضَرُورٌ signifying "narrowness," or "straitness." (TA.) [See also 4. Hence the phrase, لَأَضْطَرَّنَّكَ إِلَى أَصْلِكَ, expl. in art. اصل. See also the Ḳur ii. 120, and xxxi. 23.] — اُضْطُرَّ إِلَى كَذَا *He was,* or *became, necessitated, constrained, compelled, forced,* or *driven, to have recourse to,* or *to do, such a thing;* or *was impelled,* or *driven, against his will, to it,* or *to do it:* (Ṣ, Ḳ:) *he wanted,* or *was* or *became in need of, such a thing.* (Ḳ.)

ضَرٌّ: see the next paragraph, in two places.

ضُرٌّ *Harm, injury, hurt, mischief,* or *damage;* *contr. of* نَفْعٌ; as also ▼ضَرٌّ, (A, Ḳ,) or this is an inf. n., (Ṣ, Mṣb, Ḳ,) and the former is a simple subst.; (ADḳ, Mṣb, Ḳ;) and ▼ضَرَرٌ [which is now the most common]: (Ṣ, Mgh, Mṣb, TA:) or *an evil state* or *condition;* (ADḳ, T, Ṣ, L, Mṣb, Ḳ;) as also ▼ضَرَرٌ and ▼ضُرَّةٌ and ▼تَضُرَّةٌ; (Ḳ; for the right reading in the Ḳ is والضُّرُّ سُوْءُ الحَالِ, as in the L, &c.; not والضرر وسوء الحال, TA; [but in some of the copies of the Ḳ, and in the TA, this signification is assigned to ضرّ instead of ضُرّ; and in the latter, its pl. is said to be أَضُرٌّ;]) and *poverty;* and *bodily affliction:* but the contr. of نَفْعٌ is termed ▼ضَرٌّ, with fet-ḥ: (ADḳ, T, Mṣb, TA:*) [see also ضُرَّةٌ and ضَرُورٌ and ضَرَّاءُ and ضَرُورَةٌ and ضَارُورَآءُ, all of which have similar meanings:] and *disease;* (A, Mṣb;) thus in the Ḳur xxi. 83: (Mṣb:) or *leanness:* (Ṣ, A, TA:) the *state,* or *condition, of him who is termed* ضَرِيرٌ [q. v.]. (TA.) — See also the next paragraph, in two places.

ضِرٌّ The *taking a wife in addition to another wife;* (Ṣ;) a subst. from ضُرَّةٌ. (Ḳ.) You say, نُكِحَتِ المَرْأَةُ عَلَى ضِرٍّ *The woman was taken to wife in addition to a former wife.* (Ṣ.) And, accord. to Aboo-'Abd-Allah Eṭ-Ṭuwál, تَزَوَّجْتُ المَرْأَةَ عَلَى ضِرٍّ and ▼ضُرٍّ [*I took the woman to wife in addition to another wife*]. (Ṣ.) And تَزَوَّجَ عَلَى ضِرٍّ and ▼ضُرٍّ i. e. مُضَارَّةً, meaning *He married so as to have two or three wives together.* (Ḳ.) And Kr mentions the phrase, تَزَوَّجْتُ المَرْأَةَ عَلَى ضِرٍّ كُنَّ لَهَا [*I took to wife the woman in addition to others who were her fellow-wives*]: and if it be so, ضِرٌّ is an inf. n. [used in this instance as an epithet, and therefore applicable to a pl. number as well as to a single person], formed by the rejection of the augmentative letter [in its verb, i. e. أَضَرَّ], or it is a pl. that has no sing. (TA.) — One says also رَجُلٌ ضِرُّ أَضْرَارٍ (Ḳ, TA) i. e. *A man* [who is] *a strong one of strong ones;* like as one says صِلُّ أَصْلَالٍ and صِلُّ أَصْلَالٍ: (TA:) or *very cunning* (دَاهِيَةٌ) *in his judgment,* or *opinion.* (Ḳ, TA.)

ضُرَّةٌ [*Necessity,* or *need;*] a subst. from 8: (Ḳ, TA:) *hardness, distressfulness,* or *afflictiveness, of state* or *condition:* and *annoyance, molestation, harm,* or *hurt.* (Ṣgh, Ḳ.) See also ضُرٌّ, and] ضَرَرٌ, and ضَرَّاءُ, and ضَرُورَةٌ. — A woman's *husband's wife;* her *fellow-wife:* (Ṣ, Mṣb, Ḳ:) an appellation disliked by the Muslim; جَارَةٌ being used in preference to it; accord. to a trad.: (TA:) pl. ضَرَائِرُ (Mṣb, Ḳ) and ضَرَّاتٌ; (Mṣb;) the former extr. [with respect to rule]; (TA;) the latter regular. (Mṣb.) [See also عَلَّةٌ.] — Hence, sing. of ضَرَائِرُ signifying ‡ *Discordant things* or *affairs;* likened to fellow-wives, who will not agree. (TA.) — And [hence also, app.,] الضَّرَّتَانِ is a term applied to † *The two stones of a mill.* (Ṣ, M.) — The *flesh of the* ضَرْع [or *udder*]: (Ṣ:) or the *udder* (ضرع) *altogether,* (Ḳ, TA,) *except the* أَطْبَاء [or *teats*], *when containing milk,* but not otherwise: (TA:) or the *base of the* ضرع, *which is never,* or *scarcely ever, without milk in it:* (TA:) or the *base of the* ثَدْى [or *breast*]: and *i. q.* خِلْفٌ [q. v.]. (Ḳ.) One says ضَرَّةٌ شَكْرَى, meaning *A full* ضَرَّة: (Ṣ in this art.:) or *a* ضرّة *having much milk.* (Ṣ in art. شكر.) — ضَرَّةُ الإِبْهَامِ *The portion of flesh that is beneath the thumb, which is what corresponds to the* أَلْيَة *in the hand:* (Ṣ:) or الضَّرَّةُ signifies *the portion of the palm of the hand extending from beneath the little finger to the wrist:* (Zj, in his "Ḳhalḳ el-Insán:") or *the inner side of the hand,* (Ḳ, TA,) *over against the little finger, corresponding to the* الية *in the hand:* (TA:) or *the portion of flesh beneath the thumb:* (Ḳ:) or *the root thereof* [i. e. of the thumb]: (TA:) and *that part of the flesh of the sole of the foot upon which one treads, next the great toe.* (Ḳ.) [See أَلْيَةٌ.] — The pl. of ضَرَّةٌ (in all the senses expl. above, TA) is ضَرَائِرُ, (Ḳ, TA,) which [as said above] is extr. (TA.) — And الضَّرَّتَانِ signifies *The buttocks, on each side of the bone thereof:* (Ḳ:) or *the two flabby portions of flesh, on each side.* (M, TA.) — Also *Much property,* (Ṣ,) or *many cattle,* (Ṣ,* TA,) *exclusive of money:* (TA:) or *property,* or *cattle,* (مال,) *upon which one relies* [*for his maintenance*], *but belonging to another,* or *others,* (Ḳ, TA,) *of his relations:* (TA:) and *a detached number of cattle, of camels,* and *of sheep* or *goats.* (Ḳ, TA.)

ضُرَّةٌ: see ضَرَّاءُ.

ضَرَرٌ: see ضُرٌّ, in two places. — Also *Defect, deficiency, detriment,* or *loss,* (Mṣb, Ḳ,) and so ▼ضَرَّةٌ and ▼ضَرَارَةٌ, (TA,) *that happens to a thing,* (Ḳ,) or *to articles of property.* (Mṣb.) You say, دَخَلَ عَلَيْهِ ضَرَرٌ فِى مَالِهِ [*Defect, deficiency, detriment,* or *loss, came upon him in his property,* or *cattle*]. (TA.) And هُوَ فِى ضَرَرٍ خَيْرٍ [*He is in a state of defective,* or *little, prosperity*]. (TA.) See also ضَرَّاءُ. — Also *Narrowness,* or *straitness.* (A'Obeyd, Ṣ, Ḳ.) You say مَكَانٌ ذُو ضَرَرٍ *A narrow place.* (A'Obeyd, Ṣ.) And لَا ضَرَرَ عَلَيْكَ and ▼لَا ضَارُورَةَ and ▼لَا تَضُرَّةَ [app. *No straitness shall befall thee:* or *no evil:* or *no adversity:* or *no want*]. (Ṣ.) — And *Narrow.* (Ḳ.) You say مَكَانٌ ضَرَرٌ *A narrow place.* (TA.) And مَآءٌ ضَرَرٌ *Water in a narrow place.* (IAạr.) — And The *brink,* or *edge, of a cave,* or *cavern.* (AA, O, Ḳ.) One says, لَا تَمْشِ عَلَى هٰذَا الضَّرَرِ [*Walk not thou on this brink,* or *edge, of a cave*]. (AA, O.)

ضَرِيرٌ *i. q.* مُضَارَّةٌ [i. e. *Injurious conduct,* either *in the first instance* or *in return* or *requital:* &c.: see 3]: (Ṣ, A, Ḳ:) a subst. in this sense: (TA:) but it is mostly used in the sense here next following. (Ṣ, TA.) — ‡ *Jealousy.* (Ṣ, A, Ḳ.) One says, مَا أَشَدَّ ضَرِيرَهُ عَلَيْهَا ‡ *How great is his jealousy on her account!* (Ṣ, A.) And إِنَّهُ لَذُو ضَرِيرٍ عَلَى امْرَأَتِهِ ‡ *Verily he is jealous on account of his wife.* (TA.) — Also *Spirit* (نَفْس), and *remains of stoutness of body* (بَقِيَّةُ جِسْمٍ): (Ṣ, Ḳ:) or, as some say, *remains of spirit* (بَقِيَّةُ نَفْسٍ). (TA.) One says نَاقَةٌ ذَاتُ ضَرِيرٍ *A she-camel strong in spirit, slow in becoming fatigued:* (Ṣ, TA:) also expl. as meaning *that injures the* [*other*] *camels by the vehemence of her pace,* or *the hardness of her journeying.* (TA.) And بَاقِى ضَرِيرِهَا, referring to camels, is expl. by Aṣ as meaning *Whose strength is lasting.* (TA.) — Also *Patience,* (Ṣ, Ḳ,) and *endurance.* (Ṣ.) One says, إِنَّهُ لَذُو ضَرِيرٍ *Verily he has patient endurance of evil:* (TA:) and إِنَّهُ لَذُو ضَرِيرٍ عَلَى الشَّرِّ وَالشِّدَّةِ *Verily he has patient endurance of evil and hardship;* (Aṣ, Ṣ,* TA;) a phrase used in relation to a man and to a beast. (TA.) ═ Also [an epithet] signifying Anything *intermixed,* or *mingled, with* ضُرّ [i. e. *harm, injury,* &c.]; and so ↓ مَضْرُورٌ. (Ḳ.) — † *Blind;* (Ṣ, Ḳ;) [a more respectful epithet than أَعْمَى;] pl. أَضِرَّاءُ: (Ḳ:) † *harmed by the loss of an eye,* or *by a constant and severe disease:* (Mṣb:) ‡ *diseased:* (A, Ḳ:) and † *lean,* or *emaciated:* (Ḳ:) *affected with a malady of long continuance;* or *crippled,* or *deprived of the power to move* or *to stand* or *to walk, by disease,* or *by a protracted disease:* (TA:) fem. with ة: (A, Ḳ:) and pl. as above. (TA.) — And *Persevering,* and *strong.* (TA.) [Thus having contr. meanings.] — And *Very patient* (AA, Ṣ, Ḳ) *in endurance of everything;* applied to a beast, (AA, Ṣ,) and also to a man. (TA.) ═ Also The *brink* of a valley; (Ṣ, Ḳ;) the *side* thereof: one says, نَزَلَ فُلَانٌ عَلَى أَحَدِ ضَرِيرَىِ الوَادِى, meaning [*Such a one alighted*] *upon one of the two sides of the valley:* (Ṣ:) pl. أَضِرَّةٌ. (TA.) — [Freytag has explained it also, from the Deewán of the Hudhalees, as meaning The *last part of a journey.*]

ضَرَائِرُ Persons *in want, needy,* or *poor.* (Ṣ.) — Also pl. of ضَرَّةٌ, [q. v.,] (Mṣb, Ḳ, TA,) in various senses. (TA.)

ضَرَارَةٌ: see ضَرَرٌ: and ضَرَّاءُ, in two places. — Also † *Blindness.* (Ṣ, Ḳ, TA.) [See 1, last sentence, where it is mentioned as an inf. n.]

ضَرُورَةٌ *Necessity, necessitude, need,* or *want;* (Lth, Ṣ, Mṣb, Ḳ;) as also ↓ ضَارُورَةٌ (Ṣ, Ḳ) and ↓ ضَارُورٌ and ↓ ضَارُورَآءُ and ↓ ضَرَّةٌ: (Ḳ, TA:) pl. ضَرُورَاتٌ. (TA.) You say, حَمَلَتْنِى الضَّرُورَةُ عَلَى كَذَا وَكَذَا [*Necessity urged me to do such and such things*]. (Lth.) And ↓ رَجُلٌ ذُو ضَارُورَةٍ and ذُو ضَرُورَةٍ *A man in want.* (Ṣ.) [And hence فِى الضَّرُورَةِ as meaning *In the case of necessity* in poetry or verse: and ضَرُورَةً *by necessity;* meaning by poetic license. See also ضَرُورِيَّةٌ.] — And *Difficulty, distress, affliction, trouble, inconvenience, fatigue,* or *weariness.* (Mṣb.) [See also ضُرٌّ, and ضَرَّةٌ, and ضَرَّاءُ.]

ضَرُورِىٌّ [*Necessary* knowledge]; as opposed to اِكْتِسَابِىٌّ, [*natural, bestowed by nature, instinctive,* or] *such as the creature has by* [*divine*] *appointment;* and, as opposed to اِسْتِدْلَالِىٌّ, [*intuitive, immediate, axiomatic,* or] *such as originates without thought,* or *reflection, and intellectual examination of an evidence* or *a proof.* (Kull.) [See also بَدِيهِىٌّ.] — [ضَرُورِيَّةٌ as an epithet applied to a proposition means *Qualified by the expression* بِالضَّرُورَةِ (*by necessity*). — And the pl. ضَرُورِيَّاتٌ means *Necessary,* or *indispensable, things.*]

[ضَرُورِيَّةٌ *Necessity.* (See also ضَرُورَةٌ.) — As fem. of the epithet ضَرُورِىٌّ, see this latter word.]

ضَرَّاءُ *A hurtful state* or *condition;* (IAth;) *contr. of* سَرَّاءُ: (IAth, Mṣb:) or *hardship, distress,* or *straitness of condition* [or *of the means of subsistence,* or *of the conveniences of life*]; (AHeyth;) i. q. شِدَّةٌ; (Ṣ, A, Ḳ;) as also بَأْسَآءُ, like which it is a fem. n. without a masc.; and accord. to Fr, أَضُرٌّ and أَبْؤُسٌ may be used as pls. of these two ns.: (Ṣ:) or, accord. to Az, † *that* [*evil*] *which relates to the person;* as *disease:* whereas بَأْسَآءُ is that which relates to property; as poverty: (Bḍ in ii. 172:) or *detriment,* or *loss, with respect to property* and *with respect to persons;* (A, Ḳ;) as also ↓ ضَرَّةٌ, or ↓ ضُرَّةٌ, (accord. to different copies of the Ḳ,) and ↓ ضَرَارَةٌ: (Ḳ:) and [hence] *poverty:* and *punishment:* and *drought,* or *barrenness;* or *vehement,* or *intense, drought:* (TA: [see also ضَارُورَآءُ:]) and † *disease of long continuance;* or *such as cripples,* or *deprives of the power to move* or *to stand* or *to walk;* (A, Ḳ;) as also ↓ ضَرَرٌ, as used in the Ḳur iv. 97: or, accord. to Ibn-'Arafeh, the latter there means † *a hurtful malady that cuts one off from serving in war against unbelievers and the like;* as also ↓ ضَرَارَةٌ; *relating to sight, &c.* (TA.) ═ [Also, accord. to Freytag, *Tangled trees, in a valley:* but the word having this meaning is correctly ضَرَاءٌ, belonging to art. ضرو and ضرى, q. v. And he explains it also as meaning *a bare,* or *an open, place;* and the *contr.* i. e. *a place covered with trees;* referring to the "Kitáb el-Aḍdád."]

ضَرَّارٌ [*That harms, injures, hurts,* &c., *much*]. (TA in art. حلو.)

ضَارٌّ [act. part. n. of 1; *Harming, injuring, hurting,* &c.; or *that harms,* &c.; *noxious, injurious,* &c.]. النَّافِعُ الضَّارُّ, an appellation of God, means *He who benefiteth and who harmeth* whomsoever He will, of his creatures. (TA.)

ضَارُورٌ: see ضَرُورَةٌ.

ضَارُورَةٌ: see ضَرَرٌ; and ضَرُورَةٌ, in two places.

ضَارُورَآءُ *Drought:* and *hardship, distress,* or *adversity.* (Ḳ.) See also ضَرُورَةٌ. [And see ضُرٌّ, and ضَرَّاءُ.]

[صِفَةٌ اضْطِرَارِيَّةٌ i. q. صِفَةٌ خِلْقِيَّةٌ i. e. *A natural quality;* opposed to اِخْتِيَارِيَّةٌ.]

تَضُرَّةٌ and تَضُرَّةٌ: see ضُرٌّ: and for the former see also ضَرَرٌ.

مُضِرٌّ *Approaching* (Ḳ, TA) to a thing: and *approaching so near as to harm, injure,* or *hurt.* (TA.) سَحَابٌ مُضِرٌّ means *Clouds approaching the earth.* (Ṣ, A.) ═ Also A man *having two wives,* (Ṣ, Ḳ,*) or *having* [*several*] *wives at the same time.* (Mṣb.) And a woman *having a fellow-wife,* (TA,) or *having fellow-wives;* (Ṣ, Mṣb;) *having a fellow-wife,* or *two fellow-wives;* as also مُضِرَّةٌ. (Ḳ.) ═ And A man *having a* ضَرَّة [q.v.] *of cattle:* (TA:) or *who has a* ضَرَّة *of cattle that return to him in the afternoon,* or *evening, from the place of pasture.* (Ṣ, TA.)

مَضَرَّةٌ *A cause,* or *means, of harm, injury, hurt, mischief,* or *damage; contr. of* مَنْفَعَةٌ: (Ṣ, TA:) [and simply] *harm, injury, hurt,* &c.; syn. ضَرَرٌ: pl. مَضَارُّ. (Mṣb.)

مِضْرَارٌ A woman, and a she-camel, and a mare, *that takes fright, and runs away, and goes at random,* (تَنِدُّ وَتَرْكَبُ شِدْقَهَا,) *by reason of briskness, liveliness,* or *sprightliness.* (IAṣr, Ḳ.)

مَضْرُورٌ: see ضَرِيرٌ.

بَيْعُ المُضْطَرِّ, which is forbidden in a trad., is of two kinds: one is *The sale that one is compelled to contract against his will;* and this is null: the other is *the sale to which one is necessitated to consent in consequence of a debt that he has incurred or of a burden that has come upon him, so that he sells at a loss that which is in his possession;* and this kind of sale is valid, though disapproved by the people of knowledge. (IAth, TA.)

ضرب

1. ضَرَبَهُ, aor. ـِ, (Ṣ, O, Ḳ, &c.,) inf. n. ضَرْبٌ, (Ṣ, O, &c.,) [*He beat, struck, smote,* or *hit, him,* or *it;*] and ↓ ضَرَّبَهُ [signifies the same in an intensive sense, i. e. *he beat,* &c., *him,* or *it, much,* or *violently;* or in a frequentative sense, i. e. *several,* or *many, times:* or rather ضَرَّبَ is used in relation to several, or many, objects, as will be shown in what follows]: (Ḳ:) accord. to Er-Rághib, الضَّرْبُ signifies *the making a thing to fall upon another thing;* and, as some say, *the making it to fall with violence,* or *vehemence.* (TA.) You say, ضَرَبَهُ بِهِ [*He struck him,* or *it, with it*], i. e. with a sword, (A, Mgh, Mṣb), &c. (A, Mṣb.) And تَضْرِبُ فِى حَدِيدٍ بَارِدٍ [*Thou beatest upon cold iron*]: a prov. [expl. in art. حد]. (Ḥar p. 633.) And ضَرَبْتُ زَيْدًا سَوْطًا, meaning بِسَوْطٍ [i. e. *I struck Zeyd with a whip*], or ضَرْبَةَ سَوْطٍ [*a stroke of a whip*]: (M in art. سوط, q. v.:) and ضَرَبَهُ مِائَةَ سَوْطٍ [*He struck him a hundred strokes of the whip*]. (Ṣ and Ḳ in art. سحل, &c.) And ضَرَبْتُ عُنُقَهُ [*I smote his neck,* meaning *I beheaded him*]; and ↓ ضَرَّبْتُ الأَعْنَاقَ [*I smote the necks,* meaning *I struck off the heads*]; the teshdeed denoting muchness [of the

action] or multiplicity [of the objects]: AZ says that, when the object is one, the Arabs use only the former verb, without teshdeed; but when there is a plurality of objects, either of the verbs; (Mṣb;) [so that] one says, ضَرَبُوا أَعْنَاقَهُمْ [They smote their necks, or beheaded them], and أَمَرَ بِتَضْرِيبِ ↓ الرِّقَابِ [He gave the order to smite the necks, or to strike off the heads]: (A:) فَضَرْبَ الرِّقَابِ in the Ḳur xlvii. 4 is originally فَاضْرِبُوا الرِّقَابَ ضَرْبًا [meaning Then do ye smite the necks, i. e. strike off the heads]; (Bḍ;) the inf. n. being here put for its verb. (Jel.) [Respecting the phrase هُوَ الضُّرَيْبُكَ, see 1 in art. جدع.] — [Hence a variety of meanings and phrases here following.] — ضَرَبَ كَلْبَهُ عَلَى الصَّيْدِ † [He beat, or disciplined, or trained, his dog for the purpose of the chase]: whence the phrases ضَرَبَ عَلَيْهِ جِرْوَتَهُ and ضَرَبَ جِرْوَةَ نَفْسِهِ and ضَرَبْتُ جِرْوَتِى عَنْهُ [expl. voce جِرْوَةٌ]. (Z, and TA in art. جرو.) — لَا تُضْرَبُ أَكْبَادُ الإِبِلِ إِلَّا إِلَى ثَلَاثَةِ مَسَاجِدَ † Camels shall not be ridden, save to three mosques: [namely, that of Mekkeh, that of El-Medeeneh, and that of El-Aḳṣà at Jerusalem:] a trad. (TA. [See also 4 in art. عمل.]) — ضَرَبَ بِهِ الأَرْضَ, lit. He smote with him, or it, the ground; meaning † he cast, threw, or flung, him, or it, upon the ground. And ضَرَبَ بِسَلْحِهِ الأَرْضَ † He cast forth his excrement, or ordure, upon the ground.] And [hence] ضَرَبَ الأَرْضَ ‡ He voided excrement, or ordure; (A, TA;) and so الغَائِطَ. (TA.) [See ضَرَبَ بِنَفْسِهِ الأَرْضَ see expl. in the latter half of this paragraph.] — ضَرَبْتُ القَوْسَ بِالمِضْرَبِ. I struck the string of the bow with the wooden implement [or mallet] used in separating cotton. (Mṣb.) — ضَرَبَ العُودَ [He struck the chords of the lute; meaning he played upon the lute; and so ضَرَبَ بِالعُودِ]. (Ṣ.) — ضَرَبَ الوَتِدَ, aor. and inf. n. as above, He beat [or knocked or struck] the tent-peg, or stake, so that it became firm in the ground. (Lḥ, TA.) And [hence] ضَرَبَ الخَيْمَةَ ‡ He pitched the tent, by knocking in its pegs with a mallet: (Kull p. 231:) or he set up the tent. (Mṣb.) — ضَرَبَ الدِّرْهَمَ, aor. and inf. n. as above, ‡ He struck, coined, or minted, the dirhem, or piece of money. (TA.) And ضَرَبَ عَلَى ٱسْمِهِ † [He struck, coined, or minted, money in his name]. (ISd, TA in art. جوز.) — ضَرَبَ عَلَى المَكْتُوبِ ‡ He sealed, or stamped, the writing. (A,* TA.) [And ضَرَبَ عَلَيْهِ † He erased it; namely, anything written.] — ضَرَبَ الطِّينَ عَلَى الجِدَارِ † [He stuck, or applied, the mud upon the wall, as a plaster]. (TA.) — Hence, accord. to some, the phrase ضُرِبَتْ عَلَيْهِمُ الذِّلَّةُ, in the Ḳur ii. 58, considered as meaning † Vileness was made to cleave to them: or the meaning is, † encompassed them, like as the tent encompasses him over whom it is pitched. (Ksh, Bḍ.) And [in like manner] one says, ضُرِبَتْ عَلَيْهِمْ ضَرِيبَةٌ ‡ An impost, of the tax called جِزْيَة, &c., was imposed upon them. (A,* Mgh, Mṣb.*) And ضَرَبَ عَلَى العَبْدِ الإِتَاوَةَ ‡ He imposed upon the slave the tax according to a fixed time. (TA. [See ضَرِيبَةٌ.]) And ضُرِبَ عَلَيْهِمُ البَعْثُ † The being sent to the war was appointed them and imposed upon them as an obligation. (Mgh in art. بعث.) — ضَرَبَ الشَّبَكَةَ عَلَى الطَّائِرِ † He cast the net over the bird: (Mgh:) and ضُرِبَ الفَخُّ عَلَى الطَّائِرِ ‡ [The snare was cast over the bird]. (A, TA.) — ضَرَبَ اللَّيْلُ بِأَرْوَاقِهِ † [The night cast its folds of darkness;] meaning the night came. (TA.) [And † The night became dark, or was dark; as appears from the following verse.] Ḥomeyd says,

سَرَى مِثْلَ نَبْضِ العِرْقِ وَاللَّيْلُ ضَارِبٌ ↓ ... بِأَرْوَاقِهِ وَالصُّبْحُ قَدْ كَادَ يَسْطَعُ

† [He went on in his night-journey, like the pulsing of the vein, while the night was casting its folds of darkness over the earth, and the dawn had almost risen]. (TA. [See also ضَارِبٌ.]) You say also, ضَرَبَ عَلَيْهِ حِجَابًا † [He put, or let down, a veil, or curtain, or covering, over him, or it]. (TA.) And ضُرِبَ بَيْنَهُمَا سَدٌّ † [A barrier was set between them two]. (A in art. سد.) ضَرَبْنَا عَلَى آذَانِهِمْ [in the Ḳur xviii. 10] means ‡ We prevented their sleeping; (Ḳ, TA;) as though by putting a covering over their ears; a metonymical [and elliptical] mode of saying we made them to sleep by preventing any sound from penetrating into their ears, in consequence of which they would have awoke: (Zj, L, TA:) or ضَرَبَ عَلَى آذَانِهِمْ means † he poured upon them sleep so that they slept and did not awake: and one says also, ضَرَبْتُ النَّوْمَ عَلَى أُذُنِهِ [meaning † I poured sleep upon him by closing his ear]. (Mṣb.) — ضَرَبَتِ العَقْرَبُ, (A, Ḳ,* TA,) aor. and inf. n. as above, (TA,) ‡ The scorpion stung. (A, Ḳ,* TA.) — ضَرَبَتْهُ الرِّيحُ ‡ The wind beat it, or blew upon it; [namely, herbage, and water, &c.] And ضَرَبَهُ البَرْدُ (IKṭṭ, Ḳ, TA) † The cold smote it so as to injure it; namely, herbage; and in like manner one says of the wind: (IKṭṭ, TA:) and ↓ اضربهُ البَرْدُ (A, TA) ‡ The cold smote it by its vehemence, so that it dried up; and in like manner one says of the wind: (TA:) and ↓ اضرب الضَّرِيبُ الأَرْضَ † The hoar-frost, or rime, fell upon the land, so that its herbage became nipped, or blasted. (AZ, TA. [See also ضُرِبَ.]) And ضُرِبَ بِبَلِيَّةٍ † He was smitten with a trial, or an affliction. (L, TA.) — طَرِيقُ مَكَّةَ مَا ضَرَبَهَا العَامَ قَطْرَةٌ † [The road to Mekkeh, not a drop of rain has fallen upon it this year]. (A, TA.) — ضَرَبَ الفَحْلُ النَّاقَةَ, (Ṣ, A,* Mṣb, Ḳ,* TA,) aor. ـِ, (TA,) inf. n. ضِرَابٌ (Ṣ, A, Mṣb, Ḳ) and ضَرْبٌ also, accord. to Fr, but this latter, though agreeable with analogy, is disallowed by Sb and Akh, (TA,) ‡ The stallion leaped the she-camel; (Mṣb, TA;) i. e. (TA,) compressed (A, Ḳ, TA) her. (TA.) ضِرَابُ الجَمَلِ is used elliptically for ثَمَنُ ضِرَابِ الجَمَلِ ‡ The hire of the camel's leaping the female: the taking of which, as also the taking of the hire of any stallion for covering, is forbidden in a trad. (TA.) — ضَرَبَ الشَّىْءَ بِالشَّىْءِ ‡ He mixed the [one] thing with the [other] thing; (A, Ḳ;) as also ↓ ضَرَّبَهُ, (Ḳ,) inf. n. تَضْرِيبٌ: (TA:) accord. to some, said peculiarly in relation to milk; (MF, TA;) but [SM says,] this I have not found in any lexicon. (TA.) ضَرَبَ اللَّبَنَ فِى السِّقَآءِ means ‡ حَقَنَهُ [i. e. He collected the milk in the skin, and poured fresh milk upon that which was curdled, or thick, or upon that which was churned; or he poured the milk into the skin, and kept it therein that its butter might come forth]. (A.) In the L and other lexicons it is said that ضَرَبْتُ بَيْنَهُمْ فِى الشَّرِّ means I caused them to become confused [or I involved them] in evil or mischief. (TA. [And ضرّبت بينهم has a similar meaning: see 2.]) And ضُرِبَتِ الشَّاةُ بِلَوْنِ كَذَا means The sheep, or goat, was intermixed with such a colour. (L, TA.) — ضَرَبَ الشَّجَرُ بِعُرُوقِهِ فِى الأَرْضِ [The trees struck their roots into the earth]. (A and TA in art. عرق.) — [Hence, the saying,] ضَرَبَتْ فِيهِ فُلَانَةُ بِعِرْقٍ ذِى أَشَبٍ i. e. التِبَاسٍ; (Ṣ and TA in the present art., and in like manner, in both, in art. اشب, with the addition of ذِى before التِبَاسٍ;) ‡ [app. meaning Such a woman implanted, or engendered, in him a strain, i. e. a radical, or hereditary, quality, of a dubious kind: or the pronoun in فيه relates to a family, or people; for it is said that] the meaning is, such a woman corrupted their race by her bringing forth among them: or, as some say, عرقت فِيهِمْ عِرْقَ سَوْءٍ [i. e. عَرَّقَتْ, or, accord. to more common usage, أَعْرَقَتْ, i. e., implanted, or engendered, among them, or in them, an evil strain, or radical or hereditary disposition]. (TA. [This saying is also mentioned in the A, as tropical, but is not expl. therein.]) — ضَرَبَ بِالقِدَاحِ, (Ṣ, Mgh, Ḳ,) and ضَرَبَ القِدَاحَ, (A, TA,) ‡ He turned about, or shuffled, (أَجَالَ,) the arrows, [in the رِبَابَة (q. v.), in the game called المَيْسِر,] عَلَى الجَزُورِ [for the slaughtered camel]. (Mgh. [See حُرْضَةٌ.]) [And † He played with the gaming-arrows; practised sortilege with arrows, or with the arrows.] You say, ضَرَبْتُ مَعَ القَوْمِ بِسَهْمٍ † I practised sortilege with the people, or party, with an arrow; syn. سَاهَمْتُهُمْ. (Mṣb.) And ضَرَبَ بِالقِدْحَيْنِ † He practised sortilege with the two arrows; one of which was inscribed with the sentence "My Lord hath commanded me," and the other with "My Lord hath forbidden me:" a person between hope and despair is likened to one practising this mode of sortilege, which was used by the people of the Time of Ignorance when they doubted whether they should undertake an affair or abstain from it. (Ḥar pp. 465 and 553.) One says also, ضَرَبَ فِى الجَزُورِ بِسَهْمٍ meaning † He obtained a share, or portion, of the slaughtered camel. (Mgh.) And hence the saying of El-Ḥareeree, وَضَرَبْتُ فِى مَرْعَاهَا بِنَصِيبٍ † [And I obtained a share of its pasture]. (Mgh.) And the lawyers say, يَضْرِبُ فِيهِ بِالثُّلُثِ i. e. † He shall take thereof somewhat, according to what is due to him, of the third part. (Mgh.) They say also,

ضَرَبَ فِى مَالِهِ سَهْمًا i. e. † *He assigned* [*a share, or portion, of his property*]: and thus is expl. the saying of Aboo-Ḥaneefeh, لَا يَضْرِبُ لِلْمُوصَى لَهُ فِيمَا زَادَ عَلَى الثُّلُثِ † *He shall not assign*, or *give, to the legatee*, aught *of more than the third part*; the true objective complement being suppressed. (Mgh.) —— ضَرَبَ بِيَدَيْهِ [lit. *He beat with his arms*; meaning † *he moved his arms about*, or *to and fro; brandished, tossed*, or *swung them*]: you say, ضَرَبَ بِيَدَيْهِ وَحَرَّكَهُمَا فِى مِشْيَتِهِ † [*He swung his arms, and moved them about, in his manner of walking*]. (TA in art. جدف. [See جَدَفَ.]) And ضَرَبَ فِى المَآءِ [بِيَدَيْهِ being understood after the verb] † *He swam*. (Ḳ.) —— ضَرَبَ بِيَدِهِ إِلَى شَىْءٍ † *He made a sign*, or *pointed, with his hand, towards a thing*. (TA.) And ضَرَبَ [alone] † *He made a sign*, or *pointed*. (Ḳ.) And ضَرَبَ بِيَدِهِ إِلَى كَذَا † *He put forth his hand towards such a thing, to take it*, or *to point*, or *make a sign*. (TA.) And ضَرَبَ يَدَهُ إِلَى عَمَلِ كَذَا † [*He applied his hand to the doing of such a thing*]. (Lth, TA.) [And ضَرَبَ يَدَيْهِ فِى المَالِ a phrase expl. to me by IbrD as meaning † *He busied his hands with the property*, in the giving, or dispensing of it.] —— ضَرَبَ عَلَى يَدِهِ † [*He struck his* (i. e. another man's) *hand*; meaning] *he struck*, or *made, the bargain with him*; or *ratified the sale with him*: for it is a custom, when two persons are bargaining together, for one of them to put his hand upon the other's in ratifying the bargain. (TA, from a trad.) —— And ‡ *He prohibited*, or *prevented*, or *hindered, him, from doing a thing*, or *from doing a thing that he had begun*: (TA:) and [in like manner] ضَرَبَ عَلَى يَدَيْهِ ‡ *he withheld*, or *restrained, him*, or *it*. (Ḳ, TA.) And (i. e. the former phrase) ‡ *He* (the judge, A, Mgh, TA) *prohibited*, or *interdicted, him from the using*, or *disposing of, his property according to his own free will*. (Ṣ, A, Mgh, Mṣb, TA.) —— Also ‡ *He corrupted, vitiated, marred*, or *disordered, his affair*, or *case*, or *state*. (A, Mṣb, TA.) —— ضَرَبَ عَنْهُ † *He turned away* a person or thing *from him* [or *it*]; as also ▼ اضرب: (TA:) [or] اضرب ▼ عنه signifies, (Ṣ, Mṣb,) or signifies also, (TA,) and (Mṣb, TA) so does ضَرَبَ عنه, (Mṣb, Ḳ, TA,) [the latter app. for ضَرَبَ نَفْسَهُ عَنْهُ,] † *He turned away from, avoided, shunned*, or *left, him*, or *it*; (Ṣ,* Mṣb, Ḳ,* TA;*) namely, a person, (TA,) or a thing. (Mṣb.) أَفَنَضْرِبُ عَنْكُمُ الذِّكْرَ صَفْحًا, in the Ḳur [xliii. 4], is said to mean † *Shall we then neglect you, and not teach you what is incumbent on you?* the phrase being taken from a rider's striking his beast with his stick when he desires to turn him from the course that he is pursuing: or the meaning is, † *shall we then turn away the Ḳur-án from you*, and not invite you thereby to the faith, *turning away ourselves* from you? (TA.) One says also, ضَرَبْتُ عَنْهُ صَفْحًا meaning † *I turned away from him and left him*. (Ṣ and TA in art. صفح: see 1 in that art.) See also the saying ضَرَبَ أَخْمَاسَهُ فِى أَسْدَاسِهِ voce خُمْسٌ. —— And فُلَانٌ يَضْرِبُ أَخْمَاسًا لِأَسْدَاسٍ: see voce خِمْسٌ. —— ضَرَبَ بِنَفْسِهِ الأَرْضَ, (Ḳ,) inf. n. ضَرْبٌ, (TA,) [lit. *He smote with himself the ground*; and hence, † *he cast, threw*, or *flung, himself upon the ground*; app. often used in this sense; (a phrase similar to ضَرَبَ بِهِ الأَرْضَ expl. before;) and hence,] † *he remained, stayed*, or *abode*; (Ḳ;) and so ▼ اضرب (AZ, ISk, Ṣ, Ḳ, TA) as used in the phrase اضرب الرَّجُلُ فِى البَيْتِ ‡ *The man remained, stayed*, or *abode, in the tent*, or *house*, (AZ, ISk, Ṣ, A, TA,) *not quitting it*: (ISk, A, TA:) and [in like manner] ضَرَبَ بِذَقَنِهِ, [الأَرْضَ being understood,] † *He stayed*, or *abode, and remained fixed*. (Ḳ in art. ذقن. [See also other explanations of this last phrase in a later part of this paragraph.]) And ضَرَبَ الوَتِدَ بِمَحَلِّ كَذَا ‡ *He remained, stayed*, or *abode*, [lit., *struck the tent-peg*,] *in such a place of alighting*. (A.) And ضَرَبَتِ الإِبِلُ بِعَطَنٍ, [الأَرْضَ being understood after الابل,] † *The camels lay down* [*in a place by the water*]: (Ṣ in art. عطن:) or *satisfied themselves with drinking and then lay down around the water* or *by the watering-troughs, to be brought again to drink another time*: (IAth, TA in that art.:) and [hence,] ضَرَبَ النَّاسُ بِعَطَنٍ, occurring in a trad., † *The people's camels satisfied themselves with drinking until they lay down and remained in their place* [*at the water*]: (TA in the present art.:) or *the people satisfied their thirst and then abode at the water*. (Ḳ in art. عطن.) —— ضَرَبَ بِذَقَنِهِ الأَرْضَ ‡ *He was cowardly; and feared*; (A, O,* Ḳ, TA;) *and clave to the ground*: (O, TA:) or *he was*, or *became, affected with shame, shyness*, or *bashfulness*. (A, TA.) —— يَضْرِبُ لَهُ الأَرْضَ كُلَّهَا [lit. *He beats for it the whole land*, i. e. in journeying,] means † *he seeks it through the whole land*: so says AZ in explanation of the phrase here following. (O, TA.) يَضْرِبُ المَجْدَ † *He seeks to gain*, or *obtain, glory*: (O, Ḳ:) or *he applies himself with art and diligence to gain glory*, (يَكْتَسِبُهُ,) *and seeks it through the whole land*. (AZ, TA. [See also 8.]) —— ضَرَبَ اللَّبِنَ, (A,) or اللَّبْنَ, ‡ *He made* [or *moulded*] *bricks*. (MA.) And ضَرَبَ الخَاتَمَ ‡ *He made, fashioned*, or *moulded, the signet-ring*. (TA.) [Hence one says,] اِضْرِبْهُ عَلَى طَبْعِ هٰذَا i. e. † [*Make thou it, fashion it*, or *mould it*,] *according to the model, make, fashion*, or *mould, of this*. (IAạr, O and Ḳ in art. طبع.) And هٰذِهِ ضَرِيبَتُهُ الَّتِى ضُرِبَ عَلَيْهَا, and ضُرِبَهَا, and ضُرِبَ alone, [for ضُرِبَ عَلَيْهَا,] meaning طُبِعَ [i. e. † *This is his nature, with an adaptation*, or *a disposition, to which he was moulded*, or *created*; or *to which he was adapted*, or *disposed, by creation*]. (Lḥ, TA.) And ضُرِبَ فُلَانٌ عَلَى الكَرَمِ ‡ [*Such a one was moulded*, or *created, with an adaptation* or *a disposition, to generosity*; or *was adapted*, or *disposed, by creation*, or *nature, to generosity*]. (A.) —— ضَرَبَ مَثَلًا (Ṣ, A, O, &c.) ‡ *He rehearsed, propounded*, or *declared, a parable, a similitude, an example*, or *a proverb*; said of God [and of a man]: (Ṣ,* O,* Mṣb, TA:) or *he mentioned*, or *set forth, a parable, &c.*: or *he framed a parable*: thus expl., the verb has but one objective complement: or the phrase signifies *he made* [such a thing] *an example*, or *the subject of a parable* or *similitude &c.*; and so has two objective complements: in the saying in the Ḳur [xxxvi. 12] وَاضْرِبْ لَهُمْ مَثَلًا أَصْحَابَ القَرْيَةِ † [*And propound thou to them a parable, the people of the town*] i. e., the story of the people of the town, [or *make thou to them a parable*, or *similitude*, or *an example, the people of the town*;] مثلا may be in the accus. case as an objective complement, اصحاب القرية being a substitute for مثلا; or اصحاب القرية may be regarded as a second objective complement [i. e. second in the order of the words, but first in the order of the sense]: the phrase is differently expl. on account of the different meanings of the verb ضَرَبَ; which signifies *he described*, or *rehearsed*; and *he declared, propounded*, or *explained*; and *he made, caused to be*, or *constituted*; &c.: accord. to some, it is taken from the phrase ضَرَبَ الدِّرْهَمَ [q. v.]; because of the impression which a parable or the like makes upon the mind: accord. to some, from ضَرِيبٌ signifying "a like;" because the first thing is made like the second: accord. to some, from ضَرَبَ الطِّينَ عَلَى الجِدَارِ [q. v.; because the mud, applied as a plaster, conforms to the shape of the wall]: and accord. to some, from ضَرَبَ الخَاتَمَ [q. v.]; because of the correspondence between a parable or the like and the object to which it is applied, and the correspondence between the signet and its impression. (TA, from the M and L &c.) يَضْرِبُ اللّٰهُ الحَقَّ وَالبَاطِلَ, in the Ḳur [xiii. 18], means † *God likeneth*, or *compareth, truth and falsity*. (TA.) One says also, ضَرَبَ بِهِ مَثَلًا † [*He made him*, or *it, a subject of a parable, a similitude, an example*, or *a proverb*; *he propounded*, or *framed, a parable, &c., respecting him*, or *it*]. (TA.) And يُضْرَبُ المَثَلُ لِكَذَا [*The proverb, &c., is applied to, in relation to*, or *to the case of, such a thing*]. (Meyd &c., passim.) —— ضَرَبَ لَهُ أَجَلًا † *He specified*, or *notified, to*, or *for, him*, or *it, a term*, or *period*. (Mgh, Mṣb.*) —— ضَرَبَ لَهُمْ طَرِيقًا † *He assigned to them*, or *made for them, a way*; syn. جَعَلَ. (MA. [App. from a phrase in the Ḳur xx. 79, q. v.]) —— الضَّرْبُ as a conventional term of the accountants, or arithmeticians, means The *multiplying* a number by another number; (Mgh, Mṣb;) as when you say, [ضَرَبَ خَمْسَةً فِى سِتَّةٍ *He multiplied five by six*; and] خَمْسَةٌ فِى سِتَّةٍ بِثَلَاثِينَ [*Five* multiplied *by six is thirty*]. (Mṣb.) —— ضَرَبَ [is often intrans., and thus] signifies also تَحَرَّكَ [i. e. † *It was*, or *became, in a state of commotion, &c.*]: (Ḳ:) [see also 8, which is more commonly used in this sense:] or, *so with strength*, or *force*. (TA.) [And hence several phrases here following.] —— ضَرَبَ العِرْقُ (A, TA,) inf. n. ضَرْبٌ and ضَرَبَانٌ, (TA,) ‡ *The vein pulsed*, or *beat*, (A, TA,) and *throbbed*: (TA:) and ضَرَبَ, inf. n. ضَرَبَانٌ, ‡ *it* (the vein) *pained, and was*, or *became, in a state of strong commotion*. (TA.) And ضَرَبَ الجُرْحُ, inf. n. ضَرَبَانٌ, (Ṣ, A, Mṣb,) ‡ *The wound* [*throbbed*; or] *pained violently*: (A, Mṣb:) and so الضِّرْسُ ‡ [*the tooth*]. (A, TA.) —— ضَرَبَتِ النَّاقَةُ, (A, Ḳ,) or, as in some lexicons, المَخَاضُ, (TA,) ‡ *The she-camel*, (A, Ḳ,) or *the pregnant* camel, (TA,) *raised her tail, and smote her vulva with it,* (A, Ḳ, TA,) *and then went along.* (Ḳ, TA.) — ضَرَبَ فِى جَهَازِهِ ‡ *He* (a camel) *took fright, and ran away at random,* (Ṣ, A, L, TA,) *and ceased not to gallop and leap until he had thrown off all his furniture, or load.* (L, TA.) — جَآءَ يَضْرِبُ بِشَرٍّ ‡ *He came hastening* [*with mischief,* or] *in an evil affair.* (A.) It is said in a trad. of 'Alee, When such and such things shall happen, (mentioning faction, or sedition, or the like,) ضَرَبَ يَعْسُوبُ الدِّينِ بِذَنَبِهِ, meaning, accord. to ÁM, † *The leader of the religion shall hasten to go away through the land,* fleeing from the faction, or sedition: or, as some say, *shall go away hastily through the land, with his followers.* (O, TA. [But see يَعْسُوبٌ: and see also ذَنَبٌ.]) And you say also, ضَرَبْتُ فِى السَّيْرِ, (Mṣb,) inf. n. ضَرْبٌ, (Ṣ,) † *I hastened in journeying.* (Ṣ,* Mṣb.) And ضَرَبَ فِى الأَرْضِ, (Ṣ, A, Mgh, Mṣb, Ḳ,) aor. ـِ, (TA,) inf. n. ضَرْبٌ (Ṣ, Ḳ, TA) and مَضْرَبٌ (Ṣ, TA) and ضَرَبَانٌ, (Ḳ, TA,) † *He journeyed in the land* (Ṣ, Mgh, Mṣb) *seeking sustenance,* (Ṣ,) and *for the purpose of traffic:* (Mgh:) [and ضَرَبَ الأَرْضَ, as shown above, has a similar meaning:] or ‡ *he went forth in the land as a merchant;* (A, Ḳ;) or *warring and plundering,* (Ḳ,) or so ضَرَبَ فِى سَبِيلِ ٱللّٰهِ [meaning *in the cause of God*]: (A:) or *he hastened through the land:* (A, Ḳ:) or *he arose, and hastened in his journey through the land:* (TA:) or *he went,* or *went away, in the land:* (A, Ḳ:) or *he traversed,* or *journeyed through, the land.* (TA.) The verb is [similarly] used in relation to almost all employments: you say, ضَرَبَ فِى التِّجَارَةِ † [*He travelled for the purpose of traffic*]: (TA:) and إِنَّ لِى فِى أَلْفِ دِرْهَمٍ لَمَضْرَبًا ضَرْبًا i. e. [*Verily I have to make a journey for the sake of,* or *on account of, a thousand dirhems*]. (Ṣ, TA: but in my copies of the Ṣ, لى is omitted.) And ضَرَبَتِ الطَّيْرُ, aor. as above, ‡ *The birds went,* or *went away,* [or *migrated,*] *seeking sustenance.* (Ḳ, TA.) — ضَرَبَ said of time, † *It went, passed,* or *passed away.* (Ḳ.) And ضَرَبَ الدَّهْرُ مِنْ ضَرَبَانِهِ, or, accord. to one reading, مِنْ ضَرْبِهِ, occurring in a trad., ‡ *The time in part passed;* [*the time pursued a part of its course;*] or *a part of the time passed.* (TA.) And ضَرَبَ الدَّهْرُ ضَرَبَانَهُ † *Fortune,* or *time, produced,* or *brought to pass, its events:* (IḲṭṭ, TA:) a phrase like قُضِىَ مِنَ القَضَآءِ. (Ṣ, L, TA.) And ضَرَبَ الدَّهْرُ مِنْ ضَرَبَانِهِ أَنْ كَانَ كَذَا وَكَذَا ‡ [*Fortune,* or *time, brought to pass, among its events, that such and such things happened*]. (A, L, TA.) And ضَرَبَ الدَّهْرُ بَيْنَنَا ‡ *Fortune,* or *time, separated us:* (AO, A, TA:) or *made a wide separation between us;* syn. بَعَّدَ. (Ḳ.) — Also † *It was,* or *became, long:* (Ḳ, TA:) so in the saying, ضَرَبَ اللَّيْلُ عَلَيْهِمْ † [*The night was,* or *became, long to them*]. (TA.) — And يَضْرِبُ إِلَيْهِ † *It inclined to it.* (TA.) [One says, يَضْرِبُ إِلَى السَّوَادِ † *It inclines to blackness,* and إِلَى الحُمْرَةِ *to redness,* &c.: often occurring in the lexicons.] ═ ضَارَبَهُ فَضَرَبَهُ, aor. of the latter ـُ: see 3. ═ جَادَ ضَرْبُهَا i. q. ضَرَبَتْ يَدُهُ [meaning *Excellent,* or *how excellent, is his hand,* or *arm, in beating, striking, smiting,* or *hitting!* a phrase similar to رَمَوْتْ يَدُهُ]. (Ḳ.) ═ ضَرِبَ, (IḲṭṭ, A, Ḳ,) aor. ـَ, (Ḳ,) inf. n. ضَرَبٌ, said of herbage, ‡ *It was marred,* or *spoilt, by the cold:* (A:) or *it was smitten by the cold,* (IḲṭṭ, Ḳ, TA,) *and injured thereby,* and *by the wind.* (IḲṭṭ, TA.) And ضَرِبَتِ الأَرْضُ, inf. n. ضَرَبٌ, † *The land was smitten by hoar-frost,* or *rime, and its herbage was nipped,* or *blasted, thereby:* (AZ, TA:) and ضُرِبَتْ [in like manner] ‡ *it* (i. e. land) *was smitten by hoar-frost,* or *rime;* or *had hoar-frost,* or *rime, fallen upon it.* (Ṣ, A, TA.)

2: see 1, first sentence; and in two places in a sentence shortly after that. — ضَرَّبَ الشَّىْءَ بِالشَّىْءِ: see 1, in the second quarter of the paragraph. — [Hence,] التَّضْرِيبُ بَيْنَ القَوْمِ † *The exciting discord,* or *strife,* or *animosity, between,* or *among, the people,* or *party.* (Ṣ, TA.) — And ضَرَّبَ, inf. n. تَضْرِيبٌ, signifies also † *He excited, incited, urged,* or *instigated, and roused to ardour,* a courageous man, in war, or battle. (TA.) — ضَرَّبَ المُضَرَّبَةَ, (Ṣ, Mgh, Mṣb,) inf. n. as above, (TA,) *He sewed* (Ṣ, Mgh, Mṣb) [meaning *quilted*] *with cotton* (Mgh, Mṣb) *the* مُضَرَّبَة [q. v.]. (Ṣ, Mgh, Mṣb.) ═ ضَرَّبَتْ عَيْنُهُ *His eye became depressed in his head.* (Ḳ.) ═ ضَرَّبَ, inf. n. as above, also signifies † *He exposed himself,* or *became exposed,* (تَعَرَّضَ,) *to the snow,* (Ḳ, TA,) i. e. *the* ضَرِيب [which signifies also, and more commonly, *hoar-frost,* or *rime*]. (TA.) ═ And *He drank what is termed* ضَرِيب, (O, Ḳ, TA,) i. e. *the milk thus called,* (O,) or شَهْد [meaning *honey,* or *honey in its comb,* or *honey not expressed from its comb*]. (TA.)

3. ضَارَبَهُ, (Ṣ, A, Mgh, Mṣb, Ḳ,) inf. n. مُضَارَبَةٌ (Mṣb, TA) and ضِرَابٌ, *He contended with him in beating, striking, smiting,* or *hitting; he beat him,* &c., *being beaten,* &c., *by him;* (TA;) [*he returned him beating for beating, blow for blow,* or *blows for blows; he bandied,* or *exchanged, blows with him:* and] *he contended with him in fight.* (Ṣ, TA.) One says, ضَارَبَهُ فَضَرَبَهُ, aor. of the latter verb ـُ, (Ḳ, TA,) agreeably with the general rule respecting verbs signifying the surpassing, or overcoming, in a contest, (MF, TA,) *He contended with him in beating,* &c., *and he surpassed him,* or *overcame him, therein.* (Ḳ,* TA.) See also 6. — [Golius says, as on the authority of the KL, that ضارب signifies also "*Coivit* camelus;" and Freytag, as on the authority of the Ḳ, that it signifies "*iniit* camelus camelam:" but in the KL it is only said that ضِرَابٌ is an inf. n. of a verb having this meaning; and its verb in this sense, as is said in the Ṣ and A and Mṣb and Ḳ, is ضَرَبَ, which has been thus expl. in the first paragraph.] — ضارب فِى المَالِ and بِالمَالِ, inf. n. مُضَارَبَةٌ, means ‡ *He trafficked with the property.* (A.) And ضارب لَهُ (A, Mgh, Ḳ) فِى مَالِهِ, (A, Mgh,) or ضَارَبَهُ فِى المَالِ, (Ṣ,) inf. n. as above, (Ṣ, A, Mgh,) means ‡ *He trafficked for him with his property* [or *with the property*]; (A, Mgh;) because he who does so generally journeys in the land seeking gain; (Mgh;) app. from الضَّرْبُ فِى الأَرْضِ [the journeying in the land] for the purpose of seeking sustenance: (TA:) and is syn. with قَارَضَهُ, (Ṣ,* Mgh, Ḳ,* TA,*) *he gave him of his property for the purpose of his trafficking therewith on the condition that the gain should be between them two or that the latter should have a certain share of the gain:* and accord. to En-Naḍr, ضاربه is said of him who does thus and also of the person thus employed. (TA.)

4. اضرب الفَحْلَ النَّاقَةَ, (Ṣ,) and اضرب النَّاقَةَ الفَحْلَ, (A, TA,) inf. n. إِضْرَابٌ, (TA,) ‡ *He made the stallion to leap the she-camel.* (Ṣ,* A,* TA.) — اضرب جَأْشًا لِأَمْرِ كَذَا ‡ *He disposed,* or *accommodated, and subjected, himself to such a thing,* or *such an affair.* (A, TA.) — اضرب السَّمُومُ المَآءَ † *The* سموم [or *hot wind*] *caused the earth to imbibe the water* (أَنْشَفَهُ الأَرْضَ). (Ḳ.) — اضرب لِنَفْسِهِ خَاتَمًا ‡ [*He caused a signet-ring to be made, fashioned,* or *moulded, for himself*]. (A, TA. [See also 8.]) — اضربهُ البَرْدُ: and اضرب الضَّرِيبُ الأَرْضَ: see 1, in the former half of the paragraph. — [Accord. to the TA, أُضْرِبْنَا (there written اضربنا) seems to signify † *We were smitten by hoar-frost,* or *rime:* or *our land,* or *herbage, was smitten thereby:* thus resembling أُجْلِدْنَا and أُصْقِعْنَا: but perhaps the right reading is أُضْرِبْنَا: for] أَضْرَبَ القَوْمُ, (Ḳ, TA,) inf. n. إِضْرَابٌ, (TA,) signifies † *The people,* or *party, had hoar-frost,* or *rime, fallen upon them.* (Ḳ, TA.) — اضرب الخُبْزُ † *The bread* (Ḳ, TA) i. e. the bread baked in hot ashes (TA) *became thoroughly baked,* (Ḳ, TA,) *and in a fit state to be beaten with a stick and to have its ashes and dust shaken off.* (TA.) — اضرب عَنْهُ: see 1, near the middle of the paragraph, in two places. [اضرب عَنِ الأَمْرِ is expl. in a copy of the A as meaning عَرَفَ عَنْهُ, and in the TA, (probably from that copy of the A, as I have reason to believe that it was used by the author of the TA,) is expl. by عرف عنه; but the right reading is indubitably عَزَفَ عَنْهُ, with the dotted ز; meaning ‡ *He turned away from the thing,* or *affair;* a signification given in the first paragraph: it is said in the A to be tropical. And اضرب عَنْهُ also signifies † *He digressed from it; made a digression,* or *transition, from it;* namely, a subject of speech or discourse: and particularly † *he turned from it and retracted it.*] — اضرب الرَّجُلُ فِى البَيْتِ: see 1, in the latter half of the paragraph. — اضرب signifies also ‡ *He was silent; he spoke not:* or *he lowered his eyes, looking towards the ground:* syn. أَطْرَقَ. (Ṣ, TA.)

5. تضرّب [*He beat, struck, smote,* or *hit, himself much,* or *violently;* or *several,* or *many, times*]. One says, تضرّب بِالحَصَى [*He smote himself much with pebbles*], (Ḳ in art. كشح,) and بِالتُّرَابِ [*with earth,* or *dust, as a man sometimes does in vexation*]. (L ibid.) — See also 8, in two places.

6. تضاربوا, (A, MA, Mgh, Mṣb, Ḳ, in the Ṣ تضاربا,) and ▼ اضطربوا, (A, Mgh, Mṣb, Ḳ, in the Ṣ اضطربا,) and ▼ ضاربوا, (Ḳ,) [*They contended in beating, striking, smiting, or hitting, one another; and particularly, in fight;*] *they smote one another with the sword.* (MA.) One says, اضطرب ▼ العَبْدَانِ بِالعَصَوَيْنِ, meaning *The two slaves beat each other with the two sticks, or staves.* (Mgh.)

8. اضطرب : see 6, in two places. The inf. n. is اِضْطِرَابٌ, of which the dim. is ▼ ضُتَيْرِيبٌ, the ط being changed [back] into ت because the ض becomes movent. (Ṣ and O in art. طلق.) — [Hence, said of a thing, *Its several parts collided; or were, or became, in a state of collision:* and hence,] *i. q.* تَحَرَّكَ (Ṣ, Mṣb, Ḳ) and مَاجَ; (Ḳ;) [but more significant than either of these; meaning *he,* or more generally *it, was,* or *became, in a state of commotion, agitation, convulsion, tumult, disturbance,* or *disorder; was,* or *became, agitated, convulsed,* or *unsteady; struggled; floundered; tossed,* or *shook, about,* or *to and fro; moved,* or *went, about,* or *to and fro,* or *from side to side; wabbled; wagged; quivered, quaked, trembled,* or *shivered; fluttered; flickered;* and *the like;*] and ▼ تضرّب signifies the same. (Ḳ. [ضَرَبَ, also, is sometimes used in the sense of تَحَرَّكَ, as mentioned before.]) One says, المَوْجُ يَضْطَرِبُ *The waves* [*dash together, are tumultuous,* or] *beat one another.* (Ṣ.) And اضطرب الوَلَدُ بِالبَطْنِ [*The child was,* or *became, in a state of commotion in the belly*]; (A;) And تضرّب ▼ فِى البَطْنِ [which means the same]. (TA.) And اضطرب البَرْقُ فِى السَّحَابِ *The lightning was,* or *became, in a state of commotion in the clouds;* [or *it flickered therein;*] syn. تَحَرَّكَ. (TA.) And اضطرب فِى أُمُورِهِ *He went to and fro occupied in his affairs for the means of subsistence:* (Mgh:) and اضطرب, alone, signifies *he sought to gain;* or *applied himself with art and diligence to gain;* syn. اِكْتَسَبَ; (Ḳ, TA;) and is used by El-Kumeyt with المَجْدَ as its objective complement. (TA. [See also يَضْرِبُ المَجْدَ, in the latter half of the first paragraph.]) And اضطرب الرَّجُلُ † *The man was tall, and therewithal loose, lax, flabby, uncompact, slack,* or *shaky, in make,* or *frame.* (Ḳ,* TA.) And اضطرب حَبْلُهُمْ [properly, *Their rope was shaky, loose,* or *slack;* meaning] † *their word,* or *sentence,* or *saying, varied,* or *was discordant:* (Ḳ:) or *their words,* or *sayings,* [*conflicted,* or] *varied,* or *were discordant:* and so أَقْوَالُهُمْ [*their sayings*]. (Kull p. 56.) And اضطرب رَأْيُهُ † [*His opinion was,* or *became, confused, weak,* or *unsound*]. (TA in art. وخ.) And اضطرب عَقْلُهُ † [*His mind,* or *intellect, was,* or *became, disordered, confused,* or *unsound*]. (Ḳ, in art. توه.) And اضطرب أَمْرُهُ † *His affair,* or *state, was,* or *became, disordered, unsound,* or *corrupt;* (Ṣ, Ḳ;*) syn. اِخْتَلَّ; (Ṣ, Ḳ;) [*it was,* or *became unsound,* or *unsettled;* as is indicated in the TA in art. زل:] and اضطربت الأُمُورُ † *The affairs were,* or *became, complicated, intricate, confused, discordant,* or *incongruous;* syn. اِخْتَلَفَتْ: (Mṣb:) and اضطرب الأَمْرُ بَيْنَهُمْ † [*The affair,* or *case, was,* or *became, complicated, intricate,* or *confused, so as to be a subject of disagreement,* or *difference, between them*]. (Mṣb voce شَجَرَ, q. v.) — اضطرب خَاتَمًا † *He asked,* or *ordered, that a signet-ring should be made, fashioned,* or *moulded, for him:* (Ḳ,* TA: [see also 4:]) occurring in a trad. (TA.) — اضطرب بِنَآءً فِى المَسْجِدِ occurs in a trad. as meaning † *He set up a structure upon stakes driven into the ground in the mosque.* (TA.)

10. استضربت † *She* (a camel) *desired the stallion.* (Ḳ.) — And استضربهُ فَحْلًا *He desired,* or *demanded, of him a stallion to cover his she-camels;* like استطرقه فحلا. (TA. in art. طرق.) — استضرب العَسَلُ *The honey became* ضَرَب; (Ṣ;) i. e., *became thick;* (A;) or *became white and thick:* (Ṣ, Ḳ:) the verb in this sense is similar to اِسْتَنْوَقَ in relation to a he-camel, and اِسْتَتْيَسَتْ in relation to a she-goat. (Ṣ.)

ضَرْبٌ an inf. n. used in the sense of a pass. part. n.; (TA;) *i. q.* ▼ مَضْرُوبٌ [*Beaten, struck,* &c.]: (Ḳ, TA:) in some of the copies of the Ḳ, it is made the same as ضَرْبٌ signifying "a species" &c.: but this is a mistake. (TA.) One says دِرْهَمٌ ضَرْبٌ ‡ [*A coined dirhem*]; using the inf. n. as an epithet, as in the phrases مَآءٌ غَوْرٌ and مَآءٌ سَكْبٌ. (Ṣ.) And هٰذَا دِرْهَمٌ ضَرْبَ الأَمِيرِ, in which ضرب may be thus put in the accus. case as an inf. n., [the meaning being هٰذَا دِرْهَمٌ مَضْرُوبٌ ضَرْبَ الأَمِيرِ ‡ *This is a dirhem coined with the coining of the prince,*] which is the most common way. (L, TA.) — ‡ *A light rain;* (Ṣ, Ḳ, TA;) or so مَطَرٌ ضَرْبٌ: (A:) دِيمَةٌ signifies "a lasting, or continuous, and still, rain;" and ضَرْبٌ, *a little more than* دِيمَةٌ, or *a little above this:* and ▼ ضَرْبَةٌ [as the n. un.] signifies *a fall,* or *shower, of light rain.* (Aṣ, TA.) — † *A make, form, fashion, mould,* or *cast;* syn. صِيغَةٌ. (Ṣ, TA.) — † *A sort,* or *species;* (Ṣ, Ḳ;) as also ▼ ضَرِيبٌ; (Ḳ;) and accord. to some copies of the Ḳ ▼ مَضْرُوبٌ, but this is a mistake: the pl. of the first is ضُرُوبٌ. (TA.) — Also ‡ *A like* [of a thing and of a person]; (ISd, A, Ḳ, TA;) and so ▼ ضَرْبٌ, as related on the authority of Z; (TA;) and ▼ ضَرِيبٌ; (IAạr, Ṣ, A, TA;) as in the phrase ضَرِيبُ الشَّىْءِ *the like of the thing,* (Ṣ, TA,) and فُلَانٌ ضَرِيبُ فُلَانٍ *such a one is the like of such a one:* (IAạr, TA:) or ضَرْبٌ signifies *a like in stature and make:* (IAạr, TA:) its pl. is ضُرُوبٌ; (TA;) and the pl. of ▼ ضَرِيبٌ is ضَرَائِبُ (Ṣ) and ضُرَبَآءُ, this latter occurring in a trad., in the phrase, ذَهَبَ هٰذَا وَضُرَبَآؤُهُ *This went away, and the likes of him.* (TA.) One says also ضَرْبَ قَوْلِهِ [meaning † *In the like of his saying;* referring to a saying in the Ḳur-án, &c.; a phrase similar to نَحْوَ قَوْلِهِ]. (AZ, T voce إِنَّ in several places.) — A man *penetrating,* or *vigorous and effective; light,* or *active, in the accomplishment of an affair* or *of a want;* (Ḳ, TA;) *not flaccid,* or *flabby, in flesh.* (TA.) And (Ḳ) a man (Ṣ, TA) *light of flesh,* (Ṣ, A, Ḳ, TA,) *lean and slender.* (TA.) The pl. is ضُرُوبٌ; or, accord. to IJ, this may be pl. of ▼ ضَرْبٌ. (L, TA.) — The *last foot* of a verse: (Ḳ,* TA:) pl. [of pauc.] أَضْرُبٌ and [of mult.] ضُرُوبٌ. (TA.) — See also ضَرَبٌ. — [Reiske, as mentioned by Freytag, explains it also as meaning *Sour milk:* but this is app. a mistake for صَرْبٌ, with the unpointed ص.]

ضِرْبٌ : see the next preceding paragraph.

ضَرَبٌ (Ṣ, A, Mṣb, Ḳ) and ▼ ضَرْبٌ, but the former is the better known, (Ḳ,) *Thick honey:* (A:) or *white honey:* (Mṣb, Ḳ:) or *thick white honey:* (Ṣ:) or, as some say, *wild honey:* and ▼ ضَرَبَةٌ signifies the same: or a portion thereof: (TA:) ضَرَبٌ is masc. and fem.: (Ṣ:) [for] it is said to be pl. of ▼ ضَرَبَةٌ, or a coll. gen. n., which is in most cases masc. [but is also fem.]. (Mṣb.)

ضَرِبٌ : see مَضْرَبٌ. — Also ‡ Herbage *smitten and injured by the cold, and by the wind.* (TA.) And ‡ Herbage *smitten by hoar-frost,* or *rime.* (TA.) And أَرْضٌ ضَرِبَةٌ ‡ *Land smitten by hoar-frost,* or *rime, so that its herbage is nipped,* or *blasted, thereby.* (AZ, TA.)

ضَرْبَةٌ [inf. n. un. of ضَرَبَ; *A single act of beating, striking,* &c.: *a blow, stroke,* &c.]. — See also ضَرْبٌ, fourth sentence. — ضَرْبَةً وَاحِدَةً means † *At one time; once.* (Mgh, Mṣb.) So in the saying, لَا آخُذُ مَا لِى عَلَيْكَ إِلَّا ضَرْبَةً وَاحِدَةً † [*I will not take what is due to me on thy part save at one time,* or *once*]. (Mgh.) — ضَرْبَةُ الغَائِصِ, which is forbidden, is † *The saying of the diver for pearls, to the merchant, I will dive for thee once, and what I shall bring up shall be thine for such a price.* (T, Mgh, TA.)

ضَرَبَةٌ : see ضَرَبٌ, in two places.

ضُرُوبٌ : see مِضْرَبٌ: and see ضَرْبٌ, near the end.

ضَرِيبٌ *i. q.* ▼ مَضْرُوبٌ [*Beaten, struck,* &c.]. (Ḳ, TA.) — A tent-peg, or stake, *struck so as to be firm in the ground;* as also ▼ مَضْرُوبٌ. (Lḥ, TA.) — See also ضَرْبٌ, in three places. — Also, (Aṣ, ISd, Ḳ, TA,) or ضَرِيبُ الشَّوْلِ, accord. to Aboo-Naṣr, † *Milk of which some is milked upon other:* or, accord. to some of the Arabs of the desert, *milk from a number of camels, some of it being thin, and some of it thick:* (Ṣ:) or *milk of which some is poured upon other:* (Aṣ, TA:) or *such as is milked from a number of camels* (ISd, Ḳ, TA) *into one vessel, and mixed together, not consisting of less than the milk of three camels:* (ISd, TA:) or *milk upon which other has been milked at night, and other on the morrow, and which has been mixed together.* (TA.) [See also ضَرِيبٌ.] — And What is bad, of the kind of plants called حَمْض: or what is *broken in pieces,* thereof. (Ḳ.) — See also مِضْرَبٌ. — [Hence,] ‡ The *person who is intrusted, as deputy, with* [*the disposal of*] *the gaming-arrows* [*in the game called* المَيْسِر]: or the *person who shuffles those arrows,* or *who plays with them;* (الَّذِى يَضْرِبُ

بِالقِدَاحِ ;) as also ▼ ضَارِبٌ : (Ḳ:) or both of these epithets signify the *person who shuffles those arrows* (ٱلَّذِى يَضْرِبُ بِالقِدَاحِ) ; and he is the *person who is intrusted, as deputy, with* [*the disposal of*] *them:* (Ṣ:) the former is of the measure فَعِيلٌ in the sense of the measure فَاعِلٌ : (Sb, TA:) and the pl. is ضُرَبَآءُ. (Ṣ, A.) You say, هُوَ ضَرِيبِى, meaning ‡ *He is my playfellow with the gaming-arrows* (مَنْ يَضْرِبُ القِدَاحَ مَعِى). (A, TA.) — And الضَّرِيبُ is a name of † *The third arrow of those used in the game called* المَيْسِر : (Ḳ,* TA:) that arrow is thus called by some: by others الرَّقِيبُ [q. v.]: it has three notches; and three portions are assigned to it if successful, and three fines if unsuccessful. (Lḥ, L, TA.) — [Hence, app.,] ضَرِيبٌ signifies also † *A share,* or *portion.* (Ḳ.) — Also † *Hoar-frost,* or *rime;* (Ṣ, Ḳ;) like جَلِيدٌ and سَقِيطٌ : (Ṣ in art. جلد :) and † *snow.* (Ḳ.) — And † The *head:* (Ḳ:) so called because often in a state of agitation. (TA.) — And *i. q.* شَهْدٌ [i. e. *honey,* or *honey in its comb,* or *honey not expressed from its comb*]: and عَسَلٌ ضَرِيبٌ *honey becoming,* or *become, white and thick.* (TA. [See also ضَرَبٌ.]) — Also *Big-bellied,* (بَطِينٌ, [in some copies of the Ḳ بَطْنٌ,]) [as an epithet] of men, (Ḳ, TA,) and of others. (TA.)

ضَرِيبَةٌ *A man,* (Ḳ,) or *anything,* (T, Ṣ,* TA,) *living* or *dead,* (T, TA,) *struck,* or *smitten, with the sword:* (T, Ṣ, Ḳ, TA:) the ة is affixed, though the word has the meaning of a pass. part. n., because it becomes numbered with substs., like نَطِيحَةٌ and أَكِيلَةٌ. (Ṣ.) — [And also] The *place* [or *part*] *upon which the blow,* or *stroke, falls, of the body that is beaten,* or *struck.* (Ḥam p. 120.) — And *Wool,* or [*goats'*] *hair, separated,* or *plucked asunder, with the fingers, and then folded together, and bound with a thread, and spun:* (Ṣ: [more fully expl. voce سَلِيلَةٌ:]) and *wool that is beaten with a mallet:* (TA:) or *a portion of wool:* (Ḳ:) or *a portion of cotton,* and *of wool:* (TA:) pl. ضَرَائِبُ. (Ṣ.) — Also ‡ *An impost that is levied, of the poll-tax* or *land-tax* and *the like,* (Ṣ, A, Mgh, O, Mṣb, Ḳ, TA,) and *of* [*the tolls,* or *similar exactions, termed*] أَرْصَاد : (Ṣ, O, TA:) pl. as above. (Ṣ, A, Mgh, &c.) And (hence, TA) ‡ The غَلَّة [as meaning the *income,* or *revenue, arising from the service*] of a slave; (Ṣ, Ḳ, TA;) i. e. ضَرِيبَةُ العَبْدِ means *what the slave pays to his master, of the impost that is laid upon him:* ضَرِيبَةٌ being of the measure فَعِيلَةٌ in the sense of the measure مَفْعُولَةٌ. (TA.) — And ‡ *A nature;* or *a natural,* a *native,* or *an innate, disposition* or *temper* or *the like:* [as though signifying *a particular cast of constitution, moulded by the Creator:*] syn. طَبِيعَةٌ, (Ṣ, A, Ḳ,) and سَجِيَّةٌ : (Ṣ:) pl. as above. (A, TA.) You say, فُلَانٌ كَرِيمُ الضَّرِيبَةِ [‡ *Such a one is generous in respect of nature*]; and لَئِيمُ الضَّرِيبَةِ [‡ *mean* &c.]; (Ṣ;) and إِنَّهُ لَكَرِيمُ الضَّرَائِبِ [‡ *Verily he is generous in respect of natural dispositions*]: and خُلِقَ النَّاسُ عَلَى ضَرَائِبَ شَتَّى [*Men are created of diverse natures* &c.]. (TA.) — See also مَضْرِبٌ.

ضَرَّابٌ : see مِضْرَبٌ.

ضَارِبٌ [*Beating, striking, smiting,* or *hitting:* &c.:] act. part. n. of ضَرَبَ [in all its senses]. (Ḳ, TA.) — A she-camel *that strikes her milker:* (Ṣ, Ḳ:), or one *which, having been submissive,* or *tractable, before conceiving, afterwards strikes her milker away from before her:* or [the pl.] ضَوَارِبُ signifies she-camels *that resist after conceiving, and become repugnant, so that one cannot milk them.* (TA.) — Also, and ضَارِبَةٌ, (Ḳ, TA,) the former a possessive epithet [i. e. denoting the possession of a quality], and the latter a verbal epithet [i. e. an act. part. n.], (TA,) ‡ A she-camel *that raises her tail, and smites with it her vulva,* (Ḳ, A, in which latter only the pl. is mentioned,) *and then goes:* (Ḳ:) pl. ضَوَارِبُ. (A, TA.) And the former is like تضراب, [i. e. ▼ تِضْرَابٌ, as appears from what follows,] expl. by Lḥ as meaning † A she-camel *that has been covered by the stallion,* [*and app. that raises her tail in consequence thereof,*] *but respecting which one knows not whether she be pregnant* or *not:* (TA:) or ▼ تِضْرَابٌ signifies a she-camel *recently covered by the stallion* [*and therefore often raising her tail*]. (Mz, 40th نوع.) — The former (ضَارِبٌ) signifies also † *Swimming,* (Ṣ, TA,) in water. (TA.) Dhu-r-Rummeh says,

لَيَالِىَ ٱللَّهْوِ يَطْبِينِى فَأَتْبَعُهُ *
كَأَنَّنِى ضَارِبٌ فِى غَمْرَةٍ لَعِبُ *

[*In the nights of diversion he calls me and I follow him as though I were swimming in a deep water, sporting* therein]. (Ṣ, TA.) — طَيْرٌ ضَوَارِبُ ‡ *Birds seeking sustenance:* (Ṣ, A, TA:) or *birds traversing the land,* [or *migrating,*] *in search of sustenance.* (L, TA.) — See also ضَرِيبٌ. — ضَارِبٌ also signifies † A *dark* night: (Ḳ:) or a night *of which the darkness extends to the right and left, and fills the world.* (Ṣ, O. [So in my copies of the Ṣ and in the O and TA: but accord. to Golius, as from the Ṣ, "yet not filling the air."]) See the verse of Ḥomeyd cited in the first paragraph. [J cites as an ex. of the last of the meanings expl. above, and so does Ṣgh in the O, the verse in the sentence here next following.] — † Anything *long:* applied in this sense to a night: thus in the following verse:

وَرَابَعَتْنِى تَحْتَ لَيْلٍ ضَارِبٍ *
بِسَاعِدٍ فَعْمٍ وَكَفٍّ خَاضِبِ *

† [*And that she helped me in lifting and putting on the loads, beneath* the darkness *of a long night, with a plump fore arm and a hand dyed with ḥinnà*]. (TA.) — † *A place,* (Ṣ,) or *a depressed place,* (Ḳ, TA,) and *a valley,* (TA,) *in which are trees.* (Ṣ, Ḳ, TA.) And † *A piece of rugged ground extending in an oblong form in a plain,* or *soft, tract.* (Ḳ, TA.) And † The *like of a* رَحَبَة *in a valley* [app. meaning *where the water flows into it from its two sides:* see art. رحب]: pl. ضَوَارِبُ. (Ḳ.)

ضَارُوبٌ [an irregular instrumental noun, like طَاحُونٌ and some other words of the same measure,] ‡ *A snare for catching birds.* (A, TA.)

ضُتَيْرِيبٌ dim. of اِضْطِرَابٌ, inf. n. of 8, q. v.

تِضْرَابٌ : see ضَارِبٌ, former half, in two places.

مَضْرَبٌ is an inf. n. (Ḥam p. 129.) [See the sentence explaining the phrase ضَرَبَ فِى الأَرْضِ ; and also the sentence next following it, towards the close of the first paragraph.] — And it is also a noun of place [and of time, like مَضْرِبٌ, which is the regular form]. (Ḥam ibid.) See the next paragraph, in five places.

مَضْرِبٌ [and ▼ مَضْرَبٌ, q. v.,] *A place,* or *time,* [the latter, as is said in the explanation of a phrase mentioned in what follows,] *of beating, striking, smiting,* or *hitting:* — and also, † *a place,* or *time, of journeying.* (KL.) — مَضْرِبُ الظَّرِبَانِ means † *The line,* or *long mark, upon the face of the animal called* ظربان [as though it were a place upon which it had been struck]. (TA in art. ظرب, q. v.) — And مَضْرِبٌ, † *A place where a tent is pitched,* or *set up.* (Mṣb.) — See also مِضْرَبٌ. — Also, (thus in the TA in art. سوف, as from the A,) or ▼ مَضْرَبٌ, (thus in a copy of the A in the present art.,) ‡ *i. q.* مَسَافَةٌ [meaning *A space,* or *tract,* or *an extent, over which one journeys;* as being a place of beating the ground]: so in the saying, بَيْنَهُمْ مَضْرَبٌ ▼ بَعِيدٌ [or مَضْرِبٌ, i. e. ‡ *Between them is a far-extending space to be traversed*]. (A.) — [مَضْرِبُ عَسَلَةٍ is a euphemism for † *The place of injection of sperma:* and hence it means † *the source from which one springs; origin, ancestry,* or *parentage;* &c.] One says, مَا أَعْرِفُ لَهُ مَضْرِبَ عَسَلَةٍ (Ṣ, A) meaning أَعْرَاقَهُ [i. e. ‡ *I know not the sources* (or *the source*) *from which he has sprung;* or *his ancestry,* or *parentage*]: (Ṣ:) or مَا يُعْرَفُ لَهُ مَضْرِبُ عَسَلَةٍ ‡ *No source* or *origin* [or *parentage*], *nor people, nor ancestor* or *father, nor nobility, pertaining to him, is known.* (M, Ḳ, TA.) And مَا لِفُلَانٍ [لِزَيْدٍ, (Ṣ, A, in the latter] مَضْرِبُ عَسَلَةٍ,) i. e. ‡ [*Such a one has no source*] *of kindred* (نَسَب), *nor of cattle* or *property* (مَال). (Ṣ.) And إِنَّهُ لَكَرِيمُ المَضْرِبِ ‡ [*Verily he is generous in respect of origin*]. (A, TA.) [See also ضَرِيبَةٌ.] — One says also, أَتَتِ النَّاقَةُ عَلَى مَضْرِبِهَا, meaning † *The she-camel arrived at the time* [*of year*] *of her being leaped by the stallion;* making the time to be like the place. (Ṣ.) — مَضْرِبٌ, (Ṣ, A, O, and so in the M in art. رم,) or ▼ مَضْرَبٌ, (Ḳ,* TA,) with fet-ḥ to the ر, (Ḳ, TA,) and to the م also, (TA,) [but this is app. a mistake, as the weight of authority is in favour of the former,] † *A bone in which is marrow:* (Ṣ, O, Ḳ:) or *a bone that is broken and from which marrow is extracted* [or *sought to be extracted*]. (M in art. رم.) One says, of a sheep or goat, (Ṣ, A,) that is emaciated, (Ṣ,) مَا يَرُمُّ مِنْهَا مَضْرِبٌ ‡ [*Not a bone of her that is broken for its marrow contains any marrow*]; i. e. when a bone of her is broken, no marrow will be found in it. (Ṣ, A.) — And مَضْرِبٌ (Ṣ, Mṣb, Ḳ) and ▼ مَضْرَبٌ (Mṣb, Ḳ) and ▼ مَضْرِبَةٌ (Ṣ, Mṣb, Ḳ) and ▼ مَضْرَبَةٌ (Mṣb, Ḳ) and ▼ مَضْرُبَةٌ (Sb, TA) signify The *part* of a sword, *with which one strikes:* (Mṣb, and Ḥam p. 129:) or [the *part*] *about a span from the extremity:* (Ṣ, TA:) or the *part exclusive of,* or *below, the* ظُبَة [q. v.] (دُونَ الظُّبَةِ): (TA:) or the *edge* (حَدّ) thereof; (Ḳ, TA;) thus expl. by several of the leading lexicologists: (TA:) and so ▼ ضَرِيبَةٌ: which last also signifies *a sword:* (Ḳ:) [i. e.] a sword itself is sometimes thus called, as ISd says: (TA:) the pl. of مَضْرِبٌ is مَضَارِبُ. (Ḥam ubi suprà.) — [مَضْرِبُ مَثَلٍ means † *The secondary idea,* or *thing, signified by a parable or proverb, and compared to the primary idea,* or *thing; the thing,* or *case, to which a parable* or *proverb is applied:* correlative of مَوْرِدُ مَثَلٍ: pl. مَضَارِبُ.] — And [the pl.] مَضَارِبُ signifies † *Stratagems in war.* (IAạr, TA.)

مُضْرِبٌ [part. n. of أَضْرَبَ, q. v.]. You say, رَأَيْتُ حَيَّةً مُضْرِبًا (Ṣ, TA) and مُضْرِبَةً (TA) ‡ *I saw a serpent still, not moving.* (Ṣ, TA.)

مِضْرَبٌ [*A thing with which one beats, strikes, smites,* or *hits;*] *a thing with which the action termed* الضَّرْبُ *is performed;* as also ▼ مِضْرَابٌ. (Ḳ.) *A wooden instrument* [*a kind of mallet*] *with which the bow-string is struck in the operation of separating cotton.* (Mṣb.) — And, (Ṣ, A, Ḳ,) as an epithet applied to a man, (Ṣ, A,) it signifies شَدِيدُ الضَّرْبِ [One *who beats, strikes, smites,* or *hits, vehemently*]; (Ṣ, O;) or كَثِيرُ الضَّرْبِ [one *who beats,* &c., *much*]; as also ▼ ضَرُوبٌ (A, Ḳ) and ▼ ضَرُوبٌ (A) and ▼ ضَرِيبٌ (Ḳ, TA) and ▼ ضَرَّابٌ. (O, Ḳ, TA. [But in none of these lexicons is this signification mentioned in such a manner as to show that it necessarily relates to any but the first of these words, namely, مِضْرَبٌ: that it does so, however, is indicated by the measures of all of them.]) — Also, (O, Ḳ, TA,) or ▼ مَضْرِبٌ, with fet-ḥ to the م and kesr to the ر, (Mgh,) [thus] written like مَجْلِس by MF, and pronounced by the vulgar مَضْرَب, but both of these are [said to be] incorrect, (TA,) *A* [*tent such as is called*] قُبَّة: (Mgh:) or *a great* [*tent of the kind called*] فُسْطَاط; (O, Ḳ, TA;) the فسطاط *of a king:* (TA:) pl. مَضَارِبُ. (Mgh, TA.)

مَضْرُبَةٌ and مَضْرَبَةٌ and مَضْرِبَةٌ: see مَضْرِبٌ.

مُضَرَّبٌ *Sewed* [meaning *quilted*] *with cotton:* applied in this sense to a بِسَاط [or thing that is spread like a carpet, &c.]. (Mgh, Mṣb.)

مُضَرَّبَةٌ [a subst. signifying *A quilt; a quilted garment* and *the like:* see 2]. (Ṣ, Mgh, Mṣb.)

مِضْرَابٌ The *thing* [i. e. *plectrum*] *with which a lute* (عُود) *is struck* [or *played*]: (Ṣ:) pl. مَضَارِيبُ. (TA in art. طرب.) [See an ex. voce طَرُوب. The plectrum commonly used for this purpose in the present day is a slip of a vulture's feather, and is termed رِيشَة: see the chap. on music in my "Modern Egyptians."] — See also مِضْرَبٌ.

مَضْرُوبٌ: see ضَرْبٌ and ضَرِيبٌ, the latter in two places. Dhu-r-Rummeh says, speaking of a cake of bread (خُبْزَة),

• وَمَضْرُوبَةٍ فِى غَيْرِ ذَنْبٍ بَرِيئَةٍ •
• كَسَرْتُ لِأَصْحَابِى عَلَى عَجَلٍ كَسْرَا •

[*Many a thing* (meaning many a cake of bread) *beaten for no offence, free from blame, I have broken for my companions in haste, with a* vigorous *breaking*]. (TA, after explaining the phrase أَضْرَبَ الخُبْزَ [q. v.].) — Also † *Staying, abiding,* or *remaining,* [*fixed,* or *settled,*] *in a tent,* or *house.* (TA.)

مُضَارِبٌ *One who is employed by another to traffic for him with his (the latter's) property, on the condition of their sharing the gain together:* and also *one who employs another to traffic for him with his (the former's) property, on that condition:* thus expl. by En-Naḍr; and Az also allows the use of the word in these two senses. (TA.)

مُضْطَرَبٌ may mean اِضْطِرَابٌ [i. e. it may be used as an inf. n. of اِضْطَرَبَ (q. v.), agreeably with a general rule]: — and it may mean *A place of* اِضْطِرَاب: (Ḥam p. 142:) [thus used it often means *a place in which one goes to and fro seeking the means of subsistence:* and simply *a place in which one seeks gain:* see اِضْطَرَبَ فِى: and see also the syns. مُرَاغَمٌ (in two places) and مُتَقَلَّبٌ.] — [It is also a pass. part. n.: and hence the phrase مُضْطَرَبَاتٌ لِلْمَعَاشِ, meaning *The things that are desired to be gained for subsistence,* or *sustenance:* see مَرَاغِبُ.]

مُضْطَرِبٌ [A thing *having its several parts in a state of collision:* and hence, a thing, and a man, *in a state of commotion, agitation, convulsion,* &c.: see its verb, 8]. — One says, جَآءَ مُضْطَرِبَ العِنَانِ [lit. *He came with quivering rein*]; meaning *he came discomfited,* or *put to flight, and alone.* (Ḳ.) — And رَجُلٌ مُضْطَرِبُ الخَلْقِ ‡ *A man incongruous, unsound, faulty,* or *weak, in respect of make:* (A, TA:) *tall, and* [*loose, lax, flabby, uncompact, slack, shaky,* or] *not strong of make.* (TA.) — And حَدِيثٌ مُضْطَرِبُ السَّنَدِ † *A tradition unsound, faulty,* or *weak, in respect of the authority upon which it rests,* or *to which it is traced up* or *ascribed;* syn. مُخْتَلٌّ. (Ṣ, TA.)

ضرج

1. ضَرَجَهُ, (Ṣ, O, L, Ḳ,) aor. ـُ, (O,) or ـِ, (L,) inf. n. ضَرْجٌ, (O, L,) *He split it, slit it,* or *rent it asunder* or *open;* (Ṣ, O, L, Ḳ;) and so ▼ ضَرَّجَهُ [but app. in an intensive sense, or said of a number of things, inf. n. تَضْرِيجٌ]; namely, a garment, &c. (L.) [Hence,] ضَرَجَ النَّارَ i. q. فَتَحَ لَهَا عَيْنًا [i. e. *He made an opening in the live coals of the fire, in order that it might burn up well*]. (AḤn, TA.) — And *He smeared it, daubed it,* or *defiled it;* (O, L, Ḳ;) and so ▼ ضَرَّجَهُ [but app., in this case also, in an intensive sense, or said of a number of things]; namely, a garment, (A, L,) &c., (L,) with blood, (A, L,) or with something similar thereto, that was red, or with something yellow. (L.) — And *He threw it,* or *threw it down.* (Ḳ.) ═ ضَرَجَتْ بِجِرَّتِهَا and جَرَضَتْ [signify the same, i. e. *She was choked with her cud;* or *she swallowed her cud with difficulty;* the former verb being app. formed by transposition from the latter; but جَرَضَتْ seems to be better known than ضَرَجَتْ]; said of a camel. (O, TA.)

2: see above, in two places. — One says also, ضَرَّجَ أَنْفَهُ بِدَمٍ, (Ṣ, O,) or بِالدَّمِ, (Ḳ,) *He made his nose to bleed.* (Ṣ, O, Ḳ.) — And ضَرَّجَ الثَّوْبَ, (Ṣ, O, Ḳ,) inf. n. تَضْرِيجٌ, (Ṣ, O,) *He dyed the garment,* or *piece of cloth, of a red colour,* (Ṣ, O, Ḳ,) *making it less fully dyed than that which is termed* مُشْبَع, *and more so than that which is termed* مُوَرَّد. (Ṣ, O.) — [Hence,] ضَرَّجَ الكَلَامَ, (A, Ḳ,) inf. n. as above, (O,) ‡ *He embellished the speech,* (A, O, Ḳ,) and *amplified it,* (A,) as one does in excuses, or pleas, (O,) with truth, or with falsehood. (A, O.) — ضَرَّجَتْ جَيْبَهَا *She* (a woman) *loosened her* جَيْب [or *opening at the neck and bosom of her shift* or *the like, so that the edges were not drawn together,* or *buttoned*]. (O, Ḳ:* in the latter, ضَرَّجَ الجَيْبَ, inf. n. as above.) — ضَرَّجْنَا الإِبِلَ *We urged on the camels, in making a hostile,* or *predatory, incursion.* (O, Ḳ.*)

5: see 7, in four places. — تَضَرَّجَ also signifies *It* (a garment, A, L) *became smeared, daubed,* or *defiled,* (Ṣ, A, O, L, Ḳ,) with blood, (Ṣ, A, O, L,) or with something similar thereto, that was red, or with something yellow. (L.) — And تَضَرَّجَ الخَدُّ ‡ *The cheek became red,* (O, Ḳ, TA,) on an occasion of shame. (O.) You say, كَلَّمْتُهُ فَتَضَرَّجَ خَدَّاهُ ‡ *I spoke to him and his cheeks became red.* (A,* TA.) — And تَضَرَّجَتِ المَرْأَةُ ‡ *The woman displayed her finery,* or *ornaments, and beauties of person* or *form* or *countenance, to men,* (A, O, Ḳ, TA,) *and embellished herself.* (A, TA.)

7. انضرج *It* (a thing, or garment, &c., L) *split, slit,* or *rent asunder* or *open;* (Ṣ, O, L, Ḳ;) as also انضرح; (TA in art. ضرح;) and so ▼ تضرّج [but app. in an intensive sense, or said of a number of things]: (L:) the latter is said of a garment in the former sense; (TA;) or as meaning *it became much rent,* or *rent in several places.* (L.) When the fruits of herbs, or leguminous plants, appear, one says, اِنْضَرَجَتْ عَنْهَا لَفَائِفُهَا and أَكْمَامُهَا [i. e. *Their envelopes,* or *pericarps, and their calyxes, rent asunder* or *open, so as to disclose them*]. (A, TA. [And the like is said in the Ṣ and O.]) And one says also, ▼ تَضَرَّجَتْ عَنِ البَقْلِ لَفَائِفُهُ, meaning اِنْفَتَحَتْ [i. e.

The envelopes, or pericarps, of the herbs, or leguminous plants, opened so as to disclose what was within them]. (Ṣ, O.) And تضرّج ▼ النَّوْرُ *The blossoms opened.* (Ḳ.) And انضرج الشَّجَرُ *The buds of the trees burst open and the extremities of the leaves appeared.* (L.) And ▼ تضرّج said of lightning means تَشَقَّقَ [i. e. *It clave the clouds, and extended high, into the midst of the sky; or it was in a state of commotion in the clouds; or it spread wide and long*]. (Ṣ, A, O, Ḳ.) — Also *It was, or became, wide, or ample.* (El-Muärrij, Ṣ, O, Ḳ.) You say, انضرجت لَنَا الطَّرِيقُ *The road was, or became, wide to us.* (TA.) And انضرج مَا بَيْنَ القَوْمِ *The space between the people was, or became, far-extending:* (Aṣ, Ṣ, O, Ḳ:*) and so انضرح. (Ṣ in art. ضرح.) — انضرجت العُقَابُ *The eagle darted down upon the prey:* (O, Ḳ:) or *betook itself,* or *advanced,* to it: (O:) or *took a sidelong course to it.* (O, Ḳ.*)

ضَرْجٌ A garment, or piece of cloth, *smeared with a red,* or *yellow, colour;* as also ▼ إِضْرِيجٌ: or this latter is only [applied to a garment, or piece of cloth,] *of* [*the kind called*] خَزّ. (TA.) [And ضَرِجُ الأَنَامِلِ means *Having the ends of the fingers smeared,* or *defiled,* by blood: see Ḥam p. 709.]

ضَرْجَةٌ and ضَرَجَةٌ *A species of bird.* (TA.)

عَدْوٌ ضَرِيجٌ *A vehement running.* (Ṣ, Ḳ.)

إِضْرِيجٌ *A yellow* [*garment of the kind called*] كِسَآء; (Ḳ;) *a yellow sort of* أَكْسِيَة [pl. of كِسَآء]: (Ṣ, O:) or *a* كِسَآء *made of excellent* [*down of the kind called*] مِرْعِزَّى: (TA:) or أَكْسِيَة *made of the best of* مِرْعِزَّى: (Lth, O, TA:) and, (O, Ḳ,) accord. to Lḥ, (TA,) *red* [*cloth of the kind called*] خَزّ: (O, Ḳ, TA:) and أَكْسِيَةُ الإِضْرِيجِ signifies *the* اكسية *of red* خَزّ; (A, TA;) or *of yellow* خَزّ. (TA. See also ضَرْجٌ.) And ثَوْبٌ إِضْرِيجٌ *A garment saturated with redness.* (A.) — And *A red dye:* (O, Ḳ, TA:) so it is said to signify: and hence ▼ ثَوْبٌ مُضَرَّجٌ [meaning *A garment, or piece of cloth, dyed of a red colour in the manner expl. voce* ضرّج]. (TA.) ═ And *A horse that is swift and excellent; or swift,* or *excellent, in running;* (AO, Ṣ, O, Ḳ, TA;) *vehement in running;* (Ṣ, O, TA;) or *having a large mane:* (AO, TA:) or *wide in the* لَبَان [or *breast,* or *middle of the breast*]. (TA.)

مِضْرَجٌ: see its pl., مَضَارِجُ, below.

مُضَرَّجٌ: see إِضْرِيجٌ. — مُضَرَّجُ الخَدَّيْنِ ‡ *Having the cheeks made red.* (A,* TA.) — المُضَرَّجُ, (so in the O,) or ▼ المُضَرِّجُ, (so accord. to the Ḳ, there said to be like مُحَدِّث,) *The lion.* (O, Ḳ.)

المُضَرِّجُ: see what next precedes.

عَيْنٌ مَضْرُوجَةٌ *An eye wide in the fissure:* (Ṣ, O, Ḳ:) *a wide eye.* (A.)

مَضَارِجُ i. q. مَشَاقّ [i. e. *Fissures;* lit. *places of slitting:* pl. of مَشَقّ]. (O, Ḳ.) Himyán Ibn-Koḥáfeh Es-Saadee says, describing the tushes of a stallion-camel,

* أَوْسَعْنَ مِنْ أَشْدَاقِهِ المَضَارِجَا *

[*That widened the fissures of the sides of his mouth*]. (O.) ═ Also *Old and worn-out garments,* (A'Obeyd, Ṣ, O, Ḳ,) *that are used for service and work,* like what are called مَعَاوِز: sing. ▼ مِضْرَجٌ. (A'Obeyd, Ṣ, O.)

ضرح

1. ضَرَحَهُ, (Ṣ, O, L, Ḳ,) aor. َ, (Ḳ,) inf. n. ضَرْحٌ, (Ṣ, A, O, L,) *He removed it from its place; put it away or aside; pushed, or thrust, it away:* (Ṣ, A,* O, L, Ḳ:) *he took it, and threw it away or aside:* (L:) *he pushed it, or thrust it, away with his foot:* (Expos. of the "Amálee" of El-Ḳálee:) [and] ضَرَحَ بِالشَّىْءِ [if not a mistranscription for ضرح الشّىْءَ] *He threw* [*from him*] *the thing; and put it away or aside:* and ضَرَحَ عَنْهُ الثَّوْبَ *He cast off from him the garment.* (A.) See also 4. [And see 8.] [Hence] ضَرَحْتُ عَنِّى شَهَادَةَ القَوْمِ ‡ *I invalidated the testimony of the people or party, or annulled its claim to credibility,* (جَرَحْتُهَا,) *and cast it from me, or rejected it:* (Ṣ, A, O, Ḳ:*) said by one against whom false witness has been borne, and who has shown its falseness. (A.) — And ضَرَحَتِ الدَّابَّةُ بِرِجْلِهَا, (Ṣ, O, Ḳ,) aor. َ, (Ḳ,* TA,) inf. n. ضَرْحٌ (Ṣ, O) and ضِرَاحٌ, (Ṣ,* O, Ḳ,) this latter from Sb, (TA,) [but it seems to be implied in the Ḳ that the verb with ضِرَاحٌ for its inf. n. has its aor., as well as this inf. n., like that of كَتَبَ, which I do not think to be the case,] *The beast kicked with its hind leg:* (Ṣ, O, Ḳ:) or الضَّرْحُ is *with the fore legs;* and الرَّمْحُ, with the hind legs. (TA.) One says, فِيهَا ضِرَاحٌ [*It has a habit of kicking* with the hind leg: or, with the fore leg]; a phrase mentioned by I'Ab. (Ṣ.) — ضَرَحَ, (Ṣ, Ḳ,) or ضَرَحَ ضَرِيحًا, (A, Mṣb,) aor. َ, (Mṣb, TA,) inf. n. ضَرْحٌ, (Ṣ, Ḳ,) *He dug a* ضَرِيح [q. v.], (Ṣ, A, Mṣb, Ḳ,) لِلْمَيِّتِ [*for the corpse*]. (A,* Ḳ.) — ضَرَحَ, inf. n. ضَرْحٌ, also signifies [*He clave the* ground; (see ضَرِيح;) and] *he split, slit, or rent asunder* or *open,* anything; like ضَرَجَ, with ج: (TA:) but the phrase ضَرَحْنَا البُرُودَ, in a verse of Dhur-r-Rummeh, as some relate it, is expl. by AA as meaning *We threw off the* [garments called] برود: others relate it with ج; and in this case he says that it means "we rent asunder" or "open." (Az, O, TA.) ═ ضَرَحَ [as though quasi-pass. of ضَرَحَهُ] signifies also *He, or it, was,* or *became, distant,* or *remote;* or *removed to a distance; went far away.* (L.) [See also 7.] — And ضَرَحَتِ السُّوقُ, inf. n. ضُرُوحٌ (O, Ḳ, TA) and ضَرْحٌ, (TA,) *The market was, or became, stagnant,* or *dull, with respect to traffic.* (O, Ḳ, TA.)

3. ضارحهُ i. q. سَابَّهُ and رَامَاهُ; (O, Ḳ;) i. e. ضارحهُ and سابّهُ and راماهُ, are [all] one [in signification, app. meaning *He reviled him,* or *vilified him, being reviled,* or *vilified, by him;* so that the last seems to be here used tropically]. (TA.) — And i. q. قَارَبَهُ [*He drew him near to him*]; (O, Ḳ;) namely, his companion. (O.) — Also, inf. n. مُضَارَحَةٌ, *He, or it, resembled,* and *corresponded to, him, or it;* syn. ضَارَعَهُ and قَابَلَهُ. (TA. [See الضُّرَاحُ.])

4. اضرح i. q. أَبْعَدَ: (Ḳ:) you say, أَضْرِحْهُ عَنْكَ, (so accord. to two copies of the Ṣ,) or ▼ اِضْرَحْهُ, (so in one of my copies of the Ṣ, [i. e. اِضْرَحْهُ, from ضَرَحَهُ, in my other copy of the Ṣ اِضْرَحْهُ, so that the correct form of the verb in this sense is doubtful,]) meaning أَبْعِدْهُ [i. e. *Remove thou,* or *put far away, him, or it, from thee*]. (Ṣ.) [In the TA, it is also expl. as meaning دَفَعَ, which is likewise a signification of ضَرَحَ.] — And *He corrupted,* or *vitiated,* (O, Ḳ,) him, or it. (O.) — And أَضْرَحْتُ السُّوقَ *I made, or found, the market to be stagnant,* or *dull, with respect to traffic;* syn. أَكْسَدْتُهَا. (O, Ḳ.*)

7. انضرح *It was, or became, wide, or ample.* (TA.) You say, انضرح مَا بَيْنَ القَوْمِ *The space between the people was, or became, far-extending:* like انضرج. (Aṣ, Ṣ.) — Also *It split, slit,* or *rent asunder* or *open:* like انضرج. (TA.)

8. اضطرحوا فُلَانًا *They cast such a one aside:* (O,* L, TA: [see also 1, first sentence:]) the vulgar say اِطَّرَحُوا, thinking it to be from الطَّرْحُ, whereas it is from الضَّرْحُ: or, accord. to Az, it may be that, in اِطَّرَحُوا, the ت of the measure اِفْتَعَلَ is changed into ط, and ض incorporated into it. (L, TA.)

ضَرْحٌ inf. n. of 1. (Ṣ, A, &c.) — بَيْنِى وَبَيْنَهُمْ ضَرْحٌ means *Between me and them is a wide distance, and solitude.* (TA.) ═ Also *A skin.* (O, Ḳ.)

نِيَّةٌ ضَرَحٌ i. q. بَعِيدَةٌ [app. meaning *A distant,* or *remote, thing,* or *place, that is the object of an action or a journey:* &c.]; (O, Ḳ;) as also طَرَحٌ &c. (O.) — ضَرَحٌ applied to a man, *Bad, corrupt,* or *vitious.* (El-Muärrij, O, Ḳ.) ═ الضَّرَحُ is also used by poetic license for [the inf. n.] الضَّرْحُ. (O.)

ضَرَاحِ, like قَطَامِ, (Ḳ, TA,) is a verbal noun like نَزَالِ, (TA,) meaning اِضْرَحْ, (Ḳ, TA,) i. e. أَبْعِدْ: you say, ضَرَاحِ عَنْهُ *Remove thou to a distance,* or *go far away, from him, or it.* (TA.)

الضُّرَاحُ, (O, Ḳ, TA,) or, accord. to Mujáhid, الضَّرِيحُ ↓, (O, TA,*) [*The temple called*] البَيْتُ المَعْمُورُ, (O, Ḳ, TA,) *corresponding to,* or *over against,* [i. e. *directly over,*] *the Kaabeh,* (O, TA,) *in Heaven,* (O,) *in the Fourth Heaven,* (Ḳ, TA,) or *in the Seventh,* or *in the Sixth, and said to be beneath the* عَرْش, or *in the First Heaven:* (TA:) accord. to 'Alee, it is entered every day by seventy thousand angels. (O.)

قَوْسٌ ضَرُوحٌ *A bow that propels the arrow with vehemence;* (Ṣ, A, Ḳ;*) as also طَرُوحٌ [q. v.]. (Ṣ and O and Ḳ in art. طرح.) And دَابَّةٌ ضَرُوحٌ *A beast that kicks with its hind leg* (Ṣ, Ḳ) [or *with its fore legs:* see 1].

ضَرِيحٌ *Distant,* or *remote:* (Ṣ, Ḳ:) of the measure فَعِيلٌ in the sense of the measure مَفْعُولٌ. (TA.) — Also *A trench,* or *an oblong excavation, in the middle of a grave;* (Ṣ, A, Mgh, Mṣb, Ḳ;) and so ضَرِيحَةٌ ↓: (TA:) in this sense [likewise] of the measure فَعِيلٌ in the sense of the measure مَفْعُولٌ: (Mṣb:) what is termed لَحْدٌ is in the side: (Ṣ:) or *a grave* (Ḳ, TA) altogether: (TA:) or *a grave without a* لَحْد: (Ḳ, TA:) pl. ضَرَائِحُ. (Mṣb.) One says, نَوَّرَ اللّٰهُ ضَرِيحَهُ (A, TA) i. e. [*May God illumine*] *his grave.* (TA.) — See also الضُّرَاحُ.

ضَرِيحَةٌ: see the next preceding paragraph.

مَضْرَحِىٌّ: see مَضْرَحٌ.

مِضْرَحٌ *A garment,* or *piece of cloth,* or *other thing, used as a repository for clothes:* pl. مَضَارِحُ. (O.)

مَضْرَحِىٌّ A hawk, (Ṣ, A, O, Ḳ,) and a vulture, (A,) *having long wings;* (Ṣ, A, O, Ḳ;) as also مَضْرَحٌ ↓; (O, Ḳ;) but the former is the more common: a hawk of this description is of an excellent kind: (TA:) and to the wings of the vulture of this sort is likened the extremity of the tail of a she-camel with the coarse hairs that are upon it: (Kf, TA:) or *white,* applied to a hawk and to a vulture; (A;) or thus, applied to a vulture; and sometimes, so applied, *black:* (Ḥam p. 95:) or a vulture *intensely red* [or *brown*]: (AḤát, O:) [and a hawk *in which is redness;* otherwise it is not thus called: (so in the Deewán of Jereer, accord. to Freytag:)] or *i. q.* أَجْدَلُ and صَقْرٌ and قَطَامِىٌّ: (A'Obeyd, TA:) [it is mentioned in the Ḳ again in art. مضرح; for,] accord. to some, the م is radical: (TA in art. مضرح:) or, applied to a hawk, it means *that darts down sideways;* or *that thrusts the prey.* (Ḥam ubi suprà.) — [Hence,] ‡ *A chief,* (Ṣ, A, O, Ḳ,) *such as is generous,* or *noble,* (Ḳ,) or *of ancient* (A, O) *and generous* (O) *origin.* (A, O.) — Also *White* as an epithet applied to anything. (Ḳ.) — And ‡ *Tall,* or *long.* (Ḳ, TA.)

شَىْءٌ مُضْطَرَحٌ *A thing cast aside.* (Ṣ, Ḳ.)

Quasi ضرد

8. اِضْطَرَدَ, as though from ضَرَدَ: see 8 in art. طرد.

ضرس

1. ضَرَسَهُ, (A, TA,) aor. ـِ, (TA,) inf. n. ضَرْسٌ, (Ṣ, A, Ḳ,) *He bit it:* (TA:) or *he bit it vehemently with the* أَضْرَاس [pl. of ضِرْسٌ, q. v.]; (Ṣ, A, Ḳ;) as also ضَرَّسَهُ ↓: (A:) or *with the* ضِرْس. (T, TA.) — *He* (a beast of prey) *chewed his flesh,* (i. e., the flesh of his prey,) *without swallowing it;* (A;) as also ضَرَّسَهُ ↓. (A, TA.) — *He bit it* (namely an arrow) *to try it; to know if it were hard or weak:* (Ṣ:) *he marked it* (namely an arrow) *by biting it with his* أَضْرَاس, (M, A,) or *with his teeth.* (Az, TA.) — † *He tried him with respect to his claims to knowledge* or *courage.* (IAạr.) — ضَرَسَتْهُ الخُطُوبُ, inf. n. ضَرْسٌ, ‡ *Things* or *affairs,* or *calamities, tried,* or *tested, him;* as also ضَرَّسَتْهُ ↓. (TA.) — ضَرَسَتْهُ الحُرُوبُ, inf. n. ضَرْسٌ, ‡ *Wars tried,* or *proved, him, and rendered him expert,* or *strong;* (TA;) as also ضَرَّسَتْهُ ↓, (Ṣ, A, Ḳ,) inf. n. تَضْرِيسٌ. (Ṣ, Ḳ.) — ضَرَسَهُمُ الزَّمَانُ, (Ṣ, A, Ḳ,) inf. n. ضَرْسٌ, (Ḳ,) ‡ *Fortune became severe, rigorous, afflictive,* or *adverse, to them;* (Ṣ, A, Ḳ;*) as also ضَرَّسَهُمْ ↓. (A, TA.) — ضَرِسَ نَابُهَا ‡ *She was evil in disposition:* (TA:) and ضَرْسٌ [alone] the *being evil in disposition.* (IAạr.) — ضَرْسٌ also signifies † The *biting of blame,* or *reprehension.* (IAạr.) — And ‡ The *keeping silence during a day, until the night:* (O, Ḳ, TA:) as though biting one's tongue. (TA.) — And ضَرَسَ البِئْرَ, aor. ـِ, (O, Ḳ, TA) and ـُ, (TA,) inf. n. ضَرْسٌ, (O, TA,) † *He cased the well with stones:* (O, Ḳ, TA:) or, as some say, *he closed up the interstices of its casing with stones:* and in like manner one says of any building. (TA.) — ضَرِسَتْ أَسْنَانُهُ, (Ṣ, Ḳ,) aor. ـَ, (Ḳ,) inf. n. ضَرَسٌ, (Ṣ,) *His teeth were set on edge* (كَلَّتْ) by eating or drinking what was acid, or sour. (Ṣ, A,* Ḳ.) And ضَرِسَ الرَّجُلُ *The man's teeth were set on edge.* (TA.) It is said in a trad. of Wahb Ibn-Munebbih, that a certain bastard, of the Children of Israel, offered an offering, and it was rejected; whereupon he said, يَا رَبِّ يَأْكُلُ أَبَوَاىَ الحَمْضَ وَأَضْرَسُ أَنَا أَنْتَ أَكْرَمُ مِنْ ذٰلِكَ [*O my Lord, my two parents eat sour herbage, and are my teeth set on edge? Thou art more gracious than* to suffer *that*]: and his offering was accepted. (O in art. حمض.) [See Jer., xxxi. 29; and Ezek., xviii. 2.] — Also ضَرِسَ, inf. n. ضَرَسٌ, ‡ *He was angry by reason of hunger:* because hunger sharpens the أَضْرَاس. (TA.) — And ضَرِسُوا بِالحَرْبِ † *They persisted in war until they fought one another.* (T, O, TA.)

2. ضَرَّسَهُ, inf. n. تَضْرِيسٌ: see ضَرَسَهُ, in five places. — تَضْرِيسٌ also signifies ‡ *An indentation,* or *serration,* (Az, TA,) *like* أَضْرَاس, (TA,) in a sapphire (يَاقُوتَة) and a pearl, or in wood. (Az, TA.)

3. ضَارَسْتُ الأُمُورَ ‡ *I became experienced in affairs, and knew them.* (T, TṢ.) — ضارسوا, (Ḳ,) inf. n. مُضَارَسَةٌ and ضِرَاسٌ; so in the Tekmileh; but in the M, تضارسوا ↓; (TA;) ‡ *They warred,* or *fought, one against another, and treated one another with enmity,* or *hostility:* (Ḳ, TA:) from ضَرِسَ, [inf. n. of ضَرِسَ,] signifying the "being angry by reason of hunger." (TA.)

4. اضرسهُ *It* (acid, or sour, food, or drink,) *set his teeth on edge;* (Ibn-'Abbád, Ḳ;*) syn. أَكَلَّ أَسْنَانَهُ. (Ibn-'Abbád.) [And so, app., اضرس أَسْنَانَهُ.] — Also ‡ *He,* or *it,* (an affair, or event, Ṣ,) *disquieted him.* (Ibn-'Abbád, Ṣ, O, Ḳ, TA.) — And اضرسهُ بِالكَلَامِ † *He silenced him by speech.* (Ibn-'Abbád, O, Ḳ.)

5: see what next follows.

6. تضارس, (Ṣ, A, Ḳ,) in the M تضرّس ↓, (TA,) ‡ *It* (a building) *was,* or *became, uneven,* (Ṣ, M, A, Ḳ,) *and irregular,* (A,) *having in it what resembled* أَضْرَاس. (M.) — تضارسوا: see 3.

ضَرْسٌ † *Land of which the herbage is here and there* (IAạr, T, O, Ḳ, TA) *and on which rain has fallen here and there:* (IAạr, T, TA:) and *a portion of land upon which rain has fallen a day or part of a day.* (TA.) — See also ضِرْسٌ.

ضِرْسٌ *A tooth:* (Ṣ, Ḳ:) pl. أَضْرَاسٌ, and (sometimes, Ṣ, Mṣb) ضُرُوسٌ (Ṣ, Mṣb, Ḳ) and أَضْرُسٌ [which is a pl. of pauc., as is also, properly, the first of the pls. here mentioned]; and quasi-pl. n. ضرس [written in the TA without any syll. signs, so that it may be ضِرْسٌ, or ضَرْسٌ (like the sing.), or ضَرَسٌ]; so in the M [of which I am unable to consult the portion containing this art.]: (TA:) or [*a lateral tooth;* for] the اضراس are the *teeth, except the central incisors:* (Mgh:) or [this explanation, which I find only in the Mgh, is incomplete, and the word sometimes means the *teeth* absolutely, but properly] the *molar teeth,* or *grinders, which are twenty in number,* [*including the bicuspids,*] *next behind the canine teeth:* (Zj, in his "Khalḳ el-Insán:") or *i. q.* أَرْحَآءٌ: (Ṣ and Mṣb and Ḳ, art. رحى: [see سِنٌّ: and see also رَبَاعِيَةٌ:] ضِرْسٌ is masc.; (Mgh, Ḳ;) and sometimes fem.: (Mgh:) or what is thus called is masc. when thus called; (Ṣ, Mṣb;) but if called سِنٌّ, it is fem.: (Mṣb:) or it is properly masc.; and if found in poetry made fem., سِنٌّ is meant thereby: (Zj, Mṣb:) but Aṣ denies its being made fem.; (Mṣb, TA;) and as to the saying ascribed to Dukeyn,

* فَفُقِئَتْ عَيْنٌ وَطَنَّتْ ضِرْسُ *

[*And an eye was put out, and a tooth,* or *grinder, sounded*], he says that the right reading is وَطَنَّ الضِّرْسُ [*and the tooth,* or *grinder, sounded*], and that he who heard these words understood them not. (TA.) What are called أَضْرَاسُ العَقْلِ and أَضْرَاسُ الحُلُمِ [*The wisdom-teeth,* and *the teeth of puberty*] are four: they come forth after the [other] teeth have become strong. (TA. [See نَاجِذ.]) — [Hence,] sing. of ضُرُوسٌ (K) which signifies † The *stones with which a well is cased.* (S, O, K.) — And † *A* قِنّ [app. as meaning a *peak, or the like,*] *in a mountain.* (TA.) — And † *A rough* [*hill, or eminence, or elevated place, such as is termed*] أَكَمَة (T, O, K, TA) and [*such as is termed*] أَخْشَب: (T, TA:) or *rough ground;* written by Sgh ‡ ضَرِسٌ: (IAar, TA:) or *a portion of a* [*tract such as is termed*] قُفّ, *somewhat elevated, very rugged, rough to the tread, consisting of a single piece of stone* [or *rock*], *unmixed with clay, or soil, and not giving growth to anything:* pl. ضُرُوسٌ. (TA.) — Also ‡ *Light rain:* (IAar, TA:) or *a rain little in quantity:* (S, O:) or *a light rain:* pl. ضُرُوسٌ: (K:) or ضُرُوسٌ مِنْ مَطَرٍ means *scattered rains:* (As, TA:) or *scattered showers of rain:* (S, O:) and some say, *i. q.* جُذُر [app. a mistranscription, probably for خَدَر, which signifies *rain;* or *clouds,* or *mist, and rain*]: and [it is said that] ضِرْسٌ signifies also *a raining cloud that has not* [*much*] *width.* (TA.) — See also مُضَرَّسٌ, last sentence.

ضَرِسٌ A man *having his teeth set on edge.* (TA.) — And ‡ A man *angry by reason of hunger;* (AZ, K, TA;) because hunger sharpens the أَضْرَاس: (TA:) and ‡ ضَرِيسٌ signifies † *very hungry;* (K, TA;) *so that there is nothing that comes to him but he eats it, by reason of hunger:* (TA:) pl. of the latter ضَرَاسَى, like as حَزَانَى is a pl. of حَزِين. (K.) — And ‡ A man (S, A, O) *refractory, untractable, perverse, stubborn,* or *obstinate, in disposition:* (Yz, S, A, O, K:) *evil in disposition,* or *illnatured, and very perverse* or *cross* or *repugnant and averse;* syn. شَرِسٌ. (K.) You say رَجُلٌ ضَرِسٌ شَرِسٌ. (Yz, S, A, O.) [See ضُرُوسٌ.] — See also مُضَرَّسٌ, last sentence.

ضَرَسَةٌ *Ruggedness,* and *roughness.* (TA.)

ضُرَاسٌ *Toothache.* (MA.)

ضِرَاسٌ [seems to signify, properly, *A disposition to bite*]. — [Hence,] النَّاقَةُ بِجِنِّ ضِرَاسِهَا means † *The she-camel is in the case of the recentness of her bringing forth,* when she defends her young one; from the epithet ضَرُوسٌ; (S, Meyd, O; but in the S and O, هِيَ, referring to the she-camel, is put in the place of النَّاقَةُ;) and is a prov., applied to the man whose nature is evil on the occasion of his defending. (Meyd.) And one says, اِتَّقِ النَّاقَةَ بِجِنِّ ضِرَاسِهَا, meaning ‡ *Beware thou of the she-camel in the case of the recentness of her bringing forth, and of her evil disposition towards him who approaches her, by reason of her attachment to her young one.* (A, TA.) [In the TA, in art. جن, this saying is mentioned with ضِرَامِهَا in the place of ضِرَاسِهَا: the former may perhaps be another reading; but I rather think that it is a mistranscription for the latter. And in the present art. in the TA, it is added that Sgh has mentioned (app. in the TS, for he has not done so in the O,) El-Báhilee's having explained الضِّرَاس as meaning بِسْرٌ لَهُمْ; and that it is likewise explained in the T as meaning بِسْر: but I know no such word as بِسْر; nor do I know any word of which it is likely to be a mistranscription, though I have diligently searched for such. This word بِسْر has been altered by the copyist in each instance in the TA; so that it seems to have been indistinctly written by the author.] — [Hence also] ضِرَاسُ الحَرْبِ † *The biting of war.* (Ham p. 532.)

ضَرُوسٌ A she-camel *of evil disposition,* (S, K,) *that bites her milker:* (S, A, K:) or *that has a habit of biting to defend her young one.* (TA.) — [Hence,] حَرْبٌ ضَرُوسٌ ‡ *Devouring, biting, war:* (TA:) or *vehement war.* (Ham p. 87.) — And A she-camel *whose flow,* or *stream, of milk does not make any sound to be heard.* (TA.)

ضَرِيسٌ † *Stones resembling* أَضْرَاس [i. e. *teeth* or *lateral teeth* or *molar teeth*]: with such, a well is cased. (TA.) — And † The *vertebræ of the back.* (O, K.) — Also, and ‡ مَضْرُوسَةٌ, † A well (بِئْر) *cased with stones.* (S, K.) — See also ضَرِسٌ.

أَضْرَسُ an imitative sequent to أَخْرَسُ as an epithet applied to a man. (S, K.)

مُضَرَّسٌ † *A sort of figured cloth* or *garment,* (S, O, K,) *having upon it forms resembling* أَضْرَاس [i. e. *teeth* or *lateral teeth* or *molar teeth*], (K,) or thought by IF to be thus called because having upon it such forms: (O:) or, applied as an epithet to [the kind of garments called] رَيْط, as meaning *figured with the marks of folding:* or meaning *folded in a square form:* or, as some say, مُضَرَّسَةٌ signifies *a sort of cloths,* or *garments, upon which are lines and ornamental borders.* (TA.) — And † An arrow *that is not smooth,* or *even;* because it has in it what resemble أَضْرَاس. (TA.) — And حَرَّةٌ مُضَرَّسَةٌ and ‡ مَضْرُوسَةٌ † [*A stony tract*] *in which are stones like the* أَضْرَاس *of dogs.* (A'Obeyd, S, K.) — Also ‡ A man *who has been tried,* or *proved,* or *tried and strengthened, by experience;* (A, TA;) *whom trials have befallen, as though he had been bitten thereby:* (TA:) *who has been tried,* or *proved, and rendered expert,* or *strong, by wars,* (S, A,) and *by affairs,* or *calamities:* (A:) like مُنَجَّذ from نَاجِذ: (A, TA:) or *who has become experienced in affairs:* (AA, S:) one *who has travelled, and become experienced in affairs, and fought;* as also ‡ ضَرِيسٌ and ‡ ضَرِسٌ. (TA.)

المُضَرِّسُ *The lion, that chews the flesh of his prey without swallowing it:* (O, K:) or *the lion;* so called because he does thus. (TA.)

مَضْرُوسَةٌ: see ضَرِيسٌ: and also مُضَرَّسٌ.

ضرط

1. ضَرِطَ, aor. ـَ; (S, Msb, K;) and ضَرَطَ, aor. ـِ; (Msb;) inf. n. ضَرْطٌ (S, Msb, K, in the Msb said to be of the latter verb,) and ضَرِطٌ (Msb, K, in the Msb said to be of the former verb,) and ضَرِيطٌ and ضُرَاطٌ, (K,) or the last is a simple subst., (Msb,) [a coarse word, signifying] *He broke wind,* i. e. *emitted wind from the anus, with a sound.* (S, K.) [When it is without sound, you say فَسَا.] Hence the prov., أَوْدَى العَيْرُ إِلَّا ضَرِطًا *The ass had no power remaining except* [that of] *emitting wind from the anus, with a sound:* (S, K:) applied to a vile, or an abject, person, and to an old man; and in allusion to a thing's becoming in a bad, or corrupt, state, so that there remains of it nothing but what is of no use: (K:) the last word is in the accus. case as denoting a thing of a different kind from that signified by the preceding noun. (O.) And أَجْبَنُ مِنَ المَنْزُوفِ ضَرِطًا [*More cowardly than he who is exhausted by emitting wind from the anus, with a sound*]: another prov.: [its origin is variously related: see Freytag's Arab. Prov., i. 320:] or المَنْزُوفُ ضَرِطًا [or ضَرْطًا, for it is differently written in different copies of the K,] is *a certain beast, between the dog and the cat,* (K,) or *between the dog and the wolf,* (O,) *which, when one cries out at it, emits wind from the anus, with a sound, by reason of cowardice.* (Sgh, K.)

2: see 4, in two places.

4. اضرطهُ, and ‡ ضرّطهُ, (S, O, K,) *He made him to emit wind from the anus, with a sound:* (S:) or *he did to him that which caused him to emit wind from the anus, with a sound.* (O, K.) — اضرط بهِ; and ‡ ضرّط بهِ, (S, K,) inf. n. تَضْرِيطٌ; (K;) *He derided him, and imitated to him with his mouth the action of one emitting wind from the anus, with a sound;* (S;) *he made to him with his mouth a sound like that of an emission of wind from the anus, and derided him.* (K, TA.) اضرط بالسَّائِلِ, said in a trad., of 'Alee, means *He treated the asker with contempt, disapproving what he said; he derided him.* (TA.)

ضَرِطٌ part. n. of ضَرِطَ. (Msb.)

ضَرْطَةٌ [inf. n. un. of 1; *A single emission of wind from the anus, making a sound*]. It is said in a prov., of him who has done a deed of which he has not done the like before nor after, كَانَتْ مِنْهُ كَضَرْطَةِ الأَصَمِّ [*There proceeded from him what was like the* ضرطة *of the deaf*]. (Sgh, TA.)

ضُرَاطٌ *An emission of wind from the anus, with a sound:* (S, TA:) or the *sound thereof:* (K, TA: [in the CK, صَوْتُ الفَقْحِ is put for صَوْتُ الفَيْحِ:]) a subst. from 1. (Msb.)

ضَرُوطٌ: see ضُرَاطٌ.

ضَرِيطٌ: } see سُرَيْطَى.
ضُرَيْطَى: }
ضُرَيْطَآء: }

ضُرَاطٌ and ‡ ضَرُوطٌ and ‡ ضِرْوَطٌ are all [intensive] epithets from 1; (K;) [signifying One *who emits wind from the anus, with a sound, much,* or *frequently;*] the last mentioned by Sb, and expl. by Seer. (TA.)

ضِرْوَطٌ: see the next preceding paragraph.

ضُوَيْطٌ : } see سُوَيْطِى.
ضُوَيْطِى :
ضِوَيْطِى :

أَضْوَطُ : see أَطْوَطُ, in art. طوط.

مُضَرِّطُ الحِجَارَةِ † [as though signifying *He who makes the stones to emit sounds*, from fear:] an appellation given to 'Amr Ibn-Hind, because of his strength and hardiness and courage, (Ṣ,) or because of the awe which he inspired. (A, TA.)

ضرع

1. ضَرَعَ, said of a lamb or kid, *He took* [*with his mouth*] *the* ضَرْع [meaning *dug*] *of his mother.* (TA.) [This seems to be regarded by some as the primary signification.] — And (TA) the same, (Ṣ, Mṣb, Ḳ,) said of a man, (Ṣ,) aor. ـَ ; (Mṣb, Ḳ;) and ضَرِعَ, aor. ـَ ; and ضَرُعَ, aor. ـُ ; (Ḳ;) inf. n. (Ṣ, Mṣb, Ḳ) of the first (Ṣ, Mṣb, TA) and of the third (TA) ضَرَاعَةٌ, (Ṣ, Mṣb, Ḳ,) and (Ḳ) of the second (TA) ضَرَعٌ; (Ḳ;) *He was,* or *became, lowly, humble,* or *submissive;* (Ṣ, Ḳ;) and *low, abject,* or *abased;* (Ṣ, Mṣb, Ḳ;) إِلَيْهِ (Ḳ) and لَهُ [*to him*]: (TA:) or ضَرِعَ and ضَرَعَ signify *he lowered, humbled,* or *abased, himself,* (Ḳ,* TA,) [like تضرّع, which is more commonly used in this sense,] *and made petition for a gift:* (TA:) and ضَرُعَ, (Mṣb, Ḳ, TA,) inf. n. ضَرَعٌ, (Mṣb,) or ضَرَاعَةٌ, (TA,) *he was,* or *became, weak;* (Ḳ, TA;) and it is said that the verb in this last sense is from ضَرَعَ in the sense expl. in the first sentence: so in the "Mufradát" [of Er-Rághib]: ضَرِعَ, likewise, like فَرِحَ [in measure], signifies *he was,* or *became, weak in body, slender, spare,* or *light of flesh:* and ضُرُوعٌ, [app. as an inf. n. of which the verb is ضَرَعَ,] the *being lean,* or *emaciated.* (TA.) For another explanation of ضَرَاعَةٌ, see 5. — [ضَرَعَ is made trans. by means of ب:] one says, ضَرَعَ بِهِ فَرَسُهُ *His horse humbled him,* or *abased him:* (O, Ḳ, TA:) or, as in the L, *overcame him.* (TA.) — ضَرَعَ مِنْهُ, said of an animal of prey, (IḲṭṭ, Ḳ, TA,) inf. n. ضُرُوعٌ, (Ḳ,) *He approached* (IḲṭṭ, Ḳ, TA) *him* i. e. a man, (IḲṭṭ, TA,) or *it* i. e. a thing. (Ḳ.) — See also the next paragraph.

2. تَضْرِيعٌ signifies The *drawing near,* or *approaching, by little and little, in a deceitful,* or *guileful, manner, going this way and that,* or *to the right and left;* (Ibn-'Abbád, O, Ḳ;) as also ▼ تَضَرُّعٌ: (Ḳ:) you say ضَرَّعَ and تَضَرَّعَ. (O, TA.) — And ضَرَّعَتِ الشَّمْسُ, (Ḳ,) inf. n. as above, (Ṣ, O,) ‡ *The sun approached the setting;* (Ṣ, O, Ḳ;) [like ضجّعت;] and ▼ ضَرَعَت signifies the same; [like ضَجَعَت;] or *the sun set;* (Ḳ;) and ضَارَعَتِ ▼ الشَّمْسُ, inf. n. مُضَارَعَةٌ, signifies the same as ضَرَعَت and ضرّعت. (TA.) — And حَانَ أَنْ تُدْرِكَ i. q. ضَرَّعَتِ القِدْرُ [i. e. *The cooking-pot approached,* or *attained, to the time of the cooking of its contents;* and so, app., ▼ ضارعت, accord. to the TA, but the passage in which this is there indicated presents an obvious mistranscription]. (Ṣ, O, Ḳ, TA. [In the CḲ, تُدْرَكَ is erroneously put for تُدْرِكَ.]) — And ضَرَّعَ الرُّبُّ [app. means *The rob,* or *inspissated juice, became nearly mature;* or] *the expressed juice was cooked, but its cooking was not complete.* (O, Ḳ,* TA. [In the CḲ, الرُّبُّ is erroneously put for الرُّبُّ, and طَبَخَ for طُبِخَ, and يَتِمُّ طَبْخَهُ for يَتِمَّ طَبْخُهُ.])

3. مُضَارَعَةٌ is syn. with مُشَابَهَةٌ: (Ṣ, O, Mṣb:) accord. to Er-Rághib, its primary meaning is The *sharing* [in a thing, or particularly *in the* ضَرْع, or *udder*], like مُرَاضَعَةٌ, which is the "sharing in sucking." (TA.) You say ضارعهُ *He,* or *it, resembled him,* or *it;* was, or *became like him,* or *it.* (Ḳ, TA.) And بَيْنَهُمَا مُرَاضَعَةُ الكَأْسِ وَمُضَارَعَةُ الأَجْنَاسِ [*Between them two are the sipping of the wine-cup, and the resemblance of kinds;* or *compotation and congeniality*]: said in the A to be from الضَّرْعُ. (TA.) [See also an ex. voce تَخَلَّجَ.] — Also i. q. مُقَارَبَةٌ [meaning The *approaching* a thing]. (TA.) See 2, in two places.

4. اضرعت, said of a ewe or she-goat, *Her milk descended* [*into her udder,* i. e. *she secreted milk in her udder,* as is shown in the lexicons in many places, (see for instance, أَرْدَتْ, and رِدَّةٌ,)] *a little before her bringing forth:* (Ṣ, O, Ḳ:) and [in like manner] said of a she-camel, *her milk descended from* (مِنْ [a mistranscription for فِى i. e. *into*]) *her udder near the time of bringing forth;* and the epithet applied to her is ▼ مُضْرِعٌ [without ة]: or, as in the A, said of a she-camel and of a cow, *her udder* (ضَرْعُهَا) *became prominent before bringing forth:* (TA:) or, said of a ewe or she-goat, *she showed herself to be pregnant, and became large in her udder.* (T in art. رمد.) And أَضْرَعَتْ عَلَى رَأْسِ الوَلَدِ [*She secreted milk,* or *became large, in the udder, at the time of bringing forth,* or *when about to produce the young,* like as one says كَانَ ذٰلِكَ عَلَى رَأْسِ فُلَانٍ expl. in art. رأس], said of a ewe or goat. (Ṣ in arts. رمد and ربق [in both of which the meaning is clearly shown] and in art. دفع [in which last see several sentences].) — [Hence, app.,] أَضْرَعْتُ لَهُ مَالِى † *I gave him liberally, unsparingly,* or *freely, my property.* (O, Ḳ.*) — And اضرعهُ signifies also *He,* or *it, lowered, humbled,* or *abased, him.* (Ṣ, O, Ḳ.) Thus, in a trad. of 'Alee, أَضْرَعَ اللّٰهُ خُدُودَكُمْ *May God lower,* or *humble,* or *abase, your cheeks.* (TA.) One says also, كَانَ مَزْهُوًّا فَأَضْرَعَهُ الفَقْرُ [*He was proud, haughty,* or *insolent, and poverty lowered,* or *humbled,* or *abased, him*]. (TA.) And it is said in a prov., الحُمَّى أَضْرَعَتْنِى لَكَ, (Ṣ, Meyd, A, O,) or لِلنَّوْمِ, (Meyd, O, Ḳ,) accord. to different relations, (Meyd, O,) [meaning *The fever abased me to thee,* or *to sleep;*] asserted by El-Mufaḍḍal to have been first said by a certain man named Mureyr, to a Jinnee by whom he was carried off while sleeping under the influence of fever, after he had been making a fruitless search after his two brothers, Murárah and Murrah, who had also been carried off by Jinn: [his story is related at length in the O and TA, as well as by Meyd.; and is given in Ḥar p. 568, and in Freytag's Arab. Prov. i. pp. 364-5:] the prov. is applied to the case of abasement on the occasion of need. (Meyd, O, TA.) — One says also, اضرعهُ إِلَيْهِ *He,* or *it, constrained him to have recourse to him,* or *it.* (TA.) — And اضرعهُ الحُبُّ *Love rendered him lean,* or *emaciated.* (TA.)

5. تضرّع *He lowered, humbled,* or *abased, himself:* (O, Ḳ, TA:) or *he addressed himself with earnest,* or *energetic, supplication:* (TA:) syn. اِبْتَهَلَ, to God (إِلَى اللّٰهِ): (Ṣ, O, Ḳ:) or *he manifested* ▼ ضَرَاعَة i. e. *severe poverty,* (O, TA,) *and want,* (TA,) to God: (O, TA:) or i. q. تَعَرَّضَ بِطَلَبِ الحَاجَةِ, (Ḳ, TA,) or يَطْلُبُ الحَاجَةَ; (CḲ;) you say, جَآءَ فُلَانٌ يَتَضَرَّعُ and يَتَعَرَّضُ i. e. *Such a one came asking,* or *petitioning, to another for a thing that he wanted.* (Fr, Ṣ, O.) [See also تَضَرَّعَ.] — Also *He writhed; and asked,* or *called, for aid,* or *succour.* (TA.) — And, said of the shade, ‡ *It contracted, shrank,* or *decreased;* or *it went away;* syn. قَلَصَ: (Ibn-'Abbád, O, Ḳ, TA:) and تَضَرَّعَ is a dial. var. thereof. — See also 2.

ضَرْعٌ a word of well-known meaning; (TA;) [properly and generally, the *udder,* but sometimes applied to the *dug,* or *teat:*] the ضرع is *of every female that has a cloven hoof,* or *of the she-camel:* (Ṣ, O:) [i. e.] *of each of these:* (Ḳ:) or [*of the former only;* i. e.] *of the sheep or goat and of the cow* and *the like;* that of the camel being termed خِلْفٌ: (Lth, O, Ḳ:) it is, *to the cloven-hoofed female, like the* ثَدْى *to the woman:* (Mṣb:) or, *to cattle, like the* ثَدْى *to the woman:* (Towsheeḥ, TA:) accord. to the IF, it is *of the sheep or goat* and *of other animals:* accord. to IDrd, *of the sheep or goat* [*only*]: AZ says, *it comprises the* أَطْبَآء, *which are the* أَخْلَاف, *and in which are the* أَحَالِيل, *which are the orifices for the passing forth of the milk:* (O:) the pl. is ضُرُوعٌ. (O, Mṣb, Ḳ.) مَا لَهُ زَرْعٌ وَلَا ضَرْعٌ [lit. *He has not seed-produce nor an udder*] means ‡ *he has not anything:* (TA:) or it means *he has not land to sow, nor a ewe or she-goat or she-camel or other animal having a* ضَرْع. (O.) — See also the next paragraph, in two places.

ضَرِعٌ *A like; a similar person* or *thing;* (IAạr, O, Ḳ;) as also ▼ ضَرْعٌ: (IAạr, TA in art. صرع:) and so ضِرْعٌ (O, TA) and ضَرْعٌ. (O and Ḳ and TA in art. صرع.) — And *A sort,* or *species:* and *a state, condition,* or *manner of being:* of a thing: as also ▾ ضَرْعٌ: and so صِرْعٌ and صَرْعٌ. (TA in art. صرع.) — And *A strand of a rope:* (O, Ḳ:) and so صِرْعٌ: (O:) pl. ضُرُوعٌ. (O, Ḳ: and the CḲ adds أَضْرُعٌ.)

ضَرَعٌ *Lowly, humble, submissive,* or *in a state of abasement;* [originally an inf. n., and therefore, as an epithet,] applied to a single person and to a pl. number: (O:) and ▾ ضَارِعٌ signifies the same, applied to a single person; (O, Mṣb;) as also ▾ مُسْتَضْرِعٌ: (Ḳ,* TA:) accord. to Lth, one says, ▾ خَدُّكَ ضَارِعٌ, (O,) and ▾ أَضْرَعُ, which signifies the same, (Ḥam p. 344,) and ▾ جَنْبُكَ ضَارِعٌ, [meaning, as is implied in the O, *Thy cheek is lowly* &c., and so *thy side,* and the like is said in the Ḥam p. 590,] and ▾ أَنْتَ ضَارِعٌ [*Thou art lowly* &c.]: (O:) and the pl. of ضَارِعٌ is ضَرَعَةٌ and ضُرُوعٌ: (TA:) or ▾ ضَارِعٌ signifies, and so ▾ ضَرِعٌ, and [in an intensive sense] ▾ ضَرُوعٌ and ▾ ضَرَعَةٌ, *lowering, humbling,* or *abasing, himself:* (Ḳ:) or *thus, and making petition for a gift:* (TA:) and ضَرَعٌ signifies *weak;* (Ṣ, Mgh, Mṣb, Ḳ;) as also ▾ ضَرِعٌ; (Ḳ;) the former (Mṣb, Ḳ) originally an inf. n. (Mṣb) [and therefore, as an epithet,] applied to a single person and to a pl. number: (Ḳ:) and ضَرَعٌ and ▾ ضَارِعٌ *small;* applied to anything: or *small in age, weak,* (Ḳ, TA,) *and lean, spare,* or *light of flesh:* (TA:) and ▾ ضَارِعٌ, (Ṣ,) and ▾ ضَرِعٌ, (TA,) *lean, spare,* or *light of flesh, and weak, in the body;* ضَارِعُ الجِسْمِ (Ṣ, TA;) applied to a man: (Ṣ:) and ضَرَعٌ applied to a colt, *not having strength to run,* (Ḳ, TA,) *by reason of the smallness of his age.* (TA.) Also † *Cowardly,* or *weak-hearted:* you say, هُوَ وَرَعٌ ضَرَعٌ [both app. meaning the same]. (TA.) And, applied to a man, ‡ *Inexperienced in affairs; ignorant;* or *in whom is no profit nor judgment;* syn. غُمْرٌ. (TA.)

ضَرِعٌ: see ضَرَعٌ, in three places.

ضَرَعَةٌ: see ضَرَعٌ. — It is also a pl. of ضَارِعٌ [as mentioned above, voce ضَرَعٌ]. (TA.)

سَبَّةٌ ضُرَعَةٌ occurs in a trad. as meaning *A reviler of men, who becomes like them and equal to them.* (TA.)

ضَرُوعٌ: see ضَرَعٌ.

ضُرُوعٌ pl. of ضَرْعٌ [q. v.]. (O, Mṣb, Ḳ.) — Also *A species of grape,* (AḤn, O, Ḳ,) *growing in the Sarāh* (ٱلسَّرَاة), (AḤn, O,) *white, large in the berries,* (AḤn, O, Ḳ,) *having little juice, great in the bunches, like the sort of raisins called* طَائِفِىّ. (O.) ═ It is also a pl. of ضَارِعٌ [as mentioned above, voce ضَرَعٌ]. (TA.)

ضَرِيعٌ and ضَرِيعَةٌ (IF, Ṣ, O, Ḳ) and ▾ ضَرْعَآءُ, (O, Ḳ,) applied to a ewe or she-goat, *Large in the* ضَرْع [or *udder*]; (IF, Ṣ, O, Ḳ;) and in like manner applied to a woman: (Ḳ:) or ▾ the last is applied to a woman as meaning *large in the breasts,* and in like manner to a ewe or she-goat: (IDrd, TA:) or, accord. to the L, the second and ▾ third, as first expl. above, are applied to a ewe or she-goat, and to a camel; and the first is applied to a ewe or she-goat, as meaning *goodly in the* ضَرْع. (TA.) ═ Also, the first of these words, (O, Ḳ,) mentioned in the Ḳur lxxxviii. 6, (O,) *i. q.* شِبْرِقٌ; (O, Ḳ;) which is *A bad sort of pasture, upon which the pasturing cattle do not make* (لَا تَعْقِدُ) *fat nor flesh, and which renders them in a bad condition if they do not quit it and betake themselves to other pasture;* (AḤn, O;) or, accord. to IAth, the شبرق is *a certain plant in El-Ḥijáz, having large thorns:* (TA:) or, the *plant called* شِبْرِق *that is dried up;* (Fr, Ṣ, O, Ḳ;) شبرق being its appellation when it is in its fresh state; (Fr, Ḳ, TA;) the people of El-Ḥijáz call it ضريع in its dry state; (Fr, TA;) and it is [said to be] a plant which the beast will not approach, because of its bad quality: (Ḳ:) and (Ḳ) *what is dry of any tree;* (Ibn-'Abbád, O, Ḳ;) accord. to some, peculiarly, of the عَرْفَج and خُلَّة; (TA;) or [*any*] *dry herbage:* (TA in art. بحت:) and, (Ḳ,) accord. to Lth, (O,) *a certain plant in water that has become altered for the worse by long standing or the like, having roots that reach not to the ground:* (O, Ḳ:) or *a certain thing in Hell, more bitter than aloes, and more stinking than the carcass, and hotter than fire;* (Ḳ, TA;) *the food of the inmates of Hell;* but this was unknown to the [pagan] Arabs: (TA:) and, (Ḳ,) as some say, (O,) *a certain plant,* (Ḳ, O,) *green,* (O,) thus in the L, but in the "Mufradát" *red,* (TA,) *of fetid odour, cast up by the sea,* (O, Ḳ,) *light, and hollow:* (TA:) and, (Ḳ,) accord. to Abu-l-Jowzà, (O,) *the prickles of the palm-tree:* (O, Ḳ:) and, (Ḳ,) accord. to IAạr, (O,) the [*thorny tree called*] عَوْسَج, *in its fresh state.* (O, Ḳ.) — Also *Wine:* or *thin wine:* (Ḳ:) or *thin beverage.* (Ibn-'Abbád, O, Ḳ.) — And the *skin that is upon the bone, beneath the flesh* (Lth, O, Ḳ) *of the rib:* (Lth, O:) or the *integument upon it.* (TA.)

ضَارِعٌ: see ضَرَعٌ, in seven places. — نُجُومٌ ضَوَارِعُ means ‡ *Stars inclining to setting,* or *to the places of setting.* (A and TA in art. خضع.)

أَضْرَعُ: see ضَرَعٌ: ═ and for its fem., ضَرْعَآءُ, see ضَرِيعٌ, in three places.

مُضْرِعٌ an epithet applied to a she-camel [and app. to a ewe or she-goat]: see 4.

[مُضَرَّعٌ part. n. of the intrans. verb ضَرَّعَ. — In the TA, voce كُثْءٌ, مصرع, which is evidently a mistranscription for مُضَرَّعٌ, is expl. as an epithet applied to a preparation of أَقِط (q. v.) as meaning *Such as has become thick,* or *coagulated, and almost thoroughly cooked:* on the authority of AḤát.]

ٱلْمُضَارِعُ [as a conventional term of grammar] *The future tense;* [or rather *the aorist;* for it is properly *the present,* and tropically *the future:*] so called because it resembles nouns in admitting the desinential syntactical signs. (TA.)

مُسْتَضْرِعٌ: see ضَرَعٌ.

ضرغم

Q. 1. ضَرْغَمَتِ ٱلْأَبْطَالُ, [inf. n. ضَرْغَمَةٌ,] † *The men of valour acted like lions;* as also ▾ تَضَرْغَمَتْ: (Ḳ:) or, as some say, ٱلضَّرْغَمَةُ and ▾ ٱلتَّضَرْغُمُ signify † *the choosing of valiant men* [app. *as antagonists*] *in war,* or *battle.* (TA.) And you say, ضَرْغَمَ ٱلْأَبْطَالُ بَعْضُهَا بَعْضًا فِى ٱلْحَرْبِ † [*The men of valour attacked one another like lions in war,* or *battle*]. (Ṣ, TA.)

Q. 2. تَضَرْغَمَ: see what precedes, in two places.

ضِرْغَمٌ, or ضَرْغَمٌ: see the next paragraph.

ضِرْغَامٌ, (MA, Ḳ, and so in some copies of the Ṣ,) and ▾ ضِرْغَامَةٌ, (MA, Ḳ, and so in other copies of the Ṣ,) and ▾ ضِرْغَمٌ, (MA,) or ▾ ضَرْغَمٌ, like جَعْفَرٌ, (Ḳ, TA,) The *lion:* (Ṣ, MA, Ḳ:) or *a lion accustomed to prey, strong, and bold.* (TA.) — And ٱلضِّرْغَامُ is also applied to † *The constellation of the Lion.* (Ḥam p. 110.)

ضِرْغَامَةٌ: see ضِرْغَامٌ. — Hence, as being likened to a lion, (TA,) ‡ *Courageous;* (Ḳ, TA;) as an epithet applied to a man. (TA.) — And † A *powerful* stallion [camel]. (Ḳ.) — And ‡ A *strong* man; (Ḳ, TA;) as being likened to a lion. (TA.) — And ضِرْغَامَةٌ مِنْ طِينٍ is said in the Nawádir el-Aạráb to mean *Slime,* or *mire.* (TA.)

ضرم

1. ضَرِمَتِ ٱلنَّارُ, (Ṣ, Mṣb, Ḳ,) aor. ـَ, (Mṣb, Ḳ,) inf. n. ضَرَمٌ; (Mṣb, TA;) and ▾ اضطرمت, and [in an intensive sense] ▾ تضرّمت; (Ṣ, Mṣb, Ḳ;) *The fire became kindled;* or *it burned up, burned brightly* or *fiercely, blazed,* or *flamed;* syn. ٱلْتَهَبَتْ, (Ṣ, Mṣb,) or ٱشْتَعَلَتْ. (Ḳ.) — And ضَرِمَ ٱلشَّىْءُ ‡ *The thing was,* or *became, intensely hot.* (Ṣ, Ḳ.*) — And ضَرِمَتِ ٱلْحَرْبُ, and ▾ اضطرمت, and [in an intensive sense] ▾ تضرّمت, † *The war was,* or *became, kindled;* or *it burned fiercely,* or *raged.* (TA.) — And ضَرِمَ, (Ṣ, Mṣb, Ḳ,) inf. n. as above, (Mṣb,) said of a man, (Ṣ, Mṣb,) ‡ *He was,* or *became, vehemently hungry:* (Ṣ, Mṣb, Ḳ, TA:) or *he burned with hunger:* said by Z to be tropical: (TA:) and so تضرّم جُوعًا, syn. تَحَرَّقَ. (TA in art. حرق.) And one says of him who is vehemently hungry, ضَرِمَ شَذَاهُ † [lit. *His flies have become vehemently hungry,* or *burning with hunger*]. (Ṣ in art. شذو.) — And ضَرِمَ فِى ٱلطَّعَامِ, (Ḳ,) inf. n. as above, (TA,) ‡ *He applied himself to the eating of the food vigorously,* or *with energy, not pushing away aught thereof.* (Ḳ, TA.) — And ضَرِمَ عَلَيْهِ (Mṣb,* Ḳ) ‡ *His anger became violent* [*against him*]: (Mṣb:) or *he burned with anger against him;* as also ▾ تضرّم عليه; (Ḳ;)

or the latter signifies *he became angered against him:* (Ṣ, TA:) and ▼اضطرم عليه *he was,* or *became, angry with him.* (TA.) — And ضَرِمَ said of a horse, ‡ *He ran vehemently* [or *ardently*]: and they say also ضَرِمَ الرُّقَاقَ, [or perhaps correctly ضَرِمَ فِى الرُّقَاقِ,] meaning ‡ *He ran vehemently in a tract of soft ground:* (TA:) and ▼اضطرم جَرْيُهُ † [*His running was,* or *became, vehement,* or *ardent,*] is likewise said of a horse. (Aṣ, Ṣ* and Ḳ* in art. مصع.)

2: see the next paragraph.

4. اضرم النَّارَ, (Ṣ, Mṣb, Ḳ,) inf. n. إِضْرَامٌ; (Mṣb;) and ▼ضَرَّمَهَا, (Ṣ, Ḳ,) but this is with teshdeed to denote intensiveness [of the signification]; (Ṣ;) and ▼استضرمها, (Ḳ,) in which the prefix is not meant to denote demand; (TA;) *He kindled the fire;* or *made it to burn up, burn brightly* or *fiercely, blaze,* or *flame;* (Ṣ, Mṣb, Ḳ;) syn. أَوْقَدَهَا, (Ḳ,) or أَشْعَلَهَا. (Ṣ in art. شعل.)

5: see 1, in four places.

8: see 1, in four places. — One says also, اضطرم المَشِيبُ ‡ *Whiteness of the hair became glistening* (اِشْتَعَلَ, Ḳ, TA) *and much in degree.* (TA.) — And ▼اضطرم الشَّرُّ بَيْنَهُمْ † *Evil became excited among them.* (TA.) — [And اضطرم is said of a stallion-camel meaning † *He was,* or *became, excited by lust,* or *by vehement lust:* see its part. n., below.]

10: see 4.

ضِرْمٌ and ضَرَمٌ, (Ḳ, TA,) the former of which is that commonly known, (TA,) *A species of tree* or *plant* (شَجَر) *of sweet odour,* (Ḳ, TA,) *found in the mountains of Eṭ-Ṭáïf and El-Yemen,* (TA,) *the fruit of which is like the acorn, and the flower like that of the* [*species of marjoram called*] سَعْتَر, (Ḳ, TA,) *fed upon by bees,* (TA,) *and the honey thereof has an excellent quality,* (Ḳ, TA,) *and is called* عَسَلُ الضِّرْمَةِ: (TA: [ضِرْمَةٌ being the n. un.:]) or it is *what is called in the ancient Greek language* أَسْطُوخُودُوس [app. a mode of writing στοιχάδος, gen. of στοιχὰς; for it is applied in the present day to *stæchas,* commonly called *French lavender*]. (Ḳ, TA.)

ضَرَمٌ: see ضَرَمَةٌ, in two places: — and ضِرَامٌ.

ضَرِمٌ [part. n. of 1: *Becoming kindled;* &c. — And hence, ‡ *Burning with hunger;* or] *vehemently hungry;* (Mṣb;) [or simply] *hungering,* or *hungry:* (Ṣ, Ḳ:) or [*burning with anger;* or] *violently angry.* (Mṣb.) — And † *A beast of prey in a state of excitement by lust.* (TA.) — And ‡ A horse *that runs vehemently* [or *ardently*]; (Ṣ, Ḳ, TA;) and so ضَرِمُ العَدْوِ. (TA.) — And † The *young one of the eagle.* (Ṣ, Ḳ.)

ضَرَمَةٌ *A palm-branch with its leaves upon it,* or *a* شِيحَة [i. e. *plant of one of the species of wormwood called* شِيح], *having fire* [*kindled*] *in its extremity:* (Ṣ, Ḳ:) pl. [or rather coll. gen. n.] ▼ضَرَمٌ. (Ṣ.) [Hence,] one says, مَا بِهَا نَافِخُ ضَرَمَةٍ, [in the CḲ ضَرْمَةٍ, and in my MS. copy of the Ḳ ضِرْمَةٍ, both of which are wrong, *There is not in it* (namely, the house, الدَّار,) *a blower of a* ضَرَمَة,] meaning, ‡ *anyone.* (Ṣ, Ḳ, TA.) — Also *A live coal.* (Ḳ.) — And *Fire,* (Ḳ, TA,) itself, as some say; (TA;) or so ▼ضَرَمٌ, (Ḥam p. 77, and Ḥar p. 27,) sometimes. (Ḥam ibid.)

ضِرَامٌ [is like the inf. n. ضَرَمٌ used as a simple subst., signifying] *A kindling,* or *burning up, burning brightly* or *fiercely, blazing,* or *flaming,* of fire, (Ṣ, A, TA,) in [the species of high, coarse grass called] حَلْفَاء, and the like thereof: (Ṣ, TA:) [and] the *blazing,* or *flaming,* of the [plant called] عَرْفَج [q. v.]. (Mgh.) — [See also a phrase mentioned voce ضِرَاس.] — Also (Ṣ) *Fragments,* or *broken pieces, of firewood,* (Ṣ, Ḳ,) *in which fire quickly kindles,* or *burns up, burns brightly* or *fiercely, blazes,* or *flames:* (Ṣ:) or *such as is weak and soft* (Ḳ, TA) *thereof:* (TA:) *such as has* [i. e. *leaves*] *no live coals:* (Ḳ, TA:) pl. of ▼ضَرَمٌ; which is expl. in the A as meaning *slender firewood;* (TA;) or which means *firewood,* and *what is thrown into fire* [*as fuel*]: (Ḥar p. 27:) or ضِرَامٌ signifies *firewood that has kindled,* or *burned up,* &c.: as also ▼ضِرَامَةٌ. (Ḳ.)

ضَرِيمٌ i. q. حَرِيقٌ, (Ṣ, A, TA,) [as meaning] *Burnt with,* or *in, fire:* (KL:) in the Ḳ, the word expl. as signifying حَرِيقٌ is said to be like حَيْدَرٍ, i. e. ▼ضَيْرَمٌ. (TA.) — And † *Burning in the bowels.* (TA.)

ضَيْرَمٌ The *gum of a certain tree.* (Ḳ.)

ضِرَامَةٌ: see ضِرَامٌ, last explanation. — Also The *terebinth-tree.* (Ḳ.)

ضَيْرَمٌ: see ضَرِيمٌ.

مُضْطَرِمٌ † A stallion [camel] *excited by lust,* or *by vehement lust.* (TA.)

ضرى and ضرو

1. ضَرِىَ بِهِ, (Ṣ, M, Mṣb, Ḳ,) aor. ـَ, (Ṣ, Mṣb, Ḳ,) inf. n. ضَرَاوَةٌ (Ṣ, M, Mṣb, Ḳ) and ضَرًا (M, Mṣb, Ḳ) and ضَرْىٌ and ضَرَآءٌ, (Ḳ, TA, [the last in the CḲ written ضِرَاءٌ,]) *He was,* or *became, attached, addicted,* or *devoted, to it;* (Ṣ, M, Ḳ, TA;) and (TA) *he habituated,* or *accustomed, himself to it,* (M,* Mṣb, Ḳ,* TA,) *so that he could hardly,* or *in nowise, withhold himself from it;* (TA;) and *emboldened himself to do it* or *undertake it* or *the like:* and *he kept,* or *clave, to it;* and *became attached, addicted,* or *devoted, to it; like the animal of prey to the chase.* (Mṣb.) [And ضَرِيَهُ occurs in the M, in art. موس, in explanation of تَمَوَّسَ بِهِ, app. for ضَرِىَ بِهِ, in the same sense.] It is said in a trad., إِنَّ لِلْإِسْلَامِ ضَرَاوَةً i. e. *Verily there is a habituating and an attachment of oneself to El-Islám;* meaning, one cannot withhold himself from it. (TA.) And in a saying, (Ṣ,) or trad., (M, TA,) of 'Omar, إِيَّاكُمْ وَهٰذِهِ المَجَازِرَ فَإِنَّ لَهَا ضَرَاوَةً كَضَرَاوَةِ الخَمْرِ (Ṣ, M, TA) i. e. [*Avoid ye these places where cattle are slaughtered and where their flesh is sold, for*] *there is a habituating of oneself to them, and a yearning towards them, like the habituating of oneself to wine;* for he who habituates himself to flesh-meat hardly, or in nowise, withholds himself from it, and becomes extravagant in his expenditure. (TA. [See also مُجْزِرٌ.]) And one says of a dog, ضَرِىَ بِالصَّيْدِ, (Ṣ, M, Mgh, Ḳ,) [in Ḥar p. 579 فِى الصَّيْدِ, which I do not find elsewhere,] aor. ـَ, (Ṣ,) inf. n. ضَرَاوَةٌ, (Aṣ, Ṣ, Mgh,) or ضَرًى and ضَرَآءٌ and ضِرَآءٌ, (M, Ḳ,) the last on the authority of AZ, (M,) *He became habituated,* or *accustomed, to the chase.* (Ṣ, Mgh, TA.) And ضَرِيَتِ الجَرَّةُ بِالخَلِّ [*The jar became seasoned with vinegar*] and بِالنَّبِيذِ [*with must* or *the like*]. (TA.) And ضَرِىَ النَّبِيذُ *The* نبيذ *became strong* [by remaining several days in the jar or skin]. (TA.) — ضَرَا, (Ṣ, Ḳ,) aor. ـُ, inf. n. ضَرْوٌ, (Ṣ,) or ضُرُوٌّ, (Ḳ,) said of a vein, *It shed blood:* (Ṣ, Ḳ:) or, accord. to the T, *it quivered, and gushed with blood* or *made a sound by reason of the blood coming forth:* Z says that the form of the verb is altered because of the alteration of the meaning. (TA.) And ضَرِىَ, (M, Ḳ,) aor. ـَ, (Ḳ,) [likewise] said of a vein, (M,) signifies *It flowed,* (M, Ḳ, TA,) and *ran* [*with blood*]; on the authority of IAạr. (TA.) And ضَرَا, aor. ـِ, said of a wound, *It ceased not to flow* [*with blood*]. (IAth, TA.) — And ضَرَا, inf. n. ضرو [whether ضَرْوٌ or ضُرُوٌّ is not shown], said of a man, *He hid,* or *concealed, himself.* (IḲṭṭ, TA. [See also 10.])

2. ضَرَّاهُ بِهِ, (M, Mṣb, Ḳ,) inf. n. تَضْرِيَةٌ; (Ḳ;) and ▼اضراهُ; (Mṣb, Ḳ;) *He caused him to become attached, addicted,* or *devoted, to it;* (M, Ḳ, TA;) *he habituated,* or *accustomed, him to it,* (M,* Mṣb, Ḳ,* TA,) [*so that he could hardly,* or *in nowise, withhold himself from it;* (see 1, first sentence;)] and *emboldened him to do it* or *undertake it* or *the like.* (Mṣb.) And ضَرَّى الكَلْبَ بِالصَّيْدِ, (Ṣ,* Mgh,) inf. n. as above; (Ṣ, Mgh;) and ▼اضراهُ بِهِ, (Ṣ, Mgh, TA,*) inf. n. إِضْرَآءٌ; (Mgh;) *He habituated,* or *accustomed, the dog to the chase;* (Ṣ, Mgh, TA;) and *incited him,* or *caused him to become attached* or *addicted, thereto.* (Ṣ.)

4: see the next preceding paragraph in two places.

10. اِسْتَضْرَيْتُ لِلصَّيْدِ *I deluded,* or *circumvented, the object,* or *objects, of the chase, at unawares.* (Ṣ. [See also 1, last meaning.])

ضَرْوٌ: see the next paragraph, in three places.

ضِرْوٌ *A dog,* (M,) or *young dog,* (Ṣ, Ḳ,) *such as is termed* ضَارٍ [i. e. *habituated,* or *accustomed, to the chase*]; (Ṣ, M, Ḳ;) as also ▼ضِرِىٌّ: (Ḳ, TA: [in the CḲ, كَالضُّرَى is erroneously put for كَالضَّرِىِّ:]) the latter word is like غَنِىٌّ: (TA:) the fem. of the former is with ة: and the pl. [of pauc.] أَضْرٍ [originally أَضْرُوٌ] and [of mult.] ضِرَآءٌ. (Ṣ, M.) — And *A taint of* جُذَام [or *elephantiasis*]: (M, Ḳ:) occurring in a trad. in which it is said of Aboo-Bekr, أَكَلَ مَعَ رَجُلٍ

به ضَرْوٌ مِنْ جُذَامٍ [*He ate with a man in whom was a taint of elephantiasis*]: it is from [the inf. n.] الضَّرَاوَةُ; as though the disease became attached, or habituated, to the person: (M, TA:) mentioned by Hr in the "Ghareebeyn:" (M:) or, as some relate it, the word is with the fet-ḥ, [i. e. ↓ضَرْوٌ,] and is from ضَرَا said of a wound, the meaning being *in whom was a wound having an incessant flowing.* (TA.) — Also, and ↓ضِرْوٌ, *A species of tree, of sweet odour, with* [*the wood of*] *which the teeth are rubbed and cleansed, and the leaves of which are put into perfume;* (M, TA;) *i. q.* مَحْلَبٌ [q. v.]; so says Lth: (TA:) AḤn says, *the places of its growth are mostly in El-Yemen;* (M, TA;) and some say that the ضرو is the بُطْم [or *terebinth-tree,* or the *fruit thereof*]: (M:) AḤn says also, *it is of the trees of the mountains, and is like the great oak,* (M, TA,*) *having clusters* [*of berries*] *like those of the oak, but its berries are larger; its leaves are cooked, and, when thoroughly cooked, are cleared away, and the water thereof is returned to the fire, and coagulates,* (M, TA,) *becoming like* قُبَيْطَآء [q. v.], (M,) *and is used medicinally as a remedy for roughness of the chest and for pain of the fauces:* (M, TA:) or the *gum of a certain tree called the* كَمْكَام [i. e. the *cancamum-tree*], *brought from El-Yemen:* (Ṣ:) or this is a mistake, for it is the *tree so called, not its gum:* (Ḳ:) [but] it is said in the T, on the authority of AḤn, that كمكام signifies the bark (قِرْف) of the tree called ضرو: and some say that it is the resin (عِلْك) of the ضرو: and in the Moḥeeṭ of Ibn-'Abbád it is said that كمكام signifies the bark (قرف, or, as some say, لِحَآء,) of the tree called ضرو, and is an aromatic perfume: (TA:) and (Ḳ, TA) IAạr says, (TA,) the ضرو is the حَبَّة خَضْرَآء [or *fruit of the terebinth-tree*], (Ḳ, TA,) *which is also sometimes used for rubbing and cleansing the teeth: when a girl rubs and cleanses her teeth with a stick of the tree called* ضرو, *the saliva with which the stick is moistened from her mouth is like honey:* (TA:) and the word is also pronounced ↓ضَرْوٌ. (Ḳ.)

ضَرَآءٌ *A level tract of land in which are beasts of prey and a few trees:* (M, Ḳ:) or *a piece of land, or ground, that conceals one:* (AA, TA:) and *trees, &c., that conceal one:* (M:) or *a thicket; or tangled,* or *luxuriant,* or *abundant and dense, trees; in a valley.* (Ṣ, Ḳ.) One says, تَوَارَى الصَّيْدُ مِنِّى فِى ضَرَآءِ الوَادِى [*The game hid itself from me in the tangled,* or *luxuriant,* or *abundant and dense, trees of the valley*]. (Ṣ.) And فُلَانٌ يَمْشِى الضَّرَآءَ, with fet-ḥ, meaning *Such a one goes along lurking among the trees that conceal him.* (Ṣ.) And هُوَ يَدِبُّ لَهُ الضَّرَآءَ وَيَمْشِى لَهُ الخَمَرَ [*He creeps to him in the thicket, and walks,* or *goes along, to him in the covert of trees*]: said of a man when he deludes, or circumvents, his companion: (Ṣ:) but accord. to IAạr, ضراء here means *a low,* or *depressed, place.* (Meyd.) And فُلَانٌ لَا يُدَبُّ لَهُ الضَّرَآءَ [app. meaning *The thicket will not be crept through to such a one:* but mentioned after the last of the explanations here following]. (M.) [See also ضَرَّآء, in art. ضر.] — [It is said that] it signifies also The *hiding* or *concealing, oneself:* (AA, Ḳ, TA:) [or] the *walking,* or *going along, in that which conceals one from him whom one beguiles,* or *circumvents.* (M.)

ضُرَاةٌ, a pl. epithet, [of which the sing. is probably ↓ضَرِىٌّ,] *Courageous:* hence, in a trad., إِنَّ فِينَا ضُرَاةَ ٱللّٰهِ [*Verily among us are the champions of God*]. (TA.)

ضَرِىٌّ: see ضِرْوٌ, first sentence. — Applied to a vein, (Ṣ, M, Ḳ, TA,) ‡ *Flowing;* as also ↓ضَارٍ: (M:) or *flowing much;* (TA;) *of which the blood hardly,* or *in nowise, stops;* (Ṣ, Ḳ, TA;) as though it were habituated to the flowing. (TA.) — See also ضُرَاةٌ.

ضَارٍ *Attached, addicted,* or *devoted,* to a thing; (TA;) *habituated,* or *accustomed,* thereto, (Mṣb, TA,) *so as hardly,* or *in nowise, to withhold himself* therefrom; (TA;) and *emboldening himself* to do it or undertake it or the like: and *keeping,* or *cleaving,* thereto; *being attached, addicted,* or *devoted,* to it; *like the animal of prey* to the chase. (Mṣb.) [Hence,] كَلْبٌ ضَارٍ, (Ṣ, Mgh,) or كَلْبٌ ضَارٍ بِالصَّيْدِ, (M, Ḳ,) *A dog habituated,* or *accustomed, to the chase:* (Ṣ, Mgh, TA:) and كَلْبَةٌ ضَارِيَةٌ. (Ṣ. [See also ضِرْوٌ, first sentence.]) [كَلْبٌ ضَارٍ بِالصَّيْدِ] is also expl. in the TA by the words إِذَا تَطَعَّمَ بِلَحْمِهِ, app. meaning *A dog having his appetite excited by tasting the flesh of the game.*] ضَوَارٍ [is pl. of ضَارٍ applied to an irrational animal, and as such] signifies [*Animals accustomed to prey; rapacious,* or *ravenous, beasts;* and particularly] *lions.* (TA.) And المَوَاشِى الضَّارِيَةُ *The cattle that are in the habit of pasturing upon peoples' seed-produce.* (Nh, TA.) And بَيْتٌ ضَارٍ بِاللَّحْمِ *A house,* or *tent, in which flesh-meat is habitually found so much that its odour remains in it.* (TA.) And سِقَآءٌ ضَارٍ بِاللَّبَنِ, thus correctly, as in the M, but in [some of] the copies of the Ḳ بِالسَّمْنِ, (TA,) *A skin in which milk is long kept so that its flavour becomes good.* (M, TA.) And جَرَّةٌ ضَارِيَةٌ بِالخَلِّ and بِالنَّبِيذِ [*A jar become seasoned with vinegar and with must or the like*]. (M, TA.) الإِنَآءُ الضَّارِى, occurring in a trad. of 'Alee, is said to mean *The jar that runs* [or *leaks*]; and the drinking from it is forbidden because it renders the drinking troublesome: thus expl. by IAạr: but it is also expl. as meaning *the wine-jar that has become seasoned with wine* (ضَرِىَ بِالخَمْرِ); so that when نَبِيذ is put into it, it becomes intoxicating. (TA.) And عِرْقٌ ضَارٍ means *A vein shedding blood:* (Ṣ, Ḳ, TA:) [or *quivering, and gushing with blood* or *making a sound by reason of the blood coming forth:* (see the verb:)] or *flowing,* or *running:* (TA: see ضَرِىٌّ:) or *accustomed to be opened, and therefore when the time for it is come and it is opened, emitting its blood more quickly.* (TA.)

ضع

1. ضَعٌّ, (Ṣ, O, Ḳ,) an inf. n. of which the verb is ضَعَّ, aor. ـُ, (TḲ,) The *breaking,* or *training,* (Ṣ,) or *training well,* (IAạr, O, Ḳ,) a he-camel, (IAạr, Ṣ, O, Ḳ,) and a she-camel, not previously trained: (IAạr, O, Ḳ:) or the *saying* to a camel ↓ضَعْ *in order that he may become well trained.* (Th, Ṣ, O, Ḳ.)

R. Q. 1. ضَعْضَعَهُ, (inf. n. ضَعْضَعَةٌ, TḲ,) *He threw it down,* or *pulled it down,* [or *rased it,*] *to the ground;* (Ṣ, O, Ḳ;) namely, a building. (Ṣ, O.) — And ضَعْضَعَهُ الدَّهْرُ *Time,* or *fortune, lowered, humbled,* or *abased him;* (Ṣ, O;) and so ↓تَضَعْضَعَ بِهِ الدَّهْرُ. (TA.) [See also ضَعْضَعَةٌ below.]

R. Q. 2. تَضَعْضَعَتْ أَرْكَانُهُ, referring to a building, *i. q.* ٱتَّضَعَتْ, (Ṣ,) i. e. [*Its angles,* or *corners,* or *its sides,*] *sank down;* and *became in a state of ruin.* (PṢ.) — And تضعضع said of a man, (Ṣ, O,) *He was,* or *became, lowly, humble, submissive,* or *abased;* (Ṣ, O, Ḳ;) [or *he lowered, humbled,* or *abased, himself;*] لِآخَرَ [*to another*], (Ṣ,) or لِغَنِىٍّ [*to a rich person*]. (O.) Hence, (Ṣ,) Aboo-Dhu-eyb says,

• وَتَجَلُّدِى لِلشَّامِتِينَ أُرِيهِمُ •
• أَنِّى لِرَيْبِ الدَّهْرِ لَا أَتَضَعْضَعُ •

[*And my constraining myself to behave with hardiness to those who rejoice at my misfortune: I show them that I will not humble myself to the evil accidents of time*]. (Ṣ,* O.) — And *He became poor:* (O, Ḳ:) as though from ضَعْ: (O:) and تصعصع is a dial. var. thereof, on the authority of Aboo-Sa'eed. (TA.) — And *He became weak, and light in his body, by reason of disease,* or *of grief.* (TA.) — And تضعضع مَالُهُ *His property became little.* (TA.) — See also R. Q. 1.

ضَعْ: see the first paragraph above.

ضَعْضَعٌ: see ضَعْضَاعٌ.

ضَعْضَعَةٌ inf. n. of ضَعْضَعَهُ [q. v.]. (TḲ.) — And [as though inf. n. of ضُعْضِعَ] *Lowliness, humility,* or *submissiveness:* (TA, and Ḥam p. 369:) [as used in the present day, *a state of depression; languor; weakness;* and *poverty:*] and *hardship,* or *adversity.* (TA.)

ضَعْضَاعٌ *Weak:* applied in this sense to anything. (Ṣ, O, Ḳ.) — And A man *without judgment,* (Ṣ, O, Ḳ,) *and without prudence,* or *precaution,* or *discretion;* (O, Ḳ;) and ↓ضَعْضَعٌ signifies the same, (Ṣ, O, Ḳ,) being a contraction of the former word. (Ṣ, O.)

مُتَضَعْضِعٌ [the part. n. of R. Q. 2, q. v.,] is used by the Arabs as meaning A *poor* man. (O.)

ضعف

1. ضَعُفَ, (Ṣ, O, Mṣb, Ḳ,) and ضَعَفَ, (O, Mṣb,

Ḳ,) the latter on the authority of Yoo, (O,) or of Lḥ, (L,) aor. of each ـُ, (Mṣb, Ḳ,) inf. n. ضُعْفٌ and ضَعْفٌ (Ṣ,* O,* Mṣb, Ḳ) [and app. ضَعَفٌ (q.v. infrà) or this is a simple subst.] and ضَعَافَةٌ and ضَعَافِيَةٌ, (Ḳ,) all of which are inf. ns. of the former verb, (TA,) or the first, which is of the dial. of Ḳureysh, is of the former verb, and the second, which is of the dial. of Temeem, is of the latter verb, (Mṣb,) *He,* or *it, was,* or *became, weak, feeble, faint, frail, infirm,* or *unsound;* ضُعْفٌ and ضَعْفٌ being the *contr. of* قُوَّةٌ, (Ṣ, O, Mṣb, Ḳ,) and *of* صِحَّةٌ; (Mṣb;) and both of them may be used alike, in every relation; or, accord. to the people of El-Baṣrah, both are so used; so says Az; (TA;) but some say that the former is used in relation to the body, and the latter in relation to the judgment or opinion. (O, Mṣb, Ḳ: but this is omitted in my copy of the TA.) — ضَعُفَ عَنِ الشَّىْءِ means *He lacked strength,* or *power,* or *ability, to do,* or *accomplish,* or *to bear, the thing;* [*he was weak so as to be disabled,* or *incapacitated, from doing,* or *accomplishing,* or *from bearing, the thing;*] syn. عَجَزَ عَنْهُ, (Mṣb in art. عجز,) or عَجَزَ عَنِ ٱحْتِمَالِهِ. (Mṣb in the present art.) — [See also ضَعْفٌ below.] ═ ضَعَفَ also signifies *It* (a thing) *exceeded;* syn. زَادَ. (L, TA.) — And you say, ضَعَفْتُ القَوْمَ, (Lth, O, Ḳ,*) aor. ـَ, (O,) or ـِ, (Ḳ, TA,) inf. n. ضَعْفٌ; (O;) [and app. ضَعَفْتُ عَلَيْهِمْ, like as you say زِدْتُ عَلَيْهِمْ;] *I exceeded the people,* or *party, in number, so that I and my companions had double,* or *several-fold, the number that they had.* (Lth, O, Ḳ.*) — See also 3.

2. ضعّفهُ, inf. n. تَضْعِيفٌ: see 4: and see also المُضَعَّفُ. — Also *He reckoned,* or *esteemed, him* ضَعِيف [i. e. *weak,* &c.]; (O, Ḳ;) and so ▼استضعفهُ, (Ṣ, O, Mṣb, Ḳ,) and ▼تضعّفهُ: (O, Ḳ:) or ▼استضعفهُ signifies *he found him to be so;* (TA;) or *he asserted him to be* (جَعَلَهُ) *so;* (Mṣb;) or, as also ▼تضعّفهُ, *he* [*esteemed him to be so, and therefore*] *behaved proudly, haughtily,* or *insolently, towards him, in respect of worldly things, because of* [*his*] *poverty, and meanness of condition.* (IAth, TA.) غَلَبَنِى أَهْلُ الكُوفَةِ أَسْتَعْمِلُ عَلَيْهِمُ المُؤْمِنَ فَيُضَعَّفُ وَأَسْتَعْمِلُ عَلَيْهِمُ القَوِىَّ فَيُفَجَّرُ [*The people of El-Koofeh have overcome me: I employ as governor over them the believer, and he is esteemed weak; and I employ as governor over them the strong, and he is charged with unrighteousness:*] is a saying mentioned in a trad. of 'Omar. (TA.) — And *He attributed,* or *ascribed,* (O, Ḳ,) *to him,* i. e. a man, (O,) or ‡ *to it,* i. e. a tradition, [&c.,] ضَعْف [meaning *weakness,* app., in the case of a man, *of judgment,* and in the case of a tradition &c., *of authority*]. (O, Ḳ, TA.) ═ And *He doubled it,* or *made it double, covering one part of it with another part.* (TA.) — See also the next paragraph, in two places.

3. ضاعفهُ, (Ṣ, O, Ḳ,) inf. n. مُضَاعَفَةٌ; (Ṣ, Mṣb;) and ▼ضعّفهُ, (Ṣ, Ḳ,) inf. n. تَضْعِيفٌ; (Ṣ, O, Mṣb;) and ▼اضعفهُ, (Ṣ, O, Ḳ,) inf. n. إِضْعَافٌ; (Ṣ, Mṣb;) all signify the same; (Ṣ, Ḳ;) i. e. *He doubled it,* or *made it double,* or *two-fold;* (O, Ḳ;) [and *trebled it,* or *made it treble,* or *three-fold;* and *redoubled it,* or *made it several-fold,* or *many-fold;* i. e. *multiplied it;* for] Kh says, التَّضْعِيفُ signifies *the adding to* a thing *so as to make* it *double,* or *two-fold;* or *more* [i. e. *treble,* or *three-fold;* and *several-fold,* or *many-fold*]; (Ṣ, O, Mṣb;) and so الإِضْعَافُ, and المُضَاعَفَةُ; (Ṣ, Mṣb;) and ▼ضَعَفَهُ, without teshdeed, signifies the same as ضاعفهُ. (Ḥam p. 257.) The saying, in the Ḳur [xxxiii. 30], يُضَاعَفْ لَهَا العَذَابُ ضِعْفَيْنِ, (Mgh, O, Ḳ,) in which AA read ▼يُضَعَّفْ, (TA,) accord. to AO, (Mgh, O,) means, *The punishment shall be made to her three punishments;* (Mgh, O, Ḳ;) for, he says, she is to be punished once; and when the punishment is doubled two-fold, [or is repeated twice,] the one becomes three: (TA:) he adds, (O,) and the tropical meaning of يُضَاعَفُ (مَجَازُ يُضَاعَفُ) [for which مَجَازُ يُضَاعِفُ is erroneously put in the CḲ]) is two things' being added to a thing so that it becomes three: (O, Ḳ:) but Az disapproves this, saying that it is peculiar to the tropical and the common conventional speech, whereas the skilled grammarians state the meaning to be, *she shall be punished with twice the like of the punishment of another;* (Mgh;) [so that it may be rendered *the punishment shall be doubled to her,* made *two-fold;* and in like manner] Ibn-'Arafeh explains it as meaning *she shall have two shares of punishment.* (O.) فَيُضَاعِفُهُ لَهُ أَضْعَافًا كَثِيرَةً [*And He will multiply it to him many-fold,* or, as some read, فَيُضَاعَفُهُ, *that He may multiply it,*] is another phrase occurring in the Ḳur [ii. 246]. (O, TA.) And one says, أَضْعَفْتُ ▼ الثَّوَابَ لِلْقَوْمِ [*I doubled,* or *multiplied, the recompense to the people,* or *party*]. (Mṣb.) And أُضْعِفَ ▼ القَوْمُ *The people,* or *party, had a doubling,* or *multiplying,* [of their recompense, &c.,] *made to them;* (Mṣb;) [and so, app., أُضْعِفُوا; (see مُضْعِفٌ;)] *i. q.* ضُوعِفَ لَهُمْ. (Ṣ, O, Ḳ.)

4. اضعفهُ *He,* (God, Mṣb, or another, Ṣ,) or *it,* (disease, TA,) *rendered him* ضَعِيف [i. e. *weak,* &c.]; (Ṣ, O, Mṣb, Ḳ;) as also ▼ ضعّفهُ. (L, TA.) ═ And أَضْعَفَ, said of a man, *He became one whose beast was weak.* (Ṣ, O, Ḳ.) ═ See also 3, first sentence, and last two sentences.

5: see 2, in two places. ═ [تضعّف app. signifies also *He manifested weakness:* see تضوّر.]

6. تضاعف signifies صَارَ ضِعْفَ مَا كَانَ [i. e. *It became double,* or *two-fold;* and *treble,* or *three-fold;* and *several-fold,* or *many-fold*]. (O, Ḳ.)

10: see 2, in two places.

ضَعْفٌ an inf. n. of 1, like ▼ ضُعْفٌ, (Ṣ,* O,* Mṣb, Ḳ,) [both, when used as simple substs., signifying *Weakness, feebleness,* &c.,] but some say that the former is in the judgment or opinion, and the latter in the body; (O, Mṣb, Ḳ;) and ▼ ضَعَفٌ signifies the same, (IAṭr, Ḳ, TA,) and is in the body and also in the judgment or opinion and the intellect. (TA.) — ضَعْفُ التَّأْلِيفِ [*Weakness of construction, in language,*] is *such a construction of the members of a sentence as is contrary to the* [*generally-approved*] *rules of syntax;* as when a pronoun is introduced before its noun with respect to the actual order of the words and the order of the sense [in a case in which the pronoun is affixed to the agent in a verbal proposition]; for instance, in the phrase, ضَرَبَ غُلَامُهُ زَيْدًا ["His," i. e. Zeyd's, "young man beat Zeyd"]. (KT.) When the pronoun is affixed to the objective complement, as in خَافَ رَبَّهُ عُمَرُ ["'Omar feared his Lord"] such introduction of it is common: (I'Aḳ p. 128:) and it is [universally] allowable when the pronoun is of the kind called ضَمِيرُ الشَّأْنِ, as in إِنَّهُ زَيْدٌ قَائِمٌ; or ضَمِيرُ نِعْمَ, or ضَمِيرُ رُبَّ, as in رُبَّهُ رَجُلًا لَقِيتُهُ, as in نِعْمَهُ رَجُلًا زَيْدٌ. (Kull p. 56.) — [In the CḲ, a signification belonging to ضُعْف is assigned to ضَعْف.]

ضُعْفٌ: see ضَعْفٌ. — مِنْ ضُعْفٍ in the Ḳur xxx. 53 means *Of sperm.* (O, Ḳ, TA.) AA, reciting before the Prophet, said مِنْ ضَعْفٍ; and was told by the latter to say مِن ضُعْفٍ, [i. e.] with ḍamm. (TA.)

ضِعْفُ الشَّىْءِ signifies *The like of the thing,* (AO, Zj, Ṣ, O, Mṣb, Ḳ, TA,) *that doubles it* (يُضْعِفُهُ); (Zj, TA;) and ضِعْفَاهُ, *twice the like of it;* (AO, Ṣ, O, Mṣb, Ḳ;) and أَضْعَافُهُ, *the likes of it:* (Ṣ, Mṣb:) الضِّعْفُ in the [proper] language of the Arabs means *the like:* this is the original signification: (Az, Mṣb:) and (Ḳ, TA, but in CḲ "or,") then, by a later [and conventional] usage, (Az, Mṣb,) *the like and more, the addition being unlimited:* (Az, Mṣb, Ḳ:) one says, هٰذَا ضِعْفُ هٰذَا i. e. *This is the like of this:* and هٰذَانِ ضِعْفَاهُ i. e. *These two are twice the like of it:* and it is allowable in the language of the Arabs to say, هٰذَا ضِعْفُهُ meaning *This is twice the like* [i. e. *the double*] *of it,* and *thrice the like* [i. e. *the treble*] *of it,* [and *more,*] because the ضِعْف is an unlimited addition: (Az, Mṣb: [and the like is said in the O, on the authority of Az:]) and one says, لَكَ ضِعْفُهُ meaning *Thou shalt have twice the like of it,* (Zj, O, Ḳ,) using the sing. form, though the dual form is better, (Zj, O,) and meaning also *thrice the like of it,* and *more without limit:* (Ḳ:) and الإِثْنَانِ ضِعْفُ الوَاحِدِ [i. e. الاثنان *is the double of* الواحد]: (M and Ḳ in art. ثنى:) and if one say in his will, أَعْطُوهُ ضِعْفَ نَصِيبِ وَلَدِى, twice the like of the share of his child is given to him; and if he say ضِعْفَيْهِ, thrice the like thereof is given to him; so that if the share of the son be a hundred, he [the legatee] is given two hundred in the former case, and three hundred in the latter case; for the will is made to accord with the common conventional language, not with the niceties of the [proper] language: (Az, Mṣb: [and the like is said, but less fully, in the Mgh:]) the pl. is أَضْعَافٌ only. (TA.) إِذًا لَأَذَقْنَاكَ ضِعْفَ الحَيَاةِ وَضِعْفَ المَمَاتِ, in the Ḳur [xvii. 77], means ضِعْفَ عَذَابِ, (Ṣ,) or ضِعْفَ العَذَابِ حَيًّا وَمَيِّتًا

الحَيَاةِ وَضِعْفَ عَذَابِ المَمَاتِ, (O, Jel,) i. e. [*In that case we would assuredly have made thee to taste*] *the like* [or, as some explain it, *the double*] *of the punishment* of others *in the present world and* [*the like* or *the double thereof*] *in the world to come:* (Jel:) [Ṣgh adds, app. on the authority of Ibn-'Arafeh,] the meaning is, the punishment of others should be made two-fold, or more, (يُضَاعَف,) to thee, because thou art a prophet. (O.) In the saying, فَأُولٰئِكَ لَهُمْ جَزَآءُ الضِّعْفِ بِمَا عَمِلُوا, in the Ḳur [xxxiv. 36], by الضِّعْف is meant الأَضْعَاف [i. e. *For these shall be the recompense of the likes for what they have done*]; and it is most properly held to denote ten of the likes thereof, because of the saying in the Ḳur [vi. 161], "Whoso doth that which is good, for him shall be ten of the likes thereof." (O.) In the saying, فَآتِهِمْ عَذَابًا ضِعْفًا, in the Ḳur [vii. 36], by ضِعْفًا is meant مُضَاعَفًا [i. e. *Therefore do Thou recompense them with a doubled*, or *a double, punishment*]: عَذَابٌ ضِعْفٌ meaning *a punishment as though doubled, one part of it upon another.* (TA.) — أَضْعَافُ الكِتَابِ means ‡ *The interspaces of the lines,* (Ṣ, O, Ḳ, TA,) or *of the margin,* (Ṣ, O,) or and *of the margins,* (Ḳ, TA,) *of the writing,* or *book:* (Ṣ, O, Ḳ, TA:) so in the saying, وَقَّعَ فُلَانٌ فِى أَضْعَافِ كِتَابِهِ ‡ [*Such a one made an entry of a note* or *postil* or *the like,* or *entries of notes &c., in the interspaces of the lines, &c., of his writing,* or *book*]: (Ṣ, O, TA:) and ▼ تَضَاعِيفُ signifies the same as أَضْعَافُهُ. الكِتَابِ (TA.) — And أَضْعَافُ الجَسَدِ † *The limbs, members,* or *organs,* (أَعْضَآءُ,) *of the body:* (O, Ḳ:) or *the bones thereof:* (AA, Ḳ:) or *the bones thereof having flesh upon them:* (TA:) sing. ضِعْفٌ. (Ḳ.) Hence the saying of Ru-beh,

* وَٱللّٰهُ بَيْنَ القَلْبِ وَالأَضْعَافِ *

† [*And God is between the heart and the limbs,* &c.]. (TA.) And it is said of Yoonus, [the prophet Jonah,] كَانَ فِى أَضْعَافِ الحُوتِ ‡ [*He was amid the members of the fish*]. (TA.)

ضَعَفٌ: see ضَعْفٌ. — Also *Garments,* or *pieces of cloth, made double* (▼ مُضَعَّفَةٌ). (Ibn-'Abbád, O, Ḳ.)

ضَعْفَةٌ *Weakness of heart,* and *littleness of intelligence.* (TA.)

ضَعَفَةٌ *A party,* or *company,* or *small company,* (شِرْذِمَةٌ,) *of the Arabs.* (TA.) — Also a pl. of ضَعِيفٌ [q. v.]. (Ṣ &c.)

ضَعْفَانُ: see ضَعِيفٌ.

ضَعُوفٌ: see the next paragraph, in two places.

ضَعِيفٌ (Ṣ, O, Mṣb, Ḳ) and [in an intensive sense] ▼ ضَعُوفٌ (Ibn-Buzurj, O, Ḳ) and ▼ ضَعْفَانُ (Ḳ) *Weak, feeble, faint, frail, infirm,* or *unsound:* (Ṣ,* O,* Mṣb, Ḳ:*) pl. (of the first, Ṣ, O, Mṣb) ضِعَافٌ and ضُعَفَآءُ and ضَعَفَةٌ, (Ṣ, O, Mṣb, Ḳ,) which last is [said to be] the only instance of its kind except خَبَثَةٌ pl. of خَبِيثٌ [q. v.], (TA,) and ضَعْفَى, like جَرْحَى pl. of جَرِيحٌ: (Mṣb:) fem. ▼ ضَعُوفٌ (Ibn-Burzurj, O, Ḳ) and ضَعِيفَةٌ; pl., applied to women, ضَعِيفَاتٌ (Ḳ) and ضَعَائِفُ and ضِعَافٌ. (TA.) وَخُلِقَ الإِنْسَانُ ضَعِيفًا (in the Ḳur [iv. 32], O) means [*For man was created weak,* or] *subject to be inclined by his desire.* (O, L, Ḳ.) And الضَّعِيفَانِ [*The two weak ones*] means *the woman and the slave:* hence the trad., اِتَّقُوا اللّٰهَ فِى الضَّعِيفَيْنِ [*Fear ye God in respect of the woman and the slave*]. (TA.) — In the dial. of Ḥimyer, *Blind:* and [it is said that] thus it signifies in the phrase لَنَرَاكَ فِينَا ضَعِيفًا [*Verily we see thee to be, among us, blind*], (O, Ḳ,) in the Ḳur [xi. 93]: (O:) but Esh-Shiháb rejects this, in the 'Ináyeh. (TA.) — [As a conventional term] in lexicology, applied to a word, [*Of weak authority;*] *inferior to what is termed* فَصِيحٌ, *but superior to what is termed* مُنْكَرٌ. (Mz, 10th نوع.) — Applied to verse, or poetry, [*Weak;*] *unsound,* or *infirm;* syn. عَلِيلٌ: thus used by Kh. (TA.) — The saying of a man who had found a thing dropped on the ground (وَجَدَ لُقَطَةً), فَعَرَّفْتُهَا ضَعِيفًا, means *And I made it known in a suppressed,* or *low,* [or *weak,*] *voice.* (Mgh in art. نفر.)

ضَاعِفٌ A cow *having a young one in her belly;* (IDrd, O;) as though she were made double thereby: (TA:) but IDrd says that this is not of high authority. (O.)

تَضْعِيفٌ inf. n. of 2. (Ṣ &c.) — تَضَاعِيفُ الشَّىْءِ means *The doubles,* or *trebles,* or *multiples, of the thing;* (مَا ضُعِّفَ مِنْهُ;) in this sense, تضاعيف has no sing., like تَبَاشِيرُ &c. (TA.) — تَضَاعِيفُ الكِتَابِ: see ضِعْفٌ, near the end. — As expl. by Lth, (O,) التَّضْعِيفُ signifies حُمْلَانُ الكِيمِيَآءِ [i. e. *What is used as an alloy in chemistry* or *alchymy*]. (O, Ḳ.)

مُضْعِفٌ A man *whose beast,* (Ṣ, Ḳ, and Mgh in art. كفأ,) or *whose camel,* (O,) *is weak,* (Ṣ, Mgh, O, Ḳ,) or *untractable.* (O.) Hence the saying of 'Omar, المُضْعِفُ أَمِيرٌ عَلَى أَصْحَابِهِ [*He whose beast is weak,* or *untractable, is ruler over his companions*]; (O, Ḳ;) i. e. in journeying; (O;) because they go his pace. (O, Ḳ.) And the saying, in a trad., يَرُدُّ مُشِدُّهُمْ عَلَى مُضْعِفِهِمْ [expl. in art. شد]. (Mgh in art. كفأ.) — فَأُولٰئِكَ هُمُ المُضْعِفُونَ, in the Ḳur [xxx. 38], means *These are they who shall have their recompense doubled,* or *multiplied:* (Az, Bḍ, TA:) or *those who double,* or *multiply, their recompense* (Bḍ, Jel) and *their possessions,* (Bḍ,) by the blessing of their almsgiving: (Bḍ, Jel:*) but some read المُضْعَفُونَ. (Bḍ.) — المُضْعِفُ also signifies مَنْ فَشَتْ ضَيْعَتُهُ وَكَثُرَتْ [*He whose property has become wide-spread and abundant*]. (Ibn-'Abbád, O, L, Ḳ.)

أَرْضٌ مُضَعَّفَةٌ *Land upon which a weak rain has fallen:* (Ibn-'Abbád, O, Ḳ:) and [in like manner] ▼ مَضْعُوفٌ signifies a place *upon which has fallen only a little,* or *weak, rain.* (O in art. رك.) — المُضَعَّفُ *One of the arrows used in the game of* المَيْسِر, *that has no share,* or *portion, allotted to it;* as though it were disabled from having a share (كَأَنَّهُ ضُعِّفَ ▼ عَنْ أَنْ يَكُونَ لَهُ نَصِيبٌ): (TA:) *the second of the arrows termed* الغُفْل, *that have no notches, and to which is assigned* [*no portion and*] *no fine:* these being added only to give additional weight to the collection of arrows from fear of occasioning suspicion [of foul play]. (Lḥ, M.) [See السَّفِيحُ.] — See also ضَعَفٌ.

مُضَعَّفٌ A man *having manifold good deeds.* (TA.)

مَضْعُوفٌ, applied to a thing, (Ṣ,) or to a man, (O,) *Rendered* ضَعِيف [i. e. *weak,* &c.]: (AA, Ṣ, O, Ḳ:) by rule it should be مُضْعَفٌ. (O, Ḳ.) A man *weak in intellect:* (IAạr, TA:) or *weak-hearted and having little intellect.* (TA.) — See also أَرْضٌ مُضَعَّفَةٌ, above.

دِرْعٌ مُضَاعَفَةٌ *A coat of mail composed of double rings.* (Ṣ, O, Ḳ.) — مُضَاعَفٌ as a conventional term used by those who treat of inflection, *Having a* [*radical*] *letter doubled.* (TA.)

أَهْلُ الجَنَّةِ كُلُّ ضَعِيفٍ مُتَضَعَّفٍ [*The meet for Paradise is every weak person who is esteemed weak*]. (Ḳ,* TA. [In the CḲ, erroneously, مُتَضَعِّف: and in the Ḳ, اهل الجنّة is omitted.])

ضعو

1. ضَعَا *He hid,* or *concealed, himself.* (ISd, Ḳ.)

ضَعَةٌ, (Ṣ, Ḳ,) originally ضَعْوٌ, or ضَعَوٌ, (accord. to different copies of the Ṣ,) the ة being a substitute [for the و], because of the form of its pl. [and of the rel. n.]; or, as some say, the ة is a substitute for an initial و, and it is mentioned also in art. وضع; (Ṣ;) *A species of tree,* (Ṣ, Ḳ, TA,) *in the desert:* or it is [*a plant*] *like the* [*species of panic grass called*] ثُمَام: (TA:) accord. to Az, *a species of* ثُمَام: (TA in art. ثمر:) or *another plant:* and some pronounce it ضِعَةٌ; but this is in الحَسَب [or grounds of pretension to respect &c.], and does not belong to the present art.: (TA:) the pl. is ضَعَوَاتٌ. (Ṣ, TA.) [Golius says, on the authority of Meyd, that it also signifies The reed of which writing-reeds are made.]

ضَعَوِيٌّ *Of,* or *relating to, the* ضَعَة *above mentioned.* (Ṣ, Ḳ.)

ضغث

1. ضَغَثَ الشَّىْءَ, aor. ـَ, inf. n. ضَغْثٌ, *He collected together the thing:* whence ضِغْثٌ signifying "a handful of herbs &c." (Mṣb.) See also 2. — And [hence,] ضَغَثَ الحَدِيثَ, (A, Ḳ,) aor. as above, (Ḳ,) and so the inf. n., (Ṣ,) ‡ *He confused,*

or *confounded,* [or *related in a confused manner,*] *the tradition,* or *story,* or *the like.* (Ṣ, A, Ḳ) —— And ضَغَثَ الثَّوْبَ ‡ *He washed the garment,* or *piece of cloth, without cleansing it,* (O, Ḳ, TA,) *so that it remained in a dubious state.* (TA.) ═ ضَغَثَ السَّنَامَ, aor. as above, (Ḳ,) and so the inf. n., (Ṣ,) *He felt the camel's hump in order to know whether it were fat or not:* (Ṣ, Ḳ:) and ضَغَثَهَا *he felt her* [i. e. a she-camel] *for that purpose.* (TA.) ═ ضَغَثَ, accord. to the Ḳ, [and the O, as on the authority of Fr,] is also said of a وَرَل, meaning *It uttered a cry:* but this is correctly with ب [i. e. ضَغَبَ]. (TA.)

2. ضغّث النَّبَاتَ *He made the plants,* or *herbage, what are termed* أَضْغَاث [pl. of ضِغْثٌ]. (A, TA.) —— [Hence,] ضغّث رَأْسَهُ † *He poured water upon his head, and then divided the hair with his fingers into separate handfuls, in order that the water might reach to the skin.* (L, TA.) [But see what follows.] It is said in a trad. of 'Áisheh, كَانَتْ تُضَغِّثُ رَأْسَهَا, (TA,) or ▼ تَضْغَثُ رأسها, (so in the JM,) meaning *She used to rub about the hair of her head with her hand, in washing, as though mixing it together, in order that the water with which she washed might enter into it.* (TA.)

4. اضغث الرُّؤْيَا, said of a dreamer, ‡ *He related the dream confusedly.* (A, TA.)

8. اضطغث ضِغْثًا *He collected a handful of herbage, fresh and dry mixed together.* (Ḳ.)

ضَغْثٌ *The state of* a thing's *being confused, one part with another.* (TA.)

ضِغْثٌ *A handful of herbs,* (AḤn, Ṣ, A, Mgh, Mṣb, Ḳ,) *mixed together,* (Ṣ, A, Mṣb, Ḳ,) *fresh and dry:* (Ṣ, Mṣb, Ḳ:) or *a handful of twigs of trees* or *shrubs;* (Mgh,* Mṣb;) or *of fruit-stalks of the racemes of a palm-tree:* (Mgh, Mṣb:) originally, *a number of twigs all having one root* or *stem:* and afterwards applied to *what is collected together:* (Mṣb:) or *a thing that one collects together, such as a bundle of* [*the species of trefoil called*] رَطْبَة; and *of what has a stem, and grows tall:* (Fr, TA:) or *whatever is collected together, and grasped with the hand:* (AHeyth, TA:) or *a bundle of herbs mixed together;* or *of firewood:* pl. أَضْغَاثٌ. (TA.) In the Ḳur xxxviii. 43, it is said to mean *A bundle of rushes* (أَسَل, so in the Mgh and the O, in my copy of the Mṣb اثل [which I think a mistranscription, on account of what follows]), *a hundred in number,* (O, Mṣb,) *consisting of slender stalks without leaves,* (Mgh, Mṣb,) *whereof mats are made.* (Mṣb.) See also a prov. cited and expl. voce إِبَالَةٌ. Hence, in a trad., ضِغْثَانِ مِنْ نَارٍ, meaning ‡ *Two bundles of lighted firewood.* (TA.) And, in another trad., مِنْهُمُ الآخِذُ الضِّغْثَ, meaning † *Among them is he who obtains somewhat of worldly goods.* (TA.) —— Also † *What is confused, and without truth,* or *reality,* [of dreams, and] of news, or tidings, and of an affair. (Sh, TA.) أَضْغَاثُ أَحْلَامٍ, [occurring in the Ḳur xii. 44 and xxi. 5,] of which the sing. is ضِغْثُ حُلْمٍ, (Mṣb,) means ‡ *Complications of dreams;* (A;) or *medleys of dreams, falsely resembling true dreams:* (O, Mṣb:) or *a dream of which the interpretation will not prove true, because of its confusedness:* (ISh, Ṣ, Ḳ:) or *a false dream;* the pl. form being used to give emphasis to the meaning of unreality, or because the phrase comprehends various things: (Bḍ in xii. 44:) or أَضْغَاثُ الرُّؤْيَا means *the terrors,* or *frightful things, of the dream.* (Mujáhid, O, TA.) One says also, أَتَانَا بِأَضْغَاثٍ مِنَ الأَخْبَارِ, meaning ‡ *He brought us* [*various*] *sorts of news,* or *tidings.* (TA.) ضِغْثٌ means also † *A deed that is of a mixed kind, not pure,* or *not sincere.* (IAth and O, from a trad.) And كَلَامٌ ضِغْثٌ † *Speech in which is no good:* pl. أَضْغَاثٌ. (TA.)

ضَغُوثٌ, applied to a she-camel, *i. q.* ضَبُوثٌ; (Ṣ, Ḳ;) i. e. *Of which one doubts whether she be fat, and which one therefore feels with his hand;* (Ṣ;) or *of which one feels the hump, in order to know whether she be fat or not:* pl. ضُغُثٌ. (TA.) And A camel's hump *of which one doubts whether it be fat or not.* (Kr, TA.)

ضَغِيثَةٌ *A confused company* of men. (O.)

ضَاغِثٌ One *who hides himself in a thicket* or *the like, and frightens boys by a sound reiterated in his fauces:* (Ṣ:) the author of the Ḳ, following Ṣgh in the TṢ and O, and Az in the T, says that this is a mistake, and that the word is correctly written with ب [i. e. ضَاغِبٌ]; but IF and IM and others write it as in the Ṣ. (TA.)

تَضْغِيثٌ *Rain that moistens the earth and the herbage.* (Ḳ.)

ضغط

ضَغَطَهُ, (Ṣ, Mṣb, Ḳ,) aor. ـَ, (Ṣ, Mṣb,) inf. n. ضَغْطٌ, (Ṣ, Mgh, Mṣb,) *He pressed him; pushed him;* (Ṣ, Mṣb, Ḳ;) *squeezed him;* (Mgh,* Mṣb, Ḳ;) against (إِلَى, Ṣ, Mṣb, Ḳ, [and عَلَى,]) a thing, (Ḳ,) or a wall, (Ṣ, Mṣb,) and the like, (Ṣ,) and the ground: (TA:) *he straitened him: he overcame, subdued,* or *overpowered, him;* or *he constrained him.* (TA.) It is said in a trad., لَتُضْغَطُنَّ عَلَى بَابِ الجَنَّةِ *Ye shall assuredly be pressed,* or *pushed, against the gate of Paradise.* (TA.) You say of a tight boot, ضَغَطَ رِجْلَهُ [*It compressed,* or *pinched, his foot*]. (Ḳ in art. حزق.) And you say also, ضَغَطَ عَلَيْهِ, and ▼ اِضْتَغَطَ, (Lḥ, TA,) which latter, by rule, should be اِضْطَغَطَ, (TA,) † *He treated him with hardness, severity,* or *rigour, with respect to a debt or the like.* (Lḥ, TA.)

3. ضَاغَطُوا, (Ḳ,) inf. n. ضِغَاطٌ (IDrd, T, O, TA) and مُضَاغَطَةٌ; (IDrd, O;) and ▼ تَضَاغَطُوا; (IDrd, O, Ḳ;) *They pressed, pushed, crowded,* or *straitened, one another;* syns. زَاحَمُوا and ازدحموا. (IDrd, O, Ḳ.) You say, تَضَاغَطَ ▼ النَّاسُ فِي الاِزْدِحَامِ [*The people pressed,* or *pushed, one another in crowding together*]; and ضِغَاطٌ is like تَضَاغُطٌ. (T, TA.)

6: see 3, in two places.

7. انضغط [as quasi-pass. of 1, app. signifies *He was,* or *became, pressed, pushed,* or *squeezed:* and, accord. to a version of the Bible, as mentioned by Golius, in Num. xx. (or xxii.) 25, *he pressed,* or *squeezed, himself,* against (إِلَى) a wall: and also,] † *he* (a man) *was,* or *became, overcome, subdued,* or *overpowered;* or *constrained;* syn. اِنْقَهَرَ. (TA.)

8: see 1, last sentence.

ضَغْطَةٌ The *pressure* of the grave; (Ṣ, Mṣb, Ḳ;) because it straitens the dead: (Mṣb:) its *straitening.* (Mgh.) —— It is also expl. by En-Naḍr [ISh] as signifying مجاهرة [app. a mistake for مُجَاهَدَة, as meaning † The *exertion of one's utmost power, ability,* or *endeavour, in contending with another:* and in this sense it should perhaps be written ▼ ضُغْطَة]. (TA.) —— See also ضُغْطَةٌ, in two places.

ضُغْطَةٌ ‡ *Straitness; difficulty; distress; affliction;* (Ṣ, Mṣb, Ḳ;) as also ▼ ضَغْطَةٌ. (TA.) You say, اَللّٰهُمَّ ارْفَعْ عَنَّا هٰذِهِ الضُّغْطَةَ [*O God, withdraw, put away,* or *remove, from us this straitness,* &c.]. (Ṣ.) —— † *Force, constraint, compulsion;* (Mgh;) as also ▼ ضَغْطَةٌ: (TA: [in which one of the syns. is written قَبْر, evidently a mistake for قَهْر, one of the syns. of the former word in the Mgh:]) *constraint,* or *compulsion, against the will of the object thereof.* (Ṣ,* Ḳ.) You say, أَخَذْتُ فُلَانًا ضُغْطَةً † *I treated such a one with hardness, severity,* or *rigour, to constrain him,* or *compel him, to do the thing against his will.* (Ṣ.) And hence the trad. of Shureyḥ, كَانَ لَا يُجِيزُ الضُّغْطَةَ † *He used not to allow the constraint,* or *compulsion, of one's debtor, and the treating him with hardness, severity,* or *rigour:* or *one's saying, I will not give thee unless thou abate somewhat of my debt to thee:* or *one's having money owed to him by another, who disacknowledges it, and compounding with him for part of what is owed to him, then finding the voucher, and exacting from him the whole of the property after the compromise.* (Mgh.) —— See also ضَغْطَةٌ.

ضَغِيطٌ A well *having by the side of it another well,* (Aṣ, Ṣ, O, Ḳ,) *and one of them becomes foul with black mud,* (Aṣ, Ṣ, O,) or *and one of them becomes choked up, and foul with black mud,* (Ḳ,) *so that its water becomes stinking, and it flows into the water of the sweet well, and corrupts it, so that no one drinks of it:* (Aṣ, Ṣ, O, Ḳ:) or a well *that is dug by the side of another well, in consequence of which its water becomes little in quantity:* or a well *dug between two wells that have become choked up.* (O.) ═ And A man *weak in judgment,* (Ḳ, TA,) *that will not be roused to action with the people:* (TA:) pl. ضَغْطَى, (Ḳ, TA,) [like مَرْضَى &c.,] because it is as though it were [significant of suffering from] a disease. (TA.)

ضَاغِطٌ *A slitting in the arm-pit of a camel,* (Ṣ, Ḳ,) *and abundance of flesh* [*in that part, pressing against the side*]: (Ṣ:) and *i. q.* ضَبٌّ: (Ṣ, Ḳ) or *a thing like a bag:* (TA:) *a tumour in the armpit of a camel, like a bag, straitening him:* (Meyd: see مُعْرِكٌ:) or *skin collected together:* or the *base of the callous protuberance upon the breast of a camel pressing against the place of the arm-pit, and marking,* or *scarring, and excoriating, it.* (TA.) Accord. to IDrd, بَعِيرٌ بِهِ ضَاغِطٌ means *A camel whose arm-pit comes in contact with his side so as to mark it,* or *scar it.* (TA.) ═ ‡ *A watcher, keeper,* or *guardian; a confidential superintendent;* (Ṣ, Ḳ;) over a person; so called because he straitens him; (Ṣ;) or over a thing. (Ḳ.) You say, أَرْسَلَهُ ضَاغِطًا عَلَى فُلَانٍ ‡ *He sent him as a watcher,* &c., *over such a one.* (Ṣ, TA.) And hence what is said in the trad. of Mo'ádh, (Ṣ, L,) when his wife asked him, on his return from collecting the poor-rates in El-Yemen, where was the present which he had brought for his wife, and he answered, (L,) كَانَ عَلَىَّ ضَاغِطٌ [*There was over me a watcher*], (Ṣ,) or كَانَ مَعِى ضَاغِطٌ [*There was with me a watcher*], meaning God, who knows the secrets of men; or he meant, by ضاغط, the trust committed to him by God, which he had taken upon himself; but his wife imagined that there was with him a watcher who straitened him, and prevented his taking to please her. (L.)

ضغن

1. ضَغِنَ, (AZ, Ṣ, Mṣb, Ḳ,) aor. ـَ, (Mṣb, Ḳ,) inf. n. ضَغَنٌ (AZ, Ṣ, Mṣb, TA) and ضِغْنٌ, (AZ, TA,) or the latter is a simple subst., (Mṣb,) *He,* (Ṣ, Ḳ,) or *it,* i. e. one's bosom, (Mṣb,) *was,* or *became, affected with rancour, malevolence, malice,* or *spite;* (Ṣ, Mṣb, Ḳ;) or, said of a man, *his bosom was,* or *became, affected therewith;* (AZ, TA;) عَلَيْهِ *against him.* (Ṣ.) [See also ضِغْنٌ below.] — And, (IAạr, Ṣ, Ḳ,) aor. and inf. ns. as above, (TA,) *He inclined,* (IAạr, Ṣ, Ḳ, TA,) إِلَيْهِ *towards him,* (IAạr, TA,) and عَلَيْهِ *against him,* (TA,) and إِلَى الدُّنْيَا [*towards the present world,* or *worldly things*]. (Ṣ, Ḳ.) And ضَغِنَتِ القَنَاةُ, inf. n. ضَغَنٌ, ‡ *The spear-shaft was,* or *became, crooked.* (TA.) — Also, (Ḳ, TA,) aor. and inf. ns. as above, (TA,) *He was,* or *became, affected with desire,* or *with yearning* or *longing of the soul.* (Ḳ, TA.)

6. تَضَاغُنٌ The *conceiving,* or *being affected with, mutual rancour, malevolence, malice,* or *spite.* (KL, and Ḥar p. 43.) You say, تضاغنوا and ↓ اضطغنوا *They had,* or *held, in the heart, feelings of mutual rancour, malevolence, malice,* or *spite.* (Ṣ, Ḳ.)

8: see what next precedes. — One says also, اضطغن عَلَى فُلَانٍ ضَغِينَةً *He conceived,* or *concealed,* [*in his heart,*] *rancour, malevolence, malice,* or *spite, against such a one.* (TA.) — And اضطغنهُ *He took it* (i. e. a thing, and weapon, Ṣ) *beneath his* حِضْن [or *the part between his armpit and flank,* &c.]: (Ṣ, Ḳ:) and *he carried him* (i. e. a child) *in that part,* or *in his bosom.* (TA.) — الاِضْطِغَانُ is also *syn. with* الاِشْتِمَالُ, which is *The putting* [*a portion of*] *the garment beneath* [*and within*] *the right arm,* [app. *from behind,*] *and the other end beneath the left arm, and drawing it* [i. e. *the garment*] *together with the left hand.* (TA. [But see اِشْتَمَلَ.])

ضِغْنٌ [said by some to be an inf. n.: (see 1:)] *Rancour, malevolence, malice,* or *spite;* (Ṣ, Mṣb, Ḳ;) as also ↓ ضَغِينَةٌ: (Ṣ, Ḳ:) or both signify *vehement rancour* &c.; and *enmity;* and *violent hatred:* (TA:) the pl. of the former is أَضْغَانٌ; (MA, Mṣb;) and that of ↓ the latter is ضَغَائِنُ, (MA,) and ↓ ضَغِينٌ may be a pl. of ضَغِينَةٌ, [or rather a coll. gen. n.,] or the ة may be elided by poetic license; or these two may be dial. vars., like حَقٌّ and حُقَّةٌ [accord. to some], and بَيَاضَةٌ and بَيَاضٌ. (TA.) One says, when he has sought to gain a person's good will, or approval, سَلَلْتُ ضِغْنَ فُلَانٍ and ↓ ضَغِينَتَهُ [*I drew forth the rancour,* &c., *of such a one*]. (TA.) And a woman who hates her husband is said to be ذَاتُ ضِغْنٍ عَلَى زَوْجِهَا [*One who has a feeling of rancour,* &c., *against her husband*]. (TA.) — And *Difficulty of disposition* in a beast: so in the phrase ذَاتُ ضِغْنٍ [A beast (دَابَّةٌ) *having a difficult disposition*]. (TA.) See also the phrase ذَاتُ شَغْبٍ وَضِغْنٍ, applied to a she-ass, in art. شغب. — And *Inclination.* (Ṣ, Ḳ.) One says, ضِغْنِى إِلَى فُلَانٍ *My inclination is towards such a one.* (Ṣ.) — And *Desire;* or *yearning* or *longing of the soul.* (Ḳ, TA.) One says نَاقَةٌ ذَاتُ ضِغْنٍ meaning *A she-camel yearning towards,* or *longing for, her home,* or *accustomed place,* (Ṣ, TA,) *and her mates.* (Ṣ. [See a verse cited voce رِفَاقٌ.]) And sometimes ضِغْنٌ is thus used, metaphorically, in relation to women. (TA.) ═ Also *A side;* or *a region, quarter,* or *tract;* syn. نَاحِيَةٌ. (Ḳ.) — And The إِبْط [i. e. *foot, bottom,* or *lowest part,*] *of a mountain:* thus correctly, as in the "Nawádir:" in the copies of the Ḳ, الجَمَل is erroneously put for الجَبَل. (TA.)

ضَغِنٌ *Affected with rancour, malevolence, malice,* or *spite;* as also ↓ ضَاغِنٌ. (Mṣb.) — And قَنَاةٌ ضَغِنَةٌ ‡ *A crooked spear-shaft.* (Ṣ, Ḳ, TA.) — See also ضَاغِنٌ.

ضَغُونٌ A horse, and a mare, *that runs like him who reverts from the state in which he was,* or *from the course that he was following.* (AO, TA. [See also ضَاغِنٌ.])

ضَغِينٌ: see ضِغْنٌ.

ضَغِينَةٌ: see ضِغْنٌ, in three places.

الضَّغِينِىُّ *The lion:* (Ḳ, TA:) as though a rel. n. from الضَّغِينَةُ: because he is very rancorous, malevolent, malicious, or spiteful. (TA.)

ضَاغِنٌ: see ضَغِنٌ. — Also A horse *that will not exert his power of running unless beaten;* (Ṣ, Ḳ, TA;) and so ↓ ضَغِنٌ. (Ṣ,* TA. [See also ضَغُونٌ.])

مُضَاغِنٌ One *who treats,* or *regards, his brother with rancour, malevolence, malice,* or *spite,* or *with enmity, being so regarded,* or *treated, by him;* as also ↓ مُضْطَغِنٌ. (TA.)

مُضْطَغِنٌ: see what next precedes.

ضف

1. ضَفَّهُ, (O, Ḳ,) aor. ـُ, inf. n. ضَفٌّ, (O,) *He collected it together.* (O, Ḳ.) — And ضَفَّ, [app. for ضَفَّ أَصَابِعَهُ,] (Fr, O, Ḳ,) aor. and inf. n. as above, (Fr, O,) said of one warming himself, *He closed his fingers together and put them near to the fire.* (Fr, O, Ḳ.) — And ضَفَّ النَّاقَةَ, (Ṣ, O, Ḳ,) aor. and inf. n. as above, (TA,) *He milked the camel with the whole hand;* (Ṣ, O, Ḳ, TA;) because of the largeness of the dug; mentioned by Az, on the authority of Ks; (TA;) a dial. var. of ضَبَّهَا: (Ṣ, O:) or, accord. to Fr, the doing thus is termed الضَّفُّ; but الضَّبُّ signifies "the putting one's thumb upon the teat and then turning his fingers over the thumb and the teat together:" or, as is said on other authority, الضَّفُّ signifies *the clasping the two teats together with the hand when milking:* [but this is also said to be the meaning of الضَّبُّ:] or, as Lḥ says, *the grasping the teat with all one's fingers.* (TA.) ═ ضَفَّ القَوْمُ عَلَى الطَّعَامِ, or المَآءِ, [aor. app. ـُ or ـِ, or both,] inf. n. ضَفٌّ and ضَفَفٌ, [see the latter of these below,] *The people,* or *party, pushed, pressed, crowded,* or *thronged, together upon the food,* or *the water.* (TḲ.) [See also what next follows.]

6. تضافّوا عَلَيْهِ *They multiplied,* or *became numerous,* (Ṣ, O, Ḳ,) *and collected themselves together,* (O, Ḳ,) [*and,* accord. to an explanation of the part. n., by Lḥ, *pushed, pressed, crowded,* or *thronged, together,*] *upon it,* or *at it;* namely water, (Ṣ, O, Ḳ,) &c.; (O, Ḳ;) like تصافّوا. (TA.) — And تضافّوا signifies also, accord. to the O and Ḳ, خَفَّتْ أَحْوَالُهُمْ; but correctly, as in the "Nawádir" of AZ, أَمْوَالُهُمْ [i. e. *Their possessions became scanty*]. (TA.)

ضَفٌّ *Narrow,* or *strait, and hard:* so in the phrase رَجُلٌ ضَفُّ الحَالِ [*A man whose state,* or *condition, is narrow,* or *strait, and hard*]: (AZ, Ṣ, O, Ḳ:*) and one says also رجل ↓ ضَفَفُ الحَالِ, and قَوْمٌ ضَفَفُوا الحَالِ; but idghám is more proper. (Sb, TA.) ═ شَاةٌ ضَفَّةُ الشُّخْبِ *A ewe,* or *goat, whose stream of milk from the udder is wide.* (AA, O, L, Ḳ.)

ضُفٌّ *A little thing resembling the tick, of the colour of ashes and dust, the sting,* or *bite, of which causes the skin to break forth with the eruption termed* شَرًى [q. v.]: (Aboo-Málik, O, Ḳ:) pl. ضِفَفَةٌ, like قِرَدَةٌ. (Ḳ.)

ضَفَّةٌ A single act of pushing, pressing, crowding, or thronging, together upon water. (Ṣ, O, Ḳ. [See ضَفَفٌ.]) — دَخَلْتُ فِى ضَفَّةِ القَوْمِ and ضَفْضَفَتِهِمْ (O, Ḳ*) are phrases mentioned by Aṣ (O, TA) and Lth (TA) as meaning I entered among the company, or collective body, of the people, or party. (O, Ḳ.*) — And ضَفَّةٌ signifies also The first دُفْعَة [i. e. rush, or quantity that pours forth at once or that is poured forth at once], or دَفْعَة [i. e. single act of pouring], (accord. to different copies of the Ḳ,) of water. (Ḳ.) ═ See also the next paragraph, in five places.

ضِفَّةٌ (T, Ṣ, O, Mgh, Mṣb, Ḳ) and ضَفَّةٌ (T, O, Mgh, Mṣb, Ḳ) The side of a river (T, Ṣ, O, Mgh, Mṣb, Ḳ) and of a well: (Mṣb:) ضِفَّتَاهُ signifying its (a river's) two sides: (Ṣ:) and ضَفَّتَا الوَادِى, or الحَيْزُومِ, and ضِفَّتَاهُ, the two sides of the valley, or of the حيزوم [i. e. breast, or chest, &c.]: (IAṭr, Ḳ:) and ضَفَّةُ البَحْرِ [or ضِفَّتُهُ] the shore of the sea: (Ḳ:) and the dual of ضَفَّةٌ [or ضِفَّةٌ?] occurs in a saying of 'Alee metaphorically used as meaning † the two sides of the eyelids: (TA:) the pl. of ضِفَّةٌ is ضِفَفٌ, (Mṣb,) or ضِفَافٌ; (TA;) and that of ضَفَّةٌ is ضَفَّاتٌ. (Mṣb.)

ضَفَفٌ The pushing, pressing, crowding, or thronging, together, of people, at, or upon, water [to drink thereof or to water their beasts]. (Ṣ, O, Ḳ. [See also 1, last explanation.]) And Numerousness of the persons composing a family, or household: (Ṣ, O, Ḳ:) or, accord. to Lḥ, visitors and friends that come time after time; and one's household, or family: or, as some say, i. q. حَشَمٌ [i. e. one's dependents, &c.]. (TA.) And The taking of food with other people: (Ṣ, O, Ḳ:*) thus in a trad. in which it is said of the Prophet, مَا شَبِعَ مِنْ خُبْزٍ وَلَحْمٍ إِلَّا عَلَى ضَفَفٍ [He did not satiate himself with the eating of bread and flesh-meat except in a case of taking thereof with others], as expl. by a man of the desert in answer to a question put to him by Málik Ibn-Deenár: (Ṣ, O: but in the latter, لَمْ يَشْبَعْ:) or the case of the eaters' being too many for the food: (Th, O, Ḳ:) [or,] accord. to Kh, (Ṣ, O,) numerousness of the hands upon the food: (Ṣ, O, Mṣb:) [or,] accord. to Aṣ, the case of the property's being little, and the devourers thereof many. (Ṣ, O.) [See also حَفَفٌ.] Accord. to AZ, (Ṣ, O,) Straitness, and hardness, or hardship: (Ṣ, O, Mṣb:) accord. to Fr, (Ṣ, O,) want. (Ṣ, O, Mṣb, Ḳ.) [See two exs. voce حَفَفٌ.] Also Weakness. (Fr, O, Ḳ.) And Haste (Fr, Ṣ, O, Mṣb) in an affair: (Mṣb:) so in the saying, لَقِيتُهُ عَلَى ضَفَفٍ [I met him, or found him, in a state of haste]. (Fr, Ṣ, O.) And A quantity less than will fill the measure, and less than anything that is filled. (Sh, O, Ḳ.) And Food, or the eating, less than satiates. (TA.) ═ See also ضَفّ.

ضفاف [thus written without any syll. sign] The quality denoted by the epithet ضَفُوفٌ applied to a she-camel or a ewe or goat. (TA.)

ضَفُوفٌ Having much milk, not to be milked save with the whole hand; (O, Ḳ;*) applied to a camel, (O, Ḳ,) and to a ewe or goat: so in a verse cited voce صَوفٌ, as some relate it; but as others relate it, the word is صَفُوفٌ, with ص. (TA.) — And [hence, app.,] عَيْنٌ ضَفُوفٌ † A source abounding with water. (TA.)

هُوَ فُلَانٌ مِنْ لَفِيفِنَا وَضَفِيفِنَا, (O, TA,) in the Ḳ مِنْ ضَفِيفِنَا وَلَفِيفِنَا, but the former is the right order, (TA,) a saying mentioned by Aboo-Sa'eed, (O, TA,) means Such a one is of those whom we associate with us, and those whom we congregate with us, when events befall us. (O, Ḳ,* TA.)

ضَفَافَةٌ, (O, Ḳ,) without teshdeed, (O,) like سَحَابَةٌ, (Ḳ,) Devoid of intellect, or intelligence. (O, Ḳ.)

ضَفْضَفَةٌ: see ضَفَّةٌ.

مَآءٌ مَضْفُوفٌ A water that is thronged [so that it has become little in quantity]; (Ṣ, O, Ḳ;) like مَشْفُوهٌ; (Ṣ, O;) to which many men and cattle have come: (Lḥ, TA:) occurring in a verse cited voce مُدَارَةٌ, in art. دور: (Ṣ, O, TA:) in that verse, Aboo-'Amr Esh-Sheybánee, instead of المَضْفُوف, read المَظْفُوف; which means [the same, (Ḳ in art. ظف,) or] "occupied." (IB, TA.) — [Hence,] رَجُلٌ مَضْفُوفٌ ‡ A man exhausted of what he possessed [in consequence of much begging]; like مَثْمُودٌ: (Ṣ, O, TA:) [see also مَشْفُوهٌ:] some say مَضْفُوفٌ عَلَيْهِ. (TA.)

ضفدع

Q. 1. ضَفْدَعَ, said of water, It had in it ضَفَادِع [or frogs]. (O, Ḳ.) ═ And, said of a man, He shrank, or became contracted; syn. تَقَبَّضَ: or he voided his excrement, or ordure; or thin excrement; syn. سَلَحَ: or he emitted wind from the anus, with a sound. (TA.)

ضِفْدِعٌ (Ṣ, O, Mṣb, Ḳ) and ضِفْدَعٌ and ضُفْدَعٌ (Ḳ) and ضُفْدُعٌ, (Ṣ, O, Mṣb, Ḳ,) this last said by some, (Ṣ, O, Mṣb,) but most rare, or rejected, (Ḳ,) disallowed by Kh and a number of others, (Mṣb,) [for] accord. to Kh [and others] there are only four words of the measure فِعْلَلٌ in the language, which are دِرْهَمٌ and هِجْرَعٌ and هِبْلَعٌ and the proper name قِلْعَمٌ, (Ṣ, O,) [The frog; and app. also the water-toad;] a certain reptile (دَابَّة) of the rivers, (Ḳ, TA,) generated in the river, (TA,) the flesh of which, cooked with olive-oil, is [said to be] an antidote to the poison of venomous creatures, (Ḳ, TA,) when put upon the place of the sting, or bite: (TA:) and [a certain reptile] of the land, (Ḳ, TA,) [app. the land-toad,] that lives, or grows, in caverns and caves, (TA,) the fat of which is [said to be] wonderful for the extraction of teeth (Ḳ, TA) without fatigue, and of the skin of which, tanned, the skull-cap that renders invisible (طَاقِيَّةُ الإِخْفَآءِ) [a vulgar term]) is made, as is said by the performers of legerdemain; and the flesh of this species is said to be poisonous: (TA;) the fem., (Ṣ, O, Mṣb,) or the n. un., (Ḳ,) is with ة: and the pl. is ضَفَادِعُ (Ṣ, O, Mṣb, Ḳ) [and ضَفَادُ; in the Mṣb and Ḳ, ضَفَادِى; in the O, correctly, الضَّفَادِى is said to be a var. of الضَّفَادِعُ, like الثَّعَالِى and الأَرَانِى of الأَرَانِبُ and الثَّعَالِبُ]. — نَقَّتْ ضَفَادِعُ بَطْنِهِ [lit. The frogs of his belly croaked] means † he was, or became, hungry; (O, Ḳ;) like نَقَّتْ عَصَافِيرُ بَطْنِهِ. (O.) — الضِّفْدِعُ الأَوَّلُ is a name of † The bright star [α] on the mouth of Piscis Australis; (Ḳzw, Descr. of Aquarius;) also called فَمُ الحُوتِ: (Idem, Descr. of Piscis Australis:) and الضِّفْدِعُ الثَّانِى is the name of † The star on the southern fork of the tail of Cetus. (Idem.) — And الضِّفْدِعُ, (O, Ḳ,) thus only, (TA,) † A certain bone [or horny substance, which we, in like manner, call "the frog,"] in the interior of the horse's hoof, (O, Ḳ,) in the sole thereof. (O.) [See also نَسْرٌ.]

مُضَفْدِعَاتٌ Waters abounding with ضَفَادِع [or frogs]. (Ṣ, O.)

ضفر

1. ضَفَرَ, (A, Mṣb, Ḳ,) aor. ـِ, (Mṣb, Ḳ,) inf. n. ضَفْرٌ, (Ṣ, A, &c.,) He plaited, braided, or interwove, (Ṣ, A, Mgh, Ḳ,) hair, (Ṣ, Mgh, Ḳ,) &c., (Ṣ,) or the like, (TA,) or a [lock of hair, such as is called] ذُؤَابَة, and a [girth of thongs such as is called] نِسْع, (A,) in a wide form; (Ṣ, Mgh;) as also ضَفَّرَ, inf. n. تَضْفِيرٌ: (Ṣ, TA:) he made hair into ضَفَائِر, [pl. of ضَفِيرَة,] each ضَفِيرَة consisting of three or more distinct portions. (Mṣb.) — He twisted a rope or cord. (Ḳ.) — ضَفَرَتْ شَعَرَهَا, (Ṣ, TA,) aor. ـِ, (TA,) inf. n. as above, (Ḳ,) said of a woman, (Ṣ, TA,) She gathered together her hair. (Ḳ,* TA.) — And ضَفَرَ, from the same verb in the first of the senses expl. above, ‡ He made, or constructed, a [dam of the kind called] ضَفِيرَة. (IAṭr, TA.) — ضَفْرٌ also signifies † The building with stones without [the cement called] كِلْس and without clay. (Ḳ,* TA.) You say, ضَفَرَ الحِجَارَةَ حَوْلَ بَيْتِهِ † [He built the stones around his house, or tent, without mortar or clay]. (TA.) — ضَفَرَ البَعِيرَ العَلَفَ, (A,) inf. n. ضَفْرٌ, (Ḳ,) ‡ He put the fodder into the mouth of the camel, (A, Ḳ,*) against his will. (A.) And ضَفَرَ الفَرَسَ لِجَامَهُ, (A,) or ضَفَرَ الدَّابَّةَ, aor. ـِ, inf. n. ضَفْرٌ, (TA,) ‡ He put the bit into the mouth of the horse, (A,) or of the beast. (TA.) ═ Also ضَفَرَ, aor. ـِ, (Ṣ, Mṣb, Ḳ,) inf. n. ضَفْرٌ, (Ṣ, Mṣb,) He ran; syn. عَدَا and سَعَى: (Ṣ, Mṣb, Ḳ:) or he hastened, or went quickly: or he bounded, or sprang: (TA:) he leaped (Aṣ, Ḳ) in his running. (Aṣ, TA.)

2: see the preceding paragraph, first sentence.

3. ضافره He aided him. (A, Mṣb.) [See also 6.]

6. تضافروا They leagued together, and aided one another, (Ibn-Buzurj, Ṣ,* A,* Mṣb,* Ḳ,*) عَلَى الأَمْرِ to do the thing, (Ṣ, A,* Ḳ,) and عَلَى فُلَانٍ against such a one. (Ibn-Buzurj.)

7. انضفر الحَبْلَانِ The two ropes became twisted together. (Ṣ.)

ضَفْرٌ *A camel's girth, of plaited* [*goats'*] *hair;* (Ḳ,* TA;) as also ↑ ضِفَارٌ: (Ḳ:) the *girth of a camel's saddle:* (Ṣ:) *a wide girth of a camel's saddle;* as also ↑ ضَفِيرَةٌ: pl. [of mult.] (of the first, TA) ضُفُورٌ (Ḳ, TA) and [of pauc.] أَضْفَارٌ; (TA;) and (of the second, TA) ضُفُرٌ. (Ḳ, TA.) —— See also ضَفِيرَةٌ, in three places. —— Also † *A great quantity of sand that has become collected together:* or *a quantity of sand that has become accumulated, part upon part;* (Ḳ;) and (Ḳ) so ↑ ضَفِرَةٌ: (Ṣ, Ḳ:) pl. [of the former] ضُفُورٌ; (Ḳ;) and [coll. gen. n.] of the latter ↑ ضَفِرٌ: (Ṣ:) or *a long, broad,* حِقْف [generally expl. as meaning a *winding tract*] *of sand;* by some pronounced ↑ ضَفَرٌ: (Lth, TA:) [or] *a* حِقْف *of sand* is termed ↑ ضَفِرَةٌ. (Ṣ.)

ضَفَرٌ: see the last preceding sentence.

ضَفِرٌ and [its n. un.] ضَفِرَةٌ: see ضَفْرٌ. —— كِنَانَةٌ ضَفِرَةٌ [in the TA ضفيرة, evidently a mistranscription,] *i. q.* مُمْتَلِئَةٌ [i. e. *A full quiver*]. (Ṣ, O. [Freytag writes كِنَانَةُ ضَفِرَةٍ, and explains it as meaning "Gens Cinanah impleta est:" but in my copies of the Ṣ and in the O, it is كِنَانَةٌ.])

ضِفَارٌ: see ضَفْرٌ, first sentence.

ضَفِيرٌ *A rope of* [*goats'*] *hair,* (Mgh, Mṣb, TA,) *twisted:* of the measure فَعِيلٌ in the sense of the measure مَفْعُولٌ. (TA.) —— And † The *shore,* or *side,* of the sea or of a great river; (O, Ḳ,* TA;) as also ↑ ضَفِيرَةٌ. (TA.)

ضَفِيرَةٌ (Aṣ, Ṣ, M, A, Mgh, Mṣb, Ḳ) and ↑ ضَفْرٌ, (Ṣ, M, A, Mgh, Ḳ,) the latter an inf. n. used as a subst. [properly so termed], (Mgh,) *A single lock of hair:* (M, Mṣb, Ḳ:) and (Mṣb) *a* [*lock of hair such as is termed*] ذُؤَابَة, (Mgh, Mṣb,) or جَمِيرَة and غَدِيرَة, of a woman: (Aṣ, TA:) or *a plaited, braided,* or *interwoven,* ذؤابة: (A, TA:) or [*a plait of hair*] *consisting of three,* or *more, distinct portions:* (Mṣb:) or *i. q.* عَقِيصَةٌ [q. v.]: one says لَهَا ضَفِيرَتَانِ, and ↑ ضَفْرَانِ, meaning عَقِيصَتَانِ: (Yaạḳoob, Ṣ:) or the ضَفِيرَتَانِ pertain to a man, not to a woman; [though such is not the case accord. to modern usage;] and غَدَائِر, [pl. of غَدِيرَة,] to women; and these are مَضْفُورَة [i. e. plaited]: (AZ, TA:) the pl. of ضَفِيرَةٌ is ضَفَائِرُ (A, Mṣb) and ضُفُرٌ; (Mṣb;) and the pl. of ↑ ضَفْرٌ is ضُفُورٌ. (A.) —— See also ضَفْرٌ, in two places. —— ضَفِيرَةٌ also signifies ‡ *A dam,* (IAạr, Ṣ, A, Mgh, Mṣb,) *extending in an oblong form upon the ground, having in it wood and stones.* (IAạr, TA.) —— And † *A plain,* or *soft, tract of land, oblong, producing herbage* or *the like, extending* [*to the distance of the journey of*] *a day,* or *two days.* (TA.) —— See also ضَفِيرٌ.

الضَّافِرُ فِى الحَجِّ *He who twists,* or *plaits,* (يَعْقِصُ,) *his hair during the performance of the pilgrimage.* (TA.)

ضفو

1. ضَفَا, aor. يَضْفُو, (Ṣ, Mṣb,) inf. n. ضَفْوٌ (Ṣ, Mṣb, Ḳ) and ضُفُوٌّ, (Mṣb,) *It* (a thing, Ṣ, and a garment, Ṣ, Mṣb) *was,* or *became, complete, full, ample,* or *without deficiency.* (Ṣ, Mṣb, Ḳ.*) —— And *It was,* or *became, much in quantity;* (Ṣ, Ḳ,* TA;) said of property, or property consisting in cattle, (Ṣ, TA,) and of hair, and of wool. (TA.) [Hence,] one says, ضَفَتْ عَلَيْهِ النِّعْمَةُ, *i. q.* رَفَّتْ [i. e. *Wealth became abundantly bestowed upon him*]. (M in art. رف.) And ضَفَا العَيْشُ, meaning اِتَّسَعَ [i. e. *The means of subsistence became ample*]. (Mṣb.) —— And ضَفَا الحَوْضُ, (TA,) inf. n. ضَفْوٌ, (Ḳ, TA,) *The watering-trough overflowed* (Ḳ,* TA) *by reason of its fulness.* (TA.) == ضَفِىَ *He* (a man) *became poor:* mentioned by Az in art. ضيق. (TA.)

ضَفًا *A side:* and ضَفَوَاهُ *his,* or *its, two sides.* (Ḳ.) [ضَفَّةٌ and ضِفَّةٌ, also, have a similar meaning.]

ضَفْوٌ [an inf. n. of 1, q. v.: and as a simple subst.,] *Wealth,* or *prosperity,* and *ampleness* [*of circumstances*]. (TA.) [See also what next follows.]

ضَفْوَةُ العَيْشِ *An easy and a plentiful state,* or *condition, of life.* (Ḳ, TA.) One says, فُلَانٌ فِى ضَفْوَةٍ مِنْ عَيْشِهِ [*Such a one is in an easy and a plentiful state,* or *condition, in respect of his means of subsistence*]. (Ṣ.)

ثَوْبٌ ضَافٍ *A garment that is complete, full, ample,* or *without deficiency.* (Ṣ, Mṣb, Ḳ.*) And فَرَسٌ ضَافِى السَّبِيبِ *A horse full,* or *ample, in the* سبيب [or *hair of the forelock* or *of the mane* or *of the tail*]. (TA.) And رَجُلٌ ضَافِى الرَّأْسِ *A man having much hair of the head.* (Ṣ.) And دِيمَةٌ ضَافِيَةٌ *A lasting,* or *continuous,* or *continuous and still, rain, in consequence of which the land becomes abundant with herbage.* (TA.) And هُوَ ضَافِى الفَضْلِ ‡ [*He is abundant in excellence*]. (TA.)

ضل

1. ضَلَلْتُ, (Ṣ, Mgh,* O, Mṣb,* Ḳ,) third pers. ضَلَّ, (Mgh, Mṣb,) aor. ـِ, (Ṣ, Mgh, O, Mṣb, Ḳ,) inf. n. ضَلَالٌ and ضَلَالَةٌ; (Ṣ,* O,* Mṣb;) and ضَلِلْتُ, (Ṣ, Mgh,* O, Mṣb,* Ḳ,) third pers. as above; (Mgh;) the former of the dial. of Nejd, and the more chaste; the latter of the dial. of the people of El-'Áliyeh, (Ṣ, Mṣb, TA,) and of El-Ḥijáz, and Kr has mentioned ضَلِلْتُ for ضَلَلْتُ as heard from the tribe of Temeem; (TA;) *I erred, strayed,* or *went astray;* (Mgh, Mṣb;) *deviated from the right way* or *course,* or *from that which was right; missed,* or *lost, the right way;* or *lost my way;* ضَلَالٌ and ضَلَالَةٌ signifying the contr. of رَشَادٌ, (Ṣ, O, TA,) and of هُدًى. (Ḳ, TA.) [See ضَلَالٌ below.] Hence, in the Ḳur [xxxiv. 49], قُلْ إِنْ ضَلَلْتُ فَإِنَّمَا أَضِلُّ عَلَى نَفْسِى [*Say thou, If I err, I shall err only against myself,* i. e., to my own hurt]. (O, Mṣb. [See also x. 108 and xvii. 16 of the Ḳur.]) One says also, ضَلَّ ضَلَالُهُ [app. *His error became error indeed;* a phrase similar to جَدَّ جِدُّهُ, q. v.: or *his erring passed away;* see 4, latter part]. (TA.) And ضَلَّ عَنِ القَصْدِ *He deviated from the right way* or *course.* (TA.) And the verb is trans. as well as intrans.: you say, ضَلَّ الطَّرِيقَ, and ضَلَّ عَنْهُ, aor. ـِ and ـَ, (Mgh, Mṣb,) inf. ns. as above, meaning *He erred, strayed,* or *went astray, from the road,* or *way;* (Mṣb;) *he did not find the way to the road:* (Mgh, Mṣb:) and of anything stationary, if you miss the place thereof, you say ضَلَلْتُهُ and ضَلِلْتُهُ: (Az, Mṣb:) or you say, ضَلَلْتُ الطَّرِيقَ, (Ḳ,) or ضَلَلْتُ المَسْجِدَ, and الدَّارَ, (ISk, Ṣ, O,) [*I missed,* or *lost, the right way to the road,* or *the mosque,* and *the house,*] when you know not the place thereof: (ISk, Ṣ, O:) and in like manner, anything stationary, to which one does not find the way: (ISk, Ṣ, O, Ḳ:) and AA says the like: but that one says of a thing that falls from his hand, and a thing that quits its place, ↑ أَضْلَلْتُهُ, (IB, TA,) which means *I lost it, and knew not its place;* meaning, for instance, a horse, or she-camel, or the like: (Az, Mṣb:) [thus] one says, أَضْلَلْتُ بَعِيرِى [*I lost my camel, and knew not his place,*] (AA, ISk, Ṣ, IB, O) when his shank has been tied up to his arm and one does not find the way to him, and when he has been left loose and has gone away whither one knows not: (AA, IB, TA:) but Yoo differs from others respecting this case; for, accord. to him, one says, أَضَلَّ فُلَانٌ بَعِيرَهُ and also ضَلَّهُ, in the same sense; (O, TA;) and the like is said in the Ḳ: (TA:) and it is also said in the Bári' that when you seek an animal and miss its place and find not the way to it, it is regarded as in the category of stationary things, and therefore you say ضَلَلْتُهُ. (Mṣb.) —— ضَلَّ signifies also *He was,* or *became, confounded,* or *perplexed, and unable to see his right course.* (Ibn-Es-Seed, TA.) —— Also, aor. ـِ, (Ṣ, O, Ḳ) and ـَ, (Ḳ,) the pret. being like زَلَّ and مَلَّ, (TA,) inf. n. ضَلَالٌ, *It* (a thing, Ṣ, O, TA) *became lost;* [as though it went astray;] *it perished, came to nought,* or *passed away.* (Ṣ, O, Ḳ, TA.) Thus in the phrase ضَلَّ عَنِّى كَذَا *Such a thing became lost from me.* (Mgh.) One says to him from whom pieces of money have dropped, قَدْ ضَلَّتْ عَنْكَ [*They have become lost from thee*]. (TA.) And to him who has done a deed from which no profit has resulted, you say, قَدْ ضَلَّ سَعْيُكَ ‡ [*Thy labour has been lost*]: the like occurs in the Ḳur xviii. 104, meaning ضَاعَ. (TA, in two places.) —— And ‡ *He* (a man, TA) *died, and became dust and bones.* (Ḳ, TA.) In this sense the verb is used in the Ḳur xxxii. 9: but some there read, in the place of ضَلَلْنَا, صَلَلْنَا [q. v.], with ص: (TA:) or the verb in that instance has the meaning here next following. (Ṣ.) —— And † *He,* or *it,* (a man, Ṣ, TA, or a camel, Mṣb, and a thing, TA,) *was,* or *became, unperceived* or *imperceptible, unapparent, latent, hidden* or *concealed,* or *absent.* (Ṣ, Mṣb, Ḳ, TA.) Hence the phrase, ضَلَّ المَآءُ فِى اللَّبَنِ ‡ [*The water became unperceived,* or *concealed, in the milk*]. (TA.) One says of a road to which he has not been able to find the way, ضَلَّ عَنِّى

[*It has become hidden from me*]. (Ḳ, TA.) And hence also the saying of a man, as is related in a trad., (Ṣ, O, TA,) after his having charged his sons by saying to them, "When I die, burn ye me; and when I shall have become ashes, pound me; then scatter me in the water:" (O, TA:) لَعَلِّى أَضِلُّ ٱللّٰهَ (Ṣ, O, TA) i. e. † *May-be, I shall be unperceived by God*, or *concealed from Him:* (Ṣ:) or *may-be, I shall be hidden*, or *absent, from God's punishment:* (O, TA:) or, as El-'Otbee says, *may-be, I shall escape God, and my place will be hidden from Him.* (TA.) And ضَلَّ said of one forgetting means † *His memory became absent from him.* (O, Mṣb, TA.) أَنْ تَضِلَّ إِحْدَاهُمَا, or إِنْ تَضِلَّ, in the Ḳur [ii. 282], accord. to different readers, (TA,) in which instance أَنْ and إِنْ are syn., (Mughnee, [see أَنْ, in p. 106, cols. 1 and 2,]) means *If one of them twain* [referring to women] *be absent from her memory:* or *if the memory of one of them twain be absent from her:* [or *if one of them twain err in her memory:*] or, accord. to Zj, the meaning of the verb in this case is that which next follows. (TA.) — ضَلِلْتُ الشَّىْءَ also signifies † *I forgot the thing:* whence one says of a woman, ضَلَّتْ أَيَّامَ حَيْضِهَا † [*She forgot the days of her menstruation*]; and so أَضَلَّتْهَا ♦: (Mgh:) or ضُلَّ فُلَانًا † *He was made*, or *caused, to forget such a one.* (Ḳ. [In the CḲ, أَنْسِيَهُ is erroneously put for أُنْسِيَهُ.]) It is said that لَا يَضِلُّ رَبِّى, in the Ḳur xx. 54, means † *My Lord will not be unmindful:* or *nothing will escape Him.* (TA.) — And one says, ضَلَّنِى فُلَانٌ, (Mṣb, Ḳ,) or ضَلَّنِى فُلَانٌ فَلَمْ أَقْدِرْ عَلَيْهِ, (O,) meaning *Such a one went away from me*, (O, Mṣb, Ḳ,) *and I was unable to compass him* [or *to find him*]: so in the Bári'. (Mṣb.) — ضَلَّ, as a verb of wonder: see ضُلَّ.

2. ضَلَّلَهُ, (Ṣ, MA, O, Ḳ,) inf. n. تَضْلِيلٌ and تَضْلَالٌ, (Ḳ,) *He, or it, made*, or *caused, him to pursue a course that led to error*, or *deviation from the right way:* (Ḳ: [see also 4:]) *he, or it, led him astray; seduced him:* (MA:) [or] *he attributed*, or *imputed, to him error*, or *deviation from the right way.* (Ṣ, MA, O.) ضُلِّلَ سَعْيُهُمْ, a phrase used by a poet, means *Error, or deviation from the right way, was attributed to their labour;* because they did not reach their goal. (Ḥam p. 771.) — [Hence,] one says, ضَلِّلْ مَالَكَ *Send forth*, or *set free, thy cattle to pasture*, or *to pasture where they please, by themselves.* (O.) — See also the next paragraph.

4. اضلّهُ, inf. n. إِضْلَالٌ, *He, or it, made him*, or *caused him, to err, stray*, or *go astray; to deviate from the right way* or *course*, or *from that which was right; to miss*, or *lose, the right way;* or *to lose his way.* (Az, TA.) [See also 2, first sentence.] الإِضْلَالُ is of two sorts: one of these is the consequence of erring, or straying; either as in the case in which one says أَضْلَلْتُ البَعِيرَ (expl. above, see 1, former half); or the decreeing that one shall err, or stray, &c., because he has done so already, and this is sometimes the case when the إِضْلَال of a man is attributed to God: the other sort is the embellishing [or commending] to a man that which is false, or wrong, or vain, in order that he may err, or stray, &c.: and God's إِضْلَال of a man is of two sorts; one of which has been expl. above; the other is God's so constituting man that when he observes [and pursues] a certain course, or way, [of acting or the like], whether it be such as is commended or such as is discommended, he habituates himself to it, and esteems it pleasant, and keeps to it, and finds it difficult to turn from it, wherefore it is said that custom is a second nature. (Er-Rághib, TA.) — Also *He, or it, made*, or *caused, him*, or *it, to perish*, or *become lost;* syn. أَهْلَكَهُ, (Ṣ, TA,) and أَضَاعَهُ, (El-Fárábee, Ṣ, O, Mṣb,) or ضَيَّعَهُ; (TA;) [اضاعه and ضيّعه signifying the same; and so اضلّه and ♦ ضَلَّلَهُ; whence,] أَلَمْ يَجْعَلْ كَيْدَهُمْ فِى تَضْلِيلٍ, in the Ḳur cv. 2, means [*Did He not make their plot to be* such as ended] *in a causing to perish*, or *become lost*, (فِى تَضْيِيعٍ,) and *in annulment?* (Ksh, Bḍ.) أَضَلَّ أَعْمَالَهُمْ, in the Ḳur [xlvii. 1 and 9, which may be rendered † *He will cause their works to be lost*, or *to be of no effect*], means, accord. to Aboo-Is-ḥáḳ, *He will not recompense them for their good works;* the phrase being similar to the saying قَدْ ضَلَّ سَعْيُكَ [expl. above]. (TA.) And أَضَلَّ ٱللّٰهُ ضَلَالَكَ † [*May God make thine erring to be no more*, or *to come to an end*,] is expl. by ISk as meaning *may thine erring pass away from thee, so that thou shalt not err;* and he adds that the saying ضَلَّ ضَلَالُكَ means ذَهَبَ عَنْكَ حَتَّى لَا تَضِلَّ. (TA.) — Also ‡ *He buried, and hid*, or *concealed, him*, or *it.* (Ḳ, TA.) You say, أُضِلَّ المَيِّتُ ‡ *The dead was buried.* (Ṣ, O.) The phrase أَضَلَّتْ بِهِ أُمُّهُ, meaning ‡ *His mother buried him*, in a verse cited by IAạr, is extr., or anomalous. (TA.) — And *He found him to be erring, straying, going astray; deviating from the right way* or *course*, or *from that which was right; missing*, or *losing, the right way; losing his way; not rightly directed*, or *not finding the way to the truth:* like as one says أَحْمَدَهُ, and أَبْخَلَهُ. (TA.) — And you say, أَضَلَّنِى كَذَا, meaning † *Such a thing was*, or *became, beyond my power*, or *compass.* (IAạr, Mṣb, TA.) — See also 1, near the end.

5. تضلّل *It went away:* so in the saying, تضلّل المَآءُ مِنْ تَحْتِ الحَجَرِ [*The water went away from beneath the stone*]. (O, TA.)

6. تضالّ *He feigned himself to be erring, straying, going astray; deviating from the right way* or *course*, or *from that which was right; missing*, or *losing, the right way;* or *losing his way.* (O, TA.)

10. استضلّ ضَلَالَهُ *His erring demanded that he should err* [*the more*], *so that he did err* [*the more:* like as erring is said to be a cause of one's being made to err: see 4: and see also ضَلَّ ضَلَالُهُ, near the beginning of the art.]: so in the saying of Aboo-Dhu-eyb,

• رَآهَا الفُؤَادُ فَٱسْتُضِلَّ ضَلَالُهُ •

[*The heart beheld her, and his erring demanded that he should err* &c.]. (Skr, Ṣ, TA.)

ضَلٌّ: see ضَلَالٌ.

ضُلٌّ: see ضَلَالٌ. — [Also, app. as meaning *A lost state; a state of perishing, coming to nought*, or *passing away;*] a subst. from ضَلَّ signifying ضَاعَ and هَلَكَ. (Ṣ, TA.) — And hence [its usage, in the manner of a proper name, in] the saying, هُوَ ضُلُّ بْنُ ضُلٍّ, (Ṣ,) which means, (Ṣ, O, Ḳ,) as also ♦ هُوَ ضِلُّ بْنُ ضِلٍّ, (Ibn-'Abbád, O, Ḳ,) *He is the unknown, the son of the unknown;* (Ṣ, Z, O, Ḳ;) and in like manner, ♦ الضَّلَالُ بْنُ الثَّلَالِ; (Ṣ, O;) and ضُلُّ بْنُ ثُلٍّ: (TA:) or *he is one in whom is no good:* (Ḳ:) or *he is one who persists in error.* (M, Ḳ.) — [Hence also, perhaps, it is said that] يَا ضُلَّ مَا تَجْرِى بِهِ العَصَا [in the CḲ ضَلَّ] means يَا تَلَفَهُ and يَا فَقْدَهُ [i. e., app., *O the loss*, or *O the coming to nought, of that by reason of which the mare El-'Aṣà is running!*]: (Ḳ, TA:) a prov.; said by Ḳaṣeer Ibn-Saąd to Jedheemeh El-Abrash, when he went with him to Ez-Zebbà; for when they were within her province, he repented, and Ḳaṣeer said to him, "Mount this my horse, and escape upon him, for his dust will not be cloven [by the pursuer," i. e. he will not be overtaken]: (TA: [but the mare is thus made a male:]) or it was said by 'Amr Ibn-'Adee, when he saw El-'Aṣà, the mare of Jedheemeh, with Ḳaṣeer upon her: قَوْمِ is suppressed after يا; and ♦ ضُلَّ is of the forms [of verbs] denoting wonder, originally ضَلُلَ, with ḍamm, like حُبَّ in the phrase حُبَّ بِفُلَانٍ, originally حَبُبَ; and the meaning of the prov. is, O people, *what a case of perdition is that by reason of which El-'Aṣà is running!* i. e., the death of Jedheemeh. (Meyd.) — ضُلُّ بِتِضْلَالٍ [in CḲ ضَلَّ] means *A vain*, or *futile, thing:* (Ṣ, O, Ḳ:) [or *a vain, misleading thing;* تِضْلَال being an inf. n. of ضَلَّلَ:] 'Amr Ibn-Shás El-Asadee says,

• تَذَكَّرْتُ لَيْلَى لَاتَ حِينَ ٱدِّكَارِهَا •
• وَقَدْ حُنِىَ الأَضْلَاعُ ضُلٌّ بِتِضْلَالِ •

[*I remembered Leylà when it was not a time for remembering her, the ribs having become bent by the bending of the back with age: it was a vain, misleading thing*]. (Ṣ, O.) — ضُلُّ أَضْلَالٍ: see ضِلَّةٌ.

ضِلُّ أَضْلَالٍ: see ضُلٌّ. — هُوَ ضِلُّ بْنُ ضِلٍّ: see ضُلٌّ. see ضِلَّةٌ.

ضِلَّةٌ *Confusion*, or *perplexity, and inability to see the right course:* (Ḳ:) [or *error:* for] one says, فَعَلَ ذٰلِكَ ضِلَّةً *He did that in error* (فِى ضَلَالَةٍ): and ذَهَبَ ضِلَّةً *He went away not knowing whither he went:* (TA:) and فُلَانٌ يَلُومُنِى ضِلَّةً *Such a one blames me wrongly:* (Ṣ, O:) [or, *behind my back*, or *in my absence:* for] ضِلَّةٌ signifies also *speech respecting a person behind his back*, or *in his absence*; relating to good and to evil. (M, Ḳ, TA.) ═ [Freytag explains it as signifying also *One in whom is no good*, on the authority of Meyd.]

ضُلَّةٌ *Skill in guiding*, or *directing aright*, *in journeying*. (Fr, Ḳ,* TA.)

ضِلَّةٌ: see ضَلَالٌ. — [Hence,] هُوَ ٱبْنُهُ لِضِلَّةٍ ‡ *He is his son unlawfully begotten*, or *not trueborn*. (AZ, A, Ḳ, TA.) — ذَهَبَ دَمُهُ ضِلَّةً ‡ *His blood went unrevenged*, or *without retaliation*. (Ḳ, TA.) — And هُوَ تِبْعُ ضِلَّةٍ, (Th, O, Ḳ, TA,) with kesr to the ت and to the ض, (TA,) [in the CḲ, erroneously, تَبْعُ,] and تِبْعُ ضِلَّةٍ, (Ḳ, TA,) thus related by IAạr, (TA,) but the former only accord. to Th, (TA in art. تبع,) † *He is a follower of women*: (TA in that art.:) or *he is one in whom is no good, and with whom is no good*: (IAạr, Th, TA:) or *he is a very cunning man* (دَاهِيَةٌ), *one in whom is no good*; (IAạr, O, Ḳ, TA;) and so تِبْعُ صِلَّةٍ, (O, L, TA,) as some relate it; (L, TA;) and in like manner, ضِلُّ ▼ أَضْلَالٍ, (Lḥ, O, Ḳ, TA,) and ضُلُّ ▼ أُضْلَالٍ, (Ḳ, TA,) and صِلُّ أَصْلَالٍ, [q. v.,] which is with kesr only, (Ḳ, TA,) a phrase similar to ضِرُّ أَضْرَارٍ. (TA in art. ضر.)

ضَلَلٌ: see ضَلَالٌ. — Also Water (O, Ḳ) *running* (Ḳ) *beneath a rock, which the sun does not reach*: (O, Ḳ:) one says مَآءٌ ضَلَلٌ: (O:) or *running among trees*. (Ḳ.) [See also ضَلَّلٌ.]

ضَلَالٌ [an inf. n. of 1: used as a simple subst.,] *Error*; *contr. of* رَشَادٌ, (Ṣ, O, TA,) and *of* هُدًى; (Ḳ, TA;) as also ▼ ضَلَالَةٌ, (Ṣ, O, Ḳ,) and ▼ ضَلٌّ, and ▼ ضُلٌّ, and ▼ ضِلَّةٌ, and ▼ ضَلَلٌ, and ▼ ضَلْضَلَةٌ, (Ḳ,) and ▼ ضُلْضُلَةٌ, (O, TA,) and ▼ أُضْلُولَةٌ, (Ḳ,) of which last the pl. is أَضَالِيلُ, (Lth, O, TA,) as in the saying تَمَادَى فِى أَضَالِيلِ ٱلْهَوَى [*He persevered in the errors of love*], (TA,) or أَضَالِيلُ, as some say, has no sing., or its sing. is supposed, or has been heard, and is أُضْلُولَةٌ or أُضْلُولٌ or إِضْلِيلٌ or some other form: (MF, TA:) the primary signification of ٱلضَّلَالُ is *the going away from the right course*, or *direction*: (Ḥam p. 357:) or it signifies, accord. to Ibn-El-Kemál, *the loss*, or *missing*, *of that which brings*, or *conducts*, *to the object sought*: or, as some say, *the pursuing a way that will not bring*, or *conduct*, *to that object*: or, accord. to Er-Rághib, *the deviating from the right way*: and it is said to be *any deviation from that which is right, intentional* or *unintentional, little* or *much*; because the right and approved way is very difficult; wherefore it may be used of him who commits any mistake whatever, and is imputed to prophets and to unbelievers, though between the ضلال of the former and that of the latter is a wide difference: and in another point of view, it is of two sorts; one is in the speculative departments of knowledge, as in acquaintance with the unity of God, and with the prophetic function or office, and the like, indicated in the Ḳur iv. 135; or it is in the practical departments of knowledge, as in acquaintance with the ordinances of the law, that is, religious services. (TA.) — Also *A state of perdition*: so in the Ḳur liv. 24: (Ṣ, O:) [and in like manner ▼ ضَلَالَةٌ; for] ضَلَالَةُ ٱلْعَمَلِ signifies *The annulled and lost state of work*. (TA.) — And *Absence*, or *a state of concealment*. (Mṣb. [This is there said to be the primary signification.]) — هُوَ ٱلضَّلَالُ بْنُ ٱلتَّلَالِ: see expl. voce ضُلٌّ.

ضَلُولٌ: see ضَالٌّ.

ضَلَالَةٌ: see ضَلَالٌ, in the beginning, and near the end, of the paragraph. One says, هِىَ ٱلضَّلَالَةُ وَٱلتَّلَالَةُ; (Ṣ, O;) in which the latter noun is an imitative sequent. (Ṣ and Ḳ in art. تل.)

ضِلِّيلٌ A man (Ṣ, O) *who errs, strays, goes astray*, or *deviates from the right way* or *course, much*, or *often*: (Ṣ, O, Ḳ:) or ‡ *who errs*, &c., *much*, or *often*, *in religion*: (TA:) and ▼ مُضَلَّلٌ, (Ṣ, TA,) which in some of the copies of the Ṣ is written thus and also مُضِلَّلٌ, (TA,) signifies the same; (Ṣ, TA;) or one *who is not disposed*, or *directed*, *to good*; in the Ḳ, ٱلَّذِى لَا يُوَفَّى بِخَيْرٍ, [or يُوفِى بخير, as in the CḲ,] but correctly ٱلَّذِى لَا يُوَفَّقُ لِخَيْرٍ; or, as some say, *a committer of errors*, and *of false, wrong*, or *vain, actions*: and ضِلِّيلٌ is also expl. as signifying one *who will not desist from error*. (TA.) Imra-el-Ḳeys was called ٱلْمَلِكُ ٱلضِّلِّيلُ [*The much-erring king*], (Ṣ, O, Ḳ, TA, [in the CḲ, erroneously, ٱلضَّلِيلُ,]) and ▼ ٱلملك ٱلْمُضَلَّلُ. (Ḳ.)

ضَالٌّ *Erring, straying*, or *going astray*; *deviating from the right way* or *course*, or *from that which is right*; *missing*, or *losing*, *the right way*; or *losing his way*; (Ṣ,* Mṣb, TA;) and ▼ ضَلُولٌ is syn. therewith; (Ḳ;) [or rather with ضِلِّيلٌ, accord. to a general rule:] pl. of the former ضُلَّالٌ, [of which see an ex. in a verse cited voce رِسْلٌ,] and ضَالُّونَ: [in the Ḳur i. last verse,] some read وَلَا ٱلضَّأَلِّينَ, to avoid the concurrence of two quiescent letters. (TA.) You say ضَالٌّ تَالٌّ; (Ṣ, O;) in which the latter epithet is an imitative sequent. (Ṣ and Ḳ in art. تل.) — [Also *Becoming lost*; &c. — And *Forgetting*. It is said that] وَأَنَا مِنَ ٱلضَّالِّينَ [in the Ḳur xxvi. 19] means † *I being of those that forgot*. (Ḳ, TA.) And ٱمْرَأَةٌ ضَالَّةٌ means † *A woman forgetting the days of her menstruation*. (Mgh.)

ضَالَّةٌ an epithet in which the quality of a subst. is predominant, (IAth, TA,) *A stray*; i. e. *a beast that has strayed*: (Ṣ, O, TA:) or *a camel remaining in a place where it is lost, without an owner* (Ḳ, TA) *that is known*: (TA:) or *a lost animal* (IAth, Mṣb, TA) or *other thing, whatever it be*: (IAth, TA:) applied to the male and to the female, (Ṣ, O, Mṣb, Ḳ,) and to two and to a pl. number: (TA;) and it has for its pl. ضَوَالُّ, (Mṣb, TA,) like دَوَابُّ pl. of دَابَّةٌ. (Mṣb.) It is said in a trad., ضَالَّةُ ٱلْمُؤْمِنِ حَرَقُ ٱلنَّارِ [expl. in art. حرق]. (TA.) And one says, ٱلْحِكْمَةُ ضَالَّةُ ٱلْمُؤْمِنِ † [*Wisdom is the object of persevering quest of the believer*]; meaning that the believer ceases not to seek wisdom like as a man seeks his stray. (TA.)

ضَلَضِلٌ and ▼ ضَلَضِلَةٌ, (Aṣ, Ṣ,) as though contracted from ضَلَاضِلٌ [and ضَلَاضِلَةٌ], (Ṣ,) or أَرْضٌ ▼ ضَلَضِلَةٌ and ضَلَضِلٌ [in the CḲ ضَلَضَلَةٌ and ضَلَضَلٌ] and ▼ ضُلَضِلَةٌ and ▼ ضُلَضِلٌ (Ḳ) and ▼ ضُلَاضِلٌ (Lḥ, Ḳ) and ضُلْضُلَةٌ, (IDrd, Ḳ,) *Rugged land* or *ground*. (Aṣ, Ṣ, Ḳ.) And مَكَانٌ ضَلَضِلٌ, originally ضَلَاضِيلُ, *A hard, stony place*. (Fr, TA.) — Also, (so in the Ḳ,) i. e. (TA) ضَلَضِلٌ and ▼ ضَلَضِلَةٌ, accord. to Aṣ, (O, TA,) or ▼ ضُلَضِلَةٌ, (Ṣ, O, TA,) [said to be] the only instance of its kind among reduplicate words, (Ṣ, O, TA, [in which last the same assertion is quoted from the T, app. in relation to the last, or last but one, of these words,]) and, as in the Jm, ▼ ضُلْضُلَةٌ, (O, TA,) *A stone*, (Aṣ, Ṣ, O,) or *stones*, (Ḳ,) *such as a man can lift from the ground and carry*: (Aṣ, Ṣ, O, Ḳ:) or, accord. to the T, ضلضلة [thus in the TA, app. ▼ ضَلَضِلَةٌ or ▼ ضُلَضِلَةٌ,] signifies *any stone such as a man can lift from the ground and carry*, or *above that, smooth, found in the interiors of valleys*. (TA.)

ضُلَضِلٌ: see the next preceding paragraph. ═ Also, (IAạr, O, TA,) in the Ḳ, erroneously, ضُلَضِلَةٌ, (TA,) and ▼ ضُلَاضِلٌ, *A skilful guide of the way*. (IAạr, O, Ḳ, TA.)

ضَلْضَلَةٌ: see ضَلَالٌ.

ضُلْضُلَةٌ: see ضَلَضِلٌ, in two places. — ضَلَاضِلُ ٱلْمَآءِ, (O, Ḳ,) and صَلَاصِلُهُ, (O,) [said in the O, in this art., to be pls. of which the sings. are ضُلَضِلَةٌ and صُلَصِلَةٌ, but the sings. are correctly ضُلْضُلَةٌ and صُلْصُلَةٌ, (see the latter of these two in its proper art.,)] *The remains of water*: (O, Ḳ:) so says Lḥ. (O.)

ضَلَضِلَةٌ: see ضَلَضِلٌ, in four places.

ضُلَضِلَةٌ: see ضَلَالٌ: — and مَضَلَّةٌ: — and ضَلَضِلٌ, in three places.

ضُلَاضِلٌ: see ضَلَضِلٌ: ═ and ضُلَضِلٌ.

أُضْلُولَةٌ: see ضَلَالٌ.

وَقَعَ فِى وَادِى تُضُلِّلَ, (Ks, Ṣ, O, Ḳ,*) like تُخُيِّبَ and تُهُلِّكَ, all imperfectly decl., (Ṣ, O,) and تَضَلَّلَ, (Ibn-'Abbád, O, Ḳ,) and تَضَلَّلَ, with two fet-ḥahs, and تِضِلَّلَ, with two kesrehs, (Ibn-'Abbád, O, TA,) meaning ٱلْبَاطِلِ [i. e. † *He fell into that which was vain, unreal, nought, futile*, or *the like*, and consequently, *into disappointment*]: (Ibn-'Abbád, Ṣ, O, Ḳ, TA:) or, accord. to the A, وَقَعُوا فِى وادى تضلل means ‡ *They perished*. (TA.)

طَرِيقٌ مُضِلٌّ *A road that causes to go astray, or to deviate from the right course.* (TA.) And, accord. to Aṣ, مُضِلٌّ signifies A land (أَرْضٌ) *in which one loses his way.* (TA. [See also the next paragraph.]) [Hence,] فِتْنَةٌ مُضِلَّةٌ means [*A trial, or sedition, or discord, &c.,*] *that causes men to go astray, or to deviate from that which is right.* (TA.) And [hence also,] المُضِلُّ means *The* سَرَاب [or *mirage*]. (TA.)

مَضَلَّةٌ a subst. like مَجْبَنَةٌ and مَبْخَلَةٌ [i. e., as such, signifying *A cause of erring, straying, going astray,* or *deviating from the right way* or *course* or *from that which is right, &c.*]: (TA:) [and used in the manner of an epithet:] one says أَرْضٌ مَضَلَّةٌ *A land that causes one to err, &c.*: (TA:) or, as also ↑ مَضِلَّةٌ, (Ṣ, O, Mṣb, Ḳ, TA, [in the CḲ مِضَلَّةٌ,]) and ↑ ضُلَضِلَةٌ, (O, Ḳ,) *a land in which one errs,* or *strays, from the* [*right*] *way;* (Ṣ, O, Mṣb, Ḳ;*) *in which one does not find the right way:* and خَرْقٌ مَضَلَّةٌ [*A desert,* or *far-extending desert, &c., in which one errs, &c.*]: it is used alike as masc. and fem. and pl.: but one says also أَرَضُونَ مَضَلَّاتٌ. (TA.)

مَضِلَّةٌ: see the next preceding paragraph.

مُضَلَّلٌ: see ضِلِّيلٌ, in two places.

مُتَضَالٌّ [part. n. of 6, q. v.]. One says, إِنَّكَ تَهْدِى الضَّالَّ وَلَا تَهْدِى المُتَضَالَّ [*Verily thou wilt direct aright the erring, &c., but thou wilt not direct aright him who feigns himself to be erring, &c.*]. (Ṣ, O.)

ضلع

1. ضَلَعَ, aor. ـَ, (Ṣ, O, Mṣb, Ḳ,) inf. n. ضَلْعٌ, (Ṣ, O, Mṣb,) *It,* or † *he, inclined,* or *declined:* (Ṣ, O, Ḳ:) *it,* or † *he, declined,* or *deviated, from that which was right,* or *true:* (Ṣ, O, Mṣb, Ḳ:) † *he acted wrongfully, unjustly, injuriously,* or *tyrannically.* (Ṣ,* O,* Ḳ.) You say, ضَلَعَ عَنْهُ ‡ *He deviated,* or *turned away, from him,* or *it;* or *he did so, acting wrongfully, &c.:* and ضَلَعَ عَلَيْهِ † *he acted wrongfully, &c., against him.* (TA.) And ضَلْعُكَ مَعَ فُلَانٍ (Ṣ, O, Mṣb,* Ḳ*) † *Thy inclining,* (Ṣ, O, Mṣb, Ḳ,) and *thy love,* or *desire,* (Ṣ, O,) *is with such a one* [i. e. *in unison with that of such a one*]. (Ṣ, O, Mṣb,* Ḳ:* in the Mṣb and Ḳ, مَعَهُ is put in the place of مَعَ فُلَانٍ.) And لَا تَنْقُشِ الشَّوْكَةَ بِالشَّوْكَةِ فَإِنَّ ضَلْعَهَا مَعَهَا, (Ṣ, O, Ḳ,) or بِمِثْلِهَا [in the place of بالشوكة], (Meyd,) [lit. *Extract not thou the thorn by means of the thorn, or by means of the like of it, for its inclination is with it,*] meaning, demand not aid, in the case of thy want, of him who is more benevolent to the person from whom the object of want is sought than he is to thee: (Meyd:) a prov.: (Ṣ, Meyd, O:) applied to the man who contends in an altercation with another, and says, "Appoint thou between me and thee such a one;" pointing to a man who loves what he [i. e. the opponent of the speaker] loves: (Ṣ, O, Ḳ:) the author of the Ḳ adds, it is said that it should by rule be ضَلَعُكَ, for they say ضَلِعَ مَعَ فُلَانٍ, like فَرِحَ, [as though meaning *he inclined with such a one,*] but they have contracted it; which is wonderful, in consideration with his having mentioned shortly before, ضَلَعَ, like مَنَعَ, as signifying مَالَ. (TA.) One says also, خَاصَمْتُ فُلَانًا فَكَانَ ضَلْعُكَ عَلَىَّ i. e. † [*I contended in an altercation with such a one and*] *thy inclining* [*was against me*]. (Ṣ, O.) —— ضَلِعَ, aor. ـَ, (Mgh, Mṣb, Ḳ,) inf. n. ضَلَعٌ, (Mgh, Mṣb,) means *It* (a sword, Ḳ, or a thing, Mṣb) *was,* or *became, crooked,* or *curved:* (Mgh, Mṣb, Ḳ:) and ↑ تضلّع may mean the same: (Ham p. 80:) a poet says, (namely, Moḥammad Ibn-'Abd-Allah El-Azdee, TA,)

* وَقَدْ يَحْمِلُ السَّيْفَ المُجَرَّبَ رَبُّهُ *
* عَلَى ضَلَعٍ فِى مَتْنِهِ وَهْوَ قَاطِعُ *

[*And verily,* or *sometimes,* or *often, its owner bears the tried sword, notwithstanding crookedness in its broad side, it being sharp*]: (Ṣ, O:) and (Ḳ) ضَلَعٌ signifies the *being crooked,* or *curved, by nature;* (Ṣ, O, Ḳ;) as also ضَلْعٌ; whence the saying, لَأُقِيمَنَّ ضَلَعَكَ and ضَلْعَكَ [*I will assuredly straighten thy natural crookedness*]: (Ḳ:) thus in the copies of the Ḳ; but this is a mistake, occasioned by the author's seeing in the T and M لَأُقِيمَنَّ ضَلَعَكَ and ضَلَعَكَ meaning عَوَجَكَ, and his imagining both these nouns to be with ض and to differ in the manner stated above: (TA:) you say, ضَلِعَ, aor. ـَ, inf. n. ضَلَعٌ i. e. *he,* or *it, was,* or *became, crooked,* or *curved, by nature:* (Ṣ, O:) or ضَلَعٌ in the camel is like غَمْزٌ in horses or the like, [meaning the *limping,* or *halting,* or *having a slight lameness, in the hind leg,*] and the verb is ضَلِعَ; and the epithet [or part. n.] is ↑ ضَلِعٌ: (Ḳ:) or this is rather the explanation of ظَلَعٌ, with ظ; (TA;) [or as Mṭr says,] ضلع as meaning what resembles عَرَجٌ [or natural lameness] is correctly ظلع: (Mgh:) but when it (i. e. the crookedness, TA) is not natural, one says, ضَلَعَ, like مَنَعَ, (Ḳ, TA,) [but this seems rather to relate to the meaning of "limping," agreeably with what I have cited above from the Mgh,] and the inf. n. is ضَلْعٌ: (TA:) and the epithet [or part. n.] is ↑ ضَالِعٌ. (Ḳ.) —— ضَلُعَ, [aor. ـُ,] inf. n. ضَلَاعَةٌ, *He* (a man, Ṣ, O, Mṣb, [and app. also a horse and the like, see its part. n. ضَلِيعٌ,]) *was,* or *became, strong,* or *powerful;* (Ṣ, O, Mṣb, Ḳ;) and *strong, hard,* or *firm, in the* أَضْلَاع [or *ribs*]. (Ṣ, O, Ḳ. [The latter is said in Ḥar p. 6 to be the primary meaning; and the former, metaphorical.]) ═ ضَلَعَ as syn. with تَضَلَّعَ: see the latter. ═ ضَلَعَ فُلَانًا *He struck such a one upon his* ضِلَع [or *rib*]. (Ḳ.)

2: see 4, in two places. —— تَضْلِيعُ الأَعْمَالِ is said by some to mean † *The making deeds to deviate from the right,* or *direct, way* or *course:* and by some to mean † *the making them heavy,* or *burdensome.* (Ḥar p. 77.) —— تَضْلِيعُ الثَّوْبِ signifies *The figuring the garment,* or *piece of cloth, with the form of* أَضْلَاع [or *ribs*]. (Ṣ, O, Ḳ.) [See also the pass. part. n., below.]

4. اضلعهُ, (Ḳ,) inf. n. إِضْلَاعٌ, (Ṣ, O,) *It,* or *he, made it,* or † *him, to incline,* or *decline;* (Ṣ, O, Ḳ;) [and so ↑ ضلّعهُ; for] الإِضْلَاعُ and التَّضْلِيعُ signify الإِمَالَةُ. (Ḥar p. 77.) —— [And *It,* or *he, made it,* or *him, to be crooked,* or *curved;* and so ↑ ضلّعهُ; for] الإِضْلَاعُ and التَّضْلِيعُ signify also التَّعْوِيجُ. (Ḥar ubi suprà.) —— [Hence,] one says also, أَضْلَعَتْهُ الخُطُوبُ, meaning † [*Affairs,* or *great* or *grievous affairs,*] *burdened him* [as though making him to incline, or curving him]. (TA.) ═ See also 8.

5. تضلّع: see 1, in the middle of the paragraph. —— [Also,] (Ṣ, O, Ḳ,) and ↑ ضَلَعَ, like مَنَعَ, (Ḳ,) said of a man, (Ṣ, O,) *He became filled,* (Ṣ, O, Ḳ,) or *what was between his* أَضْلَاع [or *ribs*] *became filled,* (TA,) *with food,* (Ṣ, O, Ḳ,) or *drink:* (Ṣ, O:) or *with drink so that the water reached his* أَضْلَاع, (Ḳ, TA,) *and they became swollen out in consequence thereof:* (TA in explanation of the former verb:) and the former verb is also expl. as meaning *he drank much, so that his side and his ribs became stretched.* (TA.) And تضلّع مِنَ الطَّعَامِ *He became filled with the food;* as though it filled his ribs. (Mṣb.)

8. الإِضْطِلَاعُ is from الضَّلَاعَةُ [inf. n. of ضَلُعَ] meaning "the being strong, or powerful;" (ISk, Ṣ, O, and Ḥar p. 391;) الإِضْطِلَاعُ بِالشَّىْءِ signifying *The raising the thing upon one's back, and rising with it, and having strength,* or *power, sufficient for it.* (Ḥar ibid.) And you say, اضطلع بِحِمْلِهِ, meaning *He had strength,* or *power, to bear it,* or *carry it.* (Mgh, and Ḥar p. 645.) [See also the part. n., below.] And ↑ أَضْلَعَ بِالأَمْرِ † *He had strength,* or *power, sufficient for the affair;* as though his ribs had strength to bear it. (Mṣb.)

ضَلْعٌ: see ضِلَعٌ, first sentence.

ضِلْعٌ: see ضِلَعٌ, first and last sentences.

ضَلَعٌ The *weight,* or *burden,* of debt, *that bends the bearer thereof.* (IAth, O, Ḳ.) And *Strength,* or *power;* (Aṣ, Ṣ, O, Mṣb, Ḳ;) a subst. in this sense, from ضَلُعَ; (Mṣb;) and the *bearing,* or *endurance of that which is heavy,* or *burdensome.* (Aṣ, Ṣ, O, Ḳ.) —— Also inf. n. of ضَلِعَ [q. v.]. (Mgh, Mṣb, Ḳ.)

ضَلِعٌ *Crooked,* or *curved, by nature.* (Ṣ, O, TA.) And applied to a spear as meaning *Crooked,* or *curved; not straightened:* (TA:) or, so applied, *inclining,* or *bending:* (Ḥam p. 80:) and ↑ ضَلِيعٌ and ↑ ضَالِعٌ, so applied, [likewise] mean *crooked*, or *curved*. (TA.) — See also 1, in the last quarter of the paragraph.

ضِلَعٌ and ▼ ضِلْعٌ, (Ṣ, Mgh, O, Mṣb, Ḳ,) the former of the dial. of El-Ḥijáz and the latter of the dial. of Temeem, (Mṣb, TA,) and ▼ ضَلْعٌ, which is the only form, or almost the only one, that is used by the vulgar, is said by MF to be mentioned by some one or more of the commentators, but not known in the lexicons, (TA;) [*A rib;*] *a certain appertenance of an animal,* (Mṣb,) *well known;* (Ḳ;) the *curved thing of the side;* (TA;) *a single bone of the bones of the side:* (Mgh, Mṣb:) of the fem. gender, (Mṣb, Ḳ, TA,) accord. to common repute; or, as some say, masc.; or, accord. to some, whose opinion in this case is preferred by Ibn-Málik and others, of both genders: (TA:) pl. [of mult.] ضُلُوعٌ and [of pauc.] أَضْلَاعٌ (Ṣ, Mgh, O, Mṣb, Ḳ) and أَضْلُعٌ, (O, Mṣb, Ḳ,) and أَضَالِعُ also is a pl. of ضِلَعٌ, or, as some say, of [its pl.] أَضْلُعٌ. (TA.) ضِلَعُ الخَلْفِ [and الخِلْفِ] is [*The rib*] *in the lowest part of the side* [of a man, i. e. *the lowest rib;* and *the hindmost rib* in a beast]: (TA:) and signifies also *A burn in the part behind what is thus termed.* (O, Ḳ, TA.) — Also † *A piece of stick* or *wood;* syn. عُودٌ; [erroneously supposed by Golius and Freytag to mean here the musical instrument thus called;] (IAạr, O, Ḳ;) so in a saying of the Prophet to a woman, respecting a blood-stain on a garment, حُتِّيهِ بِضِلَعٍ † [*Scrape thou it off with a piece of stick*]: (IAạr, O:) or † *such as is wide and curved;* as being likened to the ضِلَع (O, Ḳ) of an animal. (Ḳ.) — And ‡ *An oblong piece* of a melon; (O,* Ḳ, TA;) as being likened to the ضِلَع [properly thus called]. (O, TA.) — And ‡ *A trap* for birds; because of its gibbous shape: so in the saying, نَصَبَ ضِلَعًا لِلطَّيْرِ [*He set up a trap for the birds*]. (A, TA.) — And The *base*, or *lower part, of a raceme of a palm-tree.* (TA in art. عهن.) — And † *A line that is made on the ground, after which another line is made, and then the space between these two is sown.* (TA.) — And † *A small mountain apart from others:* (Ṣ, O, Ḳ:) or *a small mountain, such as is not long:* (TA:) or *a low and narrow mountain,* (Aboo-Naṣr, Ṣ, O, Ḳ, TA,) *long and extended:* or, accord. to Aṣ, *a small mountain, extending lengthwise upon the earth, not high.* (TA.) And [the pl.] ضُلُوعٌ signifies ‡ *Curved tracts of ground:* or *tracks* (طَرَائِق) *of a* [*piece of stony ground such as is termed*] حَرَّة. (O, Ḳ, TA.) — Also † *An island in the sea;* pl. أَضْلَاعٌ: or, as some say, it is the name of a particular island. (TA.) — [In geometry, † *A side* of a rectilinear triangle or square or polygon. — And † *A square root;* called in arithmetic جَذْر: see شَىْءٌ, near the end of the paragraph.] — One says also, هُمْ عَلَىَّ ضِلَعٌ جَائِرَةٌ, (Ṣ, A, O, Ḳ, in the last of which, between هم and علىّ is inserted هٰكَذَا,) and ▼ ضِلْعٌ is allowable, (Ṣ, TA,) meaning ‡ *They are assembled against me with hostility:* (A, TA:) the origin of which is the saying of AZ, one says, هُمْ عَلَىَّ إِلْبٌ وَاحِدٌ [or أَلْبٌ وَاحِدٌ] and صَدْعٌ وَاحِدٌ and ضِلَعٌ وَاحِدٌ, meaning as above. (TA.)

ضِلَعَةٌ *A certain small fish, green* (خَضْرَآء), *short in the bone.* (Ibn-'Abbád, O, Ḳ.)

ضَلِيعٌ: see ضَلْعٌ: — and see also مَضْلُوعٌ, in three places. — Also, applied to a man, (Ṣ, O, Mṣb,) *Strong*, or *powerful;* (Ṣ, O, Mṣb, Ḳ;) and *strong, hard*, or *firm, in the* أَضْلَاع [or *ribs*]: (Ṣ, O, Ḳ:) or, as some say, *long in the* أَضْلَاع, *great in make, bulky;* applied to any animal, even to a jinnee: (TA:) pl. ضُلْعٌ, (Ḳ,) or app., ضُلُعٌ [of which the former may be a contraction]. (TA.) And, applied to a horse, *Complete*, or *perfect, in make* or *formation, large in the middle, thick in the* [*bones called*] أَلْوَاح, *having many sinews:* (ISk, Ṣ, O, Ḳ:) or, so applied, *thick in the* أَلْوَاح; *strong, hard*, or *firm, in the sinews:* (Mṣb:) or, as some say, *long in the ribs* (الأَضْلَاع), *wide in the sides, large in the breast.* (TA.) And ضَلِيعُ الفَمِ A man *large in the mouth:* (Ḳt, O, Ḳ:) or *wide therein:* (A'Obeyd, O, Ḳ:) expl. in the former sense, and in the latter, as applied to the Prophet; (O, TA;) width of the mouth, (Ḳt, O, Ḳ, TA,) and largeness thereof, (TA,) being commended by the Arabs, and smallness thereof being discommended by them; (Ḳt, O, Ḳ, TA;) whereas the Persians, or foreigners, (العَجَم,) commend smallness thereof: (TA:) or *having large teeth, closely and regularly set together;* (Sh, O, Ḳ;) and thus also expl., by Sh, as applied to the Prophet: (O, TA:) and ضَلِيعُ الثَّنَايَا a man *whose central incisors are thick.* (TA.)

ضَالِعٌ *Inclining*, or *declining:* (TA: [like ظَالِعٌ:]) *declining*, or *deviating, from that which is right*, or *true: acting wrongfully, unjustly, injuriously*, or *tyrannically.* (Ṣ, O, Ḳ, TA.) — See also ضَلْعٌ. — And see 1, in the last quarter of the paragraph.

ضَوْلَعٌ ‡ *Inclining with love* or *desire.* (IAạr, O, Ḳ, TA.)

أَضْلَعُ, applied to a man, [and accord. to the CḲ to a beast (دَابَّة) also,] *Whose tooth is like the* ضِلَع [or *rib*]; (Lth, O, Ḳ;) fem. ضَلْعَآءُ [perhaps applied to the tooth, but more probably, I think, to a woman]; (TA;) and pl. ضُلْعٌ. (Ḳ.) — Also, (O, [but accord. to the Ḳ "or,"]) *Strong, thick,* (O, Ḳ, TA,) *large in make.* (TA.) — And *Stronger*, or *more powerful.* (O,* TA.)

مُضْلِعٌ A load *heavily burdening*, or *overburdening,* (Ṣ, IAth, O, Ḳ, TA,) *to the* أَضْلَاع [or *ribs*]; (TA;) as though leaning, or bearing, upon the أَضْلَاع: (IAth, TA:) or a *heavy* load, *which one is unable to bear;* as also ▼ مُضَلِّعٌ. (Ḥar p. 77.) [See also مُضْطَلِعٌ.] And, دَاهِيَةٌ مُضْلِعَةٌ ‡ *A calamity that heavily burdens*, or *overburdens, and breaks, the* أَضْلَاع [or *ribs*]. (TA.) — And دَابَّةٌ مُضْلِعٌ *A beast whose* أَضْلَاع [or *ribs*] *have not strength sufficient for the load.* (Ibn-'Abbád, O, L, Ḳ.) — See also مُضْطَلِعٌ.

مُضَلَّعٌ A garment, or piece of cloth, *figured with stripes, like thongs*, or *straps,* (O, Ḳ, TA,) *these being of* إِبْرِيسَم, or *of* قَزّ, [i. e. *silk*, or *raw silk,*] *wide, like* أَضْلَاع [or *ribs*]: (TA:) or [simply] *figured:* (Lḥ, TA:) or *variously woven, and thin:* (TA:) or *partly woven and partly left unwoven.* (ISh, Az, O, Ḳ, TA.) — And قُبَّةٌ مُضَلَّعَةٌ [*A ribbed dome* or *cupola;* i. e.] *having the form of* أَضْلَاع. (TA.)

مُضَلِّعٌ: see مُضْلِعٌ.

مَضْلُوعٌ *Having the* ضِلَع [or *rib*] *broken.* (Ibn-'Abbád, O.) — And قَوْسٌ مَضْلُوعَةٌ *A bow in the wood of which are a bending* (عَطْف) *and an evenness* (تَقَوُّم, as in the O and Ḳ, or تَقْوِيم, as in the L), [app. *towards each extremity,*] *the rest of it* (سَائِرُهَا) *being similar to its* كَبِد [which means its *middle part*, or *part where it is grasped with the hand*, or *part against which the arrow goes*, &c., for it is variously explained]; (O, Ḳ, TA;) so accord. to Aṣ, (O, TA,) and AḤn; (TA;) as also ▼ ضَلِيعٌ, (O, Ḳ, TA,) and ▼ ضَلِيعَةٌ; for which last, مَضْلُوعَةٌ is erroneously repeated in the Ḳ; [app. from its author finding it said in the O that such a bow is termed ضَلِيع and مَضْلُوعَة; and in the TḲ, مُضَوْلَعَةٌ is substituted for it:] ▼ قَوْسٌ ضَلِيعَةٌ is also expl. as meaning *a thick bow.* (TA.)

مُضْطَلِعٌ is from الضَّلَاعَةُ [inf. n. of ضَلُعَ]: so in the saying, فُلَانٌ مُضْطَلِعٌ بِهٰذَا الأَمْرِ i. e. *Such a one is possessed of strength*, or *power, sufficient for this affair:* so says ISk: and he adds that one should not say مُطَّلِعٌ: Aboo-Naṣr Aḥmad Ibn-Ḥátim says, one says هُوَ مُضْطَلِعٌ بِهٰذَا الأَمْرِ and مُطَّلِعٌ لَهُ [also]; الاِضْطِلَاعُ being from الضَّلَاعَةُ meaning القُوَّةُ; and الاِطِّلَاعُ being from العُلُوّ, from the saying اِطَّلَعْتُ الثَّنِيَّةَ meaning عَلَوْتُهَا [I ascended upon the mountain, or mountain-road, termed ثَنِيَّة]; i. e. *he is one who has ascendancy with respect to this affair, who is master of it:* (Ṣ, O, TA:) Lth expressly allows مُطَّلِعٌ for مُضْطَلِعٌ by the incorporation of the ض into the [letter that is originally] ت, so that the two together become ط with teshdeed. (TA.) And مُضْطَلِعٌ means the same as هُوَ مُضْلِعٌ ▼ لِهٰذَا الأَمْرِ as first expl. above, i. e. *He is possessed of strength*, or *power, sufficient for this affair.* (O, Ḳ. [In both, in this instance, لِهٰذَا, not بِهٰذَا.]) In the phrase إِذَا كَانَ مُضْطَلِعًا عَلَى حَقِّهِ [*If he be possessed of power*, or *ability, to obtain his right*, or *due*], it seems that مضطلعا is made trans. by means of على because made to imply the meaning of قَادِرًا or مُقْتَدِرًا. (Mgh.) ▼ مُسْتَضْلِعٌ,

likewise, signifies *Having strength*, or *power*. (TA.)

مُسْتَضْلِعٌ : see what next precedes.

ضم

1. ضَمَّهُ, [aor. ـُ,] inf. n. ضَمٌّ, *He drew it, put it, brought it, or gathered it, together; collected it; or contracted it.* (Mṣb.) You say, ضَمَّ شَيْئًا إِلَى شَىْءٍ, (Ṣ, MA, Ḳ,) [aor. and] inf. n. as above, *He drew, put, or brought, together* [*and joined* or *adjoined*] *a thing to a thing.* (MA, Ḳ.) And ضَمَمْتُهُ إِلَى صَدْرِى [*I drew him*, or *pressed him, to my bosom;*] *I embraced him.* (TA.) And ضَمَّ القَوْمُ, [أَنْفُسَهُمْ being app. understood, or perhaps it is correctly ضُمَّ,] *The people*, or *party, collected themselves together*, or *became collected.* (TA.) And أَللّٰهُمَّ اضْمُمْ نَشْرِى † *O God, compose what is discomposed*, or *disorganized*, [lit. *bring together what is scattered*,] *of my affairs.* (Ḳ* and TA in art. نشر.) And ضُمَّ جَنَاحَكَ عَنِ النَّاسِ † [*Contract thy side from men;*] meaning *be thou gentle, courteous, easy to deal with*, or *compliant, to men.* (TA.) And ضُمَّتْ عَلَيْهِ الأَنَامِلُ *The ends of the fingers were drawn together upon it.* (Ḥam p. 21. [See also a similar phrase in what follows, with the verb in the act. form, virtually meaning the same.]) — [Also *He compacted it:* and *he compressed it.* — And *He*, or *it, comprised it;* or *enclosed it:* and *he grasped it:* as also ضَمَّ عَلَيْهِ, in both of these senses.] You say, ضَمَّتْ عَلَيْهِ الأَنَامِلُ *The ends of the fingers grasped it.* (Ḥam p. 21. [See a similar phrase above.]) And ضَمَّ عَلَى المَالِ *He took* [or *grasped*] *all the property.* (TA.) And ضَمَّ مِنْ مَالِهِ *He took of his property.* (TA.) — [ضَمَّ الحَرْفَ, aor. and inf. n. as above, a conventional phrase in lexicology and grammar, *He pronounced the letter with the vowel-sound termed* ضَمّ: and *he marked the letter with the sign of that vowel-sound.*]

3. ضَامَّهُ, (Ṣ, MA, Ḳ, TA,) inf. n. مُضَامَّةٌ, (TA,) *He became, or drew, near, or close, to him; he became conjoined with him;* (MA;) i. q. ↓ انضمّ إِلَيْهِ; (Ṣ,* MA, Ḳ;*) and ↓ تضامّ. (Ḳ.) And ضَامَمْتُ الرَّجُلَ *I continued conjoined with the man occupied in one affair.* (TA.) And ضامّ الشَّىْءُ إِلَى الشَّىْءِ *The thing became* [*adjoined to the thing*, or] *conjoined with the thing.* (TA.) See also 6.

4. أَضْمَمْتُهُ كِتَابًا إِلَى أَخِى [app. *I made him*, or *it, to be accompanied by*, or *I made it to comprise, a letter to my brother*]. (TA.)

5. تَضَمَّمْتُهُ *I took it*, or *devoured it, altogether.* (TA in art. ضب.) [See also R. Q. 1.]

6. تَضَامُّوا *They became, or drew, near*, or *close, together*, or *one to another;* or *became conjoined, one with another.* (Ṣ, MA, TA. [See also 3.]) Hence the saying in a trad., لَا تَضَامُّونَ فِى رُؤْيَتِهِ [originally تَتَضَامُّونَ]; but some relate it otherwise, saying ↓ لَا تُضَامُّونَ; and some, لَا تُضَامُونَ, from الضَّيْمُ; (TA in this art.;) and some, لَا تُضَارُّونَ; and some, لَا تُضَارُونَ, from الضَّيْرُ. (TA in art. ضر: for explanations, see 3 in that art.) See also 3 above. [Hence,] تضامّ فِى سُجُودِهِ وَجُلُوسِهِ [*He drew himself together in his prostration and his sitting*, in prayer]. (Ṣ,* and Ḳ in art. حفز.)

7. انضمّ *It was, or became, drawn, put, brought*, or *gathered, together; collected;* or *contracted.* (Mṣb.) انضمّ إِلَيْهِ is syn. with ضَامَّهُ, q. v. (Ṣ,* MA, Ḳ.*) [And it signifies also *He adjoined himself, got him* or *got himself, betook him* or *betook himself, repaired*, or *resorted, to him*, or *it.* And انضمّ عَلَيْهِ *It became drawn together upon it.*] انضمّ الى كَذَا is expl. in the TA as meaning اِنْطَوَى: but I think that الى is evidently a mistranscription for عَلَى; and that the meaning therefore is, *It infolded such a thing*, or *enclosed it*, like اضطمّ عليه, q. v.]

8. اضطمّ الشَّىْءَ *He drew, brought*, or *gathered, the thing to himself:* (Ḳ:) the ط is substituted for ت because of the ض. (Az, TA.) — Hence, in a trad., اضطمّ بَعْضُهُمْ إِلَى بَعْضٍ [*They drew near*, or *close, one to another*]. (TA. [See also 6.]) And, in another trad., اضطمّ عَلَيْهِ النَّاسُ *The people*, or *men, pushed, pressed, crowded*, or *thronged, together upon him.* (TA.) — And اضطمّ عَلَيْهِ *It comprised it*, or *enclosed it.* (Ḳ.) You say, اِضْطَمَّتْ عَلَيْهِ الضُّلُوعُ *The ribs comprised it*, or *enclosed it.* (Ṣ. [See also 7.])

R. Q. 1. ضَمْضَمَ عَلَى المَالِ *He took all the property;* (Ḳ;) as though he drew it, or gathered it, (ضَمَّهُ,) to himself. (TA.) [See also 5.] — And ضَمْضَمَ *He* (a man, TA) *encouraged his heart;* or *became courageous in heart.* (Ḳ, accord. to different copies.) — And, said of a lion, *He* [*roared*, or] *uttered a cry:* (Ḳ, TA:) inf. n. ضَمْضَمَةٌ. (TA.)

ضَمٌّ inf. n. of 1 [q. v.]. (Mṣb, &c.) — [As a conventional term of lexicology and grammar, *A certain vowel-sound, well known.*]

الضُّمُّ and ↓ الضِّمَامُ *Severe calamity* or *misfortune;* (Ḳ, TA;) accord. to Lth: (TA:) but app. mistranscriptions, and correctly with ص [i. e. الصُّمُّ and, by implication, الصِّمَامُ], but the latter is app. only صَمَامِ, without the art., like قَطَامِ; (Ḳ, TA;) so says Az. (TA.)

ضَمَّةٌ [inf. n. un. of 1 (q. v.): and as such signifying] *An embracing.* (TA.) — Also *A number of horses assembled from every quarter for a race:* (Ḳ, TA:) thus called because so assembled. (TA.) — [And, as a conventional term in lexicology and grammar, The *sign of the vowel-sound termed* ضَمّ.]

ضِمَامٌ: see what next follows.

ضِمَامٌ, (Ṣ, KL,) with kesr; (Ṣ;) or ↓ ضُمَامٌ, like غُرَابٌ; (Ḳ;) [the former app. the right, being agreeable with analogy, like رِبَاطٌ and وِثَاقٌ and عِقَالٌ and إِسَارٌ &c.;] *A thing*, (Ṣ, Ḳ,) or *thread, string, cord*, or *the like*, (KL,) *by means of which one thing is drawn, and joined*, or *adjoined, to another thing.* (Ṣ, Ḳ, KL.) One says, التَّقْوَى ضِمَامُ الخَيْرِ كُلِّهِ [*Piety is that which draws and attaches* to its possessor *every good thing*]. (TA.) — See also الضُّمّ, above.

ضُمُومٌ *Any valley along which one goes between two long hills of the kind termed* أَكَمَة: or *any valley flowing* [*with water*] *between two long hills of that kind:* (so accord. to different copies of the Ḳ:) [the former explanation is app. the right; for] AḤn says, when one goes along a valley between two long hills of the kind termed أَكَمَة, that place is termed الضُّمُوم. (TA.)

ضَمِيمٌ [i. q. ↓ مَضْمُومٌ]. One says, أَرْسَلْتُ فُلَانًا وَجَعَلْتُ ضَمِيمَهُ فُلَانًا [*I sent such a one, and made such a one his adjunct*]. (TA.)

ضِمَامَةٌ : see إِضَامَةٌ. — ضِمَامَتَا المُصْحَفِ means *The two sides* [or *boards*] *of the book, that embrace it between them.* (T and M and TA voce دَفَّةٌ.) And in like manner, ضِمَامَتَا السَّرْجِ and الرَّحْلِ [*The two boards of the horse's saddle* and *of the camel's saddle, that embrace it between them*]. (M ibid.)

ضَمَّامٌ *One who collects together the seed-produce.* (TA.)

ضَامٌّ act. part. n. of 1 [q. v.]. (TA.)

ضَامَّةٌ [a subst. from ضَامٌّ, rendered such by the affix ة]. You say, نَهَضَ فُلَانٌ لِلْقِتَالِ وَهُوَ ضَامَّةُ قَوْمِهِ [*Such a one rose and sped to fight*, or *to the fight, he being the musterer of his people*, or *party*]. (TA.) — Also *A want*, or *an object of want, that brings one and causes him to have recourse* [*to a thing*]. (Meyd, in explanation of a prov. cited voce ضَائِمٌ, in art. ضيم, q. v.)

ضَمْضَمٌ *A lion that grasps everything;* as also ↓ ضُمَاضِمٌ. (Ṣ.) [See also ضَمْضَامٌ: and see what here follows.] — Also, (Ṣ,) *Angry;* (Ṣ, Ḳ;) applied to a man: (Ṣ:) and, as also ↓ ضُمَاضِمٌ and ↓ ضُمَضِمٌ, *an angry lion:* (Ḳ, TA:) or simply *a lion:* (TA:) and *bold*, or *daring;* (Ḳ, TA;) applied to a man. (TA.) — And *Big, bulky*, or *corpulent:* (Ḳ, TA:) but it is mentioned by IAạr as with the unpointed ص. (TA.)

ضُمَضِمٌ : see ضَمْضَمٌ. — Also *Niggardly in the utmost degree.* (IAạr, TA.) [See also ضُمَاضِمٌ.]

ضِمْضِمَةٌ : see زِمْزِمَةٌ and ضِمْضِمَةٌ.

ضَمْضَامٌ *One who takes*, or *gets, everything within his grasp;* (Ḳ, TA;) *drawing it to himself.* (TA.) [See also ضَمْضَمٌ.]

ضُمَاضِمٌ : see ضَمْضَمٌ, in two places. — Also

One *who eats much; who has an inordinate appetite for food; who appropriates to himself exclusively of others:* or *who eats much, and does not become satiated.* (TA.) — And *A niggardly man.* (TA.) [See also ضَمْضَمٌ.]

إِضْمَامَةٌ *A bundle,* (حُزْمَةٌ, Mṣb,) or *number put,* or *joined, together,* (TA,) i. q. إِضْبَارَةٌ, (Ṣ, TA,) of books or writings; (Ṣ, Mṣb, TA;) as also ↓ ضِمَامَةٌ: (TA:) pl. of the former أَضَامِيمُ. (Ṣ.) You say, جَآءَ فُلَانٌ بِإِضْمَامَةٍ مِنْ كُتُبٍ [*Such a one brought a bundle of books* or *writings*]. (Ṣ.) — And *A company,* or *collection,* (Ṣ, Ḳ, TA,) of men, or people, *not of one stock, but of different tribes mixed together;* [and *of horses;*] as though collected and joined, one to another: pl. as above. (TA.) One says, فَرَسٌ سَبَّاقُ الأَضَامِيمِ i. e. [*A horse that often outstrips*] *the collections* (Ṣ, Ḳ) *of horses.* (Ḳ.) — And its pl. أَضَامِيمُ signifies also *Stones:* (TA:) or *collections of stones:* (Mgh in art. صقع:) occurring in a trad. respecting the stoning of an adulterer. (Mgh, TA.)

مَضَمٌّ *A place of assembling* of military forces. (TA.)

مَضْمُومٌ pass. part. n. of 1 [q. v.]. (TA.) See also ضَمِيمٌ.

مُنْضَمٌّ [part. n. of 7, q. v. — Hence,] *Lean;* or *slender and lean;* or *lean, and lank in the belly;* as though one part thereof were drawn and adjoined to another. (TA.)

ضمحل

Q. 4, accord. to some, but Q. Q. accord. to most. اِضْمَحَلَّ: see art. ضحل.

ضمحن

Q. 4. اِضْمَحَنَّ *i. q.* اِضْمَحَلَّ [q. v. in art. اضحل]; formed from the latter by substitution [of ن for ل: mentioned by Yaakoob. (TA: and mentioned in the Ḳ in art. ضمحل.)

ضمخ

1: see the next paragraph.

2. ضَمَّخَهُ بِالطِّيبِ, (Ṣ, A, Mgh, Mṣb,) inf. n. تَضْمِيخٌ; (Ṣ, A, Ḳ;) and ↓ ضَمَخَهُ, (ISd, TA,) aor. ـَ, (TḲ,) inf. n. ضَمْخٌ; (ISd, Ḳ;) *He daubed,* or *smeared,* (Ṣ, A, Mgh, Mṣb, Ḳ,) *him,* (Ṣ, A, Mgh, Mṣb,) or *his body,* (L, Ḳ,) *with perfume,* or *some odoriferous* or *fragrant substance,* (Ṣ, A, Mgh, L, Mṣb, Ḳ,) *copiously,* (L,) *so that it seemed to drip.* (L, Ḳ.) It is said in a trad., كَانَ يُضَمِّخُ رَأْسَهُ بِالطِّيبِ *He* [Mohammad] *used to daub,* or *smear, his head copiously with perfume.* (L.)

5. تَضَمَّخَ بِالطِّيبِ, (Ṣ, A, Mgh, Mṣb, Ḳ,) and ↓ اِضْطَمَخَ, (Ḳ,) and ↓ اِضَّمَخَ, (L,) and ↓ انضمخ, *He daubed* or *smeared himself,* or *he became daubed* or *smeared,* (Ṣ, A, Mgh, Mṣb, Ḳ,) *copiously,* (L,) *with perfume,* (Ṣ, A, Mgh, Mṣb, Ḳ,) *so that it seemed to drip.* (L, Ḳ.)

7: see what next precedes.

8. اِضْطَمَخَ, and its var. اِضَّمَخَ: see 5.

ضَمِخَةٌ *A fat* woman or she-camel. (Ḳ.) — And *Fresh ripe dates* (رُطَب [so in copies of the Ḳ, accord. to the TA رَطْب, app. a mistranscription,]) *from which something drips.*

ضمد

1. ضَمَدَ الجُرْحَ, (Ṣ, A, L, Ḳ,) aor. ـِ (Ṣ, L, Ḳ) and ـُ, (Ḳ,) inf. n. ضَمْدٌ; (Ṣ, L;) and ↓ ضَمَّدَهُ, (A, Ḳ,) inf. n. تَضْمِيدٌ; (TA;) *He bound the wound* (and in like manner one says of other things, L) *with a* ضِمَاد or ضِمَادَة i. e. a *bandage,* or *fillet,* (Ṣ, A, L, Ḳ,) or *kerchief.* (A.) This is the primary signification. (L.) And ضَمَدَ رَأْسَهُ, (L,) or ↓ ضَمَّدَهُ بِضِمَادٍ, (Lth,) *He wound a piece of rag round his head, after anointing it,* or *wetting it with water:* (Lth, L:) and ↓ ضمّد رَأْسَهُ, inf. n. تَضْمِيدٌ, *He bound his head with a fillet,* or *bandage,* (Ṣ, A,) or *a kerchief,* (A,) or *a piece of cloth, not a turban.* (Ṣ.) And ضَمَدَ الجُرْحَ, inf. n. ضَمْدٌ, also signifies *He applied a remedy* [or *dressing*] *to the wound, without bandaging it.* (L.) And ↓ ضمّد عَيْنَيْهِ بِالصَّبِرِ *He applied aloes to his eyes.* (L, from a trad.) And ضَمَدَهُ بِالزَّعْفَرَانِ وَالصَّبِرِ *He smeared him,* or *it, over,* [or *poulticed him,* or *it,*] *with saffron and aloes.* (Az, L.) — And أُضْمُدْ عَلَيْكَ ثِيَابَكَ *Bind thou upon thee thy garments,* (Ibn-Málik, A,) and عِمَامَتَكَ [*thy turban*]. (A.) And أَجِدْ ضَمْدَ هٰذَا العِدْلِ *Make thou good the binding of this half-load.* (L.) — And ضَمَدَهُ † *He struck him,* or *hit him, on his head* with a staff or stick: (Ṣ, Ḳ:) sometimes used in this sense: (Ṣ:) or *he cut,* or *wounded,* (A, L,) *him* (L,) or *it,* i. e. his head, (A,) *in the place of the turban,* with a sword; syn. عَمَّمَهُ. (A, L.) — ضَمْدٌ also signifies † The *treating with gentleness,* or *blandishment; soothing, coaxing, wheedling,* or *cajoling;* or *striving, endeavouring,* or *desiring, to do so.* (Ṣ, L, Ḳ.) — And ضَمَدَتْ, (A, L,) aor ـُ and ـِ, (L,) inf. n. ضَمْدٌ (AA, Ṣ, L, Ḳ) and ضِمَادٌ, (Fr, A, L,) ‡ *She* (a woman) *took to herself two friends,* (Ṣ, A, L, Ḳ,) or *secret friends,* or *amorous associates,* (A,) *together:* (Ṣ, A, L, Ḳ:) or *she took another man beside her husband* (AA, A, L) *as her friend,* or *secret friend,* or *amorous associate;* (A;) or *two other men:* (AA, L;) or *she associated as a friend with two or three men in a time of drought, in order that she might eat with one and then with another so as to satiate herself.* (Fr.) And ضَمَدَتْهُ, aor. as above, † *She* (a woman having a husband or a friend [or lover]) *took him* (another man) *as her friend* [or *lover*]. (L.) Aboo-Dhu-eyb says,

تُرِيدِينَ كَيْمَا تَضْمِدِينِي وَخَالِدًا
وَهَلْ يُجْمَعُ السَّيْفَانِ وَيْحَكِ فِي غِمْدِ

† [*Thou desirest to take me as thy lover together with Khálid: but can the two swords* (mercy on thee) *be combined in one scabbard?*]. (Ṣ, L.) And one says, ضَمَدَاهَا † *They both associated as friends* [or *lovers*] *with her,* or *made love to her.* (L.) = ضَمِدَ, aor. ـَ, *It dried;* (Hr, L, Ḳ;) said of blood upon the throat of a slaughtered sheep or goat. (Hr, L.) = Also, inf. n. ضَمَدٌ, *He acted wrongfully,* or *injuriously,* or *unjustly.* (L.) — And ضَمِدَ عَلَيْهِ, aor. ـَ, inf. n. ضَمَدٌ, *He bore rancour, malevolence, malice,* or *spite, against him:* (Ṣ, L, Ḳ:*) or *held fast rancour, &c., against him in his heart.* (L.) And *He was angry with him:* or *vehemently enraged against him and angry with him:* or *he was enraged against him;* i. e. one over whom he had power to vent his rage. (L.)

2: see the preceding paragraph, in four places.

4. أَضْمَدَهُمْ ‡ *He collected them together.* (Ḳ, TA.) — And اضمد العَرْفَجُ *The* [plant called] عرفج *contained its* خُوصَة [q. v.] *lying hidden within it, not yet appearing.* (Ṣ, Ḳ.*)

5. تضمّد *It* (a wound) *was bound with a bandage* or *fillet* [or *kerchief* (see 1)]. (Ḳ.) *It* (a man's head) *was bound with a bandage* or *fillet* [or *kerchief*] or *with a piece of cloth, not a turban.* (Ṣ.) — [And تضمّد بِهِ *He used it,* or *applied it, as a poultice* or *the like.*]

ضَمْدٌ *Such as is fresh,* or *moist,* of herbage or trees: and *such as is dry* thereof: (Ṣ,* L, Ḳ:*) thus having two contr. meanings: (Ḳ:) or *fresh and dry* herbage *mixed together:* and herbage *of which every twig,* or *shoot, has put forth its leaves.* (L.) ضَمْدٌ مِنَ الدَّمِ means *Such as is dry of blood; dry blood.* (L.) — Also The *better,* or *best,* and the *worse,* or *worst,* of sheep or goats: (Ṣ, L, Ḳ:) or the *young,* and the *old:* or *such as are in a sound,* or *good, state,* and *such as are in an unsound,* or *a bad, state:* or the *slender,* and the *large.* (L.) A man says to his creditor, أَقْضِيكَ مِنْ ضَمْدِ هٰذِهِ الغَنَمِ [*I will pay thee with some of the better,* or *best,* or *of the worse,* or *worst,* &c., *of these sheep or goats*]. (Ṣ.)

ضِمْدٌ † *A friend;* or *a true,* or *sincere, friend;* or *a special,* or *particular, friend.* (Ḳ.)

ضَمَدٌ *A remainder, that is due to one, of a fine for blood,* or *of any other debt.* (Ṣ, Ḳ.) One says, لَنَا عِنْدَ فُلَانٍ ضَمَدٌ *A remainder of a fine for blood, or of another debt, is owed to us by such a one.* (Ṣ.)

عَبْدٌ ضَمَدَةٌ *A bulky, thick, slave.* (El-Hejeree, TA.)

ضِمَادٌ *A bandage,* or *fillet,* (Ṣ, A, Ḳ,) or *a kerchief,* (A,) *that is bound upon a wound;* (Ṣ, A, Ḳ;) as also ↓ ضِمَادَةٌ: (Ṣ, Ḳ:) and *a piece of rag that is wound round the head, after anointing it,* or *wetting it with water:* (Lth, L:) and sometimes *put upon the head on account of a headache:* pl. ضَمَائِدُ. (L.) — Also *A remedy* [or *dressing,* such as *a poultice* and *the like,*] *that is applied to a wound.* (Ibn-Hání.)

ضِمَادَةٌ: see ضِمَادٌ. — أَنَا عَلَى ضِمَادَةٍ مِنَ الأَمْرِ

means *I have become on the point*, or *verge, of the affair*, or *event*. (Ṣ.)

ضَامِدٌ i. q. لَازِمٌ [*Cleaving, clinging, holding fast*, &c.]. (AḤn.)

مِضْمَدَةٌ [*A sort of yoke;*] *a piece of wood which is put upon the necks of the two bulls* [*in ploughing*], *having at each extremity a perforation, and between the two perforations, in its upper side, a notch* [app. *for the tying of the beam of the plough thereto so that it may not shift from the middle*], *each of the perforations having a string put into it with the two ends thereof coming forth beneath the* مضمدة, *and each end of the string having a* [*short*] *staff*, or *stick, tied to it; the neck of the bull being put between the two staves*, or *sticks*. (TA.)

ضمر

1. ضَمَرَ, (Ṣ, A, Mgh, Mṣb, Ḳ,) aor. ـُ; (Ṣ, Mṣb, Ḳ;) and ضَمُرَ; (Ṣ, Mṣb, Ḳ;) inf. n. ضُمُورٌ, of the former, and ضُمْرٌ, (Ṣ, A, Mgh, Mṣb, Ḳ,) of the former also, (A, Mgh,) or of the latter, (Mṣb,) [also written ضُمُرٌ, (see an ex., voce نَهَارٌ,)] *He* (a horse, [&c.,] Ṣ, A, &c.) *was*, or *became, lean*, or *light of flesh:* (Ṣ:) or *slender, and lean:* (Mṣb:) or *lean, and lank in the belly:* (A, Ḳ:) or *lank in the belly by reason of leanness:* (Mgh:) and ▼ اضطمر signifies the same. (Ṣ, Ḳ.) [See also 5 and 8.] — Also, inf. n. ضُمُورٌ, *He became lean and weak.* (TA.) — ضَمَرَ العِنَبُ † *The grapes became withered, so as to be neither fresh grapes nor raisins.* (Ṣgh.) — ضَمَرَتِ الحِنْطَةُ † *The wheat*, being parched over the fire, *became contracted and small.* (Mgh.)

2. ضَمَّرَهُ, inf. n. تَضْمِيرٌ, *He made him* (a horse) *lean*, or *light of flesh*; [&c.;] as also ▼ اضمرهُ. (Ṣ.) — *He prepared him* (i. e. a horse) *for racing*, [or *for a military expedition*, (see مُضَمَّرٌ,)] *by feeding him with food barely sufficient to sustain him, after he had become fat;* as also ▼ اضمرهُ. (Mṣb:) *he fed him with food barely sufficient to sustain him, after he had become fat;* as also ▼ اضمرهُ: (Ḳ:) or *he fed him with fodder so that he became fat, and then reduced him to food barely sufficient to sustain him; which is done during forty days:* (Ṣ:) or *he saddled him, and put on him a housing, in order that he might sweat under it, and so lose his flabbiness, and become firm in flesh; and then mounted upon him a light boy or young man, to make him run, but not to make him go so quick a pace as that which is termed* عَنَق; *by the doing of which, one becomes in no fear of his losing his breath in running, and a quick run does not cut him short:* this (says AM) is what I have seen the Arabs practise; and they term it تَضْمِير, and also ▼ مِضْمَار. (T, L.) — Also *He*, or *it, weakened, and subdued, and diminished, him:* and the same signification is assigned to it [tropically] when the objective complement is a word denoting a sensation or passion. (TA.) — التَّضْمِيرُ also signifies *The plaiting well*, and *the anointing well, the lock of hair termed* ضَمِيرَة. (TA.)

4: see 2, in three places. = اضمرهُ signifies also *He determined*, or *resolved, upon it*, فِى ضَمِيرِهِ *in his heart*, or *mind.* (Mṣb.) — *He conceived it* in his heart, or mind. (MA, KL.) — *He concealed it*, syn. أَسَرَّهُ, (A,) or أَخْفَاهُ, (Ḳ,) فِى قَلْبِهِ *in his heart*, (A,) or فى نَفْسِهِ *in his mind.* (Ṣ.) — [And hence, *He suppressed it*, (namely a word or the like,) *meaning it to be understood.* — And hence also اضمر meaning *He made use of a pronoun.*] — And اضمر صَرْفَ الحَرْفِ [*He suppressed the vowel of the* final *letter;*] *he made the movent* [final] *letter quiescent.* (TA.) — And أَضْمَرَتْهُ البِلَادُ ‡ *The lands*, or *countries, hid him, by his having travelled far:* (A:) and اضمرته الأَرْضُ † *the earth hid him*, either *by reason of travel*, or *by death.* (Ḳ, TA.) = اضمر is also *syn. with* اِسْتَقْصَى [q. v.]. (O, Ḳ.) [Accord. to the TḲ, one says اضمر الشَّىْءَ, meaning استقصاهُ.]

5. تضمّر وَجْهُهُ *His face became shrivelled*, or *contracted, by emaciation.* (Ṣgh, L, Ḳ.)

7. انضمر *It* (a branch, or twig,) *became dried up.* (TA.)

8. اضطمر: see 1. — Also *He*, (a horse,) *after having been fed until he had become fat, was reduced to food barely sufficient to sustain him.* (TA.) [See 2.]

ضُمْرٌ: see ضَامِرٌ, in two places. — Hence, in the opinion of ISd, as he says in the M, it is also applied to a horse as meaning دَقِيقُ الحَجَاجَيْنِ [i. e. *Thin in the bones surrounding*, or *projecting over, the cavities of the eyes:* in the TA, البجاجين, an obvious mistranscription; and in the TḲ, الحجاجتين, which is also wrong]: on the authority of Kr: in the copies of the Ḳ, الحَاجِبَيْنِ. (TA.) — And *Narrow;* (O, Ḳ;) applied to a place. (O.) — And i. q. ▼ ضَمِيرٌ [app. in the first of the senses assigned to the latter below]. (O, Ḳ: in the CḲ ضُمَيْر.) See also مُضْمَرٌ.

ضَمْرَانٌ (Ṣ, O, Ḳ) and ▼ ضُمْرَانٌ (TA) *A certain plant*, (Ṣ, O, Ḳ,) *of the shrub-kind* (مِنْ دِقِّ الشَّجَرِ): (Ḳ:) or *of the kind called* حَمْض: AM says, *it is not of the shrub-kind, and has* [what are termed] هَدَب [q. v.] *like the* هَدَب *of the* أَرْطَى: (TA:) AḤn says, *it resembles the* رِمْث, *except that it is yellow* (أَصْفَر) [app. a mistranscription for أَصْغَر i. e. *smaller*]), *and it has little wood*, [and] *the small and dry parts of its branches are fed upon* [by the camels] (يُخْتَطَبُ): he adds, on the authority of the ancient Arabs of the desert, that *it is* [*of the kind called*] حَمْض, *green, lank, pleasing to the camels:* and Aboo-Naṣr says that *it is of the kind called* حَمْض. (O.) = See also what next follows.

ضُمْرَانٌ (A'Obeyd, Ṣ, O, Ḳ, TA) and ▼ ضَمْرَانٌ, thus, with fet-ḥ, as said by Aṣ on the authority of ISk; each of the names of dogs; (TA;) a name of a male dog; (O, Ḳ;) not of a bitch, as J asserts it to be. (Ḳ.) = See also the next preceding paragraph.

ضِمَارٌ *A place*, or *a valley, that is depressed, concealing him who is journeying in it.* (O.) [Accord. to the Ḳ, الضِّمَارُ is "*A place;*" i. e. the name of a certain place.] — مَالٌ ضِمَارٌ *Property of which one hopes not for the return:* (Ḳ:) or *absent property of which one hopes not for the return:* (A'Obeyd, Mṣb, TA:) if not absent, it is not thus called. (A'Obeyd, TA.) — دَيْنٌ ضِمَارٌ *A debt of which the payment is not hoped for:* (Ṣ:) or *for the payment of which no period is fixed.* (Ḳ,* TA.) — عَطَآءٌ ضِمَارٌ *A gift that is not hoped for.* (A.) — وَعْدٌ ضِمَارٌ, (Ṣ,) and عِدَةٌ ضِمَارٌ, (A, Ḳ, [مِنَ العَذَابِ in the CḲ being a mistranscription for مِنَ العِدَاتِ, as in other copies of the Ḳ and in the TA, in which latter is added that عِدَات is pl. of عِدَة, which is syn. with وَعْد,]) *A promise of which the fulfilment is not hoped for:* (Ṣ, A:) or *of which the fulfilment is delayed.* (Ḳ.) — ضِمَارٌ also signifies *Anything of which one is not confident*, or *sure.* (Ṣ.) — And *A debt of which the payment is deferred by the creditor to a future period;* or *a sale upon credit, in which the payment is deferred to a definite period;* or *a postponement*, or *delay, as to the time of the payment of a debt* or *of the price of a thing sold* &c.; syn. نَسِيْئَة. (Fr, TA.) — Also *Unseen; not apparent; contr. of* عِيَان. (Ḳ.) A poet says, censuring a certain man,

وَعَيْنُهُ كَالكَالِئِ الضِّمَارِ *

[*And his present gift is* a thing not hoped for, *like the unseen debt of which the payment is deferred by the creditor:*] meaning, his present gift is like the absent that is not hoped for. (TA.) — ذَهَبُوا بِمَالِى ضِمَارًا means *They took away my property by gaming.* (Fr, TA.) = Also *A certain idol, which was worshipped by El-'Abbás Ibn-Mirdás.* (O, Ḳ, TA. [It is implied in the Ḳ that it is with the art. ال; but it is not so accord. to the O and TA.])

ضَمِيرٌ *A thing that thou concealest*, or *conceivest*, or *determinest upon*, (تُضْمِرُهُ,) *in thy heart*, or *mind:* (Lth, TA:) *a secret;* syn. سِرّ: (Ḳ:) a subst. from أَضْمَرَ فِى نَفْسِهِ شَيْئًا: (Ṣ:) pl. ضَمَائِرُ. (Ṣ, Ḳ.) — [Hence used as meaning *A pronoun;* which is also termed ▼ مُضْمَرٌ, and اِسْمٌ مُضْمَرٌ, lit. *a concealed noun*, i. e. a noun of which the signification is not shown by itself alone; opposed to مُظْهَرٌ: pl. of the first as above; and of the second مُضْمَرَاتٌ.] — See also ضُمْرٌ. — And الضَّمِيرُ signifies *The heart* [itself]; *the mind; the recesses of the mind; the secret thoughts;* or *the soul;* syn. قَلْبُ الإِنْسَانِ, and بَاطِنُهُ, (Mṣb,) or دَاخِلُ الخَاطِرِ: (A, Ḳ:) pl. as above, (Mṣb, Ḳ,) the sing. being likened to سَرِيرَةٌ, of which the pl. is سَرَائِرُ. (Mṣb.) [See also مُضْمَرٌ. And see an ex. in a verse cited in art. سمح, 7th conj.] = Also *Withered*, or *shrivelled, grapes*, (O, Ḳ,) *that are neither fresh grapes nor raisins.* (O.)

لَقِيتُهُ بِالضَّمِيرِ is a phrase mentioned by Ṣgh [in

the O] as meaning *I met him at sunset*: but it is correctly [بِالضُّمْرِ,] with the unpointed ص. (TA.)

ضَمِيرَةٌ *A lock*, or *plaited lock, of hair, such as is termed* ضَفِيرَةٌ and غَدِيرَةٌ: pl. ضَمَائِرُ. (Aṣ, TA.)

ضَامِرٌ *Lean, and lank in the belly*; [&c.; see 1;] (A, Ḳ;) applied to a he-camel, (Ḳ,) and to a horse, as also ▼ضُمْرٌ, and ▼مُضْمَرٌ, and ▼مُضْطَمِرٌ; (A;) and to a she-camel, (Ṣ, A, Ḳ,) as also ضَامِرَةٌ; (Ṣ;) [and to a man;] ضَامِر applied to a she-camel being regarded as a possessive epithet [signifying ذَاتُ ضُمْرٍ]: (TA:) and ▼ضُمْرٌ signifies also *lank in the belly, and small and slender in person*; applied to a man: (Ṣ, A, Ḳ:) fem. with ة: (A, Ḳ:) the pl. of ضَامِرٌ is ضُمَّرٌ. (Ḥam p. 473.) — And A horse *in a state of preparation for racing, by his having been fed with food barely sufficient to sustain him, after having become fat*: and you say خَيْلٌ ضَامِرَةٌ and ضَوَامِرُ, meaning *horses in that state*. (Mṣb.) — Applied to grain, it means *Thin*, or *slender*: (Mgh:) and to a branch or twig, *sapless*; *dried up*; as also ▼مُنْضَمِرٌ. (Ḳ.)

ضَوْمُرَانٌ (Ṣ, O, Mṣb, Ḳ) and ضَوْمَرَانٌ (Mṣb) and ▼ضَيْمُرَانٌ (O, Mṣb, Ḳ) and ضَيْمَرَانٌ (Mṣb) *A species of the* رَيَاحِين [or *sweet-smelling plants*]: (Ṣ, O:) or *of the wild* رَيْحَان: (Ḳ:) or the رَيْحَان فَارِسِى: (Mṣb, Ḳ:) Aboo-Naṣr says that the ضيمران is the شَاهَسْفَرَم [or شَاهِسْفَرَم, i. e. *basil-royal*, or *common sweet basil*, *ocimum basilicum*]: AḤn says, on the authority of an Arab of the desert, of El-Yemen, that the ضيمران is *exactly like the* حَوك [which is one of the names now applied to *sweet basil*], *of sweet odour*, and is therefore asserted by some to be the شاهسفرم, but the ضيمران is *wild*; and he says that some call it ضَوْمَرَان. (O.)

ضَيْمُرَانٌ and ضَيْمَرَانٌ: see the next preceding paragraph.

مُضْمَرٌ *Concealed*, (Ḳ,) [or *conceived*,] in the mind. (Ṣ.) You say, هَوًى مُضْمَرٌ, meaning *Concealed love*; as also ▼ضُمْرٌ; as though the latter were believed to be an inf. n. [used in the sense of a pass. part. n.] from the unaugmented, for the augmented, verb. (TA.) See also ضَمِيرٌ. — Also The *place of concealment*, (Ḳ,) [or *of conception*,] in the mind. (Ṣ.) A poet, (Ṣ,) El-Aḥwaṣ Ibn-Moḥammad El-Anṣáree, (TA,) says,

سَتَبْقَى لَهَا فِى مُضْمَرِ القَلْبِ وَالحَشَا
سَرِيرَةُ وُدٍّ يَوْمَ تُبْلَى السَّرَائِرُ

[*There will remain to her, in the hiding-place of the heart and the bowels, a secret love*, (lit. a secret of love,) *on the day when secrets shall be revealed*]. (Ṣ, TA.)

مُضْمَرٌ: see ضَامِرٌ.

مُضَمِّرٌ One *who prepares his horses, by reducing them to scanty food*, (يُضَمِّرُهَا,) *for a military expedition* or *for racing*. (TA.)

مِضْمَارٌ *A training-place in which horses are prepared for racing* [or *for military service*] *by being fed with food barely sufficient to sustain them, after they have become fat*: (Ṣ,* Mṣb, Ḳ:*) [a *hippodrome*; *a place where horses are exercised*:] pl. مَضَامِيرُ. (A.) You say, جَرَى فِى المِضْمَارِ [*He ran in the hippodrome*, or *place of exercise*]. (A.) And الغِنَآءُ مِضْمَارُ الشِّعْرِ ‡ [app. meaning *Singing is that in which the excellences of poetry are displayed, like as the excellences of a horse are displayed in the hippodrome*]. (A.) — Also The *time, of forty days, during which a horse is reduced to food barely sufficient to sustain him, after his having been fed with fodder so that he has become fat*; (Ṣ, TA;) the *time during which a horse is thus prepared for racing* or *for an expedition against the enemy*: pl. as above. (TA.) It is said in a trad., اليَوْمَ مِضْمَارٌ وَغَدًا ٱلسِّبَاقُ وَالسَّابِقُ مَنْ سَبَقَ ٱلْجَنَّةَ [*To-day is a time for training, and to-morrow is the race, and the winner is he who wins Paradise*:] i. e., to-day one is to work, in the present world, for the desire of Paradise; like as a horse is trained for racing. (Sh.) [One of the explanations of المضمار in the Ḳ is غَايَةُ الفَرَسِ فِى السِّبَاقِ, or, as in the TA, لِلسِّبَاقِ, app. meaning *The goal*, or *limit*, *of the horse in racing*: but in the TA, these words are made to form part of an explanation which I have given before, i. e., the time during which a horse is prepared for racing, &c.] = See also 2.

لُؤْلُؤٌ مُضْطَمِرٌ *Contracted pearls*: (Ḳ:) or *pearls having somewhat of contraction in the middle*. (Ṣ.) — See also ضَامِرٌ.

مُنْضَمِرٌ: see ضَامِرٌ, last sentence.

ضمن

1. ضَمِنَ الشَّىْءَ, (IAṭr, Ṣ, Ḳ,) or المَالَ, (Mgh, Mṣb,) and ضَمِنَ بِهِ, (Mṣb, Ḳ,) aor. ـَ, (Ḳ,) inf. n. ضَمَانٌ (IAṭr, Ṣ, Mṣb, Ḳ) and ضَمْنٌ, (Ḳ,) *He was*, or *became, responsible, answerable, accountable, amenable, surety*, or *guarantee*, (Ṣ, Mgh, Ḳ,) *for the thing*, (Ṣ, Ḳ,) or *for the property*: (Mgh:) or *he made himself responsible, &c., for it*; syn. اِلْتَزَمَهُ; (Mṣb;) and so, in this sense, ▼تضمّنه, (Ṣ,* Ḳ,) quasi-pass. of ضَمَّنَهُ: (Ṣ, Ḳ:) [as though he had it within his grasp, or in his possession; for] the primary signification of الضَّمَانُ is التَّحْصِيلُ: (Mṣb:) some of the lawyers say that it is from الضَّمُّ; but this is a mistake; (Mṣb, TA;) for the ن is radical. (Mṣb.) And ضَمِنَ لَهُ كَذَا *He was, or became, responsible, &c., to him for such a thing*. (MA.) And ضَمِنَ المَالَ مِنْهُ *He was, or became, responsible, &c., to him for the property* [received *from him*]. (Mgh.) — See also 5, in four places. — ضَمِنَهُ signifies also † *He learned it; acquired a knowledge of it*. (TA.) = And ضَمِنَ, (Ṣ, Mṣb, Ḳ,) aor. ـَ, (Ḳ,) inf. n. ضَمَنٌ, (Ṣ, Mṣb, Ḳ,*) † *He* (a man, Ṣ) *had*, or *was affected with, a malady of long continuance*, or *such as crippled him*; (Ṣ, Mṣb, Ḳ;) *was afflicted in his body* (Ṣ,* Ḳ, TA) *by some trial*, or *fracture*, or *other ailment*. (Ṣ,* TA.) And ضَمِنَتْ يَدُهُ, inf. n. ضَمَانَةٌ, † *His arm*, or *hand, was affected with a malady of long continuance*, or *such as crippled*. (Fr, TA.)

2. ضَمَّنَهُ الشَّىْءَ, (Ṣ, MA, Ḳ,) or المَالَ, (Mgh, Mṣb,) inf. n. تَضْمِينٌ, (Ṣ,) *He made him to be responsible, answerable, accountable, amenable, surety*, or *guarantee*, (Ṣ, MA, Mgh, Mṣb, Ḳ,) *for the thing*, (Ṣ, MA, Ḳ,) or *for the property*. (Mgh, Mṣb.) [See an ex. in a verse cited voce مُعَبَّدٌ.] — ضَمَّنْتُ الشَّىْءَ كَذَا *I made the thing to comprise, comprehend*, or *contain, such a thing*. (Mṣb.) Hence, ضَمَّنَ ٱللّٰهُ أَصْلَابَ الفُحُولِ النَّسْلَ [*God has made the loins of the stallions to comprise, in the elemental state, the progeny*]. (Mṣb.) And ضَمَّنَهُ الوِعَآءَ *He put it* (i. e. anything) *into the receptacle*. (Ṣ, Ḳ.) And ضَمَّنَ المَيِّتَ القَبْرَ *He deposited the dead body in the grave*. (TA.) And ضَمَّنَ الكِتَابَ كَذَا † *He made the writing to comprise*, or *include, such a thing*. (MA.) [And ضَمَّنَ الكَلَامَ كَذَا † *He made*, or *held, the sentence*, or *speech*, or *phrase, to imply such a thing*. And ضَمَّنَ الكَلِمَةَ مَعْنَى كَذَا † *He made the word to imply* or *import, such a meaning*.] — التَّضْمِينُ as a conventional term of those who treat of elegance of speech is † *The making poetry to comprise a verse* [*of another poet*]: (TA:) or *the introducing into poetry a hemistich, or a verse*, or *two verses, of another poet, to complete the meaning intended, and for the purpose of corroborating the meaning, on the condition of notifying it as borrowed, beforehand*, or *of its being well known, so that the hearer will not imagine it to be stolen*: and *if it is a hemistich*, or *less than that, it is termed* رَفْوٌ. (Ḥar p. 267.) And as a conventional term of those who treat of versification, † *The making a verse to be not complete otherwise than with what follows it*. (TA.)

5: see 1, first sentence. — تضمّن الشَّىْءُ كَذَا *The thing comprised, comprehended*, or *contained, such a thing*. (Mṣb.) Hence, تَضَمَّنَتْ أَصْلَابُ الفُحُولِ النَّسْلَ and ▼ضَمِنَتْهُ [*The loins of the stallions comprised, in the elemental state, the progeny*]. (Mṣb.) And تضمّن القَبْرُ المَيِّتَ *The grave had the dead body deposited in it*. (TA.) And تضمّن الكِتَابُ كَذَا [and ▼ضَمِنَهُ] † *The writing comprised*, or *included, such a thing*. (Ṣ, MA, Ḳ.) And تضمّن الكَلَامُ كَذَا [and ▼ضَمِنَهُ, as is indicated in the first sentence of this art.,] † *The sentence*, or *speech*, or *phrase, comprehended*, or *comprised, within its scope*, [or *implied*,] *such a thing*; syn. حَصَّلَهُ. (Mṣb.) [And تَضَمَّنَتِ الكَلِمَةُ مَعْنَى كَذَا and ▼ضَمِنَتْهُ † *The word implied such a meaning*.]

ضِمْنٌ ‡ The طَىّ, (Ṣ, MA, Ḳ,) i. e. the *inside*, (MA, TḲ,) [lit. the *folding*,] of a writing, or letter. (Ṣ, MA, Ḳ, TA.) You say, أَنْفَذْتُهُ ضِمْنَ كِتَابِى i. e. فِى طَيِّهِ ‡ [*I sent it*, or *transmitted it, within the folding of my writing* or *letter*; meaning *infolded*, or *enclosed*, *in it*; *included in it*; or *in the inside of it*]. (Ṣ, TA.) And فِى ضِمْنِ كَلَامِهِ [and كِتَابِهِ] means † *Among the contents*, or *implications*, *of his speech* [and *of his writing* or *letter*] (فِى مَطَاوِيهِ); and *the indications thereof.* (Mṣb.) ═ *A thing that satisfies the stomach*: thus, مَا أَغْنَى عَنِّى فُلَانٌ ضِمْنًا means *Such a one did not stand me in stead*, or *supply my want, of anything, even as much as a thing that would satisfy the stomach.* (IAạr, TA.)

ضَمَنٌ (Ṣ, Ḳ) and ↓ ضَمَانٌ and ↓ ضَمَانَةٌ (Ṣ, Mṣb, Ḳ) ‡ *A malady of long continuance*, or *such as cripples*; (Ṣ, Mṣb, Ḳ, TA;) *an affliction in the body*, (Ṣ,* Ḳ, TA,) *by some trial*, or *fracture*, or *other ailment*; (Ṣ, TA;) and ↓ ضُمْنَةٌ signifies the same; (Ḳ;) and [*simply*] *a disease*, or *malady*; (Ṣ, Ḳ;) as in the saying, كَانَتْ ضُمْنَةُ فُلَانٍ أَرْبَعَةَ أَشْهُرٍ ‡ [*The disease of such a one was four months* in duration]. (Ṣ, TA.) [See also 1, last two sentences.] —— ضَمَنٌ also signifies † *A burden*; syn. كَلٌّ: so in the saying, فُلَانٌ ضَمَنٌ عَلَى أَصْحَابِهِ [*Such a one is a burden upon his companions*]. (AZ, TA.) ═ It is also an epithet: see the next pargaraph.

ضَمِنٌ (applied to a man, Ṣ) † *Affected with a malady of long continuance*, or *such as cripples*; (Ṣ, Mṣb, Ḳ, TA;) *afflicted in the body*, (Ṣ,* Ḳ, TA,) *by some trial*, or *fracture*, or *other ailment*: (Ṣ, TA:) and ↓ ضَمَنٌ signifies [the same; or simply] *affected with a disease*, or *malady*; applied to a man [and to two and more and to a female; being originally an inf. n.]; having no dual nor pl. nor fem. form: (TA:) pl. of the former ضَمْنَى (Ṣ,* Mṣb, Ḳ,* TA) and ضَمِنُونَ, or the former of these is pl. of ↓ ضَمِينٌ [which signifies the same as ضَمِنٌ]. (TA.) اِكْتَتَبَ ضَمِنًا [in the CḲ ضَمَنًا] means † *He wrote himself down* [*as one affected with a malady of long continuance*, &c., or] *in the register of the* ضَمْنَى, i. e. *the* زَمْنَى; (Ṣ, Ḳ, TA;) i. e. he asked that he might write himself down [as such], and took for himself a billet from the commander of the army in order to excuse himself from fighting against the unbelievers: (TA:) of such it is said "that God will raise him in that state on the day of resurrection. (Ṣ, TA.) مَعْبُوطَةٌ غَيْرُ ضَمِنَةٍ, occurring in a trad., means *Slaughtered not having any disease.* (TA.) —— Also ‡ [*Loving*: (see ضَمَانَةٌ:) or] *loving excessively*, or *admiringly*. (Ḳ, TA.)

ضُمْنَةٌ: see ضَمَنٌ.

ضَمَانٌ an inf. n.: [see 1, first sentence:] (IAạr, Ṣ, Mṣb, Ḳ:) [used as a simple subst.,] *Responsibility*, *answerableness*, *accountability*, *amenability*, *suretiship*, or *guaranteeship*; syn. كَفَالَةٌ: (Mgh:) but it is more common [in signification] than كَفَالَةٌ; for it sometimes signifies what is not كَفَالَةٌ, namely, [*indemnification*; or] *restoration of the like*, or *of the value, of a thing that has perished.* (Kull.) [ضَمَانُ مَالٍ, and غُرْمٍ, signify *Responsibility*, &c., *for property*, and *for a debt, owed by another person.* And ضَمَانُ نَفْسٍ, and حُضُورٍ, signify *Responsibility*, &c., *for the appearance*, or *presence, of another person, to answer a suit.*] ضَمَان دَرَك is a vulgar phrase; correctly ضَمَانُ الدَّرَكِ [expl. in art. درك]. (TA.) ═ See also ضَمَنٌ.

ضَمِينٌ: see ضَامِنٌ: ═ and see also ضَمِنٌ.

ضَمَانَةٌ: see ضَمَنٌ. —— Also ‡ *Love*: (Ḳ, TA:) [or] *excessive*, or *admiring*, *love.* (TA.)

ضَامِنٌ and ↓ ضَمِينٌ One who is *responsible*, *answerable*, *accountable*, *amenable*, *surety*, or *guarantee*: (Ṣ, Mṣb, Ḳ:) both are mentioned by IAạr as syn., like سَامِنٌ and سَمِينٌ. (TA.) God is represented by the Prophet as saying, مَنْ خَرَجَ مُجَاهِدًا فِى سَبِيلِى وَٱبْتِغَآءَ مَرْضَاتِى فَأَنَا عَلَيْهِ ضَامِنٌ وَهُوَ عَلَىَّ ضَامِنٌ, meaning [*Whoso goes forth as a warrior in my cause, and seeking*, or *seeking earnestly, to obtain my approval*,] *I am responsible to him* for what I have promised him, to recompense him living and dead; ضامن being made trans. by means of على because it implies the meaning of مُجَامِر and رَقِيبٌ; and the last clause means nearly the same, but is rendered as meaning *and he is one who has* [*a claim to*] *responsibility on my part*, as though care and mindfulness [of him] were obligatory on me. (Mgh.) And it is said in a trad., الإِمَامُ ضَامِنٌ وَالمُؤَذِّنُ مُؤْتَمَنٌ: (Mgh, JM,* TA:) [the latter clause has been expl. in art. أمن (voce أَمِينٌ):] the former clause means, *The imám* [or *leader of prayer*] *is as though he were responsible for the correctness of the prayer of those who follow him*: (JM, TA: [and the like is said, with other, similar, explanations, in the Mgh:]) or it means, *the imám is careful*, or *mindful, for the people* [*who follow him*], *of* [*the correctness of*] *their prayer.* (TA.) —— ضَامِنٌ and ↓ مِضْمَانٌ applied to a she-camel, signify *Having a fœtus in her belly*: and the pls. are ضَوَامِنُ and مَضَامِينُ. (IAạr, L and TA in art. لقح and in the present art.) —— ضَامِنَةٌ applied to rights, or dues, (حُقُوق,) is used by Lebeed as meaning مَضْمُونَةٌ; [see مَضْمُونٌ;] like رَاحِلَةٌ is used as meaning مَرْحُولَةٌ. (TA.)

ضَامِنَةٌ [fem. of ضَامِنٌ, q. v.]. —— الضَّامِنَةُ signifies *What is included within the middle* of any town or country or the like. (TA.) الضَّامِنَةُ مِنَ النَّخْلِ, (AO, Ṣ, Ḳ,* TA,) occurring in a letter of the Prophet, (AO, Ṣ, TA,) means *What are included within the cities* or *towns* or *villages, of the palm-trees*: (AO, Ṣ, Ḳ,* TA:) or *what are surrounded, thereof, by the wall of the city*: (Ḳ:) but Az says that they are so called because their owners are responsible for their culture and keeping: (TA:) opposed to الضَّاحِيَةُ من النخل, which means what are in the open country, of the palm-trees that imbibe with their roots, without being watered. (AO, Ṣ, TA.*)

مُضَمَّنٌ Water *included in a mug* or *other vessel*: and milk *included in the udder.* (TA.) —— Also † Poetry *made to comprise a verse* [*from another poem*]. (Ṣ, Ḳ. [See 2, last sentence but one.]) And † A verse [*made to be*] *not complete otherwise than with what follows it.* (Ṣ, Ḳ. [See 2, last sentence.]) —— And † A sound [*made to comprehend with it somewhat of another*:] *upon which one cannot pause without conjoining it with another*: (Ḳ:) in the T it is said to be [*such as is exemplified in*] *a man's saying* قِفْ فُلْ [or فُلَ, for قِفْ فُلَانُ *Pause thou, such a one*], *with making the* ل *to have a smack of the vowel-sound* (بِإِشْمَامِ اللَّامِ إِلَى الحَرَكَةِ). (TA.)

مِضْمَانٌ: see ضَامِنٌ, last sentence but one.

مَضْمُونٌ pass. part. n. of 1 in the first of the senses assigned to the latter above: you say شَىْءٌ مَضْمُونٌ [meaning *A thing*, such as property, or the payment of a debt, &c., *ensured by an acknowledgment of responsibility for it*]. (TA.) —— مَضْمُونُ كِتَابٍ means مَا فِى ضِمْنِهِ and عَلَيْهِ [i. e. *The contents of a writing* or *letter*; or *what is infolded*, or *included, in a writing* or *letter*; *what is implied therein*; and *what is indicated therein*]: pl. مَضَامِينُ. (TA.) —— And المَضَامِينُ, (A'Obeyd, Ṣ, Mṣb, Ḳ,) of which the sing. is مَضْمُونٌ, (A'Obeyd, Mṣb, Ḳ,) and one may also say نَسَمَةٌ مَضْمُونَةٌ, as meaning نَسَمَةٌ, (Mṣb,) signifies *What are* [*comprised*] *in the loins of the stallions*; (A'Obeyd, Ṣ, Mṣb, Ḳ;) i. e. *the progeny* [*thereof, in the elemental state*]: (Mṣb:) or, accord. to Aboo-Sa'eed, [though the reverse is generally held to be the case,] المَلَاقِيحُ signifies what are in the backs of the he-camels, and المَضَامِينُ *what are in the bellies of the females.* (L in art. لقح.) The selling of the مضامين and the ملاقيح is forbidden. (Ṣ.) [مَضَامِينُ is also pl. of مِضْمَانٌ, q. v.] —— مَضْمُونُ اليَدِ *i. q.* مَخْبُونُهَا, (Ḳ,) meaning مَعْلُولُهَا [i. e. *Diseased in the arm*, or *hand*]; (TḲ;) applied to a man. (TA. [See 1, last sentence, which indicates a more particular meaning.])

ضن

1. ضَنَّ بِهِ, (Mgh, Mṣb,) first pers. ضَنِنْتُ بِهِ, (Ṣ, Mṣb,*) [and one may say عَلَيْهِ, and عَنْهُ, in the place of بِهِ, (see ضَنِينٌ,)] and ضَنِنُوا occurs, in a verse of Ḳaạnab Ibn-Umm-Ṣáhib, used by poetic license for ضَنُّوا, (Ṣ,) aor. ـَ; (Ṣ, Mgh, Mṣb, Ḳ;) and ضَنَّ, (Mṣb,) first pers. ضَنَنْتُ, (Ṣ, Mṣb,*) aor. ـِ, (Ṣ, Mṣb, Ḳ,) accord. to Fr, (Ṣ,) or, accord. to Th, Fr said, I have heard ضَنَنْتُ, though I have not heard أَضِنُّ, but this aor. is mentioned by Yaạkoob; (TA;) inf. n. ضِنٌّ (Ṣ, Mgh, Mṣb, Ḳ [in the CḲ ضِنَانًا is erroneously put for ضِنًّا]) and ضَنٌّ (TA) and ضَنَانَةٌ, (Ṣ, Mgh, Mṣb, Ḳ, TA,) with fet-ḥ, (Mṣb, TA,) and ضِنَّةٌ, (Mṣb,) or this last is a simple subst.; (Mgh;) *He was*, or *became, niggardly, tenacious, stingy*, or *avaricious*, (Ṣ, Mgh, Mṣb, Ḳ,) *of it.*

(Ṣ, Mgh, Mṣb. [See also 8.]) You say, ضَنَّ عَلَيْهِ بِكَذَا *He was, or became, niggardly, &c., to him, of such a thing.* (Mgh.) And إِنَّمَا يُضَنُّ بِالضَّنِينِ ↑ [*Only he who clings is to be clung to*]: a prov., meaning that you should cling to fraternizing [only] with him who clings to fraternizing with you. (Meyd, and Ḥar p. 42.) And ضَنِنْتُ بِالمَنْزِلِ, inf. n. ضِنٌّ and ضَنَانَةٌ, [*I kept tenaciously to, or*] *I did not quit, or relinquish, the place of alighting, or abode.* (TA.)

8. اِضْطَنَّ (originally اِضْتَنَّ, TA) *He* (a man, TA) *was, or became, niggardly, tenacious, stingy, or avaricious.* (Ḳ.) [See also 1.]

ضِنٌّ an inf. n. of 1 [q. v.]. (Ṣ &c.) —— Also *A thing highly esteemed, of which one is tenacious.* (TA.) —— [Hence] one says, هُوَ ضِنِّى *He is the person of whose affection I am tenacious*; as also ↑ ضِنَّتِى and ↑ ضَنِينِى: (TA:) or *he is my particular, or special, friend,* (Ḳ, TA,) مِنْ بَيْنِ إِخْوَانِى [*chosen from among my brethren*]; (Ṣ, TA;) as though I appropriated him specially to myself, and were tenacious of him because of the place that he held in my estimation: as is said in the Ṣ, it is like special appropriation [of the person to oneself]. (TA.) [And as ضِنٌّ is originally an inf. n., it is used as an epithet applied to a pl. number:] it is said in a trad., إِنَّ لِلّٰهِ ضِنًّا مِنْ خَلْقِهِ يُحْيِيهِمْ فِى عَافِيَةٍ وَيُمِيتُهُمْ فِى عَافِيَةٍ, (Ṣ, TA,) or ↑ ضَنَائِنَ مِنْ خَلْقِهِ, (Ḳ,* TA,) accord. to different relations thereof, (TA,) i. e. [*Verily God has*] *specially-distinguished individuals* [*of his creatures, whom He causes to live in a state of freedom from disease, or from disease and trial, and whom He causes to die in a state of freedom* &c.]: (Ḳ, TA:) the sing. of ضَنَائِن is ↑ ضَنِينَةٌ, of the measure فَعِيلَةٌ in the sense of the measure مَفْعُولَةٌ, and meaning *a thing that one specially appropriates to himself, and of which he is tenacious because of the place that it holds in his estimation.* (TA.)

ضِنَّةٌ an inf. n. of ضَنَّ: (Mṣb:) or a subst. therefrom signifying *Niggardliness, tenaciousness, stinginess, or avarice:* (Mgh:) or *vehement niggardliness* &c.; as also ↑ مَضَنَّةٌ. (TA.) —— See also ضِنٌّ.

ضَنَنٌ *Courageous, brave, or strong-hearted.* (Ḳ.)

ضَنِينٌ *Niggardly, tenacious, stingy, or avaricious,* (Ṣ, Mgh, Mṣb, Ḳ,) بِشَىْءٍ [*of a thing*], (Ṣ,) or بِشَىْءٍ نَفِيسٍ [*of a thing held in high estimation*]. (TA.) وَمَا هُوَ عَلَى ٱلْغَيْبِ بِضَنِينٍ, in the Ḳur [lxxxi. 24], as some read it, others reading بِظَنِينٍ [q. v.], is expl. by Zj as meaning, *And he is not a tenacious concealer of that which has been revealed to him:* and if عَن or بِ were substituted for عَلَى, it would be correct. (TA.) —— See also 1. —— And see ضِنٌّ.

ضَنَانَةٌ an inf. n. of 1 [q. v.]. (Ṣ &c.) —— [Hence,] one says, هَجَمْتُ عَلَى القَوْمِ بِضَنَانَتِهِمْ, meaning † [*I came suddenly upon the people, or party, in their close state, i. e.,*] *when they had not dispersed themselves.* (TA.) And أَخَذْتُ الأَمْرَ بِضَنَانَتِهِ † [*I took to the affair*] *in its fresh state.* (TA.)

ضَنِينَةٌ; and its pl. ضَنَائِنُ: see ضِنٌّ.

مَضِنَّةٌ: see ضِنَّةٌ. —— هٰذَا عِلْقٌ مَضَنَّةٌ and مَضِنَّةٌ [the former mentioned after the latter in the Ṣ] *This is a thing held in high estimation, of which one is tenacious,* (Ṣ, Ḳ, TA,) *and for which people vie in desire.* (TA.) [See also عِلْق, last sentence.]

المَضْنُونُ a name of [*The compound of perfumes commonly called*] الغَالِيَة; (Ez-Zejjájee, Ṣ, Ḳ, TA;) as also ↑ المَضْنُونَةُ; (Ez-Zejjájee, Ṣ,* TA;) which latter is said by Aṣ to be *a sort of perfume*; and so is the former in the A: in the M the former is said to be *the oil of ben:* it is thus called because one is tenacious of it. (TA.) —— Also, (IKh, TA,) or ↑ المَضْنُونَةُ, (Ḳ, TA,) a name of *The well Zemzem.* (Ḳ, TA.)

المَضْنُونَةُ: see the next preceding paragraph, in two places.

ضنأ

1. ضَنَأَتْ, aor. َ, (Ṣ, M, O, Mṣb, Ḳ,) inf. n. ضَنْءٌ and ضُنُوءٌ; (Ṣ, M, O, Ḳ;) and accord. to the Ḳ, ضَنِئَتْ, but MF says that this latter is unknown, i. e., it is not mentioned in the other lexicons in the sense here assigned to it in the Ḳ; (TA;) and ↑ اضنأت; (Ṣ, M, O, Ḳ;) *She* (a woman) *had many children:* (Ṣ, M, O, Mṣb, Ḳ:) [and so ضَنَتْ and ضَنِيَتْ, as mentioned in art. ضنو:] and in like manner one says of cattle; (M;) [i. e.] one says, ضَنَأَ المَالُ, (Ṣ, O, Ḳ) and ضَنِئَ, (O, Ḳ,) and ضَنَأَتِ المَاشِيَةُ and ضَنِئَت, (TA,) [and ↑ اضنأ and اضنأت as is implied in the M,] *The cattle multiplied, or became numerous or many.* (Ṣ, O, Ḳ, TA.) And ضَنَأَتْ is said to signify *She brought forth.* (TA.) —— And ضَنَأَ فِى الأَرْضِ, (M, Ḳ,) inf. n. ضَنْءٌ and ضُنُوءٌ [as above], (M, TA,) *He hid, or concealed, himself in the land, or country:* (M:) or *he went away in the land, or into the country, and hid, or concealed, himself* [*therein*]: (Ḳ:) like ضَبَأَ. (TA.)

4: see above, in two places. —— أَضْنَؤُوا signifies *Their cattle multiplied, or became numerous or many.* (Ṣ, O, Ḳ.)

8. اضطنأ لهُ and منهُ *He was abashed at, or shy of,* and *he shrank at, or from, him, or it.* (M, Ḳ. [See also اضطبأ.]) Eṭ-Ṭirimmáḥ uses اضطنأ [or اِضْطَنَى in this sense,] and يَضْطَنِى meaning اضطنأ [and يضطنئ]: or as being derived from الضَّنَى meaning "disease." (M.)

ضَنْءٌ *Children, or offspring*; as also ↑ ضِنْءٌ; (Ṣ, M, O, Ḳ; [and so ضَنْوٌ and ضِنْوٌ, as mentioned in art. ضنو;]) the former accord. to El-Umawee, and both accord. to AA: (Ṣ, O:) the former signifies the *offspring* of anything: (TA:) and also, (Ḳ, TA, [in a copy of the M ↑ the latter, but this is app. a mistranscription,]) *multitude of offspring:* it is like نَفْرٌ (M, Ḳ) and رَهْطٌ, (M,) having no n. un.: the pl. is ضُنُوءٌ. (M, Ḳ.)

ضِنْءٌ *Origin, root, race, or stock*; syn. أَصْلٌ: (El-Umawee, Ṣ, M, O, Ḳ:) and the *place in which a thing originates*; syn. مَعْدِنٌ. (El-Umawee, Ṣ, O, Ḳ.) One says, فُلَانٌ فِى ضِنْءِ صِدْقٍ [*Such a one is of an excellent origin or race or stock*], (Ṣ, O, L,) and فِى ضِنْءِ سَوْءٍ [*of a bad origin* &c.]. (L.) —— See also ضَنْءٌ, in two places.

ضُنَأَةٌ (M, O, Ḳ) and ↑ ضُنَاءَةٌ (O, Ḳ) *Necessity, need, or want*; or *difficulty, or distress*; (ضَارُورَةٌ, M, O, or ضَرُورَةٌ, Ḳ; [both meaning the same;]) *that befalls a man:* (O:) so in the saying قَعَدَ مَقْعَدَ ضُنَأَةٍ (M, Ḳ) and ↑ ضُنَاءَةٍ (Ḳ) [lit. *He sat in the sitting-place of necessity,* &c.; meaning *he was, or became, in an abject condition*]: the phrase denotes disdain, or scorn; and is thought by AM to be from اِضْطَنَأَ meaning "he was abashed, &c." (TA.)

ضُنَاءَةٌ: see the next preceding paragraph, in two places.

ضَانِئٌ (Ṣ, O, Ḳ) and ضَانِئَةٌ (Ks, Ṣ, O, Mṣb, Ḳ) A woman *having many children:* (Ṣ, O, Mṣb, Ḳ:) and in like manner, the latter, cattle (مَاشِيَةٌ) *having numerous offspring.* (TA.)

ضنك

1. ضَنُكَ, aor. ُ, inf. n. ضَنْكٌ and ضَنَاكَةٌ and ضُنُوكَةٌ, (O, Ḳ,) the first and third of these, (O,) or the first and second, (TA,) accord. to IDrd, used in relation to a place, and the second and third in relation to life, or sustenance, or means of subsistence, (O, TA,) *It was, or became, narrow, or strait.* (O, Ḳ, TA.) —— And ضَنُكَ said of a man, inf. n. ضَنَاكَةٌ, *He was, or became, weak in his judgment,* and *in his body,* and *in his soul,* and *in his intellect.* (Ḳ.) —— And ضَنُكَ السَّحَابُ *The clouds became thick, collected together, and dense.* (O, TA.) ═ ضُنِكَ, like عُنِىَ, *He was, or became, affected with a coryza, or defluxion from the head and nose.* (Ḳ.)

4. اضنكهُ *He* (God) *caused him to be affected with a coryza, or defluxion from the head and nose.* (TA.)

ضَنْكٌ an inf. n. of ضَنُكَ: (O, Ḳ:) its primary signification is *Narrowness, or straitness,* and *hardship.* (Aboo-Is-ḥáḳ, TA.) —— And *Narrow, or strait*; syn. ضَيِّقٌ; (Ṣ, M, O, Ḳ; [in the CḲ, and in a copy of the Ṣ, ضِيق, which is also a correct explanation, as shown above; but not what is here meant, as appears from what follows;]) applied to anything, (M, Ḳ,) masc.

and fem., (M, K, and Bd in xx. 123,) being an inf. n. used as an epithet. (Bd ibid.) [Like the Pers. تَنْگ.] One says مَكَانٌ ضَنْكٌ *A narrow*, or *strait, place.* (IDrd, O, TA.) And عَيْشٌ ضَنْكٌ *A strait life*; or *strait sustenance*, or *means of subsistence*; (IDrd, O, TA;) as also ▾ عَيْشٌ ضَنِيكٌ: (AA, O, K, TA:) and thus مَعِيشَةً ضَنْكًا in the Kur xx. 123; where some read ▾ ضَنْكَى, like سَكْرَى: (Bd:) or this means *such as is unlawful*; (O, TA;) every life that is unlawful being termed ضَنْكٌ, accord. to Lth, even though it be ample: (O, TA:*) Aboo-Is-hák thinks it to mean [*subsistence*] *in the fire of Hell*: but says that most explain this phrase in the Kur as meaning *the punishment of the grave*: (TA:) thus it means accord. to Ibn-Mes'ood: (O:) or, accord. to Katádeh, *Hell*: (O, TA:) or, accord. to Ed-Dahhák, *forbidden gain*: (TA:) or, as some say, الضَّرِيعُ [q. v.], and الزَّقُّومُ [q. v.]. (Bd.)

ضُنْكَةٌ: see ضُنَاكٌ.

ضَنْكَى: see ضَنْكٌ.

ضِنَاكٌ: see ضَنَاكٌ.

ضُنَاكٌ *A coryza*, or *defluxion from the head and nose*; syn. زُكَامٌ; (S, O, K;) as also ▾ ضُنْكَةٌ. (K.)

ضِنَاكٌ; (O, K, &c.;) accord. to El-Fárábee, (O, TA,) and J [in the S], (TA,) ▾ ضَنَاكٌ; but accord. to others, with kesr, and this is the right; (O, TA;) *Compact in flesh*; applied to a woman: (El-Fárábee, S, O:) or *plump, and compact in flesh*; so applied: (Lth, TA:) or *heavy in the hinder part*, (K, TA,) *and large in body*; (TA;) so applied: (K,* TA:) or *having much flesh*; applied to a male and to a female, without ة: (IAth, TA:) and *firm in make, and strong*; applied to a male and to a female; (K, TA;) of human beings, and of camels, and in like manner of palm-trees and of trees in general: (TA:) and, applied to a she-camel, *thick in the hinder part*: (TA:) and [*large*; applied to trees (شَجَرٌ): or] *large trees.* (Ibn-'Abbád, O, K.)

ضَنِيكٌ: see ضَنْكٌ. — Also *Weak in his body*, and *in his intellect*, (AZ, O, K,) and *in his judgment*, and *in his soul.* (K.) — And *A servant who works for his bread.* (AZ, O, K.) — And *i. q.* مَقْطُوعٌ [*Cut off*; &c.]. (AA, O, K.)

ضُنَاكٌ *Hard, and firm and compact in flesh*; (Lh, O, K;) applied to a man; (Lh, O;) as also ضُنَاكٌ: (K:) fem. ضُنَاكَةٌ; (Lh, O, K;) applied to a woman. (Lh, O.) And, applied to a she-camel, *Great*, (K, TA,) *and compact in make*: (TA:) as also with ة. (K.)

مُضْنَكٌ, (TA,) or ▾ مُتَضَنِّكٌ, (O,) *Affected with a constant*, or *chronic, pervading disease*; or *emaciated by disease so as to be at the point of death.* (O, TA.)

مَضْنُوكٌ *Affected with the malady termed* ضُنَاكٌ [q. v.]. (S, O.)

مُتَضَنِّكٌ: see مُضْنَكٌ.

ضنو

1. ضَنَتِ الْمَرْأَةُ, inf. n. ضَنَآءٌ (S, M, K) and ضَنًا, (M, K,) *The woman had many children*; (S, M, K;) as also ضَنِيَت: (K:) and so with ء. (S.) — And ضَنَا نَصِيبُهُ *His share*, or *portion, became redundant*; *it increased*, or *augmented.* (Sgh, K.)

ضَنْوٌ and ضِنْوٌ *Children*, or *offspring*; (AA, S, K;) like ضَنْءٌ and ضِنْءٌ; as also ▾ ضَنًا, accord. to IAar. (TA.)

ضَنًا: see what next precedes.

ضنى

1. ضَنِىَ, (S, M, Msb, K,) aor. َ, (Msb, K,) inf. n. ضَنًى; (S, M, Mgh, Msb, K;) and ▾ اضطنى signifies the same; *He was, or became, slender, and small in body*: and hence, (Ham p. 112,) *he was*, or *became, diseased, disordered*, or *sick*; (S, and Ham ibid.;) because disease occasions leanness, or emaciation: (Ham:) or *he was*, or *became, lean*, or *emaciated*: (so accord. to the explanation of the inf. n. in the Mgh:) or *he was*, or *became, affected with a disease, disorder*, or *sickness*, (M, Msb, K,) *of long continuance, and settled*, (M,) or *constant, so that he was at the point of death*, (Msb,) or *such as infected*, or *pervaded, him, and so that, whenever he thought himself to be recovering, he relapsed.* (K.) = [See also 1 in art. ضنو.]

3. مُضَانَاةٌ *i. q.* مُعَانَاةٌ, (S, K, KL,) both signifying The *suffering*, or *enduring*, [or *contending with*,] *the difficulty*, or *trouble*, or *inconvenience*, of a thing; as also مُقَاسَاةٌ. (KL.)

4. اضناه, said of a disease, disorder, or sickness, (S, M, Mgh, Msb, K,) *It rendered him such as is termed* ضَنًى or ضَنٍ: (M, Msb, K:) *rendered him lean*, or *emaciated*: (Mgh:) or *oppressed him*; *burdened him heavily*; *overburdened him*; or *overcame him, and rendered him heavy.* (S, TA.) = And أَضْنَى *He kept to the bed by reason of what is termed* ضَنًى [i. e. *leanness*, or *emaciation*; or *disease, disorder*, or *sickness*, or *such as was of long continuance*, &c.: see 1]. (TA.)

5. تضنّى *He* (a man) *feigned himself diseased, disordered*, or *sick.* (TA.)

8. اضطنى: see 1. — See also 8 in art. ضنأ.

ضَنًى inf. n. of 1. (S, M, &c.) — Also, [in some copies of the K erroneously written ضَنًى,] and ▾ ضَنٍ; (S, M, Msb, K;) the former applied alike to a man (Fr, IAar, T, S, Msb) and to a woman (IAar, T, S, Msb) and to two persons (Msb) and to a pl. number, (Fr, IAar, T, S, Msb,) because originally an inf. n., (S, Msb,) for ذَاتُ ضَنًى and ذُو ضَنًى [&c.]; (Msb;) or some do not dualize it nor pluralize it, because it is [originally] an inf. n., and others dualize it and pluralize it; (M;) but ▾ ضَنٍ has a fem. (Msb) and a dual and a pl., (S,) its fem. being ضَنِيَةٌ (Msb, TA) [and its dual ضَنِيَانِ] and the pl. is أَضْنَآءٌ; (TA;) [*Slender, and small in body*: and hence, (see 1,)] *diseased, disordered*, or *sick*: (S:) [or *lean*, or *emaciated*: (see again 1:)] or *affected with a disease, disorder*, or *sickness*, (M, Msb, K,) *of long continuance, and settled*, (M,) or *constant, so that he is at the point of death*, (Msb,) or *such as infects*, or *pervades, him, and so that, whenever he thinks himself to be recovering, he relapses.* (K.) You say, تَرَكْتُهُ ضَنًى and ▾ ضَنِيًا [*I left him lean*, or *diseased*, &c.]. (S.)

ضَنٍ; fem. ضَنِيَةٌ; and pl. أَضْنَآءٌ: see the next preceding paragraph, in three places.

ضَنًى, [written in the TA ضنا, but the final radical is ى,] with kesr, accord. to IAar, signifies *Pains that cause fear.* (TA.)

ضَنَآءٌ, like سَلَامٌ [in measure, The *state of such as is termed* ضَنًى or ضَنٍ], a subst. from ضَنِىَ. (Msb.)

مُضْنًى *Rendered lean*, or *emaciated*; [&c.;] (Mgh;) pass. part. n. of 4 [q. v.]. (Mgh, Msb.)

ضهأ

3. مُضَاهَأَةٌ is *syn. with* مُضَاهَاةٌ, (K, TA, [the و before المُضَاهَاةُ in the CK should be erased,]) *i. q.* مُشَاكَلَةٌ: (S, O, Msb, TA:) you say, ضَاهَأْتُهُ and ضَاهَيْتُهُ, ('Eyn, S,* O,* Msb,* TA,) i. e. *I resembled him*; syn. شَابَهْتُهُ: ('Eyn, TA:) [or *I conformed with him*:] or ضَاهَأَهُ, inf. n. as above, signifies *he imitated him*; syn. عَارَضَهُ and بَارَاهُ; and one says also, ضَاهَيْتُهُ, inf. n. مُضَاهَاةٌ: (Msb:) the verb is read both with and without ء in the Kur [ix. 30]. (O, Msb, TA.) — ضَاهَأَ بِهِ, (A'Obeyd, TA,) [or ضَاهَاهُ, like ضَاهَاهُ, mentioned in art. ضهى,] inf. n. as above, (K,) *He* (a man) *was*, or *became, gentle, tender*, or *courteous*, or *he acted*, or *behaved, gently*, &c., *with him*, or *to him.* (A'Obeyd, K,* TA.)

Q. Q. 1, or Q. 1. ضَهْيَأَ: } see art. ضهيأ.
ضَهْيَأَ and ضَهْيَأَةٌ: }

ضهب

1. ضَهَبَهُ بِالنَّارِ, aor. َ, (K,) inf. n. ضَهْبٌ, (TK,) *He altered it*, (K, TA,) *and changed its colour*, (TA,) *by means of fire.* (K, TA.) [See also 2.] = ضَهَبَ said of a man, (O, K,) aor. َ, (TA,) inf. n. ضُهُوبٌ, (O, K,) ‡ *He failed of fulfilling his promise* (أَخْلَفَ), *and was weak, and not like a man*: (O, K, TA:) as though likened to meat not thoroughly cooked. (TA. [See 2.]) — And ضَهْبُ القَوْمِ signifies اِخْتِلَاطُهُمْ [i. e. *The people's being mixed*, or *confused*]: (JK, O:) or أَخْلَاطُهُمْ [i. e. ▾ ضَهْبٌ is a subst., signifying *a medley*, or *mixed* or *promiscuous multitude* or *collection*, of people]. (So in the K. [But I think that this explanation is a mistranscription.]) [Or it signifies *The people's multiplying themselves, and hastening*: for] it is said in the "Nawádir" that ضَهَبَ

حُطُبُوا and ضَهَبُوا and هَلَبُوا and أَلَبُوا and الفَوْرِ all denote الإِقْتَار and الإِسْرَاع : so in the T in art. حضب. (TA.)

2. ضهّب, inf. n. تَضْهِيبٌ, *He roasted* (Lth, Ḳ, TA) flesh-meat (Lth, TA) *upon heated stones:* (Lth, Ḳ, TA:) or *he roasted,* (Ḳ,) or *put into the fire,* (AA, TA,) *but did not cook thoroughly,* (AA, Ḳ, TA,) flesh-meat. (AA, TA.) — And, (Ḳ,) inf. n. as above, (Ṣ, O,) *He exposed* a bow, (Ṣ, O, Ḳ,) and a spear, (Ṣ, O,) *to the fire,* (Ṣ, O, Ḳ,) *on the occasion of straightening it,* (Ṣ, O,) or *to straighten it.* (Ḳ.) [See also 1.] — And *He collected together* the fire; (JK;) and so ▼ ضَهْضَبَ. (JK, O, Ḳ.)

3. مُضَاهَبَةٌ signifies *Mutual reviling* or *vilifying;* (Ḳ;) *the addressing each other with bad words.* (TA.)

Q. 1. ضَهْضَبَ: see 2, last sentence. [Mentioned in this art., as though Q. Q., contr. to the rule generally observed with respect to words of four radical letters of which the first and third are identical but not the second and fourth.]

ضَهْبٌ: see the first paragraph.

قَوْسٌ ضَهْبَآءُ *A bow upon which the fire has taken effect* [*so as to alter its colour*]: (O, Ḳ:) like ضَهْيَآءُ. (TA.)

ضَيْهَبٌ i. q. مَضْهَبٌ, meaning *A place where flesh-meat is roasted* [*on the ground heated by the sun*]; (Ḳ; [in the CḲ, يُشْوِىّ اللَّحم is erroneously put for يُشْوَى اللَّحْمُ;]) accord. to Lth, *any* [*high ground such as is called*] قُفّ, or *rugged ground,* or *place on a mountain, upon which the sun shines with such heat that flesh-meat will roast upon it:* but Az says that what Lth means is صَيْهَبٌ only, with the unpointed ص; (O,* TA;) and if so, the meaning assigned here in the Ḳ is not correct. (TA.)

مُضَهَّبٌ Flesh-meat *roasted, but not thoroughly cooked:* (Ṣ, A, O:) accord. to El-Mufaddal, flesh-meat *cut in pieces;* (O;) and thus in the Ḳ; (TA;) but IF says that this is nought, unless it be *cut in pieces roasted:* (O:) it is at variance with what is said by the leading authorities, for they say that it means flesh-meat *roasted upon heated stones:* or *roasted upon the fire, but not thoroughly cooked:* (TA:) or *cooked in a frying-pan.* (TA in art. عرص.) Imra-el-Ḳeys says,

* نَمُشُّ بِأَعْرَافِ الجِيَادِ أَكُفَّنَا *

* إِذَا نَحْنُ قُمْنَا عَنْ شِوَآءٍ مُضَهَّبِ *

[*We wipe our hands with the manes of the swift horses when we rise from eating roast meat not thoroughly cooked*]. (Ṣ, O.)

ضهد

1. ضَهَدَهُ, (Ṣ, L, Ḳ,) aor. ـَ, (Ṣ, L,) inf. n. ضَهْدٌ; (L;) and ▼ اضطهدهُ, (as in the L, and in some copies of the Ḳ,) or ▼ اضهده; (as in other copies of the Ḳ;) *He overpowered him; subdued him; oppressed him:* (Ṣ, L, Ḳ:) *he treated him wrongfully, unjustly,* or *injuriously;* (L;) as also ▼ اضهد به: (L, Ḳ:) *he constrained him.* (Ṣ, L.) كَانَ لَا يُجِيزُ ٱلْإِضْطِهَادَ ▼, occurring in a trad., means *He used not to allow constraint,* or *compulsion,* or *force,* in a sale, and in an oath, &c. (L.)

4: } see each, in two places, in the preceding
8: } paragraph.

ضُهْدَةٌ *Force; constraint; compulsion.* (L.) — هُوَ ضُهْدَةٌ لِكُلِّ أَحَدٍ means *He is one who may be overpowered, subdued,* or *oppressed, by every one who desires to make him so.* (Ṣ, L, Ḳ.)

ضَهْيَدٌ *Hardy, strong, robust:* (L, Ḳ:) applied to a man: (L:) [said to be] the only word of the measure فَعْيَلٌ (Ḳ) in the language of the Arabs; but Kh asserts it to be a forged word: (TA:) ضَهْيَأٌ and عَثْيَرٌ are also mentioned as of this measure; [but the latter is disallowed in the Ṣ and O, voce عِثْيَرٌ;] and مَدْيَنُ and مَرْيَمُ [which, however, are foreign proper names]. (MF.)

مَضْهُودٌ and ▼ مُضْطَهَدٌ A man (L) *overpowered; subdued; oppressed;* (Ṣ, L;) *abased;* (L;) *constrained.* (Ṣ, L.)

مُضْطَهَدٌ: see what next precedes.

المُضْطَهِدُ *The lion.* (Ḳ.)

ضهضب

Q. 1. ضَهْضَبَ: see 2 in art. ضهب.

ضهو

ضَهْوَةٌ *A* بِرْكَة *of water;* [i. e. *a watering-trough,* or *tank,* or *the like, of water;* or *a basin, pool, pond,* or *lake, of water;* or *a place where water remains and collects,* or *collects and stagnates;*] (M, Ḳ;) as though formed by transposition from وَهْضَةٌ, which signifies *a depressed piece of ground:* (TA:) pl. أَضْهَآءٌ. (M, Ḳ.)

ضَهْوَآءُ A woman *whose breasts have not become prominent,* or *protuberant.* (Lth, Ḳ.) [See also ضَهْيَآءُ, in the next art.]

ضهى

1. ضَهِيَتْ, aor. ـَ, inf. n. ضَهًى, *She was,* or *became, such as is termed* ضَهْيَآء. (Ḳ.)

3. ضاهاهُ, (Ṣ, Mṣb, Ḳ,) inf. n. مُضَاهَاةٌ, (Ṣ, Mṣb,) *He resembled,* or *conformed with, him,* or *it;* syn. شَاكَلَهُ; (Ṣ, Mṣb, Ḳ;) like ضَاهَأَهُ [q. v.]: (Ṣ, Mṣb:) and, like the latter, *he imitated him.* (Mṣb, TA.*) It is said in a trad., أَشَدُّ ٱلنَّاسِ عَذَابًا يَوْمَ القِيَامَةِ الَّذِينَ يُضَاهُونَ خَلْقَ ٱللّٰهِ i. e. [*The most severely punished of mankind on the day of resurrection will be*] *those who imitate by what they make* [*the creation of God*]; meaning the sculptors or limners or the like. (Mṣb.) — Also, [or ضَاهَى بِهِ, like ضَاهَأَ بِهِ, q. v.,] *He was,* or *became, gentle, tender,* or *courteous,* or *he acted,* or *behaved, gently,* &c., *with him,* or *to him;* namely, a man, and other than a man. (TA.)

4. اضهى *He married,* i. e. *took to wife, a woman such as is termed* ضَهْيَآء. (AA, Ḳ.) — And *He pastured his camels upon the species of tree called* ضَهْيَآء. (Ḳ.)

ضَهْيًا: see the next paragraph, in four places.

ضَهْيَآءُ A woman *that does not menstruate:* pl. ضُهْىٌ; which necessarily implies that the former is [as above, i. e.] with the long ا: but AA mentions ▼ ضَهْيَاةٌ and ▼ ضَهْيَاءَةٌ, with ة and with ء, as having this meaning; which necessarily implies that ضهيا is with the short ا [i. e., accord. to a general rule, ▼ ضَهْيًا, with tenween, like ضَهْيَأٌ, q. v. in art. ضهأ, though (accord. to a general rule) this should be regarded as a masc. epithet]: (Ṣ:) or ضَهْيَآءُ, and also with the short ا [app. ▼ ضَهْيًا, as above, not ضَهْيَا, or, as I rather incline to think, ضَهْيَأٌ (which is mentioned in art. ضهأ) may be here meant], signify a woman *that does not menstruate nor become pregnant;* (Ḳ, TA;) so that she is as though she resembled a man: (TA: [see 3:]) or *that menstruates but does not become pregnant:* (Ḳ, TA:) or *that does not bring forth, though she menstruate:* (TA:) or *whose breasts do not grow forth;* (Ḳ, TA;) and when this is the case, she does not menstruate: or the former signifies *that does not menstruate, being pregnant.* (TA.) — And † Land *that does not give growth to anything;* as also with the short ا [i. e. ▼ ضَهْيًا or ضَهْيَأٌ]. (Ḳ. [In the TA this meaning is restricted, app. without reason, to the form with the short ا.]) — Also, (Ṣ, Ḳ,) and with the short ا [i. e. ▼ ضَهْيًا or ضَهْيَأٌ], (Ḳ,) *A species of tree* (Ṣ, Ḳ) *of the kind called* عِضَاه, (Ḳ,) *having a* بَرَمَة [q. v.] *and a pod* (عُلَّفَة) [*which succeeds the* بَرَمَة], *and many thorns.* (TA. [For further descriptions thereof, see ضَهْيَأٌ, in art. ضهأ.])

ضَهْيَاةٌ and ضَهْيَاءَةٌ: see the next preceding paragraph.

ضَهِىٌّ, (Ṣ, Ḳ,) of the measure فَعِيلٌ, (Ṣ,) *The like* of another [thing or person]: (Ṣ, Ḳ:) one says, هٰذَا ضَهِىُّ هٰذَا *This is the like of this:* (Ṣ:) or هُوَ ضَهِيُّكَ *He is the like of thee.* (Ḳ.)

ضهيأ

Q. 1. [Accord. to the O and Ḳ, Q. Q. 1, being mentioned therein in art. ضهأ.] ضَهْيَأَ أَمْرَهُ *He fell short of doing what he ought to have done in his affair,* (مَرَّضَهُ, O, Ḳ,) *and did not decide it,* (لَمْ يَصْرِمْهُ, O,) or *and did not perform it firmly,* or *soundly:* (Ḳ:) like رَهْيَأَ. (TA.)

ضَهْيَأٌ, of the measure فَعْلَلٌ, or, as some say, فَعْيَلٌ; if of the latter, [said to be] the only instance of this measure in the language; ضهيد

being a forged word; [but see this word;] and مُوْئِرٌ being a foreign proper name; (TA;) or, accord. to Sb, the hemzeh in ضَهْيَأٌ, which is with tenween, is augmentative, because it is syn. with ضَهْيَآءُ, which is with the long ا and imperfectly decl., for the ى cannot be augmentative and the hemzeh radical in the latter; (MF and TA in art. ضهى;) [a word like ضَهْيَأٌ and ضَهْيَآءُ (which see in art. ضهى) in most, or as some seem to say in all, of its meanings;] *A certain tree, resembling the* سَيَال, (AZ, O, Ḳ,) *each of which has its fruit in a* سِنْفَة [or *pod*]; *it has weak thorns, and grows in the valleys and on the mountains:* (AZ, O:) Ed-Deenawaree [i. e. AḤn] says, on the authority of some one or more of the Arabs of the desert, of El-Azd, that the ضهيأ is *a great tree of the kind called* عِضَاه, *having a* بَرَمَة [q. v.] *and a pod* (عُلَّفَة) [*which succeeds the* بَرَمَة], *and many thorns; its pods* (عُلَّف) *are intensely red, and its leaves are like those of the* [*species of acacia called*] سَمُر. (O.) ═ Also A woman *that does not menstruate:* and *that has neither milk nor breast:* as also ▼ ضَهْيَأَةٌ: (Ḳ:) or the latter is an epithet applied to a woman in these two senses: (O: [in which the former word, without ة, is not mentioned:]) Seer says, in his Expos. of "the Book" of Sb, that ضَهْيَأٌ, like ضَهْيَآءُ [which belongs to art. ضهى], is a subst. as well as an epithet, signifying *a woman whose breast has not grown forth:* and *one who has not menstruated:* — and also † *A land that has not given growth to anything:* (MF, TA:) or ▼ ضَهْيَأَةٌ signifies as above: and also † a desert (فَلَاةٌ) *having in it no water:* (O, Ḳ, TA:) or *that does not give growth to anything;* app. because it has no water. (TA.) [Accord. to those who hold the ى to be augmentative,] a woman is thus termed because she resembles men (لِأَنَّهَا ضَاهَأَتِ الرِّجَالَ). (O, TA.)

ضَهْيَأَةٌ: see the next preceding paragraph, in two places.

ضو

R. Q. 1. ضَوْضَوْا, [inf. n. ضَوْضَاةٌ and ضَوْضَآءٌ, (see the next paragraph,)] *They cried out, shouted,* or *clamoured;* first pers. sing. ضَوْضَيْتُ, the [second] و being changed into ى. (Ṣ, TA.)

ضَوَّةٌ [in the CḲ erroneously written ضَوَاةٌ] *A crying out, shouting,* or *clamouring;* (Ṣ, Ḳ;) so says Aṣ, and AZ says the like; (Ṣ;) as also ▼ ضَوْضَاةٌ (Ṣ, Ḳ) and ▼ ضَوْضَآءٌ, (TA in art. ضوض, [these two there mentioned as inf. ns., on the authority of IḲṭṭ,]) and ▼ ضَوْضَى. (Ḳ in art. ضوض.) One says, سَمِعْتُ ضَوَّةَ القَوْمِ [*I heard the crying out, shouting,* or *clamouring, of the people,* or *party*]. (Aṣ, AZ, Ṣ.)

ضَوْضَى and ضَوْضَآءٌ and ضَوْضَاةٌ: see the next preceding paragraph.

ضُوَاضِبٌ *Large, big,* or *bulky; thick;* or *large in body;* syn. ضَخْمٌ, (Ḳ, TA,) and عَظِيمٌ. (TA.)

ضُوَاضِيَةٌ: see what next follows.

ضُوَيْضِيَةٌ, (Ḳ, TA,) in the dim. form, (TA,) *A calamity,* or *misfortune;* (Ḳ, TA;) because of its greatness; (TA;) as also ▼ ضُوَاضِيَةٌ. (Ḳ, TA.) — And A stallion [camel] *excited by lust.* (Ṣgh, Ḳ.)

مُضَوْضٍ A man *crying out; shouting,* or *clamouring;* (Ḳ and TA in art. ضوض; [in the CḲ erroneously written مُضَوْضَى;]) like مُضَوْضٍ. (TA in that art.)

ضوأ

1: see 4, in two places.

2: see the next paragraph, in two places. — One says also, ضَوَّأْتُ عَنْهُ [meaning *I brought to light, made visible, discovered,* or *revealed, him,* or *it*]. (M, TA.) A sheep, or goat, belonging to an Arab of the desert strayed; whereupon he said, اَللّٰهُمَّ ضَوِّئْ عَنْهُ [*O God, bring it to light,* or *discover it*]. (A, TA.) ═ Accord. to Lth, but he is the only authority for it known by AM, ضَوَّأَ عَنِ الأَمْرِ, (TA,) inf. n. تَضْوِئَةٌ, means *He declined,* or *turned away, from the affair.* (Ḳ, TA.)

4. اضاء, (M, Mṣb, Ḳ,) said of a thing, (M,) [as, for instance,] of the moon, (Mṣb,) or اضاءت, said of fire (النَّار), (A'Obeyd, Ṣ, O,) inf. n. إِضَاءَةٌ; (Mṣb;) and ▼ ضَآءَ, (M, Mṣb, Ḳ,) or ضَآءَتْ, (Ṣ, O,) aor. يَضُوءُ, (M,) or تَضُوءُ, (Ṣ,) inf. n. ضَوْءٌ (Ṣ, M, O, Mṣb, Ḳ) and ضُوءٌ, (Ṣ, O, Ḳ,) or the latter is a simple subst.; (Mṣb;) but the former verb is preferred; (TA;) *It gave light, was light* or *bright, shone,* or *shone brightly.* (Mṣb, Ḳ,* TA.) [See also an ex. of ▼ the latter verb in a verse cited voce أُفُقٌ; and cited here in the TA.] And أَضَأْتُ لَهُ [*I gave light to him*]. (M.) ═ The former verb is also trans.: you say, أَضَاءَتْهُ النَّارُ [*The fire made it to be light* or *bright, to shine,* or *to shine brightly*]: (Ṣ, O:) and أَضَأْتُهُ and ▼ ضَوَّأْتُهُ [*I made it to give light, to be light* or *bright, to shine,* or *to shine brightly*]: (M, Mṣb,* Ḳ:) and ▼ ضَوَّأْتُ بِهِ and أَضَأْتُ بِهِ البَيْتَ [*I lighted,* or *illumined, with it* (i. e. with a lamp or the like) *the house,* or *chamber,* or *tent*]. (M.) — [Hence,] اضاء بِبَوْلِهِ ‡ *He ejected his urine* [so as to make its drops to glisten]; or *emitted it and then stopped it;* syn. حَذَفَ بِهِ; (Ḳ, TA;) or خَذَفَ; (so in a copy of the M, as on the authority of Kr;) or, as in the A, أَذْرَعَ بِهِ. (TA.) — And they said مَا أَضْوَأَهُ [*How light,* or *bright, is it!*]. (Ṣ voce أَظْلَمَ [q. v.].) — And اضاء signifies also أَصَابَ ضَوْءًا [*He saw* (lit. *lighted on,* or *found,*) *light,* or *brightness*]. (T voce أَظْلَمَ [q. v.])

5. تضوّأ *He stood in the dark to see people by the light of their fire,* (AZ, Ḳ, TA,) *without their seeing him.* (AZ, TA.) And تضوّأ آمْرَأَةً [*He stood in the dark to see a woman by the light of her fire, without her seeing him*]. (TA.)

10. اِسْتَضَأْتُ بِهِ [*I sought to obtain light by means of it; I made use of it for light*]. (M, Ḳ.) لَا تَسْتَضِيئُوا بِنَارِ أَهْلِ الشِّرْكِ [lit. *Seek not ye to obtain light by means of the fire of the people of belief in a plurality of gods*], (O, Ḳ,) a saying of the Prophet, (O,) means ‡ *seek not ye counsel,* or *advice, of the believers in a plurality of gods, in affairs:* (O, Ḳ:) because he whose affair is confused and dubious to him is as though he were in darkness. (O.)

ضَوْءٌ and ▼ ضُوءٌ and ▼ ضِيَآءٌ (Ṣ, M, O, Ḳ) and ▼ ضِوَآءٌ, (M, Ḳ,) the last of which is [erroneously] written in the L ضَوَآءٌ, (TA,) signify the same, (Ṣ, M, O, Ḳ,) i. e. *Light,* syn. نُور, (Ḳ, TA,) accord. to the leading lexicologists; but see what follows: (TA:) and ضَوْءٌ is an inf. n. of ضَآءَ, (Ṣ, M, O, Mṣb, Ḳ,) and so is ▼ ضُوءٌ, (Ṣ, O, Ḳ,) or this is a simple subst. from ضَآءَ, and so is ▼ ضِيَآءٌ, which is also, sometimes, written ▼ ضِئَآءٌ, from أَضَآءَ, as syn. with ضَآءَ: (Mṣb:) the pl. of ضَوْءٌ (M, TA) and ▼ ضُوءٌ (M) is أَضْوَآءٌ; and ▼ ضِيَآءٌ is sometimes a pl., (M, TA,) as Zj states it to be: (TA:) some say that ضَوْءٌ has a more intensive signification than نُورٌ, and that hence God has likened his direction [the Ḳur-án] to النُّور rather than to الضَّوْء; because if it were otherwise, no one had erred: and that hence, also, [in the Ḳur x. 5,] the sun is termed ▼ ضِيَآء; and the moon, نُور: it is also said that ضَوْء signifies the *rays that are diffused by what is termed* نُور: the ḳádee Zekereeyà affirms that these two words are syn. by their original application, but that ضَوْء is more forcible accord. to usage: and some say that الضَّوْء signifies *that* [*light*] *which subsists by itself,* as [that of] the sun, and fire; and النُّور, to that which subsists by some other thing [as does the light of the moon]. (MF, TA.)

ضُوءٌ: see the next preceding paragraph, in three places.

ضِوَآءٌ: see ضَوْء.

ضِيَآءٌ and ضِئَآءٌ: see ضَوْءٌ, in five places.

ضوح

2. ضَوَّحَ: see 2, in two places, in art. ضيح.

ضود

ضَادٌ *The name of one of the letters of the alphabet.* (L, Mṣb, Ḳ.) See the letter ض.

ضور

1. ضَارَهُ, aor. يَضُورُ: see ضَارَهُ, aor. يَضِيرُ, in art. ضير.

5. تضوّر *He writhed* by reason of the pain of beating, (M, A, Ḳ,) or of hunger: (Ḳ:) *he cried out and writhed* on being beaten, (Lth, Ṣ, A,) or

by reason of vehement hunger: (Ṣ, A:) *he writhed and cried out and turned over*, by reason of the vehemence of fever: (TA:) *he manifested harm, injury, or hurt, that he suffered*; and *was in a state of agitation*: (IAmb, TA:) *he manifested weakness*: (Abu-l-'Abbás, in TA: [but for تَضْعِيف, as the explanation of the inf. n., in the TA, I read تَضَعُّف:]) *he* (a wolf, and a dog, and a lion, and a fox,) *cried out* (M, Ḳ) with hunger. (M.)

ضوز

1. ضَازَهُ حَقَّهُ, aor. يَضُوزُهُ, *i. q.* ضَازَهُ, aor. يَضِيزُهُ: see art. ضيز. (Ḳ.) You say also ضَازَنِى, aor. يَضُوزُنِى, meaning نَقَصَنِى [*He made me to suffer loss*]. (Kr, M, TA.) —— And ضَازَ, aor. يَضُوزُ is also [intrans.] like ضَأَزَ, q. v. (TA in art. ضأز.)

قِسْمَةٌ ضُوزَى *i. q.* ضِيزَى: see art. ضيز. (M, TA.*)

ضوض

For words mentioned in the Ḳ under this head, see art. ضو.

ضوع

1. ضَاعَهُ, (aor. يَضُوعُهُ, Ṣ, O,) inf. n. ضَوْعٌ, *He, or it, put it, or him, into a state of motion, commotion, or agitation*; (Ṣ, O, Ḳ;) as also ▼ضَوَّعهُ, inf. n. تَضْوِيعٌ: (TA:) and *disquieted*, or *disturbed, him, or it*: and *frightened him*: (Ṣ, O, Ḳ:) and some say, *roused*, or *excited, him*: and ▼ضَوَّعهُ, also, has the last but one, or the last, of these meanings. (TA.) One says, لَا يَضُوعَنَّكَ مَا تَسْمَعُ مِنْهَا i. e. [*By no means let that which thou hearest from her move thee*, or *disquiet thee*, or *frighten thee*; or] *do not thou be moved by what thou hearest from her*; or *do not thou care for it*, or *regard it*. (TA.) And ضَاعَهُ أَمْرُ كَذَا وَكَذَا *Such and such things frightened him*. (AA, TA.) —— And, said of the wind, *It made it to incline*; namely, a branch: (Ḳ:) and *it* (the wind) *bore heavily upon it*. (TA. [The object of the verb in this sense is not there mentioned.]) —— And *i. q.* شَاقَهُ [*He, or it, excited his desire*]: (so in the O, on the authority of Ibn-'Abbád:) or *i. q.* شَاقَّهُ [*he acted with him contrariously, or adversely, and inimically*; &c.]. (So in copies of the Ḳ.) —— And ضَاعَ الإِبِلَ, (O,) or الدَّابَّةَ, (Ḳ,) said of journeying *It rendered lean, or emaciated*, (O, Ḳ,) *the camels*, (O,) or *the beast*. (Ḳ.) —— And ضاع فَرْخَهُ, (IAạr, O, Ḳ,) aor. as above, (IAạr, O,) and so the inf. n., (TA,) *It* (a bird) *fed its young one with its bill*. (IAạr, O, Ḳ.) When you command the bird to do so, you say ضُعْ ضُعْ. (IAạr, O.) —— ضَاعَ is also intrans.: see 5, in two places.

2: see 1, first sentence, in two places.

4. مَا أَضْوَعَهُ, said of odour, means *How sweet* [or *fragrant*] *is it!* (Ḥar p. 670.)

5. تضوّع said of the wind, *It became in motion*. (TA.) And تضوّعت رَائِحَةُ الطِّيبِ *The odour of the perfume diffused itself*, or *became diffused*. (O.) And تضوّع المِسْكُ, (Ṣ, Ḳ,) as also تضيّع; (Ṣ;) or تَضَوَّعَ الشَّىْءُ; (Mṣb;) and ▼ضاع, (Ṣ, O, Mṣb, Ḳ,) aor. يَضُوعُ, (O, Mṣb,) inf. n. ضَوْعٌ; (Mṣb;) and ضاع, aor. يَضِيعُ; (Ḥar p. 670;) *The musk, being put in motion, diffused its odour*, or *fragrance*; (Ṣ, O, Ḳ, TA;) or *the thing diffused its odour*: (Mṣb:) so in a verse of Imra-el-Ḳeys cited voce رَيَّا, in art. روى: [in which, in the place of تَضَوَّعَ, some read يَضَّوَّعُ, for يَتَضَوَّعُ:] (TA:) and in like manner one says of a stinking thing. (IAạr, Ḳ.) And تضوّع مِسْكًا [*It diffused the odour*, or *fragrance, of musk*]. (Ṣ, O.) —— And تضوّع مِنْهُ رَائِحَةً *He snuffed*, or *scented*, or *smelt, from him, or it, an odour*. (TA.) —— Also, said of the [bird called] ضُوَع, *It cried*, or *uttered a loud cry* or *crying*. (AḤát, O.) —— And, (O,) said of a child, (Ḳ,) *He writhed*, (Ḳ,) or *cried out and writhed*, (O, Ḳ,* TA,) *in weeping*; (Ḳ,* TA; in the former, مِنَ البُكَآءِ; but correctly, فِى البُكَآءِ; TA;) as also ▼ضاع, (Lth, O, Ḳ,) aor. يَضُوعُ, (Lth, O,) inf. n. ضَوْعٌ: (TA:) both signify *he cried*, or *uttered a loud cry* or *crying, in weeping*; as one does when beaten: or the former, mostly said of a child, signifies *he writhed in weeping with vehemence, and raising the voice*; as expl. by Lth: (TA:) or it signifies also *he* (a child) *wept vehemently*: (O:) and, said of a young bird, *it writhed*, or *cried out and writhed*; (O, Ḳ;) as when said of a child; and so ▼انضاع, said of both: (Ḳ:) or ▼انضاع, said of a young bird, (Ṣ, O, Ḳ,) as also تضوّع, (O, Ḳ,) signifies *it spread its wings to its mother in order that she might feed it with her bill*. (Ṣ, O, Ḳ.)

7. انضاع: see the next preceding sentence, in two places. —— Also *He was frightened at a thing, and cried out at it*, or *uttered a loud cry* or *crying by reason of it*. (TA.)

ضُوَعٌ (Ṣ, O, Mṣb, Ḳ) and ضِوَعٌ (AHeyth, O, Ḳ) *A certain night-bird*, (Ṣ, O, Mṣb, Ḳ,) [*a species of owl*, i. e.,] *of the kind termed* هَام: (Ṣ, O, Mṣb:) or [*a male owl*;] *the male of the* بُوم; (Ṣ, O, Mṣb, Ḳ;) accord. to El-Mufaddal: (Ṣ, O:) said by ADḳ to be *a bird that utters a scream when it perceives the daybreak*: (O:) or the كَرَوَان [a name now given to the *stone-curlew*, or *charadrius œdicnemus*]: (Ḳ:) or *a certain black bird, resembling the* غُرَاب [or *crow*], (Eṭ-Ṭáifee, O, Ḳ,) *smaller than this, but red in its wings, these being of a roseate colour*: so says AḤát, on the authority of Eṭ-Ṭáifee: accord. to others, he says, it is *a small bird, less than the* حُمَّر *and the* دُخَّل; (O;) and in like manner says Th: (TA:) also that the ▼ضُوَعَة [which may be the fem. or a n. un.] is *of a colour inclining to yellow, dusky and blackish externally, and yellow and ash-coloured within, short in the neck and tail, smaller than the sparrow*; and that it is thus called because of the cry that it utters at the commencement of daybreak: accord. to El-Ḥanashee, the ضُوَع is *a bird such as is termed* أَبْغَث [q. v.], *resembling the domestic hen*, (O,) *the flesh of which is good*: (O, Ḳ:) but he adds that it has been said by some to be *not a bird*: and in another place of the book he says that the ▼ضُوَعَة is *black, like the* غُرَاب, *a little larger than the* صُفْرَة, *red in the* خَوَافِق: (O: [but الخَوَافِق is an obvious mistranscription for الخَوَافِى: see خَافِيَةٌ:]) the pl. is أَضْوَاعٌ [a pl. of pauc.] and ضِيعَانٌ. (Ṣ, O, Mṣb, Ḳ.)

ضُوَعَةٌ: see the next preceding paragraph, in two places.

ضُوَاعٌ The *cry of the bird called* ضُوَع. (Ṣ, O, Mṣb, Ḳ.)

ضَوَائِعُ, applied to camels, (O, Ḳ,) and to other beasts, (O,) *Lean, and lank in the belly*: (O, Ḳ:) or *emaciated*: (TA:) app. from ضَاعَ said of journeying, meaning "it rendered lean, or emaciated: (O:) by rule it should be ضَائِعَةٌ. (TA.)

الضُّوَّاعُ, like شُدَّاد, [in the O erroneously written الضُّوَاعُ,] *The fox*. (Ibn-'Abbád, Ḳ.)

مَضُوعٌ pass. part. n. of ضَاعَهُ. (O, TA.)

ضوف

1. ضَافَ عَنْهُ, inf. n. ضَوْفٌ: see 1 in art ضيف.

مَضُوفٌ: } see art. ضيف.
مَضُوفَةٌ: }

ضوم

1. ضَامَ, aor. يَضُومُ, inf. n. ضَوْمٌ, a dial. var. of ضَامَ, aor. يَضِيمُ, inf. n. ضَيْمٌ: (Ḳ:) like ضُمْتُهُ, like ظَلَمْتُهُ, signifying ضِمْتُهُ [*I wronged him*, &c.]. (M, TA.)

ضون

1. ضَوْنَةٌ, (Ḳ,) an inf. n. of which the verb is ضَانَ, aor. يَضُونُ, said of a man; (TḲ,) *The having numerous offspring*; as also ▼تَضَوُّنٌ. (Ḳ.) [Probably from ضَيْوَنٌ.]

5: see the preceding paragraph.

ضَوْنٌ The إِنْفَحَة [i. e. *runnet*, or *runnet-bag, of a kid*, or *lamb*]. (Ḳ.)

ضَانَةٌ *A nose-ring of brass* (بُرَةٌ مِنْ صُفْرٍ M, Ḳ, M) *for a camel*: (Ḳ:) or a [*camel's nose-ring such as is termed*] خِزَامَة; accord. to Sh: mentioned in the Ḳ in art. ضأن; but this is its proper place, for it is without ء. (TA.)

ضَوْنَةٌ *A young female child*. (Ḳ, TA. [In the CḲ, الظَّبْيَةُ is put for الصَّبِيَّةُ.])

ضَيْوَنٌ, (Ṣ, M, Ḳ,) of the measure فَيْعَلٌ, not فَعْوَلٌ, because the former is the more common, (IB, TA,) extr. [in respect of rule], preserving its original form, (M,) without إِدْغَام [i. e. not having its و incorporated into the ى so as to become ضَيِّنٌ, as it should by rule,] because it is a primitive noun, (Ṣ,) like حَيْوَةٌ, which is a proper name of a man, (Ṣ, M,) but more extr. because that is allowable in a proper name which is not allowable in another kind of word, (M,) [*A he-cat;*] i. q. سِنَّوْرٌ [q. v.]; (M:) the *male* سِنَّوْر: (Ṣ, Ḳ:) or *a certain small beast resembling the* سِنَّوْر: (M:) pl. ضَيَاوِنُ, (Ṣ, Ḳ,) in which the و is unaltered because it is so in the sing.: (Ṣ, TA:) Sb says, the dim. is ▼ ضُيَيْنٌ, like أُسَيْدٌ [dim. of أَسْوَدُ], but he who says أُسَيْوِدٌ may say ▼ ضُيَيْوِنٌ. (Ṣ.)

ضُيَيْنٌ and ضُيَيْوِنٌ: see what next precedes.

ضوى

1. ضَوِىَ, aor. يَضْوَى, inf. n. ضَوًى, *He* (a child, Mṣb) *was,* or *became, lean,* or *emaciated,* (Ṣ, Mṣb, Ḳ,) *and small in body:* (Mṣb:) or *slender in the bones, and spare of body, naturally.* (M, Ḳ.) [See also 4.] ═ ضَوَى إِلَيْهِ, (Ṣ, M, Ḳ,) aor. يَضْوِى, (Ṣ, Ḳ,) inf. n. ضُوِىٌّ (Ṣ, M, Ḳ) and ضَىٌّ, (M, Ḳ,) *He adjoined himself, got him* or *got himself, betook him* or *betook himself, repaired,* or *resorted, to him;* syn. اِنْضَمَّ; (Ṣ, M, Ḳ;) as also ▼ انضوى; (Ḥar p. 73;) and *he had recourse,* or *betook himself, to him for protection,* or *refuge.* (Ṣ,* M, Ḳ.) — And ضَوَى إِلَىَّ مِنْهُ خَيْرٌ, inf. n. ضَىٌّ and ضُوِىٌّ, i. q. سَالَ [i. e. *Bounty flowed to me from him*]: (M, TA:) accord. to the copies of the Ḳ, ضوى الى خبره سال; which is wrong. (TA. [In my MS. copy of the Ḳ, الى خَيْرُه سَالَ.]) — And ضَوَى signifies also *It came by night:* (M, Ḳ:) you say, ضَوَى إِلَيْنَا خَبَرُهُ *The news,* or *tidings, of him,* or *it, came to us by night.* (M, TA.) ═ ضَوِىَ, said of a camel, *He was,* or *became, affected with the tumours termed* ضَوًى, (Lth, TA,) or *with what is termed* ضَوَاةٌ [q. v.]. (M.)

4. اضوى *He* (a man, TA) *was,* or *became, slender* (Ḳ, TA) *in his body.* (TA. [See also ضَوِىَ.]) And اضوى القَوْمُ *The people's cattle became lean,* or *emaciated;* like اصوى القوم. (IḲṭṭ, TA in art. صوى.) — And *He* (a man) *had offspring such as is termed* ضَاوِىٌّ *born to him:* and in like manner اضوت is said of a woman [as meaning *she brought forth such offspring*]; (M;) or *she brought forth a boy such as is so termed.* (Ḳ.) اِغْتَرِبُوا وَلَا تُضْوُوا, (Ṣ, M, Mṣb,) occurring in a trad., (Ṣ,) means *Marry ye among women that are remote in respect of relationship,* (Ṣ, M, Mṣb,*) *and not among the relations of your paternal uncles,* (Ṣ,) or *and not among your near relations, lest your offspring be such as is termed* ضَاوِىٌّ: (M, Mṣb:) for the Arabs assert that a man's offspring from his near relation is meagre, though generous, of the nature of his people. (Ṣ, Mṣb.) ═ اضواهُ *He rendered it weak.* (Ṣ, Mṣb, Ḳ.*) You say, اضوى الأَمْرَ ‡ *He rendered the affair weak;* (Ṣ, TA;) *did not render it firm,* or *sound;* or *did not perform it in a firm,* or *sound, manner.* (Ṣ, Ḳ, TA.) — And اضواهُ حَقَّهُ † *He curtailed him,* or *defrauded him, of his right,* or *due.* (IAạr, M, Ḳ.*) ═ اضواهُ اللَّيْلُ إِلَيْهِ *The night made him to have recourse,* or *to betake himself, to him for protection,* or *refuge.* (TA.)

7: see 1, second sentence.

ضَوًى inf. n. of ضَوِىَ [q. v.]. (Ṣ, M, &c.) ═ See also the next paragraph.

ضَوَاةٌ [mentioned in the TA as from the Ḳ, but not in the CḲ, and in my MS. copy of the Ḳ inserted in the margin,] *A ganglion* (غُدَدَةٌ, M, or غُدَّةٌ, Ḳ, TA) *beneath the lobe of the ear, above the* لَكَمَة [q. v.]: (M, Ḳ, TA:) or, accord. to Az, [*a thing*] *resembling a* غُدَّة. (TA.) And *A tumour occurring in the fauces of camels and other animals:* pl. ▼ ضَوًى: (M:) or this latter [is properly termed a coll. gen. n., of which ضَوَاةٌ is the n. un., and] signifies *tumours accidental to the camel, in his head, having an overpowering effect upon his eyes, and rendering it difficult to attach to him the* [*halter called*] خِطَام; *and sometimes it is in the side of the mouth.* (Lth, TA.) And (M, TA) *A* سِلْعَة [or *ganglion*] (Ṣ, M, TA) *in a camel,* (Ṣ,) or *in any part of the body.* (M, TA.) — Also *A certain thing,* or *small thing,* (هَنَةٌ,) *that comes forth from the she-camel's vulva before the coming forth of the fœtus.* (M, Ḳ, TA.)

ضَاوٍ: see the next paragraph. ═ Also *Coming by night;* syn. طَارِقٌ [which Golius here explains as meaning "Lucifer," and supposes to be for ضَاوِىٌّ]. (M, Ḳ.)

ضَاوِىٌّ, (Ṣ, M, Mṣb, Ḳ,) of the measure فَاعُولٌ, [originally ضَاوُوىٌ,] (Ṣ, Mṣb,) and ▼ ضَاوٍ, (Mṣb, TA,) applied to a boy, (Ṣ, M, Ḳ,) and with ة applied to a girl, (Ṣ, Mṣb, Ḳ,) *Lean,* or *emaciated,* (Ṣ, Mṣb, Ḳ,) *and small in body:* (Mṣb:) or *slender in the bones, and spare of body, naturally:* (M, Ḳ:) and likewise applied to any species of animal: (M:) accord. to the T, the *offspring of an incestuous union.* (TA.) الضَّاوِىُّ, (T, TA,) not without teshdeed, as the text of the Ḳ implies it to be, (TA,) was the name of *A certain horse,* (T, Ḳ, TA,) *belonging to Ghanee.* (T, TA.) — Also the former, *disordered,* or *diseased, and near to dying:* [so I render حَارِضٌ, q. v.:] and *weak; in a bad,* or *corrupt, state.* (TA.)

فِيهِ ضَاوِيَةٌ *In him is leanness* or *emaciation* [&c.]: (Ṣ:) i. q. ضَوًى [the inf. n. of ضَوِىَ, used as a subst.]. (TA.)

مُضْوِىٌّ, applied to a camel, part. n. of ضُوِىَ [q. v.]. (Lth, TA.)

ضيح

1. ضَاحَ اللَّبَنَ: see 2, in two places. ═ ضَاحَتِ البِلَادُ *The tracts of land became vacant,* (Ḳ, TA,) *by reason of drought.* (TA.)

2. ضَيَّحَ اللَّبَنَ, (Ṣ, O, Ḳ,) inf. n. تَضْيِيحٌ, (Ṣ,) *He mixed the milk with water,* (Ṣ, O, Ḳ,) *so that it became* ضَيْح; (Ṣ;) as also ضَوَّحَهُ, as heard by Az from an Arab of the desert; (TA;) and ▼ ضَاحَهُ, (O, Ḳ,) inf. n. ضَيْحٌ, but this last is said by IDrd to be obsolete: (O:) or ▼ ضَاحَهُ, inf. n. ضَيْحٌ, *he poured water into it, it being thick, and then stirred it about until it became of a uniform consistence.* (T, TA.) — And ضَيَّحَهُ *He gave him to drink thin milk, mixed with water, such as is termed* ضَيْح; (Ṣ, Ḳ;) as also ضَوَّحَهُ. (Ḳ.)

4. اضاح, said of the مُقْل [or fruit of the Theban palm] *It became what is termed* ضَيْح, *and fit to be eaten.* (O.)

5. تضيّح *It* (milk) *became what is termed* ضَيَاح; (Ḳ;) i. e. *it was diluted with water, and stirred about until it became of a uniform consistence:* and so any medicine, or poison. (TA.) — And *He* (a man) *drank what is termed* ضَيَاح. (Ḳ.)

ضَيْحٌ and ▼ ضَيَاحٌ *Thin milk, mixed* (Ṣ, O, Ḳ, TA) *with much water:* the former expl. by Aṣ as meaning *milk in which is much water:* the latter expl. in the T as *thick milk into which water is poured, and which is then stirred about until it becomes of a uniform consistence:* also, both words, *milk, whether it be fresh or such as is termed* رَائِب [q. v.], *upon which water is poured until it has become thin:* and ▼ ضَيَاحٌ and ▼ مُضَيَّحٌ any medicine or poison *having water poured into it, and then stirred about until it becomes of a uniform consistence:* or, accord. to Lth, only milk is termed ضَيَاح. (TA.) [See an ex. voce خَضَارٌ.] — ضَيْحٌ also signifies *Honey.* (O, Ḳ.) — And *Ripe* مُقْل [*or fruit of the Theban palm*]: (O, Ḳ: [see 4:]) this is of the dial. of El-Yemen, universally. (O.)

ضِيحٌ i. q. ضِحٌّ [q. v.]: (Ḳ:) ascribed by IDrd to the vulgar. (TA.) — Also an imitative sequent to ريح, (Ḳ,) [i. e.] a corroborative of ريح, (O,) in the phrase جَآءَ بِالرِّيحِ وَالضِّيحِ [expl. voce ضِحّ], and therefore having no meaning if used alone. (O,* TA.)

ضَاحَةٌ The *sight:* (O, Ḳ:) one says, مَا أَجْوَدَ ضَاحَتَهُ [*How good, or excellent, is his sight!*]: (O:) or the *eye.* (Ḳ.)

ضَيْحَةٌ *A single drink,* or *draught, of thin milk, such as is termed* ضَيْح. (TA.)

ضَيَاحٌ: see ضَيْحٌ, in two places.

مُضَيَّحٌ: see ضَيْحٌ.

عَيْشٌ مُضَيَّحٌ ‡ *A turbid life;* syn. مَمْذُوقٌ. (Fr, O, Ḳ, TA.)

مُتَضَيِّحٌ ‡ *Coming to the watering-trough when*

most of the contents thereof has been drunk and there remains but little, mixed, (IAth,* O, Ḳ, TA,) *and turbid;* (IAth, TA;) this being likened to milk mixed with water: (TA:) or *coming to water the last of the people.* (AHeyth, TA.)

ضير

1. ضَارَهُ, aor. يَضِيرُ, inf. n. ضَيْرٌ; (Ṣ, M, A, Mṣb, Ḳ;) as also ضَارَهُ, aor. يَضُورُ, inf. n. ضَوْرٌ; (Ṣ, M, Ḳ;) *It* (a thing, M, Ḳ) *harmed, injured, hurt, mischiefed,* or *damaged, him; i. q.* ضَرَّهُ, (Ṣ, M, Ḳ,) or أَضَرَّ بِهِ. (Mṣb.) You say, هٰذَا مِمَّا لَا يَضِيرُكَ [*This is of the things that will not harm thee*]: and لَوْ فَعَلْتَهُ لَمْ يَضِرْكَ [*Hadst thou done it, it had not harmed thee*]: and لَا ضَيْرَ عَلَيْكَ [*No harm shall befall thee*]. (A.) And مَا يَضِيرُكَ عَلَى الضَّبِّ ضَيْدٌ *i. q.* مَا يَضُرُّكَ q. v. (A in art. ضر.) And Ks says that he had heard (from one of the people of El-'Áliyeh, TA) the phrase لَا يَنْفَعُنِى ذٰلِكَ وَلَا يَضُورُنِى [*That will not benefit me, nor will it harm me*]. (Ṣ, TA.) See also a reading of a phrase in a trad. cited in art. ضر. conj. 3.

ضيز

1. ضَازَ, (Ṣ, Ḳ,) aor. يَضِيزُ, inf. n. ضَيْزٌ, (TA,) *He deviated from the right course; or acted unjustly, wrongfully, injuriously,* or *tyrannically;* (Ṣ, Ḳ;) فِى الحُكْمِ *in the judgment:* (Ṣ:) like ضَأَزَ. (TA in art. ضأز.) —— ضَازَهُ حَقَّهُ, aor. and inf. n. as above, *He deprived him,* or *defrauded him, of a part,* or *the whole, of his right,* or *due:* (Ṣ, M, Ḳ:) like ضَازَهُ, aor. يَضُوزُهُ: (Ḳ:) *he refused it to him,* or *withheld it from him:* (AZ, M, TA:) and sometimes one says ضَأَزَهُ, aor. يَضْأَزُهُ, inf. n. ضَأْزٌ. (Ṣ, TA.)

قِسْمَةٌ ضِيزَى *An unjust,* (Ṣ, M,) or *a defective,* (Ḳ in art. ضأز,) *division:* (Ṣ, M, Ḳ:) as also ضُوزَى: (M:) ضيزى in the Ḳur liii. 22 is read by all without hemz: (TA:) it is of the measure فُعْلَى, like طُوبَى and حُبْلَى; but the ض is with kesr in order that the ى may remain unchanged; for there is not in the language an epithet of the measure فِعْلَى; this being a measure of substantives, like الشِّعْرَى and الدِّفْلَى: (Ṣ:) or, accord. to Aboo-'Alee, it is not an epithet, but an inf. n., like ذِكْرَى, as though the meaning were قِسْمَةٌ ذَاتُ جَوْرٍ: (Ḥar p. 524:) Fr says that some of the Arabs say ضَأْزَى, and ضُؤْزَى: and AḤát mentions AZ's having heard the Arabs say ضِئْزَى, with hemz. (Ṣ.)

ضيع

1. ضَاعَ, aor. يَضِيعُ, inf. n. ضَيَاعٌ and ضَيْعَةٌ (Ṣ, Mgh, O, Mṣb, Ḳ) and ضَيْعٌ and ضِيعٌ, (Ḳ,) *It* (a thing, Ṣ, Mgh, O, Mṣb) *perished, came to nought, passed away,* or *became lost.* (Ṣ, O, Mṣb, Ḳ.) It is said in a trad. of Saad, إِنِّى أَخَافُ عَلَى الأَعْنَابِ الضَّيْعَةَ i. e. [*Verily I fear, for the grapes,*] *their* [lit. *the*] *perishing,* or *becoming lost.* (TA.) —— And ضاع, (Ḳ, TA,) inf. n. ضَيَاعٌ and ضَيْعَةٌ, (TA,) *It* (a thing) *was left; left,* or *let, alone;* or *neglected.* (Ḳ, TA.) Hence, ضاعت الإِبِلُ, and ضاع العِيَالُ, *The camels,* and *the family,* or *household, were left untended,* and *unminded;* and *were left alone,* or *neglected.* (TA.) ═ ضاع, aor. يَضِيعُ, said of perfume, or sweet odour, *i. q.* ضاع having for its aor. يَضُوعُ. (Ḥar p. 670.) [See 5 in art. ضوع: and see also 5 in the present art.]

2. ضيّع الشَّىْءَ, (O, Mṣb, Ḳ,) inf. n. تَضْيِيعٌ; (Ṣ;) and ↓ اضاعهُ, (O, Mṣb, Ḳ,) inf. n. إِضَاعَةٌ; (Ṣ;) both signify the same; (Ṣ, O, Mṣb, Ḳ;) *He made,* or *caused, the thing to perish,* or *become lost; he destroyed it, wasted it,* or *lost it.* (Mṣb, Ḳ, TA.) Hence, ضَيَّعُوا فُلَانًا is used by the vulgar as meaning *They beheaded such a one with the sword.* (TA.) It is said in a prov., الصَّيْفَ ضَيَّعْتِ اللَّبَنَ [*In the spring,* or *in the summer, thou losedst the milk*], in which the ت is with kesr when the words are addressed to a male, or to a female, or to a pl. number, because originally addressed to a woman, the wife of a wealthy man, whom she disliked because of his being aged, wherefore he divorced her, and a poor man married her, and she sent to her first husband requesting a gift, and he answered her thus; (Ṣ, O, Ḳ;*) الصيف being in the accus. case as an adv. n.: so says Yaḳoob: (Ṣ, O:) or El-Aswad Ibn-Hurmuz divorced his wife El-'Anood Esh-Shenneeyeh, (O, Ḳ,) of the Benoo-Shenn, (TA,) preferring to her a beautiful and wealthy woman of his people; (O, Ḳ;*) then there occurred between them what led to their separation, and he sought to obtain [again] El-'Anood, and sent a message to her; but in replying to him she said,

* أَنْشَأْتَ تَطْلُبُ وَصْلَنَا *
* فِى الصَّيْفِ ضَيَّعْتَ اللَّبَنْ *

[*Thou hast begun to seek our union: in the spring,* or *in the summer, thou losedst the milk*]: (O,* Ḳ:) the ت in this case being with fet-ḥ. (Ḳ. [See more in Freytag's Arab. Prov. ii. 197-8, or in Ḥar p. 577; in both of which, however, and in the O, ضيّعت is with kesr in the latter case, as in the former.]) [One says also, ضيّع عَهْدَهُ, meaning *He broke his compact, contract,* or *covenant*]. The phrase, in a trad., نَهَى عَنْ إِضَاعَةِ ↓ المَالِ means *He forbade the expending of wealth otherwise than in obedience to God, and the squandering thereof, and extravagance.* (TA.) —— See also the next paragraph.

4. اضاع الشَّىْءَ: see 2, first sentence, and last but one. —— Also, [and app. ↓ ضيّعهُ likewise, accord. to the Ḳ,] *He left the thing; left it,* or *let it, alone;* or *neglected it.* (Ḳ, TA.) You say, اضاع عِيَالَهُ *He neglected his family,* or *household; omitted taking good care of them,* or *being mindful of them.* (TA.) وَمَا كَانَ ٱللّٰهُ لِيُضِيعَ إِيمَانَكُمْ, in the Ḳur [ii. 138], means *And God will not neglect* [or *make to be lost*] *your prayer.* (TA.) أَضَاعُوا الصَّلَاةَ, in the same, [xix. 60,] means *Who neglected,* or *omitted, prayer,* (Bḍ, TA,) *altogether:* (TA:) or *deferred it:* (Bḍ:) or *who performed it in other than its right time:* but the first explanation is more suitable, for the unbelievers are meant thereby. (TA.) ═ اضاع [is also intrans., and] may signify *He found his affair to be coming to nought.* (Ḥam p. 33.) —— And *His estates* (ضِيَاعُهُ) *became wide-spread,* (Ṣ, O, Ḳ,) and *many,* or *numerous.* (Ṣ, O, Mṣb, Ḳ.)

5. تضيّع, said of the wind, *It blew:* because it [often] destroys that upon which it blows: so says Er-Rághib. (TA. [But it may be from what here follows.]) —— Said of musk, *It diffused its odour,* or *fragrance:* (Ṣ, O, Ḳ;) a dial. var. of تضوّع: (Ṣ:) or an instance of substitution [of ى for و]. (O.) [See also 1, last explanation.]

مَاتَ ضِيعًا and ضَيْعًا: see ضَيَاعٌ.

ضَيْعَةٌ an inf. n. of 1. (Ṣ, &c.) —— See ضَيَاعٌ, below, last sentence but one. —— Also *A single case,* or *occasion, of perishing, coming to nought, passing away,* or *becoming lost;* or *of being left, left* or *let alone,* or *neglected.* (TA.) —— تَرَكْتُهُ بِضَيْعَةٍ means *I left him unsought-after,* or *unminded,* or *unmissed.* (TA. [See also a similar phrase voce ضَيَاعٌ.]) ═ Also *i. q.* عَقَارٌ [meaning *An estate consisting of land,* or *of land and a house,* or *of a house* or *land yielding a revenue,* or *of a house and palm-trees,* or *the like*]; (Ṣ, O, Mṣb, Ḳ;) and [particularly] *land yielding a revenue;* (Ḳ;) or with the people of the towns and villages and cultivated lands it signifies the *property,* of a man, *consisting of palm-trees and grape-vines and land:* but the Arabs [of the desert] know not the word in this sense: (Az, TA:) IF says, I do not reckon the application of this word as a name for the عقار to be of the original language, but think it to be an innovation in speech; and I have heard it said that this is termed a ضيعة because, when frequent attention to it is neglected, it perishes; and if it be so, this is an evidence of what we have said, that it is of the innovated speech: (O, TA:) the dim. is ↓ ضُيَيْعَةٌ, for which one should not say ضُوَيْعَةٌ: (Ṣ, O, Ḳ:) the pl. is ضِيَاعٌ and ضِيَعٌ, (Ṣ, O, Mṣb, Ḳ,) as though the latter were a contraction of the former, (Mṣb,) and ضَيْعَاتٌ: (Ḳ:) accord. to Lth, the first of these pls. signifies *places of alighting* or *abode* or *settlement;* which are thus called because, when the paying frequent attention to them, or taking good care of them, and the keeping them, or putting them, in a good state, or state of repair, is neglected, they come to nought: and ضَيْعَاتٌ occurs in a trad. as meaning the *means of subsistence.* (TA.) And, (T, O, Mṣb, Ḳ,) as used by the Arabs [of the desert], who know not the word in any other sense than this, (T, O,) *A craft,* or *handicraft, by which one gains his subsistence; a mode,* or *manner, of gain;* or *any habitual work* or *occupation* of a man; (T, O, Mṣb, Ḳ;) as the *sewing of skins* or *boots* and *the like*; and the *twisting of ropes*; and the *weaving*, or *plaiting*, *of palm-leaves*; and the *culture of palm-trees* (عَمَلُ النَّخْلِ); and the *pasturing of camels*; and *the like thereof*; (T, O;) including the *sowing*, or *tilling*, *of land*: (TA:) or the ضَيْعَة of the Arabs was the *management*, or *tending*, *of camels* and *of sheep and goats*: and the term includes a man's *craft*, or *handicraft*, or *means of gain*: (Sh, O:) and his *traffic*: (Sh, O, Ḳ:) one says to a man, قُمْ إِلَى ضَيْعَتِكَ [*Arise to thy craft*, &c.]: (Sh, O:) and كُلُّ رَجُلٍ وَضَيْعَتُهُ, [*Every man* should occupy himself *with his* proper *craft*, &c.] (Mṣb.) أَفْشَى ٱللّٰهُ ضَيْعَتَهُ, occurring in a trad., means *God made* or *may God make, his means of subsistence to be abundant*. (TA.) And one says, فَشَتْ ضَيْعَتُهُ, [or, more commonly, فَشَتْ عَلَيْهِ ضَيْعَتُهُ, as in the TA in art. فشو, &c.,] which is said to mean *His property was*, or *became*, *large*, or *abundant*, [or *wide-spread*,] *so that he was unable to collect it together*: and [hence] *his means of attaining his object* [or *his affairs* (as in the TA in art. فشو)] *became disordered so that he knew not with which of them to begin*: (TA:) or *he took to doing an affair that did not concern him*: (TA, and Ḥam p. 33:) it is nearly like the saying اِتَّسَعَ الخَرْقُ عَلَى الرَّاقِعِ [expl. in art. خرق]. (Ḥam ibid.) And إِنِّى لَأَرَى ضَيْعَةً لَا يُصْلِحُهَا إِلَّا ضَجْعَةٌ [*Verily I see property that nothing but a sleep will restore to a right state*] a prov.; said by a pastor whose camels had dispersed themselves, and who, desiring to collect them together, and being unable to do so, sought aid of sleep. (O.)

مَاتَ ضِيعَةً: see the next paragraph.

ضَيَاعٌ an inf. n. of 1 [q. v.]. (Ṣ, &c.) [Hence] one says, مَاتَ ضَيَاعًا, as also ▼ ضِيعًا, and ▼ ضِيعَةً, *He* (a man, TA) *died unsought-after*, or *unminded*, or *unmissed*. (Ḳ, TA. [See also a similar phrase voce ضَيْعَة.]) — Also *A family*, or *household*: (ISh, O, Ḳ:) or the meaning is عِيَالٌ ضُيَّعٌ, (Mgh, O, Ḳ,*) i. e. *a family*, or *household*, *neglected, untended, and unminded*; (TA;) or *such as are exposed*, or *liable*, *to perish*, (بِعَرَضِ أَنْ يَضِيعَ,) *as young children, and those who are crippled*, or *deprived of the power of motion, who cannot manage their own affairs*: (Mgh:) occurring in a trad., in which it is said that when a man died leaving such as are thus termed, (تَرَكَ ضَيَاعًا,) they were to be brought to the Prophet, (Mgh, O,) to be maintained by means of the government-treasury: (Mgh:) a prefixed noun is to be understood [i. e. it is for عِيَالٌ ضَيَاعٌ or the like]: (Mgh:) or it is an inf. n. used as a subst. [properly thus termed]: (Mgh, O:) or, accord. to one relation of the trad., the word is ▼ ضَيْعَة [which is likewise an inf. n., and in this case to be expl. in the same manner]: (Mgh:) if read ضِيَاعًا, it would be pl. of ضَائِعٌ. (Mgh, O.) — Also *A sort of perfume*, or *odoriferous substance*. (Ḳ.)

ضُيَيْعَةٌ dim. of ضَيْعَةٌ, q. v. (Ṣ, O, Ḳ.)

ضَائِعٌ *Perishing, coming to nought, passing away*, or *becoming lost*: (Mgh,* Mṣb:) [and *being left*; *left*, or *let, alone*; or *neglected*:] part. n. of 1: (Mgh, Mṣb:) pl. ضِيَاعٌ (Mgh, O, Mṣb, Ḳ) and ضُيَّعٌ. (Mgh, O,* Mṣb, Ḳ.*) [See an ex. of the latter pl. in a verse cited voce دَانَ, in art. دين. See also سَائِعٌ, in art. سوع.] — And A man *in a state of poverty*: or *having a family*, or *household, to sustain*: or *in a state of circumstances by means of which he is unable to subsist*. (TA.) — جَائِعٌ فُلَانٌ يَأْكُلُ فِى مِعًى ضَائِعٍ means [i. e. *Such a one eats into a hungry*, or *an empty, gut*]: and it was said to the daughters of El-Khuss, "What is the sharpest thing? (مَا أَحَدُّ شَىْءٍ;) and she answered, نَابٌ جَائِعٌ يُلْقِى فِى مِعًى ضَائِعٍ [*A hungry canine tooth that throws* the food *into an empty gut*]. (Ṣ.)

أَضْيَعُ means أَكْثَرُ ضَيَاعًا: so in the saying, فُلَانٌ أَضْيَعُ مِنْ فُلَانٍ [*Such a one is in a more perishing state than such a one*]. (TA.)

مُضِيعٌ act. part. n. of the trans. v. اضاع. (TA.) [See مُسِيعٌ, in art. سوع.] — And part. n. of the intrans. v. اضاع; as such signifying One *whose estates* (ضِيَاعُهُ) *are becoming wide-spread, and many*, or *numerous*. (Ṣ, TA.)

مَضِيعَةٌ and مَضْيَعَةٌ *i. q.* ضَيَاعٌ [an inf. n. of 1, q. v.]. (Mgh, O, Mṣb, Ḳ.) So in the saying, تَرَكَ عِيَالَهُ بِمَضْيَعَةٍ or بِمَضِيعَةٍ [*He left his family*, or *household, in a state of perishing*, &c.]. (Mgh.) So too in the saying, السَّارِقُ لَا يُقْطَعُ فِى مَالٍ بِمَضِيعَةٍ [*The thief shall not suffer amputation* of his hand *in the case of* his stealing *property in a neglected state*]. (Mgh.) And so in the saying, هُوَ بِدَارِ مَضِيعَةٍ (Ṣ,* O, Ḳ) and مَضْيَعَةٍ (O, Ḳ) [*He is in a place* (lit. *an abode*) *of perdition*, &c.]: or as meaning in this saying, *abandonment*, and *ignominy*. (TA.) And هُوَ مُقِيمٌ بِدَارِ مَضِيعَةٍ or مَضْيَعَةٍ means [*He is dwelling in the abode of indolence*; or] *his characteristic in his affairs is indolence*. (Mṣb.) — Also, [or perhaps the latter only, as meaning *A cause of perishing* &c., this latter being app. of the class of مَجْبَنَةٌ and مَبْخَلَةٌ &c.,] *A desert*, or *waterless desert, that is cut off* [*from inhabited regions*]: or, as expl. by IJ, *a place in which a man perishes*, or *is lost*. (Mṣb.)

مُضَيِّعٌ: see what follows.

مِضْيَاعٌ لَهُ ▼ مُضَيِّعٌ *i. q.* رَجُلٌ مِضْيَاعٌ لِلْمَالِ [i. e. *A man who wastes*, or *squanders, wealth*, or *property*]. (Ṣ, O, Ḳ.)

ضيف

1. ضَافَ, (M, Ḳ,) [aor. يَضِيفُ,] inf. n. ضَيْفٌ; (TḲ;) and ▼ اضاف, (M,) and ▼ تَضَيَّفَ, and ▼ ضَيَّفَ; (Ḳ;) *He*, or *it, inclined*, (M, Ḳ,) and *approached*, or *drew near*; إِلَيْهِ [*to him*, or *it*]. (M.) — And ضَافَتِ الشَّمْسُ, (Ṣ, M, Mgh,) or ضافت الشمس لِلْغُرُوبِ, (O,) aor. تَضِيفُ, inf. n. ضَيْفٌ; (M;) and ▼ تَضَيَّفَتْ, (Ṣ, M, Mgh,) or تضيّفت للغروب; (O;) and ▼ ضَيَّفَتْ, (Ṣ, M, Mgh,) or ضيّفت للغروب; (O;) *The sun inclined*, (Ṣ, Mgh, O,) or *drew near*, (M,) *to setting*. (Ṣ, M, Mgh, O.) — And ضَافَتْ said of a woman, aor. as above, *She menstruated*; (O, Ḳ;) because she who does so inclines, or declines, from a state of pureness to menstruation. (O, TA.) — And ضَافَ السَّهْمُ عَنِ الهَدَفِ, (M,) or ضاف السهم, (Ṣ, O,) *The arrow turned aside from the butt*: (Ṣ, M, O:) like صاف. (Ṣ, O.) And ضَافَ عَنِ الشَّىْءِ, inf. n. ضَوْفٌ [and ضَيْفٌ], *He*, or *it, turned away from the thing*: like صاف, inf. n. صَوْفٌ [and صَيْفٌ]. (M in art. ضوف.) — And ضاف said of a man, † *He feared*; as also ▼ اضاف. (M.) And ▼ اضاف مِنْهُ † *He feared it*, or *was cautious of it*; namely, an event, or affair; (Ṣ, M, O, Ḳ, TA;) as also ضاف مِنْهُ: (TA:) or ‡ *he was cautious of it with the caution of one encompassed*, or *beset, thereby*. (Z, TA.) — ضِفْتُهُ, (Ṣ, M, O, Mṣb, Ḳ,) aor. أَضِيفُهُ, (O, Ḳ,) inf. n. ضِيَافَةٌ, (Ṣ,) or ضَيْفٌ, (Mṣb,) or both; (M, O, Ḳ;) and ▼ تَضَيَّفْتُهُ; (Ṣ, M, O, Ḳ;) *I alighted at his abode*; (M, Mṣb;) and *inclined to him*: (M:) or *I alighted at his abode* (Ṣ, M, O, Mṣb, Ḳ) *as a* ضَيْف [or *guest*], (Ṣ, O, Ḳ,) or *and became his* ضَيْف [or *guest*]. (M, O, Mṣb. [See also 3.]) And ضَافَ القَوْمَ, and ▼ تَضَيَّفَهُمْ, *He alighted at the abode of the people*, or *party, as a* ضَيْف [or *guest*]. (Mgh.) And ▼ تَضَيَّفْتُهُ *I came to him as a* ضَيْف [or *guest*]. (L, TA.) — [Hence,] ضَافَهُ الهَمُّ † *Anxiety befell him*. (Ṣ, M,* O. [See, again, 3.]) — And ضِفْتُهُ signifies also *I sought*, or *desired, of him entertainment as a* ضَيْف [or *guest*]; and so ▼ تَضَيَّفْتُهُ; (M;) or this latter, (L, Mṣb,) and ▼ اِسْتَضَفْتُهُ, (M,) *I asked of him such entertainment*. (M, L, Mṣb.)

2. ضيّف, intrans.: see 1, first and second sentences. — As trans.: see 4, last sentence, in four places. — [Hence,] ضَيَّفْتُهُ signifies also † *I protected him*, or *defended him, from him who sought*, or *pursued, him*: (Mṣb:) ‡ *I rendered him safe, secure*, or *free from fear*; and *became at peace with him*; thus used metaphorically. (TA.)

3. ضايفهُ [app. signifies *He straitened him*: (see 6:) or, perhaps, *he became his guest*; like ضَافَهُ, &c.]. — [Hence one says,] ضَايَفَهُ الهَمُّ ‡ [*Anxiety straitened him*: or, perhaps, *befell him*; like ضَافَهُ]. (TA.) — [And ضايفهُ, inf. n. مُضَايَفَةٌ, signifies also *It was*, or *became, correlative to it*; as, for instance, fathership to sonship. See also the next paragraph.]

4. اضاف, intrans.: see 1, in three places. — Also, said of a man, *He ran*, and *hastened, made haste*, or *sped*, (Ibn-'Abbád, O, Ḳ,) and *fled*, or *turned away and fled:* (Ḳ:) and said of a dog as meaning *he ran away,* or *fled.* (TA in art. جبن.) — And أَشْرَفَ عَلَيْهِ i. q. اضاف عَلَى الشَّىْءِ [*He looked upon,* or *viewed, the thing from above:* or *he was,* or *became, on the brink,* or *verge,* or *at the point, of the thing:* &c.]. (O, Ḳ,* TA.) — تُضِيفُ إِلَى صَوْتِ الفَحْلِ, said of a she-camel, means *She hears with desire of going to him the voice,* or *sound, of the stallion.* (M.) — And الإِضَافَةُ and ♦ التَّضَايُفُ signify *Correlation,* or *reciprocal relation, so that one of the two cannot be conceived in the mind without the other;* as in the case of الأُبُوَّةُ and البُنُوَّةُ [i. e. fathership and sonship]. (KT. [See also 3.]) = اضافهُ إِلَيْهِ *He made it to incline towards it;* (Ṣ, M,* O, Mṣb, Ḳ;*) namely, a thing (Ṣ, O) to a thing. (Ṣ, O, Mṣb.) *He made it to lean, rest,* or *stay itself, against it,* or *upon it.* (M, TA.) You say, اضاف ظَهْرَهُ إِلَى الحَائِطِ *He leaned his back against the wall.* (MA.) And اضاف إِلَيْهِ أَمْرًا ‡ *He rested,* or *stayed, upon him an affair, and desired him to do what would suffice.* (TA.) — And *He made him to have recourse to it,* or *to betake himself to it for refuge.* (Ṣ, O, Ḳ.) — And *He adjoined it to it.* (Mṣb.) — And hence الإِضَافَةُ as a conventional term of the grammarians; because the first [of two nouns in the case to which it applies] is adjoined to the second: (Mṣb:) [for] إِضَافَةُ الاِسْمِ إِلَى الاِسْمِ is [*The prefixing the noun to the noun so that the former governs the latter in the gen. case*] as when you say غُلَامُ زَيْدٍ; in which instance, غلام is termed ♦ مُضَافٌ, and زيد is termed ♦ مُضَافٌ إِلَيْهِ: and this is done for the purpose of particularizing or appropriating, and of making known or definite: therefore the إِضَافَة of a thing to itself [i. e. the prefixing a noun in this manner to one identical therewith in meaning] is not allowable, because a thing does not make known, or definite, itself; (Ṣ;) unless by an ellipsis, as when you say حَقُّ الشَّىْءِ اليَقِينِ for حَقُّ اليَقِينِ; or, accord. to Fr, the Arabs used to do so because of the difference of the two words themselves. (Ṣ voce جَامِعٌ.) [الإِضَافَةُ is also often used as meaning *The state of being prefixed in the manner explained above;* or *the connection of a noun so prefixed with its complement.* The various kinds of إِضَافَة are sufficiently explained in the grammars of De Sacy and others: they are not proper subjects of a lexicon, though much is said respecting them in the O, and more in the Mṣb. — Hence also, بِالإِضَافَةِ إِلَى كَذَا meaning *In comparison with* (lit. *to*), or *in relation to,* (like بِالنِّسْبَةِ إِلَى,) *such a thing;* as though *in juxtaposition to it:* a phrase of frequent occurrence: see an ex. in Bḍ ii. 6.] — أَضَفْتُهُ (inf. n. إِضَافَةٌ, Mṣb) and ♦ ضَيَّفْتُهُ (inf. n. تَضْيِيفٌ, O) both signify the same, (Ṣ, M, O, Mṣb, Ḳ,) from الضِّيَافَةُ; (O;) i. e. both signify *I made him a guest,* or *lodged him,* or *gave him refuge* or *asylum,* syn. أَنْزَلْتُهُ, (Ṣ, M, Mṣb,) *with me, as a* ضَيْف [or *guest*], (Ṣ,) *and entertained him:* (Ṣ, M, Mṣb:) أَضَافُوهُ and ♦ ضَيَّفُوهُ both signify أَنْزَلُوهُ: (Mgh:) accord. to Th, أَضَفْتُهُ signifies *I lodged him at my abode as a* ضَيْف: and *I gave him* (i. e. one in fear) *protection,* or *refuge* or *asylum:* (Mṣb:) and ♦ ضَيَّفْتُهُ is also expl. as meaning *I fed him:* and ♦ ضَيَّفَهُ as meaning *he made him to be in the condition of* أَضْيَاف [or *guests*]. (TA.)

5, intrans.: see 1, first and second sentences. — تَضَيُّفٌ signifies also The *being collected together.* (KL, from the Mj.) — And The *being a* تَابِع [or *follower,* &c.]. (Id.) = As trans.: see 1, latter half, in four places.

6: see 4. = تضايف as said of a valley, [from ضِيف "a side,"] *It became narrow;* syn. تَضَايَقَ. (Ṣ, M, O.) تَضَايَفْنَ عَلَيْهِ, a phrase used by a poet [describing camels following an old camel], *They became near to him,* (Ṣ, M, O,) *by his side.* (Ṣ, M.) And you say, تضايفهُ القَوْمُ *The people,* or *party, became on both sides of him* (بِضِيفَيْهِ). (TA.) And تضايفهُ السَّبُعَانِ *The two beasts of prey hemmed him in on both sides.* (TA.) And تَضَايَفَتْ عَلَيْهِ and تَضَايَفَتِ الكِلَابُ الصَّيْدَ [*The dogs hemmed in the object of the chase on both sides,* or *round about*]. (TA.) [In the TA, all these are said to be tropical; but why, I see not.]

[7. انضاف إِلَيْهِ signifies *He,* or *it, became joined,* or *adjoined,* or *added, to him,* or *it:* and *he joined himself to him:* but is perhaps post-classical.]

10: see 1, last sentence. — You say also اِسْتَضَافَنِى, meaning *He desired me,* or *asked me, to grant him protection,* or *refuge.* (Mṣb.) And استضاف فُلَانٌ إِلَى فُلَانٍ *Such a one had recourse,* or *betook himself, to such a one for protection,* or *refuge.* (IAṣr, M.)

ضَيْفٌ *A guest:* and *guests:* (MA:) so called because adjoined to the family and fed with them: (Ḥam p. 124:) it is applied to one, and to a pl. number, (Ṣ, M, MA, O, Mṣb, Ḳ,) and to a male and to a female, (Ṣ, O, Mṣb, Ḳ,) because it is originally an inf. n.: (MA, Mṣb:) [as a sing.,] i. q. ♦ مُضَيَّفٌ, (M,) which is *syn. with* نَزِيلٌ: (TA:) and applied to a pl. number, it may be pl. [or rather a quasi-pl. n.] of ♦ ضَائِفٌ, which is syn. with نَازِلٌ; thus being of the class of زَوْرٌ and صَوْمٌ: (M:) and it is also pluralized, having for its pls. أَضْيَافٌ and ضِيفَانٌ (Ṣ, M, MA, O, Mṣb, Ḳ) and ضُيُوفٌ (Ṣ, M, MA, O, Ḳ) and ضِيَافٌ, (MA, TA,) the first of which is properly a pl. of pauc., but is also used as a pl. of mult.: (M:) and a female is termed ضَيْفَةٌ as well as ضَيْفٌ: (Ṣ, M, O, Mṣb, Ḳ:) El-Ba'eeth says,

• لَقَى حَمَلَتْهُ أُمُّهُ وَهْىَ ضَيْفَةٌ •

[*A castaway with whom his mother became pregnant while she was a guest*]: (Ṣ, M, O:) or, accord. to AHeyth, the meaning here is that which follows. (O.) — ضَيْفَةٌ applied to a woman signifies also *Menstruating:* (O, Ḳ:) so says AHeyth with reference to the citation above from El-Ba'eeth. (O.)

ضِيفٌ The *side* (T, Ṣ, M, O, Ḳ) of a valley (T, M) and of a mountain (M) [&c.: see 6]: and, as metaphorically used by an anonymous poet, of the ذَكَر: (M:) and ♦ مَضَايِفُ signifies the *sides* of a valley. (TA.) — And one says, فُلَانٌ فِى ضِيفِ فُلَانٍ, meaning *Such a one is in the vicinage,* or *quarter, of such a one.* (M.)

ضَيْفَنٌ *One who comes with a guest:* (Ṣ, O:) or *who so comes intruding without invitation:* (Ḳ:) or *one who follows a guest:* derived from ضَيْف, accord. to Sb; but said by AZ to belong to art. ضفن: (M:) [accord. to J and Ṣgh] the ن is augmentative: the pl. is ضَيَافِنُ. (Ṣ, O.)

ضِيَافَةٌ an inf. n. of ضَافَهُ in the first of the senses assigned to the latter above. (Ṣ, M, O, Ḳ.) — [And] a subst. from أَضَفْتُهُ and ضَيَّفْتُهُ [as such signifying The *entertainment of a guest* or *guests;* i. e. the *act of entertaining:* and an *entertainment* as meaning *a repast, given to a guest* or *guests; a banquet,* or *feast*]. (Mṣb.) [Hence, دَارُ الضِّيَافَةِ *The house of entertainment of guests.*]

ضَائِفٌ A man *alighting as a guest;* syn. نَازِلٌ: (M, TA:) see ضَيْفٌ: its [proper] pl. is ضُيَّفٌ. (TA.)

مُضَافٌ; and مُضَافٌ إِلَيْهِ: see 4. — The former signifies also ‡ One who is *made an adjunct,* or *adherent, to a people,* or *party,* (Ṣ, M, O, Ḳ, TA,) and *made to incline to them,* (M,) *not being of them.* (M, TA.) One says, مَا هُوَ إِلَّا مُضَافٌ ‡ [*He is none other than an adjunct,* or *adherent*]. (TA.) — And ‡ One *whose origin,* or *lineage,* or *parentage, is suspected;* or *who makes a claim to relationship not having it:* (O, Ḳ, TA:) and (Ḳ) *whose origin,* or *relationship, is referred to a people,* or *party, of whom he is not a member.* (O, Ḳ, TA.) — And One *who is constrained to betake himself to a place of refuge,* (M, O, Ḳ, TA,) *to a narrow,* or *confined, place, and who is burdened with evil:* (TA:) El-Bureyḳ El-Hudhalee says,

• وَيَحْمِى المُضَافَ إِذَا مَا دَعَا •

[*And he protects him who is constrained to betake himself to a place of refuge, when he calls for aid*]. (M.) And ♦ مُسْتَضَافٌ signifies the same as مُضَافٌ [app. in the last of the senses expl. above]: so says IB; and he cites the saying of Jowwás Ibn-Ḥeiyán El-Azdee,

• وَلَقَدْ أُقْدِمُ فِى الرَّوْ • عِ وَأَحْمِى المُسْتَضَافَا •

[app. meaning *And verily I advance boldly in the case of fear, and I protect him who is constrained to betake himself to a place of refuge*]. (TA.) [See also مَضُوفٌ.] — Also One who is *beset, hemmed in,* or *encompassed,* in war, or battle: (Ṣ, O, Ḳ: said in the TA to be tropical:) or one *falling among the horsemen and men of valour, having in him no strength.* (M.) [See, again, مَضُوفٌ.] — And One *in a state of fear.* (TA.)

مَضُوفٌ *Beset by distress of mind:* (TA:) [accord. to Freytag, as from the Deewán of the

Hudhalees, *constrained to seek refuge*: (see also مُضَافٌ:)] it occurs in the saying of the Hudhalee,

أَنْتَ تُجِيبُ دَعْوَةَ ٱلْمَضُوفِ

[*Thou answerest the prayer*, or *call, of him who is beset* &c.]; and is formed after the manner of بَيْعٌ for بَوْعٌ. (M, TA.)

مَضِيفٌ a dial. var. of مَصِيفٌ [q. v.]. (TA.) [ISd says that] مَضِيفًا occurring in a verse of Aboo-Dhu-eyb [as some relate it], cited voce حَرْبَةٌ, [where the reading of مَصِيفًا is given,] is for ضَائِفًا, meaning *Turning aside; crooked.* (M.)

مُضِيفٌ *Fleeing*; or *turning away and fleeing.* (Ibn-'Abbád, O. [See also its verb.])

مُضَافَةٌ *Hardship*, or *difficulty*, or *distress.* (TA.) — See also the next paragraph.

مَضُوفَةٌ, an anomalous word, by rule مَضِيفَةٌ, (Kh, Sb, TA in art. ضوف,) *Anxiety*; and *want*, or *a want*; (O and Ḳ in that art.;) and ▼ مَضِيفَةٌ and ▼ مُضِيفَةٌ signify the same; (O in that art. and in art. ضيف;) or these two signify *anxiety*, and *grief*: (Ḳ in this art.:) or مَضُوفَةٌ signifies *an affair*, or *event, that is feared*, or *of which one is cautious*; (Ṣ and M in this art.;) thus accord. to Aṣ; and ▼ مَضِيفَةٌ and ▼ مُضَافَةٌ signify the same. (Ṣ, L, TA.)

مَضِيفَةٌ and مُضِيفَةٌ: see both in the next preceding paragraph; the former in two places.

مَضْيَفَةٌ, of the measure مَفْعَلَةٌ, *A place of* ضِيَافَة [i. e. *entertainment of a guest* or *guests*: pl. مَضَايِفُ]. (TA.)

مُضَيَّفٌ: see ضَيْفٌ.

مُضَيِّفٌ The *master of an abode in which guests are entertained*; as also ▼ مُضَايِفِيٌّ. (TA.)

مِضْيَافٌ [One *who often entertains guests*]. (Ḥar p. 579.)

مَضَايِفُ [pl. of مَضْيَفَةٌ: — and also of a sing. not mentioned]: see ضَيْفٌ.

مُضَايِفِيٌّ [from مَضَايِفُ pl. of مَضْيَفَةٌ]: see مُضَيِّفٌ.

أَسْمَآءٌ مُتَضَايِفَةٌ *Correlative nouns*; i. e. *nouns significant of the existence of persons*, or *things, whereof the existence of one necessarily indicates the existence of another*; as أَبٌ and ٱبْنٌ [father and son]. (Er-Rághib, TA.)

مُسْتَضَافٌ: see مُضَافٌ.

مُسْتَضِيفٌ [act. part. n. of 10, q. v.:] *Asking*, or *calling, for aid*, or *succour*. (Ibn-'Abbád, O, Ḳ.)

ضيق

1. ضَاقَ, aor. يَضِيقُ, inf. n. ضِيقٌ (Ṣ, O, Mṣb, Ḳ) and ضَيْقٌ, (Ṣ, O, Ḳ,) or this latter is a simple subst., (Mṣb,) *It was*, or *became, narrow*, or *strait*; contr. of ٱتَّسَعَ; (Mṣb, Ḳ;) as also ▼ تَضَيَّقَ, [or rather this signifies *it was*, or *became, rendered narrow*, or *strait*, being quasi-pass. of 2,] and ▼ تَضَايَقَ: (Ḳ:) it is said of a thing, (Ṣ, O, Mṣb,) and of a place. (Mṣb.) [See also ضَيِّقٌ below.] ضَاقَتْ عَلَيْهِمُ ٱلْأَرْضُ, in the Ḳur ix. 119, means *The earth became strait to them.* (Bḍ, Jel.) And one says, ضَاقَتْ بِهِ ٱلْأَرْضُ [meaning, in like manner, *The earth*, or *land, became narrow*, or *strait, with him*]: 'Amr Ibn-El-Ahtam says,

لَعَمْرُكَ مَا ضَاقَتْ بِلَادٌ بِأَهْلِهَا ‌ ‌ وَلٰكِنَّ أَخْلَاقَ ٱلرِّجَالِ تَضِيقُ

[*By thy life*, or *by thy religion, countries have not become narrow with their inhabitants, but the dispositions of the men become narrow*]. (O, TA.) [ضَاقَ بِهِ often signifies, and so does ▼ تَضَايَقَ بِهِ, *It was*, or *became, choked, surcharged*, or *overfilled, with it*; for instance, a water-course with water, and a place with people.] And ▼ تَضَايَقَ ضَاقَ عَلَيْهِ بِهِ ٱلْأَمْرُ means ‡ [*The affair was*, or *became, strait to him*]. (O, TA. [See an ex. in art. رحب, conj. 6.]) One says also, ضَاقَ عَلَيْهِ مَعَاشُهُ: see 4. [And ضَاقَ ٱلْوَقْتُ † *The time became strait*, or *contracted.*] And ضَاقَ صَدْرُهُ † *His bosom*, or *mind, became strait*, or *contracted*: (Mṣb:) and ضَاقَ عَنْهُ صَدْرُكَ † [*Thy mind became so contracted as to be incapable of it*: or *thy mind shrank from it*]. (Ḳ.) [And يَضِيقُ ٱلْعَقْلُ عَنْ تَقْدِيرِهِ † *The intellect is incapable of determining its limit*, or *limits*, or *the like.*] And ضَاقَ عَنِ ٱلْجَوَابِ and ضَاقَ بِٱلْجَوَابِ † [*He was straitened*, or *embarrassed, so as to be unable to reply*, or *to answer*; *he was incapable of replying*, or *answering*]: both signify the same. (TA in art. زند.) And ضَاقَ بِٱلْأَمْرِ ذَرْعًا, (Ṣ,* O,* Mṣb,) meaning † *The thing*, or *affair, was difficult*, or *distressing, to him*, (Mṣb,) originally ضَاقَ ذَرْعُهُ بِهِ, (Ṣ,* O,* Mṣb,) i. e. *his ability* [*was straitened by it*, or *was inadequate to it*]; and *his power*: (Mṣb:) or *his art*, or *artifice*, or *cunning*: or *his way, course, mode*, or *manner, of acting* (مَذْهَبُهُ) [*was straitened*, or *rendered difficult*, or *distressing, by it*]. (O. [See more voce ذَرْعٌ: and see a similar phrase in the Ḳur xi. 79 and xxix. 32.]) And hence, app., the saying ضَاقَ ٱلْمَالُ عَنِ ٱلدُّيُونِ ‡ *The property was inadequate to the debts.* (Mṣb.) And you say, ضَاقَ عَنْكَ ٱلشَّىْءُ لَمْ يَسَعْكَ † *The thing was not* [meaning *allowable to thee*]: one says, لَا يَسَعُنِى شَىْءٌ وَيَضِيقُ عَنْكَ, (Ṣ, O,* TA, [in the O, erroneously, لا يستغنى,]) i. e. وَأَنْ يَضِيقَ عَنْكَ † [*A thing will not be allowable to me conjointly with its being disallowable to thee*, وَأَنْ يَضِيقَ meaning مَعَ ضِيقِهِ]: بَلْ مَتَى وَسِعَنِى شَىْءٌ وَسِعَكَ [*but when a thing is allowable to me, it is allowable to thee*]. (Ṣ in art. وسع.) And ضَاقَ, (aor. يَضِيقُ, Ḳ, inf. n. ضِيقٌ, TA,) ‡ *He was* or *became, niggardly*, or *avaricious.* (Ṣ, O, Mṣb, Ḳ, TA.)

2. ضَيَّقَهُ, (Mṣb, Ḳ,) inf. n. تَضْيِيقٌ, (Mṣb, TA,) *He made it strait*, or *narrow*; (Mṣb, Ḳ;) namely, a place [&c.]; (Mṣb;) as also ▼ أَضَاقَهُ, (Ḳ,) inf. n. إِضَاقَةٌ. (TA.) You say, ضَيَّقْتُ عَلَيْهِ ٱلْمَكَانَ, (Ṣ,) or ٱلشَّىْءَ, i. e. *I straitened*, or *made narrow, to him* [*the place*, or *the thing*; or *I scanted it*, or *made it scanty*]; contr. of وَسَّعْتُهُ عَلَيْهِ. (O.) And ضَيَّقْتُ عَلَيْهِ [alone, used elliptically, *I straitened him*, properly speaking; and also, † his circumstances &c.]. (Mṣb.) And ضُيِّقَ عَلَى فُلَانٍ † [*Such a one was straitened*]. (TA.) لِتُضَيِّقُوا عَلَيْهِنَّ, in the Ḳur [lxv. 6, † *In order that ye may straiten them*], implies relation to expenses and to the bosom. (TA.) [See 3. ٱلتَّضْيِيقُ بَيْنَ شَيْئَيْنِ, occurring in the Ṣ and Ḳ in art. حوص, means *The making a coarctation between two things.*]

3. ضَايَقَهُ *He straitened him*: (MA:) [see also 2: or, properly, *he straitened him, being in like manner straitened by him*: see 1 in art. زحم: and] ‡ *he treated him*, or *behaved towards him, with hardness*, or *harshness*; (O,* Ḳ,* TA;) فِى كَذَا [*in*, or *in respect of, such a thing*]. (TA.)

4. اضاق ‡ *His means of living became strait* (ضَاقَ ▼ عَلَيْهِ مَعَاشُهُ); (TA;) *his property went away*; (Ṣ, O, Mṣb, Ḳ;) and *he became poor.* (TA.) — See also 2.

5: see 1, first sentence.

6: see 1, in three places. تَضَايَقُوا *They straitened one another*; *pushed*, or *pressed, one against another*; or *crowded one another*; in a place of assembly; syn. زَحَمَ بَعْضُهُمْ بَعْضًا: (Mṣb in art. زحم:) or *they became straitened* in a place, or † in disposition. (Ṣ, O.)

10. اِسْتَضَاقَتْ بِفُرْزَجَةٍ [*She endeavoured to constrict her vagina by means of a pessary*], (O, Ḳ, TA,) or بِٱلْأَدْوِيَةِ [*by means of medicaments*]; (A, TA;) said of a woman. (A, O, Ḳ.)

ضَيْقٌ an inf. n. of 1, (Ṣ, O, Mṣb, Ḳ,) as also ▼ ضِيقٌ, (Ṣ, O, Ḳ,) or the latter is a simple subst.: (Mṣb:) [both, used as simple substs., signify *Narrowness*, or *straitness*:] accord. to Fr, [both seem to signify thus; but the latter, properly; and the former, tropically; for he says that] ٱلضَّيْقُ is in that which does not [really] become wide, like the mind (ٱلصَّدْر): (O:) or it is مَا ضَاقَ عَنْهُ صَدْرُكَ [*that of which the mind by its being contracted is incapable*, or *from which the mind shrinks*; an explanation not given in the Ḳ as on the authority of Fr, and deviating from his words as given in the O; whence it appears that, for مَا, we should perhaps read فِيمَا]: (Ḳ:) but ▼ ٱلضِّيقُ is in that which may be [really] wide, like the house and the garment: (O, Ḳ:) and the former [is also used as an epithet, being a contraction of ضَيِّقٌ in this case, and as such] has a dual and a plural and a feminine; but the latter has not: (O:) or ▼ both are alike [in signification]: (Ḳ:) and ▼ ضَيْقَةٌ is syn. with ضَيْقٌ. (Ṣ.) — Also, and ▼ ضِيقٌ, accord. to AA, (O, [the latter there expressly said to be بِٱلْكَسْرِ,]) or the former and ▼ ضِيقٌ, (Ḳ, [said in the TA to be a mistake for ضَيْق, but see what follows,]) *Doubt* (AA, O, Ḳ) *in the heart:* (Ḳ:) the first is more common than the second, in this sense; and occurs in the Ḳur in xvi. last verse and xxvii. 72: (O:) [but] Ibn-Ketheer read, in both of these instances, ♦ ضِيق; and this and ضَيْق are dial. vars. signifying *straitness of mind.* (Bḍ.) — See also ضَيِّق, in two places: — and ضَيْقَة, second sentence, in two places.

ضِيق: see the next preceding paragraph, in five places.

ضَيْق: see ضَيِّق, latter part.

ضَيْقَة: see ضَيِّق, latter part. — Also (Ṣ) ‡ *Poverty;* and *an evil state* or *condition;* (Ṣ, O, Ḳ, TA;) and so ♦ ضِيقَة: (Ḳ, TA:) and the pl. [or rather coll. gen. n.] (Fr, Ṣ, Ḳ, TA) of the former (Fr, Ṣ, TA) is ♦ ضَيْق: (Fr, Ṣ, Ḳ, TA: [in the CḲ, erroneously, ضِيق:]) Fr says, when you see ♦ الضَّيْق to have occurred in the place of الضِّيق, it is in [one of] two cases; either it is the pl. [or coll. gen. n.] of الضَّيْقَة; or it means *the narrow,* or *strait, thing,* ضَيْق being a contraction of ضَيِّق. (TA.) — And الضَّيْقَة, (O,) or ضَيْقَة [without the article], (JK, O, TA,) or ♦ الضِّيقَة, (Ḳ, [app. a mistake, for in the O, in every case, whether as a proper name or not, الضيقة is written الضَّيْقَة,]) is the name of *A certain mansion of the moon,* (JK, O, Ḳ, TA,) [not one of the Twenty-eight Mansions,] *close by* الثُّرَيَّا [or *the Pleiades*]: (JK, O, TA:) or, as IḲṭ says, on the authority of Ibn-Ziyád El-Kilábee, sometimes the moon falls short of الدَّبَرَان and alights in الضيقة, i. e. *two small stars, near together, between* الثُّرَيَّا *and* الدَّبَرَان: (TA:) it is asserted by the Arabs to be an inauspicious place. (O,* TA.) Hence the saying of El-Akhṭal,

فَهَلَّا زَجَرْتَ الطَّيْرَ لَيْلَةَ جِئْتَهَا
بِضَيْقَةَ بَيْنَ النَّجْمِ وَالدَّبَرَانِ

[*And wherefore didst not thou draw an omen from the flight of birds on the night when thou camest to her,* when the moon was *in Ḍeyḳah, between the Pleiades and Ed-Debarán?*]: he notifies that the moon, in the night of their coming together, was making its abode [in the neighbourhood of] الدبران, which is inauspicious: (O, TA:) or [the latter hemistich, as J relates it, app. on the authority of A'Obeyd, is thus,]

بِضِيقَةِ بَيْنَ النَّجْمِ وَالدَّبَرَانِ

from الضِّيقَة as syn. with الضِّيق; (Ṣ;) and as AA relates the verse, it is [thus] with kesr to the ة in بضيقة; the word not being made the [proper] name of a place, but the meaning being بِضِيقَةٍ مَا بَيْنَ النجم والدبران [i. e. *in the narrow space between the Pleiades and Ed-Debarán*]. (TA.) — ضَيِّقَة is also the fem. of ضَيِّق the contracted form of ضَيْق. (Ṣ, O, TA.)

ضِيقَة: see the next preceding paragraph, former half, in two places.

ضُوقَى and ضِيقَى are fems. of ♦ أَضْيَقُ; (Ṣ, O, Ḳ;) the former [as well as the latter] is [originally] of the measure فُعْلَى, (TA,) [each being originally ضُيْقَى,] the ى being changed in the former into و because quiescent and preceded by ḍammeh: (Ṣ, O, TA:) the former occurs in the saying of a woman to her fellow-wife, contending with her for superiority,

مَا أَنْتِ بِالخُورَى وَلَا الضُّوقَى حِرًا

[*Thou art not the better nor the narrower* &c.; خُورَى being in like manner fem. of أَخْيَرُ]. (TA.) Accord. to Kr, the former is pl. of ♦ ضَيِّقَة; (TA;) and he says the same of ضِيقَى also; (TA voce كَيِّس;) but ISd says, I know not how this may be, for فُعْلَى is not of the measures of pls. except of the kind of pl. which differs not from its sing. otherwise than in the latter's having ة [as an affix], like بُهْمَاةٌ and بُهْمَى [q. v.]. (TA in the present art.)

ضِيَاق: see مِضْيَاق.

ضَائِق: see the next paragraph, in four places.

ضَيِّق and ♦ ضَيْق, (Ṣ, O, Ḳ,) the latter a contraction of the former, (Ṣ,) the two being like هَيِّن and هَيْن [&c.], (O,) and ♦ ضَائِق, (Ḳ,) *Narrow,* or *strait:* (Ṣ,* O,* Ḳ:) or ضَيِّق is an epithet used in this sense when permanence [of the attribute] is meant [and so therefore is its contracted form]; and ♦ ضَائِق as meaning [*being,* or *becoming, narrow* or *strait;* or] *temporarily narrow* or *strait:* (Mṣb:) the fem. of the first (TA) and of the second (Ṣ, O, TA) [as well as of the third] is with ة: (Ṣ, O, TA:) see also ضُوقَى: [the pls. of the first and second, applied to rational beings, is ضَيِّقُونَ and ضَيْقُونَ, like مَيِّتُونَ and مَيْتُونَ: and] the pl. of ♦ ضَائِق is ضَاقَة. (TA.) You say شَىْءٌ ضَيِّقٌ (O, Mṣb) and ♦ ضَيْقٌ (O) *A narrow,* or *strait, thing.* (O,* Mṣb.) And صَدْرٌ ضَيِّقٌ † *A strait,* or *contracted, mind;* (Mṣb;) and نَفْسٌ ضَيِّقَةٌ [meaning the same]. (TA.) And وَضَائِقٌ ♦ بِهِ صَدْرُكَ, in the Ḳur [xi. 15], means † *And thy mind is temporarily strait* or *contracted thereby.* (Mṣb.) ضَيِّق signifies also † *Niggardly,* or *avaricious.* (KL.) [And ضَيِّقُ الخُلُقِ † *Narrow,* or *illiberal, in disposition.*]

أَضْيَقُ [*More,* and *most, narrow* or *strait* or *contracted*]: (Ṣ, O, Ḳ:) see its fems. ضُوقَى and ضِيقَى, above. [See also three exs. voce اِسْتٌ, in art. سته.]

مَضِيق *A narrow,* or *strait, place:* (Ḳ:) [*a pass:* *a place of narrowness* or *straitness*] of land; and of the vulva; and † [*a place,* or *state, of straitness*] of life, or of the means of subsistence: (Ḳ in art. ازم:) and ‡ *a narrow,* or *strait, affair* or *case:* (Ḳ, TA:) pl. مَضَايِق. (TA.)

أَمْرٌ مُضَيَّقٌ † [*An affair rendered strait*]. (TA.)

مِضْيَاق, (JK, and O on the authority of Ibn-'Abbád, and TA,) or ♦ ضِيَاق, like كِتَاب [in measure], thus in all the copies of the Ḳ, (TA,) [but probably, I think, taken from a mistranscription,] *A pessary* (دُرْجَة) *of rag and perfume, with which a woman endeavours to constrict her vagina* (تَسْتَضِيقُ بِهَا). (JK, Ibn-'Abbád, O, Ḳ.)

ضيل

4. أَضْيَلَتِ الأَرْضُ and أَضَالَت *The land had in it* [*trees of the species called*] ضَال: (Fr, Ṣ, O:) or أَضْيَلَ المَكَانُ and اضال *the place gave growth to* ضَال: (AḤn, M, Ḳ:) or *had in it many* ضَال. (IḲṭṭ, TA.)

ضَالٌ The *wild* [*species of lote-tree called*] سِدْر [q.v.]: (Ṣ, O, K:) or *such of the* سدر *as are watered only by the rain;* (M, Ḳ:) the سدر *of the mountains, which is thinner in its wood than that of the rivers:* AḤn says, *it grows in the plain,* or *soft, tracts, and in the rugged; and the bow that is made of it, when it is pared, is pared so as to be thick, in order that it may be stronger, because of the lightness of its wood:* (M:) n. un. with ة: (Ṣ, M, O, Ḳ.) [See also عُبْرِىّ, and عُبْرِىّ.] — Also *Another species of tree;* (M, Ḳ;) AḤn says, it is *a tree of the shrub-kind, found in the borders of El-Yemen, rising to the height of a cubit, in its manner of growth like the cypress, and having a yellow* [*fruit of the sort called a*] بَرَمَة, *of a very pungent odour, so that its odour comes to you before you reach it: it is not of the* سدر *thus called.* (M.)

ضَالَةٌ n. un. of ضَال [q. v.]. (Ṣ, M, O, Ḳ.) — Also *Arrows,* (M, O, TA,) and *bows,* (TA,) *made of the* [*species of lote-tree called*] ضَال: (M, TA:) this is the primary signification: (TA:) or *arrows,* (IB, Ḳ,) because they are made thereof: (IB:) or it signifies, (Ḳ,) or signifies also, (O,) *all kinds of weapons.* (O, Ḳ.) One says, رَأَيْتُهُ يَرْمِى بِالضَّالَةِ [*I saw him shooting arrows*]. (TA.) And خَرَجَ وَفِى يَدِهِ ضَالَةٌ i. e. [*He went forth having in his hand*] *a bow.* (TA.) And إِنَّهُ لَكَامِلُ الضَّالَةِ *Verily he is complete in respect of weapons.* (O.) And خَرَجَ فُلَانٌ بِضَالَتِهِ *Such a one went forth with his weapons.* (O.)

ضير

1. ضَامَهُ, (Ṣ, Mṣb,) aor. يَضِيمُهُ, (Ṣ,) inf. n. ضَيْم, (Ṣ,* Mṣb,) [as also ضَامَهُ, aor. يَضُومُهُ, inf. n. ضَوْم, (see art. ضوم,)] *He wronged him; treated him wrongfully, unjustly, injuriously,* or *tyrannically:* (Ṣ:) *he harmed, injured, hurt,* or *damaged, him:* (Mṣb:) and ♦ استضامهُ signifies the same. (Ṣ.) And ضَامَهُ حَقَّهُ, (M, Ḳ,) aor. as above, (Ḳ,) and so the inf. n., (M,) *He defrauded him of his right,* or *due, partially* or *wholly;* (M, Ḳ;) as also ♦ استضامهُ. (Ḳ.) —

And ضُمْتُ *I was wronged,* &c.: of which there are three dial. vars.; one says of a man ضِيمَ; and ضُيْمَ, with [the pronunciation termed] إِشْمَام; and ضُومَ; like as we have said respecting بِيعَ. (Ṣ.) One says, مَا ضِمْتُ أَحَدًا وَمَا ضُمْتُ [*I have not wronged any one, and I have not been wronged*]; i. e. no one has wronged me. (TA.) It is said in a trad., as some relate it, لَا تُضَامُونَ فِى رُؤْيَتِهِ [or ▼ تُضَامُّونَ or ▼ تَضَامُّونَ *Ye will not be wronged in the seeing Him*]. (M. [For other readings and explanations of this trad., see 3 in art. ضم.])

3 and 6: see the preceding paragraph.

10: see 1, in two places.

ضَيْمٌ *Wrong;* i. e. *wrongdoing;* or *wrongful, unjust, injurious,* or *tyrannical, treatment:* (Ṣ, Ḳ:) an inf. n. which is pluralized; its pl. being ضُيُوم. (M, Ḳ.)

ضِيمٌ The *side of a mountain,* (Ṣ, M, Ḳ,) and *of an* [*eminence such as is termed*] أَكَمَة. (M.)

ضَائِمٌ *Wronging,* or *a wrongdoer:* pl. ضَامَةٌ: the latter occurring in the prov., تَأْتِى بِكَ الضَّامَةُ عِرِّيسَ الأَسَدِ [*The wrongdoers bring thee,* or cause *thee to come, to the covert of the lion*]; meaning, the wrong of the wrongdoers requires thee to cast thyself into destruction: applied in offering an excuse for venturing upon that which is perilous: or, as some relate it, الضَّامَّةُ, from الضَّمُّ; meaning "want, or the object of want, that brings thee and causes thee to have recourse [to a thing]." (Meyd.)

مَضِيمٌ *Wronged; treated wrongfully, unjustly, injuriously,* or *tyrannically:* as also ▼ مُسْتَضَامٌ. (Ṣ, Ḳ,* TA.)

مُسْتَضَامٌ: see what next precedes.

ط

The sixteenth letter of the alphabet; called طَآءٌ [and طَا]; the ا of which is reduced to ى [as its radical letter]: when you spell it, you make its final letter quiescent; but when you apply an epithet to it, and make it a noun, you decline it as a noun, saying, [for instance,] هٰذِهِ طَآءٌ طَوِيلَةٌ [*This is a tall* ط]: it is one of the letters termed مَجْهُورَة [or vocal, i. e. pronounced with the voice, and not with the breath only]; and of the letters termed نِطْعِيَّة, like ت and د, because originating from the نِطْع [q. v.] of the roof of the mouth. (TA.) It is substituted for the ت in the measure اِفْتَعَلَ and the forms inflected therefrom, and [sometimes] for the pronominal ت, when immediately following any of the palatal letters [ص and ض and ط and ظ]; (MF, TA;) as in اِصْطَبَرَ and اِضْطَرَبَ and اِطَّبَعَ and اِظْطَلَمَ, for اِصْتَبَرَ and اِضْتَرَبَ and اِطْتَبَعَ and اِظْتَلَمَ; and in] فَحَصْطُ and حِضْطُ and خَبَطُّ and حَفِظْطُ, for فَحَصْتُ and حِضْتُ and خَبَطْتُ and حَفِظْتُ; but some of the grammarians say that this [latter] substitution is not to be made invariably; [nor is it common;] and it is said to be a dialectal peculiarity of some of the Benoo-Temeem. (TA.) It is also substituted for د: thus Yaḳoob mentions, on the authority of Aṣ, مَطُّ الحُرُوفِ, for مَدُّ الحُرُوفِ: and AO, المُبْطَأُ, for المُبْدَأُ: and Aboo-'Amr Ez-Záhid, in the Yawáḳeet, مَا أَبْعَدَ طَارَكَ, for مَا أَبْعَدَ دَارَكَ. (TA.) — [As a numeral, it denotes *Nine*.]

طأ

R. Q. 1. طَأْطَأَ, inf. n. طَأْطَأَةٌ, *He lowered*, or *depressed*, a thing. (TA.) You say, طَأْطَأَ رَأْسَهُ *He lowered his head;* (Ṣ, Ḳ, TA;) and so ↑ تَطَأْطَأَ, alone. (TA.) And طَأْطَأَ عَنِ الشَّىْءِ *He lowered his head from the thing.* (TA.) And تَطَأْطَأْتُ ↑ لَهُمْ تَطَأْطُؤَ الدُّلَاةِ, (Ṣ, TA,) occurring in a trad. of 'Othmán, (TA,) *I stooped*, or *lowered myself*, [or *bent myself down*,] *to them, like as do the drawers of water with the bucket.* (Ṣ, TA.) And تَطَأْطَأْ ↑ لَهَا تُخْطِئْكَ, a prov., (Meyd, TA,) meaning *Stoop thy head to it*, i. e. to an accident, or a calamity, and *it will* [*miss thee*, or] *pass by thee:* applied in relation to the abstaining from exposing oneself to evil. (Meyd.) And طَأْطَأَتْ سِتْرَهَا ‡ *She* (a woman) *lowered her veil*, or *curtain.* (TA.) And طَأْطَأَ يَدَهُ بِالعِنَانِ *He lowered his hand with the rein, for the purpose of* [*the horse's*] *running and hastening.* (Ḳ,* TA.) And [hence, perhaps,] طَأْطَأَ فَرَسَهُ *He struck his horse with his thighs, to make him go quickly.* (Ḳ,* TA.) And طَأْطَأَ مِنْ فُلَانٍ † *He lowered the reputation*, or *estimation*, or *dignity*, *of such a one.* (TA.) — *He hastened*, or *was quick.* (TA.) You say, طَأْطَأَ فِى مَالِهِ *He hastened, and exceeded the usual bounds, in the expenditure of his property.* (A, Ḳ, TA.) And طَأْطَأَ فِى قَتْلِهِمْ *He hastened, and exceeded the usual bounds, in their slaughter.* (TA.) — And *He filled up a hollow, or cavity, dug in the ground.* (TA.)

R. Q. 2. تَطَأْطَأَ *It was*, or *became, low*, or *depressed.* (Ṣ, O.) *It* (the head) *was*, or *became, lowered.* (Ḳ.) See also the first paragraph, in three places. One says also, تَطَاوَلَ عَلَىَّ فَتَطَأْطَأْتُ مِنْهُ [app. meaning † *He domineered over me*, or *exalted himself above me, and I humbled*, or *abased, myself to him:* see طَأْطَأَ مِنْ فُلَانٍ, above]. (TA.)

طَأْطَأَةٌ *A low*, or *depressed, place*, (Ṣ, O, Ḳ,) of the ground, *that conceals him who is within it:* (Ḳ:) or, as some say, *a narrow, depressed place;* also called صَاعٌ and مِعًى. (TA.) — And *A short, short-necked*, camel. (O, Ḳ.)

طب

1. طَبَّ, aor. ـُ, (O, Mṣb, Ḳ, TA,) agreeably with analogy in the case of a trans. reduplicative verb [like this], (TA,) and ـِ, (Ḳ, TA,) which is irregular, (TA,) inf. n. طَبٌّ (O,* Mṣb, Ḳ,* TA) [and app. طُبٌّ and طِبٌّ also accord. to the O and Ḳ, but, accord. to the Mṣb, طِبٌّ is the subst. from this verb, and app. طُبٌّ is likewise a simple subst.], *He treated medically, therapeutically*, or *curatively*, (O,* Mṣb, Ḳ,*) another person (O, Mṣb) [or the body, and in like manner the soul: see طِبٌّ, below]. — And طَبِبْتَ, with kesr, (Ṣ, O, Ḳ,) and طَبَبْتَ, with fet-ḥ, (O, Ḳ,) [third pers. of each طَبَّ, and, accord. to analogy, the aor. of the former is ـَ, and of the latter ـِ, but from what follows it seems probable that one says also طَبُبْتَ in the same sense, aor. ـُ, unless تَطُبُّ have طَبِبْتَ as an irreg. aor.,] *Thou wast*, or *becamest a* طَبِيب [or *physician*], not having been such. (Ṣ, O, Ḳ.) One says, إِنْ كُنْتَ ذَا طِبٍّ فَطُبَّ لِعَيْنَيْكَ, (Ṣ, O, and so in copies of the Ḳ,) or لِعَيْنِكَ, (so in other copies of the Ḳ,) or لِنَفْسِكَ, (ISk, TA,) and ذَا طَبٍّ, and ذَا طُبٍّ, (Ṣ, Ḳ,) and فَطِبَّ, and فَطَبَّ; (Ḳ;) [i. e. *If thou be a possessor of the art*, or *science*, *of physic, be a physician to thine eyes*, or *thine eye*, or *thyself;*] meaning, begin by rectifying thyself. (ISk, TA. [See also Freytag's Arab. Prov. ii. 902.]) — And [hence] طَبَّ signifies also † *He acted with skill*, or *expertness:* [and in this sense likewise the second pers. is probably طَبِبْتَ and طَبَبْتَ and طَبُبْتَ, of which last the inf. n. is app. طَبَابَةٌ, occurring in one of the phrases here following:] so in the saying, اِصْنَعْهُ صَنْعَةَ مَنْ طَبَّ لِمَنْ حَبَّ i. e. † *Do thou it in the manner of him who acts with skill*, or *expertness*, *for him whom he loves:* a prov., relating to the accomplishing an object of want skilfully and well. (El-Aḥmar, TA. [See also Freytag's Arab. Prov. i. 717.]) One says also, اِعْمَلْ فِى هٰذَا عَمَلَ مَنْ طَبَّ لِمَنْ حَبَّ † [*Do thou, in this, the deed of him who acts with skill*, or *expertness*, *for him whom he loves*]. (M, Mṣb,* TA.) And مَنْ أَحَبَّ طَبَّ, (Meyd,) or مَنْ حَبَّ طَبَّ, (Ḳ,) † *He who loves is skilful*, or *intelligent*, and *exercises art*, or *ingenuity*, for him whom he loves: (Meyd:) or † *he who loves executes affairs with deliberateness and gentleness.* (Ḳ.) [That one says طَبُبْتَ, as well as طَبِبْتَ and طَبَبْتَ, seems to be indicated by the fact that ↑ طَبَابَة, as an inf. n., is thus written, in a copy of the KL in my possession, and expl. as meaning The *medical art:* Golius, however, appears to have found it written, in a copy of the same work, ↑ طِبَابَة, which is agreeable with analogy as inf. n. of a verb of the measure فَعَلَ significant of an art, and is probably correct: Freytag mentions the pl. طَبَائِب as signifying medical

arts, on the authority of the Deewán of the Hudhalees.] —— طَبَّهُ also signifies † He enchanted him, or fascinated him: (O:) and طُبَّ ‡ he (a man, Ṣ, A) was enchanted, or fascinated. (Ṣ, A, O. [See also طِبٌّ, below.]) —— طَبَّ السِّقَآءَ, aor. ـُ, (Ṣ, TA,) inf. n. طَبٌّ; (Ḳ, TA;) and ▼ طَبَّبَهُ, with teshdeed to denote muchness, (Ṣ, TA,) inf. n. تَطْبِيبٌ; (Ḳ, TA;) He covered the seams of the water-skin, or milk-skin, with a طِبَابَة [q. v.]: (Ṣ, Ḳ,* TA:) and طَبَّ الخُرَزَ he covered the seams with a طِبَابَة: (TA:) [and] طَبَّبَتِ ▼ المَزَادَةَ she (a girl, or young woman,) put [or sewed] a piece of skin called ▼ طِبَابٌ and ▼ طِبَابَةٌ, upon the place of junction [of each] of the two extremities of the loop-shaped handles of the مزادة [or leathern water-bag]; as though she rectified the مزادة thereby. (A.)

2: see the last sentence above, in two places. —— تَطْبِيبٌ also signifies The inserting a بَنِيقَة [or gore] for the purpose of widening دِيبَاج [or silk brocade]: (Ḳ, TA:) or, as in the A, one says of a tailor, طَبَّبَ الثَّوْبَ, meaning he added, in the garment, a بَنِيقَة [or gore], in order that it might become [more] wide. (TA.) —— Also The hanging a سِقَآء [or milk-skin] (Ṣ, Ḳ, TA) to a pole (عَمُود, Ṣ, this is the right word, not عُود [as in copies of the Ḳ], TA) of the tent, (Ṣ,) and then agitating it to produce the butter: (Ṣ, Ḳ, TA:) but Az says, I have not heard تطبيب explained in this sense except on the authority of Lth, and I think that it is تطنيب. (TA.)

3. مُطَابَّةٌ signifies ‡ The seeking, or labouring, to find the means of accomplishment [of an affair, like as the physician seeks to find the means of curing a disease]; syn. مُدَاوَرَةٌ. (Ḳ, TA.) One says, أَنَا أُطَابُّ هٰذَا الأَمْرَ مُنْذُ حِينٍ كَيْ أَبْلُغَهُ ‡ [I have been seeking, or labouring, to find the means of accomplishing this affair, that I might attain to it]. (A, TA.)

4. مَا أَطَبَّهُمْ How [knowing, or] skilful, or expert, are they! (Meyd, in explaining a prov. cited below, voce طَبٌّ.)

5. تَطَبَّبَ He applied himself to the science of physic: (TA:) [or he applied himself to the science of physic but did not know it well: (see the part. n., below:)] or he practised physic: and he professed physic. (KL.) —— And تَطَبَّبَ لَهُ He inquired of [or consulted] the physicians for him. (TA.)

10. اِسْتَطَبَّ لِوَجَعِهِ He asked, or sought, a medical prescription for his pain, or disease. (Ṣ, A, Mṣb, Ḳ.) —— And جَآءَ يَسْتَطِبُّ لِإِبِلِهِ ‡ He came asking, or seeking, for his she-camels, a gentle stallion, that would not injure them. (A.)

R. Q. 1. طَبْطَبَ, (Lth, Ḳ, TA,) inf. n. طَبْطَبَةٌ, (Lth, TA,) said of a valley, or water-course, (Lth, Ḳ, TA,) It flowed with water so that one heard it to make a sound like طَبْ طَبْ: (Lth, TA:) or it made a sound (Ḳ, TA) with the water. (TA.) طَبْطَبَةٌ signifies The sounding of water (IAạr, Ṣ, Ḳ, TA) when in a state of commotion and collision, (IAạr, TA,) and of the like, (Ṣ, TA,) and of the dashing of a torrent. (Ḳ.) And ▼ تَطَبْطَبَ It made a sound, or noise, [like طَبْ طَبْ,] said of water and the like, (Ṣ,) and of a woman's breast: (TA:) a poet says,

إِذَا طَحَنَتْ دُرْنِيَّةٌ لِعِيَالِهَا
تَطَبْطَبَ ثَدْيَاهَا فَطَارَ طَحِينُهَا

[When a woman of Durnà grinds for her family, her breasts make a sound by their collision, and her flour flies away]. (Ṣ, TA.) ═ طَبْطَبَ المَآءَ He put the water into a state of commotion. (TA.)

R. Q. 2. تَطَبْطَبَ: see the next preceding paragraph.

طَبٌّ: see طِبٌّ. ═ It is also an inf. n. used as an epithet: see طَبِيبٌ. (Mṣb.) —— And, (Ṣ, A, Mṣb, Ḳ,) as such, i. e. an inf. n. used as an epithet, or by original application, but the former is app. the case, and some have mentioned likewise ▼ طِبٌّ and ▼ طُبٌّ, (MF, TA,) ‡ Knowing, or possessing knowledge, (Ṣ, A, Mṣb, TA,) respecting a thing, or of a thing; (A, Mṣb, TA;) and so ▼ طَبِيبٌ: (TA:) and (TA) † skilful, or expert; (T, Ḳ;) as also ▼ طَبِيبٌ: (T, Ṣ, Ḳ:) and ‡ gentle; (Nh, TA;) and so too ▼ طَبِيبٌ. (TA.) One says, فُلَانٌ طَبٌّ بِكَذَا † Such a one is knowing with regard to, or is one possessing knowledge of, such a thing. (TA.) And القَوْمُ طَبُّونَ, or, as some relate it, القَوْمُ مَا ▼ أَطَبُّونَ, is a prov.: the former means † The people, or party, are knowing, or skilful, or expert: and [Meyd says,] I know not any way in which the latter is explainable unless ▼ أَطَبُّ be syn. with طَبٌّ, like أَخْشَنُ and خَشِنٌ, &c., and ما a connective. (Meyd.) To a man who offered to cure the [so-called] seal, or stamp, of the prophetic office between the Prophet's shoulder-blades, asserting himself to be a طَبِيب [or physician], the Prophet replied, ▼ طَبِيبُهَا الَّذِى خَلَقَهَا, meaning † He who has knowledge respecting it is He who created it. (TA.) And El-Marrár El-Faḳ'asee says,

تَدِينُ لِمَزْرُورٍ إِلَى جَنْبِ حَلْقَةٍ
مِنَ الشِّبْهِ سَوَّاهَا بِرِفْقٍ طَبِيبُهَا ▼

† [She obeys a plaited nose-rein attached to the side of a ring of brass, the skilful maker of which has fashioned it with gentleness]: (Ṣ, L:) i. e. the she-camel of which he speaks obeys her rein that is tied to her nose-ring of brass. (L.) [Hence,] فَحْلٌ طَبٌّ † A stallion [camel] expert in covering, (Ṣ, Mṣb, Ḳ, TA,) as also ▼ طَبِيبٌ; (Mṣb;) that knows the she-camel that is pregnant from her that is not, and her that desires the stallion from her that is covered without desire, and the motion of the fœtus in the womb, &c.: (TA:) or ‡ that is gentle, and does not injure the female that he covers. (A, TA.) And بَعِيرٌ طَبٌّ ‡ A camel that is mindful, or careful, as to the place of his foot, (A, Ḳ, TA,) where to tread with it: or that does not place his foot save where he sees. (TA.)

طُبٌّ: see the next paragraph: ═ and see also طَبٌّ.

طِبٌّ (Ṣ, A, O, Mṣb, Ḳ) and ▼ طَبٌّ and ▼ طُبٌّ (Ṣ, A, O, Ḳ) Medical, therapeutical, or curative, treatment, (A,* O,* Mṣb, Ḳ,*) of the body, [i. e. the physicking thereof,] (A, Ḳ,) and likewise of the soul. (Ḳ.) —— [And Knowledge]. قَرُبَ طِبٌّ [Knowledge is near], or, as some relate it, قَرُبَ طِبًّا, (Meyd, O, Ḳ, TA,) with the noun in the accus. case, as a specificative, (TA,) like the phrase نِعْمَ رَجُلًا, (Meyd, O, TA,) is a prov.: originally said by a woman to a man who asked her an indecent question which he was himself about to resolve: (Meyd, O, Ḳ, TA:) it is like the saying, أَنْتَ عَلَى المُجَرَّبِ [q. v.]: (Meyd, TA:) and is related on the authority of Ibn-Háni. (TA.) —— And Skill, or expertness. (T, ISd, Meyd, TA.) This is said in the T to be the primary signification. (TA. [But see طَبِيبٌ.]) —— And ‡ Gentleness; gentle treatment or conduct. (Ḳ, TA.) —— And ‡ Enchantment, or fascination: (Ṣ, O, Ḳ, TA: but only طِبٌّ is mentioned in this sense in the Ṣ and O:) used in this sense as ominating cure. (AO, O,* TA.) —— And طِبٌّ signifies also Desire, or appetence; syn. شَهْوَةٌ: and will, or wish; syn. إِرَادَةٌ. (Ḳ.) —— And ‡ State, condition, or case; syn. شَأْنٌ, (Ḳ, TA,) and دَأْبٌ: (A, TA:) [or by the latter of these two words may be meant what here follows:] custom, habit, or wont. (Ṣ, Ḳ, TA.) One says, مَا ذَاكَ بِطِبِّى ‡ That is not my custom, habit, or wont. (Ṣ, A, TA.) [See also another ex., in a verse (added here in the Ṣ and TA) which I have cited voce إِنَّ, page 107, col. iii.] ═ See also طَبٌّ.

طُبَّةٌ: see طِبَابَةٌ, in two places.

طِبَّةٌ An oblong piece, or portion, of a garment, or of a piece of cloth, (Ṣ, A, TA,) as also ▼ طَبِيبَةٌ; (A;) and likewise of skin: or a square piece of the latter: and a round piece in a مَزَادَة and a سُفْرَة and the like: (TA:) pl. طِبَبٌ: (Ṣ:) and, as also ▼ طِبَابَةٌ, (Aṣ, Ṣ, TA,) † a streak in sand and clouds, (Aṣ, TA,) or a streak of sand or clouds: (Ṣ:) or طُبَّةٌ and ▼ طِبَابَةٌ and ▼ طَبِيبَةٌ signify an oblong piece, or portion, of a garment or piece of cloth, and of skin, and † of land or ground, and † of clouds: (Ḳ:) or, all three words, a long strip of a garment or piece of cloth, and of skin, and † of sand, and † of clouds: (TA:) and † a long and narrow tract of land abounding with plants or herbage: (AḤn, TA; and A in explanation of the first word:) pl. [of the first] طِبَبٌ and [of the same, or of the third, or a coll. gen. n. of which the second word is the n. un.,] ▾ طِبَابٌ. (Ḳ.) And sometimes طُبَّةٌ is applied to The *piece that is sewed upon the edge of the leathern bucket* and *upon that of the* سُفْرَة: and the pl. is طُبَبٌ and ▾ طِبَابٌ. (M, TA.) طُبَبُ شُعَاعِ الشَّمْسِ (Aṣ, Ṣ, TA) and ▾ الطِّبَابُ, (Aṣ, TA,) or طُبَبُ الشَّمْسِ and ▾ طِبَابُهَا, (A, TA,) signify ‡ *The streaks that are seen in the rays,* or *beams, of the sun when it rises.* (Aṣ, Ṣ, A,* TA.) — Also ‡ *i. q.* نَاحِيَةٌ [i. e. *A side;* or *a region, quarter,* or *tract;* &c.]: (so in a copy of the A:) or *i. q.* نَاصِيَةٌ [i. e. *a forelock;* &c.]. (So in the TA.) [One of these two explanations is app. a mistranscription for the other.] — And one says, إِنَّكَ لَتَلْقَى فُلَانًا عَلَى طُبَبٍ مُخْتَلِفَةٍ, meaning, عَلَى أَلْوَانٍ ‡ [i. e. *Verily thou wilt find such a one to be of various moods, dispositions,* or *characters*]. (A, TA.)

طِبَابٌ [like عِلَاجٌ] *A thing that is used for medical,* or *curative, treatment:* so in the saying, ذَا طِبَابُ هٰذِهِ العِلَّةِ [*This,* or *that, is what is used for the medical,* or *curative, treatment of this disease*]. (A, TA.) — See also طُبَّةٌ, latter half, in four places. And see طِبَابَةٌ, in five places: and 1, last sentence.

طَبِيبٌ (Ṣ, Mṣb, Ḳ, TA) and ▾ طَبٌّ (Mṣb, TA) [*A physician;*] *one skilled in* الطِّبّ [i. e. *medical, therapeutical,* or *curative, treatment*]; (Ṣ, TA;) or *one who practises medical, therapeutical,* or *curative, treatment;* (Mṣb;) and ▾ مُتَطَبِّبٌ signifies [likewise *one who practises physic:* and *a professor of physic:* (see its verb:) or] *one who applies himself to the science of physic:* (Ṣ, Ḳ, TA:) or *one who applies himself to that science but does not know it well:* (Nh, TA:) it has been said that the طَبِيب is so called from the same epithet as signifying "skilful, or expert;" but this is not a valid assertion: (TA:) the pl. (of pauc., Ṣ) is أَطِبَّةٌ (Ṣ, Ḳ) and (of mult., Ṣ) أَطِبَّآءُ. (Ṣ, Mṣb, Ḳ.) — The first of these words (طبيب) occurs in a trad. as meaning ‡ *A judge;* being metonymically thus used, because the office of him who judges between litigants is like that of the طبيب who cures diseases of the body. (TA.) [And hence, طَبِيبُ العَرَبِ: see فَقِيهُ العَرَبِ, in art. فقه.] See also طَبٌّ, in six places.

طَبَابَةٌ: see 1, latter half.

طِبَابَةٌ: see 1, latter half. — Also *A piece of skin with which the seams of a* سِقَآء *are covered, extending across,* [so I render مُعْتَرِضَةٌ, app. meaning *from side to side,* for one edge of the skin beneath overlaps the other,] *like the finger* [*in breadth*], *doubled* [but see what is said below on the authority of AZ] *over the place of the sewing:* pl. [or rather coll. gen. n.] ▾ طِبَابٌ: (Aṣ, Ṣ, TA:) or *that which is put over the place where the two edges of the skin meet, when it is sewed, in the lower part of the* قِرْبَة *and of the* سِقَآء *and of the* إِدَاوَة: so says Aṣ: or, as also ▾ طِبَابٌ, the *piece of skin that is put over the two edges of the skin, in these things, when it is laid flat and then sewed, without being doubled:* (TA:) accord. to AZ, when the [piece of] skin, in the lower parts of these things, is doubled, and then sewed, it is called عِرَاقٌ; and when it is laid flat and then sewed, without being doubled, it is called ▾ طِبَابٌ: (TA; and the like is said in the Ṣ in art. عرق:) or طِبَابَةٌ and عِرَاقٌ both signify, accord. to Aṣ, *a piece of skin with which the punctures of the seams are covered:* (Ṣ in art. عرق:) or a طِبَابَة is *a wide strip of skin, in which is the sewing:* and the pl. [or coll. gen. n.] is ▾ طِبَابٌ: (M, TA:) or, accord. to the Ḳ, *a strip of skin that is in the lower part of a* قِرْبَة, *between the two seams;* as also ▾ طُبَّةٌ: but in this explanation, its author has confounded the words of Lth, who says that طِبَابَةٌ signifies the *strip of the skin that is between the two seams;* and ▾ طُبَّةٌ, the *strip of skin that is in the lower part of the* قِرْبَة, *and that contracts the seams* [so I render يقارب الخرز, but the meaning of this phrase is not, to me, clear]. (TA.) See also 1, last sentence. — And see طُبَّةٌ, in two places. — Also, and ▾ طِبَابٌ, (Ḳ, TA, in the CḲ طَبَاب and طَبابة,) [or the latter is a coll. gen. n.,] † *A streak,* or *narrow elongated tract,* of the sky: (Ḳ, TA:) [and app. *any portion* of the sky *not of large extent:*] an ex. of the latter word occurs in a verse cited voce مَرَاكُدُ: and in another verse, a man in a prison is described as seeing only a طِبَابَة of the sky like a shield; i. e. *a round portion* thereof. (Az, TA.)

طَبِيبَةٌ, see طُبَّةٌ, in two places.

طِبِّىٌّ *Medical, therapeutical,* or *curative;* of, or *relating to, medical, therapeutical,* or *curative, treatment.* (Mṣb.)

طَبْطَبَةٌ *A certain broad thing, one part of which is struck with another part thereof.* (TA.)

طَبْطَبِيَّةٌ *A* [*kind of whip,* or *scourge, such as is called*] دِرَّةٌ [q. v.]: (Ḳ, TA:) because the sound that is made by its fall is like طَبْ طَبْ. (TA.)

طَبْطَابٌ *A certain bird,* or *flying thing,* (طَائِرٌ,) *having large ears.* (Ḳ.)

طَبْطَابَةٌ, or طُبْطُابَةٌ, (accord. to different copies of the Ḳ,) *A broad piece of wood, with which one plays with the ball,* (Ḳ, TA,) or *with which the horseman plays with the ball.* (T, TA.)

الطُّبَاطِبُ *The* عَجَم [i. e. *Persians,* or *foreigners*]. (L, TA.)

أَطَبُّ; and its pl., أَطَبُّونَ: see طَبٌّ.

مَطْبُوبٌ ‡ A man *enchanted,* or *fascinated.* (Ṣ, A.)

مُتَطَبِّبٌ: see طَبِيبٌ.

طباهج

طَبَاهَجٌ, (so in some copies of the Ḳ, and so in the Ṣ voce كَبَابٌ,) or طَبَاهَجَةٌ, (so in other copies of the Ḳ,) with fet-ḥ to the ط and the ه, (TA,) [the latter app. a n. un.,] *Flesh-meat cut into thin slices and broiled:* (Ḳ,* TA:) or *a food composed of flesh-meat and eggs:* (MA; in which the word is written طَبَاهِجَة:) [or, accord. to Golius, as on the authority of J and El-Ḥaleemee, *a food of pieces of flesh-meat, eggs, onion, and water:* but I do not find that J has explained it otherwise than by what here follows:] *i. q.* كَبَابٌ: (Ṣ voce كَبَابٌ:) or *a kind of fry of flesh-meat:* (L:) arabicized from [the Pers.] تَبَاهَهْ. (Ḳ.) [See also De Sacy's Chrest. Arabe, sec. ed. i. 175.]

طبخ

1. طَبَخَ, (Ṣ, A, Ḳ, &c.,) aor. ـُ (L, Mṣb, Ḳ) and ـِ, (L, Ḳ,) inf. n. طَبْخٌ; (L, Mṣb, Ḳ;) and ▾ اِطَّبَخَ; (Ṣb, L;) *He cooked* (Ṣ, L, Ḳ) flesh-meat, (Ṣ, A, L,) &c., (L,) either *in a cooking-pot* [*by boiling* or *stewing* or *the like*] or *by roasting* or *broiling* or *frying;* (Ṣ,* L, Ḳ;) the former verb [accord. to some] said of one who cooks *for himself* or *for others;* and the latter, of one who cooks only *for himself:* (L: [but see an ex. in what follows, of this paragraph; and see also the latter verb below:]) or the former signifies *he cooked* flesh-meat *with broth* or *gravy.* (Az, Mṣb.) And you say also طَبَخَ القِدْرَ *He cooked* [*the contents of*] *the cooking-pot.* (Ṣ, L.) And طَبَخَ المَرَقَ [*He cooked the broth*]. (A.) — And طَبَخَ *He* (a dyer) *decocted* Brazil-wood (بَقَّم) &c. (A. [See طَبَّاخَةٌ.]) — And *He baked* bread, and wheat, and bricks [and clay and pottery]. (L.) One says, هٰذِهِ خُبْزَةٌ جَيِّدَةُ الطَّبْخِ *This is a cake of bread well baked* [*in the hot ashes*]. (Ṣ, A,* L, Mṣb.) And هٰذِهِ آجُرَّةٌ جَيِّدَةُ الطَّبْخِ *This is a brick well baked.* (L, Mṣb.) And ▾ اِطَّبِخُوا لَنَا قُرْصًا [*Bake ye for us* (app. meaning for us including yourselves) *a round cake of bread*]. (Ṣ.) — Also † *It* (the heat) *ripened* the fruit. (TA.) And طَبَخَتْهُمُ الهَوَاجِرُ ‡ [*The vehement midday-heats fevered them*]. (A.) And طَبَخَتْهُ الجُدَرِىُّ ‡ [*The small-pox affected him with a hot,* or *burning, fever*]: and in like manner one says of the حَصْبَة [i. e. measles, or spotted fever: see طَابِخٌ]. (A.) — [And † *He dressed* silk: see the pass. part. n., below.] — [طَبِخَ, aor. ـَ, inf. n. طَبَخٌ, accord. to the L, seems to signify *He was,* or *became, confirmed in stupidity:* but only the inf. n. is there mentioned; and this is doubtful: see أَطْبَخُ.]

2. طَبَّخَ, inf. n. تَطْبِيخٌ, *It* (a حِسْل [or young lizard of the species called ضَبّ]) *grew big;* syn. كَبِرَ. (Ṣ. [See مُطَبِّخٌ.]) — And *He* (a boy) *became active, and grew up,* or *became a young man;* (L, Ḳ;) *grew big;* syn. كَبِرَ; (Ḳ;) *and became intelligent.* (L.)

5. تطبّخ *He* (a man) *ate* طِبِّيخ [or *melons,* or *water-melons;* as also تبطّخ]. (A.)

7. انطبخ, (Ṣ, A, L, Mṣb, Ḳ,) and ↑ اِطَّبَخَ, (Ḳ, [but this latter seems to be a mistake, occasioned by a misunderstanding of the word اِشْتَوَى, one of the words by which it is expl. in several of the lexicons,] *It* (flesh-meat, Ṣ, A, L, and the same is said of other things, L) *was,* or *became, cooked,* either *in a cooking-pot* [*by boiling* or *stewing* or *the like*] or *by roasting* or *broiling* or *frying:* (Ṣ, L, Ḳ:) or *it* (flesh-meat) *was,* or *became, cooked with broth,* or *gravy.* (Az, Mṣb.) And you say also, انطبخت القِدْرُ [*The contents of*] *the cooking-pot became cooked.* (Ṣ, L.) And انطبخ المَرَقُ [*The broth became cooked*]. (A.) — [Said of bread, and wheat, and bricks and clay and pottery, *It was,* or *they were,* or *became, baked.* (See 1.)]

8. اِطَّبَخَ *He prepared,* or *prepared for himself,* طبيخ [i. e. *flesh-meat cooked in a pot,* &c.], syn. اِتَّخَذَ طَبِيخًا, (Ṣ, A, L, Ḳ,) or قَدِير, [which signifies *flesh-meat cooked in a pot, with,* or *without, seeds to season it, such as pepper and cumin-seeds and the like,* as expl. below, voce طَبِيخ]; (TA;) [it is said that] it particularly signifies *he cooked for himself* alone, [or it signifies *for himself with others,*] thus differing from طَبَخَ, as expl. above: (L:) see 1, in two places; and see also 7: ISk says that اِطِّبَاخ signifies the *cooking in a pot* and *by roasting* or *broiling* or *frying.* (Ṣ.) — [Also, probably, *He prepared,* or *prepared for himself, the beverage called* طَبِيخ.]

طَبْخ : see طَبِيخ.

طَبْخَة : see أَطْبَخ.

طَبَاخ, (Ṣ, A, Ḳ,) thus in the handwriting of El-Iyádee, (L,) and طُبَاخ, (Ḳ,) thus in the handwriting of Az, (L,) † *Firmness,* or *soundness;* (Ḳ;) *strength, and fatness.* (Ṣ, L, Ḳ.) One says, مَا بِهِ طَبَاخٌ ‡ *There is not in it,* or *him, strength* [*nor fatness*]: originally said of lean flesh-meat, that yields no benefit to him who cooks it. (A.) And رَجُلٌ لَيْسَ بِهِ طَبَاخٌ † *A man in whom is no strength nor fatness.* (Ṣ.) And لَا طَبَاخَ لَهُ † *He has no intelligence, nor does he possess any good:* and † *he has no companion remaining to him.* (L.) And فِى كَلَامِهِ طَبَاخٌ † *In his speech is soundness.* (TA.) And مَا فِى كَلَامِهِ طَبَاخٌ ‡ *There is no profit in his speech.* (A.)

طَبِيخ, of the measure فَعِيلٌ in the sense of the measure مَفْعُولٌ [i. e. *i. q.* ↑ مَطْبُوخ *Cooked;* &c.; but accord. to general usage, it is an epithet in which the quality of a subst. predominates, signifying *cooked flesh-meat*]: accord. to some, *flesh-meat cooked with broth or gravy;* what is cooked without broth or gravy not being thus termed: (Mṣb:) or, as El-Karkhee says, *what has broth, or gravy, and contains flesh* or *fat;* dry fried meat, and the like, not being thus termed: (Mgh:) or *i. q.* قَدِير [which signifies either *flesh-meat cooked in a pot,* or *flesh-meat cooked in a pot with seeds to season it such as pepper and cumin-seeds and the like*]: or قدير is applied to that which is with seeds to season it, and طبيخ is *that which is not seasoned with seeds such as pepper and cumin-seeds and the like:* (L, TA:) [pl. أَطْبِخَة:] and cooked flesh-meat is also called ↑ طِبْخ. (L.) — [Also *A decoction:* used in this sense in medical and other books. (See also طُبَاخَة.)] — And *A sort of* مُنَصَّف [i. e. *wine,* or *beverage, cooked until half of it has evaporated*]. (Ṣ, M, A, Ḳ.) — And *Gypsum:* and *baked bricks.* (Ḳ.) These are said to be meant by the last word in the following trad., إِذَا أَرَادَ ٱللّٰهُ بِعَبْدٍ سُوْءًا جَعَلَ مَالَهُ فِى ٱلطَّبِيخَيْنِ [*When God desires evil to befall a man* (lit. *a servant*), *He makes his property to consist in gypsum and baked bricks*]. (L.)

طُبَاخَة *The froth,* or *foam, that boils over from a cooking-pot.* (Ṣ, Ḳ.) — And *A decoction* of anything; the *extracted juice,* thereof, *that is taken after coction; such as that of Brazil-wood* (بَقَّم), and *the like:* (L:) *what one takes, of that which he requires* [*for use*], *of that which is cooked; such as* بقّم; *of which one takes the* طباخة *for dyeing, and throws away the rest.* (T.) [See also طَبِيخ.]

طِبَاخَة *The art,* or *business, of cooking.* (Ḳ.)

طَبِيخَةُ الحَرِّ, (A, L,) pl. طَبَائِخُ, (Ṣ, A, L, Ḳ,) ‡ *Hot wind* (Ṣ, A, L, Ḳ) *blowing at midday in the season of vehement heat.* (A, L.) One says, خَرَجُوا فِى طَبِيخَةِ الحَرِّ, and فى طَبَائِخِهِ ‡ *They went forth during the hot wind* &c., *and during the hot winds* &c. (A.)

اِمْرَأَةٌ طُبَاخِيَّةٌ (Ṣ, L, Ḳ) and طُبَاخِيَّةٌ, (Ḳ,) *A young woman,* (L, Ḳ,) *full,* [or *plump,*] (L,) *compact in flesh:* (Ṣ, L, Ḳ:) or the latter, (L,) or both, (Ḳ,) *an intelligent and beautiful woman.* (L, Ḳ.)

طَبَّاخ *A cook.* (Ḳ.)

طِبِّيخ, (A, L, Ḳ,) written by Aboo-Bekr طَبِّيخ, with fet-ḥ to the ط, (L,) *i. q.* بِطِّيخ [*The melon;* or particularly the *water-melon*]: (L, Ḳ:) of the dial. of El-Ḥijáz, (L,) or of El-Medeeneh. (A.) [Freytag says that, accord. to some, but he does not not name his authority, it is *a large, round melon, rough to the touch, and without a neck, different from the* بطيخ, *which is a small melon.*]

طَابِخ [act. part. n. of طَبَخَ: — and hence,] sing. of طُبَّخ, which signifies † The *angels of punishment* [*who roast the damned in Hell*]. (Ṣ, Ḳ.) — Also, (Ṣ, Ḳ,) or حُمَّى طَابِخٌ, (A,) ‡ *A* [*hot,* or *burning,*] *fever, such as is termed* صَالِب. (Ṣ, Ḳ, TA.)

طَابِخَة ‡ *i. q.* هَاجِرَة [i. e. *Midday when the heat is vehement;* or *midday in summer,* or *in the hot season;* &c.]. (Ṣ, Ḳ, TA.)

أَطْبَخ *Confirmed in stupidity;* as also ↑ طَبْخَة; (L, Ḳ;) but the word commonly known is طَبِخَة. (L.)

مَطْبَخ (Ṣ, Mgh, Mṣb, Ḳ) and ↑ مِطْبَخ, (Mgh, Mṣb,) sometimes called by the latter name as being likened to an instrument, (Mṣb,) and this latter is the only form mentioned in the A, and is said by Sb to be not a noun of place, but a subst. like مِرْبَد, (TA,) *A place of cooking; a place in which cooking is performed;* (Ṣ, A, Mgh, Mṣb, Ḳ;) *a cook's house* or *room; a kitchen.* (T.) [See also مُطَّبَخ.] One says, هُوَ أَبْيَضُ المَطْبَخِ ‡ [lit. *He is one whose kitchen,* or *cooking-place, is white;* meaning *he is inhospitable;* like as one says in the contrary case, هُوَ كَثِيرُ الرَّمَادِ]: and in like manner, هُمْ بِيضُ المَطَابِخِ. (A.)

مِطْبَخ *An implement for cooking:* or *a cooking-pot.* (Ḳ.) — See also the next preceding paragraph.

مُطَبِّخ *A young* [*lizard of the species called*] ضَبّ [*in a certain stage of its growth*]: in its first stage it is called حِسْل; then, غَيْدَاق; then, مُطَبِّخ; then, خُضَرِم; and then, ضَبّ: (Ṣ, L:) or *one that has nearly attained to the size of its parent:* or *one in its fullest state:* (ISd, L:) or the *first of the offspring of the* ضَبّ (أَوَّلُ وَلَدِ الضَّبِّ). (Ḳ. [But this is evidently a mistake, as is observed in the TḲ.]) — And *A young man that is full* [or *plump*]: (Ḳ:) a child when born is called رَضِيع and طِفْل; then فَطِيم; then, دَارِج; then, جَفْر; then, يَافِع; then شَدَخ; then, مُطَبِّخ; and then, كَوْكَب. (IAạr, TA.)

مَطْبُوخ : see طَبِيخ. — إِبْرِيسَمٌ مَطْبُوخٌ [*Dressed silk*]. (Mgh and Mṣb voce حَرِير.)

مُطَّبَخ *A place in which people cook their food.* (JK.) One says, هٰذَا مُطَّبَخُ القَوْمِ وَهٰذَا مُشْتَوَاهُمْ [*This is the people's place of cooking their food, and this is the place of their roasting* or *broiling* or *frying*]. (Ṣ.) [See also مَطْبَخ.]

طبرزن and طبرزل and طبرزذ

طَبَرْزَذ, an arabicized word, (Ṣ, L, Mṣb, Ḳ,) from the Pers. تَبَرْزَد, (L,) as though pieces were chipped from its sides with an axe, or a hatchet, (L, Mṣb, Ḳ,) تَبَر in Pers. signifying "an axe or a hatchet," (L,) [and زَد "he struck,"] originally meaning "what is chipped, or cut, or hewn, with an axe or a hatchet;" (Shifá el-Ghaleel;) [*Sugar-candy;* called in the present day طَبَرْزَد and قَنْد and قَنْدَة: see قَنْد:] or *excellent sugar:* (MF, voce نَبَات:) or *sugar:* (L, Ḳ:) as also

↑ سُكَّرٌ طَبَرْزَذِىٌّ ; (Mṣb ;) and طَبَرْزَلٌ and طَبَرْزَنٌ : (Aṣ, Ṣ, L, Mṣb, Ḳ :) and Yaạḳoob says طَبَرْزَذٌ and طَبَرْزَلٌ and طَبَرْزَنٌ : but ISd remarks upon these forms as being unknown to him. (L.)

طَبَرْزَذِىٌّ : see the preceding paragraph.

طبع

1. طَبَعَ, aor. َ, inf. n. طَبْعٌ, *He sealed, stamped, imprinted,* or *impressed;* syn. خَتَمَ : (Mṣb :) [and, as now used, *he printed* a book or the like :] طَبْعٌ and خَتْمٌ both signify the *making an impression* in, or upon, clay and the like : (Ṣ, Mgh, O, Ḳ :) or, as Er-Rághib says, the *impressing* a thing *with the engraving of the signet and stamp :* (TA in this art. and in art. ختم : [see more in the first paragraph of the latter art :]) and he says also that طَبْعٌ signifies the *figuring* a thing *with some particular figure;* as in the case of the طَبْع of the die for stamping coins, and the طَبْع of coins [themselves] : but that it is *more general in signification than* خَتْمٌ, and *more particular than* نَقْشٌ ; as will be shown by what follows : accord. to Aboo-Is-ḥáḳ the Grammarian, طَبْعٌ and خَتْمٌ both signify the *covering over* a thing, *and securing oneself from a thing's entering* it : and IAth says [in like manner] that they held طَبْعٌ to be *syn. with* رَيْنٌ [inf. n. of رَانَ] : but Mujáhid says that رَيْنٌ denotes less than طَبْعٌ ; and طَبْعٌ, less than إِقْفَالٌ [or the "closing with a lock :" this he says with reference to a phrase in the Ḳur xlvii. 26]. (TA.) You say, طَبَعَ الكِتَابَ, (Mgh, Mṣb,) and طَبَعَ عَلَى الكِتَابِ, (Ṣ, Mgh, Mṣb, Ḳ,*) *He sealed* (خَتَمَ, Ṣ, Mgh, Mṣb, Ḳ,) *the writing,* or *letter.* (Ṣ, Mgh, Mṣb.) And طَبَعَ الشَّاةَ *He branded,* or *otherwise marked, the sheep,* or *goat.* (O. [See طَابَعٌ.]) And طَبَعَ اللّٰهُ عَلَى قَلْبِهِ ‡ *God sealed* [or *set a seal upon*] *his* [i. e. an unbeliever's] *heart, so that he should not heed admonition, nor be disposed to that which is good;* (Mgh ;) or *so that belief should not enter it :* (O :) [and in like manner, خَتَمَ عَلَيْهِ, q. v. :] in this, regard is had to the طَبْع, and the طَبِيعَة, which is the natural constitution or disposition; for it denotes the characterizing of the soul with some particular quality or qualities, either by creation or by habit, and more especially by creation. (Er-Rághib, TA.) — Also *He began to make,* or *manufacture,* a thing : and *he made* [a thing] as in instances here following. (Mgh.) You say, طَبَعَ مِنَ الطِّينِ جَرَّةً *He made,* [or *fashioned,* or *moulded,*] *of the clay, a jar.* (Ṣ, O, Ḳ.) And طَبَعَ اللَّبِنَ, (Mgh, TA,) and السَّيْفَ, (Ṣ, Mgh, O, Ḳ,) and الدِّرْهَمَ, (Ṣ, O, Ḳ,) *He made* (Ṣ, Mgh, O, Ḳ) [*the crude bricks,* and *the sword,* and *the dirhem*] : or طَبَعَ الدَّرَاهِمَ *he struck* (Mgh, Mṣb) *with the die* (Mṣb) [i. e. *coined,* or *minted,*] *the dirhems,* or *money.* (Mgh, Mṣb.) And [hence] one says, طَبَعَهُ اللّٰهُ عَلَى الأَمْرِ, aor. and inf. n. as above, † *God created him with an adaptation,* or *a disposition, to the thing, affair, state, condition,* or *case;* or *adapted him,* or *disposed him, by creation,* [or *nature*], *thereto.* (TA.) And طُبِعَ عَلَى الشَّىْءِ † *He* (a man, O, TA) *was created with an adaptation,* or *a disposition, to the thing;* or *was adapted,* or *disposed, by creation* [or *nature*], *thereto;* syn. جُبِلَ, (IDrd, O, Ḳ, TA,) or فُطِرَ. (Lḥ, TA.) — Also, (aor. as above, TA, and so the inf. n., O, TA,) *He filled* (Er-Rághib, O, Ḳ, TA) a measure for corn or the like, (Er-Rághib, TA,) or a leathern bucket, (O, Ḳ, TA,) and a skin, (O, TA,) &c.; (O ;) and so ↑ طَبَّعَ, (Ṣ, O, Ḳ,) inf. n. تَطْبِيعٌ : (Ṣ, O :) because the quantity that fills it is a sign that prevents the taking a portion of what is in it [without the act's being discovered]. (Er-Rághib, TA.) — And طَبَعَ قَفَاهُ, (IAạr, O, Ḳ,) inf. n. as above, (IAạr, O,) *He struck the back of his neck with his hand;* (IAạr, O, Ḳ ;) i. e. the back of the neck of a boy : if with the ends of the fingers, one says, قَدَّ قَفَاهُ. (IAạr, O.) — مَا أَدْرِى مِنْ أَيْنَ طَبَعَ means *I know not whence he came forth;* syn. طَلَعَ. (TA.) = طَبِعَ, [aor. َ,] inf. n. طَبَعٌ, said of a sword, *It was,* or *became, rusty,* or *overspread with rust :* (Ṣ :) or *very rusty,* or *overspread with much rust.* (Ḳ, TA : from an explanation of the aor. : but this is written in the CḲ and in my MS. copy of the Ḳ, and in the O, يُطْبَعُ. [An explanation of طَبَعٌ in the O and Ḳ confirms the reading يَطْبَعُ ; and another confirmation thereof will be found in what follows in this paragraph.]) — Said of a thing, (Mṣb,) or of a garment, or piece of cloth, (TA,) inf. n. طَبَعٌ, *It was,* or *became, dirty;* (Mṣb, TA ;) and ↑ تطبّع is likewise said [in the same sense] of a garment, or piece of cloth. (M and TA voce رَانَ, in art. رين.) — Said of a man, † *He was* or *became, filthy* or *foul* [*in character*]. (Ṣ.) And † *He was,* or *became, sluggish, lazy,* or *indolent.* (Ṣ.) One says of a man, يَطْبَعُ, (O, Ḳ,) like يَفْرَحُ, (Ḳ,) meaning † *He has no penetrative energy, sharpness,* or *effectiveness, in the affairs that are the means,* or *causes, of attaining honour, like the sword that is overspread with much rust.* (O, Ḳ.) = طُبِعَ, (O, Ḳ,) inf. n. طَبْعٌ, (O,) said of a man, † *He was rendered* [or *pronounced*] *filthy* or *foul* [*in character*]; (O, Ḳ ;) on the authority of Sh; (O ;) and so طَبِعَ, like فَرِحَ ; (TA as on the authority of Sh ; [but this I think doubtful ;]) *and disgraced,* or *dishonoured :* (Ḳ :) and ↑ طُبِّعَ, (O, TA,) inf. n. تَطْبِيعٌ, (TA,) *he was rendered* [or *pronounced*] *filthy* or *foul* [*in character*], (O, TA,) *and blamed,* or *discommended.* (O.)

2. طبّع, inf. n. تَطْبِيعٌ, *He sealed well* [or *much,* or *he sealed* a number of writings &c.]. (KL : in which only the inf. n. is mentioned.) — And *He loaded* [a beast *heavily,* or] *well.* (KL.) — See also 1, a little after the middle. = تَطْبِيعٌ signifies also The *rendering unclean, dirty, filthy,* or *impure.* (O, Ḳ.) — See 1, last sentence.

5. تطبّع † *He affected what was not in his natural disposition.* (Ḥar p. 236.) You say, تطبّع بِطِبَاعِهِ ‡ *He affected,* or *feigned, his* [i. e. another's] *natural dispositions.* (O, Ḳ, TA.) — Also *It* (a vessel) *became full* or *filled :* (Ṣ, O, Ḳ :) quasi-pass. of طَبَّعَهُ. (Ṣ.) And تطبّع بِالمَآءِ *It* (a river, or rivulet,) *overflowed its sides with the water, and poured it forth abundantly.* (TA.) — See also 1, last quarter.

7. يَذُوبُ وَيَنْطَبِعُ, a phrase of Es-Sarakhsee, meaning [*It melts, and then*] *it admits of being sealed, stamped, imprinted,* or *impressed,* is allowable on the ground of analogy, though we have not heard it [as transmitted from the Arabs of pure speech]. (Mgh.) — [Golius has erroneously expl. انطبع as meaning "Mansuetus, edoctus, obsequens fuit ;" on the authority of the KL ; evidently in consequence of his having found its inf. n. (انْطِبَاعٌ) written in a copy of that work for اِنْقِيَادٌ, the reading in my own copy.]

8. الاِطِّبَاعُ for الاِضْطِبَاعُ see in art. ضبع.

طَبْعٌ, originally an inf. n., (Ṣ,) signifies † *A nature;* or *a natural, a native,* or *an innate, disposition* or *temper* or *the like;* or *an idiosyncrasy;* syn. سَجِيَّةٌ (Ṣ, O, Ḳ, TA) or جِبِلَّةٌ (Mṣb) and خَلِيقَةٌ ; (TA ;) *to which a man is adapted by creation;* (Ṣ, O, Mṣb, Ḳ, TA ;) [as though it were stamped, or impressed, upon him ;] as also ↑ طَبِيعَةٌ ; (Ṣ, O, Ḳ, TA ;) or this signifies his مِزَاج [i. e. *constitution,* or *temperament,* or *aggregate natural constituents*], *composed of the* [*four*] *humours;* (Mṣb ; [see مِزَاجٌ ;]) and ↑ طِبَاعٌ ; (Ṣ, O, Ḳ, TA ;) or this last signifies, (Ḳ,) or signifies also, (O,) with the article ال prefixed to it, *what is,* or *are, constituted in us in consequence of food and drink &c.* (مَا رُكِّبَ فِينَا مِنَ المَطْعَمِ وَالمَشْرَبِ وَغَيْرِ ذٰلِكَ [in which مطعم and مشرب are evidently used as inf. ns. agreeably with general analogy]), (O, Ḳ, TA,) by غير ذلك being meant *such as straitness and ampleness* [*of circumstances*], *and niggardliness and liberality,* (TA,) *of the natural dispositions that are inseparable from us;* (O, Ḳ, TA ;) and this word is fem., (O, TA,) like طَبِيعَةٌ, as is said in the M ; or it is sing. and masc. accord. to Abu-l-Ḳásim Ez-Zejjájee ; and it is also pl. of طَبْعٌ, as it is said to be by Az ; (TA ;) [and those who have asserted it to be fem. may have held it to be a pl. ;] and ↑ طَابَعٌ is syn. with طِبَاعٌ [as a sing.] ; (Ḳ, TA ;) or, as Lḥ says, it is syn. with ↑ طَبِيعَةٌ ; of which the pl. is طَبَائِعُ. (TA.) — Also † *Model, make, fashion,* or *mould :* as in the saying, اِضْرِبْهُ عَلَى طَبْعِ هٰذَا † [*Make thou it, fashion it,* or *mould it, according to the model, make, fashion,* or *mould, of this*]. (IAạr, O, L, Ḳ, TA.)

طِبْعٌ *A river,* or *rivulet;* (Aṣ, T, Ṣ, O, Ḳ, TA ;) so called because *first dug* [*and filled*] *by men;* having the meaning of مَطْبُوعٌ, like قِطْفٌ

in the sense of مَطْطُوقٌ; not applied to any of those cleft by God, such as the Tigris and the Euphrates and the Nile and the like thereof: (Az, TA:) pl. أَطْبَاعٌ, [properly a pl. of pauc.,] (Aṣ, Ṣ, O,) or طُبُوعٌ, as heard by Az from the Arabs, and طِبَاعٌ: (TA:) or الطِّبْعُ, as some say, is the name of *a particular river:* (Ṣ, O:) or it is also thus applied, i. e. to a particular river. (Ḳ.) — And i. q. مَغِيضُ مَآءٍ [i. e. *A place where water sinks,* or *goes away, into the earth;* or *where water enters into the earth;* and *where it collects*]: (O, Ḳ:) pl. أَطْبَاعٌ. (O, TA.) — And The *quantity sufficient for the filling of a measure for corn or the like,* and *of a skin,* (O, Ḳ, TA, [والسِّقَاءُ in the CḲ being a mistake for والسِّقَاءِ,]) *such as does not admit of any addition:* and the *quantity that a vessel holds, of water.* (TA.) — See also the next paragraph, in two places.

طَبَعٌ *Dirtiness,* (Ṣ, Mṣb,) or *dirt:* (Ṣ:) or, as also † طِبْعٌ, *rustiness,* or *rust,* (O, Ḳ, TA,) *upon iron;* (TA;) and *dirtiness,* or *dirt,* (O, Ḳ, TA,) *covering the sword:* (TA:) or the former signifies *much dirtiness* or *dirt, from rust:* (Lth, O, Ḳ:) pl. أَطْبَاعٌ. (Ḳ. [See طَبِعَ, of which طَبَعٌ is the inf. n.]) — Also ‡ *Disgrace,* or *dishonour;* (A'Obeyd, O, Ḳ, TA;) and so † طِبْعٌ; (TA;) it is *in religion,* or *in respect of worldly things.* (A'Obeyd, TA.) Thábit-Ḳuṭneh says, in a verse ascribed by Et-Tanookhee to 'Orweh Ibn-Udheyneh,

لَا خَيْرَ فِى طَمَعٍ يُدْنِى إِلَى طَبَعٍ
وَغُفَّةٌ مِنْ قِوَامِ العَيْشِ تَكْفِينِى

[*There is no good in coveting,* or *covetousness, that leads to disgrace: and a sufficiency of the means of subsistence contents me*]: (O, TA:) يُدْنِى in this case means يُؤَدِّى. (O.)

طَبِعٌ *Rusty;* applied to a sword. (TA.) — *Dirty.* (Mṣb.) — Applied to a man, (O,) ‡ *Filthy,* or *foul, base, ignoble, mean,* or *sordid, in disposition; that will not be ashamed of an evil action* or *saying.* (O, Ḳ, TA.) — And † *Sluggish, lazy,* or *indolent.* (TA.)

طُبْعَانُ الأَمِيرِ *The clay with which the prince,* or *governor, seals.* (O, Ḳ.)

طِبَاعٌ, as a sing. and a pl.: see طَبْعٌ.

طِبَاعَةٌ The *art,* or *craft, of the* طَبَّاع, or *manufacturer of swords,* (O, Ḳ, TA,) or *of knives,* or *of spear-heads,* or *the like.* (TA.) — [Also, as used in the present day, The *art of printing.*]

طَبِيعَةٌ: see طَبْعٌ, in two places. [It generally signifies] The مِزَاج [or *nature,* as meaning the *constitution,* or *temperament,* or *aggregate natural constituents,* of an animal body, or any other thing, for instance,] of medicine, and of fire, *which God has rendered subservient* [*to some purpose* or *purposes*]. (TA.) [Hence the phrase يَبِسَتْ طَبِيعَتُهُ, meaning *He became costive.* And الطَّبَائِعُ الأَرْبَعُ *The four humours* of the body: see خِلْطٌ and مِزَاجٌ.]

طَبِيعِىٌّ *Natural;* i. e. *of,* or *relating to,* the *natural, native,* or *innate, disposition,* or *temper,* or other *quality* or *property;* like جِبِلِّىٌّ; meaning *essential; resulting from the Creator's ordering of the natural disposition in the body.* (Mṣb in art. جبل.) [Hence, العِلْمُ الطَّبِيعِىُّ *Natural,* or *physical, science.*]

طَبَّاعٌ *A manufacturer of swords,* (O, Ḳ, TA,) or *of knives,* or *of spear-heads,* or *the like.* (TA.)

طَبُّوعٌ *A certain venomous* دُوَيْبَّة [or *insect*]: (El-Jáḥidh, O, Ḳ, TA:) or, (Ḳ,) as said to Az by a man of Egypt, *an insect* (دُوَيْبَّة) (O) *of the same kind as the* قِرْدَان [or *ticks*], (O, Ḳ,) *but* (O) *the bite of which occasions intense pain;* (O, Ḳ;) *and sometimes,* or *often, he that is bitten by it becomes swollen* [app. *in the part bitten*], *and is relieved by sweet things:* Az says that it is *with the Arabs* [*called,* or *what is called,*] *the* نِبْر [which is expl. as meaning the *tick;* or *an insect resembling the tick, which, when it creeps upon the camel, causes the track along which it creeps to swell;* or as being *smaller than the tick, that bites, and causes the place of its bite to swell;* &c.]: (O:) [accord. to Dmr, as stated by Freytag, i. q. قَمْقَامَةٌ, which is expl. as applied to *a small tick;* and *a species of louse, that clings tightly to the roots of the hair,* app. meaning *a crab-louse:*] what is known thereof [or by this appellation] now is *a thing of the form of a small emaciated tick, that sticks to the body of a man, and is hardly,* or *not at all, severed, except by the application of mercury.* (TA.)

طَبِيعٌ The *heart* (لُبّ) *of the* طَلْع [as meaning the *spathe of the palm-tree*]; (O, Ḳ;) so called because of its fulness; expl. in a trad. of El-Ḥasan El-Baṣree as meaning the طَلْع [i. e., in this case, agreeably with general usage, the *spadix of the palm-tree*] *in its* كُفُرَّى [i. e. *spathe*], the كُفُرَّى being the envelope of the طَلْع. (O, TA.)

طَابَعٌ and † طَابِعٌ (Ṣ, O, Mṣb, Ḳ, &c.) i. q. خَاتَمٌ (Ṣ, O) and خَاتِمٌ (O) [meaning *A signet, seal,* or *stamp;* i. e.] *a thing with which one seals, stamps, imprints,* or *impresses:* (Mṣb, TA:) [and also *a seal,* or *stamp,* as meaning *a piece of clay* or *wax* or *the like,* or *a place in a paper* &c., *impressed,* or *imprinted, with the instrument thus called:*] and accord. to ISh, the former, (O,) or each, (Ḳ,) signifies the مِيسَم [which means the *instrument for the branding* or *otherwise marking,* and the *brand* or *other mark,*] *of the* فَرَائِض [or *beasts that are to be given in payment of the poor-rate:* see طَبَعَ الشَّاةَ]. (O, Ḳ.) One says, الطَّابِعُ طَابِعٌ † [*The signet,* &c., *is a thing that seals,* &c.]; which is like the attribution of the act to the instrument. (Er-Rághib, TA.) And كَلَامٌ عَلَيْهِ طَابَعُ الفَصَاحَةِ ‡ [*Language upon which is the stamp of chasteness,* or *perspicuity,* &c.]. (TA.)

طَابِعٌ: see the next preceding paragraph, in two places: — and see also طَبْعٌ.

[مَطْبَعٌ *A place where anything is sealed, stamped, imprinted,* or *impressed.* And, as used in the present day, *A printing-house;* as also مَطْبَعَةٌ.]

مُطَبَّعَةٌ, applied to a she-camel: see the next paragraph.

مُطَبَّعٌ *Filled:* so its fem. in the phrase قِرْبَةٌ مُطَبَّعَةٌ طَعَامًا [*A skin filled with food*]. (TA.) — And مُطَبَّعَةٌ applied to a she-camel, *Filled with fat and flesh, so as to be rendered firm in make:* (Az, TA:) or [simply] *fat.* (Z, TA.) — And, (TA,) so applied, *Heavily laden;* (Ṣ, O, Ḳ, TA;) and [in like manner] † مُطَبَّعَةٌ a she-camel *heavily burdened by her load.* (TA.) — And مُهْرٌ مُطَبَّعٌ *A colt trained,* or *rendered tractable* or *manageable.* (TA.)

مَطْبُوعٌ [pass. part. n. of طَبَعَ in all its senses]. — You say, هُوَ مَطْبُوعٌ عَلَى الكَرَمِ ‡ [*He is created with an adaptation,* or *a disposition, to generosity*]. (TA.)

طبق

1. [طَبَقَهُ, aor. ـُ, accord. to Freytag, is expl. in the Ḳ as syn. with أَطْبَقَهُ in the first of the senses assigned to this latter below: but I find no authority for this in the Ḳ nor in any other lexicon.] — طَبِقَتْ يَدُهُ, (Ṣ, O, Ḳ, TA,) aor. ـَ; and طُبِقَتْ, aor. ـُ; (TA;) inf. n. (of the former, Ṣ, TA) طَبَقٌ (Ṣ, O, Ḳ, TA) and (of the latter, TA) طُبْقٌ; (Ḳ, TA;) † *His arm would not be stretched forth;* (Ṣ, O;) or ‡ *stuck to his side,* (Ḳ, TA,) *and would not be stretched forth.* (TA.) — طَفِقَ i. q. طَبِقَ يَفْعَلُ بِى كَذَا [i. e. *He set about,* or *began,* &c., *doing with me such a thing*]. (O, Ḳ.*)

2. طَبَّقَهُ, inf. n. تَطْبِيقٌ: see 4. — [Hence,] طَبَّقَ السَّحَابُ الجَوَّ *The clouds covered the mid-air between the heaven and the earth:* (Ḳ:) and طَبَّقَهَا and † أَطْبَقَ الغَيْمُ السَّمَآءَ [*The clouds covered the sky*]: (Mgh, TA:) both signify the same. (TA.) And طَبَّقَ المَآءُ وَجْهَ الأَرْضِ *The water covered the face of the earth,* or *land.* (Ḳ.) — And طَبَّقَ الشَّىْءُ, inf. n. as above, i. q. عَمَّ [*The thing was,* or *became, common,* or *general, in its relation* or *relations, operation* or *operations, effect* or *effects,* &c.]. (Ḳ.) And as syn. with عَمَّ it is trans.: so in the phrase, هٰذَا مَطَرٌ طَبَّقَ الأَرْضَ [*This is rain that has included the general extent of the land within the compass of its fall*]. (TA.) And one says also, طَبَّقَ الغَيْمُ, (Ṣ, O, TA,) inf. n. as above, (Ṣ, O, Ḳ, TA,) *The clouds rained upon the whole of the land;* (Ṣ, O;) or *made their rain common,* or *general,* (Ḳ, TA,)

to the land. (TA.) — تَطْبِيقٌ also signifies The *making* a thing *to suit, match, tally, conform, correspond,* or *agree,* with another thing. (KL.) — [And طبق بَيْنَ الشَّيْئَيْنِ *He put the two things together, face to face.* (See also 3.) — Hence,] التَّطْبِيقُ in the divinely-appointed act of prayer is *The putting the hands* [*together, palm to palm,*] *between the thighs in the act of bowing oneself;* (Ṣ, O, Ḳ;) and in like manner *in the act termed* التَّشَهُّد [q. v.]. (El-Ḥarbee, TA.) One says of a person bowing himself in prayer, طبّق, and likewise ▼ اطبق, (TA,) or طبّق كَفَّيْهِ, (Mgh,) or طبّق بَيْنَ كَفَّيْهِ ثُمَّ وَضَعَهُمَا بَيْنَ فَخِذَيْهِ, (O,) *He put his hands* [*together, palm to palm, and then put them*] *between his thighs.* (Mgh.) The doing thus is forbidden; (Mgh, O;) for the hands should be placed upon the knees. (O.) — Also *The* horse's *raising his fore feet together and putting them down together in running:* (Ṣ, O, Ḳ:) or, accord. to Aṣ, *the leaping* of a camel, or of a she-camel, *and then alighting so that the legs fall upon the ground together;* the doing of which is not approved. (TA.) — And طبّقت الإِبِلُ الطَّرِيقَ ‡ *The camels travelled the road without declining from the right direction.* (TA. [The verb is there written without any syll. signs; but is evidently thus.]) — And طبّق السَّيْفُ, (Ṣ, O, TA,) [i. e. طبّق السَّيْفُ المَفْصِلَ,] inf. n. as above, (Ḳ,) *The sword hit the joint* (Ṣ, O, Ḳ, TA) *and severed the limb:* (Ṣ, O, TA:) or *fell between two bones.* (TA.) A poet says, (Ṣ,) namely, El-Farezdaḳ, praising El-Ḥajjáj, and likening him to a sword, (O,)

• يُصَمِّمُ أَحْيَانًا وَحِينًا يُطَبِّقُ •

[expl. in art. صم]. (Ṣ, O.) Hence, يُطَبِّقُ المَفْصِلَ means † *He hits aright the argument, proof,* or *evidence:* (Ṣ, O:) and this is also said of an eloquent man. (AZ, TA voce قَالَبٌ, q. v.) Hence also, طبّق alone, † *He hit upon the right mode of judicial decision:* (O, TA:) and *the text of the tradition.* (TA.)

3. مُطَابَقَةٌ signifies The *putting a thing upon,* or *above,* or *over, another thing commensurate therewith:* whence the phrase, طَابَقْتُ النَّعْلَ [i. e., as expl. in Bḍ lxvii. 3, *I sewed another sole upon the sole* or *sandal*]. (Er-Rághib, TA.) [Hence] one says also, طَابَقْتُ بَيْنَ الشَّيْئَيْنِ *I made the two things commensurate, and stuck them together.* (Ṣ, O. [See also 2.]) And طابق بَيْنَ قَمِيصَيْنِ *He put on,* or *attired himself with, two shirts, one over,* or *outside, the other;* (Ḳ, TA;) and in like manner صَافَقَ بَيْنَهُمَا, and طَارَقَ, (TA,) and ظَاهَرَ. (A &c. in art. ظهر.) — And طابقهُ, (Ḳ, TA,) inf. n. مُطَابَقَةٌ (Ṣ, O, Ḳ, TA) and طِبَاقٌ, (Ḳ, TA,) *It suited, matched, tallied, conformed, corresponded,* or *agreed, with it;* (Ṣ,* O,* Ḳ, TA;) and *was equal to it;* or *was like it in measure, size, quantity,* or *the like.* (TA.) — [Hence,] one says, هٰذَا جَوَابٌ يُطَابِقُ السُّؤَالَ [*This is an answer,* or *a reply, that is suitable to the question*]. (TA.) — And طابقت زَوْجَهَا *She* (a woman) *complied with* [*the desire of*] *her husband:* and طابقت said of a she-camel, and of a woman, *She was,* or *became, submissive to him who desired her.* (TA.) — And طابق لِى بِحَقِّى *He obeyed me with respect to my right,* or *due, and hastened to render it;* or *he acknowledged to me my right,* or *due, willingly.* (TA.) — And طابقهُ عَلَى الأَمْرِ *He combined with him, and aided him, to do the thing:* or [simply] *he aided him to do it.* (TA.) — And طابق عَلَى العَمَلِ *He became accustomed, habituated,* or *inured, to the work.* (Ṣ,* O,* TA.) — مُطَابَقَةٌ, of a horse, (Ṣ, O, Ḳ,) in his running, (Ṣ, O,) and in like manner of a camel, as in the A, (TA,) means His *putting his hind feet in the places that were those of his fore feet.* (Ṣ, O, Ḳ.) — And (hence, TA) ‡ The *walking as one shackled;* (Ṣ, O, Ḳ, TA;) i. e., *with short steps.* (TA.) [See an ex. voce جَحْجَلٌ.]

4. اطبقهُ *He covered it;* (Ṣ, O, Ḳ;) as also ▼ طبّقهُ, inf. n. تَطْبِيقٌ; (Ḳ;) [i. e.] *he made it to be covered;* (Ṣ, O;) *he put the* طَبَق, i. e. *cover, upon it,* namely, a jar [or the like]. (Mgh. [And the like is said in several other arts. in other lexicons.]) And اطبقتُ الرَّحَى *I put the upper mill-stone upon the lower.* (TA.) — See also 2, second sentence. [This last ex. shows that اطبقهُ signifies sometimes *It covered it* as meaning *it became a cover,* or *like a cover, to it;* and اطبق عَلَيْهِ likewise has this meaning; as also ▼ انطبق عليه, and ▼ تطبّق عليه.] — [Hence,] one says, اطبق عَلَيْهِ الجُنُونُ (Mṣb, TA) † *Insanity covered* [i. e. *veiled,* or *wholly obscured,*] *his reason,* or *intellect.* (TA.) And اطبقت عَلَيْهِ الحُمَّى (Mgh, O, TA) ‡ *The fever was,* or *became, continual upon him, not quitting him night nor day.* (TA.) — اطبقوا عَلَى الأَمْرِ means ‡ *They combined consentaneously,* or *agreed together, respecting,* or *to do, the thing,* or *affair;* (Ṣ,* Mgh,* O,* Mṣb, TA;*) and so ▼ تطابقوا عَلَيْهِ. (MA.) — And اطبقوا عَلَيْهِ *They came round about him.* (MA.) — [And اطبقت عَلَيْهِ الحَيَّةُ *The serpent wound itself round upon him.* (See طَبَقٌ, last sentence.)] — And اطبقت النُّجُومُ *The stars appeared, and were numerous;* (O, Ḳ, TA;) [*as though they were like a cover;* or] *as though they were stage above stage* (طَبَقَةٌ فَوْقَ طَبَقَةٍ). (TA.) — [اطبقهُ عَلَيْهِ signifies *He made it to cover it;* i. e., *to be a cover,* or *like a cover, upon it.*] You say, أَطْبَقَ عَلَى مَخْرَجِ الحَرْفِ مِنَ اللِّسَانِ مَا حَاذَاهُ مِنَ الحَنَكِ [*He made to cover the part of the tongue which was the place of utterance of the letter what was opposite to it of the palate;* i. e. he put that part of his tongue close beneath the opposite part of the palate]. (O.) — [Hence,] أَطْبَقَ عَلَيْهِمُ العَذَابَ, said of God, † *He made punishment to fall,* or *come, upon them in common,* or *universally,* [*as though He made it to cover them,*] *so that none of them escaped.* (Jel in xci. 14.) — And أَطْبَقَ ٱللّٰهُ عَلَيْهِ الحُمَّى, and الجُنُونَ, † *God made the fever to be continual upon him,* and in like manner *insanity:* the verb being used as intrans. and trans. (Mṣb. [But its author adds that he had not found this: meaning that he had not found any classical authority for the trans. use of the verb in this and similar senses.]) — One says also, اطبق البَابَ [*He closed the door*]. (Mṣb and Ḳ in art. وصد; &c.) And أَطْبِقْ شَفَتَيْكَ [*Close thy lips;*] i. e. † *be thou silent.* (TA.) [And اطبق الكِتَابَ *He closed,* or *shut, the book.* And اطبق الثَّوْبَ *He folded together the garment,* or *piece of cloth.*] See also 2, in the middle of the paragraph. — مَا أَطْبَقَهُ لِكَذَا *How skilful is he* (O, Ḳ) [*for the performance of such a thing*]! (O) is from طَبَّقَ المَفْصِلَ. (JK.)

5. تطبّق: see 4. — تطبّق عَلَيْهِ: see 7. [Hence,] one says, لَوْ تَطَبَّقَتِ السَّمَآءُ عَلَى الأَرْضِ مَا فَعَلْتُ كَذَا [*If the heaven became as a cover upon the earth, I would not do such a thing*]. (Ṣ, O.)

6. تطابق الشَّيْآنِ *The two things suited, matched, tallied, conformed, corresponded,* or *agreed, each with the other;* (Ṣ,* O,* TA;) and *were equal, each to the other;* or *were like each other in measure, size, quantity,* or *the like.* (TA.) And تطابقوا عَلَى الأَمْرِ: see 4.

7. انطبق *It was,* or *became, covered;* (O, Ḳ;) [i. e.] *it was made to be covered;*] or *it had the* طَبَق, i. e. *cover, put upon it;*] *quasi-pass.* of أَطْبَقَهُ; (O;) and so ▼ تطبّق. (Ṣ, O, Ḳ.) — [And *It became closed;* said of a door, &c. — Hence,] يَنْغَلِقُ i. q. يَنْطَبِقُ عَلَيْهِ الكَلَامُ † [*Speech is as though it were closed against him;* i. e. *he is impeded in his speech, unable to speak,* or *tonguetied*]. (O.) — See also 4. — [Hence one says of a rule, يَنْطَبِقُ عَلَى كَذَا وَكَذَا † *It applies to such and such things* or *subjects.*]

طَبْق: see an ex. of the accus. case, in the phrase وَلَدَتِ الغَنَمُ طَبْقًا, voce طَبَقٌ, last quarter. — طَبْق is also expl., by IAạr, as meaning The *doing wrong,* or *injuring, by false pretence* or *false allegation.* (TA.)

طِبْق: see طَبَقٌ, in the latter part of the former half. — طِبَاق: see — هٰذَا الشَّىْءُ طِبْقُ الأَرْضِ. — طِبْقُ هٰذَا, (IAạr, O, Ḳ,*) and ▼ طَبَقُهُ, and ▼ طَبِيقُهُ, (IAạr,* O,* Ḳ,) and ▼ طِبَاقُهُ, (IAạr, O, Ḳ,) and ▼ طَابَقُهُ, and ▼ مُطْبَقُهُ, (IAạr, O, TA,) i. q. ▼ مُطَابِقُهُ [i. e. *This thing is the match of this;* or *what suits, matches, tallies, conforms, corresponds,* or *agrees, with this; what is equal to this;* or *the like of this in measure, size, quantity,* or *the like*]. (IAạr, O, Ḳ, TA.) — طِبْق signifies also *A space,* or *period,* (سَاعَةٌ,) of the day; and so ▼ طِبْقَةٌ: and ▼ طَبِيقٌ signifies the same of the night: (Ḳ:) you say, أَقَمْتُ عِنْدَهُ طِبْقًا مِنَ النَّهَارِ, and ▼ طِبْقَةً, *I remained at his abode during a space,* or *period,* (سَاعَةً,) *of the day:* (Ibn-'Abbád, O:) and طِبْقًا, (Ḳ, TA,) with kesr, (TA,) or ▼ طَبِيقًا, (so in the O,) and ▼ طَبِيقًا, i. e. *a while,* or *a long time,* syn. مَلِيًّا: (Ibn-'Abbád, O, Ḳ:) or, accord. to the L, one says, أَتَانَا بَعْدَ طِبْقٍ مِنَ

اللَّيْلِ, and † طِبْقٍ, *he came to us after a space, or period,* (حِينٍ,) *of the night;* and in like manner, مِنَ النَّهَارِ *of the day:* (TA:) the pl. of طِبْقٌ is طُبُقٌ. (Ḳ.) [See also طَبَقٌ, in, or near, the middle of the paragraph.] ═ Also *Bird-lime;* a dial. var. of دِبْقٌ. (IDrd, O, Ḳ.) And The *fruit of a certain kind of tree* [app. meaning the *berries of the viscum,* or *mistletoe,* of which bird-lime is mostly prepared, and which are called دِبْق in the present day]. (Ḳ.) And *Anything with which a thing is stuck,* or *made to stick.* (Ḳ.) And [particularly] *A thing* [or *substance*] *to which the exterior lamina of the pearl is stuck so that it becomes like it;* as also † مُطَبِّقٌ. (TA.) —— And *Snares for birds,* or *things with which birds are caught;* (Ibn-'Abbád, O;) *like* فِخَاخ; as also طِبْقٌ; of which [latter] the sing is † طِبْقَةٌ. (Ibn-'Abbád, O, Ḳ.) ═ Also *A road,* or *way:* ═ and *i. q.* دَسْتُور [as a Pers. word, generally meaning *Permission,* or *leave,* as expl. by Golius in this instance]. (KL. [But for these two significations I have not found any other authority.])

طَبَقٌ *A thing that is the equal* of another thing (Mṣb, Ḳ) of any kind (Ḳ) *in its measure so that it covers the whole extent of the latter like the lid:* this is its primary signification: (Mṣb:) [whence] one says, هٰذَا الشَّىْءُ طَبَقُ هٰذَا, like طِبْقُهُ, q. v.: (IAạr, O, Ḳ:) and [hence] it signifies The *cover,* or *lid,* (Mgh, Ḳ,) of a jar, (Mgh,) or of anything: (Ḳ:) pl. أَطْبَاقٌ (Ṣ,* O,* Ḳ) [and طِبَاقٌ, mentioned in the Mṣb as a pl. of طَبَقٌ in another, but similar, sense, which will be found in what follows, but better known as a pl. of طَبَقَةٌ], and أَطْبِقَةٌ is added as another pl. in the Ḳ, but [SM says] this is strange; I have not found it in the [other] lexicons; and it may be that the right reading is وَأَطْبَقَهُ, as syn. with what immediately there follows it, i. e. وَطَبَّقَهُ. (TA.) وَافَقَ شَنٌّ طَبَقَهُ is [a prov.] expl. (O, Ḳ, TA) by Aṣ (O, TA) as said of a company of men who had a receptacle of skin [i. e. a water-skin] that had become old and worn out, wherefore they made a طَبَق [or cover] for it: (O, Ḳ, TA:) [so that the meaning is, *A water-skin that had become old and worn out suited its cover:*] or شَنّ and طَبَق [in the O طبقة] were two tribes; (Ṣ,* O, Ḳ* TA;) and, as ISd says, شَنّ does not here mean a water-skin, for this has no طَبَق: (TA:) or [طَبَقَهُ is for طَبَقَةُ, and] طَبَقَةُ was an intelligent woman, whom an intelligent man took as his wife. (O, Ḳ, TA. [See Freytag's Arab. Prov., ii. 800.]) —— Also *A certain household utensil;* (Mṣb;) [i. e. *a dish,* or *plate;* perhaps thus called because the cover of a cooking-vessel is often used as a dish or plate;] the *thing upon which one eats,* (Ḳ, TA,) and *in which one eats;* and the *thing upon which fruit is placed* [i. e. a *dish, or plate, used for that purpose;* and likewise *a round tray,* and *the like*]: (TA:) pl. أَطْبَاقٌ and طِبَاقٌ. (Mṣb.) —— ‡ The *surface of the earth* [considered as a cover]. (Ḳ, TA.) [And in like manner applied to *A layer,* or *stratum,* of earth. دَفَنْتُ الشَّىْءَ is expl. in the Mṣb as meaning أَخْفَيْتُهُ تَحْتَ أَطْبَاقِ التُّرَابِ *I concealed it beneath the layers,* or *strata, of the earth,* or *dust.* See also طَبَقَةٌ.] —— ‡ The *exterior part of the pudendum muliebre* [considered as a cover]. (Ibn-'Abbád, O, Ḳ, TA.) —— *A fold, a ply,* or *an overlapping part,* of a thing. (PṢ. [See حَفْث.]) —— [And hence, app., ‡ *A roller* of the sea: see آذِىٌّ.] —— *A thin bone* [or *cartilage*] *that forms a division between any two vertebræ:* (Ṣ, O, Ḳ:) *what is between any two vertebræ* of a horse [&c.]: pl. أَطْبَاقٌ: (Kr:) and some say, the *vertebræ altogether:* and some say, *a vertebra, in any part.* (TA.) It is said in a trad. respecting the day of resurrection, تَبْقَى أَصْلَابُ المُنَافِقِينَ طَبَقًا وَاحِدًا, meaning [*The backbones of the hypocrites shall be* (lit. *continue to be*) as though they were] *one vertebra:* or, as some say, † طَبَقَةً; and [they say that] طَبَق is the pl. [or coll. gen. n.]. (O. [See also 1 in art. عقر.]) —— [And *Any of the successively-superimposed cartilages of the windpipe:* pl. أَطْبَاقٌ. (See حَنْجَرَةٌ, in art. حجر; and see also حُلْقُومٌ.)] —— *Any of the stages of Hell* [whereof every one except the lowest is imagined to be like a cover over another]. (TA.) [And in like manner, *Any of the Seven Heavens:*] one says, السَّمٰوَاتُ طِبَاقٌ, meaning *The Heavens are* [composed of *stages*] *one above another;* (Ṣ, O, Mṣb;*) every heaven [except the lowest] being like a طبق to another: (Mṣb:) or this is said because of their being conformable, one with another: (Ḳ:) and it is said in the Ḳur lxvii. 3, اَلَّذِى خَلَقَ سَبْعَ سَمٰوَاتٍ طِبَاقًا, meaning [*Who hath created seven heavens*] *placed one above another;* طباقا being the inf. n. of طَابَقْتُ النَّعْلَ [q. v.], used as an epithet; or for ذَاتَ طِبَاقٍ; or طُوبِقَتْ طِبَاقًا, pl. of طَبَقٌ or of † طَبَقَةٌ. (Bḍ.) —— [*Any of the bones* of the head; because they compose a covering: or] أَطْبَاقُ الرَّأْسِ means *the bones of the head* because they suit one another and have certain parts of them inserted and infixed into other parts. (TA. [See 8 in art. شجر.]) —— *Any joint of a limb:* pl. أَطْبَاقٌ. (Aṣ, TA.) —— *A collective number* of men, and of locusts; (Ṣ, O, Ḳ;) as also † طِبْقٌ, (Ḳ,) which is thus expl. by Aṣ in relation to men: (TA:) or *a multitude* of men, and of locusts: (Ḳ:) [app. considered as covering a space of ground:] or *a company* of men *that are equal with a company like them.* (ISd, TA.) —— *A generation of mankind;* or the *people of one time;* syn. قَرْنٌ and عَالَمٌ; as in the saying of El-'Abbás,

إِذَا مَضَى عَالَمٌ بَدَا طَبَقُ

[metre مُنْسَرِح] i. e. إِذَا مَضَى قَرْنٌ بَدَا قَرْنٌ [*When a generation passes away, a generation appears* in its place]: the قَرْن being called طَبَق because they are a طَبَق [i. e. cover] to the earth: then they pass away and another طبق comes: (O, TA:) or, as IAạr says, طَبَقٌ signifies *a people after a people.* (TA.) And (TA) *A* قَرْن [i. e. *generation*] *of time:* or *twenty years:* (Ḳ, TA:) or, as in the book of El-Hejeree, on the authority of I'Ab, † طَبَقَةٌ has this latter meaning. (TA.) —— ‡ A rain *such as fills and covers the earth,* or *land;* (TA;) or *such as is general,* (Ṣ, O, Ḳ, TA,) *and of wide extent;* termed by a poet (namely, Imra-el-Ḳeys, O, TA) طَبَقُ الأَرْضِ: (Ṣ, O, TA:) or a *lasting* rain, *consecutive in its falls.* (Mṣb.) And أَصْبَحَتِ الأَرْضُ طَبَقًا وَاحِدًا means † [*The land became,* or *became in the morning,*] *covered with water over its surface.* (TA.) —— *A main portion* of the night and of the day: (Ṣ, O, Ḳ:) or, accord. to the Mufradát [of Er-Rághib], طَبَقُ اللَّيْلِ وَالنَّهَارِ signifies سَاعَاتُهُ المطابقة [app. a mistranscription for المُتَطَابِقَةُ, and meaning *the commensurate,* or *similar,* or *equal, portions of the night and of the day*]. (TA.) See also طِبْقٌ. —— And *A state,* or *condition;* (Ṣ, O, Ḳ, TA;) as also † طَبَقَةٌ, of which the pl. is طِبَاقٌ: the pl. of the former in this sense is أَطْبَاقٌ. (TA.) Hence the phrase, لَتَرْكَبُنَّ طَبَقًا عَنْ طَبَقٍ, (Ṣ, O, Ḳ, TA,) in the Ḳur [lxxxiv. 19], meaning [*Ye shall assuredly enter upon*] *state after state,* (Ṣ,* O, TA,) and *predicament after predicament;* as in the A; (TA;) on the day of resurrection; (Ṣ;) the state being termed طَبَق because it will fill the hearts [as though the dread thereof covered them], or will be near to doing so; (O, TA;) and عَنْ being put in this instance, as it is in many others, in the place of بَعْدَ: (TA:) or the meaning is, *one after another of similar states of hardship:* or it may be, *degrees of hardship after degrees thereof;* طَبَق accord. to this rendering being regarded as pl. [or coll. gen. n.] of † طَبَقَةٌ: (Ksh and Bḍ:) or [*ye shall assuredly mount upon*] *the heaven in one state after another state;* for it (the heaven) shall be like مُهْل [i. e. molten brass or iron &c., as is said in the Ḳur lxx. 8,] and then successively in other states: (O, TA:) so says Aboo-Bekr: accord. to Er-Rághib, it points to the various successive states of man in the present world from his creation, and in the world to come until his resting in one of the two abodes [Paradise or Hell]: or, accord. to Ibn-Abi-l-Ḥadeed, it means [*ye shall assuredly enter upon*] *difficulty after difficulty;* as is related by MF; and the same is said by Az on the authority of I'Ab: (TA:) some read لَتَرْكَبَنَّ, meaning *thou,* O Mohammad, *shalt assuredly mount upon stage after stage* of the stages (أَطْبَاق) of heaven; and I'Ab and Ibn-Mes-ood read لَتَرْكِبُنَّ, with kesr to the ب, which is accord. to the dial. of Temeem, and Ḳeys and Asad and Rabee'ah pronounce the first letter of the future with kesr except when it is ى: 'Omar read لَيَرْكَبَنَّ, either as relating to the Prophet or as referring to him who is mentioned in verses 10-15 of the same chapter. (O, TA.) One says also, بَاتَ يَرْعَى طَبَقَ النُّجُومِ, meaning ‡ [*He passed the night watching*] *the state of the stars in their course:* (TA:) or طَبَقٌ

النُّجُومِ means *the falling* [or app. *setting*] *of stars after* [*other*] *stars:* or, accord. to Es-Sadoosee, *the rising of a star and the setting of another:* and *a collective number thereof after a collective number* [*of others*]: and such, he says, are termed طَبَقَاتٌ ↑ مِنَ النُّجُومِ. (O.) — جَآءَتِ الإِبِلُ طَبَقًا عَلَى خُفٍّ وَاحِدٍ وَاحِدًا means [i. e. *The camels came following one another, in a single line:* see art. خف]. (TA.) And one says, وَلَدَتِ الغَنَمُ طَبَقًا and ↑ طِبْقًا, meaning *The sheep,* or *goats, brought forth one after another:* (L:) El-Umawee says, when they do thus, one says, وَلَدْتُهَا الرُّجَيْلَآءَ and وَلَدْتُهَا طَبَقًا and ↑ طَبَقَةً [*They brought them forth* (i. e. their young ones) *one after another*]. (Ṣ, O.) — [The pl.] الأَطْبَاقُ also signifies *Those who are remote, and those who are remotely connected:* so in a trad. respecting the signs of the resurrection, or of the time thereof; in which it is said, يُوصَلُ الأَطْبَاقُ وَيُقْطَعُ الأَرْحَامُ [*Those who are remote, and those who are remotely related, shall be brought into close connection, and the ties of relationship shall be severed*]. (TA.) — بِنْتُ طَبَقٍ is an appellation of *A female tortoise,* [app. because of the cover of her back,] *which,* (Ṣ, O, Ḳ,) *as the Arabs assert,* (Ṣ, O,) *lays ninety-nine eggs, all of them* [*eventually*] *tortoises, and lays one egg which discloses* (Ṣ, O, Ḳ) *a serpent* (Ḳ) [or *a serpent such as is termed*] *an* أَسْوَد; (Ṣ, O;) or, accord. to Az, *sixty-nine* [*eggs*], *and the seventieth is* [*eventually*] *a viper.* (So in a marg. note in one of my copies of the Ṣ; in which, also, the appellation is written بِنْتُ طَبَقٍ, instead of بِنْتُ طَبَقٍ.) Hence the phrase إِحْدَى بَنَاتِ طَبَقٍ, meaning ‡ *A calamity;* (Ṣ, O, TA;) as also بِنْتُ طَبَقٍ: (TA:) بَنَاتُ طَبَقٍ meaning *calamities* [like مُطْبِقَاتٌ]: as well as *tortoises:* and *serpents:* (Ḳ:) and أُمُّ طَبَقٍ [in like manner] means *calamity:* (TA in art. طرق:) or, accord. to Eth-Tha'álibee, طَبَقٌ [thus, imperfectly decl., as written in the L,) signifies *a yellow serpent:* (L, TA:) and أُمُّ طَبَقٍ and بِنْتُ طَبَقٍ are said to signify *the serpent,* because of its coiling itself round: or بَنَاتُ طَبَقٍ is an appellation applied to *serpents* because of their winding themselves round (لِانْطِبَاقِهَا) upon him whom they bite; or, as some say, because the حَوَّآء [q. v.] confines them beneath the lids (أَطْبَاق) of the baskets (أَسْفَاط) covered with leather; or, as Z says, because they resemble the طَبَق [i. e. cover, or dish, or plate,] when they coil themselves round. (TA.)

طَبَقَةٌ: see طِبْقٌ, former half, in two places: = and also near the end of the same paragraph.

طَبَقَةٌ [generally signifying *Any one of two or more things that are placed,* or *situate, one above another; a stage, story,* or *floor; a layer,* or *stratum;* or *the like:* pl. طَبَقَاتٌ and طِبَاقٌ]: see طَبَقٌ, in seven places. — [Hence, طَبَقَاتُ العَيْنِ *The coats,* or *tunics, of the eye.* (See جُلَيْدَةٌ.)] — [Hence also,] طَبَقَاتُ النَّاسِ *The degrees, ranks, orders,* or *classes, of men.* (Ṣ,* O,* TA.) [Thus, طَبَقَاتُ الشُّعَرَآءِ means *The orders,* or *classes, of the poets.*] — كُتُبُهُ إِلَيَّ طَبَقَةٌ is a phrase mentioned by Ibn-'Abbád as meaning *His letters,* or *epistles, to me are consecutive.* (O, TA.) — A طَبَقَة of land is [*A portion*] *like a* مَشَارَة [expl. in art. شور]. (TA.)

يَدٌ طَبِقَةٌ *An arm that will not be stretched forth;* (Ṣ, O, TA;) *sticking to the side.* (Ḳ, TA.)

طِبَاقٌ [a pl. of طَبَقَةٌ, and said to be also a pl. of طَبَقٌ]. — طِبَاقُ الأَرْضِ means *What is upon the earth:* (Ṣ, O:) or *what fills,* or *would fill, the earth, extending over it in general,* or *in common,* (O, TA,) *as though it were a* طَبَق [or *cover*] *to it.* (TA.) It is said in a trad. respecting Ḳureysh, عِلْمُ عَالِمِهِمْ طِبَاقُ الأَرْضِ i. e. *The knowledge of the knowing of them is as though it extended over the earth in general,* or *in common, and were a cover to it;* (O,* TA;) or, as some relate it, طِبْقُ ↑ الأَرْضِ. (TA.) — See also طِبْقٌ. — And see مُطْبِقٌ.

طَبِيقٌ: see طِبْقٌ, in five places.

طَبَاقَآءُ ‡ A camel (Ṣ, O, Ḳ) *that will not cover;* (Ṣ, O;) *lacking strength,* or *ability, to cover.* (Ḳ, TA.) — And, applied to a man, (Ṣ, O, Ḳ,) † *Impeded in his speech; unable to speak;* or *tonguetied:* (O, Ḳ,* TA:) or *that will not perform the act of coïtus:* (TA:) or *heavy, covering the woman* (يُطْبِقُ عَلَى المَرْأَةِ, in the CḲ [erroneously] يَطْبِقُ, and in my MS. copy of the Ḳ يُطْبِقُ المَرْأَةَ,) *with his breast by reason of his heaviness:* (Ḳ, TA:) or *impotent;* syn. عَيِيٌّ: (Ṣ, O:) or *impotent* (عَيِيٌّ), *heavy, covering her whom he compresses,* or *the woman, with his breast, by reason of his littleness,* or *immature age:* accord. to Aṣ, *stupid, foolish, impotent in speech* or *actions, dull,* or *heavy:* accord. to IAạr, *whose reason is veiled,* or *wholly obscured,* (أُطْبِقَ عَلَيْهِ الجُنُونُ, [see مُطْبَقٌ ↑ عَلَيْهِ],) *by stupidity,* or *foolishness:* or, as some say, *whose affairs are veiled to him* [*so that he sees not how to accomplish them*]: or *who lacks ability to speak, his lips being closed.* (TA.) — تَحَلَّبُوا عَلَى ذٰلِكَ الإِنْسَانِ طَبَاقَآءَ means *They collected themselves together against that man, all of them.* (ISh, O.)

طُبَّاقٌ *A species of tree,* (Ṣ, O, Ḳ,) *growing upon the mountains of Mekkeh;* (Ḳ;) described to AḤn by some one or more of Azd-es-Saráh as being *about the stature of a man in height, growing near one another, scarcely ever or never seen singly, having long, slender, green leaves, which slip* [*between the fingers*] *when squeezed, applied as a dressing to a fracture, which, remaining upon it, they consolidate; it has a clustered yellow flower; is not eaten by the camels, but by the sheep* or *goats; and grows among the rocks, with the* عَرْعَر; *the bees eat from its flowers, and the mountain-goats also feed upon it:* (O:) *it is beneficial as an antidote against poisons, taken internally and applied as a dressing, and as a remedy for the mange,* or *scab, and the itch, and fevers of long continuance, and colic, and jaundice, and obstructions of the liver; and is very healing.* (Ḳ.) [طُبَاق, thus written by Golius, without teshdeed, is said by him to be *Ocimum agreste;* as on the authority of Meyd; but he has not given the syn. by which Meyd has explained it.] بَيْنَ شَثٍّ وَطُبَّاقٍ, in a trad. of Moḥammad Ibn-El-Ḥanafeeyeh, means in the places where grow these two species of trees; (O;) i. e. in the tracts of the mountains of Mekkeh. (TA.)

طَابَقٌ: see طَبَقٌ. = Also, (Ṣ, Mgh, O, Ḳ,) and طَابِقٌ, (Ḳ,) both mentioned by Ks and Lḥ, [and both in one of my copies of the Ṣ,] (TA,) and ↑ طَابَاقٌ, (Fr, O, Ḳ,) *A large brick:* (Mgh:) or *a large baked brick:* (Ṣ, O, Ḳ:) [or *a large tile,* or *flat piece of baked clay:*] and *a large* [*piece of*] *glass:* (Mgh:) arabicized, (Ṣ, Mgh, O,) from the Pers., (Ṣ, O,) i. e. from تَابَهْ: (Mgh, O:) [and particularly *a large flat piece of baked clay,* or *of stone,* &c., *that is used for a trapdoor:*] whence, بَيْتُ الطَّابَقِ [*the chamber that has a trap-door*]: (Mgh: [see also مُطْبِقٌ:]) pl. طَوَابِقُ and طَوَابِيقُ; (Mgh, O, Ḳ;) the former being pl. of طَابَقٌ, and the latter of طاباق. (O.) — And in like manner the طَابَق of iron [is from the Pers. تَابَهْ]: (O:) [i. e.] طَابَقٌ signifies also, (Ḳ, TA,) and طَابِقٌ likewise, (accord. to the Ḳ,) *A certain vessel in which one cooks,* (Ḳ, TA,) [meaning *a frying-pan,*] *of iron* or *of copper:* (TA:) arabicized from تَابَهْ. (Ḳ, TA.) — [And *A plate,* or *flat piece, of metal.*] = بِئْرٌ ذَاتُ طَابَقٍ means *A well in which are projecting edges.* (Ibn-'Abbád, O.) = And طَابَقٌ and طَابِقٌ signify also *A limb,* or *member,* (Th, O,* Ḳ, TA,) of a human being, such as the *arm,* or *hand,* and the *leg,* or *foot,* and *the like:* (Th, TA:) applied in a trad. to the *hand* of a thief, which is to be cut off: (TA:) [see طَائِفٌ, in art. طوف:] or they signify [or signify also] the *half* of a sheep, or goat: (Ḳ, TA:) or *as much* thereof *as two persons,* or *three, eat.* (TA.)

طَابَاقٌ; pl. طَوَابِيقُ: see the next preceding paragraph.

العِمَّةُ الطَّابِقِيَّةُ *The mode of disposing the turban without winding* [*a portion thereof*] *beneath the chin:* (O, Ḳ:) a mode which is forbidden. (O.) جَآءَ فُلَانٌ مُتَعَمِّمًا طَابِقِيًّا means *Such a one came having his turban disposed in the manner above described.* (IAạr, O.)

مُطْبِقٌ: see مُطْبَقٌ.

مُطْبَقٌ [pass. part. n. of 4, *Covered;* &c.]. — الحُرُوفُ المُطْبَقَةُ are *The letters* ص, ض, ط, and ظ: (Ṣ, O, Ḳ:) the part of the tongue which is the place of their utterance being [closely] covered [in their utterance] by what is opposite to it of the palate. (O, TA.) — And مُطْبَقٌ is used by the vulgar for مُطْبَقٌ عَلَيْهِ, [which is for مُطْبَقٌ عَلَيْهِ الجُنُونُ,] meaning † *Upon whom insanity is made to be continual:* (Mṣb: see also طَبَاقَآءُ [where مُطْبَقٌ عَلَيْهِ is in my opinion better rendered]:) and you say مَجْنُونَةٌ مُطْبَقٌ عَلَيْهَا [in like manner, for مُطْبَقٌ عَلَيْهَا الجُنُونُ † *an insane female whose reason insanity has veiled,* or *wholly obscured*]. (Mgh, O.) —— مُطْبَقٌ عَلَيْهِ signifies also *Affected with a swooning,* or *a fit of insensibility.* (TA.) —— بَيْتٌ مُطْبَقٌ means † *A verse of which the former hemistich ends in the middle of a word.* (Z, TA.) —— See also the next paragraph. —— And see طَبَقٌ.

مُطْبِقٌ *Covering.* (O, Ḳ, TA.) —— Hence, (Ḳ, TA,) جُنُونٌ مُطْبِقٌ (Mgh, O, Ḳ, TA) † *Insanity that covers* [i. e. *veils,* or *wholly obscures,*] *the reason,* or *intellect.* (TA.) —— حُمَّى مُطْبِقَةٌ (Ṣ, Mgh, O, Mṣb, Ḳ) ‡ *A continual fever, not quitting night nor day.* (Ṣ, Mṣb,* TA.) —— مُطْبِقَةٌ [for سَنَةٌ مُطْبِقَةٌ] means ‡ *A hard,* or *severe, year.* (TA.) And مُطْبِقَاتٌ means † *Calamities* [like بَنَاتُ طَبَقٍ]. (TA.) —— And مُطْبِقٌ may have the same meaning as ▼ مُطْبَقٌ. (TA. [But in what sense the latter is here used is not specified.]) —— It signifies also *A subterranean prison;* or *a place of confinement beneath the ground.* (TA. [The word in this sense, which is probably post-classical, is there said to be like مُحْسِنٌ; but perhaps only because of its having been found written مُطْبِقٌ; for I think that I have heard ▼ مُطْبَقٌ used in this sense; and I find an apparent authority for this in a copy of the M in arts. اصد and وصد, where الإِصَادُ and الوِصَادُ are expl. as meaning المُطْبَقُ: and likewise in the TA in art. رهن, where I find مُطْبَقٌ, thus written; see 2 in that art.: it seems also that ▼ طِبَاقٌ may have the same signification; for I find الإِصَادُ expl. as meaning الطِّبَاقُ in the Ḳ in art. اصد; and thus in the O in art. وصد, and likewise الوِصَادُ.])

مُطَبَّقٌ: see طَبَقٌ, last quarter.

جَرَادٌ مُطَبِّقٌ *Locusts extending in common* or *universally* [*over a tract* or *region*]. (TA.) And سَحَابَةٌ مُطَبِّقَةٌ *A cloud raining upon the whole of a land.* (Ṣ, O.) —— مُطَبِّقٌ signifies also [A sword *hitting the joint, and severing the limb:* or *falling between two bones.* —— And hence,] ‡ One *who takes the right course in affairs by his* [*good*] *judgment.* (Ḳ, TA.)

مُطَابِقٌ: see an ex. voce طَبَقٌ.

طبل

1. طَبَلَ, (Lth, O, Mṣb, Ḳ,) aor. ـِ (Lth, O, Mṣb) and ـُ, (Mṣb,) inf. n. طَبْلٌ, *He beat the* طَبْل [or *drum; he drummed*]; (Lth, O, Mṣb, Ḳ;) and ▼ طَبَّلَ, (Mṣb, Ḳ,) inf. n. تَطْبِيلٌ, (O, Mṣb,) signifies the same; (O,* Ḳ;) or the latter verb signifies *he did so much.* (Mṣb.)

2: see the preceding paragraph.

طَبْلٌ [*A drum;*] *a certain thing with which one beats,* (Ṣ, O, Ḳ,) [or rather *upon which one beats,*] *well known,* (Mṣb,) *having a single face,* and *having two faces:* (Mṣb, Ḳ:) pl. [of mult.] طُبُولٌ (O, Mṣb, Ḳ) and [of pauc.] أَطْبَالٌ. (Mṣb, Ḳ.) [Hence] one says, هُوَ طَبْلٌ ذُو وَجْهَيْنِ [lit. *He is a double-faced drum*]; meaning ‡ *he is of ill-omened,* or *hard, aspect.* (TA.) And فُلَانٌ يَضْرِبُ الطَّبْلَ تَحْتَ الكِسَآءِ [lit. *Such a one beats the drum beneath the* garment called كساء; meaning, † *strives to conceal what is notorious:* similar to the Pers. saying طَبْل دَرْ زِيرِ گِلِيم زَدَنْ]. (TA.) —— Also *A* رَبْعَة [or *small round basket, covered with leather,*] *for perfumes.* (TA.) And *A* سَلَّة [or *round basket*] *for food,* [app. *shallow, resembling a round tray,* for it is said to be] *like the* خِوَان; also called ▼ طَبْلِيَّة, of which the pl. is طَبَالِىّ. (TA. [See also سَدٌّ, last sentence.]) [And *A kind of tray, of wood, used for counting money, &c.;* also called ▼ طَبْلَة: this is app. what is meant by the saying in the Ṣ, طَبْلُ الدَّرَاهِمِ وَغَيْرِهَا مَعْرُوفٌ; and by the saying in the O, طَبْلَةُ الدَّرَاهِمِ مَعْرُوفٌ.] —— And *A certain sort of garments,* or *cloths,* (Lth, IDrd, O, Ḳ,*) *upon which is the form of the* طَبْل [or *drum*], (Lth, O, Ḳ,) or *figured with the like of* طُبُول [or *drums*], (T, TA,) *of the fabric of El-Yemen,* or *of Egypt,* (Ḳ,) or *brought from Egypt, and called also* ▼ الطَّبْلِيَّة and أَرْدِيَةُ الطَّبْلِ: (Lth, O:) which last appellation is expl. in the A as meaning [*garments of the kind called*] بُرُود, *worn by the lords,* or *principal personages, of Egypt.* (TA.) —— And The [*tax called*] خَرَاج: (IAạr, O, Ḳ:) [or *an instalment* thereof; for] one says, أَدَّى أَهْلُ مِصْرَ طَبْلًا مِنَ الخَرَاجِ and طَبْلَيْنِ and طُبُولًا *The people of Egypt payed an instalment of the* خراج [and *two instalments* and several *instalments*]; so called after the طَبْل [or drum] of the بُنْدَار [app. meaning the farmer-general of the tax, who, it seems from this, announced his coming by the beating of a drum]: (A, TA:) [and probably syn. with خَرَاج as meaning *revenue* in a general sense; for it is added,] hence [the saying] هُوَ يُحِبُّ ▼ الطَّبْلِيَّةَ (O, Ḳ [in the CḲ تَحْتَ is erroneously put for يُحِبُّ]) i. e. *He loves the* خَرَاج, (O,) or *the money of the* خَرَاج, (Ḳ,) *without fatigue.* (O.) ═ الطَّبْلُ signifies also الخَلْقُ and النَّاسُ [i. e. *The created beings* in general and *mankind* in particular]: one says, مَا أَدْرِى أَىُّ الطَّبْلِ هُوَ i. e. [*I know not*] *what one of mankind he is:* (Ṣ, O:) and so أَىُّ الطَّبْنِ هُوَ. (TA.)

طَبْلَةٌ [*A wooden tray;* generally *round:* like طَبْلَه in Persian. And such is app. meant by what here follows:] *A certain thing of wood, which women take for their use.* (TA.) See also طَبْلٌ.

طَبْلِيَّةٌ: see طَبْلٌ, in three places.

طِبَالَةٌ *The art,* or *occupation, of beating the* طَبْل [or *drum*]. (Mṣb, Ḳ.)

طَبَّالٌ [*A drummer;*] *a beater of the* طَبْل. (O, Ḳ.*)

طَبَّالَةٌ [fem. of طَبَّالٌ: —— and] *i. q.* طُوبَالَةٌ, q. v.

طُوبَالَةٌ *A ewe;* (Ṣ, O, Ḳ;) as also ▼ طَبَّالَةٌ: (TA:) pl. of the former طُوبَالَاتٌ: a ram is not to be called طُوبَالٌ. (Ṣ, Ḳ.) Ṭarafeh says,

* نَعَانِى حَنَانَةُ طُوبَالَةً *
* تَسَفُّ يَبِيسًا مِنَ العِشْرِقِ *

[*Ḥanáneh announced to me death* (app. meaning *predicted my death,* for otherwise it should be نَعَى لِى): *a ewe that eats dry 'ishriḳ*]: (Ṣ, O, TA:) [in explanation of which it is said,] نَعَانِى means أَخْبَرَنِى بِالمَوْتِ: and حَنَانَةُ is the name of a pastor: and طوبالة is put in the accus. case as a term of revilement, as though the poet said أَعْنِى طُوبَالَةً. (TA.)

طبن

1. طَبِنَ لَهُ, aor. ـَ, inf. n. طَبَنٌ [accord. to the CḲ طَبْنٌ, which is wrong]; and طَبَنَ له, aor. ـُ, inf. n. طَبَانَةٌ and طَبَانِيَةٌ and طُبُونَةٌ; *He understood it;* or *knew it;* or *had knowledge,* or *was cognizant, of it:* (Ṣ, Ḳ:) some say that طَبِنَ relates to good, and تَبِنَ to evil; but AO says that طَبَانَةٌ and تَبَانَةٌ are one, meaning the *being very intelligent* or *knowing;* and Lḥ says that طَبَانَةٌ and طَبَانِيَةٌ, and تَبَانَةٌ and تَبَانِيَةٌ, and لَقَانَةٌ and لَقَانِيَةٌ, and لَحَانَةٌ and لَحَانِيَةٌ [app. mistranscriptions for لَكَانَةٌ and لَكَانِيَةٌ], are one [in meaning]. (TA. [See more in the first paragraph of art. تبن.]) —— طَبِنَ لَهَا, in which the pronoun refers to a woman, a phrase occurring in a trad., is expl. as meaning *He apprehended what was the state,* or *disposition, of her mind, and that she was one who would comply with the endeavour to seduce her:* or, accord. to Sh, it is طَبَنَ لَهَا, like ضَرَبَ, and means *he deceived her,* or *corrupted her, and beguiled her:* accord. to Az, طَبِنْتُ بِهِ, aor. ـَ, inf. n. طَبَانَةٌ; and طَبَنْتُ, aor. ـُ, inf. n. طَبْنٌ; signify *I deceived him,* or *deluded him.* (TA.) —— And طَبَانِيَةٌ, accord. to IB, signifies also A man's *looking at his wife, and either debarring her from appearing* or *being angry and jealous.* (TA.) ═ طَبَنَ النَّارَ, (Ṣ, Ḳ,) aor. ـُ, (Ḳ, TA, [in the CḲ ـِ,]) inf. n. طَبْنٌ, (Ḳ,) *He covered the fire* [*in a hollow*] *in the earth, in order that it might not become extinguished.* (Ṣ, Ḳ.)

3. طَابِنْ هٰذِهِ الحُفْرَةَ (Ṣ) or الحَفِيرَةَ (Ḳ) means *Lower thou* [or *deepen thou*] *this hollow in the ground* [app. for fire to be covered over therein; see 1, last sentence]; syn. طَامِنْهَا and طَأْطِئْهَا. (The former syn. in some copies of the Ṣ and Ḳ; the latter in other copies of the Ṣ; and both in

some copies of the Ḳ.) —— And طَابَنَ ظَهْرَهُ *He lowered, or bent down, his back;* syn. طَامَنَهُ. (TA.) ═ And طَابَنَهُ, (Ḳ,) inf. n. مُطَابَنَةٌ and طِبَانٌ, (TA,) *He, or it, agreed,* or *accorded, with him, or it.* (Ḳ.)

Q. Q. 4. اِطْبَأَنَّ *i. q.* اِطْمَأَنَّ; (Ṣ, Ḳ;) formed from the latter by substitution [of ب for م]. (Ṣ in art. طمن.) So in the phrase اِطْبَأَنَّ قَلْبُهُ, meaning *His heart became quiet, at rest, at ease,* or *tranquil.* (TA.)

طَبْنٌ *A numerous collection* or *body* (Ḳ, TA) *of men;* (TA;) as also ↓ طِبْنٌ. (Ḳ, TA. [Freytag adds طِبْنٌ and طُبْنٌ in this sense; but they are mentioned in the Ḳ as syns. of طَبْنٌ meaning a certain game: and Golius adds, instead of these two, طِبِنٌ and طُبُنٌ, which are altogether wrong.]) —— And one says, مَا أَدْرِى أَىُّ الطَّبْنِ هُوَ, (Ṣ, Ḳ,*) meaning أَىُّ النَّاسِ هُوَ [i. e. *I know not what one of mankind he is*]: (Ṣ, Ḳ:) and so أَىُّ الطَّبْلِ هُوَ. (Ṣ and O in art. طبل.) ═ Also, [and it is implied in the Ḳ that the following explanation applies likewise to ↓ طَبَنٌ and ↓ طِبْنٌ and ↓ طُبْنٌ, but the TA restricts it to طَبْنٌ,] *A carcass which is placed for the purpose of capturing upon it the vultures and beasts of prey.* (Ḳ, TA. [Freytag assigns this meaning to طَبْنٌ only.]) ═ See also طَبْنَةٌ.

طِبْنٌ The [*kind of mandoline called*] طُنْبُور: (IAạr, Ḳ:) or the عُود [i. e. *lute*]. (Ḳ.) —— See also طَبْنَةٌ. —— And see طَبْنٌ.

طُبْنٌ : see طَبْنَةٌ: —— and see also طَبْنٌ. —— الطُّبْنُ also signifies *What the wind brings,* [or *bears along,*] *of firewood* [app. meaning of fragments thereof], and الثُّمْش: [but this seems to be a mistranscription; for it is immediately added,] and sometimes *the house* (البيت) *that is built,* or *constructed, therewith* is thus called. (TA.)

طَبَنٌ : see طَبْنٌ: ═ and see also طَبْنَةٌ.

طَبِنٌ and ↓ طَابِنٌ *Intelligent, understanding, skilled,* or *knowing,* (Ṣ, Ḳ,* TA,) *in everything:* (TA:) the former is syn. with تَبِنٌ [q. v.]: (M in art. تبن:) and ↓ طُبُنَّةٌ signifies [*very intelligent* &c., being of a measure proper to intensive epithets; or simply] *skilled,* or *skilful.* (TA.) ═ And for the first of these words (طَبِنٌ), see also طَبْنَةٌ.

طُبَنٌ : see طَبْنَةٌ: ═ and see also طَبْنٌ.

طَبْنَةٌ, (Ṣ,) or ↓ طَبْنٌ and ↓ طِبْنٌ and ↓ طُبْنٌ, (Ḳ) and ↓ طَبَنٌ and ↓ طَبِنٌ (TA) and ↓ طُبَنٌ, (Ḳ,) or this last is pl. of طُبْنَةٌ, (Ṣ, TA,) *A certain game,* (Ṣ, Ḳ, TA,) [said to be] *played by children, by means of a circular line,* [*drawn on the ground,* (but see what follows,)] and [also] called by them الرَّحَى; (TA;) *called in Pers.* سِهْ بَرَه, or سِيدَرَه, (accord. to different copies of the Ṣ,) or سِدَرَه, (accord. to some copies of the Ḳ, and the TA, [this and سِيدَرَه being app. for سِهْ دَرَه, which is syn. with سِهْ بَرَه,] in a MS. copy of the Ḳ سَدْ مَرَه, and in the CḲ سد مرّه, [both app. mistranscriptions for سِهْ بَرَه,]) i. e. "having three doors;" (TA;) [app. the same that is sometimes called in Pers. سِهْ دَرَك;] the game that is called in Turkish طوقورجون [and طُوقُرْجُن], and in Arabic called also قرق; (TḲ;) [i. e. قِرْق, which is said in the Ḳ and TA in art. قرق to be the *game called* سُدَّر; accord. to an explanation and diagram there given, *played by means of twenty-four lines, composed of four squares,* or *parallelograms, one of these having within it another, the latter having within it another, and this last having within it another; to which are added a line drawn from each angle of the outermost of these to the corresponding angle of the innermost and another line drawn from the middle of each side of the outermost to the middle of the corresponding side of the innermost; within which combination of twenty-four lines they place* (يَضَعُونَ, in the CḲ يَصْفُونَ,) *pebbles.* سُدَّر is evidently from the Pers. سِهْ دَرَه: it is said in the TA in art. سدر to be also pronounced سِدَّر and سُدَّر, and to be a Pers. term arabicized. Golius, without mentioning any other authority than that of the Ḳ, explains طُبَنٌ as follows: "*Pers.* سَدَرَه, *Turc.* دُقُرْجُن اُويُنِى, *Græc.* τριώδιον, Trium, *vel* novem, scruporum ludus." Freytag explains the same word as meaning "Triodii seu trivalli ludus;" adding a loose rendering of the explanation of قِرْق in the Ḳ.] ═ طَبْنَةٌ signifies also The *sound of the* [*musical instrument called*] طُنْبُر. (IAạr, Ḳ.)

طَبَانَةٌ *Intelligence, understanding, skill,* or *knowledge:* (Ṣ, Ḳ:) pl. طِبَنٌ. (Ḳ.)

طُبُنَّةٌ : see طَبِنٌ.

طُبَأْنِينَةٌ *i. q.* طُمَأْنِينَةٌ [q. v.]. (TA.)

طَابِنٌ : see طَبِنٌ.

طَابُونٌ *A place in which fire is covered* [*in a hollow*] *in the earth, in order that it may not become extinguished:* (Ṣ, Ḳ:) pl. طَوَابِينُ. (TA.)

مُطْبَئِنٌّ *i. q.* مُطْمَئِنٌّ [q. v.]. (Ṣ.)

طبو

1. طَبَاهُ, (Ṣ, Ḳ,) aor. يَطْبُوهُ, (Ṣ,) inf. n. طَبْوٌ; (Ḳ;) and طَبَاهُ, aor. يَطْبِيهِ, (Ṣ, TA,) inf. n. طَبْىٌ; (TA in art. طبى;) *He called him:* (Ṣ, Ḳ:) or, accord. to Sh, *he called him with a gentle calling:* (TA:) an ex. of the latter verb occurs in a verse of Dhu-r-Rummeh cited voce ضَارِبٌ, (Ṣ,) or, as Lḥ cited that verse, an ex. of the former verb: (TA:) and ↓ اِطَّبَاهُ, (Sh, Ṣ, Ḳ, [in the CḲ erroneously written اَطْبَاهُ,]) of the measure اِفْتَعَلَهُ, (Ṣ,) signifies the same. (Sh, Ṣ, Ḳ.) And [hence] one says, لَا أَدْرِى مِنْ أَيْنَ اطبيت, [a mistranscription for طُبِيتَ,] with ḍamm, and اطّبيت, [i. e. ↓ اُطُّبِيتَ,] meaning [*I know not whence thou hast been called;* or] *whence thou hast come.* (TA in art. طبى.)

8: see 1, in two places. —— One says also اِطَّبَى بَنُو فُلَانٍ فُلَانًا, (Ṣ, Ḳ, TA, [in the CḲ, erroneously, اَطْبَى,]) *The sons of such a one associated as friends with such a one and slew him:* (Ṣ, Ḳ, TA:) and اِطَّبَيْتُهُ *I acted with him as a friend, then I slew him.* (IḲṭṭ, TA.) —— اِطَّبَى القُلُوبَ, in a trad. of Ibn-Ez-Zubeyr, means *He showed love,* or *affection, to the hearts* [of others], *and drew them near to him.* (TA.) And اِطَّبَاهُ signifies also *He attracted him to himself;* or *sought to make him incline.* (TA.)

[طباة (thus written without any vowel-sign) is said in the TA, in art. طبى, to signify أَحْمَقُ (i. e. *Stupid,* &c.): but I think it probable that this is from a mistranscription for طَبَّاةٌ, properly meaning "a hyena;" a beast proverbial for stupidity: see ضَبُعٌ.]

طَبْوَاءُ : see طُبْيَةٌ, in the next art.

طبى

1. طَبَيْتُهُ عَنْهُ, (Ṣ, Ḳ,) aor. أَطْبِيهِ, inf. n. طَبْىٌ, (TA,) *I turned him away,* or *back, from it,* (Lth, Ṣ, Ḳ, TA,) namely, his opinion, and his affair, &c. (Lth, TA.) —— And طَبَيْتُهُ إِلَيْهِ *I called him to it;* as also ↓ اِطَّبَيْتُهُ [in the CḲ erroneously written اَطْبَيْتُهُ]. (Ḳ, TA. See also art. طبو.) —— And طَبَيْتُهُ *I led him.* (Ḳ, TA.) And thus Lḥ explains the ex. of this verb in the verse of Dhu-r-Rummeh cited voce ضَارِبٌ. (TA.) ═ طَبِيَتْ, aor. ـَ, inf. n. طَبًى; (TA;) or طَبِيَتْ طَبًى شَدِيدًا; (Ḳ; [in the CḲ, erroneously, طَبْيًا;]) said of a she-camel, *Her* طُبْى [q. v.] *was,* or *became, flaccid, flabby,* or *pendulous;* (TA;) or *very flaccid* &c.; (Ḳ;) on the authority of Fr. (TA.)

8: see the preceding paragraph: and see also the same verb in art. طبو.

طُبْىٌ (Ṣ, Mgh, Mṣb, Ḳ, &c.) and ↓ طِبْىٌ (Ṣ, Ḳ) [*A teat,* or *dug, of any of certain animals mentioned in what follows;* agreeably with an explanation of its pl. in the O, voce ضَرْعٌ, on the authority of AZ; and agreeably with a usage of its pl. in the TA, voce خِلْفٌ, on the authority of Lth: this is the most usual, if not the only proper, signification:] the ضَرْع [which sometimes means the *teat,* or *dug,* and is app. here used in this sense]; mostly, *of a beast of prey:* (Mgh:) or it is *to the beast of prey, and to the solid-hoofed animal,* (Aṣ, T, Ṣ,) *like the* ضَرْع *to others;* and sometimes *to the camel;* (Ṣ;) or that of the camel and of the cloven-hoofed animal is termed خِلْفٌ: (Aṣ, T:) or, *to the camel,* and *to the cloven-hoofed animal, like the* ثَدْى [which sometimes means the *teat*] *to the woman;* and in rare instances, *to the solid-hoofed animal,* and *to the beast of prey:* (Mṣb:) or the حَلَمَات [meaning *teats*], (Ḳ, TA,) or, accord. to the M, the حَلَمَتَانِ [meaning *pair of teats*], (TA,) *of the* ضَرْع [or *udder*], *of the camel,* and *of a cloven-hoofed animal,* and *of a solid-hoofed animal,* and *of a beast of prey:* (Ḳ:) [and ↑ طُبْيَةٌ is perhaps a dial. var.: (see خَاتِمٌ, last sentence but two:)] pl. أَطْبَآءٌ. (Ṣ, Mgh, Mṣb, Ḳ.) It is said in a prov., (Ṣ,) [and] in a letter of 'Othmán to 'Alee, (TA,) جَاوَزَ الحِزَامُ الطُّبْيَيْنِ (Ṣ, Ḳ) *The girth passed beyond the* طُبْيَان [or *two teats,* or *two pairs of teats*]; (TA;) meaning † *the affair,* or *case, became distressing,* and *formidable.* (Ḳ, TA.) — El-Ḥoseyn Ibn-Muṭeyr uses the pl. metaphorically in relation to rain, by way of comparison, saying,

كَثُرَتْ كَكَثْرَةِ وَبْلِهِ أَطْبَاؤُهُ *
فَإِذَا تَجَلَّتْ فَاضَتِ الأَطْبَآءُ *

[in which, for تَجَلَّتْ, I read تَحَلَّبَ; for the verse, literally rendered, seems to mean, ‡ *Its teats were abundant as the abundance of its heavy rain,* (or rather I would read لِكَثْرَةِ وبله *by reason of the abundance* &c.,) *so that when it flowed* with rain, as though it were milked, *the teats poured forth exuberantly*]. (TA.) — أَطْبَآءُ الكَلْبَةِ † [*Bitch's dugs*] is an appellation of *the tree called* مُخَاطَة [i. e. *the sebesten*]. (TA in art. مخط, q. v.)

طِبْىٌ : } see the next preceding paragraph.
طُبْيَةٌ : }

طَبِيَةٌ, like فَرِحَةٌ, on the authority of Fr, in the Ḳ erroneously written طَبْيَةٌ, (TA,) [and also there misplaced, for, with قَبِىَ (in the CḲ قَبُوَ) preceding it, it should follow immediately after the explanation of the phrase طَبِيَتِ النَّاقَةُ, being the part. n., and thus signifying *Whose* طُبْى *is flaccid, flabby,* or *pendulous,*] applied to a she-camel; (Fr, TA;) and طَبْوَآءُ signifies the same; (Fr, Ḳ, TA;) or this is applied to a she-goat, meaning *whose dugs* (أَخْلَافُهَا) *descend towards the ground.* (So in one of my copies of the Ṣ: in the other copy omitted.)

خِلْفٌ طَبِىٌّ *i. q.* مُجِيبٌ [meaning *Yielding milk*]; (Ṣ, Ḳ; [thus in my copies of the Ṣ, and in copies of the Ḳ; but said in the TA to be written in the Ḳ and in the copies of the Ṣ, مُجَيَّبٌ, which is evidently wrong;]) as though called, and answering the call. (JM.)

طجن

1. طَجْنٌ The act of *frying:* (Ḳ:) an adventitious word in the Arabic language. (TA.) You say, طَجَنَ الشَّىْءَ, aor. ـُ, inf. n. طَجْنٌ, *He fried the thing.* (TḲ.)

طَاجَنٌ, (Ṣ,) or طَاجِنٌ, (T,) or both, (Mṣb, TA, and in a copy of the Ṣ written طَاجِنٌ,) and ↑ طَيْجَنٌ, (Ṣ, Mṣb, Ḳ,) *A frying-pan;* syn. مِقْلًى; (Mṣb;) *a* طَابَق *upon which one fries:* (Ṣ, Ḳ:) arabicized words, (Ṣ, Mṣb, Ḳ,) because ط and ج do not occur in the original language of the Arabs: (Ṣ, TA:) [app. from the Greek τήγανον:] the pl. of طاجن is طَوَاجِنُ; (Mṣb, TA;) and that of ↑ طيجن is طَيَاجِنُ, (Mṣb,) or طَيَاجِينُ. (MA, TA.)

طَيْجَنٌ: see the next preceding paragraph, in two places.

مُطَجَّنٌ *Fried in a* طاجن. (Ḳ.)

طح

1. طَحَّهُ, aor. ـُ, (Ṣ, O,) inf. n. طَحٌّ, (Ṣ, O, Ḳ,) *He scraped it with his heel so as to remove its superficial part; grazed it with his heel:* (Ṣ, O, Ḳ:*) or *he put his heel upon it and then so scraped it.* (TA.) — And *He spread it,* or *expanded it.* (IDrd, O, K.)

4. اطحّهُ *He made it to fall, threw it down,* or *let it fall:* and *he threw it.* (Fr, O, Ḳ.)

7. انطحّ ‡ *It* (a thing, O) *became spread* or *expanded;* or *it spread,* or *expanded, itself.* (O, Ḳ.)

R. Q. 1. طَحْطَحَ بِهِمْ, (Ṣ, O,) inf. n. طَحْطَحَةٌ and طِحْطَاحٌ, (Ṣ,) *He dispersed,* or *scattered, them,* (Ṣ, O, TA,) *destroying them:* (TA:) or *he dispersed,* or *scattered, them, and overcame them.* (IF, O.) And طَحْطَحَهُ *He dispersed,* or *scattered, it, destroying it:* (Lth, TA:) or *he destroyed it:* (IDrd, O:) and *he broke it:* (Ṣ, O:) or *he broke it, destroying it:* (TA:) and *he dispersed,* or *scattered, it.* (Ṣ, O.) And طَحْطَحَهُمْ, said of time, or fortune, *It destroyed them;* and *dispersed,* or *scattered, them.* (A.) And طَحْطَحَ مَالَهُ *He dispersed,* or *scattered, his property.* (A.) — And طَحْطَحَ *He laughed slightly:* (Ḳ:) or so طَحْطَحَ فِى ضَحِكِهِ; (TA;) which means the same as طَهْلَةَ and كَتْكَتَ (O, TA) and طَخْطَخَ and كَدْكَدَ and كَرْكَرَ. (TA.)

طَحْطَحٌ *i. q.* مَسَاحِجُ [pl. of مَسْحَجٌ and of مِسْحَجٌ: see these two words]. (IAạr, O, Ḳ.)

طَحَّانٌ [*A grinder* of corn &c. *with a mill*] is said by Ks to be of the measure فَعْلَانٌ from [the inf. n.] الطَّحُّ. (O, TA.) [But see art. طحن.]

مَا عَلَى رَأْسِهِ طَحْطَحَةٌ means *There is not upon his head a single hair:* so says AZ: Lḥ says, أَتَانَا وَمَا عَلَيْهِ طَحْطَحَةٌ *He came to us not having upon him anything:* (O:) or the last word in ما عليه طحطحة signifies *anything:* or *any hair.* (Ḳ.) [See also طَحْلَبَةٌ.]

الطُّحْطَاحُ *The lion.* (IDrd, O, Ḳ.)

مِطَحَّةٌ The *hinder part of the hoof of a sheep or goat:* (Lth, IAạr, O, Ḳ:) or *a thing resembling a* فَلْكَة [generally meaning the *whirl of a spindle*], *in its foot, with which it scrapes the ground:* (Th, O, Ḳ:) Lth says that, beneath its hoof, in the place of the مِطَحَّة, is a little bone like the فَلْكَة. (O.)

طحل

1. طَحَلَهُ, (Ṣ, O, Ḳ,) aor. ـَ, inf. n. طَحْلٌ and طَحَلٌ, (Ḳ,) *He hit,* or *hurt, his* طِحَال [or *spleen*]. (Ṣ, O, Ḳ.) = And طَحَلَهُ, (O, Ḳ,) aor. ـَ, (Ḳ,) inf. n. طَحْلٌ, (O,) *He filled it;* (O, Ḳ;) namely, a vessel. (O.) = طَحِلَ, (Ṣ, O, Mṣb, Ḳ,) aor. ـَ, (Mṣb, Ḳ,) inf. n. طَحَلٌ, (Ṣ, O, Mṣb,) *He had a complaint of his* طحال [or *spleen*]: (Ṣ:) or *he became large in his* طحال: (O, Mṣb, Ḳ:) and طُحِلَ, like عُنِىَ, inf. n. طَحْلٌ, [accord. to the CḲ طَحَلٌ,] has the former of these two meanings. (Ḳ, TA.) — And طَحِلَ, (Ḳ, TA,) inf. n. طَحَلٌ, (TA,) *He was,* or *became, of the colour termed* طُحْلَة; said of a wolf; and in like manner one says of a sheep or goat. (Ḳ, TA.) — And طَحِلَ said of water, (Ṣ, O, Ḳ,) as also طَحَلَ, (Ṣ, O,) *It was,* or *became, corrupt,* (Ṣ, O, Ḳ,) *and altered in odour,* (Ṣ, O,) or *stinking, by reason of black mud.* (Ḳ.)

طَحِلٌ *Having his* طحال [or *spleen*] *large,* or *enlarged:* (Mṣb, Ḳ:) or *having pain therein;* as also ↑ مَطْحُولٌ; (O;) or this latter signifies *having a complaint of the* طحال; (TA;) or it signifies, (Ṣ,) or signifies also, (TA,) *hit,* or *hurt, therein.* (Ṣ, TA.) — And † [*Spleenful,* as meaning] *angry.* (IAạr, O, Ḳ.) — And *Black:* (O, Ḳ:) or *of a dusky,* or *dingy, black colour;* (IAạr, TA;) which, Z says, may be from [the colour of] the طحال, or from the meaning of الطُّحْلُبُ: (TA: [see also أَطْحَلُ:]) [for it signifies also] — *Overspread with* [*the green substance termed*] طُحْلُب; (IAạr, O, Ḳ;) or *having much* طحلب; applied to water: (AZ, IAạr,* O,* Mṣb, Ḳ:) and in like manner one says عَيْنٌ طَحِلَةٌ *a source having much* طحلب. (Mṣb.) = Also *Full;* (IAạr, O, Ḳ;) and so ↑ مَطْحُولٌ; applied to a vessel. (Ḳ.)

طُحْلَةٌ *A colour between that of dust and whiteness,* (Ṣ, M, O, TA,) *with a little blackness, like the colour of ashes:* (M, TA:) or *a colour between that of dust and blackness, with a little whiteness.* (Ḳ.)

طِحَالٌ [The *spleen;*] *one of the intestines,* (Mṣb,) or *a piece of flesh,* (Ḳ, TA,) *well known,* (Ṣ, O, Mṣb, Ḳ,) *black,* (or rather *blackish,*] *and broad, in the belly of man and of others, on the left, cleaving to the side,* (TA,) or *cleaving to the ribs on the left side,* (Zj in his "Khalḳ el-Insán,") *and said to pertain to every ruminant except the horse, which has none:* (Mṣb: [a strange assertion, involving a double mistake; partly originating from a saying which will be mentioned in what follows:]) it is of the masc. gender: (Lḥ,

TA:) the pl. is طُحُلٌ (Mṣb, Ḳ, TA) and أَطْحِلَةٌ and طِحَالَاتٌ. (Mṣb. [The second and third of these pls. appear to be rare; for it is said in the TA that the first is the only pl. form: and the last is anomalous.]) One says of the horse, لَا طِحَالَ لَهُ [lit. *He has no spleen*]; which is a metaphor, meaning ‡ *he is quick*, or *swift, in his running*; like as one says of the camel, لَا مَرَارَةَ لَهُ [lit. "he has no gall-bladder"]; meaning "he has no daring." (Ṣ, O.)

طَاحِلٌ: see the next paragraph, in two places.

أَطْحَلُ *Of a colour like that of the* طِحَال [or *spleen*], (Ḥam p. 96, and TA,) thus applied to a [garment of the kind called] كِسَآء, (TA,) and this is said to be the primary signification: or *of the colour of ashes*: (Ḥam ubi suprà:) or *of the colour termed* طُحْلَة expl. above, (Ṣ, O, Ḳ,) thus applied to a wolf, (O, Ḳ,) and thus the fem. طَحْلَآءُ applied to a sheep or goat (شَاة), (Ḳ,) and the masc. applied to ashes (رَمَاد): (Ṣ, O:) also, (Ṣ, O,) and (O) ▼ طَاحِلٌ, (O, Ḳ, [in the CḲ طَحِلٌ, q. v.,]) applied to beverage or wine (شَرَاب), (Ṣ, O, Ḳ,) meaning *not clear*, (Ṣ, O,) or *turbid*; and so ▼ طَاحِلٌ applied to dust (غُبَار), Ḳ, TA, [in the CḲ غُرَاب,] and قَتَام, O and TA). And one says فَرَسٌ أَخْضَرُ أَطْحَلُ meaning *A horse whose* خُضْرَة [i. e. *dingy ash-colour*, or *dark dust-colour*,] *is overspread by a little yellowness*. (Ṣ, O.)

مَطْحُولٌ: see طَحِلَ, first sentence: — and the same, also, last sentence.

طحلب

Q. 1. طَحْلَبَ المَآءُ, (Ṣ, Ḳ, TA,) inf. n. طَحْلَبَةٌ, (KL,) *The water became overspread with the green substance called* طُحْلُب: (Ṣ,* TA:) or *had much thereof*. (Ḳ, TA.) — And طَحْلَبَتِ الأَرْضُ † *The land became green with herbage*: (Ḳ, TA:) or *began to become so*. (TA.) ═ طَحْلَبَ الإِبِلَ *He sheared the camels*. (Ḳ.) — And طَحْلَبَ فُلَانًا *He slew such a one*. (Ḳ.)

طُحْلُبٌ and طُحْلَبٌ (Ṣ, Mṣb, Ḳ) and طِحْلِبٌ (Lḥ, M, Ḳ) *The green substance*, (Ṣ, Ḳ,) or *green slimy substance*, (Mṣb,) *that overspreads water* (Ṣ, Mṣb, Ḳ) *which has become stale*: (Ḳ:) or *what is upon water, resembling the web of the spider*: n. un. with ة. (TA.) [See also عَرْمَض.]

مَا عَلَيْهِ طِحْلِبَةٌ *There is not upon him a hair*. (Ḳ.) [See also طِحْطِحَة.]

عَيْنٌ مُطَحْلِبَةٌ, (Ṣ,) and مَآءٌ مُطَحْلِبٌ (IAạr, Ḳ) and مُطَحْلَبٌ, (Ḳ,) this last anomalous, like مُسْهَبٌ, or originating from the supposition of the verb's being trans., (MF,) *A source*, (Ṣ,) and *water*, (Ḳ,) *overspread with* طُحْلُب, (Ṣ,) or *having much thereof*. (Ḳ.)

طحم

1. طَحَمَهُ, [aor. ـَ,] inf. n. طَحْمٌ, *He filled it*. (TA.)

طَحْمَةٌ (Ṣ, Ḳ) and ▼ طُحْمَةٌ (Ḳ, and thus also in some copies of the Ṣ) and ▼ طِحْمَةٌ (Ḳ) The دُفْعَة [as meaning *tide*, or *rush*,] of a torrent, (Ṣ, Ḳ,) and so [as meaning *tide*] of a valley, (Ḳ,) and so [as meaning *irruption*, or *invasion*,] of night; (Ṣ, Ḳ;) and the *greater*, or *main, part* of a torrent, and of night: (Ṣ:) or the *first* دُفْعَة, and the *greater*, or *main, part*: or the *impulse*, or *driving, of the greater*, or *main, part* [of a torrent]: and accord. to Z, طَحْمَةُ اللَّيْلِ is tropical, and means ‡ *the greater*, or *main, part of the blackness of night*. (TA.) — And ‡ *A company*, or *congregated body*, of men: (Ṣ, A, Ḳ, TA:) or, as in the M, *a rush*, or *rushing body*, of men, *more in number than such as are termed* قَادِيَة, which means *the first that come to one*, or *come upon one*. (TA.) — And طَحْمَةُ الفِتْنَةِ means ‡ The جَوْلَة [or *wheeling about*, or the *defeat, and return to fight*,] *of men on the occasion of* فِتْنَة [i. e. *conflict and faction*, or *the like*]. (TA.) ═ See also طَحْمَآء.

طُحْمَةٌ: } see the next preceding paragraph.
طِحْمَةٌ: }

طُحَمَةٌ A man *vehement in conflict*. (Ṣ, Ḳ.) ═ And *Numerous camels*. (Ḳ.)

طَحْمَآءُ *A species of plant*, (Ṣ, Ḳ,) *growing in plain*, or *soft, land, of the kind called* حَمْض: (TA:) or *i. q.* نَجِيل, (AḤn, Ḳ, TA,) *which is the best of all the* حَمْض, [*herbaceous*, i. e.] *not having wood fit for fuel nor such as is fit for carpentry, and eaten by the camels*; (AḤn, TA;) as also ▼ طَحْمَة, (Ḳ, TA,) which is said by AḤn to be *of the kind called* حَمْض, *broad in the leaves, and having much juice*. (TA.)

طَحُومٌ *That impels, or propels, much*, or *vehemently*: (Ḳ:) applied to a bow; as also طَحُورٌ: or a bow *of which the arrow is swift*. (TA.)

سُيُولٌ طَوَاحِمُ *i. q.* دَوَافِعُ [i. e. *Torrents pouring as though impelling*, or *propelling, themselves*]. (TA.)

مَطْحُومٌ *Filled*. (Ḳ.)

طحن

1. طَحَنَ البُرَّ, aor. ـَ, inf. n. طَحْنٌ, (Ṣ, Mṣb, Ḳ,) said of a man, (Ṣ,) *He ground the wheat*; i. e. *he made the wheat into* دَقِيق [i. e. *flour*]; and so [but app. in an intensive sense] ▼ طَحَّنَهُ. (Ḳ.) — [Hence] one says, طَحَنَهُمْ فَأَهْلَكَهُمْ † [*He crushed them and destroyed them*]. (T and M and Ḳ in art. دمر.) And حَرْبٌ تَطْحَنُ كُلَّ شَيْءٍ † [*A war that crushes every thing*]. (TA. [See also طَحُون.]) And طَحَنَتْهُمُ المَنُونُ † [*Time*, or *death, reduced them to dust*]. (TA.) — And one says also, طَحَنَتِ الرَّحَى [*The mill-stone ground*; or *revolved*]. (Ṣ.) — And [hence,] طَحَنَتِ الأَفْعَى *The viper turned round about*; or *coiled itself*. (Ṣ, Ḳ.*)

2: see the preceding paragraph, first sentence.

طِحْنٌ: see what next follows.

طَحْنٌ *Flour*; (Ṣ, MA, Ḳ;) as also ▼ طَحِينٌ: (MA:) or *ground wheat* and *the like*; [or *meal*;] and sometimes the inf. n., ▼ طَحْنٌ, is used in this sense. (Mṣb.) Hence the prov., أَسْمَعُ جَعْجَعَةً وَلَا أَرَى طِحْنًا [*I hear a sound of the mill*, or *mill-stone, but I see not flour*]. (Ḳ.)

طَحَنٌ *A certain small creeping thing*, (دُوَيْبَّة, Ṣ, Ḳ, TA,) *in form like* [*the species of lizard*, or *reptile, called*] أُمّ حُبَيْن, [see art. حبن,] *but more slender* (أَلْطَف) *than this latter, that raises its tail like as does the pregnant camel, and, when bidden to grind, by the children of the Arabs of the desert, grinds with itself the ground until it becomes concealed in the soft soil; and one never sees it but in a tract of ground such as is termed* بَلُوقَة: Az says that ▼ طُحَنَة signifies *a certain small creeping thing* (دويبّة) *like the* [*beetle called*] جُعَل; and that طُحَن is the pl.: [but, properly speaking, the latter is a coll. gen. n., and the former is the n. un.:] Aṣ says that it is [*a creature*] *smaller than the hedge-hog, that comes into existence in the sands, appearing sometimes, and turning round as though grinding, and then diving* [*into the sand*]: (TA: [see also عَوَّانَة:]) and, (Ḳ,) accord. to Aboo-Kheyreh, (TA,) the طَحَن *is what is called* لَيْثُ عِفِرِّينَ [q. v. in art. عفر], (Ḳ, TA, in the CḲ لَيْثُ عِفْرِينَ,) *resembling the pistachio-nut, in colour like the dust, that buries itself in the earth*. (TA.) — [Hence, app.,] *Short*: (Ḳ:) [or] accord. to Zj, ▼ طُحَنَة signifies *short, having in him* لُوثَة [app. meaning *stupidity*, or *the like*]; and IB says that he who is tall, having in him لوثة, is termed عَشَنَّق: (TA:) accord. to IAạr, *short in the utmost degree*: (Az, TA:) accord. to IKh, the *shortest of the short*; and the tallest of the tall is termed سَمَرْطُول. (TA.)

طُحَنَة: see the next preceding paragraph, in two places.

طَحُونٌ † A war (حَرْب) *that crushes* (تَطْحَنُ) *everything*. (TA.) And [hence] الطَّحُونُ is a name for † *War*. (Az, Ḳ,* TA.) — And [hence also] ‡ *A* كَتِيبَة [or *troop*] *that crushes* (تَطْحَنُ) *what it meets*: (Ṣ, TA:) or *a great* كَتِيبَة: (Ḳ:) or a كَتِيبَة *of horsemen, mighty*, or *valorous, and numerous*. (TA.) — And † *Numerous camels*; as also ▼ طَحَّانَة: (Ṣ, Ḳ:) or both signify *camels when they are* [*many, and are*] *such as are termed* رِفَاق, *and have their owners with them*; (TA;) as also رَطُونٌ and رَطَّانَةٌ: (Aṣ, TA in art. رطن, q. v.:) and the former, *about three hundred sheep or goats*; (Ḳ;) accord. to Lḥ; but ISd says, I know not any other who has mentioned the طحون of sheep or goats. (TA.)

طَحِينٌ and ▼ مَطْحُونٌ (Mṣb, TA) and ▼ مُطْحَنٌ (TA) *Ground* wheat (Mṣb, TA) and the like thereof. (Mṣb.) — For the first, see also طِحْنٌ.

طِحَانَةٌ The *craft*, or *occupation*, *of the* طَحَّان [or *miller*]. (Ḳ.)

طَحِينَةٌ The *dregs of the oil of sesame*. (TA.)

طَحَّانٌ [meaning *A miller*, or *grinder of wheat* and *the like*,] is thus, perfectly decl., if you do not derive it from الطَّحّ: (Ḳ, TA:) i. e. طَحَّان, if you derive it from الطَّحْنُ, is perfectly decl.; but if you derive it from الطَّحّ, or from الطَّحَا which signifies "the expanded tract of land," it is imperfectly decl.: (Ṣ, TA:) if from الطَّحّ, it is of the measure فَعْلَانُ, not فَعَّالٌ; and if from الطَّحَا, it would be by rule طَحْوَانُ. (IB, TA.)

طَحَّانَةٌ: see طَاحُونَةٌ: — and see also طَحُونٌ.

طَاحِنٌ *The bull, of those that tread the wheat, that stands* [الَّتِى تَقُومُ, for which الَّذِى يَقُومُ is erroneously put in the Ḳ and TA,] *in the middle of the heap thereof and around which the other bulls turn:* (Ḳ, TA:) mentioned by En-Naḍr, on the authority of El-Jaạdee. (TA.)

[طَيْحَنٌ, mentioned by Freytag as meaning *A frying-pan* ("*sartago*"), is evidently a mistranscription, for طَيْجَنٌ.]

طَاحِنَةٌ, (Mṣb, TA,) in which the ة is added to give intensiveness to the signification, (Mṣb,) [or to convert the epithet طَاحِنٌ into a subst.,] sing. of طَوَاحِنُ, (Mṣb, TA,) which signifies The أَضْرَاس [as meaning the *molar teeth*, or *grinders*,] (Ṣ, Mṣb, Ḳ, TA) of a man and of others; as being likened to a mill. (TA.)

طَاحُونٌ: see what next follows.

طَاحُونَةٌ *A mill:* (Ṣ, Mṣb, Ḳ:) [also called in the present day ▼ طَاحُونٌ: and the same meaning is assigned by Golius and Freytag, by the latter as on the authority of the Ḳ, (in which I do not find it,) to ▼ مَطْحَنَةٌ, pl. مَطَاحِنُ; and by Golius to ▼ مِطْحَانٌ likewise:] or *a mill that is turned by water;* (Lth, MA, Mgh;) as also ▼ طَحَّانَةٌ: (Lth, Mgh, TA:) or this signifies *a mill that is turned by a beast* [as طاحونة and طاحون do in the present day]: (MA, Mgh:) pl. of the first طَوَاحِينُ. (Mṣb, TA.)

[مَطْحَنَةٌ is said by Golius, as on the authority of the KL, (in which however I do not find it,) to signify *A place where grinding is performed.*]

مَطْحَنَةٌ: see طَاحُونَةٌ.

مُطْحَنٌ: see طَحِينٌ.

مِطْحَانٌ A viper *turning round about;* or *coiling itself.* (Ṣ, Ḳ.) A poet says,

* بِخَرْسَآءَ مِطْحَانٍ كَأَنَّ فَحِيحَهَا *
* إِذَا فَزِعَتْ مَآءٌ هُرِيقَ عَلَى جَمْرِ *

[*With a coiling viper, as though its hissing, when it is frightened, were* the sound of *water poured upon live coals*]. (Ṣ, TA.) — See also طَاحُونَةٌ.

مَطْحُونٌ: see طَحِينٌ. — Also ‡ *Milk:* so called as being likened to corn ready-ground, and fit for food. (L in art. مسد.)

طحى and طحو

1. طَحَا, aor. يَطْحُو, inf. n. طَحْوٌ; and طَحَى, aor. يَطْحَى, inf. n. طَحْىٌ; two dial. vars., though only طَحَى, like سَعَى, is mentioned in the Ḳ; (TA;) *He spread* [a thing]; *spread* [it] *out*, or *forth; expanded* [it]; or *extended* [it]. (Ḳ, TA.) You say, طَحَوْتُهُ, like دَحَوْتُهُ, i. e. *I spread it;* &c. (Ṣ.) — And you say, الْقَوْمُ يَطْحَى بَعْضُهُمْ بَعْضًا *The people*, or *party, repel one another.* (TA.) ═ طَحَى, (Ḳ,) or طَحَا, (TA,) also signifies *It*, or *he, became spread, spread out* or *forth, expanded*, or *extended;* (Ḳ, TA;) being intrans. as well as trans. (TA.) Accord. to Aṣ, (TA,) طَحَا مِنَ الضَّرْبَةِ means *He became extended* (Ṣ, TA) *upon the ground* (TA) *in consequence of the blow:* (Ṣ, TA:) [and this is probably meant by what here follows:] طَحَا is said when one throws down a man upon his face; (Ḳ, TA;) or when he spreads, or extends, him; or when he prostrates him on the ground: (TA:) but accord. to Fr, one says, ▼ شَرِبَ حَتَّى طَحَّى i. e. [*He drank until*] *he stretched out his legs:* and ▼ طَحَّى الْبَعِيرُ إِلَى الْأَرْضِ i. e. *The camel stuck to the ground,* either from emptiness or from emaciation: and in like manner one says of a man when people call him to aid or to do an act of kindness: the verb being in all these instances with teshdeed: as though, by saying this, he contradicted Aṣ as to its being without teshdeed. (TA.) Accord. to AA, (Ṣ,) طَحَيْتُ means *I lay*, or *lay upon my side*, or *laid my side upon the ground.* (Ṣ, Ḳ.*) And you say, ▼ نَامَ فُلَانٌ فَتَطَحَّى i. e. [*Such a one slept, and*] *lay*, or *lay upon his side, in a wide space of ground.* (TA.) — Also, i. e. طَحَا, (AA, Ṣ,) or طَحَى, (Ḳ,) *He* (a man, AA, Ṣ) *went away into the country*, or *in the land:* (AA, Ṣ, Ḳ:) like طَبَا. (Ṣ in art. طبو.) One says, مَا أَدْرِى أَيْنَ طَحَا [*I know not whither he has gone away* &c.]. (Ṣ.) And طَحَا بِهِ قَلْبُهُ *His heart carried him away* (ذَهَبَ بِهِ) in [the pursuit of] anything: (Ṣ, Ḳ:) whence the saying of Alḳameh Ibn-'Abadeh,

* طَحَا بِكَ قَلْبٌ فِى الْحِسَانِ طَرُوبُ *
* بُعَيْدَ الشَّبَابِ عَصْرَ حَانَ مَشِيبُ *

[*A heart much affected with emotion has carried thee away in the pursuit of the beauties long after youthfulness, in the time when entering upon hoariness has arrived:* بُعَيْدَ being here a dim. used for the purpose of enhancement]. (Ṣ, TA.) And طَحَى بِكَ هَمُّكَ *Thy anxiety has carried thee away in a far-extending course.* (TA.) And طَحَى بِالْكُرَةِ *He threw the ball.* (TA.) And طَحَى بِفُلَانٍ شَحْمُهُ *Such a one became fat.* (TA.) — طَحَا, aor. يَطْحُو, signifies also *He*, or *it, was* or *became, distant*, or *remote.* (Ḳ.)

2: see 1, former half, in two places.

5: see 1, latter half.

طَحًا *An expanded tract of land.* (Ṣ, Ḳ.) ═ [And the same word, app., written in the TA طحى, is there expl. as meaning The *lower*, or *baser*, or the *lowest*, or *basest*, of mankind, or of the people.]

طَحْيَةٌ *A portion* of clouds; as also طُحْيَةٌ. (Ḳ.)

أَقْبَلَ التَّيْسُ فِى طَحْيَائِهِ is expl. by AZ as meaning [The *he-goat came*] *in his state of rattling at rutting-time* (فِى هَبِيبِهِ). (TA. [But probably the right expression is فِى طَخْيَائِهِ: see طَخْيَآء.])

طَحَّانٌ as derived from الطَّحَا: see طَحَّانٌ, in art. طحن.

طَاحٍ *Spread; spread out*, or *forth; expanded;* or *extended.* (Ṣ,* Ḳ. [See also مُطَحٍّ.]) And *That has filled everything by its multitude:* (Ḳ, TA:) in this sense [or in the former sense as is implied in the Ṣ] applied to an army. (TA.) And one says مِظَلَّةٌ طَاحِيَةٌ and ▼ مَطْحُوَّةٌ and ▼ مَطْحِيَّةٌ, meaning *A great* (T, Ḳ, TA) *spreading* (TA) *tent.* (T, Ḳ,* TA.) And الْمُدَوِّمَةُ الطَّوَاحِى The vultures *that circle* [*in the sky*] *around the bodies of the slain.* (Ṣ, TA.) — Also *High, elevated*, or *lofty:* so in the phrase لَا وَالْقَمَرِ الطَّاحِى [*No, by the high moon*]; an oath of some of the Arabs. (TA.) [And *Tall* as applied to a horse: so طاحى is expl. in the TA; but this, being without the article ال, is a mistake for طَاحٍ.] — And *A great congregated body of men.* (IAạr, Ḳ.)

مَطْحُوَّةٌ: / مَطْحِيَّةٌ: } see the next preceding paragraph.

مُطَحٍّ *Spread, expanded*, or *extended;* [like طَاحٍ;] or *thrown down upon his face;* or *lying, and stretching himself, upon his face, on the ground.* (TA.) And *Cleaving*, or *sticking, to the ground.* (TA.) And بَقْلَةٌ مُطَحِّيَةٌ *A herb*, or *leguminous plant, growing upon the surface of the earth,* (Ḳ, TA,) *having spread itself upon it.* (TA.)

طخى and طخو

1. طَخَا اللَّيْلُ, [aor. ـُ,] inf. n. طَخْوٌ and طُخُوٌّ; and طَخِىَ [of which the aor. is app. ـَ, and the inf. n. طَخًى]; *The night was*, or *became, dark.* (TA. [The former of these verbs, with the latter of its inf. ns., is mentioned by Golius as on the

authority of J; but I do not find it in either of my copies of the Ṣ.]) — And طَخِىَ, inf. n. طَخًى, *He was,* or *became, foolish, stupid,* or *unsound* [*as though obscured*] *in intellect* or *understanding.* (TA.)

4. أَطْخَتِ السَّمَآءُ *The sky became overspread with* طَخَآء, meaning *clouds,* and *darkness.* (TA.)

طَخًى : see طَخْيَآءُ.

طَخْوَةٌ : see the next paragraph.

طَخْيَةٌ *Darkness;* as also ▼ طُخْيَةٌ and ▼ طِخْيَةٌ: (ISd, Ḳ:) and so ▼ طَخَآءٌ. (TA.) — And *A portion* of clouds; like طَخْيَةٌ: (Ḳ:) or *a thin cloud;* (M, TA;) and so ▼ طَخْوَةٌ: (M, Ḳ, TA: [see also طَخَآءٌ:]) but, (TA,) accord. to Lḥ, one says, مَا فِى السَّمَآءِ طُخْيَةٌ ▼, with ḍamm, meaning *There is not in the sky aught of clouds.* (Ṣ, TA.) — Also *Foolish; stupid,* or *unsound* [*as though obscured*] *in intellect* or *understanding:* pl. طَخْيُونَ. (Az, ISd, Ḳ.)

طُخْيَةٌ : see the next paragraph above, in two places.

طِخْيَةٌ : see طَخْيَةٌ.

طَخْوَآءُ : see the next following paragraph.

طَخْيَآءُ The *darkness of clouds.* (Lth, Mgh, TA.) — And لَيْلَةٌ طَخْيَآءُ (Ṣ,* ISd, Mgh, Ḳ*) *A dark night;* (Ṣ, Ḳ;) as also ▼ لَيْلَةٌ طَخْوَآءُ: (TA:) or *a night intensely dark,* (ISd, Mgh, TA,) *in which the clouds have concealed the moon:* (ISd, TA:) and ▼ لَيْلٌ طَاخٍ and لَيْلٌ طَخًى [app. ▼ طَخًى, as inf. n. used as an epithet,] *dark night:* and لَيَالٍ ▼ طَاخِيَاتٌ *dark nights.* (TA.) — And كَلِمَةٌ طَخْيَآءُ [*A sentence,* or *an expression,*] *not understood.* (Ṣ, Ḳ.*) — And [hence, perhaps,] one says [of a he-goat], كَانَ ذٰلِكَ فِى طَخْيَائِهِ, meaning فِى هِبَابِهِ [i. e. *That was in his state of rattling at rutting-time*]. (JK. [See a similar phrase in art. طحو and طحى; in which طَحْيَائِهِ is probably a mistranscription for طَخْيَائِهِ.])

طَخَآءٌ : see طَخْيَةٌ. — Also *Clouds:* (TA:) or *high,* or *elevated, clouds;* (A'Obeyd, Az, Ṣ, Ḳ;) as also طَهَآءٌ: (TA:) or, accord. to the M, *thin clouds:* [see also طَخْيَةٌ:] and Lth says that ▼ طَخَآءَةٌ مِنْ غَيْمٍ signifies *any round portion of cloud that excludes the light of the moon.* (TA.) — And *Any covering,* or *envelope,* of a thing: one says, عَلَى قَلْبِهِ طَخَآءٌ, and ▼ طَخَآءَةٌ, *Upon his heart is a covering:* (M, TA:) the طَخَآء of the heart is said to be *a covering* thereof *like that of the moon:* (TA:) or طَخَآءٌ signifies كَرْبٌ, (Ḳ,) or the *like thereof,* (Ṣ,) [i. e. *grief,* or *anxiety, that presses heavily,*] upon the heart; (Ṣ, Ḳ;) as in the saying, وَجَدْتُ عَلَى قَلْبِى طَخَآءً [*I experienced, upon my heart, grief,* or *anxiety, that pressed heavily*]: (Ṣ:) or it signifies *heaviness:* or *rancour, malevolence, malice,* or *spite.* (T, TA.)

طَخَآءَةٌ : see the next paragraph above, in two places.

طَاخٍ, and the fem. pl.: see طَخْيَآءُ. You say also ظَلَامٌ طَاخٍ (Ṣ, Ḳ) *Intense darkness;* (Ḳ, TA;) [in like manner] expl. in some of the copies of the Ṣ as meaning حِنْدِسٌ. (TA.)

طدو

دِينٌ طَادٍ, (Ṣ, TA,) the latter word formed by transposition from وَاطِدٌ; (M, TA;) and عَادَةٌ طَادِيَةٌ, (Ṣ, Ḳ,) the latter word said to be formed by transposition from وَاطِدَةٌ, (Ṣ,) *A custom,* or *habit, that is constant, settled,* or *established; old,* or *inveterate.* (Ṣ, Ḳ.) طَادٍ and وَاطِدٌ are also expl. as meaning *Continuous;* or *constant and uninterrupted.* (TA in art. وطد.)

طر

1. طَرَّ, aor. ـُ, (A, Mṣb, TA,) inf. n. طَرٌّ, (Ṣ, A, Mṣb, Ḳ,) *He cut,* or *divided, lengthwise; slit;* or *rent;* (Ṣ, A, Mṣb, Ḳ;) a garment or piece of cloth: (TA:) and *he cut* [in any manner] (Ṣ, A, Ḳ) the same, (A, TA,) or some other thing. (A.) — *He cut off* a man's arm or hand, by a blow, or stroke; (A;) as also ▼ اطرّ; (Ṣ, A, Ḳ;*) and so اترّ. (TA.) *He cut,* or *clipped,* his mustache. (TA.) And one says of a woman, تَطُرُّ شَعْرَهَا *She cuts her hair short.* (A.) [And app. *She cuts her hair over the forehead so as to form what is termed a* طُرَّة: see also 2.] — And طَرَّتِ الإِبِلُ الجِبَالَ وَالآكَامَ ‡ *The camels traversed the mountains and the hills.* (A.) And طَرَرْتُ القَوْمَ † *I passed by the people, all of them.* (Yoo, TA.) = Also, طَرَّ, (Ṣ, A,) aor. as above, (TA,) inf. n. طَرٌّ (A, Ḳ) and طُرُورٌ, (Ḳ,) *He sharpened* (Ṣ, A, Ḳ, TA) a spear-head, (Ṣ,) or a knife (A, Ḳ) &c., (Ḳ,) or an iron implement. (TA.) — And طَرَّ *He polished* a sword. (O.) — And, (TA,) inf. n. طَرٌّ, (Ḳ,) *He renovated* a building. (Ḳ, TA. [In the CḲ, تَحْدِيد is put for تَجْدِيد as the explanation of the inf. n.]) — And *He plastered with clay* his watering-trough, or tank: (Ṣ, TA:) and likewise his mosque, or oratory, *and decorated* it. (TA.) — And طَرَّهُ بِثَنَآءٍ حَسَنٍ, aor. ـُ, inf. n. طَرٌّ, *He eulogized him.* (TA voce خَمَرَ.) = And, aor. as above, (TA,) inf. n. طَرٌّ, (Ṣ, A, Ḳ,) *He drove away;* syn. شَلَّ; (Ṣ, A, Ḳ, TA;) and ▼ اطرّ, inf. n. إِطْرَارٌ, signifies [the same, i. e.] طَرَدَ. (Aṣ, TA.) In some copies of the Ḳ, [and in a copy of the A,] الشَّدُّ is erroneously put for الشَّلُّ as an explanation of الطَّرُّ. (TA.) — And you say طَرَرْتُ الإِبِلَ, (Ṣ,) inf. n. طَرٌّ, (Ḳ,) *I drove,* or *brought,* or *gathered, the camels together, from their several quarters;* (Ṣ, Ḳ;*) like طَرَدْتُهَا: (Ṣ:) or, accord. to Yaḳoob, *I walked on one side of the camels, and then on the other side, to put them in right order.* (Ṣ.) — And طَرٌّ signifies also The act of *seizing,* or *carrying-off, by force;* or *snatching at unawares.* (Kr, Ḳ.) — And The act of *slapping with the palm of the hand.* (Kr, Ḳ.) = As an intrans. v., طَرَّ, aor. ـُ (Ṣ, A, Mṣb, Ḳ) and ـِ, (Mṣb, Ḳ,) the latter agreeable with analogy, (TA,) [but the former the more common,] inf. n. طُرُورٌ, (Ṣ, Mṣb,) or طَرٌّ, (Ḳ,) or both, (TA,) ‡ *It* (a plant) *clave the earth:* (A:) or *grew forth,* or *sprouted:* (Ṣ, Mṣb:) or *came up,* or *forth.* (Ḳ.) And it is likewise said of the mustache (Ṣ, A, Mṣb, Ḳ) of a boy, (Ṣ, A, Mṣb,) and of hair in general; meaning ‡ *It burst through the skin:* (A:) some say, طَرَّ شَارِبُهُ [meaning *his mustache grew forth*]; (O, TA;) but طَرَّ is more chaste. (Az, TA.) — طَرَّتِ النُّجُومُ, occurring in a trad., means † *The stars rose;* (O, TA;) from طَرَّ said of a plant: (TA:) or the phrase, as some relate it, is طَرَّتِ النجوم, which means † *the stars shone;* (O, TA;) from طَرَّ meaning "he polished" a sword. (O.) — And طَرَّتْ يَدُهُ, (Ṣ, Ḳ,* TA,) aor. ـِ and ـُ (Ḳ, TA) by common consent of the authorities on inflection, (TA,) † *His arm,* or *hand, fell off;* (Ṣ, Ḳ,* TA;) [*being severed* by a blow, or stroke;] like تَرَّتْ. (Ṣ, TA.) = See also 4. = طَرَّ said of a man, [app. of the measure فَعُلَ, originally طَرُرَ,] inf. n. طَرَارَةٌ, *He was,* or *became, beautiful, goodly,* or *comely.* (ISh, TA.) — And طَرَّتْ نَاقَتِى, [app. of the measure فَعِلَتْ, originally طَرِرَتْ,] aor. تَطَرُّ, inf. n. طَرَرٌ, *My she-camel was,* or *became, clear in colour.* (O, TA.)

2. طَرَّرَتْ, [and طرّرت شَعْرَهَا,] inf. n. تَطْرِيرٌ, *She* (a girl) *made to herself a* طُرَّة [q. v.]. (TA.) [See also 1.]

4: see 1, second sentence. — اطرّه signifies also *He made it to fall off.* (Ḳ, TA.) One says, اطرّ اللّٰهُ يَدَ فُلَانٍ *God made,* or *may God make, the arm,* or *hand, of such a one to fall off;* as also اترّه. (TA.) = And اطرّ, (Ḳ,) inf. n. إِطْرَارٌ, (AZ, Ṣ,) *He excited,* or *incited;* syn. أَغْرَى. (AZ, Ṣ, Ḳ.) — See, again, 1. = اطرّ is also *syn. with* أَدَلَّ [as meaning *He acted with boldness,* or *he emboldened himself:* in the CḲ, erroneously, أَذَلَّ]. (Ṣ, Ḳ.) Hence, [accord. to ISk,] أَطِرِّى فَإِنَّكِ نَاعِلَةٌ, (ISk, Ṣ, Ḳ,) or ▼ طِرِّى, (Ḳ,) both mentioned by Aboo-Sa'eed, (TA,) a prov., (Ṣ, TA,) meaning *Act thou with boldness,* or *embolden thyself,* (أَدِلِّى,) *for thou art wearing sandals:* (ISk, Ṣ, Ḳ:) applied alike to a male and to a female and to two and to a pl. number, for it was originally said to a woman, and is therefore used as thus said: (Ṣ:) or, (Ṣ, Ḳ,) accord. to AO, (Ṣ,) it means † *venture thou upon the affair that is difficult, for thou hast strength for it;* and was originally said by a man to a woman who was pasturing his cattle in the soft, or plain, land, and leaving the rugged; [lit.] meaning *take thou to the* طُرَر, i. e. *sides, of the valley;* and he says, I think that by the sandals he meant the roughness of the skin of her feet: (Ṣ, Ḳ:*) or it means *collect thou together the camels:* (Ḳ:) or, accord. to Aboo-Sa'eed, *take thou to the* أَطْرَار, i. e. *sides, of the camels;* i. e. *take care of them, from the most remote of them* [*inclusively*], *and keep them in safety.* (TA.) Some say أَطْرِى. (M and Ḳ in art. طرى.) — And one says, of a man, مَا أَطْرَهُ, meaning *How beautiful,* or *goodly,* or *comely, is he!* (ISh, TA.)

10. استطرّ إِتْمَامَهُ الشَّعَر *It caused the* [*downy,* or *fine,*] *hair to grow to its full,* or *complete, state:* occurring in some verses of El-Ajjáj. (O, TA.)

R. Q. 1. طَرْطَرَ, [inf. n. طَرْطَرَةٌ,] (Ḳ,) said of a man, (TA,) *He gloried,* or *boasted, vainly, and praised himself for that which was not in him;* syn. طَرْمَذَ. (Ḳ.) IDrd says, طَرْطَرَةٌ is an Arabic word, [i. e. it is genuine Arabic,] though in common use with the post-classical writers: one says, رَجُلٌ فِيهِ طَرْطَرَةٌ, meaning *A man in whom is vain-glorying &c.* (طَرْمَذَةٌ) *and loquacity.* (O, TA.) — And طَرْطَرَ بِضَأْنِهِ *He called his ewes to be milked,* (O, Ḳ, TA,) *saying to them* طَرْ طَرْ. (TA.)

Q. Q. 3. اِطْرَوْرَى *He* (a man, TA) *became filled by repletion of the stomach,* or *by anger;* (O, Ḳ, TA;) as also اِطْرَوْرَى. (O.) [But the former verb is also mentioned in the Ḳ, in art. طرو, as of the measure اِفْعَوْعَلَ; and the latter, in art. طرى.]

طَرْ طَرْ a cry by which ewes are called to be milked. (TA.) [See R. Q. 1, last sentence.]

طَرْ طَرْ is said in enjoining one to abide in the neighbourhood of the House of God [at Mekkeh], (O, Ḳ,) and to do so constantly: (Ḳ:) so says IAạr: (TA:) Az has mentioned it in this art.; but if it be a word repeated, from طَارَ, aor. يَطُورُ, its proper place is art. طور: the present art. would be its proper place only if it were طَرْطَرْ [imperative of طَرْطَرَ]: (O:) [F says,] in my opinion it should rightly be mentioned in art. طور; but Az and others have mentioned it among reduplicate words; therefore I have followed them, and notified [the case]. (Ḳ.)

طُرٌّ [The *fur,* or *soft hair, called*] وَبَر, and *hair of the ass, that comes forth after the falling off of former hair.* (Ḳ.)

طُرٌّ *A collective body* [*of men*]. (Yoo, TA.) One says, جَاؤُوا طُرًّا *They came all;* (Ṣ, TA;) and it is said that طُرًّا is here in the accus. case as a denotative of state, or as an inf. n.: Sb mentions the phrase مَرَرْتُ بِهِمْ طُرًّا *I passed by them all;* and he says that the last word is used only as a denotative of state: but Khaṣeeb En-Naṣránee used it otherwise; replying to one who said to him, How art thou? أَحْمَدُ اللّٰهَ إِلَى طُرِّ خَلْقِهِ [*I praise God to all his creatures*]; and the phrase رَأَيْتُ بَنِى فُلَانٍ بِطُرٍّ *I saw the sons of such a one, all of them,* has also been transmitted: some say that طُرًّا in the first of the phrases above is put in the place of an act. part. n., and is [originally] an inf. n. (TA.)

طِرٌّ: see طُرَّةٌ, latter half.

طَرَّةٌ *A single act of cutting* [&c.: an inf. n. of 1, q. v.]. (TA.) — And *Impregnation by a single act of initus:* (O, L, Ḳ:) [used in relation to camels:] or it signifies [simply] *a single act of initus:* thus in the phrase أَلْقَحَهَا بِطَرَّةٍ [*He* (the stallion) *impregnated her by a single act of initus*]. (TḲ.) — الطَّرَّةُ, (AHeyth, O, Ḳ,) thus with fet-ḥ, (O,) and thus written by AHeyth, (TA,) signifies also *The flank.* (AHeyth, O, Ḳ.)

طُرَّةٌ *A thing that is cut.* (TA.) — The *hair that is cut over* (lit. *over against,* حِذَآء,) *the forehead:* (Mgh, Mṣb, voce قُصَّة:) *what a girl cuts short, of the full hair upon her forehead, and forms into a row* or *rows:* (A:) [so accord. to present usage; the *hair over the forehead* of a girl or woman, *cut with a straight* or *even edge,* or *with two such edges one above the other, so as to form a kind of border;* as also قُصَّةٌ:] *what is cut, in the fore part of the* نَاصِيَة [or *hair over the forehead*] *of a girl, like the* عَلَم [or *ornamental border*], (Ḳ, TA,) or *like the* طُرَّة [which seems here to signify the same as عَلَم, or nearly so], (TA,) *which is beneath a crown:* and sometimes it is [*an imitation of a band, across the forehead,*] *made of* [*the black substance called*] رَامَك: as also طُرُورٌ ♦; (Ḳ, TA;) or طُرُورٌ ♦: (so in the O:) or the latter signifies *a* طُرَّة *made of* رَامَك: (O, TṢ:) pl. (of طُرَّة, TA) طُرَرٌ, and (of طُرُور [or طُرُور], TA [and accord. to analogy of طُرَّة also]) طِرَارٌ. (Ḳ.) — Also (Ḳ) [absolutely] The *hair over the forehead;* syn. نَاصِيَة. (Ṣ, O, Ḳ.) — [Hence, app.,] The طُرَّة of a building; also called its صُفَّة: see this latter word.] — And ‡ The طُرَّة of a garment or piece of cloth; (Ṣ, A, O, Mṣb;) i. e., (Ṣ,) the *border,* or *side,* thereof, *that has no* هُدْب [or *end of unwoven threads*]: (Ṣ, O, Ḳ:) [and the *fringed end* thereof: (see صَنِفَةٌ and هُدْبٌ:)] or the *ornamental,* or *figured,* or *variegated, border* (عَلَم) thereof: and, in like manner, of a [water-bag of the kind called] مَزَادَة: (Ḳ, TA: [وَالمَزَادَة in the CḲ is a mistake for وَالمزادة:]) or the طُرَّة of a garment or piece of cloth is *a thing resembling two ornamental,* or *figured,* or *variegated, borders* (عَلَمَانِ) *sewed upon the two sides of a* بُرْد, *upon its border:* (Lth, TA:) pl. طُرَرٌ (Mṣb, Ḳ) and طِرَارٌ. (Ḳ.) And طُرَّاتٌ [is likewise a pl. of طُرَّة, and] occurs in a trad. as meaning *Veils* (سُتُور), or *head-veils,* (O, TA,) or *pieces* [or *strips*], (Z, TA,) cut by women from a garment of the kind called سِيَرَاء. (Z, O, TA.) — And ‡ The *side,* or *edge,* of a river, and of a valley: (Ṣ, A, O, Ḳ:) the *border* of a land or country: (TA:) and the *edge* of anything; (Ṣ, O, Ḳ;) its *extremity:* (Ḳ:) pl. طُرَرٌ (Ṣ, O, Ḳ) and طِرَارٌ: (Ḳ:) and أَطْرَارٌ also signifies the *sides* of a valley; and in like manner, of a country, and of a road; (TA;) and the *extremities* of a country; (Ṣ, O, TA;) and its sing. is طُرٌّ ♦; or, accord. to the T, طُرَّةٌ: (TA:) and طُرَرٌ signifies also ‡ the *margins* of a book or writing; (A, TA;) and the sing. is طُرَّةٌ. (TA in arts. حشى and همش.) — And ‡ The *two lines,* or *streaks,* (خُطَّتَانِ,) *upon the two shoulders* (كَتِفَانِ) of the ass: (Ḳ:) or الطُّرَّتَانِ signifies the *streaked place upon each side* of that animal: (TA:) or *two black streaks* (خطّتان, as above,) *upon the two shoulders* (كتفان) of the ass: and applied by Aboo-Dhu-eyb to those of the wild bull: (Ṣ, O:) or *two stripes,* or *streaks, on the back* of the ass: (A:) and طُرَّةُ مَتْنِهِ *the streak of his back.* (Ṣ.) — ‡ *A streak* of cloud: (Ṣ, A,* O, Ḳ:) *an oblong portion* of cloud, *commencing from the horizon:* (TA:) its dim., طُرَيْرَةٌ, occurs in a trad. (O, TA.) — And † *A goodly aspect* of a man. (TA.) — And one says, رَأَيْتُ طُرَّةَ بَنِى فُلَانٍ † *I saw the mode,* or *manner, of alighting and abiding of the sons of such a one, from afar.* (TA.) — And بَدَتْ طُرَرُ الأَمْرِ ‡ *The indications,* or *signs,* or *tokens, of the affair,* or *event, appeared.* (A, TA.) — And تَكَلَّمَ بِالشَّىْءِ مِنْ طِرَارِهِ † *He spoke the thing eliciting it from his mind.* (TA.)

طُرُورٌ, or طُرُورٌ: see طُرَّةٌ.

طَرِيرٌ *Sharpened;* applied to a spear-head; (A, Ḳ, TA:) as also مَطْرُورٌ ♦: (A, TA:) or, so applied, *polished;* (O;) or thus also, applied to an arrow; and so مَطْرُورٌ ♦ applied to a sword. (TA.) — And ‡ *Goodly,* or *pleasing, in aspect;* (Ṣ, A, O, Ḳ;) applied to a man: (A:) a *beautiful, goodly,* or *comely,* man: (ISh, TA:) a man *beautiful, goodly,* or *comely,* in face: and some say, *whose prime of manhood is future:* (TA:) or *a youth,* or *young man, soft,* or *tender, fleshy, and fat:* (Ḥam p. 513:) pl. طِرَارٌ. (ISh, TA.) See also طَارٌّ.

طُرَّى A she-ass *driven away:* (O, Ḳ, TA:) or a *brisk, lively,* or *sprightly,* ass. (TA.)

طَرَّارٌ *A cutpurse; one who cuts,* or *slits, purses,* (A, Mgh, Mṣb,* TA,) *and takes people's money at unawares:* (Mṣb:) or *who slits a man's sleeve,* [*in which he carries his money and the like,*] *and gently extracts what is in it:* (TA:) from الطَّرُّ "the act of slitting" (Ṣ, Mṣb) and "cutting." (Ṣ.)

طِرِّيَانٌ *A table upon which one eats;* syn. خِوَانٌ: (Ḳ:) or *a dish,* or *plate,* (طَبَق,) *upon which food is eaten.* (O.) [But see طِرِّيَانٌ, in art. طرو.]

طَارٌّ ‡ A boy *whose mustache is growing forth:* (Ṣ, A, Mṣb:) or *whose mustache has grown forth;* (Lth, L, Ḳ;) as also طَرِيرٌ ♦. (Ḳ.) — And طَارٌّ ‡ *A sort of* [*cloth of the kind called*] خَزّ [app. *having a nap*]. (A, TA.)

طُرْطُورٌ *A sort of* قَلَنْسُوَة [q. v.], (Ṣ, Ḳ,) *worn*

by *Arabs of the desert*, (Ṣ,) *tall*, or *long, and narrow* (Ṣ, Ḳ) *in the head*, or *top:* (Ṣ:) [in the present day applied to *a sort of high, conical, cap:* and *a cowl.*] — And † *A slender and tall man.* (Ṣ, Ḳ.) — And, (Ḳ,) accord. to IAạr, (O,) *Low, ignoble, mean*, or *sordid*, (وَغْدٌ,) *and weak:* (O, Ḳ:) pl. طَرَاطِيرُ. (O.)

مُطِرٌّ A boy *having a* طُرَّة; as also ↓ مُطَرَّرٌ: and the latter with ة is applied to a girl. (So in a copy of the A.) — جَلَبٌ مُطِرٌّ † [*A thing*, or *things, brought for the purpose of traffic,*] *come from the extremities* (أَطْرَار) *of the country.* (TA.) — غَضَبٌ مُطِرٌّ *Anger that is misplaced, and for a thing that does not require it:* (Ṣ, Ḳ:) or *in which is somewhat of boldness*, or *presumptuousness:* or *such as is vehement*, or *violent.* (TA.) — جَآءَ فُلَانٌ مُطِرًّا *Such a one came domineering*, or *exalting himself; behaving boldly*, or *presumptuously.* (Aṣ, Ṣ.)

مِطَرَّةٌ, (O,) or مُطَرَّةٌ, or مُطَرَّةٌ, (accord. to different copies of the Ḳ,) with ḍamm, (Ḳ,) [and accord. to the TḲ with fet-ḥ to the ط,] *Custom, habit*, or *wont:* (O, Ḳ:) so says AZ: (O:) [the form given in the O seems to be preferable: but] F has also mentioned it as without teshdeed, [i. e. مَطْرَة,] and thus it is mentioned [in the Ḳ] in art. مطر. (TA.)

مُطَرَّرٌ: see مُطِرٌّ.

مَطْرُورٌ: see طَرِيرٌ, in two places.

طرأ

1. طَرَأَ عَلَيْهِمْ, aor. ـَ, inf. n. طُرُوْءٌ (Ṣ, Mgh, Mṣb, Ḳ) and طَرْءٌ, (Ṣ, Ḳ,) *He came to them from a place;* (Ḳ;) or *from a distant place, unexpectedly:* (Mgh:) or *he came forth upon them* (Ṣ, Mṣb, Ḳ) *from a place*, (Ḳ,) or *from a distant place*, (TA,) *unexpectedly*, (Ḳ, TA,) or *from another country*, or *territory*, or *town*, or *the like:* (Ṣ:) or *he came to them without their knowledge:* or *he came forth upon them from an opening*, or *a wide, open tract:* the original word is [said to be] دَرَأَ [q. v.: see also طَرَا, in art. طرو]. (TA.) And طَرَأَ, (Mṣb, TA,) said of a thing, (Mṣb,) aor. as above, (Mṣb, TA,) inf. n. طران [app. طَرَآنٌ], (Mṣb,) *It came*, (Mṣb, TA,) *came to pass, happened*, or *occurred*, (Mṣb,) *unexpectedly.* (Mṣb, TA.) It is said in a trad., طَرَأَ عَلَىَّ مِنَ القُرْآنِ, as though meaning *A portion of the recitation of the Ḳur-án came to my turn at an unexpected time.* (TA.) = طَرُؤَ, [aor. ـُ,] (Mgh, Mṣb, Ḳ,) inf. n. طَرَاءَةٌ (Mgh, Ḳ) and طَرَآءٌ, (Ḳ,) in some of the copies of the Ḳ طَرَآءَةٌ and طَرَاءَةٌ, (TA,) *It* (a thing, Mṣb) *was*, or *became, fresh, juicy*, or *moist;* (Mṣb;) contr. of ذَوِىَ; (Ḳ;) i. q. طَرُوَ, inf. n. طَرَاوَةٌ, (Mgh, Mṣb,) of which it is a dial. var., (Mṣb,) and which is the more common. (TA.)

2. طَرَّأَهُ, inf. n. تَطْرِئَةٌ, *He rendered it fresh, juicy*, or *moist.* (TA.)

4. أَطْرَأَهُ *He praised him:* (TA:) or *he praised him greatly*, or *extravagantly;* or *exceeded the just*, or *usual, bounds, in praising him:* (Ḳ, TA:) accord. to Es-Saraḳustee, أَطْرَأْتُهُ signifies *I praised him:* and أَطْرَيْتُهُ, [in like manner,] *I eulogized*, or *commended, him.* (Mṣb.) [See also the latter verb in art. طرو.]

طُرْأَةُ السَّيْلِ i. q. دُفْعَتُهُ [i. e. *The tide*, or *what pours forth at once, of the torrent*]: (Ḳ:) from طَرَأَ "he came forth" from a land. (TA.)

طُرْآنٌ, (O, Ḳ,) or ↓ طُرْآنِىٌّ, occurring in the poetry of El-'Ajjáj, (TA,) *A road*, or *way*, and *an affair*, or *event, unknown*, or *disapproved*, or *deemed strange* or *extraordinary:* (O, Ḳ:) [or an affair, or event,] *unknown*, &c., and *wonderful.* (TA.)

طُرْآنِىٌّ, an epithet applied to a pigeon, (O, Ḳ,) and to an event, (Ḳ,) *Of which one knows not whence it has come:* (Ḳ:) an irregular rel. n. from طَرَأَ عَلَيْنَا فُلَانٌ "Such a one came forth upon us without our knowing him:" (TA:) [or] طُرْآن is the name of a certain mountain in which are many pigeons; (O, Ḳ;) and hence the epithet above mentioned as applied to a pigeon: (O, TA:) Aboo-'Obeyd El-Bekree writes this name, in the Moạjam, with ḍamm to the first letter and teshdeed to the second: the vulgar say حَمَامٌ طُورَانِىٌّ, which is a mistake. (TA.) — See also طُرْآنٌ.

طَرِىْءٌ *Fresh, juicy*, or *moist;* (A,* Mgh,* Mṣb, TA;) a dial. var. of طَرِىٌّ. (Mṣb.)

طَارِئٌ part. n. of طَرَأَ, applied to a man, and to a thing: (Mṣb:) the pl. is طُرَّآءُ, (Ḳ, TA,) like زُهَّادٌ, (TA,) and طُرَآءُ, (Ḳ, TA,) like عُلَمَآءُ, and MF mentions, as from the M, طَرْأٌ, like خَدَمٌ, [but this is properly termed a quasi-pl. n.,] and طَرَأَةٌ, like كَتَبَةٌ, and in some copies طُرَاةٌ, like قُضَاةٌ: (TA:) and طُرًّا is applied to strangers, for طُرَّآءُ, meaning Persons *coming from a distant place.* (L, TA.) One says, هُوَ مِنَ الطُّرَّآءِ لَا مِنَ الثُّنَّآءِ [*He is of those who come from another place*, or *country; not of the settled residents*]. (A, TA.) — [It is also applied to a signification, as meaning † *Adventitious.*]

طَارِئَةٌ † *A calamity*, or *misfortune*, (O, Ḳ, TA,) *of which one knows not whence it has come.* (TA.)

مطرئ [thus written, without any syll. signs, in the TA, and there said to be the subst. (اسم) from أَطْرَأَهُ: but I think that it is evidently مُطْرِئٌ; and not the subst., but the act. part. n. (اِسْمُ الفَاعِلِ), of أَطْرَأَهُ].

طرب

1. طَرِبَ, (Ṣ, Mṣb, TA,) aor. ـَ, (Mṣb,) inf. n. طَرَبٌ, (Ṣ,* Mṣb, Ḳ,* TA,) *He was*, or *became, affected with emotion*, or *a lively emotion*, or *excitement, agitation*, or *unsteadiness*, (خِفَّة, Ṣ, Mṣb, Ḳ, TA,) [*of the heart* or *mind,*] *by reason of joy* or *of grief*, (Ḳ, TA,) or *of intense grief* or *joy*, (Ṣ,) or *of intense fear* or *joy:* (Mṣb:) or [*he was moved with joy*, or *delight;*] *he was joyful, mirthful*, or *glad:* and the contr., i. e. *he was affected with grief, sadness*, or *sorrow.* (Ḳ,* TA.) [See طَرَبٌ, below.] — And طَرِبَتِ الإِبِلُ لِلْحُدَآءِ [*The camels became excited by reason of the driver's urging them with singing*]. (A, TA.) — And طربت عَنِ الطَّرِيقِ [written in the TA without any syll. signs, app. طَرِبْتُ,] i. q. عدلت عنه [i. e. *I deviated* (عَدَلْتُ) *from the road*, or *way*]. (TA.)

2. طَرَّبَ, (TA,) inf. n. تَطْرِيبٌ, (Ḳ,) *He sang.* (Ḳ, TA.) And طَرَّبَ فِى صَوْتِهِ *He trilled*, or *quavered, and prolonged, his voice:* (Mṣb:) or التَّطْرِيبُ فِى الصَّوْتِ is *the prolonging of the voice, and modulating it sweetly.* (Ṣ, TA.) And, said of a bird, or, accord. to some, peculiarly of the مُكَّآء, *It prolonged its voice, and trilled*, or *quavered, it*, or *warbled.* (TA.) And in like manner, طرّب فِى قِرَآءَتِهِ (A, TA) *He prolonged, and trilled*, or *quavered, his voice in his reciting*, or *reading;* (TA;) and فِى غِنَائِهِ [*in his singing*]. (A.) And قَرَأَ بِالتَّطْرِيبِ [*He recited*, or *read, with a prolonging, and trilling*, or *quavering, of the voice*]. (A, TA.) — And طَرَّبُوا *They raised their voices, cried out*, or *cried aloud, time after time.* (Skr, TA.) = طَرَّبَهُ: see 4. — [Freytag adds that, in the "Fákihet el-Khulafà," p. 42, l. 5 infr., it means *He asserted him to have sung excellently.*]

4. اطربهُ *He*, (Ṣ,) or *it*, (one's voice, A,) *caused him to be affected with* طَرَب [i. e. *emotion*, or *a lively emotion*, &c.]; as also ↓ تطرّبهُ; (Ṣ, A;) [and ↓ طَرَّبَهُ; for] تَطْرِيبٌ signifies the same as إِطْرَابٌ, like ↓ تَطَرُّبٌ: (Ḳ:) [generally, *he*, or *it, rendered him lively, brisk*, or *sprightly:* and] اطربهُ is said of joy, and of grief, meaning [*it affected him with* طَرَب; or] *it rendered him restless*, or *unsteady.* (MA.)

5: see the next preceding paragraph, in two places.

10. استطرب *He*, or *it, sought*, or *demanded*, طَرَب [i. e. *emotion, or a lively emotion*, &c.], (Ḳ, TA,) *and diversion, sport*, or *play.* (TA.) — And *They* (a party, or company of men,) *became affected with intense* طَرَب. (A, TA.) = استطرب الإِبِلَ *He put in motion the camels by urging them with singing.* (Ḳ.) You say استطرب الحُدَاةُ الإِبِلَ [*The drivers, singing to them, excited, moved*, or *stirred, the camels,*] when the camels have become lively, brisk, sprightly, or agile, because of their urging them with singing. (O, TA.) Az cites the saying of Eṭ-Ṭirimmáḥ,

وَٱسْتَطْرَبَتْ ظُعْنُهُمْ لَمَّا ٱحْزَأَلَّ بِهِمْ

آلُ الضُّحَى نَاشِطًا مِنْ دَاعِبَاتٍ دَدِ

but in his poem it is وَٱسْتَطْرَفَتْ, with فاء [i. e. with the letter ف]: (O:) [this latter reading is, I doubt not, the right; and the meaning seems to be, *And their women borne in the camel-vehicles, when the mirage of the early part of the forenoon elevated them* to the eye, *elicited anew longing desire for their homes,* or *accustomed places, from jocose, sportful females,* lit., *from jesting females of sport* or *diversion:* the verse as cited by Az may admit of a similar rendering if we suppose استطربت to be there used tropically: the writer of my copy of the TA has endeavoured, in marginal notes in the present art. and in art. ددو, but in my opinion unsatisfactorily, to explain it; and has supposed استطربت to mean طَرِبَتْ: his two notes, moreover, are inconsistent:] نَاشِطًا in this verse means شَوْقًا نَازِعًا. (K in art. ددو. [The verse is there cited with two readings differing from the words given by Az; وَٱسْتَطْرَقَتْ, thus written with ق instead of ف, a manifest mistake, and مِنْ دَاعِبٍ دَدُو.]) — استطربهُ signifies also *He asked him to sing.* (A, TA.)

طَرَبٌ *Emotion,* or *a lively emotion,* or *excitement, agitation,* or *unsteadiness,* (خِفَّةٌ, Ṣ, A, Mṣb, Ḳ,) [*of the heart or mind,*] *by reason of joy* or *grief,* (A, Ḳ,) or *of intense grief* or *joy,* (Ṣ,) or *of intense fear* or *joy:* (Mṣb:) or *joy, mirth,* or *gladness:* and the contr., i. e. *grief, sadness,* or *sorrow:* (Th, Ḳ:) or, as some say, the *lodgement of joy, mirth,* or *gladness, and departure of grief, sadness,* or *sorrow:* so in the M: (TA:) the vulgar apply it peculiarly to joy; (Mṣb;) [but] the application of it peculiarly to joy is a mistake: (Ḳ:) it signifies also *motion;* syn. حَرَكَةٌ: (Ḳ:) it is said in the M, Th says that الطَّرَبُ is derived from الحَرَكَةُ; whence it seems that الطَّرَبُ is, in his opinion, syn. with الحَرَكَةُ; but [ISd adds] I know not this: (TA:) [it does, however, obviously imply the signification of motion, either ideal or actual:] also *desire,* or *yearning* or *longing of the soul:* (Ḳ:) the pl. is أَطْرَابٌ. (TA.) A poet says, (Ṣ,) namely, En-Nábighah El-Jaạdee, using it in relation to anxiety, (TA,)

* وَأَرَانِى طَرِبًا ♦ فِى إِثْرِهِمْ *
* طَرَبَ الوَالِهِ أَوْ كَالْمُخْتَبَلْ *

[*And I perceive myself to be affected with emotion,* or *a lively emotion, after them,* (i. e. after the loss of them,) *with the emotion of him who is bereft of offspring* or *friends,* or *like him who is insane in mind*]: (Ṣ, TA:) الوَالِه here signifies الثَّاكِل; and المُخْتَبَل means مَنْ جُنَّ فِى عَقْلِهِ. (TA.) — And [the pl.] أَطْرَابٌ signifies *Choice sweet-smelling plants:* (Ḳ:) or [simply] *sweet-smelling plants:* (TA:) and the *more fragrant of such plants.* (O, TA.)

طَرِبٌ *Affected with* طَرَب [i. e. *emotion,* or *a lively emotion,* &c.]: (Ṣ, A, O, Mṣb, TA:) pl. طِرَابٌ. (A, TA.) A Hudhalee says,

* بَاتَتْ طِرَابًا وَبَاتَ اللَّيْلَ لَمْ يَنَمِ *

[*They passed the night joyful,* or *glad, and he passed the night without sleeping*]: (O, TA:) meaning that the [wild] bulls or cows, thirsting, passed the night joyful on account of the lightning that they saw, and the water for which they hoped in consequence thereof. (TA.) See also another ex. in the verse cited voce إِبِلٌ. — طِرَابٌ means *Camels yearning for their accustomed places of abode:* (Ṣ, O, TA:) or they are so termed when they are *excited* (إِذَا طَرِبَتْ) *by reason of their drivers' urging them with singing.* (A, TA.) — Also The *head* [meaning the *hair of the head*]: so called because of the sound that it makes when it is twisted with fingers: occurring in the phrase حَتَّى يَرُنَّا الطَّرِبَ [*That he may dye the hair of the head with* يُرَنَّا, i. e. حِنَّآء]. (L, TA.)

طَرُوبٌ (A, O, Mṣb, Ḳ, TA) and ♦ مِطْرَابٌ (A, O, Ḳ, TA) and ♦ مِطْرَابَةٌ [which is of a very unusual form (see مِعْزَابَةٌ)], (Lḥ, Ḳ, TA,) applied to a man, (O, Ḳ, TA,) *Much,* or *often, affected with* طَرَب [i. e. *emotion,* or *lively emotion,* &c.]: (O, Mṣb, TA:) [but the last is doubly intensive, signifying *very much,* or *very often, so affected:*] pl. [of the second and third] مَطَارِيبُ. (A.) One says, إِذَا خَفَقَتِ المَضَارِيبُ خَفَّتِ المَطَارِيبُ ♦ [*When the plectra of the lutes quiver, the persons who are wont to be affected with emotion become lively,* or *light-hearted*]. (A, TA.) And حَمَامَةٌ ♦ مِطْرَابٌ [*A pigeon that cooes much* or *often*]. (A, TA.) And ♦ إِبِلٌ مَطَارِيبُ [*Camels that yearn much,* or *often, for their accustomed places of abode:* or *that are much,* or *often, excited by reason of their drivers' urging them with singing:* see طِرَابٌ]. (A, TA.)

مَطْرَبٌ and ♦ مَطْرَبَةٌ *A separate,* or *straggling, road,* or *way:* (Ṣ, O:) or *a narrow road,* or *way:* (Ḳ:) or the former, *a conspicuous road* or *way:* (IAạr, TA:) and the latter, *a small road,* or *way, leading into a great one:* or *a narrow road,* or *way, apart from others:* (TA:) or *a small road,* or *way, branching off from a main road:* (O:) pl. مَطَارِبُ: (Ṣ, O:) [it is said (but see 1, last sentence,) that] there is no verb corresponding thereto. (TA.) A poet says, (Ṣ,) namely, Aboo-Dhu-eyb, (O, TA,)

* وَمُتْلِفٍ مِثْلِ فَرْقِ الرَّأْسِ تَخْلِجُهُ *
* مَطَارِبٌ زَقَبٌ أَمْيَالُهَا فِيحُ *

(Ṣ, O, TA) i. e. *Many a desert tract, like the division of the hair of the head* in narrowness, *narrow conspicuous* [or *straggling*] *roads,* or *ways,* [*whereof the portions over which the eye can reach are far-extending,*] *protract;* some of these roads, or ways, tending this way and some that way. (TA. [مطارب is here with tenween for the sake of the measure. See also زَقَبٌ. Perhaps the poet means to liken the said roads to the ropes of a tent.]) It is said in a trad., لَعَنَ ٱللّٰهُ مَنْ غَيَّرَ المَطْرَبَةَ ♦ [*May God curse him who alters the* مطربة]; i. e., the road thus called. (TA.)

مَطْرَبَةٌ: see the next preceding paragraph, in two places.

مِطْرَابٌ, and its pl.: see طَرُوبٌ, in four places.

مِطْرَابَةٌ: see طَرُوبٌ.

طربل

Q. 1. طَرْبَلَ بَوْلَهُ *He extended* [or *emitted*] *his urine upwards.* (Ṣ, O, Ḳ.) — And طَرْبَلَ *He dragged his skirt, and walked with a proud and self-conceited gait, stretching out his arms.* (O.)

طِرْبَالٌ *A high portion of a wall;* (Ṣ, O;) whence the saying, in a trad., that when any one passes by a leaning طربال, he should quicken his pace: (O:) *it resembles a* مَنْظَرَة *of the* مَنَاظِر *of the 'Ajam, being in form like a* صَوْمَعَة [q. v.]: (AO, O, TA:) or *a sign of the way, constructed* (O, Ḳ) *upon a mountain:* (O:) and (O, Ḳ) accord. to IDrd, (O,) *a portion of a mountain,* and *of a wall, elongated in form towards the sky,* (O, Ḳ,) *and inclining:* (O:) and *any high building:* (Ḳ:) [and this seems to be meant by what here next follows:] accord. to IAạr, *a high,* or *an overtopping,* or *overlooking,* هَدَف: (TA:) and, (Ṣ, O, Ḳ,) as some say, (O,) *a great, high,* or *overtopping, rock* (Ṣ, O, Ḳ) *of a mountain:* (Ṣ, Ḳ:) ISh says that it is *a structure erected as a sign for horses to run thereto in a race, and one kind thereof is like the* مَنَارَة [q. v.]: Fr, that it signifies *a* صَوْمَعَة [q. v.]: (TA:) and [it is said that] the طَرَابِيل of Syria are *its* صَوَامِع. (Ṣ, O, Ḳ.) Az mentions his having heard [the pl.] طَرَابِيل, and عَرَازِيل likewise, applied to *Booths constructed of palm-branches, in which the watchers of the palm-trees shelter themselves from the sun.* (TA.)

طِرْبِيلٌ [perhaps from the Latin "tribula" or "tribulum"] The [*machine, or drag, called*] نَوْرَج [q. v.] *with which the heap of corn is thrashed.* (Ibn-'Abbád, O, Ḳ.)

جَرَّةٌ مُطَرْبَلَةُ الجَوَانِبِ *A jar long in the sides.* (Sh, TA.)

طرث

R. Q. 2. تَطَرْثَثَ *He gathered,* or *collected, the species of plants called* طُرْثُوث. (Ṣ, Mṣb, Ḳ.)

طَرْثٌ Any plant (نَبَات, Ḳ [so in the TA and in my MS. copy of the Ḳ, in the CḲ بِناء, which is an evident mistranscription,]) that is *fresh and juicy.* (Ḳ.)

طُرْثٌ The *extremity of the* بَظْر [q. v.]. (Ḳ.) — And *Flaccidity,* or *flabbiness.* (L.)

طُرْثُوثٌ *A species of plant, which is eaten;* (Ṣ, Ḳ;) [app. *a kind,* or *species, of fungus;* perhaps *a species of phallus;*] *a plant of the same kind as* the ذُؤْنُون and the عُرْجُون; (IAạr, T in art. ذأن;) accord. to Lth, *a slender, oblong plant, inclining to redness, and serving as a* دِبَاغ *to the stomach* [app. meaning *a stomachic*], *included among medicines, of which there is a bitter sort and a sweet sort;* (Mṣb;) in the M said to be *a plant of the sands, long and slender, similar to the* قُطْر [q. v.], *inclining to redness, which dries, and serves as a* دِبَاغ *to the stomach;* n. un. with ة; on the authority of AḤn: it is *of two sorts; one sweet, which is the red; and one bitter, which is the white;* IAạr says that it is *a plant of the length of a cubit, having no leaves, as though it were of the same kind as the truffle;* (TA;) Az says that *the* طرثوث *of the desert has no leaves* (Mṣb, TA) *nor any fruit,* (TA,) *grows in the sands* (Mṣb, TA) *and in the level grounds,* (TA,) *has in it no acidity,* (Mṣb,) *but a sweetness inclining to astringency and bitterness, and is red, with a round head,* (Mṣb, TA,) *like the glans of a man's penis:* (TA:) [Ibn-Seenà (whom we call Avicenna), in his list of medicinal simples, (book ii., p. 183 of the printed ed.,) describes طَرَاثِيث *as pieces of wood in a rotting state, of the thickness of a finger, and in length less and more, having an astringent taste, and dust-coloured; said to be brought from the desert.* See also سُوقَةٌ.] The Arabs say, طَرَاثِيثُ لَا أَرْطَى لَهَا [*Turthoothehs without arṭáhs*]: because the former grow not save with the latter: a prov., like ذَآنِينُ لَا رِمْثَ لَهَا: applied to him who is ruined, and has nothing remaining, after having had ancestry and rank and wealth. (TA. [See also art. ذأن, last sentence.]) —— Also ‡ The *glans of a man's penis:* (Ḳ, TA:) so called as being likened to [the head of] the plant above described. (TA.)

طرح

1. طَرَحَهُ, and طَرَحَ بِهِ, (Ṣ, A, Mgh, O, Mṣb, Ḳ,) the latter allowable because a verb that is syn. with another verb may have the same government as the latter, and طَرَحَ is syn. with a verb that is trans. by means of بِ, as will be shown in what follows, (Mṣb,) aor. ـَ, (Mgh, Mṣb, Ḳ,) inf. n. طَرْحٌ, (Ṣ, Mgh, O, Mṣb,) *He cast it, threw it, or flung it; or cast, threw, or flung, it away;* [and particularly *as a thing of no account;* (see طِرْحٌ;)] syn. رَمَاهُ, (Ṣ, A, O, Ḳ,) or رَمَى بِهِ (Mgh, Mṣb,) and أَلْقَاهُ; (A, Mgh;) مِنْ يَدِهِ [*from his hand*]. (Mgh.) You say, طَرَحَ لَهُ الوِسَادَةَ (A, TA) *He threw to him the pillow,* or *cushion;* syn. أَلْقَاهُ. (TA.) And طَرَحْتُ الرِّدَآءَ عَلَى عَاتِقِى *I threw the* [*garment called*] رِدَآء *upon my shoulder;* syn. أَلْقَيْتُهُ. (Mṣb.) And [hence] طَرَحَ عَلَيْهِ المَسْأَلَةَ ‡ *He put, or proposed,* (lit. *threw,*) *to him the question:* (A,* TA:) thought by ISd to be post-classical. (TA.) [And in post-classical language, طَرْحٌ signifies also The *making a throw* in the game of backgammon and the like; and the *making a move* in the game of chess &c.] —— Also, i. e. طَرَحَهُ and طَرَحَ بِهِ, *He removed it; placed it,* or *put it, at a distance; put it away,* or *far away;* [*cast it off, rejected it,* or *discarded it;*] (ISd, Ḳ, TA;) as also ↓ إِطَّرَحَهُ; (Ṣ, A, O, Ḳ;) [respecting which see 8 in art. ضرح;] and ↓ طَرَّحَهُ, (Ḳ,) inf. n. تَطْرِيحٌ; (TA;) or this last signifies *he cast it, threw it,* or *flung it,* or *he cast, threw,* or *flung, it away, much,* or *frequently.* (Ṣ, A, O.) One says, طَرَحَتِ النَّوَى بِفُلَانٍ كُلَّ مَطْرَحٍ i. e. ‡ [*Removal,* or *distance,* or *the place to which he journeyed,*] *rendered such a one* [*utterly*] *remote* [or *cast away*]. (Ṣ, O, TA. [Here مَطْرَح is an inf. n.]) And [in like manner] طَرَحَ بِهِ الدَّهْرُ كُلَّ مَطْرَحٍ i. e. ‡ [*Time,* or *fortune,*] *removed him,* or *separated him,* [*utterly,*] *from his family and kindred.* (TA.) And مَا طَرَحَكَ إِلَى هٰذِهِ البِلَادِ ‡ [*What has driven thee to these regions?*]. (A.) And اِطْرَحْ إِلَيْهِمْ عَهْدَهُمْ † [*Cast thou from thee, to them, their covenant;* i. e. *reject it,* or *renounce it, to them*]. (Bḍ in viii. 60.) And اِطْرَحْ هٰذَا الحَدِيثَ ‡ [*Dismiss thou this discourse*]. (A, TA. [See the pass. part. n., below.]) And ↓ اِطَّرِحْ شُكْرِى وَلَوْمِى † *Let thou alone,* or *abstain thou from, thanking me and blaming me.* (Ḥar p. 332.) ═══ طَرِحَ, (IAạr, O, Ḳ,) aor. ـَ, (Ḳ,) inf. n. طَرَحٌ, (TḲ,) *He* (a man, IAạr, O) *was,* or *became, evil in disposition.* (IAạr, O, Ḳ.) —— And *He enjoyed,* or *led, a life of ample ease and comfort.* (IAạr, O, Ḳ.)

2: see 1. —— طَرَّحَ, (Ṣ, A, O, Ḳ,) inf. n. تَطْرِيحٌ, (Ṣ, Ḳ,) signifies also ‡ *He made* a thing *long,* or *he made it high:* (TA:) or *he made* his building *long;* (Ṣ, Ḳ;) as also ↓ طَرْمَحَ, (Ṣ, and Ḳ in art. طرمح,) in which the م is [said to be] augmentative: (Ṣ:) or both signify *he made* his building *long and high:* (A:) or the former signifies *he made* his building *very long.* (O.) —— And *He* (a horse) *took long,* or *wide, steps in running.* (O, TA.)

3. مُطَارَحَةُ الكَلَامِ is a phrase well known: (Ṣ, Ḳ:) المُطَارَحَةُ signifies † *The bandying of words, one with another;* (KL, and Ḥar p. 190;) *the holding a colloquy,* or *a discussion, with another:* and it is [said to be] primarily used in relation to singing. (Ḥar ibid.) You say, طارحهُ الكَلَامَ † *He held a colloquy,* or *a discussion, with him.* (MA.) And طَارَحْتُهُ العِلْمَ and الغِنَآءَ ‡ [*I bandied with him scientific discourse and songs*]. (A.) [See also 6.]

4. أَطْرِحْ ‡ *Look thou:* (A, TA:) from طَرْفٌ مِطْرَحٌ and طَرْحٌ. (TA.)

[5. تطرّح *He attired himself with a* طَرْحَة: a post-classical word.]

6. تطارحوا ‡ *They bandied questions, one with another; put,* or *proposed,* (lit. *threw,*) *questions, one to another.* (A.)

8. إِطَّرَحَ: see 1, in three places.

Q. Q. 1. طَرْمَحَ: see 2; and see also art. طرمح.

طِرْحٌ (Ṣ, A, Ḳ) and ↓ طَرِيحٌ and ↓ مَطْرُوحٌ (Ḳ) A thing (Ṣ, A) *cast, thrown,* or *flung, away,* syn. مَطْرُوحٌ, (Ṣ, A, Ḳ,) *and not wanted by any one.* (Ṣ.) One says, لَوْ بَاتَ مَتَاعُكَ طِرْحًا مَا أُخِذَ [*If thy household goods passed the night,* or *remained during the night, cast away and neglected, they would not be taken*]. (A, TA.) ═══ And طِرْحٌ signifies also The *leopard:* so says Aboo-Kheyreh: pl. طُرُوحٌ. (O.)

طَرْحٌ † *Distance,* or *remoteness.* (TA.) —— See also طَرُوحٌ, in two places.

طَرْحَةٌ The [*article of apparel called*] طَيْلَسَان [q. v.]: (O, Ḳ:) it was not known to the Arabs. (O.) [See De Sacy's Chrest. Arabe, sec. ed., ii. 267-269: and Dozy's Dict. des Noms des Vêtements chez les Arabes, pp. 254-262. It is now applied in Egypt to a kind of head-veil worn by women, the two ends of which generally hang down behind, nearly reaching to the ground: but it is often worn in another manner; about a quarter of it hanging down behind, and the remainder being turned over the head, and under the chin, and over the head again, so that the middle part covers the bosom, and both ends hang down behind: it is a piece of muslin, or the like, often embroidered at each end; about three quarters of a yard in width, and in length nearly equal to twice the height of the wearer.]

طِرِّيحٌ: see طِرْحٌ.

طُرَاحٌ: see the next paragraph.

طَرُوحٌ † *A distant* place; as also ↓ طَرْحٌ, (Ṣ, Ḳ,) and ↓ طُرَاحٌ, (Ḳ,) and [app. ↓ طَارِحٌ, for] one says دِيَارٌ طَوَارِحُ ‡ *Distant dwellings* or *abodes* [as though the latter word were pl. of طَارِحَةٌ]. (A, TA.) [Hence,] عُقْبَةٌ طَرُوحٌ ‡ [*A stage of a journey*] *far-extending.* (A,* O: in a copy of the former عَقَبَةٌ.) And ↓ سَيْرٌ طُرَاحِىٌّ † *A far,* or *distant, journey:* (Aṣ, Ṣ, O, Ḳ:) or *a hard journey.* (TA.) And نِيَّةٌ طَرُوحٌ, (TA,) or ↓ طَرْحٌ, (T, Ḳ, TA, and O in art. ضرح,) like ضَرْحٌ, (O in that art.,) *i. q.* بَعِيدَةٌ [app. meaning † *A distant,* or *remote, thing,* or *place, that is the object of an action* or *a journey*]. (T, O, Ḳ.) And نَخْلَةٌ طَرُوحٌ † *A palm-tree having long racemes:* (Ṣ, O, Ḳ:) or *of which the upper part is far from the lower:* pl. طُرُحٌ, with two dammehs. (TA.) —— قَوْسٌ طَرُوحٌ ‡ *A bow that propels the arrow with vehemence;* (Ṣ, A, O;)

i. q. ضَرُوحٌ: (Ṣ, O, Ḳ:) or *that sends the arrow far:* (TA:) or *that sends it to the furthest limit.* (AḤn, TA.) And رَجُلٌ طَرُوحٌ ‡ *A man who, when he compresses, impregnates.* (Lḥ, O, Ḳ.) And فَحْلٌ طَرُوحٌ † *i. q.* مِطْرَحٌ, q. v. (O.) And زَمَنٌ طَرُوحٌ ‡ *A time that casts the people thereof into places,* or *positions, of peril:* and نَوَائِبُ طُرُحٌ [or طُرْحٌ, as above, ‡ *Accidents that cast people into such places* or *positions*]. (A.)

طَرِيحٌ: see طِرْحٌ: — and see also مِطْرَحٌ.

طَرُوحٌ: see سَيْرٌ طَرَاحِىٌّ.

طَرَّاحَةٌ: see مِطْرَحٌ.

طَارِحٌ: [fem. with ة; and pl. of the latter طَوَارِحُ:] see طَرُوحٌ.

سَنَامٌ إِطْرِيحٌ *A long,* (Ṣ, O, L, Ḳ,) or *tall,* (Ṣ,* O,* L, Ḳ,*) *camel's hump,* (Ṣ, O, L, Ḳ,) *leaning on one side.* (L.) [See an ex. voce إِسْلِيحٌ.]

أُطْرُوحَةٌ † *A question that one puts,* or *proposes,* lit. *throws.* (TA.)

فُلَانٌ يُلْقِى الأَطَارِيحَ is expl. by AO as meaning *Such a one moves both his arms up and down* [*in walking*]: denoting a proud and self-conceited manner of walking. (O.)

مَطْرَحٌ *A place where,* or *into which, a thing* [or *person is cast* or *thrown* or] *is made to be:* pl. مَطَارِحُ. (Ḥar p. 188.) — [And hence,] ‡ *A state in which a person is* [*put,* or *placed*]: so in the saying, مَا طَرَحَكَ هٰذَا المَطْرَحَ ‡ *What hath put,* or *placed, thee in this state* in which thou art? (A.)

مِطْرَحٌ *I. q.* مِفْرَشٌ [q. v.: and ▼ طَرَّاحَةٌ has the same, or a similar, meaning; applied in the present day to *a horse-cloth,* and *the like;* and to *a mattress*]: pl. مَطَارِحُ. (A, TA.) — فَحْلٌ مِطْرَحٌ ‡ *A stallion that sends his semen far into the womb;* (A,* O, Ḳ;) like ▼ طَرُوحٌ. (O.) And طَرْفٌ مِطْرَحٌ ‡ *An eye that sees far;* (A, O, Ḳ;) as also ▼ طَرِيحٌ. (A, TA.) And رُمْحٌ مِطْرَحٌ ‡ *A long spear.* (A, Ḳ.) And إِبِلٌ مَطَارِيحُ ‡ *Quick,* or *swift, camels.* (A, TA.) — [مِطْرَحٌ, as stated by Freytag, is also expl. by Reiske as meaning *Camela in cujus ventrem aqua profunda cadit:* but this explanation may have originated from a doubtful instance of the same epithet applied to a stallion camel: see above.]

قَوْلٌ مُطْرَحٌ ‡ *A* [*rejected*] *saying, to which no regard is paid.* (A, TA.)

مَشَى مُتَطَرِّحًا † *He walked,* or *went, in a slack,* or *languid, manner; as though repeatedly stumbling,* or *throwing himself down;* syn. مُتَسَاقِطًا; (IDrd, A, O;) *like one fatigued,* or *weary,* (IDrd, O, Ḳ,) *and weak.* (TA.)

طرد

1. طَرَدَهُ, aor. ـُ, (Ṣ, A, Mgh, &c.,) inf. n. طَرْدٌ (Ṣ, A, L, Mgh, Mṣb, Ḳ) and طَرَدٌ, (Ṣ, A, L, Ḳ,) or the latter is a simple subst., (Mṣb,) *He drove away him,* or *it;* as also ▼ طَرَّدَهُ and ▼ اِطَّرَدَهُ: (L:) *he drove him away, expelled him,* or *banished him,* (ISk, Ṣ, L, Ḳ,) *and said to him, Depart thou,* or *go thou away, from us:* (ISk, Ṣ, L:) *he removed him,* or *it; put,* or *placed, him,* or *it, at a distance, away,* or *far away;* (Ṣ, A, Mgh, L, Ḳ;*) with his hand, or arm, or with an instrument in his hand; as when one says طَرَدْتُ الذُّبَابَ عَنِ الشَّرَابِ [*I drove away the flies from the wine,* or *beverage*]. (Durrat el-Ghowwáṣ, in De Sacy's Anthol. Gramm. Ar., p. 60 of the Ar. text.) You say, طَرَدْتُهُ فَذَهَبَ [*I drove him away, &c., and he went away*], (Sb, Ṣ, Mṣb,) using ذهب in the place of the quasi-pass., (Mṣb,) not using [in this case] the measure اِنْفَعَلَ (Ṣ, A) nor اِفْتَعَلَ, (Ṣ,) [i. e.] you do not say ▼ انطرد nor ▼ اطّرد, (Sb, Mṣb,) except in a bad dialect. (Ṣ, A, Mṣb.) And you say, مَرَّ فُلَانٌ يَطْرُدُهُمْ *Such a one went along driving them away and pursuing them.* (Ṣ, L.) — And طَرَدَ الإِبِلَ, [aor. ـُ,] (Ṣ, L,) inf. n. طَرْدٌ and طَرَدٌ, *He drove,* or *brought,* or *gathered, the camels together, from their several quarters.* (Ṣ, L, Ḳ.*) — [And طَرَدَ, aor. and inf. n. as above, ‡ *He coursed, pursued, hunted,* or *strove to gain possession of* or *to catch,* wild animals or the like]: the inf. n. طَرْدٌ is expl. as signifying مُزَاوَلَةُ الصَّيْدِ [and طَرْدٌ is very frequently used in this sense]. (Ṣ, Ḳ.) You say, خَرَجَ يَطْرُدُ حُمُرَ الوَحْشِ ‡ *He went forth to course, pursue, hunt, snare, entrap,* or *catch, the wild asses.* (A.) And طَرَدَتِ الكِلَابُ الصَّيْدَ † *The dogs drove away, and pursued closely, the wild animals,* or *the like.* (L.) And ▼ طارد الصَّيْدَ, inf. n. طِرَادٌ, † *He circumvented, in order to snare, entrap,* or *catch, the wild animal,* or *wild animals,* or *the like;* and in like manner, a serpent. (L.) — And طَرَدْتُ القَوْمَ *I came to the people,* or *party,* or *came upon them,* or *destroyed them,* (أَتَيْتُهُمْ, Ḳ, or أَتَيْتُ عَلَيْهِمْ, T, Ṣ, L,) *and passed through them.* (T, Ṣ, L, Ḳ.) — And الرِّيحُ تَطْرُدُ الحَصَى وَالصَّفَى ‡ *The wind blows away with violence the pebbles and the dust.* (A.) — And القِيعَانُ تَطْرُدُ السَّرَابَ ‡ *The plains have the mirage running along them like water.* (A.) — And طَرَدْتُ بَصَرِى فِى أَمْرِ القَوْمِ ‡ [*I directed my observation to the affair,* or *case, of the people,* or *party*]. (A.) — And طَرَدْتُ الخِلَافَ فِى المَسْأَلَةِ † *I put forward an opposition,* or *a contradiction, in the question:* app. from المُطَارَدَةُ meaning "the making to run in a race." (Mṣb.)

2: see 1, first sentence: and see also 4; the latter, in two places. — One says also, طرّد صَوْتَهُ ‡ *He prolonged his voice;* syn. مَدَّهُ: (A, TA:*) or تَطْرِيدُ السَّوْطِ signifies مَدُّهُ [i. e. *the extending,* or *stretching forth, the whip*]. (Ḳ, TA.) [The latter I think a mistranscription.] — طرّده جَرْحَهُمْ, said of a judge, means ‡ *He bade him,* (i. e. a litigant) *to invalidate their testimony,* or *evidence,* if able to do so. (TA, from a saying of Esh-Sháfi'ee.)

3. طارد قِرْنَهُ, (A,) inf. n. مُطَارَدَةٌ and طِرَادٌ, (Ṣ, A, Ḳ,) ‡ *He charged upon,* or *assaulted,* or *attacked, his adversary,* (Ṣ, A, Ḳ,) in war (Ṣ) &c., (TA,) *the latter doing the same,* (Ṣ, Ḳ,) *and fought him,* whether he drove him away or not. (A.) One says, هُمْ فُرْسَانُ الطِّرَادِ ‡ *They are the horsemen who charge upon, assault,* or *attack, one another.* (Ṣ, Ḳ, TA.) — طارد, inf. n. مُطَارَدَةٌ, signifies [also] † *He made* [a horse] *to run in a race.* (Mṣb.) — طارد الصَّيْدَ: see 1, latter half.

4. اطردهُ *He made him,* or *caused him,* (ISh, ISk, Ṣ, Mgh,) or *he ordered him,* (L, Ḳ,) *to be driven away, expelled, banished, removed,* or *put* or *placed at a distance* or *away* or *far away,* (ISh, ISk, Ṣ, Mgh, L, Ḳ,) *so as not to be in a state of security;* (ISh, Mgh, TA;) said of the Sulṭán: (Mgh:) or *he* (the Sulṭán, Ṣ, L) *ordered that he should be expelled,* or *banished,* (Ṣ, L, Ḳ,) *from his,* (Ṣ, L,) or *from the,* (Ḳ,) *town,* or *country:* (Ṣ, L, Ḳ:) or اطردهُ عَنِ البَلَدِ, and ▼ طرّدهُ with teshdeed, *he* (the Sulṭán) *expelled him,* or *banished him, from the town,* or *country.* (Mṣb.) — And اطرد الإِبِلَ *He ordered that the camels should be driven,* or *brought,* or *gathered, together, from their several quarters.* (Ṣ, L.) — And أَطْرَدْنَا الغَنَمَ *We sent the he-goats among the herd.* (IAạr, TA.) — And اطردهُ, (L, Ḳ,) inf. n. إِطْرَادٌ, (A'Obeyd, Mgh,) *He* (i. e. a person about to race with another, L) *said to him, If thou outstrip me I will give thee such a thing, and if I outstrip thee thou shalt give me such a thing;* (A'Obeyd, Mgh, L, Ḳ;) as also ▼ طرّدهُ. (L.)

6. تطاردا ‡ *They two charged upon, assaulted,* or *attacked, and fought, each other,* whether they drove each other away or not. (A.)

7. انطرد a word of a bad dialect. (Ṣ, A, Mṣb.) See 1.

8. اِطَّرَدَ, as trans.: see 1, first sentence. — As quasi-pass.: see 1, second sentence. — اِطَّرَدَ المَآءُ ‡ *The water flowed in a regular,* or *a continuous,* or *an uninterrupted, course, one portion following another:* (A,* L, Mṣb:) and اطّردت الأَنْهَارُ † *The rivers so flowed:* (Mṣb:) or [simply] *the rivers ran,* or *flowed.* (Ṣ.) And اِضْطَرَدَ الخَيْلُ ‡ *The horses ran, following one another:* occurring in a trad.: the verb is originally اِطْتَرَدَ; the augmentative ت being changed into ط, and then the radical ط is changed into ض: (L:) and for اِطِّرَادٌ, some say اِضْطِرَادٌ, changing the ض into ل [as in اِلْطَجَعَ for اِضْطَجَعَ]. (Az, TA in art. ضجع.) And اطّردوا إِلَى السَّيْرِ ‡ *They followed one another to go on a journey.* (A.) And اطّرد الشَّىْءُ, (Ṣ, A, L,) or الأَمْرُ, (Mṣb, Ḳ,) ‡ *The thing,* or *the affair, followed a regular and continuous course, one part,* or *stage, following another*

uninterruptedly; (Ṣ, A, L, Mṣb, Ḳ:) and اطّرد الأَمْرُ signifies also *the affair followed a right, a direct, or an even, course.* (Ṣ, L, Ḳ.) And اطّرد الكَلَامُ † *The language, or speech, was consecutive, or uninterrupted, in its parts.* (L.) And اطّردت قِرَاءَتُهُ † *His recitation, or reading, continued uninterruptedly:* from يَوْمٌ طَرَّادٌ meaning "a long day." (Mgh.) And اطّرد الحَدُّ † *The definition was of uniform, undeviating, or general, application; it uniformly, or commonly, or constantly, applied, or obtained;* i. e. *all the things to which it related followed one uniform, or undeviating, way, like the course of rivers.* (Mṣb. [And in like manner one says of a rule.]) اطّرد said of a word, form or measure, construction, or government, means ‡ *It was agreeable with the common, or constant, course of speech in respect of analogy, or rule; it was agreeable with common, or constant, analogy, or rule:* and, said of the same, or of a rule, *it was agreeable with the common, or constant, course of speech in respect of usage; it was agreeable with common, or constant, usage; it commonly, or constantly, obtained:* [the verb is used absolutely to express each of these two meanings; the context in general showing clearly which meaning is intended:] the former meaning is also expressed by the phrase اطّرد فِى القِيَاسِ; and the latter, by the phrase اطّرد فِى الاِسْتِعْمَالِ. (Mz, 12th نوع. [See also the contr. شَذَّ: and see مُطَّرِدٌ, below.])

10. استطرد *He desired, or sought, to drive away, expel, banish, remove, or put or place at a distance or away or far away.* (ḲL.) — استطرد لَهُ (Ṣ, L, Mṣb, in the Ḳ اِسْتَطْرَدَهُ لَهُ,) denotes a kind of stratagem, (Ṣ, L,) or what is as though it were a kind of stratagem, (Ḳ,) meaning † *He fled, or wheeled about widely, from him,* i. e. from his adversary in fight, *to turn again, by way of stratagem, and then returned upon him; as though he drew him from a position which he could not maintain to one which he could maintain.* (Mṣb.) — And hence, app., the phrase, وَقَعَ ذٰلِكَ عَلَى وَجْهِ الاِسْتِطْرَادِ † *That occurred in the way of a digression, not being mentioned in its proper place.* (Mṣb.)

طَرْدٌ *i. q.* فِرَاخُ النَّحْلِ [as though meaning The *young ones of bees:* but app. a mistranscription for فراخ النَّخْلِ † the *suckers, or offsets, of palm-trees;* as though pushed forth; of the measure فَعْلٌ in the sense of the measure مَفْعُولٌ, like نَقْضٌ &c.]. (TA, from AḤn.)

مَآءٌ طَرِدٌ *Water in which beasts have waded, and in which they have voided their urine and dung.* (Ḳ.)

طَرْدَةٌ † *A charge, or an assault, of two horsemen, each upon the other, at one time.* (Ḳ.)

طَرْدِينٌ *A certain food of the [people called]* أَطْرَاد [pl. of طَرْدٌ]. (Ḳ.)

طَرَادٌ: see مُطْرَدٌ. — فُلَانٌ يَمْشِى مَشْيًا طرادًا [app. طَرَادًا, from طِرَادٌ meaning "a spear;" or perhaps ▼ طُرَّادًا;] † *Such a one walks in a straight, a direct, or an even, course.* (L, TA.)

طَرِيدٌ and ▼ مَطْرُودٌ (Ṣ, L, Mṣb) and ▼ مُطَرَّدٌ (A) [and ▼ مُطْرَدٌ] A man *driven away, expelled, banished,* or *outcast;* (L;) a man *removed; put, or placed, at a distance, away, or far away:* (Ṣ, L:) طَرِيدٌ is likewise applied to a female, as also طَرِيدَةٌ; and the pl. of both in this case is طَرَائِدُ. (M, L.) نَاقَةٌ طَرِيدٌ, without ة, means *A she-camel driven away, and taken away:* pl. طَرَائِدُ. (L.) — And ‡ *One who is born after another:* (Ṣ, L, Ḳ:) the second is termed the طَرِيد of the first. (Ṣ, L.) Also † *One who is born before another.* (Ḳ.) And hence, الطَّرِيدَانِ ‡ *The night and the day:* (A, L, Ḳ:) each being the طَرِيد of the other. (A, L.) — See also طَرَّادٌ. — Also ‡ *Old;* applied to a garment, or piece of cloth; syn. شَارِفٌ. (A, TA.) And ثَوْبٌ طَرَائِدُ is mentioned by Lḥ as meaning † *An old, worn-out, garment, or piece of cloth.* (TA.) — And The *base,* or *lower part, of the raceme of a palm-tree;* (Ṣ, L, Ḳ;) as also ▼ طَرِيدَةٌ. (L.)

طَرِيدَةٌ [a subst. from طَرِيدٌ, rendered so by the affix ة,] *A wild animal, or the like, that is coursed, hunted, snared, entrapped, or caught:* (Ṣ, L, Ḳ, TA:) pl. طَرَائِدُ. (TA.) The *female that is the object of the chase* of a male [wild] ass. (M* and Ḳ* and MF, all in art. الب.) — And *A number of camels driven away together,* i. e., (Ṣ,) *camels that are stolen:* (Ṣ, Ḳ:) *a number of camels attached by a troop of horsemen and driven away.* (A, L.) — † *A cane wherein is a notch* (حُزَّة), *which is put upon spindles and arrows,* (Ṣ, L, Ḳ,) *and upon a stick,* (L,) *and thus used for planing them:* (Ṣ, L, Ḳ:) ‡ *i. q.* سَفَنٌ, (AHeyth, A, L,) i. e. *a cane which is hollowed, and has some notches cut in it,* (AHeyth, L,) *through which an arrow is put* (AHeyth, A, L) *and repeatedly drawn [to smooth it]:* (AHeyth, A:) or *a small piece of wood, in the form of a water-spout, as though it were the half of a cane, of the size required by the bow or arrow [which are to be smoothed therewith].* (AḤn, L.) — ‡ *An oblong piece* (A, Ḳ) of a garment (A) or of silk: (Ḳ:) or *a long strip* (AA, IAạr, TA) of rag (AA, TA) or of silk. (IAạr, TA.) † *A piece of rag, which is moistened, or wetted, and with which the [kind of oven called]* تَنُّور *is wiped;* as also ▼ مِطْرَدَةٌ. (Ḳ.) — And ‡ *A narrow strip* of herbage (A,* Ḳ, TA) and of land. (Ḳ, TA.) — And ‡ The *line, or streak,* (خُطَّة,) *between the rump-bone and withers.* (L.) — See also طَرِيدٌ, last sentence. — الطَّرِيدَةُ is also the name of *A certain game* (Ḳ, TA) *of the boys of the Arabs of the desert,* (TA,) *called by the vulgar* المَسَّةُ, (Ḳ, TA,) *and some say* المَاسَّةُ, (TA,) and الضَّبْطَةُ: *when the hand of the player falls upon the body or head or shoulder of another, it is [said to be]* المَسَّةُ; *and when it falls upon the leg, or foot, it is* الأَسْنُ: (Ḳ, TA:) but this [app. meaning الأَسْنُ] is not of established authority: *it was also played by girls.* (TA.) — See also what here follows.

طَرَّادٌ *A small and swift kind of ship or boat:* (Ḳ, TA:) called by the vulgar ▼ تَطْرِيدَةٌ [perhaps a mistranscription for ▼ طَرِيدَةٌ, which is a post-classical term for *a vessel used for the transport of horses;* and of which طَرَائِدُ is the pl.: see Quatremère's Hist. des Sultans Mamlouks, i. 144]. (TA.) — Also † *One who prolongs a recitation, or reading, [of the Ḳur-án] to people so that he drives them away:* (Ḳ:) or *one who drives away people by the length of his standing and the muchness of his recitation, or reading.* (Mgh.) — And ‡ *Wide, spacious,* or *ample;* (A, Ḳ;) applied to a plain, (A,) or place. (Ḳ.) And ‡ An *even, wide,* roof. (Ḳ, TA.) And بِلَادٌ طَرَّادَةٌ ‡ *Wide, or spacious, regions or lands,* (A, L,) *in which the mirage [in appearance] flows.* (L.) — Also, (A, Mgh, L, Ḳ,) and ▼ طَرِيدٌ, and ▼ مُطَّرِدٌ, (L, Ḳ,) ‡ A *long* day: (L, Mgh, Ḳ, TA:) ‡ a *whole,* or *complete,* day, (A, L,) or month. (A.) And سِنُونَ طَرَّادَةٌ ‡ *Whole,* or *complete, years.* (A.) — See also طِرَادٌ.

طَارِدٌ [act. part. n. of 1: fem. with ة, and pl. of the latter طَوَارِدُ]. — [Hence] طَوَارِدُ الإِبِلِ ‡ *Those that remain behind,* [as though driving away the others,] *of the camels.* (A.)

تَطْرِيدَةٌ: see طَرَّادٌ.

مِطْرَدٌ *A spear;* so called because one hunts (يطرد) with it: (Mṣb:) or, (Ṣ, M, A, Mgh, L, Ḳ,) as also ▼ طِرَادٌ, (L, Ḳ, [in my copy of the Mgh, app., طَرَّادٌ, its pl. being there plainly written طَرَّادَات, though the sing. is doubtfully written, and it may be that Freytag, who mentions طَرَّادَةٌ as signifying *a spear,* was led to do so from his finding طِرَادَات, which I believe to be pl. of طِرَادٌ, written طَرَّادَات,]) *a short spear,* (M, A, Mgh, L, Ḳ,) so called for the reason above mentioned, (Mgh,) [i. e.] *with which one hunts* (يطرد), *or with which one hunts wild animals;* (M, L;) [*a short hunting-spear;*] or *a short spear with which one thrusts, or pierces,* (Ṣ, L,) *wild animals,* (Ṣ,) or *wild asses:* (L:) pl. مَطَارِدُ. (A.) [And Freytag mentions مَطَارِدُ as a pl. without sing., occurring in the Deewán of the Hudhalees, meaning *Long arrows.*]

مِطْرَدَةٌ *A means of driving away, removing,* &c.: so in the phrase مِطْرَدَةُ الدَّآءِ عَنِ الجَسَدِ † *A means of driving away, or removing, disease from the body.* (L, from a trad.) — And † The *beaten track;* or *main part, and middle; of a road;* as also ▼ مُطَّرِدَةٌ. (Ḳ.)

مِطْرَدَةٌ: see طَرِيدَةٌ, latter half: — and مُطَّرِدَةٌ.

مُطْرَدٌ: see طَرِيدٌ: — and طَرَّادٌ.

[مُطَّرِدٌ, accord. to Freytag, occurs in the Deewán of the Hudhalees, applied to a spear, as meaning *Altogether straight, so that the whole trembles:*

for that which is crooked does not. But this, if not a mistranscription, is app. used by poetic license, for ↑ مُطَّرِدٌ.]

مَطْرُودٌ : } see طَرِيدٌ.
مُطَّرَدٌ :

جَدْوَلٌ مُطَّرِدٌ † *A rivulet*, or *streamlet*, [*regular*, or *uninterrupted, and*] *swift in course.* (L.) — [In a copy of the A, among tropical phrases, I find جَدْوَلٌ مُطَّرِدُ الأَنَابِيبِ وَالكُعُوبِ; but it seems that there is an omission here, and that after جَدْوَل we should read مُطَّرِدٌ; and then, وَرُمْحٌ الخ, i. e. ‡ *A spear even and regular in the internodal portions and the knots.*] See مُطَّرَدٌ. — [Hoseyn Ibn-Homám El-Murree applies مُطَّرِد, as an epithet in which the quality of a subst. predominates, to *A coat of mail*, app. meaning *even and regular in texture*: see Ham p. 189.] — بَعِيرٌ مُطَّرِدٌ † *A camel that continues his pace, or course, uninterruptedly, and does not become out of breath from running.* (L.) — مُطَّرِدُ التَّسْيِيرِ is used by a poet as a name for † *The nose* of a running horse [app. meaning *uninterrupted in breathing*]. (S, L.) — مُطَّرِدٌ applied to a word, form or measure, construction, or government, means ‡ *Agreeable with the common*, or *constant, course of speech in respect of analogy*, or *rule*; *agreeable with common*, or *constant, analogy*, or *rule*: and, applied to the same, or to a rule, *agreeable with the common*, or *constant, course of speech in respect of usage*; *agreeable with common*, or *constant, usage*; *commonly*, or *constantly, obtaining*: (Mz, 12th نوع:) [but what is thus termed is not strictly speaking and in every case without exception; for, taking 24 to represent universality, 23 in comparison therewith is مُطَّرِد; 20 in comparison with 23 is غَالِب; 15 is كَثِير; 3 is قَلِيل; and 1 is نَادِر. (Mz, 13th نوع.) [See also the contr. شَاذٌّ : and see 8 in this art.])

رَمْلٌ مُتَطَارِدٌ † *Sand of which one part drives away and follows another.* (L.)

طرز

1. طَرَزَ, aor. ِ, (K,) inf. n. طَرْزٌ, (TK,) *He became goodly in shape, form*, or *aspect, after having been thick.* (Sgh,* K,* TK.) — ‡ *He became good in disposition, after having been evil.* (K.) — طَرِزَ فِى المَلْبَسِ وَفِى المَطْعَمِ, (K,) and (TA,) ‡ *He was nice*, or *dainty* (تَأَنَّقَ, K, or تَنَوَّقَ, A) *in apparel*, (K,* TA,) *and in diet*; (TA;) *not wearing*, (K, TA,) *and not eating*, (TA,) *aught but what was good*: (K, TA:) as also ↑ تطرّز فيهما. (TA.) — Accord. to IAar, الطَّرْزُ signifies الرفع بالكز; [thus in the L and TA; but, I think, incorrectly, for الدَّفْعُ بِالْكَزِّ;] and one says, طَرَزَهُ, inf. n. طَرْزٌ [app. meaning *He repelled him by striking with his fist*]. (L, TA.)

2. طرّز الثَّوْبَ, (S, K, &c.,) inf. n. تَطْرِيزٌ, (Msb, K,) *He embroidered*, or *variegated*, or *figured, the garment*, or *piece of cloth.* (S, A, Msb, K.) [See طِرَازٌ.]

5. تطرّز *It* (a garment, or a piece of cloth,) *was embroidered*, or *variegated*, or *figured.* (K.) — See also 1.

طَرْزٌ, (Msb, and so in two copies of the K, and in the TK,) like فَلْسٌ [in measure], (Msb,) or ↑ طِرْزٌ, (so in the K accord. to the TA, and so in a copy of the A,) *Form; shape; outward appearance*; or *garb*; syn. شَكْلٌ; (IAar, Msb, TA;) and هَيْئَةٌ; (K;) and بِزَّةٌ: (TA:) as also ↑ طِرَازٌ; syn. هَيْئَةٌ. (S.) You say, هٰذَا طَرْزُ هٰذَا *This is of the form*, or *shape, of this.* (Msb.) — ‡ *A way*, or *manner, of acting*; (A, TA;) as also ↑ طِرَازٌ; syn. of the latter نَمَطٌ, (S, Msb, K,) and أُسْلُوبٌ. (TK.) You say, مَا أَحْسَنَ طَرْزَ ↑ فُلَانٍ ‡ *How good is the way of acting of such a one!* and طِرْزُهُ ↑ طِرْزٌ حَسَنٌ ‡ *His way of acting is a good way of acting.* (A, TA.) And مِنَ الطِّرَازِ ↑ الأَوَّلِ, (S, Msb,) occurring in a verse of Hassán Ibn-Thábit, (S,) signifies *Of* [the people of] *the first* [*and best*] *way of acting*; i. e., مِنَ النَّمَطِ الأَوَّلِ. (S, Msb.) [But see a different explanation of this phrase below, voce طِرَازٌ.] — Anything *good, goodly*, or *excellent*; as also ↑ طِرَازٌ. (TA.)

طِرْزٌ : see طَرْزٌ, in three places. — Also *A house*, or *chamber*, (بَيْتٌ,) *somewhat long*; [said to be] a Pers. word arabicized: or *a summer-house*, or *summer-chamber.* (TA.)

طِرَازٌ The *embroidery*, or *variegated* or *figured work*, (عَلَمٌ,) *of a garment*, or *piece of cloth*: (S, A, Mgh, Msb, K:) a Pers. word, (S, A, TA,) arabicized: (S, A, Msb, K:) said to be originally تَرْز, meaning, in Pers., "even measurement:" (TA:) [or originally طِرَاز, which has the same meaning in Pers. as the arabicized form has in Arabic:] pl. طُرُزٌ. (Msb.) — And *A garment*, or *piece of cloth, woven for the Sultán*: (K:) also arabicized [from the Pers. طِرَاز, meaning, *a royal robe*, or *rich embroidered garment*]: and one also says, ↑ ثَوْبٌ طِرَازِىٌّ: (TA:) or this last is so called from a place named طِرَاز. (Mgh.) — And *A place in which goodly garments* or *cloths are woven*: (Lth, Az, A, K:) and this also is arabicized [from the Pers. طِرَاز, which has the same meaning]. (TA.) You say, عُمِلَ هٰذَا الثَّوْبُ فِى طِرَازِ فُلَانٍ *This garment*, or *piece of cloth, was made in such a one's place for weaving goodly garments* or *cloths.* (A.) And هُوَ مَا عُمِلَ فِى طِرَازِ اللّٰهِ ‡ [*It is what has been made in God's place of creation of goodly things*]: said of a beautiful face. (A, TA.) And هٰذَا الكَلَامُ الحَسَنُ مِنْ طِرَازِ فُلَانٍ ‡ [*This beautiful language is of the elegant composition of such a one*]. (A, TA.) And هُوَ مِنَ الطِّرَازِ الأَوَّلِ ‡ [app. *He is of the first noble extraction*]. (A, TA. [See also طَرْزٌ.]) And one says of a man, when he utters a good thing of his own excogitation, هٰذَا مِنْ طِرَازِهِ † [*This is of his clever excogitation*]. (Sgh, TA.) And in like manner is expl. the phrase, in a trad., لَيْسَ هٰذَا مِنْ طِرَازِكَ † *This is not of thine own authorship and excogitation.* (TA.) — See also طَرْزٌ, in four places.

طِرَازِىٌّ *An embroiderer; one who does figured work upon garments* or *cloths*; as also ↑ مُطَرِّزٌ (TA) [and ↑ طَرَّازٌ]. — ثَوْبٌ طِرَازِىٌّ: see طِرَازٌ.

طِرْزَدَانٌ, or طِرَازْدَانٌ, or طِرَزْوَدَانٌ, (accord. to different copies of the Mgh and K,) The *case* (غِلَافٌ) *of the balance* (المِيزَان); an arabicized word; (Mgh, K;) mentioned by Sgh; in Pers. تَرَازُودَانٌ [but this is expl. in Pers. dictionaries as meaning the *scale of a balance*]. (TA.)

طَرَّازٌ : see the paragraph next but one above.

مُطَرَّزٌ A garment, or piece of cloth, *embroidered*, or *variegated*, or *figured.* (S, Msb.)

مُطَرِّزٌ : see طِرَازِىٌّ.

طرس

1. طَرَسَهُ, inf. n. طَرْسٌ, *He wrote it*; namely, a writing or book; as also سَطَرَهُ. (TA.) — See also 2. — طَرِسَ, a verb like فَرِحَ, *He* (a man) *became worn out in body, and aged.* (Sgh, TA.)

2. طرّسهُ, (M, A,) so written by El-Urmawee, (TA,) inf. n. تَطْرِيسٌ; (A;) or ↑ طَرَسَهُ, aor. ُ; (K;) *He obliterated it*, or *effaced it*; (K, TA; [compare دَرَسَهُ;]) and (TA) *he marred*, or *spoiled, it*: (M, TA:) or *he obliterated it*, or *effaced it, well.* (A.) — Also, the former, (M,) inf. n. as above, (K,) *He blackened it*; namely, a door. (M, K.) — And طرّس, (TK,) inf. n. as above, (Lth, K,) *He restored the writing upon a thing whereon the writing had been obliterated*, or *effaced.* (Lth, K.*)

5. تطرّس *He ate not, nor drank, aught save what was good*; (K, TA;) like تنطّس: so says IF. (TA.) — تطرّس عَنْهُ *He shunned it; kept aloof*, or *preserved himself, from it*; (Sgh, K, TA;) and *held himself above the commission of it.* (Sgh, TA.)

طِرْسٌ *A written paper* or *the like*; syn. صَحِيفَةٌ, (S, A, Msb, K;) or صَحِيفَةٌ إِذَا كُتِبَتْ; as also طِلْسٌ: (Sh, TA:) or *one of which the writing has been obliterated*, or *effaced, and which has then been written upon* [*again*]; (S, A, Msb, K;) [*a palimpsest*;] as also طِلْسٌ: (S:) or *one of which the writing has been obliterated*, or *effaced, well*: (Az, in TA, art. طلس:) or *a writing that has been obliterated*, or *effaced, and then written* [*again*]; as also طِرْصٌ: (M:) or *an obliterated*, or *effaced, writing upon which one is able to renew the writing*: (Lth, TA:) pl. [of pauc.] أَطْرَاسٌ (S, M, Msb, K) and [of mult.] طُرُوسٌ. (M, A, Msb, K.)

مُتَطَرِّسٌ One *who seeks, pursues*, or *desires, the*

most pleasing of things; who picks, or chooses. (T, Ḳ, TA.)

طرش

1. طَرِشَ, aor. ـَ, (Mgh, Mṣb, Ḳ,) inf. n. طَرَشٌ, (Ṣ, A, Mgh, Mṣb, Ḳ,) *He was,* or *became, deaf:* or *affected with something less than* صَمَمٌ [or *deafness*]: (Mṣb:) or *like deafness:* (Mgh:) [meaning, *heaviness,* or *dulness, of hearing:* (see أَطْرَشُ:)] or طَرَشٌ is *the slightest deafness:* (Ṣ, A, Ḳ: [in the CḲ it is erroneously written طَرْش:]) but some say that it is not pure Arabic: (Mṣb:) and some say that it is post-classical: (Ṣ, Mṣb, Ḳ:) so says IDrd: (O:) AḤát disallows the root and its derivatives, and says that they have not been content with the barbarousness of saying طَرَشٌ, but have formed from it a verb, namely, طَرِشَ: (O, TA:) El-Ma'arree says that the verb has been formed by the vulgar from أُطْرُوشٌ, which is an Arabic word. (TA.)

5. تطرّش *He stood and sat;* said of one who is convalescent: (O:) or *he became convalescent, and nearly recovered, and arose and walked;* syn. ابْرَغَشَّ. (Ḳ.) —— تطرّش بِالبَهْمِ *i. q.* اخْتَلَفَ بِهَا [i. e. *He went to and fro, repeatedly, with the young lambs* or *kids:* strangely expl. in the TḲ as said of a camel, and as meaning *he became mixed,* or *confounded, among the beasts*]. (O, Ḳ.)

6. تطارش *He feigned himself deaf:* (O, Ḳ:) or *heavy,* or *dull, of hearing.* (Mgh.)

بِهِ طُرْشَةٌ *In him is the slightest deafness.* (Ibn-'Abbád, O, Ḳ.)

أَطْرَشُ, (Mṣb,) or ▾ أُطْرُوشٌ, (Az, A, Mgh, O, Mṣb, Ḳ,) of which Az says, I know not whether it be Arabic or adventitious, (Mṣb,) and IDrd says that it is not genuine Arabic, (Mgh,) and AḤát disallows it, but El-Ma'arree says that it is Arabic, though the verb is a barbarism, (TA,) *Deaf;* (Mṣb, Ḳ;) and in some of the copies of [the work of] Yaḳoob, ▾ أُطْرُشٌ is found, thus expl.: (TA:) or *heavy,* or *dull, of hearing:* (Mgh:) or *affected with something less than deafness:* (Mṣb:) or *with the slightest deafness:* (A:) the fem. of أَطْرَشُ is طَرْشَآءُ: (Mṣb:) and the pl. is طُرْشٌ. (Mgh, O, Mṣb, Ḳ.*) ═ Accord. to Z, [in the A,] أَطْرَشُ, applied to a man, signifies *Having thin eyebrows.* (TA. [But I think that this is a mistranscription for أَطْرَطُ.])

أُطْرُشٌ : } see the next preceding paragraph.
أُطْرُوشٌ : }

طرط

1. طَرِطَ, [aor. ـَ,] inf. n. طَرَطٌ, *He had thin eyebrows:* (Ibn-'Abbád, O:) or *he had light, thin,* or *scanty, hair of the eyes, of the eyebrows,* and *of the eyelashes.* (Ḳ.) —— And *He was,* or *became, foolish, stupid, unsound in intellect* or *understanding,* or *deficient therein.* (Ḳ.)

طَرَطٌ *Thinness of the hair* in the eyebrow. (IAạr, TA.)

طَرِطٌ : see أَطْرَطُ. —— Also *Foolish, stupid, unsound in intellect* or *understanding,* or *deficient therein.* (Ḳ.)

طَارِطٌ *Light, thin,* or *scanty, in the hair;* (IAạr, O, L, Ḳ;) applied to an eyebrow. (L.)

أَطْرَطُ الحَاجِبَيْنِ A man *destitute of eyebrows;* (AZ, Ṣ, O;) as also أَمْرَطُ الحاجبين; (O;) and some say أَضْرَطُ, but Abu-l-Ghowth knew it not: (Ṣ, O:) or *having light, thin,* or *scanty, hair of the eyebrows;* and so ▾ طَرِطُ الحَاجِبَيْنِ: (Ḳ:) the mention of the حَاجِبَانِ is indispensable; (AZ, Ṣ, O, Ḳ;) but sometimes omitted, on the ground of a weak authority: (Ḳ, TA:) and accord. to Ibn-'Abbád, أَطْرَطُ signifies *having thin eyebrows.* (O.) And طَرْطَآءُ العَيْنِ A woman *having scanty eyelashes.* (O, Ḳ.)

طرطب

Q. 1. طَرْطَبَ بِالمِعْزَى, inf. n. طَرْطَبَةٌ, *He* (the milker) *called the goats,* [app. *by making a sound with the lips;* for,] accord. to AZ, طَرْطَبَةٌ is with the lips: (Ṣ:) *he called the goats:* (IḲṭṭ, TA:) and طَرْطَبَ بِالنَّعْجَةِ *he called the ewe:* (AZ, TA:) [and Freytag says, on the authority of the "Kitáb el-Aḍdád," that طَرْطَبَ signifies also *he drove away* sheep from himself:] the inf. n. signifies the milker's *making a sound* to the goats *with his lips,* (ISd, Ḳ, TA,) *to quiet them,* or *appease them:* (ISd, TA:) and the *calling* sheep or goats *to be milked,* (Ḳ, TA,) as some say, *with the lips:* (TA:) also the *calling* of asses: (Az, TA:) and, accord. to some, the *whistling with the lips* to sheep. (TA.) —— يُطَرْطِبُ شُعَيْرَاتٍ لَهُ, occurring in a trad., means *Putting in motion his mustache* [lit. *some small hairs that he had*] *in his speech:* or, as some say, *blowing with his lips into his mustache* by reason of rage and pride. (O.) —— And طَرْطَبَةٌ signifies also The *agitation,* or *commotion,* of water in the belly (IḲṭṭ, Ḳ, TA) and in a skin. (IḲṭṭ, TA.) —— And The act of *fleeing.* (IḲṭṭ, TA.)

طُرْطُبٌ : see طُرْطُبٌّ, in two places.

طُرْطُبَةٌ : see طُرْطُبٌّ : —— and طُرْطُبَّةٌ.

طُرْطُبٌّ *A long breast:* (Ṣ:) or, as also ▾ طُرْطُبٌ, and, accord. to him who makes ثَدْىٌ [the "breast"] fem., ▾ طُرْطُبَّى, *a large, flabby breast:* (Ḳ:) or *a large, flabby, long breast:* (TA:) and the first word, *a long udder;* (Ḥam p. 809;) [and] so ▾ طُرْطُبَةٌ, written without tenween, in the dial. of El-Yemen; on the authority of Kr. (TA.) One says, أَخْزَى اللّٰهُ طُرْطُبَّيْهَا *May God expose to shame her long breasts.* (A, TA.) —— Also, and ▾ طُرْطُبٌ, † *The penis:* (Ḳ:) [not found by SM in any work except the Ḳ; but the former word is mentioned in this sense in the O:] app. so called as being likened to a long and flabby breast. (TA.) —— دُهْدُرَّيْنِ وَطُرْطُبَّيْنِ [or each of these two words by itself] is said to, or in reference to, a man whom one derides. (AZ, Ṣ, O, Ḳ. [See art. دهدر.])

طُرْطُبَّةٌ A woman *having long breasts:* (Ṣ, TA:) or *having large breasts:* or *having flabby breasts.* (TA.) And, or accord. to the TA and some copies of the Ḳ ▾ طُرْطُبَةٌ, (said in the TA to be without teshdeed,) as also ▾ طُرْطُبَانِيَّةٌ, *Having a long udder:* (Ḳ:) or a she-goat *having long teats.* (TA.)

طُرْطُبَّى : see طُرْطُبٌّ.

طُرْطُبَانِيَّةٌ : see طُرْطُبَّةٌ.

This art. is included in some of the lexicons in art. طرب.

طرف

1. طَرَفَ, aor. ـُ, inf. n. طَرْفٌ, *He looked from the outer angle of the eye:* or [*he twinkled with his eye,* i. e.] *he put the edge of his eyelid in motion,* or *in a state of commotion, and looked:* (M, TA:) or الطَّرْفُ signifies *the putting the eyelids in motion,* or *in a state of commotion, in looking:* (Mgh,* TA:) one says, شَخَصَ بَصَرُهُ فَمَا يَطْرِفُ [*His eye,* or *eyes, has,* or *have, become fixedly open,* or *raised, and he does not put his eyelids in motion,* or *does not twinkle with his eye,* or *eyes, in looking*]: (TA:) [or] one says, طَرَفَ البَصَرُ, aor. and inf. n. as above, meaning *the eye,* or *eyes,* [*twinkled,* or] *became in a state of commotion:* (Mṣb:) [or] طَرَفَ بَصَرَهُ, (O, Ḳ, TA, and so in a copy of the Ṣ,) or بَصَرُهُ, (so in one of my copies of the Ṣ,) aor. and inf. n. as above, [*he winked,* i. e.] *he closed one of his eyelids upon the other:* (Ṣ, O, Ḳ: [see also 4:]) or طَرَفَ بِعَيْنِهِ [in the CḲ بِعَيْنَيْهِ] *he put his eyelids in motion,* or *in a state of commotion:* (Ḳ, TA:) and طَرَفَتْ عَيْنُهُ, aor. تَطْرِفُ, inf. n. as above, *his eyelids were put in motion* or *in a state of commotion, by looking.* (Aṣ, TA.) [Another meaning of طَرَفَ بَصَرَهُ, and another of طَرَفَتْ said of the eye, will be found below.] عَيْنٌ تَطْرِفُ, signifying *An eye that* [*twinkles,* or] *puts the eyelid in motion,* or *in a state of commotion, with looking,* is used for ذُو عَيْنٍ تَطْرِفُ, meaning † *a living being.* (Mgh.) مَا بَقِيَتْ مِنْهُمْ عَيْنٌ تَطْرِفُ [*There remained not of them* one having *an eye twinkling*] means ‡ *they died,* (O, Ḳ, TA,) or (O, in the Ḳ erroneously "and," TA) *they were slain.* (O, Ḳ, TA.) —— [Also *He looked:* for] الطَّرْفُ is used as meaning *the act of looking* (Er-Rághib, Mṣb, TA) because the putting in motion of the eyelid constantly attends that act: (Er-Rághib, TA:) and طَرَفْتُهُ, inf. n. as above, signifies *I saw,* or *I looked at* or *towards, him,* or *it;* syn. أَبْصَرْتُهُ. (Ḥam p. 111.) It is said in the Ḳur [xiv. 44] لَا يَرْتَدُّ إِلَيْهِمْ طَرْفُهُمْ [*Their look shall not revert to them;* i. e., *shall not be withdrawn by them* from that upon which they shall look]. (Ṣ, O.) And in the same [xxvii. 40], أَنَا آتِيكَ بِهِ قَبْلَ أَنْ يَرْتَدَّ إِلَيْكَ طَرْفُكَ, [meaning, in like manner, *I will bring it to thee before thy look* at a thing *shall revert to thee,* or *be withdrawn by thee* therefrom: or,] accord. to Fr, meaning *before a thing shall be brought to thee*

from the extent of thy vision: or, as some say, *in the space in which thou shalt open thine eye and then close it:* or *in the space in which one shall reach the extent of thy vision.* (O.) And one says, نَظَرَ فُلَانٌ بِطَرْفٍ خَفِيٍّ [*Such a one looked with a furtive glance*], meaning, *contracted his eyelids over the main portion of his eye and looked with the rest of it,* by reason of shyness or fear. (Ḥar p. 565.) And تَطْرِفُ الرِّجَالَ [app. meaning *She looks at the men*] is said of a woman who does not keep constantly to one. (TA. [See مَطْرُوفَةٌ.]) And تَطْرِفُ الرِّيَاضَ رَوْضَةً بَعْدَ رَوْضَةٍ [app. meaning *She looks at the meadows, meadow after meadow,* to pasture upon them in succession,] is said of a she-camel such as is termed طَرِفَةٌ [q. v.]. (Aṣ, TA.) — طَرَفْتُ عَيْنَهُ, (Ṣ, O, Mṣb, in the Ḳ طَرَفَ عَيْنَهُ,) aor. and inf. n. as above, (Mṣb, TA,) *I* (Ṣ, O, Mṣb) *hit, struck, smote,* or *hurt, his eye with a thing,* (Ṣ, O, Mṣb, Ḳ, [in the CḲ شَىْءٌ is put for بِشَىْءٍ,]) such as a garment or some other thing, (TA,) *so that it shed tears:* and one says of the eye, طُرِفَتْ. (Ṣ, O, Ḳ. [See another explanation of the latter in the first sentence.]) Ziyád, in reciting a خُطْبَة, said, قَدْ طَرَفَتْ أَعْيُنَكُمُ الدُّنْيَا وَسَدَّتْ مَسَامِعَكُمُ الشَّهَوَاتُ [*The good of the present world hath smitten your eyes, and appetences have stopped your ears*]. (O.) And one says طَرَفَهُ and ▼ طرّفه meaning *He,* or *it, struck, smote,* or *hurt, his eye.* (TA.) And طَرَفَهَا الحُزْنُ وَالبُكَآءُ *Grief and weeping hurt it* (the eye), *so that it shed tears.* (TA.) And طَرَفَهَا حُبُّ الرِّجَالِ *The love of the men smote her eye, so that she raised her eyes and looked at every one that looked at her;* as though a طَرْفَة [or red spot of blood], or a stick or the like, hurt her eye. (Az, TA.) — الطَّرْفُ signifies also *The slapping with the hand* (Ḳ, TA) *upon the extremity of the eye.* (TA.) — Then it became applied to signify *The striking upon the head.* (TA.) — طَرَفَهُ عَنْهُ signifies *He turned him,* or *it, away,* or *back, from him,* or *it.* (Ṣ, O, Ḳ.) Hence the saying of a poet, (Ṣ, O, TA,) 'Amr Ibn-Abee-Rabee'ah, (TA,) or a young woman of the Anṣár, (O,)

• إِنَّكَ وَٱللّٰهِ لَذُو مَلَّةٍ •
• يَطْرِفُكَ الأَدْنَى عَنِ الأَبْعَدِ •

so in the Ṣ; but the right reading is عَنِ الأَقْدَمِ, for the next verse ends with تَصْرِمِى: (IB, TA:) [i. e. *Verily thou, by Alláh, art one having a weariness: the nearer turns thee away,* or *back, from the older:*] meaning, he turns away, or back, thy sight from the latter: i. e. thou takest the new (تَسْتَطْرِفُ ▼ الجَدِيدَ), and forgettest the old. (Ṣ, TA.) You say, طَرَفْتُ البَصَرَ عَنْهُ (Ṣ,* Mṣb) *I turned away,* or *back, the sight from him,* or *it.* (Mṣb.) And اِطْرِفْ بَصَرَكَ *Turn away,* or *back, thy sight* from that upon which it has fallen and to which it has been extended. (TA.) — And طَرَفَهُ عَنَّا شُغْلٌ *Business,* or *occupation, withheld him from us.* (TA.) — And طَرَفَهُ *He drove him away.* (Sh, TA.) ═ طَرِفَتْ, (Ṣ, O, Ḳ,) [aor. ـَ,] inf. n. طَرَفٌ; (TA;) and ▼ تطرّفت; *She* (a camel) *depastured the sides,* or *lateral parts,* (أَطْرَاف,) *of the pasturage, not mixing with the other she-camels,* (Ṣ, O, Ḳ,) *tasting, and not keeping constantly to one pasturage.* (Ḥar p. 569.) ═ طَرُفَ, (Ṣ, O, Mṣb, Ḳ,) inf. n. طَرَافَةٌ, (O, TA,) *It* (property) *was recently,* or *newly, acquired:* (Ṣ, O, Ḳ:*) or *it* (a thing) *was good* [*and recent* or *new* or *fresh*]. (Mṣb.) — And the same verb, (Ṣ, Ḳ,) inf. n. as above, (Ṣ, TA,) *He was such as is termed* طَرِيفٌ [and طَرْفٌ q. v.] as meaning the *contr. of* قُعْدُدٌ. (Ṣ, Ḳ.)

2. طرّفهُ [from the subst. الطَّرْفُ meaning "the eye"]: see 1, latter half. ═ طرّف [from الطَّرَفُ], (Ṣ, O, Ḳ,) inf. n. تَطْرِيفٌ, (Ḳ,) *He* (a man, Ṣ, O) *fought around the army;* because he charges upon, or assaults, those who form the side, or flank, or extreme portion, of it, (Ṣ, O, Ḳ,) and drives them back upon the main body: (Ṣ, O:) or, as in the M, *he fought the most remote thereof, and those that formed the side,* or *flank, thereof.* (TA.) — And طرّف عَلَىَّ الإِبِلَ *He drove,* or *sent, back to me those that formed the sides,* or *extreme portions, of the camels.* (O, Ḳ.) And طرّف الخَيْلَ *He drove back the foremost of the horsemen* (O, Ḳ, TA) *to,* or *upon, the hindmost of them.* (TA.) Accord. to El-Mufaḍḍal, تَطْرِيفٌ, signifies a man's *repelling* another man from the hindmost of his companions: (O, TA:*) one says, طَرِّفْ عَنَّا هٰذَا الفَارِسَ [*Repel thou from our rear this horseman*]. (O, TA.) — For another signification [from الطَّرَفُ] see 4. — [Hence also,] طرّفت بَنَانَهَا *She* (a woman) *tinged,* or *dyed, the ends* (أَطْرَاف, O, Mṣb, TA) *of her fingers with* حِنَّآء. (O, Mṣb, Ḳ,* TA.) — And تَطْرِيفُ الأُذُنِ *The making the ear* of a horse *to be pointed, tapering,* or *slender at the extremity.* (TA.) [Hence,] Khálid Ibn-Ṣafwán said, خَيْرُ الكَلَامِ مَا طُرِّفَتْ مَعَانِيهِ وَشُرِّفَتْ مَبَانِيهِ † [*The best of language is that of which the meanings are pointed, and of which the constructions are crowned with embellishments as though they were adorned with* شُرَف, pl. of شُرْفَةٌ, q. v.]. (TA: there mentioned immediately after what here next precedes it.) — And طرّف الشَّىْءَ [from طَرَفٌ signifying "anything chosen or choice"] means *He chose,* or *made choice of, the thing;* as also ▼ تطرّفه. (TA. [See also 10.]) — طرّف said of a camel means *He lost his tooth* [or *teeth*] (O, Ḳ, TA) *by reason of extreme age.* (TA.)

4. اطرف *He* (a man, Ḳ) *closed his eyelids.* (Ibn-'Abbád, O, Ḳ. [See also 1, first sentence.]) ═ اطرف الثَّوْبَ, inf. n. إِطْرَافٌ, *He made two ornamental* or *coloured* or *figured borders* (عَلَمَيْنِ) *in the ends,* or *sides, of the garment* (فِى طَرَفَيْهِ); as also ▼ طرّفه, inf. n. تَطْرِيفٌ. (Mṣb: and in like manner the pass. of the former verb is expl. in the Ṣ and O, as said of a رِدَآء, of خَزّ.) ═ اطرف فُلَانًا *He gave to such a one what he had not given to any one before him:* (L, Ḳ,* TA:) or *he gave him a thing of which he did not possess the like, and which pleased him:* (TA:) [and *he gave him property newly,* or *recently, acquired.*] You say, أَطْرَفَهُ كَذَا and بِكَذَا, meaning أَتْحَفَهُ [*He gave him such a thing as a* تُحْفَة, i. e. طُرْفَة, q. v.]. (Ḥar p. 54.) — [Hence,] اطرف فُلَانٌ signifies جَآءَ بِطُرْفَةٍ, (Ṣ, and Ḥar p. 54,) as meaning *Such a one brought something newly found,* or *gained,* or *acquired:* (Ḥar p. 54:) and as meaning *he brought a thing that was strange,* or *extraordinary, and approved,* or *deemed good:* (Id. p. 615:) and as meaning *he brought new information* or *tidings.* (Id. p. 32.) And one says, اطرفهُ خَبَرًا [and بِخَبَرٍ (see Ḥar p. 529)] meaning *He told him new information* or *tidings.* (Az, TA.) — أُطْرِفَ بِهِ مَنْ حَوَالَيْهِ [a phrase used by El-Ḥareeree] means *They who were around him became possessors, thereby, of a new and strange piece of information,* (صَارُوا بِسَبَبِهِ ذَوِى طُرْفَةٍ,) *and said,* مَا أَطْرَفَهُ [*How novel and strange is it!*], by reason of their wonder at it; so that the verb is intrans., and من is its agent: or it may mean *he made to wonder by reason of it those who were around him.* (Ḥar p. 474.) ═ الإِطْرَافُ signifies also كَثْرَةُ الآبَآءِ [i. e., app., *The being numerous,* as said of ancestors, meaning ancestors of note]. (TA.) ═ اطرف البَلَدُ, (Ṣ, O, Ḳ, TA,) and اطرفت الأَرْضُ, (TA,) *The country,* and *the land, abounded with* [*the kinds of pasture called*] طَرِيفَة [q. v.]. (Ṣ, O, Ḳ, TA.)

5. تطرّف [as quasi-pass. of 2 signifies *It became pointed, tapering,* or *slender at the extremity:* see ذُبَابُ السَّيْفِ in art. ذب]. — [And] *i. q.* صَارَ طَرَفًا [*It became an extremity,* or *a side;* or *at,* or *in, an extremity* or *a side*]. (TA.) — كَانَ لَا يَتَطَرَّفُ مِنَ البَوْلِ, in a trad. respecting the punishment of the grave, means *He used not to go far aside from urine.* (L, TA.*) — تطرّفت said of a she-camel: see 1, near the end. — Said of the sun, *It became near to setting.* (TA.) — تطرّف عَلَى القَوْمِ *He made a sudden,* or *an unexpected, attack upon the territory,* or *dwellings, of the people.* (TA.) ═ تطرّف الشَّىْءَ *He took from the side of the thing:* [and] *he took the side of it.* (MA.) — See also 2, last signification but one.

8. اِطَّرَفْتُ الشَّىْءَ, of the measure اِفْتَعَلْتُ, *I purchased the thing new.* (Ṣ, O, Ḳ. [See also 10.])

10. استطرفهُ *He counted, accounted, reckoned,* or *esteemed, it new;* (PṢ;) or طَرِيف [as meaning *newly,* or *recently, acquired*]. (Ṣ, O, Ḳ.) One says of good discourse, يَسْتَطْرِفُهُ مَنْ سَمِعَهُ [*He who has heard it esteems it new*]. (Ḳ.) — And استطرف الشَّىْءَ *He found, gained,* or *acquired, the thing newly.* (Ṣ, O, Ḳ. [See also 8.]) — You say of a woman who does not keep constantly to a husband, تَسْتَطْرِفُ الرِّجَالَ † [*She takes,* or *chooses, new ones of the men*]: she who does thus being likened to the she-camel termed طَرِفَةٌ, that depastures the extremities, or sides, of the pasturage, and tastes, and does not keep constantly

to one pasturage. (Ḥar p. 569.) See also 1, last quarter. — And one says of camels, اسْتَطْرَفَتِ المَرْتَعَ *They chose*, or *selected*, *the pasturage*: or *they took the first thereof*. (TA. [See also 2, last signification but one.])

طَرْفٌ The *eye*; a word having no pl. in this sense because it is originally an inf. n., (Ṣ, O, Ḳ,) therefore it may denote a sing. and may also denote a pl. number [i. e. may signify also *eyes*]: (Ṣ, O, Mṣb:) or, (Ḳ,) as Ibn-'Abbád says, (O,) it is a coll. n. signifying the بَصَر [which has the sing. and the pl. meanings mentioned above, as well as the meaning of the *sense of sight*], and is not dualized nor pluralized: or, as some say, it has for pl. أَطْرَافٌ: (O, Ḳ:) but this is refuted by the occurrence of طَرْف in a pl. sense in the Ḳur xxxvii. 47 and xxxviii. 52 and lv. 56: (O:) and though الأَطْرَاف is said to occur as its pl. in a trad. of Umm-Selemeh, this is a mistake for الإِطْرَاق: (Z, O:) it is said, however, that its being originally an inf. n. is not a reason for its not being allowable to pluralize it when it has become a subst., and especially when it is not meant to convey the signification of an epithet: (MF:) [but it may be regarded as an epithet, meaning *seer*, and, being originally an inf. n., *seers* also; and this is the more probable because] الطَّوَارِفُ ♦ [is an epithet used as a subst., and thus] signifies *the eyes*, (Ṣ, O, Ḳ,) as in the saying هُوَ بِمَكَانٍ لَا تَرَاهُ الطَّوَارِفُ [*He is in a place in which the eyes will not see him*]; (Ṣ,* O,* TA;) pl. of ♦ طَارِفَةٌ. (TA.) — [Hence,] الطَّرْفُ is the name of † *Two stars, which precede* الجَبْهَة, (Ṣ, O, Ḳ,) so called because (Ḳ) they are [regarded as] *the two eyes of Leo; one of the Mansions of the Moon*: (Ṣ, O, Ḳ:) [often called الطَّرْفَة, q. v.:] *the* طَرْف *of Leo, consisting of two small stars in front of* الجَبْهَة, *like the* فَرْقَدَانِ, *but inferior to them in light, and having somewhat of obliquity; the Ninth Mansion of the Moon*: (Ḳzw in his descr. of that Mansion:) or *the star* [app. λ] *in the face of Leo, together with that which is outside* [app. α] *on the figure of Cancer*: (Ḳzw in his descr. of Leo:) or *the bright star* [α] *on the hinder, southern, leg, or foot*, [i. e. *claw*,] *of Cancer*. (Ḳzw in his descr. of Cancer.) [See مَنَازِلُ القَمَرِ, in art. نزل.] — And طَرْفُ العَيْنِ signifies *The eyelid*. (TA.) = Also طَرْفٌ, A man *generous*, or *noble*, (Ḳ, TA, [see also طِرْفٌ,]) *in respect of ancestry, up to the greatest* [i. e. *most remote*] *forefather*. (TA.) = See also طَرَفٌ, first sentence.

طُرْفٌ: see طَرِيفٌ, with which it is syn., and of which it is also a pl.

طِرْفٌ A *generous* horse: (Aṣ, Ṣ, O, Ḳ:) or, accord. to Er-Rághib, one *that is looked at* (يُطْرَفُ) *because of his beauty*; so that it is originally مَطْرُوفٌ, i. e. مَنْظُورٌ; like نِقْضٌ in the sense of مَنْقُوضٌ: (TA:) pl. طُرُوفٌ (Aṣ, Ṣ, O, Ḳ) and أَطْرَافٌ: (O, Ḳ:) accord. to AZ, an epithet applied peculiarly to the *males*: (Ṣ, O, Ḳ:*) or *generous in respect of the sires and the dams*: (Lth, O, Ḳ:) or *recently acquired; not of his owner's breeding*; fem. with ة, (O, Ḳ,) occurring in a verse of El-'Ajjáj: Lth says that they sometimes apply the epithets طِرْفٌ and طِرْفَةٌ as syn. with نَجِيبٌ and نَجِيبَةٌ, in a manner unusual in the language: (O:) accord. to Ks, طِرْفَةٌ is applied as an epithet to a mare: (TA:) and طِرْفٌ signifies also a horse *long in the legs* or *the neck, having the ears pointed, tapering*, or *slender at the extremities*. (TA in the supplement to this art.) — And ‡ *Generous* (Ṣ, O, TA) as an epithet applied to a young man (Ṣ, TA) or to a man; (O, TA;) as also ♦ طَرْفٌ: (O, Ḳ:) or a man *generous in respect of his male and his female ancestors*: (Ḳ,* TA:) pl. أَطْرَافٌ: (O, Ḳ:) when applied to other than man, its pl. [or rather one of its pls.] is طُرُوفٌ. (Ḳ.) — See also طَرَفٌ, latter half. — And رَجُلٌ طِرْفٌ فِى نَسَبِهِ, (Ḳ, TA,) with kesr, (TA,) [in the CḲ, erroneously, طَرْف,] † *A man whose nobility is recent*: as though a contraction of ♦ طَرِيف. (Ḳ, TA.) — And امْرَأَةٌ طِرْفُ الحَدِيثِ, (Ḳ, TA,) with kesr, (TA,) [in the CḲ طَرْف,] *A woman whose discourse is good; every one who has heard it esteeming it new* (يَسْتَطْرِفُهُ). (Ḳ,* TA.) = And One *desirous of possessing everything that he sees*. (Ḳ.) — See also طَرْف, in two places. — And see طَرِيف. = Also *Anything of the produce of the earth still in the calyxes thereof*. (Ibn-'Abbád, O, Ḳ.*)

طَرَفٌ The *extremity*, or *end*, of anything; [as of a sword, and of a spear, and of a rope, and of the tongue, &c.;] thus accord. to ISd; but in the Ḳ this meaning is assigned to ♦ طَرْف: (TA: [several evidences of the correctness of the former word in this sense will be found in the present art.; and countless instances of it occur in other arts. &c.: it seems to have been generally regarded by the lexicographers as too notorious to need its being mentioned:]) and *a side; a lateral*, or *an outward*, or *adjacent, part* or *portion*; *a region, district, quarter*, or *tract*; syn. نَاحِيَةٌ: (Ṣ, O, Mṣb, Ḳ:) and *a part, portion, piece*, or *bit*, (syn. طَائِفَةٌ,) of a thing: (Ṣ, O, Ḳ:) it is used in relation to bodies, or material things, and to times &c.; (Er-Rághib, TA;) and is thus used in the sense of طَائِفَة of a people, in the Ḳur iii. 122; (Ksh;) [and may often be rendered *somewhat* of a thing, whether material (as land &c.) or not material (as in the T and Ṣ voce ذَرْوٌ, where it is used of a saying, and as in the Ṣ and A and Ḳ in art. هوس &c., where it is used of madness, or insanity, or diabolical possession):] the pl. is أَطْرَافٌ. (O, Mṣb, Ḳ.) — [Hence,] الأَطْرَافُ signifies *The fingers*: and [when relating to the fingers] has no sing. unless this is used as a prefixed noun, as in the saying أَشَارَتْ بِطَرَفِ إِصْبَعِهَا [*She made a sign with the end of her finger*]: but the pl. is said by Az to be used in the sense of the sing. in the following ex. cited by Fr,

* يُبْدِينَ أَطْرَافًا لِطَافًا عَنَمَهْ *

[so that the meaning is, *They show an elegant finger* like *a fruit of the species of tree called* عَنَم]; therefore the poet says عَنَمَهْ [which is a n. un.: but I think that it is much more reasonable, and especially as the verb is pl., to regard the ه in this case as the ه of pausation, of which see an ex. voce حِينٌ; and accordingly to render the saying, *they show elegant fingers* like *fruits of the* عَنَم]. (TA.) It is said in a trad. of Abraham, when he was a little child, جُعِلَ رِزْقُهُ فِى أَطْرَافِهِ [*His sustenance was made to be in his fingers*]; meaning that he used to suck his fingers and find in them that which nourished him. (TA.) — And [hence] أَطْرَافُ العَذَارَى ‡ *A species of grapes*, (A, Ḳ, TA,) *white and slender, found at Eṭ-Ṭáïf*: (A, TA:) or, as in the L, *black and long, resembling acorns, likened to the fingers of virgins, that are dyed* [*with* حِنَّاء], *because of their length; and the bunch of which is about a cubit long*. (TA.) — ذُو الطَّرَفَيْنِ is an appellation of *A sort of serpent*, (Ḳ,) *a sort of black serpent*, (TA,) or *the* [*serpent called*] أَسْوَد, (O,) *having two stings, one in its nose and the other in its tail, with both of which*, (O, Ḳ, TA,) *so it is said*, (O, TA,) *it smites, and it suffers not him whom it smites to linger, killing at once*. (O, Ḳ, TA.) — طَرَفَا الدَّابَّةِ sometimes means *The fore part and the hinder part of the beast*. (TA.) — And أَطْرَافُ الجَسَدِ (O) or البَدَنِ (Ḳ) means [*The extremities of the body*; i. e.] *the arms* or *hands, and the legs* or *feet, and the head*: (O, Ḳ:) or, as in the L, أَطْرَاف is pl. of طَرَف *as syn. with* شَوَاة [n. un. of شَوًى, q. v.]. (TA.) — [And the dual has various other meanings assigned to it, derived from the first of the significations mentioned in this paragraph.] It is said in a trad. (O, Ḳ) of the Prophet, (O,) كَانَ إِذَا اشْتَكَى أَحَدٌ مِنْ أَهْلِهِ لَمْ تَزَلِ البُرْمَةُ عَلَى النَّارِ حَتَّى يَأْتِىَ عَلَى أَحَدِ طَرَفَيْهِ [*It was the case that when any one of his family had a complaint, the cooking-pot did not cease to be on the fire but he arrived at one of his two limits*]; meaning † *convalescence or death*; because these are the two terminations of the case of the diseased. (O, Ḳ.) — And one says, لَا يَمْلِكُ طَرَفَيْهِ † *He will not have control over his mouth and his anus*: referring to him who has drunk medicine or become intoxicated. (AO, ISk, Ṣ, O, Ḳ.) — And فُلَانٌ فَاسِدُ الطَّرَفَيْنِ † *Such a one is corrupt in respect of the tongue and the* فَرْج. (TA.) — And لَا يَدْرِى أَىُّ طَرَفَيْهِ أَطْوَلُ, (in the CḲ يَدْرَى,) [*He will not*, or *does not, know which of his two extremities is the longer*,] meaning ‡ *his* ذَكَر *and his tongue*; (Ṣ, O, Ḳ, TA;) whence طَرَف is used as signifying † *the tongue*: (TA:) or the meaning is, as some say, † *which of his two halves is the longer*; the lower or the upper: (TA:) or † *the lineage of his father or that of his mother* (O, Ḳ, TA) *in respect of generosity*, or *nobility*: (O, TA:) i. e., which of his two parents is the more generous, or noble: so says Fr. (TA.) — كَرِيمُ الطَّرَفَيْنِ means

‡ *Generous*, or *noble*, [*on both sides*, i. e.] *in respect of male and female ancestors.* (Ṣ, O, TA.) — And أَطْرَافٌ means also † A man's *father and mother* and *brothers* and *paternal uncles* and *any relations whom it is unlawful for him to marry.* (AZ, Ṣ, O, Ḳ.) — And † *Noble*, or *exalted, men:* (Th, Ṣ:) or أَطْرَافُ الأَرْضِ means ‡ *the noble*, or *exalted, men*, and *the learned men, of the earth*, or *land:* (O, Ḳ, TA:) one of whom is termed طَرَفٌ, or ♦ طِرْفٌ. (O. See the latter of these words.) And hence, as some explain it, the saying in the Ḳur [xiii. 41, like one in xxi. 45], أَوَلَمْ يَرَوْا أَنَّا نَأْتِى الأَرْضَ نَنْقُصُهَا مِنْ أَطْرَافِهَا † [*Have they not seen that we visit*, or *bring destruction upon, the land, curtailing it of its learned men?*]; the meaning being, the death of its learned men: (O, TA:) or, as some say, [*curtailing it of its inhabitants and its fruits*; for they say that] the meaning is, the death of its inhabitants and the diminution of its fruits: (TA:) or it means, *curtailing it of its sides*, or *districts*, one by one: (Az, O, L:) Ibn-'Arafeh says that the meaning is, we lay open by conquest, to the Prophet, (نَفْتَحُ عَلَى النَّبِىِّ,) the country around Mekkeh. (O, TA.) [— أَطْرَافُ النَّاسِ also means † *The lower orders of the people:* but this I believe to be post-classical.] — طَرَفَىِ النَّهَارِ, in the Ḳur xi. 116, means غُدْوَةً وَعَشِيَّةً [i. e. *Morning and afternoon*]; by the former being meant *daybreak*; and by the latter, *noon and the* عَصْر [q. v.], (Ksh, Bḍ,) or *the* عَصْر [only]. (Bḍ.) And أَطْرَافَ النَّهَارِ, in the Ḳur xx. 130, means *At daybreak and at sunset:* (Ksh, Bḍ:) or *at noon and at the* عَصْر; so says Zj: or, accord. to IAạr, *in the hours* (سَاعَات) *of the day:* Abu-l-'Abbás says that it means طَرَفَىِ النَّهَارِ. (TA.) — [عَلَى طَرَفٍ often occurs as meaning *Beside, aside*, or *apart*; like عَلَى نَاحِيَةٍ, and عَلَى جَانِبٍ: and in like manner the Persians say بَرْ طَرَفْ. — And مِنْ طَرَفِ فُلَانٍ is often used as meaning *On the part of such a one*; but is perhaps post-classical.] — And you say, لِلأَمْرِ طَرَفَانِ [meaning † *There are two ways of performing the affair, either of which may be chosen*; as though it had two ends, or two sides]. (TA voce صَرْعٌ.) And جَعَلَهُ مُطْلَقَ الطَّرَفَيْنِ † [*He made it allowable*, or *free, in respect of both the alternatives, either way one might choose to take*]. (Mṣb in art. بوح.) — [And hence, perhaps,] طَرَفٌ signifies also † *Anything chosen* or *choice:* pl. أَطْرَافٌ: [whence] أَطْرَافُ الحَدِيثِ means † *Chosen*, or *choice, subjects of discourse*; as also ♦ طَرَائِفُ الحَدِيثِ: and أَطْرَافُ الأَحَادِيثِ means [the same, or] *colloquies of friends, consisting of mutual communications, and oblique expressions, and allusions:* so says ISd: and this is likewise a meaning of ♦ الطِّرَافُ and السِّبَابُ, which latter [properly signifying "mutual reviling"] is given in the Ḳ as an explanation of the former. (TA.) — Also *Flesh*, or *flesh-meat*; syn. لَحْمٌ. (TA.)

طَرِفٌ, in the Ḳ ♦ طَرْفٌ, but the former is the right, (TA,) A male camel *that removes from one pasturage to another*; (Ḳ, TA;) *not keeping constantly to one pasturage.* (TA.) And طَرِفَةٌ A she-camel *that does not keep constantly to one pasturage*; (Ṣ, O, Ḳ;) *that depastures the extremities*, or *sides, of the pasturage, and tastes, and does not keep constantly to one pasturage:* (Ḥar p. 569:) or, accord. to Aṣ, *that looks at the meadows* (تَطَّرِفُ الرِّيَاضَ), *meadow after meadow* [app. *to pasture upon them in succession*]: (TA:) and ♦ مُسْتَطْرِفَةٌ, so applied, signifies the same as طَرِفَةٌ: (TA, but not as on the authority of Aṣ:) and ♦ مِطْرَافٌ, so applied, *that will not feed upon a pasturage unless she choose anew*, or *take the first of*, (حَتَّى تَسْتَطْرِفَ,) *another.* (Aṣ, Ṣ, O, Ḳ.) — And [hence (see 10)] طَرِفٌ applied to a man signifies † *That does not keep constantly to a wife*, or *woman, nor to a companion:* (Ṣ, O, Ḳ:) and ♦ طِرْفٌ, thus accord. to the Ḳ, (TA, [in which it is said that by rule it should be طَرِفٌ, as above,]) a man *who does not keep constantly to the companionship of one person, by reason of his weariness.* (Ḳ.) And ♦ مُتَطَرِّفَةٌ applied to a woman, † *That chooses new ones of the men* (تَسْتَطْرِفُ الرِّجَالَ), *not keeping constantly to a husband*; as being likened to the she-camel termed طَرِفَةٌ. (Ḥar p. 569.) ═ And طَرُوفٌ, applied to a she-camel, (O, Ḳ, [but in some of the copies of the latter, where it follows next after another explanation of the epithet thus applied, mentioned above, "or,"]) accord. to IAạr, *Whose fore part of the head has gradually shed its hair* (الَّتِى تَحَاتَّ مُقَدَّمُ الرَّأْسِ فِيهَا, O) or *whose fore part of her mouth has shed its teeth one after another* (الَّتِى تَحَاتَّ مُقَدَّمُ فِيهَا, Ḳ) *by reason of extreme age.* (O, Ḳ. [See 2, last sentence.]) ═ Also, and ♦ طَرِيفٌ † *Contr. of* قُعْدُدٌ; (Ṣ, M, Ḳ, TA;) i. e., as the latter is further expl. in the Ṣ, and each in the M, *having many ancestors, up to the greatest* [i. e. *most remote*] *forefather*; and J adds that sometimes it is used in praise: thus also Aṣ explains ♦ طَرِيفُ النَّسَبِ: accord. to IAạr, طَرِيفٌ signifies مُنْحَدِرٌ فِى النَّسَبِ [app. مُنْحَدِرٌ, as though meaning *of long descent*]; and he says that it is with the Arabs more noble than قُعْدُدٌ: the pl. of طَرِفٌ as meaning the contr. of قُعْدُدٌ is طَرِفُونَ; and the pl. of ♦ طَرِيفٌ in the same sense is طُرُفٌ and طَرْفٌ and طُرَّافٌ, the second and third of which pls. are anomalous. (TA.) — [طَرِفٌ seems also to have the contr. meaning; or † One *whose nobility is recent:* and the like is said of قُعْدُدٌ; that it has two contr. meanings:] see طَرْفٌ.

طَرْفَةٌ [*A wink*, i. e.] *a closing of one of the eyelids upon the other:* (Ṣ, O, Ḳ:) or [*a twinkling of the eye*, i. e.] *a putting the eyelids in motion* or *in a state of commotion.* (Ḳ.) One says أَسْرَعُ مِنْ طَرْفَةِ عَيْنٍ [*Quicker than a wink*, or *a twinkling of an eye*]. (Ṣ, O.) And مَا يُفَارِقُنِى طَرْفَةَ عَيْنٍ [*He does not separate himself from me during a wink*, or *a twinkling of an eye*]. (TA.) — Also *A red spot of blood, in the eye, occasioned by a blow* or *some other cause.* (Ṣ, O, Ḳ.) — And *A brand*, or *mark made with a hot iron, having to it no* أَطْرَاف [or *sides*, or *lateral portions*], *being only a line.* (Ibn-'Abbád, O, Ḳ.) ═ And الطَّرْفَةُ *A certain star* or *asterism* (نَجْمٌ). (Ḳ. [There thus mentioned as though different from the asterism commonly called الطَّرْفُ, which I do not believe to be the case: see the latter appellation.])

طُرْفَةٌ *A hurt of the eye, occasioning its shedding tears.* (Ḳ.) ═ And *Newly-acquired property*; (Ṣ, O, Ḳ;) *anything that one has newly acquired, and that pleases him*; as also ♦ أُطْرُوفَةٌ; (TA;) *a thing newly acquired*; (Ḥar p. 54;) and *a thing that is strange and deemed good*; (Id. p. 615;) [*a pleasing rarity*;] *a welcome*, or *pleasing, thing*; (KL;) and *a gift not given to any one before*; (Ḳ,* TA;) and *a gift of which the recipient did not possess the like, and which pleases him*; (TA;) [generally, *a novel*, or *rare, and pleasing, present*; like تُحْفَةٌ and نُزْلَةٌ:] pl. طُرَفٌ. (Ḥar p. 32.) [See also طَرِيفٌ and طَرِيفَةٌ.]

طَرْفَةٌ *A single tree of the species called* طَرْفَآءُ, q. v. (AḤn, Ṣ, O, Ḳ.)

طُرْفَى *Remoteness* in lineage *from the* [*chief*, or *oldest*,] *ancestor:* قُعْدَى is nearer therein. (IB, TA.) [See طَرِفٌ.]

طَرْفَآءُ [accord. to some طَرَفَآءُ and accord. to others طَرْفَاءُ, as will be seen from what follows,] *A kind of trees*, (Ṣ, O, Ḳ,) *of which there are four species, one of these being the* أَثْل [q. v.]: (Ḳ:) [or it is *different from the* أَثْل: the name is now generally applied to the *common*, or *French, tamarisk*; *tamarix gallica* of Linn.: (Forskål's Flora Aegypt. Arab. p. lxiv. no. 181; and Delile's Floræ Aegypt. Illustr. no. 349:)] AḤn says, *it is of the kind called* عِضَاه; *its* هَدَب [q. v.] *are like those of the* أَثْل; *it has no wood fit for carpentry, coming forth only as even and smooth rods towards the sky; and sometimes the camels eat it as* حَمْض [q. v.] *when they find no other* حَمْض: AA, he adds, says that *it is a sort of* حَمْض: (TA:) the n. un. is ♦ طَرْفَةٌ, (AḤn, Ṣ, O, Ḳ,) [which is irreg.,] and طَرْفَآءَةٌ, (AḤn, O, Ḳ, [in the CḲ, erroneously, طَرْفَاةٌ,]) [and this requires طَرْفَآء to be with tenween, as a coll. gen. n.,] or, accord. to Sb, طَرْفَآء is sing. and pl.: (Ṣ, O:) or it is a pl. [or quasi-pl. n.] of طَرْفَةٌ, like as شَجْرَآء is of شَجَرَةٌ: (Ṣ in art. شجر: [see شَجْرَآء:]) or it is a coll. gen. n.: accord. to IJ, the ء in طَرْفَآء is a denotative of the fem. gender; but in طَرْفَآءَة, the ة is a denotative of the fem. gender, and the ء is augmentative. (M, TA.) — Also *A place of growth of the* طَرْفَآء. (TA.)

طِرَافٌ *The portion that is taken* [app. meaning *cut*] *from the extremities* (أَطْرَاف) *of corn*, or *seed-produce.* (Ibn-'Abbád, O, Ḳ.) — تَطَارَفُوا

وَرِثُوا المَجْدَ طَرَافًا means عَنْ شَرَفٍ [i. e. *They inherited, one after another, glory from nobility of ancestry*]. (Ibn-'Abbád, O, Ḳ.) — See also طَرِيفٌ. — And see طَرَفٌ, last sentence but one. — Also *A tent of skin*, or *leather*, (Ṣ, Ḳ, TA,) *without a* كِفَآء [q. v., for it is variously explained]; *of the tents of the Arabs of the desert*. (TA.)

طَرِيفٌ: see مَطْرُوفٌ. — Also, (Ṣ, O, Mṣb, Ḳ,) and ▼ طَارِفٌ, (Ṣ, O, Ḳ,) and ▼ طِرَافٌ, (Ḳ,) [of which last it seems to be said in the supplement to this art. in the TA, that it may be either a pl. or a syn. of طَرِيفٌ,] Property *newly acquired*; (Ṣ, O, Mṣb, Ḳ;) as also ▼ طُرْفٌ and ▼ طَرَفٌ and ▼ مُطْرِفٌ (Ḳ) and ▼ مُسْتَطْرَفٌ; (TA;) [and it is said in one place in the TA that ▼ مُطْرَفٌ and ▼ مُطَرَّفٌ are dial. vars. of مُطْرِفٌ; but I think that this last word is probably a mistake for ▼ مُطْرَفٌ;] contr. of تَلِيدٌ (Ṣ, O, Mṣb) and تَالِدٌ (Ṣ, O) [and إِتْلَادٌ]: pl. of the first and third طُرُفٌ. (Ḳ.) — Also, the first, A thing that is *good* [*and recent* or *new* or *fresh*]: (Mṣb:) what is *strange*, (IAạr, Ḳ, TA,) [or *rare*,] *and coloured*, or *of various colours*, (IAạr, TA,) [or *pleasing to the eye*,] of fruits and other things, (IAạr, Ḳ, TA,) مِمَّا يستطرف بِهِ [in which يستطرف is evidently a mistranscription for يُطْرَفُ, i. e., *of such things as are given as* طُرَف (pl. of طُرْفَةٌ) meaning *rare and pleasing gifts*]. (TA, from IAạr.) — See also طَرَفٌ, latter part, in three places.

طَرِيفَةٌ The *plant called* نَصِيٌّ *when it has become white* (Ṣ, O, Ḳ, TA) *and dry*: (TA:) or *when it has attained its full perfection*; (ISk, Ṣ, O, Ḳ, TA;) and the *plant called* صِلِّيَان *in this same state*: (ISk, Ṣ, O, TA:) or the *first of any herbage that the cattle choose and depasture*: (TA:) or the *best of pasturage, except such as is termed* عُشْب; *including the sorts termed* نَصِيّ and صِلِّيَان and عَنْكَث and هَلْتَى and سَحَم and ثَغَام. (O, TA.) — [As a subst. from طَرِيفٌ, rendered such by the affix ة, it signifies *Anything new, recent*, or *fresh*: and *anything choice*: pl. طَرَائِفُ. (See also طُرْفَةٌ.) Hence, طَرَائِفُ البَيْتِ *The choice articles*, such as vessels &c., *of the house*: see رَفٌّ. And hence also,] طَرَائِفُ الحَدِيثِ: see طَرَفٌ, last sentence but one.

طَارِفٌ: see طَرِيفٌ.

طَارِفَةٌ [a subst. from طَارِفٌ, rendered such by the affix ة]: pl. طَوَارِفُ: see طَرْفٌ, in two places. — [Also, app., *A thing that causes a twinkling*, or *winking*, of the eye. Whence, app.,] one says, جَآءَ بِطَارِفَةِ عَيْنٍ, meaning ‡ *He* (a man, Ṣ, O) *brought much property*, or *many cattle*. (Ṣ, O, Ḳ, TA.) — The phrase مَا أَبْرَزَتْهُ طَوَارِفُ القَرَائِحِ, in which طَوَارِف is pl. of طَارِفَة, from طَارِف signifying property "newly acquired," means مَا أَحْدَثَتْهُ القَرَائِحُ المُتَأَخِّرَةُ [i. e. *What the modern excogitative faculties have originated*]. (Ḥar p. 63.) — طَوَارِفُ الخِبَآءِ means *The portions of the sides of the tent that are raised for the purpose of one's looking out*: (Ṣ, O, Ḳ:) or, as some say, *rings attached to the skirts* (رُفُوف) *of the tent, having ropes by which they are tied to the tent-pegs*. (TA.) — And سِبَاعٌ طَوَارِفُ means *Beasts of prey that seize*, or *carry off by force, the animals that are the objects of the chase*. (O, Ḳ.)

هُوَ أَطْرَفُهُمْ *He is the most remote of them from the greatest* [or *earliest*] *ancestor*. (Lḥ, TA.)

أُطْرُوفَةٌ: see طُرْفَةٌ.

اِخْتَضَبَتْ تَطَارِيفَ *She* (a woman) *dyed* [with حِنَّآء] *the ends of her fingers*. (O, Ḳ.)

مُطْرَفٌ: see مِطْرَفٌ: — and see also طَرِيفٌ.

مُطْرِفٌ: see مِطْرَفٌ: and مُطْرِفٌ: and see also طَرِيفٌ.

مُطْرِفٌ [act. part. n. of 4, q. v.]. — أَنْشِدِ البَيْتَيْنِ المُطْرِفَيْنِ, a phrase used by El-Ḥareeree, means *Recite thou the two verses that adduce what is strange*, or *extraordinary, and approved*, or *deemed good*: or, as some relate it, ▼ المُطْرَفَيْنِ, expl. by Mṭr as meaning *that are ornamented at their two extremities*; like the رِدَآء called مُطْرَف: or ▼ المُطَرَّفَيْنِ, meaning, if correctly related, *that are beautified, and excite admiration, in the first and last foot*; as being likened to the horse termed مُطَرَّف, that is white in the head and the tail: and المطرفين [i. e. المُطَرِّفَيْنِ] may mean المستطرفين [i. e. المُسْتَطْرَفَيْنِ]. (Ḥar p. 615: in the next p. of which, an ex. is given.) — See also طَرِيفٌ.

مِطْرَفٌ (Ṣ, O, L, Mṣb, TA) and ▼ مُطْرَفٌ, (Ṣ, O, L, Mṣb, Ḳ, TA,) the latter, only, mentioned in the Ḳ, (TA,) and this is the original form, because it is from أُطْرِفَ, but the ḍammeh was deemed difficult of pronunciation, and therefore kesreh was substituted for it, (Fr, Ṣ, O, TA,) like as is the case in مِصْحَف [q. v.], (Fr, TA,) and IAth mentions also ▼ مَطْرَفٌ, (TA,) *A garment*, (Mṣb,) or [*such as is termed*] رِدَآء, (Ṣ, O, Ḳ,) *of* [*the kind of cloth called*] خَزّ, (Ṣ, O, Mṣb, Ḳ,) *square*, or *four-sided*, (Ṣ, O, Ḳ,) *having ornamental* or *coloured* or *figured, borders* (أَعْلَام): (Ṣ, O, Mṣb, Ḳ:) or *a garment having, in its two ends*, or *sides*, (فِى طَرَفَيْهِ,) *two such borders* (عَلَمَانِ): (Fr, TA:) or *a square*, or *four-sided, garment of* خَزّ: (Mṣb:) pl. مَطَارِفُ. (Ṣ, O, Mṣb, Ḳ.) — مَطَارِفُ is also applied to † *Clouds* [as being likened to the garments thus called]. (TA in art. دكن.) — See also طَرِيفٌ.

مُطَرَّفٌ A horse *white in the head and the tail, the rest of him being of a different colour*: and in like manner *black in the head and the tail*. (Ṣ, O, Ḳ.) And, accord. to AO, أَبْلَقُ مُطَرَّفٌ A horse *white in the head*: and likewise *white in the tail and the head*. (TA.) And شَاةٌ مُطَرَّفَةٌ A sheep or goat *black in the end of the tail, in other parts white*: (Ṣ, O, Ḳ:) or *white in the ends of the ears, and for the rest part black*: or *black in the ends of the ears, and for the rest part white*. (TA.) — See also مُطْرَفٌ. And see سَبْغ. — In a verse of Sá'ideh the Hudhalee, as some relate it, but accord. to others it is مُطَرِّفٌ [q. v.], (O, TA,) describing a horse, (O,) it signifies مُرَدَّدٌ فِى الكَرَمِ [app. meaning *Repeatedly improved in generosity by descent from a number of generous sires and dams*]. (O, TA.) — See also مُسْتَطْرَفٌ.

مُطَرِّفٌ A man *who fights around the army*: (O, Ḳ, TA: [see 2, second sentence:]) or, as some say, *who fights the* أَطْرَاف [app. meaning *noble*, or *exalted*, pl. of طَرَفٌ q. v., or of طِرْفٌ,] *of men*. (TA.) — In a verse of Sá'ideh the Hudhalee, (O, TA,) describing a horse, (O,) *That repels those that form the side*, or *flank, of the horses and of the* [*hostile*] *company of men*: but as some relate it, the word is مُطَرَّفٌ [q. v.]. (O, TA.)

مِطْرَافٌ: see طَرِفٌ, former half.

مَطْرُوفٌ [pass. part. n. of طَرَفَ, q. v.]. You say, فُلَانٌ مَطْرُوفُ العَيْنِ بِفُلَانٍ, meaning *Such a one is, exclusively of others, looked at by such a one*. (Ṣ, O.) — And عَيْنٌ مَطْرُوفَةٌ *An eye of which the lids are put in motion* or *in a state of commotion, by looking*. (Aṣ, TA.) [And] *An eye, hit, struck, smitten*, or *hurt, with a thing, so that it sheds tears*. (Ṣ, O, Ḳ.) And ▼ طَرِيفٌ applied to an eye signifies the same as مَطْرُوفَةٌ [in one of these senses, but in which of them is not said]. (TA.) — مَطْرُوفَةٌ applied to a woman means *As though her eye were hit, struck, smitten*, or *hurt, with something*, (O, and EM p. 83,) *so that it shed tears*, (O,) *by reason of the languish of her look*; (EM ibid;) and this is said to be its meaning in the saying of Ṭarafeh,

إِذَا نَحْنُ قُلْنَا أَسْمِعِينَا انْبَرَتْ لَنَا •

عَلَى رِسْلِهَا مَطْرُوفَةً لَمْ تَشَدَّدِ •

(O, EM,) i. e. *When we say, "Sing thou to us," she betakes herself to us in her gentle way, as though her eye were hurt by something, by reason of the languish of her look, not straining herself* in her singing; but as some relate the verse, the word is مَطْرُوقَةً, meaning "weakly:" (EM:) or it means *whose eye the love of men has smitten, so that she raises her eyes and looks at every one that looks at her*; as though a طَرْفَة [or red spot of blood], or a stick or the like, hurt her eye: (Az, TA:) or *having a languishing eye*; as though it were turned away, or back, (طُرِفَتْ,) from everything at which it looked: (IAạr, TA:) or *as though her eye were turned away, or back, so that it, or she, is still*: (TA:) or † *who looks at the men* (تَطْرِفُ الرِّجَالَ); i. e. † *who does not keep constantly to one*; the pass. part. n. being put in the place of the act.; but Az says that this explanation is at variance with the original purport of the word: (TA:) or مَطْرُوفَةٌ بِالرِّجَالِ means ‡ a woman *who raises*, or *stretches and raises, her* eye at men, (Ṣ, O, Ḳ, TA,) and turns away her look from her husband, to others, (Ṣ, TA,*) and in whom is no good: (TA:) or † who looks not at any but the men; (Ḳ;) or مَطْرُوفَةُ العَيْنِ بِالرِّجَالِ has this meaning. (AA, TA.) — أَرْضٌ مَطْرُوفَةٌ Land abounding with the herbage called طَرِيفَة. (Ṣ, O, Ḳ.)

مُطْرَفٌ A camel newly purchased: (Ṣ:) or purchased from another part of the country, and therefore yearning for his accustomed place. (IB, TA.)

مُتَطَرِّفٌ A man who does not, or will not, keep constantly to an affair; [but I think that امر (which I have rendered "an affair") in my original is evidently a mistranscription for امرأة, i. e. a woman, or wife;] as also ↑ مُسْتَطْرِفٌ. (TA.) See also طَرِفٌ.

مُسْتَطْرَفٌ: see طَرِيفٌ. — فَعَلْتُهُ فِى مُسْتَطْرَفِ الأَيَّامِ I did it in the first, or first part, of the days; (فِى مُسْتَأْنَفِهَا;) as also ↑ فِى مُطْرَفِ الايام. (Ṣ, O, Ḳ.)

مُسْتَطْرِفٌ: see مُتَطَرِّفٌ. See also طَرِفٌ.

طرق

1. طَرْقٌ signifies The beating [a thing], or striking [it, in any manner, and with anything]; (Ḳ, TA;) this being the primary meaning: (TA:) or with the مِطْرَقَة, (Ḳ, TA,) which is the implement of the blacksmith and of the artificer [with which he beats the iron], and the rod, or stick, with which one beats wool [or hair] to loosen or separate it: (TA:) and the slapping (Ḳ, TA) with the hand. (TA.) You say, طَرَقَ البَابَ, aor. ـُ, inf. n. طَرْقٌ, He knocked [or (as we say) knocked at] the door. (Mṣb.) طَرَقَ الصُّوفَ, (Ṣ, O, TA,*) or الشَّعَرَ, (TA,) aor. as above, (Ṣ, O,) and so the inf. n., (Ṣ, O, Ḳ,) He beat the wool, (Ṣ, O, Ḳ, TA,) or the hair, (TA,) with the rod, or stick, called مِطْرَقَة, (Ṣ, O,) to loosen it, or separate it: (Ṣ,* O,* TA:) or he plucked it [so as to loosen it, or separate it]. (Ḳ, TA.) أَطْرِقِى وَمِيشِى, a prov., and occurring in a verse of Ru-beh, [originally addressed to a woman,] and [lit.] meaning Beat thou the wool with the stick, and mix the hair with the wool, is said to him who confuses or confounds, in his speech, and practises various modes, or manners, therein. (Az, TA. [See Freytag's Arab. Prov. ii. 28.]) And you say also, طَرَقَ الحَدِيدَةَ He beat the piece of iron [with the مِطْرَقَة]: (Mgh,* Mṣb:) and ↑ طَرَّقَهَا he beat it much, or vehemently. (Mṣb.) And طَرَقَهُ بِكَفِّهِ, inf. n. as above, He slapped him with his hand. (TA.) And طَرَقْتُ الطَّرِيقَ I travelled [or beat] the road. (Mṣb.) [And hence, app.,] طَرْقٌ signifies also The being quick of pace; [probably as an inf. n.;] or quickness of going along. (Sh, TA.) And طَرَقَتِ الأَرْضُ The ground was beaten so as to be rendered even, or easy to be travelled; and trodden with the feet. (TA.) And طَرَقَ الدَّوَابُّ المَآءَ بِالرِّجْلِ حَتَّى تُكَدِّرَهُ [The beasts beat the water with the foot so as to render it turbid, or muddy]: (Er-Rághib, TA:) or طَرَقَتِ الإِبِلُ المَآءَ, (Ṣ, O, TA,) aor. as above, (O,) ‡ the camels staled and dunged in the water. (Ṣ, O, TA.) — Also † The coming by night; (Ḳ, TA;) because he who comes by night [generally] needs to knock at the door; as some say; (TA;) and so طُرُوقٌ [which is the more common in this sense]. (Ḳ, TA.) You say, طَرَقَ, aor. ـُ, inf. n. طُرُوقٌ, He came by night. (Ṣ.) أَتَانَا فُلَانٌ طُرُوقًا † Such a one came to us by night. (Ṣ.) And طَرَقَ القَوْمَ, aor. ـُ, inf. n. طَرْقٌ and طُرُوقٌ, † He came to the people, or party, by night. (TA.) And طَرَقَ أَهْلَهُ لَيْلًا, (Ṣ, O,) or طَرَقَ أَهْلَهُ, (TA,) inf. n. طُرُوقٌ, (TA,) † He came to his اهل [meaning wife] by night: (Ṣ,* O, TA:) the doing of which by him who has been long absent is forbidden by the Prophet. (O, TA.*) And طَرَقَ النَّجْمُ, aor. ـُ, inf. n. طُرُوقٌ, † The star, or asterism, rose: and of anything that has come by night, one says طَرَقَ. (Mṣb.) One says also, طُرِقَ فُلَانٌ † Such a one was made an object of [or was visited by or was smitten by] nocturnal accidents or calamities. (TA.) And طَرَقَهُ الزَّمَانُ بِنَوَائِبِهِ † [Time, or fortune, visited him, or smote him, with its accidents, or calamities; or did so suddenly, like one knocking at the door in the night]. (TA.) And طَرَقَنِى خَيَالٌ † [An apparition, or a phantom, visited me in the night]. (TA.) And طَرَقَنِى هَمٌّ † [Anxiety came upon me; or did so suddenly, like one coming in the night]. (TA.) And [hence, app.,] طَرَقَ سَمْعِى كَذَا † [Such a thing struck my ear]: and طَرَقَتْ مَسَامِعِى بِخَيْرٍ † [My ears were struck by good tidings]. (TA.) — Also The stallion's covering the she-camel; (Mṣb, Ḳ;*) and so طُرُوقٌ; (Ḳ, TA;) and طِرَاقٌ likewise [app. another inf. n. of طَرَقَ, as its syn. ضِرَابٌ is of ضَرَبَ]: (TA:) or his leaping her, (Ṣ, O, TA,) and covering her. (TA.) You say, طَرَقَ الفَحْلُ النَّاقَةَ, (Ṣ, O, Mṣb, TA,) aor. ـُ, (Ṣ, O, TA,) inf. n. طَرْقٌ, (Mṣb,) or طُرُوقٌ, (Ṣ,) or both, (O, TA,) The stallion covered the she-camel: (Mṣb:) or leaped the she-camel, (Ṣ, O, TA,) and covered her. (TA.) — And [The practising of geomancy;] i. q. ضَرْبٌ بِالحَصَى, (Ṣ, IAth, O, Ḳ,) which is performed by women, (IAth, TA,) or by a diviner; (Ḳ;) a certain mode of divination: (Ṣ:) or [the practising of geomancy; i. e.] a man's making lines, or marks, upon the ground, with two fingers, and then with one finger, and saying, اِبْنَىْ عِيَانْ أَسْرِعَا البَيَانْ: (AZ, O, TA: [see this saying explained, with another description of the process, in the first paragraph of art. خط:]) or it is the making lines, or marks, upon the sand: (TA:) you say, طَرَقَ, aor. ـُ, inf. n. طَرْقٌ, He made lines, or marks, with a finger, [&c.,] in divining. (JK.) [See the last sentence in art. جبت.] Also The diviner's mixing cotton with wool when divining. (Lth, Ḳ.) — And طَرَقْنَا النَّعْجَةَ, aor. ـُ, inf. n. طَرْقٌ, We branded the ewe with the mark called طِرَاق. (ISh, O.) — طَرِقَ, (Ḳ, TA,) like عَنِىَ, (TA,) [inf. n., app., طَرْقٌ, q. v.,] ‡ He was, or became, weak in intellect, (Ḳ, TA,) and soft. (TA.) — طَرِقَ, aor. ـَ, (Ḳ,) inf. n. طَرَقٌ, (Fr, Ṣ, O, Ḳ,) He (a camel) had a weakness in his knees: (Fr, Ṣ, O, Ḳ: [see حَلِلَ:]) or, said of a human being and of a camel, he had a weakness in the knee and in the arm or the fore leg: (TA:) or, said of a camel, he had a crookedness in the سَاق (Lth,* O,* Ḳ) of the hind leg, [app. meaning in the thigh,] without the [kind of straddling termed] فَحَج, and with an inclining in the heel. (Lth, O.) — [See also طَرَقٌ below.] — طَرِقَ signifies also He drank turbid, or muddy, water, (O, Ḳ, TA,) such as is termed [طَرْقٌ and] مَطْرُوقٌ. (TA. [In the Ḳ it is said to be, in this sense, like سَمِعَ; which seems to indicate that the inf. n. is طَرَقٌ, not طَرْقٌ.])

2. طَرَّقَ الحَدِيدَةَ: see 1, former half. — طَرَّقَ طَرِيقًا He made a road plane, or even, so that people travelled it [or beat it with their feet] in their passing along. (TA.) The saying لَا تُطَرِّقُوا المَسَاجِدَ means Make not ye the mosques to be roads [or places of passage]. (TA.) طَرَّقْتُ لَهُ is from الطَّرِيقُ: (Ṣ, O:) you say, طَرِّقْ لَنَا [app. referring to camels] He made for them a road, or way: (Ḳ:) or طَرَّقَ لَهُ he gave a way to, or admitted, him, or it. (MA.) — طَرَّقَتْ said of the [bird called] قَطَاة, peculiarly, (inf. n. تَطْرِيقٌ, O, Ḳ,) She arrived at the time of her egg's coming forth: (Aṣ, A'Obeyd, Ṣ, O, Ḳ:) or she (a قطاة) hollowed out in the ground a place wherein to lay her eggs; as though she made a way for them: so says AHeyth: but the verb may be similarly used of other than the قطاة, metaphorically; whence the saying,

* قَدْ طَرَّقَتْ بِبِكْرِهَا أُمُّ طَبَقْ *

i. e. ‡ Calamity [has prepared to bring forth her first-born]. (Az, TA.) [Hence, app.,] one says also, ضَرَبَهُ حَتَّى طَرَّقَ بِجَعْرِهِ [He beat him until he gave passage, or was about to give passage, to his ordure]. (Aṣ, Ṣ, O.) And طَرَّقَ لِى, inf. n. تَطْرِيقٌ, signifies أَخْرَجَ [app. meaning He gave forth, or produced, to me something]. (TA.) — طَرَّقَتْ بِوَلَدِهَا, said of a camel, means She brought forth with difficulty, her young one sticking fast, and not coming forth easily; and in like manner it is said of a woman: (Aṣ, Ṣ, O, Ḳ:) so in a verse of Ows Ibn-Ḥajar, cited voce نفاس: (O:) or طرّقت said of a woman and of any pregnant female, means the half of her young one came forth, and then it stuck fast. (Lth, TA.) [Hence,] طَرَّقَ فُلَانٌ بِحَقِّى ‡ Such a one acknowledged my right, or due, after disacknowledging it. (Aṣ, Ṣ, O, Ḳ, TA.) — Accord. to AZ, (TA,) طرّق الإِبِلَ means He withheld the camels from pasture, (Ṣ, O, Ḳ, TA,) or from some other thing: (Ṣ, O, TA:) Sh, however, says that he knew not this; but that IAạr explained طَرَّقْتُ, with ق, as meaning "I repelled." (TA.) —

أَخَذَ فُلَانٌ فِى التَّطْرِيقِ means † *Such a one practised artifice and divination.* (TA.) — طَرَّقْتُ التُّرْسَ *I sewed the shield upon another skin:* and طَرَّقْتُ النَّعْلَ, inf. n. تَطْرِيقٌ, *I made the sole of two pieces of skin, sewing one of them upon the other.* (Mṣb. [See also the next paragraph.])

3. طَارَقْتُ النَّعْلَ [meaning *I sewed another sole upon the sole*] is an instance of a verb of the measure فَاعَلَ relating to the act of a single agent. (AAF, TA in art. خدع.) [See also 2, last sentence.] You say also, طارق الرَّجُلُ نَعْلَيْهِ, [inf. n. مُطَارَقَةٌ,] *The man put one of his two soles upon the other and sewed them together.* (Aṣ, TA.) And طارق بَيْنَ نَعْلَيْنِ *He sewed one sole upon another.* (Ṣ, O, Ḳ.) And طارق بين الثَّوْبَيْنِ, (Ṣ,) or بَيْنَ ثَوْبَيْنِ, (O, Ḳ,) and بين الدِّرْعَيْنِ, (TA,) *i. q.* طَابَقَ, (Ḳ,) or ظَاهَرَ, i. e. *He put on himself one of the two garments,* or *one of two garments,* [and *one of the two coats of mail,*] *over the other.* (Ṣ, O.) طُورِقَ is said of anything as meaning *It was put one part thereof upon,* or *above, another;* and so ▼ اِطَّرَقَ; (TA;) [and in like manner ▼ أُطْرِقَ; for] one says of shields, يُطْرَقُ بَعْضُهَا عَلَى بَعْضٍ *One of them is sewed upon another:* (Ṣ, O, Ḳ:) and أُطْرِقَتْ بِالجِلْدِ وَالعَصَبِ *They were clad* [or *covered*] *with skin and sinews.* (Ṣ, O.) — طارق الغَمَامُ الظَّلَامَ *The clouds followed upon the darkness.* (TA.) — And طارق الكَلَامَ ‡ *He practised,* or *took to, various modes,* or *manners, in speech;* syn. تَفَنَّنَ فِيهِ. (TA.)

4. اطرقهُ فَحْلَهُ *He lent him his stallion* [*camel*] *to cover his she-camels.* (Ṣ, O, Ḳ.) — لَا أَطْرَقَ ٱللّٰهُ عَلَيْكَ, (O,) or عَلَيْهِ, (Ḳ, TA,) means ‡ *May God not cause thee,* or *him, to have one whom thou mayest,* or *whom he may, take to wife,* or *compress.* (O, Ḳ, TA.) — See also 3, latter part. — اطرق رَأْسَهُ *He inclined his head* [*downwards*]. (TA.) And أَطْرِقْ بَصَرَكَ *Lower thine eyes towards thy breast, and be silent:* occurring in a trad. respecting the looking unexpectedly [at one at whom one should not look]. (TA.) And أَطْرَقَ, alone, *He bent down his head:* (MA:) or *he lowered his eyes, looking towards the ground;* (Ṣ, O, Ḳ;) and sometimes the doing so is natural: (TA: [and the same is indicated in the Ṣ:]) and it may mean *he had a laxness in the eyelids:* (A'Obeyd, TA:) or *he contracted his eyelids, as though his eye struck the ground:* (Er-Rághib, TA:) and *he was,* or *became, silent,* (ISk, Ṣ, O, Ḳ,) accord. to some, *by reason of fright,* (TA,) *not speaking.* (ISk, Ṣ, O, K.) It is said in a prov.,

• أَطْرِقْ كَرَا أَطْرِقْ كَرَا •
• إِنَّ النَّعَامَ فِى القُرَى •

[*Lower thine eyes karà: lower thine eyes karà:* (كرا meaning the *male of the* كَرَوَان, a name now given to the *stone-curlew,* or *charadrius œdicnemus:*) *verily the ostriches are in the towns,* or *villages*]: applied to the self-conceited; (Ṣ, O;) and to him who is insufficient, or unprofitable; who speaks and it is said to him, "Be silent, and beware of the spreading abroad of that which thou utterest, for dislike of what may be its result:" and by the saying انّ النعام فى القرى is meant, they will come to thee and trample thee with their feet: (O:) it is like the saying نُغَضُ الطَّرْفَ. (Ṣ. [See also كَرَوَانٌ: and see also Freytag's Arab. Prov. ii. 30-31.]) It is asserted that when they desire to capture the كرا, and see it from afar, they encompass it, and one of them says, أَطْرِقْ كَرَا إِنَّكَ لَا تُرَى [or لَنْ تُرَى (Meyd in explanation of the preceding prov.) i. e. *Lower thine eyes,* or *be silent, karà: thou wilt not be seen:*] until he becomes within reach of it; when he throws a garment over it, and takes it. ('Eyn, TA.) And أَطْرِقْ كَرَا يُحْلَبْ لَكَ [*Lower thine eyes,* or *be silent, karà: milk shall be drawn for thee:*] is [a prov., mentioned by Meyd,] said to a stupid person whom one incites to hope for that which is vain, or false, and who believes [what is said to him]. (O.) — One says also, اطرق إِلَى اللَّهْوِ ‡ *He inclined to diversion, sport,* or *play.* (IAạr, Ḳ, TA.) — اطرق اللَّيْلُ عَلَيْهِ: see 8: — and اطرقت الإِبِلُ: see 6. — اطرق الصَّيْدَ *He set a snare for the beasts,* or *birds, of the chase.* (TA.) — And hence, اطرق فُلَانٌ لِفُلَانٍ † *Such a one plotted against such a one by calumny,* or *slander, in order to throw him into destruction,* or *into that from which escape would be difficult.* (TA.)

5. تطرّق إِلَى كَذَا *He found a way to such a thing:* (MA:) or *he sought to gain access to such a thing.* (Er-Rághib, TA.)

6. تَطَارُقٌ signifies The *coming consecutively,* or *being consecutive.* (TA.) You say, تطارقت الإِبِلُ *The camels came following one another, the head of each* [*except the first*] *being at the tail of the next* [*before it*], *whether tied together in a file* or *not:* (TA:) or *went away, one after another;* (Ṣ, O, Ḳ;) as also ▼ اِطَّرَقَت; (O, Ḳ, TA;) in the Ṣ, incorrectly, ▼ أُطْرِقَت; which is also mentioned in the Ḳ, in another part of the art., and there expl. as meaning *they followed one another;* but the verb in this sense is ▼ اِطَّرَقَت: (TA:) and, (O, Ḳ, TA,) as some say, (O, TA,) this last signifies *they scattered,* or *dispersed, themselves upon the roads, and quitted the main beaten tracks:* (O, Ḳ, TA:) Aṣ cited as an ex., (from Ru-beh, TA,) describing camels, (O,)

• جَاءَتْ مَعًا وَٱطَّرَقَتْ ▼ شَتِيتَا •

meaning *They came together, and went away in a state of dispersion.* (Ṣ, O, TA.) And you say, تطارق الظَّلَامُ وَالغَمَامُ *The darkness and the clouds were,* or *became, consecutive.* (TA.) And تطارقت عَلَيْنَا الأَخْبَارُ [*The tidings came to us consecutively*]. (TA.)

8. اِطَّرَقَ: see 3. Said of the wing of a bird, (Ṣ, TA,) *Its feathers overlay one another:* (TA:) or *it was,* or *became, abundant and dense* [*in its feathers*]. (Ṣ, TA.) And اطّرقت الأَرْضُ *The earth became disposed in layers, one above another, being compacted by the rain.* (TA.) And اطّرق الحَوْضُ *The watering-trough,* or *tank, had in it* [*a deposit of*] *compacted dung,* or *dung and mud* or *clay, that had fallen into it.* (TA.) And اطّرق عَلَيْهِ اللَّيْلُ, as in the O and L; in the Ḳ, erroneously, ▼ أَطْرَقَ; *The night came upon him portion upon portion.* (TA.) See also 6, in three places.

10. استطرقهُ فَحْلًا *He desired,* or *demanded, of him a stallion to cover his she-camels;* (Ṣ, O, Ḳ;) like استضربهُ. (TA.) — And استطرقهُ *He desired,* or *demanded, of him the practising of pessomancy* (الضَّرْبَ بِالحَصَى), *and the looking* [or *divining*] *for him therein.* (Ḳ,* TA.) — And *He desired,* or *demanded, of him the* [*having,* or *taking, a*] *road,* or *way, within some one of his boundaries.* (TA.) — مِنْ غَيْرِ أَنْ يَسْتَطْرِقَ نَصِيبَ الآخَرِ, a phrase used by El-Ḳudooree, means *Without his taking for himself the portion of the other as a road* or *way* [or *place of passage*]. (Mgh.) And الإِسْتِطْرَاقُ بَيْنَ الصُّفُوفِ, a phrase used by Khwáhar-Zádeh [commonly pronounced Kháhar-Zádeh], means *The going* [or *the taking for oneself a way*] *between the ranks* [of the people engaged in prayer]: from الطَّرِيقُ. (Mgh.) And إِسْتَطْرَقْتُ إِلَى البَابِ *I went along a road,* or *way, to the door.* (Mṣb.) [Hence a phrase in the Fákihet el-Khulafà, p. 105, line 15.] — [آسْتَطْرَقَتْ in a verse cited in the Ḳ in art. دد is a mistake for استطرفت, with فاء: see 10 in art. طرب.]

طَرْقٌ [originally an inf. n., and as such app. signifying *An act of striking* the lute &c.: and hence,] *a species* (ضَرْبٌ) *of the* أَصْوَات [meaning *sounds,* or *airs,* or *tunes,*] *of the lute:* (TA:) or *any* صَوْت [i. e. *air,* or *tune*], (Lth, O, Ḳ, TA,) or *any* نَغْمَة [i. e. *melody*], (Ḳ, TA,) *of the lute* and *the like, by itself:* (Lth, O, Ḳ, TA:) you say, تَضْرِبُ هٰذِهِ الجَارِيَةُ كَذَا وَكَذَا طَرْقًا [*This girl,* or *young woman,* or *female slave, plays such and such airs* or *tunes,* or *such and such melodies, of the lute* or *the like*]. (Lth, O, Ḳ.*) — [Hence, probably,] عِنْدَهُ طُرُوقٌ مِنَ الكَلَامِ, sing. طَرْقٌ, a phrase mentioned by Kr; thought by ISd to mean *He has* [*various*] *sorts,* or *species, of speech.* (TA.) — See also طَرْقَةٌ, in four places. — Also ‡ *A stallion* [*camel*] *covering:* (O, Ḳ, TA:) pl. طُرُوقٌ and طِرَاقٌ: (TA:) an inf. n. used as a subst. [or an epithet]: (O, Ḳ, TA:) for ذُو طَرْقٍ. (TA.) — And † The *sperma* of the stallion [camel]: (Ṣ, Ḳ:) a man says to another, أَعِرْنِى طَرْقَ فَحْلِكَ العَامَ i. e. [*Lend thou to me*] *the sperma,* and *the covering,* (Aṣ, TA,) which latter is said to be the original meaning, (TA,) *of thy stallion* [*camel this year*]. (Aṣ, TA.) And it is said to be sometimes applied metaphorically to † The *sperma* of man: or in relation to man, it may be an epithet, [like as it is sometimes in relation to a stallion-camel, as mentioned above,] and not metaphorical. (TA.) And طَرْقُ الجَمَلِ means also *The hire that is given for the camel's covering of the female.* (TA in art. شبر.) — Also, and ▼ مَطْرُوقٌ, ‡ *Water* (Ṣ, O, Ḳ, TA) *of the rain* (Ṣ, O, TA) *in which camels* (Ṣ, O, Ḳ) *and others* [i. e. *other beasts*] *have staled,* (Ṣ,) or *waded and staled,* (Ṣ,* O, Ḳ, TA,) *and dunged:* (Ṣ, O, TA:) or *stagnant water in which beasts have waded and staled:* (Mgh:) and ▼ طَرْقٌ [expressly stated to be مُحَرَّكَة] signifies [the same, or] *water that has collected, in which there has been a wading and staling, so that it has become turbid;* (TA;) or *places where water collects and stagnates* (Ṣ, O, Ḳ, TA) *in stony tracts of land;* (TA;) and the pl. of this is أَطْرَاقٌ. (TA.) — طَرْقٌ also signifies *A* [*snare, trap, gin,* or *net, such as is commonly called*] فَخّ, (IAạr, O, Ḳ,) or the *like thereof;* and so ▼ طِرْقٌ: (Ḳ: [by Golius and Freytag, this meaning has been assigned to طَرْقَةٌ; and by Freytag, to طُرْقَةٌ also; in consequence of a want of clearness in the Ḳ:]) or *a snare,* or *thing by means of which wild animals are taken,* like the فَخّ; (Lth, O;) and ▼ طَرَقَةٌ, (Ṣ, O, Ḳ,) of which the pl. [or coll. gen. n.] is ▼ طَرَقٌ, (Ṣ, Ḳ,) signifies [the same, or] the *snare* (حِبَالَة) *of the sportsman,* (Ṣ, O, Ḳ,) *having* [*what are termed*] كِفَف [pl. of كِفَّةٌ, q. v.]. (Ṣ, O.) — And *A palm-tree:* of the dial. of Ṭeiyi. (AḤn, Ḳ.) — And ‡ *Weakness of intellect,* (Ḳ, TA,) *and softness.* (TA [See طَرِقٌ.])

طُرْقٌ: see طُرْقَةٌ. — [Also a contraction of طُرُقٌ, pl. of طَرِيقٌ, q. v.] — And pl. of طِرَاقٌ [q. v.]. (Ḳ.)

طِرْقٌ *Fat,* as a subst.: (Ṣ, O, Ḳ:) this is the primary signification. (Ṣ, O.) [See an ex. voce بِنٌّ.] — And *Fatness.* (AḤn, Ḳ.) One says, هٰذَا البَعِيرُ مَا بِهِ طِرْقٌ i. e. *This camel has not in him fatness,* and *fat.* (AḤn, TA.) It is said to be mostly used in negative phrases. (TA.) — And *Strength:* (Ṣ, O, Ḳ:) because it mostly arises from fat. (Ṣ, O.) One says, مَا بِهِ طِرْقٌ, meaning *There is not in him strength.* (TA.) The pl. is أَطْرَاقٌ. (TA.) — See also طَرْقٌ, last quarter.

طَرَقٌ: see طَرْقٌ, third quarter. — Also *i. q.* مُذَلَّل [applied to a beast, app. to a camel,] meaning *Rendered submissive,* or *tractable;* or *broken.* (TA.) — It is also pl. of ▼ طَرَقَةٌ, [or rather is a coll. gen. n. of which the n. un. is طَرَقَةٌ,] (Ṣ, O, Ḳ,) which latter signifies *A row* of bricks in a wall, or of other things, (Ṣ, O,) or [particularly] of palm-trees. (Aṣ, TA.) — Also, ▼ the latter, [as is expressly stated in the TA, and indicated in the Ṣ and O, (آثَارُ and بَعْضُهَا in the CḲ being mistakes for آثَارٍ and بَعْضِهَا,)] The *foot-marks* [or *track*] *of camels following near after one another.* (Ṣ, O, Ḳ.) You say, جَآءَتِ الإِبِلُ عَلَى طَرَقَةٍ ▼ وَاحِدَةٍ *The camels came upon one track* [or *in one line*]; like as you say, عَلَى خُفٍّ وَاحِدٍ. (Ṣ, O. [See also a similar phrase voce مِطْرَاقٌ.]) And Aboo-Turáb mentions, as a phrase of certain of Benoo-Kiláb, عَرَقْتُهَا and مَرَرْتُ عَلَى طَرَقَةِ ▼ الإِبِلِ, meaning *I went upon the track of the camels.* (TA.) — See also طَرْقٌ, last quarter. — Also, i. e. طَرَقٌ, *A duplicature,* or *fold,* (ثِنْي,) in the CḲ [erroneously] (ثَنْى,) of a water-skin: (Ṣ, O, Ḳ:) and أَطْرَاقٌ is its pl., (Ṣ, O,) signifying its *duplicatures,* or *folds,* (Ṣ, O, Ḳ,) *when it is bent,* (O,) or *when it is doubled,* or *folded,* (Ṣ, Ḳ,) *and bent.* (Ṣ.) — And أَطْرَاقُ البَطْنِ *The parts of the belly that lie one above another* (Ḳ, TA) *when it is wrinkled:* pl. of طَرَقٌ. (TA.) — طَرَقٌ in the feathers of a bird is their *Overlying one another:* (Ṣ, O, Ḳ, TA:) or, accord. to the A, it is *softness and flaccidity* therein. (TA.) — [Also inf. n. of طَرِقَ, q. v.]

طَرْقَةٌ *A time; one time;* syn. مَرَّةٌ: (Ṣ, O, Ḳ;) as also ▼ طَرْقٌ, (O, Ḳ,) and ▼ طُرْقَةٌ and ▼ طُرْقٌ. (Ḳ.) You say, اِخْتَضَبَتِ المَرْأَةُ طَرْقَةً, (Ṣ, O,) or طَرْقَتَيْنِ, (Ṣ,) or ▼ طَرْقًا, (Ḳ,) or ▼ طَرْقَيْنِ, (O, Ḳ,) [&c.,] i. e. [*The woman dyed her hands* with ḥinnà] *once,* or *twice.* (Ṣ, O, Ḳ.) And أَنَا آتِى فُلَانًا فِى اليَوْمِ طَرْقَتَيْنِ, (Ṣ, Ḳ,) and ▼ طَرْقَيْنِ, (O, Ḳ,) &c., (Ḳ,) i. e. ‡ [*I come to such a one in the day*] *twice.* (Ṣ, O, TA.) And هُوَ أَحْسَنُ مِنْ فُلَانٍ بِعِشْرِينَ طَرْقَةً † [*He is better than such a one by twenty times*]. (A, TA.) — طَرْقَةُ الطَّرِيقِ means *The main and middle part,* or *the distinct* [*beaten*] *track, of the road.* (TA.) — And هٰذِهِ النَّبْلُ طَرْقَةُ رَجُلٍ وَاحِدٍ [*These arrows are*] *the work,* or *manufacture, of one man.* (Ṣ, O, Ḳ.*) — See also طَرِيقَةٌ.

طُرْقَةٌ *i. q.* طَرِيقٌ, q. v. (Ḳ.) — And sing. of طُرَقٌ signifying The *beaten tracks in roads;* and of طُرُقَاتٌ in the phrase طُرُقَاتُ الإِبِلِ meaning *the tracks of the camels following one another consecutively.* (TA.) — Also *A way,* or *course, that one pursues* (طَرِيقَةٌ) *to a thing.* (Ḳ.) — And † *A custom, manner, habit,* or *wont.* (Ṣ, O, K.) One says, مَا زَالَ ذٰلِكَ طُرْقَتَكَ † *That ceased not to be thy custom,* &c. (Ṣ, O.) — And *A line,* or *streak,* (طَرِيقَةٌ,) *in things that are sewed,* or *put, one upon another.* (Ḳ,* TA: [المُطَارَقَةُ in the CḲ is a mistake for المطارقة:]) as also ▼ طُرْقَةٌ. (Ḳ.) — And *A line,* or *streak, in a bow:* or *lines,* or *streaks, therein:* pl. طُرَقٌ: (Ḳ:) or its pl., i. e. طُرَقٌ, has the latter meaning. (Ṣ, O.) — And *Stones one upon another.* (O, Ḳ.) — Also *Darkness.* (Ibn-'Abbád, O, Ḳ.) One says, جِئْتُهُ فِى طُرْقَةِ اللَّيْلِ [*I came to him in the darkness of night*]. (TA.) — And *i. q.* مَطْمَعٌ [app. as meaning *Inordinate desire,* though it also means *a thing that is coveted*], (Ibn-'Abbád, O,) or طَمَعٌ [which has both of these meanings]. (Ḳ.) [That the former is the meaning here intended I infer from the fact that Ṣgh immediately adds what here follows.] — IAạr says, (O,) فِى فُلَانٍ طُرْقَةٌ means *In such a one is* تَخْنِيث [i. e., app., *a certain unnatural vice;* see 2 (last sentence) in art. خنث]: (O, TA:) and so فِيهِ تَوْضِيعٌ. (TA.) — See also طَرَقَةٌ. — Also *Foolish; stupid;* or *unsound,* or *deficient, in intellect* or *understanding.* (O, Ḳ.) — [Freytag adds, from the Deewán of the Hudhalees, that it signifies also *A prey* (*præda*).]

طِرْقَةٌ: see the next preceding paragraph.

طَرَقَةٌ: see طَرْقٌ, in four places: — and see also طَرْقٌ, last quarter. — One says also, وَضَعَ الأَشْيَآءَ طَرَقَةً طَرَقَةً i. e. *He put the things one upon another;* and so ▼ طَرِيقَةً طَرِيقَةً. (TA.)

طُرَقَةٌ ‡ A man *who journeys by night in order that he may come to his* أَهْل [meaning *wife*] *in the night:* (Ṣ, O, TA:) or one *who journeys much by night.* (L in art. خشف.)

طِرَاقٌ (of which طُرُقٌ is the pl. [app. in all its senses]) *Any sole that is sewed upon another sole so as to make it double,* (Ṣ,* O, Ḳ,) *matching the latter exactly:* (O, Ḳ:) [this is called طِرَاقُ نَعْلٍ; for it is said that] طِرَاقُ النَّعْلِ signifies *that with which the sole is covered, and which is sewed upon it.* (Ṣ.) — And The *skin* [meaning *sole*] *of a sandal,* (Lth, O, Ḳ,) *when the* [*thong,* or *strap, called*] شِرَاك *has been removed from it.* (Lth, O.) El-Ḥárith Ibn-Ḥillizeh [in the 13th verse of his Mo'allaḳah, using it in a pl. sense,] applies it to the *Soles that are attached to the feet of camels:* (TA:) or he there means by it the *marks left by the* طراق *of a she-camel.* (EM p. 250.) And *A piece of skin cut in a round form, of the size of a shield, and attached thereto, and sewed.* (O, Ḳ.) — And *Anything made to match,* or *correspond with, another thing.* (Lth, O, Ḳ.) — *Iron that is expanded, and then rounded, and made into a helmet* (Lth, O, Ḳ) or *a* [*kind of armlet called*] سَاعِد (Lth, O) and *the like.* (Lth, O, Ḳ.) And *Any* قَبِيلَة [i. e. *plate,* likened to a قبيلة of the head,] *of a helmet, by itself.* (Lth, O.) And *Plates,* of a helmet, *one above another.* (TA) — رِيشٌ طِرَاقٌ *Feathers overlying one another.* (Ṣ.) And طَائِرٌ طِرَاقُ الرِّيشِ *A bird whose feathers overlie one another.* (TA.) — Also *A brand made upon the middle of the ear of a ewe,* (En-Naḍr, O, Ḳ,) *externally; being a white line, made with fire, resembling a track of a road:* (En-Naḍr, O:) there are two such brands, called طِرَاقَانِ. (TA.) — See also طَرِيقَةٌ.

طَرِيقٌ *A road, way,* or *path;* syn. سَبِيلٌ: (Ṣ;) [i. e. *a beaten track,* being of the measure فَعِيلٌ in the sense of the measure مَفْعُولٌ; and applied to *any place of passage;*] and ▼ طُرْقَةٌ signifies the same: (Ḳ:) [see also مُسْتَطْرَقٌ:] it is masc. (Ṣ, O, Mṣb, Ḳ*) in the dial. of Nejd, and so in the Ḳur xx. 79; (Mṣb;) and fem. (Ṣ, O, Mṣb, Ḳ) in the dial. of El-Ḥijáz: (Mṣb:) the latter accord. to general usage: (MF:) [see زُقَاقٌ:] the pl. [of pauc.] is أَطْرِقَةٌ (Ṣ, Mṣb, Ḳ) with those who make the sing. masc. (Mṣb) and أَطْرُقٌ (O, Ḳ) with those who make the sing. fem. (TA) and [of mult.] طُرُقٌ (Ṣ, O, Mṣb, Ḳ) and طُرُقٌ [of which see an ex. voce دِلَالَةٌ] (Ḳ) and أَطْرِقَةٌ, (O, Ḳ,) and طُرُقَاتٌ is a pl. pl. (Mṣb, Ḳ) i. e. pl. of طُرُقٌ. (Mṣb, TA.) — In the saying بَنُو فُلَانٍ يَطَؤُهُمُ الطَّرِيقُ, accord. to Sb, الطَّرِيقُ is for أَهْلُ الطَّرِيقِ: [the meaning therefore is, † *The sons of such a one* sojourn, or encamp, *where the people of the road tread upon them,* i. e., *become their guests:* (see more in art. وطأ:)] or, as some say, الطريق here means *the wayfarers* without any suppression. (TA.) — حَقُّ الطَّرِيقِ [*The duty relating to the road*] is *the lowering of the eyes; the putting away,* or *aside, what is hurtful,* or *annoying; the returning of salutations; the enjoining of that which is good; and the forbidding of that which is evil.* (El-Jámi' eṣ-Ṣagheer. See جَلَسَ.) — قَطَعَ الطَّرِيقَ [*He intercepted the road*] means *he made the road to be feared, relying upon his strength, robbing, and slaying men* [or *passengers*]. (Mṣb in art. قطع.) [And أَصَابَ الطَّرِيقَ means the same; or, as expl. by Freytag, on the authority of Meyd, *He was,* or *became, a robber.*] — [Hence,] ابْنُ الطَّرِيقِ means † *The robber* [*on the highway*]. (T in art. بنى.) — [But أَهْلُ طَرِيقِ ٱللّٰهِ means † *The devotees.*] — أُمُّ طَرِيقٍ, thus correctly in the 'Eyn, [and shown to be so by a verse there cited, q. v. voce عَشَبٌ,] † *The hyena:* erroneously written by Ṣgh, ▼ امّ طُرَيْقٍ; and the author of the Ḳ has copied him in this instance accord. to his usual custom. (TA.) — See also أُمُّ الطَّرِيقِ and أُمَّةُ الطَّرِيقِ in art. امّ. — بَنَاتُ الطَّرِيقِ means † *The branches of the road, that vary, and lead in any,* or *every, direction.* (TA.) — طَرِيقٌ signifies also The *space between two rows of palm-trees;* as being likened to the طَرِيق [commonly so called] in extension. (Er-Rághib, TA.) — أَخَذَ فُلَانٌ فِى الطَّرِيقِ means the same as أَخَذَ فِى التَّطْرِيقِ [expl. before: see 2, near the end]. (TA.) — طَرِيقٌ as *syn. with* طَرِيقَةٌ: see the latter word, first sentence. — [بِالطَّرِيقِ الأَوْلَى is a phrase of frequent occurrence, app. post-classical; lit. *By the fitter way;* meaning *with the stronger reason; à fortiori:* see an ex. in Beyḍ xlii. 3, and De Sacy's Anthol. Gr. Ar. p. 467.] == Also *A sort of palm-tree.* (TA.) — See also طَرِيقَةٌ (of which it is said to be a pl.), last sentence.

طُرَيْقٌ: see أُطْرُوقٌ.

طَرُوقَةٌ *A she-camel covered by the stallion;* of the measure فَعُولَةٌ in the sense of the measure مَفْعُولَةٌ. (Mṣb.) طَرُوقَةُ الفَحْلِ means *The female of the stallion* [*camel*]. (Ṣ, O.) And (Ṣ, O) *A she-camel that has attained to the fit age for her being covered by the stallion:* (Ṣ, O, Mṣb, Ḳ:) it is not a condition of the application of the term that he has already covered her: (Mṣb:) or *a young,* or *youthful, she-camel that has attained to that age and kept to the stallion and been chosen by him.* (TA.) And one says to a husband, كَيْفَ طَرُوقَتُكَ, meaning † *How is thy wife?* (TA:) every wife is termed طَرُوقَةُ زَوْجِهَا, (O,) or طروقة بَعْلِهَا, (Mṣb,) or طروقة فَحْلِهَا; (Ḳ,* TA;) which is thought by ISd to be metaphorical. (TA.) — One says also, نَوَّخَ ٱللّٰهُ الأَرْضَ طَرُوقَةً لِلْمَآءِ i. e. † *God made,* or *may God make, the land capable of receiving the water* [of the rain *so as to be impregnated,* or *fertilized,* or *soaked, thereby*]; expl. by جَعَلَهَا مِمَّا تُطِيقُهُ. (Ṣ in art. نوخ.) [See also a verse cited in art. سعد, conj. 4.]

طَرِيقَةٌ *A way, course, rule, mode,* or *manner, of acting* or *conduct* or *the like,* (syn. مَذْهَبٌ, Ṣ, TA, and سِيرَةٌ, and مَسْلَكٌ, TA,) of a man, (Ṣ, TA,) whether it be *approved* or *disapproved;* (TA;) as also ▼ طَرِيقٌ, which is metaphorically used in this sense: (Er-Rághib, TA:) [like مَذْهَبٌ, often *relating to the doctrines and practices of religion:* and often used in post-classical times as meaning the *rule* of a religious order or sect:] and meaning also *a manner of being; a state,* or *condition;* (syn. حَالَةٌ, Ṣ, or حَالٌ, O, Ḳ;) as in the saying, مَا زَالَ فُلَانٌ عَلَى طَرِيقَةٍ وَاحِدَةٍ [*Such a one ceased not to be in one state,* or *condition*]; (Ṣ;) and it is applied to such as is good and to such as is evil. (O.) One says also, هُوَ عَلَى طَرِيقَتِهِ [*He is following his own way,* or *course*]. (TA voce جَدِيَّةٌ.) — لَوِ ٱسْتَقَامُوا عَلَى الطَّرِيقَةِ, in the Ḳur [lxxii. 16], means, accord. to Fr, [*If they had gone on undeviating in the way*] *of polytheism:* but accord. to others, *of the right direction.* (O.) [The pl. is طَرَائِقُ.] — [It is also used for أَهْلُ طَرِيقَةٍ: and in like manner the pl., for أَهْلُ طَرَائِقَ. Thus,] كُنَّا طَرَائِقَ قِدَدًا, in the Ḳur [lxxii. 11], means † *We were sects differing in our desires.* (Fr, Ṣ, O. [See also قِدَّةٌ.]) And طَرِيقَةُ القَوْمِ means ‡ *The most excellent,* (Ṣ, O, Ḳ, TA,) and *the best,* (Ṣ, O,) and *the eminent,* or *noble, persons,* (Ḳ, TA,) *of the people:* (Ṣ, O, Ḳ, TA:) and you say, هٰذَا رَجُلٌ طَرِيقَةُ قَوْمِهِ ‡ [*This is a man the most excellent,* &c., *of his people*]: and هٰؤُلَآءِ طَرِيقَةُ قَوْمِهِمْ and طَرَائِقُ قَوْمِهِمْ ‡ *These are* [*the most excellent,* &c., or] *the eminent,* or *noble, persons of their people:* (Ṣ, O, Ḳ,* TA:) so says Yaạḳoob, on the authority of Fr. (Ṣ, O, TA.) وَيَذْهَبَا بِطَرِيقَتِكُمُ المُثْلَى, in the Ḳur [xx. 66], means [*And that they may take away*] *your most excellent body of people:* (O:) or *your eminent,* or *noble, body of people who should be made examples to be followed:* and Zj thinks that بطريقتكم is for بِأَهْلِ طَرِيقَتِكُمْ: (TA:) or, accord. to Akh, the meaning is, *your established rule* or *usage,* and *your religion,* or *system of religious ordinances.* (O, TA.) — [Also † The *way,* or *course,* of an event: and hence,] طَرَائِقُ الدَّهْرِ means † *The vicissitudes of time* or *fortune.* (TA.) — [And † The *air* of a song &c.: but this is probably post-classical.] — Also *A line, streak,* or *stripe,* in a thing: (Ḳ, TA:) [and *a crease,* or *wrinkle;* often used in this sense:] and [its pl.] طَرَائِقُ signifies the *lines,* or *streaks, that are called* حُبُك, of a helmet. (TA.) The طَرِيقَة [or *line*] *that is in the upper part of the back:* and the *line,* or *streak, that extends upon* [i. e. *along*] *the back of the ass.* (TA.) [*A vein,* or *seam,* in a rock or the like. *A track* in stony or rugged land &c. *A narrow strip* of ground or land, and of herbage.] *An extended piece* or *portion* [i. e. *a strip*] of sand; and likewise of fat; and [likewise of flesh; or] *an oblong piece* of flesh. (TA.) — [Hence, app.,] ثَوْبٌ طَرَائِقُ *A garment old and worn out* [as though *reduced to strips* or *shreds*]. (Lḥ, Ḳ.) — ذَاتُ طَرَائِقَ and فِيهَا طَرَائِقُ are phrases used, the latter by Dhu-r-Rummeh, in describing a spear-shaft (قَنَاة) shrunk by dryness [app. meaning *Having lines,* or *what resemble wrinkles, caused by shrinking*]. (TA.) — And طَرَائِقُ signifies also The *last remains of the soft and best portions of pasturage.* (TA.) — And The *stages of Heaven;* so called because they lie one above another: (TA:) [for] السَّمٰوَاتُ سَبْعُ طَرَائِقَ بَعْضُهَا فَوْقَ بَعْضٍ [*The Heavens are seven stages, one above another*]: (Lth, O, TA:) and they have mentioned [likewise] the stages of the earth [as seven in number: and of hell also: see دَرَكٌ]. (TA.) See also طَرَقَةٌ. — Accord. to Lth, (O, TA,) طَرِيقَةٌ signifies also *Any* أُخْدُورَةٌ, (so in the O and in copies of the Ḳ and accord. to the TA, and thus also in the JḲ,) or أُخْدُودَةٌ, (thus accord. to the CḲ,) [neither of which words have I found in any but this passage, nor do I know any words nearly resembling them except أُخْدُور and أُخْدُود, of which they may be mistranscriptions, or perhaps dial. vars., the former signifying a *declivity, slope,* or *place of descent,* and the latter a *furrow, trench,* or *channel,*] *of the earth* or *ground:* (O, Ḳ, TA:) or [*any*] *border,* or *side,* (صَنِفَةٌ,) *of a garment,* or *piece of cloth;* or *of a thing of which one part is stuck upon another,* or *of which the several portions are stuck one upon another;* and in like manner *of colours* [*similarly disposed*]. (O, TA.) — And *A web,* or *thing woven, of wool,* or *of* [*goats'*] *hair, a cubit in breadth,* (Ṣ, O, Ḳ, TA,) or *less,* (Ṣ, O, TA,) *and in length four cubits,* or *eight cubits,* (TA,) [or] *proportioned to the size of the tent* (Ṣ, O, Ḳ, TA) *in its length,* (Ṣ, O,) *which is sewed in the place where the* شُقَاق [or *oblong pieces of cloth that compose the main covering of the tent*] *meet, from the* كِسْر [q. v.] *to the* كِسْر; (Ṣ, O, Ḳ, TA:) [*it is app. sewed beneath the middle of the tent-covering, half of its breadth being sewed to one* شُقَّة *and the other half thereof to the other middle* شُقَّة; (see Burckhardt's "Bedouins and Wahábys," p. 38 of the 8vo ed.;) *and sometimes, it seems, there are three* طَرَائِق, *one in the middle and one towards each side;* for it is added,] *and in them are the heads of the tent-poles,* [*these generally consisting of three rows, three in each row,*] *between which and the* طرائق

are pieces of felt, in which are the nozzles (أُنُوف) of the tent-poles, in order that these may not rend the طرائق. (TA.) — Also A tent pole; any one of the poles of a tent: a خِبَآء has one طريقة: a بَيْت has two and three and four [and more]: and the part between two poles is called مَتْن: (AZ, TA in art. ربع:) or the pole of a [large tent such as is called] مِظَلَّة, (Ḳ, TA,) and of a خِبَآء. (TA.) — And A tall palm-tree: (Ḳ:) or the tallest of palm-trees: so called in the dial. of El-Yemámeh: (AA, ISk, Ṣ, O:) or a smooth palm-tree: or a palm-tree [the head of] which may be reached by the hand: (TA:) pl. [or rather coll. gen. n.] ↓ طَرِيقٌ. (AA, ISk, Ṣ, O.)

طِرْيَاقٌ: see طِرَاقٌ.

أُمُّ طُرَيْقٍ: see طَرِيقٌ, latter part.

طَرِّيقٌ means كَثِيرُ الإِطْرَاقِ [i. e. One who lowers his eyes, looking towards the ground, much, or often; or who keeps silence much, or often]; (Lth, O, Ḳ;) applied to a man: (Lth, O:) and ↓ مِطْرَاقٌ signifies [the same, or] one who keeps silence much, or often; as also ↓ مُطْرِقٌ [except that this does not imply muchness or frequency]. (TA.) — And The male of the [bird called] كَرَوَان; (Lth, O, Ḳ;) because, when it sees a man, it falls upon the ground and is silent. (Lth, O.) [See 4.] — أَرْضٌ طَرِيقَةٌ Soft, or plain, land or ground; (O, Ḳ;) as though beaten so as to be rendered even, or easy to be travelled, and trodden with the feet. (TA.)

طَرِيقَةٌ [fem. of طَرِيقٌ: see what next precedes. — And also a subst., signifying] Gentleness and submissiveness: (Ṣ, O:) or softness, or flaccidity, and gentleness: (O, Ḳ:) and softness, or flaccidity, and languor, or affected languor, and weakness, in a man; as also ↓ طَرْقَةٌ and ↓ طِرَاقٌ. (TA.) One says, تَحْتَ طَرِيقَتِكَ لَعِنْدَأْوَةٌ (Ṣ, O, Ḳ) i. e. Beneath thy gentleness and submissiveness is occasionally somewhat of hardness: (Ṣ, O, TA:) or beneath thy silence is impetuosity, and refractoriness: (TA:) or beneath thy silence is deceit, or guile. (Ḳ, voce عِنْدَأْوَةٌ, q. v.)

طِرْيَاقٌ i. q. تِرْيَاقٌ [q. v.], (O, Ḳ,) as also دِرْيَاقٌ; (O;) and so ↓ طِرَاقٌ. (O, Ḳ.)

طَارِقٌ [act. part. n. of طَرَقَ; and, as such, generally meaning] Coming, or a comer, (Ṣ,) [i. e.] anything coming, (O, Mṣb,) by night: (Ṣ, O, Mṣb:) one who comes by night being thus called because of his [generally] needing to knock at the door: in the Mufradát [of Er-Rághib] said to signify a wayfarer (سَالِكٌ لِلطَّرِيقِ): but in the common conventional language particularly applied to the comer by night: its pl. is أَطْرَاقٌ, like أَنْصَارٌ pl. of نَاصِرٌ, [and app., as in a sense hereafter mentioned, طُرَّاقٌ also, agreeably with analogy,] and the pl. of [its fem.] طَارِقَةٌ is طَوَارِقُ. (TA.) [دَاعِي المَنَايَا, like طَارِقُ المَنَايَا, means The summoner of death, lit., of deaths; because death makes known its arrival or approach suddenly, like a person knocking at the door in the night.] — Hence الطَّارِقُ, mentioned in the Ḳur [lxxxvi. 1 and 2], The star that appears in the night: (Er-Rághib, O:) or the morning-star; (Ṣ, O, Ḳ;) because it comes [or appears] in [the end of] the night. (O.) — Hence the saying of Hind (Ṣ, O) the daughter of 'Otbeh the son of Rabee'ah, on the day [of the battle] of Oḥud, quoting proverbially what was said by Ez-Zarḳà El-Iyádeeyeh when Kisrà warred with Iyád, (O,)

• نَحْنُ بَنَاتُ طَارِقِ • لَا نَنْثَنِي لِوَامِقِ •
• نَمْشِي عَلَى النَّمَارِقِ •

† [We are the daughters of one like a star, or a morning-star: we bend not to a lover: we walk upon the pillows]: (Ṣ,* O,* TA:) meaning we are the daughters of a chief; likening him to the star in elevation; (O, TA;) i. e. our father is, in respect of elevation, like the shining star: (Ṣ:) or بَنَاتُ طَارِقٍ means † the daughters of the kings. (T and TA in art. بنى.) — And طَارِقٌ signifies also [A diviner: and particularly, by means of pebbles; a practiser of pessomancy: or] one who is nearly a كَاهِن; possessing more knowledge than such as is termed حَازٍ: (ISh, TA in art. حزى:) طُرَّاقٌ [is its pl., and] signifies practisers of divination: and طَوَارِقُ [is pl. of طَارِقَةٌ, and thus] signifies female practisers of divination: Lebeed says,

• لَعَمْرُكَ مَا تَدْرِى الطَّوَارِقُ بِالحَصَى •
• وَلَا زَاجِرَاتُ الطَّيْرِ مَا اللّٰهُ صَانِعُ •

[By thy life, or by thy religion, the diviners with pebbles know not, nor the diviners by the flight of birds, what God is doing]. (Ṣ, O.)

طَارِقَةٌ [a subst. from طَارِقٌ, made so by the affix ة, † An event occurring, or coming to pass, in the night: pl. طَوَارِقُ]. One says, نَعُوذُ بِٱللّٰهِ مِنْ طَوَارِقِ السُّوْءِ ‡ [We seek protection by God from] the nocturnal events or accidents or casualties [that are occasions of that which is evil]. (Er-Rághib, TA.) And طَارِقَةٌ occurring in a trad. of 'Alee is expl. as signifying طَرَقَتْ بِخَيْرٍ [app. meaning An event that has occurred in the night bringing good, or good fortune]. (TA.) — Also A man's [small sub-tribe such as is called] عَشِيرَة, (Ṣ, O, Ḳ,) and [such as is called] فَخِذ. (Ṣ, O.) — And A small couch, (IDrd, O, Ḳ,) of a size sufficient for one person: of the dial. of El-Yemen. (IDrd, O.) — [El-Maḳreezee mentions the custom of attaching طَوَارِق حَرْبِيَّة upon the gates of Cairo and upon the entrances of the houses of the أُمَرَآء; and De Sacy approves of the opinion of A. Schultens and of M. Reinaud that the meaning is Cuirasses, from the Greek θώραξ: (see De Sacy's Chrest. Arabe, sec. ed., vol. i. pp. 274-5:) but I think that the meaning is more probably large maces; for such maces, each with a head like a cannon-ball, may still be seen, if they have not been removed within the last few years, upon several of the gates of Cairo; and if so, طَوَارِق in this case is app. from طَرَقَ "he beat:" see also عَمُودٌ.]

طَارِقِيَّةٌ A قِلَادَة [i. e. collar, or necklace]: (Ḳ:) [or rather] a sort of قَلَائِد [pl. of قِلَادَة]. (Lth, O.)

أَطْرَقُ A camel having the affection termed طَرَقٌ, inf. n. of طَرِقَ [q. v.]: fem. طَرْقَآءُ: (Ṣ, O, Ḳ:) and the latter is said by Lth to be applied to the hind leg as meaning having the crookedness termed طَرَقٌ in its سَاق. (O.)

أُطَيْرِقٌ and ↓ طُرَيْقٌ A sort of palm-tree of El-Ḥijáz, (AḤn, O, Ḳ,) that is early in bearing, before the other palm-trees; the ripening and ripe dates of which are yellow: (O:) AḤn also says, in one place, the اطيرق is a species of palm-trees, the earliest in bearing of all the palm-trees of El-Ḥijáz; and by certain of the poets such are called الأُطَيْرِقُونَ and الطُّرَيْقُونَ. (TA.)

تُرْسٌ مُطْرَقٌ [A shield having another sewed upon it: or covered with skin and sinews]: (Ṣ:) and مَجَانٌّ مُطْرَقَةٌ, (Ṣ, Mṣb, Ḳ,) or ↓ مُطَرَّقَةٌ, (O, Mṣb, Ḳ,) Shields sewed one upon another; (Ṣ, O, Ḳ;) formed of two skins, one of them sewed upon the other; (Mṣb;) like نَعْلٌ مُطْرَقَةٌ a sole having another sole sewed upon it; as also ↓ مُطَارَقَةٌ: (Ṣ, O, Ḳ:) or shields clad [i. e. covered] with skin and sinews. (Ṣ, O.) كَأَنَّ وُجُوهَهُمُ المَجَانُّ المُطْرَقَةُ, or ↓ المُطَرَّقَةُ, occurring in a trad., (Mṣb, TA,) i. e. [As though their faces were] shields clad with sinews one above another, (TA,) means † having rough, or coarse, and broad, faces. (Mṣb, TA.) — And رِيشٌ مُطْرَقٌ Feathers overlying one another. (TA.)

مُطْرِقٌ Having a natural laxness of the eye [or rather of the eyelids, and a consequent lowering of the eye towards the ground]: (Ṣ, O:) [or bending down the head: or lowering the eyes, looking towards the ground; either naturally or otherwise: (see its verb, 4:)] and silent, or keeping silence. (TA. See also طَرِّيقٌ.) — It is also applied as an epithet to a stallion-camel: and to a [she-camel such as is termed] جُمَالِيَّة [i. e. one resembling a he-camel in greatness of make], and, thus applied, [and app. likewise when applied to a stallion-camel,] it may mean That does not utter a grumbling cry, nor vociferate: or, accord. to Khálid Ibn-Jembeh, [quick in pace, for he says that] it is from طَرْقٌ signifying "quickness of going." (Sh, TA.) — See also مِطْرَاقٌ, last sentence. — And, applied to a man, ‡ Low, ignoble, or mean, (Ḳ, TA,) in race, or parentage, or in the grounds of pretension to respect or honour. (TA.) — Also An enemy: from أَطْرَقَ فُلَانٌ لِفُلَانٍ expl. above [see 4, last sentence]. (TA.)

مِطْرَقٌ: see the next paragraph.

مِطْرَقَةٌ The rod, or stick, with which wool is beaten, (Ṣ, O, Ḳ, TA,) to loosen it, or separate it; (Ṣ,* O,* TA;) as also ↓ مِطْرَقٌ. (O, Ḳ, TA.) And A rod, or stick, or small staff, with which *one is beaten*: pl. مَطَارِقُ: one says, ضَرَبَهُ بِالْمَطَارِقِ *He beat him with the rods*, &c. (TA.) — And The *implement* [i. e. *hammer*] (Ṣ, Mgh, O, Mṣb) *of the blacksmith*, (Ṣ, O,) *with which the iron is beaten.* (Mgh, Mṣb.)

ذَهَبٌ مُطَرَّقٌ *Stamped*, or *minted, gold*; syn. مَسْكُوكٌ. (TA.) — And نَاقَةٌ مُطَرَّقَةٌ [like مَطْرُوقَةٌ (q. v.)] † *A she-camel rendered tractable, submissive*, or *manageable.* (TA.) — And جُلٌّ مُطَرَّقٌ [*A horse-cloth*] *in which are* [*various*] *colours* [app. *forming* طَرَائِق, i. e. *lines, streaks*, or *stripes*]. (O.) — See also مُطْرِقٌ, in two places.

قَطَاةٌ مُطَرِّقٌ [thus without ة] *A bird of the species called* قَطًا *that has arrived at the time of her egg's coming forth.* (Ṣ.) [See also مُعَضِّلٌ.]

مِطْرَاقٌ: see طَرِيقٌ. — Also A she-camel *recently covered by the stallion.* (O, TA.) — And pl. of مَطَارِيقُ in the saying جَآءَتِ الإِبِلُ مَطَارِيقَ (TA) which means *The camels came in one* طَرِيق [i. e. *road*, or *way*]: (Er-Rághib, TA:) or *the camels came following one another* (Ṣ, O, Ḳ,* TA) *when drawing near to the water.* (O, Ḳ, TA. [See also a similar phrase voce طَرَقٌ.]) — [Hence,] مِطْرَاقُ الشَّىْءِ signifies *That which follows the thing*; and *the like of the thing*: (Ḳ:) one says, هٰذَا مِطْرَاقُ هٰذَا *This is what follows this*; and *the like of this*: (Ṣ, O:) and the pl. is مَطَارِيقُ. (Ṣ.) — And مَطَارِيقُ signifies also Persons *going on foot*: (Ḳ:) one says, خَرَجَ القَوْمُ مَطَارِيقَ *The people*, or *party, went forth going on foot*; *having no beasts*: and the sing. is مِطْرَاقٌ, (O,) or ↑ مُطْرِقٌ, ('Eyn, L,* TA,*) accord. to A'Obeyd; the latter, if correct, extr. (TA.)

مَطْرُوقٌ [pass. part. n. of طَرَقَ; *Beaten*, &c.]. هُوَ مَطْرُوقٌ means *He is one whom every one beats* or *slaps* (يَطْرُقُهُ كُلُّ أَحَدٍ). (TA.) — And ‡ A man *in whom is softness*, or *flaccidity*, (Aṣ, Ṣ, O, Ḳ, TA,) *and weakness*: (Aṣ, Ṣ:) or *weakness and softness*: (TA:) or *softness and flaccidity*: from the saying هُوَ مَطْرُوقٌ i. e. اصابته حادثة كتفته [which, if we should read كَتَّفَتْهُ, seems to mean *he is smitten by an event*, or *accident, that has disabled him as though it bound his arms behind his back*; but I think it probable that كتفته is a mistranscription]: or because he is مصروف [app. a mistake for مَضْرُوب], like as one says مَقْرُوعٌ and مَدْمُوغٌ [app. meaning *beaten* and *subdued*, or *rendered submissive*]: or as being likened, in abjectness, to a she-camel that is termed مَطْرُوقَةٌ [like مُطَرَّقَةٌ (q. v.)]. (Er-Rághib, TA.) مَطْرُوقَةٌ applied to a woman means [app. *Soft and feminine*;] *that does not make herself like a man.* (TA.) [See also a reading of a verse cited voce مَطْرُوفٌ.] — Also ‡ *Weak in intellect*, (Ḳ, TA,) *and soft.* (TA.) — Applied to herbage, *Smitten by the rain after its having dried up.* (Ibn-'Abbád, L, Ḳ.) — See also طَرْقٌ, latter half. Applied to a ewe, مَطْرُوقَةٌ signifies *Branded with the mark called* طِرَاق *upon the middle of her ear.* (ISh, O, Ḳ.)

مُطَارِقٌ: see its fem., with ة, voce مُطْرِقٌ.

مُسْتَطْرَقٌ ‡ i. q. سِكَّةٌ [app. as meaning *A road*, like طَرِيقٌ; or *a highway*]. (TA.)

مُنْطَرِقَاتٌ *Mineral substances.* (TA.)

طرمح

Q. 1. طَرْمَحَ *He made* his building *long*; (Ṣ, Ḳ; in the former in art. طرح;) like طَرَّحَ: (Ṣ and Ḳ in art. طرح:) or *he made it long and high*: (A, TA:) accord. to J, the م is augmentative. (TA.) A poet says, describing camels which herbage produced by the نَوْء [here meaning the rain of the auroral setting] of the constellation Leo had filled with fat,

طَرْمَحَ أَقْطَارَهَا أَحْوَى لِوَالِدَةٍ
صَحْمَآءَ وَالفَحْلُ لِلضِّرْغَامِ يَنْتَسِبُ

[*Dark green* herbage, *the offspring of a mother* (meaning, as is said in the TA, of a cloud) *of a yellowish black hue, the stallion* (meaning the star or asterism supposed to be the cause of its giving rain) *tracing his origin to the lion, extended*, or *stretched out, their sides*]. (Ṣ and TA, the former in art. طرح.)

طِرْمَحٌ One *who takes*, or *walks with, long steps*: (Ḳ, TA:) accord. to IḲṭṭ, the م is augmentative. (TA.)

طَرْمَحَانِيَّةٌ *Pride.* (Ḳ.) — مِشْيَةٌ طَرْمَحَانِيَّةٌ A *proud walk* or *gait.* (TA.)

طُرْمُوحٌ (Ḳ, TA) and ↑ طِرِمَّاحٌ, as also طُرْحُومٌ, which last is thought by IDrd to be formed by transposition, (TA,) *Long*, or *tall.* (Ḳ, TA.)

طِرِمَّاحٌ, of the very rare measure فِعِلَّالٌ, of which there can hardly, or cannot at all, be found any other example, except سِنِمَّارٌ, a foreign word, and سِجِلَّاطٌ, also said to be of foreign origin, (TA,) A man *of high ancestry* or *family, and celebrated*; (Ḳ, TA;) *of high renown.* (TA.) — And One *who goes*, or *penetrates, far*, or *deeply, into an affair.* (AZ, Ḳ, TA.) — And accord. to Abu-l-'Omeythil El-Aạrábee, One *who elevates his head in pride.* (TA.) — See also طُرْمُوحٌ.

طرمذ

Q. 1. طَرْمَذَ, inf. n. طَرْمَذَةٌ, *He gloried*, or *boasted, vainly, and praised himself for that which was not in him*: (AHeyth, L:) Th says, in his "Amálee," that طَرْمَذَةٌ is a genuine Arabic word; (L;) and so says El-Ḳálee: (TA:) but in the Ṣ it is said to be not of the language of the people of the desert. (L, TA.) [See this word below.] — طَرْمَذَ عَلَيْهِ *He gloried over him, and praised himself for that which he did not possess.* (L, Ḳ.)

فِيهِ طَرْمَذَةٌ *In him is pride*: (Abu-l-'Abbás, L:) [or *vain-glorying*: see 1.]

طِرْمِذَةٌ: see the last paragraph below.

طَرْمَذَارٌ and طِرْمِذَانٌ: see the next paragraph.

طِرْمَاذٌ One *who glories*, or *boasts, vainly, and praises himself for that which is not in him*; (L, Ḳ;) as also ↑ طِرْمِذَانٌ, (L, Ḳ,) and طِرْمِذَارٌ, (L,) or طَرْمَذَارٌ, (Ḳ, in which it is mentioned in a separate art.,) but طرمذار is said to have been unknown by IAạr: (TA:) or one *who boasts of abundance which he does not possess*; as also the last of the above-mentioned epithets, which also signifies one *who boasts of that which he does not perform.* (L.) — Also A horse *of generous breed.* (Th, L.)

مُطَرْمِذٌ (Ṣ, L, Ḳ) and ↑ طِرْمِذَةٌ (Ḳ) A man *who says but does not act*, or *perform*; (Ṣ, L, Ḳ;) and *who does not act seriously*, or *in earnest*, (لَا يُحَقِّقُ,) *in affairs*: (Ḳ:) or, accord. to some copies of the Ḳ, *who does not verify things.* (TA.)

طرو

1. طَرُوَ, [aor. يَطْرُو,] (Ḳṭr, Ṣ, Mgh, Mṣb, Ḳ,) and طَرِىَ, [aor. يَطْرَى,] (Ḳṭr, Ṣ, Ḳ,) inf. n. طَرَاوَةٌ (Ḳṭr, Ṣ, Mgh, Mṣb, Ḳ) and طَرَآءَةٌ (Ṣ, Ḳ,) and طَرَاةٌ, (TA, and so in some copies of the Ṣ and of the Ḳ,) like حَصَاةٌ, (TA,) and طَرَآءٌ, (so in some copies of the Ḳ,) or طَرًا, (TA as from the Ḳ,) with the shortened alif, (TA,) [the last agreeable with analogy as inf. n. of طَرِىَ,] said of a thing, (Mgh, Mṣb,) or of flesh-meat, (Ḳṭr, Ṣ,) *It was*, or *became, fresh, juicy*, or *moist*: (Ḳṭr, Ṣ, Mṣb, Ḳ:) and طَرُؤَ signifies the same; (Mgh, Mṣb;) but طَرُوَ is more common. (TA in art. طرأ.) — And طَرِىَ signifies also تَجَدَّدَ [*It became new*; *was newly made* or *done*; or *was renewed*]. (TA.) — طَرَا, [aor. يَطْرُو,] inf. n. طُرُوٌّ, (Ḳ,) or, as written in the M, طَرْوٌ, (TA,) *He came from a distant place*: (Ḳ:) you say طَرَا عَلَيْهِمْ *he came*, or, accord. to Lth, *he came forth, upon them from a distant place*: or, accord. to AZ, *he came upon them without their knowledge*: it is a dial. var. of طَرَأَ [q. v.]. (TA.) — And طَرَا signifies also مَضَى [*He went*, or *went away*, &c.]. (TA.) — And طَرِىَ, aor. يَطْرَى, (IAạr, Ḳ,) in which, accord. to the Ḳ, the last radical letter is ى, [not و changed into ى by reason of the kesreh before it,] but ISd says that there is no word of which the radical letters are ط and ر and ى, (TA,) *He advanced*, or *came forward*: or *he passed, passed by, went*, or *went away.* (IAạr, Ḳ,* TA.)

2. طَرَّاهُ, inf. n. تَطْرِيَةٌ, *He rendered it fresh, juicy*, or *moist.* (Ḳ.) You say, طَرَّيْتُ الثَّوْبَ inf. n. as above, (Ṣ,) [app. meaning *I refreshed*,

or *I moistened, the garment*, or *piece of cloth.*] — And طرّى, (Ḳ,) inf. n. as above, (TA,) *He rendered* perfume *fragrant* [as though he refreshed it] *by admixtures;* (Ḳ, TA;) and aloes-wood *with* [*other*] *perfume*, or *ambergris*, or *some other thing:* (Az, TA:) and in like manner, food, (Ḳ, TA,) *by mixing it with aromatics.* (TA.) — And *He plastered*, or *coated*, a building *with clay*, or *mud:* of the dial. of Mekkeh. (Z, TA.)

4. اطراهُ *He praised him;* thus in the Ṣ, and in like manner expl. by Zbd and IḲṭṭ; (TA;) and thus اطرأهُ [with ء] is expl. by Es-Saraḳusṭee: (Mṣb:) *he eulogized*, or *commended, him;* (Ḳ;) thus in the M; (TA;) and thus it is expl. by Es-Saraḳusṭee: (Mṣb:) or *he praised him renewing the mention of him:* (Er-Rághib, TA:) or *he praised him exceedingly:* (AA, TA:) or *he praised him for the best of the qualities that he possessed;* (Mṣb, TA;) thus expl. by IF, and in like manner by Z: (TA:) or *he praised him for that which was not in him:* (Az, TA:) or *he praised him greatly*, or *extravagantly; exceeded the just*, or *usual, bounds in praising him:* (Mṣb:) or, accord. to Hr and IAth, *he exceeded the just*, or *usual bounds in praising him, and lied therein.* (TA.) — And اطرى العَسَلَ *He made the honey to thicken*, or *coagulate.* (Ṣ, Mṣb, TA.)

12. اِطْرَوْرَى, (Ḳ, TA,) inf. n. اِطْرِيرَآءٌ, (TA,) *He suffered from indigestion*, or *heaviness of the stomach,* (Ḳ, TA,) *in consequence of much eating,* (TA,) *and became inflated in his belly:* (Ḳ, TA:) and so اِطْرَوْرَى: thus correctly; but mentioned by J and IḲṭṭ as with ض. (TA.) [See also Q. Q. 3 in art. طر.]

الطُّرَا [without the article طُرًا] *What is not of the nature of the earth;* (Ḳ;) or *whatever is upon the surface of the earth, of such things as are not of the nature of the earth, consisting of pebbles;* or *small pebbles;* [and *the like;*] and *dust* and *the like:* (TA:) and, (Ḳ, TA,) as some say, (TA,) *the sorts of created things whereof the number cannot be reckoned;* (Ḳ, TA;) or *any created things whereof the number and the sorts cannot be reckoned.* (TA.) One says, هُمْ أَكْثَرُ مِنَ الطُّرَى وَالثَّرَى [or الطُّرَا والثَّرَا] i. e. *They are more in number*, or *quantity, than the pebbles, &c., and than the moist earth*]. (TA.)

طَرِىٌّ *Fresh, juicy*, or *moist:* (Ṣ, Mṣb, Ḳ, TA:) and طَرِىءٌ is a dial. var. thereof. (Mṣb.) It is expl. as meaning thus in the Ḳur [xvi. 14 and] xxxv. 13 [as an epithet applied to the flesh of fish]. (TA.) And الطَّرِيَّانِ [used as a subst.] means *Fish and fresh ripe dates.* (A, TA.) — Also *Strange*, or *a stranger;* syn. غَرِيبٌ: and AA has mentioned ▼ رَجُلٌ طَارِىٌّ, [said to be] with teshdeed, [otherwise I should think it might be a mistranscription for طَارِئٌ,] as meaning *a man that is a stranger.* (TA.)

طِرِيَّانٌ, with two kesrehs, and with the ى musheddedeh, The خِوَان [or *table*] *upon which one eats;* thus accord. to ISk: or, accord. to IAṭr, the طَبَق [i. e. *dish*, or *plate*]: occurring in a trad.; as some relate it, thus; and as others relate it, طِرْيَان, with the ر musheddedeh, like صِلِّيَان; [and thus it is mentioned in the O and Ḳ in art. طر;] but Fr says that this latter is of the dial. of the vulgar. (TA.)

طَارِىٌّ: see طَرِىٌّ.

إِطْرِيَةٌ *A sort of food, called in Pers.* لَاخْشَهْ; (Ṣ;) [i. e.] *a certain food, like threads, made of flour;* (Ḳ, TA;) an explanation necessarily implying that it is *what is called in Egypt* غَزْلُ البَنَات: accord. to Sh, *a thing made of softened starch;* and said by Lth to be *a food made by the people of Syria;* a word having no n. un.; and what these two say indicates that it is *what is called* كُنَافَة: Lth and Z mention the word as pronounced also with fet-ḥ; but Az says that the pronunciation with fet-ḥ is incorrect. (TA.)

أُطْرُوَانٌ The *first stage*, and the *quickness,* (غُلَوَآء, in the CḲ [erroneously] غُلُوّ,) of youth: (Ḳ, TA:) like عُنْفُوَانٌ in measure and in meaning. (TA.) One says also, ▼ لِكُلِّ شَىْءٍ أُطْرُوَانِيَّةٌ i. e. [*To everything there is*] *a state of youthfulness.* (TA.)

أُطْرُوَانِيَّةٌ: see what next precedes.

عُودٌ مُطَرًّى [*Aloes-wood*] *such as is termed* مُطَيَّر, *with which one fumigates himself:* (Ṣ, TA:) and أَلُوَّةٌ مُطَرَّاةٌ [signifies the same, i. e. *aloes-wood*] *rendered fragrant* [as though refreshed] *by the admixture of* [*other*] *perfume*, or *of ambergris,* or *some other thing:* المُطَرَّاةُ is said by Lth to mean *a sort of perfume.* (TA.) And غِسْلَةٌ مُطَرَّاةٌ *A preparation for washing the head* or *hand, compounded with aromatics.* (Ṣ, TA.) — And one says, هُوَ مُطَرًّى فِى نَفْسِهِ, meaning مُتَخَيِّرٌ [i. e. † *He is restored to a good state*, or *condition, of body*, or *of property*]. (TA.)

طس

طَسٌّ and ▼ طَسَّةٌ (Ṣ, M, Ḳ) and ▼ طِسَّةٌ (M, Ḳ) *i. q.* طَسْتٌ, (Ṣ, Ḳ,) which is expl. in its proper place: (TA:) [see art. طست: or] طَسَّةٌ is the original of طَسْتٌ: (Lth, TA:) the pl. (of طَسٌّ, M) is أَطْسَاسٌ [a pl. of pauc.] (M) and طُسُوسٌ (Ṣ, M, Ḳ) and طَسِيسٌ (M, Ḳ) [or rather this is a quasi-pl. n.] and (of طَسَّةٌ and طِسَّةٌ, M) طِسَاسٌ and [of طَسَّةٌ also] طَسَّاتٌ, (Ṣ, Ḳ,) and طِسَّةٌ may also have for its pl. طِسَسٌ, accord. to rule. (M.) The dim. [of طَسٌّ] is طُسَيْسٌ; (Ṣ in art. طست;) and [of طَسَّةٌ and طِسَّةٌ,] طُسَيْسَةٌ. (IḲt and Mṣb in art. طست.)

طَسَّةٌ:
طِسَّةٌ: } see the preceding paragraph.

طِسَاسَةٌ The *trade of selling*, (M,) or the *art of making,* (Ḳ,) [*the kind of basins called*] طُسُوس [pl. of طَسٌّ]. (M, Ḳ.*)

طَسَّاسٌ *A seller*, (M,) or *maker,* (Ḳ,) *of* [*the kind of basins called*] طُسُوس. (M, Ḳ.*)

طست

طَسْتٌ (Ṣ, M, Ḳ, &c.) *A kind of vessel of* صُفْر [or *brass*]: (M, TA:) [generally pronounced in the present day طِشْت and طَشْت: and mostly applied to *a kind of basin of tinned copper*, or *of brass*, or *of silver, used for washing the hands &c.*, figured and described in my work on the Modern Egyptians:] *i. q.* طَسٌّ, [q. v.,] (IḲt, Ṣ, Mgh, Mṣb, Ḳ,) which is [said to be] arabicized from طَشْت, the latter being a foreign word; (Mgh;) [but it is from the Pers., طَشْت;] it is of the dial. of Ṭeiyi; (Ṣ;) and [said to be] formed from طَسٌّ, one of the two س being changed into ت, (IḲt, Ṣ, Mṣb, Ḳ,) because they are deemed difficult of pronunciation; (IḲt, Ṣ, Mṣb;) but in forming the pl. and the dim., the second س is restored, because separated from the former; (Ṣ;) for (IḲt, Ṣ, Mṣb) the pl. is طِسَاسٌ (Ṣ, Mgh, Mṣb) and طُسُوسٌ, though it has also for its pl. طُسُوتٌ, (IḲt, Mgh, Mṣb,) or, accord. to Zj, طَسَاتٌ; (Mṣb;) and the dim. is طُسَيْسٌ, (Ṣ,) or طُسَيْسَةٌ: (IḲt, Mṣb:) it is also pronounced طِسْتٌ; (MF;) and طَشْتٌ also has been mentioned; (Ḳ;) but some say that this is a mistake; and others, that طَشْت is the original word from which طَسْت is arabicized: (TA:) Zj says that, with most of the Arabs, (Mṣb,) it is fem.: (Mgh, Mṣb:) sometimes it is masc.: (Lḥ, M:) IAmb says, on the authority of Fr, that the word used by the Arabs was طَسَّة, save that some said طَسٌّ, without ة; and that the tribe of Ṭeiyi said طَسْتٌ, like as they said لِصْتٌ for لِصٌّ: Es-Sijistánee says that it is a foreign word arabicized: and Az, that it is a word adopted into the Arabic language, because ط and ت do not both occur in an Arabic word. (Mṣb.)

طسق

طَسْقٌ, incorrectly pronounced by the people of Baghdád طَشْق, (O, Ḳ,) *A certain measure of capacity,* (Lth, M, O, Ḳ,) *well known:* (M:) and (Lth, M, O, in the Ḳ "or") the *portion of the* [*tax called*] خَرَاج *that is levied on the* [*quantities of land termed*] جُرْبَان, (Lth, M, O, Ḳ,) pl. of جَرِيب: (TA:) *an assessed rate* (وَظِيفَة) *of the land-tax:* (Ṣ:) it is *like the* خَرَاج, *having a certain amount:* (Az, TA:) or it is *like an impost of a certain amount:* (O, Ḳ:) not a pure Arabic word: (Az, O:) app. post-classical: (Ḳ:) or (Ḳ) a Pers. word (Ṣ) arabicized: (Ṣ, Ḳ:) from the Pers. تَشْه [or تَشْتَه] originally signifying "an oil-measure:" (TḲ:) it occurs in a letter of 'Omar to 'Othmán. (Ṣ, O, Ḳ.)

طسوج

طَسُّوجٌ *A certain weight;* (T, TA;) *two grains*, i. e. *grains of barley;* (حَبَّتَانِ;) (Ṣ;) the *quarter* of a دَانِق ; (Ṣ, Ḳ;) i. e. the *twenty-fourth part of a* دِرْهَم ; the دانق being the sixth of a درهم : (TA:) pl. طَسَاسِيجُ : (Ṣ:) an arabicized word [from the Pers. تَسُو]. (Ṣ, Ḳ.) — Also i. q. نَاحِيَةٌ [as meaning *A district*, or *province*, or *the like*]; (Ṣ, Mgh, Ḳ;) such as *a* قَرْيَة [here app. meaning *township*], and *the like*: for instance, Ardabeel is of the طَسَاسِيج of Ḥulwán: (Mgh:) *one of the* طَسَاسِيج *of the Sawád*: (T, TA:) the طساسيج of the people of El-Ahwáz are like the مَخَالِيف of the people of El-Yemen and the أَجْنَاد of the people of Syria and the كُوَر of the people of El-'Irák and the رَسَاتِيق of the people of El-Jibál: (IB voce مِخْلَاف:) in this sense likewise (Ṣ) an arabicized word. (Ṣ, Mgh, Ḳ.*)

طش

1. طَشَّتِ السَّمَآءُ, (Ṣ, A, O, Ḳ,) aor. ُ and ِ, (O, Ḳ,) inf. n. طَشٌّ, (TḲ,) *The sky let fall rain such as is called* طَشّ [q. v.]; as also ▼ اطشّت. (Ṣ, A, O, Ḳ.) — [Hence,] طَشَّ [as meaning † *He sprinkled the moisture from his nose like fine rain*] is said of one affected with the malady termed طُشَّة, when he blows his nose. (O.) — And طُشَّ, (O, Ḳ,) with ḍamm, (Ḳ,) *He* (a man) *was*, or *became, affected with the malady termed* طُشَّة: (O, Ḳ:) but Az says that the [better] known word is طُشِىَ. (TA.)

4: see the preceding paragraph.

طَشٌّ and ▼ طَشِيشٌ *Weak* [or *fine*] *rain*, (Ṣ, A, O, Ḳ,) *but exceeding what is termed* رَذَاذ: (Ṣ, O, Ḳ:) or the former is *less than* رذاذ: (El-Khaṭṭábee, and Suh in TA art. رذ:) or *rain exceeding what is termed* رَكّ, *but less than what is termed* قِطْقِط: (TA:) or the *first of rain*; (L, TA;) *next to which is what is termed* رَشّ: (L:) [but see these other terms for rain: طِشَاش and طُشُوش are pls. of طَشّ; both mentioned in the O, though not there said to be pls. of طَشّ:] one says, أَصَابَنَا طِشَاشٌ وَرِشَاشٌ [*Rains such as are termed* طشاش *and* رشاش *fell upon us*]. (O.)

طُشَّةٌ and ▼ طُشَاشٌ, both with ḍamm, *A malady like the* [*rheum termed*] زُكَام, (O, Ḳ,) *incident to human beings*: said by El-Ḳutabee to be termed طُشَّة because when he who is affected with it blows his nose he sprinkles the moisture from it like fine rain (إِذَا اسْتَنْثَرَ طَشَّ): but the [better] known word is طُشَآة. (O.) [See also the next paragraph.]

طُشَّة is said in the Ḳ to signify *A young child*; its author having app. understood a young child to be meant thereby in a trad. respecting the [plant called] حَزَآة, in which it is said, يَشْتَرِيهَا أَكَايِسُ الصِّبْيَانِ لِلطُّشَّةِ [evidently meaning, *Intelligent children purchase it for the malady termed* طُشَة, this word being doubtless either a dial. var. of طُشَّة, or a mistranscription]: that طشّة here denotes children is refuted by another relation of the trad., يَشْرَبُهَا أَكَايِسُ النِّسَآءِ لِلطُّشَّةِ [i. e. *intelligent women drink* a preparation of *it for the* طُشَّة]. (TA.)

طَشَاشٌ *i. q.* رَشَاشٌ [i. e. *Such as is sprinkled*, or *scattered*,] (Ḳ, TA) of rain: or *such as is weak*. (TA.) [Not to be mistaken for the pls. طِشَاش and رِشَاش: see طَشّ.] — And hence, app., and, if so, tropical, *Weakness of sight*: whence the prov., الطَّشَاشُ وَلَا الْعَمَى [*Weakness of sight, and not blindness*]. (TA.)

طُشَاشٌ: see طُشَّةٌ.

طَشِيشٌ: see طَشٌّ.

أَرْضٌ مَطْشُوشَةٌ *Land upon which has fallen rain such as is termed* طَشّ. (Ṣ, A, O.) — And رَجُلٌ مَطْشُوشٌ *A man affected with the malady termed* طُشَّة. (TA.)

طشت

طَشْتٌ: see طَسْتٌ.

طعم

1. طَعِمَهُ, aor. َ, inf. n. طُعْمٌ and طَعَامٌ, *He ate it*; namely, food: (Ḳ,* TA:) and طَعِمَ, aor. as above, inf. n. طُعْمٌ, with ḍamm, *he tasted* [a thing]: (Ḳ:) or طَعِمَ, aor. as above, (Ṣ, Mgh,* Mṣb,) inf. n. طُعْمٌ, with ḍamm, (Ṣ,) or طَعْمٌ, with fet-ḥ, (Mṣb,) or both, (Mgh,) and مَطْعَمٌ also is an inf. n. of the same verb, (TA,) signifies *he ate*, (Ṣ, Mgh, Mṣb,*) a thing, (Mgh,) and [app. also *he swallowed*, for it is said that] it applies to anything that is swallowed easily or agreeably, even to water: (Mṣb:) and *he tasted* (Ṣ, Mgh, Mṣb) a thing; (Mgh, Mṣb;) as also ▼ تطعّم; (Ṣ, Mgh, Ḳ;) [i. e.] this latter verb signifies *he tasted* food *in order that he might know its flavour*; and so ▼ استطعم: (Mṣb:) and طَعِمَ as meaning *he tasted* may be used in relation to that which is eaten and to that which is drunk. (L.) Hence, in the Ḳur [xxxiii. 53], فَإِذَا طَعِمْتُمْ فَانْتَشِرُوا *And when ye shall have eaten* [*disperse yourselves*]. (Ṣ,* TA.) And you say, فُلَانٌ قَلَّ طُعْمُهُ, meaning [*Such a one,*] *his eating* [*was*, or *became, little*]. (Ṣ.) The saying in the Ḳur [ii. 250], وَمَنْ لَمْ يَطْعَمْهُ فَإِنَّهُ مِنِّى means *But whoso does not taste it*, (Ṣ, Mṣb,* TA,) *he is of my followers*, (Bḍ, Jel,) or *is at one*, or *in union, with me*: (Bḍ:) or, accord. to Zj, the meaning is, لَمْ يَتَطَعَّمْ ▼ بِهِ [app. meaning *does not refresh himself with it as though with food*]: (TA:) or, as some say, the passage in which it occurs denotes a prohibition to take aught save as much as is laded out with the hand; and when water has with it something that is chewed, one says of it يُطْعَمُ. (Er-Rághib, TA.) تَطَعَّمْ ▼ تَطْعَمْ i. e. *Taste thou*, (Ṣ, Mgh, Ḳ,) *then thou wilt have desire*, or *appetence*, (Mgh,) or *so that thou mayest have desire*, or *appetence, and mayest eat*; (Ṣ, Ḳ;) or *taste thou the food, for it will induce thee to eat it*; (IB, TA;) is a prov., (IB, Mgh, TA,) said to him who refrains from an affair; meaning, commence it, for thy doing so will invite thee to finish it. (IB, TA.) — الطُّعْمُ signifies also *The eating with the central incisors*: one says, إِنَّهُ لَيَطْعَمُ طُعْمًا حَسَنًا [*Verily he eats well with the central incisors*]. (TA.) — مَا يَطْعَمُ آكِلُ هٰذَا الطَّعَامِ, (Ḳ,* TA,) a phrase mentioned by ISh, (TA,) means ‡ *The eater of this food does not become satisfied in stomach*. (Ḳ,* TA.) — طَعِمَ said of a branch, or shoot, ‡ *It received ingraftment*. (ISh, Ḳ, TA.) — And [hence, perhaps,] طَعِمَتْ عَيْنُهُ † [*His eye had a mote cast into it*: see 4]. (TA.) — طَعِمَ عَلَيْهِ, (Ḳ, TA,) inf. n. طُعْمٌ, (Ḳ,* TA,) which, in the Ḳ, is improperly disjoined from its verb, [as though it were a simple subst.,] (TA,) *i. q.* قَدَرَ [i. e. *He had power over him*, or *it*; or *he had power*, or *ability, to do it*, &c.]. (Ḳ, TA.)

2: see 4, in three places. — طَعَّمَ, (Ḳ, TA,) inf. n. تَطْعِيمٌ, (TA,) said of a bone, means † *It had*, or *contained, marrow*. (Ḳ, TA.) [Used in this sense, it may be regarded as a trans. v. of which the objective complement is understood; as though signifying *It fed*.]

3. طَاعَمْتُهُ *I ate with him*. (TA.) — And [hence] طَاعَمَا, said of two pigeons, ‡ *They billed; the male bird inserting his mouth* [or *bill*] *into that of his female*; as also ▼ تَطَاعَمَا. (Ḳ, TA.)

4. اطعمهُ, (Mṣb, Ḳ,) or اطعمهُ الطَّعَامَ, (Ṣ,) [inf. n. إِطْعَامٌ,] *He fed him*; or *gave him to eat*, or *gave him food*; (Mṣb, Ḳ;) [and so, accord. to modern usage, ▼ طعّمهُ.] — And [hence] اطعمهُ signifies also ‡ *He supplied him with the means of subsistence*: whence, in the Ḳur [li. 57], وَمَا أُرِيدُ أَنْ يُطْعِمُونِ i. e. ‡ *And I desire not that* [*they*, meaning] any of my servants *should supply me with the means of subsistence*; for I am the supplier of the means of subsistence. (TA.) — And أَطْعَمْتُكَ هٰذِهِ الْأَرْضَ † *I have assigned to thee as a* طُعْمَة [q. v.] *this land*. (TA.) It is said of the Prophet, أَطْعَمَهُمْ طُعْمَةً † [*He assigned to them*, or *gave them, a* طعمة]: accord. to Aboo-Ḥaneefeh, الإِطْعَامُ signifies peculiarly † *the lending of land for cultivation*: but it is said on the authority of Mo'áwiyeh, إِنَّهُ أَطْعَمَ عَمْرًا خَرَاجَ مِصْرَ, meaning † *that he gave 'Amr as a* طُعْمَة *the* خراج [or *land-tax*] *of Egypt*. (Mgh.) — See also 10. — اطعم الغُصْنَ, (ISh, Ḳ,) inf. n. إِطْعَامٌ, (TA,) ‡ *He ingrafted upon the branch*, or *shoot, a branch*, or *shoot, of another tree*; (ISh, Ḳ, TA;) as also ▼ طعّمهُ, [which is more commonly used in this sense,] (Ḳ,) inf. n. تَطْعِيمٌ. (TA.) [And ▼ طعّمهُ is now used as meaning also † *He inoculated him*.] — And أَطْعَمْتُ عَيْنَهُ قَذًى † [*I cast a mote into his eye*]. (TA.)

[— See also a verse cited voce عَقَبَةٌ.] — اطعم النَّخْلُ ‡ *The palm-trees had ripe fruit,* (Ṣ, Ḳ, TA,) *such as might be eaten:* or *bore fruit:* (TA:) or اطعمت الشَّجَرَةُ *the tree had ripe fruit:* (Mṣb:) or اطعمت الثَّمَرَةُ *the fruit became ripe.* (Mgh.)

5: see 1, in three places: and see also an ex. voce ضَارٍ, in art. ضرو and ضرى.

6. تطاعموا *They* (a party on a journey) *ate with,* or *at the tent of,* [meaning, *of the food of,*] *this man on one occasion of alighting, and another man on another occasion of alighting; each one of them having his turn to supply the food of one day:* like تناوبوا and تنازلوا. (ISh, TA in art. نوب.) — See also 3. — [Hence,] one says of two persons in conformity, تَطَاعَمَا, meaning † *They acted as do the two* [*billing*] *pigeons.* (TA.)

8. اِطَّعَمَ البُسْرُ, (Ḳ,) or اِطَّعَمَتِ البُسْرَةُ, (Ṣ,) † *The ripening dates,* or *the ripening date, acquired flavour,* (Ṣ, Ḳ, TA,) *and became ripe, so as to be eaten.* (TA.) — [Hence,] one says, هُوَ رَجُلٌ لَا يَطَّعِمُ ‡ *He is a man who will not become well disciplined, in whom that which should improve him will not produce an effect,* (Ḳ,* TA,) *and who will not become intelligent.* (TA.)

10. استطعمهُ *He asked him to feed him.* (Ṣ, Mgh, Mṣb.) — [Hence,] اِسْتَطْعَمْتُهُ الحَدِيثَ † *I asked him to relate to me the narrative,* or *tradition:* or *to make me to taste the savour of his discourse.* (TA.) — And إِذَا ٱسْتَطْعَمَكُمُ الإِمَامُ فَأَطْعِمُوهُ ‡ *When the* امام [or *leader in prayer*] *desires you to tell him what he should say,* (Ṣ, Mgh, Ḳ, TA,) being unable to proceed (Mgh, TA) in reciting the prayer, (TA,) *do ye tell him what he should say,* (Ṣ, Mgh, Ḳ, TA,) and *prompt him,* as though putting the recitation into his mouth like as food is put in: (TA:) a saying of 'Alee. (Ḳ.) — And اِسْتَطْعَمْتُ الفَرَسَ † *I desired the horse's running.* (TA.) — See also 1, first sentence.

طَعْمٌ [as an inf. n.: see 1. — As a simple subst.,] *Taste, flavour,* or *savour;* (Ṣ, Mṣb, TA;) *sweetness,* and *bitterness,* and *a quality* [*of any kind*] *between these two,* in food and in beverage: pl. طُعُومٌ. (Ḳ.) One says, طَعْمُهُ مُرٌّ [*Its taste is bitter*], (Ṣ, TA,) and حُلْوٌ [*sweet*], (Mṣb, TA,) and حَامِضٌ [*acid*]: and تَغَيَّرَ طَعْمُهُ *Its taste became altered from its natural quality.* (Mṣb.) — And [*Relish,* i. e.] *a desired quality* of food. (Ṣ, Mṣb, Ḳ.) One says, لَيْسَ لَهُ طَعْمٌ [*It has no relish*]: (Ṣ:) and لَيْسَ لِلْغَثِّ طَعْمٌ [*What is lean has no relish*]: and ↓ طُعْمٌ signifies the same in the dial. of Kiláb. (Mṣb.) — [Hence, † *An approvable quality* in a man.] One says رَجُلٌ ذُو طَعْمٍ † *A man possessing intelligence,* and *prudence,* or *discretion:* and مَا بِفُلَانٍ طَعْمٌ وَلَا نَوِيصٌ † *There is not in such a one intelligence nor activity:* and لَيْسَ لِمَا يَفْعَلُ فُلَانٌ طَعْمٌ † *There appertains not to what such a one does any pleasing quality, nor any place of honour in the heart,* or *mind:* and it is said in a trad., مَا قَتَلْنَا أَحَدًا بِهِ طَعْمٌ مَا قَتَلْنَا إِلَّا عَجَائِزَ صُلْعًا † *We slew not any one of account, any known person,* or *any one of rank,* or *station;* [*we slew not any but bald-headed old women;*] and one may also say in this case ↓ طُعْمٌ, with ḍamm. (TA.) — Also *A thing that is swallowed easily* or *agreeably,* whether *solid, as grains* [*&c.*], or *liquid, as expressed juice* and *oil* and *vinegar* [*&c.*]; differing from طَعَامٌ, which does not apply to liquids. (Mṣb.)

طُعْمٌ [as an inf. n.: see 1: —] as a subst.: see طَعَامٌ. — Also *Grain that is thrown to birds.* (T, Mṣb, TA.) And *A bait that is thrown to fish.* (TA.) — طَعَامُ طُعْمٍ means *Food that satisfies the stomach of its eater:* (ISh, Ḳ, TA:) and is said by MF to be for طَعَامُ شَىْءٍ طُعْمٍ. (TA.) The Prophet said of the well Zemzem, إِنَّهَا طَعَامُ طُعْمٍ, meaning *Verily it is a satisfier of the stomach of man,* (ISh, Mṣb, TA,) *like as is food.* (TA.) — See also طَعْمٌ.

طَعَمٌ ; see طَعْمٌ.

طَعِمٌ : see طَاعِمٌ.

طُعْمَةٌ i. q. مَأْكَلَةٌ, (Ṣ, Mṣb, Ḳ, TA,) or رِزْقٌ; (Mgh;) i. e. † *An assigned,* or *appointed, means of subsistence; such as a grant of a tract of land;* [*an allodium so granted;*] and *a tax,* or *a portion of a tax* or *of taxes;* and *the like:* (Mgh, TA:) pl. طُعَمٌ. (Mgh, Ḳ.) One says, جَعَلْتُ هٰذِهِ الضَّيْعَةَ طُعْمَةً لِفُلَانٍ † [*I have assigned this estate as a means of subsistence to such a one*]. (Ṣ.) [For other exs., see 4.] And it is said in a trad. respecting the inheritance of the grandfather, إِنَّ السُّدُسَ الآخَرَ طُعْمَةٌ لَهُ i. e. † *The other sixth is a surplus for him beyond his* [*regular*] *due.* (TA.) — Also *An invitation to food.* (Ḳ.) — And ‡ *A mode,* or *manner, of gain;* (Ṣ, Ḳ, TA;) as also ↓ طِعْمَةٌ: (TA:) it is like حِرْفَةٌ. (A, TA.) One says, فُلَانٌ عَفِيفُ الطُّعْمَةِ ‡ [*Such a one is uncorrupt in respect of the mode of gain*]: and خَبِيثُ الطُّعْمَةِ i. e. *corrupt in respect of the means of gain.* (Ṣ, TA.)

طِعْمَةٌ *A way, mode,* or *manner, of eating:* (Ḳ, TA:) Lḥ explains it as meaning *a way, mode,* or *manner, of acting* or *conduct,* without saying in eating or in any other thing. (TA.) One says, فُلَانٌ حَسَنُ الطِّعْمَةِ وَالشِّرْبَةِ [*Such a one is good,* or *comely, in respect of the way, mode,* or *manner, of eating and of drinking*]. (A'Obeyd, Ṣ, TA.) And فُلَانٌ طَيِّبُ الطِّعْمَةِ ‡ [*Such a one is accustomed to eat nothing but what is lawful*], and خَبِيثُ الطِّعْمَةِ *accustomed to eat nothing but what is unlawful.* (TA.) See also طُعْمَةٌ.

طَعَامٌ [as an inf. n.: see 1. — As a subst.,] *Food,* (Ṣ, Nh, Mgh, Mṣb, Ḳ,) *of any kind;* (Nh, TA;) like as شَرَابٌ signifies beverage [of any kind]: (Mgh, Mṣb:) and especially *wheat,* (Ṣ, Nh, Mgh, Mṣb, Ḳ,) to which it is applied by the people of El-Ḥijáz; (Mṣb, TA;) and *barley;* (Nh, TA;) [and *corn* in general; thus applied to *millet* in the present day in some parts of Arabia, as, for instance, in El-Yemen; (see مِيرَةٌ;)] and *dates,* (Nh, Mgh, TA,) when said not to mean wheat; (Mgh, TA;) *&c.:* (Nh, TA:) and in the Expos. of the "Shifà," it is said to be applied to ‡ *other than food* tropically: (TA:) and ↓ طُعْمٌ signifies the same; (Ṣ, Mgh, Mṣb, Ḳ;) as also ↓ مَطْعَمٌ; (Ḥam p. 166, and Ḳ;*) of which the pl. is مَطَاعِمُ: (Ḥam ubi suprà:) one says, هُوَ يَحْتَكِرُ المَطَاعِمَ, meaning [*He collects and withholds*] *wheat* [*waiting for a time of scarcity and dearness*]: (A, TA:) the pl. of طَعَامٌ is أَطْعِمَةٌ, (Mgh, Mṣb, Ḳ,) and pl. pl. أَطْعِمَاتٌ. (Ḳ.) [It often means *A meal,* or *repast.*] طَعَامُ البَحْرِ means *That from which the water* [*of the sea,* or *of the great river,*] *has receded, leaving it, so that it is taken without fishing:* or, as some say, *anything that is irrigated by the water of the* بحر [i. e. *great river*], *and consequently vegetates:* so says Zj. (TA. [See the Ḳur v. 97.])

طَعُومٌ and ↓ طَعِيمٌ, applied to a slaughtered camel or she-camel, † *Such as is between the lean and the fat:* (Fr, Ṣ, Ḳ:) or the former, so applied, signifies *fat:* and each, applied to a sheep or goat (شاة), *having somewhat of fat:* (TA:) and the former, as also ↓ مُطْعِمٌ and ↓ مُطَّعِمٌ [in the CḲ مُطْعَمٌ], signifies ‡ thus, applied to a he-camel and to a she-camel, (Ḳ,* TA,) as also ↓ طَعِيمٌ: or a she-camel *having in her a little marrow:* or *in the flesh of which is found the flavour of fat, by reason of her fatness.* (TA.) Accord. to Aboo-Sa'eed, one says, لَكَ غَثُّ هٰذَا وَطَعُومُهُ i. e. † [*Thine is,* or *shall be, the lean of this*] *and the fat thereof.* (TA.) And مُخٌّ طَعُومٌ means † *Marrow in which is found the flavour of fatness.* (TA.)

طَعِيمٌ: see the next preceding paragraph, in two places. — Also, applied to water, i. q. شَرُوبٌ [q. v.]. (TA in art. شرب.)

طَعُومَةٌ *A sheep,* or *goat* (شاة) *that is confined to be eaten.* (Ḳ.)

طَعَامِيٌّ *A seller of* طعام [app. as meaning *wheat,* or *corn*]. (TA.)

طَاعِمٌ *Eating:* and *tasting.* (Ṣ.) — And ‡ *A man having a good state,* or *condition, in respect of food;* as also ↓ طَعِمٌ; (Ḳ, TA;) [each] a possessive epithet in this sense; on the authority of Sb. (TA.) — أَنَا طَاعِمٌ عَنْ طَعَامِكُمْ, thus in the A and Ḳ, but in the L غَيْرُ طعامكم, (TA,) means ‡ *I am in no need of your food.* (Ḳ, TA.)

مَطْعَمٌ [as an inf. n.: see 1. — As a subst.,] *A place of eating:* (Ḥar p. 345:) [and *a time thereof:*] syn. مَأْكَلٌ. (TA.) — See also طَعَامٌ. — And see also مُسْتَطْعَمٌ.

مُطْعَمٌ [*Fed.* — And hence,] ‡ *Supplied with the means of subsistence.* (Ṣ, Ḳ, TA.) — [Hence,] one says, إِنَّكَ مُطْعَمٌ مَوَدَّتِى, meaning مَرْزُوقٌ مَوَدَّتِى [i. e. ‡ *Verily thou art gifted with my love,* or *affection*]. (TA.)

مِطْعَمٌ *That eats vehemently:* (Ṣ, Ḳ:) fem. with ة: (Ḳ:) the former applied to a man; (Ṣ, TA;) and the latter, to a woman, and extr., [saidto be] the only instance of the kind except مِصَكَّةٌ. (TA.)

مُطْعَمَةٌ or مُطْعِمَةٌ: see the next paragraph, each in two places.

مُطْعِمَةٌ, (Ṣ, Ḳ,) like مُحْسِنَةٌ, (Ḳ,) [i. e.] with kesr to the ع, accord. to IAạr, (Ṣ,) and like مُكْرَمَةٌ, (Ḳ, [i. e. ▾ مُطْعَمَةٌ, but I think it most probable that it is correctly ▾ مِطْعَمَةٌ, like مِكْنَسَةٌ &c., as being the name of an instrument, agreeably with a remark respecting it in what follows,]) ‡ *A bow:* (Ṣ, Ḳ, TA:) called by the former appellation because it feeds its owner with the game: (IAạr, Ṣ, TA:) and by the latter appellation because one takes the game by means of it, and often shoots with it. (TA.) — And المُطْعِمَةُ, (Ḳ, TA,) or, as written by Z, with fet-ḥ, [i. e. ▾ المُطْعَمَةُ, or, as I think more probable, ▾ المِطْعَمَةُ,] ‡ *The* غَلْصَمَة [or *epiglottis;* because it is said to throw the meat and drink into the gullet]. (Ḳ, TA.) And ‡ [*The place thereof;* i. e.] *the* حَلْق [or *fauces;* or *upper part of the throat*]: so in the saying, أَخَذَ فُلَانٌ بِمُطْعِمَةِ فُلَانٍ i. e. ‡ *Such a one seized the* حَلْق *of such a one, squeezing it;* said only in a case of throttling and fighting. (AZ, TA.) — And المُطْعِمَتَانِ ‡ *The two corresponding anterior toes of a bird;* (Ṣ, Ḳ, TA;) i. e. *the two talons with which the bird seizes the flesh-meat.* (TA.)

مُطَّعِمٌ: see طَعُومٌ. — Also † Milk *that has acquired in the skin a flavour and a pleasant odour:* (AḤát, Ḳ, TA:) and ▾ مُطْعِمٌ signifies [the same, or] milk *that has acquired the flavour of the skin.* (TA.)

مُطْعِمٌ: see طَعُومٌ: — and see also مُطَّعِمٌ.

مِطْعَامٌ One *who feeds others much,* (Ṣ,) or *who has many guests,* (Ḳ,) *and who entertains guests much;* (Ṣ, Ḳ;) applied to a man, (Ṣ, TA,) and to a woman: (TA:) [and app. one *who eats much:* for] قَوْمٌ مَطَاعِيمُ signifies *a people,* or *party, that eat much:* or *that feed others much.* (TA.)

مُتَابَعُ الخَلْقِ i. q. مُطَاعَمُ الخَلْقِ [app. † *Sound,* or *free from defect, in make*]. (TA.)

مُسْتَطْعَمٌ The *lips* of the horse: (Ṣ, Ḳ, TA:) Aṣ says that thinness of the مستطعم of the horse is approved: (Ṣ, TA:) but some say that it is the *part beneath the* مَرْسِن [or *place of the halter*] *of the horse, extending to the extremities of his lips:* and مطعم [thus in my original, app. ▾ مَطْعَمٌ, as being the "place of eating,"] signifies the same. (TA.)

طعن

1. طَعَنَهُ بِالرُّمْحِ, aor. ُ and َ, (Ṣ, Mṣb, Ḳ,) the latter allowed by Fr as aor. of the verb in all its senses, (Ṣ, Mṣb,) because of the faucial letter, (Mṣb,) and heard by him as aor. of the verb in this phrase, but not by Ks in this case nor in relation to the grounds of pretension to respect or honour, (TA,) inf. n. طَعْنٌ, (Ṣ, Mṣb, Ḳ,) and مَطْعَنٌ, (Mṣb,) and Lth authorizes طَعَنَانٌ also in this case as well as in the case of طَعَنَ بِالقَوْلِ, (TA,) *He smote him and pierced him,* or *he smote him and he pierced him,* [for it does not always signify the causing the weapon to enter,] *with the spear;* (Ḳ;) *he pierced him, smote him,* or *wounded him, with the spear:* (MA:) [sometimes طَعَنَهُ means *he pierced, stabbed, stuck,* or *gored, him* with a spear, &c.; and sometimes, *he thrust, goaded,* or *poked, him:*] you say, طَعَنَ الدَّابَّةَ بِعُودٍ أَوْ نَحْوِهِ [*He goaded the beast with a stick or the like*]. (Mgh and Mṣb in art. نخس.) — [Hence,] طُعِنَ ‡ *He was smitten by the* طَاعُون i. e. *plague,* or *pestilence;* (Z, Mṣb, Ḳ, TA;) said of a man, (Mṣb, TA,) and of a camel. (TA.) — And طَعَنَ فِيهِ بِالقَوْلِ, (Ṣ, Mṣb, Ḳ,) and عَلَيْهِ, (Mṣb, TA,) and طَعَنَهُ بِلِسَانِهِ, (TA,) [and طَعَنَ فِى عِرْضِهِ,] aor. ُ, (Lth, TA,) or, accord. to some, in this case َ, (TA,) or both, (Mṣb,) inf. n. طَعْنٌ and طَعَنَانٌ, (Ṣ, Mṣb, Ḳ, TA, [the latter in the CḲ, erroneously, طَعْنان, but expressly said in the TA to be بِالتَّحْرِيك,]) ‡ [*He wounded him,* or *attacked him, with words,* and *with his tongue;* and *wounded,* or *attacked, his reputation;*] *he blamed, censured,* or *reproached, him; attributed* or *imputed to him, charged him with,* or *accused him of, a vice, fault,* or *the like;* or *spoke against him.* (Mṣb, TA.) A poet says, (Ṣ,) namely, Aboo-Zubeyd, (TA,)

وَأَبِى ظَاهِرُ الشَّنَاءَةِ إِلَّا
طَعَنَانًا وَقَوْلَ مَا لَا يُقَالُ

[*And my father is one in whom hatred is manifest,* (or, as in the TA, المُظْهِرُ العَدَاوَةَ, *he who manifests enmity,*) *except in censuring, and saying what should not be said*]. (Ṣ.) طَعَنَانٌ is of a measure of inf. ns. of verbs denoting that in which is prolongation and perseverance; and aptly applies to deviation from the right course. (TA.) — طَعَنَ إِلَى أُمِّهِ is said of a child, meaning *He raised his head* [or *thrust with it*] *towards the breast of his mother.* (L.) — And طَعَنَ فِى الدَّارِ, said of a branch of a tree, (L, Mṣb,) means *It inclined into, or against, the house, rising:* (L:) or *it inclined towards the house, extending sideways.* (Mṣb.) — طَعَنَتْ فِى الخِدْرِ, said, in a trad., of any one of the Prophet's daughters, when demanded in marriage, as denoting her disapproval, means † *She entered within the* خدر [or *curtain*]: or, as some say, *she struck the* خدر *with her hand.* (TA in art. خدر.) — And you say, طَعَنَ فِى المَفَازَةِ, (Ṣ, Mṣb, Ḳ,) aor. ُ and َ, (Ṣ,) inf. n. طَعْنٌ, (Mṣb,) ‡ *He went away in,* or *into, the desert,* (Ṣ, Mṣb, Ḳ, TA,) *penetrated into it,* (TA,) and *traversed it.* (So in a copy of the Ṣ.) — And طَعَنَ اللَّيْلَ ‡ *He journeyed throughout the whole of the night.* (Ḳ, TA.) One says, خَرَجَ يَطْعَنُ اللَّيْلَ ‡ *He went forth journeying in the night.* (TA.) And طَعَنَ بِالقَوْمِ † *He journeyed by night with the people,* or *party.* (TA.) — And طَعَنَ فِى السِّنِّ, (Ṣ, Mṣb,) aor. ُ, (Ṣ,) † *He became old,* or *advanced* [or *far-advanced*] *in age:* (Mṣb:) or *he rose* (شَخَصَ) *in age.* (TA.) — And طَعَنَ فِيهِ means also † *He began it,* or *entered upon it,* namely, a thing, (Mṣb, TA,) or an affair, of any kind. (Mṣb.) Hence one says of a woman, طَعَنَتْ فِى الحَيْضَةِ, for طعنت فى أَيَّامِ الحَيْضَةِ i. e. † *She entered upon the days of the menstruation.* (Mṣb.) — طَعَنَ فِى العِنَانِ, (Ḳ,) aor. ُ, (Ṣ,) said of a horse, means ‡ *He strained the rein* [*by thrusting forward his head*], *and hastened,* or *was quick* (تَبَسَّطَ, so in copies of the Ṣ, in the Ḳ تَنَشَّطَ,) *in going,* or *pace.* (Ṣ, Ḳ, TA.) — And طَعَنَ فِى جِنَازَتِهِ means † *He died;* (Lth and Mgh and TA in art. جنز;) [lit. *he was thrust into his bier:*] or *he was at the point of death:* and طَعَنَ فِى نَيْطِهِ signifies the same. (TA in the present art.)

3: see 6. — الطِّعَانُ is metonymically used as meaning المُجَامَعَةُ. (Ḥar p. 601.)

6. تَطَاعَنُوا فِى الحَرْبِ, (Ṣ, Ḳ,) inf. n. تَطَاعُنٌ, (Ḳ, TA,) and accord. to the Ḳ طعنان, app. طَعَنَانٌ, [in the CḲ with the ع quiescent,] but correctly ▾ طِعِنَّانٌ, with two kesrehs and with a sheddeh to the نّ, which is anomalous; and to this the Ḳ adds طِعَانٌ, with kesr, [in the CḲ written with fet-ḥ,] but this is the inf. n. of ▾ طَاعَنُوا, not of تطاعنوا, as also مُطَاعَنَةٌ; (TA;) and ▾ اِطَّعَنُوا, (Ṣ, Ḳ,) of the measure اِفْتَعَلُوا; (Ṣ;) [*They pierced,* or *thrust, one another in war:*] Az says that التَّفَاعُل and الاِفْتِعَال scarcely ever signify otherwise than the participation of two agents. (TA.)

8: see the next preceding paragraph.

طَعْنٌ: see what next follows.

طَعْنَةٌ [as an inf. n. of un., *A single act of piercing* or *thrusting;* i. e. *a piercing thrust* or *a stab,* or simply *a thrust;* with a spear or the like: and *a wound made by piercing* or *thrusting* with a spear or the like; i. e.] the *effect of* الطَّعْن: pl. [or rather coll. gen. n.] ▾ طَعْنٌ, thus used by a Hudhalee poet in the phrase طَعْنٌ جَوَائِفُ [*spear-wounds penetrating into the interior of the body,* or *into a vital part*]. (TA.) — [It is also an inf. n. of un. in other senses. — Golius assigns also to this word and to طُعْنَةٌ and طِعْنَةٌ, as from the Ḳ, the meaning of *A woman of evil disposition:* but this is evidently a mistake, and taken from an art. (next after the present one) in the Ḳ, in which الطَّعْثَنَةُ, there said to be بِالمُهْمَلَةِ وَالمُثَلَّثَةِ, is expl. as meaning "the woman evil in disposition."]

طِعِنَّانٌ an anomalous inf. n. of 6, q. v. (TA.)

طَعِينٌ : see مَطْعُونٌ, in two places.

طَعَّانٌ, (Ṣ, TA,) occurring in a trad., (Ṣ,) means *Wont* [*to wound, or attack, the reputations of men;*] *to attack men with blame, censure,* or *reproach,* and *with backbiting,* and *the like:* (TA:) it is for طَعَّانٌ فِى أَعْرَاضِ النَّاسِ [a phrase mentioned in the Mṣb]. (Ṣ, TA.*)

طِعِّينٌ *Skilled in piercing,* or *thrusting,* [*with the spear,*] *in war.* (TA.)

طَاعُونٌ † *An epidemic disease;* (TA;) [i. e.] *plague,* or *pestilence,* syn. وَبَأٌ or وَبَآءٌ, (Ḳ, TA,) *by reason of which the air is vitiated, and by it the constitutions and the bodies are vitiated:* (TA:) or the *kind of* وَبَأ *with which men are smitten by the jinn,* or *genii:* (TA voce وَبَأٌ, q. v.:) or *a mortality in consequence of* وَبَأ: (Ṣ, Mṣb:) pl. طَوَاعِينُ: (Ṣ, Mṣb, Ḳ:) it is a tropical term from الطَّعْنُ, because the طَوَاعِين are called by them رِمَاحُ الجِنّ [*the spears of the jinn,* or *genii*]. (Z, TA.)

مَطْعَنٌ is a noun of place [signifying *A place of piercing* or *thrusting* &c.]; as well as an inf. n. (Mṣb.) مَا فِيهِ مَطْعَنٌ means † *There is not in him anything* [*for which his reputation is to be wounded,* or *attacked,* or] *for which he is to be blamed, censured,* or *spoken against:* (TA in art. غمز:) and you say, لَهُ فِيهِ مَطْعَنٌ † [*He has* (meaning *he finds*) *in him something for which his reputation may be wounded,* &c.]: pl. مَطَاعِنُ. (TA in the present art.)

مِطْعَنٌ : see what next follows.

مِطْعَانٌ One *who pierces,* or *thrusts, the enemy much;* (Ṣ, Ḳ;) as also ↓ مِطْعَنٌ: (Ḳ:) pl. of the former مَطَاعِينُ; (Ṣ, Ḳ;) and of the latter مَطَاعِنُ. (Ḳ.)

مَطْعُونٌ *Smitten and pierced* [&c.; see 1, first sentence]; as also ↓ طَعِينٌ: (Ḳ:) AZ says, (TA,) the pl. [of the latter] is طُعُنٌ, (Ḳ, TA,) and not طَعْنَى [like قَتْلَى]. (TA.) — Also ‡ *Smitten by the* طَاعُون [i. e. *plague,* or *pestilence*]; (Mṣb, TA;) and so ↓ طَعِينٌ. (TA.)

طغم

5. تطغم [in Freytag's Lex. تَطَاغَمَ] *He feigned ignorance* (Ḳ, TA) عَلَيْهِ [*to him*]; *as though he did as do the* طَغَام. (TA.)

طَغْمٌ *A sea.* (Ḳ.) And *Much water.* (Ḳ.)

طَغَامٌ *Low, ignoble, mean,* or *sordid, and weak, persons, such as serve for the food of their bellies;* or *stupid, weak in intellect, low, ignoble, mean,* or *sordid:* (Ṣ, Ḳ, TA:) and applied to a single person as well as to a pl. number. (Ṣ, TA.) — And The *inferior,* or *meaner, sorts of birds,* (Ṣ, Ḳ, TA,) [*contr. of* عِتَاقُ الطَّيْرِ,] and some add, and *of beasts,* or *birds, of prey:* (TA:) n. un. with ة; (Ṣ, Ḳ;) applied to the male and the female. (Yaạḳoob, Ṣ.) It has no verb; and its derivation is not known. (Ṣ.) — يَا طَغَامَ الأَحْلَامِ, said by 'Alee to the people of El-'Irák, is a phrase of the same class as إِشْفَى المِرْفَقِ, [i. e. an instance of a subst. used as an epithet,] as though he said يَا ضِعَافَ الأَحْلَامِ [*O ye weak in respect of the qualities of forbearance*]. (TA.) — طَغَامُ الكَلَامِ means ‡ *Low,* or *vile, speech:* one says, كَلَامُ الطَّغَامِ طَغَامُ الكَلَامِ ‡ [*The speech of the low, ignoble,* &c., *is low,* or *vile, speech*]. (TA.)

طَغَامَةٌ *Foolish; stupid;* or *having little,* or *no, intellect* or *understanding;* (Az, Ḳ;) as also دَغَامَةٌ. (Az, TA.) — [See also طَغَامٌ, of which it is a n. un.]

طُغُومَةٌ and طُغُومِيَّةٌ *Foolishness; stupidity;* or *paucity,* or *want, of intellect* or *understanding:* and *lowness, ignobleness,* or *meanness.* (Ḳ.)

طغى and طغو

1. طَغَى, aor. يَطْغَى; (Ṣ, M, Mṣb, TA, &c.;) not mentioned in the Ḳ [in art. طغى, but in some copies thereof mentioned in art طغو]; perhaps dropped by the copyist; (TA;) and طَغَا, aor. يَطْغُو; and طَغِىَ, aor. يَطْغَى; (Ṣ, Mṣb, Ḳ;) inf. n. طُغْىٌ, which is of the first, though mentioned in the Ḳ as being of the last; (TA;) and طُغْيَانٌ, (Ṣ, Ḳ,) which is also of the first, and second, (Ṣ,) or of the last, as also طِغْيَانٌ, (Ḳ,) mentioned by Ks as from some of the tribe of Kelb; (TA;) or طُغْيَانٌ is a simple subst.; (Mṣb;) and طَغْيًا, mentioned by Az as an inf. n. [app. of the first]; (TA;) and the inf. n. of the second is طُغُوٌّ, (Mṣb,) or طُغْوٌ, (Ḳ accord. to the TA,) like عُلُوٌّ, (TA,) or طَغْوَى, (so in some copies of the Ḳ,) and طُغْوَى, mentioned as an inf. n. by Az, (TA,) and طُغْوَانٌ; (Ḳ, and mentioned in the Ṣ as syn. with طُغْيَانٌ;) and the inf. n. of طَغِىَ is طَغًى; (Mṣb, TA;) *He exceeded the just,* or *common, limit* or *measure; was excessive, immoderate, inordinate,* or *exorbitant;* (Ṣ, Mṣb, Ḳ, TA;) [and particularly] *in disobedience:* (Ṣ,* Mṣb,* TA:) *he exalted himself, and was inordinate in infidelity:* *he was extravagant in acts of disobedience and in wrong-doing:* (Ḳ:) accord. to El-Ḥarállee, الطُّغْيَانُ signifies *the acting wrongfully in respect of the limits of things* and *the measures thereof.* (TA.) — [Hence,] طَغَى, in the Ḳ طَغِىَ, but the former is the right, (TA,) or طَغَا, (Mṣb,) said of a torrent, (Mṣb,) or of water, (Ḳ, TA,) ‡ *It rose high,* (Mṣb, Ḳ, TA,) *so as to exceed the ordinary limit in copiousness:* (Mṣb:) or طَغَى or طَغَا, (accord. to different copies of the Ṣ,) said of a torrent, † *it brought much water:* and, said of the sea, † *its waves became raised,* or *in a state of commotion:* and, said of the blood, † *it became roused,* or *excited.* (Ṣ.) [Hence also the phrase طَغَا مِرْقَمُكَ † *Thy pen has exceeded its due limit:* see art. رقم.] — طَغَتِ البَقَرَةُ, (Ḳ,) aor. ـَ, (TA,) means *The* بَقَرَة [i. e. the *bovine antelope called* بَقَرَةُ الوَحْشِ (see طُغْيَا)] *uttered a cry* or *cries.* (Ḳ.)

4. اطغاهُ *It,* (i. e. wealth, Ṣ,) or *he,* (a man, Mṣb,) *made him to exceed the just,* or *common, limit* or *measure; to be excessive, immoderate, inordinate,* or *exorbitant.* (Ṣ, Mṣb, Ḳ.)

6. تطاغى المَوْجُ [app. *The waves conflicted,* or *dashed together, with excessive vehemence*]: a phrase mentioned by Z. (TA.)

طَغًا : see what next follows.

طَغْىٌ; accord. to the copies of the Ḳ ↓ طَغًا, but this is incorrect; *A sound,* or *voice;* of the dial. of Hudheyl: one says, سَمِعْتُ طَغْىَ فُلَانٍ *I heard the sound,* or *voice, of such a one:* and, as in the "Nawádir," سَمِعْتُ طَغْىَ القَوْمِ, and طَغْيَهُمْ, and دَغْيَهُمْ, *I heard the sound,* or *voice,* [or *voices,*] *of the people,* or *party.* (TA.)

طَغْوَةٌ : see what next follows.

طَغْيَةٌ The *top,* or *upper part, of a mountain:* (Ṣ, TA:) and *any high,* or *elevated, place;* as also ↓ طَغْوَةٌ. (TA as from the Ṣ: but only the latter word is mentioned in this sense in my copies of the Ṣ.) — And (Ṣ) *A small quantity* (نُبْذَةٌ) of anything: (Ṣ, Ḳ:*) so says AZ. (Ṣ. [In this sense, and in the two senses following, erroneously written in the CḲ طُغْيَة.]) — And *A smooth stone* or *rock.* (Ḳ.) — And, accord. to the copies of the Ḳ, الطَّغْيَةُ signifies المُسْتَصْعَبُ مِنَ الجَبَلِ [as though meaning *What is deemed,* or *found, difficult, of the mountain*]: but [SM says, though I think this doubtful,] it is correctly مِنَ الخَيْلِ [meaning *what is refractory,* or *untractable, of horses*], as in the M. (TA.)

طَغْوَى a subst. from the verb طَغَا, (Ḳ, TA,) [and] so is ↓ طُغْيَانٌ, (Mṣb,) or the latter is an inf. n., (Ṣ, Ḳ,) and, accord. to Az, so is طَغْوَى, and so too is ↓ طُغْيَا, which latter is said by Zj to be the original of طَغْوَى: (TA:) it is like طُغْوَانٌ and طُغْيَانٌ. (Ṣ.) Hence, in the Ḳur [xci. 11], كَذَّبَتْ ثَمُودُ بِطَغْوَاهَا [*Thamood disbelieved by reason of their exorbitance*]; (Ḳ,* TA;) meaning that they did not believe when they were threatened with the punishment of their طُغْيَان: or, as is said in the Expos. of Bkh, the meaning is, *by reason of their acts of disobedience.* (TA.)

طُغْيَا : see the next preceding paragraph. — It is also a proper name for [*The bovine antelope called*] بَقَرَةُ الوَحْشِ; (Ḳ, TA;) from طَغَتِ البَقَرَةُ [expl. above: see 1, last sentence]: (TA:) [or, as it appears from a citation in the TA, partly mistranscribed so as to be unintelligible, طُغْيَا or ↓ طَغْيَا signifies, accord. to IAạr, *a* بَقَرَة *uttering a cry* or *cries*, or *a loud cry* or *loud cries*:] or ▼ طُغْيَا with ḍamm accord. to Aṣ, or طَغْيَا with fet-ḥ accord. to Th, signifies *a youngling of the* بَقَر الوَحْش. (Ṣ.)

طُغْيَا: see what next precedes, in two places.

طُغْيَانٌ: see طَغْوَى.

طَاغٍ Any *exceeding his*, or *its, just limit* [*in an absolute sense* or] *in disobedience.* (Ṣ, Mṣb.)

طَاغِيَةٌ *i. q.* جَبَّارٌ [i. e. *Insolent, tyrannical, &c.*]; (Ḳ, TA;) *who deviates from the right way* or *course*, or *trangresses the just limit*: (TA:) and *stupid*, or *foolish*; *proud*; (Ḳ, TA;) *wrongful, unjust*, or *injurious, in conduct*: (TA:) or one *who cares not what he does, devouring* [*the property of*] *men, and oppressing them, and who is not turned from his course by a disposition to shun sin* or *crime, nor by fear.* (Sh, TA.) [Hence,] الطَّاغِيَةُ is an appellation of *The king of the* رُوم [or *Greeks of the Lower Empire*]; (Ṣ, Ḳ, TA;) applied to him as a surname because of his much exorbitance, and corrupt conduct. (TA.) — And *A thunderbolt*; syn. صَاعِقَةٌ. (Ṣ, Ḳ.) — And The *cry of punishment*; by which Thamood were destroyed, as mentioned in the Ḳur [lxix. 5]: (Ṣ, TA:) or, accord. to Zj, it there means their طُغْيَان [or *exorbitance*]; being a subst. like عَافِيَةٌ and عَاقِبَةٌ. (TA.) — Also The *flood denoted by the words of the Ḳur* [lxix. 11] إِنَّا لَمَّا طَغَى المَآءُ. (Er-Rághib, TA.)

طَاغُوتٌ is of the measure فَلَعُوتٌ, from طَغَوْتُ; (M, Ḳ;) formed by transposition, though like لَاهُوتٌ which is not so formed: (Ṣ:) it is originally of the measure فَعَلُوتٌ, which is changed to فَلَعُوتٌ, so that it becomes طَوَغُوتٌ, and this is then altered to طَاغُوتٌ: (Mṣb, TA:) it is held to be altered from طَوَغُوت rather than from طَغَيُوت because the transposition of و is more common than that of ى, as in شَاكٍ &c.: (M, TA:) or, as some say, the ت is a substitute for و, and the measure is فَاعُولٌ: and some say that the measure is فَاعَلُوتٌ, and that it is originally طَاغَيُوتٌ: (TA:) the pl. is طَوَاغِيتُ (Ṣ, Ḳ) and طَوَاغٍ, (Ḳ,) the latter mentioned by ISd. (TA.) It signifies *A devil*; (Ṣ, Mṣb, Ḳ, TA;) thus expl. by Abu-l-'Áliyeh and others, and said to be on the authority of 'Omar: (TA:) or *one that is exorbitant in pride* or *corruptness* or *disbelief* or *disobedience, of the jinn*, or *genii*: (Er-Rághib, TA:) or الطَّاغُوتُ means [*the idol called*] اللَّاتُ and [*that called*] العُزَّى; (Ḳ;) or thus some expl. الجِبْتُ and الطَّاغُوت [together, in the Ḳur iv. 54]: (TA:) or *whatever is worshipped instead*, or *to the exclusion, of God*; (Zj, Ḳ, TA;) as also الجِبْتُ: (Zj, TA:) and *the idols* [*in general*]: (Ḳ:) or it is *of the idols*, and *of the jinn*, or *genii*, and *of mankind*: (Akh, TA:) or *he who turns from the good way*: (Er-Rághib, TA:) and *the diviner*: (Ṣ, Ḳ, TA:) and *the enchanter*: thus expl. by 'Ikrimeh; and said to mean thus in the Ḳur iv. 63: and so الجِبْتُ accord. to Zj: (TA:) and *any head*, or *leader, of error*: (Ṣ, Ḳ:) and *the exorbitant in pride* or *corruptness* or *disbelief* or *disobedience, of the people of the Scripture*: (Ḳ:) it is used as a sing., (Ṣ, Ḳ,) as in the Ḳur iv. 63; (Ṣ;) and as a pl., (Ṣ, Ḳ,) as in the Ḳur ii. 259; (Ṣ;) and masc. and fem., (Mṣb, TA,) as fem. in the Ḳur xxxix. 19: (TA:) or by الجِبْتُ is meant Ḥoyeí Ibn-Akhṭab; and by الطَّاغُوت, Kaab Ibn-El-Ashraf: (I'Ab, Ḳ:) and [the pls.] طَوَاغِيتُ and طَوَاغٍ signify [sometimes] *idol temples*: so says El-Ḥáfidh in the preface to the "Fet-ḥ" [i. e. his celebrated work entitled "Fet-ḥ el-Bári"]. (TA.)

طف

1. طَفَّ, (Aṣ, O, Ḳ,) [aor., app., ـُ,] inf. n. طَفٌّ, (TḲ, [or, accord. to Freytag طُفُوفٌ, which see in what follows,]) *It* (a thing) *was*, or *became, near*. (Aṣ, O, Ḳ.) You say, أَخَذْتُ مِنْ مَتَاعِي مَا خَفَّ وَطَفَّ i. e. [*I took, of my goods,*] *what* [*was light, and*] *was near* to me. (Aṣ, O.) And طَفَّ الشَّىْءُ مِنَ الشَّىْءِ *The thing was*, or *became, near to the thing.* (O, Ḳ.*) And خُذْ مَا طَفَّ لَكَ, and أَطَفَّ ▼ لَكَ, (Ṣ, Meyd, O, Ḳ,) and اسْتَطَفَّ ▼ لَكَ, (Meyd, O, TA,) *Take thou what has risen to thee, and become within thy power* or *reach*, (Ṣ, O, Ḳ, TA,) *and become attainable* [*to thee*], or *prepared* [*for thee*], (AZ, Meyd, TA,) *and become near to thee*: (Ḳ, TA:) or *what has risen to view, and has appeared,* [*to thee,*] *to be taken*: (TA:) [for] طَفَّ, inf. n. طُفُوفٌ, signifies *it rose* [app. *so as to become visible*]: and *it was*, or *became, little in quantity*: the saying is a prov., relating to a man's being content with a part of that which he wants: (Meyd:) and in like manner one says, خُذْ مَا دَقَّ لَكَ, and اسْتَدَقَّ: (AZ, Meyd, TA:) and Ks mentions, in relation to a man's being content with a part of that which he wants, the saying, خُذْ مَا طَفَّ لَكَ وَدَعْ مَا اسْتَطَفَّ ▼ لَكَ [app. meaning, if the saying be correctly thus related, *Take what is within thy power*, or *reach, and leave what has risen to thy view so as to invite approach*]; i. e. be content with what is within thy power. (TA.) — طَفَّتِ الشَّمْسُ: — and طَفَّ said of a bird: see 2. — مَرَّ يَطِفُّ [app. يَطُفُّ] *He passed by hastening*, or *going quickly*. (O.) — طَفَّ النَّاقَةَ, (O, Ḳ,) aor. ـُ, (O, TA,) inf. n. طَفٌّ, (TA,) *He* (a man, O) *bound the legs of the she-camel*, (O, Ḳ,) *all of them.* (O.) — طَفَّهُ *He* (a man, O) *raised it* (i. e. a thing, O) with his leg or foot, or with his arm or hand. (O, Ḳ.) And طَفَّ بِفُلَانٍ مَوْضِعَ كَذَا *He raised such a one to such a place*; and *made him to be on a level with it.* (TA.) — And طَفَّ الحَائِطَ, inf. n. طَفٌّ, *He mounted upon the wall.* (TA.)

2. طفّف *He made defective*, or *deficient*. (TA.) You say, طَفَّفَ المِكْيَالَ, (Ḳ,) or طَفَّفَ المِيزَانَ, and المِيزَانَ, (Mṣb,) inf. n. تَطْفِيفٌ, (Ṣ, O, Mṣb,) *He gave short measure*, and *short weight*; (Mṣb;) *he made the contents of the measure to be defective*, (Ṣ, O, Mṣb, Ḳ,) and in like manner, *of the balance*; (Mṣb;) *not filling the former to its uppermost parts*: (Ṣ, TA:) i. e. *he did thus, cheating his companion in measure* or *in weight*. (TA.) [Hence,] طفّف عَلَى عِيَالِهِ ‡ *He scanted his household, stinted them*, or *was niggardly* or *parsimonious towards them, in expenditure*. (TA.) And طفّف عَلَى الرَّجُلِ † *He gave to the man less than he had taken from him.* (TA.) And طفّف الإِنَآءَ *He took what was upon* [or *above*] *the vessel* [i. e. *its* طُفَاف, or طُفَافَة]. (TA. [See also 4, last sentence.]) — Also *He made full*, or *complete*. (TA.) [Thus it has two contr. significations.] — طفّفت الشَّمْسُ ‡ *The sun drew near to setting*: (TA:) [but this may be a mistranscription for ▼ طَفَّتْ, mentioned by Golius in this sense on the authority of Z: or each may be correct: that the latter is correct, and that ▼ طُفَافٌ or ▼ طِفَافٌ is its inf. n., seems to be indicated by the fact that SM adds immediately after the explanation of the former phrase,] أَتَانَا عِنْدَ طِفَافِ الشَّمْسِ means ‡ [*He came to us*] *at the sun's drawing near to setting.* (TA.) — طفّف, said of a bird, [or ▼ طَفَّ, mentioned by Freytag from Hamaker's Specim. catal. p. 49, l. 4, of the Arabic text, or both may be correct,] *The bird expanded his wings*: (O, Ḳ:) so says Ibn-'Abbád. (O.) — And طفّف بِهِ الفَرَسُ ‡ *The horse leaped with him.* (Ibn-'Abbád, O, Ḳ. [Golius has omitted this; and has assigned to طفّف, followed by ب with the person who is the object, as on the authority of the Ṣ and Ḳ, the signification of ادنا (properly أَدْنَى), meaning "prope admovit," a signification belonging to أَطَفَّ, but not assigned to either of these verbs in the Ṣ nor in the Ḳ.]) طفّف بِىَ الفَرَسُ مَسْجِدَ بَنِى زُرَيْقٍ, in a saying of Ibn-'Omar respecting a horse-race, means ‡ *The horse leaped with me* (Ṣ, O, TA) *so that he passed beyond the mosque of the Sons of Zureyḳ.* (O, TA.)

4. اطفّ لَهُ: خُذْ مَا أَطَفَّ لَكَ: see 1. — And اطفّ لَهُ *He had knowledge of it*, i. e. an affair; (Lth, O, Ḳ;) and *of him*, i. e. a person. (O.) — And *He desired to deceive him*: (O, Ḳ:) or *he had knowledge of him, and desired to deceive him.* (O.) — And اطفّ عَلَيْهِ *i. q.* أَشْرَفَ (O, Ḳ) i. e. أَشْرَفَ عَلَيْهِ [meaning *He looked upon it, looked upon it from above, looked down upon it, got a view of it, saw it*, or *got knowledge of it*]; namely, a thing; as also أَطَلَّ عَلَيْهِ. (O.) — And, (AZ, O, Ḳ, TA,) as also أَطَلَّ عَلَيْهِ, (AZ, TA,) *He got possession of it*, (AZ, O, Ḳ, TA,) *and took it away*, or *went away with it*; (AZ, O, TA;) namely, the property of another person. (AZ, TA.) — اطفّ عَلَيْهِ بِحَجَرٍ *He reached*, or *hit, him*, or *it*, (تَنَاوَلَهُ,) *with a stone.* (Ibn-'Abbád, O, Ḳ.) — اطفّت النَّاقَةُ *The she-camel cast*, (Ibn-

'Abbád, O,) or *brought forth,* (Ḳ,) *her young one in an imperfect state.* (Ibn-'Abbád, O, Ḳ.) ═ اطفّه *He put it,* or *brought it, near:* 'Adee Ibn-Zeyd says, [using the verb in this sense,]

أَطَفَّ لِأَنْفِهِ المُوسَى قَصِيرُ

[*Kaseer put the razor near to his nose*]: (Ḥam p. 436:) or this means *Kaseer put the razor near to his nose and cut it off.* (TA.) — And i. q. مَكَّنَهُ. (TA.) [You say, مَكَّنَهُ مِنَ الشَّىْءِ, and app., in like manner, اطفّهُ مِنَ الشَّىْءِ, i. e. *He made him to have power over the thing;* or *to have the thing within his power* or *reach;* and so, perhaps, اطفّهُ لِلشَّىْءِ.] — And اطفّ لَهُ السَّيْفَ *He held forth the sword towards him, and struck him with it.* (TA.) — And اطفّ الكَيْلَ *He made the contents of the measure to reach to its uppermost parts:* (Ṣ, Ḳ:) or, as some say, *he took what was upon* [or *above*] *the measure.* (TA. [See also طَفَّفَ الإِنَآءَ.])

10. استطفّ, said of a camel's hump, *It rose,* or *became high.* (TA.) — And استطفّت حَاجَتُهُ *The thing that he wanted became prepared, and easy of attainment.* (TA.) See also 1, in two places.

R. Q. 1. طَفْطَفَ *He* (a man, TA) *became lax* [or *weak*] (Ibn-'Abbád, O, Ḳ) *in the hands of his adversary* (Ibn-'Abbád, O) or *in the hand of his adversary.* (Ḳ.)

طَفٌّ The *side* (O, Ḳ) of a thing: (O:) [like دَفٌّ:] and the *bank,* or *shore,* (O, Ḳ,) of a great river or a sea; (O;) as also ↓ طَفْطَافٌ: (O, Ḳ:) accord. to Lth, of the Euphrates: (O:) or, as some say, the *elevated part of the side* of the Euphrates. (TA.) And الطَّفُّ is applied to *The part of the land of the Arabs that overlooks the cultivated region of El-'Irák:* (IDrd, O, Ḳ:) said by Aṣ to be so called because it is near to the cultivated region: (O:) or it is *a place in the district of El-Koofeh.* (Ṣ, O, Ḳ.*) — And The *exterior court* or *yard of a house.* (TA.) — See also طَفَافٌ, in two places. ═ And see طَفَاف.

طَفَفٌ: see طَفَافٌ.

طَفَفَةٌ: see طُفَافَةٌ.

طَفَافُ المَكُّوكِ (Ṣ, O, Mṣb,* Ḳ) and الإِنَآءِ, (Ḳ,) and ↓ طُفَافَةٌ, (Ṣ, Mgh,* O, Mṣb, Ḳ,) and ↓ طَفَّةٌ, and ↓ طَفَفَةٌ, (Ṣ, Mgh,* O, Ḳ,) *The quantity sufficing for the filling* (Ṣ, O, Mṣb, Ḳ) *of the* [*measure called*] مكّوك (Ṣ, O, Ḳ) and *of the vessel* (Ḳ) *to its uppermost parts:* (Ṣ, O, Mṣb, Ḳ:) or *what remains in it after the wiping off of the head thereof:* (M, Ḳ: [the measure being generally in the form of a truncated cone, much smaller at the top than at the base, the quantity rising above the top is not much:]) or *the* جُمَام or جِمَام or جَمَام (accord. to different copies of the Ḳ [generally meaning the *quantity that rises above the top after the filling*]) *thereof:* or *the quantity sufficing for the filling thereof:* (Ḳ:) or *the quantity nearly sufficing for the filling thereof:* (TA: [and the like explanation is given of the third word in the Ṣ &c., as will be shown by what follows:]) or *the quantity that falls short of the filling thereof.* (Mgh. [See also طُفَافَةٌ.]) It is said in a trad. (Ṣ, Mgh, O) of the Prophet, (Mgh, O,) كُلُّكُمْ بَنُو آدَمَ طَفُّ الصَّاعِ, (Ṣ, O,) or طَفَّ ↓ الصَّاعِ, (so in my copy of the Mgh,) *All of you, sons of Adam, are like the quantity nearly sufficing for the filling of the* صاع; (Ṣ,* Mgh, O;) i. e. ye are all nearly alike; so says Az: (Mgh:) meaning, all of you, in being related to one father, are in one predicament in respect of defectiveness, like the thing measured that falls short of filling the measure: (IAth, Mgh, O:) the Prophet then proceeded to inform them that there is no excellence of one above another except by piety. (O.) ═ طَفَافٌ signifies also The *blackness of night;* (O, Ḳ;) and so ↓ طِفَافٌ. (Ḳ.) — See also 2.

طُفَافٌ: see طَفَافَةٌ, in two places.

طِفَافٌ: see طَفَافٌ, in two places: — and see 2.

طَفِيفٌ *Little in quantity:* (Ṣ, O, Mṣb, Ḳ:) and *incomplete:* (IDrd, O, Ḳ:) applied to a thing in this sense, (IDrd, O,) and in the former sense. (TA.) [See تَفِلٌ.] — Also *Low, base, vile, mean, paltry,* or *contemptible.* (TA.)

طُفَافَةٌ The *quantity that is above the measure;* (Ṣ, O, Mṣb, Ḳ;) as also ↓ طُفَافٌ (Ṣ) or ↓ طَفَفَةٌ: (O, Ḳ:) or the *quantity that falls short of filling the vessel,* (IDrd, O, Ḳ,) of beverage or wine, &c. (IDrd, O. [See also طَفَافٌ.]) And *Somewhat, little in quantity, remaining in a vessel.* (TA.) — And طُفَافَةُ الإِنَآءِ and ↓ طُفَافُهُ *The uppermost part of the vessel.* (Ḳ.)

طَفَّافٌ (O, Ḳ) and ↓ طَفٌّ (Ḳ) and خَفٌّ and دَفٌّ, as epithets applied to a horse, are alike (O, Ḳ) in meaning (Ḳ) [app. signifying *Light, brisk,* or *quick:* (see طَفَّفَ بِهِ الفَرَسُ:) in the TḲ, and hence by Freytag, expl. as meaning thus, but as an epithet applied to a man].

إِنَآءٌ طَفَّانُ [in the CḲ طَفَّانٌ] *A vessel in which the measuring* [or *thing measured*] *has reached its uppermost parts:* (Ṣ, O, Ḳ:) [or] *a full vessel.* (IAạr, TA.)

الطَّافَّةُ *What is between mountains and plains.* (Ibn-'Abbád, O, Ḳ.) — And طَافَّةُ البُسْتَانِ *What surrounds the garden:* (Ibn-'Abbád, O, Ḳ:) pl. طَوَافُّ. (Ibn-'Abbád, O.)

طَفْطَفَةٌ (Ṣ, O, Ḳ) and طِفْطِفَةٌ, (O, Ḳ,) the latter mentioned on the authority of AZ, (O,) The خَاصِرَة [or *flank*]: (Ṣ, O, Ḳ:) or *any quivering flesh:* (Az, O, Ḳ: [see شَدْقٌ:]) or the *flaccid flesh of the soft parts of the belly;* (O, Ḳ;) thus the former word is expl. by IDrd: (O:) or the *extremities of the side, adjoining the ribs:* (Ḳ:) and said to mean the *soft part of the liver;* the pl. being used by Dhu-r-Rummeh in relation to the liver: (L, TA:) the pl. is طَفَاطِفُ. (O, Ḳ.)

طَفْطَافٌ The *extremities of trees:* (Ṣ, O, Ḳ:) or the *soft,* or *tender, and succulent,* of plants, or herbage: or, accord. to El-Mufaddal, the *leaves of the branches.* (TA.) — See also طَفٌّ.

مُطَفِّفٌ One *who gives short measure,* and *short weight,* (Zj, Mṣb, TA,) *thus cheating his companion;* but this epithet is not applied unrestrictedly except in the case of exorbitant deficiency: [or] accord. to Aboo-Is-ḥáḳ [i. e. Zj], the مطفّف is thus called because he seldom or never steals from the measure or balance save what is paltry, i. e. طَفِيف; for it is from طَفُّ الشَّىْءِ, meaning "the side of the thing:" the pl. occurs in the Ḳur lxxxiii. 1. (TA.)

طفأ

1. طَفِئَتِ النَّارُ, aor. ـَ, inf. n. طُفُوْءٌ (Ṣ, Mṣb, Ḳ) and طَفَأٌ; (TA;) and ↓ انطفأت; (Ṣ, Ḳ;) *The fire became extinguished,* or *quenched:* (Mṣb:) or *ceased to flame:* (Ḳ, TA:) [or rather, *ceased to flame and its live coals became cool;* for] when the flame of the fire has become allayed but its coals still burn, it is said to be خَامِدَة; and when its flame is extinct and its coals have become cool, it is said to be هَامِدَة and ↓ طَافِئَة. (TA.)

4. اطفأ النَّارَ *He extinguished,* or *quenched, the fire.* (Ṣ,* Mṣb, Ḳ,* TA.) Hence, اطفأ الحَرْبَ ‡ *He extinguished the fire of the war.* (TA.) And أَطْفَأْتُ الفِتْنَةَ ‡ *I allayed the sedition,* or *conflict and faction,* or *the like.* (Mṣb.)

7: see the first paragraph.

نَارٌ طَافِئَةٌ [*Fire becoming,* or *become, extinguished*]: see 1.

مُطْفِئُ الجَمْرِ [*The extinguisher of the live coals;*] *one of the* [seven] *days called* أَيَّامُ العَجُوزِ; (Ṣ, O;) *the fifth of those days;* (Ḳ;) so in the M &c.: (TA:) or *the fourth thereof:* (O, Ḳ:) or *the last thereof.* (Ḥar p. 295.) [Accord. to modern Egyptian almanacs, it is the fourth of those days on which the last of the three جَمَرَات becomes extinct: see جَمْرَةٌ: and see also عَجُوزٌ.] — مُطْفِئَةُ الرَّضْفِ (so in the M and O and L and in some copies of the Ḳ, in other copies of the Ḳ مُطْفِئُ, TA) *A piece of fat which, when it falls upon the* رَضْف [or *heated stones*], *melts, and quenches them.* (Lth, O, Ḳ.) And in the M and L, it is said to signify *A lean sheep* or *goat:* the Arabs, as is related by Lḥ, used to say, حَدَسَ لَهُمْ بِمُطْفِئَةِ الرَّضْفِ (TA) i. e. *He slaughtered for them a lean sheep* or *goat, which extinguished the fire and did not become thoroughly cooked:* (M and L and Ḳ in art. حدس:) or *a fat sheep* or *goat,* (AO and T, TA in that art.,) *which quenched the* رَضْف *by its fat.* (T, TA ibid. [See also دَمَغ.]) — Also *A serpent, the poison of which, as it passes by the* رَضْف, *extinguishes their fire:* (O, Ḳ:) in a verse of El-Kumeyt, [for the sake of the metre,] the former word is [altered to] ▼ مُطَفِّئَة. (O.) — And ‡ *A calamity,* or *misfortune:* (O, Ḳ, TA:) said by AO to mean originally *such as has made one to forget that which was before it, and extinguished its heat.* (O, TA.)

مُطَفِّئَةُ الرَّضْفِ: see the next preceding paragraph.

طفح

1. طَفَحَ, (Ṣ, A, Ḳ,) aor. ـَ, (TA,) inf. n. طُفُوحٌ (Ṣ, A, Ḳ) and طَفْحٌ, (Ḳ,) *It* (a vessel, Ṣ, A, Ḳ, and a river, A, TA, and a watering-trough, or tank, A) *was,* or *became, full, so as to overflow:* (Ṣ, A:) *was,* or *became, full, and high* [*in its contents*], (Ḳ, TA,) *so as to overflow.* (TA.) [See also مِرْقَمٌ.] — طَفَحَ said of one intoxicated, ‡ *He was full of wine.* (T, Ṣ, TA.) — طَفَحَتْ بِالأَوْلَادِ ‡ *She* (a woman) *brought forth children abundantly; brought forth many children:* (A:) [or] طَفَحَتْ بِالوَلَدِ *she brought forth the child at the full period of gestation,* or *fully formed.* (Ḳ.) — طَفَحَ عَقْلُهُ † *His understanding,* or *intellect, became eminent* [or, app., *exuberant*]. (TA.) — طَفَحَ, aor. as above, also signifies † *He ran.* (Aṣ, TA.) — And one says, اِطْفَحْ عَنِّى, meaning † *Go thou away,* or *depart, from me.* (Ṣ, Ḳ.) ═ طَفَحَ as trans.: see 4. — طَفَحَتِ الرِّيحُ القُطْنَةَ *The wind raised,* or *carried up, the portion of cotton:* (Ṣ, Ḳ:) and in like manner, a similar thing. (Ṣ.)

2: see the next paragraph.

4. اطفحهُ; (Ṣ, A, Ḳ;) and ▼ طفحهُ, (Ṣ, Ḳ,) inf. n. تَطْفِيحٌ; (Ṣ;) and ▼ طَفَحَهُ, (Ḳ,) inf. n. طَفْحٌ; (TA;) *He filled it so that it overflowed:* (Ṣ, A:) or *he filled it so that it became high* [*in its contents*]: (Ḳ:) namely, a vessel, (Ṣ, A, Ḳ,) and a river, or rivulet, and a watering-trough, or tank. (A.)

8. اِطَّفَحَ القِدْرَ, (Ṣ, Ḳ, in the CḲ [erroneously] القِدْرُ) *He took off the* طُفَاحَة (i. e. *scum*) *of the cooking-pot.* (Ṣ.)

طَفْحَانُ; fem. طَفْحَى: see طَافِحٌ.

طِفَاحُ الأَرْضِ *What would fill the earth* (T in art. طف, and Ḳ,) *so that it would overflow:* (T:) so in the saying, in a trad., وَإِنْ كَانَ عَلَيْهِ طِفَاحُ الأَرْضِ ذُنُوبًا [*Though there be upon him,* or *imputable to him, what would fill the earth so that it would overflow, of sins,* or *crimes*]. (T.)

طُفَاحَةٌ *What has come forth upon the surface of a thing, such as the scum of the cooking-pot,* (Ṣ,) which is termed طُفَاحَةُ القِدْرِ. (A, Ḳ.)

طَفَّاحُ القَوَائِمِ ‡ A horse *that runs much.* (A.) And طَفَّاحَةُ القَوَائِمِ ‡ A she-camel *having swift legs.* (Ḳ, TA.)

طَافِحٌ *Full, so as to overflow;* applied to [a vessel, and] a river, and a watering-trough, or tank: (A, TA:) or *full:* and *full and high.* (A'Obeyd, T, TA.) And ▼ إِنَآءٌ طَفْحَانُ, and قَصْعَةٌ طَفْحَى *A vessel,* and *a bowl, of which the contents flow over the sides.* (Ḳ.) — Applied to one intoxicated, ‡ *Full of wine.* (T, Ṣ, A, Ḳ.) — And † *Running,* or one *that runs.* (Aṣ, TA.) ═ And [the fem.] طَافِحَةٌ signifies *Dry,* or *tough,* or *rigid:* whence the phrase رُكْبَةٌ طَافِحَةٌ meaning *A knee which he to whom it belongs cannot grasp with his hand.* (Ḳ.)

مِطْفَحَةٌ *A skimmer,* or *ladle with which the scum of the cooking-pot is taken off;* (Ḳ;) called in Pers. كَفْكِير. (TA.)

طفر

1. طَفَرَ, (Ṣ, A, Mgh, Mṣb,) aor. ـِ, (Ṣ, Mgh, Mṣb,) inf. n. طُفُورٌ (Ṣ, A, Mgh, Mṣb, Ḳ) and طَفْرٌ, (Ṣ, A, Mgh, Mṣb,) or طَفْرَةٌ, (Ḳ,) [but] this has a more particular signification than طَفْرٌ, (Mṣb,) [being an inf. n. un.,] *He leaped:* (Ṣ:) or *he leaped upwards,* (Lth, T, A, Mgh, Mṣb, Ḳ,) *as when one leaps over a wall to what is behind it.* (Lth, T, Mgh, Mṣb.) One says, طَفَرَ الحَائِطَ, (TA,) or طَفَرَ الحَائِطَ إِلَى مَا وَرَآءَهُ, (A,) *He leaped over the wall to what was behind it.* (TA.) And طَفَرَ الفَرَسُ النَّهْرَ [*The horse leaped over the river,* or *rivulet*]. (A, TA.)

2. طفّر الفَرَسَ النَّهْرَ *He made the horse to leap over the river,* or *rivulet.* (A, TA.)

8. اِطَّفَرَ فَرَسَهُ, inf. n. اِطِّفَارٌ; (O, TA;) accord. to the Ḳ, اُطْفُرَ, inf. n. اِطْفَارٌ, but the former is the right; (TA;) *He thrust his feet into the groins of his horse:* the doing of which is a fault in the rider. (O, Ḳ, TA.) And in like manner one says of a man when he makes his camel to run: (O, TA:) i. e. اِطَّفَرَ بَعِيرَهُ, inf. n. اِطِّفَارٌ, *He thrust his feet into the groins of his camel.* (L.) [It seems to be tropical, from what here follows.] — اِطَّفَرَ الرَّجُلُ, meaning *He stuck his nails* [into a thing] is originally اِظَّفَرَ; (TA; [in which it is said to be tropical; but for this I see no reason;]) as also اِطَّفَرَهُ *he stuck his nail into it.* (TA in art. ظفر.)

طَفْرَةٌ *A leap:* (Ṣ:) or *a leap upwards,* (T, A,* Mgh, Mṣb, Ḳ,*) *as when one leaps over a wall;* (T, Mgh, Mṣb;) said to be thus distinguished from وَثْبَةٌ, which is downwards. (Mgh, Mṣb.) Hence طَفْرَةُ النِّظَامِ [app. meaning *An overleaping the right order,* or *method:* I have not found any explanation of it]. (A.)

هُوَ طَفَّارُ الأَنْهَارِ [*He is the leaper over rivers,* or *rivulets*]. (A.)

طفس

طِنْفِسَةٌ and its variations: see art طنفس.

طفق

1. طَفِقَ يَفْعَلُ كَذَا, (Ṣ, Mgh, O, Ḳ,) aor. ـَ; (Ṣ, Ḳ;) and طَفَقَ, aor. ـِ, (Ṣ, O, Ḳ,) mentioned by Akh, (Ṣ, ISd, O,) and by Zj, (ISd, TA,) as said by some, (Ṣ, O,) but pronounced by Lth to be bad; (TA;) inf. n. طَفَقٌ, (Ṣ, Ḳ, TA, [in some copies of the Ḳ, erroneously, طَفْقٌ,]) of the former verb; (Ṣ, TA;) and طُفُوقٌ, (Ṣ, O, Ḳ,) of the latter verb; (Ṣ, O;) *He set about, began, commenced, took to,* or *betook himself to, doing such a thing:* (Ṣ, Mgh, O, TA:) expl. in the Ḳ as meaning *he continued uninterruptedly the doing of such a thing* (وَاصَلَ الفِعْلَ [or in some copies وَصَلَ الفِعْلَ]), and by El-Ḥáfidh Ibn-Ḥajar, in the "Fet-ḥ el-Bárì," as meaning *he entered upon, began,* or *commenced, and went on continually, doing such a thing;* but it denotes the entering upon the doing of a thing irrespectively of the going on continually or not, and therefore it is not allowable to prefix أَنْ to its predicate: (MF, TA:) it is followed by a future [or an aor., as in the ex. above]: the saying فَطَفِقَ مَسْحًا بِالسُّوقِ وَالأَعْنَاقِ, in the Ḳur [xxxviii. 32], (TA,) i. e. *He took to severing* with the sword [*the thighs and the necks*], or, as some say, *to wiping* [or *stroking*] with his hand [*the thighs and the necks*], (Bḍ,) is for طَفِقَ يَمْسَحُ مَسْحًا: (Bḍ,* TA:) the verb is used only in an affirmative phrase: they do not say مَا طَفِقَ. (IDrd, O, Ḳ.) — طَفِقَ فُلَانٌ بِمَا أَرَادَ, (Aboo-Sa'eed, O, Ḳ,*) a phrase of the Arabs of the desert, (Aboo-Sa'eed, O,) means *Such a one attained that which he desired.* (Aboo-Sa'eed, O, Ḳ.*) — And one says طَفِقَ المَوْضِعَ, aor. ـَ, *He kept,* or *clave, to the place.* (ISd, Ḳ.)

4. اطفقهُ ٱللّٰهُ بِهِ *God caused him to attain him,* or *it.* (Aboo-Sa'eed, O, Ḳ.) One says, لَئِنْ أَطْفَقَنِى ٱللّٰهُ بِهِ لَأَفْعَلَنَّ بِهِ [*Verily if God cause me to attain him,* or *it, I will assuredly do something with him,* or *it*]. (TA.)

طفل

1. طَفُلَ, aor. ـُ, inf. n. طَفَالَةٌ and طُفُولَةٌ, *It* (anything) *was,* or *became, soft,* or *tender;* [as though resembling a طِفْل;] (Ḳ, TA;) syn. رَخُصَ. (TA.) ═ طَفَلَتْ said of a she-camel: see 2. — طَفَلَ, (Ḳ, TA,) inf. n. طُفُولٌ, said of a man, (TA,) *He entered upon the* [*time called*] طَفَل, (Ḳ, TA,) which has two contr. meanings; (TA;) as also ▼ اطفل. (Ḳ.) — And طَفَلَتِ الشَّمْسُ *The sun rose:* (O, Ḳ:) so says Fr in his "Nawádir." (O.) — And, (O, Ḳ,) accord. to Zj, (O,) *The sun became red on the occasion of setting;* and so ▼ أَطْفَلَتْ: (O, Ḳ:) thus the former has two contr. meanings: (Ḳ:) and

طَفَّلَتِ ▼ الشَّمْسُ, (Ṣ, Ḳ,) or طَفَّلَتْ لِلْغُرُوبِ, (Ṣ,) inf. n. تَطْفِيلٌ, (Ṣ, O,) *The sun inclined to setting:* (Ṣ, O:) or *approached the setting;* as also طَفَلَتْ, (Ḳ, TA,) aor. ـُ, inf. n. طُفُولٌ. (TA.) ═ طَفَلَتِ الحُمُرُ العُشْبَ *The asses depastured the herbs so as to raise the dust upon them.* (Ibn-'Abbád, O.) ═ And طَفَلَ النَّبْتُ ; (Ibn-'Abbád, O, Ḳ;) and طُفِلَ ; (Ibn-'Abbád, O, TA;) or, accord. to the Ḳ, ▼ طَفَّلَ, inf. n. تَطْفِيلٌ ; (TA;) *The herbage became soiled by dust,* (Ibn-'Abbád, O, Ḳ, TA,) *and thereby marred,* or *injured.* (Ibn-'Abbád, O, TA.)

2. طفّلت النّاقة i. q. رَشَّحَتْ طِفْلَهَا or رَشَّحَتْهُ [i. e. *The she-camel rubbed the root of her young one's tail, and pushed him on with her head; and went before him, and waited for him until he overtook her; and sometimes gently urged him on, and followed him*]; (Ḳ accord. to different copies; [but both of these verbs signify the same, as expl. in the L;]) and so ▼ طَفَلَتْ, (Ḳ, TA,) aor. ـُ, inf. n. طُفُولٌ. (TA.) — طفّلت الشَّمْسُ : see 1. — طَفَّلَ اللَّيْلُ *The night began to be dark:* (Ṣ, O:) or *drew near.* (Ḳ.) ═ طَفَّلَ الإِبِلَ, (Ṣ, O, Ḳ,) inf. n. تَطْفِيلٌ, (Ṣ, O,) *He treated the camels gently, in journeying, in order that their young ones* (أَطْفَالَهَا) *might come up to them.* (Ṣ, O, Ḳ.) — And طَفَّلَ الكَلَامَ, ‡ *He considered,* or *forecast, the results of the speech,* or *saying; he looked to what would,* or *might, be its result;* or *he thought,* or *meditated, upon it, and endeavoured to understand it;* syn. تَدَبَّرَهُ ; (Ḳ, TA;) and (TA) so ▼ اطفله. (O, TA.) ═ See also 1, last sentence. ═ And see 5, in two places.

4. اطفلت, said of a woman, (Ṣ, O, TA,) and of a girl, or young woman, (صَبِيَّة, [but this, I doubt not, is a mistranscription for ظَبْيَة, i. e. a doe-gazelle,]) and of a she-camel, (TA,) or of any female, (Mṣb,) *She had a* طِفْل [or *young one of tender age*]: (Ṣ, O, TA:) or *she brought forth.* (Mṣb.) — See also 1, in two places. ═ And see 2.

5. تطفّل *He was,* or *became, an intruder at feasts, uninvited;* (Ṣ, Mṣb, Ḳ;) as also ▼ طفّل, (Ḳ,) inf. n. تَطْفِيلٌ : (TA:) or *he imitated Ṭufeyl:* (Ḥar p. 179: [see طُفَيْلِىٌّ :]) and تطفّل عليه and ▼ طفّل عَلَيْهِ *he intruded upon him at a feast, uninvited.* (TA.) It is of the speech of the people of El-'Irák. (Lth, Mṣb.)

طَفْلٌ *Soft,* or *tender;* (Ṣ, O, Ḳ;) applied to anything: (Ḳ:) fem. with ة ; (Ṣ, O, Ḳ;) applied to a girl, or young woman, (Ṣ,) or to a woman: (O:) and pl. طِفَالٌ and طُفُولٌ. (Ḳ.) One says بَنَانٌ طَفْلٌ [*Soft,* or *tender, fingers,* or *ends of fingers*]; this being allowable, though بنان is a [kind of] pl. and طفل is a sing., because every pl. [of the kind] that differs not from its sing. save in the ة [affixed to the latter] is made sing. and masc. [as well as fem.]: and therefore Homeyd says,

فَلَمَّا كَشَفْنَ اللِّبْسَ عَنْهُ مَسَحْنَهُ *
بِأَطْرَافِ طَفْلٍ زَانَ غَيْلًا مُوَشَّمَا *

[*And when they* (referring to females) *removed from over him the clothing, they wiped him with the extremities of soft,* or *tender, fingers, that adorned a plump fore arm, tattooed*]; meaning, بِأَطْرَافِ بَنَانٍ طَفْلٍ. (Ṣ, O.) ═ Also [*Fullers' earth, which is used for scouring cloths, and is sometimes used in the bath, instead of soap;*] *a certain yellow* [or rather *yellowish*, and sometimes *white*, or *whitish*,] *earth, well known in Egypt, with which cloths are dyed* [or rather *scoured*]; (TA;) *also called* بَيْلُونٌ. (Esh-Shiháb El-'Ajamee, TA in art. بلن.)

طِفْلٌ *A young one,* or *youngling,* or the *young,* (Mṣb, Ḳ,*) of anything, (Ḳ,) [or] of a human being and of a beast: (Mṣb:) or (Ḳ) *a new-born child,* or *young infant:* and also *a young one,* or the *young,* of any wild animal: (Ṣ, O, Ḳ:) or it is applied to *a child until he discriminates;* (Mṣb, TA;) after which he is called صَبِىٌّ ; thus some say, (Mṣb,) [and] thus says El-Munáwee: (TA:) or, accord. to Az, (Mṣb, TA,) on the authority of AHeyth, (TA,) *a child from the time of his birth* (Mgh, TA) *until he attains to puberty:* (Mgh, Mṣb, TA:) fem. طِفْلَةٌ : (Zj, Mgh, Mṣb, TA:) and pl. أَطْفَالٌ : (Zj, Ṣ, O, Mṣb, TA:) but طِفْلٌ is also used as fem., (Zj, Mgh, O, Mṣb, TA,) and dual, (Zj, TA,) and pl., (Zj, Ṣ, O, Mṣb, TA,) occurring as pl. in the Ḳur xxiv. 31, (Ṣ, O, Mṣb,) and [xxii. 5 and] xl. 69: (Zj, TA:) and ▼ طِفْيَلٌ signifies the same as طِفْلٌ ; (Ḳ, TA;) used in this sense by a rájiz; but accord. to some, by poetic license, for the dim. ▼ طُفَيْلٌ. (TA.) — [Hence,] † *Any part* or *portion* of anything, whether a substance or an accident: (Ḳ, TA:) pl. أَطْفَالٌ : whence they say طِفْلُ الهَجْرِ and الحُبِّ † [*The portion of anxiety* and *of love*]. (TA.) — ‡ *A falling spark* or *portion* (سِقْط [in the CḲ سَقْط]) of fire: (M, Ḳ, TA:) or *a live coal:* (A, TA:) or *fire when just struck;* as also ▼ طِفْلَةٌ : (T, TA: [but this latter is the n. un.:]) and the pl. is أَطْفَالٌ : one says, تَطَايَرَتْ أَطْفَالُ النَّارِ, meaning ‡ *The sparks of the fire* [*became scattered*]. (TA.) — † *Small clouds:* so in a verse of Aboo-Dhu-eyb. (TA.) — ‡ *An object of want:* (Ḳ:) or *a small object of want.* (TA.) One says, هُوَ يَسْعَى فِى أَطْفَالِ الحَوَائِجِ, i. e. [‡ *He labours in the accomplishment of*] *small objects of want.* (A, TA.) ═ ‡ *Night:* (Ḳ, TA:) or the *first part thereof.* (A, TA.) — And † The *sun when near to the setting.* (ISd, Ḳ, TA.)

طَفَلٌ : see طُفُولِيَّةٌ. — Also The *period* [*next*] *after sunrise:* from طِفْلٌ signifying "a young one" or "youngling:" (O:) or طَفَلُ الغَدَاةِ signifies *the period from that when the sun is about to rise,* or *appear, until its light has ascendancy over the earth:* (T, TA:) or *when the sun is about to rise,* or *appear, and has not yet ascendancy in,* or *upon, the earth:* (Er-Rághib, TA:) or *the period from the rising,* or *appearing, of the sun, until its having ascendancy* [for إِلَى ٱسْتِكْمَالِهَا in a copy of the M, and استكمانها and استكنانها in different copies of the Ḳ, I read إِلى ٱسْتِمْكَانِهَا, agreeably with the explanation in the the T and with that of Er-Rághib, in both of which the verb used is يَسْتَمْكِنُ,] *in,* or *upon, the earth.* (M, Ḳ.) And (O) The *period after* [that called] the عَصْر [q. v.] *when the sun inclines to the setting:* (Ṣ, O:) or طَفَلُ العَشِىِّ signifies *the last part of the afternoon, at sunset,* (Ḳ, TA,) and *at the time of the sun's becoming yellow, when it is about to set.* (TA.) One says, أَتَيْتُهُ طَفَلًا [*I came to him at one of the periods termed* طَفَل]. (Ṣ, O.) — Also The *coming of the night with its darkness.* (TA.) — And The *darkness* itself. (O, Ḳ.) ═ Also *Rain:* so in the phrase طَفَلُ الثُّرَيَّا [*The rain of the auroral setting of the Pleiades*]. (Ṣ, O.) [Or *A shower of rain:* for] one says, وَقَعَتْ أَطْفَالُ الوَسْمِىِّ *The showers of the* [rain called] وسمىّ [q. v.] *fell:* and جَادَهُ طَفَلٌ مِنْ مَطَرٍ [*A shower of rain descended copiously upon him,* or *it*]. (A, TA.) — And رِيحٌ طَفَلٌ *A wind that blows gently,* or *softly.* (TA.)

طَفِلٌ Herbage *that does not become tall* (TA.)

طُفَالٌ and طَفَالٌ *Dry clay:* (Ḳ:) of the dial. of El-Yemen. (TA.)

طَفِيلٌ, like أَمِيرٍ, (Ḳ,) or, accord. to the L, ▼ طِفْئِلٌ, mentioned in the L in art. طفال, (TA,) *Turbid water remaining in a watering-trough:* (Ḳ, TA:) n. un. with ة ; (Ḳ;) accord. to the L, طِفْئِلَةٌ ; meaning *a portion thereof.* (TA.)

طُفَيْلٌ dim. of طِفْلٌ, q. v.

طِفْئِلٌ : see طَفِيلٌ.

طِفْيَلٌ : see طِفْلٌ.

طَفَالَةٌ : } see what next follows.
طُفُولَةٌ : }

طُفُولِيَّةٌ, mentioned by ISd and the expositors of the Fṣ and others, as well as in the Ḳ, and also pronounced without teshdeed, [i. e. طُفُولِيَةٌ,] which shows, as do several other reasons, that the ى therein is not that which is the characteristic of rel. ns., though it has been asserted to be so, (MF, TA,) The *state,* or *condition, of the* طِفْل ; [i. e. *early infancy:* or, in a larger sense, *childhood;*] as also ▼ طُفُولَةٌ and ▼ طَفَالَةٌ and ▼ طَفَلٌ ; (Ḳ;) [inf. ns.] having no verb [corresponding to them]. (TA.)

طُفَيْلِىٌّ *One who intrudes at feasts, uninvited;* (Ṣ, O, Mṣb, Ḳ;) as also ▼ طِفْلِيلٌ : (Ḳ:) the former is a rel. n. from طُفَيْلٌ, the name of a certain man of El-Koofeh, (ISk, Ṣ, O, Mṣb, Ḳ,) who used to intrude at feasts, uninvited, (ISk, Ṣ, O, Mṣb,) and who was called طُفَيْلُ الأَعْرَاسِ and طُفَيْلُ العَرَائِسِ : (ISk, Ṣ, O: [two other derivations are mentioned in the TA; but they are too far-fetched to deserve notice:]) such the Arabs [in their proper language] called وَارِشٌ. (ISk, Ṣ, O, Mṣb.)

طَفَّالٌ *One who sells* طَفْل [or *fullers' earth*]. (TA.)

طُفَيْلِىٌّ : see طِفْلِيلٌ.

[طَافِلَةٌ, which Golius explains as meaning "i. q. فَايِدَةٌ et خَيْرٌ, utilitas, bonum," referring to the KL as his authority, is evidently a mistake for طَائِلٌ, expl. as meaning فَائِدَةٌ and خَيْرٌ in my copy of the KL, which does not mention طَافِلَةٌ in any sense.]

أَطْفَلُ [*More, or most, like to the* طُفَيْلِىّ: and hence, *more, and most, intrusive, uninvited*]. أَطْفَلُ مِنْ لَيْلٍ عَلَى نَهَارٍ [*More intrusive, uninvited, than night upon day*], and مِنْ شَيْبٍ عَلَى شَبَابٍ [*than hoariness upon youthfulness*], and مِنْ ذُبَابٍ [*than flies*], are proverbs. (Meyd.)

مُطْفِلٌ, (A'Obeyd, Ṣ, O, Mṣb, Ḳ,) and مُطْفِلَةٌ also, (TA,) applied to a female, of human beings and of wild animals, (Ḳ, TA,) and of camels, (A'Obeyd, TA,) *i. q.* ذَاتُ طِفْلٍ [*Having a young one, or youngling, &c.*], (A'Obeyd, Ḳ, TA,) *with her*: (A'Obeyd, TA:) or applied to a she-gazelle and camel, (Ṣ, O,) or to any female, (Mṣb,) *that has recently brought forth*: (Ṣ, O, Mṣb:*) pl. مَطَافِلُ and مَطَافِيلُ. (A'Obeyd, Ṣ, O, Ḳ.) [See also عَائِذٌ, in art. عوذ.] سَارَتْ قُرَيْشٌ بِالعُوذِ المَطَافِيلِ i. e. *Kureysh journeyed with the camels that had recently brought forth having with them their young ones*, occurring in a trad., means, † *with their collective company, their old and their young*. (TA.) [See, again, عَائِذٌ.] — [It is also said by Freytag to be applied in the Deewán of the Hudhalees to clouds followed by small ones.] — And لَيْلَةٌ مُطْفِلٌ means *A night that kills the young ones by its cold*. (Ḳ, TA.)

طفو and طفى

1. طَفَا فَوْقَ المَآءِ, (Ṣ, Mgh, Mṣb, Ḳ,) aor. يَطْفُو, (Ṣ, Mgh, Mṣb,) inf. n. طُفُوٌّ (Ṣ, Mgh, Mṣb, Ḳ) and طَفْوٌ, (Ṣ, Mṣb, Ḳ,) *It* (a thing, Ṣ, Mgh, Mṣb) *floated upon the water*, (Ṣ, Mgh, Mṣb, Ḳ,) *and did not sink*. (Ṣ, Mṣb.) — [Hence,] one says, † الظُّعُنُ تَطْفُو وَتَرْسُبُ فِى السَّرَابِ [*The women's camel-vehicles appear, as though floating, and disappear, as though sinking, in the mirage*]. (TA.) — And طَفَتِ الخُوصَةُ فَوْقَ الشَّجَرِ ‡ [*The leaf of the date-palm, or of the Theban palm, &c.,*] *appeared* [*above the trees*]. (Ḳ, TA.) — And طَفَا said of a bull, (Ḳ,) or of a wild bull, (TA,) ‡ *He mounted upon the hills* (Ḳ, TA) and *upon the sands*. (TA. [In the CḲ, على الاَكَمِ is erroneously put for عَلَا الأَكَمَ.]) — And طَفَوْتُ فَوْقَهُ † *I leaped upon it*. (TA.) The saying

عَبْدٌ إِذَا مَا رَسَبَ القَوْمُ طَفَا

is expl. by IAạr as meaning [*A slave*] *who, when the people are grave, leaps* by reason of his ignorance. (TA.) — And طَفَا المَآءُ [not a mistranscription for طَغَا] † *The water rose*, or *became high*. (TA voce طُوفَانٌ, q. v.) — And طَفَا said of a gazelle, † *He ran vehemently*. (Ḳ.) One says of a gazelle, مَرَّ يَطْفُو, meaning ‡ *He passed by*, or *along*, or *away, going lightly*, or *briskly, upon the ground, and running vehemently*. (Ṣ, TA.) — And, said of a man, (Ḳ, TA,) by way of comparison [to a floating fish], (TA,) ‡ *He died*. (Ḳ, TA.) — And † *He* (i. e. a man) *entered into* [or *upon*] *an affair*: (Ḳ, TA:) [or,] accord. to the "Nawádir," one says, طَفَا فِى الأَرْضِ *he entered into the earth*, either وَاغِلًا [app. as meaning *penetrating, and becoming concealed*], or رَاسِخًا [app. as meaning *becoming firmly fixed* therein]. (TA.) = [طَفَا is made trans. by means of بِ: see an ex. voce أَرْسَبَ.]

4. اطفى *He kept continually*, or *constantly, to the eating of fish found floating upon the water*. (TA.)

طُفْىٌ : see طُفْيَةٌ.

طَفْوَةٌ, (Ḳ,) thus it should app. be accord. to the Ḳ, but in copies of the M, ▼ طُفْوَةٌ, with ḍamm, (TA,) *A thin*, or *slender, plant*. (Ḳ.)

طُفْوَةٌ : see what next precedes: — and see also the paragraph next following.

طُفْيَةٌ The *leaf of the* مُقْل [or *Theban palm*]; (Ṣ, Mgh, Mṣb, Ḳ;) and so ▼ طُفْوَةٌ: (Aṣ, TA:) pl. ▼ طُفًى (Ṣ,* TA) or [rather this is a coll. gen. n., and the pl. properly so termed is] طُفًى, (Mṣb,) which is [also] pl. of طُفْوَةٌ. (Aṣ, TA.) [Accord. to Forskål (Flora Ægypt. Arab., p. cxxvi.), the Theban palm itself, which he terms "borassus flabelliformis," is called طفى, as well as دوم.] — And [hence] ذُو الطُّفْيَتَيْنِ, (Ḳ,) or الطُّفْيَةِ, (Ṣ, Mgh, Mṣb, TA,) is the name of † *A serpent* (Ṣ, Mgh, Mṣb, Ḳ) *of a foul*, or *malignant, sort*, (Ḳ,) *having upon its back two lines*, or *stripes*, (Ṣ, Mgh, Mṣb, Ḳ,) *which are black*, (Ṣ, Mgh, Mṣb,) *resembling two leaves such as are termed* طُفْيَتَانِ: (Ṣ, Mgh, Mṣb, Ḳ:) and sometimes it is termed طُفْيَةٌ, meaning ذَاتُ طُفْيَةٍ: and الطُّفَى is used as the pl., meaning ذَوَاتُ الطُّفَى. (Ṣ.)

طُفَاوَةٌ The *floating froth* or *scum* (Ḳ, TA) *and grease* (TA) *of the cooking-pot*. (Ḳ, TA.) — And *A halo around the sun*, (Ṣ, Ḳ,) and also *around the moon* [like هَالَةٌ]: (Ḳ:) the former accord. to Fr, and the latter accord. to AHát. (TA.) — And one says, أَصَبْنَا طُفَاوَةً مِنَ الرَّبِيعِ meaning شَيْئًا مِنْهُ [i. e. *We obtained somewhat of the herbage*, or perhaps *of the rain, of the season called* رَبِيع]. (Ṣ, TA.)

سَمَكٌ طَافٍ *Fish floating upon the surface of the water, having died therein*. (Mgh, Mṣb, TA.) — [Hence,] فَرَسٌ طَافٍ † *A horse elevating his head*. (TA.) — كَأَنَّ عَيْنَهُ عِنَبَةٌ طَافِيَةٌ [*As though his eye were a floating grape*], in a trad. respecting Ed-Dejjál, is expl. by Th as meaning his eye's being prominent and conspicuous. (TA.)

طق

R. Q. 1. طَقْطَقَ [*He caused a thing to make a sound such as is termed* طَقْطَقَةٌ]. (Ḳ voce طَرَّبَ.)

طَقْ a word imitative of a sound; and sometimes they said ▼ طَقْطَقْ: (IDrd, O, TA:) or the former is a word imitative of The *sound of stones*; and ▼ the latter is its noun: (Ḳ:) one says, سَمِعْتُ طَقْطَقَةَ ▼ الحِجَارَةِ *I heard* [*the sound of*] *the falling of the stones, one upon another*, when they rolled down from a mountain: (IDrd, O:) or طَقْ is a word imitative of the *sound of the stone and of the solid hoof*; and ▼ طَقْطَقَةٌ signifies the *action thereof*: (M, TA:) or this latter is a word imitative of the *sound of the successive falling of stones, one upon another*: (IDrd, O:) or this word signifies the *sound of the legs of horses upon the hard ground*; (IAạr, TA;) [or] sometimes it signifies also the *sound of the solid hoofs upon the ground*; (IDrd, O;) or the *sounds of the hoofs of horses* or *similar beasts* [*with quick reiteration*]; like دَقْدَقَةٌ; and sometimes they said ▼ حَبَطِقْطِقْ, of which El-Mázinee cites an ex.; (Ṣ, O;) but [J says] I have not seen this except in his book: (Ṣ:) another ex. of it, however, is cited by Lth. (TA.)

طِقْ The *sound of a frog leaping from the margin of a river* or *rivulet*. (M, Ḳ.) One says, لَا يُسَاوِى طِقْ [*It is not*, or *will not be, equal to the sound of a frog* &c.]. (M.)

طَقْطَقَةٌ : see طَقْ, in four places. — In the language of the common people, it means *Lightness*, or *promptness, in speech*. (TA.) — And † The *death that results from the jinn's piercing* or *thrusting* [i. e. *from the* طَاعُون]. (TA.)

طُقْطُوقٌ and ▼ مُطَقْطِقٌ in the language of the common people, *Light in person*; and *light*, or *prompt, in speech*. (TA.)

مُطَقْطِقٌ : see what next precedes.

حَبَطِقْطِقْ : see طَقْ.

طل

1. طَلَّتِ السَّمَآءُ الأَرْضَ, [aor. ـُ,] inf. n. طَلٌّ, *The sky rained small rain upon the earth*, or *land*. (MA.) And طُلَّتِ الأَرْضُ, (Ṣ, O, Ḳ,) inf. n. as above, (TA,) [meaning, as is implied in the Ṣ and O, *The earth*, or *land, was rained upon by the weakest of rain*; or *was rained upon*, or *bedewed, by the* طَلّ, q. v.; or] *the* طَلّ *descended upon the earth*, or *land*: (Ḳ:) and طَلَّهَا النَّدَى [*The rain, or dew, moistened it*]: (Ṣ, O, TA:) and طَلَّتْ, with fet-ḥ, signifies [accord. to some] *It became*

moist, or *moistened:* one says, طُلَّتْ بِلَادُكَ, and طُلَّتْ; the former meaning *May thy countries*, or *tracts of country, be rained upon;* and the latter, *become moist*, or *moistened:* or, accord. to Aboo-Is-ḥák, [i. e. Zj,] طُلَّتْ only, with ḍamm; [and he adds,] one says, رَحُبَتْ بِلَادُكَ وَطُلَّتْ, with ḍamm, [i. e. *May thy tracts of country be spacious to thee, and be moistened by the* طَلّ,] (or, as in art. رحب in the TA, أَرْحَبَتْ عَلَيْكَ وَطُلَّتْ,) not طَلَّتْ; because the طلّ is not from them, [i. e. it is not from the tracts of country,] but they are the objects thereof. (TA.) [Golius mentions, among the significations of طَلَّ, as on the authority of Z, *i. q.* رحب, said of land, or the earth, and followed by على relating to a person: but I think it most probable that he inferred this signification from his finding, in a copy of the A, the phrase رَحُبَتْ عَلَيْكَ الأَرْضُ وَطَلَّتْ (for وَطُلَّتْ), without any explanation. And Freytag mentions ▼ أُطِلَّ as meaning *It was watered by fine rain;* from the Deewán of the Hudhalees.] And [it is said that] طَلَّتِ السَّمَآءُ signifies اِشْتَدَّ وَقْعُهَا [i. e. *The rain fell vehemently*]. (TA.) ═ طَلَّ دَمَهُ, (AZ, Ṣ, O, Mṣb,) said of God, (Ṣ,) or of the ruling power, (Mṣb,) first pers. طَلَلْتُهُ, (Ḳ,) aor. ـُ, (Mṣb,) inf. n. طَلٌّ (Mṣb, Ḳ) and طُلُولٌ, (Ḳ,) *He made his blood to go for nought, unretaliated, and uncompensated by a mulct; made it to be of no account:* (AZ, Ṣ, O, Mṣb, Ḳ, TA:) or *held it to be of little account, as though it were but* [*the rain, or dew, termed*] طَلّ, *in its result;* this, accord. to Er-Rághib, being the proper meaning: (TA:) and ▼ اطلّه signifies the same. (AZ, Ṣ, O, Mṣb, Ḳ.) And طُلَّ دَمُهُ *His blood was made to go for nought*, &c.; (AZ, Ṣ, Mgh, O, Mṣb, Ḳ;) as also ▼ أُطِلَّ دَمُهُ: (AZ, Ṣ, O, Mṣb, Ḳ:) and طَلَّ دَمُهُ, (Ṣ, O, Mṣb, Ḳ,) with fet-ḥ, accord. to Ks and AO, (Ṣ, O, Mṣb,) aor. ـُ [contr. to analogy], (Mṣb,) or ـِ [agreeably with analogy]; (Ḳ;) and طَلَّ, originally طَلِلَ, (Mṣb, Ḳ,*) aor. ـَ; (Mṣb, Ḳ;) [*his blood went for nought*, &c.;] but this is disallowed by AZ; (Ṣ, O, Mṣb;) and it is more commonly with ḍamm. (Ḳ.) — And طَلَّهُ حَقَّهُ, aor. ـُ, *He diminished*, or *impaired, to him his right*, or *due;* or *deprived*, or *defrauded him of it, partly*, or *wholly:* (Ḳ, TA:) or, accord. to Khálid Ibn-Jembeh, (TA,) *he denied him*, or *refused him, his right*, or *due;* (Ḳ, TA;) and *withheld it* [*from him*]: (TA:) and *he annulled it;* or *made it to go for nought, as a thing of no account*, or *as a thing that had perished* or *become lost.* (Ḳ, TA.) You say, طَلُّوا فُلَانًا حَقَّهُ, aor. ـُ, inf. n. طَلٌّ, *They denied*, or *refused, such a one his right*, or *due:* so says Khálid Ibn-Jembeh. (O.) — And طَلَّ غَرِيمَهُ, (Ḳ,) aor. ـُ, (TA,) inf. n. طَلٌّ, (O, Ḳ,) *He delayed*, or *deferred, with his creditor*, or *put him off, by promising time after time to pay him.* (O,* Ḳ.) — And طَلٌّ signifies also The *driving* of camels *roughly*, or *rigorously.* (Ḳ.) You say, طَلَّ الإِبِلَ, inf. n. طَلٌّ, *He drove the camels roughly*, or *rigorously!* (TḲ.) ═ طَلَّ, [sec. pers. طَلِلْتَ, aor. ـَ,] inf. n. طَلَالَةٌ; like مَلَّ, [sec. pers. مَلِلْتَ, aor. ـَ,] (Ḳ, TA,) inf. n. مَلَالَةٌ; (TA;) [accord. to Freytag, followed by لَهُ, and in the Deewán of the Hudhalees by إِلَيْهِ; and so, accord. to him, ▼ استطلّ, followed by لَهُ;] *He*, or *it, was*, or *became, pleasing*, (Ḳ, TA,) and *goodly.* (TA.) ═ And طَلَّهُ, (Ḳ,) inf. n. طَلٌّ, (TA,) is also *syn. with* طَلَاهُ: (Ḳ:) so in the phrase طَلَّهُ بِالوَرْسِ [*He smeared it*, or *rubbed it over, with* ورس, q. v.]; namely, a thing. (Ibn-'Abbád, O.)

4: see 1, former half: ═ and the same, latter half, in two places. ═ اطلّ عَلَيْهِ *He* (a man, Mṣb) *looked upon it, looked upon it from above, looked down upon it, got a view of it*, or *saw it;* syn. أَشْرَفَ, (Ṣ, O, Ḳ,) [i. e.] أَشْرَفَ عَلَيْهِ, (Mṣb,) or أَوْفَى عليه; (Ḥam p. 208;) properly أَوْفَى عَلَيْهِ بِطَلَلِهِ, i. e. بِشَخْصِهِ [meaning *he looked upon it, &c., with his body;* not in imagination]; (Er-Rághib, TA;) and ▼ استطلّ signifies the same: (Ḳ:) and so أَطَفَّ عليه. (O in art. طف.) [See also 6.] Hence, in a trad., the saying of Ṣafeeyeh the daughter of 'Abd-El-Muṭṭalib, فَأَطَلَّ عَلَيْنَا يَهُودِىٌّ فَقُمْتُ فَضَرَبْتُ رَأْسَهُ بِالسَّيْفِ ثُمَّ رَمَيْتُ بِهِ عَلَيْهِمْ [*And a Jew looked upon us, and I arose, and smote off his head with the sword, then cast it upon them*]. (O.) — [Hence, perhaps,] اطلّ الزَّمَانُ † *The time drew near.* (Mṣb.) — And اطلّ عَلَى حَقِّى فَذَهَبَ بِهِ † *He got possession of my right*, or *due, and took it away*, or *went away with it.* (Ibn-'Abbád, O.) [See also أَطَفَّ.] — And اطلّ عَلَيْهِ ‡ *He importuned him*, (Ibn-'Abbád, O, TA,) حَتَّى غَلَبَهُ [*so that*, or *until, he overcame him*]. (TA.) And اطلّ فُلَانٌ عَلَى فُلَانٍ بِالأَذَى † *Such a one kept continually*, or *constantly, to the annoying*, or *molesting*, or *hurting, of such a one.* (TA.) ═ An Arab woman of the desert is related to have said, مَا أَطَلَّ شِعْرَ جَمِيلٍ وَأَحْلَاهُ [*How pleasing is the poetry of Jemeel, and how sweet is it!*]. (TA.)

5. هٰذِهِ الأَرْضُ قَدْ تَطَلَّلَتْ *This land has produced herbage, and become replete*, [for تَنَحَّبَتْ (to which I cannot assign any apposite meaning), in my original, I read تَحَيَّرَتْ,] *and has not been trodden by any one:* so says AA. (O.)

6. تَطَالَّ (Ṣ, O, in the Ḳ in art. طول written تَطَاالَّ,) (O) إِلَى الشَّىْءِ *He stretched out his neck, looking at the thing, it being far from him:* (Ṣ, O:) or *he stretched out his neck to look:* (TA in art. دمع:) or تَطَالَلْتُ signifies *I stood upon my toes, and stretched my stature, to look at a thing*, (تَطَاوَلْتُ, Ḳ, TA, both of these verbs meaning thus, TA in art. طول,) *and looked:* (Ḳ, TA:) or, accord. to AA, التَّطَالُّ signifies *the looking from above a place*, or *from a curtain* or *the like.* (TA.) [See an ex. in a verse cited in art. شرف, conj. 10: and see also 4 in the present art.]

10: see 4. — استطلّ الفَرَسُ بِذَنَبِهِ is expl. by Ibn-'Abbád as signifying مَرَّ مُطِلًّا بِهِ إِذَا نَاصَبَهُ فِى السَّمَآءِ [app. meaning *The horse went along raising his tail toward the sky:* for I think that إِذَا نَاصَبَهُ should be إِذَا كَانَ نَاصِبَهُ, or أَىْ نَاصِبَهُ]. (O.) ═ See also 1, last sentence but one.

R. Q. 1. طَلْطَلَهُ *He moved him, agitated him, shook him*, or *put him into a state of motion* or *commotion;* (Ḳ, TA;) like تَلْتَلَهُ: (TA:) [or,] accord. to Ibn-'Abbád, الطَّلْطَلَةُ signifies *the moving about the arms in walking.* (O.)

طَلٌّ *Light*, (Mṣb,) or *weak*, (Ḳ,) [i. e. *drizzling*,] *rain:* (Mṣb, Ḳ:) or the *lightest*, (Ḳ,) or *weakest, of rain:* (Ṣ, O, Mṣb, Ḳ:) or *dew* (نَدًى, Ḳ, TA) *that descends from the sky in cloudless weather:* (TA:) or *above* نَدًى *and less than* مَطَرٌ: (Ḳ:) or, accord. to Er-Rághib, *rain that has little effect;* and so in the Ḳur ii. 267: (TA:) pl. طِلَالٌ (Ṣ, O, Ḳ) and طَلَلٌ, (O, Ḳ,) the latter mentioned by Fr, and said by him to be the only instance of the kind that has been heard except حِرَفٌ pl. of حَرْفٌ as meaning the حَرْف of a mountain; (O;) [or] طِلَلٌ is a contraction of طِلَالٌ: in a saying of a poet, cited by IAar, (TA,) ▼ الطَّلَل occurs for الطَّلّ [in the CḲ الطُّلَل]: or in this instance, as some relate it, the word is الطِّلَل. (Ḳ, TA.) — And *Milk:* (Ḳ:) or so ▼ طُلٌّ, with ḍamm, in the saying مَا بِالنَّاقَةِ طُلٌّ [*There is not in the she-camel any milk*], as Yaạkoob says, and as is related on the authority of AA, (Ṣ,) and thus in the saying مَا بِالدَّارِ طُلٌّ [*There is not in the house any milk*]: (O:) or طُلٌّ signifies thus: or *blood.* (Ḳ. [But see this word below.]) — And *Paucity of milk of a camel;* as also ▼ طُلٌّ. (Ḳ.) — And *Fat*, or *fatness;* syn. طِرْقٌ [in the CḲ طَرْقٌ, and in my MS. copy of the Ḳ طُرْقٌ]: thus in the saying مَا بِالنَّاقَةِ طَلٌّ [*There is not in the she-camel any fat*, or *fatness*]. (M, Ḳ, TA: in the CḲ طُلٌّ.) ═ [It is also used as an epithet.] You say يَوْمٌ طَلٌّ, meaning ذُو طَلٍّ, i. e. [*A day having drizzling rain*, or *dew;* or] *moist*, or *humid.* (TA.) And أَرْضٌ طَلَّةٌ *Land moistened by dew* [or *by drizzling rain*]; (TA;) as also ▼ مَطْلُولَةٌ: (Ṣ, TA:) and [in like manner] طَلَّةٌ signifies a meadow (رَوْضَةٌ) *moistened by* طَلّ. (Ḳ.) And طَلٌّ signifies Anything *moist.* (TA.) — [Hence, app.,] *Goodly*, or *good*, or *beautiful*, and *pleasing:* thus applied to a night, and to poetry (شِعْرٌ [in the CḲ شَعْرٌ]), and to water, &c.: (Ḳ, TA:) applied to these as meaning *good*, or *beautiful;* and so to discourse; (TA;) and thus ▼ طَلَّةٌ applied to a خُطْبَة. (Ibn-'Abbád, O, TA.) And اِمْرَأَةٌ طَلَّةٌ means *A beautiful, elegant*, or *graceful, woman.* (TA.) And خَمْرٌ طَلَّةٌ *Pleasant*, or *delicious, wine:* (Ṣ, O, Ḳ:*) or, as some say, *such as descends easily* [or *pleasantly down the throat*]. (TA.) And طَلَّةٌ applied to an odour (رَائِحَةٌ, Ḳ, TA, or رِيًّا, TA) likewise signifies *Pleasant*, or *delicious*. (Ḳ, TA.) ═ Also An *aged* man: (Kr, Ḳ:) and طَلَّةٌ signifies an *old* woman: (Ḳ, TA:) and a woman *foul, unseemly*, or *obscene, in tongue*; (Ḳ,* TA;) *annoying*, or *molesting*. (TA.) — And *A serpent*; (Ḳ;) thus accord. to IAạr: (O:) and so ▼ طِلٌّ; (Ḳ;) thus accord. to AA; (O;) like طِلْعٌ. (TA in art. طلع.)

طُلٌّ: see طَلٌّ, in two places. [But the signification of "blood" there mentioned requires consideration; for Ṣgh adds immediately after explaining the saying مَا بِالدَّارِ طُلٌّ what here follows.] — ذَهَبَ دَمُهُ طُلًّا and ▼ طِلًّا means هَدَرًا [i. e. *His blood went for nought, unretaliated, and uncompensated by a mulct*]. (Ibn-'Abbád, O. [Then follows immediately in the O الطُّلَّآءُ, expl. as below.])

طِلٌّ: see طَلٌّ, last sentence: ═ and see also طُلٌّ.

طَلَّةٌ [fem. of طَلٌّ, q. v. — And also used as a subst.: signifying] *A wife*. (Ṣ, O, Ḳ.) ═ And *Daintiness*, or *delicacy, in food and clothing*. (Ḳ, TA. [In the CḲ, النَّعْمَةُ is erroneously put for النِّعْمَةُ.])

طُلَّةٌ The *neck*. (Ḳ.) ═ And *A draught of milk*; (Az, Ḳ, TA;) as also ▼ طُلَّى: (Az, TA:) pl. of the former طُلَلٌ. (Ḳ.)

طَلَلٌ *A portion still standing of the remains of a dwelling* or *house*; (Ṣ, O, Mṣb,* Ḳ;) as also ▼ طَلَالَةٌ: (Ḳ:) pl. أَطْلَالٌ and طُلُولٌ, (Ṣ, O, Mṣb, Ḳ,) the latter pl. sometimes used: (Mṣb:) what cleaves to the ground is termed رَسْمٌ: (TA:) the people of the towns or villages apply the term أَطْلَالٌ to the *remains of walls* and *of places of worship*; and the people of the tents to [the *remains of*] *places of eating* and *of drinking* and *of sleeping*: (Ḥam p. 541:) [and] as pl. of طَلَلٌ it signifies *elevated places*: one says, رَأَيْتُ طَلَلَ القَرْيَةِ, meaning *I saw what was elevated of the land of the town*, or *village*. (Ḥar p. 139.) — And The شَخْص [or *body*, or *bodily* or *corporeal form* or *figure* or *substance, such as one sees from a distance*,] of a thing, (Mṣb, Ḳ,) whatever it be; as also ▼ طَلَالَةٌ: pl. of the former as above: (Ḳ:) the شَخْص [as meaning *body*, or *person*,] of a man; as also ▼ طَلَالَةٌ: (Ṣ, O:) or, of a man, the *erect* شَخْص. (Mṣb voce جُثَّةٌ.) And ظَلَالَةٌ, with ظ, signifies the same. (O and Ḳ in art. ظل.) One says, حَيَّا ٱللّٰهُ طَلَلَكَ and ▼ طَلَالَتَكَ, meaning [*May God preserve*, or *save*,] *thy* شَخْص [i. e. *body*, or *person*]. (Ṣ, O.) And حَيَّا ٱللّٰهُ طَلَلَكَ and أَطْلَالَكَ, meaning مَا شَخَصَ مِنْ جَسَدِكَ [i. e. *May God preserve*, or *save, what has risen into view of thy body*, or *person*]. (TA.) — Also *A place in the* صَحْن [or *court*] of a house, *prepared for the household to sit upon*: ADḳ says that there was *a place on which to eat and drink in the* فِنَآء [or *yard*] of every house, called the طَلَل: (Az, TA:) accord. to ISd, (TA,) the طَلَل of a house is, or was, *like the* [*kind of wide bench, of stone or brick &c., generally built against a wall, called*] دُكَّانَة [or دُكَّان], *upon which to sit*. (Ḳ, TA.) — And The جِلَال [or *deck*] of a ship or boat; (M, Mgh, O, Ḳ;) i. e. (Mgh) the *covering* thereof, *which is like the roof* (Mgh, Mṣb) *of a house* or *chamber*: (Mgh:) pl. أَطْلَالٌ. (Mgh, Mṣb, TA.) [In the TA it is said to mean the شِرَاع of a ship or boat; which is a mistake, as is sufficiently shown by its being there immediately added, "hence the trad. of Aboo-Bekr, that he used to pray upon the اطلال of the ship or boat."] — [Hence, app.,] one says, (of a man, Ibn-'Abbád, O,) مَشَى عَلَى طَلَلِ المَآءِ i. e. على ظَهْرِهِ, (Ibn-'Abbád, O, Ḳ,) which, Z says, means على وَجْهِهِ [i. e. ‡ *He walked*, or *went along, upon the surface of the water*: but whether this relates to a pretended miracle or to sliding upon ice, I know not]: and he adds that it is a tropical phrase. (TA.) ═ Also Anything *fresh*, or *juicy*, or [like طَلٌّ] *moist*; syn. طَرِىٌّ. (Ḳ.) — See also طَلٌّ, first sentence.

طَلِيلٌ: see مَطْلُولٌ. ═ Also *Sweet*; syn. حُلْوٌ: (so accord. to the O and some copies of the Ḳ: accord. to other copies of the Ḳ, *i. q.* خَلَقٌ; i. e., accord. to some of these copies, خَلَقٌ; accord. to some, خَلَقٌ; and accord. to some, خَلَقٌ:) thus expl. by Ibn-'Abbád; and said by him to be of the dial. of Hudheyl. (O.) [The explanation in the O is, I doubt not, the right: and hence] — طَلِيلَةٌ applied to a خُطْبَة: see طَلٌّ, latter part. ═ Also *A mat*; syn. حَصِيرٌ: (IAạr, O, Ḳ:) or *such as is woven of* [*the leaves of the*] دَوْم [or *Theban palm-tree*]; or *of the leaves of the date-palm*; or *of the* قُشُور [app. meaning the *peels of the branches*] *thereof*: (Ḳ, TA:) so in the M: in the T it is said that ▼ طَلِيلَةٌ means, accord. to AA, *a* [*mat of the kind called*] بُورِيَآء; and accord. to Aṣ, *a* بَارِىّ [which signifies the same as بُورِيَآء]: (TA:) pl. أَطِلَّةٌ and طِلَّةٌ and طُلُلٌ. (Ḳ.)

طَلَالَةٌ [an inf. n.: see 1, last sentence but one. And, as a simple subst.,] *A good*, or *goodly, state* or *condition*; and *a beautiful aspect, appearance, mien*, or *guise*. (IAạr, O, Ḳ.) And *Beauty*, or *beauty of colour*, or *brightness*: (O, Ḳ:) so in the saying, عَلَى مَنْطِقِهِ طَلَالَةُ الحُسْنِ [*Upon his diction is the glow of beauty*]. (O.) Accord. to Aṣ, *i. q.* حُسْنٌ and مَآءٌ [i. e. *Goodliness*, or *beauty*, and, app., *lustre*]. (TA.) — Also, (AA, O, Ḳ,) and some say ▼ طُلَالَةٌ, (AA, O,) *Joy, gladness*, or *happiness*. (AA, O, Ḳ.) ═ See also طَلَلٌ, in four places. — [Hence,] one says فَرَسٌ حَسَنُ الطَّلَالَةِ, meaning [*A horse goodly*, or *beautiful*,] *in what is high*, or *elevated, of his frame*, or *make*. (TA.)

طُلَالَةٌ: see the next preceding paragraph.

طَلِيلَةٌ: see طَلِيلٌ.

طُلَّى: see طُلَّةٌ.

طُلَّآءُ, (Ibn-'Abbád, O, Ḳ,) like سُلَّآءُ, (Ḳ, TA,) [in the CḲ, طَلَآءُ, like سَلَآءُ, and] in some copies of the Ḳ, erroneously, طِلَآءُ, (TA,) *Blood*, itself: and some say, *a pellicle upon the surface thereof*: (O:) [and in like manner طُلَّآءُ is expl. in the Ḳ in art. طلا:] or *blood that has been made to go for nought, unretaliated, and uncompensated by a mulct*: (Ḳ: [and from the context in the O, it seems that this is probably meant by Ibn-'Abbád: see طُلٌّ:]) accord. to AAF, (TA,) the ء in this word is originally ل. (Ḳ, TA.)

طُلْطُلٌ *A chronic*, or *permanent, disease*. (IAạr, Az, Ḳ.)

طُلْطُلٌ: see طُلَاطِلَةٌ.

طُلْطُلَةٌ: } see طُلَاطِلَةٌ: each in two places.
طَلَاطِلٌ: }

طُلَاطِلٌ: see the next paragraph, in three places.

طُلَاطِلَةٌ *A calamity*, or *misfortune*; (Ṣ, O, Ḳ;) as also ▼ طُلْطُلَةٌ [in the CḲ طَلْطَلَةٌ] and ▼ طُلْطُلٌ [in the CḲ طَلْطَلٌ]. (Ḳ, TA.) — Also, (Ṣ, O,) or ▼ طُلَاطِلٌ, (M, Ḳ,) *A disease that wearies the physicians*, (Ṣ, M, O, Ḳ,) *for which there is no remedy*: (Ṣ, O:) and said in the M to be *a pain in the back*. (TA.) And the former, *A disease that attacks a man in his belly*; as also ▼ طُلْطُلَةٌ. (O.) And *A disease in the backs of asses, that breaks their backs*; (Ḳ,* TA;) so in the M; (TA;) as also طلاطل with ḍamm and fet-ḥ [i. e. ▼ طُلَاطِلٌ and ▼ طَلَاطِلٌ]. (Ḳ.) — And *Death*; as also ▼ طُلَاطِلٌ; (Ḳ, TA;) so in the M, with ḍamm; and with fet-ḥ [i. e. ▼ طَلَاطِلٌ]. (TA.) — And *A certain piece of flesh in the fauces*; (ISd, Ḳ, TA:) or the *piece of flesh extending downwards upon* [*the upper extremity of*] *the* مُسْتَرَط [or مَسْرَط, i. e. the *gullet*]; (Aṣ, Az, O, Ḳ,* TA;) [meaning] the لَهَاة [or *uvula*]: (TA:) or, (O, Ḳ,) accord. to AHeyth, (O,) the *falling of the* لَهَاة [or *uvula*], *so that neither food nor beverage passes the fauces easily by reason of it*. (O, Ḳ.)

أَطْلَالٌ is the name of a certain mare, (O, Ḳ,) or of a she-camel, (Ḳ,) which, in reply to her rider's commanding her to leap a river, on the day of El-Ḳádiseeyeh, is asserted to have spoken, saying, وَثْبٌ وَسُورَةُ البَقَرَةِ [A leap, by the Chapter of the Cow!]. (O, Ḳ.) [Freytag has erroneously said, as on the authority of the Ḳ, that it is a name of the chapter of the Ḳur-án otherwise called بقرة.]

مُطَلٌّ: see مَطْلُولٌ.

أَمْرٌ مُطِلٌّ *An affair not settled*, or *not established*. (So accord. to some copies of the Ṣ and Ḳ, expl. by the words لَيْسَ بِمُسْتَقِرٍّ: in other copies of both, and in the O, لَيس بِمُسْفِرٍ [to which I am unable to assign any probable meaning].)

مُطَلْطَلٌ *i. q.* ضَبَابٌ [*Mist; or moisture like clouds, or like dust, covering the earth in the early mornings; or thin clouds, like smoke;* &c.: see art. ضب]. (TA.)

مَطْلُولٌ : see its fem., with ة, voce طَلٌّ. — Also Blood *made to go for nought, unretaliated, and uncompensated by a mulct;* (Ṣ, O, Ḳ;) and so ▼ طَلِيلٌ and ▼ مُطَلٌّ. (Ḳ.) — Also [or لَبَنٌ مَطْلُولٌ] *Pure milk with froth upon it, upon which water has been poured, and which one imagines to be good,* or *pleasant, whereas there is no goodness in it;* and so ▼ مَطْلُولَةٌ : or this latter, some say, signifies *a piece of skin soaked and softened* [for مَوْزُونَةٌ in my original, which I think a mistranscription, I read مَوْدُونَةٌ] *with pure milk, which they eat* [app. in a time of scarcity].

مَطْلُولَةٌ : see the next preceding paragraph.

طلب

1. طَلَبَهُ, (Ṣ, A, O, &c.,) aor. ـُ, (Mṣb,) inf. n. طَلَبٌ (Ṣ, A, MA, O, Mṣb, Ḳ &c.) and مَطْلَبٌ (A, MA, Mṣb) and طِلَابٌ and طِلَابَةٌ (A, MA) and طَلِبَةٌ (MA) and تَطْلَابٌ [which is of a measure denoting intensiveness]; (TA;) and ▼ اِطَّلَبَهُ; (Ṣ, A, O, Mṣb, Ḳ;) and ▼ تطلّبهُ; (A, Ḳ;) [but see this last below;] *He sought it, desired it, demanded it,* or *asked for it;* (MA;) [*he pursued it, pursued after it,* or *prosecuted it;*] *he sought, desired,* or *endeavoured, to find it and to get* or *take it:* (A, Ḳ, TA:) *and* طَلَبَ is also expl. as signifying اتبع [i. e. أَتْبَعَ *he followed in pursuit,* &c.]. (TA.) One says, أُطْلُبْ لِى شَيْئًا *Seek thou,* &c., *for me, a thing.* (Lḥ, TA.) And طَلَبَهُ مِنْهُ and إِلَيْهِ, inf. n. as above, *He sought it, desired it, demanded it,* or *asked for it, of him.* (MA.) And طَلَبَ إِلَىَّ means رَغِبَ [i. e. *He petitioned me,* or *made petition to me,* &c.]: (Ḳ, TA:) or طَلَبَ إِلَيْهِ means سَأَلَهُ [*he asked him*]: or [it means] طَلَبَهُ رَاغِبًا إِلَيْهِ [*he sought him, petitioning him*]; for it is generally held that طَلَبَ is not trans. by means of a prep., therefore they explain the like of this phrase as implicative. (MF, TA.) See also 4, in two places: and see 5. You say also, طَلَبَهُ بِحَقٍّ, meaning طَالَبَهُ, q. v. (Ḳ.) And طَلَبَ بِثَأْرِهِ and بِذَحْلِهِ [*He sought to obtain his blood-revenge,* or *retaliation;* and in like manner, طَلَبَ بِدَمِهِ]. (Ṣ and Mṣb in art. ذحل.) — [Hence,] one says also, السِّرَاجُ يَطْلُبُ أَنْ يَنْطَفِئَ ‡ [*The lamp,* or *lighted wick, is near,* or *about, to become extinguished*]; like as one says, جِدَارٌ يُرِيدُ أَنْ يَنْقَضَّ. (A.) ═ طَلِبَ, aor. ـَ, (O, Ḳ,) inf. n. طَلَبٌ, (TḲ,) *He,* or *it,* [accord. to the TḲ said of a man,] *was,* or *became, distant,* or *remote.* (O, Ḳ. [See also 4.])

2 : see 5.

3. طَالَبَهُ, inf. n. مُطَالَبَةٌ and طِلَابٌ, (Mṣb, Ḳ,) *He sought* or *demanded of him a thing* [*as being due to him;* i. e. *he sued* or *prosecuted him for it*]; (Mṣb;) *i. q.* ▼ طَلَبَهُ بِحَقٍّ [*he sought* or *demanded of him,* &c., *a right,* or *due*]: (Ḳ:) and you say, طالبهُ بِحَقٍّ لَهُ عَلَيْهِ [*he sought* or *demanded of him,* &c., *a thing due to him on his part*]. (A.) مُطَالَبَةٌ is used in relation to a real thing: [but it does not necessarily imply the justice of the act:] one says, طالب زَيْدٌ عَمْرًا بِالدَّرَاهِمِ [*Zeyd sought* or *demanded of 'Amr,* or *sued* or *prosecuted him for, the money*]. (Kull p. 349.) And طالبهُ بِالدَّيْنِ *He sought* or *demanded of him* [&c.] *the debt.* (MA.) And طالبهُ بِكَذَا, (Ṣ, O,) inf. n. مُطَالَبَةٌ, (Ṣ,) [*He sought or demanded of him,* &c., *such a thing;* or *he prosecuted him for such a thing,* as, for instance, blood, or mutilation, or a wound: see exs. voce خَبْلٌ.]

4. اطلبهُ *He performed,* or *accomplished, for him,* (Ṣ, A, O, Mṣb, TA,) *that which he sought,* or *demanded,* (Ṣ, A,* O, Mṣb,) or *the object of his want:* (TA:) or *he gave him that which he sought,* or *demanded.* (Ḳ.) A man said to the Prophet, أُطْلُبْ ▼ إِلَىَّ طَلِبَةً فَإِنِّى أُحِبُّ أَنْ أُطْلِبَكَهَا i. e. [*Ask thou of me*] *an object of want,* [*for I love*] *to perform it,* or *accomplish it, for thee.* (TA.) And one says, طَلَبَ ▼ إِلَىَّ فَأَطْلَبْتُهُ i. e. [*He asked of me* a thing] *and I performed,* or *accomplished, for him that which he sought,* or *demanded.* (TA.) And اطلبهُ الشَّىْءَ *He aided him,* or *helped him, to seek the thing.* (TA.) And أَطْلِبْنِى *Aid thou me to seek.* (Lḥ, TA.) — Also *He,* or *it,* (said of a man, Mṣb, and of poverty, A,) *necessitated his seeking,* or *demanding.* (Ṣ, A, O, Mṣb, Ḳ.) Thus it has two contr. significations. (Ṣ, O, Ḳ.) — And hence, (Ṣ, O,) أَطْلَبَ said of water, and of pasture, or herbage, (Ṣ, A, O,) &c., (Ṣ, O,) *It was distant,* or *remote,* (Ṣ, A, O,) *so as to be not attainable but by seeking,* (Ṣ, O,) or *so that it was sought.* (A.)

5. تطلّبهُ *He sought it,* or *demanded it, repeatedly,* or *time after time:* (Ṣ, O:) [*he made repeated,* or *successive, endeavours to obtain it,* or *to attain it: he prosecuted a search after it:*] or *he sought it diligently, studiously, sedulously,* or *earnestly;* syn. اِبْتِغَاءٌ: (Mṣb:) or *he sought, desired,* or *endeavoured, leisurely, to find it and to get* or *take it;* (O, TA;) and (TA) so ▼ طَلَّبَهُ, inf. n. تَطْلِيبٌ; (Ḳ, TA;) and ▼ طَلَبَهُ; (TA;) *from* [*various*] *places.* (O, TA.) — See also 1, first sentence.

7. انطلب لَهُ is quasi-pass. of طَلَبَهُ, and means *It* (an action [&c.]) *was,* or *became, suitable to him;* or *fit, meet,* or *proper, for him:* [as though it were sought, or desired, or desirable:] but they have been content to use اِنْبَغَى in the place of this verb. (Zj, TA in art. بغى. [يَنْبَغِى, in the Ḳur xix. 93, is expl. by يَنْطَلِبُ in the Ksh and in the Expos. of Bḍ.])

8 : see 1, first sentence.

طَلَبٌ : see طَلِبَةٌ, in two places: — and طَالِبٌ.

طَلَبٌ an inf. n. of 1 [q. v.]. (Ṣ, A, &c.) — See also طِلَابٌ, in two places. — And see طَلِبَةٌ.

طَلَبَةٌ *A far-extending journey:* (O, Ḳ:) and so ▼ سَفَرٌ طَلُوبٌ. (A.)

طِلْبَةٌ [*A mode,* or *manner, of seeking* &c.: an inf. n. of modality, like جِلْسَةٌ &c. — And] a subst from طَالَبَهُ: (Ḳ:) see طَلِبَةٌ, in three places. — أُمُّ طِلْبَةَ *The eagle.* (O, Ḳ.)

طَلِبَةٌ an inf. n. of طَلَبَهُ [q. v.]. (MA.) — [It generally signifies] *A thing that one seeks, desires, demands,* or *asks for; a thing that one seeks, desires,* or *endeavours, to find and to get* or *take; an object of quest,* or *desire;* (Ṣ, O, Mṣb, Ḳ;) as also ▼ طِلَابٌ, which is originally an inf. n. of طَالَبَهُ; (Mṣb;) and so ▼ طَلَبٌ; (Ḥar p. 560;) and ▼ طِلْبَةٌ and ▼ طَلَبٌ are substs. from طَالَبَهُ, (Ḳ,) signifying [the same, or] *a right,* or *due, sought,* or *demanded:* (TḲ:) and طَلِبَةٌ signifies also *an object of want,* or *need; a needful thing:* (TA:) its pl. is طَلِبَاتٌ. (Mṣb.) One says, لِى عِنْدَهُ ▼ طِلْبَةٌ [or طَلِبَةٌ] *I have an object of quest,* or *desire,* or *of want,* or *a right,* or *due, necessary to be sought,* or *demanded, of him.* (A.) And هِىَ طَلَبُ ▼ فُلَانٍ *She is the object of love of such a one;* as also ▼ طِلْبَتُهُ: (A, Ḳ:) or the former, (O,) or each, the latter mentioned by Lḥ, (TA,) means *she is the object of quest,* or *desire,* and *the object of love, of such a one.* (O, TA.) ═ And it is said on the authority of IAạr that طلبة [app., accord. to the context, طَلَبَةٌ] signifies *A company,* or *an assembly, of men.* (TA.)

طِلَابٌ : see the next preceding paragraph.

طَلُوبٌ, of which the pl. is طُلُبٌ, (Ḳ, TA,) and, as is said in the Mṣb, [but not in my copy of it,] طُلْبٌ; (TA;) and ▼ طَلَّابٌ, of which the pl. is طَلَّابُونَ; and ▼ طَلِيبٌ, of which the pl. is طُلَبَآءُ; *Seeking, desiring,* or *demanding;* or *seeking, desiring,* or *endeavouring, to find and to get* or *take;* (Ḳ, TA;) *much,* or *often;* all are intensive in signification. (TA.) — And بِئْرٌ طَلُوبٌ (O, TA) [and] ▼ طَلِيبٌ (thus in a copy of the A) *A well of which the water is remote:* (A, O, TA:) pl. of the former آبَارٌ طُلُبٌ. (O, TA.) See also طَلَبَةٌ.

طَلِيبٌ : see the next preceding paragraph, in two places.

طَلَّابٌ : see طَلُوبٌ.

طَالِبٌ *Seeking, desiring,* or *demanding;* or *seeking, desiring,* or *endeavouring, to find and to get* or *take;* or *a seeker,* &c.: (Mṣb,* Ḳ, TA:) [and used for طَالِبُ عِلْمٍ *a student of science* or *knowledge:*] pl. طُلَّابٌ and طَلَبَةٌ (Mṣb, Ḳ, TA) and طَلَبٌ (Ḳ) and طَالِبُونَ (Mṣb) and أَطْلَابٌ [a pl. of pauc., like أَصْحَابٌ,] (A) and ↓ طَلَبٌ, (Ṣ, A, O, Ḳ,) or this last, as is said in the M, is [properly speaking] a quasi-pl. n., (TA,) or, (Mgh, TA,) as IAth says, (TA,) it is either a pl. of طَالِبٌ or an inf. n. used as such, (Mgh, TA,) for أَهْلُ الطَّلَبِ: (TA:) fem., applied to a woman, طَالِبَةٌ; of which the pl. is طَالِبَاتٌ and طَوَالِبُ. (Mṣb.) You say, هُوَ طَالِبٌ لِلشَّىْءِ *He is a seeker*, &c., *of the thing*. (TA.) And هٰؤُلَآءِ أَطْلَابُهُمْ and ↓ طَلَبُ أَعْدَائِهِمْ *These are* the troops that are *the seekers* [or *pursuers*] *of their enemies*. (A.) And هُوَ طِلْبُ ↓ نِسَآءٍ, (A, Ḳ,) with kesr, (Ḳ,) *He is a seeker*, or *desirer*, *of women*: (A, Ḳ:) pl. أَطْلَابٌ and طِلَبَةٌ. (Ḳ.)

مَطْلَبٌ *A place*, (Mṣb, KL,) or *time*, (KL,) *of seeking*: (Mṣb, KL:) [and so ↓ مَطْلِبٌ:] pl. مَطَالِبُ. (KL.) [And particularly applied to *A place in which treasure is buried and sought*. And *A place where anything remarkable is to be sought*, or *looked for*, *in a book*.] — [And hence, † *A person from whom one seeks a thing*.] لَيْسَ لِى مَطْلَبٌ سِوَاكَ † [*I have none from whom to seek the accomplishment of my desires but Thee*] occurs in a trad. respecting prayer. (TA.) — See also مَطْلُوبٌ. — It is also an inf. n. of 1 [q. v.]. (A, MA, Mṣb.)

مُطْلِبٌ, applied to water, and to pasture, or herbage, *Distant*, or *remote*, (Ṣ, A, O,) *so as not to be attainable but by seeking*, (Ṣ, O,) or *so that it is sought*: (A:) or, applied to pasture, or herbage, *distant*, or *remote*: and, applied to water, *distant*, or *remote*, *from the pasture* or *herbage*: or *between which and the pasture*, or *herbage*, *is twice the space termed a* ميل, (Ḳ, TA,) or *thrice that space*, the ميل being *the space from one* عَلَم [or *sign of the way*] *to another*; (TA;) or *a day*, or *two days*, (Ḳ, TA,) i. e. *a day's journey*, or *two days' journey*; in the latter case being termed مُطْلِبٌ إِبِلٍ [i. e. *distant to be sought of camels*]. (TA.) It is also applied to other things: a poet says,

• أَهَاجَكَ بَرْقٌ آخِرَ اللَّيْلِ مُطْلِبُ •

[*Has distant lightning, in the latter part of the night, excited thee?*]. (Ṣ, O.)

مَطْلُوبٌ *Sought*, *desired*, or *demanded*; and so ↓ مَطْلَبٌ [but app. as an epithet in which the quality of a subst. is predominant, and used in the sense of طَلِبَةٌ]. (KL.)

مَطْلِبٌ: see مَطْلَبٌ.

طلح

1. طَلِحَتِ الإِبِلُ, (Ṣ, A,) [aor. ـَ,] inf. n. طَلَحٌ, (TA,) *The camels had a complaint* (Ṣ, A) *of their bellies* (Ṣ) *from eating of the trees called* طَلْح. (Ṣ, A. [But see إِبِلٌ طَلِحَةٌ.]) — And طَلِحَ, aor. ـَ, (Ḳ,) inf. n. as above, (TḲ,) *He* (a man, TḲ,) *was*, or *became*, *empty*, or *void of food*, *in his belly*; as also طَلُحَ, like غَنِىَ. (Ḳ.) = طَلَحَ, (Ṣ, M, A, Ḳ,) aor. ـَ, inf. n. طَلْحٌ and طَلَاحَةٌ, (M, Ḳ,) said of a camel, (Ṣ, M, A, Ḳ,) *He was*, or *became*, *lean*, or *emaciated*, *by reason of fatigue*, or *of disease*: (A:) or *fatigued*, or *wearied*: (ISk, Ṣ, Ḳ:) or *injured*, or *hurt*, *by fatigue*: (AZ, T, TA:) or *he was*, or *became*, *fatigued*, *and fell down by reason of travel*: (M, TA:) or طَلِحَ, aor. ـَ, inf. n. طَلَحٌ; and طَلُحَ, aor. ـُ, inf. n. طَلْحٌ; *he was*, or *became*, *fatigued*: or *lean*, *by reason of fatigue*, or *of disease*. (MA.) — And طَلُحَ, inf. n. طَلَاحٌ, ‡ *He* (a man) *was*, or *became*, *bad*, *corrupt*, or *vicious*. (A, L. [See طَلَاحٌ below.]) = طَلَحَهُ, aor. ـَ, [inf. n. طَلْحٌ,] *He*, or *it*, (a man, MA, Mṣb, or journeying, A,) *rendered him lean*, or *emaciated him*; (A, MA, Mṣb;) namely, a camel: (A, Mṣb:) [or] *he fatigued him*; (MA, Ḳ;) i. e., a camel; (Ṣ, Ḳ;) and (Ḳ) so ↓ اطلحه; and ↓ طلّحه, (Ṣ, Ḳ,) inf. n. of the latter تَطْلِيحٌ. (TA.)

2: see the last sentence above. — [Hence, app.,] طلّح عَلَيْهِ, (A, Ḳ,) inf. n. تَطْلِيحٌ, (Ḳ,) ‡ *He importuned him*, (A, Ḳ,) i. e., his debtor, *so that he wearied him*. (A.)

4: see 1, last sentence.

طَلْحٌ, [a coll. gen. n.,] (Ṣ, A, Mṣb, Ḳ, &c.,) and طِلَاحٌ; (Ṣ, A, Ḳ;) the latter said to be pl. of طَلْحَةٌ, (TA,) which is the n. un. of طَلْحٌ, (Ṣ,) or, accord. to Sb, the pl. of طَلْحَةٌ is طُلُوحٌ, like as صُخُورٌ is pl. of صَخْرَةٌ; and طِلَاحٌ also; and the pl. of طَلْحٌ is أَطْلَاحٌ; (M;) [The *acacia*, or *mimosa*, *gummifera*; an appellation applicable also to the سَنْط, which produces the gum-arabic: (see صَمْغٌ:) the former tree is termed by Forskål (Flora Ægypt. Arab. p. cxxiv.) "mimosa gummifera;" but it is more commonly termed an "acacia:" its pods are termed غُلُفٌ, q. v.:] *a species of large trees*, (Ṣ, Ḳ,) *of the kind called* عِضَاه; (Ṣ, Mṣb;) *growing in El-Ḥijáz* [*and Egypt and Nubia and other countries*]; *the fruit of which is like that of the* سَمُرَة; *having curved thorns*: *the places in which it grows are the interiors of valleys*; *and it is that species of the* عضاه *which is the largest in its thorns, and the hardest in respect of its wood, and the best in respect of its gum*: Lth describes it as above, and says that it is *the same as the* أُمُّ غَيْلَانَ [and the like is said in the A]: ISh says that it is *a tall tree, affording a shade in which men and camels repose, with few leaves, long and large branches, with many thorns,* [*more*] *than the prickles of the palm-tree, and a great trunk, which a man's arm cannot embrace*; *the same as the* ام غيلان; *and grows in the mountains*: AḤn says that *it is, of the trees called* عضاه, *the largest, and that which has most leaves, and the greenest, and has thick and long thorns, but these are of the least hurtful of thorns, producing no heat in the foot*; *it has a fruit* (بَرَمَة) *of pleasant odour*; *and there is not among the trees called* عضاه *any that produces more gum than it, nor any more bulky*; *and it grows only in rugged, hard, fertile ground*. (TA.) By طلح in the Ḳur lvi. 28 may be meant the trees called ام غيلان, because they have a blossom of a very pleasant odour. (Zj.) [But see below.] — طَلْحٌ signifies also *Banana-trees*; syn. شَجَرُ المَوْزِ; and is said [by some] to have this meaning in the Ḳur lvi. 28: (Zj, T, TA:) or *i. q.* مَوْزٌ [which some expl. as meaning the trees above-mentioned; but others as meaning the *fruit of those trees*]: (Mṣb, Ḳ:) this, however, is said to be unknown in the [classical] language. (TA.) — And *i. q.* طَلْعٌ [generally meaning The *spadix of the palm-tree*; but sometimes the *spathe thereof*]: (Ḳ:) a dial. var. of the latter word: (Ṣ:) mentioned by ISk among words formed by the substitution of one letter for another: and this meaning, also, it is said [by some] to have in the Ḳur lvi. 28. (TA.) = And *Remains of turbid water in a watering-trough* or *tank*. (Ḳ.) = And *Having the belly void of food*. (Ḳ.) — See also طَلِيحٌ.

طِلْحٌ The *tick*; syn. قُرَادٌ; (Ṣ, A, Ḳ;) sometimes applied thereto; (Ṣ;) as also ↓ طَلِيحٌ: (Ṣ, Ḳ:) or *a large tick*. (TA. [See حَمْنَانٌ.]) — [Hence,] طِلْحُ مَالٍ ‡ *One who keeps to camels*, or *cattle*, *and to the care of them, like as cleaves the* طلح, i. e. *tick*: (A:) *a manager*, *tender*, or *superintendent*, *of camels*, or *cattle*; or *a good pastor thereof*. (Ḳ.) — And طِلْحُ نِسَآءٍ ‡ *One who follows*, or *goes after*, *women* (Ḳ, TA) *much*, or *often*. (TA.) — And طِلْحٌ is also expl. as signifying *A pastor fatigued*, or *wearied*: (Ḳ, TA:) and [its pl.] طُلُحٌ, as signifying [simply] *pastors*. (L.) El-Ḥoṭei-ah says, after mentioning certain camels and their pastors,

• إِذَا نَامَ طِلْحٌ أَشْعَثُ الرَّأْسِ خَلْفَهَا •
• هَدَاهُ لَهَا أَنْفَاسُهَا وَزَفِيرُهَا •

When a pastor, dusty and shaggy or *matted in the hair of the head, sleeps behind them,* [and they become lost to him,] *their breathing and their vehement respiration* occasioned by the fulness of their bellies *guides him to them*, so that he finds them, even if they be distant. (Ṣ,* L.) — See also طَلِيحٌ, in four places.

طَلَحٌ (thus correctly written, not طَلْحٌ as in [some of the copies of] the Ṣ, TA) *Enjoyment of a life of ease and plenty*. (Ṣ, Ḳ.)

طَلِحٌ an epithet applied to a camel. (A.) You say إِبِلٌ طَلِحَةٌ and طَلَاحَى [the latter being the pl.] *Camels having a complaint* (Ṣ, A, Ḳ) *of* their bellies (Ṣ, Ḳ) *from eating of the trees called* طَلْح: (Ṣ, A, Ḳ:) but [the meaning seems to be, *from eating thereof immoderately*, for] Aboo-Sa'eed disapproves of the phrase ابل طلاحى as meaning *camels that have eaten of the* طلح [*and become disordered thereby*, though it appears from what is said in art. عضه that camels are sometimes disordered by eating of any of the trees called عِضَاه], asserting it to signify *camels that are fatigued*, or *wearied*; for [he says that] the طلح do not disorder camels, but are wholesome food for them. (TA.) See also طَلِيحٌ, in two places. — And أَرْضٌ طَلِحَةٌ *Land abounding with the trees called* طَلْح. (Ḳ.)

طَلْحَةٌ n. un. of طَلْحٌ [q. v.]. (Ṣ.) — أُمُّ طَلْحَةَ *The louse.* (TA.)

طَلْحِيَّةٌ meaning *A piece of paper* is a post-classical word. (Ḳ.)

طَلَاحٌ, as an attribute of a man, ‡ *Badness, corruptness*, or *viciousness*: (A:) *contr. of* صَلَاحٌ. (Ṣ, L, Ḳ.)

طَلِيحٌ, (A, Mgh, Mṣb,) of the measure فَعِيلٌ in the sense of the measure مَفْعُولٌ, (Mgh, Mṣb,) *Rendered lean*, or *emaciated*, (A, Mgh, Mṣb,) applied to a camel; (A, Mṣb;) as also ↓ طَلِحٌ, (A,) or ↓ طِلْحٌ, (Ḳ,) and ↓ طَالِحٌ, so applied, *by reason of fatigue*, or *of disease*. (A.) Also, (Ṣ, Mgh, Ḳ,) applied to a camel, and ↓ طِلْحٌ, (Ṣ, Ḳ,) the latter, (Ṣ, MF,) and the former likewise, (MF,) applied to the male and to the female of camels and of other animals, (Ṣ, MF,) and ↓ طَلْحٌ, (Ḳ,) and ↓ طَلِحٌ, (L, TA,) *Fatigued*: (Ṣ, Mgh, Ḳ, TA:) and in like manner, applied to a she-camel, طَلِيحَةٌ and ↓ طِلْحَةٌ, (Ḳ, in the CḲ طَلْحَةٌ,) but the forms commonly known of these two epithets thus applied are without ة, because each has the signification of a pass. part. n., (MF,) and ↓ طَالِحٌ: (IAạr, Ḳ:) the pls. are طُلَّحٌ and طَلَائِحُ, (Ṣ, Ḳ,) [both pls. of طَلِيحٌ,] meaning *fatigued*, or *jaded, and rendered lean, by travel*, (Ṣ,) and طَلْحَى, which last is [said by SM to be] anomalous, because [he holds that] it has the meaning of an act. part. n., [app. on the ground that some expl. طَلِيحٌ as syn. with مُعْيٍ and تَعِبٌ,] (TA,) and طُلُحٌ is another pl., [app. of the second and third and fourth of the sings. mentioned above,] signifying *fatigued*; (L, TA;) and أَطْلَاحٌ is pl. [of pauc.] of طِلْحٌ. (Ṣ.) One says نَاقَةٌ طَلِيحُ أَسْفَارٍ meaning *A she-camel jaded, and rendered lean, by journeys*: (T, Ṣ:) and طَلِيحُ سَفَرٍ, and ↓ طِلْحُ سَفَرٍ. (IAạr, TA.) رَاكِبُ النَّاقَةِ طَلِيحَانِ means *The rider of the she-camel and the she-camel are both fatigued*, or *jaded*: (L, Ḳ:) for رَاكِبُ النَّاقَةِ وَالنَّاقَةُ طَلِيحَانِ: or for رَاكِبُ النَّاقَةِ أَحَدُ الطَّلِيحَيْنِ. (L.) — See also طِلْحٌ.

إِبِلٌ طِلَاحِيَّةٌ and طُلَاحِيَّةٌ, (Ṣ, Ḳ,) the latter anomalous, (Ṣ,) or the latter is a dial. var. of the former, which is not a rel. n. from the pl. طِلَاحٌ, because, when a rel. n. is formed from a pl., the pl. is reduced to its sing. form, unless it is used as a name of a particular thing, (from a marginal note in copies of the Ṣ, [see also Ḥam pp. 791-2,]) *Camels feeding upon the trees called* طِلَاح [or طَلْح]. (Ṣ, Ḳ.)

طَالِحٌ: see طَلِيحٌ, in two places. — Also, as an epithet applied to a man, ‡ *Bad, corrupt*, or *vicious*; (A, L;) *in whom is no good*: (L:) *contr. of* صَالِحٌ. (Ṣ, L.)

مُطَلِّحٌ † One *who acts wrongfully, unjustly*, or *injuriously*, فِى المَالِ [*with respect to property*, or *camels*, or *cattle*]. (Az, L.) — And, accord. to Az, One *who breathes hard*, or *emits the voice with a moaning sound*, فِى الكَلَامِ [*in speaking*]; syn. نَثَّاثٌ [but the first letter in this word is written in the L without any diacritical point; so that the word may perhaps be بَهَّاتٌ, meaning *a great*, or *frequent, calumniator, slanderer*, or *false-accuser*: see art. بهت]. (L, TA.)

طلس

1. طَلَسَهُ, (Ṣ, M, A, Ḳ,) aor. ـِ, (Ḳ, MṢ, O, TA, but in a copy of the A, ـُ,) inf. n. طَلْسٌ; (Ṣ, M, A, Ḳ;) and ↓ طَلَّسَهُ, (M, A, Ḳ,) inf. n. تَطْلِيسٌ; (A;) *He obliterated it*, or *effaced it*, namely, a writing; (Ṣ, O, Ḳ;) *i. q.* طَرَسَهُ: (M:) or *he obliterated it*, or *effaced it*, namely a writing, [*so far as*] *to mar*, or *spoil, its characters*; thus differing from طَرَّسَهُ, which signifies "he obliterated it, or effaced it, well." (T, A.) — [Hence,] طَلَسَ بَصَرَهُ ‡ *He took away*, or *destroyed, his sight*: (A, TA:) in the Ḳ [and O] طَلَسَ بَصَرُهُ *his sight went away*, or *became destroyed*; on the authority of Ibn-'Abbád. (TA.) — طَلِسَ, aor. ـَ, inf. n. طَلَسٌ, *It* (a garment, or piece of cloth,) *was*, or *became, old and worn-out*. (IKṭṭ.) — طَلِسَ, aor. ـَ, inf. n. طَلَسٌ; and طَلُسَ, aor. ـُ, inf. n. طُلْسَةٌ; *He*, or *it, was*, or *became, of a dusty colour, inclining to black*. (IKṭṭ: the inf. ns., only, are mentioned in the M.)

2: see above, first sentence.

5. تطلّس *It* (a writing) *became obliterated*, or *effaced*. (Ṣ.) [See also 7.] — تطلّس بِطَيْلَسَانٍ, and ↓ تَطَيْلَسَ, *He clad*, or *attired, himself with a* طَيْلَسَان. (M, TA.) [The former verb is used by El-Hemedhánee transitively, as meaning, *He put on*, or *made use of*, a napkin *as a* طيلسان: (see De Sacy's Chrest. Arabe, sec. ed., vol. iii., p. 90 of the Arabic text:) but perhaps this usage is only post-classical.]

7. انطلس أَثَرُهُ *His trace*, or *track*, or *footsteps, became concealed*, or *unapparent*: said of a beast: (Ibn-'Abbád, TṢ, O, TA:) أُمْرُهُ, in the copies of the Ḳ, is a mistake. (TA.) [See also 5.]

Q. Q. 2. تَطَيْلَسَ: see 5.

طِلْسٌ *Black*; as also ↓ طَيْلَسَانٌ: (IAạr, Az, TA:) accord. to the O and Ḳ, the former signifies *a black* طَيْلَسَان; but this is a mistake. (TA.)

طِلْسٌ *i. q.* طِرْسٌ: (Ṣ in art. طرس, M, Mṣb, TA:) i. e., (TA,) *A written paper* or *the like*; syn. صَحِيفَةٌ: (Ḳ, TA:) or *one of which the writing has been obliterated*, or *effaced*, (A, Ḳ, TA,) *but not well obliterated*; thus differing from طِرْسٌ, accord. to the T: (TA:) pl. طُلُوسٌ. (Mṣb, TA.) See طِرْسٌ. — Also The *skin of the thigh of the camel* (T, M, Ḳ) *when the hair has fallen off*. (T, Ḳ.) — See also أَطْلَسُ, in three places.

طَلِيسٌ, of the measure فَعِيلٌ in the sense of the measure مَفْعُولٌ, † *Having the eye blinded*: in the O and Ḳ erroneously said to be طِلِّيسٌ, like سِكِّيتٌ: but in the Tekmileh, correctly, طَلِيسٌ, like أَمِيرٌ. (TA.)

طَلَّاسَةٌ *A piece of rag with which one wipes a tablet* (A, Ḳ, TA) *upon which is writing, and with which the writing is obliterated*, or *effaced*. (A, TA.)

طَيْلَسٌ }
طَالَسَانٌ } see طَيْلَسَانٌ.

طَيْلَسَانٌ (El-Fárábee, Ṣ, M, Mgh, O, Mṣb, Ḳ) and طَيْلِسَانٌ, (M, O, Ḳ,) the latter form used by some, (El-Fárábee, Mṣb,) or by the vulgar, (Ṣ,) and disallowed by Aṣ, (M, Mṣb,) and طَيْلُسَانٌ, all these three forms being mentioned by 'Iyáḍ and others, (Ḳ,) [accord. to the TA, following Lth; but the words of Lth, as cited in the TA, and in the O, rather signify that, if, instead of طَيْلِسَانٌ, with kesr to the ل, one said طَيْلُسَانٌ, with ḍamm to the ل, like خَيْزُرَانٌ and خَيْسُمَانٌ, it would be more agreeable with analogy; and the like is said in the Mṣb, as on the authority of Az;] and ↓ طَيْلَسٌ (M, Mgh, O, Ḳ) and ↓ طَالَسَانٌ; (M, TA;) arabicized words, (Ṣ, Mgh, Mṣb, Ḳ,) from the Pers., (Ṣ, Mṣb,) originally تَالَشَانٌ, (as in some copies of the Ḳ,) or تَالَسَانٌ; (as in other copies of the Ḳ, and in some copies of the T, and thus written by El-Urmawee, as is said in the TA, and thus written also in the Mgh;) differently expl. by different persons; (TA;) [app. accord. to the fashions of different times and countries;] accord. to some, (TA,) *A certain kind of* كِسَآء: (M, TA:) or *a certain article of apparel worn by the* عَجَم [*Persians* or *other foreigners*], (Mgh, Mṣb,) *of a round form, and black*; accord. to the "Jemạ et-Tefáreeḳ," *having its woof and warp both of wool*: (Mgh:) or *a* كِسَآء, *of a dark*, or *an ashy, dust-colour*, (أَخْضَر,) *worn by persons of distinction*: (Esh-Shereeshee, in Ḥar, p. 238:) [see also بَتٌّ, and سَاجٌ: El-Maḳreezee mentions a kind of طيلسان

having a round piece cut out from the middle of it (مُقَوَّر) worn by the Egyptian Wezeer, and called, in his time, (the 14th and 15th centuries of our era,) طَرْحَة: (see this word: and see De Sacy's Chrest. Arabe, sec. ed., ii. 267—269; and Dozy's Dict. des Noms des Vêtements chez les Arabes, 278—90:) it seems to have resembled our academic hood, of which it was perhaps the original: the term طيلسان is now commonly applied to *an oblong piece of drapery*, or *a scarf*, or *an oblong shawl, worn in such a manner that one end hangs down upon the side of the bosom, the middle part being turned over the head and under the chin, and the other end being thrown over the shoulder, and hanging down upon the back*: this is worn by many of the professional learned men in winter, in Arabian countries: it is also used in the sense of the word عَذَبَة, meaning *an end of a turban, when made to hang down between the shoulders*: see عَذَبٌ:] the pl. (of طَيْلَسَانٌ and طَيْلِسَانٌ and طَيْلَسٌ, M) is طَيَالِسَةٌ, (Ṣ, M, A, Mgh, Mṣb, Ḳ,) in which the ة is added because it is a foreign word, (Ṣ, M, Ḳ,) and طَيَالِسُ; (M, A;) or the latter is pl. of طَيْلَسٌ: (TA:) I do not know (says ISd) any pl. of طَالَسَانٌ: (M, TA:) it is not allowable to form an abbreviation of طَيْلِسَانٌ, with kesr to the ل, as a compellation, because there is no instance of the measure فَيْعِلٌ, with kesr to the ع, except in infirm words such as سَيِّدٌ and مَيِّتٌ. (Ṣ.) Hence the expression, (Mgh,) يَا ٱبْنَ ٱلطَّيْلَسَانِ, [lit., *O son of the ṭeylesán*,] meaning, *O 'Ajamee*, (A, Mgh,) or *Aajamee*, (Ḳ,) [i. e., *Persian*, or *foreigner*,] used in reviling another; (Mgh, Ḳ;) for the عَجَم are those who [most commonly] attire themselves with the طيلسان. (TA.) ═ See also طَلْسٌ.

أَطْلَسُ *Old and worn-out*; (Ṣ, M, Ḳ;) applied to a garment, or piece of cloth: (M, Ḳ:) as also ▼ طِلْسٌ; pl. أَطْلَاسٌ. (Ṣ.) You say, رَجُلٌ أَطْلَسُ الثَّوْبِ *A man whose garment is old and worn-out*. (Ṣ.) — A dirhem [*of which the impression is obliterated*;] *having no impression*. (Mṣb, voce مَمْسُوحٌ.) — A wolf *whose hair has fallen off by degrees*; (Az, TA;) as also ▼ طِلْسٌ: (IAạr, A, Ḳ:) or a wolf *of a dusty colour inclining to blackness*; (Ṣ, M, A, Ḳ;) and anything of that colour; (Ṣ, Ḳ;) whether a garment or any other thing: (TA:) fem. طَلْسَآءُ: (M:) pl. طُلْسٌ. (A.) — A man *having little hair upon the side of the cheek*; pl. طُلْسٌ: or *i. q.* كَوْسَجٌ [q. v.]: of the the dial. of El-Yemen. (TA.) — *Dirty*, or *filthy*; as also ▼ طِلْسٌ: (Ḳ:) the latter applied to a garment, or piece of cloth, (Ḳ, TA,) *in the colour of which is a dusty hue*: (TA:) and طَلْسَآءُ *a dirty rag*. (O.) — A man ‡ *dirty*, or *filthy, in apparel*: likened to a wolf in respect of the dusty hue of his clothes: (M:) or *black and dirty*. (O.) — [Hence,] † A man *who is accused of foul, or evil, conduct*; (Sh, O, Ḳ;) and so أَطْلَسُ الثَّوْبَيْنِ, an expression used by Ows Ibn-Hajar. (Sh, O.) — ‡ *Black, as an Abyssinian and the like*: (O, Ḳ:) as being likened in colour to a wolf. (TA.) [See also طَلْسٌ.] — ‡ *A thief*: (O, Ḳ:) because of his evil nature, (TA,) being likened to a wolf. (O, TA.) ═ [*Satin*; so called in the present day;] a garment, or piece of cloth, *of woven silk*: [app. because of its smoothness:] but this is not [of the classical] Arabic: pl. طُلْسٌ. (TA.) ═ فَلَكُ الأَطْلَسِ: see أَثِيرٌ, last sentence.

طلسم

Q. 1: طَلْسَمَ *He* (a man) *made his face to be displeasing*, or *odious*; (M, L, TA;) *he contracted it*; or *made it austere*, or *morose*: and so طَرْمَسَ, and طَلْمَسَ, (L, TA,) and طَرْسَمَ. (TA in art. طلمس.) — And *He* (a man) *bent down his head*; or *lowered his eyes, looking towards the ground*; or *was*, or *became, silent*; syn. أَطْرَقَ: and so طَرْسَمَ. (Ṣ in art. طرسم; and TA.) — [And, accord. to Golius, *He receded*, or *drew back*, from fight; followed by عَنْ: (one of the significations assigned in the Ḳ to طَرْسَمَ:) he mentions this as on the authority of J: perhaps he found it in a copy of the Ṣ in art. طرمس (in which الطَّرْمَسَةُ is expl. as meaning الاِنْقِبَاضُ and النُّكُوصُ), or in some other art. of that work in which I do not remember to have seen it. ═ Also *He sculptured, engraved*, or *inscribed*, a thing *with talismanic devices* or *characters*. And *He charmed*, or *guarded*, or *preserved, by means of a talisman*. See what follows.]

طِلَسْمٌ, or, accord. to MF, طِلَّسْمٌ, [also written طَلْسَمٌ, and طِلَّسَمٌ, and طَلَّسْمٌ, and طِلِّسْمٌ, and طَلَّسَمٌ,] said by MF to be a Pers., or foreign, word; [perhaps from a late usage of the Greek τέλεσμα;] but [SM says] in my opinion it is Arabic; a name for *A concealed secret*; [i. e. *a mystery*: hence our word *talisman*: accord. to common modern usage, it signifies *mystical devices or characters, astrological* or *of some other magical kind*: and *a seal, an image*, or *some other thing, upon which such devices*, or *characters, are engraved* or *inscribed*; *contrived for the purpose of preserving from enchantment* or *from a particular accident* or *from a variety of evils*, or *to protect a treasure with which it is deposited*, or (generally by its being rubbed) *to procure the presence and services of a Jinnee*, &c.:] pl. طَلَاسِمُ (TA) [and طِلَسْمَاتٌ or طِلَّسْمَاتٌ &c.].

طلع

1. طَلَعَتِ ٱلشَّمْسُ, (Ṣ, O, Mṣb, Ḳ,) aor. ـُ [notwithstanding the faucial letter], (Mṣb, JM, TA,) inf. n. طُلُوعٌ and مَطْلَعٌ and مَطْلِعٌ, (Ṣ, O, Mṣb, Ḳ,) the second and third both used as inf. ns., and also as ns. of place [and of time], (Ṣ, O, Ḳ,) but the former of them is preferable on the ground of analogy as an inf. n., and the latter as a n. of place (Fr, O) or of time, (Zj, O,) *The sun rose*, (MA,) or *appeared*; (Ḳ;) and in like manner طَلَعَ is said of the moon, (TA,) and of a star, or an asterism; (Ṣ, O, Ḳ;) and so ▼ اِطَّلَعَ; (Ḳ;) [and ▼ أَطْلَعَ, for] أَطْلَعَتِ الثُّرَيَّا means طَلَعَت [i. e. *The Pleiades rose*], as in a verse of El-Kumeyt [in which, however, the verb may, consistently with the metre, be a mistranscription for اِطَّلَعَتْ]; (IB, TA); and أَطْلَعَ is syn. with طَلَعَ in the saying of Ru-beh,

* كَأَنَّهُ كَوْكَبُ غَيْمٍ أَطْلَعَا *

[*As though it*, or *he, were a star* in the midst *of clouds, that had risen*]. (TA.) One says also, آتِيكَ كُلَّ يَوْمٍ طَلَعَتْهُ الشَّمْسُ, meaning طَلَعَتْ فِيهِ [i. e. *I will come to thee every day in which the sun rises*]: and it is said in a prayer, طَلَعَتِ الشَّمْسُ وَلَا تَطْلُعُ بِنَفْسِ أَحَدٍ مِنَّا [meaning *The sun has risen, and may it not have risen with the soul of any one of us*]; i. e., may not any one of us have died with its rising: the future being put in the place of the preterite. (TA.) — And طَلَعَ is said of anything that appears to one from the upper part [of a thing, or that comes up out of a thing and appears]. (Mgh, Mṣb.) It is said in the Ksh that الطُّلُوعُ signifies *The appearing by rising*, or *by becoming elevated*. (TA.) One says, طَلَعَتْ سِنُّ الصَّبِىِّ ‡ *The tooth of the child showed its point*. (Ḳ, TA.) And طَلَعَ الزَّرْعُ, [aor. ـُ,] inf. n. طُلُوعٌ, ‡ *The seed-produce began to come up, and showed its sprouting forth*: (T, TA:) and ▼ أَطْلَعَ الزَّرْعُ ‡ *The seed-produce appeared*: (TA:) and ▼ أَطْلَعَ نَبْتُ الأَرْضِ † *The plants*, or *herbage, of the earth*, or *land, came forth*: (Mgh:) and ▼ أَطْلَعَ الشَّجَرُ ‡ *The trees put forth their leaves*. (TA.) And طَلَعَ النَّخْلُ, (O, Ḳ,) aor. ـُ, inf. n. طُلُوعٌ; (TA;) and (O, Ḳ) ▼ أَطْلَعَ; (Zj, Ṣ, Mgh, O, Ḳ;) or أَطْلَعَتِ النَّخْلَةُ; (Mṣb;) † *The palm-trees*, or *-tree, put forth the* طَلْع [q. v.]; (Zj, Ṣ, Mgh, O, Mṣb, Ḳ;) as also ▼ طلّع, (L, Ḳ, TA,) inf. n. تَطْلِيعٌ. (L, TA. [These verbs, in this sense, are app. derived from the subst. طَلْعٌ; but this is obviously from طَلَعَ.]) — One says also, مَلَأْتُ لَهُ القَدَحَ حَتَّى يَكَادَ يَطْلُعُ مِنْ نَوَاحِيهِ [*I filled for him the drinking-vessel until it nearly overflowed from its sides*]. (TA.) And ▼ تَطَلَّعَ المَآءُ فِى الإِنَآءِ † *The water in the vessel poured forth* [or *overflowed*] *from its sides*. (TA.) — And طَلَعَ الجَبَلَ, (Mgh, Mṣb, Ḳ,) aor. ـُ, (TA,) inf. n. طُلُوعٌ, (Mṣb, TA,) ‡ *He ascended upon the mountain*; (Mgh, Mṣb, Ḳ, TA;) the prep. [عَلَى] being suppressed; (Mgh;) as also طَلِعَ, with kesr; (Ḳ;) and ▼ اِطَّلَعَ الجَبَلَ signifies the same as طَلَعَهُ: (TA: [see also مُطَّلَعٌ, in art. ضلع:]) accord. to ISk, one says, طَلِعْتُ الجَبَلَ, with kesr, meaning † *I ascended upon the mountain*; (Ṣ, O;) but others say, طَلَعْتُ, with fet-ḥ. (O.) And ‡ *He ascended the mountain:* (TA:) [or] طَلَعْتُ فِى الجَبَلِ means † *I ascended the mountain.* (Mṣb. [See also another explanation of this latter phrase in what follows.]) — And طَلَعَ عَلَيْنَا, aor. ـُ and ـَ; and ▼ اِطَّلَعَ; † *He* (a man) *came to us;* (Ḳ;) and *came upon us suddenly,* or *at unawares:* (TA:) and طَلَعَ عَنْهُمْ *he became absent,* or *absented himself,* or *departed, from them:* (Ḳ:) or طَلَعَ عَلَى القَوْمِ *he came forth upon the people,* or *party:* and *he looked upon them:* (MA:) accord. to ISk, طَلَعْتُ عَلَى القَوْمِ means *I came to the people,* or *party:* and طَلَعْتُ عَنْهُمْ *I became absent,* or *absented myself,* or *departed, from them:* (Ṣ, O:) and ▼ أَطْلَعْتُ عَلَيْهِمْ signifies the same as طَلَعْتُ: (O:) and طَلَعْتُ عَلَيْهِمْ has the same meaning [also] as طَلَعْتُ عَنْهُمْ expl. above, accord. to ISk; عَلَى being put in the place of عَن: accord. to AZ [likewise], طَلَعْتُ عَلَى القَوْمِ, inf. n. طُلُوعٌ, means *I became absent from the people,* or *party, so that they did not see me:* and also *I advanced,* or *approached, towards them, so that they saw me:* thus having two contr. meanings: and accord. to Az, the Arabs said, طَلَعْتُ فِى الجَبَلِ, inf. n. طُلُوعٌ, as meaning *I retired,* or *went back, into the mountain, so that my companion did not see me:* [see another explanation of this phrase in what precedes:] and طَلَعْتُ عَنْ صَاحِبِى, inf. n. طُلُوعٌ, *I retired,* or *went back, from my companion:* and طَلَعْتُ عَنْ صَاحِبِى [in which عَنْ seems to be evidently a mistranscription for عَلَى] *I advanced,* or *approached, towards my companion.* (TA.) [In all of these phrases, طَلَعَ and طَلَعْتُ may be correctly rendered *He,* and *I, came forth,* or *went forth.* And hence,] it is said in a prov., هٰذِهِ يَمِينٌ قَدْ طَلَعَتْ فِى المَخَارِمِ [expl. in art. خرم, voce مَخْرِمٌ]. (AZ, TA.) — For another meaning of طَلَعَ followed by عَلَى, see اِطَّلَعَ [which is more common as having that meaning]. — طَلَعَ is also *syn. with* قَصَدَ: so in the phrase طَلَعَ بِلَادَهُ ‡ [*He tended, repaired, betook himself,* or *went, to,* or *towards, his country*]: (Ḳ, TA:) and so in the saying, in a trad., هٰذَا بُسْرٌ قَدْ طَلَعَ اليَمَنَ, (so in the O,) or هٰذَا بُرٌّ, (so in the TA,) ‡ [*These are ripening dates,* or *this is wheat, that have,* or *has, gone to,* or *towards, El-Yemen,*] meaning from Nejd. (TA.) — And *syn. with* بَلَغَ; as also ▼ اِطَّلَعَ: (O, Ḳ:) so the former in the saying, طَلَعَ أَرْضَهُمْ ‡ [*He reached,* or *arrived at, their land*]; (Ḳ, TA;) and مَتَى طَلَعْتَ أَرْضَنَا ‡ [*When didst thou reach,* or *arrive at, our land?*]: (O, TA:) and so the latter verb in the saying, اطّلع ▼ هٰذِهِ الأَرْضَ [*He reached,* or *arrived at, this land*]: (O, Ḳ:) and hence, (TA,) ▼ الَّتِى تَطَّلِعُ عَلَى الأَفْئِدَةِ, in the Ḳur [civ. 7], means † *Whereof the pain shall reach the hearts:* (Fr, O, TA:) or *which shall rise above the hearts,* (O, TA,) [or *overwhelm them,*] *and burn them.* (TA.)

2. طلّع said of the palm-tree: see 1, former half. — طلّعهُ, inf. n. تَطْلِيعٌ, meaning *He put it forth,* or *produced it,* is a vulgar word. (TA.) — طلّع كَيْلَهُ, inf. n. as above, † *He filled his measure.* (O, Ḳ.)

3. طالعهُ, (Ṣ, O, Ḳ,) inf. n. مُطَالَعَةٌ and طِلَاعٌ, (Ḳ,) *i. q.* اِطَّلَعَ عَلَيْهِ; (Ṣ, O, Ḳ;) i. e., a thing: (Ṣ, O:) Lth says that طِلَاعٌ is syn. with اِطِّلَاعٌ; but Az disapproves this: (O:) [the verb is correctly explained in what here follows:] one says, طَالَعْتُ ضَيْعَتِى, meaning نَظَرْتُهَا وَاطَّلَعْتُ عَلَيْهَا [*I inspected,* or *considered with my eye, my estate, and obtained a knowledge of it,* or *acquainted myself with its condition*]: (TA:) or مُطَالَعَةٌ signifies the *inspecting* a thing *well, in order to obtain a knowledge of it.* (KL.) [Hence, مُطَالَعَةُ الكُتُبِ † *The studying,* and *perusing, of books.*] — See also the next paragraph, latter half, in three places.

4: see 1, former half, in five places. — اطلعت النَّخْلَةُ signifies also † *The palm-tree became tall.* (Mṣb.) — And اطلع, also, ‡ *He made his arrow to pass above the butt.* (Ṣ, O, Ḳ, TA.) — And ‡ *He vomited.* (Ṣ, O, Ḳ, TA.) — And اطلعت السَّمَآءُ *i. q.* أَقْلَعَتْ [i. e. † *The rain cleared away*]. (TA.) — اطلع followed by عَلَى: see 1, latter half: — and see also 8. — And اطلع as *syn. with* أَشْرَفَ: see 8, in two places. — اطلع رَأْسَهُ † [*He raised his head, looking at a thing;* or] *he looked at a thing from above;* syn. أَشْرَفَ عَلَى شَىْءٍ. (TA.) — اطلعهُ عَلَى كَذَا † *He made him acquainted with such a thing; acquainted him with it,* or *made him to know it.* (Mṣb.) إِطْلَاعٌ signifies † The *making to know,* and *to see.* (KL.) For an ex. [of the latter meaning], in the pass. form of the verb, see 8. You say, اطلعهُ عَلَى سِرِّهِ, (Ṣ, O, Ḳ, TA,) ‡ *He made him to know,* (TA,) or *revealed,* or *showed, to him,* (O, Ḳ, TA,) *his secret.* (O, Ḳ, TA.) [See also 8, last sentence.] And أَنَا أُطَالِعُكَ ▼ بِحَقِيقَةِ الأَمْرِ means أُطْلِعُكَ عَلَيْهِ ‡ [*I will acquaint thee with the truth of the case*]. (TA.) And similar to this is the saying, طَالِعْنِى ▼ بِكُتُبِكَ (TA [and a similar phrase is mentioned without explanation in the Ṣ]) [meaning † *Acquaint thou me with thy letters:* and also, *by means of thy letters;* for] one of the meanings of مُطَالَعَةٌ is The *making* one *to know* a thing *by writing.* (KL.) [And in like manner,] one says also, طالع ▼ بِالحَالِ, (O, Ḳ,) inf. n. مُطَالَعَةٌ and طِلَاعٌ, (TA,) † *He showed, exhibited,* or *manifested, the case.* (O, Ḳ.) — You say also, اطلع إِلَيْهِ مَعْرُوفًا † *He did to him,* or *conferred upon him, a benefit, benefaction,* or *favour.* (O, Ḳ.) — And اطلع فُلَانًا ‡ *He made such a one to hasten,* or *be quick.* (O, Ḳ, TA.)

5. تطلّع ‡ *It became full* [*to the top,* or *so as to overflow*]; said of a measure for corn or the like. (O, Ḳ, TA.) — See also 1, former half. — And † *He was proud,* or *self-conceited,* [or *lofty,*] or *was quick, with an affected inclining of his body from side to side,* (زَافَ,) *in his gait:* (O:) or so تطلّع فِى مِشْيَتِهِ: (Ḳ:) app. syn. with تَتَلَّعَ, meaning *he advanced his neck, and raised his head.* (TA.) — And ‡ *He raised his eyes, looking* [for a thing, or towards a thing]. (Ḳ, TA.) You say, تطلّع إِلَى وُرُودِهِ ‡ *He raised his eyes, looking for its,* or *his arrival.* (Ḳ, TA.) And تَطَلَّعْتُ إِلَى وُرُودِ كِتَابِكَ (Ṣ, O, TA) ‡ *I raised my eyes, looking,* (TA,) or *I looked continually,* (PṢ,) *for the arrival of thy letter:* (TA, PṢ:) or *i. q.* اِنْتَظَرْتُ [agreeably with what here follows, and with an explanation of the inf. n. in the KL]. (PṢ.) And تطلّع إِلَى لِقَائِهِ † *He looked for the meeting him.* (MA.) And [hence] one says, عَافَى ٱللّٰهُ رَجُلًا لَمْ يَتَطَلَّعْ فِى فِيكَ, meaning ‡ [*May God preserve* from disease, or harm, *a man*] *who has not sought to find some slip,* or *fault, in thy speech:* (O, Ḳ, TA:) mentioned by AZ, (O, TA,) and by Z. (TA.) [Hence likewise,] التَّطَلُّعُ signifies also الإِشْرَافُ [as meaning ‡ *The being eager,* or *vehemently eager,* agreeably with what here follows]. (TA.) And التَّطَلُّعُ إِلَى الشَّىْءِ ‡ *The inclining* of the soul *to the love of the thing,* and *the desiring it so that the man perishes.* (TA.) And تَطَلُّعُ النَّفْسِ † *The desiring,* or *yearning,* or *longing, of the soul.* (TA.) [See an ex. in a verse cited in the first paragraph of art. صبر.] — تطلّعهُ ‡ *He looked at him with a look of love* or *of hatred.* (TA.) — And ‡ *He overcame him,* and *overtook him;* namely, a man. (TA.) — See also 6. — And see 8.

6. تَطَالَعَتْهُ *i. q.* طَرَقَتْهُ [i. e. † *She,* or *it,* or *they* (referring to irrational things), *came to him in the night*]: Aboo-'Alee cites [as an ex.],

* تَطَالَعُنِى خَيَالَاتٌ لِسَلْمَى *
* كَمَا يَتَطَالَعُ الدَّيْنَ الغَرِيمُ *

[*Apparitions of Selmà come to me in the night, like as the creditor comes in the night to exact the debt*]: but accord. to another, or others, it is only ▼ يَتَطَلَّعُ, because تَفَاعَلَ is generally intrans.: so that accord. to Aboo-'Alee, it is like تَفَاوَضْنَا الحَدِيثَ and تَعَاطَيْنَا الكَأْسَ and تَنَاشَدْنَا الأَشْعَارَ. (IB, TA.)

8. اِطَّلَعَ: see 1, first sentence: — and near the middle of the paragraph, in two places: — and last sentence, in three places. — Also † *i. q.* أَشْرَفَ [meaning as expl. in the next sentence]; as also ▼ أَطْلَعَ, of the class of أَكْرَمَ. (Mgh.) One says, اِطَّلَعْتُ مِنْ فَوْقِ الجَبَلِ and ▼ أَطْلَعْتُ † [*I looked,* or *looked down, from above the mountain*]. (TA.) And اِطَّلَعْتُ الفَجْرَ ‡ *I looked at the dawn when it rose.* (O, TA.*) And اِطَّلَعْتُ عَلَيْهِ ‡ *I looked down,* or *from above, upon him,* or *it;*

syn. أَشْرَفْتُ. (TA.) [Hence,] هَلْ أَنْتُمْ مُطَّلِعُونَ فَاطَّلَعَ, in the Ḳur [xxxvii. 52 and 53], means † *Would ye* [*be of those who*] *look to see* (تُحِبُّونَ أَنْ تَطَّلِعُوا) where is your place of abode among the people of Hell? *and he* (i. e. the Muslim) *shall look* (فَاطَّلَعَ المُسْلِمُ) and see his [former] associate in the midst of Hell-fire: but some read هل انتم مُطْلِعُونَ فَأُطْلِعَ ▼ [in the CḲ فاطَّلَعَ], but it is expressly said in the O that the hemzeh is with ḍamm and the ط quiescent and the ل with kesr; the meaning being † *Are ye of those who will make me to see? and he shall be made to see*; as is indicated in the O and TA]. (Ḳ, O.) —— And † *He saw.* (KL.) You say, اطّلع عَلَيْهِ meaning † *He saw it.* (MA.) [Hence,] it is said in a prov., بَعْدَ ٱطِّلَاعٍ إِينَاسٌ (O, TA) i. e. † *After appearance* [or rather *sight, is knowledge*, or *certain knowledge*]. (Fr, TA in art. انس. [See Freytag's Arab. Prov. i. 181.]) —— And اطّلع عَلَيْهِ, (Mṣb, TA,) and اطّلعهُ, and ▼ تطلّعهُ, and ▼ أَطْلَعَ عليه, ▼ طَلَعَ عليه, inf. n. طُلُوعٌ, (Ḳ, TA,) and عليه, (TA,) ‡ *He got*, or *obtained, sight and knowledge of it:* (Mṣb, TA:*) or [simply] *he knew it*; namely, an affair, or a case, or an event. (Ḳ, TA.) One says, اطّلع عَلَى بَاطِنِهِ, (Ḳ,) or اطّلع عَلَى بَاطِنِ أَمْرِهِ, (Ṣ, O,) ‡ *He became acquainted with*, or *obtained knowledge of*, or *knew, his inward*, or *intrinsic, state or circumstances*, or *the inward*, or *intrinsic, state* or *circumstances of his affair* or *case.* (Ḳ,* TA.) And accord. to some, اِطِّلَاعُ الحِجَابِ means † *The stretching out the head* [*and looking over the veil* of Paradise or of Hell]; for he who examines into a thing stretches out his head to see what is behind the veil, or covering. (TA voce حِجَابٌ, q. v.) [And one says also, اطّلع فِيهِ, meaning † *He looked into it:* see an ex. voce هَدَرَ.] —— اِطَّلَعَتْهُ عَيْنِى means ‡ *My eye regarded him with contempt.* (TA.) ▬ [اِطَّلَعَ is used sometimes for اِضْطَلَعَ, as is shown in art. ضلع: see مُضْطَلِعٌ: and see an instance in the first paragraph of art. علو.] ▬ And accord. to Kr, الإِطِّلَاعُ signifies also النَّجَاةُ. (TA. [But I think that both words are mistranscribed, and that Kr explained الإِطِّلَاعُ as meaning النِّجَآءُ, i. e. *The acquainting with a secret.*])

10. استطلعهُ signifies طَلَبَ طُلُوعَهُ † [*He sought*, or *desired, its*, or *his, coming forth*, or *appearance*]. (Ḥar p. 47.) [And hence, † *He sought*, or *desired, to elicit*, or *to discover, it: he sought*, or *desired, information respecting it*, مِنْهُ *of him:* and *he asked him to tell him* a thing. (See Ḥar pp. 134 and 82.)] You say, استطلع رَأْىَ فُلَانٍ (Ṣ, O, Ḳ, TA) ‡ *He looked to see what was the opinion*, or *advice, of such a one*, (O, Ḳ, TA,) and *what would be shown to him* [*thereof*] *respecting his affair*, or *case.* (O, Ḳ.) It is doubly trans. [as shown above]: you say, استطلعت رَأْىَ زَيْدٍ; as well as اِسْتَطْلَعْتُ زَيْدًا رَأْيَهُ. (Ḥar p. 322.) —— And † *He took it away*, or *went away with it.* (Ibn-'Abbád, O, Ḳ.) You say, استطلع مَالَهُ † *He took away*, or *went away with, his property.* (TA.)

طَلْعٌ † The طلع [i. e. *spadix*, or *spadix in its spathe*, and sometimes, the *spathe* alone,] *of the palm-tree:* (Ṣ, O:) the إِغْرِيض [or *spadix*] *of the palm-tree, from over which the* كافور [or *spathe*] *bursts open longitudinally*; or the *flowers of the palm-tree, while in the* كافور; (TA;) *a thing that comes forth from the palm-tree, as though it were two soles*, or *sandals, closed together, with the* حَمْل [meaning *flowers*] *compactly disposed between them, and having the extremity pointed*; or the ثَمَرَة [or *produce*] *of the palm-tree, in the first stage of its appearance, the covering* [or *spathe*] *of which is called the* كُفُرَّى (Ḳ, TA) *and the* كَافُور, (TA,) *and what is within this the* إِغْرِيض, *because of its whiteness*; (Ḳ, TA;) or the طلع is *what comes forth from the palm-tree and becomes dates if the tree is female; and if the tree is male it does not become dates, but is eaten in its fresh state, or is left upon the palm-tree a certain number of days until there becomes produced in it a white substance like flour*, [i. e. *the pollen*,] *having a strong odour, and with this the female is fecundated*; (Mṣb;) or *a certain white thing that appears from the* كُمّ [or *spathe*] *of the palm-tree, to the colour of which* [*that of*] *the teeth are likened, and to the odour thereof* [*that of*] *the sperma:* and also, [sometimes,] the كُمّ [or *spathe*] *that comes forth from the palm-tree, before it bursts open longitudinally:* [and this is also called the كُفُرَّى, for] the phrase طَلْعُ الكُفُرَّى is an instance of the prefixing of a noun to an explicative thereof: (Mgh:) [or this phrase may mean *the spadix of the spathe of a palm-tree:* طَلْعٌ, it should be added, is sometimes used as a coll. gen. n.: and its n. un. is with ة: thus in explanations of إِغْرِيض &c.] In the Ḳur xxxvii. 63, it is applied to ‡ The *fruit*, or *produce*, of the tree called الزَّقُّوم, in the bottom of Hell, metaphorically, because partaking of the form of the طلع of dates, or because coming forth from the tree. (Bḍ.) ▬ Also † i. q. مِقْدَارٌ [as meaning *Number*, or *quantity*]: (Ḳ, TA:) so in the phrase الجَيْشُ طَلْعُ أَلْفٍ [*The army consists of the number of a thousand*]. (Ḳ,* TA). ▬ See also the next paragraph, in three places.

طِلْعٌ ‡ a subst. from الإِطِّلَاعُ: [meaning *Knowledge:*] whence the saying, اِطَّلَعَ طِلْعَ العَدُوِّ ‡ [*He learned the knowledge of the enemy*; meaning *he obtained knowledge of the state*, or *case*, or *tidings*, or *of the secret*, or *of the inward*, or *intrinsic*, or *secret, state or circumstances, of the enemy*]; (Ṣ, O, Ḳ, TA;) [for] طِلْعُ العَدُوِّ means خَبَرُهُ, (Mṣb,) or بَاطِنُ أَمْرِهِمْ, (PṢ,) or سِرُّهُ: (Ḥar p. 82:) and [hence also] one says, أَطْلَعْتُهُ طِلْعَ أَمْرِى, meaning ‡ *I revealed*, or *showed, to him my secret.* (O, Ḳ, TA.) ▬ Also † *An elevated place, above what is around it, from which one looks down* (يُطَّلَعُ [in the CḲ erroneously يُطْلَعُ]); as also ▼ طَلْعٌ. (Ḳ, TA.) You say, عَلَوْتُ طِلْعَ الأَكَمَةِ, meaning † *I ascended upon a part of the hill from which I overlooked what was around it.* (IDrd, O, TA.) —— And † i. q. نَاحِيَةٌ [*A side*, or *an adjacent tract*, or *a region*, &c.]; as also ▼ طَلْعٌ. (Ḳ.) One says, كُنْ بِطِلْعِ الوَادِى and ▼ بِطَلْعِ الوادى [i. e. بِطَلْعِ الوادى also, meaning, as is indicated in the TA, † *Be thou in the side*, &c., *of the valley*]: (Ṣ, O:) and one says also, فُلَانٌ طِلْعَ الوَادِى, without ب [† *Such a one is in the side*, &c., *of the valley*]. (O.) —— And † *Any depressed piece of ground:* or *such as has in it a hill:* (Ḳ:) [i. e.,] as expl. by Aṣ, *any depressed piece of ground having in it a hill from which, when you ascend upon it, you see what is in it.* (O.) ▬ Also the *serpent:* (AA, O, Ḳ:) like طِلٌّ. (TA.)

طَلِعٌ ‡ [*Desirous, eager*, or *vehemently eager*]. نَفْسٌ طَلِعَةٌ and نُفُوسٌ طَلِعَةٌ, like فَرِحَةٌ [in form], mean ‡ *A soul*, and *souls, desirous, eager*, or *vehemently eager.* (TA.) [See also طُلَعَةٌ.]

طُلْعَةٌ ‡ The *aspect*; or *countenance*; syn. رُؤْيَةٌ: (Ṣ, O, Ḳ, TA:) or *person and aspect:* (L, TA:) or *face:* (Ḳ:) so in the saying, حَيَّا ٱللّٰهُ طُلْعَتَهُ ‡ [*May God preserve his aspect*, &c.]. (O, Ḳ.)

طُلَعَةٌ : نَفْسٌ طُلَعَةٌ, means نَفْسٌ تُكْثِرُ التَّطَلُّعَ لِلشَّىْءِ, (Ṣ, O,) or إِلَى الشَّىْءِ, (Ḳ, TA,) i. e. ‡ *A soul that inclines much to the love of the thing* [that it would obtain], *and desires it so that the man perishes:* and طُلَعَةٌ is used also as applied to a pl., so that one says also نُفُوسٌ طُلَعَةٌ, (TA,) or أَنْفُسٌ طُلَعَةٌ, meaning *souls eager*, or *vehemently eager, for the objects of their love and appetence.* (O.) [See also طَلِعٌ.] And in like manner one says اِمْرَأَةٌ طُلَعَةٌ, (Ṣ,) or اِمْرَأَةٌ طُلَعَةٌ خُبَأَةٌ: (TA:) or this latter means ‡ *A woman that comes forth* (تَطَّلِعُ [in the CḲ erroneously تَطْلُعُ]) *at one time* (مَرَّةً [omitted in the CḲ]) *and conceals herself at another:* (O, Ḳ, TA:) and in like manner one says اِمْرَأَةٌ طُلَعَةٌ قُبَعَةٌ. (TA.)

طُلَعَآءُ, (Ṣ, O, Ḳ,) like عُلَوَآءُ [in form], (Ṣ, O,) ‡ *Vomit:* (Ṣ, O, Ḳ, TA;) as also ▼ طَوْلَعٌ: (IAạr, O, Ḳ:) or the former signifies *a little vomit.* (Ḳ voce قَلْس.)

طَلَاعٌ, like سَحَابٌ [in form], the subst. from الاطلاع [app. الإِطِّلَاعُ, i. e. a subst. *syn. with* إِطْلَاعٌ]; like as صَلَاحٌ is with إِصْلَاحٌ, and فَسَادٌ with إِفْسَادٌ. (TA.)

طِلَاعٌ ‡ *A thing sufficient in quantity*, or *dimensions, for the filling* of another thing, (Ṣ, O, Ḳ, TA,) accord. to A'Obeyd, *so as to overflow* [an addition not always agreeable with usage]: (TA:) pl. طُلُعٌ. (Ḳ.) طِلَاعُ الأَرْضِ ذَهَبًا means

‡ *What would suffice for the filling of the earth, of gold:* (Aṣ, Ṣ, O, TA:) or, accord. to Lth, *what the sun has risen,* or *appeared, upon,* to which Er-Rághib adds *and man.* (TA.) And you say قَوْسٌ طِلَاعُ الكَفِّ ‡ *A bow of which the part that is grasped is sufficient in size for the filling of the hand.* (Ṣ,* O,* TA.) And هٰذَا طِلَاعُ هٰذَا † *This is of the quantity,* or *measure,* or *size, of this.* (TA.)

طَلُوعٌ † *Aspiring to,* or *seeking the means of attaining, lofty things,* or *eminence.* (Ḥam p. 655.)

طَلِيعَةٌ, of an army, † [*A scout;* and *a party of scouts;*] *a man,* (Ṣ, O, Ḳ, TA,) and *a party of men,* (O, Ḳ, TA,) *that is sent,* (Ṣ, O, Ḳ, TA) *and goes forth,* (TA,) *to obtain knowledge of the state,* or *case,* or *tidings,* or *of the secret,* or *of the inward,* or *intrinsic,* or *secret, state* or *circumstances, of the enemy,* (لِيَطَّلِعَ طِلْعَ العَدُوِّ, Ṣ, O, Ḳ, TA,) *like the* جَاسُوس; (TA;) *a man,* (Mgh,) or *a party of men,* (Mgh, Mṣb,) *sent* (Mgh, Mṣb) *before another party* (Mṣb) *to acquaint himself,* or *themselves, with the tidings,* or *state,* or *case, of the enemy;* (Mgh, Mṣb;) accord. to the 'Eyn, applied to *a single man,* and to *a number of men when they are together;* and as used by [the Ḥanafee Imám] Moḥammad, *three,* and *four;* more than these being termed سَرِيَّةٌ: (Mgh:) pl. طَلَائِعُ. (Mgh, O, Mṣb, Ḳ.)

طَلَّاعُ الأَنْجُدِ and طَلَّاعُ الثَّنَايَا ‡ [lit. A man *wont to ascend mountain-roads;* meaning] a man *experienced in affairs; wont to surmount them by his knowledge and his experience and his good judgment:* or *who aspires to lofty things,* or *the means of attaining eminence:* (O, Ḳ, TA: [see also ثَنِيَّةٌ:]) أَنْجُدٌ being pl. of نَجْدٌ; which means "a road in a mountain," like ثَنِيَّةٌ [of which ثَنَايَا is the pl.]. (TA.) An ex. of the former phrase is presented by a verse of Soḥeym Ibn-Wetheel cited in art. جلو: and an ex. of the latter by the saying of Moḥammad Ibn-Abee-Shiḥádh Eḍ-Ḍabbee, said by ISk to be of Ráshid Ibn-Dirwás,

* وَقَدْ يَقْصُرُ القُلُّ الفَتَى دُونَ هَمِّهِ *
* وَقَدْ كَانَ لَوْلَا القُلُّ طَلَّاعَ أَنْجُدِ *

[*Certainly,* or *sometimes,* or *often, poverty withholds the young man from attaining his purpose; and certainly,* or *sometimes,* or *often, but for poverty, he would be a surmounter of affairs by his knowledge* &c.]. (O, TA.) ═ قَدَحٌ طَلَّاعٌ ‡ *A full drinking-vessel.* (TA.) And عَيْنٌ طَلَّاعٌ [or طَلَّاعَةٌ?] ‡ *An eye filled with tears.* (TA.)

طَالِعٌ [*Rising,* or *appearing,* as a star &c.:] anything *appearing from the upper part* [*of a thing,* or *that comes up out of a thing and appears*]: (TA:) [or *appearing by rising,* or *by becoming elevated.* (See 1.)] — [Hence,] one says, طَالِعُهُ سَعِيدٌ, meaning *His star* [*is fortunate*]. (TA.) — [Hence also,] الطَّالِعُ means *The false dawn:* (Ṣ:) or so الطَّالِعُ المُصْعِدُ. (O.) — And *The* هِلَال [or *moon when near the sun, showing a narrow rim of light;* probably *the new moon,* from the sight of which the commencement of the month was reckoned; as appears from what follows]. (O, Ḳ.) مَا رَأَيْتُكَ مُنْذُ طَالِعَيْنِ is mentioned as heard from some of the Arabs of the desert, meaning مُنْذُ شَهْرَيْنِ [i. e. *I have not seen thee for two months,* or *during the period since two new moons*]. (O.) — Also *The arrow that falls behind the butt:* (Az, O, Ḳ:) or *that passes beyond the butt, going over it:* (TA:) and Ḳt says that they used to reckon that falling above the mark as that which hit the butt: pl. طَوَالِعُ. (O, TA.) It is said of one of the kings, accord. to Ṣgh, [in the O,] كَانَ يَسْجُدُ لِلطَّالِعِ, (TA,) meaning as expl. in art. سجد: (O, TA:*) or it may mean that *he used to lower himself,* or *bend himself down, to the rising* هِلَال, by way of magnifying God. (O, TA.) — طَالِعَةُ الإِبِلِ means † *The first,* or *foremost, of the camels.* (TA.)

طَوْلَعٌ: see طُلَعَآءُ.

مَطْلَعٌ and مَطْلِعٌ are inf. ns.: and signify also The *place* [and the *time*] *of rising* of the sun [&c.]: (Ṣ, O, Ḳ: [see 1, first sentence:]) but by Fr the former is explained as meaning the *rising,* and the latter as meaning the *place of rising:* and some of the Baṣrees say that when one reads حَتَّى مَطْلِعِ الفَجْرِ [in the last verse of ch. xcvii. of the Ḳur], with kesr to the ل, the meaning is, [*until*] *the time of rising* [*of the dawn*]: (O, TA:) [the pl.] مَطَالِعُ signifies the *places* [and the *times*] *of rising* of the sun [&c.]. (TA.) — مَطْلَعُ الجَبَلِ means † *The place of ascent of the mountain.* (TA.) And you say, هٰذَا لَكَ مَطْلَعَ الأَكَمَةِ, meaning † *This is present before thee;* i. e. *as near to thee as if thou hadst to ascend for it the hill.* (TA.) — مَطْلَعُ القَصِيدَةِ means ‡ *The beginning of the* قصيدة [or *ode*]. (TA.) — See also مُطَّلَعٌ.

مُطْلِعٌ † A palm-tree (نَخْلَةٌ) *putting forth its* طَلْع [q. v.]; and sometimes they said مُطْلِعَةٌ. (Mṣb.) — And the latter, † A palm-tree *taller than the other palm-trees* [*around it* or *adjacent to it*]. (Ṣ, O, Ḳ.)

مُطَّلَعٌ † [*A place to which one ascends:* or] *a place of ascent from a low spot to a place that overlooks.* (Aṣ, TA.) Hence, (TA,) it is said in a trad. (O, Ḳ) of the Prophet, (O,) مَا نَزَلَ مِنَ القُرْآنِ آيَةٌ إِلَّا لَهَا ظَهْرٌ وَبَطْنٌ وَلِكُلِّ حَرْفٍ حَدٌّ وَلِكُلِّ حَدٍّ مُطَّلَعٌ i. e. (O, Ḳ) † *Not a verse of the Ḳur-án has come down but it has an apparent and known* [or *exoteric*] *interpretation and an intrinsic* [or *esoteric*] *interpretation,* (TA voce ظَهْرٌ, where see more,) [*and every word has a scope, and every scope has*] *a place* [meaning *point*] *to which the knowledge thereof may ascend,* (O, Ḳ, TA,) or, as some say, *something that may be violated,* God not having forbidden a thing that should be held sacred without his knowing that some one would seek to elicit it. (TA.) — And *i. q.* مَأْتًى; (Ṣ, O, Ḳ, TA;) مُطَّلَعُ الأَمْرِ meaning مَأْتَاهُ; (Ṣ, O, TA;) as also ↓ مُطْلَعُ الأَمْرِ; (TA;) i. e. † *The way,* or *manner, of attaining to the doing,* or *performing, of the affair.* (TA.) One says, مَا لِهٰذَا الأَمْرِ مُطَّلَعٌ † *There is no way,* or *manner, of attaining to the doing,* or *performing, of this affair.* (TA.) And أَيْنَ مُطَّلَعُ هٰذَا الأَمْرِ i. e. مَأْتَاهُ † [*Where is the way of attaining to the doing,* or *performing, of this affair?*]. (Ṣ, O, TA.) — And ‡ *An elevated place from which one looks towards a low place.* (Ṣ, O, Mṣb, Ḳ, TA.) To this is likened the scene of the events of the world to come, (Ṣ, O, Mṣb, Ḳ, TA,) after death, i. e. the station of the day of resurrection, (TA,) in the saying of 'Omar, لَوْ أَنَّ لِي مَا فِي الأَرْضِ جَمِيعًا لَافْتَدَيْتُ بِهِ مِنْ هَوْلِ المُطَّلَعِ ‡ [*If all that is in the world belonged to me, assuredly I would ransom myself therewith from the terror of the place whence one will look down* on the day of resurrection]: (Ṣ,* O, Mṣb,* Ḳ,* TA:) or المُطَّلَعُ means *that which is looked upon of* such hardships as the interrogation of [the angels] Munkar and Nekeer, and the pressure of the grave, and its solitude, and the like; and is [for المُطَّلَعُ عَلَيْهِ, or] originally an inf. n. in the sense of الاِطِّلَاعُ: or it may be a noun of time, and thus applied to the day of resurrection. (Ḥar p. 344-5.)

مُطَّلِعٌ *Strong,* or *powerful; high,* or *eminent; one who subdues,* or *overcomes:* (Ḳ:) or *strong,* or *powerful;* as also مُضْطَلِعٌ: or the latter has this meaning, from الضَّلَاعَةُ; and the former signifies *high,* or *eminent;* one *who subdues,* or *overcomes:* (O:) accord. to ISk, one says, هُوَ مُضْطَلِعٌ بِحَمْلِهِ ["he is one who has strength to bear it"]; but not مطّلع بحمله. (TA.) [See, however, مُضْطَلِعٌ, in art. ضلع.]

مُطَالَعٌ [pass. part. n. of 3, q. v.]. One says, الشر تلقى مُطَالَعَ الاِسْمِ, [thus in my original, app. الشَّرَّ تَلْقَى الخ] meaning بَارِزًا مَكْشُوفًا [i. e., if I rightly read it, † *Evil thou wilt find to be that whereof the name is manifest,* or *overt;* so that, when it is mentioned, it is well known]. (TA.)

طلف

2. طَلَّفَ عَلَيْهِ, inf. n. تَطْلِيفٌ; (O, Ḳ;) and ظَلَّفَ is a dial. var. thereof; (TA;) *He exceeded it;* (O, Ḳ;) [meaning a certain number of years; for] it is like ذَرَّفَ and رَمَّثَ and طَلَّثَ. (IAạr, TA in art. ظلف.)

4. اطلف [*He escaped being a victim of his adversary's blood-revenge;* expl. as meaning] *the blood-revenge of his adversary was ineffectual,* or *had not effect.* (Ibn-'Abbád, O, Ḳ.) ═ اطلفهُ *He made it* [i. e. a man's blood] *to go for nothing* [i. e. *unretaliated, or uncompensated by a mulct*]; or *to be of no account.* (Ṣ, O, Ḳ.) — And *He gave him* (Ṣ, O, Ḳ) a thing (O) *as a free gift.* (Ṣ, O, Ḳ.)

طَلْفٌ : see the next paragraph in two places.

طَلَفٌ *A thing that goes for nothing*; [as blood *that is unretaliated, or uncompensated by a mulct*;] *that is of no account, ineffectual,* or *null*; syn. هَدَرٌ; (Ṣ, O, Ḳ;) [and so ▼ طَلْفٌ, as shown by what follows;] as also ▼ طَلِيفٌ. (O, Ḳ.) You say, ذَهَبَ دَمُهُ طَلَفًا, (AA, Ṣ, O, Ḳ,) and ▼ طَلْفًا, (AA, O, Ḳ,) and طَلَفًا and طُلْفًا, (AA, O,) *His blood went for nothing; as a thing of no account; ineffectually;* or *in vain; unretaliated,* or *uncompensated by a mulct;* syn. هَدَرًا, (AA, Ṣ, O, Ḳ, TA,) and بَاطِلًا: and in like manner, مَالُهُ [*his property*]. (TA. [See also تَلَفٌ.]) And Ru-beh says,

كَمْ مِنْ عِدًى أَمْوَالُهُمْ طَلِيفُ ▼

[*How many enemies are there whose possessions are things that have gone for nought!*]. (O, as an ex. of the last word in the sense of هَدَرٌ.) — And (Ṣ, O, Ḳ) hence (O) *A gift*; (Ṣ, O, Ḳ;) *a gift freely bestowed, not for any compensation.* (Ṣ, TA.) — And *A thing that is easy*; or *of light estimation, paltry,* or *despicable*; [as also طَلَفٌ;] syn. هَيِّنٌ. (IF, O, Ḳ.) — And *A redundant portion of a thing*: (IF, O, Ḳ:) if this be not what is meant by the saying that طَلَفٌ is syn. with فَضْلٌ, this saying is of no account. (IF, O.)

طَلِيفٌ : see طَلَفٌ, in two places. — Also *A thing that is taken.* (O, Ḳ.*) [And hence, perhaps, the saying of Ru-beh cited above.] — One says also, ذَهَبَ فُلَانٌ بِالمَالِ طَلِيفًا and طَلِيفًا i. e. *Such a one went away with the property without compensation.* (Yoo, O.) — And أَكَلَ مَالَهُ فِى طَلِيفٍ *He devoured his property in a vain, or an ineffectual, procedure.* (O.)

طلق

1. طَلَقَتِ النَّاقَةُ, (Ṣ, Mgh, Mṣb,) aor. ـُ, inf. n. طُلُوقٌ, (Mṣb,) *The she-camel was,* or *became, loosed from her bond,* (Ṣ, Mgh, Mṣb,) or *cord, by which her fore shank and her arm had been bound together.* (Ṣ, Mgh.) And طَلَقَتِ النَّاقَةُ إِلَى المَآءِ [*The she-camel was,* or *became, loosed from her bond to repair to the water*]: (Mṣb:) or طَلَقَتِ الإِبِلُ إِلَى المَآءِ, (AZ, Aṣ, Ṣ, TA) (AZ, TA,) aor. as above, (Aṣ, TA,) inf. n. طَلْقٌ (AZ, Aṣ, Ṣ, TA) and طُلُوقٌ, (AZ, Ṣ, TA,) *the camels were,* or *became, loosed to repair to the water, it being distant two days' journeys,* (AZ, Aṣ, Ṣ, TA,) *and were left to pasture while going thither*: and the subst. is طَلَقٌ [q. v.]. (AZ, Ṣ, TA.) — [Hence,] طَلَقَتْ, (IAạr, Th, Ṣ, Mgh, O, Mṣb,) or طَلَقَتْ مِنْ زَوْجِهَا, (Ḳ,) aor. ـُ; (Th, Ṣ, O, Mṣb, Ḳ;) and طَلُقَتْ also; (IAạr, Th, Mgh, Mṣb;) the latter of which is preferable, but the former is allowable; (IAạr, TA;) or the latter is the more common; (Th, TA;) but accord. to Akh, the latter is not allowable; (Ṣ, O, TA;) inf. n. طَلَاقٌ, (Th, Ṣ, Mgh, O, Ḳ,) or [properly طَلْقٌ, for it is said that] طَلَاقٌ is the subst., (Mṣb,) [or] طَلَاقٌ is also a subst. syn. with تَطْلِيقٌ, [as will be expl. below,] as well as inf. n. of طَلَقَتْ and طَلُقَتْ;) (Mgh;) said of a woman; (IAạr, Th, Ṣ, &c.;) ‡ *She was,* or *became,* [*divorced,* or] *left to go her way,* (O,) or *separated from her husband* [*by a sentence of divorce*]. (Ḳ, TA.) — And طَلُقَ لِسَانُهُ, inf. n. طُلُوقٌ and طُلُوقَةٌ, † *His tongue was,* or *became, eloquent,* or *chaste in speech, and sweet therein.* (Mṣb. [See also طَلْقٌ: and see 7.]) — And طَلُقَ, (Ṣ, O, Ḳ, TA,) inf. n. طَلَاقَةٌ, (Ṣ, O,) or طُلُوقَةٌ and طُلُوقٌ, (TA,) ‡ *He was,* or *became, laughing,* or *happy,* or *cheerful, and bright,* (Ḳ, TA,) *in face,* or *countenance*: (Ṣ, O, Ḳ, TA:) or, inf. n. طَلَاقَةٌ, † *it* (the face, or countenance,) *was,* or *became, cheerful,* or *happy,* (MA, Mṣb,) *the contr. of frowning* or *contracted,* (Mgh,) *displaying openness and pleasantness*; (Mṣb;) and ▼ تطلّق signifies the same; (MA, Mgh;) as also ▼ انطلق; (Mgh;) syn. انبسط; (Ḳ;) whence the saying, يَنْبَغِى لِلْقَاضِى أَنْ يُنْصِفَ الخَصْمَيْنِ وَلَا يَنْطَلِقَ ▼ بِوَجْهِهِ إِلَى أَحَدِهِمَا, meaning † [*It behooves the judge to treat with equity the two adversaries in litigation, and*] *he shall not speak to one of them with a cheerful countenance* (بِوَجْهٍ طَلْقٍ) *and with sweet speech,* not doing this to the other: or it may be from الإِنْطِلَاقُ signifying "the going away," and may hence mean, *and he shall not turn his face,* or *pay regard, to one of them* [in preference to the other]. (Mgh.) — And طَلُقَ, inf. n. طُلُوقَةٌ and طَلَاقَةٌ, said of a day, ‡ *It was,* or *became, such as is termed* طَلْقٌ; i. e. [*temperate,*] *neither hot nor cold*; [&c.; see طَلْقٌ;] and in like manner طَلُقَتْ is said of a night (لَيْلَةٌ). (Ḳ, TA.) — طَلِقَ, (O, Ḳ,) with kesr, (O,) like سَمِعَ, (Ḳ,) signifies تَبَاعَدَ [*He,* or *it, was,* or *became, distant,* or *remote*; &c.]. (O, Ḳ.) — طَلَقَ is also trans., syn. with أَطْلَقَ: see the latter verb, former half, in two places. — [Hence,] طُلِقَتْ, (Ṣ, Mgh, O, Mṣb, Ḳ,) aor. تُطْلَقُ, (Ṣ,) inf. n. طَلْقٌ, (Ṣ, Mgh,* O,* Mṣb, Ḳ,) and inf. n. un. طَلْقَةٌ, (TA,) † *She* (a woman, Ṣ, O, Mṣb) *was taken with the pains of parturition*: (Ṣ, Mgh, O, Mṣb, Ḳ:) a phrase implying a presage of good [i. e. of speedy and safe delivery]. (Mgh.) [And طُلِقَتْ بِهِ † *She was,* or *became, in labour with him.*]

2. طلّق نَاقَتَهُ *He left, left alone,* or *let go, his she-camel.* (TA.) See also 4, second sentence. — [Hence,] طلّق آمْرَأَتَهُ, (Ṣ, Mṣb, Ḳ,) inf. n. تَطْلِيقٌ, (Ṣ, Mgh, O, Mṣb,) from طَلَاقٌ [q. v.]; (O;) and ▼ اطلقها, (Ḳ,) inf. n. إِطْلَاقٌ; (TA;) ‡ [*He divorced his wife*;] *he separated his wife from himself* [*by a sentence of divorce*]. (Ḳ, TA.) [طلّق in this sense is opposed to رَاجَعَ: and hence the meanings of these two verbs in a verse of En-Nábighah which I have cited in art. نذر, (see conj. 6 in that art.,) and which is also cited in the Ṣ and O and TA in the present art.] — And طلّق البِلَادَ ‡ *He left,* or *quitted, the country.* (IAạr, TA.) El-'Okeylee, being asked by Ks, أَطَلَّقْتَ آمْرَأَتَكَ [*Hast thou quitted thy wife?*], answered, نَعَمْ وَالأَرْضَ مِنْ وَرَائِهَا † [*Yes, and the land behind her*]. (IAạr, TA.) And one says, طَلَّقْتُ القَوْمَ † *I left,* or *quitted, the people,* or *party*: and طلّق العِيَالَ † *He left* [or *deserted*] *the household, like as the man leaves* [or *divorces*] *the woman,* or *wife.* (TA.) And طلّق العَيْرُ عَانَتَهُ † *The he-ass passed by,* or *beyond, his she-ass, and then left her*: and طَلَّقَتْهُ العَانَةُ † *The she-ass submitted herself* [the verb which I thus render has been altered to انقدت, for which I read آنْقَادَتْ,] *to him, after having been incompliant.* (TA.) — And طُلِّقَ السَّلِيمُ † *The person bitten by a serpent became rid of the pain*: (Er-Rághib, TA:) or *recovered himself, and his pain became allayed,* (Ṣ, O, Ḳ,) *after the paroxysm*: (Ṣ, O:) inf. n. as above. (Ḳ.) — طلّق نَخْلَهُ: see 4, last sentence.

4. الإِطْلَاقُ signifies *The loosing,* or *setting loose* or *free,* and *letting go.* (TA.) You say, اطلق النَّاقَةَ مِنَ العِقَالِ, (Ṣ, O, Mṣb, TA,) or مِنْ عِقَالِهَا, i. e. *He loosed the she-camel from the bond,* or *cord, by which her fore shank and arm were bound together*; (Mgh;) as also ▼ طلّقها. (TA.) And اطلق الأَسِيرَ, (Ṣ, Mgh, O, Mṣb, Ḳ, TA,) and اطلق عَنْهُ, (O, TA,) *He let go the captive*; (Ṣ, O, Ḳ, TA;) and *set him free*; (TA;) *he loosed the bond of the captive, and let him go*: (Mgh, Mṣb:) and أُطْلِقَ عَنْهُ إِسَارُهُ [*His bond was loosed from him*], namely, the captive. (Ṣ.) And اطلق خَيْلَهُ فِى الحَلْبَةِ *He made his horses to run* [*in the race-ground*]. (TA.) And اطلق النَّاقَةَ *He drove the she-camel to the water*: (TA:) or أَطْلَقْتُ النَّاقَةَ إِلَى المَآءِ [*I loosed the she-camel from her bond to repair to the water*]: (Mṣb:) or أَطْلَقْتُ الإِبِلَ إِلَى المَآءِ (AZ, Ṣ, O, TA) (AZ, Ṣ,* TA) *I loosed the camels to repair to the water, it being distant two days' journeys, and left them to pasture while going thither.* (AZ, Ṣ, O,* TA.) And اطلق القَوْمُ means *The people,* or *party, had their camels loosed to repair to the water, it being distant two days' journeys, and the camels being left to pasture while going thither.* (Ṣ, Ḳ,* TA.) — اطلق آمْرَأَتَهُ: see 2, third sentence. — اطلق الدَّوَآءُ بَطْنَهُ *The medicine loosened,* or *relaxed, his belly* [or *bowels*]; (Mṣb;) or *moved his belly.* (TA.) — [اطلق عِنَانَهُ *He let loose,* or *slackened, his* (a horse's) *rein*; and so † *made him to quicken his pace.* (See Ḥar p. 356.)] And اطلق رِجْلَهُ † *He hastened him*; or *desired,* or *required, him to hasten,* or *be quick*; as also ▼ استطلقهُ. (TA. [Whether the pronoun relate to a beast or a man is not shown. By استطلقه is not meant استطلق رِجْلَهُ, as رِجْل is fem.]) — اطلق يَدَهُ بِخَيْرٍ, (Ṣ, O,

Ḳ, TA) and فِى خَيْرٍ, and بِمَالٍ and فِى مَالٍ; (TA;) and ↓ طَلَّقَهَا, (Ṣ, O, Ḳ,) aor. ـُ, (Ṣ,) or ـَ, (Ḳ,) but expressly said in the Ṣ to be with ḍamm, inf. n. طَلْقٌ; (TA;) † *He opened his hand* [*freely*] *with good,* (Ḳ, TA,) and *with property.* (TA.) And اطلق لَهُ مَالًا † *He gave him property:* (MA:) and ↓ طَلَّقَ † *he gave* (Ibn-'Abbád, O, Ḳ) a thing. (Ḳ.) And اطلق صَاحِبُ الدَّيْنِ كَذَا † [*The creditor remitted so much* of the debt; being asked, or desired, to do so: see 10]. (Mṣb.) — [اطلقهُ also signifies † *He made it allowable,* or *free,* to be done, or taken, &c.] You say, اطلق لَهُ فِعْلَ كَذَا † *He permitted him,* or *gave him permission* or *leave, to do such a thing; i. q.* أَذِنَ لَهُ فِيهِ. (Mṣb in art. اذن.) — [And † *He made it to be unrestricted.* Hence the saying, اطلق بِهِمُ السَّيْفَ † *He made the sword to have unrestricted scope with them;* i. e. *he slew them without restriction.*] And أَطْلَقْتُ البَيِّنَةَ † *I made the evidence, proof,* or *voucher, to be without any mention of the date; contr. of* أَرَّخْتُهَا; (Mṣb in art. ارخ;) or *I gave the evidence without restricting it by a date:* from أَطْلَقْتُ الأَسِيرَ. (Mṣb in the present art.) And hence also أَطْلَقْتُ القَوْلَ † *I made the saying to be unrestricted,* and *unconditional.* (Mṣb.) [And اطلق لَفْظًا † *He uttered,* or *mentioned,* or *used, a word,* or *an expression, without restriction:* and in like manner, اطلق alone is often employed. And † *He used,* or *applied, a word,* or *an expression, without restriction,* عَلَى مَعْنًى *to signify a* particular *meaning:* thus in the saying اطلق المَصْدَرَ عَلَى الفَاعِلِ † *He used,* or *applied, the infinitive noun without restricting it* by the prefix ذُو, or the like, *to signify the active participial noun;* as عَدْلًا to signify عَادِلًا: and thus in the saying اطلق اسْمَ الكُلِّ عَلَى الجُزْءِ † *He used,* or *applied, the name of the whole without restricting it* by a prefix *to signify the part;* as القُرْآن to signify الآيَة: and many similar exs. might be added: but this usage of the verb is conventional: see Kull p. 57. Hence also أَلِفُ الإِطْلَاقِ: see art. ا, p. 1, col. 3.] — الإِطْلَاقُ فِى القَائِمَةِ [in which الاطلاق is inf. n. of the pass. v., أُطْلِقَ,] is † *The freedom from* [*the whiteness termed*] وَضَح [meaning تَحْجِيل, q. v.,] *in the leg* [of a horse]: and some make الإِطْلَاق to signify *the having a fore leg and a hind leg in one side with* تحجيل; and الإِمْسَاك [as inf. n. of أُمْسِكَ], the having a fore leg and a hind leg without تحجيل. (TA.) — اطلق عَدُوَّهُ † *He dosed his enemy with poison.* (IAạr, O, Ḳ.) — And اطلق نَخْلَهُ ‡ *He fecundated his palm-trees;* (IAạr, O, Ḳ, TA;) said when they are tall; (IAạr, O, TA;) as also ↓ طلّقهُ, (IAạr, O, Ḳ,) inf. n. تَطْلِيقٌ. (Ḳ.)

5. تطلّق, said of a gazelle, *He went along,* (Ṣ, O, Mṣb, Ḳ,) or *bounded in his running,* or *ran briskly in one direction,* (اِسْتَنَّ فِى عَدْوِهِ,) *and went along,* (TA,) *not pausing nor waiting for anything;* (Ṣ, O, Mṣb, Ḳ, TA;) as also ↓ استطلق. (TA.) And تطلّقت الخَيْلُ *The horses went* [or *ran*] *a heat without restraining themselves, to the goal.* (TA.) — And, said of a horse, ‡ *He staled after running.* (AO, O, Ḳ.) — Said of the face: see 1, latter half.

7. انطلق, inf. n. اِنْطِلَاقٌ, of which the dim. is ↓ نُطَيْلِيقٌ, the conjunctive ا being rejected, so that it becomes نطلاق, (Ṣ, O,) [*He was,* or *became, loosed from his bond:* whence,] اِنْطِلَاقُ العِنَانِ [*The rein's being let loose,* or *slackened,*] is a phrase metonymically used to denote quickness in going along. (Ḥar pp. 355-6.) — [Hence,] † *He* (a captive loosed from his bond) *went his way:* (Mṣb:) or [simply] *he went away,* or *departed:* (Ṣ, Mgh, O, Ḳ:) or *he went removing from his place.* (Er-Rághib, TA.) Thus in the Ḳur [lxxvii. 29], اِنْطَلِقُوا إِلَى مَا كُنْتُمْ بِهِ تُكَذِّبُونَ † [*Depart ye to that in which ye disbelieved*]; (TA;) meaning to the punishment: (Bḍ, Jel:) or, accord. to IAth, [it seems to mean *go ye away quickly* into the lowest depth of misery or affliction; for he says, app. in explanation of this verse of the Ḳur, that] الاِنْطِلَاقُ means سُرْعَةُ الذَّهَابِ فِى أَصْلِ المِحْنَةِ. (TA.) And one says also, انطلق يَفْعَلُ كَذَا ‡ *He went away doing,* or *to do, such a thing.* (TA.) وَانْطَلَقَ المَلَأُ مِنْهُمْ أَنِ امْشُوا [in the Ḳur xxxviii. 5 may be expl. in a similar manner; أَنْ being here used in the place of يَقُولُونَ: or this] means [*And the chief persons of them*] *broke forth,* or *launched forth, with their tongues,* [*saying,*] *Go ye on,* or *continue ye, in your course of action* &c. (Mughnee, voce أَنْ.) And one says, اُنْطُلِقَ بِهِ, (Ṣ, O, Ḳ,) meaning *He,* or *it, was taken away;* (Ḳ;) like as one says, اُنْقُطِعَ بِهِ. (Ṣ, O.) — انطلق لِسَانُهُ means † *His tongue was,* or *became, free from impediment;* and hence, *eloquent,* or *chaste in speech.* See an ex. in the Ḳur xxvi. 12: and see also طَلُقَ لِسَانُهُ. — انطلق said of the face: see 1, latter half, in two places.

8. مَا تَطَّلِقُ نَفْسِى لِهٰذَا الأَمْرِ, (Ṣ, O, Ḳ,*) of the measure تَفْتَعِلُ, (Ṣ, O, Ḳ,) inf. n. اِطِّلَاقٌ, of which the dim. is ↓ طُتَيْلِيقٌ, the [latter] ط being changed [back] into ت because the former ط becomes movent, (Ṣ, O,) † *My mind does not become free from straitness* [*for,* or *with respect to, this thing,* or *affair*]. (Ṣ, O, Ḳ.*)

10. اِسْتِطْلَاقٌ [primarily signifies The *desiring to be loosed, unbound, set loose* or *free,* and *let go*]: its dim. is ↓ تُطَيْلِيقٌ. (Ṣ, O.) — [Hence,] استطلق بَطْنُهُ † *His belly* [or *bowels*] *became* [*unbound,*] *loosened,* or *relaxed;* (Mṣb, TA;) or *became moved;* (Ṣ, O, Ḳ, TA;) and *the contents thereof came forth.* (TA.) — Said of a gazelle, *i. q.* تطلّق, q. v. (TA.) ═ [It is also trans., as such primarily signifying The *desiring* a person or thing *to be loosed, unbound, set loose* or *free,* and *let go.* — Hence,] one says, استطلق الرَّاعِى نَاقَةً لِنَفْسِهِ (Ṣ, O) [meaning *The pastor desired a she-camel to be left,* or *he left a she-camel, for himself, not milking her at the water;* as is plainly indicated by what immediately precedes it in the Ṣ: or] *the pastor took,* (PṢ,) or *retained,* [which is virtually the same,] *a she-camel for himself.* (PṢ, TA.) — And اِسْتَطْلَقْتُ مِنْ صَاحِبِ الدَّيْنِ كَذَا † [*I desired,* or *demanded, of the creditor, the remission of so much* of the debt]. (Mṣb.) — See also 4, former half.

طَلْقٌ [*Loosed from his bond, set loose* or *free,* or], as expl. by IAạr, *let go;* as also ↓ طَلِيقٌ and ↓ مُطْلَقٌ: and a man *not having anything upon him,* as expl. by Ks: and طَلْقُ اليَدَيْنِ a camel *not having the fore legs bound.* (TA.) You say, حُبِسَ طَلْقًا, (so in the CḲ,) or ↓ طَلَقًا, (Ḳ accord. to the TA, [and this is agreeable with the preceding context in the Ḳ, but it requires confirmation which I do not find,]) and with ḍamm, [i. e. طُلْقًا,] accord. to the Ḳ, but correctly with two ḍammehs, [i. e. ↓ طُلُقًا,] (TA, and thus in the Ṣ,) *He was imprisoned without shackle and without bond.* (Ḳ, TA) See also طُلُقٌ, first sentence. — [Hence,] طَلْقُ اللِّسَانِ, and ↓ طَلِيقُ اللسان, (Ṣ, O, Mṣb, Ḳ,) and ↓ طُلُقُ اللسان, (Ḳ,) and ↓ طَلَقُ اللسان, (TA,) ‡ *Eloquent,* or *chaste, in speech, and sweet therein:* (Mṣb:) and ↓ مُنْطَلِقُ اللِّسَانِ and ↓ مُتَطَلِّقُهُ ‡ [*free from impediment of the tongue;* or] *eloquent,* or *chaste in speech.* (TA.) And لِسَانٌ طَلْقٌ ذَلْقٌ, and ↓ طُلُقٌ ↓ ذُلُقٌ, and ↓ طَلِيقٌ ↓ ذَلِيقٌ, (Ṣ, O, Ḳ,) but the last two of these were unknown to Aṣ, and the latter of them was disallowed by IAạr, (TA,) and ↓ طُلُقٌ ↓ ذُلُقٌ, (O, Ḳ,) [expl. in the Ḳ as meaning *A tongue having sharpness;* but correctly] meaning ‡ *a tongue free from impediment,* or *eloquent,* or *chaste in speech,* (ذُو انْطِلَاقٍ,) *and sharp.* (O, TA.) — And طَلْقُ اليَدَيْنِ, (Ṣ, Mgh, O, Mṣb, Ḳ,) and ↓ طُلُقُ اليدين, (O, Ḳ,) and ↓ طَلِيقُ اليدين, (L, TA,) ‡ *Liberal, bountiful, munificent,* or *generous;* (Ṣ, Mgh, O, Mṣb, Ḳ;) applied to a man: (Ṣ, Mgh, O, Mṣb:) and in like manner, a woman: (TA:) [or] a woman is termed طَلْقَةُ اليَدَيْنِ: (Ṣ:) and so, accord. to AZ, طَلْقُ الوَجْهِ; which [generally] has another meaning, expl. in what follows. (TA.) And يَدُهُ طَلْقٌ ‡ *His hand is liberal;* syn. بُسُطٌ; (TA in art. بسط;) and so ↓ مُطْلَقَةٌ: (Ṣ and Ḳ and TA in that art.:) or the latter signifies *opened;* and so ↓ مَطْلُوقَةٌ. (TA in the present art.) — And طَلْقُ الوَجْهِ, (Ṣ, O, Mṣb, Ḳ,) and ↓ طَلِقُ الوجه, (IAạr, O, Ḳ,) and ↓ طُلُقُ الوجه, (IAạr, Ḳ,) and ↓ طَلِيقُ الوجه, (Ṣ, O, Ḳ,) ‡ *Laughing,* or *happy,* or *cheerful, and bright, in the face,* or *countenance:* (Ḳ, TA:) or *cheerful,* or *happy, displaying openness and pleasantness, in the face;* and so طَلْقٌ alone: (Mṣb:) and ↓ طَلِيقُ الوجه *open and pleasant, and goodly, in countenance:* (AZ, TA:) and طَلِيقٌ alone, *joyful,* and *open* or *cheer-*

ful, in countenance. (TA. [And it is there said that the pl. of طَلْقٌ is طَلْقَات: but this is app. a mistranscription for طُلْقَانٌ or طِلْقَانٌ.]) أَوْجُهٌ ↑ طَوَالِقُ is not allowable, except in poetry. (IAạr, TA.) —— And يَوْمٌ طَلْقٌ, (Lth, Ṣ, Mgh, O, Ḳ,) and لَيْلَةٌ طَلْقَةٌ (Lth, Ṣ, Mgh, O, Mṣb, Ḳ) and طَلْقٌ, (O, Mṣb, Ḳ,) ‡ *A day,* and *a night, in which is neither heat nor cold:* (Lth, Mgh, O, Mṣb, Ḳ:) or *in which is no cold nor anything hurtful:* (Ṣ:) or *in which is no rain:* or *in which is no wind:* or *in which the cold is mild:* (TA: [after which is added, من ايام طَلْقَات: but the last word seems, as in an instance before mentioned, to be mistranscribed, or ايام (i. e. أَيَّام) may be a mistake for لَيَالٍ:]) or لَيْلَةٌ طَلْقٌ means *a night in which is no cold:* (AA, TA:) or *in which the wind is still:* (O, TA:) and لَيْلَةٌ طَلْقَةٌ sometimes means *a moon-lit,* or *a light,* or *bright, night:* (IDrd, O, TA:) and one says also ↑ لَيْلَةٌ طَالِقَةٌ, (Ḳ, TA,) meaning *a still,* or *calm,* and *light,* or *bright, night:* (TA:) and ↑ لَيَالٍ طَوَالِقُ, (Ḳ,* TA,) meaning *pleasant nights in which is neither heat nor cold.* (TA.) Er-Rá'ee says,

• فَلَمَّا عَلَتْهُ الشَّمْسُ فِى يَوْمِ طَلْقَةٍ •

meaning يَوْمِ لَيْلَةٍ طَلْقَةٍ [*And when the sun came upon him,* or *it,*] *in a day of a night in which was neither cold nor wind;* i. e., in a day after such a night; for the Arabs commence with the night, before the day: and the phrase فِى يَوْمِ طَلْقَةٍ occurs in like manner in a verse of Dhu-r-Rummeh. (Az, TA.) —— For the epithet طَلْقُ الْيَدِ الْيُمْنَى, (applied to a horse, accord. to the K,) see طُلُقٌ. —— And for other meanings assigned in the Ḳ to طَلْقٌ, see طِلْقٌ, in two places. ═ طَلْقٌ signifies also The *pain of childbirth.* (Ṣ, O.) One says, ضَرَبَهَا الطَّلْقُ [*The pain of childbirth smote her*]. (O.) [See also طُلِقَتْ, of which it is the inf. n.] ═ And [it is said to signify] *A sort of medicine.* (Ṣ.) See طَلَقٌ, latter half, in two places.

طَلْقُ الوَجْهِ and —— طَلْقُ اليَدَيْنِ: see the next preceding paragraph.

طِلْقٌ: see طَلْقُ الوَجْهِ and —— طَلْقُ اللِّسَانِ. —— طِلْقٌ signifies also ‡ *Lawful, allowable,* or *free:* (Ṣ, Mgh, O, Mṣb, Ḳ, TA:) or it signifies, (Mṣb, TA,) or signifies also, (Mgh,) ↑ مُطْلَقٌ, (Mgh, Mṣb, TA,) [i. e.] a thing *unrestricted,* (TA,) i. e. any affair *in which one has power,* or *authority, to act according to his own judgment* or *discretion* or *free will.* (Mṣb.) One says, هٰذَا حَلَالٌ طِلْقٌ ‡ [*This is lawful, &c., unrestricted;* using the latter epithet as a corroborative]: and [in the contr. case] حَرَامٌ غِلْقٌ. (TA.) And هُوَ لَكَ طِلْقًا ‡ [*It is thine lawfully* &c.]. (Ṣ, O, Ḳ, TA.) And اِفْعَلْ هٰذَا طِلْقًا لَكَ † *Do thou this as a thing lawful &c. to thee.* (Mṣb.) And أَعْطَيْتُهُ مِنْ طِلْقِ مَالِى † *I gave him of what was lawful* &c., i. e. *free to be disposed of by me, of my property:* (Mṣb:) or ‡ *of what was clear* [*from any claim or the like*], and *good,* or *lawful, of my property.* (TA.) And الخَيْلُ طِلْقٌ, occurring in a trad. as meaning ‡ *Horses are allowable* to be betted upon. (TA.) And أَنْتَ طِلْقٌ مِنْ هٰذَا الأَمْرِ ‡ *Thou art clear of this affair;* (Ṣ, O, Ḳ,* TA;*) *quit of it,* or *irresponsible for it.* (Ḳ, TA.) —— [In consequence of a misplacement in some copies of the Ḳ, several meanings belonging to طَلَقٌ are assigned to طِلْقٌ.] ═ See also طَلْقٌ, latter half.

طَلَقٌ: see طَلْقٌ, second sentence. —— Also the subst. from طَلَقَتِ الإِبِلُ: (AZ, Ṣ, TA: [see 1, second sentence:]) and [as such] signifying The *journeying* [of camels] *during the night to arrive at the water in the next night, there being two nights between them and the water; the first of which nights is termed* الطَّلَقُ [or لَيْلَةُ الطَّلَقِ (see حَوْزٌ)]; *the pastor loosing them to repair to the water,* [in the CḲ يَجْلِبُهَا is put for يُخَلِّيهَا,] *and leaving them to pasture while going thither: the camels after the driving, during the first night, are said to be* ↑ طَوَالِقُ; and in the second night, قَوَارِبُ: (Ṣ, O, Ḳ, TA:) or الطَّلَقُ signifies *the first of two days intervening between the camels and the water;* and القَرَبُ, the second: and لَيْلَةُ الطَّلَقِ, *the night in which the faces of the camels are turned towards the water and during which they are left to pasture;* and لَيْلَةُ القَرَبِ, the second night: (Aṣ, TA:) but it has been said that لَيْلَةُ الطَّلَقِ means *the second of the nights in which the camels repair to the water:* Th says that الطَّلَقُ signifies *the second of two days during which the camels seek the water when it is two days distant from them;* and القَرَبُ, the first of those days: and it is said that لَيْلَةُ الطَّلَقِ means [*the night of*] *the turning of the faces of the camels towards the water:* but this explanation was not pleasing to ISd. (TA.) [See an ex. voce حَوْزٌ, in which it is used tropically.] —— Also *A heat;* i. e. *a single run,* or *a run at once, to a goal,* or *limit;* syn. شَوْطٌ: (Ṣ, IAth, O, Mṣb, Ḳ, TA;) meaning *a running,* of a horse, *without restraining himself,* [or *without stopping,*] *to a goal,* or *limit:* (Mṣb:) and the *utmost extent to which a horse runs.* (TA.) One says of a horse, عَدَا طَلَقًا or طَلَقَيْنِ [*He ran a heat* or *two heats*]. (Ṣ, O, Mṣb, Ḳ. [In the CḲ, erroneously, طَلْقًا and طَلْقَيْنِ.]) —— And (hence, TA) ‡ *A share,* or *portion,* (Ibn-'Abbád, A, O, Ḳ, TA,) of property [&c.]. (A, TA.) ═ Also *A shackle,* or *pair of shackles,* (قَيْدٌ,) *of skins:* (Ṣ, M, O, Ḳ, TA:) or *a rope strongly twisted, so that it will stand up.* (TA.) —— And sing. of أَطْلَاقٌ which signifies The [*intestines into which the food passes from the stomach, termed the*] أَمْعَآء, or the أَقْتَاب *of the belly;* (IDrd, O, Ḳ;* [in some copies of the last of which, القُتْبُ is erroneously put for القَتَبُ as one of the words explaining الطَّلَقُ;]) so in one or more of the dialects: AO says, in the belly are أَطْلَاقٌ, of which the sing. is طَلَقٌ; (O, TA;) meaning the *lines,* or *streaks,* (طَرَائِق,) *of the belly:* and طَلَقُ البَطْنِ is also expl. [in like manner] as meaning the جُدَّة *of the belly;* pl. as above. (TA.) ═ Also The [*plant called*] شُبْرُم: [but what plant is meant by this is doubtful:] or *a plant that is used in dyes:* or this is a mistake: (Ḳ:) [or] accord. to Ibn-'Abbád, ↑ الطُّلَقُ is *what is used in dyes;* and is said to be *the* شُبْرُم: (O, TA:*) and (Ḳ) accord. to Aṣ, (O,) طَلَقٌ signifies *a sort of medicament,* (O, Ḳ,) *which, when one is anointed therewith,* (Ḳ,) i. e. *with the extract thereof,* (TA,) *prevents the burning of fire:* (Ḳ:) or *a species of plant:* so says Aṣ: (O:) the appellation by which it is generally known is ↑ طَلْقٌ, with the ل quiescent; (O, Ḳ;) or this pronunciation is incorrect: (Ḳ:) and AḤát mentions, (Ḳ, TA,) on the authority of Aṣ, (TA,) its being termed ↑ طَلَّق: (Ḳ, TA:) *but it is not a plant: it is of the nature of stones, and of* [*what are termed*] لِخَاف [thin white stones]; and probably he [referring to Aṣ] heard that it is called كَوْكَبُ الأَرْضِ, and therefore supposed it to be a plant; for if it were a plant, fire would burn it; but *fire does not burn it, unless by means of artful contrivances:* (O, TA:) the word is arabicized, from تَلْكْ: (Ḳ, TA: in the O written تلك:) [it is the well-known mineral termed *talc:*] the Ra-ees [Ibn-Seenà, whom we call "Avicenna,"] says, (TA,) *it is a brightly-shining stone, that separates, when it is bruised, into several laminæ and split pieces, of which are made* مضاوى [correctly مَضَاوِئُ, meaning *small circular panes which are inserted in apertures to admit light,*] *for the* [*cupolas of*] *hot baths, instead of glass: the best is that of El-Yemen; then that of India; then that of El-Undulus* [or *El-Andalus*]: the art employed in dissolving it consists in putting it into a piece of rag with some pebbles and immersing it in tepid water, then moving it about gently until it becomes dissolved and comes forth from the piece of rag into the water, whereupon the water is strained from it, and it is put in the sun to dry. (Ḳ, TA.)

طَلِقُ الوَجْهِ and —— طَلِقٌ ذَلِقٌ: } see طَلْقٌ.
لِسَانٌ طَلِقٌ ذَلِقٌ and طَلِقُ اللِّسَانِ: }

طُلُقٌ, (Ṣ, O, Mṣb, TA,) with two ḍammehs, (Mṣb, TA,) or ↑ طُلْقٌ, (Ḳ,) but this requires consideration, (TA,) *Not shackled;* applied to a she-camel, (Ṣ, O, Mṣb, TA,) and to a he-camel, (Ṣ, O, TA,) and to a person imprisoned; (O, TA;) as also ↑ طَالِقٌ applied to a she-camel; but طُلُقٌ is more common: (Aboo-Naṣr, TA:) the pl. of طُلُقٌ is أَطْلَاقٌ. (Ṣ, TA.) See also طَلْقٌ, second sentence. —— لِسَانٌ طُلُقٌ ذُلُقٌ: —— and طُلُقُ اليَدَيْنِ: see طَلْقٌ again. —— And طُلُقٌ إِحْدَى القَوَائِمِ † A horse *having one of the legs without* [*the whiteness termed*] التَّحْجِيل. (Ṣ.) And طُلُقُ ↑ اليَدِ اليُمْنَى, (O,) or طَلْقُ اليَدِ اليُمْنَى, (Ḳ, [in this case again deviating from other authorities,]) ‡ A horse *without* تَحْجِيل *in the right fore leg;* (TA;) i. q. مُطْلَقُ ↑ اليَدِ اليمنى. (O, Ḳ, TA.) And مُطْلَقُ ↑ اليَدَيْنِ † A horse *having the fore legs free from* تحجيل. (Mṣb.)

— [As an epithet in which the quality of a subst. is predominant,] طَلُوقٌ, (Ibn-'Abbád, O,) or † طَلَقٌ, (Ḳ, [but this, as in the instances above, is questionable,]) signifies † *A gazelle:* (Ibn-'Abbád, O, Ḳ:) so called because of the quickness of its running: (O,* TA:) pl. أُطْلَاقٌ. (Ibn-'Abbád, O, Ḳ.) — And † *A dog of the chase:* (Ḳ:) because he is let loose; or because of the quickness of his running at the chase: (TA:) أُطْلَاقٌ is mentioned by Ibn-'Abbád as signifying *dogs of the chase.* (O.)

طَلْقَةٌ [*A single divorce:* used in this sense in law-books]. (T and Mṣb in art. بت, &c.)

طَلَقَةٌ: see مِطْلَاقٌ.

طَلَاقٌ is the inf. n. of طَلَقَتْ said of a woman: (Th, Ṣ, Mgh, O, Ḳ:) or the subst. therefrom: (Mṣb:) or [rather] it is also a subst. in the sense of تَطْلِيقٌ; (Mgh;) [whence,] طَلَاقُ المَرْأَةِ signifies † *The letting the wife go her way:* (Lth, O:) and it has two meanings: one is [*the divorcing of the woman;* i. e.] *the dissolving of the wife's marriage-tie:* and the other is *the leaving,* and *dismissing, of the wife* [either in an absolute sense or as is done by a single sentence of divorce]. (O, TA.) Some of the lawyers hold that the free woman whose husband is a slave is not separated but by three [sentences, as is the case when both husband and wife are free]; and the female slave whose husband is free, by two: some, that the wife in the former case is separated by two [sentences]; and in the latter case, by not less than three: and some, that when the husband is a slave and the wife is free, or the reverse, or when both are slaves, the wife is separated by two [sentences]. (TA.)

طَلِيقٌ A captive *having his bond loosed from him,* (Ṣ, O, Ḳ, TA,) *and let go.* (TA.) See also طَلْقٌ, first sentence. — And † A man *freed from slavery; emancipated;* i. q. عَتِيقٌ; i. e. *who has become free:* pl. طُلَقَآءُ. (TA.) — It is said in a trad., الطُّلَقَآءُ مِنْ قُرَيْشٍ وَالعُتَقَآءُ مِنْ ثَقِيفٍ † [*The* طلقاء *are of Kureysh; and the* عُتَقَآء, *of Thakeef*]: الطلقاء being app. applied to Kureysh as it has a more special signification than العتقاء: but accord. to Th, الطُّلَقَآءُ signifies *those who have been brought within the pale of El-Islám against their will.* (TA.) — طَلِيقُ اللِّسَانِ: and — طَلِيقُ اليَدَيْنِ and — لِسَانٌ طَلِيقٌ ذَلِيقٌ: and — طَلِيقُ الوَجْهِ: see طَلْقٌ again; the last in two places. — طَلِيقُ الإِلٰهِ means ‡ *The wind.* (O, Ḳ, TA.)

طُلَّاقٌ: } see مِطْلَاقٌ.
طِلِّيقٌ:

طَالِقٌ A she-camel *not having having her fore shank and her arm bound together:* (TA:) or *not having upon her a* خِطَام [or halter]: (IDrd, O, Ḳ:) or *repairing to the water;* and so † مِطْلَاقٌ; (Aboo-Nasr, Ḳ, TA;) of which latter the pl. is مَطَالِيقُ: (TA:) or *that is left a day and a night and then milked:* (Ḳ:) pl. طَوَالِقُ and أَطْلَاقٌ and طُلَّقٌ; which last is expl. by AA as meaning she-camels *that are milked in the place of pasturing.* (TA.) See also طَلْقٌ, first sentence: and for an explanation of the pl. طَوَالِقُ applied to camels, see طَلَقٌ, second sentence. Also (O) طَالِقٌ, (Ṣ, O,) or طَالِقَةٌ, (Ḳ,) signifies A she-camel *which the pastor leaves for himself, not milking her at the water:* (Ṣ, O, Ḳ:) the former is expl. by Esh-Sheybánee as meaning one *which the pastor leaves* [*with her udder bound*] *with her* صِرَار, *not milking her in the place where she lies down to rest:* (TA:) or the latter signifies, (Lth, O, Ḳ,) and the former also, (Lth, O,) a she-camel *that is set loose among the tribe to pasture where she will in any part of the tract adjacent to their place of alighting* or *abode,* (Lth, O, Ḳ, [مِنْ جَنَابِهِمْ in the CḲ being erroneously put for مِنْ جَنَائِبِهِمْ,]) *that has not her fore shank and her arm bound together when she returns in the afternoon* or *evening, nor is turned away* [*from the others*] *in the place of pasturage:* (Lth, O:) or طَالِقٌ signifies a she-camel, (Ṣ, Mṣb,) and a ewe, (Ṣ,) *that is set loose,* or *dismissed, to pasture where she will:* (Ṣ, Mṣb:) and also as first expl. in this sentence: (Ṣ:) it is mentioned by El-Fárábee as signifying a ewe *left to pasture by herself, alone.* (Mṣb.) — [Hence,] طَالِقٌ and طَالِقَةٌ, (Ṣ, Mgh, O, Mṣb, Ḳ,) the former, without ة, used by all, (Mṣb,) the latter occurring in a verse of El-Aạshà, (Ṣ, Mgh,* O, Mṣb,) ending a hemistich, and pronounced طَالِقَهْ, (Ṣ, O, Mṣb, [which cite the verse somewhat differently,]) ‡ A woman [*divorced,* or] *left to go her way,* (Ṣ,* Mgh,* O, Mṣb,*) or *separated from her husband* [*by a sentence of divorce*]: (Ṣ,* Mgh,* Mṣb,* Ḳ, TA:) both mentioned by Akh: (O, TA:) accord. to IAmb, one says طَالِقٌ only, because it applies only to a female: accord. to Lth and IF, طَالِقَةٌ means طَالِقَةٌ غَدًا [*divorced, &c., to-morrow*]; and Lth adds that it is thus to accord with its verb, طَلَقَتْ: some, however, say that the ة is affixed in the verse of El-Aạshà by poetic license, to complete the hemistich; but an Arab of the desert, in reciting this verse to Aṣ, is related to have said طَالِقٌ [which equally completes the hemistich]: and the Basrees hold that the sign of the fem. gender is elided in طَالِقٌ because it is a possessive epithet, meaning ذَاتُ طَلَاقٍ [*having divorce*]. (Mṣb.) — أَوْجُهٌ طَوَالِقُ: and — نَيْلَةٌ and — لَيَالٍ طَوَالِقُ and طَالِقَةٌ: see طَلْقٌ, latter half.

طُتَيْلِيقٌ dim. of اِطِّلَاقٌ. (Ṣ, O.) See 8.

تُطَيْلِيقٌ dim. of اِسْتِطْلَاقٌ. (Ṣ, O.) See 10.

مُطْلَقٌ: see طَلْقٌ, first sentence. — [Hence,] يَدُهُ مُطْلَقَةٌ: see طَلْقٌ again, former half. — See also طَلْقٌ. مَآءٌ مُطْلَقٌ means † *Water that is unrestricted.* (TA.) And حُكْمٌ مُطْلَقٌ means † [*A judicial decision,* or *an ordinance* or *the like,* or *a rule, that is unrestricted,* or *absolute,* or] *in which is no exception.* (TA.) — مُطْلَقُ اليَدَيْنِ: and مُطْلَقُ اليَدِ اليُمْنَى: each applied to a horse: see طَلْقٌ. ═ [Golius, as on the authority of Meyd, explains it as signifying also *A place where horses meet to be sent forth to run,* or *race:* but what here next follows inclines me to think that it may be correctly مُطَلِّقٌ.]

مُطَلِّقٌ One *desiring to outstrip with his horse in a race.* (Ḳ.)

مِطْلَاقٌ: see طَالِقٌ. ═ Also, (Ṣ, O, Mṣb, Ḳ,) and † مِطْلِيقٌ, (O, Mṣb, Ḳ,) and † طُلَقَةٌ, (Ṣ, O, Ḳ,) and † طِلِّيقٌ, (Ḳ,) and † طُلَّاقٌ, this last mentioned by Z, (TA,) ‡ One *who oftentimes divorces,* or *dismisses, wives.* (Ṣ, O, Mṣb, Ḳ, TA.)

مِطْلِيقٌ: see what next precedes.

مَطْلُوقَةٌ: see طَلْقٌ. — اِمْرَأَةٌ مَطْلُوقَةٌ † *A woman taken with the pains of parturition.* (Mgh, Mṣb.)

مُطَيْلِقٌ and مُطَيْلِيقٌ dims. of مُنْطَلِقٌ. (Ṣ.)

مُتَطَلِّقُ اللِّسَانِ: } see طَلْقٌ, former half.
مُنْطَلِقُ اللِّسَانِ:

نُطَيْلِيقٌ: dim. of اِنْطِلَاقٌ. (Ṣ, O.) See 7.

طلم

1. طَلَمَ الخُبْزَةَ, (Ḳ,) aor. ِ, (TḲ,) inf. n. طَلْمٌ, (TA,) *He made the cake of bread even,* or *equable.* (Ḳ.)

2. طلّم, inf. n. تَطْلِيمٌ, *He beat* a cake of bread baked in hot ashes *with his hand,* (Ḳ, TA) *in order that it might become cool.* (TA.) Hence the saying of Ḥassán,

• تَظَلُّ جِيَادُنَا مُتَمَطِّرَاتٍ •
• يُطَلِّمُهُنَّ بِالخُمُرِ النِّسَآءُ •

(Ḳ,* TA:) or, as some relate it, يُلَطِّمُهُنَّ; but this is weak, or repudiated: (Ḳ:) or this is the correct reading, and the more obviously appropriate in meaning, accord. to MF; and accord. to IAth, it is the reading commonly known, and the same as the former in meaning: (TA:) the meaning is, [*Our coursers passing the day running like the pouring of rain,*] *the women wiping the sweat from them with the mufflers:* (Ḳ, TA:) or, as some say, [*the women with the mufflers*] *beating them with the hands* in removing the dust that was upon them. (TA.)

طُلْمٌ *A table upon which the bread is expanded* [*previously to the baking*]. (Ḳ.)

طُلْمٌ *Dirt of the teeth in consequence of neglect* [*of the use*] *of the* سِوَاك [or *tooth-stick*]. (Ḳ.)

طُلْمَةٌ *A* خُبْزَة, (Ṣ, Ḳ, TA,) [i. e. a *cake of bread,* or *lump of dough,*] *baked in hot ashes in a hollow in the ground;* what people [now] call a مَلَّة; but this is the name of the hollow itself: what is baked in this is [properly called] the

طُلْمَة and خُبْزَة and مَلِيل: (Ṣ, TA:) pl. طُلَمٌ. (L, TA.) It is said in a prov., إِنَّ دُونَ الطُّلْمَةِ خَرْطَ قَتَادِ هَوْبَرٍ (Meyd, TA) [i. e. *Before the attainment of the cake of bread baked in hot ashes is the stripping of the leaves, by grasping each branch and drawing the hand down it, of the tragacanth of Howbar*]: the طُلْمَة is the *cake of bread that is put in hot ashes;* and Howbar is a place abounding with the tragacanth: the prov. is applied in relation to a thing that is unattainable. (Meyd.)

طُلَّامٌ The [*tree called*] تَنُّوم [q. v.]; which is [erroneously said to be] *hemp-seed* (حَبُّ الشَّهْدَانِجِ). (Ḳ.)

مِطْلَمَةٌ The *implement with which bread is expanded.* (KL.)

طلو and طلى

1. طَلَوْتُ الطَّلَا, (Ṣ, TA,) or الطَّلِىَّ, aor. أَطْلُو; (TA;) and طَلَيْتُهُ, (Ṣ, Ḳ, TA,) aor. أَطْلِى, inf. n. طَلْىٌ; (TA;) *I tied the young lamb* or *kid,* (Ṣ, Ḳ,* TA,) *by its leg,* (Ṣ, TA,) *to a peg,* or *stake;* (TA;) and *confined, restrained,* or *withheld, it.* (Ṣ.) And طَلَيْتُ الشَّىْءَ *I confined, restrained,* or *withheld, the thing.* (Ṣ, Ḳ,* TA.) ═ طَلَيْتُهُ بِهِ, (Ṣ, Mgh, Mṣb,) aor. أَطْلِى, (Mṣb,) inf. n. طَلْىٌ, (Ṣ, Mṣb,) *I daubed, bedaubed, smeared,* or *besmeared, it;* (Mgh;) [*rubbed,* or *did, it over; anointed, painted, varnished, plastered, coated, overspread,* or *overlaid, it; with it;* i. e. with any fluid, semifluid, liniment, unguent, or the like; as, for instance,] with oil, (Ṣ,) or tar, (Mgh,) or clay, or mud, (Mṣb,) &c. (Ṣ, Mgh, Mṣb.) You say, طَلَى البَعِيرَ الهِنَآءَ, and بِالهِنَآءِ, [the latter of which is the more common,] aor. يَطْلِى, (Ḳ,) inf. n. as above, (TA,) *He daubed, bedaubed, smeared,* or *besmeared, the camel with tar;* as also ↓ طَلَّاهُ, [but app. in an intensive sense, or relating to several objects,] (Ḳ, TA,) inf. n. تَطْلِيَةٌ. (TA.) [And طَلَاهُ بِالذَّهَبِ *He gilded it.* And طَلَاهُ بِالفِضَّةِ *He silvered it.*] — Hence, طَلَى اللَّيْلُ الآفَاقَ † *The night covered* [*with its darkness*] *the adjacent regions,* or *the tracts of the horizon;* like as when a camel is daubed with tar. (TA.) — And طَلَى, aor. يَطْلِى, † *He reviled* [another], or *vilified* [him]; (TA;) as also ↓ طَلَّى, (Ḳ,* TA,) inf. n. تَطْلِيَةٌ; (Ḳ;) or تَطْلِيَةٌ signifies the *reviling,* or *vilifying, in a foul manner.* (IAạr, TA.) — And طَلَى البَقْلُ † *The herbs,* or *leguminous plants, appeared upon the surface of the earth* [as though they overspread it with a coating of colour]. (TA.) ═ طَلِىَ فُوهُ, aor. يَطْلَى, inf. n. طَلًا, *His mouth had a yellowness in the teeth.* (Ṣ, TA.) طَلًا [in relation to the mouth but in a somewhat different sense] is mentioned in the Ḳ in art. طلو and not in art. طلى; but it belongs to both of these. (TA.)

2: see the preceding paragraph, in two places. — طَلَّيْتُ فُلَانًا, (Ṣ,) inf. n. تَطْلِيَةٌ, (Ṣ, Ḳ,) signifies also *I tended,* or *took care of, such a one in his sickness; undertook,* or *managed,* or *superintended, the treatment of him therein.* (Ṣ, Ḳ,* TA.) ═ And التَّطْلِيَةُ also signifies *The act of singing.* (AA, Ḳ.)

4. اطلت *She* (a wild animal) *had with her a young one,* which is termed طَلًا. (IḲṭṭ, TA.) ═ اطلى (said of a man, Ṣ, TA, and of a camel, TA) *He had an inclining of the neck* (Ṣ, Ḳ, TA) *towards one side* when said of a man, (TA,) on the occasion of death, (Ṣ, Ḳ, TA,) or on some other occasion. (Ṣ, TA.) — Hence, (IAth, TA,) مَا أَطْلَى نَبِىٌّ قَطُّ, (Ḳ, TA,) occurring in a trad., (TA,) means مَا مَالَ إِلَى هَوَاهُ [i. e. † *No prophet ever inclined to his natural desire*]: (Ḳ, TA:) as some relate it, مَا آطَّلَى; but this is a mistake. (TA.)

5. تطلّى: see 8. — Also, (said of a man, TA,) *He kept to diversion, sport,* or *play, and mirth.* (Ḳ, TA.)

8. اِطَّلَى, (Ṣ, Mgh, Mṣb, Ḳ,) of the measure اِفْتَعَلَ, (Ṣ, Mgh, Mṣb,) and ↓ تطلّى, (Ṣ, Ḳ,) [*He,* or *it, was,* or *became, daubed, bedaubed, smeared,* or *besmeared; rubbed,* or *done, over; anointed, painted, varnished, plastered, coated, overspread,* or *overlaid:* or] *he daubed,* &c., *himself:* (Ṣ,* Mgh, Mṣb, Ḳ:*) بِهِ [*with it*]; (Ṣ, Ḳ;) i. e. [with any fluid, semifluid, liniment, unguent, or the like; as, for instance,] with oil, (Ṣ,) or tar, (Mgh, Ḳ,) or clay, or mud, (Mṣb,) &c. (Ṣ, Mgh, Mṣb.)

12. اِطْلَوْلَى *He was good in speech:* ═ and *He was defeated,* or *put to flight.* (IAạr, TA in art. حلى.)

طَلًا The *young one of any of the cloven-hoofed animals:* (Ṣ, TA: [in the latter of which is added, as from the Ṣ, وَالخُفِّ; but this is app. a mistake:]) or the *young one of the gazelle, when just born:* (M, Mṣb, Ḳ: [see شَصْرٌ:]) and the *youngling, of any kind;* as also ↓ طَلْوٌ; (Ḳ, TA;) which latter is mentioned by IDrd; but expl. by him as meaning the *young one of a wild animal:* (TA:) and ↓ طِلْوَةٌ has this last meaning (Ḳ, TA) likewise accord. to IDrd: (TA:) the pl. [of pauc.] of طَلًا is أَطْلَآءٌ (Ṣ, Mṣb, Ḳ) and [of mult.] طِلَآءٌ (Ḳ) and طُلِىٌّ (Ḳ, TA, but omitted in the CḲ) and طِلِىٌّ (Lth, TA) and طُلْيَانٌ (Ḳ) and طِلْيَانٌ. (Lth, Ḳ.) [See also طُلِىٌّ.] — [And, accord. to Freytag (in art. طلى), *An infant until a month old or more:* but for this he has named no authority.] ═ And The *person;* syn. شَخْصٌ. (Ṣ, Ḳ.) So in the saying, إِنَّهُ لَجَمِيلُ الطَّلَا [*Verily he is goodly,* or *comely, in person*]. (Ṣ.) ═ Also *Daubed,* or *smeared,* (↓ مَطْلِىٌّ,) *with tar.* (Ṣ, Ḳ.) [See also طَلِيَّا.] — And A man *having a severe disease:* (Ḳ, TA:) having no dual nor pl., or, as some say, (TA,) the pl. is أَطْلَآءٌ, and the dual is طَلَيَانِ. (Ḳ, TA.) [See also مُطَلًّى.] ═ And *Desire;* syn. هَوًى. (Ḳ, TA.) So in the saying, قَضَى طَلَاهُ مِنْ حَاجَتِهِ [*He accomplished his desire of that which he wanted*]. (Ḳ, TA.) [Or, as Freytag says, on the authority of the Deewán of the Hudhalees, accord. to some it signifies *Pleasure* (*voluptas*): and accord. to others, *thirst.* But see طِلًا.] — See also طُلَاوَةٌ, in two places. ═ And see also طِلَآءٌ, last sentence.

طِلًا *Pleasure,* or *delight.* (Ḳ.) ═ See also طِلَآءٌ.

طَلْوٌ: see طَلًا, first sentence.

طِلْوٌ The *wolf.* (Ḳ.) — And *A hunter,* or *pursuer of wild animals or the like, slender in body:* (Aboo-Sa'eed, Ḳ, TA: [in the CḲ, القَابِضُ is erroneously put for القَانِصُ:]) said to be [so called as being] likened to the wolf. (Aboo-Sa'eed, TA.) Eṭ-Ṭirimmáḥ says,

صَادَفَتْ طِلْوًا طَوِيلَ الطَّوَى •
حَافِظَ العَيْنِ قَلِيلَ السَّأَمْ •

[*She,* or *they,* (app. referring to one or more of the objects of the chase,) *encountered a hunter slender in body, a long endurer of hunger, one whom sleep did not overcome, little,* or *seldom, subject to disgust*]. (Aboo-Sa'eed, TA.) ═ See also طِلَآءٌ, last sentence.

طُلَاةٌ (Ṣ, Ḳ, TA) accord. to AA and Fr, (Ṣ, TA,) and so says Sb on the authority of Abu-l-Khaṭṭáb, (TA,) or ↓ طُلْيَةٌ (Ṣ, Ḳ, TA) accord. to Aṣ, (Ṣ, TA,) each with ḍamm, (TA,) is sing. of طُلًا or طُلًى; which signifies *Necks:* (Ṣ, Ḳ:) or the *bases of the necks:* (M, Ḳ:) or the *broad part* [or *parts*] *beneath the protuberant bone behind the ear:* or, accord. to ISk, the *sides of the neck:* Sb says that طُلَاةٌ and طُلًا are of the class of رُطَبَةٌ and رُطَبٌ, not of the class of تَمْرَةٌ and تَمْرٌ: (TA:) [but see art. رطب, in which it is said, as on the authority of Sb, that رُطَبٌ is not a broken pl. of رُطَبَةٌ, being masc. like تَمْرٌ:] ↓ طُلْوَةٌ, also, signifies the *side of the neck,* as a dial. var. of [طُلَاةٌ or of] طُلْيَةٌ. (TA.)

طُلْوَةٌ The *whiteness of the dawn,* (Ḳ, TA,) and *of blossoms,* or *flowers.* (TA.) ═ See also طُلَاةٌ.

طِلْوَةٌ: see طَلًا: ═ and see also طِلَآءٌ, last sentence.

طَلْيَةٌ *A single act of daubing* or *smearing* or *the like:* pl. طَلَيَاتٌ. (Mgh.) ═ See also طِلَآءٌ, last sentence.

طُلْيَةٌ: see طُلَاةٌ. ═ Also *A portion, tuft,* or *wisp, of wool, with which mangy camels are daubed* [*with tar*]; also called رِبْذَةٌ: whence the saying, مَا يُسَاوِى طُلْيَةً [*It is not worth a* طلية]. (TA.) — See also طَلِيَّا. — And see طِلَآءٌ, last sentence.

طَلْيَاءُ A she-camel *daubed*, or *smeared*, (↓ مُطْلِيَّةٌ, Ḳ, TA,) *with tar*. (TA.) [See also طَلًا.] — And A *mangy* she-camel: (Ḳ:) app. so called because the she-camel is not daubed, or smeared, [with tar] unless mangy. (TA.) — And The *rag of a menstruous woman*: (Ḳ, TA:) whence the prov., أَهْوَنُ مِنَ الطَّلْيَاءِ [*More despicable than the* طلياء]: or, accord. to IAạr, this is called ↓ طَلِيَّةٌ. (TA.) — [In some copies of the Ḳ, this word is erroneously put for طُلَيًّا, q. v.]

طُلَوَاءُ: see طَلَوَانٌ. ═ Also [The *green substance that overspreads stale water, called*] طُحْلُب; and so ↓ طُلَاوَةٌ. (Ṣgh, TA.)

طُلْوَانٌ: see طُلَاوَةٌ.

طَلَوَانٌ and ↓ طُلْوَانٌ and ↓ طُلَوَاءُ [or app. the last only accord. to some copies of the Ḳ] *Expectation*: and *slowness*, or *tardiness*; as also ↓ طَلَاوَةٌ, (Ḳ, TA,) with fet-ḥ. (TA.) See also طُلَاوَةٌ.

طَلَوَانٌ: see the next preceding paragraph: and see also طُلَاوَةٌ.

طَلِيٌّ: see طِلْيَانٌ.

طَلَيَانٌ: see طُلَاوَةٌ.

طُلَاةٌ The *coat upon the surface of blood*. (Ḳ.) [See also طُلَاوَةٌ. And see طُلَّاةٌ.]

طِلَاءٌ *Tar*: and *anything* (Ṣ, Mgh, Mṣb, Ḳ) *of the like kind* (Mgh, Mṣb) *with which one daubs* or *smears* or *the like*; [i. e. *any fluid, semifluid, liniment, unguent, oil, varnish, plaster*, or *the like, with which a thing is daubed, smeared, rubbed* or *done over, anointed, painted, varnished, plastered, coated, overspread*, or *overlaid*;] (Ṣ, Mgh, Mṣb, Ḳ;) as also ↓ طِلَاوَةٌ, which by rule should be ↓ طِلَايَةٌ, for it is from طَلَيْتُ. (TA, in which طِلَايَةٌ is afterwards mentioned as having the same meaning.) — And, as being likened thereto, † *Any thick beverage* or *wine*: (Mgh:) *expressed juice of grapes cooked until the quantity of two thirds has gone by evaporation*; (Ṣ, A, Mgh;) *called by the Persians* مَيْبُخْتَج [or مَىْ بُخْتَه]; called by the Arabs طِلَاء as being likened to tar: (A, Mgh:*) or *thick expressed juice*, or *wine, cooked until half of it has gone*: (Ḳ:) in a verse of Ibn-Sukkarah, shortened to ↓ طِلًا, for the sake of the metre. (Ḥar p. 302.) — And † *Wine* [in an absolute sense] (Ṣ, Ḳ) is thus called by some of the Arabs, for the purpose of euphemism. (Ṣ.) 'Obeyd Ibn-El-Abraṣ said to El-Mundhir when he [the latter] desired to slay him, هِىَ الخَمْرُ تُكْنَى الطِّلَاءَ كَمَا الذِّئْبُ يُكْنَى أَبَا جَعْدَةٍ [*It is wine: it is surnamed* الطلاء *like as the wolf is surnamed* ابو جعدة]: i. e. thou pretendest to show honour to me while desiring to slay me; like the wolf, whose acting is not good though his surname is good: (Ṣ:) or, as cited by IḲt, عَنِ الخَمْرِ تُكْنَى الطِّلَاءَ: and in the M,

هِىَ الخَمْرُ يُكْنُونَهَا بِالطِّلَاءِ

[forming a hemistich; the words كَمَا الذِّئْبُ الخ, cited above, completing the verse]. (TA.) — And † The *ashes between the three stones upon which the cooking-pot is placed*: so called by way of comparison [to tar]. (TA.) — And *Pure silver*. (TA.) — And † *Revilement*, or *reproach*. (Ḳ.) ═ Also The *cord with which the leg of the lamb*, or *kid, is tied* (Ṣ, Ḳ) *to a peg*, or *stake*; (Ṣ;) and so ↓ طِلْوٌ and ↓ طِلْوَةٌ: (TA:) or the *string with which the leg of the kid is tied as long as he is little*; (Lḥ, TA;) and so ↓ طَلِيَّةٌ and ↓ طُلْيَةٌ and ↓ طَلًى [or طَلًا]. (TA.)

طَلِىٌّ *Confined, restrained*, or *withheld*; [and particularly *tied by the leg*, as is shown by what follows;] as also ↓ مَطْلِىٌّ. (Ṣ.) — And *A young lamb* or *kid*: (ISk, Ṣ, Ḳ:) so called because it is tied by the leg for some days to a peg, or stake: (ISk, Ṣ:) pl. طُلْيَانٌ; like رُغْفَانٌ, (ISk, Ṣ, Ḳ,) pl. of رَغِيفٌ: (ISk, Ṣ:) it is thus pluralized like a subst. because it is an epithet in which the quality of a subst. is predominant. (AAF, TA.) [See also طَلًا.] — [Hence الطَّلِىُّ meaning † *The sign of Aries*: see an ex. voce حَمَلٌ.] ═ Also *A yellowness in the teeth*; and so ↓ طِلْيَانٌ: like صَبِىٌّ and صِبْيَانٌ [in form]. (Ṣ.) [See also طُلَاوَةٌ.]

طِلَاوَةٌ: see the next paragraph, in two places: ═ and see also طُلْوَانٌ.

طُلَاوَةٌ, and ↓ طَلَاوَةٌ, (Az, Ṣ, ISd, Mṣb, Ḳ,) the former preferred by Az, (TA, and this, only, mentioned in the Mgh,) and ↓ طِلَاوَةٌ, (Ḳ,) *Beauty, goodliness, grace, comeliness*, or *pleasingness*: (Az,* ISd,* Ṣ, Mgh, Mṣb,* Ḳ:) ISd says, it is in that which has growth and that which has not growth. (TA.) One says, عَلَيْهِ طُلَاوَةٌ [*Upon him*, or *it, is an appearance of beauty*, &c.]. (Mṣb.) And مَا عَلَيْهِ طُلَاوَةٌ [*There is not upon him*, or *it*, &c.]. (Ṣ.) And إِنَّ لِلْقُرْآنِ لَطُلَاوَةً [*Verily to the Ḳur-án pertains beauty*, &c.]. (Mgh, from a trad.) And مَا عَلَى وَجْهِهِ حَلَاوَةٌ وَلَا طُلَاوَةٌ [*There is not upon his face an appearance of sweetness nor an appearance of beauty*, &c.]. (TA.) — Also, (Ḳ,) or the first, with ḍamm, (TA,) *Enchantment*, or *fascination*: (Ḳ:) a meaning mentioned by ISd. (TA.) ═ And (the first, TA) The *thin skin that overspreads the surface of milk*, (T, ISd, Ḳ, TA,) as also ↓ طُلَايَةٌ, (Kr, TA,) or *of blood*. (ISd, Ḳ, TA. [See also طُلَاةٌ.]) — And *Remains of food in the mouth*. (Lḥ, Ḳ, TA.) — And *Saliva becoming dry* (Ḳ, TA) *and thick* (TA) *in the mouth, by reason of some accident*, (Ḳ, TA,) or, as in the M, *from thirst*, (TA,) or *disease*; (Ḳ, TA;) the first and ↓ second have this meaning; (TA;) as also ↓ طُلًا (Ḳ) [and app. ↓ طُلْوَانٌ and ↓ طَلَوَانٌ also accord. to the copies of the Ḳ followed in the TA; but see طَلَوَانٌ above]: it is also said that ↓ طَلَوَانٌ, with fet-ḥ, signifies *saliva becoming dry upon the teeth from hunger*; and has no pl.: ↓ طَلًا is the inf. n. of طَلِىَ فُوهُ: and signifies also *a whiteness that comes upon the teeth from disease* or *thirst*; and so ↓ طَلَيَانٌ. (TA.) [See also طَلِىٌّ.] — For other meanings of طُلَاوَةٌ, see طَلَوَانٌ,— and طِلَاءٌ. — It signifies also *A small quantity* of herbage or pasture. (TA.)

طَلَاوَةٌ: see طُلَاوَةٌ, first sentence.

طُلَايَةٌ: see طُلَاةٌ: — and see also طُلَاوَةٌ.

طُلَيًّا, thus correctly, as written by Ṣgh in the TṢ, not, as in the copies of the Ḳ, طَلْيَا [or طَلْيَاءُ], (TA,) The *mange*, or *scab*. (Ḳ, TA.) And *A certain purulent pustule*, [or *eruption*,] *resembling the* قُوبَاء [or *ringworm*], (Ḳ, TA,) *that comes forth in a man's side*; whereupon one says to him, "It is only قُوبَاء, and not طُلَيًّا;" thus making light of it to him. (TA.)

طُلَّى *A draught of milk*: (Ḳ:) but this is of the measure فُعْلَى, belonging to art. طل. (TA. [See طُلَّة in that art.])

طَلَّاءٌ *A seller of the thickened juice called* طِلَاء. (MA.)

طُلَّاةٌ *Blood*, (A'Obeyd, Ṣ, Ḳ, TA,) itself; applied to that of a slain person: or, accord. to Aboo-Sa'eed, *a thing* [or *fluid*] *that comes forth after the flow of the blood, differing from blood in colour, on the occasion of the exit of the soul of the slaughtered animal*: and the *blood with which one daubs*, or *smears*. (TA.) [See also طُلَاةٌ.]

طَالٍ A water to which camels come to drink *overspread with* [*the green substance called*] طُحْلُب [and طُلَوَاء]. (Ḳ, TA.) — And ‡ *A dark* night: (AA, Ḳ, TA:) as though it smeared [with tar] the forms, or persons, of men, and obscured them. (AA, TA.)

مِطْلًى: see what next follows.

مَطْلَاةٌ (Ṣ, Ḳ) and ↓ مِطْلًى (Ḳ) *A narrow tract of ground in which water flows*: (Ḳ:) or *soft ground that gives growth to the trees called* غَضَاء, (as in the Ṣ and in some copies of the Ḳ,) or غَضًا: (so in other copies of the Ḳ and in copies of the T and M:) and المَطَالِى, which is the pl. [of the latter, or المَطَالِى pl. of the former], signifies *the soft places*: (TA:) or *the places in which the wild animals feed their younglings*: (Ṣ, Ḳ, TA:) so it is said. (Ṣ.)

مَطْلِىٌّ: see طَلِىٌّ: ═ see also طَلًا; and see the fem., with ة, voce طَلْيَاءُ. — [Hence,] أَمْرٌ مَطْلِىٌّ † *A dubious and obscure affair*, or *case*: as though it were smeared over with that which involved it. (TA.) — And عُودٌ مَطْلِىٌّ † *A stick*, or *rod*, or *branch, not stript of the peel* or *bark*. (TA.)

مُطَلًّى *Having a constant*, or *chronic, disease*, (Ḳ, TA,) *and bent thereby*. (TA.) [See also

[طلًا.] — And *Imprisoned without hope of liberation.* (Ḳ.)

طمر

1. طَمَرَ, (MA, Ḳ, TA,) aor. ـِ, (TA, [by rule it should be ـُ,]) inf. n. طُمُورٌ (MA, Ḳ, TA) and طَمْرٌ, (Ḳ, TA,) said of water, *It was,* or *became, abundant,* (MA, Ḳ, TA,) *and rose high,* or *to a high pitch.* (TA.) [See also طَمَى.] And طَمَرَ الوَادِى means [طَمَرَ سَيْلُ الوَادِى i. e. *The torrent of the valley* or *water-course*] *rose high,* or *to a high pitch, and predominated:* whence the prov., جَرَى الوَادِى فَطَمَّ عَلَى القَرِىّ; in explanation of which Meyd says, i. e., [*The torrent of the valley* or *water-course* (سَيْلُ الوَادِى) *flowed,* (so in the Provs. of Meyd,)] *and filled up,* or *choked up,* meaning *destroyed by filling up,* or *choking up, the channel by which the water ran into the meadow:* and he says that the prov. is applied to the case in which evil exceeds the ordinary limit: (Ḥar p. 127:) [or, accord. to Z, it means a man's overcoming his adversary: (Freytag's Arab. Prov. i. 278:) but it should be observed that طَمَرَ in this sense is trans. without a prep.:] one says of a torrent, (Ṣ, Meyd, and Ḥar ubi suprà,) طَمَرَ الرَّكِيَّةَ, (Ṣ, Meyd, Ḳ, Ḥar,) aor. ـِ and ـُ, (Ḳ, TA,) the latter on the authority of IAạr, inf. n. طَمْرٌ, (TA,) *It filled up,* or *choked up, the well,* syn. دَفَنَهَا, (Ṣ, Meyd, Ḳ, Ḥar,) or كَبَسَهَا, (IAạr, TA,) *and made it even* or *level* (سَوَّاهَا) [*with the ground around it*]: (Ṣ, Ḳ:) and طَمَرَ الشَّىْءَ بِالتُّرَابِ, inf. n. طَمْرٌ, *He covered over the thing with earth,* or *dust;* syn. كَبَسَهُ: (TA:) and طَمَرَ الإِنَآءَ, (Ḳ, TA,) inf. n. طَمْرٌ, (TA,) *He filled the vessel* (Ḳ, TA) *so that the contents overflowed its edges:* (TA:) and طَمَرَ البِئْرَ وَغَيْرَهَا بِالتُّرَابِ, aor. ـِ, inf. n. طَمْرٌ, *He filled the well &c. with earth,* or *dust, so that it became even with the ground:* (Mgh,* Mṣb:) and طَمَّهَا التُّرَابُ *The earth,* or *dust, so filled it.* (Mṣb.) — [Hence, i. e. from طَمَرَ الوَادِى meaning as expl. in the beginning of the next preceding sentence,] one says, طَمَرَ الشَّىْءُ, (Ṣ, Ḳ,) aor. ـِ, (Ṣ, TA,) [inf. n. طَمْرٌ and طُمُورٌ,] † *The thing abounded so that it rose to a high pitch,* or *had ascendency, and overcame.* (Ṣ, Ḳ.) And طَمَرَ الأَمْرُ, inf. n. طَمْرٌ, † *The affair,* or *event, rose to a high pitch,* or *had ascendency, and overcame:* (Mṣb:) or *was,* or *became, great,* or *formidable.* (Ḥar p. 127.) And أَمْرٌ يَطِمُرُ وَلَا يَتِمُّ [app. يَطْمُرُ, agreeably with analogy, in order to وَلَا يَتِمُّ, assimilate the former verb with the latter, as is often done; meaning † *An affair that is great,* or *formidable, and that will not become accomplished*]. (TA.) And طَمَّتِ الفِتْنَةُ † *The sedition,* or *conflict and faction,* or *the like, was,* or *became, vehement,* or *severe.* (TA.) And دَاهِيَةٌ تَطِمُرُ عَلَى الدَّوَاهِى [i. e. تَطْمُرُ or تَطْمِرُ], meaning † [*A calamity*] *that predominates over* [*the other calamities*]. (Ḥar p. 127.) — طَمَرَ عَلَيْهَا and طَمَرَ الفَرَسَ *He* (the stallion) *leaped the mare.* (TA.) And طَمَرَ الشَّجَرَةَ, (Ḳ,) inf. n. طَمْرٌ, (JM,) *He* (a bird) *mounted upon the top of the tree.* (Ḳ.) — طَمَرَ said of a man and of a horse, aor. ـُ and ـِ, inf. n. طَمِيرٌ and طَمْرٌ, *He was,* or *became, light,* or *active,* (Ḳ, TA,) *and quick:* (TA:) or *he went away upon the face of the earth:* (Ḳ, TA:) or *he went away in any way.* (TA.) And *He ran in an easy manner:* (Ḳ:) or so طَمَرَ, aor. ـُ, inf. n. طَمِيرٌ: (TA:) and مَرَّ يَطْمِرُ, with kesr, inf. n. طَمِيرٌ, *He passed along running in an easy manner:* (Ṣ:) and so, accord. to Aṣ, طَمَرَ, inf. n. طُمُورٌ. (TA.) [See also طَمَى.] — طَمَرَ رَأْسَهُ, (Ḳ,) aor. ـِ, inf. n. طَمْرٌ, (TA,) *He took somewhat from* [*the hair of*] *his head;* غَضَّ مِنْهُ. (Ḳ. [So in my MS. copy: in the CḲ and TA, erroneously, عَضَّ, with the unpointed ع; and thus in the TḲ, in which, however, the phrase is well expl., on the authority of the A, as meaning *he shaved a portion of his head:* see also the pass. part. n.]) And طَمَرَ شَعْرَهُ, (Ṣ, Ḳ,) aor. ـِ, inf. n. طَمْرٌ, (TA,) *He cut his hair;* (Ṣ, Ḳ, TA;) and *he cut it off entirely.* (TA.) And طَمَرَ شَعْرَهُ عَقَصَهُ, (Ṣ, Ḳ,) inf. n. طُمُورٌ, (Ṣ,) i. q. عَقَصَهُ [i. e. *He plaited his hair:* or *twisted it:* &c.]. (Ṣ, Ḳ.)

2. طَمَّرَ, inf. n. تَطْمِيرٌ, *He* (a bird) *alighted upon a branch.* (Aboo-Naṣr, Ṣ, Ḳ.)

4. اطمر شَعْرُهُ *His hair attained,* or *drew near, to the time for its being cut;* as also ↓ استطمر. (Ṣ, Ḳ.)

7. انطمر, said of a rivulet, [and in like manner of a well, &c.,] *It became filled up* with earth, or dust, *so as to be even with the ground* [*around it*]. (Mgh.)

10: see 4.

R. Q. 1. طَمْطَرَ *He swam in the midst of the sea.* (IAạr, Ḳ.) — And *It* (the sea) *became full.* (TA.) = *He had a barbarousness,* or *vitiousness,* or *an impotence,* or *impediment, in his speech,* or *utterance, not speaking clearly,* or *correctly.* (TA.)

طَمْرٌ [as an inf. n.: see 1. — As a subst.,] see the next paragraph.

طِمْرٌ *The sea:* (Ṣ, Ḳ, TA:) said to be so called because of its overwhelming what is in it (لِأَنَّهُ طَمَرَ عَلَى مَا فِيهِ): but in this sense the word is said to be ↓ طِمٌّ, and to be pronounced with kesr for the purpose of assimilating it to رِمٌّ. (TA.) One says, جَآءَ بِالطِّمِّ وَالرِّمِّ, meaning *He brought much wealth:* (Ṣ, TA:) or the meaning in this instance is الامر الكثير [app. a mistranscription for الأَمْرُ الكَبِيرُ i. e. *that which was a great event*]: so says Aṣ: or *much of everything:* or *much and little:* thus accord. to Aboo-Ṭálib: or *what was moist and what was dry:* or *the leaves of trees, and what had fallen off from them.* (TA. [See more voce رِمٌّ: and see also what here follows.]) — And *Water:* (Ḳ, TA:) or *much water;* as also ↓ طَامِرٌ [or مَآءٌ طَامِرٌ]: (TA:) or the *rubbish and scum,* and *the like, that is upon its surface;* or *that is driven along by it:* (Ḳ,* TA:) and thus expl. as used in the saying above-mentioned. (TA.) — And *A large number:* (Ḳ:) and this also is said to be meant in the phrase above. (TA.) — And *A wonderful thing;* syn. عَجَبٌ and عَجِيبٌ [which here, as in many other instances, evidently signify the same]: (Ḳ:) and this too is said to be meant in the phrase above. (TA.) — And *A male ostrich:* (Ḳ:) because of the lightness of his pace. (TA.) — And *A courser,* or *swift horse;* as also ↓ طَمِيمٌ: (Ḳ,* TA: [see also طَمُومٌ:]) called طِمٌّ because of his light and quick, or easy, running (لِطَمِيمِ عَدْوِهِ); or as being likened to the sea, as a horse is termed بَحْرٌ and سَكْبٌ and غَرْبٌ. (TA.) — And *A large* ذَكَر: (Ḳ:) because its head is مَطْمُومٌ [as though this epithet meant "bare"]. (TA.) — الطِّمُّ is also said in the Ḳ to signify الكَيِّسُ; but [SM says] I think that this is a mistranscription for الطَّمْرُ meaning الكَبْسُ [see طَمَرَ الرَّكِيَّةَ, in the first paragraph]. (TA.)

طُمَّةٌ *A company,* or *congregated body,* of men: and the *middle* of them: one says, لَقِيتُهُ فِى طُمَّةِ القَوْمِ [*I met him,* or *found him, in the company of people,* or *in the midst of the people*]. (TA.) = Also *Error;* or *deviation from the right course:* and *confusion,* or *perplexity, and inability to see the right course.* (TA.) — And *Dirt,* or *filth;* syn. قَذَرٌ. (TA.) — And *Human dung.* (Ḳ.) AZ says, When thou givest good advice to a man and he refuses to do aught but follow his own opinion alone, دَعْهُ يَتَرَمَّعُ فِى طُمَّتِهِ [*Leave him wallowing in his dung*]. (TA.) — And *A portion* (Ḳ, TA) *of herbage,* mostly (TA) *of what is dry,* or *dried up.* (Ḳ, TA.)

طَمِيمٌ *Hardy, strong,* or *sturdy:* occurring thus, without idghám, in a verse of 'Adee Ibn-Zeyd; applied to a beast such as is termed قَارِحٌ. (TA.)

فَرَسٌ طَمُومٌ *A swift horse.* (TA. [See also طِمٌّ.])

طَمِيمٌ: see طِمٌّ. — Also *A medley* of men, or people: and *a multitude* thereof. (TA.)

طَامٌّ [part. n. of 1]: see طِمٌّ: — and see the paragraph here following.

طَامَّةٌ *A calamity that predominates over others:* (Ḳ, and Ḥar p. 127:) or simply *a calamity.* (TA.) It is said in a trad. of Aboo-Bekr En-Nessábeh, مَا مِنْ طَامَّةٍ إِلَّا وَفَوْقَهَا طَامَّةٌ (Ṣ,* TA) i. e. *There is no calamity but above it is a calamity.* (TA.) — And *A great,* or *formidable, thing;* as also ↓ طَامٌّ. (TA.) — And *A cry,* or *vehement cry, that overcomes everything.* (TA.) — And الطَّامَّةُ signifies

The resurrection: (Ṣ, Mṣb, Ḳ:) so called because it surpasses, or predominates over, everything: (Ṣ,* Mṣb,* TA:) and also called الطَّامَّةُ الكُبْرَى. (Ḥar p. 346.)

طِمْطِمِىٌّ and ↓ طُمْطُمَانِىٌّ (Ṣ, Ḳ) and ↓ طِمْطِمٌ (Ḳ) and ↓ طُمَاطِمٌ (TA) A man *having a barbarousness,* or *vitiousness,* or *an impotence,* or *impediment, in his speech,* or *utterance, not speaking clearly,* or *correctly:* (Ṣ, Ḳ, TA:) and Aboo-Turáb explains [the pl. of the first] طَمَاطِمُ as meaning *foreigners* (عَجَم). (TA.) Hence the saying of the poet, (Ṣ,) 'Antarah, (TA,)

* تَأْوِى لَهُ قُلُصُ النَّعَامِ كَمَا أَوَتْ *

* حِزَقٌ يَمَانِيَةٌ لِأَعْجَمَ طِمْطِمِ *

(Ṣ, TA;) respecting which Fr relates his having heard El-Mufaḍḍal say that one of the most learned of men explained to him الخِرَقُ اليَمَانِيَةُ as meaning *the clouds* [app. likened to rags of cloth of El-Yemen], and الأَعْجَمُ الطِّمْطِمُ as meaning *the sound of thunder:* (TA:) or the latter hemistich is thus:

* حِزَقٌ يَمَانِيَةٌ لِأَعْجَمَ طِمْطِمِ *

and the verse means, *To whom* (referring to a male ostrich) *repair the young ostriches, like as herds* of camels *of El-Yemen repair to one who is impotent, and indistinct,* or *incorrect, in speech:* he likens the male ostrich, in respect of blackness, and want of speech, to an Abyssinian pastor impotent, and indistinct, or incorrect, in speech. (EM p. 231.) — طِمْطِمٌ signifies also *A sort of sheep, having small ears, and* أَغْبَاب [or *what resemble dewlaps*], *like the* اغباب *of oxen: they are in the region of El-Yemen.* (IDrd, TA.)

طِمْطِمَةٌ *A barbarousness,* or *vitiousness,* or *an impotence,* or *impediment, in speech,* or *utterance, so that the speech is not clear,* or *correct.* (TA. [See R. Q. 1, of which it is the inf. n.])

طِمْطِمِىٌّ : } see طِمْطِمٌ.
طُمْطُمَانِىٌّ :

طُمْطُمَانِيَّةُ حِمْيَرَ *The disapproved phraseology* [or *pronunciation*] *of the dialect of Ḥimyer,* (Ḳ, TA,) *resembling the speech of the foreigners:* thus expl. by Mbr and Eth-Tha'álibee and others: or, as some say, *their change of* ل *into* م [in امْ for الْ; of which see several exs. voce أَمْ]. (TA.)

طُمْطَامٌ The *middle of the sea.* (Ḳ, TA.) — And hence, ‡ *Much fire:* or the *midst of fire:* or the *main part thereof:* occurring in a trad. of Aboo-Ṭálib. (TA.)

طُمَاطِمٌ : see طِمْطِمٌ.

[أَذًى أَطْمَرُ *Vehement,* or *severe, annoyance, molestation, harm,* or *hurt:* in the TA carelessly written اذا اطمر; and there said to be from طَمَّت الفِتْنَةُ, q. v. See also an ex. in the Ḥam p. 363; where أَطَمُّ occurs at the end of a verse for أَطَمُّ used in a like sense; i. e. as an epithet, not as a verb.]

أُطَامِيمُ is said in the Ḳ to signify The *legs* of a beast: but AA says, respecting the phrase مُسْتَعِدَّاتٌ أَطَامِيمُ in a verse of Ibn-Muḳbil describing a she-camel, that the former of these words is used as meaning *legs,* and اطاميم means *brisk, active,* or *quick:* and by another, or others, this latter word is said to mean تَطِمُّ فِى السَّيْرِ, i. e. *that are quick in pace.* (TA.)

شَعَرٌ مَطْمُومٌ means مَعْقُوصٌ [i. e. *Hair plaited:* or *twisted:* &c.]. (Ṣ, TA.) — And رَأْسٌ مَطْمُومٌ *A head of which all the hair is cut off.* (Ḳ* and TA in art. زق.) And مَطْمُومُ الرَّأْسِ A man *having all the hair of his head cut off.* (TA in that art.)

طمث

1. طَمَثَتْ, (Ṣ, Mṣb, Ḳ,) aor. ـِ, (Ṣ, Ḳ,) or ـُ, (Mṣb,) inf. n. طَمْثٌ; (Mṣb, TA;) and طَمِثَتْ, (Ṣ, Mṣb, Ḳ,) aor. ـَ; (Mṣb, Ḳ; [accord. to the former of which, the inf. n. of the latter verb seems to be طَمَثٌ; but accord. to the Ḳ, it seems to be طَمْثٌ;]) *She menstruated;* said of a woman: (Ṣ, Mṣb, Ḳ:) the primary signification, accord. to Th; that of "devirgination," i. e. "coition with the causing to bleed," being one subsequently given to طَمْثٌ: (TA:) or, as some say, *for the first time:* (Mṣb, TA:) and accord. to Lḥ, used peculiarly in relation to a girl, or young woman. (TA.) — طَمَثَهَا, aor. ـُ, (Ṣ, Mgh, Mṣb, Ḳ) and ـِ, (Ṣ, Mṣb, Ḳ,) the former accord. to most of the readers in the Ḳur [lv. 56 and 74], (TA,) inf. n. طَمْثٌ, (Ṣ, Mṣb,) *He devirginated her,* (Fr, Ṣ, Mgh, Mṣb, Ḳ,) namely, a woman, (Mgh,) or his wife, (Mṣb,) *causing her to bleed;* (Fr, Mgh, Mṣb;) not otherwise: (Mṣb:) or, accord. to some, i. q. جَامَعَهَا, in a general sense: (TA:) in this sense the verb is used in the Ḳur; (Mṣb;) or, as some say, in the sense expl. in the next sentence: (TA:) and طُمِثَتْ, aor. تُطْمَثُ, *she was caused to bleed by devirgination.* (AHeyth, TA.) — طَمَثَ, (AA, Ṣ, TA,) inf. n. طَمْثٌ, (AA, Ṣ, Ḳ, TA,) signifies also ‡ *He,* or *it, touched* a thing: (AA, Ṣ, Ḳ,* TA:) said in relation to anything that is touched: one says, مَا طَمَثَ ذَا المَرْتَعَ قَبْلَنَا أَحَدٌ ‡ *No one touched this place of pasturing,* or *this pasture, before us:* and مَا طَمَثَ هٰذِهِ النَّاقَةَ حَبْلٌ قَطُّ ‡ *A rope* such as is called عِقَال *never touched this she-camel:* (AA, Ṣ, TA:) and هٰذَا جَمَلٌ مَا طَمَثَهُ حَبْلٌ قَطُّ ‡ *This is a camel which a rope has never touched.* (TA.) — And طَمَثَ البَعِيرَ, inf. n. طَمْثٌ † *He bound the camel's fore shank to his* (the camel's) *arm.* (TA.)

طَمْثٌ *Blood:* (Fr, TA: [the context in the TA seems to indicate that it means *blood that flows when a woman,* or *girl, is devirginated:*] or the *blood of the menses;* (KL, and TA in art. جزر;) as also ↓ طَمَثٌ. (KL.) — And *Dirt, filth,* or *pollution.* (Ḳ.) — And *A thing that induces suspicion,* or *evil opinion:* one says, مَا بِفُلَانٍ طَمْثٌ *There is not, in such a one, anything that induces suspicion,* or *evil opinion.* (TA.) — And *Corruption.* (L, Ḳ; but not in the CḲ.)

طَمَثٌ : see the next preceding paragraph.

طَامِثٌ, (Ṣ, Mṣb, Ḳ,) without ة, (Mṣb, TA,) A woman, (Ṣ, Mṣb, Ḳ,) or, accord. to Lḥ, peculiarly a girl, or young woman, (TA,) *menstruating:* (Ṣ, Mṣb, Ḳ, TA:) or, as some say, *for the first time.* (Mṣb, TA.)

طمح

1. طَمَحَ بَصَرُهُ إِلَيْهِ, (Ṣ, L, Ḳ,) aor. ـَ, (Ḳ,) inf. n. طُمُوحٌ (Ḳ in art. مد, and TḲ) and طِمَاحٌ and طَمْحٌ, (TḲ,) *His sight,* or *eye, became raised towards it,* (Ṣ, Ḳ,) i. e., a thing: (Ṣ:) or *became stretched and raised towards it.* (L.) And طَمَحَ بِبَصَرِهِ, aor. ـَ, (L, Mṣb,) inf. n. طَمْحٌ, (L,) or طُمُوحٌ, (Mṣb,) *He raised his eyes;* (L, Mṣb;) [and] so أَطْمَحَ ↓ بَصَرَهُ: (Ṣ, Ḳ:) or *cast his eyes:* (L:) towards a thing (إِلَى شَىْءٍ, L, or نَحْوَ شَىْءٍ, Mṣb): [said to be] from the phrase جَبَلٌ طَامِحٌ. (Mṣb.) And طَمَحَ بِعَيْنِهِ, said of a proud man, *He raised his eye.* (A.) And طَمَحَتْ بِعَيْنِهَا *She* (a woman) *cast her eye* at a man. (L.) And طَمَحَتْ [alone], said of a woman, *She raised her eyes.* (L.) And تَطْمَحُ إِلَى الرِّجَالِ [*She raises her eyes towards,* or *looks at, men*]. (Ṣ.) — And طَمَحَ, inf. n. طِمَاحٌ and طُمُوحٌ, (A, L, TA,) *He* (a horse) *raised his head and his eyes* in his running: (A, TA:) or *he raised his fore legs;* (L;) and so ↓ طَمَّحَ, inf. n. تَطْمِيحٌ: (T, L, Ḳ:) [or the former, *he was,* or *became, refractory, and overcame his rider, running away with him:* for] طِمَاحٌ is *syn. with* جِمَاحٌ, (Ḳ,) or *like* جِمَاحٌ: (Yz, Ṣ:) one says, فَرَسٌ فِيهِ طِمَاحٌ [*a horse in which is refractoriness,* &c.]. (Ṣ.) — طَمَحَتْ, aor. ـَ, (L,) inf. n. طِمَاحٌ, (L, Ḳ,) is also said of a woman, meaning † *She was,* or *became, disobedient to her husband, resisting him, hating him, and deserting him:* (L, Ḳ:*) and, thus said of a woman, طَمَحَتْ, (Ṣ, Ḳ,) or طَمَحَتْ عَلَى زَوْجِهَا, (A,) is *syn. with,* (A, Ḳ,) or *like,* (Ṣ,) جَمَحَتْ ‡ [*she went forth from the place where she used to pass the night, in anger, without the permission of her husband*]: (Ṣ, A, Ḳ:) and طَمَحَتْ مِنْ زَوْجِهَا and جَمَحَتْ ‡ *she went forth from the house,* or *tent, of her husband, to her own family, before he divorced her.* (TA in art. جمح.) And طَمَحَ إِلَيْهِ, like جَمَحَ اليه, said of a man, † *He hastened,* or *went*

quickly, to him, or it, so that his course was not turned for anything. (TA in art. طمح.) — طَمَحَ, inf. n. طِمَاحٌ, also signifies † He was proud, and boastful; because he who is so exalts himself. (L.) — And طَمَحَ فِى السَّوْمِ † He went far beyond what was right, or just, in making a bargain for his merchandise. (Lh, L.) And طَمَحَ, (Ṣ,) or طَمَحَ فِى الطَّلَبِ, (Ḳ,) † He went far in search; (Ṣ, Ḳ;) so accord. to some. (Ṣ.) [طَمَحَ إِلَى كُلِّ شَىْءٍ, said of the heart, app. means † It aspired to everything: see its part. n., طَامِحٌ.] — طَمَحَ الشُّخْبُ † The extended stream of milk from the udder fell upon the ground so as to be unprofitable. (Provs. of Meyd, section ش: see شُخْبٌ.) — طَمَحَ بِهِ † He made, or caused, him, or it, to go, go away, or pass away; took away, carried off, or went away with, him, or it. (Ḳ.) — And طَمَحْتُ الشَّىْءَ [if not a mistranscription for طَمَّحْتُ بِالشَّىْءِ] ‡ I cast the thing in the air. (A.)

2: see 1. — طَمَّحَ بِبَوْلِهِ, (Ṣ, Ḳ, TA,) and طَمَّحَ بَوْلَهُ, (L, TA,) and طَمَّحَ بِالشَّىْءِ, inf. n. تَطْمِيحٌ, (T, TA,) ‡ He cast forth his urine, (Ṣ, L, Ḳ, TA,) and the thing, (T, TA,) in the air. (T, Ṣ, L, Ḳ, TA.) [See also 1, last sentence.]

4: see 1, second sentence.

طَمْحٌ, or طَمَحٌ, (accord. to different copies of the Ḳ,) expl. by Ibn-'Abbád, (Ḳ, TA,) in the Moheeṭ, (TA,) as the name of A species of tree, is a mistake, being correctly with ظ and خ; (Ḳ, TA;) or it is also called طمح as well as طمخ. (TA in art. طمخ.)

نِيَّةٌ طَمْحٌ i. q. بَعِيدَةٌ [app. meaning † A distant, or remote, thing, or place, that is the object of an action or a journey]; like طَرْحٌ and ضَرْحٌ. (O in art. ضرح.)

طَمَحَاتُ الدَّهْرِ, (Ṣ, A, Ḳ,) and طَمَحَاتُهُ, (Ḳ,) the latter used by poetic license, (TA,) ‡ The hard, or distressing, events, or the calamities, or afflictions, of time, or fortune. (Ṣ, A, Ḳ.)

طَمُوحُ البَصَرِ: see طَامِحٌ. — بَحْرٌ طَمُوحُ المَوْجِ (A, TA) ‡ A sea of which the waves rise high. (TA.) And بِئْرٌ طَمُوحُ المَآءِ ‡ A well of which the water has collected and risen high. (TA.)

سَيْرٌ طُمَاحِىٌّ † A far, or distant, journey; like طُرَاحِىٌّ. (Aṣ, O in art. طرح.)

طَمَّاحٌ A long-sighted man. (L.) And طَمَّاحَةٌ A woman who looks much to the right and left at strange men, or at a man who is not her husband. (L.) — Also † Vehemently desirous, or greedy; or very vehemently desirous, or very greedy: (Ṣ, Ḳ:) applied to a man. (Ṣ.)

طَامِحٌ [part. n. of 1: fem. with ة: pl. of the latter طَوَامِحُ]. You say نِسَآءٌ طَوَامِحُ إِلَى الرِّجَالِ [Women who raise their eyes towards, or look at, men]. (A.) And فَرَسٌ طَامِحُ الطَّرْفِ, (A, L,) and طَامِحُ البَصَرِ, and ▼ طَمُوحُهُ, (L,) A horse that raises, or elevates, his eye. (L.) — طَامِحٌ [without ة] is also an epithet applied to a woman, from طَمَحَتْ as syn. with, or similar to, جَمَحَتْ; [i. e. an epithet meaning That goes forth from the place where she has been accustomed to pass the night, in anger, without the permission of her husband; or that goes forth from the house, or tent, of her husband, to her own family, not having been divorced by him;] (Ṣ, Ḳ;) that raises her eyes towards, or looks at, men (تَطْمَحُ إِلَى الرِّجَالِ): (Ṣ:) or that hates her husband, and looks towards other men: (Aboo-'Amr Esh-Sheybánee, T:) a woman disobedient to her husband, resisting him, hating him, and deserting him. (L.) — Also A high, overlooking, mountain. (Mṣb.) Anything high, lofty, or elevating itself. (Ṣ, Ḳ.) And † Anyone lofty, or elevating himself, in excessive pride. (T, TA.) And one says قَلْبٌ طَامِحٌ إِلَى كُلِّ شَىْءٍ [app. meaning † A heart aspiring to everything]. (Lth, O, Ḳ, TA, voce شَنِقٌ.)

طمر

1. طَمَرَ, (Ṣ, O, Mṣb, Ḳ,) aor. ِ, (O, Mṣb,) or ُ, (Ḳ,) inf. n. طَمْرٌ, (A, O, Mṣb, Ḳ,) He buried (A, Mṣb, Ḳ) a corpse, in the earth: (Mṣb:) he hid, or concealed, (Ṣ, A, O, Mṣb, Ḳ,) a thing, (Mṣb,) or wheat, in a مَطْمُورَة, (Ṣ, O,) or himself, or his goods, (A, TA,) in a place where he, or they, could not be known. (TA.) — He filled a مَطْمُورَة. (Ṣ, Ḳ.) And He filled up a well. (TA.) — Az heard a man of 'Okeyl say of a stallion-camel that had covered a female, قَدْ طَمَرَهَا [meaning He inserted the whole of his veretrum into her; as is indicated by the context]: and إِنَّهُ لَكَثِيرُ الطَّمْرِ; and thus one says of a man, meaning Verily he is one who compresses much. (L, TA. [See also 4.]) = طَمَرَ signifies also He built. (O.) And [hence] one says, هُوَ يَطْمُرُ عَلَى مِطْمَارِ ▼ أَبِيهِ, (A, Ḳ, in the latter of which the verb is omitted,) meaning ‡ He imitates the actions of his father: (A, TA:) or he resembles his father in make and disposition. (Ḳ.) = And طَمَرَ, aor. ُ (Ṣ, O, Ḳ) and ِ, (O,) inf. n. طُمُورٌ (Ṣ, A, O, Ḳ) and طَمْرٌ (Ḳ) and طِمَارٌ (Ḳ, TA, in the CḲ طَمار) and طَمَرَانٌ, (TA,) He leaped: (TA:) or he leaped downwards: (A, Ḳ:) or upwards (lit. in, or into, the sky): (A, Ḳ:) or he did what resembled leaping (Ṣ, O) upwards (lit. in, or into, the sky); (Ṣ;) thus does a horse; and the [bird called] أَخْيَل, in flying. (Ṣ, O.) And طَمَرَ فِى الرَّكِيَّةِ, inf. n. طُمُورٌ and طَمْرٌ, He leaped into the well, from the top of it to the bottom. (Mṣb.) [It is said that] طَمَرَ signifies He, or it, became, or rose, high: and also, became, or descended, low. (TA. [But perhaps it is a mistranscription for طَمِرَ: see مَطْمُورٌ.]) — And طَمَرَ فِى الأَرْضِ, (TA,) inf. n. طُمُورٌ, (Ḳ,) He went away into, or in, the country, or land: (Ḳ, TA:) he became absent, or hidden, or concealed; or he absented, or hid, or concealed, himself. (TA.) = طَمِرَ said of a wound, It became inflated, or swollen. (O, Ḳ.) — And طَمِرَتْ يَدُهُ, the verb in this case being of the class of فَرِحَ, His arm, or hand, became swollen, (Ḳ,) and inflated. (TA.) — And طَمِرَ فِى ثَدْيِ المَرْأَةِ The woman's breast became swollen. (O.) — And طَمِرَ فِى ضِرْسِهِ Pain became excited in his tooth, or his lateral, or molar, tooth: (O, Ḳ:) the verb in this phrase [and in that next preceding] is like عَنِىَ. (Ḳ.)

2. طَمَّرَ, (O,) inf. n. تَطْمِيرٌ, (O, Ḳ,) He made his building high. (O.) — And i. q. طَوَى [meaning He folded a written paper &c.; or rolled up a طُومَار, or scroll: and † He (the Creator) made the limbs, or shanks, of an animal, compact, or round; as though rolled up like scrolls]. (O, Ḳ, TA.) طُمِّرَتْ, in a verse of Kaab Ibn-Zuheyr, [referring to a wild she-ass, or to her legs,] means † She was, or they were, rendered compact in make; or rounded, as though rolled up like as are طَوَامِير [or scrolls]. (TA.) — And He let down a curtain. (Ḳ, TA.) One says, طَمَّرُوا بُيُوتَهُمْ They let down their curtains over their doors. (O, TA.)

4. اطمر غُرْمُولَهُ فِى الحِجْرِ He (a horse) inserted the whole of his veretrum into the mare. (Ḳ. [See also 1, fourth sentence.])

8. اِطَّمَرَ عَلَيْهِ, of the measure اِفْتَعَلَ, [originally اِطْتَمَرَ,] He leaped upon him, namely, a horse, (Ḳ,) and a camel, (TA,) from behind, (Ḳ, TA,) and mounted him. (TA.)

طِمْرٌ An old and worn-out garment: (Ṣ, A, O, Mgh, Mṣb, Ḳ:) this is the meaning commonly known: (TA:) or an old and worn-out [garment of the kind called] كِسَآء, not of wool: (IAạr, A, Ḳ:) and ▼ طُمْرُورٌ signifies the same: (Ibn-'Abbád, O, Ḳ:) pl. of the former أَطْمَارٌ, (Ṣ, Mgh, O, Mṣb, Ḳ,) the only pl. form. (Sb, TA.) = See also the next paragraph. [Freytag has assigned to this word, as on the authority of the Ḳ, three meanings which the Ḳ assigns to طُمْرُورٌ.]

طِمِرٌّ (Ṣ, O, Ḳ) and ▼ طِمْرٌ (O) and ▼ طِمِرُّ and ▼ طُمْرُورٌ (O, Ḳ) and ▼ طِمْرِيرٌ (Ḳ) and ▼ أُطْمُرٌّ (O, Ḳ) A horse in a state of excitement (مُسْتَفِزٌّ) [so accord. to my copies of the Ṣ, as though for مُسْتَفِزٌّ نَفْسَهُ, or probably a mistranscription for مُسْتَفَزٌّ,]) to leap and run: (Ṣ, O: [accord. to my copies of the former, مُسْتَفِزٌّ لِلْوَثْبِ وَالعَدْوِ: in the O, مُسْتَفِزٌّ الوَثْبِ وَالعَدْوِ:]) or, accord. to AO, contracted [or compact] in make: (Ṣ, O:) and (O) a fleet, or swift, and excellent, horse: (O, Ḳ:) and the first, that leaps much; as also ضِبِرٌّ: (O in art. ضبر:) or ▼ طُمْرُورٌ signifies long-legged, and light, or active: or ready, or in a state of preparation, for running: (Ḳ:) the fem.

طِمِرَّةٌ is applied metaphorically by a poet to a she-ass as meaning *vehement in running.* (TA.) — And مَكَانٌ طِمِرٌّ *A high place.* (O.)

طُمُرٌ : see طُمْرٌ.

طُمُرَّةٌ : see طُمْرَةٌ.

طُمْرُورٌ : see طِمِرٌّ.

طُمْرُورٌ : see طُمْرٌ: — and see طِمِرٌّ, in two places. — Also A man (O) *possessing nothing:* (O, Ḳ:) accord. to IDrd, *a low, vile,* or *mean, person,* [so I render قَانِصٌ, q. v.,] *in evil condition:* a dial. var. of طُمْلُولٌ. (O.) And *A stranger.* (O.) — And *Dry wood.* (O.) — And The [*bird called*] شِقِرَّاق. (O, Ḳ.)

طِمْرِيرٌ : see طِمِرٌّ.

طَمَارِ, like قَطَامِ, [indecl.,] (Ṣ, O, Ḳ,) a proper name, (IAạr, O,) *The high place;* (IAạr, Ṣ, O, Ḳ;) as also طَمَارٌ, with fet-ḥ. (Ṣ, O, Ḳ.) One says, اِنْصَبَّ عَلَيْهِ مِنْ طَمَارِ [*He,* or *it, descended upon him from the high place*]: (Aṣ, Ṣ, O:) Ks said وَقَعَ فِى بَنَاتِ طَمَارِ and مِنْ طَمَارَ. (Ṣ, O.) — وَقَعَ فِى بَنَاتِ طَمَارِ (A, Ḳ,* TA) means ‡ *He fell into calamities,* and *hardships,* or *difficulties:* (A:) or *calamity:* (Ḳ, TA:) or *trial:* and *hardship,* or *difficulty.* (TA.)

طُمْرٌ i. q. أَصْلٌ; as also ▼ طُمْرُورٌ: (O, Ḳ:) so the former signifies in the saying, لَأَرُدَّنَّهُ إِلَى طُمْرِهِ [app. meaning *I will assuredly reduce him to the utmost point,* or *degree, to which he can be reduced:* see a similar phrase voce أَصْلٌ]. (O, TA.) — And one says, فُلَانٌ طُمْرُ شَرٍّ *Such a one is evil in the utmost degree.* (IAạr, T in art. دون.) — And أَنْتَ فِى طُمْرِكَ الَّذِى كُنْتَ فِيهِ, (so in copies of the Ḳ and in the TA,) or ▼ طُمُرِكَ, (so in the O,) i. e. فِى غِرَّتِكَ وَجَهْلِكَ [*Thou art in thy state of inexperience and ignorance in which thou wast formerly*]: (O, Ḳ:) but [SM says] the right reading is فِى غَرْبِكَ i. e. *in thy* [*state of*] *sharpness, and briskness, liveliness,* or *sprightliness:* in some copies of the Ḳ, عَزْمِكَ وَجَهْدِكَ; and in some, عُزْبِكَ وَجَهْدِكَ; which are both mistranscriptions: (TA:) a saying mentioned by Fr. (O.)

طُمْرَةٌ, (so in copies of the Ḳ and accord. to the TA,) with ḍamm to the ط, and teshdeed and fet-ḥ to the م; (TA;) or ▼ طُمُرَّةٌ, with two ḍammehs, and teshdeed to the ر; (O, and so accord. to the TḲ; [and this I think most probably the right;]) The *first period* of شَبَاب [i. e. youthfulness, or young manhood, &c.]: (O, Ḳ:) so in the saying mentioned and expl. by Fr, كَانَ ذٰلِكَ فِى طُمُرَّةِ شَبَابِهِ [*That was in the first period of his youthfulness,* &c.]. (O.)

طُمْرُورٌ : see طُمْرٌ.

طَامِرٌ ‡ *The flea;* (Ṣ, O;) [because of its leaping;] and (O) so طَامِرُ بْنُ طَامِرٍ: (A, O, Ḳ:) pl. طَوَامِرُ. (TA.) One says, أَشْهَرُ مِنْ طَامِرِ بْنِ طَامِرٍ i. e. ‡ [*More commonly known*] *than the flea.* (A, TA.) — And طَامِرُ بْنُ طَامِرٍ means also † *The remote, who, as well as his father, is unknown:* (Ḳ:) or *the man* (Ṣ, O) *who is unknown,* (O,) or *whose place whence he comes is unknown.* (Ṣ.)

طَامُورٌ : see what next follows.

طُومَارٌ (Ṣ, A, Ḳ) and ▼ طَامُورٌ (Ḳ) *A piece of paper,* or *skin, on which something is written;* syn. صَحِيفَةٌ: (A, Ḳ:) [generally, *a roll,* or *scroll;*] *a paper folded* or *rolled up* (MA, and Har p. 254, each in explanation of the former word,) *and written upon:* (Ḥar ibid.:) [a مِسَرَّةٌ (an instrument in which one speaks secretly) is described in the Ṣ and Ḳ as being like a طُومَار: and this word is particularly applied, but perhaps as a post-classical term, to *a roll of papyrus,* or to *paper made of papyrus;* being *syn. with* قِرْطَاس used in this sense: (see De Sacy's "Rel. de l'Égypte par Abd-Allatif," p. 109, where El-Kindee is cited to this effect:) see also سِجِلٌّ:] طُومَارٌ is said to be a foreign word introduced into the Arabic language; but ISd thinks it to be genuine Arabic, because Sb reckons it among the words that are Arabic in form, and asserts it to be quasi-coordinate to فُسْطَاط: (TA:) the pl. is طَوَامِيرُ. (Ṣ, A, Ḳ, &c.) [قَلَمُ طُومَارٍ is a modern term for *A sort of large handwriting.*]

أُطْمُرٌ : see طِمِرٌّ.

مِطْمَرٌ The *builder's* زِيج, (Ṣ, O,) also called تُرٌّ and إِمَامٌ; (O;) [i. e.,] like these two words, it signifies the *cord which the builder extends to make even, thereby, the row of stones or bricks of the building;* (T in art. امر;) the *builder's cord,* or *line, with which he proportions* (Ḳ, TA) *the building;* (TA;) as also ▼ مِطْمَارٌ: (Ḳ, TA:) ▼ the مِطْمَار in the dial. of the people of El-Ḥijáz is the شَاقُول, (O,) which is *a wooden implement, used by the sowers of the land at El-Basrah,* (Lth, Ḳ, TA, all in art. شقل,) *two cubits long,* (Lth and TA ibid.,) or *a staff a cubit long,* (A and TA in art. بقل,) *having upon its head* [or rather *end*] *a* زُجّ [or *pointed iron*], (Lth and Ḳ and TA in art. شقل, and A and TA in art. بقل,) *upon which one of them puts the end of a rope, and then he sticks it in the ground, and keeps it in its place firmly by stretching the rope* [app. *for the purpose of making even a row of seeds* or *the like*]. (Lth and TA in art. شقل.) Hence, (O,) أَقِمِ الْمِطْمَرَ, said to one relating a trad., means ‡ *Rectify thou the tradition, and correct its expressions,* (O, Ḳ, TA,) *and trim it, and be veracious in it.* (O, TA.) And ▼ هُوَ يَطْمُرُ عَلَى مِطْمَارِ أَبِيهِ, expl. in the first paragraph. (A, Ḳ.*)

المُطَمِّرَاتُ : see المُطْمِرَاتُ.

مُطَمَّرٌ ‡ *Accumulated;* applied to household-goods (مَتَاع): and also applied to property (مَال) [in the same sense]. (A, TA.) — And, with ة, applied to a she-ass, ‡ *Long, and firm in make,* (A, O, Ḳ, TA,) *as though rounded,* or *rolled up, like as is the* طُومَار [or *scroll*]. (A,* TA.) — الْعَظَائِمُ الْمُطَمَّرَاتُ, occurring in a trad., (O, TA,) as some relate it, (TA,) means *The* [*great*] *sins that are hidden,* or *concealed:* (O, TA:) or, as others relate it, the latter word is ▼ الْمُطْمِرَاتُ, (TA,) which means *that destroy* [the sinner]. (Ḳ, TA.)

الْأُمُورُ الْمُطْمِرَاتُ (so in two copies of the Ṣ, in the PṢ ▼ الْمُطَمِّرَات, in one of my copies of the Ṣ الْمُطْمِرَاتُ, and in the other of those copies omitted,) *The affairs,* or *events, that destroy,* or *cause destruction.* (Ṣ.) See also the next preceding paragraph.

مِطْمَارٌ : see مِطْمَرٌ, in three places. — Also A man (Ḳ) *wearing* أَطْمَار [i. e. *old and worn-out garments*]. (O, Ḳ.)

مَطْمُورٌ [pass. part. n. of طَمَرَ, q. v. — Also] *High:* and *low:* thus having two contr. meanings. (TA.)

مَطْمُورَةٌ *A hollow,* or *cavity, dug in the ground,* (Ṣ, A, Mgh, Mṣb, Ḳ,) *widened in the lower part,* (TA,) *in which wheat is hidden,* (Ṣ, Mgh,) or *grain:* (TA:) *a house, chamber, cell,* or *cellar, constructed in the ground:* (IDrd, Mgh, Mṣb:) pl. مَطَامِيرُ. (A, Mgh.) — And *A prison,* or *place of confinement.* (TA.)

طمس

1. طَمَسَ, aor. ـِ and ـُ, (Ṣ, M, Mṣb, Ḳ,) inf. n. طُمُوسٌ (Ṣ, M, A, Mṣb, Ḳ) and طَمْسٌ, (Zj;) *It* (a thing, as, for instance, a road, or path, T, Ṣ, M, Mṣb, and a writing, T, or a relic, trace, or vestige, A) *became effaced,* or *obliterated;* (T, Ṣ, M, A, Mṣb, Ḳ;) *the trace,* or *mark, thereof* (i. e. of a road &c.) *became effaced,* or *obliterated:* (M:) or *it* (a thing) *quitted,* or *went from, its form,* or *shape:* (Zj:) and ▼ انطمس (said of a relic, or remain, or of a mark, or trace, and of a writing, TA, or other thing, Ṣ) has the first of the significations above; (Ṣ, A, Ḳ;) and so ▼ تطمّس. (Ṣ, Ḳ.) — *It* († a star, T, M, and † the moon, and the sight, or eye, M) *lost,* or *became deprived of, its light.* (T, M.) [See also the pass. form in what follows.] — طُمُوسُ الْقَلْبِ means *The heart's becoming in a bad,* or *corrupt, state.* (O. [See also the last sentence of this paragraph.]) — طَمَسَ الرَّجُلُ *The man was,* or *became, distant,* or *remote;* or *went to a distance,* or *far away.* (T, M, O, Ḳ.) — And طَمَسَ بِعَيْنِهِ, (M, O, Ḳ,) inf. n. طَمْسٌ, (IDrd, O,) *He looked far:* (M, O, Ḳ:) or *he looked at a thing from afar.* (IDrd, O.) — طَمَسَهُ, (Ṣ, IḲṭṭ, Mṣb, Ḳ,) and طَمَسَ عَلَيْهِ, (M, TA,) aor. ـِ, (M, Mṣb,) inf. n. طَمْسٌ, (Ṣ, Mṣb, Ḳ,) *He effaced it,* or *obliterated it;* (Ṣ, M, Mṣb, Ḳ;) *he effaced,* or *obliterated,* (M,) or *removed,* (TA,) or *extirpated,*

(Ḳ,) *the trace,* or *mark, thereof;* (M, Ḳ, TA;) as also ▾ طَمَّسَهُ, (M, TA,) inf. n. تَطْمِيسٌ: (TA:) or *he destroyed it:* (IḲṭṭ:) and طَمَسَ المَكْتُوبَ is also expl. as signifying *he covered the writing by folding.* (Ḥar p. 505.) You say, طَمَسَتْهُ الرِّيحُ *The wind effaced,* or *obliterated, it;* namely, the trace, or mark, of a thing. (A.) And it is said in the Ḳur [lxxvii. 8], فَإِذَا النُّجُومُ طُمِسَتْ *And when the stars shall have their traces extirpated:* (O, Ḳ:) or *shall lose their light.* (T, TA.) — طَمَسَ أَعْيُنَهُمْ, [as in the Ḳur liv. 37,] (A,) and عَلَى أَعْيُنِهِمْ, (T, A,) as in the Ḳur xxxvi. 66, (T,) *He* (God) *blinded them.* (T, TA.) — [Hence, app.,] طَمَسَ الغَيْمُ النُّجُومَ ‡ [*The clouds,* or *mist, covered,* or *concealed, the stars;* as though it put out their light]. (A.) — And [hence also,] طَمَسَ, aor. ـِ, (O, Ḳ,) inf. n. طَمَاسَةٌ, (O,* Ḳ,* TḲ,) † *He conjectured,* or *computed by conjecture,* (O, Ḳ, TA, TḲ,) a thing: (TḲ:) because the doing so is generally accompanied by the putting of the eyelids together, as though one were blinded. (TA.) — طَمَّسَهُ, inf. n. تَطْمِيسٌ, also signifies *He* (God) *transformed,* or *metamorphosed, him* or *it.* (TA.) Hence the saying in the Ḳur [x. 88], رَبَّنَا ٱطْمِسْ عَلَى أَمْوَالِهِمْ *O our Lord, transform their possessions:* (TA:) they say that they became stones: (O, TA:) or *change,* or *alter, their possessions:* (Ṣ, O:) or *destroy their possessions:* (Ibn-Arafeh, O, Bḍ, Ḳ:) the verb is also read ٱطْمُسْ. (Bḍ.) This طَمْس was the last of the nine signs which were given to Moses, when the property of Pharaoh was transformed at his prayer, and became stones. (M.) [See the Ḳur xvii. 103, and xxvii. 12.] In like manner, it is said in the Ḳur [iv. 50], مِنْ قَبْلِ أَنْ نَطْمِسَ وُجُوهًا *Before we change,* or *alter, faces:* (Ṣ:) or these words, with what immediately follows, فَنَرُدَّهَا عَلَى أَدْبَارِهَا, are expl. in three different ways: *before we make faces to be like the backs of necks:* or *before we make faces to be places in which hair shall grow like the backs of necks:* or ‡ *before we make them to err,* in requital of their opposition. (Zj, TA.) — طَمْسٌ also signifies *i. q.* فَسَادٌ [as though in the sense of إِفْسَادٌ The *making,* or *rendering, bad, corrupt,* &c.: but see طَمُوسُ القَلْبِ, above]. (TA.)

2: see طَمَسَهُ, in the paragraph above.

5:
7: } see 1, first sentence.

طَمِيسٌ: see طَامِسٌ, in four places.

طَمَاسَةٌ *Conjecture;* or *computation by conjecture.* (Fr, Mgh, O, Ḳ. [Accord to the TḲ, an inf. n.: see 1.])

رَسْمٌ طَامِسٌ [*A relic,* or *remain,* or *a mark,* or *trace, becoming,* or *become, effaced,* or *obliterated*]; (A;) [and so, app., ▾ طَمِيسٌ and ▾ مَطْمُوسٌ:] and أَرْبُعٌ طِمَاسٌ [pl. of رَبْعٌ طَمِيسٌ ▾ or طَامِسٌ] *dwellings of which the remains are becoming,* or *become, effaced,* or *obliterated.* (M.) — [عَيْنٌ طَامِسَةٌ *An eye of which the sight is going,* or *gone:* and] رَجُلٌ مَطْمُوسٌ ▾ *a man whose sight is going,* or *gone;* as also ▾ طَمِيسٌ: (Ḳ:) or *a blind man,* (Zj, M,) *the edge of whose eyelid is not apparent:* (Zj, T, M:) or *a man who has no slit between his two eyelids;* as also ▾ طَمِيسٌ: (A:) and نَجْمٌ طَامِسٌ ‡ *a star* [*that is evanescent,*] *of which the light is going,* or *gone:* (A:) and نُجُومٌ طَوَامِسُ ‡ *stars that become hidden,* or *concealed,* or *that set:* (TA:) or † *stars that are covered by the* سَرَاب [app. a mistranscription for سَحَاب or *clouds*], *so that they are not seen.* (Az, TA.) And طَامِسٌ signifies also *Distant,* or *remote:* (T, Ḳ, TA:) or a mountain *not plainly discernible from afar:* (TA:) pl. طَوَامِسُ. (Ḳ, TA.) And A desert *far-extending and pathless.* (M, TA.) — رَجُلٌ طَامِسُ القَلْبِ ‡ *A man dead in heart,* (A, Ḳ,) *who keeps nothing in mind:* (A:) or *a man of bad, corrupt,* or *depraved, heart.* (IḲṭṭ.) — رِيَاحٌ طَوَامِسُ [pl. of رِيحٌ طَامِسَةٌ] (A, TA) *Winds that efface,* or *obliterate,* things, *by repeatedly passing over* them; syn. دَوَارِسُ. (TA.)

مَطْمُوسٌ: see طَامِسٌ, in two places.

طمع

1. طَمِعَ فِيهِ (Ṣ, O, Mṣb, Ḳ, &c.) and بِهِ, (O, Ḳ,) aor. ـَ, (O, Ḳ,) inf. n. طَمَعٌ (Ṣ, O, Mṣb, Ḳ) and طَمَاعَةٌ, (Ṣ, O, TA,) accord. to all the copies of the Ḳ [and my copy of the Mṣb] طَمَاعٌ, but this is wrong, (TA,) and طَمَاعِيَةٌ, (Ṣ, O, Mṣb, Ḳ,) without teshdeed, (Ṣ, Mṣb,) and طَمَاعِيَّةٌ, with teshdeed, as in the L, but some disapprove this last, (TA,) *He coveted it;* i. e. *desired it vehemently, eagerly, greedily, very greedily, excessively, inordinately,* or *culpably;* or *he strove to acquire, obtain,* or *attain, it;* syn. حَرَصَ عَلَيْهِ: (Ḳ, TA:) طَمَعٌ signifying the *longing,* or *yearning,* for a thing; or *lusting* after it; mostly, *for the gratification of animal appetite, without any lawful incitement:* (Er-Rághib, TA:) and it is mostly used in relation to that of which the occurrence, or coming to pass, is [deemed] near: but sometimes طَمِعَ فِيهِ signifies *he hoped for it.* (Mṣb.) [See also طَمَعٌ below. One says also, طَمِعَ فِى فُلَانٍ, meaning *He eagerly desired,* or *he hoped, to make himself master of,* or *to overcome, such a one:* (see an ex. voce خَارِقٌ:) and طَمِعَ فِى فُلَانَةَ *he eagerly desired,* or *he hoped, to gain possession of,* or *to win, such a woman;* or *he lusted after her.*] — طَمُعَ, said of a man, means *He became very covetous;* (صَارَ كَثِيرَ الطَّمَعِ: Ṣ, O, Ḳ:) [or rather *how covetous is he!* for] it is a verb of wonder; the verbs of wonder being of three forms, accord. to rule; as in the exs. مَا أَحْسَنَ and أَسْمِعْ بِهِ and كَبُرَتْ كَلِمَةً; from which نِعْمَ and بِئْسَ are anomalous exceptions. (Ṣ, O.)

2: see what next follows. — [See also تَطْمِيعٌ below.]

4. اطمعهُ *He made him to covet,* &c.; (Ṣ,* O,* Mṣb,* Ḳ, TA;) and so ▾ طَمَّعَهُ, inf. n. تَطْمِيعٌ: (TA:) the verb is followed by فِى [and app. by بِ also] before the object. (Ṣ.)

5. تَطَمَّعَ فِى المَرْأَةِ [*He became excited to feel an eager desire for the woman;* or *to lust after her*]. (TA in art. ضعضع.)

طَمَعٌ an inf. n. of طَمِعَ. (Ṣ, O, Mṣb, Ḳ.) It is said in a trad. of 'Omar, الطَّمَعُ فَقْرٌ وَالْيَأْسُ غِنًى [meaning *Coveting,* or *covetousness,* or *greed, is a cause of poverty,* and *despair is a cause of freedom from want*]. (TA.) And one says, الطَّمَعُ طَبَعٌ [*Coveting,* or *covetousness,* or *greed, is a cause of disgrace,* or *dishonour*]. (TA. See أَطْمَعُ.) [See also an ex. in a verse cited voce طَبَعٌ. And see an ex. voce خَائِفٌ.] — And *A thing that is coveted,* or *desired vehemently* &c.: (Ḥam p. 517:) [pl. أَطْمَاعٌ. See also مَطْمَعٌ.] — And hence, (Ḥam ibid.,) The *daily,* or *monthly, allowance of food* or *the like, subsistence-money,* or *pay,* (syn. رِزْقٌ,) of soldiers: pl. أَطْمَاعٌ: (Ṣ, O, Mṣb, Ḳ:) or their أَطْمَاع are their *times of receiving such allowances.* (Ḳ.)

طَمُعٌ: see the next paragraph.

طَمِعٌ (Ṣ, O, Mṣb, Ḳ) and ▾ طَامِعٌ (O, Mṣb, Ḳ) and ▾ طَمُعٌ (Ṣ, O, Ḳ) and ▾ طَمَّاعٌ and ▾ طَمُوعٌ (TA) epithets from طَمِعَ: (Ṣ, O, Mṣb, Ḳ:) [the first and second signify *Coveting,* &c.: and the rest, *coveting* &c. *much,* or *very covetous* &c.:] pl. [of the first] طَمِعُونَ and [of the second or of the first] طَمَعَاءُ and [of the first] طَمَاعَى and [of the first or third or second] أَطْمَاعٌ. (Ḳ.)

طَمُوعٌ:
طَمَّاعٌ:
طَامِعٌ: } see the next preceding paragraph.

أَطْمَعُ [*More,* and *most, covetous* &c.]. أَطْمَعُ مِنْ قَالِبِ الصَّخْرَةِ [*More covetous than the turner-over of the great mass of stone*] is a prov., of which the origin was this: a man of Ma'add saw a stone in the land of El-Yemen, on which was inscribed, ٱقْلِبْنِى أَنْفَعْكَ ["Turn me over, I will benefit thee"]: and he exercised his skill in turning it over, and found [inscribed] on the other side, رُبَّ طَمَعٍ ▾ يَهْدِى إِلَى طَبَعٍ [*Many a coveting leads to disgrace*]: and he ceased not to beat with his head the great mass of stone, by reason of regret, until his brains issued and he died. (Meyd.)

تَطْمِيعٌ inf. n. of 2. (TA.) — [Hence,] تَطْمِيعٌ

الْقَطْرِ † *The first of rain, when it begins, and little thereof comes:* so called because it causes to covet more. (IAạr, TA.)

مَطْمَعٌ *A thing that is* [or *that is to be*] *coveted,* or *desired vehemently* &c.: (O, Ḳ: [see also طَمَعٌ:]) pl. مَطَامِعُ. (O, TA.) One says, طَمِعَ فِى غَيْرِ مَطْمَعٍ [*He coveted a thing not to be coveted;* or] *he hoped for a thing of which the attainment was remote,* or *improbable.* (Mṣb.) — And [hence,] ‡ *A bird that is put in the midst of the fowler's net in order to ensnare thereby other birds:* pl. as above. (TA.) — [And it is also used as an inf. n., agreeably with general analogy.] One says, لَا مَطْمَعَ فِى بُرْئِهِ [*There is no hope for its cure*]. (Ḳ in art. سرط.)

مَطْمَعَةٌ [*A cause of coveting,* or *desiring vehemently* &c.;] *a thing on account of which one covets,* &c. (O, Ḳ.) En-Nábighah Edh-Dhubyánee says,

* وَالْيَأْسُ مِمَّا فَاتَ يُعْقِبُ رَاحَةً *
* وَلَرُبَّ مَطْمَعَةٍ تَعُودُ ذُبَاحَا *

[*And despair of what has become beyond reach occasions, as its result, rest: and assuredly many a cause of coveting is, in its result,* (*like*) *a disease in the fauces, or a poisonous plant*]. (O.)

اِمْرَأَةٌ مِطْمَاعٌ *A woman that causes vehement desire* (تُطْمِعُ) *but does not grant attainment.* (Ṣ, O, Ḳ.)

طمن

3. طَامَنَ: see Q. Q. 1, in three places.

6. تَطَامَنَ: see Q. Q. 2: and also Q. Q. 4, in two places.

Q. Q. 1. طَأْمَنَ ظَهْرَهُ, (Ṣ, Mṣb, and so in some copies of the Ḳ,) with ء, (Mṣb,) or ▼ طَامَنَهُ, (TA, and so in some copies of the Ḳ,) without ء, for the ء in اِطْمَأَنَّ [q. v. infrà] is [said to be] for the purpose of preventing the combination of two quiescent letters, (TA,) or طَامَنَهُ also, the former being the original, (Mṣb,) *He* (a man, Mṣb) *bent down his back;* (Mṣb, TA;) *he lowered it;* (Mṣb;) and طَمْأَنَهُ signifies the same. (Ṣ, Ḳ.) [And in like manner one says of other things.] — And طَأْمَنَهُ [or طَمْأَنَهُ], and ▼ طَامَنَ الشَّىْءَ, *He caused the thing to be, or become, still, in a state of rest, quiet,* or *calm.* (TA.) = And طَأْمَنَ مِنْهُ [or ▼ طَامَنَ], (Ṣ,) or طَمْأَنَ منه, (Ḳ, TA,) *He* (a man, Ṣ) *was,* or *became, at rest from it,* (Ṣ, Ḳ,) namely, an affair, or event. (Ḳ.) [The inf. n. of طأمن is طَأْمَنَةٌ, said in the TA to be syn. with اِطْمِئْنَانٌ. See also Q. Q. 4.]

Q. Q. 2. تَطَأْمَنَ [more commonly written ▼ تَطَامَنَ], without ء, and ▼ اِطْمَأَنَّ also (see رَكَعَ) *He stooped,* [*bent himself down,*] or *lowered himself;* syn. تَطَاطَأَ. (Ṣ and TA in art. طأ, &c.; and R and TA in the present art.) — And † *He was,* or *became, lowly, humble,* or *submissive;* syn. خَضَعَ. (Ṣ and Ḳ in art. خضع, &c.: in some copies of each written with, and in others without, ء.) — See also the next paragraph, in two places.

Q. Q. 4. اِطْمَأَنَّ is said by some to be originally [اِطْمَانَّ] like اِحْمَارَّ, (Mṣb,) as Esh-Shiháb states in the Expos. of the Shifá, (TA,) and to be pronounced with ء for the purpose of avoiding [the combination of] the two quiescent letters, (Mṣb, TA,) anomalously: (Mṣb:) and some say that it is originally اِطْأَمَنَّ, (Mṣb, TA,) because you say طَأْمَنَ الرَّجُلُ ظَهْرَهُ, with ء, (Mṣb,) or, as Suh says, in the R, because it is from تَطَأْمَنَ, the م being put before the ء in order to render the word more easy of pronunciation, (TA,) therefore it is anomalous; (Mṣb;) Sb [likewise] held it to be formed by transposition, and derived from طَأْمَنَ; but AA held the contrary to be the case. (TA.) — You say, اِطْمَأَنَّتِ الْأَرْضُ, and ▼ تَطَامَنَتْ [or ▼ تَطَأْمَنَتْ], meaning *The land,* or *ground, was,* or *became, low,* or *depressed.* (TA.) — See also Q. Q. 2. — اطمأنّ, (Ṣ, Mgh, Ḳ,) inf. n. اِطْمِئْنَانٌ and طُمَأْنِينَةٌ, (Ṣ, Ḳ,) or the latter is a simple subst., (Mgh, Mṣb,) signifies [also] *He* (a man, Ṣ) *was,* or *became, still, in a state of rest* or *ease, quiet,* or *calm;* syn. سَكَنَ; (Ṣ, Mgh;) as also اِطْبَأَنَّ, which is formed by permutation. (Ṣ.) And thus it signifies as said of the heart, i. e. *It was,* or *became, still, in a state of rest* or *ease, quiet, calm, tranquil, unruffled,* or *free from disquietude.* (Mṣb.) Thus too in the saying, اطمأنّ إِلَى كَذَا, i. e. ‡ *He trusted to such a thing,* or *relied upon it, so as to become at rest* or *ease,* or *quiet, in mind.* (Ḳ,* TA.) And one says also, اطمأنّ جَالِسًا [*He became still,* or *at rest,* or *at ease, sitting*]: (TA:) and اطمأنّ بِنَا الْجُلُوسُ [lit. *The sitting became still,* or *free from disquiet, with us*]; meaning اِسْتَقْرَرْنَا وَسَكَنَّا فِى الْجُلُوسِ [i. e. *we became settled,* or *at rest* or *ease, and still, in the sitting;* or *became seated at ease*]. (Ḥar p. 280.) And اطمأنّ بِالْمَوْضِعِ [*He settled in the place;* i. e.] *he remained, stayed, abode,* or *dwelt, in the place, and took it as his home.* (Mṣb.) And اطمأنّ عَمَّا كَانَ يَفْعَلُهُ † [*He became at rest from that which he was doing;*] i. e. *he desisted from that which he was doing.* (TA.) And ▼ فِيهِ تَطَامُنٌ [or ▼ تَطَأْمُنٌ] *In him is quietness, calmness,* or *sedateness.* (TA.)

مُطْمَئِنٌّ: see طَمْنٌ.

طُمَيْئِنٌ dim. of مُطْمَئِنٌّ; (Ṣ, Ḳ;) formed by rejecting the م at the beginning, and one of the two ن at the end, of the latter word. (Ṣ.)

طُمَأْنِينَةٌ an [irreg.] inf. n. of اِطْمَأَنَّ, (Ṣ, Ḳ,) or a subst. therefrom; as such signifying [*A depression in the ground;* as, for instance, in the Ṣ and Ḳ voce رَزْنٌ: (comp. مُطْمَأَنٌّ:) — and also] *Stillness, a state of rest* or *ease, quietness, calmness, tranquillity,* or *freedom from disquietude.* (Mgh, Mṣb.)

طُمَيْئِنَةٌ dim. of طُمَأْنِينَةٌ; formed by the rejection of one of the two ن in the latter word, because it is augmentative. (Ṣ.)

مُطْمَأَنٌّ *A place of depression* or *lowness* in the land or ground. (Mgh. [See also the following paragraph.]) = مُطْمَأَنٌّ إِلَيْهِ ‡ A thing *to which one trusts,* or *upon which one relies, so as to become at rest* or *ease,* or *quiet, in mind.* (Ṣ, Ḳ,* TA.)

مُطْمَئِنٌّ A place *low,* or *depressed.* (Mgh, Mṣb.) — And A man (Ṣ) *still, in a state of rest* or *ease, quiet,* or *calm;* (Ṣ, Mgh, Ḳ;) as also ▼ طَمْنٌ, (Ḳ,) but this is a word unused in the [genuine] language, (TA,) pl. طُمُونٌ. (Ḳ.) Hence one says, هُوَ مُطْمَئِنٌّ إِلَى كَذَا ‡ *He is trusting to such a thing,* or *relying upon it, so as to be at rest* or *ease,* or *quiet, in mind.* (Ṣ, Ḳ,* TA.) And [it is said that] النَّفْسُ الْمُطْمَئِنَّةُ means † *The soul that has become at rest* or *ease, quiet,* or *calm, by belief; and lowly, humble,* or *submissive, to its Lord.* (TA. [See the Ḳur lxxxix. 27.]) — Also *Taking for oneself a place in the earth,* or *in a country, as a home,* or *settled place of abode.* (TA.)

طمو and طمى

1. طَمَا, aor. يَطْمُو, inf. n. طُمُوٌّ; and طَمَى, aor. يَطْمِى, (Ṣ, Ḳ,) inf. n. طُمِىٌّ, (Ṣ,) thus in the M [as well as in the Ṣ], or طَمْىٌ, thus in the Ḳ and in the book of ISk; (TA;) said of water, (Ṣ, Ḳ,) *It became high,* (Ḳ,) or *it rose high, and filled the channel in which it flowed.* (Ṣ.) [See also طَمَّ.] — And, both verbs, said of a plant, *It became tall.* (Ḳ.) — Also, (Ḳ, TA,) said of the sea, and of a river, and of a well, (TA,) *It became full:* (Ḳ, TA:) so says Lth. (TA.) — And طَمَتْ بِزَوْجِهَا ‡ *She* (a woman) *exalted herself with her husband;* syn. اِرْتَفَعَتْ بِهِ; (Ṣ, TA;) from طَمَا or طَمَى said of water: (Ṣ:) or *she grinned at her husband.* (Z, TA.) — طَمَتْ بِهِ هِمَّتُهُ, aor. ـُ and ـِ as above, † *His ambition elevated him.* (Ḳ,* TA.) — And طَمَا بِهِ said of anxiety, and of grief, and of fear, † *It became vehement in him:* the following verse by himself is quoted by Z:

* قَدْ طَمَا بِى خَوْفُ الْمَنِيَّةِ لٰكِنْ *
* خَوْفُ مَا يَعْقُبُ الْمَنِيَّةَ أَطْمَى ▼ *

[† *The fear of death has become vehement in me, but the fear of what will follow death is more vehement.*] (TA.) — And طَمَى, aor. يَطْمِى,

like طَمَرَ, aor. يَطْمِرُ, signifies *He passed by, or along, hastening, or going quickly:* (Ṣ, TA:) and hence, طَمَا [or طَمِى], said of a horse, *He hastened, or went quickly.* (TA.)

[طَمَايَةٌ is said by Golius, as on the authority of Z, to signify *Solicitude, and fear:* but probably, I think, from his having found طَمَايَةُ هَمٍّ وَخَوْفٍ erroneously written for طَمَا بِهِ هَمٌّ وَخَوْفٌ meaning "fear became vehement in him."]

مَآءٌ طَامٍ *Water rising high, and filling its channel.* (Ṣ.) And بَحْرٌ طَامٍ *A* [*high or*] *copious sea.* (TA.)

أَطْمَى [*More, and most, vehement*]: see the verse cited above.

طن

1. طَنَّ, (MA, Mṣb, Ḳ, TA,) aor. ـِ, (Mṣb, TA,) inf. n. طَنِينٌ [q. v. infrà], (MA, Mṣb,) *It made a sound* [*of a continued or a reiterated kind, and either low or sharp*]; (MA, Mṣb, Ḳ, TA;) as also ↓ طَنَّنَ, and ↓ طَنْطَنَ. (Ḳ.) You say, طَنَّ الذُّبَابُ [and ↓ طَنْطَنَ, as also دَنَّ and دَنْدَنَ,] *The flies made a* [*humming, or buzzing,*] *sound.* (MA, Mṣb.) And in like manner طَنَّ is said of other things than flies. (Mṣb.) [Thus,] طَنَّ الطَّسْتُ, (MA,) or طَنَّتِ الطَّسْتُ, (Ṣ,) *The basin of brass or other metal made a* [*ringing, or tinkling,*] *sound.* (Ṣ, MA.) And البَطَّةُ تَطِنُّ *The duck, or goose, utters a sound or sounds* [i. e. *quacks*]. (Ṣ.) — [Hence,] one says also, طَنَّ ذِكْرُهُ فِى البِلَادِ † [*His fame resounded through the countries*]. (TA.) — And طَنَّتِ الإِبِلُ † *The camels thirsted* [app. because thirst is often attended with a ringing, or tingling, in the ears]. (TA.) — And طَنَّتْ سَاقُهُ ‡ *His shank was quickly cut off:* the verb being imitative of the sound of the shank in its falling. (TA.) — And طَنَّ † *He* (a man, TA) *died:* (Ṣ, Ḳ:) so in the "Muṣannaf" [of Aboo-'Amr Esh-Sheybánee]. (Ṣ.) — And † *He licked his finger.* (TA.)

2: see the foregoing paragraph, first sentence.

4. اطنّ الطَّسْتَ *He caused the basin of brass or other metal to make a* [*ringing, or tinkling,*] *sound.* (Ṣ, Ḳ.) — And اطنّ سَاقَهُ (Ṣ, Ḳ) ‡ *He cut off his shank* (Ṣ, Ḳ, TA) *quickly;* (TA;) or اطنّ يَدَهُ *he made his arm, or hand, to fall off;* (so in a copy of the Ṣ;) by a stroke [of a sword or the like]; the verb being meant to imitate the sound of the cutting, (Ṣ,) or the sound of the limb in its falling; and in like manner one says أَتَنَّهَا [and أَطَرَّهَا] and أَتَرَّهَا, meaning the same. (TA.)

8. هُوَ يُطَّنُّ بِكَذَا, meaning *He is suspected of such a thing,* is originally يُظْتَنُّ; as also يُظَّنُّ. (TA.)

R. Q. 1. طَنْطَنَ: see 1, first and second sentences.

طَنٌّ [accord. to the CḲ طِنٌّ, being there said to be with kesr, but not so in other copies of the Ḳ, nor in the TA,] *Fresh, ripe, red dates, very sweet,* (Ḳ, TA,) *and having much flowing juice;* as also ↓ طُنٌّ, with ḍamm. (TA.) — Also, [if not a mistranscription for طُنٌّ,] *A half-load, such as is borne on one side of a beast, of cotton that has been separated, or loosened, and cleared of its seeds:* from El-Hejeree. (TA.)

طُنٌّ *A bundle of reeds or canes,* (Ṣ, M, Ḳ,) or (so accord. to the Mṣb, but in the TA "and") *of firewood:* (Mṣb, TA:) thought by IDrd to be not genuine Arabic: and pronounced by the vulgar طِنّ, with kesr: (TA:) n. un. with ة; (Ḳ;) [i. e.] ↓ طُنَّةٌ signifies *a single reed or cane* [or *piece of firewood*] *of a bundle:* (Ṣ:) and the pl. is أَطْنَانٌ: (Mṣb:) [or,] accord. to AḤn, a طُنّ of reeds or canes, and of fresh branches, is a وريقة [app. meaning *a leafy bundle*] *put together and bound round, and having flowers, or blossoms, and plucked fruits put in the interior thereof.* (TA.) — And *A thing that is put between the two half-loads that are upon the sides of a beast.* (AHeyth, Ḳ.) — And *The stature* [of a man]: or, accord. to IAạr, (TA,) the *body* of a man and of any animal: pl. أَطْنَانٌ and طِنَانٌ: (Ḳ, TA:) whence, he says, the saying, فُلَانٌ لَا يَقُومُ بِطُنِّ نَفْسِهِ فَكَيْفَ بِغَيْرِهِ [*Such a one will not rise with his own body: how then with another?*]: but accord. to IDrd, this is a saying of the vulgar; and he does not think it to be genuine Arabic. (TA.) — See also طَنٌّ.

طُنَّةٌ: see the next preceding paragraph.

طِنَّةٌ: see ظِنَّةٌ.

طِنِّىٌّ A *large-bodied* man. (Ḳ, TA.)

طَنِينٌ an inf. n.: (MA, Mṣb: [see 1:]) [as a simple subst.,] The *sound of flies* [i. e. *a humming, or buzzing*]: and *of a basin of brass or other metal* [i. e. *a ringing, or tinkling*]: (Ṣ, Ḳ, TA:) and *of the ear* [i. e. *a ringing, or tingling*]: and *of a mountain:* and *of a hard thing* [*of any kind*]: and ↓ طَنْطَنَةٌ has a similar meaning. (TA.)

قَصِيدَةٌ طَنَّانَةٌ [*A sonorous ode.*] (TA.)

طَنْطَنَةٌ: see طَنِينٌ. It is an onomatopœia, meaning The *sound of the* [*kind of mandoline called*] طُنْبُور, *and the like,* (Ḳ, TA,) *such as the lute.* (TA.) And *Low, faint, or soft, speech.* (TA.) And *Loquacity, and a sounding utterance of speech.* (TA.)

رَجُلٌ ذُو طَنْطَانٍ *A clamorous man.* (Ḳ.)

طنأ

1. طَنِئَ, aor. ـَ, said of a camel, *He had his spleen adhering to his side.* (Ḳ.) And, said of a man, *He had a tertian fever, and his spleen in consequence became enlarged.* (Lḥ, TA.) Thus pronounced by some with ء [for طَنِىَ, q. v.]. (TA.)

4. أَطْنَأَ [*He suffered not to retain the last remains of life*]. One says, هٰذِهِ حَيَّةٌ لَا تُطْنِئُ *This is a serpent that will not suffer one to survive;* (Ṣ, O, Ḳ;*) *that kills instantly:* also without ء, but originally with ء; from طِنْءٌ in the first of the senses assigned to it below. (Ṣ, O.)

طِنْءٌ The [*last*] *remains of the vital spirit.* (Ṣ, O, Ḳ.) One says, تَرَكْتُهُ بِطِنْئِهِ *I left him with the* [*last*] *remains of life.* (Ṣ, O.) — And The *remains of water in a watering-trough, or tank.* (O, Ḳ, TA.) And it is said that رَوْضَةٌ, by which it is also expl. in the Ḳ [and in the O], has this meaning [as well as that of *A meadow, &c.*]; and therefore this explanation without the former is given in the L. (TA.) — And *Ashes in a state of extinction:* (O, Ḳ:) and so طِنًى. (Ḳ and TA in art. طنى.) — [And app. *A bier;* for this is a meaning assigned to نَبْطٌ; and] one says, رُمِىَ فُلَانٌ فِى طِنْئِهِ [and فى طِنْيِهِ] and فى نَبْطِهِ [*Such a one was cast into his bier*]; meaning, when he died. (AZ, TA.) — And *A disease, or malady.* (Ḳ.) — And *Doubt, or suspicion, or evil opinion; or a thing that occasions doubt or suspicion or evil opinion;* syn. رِيبَةٌ; (Ṣ, O, Ḳ, TA; in the CḲ زِنْيَةٌ;) and تُهَمَةٌ: (TA:) and so طِنًى. (TA in art. طنى.) Fr. cites,

كَأَنَّ عَلَى ذِى الطِّنْءِ عَيْنًا بَصِيرَةً

meaning, عَلَى ذِى الرِّيبَةِ [i. e. *As though there were a discerning eye upon him in whom is that which occasions doubt, &c.*]. (TA.)

طنب

1. طَنِبَ, aor. ـَ, inf. n. طَنَبٌ, *He* (a horse) *was long in the back.* (O, Mṣb, TḲ.) [See أَطْنَبُ below: and see also 2.] — [And app., in like manner said of a horse, *He was long and lax in the hind legs.* See, again, أَطْنَبُ below.] — And *It* (a spear) *was, or became, crooked.* (TḲ.)

2. طَنَّبَهُ, inf. n. تَطْنِيبٌ, *He extended it,* (Ḳ, TA,) namely, a tent, (A, TA,) *by means of its* أَطْنَاب [or *tent-ropes*], *and tied it, or made it fast.* (Ḳ, TA.) And طَنَّبَ [alone] *He stretched his tent-ropes and pitched his tent.* (TA voce رَافِضٌ, q. v.) — [Hence,] طَنَّبَ بِالمَكَانِ, (Ṣ, Ḳ,) or بِالبَلَدِ, (A,) ‡ *He remained, stayed, dwelt, or abode, in the place, or in the country or town.* (Ṣ, A, Ḳ.) — And طَنَّبَ القَوْسَ *He attached an* إِطْنَابَة [q. v.] *to the bow.* (TA.) — And تَطْنِيبُ السِّقَآءِ means تَطْبِيبُهُ [q. v.], (Ḳ,) i. e. *The hanging the milk-skin to a pole of the tent, and then agitating it to produce the butter.* (AA, TA.) — طَنِبَ said of a horse, *He was long in the* مَتْن [i. e. the *back,* or the *portion of flesh and sinew on either*

side of the back-bone]. (Ṣ, O. [See also 1.]) —— And, said of a wolf, *He howled.* (Ḳ.)

3. طَانَبْتُهُمْ فِى المَحَالِّ *I had my tent-ropes* (طُنُب) *next to theirs in the places of alighting.* (A.)

4. اطنبت الرِّيحُ, (inf. n. إِطْنَابٌ, Mṣb,) *The wind blew violently, and was accompanied with dust.* (Ṣ, O, Mṣb, Ḳ.) —— And hence, اطنب said of a man, (Mṣb,) inf. n. as above, (TA,) † *He exerted himself much,* or *beyond measure,* or *to the utmost,* or *was extravagant,* or *immoderate,* (Mṣb, TA,) and *profuse,* (TA,) *in praising* or *blaming:* (Mṣb, TA:) or اطنب فِى الكَلَامِ *he so exerted himself,* or *was extravagant* or *immoderate, in speech:* (Ṣ, O, TA:) or *he was eloquent in description,* whether *praising* or *blaming;* (Ḳ, TA;) and so *in speech:* (TA:) and اطنب فِى الوَصْفِ *he exerted himself much,* or *beyond measure,* or *to the utmost, in description.* (IAmb, TA.) And اطنب فِى عَدْوِهِ † *He exerted himself much,* or *beyond measure,* or *to the utmost, in his running.* (IAmb, TA.) —— اطنبت الإِبِلُ † *The camels followed one another in journeying.* (Ṣ, O, Ḳ.) —— And اطنب النَّهْرُ † *The river went* [or *flowed*] *far away.* (Ḳ.)

طُنْبٌ: see طُنُبٌ.

طَنَبٌ inf. n. of 1 [q. v.]. (O, Mṣb, TḲ.) *Length in the back* of a horse; (A, O, Mṣb, Ḳ;) which is a fault (A, O, Mṣb, Ḳ, TA) in the male, but not in the female: (TA:) one says, فِيهِ طَنَبٌ (A) or فِى ظَهْرِهِ طَنَبٌ (TA) *In him is length in the back* (A) or *in his back is length.* (TA.) And *Length in the hind legs* [of a horse], *together with laxness.* (Ḳ, TA.) —— And *Crookedness* in a spear. (Ṣ, O, Ḳ.)

طُنُبٌ (Ṣ, A, O, L, Mṣb, Ḳ) and ♦ طُنْبٌ (L, TA) *A tent-rope:* (Ḥam p. 687:) *a rope with which the* خَيْمَة *and the like are tied,* or *made fast:* (Mṣb:) *a rope of the* خِبَآء (Ṣ, O, L, TA) and *of the* سُرَادِق [q. v.] and *the like:* (L, TA:) *a long rope with which the* سرادق *of the tent is tied,* or *made fast;* (A, Ḳ, TA;) or, as in the M, *with which the tent and the* سرادق *are tied,* or *made fast,* [*extending*] *between the ground and the* طَرَائِق [pl. of طَرِيقَةٌ, q. v.]: (TA:) and also *a* وَتِد [app. meaning *a tent-peg*]; thus in the Ḳ, and the like is said in the M; those who make الوَتِدُ in the Ḳ to be conjoined with سرادق [as though the author meant that طنب signifies *a long rope with which the* سرادق *of the tent, and the peg, are tied,* or *made fast,*] being in error: (TA: [but in my opinion, this reading which is disallowed in the TA is more probably correct than the other: in the CḲ, and in my MS. copy of the Ḳ, instead of وَالوَتِدُ, we find او الوتد: in a copy of the A, او الوَتَرُ, an obvious mistranscription:]) the pl. is أَطْنَابٌ (Ṣ, O, Mṣb, Ḳ) and طِنَبَةٌ; (Ḳ;) and some of the lexicologists assert that طنب is used as a sing. like عُنُقٌ, and as a pl. like كُتُبٌ; (MF, TA;) and Ibn-es-Sarráj says, in one place of his book, that it has no other pl. than أَطْنَابٌ; but in another place he says that it has this pl. accord. to those who give it a pl., thus giving to understand that there is a difference of opinion as to the plural's being allowable, and that it is used in one form as sing. and pl., which is the case: (Mṣb, TA:) the أَطْنَاب are the أَوَاخِىّ [pl. of آخِيَّةٌ], i. e. the *long ropes of the* أَخْبِيَة [pl. of خِبَآء]; the short ropes being called أُصُرٌ, sing. إِصَارٌ: the former are the ropes with which the tent is tied, or made fast, between the ground and the طَرَائِق. (TA.) As an instance of a tropical usage, (A, TA,) it is related that when El-Ash'ath contracted marriage with a woman, (A, Nh, O, Mṣb, L,) namely, Meleekeh Bint-Zurárah, (Nh, Mṣb, L,) on the terms upon which she should decide, (A, Nh, O, &c.,) and she decided upon a hundred thousand dirhems, (A, Nh, Mṣb, L,) رَدَّهَا عُمَرُ إِلَى أَطْنَابِ بَيْتِهَا, meaning ‡ *'Omar reduced her to the dowry of the like of her among the women of her family;* (A, Nh, O, Mṣb, L;) [lit., *to the ropes of her tent,* or *to the tent-ropes of her family;*] i. e., to the ground whereon was built the condition of her family, and over which their tent-ropes extended. (Nh, L.) And another tropical usage occurs in the saying, مَا بَيْنَ طُنُبَىِ المَدِينَةِ أَحْوَجُ مِنِّى إِلَيْهَا, (TA,) a saying ascribed to the Prophet, (O,) meaning ‡ *What is between the two extremities,* (O, TA,) and *the two sides,* (TA,) *of the city is more in need of it than I.* (O, TA.) —— [Hence,] ‡ *A sinew,* or *tendon,* (Ṣ, O, Ḳ,) or *ligament,* (M, A,) of the body, (Ṣ, M, O, Ḳ,) *that ties the joints and bones:* (M:) pl. أَطْنَابٌ. (M, A.) أَطْنَابُ الأَصَابِعِ means ‡ *The tendons of the fingers,* [or *the interossei,*] *on the outer side of the hand, extended above the* سُلَامَى, *from the wrist to the lowest parts of the fingers.* (A,* and TA voce أَشْجَعُ, q. v.) —— And † *A certain tendon in the uppermost part of the chest:* (Ḳ, TA:) [or,] accord. to the L, the طُنُبَانِ [or طُنْبَانِ?] are *two tendons* [or *the sterno-mastoides*] *next the pit of the throat, that extend,* or *stretch, when a man turns his head aside.* (TA.) —— And ‡ The *root of a tree:* (Ṣ, A, O, K:) pl. أَطْنَابٌ: (A:) or this (the pl.) signifies the *minor roots that branch off from the root-stock* or *main body of the root.* (TA.) You say, تَقَبَّضَتْ أَطْنَابُهَا ‡ [*Its roots contracted;*] meaning *it was planted.* (A.) —— And أَطْنَابُ الشَّمْسِ ‡ *The rays,* or *beams, of the sun, that extend like sinews,* or *tendons, at the time of its rising.* (TA.) You say, مَدَّتِ الشَّمْسُ أَطْنَابَهَا [and امْتَدَّتْ أَطْنَابُهَا] ‡ [*The sun extended its beams* and *its beams became extended*], meaning *the sun rose.* (A.) —— See also إِطْنَابَةٌ.

مُطَانِبٌ: see طُنُبٌ.

أَطْنَبُ *Having the quality termed* طَنَبٌ; *long in the back;* [&c.;] (A, O, Mṣb, Ḳ;) applied to a horse: (A, O, Mṣb:) fem. طَنْبَآءُ. (Mṣb, Ḳ.)

إِطْنَابَةٌ *A* مِظَلَّة; (Ṣ, O, Ḳ, TA; [in one of my copies of the Ṣ مُظَلَّة, and in the CḲ مَظَلَّة, but, as is said in the TA, it is with kesr;]) meaning *a large tent of* [*goats'*] *hair.* (KL.) —— And *A thong at the head of the bow-string;* (Aṣ, TA;) *a thong that is bound to the end of the string of the Arabian bow:* (Ṣ, O:) or the *thong that is at the lower curved extremity of the bow and that binds the string to the notch:* (TA:) or, as also ♦ طُنُبٌ, *a thong that is connected with the bow-string, and then wound round the* كُظْر, (Ḳ, TA,) which is the *notch of the bow, into which the ring of the bow-string goes.* (TA.) —— And *A thong,* or *strap, that is bound to the end of the girth, as an aid to its* [*main*] *strap when it becomes loose,* or *unsteady:* (TA:) or *a thong,* or *strap, of the girth, that is tied in a knot to the buckle:* pl. أَطَانِيبُ. (O, TA.) En-Nábighah [Edh-Dhubyánee (O)] says, (O, TA,) describing horses, and the same words occur in a verse of Selámeh, (TA,)

* يَرْكُضْنَ قَدْ قَلِقَتْ عُقَدُ الأَطَانِبِ *

which is said to mean, [*Striking the ground with their hoofs,*] *the knots of the breast-girths* (الأَلْبَاب) and (الحُزُم) *having become loose.* (O, TA. [عُقَدُ is here put for عُقَدُ for the sake of the metre.]) —— One says also غَارَاتٌ, خَيْلٌ أَطَانِيبُ, (O,) and أَطَانِيبُ, (A, O,) meaning ‡ [*Horses* or *horsemen,* and *horsemen making a raid,*] *following one another* (A, O) *continuously, without* [*visible*] *end.* (A.) And رَأَيْتُ إِطْنَابَةً مِنْ خَيْلٍ and مِنْ طَيْرٍ † [*I saw a number following one another of horses* or *horsemen* and *of birds*]. (O.)

مِطْنَبٌ The *shoulder,* syn. مَنْكِب; and the *part between the shoulder-joint and the neck,* syn. عَاتِق: (Ṣ, O, Ḳ:) and accord. to a marginal note in a copy of the L, ♦ مِطْنَبٌ signifies the same: (TA:) pl. مَطَانِبُ. (Ṣ, O.) —— Also, with the article, *i. q.* حَبْلُ العَاتِقِ: [see حَبْلٌ and عَاتِق:] pl. as above. (TA.)

مُطْنِبٌ [part. n. of 4, q. v. As such signifying] † *A great praiser of every one.* (TA.) —— And نَهْرٌ مُطْنِبٌ ‡ *A river that goes* [or *flows*] *far away.* (A, O.) [See also مُطَنِّبٌ.]

مُطَنَّبٌ: see مُطْنِبٌ.

مُطَنَّبٌ A tent, (بَيْت, O, or خِبَآء, Ṣ,) and a رِوَاق, (Ṣ,) *tied,* or *made fast, with* أَطْنَاب [or *tent-ropes*]. (Ṣ, O.) A man is related to have said to Ubei Ibn-Kaab, in reply to the latter's advising him to buy a beast to convey him to the place of prayer of the Prophet, مَا أُحِبُّ أَنَّ بَيْتِى مُطَنَّبٌ بِبَيْتِ مُحَمَّدٍ i. e. [*I do not like*] *that my tent should be tied with tent-ropes to the tent of Mohammad:* as though he reckoned upon a reward for his many foot-steps to the mosque. (O.) —— And قَوْسٌ مُطَنَّبَةٌ *A bow having an* إِطْنَابَة [q. v.] *attached to it.* (TA.)

عَسْكَرٌ مُطَنِّبٌ [perhaps correctly مُطْنِبٌ, q. v.,]

† *An army of which the remotest part is not seen, by reason of its multitude.* (TA. [See also what next follows.])

جَيْشٌ مِطْنَابٌ † *A great army;* (Ḳ;) *an army of which the two extremities are far apart, that is not near to ending.* (O, TA. [See also what next precedes.])

مُطَانِبٌ and ♦ طَنِيبٌ, of which latter the pl. is طُنَائِبُ, signify the same; the latter having the meaning assigned to the former in what here follows. (TA.) One says, هُوَ جَارِى مُطَانِبِى *He is my neighbour whose ropes* (طُنُب) *of his tent are next to those of my tent.* (Sh, A, O, Ḳ.*)

حَىٌّ مُتَطَانِبٌ [*A tribe of which the ropes of the tents, and therefore the tents themselves, are near together:* see the next preceding paragraph]. (A.)

طنبر

طِنْبَارٌ: see the next paragraph.

طُنْبُورٌ (Ṣ, O, Mṣb, Ḳ) and ♦ طِنْبَارٌ (Ṣ, O, Ḳ) [the former vulgarly pronounced طَنْبُور] *A certain musical instrument;* (O, Mṣb;) [*a kind of mandoline with chords of brass wire, which is played with a plectrum;*] arabicized, (Ṣ, O, Mṣb, Ḳ,) from the Pers., (Ṣ, O, Mṣb,) originally دُنْبَهْ بَرَّهْ, (Ḳ, TA,) [correctly دُنْبَهٔ بَرَّهْ, or] دُنْبِ بَرَّهْ, (O,) being likened to the tail (أَلْيَة) of a lamb: (O, Ḳ, TA:) so says Aṣ: (O:) pl. طَنَابِيرُ. (MA.) [Accord. to the Mṣb, طُنْبُور is of the measure فُنْعُول: but accord. to the derivation mentioned above, the ن is a radical letter.]

طُنْبُورِىٌّ [or, accord. to Golius, on the authority of Meyd, طُنْبُورَانِىٌّ,] *A player on the* طُنْبُور. (MA.)

طنجر

طِنْجِرَةٌ: see the following paragraph.

طِنْجِيرٌ *A certain vessel* (O, Mṣb) *of copper* or *brass,* (Mṣb,) *in which one cooks,* (O, Mṣb,) *nearly resembling a* طَبَق, (Mṣb,) *without a cover;* (O;) also called ♦ طِنْجِرَةٌ [vulgarly pronounced طَنْجَرَة and تَنْجَرَة, and now applied to *a saucepan*]: (TA:) خَبِيص [q. v.] is made in it: (Ḳ in art. خبص:) an arabicized word; in Pers. پَاتِيلَهْ: (Ḳ: [in some copies of the Ḳ, and in the O, بَاتِيلَهْ:]) pl. of the former طَنَاجِيرُ (Mṣb) [and of the latter طَنَاجِرُ. Accord. to the Mṣb, it is of the measure فِنْعِيل: but accord. to the O and Ḳ, the ن is a radical letter.] — It is also used by the Arabs of our time as a metonymical appellation of ‡ *A coward:* or *a low, vile,* or *mean, person:* as though they meant thereby a townsman, or villager, who constantly eats in cooking-pots and bowls of copper; differing from the people of the desert. (TA.)

طنخ

1. طَنِخَ, (Ṣ, L, Ḳ,) aor. ـَ, (Ḳ,) inf. n. طَنَخٌ, (Ṣ,) *His* (a man's, Ṣ) *heart* (قَلْب [meaning *stomach,* which is often thus termed in the present day,]) *became overpowered by grease* [or *greasy food*], *and he suffered indigestion,* (Ṣ, L, Ḳ,) *in consequence thereof;* (Ṣ, L;) as also تَنِخَ, aor. ـَ, inf. n. تَنَخٌ. (L.) And طَنِخَتْ said of camels, *They suffered indigestion.* (TA in art. طنخ.) And طَنِخَتْ نَفْسُهُ *His soul* [or *stomach*] *became heavy;* or *heaved,* or *became agitated by a tendency to vomit.* (L.) — And *He became fat.* (L, Ḳ.)

2. طَنَّخَهُ, (Ḳ,) inf. n. تَطْنِيخٌ; (TA;) and ♦ اطنخهُ, (Ḳ,) inf. n. إِطْنَاخٌ; (TA;) *It* (grease [or greasy food], TA) *caused him to suffer indigestion.* (Ḳ, TA.) — Sh says, I heard El-Faḳ'asee say, نَشْرَبُ هٰذِهِ الأَلْبَانَ فتطنخنا عَنِ الطَّعَامِ, [i. e. فَتُطَنِّخُنَا or ♦ فَتُطْنِخُنَا] meaning [*We drink these milks and*] *they render us in no need,* or *serve us in stead, of* [*other*] *food.* (L.) — And one says, طَنِخَتِ النَّاقَةُ, and الدَّابَّةُ, meaning *The she-camel,* and *the beast, became* [or *was rendered*] *very fat.* (L.)

4: see 2, in two places.

طِنْخٌ [is said to signify] *A part,* or *portion,* of the night: so in the saying, مَرَّ طِنْخٌ مِنَ اللَّيْلِ [*A part,* or *portion, of the night passed*]: (Ḳ:) but IDrd doubted its correctness. (TA.)

طَنِخٌ A man *whose heart* [or *stomach*] *is overpowered by grease* [or *greasy food*], *and who suffers indigestion in consequence thereof;* as also ♦ طَانِخٌ. (L.) [See also 1, of which each is a part. n.]

طَنِخَةٌ, expl. in the Ḳ [and in the JK, app. from the 'Eyn,] as syn. with أَحْمَقُ, is a mistranscription, correctly طيخة [i. e. طَيِخَةٌ]. (TA.)

طَانِخٌ: see طَنِخٌ.

طنز

1. طَنَزَ بِهِ, (Ṣ,* A, MA, Ḳ,) aor. ـُ, (Ṣ, A, TA,) inf. n. طَنْزٌ, (Ṣ,* MA, Ḳ,*) *He mocked at, scoffed at, laughed at, derided,* or *ridiculed, him.* (Ṣ, A, MA, Ḳ.) [See also طَنْزٌ below.]

3. طَانَزَهُ, (A, TA,) inf. n. مُطَانَزَةٌ, (TA,) [*He mocked at, scoffed at, laughed at, derided,* or *ridiculed, him, being mocked at,* &c., *by him.*]

6. تطانزوا [*They mocked at, scoffed at, laughed at, derided,* or *ridiculed, one another*]. (A, TA.)

طَنْزٌ *Mockery, scoff, derision,* or *ridicule:* (Ṣ, Ḳ:) [J says,] I think it to be post-classical or arabicized. (Ṣ.) [Golius says, it is termed in Armenian "dnâs."] — Also *A species of fish.* (Ḳ.)

طَنَّازٌ *A mocker, scoffer,* or *derider.* (Ṣ, Ḳ.)

هُمْ مَطْنَزَةٌ *They are* [*such as occasion mockery, scoff, derision,* or *ridicule;* or] *persons in whom is no good; held in light,* or *mean, estimation* [*by others* or] *by themselves.* (Ḳ.)

طنف

1. طَنِفَ, aor. ـَ, (Ḳ,) inf. n. طَنَفٌ, (TḲ,) the verb of الطَّنِفُ signifying التُّهَمَةُ, (Ḳ,) [app., as such, meaning *He was suspicious,* agreeably with the rendering of Golius; or *he suspected;* as is indicated by its being said of طَنِف meaning مُتَّهَم, in the TA, that it is app. a possessive epithet; for if it were a part. n., طَنِف would signify *he was suspected;* as it is said to do in the TḲ and by Freytag; in my opinion, erroneously, on the supposition that طَنِف meaning مُتَّهَم is its part. n.] — And طَنُفَ, aor. ـُ, inf. n. طَنَافَةٌ and طُنُوفَةٌ and طَنَفٌ, *He was,* or *became, intrinsically corrupt.* (Ḳ.)

2. طَنَّفَهُ, inf. n. تَطْنِيفٌ, *He suspected him.* (O, Ḳ.) One says فُلَانٌ يُطَنَّفُ بِهٰذِهِ السَّرِقَةِ *Such a one is suspected of this theft.* (TA.) — طَنَّفَ نَفْسَهُ إِلَى كَذَا *He made his mind to approach a coveting of such a thing.* (IDrd, O, Ḳ.) — And طَنَّفَ لِلْأَمْرِ, inf. n. as above, *He was,* or *became, near to the affair.* (TA.) [See an ex. voce رَايَفَ.] — طنّف جِدَارَهُ *He put above his wall thorns* or *branches of trees,* (O,) or *thorns and sticks and branches,* (Ḳ,) *in order to make the climbing,* or *scaling, of it difficult:* (O:) so says Az. (TA.) [And it probably signifies *He made a* طُنُف, or طُنْف, *of any kind to his wall.*]

4. اطنف *He ascended upon the* طُنُف [or طُنْف i. e. *ledge,* or *projecting part, of a mountain*]. (O.) — مَا أَطْنَفَهُ *How abstinent is he!* (O, Ḳ.)

5. مَا تَطَنَّفَتْ نَفْسِى إِلَى هٰذَا i. q. مَا أَشْفَتْ [app. meaning *My mind did not come to the point,* or *verge, of this*]. (O, Ḳ.) — And هُوَ يَتَطَنَّفُ النَّاسَ *He comes upon people overwhelmingly;* syn. يَغْشَاهُمْ. (Ibn-'Abbád, O, Ḳ.*)

طَنْفٌ: } see what next follows.
طِنْفٌ: }

طُنُفٌ and ♦ طُنْفٌ (Ṣ, O, Ḳ) and ♦ طَنْفٌ and ♦ طِنْفٌ (Ḳ) *A* حَيْد [or *ledge*] *of a mountain;* (Ṣ, O, Ḳ;) *a projecting portion thereof;* (Ḳ;) *a portion projecting therefrom, resembling a wing:* (TA:) [all these are meanings assigned to the حَيْد of a mountain:] and *a head, of the heads of a mountain:* (Ṣ, O, Ḳ:) pl. [of pauc.] أَطْنَافٌ and [of mult.] طُنُوفٌ. (O, Ḳ.) — Also, (Ḳ,) or the first and second, (Ṣ, O,) The إِفْرِيز [i. e., app., the *projecting coping,* or *ledge,* or *cornice,* (see زَنْف, and طَاق,)] *of a wall:* (Ṣ, O, Ḳ:) and *a projecting appertenance of a building:* (Ḳ:) and *a roof,* or *covering, made to project towards the road, over the door of a house;* (Ṣ, O, Ḳ;) i. q. كُنَّةٌ. (IAạr, TA.) — And طُنُفٌ is also applied to *A low wall built on the house-top* by the people of Mekkeh. (Z, TA.) ═ And طُنُفٌ signifies also *Thongs*, or *straps*; syn. سُيُورٌ; (A'Obeyd, Ṣ, O, Ḳ;) and so ▼ طُنْفٌ: (Ṣ, O:) or the *red skins that are* [*put as coverings*] *upon* [*receptacles of the kind called*] أَسْفَاط [pl. of سَفَطٌ, q. v.]: (Ḳ:) or ▼ طُنُفٌ has this meaning as well as that next preceding. (O.) El-Afwah El-Owdee likens a woman's fingers to ▼ طُنُفٌ, (O,) or طَنَفٌ, (TA,) used in the sense last mentioned above (O, TA) [or, more probably, I think, in the sense here next following]. — Also (i. e. طَنَفٌ [and probably ▼ طُنُفٌ likewise]) *A kind of red tree* (شَجَرٌ [or perhaps *fruit*, ثَمَرٌ,]) *resembling the* عَنَم [q. v.]. (TA.) ═ And *Suspicion*. (O, Ḳ.) [See also 1.]

طَنِفٌ *Suspected* (O, Ḳ, TA) of a thing (بِأَمْرٍ); app. a possessive epithet; and ▼ مُطَنَّفٌ signifies the same. (TA.) — And *Intrinsically corrupt*. (Ḳ.) — And One *who eats little*: (O, Ḳ:) thus expl. by Esh-Sheybánee. (O.)

طُنْفٌ: see طَنَفٌ, in five places.

طِنَافٌ: see طِيَافٌ, in art. طيف.

مُطْنِفٌ, (Ṣ, O, Ḳ,) applied by Esh-Shenfarà as an epithet to bees (نَحْل) that have missed the cavity in a mountain [in which they are accustomed to hive], (Ṣ, O,) *That ascend upon a* طَنَف [*of a mountain*]: (Ṣ, Ḳ:* [in the latter, مَنْ is erroneously put for اَلَّذِى: and so in the explanation here following:]) or it signifies, (O,) or signifies also, (Ḳ,) *having a* طَنَف (O, and so in some copies of the Ḳ) or طَنَف. (So in other copies of the Ḳ.)

مُطَنَّفٌ: see طَنِفٌ. ═ Also, [if not a mistake for مُطَلَّفٌ,] *i. q.* مُهْدَرٌ [*Made to go for nothing, unretaliated*, or *uncompensated by a mulct*; or *to be of no account*]. (TA.)

طنفس

طِنْفِسَةٌ and طَنْفَسَةٌ, (M, Mṣb, Ḳ,) the former of which is the more approved, (Mṣb,) and طُنْفُسَةٌ (Kr, M, Ḳ) and طِنْفَسَةٌ, [which is a form often occurring,] (M, Ḳ,) and طَنْفِسَةٌ, (Ḳ,) [variously written in different copies of the Ṣ, and in that lexicon, and in the Mṣb, mentioned in art. طفس, indicating that the ن is augmentative in the opinion of the authors of those two works,] *A carpet*: and *a piece of cloth* (ثَوْبٌ): and *a mat of palm-leaves, a cubit in width*: (Ḳ:) or *a kind of carpet called in Persian* طَنْبَسَة (Ḥar p. 376) [*and* تَنْبَسَه]: or *a carpet having a fine nap*, or *pile*: or, as some say, *what is put beneath the* رَحْل [*or camel's saddle*], *upon the shoulders of the camel*: (Mṣb:) or the نُمْرُقَة [q. v.] *above the* رَحْل: (M:) pl. طَنَافِسُ. (Ṣ, Mṣb, Ḳ.)

طنى

1. طَنِيَ, aor. ـَ, (Ṣ, Ḳ,) inf. n. طَنًى, (Ṣ,) said of a camel, *He had his spleen adhering to his side in consequence of vehement thirst*: (Ṣ:) or, said of a man, *he had his spleen and his lungs adhering to the ribs on the left side*, (Ḳ, TA,) *so that, sometimes, they become putrid and black*; but mostly this is the case in camels; (TA;) as also ▼ اطنى: (Ḳ:) or *he* (a man) *had a tertian fever, and his spleen in consequence became enlarged*: (Lḥ,* TA:) and, said of a camel, *his spleen became enlarged in consequence of the* [*disease of the lungs called*] نُحَاز. (Lḥ, TA.) [And طَنِئَ is a dial. var. thereof.] — And, said of a man, *i. q.* ضَنِيَ [i. e. *He was*, or *became, slender, and small in body*: or *diseased, disordered*, or *sick*: or *lean*, or *emaciated*: &c.]. (TA.)

2. طنّاهُ, inf. n. تَطْنِيَةٌ, *He treated him to cure him of the disorder of the spleen mentioned above*; (Ṣ, Ḳ;) namely, a camel, (Ṣ,) or a man: (Ḳ:) and *he cauterized him* (i. e. his camel) *in his side*; (Ḳ, TA;) or, as in the Nawádir of Lḥ, طنّى بَعِيرَهُ فِى جَنْبَيْهِ *he cauterized his camel* [*in his sides*] *by reason of the disorder above mentioned*: and the cure [or curing] of that disorder is [also] the *taking a wooden peg, and laying him* [i. e. the camel] *upon his side on the ground, and making, between his ribs, incisions* [*therewith*], *not penetrating through*. (TA.)

4. اطنى: see 1. — Also *He inclined to suspicion*, or *evil opinion*: (Ḳ, TA:) and sometimes pronounced أَطْنَأَ. (TA.) ═ اطناهُ *He* (a man) *hit him* (i. e. another man) *in that which was not a vital part*. (Ḳ, TA. In some copies of the Ḳ, فِى المَقْتَلِ is [erroneously] put for فِى غَيْرِ المَقْتَلِ.) And, said of a disease, *It left him* (i. e. a sick man) *with somewhat of life remaining in him*. (IAạr, TA.) One says هٰذِهِ حَيَّةٌ لَا تُطْنِى *This is a serpent that will not suffer him who is bitten by it to survive*; (ISk,* Ṣ,* Ḳ;) *that kills instantly*: (ISk, Ṣ:) or *that will not miss*: (AHeyth, TA:) originally لَا تُطْنِئُ. (ISk, Ṣ.) And ضَرَبَهُ ضَرْبَةً لَا تُطْنِى *He struck him a blow that would not be slow in killing him*. (TA.) And لَدَغَتْهُ حَيَّةٌ فَأَطْنَتْهُ [*A serpent bit him and suffered him to survive*]. (TA.) And the subst. [used in the sense of the inf. n.] from this verb as expl. in all these phrases is ▼ طَنًى. (TA.)

طِنْىٌ *A bier*: [like طِنْءٌ:] one says, رُمِىَ فُلَانٌ فِى طِنْيِهِ [and فِى طِنْئِهِ] and فِى نَبْطِهِ, *Such a one was cast into his bier*; meaning, when he died. (TA.) ═ See also the next paragraph.

طَنًى The *adhering of the spleen to the side in consequence of vehement thirst*. (Ṣ.) [See also طَنِيَ, of which it is the inf. n.] — And *Disease* [in a general sense]. (Ḳ, TA.) [Accord. to the CḲ, in this sense, and in other senses mentioned in this paragraph, طَنْىٌ, which is wrong.] — And *Ashes in a state of extinction*: (Ḳ, TA:) and so طِنْءٌ. (O and Ḳ in art. طنأ.) ═ And *Doubt*, or *suspicion*, or *evil opinion*; or *a thing that occasions doubt* &c.; (Ḳ,* TA;) as also ▼ طِنْىٌ: and so طِنْءٌ, with ء. (TA.) — And *Opinion*, of any kind. (TA.) ═ See also 4, last sentence. ═ And see the next paragraph.

طَنٍ A camel *having his spleen adhering to his side in consequence of vehement thirst*: (Ṣ:) or a man *having a tertian fever, and his spleen in consequence having become enlarged*: (Lḥ,* TA:) or a man *having his spleen and his lungs adhering to the ribs on the left side*, (Ḳ, TA,) *so that, sometimes, they become putrid and black*; but mostly this is the case in camels; (TA;) and so ▼ طَنِىٌّ. (Ḳ, TA.)

طه

R. Q. 1. طَهْطَهَ *He laughed immoderately*: (L voce كَدْكَدَ:) or you say طَهْطَهَ فِى ضَحِكِهِ, meaning *he laughed slightly*; like طَخْطَخَ. (O and TA in art. طخ.)

طٰهٰ [at the commencement of the 20th chapter of the Ḳur-án] means اِطْمَئِنّ [*Be thou still*, &c.]: (Ḳ, TA:) and thus it is expl. as occurring in a trad. respecting Moses' hearing the speech of the Lord of Might: (TA:) or, as some say, it is for طَأْ [imperative of وَطِئَ], meaning *tread upon the ground with the soles of both thy feet*; because the Prophet raised one of his feet in prayer: (TA in art. وطأ:) or it means *O man*, in the Abyssinian language; (Lth, Ḳ, TA;) or so in Syriac, accord. to Ḳatádeh; or so in Nabathæan, accord. to other authorities: (TA:) read طٰهٰ, with the two fet-ḥahs pronounced fully, it is two letters of the alphabet (مِنَ الهِجَآءِ [strangely misunderstood by Freytag as meaning "quibus maledicitur"]): (Lth, Ḳ, TA:) Ibn-Mes'ood is related to have read طِهِ, with the two kesrehs pronounced fully: and Fr says that some divided it, reading طِ هِ: (TA:) Abu-n-Nejm has called it طَهَا. (TA in art. طهو, q. v.)

طَهْطَهَةٌ sing. of طَهَاطِهُ, (TA,) which signifies The *voices* [or *neighings*] of horses. (Ḳ, TA.)

طُهْطُهَاهُ, as an epithet applied to a horse, *That excites admiration by his beauty*, or *swift and excellent*; *youthful*; *excelling in beauty*. (Lth, L, Ḳ, TA.)

طهر

1. طَهَرَ and طَهُرَ, (Ṣ, A, Mṣb, Ḳ,) aor. of each ـُ, (Mṣb, Ḳ,) inf. n. طَهَارَةٌ, (Ṣ, Mṣb, Ḳ,) which is of each verb, (Ṣ, Mṣb,) and طُهْرٌ, (Sb, Ḳ,) or the latter is a simple subst., (Ṣ, Mṣb,) *It was*, or *became, clean, free from dirt* or *filth*, or *pure*. (A,* Mṣb, Ḳ.*) طهارة is of two kinds; [properly] corporeal and [tropically] spiritual. (TA.) — And طَهَرَتْ, (M, Mgh, Ḳ,) or طَهَرَتْ مِنَ الحَيْضِ, aor. ـُ; (Mṣb;) and طَهُرَتْ, (M, Mṣb, Ḳ,) which is allowable, (IAạr,) but of rare occurrence, (Mṣb,) and طَهِرَتْ, [which is of more rare occurrence;] (M, El-Isnawee;) inf. n. طُهْرٌ and طَهَارَةٌ and طُهُورٌ and طَهُورٌ; (TA;) *She was*, or *became, pure from the menstrual discharge*; (Mgh;) *her discharge of blood stopped*. (Mgh, Ḳ.) See also 5. The saying, إِنَّ الشَّاةَ تَقْذِى عَشْرًا ثُمَّ تَطْهُرُ

[*Verily the ewe, or she-goat, emits a white fluid from her womb during ten* nights, *and then becomes pure,*] is mentioned on the authority of Lḥ: but ISd says, whether he mentioned this as heard from the Arabs, or did so presumptuously, I know not. (TA.) ═ طَهَرَهُ, aor. ـَ, (Ḳ,) inf. n. طَهْرٌ,) (TḲ,) signifies *He made it,* or *caused it, to be,* or *become, distant,* or *remote;* syn. أَبْعَدَهُ: (O, Ḳ:) and so طَحَرَهُ; (O, TA;) the ح being substituted for ه. (TA.)

2. طَهَّرَهُ, inf. n. تَطْهِيرٌ, [*He cleansed,* or *purified, him,* or *it:*] (Ṣ:) and طَهَّرَهُ بِالمَآءِ *he washed him,* or *it, with water:* (Ḳ:) and ↓ أَطْهَرَهُ signifies the same as طَهَّرَهُ. (Bḍ in lvi. 78.) — طَهِّرَا بَيْتِىَ, in the Ḳur [ii. 119], *Cleanse ye my house* [the Kaạbeh] *of the idols* (Aboo-Is-ḥáḳ, Bḍ, Jel) *and impurities; and what does not become it:* (Bḍ:) or *clear ye it:* (Bḍ:) or *cleanse ye my house from* [*pollution by*] *disobediences and forbidden actions:* (Az:) or, accord. to some, it means an incitement to purify the heart. (TA.) — وَثِيَابَكَ فَطَهِّرْ, in the Ḳur [lxxiv. 4], means *And cleanse thy clothes from dirt:* (Jel:) or *shorten thy clothes,* to prevent their being rendered dirty by trailing along the ground: (Jel, TA:) or † *purify thy heart:* or † *thy soul:* or † *make thy conduct right:* (TA:) and see other explanations voce ثَوْبٌ. — طَهَّرَ وَلَدَهُ † *He performed the rite of circumcision upon his son* [*and so purified him*]. (TA.) — طَهَّرَهُ ٱللّٰهُ ‡ [*God purified him from sin*]. (A.) — طَهَّرَهُ الحَدُّ † *The prescribed punishment, such as stoning &c., cleansed him from his sin.* (TA.) — لَمْ يُرِدِ ٱللّٰهُ أَنْ يُطَهِّرَ قُلُوبَهُمْ, in the Ḳur [v. 45], means † *God hath not pleased to cleanse their hearts from infidelity:* (Bḍ, Jel:) or *to direct.* (TA.)

4: see 2, first sentence.

5. تَطَهَّرَ, inf. n. تَطَهُّرٌ, is sometimes changed into اِطَّهَّرَ, inf. n. اِطَّهُّرٌ, the ت being incorporated into the ط, and this requiring a conjunctive ا, (Ṣgh, Ḳ,) in order that the word may not begin with a quiescent letter: (Ṣgh:) and طَهُورٌ is also an inf. n. [or rather a quasi-inf. n.] (Sb, Ḳ) of تَطَهَّرَ, (Mgh, TA,) like as وَضُوْءٌ is [said to be] of تَوَضَّأَ. (TA.) The meaning is, [*He became cleansed,* or *purified:* or *he cleansed,* or *purified, himself:* and] *he washed himself.* (Mgh.) You say, تَطَهَّرَ بِالمَآءِ [*He cleansed,* or *purified,* or *washed, himself with water*]: (Ṣ:) *he performed the ablution termed* الوُضُوْء: and *that termed* الاِسْتِنْجَآء; (A;) as also تطهّر alone, as used in the Ḳur ix. 109: (Mgh, TA:) and the same verb, alone, is expl. as signifying *he made use of water,* or *what supplied its place;* thus used in the Ḳur v. 9. (TA.) In the Ḳur vii. 80 and xxvii. 57, the verb is used derisively. (TA.) You say also, تَطَهَّرَتْ, (Mgh, Mṣb, Ḳ,) and اِطَّهَّرَتْ, (Mgh,) meaning, *She cleansed,* or *purified, herself by washing, from* [*the pollution of*] *the menstrual discharge,* (Mgh, Mṣb, Ḳ,) *&c.;* (Ḳ;) as also ↓ طَهَرَتْ and طَهُرَتْ; (Mṣb,* Ḳ;) agreeably with what is said in the B, that طَهَرَ and طَهُرَ and اِطَّهَّرَ and تطهّر have the same signification: (TA:) or تطهّرت and اطّهّرت have this signification; but the unaugmented verb has the signification first assigned to it, or "her discharge of blood stopped:" (Abu-l-'Abbás, IAạr:) in the Ḳur ii. 222, some read حَتَّى يَطْهُرْنَ; and others, حَتَّى يَطَّهَّرْنَ: but the latter reading is the preferable, on account of the difference between the two forms of the verb, just mentioned: (Abu-l-'Abbás:) or the law which allows not the touching a woman until she has performed the ablution mentioned above shows the two forms of the verb to be the same in signification. (TA.) — Also ‡ *He removed himself far from unclean things,* or *impurities.* (Ṣ, Mgh, Ḳ.*) — ‡ *He refrained from sin,* (Ḳ, TA,) *and from what was not good:* (TA:) *he removed himself far from low,* or *ignoble, habits:* and in this sense, accord. to some, it is used in the Ḳur vii. 80 and xxvii. 57. (TA.) And تطهّر مِنَ الإِثْمِ ‡ *He removed himself far from sin.* (A.)

طُهْرٌ [see 1: —] *Cleanness; freedom from dirt* or *filth;* or *pureness.* (Ṣ,* Mṣb.) — The *state of pureness from the menstrual discharge:* (S, A, Mgh, Mṣb:) pl. أَطْهَارٌ. (A, Mṣb.) And the pl. signifies The *days of a woman's state of pureness from the menstrual discharge.* (Ḳ.)

طَهِرٌ: see طَاهِرٌ, in three places.

طُهْرَةٌ a subst. from التَّطْهِيرُ [and signifying *A cleansing,* or *purification:* and in this sense it was applied by the Christians to baptism]: (Mgh:) or from طَهَّرَهُ بِالمَآءِ [and signifying *a cleansing,* or *purification, by water*]: (Ḳ:) or *cleanness,* or *pureness.* (TḲ.)

طَهُورٌ inf. n. of 1; as also طُهُورٌ: (TA:) and inf. n. [or rather quasi-inf. n.] of 5. (Sb, Mgh, TA.) — *A thing* [such as water] *with which one cleanses* or *purifies:* (T, Ṣ, Mgh, Mṣb, Ḳ:) a word similar to فَطُورٌ and سَحُورٌ and وَقُودٌ: (Ṣ:) and the author of the "Maṭáli' el-Anwár" mentions طُهُورٌ also in this sense; but this is strange and anomalous: (En-Nawawee:) the former occurs in the Ḳur xxv. 50: (Ṣ:) or it signifies *water with which the ablution termed* وُضُوْء *is performed:* (A, IAth:) or it has the signification next following. (Ḳ.) It is said, التَّوْبَةُ طَهُورٌ لِلْمُذْنِبِ ‡ [*Repentance is a means of purifying the sinner,* or *criminal*]. (A.) Lth says that it is that which is [accompanied] by the execution of the prescribed punishment, such as stoning &c. (TA.) [See also مَطْهَرَةٌ.] ═ It is also an epithet, (Mgh, TA,) and signifies *Clean and cleansing,* or *pure and purifying:* (Th, T, Mgh, Mṣb:) whatever God has created descending from the sky, or welling forth from the earth as a spring or river or sea, in which a human being does nothing but drawing water, and of which the colour is not changed by anything mixing with it, nor the taste thereby, is طَهُور: and what is otherwise, as the water of roses and of the leaves of trees, and what flows from the grape-vine, though it be طَاهِر, is not طَهُور: (Esh-Sháfi'ee:) the former removes impurities: the latter, if not at the same time طَهُور, does not: (TA:) or *very clean* or *pure:* (A, Mṣb:) the explanation by Th, if meant to show that the word signifies *of the utmost cleanness* or *pureness,* is correct and good: otherwise, it is not so; for فَعُولٌ is not formed from تَفْعِيلٌ: (Mgh, O:) it is also explained as signifying, simply, *cleansing,* or *purifying:* (B, TA:) also as *syn. with* طَاهِرٌ, as in the phrase رِيقُهُنَّ طَهُورٌ [*their saliva is pure*]: but here it is either an intensive epithet or used for طَاهِرٌ for the sake of the measure. (Mṣb.)

طَهِيرٌ: see طَاهِرٌ, in two places.

طَهَارَةٌ [see 1. —] The *act of performing the ablution termed* الغُسْل, and *that termed* الوُضُوْء, and *that termed* الاِسْتِنْجَآء. (Mṣb, TA.)

طُهَارَةٌ *What remains of that with which one has performed the ablution termed* طَهَارَة. (TA.)

طَهُورِيَّةٌ The *quality of being* طَهُور. (Mṣb.)

طَاهِرٌ *Clean; free from dirt* or *filth;* or *pure;* (Mṣb, Ḳ;) as also ↓ طَهِرٌ (IAạr, Ḳ) and ↓ طَهِيرٌ: (M, Ḳ:) fem. طَاهِرَةٌ: (Ṣ, A, Mṣb:) pl. (of طَاهِرٌ, TA) أَطْهَارٌ (Ḳ) and طَهَارَى, (Ṣ, Ḳ,) which latter is anomalous, as though its sing. were طَهْرَانُ, (Ṣ,) and, applied to men, طَاهِرُونَ: (TA:) and (of ↓ طَهِرٌ, TA) طَهِرُونَ; (Ḳ;) the only form; there being no broken pl.: (TA:) and of طَاهِرَةٌ, طَاهِرَاتٌ (TA) and طَوَاهِرُ. (A.) You say, رَجُلٌ طَاهِرٌ and ↓ طَهِيرٌ [*A clean, or pure, man*]. (O.) And اِمْرَأَةٌ طَاهِرَةٌ مِنَ النَّجَاسَةِ [*A woman pure from dirt* or *filth*]. (Ṣ.) And مَآءٌ طَاهِرٌ *Clean,* or *pure, water:* and also, *fit to cleanse* or *purify with.* (Mṣb.) And ثِيَابٌ طَهَارَى [*Clean clothes*]. (Ṣ.) [See also طَهُورٌ.] — *Pure from the menstrual discharge;* in this sense without ة: (IAạr:) as also طَاهِرٌ مِنَ الحَيْضِ. (Ṣ, Mṣb.) — هُوَ طَاهِرُ العِرْضِ † *He is clear from vice,* or *fault.* (Mṣb.) اِمْرَأَةٌ طَاهِرَةٌ مِنَ العُيُوبِ † [*A woman pure from vices,* or *the like*]. (Ṣ.) And رَجُلٌ طَاهِرُ الثِّيَابِ, (Ṣ, A, TA,) and طَاهِرُ الأَثْوَابِ, (TA,) ‡ *A man free,* or *far-removed, from low,* or *ignoble, habits:* (Ṣ,* A, TA:) and in like manner, طَاهِرُ الخُلُقِ, and ↓ طَهِرُ الخُلُقِ: fem. طَاهِرَةٌ. (TA.)

أَطْهَرُ [*More,* and *most, clean* or *pure*]. — [Hence,] هُنَّ أَطْهَرُ لَكُمْ [Ḳur xi. 80] † *They are more lawful to you.* (O, TA.)

مَطْهَرَةٌ and مِطْهَرَةٌ, (Ṣ, A, Ḳ, &c.,) the former of which is the more approved, (Ṣ,) *A vessel,* (A, Ḳ,) or *any vessel,* (Mgh, Mṣb,) [*for purification,*

i. e.,] *with which one washes himself,* (A, Mgh, Mṣb, Ḳ,) *and performs the ablution termed* وُضُوء, such as a سَطْل, or رَكْوَة: (TA:) and (A, Mgh, Mṣb, Ḳ) *i. q.* إِدَاوَة [*a kind of leathern vessel for water*]: (Ṣ, A, Mgh, Mṣb, Ḳ:) pl. مَطَاهِرُ. (Ṣ, Mṣb.) Hence, [or from مَطْهَرَة as signifying, agreeably with analogy, *A means of cleansing* or *purifying,*] the saying, (Mṣb,) السِّوَاكُ مَطْهَرَةٌ لِلْفَمِ [*The tooth-stick is a means of purifying to the mouth*]. (Ṣ, Mṣb.) — Also *A house,* or *chamber, in which one washes himself,* (Ḳ, TA,) *and performs the ablutions termed* وُضُوء *and* غُسْل *and* اِسْتِنْجَآء. (TA.)

صُحُفًا مُطَهَّرَةً, in the Ḳur [xcviii. 2], signifies *Writings cleansed from impurities and falsehood.* (TA.) — And أَزْوَاجٌ مُطَهَّرَةٌ, in the same [ii. 23], *Wives purified from the pollution of the menstrual discharge and the other natural evacuations.* (O, TA.) — And لَا يَمَسُّهُ إِلَّا المُطَهَّرُونَ, in the same [lvi. 78], is said by some to mean, † *None shall attain to the knowledge of its true meanings except those who have purified themselves from the filth of corrupt conduct, and ignorances, and acts of disobedience.* (TA.)

وَمُطَهِّرُكَ مِنَ الَّذِينَ كَفَرُوا, in the Ḳur [iii. 48], signifies *And will take thee forth from those who have disbelieved, and make thee to be far from doing as they do.* (TA.)

وَيُحِبُّ المُتَطَهِّرِينَ, in the Ḳur [ii. 222], signifies *And He loveth those who purify their spirits.* (TA.)

طهى and طهو

1. طَهَا, aor. يَطْهُو and يَطْهَى, inf. n. طَهْوٌ (Ṣ, Ḳ) and طُهُوٌّ (Ḳ) and طَهْىٌ, (Ṣ, [so in both of my copies,]) or طُهِىٌّ, (Ḳ,) and طَهَايَةٌ, thus app. accord. to the Ḳ, [and thus in my MS. copy and in the CḲ,] but in the M with kesr [i. e. طِهَايَةٌ], (TA,) *He cooked* flesh-meat *in the manner termed* طَبْخ [meaning *by boiling* or *stewing* or *the like*], (Ṣ, Ḳ,) or *by roasting* or *broiling* or *frying:* (Ḳ:) and [*he made,* or *kneaded and baked,* bread; for] الطَّهْوُ signifies also الخَبْزُ. (TA.) — [And hence, † *He performed,* or *executed,* an affair *firmly, soundly,* or *thoroughly;* and *matured* it: see the pass. part. n., below; and see also طَهْوٌ.] — And طَهَا, (Ṣ, Ḳ,) inf. n. طُهُوٌّ, (TA,) said of a man, (Ṣ,) *He went away into the country,* or *in the land:* (Ṣ, Ḳ:) like طَحَا: (Ṣ:) [or] you say, طَهَا فِى الأَرْضِ, inf. n. طُهُوٌّ; and طَهَى فِى الأَرْضِ, inf. n. طَهْىٌ: both signify the same. (TA.) And in like manner, طَهَتِ الإِبِلُ, (Ṣ, TA,) aor. تَطْهَى, inf. n. طَهْوٌ and طُهُوٌّ, (TA,) *The camels went away into the country,* or *in the land,* (Ṣ, TA,) *having become scattered,* or *dispersed:* (TA:) or *went away at random into the country,* or *in the land.* (Ḥam p. 12.) — And طَهَا, inf. n. طَهْوٌ, *He leaped.* (IAạr, TA.) — And طَهِىَ, inf. n. طَهًى, *He committed a sin, crime, fault,* or *misdemeanour.* (TA. [See also طَهًى.])

4. اطهى *He was,* or *became, skilled in his work, art,* or *craft.* (Az, Ḳ.)

طَهَا is used by Abu-n-Nejm for طٰهٰ meaning the Chapter of the Ḳur-án [thus called, because commencing with these two letters, namely, the 20th,] in his saying,

• مَدَّ لَنَا فِى عُمْرِهِ رَبُّ طَهَا •

[*May the Lord of* طٰهٰ *lengthen for us his life*]. (TA.) [See art. طه.]

طَهْوٌ [The *cooking* of flesh-meat: see 1, first sentence. — And hence,] † *A deed,* or *a performance.* (Ṣ, Ḳ, TA.) Thus in a trad., (Ṣ, TA,) in which it is related that it was said to Aboo-Hureyreh, "Didst thou hear this from the Apostle of God?" and he replied وَمَا كَانَ طَهْوِى i. e. † *And what was my deed,* or *performance?* or, accord. to A'Obeyd, أَنَا مَا طَهْوِى [*I, what is my deed,* or *performance?*] (TA) or فَمَا طَهْوِى *What then is my deed,* or *performance,* (Ṣ,) if I have not made that relation to be soundly, or well, performed, (Ṣ,* TA,) like as the cook does the cooking of food? (TA.) See also طُهًى.

طَهْىٌ: see طَهًى. — Also *Thin clouds.* (TA.) [See also طَهَآءٌ.] — And it is said in the "Nawádir" that سَمِعْتُ طَهْيَمَةً, as also دَغْيَمَةً and طَغْيَمَةً, means *I heard their sound,* or *voice:* [or *their sounds,* or *voices:*] and one says, فلان فى طهى ونهى [app. فِى طَهْىٍ وَنَهْىٍ, as though meaning *Such a one is engaged in clamour and prohibition*]. (TA.)

طَهًى *Broken bits of straw.* (Ḳ, TA.)

طُهًى *Cooked flesh-meat.* (IAạr, Ḳ.) [It is said in one place in the TA that الطُّهَى, with ḍamm, (as though it were الطُّهْىُ, but I suppose الطَّهْىُ to be meant,) is the subst. from طَهَا اللَّحْمَ.] — Also *A sin, crime, fault, misdemeanour,* or *misdeed;* syn. ذَنْبٌ; (Ḳ, TA; [in some copies of the Ḳ, الذِّنْبُ is put (erroneously, as is said in the TA,) in the place of الذَّنْبُ; and in the CḲ, الذُّنْبُ;]) as also ↓ طَهْىٌ: and ↓ مَا طَهْوِى in the trad. of Aboo-Hureyreh [mentioned above] is expl. by some as meaning مَا ذَنْبِى [*What is my fault?*]. (TA.)

طَهَآءٌ, (Ṣ, Ḳ, TA,) with the lengthened ا, (Ṣ, TA,) is like طَخَآءٌ; (Ḳ, TA; [in some copies of the Ḳ, each of these is erroneously written with the shortened ا, without ء;]) i. e. it is a dial. var. of the latter word, signifying *High,* or *elevated, clouds:* (Ṣ, TA:) or *thin clouds:* (Ḥam p. 12: [see also طَهْىٌ:]) [and طَهَآءَةٌ is the n. un.:] one says, مَا فِى السَّمَآءِ طَهَآءَةٌ, meaning *There is not in the sky a portion of cloud.* (Ṣ.)

طُهَاوَةٌ *The thin skin that is upon milk* or *blood.* (ISd, Ḳ.)

مَا أَدْرِى أَىُّ الطُّهَيَآءِ هُوَ means *I know not what one of mankind,* or *of the people, he is:* (Ḳ, TA:) like أَىُّ الضُّحْيَآءِ: mentioned by Az. (TA.)

طُهْيَانٌ The *top of a mountain.* (Ḳ.) — And *A* بَرَّادَة [meaning a *stand,* or *shelf, upon which vessels of porous earth, containing water, are placed, in order that the water may become cool*]. (Ḳ, TA. [In the CḲ, erroneously, بُرادَة: as is said in the TA, and shown by what here follows, it is with teshdeed; and it is written in my MS. copy of the Ḳ بَرَّادَة.]) — In the saying of El-Aḥwal El-Kindee,

• فَلَيْتَ لَنَا مِنْ مَآءِ زَمْزَمَ شَرْبَةً •

• مُبَرَّدَةً بَاتَتْ عَلَى الطُّهْيَانِ •

[*And would that there were for us, of the water of Zemzem, a cooled draught that had passed the night upon the* طُهْيَان], it has been expl. as having the former of these meaning, and as having the second thereof, and as meaning a certain mountain in El-Yemen. (TA.)

طَاهٍ *A cook;* (Ṣ, Ḳ;) *a roaster, broiler,* or *fryer:* and *a maker,* or *kneader and baker, of bread:* (Ḳ:) and, (Ḳ, TA,) as some say, (TA,) *any dresser,* or *preparer, of food,* (Ḳ, TA,) &c., *who qualifies it well, rightly,* or *properly:* (TA:) pl. طُهَاةٌ and طُهِىٌّ: (Ḳ, TA: [in the CḲ the latter is written طُهًى, which is evidently wrong; whereas طُهِىٌّ is agreeable with analogy, being originally طُهُوْىٌ:]) the fem. is طَاهِيَةٌ, and its pl. is طَوَاهٍ. (TA.) — لَيْلٌ طَاهٍ *A dark night.* (TA.)

أَمْرٌ مَطْهُوٌّ ‡ *An affair performed,* or *executed, firmly, soundly,* or *thoroughly;* and *matured.* (TA.)

طوب

طُوبٌ *Baked bricks;* syn. آجُرٌّ: (Ṣ, O, Mṣb, Ḳ:) n. un. with ة: so says Az, and El-Fárábee says the like; and accord. to them it seems to be [genuine] Arabic: accord. to IDrd, it is of the dial. of Syria; but [Fei adds] I think it to be of the dial. of Room: (Mṣb:) or it is of the dial. of Egypt: (Ṣ, O:) [probably of Coptic origin. It is mentioned in the Ṣ and Ḳ in art. طيب.]

أَوْبَةٌ وَطَوْبَةٌ, [the latter word] meaning الطَّيِّبُ, [and both together *A return and perfume,*] is a phrase which one says to the person entering and to him coming [as though he who said this meant I experience a return that is to me like perfume]. (O.)

طُوبَى: see art. طيب.

[طَوَّابٌ *A baker of bricks:* from طُوبٌ: mentioned by Golius, in art. طيب, as occurring in the Hist. Sar.: and it is used in this sense in the present day.]

طوح

1. طَاحَ, (Ṣ, A, L, Ḳ,) aor. يَطُوحُ and يَطِيحُ, (Ṣ, L, Ḳ,) inf. n. of the former طَوْحٌ, and of the latter طَيْحٌ, (L,) *He,* or *it, perished,* or *came to nought;* (Ṣ, A, Ḳ;) as also ↓ تطوّح: (A:) or

was, or became, at the point of perishing: (Ḳ:) and *he, or it,* (i. e. anything, TA,) *went away; passed away;* (Ḳ, TA;) *came to nought.* (TA.) — And (as some say, TA) *He, or it, fell;* (Ṣ, A, Ḳ;) and so ▼ تطوّح, as in the phrase تطوّح فِى البِئْرِ [*It fell into the well*], said of a bucket. (TA.) — And *He lost his way,* syn. تَاهَ, (Ṣ, A, Ḳ,) in the land, (Ṣ, Ḳ,) or in the desert; as also ▼ تطوّح and ▼ تطيّح. (TA.) And, said of an arrow, *It missed its aim.* (Ḥar p. 126.) ═ And أَيْنَ طِيحَ بِكَ *Whither hast thou been taken,* or *carried, away?* (A.) And طَاحَ بِهِ فَرَسُهُ *His horse went away with him* [or *carried him away*] *like an arrow.* (A.) And مَا كَانَتْ إِلَّا مَزْحَةً طَاحَ بِهَا لِسَانِى [*It was nought but a jest,* or *joke, which my tongue hastily uttered,* or *which my tongue let fall*]. (A.) — See also the next paragraph.

2. طوّحهُ *He caused him,* or *it, to perish,* or *come to nought;* as also طوّح بِهِ, (A,) and طيّحهُ; (A, and Ḳ in art. طيح;) and ▼ اطاحهُ signifies the same, (IAạr, Ḳ,) said of a thing, (Ḳ,) or of property, (IAạr, and Ḳ in art. طيح,) as is also طوّحهُ, (IAạr,) and *he made it pass away.* (Ḳ.) And *He sent him to a land from which he should not return.* (Ḳ.) And طوّح بِثَوْبِهِ *He cast his garment* [app. meaning *himself* (see a verse of Esh-Shemmákh, or of Leylà, cited voce ثوب)] *into a place of destruction;* as also طيّح به. (L, and Ḳ in art. طيح.) And قَذَفَتْهُ القَوَاذِفُ i. q. ▼ طَوَّحَتْهُ الطَّوَائِحُ (Ṣ, Ḳ) i. e. *Accidents,* or *events, that cast into places of perdition* [*cast him thereinto*]: (MF,* TḲ:) one should not say المُطَوِّحَاتُ: it is an extr. phrase, (Ṣ, Ḳ,) like the phrase in the Ḳur [xv. 22], وَأَرْسَلْنَا الرِّيَاحَ لَوَاقِحَ accord. to one of the two interpretations thereof: (Ṣ:) and أَطَاحَتْهُ ▼ المَطَاوِحُ and قَذَفَتْهُ القَوَاذِفُ signify the same, i. e. الطَّوَائِحُ; (A;) or [rather] the former of these two phrases has a similar meaning [i. e. *the places of perdition caused him to fall thereinto;* unless مَطَاوِح have a signification which I do not find explained]. (TA.) And طوّح بِهِ *He incited him, induced him,* or *made him, to venture upon a desert in which perdition was to be feared.* (Ḳ,* TA.) — Also *He,* or *it, caused him to lose his way,* syn. تَوَّهَهُ, (Ṣ, Ḳ,) and so ▼ طاح بِهِ, (Ḥar p. 126,) and طيّحهُ, (Ḳ in art. طيح,) *and carried him away hither and thither,* (Ṣ,) or *so that he cast himself hither and thither,* (Ḳ, TA,) and so طوّح بِهِ. (TA.) And طوّح نَفْسَهُ *He made himself to be,* or *become, confounded,* or *perplexed, and unable to see his right course;* like تَوَّهَهَا and تَيَّهَهَا. (Ṣ in art. تيه.) — طوّح بِهِ also signifies *He threw it,* or *cast it, in the air.* (Ḳ, TA. [For الهَوَآءِ, Golius and Freytag have read الهَوَى. See 5.]) — And طوّحهُ *He beat him,* or *struck him, with a staff,* or *stick.* (Ḳ.) ═ طوّح فِى الجِبَالِ *He went round about much,* or *often, in the mountains;* i. q. طَوَّفَ and طَوَّدَ. (Ṣ in art. طود.)

3. طاوحهُ *He contended with him in casting,* or *shooting.* (L, Ḳ.) A poet says,

* فَأَمَّا وَاحِدٌ فَكَفَاكَ مِثْلِى *
* فَمَنْ لِيَدٍ تُطَاوِحُهَا الأَيَادِى *

Now as for one, what would proceed from me would suffice thee: but who will be responsible for a hand with which several hands contend in casting, or *shooting?* (L.)

4: see 2, in two places. — One says also, اطاح شَعْرَهُ *He,* or *it, caused his hair to fall off.* (Ḳ.) [And اطاح قَوَائِمَهُ is said of a horse, or of a man in relation to a horse, app. meaning *He made his legs to fall* in a particular manner: see مُسْعَرٌ.] — مَا أَطْوَحَهُ and مَا أَطْيَحَهُ i. q. مَا أَتْوَهَهُ and مَا أَتْيَهَهُ: see 4 in art. توه.

5. تطوّح: see 1, in four places. — Also [*He lost his way,* or *was made to lose his way, and*] *he cast himself hither and thither* (Ṣ, Ḳ) فِى البِلَادِ *in the countries.* (Ṣ.) — And *He,* or *it, went and came,* or *moved to and fro, in the air:* and *he moved to and fro* in sleep, upon the back of a camel. (L.)

6. تَطَاوُحٌ signifies The *casting,* or *throwing,* a thing [*to and fro,*] *one with another;* or *one to,* or *at, another.* (KL.) — [Hence,] تَطَاوَحَتْ بِهِمُ النَّوَى i. q. تَرَامَتْ [i. e. † *Distance cast them away, one from another*]. (Ṣ, A, Ḳ.) — And تَطَاوَحُوهُ بِالضَّرْبِ, and بِالأَمْرِ, *They contended with him* [*in beating,* and *in the affair*]. (A.)

نِيَّةٌ طَوْحٌ i. q. بَعِيدَةٌ [app. meaning *A distant,* or *remote, thing,* or *place, that is the object of an action* or *a journey*]; (Ḳ, and O in art. ضرح;) like طَرْحٌ and طَمْحٌ and ضَرْحٌ. (O.)

طَوَائِحُ i. q. قَوَاذِفُ, (Ṣ, A, Ḳ,) i. e. *Accidents,* or *events, that cast into places of perdition:* (MF,* TḲ:) said in the 'Ináyeh to be an anomalous pl. of ▼ مُطِيحَةٌ, from أَطَاحَ meaning "he, or it, caused to pass away," and "to perish, or come to nought." (MF.) See 2.

[طَوَّاحٌ is expl. by Freytag as signifying *Evil-affecting:* but he names no authority.]

طُوَّاحَةٌ *A child's swing, of rope.* (TA voce رُجَّاحَةٌ.)

طَائِحٌ [part. n. of 1] *Perishing* [&c.]. (L.) — See also art. طيح.

[طايحة, correctly طَائِحَةٌ, is expl. by Freytag, on the authority of the Deewán of the Hudhalees, as meaning *An army.*]

مُطِيحَةٌ: see طَوَائِحُ.

مِطْوَاحٌ *A staff,* or *stick,* (Ḳ, TA,) [as being] *an instrument of destruction.* (TA.)

مَطَاوِحُ i. q. مَقَاذِفُ, (Ṣ, Ḳ,) which means *Places of perdition;* (TA in art. قذف;) like مَطَاوِدُ [pl. of مَطَادَةٌ]. (Ṣ and TA in art. طود.)

[مُتَطَاوِحٌ, app. a mistranscription for مُتَطَاوَحٌ, which lit. means *A place of casting,* or *throwing, to and fro,* is expl. by Freytag, on the authority of the Deewán of Jereer, as meaning *the intermediate part between the top and bottom of a well.*]

طوخ

1. طَاخَهُ, (Ḳ,) aor. يَطُوخُهُ, (TA,) inf. n. طَوْخٌ; (Ḳ;) as also طَاخَهُ, aor. يَطِيخُهُ, inf. n. طَيْخٌ; which is the more common; (TA;) *He charged, reproached,* or *upbraided, him with something bad, evil, abominable,* or *foul,* either said or done. (Ḳ.) [See also art. طيخ.]

طود

1. طَادَ, (aor. يَطُودُ, inf. n. طَوْدٌ, TḲ,) *It* (a thing, TḲ) *was,* or *became, firm,* or *steadfast.* (Fr, L, Ḳ.)

2. طوّد, (Ṣ, L, Ḳ,) inf. n. تَطْوِيدٌ and تَطْوَادٌ; and ▼ تطوّد; (Ḳ;) *He went round about much,* or *often,* syn. طَوَّفَ (Ṣ, L, Ḳ) and طَوَّحَ, (Ṣ,) فِى الجِبَالِ *in the mountains:* (Ṣ:) or the former, he went *round about much,* or *often, in the countries to seek the means of subsistence.* (IAạr, L.) And one says also, طوّد بِنَفْسِهِ [*He went round about &c. by himself*], and بِفُلَانٍ [*with such a one*]. (L.) ═ طوّدهُ, inf. n. تَطْوِيدٌ, *He* (God) *made it high,* or *tall.* (A.)

[4. اطاد *He made,* or *rendered, firm,* or *steadfast:* so accord. to Freytag; but he names no authority.]

5: see 2.

7. انطاد *It rose,* or *ascended, in the air.* (Ḳ.)

طَادٌ *Heavy:* (Ḳ:) and ▼ طَادِىٌّ *firm,* or *steadfast:* (L:) or both signify *heavy and firm* or *steadfast.* (TA.) — Also the former, *A stallion excited by lust.* (Ḳ.)

طَوْدٌ *A mountain:* (Ḳ:) or *a great mountain* (Ṣ, A, L, Ḳ) *rising high into the sky:* (A:) or i. q. هَضْبَةٌ [either as denoting a hill or mountain or a tract of sand: see the next sentence]: (IAạr:) pl. أَطْوَادٌ (A, L, Ḳ) and طِوَدَةٌ. (Ḳ.) — And *An elevated,* or *overlooking, tract of sand;* (Ḳ, TA;) as also هَضْبَةٌ. (TA.) — And the pl. أَطْوَاد is applied by a poet to signify ‡ *Camels' humps;* as being likened to mountains because of their height. (IAạr, L.) — اِبْنُ الطَّوْدِ means † *The mass of rock* (الجُلْمُودُ) *that falls from the upper part of a mountain:* (A, L,* Ḳ:*) or *the echo.* (A.) One says, أَسْرَعُ مِنِ ابْنِ الطَّوْدِ † *Quicker,* or *swifter, than the mass of rock that falls* &c.: or *than the echo.* (A.)

طَادِىٌّ: see طَادٌ.

مَطَادَةٌ *A desert, or waterless desert, far-extending:* (Ḳ:) pl. مَطَاوِدُ. (TA.) And the latter (i. e. the pl.), *Places of perdition;* (Ḳ, TA;) it is like مَطَاوِحُ. (Ṣ, TA.)

مُطَوَّدٌ *Remote,* or *distant.* (Ḳ.)

بِنَآءٌ مُنْطَادٌ *A lofty building,* (Ḳ, TA,) *rising high in the air.* (TA.)

طور

1. طَارَ حَوْلَهُ, aor. يَطُورُ, (TA,) inf. n. طَوْرٌ and طَوَرَانٌ, (Ḳ,) *He went,* or *hovered,* (حَامَ,) *round about it.* (Ḳ,* TA.) — Hence, لَا يَطُورُنِى *He will not approach my immediate vicinage.* (TA.) And لَا تَطُرْ حَرَانَا *Approach thou not our environs.* (Ṣ, O, TA.) And لَا أَطُورُ بِهِ *I will not approach him, or it:* (Ṣ, O, TA:) occurring in a trad. (TA.) And فُلَانٌ يَطُورُ بِفُلَانٍ *Such a one as it were hovers round about such a one, and draws near to him.* (TA.)

مَا أَبْعَدَ طَارَكَ for مَا ابعد دَارَكَ: see the remarks on letter ط.

طَوْرٌ *A time; one time; like the French "fois;"* syn. تَارَةٌ: (Ṣ, A, O, Mṣb, Ḳ:) pl. أَطْوَارٌ. (Ṣ, Ḳ, A.) You say, أَتَيْتُهُ طَوْرًا بَعْدَ طَوْرٍ *I came to him time after time.* (A.) فَعَلَ ذٰلِكَ طَوْرًا بَعْدَ طَوْرٍ *He did that time after time.* (Mṣb.) And جِئْتُهُ أَطْوَارًا *I came to him several times.* (A.) — And *State; condition; quality, mode,* or *manner; form,* or *appearance:* pl. أَطْوَارٌ. (Mṣb.) You say, النَّاسُ أَطْوَارٌ *Mankind are of divers sorts and conditions.* (Ṣ, A.*) It is said in the Ḳur [lxxi. 13], وَقَدْ خَلَقَكُمْ أَطْوَارًا *And He hath created you of divers sorts and conditions:* (TA:) or *of different forms, every one of his proper form:* (Th, TA:) or *of various aspects and dispositions:* (TA:) or *one time, a clot of blood; and one time, a lump of flesh:* (Akh, Ṣ:) or [*one time,*] *seed; then, a clot of blood; then, a lump of flesh; then, bone.* (Fr, TA.) — And *Quantity; measure; extent:* (Ḳ:) *limit:* (Ṣ, A:) *a limit between two things.* (O, Ḳ.) You say, عَدَا فُلَانٌ طَوْرَهُ *Such a one exceeded his proper measure,* or *extent:* (TA:) or *his proper limit:* (Ṣ, A, O, TA:) and تَعَدَّى طَوْرَهُ *he transgressed the limits of his proper state, or condition.* (Mṣb, TA.) — *A thing that is commensurate,* (L, Ḳ, TA,) or *equal in length* [*and breadth* (see عَدَآءٌ)], (TA,) or *correspondent, to a thing;* (L, Ḳ, TA;) as also ↓ طِوَارٌ and ↓ طُورٌ. (Ḳ.) You say of anything that is the equal of another thing, هُوَ طُورُهُ, and ↓ طِوَارُهُ *It is the equal of it.* (Aboo-Bekr, TA.) You say also, رَأَيْتُ حَبْلًا بِطِوَارِ هٰذَا الحَائِطِ *I saw a rope of the length of this wall.* (TA.) And هٰذِهِ الدَّارُ بِطِوَارِ ↓ هٰذِهِ الدَّارِ *This house has its wall contiguous to the wall of this* [*other*] *house, in one rank,* or *series.* (TA.) And ↓ طَوَارُ دَارٍ, (Ṣ, O, Ḳ,) and ↓ طِوَارُ دار, (Ḳ,) and طُورُهَا, and ↓ طُورَتُهَا, (O,) *The part of the* فِنَآء [*or exterior court,* or *yard*], *of a house, that is coextensive with the house;* (Ṣ, A, O, Ḳ;*) i. q. جَوَارُهُ. (Ḳ in art. جور.) [See also the next paragraph.]

طُورٌ: see طَوْرٌ, latter part, in two places. — *The yard* (فِنَآء) *of a house;* (Ḳ;) as also ↓ طُورَةٌ. (TA.) [See also طَوَار, voce طَوْرٌ, last signification.] — *A mountain:* (Ṣ, O, Ḳ:) or *any mountain that produces trees,* otherwise a mountain is not so called. (R, TA.) [Hence الطُّورُ is applied to Mount Sinai, which is also called طُورُ سِينَآءَ, and طُورُ سِينِينَ; and to the Mount of Olives, and to several other mountains; as is said in the Ḳ &c.]

طُورَةٌ: see طَوْرٌ, last signification: and also طُورٌ.

طُورَةٌ i. q. طِيرَةٌ [q. v.]; (Ḳ;) a dial. var. of the latter word. (O.)

طُورِىٌّ *Wild; that estranges himself,* or *itself, from mankind;* (Ṣ, A, O, Ḳ;) applied to a bird, (Ṣ, O,) and to a man; (Ṣ, A, O;) as also ↓ طُورَانِىٌّ. (O.) You say, حَمَامٌ طُورِىٌّ, and ↓ طُورَانِىٌّ, *Wild pigeons:* (Ṣ, TA:) so called in relation to الطُّورُ, a certain mountain; or the mountain is called طُرَانُ, and [if so] it is an irreg. rel. n.: or *that have come from a distant country.* (TA.) [See also عُزْفٌ.] And أَعَارِيبُ طُورِيُّونَ *Wild Arabs of the desert,* that avoid the towns and villages, from fear of epidemic disease, and of perdition: as though they were thus called in relation to the mountain named الطُّور, in Syria. (TA.) And رَجُلٌ طُورِىٌّ *A stranger.* (O, TA.) — مَا بِهَا طُورِىٌّ, (Ṣ, A, O, Ḳ,) and ↓ طُورَانِىٌّ, (Lth, O, Ḳ,) *There is not in it* (i. e. بِالدَّارِ *in the house,* A, TA) *any one:* (Lth, Ṣ, A, O, Ḳ:) as also دُورِىٌّ. (TA.)

طُورَانِىٌّ: see طُورِىٌّ, in three places.

طَوَارٌ and طِوَارٌ: see طَوْرٌ, latter part, in six places.

بَلَغَ فُلَانٌ فِى العِلْمِ أَطْوَرَيْهِ *Such a one attained the two extremes of science,* or *learning;* (Ṣ, O;) *the beginning and the end thereof;* (Ṣ, O, Ḳ;) as also أَطْوَرِيهِ: (Ḳ:) or the latter, which is the form mentioned by AZ, (Ṣ, O,) and by IAạr, (Sh, TA,) signifies *the utmost point thereof;* accord. to AZ, as related by A'Obeyd: (Ṣ, O:) or *he attained, in science,* or *learning, his utmost, and his ambition;* accord. to IAạr: (Sh, TA:) or بَلَغَ أَطْوَرِيهِ *he attained the utmost of his endeavour.* (L.) — بَلَغْتُ مِنْ فُلَانٍ أَطْوَرَيْهِ *I did the utmost in the case of such a one.* (ISk, TA.) — رَكِبَ فُلَانٌ الدَّهْرَ وَأَطْوَرَيْهِ [*Such a one encountered fortune and*] *its two extremes.* (Aṣ, TA.) — لَقِىَ مِنْهُ الأَطْوَرِينَ, with kesr to the ر, *He experienced from him,* or *it, calamity.* (Aṣ, O, Ḳ.)

طوس

1. طَاسَ, aor. يَطُوسُ, (Ṣ, TA,) inf. n. طَوْسٌ, (Ṣ, A, Ḳ, TA,) *He was,* or *became, beautiful,* (Ṣ, A, Ḳ, TA,) *and bright,* or *fresh,* (Ḳ, TA,) *in face,* (Ṣ, A, Ḳ, TA,) *after illness:* (Ḳ, TA:) from الطُّوسُ signifying "the moon:" so in the T: ascribed by Ṣgh to AA. (TA.) [In one copy of the Ṣ, this verb is omitted.] — طاس الشَّىْءَ, (M, O,) aor. as above, (O,) inf. n. طَوْسٌ, (M, A, O, Ḳ,) *He trod,* or *trod upon, the thing;* (M, A,* O, Ḳ;*) [like دَاسَهُ;] *and broke it:* (M, O:) so says IDrd: (O:) and الوَطْسُ is like الطَّوْسُ. (TA.)

2. مَا أَدْرِى أَيْنَ طَوَّسَ بِهِ *I know not whither he has gone* (T, O, Ḳ) [*with him, or it*]. (Ḳ.)

5. تَطَوَّسَتْ *She* (a woman, A, Ḳ, or a girl, M) *adorned herself:* (M, A, Ṣgh, Ḳ:) [*as though she made herself like a* طَاوُوس, or *peacock.*] — تطوّس *He* (a pigeon) *shook,* or *ruffled, his feathers:* you say, الحَمَامُ يَكْسَحُ بِذَنَبِهِ حَوْلَ الحَمَامَةِ وَيَتَطَوَّسُ لَهَا *The male pigeon sweeps with his tail around the female pigeon, and shakes,* or *ruffles, his feathers to her.* (A, TA.)

طَاسٌ [*A drinking-cup;* also vulgarly called طَاسَة;] *a certain thing in which one drinks;* (Ṣ, Ḳ;) or *with which one drinks;* accord. to AḤn, *also called* قَاقُزَّة. (M.)

طُوسٌ *The moon:* (IAạr, T, Ṣ, Ḳ: but omitted in one copy of the Ṣ:) or *the moon a little after,* or *before, the change;* i. q. هِلَالٌ: pl. أَطْوَاسٌ. (M.)

طُوَاسٌ, (M, TA,) thus correctly, as written by El-Urmawee, with ḍamm; not with fet-ḥ, as in the Ḳ and as written by Ṣgh; (TA;) [in the O, طَوَاسٌ;] *One of the nights of the last part of the* [*lunar*] *month;* (M;) *one of the nights called* لَيَالِى المُحَاقِ. (O, Ḳ.)

طَاوُوسٌ, (Ṣ, M, A, &c.,) of the measure فَاعُولٌ, (M,) the hemzeh being a substitute for و, (Mṣb,) [*The peacock;*] *a certain bird,* (Ṣ, M, A, O, Ḳ,) *beautiful,* (M, TA,) *and well known:* (O, Mṣb, Ḳ:) dim. طُوَيْسٌ, formed after the rejection of the augmentative letters: (Ṣ, O, Mṣb, Ḳ:) pl. أَطْوَاسٌ (M, A, K) and (sometimes, M) طَوَاوِيسُ, (M, O, Ḳ,) by the rejection of what is augmentative: (M:) the former pl. is the more known. (TA.) — † *A goodly,* or *beautiful, man;* (El-Muärrij, O, Ḳ;) in the dial. of Syria. (El-Muärrij, O.) — † *Silver;* (A, O, Ḳ;) in the dial. of El-Yemen. (A, O.) — † *Verdant land, wherein,* (O, Ḳ,) or *whereon,* (T, O,) *is every kind of plant,* (O, Ḳ,) or *of flowers, in the days of spring.* (T, O.)

مُطَوَّسٌ *Goodly,* or *beautiful;* (M, A, Mṣb, Ḳ;) applied to a face, (A, TA,) or other thing. (Mṣb, Ḳ.)

طوع

1. طَاعَ لَهُ, (T, Ṣ, O, Mṣb, Ḳ,) and طَاعَهُ, (Mṣb,) first pers. طُعْتُ, (Zj, O, Mṣb,*) aor. يَطُوعُ, (T, Ṣ, O, Mṣb, Ḳ,) inf. n. طَوْعٌ; (T, Mṣb, TA;) and, first pers. طِعْتُ, (Zj, O, Mṣb,*) aor. يَطَاعُ, (T, O, Mṣb, Ḳ,) a good dial. var., (T, TA,) and طَاعَ, يَطِيعُ, (Mṣb, and Ḳ in art. طيع,) inf. n. طَيْعٌ; (TA in art. طيع;) three dial. vars., coordinate to

قَالَ and خَافَ and بَاعَ; (Mṣb;) *He was,* or *became, submissive to him;* (Ṣ, O, Mṣb, Ḳ;) as also ↓ انطاع له; (AO, Ṣ, O, Mṣb;) and ↓ اطاعه, inf. n. إِطَاعَةٌ, and subst. [i. e. quasi-inf. n.] ↓ طَاعَةٌ: (Mṣb:) or i. q. ↓ اطاع; (T, TA;) which is expl. by ISd as meaning *he was,* or *became, gentle, and submissive;* as also طَاعَ, aor. يَطَاعُ: (TA:) [or each of these two verbs may be rendered *he was,* or *became, obedient;* or *he obeyed;* when by this is meant compliance with another's will or wish, not with a command: but] one says, ↓ أَمَرَهُ فَأَطَاعَهُ [*He commanded him and he obeyed him*], with ا, not otherwise; (Ṣ;) or أَمَرَهُ فَأَطَاعَ [*he commanded him and he obeyed*]; for it is said that ↓ الطَّاعَةُ is never otherwise than a consequence of a command; and IF says that when one goes by command of another you say of him اطاعه: (Mṣb:) Er-Rághib says that ↓ الطَّاعَةُ is like الطَّوْعُ; but is mostly used as meaning *obedience* to a command [or the like; whence the saying, اَللَّهُمَّ لَا تُطِيعَنَّ بِى شَامِتًا, expl. in art. شمت]: (TA:) and ↓ طاوعه, also, signifies *he obeyed him;* like ↓ اطاعه: you say, طاوعه ↓ عَلَى أَمْرِ كَذَا *he obeyed him in respect of such an affair.* (MA. [But see 3 below.]) — [Hence,] لِسَانُهُ لَا يَطُوعُ بِكَذَا † *His tongue will not aid,* or *assist,* him *with such a thing.* (Ṣ, O.) See also 2. [And see 3.] — And sometimes (Ṣ) one says, طَاعَ لَهُ المَرْتَعُ, (Ṣ, O, Ḳ,) like ↓ اطاع له, (ISk, Ṣ, O,) or like اطاعه, (Ḳ,) meaning ‡ *The pasturage enabled him to pasture his cattle upon it* (Ṣ, O, Ḳ,* TA) *wheresoever he would,* (TA,) *and was ample to him;* (O, TA;) and *it was not inaccessible to him.* (TA.)

2. تَطْوِيعٌ [primarily] signifies The *making obedient;* or the *causing to obey.* (KL.) — فَطَوَّعَتْ لَهُ نَفْسُهُ قَتْلَ أَخِيهِ, (Ṣ, O, Mṣb,* Ḳ,*) in the Ḳur [v. 33], means ‡ *And his soul,* or *mind, facilitated to him* [*the slaying of his brother*]; (Akh, Ṣ, O, Mṣb, TA;) like طَوَّقَتْهُ; (Akh, Ṣ, O, TA;) and like ↓ طَاوَعَتْهُ, [which is one of the explanations in the O and Ḳ, and] which means the same; (Mṣb;) and accord. to this explanation it is tropical: Mbr says that it is an instance of فَعَّلَتْ from الطَّوْعُ; and ↓ طَاعَتْ and طَوَّعَتْ are said to signify alike: (TA:) or the meaning is, *aided him,* or *assisted him;* (Fr, O, Ḳ;) accord. to which explanation, and that of Mbr, فِى is said by Az to be suppressed; the meaning being, لِقَتْلِ أَخِيهِ, or فِى قَتْلِ أَخِيهِ; and he prefers the explanation of Akh: (TA:) or the meaning is, (O, Ḳ,) accord. to Mujáhid, (O,) *encouraged him,* and (O, Ḳ) A'Obeyd says that by this Mujáhid meant (TA) *aided him, and complied with his wish.* (O, Ḳ, TA,)

3. طاوعه, (IF, Mṣb, Ḳ, TA,) inf. n. مُطَاوَعَةٌ, (Ṣ, O, TA,) and quasi-inf. n. طَوَاعِيَةٌ, (TA,) i. q. وَافَقَهُ [as meaning *He complied with him*]. (IF, Ṣ,* O,* Mṣb, Ḳ,* TA.) You say, طاوعت المَرْأَةُ زَوْجَهَا, quasi-inf. n. طَوَاعِيَةٌ, *The woman complied with her husband.* (TA.) It is said that طاوعه differs from أَطَاعَهُ. (Mṣb, TA.) But see 1, latter half, in two places. — See also 2. — One says also, طاوع لَهُ المُرَادُ ‡ *The thing wished,* or *desired,* or *sought after,* [*was,* or *became, easy of attainment to him;* or] *came to him easily.* (TA.)

4. اطاع, inf. n. إِطَاعَةٌ, and quasi-inf. n. طَاعَةٌ: see 1, in four places. It also signifies *He consented;* or *complied with what was desired of him;* and so ↓ استطاع. (TA.) — [Hence,] اطاع لَهُ المَرْتَعُ: see 1, last sentence. One says also, اطاع النَّخْلُ, (Ṣ, O,) and الشَّجَرُ, (Ṣ, O, Ḳ,) ‡ *The palm-trees,* (Ṣ, O, TA,) and *the trees,* (Ṣ, O, Ḳ, TA,) *had ripe fruit, that might be gathered.* (Ṣ, O, Ḳ, TA.) And اطاع التَّمْرُ † *The dates attained,* or *were near, to the time,* or *season, for their being cut off.* (TA.)

5. تطوّع لِلشَّىْءِ and تطوّعه *He desired the thing;* or *sought it;* or *sought it by artful,* or *skilful, management:* or *he constrained himself to do it:* or *he took it,* or *imposed it, upon himself submissively.* (TA.) You say, تَطَوَّعْ لِهٰذَا الأَمْرِ حَتَّى تَسْتَطِيعَهُ, (Ṣ,) and ↓ تَطَاوَعْ, (Ṣ, Ḳ,*) *Constrain thyself to acquire ability to perform this affair until thou shalt be able to perform it.* (Ṣ.) And تطوّع بِالشَّىْءِ *He did the thing without its being incumbent,* or *obligatory, on him;* syn. تَبَرَّعَ بِهِ. (Ṣ, O,* Mṣb.) مَنْ تَطَوَّعَ خَيْرًا, in the Ḳur ii. 153 [and 180], means *Whoso does good that is not obligatory on him:* (Jel:) or *does good in obedience,* whether obligatory or supererogatory: or *does good beyond what is obligatory on him:* (Bḍ:) خَيْرًا being for بِخَيْرٍ: (Bḍ,* Jel:) or it is an epithet qualifying an inf. n. suppressed: or the verb is made trans. as implying the meaning of فَعَلَ or أَتَى: (Bḍ:) and the Koofees, except 'Áṣim, read يَطَّوَّعْ, for يَتَطَوَّعْ. (Az,* O, TA.*) [Hence,] صَلَاةُ التَّطَوُّعِ *The supererogatory prayer;* syn. النَّافِلَةُ. (O, Ḳ.) And Az says that تَطَوُّعٌ signifies *A thing that one does spontaneously, not made obligatory on him by an ordinance of God;* as though it were made a subst. (TA.)

6: see the next preceding paragraph.

7: see 1, first sentence.

10. استطاع, (Ṣ, O, Mṣb, Ḳ,) inf. n. اِسْتِطَاعَةٌ, (Ṣ, O, Mṣb,) originally اِسْتِطْوَاعٌ, (O, B, TA,) i. q. أَطَاقَ [meaning *He was able;* and *he was able to do,* or *accomplish,* a thing, and *to acquire* or *obtain* it, and *to have* it, &c.]; (Ḳ, TA; [in the CḲ, erroneously, أَطَاعَ, which, however, correctly explains one meaning of استطاع, as will be seen by what follows;]) the inf. n. being *syn. with* إِطَاقَةٌ, (Ṣ, O, TA,) or طَاقَةٌ, (Mṣb,) and قُدْرَةٌ: (Mṣb, TA:) but it is said peculiarly of a human being [or a rational creature], whereas اطاق is used in a general manner: (IB, TA:) and the application of the former requires a peculiar constitution of the agent, and the conception of the act, and the fitness of the object to be acted upon or effected, and the possession of an instrument when the action is instrumental as in the case of writing: (Er-Rághib, TA:) and one says also, (Ḳ,) or sometimes they said, (Ṣ, O, Mṣb,) اِسْطَاعَ, (Ṣ, O, Mṣb, Ḳ,) aor. يَسْطِيعُ, (Ṣ, O, Mṣb,) with fet-ḥ [to the first letter]; (Mṣb;) rejecting the ت, deeming it difficult of utterance with the ط, and disliking to incorporate it into the ط because the س would then become movent, which it never is: Ḥamzeh (i. e. Ez-Zeiyát, TA, not Khallád, O, Ḳ, TA) read, [in the Ḳur xviii. 96,] فَمَا اسْطَّاعُوا, with idghám, combining two quiescent letters: (Ṣ, O, Ḳ:) this reading is said by Zj, as on the authority of Kh and Yoo and Sb and others, to be incorrect; but Abu-l-'Abbás Aḥmad Ibn Moḥammad Ibn-'Abd-El-Ghanee Ed-Dimyáṭee, who died in the year [of the Flight] 1116, and Ibn-El-Jezeree, and El-Ḥáfidh Aboo-'Amr, contradict him, affirming it to be allowable: (TA:) and Akh says, (Ṣ, O,) and some of the Arabs say اِسْتَاعَ, aor. يَسْتِيعُ, (Ṣ, O, Ḳ,) rejecting the ط; (Ṣ, O;) which Zj holds to be not allowable in reading [the Ḳur-án]: (TA:) and some of the Arabs say أَسْطَاعَ, aor. يُسْطِيعُ, [in the CḲ, erroneously, يَسْطِيعُ,] with the disjunctive ا [in the former], meaning أَطَاعَ, aor. يُطِيعُ, (Akh, Ṣ, O, Ḳ,) making the س to be a substitute for the suppressed vowel of the medial radical letter of the verb [اطاع], (Akh, Ṣ, O,) for, as is said by Kh and Sb, أَطَاعَ is originally أَطْوَعَ; (TA;) or, as AZ says, the verb in this case, with ḍamm to the aor., is likened to أَفْعَلَ, aor. يُفْعِلُ, inf. n. إِفْعَالٌ: (Mṣb:) but Zj says that he who reads فَمَا اسْطَّاعُوا errs; for the س of اِسْتَفْعَلَ is never movent: and Sb mentions مَا أَسْتَيِعُ; holding it to be an instance of substitution. (TA.) — See also 4. Some say that هَلْ يَسْتَطِيعُ رَبُّكَ أَنْ يُنَزِّلَ عَلَيْنَا مَائِدَةً مِنَ السَّمَآءِ, in the Ḳur [v. 112], means هَلْ يُجِيبُ [i. e. *Will thy Lord consent,* or *comply with the desire, that He should send down to us a table with food upon it from Heaven?*]: (Er-Rághib, TA:) — and Ks read هَلْ تَسْتَطِيعُ رَبَّكَ, meaning *Wilt thou demand of thy Lord that He consent,* or *comply with the desire?* (O, TA:) for استطاعه signifies also *He demanded his obedience,* and *his consent,* or *compliance with what he desired of him.* (TA.)

طَاعٌ accord. to the copies of the O and Ḳ; but some say طَاعٍ accord. to the O: see طَائِعٌ, in three places.

طَوْعٌ: see طَائِعٌ, in seven places.

طَاعَةٌ [quasi-inf. n. of 4: as a simple subst., sometimes meaning *Submission,* or *submissiveness:* but mostly, *obedience to a command*]: see 1, in three places; and see also طَوَاعِيَةٌ. = [See also طَائِعٌ, of which it is a pl.]

طَوَاعَةٌ: see what next follows.

طَوَاعِيَةٌ i. q. ↓ طَاعَةٌ: (Ṣ, O, Ḳ:) so in the saying فُلَانٌ حَسَنُ الطَّوَاعِيَةِ لَكَ [*Such a one is good in obedience to thee*]: (Ṣ, O, TA:) or it is a subst. from 3 [q. v.]; and so ▼ طَوَاعَةٌ [app. طُوَاعَةٌ]. (L, TA.)

طَائِعٌ (Ṣ, O, Mṣb, Ḳ) and ▼ طَاعٍ, (O, Ḳ,) and some say ▼ طَاعٍ, formed from طَائِعٌ by transposition, (O,) and ▼ طَيِّعٌ, signify the same, (Ṣ, O, Mṣb, Ḳ,) i. e. *Being*, or *becoming, submissive*; [or, simply, *submissive*; and *obeying*; or *obedient*;] (Mṣb;) and ▼ طَوْعٌ, originally an inf. n., is likewise used as syn. with طَائِعٌ: (Ḥam p. 408:) the pl. is طُوَّعٌ, (Ṣ, O, Ḳ,) i. e. pl. of طَائِعٌ, (Ṣ, O,) and طَاعَةٌ is [also a pl. of طَائِعٌ, like as بَاعَةٌ is of بَائِعٌ; or] *syn. with* مُطِيعُونَ: (TA in art. سوع:) [whence one says, دَخَلَ فِى طَاعَتِهِ, and خَرَجَ مِنْ طَاعَتِهِ, *He entered among*, and *he quitted, his obeyers*, or *those who obeyed him*; i. e. *he became obedient*, and *he became disobedient, to him*:] and ▼ مِطْوَاعٌ, (Ṣ, O, Ḳ,) pl. مَطَاوِيعُ, (TA,) is [app., agreeably with analogy, an intensive epithet, meaning *very submissive* or *obedient*, but is said to be, in like manner,] *syn. with* مُطِيعٌ, (Ṣ, O, Ḳ,) applied to a man: (Ṣ, O:) and ▼ مِطْوَاعَةٌ, applied to a man, [is app. a doubly intensive epithet; or] is *syn. with* مِطْوَاعٌ: (TA:) and is applied to a pl. number, as meaning *compliant* and *submissive*. (Ḥar p. 237.) One says, جَآءَ فُلَانٌ طَائِعًا *Such a one came* [*submissively*, or *obediently*, or *willingly*,] *not being compelled against his will*. (Ṣ, O.) And a poet says,

* حَلَفْتُ بِالبَيْتِ وَمَا حَوْلَهُ *

* مِنْ عَائِذٍ بِالبَيْتِ أَوْطَاعِ▼ *

[*I swore*, or *have sworn, by the House* of God (i. e. the Kaabeh), *and what are around it, of such as betakes himself for refuge to the House or of such as renders obedience* by visiting it]. (O.) And one says also, ▼ جَآءَ طَيِّعًا [*He came of his own accord*, or *willingly*]. (M and TA voce ذو.) And طَيِّعُ ▼ اللِّسَانِ ‡ A man *chaste*, or *eloquent, in speech*. (TA.) And نَاقَةٌ طَيِّعَةٌ ▼ القِيَادِ and طَوْعُ ▼ القِيَادِ † *A she-camel that is gentle*; [or *tractable*;] *that does not contend with her leader*. (TA.) And فَرَسٌ طَوْعُ ▼ العِنَانِ ‡ *A tractable horse*. (Ṣ, O, Ḳ, TA.) And فُلَانٌ طَوْعُ ▼ يَدِكَ ‡ *Such a one is submissive to thy hand*. (Ṣ, O, Ḳ, TA.) And اِمْرَأَةٌ طَوْعُ ▼ الضَّجِيعِ *A woman submissive to the bedfellow*. (TA.) And فُلَانٌ طَوْعُ ▼ المَكَارِهِ † *Such a one is submissive to misfortunes*, [*being*] *subject thereto*. (T, TA.) [See also an ex. of ▼ طَوْع in a verse cited in art. شمت voce شَامِتَةٌ.] هُوَ أَطْوَعُ ▼ السِّنَانِ means † *He is one to whom the spear-head is subservient, howsoever he will*. (Ḳ in art. سن.)

طَيِّعٌ: see the next preceding paragraph, in four places.

أَطْوَعُ [as signifying *More*, and *most, submissive* or *obedient* is regularly formed from طَاعَ; or] is from الطَّاعَةُ [i. e. from أَطَاعَ], and similar to أَجْوَبُ [from أَجَابَ, and therefore anomalous]. (M and L in art. جوب.) أَطْوَعُ مِنْ فَرَسٍ, and مِنْ كَلْبٍ, [*More submissive*, or *obedient, than a horse*, and *than a dog*,] are provs. (Meyd.) — [It app. signifies also *Very submissive* or *obedient*: see an ex. in a verse cited voce تَبَدَّعَ. — And it is also a simple epithet, like أَهْوَنُ &c.:] see طَائِعٌ, last sentence.

شُحٌّ مُطَاعٌ means *A niggardliness that is obeyed by him who is characterized thereby, by the refusing rights*, or *dues*, (O, Ḳ,) *which God has rendered obligatory on him, in respect of his property*: occurring in a trad. of the Prophet. (O.) And المُطَاعُ, as a name of the Prophet, means *He whose prayer is answered; whose intercession for his people is accepted*. (TA.)

مِطْوَاعٌ: see طَائِعٌ, first sentence.

مِطْوَاعَةٌ [an epithet of a very rare form, like مِعْزَابَةٌ, q. v.]: see طَائِعٌ.

مُطَاوِعٌ an epithet applied by the grammarians to ‡ *A verb that is intransitive* [such as I term *quasi-passive*; expl. as meaning a verb *whose* (*grammatical*) *agent receives the effect of the action of the agent of another verb*] (فِعْلٌ يَقْبَلُ فَاعِلُهُ أَثَرَ فِعْلِ فَاعِلِ فِعْلٍ آخَرَ). (Ṣ, O, TA.)

المُطَّوِّعَةُ and المُطَّوِّعِينَ: see what follows.

مُتَطَوِّعٌ *A supererogator in any good act*. (O, Ḳ.) One says, فَعَلَهُ مُتَطَوِّعًا [*He did it without its being incumbent*, or *obligatory, on him*; *supererogatorily*: or *gratuitously, unasked*, or *unbidden*: or *disinterestedly*; *not seeking*, or *desiring, a compensation*: syn. مُتَبَرِّعًا]. (Ṣ and Ḳ in art. برع.) And ▼ المُطَّوِّعَةُ means *Those who exceed what is obligatory on them in fighting*, or *warring, against unbelievers* or *the like*; (Ṣ, O, Mṣb;) originally المُتَطَوِّعَةُ: (Mṣb:) hence ▼ المُطَّوِّعِينَ in the Ḳur ix. 80; originally المُتَطَوِّعِينَ. (Ṣ, O.)

طوف

1. The inf. n. طَوَافٌ primarily signifies, accord. to Er-Rághib, The act of *going*, or *walking*, in an absolute sense: or the *going*, or *walking, around*, or *otherwise*. (MF, TA.) [Hence,] طَافَ حَوْلَ الكَعْبَةِ, (Ṣ,) or بِالشَّىْءِ, (Mṣb,) or الشَّىْءَ, (O, Ḳ,) and بِهَا, (Ḳ,) aor. يَطُوفُ, (Ṣ, O, Mṣb,) inf. n. طَوْفٌ (Ṣ, O, Mṣb, Ḳ) and طَوَافٌ (O, Mṣb, Ḳ, and mentioned also in the Ṣ but not there said to be an inf. n.) and طَوَفَانٌ, (Ṣ, O, Ḳ,) [and perhaps طُوفَانٌ, q. v.,] *He went round* or *round about, circuited*, or *circuited around*, or *compassed*, (Mṣb, TA,) *the thing*, (Ṣ, Mṣb,) or *the Kaabeh*; (O, Ḳ;) and so طَافَ, aor. يَطِيفُ; (Mṣb; [but this I think doubtful;]) and ▼ تطوّف, (Ṣ, Mṣb, Ḳ,) and ▼ اِطَّوَّفَ, a variation of that next preceding, (Mṣb, TA,) inf. n. اِطِّوَافٌ; (TA;) and ▼ استطاف, (Ṣ, Mṣb, Ḳ,) as also ▼ استطافهُ; (TA;) and اطاف ▼ بِهِ, (Mṣb,) or عَلَيْهِ; (TA;) and ▼ طوّف, inf. n. ▼ تَطْوِيفٌ; (Ḳ;) or this last signifies *he did so much*, or *often*. (Ṣ, TA.) And طَافَ بِالقَوْمِ, aor. يَطُوفُ, inf. n. طَوْفٌ and طَوَفَانٌ and مَطَافٌ, *He went round about* [or *round about among*] *the people*, or *party*; as also ▼ اطاف: the aor. of the former verb occurs in the Ḳur lvi. 17 and lxxvi. 19, trans. by means of عَلَى. (TA.) And طُفْتُ بِهِ عَلَى البَيْتِ [*I went round the House* of God, i. e. the Kaabeh, *with him*; or] *I made him to go round*, or *to circuit*, or *compass, the House*. (Mṣb. [The vulgar in the present day say ▼ طَوَّفْتُهُ: and they apply the appellation ▼ مُطَوِّف to *One who makes the circuits round the Kaabeh with a pilgrim, and serves to conduct him round about to the other sacred objects, or places*.]) You say also, طاف فِى البِلَادِ, inf. n. طَوْفٌ and تَطْوَافٌ, *He journeyed* [or *journeyed round about*] *in the countries*, or *tracts of country*; and so [or as meaning *he did so much* or *often*] ▼ طوّف, inf. n. تَطْوِيفٌ and تَطْوَافٌ. (TA. [In one place in the TA, the latter inf. n. is said to be with kesr, so that it is like تِبْيَانٌ; but see this latter, which is very extr.: see also تَطْوَافٌ below.]) — لَأَطُوفَنَّ طَوْفَهُ means the same as لَأَسْعَرَنَّ سَعْرَهُ [app. *I will assuredly practise circumvention like his practising thereof*]. (Fr, O and Ḳ in art. سعر, q. v.) — See also 4, in two places. — طَافَ, (Ṣ, Mgh, O, Mṣb, Ḳ,) aor. as above, (Ṣ, O, Mṣb,) inf. n. طَوْفٌ, (Ṣ, Mgh, O, Mṣb,) from طَوْفٌ signifying غَائِطٌ; (Ṣ, O;) as also ▼ اِطَّافَ, (IAạr, Ṣ, Ḳ, TA, [in the CḲ, erroneously, اُطَّافَ,]) *He voided his excrement*, or *ordure*; (Mgh, Mṣb;*) or *he went away* (Ṣ, O, Ḳ) *to the field*, or *open tract*, (Ṣ, O,) *to void his excrement*, or *ordure*. (Ṣ, O, Ḳ.)

2: see 1, in three places. — You say also, طوّف النَّاسُ, and الجَرَادُ, *The men*, or *people*, and *the locusts, filled the land like the* طُوفَان [or *flood*]. (TA.)

4: see 1, in two places. — اطاف بِالشَّىْءِ signifies also *He*, or *it, surrounded*, or *encompassed, the thing*. (Mṣb.) — And اطاف بِهِ *He came to him*; *visited him*; or *alighted at his abode as a guest*; syn. أَلَمَّ بِهِ: and *he approached him*; or *drew*, or *was*, or *became, near to him*; syn. قَارَبَهُ. (Ṣ, Ḳ.) [And] طَافَ ▼ بِالنِّسَآءِ, aor. يَطُوفُ; and اطاف; *He came to women*, or *the women*; *visited them*; or *alighted at their abodes as a guest*; syn. أَلَمَّ. (Mṣb.) And اطاف بِهِ and عَلَيْهِ *He came to him by night*: and sometimes improperly used as meaning by day: a poet says,

أَطَفْتُ بِهَا نَهَارًا غَيْرَ لَيْلٍ

وَأَلْهَى رَبَّهَا طَلَبُ الرِّحَالِ

[*I came to her by day, not by night, while the seeking for the camels' saddles*, or *for the things necessary for his journey*, or *for the places of alighting, diverted her lord*, or *husband*, from attending to her]. (TA.) And طَافَ ▼ بِهِ الخَيَالُ, aor. يَطُوفُ, inf. n. طَوْفٌ; and, as Aṣ used to say, طَافَ, aor. يَطِيفُ, inf. n. طَيْفٌ; *The* خيال [i. e. *apparition*, or *phantom*,] *came to him*, or *visited him*, (أَلَمَّ بِهِ,) *in sleep*. (TA.)

5. تطوّف and اِطَّوَّفَ: see 1, first sentence.

8. اِطَّافَ: see 1, last sentence.

10: see 1, first sentence, in two places.

طَافٌ A man *who goes round*, or *round about, much*, or *often*; (Ṣ, O, Ḳ;) [and] so ▼ طَوَّافٌ: and ▼ طَوَّافَةٌ a woman *who goes round*, or *round about, much*, or *often, to the tents*, or *houses, of her female neighbours*. (Mṣb.) ═ See also طَوْفٌ.

طَوْفٌ in the phrase أَصَابَهُ مِنَ الشَّيْطَانِ طَوْفٌ, *i. q.* طَائِفٌ. (TA. See طَائِفٌ below, and in art. طيف.) — [Also *A kind of float composed of*] *inflated water-skins bound together*, (Ṣ, O, Mṣb, Ḳ,) *with wood* [or *planks*] *laid upon them*, (Mṣb,) *so as to have the form of a flat roof*, (Ṣ, O, Mṣb, Ḳ,) *upon the water*; (Mṣb;) *used for embarking thereon upon the water and for carriage thereon* (Ṣ, O, Ḳ, TA) *of wheat or other provisions and of men, and for the crossing* [*of rivers*] *thereon*: (TA:) *i. q.* رَمَثٌ: and *sometimes it is of wood*, or *timber*: (Ṣ, O:) accord. to Az, *a thing upon which large rivers are crossed, made of canes and of pieces of wood bound together, one upon another, and then bound round with ropes of the fibres or leaves of the palm-tree so as to be secure from its becoming unbound; after which it is used for embarking thereon and crossing, and sometimes it is laden with a load proportionate to its strength and its thickness*: and it is *also called* عَامَةٌ, without teshdeed to the م: (TA:) pl. أَطْوَافٌ. (Mṣb, TA.) — And The *bull* (ثَوْر) *around which turn the oxen in the treading* [*of corn*]. (TA.) [See طَائِفٌ.] — And *i. q.* قَلْدٌ [app. as meaning *A portion of water for irrigation*: for it is immediately added], and طَوْفُ القَصَبِ signifies *the quantity of water with which the canes are irrigated*. (TA.) ═ Also The *foul matter that comes forth from the child after suckling*: (El-Aḥmar, Mṣb, TA:) and by a secondary application, (Mṣb,) *human excrement*, or *ordure*, (Ṣ, Mgh, O, Mṣb, Ḳ,) in an absolute sense: (Mṣb:) what Er-Rághib says respecting it indicates that this is metonymical. (TA.)

بِطَافِ رَقَبَتِهِ *i. q.* بِصُوفِ رقبته and أَخَذَهُ بِطُوفِ رَقَبَتِهِ (Ṣ, Ḳ) and بِصَافِهَا رقبته. (Ḳ.)

طُوفَانٌ *An overpowering rain*: and *overpowering water*, [a meaning erroneously assigned in the CḲ to طَوَّاف instead of طُوفَان,] *that covers* [or *overwhelms*] *everything*; (Ṣ, Ḳ, TA;) in the common conventional acceptation, *water abounding to the utmost degree*; [i. e. *a flood*, or *deluge*;] such as befell the people of Noah; (TA;) or طُوفَانُ المَآءِ signifies *the water that covers* [or *overwhelms*] *everything*: (Mṣb:) and *a drowning torrent*: (Ḳ:) and † *much* of anything, [like as we say *a flood* of anything,] *such as includes the generality of persons, or things, within its compass*: (Ḳ, TA:) and particularly † *death*; or *quick*, or *quick and wide-spreading, death*; or *death commonly*, or *generally, prevailing*; (TA;) or *quick*, or *quick and wide-spreading, death, commonly*, or *generally, prevailing*: and † *quick* [*and extensive*] *slaughter*: (Ḳ:) and † *any accident* [or *evil accident*] *that besets a man*: and † *trial*, or *affliction*: (TA:) and El-'Ajjáj likens to the rain, or water, thus called, the darkness of night; using the phrase طُوفَانُ الظَّلَامِ; (Kh, Ṣ;) by which he means † *the intensity of the darkness of the night*: (TA:) طُوفَانٌ is said to be a pl. [or coll. gen. n.]; (Mṣb, TA;) and its sing. [or n. un.] is طُوفَانَةٌ, (Ṣ, Mṣb, Ḳ, TA,) accord. to analogy: (Ṣ:) thus says Akh: (Ṣ, TA:) or it is an inf. n., like نُقْصَانٌ and رُجْحَانٌ; and is from طَافَ, aor. يَطُوفُ: (Mṣb, TA:) thus says Abu-l-'Abbás; and he says that there is no need of seeking for it a sing.: some say that it is of the measure فُلْعَانٌ, from طَفَا المَآءُ, aor. يَطْفُو, meaning "the water rose," or "became high;" the ل being transposed to the place of the ع; but this is strange. (TA.)

طَوَافٌ [is an inf. n. of 1, q. v., sometimes used as a simple subst., and] has for its pl. أَطْوَافٌ [which is regularly pl. of طَوْفٌ]. (TA.)

طَوَّافٌ; and its fem., with ة: see طَافٌ. — The former signifies also *A servant who serves one with gentleness and carefulness*: (Ḳ, TA:) pl. طَوَّافُونَ: so says AHeyth: IDrd explains the pl. as meaning *servants*, and *male slaves*. (TA.) It is said in a trad., respecting the she-cat, that it is not unclean, but is مِنَ الطَّوَّافِينَ عَلَيْكُمْ, or الطَّوَّافَاتِ; [i. e. *of those that go round about waiting upon you*;] she being thus put in the predicament of the slaves: whence the saying of En-Nakha'ee, that the she-cat is like some of the people of the house, or tent. (TA.) [In the CḲ, a meaning belonging to طُوفَان is erroneously assigned to طَوَّاف.] ═ Also *A maker of the* طَوْف *that is composed of* [*inflated*] *water-skins* [*&c.*] *upon which one crosses* [*rivers &c.*]. (TA.)

طَائِفٌ part. n. of طَافَ, signifying *Going round* or *round about*, &c. (Mṣb.) — [And hence,] The عَسَس [quasi-pl. n. of عَاسٌّ]; (Ṣ, O, Ḳ, TA;) [i. e.] the *patrol*, or *watch that go the round of the houses*; thus expl. by Er-Rághib; and said to mean particularly those who do so *by night*. (TA.) — And The *bull that is next to the extremity*, or *side, of the* كُدْس [or *wheat collected together in the place where it is trodden out*]. (Ibn-'Abbád, Ḳ.) [See طَوْفٌ.] — The طَائِف of the bow is The *part between the* سِيَة [or *curved portion of the extremity*] *and the* أَبْهَر [q. v.]: (Ṣ, Ḳ:) or *near* [*the length of a cubit* or] *the bone of the fore arm from its* [*middle portion called the*] كَبِد [thus I render قَرِيبٌ مِنْ عَظْمِ الذِّرَاعِ مِنْ كَبِدِهَا, which, I think, can have no other meaning]: or the طَائِفَانِ are [*two parts*] *exclusive of the two curved ends* (دُونَ السِّيَتَيْنِ): (Ḳ: [this last explanation seems to leave one of the limits of each طائف undefined:]) or, accord. to AḤn, the طائف of the bow is the *part beyond its* كُلْيَة [q. v.], *above and below*, [*extending*] *to the place of the curving of the end of the bow*: the pl. is طَوَائِفُ. (TA.) — لَأَقْطَعَنَّ مِنْهُ طَائِفًا occurs in a trad. respecting a runaway slave, as meaning [*I will assuredly cut off*] *some one*, or *more, of his* أَطْرَاف [app. meaning *fingers*]: or, as some relate it, the word is طَابِقًا. (TA.) And Aboo-Kebeer El-Hudhalee says,

تَقَعُ السُّيُوفُ عَلَى طَوَائِفَ مِنْهُمُ

meaning, it is said, [*The swords fall upon*] *arms and legs* or *hands and feet* [*of them*: but in this case, طَوَائِف may be pl. of ▼ طَائِفَةٌ]. (TA.) ═ One says also, أَصَابَهُ مِنَ الشَّيْطَانِ طَائِفٌ [*A visitation from the Devil befell him*]; and ▼ طَوْفٌ likewise, in the same sense. (TA. [See also طَيْفٌ.])

طَائِفَةٌ *A detached*, or *distinct, part* or *portion*; *a piece*, or *bit*; [or *somewhat*;] of a thing: (Ṣ, Mṣb, Ḳ:) and *a* فِرْقَة of men [i. e. *a party, portion, division*, or *class*, thereof; as those *of one profession* or *trade*: *a body*, or *distinct community*: *a sect*: *a corps*: and sometimes *a people*, or *nation*]: (Mṣb:) and *a company*, or *congregated body*, (Mṣb, KL,) of men, *at least consisting of three*; and sometimes applied to *one*; and *two*: (Mṣb:) or *one*: and *more than one*: (Ṣ, Ḳ:) so, accord. to I'Ab, in the Ḳur xxiv. 2: (Ṣ:) or *up to a thousand*: (Mujáhid, Ḳ:) or *at least two men*: ('Aṭà, Ḳ:) or *one man*; (Ḳ;) as is said also on the authority of Mujáhid; (TA;) so that it is syn. with نَفْسٌ [as meaning *a single person*, or *an individual*]: (Ḳ:) [and sometimes it is applied to *a distinct number*, or *herd* &c., of animals:] Er-Rághib says that when a plural or collective number is meant thereby, it is [what lexicologists term] a pl. of طَائِفٌ; and when one is meant thereby, it may be a pl. metonymically used as a sing., or it may be considered as of the class of رَاوِيَةٌ and عَلَّامَةٌ and the like: (TA:) [pl. طَوَائِفُ.] — See also طَائِفٌ, last sentence but one.

طَائِفِيٌّ *A sort of raisins, of which the bunches are composed of closely-compacted berries*: app. so called in relation to [the district of] Eṭ-Ṭáïf. (AḤn, TA.)

تِطْوَافٌ, (JM, TA,) with kesr, (TA,) [and app. تَطْوَافٌ also, as it is sometimes written,] for ذُو تطواف, (JM,) *A garment in which one goes round*, or *circuits*, (JM, TA,) *the House* [*of God*, i. e. *the Kaabeh*]. (JM.)

مَطَافٌ *A place of* طَوَاف (O, Mṣb, Ḳ*) i. e. *of going round* or *round about*, or *circuiting*. (Mṣb.)

مُطَوَّفٌ: see 1, latter half.

طوق

1. طَاقَهُ, inf. n. طَوْقٌ: see 4.

2. طَوَّقَهُ, (Ṣ, TA,) or طَوَّقَهُ طَوْقًا, (O, Ḳ, TA,) inf. n. تَطْوِيقٌ, (TA,) *He attired him with a* طَوْق [*or neck-ring*]. (Ṣ, TA.) —— [Hence,] طَوَّقْتُهُ الشَّىْءَ means † *I made the thing to be* [*as though it were*] *his* طَوْق [*or neck-ring*]: and thereby is expressed the imposing [upon one] a thing that is difficult, troublesome, or inconvenient: (Mṣb:) [i. e.] طَوَّقْتُكَ الشَّىْءَ means † *I imposed*, or *have imposed, upon thee the thing as one that is difficult, troublesome*, or *inconvenient*. (Ṣ, O, Ḳ.*) سَيُطَوَّقُونَ مَا بَخِلُوا بِهِ, in the Ḳur [iii. 176], means † *They shall have that whereof they were niggardly made to cleave to their necks* [*like the neck-ring*]: (O, TA:) as is said in a trad., it shall be made a biting snake upon the neck. (Jel.) And [in the Ḳur ii. 180] some read, وَعَلَى الَّذِينَ يُطَوَّقُونَهُ, [in the CḲ, erroneously, يُطَوِّقُونَهُ,] meaning, † *And upon those who shall have it put* [*upon them*] *like the* طَوْق *upon their necks* [*shall be incumbent* &c.]: (Ḳ, TA:) which is like the saying يُجَشَّمُونَهُ and يُكَلَّفُونَهُ [i. e. *shall have it imposed upon them as a thing that is difficult, troublesome*, or *inconvenient*]: (TA:) another reading is ▼ يَطَّوَّقُونَهُ, [in the CḲ, erroneously, يُطَوِّقُونَهُ,] originally يَتَطَوَّقُونَهُ [meaning the same as the former reading]: and another, ▼ يُطَيَّقُونَهُ, originally يُطَيْوَقُونَهُ [also meaning the same; in the CḲ, erroneously, يُطَيِّقُونَهُ]: and another, ▼ يَطَّيَّقُونَهُ, [in the CḲ, erroneously, with ḍamm to the first letter, and so in what follows,] originally يَتَطَيْوَقُونَهُ [also meaning the same]. (Ḳ, TA.) One says also, طَوَّقَهُ إِيَّاهُ and طَوَّقَهُ بِهِ, meaning † *He made it*, namely, a sword, &c., *to be to him a* طَوْق [or *thing encircling*, or *going round, his neck*]. (TA.) And طَوَّقَنِى نِعْمَةً ‡ [*He conferred upon me a permanent badge of favour*]: and طُوِّقْتُ مِنْهُ أَيَادِىَ ‡ [*I had permanent badges of favours from him conferred upon me*]: and the verb is also used [in like manner] to denote dispraise, to which it has been erroneously said by some to be restricted. (TA.) [See also 2 in art. قلد: and see طَوْق.]) —— طَوَّقَتِ الحَيَّةُ: see 5. —— طَوَّقَنِى اللّٰهُ أَدَآءَ حَقِّكَ, (Ṣ, O,) or حَقِّهِ, (Ḳ,) means *God strengthened me*, or *empowered me, sufficiently for the giving*, or *paying, of thy due*, or *of his due*: syn. قَوَّانِى (Ṣ, O, Ḳ) عَلَيْهِ. (Ḳ.) And طَوَّقَهُ *He was enabled to do it*. (TA.) —— طَوَّقَتْ لَهُ نَفْسُهُ (Akh, Ṣ, O, Ḳ) is syn. with طَوَّعَتْ, (Akh, Ṣ, O,) meaning *His soul*, or *mind, facilitated to him* [the doing of a thing]. (Akh, Ṣ, O, Ḳ.)

اطاق الشئ, (Ṣ, O, Mṣb, Ḳ,) and اطاق عَلَيْهِ, (Ḳ,) inf. n. إِطَاقَةٌ, (Ṣ, O, Mṣb, Ḳ,) and طَاقَةٌ is the subst. (Az, Mṣb, Ḳ) used in the place of the inf. n. like طَاعَةٌ in the place of إِطَاعَةٌ, (Az, TA,) *He was*, or *became, able to do*, or *accomplish*, or *to bear, the thing*; (Ṣ, Mṣb, Ḳ;) as also ▼ طَاقَهُ, (Az,* Ḳ,) aor. يَطُوقُ, (Az, TA,) inf. n. طَوْقٌ. (Az, Ḳ.) It is not used exclusively of a human being, as some assert it to be; but is used in a general manner. (TA.) [One says لَا يُطَاقُ meaning *He will not be*, or *is not to be, coped with*: and also as meaning *it is not to be done*, or *to be borne, endured*, or *tolerated*: and so مَا يُطَاقُ: see an ex. voce حَمُضَ.]

5. تطوّق *He put on*, or *attired himself with, a* طَوْق [or *neck-ring*]. (Ṣ, O, Ḳ.) —— [Hence,] تطوّقهُ, and تطوّق بِهِ, † *He had it put upon him, and he bore it, and he took it upon himself, like the* طَوْق *upon the neck*: and *he had it imposed upon him, and he imposed it upon himself, as a thing that was difficult, troublesome*, or *inconvenient*]. See 2. [See also Ḥar p. 310. And see 5 in art. قلد.] —— And تطوّقت الحَيَّةُ عَلَى عُنُقِهِ ‡ *The serpent became like the* طَوْق *upon his neck*; as also ▼ طوّقت. (TA.)

Q. Q. 1. يُطَيَّقُونَهُ, originally يُطَيْوَقُونَهُ: see 2.

Q. Q. 2. يَطَّيَّقُونَهُ, originally يَتَطَيْوَقُونَهُ: see 2.

طَاقٌ *A curved construction* or *structure*; (Ṣ, O, Ḳ;) [said to be] a Pers. word arabicized; (Ṣ, O;) and its pl. is طَاقَاتٌ and طِيقَانٌ: (Ṣ, O, Ḳ:) or *an arch* of a building, wherever it is; and the pl. is أَطْوَاقٌ and طِيقَانٌ: (JḲ, TA:) and as signifying [thus, or] *an arch constructed with bricks*, it is [said to be] originally ▼ طَائِقٌ; and therefore to have for its pl. طَوَائِقُ: so says Az. (TA.) [It is often applied to *An arched gateway* or *doorway*: and to *a vault*. And] i. q. كُوَّةٌ [i. e. *A mural aperture*; *a hole*, or *an aperture, in a wall*; a meaning also assigned to إِفْرِيزٌ, by which طَاقٌ will be found to be expl. in what follows: or *a niche in a wall*; which, as also *a window*, is now often called ▼ طَاقَة]. (So in the Munjid of Kr.) [And app. *A kind of arched construction with a flat top which forms a shelf, against a wall*. (See رَفٌّ and سَهْوَةٌ.)] And i. q. إِفْرِيزٌ [which is expl. as meaning *a projecting roof* or *covering* of a wall: and *a projecting coping*, or *ledge*, or *cornice, surrounding the upper part of a wall*: and in the KL as meaning *a hole*, or *an aperture, of a wall*; (as mentioned above;) but its author adds "so we have heard"]: (MA voce إِفْرِيزٌ:) or so أَطْوَاقٌ. (JK, and O on the authority of Ibn-'Abbád. [But this I think doubtful, and the more so as it will be seen in what follows that another meaning assigned in these same lexicons to أَطْوَاقٌ is said by IB to be a meaning of طَاقٌ.]) —— See also طَائِقٌ, in two places. —— [Also *A layer, stratum, lamina*, or *the like*; or *any flat piece*, or *portion*, of a thing, *such as is in some cases placed over*, or *under, a similar piece* or *portion*: and *anything such as is in some cases lined*, or *faced*, or *otherwise combined, with another similar thing*: pl. طَاقَاتٌ.] You say طَاقُ نَعْلٍ [*A single piece of leather of a sole* that consists of two or more of such pieces]; (Ṣ, O, Ḳ;) and طَاقَةُ ▼ نَعْلٍ [which means the same]. (Ḳ.) And نَعْلٌ طَاقٌ وَاحِدٌ *A single sole*; i. e. *a sole of a single piece*; *not made of two pieces sewed together, one upon the other*. (TA in art. نعل.) And [in like manner] a garment is said to be طَاقٌ وَاحِدٌ [i. e. *Single, not double, not lined nor faced nor stuffed*]. (Az, in TA in art. سمط, [where this meaning is clearly indicated,] and Th, in M, same art.) Thus one says سَرَاوِيلُ طَاقٌ وَاحِدٌ [*Trousers*, or *drawers, of single cloth*]. (Th, M and Ḳ in art. سمط.) [See also what is said of the phrase رِجْلُ السَّرَاوِيلِ الطَّاقُ voce رِجْلٌ.] One says also غَزْلٌ طَاقٌ وَاحِدٌ [*Spun thread that is a single yarn*]: and غَزْلٌ مَفْتُولٌ طَاقَيْنِ [*Spun thread twisted of two yarns*]. (Ṣ and TA in art. سحل.) See also طَاقَة, which has a similar meaning. [And see an ex. of the pl. طَاقَات voce رُبْعَةٌ.] —— Also *A certain sort of garment*, (Ṣ, O, Ḳ,) *having sleeves*. (Ṣ, O.) [And] accord. to Esh-Shereeshee, *A garment worn by a new-born child*, or *young infant, without an opening at the bosom*. (Ḥar p. 502.) —— And (O, Ḳ) accord. to IAạr, (O,) *A* [*garment of the kind called*] طَيْلَسَان [q. v.]: (O, Ḳ:) or *such as is* أَخْضَر [properly meaning *green*; but when applied to a garment commonly meaning, as used by the Arabs, *of a dark*, or *an ashy, dust-colour*; or *a dingy ash-colour*]: (Kr, Ḳ:) pl. طِيقَانٌ, like سِيجَانٌ pl. of سَاجٌ. (TA.) —— And *A* [*garment of the kind called*] كِسَآء: (IB, TA:) and (TA) so أَطْوَاقٌ. (JK, and O and TA on the authority of Ibn-'Abbád. [But this, as I have shown above, I think doubtful.]) —— And *A* [*woman's muffler*, or *head-covering, such as is called*] خِمَار. (IAạr, TA.) —— And one says, رَأَيْتُ أَرْضًا كَأَنَّهَا الطِّيقَانُ ‡ [*I saw a land as though it were* spread with *the garments called* طيقان]; meaning, *whereof the herbage was abundant*. (TA.)

طَوْقٌ [*A neck-ring*;] *a certain ornament for the neck*; (Ḳ;) *a thing well known*: (Mṣb:) [its most usual form is figured in my work on the Modern Egyptians, Appendix A:] pl. أَطْوَاقٌ. (Ṣ, O, Mṣb, Ḳ.) It is said in a prov., كَبِرَ عَمْرٌو عَنِ الطَّوْقِ ['*Amr has become too much advanced in age for the neck-ring*]: (A'Obeyd, O, Ḳ, TA: in some copies of the Ḳ [erroneously] كَبُرَ:) or شَبَّ عَمْرٌو عَنِ الطَّوْقِ, [which has the like meaning,] as in most of the books of proverbs: (TA:) applied to him who occupies himself with a thing that is beneath his ability. (Ḳ. [For the story of the origin of this prov., see Freytag's Arab. Prov. ii. 319-21, or Ḥar pp. 502-3; as it is too long to be quoted here.]) —— And *Anything that surrounds another thing* (Mṣb, Ḳ) is called its طَوْق. (Mṣb.) —— Hence ذَاتُ الطَّوْقِ as an appellation of *The* [*ringed*] *pigeon* [or *ring-dove*]. (Mṣb.) —— [And hence] one says, تَقَلَّدْتُ النِّعْمَةَ طَوْقَ الحَمَامَةِ ‡ [*I bore the favour as the ring of the pigeon;* meaning, *as a permanent badge* or *decoration*]: and فِى عُنُقِى طَوْقٌ مَا لِى بِأَدَآءِ شُكْرِهِ طَوْقٌ ‡ [*Upon my neck is a permanent badge* or *decoration, for which I have not ability to render due acknowledgment*]: so in the A: hence also the saying of El-Mutanebbee,

* أَقَامَتْ فِى الرِّقَابِ لَهُ أَيَادٍ
* هِىَ الأَطْوَاقُ وَالنَّاسُ الحَمَامُ

[*Favours of his have remained upon the necks: they are the neck-rings, and the men are the pigeons*]. (TA. [See, for this verse, p. 164 of Dieterici's ed. of the Deewán of El-Mutanebbee.]) — الطَّوْقُ signifies also *The neck* [itself]. (TA.) — And *The* كَرّ, (O,) or حَابُول, (Ḳ,) [i. e. the *rope in the form of a loop*] *by means of which one ascends the palm-tree.* (O, Ḳ.*) = See also the next paragraph, first and second sentences.

طَاقَةٌ is the subst. from أَطَاقَ, (Az, Mṣb, Ḳ,) and is used in the place of the inf. n., (Az, TA,) and [when used as a simple subst.] signifies *Ability,* or *power;* (Ṣ, O,* Mṣb, Ḳ;) and so ▼ طَوْقٌ, (Ṣ, O, Ḳ,) which is [originally] an inf. n., (Az, Ḳ,) and is also expl. as meaning the *utmost that one can do, with difficulty, trouble,* or *inconvenience.* (TA.) One says, [لَا طَاقَةَ لِى بِهِ *I have not ability,* or *power, to do it,* or *to bear* or *endure* or *tolerate it:* and, *to cope with him:* (see Ḳur ii. last verse: and verse 250:) and] ▼ هُوَ فِى طَوْقِى *It is within my ability,* or *power.* (Ṣ.) In the phrase طَلَبْتَهُ طَاقَتَكَ, [as meaning *Thou soughtest him,* or *it, in thy state of ability,* or *power,*] Sb says, the [quasi-] inf. n. is prefixed [to the pronoun, and thus rendered determinate], though occupying the place of a denotative of state; in like manner as the article ال is prefixed [to عِرَاك] in the phrase أَرْسَلَهَا العِرَاكَ. (TA.) = [Also *A slender and small bundle* or *fascicle of fibres* or *filaments* or *the like; one of those whereof two or more, twisted together, compose a rope; a strand, a yarn, a single twist,* or *single thread,* of a rope or cord or fringe &c.] You say طَاقَةٌ مِنْ حَبْلٍ *A strand, yarn,* or *single twist, of a rope;* syn. قُوَّةٌ; (Ṣ voce قُوَّةٌ;) and so ▼ طَاقٌ مِنْ حَبْلٍ: (JK voce قُوَّةٌ:) [the pl. of طَاقَةٌ in this sense is طَاقَاتٌ: طَاقَاتُ الحَبْلِ means قُوَاهُ, as is said in the A. (TA.) — And *A* شُعْبَة [i. e. *sprig, spray, bunch,* or *branchlet,*] of sweet basil, or of sweet-smelling plants: and likewise [*a lock,* or *flock,*] of hair: (JK, TA:) [and so of wool, and the like;] you say طَاقَةُ رَيْحَانٍ, (Ṣ, O, Ḳ, TA,) [or مِنْ رَيْحَانٍ, &c.,] meaning شُعْبَةٌ مِنْهُ, as in the A. (TA.) — طَاقَةُ نَعْلٍ: see طَاقٌ, latter half. — See also another meaning of طَاقَةٌ voce طَاقٌ, first quarter.

طُوقَةٌ *A round, and plain,* or *soft, piece of ground, amid rugged tracts of ground:* (O, Ḳ:) mentioned by IDrd as occurring in some poem of the Time of Ignorance but not heard by him from his companions. (O.)

طَائِقٌ (Ṣ, O, Ḳ) and ▼ طَاقٌ (O, Ḳ) *A prominence* [app. meaning a *ledge* or *ridge*] *projecting from a mountain:* (Ṣ, O, Ḳ:) and the former, (Ṣ,) or the latter, (Ḳ,) or each, (O,) also the *like thereof in a well;* (Ṣ, O, Ḳ; [in the CḲ, التِّيرِ is erroneously put for البِئْرِ;]) i. e., *in the wall that surrounds the interior of a well;* and its pl. is طَوَائِقُ: (TA:) and *between any two pieces of wood* [or *planks*] *of a ship,* or *boat:* (Ṣ, O, Ḳ:) or طَائِقٌ signifies *one of the pieces of wood* [or *planks*] *of the interior of a* زَوْرَق [or *skiff*]: accord. to Aboo-'Amr Esh-Sheybánee, it is the *middle,* or *in the middle, of a ship* or *boat:* and accord. to Aṣ, *a prominence projecting from a ship,* or *boat, like a ledge swelling out from a mountain:* and also, he says, *a ridge,* or *ledge, in a* [*mountain,* or *portion of a mountain, such as is termed*] قُنَّة: accord. to Lth, طَائِقُ كُلِّ شَىْءٍ signifies *any mountain,* or [*hill such as is termed*] أَكَمَة, *that surrounds anything:* and its pl. is أَطْوَاقٌ [like أَصْحَابٌ pl. of صَاحِبٌ]. (TA.) — طَائِقٌ also signifies, accord. to Ibn-Ḥamzeh, The *curved extremity* of a bow; which is said to be called its ▼ طَاقٌ; but this he disallows. (TA.) — See also طَاقٌ, first sentence.

أَطْوَاقٌ [a pl. of طَاقٌ: and of طَوْقٌ: and of طَائِقٌ. = Also] The *milk of the cocoa-nut:* (O, Ḳ, TA:) AḤn says, (O, TA,) *it is very intoxicating;* (O, Ḳ, TA;) *moderately as long as its drinker does not go forth to the wind; but if he does so, his intoxication becomes excessive;* (Ḳ, TA;) *and when he who is not accustomed to it,* (O, Ḳ, TA,) *and is not suited to it,* (O, TA,) *continues constantly the drinking of it, it vitiates his intellect,* (O, Ḳ, TA,) *and confuses his understanding:* (O, TA:) *when it remains until the morrow, it becomes most acid vinegar.* (Ḳ, TA.)

حَمَامٌ مُطَوَّقٌ, (O,) and حَمَامَةٌ مُطَوَّقَةٌ, (Ṣ, O, Ḳ,) [*Pigeons, and a pigeon,*] *having* [i. e. *marked with*] *a ring upon the neck.* (Ṣ, O, Ḳ.) — And مُطَوَّقَةٌ signifies *A large* قَارُورَة [i. e. *flask,* or *bottle,*] *having a ringed neck:* (O, Ḳ:) thus called by the people of El-'Irák. (O.)

طول

1. طَالَ, (Ṣ, O, Mṣb, Ḳ,) said by some to be of the class of قَرُبَ, being made by them to accord in form with its contr., which is قَصُرَ, and by others said to be of the class of قَالَ, (Mṣb,) first pers. طُلْتُ, [said to be] originally طَوُلْتُ, because one says طَوِيلٌ, [not طَائِلٌ, when using it as an intrans. v.,] (Ṣ, O,) aor. يَطُولُ, (TA,) inf. n. طُولٌ, (Ṣ,* O,* Mṣb, Ḳ,) *It* (a thing, Ṣ, O, Mṣb) *was,* or *became, elongated,* or *extended;* [i. e. *it was,* or *became, long;* and *it was,* or *became, tall,* or *high;* which meanings are sometimes more explicitly denoted in order to avoid ambiguity, as when one says طَالَ عَلَى وَجْهِ الأَرْضِ *it was,* or *became, elongated,* or *extended, upon the surface of the earth* or *ground;* and طَالَ فِى السَّمَآءِ *it was,* or *became, elongated,* or *extended, towards* (lit. *into*) *the sky;*] (Ṣ, O, Mṣb, Ḳ;) and ▼ اِسْتَطَالَ signifies the same. (Ṣ, O, Ḳ.) It is also said of any time that is extended; and of anxiety that cleaves to one continually; and the like: [see طُولٌ, below:] thus one says طَالَ اللَّيْلُ [*The night became long,* or *protracted*]: (TA:) [and thus طَالَ عَلَيْهِمُ الأَمَدُ, in the Ḳur lvii. 15, means *The time became extended,* or *prolonged, unto them:*] and ▼ تَطَاوَلَ عَلَيْهِمُ العُمُرُ, in the Ḳur xxviii. 45, means, in like manner, [*Life was prolonged unto them;* or] *their lives became long,* or *prolonged:* (Jel:) and طال المَجْلِسُ *The time of the assembly was,* or *became, extended,* or *prolonged:* (Mṣb:) and طال الهَمُّ [*Anxiety became protracted*]. (TA.) [One says also طَالَمَا فَعَلَ كَذَا *Long time did he thus;* and the like; with the restrictive ما: see Ḥar p. 17.] = When trans. [without a particle] it is of the class فَعَلَ; not فَعُلَ, because this is not trans.: (TA:) one says طُلْتُهُ meaning *I exceeded him,* or *surpassed him, in* الطُّول [i. e. *tallness;* or *I overtopped him*]: and also *in* الطَّوْل [i. e. *beneficence, and excellence,* &c.]. (Ṣ, O, Ḳ.) See 3. A poet says,

* إِنَّ الفَرَزْدَقَ صَخْرَةٌ عَادِيَّةٌ
* طَالَتْ فَلَيْسَ تَنَالُهَا الأَوْعَالُ

[*Verily El-Farezdaḳ is a bare rock that has exceeded in height* the mountain-goats *so that the mountain-goats do not reach it*]: he means طَالَتِ الأَوْعَالَ. (TA.) And it is said in a trad., فَطَالَ العَبَّاسُ عُمَرَ i. e. *And El-'Abbás exceeded 'Omar in tallness of stature.* (TA.) And you say, طَالَهُ فِى الحَسَبِ [*He excelled him in the grounds of pretension to respect* or *honour*]. (Ḳ and TA in explanation of شَرُفَهُ: in the CḲ [erroneously] طاوَلَهُ.) = One says also, طال عَلَيْهِ, (Ṣ,) or عَلَيْهِمْ, (Mṣb, Ḳ,) the verb in this case being of the class of قَالَ, aor. يَطُولُ, (Mṣb,) inf. n. طَوْلٌ; (Ṣ,* Mṣb;) and ▼ تطوّل; (Ṣ, Mṣb, Ḳ;) and ▼ اطال; (Mṣb;) *He bestowed,* or *conferred, a benefit* or *benefits,* or *a favour* or *favours,* (Ṣ, Mṣb, Ḳ,) *upon him,* (Ṣ,) or *upon them.* (Mṣb, Ḳ.) And ▼ تطوّل عَلَيْنَا بِشَىْءٍ *He gave to us a thing;* like تَنَوَّلَ; but the latter is said by Aboo-Miḥjen to be used only in relation to good; and the former, sometimes, in relation to good and to evil. (TA in art. نول.)

2. طوّلهُ, (Ṣ, O, Mṣb, Ḳ,) inf. n. تَطْوِيلٌ; (O;) and ▼ اطالهُ, (Ṣ, O, Mṣb, Ḳ,) and ▼ أَطْوَلَهُ, (Ṣ, O, Ḳ,) inf. n. إِطَالَةٌ; (O;) both signify the same; (Ṣ, O, Mṣb, Ḳ;) *He elongated it; extended it; lengthened it;* or *made it long,* or *tall* or *high;* (Ṣ,* O, Mṣb;) syn. مَدَّهُ, (Ṣ,* O,* Mṣb,) and جَعَلَهُ طَوِيلًا. (O, TA.) You say, طَوَّلْتُ الحَدِيدَةَ *I elongated,* or *lengthened, the piece of iron.* (Mṣb.) And ▼ اطال ٱللّٰهُ بَقَآءَهُ *God extended,* or *prolonged, his continuance* [*in life*]; or *may God extend,* &c.

(Mṣb.) And اطال ♦ المَجْلِسَ *He extended*, or *prolonged, the time of the assembly.* (Mṣb.) And طوّل لِلفَرَسِ, (Ṣ, O,) or لِلدَّابَّةِ, (Mṣb, Ḳ,) *He slackened* [or *lengthened*] (Ṣ, O, Mṣb, Ḳ) *the tether*, (Ṣ, O, Ḳ,) or *rope*, (Mṣb,) *of the horse*, (Ṣ, O,) or *of the beast*, (Mṣb, Ḳ,) in the place of pasture, (Ṣ, O, Ḳ,) or that it might pasture [more largely]: (Mṣb:) and اطال ♦ لَهَا الطِّوَلَ and الطِّيَلَ [signify the same]. (TA, from a trad.) And [hence] طوّل لَهُ (inf. n. as above, Ṣ) *He granted him a delay*, or *respite*; (Ṣ, O, Mṣb, Ḳ;) said of God: (Ṣ:) and المُطَاوَلَةُ ♦ فِى طاولهُ means التَّطْوِيلُ فِيهِ الأَمْرِ; (Mṣb;) [i. e.] signifies *he delayed*, or *deferred, with him*, (Ṣ, O, Ḳ, TA,) فِى الأَمْرِ [*in the affair*], (Ṣ, O,) or فِى الدَّيْنِ [*in the case of the debt*] and العِدَةِ [*the promise*]. (TA.) [And طوّل عَلَيْهِ and ♦ تطوّل *He was prolix*, or *tedious, to him*: see 2 in art. بسق; and see an ex. of the former voce حُوزٌ.]

3. ♦ طَاوَلَنِى فَطُلْتُهُ *He contended with me for superiority* (Ks, O, TA) *in* الطُّول [i. e. *tallness*], and also *in* الطَّوْل [i. e. *beneficence*, and *excellence*, &c.], *and I exceeded him*, or *surpassed him, therein.* (Ṣ, O, Ḳ.) بِكَ أُطَاوِلُ occurs in a prayer of the Prophet, and is from الطَّوْل, meaning [*By means of Thee I contend for*] *superiority* over the enemies. (O.) One says also, طَاوَلَهُ بِالكِبَرِ وَقَالَ أَنَا أَكْبَرُ مِنْكَ [*He contended, or disputed, with him for superiority in greatness, and said, I am greater than thou*]. (A in art. كبر.) [And المُطَاوَلَةُ فِى الحُظْوَةِ, occurring in the TA in art. سمو, means *The contending*, or *vying*, or *competing, for superiority, in highness of rank.*] —— See also 2, last sentence but one.

4. اطال and اطول, as trans.: see 2, in five places. ═ اطالت المَرْأَةُ *The woman brought forth tall children*, (Ṣ, A, O, Ḳ,) or *a tall child.* (Ḳ.) It is said in a trad., (Ṣ,) or in a prov., not a trad., (Ḳ,) but IAth declares it to be a trad., and in the trads. of the Prophet are many celebrated provs., (MF,) إِنَّ القَصِيرَةَ قَدْ تُطِيلُ [*Verily the short woman sometimes brings forth tall children*], (Ṣ, O, Ḳ,) وَإِنَّ الطَّوِيلَةَ ♦ قَدْ تُقْصِرُ [*and verily the tall woman sometimes brings forth short children*]. (O.) —— See also 1, last sentence but one. —— One says also, اطال لِفَرَسِهِ *He tied his horse with the rope* [or *tether*, called طِوَل]. (TA.)

5: see 2, last sentence: —— and see also 1, last two sentences.

6. تطاول: see 1, former half. —— Also *It became high by degrees*; said of a building. (L in art. شيد.) —— And *i. q.* تَعَالَ or تَطَاوَلَ, (Ṣ, Ḳ, TA,) meaning *He* (a man, Ṣ, TA) *stood upon his toes, and stretched his stature, to look at a thing*: (TA:) or تَطَاوَلْتُ فِى قِيَامِى *I stretched my legs, in my standing, to look.* (O.) One says, يَتَطَاوَلُ لِلْأَفْنَانِ وَيَجْتَذِبُهَا بِالمِحْجَنِ [*He stretches himself up towards the branches, and draws them to him with the hooked-headed stick*]. (Ṣ in art. حرق.) And it is said in a trad., تطاول عَلَيْهِمُ الرَّبُّ بِفَضْلِهِ *The Lord looked down upon them*, or *regarded them compassionately*, (أَشْرَفَ,) *with his favour.* (O.) —— Also *He made a show of* الطُّول [i. e. *tallness*], or الطَّوْل [i. e. *beneficence*, and *excellence*, &c.]. (TA.) —— تطاول عَلَيْهِ and ♦ استطال signify the same; (Az, Ṣ, O, Mṣb, Ḳ, TA;) *He held up his head with a show of superiority over him*; (Az, TA;) [i. e. *he behaved haughtily, arrogantly, overweeningly, overbearingly, domineeringly*, or *proudly, towards him*; *domineered over him*; or *exalted himself above him*;] or *he overbore, overpowered, subdued*, or *oppressed, him*: (Mṣb:) استطال ♦ عليه is also expl. as meaning *he arrogated to himself excellence over him*, syn. تَفَضَّلَ; (Ḳ, TA;) *and exalted himself above him*: (TA:) and استطالوا ♦ عَلَيْهِمْ as meaning *they slew of them more than they* [the latter] *had slain* (Ṣ, O, Ḳ) *of them* [the former]: (O:) and الِاسْتِطَالَةُ ♦ فِى عِرْضِ النَّاسِ occurs in a trad. as meaning *the contemning of men*, and *exalting oneself above them*, and *reviling them, vilifying them*, or *detracting from their reputation.* (TA.) One says also تطاول بِمَا عِنْدَهُ *He exalted*, or *magnified*, or *boasted, himself in*, or *he boasted of, what he possessed.* (TA in art. فتح.) And الفَحْلُ يَتَطَاوَلُ عَلَى إِبِلِهِ *The stallion* [*overbears*, or] *drives as he pleases, and repels the other stallions from, his she-camels.* (O.) —— And تَطَاوَلُوا *They vied, competed*, or *contended for superiority, each with the other* [*in* الطُّول i. e. *tallness*, or *in* الطَّوْل i. e. *beneficence*, and *excellence*, &c.: see 3]. (TA.)

10. استطال: see 1, first sentence. —— Also *It extended and rose*; (Ḳ, TA;) said of a crack [in a wall]; like استطار: mentioned by Th. (TA.) [And likewise said, in the same sense, of the dawn, i. e., of the false dawn; in which case it is opposed to استطار: see مُسْتَطِيلٌ.] —— See also 6, in four places. ═ This verb is also used, by Z and Bḍ, in a trans. sense; and استطالهُ, occurring in the "Mufaṣṣal" [of Z] is expl. as meaning عَدَّهُ طَوِيلًا [*He reckoned it long*, &c.]; and in like manner it is used by Es-Saad in the "Muṭowwal:" but this usage is on the ground of analogy [only]; for, accord. to the genuine lexical usage, it is intransitive. (TA.)

طَوْلٌ [is originally an inf. n.: (see طَالَ عَلَيْهِ:) and, used as a simple subst.,] signifies *Beneficence*; and *bounty*: (Ṣ, TA:) and [*a benefit, a favour, a boon*, or] *a gift.* (Ḥar p. 58.) —— And, (O, Ḳ, TA,) as also ♦ طَائِلٌ and ♦ طَائِلَةٌ, (Ḳ, TA,) *Excellence, excess*, or *superabundance*: and *power*, or *ability*: and *wealth*, or *competence*: and *ampleness of circumstances*: (O, Ḳ, TA:) and *superiority*, or *ascendancy.* (O, TA.) One says, لِفُلَانٍ عَلَى فُلَانٍ طَوْلٌ *To such a one belongs excellence*, or *superabundance, above such a one.* (O. [And the like is said in the Mgh.]) And it is said in the Ḳur [iv. 29], وَمَنْ لَمْ يَسْتَطِعْ مِنْكُمْ طَوْلًا أَنْ يَنْكِحَ المُحْصَنَاتِ, meaning *And such of you as is not able to obtain superabundance so that he may marry the free women*, let him marry a female slave; (Mgh;) i. e. such as is not able to give the dowry of the free woman, (Mgh, O, TA,) as expl. by Zj. (Mgh, TA.) In the phrase طَوْلُ الحُرَّةِ, the former word is originally the inf. n. of the verb in طَالَ عَلَيْهَا meaning "he benefited her;" because, when one is able to give the dowry of the free woman, and pays it, he benefits her: or, as some of the lawyers say, this phrase means *The superabundance of the means of sustenance that suffices for the marrying of the free woman*, agreeably with a saying of Az: or, as some say, طول means *wealth*, or *competence*; and the phrase is originally طَوْلٌ إِلَى الحُرَّةِ, i. e. *ampleness of wealth such as supplies the means of attaining to the free woman*: or originally طَوْلٌ عَلَى الحُرَّةِ, meaning *power*, or *ability, for the marrying of the free woman*: (Mṣb:) Esh-Shaabee is related to have used the phrase الطَّوْلُ إِلَى الحُرَّةِ; and in like manner are IAb and Jábir and Sa'eed Ibn-Jubeyr. (Mgh.) ذِى الطَّوْلِ in the Ḳur xl. 3 means *The Possessor of all-sufficiency*, and *of superabundance*, or *of bounty*: (O:) or *the Possessor of power*: or *of bounty*, and *beneficence.* (TA.) And أُولُو الطَّوْلِ مِنْهُمْ in the Ḳur ix. 87 means *Those, of them, who are possessors of superabundance*, and *of opulence.* (Bḍ.) —— See also طِوَلٌ, latter half, in two places.

طُولٌ [is originally an inf. n.: (see 1, first sentence:) and, used as a simple subst.,] signifies *Length*; and *tallness*, or *height*; *contr. of* عَرْضٌ; (Ṣ, O, Mṣb;) or *of* قِصَرٌ: (M, TA:) pl. أَطْوَالٌ: (Mṣb:) it is in man and other animals, and in inanimate things: (TA:) in real things, or substances; and also in ideal things, or attributes, as time and the like. (Er-Rághib, TA.) [One says, قَطَعَهُ طُولًا and بِالطُّولِ *He cut it lengthwise.*] —— And The *utmost extent* of time. (TA.) You say, لَا أُكَلِّمُهُ طُولَ الدَّهْرِ, (Ṣ, O, TA) and ♦ طَوَالَ الدَّهْرِ, (Ṣ, O, Ḳ,* TA,) both meaning the same, (Ṣ, O, TA,) i. e. [*I will not speak to him*] *during the utmost extent of time.* (Ḳ,* TA.) —— [In geography, The *longitude* of a place: pl. as above.] —— See also طِوَلٌ, in two places.

طَوَلٌ *Length in the upper lip* of the camel, (M, Ḳ, TA,) *beyond the lower.* (M, TA.)

طُوَلٌ: see طِوَلٌ. ═ Also pl. of طُولَى, fem. of أَطْوَلُ [q. v.].

طِوَلٌ, for which ♦ طُوَلٌ occurs in poetry, (Ṣ, O, Ḳ,) and ♦ طِيَلٌ, for which also ♦ طِيَلٌ occurs in poetry, (Ḳ,) and ♦ طِوِيلَةٌ, (Lth, O, Ḳ,) but this is disapproved by Az, (TA,) and ♦ تِطْوَلٌ, (Ḳ,) *A tether*; i. e. the *rope that is extended for a horse or similar beast, and attached to which he pastures:* (Ṣ, O:) *a rope with which the leg of such a beast is bound:* (Ḳ:) *a long rope thus used:* (TA:) or *with which one binds him, holding its extremity, and letting the beast pasture:* (Ḳ, TA:) or *of which one of the two ends is bound to a stake, and the other to the fore leg of a horse, in order that he may go round about bound thereby, and pasture, and not go away at random.* (TA.) An ex. of the first of these words occurs in a verse of Ṭarafeh cited voce ثِنْىٌ. (Ṣ, O.) And it is said in a trad. that when a man of an army alights in a place, he may debar others from the extent of the طِوَل of his horse. (TA.) — أَرْخَى لَهُ الطِّوَلَ [lit. meaning *He relaxed,* or *slackened, to him the tether*] means [also] ‡ *he left him to his own affair.* (A and TA in art. رخو.) — And one says, طَالَ طِوَلُكَ and ▼ طِيَلُكَ and ▼ طِيلُكَ and ▼ طُوَلُكَ and ▼ طُولُكَ and ▼ طِوَالُكَ and ▼ طِيَالُكَ (ISk, Ṣ, O, Ḳ) and ▼ طَوَلُكَ (Ḳ) meaning † *Thy life* [*has become long; or may thy life become long*]: (ISk, Ṣ, O, Ḳ: [see also طِيلَةٌ:]) or *thine absence:* (Ṣ, Ḳ:) or ‡ *thy tarrying,* (A, Ḳ, TA,) and *thy flagging in an affair.* (A, TA.) Ṭufeyl says,

أَتَانَا فَلَمْ نَدْفَعْهُ إِذْ جَآءَ طَارِقًا •
وَقُلْنَا لَهُ قَدْ طَالَ ▼ طُولُكَ فَانْزِلِ •

meaning [*He came to us, and we did not repel him since he came as a nightly visiter, and we said to him,*] *Thy case in respect of the length of the journey and the endurance of travel* [*has been long, therefore alight thou:* or the right reading may be ▼ طُولُكَ, which is better known]: or, as some relate it, ▼ طِيلُكَ. (TA.) [It is also said that] طِوَلٌ is a pl. [or rather a coll. gen. n.] of which the sing. [or n. un.] is ▼ طِوَلَةٌ; and in like manner, ▼ طِيَلٌ, of ▼ طِيَلَةٌ. (TA.)

طِيلٌ: see the next preceding paragraph, latter half, in two places. — [In the phrases طِيلُ يَوْمٍ and طِيلُ لَيْلَةٍ, it app. means *A tedious period,* or *length of time.*]

طِيَلٌ: see طِوَلٌ, in three places.

طَالَةٌ *A she-ass:* (O, Ḳ:) said to occur [as meaning *a wild she-ass*] in a poem of Dhu-r-Rummeh, who likens thereto his she-camel: but unknown to Az. (TA.)

طِيلَةٌ *Life; the period of life.* (Ḳ, TA.) One says, أَطَالَ ٱللّٰهُ طِيلَتَهُ [*God prolonged,* or *may God prolong, his life*]. (TA.) [See also طِوَلٌ.]

طِوَلَةٌ: } طِيَلَةٌ: } see طِوَلٌ, last sentence.

طُولَى [fem. of أَطْوَلُ: used as a subst.,] *A high,* or *an elevated, state* or *condition:* pl. طُوَلٌ. (Ḳ.)

طُوَّالَنِىٌّ: see طُوَّالٌ.

طِوَالٌ: } طِيَالٌ: } see طِوَلٌ, first sentence.

طَوَالٌ: see طُولٌ: — and see also طِوَلٌ.

طُوَالٌ: see طَوِيلٌ: — and see also طُوَّالٌ.

طِيَالٌ: see طِوَلٌ.

طَوِيلٌ *Elongated,* or *extended;* [i. e. *long;* and *tall,* or *high;*] (Ṣ, O, Mṣb, Ḳ;) as also ▼ طُوَالٌ; (Ṣ, O, Ḳ; but see طُوَّالٌ;) and ▼ مُسْتَطِيلٌ: and ▼ أَطْوَلُ is used in the sense of طَوِيلَةٌ, [being syn. sometimes with طَوِيلٌ and طَوِيلَةٌ,] in a verse of El-Farezdaḳ cited voce عَزِيزٌ: (O, TA:) [it seems, from a comparison of explanations of سُرْحُوبٌ and سَلْهَبٌ &c. in the Ṣ and Ḳ, that طَوِيلٌ applied to a horse or the like generally signifies *long-bodied:*] طَوِيلٌ is the only epithet, known to IJ, of the measure فَعِيلٌ having the ف and ل sound and having و for its ع, except صَوِيبٌ and قَوِيمٌ; for عَوِيصٌ is [held by him to be only] used as a subst.: (M in art. صوب:) the pl. (of طَوِيلٌ and طُوَالٌ, TA) is طِوَالٌ (Ṣ, O, Mṣb, Ḳ) and طِيَالٌ; (Ṣ, O, Ḳ;) the latter anomalous, and said by IJ to occur only in one verse: (TA:) the fem. is طَوِيلَةٌ (Mṣb, Ḳ) and طُوَالَةٌ; (Ḳ,* TA;) and the pl. of the former of these is طَوِيلَاتٌ. (Mṣb.) — They said, إِنَّ ٱللَّيْلَ طَوِيلٌ وَلَا يَطُلْ إِلَّا بِخَيْرٍ [*Verily the night is long, and may it not be long save with good fortune*]: mentioned by Lḥ, as expressing a prayer. (TA.) And قَصِيرَةٌ مِنْ طَوِيلَةٍ [*A short thing from a tall thing*]; meaning *a date from a palm-tree:* a prov., alluding to the abridging of speech, or language. (IAạr, Meyd, Ḳ.) See also 4. — ٱلطَّوِيلُ is also the name of *A certain kind of metre of verse;* (Ṣ, O, Ḳ;) [namely, *the first;*] *consisting of* فَعُولُنْ مَفَاعِيلُنْ *eight* [a mistake for *four*] *times:* (O, TA:) so called because it is the longest of all the metres of verse; originally comprising forty-eight letters: (TA:) a post-classical term. (Ṣ, O, Ḳ.)

طَوِيلَةٌ as a subst.: see طِوَلٌ.

طُوَّلٌ *A certain bird,* (Ṣ, O, Ḳ,) *of the aquatic kind, having long legs.* (O, Ḳ.)

طِيَلَةُ ٱلرِّيحِ *The wind's counterwind.* (Ṣ, O, Ḳ.)

طُوَّالٌ *Very,* or *exceedingly, tall;* (Ṣ, O, Ḳ, TA;) applied to a man; as also, in the same sense, ▼ طُوَالٌ, (TA,) the latter having a stronger signification than طَوِيلٌ, [with which it is mentioned above as syn.,] (TA voce رَكِيكٌ,) or it denotes less than طُوَّالٌ; (O in art. طرف;) and so ▼ طُوَّلَانِىٌّ and ▼ مُطَاوِلٌ, in the dial. of the vulgar: طُوَّالٌ has no broken pl., its pl. being only طُوَّالُونَ: its fem. is with ة, and so is that of طُوَالٌ; each applied to a woman. (TA.)

طَائِلٌ *Benefiting; bestowing,* or *conferring, a benefit* or *benefits,* or *a favour* or *favours.* (Mṣb.) — [Hence its usage in the following exs.] One says of that which is vile, or contemptible, (Mṣb, Ḳ, TA,) هُوَ غَيْرُ طَائِلٍ, (Mṣb,) or مَا هُوَ بِطَائِلٍ, (Ḳ, TA,) [*It is not good for anything; it is unprofitable, useless,* or *worthless*]; and in this manner it is used alike as masc. and fem. (TA.) And it is said in a trad., ضَرَبْتُهُ بِسَيْفٍ غَيْرِ طَائِلٍ, meaning *I smote him with a sword that was not sharp.* (TA.) And in another trad., كُفِّنَ فِى كَفَنٍ غَيْرِ طَائِلٍ i. e. [*He was shrouded in grave-clothing*] *not of delicate texture,* and *not of a goodly kind.* (TA.) — And [hence] it signifies [also] *Benefit, profit, utility,* or *avail;* and *excellence:* thus in the saying, هٰذَا أَمْرٌ لَا طَائِلَ فِيهِ [*This is an affair in which is no benefit,* &c.]: (Ṣ, O, TA:) and لَمْ يَحْلَ مِنْهُ بِطَائِلٍ [*He did not find* or *experience,* or *get* or *obtain, from it,* or *him, any benefit,* &c.]: it is only used in negative phrases [in this sense]: (Ṣ, O, Ḳ, TA:) and [thus] one says also, نَطَقَ بِمَا لَا طَائِلَ تَحْتَهُ [*He spoke that in which was no profit*]. (TA in art. بوق.) See also طَوْلٌ, second sentence.

طَائِلَةٌ: see طَوْلٌ, second sentence. — Also *Enmity:* and *blood-revenge:* (Ṣ, O, Ḳ, TA:) pl. طَوَائِلُ. (TA.) You say, فُلَانٌ يَطْلُبُ بَنِى فُلَانٍ بِطَائِلَةٍ i. e. *Such a one seeks to obtain of the sons of such a one blood-revenge.* (TA.) [See also an ex. in art. عقل, conj. 8.]

أَطْوَلُ *Exceeding,* or *surpassing, in* ٱلطُّول [i. e. *length,* and *tallness* or *height*]: (Ṣ, O, Mṣb,* Ḳ:) and also *in* ٱلطَّوْل [i. e. *beneficence,* and *excellence,* &c.]: (Ṣ, O, Ḳ:) fem. طُولَى: (Ṣ, O, Mṣb, Ḳ:) pl. of the former, applied to men, أَطَاوِلُ; (Ṣ, O;) and of the latter طُوَلٌ. (Ṣ, O, Mṣb, Ḳ.*) — ٱلسَّبْعُ ٱلطُّوَلُ, i. e. *The seven longer* chapters of the Ḳur-án, (O, TA,) are *the chapter of* ٱلْبَقَرَة *and the next five chapters of which the last is* ٱلْأَعْرَاف, *and one other, which is the chapter of* يُونُس, or ٱلْأَنْفَال *and* بَرَآءَة *together,* these being regarded as one chapter, (O, Ḳ, TA,) or, as some say, ٱلْكَهْف, and some say ٱلتَّوْبَة [which is the same as بَرَآءَة]; and some say [*the chapters vulgarly called*] *the* حَوَامِيم [which are *the fortieth and six following chapters*]: but the first of all these sayings is the right. (TA.) And طُولَى ٱلطُّولَيَيْنِ [*The longer of the two longer* chapters of the Ḳur-án], occurring in a trad. of Umm-Selemeh, was expl. by her as meaning *the chapter of* ٱلْأَعْرَاف: (O:) ٱلطُّولَيَانِ meaning ٱلْأَنْعَام *and* ٱلْأَعْرَاف. (TA.) أَسْرَعُكُنَّ لُحُوقًا بِى أَطْوَلُكُنَّ يَدًا, or, as some relate it لَحَاقًا, a saying of the Prophet to his wives, means [*The quickest of you in attaining to me is,* or *will be,*] *the most extensive of you in giving.* (O.) — See also طَوِيلٌ. — Also A camel *whose upper lip is long,* (Ṣ, O, Ḳ, TA,) *extending beyond the lower.* (TA.)

تِطْوَلٌ: see طَوْلٌ, first sentence.

مِطْوَلٌ The *penis.* (O, Ḳ.) — And *A halter;* syn. رَسَنٌ: (Ḳ:) pl. مَطَاوِلُ, signifying the *halters* (أَرْسَان) of horses. (O, Ḳ.)

مُطَاوِلٌ: see طُوَّالٌ. [And see also its verb.]

مَدًى مُتَطَاوِلٌ *A distant limit*, or *far-extending space.* (W p. 50.)

مُسْتَطَالٌ is used by Z and Bḍ as meaning *Reckoned long*, on the ground of analogy. (TA. [See its verb.])

مُسْتَطِيلٌ : see طَوِيلٌ. الفَجْرُ المُسْتَطِيلُ is *The first dawn*; also called *the false*; and termed ذَنَبُ السِّرْحَانِ [the *tail of the wolf*], because *it appears rising without extending laterally*: (Mṣb:) opposed to المُسْتَطِيرُ. (TA in art. طير.)

طوى

1. طَوَى الشَّىْءَ, (Ṣ, Mṣb,*) or الصَّحِيفَةَ, (Ḳ,) aor. يَطْوِى, (Mṣb, Ḳ,) inf. n. طَىٌّ, (Ṣ, Mṣb,) [*He folded, folded up*, or *folded together*, and *he rolled up, the thing*, such as a garment, or piece of cloth, or the like, or *the written piece of paper*:] طَوَى الصَّحِيفَةَ meaning *the contr. of* نَشَرَهَا. (TA.) And one says also, طَوَى الثَّوْبَ, inf. n. طِيَّةٌ, with kesr, and طِيَةٌ, like عِدَةٌ, this latter on the authority of Lḥ, and extr., [meaning *He folded, &c., the garment*, or *piece of cloth*:] and the phrase صَحِيفَةٌ جَافِيَةُ الطَّىِّ has been mentioned as meaning [i. e. *A written piece of paper thick*, or *rude, in respect of the folding, &c.*]. (TA.) [And طَوَيْتُ السِّقَآءَ عَلَى بُلُلَتِهِ, and بَلَلَتِهِ, or بَلَلِهِ, *I folded the skin while it was moist*: whence the phrases طَوَيْتُ فُلَانًا عَلَى بُلُلَتِهِ, and بَلَلَتِهِ, &c., and طَوَاهُ عَلَى بِلَالِهِ, and بُلُولِهِ, expl. voce بَلَلٌ; and a similar phrase in a verse cited voce ذَرِبَ, q. v.: see also a similar phrase in art. دمل, conj. 3: and see طَوًى.] — [Hence, طَوَى signifies also † *He*, or *it, made* a thing *compact*, as though folded; or *round*, like a scroll.] One says, طُوِىَ جِسْمُهُ طَيًّا حَتَّى ٱكْتَنَزَ لَحْمُهُ † [*His body was*, or *became, compacted*, or *rounded, so that his*, or *its, flesh was firm*, or *hard*]. (Lḥ, TA in art. دملج.) And سَاقٌ حَسَنَةُ الطَّىِّ † [*A shank goodly in respect of the compacture*, or *rounding; well compacted, well rounded*, or *well turned*]. (Ḳ in art. جدل, &c.) And [hence likewise,] طَوَاهُ means also † *It rendered him lean, lank, light of flesh, slender*, or *lank in the belly*. (L in art. مسد.) One says, طَوَاهُ السَّيْرُ † *Journeying*, or *travel, rendered him lean*, or *emaciated him*. (TA.) — طَوَى عُنُقَهُ وَنَامَ آمِنًا is said of a gazelle [as meaning *He folded*, or *bent, his neck, and slept free from fear*]. (TA.) — طَوَى كَشْحَهُ [lit. *He folded*, or *bent, his flank*,] means ‡ *he turned away his love*, or *affection*: (Ṣ, TA:) or, as in the M, ‡ *he withdrew his countenance*: and the following ex. is cited:

* وَصَاحِبٍ قَدْ طَوَى كَشْحًا فَقُلْتُ لَهُ *

* إِنَّ ٱنْطِوَآءَكَ ▾ هٰذَا عَنْكَ يَطْوِينِى *

‡ [*Many a companion has withdrawn countenance, and I have said to him, Verily this thy withdrawing withdraws me from thee*]: (TA:) or طَوَى كَشْحَهُ عَنِّى means ‡ *he turned away from me, forsaking*, or *abandoning*. (Ḳ, TA. [See also art. كشح.]) — And طَوَى كَشْحَهُ عَلَى أَمْرٍ ‡ *He concealed an affair*, or *a case*: (Ḳ, TA:) or, as in the M, † *he determined*, or *resolved, upon an affair*: (TA:) or, as in the L, and other lexicons, † *he persevered in an affair*. (TA in art. كشح.) — And طَوَى, [for طَوَى أَحْشَآءَهُ,] (Ṣ, Ḳ,) aor. يَطْوِى, inf. n. طَىٌّ, (Ṣ,) † *He suffered hunger intentionally*, or *purposely*. (Ṣ, Ḳ. [See also طَوِىَ.]) — And طَوَى عَنِّى الحَدِيثَ, (Ḳ,* TA,) and السِّرَّ, (TA,) ‡ *He concealed from me the story*, (Ḳ,* TA,) and *the secret*. (TA.) One says, ٱطْوِ هٰذَا الحَدِيثَ ‡ *Conceal thou this story*. (TA.) — And طَوَى حَدِيثًا إِلَى حَدِيثٍ † *He concealed in his mind a story and passed on from it to another story*; like as is said of the traveller in the sentence next following: and similar to this is the phrase طَىُّ الصَّوْمِ † [*the passing on from the fasting* to the next fasting]. (TA.) One says of the traveller, يَطْوِى مَنْزِلًا إِلَى مَنْزِلٍ فَلَا يَنْزِلُ † [*He passes on from one place of alighting to another so that he does not alight*]. (TA.) And طَوَى المَكَانَ إِلَى المَكَانِ † *He passed on from the place to the place*. (TA.) And طَوَى البِلَادَ, (Ḳ, TA,) inf. n. طَىٌّ, (TA,) ‡ *He traversed the countries*, (Ḳ, TA,) *country after country*. (TA.) — طَوَى القَوْمَ means † *He came to the people*, or *party*: or *he passed by them*: (IAạr, K, TA:) or *he sat by them*, or *at their place of abode*. (Ḳ, TA.) — طَوَى ٱللّٰهُ البُعْدَ لَنَا, accord. to the Ḳ, means ‡ *May God contract* (lit. *make near*) *the distance to us*: but accord. to the T, البَعِيدَ [i. e., *make near the remote*]. (TA.) — الطَّىُّ also denotes the passing away of life: [or rather the making life to pass away:] one says, طَوَى ٱللّٰهُ عُمْرَهُ † [*God made*, or *may God make, his life to pass away*]: and a poet says,

* طَوَتْكَ خُطُوبُ دَهْرِكَ بَعْدَ نَشْرٍ *

† [*Thy misfortunes have exanimated thee after vivifying*, or *reviving*]: طُوِىَ فُلَانٌ وَهُوَ مَنْشُورٌ ‡ [*Such a one has been exanimated but he is revived*] is said of a person when [he has died and] a good reputation of him remains, or a good memorial. (TA.) [It is also implied in the TA that, in accordance with this usage of the verb, طَوَاهُ may be rendered † *He caused it to pass away*, or *come to nought* or *to an end; destroyed it*; or *annihilated it*: (see the pass. part. n.:) and, accord. to Bḍ, يَوْمَ نَطْوِى ٱلسَّمَآءَ, in the Ḳur xxi. 104, may mean *On the day when we shall efface the heaven*: but this phrase is better rendered *on the day when we shall fold*, or *roll up, the heaven*.] — One says also, طَوَى الغَزْلَ عَلَى المِطْوَى [*He wound the spun thread upon the winder*]. (TA.) — And طَوَى الرَّكِيَّةَ, (TA,) or البِئْرَ, (Mṣb,) inf. n. طَىٌّ, *He cased the well with stones, and with baked bricks*: and in like manner, طَوَى اللَّبِنَ فِى البِنَآءِ [*He cased the bricks*, or *crude bricks, in the building*]. (TA.) — طَوِىَ السِّقَآءُ, [aor. يَطْوَى,] inf. n. طَوًى, *The skin was folded having in it moisture*, or *some remains of milk, in consequence of which it became altered, and stinking, and dissundered by putrefaction*. (TA. [See also the third sentence of this paragraph.]) — And طَوِىَ, aor. يَطْوَى, inf. n. طَوًى (Ṣ, Ḳ) and طَوَآءٌ also, on the authority of Sb, (TA,) † *He was hungry*; (Ṣ, Ḳ;*) as also ▾ أَطْوَى. (Ḳ. [See also طَوَى, above.]) — And طَوِيَتْ طِيَّتُهُ *The place to which*, or *towards which, he would repair*, or *betake himself, was*, or *became, remote*. (Lḥ, TA.)

2. طَوَّيْتُهُ [*I folded it with several*, or *many, foldings*; or *wound it*, or *coiled it*: see the quasi-pass., تطوّى]. TA.)

4: see 1, last sentence but one.

5. تطوّى [*It became folded with several*, or *many, foldings*; or *wound*, or *coiled*;] quasi-pass. of 2. (TA.) You say, تَطَوَّتِ الحَيَّةُ *The serpent wound*, or *coiled, itself*. (Ṣ, TA.) And Sb mentions the phrase تَطَوَّى ▾ ٱنْطِوَآءً; citing, as an ex.,

* وَقَدْ تَطَوَّيْتُ ٱنْطِوَآءَ الحِضْبِ *

[*And I had writhed with the winding of the* حضب], meaning [by this last word] a species of serpent, or the bow-string. (TA.)

6. [This verb, said of several agents, (i. e., app. تَطَاوَوْا said of several persons, or تَطَاوَتْ said of several things,) accord. to Freytag on the authority of the Deewán of the Hudhalees signifies *They mutually folded together*.]

7. انطوى [*It was*, or *became, folded, folded up*, or *folded together*, and *rolled up*,] quasi-pass. of طَوَى (Ṣ, Ḳ, TA) as signifying the contr. of نَشَرَ; (TA;) as also ▾ اِطَّوَى, (Ḳ, TA,) of the measure اِفْتَعَلَ, mentioned by Az and ISd. (TA.) See also 5. — [Hence,] انطوى بَطْنُهُ † [*His belly became lean*, or *lank*]; said of a camel, and of a sheep or goat. (JK voce اِرْتَقَى.) And ٱنْطِوَآءُ الحَشَا † [*The state of being lean*, or *lank, in the belly*]. (Ṣ and TA voce أَخْطَفُ, q. v.) — See also a verse cited in the first paragraph. — [Hence also,] انطوى عَلَى الحِقْدِ, and الوُدِّ, † *He conceived* [*as though he infolded*] *in the heart rancour, malevolence, malice*, or *spite*, and *love*, or *affection*. (MA.) And انطوى قَلْبُهُ عَلَى غِلٍّ † [*His heart conceived, as though it infolded, rancour, malevolence, malice*, or *spite*]. (TA.)

8. see the next preceding paragraph.

طَوٌ : see طَوًى.

طَىٌّ [originally an inf. n., of طَوَى, q. v.,] and ▾ طِىً and ▾ طِوًى, [said in one place in the TA to be like إِلًى, but I think that this is only said to show that its first vowel is kesr and the second fet-ḥ, and that it is correctly طِوًى, for there is no reason for its being imperfectly decl.,] accord. to the M, are sings. of أَطْوَآء, which it explains as signifying The *lines*, or *streaks*, and *creases*, *of the folding* of a garment, or piece of cloth, and of a written piece of paper, and of the belly, and of fat, and of the guts, and of a serpent, and of other things; and it is said in the T and Ḳ that ▼ مَطَاوٍ, of which the sing. is ▼ مَطْوًى, signifies the أَطْوَآء of the serpent, and of the guts, and of fat, and of the belly, and of a garment, or piece of cloth: (TA:) one says, مَا بَقِيَتْ فِى مَطَاوِى ▼ أَمْعَائِهَا ثُمِيلَةٌ [*There remained not in the creases of her*, or *their, guts any relic of food*]: (A, TA:) and ▼ مَطَاوِى الدِّرْعِ signifies *the creases of the coat of mail when it is drawn together*, or *contracted*. (TA.) [Hence,] one says, عَلَى جَبِينِهَا أَطْوَآءُ النُّجُومِ, i. e. طَرَائِقُهُ [app. meaning *Upon her forehead* (for so جَبِين sometimes signifies) *are the wrinkles indicative of the time for the payment of the debt of nature*]. (TA.) The أَطْوَآء in the she-camel are The طَرَائِق [i. e. *lines*, or *streaks*, or perhaps *creases*, or *wrinkles*,] *of the fat* (Ṣ, Ḳ, TA) *of the hump*: (Ḳ, TA:) [or the *creases*, or *wrinkles*, *one above another*, *of the side* and *of the hump*; for] Lth says, طَرَائِقُ جَنْبِهَا وَسَنَامِهَا طَىٌّ فَوْقَ طَىٍّ [*the creases*, or *wrinkles*, *of her side and of her hump are*, or *consist of*, طَىّ *above* طَىّ]. (TA.) And AḤn says that أَطْوَآء signifies The *bending* [or rather he should have said, or perhaps he did say, the *places of bending*] *in the tail of the locust*, [*which are*] *like* عُقَد [or *articulations*]: and the pl. [of mult.] is ▼ طُوِىّ [said to be like إِلَى, but I think that it is correctly طُوِىّ, as I have observed above]. (TA.) — One says also, وَجَدْتُ فِى طَىِّ الكِتَابِ كَذَا [lit. *I found within the folding of the writing*, or *letter, such a thing*; meaning, *infolded*, or *enclosed*, or *included*, *in it*; or *among the contents*, or *implications*, *of it*]: and فِى أَطْوَآءِ الكُتُبِ and ▼ مَطَاوِيهَا [lit. *within the folds*, or *places of folding*, *of the writings*, or *letters*]. (A, TA.) And الغِلُّ فِى طَىِّ قَلْبِهِ ‡ [*Rancour, malevolence, malice*, or *spite, is conceived, as though it were infolded, in his heart*]. (TA. [See 7.]) And أَدْرَجَنِى فِى طَىِّ النِّسْيَانِ ‡ [*He*, or *it, infolded me within the folding of oblivion*]. (TA.) — See also طَوًى. — And see طُوًى. — [Also *A casing of stones* or *of baked bricks*; and particularly such a casing of a well; an inf. n. used as a subst. properly so called; and often occurring in the lexicons &c. in this sense.]

طِىٌّ: see the next preceding paragraph, first sentence.

طَيَّةٌ [inf. n. of un. of طَوَى]. You say, طَوَاهُ طَيَّةً وَاحِدَةً [*He folded it*, &c., *with one folding* &c.]. (TA.)

طِيَّةٌ, (Ṣ, TA,) from طَوَيْتُ الشَّىْءَ, (Ṣ,) is like جِلْسَةٌ (Ṣ, TA) and رِكْبَةٌ (Ṣ) and مِشْيَةٌ, signifying *A mode*, or *manner*, *of folding* &c.; and *a mode*, or *manner*, *of being folded* &c. (TA.) One says, إِنَّهُ لَحَسَنُ الطِّيَّةِ [*Verily he is good in respect of the mode*, or *manner*, *of folding*, &c.]. (Ḳ, TA.) And طَوَاهُ طِيَّةً جَيِّدَةً [*He folded it*, &c., *in a good mode*, or *manner*, *of doing so*]. (TA.) And hence the saying of Dhu-r-Rummeh,

كَمَا تُنْشَرُ بَعْدَ الطِّيَّةِ الكُتُبُ

[*Like as the writings*, or *letters*, *are unfolded after the folding in a particular manner*]: (Ṣ, TA:) he said طِيَّة, with kesr, because he did not mean a single time [of folding]. (TA.) — [See also 1, second sentence, where it is mentioned as a simple inf. n., and sometimes pronounced طِيَة, without teshdeed.] — Also *i. q.* نِيَّةٌ; (Ṣ, Ḳ;) and so ▼ طَوِيَّةٌ; (Ḳ;) and [agreeably with this explanation] Kh says that it may mean *A place of alighting* or *abode* [*to which one purposes repairing*, or *betaking himself*], and it may mean *an object of aim* or *purpose* or *intention* [*whatever it be*]: (Ṣ:) and in the A it is expl. as meaning the *direction towards which countries are traversed*: (TA:) one says طِيَّةٌ بَعِيدَةٌ i. e. [*A place of alighting* or *abode* &c.] *that is distant*, or *remote*: and بَعُدَتْ عَنَّا طِيَّتُهُ i. e. *The place of alighting*, or *of abode*, *to which he purposed repairing* [*was distant*, or *remote*]: and مَضَى لِطِيَّتِهِ i. e. [*He went*] *to his* نِيَّة [meaning either *place of alighting* &c. or *object of aim* &c.] *that he purposed*: (Ṣ:) and لَقِيتُهُ بِطِيَّاتِ العِرَاقِ i. e. [*I met him in*] *the regions*, or *quarters*, or *directions*, *of El-'Irák*: and sometimes it is pronounced طِيَة, without teshdeed. (TA.) — Also *An object of want* or *need*. (TA.) [Therefore مَضَى لِطِيَّتِهِ may be rendered *He went to accomplish his object of want or need*.] — آخِرُ طِيَّةٍ is *syn. with* آخِرُ مَخْطَرٍ [expl. voce خَطْرَةٌ, q. v.]. (TA in art. خطر.)

طَوِىٌّ *A skin for water* or *milk*; syn. سِقَآءٌ; (Ḳ;) as also ▼ طَوًى: or the former signifies *a skin* (سِقَآء) *that has been folded having in it its moisture, and has consequently become dissundered*; app. an inf. n. [of طَوِىَ] used as a subst. [properly so called]: and ▼ سِقَآءٌ طَوٍ signifies [the same, or] *a skin that has been folded having in it moisture, or some remains of milk, in consequence of which it has become altered, and stinking, and dissundered by putrefaction*. (TA.) — Also *Hunger*; (Ṣ;) [and] so ▼ طَوٌ [if not a mistranscription]. (TA. [See طَوًى, of which the former is an inf. n., as also طَوًى.])

طُوًى is said by some to be like ▼ طَوًى, meaning *A thing twice done* [as though folded]; and to be thus in the Ḳur [xx. 12 and lxxix. 16]; meaning *twice* sanctified [referring to the valley there mentioned]; (Ṣ, TA; [and thus expl., and said to be like ثِنًى, in the Ksh and by Bḍ;]) or, as El-Ḥasan says, *twice* blest and sanctified: (Ṣ, TA:) or meaning *twice* called [referring to the calling of Moses mentioned in the context]. (Ksh and Bḍ in xx. 12, and in like manner says Er-Rághib.) [But طُوًى (as most pronounce it) or طِوًى, in the Ḳur, is generally held to be the name of a certain valley. Golius explains طُوًى and طِوًى as meaning "Plicata, plicabilis, res;" which is a mistake: and he adds, "Ambulatio, incessus reciprocatus, ultro citroque in se rediens:" for the latter of these explanations, both of which he gives as on the authority of J and the Ḳ, I am quite unable to account.]

طِوًى: see the next preceding paragraph: — and see also طِىٌّ, in two places.

طَوِى البَطْنِ A man *lean*, or *lank*, *in the belly*; (Ṣ, TA; [in the Ḥam, p. 708, erroneously written طَوَى البَطْنِ, and there expl. as meaning *naturally small in the belly*;]) as also ▼ مُنْطَوٍ [or rather مُنْطَوِى البَطْنِ]; (TA;) and so ▼ طَيَّانُ. (Ḥam p. 495.) — And [hence], (Ḳ, TA,) as also ▼ طَاوٍ, and ▼ طَيَّانُ, (Ṣ, Ḳ, TA,) † *Hungry*: (Ṣ, TA:) or *having eaten nothing*: fem. [of the second] طَاوِيَةٌ (Ḳ) and [of the third] طَيَّا or طَيَّآءُ [like خَزْيَا and خَزْيَآءُ pls. of خَزْيَانُ]. (Ḳ accord. to different copies.) — See also طَوًى.

طَوِىٌّ *A bundle of* بَزّ [meaning *cloths* or *stuffs* or *garments*, or *a kind*, or *kinds, thereof*: so called as being folded together]: thus in the Tekmileh [and in copies of the Ḳ]: in [some of] the copies of the Ḳ, مِنَ البُرِّ in the place of مِنَ البَزِّ. (TA.) — And *A well that is cased* (Ṣ, M, Mṣb,* TA) *with stones*, or *with baked bricks*; as also ▼ طِىٌّ: (TA:) of the measure فَعِيلٌ in the sense of the measure مَفْعُولٌ: (Mṣb:) it is masc., but may be made fem. to accord. with the meaning [i. e. بِئْرٌ]: (M, TA:) pl. أَطْوَآءٌ: accord. to the Ḳ, ▼ طَوِيَّةٌ signifies *a well*; but [SM says] I have not seen that any one has mentioned this. (TA.) — And *A* سَاعَة [meaning *short portion*] of the night: (Ḳ:) one says, أَتَيْتُهُ بَعْدَ طَوِىٍّ مِنَ اللَّيْلِ [*I came to him after a short portion of the night*]: mentioned by ISd. (TA.)

طَوِيَّةٌ † The ضَمِير [meaning *heart*, or *mind*]: (Ṣ, Ḳ, TA:) so called because it is [as though it were] folded upon the secret, or because the secret is [as though it were] infolded in it. (TA.) — See also طِيَّةٌ. — And see طَوِىٌّ.

مَا بِالدَّارِ طُوِىٌّ [like دُوِىٌّ or دُوُوِىٌّ, if not a mistranscription for طُورِىٌّ,] means [*There is not in the house*] *any one*. (TA.)

طَيَّانُ: see the paragraph commencing with طَوِى البَطْنِ, in two places. [طَيَّانٌ, perfectly decl., belongs to art. طين, q. v.]

طَايَةٌ: see art. طى.

طَايَةٌ *A* سَطْح [or *flat top* or *roof* of a house] (Az, Ṣ, Ḳ) *upon which one sleeps*. (Az, TA.) — And *A place in which dates are put to dry in the sun*. (Ṣ, Ḳ.) — And *A great rock in land containing sand,* (Ḳ, TA,) or *in which are no stones:* mentioned by ISd. (TA.) ═ جَآءَتِ الإِبِلُ طَاوَايَاتٍ means [*The camels came*] *in herds;* syn. قُطْعَانًا: the sing. is طَايَةٌ. (TA.)

طَاوٍ A gazelle *that bends,* [or *is bending,*] or *has bent, his neck, on the occasion of lying down, and then lies down,* or *has* [*lain down and*] *slept free from fear.* (TA.) — And طَاوِى الكَشْحِ *Rendered lean* or *lank; not large in the sides.* (Ḥam p. 495.) — See also the paragraph commencing with طَوِى البَطْنِ.

شِعْرٌ طَاوِىٌّ *Verses of which the* [*fundamental*] *rhyme-letter is* ط: [but] Kh says that its ا is originally ى. (TA.)

مَطْوًى; and its pl. مَطَاوٍ, and as a prefixed n. مَطَاوِى: see طَىٌّ, in five places. مَطْوًى may be used as an inf. n., meaning The *folding* of a garment, or piece of cloth: and as meaning the *place of folding* thereof: and signifies also the *inside* thereof. (Ḥar p. 160.)

مِطْوًى [*A winder for thread;*] *a thing upon which spun thread is wound.* (TA.) — And, as a word used by the vulgar, [but by them generally pronounced مَطْوَى, with fet-ḥ, and without tenween,] *A small* [*clasp-*] *knife.* (TA.)

مَطْوِىٌّ [*Folded, folded up,* or *folded together,* and *rolled up:* see 1, first sentence. — And hence, † *Made compact,* as though folded; and *round,* like a scroll]. You say اِمْرَأَةٌ مَطْوِيَّةٌ الخَلْقِ (Ṣ and Ḳ in art. مكر) [meaning, accord. to the PṢ in that art., † *A plump woman;* and the same seems to be indicated by what immediately follows it in the Ṣ itself: but it is more correctly rendered † *a woman compacted,* or *rounded, in make:* see طَوِىُّ جِسْمُهُ. It may, however, signify also † *A woman lean, lank,* or *slender, in make;* lit., *rendered lean,* &c.: see طَوَاهُ]. — بِئْرٌ مَطْوِيَّةٌ (Ṣ, TA) *A well cased* with stones [or with baked bricks]. (TA.) — وَالسَّمٰوَاتُ مَطْوِيَّاتٌ بِيَمِينِهِ, in the Ḳur [xxxix. 67, generally understood to mean *And the heavens* shall be *folded together,* or *rolled up, by his right hand*], has been expl. as meaning [that they shall be] *destroyed:* so says Er-Rághib. (TA.)

مُنْطَوِى البَطْنِ, or مُنْطَوٍ: see the paragraph commencing with طَوِى البَطْنِ.

طى

2. طَيَّيْتُ طَآءً *I wrote a* ط. (TA.)

طَآءٌ, also pronounced طَا, *One of the letters of the alphabet* [i. e. *the letter* ط]: masc. and fem.: Kh says that its ا is originally ى. (TA.) [See art. ط.] ═ It is also an epithet applied to a man, meaning *Multum coiens.* (KL, TA.)

طَىٌّ: and طِىٌّ: and طَيَّةٌ: and طِيَّةٌ (also pronounced طِيَةٌ): and طَيَّانُ, fem. طَيَّا or طَيَّآءُ: see in art. طوى.

طيب

1. طَابَ, aor. يَطِيبُ, (Ṣ, Mṣb, Ḳ, &c.,) inf. n. طِيبٌ (Ṣ [but there mentioned app. as a subst.], O, Mgh, Mṣb, Ḳ) and طِيبَةٌ (Ṣ, O, Ḳ) and طَابٌ (Ḳ) and طُوبَى [q. v. infrà] (Ksh and Bḍ in xiii. 28) and تَطْيَابٌ, (Ṣ, Ḳ,) [the last of which is of a measure denoting intensiveness, and is said in the TA to be with fet-ḥ because it is unsound, whereas the inf. n. of a sound verb, if of the measure تفعال, is with kesr, but this is a strange mistake, (see 2 in art. بين,)] *It was,* or *became, the contr. of* خَبُثَ, (Ṣ, Mgh,) *in two senses:* (Mgh:) [i. e.] *it was,* or *became,* [*good,*] *pleasant, delightful, delicious, sweet,* or *savoury;* syn. لَذَّ; (A, Ḳ;) or كَانَ لَذِيذًا; (Mṣb;) or *it was esteemed* [*good,*] *pleasant, delightful, delicious, sweet,* or *savoury, in taste,* and *in odour:* (Mgh:) and *it was,* or *became, pure,* (Mgh, Ḳ,) or *clean.* (Mgh.) [See also طَيِّبٌ.] — [Hence,] طَابَتْ نَفْسُهُ † *His mind* [or *he* himself] *was,* or *became,* [*cheerful, happy, pleased,*] *dilated,* or *free from straitness.* (Mṣb.) And طِبْتُ بِهِ نَفْسًا *i. q.* طَابَتْ بِهِ نَفْسِى † [i. e. *I,* or *my mind, was,* or *became, cheerful, happy, pleased,* or *dilated, by means of it;* agreeably with what next precedes: or *pleased, content,* or *willing, to grant, concede, give,* or *do, it*]: (Ṣ, O, Ḳ:) [for] طَابَتْ نَفْسُهُ بِالشَّىْءِ [often] signifies ‡ *He granted, conceded,* or *gave, the thing, liberally,* [*willingly,* or *of his own good pleasure,*] *without constraint,* and *without anger.* (TA.) And فَعَلْتُ ذٰلِكَ بِطِيبَةِ نَفْسٍ † *I did that* [*of my own free will; willingly;*] *not being constrained by any one.* (Ṣ, O.) And طَابَتْ نَفْسِى عَلَيْهِ † [*My mind was agreeable to it*]; said when a thing is agreeable, or suitable, to one's mind; and [in like manner] طِبْتُ نَفْسًا عَلَيْهِ. (TA.) And طَابَتْ نَفْسُهُ لِلْعَمَلِ وَغَيْرِهِ [*He was cheerful, happy, pleased,* or *willing, to do work &c.*]. (Ḳ in art. نشط.) And طَابَتْ نَفْسِى عَنْ ذٰلِكَ تَرْكًا † [*I was pleased, willing,* or *content, to leave, give up, relinquish,* or *be without, that*]; and [in like manner] طِبْتُ نَفْسًا عَنْهُ: whence, in the Ḳur [iv. 3], فَإِنْ طِبْنَ لَكُمْ عَنْ شَىْءٍ مِنْهُ نَفْسًا † [*But if they be pleased,* or *willing,* or *content, to give up,* or *relinquish,* or *remit, unto you somewhat thereof*]. (TA.) — And طَابَ, (A, O, Mṣb, TA,) inf. n. طِيبٌ (Mṣb, Ḳ) and طِيبَةٌ, (Ḳ,) ‡ *It was,* or *became, lawful, allowable,* or *free.* (A, O, Mṣb, Ḳ,* TA.) [In the Ḳ, الطِّيبُ and الطِّيبَةُ are expl. as meaning الحِلُّ, which Golius has supposed to mean in this case "quod licitum, legitimum;" and which Freytag has in like manner expl. as meaning "res licita," and "licitum:" but it is here an inf. n., of حَلَّ; not syn. with the epithet الحَلَالُ, which is given as an explanation of الطَّيِّبُ.] You say, طَابَ لِى كَذَا ‡ *Such a thing became,* or *has become, lawful,* &c., *to me.* (A.) Hence the saying of Aboo-Hureyreh, اَلْآنَ طَابَ الضِّرَابُ, (TA,) or طَابَ آمْضَرْبُ, (O, TA,) as some relate it, accord. to the dial. of Ḥimyer, (TA,) meaning طاب الضَّرْبُ, i. e. † *Now fighting has become lawful.* (O, TA.) فَانْكِحُوا مَا طَابَ لَكُمْ مِنَ النِّسَآءِ, in the Ḳur [iv. 3], means † [*Then take ye in marriage*] *such as are lawful to you* [*of women*]. (Mgh.) — And طَابَتِ الأَرْضُ, (Ḳ, TA,) inf. n. طِيبٌ, (TA,) † *The land became abundant in herbage.* (Ḳ, TA.) ═ See also 2, in two places: — and see 10.

2. طَيَّبَهُ, (Ṣ, M, A, MA, O, Mṣb, Ḳ,) inf. n. تَطْيِيبٌ; (KL;) and ↓ اطابهُ; (Ṣ, O, Ḳ;) and ↓ طَابَهُ; (IAạr, M, Ḳ;) *He,* or *it, made it,* or *rendered it, good, pleasant, delightful, delicious, sweet,* or *savoury: perfumed,* or *rendered fragrant, him,* or *it:* (Ṣ, MA, O,* Ḳ,* KL:) [and *made it* or *rendered it, pure,* or *clean:* (see 1, first sentence:)] you say, طَيَّبَ جُلَسَآءَهُ *He perfumed his companions with whom he was sitting:* (A:) and طَيَّبَ الثَّوْبَ and ↓ طَابَهُ [*He perfumed the garment*]: (IAạr, M, TA:) or طَيَّبْتُهُ *I daubed,* or *smeared, him,* or *it, with perfume,* or *some odoriferous* or *fragrant substance:* (Mṣb:) and طَيَّبَهُ بِالطِّيبِ [*He perfumed him,* or *daubed him,* or *smeared him, with some odoriferous* or *fragrant substance*]. (TA.) — [Hence,] طَيَّبَ بِنَفْسِهِ [and طَيَّبَ نَفْسَهُ, which latter is a phrase of frequent occurrence, † *He placated,* or *soothed, his mind;*] *he spoke to him pleasantly, sweetly,* or *blandly.* (TA.) And طَيَّبْتَ نَفْسِى عَنْكَ † [*Thou hast made me to be pleased,* or *happy,* or *content, without thee*]. (Ṣ in art. سلو.) — And طَيَّبَهُ † *He made it lawful, allowable,* or *free.* (TA, from a trad.) [Hence,] طَيَّبَ لِغَرِيمِهِ نِصْفَ المَالِ ‡ *He acquitted his debtor of the half of the property; gave up, resigned,* or *remitted, it to him.* (A.) — See also 10.

3. طَايَبَهُ, (Ṣ, O, Ḳ,) inf. n. مُطَايَبَةٌ, (KL,) *He jested,* or *joked, with him;* (Ṣ, O, Ḳ;) *indulged in pleasantry with him.* (KL.)

4: see 2: — and see also 10, in four places. ═ اطاب signifies also *He brought, brought forward, offered,* or *proffered, good, pleasant, delicious,* or *savoury, food.* (O, Ḳ.) — † *He spoke good, pleasant,* or *sweet, words.* (O, Ḳ.) — † *He begat good children.* (Ḳ.) — And † *He wedded lawfully.* (O, Ḳ.) ═ مَا أَطْيَبَهُ, and مَا أَيْطَبَهُ, the latter formed by transposition, (Ṣ, TA,) or a dial. var. of the former, (TA in art. يطب,) and أَطْيِبْ بِهِ, and أَيْطِبْ بِهِ, are all allowable [as meaning *How good, pleasant, delightful, delicious,* or *sweet, is he,* or *it!* or *how pure,* or *clean,* &c.!]. (TA.) — And one says, مَا أَطْيَبَ نَفْسَهُ عَنْكَ ‡ [*How pleased,* or *happy,* or *content is he to be without thee,* or *to give thee up,* or *to relinquish thee!*]. (IAạr, Ḳ in art. سفط.)

5. تطيّب [quasi-pass. of 2, as such signifying *It became,* or *was made* or *rendered, good,*

pleasant, &c.: and] *he perfumed himself*, or *made himself fragrant*, (A, Mṣb, TA,) بِالطِّيبِ [*with perfume*], (Mṣb,) or بِالشَّىْءِ [*with the thing*]. (TA.)

10. استطابهُ, (Ṣ, Ḳ,) and اِسْتَطْيَبَهُ, (Sb, Mṣb, Ḳ,) and ▼ اطابهُ, (TA,) and ▼ أَطْيَبَهُ, and ▼ طيّبهُ, (Ḳ,) and ▼ طَابَهُ, (TA, [but this last I think doubtful,]) *He found it*, (Ṣ, Ḳ,) or *saw it*, (Mṣb,) *to be* طَيِّب [i. e. *good, pleasant*, &c.]. (Ṣ, Mṣb, Ḳ.) One says, استطاب فُلَانٌ الدِّيمَةَ [*Such a one found*, or *saw, to be good*, or *pleasant, the lasting and still rain*]. (A.) — And استطاب, (Ṣ, A, O, Mṣb, Ḳ,) or استطاب نَفْسَهُ, (TA,) and ▼ اطاب, (A, O, Ḳ,) or ▼ اطاب نَفْسَهُ, (TA,) i. q. اِسْتَنْجَى [i. e. *He washed*, or *wiped with a stone*, or *a piece of dry clay, the place of exit of his excrement*]. (Ṣ, A, O, Mṣb, Ḳ.) [This signification is said in the TA to be tropical; but it is not so accord. to the A.] — And استطاب *He shaved his pubes*. (O, Ḳ, TA.) — And *He asked* people *for sweet water*. (Ḳ.) Thus, accord. to IAạr, the saying [of a poet]

فَلَمَّا ٱسْتَطَابُوا صُبَّ فِى ٱلصَّحْنِ نِصْفُهُ

means *And when they asked for sweet water* [*the half of it was poured forth into the bowl*]: but it is also expl. agreeably with what here follows. (TA.) — *He* (a man) *drank* طَابَة [i. e. *wine*]: so in the M. (TA.)

طَابٌ is an inf. n. of طَابَ, (Ḳ,) and *syn. with* طِيبٌ and also *with* طَيِّبٌ, q. v.: a poet says, praising 'Omar Ibn-'Abd-El-'Azeez,

مُقَابَلُ ٱلْأَعْرَاقِ فِى ٱلطَّابِ ٱلطَّابْ
بَيْنَ أَبِى ٱلْعَاصِى وَآلِ ٱلْخَطَّابْ

[i. e. *Rooted by the father's and the mother's side in unsullied goodness*, or the like, *between Abu-l-'Áṣee* on the one side *and the family of El-Khaṭṭáb* on the other: for it is evidently cited as an ex. of الطاب used as a subst. and as an epithet; so that by فى الطاب الطاب is meant فى الطَّيِّبِ الطَّيِّبِ: otherwise it might be supposed that the literal repetition is meant to denote simply corroboration, as appears to be the case in an instance which will be mentioned in what follows:] the object of praise being the son of 'Abd-El-'Azeez the son of Marwán the son of El-Ḥakam the son of Abu-l-'Áṣ [or 'Áṣee], and his mother being Umm-'Áṣim the daughter of 'Áṣim the son of 'Omar the son of El-Khaṭṭáb. (Ṣ, O.) — عَذْقُ ٱبْنِ طَابٍ is the name of *A sort of palm-trees in El-Medeeneh* [app. so called because of the sweetness of their fruit, or طاب may in this instance be for طَابَة, a name of El-Medeeneh]: (Ḳ:) or, as also رُطَبُ ٱبْنِ طَابٍ, *a sort of dates of El-Medeeneh*: (Ṣ, O:) or ٱبْنُ طَابٍ is a name of *a sort of fresh ripe dates*: (Ḳ:) and عَذْقُ ٱبْنِ زَيْدٍ and عَذْقُ ٱبْنِ طَابٍ are *two sorts of dates*: (Ṣ:) accord. to IAth, رُطَبُ ٱبْنِ طَابٍ is the name of *a sort of dates of El-Medeeneh* so called in relation to Ibn-Ṭáb, a man of its inhabitants. (TA.) — طَابْ طَابْ is [asserted to be] *One of the names of the Prophet in the Gospel*; [but where said to occur, I know not;] the interpretation of مَأذْ مَأذْ; [app. a mistranscription for مَاذْ مَاذْ, meaning "very good in disposition," &c.;] the second word corroborating, and denoting intensiveness of signification. (TA.)

طُوبٌ, mentioned in this art. in the Ṣ and Ḳ, [as though it were originally طُيْبٌ,] see in art. طوب.

طِيبٌ an inf. n. of طَابَ. (O, Mgh,* Mṣb, Ḳ.) [Used as a simple subst., *Goodness, pleasantness*, &c.] You say, مَا بِهِ مِنَ ٱلطِّيبِ [*There is not in him aught of goodness*, &c.]: you should not say, مِنَ ٱلطِّيبَةِ. (Ṣ, O.) [See also طَابٌ: and طُوبَى.] — [Also] a word of well-known meaning; (Ḳ;) [*A perfume; a fragrant*, or *an odoriferous, substance*;] *a substance with which one perfumes himself*, (Ṣ, O, Mṣb,) *of what is termed* عِطْر. (Mṣb.) [The pl. accord. to Golius and Freytag is أَطْيَاب.] Hence, جَوْزُ ٱلطِّيبِ *The nutmeg*: see جوز. — Also The *most excellent* of any sort of thing. (Ḳ.) [See also أَطْيَبُ: and طَيِّبَة.]

طَابَةٌ *Wine*: (Ṣ, O, Ḳ:) as though meaning طَيِّبَة; and originally طَيِّبَة: (AM, TA:) or i. q. عَصِير [i. e. *expressed juice*]. (TA, from an explanation of a trad.) — طَابَةُ: see what next follows.

طَيْبَةُ a name of *The city of the Prophet*; (Ṣ, O, Mṣb, Ḳ;) as also ▼ طَابَةُ, (O, Mṣb, Ḳ,) and ▼ ٱلطَّيِّبَةُ, and ▼ ٱلْمُطَيَّبَةُ, (Ḳ,) which last may be also written ▼ ٱلْمُطَيِّبَةُ. (TA.)

طِيبَةٌ an inf. n. of طَابَ. (Ṣ, O, Ḳ.) — Also The *clearest* of wine: (Ḳ:) and the *choicest* of herbage. (TA.) — طِيبَةُ is a name of *The well Zemzem*. (O, Ḳ.)

سَبْىُ طِيَبَةٍ ‡ *Persons* (Aṣ, TA) *made captive lawfully*, (Aṣ, Ṣ,* A, O,* Ḳ,* TA,) *without perfidy and breach of covenant*, (Ṣ, A, O, Ḳ,) *not made so when a covenant is existing with them*, (Aṣ, TA,) *nor when there is any doubt respecting their state of slavery*: (O:) طِيَبَةٌ, in the sense of طَيِّبٌ, is [said to be] the only instance among nouns, (TA,) or rather among epithets, (MF, TA,) of فِعَلَةٌ, with kesr and then fet-ḥ, (TA,) i. e. with only fet-ḥ to the ع. (MF, TA.)

طُوبَى, of the measure فُعْلَى from ٱلطِّيبُ, originally طُيْبَى, (Zj, Ṣ, O, Mṣb,) an inf. n. of طَابَ, (Ksh and Bḍ in xiii. 28,) *syn.* with طِيبٌ: (Seer, Ḳ: [in my MS copy of the Ḳ طَيِّب, a manifest mistake:]) and fem. of أَطْيَبُ: (ISd, Ḳ:) and pl. of طَيِّبَة, (Ḳ,) accord. to Kr, who says that there is no word like it except كُوسَى pl. of كَيِّسَة, and ضُوقَى pl. of ضَيِّقَة; but ISd says that, in his opinion, طُوبَى and كُوسَى and ضُوقَى are fems. of أَطْيَبُ and أَكْيَسُ and أَضْيَقُ, because فُعْلَى is not a pl. measure: Kr also adds that they did not say ▼ طِيبَى, like as they said كِيسَى and ضِيقَى; (TA; [see ضُوقَى, in art. ضيق;]) [but Ṣgh says that] ▼ طِيبَى is a dial. var. of طُوبَى: (O:) Aboo-Ḥátim Sahl Ibn-Moḥammad Es-Sijistánee relates that an Arab of the desert, reciting as a pupil to him, persisted in pronouncing طِيبَى for طُوبَى: (TA:) it signifies حُسْنَى [as meaning *A good final*, or *ultimate, state* or *condition*]: and (some say, O, Mṣb) خَيْر [meaning *good, good fortune*, and *the like*]: (O, Mṣb, Ḳ:) and خِيرَة [meaning *God's blessing* or *favour*, &c.]; (Ḳ;) as some say: (TA:) or *eternal life*: (Zj, TA:) or *a pleasant life*: (Mṣb:) and (O, Ḳ) *a certain tree in Paradise*; (Ṣ, O, Ḳ;) thus the Prophet is related to have said; and MF says that it is a proper name thereof, not admitting the article ال, and the like is said in the M: (TA:) or it signifies *Paradise* in the Indian language; (O, Ḳ;) or, accord. to Sa'eed Ibn-Jubeyr, in the Abyssinian language: (O:) as also ▼ طِيبَى. (Ḳ.) These different significations are assigned by different persons to this word in the phrase in the Ḳur [xiii. 28] طُوبَى لَهُمْ [which seems to be best rendered as an announcement, meaning *A good final state*, &c., *shall be to them*, or *be their lot*]: (Mṣb, TA:) Sb holds that it is an invocation of good, or a prayer, [as though قُلْ i. e. "say thou" were understood before it,] and that طوبى is virtually in the nom. case, i. e. مَرْفُوع, as is shown by the words immediately following وَحُسْنُ مَآبٍ: but Th, who makes طوبى to be an inf. n. like رُجْعَى, says that one reading is طُوبَى لَهُمْ وَحُسْنَ مَآبٍ, like the phrase سَقْيًا لَهُ: MF, however, [supposing Th to have said طُوبًى, though I think it indubitable that he said طُوبَى, and only meant that it was used as virtually, not literally, with tenween,] observes that رُجْعًى, with tenween, is not known to have been transmitted from any one of the leading authorities on the Arabic language. (TA.) Ḳatádeh says that طُوبَى لَهُمْ is a phrase of the Arabs; who say, طُوبَى لَكَ إِنْ فَعَلْتَ كَذَا وَكَذَا [*A good final state* &c., *be to thee*, or *be thy lot*, or *shall be to thee, if thou do such and such things*]: and it is said in a trad., طُوبَى لِلشَّأْمِ [*May good*, &c., *betide Syria*]; in which case, طوبى is of the measure فُعْلَى from ٱلطِّيبُ, and does not mean "Paradise," nor "the tree." (L, TA.) One says, طُوبَى لَكَ and طُوبَاكَ; (Ṣ, Ḳ;) but not طُوبَيْكَ: (Yaạḳoob, Ṣ, O: [in one of my copies of the Ṣ طوبيك:]) or طوباك is a barbarism: (O, Ḳ:) it is disallowed by the T, and by most of the grammarians: but Akh says that it is used by some of the Arabs; and Ibn-El-Moạtezz uses it in the following verse:

مَرَّتْ بِنَا سَحَرًا طَيْرٌ فَقُلْتُ لَهَا
طُوبَاكِ يَا لَيْتَنَا إِيَّاكِ طُوبَاكِ

[*A flock of birds passed by us a little before daybreak, and I said to them, Good betide you: would that we were you: good betide you*]: Esh-

Shiháb El-Khafájee says that ل is understood [before the ك] in طوباك; but MF has argued well against this assertion. (TA.)

طيمى: see the next preceding paragraph, former half, in three places.

طِيَابٌ *A sort of palm-trees of El-Basrah,* (L, Ḳ, TA,) *the dates of which, when the gathering has been delayed beyond the usual time, fall, one after another, from their stones, so that the raceme remains with nothing upon it but the stones hanging to the bases of the dates; though they are large; and if the fruit is gathered when fully ripe, the stone does not come off with it.* (L, TA.)

طَيِّبٌ (Ṣ, M, Mgh, O, Mṣb, Ḳ) and ‡ طَابٌ, (Ṣ, M, O, Ḳ,) the latter originally طَائِبٌ and deprived of its medial radical letter, or of the measure فَعَلٌ, (M, TA,) *Contr. of* خَبِيثٌ, (Ṣ, Mgh, O,) *in two senses:* (Mgh:) [i. e. *good,*] *pleasant, delightful, delicious, sweet,* or *savoury;* syn. لَذِيذٌ; (Mṣb, Ḳ;*) or *esteemed* [*good,*] *pleasant, delightful, delicious, sweet,* or *savoury,* (مُسْتَلَذٌّ,) *in taste,* and *in odour:* (Mgh:) and *pure,* (Mgh, Ḳ,) or *clean.* (Mgh.) You say طَعَامٌ طَيِّبٌ *Food* [*pleasant in taste;* or] *that descends easily* [*and agreeably*] *down the throat.* (TA.) And مَآءٌ طَيِّبٌ *Sweet water;* (O, TA;) or *pure water.* (TA.) [And رَائِحَةٌ طَيِّبَةٌ *A pleasant, sweet,* or *fragrant, odour.*] And بَلَدٌ طَيِّبٌ *A country that has no salsuginous places in it:* (O, TA:) or *a land of good and fertile soil.* (Mgh.) And صَعِيدٌ طَيِّبٌ *Pure ground.* (Zj, Mgh, O.) And ٱلْكَلِمُ ٱلطَّيِّبُ † [*The good saying*] i. e. لَا إِلٰهَ إِلَّا ٱللّٰهُ [*There is no deity but God*]. (TA.) And فُلَانٌ فِى بَيْتٍ طَيِّبٍ i. e. ‡ [*Such a one is of a good house,* or *family;* meaning,] *of high,* or *noble, birth.* (TA.) And فُلَانٌ طَيِّبُ الإِزَارِ † *Such a one is continent,* or *chaste.* (O.) And فُلَانٌ طَيِّبُ الأَخْلَاقِ † *Such a one is* [*of good,* or *pleasant, dispositions;*] *easy in converse, conversable,* or *affable.* (O, TA.) [And طَيِّبُ النَّفْسِ † *Cheerful, happy, pleased,* or *dilated, in mind.* (See طَابَتْ نَفْسُهُ.) And نَفْسٌ طَيِّبَةٌ بِشَىْءٍ † *A mind cheerful, happy, pleased,* or *dilated, by means of a thing:* or *pleased, content,* or *willing, to grant, concede, give,* or *do, a thing:* and طَيِّبَةٌ عَنْ شَىْءٍ † *pleased, willing,* or *content, to leave, give up, relinquish,* or *be without, a thing.* (See, again, 1.)] —— Also † *Lawful; allowable; allowable by,* or *agreeable to, law; legitimate; legal;* or *free.* (Mgh, Mṣb, Ḳ.) لَا يَسْتَوِى ٱلْخَبِيثُ وَٱلطَّيِّبُ, in the Ḳur [v. 100], means † *The unlawful and the lawful* of property and *the unrighteous and the righteous* of deeds and *the sound and the unsound* of tenets or the like and *the good and the bad* of mankind [*shall not be equal* in your estimation]. (Mgh.) [See also the next paragraph.]

طَيِّبَةٌ [fem. of طَيِّبٌ: and also a subst., made so by the affix ة; meaning *A good, pleasant, delightful, delicious, sweet* or *savoury, thing:* and *a pure,* or *clean, thing:* pl. طَيِّبَاتٌ.] وَٱلطَّيِّبَاتِ مِنَ ٱلرِّزْقِ, in the Ḳur [vii. 30], means *And what are esteemed* [*good,*] *pleasant, delicious, sweet,* or *savoury, of foods and beverages.* (Mgh.) And أَنْفِقُوا مِنْ طَيِّبَاتِ مَا كَسَبْتُمْ, in the same [ii. 269], *Expend ye of the good things that ye have gained:* (Mgh:) or † *of your lawful gains.* (Mgh, O.) And كُلُوا مِنَ ٱلطَّيِّبَاتِ, in the same [xxiii. 53], † *Eat ye of the things that are lawful; of any such lawful things as are esteemed good,* or *pleasant.* (TA.) ٱلطَّيِّبَاتُ مِنَ ٱلْكَلَامِ means † *The most excellent of words,* or *speech;* (Mṣb, TA;) *the best thereof:* (Mṣb:) and is meant by ٱلطَّيِّبَاتُ in [the words of] the تَشَهُّد, [commencing with] ٱلتَّحِيَّاتُ لِلّٰهِ وَٱلصَّلَوَاتُ وَٱلطَّيِّبَاتُ: [see تَحِيَّةٌ, in art. حى:] and likewise in the Ḳur [xxiv. 26], where it is said, ٱلطَّيِّبَاتُ لِلطَّيِّبِينَ; by the طَيِّبِين being meant *the pure of men;* accord. to Fr.: but these words of the Ḳur are otherwise expl., as meaning *the good women are for the good men.* (O.) —— See also طَيِّبَةٌ.

طُيَّابٌ, with ḍamm, means طَيِّبٌ جِدًّا [i. e. *Very good, pleasant, delightful, delicious, sweet,* or *savoury*]. (Ṣ, O, TA. [In the Ḳ it is implied that it is simply syn. with طَيِّبٌ; like as many other intensive epithets are confounded therein with those that are not intensive.]) A poet says,

• إِنَّا وَجَدْنَا مَآءَهَا طُيَّابَا •

[*Verily we found its water to be very good, pleasant,* or *sweet*]. (Ṣ, O.)

أَطْيَبُ [*Better,* and *best; more,* and *most, pleasant, delightful, delicious, sweet,* or *savoury*]: its fem. is طُوبَى: (ISd, Ḳ:) and أَطَايِبُ is its pl.: (Ṣ:) and أَيْطَبُ is a dial. var. of أَطْيَبُ, or is formed from the latter by transposition. (TA in art. يطب.) —— ٱلأَطْيَبَانِ [*The two best,* or *most pleasant, &c., of things,*] means † *Eating and coïtus:* (IAạr, Ṣ, A, O, Ḳ:) or *sleep and coïtus:* (ISk, O, TA:) or *the mouth and the vulva of a woman:* (Yaạḳoob, A, O, Ḳ:) or *fat and youthfulness:* (A, Ḳ:) or *strength and appetence:* or *youthfulness and briskness* or *liveliness* or *sprightliness:* (Ḥar p. 88:) or *fresh ripe dates and the* خِرْبِز [or *water-melon*]: or *milk and dates.* (TA.) —— And أَطَايِبُ signifies The *best,* or *best parts,* of a thing, (Ḳ, TA,) as of flesh-meat, &c.; (TA;) as also ‡ مَطَايِبُ, a pl. which has no sing., (Ḳ, TA,) of the same class as مَحَاسِنُ and مَلَامِحُ, (TA,) or its pl. is ‡ مَطْيَبٌ, (Ks, O, Ḳ,) or ‡ مَطَابٌ and ‡ مَطَابَةٌ: (M, Ḳ:) or you say, أَطْعَمَنَا مِنْ أَطَايِبِ الجَزُورِ [*He fed us from the best parts of the slaughtered camel*], but not مِنْ مَطَايِبِ ‡ الجزور; (Ṣ, O;) or you say, مِنْ أَطَايِبِهَا and ‡ مَطَايِبِهَا; (Aṣ, A, O;) or the latter, but not the former; (Yaạḳoob, TA;) or you say أَطَايِبُ الجَزُورِ, and مَطَايِبُ ‡ الرُّطَبِ [*the best of fresh ripe dates*]; (IAạr, Ḳ;) and AḤn uses the phrase أَطَايِبُ الكَلَإِ [*the best portions of the herbage*]. (TA.)

أَيْطَبْتُهَا and أَيْطَبَةُ العَنْزِ [mentioned in this art. because held to be formed by transposition (in Freytag's Lex. with ط in each case)] *The she-goat's lusting for the male.* (AZ, O, Ḳ.)

مَطَابٌ: } see أَطْيَبُ.
مَطْيَبٌ: }

مُطِيبٌ [part. n. of 4: as such signifying] *A lawful wedder:* a woman said to her beloved,

• وَلَا زُرْتَنَا إِلَّا وَأَنْتَ مُطِيبُ •

[*Nor didst thou visit us save when thou wast a lawful wedder*]: because, in the estimation of excessive lovers, what is unlawful is more sweet. (TA.)

مَطَابَةٌ: see أَطْيَبُ.

مَطْيَبَةٌ [*A cause of pleasure* or *delight*]. One says, هٰذَا شَرَابٌ مَطْيَبَةٌ لِلنَّفْسِ *This is a beverage* [*which is a cause of pleasure to the soul,* or] *with which the soul is pleased when drinking it.* (Ṣ, O.) And in like manner one says of food. (TA.)

مُطَيَّبٌ pass. part. n. of 2. (TA.) Hence, (TA,) حِلْفُ المُطَيَّبِينَ [*The covenant of the perfumed men*]: (Ḳ, TA:) these were five tribes; Benoo-'Abd-Menáf and Benoo-Asad-Ibn-'Abd-El-'Ozzà and Benoo-Teym and Benoo-Zuhrah and Benu-l-Ḥárith and Benoo-Fihr: (TA:) and they were so called for the following reason: when Benoo-'Abd-Menáf desired to assume [the offices of] the حِجَابَة and the رِفَادَة and the لِوَآء and the سِقَايَة, [see arts. حجب &c.,] which belonged to Benoo-'Abd-ed-Dár, and these refused their consent, all of the above-mentioned, (Ḳ, TA,) having assembled in the house of Ibn-Jud'án, in the Time of Ignorance, (TA,) concluded a ratified covenant for the accomplishment of their affair, engaging not to fail in aiding one another: then they mixed some perfumes, and dipped their hands therein; after which they wiped their hands upon the Kaabeh in token of confirmation of the covenant: and Benoo-'Abd-ed-Dár, also, and their confederates, (Ḳ, TA,) composing six tribes, Benoo-'Abd-ed-Dár and Jumaḥ and Makhzoom and 'Adee and Kaab and Sahm, (TA,) concluded together another covenant, and were thence called الأَحْلَاف: (Ḳ, TA:) this is the account commonly known and received: another account is the following: there came a man of the Benoo-Zeyd to Mekkeh for the purpose of [the religious visit termed] the عُمْرَة, having with him merchandise, and a man of Sahm bought this of him, and refused to pay him for it; whereupon he called to them from the summit of Aboo-Ḳubeys, and they arose, and entered into a covenant together to do him justice: thus relates Eth-Tha'álibee: (TA:) Moḥammad was one of the مُطَيَّبُون, (Ḳ, TA,) being then twenty-five years old; and so was Aboo-Bekr: and 'Omar was an أَحْلَافِىّ. (TA.) —— المُطَيَّبَةُ: see طَيْبَةُ.

المُطَيِّبَةُ: see طَيْبَةُ.

مَطْيُوبٌ pass. part. n. of طَابَهُ [as syn. with طَيَّبَهُ]; like مَخْيُوطٌ [from خَاطَهُ]. (TA.)

مَطَايِبُ: see أَطْيَبُ, in four places.

طيح

1. طَاحَ, aor. يَطِيحُ, inf. n. طَيْحٌ: see 1 in art. طوح. Sb says that this verb is [originally طَوِحَ, aor. يَطْوَحُ, i. e.,] of the measure فَعِلَ, aor. يَفْعِلُ; like وَلِىَ, aor. يَلِى; accord. to those who say طَوَّحَهُ, and not طَيَّحَهُ: but accord. to those who say طَيَّحَهُ, it is [originally طَيَحَ, aor. يَطْيِحُ, of the measure فَعَلَ, aor. يَفْعِلُ,] like بَاعَ, aor. يَبِيعُ. (L, TA.)

2. طَيَّحَ: see 2 in art. طوح.

4. مَا أَطْيَحَهُ: see 4 in arts. طوح and توه.

5. تَطَيَّحَ, syn. with تَطَوَّحَ: see 1 in art. طوح.

6. تطايح *It became scattered,* or *dispersed;* or *it flew away* or *about;* syn. تَطَايَرَ. (Ḥam p. 615.)

طَيْحٌ *A piece of wood that is in the* أَصْل [app. meaning *lower part*] *of the plough.* (Ḳ.)

أَصَابَتْهُمْ طَيْحَةٌ (A, Ḳ) means *Events that caused divisions between them,* or *that dispersed them, befell them:* (Ḳ, TA:) so says Aboo-Sa'eed. (TA.) And one says, طَوَّحَتْهُمْ طَيْحَاتٌ *Calamities destroyed them.* (TA.) And ذَهَبَتْ أَمْوَالُهُمْ طَيْحَاتٍ *Their possessions, or cattle, went away dispersed,* or *scattered, and remote.* (TA.) [See also طَيْخَةٌ.]

طَائِحٌ: see art. طوح. — كَفٌّ طَائِحَةٌ occurs in a trad. of Aboo-Hureyreh as meaning *A hand flying from its wrist.* (TA.)

مُطَيَّحٌ, accord. to the Ḳ, signifies *Bad, corrupt,* or *vitious:* but it may be a mistranscription, for مُطَيَّخٌ [or this is a mistranscription for مُطَيَّحٌ, which is expl. as having this meaning]. (TA.)

طيخ

1. طَاخَ, aor. يَطِيخُ, (Ṣ, L, Ḳ,) inf. n. طَيْخٌ; (L;) as also ↓ تَطَيَّخَ; *He became charged, reproached,* or *upbraided, with something bad, evil, abominable,* or *foul,* (Ṣ, L, Ḳ,) either *said* or *done.* (L.) — And طاخ, aor. as above, (Ṣ, L, Ḳ,) and so the inf. n., (L,) *He magnified himself,* or *was proud.* (Ṣ, L, Ḳ.) — And *He exerted himself,* or *strove, and persisted,* or *persevered, in that which was vain.* (Ḳ.) = طَاخَهُ, aor. يَطِيخُهُ, (Ṣ, L, Ḳ,) inf. n. طَيْخٌ; as also طاخه, aor. يَطُوخُهُ, inf. n. طَوْخٌ; but the former is the more common; (TA in art. طوخ;) and ↓ طَيَّخَهُ; *He charged, reproached,* or *upbraided, him with something bad, evil, abominable,* or *foul,* (Ṣ, L, Ḳ,) either *said* or *done.* (L.) And ↓ طَيَّخَ أَصْحَابَهُ *He reviled and harassed his companions.* (Aboo-Málik, TA.) — And طاخ الأَمْرَ, inf. n. as above, *He corrupted, vitiated,* or *marred, the affair.* (ISd, TA.)

2: see above, in two places. — طَيَّخَ العَذَابُ عَلَيْهِ, (Ḳ,) or rather (TA) طَيَّخَهُ العَذَابُ, (AZ, TA,) *Punishment pressed severely,* or *persistently, upon him, so that it killed him.* (AZ, Ḳ, TA.) — And طَيَّخَهُ السِّمَنُ *Fatness filled him with fat and flesh.* (AZ, Ḳ, TA.)

5: see 1, first sentence.

طَيْخٌ: see the next paragraph.

طِيخِ a word imitative of the sound of laughing. (Sb, Ḳ.) قَالُوا طِيخِ طِيخِ, the word طيخ being in this case indecl., with kesr for its termination, means *They uttered a reiterated laughing* [*like a repeating of* طيخ]. (Lth, Ḳ, TA.) = Also, and ↓ طَيْخٌ, *Ignorance.* (TA.)

طَيْخَةٌ (L, Ḳ) and ↓ طَائِخٌ and ↓ طَيَّاخَةٌ [which last is a doubly intensive epithet] (L) *Stupid, in whom is little good:* (L, Ḳ:) or *stupid and dirty:* pl. of the first طَيْخَاتٌ: it has no known broken pl. (L.) [See also طَيْخَةٌ and طَنْخَةٌ.] = Also the first, *Trial; sedition,* or *conflict and faction;* or *the like;* syn. فِتْنَةٌ; (Ḳ, TA;) and *war.* (TA.) [See also طَيْحَةٌ.]

طَيُّوخٌ A she-camel *that goes to the right and left, and crops the extremities of the trees.* (TA.)

طَيَّاخَةٌ: }
طَائِخٌ: } see طَيْخَةٌ.

مُطَيَّخٌ [app. applied to a camel] *Smeared with tar.* (Ḳ.) — And *Bad, corrupt,* or *vitious.* (Ḳ.)

طير

1. طَارَ, aor. يَطِيرُ, (Ṣ, Mṣb,) inf. n. طَيَرَانٌ (Ṣ, A, Mṣb, Ḳ) and طَيْرُورَةٌ (Lḥ, Ṣ, Ḳ, &c.) and طَيْرٌ, (Ḳ,) *He* (a winged creature) *moved in the air by means of his wings; flew;* (A, Ḳ;) *moved in the air as a beast does upon the ground.* (Mṣb.) — It is also said of other things than those which have wings; as in the saying of El-'Amberee (Ḳureyṭ Ibn-Uneyf, Ḥam p. 3):

* طَارُوا إِلَيْهِ زَرَافَاتٍ وَوُحْدَانَا *

[*They fly to it in companies and one by one*]; (TA;) i. e. *they hasten to it:* for طِرْتُ إِلَى كَذَا means † *I hastened to such a thing:* and طِرْتُ بِكَذَا † *I outstripped,* or *became foremost, with such a thing.* (Ḥam p. 6.) And طار عَلَى مَتْنِ فَرَسِهِ ‡ *He fled upon the back of his horse.* (TA, from a trad.) And طار القَوْمُ † *The people took fright and ran away quickly.* (Mṣb.) And طَارُوا سِرَاعًا † *They went away quickly.* (TA.) — [One says also, طار عَقْلُهُ † *His reason fled.* And طار فُؤَادُهُ ‡ *His courage* (lit. *his heart*) *fled away:* see also 10: and see شَعَاعٌ. (Both are phrases of frequent occurrence.)] — And طار طَائِرُهُ: see طَائِرٌ. — طار قَلْبِى مَطَارَهُ [And see an ex. voce شُقَّةٌ.] means † *My heart inclined towards that which it loved, and clung to it.* (TA, from a trad.) And طِيرِى بِهِ, addressed to a woman, is expl. by IAạr as meaning † *Love thou,* or *become attached, to him.* (TA.) — طارت عَيْنُهُ (Ṣ and K in art. خلج) † *His eye throbbed.* (PṢ and TḲ in that art.) — طار لَهُ صِيتٌ فِى النَّاسِ ‡ [*He became famous among the people;* lit. means *fame among the people became,* or *came to be,* (صَارَ,) *his*]. (A.) [And in like manner one says,] طار لَهُ مِنْ نَصِيبِهِ كَذَا ‡ *Such a thing became his,* or *came to him, of his lot,* or *portion;* syn. صَارَ, and حَصَلَ. (Mgh.) And طار لَنَا ‡ *It came to our lot,* or *portion.* (TA.) And طار لِكُلٍّ مِنْهُمْ سَهْمُهُ ‡ *The share of each came to him.* (TA.) — See also 6, in two places. = طَارَ بِهِ is also syn. with طَيَّرَهُ, q. v. (TA.) — [Hence the metaphorical phrase طارت الإِبِلُ بِآذَانِهَا, (TA,) or بِأَذْنَابِهَا, (O, TA,) thus [correctly] in the TṢ, (TA,) [like شَالَتْ بِأَذْنَابِهَا,] means † *The she-camels conceived.* (O, TA.) — طارت بِهَا العَنْقَاءُ expl. voce عَنْقَاءُ.]

2. طَيَّرَهُ, (Ṣ, A, Mṣb, Ḳ,) and طَيَّرَ بِهِ, (Ḳ,) and ↓ اطارهُ, (Ṣ, A, Mṣb, Ḳ,) and ↓ طايرهُ, (Ṣ, Ḳ,) and ↓ طَارَ بِهِ, (TA,) *He made him to fly.* (A, Mṣb, Ḳ.) [See also 10.] — طَيَّرَ العَصَافِيرَ عَنِ الزَّرْعِ *He made the sparrows to fly away,* [*scared them,* or *dispersed them,*] *from the seed-produce.* (A.) — هُمْ فِى شَىْءٍ لَا يُطَيَّرُ غُرَابُهُ [*They are in that whereof the crow is not made to fly away,* because of its abundance]: a prov. alluding to a state of plenty. (Ṣ, TA.) [See also غُرَابٌ.] One says also أُطِيرَ الغُرَابُ [*The crow was made to fly away*]. (Ṣ.) [See مُطَارٌ.] — طَيَّرَ فُؤَادَهُ ‡ [*He, or it, made his courage* (lit. *his heart*) *to fly away*]. (Ṣ in art. فز, &c.) — طَيَّرَ المَالَ بَيْنَ القَوْمِ, and ↓ اطارهُ, *He divided the property into lots,* or *shares, among the people:* (O, Ḳ,* TA:) أَطَرْتُ, signifying *I divided into lots,* or *shares,* occurs in a trad.; but some say that the ا is a radical letter. (IAth, TA.) — طَيَّرَ الفَحْلُ الإِبِلَ means † *The stallion made all the she-camels to conceive:* (Ḳ, TA:) or, *to conceive quickly.* (TA.) And طَيَّرَتْ هِىَ [or طَيَّرَتْ ?] *They conceived quickly.* (TA.)

3: see 2, first sentence.

4: see 2, in two places. = اطارت أَرْضُنَا *Our land abounded,* or *became abundant, in birds.* (TA.)

5. تَطَيَّرَ مِنْهُ, (Ṣ, A, Mṣb, Ḳ,) and بِهِ, (Ṣ, Ḳ,) sometimes changed to اِطَّيَّرَ, (Ṣ, A, Mṣb,) as in the Ḳur xxvii. 48, the ت being incorporated into the ط, and this requiring a conjunctive ا that the word may begin with it [and not with a

quiescent letter], (Ṣ,) inf. n. [or rather quasi-inf. n.] طِيَرَةٌ, the only instance of the kind except خِيَرَةٌ, which is the same in relation to تَخَيَّرَ, (IAth,) *He augured evil from it; regarded it as an evil omen.* (Ṣ, Mṣb, Ḳ.) The Arabs, when they desired to set about an affair, passed by the places where birds lay upon the ground, and roused them, in order to learn thence whether they should proceed or refrain: but the law forbade this. (Mṣb.) They augured evil from the croaking of the crow, and from the birds' going towards the left; and in like manner, from the motions of gazelles. (TA.) تَفَآءَلَ signifies the contr. of تطيّر. (TA.)

6. تطاير † *It became scattered,* or *dispersed;* (Ṣ, Ḳ, TA;) *flew away* or *about; went away; became reduced to fragments;* (TA;) as also ▼ استطار, (Ḳ, TA,) and ▼ طَارَ. (TA.) —— ‡ *It became long,* or *tall;* (Ṣ, Ḳ;) as also ▼ طَارَ, (Ṣgh, Ḳ,) which is said of hair, (TA,) as is also the former, (Ṣ, TA,) and of a camel's hump. (Ṣgh, TA.) It is said in a trad., خُذْ مَا تَطَايَرَ مِنْ شَعْرِكَ (Ṣ, TA) [*Clip thou*] *what has become long and dishevelled* [*of thy hair*]. (TA.) —— تطاير السَّحَابُ فِى السَّمَآءِ † *The clouds became spread throughout the sky.* (Ḳ, TA.) [See also 10.]

7. انطار *It became split, slit,* or *cracked.* (Ḳ, TA.) [See also 10, latter part.]

10. استطار [*He made* a thing *to fly.* See also 2. —— Hence,] † *He drew forth* a sword *quickly from its scabbard.* (Ḳ,* TA.) —— أُسْتُطِيرَ † *It* (for ex., dust, Ṣ) *was made to fly.* (Ṣ, Ḳ.) You say, كَادَ يُسْتَطَارُ مِنْ شِدَّةِ عَدْوِهِ ‡ [*He was almost made to fly by reason of the vehemence of his running*]. (A.) And أُسْتُطِيرَ فُؤَادُهُ مِنَ الفَزَعِ ‡ [*His courage* (lit. *his heart*) *was made to fly away by reason of fright*]. (A.) —— † *He was taken away quickly, as though the birds carried him away.* (TA.) —— † *He hastened,* or *was quick, in running;* (Ḳ;) *he ran quickly;* (O, L;) said of a horse. (O, L, Ḳ.) [A signification of the pass. form; as though meaning he was made to fly.] —— † *He was* [*flurried,* or] *frightened.* (O, Ḳ.) [As though meaning originally he was made to fly by reason of fright.] ══ استطار ‡ *It* (the dawn) *spread;* (Ṣ, A, Mṣb, Ḳ;) *its light spread in the horizon:* (TA:) [see مُسْتَطِيرٌ:] and the verb is used in the same sense in relation to other things: (Ṣ:) said of lightning, *it spread in the horizon:* and of dust, *it spread in the air:* and of evil, *it spread.* (TA.) See also 6. —— ‡ *It* (a crack in a wall) *appeared and spread.* (A. [See also استطال.]) *It* (a slit, or crack, for السُّوقُ in the Ḳ is a mistake for الشَّقُّ, or, accord. to the L, a crack in a wall, TA) *rose,* (Ḳ,) *and appeared.* (TA.) † *It* (a crack in a glass vessel, and wear in a garment,) *became apparent in the parts thereof.* (TA.) —— ‡ *It* (a wall) *cracked* (Ḳ, TA) *from the beginning thereof to the end.* (TA.) † *It* (a glass vessel) *showed a crack in it from beginning to end.* (TA.) [See also 7.] ══ استطارت said of a bitch, *She desired the male.* (O, Ḳ.)

طَيْرٌ: see طَائِرٌ, in seven places: —— and see also طَيْرَةٌ, in two places. ══ طَيْرْ طَيْرْ, (O,) or طِيرْ طِيرْ, (TA,) is a cry by which a sheep or goat is called. (O, TA.)

طَيْرَةٌ and ▼ طَيْرُورَةٌ (Ṣ, Ḳ) and ▼ طَيْرٌ (Ṣ) ‡ *Levity; inconstancy.* (Ṣ, Ḳ, TA.) You say, فِى فُلَانٍ طَيْرَةٌ and ▼ طَيْرُورَةٌ, ‡ *In such a one is levity,* or *inconstancy.* (Ṣ.) And ▼ أَزْجُرْ أَحْنَآءَ طَيْرِكَ ‡ [alluding to the original signification of طَيْرٌ, namely, "birds,"] means جَوَانِبَ خِفَّتِكَ وَطَيْشِكَ [agreeing with an explanation of the same saying voce حِنْوٌ, q. v.]. (Ṣ.) —— Also طَيْرَةٌ † *A slip; a stumble:* hence the trad., إِيَّاكَ وَطَيْرَاتِ الشَّبَابِ † *Beware thou of the slips and stumbles of youth.* (TA.)

طِيرَةٌ and طِيَرَةٌ and طُوَرَةٌ; see طَائِرٌ; the second, in four places.

طَيْرُورَةٌ: see طَيْرَةٌ, in two places.

طَيَّارٌ ‡ *A sharp, spirited, vigorous,* horse, (Ḳ, TA,) *that is almost made to fly by reason of the vehemence of his running;* (TA;) as also ▼ مُطَارٌ. (Ḳ, TA. [The latter word in the CḲ written مَطَار; but said in the TA to be with ḍamm, and so written in a copy of the A.]) [See also طَيُورٌ.] —— See also مُسْتَطِيرٌ. ══ Also *A company* of men. (O.) ══ As applied to *A balance,* it is not of the language of the Arabs: (O:) [i. e., it is post-classical:] it means *an assay-balance* (مِعْيَارٌ and مِيزَانٌ) *for gold;* so called because of the form of a bird, or because of its lightness: or the *balance for dirhems* [or moneys] *that is known among them* [*who use it*] *by the appellation of the* قارسطون [meaning the χαριστίων of Archimedes, (as is observed in a note in p. 178 of vol. ii. of the sec. ed. of Ḥar,) i. e. the *hydrostatic balance*]: or, accord. to El-Fenjedeehee, the *tongue* (لِسَان) *of the balance.* (Ḥar pp. 549-50.)

هُوَ طَيُورٌ فَيُورٌ † *He is sharp, and quick in returning* [to a good state], or *recovering* [from his anger]. (Ḳ.) [See also طَيَّارٌ.]

طَائِرٌ *A flying thing* [*whether bird* or *insect*]: (Mṣb,* TA:) pl. ▼ طَيْرٌ, (Ṣ, Mṣb, Ḳ,) like as صَحْبٌ is pl. of صَاحِبٌ: (Ṣ, Mṣb:) or طَيْرٌ is originally an inf. n. of طَارَ: or an epithet contracted from طَيِّرٌ: (TA:) or a quasi-pl. n.; (Mgh, TA;) and this is the most correct opinion: (TA:) [but see, below, a reason for considering it originally an inf. n.:] and طَائِرٌ may also be quasi-pl. n., like جَامِلٌ and بَاقِرٌ: (TA:) ▼ طَيْرٌ is also sometimes used as a sing.; (Ḳtr, AO, Ṣ, Mgh, Mṣb, Ḳ;) as in the Ḳur iii. 43 [and v. 110], accord. to one reading: (Ṣ:) but ISd says, I know not how this is, unless it be meant to be [originally] an inf. n.: (TA:) [for an inf. n. used as an epithet is employed as sing. and pl.:] or طَائِرٌ, only, is used as a sing., (Th, IAmb, Mṣb,) by general consent; and AO once said so in common with others: (Th:) but ▼ طَيْرٌ has a collective, or pl., signification: (IAmb, Mṣb:) and is fem.: (Mgh:) or is more frequently fem. than masc.: (IAmb, Mṣb:) the pl. of طَيْرٌ is طُيُورٌ [a pl. of mult.] and أَطْيَارٌ [a pl. of pauc.]: (Ṣ, Mṣb, Ḳ:) or طُيُورٌ may be pl. of طَائِرٌ, like as سُجُودٌ is pl. of سَاجِدٌ: (TA:) طَائِرَةٌ is seldom applied to the female. (IAmb, Mṣb.) —— [الطَّائِرُ is a name of † *The constellation Cygnus;* also called الدَّجَاجَةُ.] —— هُوَ سَاكِنُ الطَّائِرِ means ‡ *He is grave, staid, sedate,* (Ḳ,) or *motionless;* so that if a bird alighted upon him, it would be still; for if a bird alight upon a man, and he move in the least, the bird flies away. (TA.) Of the same kind also is the saying, رُزِقَ فُلَانٌ سُكُونَ الطَّائِرِ وَخَفْضَ الجَنَاحِ ‡ [*Such a one was endowed,* or *has been endowed, with gravity and gentleness*]. (TA.) And طُيُورُهُمْ سَوَاكِنُ ‡ *They are remaining fixed, settled,* or *at rest:* and شَالَتْ نَعَامَتُهُمْ signifies the contrary. (A, TA.) And ▼ كَأَنَّ عَلَى رُؤُوسِهِمُ الطَّيْرَ ‡ [*As though birds were on their heads*] is said of a people, meaning them to be *motionless by reason of reverence:* (Ṣ, Ḳ:) it was said of the Companions of Moḥammad, describing them as quiet and grave [in his presence], without levity: and the origin of the saying is this: that birds alight only upon a thing that is still and inanimate: (TA:) or that the crow alights upon the head of the camel, and picks from it the ticks, (Ṣ, Ḳ,) and the young ones thereof, (Ṣ,) and the camel does not move (Ṣ, Ḳ) his head, (Ṣ,) lest the crow should take fright and fly away. (Ṣ, Ḳ.) In like manner, وَقَعَ طَائِرُهُ means ‡ *He became grave,* or *sedate.* (Meyd.) And ▼ طَارَ طَائِرُهُ ‡ *He became light,* or *inconstant:* (Meyd:) and *he became angry;* (O, Ḳ, TA;) like فَارَ فَائِرُهُ and ثَارَ ثَائِرُهُ: (TA:) or *he hastened, and was light,* or *active,* or *agile.* (Ḥar p. 561.) —— And it is said in a trad., الرُّؤْيَا عَلَى رِجْلِ طَائِرٍ مَا لَمْ تُعَبَّرْ (O, TA) † *A dream is unsettled as to its result,* or *final sequel, while it is not interpreted.* (TA.) [The Arabs hold that the result of a dream is affected by its interpretation: wherefore it is added in this tradition, and said in others also, that the dreamer should not relate his dream, unless to a friend or to a person of understanding.] —— ▼ عَيْثَ طِيَرَةٌ see expl. in art. عيث. —— طَائِرٌ also signifies *A thing from which one augurs either good or evil; an omen, a bodement, of good* or *of evil:* (Ḳ:) and ▼ طِيَرَةٌ (Ṣ, Ḳ) and ▼ طِيرَةٌ (Ḳ) and ▼ طُورَةٌ (IDrd, Ṣgh, Ḳ, TA [in the CḲ, in this art., erroneously, طُورَةٌ, but in art. طور it is طُورَةٌ,]) *a thing from which one augurs evil; an evil omen* or *bodement;* (Ṣ, Ḳ, &c.;) *contr. of* فَأْلٌ: (TA:) and طَائِرٌ signifies *fortune,* (A'Obeyd, Ḳ, TA,) *whether good or evil:* (TA:) and especially *evil fortune; ill luck;* as also ▼ طَيْرٌ and ▼ طِيَرَةٌ: for the Arabs used to augur evil from the croaking of the crow, and from birds going towards the left: [see 5:] (TA:) and ▼ طِيَرَةٌ is an inf. n. [or rather a quasi-inf. n.] of تَطَيَّرَ, [q. v.,] (IAth,) and signifies *auguration of evil.* (Mṣb.) The Arabs used to say, to a man or other thing from which they augured evil, (TA,) طَائِرُ ٱللّٰهِ لَا طَائِرُكَ, (ISk,

Ṣ, IAmb,) and طَائِرُ ٱللّٰهِ لَا طَائِرُكَ, meaning *What God doth and decreeth, not what thou dost and causest to be feared:* (IAmb:) accord. to ISk, one should not say طَيْرُ ▼ ٱللّٰهِ: (Ṣ:) but the Arabs are related to have said, also, لَا طَيْرَ إِلَّا طَيْرُ ٱللّٰهِ [*There is no evil fortune but that which is of God*]; like as one says, لَا أَمْرَ إِلَّا أَمْرُ ٱللّٰهِ. (Aṣ, Ṣ.) They also used to say, جَرَى لَهُ ٱلطَّائِرُ بِأَمْرِ كَذَا [*Fortune brought to him such an event*]: and hence fortune, whether good or evil, is called طَائِر. (TA.) And it is said in the Ḳur [vii. 128], إِنَّمَا طَائِرُهُمْ عِنْدَ ٱللّٰهِ, meaning *Their evil fortune,* which will overtake them, *is only* that which is threatened to befall them in the latter state, [*with God,*] and not that which befalls them in the present state of existence: (TA:) or *the cause of their good and evil is only with God;* i. e., it is his decree and will: or *the cause of their evil fortune is only with God;* i. e., it is their works, which are registered with Him. (Bḍ.) It is said in a trad., that Moḥammad liked what is termed فَأْل, and disliked what is termed ▼ طِيَرَة: (Ṣ:) and in another, that he denied there being any such thing as the latter. (TA.) ═ Also *The means of subsistence;* syn. رِزْق. (Ḳ:) or *misery:* or *happiness:* every one of these three significations has been assigned to it in the Ḳur xvii. 14: in which, accord. to AM, it is meant that God has decreed to every man happiness or misery, according as He foresaw that he would be obedient or disobedient. (TA.) [See also what immediately follows.] ═ Also *The actions of a man which are* [*as it were*] *attached as a necklace to his neck.* (Ṣ, Mṣb, Ḳ.) And this is [also said by some to be] its signification in the Ḳur xvii. 14. (Jel.) [The actions of a man are the cause of his happiness or misery.] ═ ٱلطَّائِرُ signifies also *The brain.* (AAF, L, Ḳ.)

أَطْيَرُ مِنْ عُقَابٍ [*More swift of flight than an eagle*] is a prov. said of an عقاب because it may be in the morning in El-'Irák and in the evening in El-Yemen. (Meyd.)

مَطَارٌ [*A place to* or *from which a bird* or *other thing flies:* in the phrase طَارَ قَلْبِى مَطَارَهُ, (see 1,) it lit. signifies *a place to which one would fly:*] *a place of flying.* (TA.) — أَرْضٌ مَطَارَةٌ [and ▼ مُطِيرَةٌ (see 4)] *A land abounding with birds.* (Ṣ, Ḳ.) ═ حَفْرٌ مَطَارٌ, (O,) and بِئْرٌ مَطَارَةٌ, (O, Ḳ,) [*A pit,* or *cavity,* and *a well,*] *wide in the mouth.* (O, Ḳ.)

مُطَارٌ *Made to fly away:* En-Nábighah says,

وَلِرَهْطِ حَرَّابٍ وَقَدٍّ سَوْرَةٌ
فِى ٱلْمَجْدِ لَيْسَ غُرَابُهَا بِمُطَارِ

[*And to the family of Ḥarráb and Ḳadd belongs an eminence in glory of which they fear not any diminution:* lit., *of which the crow is not made to fly away;* the greatness of their glory being likened to abundant seed-produce, as has been shown above: see 2]: (Ṣ:) A'Obeyd says that Ḥarráb and Ḳadd were two men of the Benoo-Asad. (TA in art. قد.) — See also طَيَّارٌ.

مُطِيرَةٌ: see مَطَارٌ.

مُطَيَّرٌ *A sort of* [*garment of the kind called*] بُرْد (O, Ḳ) *having upon it the forms of birds.* (O.) ═ And *Aloes-wood:* (Ḳ:) or *a certain preparation thereof:* (AḤn, TA:) or *such as is* مُطَرًّى [i. e. *mixed with some other odoriferous substance*]; formed by transposition from the latter word; (O, Ḳ;) but this pleased not ISd: (TA:) or aloes-wood *split and broken in pieces.* (O, Ḳ.*)

مُسْتَطَارٌ [*Made to fly.* — And hence,] † A horse *that hastens,* or *is quick, in running:* (Ḳ:) *that runs quickly.* (TṢ, L.) It is contracted by the poet 'Adee into مُسْطَار, or مُصْطَار. (TA.) And مُسْطَار for مُسْتَطَار is applied as an epithet to wine. (TA. [No ex. is there given to indicate the meaning.])

مُسْتَطِيرٌ ‡ *Spreading;* applied to dust; as also ▼ طَيَّارٌ; (TA;) and to hoariness; and to evil: (L:) *rising and spreading;* (Ḳ;) *whereof the light spreads in the horizon;* applied to the true dawn, which renders it unlawful to the faster to eat or drink or indulge in other carnal pleasure, and on the appearance of which the prayer of daybreak may be performed, and which is termed ٱلْخَيْطُ ٱلْأَبْيَضُ: that to which the epithet مُسْتَطِيل is applied is [the false dawn,] that which is likened to the tail of the wolf (ذَنَبُ ٱلسِّرْحَانِ), and is termed ٱلْخَيْطُ ٱلْأَسْوَدُ; and this does not render anything unlawful to the faster. (TA.) — Also A dog *excited by lust;* (Lth, O, Ḳ;) and so a camel; (Ḳ;) or the epithet applied in this sense to the latter is هَائِجٌ. (Lth, O, TA.)

طيش

1. طَاشَ, aor. يَطِيشُ, (O, Mṣb, Ḳ,) inf. n. طَيْشٌ (Ṣ, A, O, Mṣb, Ḳ) and طَيَشَانٌ, (TA, [there only said to be syn. with طَيْش, but it is well known, and often occurring, as an inf. n. of طاش in the first of the senses here explained,]) *He was,* or *became, light, inconstant, unsteady, irresolute,* or *fickle,* syn. of the inf. n. خِفَّةٌ, (Ṣ, A, Mṣb, Ḳ,) or *contr.* of حِلْمٌ, (IDrd, O,) and *i. q.* نَزَقٌ, (Ṣ, Ḳ,) *after gravity,* or *sedateness:* (TA:) or *light of intellect; lightwitted:* (TA:) and *he became bereft of his reason,* or *intellect,* (Sh, A, O, Ḳ,) *so as to be ignorant of that which he would endeavour to do.* (Sh, O.) [And, said of a beast, *He was,* or *became, restless,* or *unsteady.*] — طَاشَتْ يَدُهُ فِى ٱلصَّحْفَةِ *His hand was light,* or *active, in the bowl, and took from every side.* (TA.) — طَاشَتْ رِجْلَاهُ *His legs were in a state of commotion.* (TA.) — طَاشَ ٱلسَّهْمُ, (Ṣ, Mṣb,) inf. n. طَيْشٌ, (A, Mṣb, Ḳ,) *The arrow passed beyond the butt:* (A, Ḳ:) or *declined,* or *turned aside,* عَنِ ٱلْهَدَفِ *from the butt;* (Ṣ, Mṣb;) *and did not hit it.* (Mṣb.) — طَاشَتْ عَنِ ٱلْأَمْرِ رِجْلُهُ *His leg turned aside* [*from the root* thereof]: a phrase used by Aboo-Sahm El-Hudhalee, whose leg had been cut off. (TA.)

4. اطاشهُ [*He,* or *it, rendered him light, inconstant, unsteady,* &c.]. (TA in art. سفه.) — اطاش ٱلسَّهْمَ *He made the arrow to decline,* or *turn aside,* عَنِ ٱلْهَدَفِ *from the butt.* (Ṣ, Ḳ.)

[طَيْشَةٌ *A fit of* طَيْش, i. e. *lightness,* or *levity, inconstancy, unsteadiness, irresoluteness,* or *fickleness;* &c. See 1.]

طَيَّاشٌ: see طَائِشٌ, in three places.

طَائِشٌ (A, O, Ḳ) and ▼ طَيَّاشٌ, (Ṣ, A, O, Ḳ,) [but the latter has an intensive signification,] applied to a man, (Ṣ, O,) *Light, inconstant, unsteady, irresolute,* or *fickle,* (Ṣ, A, O, Ḳ,) *after gravity,* or *sedateness:* (TA:) or *light of intellect; lightwitted:* [&c.: see 1:] (TA:) and [so] طَائِشُ ٱللُّبِّ: (A:) and for the pl. you say قَوْمٌ طَاشَةٌ, (A, TA,) and ▼ طَيَّاشَةٌ: (TA:) and ▼ طَيَّاشٌ signifies one *who does not pursue one course,* (A, O, Ḳ,) *in consequence of the lightness of his intellect.* (TA.) — [Also, applied to a beast, *Restless,* or *unsteady.*] — Also, both epithets, but the latter has an intensive signification, An arrow *that declines,* or *turns aside,* عَنِ ٱلْهَدَفِ *from the butt; and does not hit it.* (Mṣb.)

ٱلْأُطَيْشُ *A certain bird:* (Aboo-Málik, Ḳ:) app. because of its lightness, or activity, and frequent state of commotion. (TA.)

طيع

1. طَاعَ, aor. يَطِيعُ, inf. n. طَيْعٌ: see 1 in art. طوع.

طيف

1. طَافَ ٱلْخَيَالُ, aor. يَطِيفُ, inf. n. طَيْفٌ (Ṣ, O, Mṣb, Ḳ) and مَطَافٌ; (Ṣ, O, Ḳ;) thus says Aṣ: (TA:) and طَافَ, aor. يَطُوفُ, inf. n. طَوْفٌ; (O, Ḳ;) thus says El-Mufaḍḍal: (O, TA:) *The* خيال [i. e. *apparition,* or *phantom,*] *came* (Ṣ, O, Mṣb, Ḳ) *in sleep.* (Ṣ, O, Ḳ.) And طاف بِهِ ٱلْخَيَالُ *The* خيال *came to him,* or *visited him,* (ٱلْمَرِيهِ,) *in sleep.* (TA in art. طوف.)

2. طيّف, inf. n. تَطْيِيفٌ, *He went round* or *round about,* or *circuited, much,* or *often;* as also ▼ اطاف: (Ḳ:) but, (TA,) IDrd says, طوّف and طيّف and ▼ تطيّف are the same in meaning: (O, TA:) therefore what is said in the Ḳ requires consideration: ▼ تطيّف signifies as above. (TA.)

4. اطاف: see the next preceding paragraph: and see also art. طوف.

5: see 2, in two places.

طَيْفٌ *An apparition, a phantom, a spectre,* or *an imaginary form,* (خَيَالٌ,) *coming in sleep;* (IDrd, O, Ḳ;) one says طَيْفُ خَيَالٍ and ▼ طَائِفُ خَيَالٍ [meaning thus]: (IDrd, O:) or *anything that obscures the sight,* [*arising*] *from a vain suggestion of the Devil:* (Lth, TA:) or *a jinnee,* and *a human being,* and *a* خَيَال, *that comes to,* or *visits, a man* [generally *in sleep*]; as also

▼ طَائِفٌ; so says IF in art. طوف: (Mṣb:) both of these words signify alike; i. e. *a thing like the* خَيَال; and *a thing that comes to one*, or *visits one*: (Fr, TA:) and ▼ طِيفٌ, with kesr, signifies *a* خَيَال *itself*: (Kr, TA:) or [طَيْفٌ is properly, or originally, an inf. n.; and] طَيْفُ الخَيَالِ signifies *the coming of the* خيال *in sleep*: (Ṣ, O, Ḳ:*) accord. to El-Mufaddal, (O,) one says طَيْفٌ as meaning طَائِفُ خَيَالٍ because it is originally [طَيِّفٌ, and then] طَيْفٌ; like مَيِّتٌ and مَيْتٌ from مَاتَ, aor. يَمُوتُ. (O, Ḳ.) طَيْفُ الشَّيْطَانِ and ▼ طَائِفُهُ signify *The Devil's visitation, by touch*, or *madness* or *insanity*, (بِاللَّمْسِ,) or *by vain prompting* or *suggestion*: (Mṣb:) or طَيْفٌ مِنَ الشَّيْطَانِ signifies *A touch*, or *slight degree*, or *somewhat* [*of a taint* or *an infection*], *of insanity* or *possession, from the Devil*; syn. لَمَمٌ; occurring in the Ḳur vii. 200, accord. to one reading; another reading being ▼ طَائِفٌ مِنَ الشَّيْطَانِ, which signifies the same. (Ṣ, O. [See also طَوْفٌ.]) One says also طَيْفُ جُنُونٍ [*A touch*, or *slight degree, of insanity*, or *diabolical possession*]. (Ṣ, O.) And طَيْفٌ [alone] signifies *Insanity*, or *diabolical possession*: (O, Ḳ:) so says A'Obeyd, on the authority of El-Aḥmar: (TA:) and this is said by Az to be the meaning of the word in the language of the Arabs. (O, TA.) — And † *Anger*: (I'Ab, Mujáhid, O, Ḳ:) because the intellect of the angry departs [for a time] so that he assumes the the likeness of the insane, or possessed: (O, TA:) said by I'Ab to mean thus in the Ḳur vii. 200. (TA.)

طِيفٌ: see the next preceding paragraph.

طِيَافٌ The *blackness of night*: or this is [طِنَافٌ,] with ن. (TA.)

طَائِفٌ: see طَيْفٌ, in four places: and see art. طوف.

Quasi طيل

طِيَالٌ: طِيَلٌ: طِيَلَةٌ: طِيَلٌ: طِيلٌ: and طِيَلَةٌ: see in art. طول.

طين

1. طَانَهُ, aor. يَطِينُ, (Ṣ,* Mṣb,) inf. n. طَيْنٌ; (Mṣb;) or ▼ طَيَّنَهُ, (Ṣ, MA, Ḳ,) but some disapprove this, (Ṣ,) or this denotes intensiveness and muchness; (Mṣb;) *He plastered it*, or *coated it, with* طين [i. e. *clay*, or *mud*], (Ṣ,* MA, Mṣb, Ḳ,*) namely, a roof, or flat house-top, (Ṣ, Mṣb, Ḳ,) and a house, or chamber, (Mṣb,) or a wall. (MA.) — And the former, (Ṣ, Ḳ,) and ▼ the latter also, (TA,) *He sealed it with* طين [i. e. *clay*], namely, a writing; (Ṣ, Ḳ, TA;) and so ▼ أَطَانَهُ. (TA in art. عنى.) — And [hence,] طَانَهُ ٱللّٰهُ عَلَى الخَيْرِ † *God created him with an adaptation*, or *a disposition, to that which is good; adapted him*, or *disposed him, by creation*, or *nature, thereto*; (Ṣ, Mṣb;) as also طَامَهُ: so says ISk, and he cites as an ex.,

أَلَا تِلْكَ نَفْسٌ طِينَ فِيهَا حَيَاؤُهَا

(Ṣ) meaning [*Verily that is a soul*] *of which the sense of shame is the natural quality*. (TA.) — And طان, said of a man, signifies also حَسَّنَ عَمَلَهُ [i. e. *He made his work*, or *deed, good; he performed*, or *executed, his deed*, or *work, well*]; as also طَامَ: thus expl. by IAar: in the Ḳ, the former is erroneously expl. as meaning حَسَّنَ عَمَلَ الطِّينِ. (TA.)

2: see the foregoing paragraph, in two places.

4: see the first paragraph.

5. تطيّن *He* (a man, TA) *became defiled*, or *besmeared, with* طين [i. e. *clay, earth*, or *mud*]. (Ḳ, TA.)

يَوْمٌ طَانٌ, (Ṣ,) and مَكَانٌ طَانٌ, (Ṣ, Ḳ,) and أَرْضٌ طَانَةٌ, (Ṣ,) *A day*, and *a place*, and *a land*,] *in which is much* طين [meaning *mud*]. (Ṣ, Ḳ.) ▬ See also what next follows.

طِينٌ a word of well-known meaning, (Ṣ, Mṣb, Ḳ, TA,) of which ▼ طَانٌ is a dial. var.; (TA;) *Clay, earth, mould, soil*, or *mud*: (MA, KL, &c.:) it differs in different layers, or strata, of the earth; the best is the pure, unmixed with sand, remaining after the subsiding of the waters; and the best of this is that of Egypt, which has a peculiar property of preventing plague, or pestilence, and the corruption of water into which it is thrown: it is of several sorts; among which are الطِّينُ المَخْتُومُ [*Terra sigillata*, or *Lemnian earth*], and الطِّينُ الأَرْمَنِىُّ [*Armenian bole*], &c.: (TA:) ▼ طِينَةٌ has a more particular signification, (Ṣ, Mṣb,) meaning *a piece*, or *portion, thereof*, (Ḳ, TA,) [as *a piece of clay*] *with which a* [*writing of the kind termed*] صَكّ *and the like are sealed*. (TA.) [Hence,] شَهْوَةُ الطِّينِ [*The longing for clay; a sort of malacia*]. (TA voce حُمَّاض.) And ابْنُ الطِّينِ *Adam*. (T in art. بنى.)

طِينَةٌ: see the next preceding paragraph. — Also [† *A material substance considered as that of which a thing having form consists*. — And hence,] ‡ The *natural*, or *native, constitution* or *disposition*. (Ṣ, Mṣb, Ḳ.) One says, هُوَ مِنَ الطِّينَةِ الأُولَى ‡ [app. meaning *He is of the primitive kind of natural constitution* or *disposition*]. (Ṣ, TA.) And إِنَّهُ لَيَابِسُ الطِّينَةِ ‡ [*Verily he is tough in respect of natural constitution* or *disposition*;] meaning *he is not easy* [*in disposition*]. (TA.)

[طِينِىٌّ *Of*, or *relating to*, الطِّين i. e. *clay* &c.; *clayey, earthy*, &c. — And † *Of*, or *relating to* الطِّينَة i. e. *the natural*, or *native, constitution* or *disposition; natural*, or *native*.]

طِيَانَةٌ The *art of working in*, or *with*, طين [or *clay* &c.; and particularly the *art of plastering with clay*, or *mud*]. (Ḳ.)

طَيَّانٌ *A worker in*, or *with*, طين [or *clay* &c.; and particularly *a plasterer with clay* or *mud*]. (TA.) [طَيَّانٌ, imperfectly decl., belongs to art. طوى.]

مُطَيَّنٌ A roof, or flat house-top, [&c.,] *plastered*, or *coated, with* طين [i. e. *clay*, or *mud*]. (Ṣ, Ḳ.)

ظ

The seventeenth letter of the alphabet: called ظَآءٌ [and ظَا]. (TA.) It is a letter peculiar to the Arabic language; and is one of the letters termed مَجْهُورَة [or vocal, i. e. pronounced with the voice, not with the breath only]; and of the letters termed لِثَوِيَّة [or gingival], like ث and ذ. (TA.) As it does not exist in the language of the Nabathæans, they change it into ط. (IF, TA.) [It is substituted for the ت in the measure اِفْتَعَلَ and the forms inflected therefrom when immediately following ظ; as in اِظَّلَمَ, for اِظْطَلَمَ, for اِظْتَلَمَ: and it is substituted for ذ; as in تَرَكْتُهُ وَقِيذًا and وَقِيظًا; as is related on the authorities of ISk and Kr; and as in جِلْظَآءٌ and أَرْضٌ جِلْذَآءٌ, as is mentioned in the Nawádir el-Aaráb. (TA.) — [As a numeral, it denotes *Nine hundred.*]

ظأ

R. Q. 1. ظَأْظَأَ, inf. n. ظَأْظَأَةٌ (L, Ḳ) and ظَأْظَآءٌ, (Ḳ, TA, [in the CḲ ظَأْواء,]) the latter allowable in the case of a R. Q. verb, as in the instances of وَسْوَاسٌ and the like, (MF, TA,) [accord. to some, but وسواس and the like are generally held to be inf. ns. if with kesr, and simple substs. if with fet-ḥ,] *He* (a goat) *made a* [*rattling*] *sound,* or *cry, when excited by lust,* or *at rutting-time;* syn. نَبَّ. (AA, L, Ḳ.) — And ظَأْظَأَ, (M, Ḳ,) inf. n. ظَأْظَأَةٌ, (M,) *He* (a person whose upper lip was slit, M, Ḳ, and one whose fore teeth were broken at the roots, Ḳ,* TA) *spoke unintelligible speech, and with a nasal sound.* (M, Ḳ.)

ظأر

1. ظَأَرَهَا, (Ṣ, Mgh, Ḳ,) or ظَأَرَهَا عَلَى وَلَدِ غَيْرِهَا, (M,) aor. َ, (M, Ḳ,) inf. n. ظَأْرٌ (Ṣ, M, Ḳ) and ظِئَارٌ, (M, Ḳ,) *He made her* (a camel, Ṣ, Mgh) *to incline to,* or *to affect, a young one not her own,* (Ṣ, M, Mgh, Ḳ,) *and to suckle it;* (M, Ḳ;) as also ▼أَظْأَرَهَا, and ▼ظَاءَرَهَا: (Ḳ:) and [it is also said that] ظِئَارٌ signifies the *making a she-camel to incline to,* or *to affect, and suckle, the young one of another, by the application of a* غِمَامَة *in her nose,* (Ṣ,* Ḳ,* TA,) i. e. *by stopping her nose, and also her eyes,* (TA,) *and by the insertion of a* دُرْجَة [q. v.] *composed of rags into her vulva,* (رَحِم, T, TA, or حَيَآء, Ṣ), *and closing its* [i. e. the vulva's] *edges by means of two pointed pieces of wood stuck through, and putting upon her a* غِمَامَة *covering her head, and leaving her in this state until it distresses her,* (T, TA,) *and she imagines herself to be in labour;* (TA;) *when the* درجة *is pulled out from her vulva* (حَيَآء), *and the young one of another is brought near to her, having its head and skin bedaubed with what has come forth with the* درجة *from the lower part of the vulva;* (T,* TA;) *then they open her nose and her eyes;* (TA;) *and when she sees and smells the young one, she imagines that she has brought it forth, and yields it milk: moreover, when the* درجة *is inserted, the space between the two edges of her vulva is closed by a thong* [*passed round the extremities of the two pointed pieces of wood*]. (T, TA.) It is said in a trad., of 'Omar, (T,) or Ibn-'Omar, (Ṣ, TA,) that he purchased a she-camel, and, seeing in her the laceration on the occasion of ظِئَار, returned her. (T, Ṣ,* TA.) — [Hence,] ظَأَرَهُ عَلَى أَمْرٍ, كَذَا, and ▼أَظْأَرَهُ, and ▼ظَاءَرَهُ, ‡ *He made him to incline to such a thing:* (Lth, T, TA:) and ظَاءَرَنِى عَلَى الأَمْرِ, (so in the CḲ,) or ▼ظَاءَرَنِى عَلَيْهِ, (M, TA, and so in some copies of the Ḳ,) inf. n. مُظَاءَرَةٌ, (TA,) *he endeavoured to turn me,* or *to entice me, to do the thing;* (M, Ḳ, TA;) it not being in my mind: (TA:) or *he compelled me to do the thing, against my will;* (Ḳ, TA;) I having refused to do it. (TA.) It is said in a prov., الطَّعْنُ يَظْأَرُ, meaning, *Thrusting,* or *piercing, with the spear inclines* [one's enemies] *to peace:* (Aṣ, T, A, Ḳ:) J says يَظْأَرُهُ, as also IḲṭṭ, which F disapproves; but others approve it: or the reading of the Ṣ is ▼يُظْئِرُهُ. (TA.) The Arabs also said, الطَّعْنُ ظِئَارُ قَوْمٍ (M, Ḳ) *Thrusting,* or *piercing, with the spear is a means of inclining a people to peace;* (Ḳ;) meaning, make people to fear, that they may love thee. (M, Ḳ.) It is also said, in a trad. of 'Alee, أَظْأَرُكُمْ إِلَى الحَقِّ وَأَنْتُمْ تَفِرُّونَ مِنْهُ, [perhaps a mistake for عَلَى الحَقِّ,] *I incline you* [or *I endeavour to turn you*] *to the truth, and ye flee from it.* (TA.) — ظَأَرَتْ, (Ṣ, Ḳ,) [of which ظُؤُورَة, q. v., appears to be an inf. n.; or you say ظَأَرَتْ عَلَى وَلَدِ غَيْرِهَا, and عَلَى بَوٍّ;] and ▼اِظَّأَرَتْ; (T, M, Ḳ; in one copy of the Ḳ اِظْأَرَتْ;) *She* (a camel, T, Ṣ, M) *inclined to,* or *affected, a young one not her own,* (T, M, Ḳ,) *and suckled it:* (Ḳ:) or *inclined to,* or *affected, the stuffed skin of a young camel.* (Ṣ.) — [Hence,] ظَأَرَ عَلَى عَدُوِّهِ ‡ *He returned against his enemy.* (A, TA.) — And ظَأَرَ, aor. َ; (Mṣb;) or ▼ظَاءَرَ, inf. n. مُظَاءَرَةٌ, (AZ, Ṣ;) *He took to himself a* ظِئْر [or *nurse*]. (AZ, Ṣ, Mṣb.) [See also 8.]

3: see 1, in four places. — One says also, ظَاءَرَتْ, (inf. n. مُظَاءَرَةٌ, T, A,) *She took to herself a child to suckle.* (T, M, A, Ḳ.) — And بَيْنَهُمَا مُظَاءَرَةٌ *There is between them two that relation which consists in each one's being the* ظِئْر [or rather the *fosterer of the child*] *of the other.* (M, Ḳ.) — ظَاوِرٌ occurs in a trad. for ظَائِرٌ. (TA.) [But in what sense is not explained.]

4: see 1, in three places.

8: see 1, near the end. — اِظَّأَرَ لِوَلَدِهِ ظِئْرًا, (Ṣ, and so in some copies of the Ḳ,) or اِطَّأَرَ, (M, and so in some copies of the Ḳ,) the former being similar to اِظَّلَمَ, (Ṣ,) means *He took a nurse for his child.* (Ṣ, M, Ḳ.)

10. اِسْتَظْأَرَتْ *She* (a bitch) *desired the male:* (Ḳ:) mentioned by AM; but he says, "I hesitate respecting it." (TA.) [I think it is probably a mistake for اِسْتَطَارَتْ, mentioned in art. طير. See also ظُؤْرَى.]

ظَأْرٌ Anything *accompanied by the like thereof:* thus applied to a run (عَدْوٌ): (Aṣ, T, TA:) in the Ḳ, and in the Tekmileh, عَدُوٌّ is erroneously put for عَدْوٌ: (TA:) and عَدْوٌ ظَأْرٌ is used by the poet El-Arkaṭ, in describing [wild] asses, as meaning *a run not unsparingly performed.* (T, TA.)

ظِئْرٌ One *that inclines to,* or *affects, the young one of another, and suckles* [or *fosters*] *it;* applied to a human being, (M, A, Ḳ,) and to a camel, (M,) or other [animal]; (A, Ḳ:) to a female and to a male: (M, A, Ḳ:) or a she-camel *that inclines to,* or *affects, the young one of another;*

(Mṣb;) as also ↑ ظُؤُورٌ: (Ṣ:) and hence applied also to a strange woman *that nurses,* or *fosters, the child of another:* and likewise to a man *who fosters the child of another:* and also pronounced ظِيرٌ, with the ء suppressed: (Mṣb:) and the epithet ظِئْرَةٌ is also applied to a female: (A:) the pl. [of pauc.] is أَظْؤُرٌ (M, Ḳ) and أَظْآرٌ, (Ṣ, M, A, Mṣb, Ḳ,) [which latter is also used as a pl. of mult., accord. to an ex. given in the A;] and [the proper pls. of mult. are] ظُؤُورٌ and ↑ ظُؤَارٌ, (Ṣ, M, Ḳ,) which last is an extr. form, (M,) and ↑ ظُؤْرَةٌ, (M, Ḳ,) or, accord. to Sb, this is a quasi-pl. n., (M,) and ظُؤُورَةٌ, (M, Ḳ,) like فُحُولَةٌ and بُعُولَةٌ: (M:) or the pl., applied to camels, is ↑ ظُؤَارٌ; and to women, ظُؤُورَةٌ: (M:) or to women, ظُؤَارٌ and ↑ ظُؤَارٌ: (Mṣb:) ↑ ظُؤُورَةٌ also signifies *a nurse:* (IAạr:) and ↑ ظُؤُورٌ signifies the same as ظِئْرٌ: (TA:) or a she-camel *made to incline to,* or *affect, the young one of another;* (M;) as also ↑ مُظْؤُورَةٌ: (Ṣ:) or *that keeps close to the young one,* or *to the stuffed skin of a young one.* (M.) — [The pl.] ↑ ظُؤَارٌ is also applied (by a poet, M, TA) to ‡ *The three stones upon which the cooking-pot is placed:* (Ṣ, M, Ḳ, TA:) likened to camels; (M, TA;) because of their inclining (Ṣ, M, TA) towards, (Ṣ,) or around, (M, TA,) the ashes. (Ṣ, M, TA.) — And ظِئْرٌ signifies also ‡ *An angle,* or *a corner, of a* قَصْر [or *pavilion, &c.*]. (Ḳ.) — And † *A buttress built against a wall;* (Ḳ,* TA;) likewise called ↑ ظِئْرَةٌ. (TA.)

ظُؤْرَةٌ: } see the next preceding paragraph.
ظِئْرَةٌ: }

ظُؤْرَى A cow *desiring the male:* (Ḳ:) mentioned by Az, on the authority of AḤát; and said to have no verb. (TA. [But see 10, above.])

ظُؤَارٌ: see ظِئْرٌ, in four places.

ظِئَارٌ *A* خِمَامَة [q. v.] *that is put into the nose of a she-camel to make her to incline to,* or *affect, the young one of another, in order that she may not perceive the smell of her young one.* (A.) [See also 1.]

ظُؤُورٌ: see ظِئْرٌ, in two places.

ظُؤُورَةٌ *Inclination to,* or *affection for, the young one of another:* (M, Ḳ:) it may be an inf. n., as well as a pl. [of ظِئْرٌ]. (M.) — Also [The *relation in which one stands by being a* ظِئْر, or *nurse:*] like عُمُومَة and خُؤُولَة &c. (TA.) — See also ظِئْرٌ, latter half.

مَظْؤُورَةٌ: see ظِئْرٌ, latter half.

هُوَ مُظَائِرٌ لَنَا *He is the father of the child which she is nursing.* (T, TA.*)

ظبو

ظُبَةٌ The حَدّ, (T, M, Mṣb, Ḳ,) or طَرَف, (Ṣ,) [both of which mean the *end,* or *extremity,* but the former means also the *edge,*] of a sword, (T, Ṣ, M, Mṣb, Ḳ,) or of a spear-head and the like, (Ḳ,) or also of a spear-head and of an arrow-head and of a dagger and the like; (M;) or the *part next to the* طَرَف [or *extremity*] of the sword; also called its ذُبَاب: (T:) or the ظُبَتَانِ are the *parts of the two edges that are on either side of the* ذُبَاب [by which last word is here app. meant the *point*] of the sword: (AZ, T and TA voce ذُبَابٌ, q. v.:) [for the swords of the Arabs, in the older times, were generally straight, two-edged, and tapering to a point:] or, accord. to Aboo-Riyásh, the ظُبَة of the sword is the *part that is four digits' measure below,* or *within,* (دُونَ,) *the* ذُبَاب thereof; and is the *striking-place* thereof: and it is also its حَدّ; and the ظُبَة of the spear-head is likewise its حَدّ: (Ḥam p. 48:) the ة in ظُبَة is a substitute for و, which is the final radical, (Ṣ, M, Mṣb, Ḳ,) the word being originally ظُبَوٌ: (Ṣ, TA:) the pl. is أَظْبٍ, (Ṣ, Ḳ,) a pl. of pauc., (Ṣ,) and ظُبَاتٌ (T, Ṣ, M, Mṣb, Ḳ) and ظُبَاةٌ [which is originally ظُبَوَةٌ] (Ṣ,* TA) and ظُبُونَ (T, Ṣ, M, Mṣb, Ḳ) and ظِبُونَ and ظُبًى or ظِبًا. (M, Ḳ.) In the saying of Es-Semow-al Ibn-'Ádiyà,

تَسِيلُ عَلَى حَدِّ الظُّبَاتِ نُفُوسُنَا ✱ وَلَيْسَتْ عَلَى غَيْرِ الظُّبَاتِ تَسِيلُ

[*Our bloods flow upon the edge of the* ظبات, *and upon other than* the edge of *the* ظبات *they flow not*], by the ظبات may be meant the *swords,* altogether, or the *striking-places of the swords.* (Ḥam p. 52. [See also a similar ex. in p. 48 of the same.]) — Also *A kind of* مَزَاد [or *leathern water-bag*]. (M.) — And *A place of bending,* or *turning, of a valley;* like ظَبْيَة [which belongs to art. ظبى]: pl. of the former ظُبَاءٌ, a pl. of a rare form. (M in art. ظبى.)

ظبى

[5. تظبّى, if used, means *He acted like the* ظَبْى, or *gazelle;* being similar to تَذَأَّبَ and تَنَمَّرَ &c.: its part. n. is mentioned in the first paragraph of art. ربض.]

ظَبْىٌ *A certain animal,* (TA,) *well known;* (Ṣ, Mṣb, Ḳ, TA;) the غَزَال [or *gazelle;* to which the former word is applied when used unrestrictedly, and which is app. here meant by the latter word, though this seems properly to signify "a young gazelle"]; (M;) [it is the *gazella dorcas,* also called *antilope dorcas,* of which the *ariel,* or *antilope Arabica,* is said to be a variety; or, accord. to some, each is a distinct species of gazelle: the name seems to be properly, but not always (as is shown by an explanation of وَلْدٌ), applied only to the *true antelope* of Arabia and adjacent countries, *as distinguished from the cervine and bovine antelopes:*] it is a name for the male; which is also called تَيْسٌ, when he has become what is termed a ثَنِىّ [q. v.], which he continues to be termed until he dies: (AḤát, Mṣb, TA:) the *female* is called ظَبْيَةٌ, (AḤát, T, M, Mṣb, Ḳ, TA,) and عَنْزٌ and مَاعِزَةٌ: (AḤát, Mṣb, TA:) the dual is ظَبْيَانِ: (Mṣb, TA:) and the pl. is أَظْبٍ, (Ṣ, M, Mṣb, Ḳ,) originally أَظْبُىٌ, (Ṣ, Mṣb,) a pl. of pauc., (Ṣ,) and ظُبِىٌّ and ظِبَاءٌ, (Ṣ, M, Mṣb, Ḳ,) which last is of the masc. and fem., (M, Mṣb,) and ظَبَيَاتٌ, (Ṣ, M, Mṣb, Ḳ,) which is of the fem. (M, Mṣb.) One says, بِهِ دَآءُ ظَبْىٍ [lit. *In him is the disease of a gazelle*]; meaning *in him is no disease;* as there is [said to be] no disease in the ظبى. (AA, T.) And لَكَ عِنْدِى مِائَةٌ سِنَّ الظَّبْىِ [*To thee I owe a hundred* camels *of the age of the gazelle*], i. e., all of them ثُنْيَان [pl. of ثَنِىٌّ, q. v.], because the ظبى does not exceed what is termed إِثْنَآءٌ. (M.) [See also a verse cited voce سِنٌّ; in which the phrase فَجَآءَتْ كَسِنِّ الظَّبْىِ means *And they came; like the age of the gazelle* was the age of every one of them.] It is said in a prov., ↑ لَأَتْرُكَنَّهُ تَرْكَ ظُبَىٍّ ظِلَّهُ [*I will assuredly forsake him as a little gazelle forsakes the place of its shade*]; because the ظبى, when it leaves its covert, does not return to it: it is said in confirming the relinquishing of anything. (T. [See ظِلٌّ, where other relations of this prov. are mentioned.]) And in another prov., الظِّبَاءَ عَلَى البَقَرِ, said when the tie of relationship and friendship between two men is severed, and it was used in the Time of Ignorance as a form of divorce: الظباء is in the accus. case by reason of اِخْتَرْتُ, or اِخْتَارَ, understood, [so that the meaning is I have preferred, or he has preferred, *the gazelles to the* wild *cows,*] by the بقر being meant the women: whence the saying, جَآءَ يَجُرُّ بَقَرَهُ [expl. in art. بقر]. (Meyd. [See also Freytag's Arab. Prov. ii. 61.]) And one says, أَتَيْتُهُ حِينَ شَدَّ الظَّبْىُ ظِلَّهُ i. e. [*I came to him when its shade*] *confined the* ظبى [or *gazelle*] by reason of the vehemence of the heat: or, as some relate it, حِينَ نَشَدَ الظَّبْىُ ظِلَّهُ, meaning طَلَبَهُ [i. e., *when the gazelle sought its shade*]. (TA.) And it is said in a trad., إِذَا أَتَيْتُمْ فَارْبِضْ فِى دَارِهِمْ ظَبْيًا [expl. voce رَبَضَ]. (T, TA.) بِهِ لَا بِظَبْىٍ, (Ṣ, TA,) or بِهِ لَا بِظَبْىٍ أَعْفَرَ, a prov., meaning May this accident befall *him,* (لِيَنْزِلْ بِهِ هٰذِهِ الحَادِثَةُ,) *not a white antelope,* (Meyd,) is said on an occasion of rejoicing at another's affliction, (Ṣ, Meyd, TA,) by way of imprecation, i. e. may God make that which has befallen him to cleave to him. (Ṣ, TA. [See also Freytag's Arab. Prov. i. 148.]) — [أَوْلَادُ الظِّبَآءِ and الظِّبَآءُ are mentioned by Freytag as names of *Certain stars:* in relation to the former of which he refers to Ideler's "Unters." pp. 20-21; and in relation to the latter, to the same work p. 21.] — And الظَّبْىُ is the name of *A brand,* or *mark made with a hot iron, peculiar to some of the Arabs.* (T, Ḳ.)

ظَبْيَةٌ fem. of ظَبْىٌ [q. v.]. (AḤát, T, &c.) — Also a name for † *A woman;* [or, app. *a young* woman;] and so أُمُّ ظَبْيَةَ. (Mṣb, TA.) — And † A man who is stupid, dull, wanting in intelligence, inert, or wanting in vigour. (Ḳ, TA: but not in the CḲ.) — And accord. to the Ḳ, i. q. شَاةٌ: and بَقَرَةٌ: but this is a great mistake, caused by a misunderstanding of what is cited in the passage here next following from the M. (TA.) — Also The vulva of a woman: (Lth, T, Ṣ, M, Ḳ:) and, (M,) accord. to Aṣ, (T, Ṣ,) of any solid-hoofed beast: (T, Ṣ, M:) accord. to some, (M,) or accord. to Fr, (T, Ṣ,) of the bitch: (T, Ṣ, M:) and accord. to Lth, of the she-camel: (T:) IAạr makes it to be peculiarly of the she-ass, and of the ewe or she-goat, and of the cow; (M;) meaning that it signifies the vulva of these: (TA:) and it signifies also the vagina of the mare. (M.) — Also A [bag for travelling-provisions &c., such as is called] جِرَاب: (M, Ḳ:) or peculiarly a small جراب: (M, Ḳ:*) or one made of the skin of the ظَبْى [or gazelle]: (M:) or a thing [i. e. a pouch] like the خَرِيطَة and the كِيس: dim. ↓ ظُبَيْبَةٌ: and pl. ظِبَآءٌ. (T.) — And A [tent such as is called] خِبَآء. (TA.) — And A place of bending, or turning, of a valley; (M, Ḳ;) as also ظُبَةٌ [mentioned in art. ظبو]: pl. of the former ظِبَآءٌ. (M.) — ظَبْيَةُ is one of the names of The well Zemzem. (TA.)

ظُبَىٌّ: see ظَبْىٌ [of which it is the dim.].

ظُبَيْبَةٌ dim. of ظَبْيَةٌ, q. v.

أَرْضٌ مَظْبَاةٌ A land abounding with ظِبَآء [or gazelles]. (M.)

ظر

1. ظَرَّ He cut [or split off] a مِظَرَّةٌ [i. e. a fragment of hard stone, with a sharp edge, to be used as a knife]. (Lth, T, M, Ḳ. [In some copies of the Ḳ, مَظَرَّة; and in one place, in a copy of the M, مَظَرَّة: but correctly مِظَرَّة, as is said in the TA.]) This the pastor does for the purpose of cutting off therewith a thing resembling a wart within the belly of a she-camel, (Lth, T, M,) at the orifice of the womb, when she is affected by a disease occasioned by lusting for the male. (Lth, TA.) — And He slaughtered a she-camel, (Ḳ, TA,) or, as in the "Tekmileh," an animal, with the [stone called] ظُرَر. (TA.)

4. أَظِرِّى فَإِنَّكِ نَاعِلَةٌ (M, Ḳ) is a prov., meaning Tread thou upon the ظُرَر [for thou art furnished with leathern shoes or sandals]: (M:) but the phrase commonly known is with the unpointed ط [i. e. أَطِرِّى: see 4 in art. طر]. (M, Ḳ.)

ظِرٌّ: see the next paragraph.

ظُرَرٌ A sharp-edged hard stone: (Aṣ, T, Mgh, TA:) a stone having an edge like that of the knife: (Ṣ:) or a [kind of] smooth and broad stone which a man breaks and with which he slaughters a camel; (ISh, T, Mgh,* TA;) and it is of any colour; and is also thus called before it is broken: (ISh, T, TA:) and the n. un. is ↓ ظُرَرَةٌ: (T:) or, as also ↓ ظُرَّةٌ and ↓ ظِرٌّ, a stone, (M, Ḳ,) in a general sense: (M:) or a round stone: (TA:) or a round sharp-edged stone: (M, Ḳ:) or a piece of stone having a sharp edge: (M:) the pl. is ظِرَارٌ and ظِرَّانٌ; (Aṣ, T, Ṣ, Mgh;) or the pl. is ظِرَّانٌ and ظُرَّانٌ; (Th, M, and so in the Ḳ accord. to the TA; [in the CḲ ظرار and ظُرّار;]) and Th says that the former of these is pl. of ظُرَر, or both may be pls. of ظِرّ; (M;) and another pl. is أَظِرَّةٌ, (T, TA,) [a pl. of pauc.,] occurring in a trad.; (TA;) or, accord. to ISh, ↓ ظِرَارٌ [mentioned above as a pl.] is a sing., and أَظِرَّةٌ is its pl.: (Mgh:) and ↓ ظُرْظُورٌ and ↓ أُظْرُورٌ and ↓ مُظْرُورٌ, of which last the pl. is مَظَارِيرُ, (Ṣgh, Ḳ, TA,) and all of which are with ḍamm, thus in the handwriting of Ṣgh, (TA,) signify the same [as ظُرَر &c.]. (Ṣgh, Ḳ, TA.)

ظُرَّةٌ: see the next preceding paragraph, in two places.

ظِرَارٌ: see ظُرَر: and see also مِظَرَّةٌ.

ظَرِيرٌ: see مِظَرَّةٌ. — Also A sign set up whereby one is guided to the right way: pl. أَظِرَّةٌ (M, Ḳ) and ظُرَّانٌ: (TA, and so in the CḲ: [in some copies of the Ḳ ظِرَار, which is said in the TA to be wrong:]) أَظِرَّةٌ signifies signs set up whereby one is guided to the right way, like the امرة [thus in a copy of the T, a mistranscription for أَمَرَة]; some of which are extended and hard, and millstones are made from them. (T.)

ظِرَارَةٌ: see مِظَرَّةٌ.

ظُرْظُورٌ: } see ظُرَر.
أُظْرُورٌ: }

أَرْضٌ مَظَرَّةٌ, (Ṣ, M, K,) thought to be thus by AAF; (M;) or مَظِرَّةٌ, (T, M,) with kesr to the ظ, accord. to Th; (M;) Land containing, (T, Ṣ,) or abounding with, (Ḳ,) stones of the kind called ظُرَر: (T, Ṣ, Ḳ:) or stony land: (Th, M:) and ↓ ظَرِيرٌ also has the former meaning: (Ḳ:) or this latter is an epithet applied to a place as meaning rugged, or rugged and hard: (Ṣ:) or meaning a place abounding with stones: (M:) and its pl. is أَظِرَّةٌ and ظُرَّانٌ. (Ṣ.) — See also the next paragraph.

مِظَرَّةٌ A stone with which one strikes fire. (TṢ, Ḳ.) — And also, (TṢ, TA,) or, accord. to the Ḳ, with fet-ḥ, [i. e. ↓ مَظَرَّةٌ,] but this requires consideration, (TA,) Fragments [or a fragment, agreeably with an explanation in the Mgh, in my copy of which مَظَرَّةٌ is erroneously put for مِظَرَّةٌ,] of sharp-edged stone: (TṢ, Ḳ, TA:) pl. مَظَارُّ: (TṢ, TA:) or مِظَرَّةٌ signifies a piece split off from ظِرَّان [pl. of ظُرَر or ظِرّ], (Sh, TA,) or [simply] a stone, (M, TA,) with which one cuts: (Sh, M, TA:) as also ↓ ظِرَارٌ, (M,) or ↓ ظِرَارَةٌ. (TA.)

مُظْرُورٌ: see ظُرَرٌ.

ظرب

1. ظَرِبَ بِهِ, aor. ـَ, He, or it, stuck, adhered, or clave, to him, or it. (Ḳ.)

2. ظَرَّبَتِ الحَوَافِرُ, inf. n. تَظْرِيبٌ, The solid hoofs became hard and strong. (T, Ḳ.)

ظَرِبٌ A stone projecting (Lth, T, M, Mṣb, Ḳ) from a mountain or from rugged ground (Lth, T) and having a sharp point: (Lth, T, M, Ḳ:) or an expanded mountain, (M, Ḳ, TA,) accord. to some, that is not high: (TA:) or a small mountain: (M, Ḳ:) or a small hill: (T, Ṣ, Mṣb:) pl. ظِرَابٌ (T, Ṣ, M, Mṣb, Ḳ) and أَظْرُبٌ, (Nh, TA,) [the latter a pl. of pauc.,] the former pl. of a rare kind, for by rule it should be أَظْرَابٌ, and it seems as though they had imagined the sing. to be ظَرْبٌ, and so made the pl. like سِهَامٌ, pl. of سَهْمٌ: (Mṣb, TA:) or, accord. to En-Naḍr, ظَرِبٌ signifies the smallest of [hills such as are termed] آكَام, and the sharpest in stones, all its stones being sharp like knives, the white thereof and the black and of every colour: and the pl. is أَظْرَابٌ. (T.) [See also this pl. below.]

ظُرُبٌّ Short, and thick, (M, Ḳ, TA,) and fleshy: (Lḥ, TA:) or a short and fleshy man. (Ṣ.)

ظَرِبَى and ظِرْبَى: see ظَرِبَانٌ, in three places.

ظِرْبَآءُ and ظَرِبَآءُ: see the next paragraph, in four places.

ظَرِبَانٌ (Ṣ, M, Mṣb, Ḳ, &c.) and ظِرْبَانٌ (AA, AZ, Mṣb, TA) and ظَرْبَانٌ (IJ, TA) and ↓ ظَرِبَآءُ (M, CḲ, TA, or ↓ ظِرْبَآءُ or ↓ ظَرِبَآءُ accord. to two different copies of the Ḳ) A small, stinking beast, (AZ, S, M, Mṣb, Ḳ,) resembling a cat, (AZ, Ṣ, M, Ḳ,) or resembling a short Chinese dog, (Mṣb,) or resembling an ape or a monkey, (AA, T, M, TA,) or above the whelp of a dog, (El-Mustaḳṣee, TA,) that often emits a noiseless wind from the anus; (M, Mṣb,* TA;) said by Az, on the authority of the handwriting of AHeyth, to be a beast that has small legs, their length being that of half a finger, but which is broad, its breadth being equal to the space measured by the extension of the thumb and the little finger, or of the thumb and the fore finger, and its length being a cubit, having a compact head, and its ears [for ادناه, in my original, I read أُذُنَاهُ] being like the cat's; (TA;) it is small and short in the ears, (أَصْلَمُ الأُذُنَيْنِ, M, Mṣb,) or having a stoppage of the ears, (أَصَمُّ الاذنين, TA,) its earholes [only] hearing a confused, or humming, or ringing, sound; (M, TA;) long in the snout, [but El-Farezdaḳ speaks of it as having a short nose, as is shown in the Ṣ,] black in the back, white in the belly; (M, Mṣb, TA;) it is said that its back is [or rather contains] one single bone, without any قَفَص

[or cage-formed structure of ribs, &c.], and that the sword has no effect upon it by reason of the hardness of its skin, unless striking its nose: (TA:) the pl. is ظَرَابِينُ, (M, Ḳ,) or ظَرَابِىُّ, (AZ, T, Ṣ, Mṣb,) sometimes, (Ṣ,) or this latter also, (M, Ḳ,) as though it were pl. of ظِرْبَآءٌ, (Ṣ,) or the first ى is a substitute for the ا [of the sing. ظَرِبَانٌ] and the second for the ن, (M,) and (quasi-pl. ns., M, Ḳ) ▼ ظِرْبَى (AZ, T, M, Mṣb, Ḳ) and ▼ ظِرْبَآءُ, (M, Ḳ,) or ▼ ظِرْبَى, is a pl. like حِجْلَى pl. of حَجَلٌ, (Ṣ, TA,) and these two are [said to be] the only pls. of this measure, (AḤei, TA,) and Lth and AHeyth say that ظِرْبَآءُ is incorrect, and is rightly ▼ظِرْبَى. (T, TA.) A poet says, (namely, 'Abd-Allah Ibn-Ḥajjáj Ez-Zebeedee, M, TA,)

أَلَا أَبْلِغَا قَيْسًا وَخِنْدِفَ أَنَّنِى
ضَرَبْتُ كَثِيرًا مَضْرِبَ الظَّرِبَانِ

[Now tell ye Ḳeys and Khindif that I have struck Ketheer in the place of striking of the ظربان], meaning that he had struck Ketheer Ibn-Shiháb (Ṣ, M, TA) El-Medh-ḥijee upon his face; for the ظربان has a line, or long mark, upon his face; and he likens the blow that he inflicted upon his face to that mark: [see مَضْرِبٌ:] and the same words of the latter hemistich, except that عُبَيْدًا is substituted in them for كَثِيرًا, occur in a verse of Asad Ibn-Nághiṣah, who slew 'Obeyd by order of En-Noamán. (TA.) One says, فَسَا بَيْنَنَا الظَّرِبَانُ, (Ṣ,) or بَيْنَهُمْ, (Mṣb, Ḳ,) [lit. The ظربان emitted a noiseless wind from its anus among us, or among them,] a prov., (Ṣ,) meaning that we, or they, became disunited, and alienated, one from another: [for] when this animal emits a noiseless wind from its anus in the garment of a man, the stink does not go away until the garment wears out: (Ṣ, Mṣb, Ḳ:) the Arabs of the desert assert that it does so in the garment of him who hunts it: (Ṣ:) and it is said to do so in the hole of the [lizard called] ضَبّ, which, being stupified by the foulness of the stink, is taken and eaten by it. (M, Ḳ, TA.) One says also, تَشَاتَمَا فَكَأَنَّمَا جَزَرَا بَيْنَهُمَا ظَرِبَانًا [They reviled each other, and it was as though they slaughtered between them a ظربان]: the foulness of their reviling being likened to the stink of that animal. (M, TA.) And يَتَنَازَعَانِ جِلْدَ الظَّرِبَانِ They two contend in pulling at the skin of the ظربان, meaning † they revile each other: (M, TA:) and يَتَمَاشَنَانِ جِلْدَ الظَّرِبَانِ They wipe their hands together upon the skin of the ظربان, [likewise] meaning † they revile each other. (IAạr, T, TA.)

الأَظْرَابُ [accord. to some] signifies Four teeth behind the نَوَاجِذ [or other grinders; app. meaning, of a horse]: (Ḳ:) or the sockets (أَسْنَاخ) of the teeth: (Ṣ, Ḳ:) [and it is said that] أَظْرَابُ اللِّجَامِ signifies the knots that are at the extremities of the bit. (M, TA.) J cites the following verse, ascribing it to 'Ámir Ibn-Eṭ-Ṭufeyl,

وَمُقَطِّعٍ حَلَقَ الرِّحَالَةِ سَابِحٍ
بَادٍ نَوَاجِذُهُ عَنِ الأَظْرَابِ

[thus in the Ṣ, (but in the M and TA عَلَى الأَظْرَابِ,) as though meaning And breaking in pieces the rings of the girth of the saddle, running with the fore legs well stretched forth, his grinders appearing from the sockets]: but IB says, [following the reading in the M and TA,] the verse is by Lebeed; and the poet is describing a horse that breaks in pieces the rings of the saddle by his springing forward, and whose grinders (نَوَاجِذُه) appear when he treads upon the [stones, or hills, called] ظِرَاب: [see ظَرِبٌ, of which both ظِرَابٌ and أَظْرَابٌ are said to be pls.:] also that the right reading is وَمُقَطَّعٍ [and سَابِحٌ]: and by the نواجذ are meant the ضَوَاحِك [or teeth next behind the canine teeth], accord. to Hr. (TA.)

حَوَافِرُ مُظَرَّبَةٌ [accord. to the TA مُظْرِبَةٌ, but this is evidently a mistake (see 2),] means [Solid hoofs] that have become hard and strong: (Ḳ, TA:) [but] accord. to El-Mufaḍḍal, المُظَرَّبُ, like مُعَظَّم [in measure], signifies الَّذِى قَدْ لَوَّحَتْهُ الظِّرَابُ [app. meaning that which the stones, or hills, called ظِرَاب have altered, or, perhaps, heated, in its treading upon them]. (TA.)

ظرف

1. ظَرُفَ, (T, Ṣ, M, &c.,) inf. n. ظَرَافَةٌ, (Ṣ, Mṣb,) or ظَرْفٌ and ظَرَافَةٌ, (T, M, Mgh,* O, Ḳ,) but the latter is rare, (Ḳ,) allowable in poetry, (T, M,) or, as some say, is of frequent occurrence, and confirmed by analogy, (MF, TA,) said of a man, (Ṣ, O,) [or only of a young man, and ظَرُفَتْ of a young woman,] He possessed the quality, or qualities, termed ظَرْف meaning as expl. below [i. e. excellence, or elegance, in mind, manners, and address or speech; and in person, countenance, or garb, guise, or external appearance; or all of these qualities combined: he was, or became, clever, ingenious, intelligent, or acute in intellect; well-mannered, well-bred, accomplished, or polite; beautiful in person or countenance; elegant, or graceful; or elegant in garb, guise, or external appearance]. (T, Ṣ, O, Mṣb, Ḳ.) — See also what here follows.

3. ▼ ظَارَفَنِى فَظَرُفْتُهُ [He vied, or contended, with me in ظَرْف] and I was more ظَرِيف (كُنْتُ) ▼ (أَظْرَفَ) than he. (IḲṭṭ, TA.)

4. اظرف He (a man) had many [ظُرُوف, or] receptacles [of any kind]. (TA.) — And He begat, (Ṣ, Mgh, O, Ḳ,) or had born to him, (M,) children that were ظُرَفَآء (Ṣ, M, O, Ḳ) or ظِرَاف [pls. of ظَرِيف, q. v.]. Mgh.) — اظرف بِالرَّجُلِ He mentioned the man as possessing ظَرْف. (M, TA.) — And اظرف فِى العِبَارَةِ is explainable [as meaning He was elegant, or eloquent, in the expression, or phrase, or speech], if the saying be received from those who are trustworthy: if not, it is correctly أَطْرَفَ, with the unpointed ط; meaning "he said what was novel and pleasing." (Mgh.) — اظرف المَتَاعَ, (O,) in the Ḳ, erroneously, فُلَانًا, (TA,) He put, or assigned, or made, a ظَرْف [or receptacle] for the goods. (O, TA.)

5. تظرّف He affected ظَرْف; (Ṣ, O, Ḳ;) as also ▼ تظارف. (TA.) One says, فُلَانٌ يَتَظَرَّفُ وَلَيْسَ بِظَرِيفٍ [Such a one affects ظَرْف and he is not ظَرِيف]. (TA.)

6: see the next preceding paragraph.

10. استظرفهُ He found him [or held him] to be ظَرِيف. (O,* TA.)

ظَرْفٌ A receptacle (Lth, T, Ṣ, M, Mgh, O, Mṣb, Ḳ) of anything; (Lth, T, M;) [a vessel, or vase;] an إِبْرِيق is thus termed as being a ظرف for what is in it: (Lth, T, TA:) and AḤn applies it to a seed-vessel, or pericarp, or a cell of a pericarp: (M, TA:) [and it is also applied to a case, or cover, for a book or the like:] the pl. is ظُرُوفٌ: (T, Ṣ,* M, Mgh, O, Mṣb, Ḳ:) أَظْرَافٌ is a mistake. (Mgh.) [Applying it to a vessel of silver,] Ḥar uses it as meaning "silver." (P. 614 [referring to a phrase in p. 213].) One says, أَخَذْتُ المَتَاعَ بِظَرْفِهِ [I took the goods with the receptacle thereof]. (A, TA.) And hence, (A, TA,) رَأَيْتُهُ بِظَرْفِهِ ‡ I saw him himself. (A, O, Ḳ, TA.) And هُوَ نَقِىُّ الظَّرْفِ ‡ He is faithful, (O, Ḳ, TA,) not treacherous. (M, O, Ḳ, TA.) — And hence † [An adverbial noun of place or of time, implying the meaning of the preposition فِى; and also by some applied to a noun of place or of time together with that preposition; i. e.] what are termed ظَرْفُ المَكَانِ and الزَّمَانِ, (O,) pl. ظُرُوفُ الزَّمَانِ and المَكَانِ: (Ṣ, M:*) the descriptive terms that denote the places [or times] of things are called ظُرُوفٌ: (Lth, T:) they are thus termed by Kh; and by Ks, مَحَالٌّ; and by Fr, صِفَاتٌ. (T.) — Also [Excellence, or elegance, in mind, manners, and address or speech; and in person, countenance, or garb, guise, or external appearance; or all of these qualities combined:] a term denoting a condition that combines the generality of mental and bodily and extrinsic excellences; likened [by reason of its comprehensiveness] to the receptacle thus called: (Er-Rághib, TA:) or cleverness, ingeniousness, intelligence, or acuteness in intellect; syn. كِيَاسَةٌ, (Ṣ, O, Ḳ,) or كَيْسٌ, (Mgh, Mṣb,) and ذَكَآءٌ: (Mgh:) or i. q. بَرَاعَةٌ, and ذَكَآءُ قَلْبٍ; [the former meaning excellence in knowledge, or other qualities; or accomplishment, or perfection, in every excellence, and in goodliness;] ('Eyn, M, O, Mṣb, Ḳ;*) thus accord. to most of the copies of the Ḳ [as well as the 'Eyn and M and O and Mṣb], but correctly بَزَاعَةٌ, with the letter زاى: (TA:) [if so, these two explanations (بَزَاعَةٌ and ذَكَآءُ قَلْبٍ) add nothing to others here given:] or *skilfulness* (M, Ḳ, TA) *in a thing* (M, TA) is thus termed by the people of El-Yemen: (TA:) or *it is in the tongue*, (IAạr, T, Ḳ,) *only*; (Ḳ;) meaning *beauty of expression*, (M, L, TA,) and *eloquence*; (L, TA;) and حَلَاوَةٌ is in the eyes, and مَلَاحَةٌ is in the mouth, and جَمَالٌ is in the nose: (IAạr, T:) or *beauty of garb, guise*, or *external appearance*: (M:) or *beauty of face*, and *of garb, guise*, or *external appearance*: (O, Ḳ:) or *it is in the face* and *in the tongue*: (Ks, O, Ḳ:) or *goodliness*, or *beauty*; and أَدَب [as having the meaning first assigned to ظَرْفٌ in this sentence, i. e. *excellence*, or *elegance*, *in mind, manners*, or *address* or *speech*; or as meaning *good breeding, good manners, politeness*, or *polite accomplishments*]: (Mṣb:) or, as an inf. n., the *being elegant, graceful*, or *beautiful*: and the *being intelligent, sagacious*, or *acute in intellect*: (KL:) accord. to the author of the 'Eyn, (O,) it is only an attribute of young men and young women (M, O, Mṣb,* Ḳ) that are acute in intellect, clever, or skilful; (M, O, Ḳ;) not of elders, nor of lords, or chiefs: (M, Ḳ:) but as meaning كَيْس, it is common to young persons and elders: (Mṣb:) some of those who affect distinctness of speech by twisting the sides of the mouth say that the word is ▼ ظُرْفٌ, with ḍamm, to distinguish it from ظَرْفٌ meaning "a receptacle;" but this is a sheer mistake. (MF, TA.)

ظُرْفٌ: see what immediately precedes.

[ظَرْفِيَّةٌ, a term of grammar, The *quality of denoting place*, or *time, adverbially, by a noun implying the meaning of the preposition* فِى; and also, accord. to some, *by a noun together with that preposition*. One says مَنْصُوبٌ عَلَى الظَّرْفِيَّةِ, meaning *Put in the accusative case as denoting place*, or *time, adverbially*.]

ظُرَافٌ: see ظَرِيفٌ, near the beginning and near the end.

[ظَرُوفٌ perhaps signifies *Possessing the quality*, or *qualities, termed* ظَرْف, *in a great*, or *an extraordinary degree*: used alike as masc. and fem.: for I find it stated that] one says قَيْنَةٌ ظَرُوفٌ [*A female slave*, or *slave-songstress, that is very intelligent* or *skilful* or *elegant* &c.]. (TA. [But I think it most probable that this is a mistranscrip- for فِتْيَةٌ ظُرُوفٌ, a phrase which I find in the T, and there expl. as meaning ظُرَفَآءُ.])

ظَرِيفٌ *Possessing the quality*, or *qualities, termed* ظَرْف; (T, Ṣ, M, O, Mṣb, Ḳ;) as also ▼ ظُرَافٌ; the two being like طَوِيلٌ and طُوَالٌ, (O,) [or the latter has an intensive signification, (see طُوَالٌ, and see also the "Durrat el-Ghowwáṣ," in De Sacy's Anthol. Gramm. Arabe, p. 48 of the Ar. text,)] and ▼ ظُرَّافٌ, (M, Ḳ,) or this last, which is like طُوَّالٌ, denotes more than ظُرَافٌ without teshdeed: (O:) accord. to Mbr, it is derived from ظَرْف signifying "a receptacle," as though meaning a receptacle for excellence, or elegance, in mind, manners, or address or speech: (TA:) [it may be rendered, agreeably with explanations of ظَرْف, *excellent*, or *elegant, in mind, manners*, and *address* or *speech*; and *in person, countenance* or *garb, guise*, or *external appearance*: or *clever, ingenious, intelligent*, or *acute in intellect*; *well-mannered, well-bred, accomplished*, or *polite*; *beautiful in person* or *countenance*; *elegant*, or *graceful*; &c.:] and is expl. as meaning *eloquent*; thus by Aṣ and IAạr: and *possessing knowledge and courage*: and *goodly*, or *beautiful, in clothing*, and *in outer apparel*: (TA:) and is used by the people of El-Yemen as meaning *skilful*: (O:) and, as Ks says, it is applied as an epithet to a tongue, and to a face: (TA:) the pl. of ظَرِيفٌ is ظِرَافٌ (Ṣ, M, O, Mṣb, Ḳ) and ظُرَفَآءُ (T, Ṣ, O, Mṣb, Ḳ) and ظَرِيفُونَ (O, Ḳ) and ظُرُفٌ, (Ṣ, M, IB, Ḳ,) a form sometimes used, (IB, TA,) and ظُرُوفٌ, (T, Ṣ, M, O, Ḳ,) also a form sometimes used, (Ṣ, O,) approvable in poetry, (T,) as though formed from ظَرْفٌ, or [anomalous] like مَذَاكِيرُ (Ṣ, O, Ḳ) accord. to Kh (Ṣ, O) and Sb: (TA:) the pl. of ▼ ظُرَافٌ is ظُرَفَآءُ: (Lḥ, M, Ḳ:) and the pl. of ▼ ظُرَّافٌ is ظُرَّافُونَ: (M, Ḳ:) the fem. of ظَرِيفٌ is ظَرِيفَةٌ; and the pl. of this is ظِرَافٌ, (Sb, T, M, Mṣb, TA,) like a pl. of the masc., (Sb, M, TA,) and ظَرَائِفُ. (T, M, TA.) It is said in a trad. of 'Omar, mentioned by IAạr, (Mgh, O, TA,) and by Aṣ, (TA,) إِذَا كَانَ ٱللِّصُّ ظَرِيفًا لَا يُقْطَعُ, (Mgh,) or لَمْ يُقْطَعْ, (O, TA,) meaning *When the thief is eloquent* (Mgh, O, TA) *and intelligent*, (Mgh,) he averts from himself the prescribed punishment by his pleading [so that *he will not be*, or *is not, mutilated* by amputation of the hand]. (Mgh, O, TA.)

[ظَرِيفَةٌ, as a subst., *A thing*, and *a saying, that is* ظَرِيف, meaning *elegant*, &c.: pl. ظَرَائِفُ.]

ظُرَّافٌ: see ظَرِيفٌ, near the beginning and near the end.

ظَارِفٌ [is distinguished from ظَرِيفٌ like as شَارِفٌ is from شَرِيفٌ, q. v.]. Lḥ mentions the saying أَظْرُفْ إِنْ كُنْتَ ظَارِفًا [*Possess thou* ظَرْف *if thou be one who will possess it*]: in meaning the actual state, they said إِنَّهُ لَظَرِيفٌ [*Verily he is one who possesses* ظَرْف]. (M.)

أَظْرَفُ: see 3. Ks allows the saying, interrogatively, مَا أَظْرَفُ زَيْدٍ أَلِسَانُهُ أَظْرَفُ أَمْ وَجْهُهُ [*What is the part that is the more excellent in* ظَرْف (or *elegance*, &c.), *of Zeyd? is his tongue the more so*, or *his face?*]. (TA.)

يَا مَظْرَفَانُ is an expression similar to يَا مَلْكَعَانُ [and مَكْذَبَانُ &c.; meaning *O thou who possessest the quality*, or *qualities, of* ظَرْف *in a great*, or *an extraordinary degree*]. (A, TA.)

ظعن

1. ظَعَنَ, (Ṣ, Mṣb, Ḳ,) aor. ـَ, (Mṣb, Ḳ,) inf. n. ظَعْنٌ (Ṣ, Mṣb, Ḳ) and ▼ ظَعَنٌ, (Ṣ, Ḳ,) or the latter is a simple subst., (Mṣb,) and ظُعُونٌ (TA) [and مَظْعَنٌ, occurring in a verse of Zuheyr cited in art. بلو, conj. 3], *He journeyed, went away, departed*, (Ṣ,* Mṣb, Ḳ,* TA,) or *removed*; (Mṣb;) *he journeyed to seek after herbage*, or *to water*; or *he removed from water to water*, or *from one country*, or *tract of land, to another*. (TA. [See also the part. n., ظَاعِنٌ.]) — ظَعَنَ بِهِ: see what next follows.

4. أَظْعَنَهُ *He made him to journey, go away, depart*, (Ṣ, Mṣb, Ḳ,) or *remove*; and ▼ ظَعَنَ بِهِ signifies the same [or *he journeyed*, &c., *with him*]. (Mṣb.)

8. اِظَّعَنَتْهُ *She rode him*, (Ṣ, Ḳ, TA,) namely, a camel: you say, هٰذَا بَعِيرٌ تَظَّعِنُهُ المَرْأَةُ *This is a camel that the woman rides* (Ṣ, TA) *in her journeying*, and *in the day of her departure*. (TA.)

ظَعَنٌ: see 1: — and see also ظَاعِنٌ.

ظَعْنَةٌ *A short journey*. (TA.)

ظِعْنَةٌ *A state* or *condition*, or *a mode* or *manner, of journeying* or *departing*. (TA.)

ظِعَانٌ *A rope with which a* هَوْدَج [or *woman's camel-vehicle*] *is bound*; (Ṣ, Ḳ;) or *with which a load is bound*, accord. to the T: and ▼ ظَعُونٌ signifies the same. (TA.)

ظَعُونٌ A camel *used for work and for bearing burdens*: (Ṣ, Ḳ, TA:) or, as some say, peculiarly, [like ظَعِينَةٌ,] a camel *that is ridden by a woman*. (TA.) — See also ظِعَانٌ.

ظَعِينَةٌ *A* هَوْدَج [or *woman's camel-vehicle*] (Ṣ, Mgh, Mṣb, Ḳ, TA) *in which is a woman*, (TA,) or *whether there be in it a woman or not*: (Ṣ, Mṣb, Ḳ, TA:) this is [said to be] the primary signification: (Mgh:) pl. ظَعَائِنُ and ظُعُنٌ (Ṣ, Mgh, Mṣb, Ḳ) and ظُعْنٌ (Ṣ, Ḳ) and [pl. of pauc.] أَظْعَانٌ (Ṣ, Mgh, Ḳ) and pl. pl. ظُعُنَاتٌ. (TA. [But see, in what follows, an assertion of AZ respecting the pl. ظُعُنٌ.]) — And *A woman*, (ISk, Mgh, Mṣb, TA,) *whether in a* هَوْدَج *or elsewhere*; (ISk, TA;) the word being used in the sense of مَظْعُونَةٌ [for مَظْعُونٌ بِهَا]; because her husband journeys (يَظْعَنُ) with her: (Mṣb:) or a man's *wife*; because she journeys with her husband: (TA:) or a *woman as long as she is in the* هودج; (Ṣ, Mṣb, Ḳ;) when not in it she is not thus called: (Ṣ:) or this is the primary meaning: then it was applied to her though in her tent, because she might become مَظْعُونَة [i. e. مَظْعُونٌ بِهَا]: (Mṣb:) it is mostly applied to *a woman riding* [*in a* هودج]: then, to *a* هودج *without a woman*: and to *a woman without a* هودج. (TA.) 'Amr Ibn-Kulthoom says,

قِفِى قَبْلَ التَّفَرُّقِ يَا ظَعِينَا •
• نُخَبِّرْكِ اليَقِينَ وَتُخْبِرِينَا

[*Pause thou before separation, O woman in the*

camel-vehicle: we will inform thee of the real truth respecting our case, *and thou shalt inform us* respecting thy case]: (Ṣ:) يَا ظَعِينَا is for يَا ظَعِينَةُ. (EM p. 185.) — And, accord. to Lth, *A camel that is ridden by women:* [like ظَعُونٌ:] and applied to signify *a woman* because she rides it: or, accord. to IAmb, *a camel upon which one journeys:* and hence the trad., لَيْسَ فِى جَمَلٍ ظَعِينَةٍ صَدَقَةٌ i. e. [*There is no poor-rate in the case of*] *the camel upon which one journeys;* if the phrase be thus: but if it be فِى جَمَلِ ظَعِينَةٍ, by the last word is meant a woman: (TA:) AZ says, one should not say حُمُولٌ nor ظُعُنٌ except as meaning the *camels upon which are* هَوَادِج, *whether there be in them women or not.* (Ṣ.)

ظَاعِنٌ *Journeying, going away, departing,* or *removing:* (Mṣb:) [*a traveller:*] any one *going forth on a journey, on pilgrimage,* or *on a warring and plundering expedition,* or *journeying from one city* [or *town* &c.] *to another: contr. of* خَافِضٌ [and *of* مُقِيمٌ]: one says, أَظَاعِنٌ أَنْتَ أَمْ مُقِيمٌ [*Art thou journeying* or *abiding?*]: the pl. is ظَاعِنُونَ and ظُعْنٌ, and ↓ ظَعْنٌ is a quasi-pl. n. syn. with ظَاعِنُونَ. (TA.)

مِظْعَانٌ, applied to a horse or mare, and to a she-camel, *Easy in pace.* (TA.)

مَظْعُونٌ *Made to journey, go away, depart,* or *remove;* originally مَظْعُونٌ بِهِ; the complement being suppressed because of frequency of usage. (Mṣb.)

ظفر

1. ظَفِرَهُ: see 2. ═ [See also ظَفِرَتْ.] — ظَفِرَتْ عَيْنُهُ, (T, Ṣ, O, Ḳ,) aor. ـَ, inf. n. ظَفَرٌ (Ṣ, O) and ظَفَارَةٌ; (O;) and, as some say, ظُفِرَتْ; (T;) *His eye had what is termed a* ظَفَرَة or ظُفُر. (T, Ṣ, O, Ḳ.) — And ظَفِرَ *He* (a man) *had upon his eye what is termed a* ظَفَرَة or ظُفُر. (T, O, Ḳ.) ═ ظَفِرَهُ, aor. ـَ, (Mṣb,) inf. n. ظَفَرٌ, *He attained, got, got possession of,* or *acquired, what he desired,* or *sought:* (Lth,* Ṣ,* M,* A,* Mṣb, Ḳ:*) *he succeeded,* or *was successful:* (Mṣb:) *he won, was victorious,* or *gained the victory:* (Lth, T:) and ↓ اِظَّفَرَ [originally اِظْتَفَرَ] signifies the same as ظَفِرَ. (Ṣ.) You say, ظَفِرَ بِهِ and عَلَيْهِ, and ظَفِرَهُ, *He attained it, got it, got possession of it,* or *acquired it;* (M, Ḳ;) and in like manner ↓ اِظَّفَرَ, of the measure اِفْتَعَلَ. (Ḳ.) And ظَفِرْتُ بِالضَّالَّةِ *I found the stray,* or *lost beast.* (Mṣb.) And ظَفِرَ بِعَدُوِّهِ (Ṣ, A, Mṣb) and عَلَيْهِ, (Akh, Ṣ, A,) and ظَفِرَهُ, (Ṣ,) *He gained the victory,* or *mastery, over his enemy; he overcame him.* (Ṣ,* A, Mṣb.*) — [Hence,] ظَفِرَتِ النَّاقَةُ لَقْحًا ‡ *The she-camel took,* or *received, impregnation.* (A, TA.) And مَا ظَفِرَتْكَ عَيْنِى (AZ, T, Ṣ, A, Ḳ) مُنْذُ حِينٍ (AZ, T) or مُنْذُ زَمَانٍ (Ṣ, A) ‡ *My eye hath not seen thee* [*for some time*]: (AZ, T, Ṣ, A, Ḳ:) like مَا أَخْطَأَتْكَ. (AZ, T.) ═ [ظَفَرَ in the dial. of Ḥimyer is said by Freytag, on the authority of the Kitáb el-Aḍdád, to signify *He sat.*]

2. ظَفَّرَ فِيهِ, (A, Ḳ,) inf. n. تَظْفِيرٌ, (Ṣ,) *He inserted his nail into it;* (Ṣ, A, Ḳ;) namely, an apple, and the like, (Ṣ, Ḳ,) a cucumber, and a melon: (A:) and [in like manner] ↓ اِظَّفَرَ, of the measure اِفْتَعَلَ, *he stuck,* or *fixed, his nail* [into a thing]; (Ṣ, Ḳ, TA;) and so اِطَّفَرَ, with the unpointed ط. (TA.) You say, ظَفَّرَ فُلَانٌ فِى وَجْهِ فُلَانٍ *Such a one stuck his nail into the flesh of the face of such a one, and wounded it.* (TA.) And نَيَّبَ فِى لَحْمِهِ وَظَفَّرَ *He stuck his dog-tooth and his nail into his flesh, and wounded it.* (A.) And ظَفَّرَ فُلَانٌ فِى كَذَا وَنَيَّبَ ‡ *Such a one clung to, caught to,* or *took fast hold upon, such a thing.* (A in art. نيب.) Also ظَفَّرَهُ; and ↓ ظَفَرَهُ, aor. ـِ; (M, Ḳ;) and ↓ اِظَّفَرَهُ, in the Ḳ erroneously written أَظْفَرَهُ; (TA;) *He stuck his nail into his face;* (M, Ḳ;) and so اِطَّفَرَهُ, with ط. (TA.) And ظَفَّرَهُ [*He clawed it;*] *he stuck his nail into it,* (namely, anything,) *and broke it,* or *made a mark* [or *scratch*] *upon it.* (M.) And ↓ اِظَّفَرَ الصَّقْرُ الطَّائِرَ *The hawk seized the bird with his talons.* (Ḳ.) — ظَفَّرَ, said of بَقْل [or herbs, or leguminous plants,] ‡ *They put forth what resembled the* أَظْفَار [or *talons*] *of the bird.* (M, TA.) And said of the عَرْفَج, (Ḳ, TA,) and of the أَرْطَى, (TA,) ‡ *It put forth what resembled* أَظْفَار, (Ḳ, TA,) *when it put forth its* [*leaves termed*] خُوص. (TA.) And said of the نَصِىّ, and of the وَشِيج, and of the بَرْدِىّ, and of the ثُمَام, and of the صِلِّيَان, and of the غَرَز, and of the هَدَب, ‡ *It,* or *they, put forth yellow shoots, resembling the* ظُفُر [or *talon*], *which are the* خُوص *thereof, that come forth therefrom having a dust-coloured flower.* (M, TA.) [Or,] said of a plant, (Ks, T, Ṣ,) inf. n. as above, (Ks, T,) † *It came forth;* (Ks, T;) from الأَظْفَار: (T:) or *it came forth of the measure of the* ظُفُر [or *nail*]. (Ṣ.) And ظَفَّرَتِ الأَرْضُ † *The land put forth plants,* or *herbage, that might be uprooted* (يُمْكِنُ اِحْتِفَارُهُ, so in the M, in the Ḳ اِخْتِفَاؤُهُ,) *with the nail,* (M,) or *with the fingers.* (Ḳ.) — ظَفَّرَ ثَوْبَهُ, (M, and so in a copy of the Ḳ,) inf. n. as above, (Ḳ,) † *He perfumed his garment* (M, and thus in that copy of the Ḳ) *with what is termed* ظُفُر: (M:) or ظَفَّرَ ثَوْبَهُ بِالأَظْفَارِ *he perfumed his garment with what are termed* أَظْفَار. (So accord. to other copies of the Ḳ.) — And ظَفَّرَ الجِلْدَ, (Ḳ,) or ظَفَّرْتُ الجِلْدَ, (M,) † *He,* (Ḳ,) or *I,* (M,) *rubbed the skin in order that its* أَظْفَار (M, Ḳ) which means its *creased parts* (M) *might become smooth.* (M, Ḳ.) ═ ظَفَّرَهُ also signifies, and so ↓ أَظْفَرَهُ, [*He caused him to attain, get, get possession of,* or *acquire, what he desired,* or *sought: he caused him to succeed,* or *to be successful:* and] *He* (God) *caused him to be victorious, to gain the victory,* or *to overcome.* (A.) You say, ظَفَّرَهُ بِهِ (Ṣ, M) and عَلَيْهِ, (M, TA,) inf. n. as above; (Ṣ;) and ↓ أَظْفَرَهُ بِهِ (Ṣ, M, Mṣb) and عليه; (M, Mṣb;) *He* (God, Ṣ, M, or a man, Mṣb) *caused him to gain the victory over him,* or *to overcome him,* (M, Mṣb,) namely, his enemy. (Ṣ, Mṣb.) — And ظَفَّرَهُ عَلَيْهِ *He declared him to have overcome him:* said of one who has been asked which of two persons had overcome. (T.) — And ظَفَّرَهُ, (M, Ḳ,) inf. n. as above, (Ḳ,) *He prayed for him that he might attain what he desired,* or *sought;* or *that he might be successful,* or *victorious.* (M, Ḳ.)

4: see the next preceding paragraph, latter part, in two places.

6. تَظَافَرُوا عَلَيْهِ and تَضَافَرُوا and تَظَاهَرُوا all signify the same; so says Ibn-Buzurj; (T, TA;) explaining the meaning to be, *They leagued together, and aided one another, against him;* i. e. عَلَى فُلَانٍ [*against such a one*]: (TA in art. ضفر:) the first of these has been said to be incorrect; but it is mentioned also by Ṣgh, as syn. with the third; and by Ibn-Málik, among words that are with ض and with ظ. (TA in the present art.)

8: see 2, in three places: ═ and see also 1, in two places.

ظَفْرٌ: see the next paragraph.

ظُفْرٌ (T, Ṣ, M, A, Mṣb, Ḳ, &c.) and ↓ ظُفُرٌ, (Mṣb, Ḳ,) which latter is the most chaste form, and the form adopted by the seven readers in the Ḳur vi. 147, and the former is a contraction of this, [but is the most common form,] (Mṣb,) and ↓ ظَفْرٌ, which is extr., (M, Mṣb, Ḳ,) and disallowed by IDrd, (O,) and ↓ ظِفِرٌ, which is also extr., (Mṣb,) and ↓ أُظْفُورٌ, (T, M, A, Mṣb, Ḳ,) which is erroneously mentioned in the Ṣ as a pl. of ظُفْرٌ, (Ṣgh, Mṣb, Ḳ,) by an anticipation of the pen; (Mṣb;) or, accord. to MF, it is said in most of the copies of the Ṣ, (but this is not the case,) ظُفْرٌ has for its pl. أَظْفَارٌ; and أُظْفُورٌ [has for its pl.] أَظَافِيرُ; (TA;) [and this, being the reading in most of the copies of the Ṣ seen by MF, is probably what J wrote;] *A certain well-known thing;* (M;) [i. e. *a nail;* and *a talon,* or *claw;*] *pertaining to a human being,* (M, Ibn-Es-Seed, Mṣb, Ḳ,) and *to others;* (M, Ḳ;) *to the beasts and birds mentioned in the next following sentence,* [as well as to man,] accord. to the authorities there cited; (TA;) and *to every ruminant,* as syn. with ظِلْفٌ [i. e. *a cloven hoof*]: (T and M in art. ظلف:) or *to a beast,* or *bird, that does not prey;* [as well as to man;] that of such as preys being termed مِخْلَبٌ: (M:) [and in the present day applied also to the *spur* of a cock:] it is of the masc. gender: (Lḥ, M, Mṣb:) the pl. (of ظُفْرٌ, Ṣ, M, Mṣb, &c.) is أَظْفَارٌ (Ṣ, M, Mṣb, Ḳ, &c.) and sometimes أَظْفُرٌ, (Mṣb,) [both of which are pls. of pauc., but the former is used as a pl. of mult. also,] and (of أُظْفُورٌ, M, Mṣb, or of أَظْفَار, and therefore a pl. pl., M) أَظَافِيرُ: (M, Mṣb, Ḳ:) that ↓ أُظْفُورٌ is a sing. [and not like أُبْكُور which is a quasi-pl. n.] is shown by the saying of a poet,

* مَا بَيْنَ لُقْمَتِهَا الأُولَى إِذَا ٱنْحَدَرَتْ *
* وَبَيْنَ أُخْرَى تَلِيهَا قِيسُ أُظْفُورِ *

(Ḳ) or قِيدُ أُظْفُورِ (Mṣb) [i. e. *What is between her first morsel, when it descends* into her throat, *and another that follows it, is the measure of a finger-nail*]: or, as some relate it, إِذَا ٱزْدَرَدَتْ [*when she swallows*]; and it is thus cited [in the T and] in the "Baṣáïr" of the author of the Ḳ. (TA.) The phrase كُلّ ذِى ظُفُرٍ in the Ḳur vi. 147 comprises camels and ostriches; (so in the T and TṢ and L; but in the Ḳ, الأَنْعَام is erroneously put for النَّعَام; TA;) because their مَنَاسِم are like أَظْفَار to them: (T, Ḳ, TA:) I'Ab says that it comprises camels; and also ostriches, because they have nails like camels: or any bird that has a مِخْلَب, and any beast that has a solid hoof: or, accord. to Mujáhid and Ḳatádeh, every beast and bird that has not divided toes; as the camel and ostrich and goose and duck. (TA.) — [Hence,] الأَظْفَارُ is the name of † *Certain small stars*; (Ṣ;) *certain stars before* النَّسْر [meaning النَّسْرُ الوَاقِعُ i. e. *the star α of Lyra*: app. because regarded as the talons of the نسر]: (Ḳ:) or *a certain dim star in* الشَّلْيَاق [q. v., i. e. *the constellation Lyra*]. (Ḳzw.) — [Hence also,] إِنَّهُ لَمَقْلُومُ الظُّفُرِ, (T,) or إِنَّهُ لَكَلِيلُ الظُّفُرِ, (TA,) ‡ *Verily he is one who does not slay* or *wound an enemy*: (T, TA:) and إِنَّهُ مَقْلُومُ الظُّفُرِ عَنْ أَذَى النَّاسِ ‡ *Verily he is one who does little hurt to mankind.* (T, A, TA.) And هُوَ كَلِيلُ الظُّفُرِ ‡ *He is weak*, or *abject*, or *despicable*; (T, Ṣ, Ḳ, TA;) said of a man; (Ḳ, TA;) or so مُقَلَّمُ الظُّفُرِ (Ḳ: [in the TA, as from the Ḳ, مُقَلَّمُ الأَظْفَارِ:]) or ‡ *he is sick*, or *diseased.* (A.) And بِهِ ظُفُرٌ مِنْ مَرَضٍ ‡ [app. meaning *In him is an evil result of a disease, that has clung to him*]. (A, TA. [In the A, this immediately follows what here next precedes it; and is immediately followed by the words وَذُبَابُ ظُفُرٍ مِنْهُ, which seem to be added by way of explanation; thus in my copy; but I think that ظُفُرٌ مِنْهُ here is a mistake for ظُفُرٌ فِيهِ, and have assumed this to be the case in rendering the phrase.]) — And قَرَحْتُهُ مِنْ ظُفُرِهِ إِلَى شُفْرِهِ ‡ [lit. *I wounded him much, from his nail to the edge of his eyelid*; but mentioned as tropical; app. meaning *from toe to head*]; like as one says, مِنْ قَرْنِهِ. (A.) — And مَا بِالدَّارِ ظُفُرٌ, (Ḳ,) or مَا بِالدَّارِ ظُفُرٌ وَلَا شُفْرٌ, (A, O,) ‡ *There is not in the house any one.* (A, O, Ḳ.) And مَا تَرَكَتِ السَّنَةُ ظُفُرًا وَلَا شُفْرًا ‡ *The year of drought left not anything*: and sometimes they said شَفْرًا, with fet-ḥ, and in this case they said ↓ ظَفْرًا, for assimilation. (A in art. شفر.) And رَأَيْتُهُ بِظُفُرِهِ ‡ *I saw him himself.* (O, Ḳ, TA.) — ظُفُرُ النَّسْرِ is the name of † *A certain plant*, (Ḳ, TA,) *resembling what is* [*properly*] *thus termed* [i. e. *the talon of the vulture*]. (TA.) And ظُفُرُ القِطِّ is the name of † *Another plant.* (Ḳ, TA.) — And الظُّفُرُ, (M,) or الأَظْفَارُ, (T, M, A, Mgh, O, Ḳ, &c.,) for this word in the sense here following has no sing. (T, M, O, Ḳ) accord. to the author of the 'Eyn, (M,) but sometimes one said أَظْفَارَةٌ ↓ وَاحِدَةٌ, which is not allowable by rule, and made the pl. of this to be أَظَافِير, (T, O, Ḳ,* [mentioned in the M as a pl. of الظُّفُر,]) though, if they formed a sing. from it, it should be ظُفْر, (T, O, Ḳ,) signifies ‡ *A certain odoriferous substance*, (T, Mgh, O, Ḳ,) or *a sort thereof*, (M,) [i. e. *unguis odoratus*, (called in the present day ظُفْرُ الطِّيبِ and ظُفْرُ العِفْرِيتِ,) or *ungues odorati*,] *black*, (T, M, O,) *resembling a* ظُفُر [or *nail*] (T, M, Mgh, O, Ḳ) *of a man* (M) *pulled out* (in the M and O and Ḳ مُقْتَلَف, and in the T مُقَلَّف,) *from the root thereof*, (T, M, O, Ḳ, [but in the M, the words which I have rendered "pulled out" &c. immediately follow the words ضَرْبٌ مِنَ العِطْرِ أَسْوَدُ,]) or *resembling the* أَظْفَار [or *finger-nails*], (A,) *and put into* دُخْنَة [or *incense*]: (T, M, O:) and, accord. to the Ḳ, ↓ ظَفَارِ, sometimes imperfectly decl., i. e. ↓ ظَفَارُ, signifies the same; but this is very strange, for [SM says] I have referred to the M and T and O and other lexicons without finding them to have mentioned in this sense any term but الأَظْفَارُ or الظُّفُرُ: accord. to the "Minháj," أَظْفَارُ الطِّيبِ are *pieces of an odoriferous substance resembling the* أَظْفَار [properly so called]; they are said by [the Arabic translator of] Dioscorides to be *of the nature of the shards of shells*, [so I render مِنْ جِنْسِ أَخْزَافِ الصَّدَفِ, supposing اخزاف to be here used tropically,] *found in an island of the Sea of India where is the* سُنْبُل [or *spikenard*], *a sort whereof is* [*called*] قُلْزُمِىّ [i. e. *of El-Ḳulzum*], *and another which is* [*called*] بَابِلِىّ [i. e. *of Bábil*], *black and small, and the best is that which inclines to whiteness, which drifts to El-Yemen and El-Baḥreyn.* (TA.) [Forskål, in his "Descr. Animalium" &c., mentions what here follows, among the animal substances of the materia medica of Cairo, in page 143: "*Unguis odoratus.* (Opercula Cochl.) *Dofr el afrit*, ضفر العفريت, i. e. *unguis dæmonis.* E Mochha per Suês. Arabes etiam afferunt. Nigritis fumigatorium est." (ضفر is here written, agreeably with the usual vulgar pronunciation, for ظفر.) See also قُسْط.] — أَظْفَارٌ signifies also † *Large* قِرْدَان [or *ticks*]. (Ṣ, O, Ḳ.) — And † The *creased parts* of a skin. (M, TA.) — And the ظُفُر of a bow is ‡ The *part* in the curved end *that is beyond the place where the string is tied, to the extremity*: (Aṣ, T, Ṣ, M,* O, Ḳ:*) or the *end* of the bow: (Ḳ:) or *each end* of the bow, *beyond the place where the string is tied*: (A:) pl. ظِفَرَةٌ. (M, TA.) — See also ظَفَرَةٌ.

ظِفْرٌ: see the next preceding paragraph.

ظَفَرٌ, in a man, The *quality of having long nails.* (ISk, Ṣ, O.) [App., in this sense, an inf. n. of which the verb is ظَفِرَ; as it is in other senses: see 1.] — See also ظَفَرَةٌ. — Also *Low*, or *depressed, ground*, (Ṣ, O, Ḳ,) *that produces plants*, or *herbage.* (Ṣ, O.)

ظَفِرٌ *Sharp in the nail* [or *having sharp nails*]. (A.) — And A man *having upon his eye what is termed a* ظَفَرَة; (A;) and so ↓ مَظْفُورٌ. (T, A, Mgh, Ḳ.) — And عَيْنٌ ظَفِرَةٌ *An eye having what is termed a* ظَفَرَة; (T, M, A, Ḳ;) as also ↓ مَظْفُورَةٌ. (A.) — Also [*Successful*;] *victorious*; applied to a man; (Ṣ;) and so ↓ ظَافِرٌ: (Mṣb, TA:) or ظَفِرٌ (IDrd, M, A, Ḳ) and ↓ ظَفِيرٌ (IDrd, M, Ḳ) and ↓ ظِفِّيرٌ, (IDrd, Ṣgh, Ḳ,) but this is said by IDrd to be not of established authority, (TA,) and ↓ مُظَفَّرٌ (IDrd, M, A, Ḳ) and ↓ مِظْفَارٌ, (IDrd, O, Ḳ,) all signify a man *very*, or *often, successful* or *victorious*: (IDrd, O, TA:) or ‡ one *who does not endeavour after a thing without attaining it.* (M, A, Ḳ.)

ظُفُرٌ and ظَفِيرٌ: see ظَفِرٌ.

ظُفْرَةٌ *A certain plant, burning*, or *biting, to the tongue*, (Ḳ, TA,) *resembling the* ظُفْر [or *nail*] *in its coming forth*, (TA,) *that has a beneficial effect upon foul ulcers, and warts.* (Ḳ, TA.) — And ظُفْرَةُ العَجُوزِ *The rounded head of prickles of the* [*thistle called*] حَسَك. (Ḳ,* TA.) — See also the next paragraph.

ظَفَرَةٌ *A pellicle that comes over the eye*, (T, Ṣ, Mgh, O, Ḳ,) *growing from the side next the nose*, (T, Ṣ, O,) *upon the white of the eye*, (Ṣ, Mgh, O,) *extending to the black*: (Ṣ, O:) sometimes it is cut off: if left, it covers the eye, and obscures the sight: (T:) or *a certain disease in the eye, which causes a tegument like the nail to come over it*: or *a piece of flesh that grows at the inner angle of the eye, extending to the black, and sometimes encroaching upon the black*: (M:) it is also called ↓ ظُفْرٌ (A'Obeyd, T, Ṣ, M, Mgh, O, Ḳ) and ↓ ظُفْرَةٌ, (T, Mgh,) these two terms being applied to it by the physicians, (Mgh,) and ↓ ظَفَرٌ (TA) and ↓ ظُفَارَةٌ, (so in a copy of the T, as on the authority of Ibn-Buzurj,) or ↓ ظِفَارَةٌ. (So in the O.)

ظَفَارِ and ظَفَارُ: see ظُفُرٌ. — [ظَفَارِ is well known as the name of a city in El-Yemen; or, accord. to the O, of two cities and two fortresses in El-Yemen. And accord. to the TA, it signifies *Any land that is* ذَات مَغَرَة: but the latter of these two words has been altered by an erasure over the second letter, and is perhaps incorrect: if not, it may mean, agreeably with the analogy of many words of the measure مَفْعَلَة, as مَقْدَرَة and مَمْلَحَة and مَنْجَاة &c., *such as possesses means of overcoming*, or *withstanding, invaders*: and it may be that hence ظَفَار is in two instances the name of a fortress.]

ظَفُورٌ [app. syn. with ظَفِرٌ and ظَفِيرٌ] is one of the appellations of the Prophet. (MF, TA.)

ظَفِيرٌ : see ظُفْرٌ.

ظُفَارَةٌ or ظِفَارَةٌ : see ظَفَرَةٌ.

جَزْعٌ ظَفَارِىٌّ [*Onyx of Dhafári*] is so called in relation to ظَفَارِ, a city of El-Yemen, (T, Ṣ, Mgh, O, Ḳ,) near صَنْعَآء, (Ḳ,) two days' journey from the latter. (O.) And in like manner, عُودٌ ظَفَارِىٌّ [*Aloes-wood of Dhafári*]: i. e. the عود *with which one fumigates:* (Ṣ:) or قُسْط, (O, Ḳ, TA,) which means the same, (TA, [but see this word,]) is called [قُسْطُ ظَفَارِ and قُسْطٌ ظَفَارِىٌّ] in relation to ظَفَارِ, another city of El-Yemen, near مِرْبَاط, (O, Ḳ, TA,) described by Yákoot as in the furthest part of El-Yemen, on the shore of the Sea of India, near الشِّحْر; (TA;) because it is brought thither from India. (O, Ḳ, TA.)

ظُفُرٌ : } see ظُفْرٌ.
ظَافِرٌ : }

أَظْفَرُ A man *having long nails:* (ISk, Ṣ, A:) or *having long and broad nails:* (M, Ḳ:) and in like manner applied to a مَنْسِم [or foot of a camel]: ظَفْرَآء [the reg. fem.] has not been heard. (M.)

أُظْفُورٌ : see ظُفْرٌ, in two places. — Also † The *slender thing* [or *tendril*] *that twines upon the branch of a grape-vine.* (Ḳ.)

أُظْفَارَةٌ : see ظُفْرٌ, latter half.

مُظَفَّرٌ : see ظُفْرٌ. — قَوْسٌ مُظَفَّرَةٌ † *A bow having somewhat cut off from each of its two ends* [which are called its ظُفْرَانِ]. (O, Ḳ, TA. [In the CḲ, فَرَسٌ is erroneously put for قَوْسٌ.])

مِظْفَارٌ : see ظُفْرٌ. — Also The [*instrument called*] مِنْقَاش [q. v.]. (Fr, O, Ḳ.)

مَظْفُورٌ بِهِ; and its fem.: see ظَفِرٌ. — *Overcome,* or *conquered;* [as also مَظْفُورٌ عَلَيْهِ, and مَظْفُورٌ alone; (see 1;)] applied to a man. (TA.)

ظل

1. ظَلَّ, aor. يَظَلُّ, inf. n. ظَلَالَةٌ: see 4. — ظَلَّ, (T, M, Mṣb, Ḳ,) first pers. ظَلِلْتُ, (T, Ṣ, M, O, Mṣb, Ḳ,) [and accord. to SM ظَلَلْتُ also, for he says that] the verb is of the class of مَنَعَ as well as of the class of تَعِبَ, (TA,) and ظَلْتُ, (T, Ṣ,* M, O, Ḳ,) likened to نَسْتُ, (M, Ḳ,*) formed by rejecting the former ل in ظَلِلْتُ, (T, O,) and ظِلْتُ, which is [also] originally ظَلِلْتُ, (Sb, T, M, O, Ḳ,) formed by transferring to the ظ the vowel of the rejected ل, (Sb, T, M, O,) anomalously, (Sb, M,) the latter of the dial. of the people of El-Ḥijáz; (T;) aor. يَظَلُّ; (Ṣ,* M, O,* Mṣb, Ḳ;) imperative اِظْلَلْ and (T) ظَلَّ [and it is implied in the M voce قَرَّ that one says also اِظِلْلْ and ظِلَّ, which indicates that the aor. is also يَظِلُّ, but this requires confirmation, which I have not anywhere found]; inf. n. ظُلُولٌ (T, Ṣ, M, O, Mṣb, Ḳ) and ظَلٌّ (M, Ḳ) and ظِلٌّ; (thus also in a copy of the M; [but this I think doubtful;]) accord. to Lth, (T,) or Kh, (Mṣb,) [i. e. accord. to the author of the 'Eyn,] is said only of a thing that is done in the day, or daytime; (T, Ṣ, M, O, Mṣb;) like as بَاتَ, aor. يَبِيتُ, is said only of a thing that is done in the night: (T:) it is an incomplete [i. e. a non-attributive] verb, relating to a time in which is a shade from the sun, from morning to evening, or from sunrise to sunset: (Esh-Shiháb, TA:) one says, ظَلَّ فُلَانٌ نَهَارَهُ صَائِمًا [*Such a one was during his day fasting;* or *he passed his day fasting*]: (Lth, T:) and ظَلَّ نَهَارَهُ يَفْعَلُ كَذَا [*He was in,* or *during, his day doing such a thing;* or *he passed his day doing such a thing*]: (M, Ḳ:) and ظَلِلْتُ أَعْمَلُ كَذَا [*I was in the day* or *daytime,* or *I passed the day, doing such a thing;* or] *I did such a thing in the day* or *daytime.* (Ṣ, O, Mṣb.*) In the saying of 'Antarah,

• وَلَقَدْ أَبِيتُ عَلَى الطَّوَى وَأَظَلُّهُ •
• حَتَّى أَنَالَ بِهِ كَرِيمَ الْمَأْكَلِ •

[app. meaning *And verily I pass the night in hunger, and I pass the day in it, that I may attain thereby plentiful eating*], أَظَلُّهُ is for أَظَلُّ عَلَيْهِ. (Ṣ, O.) And accord. to some, (TA,) ظَلَّ لَيْلَهُ occurs in poetry; (M, Ḳ, TA;) so that one says, ظَلَّ لَيْلَهُ يَفْعَلُ كَذَا [*He was in,* or *during, his night,* or *he passed his night, doing such a thing*]: but it is said that in this case the verb has the meaning next following. (TA.) — And it signifies also *He,* or *it, became;* syn. صَارَ: (Er-Rághib, TA:) being in this sense likewise an incomplete [i. e. a non-attributive] verb, divested of that meaning of time which it radically denotes; as in the phrase in the Ḳur [xvi. 60 and xliii. 16], ظَلَّ وَجْهُهُ مُسْوَدًّا [*His face becomes black*]: so says Ibn-Málik: (TA:) or this may mean *his face continues all the day black:* (Bḍ in xvi. 60:) and one says also, ظَلَّ يَفْعَلُ كَذَا meaning *He continued doing such a thing:* this too is mentioned by Ibn-Málik, and is of the dial. of the people of Syria. (TA.) — It is also a complete [i. e. an attributive] verb as meaning *He,* or *it, continued;* as is said in the Expos. of the "Shifè," and by Ibn-Málik; and, as Ibn-Málik likewise says, *it was,* or *became, long.* (TA.)

2. ظَلَّلَهُ عَلَيْهِ [*He made it to give shade over him,* or *it,*] (M,) inf. n. تَظْلِيلٌ. (O.) It is said in the Ḳur [vii. 160, and the like is said in ii. 54], وَظَلَّلْنَا عَلَيْهِمُ الْغَمَامَ *And we made the clouds to give shade over them.* (M.) — [And ظَلَّلَهُ signifies *He shaded him,* or *it.* See an ex. in a verse of Jereer in art. ردف, conj. 3.] لٰكِنْ عَلَى الْأَثْلَاثِ لَحْمٌ لَا يُظَلَّلُ [*But at the tamarisk-trees is flesh that will not be shaded,* or, accord. to the reading given by Meyd, بِالْأَثْلَاثِ,] is a prov., said by Beyhes, in allusion to the flesh of his slain brothers, on the occasion of persons saying, ظَلِّلُوا لَحْمَ جَزُورِكُمْ [*Shade ye the flesh of your slaughtered camel*]. (Ṣ, O.) — See also 4. — One says also ظَلَّلَ بِالسَّوْطِ, meaning *He made a sign with the whip for the purpose of frightening.* (Ibn-'Abbád, O, Ḳ.)

4. اظلّ, said of a day, *It was,* (Ṣ, O,) or *became,* (M, Ḳ,) *shady,* or *a day having shade:* (Ṣ, M, O, Ḳ:) or *it was a day having clouds,* or *other* [*causes of shade*]: (T:) or *it was continually shady;* as also † ظَلَّ, aor. يَظَلُّ, inf. n. ظَلَالَةٌ. (Mṣb.) — And, said of a thing, [*It extended its shade;* or] *its shade extended;* as also † ظلّل. (Mṣb.) — أَظَلَّتْنِى الشَّجَرَةُ [*The tree shaded me,* or *afforded me shade*]: and in like manner one says of other things than trees. (Ṣ, O.) أَظَلَّكَ said of a building, or of a mountain, or of a cloud, means *It protected thee,* and *cast its shade upon thee.* (Mgh.) — [Hence,] اظلّهُ † *He took him into his shelter,* or *protection:* (TA:) or *he guarded,* or *protected, him,* and *placed him within the scope of his might,* or *power of resistance* or *defence.* (Er-Rághib, TA.) — And أَظَلَّنِى † *It* (a thing) *covered me:* (M, Ḳ:) or *it approached me,* or *drew near to me, so as to cast its shade upon me:* (Ḳ:) or it has both of these meanings: (M:) or أَظَلَّكَ means *he,* (T, Ṣ,) or *it,* (O,) *approached thee,* or *drew near to thee, as though he,* or *it, cast his,* or *its, shade upon thee.* (T, Ṣ, O.) And hence one says, أَظَلَّكَ أَمْرٌ † *An event approached thee,* or *drew near to thee:* (Ṣ, O:) and in like manner one says of a month. (T, Ṣ, O.) And اظلّ [alone] † *It* (a thing) *advanced:* or *approached,* or *drew near.* (Mṣb.) And i. q. أَشْرَفَ [app. as meaning † *He,* or *it, became within sight,* or *view*]. (Mṣb.)

5: see the next paragraph. It is also pronounced تَظَلَّى: (IAạr, T:) and signifies *He kept to shady places, and to ease,* or *repose:* (IAạr, T and Ḳ in art. ظلى:) it is like تَقَضَّيْتُ from الظَّنُّ. (T in that art.)

10. استظلّ, (T,) or استظلّ بِالظِّلِّ, (Mṣb, TA,) *He* (a man, T) *sheltered,* or *protected, himself by means of the shade:* (T, TA:) or the latter means *he inclined to the shade and sat in it.* (M, Ḳ.) And استظلّ مِنَ الشَّىْءِ and بِهِ means † تَظَلَّلَ [i. e. *he shaded himself* (تظلّل being quasi-pass. of ظَلَّلَهُ) *from the thing* and *by means of it*]. (M, Ḳ.) You say, استظلّ بِهِ مِنَ الشَّمْسِ [*He shaded himself with it,* or *by means of it, from the sun*]. (T.) And استظلّ بِالشَّجَرَةِ *He shaded and sheltered himself by means of the tree.* (Ibn-'Abbád, Ṣ, O.) — استظلّ الدَّمُ *The blood was in the* جَوْف [or *belly,* or *interior of the belly,* or the *chest*]. (T, O, Ḳ, TA. [In the CḲ, مِن الجَوْفِ is put for فِى الجَوْفِ.]) — استظلّت العَيْنُ,

(T, Ibn-'Abbád, O,) or العُيُونُ, (Ḳ,) *The eye,* (T, Ibn-'Abbád, O,) meaning that of a she-camel, (Ibn-'Abbád, O,) or *the eyes,* (Ḳ,) *sank,* or *became depressed, in the head.* (T, Ibn-'Abbád, O, K.) —— And اسْتَظَلَّ الكَرْمُ *The grape-vine became luxuriant,* or *abundant and dense, in its branches whereon were the bunches.* (M, Ḳ.)

ظِلٌّ properly signifies *Shade;* i. e. the *light of the sun without the rays:* when there is no light, it is ظُلْمَةٌ, not ظِلٌّ: (Ṣ, O:) *contr. of* ضِحٌّ: (M, Ḳ:) or *i. q.* فَىْءٌ: (Ḳ:) so some say: (M:) or so the [common] people say: (IḲt, Mṣb:) or the former is [*shade*] *in the morning;* and the latter is in the evening: (M, Ḳ:) or, accord. to IḲt, the former is *in the morning and in the evening;* but the latter is only after the declining of the sun from the meridian: ISk says that the former is *from the rising of the sun to its declining;* and the latter, from the declining to the setting: Th says that the ظِلّ of a tree &c. is *in the morning;* and the فَىْء, in the evening: (Mṣb:) Ru-beh says, (M, Mṣb,) *any place,* (M,) or *any thing,* (Mṣb,) *upon which the sun has been and which it has quitted* is termed ظِلّ and فَىْء; (M, Mṣb;) but *a thing* [or *place*] *upon which the sun has not been* is termed ظِلّ [only]; and hence it is said that the sun annuls, or supersedes, the ظِلّ, and the فَىْء annuls, or supersedes, the sun: (Mṣb:) AHeyth says, the ظِلّ is *anything upon which the sun has not come;* and the term فَىْء is applied only after the declining of the sun; the فَىْء being eastwards and the ظِلّ being westwards; and the ظِلّ being termed ظِلّ *from the beginning of the day to the declining of the sun;* after which it is termed فَىْء until the night: (T, TA:) one says the ظِلّ of Paradise, but not its فَىْء, because the sun will never replace its ظِلّ; but En-Nábighah El-Jaadee has assigned to Paradise فَىْء having ظِلَال: (M, TA:) in a verse of Aboo-Ṣakhr El-Hudhalee, ظِلّ is made fem. as meaning مَنِيَّة [i. e. *death*]: (Ḥam p. 161:) the pl. [of mult.] is ظِلَالٌ (Ṣ, M, O, Ḳ) and ظُلُولٌ and [of pauc.] أَظْلَالٌ. (M, O, Ḳ.) The saying of a rájiz,

كَأَنَّمَا وَجْهُكَ ظِلٌّ مِنْ حَجَرْ

[*As though thy face were a shade of a stone*] is said to mean hardness of face, and shamelessness: or the being black in the face: (T, TA:) for the Arabs say that there is nothing more dense in shade than a stone. (TA.) قَدْ ضَحَا ظِلُّهُ [*His shade,* or *shadow, has become sun*] is said of the dead. (TA.) مَرَّ بِنَا كَأَنَّهُ ظِلُّ ذِئْبٍ [*He passed by us as though he were the shadow of a wolf*] means swiftly, as does a wolf. (M.) اِنْتَعَلَتْ ظِلَالَهَا † [*They made their shadows to be as though they were sandals to them*] is said of camels or other beasts when it is midday in summer and they have no shadow [but such as is beneath them]: a rájiz says,

قَدْ وَرَدَتْ تَمْشِى عَلَى ظِلَالِهَا
وَذَابَتِ الشَّمْسُ عَلَى قِلَالِهَا

[*They came to the water walking upon their shadows, and the sun was intensely hot upon the tops of their heads and humps*]. (T.) And one says, هُوَ يَتْبَعُ ظِلَّ نَفْسِهِ ‡ [*He follows the shadow of himself;* i. e. a thing that he will not overtake; for], as a poet says, the shadow that goes with thee thou wilt not overtake by following: and هُوَ يُبَارِى ظِلَّ نَفْسِهِ ‡ [*He strives to outstrip the shadow of himself*], meaning that he walks with a proud and self-conceited gait: so in the A. (TA.) And اِنْتَقَلْتُ عَنْ ظِلِّى ‡ *I left my state,* or *condition.* (TA.) And تَرَكَ الظَّبْىُ ظِلَّهُ: so in the T and Ṣ and O: (TA:) but [said to be] correctly, لَأَتْرُكَنَّهُ تَرْكَ الظَّبْىِ ظِلَّهُ, (Ḳ,) or لَأَتْرُكَنَّهُ, (M, TA,) i. e. [*I will forsake him,* or *I will assuredly forsake him, as the gazelle forsakes*] *the place of its shade:* (O, TA:) [each, however, is app. right; and the former is the more agreeable with the following explanations:] a prov., (M,) applied to the man who is wont to take fright and flee; for the gazelle, when it takes fright and flees from a thing, never returns to it: (Ṣ, O, Ḳ:) by the ظِلّ is here meant the covert in which it shades and shelters itself in the vehemence of the heat; then the hunter comes to it and rouses it, and it will not return thither; and one says, تَرَكَ الظَّبْىُ ظِلَّهُ, meaning the place of its shade: it is applied to him who takes fright and flees from a thing, and forsakes it so as not to return to it; and to the case of a man's forsaking his companion. (Meyd.) [ثَقِيلُ الظِّلِّ as applied to a man, see expl. in art. ثقل: see also Ḥar p. 250, where it is indicated that it may be rendered One *whose shadow,* even, *is oppressive,* and therefore much more so is his person.] In the phrase وَلَا الظِّلُّ وَلَا الْحَرُورُ, (M, Ḳ) in the Ḳur [xxxv. 20], Th says, accord. to some, (M,) الظِّلّ means *Paradise;* (M, Ḳ;) and الحَرُور, the fire [of Hell]: but he adds, I say that الظِّلّ is the ظِلّ itself [i. e. *shade*], and الحَرُور is the حَرّ itself [i. e. *heat*]: (M: [see also حَرُور:]) and Er-Rághib says that ظِلّ is sometimes assigned to anything; whether it be approved, as in the phrase above mentioned; or disapproved, as in وَظِلٍّ مِنْ يَحْمُومٍ in the Ḳur [lvi. 42, meaning *And shade of smoke,* or *black smoke*]. (TA.) And الظِّلَال means ظِلَالُ الجَنَّةِ [*The shades of Paradise*]: (Fr, T, O, Ḳ, TA:) in some copies of the Ḳ, وَالظِّلَالُ الجَنَّةُ, which is a mistake: (TA:) [but this requires consideration; for] El-'Abbás Ibn-'Abd-El-Muṭṭalib says,

مِنْ قَبْلِهَا طِبْتَ فِى الظِّلَالِ وَفِى
مُسْتَوْدَعٍ حَيْثُ يُخْصَفُ الوَرَقُ

[*Before it thou wast good in,* or *in the shades of, Paradise, and in a depositary in the part where leaves are sewed together to conceal the pudenda*]; (T, O, TA;) i. e. before thy descent to the earth (to which the pronoun in قبلها relates), thou wast good in the loins of Adam when he was in Paradise. (TA.) الجَنَّةُ تَحْتَ ظِلَالِ السُّيُوفِ [*Paradise is beneath the shades of the swords*] is a trad., meaning that fighting against unbelievers is a way of attaining to Paradise. (Marg. note in a copy of the "Jámi' eṣ-Ṣagheer.) مُلَاعِبُ ظِلِّهِ is an appellation of *A certain bird;* [see art. لعب;] and one says مُلَاعِبَا ظِلِّهِمَا; and مُلَاعِبَاتُ ظِلِّهِنَّ: but when you make them indeterminate, you say مُلَاعِبَاتُ أَظْلَالِهِنَّ. (T, O, Ḳ. [But in the TA in art. لعب, it is said that one dualizes and pluralizes both nouns, because the appellation becomes determinate.]) —— ظِلُّ اللَّيْلِ means ‡ *The blackness of the night:* (T, Ṣ, O, Mṣb;) metaphorically thus termed; (Ṣ;) as in the saying, أَتَانَا فِى ظِلِّ اللَّيْلِ [*He came to us in the blackness of the night*]: (Ṣ, O:) or it signifies جُنْحُ اللَّيْلِ [app. as meaning the *darkness,* and *confusedness, of the night;* see جُنْح]; (M, TA;) or so الظِّلّ: (Ḳ:) or this means *the night,* (M, Ḳ, TA,) *itself;* (M, TA;) so the astronomers say: (TA:) *all the night* is ظِلّ: and so is *all the period from the shining of the dawn to the rising of the sun.* (T.) —— ظِلُّ النَّهَارِ is *The colour of the day when the sun predominates over it* [app. meaning *when the light of the sun predominates over that of the early dawn*]. (Ḳ.) —— ظِلُّ السَّحَابِ means *Such, of the clouds, as conceal the sun:* or *the blackness of the clouds.* (M, Ḳ.) —— And ظِلَالُ البَحْرِ means *The waves of the sea;* (O, Ḳ, TA;) because they are raised so as to shade the ship and those that are in it. (TA.) —— ظِلٌّ also signifies *A* خَيَال (M, O, Ḳ) *that is seen,* (M, Ḳ,) [i. e. *an apparition, a phantom,* or *a thing that one sees like a shadow,* i. e. what we term *a shade,*] *of the jinn,* or *genii,* and *of others:* (M, O, Ḳ:) or the *like of a* خَيَال *of the jinn.* (T.) —— Also *Anything that shades one.* (TA.) —— And it is the subst. from أَظَلَّنِى الشَّىْءُ meaning "the thing covered me;" (M, Ḳ;) [i. e. it means *A covering;*] in which sense Th explains it in the phrase إِلَى ظِلٍّ ذِى ثَلَاثِ شُعَبٍ [in the Ḳur lxxvii. 30, *Unto a covering having three parts,* or *divisions*]; saying, the meaning is that the fire will have covered them; not that its ظِلّ will be like that of the present world. (M. [See شُعْبَة.]) And ظِلُّ الشَّىْءِ means † *That which serves for the veiling, covering,* or *protecting, of the thing;* syn. كِنُّهُ. (M.) [Hence] one says, فُلَانٌ يَعِيشُ فِى ظِلِّ فُلَانٍ i. e. † [*Such a one lives*] *in the shelter,* or *protection, of such a one.* (T,* Ṣ, O, Mṣb,* Ḳ.*) And السُّلْطَانُ ظِلُّ اللّٰهِ فِى الأَرْضِ, (O, TA,) a saying of the Prophet, (O,) [meaning † *The sovereign,* or *ruling, power is God's means of defence in the earth,*] because he wards off harm from the people like as the ظِلّ [properly so called] wards off the harm of the heat of the sun: (TA:) or the meaning is, † *God's means of protection:* or *God's* خَاصَّة [or *special servant*]. (O, TA.) — Also † *Might;* or *power of resistance* or *defence:* (M, Ḳ, TA:) whence [as some say] its usage in the Ḳur xiii. 35, and the usage of [the pl.] ظِلَال in xxxvi. 56 and in lxxvii. 41: [but the primary signification is more appropriate in these instances:] and so in the saying, جَعَلَنِى فِى ظِلِّهِ [i. e. † *He placed me within the scope of his might,* or *power of resistance* or *defence*]: so says Er-Rághib. (TA.) — And † *A state of life ample in its means* or *circumstances, unstraitened,* or *plentiful, and easy, pleasant, soft,* or *delicate.* (TA.) — Also † The *beginning* of winter. (T, O. [Accord. to the copies of the Ḳ, of youthfulness: but I think that الشَّبَاب in this instance, in the Ḳ, is evidently a mistranscription for الشِّتَآء.]) And † The *vehemence* (T, O, Ḳ) *of the heat* (T, O) of summer. (T, O, Ḳ.) — Also † The شَخْص [as meaning *person* of a human being, and as meaning the *bodily* or *corporeal form* or *figure* or *substance which one sees from a distance,* or the *material substance,*] of anything; (M, Ḳ, TA; [in the second and third of which is added, "or its كِنّ," a signification which I have mentioned above on the authority of the M;]) because of its [apparent] blackness [or darkness, resembling that of a shade or shadow]: (M, TA:) whence the saying, لَا يُفَارِقُ ظِلِّى ظِلَّكَ † [*My person will not quit thy person*]; like the saying, لَا يُفَارِقُ سَوَادِى سَوَادَكَ: and the following exs. have been cited as instances of ظِلّ in the sense of شَخْص: the saying of a poet,

لَمَّا نَزَلْنَا رَفَعْنَا ظِلَّ أَخْبِيَةٍ

[as though meaning *When we alighted, we raised the material fabric of tents*], for it is said that they do not set up the ظِلّ which is the فَىْء, but they only set up the tents; and the saying of another,

تَتْبَعُ أَفْيَآءَ الظِّلَالِ عَشِيَّةً

[as though meaning *He followed the shadows of the material objects in the evening*]: but Er-Rághib says that the former means, we raised the tents, and so raised the ظِلّ thereof; and in the other ex., الظلال is a general term, and الفىء [or افيآء] is a special term, so that it is an instance of the إِضَافَة of a thing to its kind [i. e. of prefixing a noun to one significant of its kind]. (TA.) [See also ظِلَالَة.] — And accord. to Ibn-'Abbád, (O,) it signifies also The *nap,* or *villous substance, upon the surface of a garment,* or *piece of cloth;* syn. زِئْبِر. (O, Ḳ.)

ظَلَّة *i. q.* إِقَامَة [*Continuance, residence, abode,* &c.]. (Ḳ:) — And *i. q.* صِحَّة: thus accord. to the copies of the Ḳ; but this may be a mistranscription; for Az and others mention, among the significations of ظَلَّة, [in a copy of the T written in this case, as in others, ظُلَّة ↓,] that of صُبْحَة [q. v.]. (TA.)

ظُلَّة *A thing that covers,* or *protects,* [or *shades,*] *one, overhead:* accord. to Lth, *i. q.* مَظَلَّة ↓ or مِظَلَّة meaning *a thing that shades one from the sun:* (T:)* see an ex. voce مِظَلَّة: *a covering:* and *i. q.* بُرْطُلَّة: (M, Ḳ:) this latter word correctly signifies *a* مِظَلَّة *for the summer:* (TA in art. برطل:) and *a thing by which one is protected from the cold and the heat:* (M:) *anything that protects and shades one, as a building* or *a mountain* or *a cloud:* (Mgh:) the *first portion that shades* (AZ, Ṣ, Ḳ) *of a cloud* (AZ, Ṣ) or *of clouds;* (Ḳ;) accord. to Er-Rághib, mostly said of that which is deemed unwholesome, and which is disliked; whence the use of the word in the Ḳur vii. 170: (TA:) and *what shades one, of trees:* (Ḳ:) or *anything that forms a covering over one,* (T, TA,) or *shades one:* (T:) and [particularly] *a thing like the* صُفَّة [q. v.], (Ṣ, M, O, Ḳ,) *by which one protects himself from the heat and the cold:* (Ḳ:) or, accord. to the lawyers, ظُلَّةُ الدَّارِ means *the* سُدَّة [or *projecting roof*] *over the door of the house:* or *that of which the beams have one end upon the house and the other end upon the wall of the opposite neighbour:* (Mgh:) pl. ظُلَل (Ṣ, M, O, Ḳ) and ظِلَال. (M, Ḳ.) [See also ظِلَال.] One says also, دَامَتْ ظُلَّتُهُ and الظِّلُّ الظَّلِيلُ ↓ ظِلَالَتُهُ, meaning *That whereby one shades himself,* (Ḳ, TA,) *of trees,* or *of stones,* or *of other things,* (TA,) [*continued.*] عَذَابُ يَوْمِ الظُّلَّةِ, in the Ḳur. [xxvi. 189], is said to mean [*The punishment of the day of*] *clouds beneath which was a hot wind* (سَمُوم): (Ṣ, O, Ḳ:) or *an overshadowing cloud, beneath which they collected themselves together, seeking protection thereby from the heat that came upon them, whereupon it covered them,* (T,* Ḳ, TA,) *and they perished beneath it:* (T, TA:) or, accord. to some, *i. q.* عَذَابُ يَوْمِ الصُّفَّةِ. (T: see art. صف.) And لَهُمْ مِنْ فَوْقِهِمْ ظُلَلٌ مِنَ النَّارِ وَمِنْ تَحْتِهِمْ ظُلَلٌ, in the Ḳur [xxxix. 18], means *To them* shall be *above them coverings of fire, and beneath them coverings* to those below them; Hell consisting of stages, one beneath another. (T, TA.) Seditions, or conflicts and factions, are mentioned in a trad. as being like ظُلَل, by which are meant *Mountains,* and *clouds:* and El-Kumeyt likens waves of the sea to ظُلَل. (TA.) And [the pl.] ظُلَل is used as meaning The *chambers of a prison.* (M, TA.) — See also ظَلَّة.

ظِلَّة *i. q.* ظِلَال; (T, Ḳ, TA;) app. a pl. of ظَلِيل, like as قِلَّة is of قَلِيل. (TA.)

ظُلَل *Water that is beneath a tree,* (O,) or *beneath trees,* (Ḳ,) *upon which the sun does not come.* (O, Ḳ.) [See also ضَلَل.]

ظَلَال, like سَحَاب, [so accord. to the Ḳ, but in my copies of the Ṣ, ظِلَال ↓,] *A thing that shades one,* (IAạr, Ṣ, O, Ḳ, TA,) *such as a cloud,* (IAạr, Ṣ, TA,) and *the like.* (IAạr, TA.) [See also ظُلَّة.]

ظِلَال pl. of ظِلّ: (Ṣ, M, O, Ḳ:) — and of ظُلَّة. (M, Ḳ.) — [Also, app., pl. of ظَلِيل: see ظِلَّة. — Freytag has app. understood it to be expl. in the Ḳ as syn. with مَظَلَّة; though it certainly is not.] — See also ظَلَال.

مَكَانٌ ظَلِيلٌ *A place having shade:* (M, Ḳ:) or *having constant shade.* (T, Ṣ, M, O, Ḳ.) And hence ظِلٌّ ظَلِيلٌ (M, Ḳ) *Constant shade:* (Ṣ:) or *extensive shade:* (O:) or in this case the latter word denotes intensiveness [meaning *dense*]; (M, Ḳ, TA;) being like شَاعِرٌ in the phrase شِعْرٌ شَاعِرٌ. (TA.) ظِلًّا ظَلِيلًا in the Ḳur iv. 60 is said by Er-Rághib to be an allusion to ease and pleasantness of life. (TA.) One says also أَيْكَةٌ ظَلِيلَةٌ *A collection of trees tangled,* or *luxuriant,* or *abundant and dense.* (TA.) In the saying of Uḥeyḥah Ibn-El-Julááḥ, describing palm-trees,

هِىَ الظِّلُّ فِى الحَرِّ حَقُّ الظَّلِيـ
لِ وَالمَنْظَرُ الأَحْسَنُ الأَجْمَلُ

[ISd says] in my opinion, he means الشَّىْءُ الظَّلِيلُ; [so that the verse should be rendered *They are the shade in the heat,* the shady thing, *the extremely shady, and the most goodly, the most beautiful, thing at which one looks;* (see the phrase هٰذَا العَالِمُ حَقُّ العَالِمِ, voce حَقّ;)] the inf. n. being put in the place of the subst. (M.) لَا ظَلِيلٌ in the Ḳur [lxxvii. 31] means *Not profitable as the shade in protecting from the heat.* (TA.)

ظَلَالَة, (M, TA,) with fet-ḥ, (TA,) the subst. from the verb in the phrase ظَلَّلْنَا عَلَيْهِمُ الغَمَامَ [expl. above, see 2; as such app. meaning either The *making to give shade,* like the inf. n. تَظْلِيل, or *a thing that gives shade,* like ظِلَالَة]. (M, TA.) — And *i. q.* شَخْص [expl. above, see ظِلّ, last quarter]: (O, K:) and so ظَلَالَة, with ط. (O.)

ظِلَالَة: see ظُلَّة. — Also *A cloud that one sees by itself, and of which one sees the shadow upon the earth.* (Ḳ.) — And one says, رَأَيْتُ ظِلَالَةً i. e. غَيَابَةً مِنَ الطَّيْرِ [app. meaning *I saw a covert,* or *place of concealment, of birds*]. (TA.)

ظَلِيلَة *A place in which a little water collects and stagnates in a water-course and the like:* (Lth, T:) or *a place in which water collects and stagnates in the lower part of the torrent of a valley:* (M, Ḳ:) or the *like of an excavated hollow in the interior of a water-course, such that the water stops, and remains therein:* (AA, O:) pl. ظَلَائِل. (Lth, AA, T, O.) And *A meadow* (رَوْضَة) *abounding with collections of trees,* or *of dense and tangled trees:* (AA, T, O, Ḳ:) pl. as above. (Ḳ.)

ظُلَّيْلَة *A thing which a man makes for himself,*

of trees, or *of a garment*, or *piece of cloth, by which to protect himself from the heat of the sun*: a vulgar word. (TA.)

ظُلْظُلٌ i. q. سُعْنٌ, i. e. *A* ▼ مِظَلَّة [q. v.; or as expl. in the L, in art. سعن, *a* ظُلَّة (q. v.), or *a thing like the* ظُلَّة, *which is made upon the flat house-tops, for the purpose of guarding against the dew that comes from the direction of the sea in the time of the greatest heat*]; on the authority of IAar. (T. [Accord. to the O and Ḳ, *i. q.* سُغْنٌ, which is evidently a mistranscription.])

أَظَلُّ [*More, and most, dense in shade*]. The Arabs say, لَيْسَ شَىْءٌ أَظَلَّ مِنْ حَجَرٍ [*There is not anything more dense in shade than a stone*]. (TA.) —— And أَظَلُّ, [as a subst., i. e. أَظَلُّ accord. to a general rule, or, if regarded as originally an epithet, it may be أَظَلُّ,] by poetic license أَظْلَلُ, (Ṣ, M, O, Ḳ,) signifies The *under part*, (Ṣ, O,) or the *concealed part*, (M, AHei, Ḳ,) *of the* مَنْسِم, (Ṣ, M, O, Ḳ,) or *of the* خُفّ, (AHei, TA,) [the former app. here used, as it is said to be in other cases, in the same sense as the latter, meaning the *foot*,] of the camel; (Ṣ, M, O, AHei, Ḳ;) so called because of its being concealed: (AHei, TA:) and, (M, Ḳ,) in a human being, (M,) الأَظَلُّ signifies بَطْنُ الإِصْبَعِ; (M, Ḳ;) and [ISd says] this is in my opinion the right explanation; but it is said that أَظَلُّ signifies بُطُونُ أَصَابِعِ الإِنْسَانِ, which means *the portion, of what is next to the fore part* [*of the bottom*] *of the foot, from the root of the great toe to the root of the little toe, of the human being*: (M:) the pl. is ظُلُّ, which is anomalous, (M, Ḳ,) or formed after the manner of the pl. of an epithet: (M:) or الظُّلُّ فِى الإِنْسَانِ means *the roots*, or *bases*, (أُصُول) *of what are termed* بُطُون الأَصَابِع, *next to the fore part* [*of the bottom*] *of the foot*. (Ibn-'Abbád, O.) Hence the prov., إِنْ يَدْمَ أَظَلُّكَ فَقَدْ نَقِبَ خُفِّى [*If the fore part of the sole of thy foot be bleeding, the sole of my foot has become worn through, in holes*: see نَقِب]: said to the complainer to him who is in a worse condition than he. (AHei, TA.)

مَظَلّ [app. مَظِلّ, being from ظَلَّ of which the aor. is يَظَلُّ; *A place of shade*, or *of continual shade*]. One says, هٰذَا مُنَاخِى وَمَحَلِّى وَبَيْتِى وَمَظَلِّى [*This is my nightly resting-place for the camels, and my place of abode, and my tent, and my place of shade*, or *of continual shade*]. (TA.)

مُظِلٌّ A thing *having shade; by means of which one shades himself*; as also ▼ مُظَلَّلٌ. (Mṣb.) And [A *cloudy* day;] a day *having clouds*: or *having continual shade*. (TA.)

مِظَلَّةٌ (T, Ṣ, M, Mṣb, Ḳ) and مَظَلَّةٌ, (T, M, Mṣb, Ḳ,) the former with kesr to the م as an instrumental noun, (Mṣb,) [and the latter with fet-ḥ as a noun of place,] *A large tent of* [*goats'*] *hair*; (Ṣ, O, Mṣb;) *more ample than the* خِبَآء; so says El-Fárábee: (Mṣb:) *one of the kinds of tents of the Arabs of the desert, the largest of the tents of* [*goats'*] *hair*; next after which is the وَسُوط; and then, the خِبَآء, which is the smallest of the tents of [goats'] hair; so says AZ: but Aboo-Málik says that the مظلّة and the خباء are *small* and *large*: IAar says that the خَيْمَة is of poles roofed with [the panic grass called] ثُمَام, and is not of cloths; but the مظلّة is *of cloths*: (T:) or it is *of the tents called* أَخْبِيَة; (M;) *such as is large, of the* أَخْبِيَة; (Ḳ;) and it is said to be *only of cloths*; and it is *large, having a* رِوَاق [q. v.]; but *sometimes it is of one oblong piece of cloth* (شُقَّة), and *of two such pieces*, and *of three*; *and sometimes it has a* كِفَآء, *which is its hinder part*: or, accord. to Th, *it is peculiarly of* [*goats'*] *hair*: (M:) see also ظُلَّة, and ظُلْظُلٌ: the pl. is مَظَالٌّ; (M, Mṣb;) and مَظَالِى or مَظَالِ occurs at the end of a verse of Umeiyeh Ibn-Abee-'Áïdh El-Hudhalee, for مَظَالّ; the [latter] ل being either elided, or changed into ى. (M.) عِلَّةٌ مَا عِلَّةٌ أَوْتَادٌ وَأَخِلَّةٌ وَعَمَدُ المِظَلَّةِ أَبْرِزُوا لِصِهْرِكُمْ ▼ ظُلَّةً [*A pretext: what is the pretext of tent-pegs, and of pins for fastening together the edges of the pieces of the tent-cloth, and of the poles of the large tent? go ye forth: he who has married among you has a tent for shade from the sun*:] is a prov., and was said by a girl who had been married to a man, and whose family delayed to conduct her to her husband, urging in excuse that they had not the apparatus of the tent: she said this to urge them, and to put a stop to their excuse: (Meyd, TA:*) and the prov. is applied in attributing untruth to pretexts. (Meyd.) —— Hence, as being likened thereto, † *A booth*, or *shed, made of palm-sticks, and covered with* [*the panic grass called*] ثُمَام. (Mṣb.) —— And The *thing* [i. e. *umbrella*] *by means of which kings are shaded on the occasion of their riding*; called in Pers. چتر. (TA.)

عَرْشٌ مُظَلَّلٌ [*A booth, or shed, shaded over*] is from الظِّلّ. (Ṣ.)

مُظَلَّلٌ: see مُظِلٌّ.

مُسْتَظِلٌّ Blood *that is in the* جَوْف [or *belly*, or *interior of the belly*, or the *chest*]. (T, O.) —— And [Az says,] I heard a man of the tribe of Ṭeiyi apply the term المُسْتَظِلَّاتُ [so accord. to a copy of the T, but in the TA المُسْتَظِلُّ,] to *Certain thin flesh, adhering to the interior of the two fetlock-joints of the camel, than which there is in the flesh of the camel none thinner, nor any softer, but there is in it no grease*. (T.)

ظلع

1. ظَلَعَ, aor. َ, inf. n. ظَلْعٌ, (Ṣ, Mgh, O, Mṣb, Ḳ,) said of a camel, (Ṣ, O, Mṣb, Ḳ,) and of a man also, (Mṣb, TA,) and, by Aboo-Dhu-eyb, of a horse, (Ṣ, TA,) [and likewise said of a dog, (see ظَالِعٌ,)] *He limped*, or *halted*, syn. غَمَزَ فِى مَشْيِهِ, (Ṣ, O, Mṣb, Ḳ, TA,) and عَرِجَ; (TA;) or *was slightly lame*: (Mgh:) what it signifies resembles عَرَج [or natural lameness], and therefore it is said to be a slight عَرَج. (Mṣb.) One says, اِرْقَ عَلَى ظَلْعِكَ, (Ṣ, O, L, Ḳ,) a prov., (O, L,) meaning *Ascend thou* the mountain *with knowledge* [or *because*] *of thy limping*, or *slight lameness, not jading thyself*: (L:) or *deal gently with thyself, and burden not thyself with more than thou art able to do*: (Ṣ:) or *impose upon thyself, of what is difficult*, [*only*] *what thou art able to do*; for he who ascends a ladder or stair, or a mountain, when he is one who limps, or has a slight lameness, deals gently with himself; i. e. *exceed not thy proper limit in thy threatening, but see thy deficiency, and thine impotence to execute it*: (O, Ḳ:*) and some say اِرْقَأْ, with ء, meaning *rectify thine affair first*; (O, Ḳ;) or as meaning *abstain, and restrain thyself*; (O;) or, accord. to AZ, *abstain thou, for I know thy vices*, or *faults*: (TA:) or the meaning of both is, *be silent, because*, or *in consideration, of the fault that is in thee*. (Ks, O, Ḳ.*) One says also, اِرْقِ عَلَى ظَلْعِكَ, with kesr to the ق, [meaning *Charm thou thy slight lameness, to cure it*,] from الرُّقْيَة: and it is said in another prov.,

اِرْقِ عَلَى ظَلْعِكَ أَنْ يُهَاضَا

[app. meaning *Charm thou thy slight lameness that it may become mitigated*: see art. هيض: the final ا in يهاضا being what is termed أَلِفُ الإِطْلَاقِ, not a radical]. (O, Ḳ.) And قِ عَلَى ظَلْعِكَ [*Be cautious, because*, or *in consideration, of thy limping*]: said when there is a vice, or fault, in a man, and you chide him in order that it may not be called to mind: (O, Ḳ: [for يَذْكُرَ in the CḲ, I read يُذْكَرَ, as in other copies of the Ḳ and in the O:]) and to this he replies, or may reply, وَقَيْتُ. (TA. [See also art. وقى.]) And اِرْبَعْ عَلَى ظَلْعِكَ [*Act gently*, or *with deliberation*, or *restrain thyself, because of thy limping*]; meaning thou art weak; therefore refrain from that which thou art not able to do. (O, Ḳ. [See also art. ربع.]) And لَا يَرْبَعُ عَلَى ظَلْعِكَ مَنْ لَيْسَ يَحْزُنُهُ أَمْرُكَ, meaning *He will not mind thine affair* (Hr, O, Ḳ) *whom thy condition does not grieve*: (Hr, O:) or, originally, *he will not pause because of thy limping*, when thou laggest behind thy companions on account of thy weakness, *who does not care for thy case*. (Hr, O, Ḳ.* [See, again, art. ربع.]) —— Also, said of a man, ‡ *He stopped short*, and *lagged behind*. (TA.) —— ظَلَعَتِ الأَرْضُ بِأَهْلِهَا ‡ *The land became straitened with its inhabitants, by reason of their multitude*; (A'Obeyd, Ṣ, O, Ḳ;) *it would not bear them, by reason of their multitude, like the beast that limps with its load because of its heaviness*. (Z, TA.)

— ظَلَعَتْ said of a bitch, ‡ *She desired copulation.* (Aṣ, O, Ḳ, TA.) And ظَلَعَ said of a dog, † *He desired to copulate.* (TA.) ═ ظَلَعَتْ عَيْنَهَا *She* (a woman) *contracted and inclined her eye.* (TA.)

4. اظلع *He made* his camel, or beast, that he rode, *to limp,* or *become lame.* (A, TA.)

5. In the following saying of a poet,

• وَمَا ذَاكَ مِنْ جُرْمٍ أَتَيْتُهُمْ بِهِ •
• وَلَا حَسَدٍ مِنِّى لَهُمْ يَتَظَلَّعُ •

ISd thinks the meaning to be, [*And that was not a crime,* or *an offence, that I committed against them, nor envy on my part*] *arising in their minds, and occurring hastily to their understandings.* (TA.)

ظَلَعٌ, thus with fet-ḥ to the ل, *A declining from the truth,* or *from that which is right;* and *a sin, crime, fault,* or *misdeed.* (TA.)

ظُلَاعٌ *A disease in the legs of a beast, not from journeying nor from fatigue,* (Lth, Ḳ, TA, [in the O inadvertently written ضُلَاع,]) *in consequence of which it limps.* (Lth, TA.)

ظَالِعٌ *Limping,* or *halting;* [or *slightly lame;*] applied to a camel, and a horse, [&c.,] (Ṣ,) [i. e.,] to a beast, (TA,) to the male and the female alike, (Lth, O, Ḳ, TA,) to the former as a part. n., and to the latter as a possessive noun, (TA,) like ضَامِرٌ; (Lth, O, TA;) or the fem. of ظَالِعٌ is ظَالِعَةٌ, (Ṣ, O, Ḳ, TA,) but one does not say ضَامِرَةٌ: (O, TA:) [pl. ظُلَّعٌ.] One says, لَا أَنَامُ حَتَّى يَنَامَ ظَالِعُ الكِلَابِ [*I will not sleep until the limping dog sleeps*]; (O, Ḳ;) a prov., (O,) meaning, until the dogs become still; (O, Ḳ;) because the ظالع, of dogs, waits until there remains none other, and then copulates, and sleeps: (Aṣ, O, Ḳ:) — or the ظالع is *the dog that is lusting for the female;* for such does not sleep; and the saying is applied to him who is mindful of his affair, who does not neglect it: — or *the bitch that is lusting for the male;* because the dogs follow her, and will not let her sleep. (O, Ḳ.) — Also *Inclining,* or *declining:* (O, Ḳ:) like ضَالِعٌ. (TA.) — And [*Declining from the truth, or from that which is right;* (see ظَلَعٌ;)] *committing a sin, crime, fault,* or *misdeed.* (TA.) — And *Suspected.* (Ṣ, O, Ḳ.) ═ In the saying of Ru-beh,

• فَإِنْ تَخَالَجْنَ العُيُونَ الظُّلَّعَا •

[*And if ye women vie with the contracted and inclined eyes*], he means المَظْلُوعَةَ, [see 1, last sentence,] using the word in the manner of a possessive noun. (TA.)

مُظْلِعٌ, applied to a load, *i. q.* مُضْلِعٌ [i. e. *Heavily burdening,* or *overburdening,* &c.; or *causing to limp*]. (TA.)

مِظْلَاعٌ an epithet applied to a horse [and the like, as meaning *That limps,* or *halts, much*]. (TA.)

ظلف

1. ظَلَفَ الصَّيْدَ, (Ṣ, M, O,) or الشَّاةَ, (Ḳ,) aor. ـِ, inf. n. ظَلْفٌ, (M,) *He hit in his* ظلف [or *cloven hoof*] (Ṣ, M, O, Ḳ) *the animal of the chase* (Ṣ, M, O) at which he had shot or cast, (Ṣ, O,) or *the* شاة [a term including the *antelope* and *the like*]. (Ḳ.) ═ ظَلَفَ أَثَرَهُ, (Ṣ, M, O, Ḳ,) aor. ـِ and ـُ, (M, Ḳ,) inf. n. ظَلْفٌ, (M, TA,) *He made his foot-marks to be unapparent, in order that he might not be tracked:* (Ḳ:) or *he went,* or *walked, upon hard and rugged ground, in order that his foot-marks might not be visible* (Ṣ, M, O, Ḳ) *upon it;* (Ṣ, O;) as also ▼ اظلفهُ; (Ṣ, M, L, TA;) in the Ḳ, erroneously ▼ ظالفهُ. (TA.) — And ظُلِفَ *It* (a herd of camels driven together) *was taken along ground such as is termed* ظَلَفٌ, (which means *rugged* ground, *such as does not show foot-marks,* M,) *in order that the foot-marks thereof might not be followed.* (Ṣ, O.) — And ظَلَفَهُمْ, (M, Ḳ,) aor. ـُ, (M,) or ـِ, (TA,) inf. n. ظَلْفٌ, (M, TA,) *He followed their foot-marks.* (M, Ḳ.) ═ ظَلَفَ نَفْسَهُ عَنْهُ, (T, Ṣ, M, O, Ḳ,) aor. ـِ, (Ṣ, O, Ḳ,) inf. n. ظَلْفٌ, (Ṣ, O,) *He withheld himself from doing it,* or *coming to it;* (Ṣ, O, Ḳ;) namely, a thing: (Ṣ, O:) or *he restrained himself from it;* (T, Ḳ;) namely, a thing that would disgrace him: (T:) or *he withheld himself from the love,* or *blamable love, of it;* namely, a thing. (M.) And ظَلَفَهُ عَنْهُ, (T, M,) aor. ـِ, inf. n. ظَلْفٌ, *He withheld him from it;* namely, an affair: (M:) or *he made him to be,* or *become, far,* or *aloof, from it;* or *to avoid it;* namely, a thing; as also ▼ اظلفهُ. (T, TA.) And ظَلَفَهُ [alone] *He withheld him from that in which was no good.* (M.) ═ ظَلِفَتِ الأَرْضُ, (M, Ḳ,) [aor. ـَ,] inf. n. ظَلَفٌ, (Ṣ,* M, TA,) *The ground was rugged, not showing a foot-mark.* (Ṣ,* M, Ḳ.) And ظَلِفَتْ مَعِيشَتُهُ, inf. n. ظَلَفٌ, *His means of subsistence became hard, strait,* or *difficult.* (TḲ.) ═ ظَلِفَتْ نَفْسِى عَنْ كَذَا, aor. ـَ, inf. n. ظَلَفٌ, *My mind,* or *soul, abstained,* or *refrained, from such a thing.* (Ṣ.) ═ [And accord. to the KL, ظَلَفٌ as an inf. n. signifies The *being ineffectual* (i. e. *unretaliated,* or *uncompensated by a mulct,* as expl. below); said of blood; and so ظَلْفٌ (which is also expl. below): — and the *being concealed*].

2. ظلّف عَلَيْهِ, (IAạr, T, O, Ḳ,) inf. n. تَظْلِيفٌ, (O,) *He exceeded it;* (IAạr, T, O, Ḳ;) i. e. [a certain number of years in age, as, for instance,] السِّتِّينَ [*sixty*], (T,) or الخَمْسِينَ [*fifty*]: (O:) and so ظَلَّفَ and طَلَّثَ and ذَرَّفَ &c. (T, TA.)

3. ظالفهُ: see 1, former half: it is a mistake, in the Ḳ, for اظلفهُ. (TA.)

4. اظلف, said of a man, (IAạr, T, O,) or of a company of men, (M,) *He,* or *they, became,* or *came to be,* (IAạr, T, M, O, Ḳ,) *in,* or *upon, a hard place,* (IAạr, T, O,) or *in,* or *upon, what is termed* أُظْلُوفَة (M, Ḳ) and ظَلَف. (M.) ═ اظلفهُ: see 1, in two places.

ظَلْفٌ, of ground, or land, *Such as is rugged, that will not show any foot-mark;* (M;) as also ▼ ظَلَفٌ: (Ṣ,* M:) or so ▼ ظَلِفَةٌ (Ṣ, Ḳ) and ▼ ظَلَفَةٌ and ▼ ظَلِفَةٌ: (Ḳ:) and ▼ ظَلِفٌ signifies ground *such as horses like to run upon:* (T:) or (i. e. the last) a place *elevated above the water and the mud;* and so ▼ ظَلَفٌ; (Ḳ;) this last thus expl. by Ibn-'Abbád: (O:) or this last and ▼ ظَلَفَةٌ, accord. to ISh, (TA,) or ▼ ظَلَفٌ and ▼ ظَلِفَةٌ, (so accord. to a copy of the T, in which the authority is not mentioned,) signify ground, or land, *in which the foot-mark will not appear, and which is high and rugged:* and accord. to Fr, ▼ ظَلِفٌ and ▼ ظَلِفَةٌ signify ground, or land, *that will not show a foot-mark;* as though it were prevented from doing so: (T, TA:) and ▼ ظَلْفٌ, (so in a copy of the T,) or ▼ ظَلَفٌ, (so in the TA,) accord. to Fr, signifies *such as is soft,* of ground, or land: but accord. to IAạr, *such as is hard, and does not show a foot-mark; in which is no softness, so as to be difficult to him who walks upon it; nor sand, so that the camels would have their feet burnt upon it; nor stones, so that they would be chafed,* or *abraded, in the soles of their feet, upon it:* and it is also expl. (by IAạr, TA) as meaning *such as is rugged and hard,* of ground, or land: (T, TA:) and ▼ ظَلِفَةٌ signifies *high* ground, or land, *that will not show a foot-mark.* (M.) [See also ظَلِيفٌ.] — [In the CḲ, الظَّلْفُ is erroneously put for الظَّلَفُ as relating to the means of subsistence.] ═ ظَلْفٌ also signifies *Ineffectual, null,* or *void:* and *allowable.* (TḲ.) One says, ذَهَبَ دَمُهُ ظَلْفًا, (AA, Ṣ, M, O, Ḳ,) and ▼ ظَلَفًا, (AA, T, Ṣ, M, O, Ḳ,) and ▼ ظَلِيفًا, (M,) as also طَلْفًا and طَلَفًا (AA, O) [and طَلِيفًا], *His blood went for nothing; as a thing of no account; ineffectually;* or *in vain; unretaliated,* or *uncompensated by a mulct.* (AA, T, Ṣ, M, O, Ḳ.)

[الظَّلْفُ in Ḥar p. 312, there said to be used as meaning *Continence,* and *disdain of base actions,* is app. a mistake for الظَّلَفُ, inf. n. of 1 in the phrase ظَلَفَ نَفْسَهُ.]

ظِلْفٌ The ظُفْر [meaning *cloven hoof*] *of any ruminant* (T, M) *of the bovine kind and the like;* (T;) [i. e.] it is *an appertenance of the bovine kind* and *of the sheep* and *goat* (Ṣ, O, Mṣb, Ḳ) and *of the gazelle* or *antelope* (Ṣ, O, Ḳ) and *the like,* (O, Mṣb, Ḳ,) *which is to them like the* ظُفْر *to man,* (Mṣb,) or *like the* قَدَم *to us:* (Ḳ:) one says the قَدَم of a man, and the حَافِر of a horse, and the خُفّ of a camel and of an ostrich, and the ظِلْف of a bovine animal and of a sheep or goat [and the like]: (ISk, T, TA:) pl. أَظْلَافٌ (Ṣ, M, O, Mṣb, Ḳ) and ظُلُوفٌ: (Ṣ, O, Ḳ:) and

أَظْلَافٌ is applied, by 'Amr Ibn-Maadee-kerib, to the *hoofs of horses*, (Ṣ, M, O,) as is said by Lth and Az and IF, by poetic license, (O,) metaphorically: (Ṣ, O:) and by El-Akhṭal, metaphorically, to the *feet of men*. (M, IB, TA.) [Its dual is used in the Ḳ, in explanations of the words شَعْرَةٌ and أَشْعَرُ, in the latter instance on the authority of Lḥ, as meaning The *two halves of a cloven hoof*.] And one says, مَا جَشِمْتُ إِلَيْكَ ظِلْفًا [app. meaning *I have not had the trouble of bringing to thee* so much as *the hoof of a gazelle* or *the like*]. (AZ, TA in art. جشم, q. v.) And هُوَ يَأْكُلُهُ بِضِرْسٍ وَيَطَؤُهُ بِظِلْفٍ [*He eats it with a lateral tooth, and treads it with a cloven hoof*; app. meaning, *vehemently*]. (TA.) — It is sometimes used as meaning ‡ *Cloven-hoofed animals*. (TA.) One says, مَا لَهُ خُفٌّ وَلَا حَافِرٌ وَلَا ظِلْفٌ ‡ [*He possesses not camels, nor horses* or *asses* or *mules, nor sheep* or *goats* or *other cloven-hoofed beasts*]. (TA in art. خف.) — It also signifies [or implies] The *making consecutive progressions* in walking and in other actions, (T, Ḳ,) or, accord. to the L, in a thing. (TA.) One says, جَآءَتِ الإِبِلُ عَلَى ظِلْفٍ وَاحِدٍ (T, A, O, TA) i. e. *The camels came following one another*. (A, TA. [See also a similar phrase voce خُفٌّ.]) And غَنَمُ فُلَانٍ عَلَى ظِلْفٍ وَاحِدٍ and ظَلَفٍ ↓ وَاحِدٍ *The sheep*, or *goats, of such a one, have all of them brought forth* [app. *one after another*]. (M.) — Also *A thing that is suitable to the requirements* of a man, and of a beast: (M:) and *an object of desire*: (M, O, Ḳ:) and *an object of want*. (T, Ḳ.) One says, أَصَابَ فُلَانٌ ظِلْفَهُ *Such a one attained what was suitable to his requirements*, and *what he desired*: and sometimes one says the like of any beast that finds, or lights on, or meets with, that which he likes. (M.) وَجَدَتِ الدَّابَّةُ ظِلْفَهَا is a prov., (M, O,) applied to him who finds the means of attaining that which he seeks; (Meyd;) meaning [*The beast found what was suitable to its requirements*; or,] *what withheld it* [*from other things*] *and prevented its desire* [*thereof*]. (A, TA. [See also Freytag's Arab. Prov., ii. 807.]) And one says, وَجَدَتِ الشَّاةُ ظِلْفَهَا *The sheep*, or *goat, found suitable pasturage, and therefore did not quit it*: (Ḳ, TA:) a prov. mentioned by Fr; applied to him, of men and of beasts, that finds what is suitable to him. (TA.) And بَلَدٌ مِنْ ظِلْفِ الغَنَمِ *A country of such as are suitable to sheep* or *goats*. (M.) And وَجَدَ ظِلْفَهُ *He found what he loved*, (O,) or *what he desired*, (Ḳ,) and *what was suitable to him*; (TA;) said of a man. (O.) And مَا وَجَدْتُ عِنْدَهُ ظِلْفِى *I did not find with him the object of my want*. (TA.) — See also ظَلْفٌ, near the middle of the paragraph. — [In some copies of the Ḳ, الظَّلِفُ is erroneously put for الظَّلَفُ as relating to the means of subsistence. And in the CḲ ظِلْفُهَا is erroneously put for ظَلَفُهَا as meaning ظَلِفُ النَّفْسِ.]

ظَلَفٌ [as an inf. n.: see 1, last quarter. — Also] *Hardness*, or *difficulty*, (Ṣ, O, Ḳ,) or *coarseness*, (M,) *in the means of subsistence*: (Ṣ, M, O, Ḳ:) thus the word is correctly written: not ظَلْفٌ, as we find it written in [copies of] the Ḳ: [nor ظَلِفٌ, as in the CḲ:] and ظَلَفُ العَيْشِ occurs in a trad., (O, TA,) meaning *straitness*, and *hardness* or *difficulty*, and *coarseness, of the means of subsistence*. (TA.) — See also ظَلْفٌ, in three places, near the beginning of the paragraph. — And see the last sentence of that paragraph. — Also *Anything that is easy*, or *of light estimation, paltry*, or *despicable*; [as also ظَلِفٌ;] syn. كُلُّ هَيِّنٍ, (M,) or هَيِّنٍ. (TA.) — See also ظِلْفٌ, latter half. — And see ظَلِيفَةٌ.

ظَلِفٌ: see ظَلْفٌ, former half, in three places. — ظَلِفُ النَّفْسِ, [accord. to the CḲ ظَلِيفُ النَّفْسِ, but this is a mistranscription,] and ظَلِيفُ ↓ النَّفْسِ, (M, O, Ḳ,) A man *who withholds himself from the love*, or *blamable love, of a thing*: (M:) or one *who abstains from that which is indecorous*; syn. نَزِهُ النَّفْسِ. (O, Ḳ.) And اِمْرَأَةٌ ظَلِفَةُ النَّفْسِ i. q. عَزِيزَةٌ عِنْدَ نَفْسِهَا [app. *A woman strong to resist, in her own estimation*; and therefore meaning *one who abstains from that which is indecorous*: Golius renders it *mulier pudica, et de honore suo sollicita*]. (Ṣ, TA.) — See also ظَلِفَةٌ.

[الظُّلُفُ in Ḥar p. 623, there said to mean *The restraining the soul from its desire*, or *blamable inclination*, is app. a mistranscription for الظَّلَفُ, inf. n. of ظَلِفَتِ النَّفْسُ.]

ظَلْفَةٌ: see ظَلْفٌ. — Also *A certain brand*, or *mark made with a hot iron, upon a camel*; and so ↓ ظَلِفَةٌ. (O, Ḳ.)

ظَلَفَةٌ: see ظَلْفٌ, in two places, near the beginning. — [Hence, perhaps,] one says, أَقَامَهُ اللّٰهُ عَلَى الظَّلَفَاتِ, (TA, [there said to be مُحَرَّكَة,]) or الظلفات, (so in a copy of the T, [i. e. ↓ الظَّلِفَاتِ,]) meaning [*God made him to keep to*] *a state of hardship and straitness*. (T, TA.)

ظَلِفَةٌ: see ظَلْفٌ, in four places: — and see ظَلْفَةٌ: — and ظَلَفَةٌ. — Also The [*lower*] *end of the* [*curved piece of wood called the*] حِنْو [*that lies against the side, at the fore part and at the hinder part*,] *of the* [*kind of saddle called*] قَتَب, and *of the* [*kind called*] إِكَاف, and *the like*; *being in what is next to the ground, of the sides thereof*: (Lth, T, TA:) or its pl., which is ظَلِفَاتٌ (Ṣ, M, O, Ḳ) and ↓ ظَلِفٌ, (O, Ḳ, [or rather the latter is a coll. gen. n.,]) signifies the *four pieces of wood*, (Ṣ, M, O, Ḳ,) *of the* [*saddle called the*] رَحْل and *of the* [*saddle called the*] قَتَب, (Ṣ, O,) *that are upon the two sides of the camel*, (Ṣ, M, O, Ḳ,) *the lower ends of which touch the ground when they are put down upon it*; *in the* وَاسِط [or *fore part of the saddle*] *are two* (i. e. ظَلِفَتَانِ), *and so in the* مُؤْخِرَة [or *hinder part*], *and they are the lower portions of the* حِنْوَانِ; (Ṣ, O, Ḳ;) *for the parts above them, next to the* [*pieces of wood called the*] عَرَاقِى, *are* [*called*] *the* عَضُدَانِ, *and the elongated pieces of wood upon the sides of the camel are the* أَحْنَآء [pl. of حِنْوٌ]: (Ṣ, O:) AZ says that the upper portions of the ظَلِفَتَانِ, [a mistake for the حِنْوَانِ, as is shown by what follows,] next to the عَرَاقِى, are [called] the عَضُدَانِ; below them being the ظَلِفَتَانِ, which are the *lower parts of the* حِنْوَانِ *of the* وَاسِط *and of the* مُؤْخِرَة. (T, TA.) — [Hence] one says, قَامُوا عَلَى ظَلِفَاتِهِمْ, meaning عَلَى أَطْرَافِهِمْ ‡ [*They stood upon their extremities*, i. e. *their feet*]. (TA.) — And نَحْنُ عَلَى ظَلِفَاتِ أَمْرٍ ‡ *We are on the verge of an affair*, or *event*. (TA.) — See also ظَلِيفَةٌ.

ظَلْفَاةٌ *A smooth stone* or *rock*, or *a hard, smooth, large stone*, (صَفَاةٌ,) *even with the ground*, (T, O, Ḳ,) *round* (مدورة), (so in a copy of the T, [i. e. مُدَوَّرَةٌ,]) or *extended* (مَمْدُودَةٌ). (O, Ḳ.)

ظُلُفٌ [a pl. of which the sing. is not mentioned: accord. to general analogy, the sing. should be ظَالِفٌ]. ظُلُوفٌ ظُلُفٌ means *Hard* ظُلُوف [or *divided hoofs*]: (Ṣ, O, Ḳ:) the latter word being a corroborative. (Ṣ, O.)

ظَلِيفٌ A *rough*, or *rugged*, place, (Ṣ, M, O, Ḳ, TA,) *in which is much sand*. (M, TA. [See also ظَلِفٌ.]) — And A man (Ṣ, O) *evil in condition* (T, Ṣ, M, Ḳ) *in respect of his means of subsistence*: (T:) and *low, abject*, or *abased, and weak*. (M, O, Ḳ.) — And An affair that is *hard*, or *difficult*: (Ḳ:) anything *difficult to one to seek*: (IDrd, M, O:) and evil *hard to be borne*, or *severe*. (Ṣ, O.) — See also ظَلَفٌ. — Also *Hardship*, or *difficulty*. (O, Ḳ.) — ذَهَبَ بِهِ ظَلِيفًا *He went away with it*, or *took it away, without compensation*, or *without price*: (T, Ṣ, M, Ḳ:) and so ظَلَفًا. (Yoo, TA in art. طلف.) And ذَهَبَ بِغُلَامِى ظَلِيفًا *He went away with*, or *took away, my young man*, or *slave, without price*. (AZ, Ṣ, O.) — See also ظَلَفٌ, last sentence. — أَخَذَهُ بِظَلِيفِ رَقَبَتِهِ *He took him by the base of his neck*. (O, Ḳ,* TA.) — See also what here follows.

ظَلِيفَةٌ: أَخَذَهُ بِظَلِيفَتِهِ, (Ṣ, M, O, L,) or ↓ بِظَلِيفِهِ, (Ḳ,) and ↓ بِظَلَفِهِ, (Ṣ, O, Ḳ,) ↓ بِظَلِفَتِهِ, (T, M, L,) *He took it altogether*, or *wholly*, (T,* Ṣ, O, Ḳ,) or *with its root*, or *base, and wholly*, (M, L,) *not leaving of it anything*: (T, Ṣ, M, O, L, Ḳ:) so says AZ. (Ṣ.)

أُظْلُوفَةٌ *A piece of rugged*, or *rough, ground*: (T:) or *ground*, (Ṣ, O, Ḳ,) or *hard ground*, (TA,) *in which are sharp stones, as though its composition were that of a mountain*: (Ṣ, O, Ḳ, TA:) pl. أَظَالِيفُ. (T, Ṣ, &c.)

مَظْلُوفٌ An animal of the chase, at which one

has shot or cast, *hit in his* ظِلْف [or *cloven hoof*]. (Yaạḳoob, Ṣ.)

ظلم

1. ظَلَمَ, aor. ـِ , has for its inf. n. ظُلْمٌ, (M, Mṣb, Ḳ, and so in some copies of the Ṣ,) or ✱ ظَلْمٌ, (so in other copies of the Ṣ,) or both, (T,) or the latter is a simple subst., (T, M, Mṣb, TA,) which is put in the place of the inf. n., (TA, [and the same is indicated in the T and Ḳ by the saying that the proper inf. n. is with fet-ḥ,]) and ✱ مَظْلَمَةٌ, (Ṣ, TA,) or this is likewise a simple subst., (Mṣb,) and ✱ مَظْلِمَةٌ, [or this also is a simple subst.,] and ✱ ظِلَامٌ also is said to be an inf. n. like ظُلْمٌ, these two being like بِئَاسٌ and بُؤْسٌ, [or it is a simple subst. like as ظُلْمٌ is said to be, or it is an inf. n. of 3, as such occurring in the middle of this paragraph,] or, accord. to Kr, it is pl. of ظُلْمٌ [like as رِمَاحٌ is pl. of رُمْحٌ]: (TA:) [ظَلَمَ when intrans. generally means *He did wrong; or acted wrongfully, unjustly, injuriously, or tyrannically:* and when trans., *he wronged; or treated, or used, wrongfully, unjustly, injuriously, or tyrannically; or he misused:*] accord. to most of the lexicologists, (Er-Rághib, TA,) primarily, (Aṣ, T, Ṣ, Mṣb,) ✱ الظُّلْمُ signifies *the putting a thing in a place not its own; putting it in a wrong place; misplacing it:* (Aṣ, T, Ṣ, M, Er-Rághib, Mṣb, Ḳ:) and it is *by exceeding* or *by falling short,* or *by deviating from the proper time and place:* (Er-Rághib, TA:) or *the acting in whatsoever way one pleases in the disposal of the property of another:* and *the transgressing the proper limit:* (El-Munáwee, TA:) [i. e.] *the transgressing the proper limit much or little:* (Er-Rághib, TA:) or, accord. to some, it primarily signifies النَّقْصُ [as meaning *the making to suffer loss,* or *detriment*]: (MF, TA:) and it is said to be of three kinds, *between man and God,* and *between man and man,* and *between a man and himself;* every one of which three is really ظُلْمٌ لِلنَّفْسِ [i. e. *a wrongdoing to oneself*]: (Er-Rághib, TA:) [when it is used as a simple subst.,] the pl. of ظُلْمٌ, accord. to Kr, is ظِلَامٌ, as mentioned above, and ✱ ظُلَامٌ, with ḍamm, is said to be syn. with ظُلْمٌ, or a pl. thereof, [of an extr. form, commonly regarded as that of a quasi-pl. n.,] like رُخَالٌ. (TA.) One says, مَنِ ٱسْتَرْعَى الذِّئْبَ فَقَدْ ظَلَمَ [*He who asks,* or *desires, the wolf to keep guard surely does wrong,* or *puts a thing in a wrong place*]: a prov. (Ṣ, Mṣb.) And مَنْ أَشْبَهَ أَبَاهُ فَمَا ظَلَمَ, (Aṣ, T, Ṣ,) a prov., meaning [*Whoso resembles his father* in a quality, or an attribute,] *he has not put the likeness in a wrong place.* (Aṣ, T. [See art. شبه.]) وَلَمْ تَظْلِمْ مِنْهُ شَيْئًا, in the Ḳur [xviii. 31], means وَلَمْ تَنْقُصْ [i. e. *And made not aught thereof to suffer loss,* or *detriment*]: (M, Ḳ:) and in like manner Fr explains the saying in the Ḳur [ii. 54 and vii. 160], وَمَا ظَلَمُونَا وَلٰكِنْ كَانُوا أَنْفُسَهُمْ يَظْلِمُونَ *And they made not us to suffer loss,* or *detriment,* by that which they did, *but themselves they made to suffer loss,* or *detriment:* (T, TA:) in which sense it seems to be indicated in the A that the verb is tropical. (TA.) — It is also trans. by means of بِ; as in the phrase in the Ḳur [vii. 101 and xvii. 61] فَظَلَمُوا بِهَا, because the meaning is كَفَرُوا [i. e. *And they disbelieved in them*], referring to the آيَات [or *signs*]; (M, TA;*) the verb having this meaning tropically or by implication; or being thus made trans. because implying the meaning of التَّكْذِيب: or [the meaning is, and *they wronged* themselves, or the people, *because of them;* for], as some say, the ب is causative, and the objective complement, i. e. أَنْفُسَهُمْ, or النَّاسَ, is suppressed. (TA.) — And it is doubly trans. by itself: (TA:) one says, ظَلَمَهُ حَقَّهُ [*He made him to suffer loss,* or *detriment, of his right,* or *due;* or *defrauded,* or *despoiled,* or *deprived, him of it*]; and ✱ تَظَلَّمَهُ حَقَّهُ: (M, Ḳ:) [and] you say, تَظَلَّمَنِى ✱ فُلَانٌ, [as well as تَظَلَّمَنِى مَالِى, occurring in a verse cited in the M,] meaning ظَلَمَنِى مَالِى [i.e. *Such a one caused me to suffer loss, &c., of my property*]. (Ṣ.) It is said in the Ḳur [iv. 44], إِنَّ ٱللّٰهَ لَا يَظْلِمُ مِثْقَالَ ذَرَّةٍ, for لَا يَظْلِمُهُمْ مِثْقَالَ ذَرَّةٍ, and the verb is made doubly trans. because the meaning is لَا يَسْلُبُهُمْ [i. e. *Verily God will not despoil them,* or *deprive them, of the weight of one of the smallest of ants,* or *a grub of an ant,* &c.]: or مِثْقَالَ ذَرَّةٍ, may be put in the place of the inf. n., for ظُلْمًا حَقِيرًا كَمِثْقَالِ ذَرَّةٍ [i. e. *with a paltry spoliation* or *deprivation, such as the weight of one of the smallest of ants,* &c.]. (M.) — One says also, أَرَادَ ظِلَامَهُ and مُظَالَمَتَهُ, [these two nouns being inf. ns. of ✱ ظَالَمَهُ, or the former, as mentioned above, is, accord. to some, an inf. n. of ظَلَمَ,] meaning ظُلْمَهُ or ظَلْمَهُ [i. e. *He desired the wronging,* &c., *of him*]. (M, Ḳ.) — ظَلَمَهُ, inf. n. ظَلْمٌ [or ظُلْمٌ?], also means *He imposed upon him a thing that was above his power,* or *ability.* (TA.) And يُظْلَمُ *He is asked for a thing that is above his power,* or *ability.* (Ṣ.) — And one says, ظَلَمَ البَعِيرَ ‡ *He slaughtered the camel without disease.* (Ṣ, Ḳ, TA.) And ظُلِمَتِ النَّاقَةُ † *The she-camel was slaughtered without disease:* or *was covered without her desiring the stallion.* (M.) And ظَلَمَ الحِمَارُ الأَتَانَ ‡ *The he-ass leaped the she-ass* (Ḳ, TA) *before her time:* (TA:) or *when she was pregnant:* (Ḳ, TA:) so in the A. (TA.) — And ظَلَمَ الوَطْبَ, (Ṣ, Ḳ,) inf. n. ظَلْمٌ [or ظُلْمٌ?], (Ṣ,) ‡ *He gave to drink of the milk of his skin before its becoming thick* (Ṣ, Ḳ, TA) *and its butter's coming forth.* (TA. [And the like is said in the T and M.]) And ظَلَمَ القَوْمَ † *He gave to drink to the people,* or *party,* (T, M, Ḳ,) *milk before it had attained to maturity,* (T, Ḳ,) as related on the authority of A'Obeyd, (T,) or [*milk such as is termed*] ظَلِيمَة: (M:) but this is a mistake: it is related on the authority of Aḥmad Ibn-Yaḥyà [i. e. Th] and AHeyth that one says, ظَلَمْتُ السِّقَآءَ, and اللَّبَنَ, meaning *I drank,* or *gave to drink, what was in the skin,* and *the milk, before its attaining to maturity and the extracting of its butter:* accord. to ISk, one says, ظَلَمْتُ وَطْبِى القَوْمَ, [but I think that it is correctly ظَلَمْتُ وَطْبِى لِلْقَوْمِ, agreeably with a verse cited in the T and M,] meaning *I gave to drink* [*to the people,* or *party,*] *the contents of my milk-skin before the thickening thereof.* (T.) And ظَلَمْتُهُ is said of anything as meaning † *I did it hastily,* or *hurriedly, before its proper time,* or *season.* (M, TA.) — ظَلَمْتُ الحَوْضَ means † *I made the watering-trough in a place in which watering-troughs should not be made.* (ISk, T.) And ظَلَمَ الأَرْضَ means ‡ *He dug the ground in what was not the place of digging:* (M, Ḳ, TA:) or *when it had not been dug before.* (M.) And, said of a torrent, † *It furrowed the earth in a place that was not furrowed.* (T.) And ظَلَمَ البِطَاحَ, said of a torrent, ‡ *It reached the* بطاح [or *wide water-courses containing fine,* or *broken, pebbles,* &c.], *not having reached them before.* (A, TA.) And ظَلَمَ الوَادِى ‡ *The water of the valley reached a place that it had not reached before.* (Fr, T, Ṣ, Ḳ, TA.) — When men have added upon the grave other than its own earth, لَا تَظْلِمُوا ‡ [*Transgress not ye the proper limit*] is said to them. (TA.) — And one says, لَا تَظْلِمْ وَضَحَ الطَّرِيقِ † *Turn not thou from the main part,* or *the beaten track, of the road.* (M.) And لَا تَظْلِمْ عَنْهُ شَيْئًا † *Turn not thou from it at all.* (T.) And لَزِمَ الطَّرِيقَ فَلَمْ يَظْلِمْهُ † [*He kept to the road, and*] *did not turn from it to the right and left.* (TA.) — And مَا ظَلَمَكَ أَنْ تَفْعَلَ (T, Ḳ, TA) ‡ *What has prevented thy doing* (Ḳ, TA) such a thing? (TA.) A man complained to Abu-l-Jarráḥ of his suffering indigestion from food that he had eaten, and he said to him, مَا ظَلَمَكَ أَنْ تَقِىْءَ † [*What has prevented thy vomiting?*]. (Fr, T.) And one says, مَا ظَلَمَكَ عَنْ كَذَا † *What has prevented thee from such a thing?* (T.) Respecting the saying

• قَالَ بَلَى يَا مَىَّ وَاليَوْمُ ظَلَمْ •

[addressed by a man to a woman who had invited him to visit her], Fr says, they say that the meaning is حَقًّا [*Truly,* or *in truth;* i. e. *He said, Yes, O Meiya, truly,* or *in truth,* I will visit thee]; and it is a prov.; (T;) or اليَوْمُ ظَلَمْ, or بَلَى وَاليَوْمُ ظَلَمْ, is a prov.; (Meyd;) and thus it was expl. by IAạr, as used in the manner of an oath: but Fr says, in my opinion the meaning is, *and a day in which is a cause of prevention shall not prevent me:* [so that the words of the hemistich above may be rendered, *he said, Yes, O Meiya, though the day present an obstacle, for I will overcome every obstacle*]: (T:)

accord. to Kr, قَدِمَ فُلَانٌ وَالْيَوْمُ ظَلَمٌ means *Such a one came truly*, or *in truth:* [or it may be rendered *such a one came though the day presented an obstacle:*] but in the saying

• إِنَّ الفِرَاقَ اليَوْمَ وَاليَوْمُ ظَلَمْ •

the meaning is said by some to be وَالْيَوْمُ ظَلَمَنَا [i. e. *Verily separation is to-day, and the day has wronged* (us)]: or, as some say, ظلم here means, *has put the thing in a wrong place:* (M:) accord. to ISk, the phrase وَالْيَوْمُ ظَلَمْ means [*And,* or *but,* or *though,*] *the day has put the affair in a wrong place.* (T.) [See also Freytag's Arab. Prov. ii. 911.] ══ ظَلِمَ, said of the night: see 4.

2. ظَلَّمَهُ, inf. n. تَظْلِيمٌ, (T, Ṣ, &c.,) *He told him that he was* ظَالِم [i. e. *doing wrong* or *acting wrongfully* &c., or *a wrongdoer*]: (T:) or *he attributed,* or *imputed, to him* ظُلْم [i. e. *wrongdoing,* &c.]. (Ṣ, M, Mṣb, Ḳ.) — And *He* (a judge) *exacted justice for him from his wronger, and aided him against him.* (T.)

3: see 1, in the middle of the paragraph.

4. اظلم, said of the night, (Fr, T, Ṣ, M, Mṣb, Ḳ,) and ظَلِمَ ♦, (Fr, T, Ṣ, Ḳ,) the latter with kesr, (Ṣ,) like سَمِعَ, (Ḳ,) [erroneously written in the TT as from the M ظَلَمَ,] *It became dark;* (Ṣ, Ḳ;) or *it became black;* (M;) or *it came with its darkness.* (Mṣb.) It is said in the Ḳur [ii. 19], وَإِذَا أَظْلَمَ عَلَيْهِمْ قَامُوا [*And when it becomes dark to them they stand still*]; the verb being intrans.: or, accord. to the Ksh, and Bḍ follows it, it may be trans. [so that the meaning is, *and when He makes* their place *dark* &c.]; as is shown by another reading, which is أُظْلِمَ: accord. to AḤei, it is known by transmission as only intrans.; but Z makes it to be trans. by itself; Ibn-Eṣ-Ṣaláḥ affirms it to be trans. and intrans.: and Az [so in the TA, but correctly ISd, in the M,] mentions the saying, تَكَلَّمَ فَأَظْلَمَ عَلَيْنَا البَيْتَ † [*He spoke, and made dark to us the house,* or *chamber,* or *tent*], meaning he made us to hear what we disliked, or hated, the verb being trans. (TA.) — And أَظْلَمُوا *They entered upon the* ظَلَام [or *darkness,* or *beginning of night*]: (Ṣ, M, Mṣb, Ḳ:) or, as in the Mufradát [of Er-Rághib], *they became in darkness.* (TA.) — And they said, مَا أَظْلَمَهُ and مَا أَضْوَأَهُ [*How dark is it!* and *How light,* or *bright, is it!*]; which is anomalous. (Ṣ, TA.) ══ And اظلم الثَّغْرُ *The front teeth glistened.* (T, Ḳ.) Hence the saying [of a poet],

• إِذَا مَا ٱجْتَلَى الرَّائِي إِلَيْهَا بِطَرْفِهِ •
• غُرُوبَ ثَنَايَاهَا أَضَاءَ وَأَظْلَمَا •

[as though meaning, *When the beholder of her with his eye looks at the fineness,* or *sharpness,* (but غُرُوب is variously explained,) *of her central teeth, it shines brightly, and glistens:* but Az plainly indicates another meaning; i. e., *he sees* (lit. *lights on,* or *finds,*) *brightness and lustre;* for he immediately adds, without the intervention of أَوْ or وَ, evidently in relation to this verse,] أَضَاءَ : أَىْ أَصَابَ ضَوْءًا وَأَظْلَمَ أَصَابَ ظَلْمًا (T:) [and ISd cites the verse above with the substitution of بِعَيْنِهِ for بِطَرْفِهِ and of أَنَارَ for أَضَاءَ immediately after saying that] أَظْلَمَ signifies *he looked at the teeth and saw lustre* (الظَّلْم). (M.) [In the Ḳ, next after the explanation of اظلم الثَّغْرُ given above, it is added that اظلم said of a man signifies أَصَابَ ظَلْمًا: thus, with fet-ḥ, to the ظ, accord. to the TA: in my MS. copy of the Ḳ and in the CḲ, ظُلْمًا, which is doubtless a mistranscription.]

5 تظلّم مِنْهُ (T, Ṣ, M, Ḳ, [but in some copies of the Ṣ, منه is omitted,]) *He complained of his* ظُلْم [or *wrongdoing,* &c.], (Ṣ, M, Ḳ,) إِلَى الحَاكِمِ [*to the judge*]: (T:) in some copies of the Ṣ, تَظَلَّمَ. (TA.) — And تظلّم signifies also *He transferred the responsibility for the* ظُلْم [or *wrongdoing,* &c.,] *upon himself,* (M, Ḳ,) accord. to IAạr, who has cited as an ex.,

• كَانَتْ إِذَا غَضِبَتْ عَلَىَّ تَظَلَّمَتْ •

[as though meaning *She used, when she was angry with me, to transfer the responsibility for the wrongdoing upon herself;* which may mean that she finally confessed the wrongdoing to be hers]; but [ISd says] I know not how that is: the تَظَلُّم in this case is only the complaining of الظُّلْم; for when she was angry with him, it was not allowable [to say] that she attributed the ظُلْم to herself. (M.) — See also 1, former half, in two places.

6. تظالم القَوْمُ (Ṣ, M, Mṣb) *The people,* or *company of men, treated,* or *used, one another wrongfully, unjustly, injuriously,* or *tyrannically* (ظَلَمَ بَعْضُهُمْ بَعْضًا). (M, Mṣb.) — And [hence] تَظَالَمَتِ المِعْزَى ‡ *The goats smote one another with their horns* by reason of their being fat and having abundance of herbage. (IAạr, M, TA.) One says, وَجَدْنَا أَرْضًا تَظَالَمُ مِعْزَاهَا ‡ *We found a land whereof the goats smote one another with their horns* by reason of satiety and liveliness. (T, TA.)

7: see the next paragraph.

8. اِظَّلَمَ (T, Ṣ, M, Ḳ) and اِظْطَلَمَ and اِطَّلَمَ, (Ṣ, M,) which last is [said to be] the most usual, (Ṣ,) [but I have mostly found the first to be used,] of the measure اِفْتَعَلَ, (Ṣ, M,) *He took upon himself* [*the bearing of*] ظُلْم [or *wrong,* &c.,] *in spite of difficulty, trouble,* or *inconvenience:* (Ṣ, TA:) or *he bore* الظُّلْم [or *wrong,* &c.,] (T, M, Ḳ, TA,) *willingly, being able to resist;* (T, TA;) and انظلم ♦ signifies [thus likewise, or] *he bore* الظُّلْم. (Ṣ, M, Ḳ.)

ظَلْمٌ The *lustre,* and *brightness, of gold.* (Z, TA.) — And hence, (Z, TA,) The *lustre* (lit. *running water*) upon the teeth; (Lth, T, Z, TA;) the *lustre* (مَآء, Ṣ, M, Ḳ, and بَرِيق, Ṣ, Ḳ) *of the teeth,* (Lth, T, Ṣ, M, Z, Ḳ, TA,) *from the clearness of the colour, not from the saliva,* (Lth,* T,* M,) *like blackness within the bone thereof, by reason of the intense whiteness,* (Ṣ, Ḳ,) *resembling the* فِرِنْد [q. v.] *of the sword,* (Ṣ, Ḳ,) or *appearing like the* فرند [*of the sword*], *so that one imagines that there is in it a blackness, by reason of the intense lustre and clearness:* (M:) or, accord. to Sh, *whiteness of the teeth, as though there were upon it* [*somewhat of*] *a blackness:* or, as Abu-l-'Abbás El-Aḥwal says, in the Expos. of the "Kaạbeeyeh," *lustre* (lit. *running water*) *of the teeth, such that one sees upon it, by reason of its intense clearness* [app. meaning *transparency*], *what resembles dust-colour and blackness:* or, accord. to another explanation, *fineness,* or *thinness, and intense whiteness, of the teeth:* (TA:) pl. ظُلُومٌ. (Ṣ, M.) — Also *Snow:* (M, Ḳ:) it is said to have this meaning: and the phrase مُشْرَبَةُ الثَّنَايَا بِمَآءِ الظَّلْمِ, used by a poet, may mean [*Having the central teeth suffused with the lustre termed* ظَلْم, as is indicated in the T and Ṣ, or] *with the water of snow.* (Lth, T.)

ظُلْمٌ [as a simple subst. generally means *Wrong, wrongdoing, injustice, injuriousness,* or *tyranny*]: see 1, first sentence, in two places. — [ظُلْمُ الارضِ in the CḲ is a mistranscription for ظَلَمُ الأَرْضِ. — And الظُّلْمُ in one place in the CḲ, as syn. with الظَّلْمَآءُ, is a mistake for الظُّلْمَةُ.]

لَقِيتُهُ أَدْنَى ظَلَمٍ, (Ṣ, M, Ḳ,) or أَدْنَى ذِى ظَلَمٍ, (Ḳ, TA, [in the CḲ أَوَّلَ ذِى ظَلَمٍ,]) means ‡ *I met him the first of everything:* (Ṣ, Ḳ, TA:) or *the first thing:* (M:) or *when the darkness was becoming confused:* (M, Ḳ:) or أَدْنَى ظَلَمٍ means *near;* (El-Umawee, Ṣ, M, Ḳ;) or *nearness:* (M, Ḳ:) and one says, هُوَ مِنْكَ أَدْنَى ذِى ظَلَمٍ [app. *He is near thee*], and رَأَيْتُهُ أَدْنَى ذِى ظَلَمٍ [app. *I saw him near*]: (M:) and ظَلَمٌ is also syn. with شَخْصٌ [as meaning *an object seen from a distance,* or *a person*]; (Ḳ;) or, as some say, it has this meaning in the phrase أَدْنَى ظَلَمٍ [so that لَقِيتُهُ أَدْنَى ظَلَمٍ may mean *I met him the nearest object seen from a distance,* or *the nearest person*]: (M:) and accord. to Kh, one says, لَقِيتُهُ أَدْنَى ظُلْمَةٍ, or أَوَّلَ ذِى ظُلْمَةٍ ♦, (as in different copies of the Ṣ,) meaning *I met him the first thing that obstructed my sight.* (Ṣ.) — ظَلَمٌ signifies also *A mountain:* and the pl. is ظُلُومٌ. (M, Ḳ.)

ظُلَمٌ an appellation of *Three nights* (T, Ṣ, Ḳ) *of the lunar month* (T, Ṣ) *next after the three called* دُرَعٌ; (T, Ṣ,* Ḳ;*) so says A'Obeyd: (T:) thus called because of their darkness: (Ṣ:) the sing. is ظَلْمَآءُ ♦; (T, Ṣ;) so that it is anomalous; for by rule it should be ظُلْمٌ; (Ṣ;) and the sing. of دُرَعٌ is دَرْعَآءُ: so says A'Obeyd: but accord. to AHeyth and Mbr, the sings. are ظُلْمَةٌ ♦ and

دَرِعَة, agreeably with rule; and this is the correct assertion. (T. [See more in art. درع, voce أَدْرَعُ.])

ظُلَمٌ: see ظَلَّامٌ.

ظُلْمَةٌ (T, Ṣ, M, Mṣb, Ḳ) and ▼ ظُلُمَةٌ (Ṣ, M, Ḳ) [accord. to the CḲ ظُلْمٌ and ظُلُمٌ, both of which are wrong,] and ▼ ظَلْمَآءُ (Ṣ, M, Mṣb, Ḳ) *Darkness; contr. of* نُورٌ: (Ṣ, Mṣb:) or *nonexistence of* نور [or *light*]: or *an accidental state that precludes the coëxistence therewith of* نور: (Er-Rághib, TA:) or the *departure of light*; as also ▼ ظَلَامٌ; (M, Ḳ;) which last has no pl.; (T, TA;) or this last signifies the *beginning*, or *first part, of night*, (Ṣ, M, Mṣb,) *even though it be one in which the moon shines*; and is said by Sb to be used only adverbially; one says, أَتَيْتُهُ ظَلَامًا, meaning *I came to him at night*, and مَعَ الظَّلَامِ i. e. *at the time of the night*: (M, TA:) the pl. of ظُلْمَةٌ is ظُلَمٌ and ظُلُمَاتٌ and ظُلْمَاتٌ (T, Ṣ, Mṣb) and ظُلَمَاتٌ, (Ṣ, Mṣb,) or, accord. to IB, the first of these pls. is of ظُلْمَةٌ and the second is of ظُلُمَةٌ. (TA.) One says, ▼ هُوَ يَخْبِطُ الظَّلَامَ or فِى الظَّلَامِ, expl. in art. خبط], and الظُّلْمَةَ [which means the same] and ▼ الظَّلْمَآءَ [which is also expl. in art. خبط]. (TA.) — ظُلْمَةٌ is also [tropically] used as a term for † *Ignorance*: and † *belief in a plurality of gods*: and † *transgression*, or *unrighteousness*: like as نُورٌ is used as a term for their contraries: (Er-Rághib, TA:) and it is said in the A that الظُّلْمُ is ظُلْمَةٌ, like as العَدْلُ is نُورٌ. (TA.) ظُلُمَاتُ البَحْرِ means † *The troubles, afflictions, calamities*, or *hardships, of the sea*. (M.) ═ And one says لَيْلَةٌ ظُلْمَةٌ, [using the latter word as an epithet, (in the CḲ, erroneously, ظَلِمَةٌ,)] and ▼ لَيْلَةٌ ظَلْمَآءُ, both meaning *A night intensely dark*; (M, Ḳ;) or the latter means مُظْلِمَةٌ [i. e. *dark*, or *black*]: (Ṣ:) and ▼ لَيْلٌ ظَلْمَآءُ also, (M, Ḳ,) which is anomalous, (Ḳ,) mentioned by IAạr, but [ISd says] this is strange, and in my opinion he has put لَيْل in the place of لَيْلَة, as in his mentioning لَيْلٌ قَمْرَآءُ [q. v.]. (M.) — See also ظُلْمٌ: — and see the paragraph next preceding it.

ظُلْمَةٌ sing. of ظُلَمٌ: see ظَلَّامٌ.

ظُلُمَةٌ: see ظُلْمَةٌ.

ظَلْمَآءُ: see ظُلْمَةٌ, in four places: and see also ظُلْمٌ.

ظَلَامٌ: see ظُلْمَةٌ, in two places.

ظَلَامٌ: see 1, in the first quarter of the paragraph.

ظُلَامٌ: see 1, near the beginning: ═ see also ظَلَّامٌ. ═ It signifies also *Little*, or *small, in quantity*: or *mean, contemptible, paltry*, or *of no weight* or *worth*: — whence the saying, نَظَرَ إِلَىَّ شَزْرًا ظُلَامًا, meaning [i. e. *He looked at me from the outer angle of the eye, with anger*, or *aversion*]. (Ḳ.)

ظَلُومٌ: see ظَلَّامٌ. — [Hence,] one says اِمْرَأَةٌ ظَلُومٌ لِلسِّقَآءِ † [*A woman wont to give to drink the milk of the skin before its attaining to maturity and the extracting of its butter*: see ظَلَمَ الوَطْبَ, and what follows it, in the first paragraph]. (M.)

ظَلِيمٌ [as syn. with مَظْلُومٌ in the primary sense of the latter I have not found: but as an epithet in which the quality of a subst. predominates it signifies] ‡ *Milk that is drunk before its becoming thick and its butter's coming forth* or *being extracted*; (Ṣ,* M;) as also ▼ ظَلِيمَةٌ, (T, Ṣ, M,) and ▼ مَظْلُومٌ. (T, Ṣ.) — And † *A place that is* ▼ مَظْلُوم [i. e. *dug where it should not be dug*]: (M, TA:) used in this sense by a poet describing a person slain in a desert, for whom a grave was dug in a place not proper for digging [it]. (M.) — And ‡ The *earth of land that is* ▼ مَظْلُومَة (Ṣ, Ḳ, TA) i. e. *dug*, (TA,) or *dug for the first time*. (Ṣ.) And † The *earth of the* لَحْد [or *lateral hollow*] *of a grave; which is put back, over it, after the burial of the dead therein*. (T, TA.) ═ Also The *male ostrich*: (T, Ṣ, M, Ḳ:) said (by IDrd, TA) to be so called because he makes a place for the laying and hatching of the eggs (يُدَحِّى, inf. n. تَدْحِيَةٌ,) where the doing so is not proper: (M, TA:) or, accord. to Er-Rághib and others, because he is believed to be deaf: (TA:) pl. ظِلْمَانٌ (T, M, Ḳ) and ظُلْمَانٌ (M, Ḳ) and أَظْلِمَةٌ, (T, M,) which last is a pl. of pauc. (T.) — And الظَّلِيمَانِ is an appellation of *Two stars*; (M, Ḳ,* TA;) *the two stars of* القَوْس [or *Sagittarius*] *that are on the northern curved end of the bow* [i. e. λ and μ, *above the nine stars called* النَّعَائِم, or "*the ostriches*"]. (Ḳzw in his descr. of Sagittarius.) And الظَّلِيمُ is the name of *The bright star* [α] *at the end of* النَّهْر [i. e. *Eridanus*]: and *A star upon the mouth of* الحُوت [i. e. *Piscis Australis*]. (Ḳzw in his descr. of Eridanus.) [It seems to be implied in the Ḳ that الظَّلِيمُ is the name of two stars; or it may be there meant that each of two stars is thus called. Freytag represents the sing. as "a name of stars," and the dual also as "a name of stars;" referring, in relation to the former, to Ideler's "Untersuch," pp. 201, 228, and 233; and in relation to the latter, to the same work, pp. 106 and 184.]

ظُلَامَةٌ: see مَظْلِمَةٌ.

ظَلِيمَةٌ: see مَظْلِمَةٌ: — and see also ظَلِيمٌ.

ظَلَّامٌ (TA) and ▼ ظَلِيمٌ (Ṣ, TA) [and ▼ ظَلُومٌ, mentioned in the M and Ḳ with ظَالِمٌ, as though syn. therewith, but it is an intensive epithet,] *One who acts wrongfully, unjustly, injuriously*, or *tyrannically, much*, or *often*; i. q. كَثِيرُ الظُّلْمِ. (Ṣ, TA.) — ظَلَّامُونَ لِلْجُزُرِ occurs in a verse of Ibn-Muḳbil [meaning † *Men often slaughtering camels without disease*]. (T, Ṣ.) ═ See also what next follows.

ظُلَّامٌ (AḤn, T, M, Ḳ) and ▼ ظُلَّامٌ (T) and ▼ ظُلَامٌ (Ḳ) and ▼ ظَالِمٌ and ▼ ظُلَمٌ, (T, Ḳ,) the last mentioned by IAạr, and its sing. is ▼ ظُلْمَةٌ, (T,) accord. to AḤn, *A certain herb*, (M, Ḳ, TA,) *which is depastured*; (M, TA;) accord. to IAạr, *a strange kind of tree*; (T, TA;) accord. to Aṣ, *a kind of tree* (T, TA*) *having long* [*shoots such as are termed*] عَسَالِيج [pl. of عُسْلُوجٌ q. v.], (T, Ḳ, TA,) *which extend so that they exceed the limit of the* أَصْل [i. e. either *root* or *stem*] *thereof*; for which reason the tree is called ظُلَّام. (T, TA.)

ظُلَيْمٌ: see ظَلَّامٌ.

ظَالِمٌ [*Acting wrongfully, unjustly, injuriously*, or *tyrannically*: and *wronging*; or *treating*, or *using, wrongfully*, &c.:] part. n. of ظَلَمَ: (M, Ḳ:) and ▼ مُتَظَلِّمٌ signifies the same; as well as *complaining of his wrongdoer*: (T:) [the pl. of the former is ظَالِمُونَ and ظَلَمَةٌ:] and ظَلَمَةٌ signifies those *who debar men from*, or *refuse to them, their rights*, or *dues*. (IAạr, T, TA.) ═ See also ظُلَّامٌ.

أَظْلَمُ [*More*, and *most, wrongful, unjust, injurious*, or *tyrannical, in conduct*]. El-Muärrij says, I heard an Arab of the desert say to his companion, أَظْلَمِى وَأَظْلَمُكَ فَعَلَ ٱللّٰهُ بِهِ, meaning *The more wrongful in conduct of me and of thee* [*may God do to him* what He will do; i. e. may God punish him]. (T.) [And] one says, لَعَنَ ٱللّٰهُ أَظْلَمِى وَأَظْلَمَكَ i. e. [*May God curse*] *the more wrongful in conduct of us*. (Ḳ. [But in the TA, a doubt is intimated as to the correctness of this latter saying.]) One says also, لَهُوَ أَظْلَمُ مِنْ حَيَّةٍ [i. e. *Verily he is more wrongful in conduct than a serpent*]: because it comes to a burrow which it has not excavated, and makes its abode in it: (Fr, T:) for it comes to the burrow of the [lizard called] ضَبّ, and eats its young one, and takes up its abode in its burrow. (TA voce حَيَّةٌ.) — And الأَظْلَمُ is an appellation of *The* ضَبّ; because it eats its young ones. (TA.)

مُظْلِمٌ [*Becoming dark*, &c.: see its verb, 4]. — [Hence,] شَعَرٌ مُظْلِمٌ ‡ *Hair intensely black*. (M, Ḳ, TA.) And نَبْتٌ مُظْلِمٌ ‡ *A plant intensely green, inclining to blackness by reason of its* [*deep*] *greenness*. (M, Ḳ, TA.) And يَوْمٌ مُظْلِمٌ ‡ *A day of much evil*: (Ḳ, TA:) or *a very evil day*: and *a day in which one finds hardship*, or *difficulty*. (M.) And أَمْرٌ مُظْلِمٌ ‡ *An affair such that one knows not how to enter upon it*; (AZ, M, Ḳ;) and so ▼ أَمْرٌ مُظْلَامٌ: (Ḳ:) [or,] accord. to Lḥ, one says ▼ يَوْمٌ مُظْلَامٌ, meaning † *a day such that one knows not how to enter upon it*. (M.)

مَظْلِمَةٌ and مَظْلَمَةٌ: see 1, near the beginning. — Also the former, (T, Ṣ, M, Mgh, Mṣb, Ḳ,) and the latter likewise, mentioned by Ibn-Málik and ISd and IḲṭṭ, and مَظْلُمَةٌ, which is disallowed by several but mentioned on the authority of Fr, and all three are mentioned in the Towsheeh and in copies of the Ṣ, (MF, TA,) and ↑ ظُلَامَةٌ, (T, Ṣ, M, Mgh, Mṣb, Ḳ,) and ↑ ظَلِيمَةٌ, (Ṣ, TA,) *A thing of which one has been defrauded;* (M, Ḳ; [in the CḲ, تَظَلَّمَةٌ is erroneously put for تُظْلِمَةٌ;]) *a thing of which thou hast been defrauded,* (الَّتِى ظُلِمْتَهَا, T,) or *a thing that thou demandest,* (مَا تَطْلُبُهُ, Ṣ, Mṣb,) *in the possession of the wrongdoer;* (T, Ṣ, Mṣb;) a term for *a thing that has been taken from thee;* (Ṣ; [thus, as is said in the M, the first is expl. by Sb;]) *a right,* or *due, that has been taken from one wrongfully:* (A, Mgh:) the pl. of مظلمة is مَظَالِمُ. (Mgh, TA.) In the phrase يَوْمُ المَظَالِمِ, [meaning *The day of the demand of things wrongfully taken,* and particularly applied to the great day of judgment,] the prefixed noun [i. e. طَلَب] is suppressed. (Mgh.) [Respecting the office termed النَّظَرُ فِى المَظَالِمِ *The examination into wrongful exactions,* see De Sacy's Chrest. Ar., sec. ed., i. 132.]

مُظَلَّمٌ † A house, or chamber, *decorated with pictures;* (M, TA;) as though the pictures were put therein where they should not be: it is related in a trad. that the Prophet, having been invited to a repast, saw the house, or chamber, to be مُظَلَّم, and turned away, not entering: (M:) or *adorned with gilding and silvering;* an explanation disapproved by Az, but pronounced by Z to be correct, from الظُّلْمُ signifying "the lustre, and brightness, of gold." (TA.) — And † Herbage *spreading* (مُنْبَتٌّ [in the CḲ مُنْبَت]) *upon the ground, not rained upon.* (Ḳ, TA.) — Also, of birds, † The رَخَم [or *vultur percnopterus*], and *crows,* or *ravens.* (IAạr, M, Ḳ.*)

مِظْلَامٌ: see مُظْلِمٌ, in two places.

مَظْلُومٌ [*Wronged; treated,* or *used, wrongfully, unjustly, injuriously,* or *tyrannically:* — and hence used in other senses]: see ظَلِيمٌ, in three places. أَرْضٌ مَظْلُومَةٌ is also expl. as meaning ‡ *Land that is dug in a place not proper for digging:* (TA:) or *land in which a watering-trough has been dug, not being a proper place for digging it:* (ISk, M:) or *land in which a well,* or *a watering-trough, has been dug, when there had not been any digging therein:* (A, TA:) or *hard land, when it is dug.* (Ḥam p. 56.) Also † *Land upon which rain has not fallen.* (T.) And بَلَدٌ مَظْلُومٌ † *A country upon which rain has not fallen, and wherein is no pasturage for the camels upon which people journey.* (T.)

مُتَظَلِّمٌ: see ظَالِمٌ.

Quasi ظلى

5. تَظَلَّى: see 5 in art. ظل.

ظمأ

1. ظَمِئَ, (T, Ṣ, M, &c.,) aor. َ, (Mṣb, Ḳ,) inf. n. ظَمَأٌ (T, Ṣ, M, Mṣb, Ḳ) and ظَمْءٌ (TA) and ظَمَآءٌ (T, M, Ḳ) and ظَمَآءَةٌ, (M, Ḳ, TA,) in one copy of the Ḳ ظَمَآءَةٌ, (TA,) *He thirsted,* or *was thirsty:* (Ṣ, M, Mṣb, Ḳ:) or *he thirsted most vehemently:* (Zj, T, M, Ḳ:) or, as some say, *he thirsted in the slightest degree.* (M, TA.) — Hence, (M,) ظَمِئَ إِلَى لِقَائِهِ ‡ *He desired,* or *longed,* [or, as we often say, *thirsted,*] *to meet with him.* (Ṣ, M, Ḳ,* TA.)

2: see the next paragraph.

4. اظمأهُ, (T,* Ṣ, Mṣb, Ḳ,) inf. n. إِظْمَآءٌ; (T;) and ↑ ظمّأهُ, (T,* Mṣb, Ḳ,) inf. n. تَظْمِئَةٌ; (T, Ṣ;) *He made him to thirst:* (Ṣ, Mṣb, Ḳ:) [or *to thirst most vehemently:* or *to thirst in the slightest degree:* see 1.] — And (Ḳ) ‡ *He made him lean,* or *lank,* namely, a horse, (T,* Ḳ, TA,) *by sweating him.* (TA.) [See also 4 in art. ظمى.]

5. تظمّأ *He constrained himself to endure with patience a state of thirst.* (A, TA.)

ظِمْءٌ a subst. from ظَمِئَ (Ṣ, M, Ḳ) in both of its senses; (M, Ḳ;) [i. e.] it signifies *Thirst:* (MA:) [or *most vehement thirst:* or the *slightest degree of thirst:*] pl. أَظْمَآءٌ. (MA.) — [And ‡ *Desire,* or *a longing,* (or, as we often say, *a thirsting,*) to meet with a person. See 1.] — And (Ṣ, M, Ḳ) The *time,* or *interval,* or *period, between two drinkings,* or *waterings,* (T, Ṣ, M, Ḳ,) *in the coming of camels to water:* (T:) and the *keeping of camels from the water* [*during that interval,* i. e.] *until the extreme limit of the coming thereto:* (Ṣ:) pl. أَظْمَآءٌ. (T, Ṣ, M.) The shortest ظِمْء of camels is that termed غِبّ, i.e., when they come to the water one day and return, and are in the place of pasture a day, and come to the water [again] on the third day; the interval between their two drinkings being termed a ظِمْء: this is during the greatest heat: but when Suheyl [i. e. Canopus] rises [aurorally, which it did in Central Arabia, about the commencement of the era of the Flight, on the 4th of August, O.S.], they increase the ظِمْء, so that the camels remain in the place of pasture two days, and come to the water on the fourth; and one says, وَرَدَتْ رِبْعًا: then follow the خِمْس and the سِدْس to the عِشْر: and the interval between their two drinkings is termed ظِمْء, whether long or short. (T.) One says, مَا بَقِىَ مِنْ عُمْرِهِ إِلَّا ظِمْءُ الحِمَارِ, (T, Ṣ,* Ḳ,* TA,) meaning *There remained not of his life save a little;* [lit., *save the period between the two drinkings of the ass;*] (Ṣ, Ḳ,* TA;) because there is no beast that bears thirst for a shorter time than the ass; (T, Ṣ,* Ḳ,* TA;) for he comes to the water in summer every day twice. (T, TA.) — الظِّمْءُ also signifies † *The period from birth to death;* (Ḳ;) or so ظِمْءُ الحَيَاةِ. (Ṣ, M, TA.) — ظِمْوٌ is a dial. var. of ظِمْءٌ. (T and M in art. ظمو.)

ظَمِئٌ: see the next paragraph.

ظَمْآنُ, (T, Ṣ, M, Mṣb, &c.,) fem. ظَمْأَى, (T, Ṣ, M, A, L, Mṣb,) both imperfectly decl.; (T;) or ظَمْآنٌ, fem. ظَمْآنَةٌ; (Ḳ; [but this requires consideration, for its correctness is extremely doubtful;]) and ↑ ظَمِئٌ, (so in the Ḳ accord. to the TA, and so in my MS. copy of the Ḳ,) like كَتِفٌ, [agreeably with analogy as part. n. of ظَمِئَ, and therefore probably correct,] (TA,) or ↑ ظَمِىءٌ, (so in a copy of the M and in the CḲ,) fem. [of the former] ظَمِئَةٌ, like فَرِحَةٌ, mentioned by Ibn-Málik, but generally held to be disused; (MF, TA;) and ظَامٍ, like رَامٍ; (TA; [app. for ↑ ظَامِئٌ;]) *Thirsty:* (Ṣ, M, Mṣb, Ḳ:) or *most vehemently thirsty:* (T, M, Ḳ:) or *thirsty in the slightest degree:* (M, TA:) pl. (of the first, M, Mṣb, and of the second, M, or of all, masc. and fem., TA) ظِمَآءٌ (T, Ṣ, M, Mṣb, Ḳ) and ظُمَآءُ, which is extr., (Ḳ, TA,) being of a form applying to only about ten words, (TA,) mentioned on the authority of Lḥ, (Ḳ, TA,) by ISd in the "Mukhaṣṣaṣ." (TA.) — [Hence,] one says, أَنَا ظَمْآنُ إِلَى لِقَائِكَ ‡ *I am desirous,* or *longing,* [or, as we often say, *thirsting,*] *to meet with thee.* (A, TA.) — And وَجْهٌ ظَمْآنُ ‡ *A face having little flesh,* (T, TA,) *the skin of which adheres to the bone, and the sap of which is little:* (TA:) an expression of praise: *contr. of* وَجْهٌ رَيَّانُ, which is [said to be] an expression of dispraise. (A, TA.) And فَرَسٌ ظَمْآنُ الشَّوَى † *A horse having little flesh upon the legs:* (T in art. روى:) and so أَظْمَى الشَّوَى. (T in art. ظمى.) And سَاقٌ ظَمْأَى † *A lean shank:* (T, TA:) and so سَاقٌ ظَمْيَآءُ. (Ṣ and M and Ḳ in art. ظمى.) And عَيْنٌ ظَمْأَى † *An eye having a thin,* or *delicate, lid:* (M, TA:) and so عين ظَمْيَآءُ. (Ṣ and M and Ḳ in art. ظمى.) And فُصُوصُهُ ظِمَآءٌ (said of a horse, T, Ṣ, TA) ‡ *His joints are* [*firm,*] *not flabby,* or *lax,* (T, Ṣ, Ḳ, TA,) *nor fleshy;* (Ṣ, Ḳ, TA;) *and are well braced;* an expression of commendation: (T:) and مَفَاصِلُ ظِمَآءٌ ‡ *Hard* [or *firm*] *joints, without flabbiness,* or *laxness:* (A, TA:) accord. to IB, belonging to art. ظمى; but said in the T to be originally from ظمأ. (TA.) — And رِيحٌ ظَمْأَى † *A wind that is hot,* (Aṣ, T, Ḳ,) *thirsty, not gentle,* (Ḳ,) *and without moisture.* (Aṣ, T.)

ظَمِىءٌ: see ظَمْآنُ, first sentence.

ظَمَآءَةٌ † *Evilness of nature,* of a man, *and meanness of disposition, and deficiency of equity to associates:* (En-Naḍr, T, Ḳ:) originating from the fact that he who is given to drink, if of an evil nature, does not act equitably to his associates. (T.)

ظَامِئٌ: see ظَمْآنُ, first sentence.

أَظْمَأُ *Tawny;* applied to a spear: (A, TA:) and so أَظْمَى. (TA in art. ظمى.) — And *Black;*

applied to an antelope and to a camel: pl. ظُمْءٌ. (A, TA.)

مَظْمَأٌ A thirsty place of the earth or ground. (M, Ḳ.)

مِظْمَآءٌ A very thirsty man. (Ḳ.)

مَظْمِىٌّ Watered [only] by the rain: contr. of مَسْقَوِىٌّ: (Ḳ:) and so مَظْمِىٌّ: applied to seed-produce. (Ṣ and Ḳ in art. ظمى.)

ظمخ

ظِمْخٌ, (Ḳ,) or ظُمْخٌ, (AA, TA,) A tree having the form of the دُلْب [or plane-tree], (AA, T, Ḳ,) from which is cut the wood of the beaters and washers and whiteners of clothes, which is buried, [and is used for tanning,] and which is also called عِرْنٌ, n. un. عِرْنَةٌ, and the spathe, or spadix, (طَلْع,) whereof is called سَعْفٌ: (AA, T:) and in the dial. of Ṭeiyi, the fig-tree; n. un. with ة: or the sing. is ظِمْخَةٌ, and the pl. is ظِمَخٌ, sometimes contracted into ظِمْخٌ: (Ḳ:) and some say that it is the tree called سُمَّاق: (TA, and so in one of my copies of the Ṣ, in which it is written طمخ:) it is also called ظنخ and زمخ and طمخ. (TA.)

ظمو

ظِمْوٌ, relating to the أَظْمَآء of camels, is a dial. var. of ظِمْءٌ, (M,) signifying The interval between two drinkings in the coming of camels to water. (T.) [See art. ظمأ.]

ظمى

1. ظَمِىَ, [and ظَمِيَتْ, aor. ـَ,] inf. n. ظَمًى, He, or it, [and she, or it,] had any of the qualities denoted by the epithet أَظْمَى [and its fem. ظَمْيَآءُ]. (M, TA. [See أَظْمَى, and see also ظَمًى expl. below.])

2: see the next paragraph.

4. أَظْمَى, inf. n. إِظْمَآءٌ, He (a horse) was made lean, or lank; as also ▼ ظَمَّى, inf. n. تَظْمِيَةٌ. (T, TA. [See also 4 in art. ظمأ.])

ظَمًى is the inf. n. of 1 [q. v.]: and [it is said that it] signifies The withering, or drying up, of the lip, from thirst: (M:) so says Lth: but it signifies paucity of the flesh and blood of the lip; not the withering, or drying-up, in consequence of thirst: it is a quality that is commended: (T:) or a tawny, or brownish, or dusky, colour, and a withering, or drying-up, in the lip. (Ṣ.) — And Paucity of the blood of the gum: (Lth, T:) or paucity of the blood and flesh of the gum. (M.) [In the T is added ويعتريه الحُسْنُ: and in the M, وهو يعترى الحُبْسُ, in which الحُبْسُ seems to be evidently a mistranscription for الحُبْشُ: I therefore think it most probable that in the T, as well as in the M, the right reading is وَهُوَ يَعْتَرِى الحُبْشَ, meaning and it is incidental to the Abyssinians.] — And Tawniness of a spear-shaft. (T.)

ظَمٍ: see أَظْمَى.

ظَمْآنُ: } see ظَمْآنُ, in art. ظمأ.
ظَامٍ: }

أَظْمَى Anything withering, or withered; or becoming, or become, dried up; from heat; as also ▼ ظَمٍ. (M.) — [Hence,] شَفَةٌ ظَمْيَآءُ A lip that is not swollen, [not] having much blood; (T;) accord. to Lth, from thirst; but AZ says that it is not so: (TA: [see ظَمًى:]) or a lip in which is a tawny, or brownish, or dusky, colour, and a withering, or lack of moisture: (Ṣ:) or a lip withering, or withered, or lacking moisture, inclining to a tawny, or brownish, or dusky, colour. (Ḳ.) — And لِثَةٌ ظَمْيَآءُ A gum having little blood: (Ṣ, Ḳ:) or, accord. to the M, having little blood and flesh. (TA.) — And عَيْنٌ ظَمْيَآءُ An eye having a thin, or delicate, lid: (T, Ṣ, M, Ḳ:) and so عين ظمْآى. (M and TA in art. ظمأ.) — And سَاقٌ ظَمْيَآءُ A lean shank: (Ṣ, M, Ḳ:) and so ساق ظَمْآى. (T and TA in art. ظمأ.) And أَظْمَى الشَّوَى means A horse having little flesh upon the legs: (TA:) and so ظَمْآنُ الشَّوَى. (T in art. روى.) — أَظْمَى is also applied to a man, as signifying Black in the lip: (M:) and so ظَمْيَآءُ applied to a woman. (T, M.) — And the former applied to a man, and the latter to a woman, Having the quality of the gum termed ظَمًى expl. above. (M.) — Both also, accord. to Lḥ, signify Tawny, brownish, or dusky; the former as applied to a man, and the latter to a woman: (M:) and thus the former applied to a spear, (Aṣ, T, Ṣ, M,) and the latter to a spear-shaft (قَنَاة). (TA.) — And أَظْمَى signifies also Black: (T:) thus as applied to shade: (Ṣ:) and so the fem. applied to a she-camel: (Ḳ:) or the latter applied to a she-camel, and [the pl.] ظُمْىٌ applied to camels, in the colour of which is a blackness. (T.) [See also أَظْمَأُ, in art. ظمأ.]

مَظْمِىٌّ Land, (M,) or [rather] seed-produce (زَرْع), (Ṣ, Ḳ,) watered only by the rain: (Ṣ, M, Ḳ:) and so مَظْمِئٌّ: (Ḳ in art. ظمأ:) such as is irrigated by running water is termed مَسْقَوِىٌّ. (Ṣ.)

ظن

1. ظَنَّ, aor. ـُ, inf. n. ظَنٌّ, (Mṣb,) [He thought, opined, supposed, or conjectured: and he doubted: and he knew, but not by ocular perception: see ظَنٌّ below:] you say, ظَنَنْتُ الشَّىْءَ, aor. أَظُنُّهُ, inf. n. ظَنٌّ; and ▼ اِظَّنَنْتُهُ and اِظْطَنَنْتُهُ; and ▼ تَظَنَّنْتُهُ and تَظَنَّيْتُهُ, this last formed by changing the last ن into ى: [i. e. I thought the thing, &c.:] and Lḥ mentions, as heard from the Benoo-Suleym, ظَنْتُ ذَاكَ i. e. ظننت ذاك [I thought that, &c.] like ظَلْتُ and other instances of the dial. of Suleym. (M.) [In the first of the senses expl. above, it governs two objective complements, which are originally an inchoative and an enunciative:] you say, ظَنَنْتُكَ زَيْدًا [I thought thee Zeyd, originally I thought thou wast Zeyd], and ظَنَنْتُ زَيْدًا إِيَّاكَ [I thought Zeyd thee, originally I thought Zeyd was thou], denoting by a pronoun what is originally an inchoative [in the former phrase] and what is originally an enunciative [in the latter phrase]. (Ṣ, TA.) It is also used [in this sense] in the same manner as a verb signifying an oath, the Arabs giving it the same kind of complement, saying, ظَنَنْتُ لَعَبْدُ ٱللّٰهِ خَيْرٌ مِنْكَ [I thought surely 'Abd-Allah was better than thou]. (Ṣ in art. درد.) [ظَنَّ بِهِ كَذَا means I thought of him, or it, such a thing: and I thought such a thing to be in him, or it: and is used in relation to good and to evil.] It is said in the Ḳur [xxxiii. 10], وَتَظُنُّونَ بِٱللّٰهِ ٱلظُّنُونَا [And ye were thinking, of God, various thoughts]. (M.) Accord. to Sb, ظَنَنْتُ بِهِ means I made him, or it, the place [i. e. object] of my ظَنّ [or thought, &c.]. (M.) [In all these exs. the verb denotes a state of mind between doubt and certainty, but the latter is predominant: and hence ظَنَّ sometimes means He doubted: and sometimes, he knew, by considering with endeavour to understand, not by ocular perception; being more frequently used in this sense than as meaning "he doubted," though not so frequently as it is in the sense of "he thought," whence the meaning "he knew" is held by some to be tropical.] إِنِّى ظَنَنْتُ أَنِّى مُلَاقٍ حِسَابِيَهْ, in the Ḳur [lxix. 20], means Verily I knew [that I should meet with my reckoning]. (T.) And ٱلَّذِينَ يَظُنُّونَ أَنَّهُمْ مُلَاقُو رَبِّهِمْ, in the same [ii. 43], means Who know [that they shall meet their Lord, lit., be meeters of their Lord]. (Mṣb.) And ظَنَنْتُ مَا قَالَ, occurring in a trad., means I knew [what he meant to say by his making a sign with his hand]. (TA.) — ظَنَنْتُهُ, (M, Mgh, Mṣb,) aor. as above, (Mṣb,) and so the inf. n., (M,) signifies also I suspected him; thought evil of him; (M, Mgh, Mṣb;) and (M) so ▼ اِظَّنَنْتُهُ (Ṣ, M, Mgh, Ḳ) and اِظْطَنَنْتُهُ (M, TA) and اِطَّنَنْتُهُ. (TA.) [Thus, too, ▼ أَظْنَنْتُهُ accord. to several copies of the Ṣ and accord. to the CḲ; but this is app. a mistranscription.] In the saying of Ibn-Seereen, لَمْ يَكُنْ عَلِىٌّ يُظَّنُّ ▼ فِى قَتْلِ عُثْمَانَ, (T, Ṣ, Ḳ, but in the T مَا كَانَ,) meaning 'Alee was not suspected [in the case of the slaying of 'Othmán], (T,) يُظَّنُّ is of the measure يُفْتَعَلُ, originally يُظْتَنُّ: (T, Ṣ, Ḳ:) so says A'Obeyd: (T:) or, as some relate it, the word is يُظَنُّ. (TA.) One says, هُوَ يُظَنُّ ▼ بِكَذَا and يُظَّنُّ, meaning He is suspected of such a thing. (TA in art. طن.) And ظَنَنْتُ زَيْدًا and ظَنَنْتُ بِزَيْدٍ I suspected Zeyd: in

this sense the verb has a single objective complement. (TA.)

4. أَظْنَنْتُهُ الشَّىْءَ *I made him to think the thing.* (M, TA.) —— And أَظْنَنْتُ بِهِ النَّاسَ [*I made the people to suspect him:* or] *I exposed him to suspicion;* (M, Mṣb, TA;) [and] so أَظْنَنْتُهُ [alone]. (Ḳ.) —— See also 1, last quarter.

5. التَّظَنِّى means *The exercising, employing,* or *using, of* الظَّنّ [i. e. *thought,* &c.]; originally التَّظَنُّنُ. (Ṣ, Ḳ.) A'Obeyd says, تَظَنَّيْتُ is from ظَنَنْتُ, and is originally تَظَنَّنْتُ; the ن being many, one of them is changed into ى: it is like قَصَّيْتُ, which is originally قَصَّصْتُ. (T.) ═ See also 1, first sentence.

8: see 1, first sentence: —— and again, in the last quarter, in three places.

ظَنٌّ is a simple subst. as well as an inf. n.; (TA;) and signifies *Thought, opinion, supposition,* or *conjecture:* (Er-Rághib, Mgh, TA:) or *a preponderant belief, with the admission that the contrary may be the case:* (KT, El-Munáwee, TA:) or *a preponderating wavering between the two extremes in indecisive belief:* (Ḳ:) or *an inference from a sign,* or *mark,* or *token; when strong, leading to knowledge; and when weak, not exceeding the limit of* وَهْم: (Er-Rághib, TA:) or *doubt* or *uncertainty;* (T, M;) or it has this meaning also; (Er-Rághib, TA;) *contr. of* يَقِين: (Mṣb:) and sometimes it is put in the place, (Ṣ, Ḳ,) or used in the sense, (Mgh, Mṣb,) of عِلْم, (Ṣ, Mgh, Ḳ,) or يَقِين, (Mṣb,) [i. e. *knowledge,* or *certainty,*] in which sense it is [held by some to be] tropical; (Mgh;) or it signifies also *knowledge,* or *certainty,* (يَقِين, T, M,) *such as is obtained by considering with endeavour to understand, not by ocular perception,* (M,) or *not such as relates to an object of sense:* (MF:) and it also means *suspicion,* or *evil opinion:* (Er-Rághib, TA: [but in this last sense, ظِنَّةٌ is more common:]) as a subst., (TA,) its pl. is ظُنُونٌ and أَظَانِينُ, (M, Ḳ, TA,) the latter anomalous, or (as ISd says, TA) it may be pl. of ▼ أُظْنُونَةٌ, but this I do not know. (M, TA.) One says, هُوَ سَيِّئُ الظَّنِّ بِكُلِّ أَحَدٍ [*He is evil in opinion of everyone*]. (M.) [And سَآءَ ظَنُّهُ بِفُلَانٍ *His opinion of such a one was evil.*] And عِلْمُهُ بِالشَّىْءِ ظُنُونٌ [*His knowledge is* but *opinions*]; meaning that no confidence is to be placed in him. (TA.)

ظِنَّةٌ *Suspicion,* or *evil opinion;* (T, Ṣ, M, Mgh, Mṣb, Ḳ;) as also طِنَّةٌ; the ظ being changed into ط, though there is no إِدْغَام in this case, because of their being accustomed to say اِطَّنَّ [for اِظَّنَّ, which is for اِظْطَنَّ]; an instance like الدِّكْرُ, which is made to accord with اِدَّكَرَ [for اِذَّكَرَ, which is for اِذْتَكَرَ], as mentioned by Sb; (M;) and ▼ ظَنَانَةٌ, (so accord. to a copy of the M,) or ▼ ظِنَانَةٌ, like كِتَابَةٌ, (TA,) signifies the same: (M, TA:) the pl. of ظِنَّةٌ is ظِنَنٌ. (Ṣ, Ḳ.) One says, عِنْدَهُ ظِنَّتِى and هُوَ ظِنَّتِى, meaning *He is the place* [i. e. *object*] *of my suspicion.* (TA.) —— And [hence] † *A little* [like the French "soupçon"] of a thing. (TA.)

ظُنَنٌ: see ظَنَّانٌ.

ظَنُونٌ A man *who thinks evil* (Ṣ, M) *of everyone.* (M.) —— A man *possessing little good* or *goodness:* or, as some say, *of whom one asks* [a thing] *thinking that he will refuse, and who is as he was thought to be:* (M:) [or] ▼ ظَنِينٌ has this latter meaning. (TA.) —— A man *in whose goodness no trust,* or *confidence, is to be placed.* (M.) And Anything *in which no trust,* or *confidence, is to be placed,* (M, TA,) of water, and of other things; (TA;) as also ▼ ظَنِينٌ. (M, TA.) A well (بِئْر) *having little water,* (Ṣ, M, Ḳ,) *in the water of which no trust,* or *confidence, is to be placed:* (M:) or a well, (Ṣ, Ḳ,) or a drinking-place, (M,) *of which one knows not whether there be in it water or not:* (Ṣ, M, Ḳ:) or water *which one imagines,* or *supposes, to exist, but of which one is not sure.* (TA.) كُلُّ مَنِيَّةٍ ظَنُونٌ إِلَّا الْقَتْلَ فِى سَبِيلِ ٱللّٰهِ is a saying mentioned, but not expl., by IAạr; [app. meaning *Every death is doubtful as to its consequence except slaughter in the way,* or *cause, of God;* but ISd says,] in my opinion the meaning is that it *is of little good and profit.* (M.) دَيْنٌ ظَنُونٌ means *A debt of which one knows not whether he who owes it will pay it or not:* (A'Obeyd, T, Ṣ, M,* Ḳ:) it is said in a trad. of 'Omar that there is no poor-rate in the case of such a debt. (TA.) —— Also A man *suspected in relation to his intellect,* or *intelligence.* (Aboo-Tálib, TA.) And A woman *suspected in relation to her grounds of pretension to respect,* or *honour, on account of lineage &c.* (TA.) And A woman *of noble rank or quality, who is taken in marriage,* (M, Ḳ,) *from a desire of obtaining offspring by her, when she is advanced in age.* (M.) —— Also A *weak* man. (Ḳ. [See also ظَنِينٌ.]) —— And A man *having little artifice, cunning, ingenuity,* or *skill.* (Ḳ.)

ظَنِينٌ *Suspected;* (T, Ṣ, M, Mgh, Mṣb, Ḳ;) applied to a man; (Ṣ, M;) *i. q.* ▼ مَظْنُونٌ, (Mbr, Mṣb,) in this sense: (Mṣb:) pl. أَظِنَّآءُ. (M, TA.) Thus in the saying in the Ḳur [lxxxi. 24], وَمَا هُوَ عَلَى الْغَيْبِ بِظَنِينٍ, (T, M, Mṣb,) meaning *And he is not suspected as to* what he makes known from God, of the knowledge of *that which is undiscoverable,* as is related on the authority of 'Alee: or, accord. to Fr, it may mean *weak;* for ظَنِينٌ may have this meaning like as ظَنُونٌ has: (T:) some read بِضَنِينٍ. (TA in art. ضن, q. v.) شَهَادَةُ ظَنِينٍ, which is said in a trad. to be not allowable, is *The testimony of one who is suspected* as to his religion. (TA.) And نَفْسٌ ▼ ظَنَّآءُ means [*A soul,* or *person,*] *suspected.* (TA.) —— Also One *who treats,* or *regards, another,* or *others, with enmity,* or *hostility;* (T, M;) because of his evil opinion and the evil opinion of which he is an object. (M.) —— See also ظَنُونٌ, in two places.

ظَنَانَةٌ or ظِنَانَةٌ: see ظِنَّةٌ.

ظَنَّآءُ: see ظَنِينٌ.

ظَنَّانٌ One *who opines,* or *conjectures, much* [and] *in an evil manner;* as also ▼ ظُنَنٌ. (TA.)

أَظَنُّ [*Such as is more,* or *most, fit that one should think of him* to do a thing]. You say, نَظَرْتُ إِلَى أَظَنِّهِمْ أَنْ يَفْعَلَ ذٰلِكَ *I looked towards him who was the most fit of them that I should think of him to do that.* (M, TA.)

أُظْنُونَةٌ: see ظَنٌّ, near the end.

مَظِنَّةٌ, (M, Mgh, Mṣb, TA,) of which مَظَنَّةٌ, mentioned by Ibn-Málik and others, and مِظَنَّةٌ, are dial. vars., (TA,) or [rather] مَظِنَّةُ شَىْءٍ, (IF, Ṣ, Mṣb, Ḳ, TA,) signifies The place, (IF, Ṣ, Mṣb, Ḳ, TA,) and the *accustomed place,* (IF, Ṣ, Mṣb, TA,) *in which is thought to be the existence,* (Ṣ, Ḳ, TA,) *of a thing;* (IF, Ṣ, Mṣb, Ḳ, TA;) [*a place*] *where a thing is thought to be:* (M:) or it signifies, (Mgh, Mṣb,) or signifies also, (Ṣ,) *a place where a thing is known to be:* (Ṣ, Mgh, Mṣb:) [*a thing,* and *a person, in which,* or *in whom, a thing,* or *quality, is thought, supposed, presumed, suspected, inferred, known,* or *accustomed, to be,* or *exist:*] accord. to IAth, by rule it should be مَظَنَّةٌ: (TA:) [it may therefore be properly rendered *a cause of thinking,* &c., *the existence* of a thing; and مَظِنَّةٌ لِكَذَا may be well expl. as meaning *a thing,* and *a person, that occasions one's thinking, supposing, presuming, suspecting, inferring,* or *knowing, the existence of such a thing* or *quality, in it,* or *in him:* and hence, *an indication,* or *evidence,* or *a symptom, diagnostic, characteristic, sign, mark,* or *token, of the existence of such a thing* or *quality:*] the pl. is مَظَانُّ. (M, Mgh, Mṣb, TA.) One says, مَوْضِعُ كَذَا مَظِنَّةٌ مِنْ فُلَانٍ i. e. *Such a place is a place in which such a one is known* [&c.] *to be.* (Ṣ, TA.) And فُلَانٌ مَظِنَّةٌ مِنْ كَذَا i. e. *Such a one is one in whom such a thing,* or *quality, is known* [&c.] *to be.* (Lḥ, T.) And فُلَانٌ مَظِنَّةٌ لِلْخَيْرِ i. e. *Such a one is one in whom good,* or *goodness, is thought* [&c.] *to be.* (Ḥam p. 437.) And En-Nábighah says,

* فَإِنْ يَكُ عَامِرٌ قَدْ قَالَ جَهْلًا *
* فَإِنَّ مَظِنَّةَ الْجَهْلِ الشَّبَابُ *

[*And if 'Ámir has spoken ignorantly, verily youthfulness is a state in which ignorance is usually found to exist*]: (Ṣ, Mṣb:*) or, as some relate the verse, السِّبَابُ [so that the meaning is, *mutual reviling is an act in which* &c.]: (Ṣ:) or, accord. to another relation, the latter hemistich is

* فَإِنَّ مَطِيَّةَ الْجَهْلِ الشَّبَابُ *

(Ṣ,* TA;) because one finds it [i. e. youthfulness] to be easy like as he does the beast on which one rides. (TA.) And one says also, طَلَبْتُهُ مَظَانَّهُ [*He sought him, or it, in the places where he, or it, was thought to be;*] meaning, *by night and by day.* (TA.) And إِنَّهُ لَمَظِنَّةٌ أَنْ يَفْعَلَ ذٰلِكَ i. e. *Verily he is apt, meet, fitted,* or *suited, for one to think of his doing that:* and in like manner one says of two, and of a pl. number, and of a female. (Lḥ, M.)

مَظْنُونٌ [*Thought, opined,* &c.: see its verb: and] see ظَنِينٌ. Applied to a narrative, or story, it means [*Doubted;* or] *of which one is not to be made to know the real state.* (TA in art. وجم.) In lexicology, A word *of the class termed* آحَاد [q. v.]. (Mz 3rd نوع.)

ظنب

ظِنْبٌ The *root,* or *lower part,* or *stem,* (أَصْل,) of a tree. (IAạr, T, Ḳ.)

ظِنْبَةٌ *A sinew* (عَقَبَة) *that is wound over the extremities of the feathers of an arrow, next the notch.* (AḤn, M, Ḳ.)

ظُنْبُوبٌ The *edge of the shin:* (Ḳ:) or the *tough edge of the shin:* or the *external part of the shank:* (M, TA:) or the *shin-bone:* or the *edge of the shin-bone:* (M, Ḳ:) or the *tough bone in the fore part of the shank:* (Ṣ:) but accord. to AZ, this term is not used in relation to animals that have أَوْظِفَة: [see وَظِيفٌ:] (T, TA:) pl. ظَنَابِيبُ. (Ṣ, M, Ḳ.) عَارِى الظَّنَابِيبِ *Without flesh upon the shins* (TA) is an epithet applied to a male ostrich. (Ṣ, TA.) قَرَعَ ظُنْبُوبَ البَعِيرِ means *He knocked,* or *struck, the shin of the camel,* that he might lie down, and he might mount him: or قَرْعُ الظُّنْبُوبِ signifies a man's *knocking,* or *striking, the shin* of his camel with his stick when he makes him lie down that he may mount him, as one in haste to betake himself to a thing: or *striking the shin* of his beast with his whip, [in the TA is here added ليبرقه, which I can only suppose to be put for لِيُبْرِكَهُ, to make him lie down,] when he desires to mount him. (TA.) [See an ex. voce عُرْقُوبٌ. Hence,] قَرَعَ فُلَانٌ لِأَمْرِهِ ظُنْبُوبَهُ † [*Such a one struck his shin to betake himself to his affair*] means *such a one applied himself to his affair with diligence,* or *energy.* (T, L, TA.) Selámeh Ibn-Jendel says,

كُنَّا إِذَا مَا أَتَانَا صَارِخٌ فَزِعٌ *
كَانَ الصُّرَاخُ لَهُ قَرْعَ الظَّنَابِيبِ *

[*We were (such that), when there came to us one crying aloud, in terror, the clamour (returned) to him was the striking of the shins;*] by which he is said to mean that a quick reply was given; calling the striking of the whip upon the leg of the boot, in urging on the horse, "the striking of the shin." (Ṣ.) You also say, قَرَعَ لِذٰلِكَ الأَمْرِ ظُنْبُوبَهُ meaning † *He prepared himself for that affair,* or *thing:* and agreeably with this signification the verse of Selámeh cited above has been explained. (M, TA.) And قَرَعَ ظَنَابِيبَ الأَمْرِ ‡ *He made,* or *rendered, the affair manageable.* (M, Ḳ, TA.) A poet, cited by IAạr, says,

* قَرَعْتُ ظَنَابِيبَ الهَوَى يَوْمَ عَالِجٍ *

‡ *I subdued love,* or *subjected it to my will, on the day of 'Álij;* as though I struck it on the shins; as a camel's shin is struck when one desires him to lie down, that he may mount him. (M, TA.) — ظُنْبُوبٌ also signifies *A nail that is in the* جُبَّة *of a spear-head,* [i. e., *in the part into which the shaft enters,*] (M, Ḳ,) *where it is fixed upon the upper extremity of the shaft:* and ظَنَابِيب has been said to be the pl. of the word in this sense in the verse of Selámeh cited above. (M, TA.)

Quasi ظنى

5. تَظَنَّى; originally تَظَنَّنَ: see the latter, in art. ظن.

ظهر

1. ظَهَرَ, (Ṣ, Mṣb, Ḳ, &c.,) aor. َ, (Mṣb,) inf. n. ظُهُور, (Ṣ, Mgh, Mṣb, Ḳ, &c.,) [*It was,* or *became, outward, exterior, external, extrinsic,* or *exoteric:* and hence,] *it appeared; became apparent, overt, open, perceptible* or *perceived, manifest, plain,* or *evident;* (Ṣ, Mgh, Mṣb, Ḳ, TA;) *after having been concealed,* or *latent:* (Mṣb, TA:) and ↓ تظاهر signifies the same. (Ḥar p. 85.) Hence the phrase ظَهَرَ لِى رَأْىٌ † [*An idea,* or *opinion, occurred to me*], said when one knows what he did not know before. (Mṣb.) [And هٰذَا مَا يَظْهَرُ لِى † *This is what appears to me* to be the case, or to be the right way or course; or *this is my opinion.*] ظَهَرَ الحَمْلُ, inf. n. as above, means *Pregnancy became apparent,* or *manifest:* it is said that this is not the case in less than three months. (Mṣb.) And it is said in a trad. of 'Áïsheh, كَانَ يُصَلِّى العَصْرَ فِى حُجْرَتِى قَبْلَ أَنْ تَظْهَرَ i. e. [*He used to perform the prayer of the afternoon in my chamber*] *before it* (meaning the sun) *became high and apparent:* (TA:) or وَالشَّمْسُ فِى حُجْرَتِى لَمْ تَظْهَرْ بَعْدُ i. e. [*when the sun was in my chamber,*] *it not having risen high* so as to be on the flat roof [thereof]: referring to the Prophet. (O. [But العَصْر must be a mistranscription for الفَجْر, i. e. *the prayer of the dawn.*]) The saying in the Ḳur [xxiv. 31] وَلَا يُبْدِينَ زِينَتَهُنَّ إِلَّا مَا ظَهَرَ مِنْهَا [which is app. best rendered *And that they discover not their ornature except what is external thereof*] has been expl. in seven different ways, most correctly as meaning the clothes: (O, TA;) accord. to 'Áïsheh, it means the bracelet (القُلْب) and the ring (الفَتَخَة): and accord. to I'Ab, the hand and the signet-ring and the face. (TA.) — Also *He went forth,* or *out,* (Mgh, TA,) *to the outside of a place.* (O, TA.) — And *He* (a bird) *migrated,* or *went down,* from one country or region to another: used in this sense by AḤn in relation to the vulture, migrating to Nejd. (L.) — ظَهَرَ عَنْهُ, said of a vice, or fault, (O, TA,) or a disgrace, (JK, A, O,) ‡ *It did not cleave to him;* (A, O, TA;) *it was remote from him;* (TA;) *it quitted him,* or *departed from him.* (JK.) — ظَهَرْتُ بِهِ, (O, TA,) inf. n. ظُهْر, (Ḳ,) † *I gloried,* or *boasted, by reason of it.* (O, Ḳ* TA.) [Respecting a meaning assigned to ظَهَرَ بِفُلَانٍ in the Ḳ, see 4.] — أَكَلَ الرَّجُلُ أُكْلَةً ظَهَرَ مِنْهَا ظَهْرَةً means † [*The man ate some food*] *in consequence of which*] *he became fat.* (TA.) = ظَهَرَهُ *He mounted it; went,* or *got, upon it,* or *upon the top of it;* (Ṣ, A,* Mgh, O, Mṣb, Ḳ;) as also ظَهَرَ عَلَيْهِ; (O;) namely, a house, (Ṣ,) or a house-top, (A, Mgh, O,) and a mountain, (A,) and a wall; (O, Mṣb;) properly, *he became upon its back:* (Mgh:) and [in like manner] one says, ظَهَّرَ ↓ فُلَانٌ نَجْدًا, inf. n. تَظْهِيرٌ, *Such a one mounted,* or *went up, upon the high region* (ظَهْر) *of Nejd.* (O.) — Hence, (Mgh, Mṣb,) ظَهَرَ عَلَيْهِ (Ṣ, Mgh, O, Mṣb, Ḳ) and بِهِ, (Ḳ,) inf. n. ظُهُورٌ (Bḍ in xxiv. 31) and ظَهْرٌ also, (Ḥam p. 301,) *He overcame, conquered, subdued, overpowered,* or *mastered, him; gained the mastery* or *victory,* or *prevailed, over him;* (Ṣ, Mgh, O, Mṣb, Ḳ;) namely, his enemy; (Mṣb;) and in like manner, [*he conquered, won, achieved,* or *attained, it,* i. e.] a thing. (O, TA.) [The saying فُلَانٌ لَا يَظْهَرُ عَلَيْهِ أَحَدٌ is expl. in the L and TA by the words اى لا يُسْلَمُ, and said to be tropical: but IbrD thinks that the correct reading is لا يُسَلِّمُ, from التَّسْلِيم; and that it is said of one who will not give up, or resign, what is in his hand; so that the meaning is, ‡ *Such a one is a person whom no one will overcome in respect of that which he holds in his possession.*] — And [hence also] ظَهَرَ عَلَيْهِ, (Mṣb, TA,) inf. n. ظُهُورٌ, (TA,) *He knew, became acquainted with,* or *got knowledge of, him,* or *it.* (Mṣb, TA.) So in the Ḳur xxiv. 31, وَالطِّفْلِ الَّذِينَ لَمْ يَظْهَرُوا عَلَى عَوْرَاتِ النِّسَاءِ [*And the young children*] *who have not attained knowledge of the* عورات, (Bḍ, Jel,) meaning [*pudenda,* or] *parts between the navel and the knees,* (Jel,) *of women,* by reason of their want of discrimination: (Bḍ:) or ‡ *who have not attained to the generative faculty;* (O, Bḍ,* TA;) from الظُّهُور in the sense of الغَلَبَة. (Bḍ.) So too in the Ḳur [xviii. 19], إِنْ يَظْهَرُوا عَلَيْكُمْ *If they get knowledge of you.* (O, TA.) — And [hence] ظَهَرَ عَلَيْهِ, (Fr, A, O, TA,) and ↓ استظهره, (Ṣ, A, O, Ḳ,) ‡ *He knew it,* or *learned it, by heart;* namely, the Ḳur-án; (A, O, TA;) and *he recited it by heart:* (A,* TA; and so in the Ṣ and O in explanation of the latter:) or [simply] *he recited it by heart;* namely, the Ḳur-án; as also ↓ اظهره: (O, Ḳ, TA:) in the copies of the Ḳ we find أَظْهَرْتُ عَلَى القُرْآنِ and أَظْهَرْتُهُ; but the former is a mistake for ظَهَرْتُ, aor. َ. (TA.) = For another signification of ظَهَرَ عَلَيْهِ, see 3. = ظَهَرَ بِحَاجَتِى, (Ṣ, A, Ḳ,)

aor. ـَ, (TA,) inf. n. ظَهْرٌ; (TḲ;) and ↓ ظهّرها, (Ḳ, TA,) in some copies of the Ḳ ظَهَرَهَا; (TA;) and ↓ اظهرها, (Ḳ,) inf. n. إِظْهَارٌ; (TA;) and ↓ اِظَّهَرَهَا, (Ḳ,) of the measure اِفْتَعَلَ; (TA;) ‡ *He held the object of my want in little, or light, estimation, or in contempt;* (Ṣ, A;) [lit.] *he put it behind* [*his*] *back;* (Ṣ, Ḳ;) *as though he put it away,* [*out of his sight,*] *and paid no regard to it.* (Ṣ, TA.) One says also, يَظْهَرُونَ بِهِمْ وَلَا يَلْتَفِتُونَ إِلَى أَرْحَامِهِمْ [*They hold them in contempt, and do not pay any regard to their ties of relationship*]. (Ṣ.) — See also 10, in three places. ═ ظَهَرَهُ, (O, Ḳ,) aor. ـَ, inf. n. ظَهْرٌ, (Ḳ,) *He struck, or smote,* (TA,) *or hit, or hurt,* (O, Ḳ,) *his back.* (O, Ḳ, TA.) ═ ظَهِرَ, (Ṣ, O, Ḳ,) aor. ـَ, (Ḳ,) inf. n. ظَهَرٌ, (O, Ḳ,) *He* (a man, Ṣ, O) *had a complaint of his back.* (Ṣ, O, Ḳ.) ═ ظَهُرَ, (JK, O, L,) or ظَهَرَ, (Ḳ, [but this is app. a mistranscription,]) inf. n. ظَهَارَةٌ, (Ṣ, O, L, Ḳ,) said of a camel, (JK, Ṣ, O,) *He was, or became, strong* (JK, Ṣ, O, L, Ḳ) *in the back.* (L, Ḳ.)

2: see 1, near the middle: — and again, in the last quarter: — and see also 3. — ظَهَّرَ الثَّوْبَ [and ↓ اظهرهُ, *contr. of* بَطَّنَهُ and ابطنهُ,] *He faced the garment, or piece of cloth; put a facing, or an outer covering,* (ظِهَارَة,) *to it.* (TA.) ═ See also 4, last sentence.

3. ظاهرهُ, (A,) inf. n. مُظَاهَرَةٌ, (Ṣ, O, Mṣb,) *He aided, or assisted, him;* (Ṣ, A, O, Mṣb;) as also ↓ ظَهَّرَ عَلَيْهِ. (Th, Ḳ.) And ظاهر عَلَيْهِ *He aided, or assisted, against him.* (TA.) — ظاهر به: see 10. — ظاهر بَيْنَهُمَا, (Ḳ,) i. e. (TA) بَيْنَ ثَوْبَيْنِ, (Ṣ, A, Mgh, TA,) and دِرْعَيْنِ, (A, Mgh, TA,) and نَعْلَيْنِ, (TA,) *i. q.* طَارَقَ بَيْنَهُمَا, (Ṣ, TA,) or طَابَقَ, (A, Ḳ, TA,) i. e. (TA) *He put them on, or attired himself with them,* [namely, *two garments,* and *two coats of mail,* and *two sandals* or *soles,* or rather, when relating to two soles, *he sewed them together,*] *one over, or outside, the other:* (Mgh, TA:) app. from تَظَاهُرٌ in the sense of "mutual aiding or assisting." (IAth.) The phrase ظاهر بدِرْعَيْنِ requires consideration; and the ب in it should be regarded as meant to denote conjunction; not as a part of the necessary complement of the verb. (Mgh.) ظاهر الدِّرْعَ is said to signify لَأَمَ بَعْضَهَا عَلَى بَعْضٍ [app. meaning *He folded over and fastened one part of the coat of mail upon another*]. (TA.) And ظاهر عَلَيْهِ جِلَالًا means *He threw upon him* (i. e. a horse) *housings or coverings* [*one over another*]. (TA in art. حنذ.) ═ ظاهر مِنِ آمْرَأَتِهِ, (Ṣ, Mgh, O, Mṣb, Ḳ,) inf. n. ظِهَارٌ (Ṣ, Mgh, Mṣb, Ḳ) and مُظَاهَرَةٌ; (JK, TA;) and ↓ تظاهر مِنْهَا, (A, Mgh, O, TA,) and ↓ اِظَّاهَرَ; (Mgh;) and ↓ تظهّر منها, (Ṣ, Mṣb, Ḳ,) and ↓ اِظَّهَّرَ; (O, TA;) and ↓ ظهّر منها, (Ṣ, O, Ḳ,) inf. n. تَظْهِيرٌ; (Ṣ;) signify the same; (O;) *He said to his wife* أَنْتِ عَلَيَّ كَظَهْرِ أُمِّي [*Thou art to me like the back of my mother*]; (Ṣ, Mgh, Mṣb, Ḳ;) [as though he said رُكُوبُكِ لِلنِّكَاحِ حَرَامٌ عَلَيَّ;] meaning رُكُوبُكِ لِلنِّكَاحِ حَرَامٌ عَلَيَّ كَرُكُوبِ أُمِّي لِلنِّكَاحِ; the back being specified in preference to the بَطْن or فَخِذ or فَرْج because the woman is likened to a beast that is ridden, and the act of نِكَاح to that of رُكُوب: the phrase being a form of divorce used by the Arabs in the Time of Ignorance. (Mṣb,* TA.) In the Ḳur lviii. 2 [and 4], some read ↓ يَظَّهَّرُونَ; some ↓ يَظَّاهَرُونَ; and 'Áṣim read يُظَاهِرُونَ. (Bḍ.) The verb is made trans. by means of مِن because the man who uttered this sentence estranged himself from his wife. (IAth.)

4. اظهرهُ *He made it apparent, overt, open, perceptible or perceived, manifest, plain, or evident; he showed, exhibited, manifested, displayed, discovered, revealed, or evinced, it; or put it forth:* (Ṣ, O, Ḳ:) [it is also used in relation to a saying, and an action, and the like, as meaning *it showed,* &c., as above, or *it bespoke, it:*] and Mṭr relates his having heard from one worthy of reliance of the people of Baghdád, that they say ↓ تظاهرتُ بِهِ in the place of أَظْهَرْتُهُ, and scarcely ever employ اظهر in its usual sense. (Ḥar p. 85.) [Hence, اظهر التَّضْعِيفَ *He made the doubling of a letter distinct;* as in تَحَحَّتْ; which, accord. to a general rule, should be تَحَتَّ: opposed to أَدْغَمَ. And اظهر لَهُ كَذَا *He showed,* &c., *to him such a thing:* and *he made a show of, professed, pretended,* or *feigned, to him such a thing:* as, for instance, love.] — أَظْهَرْتُ بِفُلَانٍ means أَعْلَيْتُ بِهِ [a phrase which I have not found except in this instance, app. *I elevated,* or *exalted, such a one:* like أَعْلَيْتُهُ, which has this meaning]: (Ṣ, IḲṭṭ, L, TA:) or أَعْلَنْتُ بِهِ [app. meaning *I made such a one to be, or become, publicly known*]: (so in the O:) [but the former explanation seems to be regarded by SM as the right; for he remarks that,] accord. to all the copies of the Ḳ, the explanation is أَعْلَنَ بِهِ, and refers to ظَهَرَ بِفُلَانٍ [instead of أَظْهَرَ]; so that what its author says in this case differs in two points of view from what is found in the "Kitáb el-Abniyeh" of IḲṭṭ, in which the ى in أَعْلَيْتُ has been marked as correct, and in the L [as well as in the Ṣ]. (TA.) ═ اظهرهُ ٱللّٰهُ عَلَى عَدُوِّهِ means *God made him to overcome, conquer, subdue, overpower, master, gain the victory over,* or *prevail over, his enemy.* (Ṣ, A, O, TA.) — And [hence] اظهرهُ عَلَيْهِ *He* (God) *made him to know it,* or *become acquainted with it:* you say, أَظْهَرَنِى ٱللّٰهُ عَلَى مَا سُرِقَ مِنِّى *God made me to know* [or *discover*] *what had been stolen from me.* (TA.) ═ See also 1, last quarter, in two places. ═ And see 2. ═ اظهر signifies also *He entered upon the time called the* ظَهِيرَة: (A, Mṣb, Ḳ:) or *the time called the* ظُهْر. (Mṣb.) And *He went,* or *journeyed, in the time called the* ظَهِيرَة; as also ↓ ظَهَّرَ, (Ḳ,) inf. n. تَظْهِيرٌ: (TA:) or *the time called the* ظُهْر. (Ṣ, O,)

5. تظهّر and اِظَّهَّرَ: see 3, latter half, in three places.

6: see 1, first sentence: — and see also 4, first sentence. — تظاهروا *They aided,* or *assisted, one another.* (Ṣ, O,* Ḳ.) And تظاهروا عَلَى فُلَانٍ *They leagued together, and aided one another, against such a one.* (Ibn-Buzurj, TA in art. ضفر.) — Also *They regarded,* or *treated, one another with enmity,* or *hostility;* or *severed themselves, one from another:* (Ṣ, Mṣb, Ḳ:) as though they turned their backs, one upon another: (Ṣ:) or, because they who do so turn their backs, one upon another. (Mṣb.) Thus the verb has two contr. meanings. (Ḳ.) — تظاهر مِنِ آمْرَأَتِهِ and اِظَّاهَرَ: see 3, latter half, in three places.

8. اِظَّهَرَ: see 1, last quarter.

10. استظهر بِهِ *He sought aid,* or *assistance, in,* or *by means of, him,* or *it,* (Ṣ, O, Mṣb, Ḳ, TA,) عَلَيْهِ [*against him, or it*]; as also استظهرهُ. (TA.) [In the CḲ, after the explanation of استظهر به, is an omission, to be supplied by the insertion of وَقُرَّاهُ.] One says, استظهر بِٱلْغِنَى عَلَى النَّوَائِبِ [*He sought aid in wealth against calamities,* or *afflictions*]. (Mṣb.) And ↓ ظاهر بِهِ signifies the same as استظهر [in this sense or in another of the senses expl. in what follows]. (TA.) — And ↓ ظَهَرْتُ بِهِ, and استظهرتُ بِالشَّىْءِ, and ↓ ظَهَرْتُهُ, *I put the thing behind my back for protection,* or *security.* (Ḥar p. 265.) — And استظهر *He prepared for himself a camel,* or *two camels,* or *more, for future need:* (T:) and استظهرهُ, and ↓ ظَهَرَ بِهِ, *He prepared him,* namely, a camel, *for future need:* (Ḳ:) and استظهر بِبَعِيرَيْنِ ظَهْرِيَّيْنِ *He prepared for himself two camels for future need.* (T. [See ظِهْرِىٌّ.]) — Hence, (T,) استظهر signifies also *He used precaution* (T, Mṣb) with respect to anything: (T:) *he secured himself,* (اِسْتَوْثَقَ,) *by using precaution;* as, for instance, a woman does by remaining three days, before she performs the ablution termed غُسْل, and prays, after the usual period of the menses. (T, L.) One says, يُسْتَحَبُّ الِاسْتِظْهَارُ بِغَسْلَةٍ ثَانِيَةٍ وَثَالِثَةٍ *The using precaution by a second and a third washing,* to make sure of being pure, *is approved.* (Er-Ráfi'ee, Mṣb.) And استظهرتُ فِى طَلَبِ الشَّىْءِ *I adopted the most fit,* or *proper, way, and used precaution, in seeking to attain the thing.* (Mṣb.) — See also 1, in the middle of the latter half.

ظَهْرٌ The *back; contr. of* بَطْنٌ: (Ṣ, A, O, Mṣb, Ḳ:) in a man, *from the hinder part of the* كَاهِل [or *base of the neck*] *to the nearest part of the buttocks, where it terminates:* (TA:) in a camel, the *part containing six vertebræ on the right and left of which are* [*two portions of flesh and sinew called the*] مَتْنَانِ: (AHeyth, T, O:) of the masc. gender: (Lḥ, A, Ḳ:) pl. [of pauc.] أَظْهُرٌ, and [of mult.] ظُهُورٌ and ظُهْرَانٌ. (Mṣb, Ḳ.) — رَجُلٌ خَفِيفُ الظَّهْرِ ‡ *A man having a small household to maintain:* and ثَقِيلُ الظَّهْرِ ‡ *having a large household to maintain.* (Ḳ,* TA.) — أَنْتِ عَلَيَّ كَظَهْرِ

أُمِّى *Thou art to me like the back of my mother:* said by a man to his wife. (Ṣ, Mgh, Mṣb, Ḳ.) [This has been expl. above: see 3.] — عَدَا فِى ظَهْرِهِ ‡ *He stole what was behind him:* (A:) [or *he acted wrongfully in respect of what was behind him:* for] لِصٌّ عَادِى ظَهْرٍ is expl. by the words عَدَا فِى ظَهْرٍ فَسَرَقَهُ [so that it app. means ‡ *A thief who has acted wrongfully in respect of what was behind one, and stolen it*]. (O, Ḳ.) — أَقْرَانُ الظَّهْرِ (Ṣ, O, Ḳ) and الظُّهُورِ (O, TA) *Adversaries who come to one from behind his back, in war,* or *fight.* (Ṣ, O, Ḳ,* TA.) In the copies of the Ḳ, يُحِبُّونَكَ is erroneously put for يَجِيئُونَكَ. (TA.) You say also, فُلَانٌ قِرْنُ الظَّهْرِ *Such a one is an adversary who comes to one from behind, unknown.* (IAạr, Aṣ.) — قَتَلَهُ ظَهْرًا *He slew him unexpectedly; he assassinated him;* syn. غِيلَةً. (IAạr, TA.) — جَعَلَنِى بِظَهْرٍ ‡ *He cast me off.* (TA.) And جَعَلْتُ حَاجَتَهُ بِظَهْرٍ ‡ *I cast his want behind my back:* (AO, Ḳ:) and † جَعَلَهَا ظِهْرِيَّةً signifies the same: (Ṣ:) and † اِتَّخَذَهَا ظِهْرِيًّا, (Ḳ,) and † ظِهْرِيَّةً: (TA:) or the former of the last two phrases signifies *he held it in contempt;* as though ظهريا were an irreg. rel. n. from ظَهْرٌ: (TA:) or † اِتَّخَذَهُ ظِهْرِيًّا signifies *he neglected,* or *forgot,* (Ṣ, O,* Mṣb,) *him,* as in the Ḳur xi. 94, (Ṣ, O,) or *it,* namely, what was said. (Mṣb.) And لَا تَجْعَلْ حَاجَتِى بِظَهْرٍ ‡ *Forget not thou,* or *neglect not, my want:* (Ṣ:) and † جَعَلَهُ ظِهْرِيًّا signifies *he forgot it;* as well as جعله بظهر. (A.) And جَعَلْتُ هٰذَا الأَمْرَ بِظَهْرٍ, and رَمَيْتُهُ بِظَهْرٍ, ‡ *I cared not for this thing.* (Th, O.) — فُلَانٌ مِنْ وَلَدِ الظَّهْرِ † *Such a one is of those who do not belong to us:* or *of those to whom no regard is paid:* (TA:) or *of those who are held in contempt, and to whose ties of relationship no regard is paid.* (Ṣ, TA.) — هُوَ ٱبْنُ عَمِّهِ ظَهْرًا ‡ [*He is his cousin on the father's side,*] *distantly related:* contr. of دِنْيًا [*and* لَحًّا]. (Aṣ, A, O, TA.) — رَجَعَ عَلَى ظَهْرِهِ [*He receded, retired,* or *retreated*]. (Ḳ in art. لبجو.) — هُوَ نَازِلٌ بَيْنَ ظَهْرَيْهِمْ, and † بين ظَهْرَانَيْهِمْ, (Ṣ, A, O, Mṣb, Ḳ,*) in which latter the ا and ن are said by some to be added for corroboration, (Mṣb,) and for which one should not say بين ظَهْرَانِيهِمْ, (IF, Ṣ, O, Mṣb, Ḳ,) and بين أَظْهُرِهِمْ, (Mṣb, Ḳ,) ‡ *He is making his abode in the midst of them; in the main body of them:* (Ḳ, TA:) originally meaning he is making his abode among them for the purpose of seeking aid of them and staying himself upon them: as though it meant that the back of one of them was before him, and that of another behind him, so that he was defended in either direction: afterwards, by reason of frequency of usage, it came to be employed to signify abiding among a people absolutely. (IAth, Mṣb.) You say also هُوَ بَيْنَ ظَهْرَيْهِ, and † بَيْنَ ظَهْرَانَيْهِ, meaning *It* (anything) *is in the midst,* or *main part, of it,* namely, another thing. (TA.) — لَقِيتُهُ بَيْنَ الظَّهْرَيْنِ, and † بَيْنَ الظَّهْرَانَيْنِ, (Ṣ, O, Mṣb, Ḳ,) ‡ *I met him during the day,* (Mṣb,) or *during the two days,* (Ṣ, O, Ḳ,) or *during the three days,* (Ḳ,) or *the days:* (Ṣ, O, Mṣb:) from the next preceding phrase. (TA.) And أَتَيْتُهُ مَرَّةً بَيْنَ الظَّهْرَيْنِ ‡ *I came to him one day:* or, accord. to Aboo-Faḳ'as, *on a day between two years.* (Fr.) And رَأَيْتُهُ بَيْنَ ظَهْرَانَيِ † اللَّيْلِ ‡ *I saw him between nightfall and daybreak.* (TA.) And جِئْتُهُ بَيْنَ ظَهْرَانَيِ † النَّهَارِ ‡ [*I came to him between the beginning and end of the day*]. (A.) — تَقَلَّبَ ظَهْرًا لِبَطْنٍ † *It turned over and over,* or *upside down,* (lit. *back for belly,*) as a serpent does upon ground heated by the sun. (Ṣ and TA in art. قلب.) [Hence,] قَلَبْتُ الأَرْضَ ظَهْرًا لِبَطْنٍ ‡ [*I turned the earth over, upside-down*]. (A.) And [hence,] قَلَّبَ أَمْرَهُ ظَهْرًا لِبَطْنٍ, (O,* TA,) and ظَهْرَهُ لِبَطْنٍ, and ظَهْرَهُ لِبَطْنِهِ, and ظَهْرَهُ لِلْبَطْنِ, which last form is preferred by El-Farezdaḳ to the second, because [as in the third form] the second of the two words is determinate like the first word, ‡ *He meditated,* or *managed, the affair with forecast, and well.* (O,* TA.) — The Arabs used to say, هٰذَا ظَهْرُ السَّمَآءِ and هذا بَطْنُ السَّمَآءِ, both meaning ‡ *This is the apparent, visible, part of the sky.* (Fr, Az.) And the like is said of the side of a wall, which is its بَطْن to a person on the same side, and its ظَهْر to one on the other side. (Az.) — مَا نَزَلَ مِنَ القُرْآنِ آيَةٌ إِلَّا لَهَا ظَهْرٌ وَبَطْنٌ, [part of] a saying of Mohammad, [of which see the rest voce مُطَّلَعٌ,] means † *Not a verse of the Ḳur-án has come down but it has a verbal expression and an interpretation:* (Ḳ,* TA:) or *a verbal expression and a meaning:* or *that which has an apparent and a known* [or *an exoteric*] *interpretation and that which has an intrinsic* [or *esoteric*] *interpretation:* (TA:) or *narration* (Ḳ, TA) *and admonition:* (TA:) or [*it is to be read and to be understood and taught;* for] by the ظهر is meant the reading; and by the بطن, the understanding and teaching. (TA.) [See also بَطْنٌ.] — ظَهْرٌ signifies also ‡ *Camels on which people ride, and which carry goods;* (Ṣ,* A,* O, Ḳ,* TA;) *camels that carry burdens upon their backs in journeying:* (TA:) [or] *a beast:* or *a camel for riding:* (Mgh:) pl. ظُهْرَانٌ. (TA.) It is said in a trad. of 'Arfajeh, فَتَنَاوَلَ السَّيْفَ مِنَ الظَّهْرِ *And he reached,* or *took in his hand, the sword from the camels for carrying burdens and for riding:* and in another, أَتَأْذَنُ لَنَا فِى نَحْرِ ظَهْرِنَا *Dost thou permit us to slaughter our camels which we ride?* (TA.) And one says also, هُوَ عَلَى ظَهْرٍ ‡ *He is determined upon travel:* (Ḳ:) as though he had already mounted a beast for that purpose. (TA.) — [Hence, app.,] † *Property consisting of camels and sheep* or *goats:* (TA:) or *much property.* (Ḳ, TA.) — † The *short side* [or *lateral half*] *of a feather:* (Ṣ, O, Ḳ:) pl. ظُهْرَانٌ: (Ṣ, M, Ḳ, TA, &c.:) opposed to بَطْنٌ, sing. of بُطْنَانٌ, (TA,) which latter signifies the "long sides:" (Ṣ, TA:) and † ظُهَارٌ signifies the same as ظَهْرٌ, (Ḳ,) or the same as ظُهْرَانٌ, being an irregular pl.; and this is meant by the saying الظُّهَارُ بِالضَّمِّ الجَمَاعَةُ, mentioned in a later place in the Ḳ [in such a manner as to have led to the supposition that ظُهَارٌ is also syn. with جَمَاعَةٌ]: (TA:) AO says that among the feathers of arrows are the ظُهَار, which are *those that are put* [*upon an arrow*] *of the* ظَهْر [or *outer side*] *of the* عَسِيب [app. here meaning the *shaft*] *of the feather;* (Ṣ, TA;) i. e., the *shorter side,* which is the best kind of feather; as also ظُهْرَانٌ: sing. ظَهْرٌ: (TA:) ISd says that the ظُهْرَان are *those parts of the feathers of the wing that are exposed to the sun and rain:* (TA:) Lth says that the ظُهَار are *those parts of the feathers of the wing that are apparent.* (O, TA.) One says, رِشْ سَهْمَكَ بِظُهْرَانٍ وَلَا تَرِشْهُ بِبُطْنَانٍ [*Feather thine arrow with short sides of feathers, and feather it not with long sides of feathers*]. (Ṣ, TA.) [De Sacy supposes that ظُهُورٌ and بُطُونٌ are also pls. of ظَهْرٌ and بَطْنٌ thus used: (see his "Chrest. Arabe," sec. ed., tome ii., p. 374:) but his reasons do not appear to me to be conclusive.] † ظُهَارٌ and ظُهْرَانٌ are also used as epithets: you say, رِيشٌ ظُهَارٌ and رِيشٌ ظُهْرَانٌ. (TA.) — [ظَهْرُ الكَفِّ and † ظَاهِرُهَا mean † *The back of the hand.* And in like manner, ظَهْرُ القَدَمِ and † ظَاهِرُهَا mean † *The upper,* or *convex, side,* or *back, of the human foot, corresponding to the back of the hand, including the instep:* opposed to بَطْن and بَاطِن. And ظَهْرُ اللِّسَانِ means † *The upper surface of the tongue.*] — And ظَهْرٌ also signifies ‡ *A way by land.* (Ṣ, M, O, Mṣb, Ḳ.) This expression is used when there is a way by land and a way by sea. (M.) You say, سَارُوا فِى طَرِيقِ الظَّهْرِ ‡ *They journeyed by land.* (A.) — And † *An elevated tract* of land or ground; as also † ظَاهِرَةٌ: (A:) or *rugged and elevated land* or *ground;* (JK, Ḳ;) as also † ظَاهِرَةٌ: (JK:) opposed to بَطْنٌ, which signifies "soft and plain and fine and low land or ground:" (TA:) and † ظَوَاهِرُ [pl. of ظَاهِرَةٌ] signifies † *elevated tracts* of land or ground: (Ṣ, Ḳ:) you say, هَاجَتْ ظَوَاهِرُ الأَرْضِ, meaning, † *the herbs,* or *leguminous plants, of the elevated tracts of land,* or *ground, dried up:* (Aṣ, Ṣ, L:) and † ظَاهِرٌ signifies † *the higher,* or *highest, part* of a mountain; (ISh, L, TA;) whether its exterior be plain or not: (TA:) and † ظَاهِرَةٌ, the same, of anything: (L:) when you have ascended upon the ظَهْر of a mountain, you are upon its ظَاهِرَة. (TA.) — سَالَ وَادِيهِمْ ظَهْرًا means † *Their valley flowed with the rain of their own land:* opposed to دَرْأً, meaning, "from other rain:" (IAạr, O, Ḳ:*) or the former signifies *their valley flowed* with its own rain: and the latter, "with other than its own rain:" (TA:) and some say ▼ ظُهْرًا, which Az thinks the better form. (O, TA.) —— [Hence, probably,] أَصَبْتُ مِنْهُ مَطَرَ ظَهْرٍ † *I obtained from him, or it, much good.* (Ṣgh, O, Ḳ.) —— And another signification of ظَهْر is *What is absent,* or *hidden,* or *concealed, from one.* (O, Ḳ.) —— It is sometimes prefixed to another noun to give plainness and force to the expression; as in ظَهْرُ الغَيْبِ and ظَهْرُ القَلْبِ, meaning نَفْسُ الغَيْبِ and نَفْسُ القَلْبِ: (Mṣb:) or it is redundant in these instances. (Mgh.) Lebeed says, describing a [wild] cow going about after a beast of prey that had eaten her young one,

• وَتَسَمَّعَتْ رِزَّ الأَنِيسِ فَرَاعَهَا •
• عَنْ ظَهْرِ غَيْبٍ وَالأَنِيسُ سَقَامُهَا •

[*And she heard the sound of man, and it frightened her, from a place that concealed what was in it; for man is her malady;* i. e., *a cause of pain and trouble and death to her*]: (TA:) meaning, she heard the sound of the hunters, &c. (TA in art. غيب.) And you say, تَنَاوَلَهُ بِظَهْرِ الغَيْبِ بِمَا يَسُوْؤُهُ *He carped at him behind the back,* or *in absence, by saying what would grieve him.* (TA in art. غيب.) And تَكَلَّمْتُ بِهِ عَنْ ظَهْرِ الغَيْبِ (A, O) or عن ظهرِ غيبٍ (TA) [app., ‡ *I spoke it by memory; in the absence of a book* or *the like;* as one says in modern Arabic, عَلَى الغَائِب. See also غَيْبٌ.] And قَرَأَهُ عَنْ ظَهْرِ القَلْبِ ‡ *He recited it by heart,* or *memory; without book:* (L, Ḳ: [in the latter, مِنْ is put in the place of عَنْ; but the right reading is that in the L: and in the CḲ is an omission here, to be supplied by the insertion of وَقَرَأَهُ:]) and قرأه عَلَى ▼ ظَاهِرًا and حَمَلَ ظَهْرِ لِسَانِهِ [signify the same]. (Ḳ.) And حَفِظَهُ عَلَى ظَهْرِ قَلْبِهِ like القُرْآنَ عَلَى ظَهْرِ لِسَانِهِ ‡ [*He knew the Ḳur-án by heart*]. (A,* O, TA.) —— One says also, فُلَانٌ يَأْكُلُ عَلَى ظَهْرِ يَدِ فُلَانٍ ‡ *Such a one eats at the expense of such a one.* (A, O, Ḳ.*) And in like manner, الفُقَرَآءُ يَأْكُلُونَ عَلَى ظَهْرِ أَيْدِى النَّاسِ ‡ *The poor eat at the expense of the people.* (A, TA.) And أَعْطَاهُ عَنْ ظَهْرِ يَدٍ ‡ *He gave him originally; without compensation.* (O,* Ḳ; but in some copies of the Ḳ we find مِنْ in the place of عَنْ.) It is said [in a trad.], أَفْضَلُ الصَّدَقَةِ مَا كَانَ عَنْ ظَهْرِ غِنًى ‡ *The most excellent of alms is that which is* [*derived*] *from competence;* عَنْ نَفْسِ الغِنَى: (Mṣb:) or simply عَنْ غِنًى, the word ظهر being here redundant: (Mgh:) or *from manifest competence upon which one relies, and in which he seeks aid against calamities,* or *afflictions:* or *from what remains after fight:* (Mṣb:) or *from superfluous property.* (TA.) ══ See also ظَهِيرٌ. ══ قِدْرٌ ظَهِرٌ means † *An old cooking-pot:* (O, Ḳ:*) pl. قُدُورٌ ظُهُورٌ: (O:) as though, because of its oldness, it were thrown behind the back. (TA.)

ظُهْرٌ *Midday,* or *noon:* (IAth, TA:) or *the time when the sun declines from the meridian:* (Mṣb,* Ḳ,* O,* TA:) or [*the time immediately*] *after the declining of the sun:* (Ṣ, Mgh:) masc. and fem.; unless when the word صَلَاة is prefixed to it, in which case it is fem. only: (Mṣb:) [pl. أَظْهَارٌ. See also ظَهِيرَةٌ.] صَلَاةُ الظُّهْرِ means *The prayer* [i. e. *the divinely-ordained prayer*] *of midday,* or *noon:* (IAth, TA:) or *of the time after the declining of the sun.* (Ṣ, O.) In the phrases أَبْرِدُوا بِالظُّهْرِ [*Defer ye the prayer of midday until the cooler time of day*] and صَلَّى الظُّهْرَ [*He performed the prayer of midday*], the prefixed noun (صَلَاة) is suppressed. (Mgh.) ══ سَالَ وَادِيهِمْ ظُهْرًا: see ظَهْرٌ, last quarter.

ظَهِرٌ, (Ṣ,) or ▼ ظَهِيرٌ, (Ḳ,) [the former agreeable with analogy, being derived from ظَهَرَ,] A man (Ṣ,) *having a complaint of the back:* (Ṣ, Ḳ:) or *having a pain in the back:* as also ▼ مَظْهُورٌ. (O, TA.)

ظُهْرَةٌ: see ظَهِيرٌ, in three places. ══ Also *The tortoise.* (O, Ḳ.)

ظِهْرَةٌ: see ظَهِيرٌ, in six places.

ظَهَرَةٌ The *goods,* or *furniture and utensils, of a house* or *tent;* (IAạr, Ṣ, O, Ḳ, TA;) as also ▼ أَهَرَةٌ: (IAạr, TA:) or the former signifies the *exterior of a house,* or *tent;* and the latter, the "interior thereof." (Th, TA.) —— And *Abundance of* مَال [i. e. property, or cattle]. (TA.) ══ See also ظَهِيرٌ.

ظِهْرِيٌّ A camel *prepared for future need;* (T, Ṣ, O, Ḳ;) *taken, by way of precaution, to bear the burden of any camel that may happen to fail in a journey:* sometimes two or more unladen camels are taken for this purpose: some say that such a camel is thus called because its owner puts it behind his back, not riding it nor putting any burden upon it: (T, TA:) the word appears to be an irreg. rel. n. from ظَهْرٌ: (ISd, TA:) pl. ظَهَارِيُّ, imperfectly decl., because the rel. ى retains its place in the sing. [inseparably; there being no such word as ظَهْرٌ: but if it be a rel. n., this pl. is irreg., like مَهَارِيُّ]. (Ṣ, O, Ḳ.) —— See ظَهْرٌ, first quarter, in five places, for examples of ظِهْرِيٌّ and ظِهْرِيَّةٌ used tropically.

ظُهْرَانٌ [app. ظُهْرَانٌ (which is also a pl. of ظَهْرٌ used in several senses), or, perhaps ظُهْرَانِ, as having a dual meaning,] The *upper, thick, pair of wings of the locust.* (AḤn, TA.) —— [See also ظَهْرٌ.]

بَيْنَ ظَهْرَانَيْهِمْ, and ظَهْرَانَيْهِ, and الظَّهْرَانَيْنِ, &c.: see ظَهْرٌ, former half, in five places.

ظَهَارٌ The *exterior* (Ḳ, TA) *and elevated* (TA) *part of a* [*stony tract such as is called*] حَرَّة. (Ḳ, TA.)

ظُهَارٌ *Pain in the back.* (Az, O, TA.) ══ See also ظَهْرٌ, third quarter, in two places.

ظَهِيرٌ: see ظَاهِرٌ. ══ Also *An aider,* or *assistant;* (Ṣ, A, O, Mṣb, Ḳ;) and so ▼ ظِهْرَةٌ (Ṣ, Ḳ) and ▼ ظُهْرَةٌ: (Ḳ:) [in one place, in the Ḳ, ظِهْرَةٌ is expl. by عَوْنٌ; but by this is meant, as will be seen below, the same as is meant by مُعِينٌ, by which all the three words are expl. in another place in the Ḳ, as well as in the Ṣ &c.:] and *aiders,* or *assistants;* (Ṣ, Mṣb;) as also ▼ ظِهْرَةٌ and ▼ ظُهْرَةٌ and ▼ ظَهْرٌ: (TA:) the pl. of ظَهِيرٌ is ظُهَرَاءُ. (O.) It is said in the Ḳur [xxv. 57], وَكَانَ الكَافِرُ عَلَى رَبِّهِ ظَهِيرًا *And the unbeliever is an aider* of the enemies of God [*against his Lord*]. (Ibn-'Arafeh.) You say also, فُلَانٌ ظِهْرَتِى ▼ عَلَى فُلَانٍ *Such a one is my aider* (عَوْن) *against such a one:* and أَنَا ظِهْرَتُكَ ▼ عَلَى هٰذَا الأَمْرِ *I am thine aider against this thing,* or *affair.* (Ṣ, O.) And it is also said in the Ḳur [lxvi. 4], وَالْمَلَائِكَةُ بَعْدَ ذٰلِكَ ظَهِيرٌ [*And the angels after that* will be his *aiders*]: an instance of ظهير in a pl. sense: (Ṣ, O, Mṣb:) for words of the measures فَعُولٌ and فَعِيلٌ are sometimes masc. and fem. [and sing.] and pl. (Ṣ.) You also say, جَآءَ فُلَانٌ فِى ظَهْرَتِهِ ▼, (Ṣ, A, Ḳ,) and ▼ ظِهْرَتِهِ, (A, Ḳ,) and ▼ ظُهْرَتِهِ, and ▼ ظَاهِرَتِهِ, (Ḳ,) *Such a one came among his people,* (Ṣ,) or *kinsfolk,* (Ḳ,) *and those who performed his affairs for him,* (Ṣ, A,) i. e., *his aiders,* or *assistants.* (A.) And هُمْ فِى ظِهْرَةٍ ▼ وَاحِدَةٍ *They aid one another against the enemies.* (TA.) —— Also *Strong in the back;* (Ḳ;) *sound therein:* (Lth:) and so ▼ مُظْهِرٌ: (Ṣ, O, Ḳ:) applied to a man: (Ṣ:) or *hard and strong;* whether in the back or any other part is not said: (TA:) in this sense, (TA,) or as signifying *strong,* (Ṣ, O,) applied to a camel: fem. with ة. (Ṣ, O, TA.) —— Also A camel *whose back is not used, on account of galls,* or *sores, upon it:* or *unsound in the back by reason of galls,* or *sores,* or *from some other cause.* (Th.) Thus it has two contr. significations. (TA.) ══ See also ظَهِرٌ.

ظِهَارَةٌ [The *facing,* or *outer covering,* or] *what is uppermost,* (TA,) *what is apparent* (Mṣb, TA) *to the eye,* (Mṣb,) *not next the body,* of a garment; (TA;) and in like manner, *what is uppermost and apparent, not next the ground,* of a carpet; (TA;) as also ▼ ظَاهِرَةٌ: (JK:) *contr. of* بِطَانَةٌ: (Ṣ, O, Mṣb, Ḳ:) pl. ظَهَائِرُ. (TA.)

ظَهِيرَةٌ The *point of midday:* (M, A, Ḳ:) or only *in summer:* (M, Ḳ:) or *i. q.* هَاجِرَةٌ [i. e. *midday in summer* or *when the heat is vehement:* or the *period from a little before, to a little after, midday in summer:* or *midday, when the sun declines from the meridian, at the* ظُهْر: or *from its declining until the* عَصْر]: (Ṣ, O, TA:) or the هَاجِرَة, which is *when the sun declines from the meridian:* (Mṣb:) or the *vehement heat of midday:* (IAth, TA:) or i. q. ظُهْر [q. v.]: (Az, TA:)

pl. ظَهَائِرُ. (TA.) You say, أَتَيْتُهُ حَدَّ الظَّهِيرَةِ [*I came to him at the point of midday in summer*; &c.]: and حِينَ قَامَ قَائِمُ الظَّهِيرَةِ [*when the sun had become high, and the shade had almost disappeared*: so expl. in art. قوم]. (Ṣ, O.) And أَبْرِدْ عَنْكَ مِنَ الظَّهِيرَةِ *Stay thou until the midday-heat shall have become assuaged, and the air be cool.* (L in art. فيح.) And hence, in a trad. of 'Omar, when a man came to him complaining of gout in the feet, he said, كَذَبَتْكَ الظَّهَائِرُ, meaning *Take thou to walking during the heat of the middays in summer.* (TA.)

ظُهَارِيَّةٌ *One of the modes of seizing* [and throwing down] *in wrestling*: or i. q. شَغْزَبِيَّةٌ: (Ḳ:) the *twisting one's leg with the leg of another in the manner that is termed* شَغْزَبِيَّة, *and so throwing him down*: one says, أَخَذَهُ الظُّهَارِيَّةَ and الشَّغْزَبِيَّةَ [*He seized him and threw him down by the trick above described*]: both signify the same: (ISh, O:) or ظُهَارِيَّةٌ signifies the *throwing one down upon the back.* (Ibn-'Abbád, O, Ḳ.) — And (hence, as being likened thereto, TA) ‡ *A certain mode*, or *manner, of compressing*, or *coitus.* (O, Ḳ, TA.) — And أَوْثَقَهُ الظُّهَارِيَّةَ *He bound his hands behind his back.* (Ibn-Buzurj, O, Ḳ, TA.)

ظَاهِرٌ [*Outward, exterior, external, extrinsic*, or *exoteric*: and hence, *appearing, apparent, overt, open, perceptible* or *perceived, manifest, conspicuous, ostensible, plain*, or *evident*: in all these senses] *contr. of* بَاطِنٌ: (Ṣ, Ḳ, TA:) and so ↓ ظَهِيرٌ. (TA.) [Hence, ظَاهِرًا *Outwardly*, &c.: and *apparently*; &c.: and فِى الظَّاهِرِ *in appearance.* And الظَّاهِرُ أَنَّهُ كَذَا *It appears*, or *it seems*, or *what seems to be the case is, that it is so*, or *thus.* And ظَاهِرٌ فِيهِ كَذَا for ظَاهِرٌ كَذَا meaning A person, or thing, *in whom*, or *in which, such a quality is apparent*, or *manifest*, &c.: see an ex. in a verse cited in the first paragraph of art. طعن.] See also مُظْهَرٌ. — [Hence also,] عَيْنٌ ظَاهِرَةٌ *A prominent eye*; (Ṣ, O, Ḳ, TA;) *that fills its cavity.* (TA.) — And هٰذَا أَمْرٌ ظَاهِرٌ عَنْكَ عَارُهُ ‡ *This is a thing*, or *an affair, of which the disgrace is remote from thee*: (Ṣ, TA:) or *does not cleave to thee.* (TA.) And هٰذَا عَيْبٌ ظَاهِرٌ عَنْكَ ‡ *This is a vice*, or *fault, that does not cleave to thee.* (A.) A poet says, (namely, Kutheiyir, accord. to a copy of the Ṣ, or Aboo-Dhu-eyb, TA,)

وَعَيَّرَهَا الوَاشُونَ أَنِّى أُحِبُّهَا •
وَتِلْكَ شَكَاةٌ ظَاهِرٌ عَنْكَ عَارُهَا •

‡ [*And the slanderers taunted her with the fact of my loving her; but that is a fault of which the disgrace is remote from thee*]. (Ṣ, TA.) — [الظَّاهِرُ also signifies *The outside*, or *exterior*, of a thing. You say, نَزَلَ ظَاهِرَ المَدِينَةِ *He alighted*, or *took up his abode, outside the city*: comp. ظَاهِرَةٌ. Hence,] ظَاهِرُ الكَفِّ and ظَاهِرُ القَدَمِ; and another signification of ظَاهِرٌ: for all of which see ظَهْرٌ, third quarter. — [Also *The external, outward*, or *extrinsic, state, condition*, or *circumstances*, of a man: and *the outward*, or *apparent, character*, or *disposition of the mind*: opposed to البَاطِنُ.] — One says also, فُلَانٌ ظَاهِرٌ عَلَى فُلَانٍ *Such a one has the ascendancy*, or *mastery, over such a one*; *is conqueror of him*, or *victorious over him.* (TA.) And هٰذَا أَمْرٌ ظَاهِرٌ بِكَ *This is a thing*, or *an affair, that overcomes*, or *overpowers, thee.* (TA.) And هٰذَا أَمْرٌ أَنْتَ بِهِ ظَاهِرٌ *This is an affair which thou hast power to do.* (TA.) [And هُوَ ظَاهِرٌ عَلَى كَذَا *He is a conqueror, a winner, an achiever*, or *an attainer, of such a thing*: see an ex. voce غُرُوب, near the end.] And الظَّاهِرُ is one of the names of God, meaning *The Ascendant*, or *Predominant, over all things*: or, as some say, *He who is known by inference of the mind from what appears to mankind of the effects of his actions and his attributes.* (IAth, TA.) — حَاجَتُهُ عِنْدَكَ ظَاهِرَةٌ means ‡ *His want is in thine estimation* [*an object of contempt*, or *neglect, as though*] *cast behind the back.* (O,* TA.) — قَرَأَهُ ظَاهِرًا: see ظَهْرٌ, towards the end of the paragraph. ═ شَآءٌ ظَوَاهِرُ *Sheep*, or *goats, that come to the water every day at noon.* (TA.)

ظَاهِرَةٌ as a subst.; and its pl. ظَوَاهِرُ: see ظَهْرٌ, in four places, in the third quarter of the paragraph. [Hence,] قُرَيْشُ الظَّوَاهِرِ *Those, of Ḳureysh, that dwell in the exterior of Mekkeh*, (O,) *upon the mountains thereof*, (Ḳ,* TA,) or *upon the higher parts of Mekkeh*: (TA:) those who dwell in the lower parts are called قُرَيْشُ البِطَاحِ; (O,* TA;) and these are the more honourable, (O, TA,*) because they are neighbours of the House of God. (O.) — See also ظُهَارَةٌ. ═ And see ظَهِيرٌ. ═ Also The *coming* of camels, (Ṣ, O, Ḳ, TA,) and of sheep or goats, (TA,) *to the water every day, at noon.* (Ṣ, O, Ḳ, TA.) One says, of camels, [and of sheep or goats,] تَرِدُ الظَّاهِرَةَ [*They come to the water every day, at noon*]: and Sh says that they return from the water at the عَصْر. (TA.) And شَرِبَ الفَرَسُ ظَاهِرَةً *The horse drank every day, at noon.* (TA.) ظَاهِرَةُ الغِبِّ [*The coming to the water at noon on alternate days*] is for sheep or goats; scarcely ever, or never, for camels; and is a little shorter [in the interval] than what is called [simply] الغِبّ. (O, TA.)

مَظْهَرٌ i. q. مَصْعَدٌ [i. e. *A place of ascent*, or *a place to which one ascends*]; (O, Ḳ; in some copies of the latter of which, both words are erroneously written with ḍamm to the م; TA;) and دَرَجَةٌ [as meaning *a degree, grade, rank, condition*, or *station*, or *an exalted*, or *a high, grade*, &c.]: (O:) used by En-Nábighah El-Jaadee as meaning *Paradise.* (O, TA.)

[مُظْهَرٌ *Made apparent*, &c. — And hence, as also ↓ ظَاهِرٌ, but the former more commonly, applied to a noun, *Explicit*; and, elliptically, *an explicit noun*; opposed to مُضْمَرٌ and ضَمِيرٌ (a concealed noun, i. e. a pronoun); and to مُبْهَمٌ (a noun of vague signification).]

مُظْهِرٌ *Possessing camels for riding* or *for carrying goods*: pl. مُظْهِرُونَ. (Ṣ,* Ḳ,* TA.) ═ And A camel *made to sweat by the* ظَهِيرَة [or *vehement heat of midday in summer*]. (Ṣgh, Ḳ, TA.) And accord. to Aṣ, one says, ↓ أَتَانَا فُلَانٌ مُظَهِّرًا, meaning *Such a one came to us in the time of the* ظَهِيرَة [or *midday in summer*, &c.]: but accord. to A'Obeyd, others say مُظْهِرًا, without teshdeed; and this is the proper form: (Ṣ:) or both mean, *in the time of the* ظُهْر. (O.)

مُظَهِّرٌ: see مُظْهِرٌ, near the end of the paragraph.

مُظَهَّرٌ: see مُظْهَرٌ.

مَظْهُورٌ pass. part. n. of ظَهَرَ [q. v.]. — See also ظَهْرٌ.

Quasi ظور

3. ظَاوَرَ, occurring in a trad. for ظَائَرَ: see 3 in art. ظأر.

ظوف

1. جَآءَ يَظُوفُهُ *He came driving him away*; as also يَظْأَفُهُ. (Ibn-'Abbád, O, Ḳ.)

ظَافٌ: see what follows, in three places.

أَخَذَهُ بِظُوفِ رَقَبَتِهِ and ↓ بِظَافِهَا (Ṣ, O, Ḳ) i. e. [*He took him*, or *laid hold upon him*,] *by the skin of his neck*: (O, Ḳ:) or أَخَذَ بِظُوفِ رَقَبَتِهِ and ↓ بِظَافِهَا i. e. [*he laid hold upon*] *the whole of his neck*: or *the pendent hair in the hollow of the back of his neck*: (M:) i. q. بِصُوفِ رَقَبَتِهِ [&c.]. (Ṣ. [See more voce صُوفٌ: and see ظَلِيفٌ, last sentence.]) And تَرَكْتُهُ بِظُوفِ رَقَبَتِهِ (Ibn-'Abbád, O, Ḳ) and ↓ بِظَافِهَا, (Ḳ,) and بِظُوفِ قَفَاهُ, (Ibn-'Abbád, O,) *I left him alone.* (Ibn-'Abbád, O, Ḳ.) [And نَجَا بِظُوفِ نَفْسِهِ *He hardly escaped.* (Freytag from the Deewán of the Hudhalees.)]

ظى

2. ظَيَّيْتُ ظَاءً حَسَنَةً and حَسَنًا *I made* [or *wrote*] *a beautiful* ظ. (M,* TA.)

ظَآءٌ, also pronounced ظَا, (TA,) *A letter peculiar to the Arabic language* [i. e. *the letter* ظ]: (Kh, T, TA, &c.:) masc. and fem.: as masc., its pl. is أَظْوَآءٌ; and as fem., ظَاآتٌ. (TA. [See art. ظ.])

Quasi ظير

ظِيرٌ, for ظِئْرٌ: see the latter, in art. ظأر.

ع

The eighteenth letter of the alphabet: called عَيْنٌ. It is [one of the letters termed مَجْهُورَة, or vocal, i. e. pronounced with the voice, not with the breath only; and] of the letters termed حَلْقِيَّة [or faucial]; these being ع and ح and ه and خ and غ [and أ]; the lowest of which in its place of utterance is ع; wherefore Kh [in the composition of his lexicon entitled "Kitáb el-'Eyn"] and several other lexicographers [after him] began their books with [words having] this letter [in their roots], giving the next place to ح, the next to ه, the next to خ, and the next to غ. (L, TA.) It is substituted for ء [in what is termed the عَنْعَنَة of Temeem]; as in عَنْ for أَنْ: and for ح; as in عَتَّى for حَتَّى, and صَبْعٌ for صَبْحٌ: and for غ; as in عُلَامٌ for غُلَامٌ. (MF, TA.) It is never consociated with ح in any word of which the letters are all radicals; unless it be a word compounded of two words, as حَيْعَلَ from حَيَّ عَلَى. (Kh, TA.) ═ [As a numeral, it denotes *Seventy.*]

عب

1. عَبَّ, aor. ـُ, (Ṣ, Mgh, O, Mṣb,) inf. n. عَبٌّ, (Ṣ, Mgh, O, Mṣb, Ḳ,) *He* (a man, Mṣb) *drank water without taking breath:* (O, Mṣb, TA; and T in art. غنث: [this is the sense in which it is generally used:]) or *he drank water without sipping or sucking in* (مِنْ غَيْرِ مَصٍّ): (Ṣ, O:) thus, (Ṣ, O, Mṣb,) in the manner termed عَبّ, (Ṣ, O,) i. e. مِنْ غَيْرِ مَصٍّ, (Mṣb,) the pigeon drinks water, like horses and similar beasts; (Ṣ, O, Mṣb;) whereas other birds take it sip after sip: (Mṣb:) or *he drank water at once, without interrupting the swallowing:* AA says, the pigeon drinks thus; differing from the other birds; for these drink by little and little: (Mgh:) [in like manner also] Esh-Sháfi'ee says, the pigeon is a bird that drinks in the manner termed عَبّ, and coos; for it does not drink like other birds, by little and little: (TA:) and it is said in a trad. that the liver-complaint (الكُبَاد) is occasioned by drinking in the manner termed عَبّ: (Ṣ, O, TA:) or عَبٌّ signifies [simply] the *drinking* water: or the *gulping,* or *swallowing down:* or the *doing so uninterruptedly:* (Ḳ, TA:) or the *drinking* water *in a single stream, without interruption:* (TA:) and the *drinking with the mouth from a place,* or *vessel, containing water, not with the hands nor with a vessel:* (Ḳ, TA:) you say, عَبَّ فِى المَآءِ, and فِى الإِنَآءِ, *he so drank of the water,* and *from the vessel:* and [accord. to some] one says of a bird, عَبَّ; not شَرِبَ: (TA:) [but] Es-Sarakustee says, one does not say of a bird شَرِبَ المَآءَ, but يَعُبُّ فِيهِ مِيزَابَانِ ـــ (.Mṣb in art. شرب.) حَسَاهُ. in a trad. respecting the حَوْض [i. e. Mohammad's pool], as some relate it, means [*Two spouts*] *were pouring forth into it with an uninterrupted pouring:* but accord. to the relation commonly known, the verb is يَغُتُّ, [i. e. يَغُتُّ in this sense, but يَغُتُّ in another sense, as meaning the making a murmuring sound,] with غ and ت. (TA.) ـــ عَبَّتِ الدَّلْوُ, (Ḳ,) [aor., app. تَعُبُّ,] inf. n. عَبٌّ, (TḲ,) *The bucket made a sound in lading out the water.* (Ḳ.) ـــ And عَبَّ البَحْرُ, inf. n. عُبَابٌ, *The sea rose high, with multitudinous waves.* (A.) [Accord. to Golius, عَبَّ said of the sea means *It had broken waves:* but for this he has named no authority.] ـــ And [hence,] ▼ عَبَّ عُبَابُهُ ‡ *His speech was continual and abundant.* (A.) ـــ عَبْعَبٌ [an inf. n., of which the verb, accord. to general analogy, is app. عَبَّ, first pers. عَبِبْتُ, aor. يَعَبُّ,] means [The *interrupting in swallowing;* or] the *interrupting the swallowing.* (TA.) ═ عَبَّ, [aor., app., ـِ,] said of a plant, *It became tall.* (Ṣ.) ـــ And [said of a man] *His face became beautiful,* or *comely, after having become altered.* (TA.)

5. تعبّب العَبِيبَةَ *He drank the* عَبِيبَة [q. v.]. (L, TA.) ـــ And تعبّب النَّبِيذَ *He persevered,* or *persisted, in drinking the* [*beverage called*] نَبِيذ. (Lḥ, Ḳ.) And *He swallowed in consecutive portions the* نَبِيذ, (A, TA,) *and in large quantity.* (A.)

R. Q. 1. عَبْعَبَ *He was put to flight.* (O, Ḳ.)

R. Q. 2. تَعَبْعَبْتُهُ *I took it,* or *devoured it, altogether.* (O, Ḳ.)

عَبُّ الشَّمْسِ: see the next paragraph. ═ عَبْ is said when one orders another to conceal himself. (IAạr, TA.)

عَبُّ الشَّمْسِ, (O, Ḳ, TA,) as some say, (TA,) and ▼ عَبُّ الشَّمْسِ, (O, Ḳ, TA,) which is the form commonly known and obtaining, (TA,) *The light of the sun:* (O, Ḳ, TA:) or *the light of the dawn.* (Az, TA.) By عَبْشَمْس as a proper name, is meant عَبْدُ شَمْسٍ: ISh says, among Saạd are بَنُو عَبْدِ الشَّمْسِ; and among Ḳureysh, بَنُو عَبِّ الشَّمْسِ. (TA.) [See also عَبْءٌ.] ═ عَبُّ قُرٍّ is for حَبُّ قُرٍّ, meaning *Hail.* (Ḳ in art. حبقر.)

عُبٌّ *i. q.* رُدْنٌ, (O, Ḳ,) which means The *base* (أَصْل) *of the sleeve:* (Ṣ and Ḳ in art. ردن:) or the *fore part of the sleeve of the shirt:* (M in that art.:) or the *lower part thereof:* (M in that art., and Ḥar pp. 149 and 390:) or the *sleeve altogether:* (M in that art.:) but, as MF says, it is a vulgar word. (TA.)

عِنَبٌ The *berries* (حَبّ) *of the* كَاكَنَج or كَاكَنْج [thus differently written, from the Pers. كَاكُنْج], (Ḳ,) which, accord. to more than one of the leading authorities, is a tree, but is expl. by the author of the Ḳ [in its proper art.] as meaning a gum: (TA:) [what is here meant by it is the *physalis alkekengi,* or *common winter-cherry:* accord. to Forskål (Flora Aegypt. Arab p. cvi.) the name عِنَب is applied to the *physalis somnifera:* and also (pp. cxxi. and cxxii. and 163) to the *croton lobatum* and *croton villosum:*] or it is applied by the physicians to the [*plant itself called*] كاكنج: (O:) or *i. q.* عِنَبُ الثَّعْلَبِ; (IAạr, O, Ḳ;) which is said by Ibn-Ḥabeeb to be an incorrect appellation, (O, TA,) being correctly عِنَب, but AM denies that the former is incorrect: (TA:) or *i. q.* رَآء; (Ḳ;) i. e. the *tree called* رَآء: (TA:) or *a tree,* or *plant,* (شَجَرَة,) *of the* [*kind called*] أَغْلَاث: (Ḳ:) AḤn says, on the authority of Aboo-Ziyád, *it is of the* أَغْلَاث, *and is a tree,* or *plant,* (شَجَرَة,) *resembling the* حَرْمَل [*peganum harmala* of Linn.], *except that it is taller, coming forth in the form of strings, and having pods* (سِنَفَة) *like those of the* حَرْمَل, *and sometimes the goats nibble from its leaves and from its pods when they dry up; it has also berries, intensely red, like beads of carnelian, smaller than the* نَبِق [or *fruit of the lote tree*], *and larger than the grape; and people seek out the leaves thereof that have not been rendered foraminous, which leaves are then bruised, and used beneficially as a dressing for maladies attended with pain:* the people assert that the jinn, or genii, perforate them in envy of mankind. (O.)

عُبُبٌ *Waters pouring forth copiously.* (IAạr, O, Ḳ.) [It may be a pl. of عُبَابٌ (as Golius says), like as قُرُدٌ is of قُرَادٌ.]

عَبَابِ [a quasi-inf. n., of the class of فَجَارِ and حَمَادِ, indecl.]. لَا عَبَابِ [app. as used in the prov. here following] means لَا تَعُبَّ فِى المَآءِ. (Ṣ. [Thus in one of my copies of the Ṣ: in the other copy the explanation is written لا تَعُبَّ فى الماء, as though عَبَابِ were an imperative verbal noun: and so in the O, in which the phrase is written لَا عَبَابِ: but تَعُبَّ I think a mistranscription.]) The saying إِذَا أَصَابَتِ الظِّبَآءُ المَآءَ فَلَا عَبَابِ وَإِنْ لَمْ تُصِبْهُ فَلَا أَبَابِ means *When the gazelles find water, they do not drink in the manner termed* عَبّ; *and when they do not find it, they do not prepare to seek it and to drink it:* (Ḳ, TA; and thus (أَبَابِ and عَبَابِ) accord. to the Mz, 40th نوع: but in the CḲ عَبابٌ and أَبابٌ:) it is a prov., frequently used by the Arabs in an abridged manner, لا عباب ولا اباب, as in the works of Meyd and others; (TA;) and is applied to a man who turns from a thing, not needing it. (Meyd.)

عُبَابٌ The *main body* of a torrent, or flow of water: and the *height and abundance* thereof: (O, Ḳ:) or the *waves, billows,* or *surges,* thereof: (Ḳ:) and the *first portion* (O, Ḳ) thereof (O) or of a thing: (Ḳ:) and the *first and main portion* of water: and the *vehemence of running* thereof. (TA.) — [Hence,] عَبَّ عُبَابُهُ: see 1, near the end. — It is said in a trad., إِنَّا حَىٌّ مِنْ مَذْحِجٍ عُبَابُ سَلَفِهَا وَلُبَابُ شَرَفِهَا, meaning † [*Verily we are a tribe* sprung *from Medh-hij, the chief of their nobility,* or *nobles, and the purest,* or *best,* issue] *of their ancestry,* or [*the purest,* or *best,* inheritors] *of their ancestral might and glory.* (TA: only سَلَفِهَا in this saying being there explained.) And in a trad. of 'Alee, relating to Aboo-Bekr, طِرْتَ بِعُبَابِهَا وَفُزْتَ بِحَبَابِهَا, expl. voce حَبَابٌ. (TA.) And one says, جَاؤُوا بِعُبَابِهِمْ † *They came* [*with their whole company,* or] *all together.* (TA.) ═ Also *A* خُوصَة [or *leaf of a palm-tree &c.*]. (Ḳ.)

عُبَيْبَةٌ *A certain food,* (Ḳ,) or *sort of food,* (TA,) and *a beverage,* (Ḳ, TA,) *obtained* (TA) *from the* [*species of mimosa called*] عُرْفُط, *of sweet flavour:* (Ḳ, TA:) or the *exudation* [or *matter exuded in the form of drops*] *of gum;* (عِرْقُ الصَّمْغِ; [written in the TA without any syll. signs; in the CḲ عِرْقُ الصَّمْغِ, and so in my MS. copy of the Ḳ; but in the latter, the former word has been altered, app. from عَرَقُ, which is evidently the right reading;]) *it is of sweet flavour, and is beaten with* [*the implement called*] *a* مِجْدَح *until it becomes thoroughly fit for use* (حَتَّى يَنْضَجَ), [app., from what here follows, *over a fire,*] *and is then drunk:* (TA:) or *what drops,* or *distils, of the exudations* (مَغَافِير) *of the* عُرْفُط: or عُبَيْبَةٌ اللَّثَى, accord. to ISk, is *the infusion* (غُسَالَة) *of* لَثًى; (Ṣ, TA;) لَثًى being *a substance which the* [*plant called*] ثُمَام *exudes, of sweet flavour;* what falls thereof upon the ground is taken, and put into a garment, or piece of cloth, and water is poured upon it, and when it flows from the garment, or piece of cloth, it is drunk, in a sweet state, and sometimes it is made thick; (Ṣ;) or لَثًى is a substance which the ثُمَام exudes, sweet like نَاطِف [q. v.]; and when any of it flows upon the ground, it is taken, and put into a vessel, or sometimes it is poured upon water, and then drunk, in a sweet state, and sometimes it is made thick: (TA:) [or عُبَيْبَةُ اللَّثَى is *a decoction of the matter exuded by a species of* ثُمَام; for] AM says, I have seen, in the desert, a species of ثُمَام that exudes a sweet gum, which is gathered from its shoots, and eaten, and is called لَثَى الثُّمَامِ: when it has remained for some time, it is found scattered at the foot of the ثُمَام, and is taken with its dust, and put into a garment, or piece of cloth, and cleansed by water poured upon it; then it is boiled over a fire until it thickens; when it is eaten: what flows from it [or the fluid part of it] is called عُبَيْبَةٌ: and تَعَبَّبْتُ عُبَيْبَةً means "I drank عُبَيْبَة." (L, TA.) It is stated in a marginal note in the L, that A'Obeyd [is related to have] said that عُبَيْبَة is "milk such as is termed رَائِب:" but AM observes that this is a disgraceful mistake, and that A'Obeyd is related on the authority of Sh to have assigned this meaning to عُبَيْبَة. (TA.) — Also The [*shrub called*] رِمْث, (Ḳ, TA,) *on which camels feed,* (TA,) *when it is in a depressed tract of land.* (Ḳ, TA.)

عُبَّى A woman *of whom a child scarcely ever,* or *never, dies.* (Kr, Ḳ.)

عُبِّيَّةٌ and عِبِّيَّةٌ, (Ṣ, O, Ḳ, TA,) [like أُبِّيَّة and إِبِّيَّة,] and عُبِيَّةٌ and عِبِيَّةٌ, in the CḲ (erroneously) without the sheddeh to the ب,] also written غُبِّيَّةٌ, with غ, (Abu-l-Ḥasan 'Alee Esh-Shádhilee,) *Pride; haughtiness:* (Ṣ, O, Ḳ:) and *glorying.* (Ḳ.) One says رَجُلٌ فِيهِ عُبِّيَّةٌ *A man in whom is pride,* or *haughtiness.* (Ṣ, O.) And عُبِّيَّةُ الجَاهِلِيَّةِ means *The pride,* or *haughtiness, of the people of the Time of Ignorance.* (Ṣ, O.) عُبِّيَّة may be of the measure فُعْلِيَّة or فُعُّولَة: if the former, from عُبَابُ المَآءِ, meaning "the height of water:" if the latter, [originally عُبُّويَة,] from عَبَاهُ, without ء, meaning "he prepared it;" because the proud is characterized by affectation and preparation. (O.)

عَبَّابٌ [app. One *that drinks in the manner termed* عَبّ]. بَنُو العَبَّابِ is an appellation of a people of the Arabs who were thus called because they intermixed with the Persians so that their horses drank (عَبَّتْ, Ḳ, TA, i. e. شَرِبَتْ, TA) of the water of the Euphrates. (Ḳ,* TA.)

عَبْعَبٌ The *softness, tenderness, bloom,* or *flourishing freshness, of youth.* (Ṣ, O, Ḳ.) — And Youth, or youthfulness, *in its state of full growth,* or *maturity:* (TA:) or *a full-grown,* or *mature, youth:* (O:) or *i. q.* شَابٌّ مُمْتَلِئٌ, (Ḳ, TA,) meaning مُمْتَلِئُ الشَّبَابِ [i. e. *a youth full of the sap,* or *vigour, of youthfulness*]. (TA.) — And *A buck-gazelle.* (Ṣ, O.) — عَبْعَبُ التَّصْوِيرِ means *Bulky in form, big* (جَلِيل) *in speech.* (TA. [But the addition "big in speech" is app. a mistake, occasioned by an omission or a transposition: see عَبْعَابٌ.]) — See also another meaning voce عَبْعَابٌ. — And العَبْعَبُ, (O, Ḳ, TA,) not a mistranscription for الغبغب, (O,) but sometimes pronounced with غ, (TA,) is the name of *A certain idol,* (O, Ḳ, TA,) *belonging to Ḳuḍá'ah* (O, TA) *and those dwelling near to them.* (TA.) And *The place of the idol* [app. of the idol above mentioned] (Ḳ, TA) is also sometimes thus called. (TA.) See also الغَبْغَبُ. ═ Also *A woollen* [*garment of the kind called*] كِسَآء: (Ṣ, O:) or *a soft* كساء, (Ḳ, TA,) *thickly woven,* (TA,) *of soft camels' hair:* (Ḳ, TA:) or *a soft and thin* كساء: (Lth, TA:) or *a striped* كساء. (TA.) — And A garment *wide,* or *ample.* (O, Ḳ.*)

عَبْعَبَةٌ *A flock,* or *small portion, of red* [or *brown*] *wool.* (O, Ḳ.) ═ And *Briskness, liveliness,* or *sprightliness:* and *insanity,* or *madness.* (TA voce عَتْعَتَةٌ.)

عَبْعَابٌ A *tall* man; (Ṣ, O, Ḳ;) as also ↓ عَبْعَبٌ. (O, Ḳ.) — And A man *having an ample throat and chest.* (O, Ḳ.) One says رَجُلٌ عَبْعَابٌ قَبْقَابٌ *A man having an ample throat and chest, big* (جَلِيل) *in speech.* (O.) — And A youth, or young man, (TA,) or an ass, (O, [in which this application is confirmed by the citation of a verse wherein the epithet is evidently applied to a swift beast such as the wild ass,]) *full-grown, and goodly in make.* (O, Ḳ, TA.)

عُنْبُبٌ *Abundance of water.* (IAạr, O, Ḳ. [See also عُبَابٌ.]) The ن is said by AM [and in the O] to be augmentative. (TA.) [But it is also mentioned in the Ḳ in art. عنب.] — And The *foremost portion of a torrent;* (Ḳ in art. عنب;) as also عُنْبُبٌ. (So in some copies of the Ḳ and in the TA in that art.) ═ And *A certain plant.* (Ḳ.)

أَعَبُّ *Poor.* (O, Ḳ.) — And *Thick-nosed.* (O, Ḳ.)

يَعْبُوبٌ *A river,* or *rivulet, that runs in a vehement manner:* (Ṣ, A, O:) or *a rivulet,* or *streamlet, abounding in water.* (Ḳ.) — And hence, (A, and Ḥar p. 68,) or from عُبَابُ المَآءِ (A,* TA) meaning "the vehemence of the running of water," and therefore tropical, (TA,) ‡ A horse *that runs much* (Ṣ, O, TA, and Ḥar ubi suprà) *and vehemently:* (TA:) or a horse that is *swift* (Ḳ, TA) *in his running,* (TA,) and, (Ḳ,) or, as some say, (TA,) *long,* or *tall,* syn. طَوِيل: (Ḳ, TA:) or *a courser easy in his running:* or *that takes long*, or *wide, steps*, (Ḳ,) *in running*, or *that runs far*. (Ḳ accord. to different copies.) [Golius, who writes the word يُعْبُوبٌ, gives among its significations that of *A locust that leaps far* or *rapidly*, as from the Ḳ; in a copy of which he probably found جَرَاد written by mistake for جَوَاد.] —— It is also used as an epithet meaning *Long*, in the saying of Ḳuss,

* عَذْقٌ بِسَاحَةِ حَائِرٍ يَعْبُوبِ *

i. e. [*A palm-tree bearing fruit, by the side of*] *a long tract depressed in the middle, with elevated borders, containing water*. (TA.) —— Also *Clouds*. (Ḳ.) —— And اليَعْبُوبُ is the name of *A certain idol*. (O.)

عبأ

1. عَبَأَ, aor. ـَ, inf. n. عَبْءٌ, *He packed up goods, or utensils; put them one upon another*: (TA:) you say, عَبَأْتُ الشَّىْءَ فِى الوِعَآءِ [*I packed the thing in the repository*], aor. as above: and some allow also عَبَّيْتُ with teshdeed and ى [which is commonly used in the present day]: (Mṣb:) [and عَبَوْتُ also, inf. n. عَبْوٌ:] or عَبَأَ, (Ṣ, O, Ḳ,) aor. as above, (Ḳ,) and so the inf. n.; (Ṣ, O;) and ↓ عَبَّأَ, inf. n. تَعْبِئَةٌ and تَعْبِىْءٌ; (Ṣ, O, Ḳ;) *he prepared, set in order, disposed*, or *arranged*, goods, or utensils: (Ṣ, O, Ḳ:) and each, (Ḳ,) or the former, (Mṣb,) or the latter, (Ṣ, O,) and عَبَّى, with teshdeed and ى, (Mṣb,) [agreeably with the authority of Yoo, for] Yoo used to say تَعْبِيَةُ الجَيْشِ, without ء, (Ṣ, O,) *he fitted out with the requisite equipage &c.*, (Ḳ,) or *prepared*, (O,) or *set in order, disposed*, or *arranged*, (O, Mṣb,) or *set in order, disposed*, or *arranged, in their places, and prepared for war* or *fight*, (TA,) the horsemen, (Ṣ, O,) or the army. (Mṣb, Ḳ, TA.) And عَبَأْتُ لَهُ شَرًّا *I prepared for him evil*, or *mischief*. (TA.) —— عَبَأَ, (AZ, Ṣ, O, Ḳ,) aor. as above, (TA,) and so the inf. n., (AZ, Ṣ, O,) also signifies *He made*, (Ḳ,) or *prepared and made*, (AZ, Ṣ, O,) and *mixed*, perfume; (AZ, Ṣ, O, Ḳ;) and so ↓ عَبَّأَ, inf. n. تَعْبِئَةٌ and تَعْبِىْءٌ; and عَبَّى. (TA.) [And accord. to an explanation of the inf. n. in the KL, it seems that عَبَأَ signifies *He excited a good*, or *pleasant, odour*; as rendered by Golius: but this I think doubtful.] —— مَا أَعْبَأُ بِهِ means *What shall I do with it?* (T, Ḳ, TA,) namely, the affair. (T, TA.) مَا يَعْبَأُ بِكُمْ رَبِّى, in the Ḳur [xxv. last verse], is said by Mujáhid to mean *What will my Lord do with you?* but see another explanation of this in what follows. (TA.) —— And it signifies also *I do not care for, mind, heed*, or *regard, him*: (Ṣ, O, Mṣb, Ḳ:) or *I do not receive with approbation anything from him, nor anything of his discourse*: (Aboo-'Adnán, TA:) or, accord. to Aboo-Is-ḥáḳ [i. e. Zj], *I do not hold him to be of any weight or worth; do not esteem him*: and he says that مَا يَعْبَأُ بِكُمْ رَبِّى, of which an explanation has been given above, means *What weight have ye in the estimation of my Lord?* (TA.) One says also, مَا عَبَأْتُ بِهِ شَيْئًا, meaning *I did not reckon him as anything; or did not esteem him at all*. (Aboo-'Abd-Er-Rahmán, TA.) And مَا عَبَأْتُ لَهُ شَيْئًا *I did not care for, mind, heed*, or *regard, him*: (T, TA:) or so مَا عَبَأْتُ بِهِ. (Mṣb.) And قَدْ عَبَأَ ٱللّٰهُ عَنْهُ *God has received with approbation everything from him*. (Aboo-'Adnán, TA.) —— And عَبَأَ لَهُ *He thought it*, or *opined it, and held it*, or *took to it as a tenet*. (O, TA.) ═ عَبَأَ وَجْهُهُ, aor. ـَ, *His face shone*: (IAạr, TA:) and so عَبَا, aor. يَعْبُو. (Ḳ in art. عبو.)

2: see 1, former half, in two places.

8. الاِعْتِبَآءُ is *syn. with* الاِحْتِشَآءُ: (Ṣ, Ḳ, TA:) one says, of a woman, اِعْتَبَأَتْ بِالْمِعْبَأَةِ [or اعتبأت alone, as indicated in the Ṣ and Ḳ, meaning *She stuffed her vulva with the* مِعْبَأَة, q. v.]. (TA.) —— And [اعتبأ app. signifies *He put together for himself*; or *grasped*; or *got*, or *gained, possession of*; property,] one says, اِحْتَوَيْتُ مَا عِنْدَهُ وَٱمْتَخَرْتُهُ وَٱعْتَبَأْتُهُ وَٱزْدَلَعْتُهُ. (Ibn-Buzurj, TA.)

عَبْءٌ: see the next paragraph. ═ Also *The light of the sun*: (IAạr, O, Ḳ:) and so عَبٌ, (IAạr, O, Ḳ, &c.,) of the former of which IAạr says that it is not known whether it be a dial. var. of the latter or the original thereof; and he says also that عَبْوَةٌ signifies the same; (TA;) or so عَبْوٌ; (TA in art. عبو;) the pl. of which is عَبًى: (TA in that art. and in the present also:) so too does عُبٌّ, (Ḳ in art. عب,) accord. to some. (TA in that art.)

عِبْءٌ *A load*, or *burden*, (Ṣ, O, Mṣb,* Ḳ, TA,) of goods, or merchandise, &c.; (TA;) or *such as a debt, or some other reponsibility that one takes upon himself*: (Lth, TA:) *a weight*, (Mṣb, Ḳ,) *of debt, &c.*, (Mṣb,) or *of anything*: (Ḳ:) pl. أَعْبَآءٌ. (Ṣ, O, Mṣb.) One says, حَمَلْتُ أَعْبَآءَ القَوْمِ, i. e. [*I bore*] *the weights*, or *burdens, of debt, &c., of the people*, or *party*. (Mṣb.) —— And *A half-load*; or *burden borne on one side of a beast, equiponderant to another on the other side*; syn. عِدْلٌ; (Ṣ, O, Ḳ;) *of goods* [*&c.*]: *each of what are termed* عِبْآنِ: pl. as above. (Ṣ, O.) —— And [hence] *A like*; as also ↓ عَبْءٌ: (Ṣ, O, Ḳ:) pl. as above. (TA.) One says, هٰذَا عِبْءُ هٰذَا *This is the like of this*. (TA.)

عَبَآءٌ: see the next paragraph. ═ Also, (Ḳ, TA,) applied to a man, (TA,) *Stupid, dull*, or *heavy*: (Ḳ, TA:) like عَبَامٌ. (TA.) [But see عَبًا, in art. عبى.]

عَبَآءَةٌ, (Mṣb, Ḳ, TA,) as also عَبَايَةٌ, (Mṣb, TA,) a dial. var., with ى in the place of the ء, (Mṣb,) or the ء is a substitute for ى, (TA,) and ↓ عَبَآءٌ, (Ḳ,) or this is a pl., like عَبَآءَاتٌ, (Mṣb,) [or rather the former of these two is a coll. gen. n. of which عَبَآءَةٌ is the n. un.,] *A well-known* [*sort of woollen garment of the kind called*] كِسَآء, (L, Ḳ, TA,) *in which are* [*generally*] *stripes*; and said to be *a* جُبَّة [q. v.] *of wool*. (TA.) [See also art. عبى: and for a description and representation of the عباية now most commonly worn in Egypt and Arabia and Syria, see my "Modern Egyptians."]

مَعْبَأٌ i. q. مَذْهَبٌ [as meaning *A way of thinking to which one takes as a tenet*]: (O, Ḳ:) from عَبَأَ لَهُ "he thought it," &c. (O.)

مِعْبَأَةٌ *The piece of rag used by a woman menstruating*. (IAạr, O, Ḳ. [See 8.])

عبث

1. عَبَثَهُ, aor. ـِ, (Ṣ, A,* O, Ḳ,*) inf. n. عَبْثٌ, (Ṣ, O,) *He mixed*, or *mingled*, (Ṣ, A, O, Ḳ,) *it*. (Ṣ, O.) —— [Hence,] عَبَثَ, aor. as above, (Ḳ,) and so the inf. n., (Ṣ, O,) *He made*, or *prepared*, عَبِيثَة [q. v.]: (Ṣ, O, Ḳ:) or so عَبَثَ عَبِيثَةً; as also ↓ اِعْتَبَثَهَا. (O.) One says, عَبَثَتِ المَرْأَةُ, meaning *The woman poured out what was moist of the* [*preparation of curd called*] أَقِط, *when it was cooked, on what was dry thereof, upon the* [*mat*, or *cloth, called*] مِشْرَ, or مَشْرَ, [the former accord. to the O and a copy of the Ṣ, and the latter accord. to another copy of the Ṣ,] *in order that what was dry thereof might bear* [*and not suffer to pass through the* مشر] *what was moist*. (Aboo-Ṣá'id El-Kilábee, Ṣ, O.) And عَبَثَ الأَقِطَ, aor. and inf. n. as above, *He dried the* أقط *in the sun*: or *he mixed it with clarified butter*: and عَبَتَهُ, with ت, is a dial. var. thereof. (TA.) ═ عَبِثَ, aor. ـَ, (Ṣ, Mgh, O, Mṣb, Ḳ,) inf. n. عَبَثٌ, (Ṣ, Mgh, O, Mṣb,) *He played*, or *sported*; (Ṣ, Mgh, O, Mṣb, Ḳ;) *and mingled together unprofitable actions*; (Mgh;) or *and did that in which was no profit*; (Mṣb;) or *he played with that which did not concern him and for which he did not care*. (TA.) You say, عَبِثَ بِهِ *He played*, or *sported*, [or *amused himself*,] *with him*, or *it*; (TA;) and ↓ تعبّث به [which signifies the same]. (Ḥam p. 710.) —— And عَبِثَ بِهِ الدَّهْرُ † [*Fortune made sport with him*]; a phrase alluding to the mutability of fortune. (Mṣb.) —— And عَبِثَ فِى مَنَامِهِ, occurring in a trad., means † *He moved his hands*, or *arms, in his sleep, like him who is pushing away or taking, or giving or receiving*. (TA.)

4: see 1, second sentence.

5: see 1, last sentence but two.

عَبَثٌ *Play*, or *sport*, (Ṣ, O, TA,) *in which is no profit to be reckoned*, or *of which no account is to be made*. (TA.) [See also عَبِثَ, of which it is the inf. n.]

عَبْثَةٌ, with the ب quiescent, *A single act of* عبث [or *play, sport, &c.*]. (Ṣ, O.)

عَبِيثٌ: see عَبِيثَةٌ. —— Also, in a certain dial., i. q. مَصْلٌ [q. v.: accord. to ISk, this latter means The *fluid that flows from* أقط *when it is cooked*]. (L, TA) — Also *A certain sweet-smelling plant.* (O, Ḳ.)

عَبِيثَةٌ [The *preparation of curd called*] أقط *whereof what is moist is poured out, when it is cooked, upon what is dry thereof, and mixed with it:* (Aboo-Ṣá'id El-Kilábee, Ṣ, O:) or أَقِطٌ مُعَالَجٌ [i. e. اقط *prepared by mixing,* or *otherwise,* app. *in the manner described above*]: (Ḳ: [see also 1, third sentence:]) and أقط *and* سَوِيق [or *meal of parched barley* or *wheat*] *mixed with clarified butter, and then eaten:* (Ṣ, O:) or أقط *mixed with clarified butter:* and أقط *pounded with dates,* or *with dried dates, and then eaten,* and *drunk;* as also ▼ عَبِيثٌ: (TA:) or it signifies, (Ḳ,) or signifies also, (Ṣ, O,) طَعَام [app. meaning *wheat*] *which is cooked, and in which locusts* (جَرَاد) *are put:* (Ṣ, O, Ḳ:) and *wheat and barley mixed together:* so in the saying, جَآءَ فُلَانٌ بِعَبِيثَةٍ فِى وِعَائِهِ [*Such a one came with wheat and barley mixed together in his provision-bag*]: pl. عَبَائِثُ. (Ṣ, O.) — Also † *Sheep,* or *goats, mixed together.* (TA.) One says, ظَلَّتِ الغَنَمُ عَبِيثَةً وَاحِدَةً † [*The sheep,* or *goats, became one mixed flock* or *herd*]; and so بَكِيلَةً وَاحِدَةً: this is when sheep, or goats, meet others and enter among them and become mixed with them: it is a proverb. (Ṣ, O.) — And عَبِيثَةُ النَّاسِ † *The mixed sorts of men* or *of the people,* (Ṣ, O, Ḳ, TA,) *who are not from one ancestor, and who are congregated from various,* or *sundry, places.* (TA.) — And عَبِيثَةٌ signifies also ‡ *One whose line of ancestors is mixed* (AO, Ṣ, O, Ḳ, TA) *and vitiated.* (Ṣ, O.)

عَبَّيثٌ One *who plays,* or *sports, much,* or *often.* (Ḳ. [In the O written عَبِيثٌ, but said in the Ḳ to be like سِكِّينٌ, perhaps a mistranscription for سِكِّيتٌ.])

عَابِثٌ [as part. n. of عَبِثَ] *Playing,* or *sporting,* (Mṣb, TA,) *with that which does not concern him and for which he does not care,* (TA,) *and doing that in which is no profit.* (Mṣb.)

خَصِيفٌ عَوْبَثَانِىٌّ *Flour and clarified butter and dates mixed with fresh milk:* so it is said to mean in the following verse:

إِذَا مَا الخَصِيفُ العَوْبَثَانِىُّ سَآءَنَا
تَرَكْنَاهُ وَٱخْتَرْنَا السَّدِيفَ المُسَرْهَدَا

[*When the mess of flour and clarified butter and dates mixed with fresh milk displeases us, we leave it, and choose the fat camel's hump,* or *the camel's hump cut in pieces*]: (Ṣ, O: [see also خَصِيفٌ:]) this verse is by Náshireh Ibn-Málik, replying to El-Mukhabbal, who reproached him for feeding upon milk. (IB, TA.)

عبد

1. عَبَدَ ٱللّٰهَ, aor. ـُ, inf. n. عِبَادَةٌ (IḲṭṭ, L, Mṣb, &c.) and عُبُودَةٌ and عُبُودِيَّةٌ (IḲṭṭ) and مَعْبَدٌ and مَعْبَدَةٌ, (L,) *He served, worshipped,* or *adored, God; rendered to Him religious service, worship,* or *adoration:* (L:) or *he obeyed God:* (IḲṭṭ:) or *he obeyed God with humility* or *submissiveness; rendered to Him humble,* or *submissive, obedience:* (IAth, L, Mṣb:) [or, inf. n. عِبَادَةٌ, *he did what God approved:* and, inf. n. عُبُودَةٌ, *he approved what God did:* (see the former of these ns. below:)] the verb is used in these senses only when the object is God, or a false god, or the Devil. (TA.) — عَبِدْتُ بِهِ أُوذِيهِ *I was excited against him to annoy, molest, harm,* or *hurt, him.* (O, Ḳ.) — And مَا عَبَدَكَ عَنِّى *What has withheld thee from me?* (IAạr, L.) — عَبُدَ, aor. ـُ, inf. n. عُبُودَةٌ and عُبُودِيَّةٌ, accord. to Lḥ and IḲṭṭ, but A'Obeyd held that there is no verb to these two ns., *He was,* or *became, a slave,* or *in a state of slavery:* or *he was,* or *became, in a state of slavery, his fathers having been so before him;* as also ▼ عُبِدَ. (L.) — Lth read [in the Ḳur v. 65] وَعَبُدَ الطَّاغُوتُ; explaining the meaning to be, *Et-Ṭághoot having become an object of worship;* and saying that عَبُدَ, here, is a verb similar to ظَرُفَ and فَقُهَ: but Az says that in this he has committed a mistake. (L.) — عَبِدَ, aor. ـَ, inf. n. عَبَدٌ (and عَبَدَةٌ, or this is a simple subst., L), *He was,* or *became, angry;* (Fr, Ṣ, O,* L, Mṣb, Ḳ;) [and so ▼ تعبّد, in the Deewán of Jereer, accord. to Freytag;] like أَمِدَ and أَبِدَ and أَحِنَ: (Fr:) and *he was long angry.* (L.) You say, عَبِدَ عَلَيْهِ *He was angry with him.* (Fr.) And El-Farezdaḳ makes it trans. without a prep., saying يَعْبَدُنِى. (L.) — *He disdained,* or *scorned.* (AZ, Ṣ, O, L.) El-Farezdaḳ says,

وَأَعْبَدُ أَنْ أَهْجُو كُلَيْبًا بِدَارِمِ

[*And I disdain to satirize Kuleyb with Dárim:* the former being unworthy to be coupled with the latter even as an object of satire]. (Ṣ, O, L.) [See also عَبِدَ.] — *He denied, disacknowledged,* or *disallowed.* (O, Ḳ.) [See, again, عَبِدَ.] — *He repented, and blamed himself,* (O, Ḳ, TA,) *for having been remiss,* or *having fallen short of doing what he ought to have done.* (TA.) — *He mourned, grieved,* or *was sorrowful.* (L.) — *He was covetous;* or *inordinately,* or *culpably, desirous.* (O, Ḳ.) And عَبِدَ بِهِ *He clave,* or *kept, to it,* or *him, inseparably.* (L.) — And, (O, L, Ḳ,) said of a camel, (L,) *He was,* or *became, affected with mange,* or *scab:* (L:) or *with incurable mange* or *scab:* (O, L:) or *with severe mange* or *scab.* (Ḳ.)

2. عَبَّدَهُ, (Ṣ,* A, O,* Mṣb, Ḳ,*) inf. n. تَعْبِيدٌ; (Ṣ, O, Ḳ;) and ▼ اعبدهُ, (Ṣ, A, O, Ḳ,) inf. n. إِعْبَادٌ; (Ṣ;) and ▼ تعبّدهُ, and ▼ اعتبدهُ, (Ṣ, O, Ḳ,) and ▼ استعبدهُ; (Ṣ,* O,* Mṣb, Ḳ;*) *He made him,* or *took him as, a slave; he enslaved him:* (Ṣ, A, O, Mṣb, Ḳ:) or عَبَّدَهُ and ▼ اعبدهُ (TA) and ▼ تعبّدهُ and ▼ اعتبدهُ (A) *he made him to be as a slave to him.* (A, TA.) See also 1, former half. You say [also] استعبدهُ ▼ الطَّمَعُ *Covetousness made him a slave.* (A.) And أَعْبَدَنِى ▼ فُلَانًا *He made me to possess such a one as a slave:* (A, O, Mṣb, Ḳ:) so accord. to Lth: but Az says that the meaning of أَعْبَدْتُ فُلَانًا as commonly known to the lexicologists is ٱسْتَعْبَدْتُهُ: he adds, however, that he does not deny the meaning assigned by Lth if it can be verified. (L.) ▼ اِعْتَبَدَ مُحَرَّرًا, occurring in a trad., or as some relate it, ▼ أَعْبَدَ, means *He took an emancipated man as a slave:* i. e. he emancipated a slave, and then concealed the act from him, or confined him, and made him to serve him by force; or he took a freeman, and pretended that he was a slave, and took possession of him by force. (L.) — عبّدهُ also signifies *He brought him under,* (namely, a man,) *subdued him,* or *rendered him submissive, so that he did the work of slaves.* (AZ, TA.) عبّد, inf. n. as above, is *syn. with* ذَلَّلَ. (Ṣ, O.) [And hence it has also the following significations, among others indicated by explanations of its pass. part. n. below. — *He rendered* a camel *submissive,* or *tractable.* — And *He beat,* or *trod,* a road, or path, *so as to make it even,* or *easy to walk or ride upon.*] — عبّد [as intrans.], inf. n. as above, *He departed, taking fright, and running away,* or *going away at random:* (O, Ḳ:) or *he hastened,* or *went quickly.* (TA.) And عبّد يَعْدُو *He hastened time after time, running.* (TA.) — مَا عَبَّدَ أَنْ فَعَلَ ذَاكَ, (inf. n. as above, Ṣ,) *He delayed not,* or *was not slow, to do,* or *in doing, that.* (Ṣ, O, Ḳ.*)

4. اعبد as trans.: see 2, former half, in four places. — اعبدوا *They collected themselves together; assembled together.* (Ḳ.) — اعبد القَوْمُ بِالرَّجُلِ *The people,* or *party, beat the man:* (O, Ḳ:) or *collected themselves together and beat him.* (TA.) — أُعْبِدَ بِهِ *His riding-camel became fatigued:* (Ṣ, O, Ḳ:) or *perished;* or *flagged,* or *became powerless;* or *stopped with him:* (Ṣ, O:) or *died,* or *became ill,* or *went away, so that he was obliged to stop:* (L:) *i. q.* أُبْدِعَ بِهِ [q. v.], (Ṣ, O, L, Ḳ,) from which it is formed by transposition. (TA.)

5. تعبّد *He became,* or *made himself, a servant of God; devoted himself to religious services* or *exercises; applied himself to acts of devotion.* (Ṣ, A, O, L, Mṣb, Ḳ.) And تعبّد بِٱلْإِسْلَامِ *He became,* or *made himself, a servant of God by* [*following the religion of*] *El-Islám;* [i. e. *he followed El-Islám as his religion;*] syn. دَانَ بِهِ. (Mṣb in art. دين.) — Also, *He* (a camel) *became refractory, and difficult to manage,* (Ḳ,) *like a wild animal.* (L.) — See also عَبِدَ, first sentence. — تعبّدهُ: see 2, first sentence, in two places. — Also *He called him,* or *invited him, to obedience.* (Mṣb.) — تعبّد البَعِيرَ *He drove away the camel until he became fatigued* (O, Ḳ, TA) *and was obliged to stop.* (TA.)

8: see 2, former half, in three places.

10: see 2, in two places.

R. Q. 2. تَعَبْدَدُوا *They* (a people) *went away*

in parties in every direction. (TA.) [See عَبَادِيدُ.]

عَبْدٌ, originally an epithet, but used as a subst., (Sb, TA,) *A male slave;* (Ṣ, A, O, L, Mṣb, Ḳ;) *i. q.* مَمْلُوكٌ; (L, Ḳ;) [but عَبْدٌ is now generally applied to *a male black slave;* and مَمْلُوكٌ, to *a male white slave;* and this distinction has long obtained;] *contr. of* حُرٌّ; (Ṣ, A, O, L, Mṣb;) as also ▼ عَبْدَلٌ, (L, Ḳ,) in which the ل is augmentative: (IF:) and *a servant,* or *worshipper,* of God, and of a false god, or of the Devil: (Lth, L, &c.:) [you say عَبْدُ ٱللّٰهِ and عَبْدُ الشَّمْسِ &c.: see also عَابِدٌ, which signifies the same; and see the remarks in this paragraph on the pls. عَبِيدٌ and عِبَادٌ and عَبَدَةٌ &c.:] and *a man,* or *human being;* (M, A, L, Ḳ;) as being *a bondman* (مَرْبُوبٌ) *to his Creator;* (L;) applied to *a male* and to *a female;* (Ibn-Ḥazm, TA;) *whether free or a slave:* (Ḳ:) pl. أَعْبُدٌ (Ṣ, O, Mṣb, Ḳ) and أَعْبِدَةٌ and أَعْبَادٌ, (IḲṭṭ, TA,) [all pls. of pauc.,] of which the first is the most commonly known, (Mṣb,) and ▼ عَبِيدٌ and عِبَادٌ, (Ṣ, O, Mṣb, Ḳ,) which two and the first are the most commonly known of all the many pls. of عَبْدٌ, (Mṣb,) عَبِيدٌ being like كَلِيبٌ as pl. of كَلْبٌ, a rare form of pl.; (Ṣ, O;) or, accord. to some, it is a quasi-pl. n.; accord. to Ibn-Málik, فَعِيلٌ occurs as a pl. measure, but sometimes they use it in the manner of a pl. and make it fem., as in the instance of عَبِيدٌ, and sometimes they use it in the manner of quasi-pl. ns. and make it masc., as in the instances of حَجِيجٌ and كَلِيبٌ; (MF;) [accord. to the general and more approved opinion, it is a quasi-pl. n., and therefore fem. and masc., but most commonly fem.;] and further it should be remarked that the common people agree in making a difference between عَبِيدٌ and عِبَادٌ, by the former meaning *slaves* [and by the latter meaning *servants* of God and also simply, with the article ال, *mankind*], saying, هٰؤُلَاءِ عَبِيدٌ *these are slaves,* and هٰذَا عَبْدٌ مِنْ عِبَادِ ٱللّٰهِ [*this is a servant, of the servants of God*]: (Az, L:) [and a distinction is also made between عِبَادٌ and عَبَدَةٌ, respecting which see what follows:] other pls. of عَبْدٌ are عِبْدَانٌ, (Ṣ, O, Ḳ,) like تُمْرَانٌ pl. of تَمْرٌ, (Ṣ, O,) and عُبْدَانٌ, (Ṣ, O, Ḳ,) like جِحْشَانٌ pl. of جَحْشٌ, (Ṣ, O,) and عُبُدٌ, (Ṣ, O, Ḳ,) like سُقُفٌ pl. of سَقْفٌ, (Ṣ, O,) or this is pl. of عَبِيدٌ, like رُغُفٌ pl. of رَغِيفٌ, (Zj,) and is also a pl. of عَابِدٌ, (L,) and some read [in the Ḳur v. 65] عُبُدَ الطَّاغُوتِ, (Akh, Ṣ, O,) and عُبْدٌ (MF) and عُبُودٌ and عُبَّدٌ and عُبَّادٌ and عَبَدَةٌ, (IḲṭṭ, TA,) the last three of which are also pls. of عَابِدٌ: (L:) one says of the worshippers of a plurality of gods, هُمْ عَبَدَةُ الطَّاغُوتِ [*they are the servants of Eṭ-Ṭághoot*]; but the Muslims one calls عِبَادُ ٱللّٰهِ, meaning *the servants,* or *worshippers, of God:* (Lth, L:) [all these are pls. in the proper sense of the term, of the broken class:] and عَبْدُونَ, (O, Ḳ,) a pl. of the sound class, adopted because عَبْدٌ is originally an epithet: (TA:) and [the following, with the exception of the first, and of some which are particularized as being pls. of pls., are also said to be pls., but are properly speaking quasi-pl. ns., namely,] ▼ عَبُدٌ, (O, Ḳ,) accord. to some, who read [in the Ḳur ubi suprà] عَبُدَ الطَّاغُوتِ, making the former a prefixed noun, as meaning *the servants* (خَدَم) *of Eṭ-Ṭághoot;* but it is a n. of the measure فَعُلٌ, like حَذُرٌ and نَدُسٌ, not a pl.; the meaning being *the servant* (خَادِم) *of Eṭ-Ṭághoot;* (Akh, Ṣ, O;) and it is also used by poetic license for عَبْدٌ; (Fr, T, Ṣ, O;) and ▼ عِبِدَّانٌ and ▼ عِبِدَّآءٌ and ▼ عِبِدَّى; (Ṣ, O, Ḳ;) or, accord. to some, the last of these signifies *slaves born in a state of slavery;* and the *female* is termed ▼ عَبْدَةٌ; and Lth says that ▼ عِبِدَّى signifies *a number of slaves born in a state of slavery, generation after generation;* but Az says that this is a mistake, that عِبِدَّى ٱللّٰهِ signifies the same as عِبَادُ ٱللّٰهِ, that it is thus used in a trad., and that عِبِدَّى is applied in another trad. to poor men of the class called أَهْلُ الصُّفَّةِ; (L;) and ▼ عُبُدَّآءٌ and ▼ عِبِدَّةٌ and ▼ عِبَادٌ (IḲṭṭ, TA) and ▼ مَعْبَدَةٌ, like مَشْيَخَةٌ, (T, O, Ḳ,) and ▼ مَعْبُودَآءُ (Yaạkoob, Ṣ, O, Ḳ) and ▼ مَعْبُودَى, (IḲṭṭ, TA,) and [pl. pl.] ▼ مَعَابِدُ, (O, Ḳ,) said to be pl. of مَعْبَدَةٌ; (TA;) and pl. pl. أَعَابِدُ, (Ḳ,) pl. of أَعْبُدٌ; (TA;) and عَبِيدُونَ, (Es-Suyooṭee, MF,) app. pl. of ▼ عَبِيدٌ. (MF.) فَٱدْخُلِي فِي عِبَادِي, in the Ḳur lxxxix. 29, means *Then enter thou among my righteous servants:* (Ksh, Bḍ, Jel:) or it means فِي حِزْبِي [*among my peculiar party*]. (Ṣ, O.) — Also ‡ *Ignoble,* or *base-born;* like as حُرٌّ is used to signify "generous," "noble," or "well-born." (Mgh in art. حر.) = Also *A certain plant, of sweet odour,* (O, Ḳ, TA,) *of which the camels are fond because it makes the milk to become plentiful, and fattens; it is sharp,* or *hot,* (حَادٌّ O, or حَارٌّ TA,) *in temperament; and when they depasture it they become thirsty, and seek the water:* (O, TA:) so says IAạr. (O.) = And *A short and broad* نَصْل [or *arrow-head,* or *spear-head,* or *blade*]. (AA, O,* Ḳ.)

عَبَدٌ: see عَابِدٌ.

عَبُدٌ: see the paragraph commencing with عَبْدٌ, latter half.

عَبِدٌ and ▼ عَابِدٌ (but the latter is rarely used, Ibn-'Arafeh) *Angry.* (L.) And (both words) *Disdaining,* or *disdainful; scorning,* or *scornful.* (L.) Accord. to AA, العَابِدِينَ in the words of the Ḳur [xliii. 81], إِنْ كَانَ لِلرَّحْمٰنِ وَلَدٌ فَأَنَا أَوَّلُ ▼ العَابِدِينَ, means *The disdainers,* or *scorners,* and *the angry:* (Ṣ,* L:) but Ibn-'Arafeh rejects this assertion: (TA:) these words are variously explained; as meaning *There is not to the Compassionate a son; and I am the first of the angry disdainers* or *scorners* of the assertion that there is: or, *and I am the first of the deniers* of this assertion: or, *and I am the first of the worshippers* of God according to the unitarian doctrine, or, *of the worshippers of God* of this people: or *if there were to the Compassionate a son, I would be the first of* his *worshippers:* or *if there be to the Compassionate a son, I am the first of worshippers;* but I am not the first worshipper of God: or, accord. to Az, the best interpretation is one ascribed to Mujáhid; i. e. *if there be to the Compassionate a son* in your opinion, *I am the first of those who have worshipped* God alone, and who have thus charged you with uttering a falsehood in this your assertion. (L.)

عَبْدَةٌ: see عَبْدٌ, latter half.

عَبَدَةٌ [as a subst. from عَبِدَ (q. v.), *Anger.* —] *Disdain,* or *scorn;* (Ṣ, O, L, Ḳ;) *disdain occasioned by a saying at which one is ashamed, and from which one abstains through scorn and pride:* (L:) or *intense disdain* or *scorn.* (A.) — *Strength:* so in the saying مَا لِثَوْبِكَ عَبَدَةٌ [*There is not any strength to thy garment*]. (Ṣ, O.) — *Strength and fatness:* (Ṣ, O, Ḳ:) thus in the phrase نَاقَةٌ ذَاتُ عَبَدَةٍ [*A she-camel possessing strength and fatness*]. (Ṣ, O.) And one says [also] نَاقَةٌ عَبَدَةٌ [if this be not a mistake for the phrase here next preceding] meaning *A strong she-camel.* (L, Mṣb.) — And *Lastingness,* or *continuance;* syn. بَقَآءٌ; (O, L, Ḳ, TA;) in some lexicons نَقَآءٌ; (TA;) *and strength.* (L.) One says, لَيْسَ لِثَوْبِكَ عَبَدَةٌ meaning *There is not to thy garment any lastingness, or continuance, and strength.* (Lḥ, L.) = Also *A stone with which perfume is bruised,* or *pounded.* (O, L, Ḳ.)

عَبْدِىٌّ [a rel. n. from عَبْدٌ]. الدَّرَاهِمُ العَبْدِيَّةُ *Certain Dirhems, which were superior to those of late times, and of greater weight.* (O, Ḳ, TA.)

عَبْدِيَّةٌ, as a subst.: see عِبَادَةٌ: — and عُبُودِيَّةٌ.

عِبِدَّةٌ: see عَبْدٌ, last quarter.

عِبِدَّى: see عَبْدٌ, latter half, in two places.

عِبِدَّآءٌ / عِبِدَّانٌ } see عَبْدٌ, latter half.

عَبْدَلٌ: see عَبْدٌ, near the beginning.

عَبْدَلِىٌّ and عَبْدَلَاوِىٌّ [both post-classical, the latter, which is the more common, said by Forskål to be an appellation of the *Cucumis chate,* which is app. from قِثَّآء, denoting several species of cucumber; but it is] *a sort of melon,* [*abounding in Egypt, of little flavour, eaten with sugar,*] said to be thus called in relation to 'Abd-Allah Ibn-Ṭáhir, a governor of Egypt on the part of El-Ma-moon. ('Abd-El-Laṭeef: see pp. 52 and 54 of the Ar. text, and pp. 34 and 35, and 125-7, of De Sacy's Transl. and Notes: and see also Forskål's Flora Ægypt. Arab. pp. lxxvi. and 168.) [See also عَجُّورٌ.]

عَبِيدٌ: see عَبْدٌ, first and last quarters.

عُبَيْدٌ [dim. of عَبْدٌ. — And, used as a proper name,] *The son of the desert,* or *of the waterless desert:* thus expl. by El-Ḳanánee to Fr. (O.) — And [hence] أُمُّ عُبَيْدٍ *The desert,* or *waterless desert,* (Fr, O, Ḳ,) *that is vacant,* or *desolate:* (Ḳ:) or *the land that is vacant,* or *desolate:* (El-Ḳanánee, Fr, O:) or *the land that the rain has missed.* (O, Ḳ.) And sometimes it is used as meaning † *Great calamity:* (TA:) it is said in a prov., وَقَعُوا فِى أُمِّ عُبَيْدٍ تَصَايَحُ حَيَّاتُهَا [for تَتَصَايَحُ, lit. *They became,* or *found themselves, in the desert,* &c., *of which the serpents were hissing, one at another*], meaning † [*they fell*] *into a great calamity.* (Meyd, TA.)

عِبَادَةٌ (Ṣ, IḲṭṭ, A, IAth, L, Ḳ) and ▼ عُبُودِيَّةٌ and ▼ عُبُودَةٌ (IḲṭṭ, Ḳ) and ▼ عَبْدِيَّةٌ (Fr, Ḳ) and ▼ مَعْبَدٌ and ▼ مَعْبَدَةٌ (L) [all said by some to be inf. ns., except the fourth,] *Religious service, worship, adoration,* or *devotion;* (L;) *obedience:* (Ṣ, IḲṭṭ, A, Ḳ:) *obedience with humility* or *submissiveness; humble,* or *submissive, obedience:* (IAth, L:) or عِبَادَةٌ signifies the *Doing what God approves:* and ▼ عُبُودَةٌ, the *approving what God does:* and the primary signification of ▼ عُبُودِيَّةٌ is *humility,* and *submissiveness:* (Ṣ, A, O:) عِبَادَةٌ is rendered only to God, or a false god, or the Devil. (TA.)

عُبُودَةٌ: see the next preceding paragraph, in two places: — and see عُبُودِيَّةٌ.

الْعُبَيْدَةُ *The* [*portion,* or *appertenance, of the stomach, of a ruminant, called*] فَحِث, (O, Ḳ, TA,) also called حَفِث [q. v.]. (TA.)

عُبُودِيَّةٌ The *state,* or *condition, of a slave; slavery; servitude;* (Ṣ, O, L, Mṣb;) as also ▼ عُبُودَةٌ (Ṣ, O, L) and ▼ عَبْدِيَّةٌ (O, Mṣb) and ▼ تَعْبِدَةٌ. (L.) — See also عِبَادَةٌ, in two places.

عَبَّادٌ: see عَبْدٌ, last quarter.

عَبَابِيدُ and عَبَادِيدُ, each a pl. having no sing., *Parties of people* (Ṣ, O, Ḳ) *going in every direction:* (Ṣ, O:) and *horsemen going in every direction.* (Ḳ.) One says, صَارَ الْقَوْمُ عَبَادِيدَ and عَبَابِيدَ *The people became divided into parties going in every direction.* (Ṣ, O.) And ذَهَبُوا عَبَادِيدَ and عَبَابِيدَ *They went away in parties in every direction.* (TA.) — Also (both words, Ḳ, or the latter [only], TA,) *Far-extending roads:* (Ḳ:) or *diverse and far-extending roads:* said to be used in this sense not with respect to coming, but only with respect to dispersion, and going away. (TA.) — Also (or the former [only], TA) *Hills such as are called* آكَام or إِكَام [pls. of أَكَمَةٌ]. (Ḳ, TA.) — And one says, مَرَّ رَاكِبًا عَبَادِيدَهُ *He passed,* or *went away, riding upon the extremities of his buttocks.* (O, Ḳ.)

عَبَادِيدِىٌّ (Ṣ, O) and عَبَابِيدِىٌّ (O, TA) rel. ns. from عَبَادِيدُ (Ṣ, O) and عَبَابِيدُ (O, TA) thus formed because the said ns. have no sings., (Sb, Ṣ, O, TA,) *Of,* or *relating to, parties of people going in every direction.* (Ṣ, O.)

عَابِدٌ *A server, a worshipper,* or *an adorer,* of God: (L:) *an obeyer* of God *with humility,* or *submissiveness:* (L, Mṣb:) [*a devotee:*] *a unitarian:* (L:) by a secondary application, used of him who takes for his god other than the True God, such as an idol, and the sun, &c.: (Mṣb:) pl. عُبَّادٌ and عَبَدَةٌ (L, Mṣb) and عُبُدٌ and عُبَّدٌ, all of which are also pls. of عَبْدٌ [q. v.]: (L:) [and quasi-pl. n. ▼عَبَدٌ (like as خَدَمٌ is of خَادِمٌ), accord. to a reading of a phrase in the Ḳur v. 65, as expl. by some.] — And *A servant:* a meaning said to be tropical. (TA.) — See also عَبِدٌ, in two places.

تَعْبِدَةٌ: see عُبُودِيَّةٌ.

مَعْبَدٌ: see عِبَادَةٌ: — and see also مُتَعَبَّدٌ.

مِعْبَدٌ *A shovel,* or *spade, of iron;* syn. مِسْحَاةٌ: (Ḳ:) pl. مَعَابِدُ. (TA.)

مَعْبَدَةٌ, and the pl. مَعَابِدُ: see عَبْدٌ, last quarter: — and for the former see also عِبَادَةٌ.

مُعَبَّدٌ, applied to a camel, *Rendered submissive,* or *tractable; broken,* or *trained;* syn. مُذَلَّلٌ: (A, L:) or *anointed with tar,* (Ṣ, O, Ḳ,) *and rendered submissive,* or *tractable:* (Ṣ, O:) or *whose whole skin is anointed with tar:* (Sh:) or *mangy,* or *scabby, whose fur has fallen off by degrees, and which is set apart from the other camels to be anointed with tar:* or *rendered submissive by the mange,* or *scab:* or *affected with the mange,* or *scab;* or *with incurable mange* or *scab.* (L. [And, applied to a camel, it has other meanings, which see in what follows.]) [And hence, app.,] سَفِينَةٌ مُعَبَّدَةٌ *A ship,* or *boat, tarred:* (AO, Ṣ, O, L, Ḳ:) or *smeared with fat,* or *oil.* (AO, L.) — Applied to a road, *Beaten;* syn. مُذَلَّلٌ; (Ṣ, A, O, Ḳ;) *trodden;* (Az, TA;) or *travelled by many passengers going to and fro:* (TA:) and *syn. with* مُذَلَّلٌ as applied to other things also. (Ḳ.) — And [hence] *A wooden pin, peg,* or *stake.* (Az, O, Ḳ, TA. [In the CḲ, الْمُوَتَّدُ is erroneously put for الوَتِدُ.]) So in the following verse of Ibn-Muḳbil:

• وَضَمَّنْتُ أَرْسَانَ الجِيَادِ مُعَبَّدًا •
• إِذَا مَا ضَرَبْنَا رَأْسَهُ لَا يُرَنَّحُ •

[*And I made a wooden peg to be a guarantee for the ropes of the coursers: when we beat its head, it did not wabble*]. (Az, O, TA.) — Also *Honoured,* or *treated with honour,* (L, Ḳ,) *and served;* applied to a camel. (L.) Thus it has two contr. significations. (Ḳ.) — And A camel *left unridden.* (O, L.) — And, applied to a stallion [camel], *Excited by lust,* or *by vehement lust.* (O, Ḳ.) — Also, applied to a country, or tract of land, *In which is no footprint,* or *track, nor any sign of the way, nor water:* (O, Ḳ:) you say بَلَدٌ مُعَبَّدٌ. (O.)

مَعْبُودَى and مَعْبُودَآءُ: see عَبْدٌ, last quarter.

مُتَعَبَّدٌ [and ▼ مَعْبَدٌ] *A place appropriated to religious services or exercises, or acts of devotion.* (TA.)

عبر

1. عَبَرَهُ, aor. ـُ, (Ṣ, Mgh, O, Mṣb, Ḳ,) inf. n. عَبْرٌ and عُبُورٌ, [the latter of which is the more common,] (Ṣ, O, Mṣb, Ḳ,) *He crossed it, went across it,* or *passed over it,* (Mgh, Mṣb, Ḳ,) *from one side thereof to the other;* (Mṣb, Ḳ;) namely, a river, (Ṣ, Mgh, O, Mṣb, Ḳ,*) and a valley, (Ḳ, TA,) &c. (Ṣ, Mgh.) — [Hence,] عَبَرَ بِهِ الْمَآءَ: see 2. — عَبَرَ السَّبِيلَ, (Mṣb, Ḳ,) aor. ـُ, inf. n. عُبُورٌ, (TA,) *He travelled,* or *passed along, the way,* or *road;* (Mṣb, Ḳ;*) as though he cut it, or furrowed it. (Ḳ,* TḲ.) — And hence, (TA,) عَبَرَ, (aor. as above, Ṣ,) ‡ *He died:* (Ṣ, O, Mṣb, Ḳ:) as though he travelled the road of life: or, as F says in the B, as though he crossed over the bridge of the present world or life. (TA.) A poet says,

• فَإِنْ نَعْبُرْ فَإِنَّ لَنَا لُمَاتٍ •
• وَإِنْ نَغْبُرْ فَنَحْنُ عَلَى نُذُورِ •

i. e. ‡ *So if we die, there are others like to us; and if we remain alive, we are* waiting for that which must necessarily come to pass, as though we were *bound by vows* to meet it. (Ṣ, O.) — And عَبَرَتِ السَّحَائِبُ, aor. as above, inf. n. عُبُورٌ, *The clouds travelled,* or *passed along, quickly.* (TA.) — عَبَرَ الرُّؤْيَا: see 2, in two places. — And [hence, perhaps,] عَبَرْتُ الطَّيْرَ, aor. ـُ and ـِ, (O, Ḳ,) inf. n. عَبْرٌ, (TA,) i. q. زَجَرْتُهَا [*I augured from the flight,* or *alighting-places,* or *cries,* &c., *of the birds;* or *I made the birds to fly away in order that I might augur from their flight,* &c.]. (O, Ḳ.) — And عَبَرَ الكِتَابَ, aor. ـُ, inf. n. عَبْرٌ, (Aṣ, Ṣ, A,* O, Ḳ,*) *He meditated upon, endeavouring to understand it,* or *he considered, examined,* or *studied,* (Aṣ, Ṣ, O, Ḳ,) or *he read mentally,* (A,) *the book,* or *writing, not raising his voice in doing so,* (Aṣ, Ṣ, A, O, Ḳ,) i. e. *in reading it.* (Ḳ.) And you say, ▼ اِعْتَبَرَ بَعْضَ الكِتَابِ بِبَعْضٍ, meaning عَبَرَهُ [i. e. *He considered and compared one part of the book,* or *writing, with another part, in order to understand it*]. (TA.) — And عَبَرَ الْمَتَاعَ, and الدَّرَاهِمَ, (Ḳ, TA,) aor. ـُ, inf. n. عَبْرٌ, (TA,) *He examined what was the weight of the goods,* and *of the dirhems, and what they were.* (Ḳ, TA.) And you say, ▼ اِعْتَبَرْتُ الدَّرَاهِمَ فَوَجَدْتُهَا أَلْفًا, meaning عَبَرْتُهَا, i. e. *I tried,* or *examined, the dirhems, and found them to be a thousand.* (Mṣb.) — See also 8, second sentence. — عَبِرَ, with kesr, aor. ـَ, inf. n. عَبَرٌ; (Ṣ;) or عَبَرَ, inf. n. عَبْرٌ; (Ḳ;) [but the former seems to be the more correct, as will be seen from what follows;] and ▼ استعبر; (A, O, Ḳ;) *He shed tears; his eyes,* or *eye, watered.* (Ṣ, A, Ḳ, TA.) And عَبِرَتْ عَيْنُهُ *His eye shed tears,* or *watered;* (Ṣ, O;) as also ▼ استعبرت. (Ṣ.) — And عَبِرَ, aor. ـَ, inf. n. عَبَرٌ; (AZ, T, O,* L, TA;) or عَبَرَ, inf. n. عَبْرٌ; (Ḳ; [but see above;]) *He grieved,* or *mourned; was sorrowful, sad,* or *unhappy.* (AZ, T, O, L, Ḳ, TA.) مَا لَهُ سَهِرَ وَعَبِرَ [*What aileth him? May he be sleepless by night, and may he grieve,* or *mourn:*]

is a form of imprecation against a man, used by the Arabs. (TA.) And عَبِرَتْ, inf. n. عَبَرٌ, means *She became bereft of her child*, or *children, by death.* (A.) [See عُبْرٌ.]

2. عَبَّرَهُ بِالمَآءِ, (Lḥ, Ḳ,) inf. n. تَعْبِيرٌ; (TA;) and عَبَّرَ ▼ بِهِ المَآءَ, (Lḥ, Ḳ,) and النَّهْرَ; (TA;) *He made him to cross, go across,* or *pass over,* or *he conveyed him across, the water,* (Lḥ, Ḳ, TA,) and *the river.* (TA.) ═ عَبَّرَ الرُّؤْيَا, (Ṣ, O, Mṣb, Ḳ,) inf. n. as above; (Ṣ, O;) and ▼ عَبَرَهَا, (Ṣ, A, O, Mṣb, Ḳ,) [which is less common, but more chaste,] aor. ـُ, (Ṣ, O,) inf. n. عِبَارَةٌ (Ṣ, A, O, Mṣb, Ḳ) and عَبْرٌ; (A, Mṣb, Ḳ;) *He interpreted,* or *explained, the dream,* (Ṣ, A, O, Mṣb, Ḳ,) *and told its final sequel* or *result:* (A, O, Ḳ:) or the former verb has an intensive signification: (Mṣb:) and تَعْبِيرٌ has a more particular [or more restricted] meaning than تَأْوِيلٌ: it is said to be from عَبَرَ الكِتَابَ [q. v.]; or, as some say, it is from عِبْرٌ signifying the "side" of a river, because the interpreter of the dream considers the two sides thereof, and meditates upon every particular of it from its beginning to its end. (TA.) In the phrase of the Ḳur [xii. 43], إِنْ كُنْتُمْ لِلرُّؤْيَا تَعْبُرُونَ ▼, the ل is termed لَامُ التَّعْقِيبِ [the ل of succedaneousness], because it is succedaneous to the connection termed إِضَافَة [i. e. the phrase is succedaneous to إِنْ كُنْتُمْ عَابِرِى الرُّؤْيَا *If ye be interpreters of the dream*]: (O, TA:) or it is inserted as an explicative: (Zj, TA:) the phrase is similar to إِنْ كُنْتَ لِلْمَالِ جَامِعًا. (Ṣ, O.) — عَبَّرَ عَمَّا فِى نَفْسِهِ, (A, Ḳ, TA,) inf. n. as above, (TA,) *He declared, spoke out clearly* or *plainly,* or *explained, what was in his mind.* (A,* Ḳ,* TA.) And اللِّسَانُ يُعَبِّرُ عَمَّا فِى الضَّمِيرِ *The tongue declares,* or *explains, what is in the mind.* (Ṣ,* O,* Mṣb.) And عَبَّرَ عَنْهُ غَيْرُهُ *Another spoke,* or *spoke out,* or *explained, for him;* (L, Ḳ,* TA;) he (the latter) being unable to say what he would. (L, TA.) And عَبَّرْتُ عَنْ فُلَانٍ *I spoke for such a one.* (Ṣ, O, Mṣb.) [Hence, يُعَبِّرُ عَنْ كَذَا, said of a word or phrase, *It expresses the meaning of, signifies,* or *denotes, such a thing.* And يُعَبَّرُ بِهِ عَنْ كَذَا *The meaning of such a thing is expressed thereby;* or *such a thing is signified,* or *denoted, thereby.*] — عَبَّرَ الدَّنَانِيرَ, (A,) or الذَّهَبَ, (Ḳ,) inf. n. as above, (A, Ḳ,) *He weighed the deenárs,* (A,) or *the gold,* (Ḳ,) *deenár by deenár:* (A, Ḳ:) or عَبَّرَهُ signifies *he weighed it* (a thing), or *measured it, without extraordinary care:* (Ḳ,* TA:) and تَعْبِيرُ الدَّرَاهِمِ, *the weighing of the dirhems collectively, after making divisions of them.* (Ṣ, O, TA.) ═ عَبَّرَ بِهِ, (Ḳ, TA,) inf. n. as above, (TA,) signifies أَرَاهُ عُبْرَ عَيْنِهِ (Ḳ, TA, in the CḲ عَيْنَيْهِ,) i. e. *He showed him what would make his eye to weep:* or *what would make his eye hot.* (TA.) Dhu-r-Rummeh says,

• عَلَى مَلْقِيَاتٍ يُعَبِّرْنَ بِالعُفْرِ •

[*Upon swiftly-running mares that show the mountain kids,* in the swiftness of their pace, *what makes their eyes to weep* from envy]. (TA.) And you say also, عَبَّرَ عَيْنَيْهِ, meaning *He made his eyes to weep.* (TA.) — Also *He destroyed him:* (Ḳ, TA:) as though he showed him what would make his eye to weep, or make it hot. (TA.) — And *He caused him to fall into difficulty,* or *distress.* (A.) And *It* (an affair, or event,) *was,* or *became, difficult,* or *distressing, to him.* (O, Ḳ.)

8. اعتبر *He became admonished,* or *reminded; he took warning,* or *example:* in this sense the verb is used in the Ḳur lix. 2: and you say, اِعْتَبَرَ بِمَا مَضَى *He became admonished* or *reminded,* or *he took warning* or *example, by what passed:* (Mṣb:) and السَّعِيدُ مَنِ اعْتَبَرَ بِغَيْرِهِ وَالشَّقِىُّ مَنِ اعْتَبَرَ بِهِ غَيْرُهُ [*The fortunate is he who takes warning by others, and the unfortunate is he by whom others take warning*]. (Kull p. 60.) And عَبْرٌ [as inf. n. of ▼ عَبَرَ, aor. ـُ,] signifies the same as اِعْتِبَارٌ [as inf. n. of اِعْتَبَرَ in the sense expl. above]: (Fr, O, L, Ḳ, TA:) whence the saying of the Arabs, اَللّٰهُمَّ ٱجْعَلْنَا مِمَّنْ يَعْبُرُ الدُّنْيَا وَلَا يَعْبُرُهَا, (Fr, O, L, TA,) with fet-ḥ to the ب of يعبر in the first case, and with ḍamm to it in the second case, (TA,) meaning *O God, make us to be of those who take warning,* or *example, by the present world, and do not* [*pass through it* or] *die quickly,* or *soon,* until they content Thee by obedience: (Fr, O, L, TA:) in the copies of the Ḳ, مِمَّنْ يَعْبُرُ الدُّنْيَا وَلَا يَعْمُرُهَا, the former verb with ب [and ḍamm], and the latter with م [and ḍamm]: and in the A is given, as a trad., أَعْبُرُوا الدُّنْيَا وَلَا تَعْمُرُوهَا: but the reading given by Ṣgh and in the L is pronounced by MF to be the right. (TA.) See also عِبْرَةٌ. [And see 10, last sentence.] — Also *He took,* or *regarded, what he witnessed,* or *saw,* or *beheld, as an indication,* or *evidence, of what was concealed from him:* (O:) *he compared what was unapparent with what was apparent* [*and so judged of the former from analogy*]: or *he considered the essential properties of things, and their modes of indication, in order that, by the consideration thereof, another thing, of their kind, might become known.* (Kull p. 60.) See, again, عِبْرَةٌ. Ibn-Seereen used to say, أَعْتَبِرُ الحَدِيثَ [*I judge by comparison with what has been transmitted by tradition* from the Prophet]; meaning I interpret a dream according to what has been transmitted by tradition, like as I do according to the Ḳur-án; as when a crow is interpreted as meaning an unrighteous man, and a rib as meaning a woman, in imitation of forms of speech used by the Prophet. (O,* TA.) — See also 1, latter half, in two places. — Also *He accounted,* or *esteemed,* or *regarded,* a thing, *in respect of predicamental order.* (Mṣb.) See, again, عِبْرَةٌ. — [And *He esteemed* a person, or thing; *held* him, or it, *in high estimation* or *regard.* — And *He took* a thing *into account, regarded* it, or *included* it *in a mental view* or *an examination.* Hence the phrase بِٱعْتِبَارِ كَذَا *With regard,* or *respect,* or *with regard had, to such a thing;* in consideration *of such a thing,* or *of the implication thereof;* and *having regard,* or *respect, to such a thing;* as also بِكَذَا and اِعْتِبَارًا لِكَذَا. And بِٱعْتِبَارٍ وَاحِدٍ *Considered in one respect; in one and the same light.* Hence also the phrase,] يُعْتَبَرُ كَذَا لِصِحَّةِ العَقْدِ *Such a thing is made a condition* [or *is taken into account*] *for the soundness,* or *validity, of the contract.* (Mṣb.) — اعتبر مِنْهُ means *He wondered at him,* or *it.* (Ḳ, TA. In the CḲ, منه is omitted.)

10. استعبر [*He desired to cross, go across,* or *pass over,* a river or the like. (See المُسْتَعْبَرُ.)] ═ استعبره الرُّؤْيَا *He asked him to interpret,* or *explain, the dream;* (Ḳ;) *he related to him the dream in order that he might interpret,* or *explain, it.* (Ṣ, O.) — لَقَدْ أَسْرَعْتَ ٱسْتِعْبَارَكَ الدَّرَاهِمَ is a saying mentioned by Aṣ as meaning [*Assuredly thou hast hastened*] *thy drawing forth of the dirhems.* (O.) ═ See also 1, last quarter, in two places. — [Accord. to Golius, استعبر is also syn. with اعتبر in the first of the senses assigned to the latter above; but for this I do not find any authority.]

عُبْرٌ: see عَبْرٌ. ═ عُبْرُ أَسْفَارٍ and عُبْرُ سَفَرٍ: see what here follows.

عُبْرُ ▼ أَسْفَارٍ and عِبْرُ ▼ أَسْفَارٍ (Ṣ, Ḳ) and عُبْرُ أَسْفَارٍ (Ḳ) and عُبْرُ ▼ سَفَرٍ and عِبْرُ ▼ سَفَرٍ and عُبْرُ سَفَرٍ (TA) *A he-camel, and a she-camel, and camels, like a ship* [or *ships*], i. e. *upon which journeys are continually made:* (Ṣ:) or a she-camel *that is strong* (Ḳ, TA) *to journey,* (TA,) [*as though*] *cutting,* or *furrowing, what she passes over,* (Ḳ, TA,) *and upon which journeys are made:* (TA:) and likewise a man (Ḳ, TA) *bold to undertake journeys, vigorous and effective therein, and strong to make them:* and in like manner a he-camel, and camels: (TA:) applied to a sing. and to a pl. (Ḳ, TA) and to a fem.: (TA:) and in like manner also ▼ عُبَارٌ, applied to a he-camel, (Ḳ,) meaning *strong* (O, TA) *to journey;* and so ▼ عِبَارٌ, with kesr, [app. pl. of عَبْرٌ,] applied to camels. (TA.) — Hence one says, إِنَّ فُلَانًا عُبْرٌ ▼ لِكُلِّ عَمَلٍ *Verily such a one is fit, and sufficiently strong, for every work.* (A.) — [Hence likewise] عُبْرٌ signifies Clouds *that travel,* or *pass along, vehemently* [or *quickly*]. (Ḳ.) ═ See also عَبْرٌ. ═ And عُبْرٌ and ▼ عَبَرٌ (Ṣ, O, Ḳ, TA, in the CḲ عُبْرَة and عَبَرَة,) and ▼ عَبْرٌ signify *A weeping with grief:* (TA:) or *heat in the eye, causing it to weep:* (Ṣ, O:) or *heat of the eye.* (Ḳ.) One says, لِأُمِّهِ العُبْرُ, and ▼ العَبَرُ, (Ṣ, A, O, TA,) and ▼ العَبْرُ, meaning *May his mother have weeping with grief:* (TA:) or *heat in the eye, causing it to weep:* (Ṣ, O:) or *may his mother be bereft of her child,* or *children, by death.* (A.) And أَرَاهُ عُبْرَ عَيْنِهِ (Ḳ, TA, in the CḲ عَيْنَيْهِ,) *He showed him what would make his eye to weep:* or *what would make his eye hot.* (TA.) And رَأَى فُلَانٌ عُبْرَ عَيْنَيْهِ *Such a one saw what made his eyes hot.* (Ṣ, O.) And إِنَّهُ لَيَنْظُرُ إِلَى عُبْرِ عَيْنَيْهِ *Verily he looks at that which he dislikes,* or *hates, and at which he weeps.* (A.) And the phrase وَعَبْرُ جَارَتِهَا occurs in the trad. of Umm-Zara, meaning *And, by reason of her chastity and beauty, a cause of weeping to her fellow-wife.* (TA.) ═ عُبْرٌ also signifies Women *bereft of their children by death*; syn. ثُكْلَى: (Ḳ, TA:) as though pl. of عَابِرٌ. (TA.)

عِبْرٌ, (Ṣ, O, Ḳ, TA, in the CḲ عِبْرَة,) and ▼عُبْرٌ, (Ṣ, O,) or ▼عَبْرٌ, (Kr, A, Ḳ, TA, accord. to the CḲ عَبْرَة,) The *bank*, or *side*, (Ṣ, A, O, Ḳ,) of a river, (Ṣ, A, O,) and of a valley. (A, Ḳ.) En-Nábighah Edh-Dhubyánee says, of the Euphrates,

• تَرْمِى أَوَاذِيُّهُ العِبْرَيْنِ بِالزَّبَدِ •

[*Its waves casting foam upon the two banks*]. (Ṣ, O.) And one says, فُلَانٌ فِى ذٰلِكَ العِبْرِ *Such a one is upon that side.* (TA.) ═ See also the next preceding paragraph, in three places.

عَبْرٌ inf. n. of عَبَرَ [q. v.]. (AZ, T, &c.) — See also عِبْرٌ, in two places: — and عَبْرَةٌ.

عُبُرٌ; and its fem., with ة; see عَابِرٌ.

عُبْرٌ: see عُبْرٌ, in two places.

عَبْرَةٌ: see عِبَارَةٌ. ═ Also *A tear*: (TA:) or *a tear before it overflows*: or *a* [*sobbing, or*] *reiteration* [*of the sound*] *of weeping in the bosom*: (A, Ḳ:) or *an overflowing of tears without the sound of weeping*: (TA:) or *a flowing*, or *an oozing, of tears*: (Ṣ, O:) or *grief without weeping*: (A, Ḳ:) pl. عَبَرَاتٌ (O, Ḳ) and ▼عَبَرٌ, (so in the O, [but this, if correct, is a quasi-pl. n.,]) or عِبَرٌ. (Thus in copies of the Ḳ.) Of the first meaning, the following is an ex.:

• وَإِنَّ شِفَائِى عَبْرَةٌ لَوْ سَفَحْتُهَا •

[*And verily my cure would be a tear if I shed it*]: and of the last, the following is an ex.:

• لَكَ مَا أَبْكِى وَلَا عَبْرَةَ بِى •

or, as some relate it, ولا عبرة لى; and the meaning is, *For thy sake I weep, but there is grief in me for myself*: so says Aṣ: (TA:) or in this saying, which is a prov., ما may be redundant, or it may be what is termed مَصْدَرِيَّة; and the meaning is, *For thee I weep*, or *for thee is my weeping, I* [myself] *having no need of weeping.* (Meyd.)

عِبْرَةٌ a subst. from الاِعْتِبَارُ; *An admonition*, or *exhortation*: (Bḍ in iii. 11): *an admonition*, or *exhortation, by which one takes warning* or *example*: (Jel in xxiii. 21:) *a thing by the state*, or *condition, of which one is admonished*, or *reminded, and guided*, or *directed*: (Bḍ in xxiii. 21:) i. q. ▼اِعْتِبَارٌ [lit. *a being admonished*, or *reminded*, &c.; but meaning *a cause of being admonished*, &c.; i. e. *a warning*, or *an example*]: (Jel in xvi. 68:) or اِعْتِبَارٌ بِمَا مَضَى i. e. اِتِّعَاظٌ and تَذَكُّرٌ [meaning, in like manner, *a cause of being admonished*, or *reminded, by what has passed*]: (Mṣb:) *an indication*, or *evidence*, (Bḍ and Jel in xxiv. 44, and Bḍ in xvi. 68,) *whereby one passes from ignorance to knowledge*: (Bḍ in xvi. 68:) *a state* [*of things* or *circumstances*] *whereby, from the knowledge of what is seen, one arrives at the knowledge of what is not seen*; as also ▼اِعْتِبَارٌ: (B, TA:) and *a wonderful thing* [app. *such as serves as a warning* or *an example*]: (A, Ḳ:) pl. عِبَرٌ. (Mṣb, TA.) — And The *account*, or *estimation*, or *regard, in which a thing is held in respect of predicamental order*; as also ▼اِعْتِبَارٌ. (Mṣb.) [Hence the common phrase لَا عِبْرَةَ بِهِ, meaning *No regard is due to it.*] ═ See also عِبَارَةٌ.

عُبْرِىٌّ, applied to the [species of lote-tree called] سِدْر, means *That grows on the banks of rivers, and becomes large*: (Ṣ, O:) an anomalous rel. n. from عِبْرٌ: (TA:) [or a regular rel. n. from عُبْرٌ as syn. with عِبْرٌ:] or, accord. to 'Omárah, *such as is large in the leaves, having few thorns, and taller than the* ضَال: or, as Aboo-Ziyád says, *that has no thorns except such as hurt* [*not* (see سِدْر)]; the thorns [that hurt] being of the سدر called ضال: he does not say, as others do, that it is that which grows upon the water: some assert that *it is also called* عُمْرِىٌّ, the ب being changed into م: (O:) or, as some say, *such as has no trunk*; *and such is only of those that are near to the* عِبْر [or *bank of a river*]: Yaḳoob says that the terms عُبْرِىٌّ and عُمْرِىٌّ are applied to the سدر *that imbibes water*; and that such as does not this is that of the desert, and is the ضَال: AZ says that the سدر, and *such as is large of the* عَوْسَج, are called عُبْرِىٌّ; and عُمْرِىٌّ is applied to the سدر that is old. (TA.) [See also عُمْرِىٌّ.]

عِبْرِىٌّ [*Hebrew*: and *a Hebrew*]. العِبْرِيُّونَ is an appellation of *The Jews* [i. e. *the Hebrews*]. (O.) — And العِبْرِىُّ and ▼العِبْرَانِىُّ, (Ṣ, A, Ḳ,) or العِبْرِيَّةُ (O) and ▼العِبْرَانِيَّةُ, (O, TA,) [*The Hebrew language*;] *the language of the Jews.* (Ṣ, A, O, Ḳ, TA.)

عَبْرَانُ; and its fem. عَبْرَى: see عَابِرٌ, in six places.

العِبْرَانِيَّةُ and العِبْرَانِىُّ: see عِبْرِىٌّ.

عَبْرُ أَسْفَارٍ: see عَبَّارٌ.

الشِّعْرَى العَبُورُ [*The star Sirius*;] *a certain bright star*; (TA;) *one of the* شِعْرَيَانِ, *which* [*in the order of rising*] *is after*, or *behind*, [in the TA, erroneously, "with,"] الجَوْزَآء [here meaning *Gemini*]: (Ṣ, O:) called العبور because of its having crossed the Milky Way. (Ṣ, O, TA.) [See also الشِّعْرَى in art. شعر.] — Hence the saying, عَصَفَتْ دَبُورُهُ وَسَقَطَتْ عَبُورُهُ, expl. in art. دبر.]

عَبِيرٌ *A certain mixture* (Aṣ, Ṣ, O, Mṣb, Ḳ) *of perfumes*, (Mṣb, Ḳ,) *compounded with saffron*: (Aṣ, Ṣ, O:) or, (Ḳ,) with the Arabs (Ṣ, O, TA) of the Time of Ignorance, (TA,) accord. to AO, it means *saffron* (Ṣ, O, Ḳ, TA) *alone*: but in a trad., mention is made of smearing with عبير or with saffron; and this shows عبير to be different from saffron: (Ṣ, O, TA:) IAth says that it is *a sort of perfume, having colour, compounded of certain mixtures.* (TA.) [See a verse cited voce ذَبِيحٌ; and another cited voce رَقْرَقَ.]

عِبَارَةٌ: see the next paragraph, in two places.

عِبَارَةٌ *Speech that passes from the tongue of the speaker to the ear of the hearer.* (TA.) — [And hence, *A passage in a book* or *writing*.] — [Hence also,] *A word, an expression*, or *a phrase.* (Kull p. 60.) — And [*An explanation*, or *interpretation*;] a subst. from عَبَّرَ عَنْهُ; as also ▼عَبَارَةٌ, (L, Ḳ, TA, [the former only in the CḲ,]) and ▼عَبْرَةٌ or ▼عِبْرَةٌ, accord. to different copies of the Ḳ. (TA.) You say, هُوَ حَسَنُ العِبَارَةِ, and, accord. to the M, ▼العَبَارَةِ also, i. e. *He has a good faculty of explaining*, or *of diction*, or *of speaking perspicuously.* (Mṣb.) [And هٰذَا عِبَارَةٌ عَنْ كَذَا *This is a word*, or *an expression*, or *a phrase, for*, or *denoting, such a thing*; lit., *an explanation of such a thing.*] ═ Also *A thing that is made a condition*: or *a thing that is made account of*, or *esteemed*, or *regarded as being of importance.* (Mṣb.)

عَبَّارٌ: see عَبْرُ أَسْفَارٍ. ═ Also *An interpreter*, or *explainer, of dreams.* (TA.)

عَابِرُ سَبِيلٍ *A wayfarer*; *a passenger*; *a person passing along a way* or *road*; (Ṣ, O, TA;) *a traveller*: (TA:) or *one who passes through without abiding*: (Mgh:) pl. عَابِرُو سَبِيلٍ and عُبَّارُ سَبِيلٍ. (TA.) And عَابِرُ السَّبِيلِ *The wayfarer*; *the passer along the way* or *road.* (Mṣb.) إِلَّا عَابِرِى سَبِيلٍ, in the Ḳur [iv. 46], means *Except those who*, wanting something in the mosque, and their houses or tents being distant, [merely *pass through*, or] *enter* the mosque *and go forth* quickly: (TA:) or *except travellers*; for the traveller sometimes wants water [which is found in the mosque]: or, as some say, *except passers through* the mosque, not meaning to pray. (Mṣb, TA.) — Hence عَابِرٌ signifies ‡ *Dying*, or *dead.* (TA. [See 1.]) — [And *Passing*, or *having currency.* Hence,] لُغَةٌ عَابِرَةٌ *An allowable form of word* or *expression*: (Ṣ, Ḳ, TA:) from عَبَرَ signifying "he passed over" a river. (TA.) ═ عَابِرٌ also signifies *Examining* a thing: *examining* a book, or writing, *and considering and comparing one part of it with another, so as to understand it.* (TA.) ═ Also *Shedding tears*, (Ṣ, O,*) applied to a man, and likewise to a woman: and ▼عَبْرَانُ *weeping*, applied to a man; and so [its fem.] ▼عَبْرَى applied to a woman: (Ṣ, O:) or ▼عَبْرَانُ signifies *weeping and grieving*, applied to a man; as also ▼عَبِرٌ; (Ḳ,* TA;) and عَابِرٌ and ▼عَبْرَى and ▼عَبِرَةٌ are applied to a woman in the same sense, (Ḳ,) or as meaning *grieving*: (TA:) pl. [of ▼عَبْرَانُ and عَبْرَى] عَبَارَى, (Ḳ, TA,) like سَكَارَى: (TA:) and عَيْنٌ ▼عَبْرَى means *a weeping eye.* (O, Ḳ,* TA.)

عَنْبَرٌ: see art. عنبر.

مَعْبَرٌ *A place where a river is crossed*; *a ferry*:

(Mgh:) *a bank, or side, of a river, prepared for crossing:* (O, Mṣb, Ḳ:) pl. مَعَابِرُ. (Mgh.)

مَعْبَرٌ *A thing upon which,* (Ṣ, O, Mṣb,) or *by means of which,* (Ḳ,) *one crosses a river;* (Ṣ, O, Mṣb, Ḳ;) whether it be *a boat* [i. e. *a ferry-boat*], (Ṣ, O, Mṣb,) which is also called ▼ مِعْبَرَةٌ, (Az, TA,) or *a bridge,* (Ṣ, O, Mṣb,) or *some other thing:* (TA:) [pl. مَعَابِرُ.]

مِعْبَرَةٌ: see what next precedes.

عبس

1. عَبَسَ, (Ṣ, L, Mṣb,) or عَبَسَ وَجْهَهُ, (A, O, Ḳ, TA,) or وَجْهُهُ, (Bḍ in lxxvi. 10,) aor. ـِ, inf. n. عُبُوسٌ [app. properly used only when the verb is intrans.] (Ṣ, A, O, Mṣb, Ḳ) and عَبْسٌ [app. only when the verb is trans.]; (A, O, Ḳ;) and ▼ عَبَّسَ, (L, Ḳ, TA,) inf. n. تَعْبِيسٌ; (TA;) *He frowned;* [*looked sternly, austerely,* or *morosely;*] or *contracted his face:* (Mṣb:) or *he contracted the part between his eyes:* (L, TA:) or *he grinned,* or *displayed his teeth, frowning,* or *contracting his face,* or *looking sternly, austerely,* or *morosely;* syn. كَلَحَ: (Ṣ, A, O, Ḳ:) or ▼ عبّس has an intensive signification; (Ṣ, O, TA;) عبّس وَجْهَهُ meaning *he did so much:* (Ṣ, O:) or عبّس [alone], *he had* [or *made*] *a hateful face:* but when one displays his teeth, or grins, the epithet كَالِحٌ is applied to him: (TA:) and [in like manner] ▼ تعبّس signifies تَجَهَّمَ, (Ṣ, O, Ḳ,) i. e. *he showed a sour, a crabbed,* or *an austere, face;* (TḲ;) and تَقَطَّبَ [which is syn. with عبّس]. (TA.) — [Hence,] عَبَسَ اليَوْمُ [for عَبَسَ مَنْ شَهِدَ اليَوْمَ *He who witnessed the day frowned,* or *contracted his face,* &c., (see يَوْمٌ عَبُوسٌ,)] means † *the day was,* or *became, distressful, afflictive,* or *calamitous.* (Mṣb.) = عَبِسَ said of camels: see 4. — [Hence,] عَبِسَ said of a man, *He was,* or *became, dirty,* or *filthy.* (TA.) — And said of a garment, *It had dirt,* or *filth, that had dried upon it.* (TA.) — And عَبِسَ الوَسَخُ فِى يَدِهِ (Ṣ, Ḳ, TA) and عَلَى يَدِهِ (TA) *The dirt,* or *filth, dried upon his hand,* or *arm.* (Ṣ, Ḳ, TA.) — And [the inf. n.] عَبَسٌ signifies *A slave's voiding his urine in,* or *on, his bed, when he has a habit of doing so and the effect thereof appears upon his person,* (O, TA,) *by reason of its muchness,* (O,) *and upon his bed:* (TA:) for doing this he may be returned; (O, TA;) but not if it is little and rare. (O.)

2: see the first sentence above, in two places.

4. أَعْبَسَتِ الإِبِلُ *The camels had dried urine and dung clinging upon their tails;* (Ṣ, O, Ḳ;) as also ▼ عَبِسَت, inf. n. عَبَسٌ; (A'Obeyd, TA;) whence, (TA,) عَبِسَتْ فِى أَبْوَالِهَا وَأَبْعَارِهَا, [meaning the same,] a phrase occurring in a trad. (O, TA.)

5: see 1, first sentence.

عَبَسٌ [an inf. n.: see 1, latter part; and see also 4. — Also a subst. signifying] *Urine and dung that have clung to the tails of camels, drying thereon,* (Ṣ, O, Ḳ, TA,) *and on their thighs;* occasioned only by fat: (TA:) and also *dung and urine that have clung to the wool of sheep, or to their tails and the inner sides of the roots of their thighs, becoming dry* [thereon]; syn. وَذَحٌ: (TA:) or *dung and urine that have dried upon the thighs of camels:* (Mgh:) or *urine and dung that dry upon the tails of sheep* or *goats* and *the like:* n. un. with ة. (Mṣb.)

عَبِسٌ [part. n. of عَبِسَ. — And occurring in the A, art. دعب, in the phrase المُنَافِقُ عَبِسٌ قَطِبٌ, in which both of the epithets are app. altered in form to assimilate them to دَعِبٌ and لَعِبٌ by which they are there preceded]: see عَابِسٌ.

عَبُوسٌ: see عَابِسٌ, in two places. — [Hence,] يَوْمٌ عَبُوسٌ † *A distressful, an afflictive,* or *a calamitous, day;* (Ṣ, Mṣb, TA;) as also يَوْمٌ ▼ عَابِسٌ: (TA:) or *a hateful day, on account of which faces frown, or contract themselves,* &c.: (O, Ḳ:) or *a day in which one frowns,* or *contracts his face,* &c. (TA.)

عَبَّاسٌ: see عَابِسٌ, in three places.

عَبَّابِسِىٌّ: see the next paragraph.

عَابِسٌ [and ▼ عَبِسٌ, mentioned above,] A man *frowning,* or *contracting his face:* (Mṣb:) [*grim-faced;* or *looking sternly, austerely,* or *morosely:*] or *contracting the part between his eyes;* &c.: (TA:) and ▼ عبّاس one *who does so much* [or *habitually; stern, austere,* or *morose, in look* or *countenance;* as also ▼ عَبُوسٌ and ▼ مُعَبِّسٌ]: (Mṣb:) or ▼ عَبَّاسٌ and ▼ مُعَبِّسٌ signify a man *having a hateful face:* and ▼ عَبَّابِسِىٌّ, *hateful to encounter* or *meet; stern, austere,* or *morose, in countenance.* (TA.) — [Hence,] العَابِسُ signifies *The lion;* (O, Ḳ;) as also ▼ العَبُوسُ, and ▼ العَبَّاسُ, (IAạr, O, Ḳ,) and ▼ العَنَبَّسُ, (Ṣ, and mentioned in the Ḳ in art. عنبس, q. v.,) [accord. to some,] of the measure فَنَعَّل, (Ṣ,) and ▼ العُنَابِسُ: (Ḳ in art. عنبس:) or *the lion from whom other lions flee.* (TA.) — See also عَبُوسٌ.

العَنَبَّسُ and العُنَابِسُ: see the next preceding paragraph.

مُعَبِّسٌ: see عَابِسٌ, in two places.

عبط

1. عَبَطَ, aor. ـِ, (Ṣ, O, Mṣb, Ḳ,) inf. n. عَبْطٌ, (Ṣ, O, Mṣb, TA,) *He* (a man) *took* a thing [app. *in a sound, or whole, state;* for such a restriction seems to be indicated by what follows, and may have been omitted in the TA by inadvertence]: this is the primary signification. (TA: but only the inf. n. of the verb in this sense is there mentioned.) You say also, عَبَطَهُ المَوْتُ, (Mṣb,) or ▼ اعبطهُ, (Ḳ,) and ▼ اعتبطهُ, (Mṣb, Ḳ,) *Death took him in a youthful, and sound,* or *healthy, state; not diseased, nor old and weak.* (Mṣb,* Ḳ,* TA.) — *He slaughtered* (Ṣ, O, Mṣb) a she-camel, (Ṣ, O,) or a sheep or goat, (Mṣb,) or *stabbed,* or *stuck,* (نَحَرَ,) a beast, [i.e. a camel,] (Ḳ,) *in a sound,* or *healthy, state,* (Mṣb,) *in a state of freedom from disease,* (Ṣ, O, Ḳ,) *and from fracture,* (TA,) [but see عَبِيطٌ,] *and in a fat and youthful condition;* (Ḳ;) as also ▼ اعتبط. (Ṣ, O, Ḳ.) And hence ▼ the latter is used to signify ‡ *He slew* a man *for no crime;* (O;) *he slew* a man *wrongfully, not in retaliation:* (El-Khaṭṭábee:) and †*he wounded.* (O, TA.) [Hence also,] عَبَطَ, (Ṣ,) or عَبَطَ نَفْسَهُ فِى الحَرْبِ, (O, Ḳ,) and بِنَفْسِهِ, (TA,) inf. n. عَبْطٌ, (O,) ‡ *He threw himself, not constrained against his will, into war,* or *fight.* (Ṣ, O, Ḳ, TA.) [And] عَبَطَتْهُ الدَّاهِيَةُ, (Ṣ, O,) or الدَّوَاهِى, (Ḳ,) ‡ *Calamity,* or *calamities, befell him,* (Lth, Ṣ, O, Ḳ,) *without his deserving the same.* (Lth, O, Ḳ, TA.) — ‡ *He made* an udder *to bleed:* (O, Ḳ, TA:) or *he wounded* it, or *made it to bleed, by vehement milking, and squeezing;* from عَبِيطٌ applied to blood, and signifying "fresh:" or *milked* it *to the uttermost, so that blood came forth after the milk.* (L, TA.) And عَبَطَ عَرَقَ الفَرَسِ, (Ḳ,) or عَبَطَ الفَرَسَ, (O, L, TA,) ‡ *He made the horse to run until he sweated.* (O, L, Ḳ, TA.) — *He slit,* or *rent* a garment, or piece of cloth, (Ṣ, O, and so in some copies of the Ḳ and in the TA,) or a thing, (so in other copies of the Ḳ and in the TA,) *when it was whole,* or *sound;* (Ḳ, TA;) aor. ـِ, inf. n. عَبْطٌ and مَعْبَطٌ. (O.) — † *It* (a plant, or herbage,) *clave* the ground. (TA.) — ‡ *He dug* the ground *in a place where it had not been dug before;* (IAạr, O, Ḳ;) as also ▼ اعتبط; (O, Ḳ, TA;) which latter also signifies [simply] † *he dug* the ground. (TA.) — عَبَطَتِ الرِّيحُ وَجْهَ الأَرْضِ ‡ *The wind stripped the surface of the ground;* (O, Ḳ;) as also ▼ اعتبطتهُ. (Ḳ, TA.) — عَبَطَ التُّرَابَ † *He* (an ass, O, TA) *raised the dust* (O, Ḳ, TA) with his hoofs; (O, TA;) as also ▼ اعتبطهُ. (O,* TA.) — عَبَطَ عِرْضَهُ ‡ [*He rent his honour, or reputation;*] *he reviled him; he detracted from his reputation, spoke against him,* or *impugned his character;* as also ▼ اعتبط عرضه: (TA:) عَبَطَ is ‡ *syn. with* غَابَ, (IAạr, O,* Ḳ, TA,) from الغِيبَةُ, not from الغَيْبُوبَةُ; (IAạr, TA;) as also ▼ اعتبط, (Ḳ, TA,) i. q. اِغْتَابَ. (TA.) — And عَبَطَ الكَذِبَ عَلَىَّ *He forged what was false against me;* as also ▼ اعتبطهُ. (Ḳ. [See also the latter below.]) = Also, aor. as above, *It* (a garment, or piece of cloth, or a thing, accord. to different copies of the Ḳ,) *became slit,* or *rent:* thus intrans. as well as trans. (Ḳ.)

4: see 1, near the beginning.

8: see 1, in nine places. — اعتبط عَلَىَّ الكَذِبَ † *He forged against me what was purely false, without excuse.* (Ṣ, O,* TA.) See also 1, last sentence but one. — [Hence the phrase حُذِفَتْ اِعْتِبَاطًا, in the Mughnee, voce إِنْ, expl. in a marginal note in my copy of that work as meaning † *It* (a letter) *is elided for no reason in itself.*]

عَبْطٌ *A pure, an unmixed, lie, without excuse.* (Ṣ, O.) — †*I. q.* رِيبَةٌ [app. here meaning *A thing that induces suspicion, or evil opinion*]. (TA.)

مَاتَ عَبْطَةً *He* (a man, Ṣ, O) *died in a sound,* or *healthy, state, and being a youth,* or *young man.* (Ṣ, O, Mṣb, Ḳ.) — عَبْطَةٌ also signifies ‡ *Evil speech of another; detraction; defamation.* (TA.)

عُبْطَةٌ *Freedom from anything injurious, except a fracture of a bone,* in flesh meat: (Ibn-Buzurj:) or *freshness* therein, and in blood, and in saffron: (Ḳ:) or *pureness,* or *freedom from admixture, and freshness,* in blood. (TA.)

عَبِيطٌ, (A, O, Ḳ,) or عَبِيطَةٌ, (T, Ṣ, Mṣb,) and ↓ مُعْتَبَطَةٌ, (T, Mṣb, TA,) A beast, [meaning a camel,] (Ḳ,) or a she-camel, (Ṣ, TA,) or the second and third applied to a sheep or goat, (T, Mṣb,) *stabbed,* or *stuck,* (A, O, Ḳ,) or *slaughtered,* (T, Ṣ, Mṣb,) *in a sound,* or *healthy, state,* (A,) *in a state of freedom from disease,* (Ṣ, O, Ḳ,) *and from fracture,* (TA,) *and in a fat and youthful condition,* (Ḳ,) or *free from anything injurious except a fracture:* (T, Mṣb:) [*contr. of* عَارِضٌ *and* عَارِضَةٌ: (see the latter of these two words:)] pl. عُبُطٌ (Ḳ) and عِبَاطٌ: (O, Ḳ:) and ↓ مَعْبُوطَةٌ, also, applied to a sheep or goat, signifies *slaughtered in a sound,* or *healthy, state.* (TA.) Also عَبِيطٌ, applied to flesh-meat, signifies *the same:* (Ṣ:) or *in a sound,* or *healthy, state:* (Mṣb:) or *free from anything injurious, except a fracture of a bone;* (T, Mṣb;) so says Ibn-Buzurj: (TA:) or *fresh;* (O, Ḳ;) and so applied to blood, (Mgh, Ḳ,) and to saffron: (Ḳ:) or, applied to blood, *pure; free from admixture;* (Ṣ, O, Mṣb;) *and fresh:* (Ṣ, O:) also, applied to flesh-meat, *fresh,* as meaning *not cooked:* (IAth:) and ↓ مَعْبُوطٌ, applied to the same, *not such as a beast or bird of prey has fastened upon, nor affected by disease.* (Az, L.) — عَبِيطٌ also signifies *Slit,* or *rent,* (Ṣ, O, TA,) *when whole,* or *sound;* (TA;) applied to a garment, or piece of cloth; (Ṣ, O, TA;) and to leather; &c.; (TA;) and so ↓ مَعْبُوطٌ: pl. of the former, عُبُطٌ. (Ṣ, O, TA.) — And *Dust raised* by the hoofs of an ass. (TA.)

عَابِطٌ † *A liar.* (TA.)

عَوْبَطٌ, (O, Ḳ, TA,) like جَوْهَرٌ, (O, TA,) [in the CḲ, عَوْبَطَةٌ,] *A calamity,* or *misfortune:* (O, Ḳ:) pl. عَوَابِطُ. (TA.) — And The *main part,* or *fathomless deep, of the sea.* (Ḳ.) Formed by transposition from عَوْطَبٌ. (TA.)

مَعْبُوطٌ, and its fem.: see عَبِيطٌ, in three places.

مُعْتَبَطَةٌ: see عَبِيطٌ.

عبق

1. عَبِقَ بِهِ الطِّيبُ, [aor. ـَ,] inf. n. عَبَقٌ (Ṣ, Mgh, O, Mṣb, Ḳ) and عَبَاقِيَةٌ (Ṣ, O, Ḳ) and عَبَاقَةٌ, (O, Ḳ,) *The perfume clung to him,* or *it,* (Ṣ, Mgh, O, Ḳ, TA,) *and remained;* and so عَسِقَ بِهِ; (TA;) and *the odour of the perfume clung to him,* or *it:* (Mgh:) or *the odour of the perfume was,* or *became, perceptible in his garment* or *his person:* and it is said to relate only to fragrant odour. (Mṣb.) — And in like manner one says of a garment, عَبِقَ بِالجِسْمِ [*It clung to the body*]. (TA.) And عَبِقَ الشَّىْءُ بِغَيْرِهِ *The thing clave,* or *kept, to another.* (Mṣb.) And عَبِقَ الشَّىْءُ بِقَلْبِى ‡ *The thing stuck to my heart.* (TA.) And عَبِقَ بِالمَكَانِ *He remained, stayed, dwelt,* or *abode, in the place.* (O, Ḳ.) And عَبِقَ بِهِ ‡ *He became attached to him,* or *it.* (O, Ḳ, TA.) [See also رَصِعَ بِالطِّيبِ.]

2. التَّعْبِيقُ signifies التَّذْكِيَةُ [used in relation to wine, app. as meaning *The becoming old;* though the latter word, thus used, is probably tropical]. (O, Ḳ.) 'Adee Ibn-Zeyd says, describing wine,

صَانَهَا التَّاجِرُ الْيَهُودِىُّ حَوْلَـ *
ـنِ فَأَذْكَى مِنْ نَشْرِهَا التَّعْبِيقُ *

[which seems to be cited as meaning, *The Jewish merchant kept it two years, and the becoming old enhanced its fragrance:* but I think that the last word may be more properly rendered *the making it to remain long* in its jar]. (O.)

Q. Q. 3. اِعْبَنْقَى *He* (a man, Ṣ) *became cunning,* or *very cunning:* (صَارَ دَاهِيَةً: Ṣ, O, Ḳ:) or *became evil in disposition:* (Ḳ:) and in like manner signifies اِبْعَنْقَى. (TA.)

عَبَقٌ: see what next follows.

عَبِقٌ Perfume [*clinging* to a person or thing, *and remaining;* and *of which the odour clings:* (see 1, first sentence:) or] *of which the odour is perceptible in the garment* or *person:* (Mṣb:) it is applied as an epithet to an odour; and ↓ عَبَقٌ also, as the inf. n., meaning ذُو عَبَقٍ. (Ḥam p. 710.) — Applied to a man, *Such that, when he has perfumed himself with the least perfume, it does not leave him for days:* and in like manner with ة applied to a woman. (Lth, O, Ḳ.) — عَبِقَةٌ لَبِقَةٌ, applied to a woman, means *Whom every dress and perfume suits.* (TA.) — And the Khuzá'ees, who were the most chaste speakers of Arabic, said رَجُلٌ عَبِقٌ لَبِقٌ as meaning ظَرِيفٌ [i. e. *A man excellent,* or *elegant, in mind, manners,* and *address* or *speech;* and *in person, countenance,* or *garb:* &c.]. (TA.)

عَبِقَةٌ *Feculence* (وَضَرٌ) *of clarified butter,* [*adhering to the interior*] *in a skin;* (IDrd, Ṣ, O, Ḳ;) also termed عَبِكَةٌ; (IDrd, O, TA;) and عَمِقَةٌ, in which the م is asserted by Lḥ to be a substitute for ب. (TA.) And one says, مَا فِى النِّحْيِ عَبِقَةٌ, meaning *There is not aught* [*remaining*] *of clarified butter in the skin;* (Ṣ, O;) as also عَبِكَةٌ. (Ṣ and O in art. عبك.) — [Hence,] one says also, مَا بَقِيَتْ لَهُمْ عَبِقَةٌ مِنْ أَمْوَالِهِمْ, meaning † [*There remained not to them*] *any relic* [*of their possessions*]. (TA.)

عِبِقَّانٌ رِبِقَّانٌ, [in the CḲ, erroneously, عَبْقانٌ رِبْقانٌ,] and with ة [affixed to each], applied to a man, *Evil in disposition:* and with ة applied to a female: so in the Ḳ; but this is inconsistent with what here follows: (TA:) accord. to As, عِبِقَّانَةٌ رِبِقَّانَةٌ and عِبِقَّانٌ رِبِقَّانٌ are applied to a man, meaning as above; and to the woman in like manner. (O, TA.)

رَجُلٌ عَبَاقَاةٌ *A man who sticks to another.* (O, Ḳ.)

عَبَاقِيَةٌ, applied to a man, (Ṣ, O, Ḳ,) *Guileful,* or *crafty;* (Ḳ;) *cunning,* or *very cunning;* (Ṣ, O, Ḳ;) *evil,* or *mischievous.* (O.) — And *A thief,* (O, Ḳ,) *who steals camels,* (خَارِبٌ, Ḳ,) or *who strips people forcibly of their clothes,* (حَارِبٌ, O,) *who will not refrain from anything:* thus expl. by ISh. (O.) — Also *A scar caused by a wound in the ball,* or *most elevated part, of the cheek.* (Ṣ, O, Ḳ.) So in the saying, بِهِ شَيْنٌ عَبَاقِيَةٌ [*In him is a blemish, a scar* &c.], (Ṣ,) or شَيْنٌ وَعَبَاقِيَةٌ [*a blemish and a scar* &c.]. (O.) — And *A certain thorny tree,* (O, Ḳ, TA,) *that hurts* (O, TA) *him who is caught by its thorns;* said by AḤn to be *of the* [*kind called*] عِضَاه. (TA.)

عُقَابٌ عَبَنْقَاةٌ (Ṣ, O, Ḳ) and عَبَنْقَاةٌ (Ḳ) and عَقَنْبَاةٌ, (Ṣ, O,) like قَعَنْبَاةٌ, (O, Ḳ,) *An eagle having sharp talons:* (Ṣ, O:) or, accord. to IDrd, *hard and strong* [*in the talons*]. (O.) [See also art. عقب.]

عبقر

عَبْقَرٌ: see the following paragraph, in two places.

عَبْقَرِىٌّ a rel. n. from ↓ عَبْقَرٌ, a place which the Arabs assert to be of the lands of the Jinn, or Genii: (Ṣ, O, Mṣb:) or a certain place, (Ḳ,) in the desert, (TA,) abounding with Jinn: (Ḳ:) AO says, We have not found any one who knows where this country is, or when it existed. (TA.) Hence it is applied as an epithet to anything wondered at, or admired, for the skilfulness which it exhibits, or the excellence of its manufacture, and its strength: (Ṣ, O:) or to any work great in estimation, and fine, and delicate: (Mṣb:) it is both sing. and pl.; and the fem. is عَبْقَرِيَّةٌ: you say, ثِيَابٌ عَبْقَرِيَّةٌ [*Cloths,* or *garments, of admirable manufacture*]: (Ṣ, O:) [or such are so called in relation to a certain town; for] ↓ عَبْقَرٌ is also a town (M, Ḳ) in El-Yemen, (M,) or, accord. to the Moajam, in El-Jezeereh, in which cloths or garments, and carpets, are variegated, or figured, (TA,) and of which the cloths or garments are of the utmost beauty. (Ḳ.) — And *A kind of carpets,* (Ṣ, O, Ḳ,) *variously dyed and figured:* upon such the Prophet used to prostrate himself when he prayed: (Ṣ, O:) as also ↓ عَبَاقِرِىٌّ: (Ḳ:) and some read عَبَاقِرِىّ in the Ḳur lv. 76: (Ṣ, O:) as pl. of عَبْقَرِىٌّ: (TA:) but this is a mistake; for a rel. n. has no such pl.; (Ṣ;) unless it be from a sing. n. of a pl. form, like حَضَاجِرِىٌّ from

حَضَاجِرُ, and so be a rel. n. from عَبَاقِرُ: so say the skilful grammarians, Kh and Sb and Ks: Az mentions the reading ▼ عَبَاقَرِىّ, with fet-h to the ق; as though it were a rel. n. from عَبَاقَرُ: Fr says that عَبْقَرِىٌّ signifies *thick* [*carpets of the kind called*] طَنَافِس: and also *silk brocade*; syn. دِيبَاج: Ḳt, that it signifies *what are called* زَرَابِىّ: Sa'eed Ibn-Jubeyr, that it signifies *excellent* زرابى: (TA:) the n. un. is عَبْقَرِيَّةٌ. (Fr, TA.) — Also *Good*, or *excellent*; applied to an animal, and to a jewel. (TA.) — *Perfect*, or *complete*; applied to anything. (Ḳ.) — *A pure, unmixed*, lie; (O, Ḳ,* TA;) *that has no truth mixed with it*. (O, TA.) — *A lord*, or *chief*, (O, Ḳ,) of men: (TA:) or (TA, in the Ḳ, "and") *one who has none above him*: and *strong*. (Ḳ.) You say of a strong man, هٰذَا عَبْقَرِىُّ قَوْمٍ: (Ṣ, O:) or this means *This is a chief*, or *lord*, *of a people*: (Aṣ, on the authority of 'Amr Ibn-El-'Alà:) and in a trad. it is said that the Prophet related a dream, mentioning 'Omar, and said, فَلَمْ أَرَ عَبْقَرِيًّا يَفْرِى فَرِيَّهُ [*And I have not seen a chief of a people do his wonderful deeds*]. (Ṣ,* O, TA.) — It is also applied as an epithet denoting superlativeness [of any quality]. (TA.) They even said ظُلْمٌ عَبْقَرِىٌّ [*Excessive*, or *extreme*, *wrongdoing*]. (Ṣ, O.)

عَبَاقِرِىٌّ and عَبَاقَرِىٌّ: see the preceding paragraph.

عبك

1. عَبَكَهُ, (IDrd, O, Ḳ,) aor. ـِ, (TA,) inf. n. عَبْكٌ, (IDrd, O,) *He mixed it*, namely, a thing, (IDrd, O, Ḳ,) with a thing; (Ḳ;) syn. خَلَطَهُ, (IDrd, O,) or لَبَكَهُ. (Ḳ.) ═ See also 1 in art. عتك.

عَبَكَةٌ *A morsel of* سَوِيق [or *meal of parched barley*]; (Ṣ, O;) *i. q.* حَبَكَةٌ; (Ṣ, Ḳ;) but this last word was not known to Az on any other authority than that of Lth. (TA in art. حبك.) One says, مَا ذُقْتُ عَبَكَةً وَلَا لَبَكَةً, meaning *I tasted not a morsel of* سَوِيق *nor a bit of* ثَرِيد [or *crumbled bread moistened with broth*]. (Ṣ, O.) — And *Somewhat of clarified butter*; like عَبَقَةٌ: so in the phrase, مَا فِى النِّحْىِ عَبَكَةٌ [*There is not aught remaining of clarified butter in the skin*]: and hence the saying, مَا أُبَالِيهِ عَبَكَةً [*I do not care for him as for a little clarified butter*; meaning, *at all*]. (Ṣ, O.) And, (Ḳ,) accord. to IAạr, (O,) *Feculence* (وَضَر) [*of clarified butter* (IDrd and O voce عَبَقَةٌ)] *adhering to* [*the interior of*] *a skin*. (O, Ḳ.) — And *A fragment of a thing*: (Ḳ:) or *a piece of* جبس [app. جِبْس, which means *gypsum*, but probably a mistranscription for جُبْن, i. e. *cheese*]. (TA.) — And *A portion of compacted dung and urine that has clung to the wool*, or *tail*, &c., *of a sheep, and dried thereon*. (O.) — And *A paltry, despicable, thing*. (O, Ḳ.) Hence the saying, مَا أَغْنَى عَنِّى عَبَكَةً [*It did not stand me in stead of a paltry thing*; meaning, *in any stead*]. (TA.) ═ Also *Impotent in speech or actions*; *heavy, dull*, or *stupid*. (IB, Ḳ,* TA.) ═ And *A knot that remains in a rope when the latter becomes old and worn out*. (AA, O.)

عبل

1. عَبُلَ, [aor. ـُ,] (Ṣ, O, Mṣb, Ḳ,) inf. n. عَبَالَةٌ, (Ṣ, O, Mṣb,) *He*, or *it*, *was*, or *became*, *large, big, bulky*, or *thick*; (Ṣ, O, Mṣb, Ḳ;) as also عَبِلَ, aor. ـَ, (Ḳ,) inf. n. عُبُولٌ; (TḲ;) and عَبَلَ, aor. ـُ, (Ḳ,) inf. n. عَبْلٌ. (TA.) ═ عَبَلَهُ, (Az, O,* Ḳ,) [aor., app., ـِ, as in other senses of the trans. verb,] inf. n. عَبْلٌ, (Az, TA,) *He cut it*, or *cut it off*, (Az, O,* Ḳ,) *so as to extirpate it*: this is the primary signification [of the trans. verb]. (Az, TA.) ▼ عَبَلَتْهُ عَبُولُ, (O, Ḳ, [but in the copies of the Ḳ erroneously written عَبُولٌ,]) said of a man when he has died, (O,) means, (Ḳ,) or is like, (O,) شَعَبَتْهُ شَعُوبُ [*Death separated him from his companions*; or, accord. to the primary signification of the verb, *death cut him off*, or *extirpated him*]; (O;) or اِشْتَعَبَتْهُ شَعُوبُ. (Ḳ. [But correctly as in the O.]) — عَبَلَ الشَّجَرَةَ, aor. ـِ, (Ṣ, O, Ḳ,) inf. n. عَبْلٌ, (Ṣ, O,) *He removed the leaves from the tree*; (Ṣ, O, Ḳ;) as also ▼ عَبَّلَهَا. (CḲ: but not in my MS. copy of the Ḳ, nor in the TA.) — And عَبَلَهُ, (IAạr, O, Ḳ,) aor. and inf. n. as above, (TA,) *He repelled it*; (IAạr, O, Ḳ;) namely, a thing. (Ḳ.) [See also the pass. part. n., below.] — And *He*, or *it*, *hindered*, *prevented*, *impeded*, or *withheld*, *him*; (O, Ḳ, TA;) and *diverted him by occupying him otherwise*. (TA.) One says, مَا عَبَلَكَ i. e. *What diverted thee by occupying thee otherwise? and hindered thee*, &c.? (TA.) — And عَبَلْتُ الحَبْلَ, inf. n. عَبْلٌ, *I twisted the rope*. (Ṣ, O.) ═ عَبَلْتُ السَّهْمَ, (Ks, Ṣ, O, Ḳ,) aor. ـُ, (Ks, O, TA,) inf. n. عَبْلٌ, (TA,) *I put*, or *made*, *to the arrow a* مِعْبَلَة. (Ks, Ṣ, O, Ḳ.) — And عَبَلْتُهُ *I shot him*, or *shot at him*, *with a* مِعْبَلَة. (O.) ═ عَبَلَ بِهِ *He went away with*, or *took away*, *him*, or *it*. (O, Ḳ.) ═ عبل الشَّجَرُ [app. عَبَلَ, but perhaps a mistranscription for أَعْبَلَ, q. v.,] *The trees put forth their leaves*: on the authority of Az. (TA.)

2: see the preceding paragraph.

4. اعبل *He*, or *it*, *was*, or *became*, *thick and white*: (Ḳ:) originally used in relation to the fore arms. (TA.) ═ اعبل الشَّجَرُ *The trees put forth their* [*leaves termed*] عَبَل: and *the trees dropped their leaves*: thus having two contr. significations: (O, Ḳ:*) or اعبل الأَرْطَى *the* [*trees called*] *became in the state in which their* هَدَب [or عَبَل (q. v.)] *were thick, in the hot season, and red, and fit to be used for tanning therewith*: and, accord. to Aṣ, اعبلت الشَّجَرَةُ signifies *the tree dropped its leaves*: (Ṣ:) accord. to En-Naḍr, اعبلت الأَرْطَاةُ signifies *the* ارطاة *put forth its leaves*: and also, *dropped its leaves*: (Az, TA:) and ISd mentions, on the authority of AḤn, اعبل الشَّجَرُ as meaning *the trees put forth their fruit*; but he says, "I have not found this to be known." (TA.) [See also 1, last sentence.]

عَبْلٌ *Large, big, bulky*, or *thick*; (Ṣ, O, Mṣb, Ḳ;) as also ▼ عَبِلٌ: (Ḳ:) fem. of the former with ة: and pl. [masc.] عِبَالٌ, (Ṣ, O, Ḳ, TA,) like ضِخَامٌ [pl. of the syn. ضَخْمٌ]: and the pl. of عَبْلَةٌ is عَبْلَاتٌ, (Ṣ, O, TA,) [with the ب quiescent,] because it is an epithet. (TA.) It is applied in this sense to anything. (Ḳ.) Thus, in a trad., it is applied to a man. (TA.) And one says رَجُلٌ عَبْلُ الذِّرَاعَيْنِ *A man large*, &c., *in the fore arms*. (Ṣ, O, Mṣb.*) And فَرَسٌ عَبْلُ الشَّوَى *A horse thick in the legs*. (Ṣ, O.) And اِمْرَأَةٌ عَبْلَةٌ *A woman complete*, or *perfect*, *in make* or *formation*. (Ṣ, O, Mṣb.) And ▼ اِمْرَأَةٌ عَبَيْلَةٌ *A large, big, bulky*, (Ibn-'Abbád, O,) or *thick*, *woman*. (Ibn-'Abbád, O, Ḳ.*) And ▼ عَابِلٌ applied to a boy, or young man, signifies *Fat*: and [so] ▼ عَبُولٌ applied to a woman: pl. of both عُبْلٌ. (TA.)

عَبَلٌ *i. q.* هَدَبٌ i. e. (Ṣ, O) *Any leaves that are* [*as though they were*] *twisted*, (Ṣ, O, Ḳ,) *not expanded*, (Ḳ,) [generally meaning *slender sprigs, like strings, garnished with minute, amplexicaul, appressed, acute leaves, overlying one another like the scales of a fish*,] *such as those of the* طَرْفَآء (Ṣ, O, Ḳ) *and of the* أَرْطَى *and of the* أَثْل *and the like of these*: (Ṣ, O:) and, (Ḳ,) as some say, (TA,) the *fruit of the* ارطى: (Ḳ, TA:) and, (Ḳ,) as some say, (TA,) the هَدَب *thereof, when they have become thick*, (Ḳ, TA,) *in the hot season, and red*, (TA,) *and fit to be used for tanning therewith*: or *slender leaves*: (Ḳ, TA:) or the *like of leaves, but not* [*what are commonly called*] *leaves*: (TA:) or *such as are falling thereof*; (Ḳ, TA;) i. e., of leaves: (TA:) and [in the CḲ "or"] *such as are coming forth* (Ḳ, TA) *thereof*: (TA:) thus having two contr. significations. (Ḳ, TA.)

عَبِلٌ: see عَبْلٌ, first sentence.

عَبَالٌ The *mountain-rose* (وَرْدٌ جَبَلِىٌّ) [one of the appellations now applied to the *eglantine*, or *sweet brier*, more commonly called the نِسْرِين]: (Ṣ, Mṣb, Ḳ:) AḤn says, an Arab of the desert informed me that the عَبَال is the *rose of the mountain* (وَرْدُ الجَبَلِ), *of which is the white, and the red, and the yellow*; (O, TA;) *having a goodly hip* (دَلِيك [thus correctly written in the O, but afterwards altered to دُلَيك,]) *in size and redness like the full-grown, unripe date, which, when it becomes ripe, is sweet, and delicious, like the fresh ripe date, and is sent from one to another as a present*: (O:) [n. un. with ة:] *the* عَبَالَة, he says, *has short, curved thorns, its rose is sweet-scented, and it grows so as to compose thickets*, (O, TA,) *and is depastured*, (O,) *and it becomes thick*, (Ḳ,) *and staves* (O, Ḳ) *thick and good*, (O,) or *thick and strong*, (TA,) *are cut from it*: (O, Ḳ, TA:) the staff of Moses is said to have been from it: (Ḳ, TA:) or, as AḤn says, the people assert that the staff of Moses was an عَبَالَة. (O.)

عَبُولٌ: see عَبْلٌ, last sentence. ═ عَبُولُ [said in

the Ḳ to be like صَبُور, but it is imperfectly decl., as a fem. proper name,] *Death*; or *the decree of death*; syn. المَنِيَّةُ. (Ḳ.) See 1, third sentence: and see also عَابِلُ.

عَبَالَّةٌ : see عَبَالَّتَهُ.

اِمْرَأَةٌ عَبِلَةٌ : see عَبْلٌ.

أَلْقَى عَلَيْهِ عَبَالَّتَهُ, with teshdeed to the ل, (Ṣ, O, Ḳ,) [of a rare form, like حَمَارَّةٌ, q. v.,] and ▼ عَبَالَتَهُ, without teshdeed, (Lh, Ḳ,) *He threw upon him his weight*. (Ṣ, O, Ḳ.)

عَابِلٌ : see عَبْلٌ, last sentence. ═ عَابِلَتِى ▼ عَبُولٌ is a saying of the Arabs like their saying شَاجِنَتِى شَجُونٌ [i. e., app., meaning *My separater* from my companions *is death*, or *shall be death alone*]. (L in art. شجن : see شَجُونٌ.)

عَبَنْبَلٌ *Great*, (AA, O, Ḳ, TA,) *big*, or *bulky*, (TA,) *and strong*. (Ḳ, TA.)

أَعْبَلُ *A mountain of which the stones are white*: (Ḳ:) or *rough, rugged*, or *thick, stone, which may be red, and may be white, and may be black*, (ISh, O, Ḳ,*) *and may be a rugged, high mountain*: (ISh, O:) expl. in the Ṣ as meaning *white stones*; but correctly, as IB says, *white stone*: and أَعْبِلَةٌ is an irreg. pl. thereof. (TA.) —— And [the fem.] عَبْلَاءُ signifies *A rock*: (Ḳ, TA: [in the CḲ, أَوْ should be inserted after الصَّخْرَةُ:]) or a *white* rock: (Th, Ṣ, Ḳ, TA:) or a *white, hard* rock: (TA:) pl. عِبَالٌ, like بِطَاحٌ pl. of بَطْحَاءُ. (Ṣ, TA.) And A *white* [hill, or eminence such as is termed] أَكَمَة. (TA.) And *A narrow strip* (طَرِيدَةٌ) *in the midst of a land, the stones of which are white, resembling the stones from which fire is struck*, and sometimes *people do strike fire with some of them: they are not what are called* مَرْو ; [*but*] *resembling* بِلَّوْر [i. e. *crystal*]. (TA.)

مِعْبَلٌ *An implement with which trees are cut* [*down*]. (TA.)

مِعْبَلَةٌ *A broad and long arrow-head*: (Aṣ, Ṣ, O, Ḳ:) or an *iron* [*arrow-head*] *made broad, and having no* عَيْر [*or central ridge*]: (AḤn, TA:) pl. مَعَابِلُ. (O, Ḳ.) [See also سَرْوَةٌ. —— Also *An arrow having a broad head*. (Freytag, from the Deewán of the Hudhalees.)]

مُعْبِلٌ One *having with him* مَعَابِل [pl. of مِعْبَلَة *of arrows*. (Ibn-'Abbád, O, Ḳ.)

مَعْبُولٌ [pass. part. n. of عَبَلَهُ; as such, *Cut*, &c.: —— and] *Repelled*: thus in the following verse, cited by IAạr:

هَا إِنَّ رَمْيِى عَنْهُمُ لَمَعْبُولْ
فَلَا صَرِيخَ اليَوْمَ إِلَّا المَصْقُولْ

[*Now verily my shooting in defence of them is repelled; so there is no aider to-day but the polished* sword]: the speaker was shooting at his enemy, and the shooting availed not at all; so he fought with the sword. (O.)

عبهل

Q. 1. عَبْهَلَ الإِبِلَ (inf. n. عَبْهَلَةٌ, TḲ) *He left the camels to pasture by themselves*, (Lth, Ṣ, O, Ḳ,) *and to go to the water when they pleased*: (TA:) like أَبْهَلَهَا; (Ṣ, O;) the ع being substituted for the أ. (Ṣ.) ═ And عَبْهَلَةٌ and عِبْهَالٌ signify The act of *reproving, blaming*, or *censuring*: (Ḳ:) inf. ns. of عَبْهَلَهُ *he reproved him*, &c. (TḲ.)

عَبْهَلٌ : see العَبَاهِلَةُ.

إِبِلٌ عَبَاهِلُ (Ṣ,* Ḳ) and ▼ مُعَبْهَلَةٌ *Camels left to pasture by themselves*, (Ṣ, Ḳ,) *without a pastor and without a keeper*. (TA.) —— See also the next paragraph.

العَبَاهِلَةُ, (Ḳ,) or عَبَاهِلَةُ اليَمَنِ (Ṣ, O) and ▼ عَبَاهِلُ اليَمَنِ, (O,) *The kings of El-Yemen who have been established*, or *confirmed, in their dominion*, (Ṣ, O, Ḳ,) *not being displaced therefrom*, (Ṣ, O,) or *and who have not been displaced therefrom*: (Ḳ:) [and SM adds, referring to العَبَاهِلَة,] A'Obeyd says, and in like manner [it denotes] anything *left to itself, not prevented*, or *withheld, from doing what it desires*: (TA: [but in this explanation the sing. is evidently put for the pl.:] the sing. of عَبَاهِلَة is most probably ▼ عَبْهَلٌ, like قَشْعَمٌ, of which قَشَاعِمَةٌ is a pl.: in the "Tahkeef el-Lisán" [of IḲṭṭ], العَبَاهِلَةُ is expl. as signifying *those over whom no one has authority*. (TA.)

مُعَبْهَلَةٌ : see عَبَاهِلُ.

مُتَعَبْهِلٌ i. q. مُمْتَنِعٌ [app. as meaning One *who resists*, or *withstands*; or *who is incompliant*, or *unyielding*]: (Ḳ:) and [so in copies of the Ḳ and in the TA, but in the CḲ "or,"] one *who will not be prevented*, or *withheld, from a thing*. (O, Ḳ.)

عبو

1. عَبَا, aor. يَعْبُو, *His face shone*: (Ḳ, TA:) [or so عَبَا وَجْهُهُ; for] عَبَأَ وَجْهُهُ signifies thus accord. to IAạr: (TA in art. عبأ:) app. from عَبٌ signifying the "light" of the sun; this being originally عَبْوٌ. (TA.) ═ And عَبْوُ المَتَاعِ is *syn. with* ▼ تَعْبِيَتُهُ, (Ḳ, TA,) mentioned by ISd, and said by IḲṭṭ to be of the dial. of El-Yemen, (TA,) signifying *The putting of the goods*, or *utensils, one upon another*: [or *packing them up* in a repository: as also عَبْوَةٌ: see 1, in art. عبأ:] IDrd says, عَبَوْتُ المَتَاعَ is of the dial. of El-Yemen, *syn. with* ▼ عَبَّيْتُهُ. (TA in art. عبى.)

2: see the preceding paragraph, in two places. —— And see also art. عبى.

عَبٌ The *light* of the sun; (IAạr, TA, and O and Ḳ in art. عبأ;) as also ▼ عَبْوٌ, which is the original form; (TA;) and so عَبْءٌ, (IAạr, and O and Ḳ in art. عبأ,) and عُبٌّ; (O and Ḳ in art. عب;) and IAạr says that ▼ عَبْوَةٌ signifies the same: (TA in art. عبأ:) or the *light and beauty* thereof: (TA in art. عبى:) pl. عِبِىٌّ. (TA.)

عَبًا, applied to a man, [like عَبَاءٌ mentioned in art. عبأ,] *Heavy, dull*, or *stupid*; or *coarse*, or *rude*; and *impotent*. (ISd, TA.) [But see this word in art. عبى.]

عَبْوٌ : see عَبٌ, above.

عِبْوٌ *A weight*, or *load*, or *burden*: or *any load*, or *burden, consisting of a debt*, or *some other responsibility that one takes upon himself*. (TA.) [See also عِبْءٌ (which signifies the same) in art. عبأ.]

عَبْوَةٌ : see عَبٌ, above.

عَابِيَةٌ *Beautiful*; (Ḳ, TA;) applied to a woman; from عَبٌ, expl. above. (TA.)

عبى

2. عَبَّيْتُ الجَيْشَ, (Ṣ, Mṣb,) inf. n. تَعْبِيَةٌ (Ṣ, Ḳ) and تَعْبِئَةٌ and تَعْبِىٌّ, so said Yoo; but AZ said عَبَّأْتُهُ; (Ṣ; [see art. عبأ;]) *I prepared*, or *made ready*, (Ṣ, Ḳ,*) or *set in order, disposed*, or *arranged*, (Mṣb,) *the army* (Ṣ, Mṣb, Ḳ) *in their places*. (Ṣ, Ḳ.) —— See also 2 in art. عبو.

6. التَّعَابِى signifies *The aiding*, or *assisting, of one party by one man, and of another party by another man, when they prepare a repast, one of the two parties making bread for this, and the other for another*. (Ḳ.)

8. الاِعْتِبَآءُ, mentioned here in the TA, as *syn. with* الاِحْتِشَآءُ, see 8 in art. عبأ.

عَبًا and ▼ عَبَايَةٌ, but the former the more chaste, are said to signify, as epithets applied to a man, *Coarse*, or *rude, heavy, dull*, or *stupid*, (Ḳ,* TA,) and *impotent*: but this requires correction; for Lth mentions العَبَا, and ▼ العَبَآءُ as used by a poet, and says that they signify *the coarse*, or *rude, impotent*, man; but Az says that he had not heard العَبَآءُ in this sense on any authority other than that of Lth, and that he held the right reading in the verse cited as an ex. by Lth to be العَيَآءُ, with ى, meaning, as also العَيَايَآءُ, "the coarse, or rude, or the heavy, dull, or stupid, and impotent, who has no need of women." (TA.)

عَبَآءٌ : see عَبَايَةٌ, in two places. ═ And see also عَبًا, above.

عباة [app. عَبَاةٌ] The [*kind of plant called*] سُطَّاح *that spreads upon the ground*. (TA.)

عَبِىٌّ One's *share* of the جَزُور [or slaughtered camel for portions of which the players at the game called المَيْسِر contend]. (Ḳ, TA.)

عَبَايَةٌ and عَبَاءَةٌ (Ṣ, Mgh, Mṣb, Ḳ, TA) *A sort of* [*the kind of garments called*] أَكْسِيَة [pl. of كِسَاء], (Ṣ, Mgh,* Ḳ, TA,) *wide*, (Mgh, TA,) *and* [*generally*] *having in it large black* [or *brown*] *stripes*: (TA:) pl. [of the latter] عَبَاءَاتٌ (Ṣ, Mṣb) and ▼ عَبَآءٌ, (Mgh, Mṣb,) formed by the elision of the ة, (Msb,) [or rather this is a coll. gen. n.,] and the pl. of عَبَايَةٌ is عُبِىٌّ, like عُتِىٌّ: or, accord. to some, ▼ عَبَآءٌ is a sing.; for they say that it signifies *a sort of* أَكْسِيَة, and that its pl. is أَعْبِيَةٌ. (TA.) See عَبَآءَةٌ in art. عبأ. ═ See also عَبًا, above.

عتب

1. عَتَبَ عَلَيْهِ, (Ṣ, Mgh, O, Ḳ,*) aor. ـِ, (Ṣ, Mgh, O, Ḳ) and ـُ, (Ṣ, O, Ḳ,) inf. n. عَتْبٌ (Ṣ, Mgh, O, Ḳ) and عِتْبَانٌ or عَتَبَانٌ or عُتْبَانٌ (accord. to different copies of the Ḳ) and مَعْتَبٌ, (Ṣ, O, Ḳ,) with which ▼ مَعْتِبَةٌ and ▼ مَعْتَبَةٌ are syn., (Ḳ,) but these two are simple substs.; (Ṣ, O; [see, however, حُمْصٌ;]) and ▼ تعتّب عليه; (Ṣ, O, TA;) *He was angry with him,* (Ṣ, Mgh, O, Ḳ, TA,) *with the anger that proceeds from a friend.* (Ṣ,* Mgh,* O,* Ḳ,* TA.) It is said in a trad., كَانَ يَقُولُ لِأَحَدِنَا عِنْدَ المَعْتَبَةِ ▼ مَا لَهُ تَرِبَتْ يَمِينُهُ [*He used to say of one of us, from a motive of friendly anger, What aileth him? May his right hand* (meaning he himself) *cleave to the dust:* see تَرِبَ]. (TA.) — And [sometimes] عَتَبَ عَلَيْهِ signifies [simply] *He was angry with him.* (Mgh, TA.*) A poet says, (Ṣ, O, TA,) namely, El-Ghatammash (O, TA) Ed-Dabbee, (TA,)

أَخِلَّاىَ لَوْ غَيْرُ الحِمَامِ أَصَابَكُمْ
عَتَبْتُ وَلٰكِنْ مَا عَلَى الدَّهْرِ مَعْتَبُ

(Ṣ, O, TA; but in the O, عَلَى المَوْتِ, and أَخِلَّآءَ, as well as أَخِلَّاىَ, as in the Ḥam p. 406;) meaning [*O my friends, had some other event than the decreed case of death befallen you,*] *I had been angry:* [*but there is no being angry with fortune:*] i. e., had ye fallen in war, we had taken your blood-revenge: but one cannot revenge himself upon fortune. (TA.) — And عَتَبَ عَلَيْهِ, (Msb, Ḳ,* TA,*) aor. ـِ and ـُ, inf. n. عَتْبٌ (Msb, Ḳ, TA) and عِتِّيبَى [an intensive form] (Ḳ, TA) and عِتْبَانٌ (Az, TA) and مَعْتَبٌ, (Msb,) signifies also *He reproved, blamed,* or *censured, him;* (Ḳ, TA;) and so ▼ عاتبهُ, (TA,) inf. n. مُعَاتَبَةٌ and عِتَابٌ: (Ḳ, TA:) or *he reproved, blamed,* or *censured, him, in anger,* or *displeasure.* (Msb.) A poet says,

إِذَا ذَهَبَ العِتَابُ ▼ فَلَيْسَ وُدٌّ
وَيَبْقَى الوُدُّ مَا بَقِىَ العِتَابُ

[*When reproof departs, there is no love: but love lasts as long as reproof lasts*]. (Ṣ,* O, TA.) عَتْبٌ and عِتْبَانٌ signify Thy *reproving a man for evil conduct that he has shown towards thee, and from which thou hast desired him to return to what will please thee,* or *make thee happy.* (Az, TA. [See also the latter word below.]) ═ مَا عَتَبْتُ بَابَهُ means *I did not tread,* or *have not trodden, upon the threshold* (عَتَبَة) *of his door;* (A, Ḳ, TA;) and so ▼ مَا تَعَتَّبْتُهُ. (A, TA.) — And [hence,] عَتَبَ, aor. ـُ and ـِ, inf. n. عَتَبَانٌ (Ṣ, O, Ḳ) and عَتْبٌ and تَعْتَابٌ, [this last an intensive form,] (Ḳ,) ‡ *He* (a stallion [camel], TA) *limped,* or *halted:* (Ḳ, TA:) or *knocked his knees together,* or *had a distortion in a hind leg:* or *was hamstrung:* (TA:) and *he* (a camel, Ṣ, O, or a stallion [camel], TA) *walked upon three legs,* (Ṣ, O, Ḳ, TA,) *in consequence of his having been hamstrung,* (Ḳ, TA,) or *in consequence of his knees' knocking together,* or *of his having a distortion in a hind leg; as though he leaped:* (TA:) and *he* (a man) *leaped on one foot,* or *hopped,* (Ṣ, O, Ḳ,) *raising the other:* (Ḳ:) in each of these cases, the beast or man is likened to one walking upon a series of steps, or the like, of stairs, (O, TA,) or of a mountain, or of rugged ground, (TA,) and leaping from one of these to another. (O, TA.) — And عَتَبَ البَرْقُ, aor. ـُ and ـِ, inf. n. عَتَبَانٌ, † *The lightning flashed in continued succession.* (TA.) — And عَتَبَ مِنْ مَوْضِعٍ إِلَى مَوْضِعٍ, aor. ـِ [and app. ـُ also], † *He passed* [*from place to place*], and ▼ مِنْ قَوْلٍ إِلَى قَوْلٍ [*from saying to saying*]. (O, TA.) — And عتب القَوْمُ فِى السَّيْرِ [i. e. عَتَبَ, though Freytag assigns this meaning to عَتَّبَ,] † *The people,* or *party, turned aside in journeying, and alighted in a place not in the right,* or *intended, direction.* (Ḥam p. 18. [See also 4 and 8.]) ═ See also أَعْتَبَ, said of a bone.

2. تَعْتِيبٌ The *making an* عَتَبَة [meaning *a threshold*]. (Ḳ, TA.) تَعْتِيبُ البَابِ means *The making a threshold* (عَتَبَة) *to the door.* (TA.) — [And The *making an* عَتَبَة (meaning *a step*):] or so تَعْتِيبُ عَتَبَةٍ.] You say, عَتِّبْ لِى عَتَبَةً فِى هٰذَا المَوْضِعِ [*Make thou for me a step in this place*] when you desire to ascend thereby to a place. (O, TA.) — And The *drawing together the* حُجْزَة [of the drawers, or trousers, i. e. the *tuck,* or *doubled upper border, through which passes the waist-band*], *and folding it, in front:* [app. meaning the *turning up a portion, drawn together in front, inside the band,* to prepare for some active employment:] (IAth, O, Ḳ, TA:) you say, عَتَّبَ سَرَاوِيلَهُ فَتَشَمَّرَ [*He drew together the tuck of his drawers,* or *trousers, &c., and prepared himself for active employment*]: (O and TA, from a trad.:) and the part so drawn together &c. is called the ثُبْنَة. (IAṣr, O.) ═ See also أَعْتَبَ, said of a bone. ═ عتّب is also said of a man as meaning *He was,* or *became, slow, tardy, dilatory, late,* or *backward:* in which sense, its ب is thought by ISd to be a substitute for the م in عَتَّمَ. (TA.)

3. عاتبهُ, inf. n. مُعَاتَبَةٌ and عِتَابٌ, (Ṣ, O, Msb,) *He reproved him, &c.,* as expl. above; see 1, in the middle of the paragraph; in two places: (TA:) or عِتَابٌ and مُعَاتَبَةٌ signify two persons' *reproving, blaming,* or *censuring, each other; each of them reminding the other of his evil conduct to him:* (Az, TA:) [or the *expostulating,* or *remonstrating, of each with the other:*] or, (Kh, T, Ṣ, O, Msb, Ḳ,) as also ▼ تَعَاتُبٌ, (Az, T, O,* Ḳ,) and ▼ تَعَتُّبٌ, (Az, Ḳ,) the *conversing,* or *talking, together, as persons confiding in their reciprocal love, and therefore acting presumptuously, one towards another; and reminding one another of their anger,* or *friendly anger;* (Kh, Ṣ, O, Msb, Ḳ;) or *desiring to discuss, in a good-humoured way, things by which they had been displeased, and which had occasioned them anger,* or *friendly anger:* (Az, Ḳ,* TA:) the language meant is that of one friend to another. (TA.) — And مُعَاتَبَةٌ signifies also The act of *disciplining, training, exercising,* or *making tractable:* it is said in a trad., ▼ عَاتِبُوا الخَيْلَ فَإِنَّهَا تُعْتِبُ i. e. *Train ye horses* for war and for riding, *for* [*they will turn from their evil habits,* or] *they will become trained, and will accept reproof.* (TA.) — And you say, عاتب الأَدِيمَ, meaning † *He put the hide again into the tan.* (T in art. ادم.) [See an ex. in a prov. cited voce أَدِيمٌ.]

4. اعتبهُ, (Ḳ, TA,) inf. n. إِعْتَابٌ, with which ▼ عُتْبَى [q. v.] is syn.; (TA;) and ▼ استعتبهُ; *He granted him his good will,* or *favour; regarded him with good will,* or *favour; became well pleased, content,* or *satisfied, with him.* (Ḳ, TA.) In the following verse of Sá'ideh Ibn-Ju-eiyeh,

شَابَ الغُرَابُ وَلَا فُؤَادُكَ تَارِكٌ
ذِكْرَ الغَضُوبِ وَلَا عِتَابُكَ يُعْتَبُ

[*The raven may become hoary but thy heart will not relinquish the remembrance of Ghadoob, nor will the reproof of thee be met with good will*], the last word is expl. by يُسْتَقْبَلُ بِعُتْبَى [meaning as rendered above, or *be regarded with favour,* or *be met by a return to such conduct as will make thy reprover well pleased with thee*]. (TA.) — [Or] *He made him to be well pleased, content,* or *satisfied:* (Ṣ, A, O:) and the former verb is used in a contr. sense [or ironically] in the following verse of Bishr Ibn-Abee-Kházim,

غَضِبَتْ تَمِيمٌ أَنْ يُقَتَّلَ عَامِرٌ
يَوْمَ النِّسَارِ فَأُعْتِبُوا بِالصَّيْلَمِ

[*Temeem were angry because 'Ámir was slaughtered on the day of En-Nisár; so they were made contented by the sword:*] i. e., we contented them by slaughter: (Ṣ,* O,* TA: [see also the Ḥam p. 196:]) [but the meaning may be, *so they were made to return* from their anger *by the sword:* that أُعْتِبَ sometimes signifies *He was made to return* appears from an explanation, in the Ḳ, of a phrase in the Ḳur xli. 23: see 10:] and أَعْتَبَنِى and ▼ اسْتَعْتَبَنِى signify also *He returned to making me happy,* or *doing what was pleasing to me, from doing evil to me:* (Ṣ, O:) or *he left off doing that for which I was angry with him, and returned to that which made me to be well pleased with him:* (TA:) or the former signifies *he removed,* or *did away with,* [my] *complaint and reproof;* the ا having a privative effect: (Msb:) and أَعْتَبَهُ مِنْ شَكْوَاهُ means *He caused him to be pleased* or *contented* [*and so relieved him from his complaint*]. (Ḥar p. 337. [See also

أَشْكَاهُ.]) — And [hence, app.,] أَعْتَبَنِى signifies *He cancelled a bargain, or contract, with me.* (TA.) ═ اعتب and ▼ استعتب also signify *He returned from doing an evil action, a crime, a sin, a fault, or an offence:* or the former signifies *he returned from doing evil to do that which made him who reproved* or *blamed him,* or *who was angry with him, to be well pleased with him.* (TA.) It is said in a prov., مَا مُسِىْءٌ مَنْ أَعْتَبَ [*He is not an evildoer who returns from his evil conduct*]. (TA.) — And اعتب (Ḳ) and ▼ اعتتب (Ṣ, Ḳ) likewise signify *He turned away,* or *turned back,* or *reverted,* from a thing: (Ṣ, O, Ḳ:) and the latter is also expl. as meaning *he turned back* from a thing, or an affair in which he was engaged, to another thing, or affair: (Ṣ, O, Ḳ:) so accord. to Fr, (Ṣ, O, TA,) from the phrase لَكَ العُتْبَى signifying as expl. below (voce عُتْبَى) on his authority. (TA.) See also 3. ═ أُعْتِبَ said of a bone that has been set is like أُتْعِبَ [meaning *It was caused to have a defect in it, so that there remained in it a constant swelling,* or *so that a lameness resulted:* see عَتْبٌ]: and تَعْتَابٌ [of which the verb may be either ▼ عَتَّبَ or ▼ عَتَبَ] has the meaning of its inf. n., إِعْتَابٌ. (TA.)

5. تعتّب عَلَيْهِ: see 1, first sentence. — Also *He accused him of a crime, an offence,* or *an injurious action, that he had not committed.* (TA.) — And you say, لَا يُتَعَتَّبُ بِشَىْءٍ *He is not to be reproved, blamed,* or *censured, with anything* [i. e. *with any reproof* &c.]. (Ḳ,* TA.) And لَا يُتَعَتَّبُ عَلَيْهِ فِى شَىْءٍ [*No reproof, blame,* or *censure, is to be cast upon him in respect of anything*]. (ISk, O, TA.) — See also 3. ═ تعتّب also signifies *He kept to,* or *was constantly at, the* عَتَبَة [or *threshold*] *of the door.* (A, TA.) — And you say, تَعَتَّبْتُ بَابَهُ: see 1, latter half.

6: see 3. One says, بَيْنَهُمْ أُعْتُوبَةٌ ▼ يَتَعَاتَبُونَ بِهَا [*Between them is speech with which they reprove, blame,* or *censure, one another*]. (Ṣ.) And إِذَا تَعَاتَبُوا أَصْلَحَ مَا بَيْنَهُمُ العِتَابُ [*When they reprove one another in a friendly manner, the reproof rectifies,* or *sets right, what is* amiss *between them*]. (Ṣ.)

8: see 4, latter part: and see also مُعْتَتَبٌ. — اعتتب فِى طَرِيقِهِ *He receded,* or *retreated, in his way, after proceeding therein for a while;* as though in consequence of a difficulty (عَتَب) presenting itself. (TA.) — And اعتتب الطَّرِيقَ *He quitted the even,* or *easy, part of the way, and took to the rugged part.* (Ṣ, O, Ḳ.) — And اعتتب مِنَ الجَبَلِ *He ascended the mountain.* (Ṣ, O, Ḳ. [In the Ḳ is added, "and did not recoil from it:" but this is a portion of the explanation of the verse here following.]) El-Ḥoṭei-ah says,

• إِذَا مَخَارِمُ أَحْنَاءٍ عَرَضْنَ لَهُ •
• لَمْ يَنْبُ عَنْهَا وَخَافَ الجَوْرَ فَاعْتَتَبَا •

i. e. [*When prominences of bends of mountains present themselves to him,*] *he does not recoil from them,* [*but fears the turning aside,*] *and so ascends* the mountain. (Ṣ, O.) — And اعتتب signifies also *He pursued a right,* or *direct, course,* syn. قَصَدَ, (Ṣ, IAth, O, Ḳ, [perhaps thus expl. in relation to the verse cited above,]) فِى الأَمْرِ [*in the affair*]. (Ḳ.)

10. استعتبهُ *He asked him, petitioned him,* or *solicited him, to grant him his good will,* or *favour; to regard him with good will,* or *favour; to become well pleased, content,* or *satisfied, with him;* (Ṣ, O, Ḳ;) or *he desired,* or *sought, of him that he should return to making him happy,* or *to doing what was pleasing to him, from doing evil to him.* (Ṣ.) And استعتب, alone, *He asked, solicited, sought,* or *desired, good will,* or *favour;* or *to be regarded with good will,* or *favour.* (Ṣ, Mṣb.) وَلَا هُمْ يُسْتَعْتَبُونَ, in the Ḳur xvi. 86, and xxx. 57, and xlv. 34, means *Nor shall they be asked to return to what will please God.* (Jel.) And وَإِنْ يَسْتَعْتِبُوا فَمَا هُمْ مِنَ المُعْتَبِينَ, in the Ḳur xli. 23, means *And if they solicit* God's *favour, they shall not be regarded with favour:* (Jel:) or *if they petition* their Lord *to cancel their compact,* [*or to restore them to the world, He will not do so;* i. e.,] *He will not restore them to the world;* (O, Ḳ, TA;) knowing that, if they were restored, they would return to that which they have been forbidden to do: this is the meaning if we read the verb in the active form: otherwise, (O, TA,) reading يُسْتَعْتَبُوا [and مُعْتَبِينَ], as 'Obeyd Ibn-'Omeyr did, (O,) the meaning is, *If God cancelled their compact, and restored them to the world, they would not* [*return from their evil ways, and*] *act obediently to God:* (O, TA:) [for] — اِسْتَعْتَبْتُهُ also signifies *I asked him,* or *desired him, to cancel a bargain,* or *compact, with me.* (TA.) ═ See also 4, in three places.

عَتْبٌ: see عُتْبَانٌ, in four places.

عَتِبٌ One *who reproves, blames,* or *censures,* (O, Ḳ, TA,) *his companion,* or *his friend,* (O, TA,) *much,* or *frequently,* (O, Ḳ, TA,) *in respect of everything,* (O, TA,) *from a motive of solicitous affection for him, and to give him good advice.* (TA.) [See also عَتَّابٌ.]

عَتَبٌ: see عَتَبَةٌ, in five places. — Also The دَسْتَانَات [or *frets*] (O, TA) *that are bound upon the* عُمُود [meaning *neck*] (O) of a lute: (O, TA:) [app. as likened to a series of steps:] or the *transverse pieces of wood upon the face* of a lute, [i. e., app., *upon the face of the neck,*] from which the chords *are extended to the extremity* of the lute: (O, Ḳ, TA:) or, accord. to IAạr, the *thing* [app. the *small ridge at the angle of the neck*] *upon which are* [or *lie*] *the extremities of the chords, in the fore part,* of the lute. (TA.) [See an engraving and a description of a lute in my work on the Modern Egyptians.] — And The *places of ascent* of mountains, and of rugged and hard pieces of ground. (TA.) — And *Ruggedness of ground.* (O, Ḳ.) — And The *space between two mountains.* (TA.) — And The *space between the fore finger and middle finger* [*when they are extended apart*]: (Mṣb in art. شبر, and Ḳ:) or the *space between the middle finger and third finger:* (Ṣ, O, Ḳ:) or the [*space that is measured by*] *placing the four fingers close together.* (Mṣb ubi suprà.) [See also بُصْمٌ, and رَتَبٌ.] — Also *A bending at the* ضَرِيبَة [or *part with which one strikes*], *and a bluntness,* of a sword. (TA.) One says, مَا فِى طَاعَةِ فُلَانٍ عَتَبٌ † *There is not in the obedience of such a one any bending nor a recoiling.* (TA.) — And *A defect in a bone, when it has not been well set, after a fracture, and there remains a constant swelling in it,* or *a lameness.* (TA.) — And *An unsoundness* (O, Ḳ, TA) in an animal's leg, (O, TA,) and † in an affair. (TA.) One says, مَا فِى مَوَدَّتِهِ عَتَبٌ † *There is not in his love,* or *affection, anything mingling with it that vitiates it, impairs it,* or *renders it unsound.* (TA.)

عَتَبَةٌ The أُسْكُفَّة [meaning *threshold*] of a door, (Ṣ, A, Mgh, O, Mṣb, Ḳ,) *upon which one treads:* (TA:) or the *upper of the two* [*transverse pieces of wood,* of a door-way, *whereof each is called* أُسْكُفَّة; i. e. the *lintel*]: (Ḳ:) [for it is said that] the upper [piece of wood] in a door-way is the عَتَبَة; and the piece of wood that is above this is the حَاجِب; (Az, TA in this art. and in art. حجب;) and the أُسْكُفَّة is the lowest [or threshold]; and the عَارِضَتَانِ are the عِضَادَتَانِ [or two side-posts]: (TA:) the pl. is ▼ عَتَبٌ [improperly termed a pl., for it is a coll. gen. n.,] (Ṣ, O, Ḳ) and عَتَبَاتٌ. (TA.) [It is mostly used in the former of the two senses expl. above.] — And [hence,] ‡ *A wife* is thus termed, (O, Ḳ,) metonymically, in like manner as she is termed نَعْل, &c. (O.) — And *A step; a single step of a series:* (Ṣ, O, Mṣb:) or *a single step of a series made of wood:* (TA:) pl. ▼ عَتَبٌ [improperly termed a pl., as observed above,] (Ṣ, O, Mṣb) and عَتَبَاتٌ. (Ṣ, O.) — العَتَبَتَانِ † [*The two thresholds* or *lintels* or *steps*] termed الخَارِجَة [or *the outer*] and الدَّاخِلَة [or *the inner*] are *two well-known figures of* [*the science of*] الرَّمْل [i. e. *geomancy*]. (TA.) — عَتَبَةُ وَادٍ *The extreme side of a valley, that is next the mountain:* (O, TA:) or, as some say, العتبة [i. e. العَتَبَة, supposed by Freytag to be العُتْبَة,] signifies *the place of bending of the valley.* (Ḥam p. 18.) — And عَتَبَة signifies also *A hardship,* or *difficulty;* and *a hateful,* or *disagreeable, thing,* or *affair,* or *case,* or *event;* and so ▼ عَتَبٌ. (Ḳ.) One says, حُمِلَ فُلَانٌ عَلَى عَتَبَةٍ *Such a one was incited, urged, induced,* or *made, to do,* or *to suffer, a disagreeable,* or *hateful, thing, of a trying,* or *an afflictive, kind.* (Ṣ, O.) And حُمِلَ عَلَى عَتَبٍ ▼ مِنَ الشَّرِّ, and عَتَبَةٍ, *He was incited,* &c., *to do,* or *to suffer, a hardship,* or *difficulty.* (TA.) And مَا فِى هٰذَا الأَمْرِ ▼ عَتَبٌ وَلَا رَتَبٌ *There is not in this thing,* or *affair,* or *case, any hardship,* or *difficulty.* (Ṣ, O.) And عَتَبَاتُ المَوْتِ means *The severities* [or *pains* or *agonies*] *of death.* (TA, from a trad.)

عُتْبَى The *being well pleased, content,* or *satis-*

fied, [with a person,] or the *regarding with good will*, or *favour*: (M, A, Ḳ:) or *good pleasure, content, satisfaction, good will*, or *favour*: (MA, Ḳ, KL:) its primary signification is the *returning of one whose good will, or favour, has been solicited, or desired, to the love of his companion*: (TA:) it is the subst. from أَعْتَبَنِى as meaning "he returned to making me happy," &c.; (Ṣ; see 4;) a subst. from الإِعْتَابُ; (Mṣb;) [i. e.] it is put in the place of اعتاب; and [thus] it signifies [the *returning to making one happy*, or *doing what is pleasing to him, from doing evil to him*: or] the *returning, from doing evil, to that which makes the person who has reproved*, or *blamed*, or *been angry, to be well pleased, content*, or *satisfied*: and [simply] the *returning from doing a crime, a misdeed, an offence*, or *an evil action*. (TA.) One says, أَعْطَانِى العُتْبَى *He granted me his good will*, or *favour*. (A.) And إِنَّمَا يُعَاتَبُ مَنْ تُرْجَى عِنْدَهُ العُتْبَى *Only he should be reproved in whom the* [finding a disposition to a] *return from his evil conduct may be hoped for*. (TA.) And العُتْبَى is [said to be] used when one does not mean thereby الإِعْتَابُ, (Ṣ, O, TA,) i. e. in the contr. of its primary sense, (TA,) in the prov. لَكَ العُتْبَى بِأَنْ لَا رَضِيتَ i. e. [بِلَا رِضَاكَ, as though meaning *Thou shalt have content*, or *satisfaction, without thy being well pleased*; or] *I will content thee with the contrary of what thou likest*: and in like manner the corresponding verb is [said to be] used in the verse of Bishr Ibn-Abee-Kházim cited above in the explanations of that verb: (Ṣ, O, TA:) [but the prov. here mentioned may be well rendered *thou shalt return from thine evil way against thy wish*; for,] accord. to Fr, العُتْبَى in the phrase لَكَ العُتْبَى signifies *the returning, from what one likes, to what he dislikes*: (MF:) and it signifies also [as expl. above] *the returning from doing a crime, a misdeed*, &c. (TA.)

عِتْبَانٌ and ▼ عَتْبٌ and ▼ عِتَابٌ [all mentioned before as inf. ns.] are said to be *syn. with* إِعْتَابٌ: [see 4, and عُتْبَى:] it is asserted that you say, مَا وَجَدْتُ فِى قَوْلِهِ عِتْبَانًا [meaning *I did not find in what he said any* evidence of a *return to be favourable*, or *to do what would be pleasing* to me], when a man has mentioned his having granted you his good will, or favour, and you see not any proof thereof: and some say, مَا وَجَدْتُ عِنْدَهُ عَتْبًا ▼ وَلَا عِتَابًا ▼ [in the like sense]: but Az says, I have not heard ▼ عَتْبٌ nor عِتْبَانٌ nor ▼ عِتَابٌ in the sense of إِعْتَابٌ; but ▼ عَتْبٌ and عِتْبَانٌ signify thy *reproving* a man *for evil conduct*, &c., as stated above; [see 1;] and ▼ عِتَابٌ and مُعَاتَبَةٌ, *mutual reproving for such conduct*. (TA.) — العِتْبَانُ *The male hyena*: (Kr, TA:) and أُمُّ عِتْبَانَ and ▼ أُمُّ عِتَابٍ [the latter of the measure كِتَانٍ, accord. to the CḲ and my MS. copy of the Ḳ, but in the TA of the measure كِتَابٍ, and therefore ▼ عِتَابٍ,] *the female hyena*: (Ḳ:) said to be so called because of her limping: but ISd says, I am not sure of this. (TA.)

عِتَابٌ: see the next preceding paragraph, in five places.

عَتُوبٌ One *upon whom reproof, blame*, or *censure, does not operate*. (O, Ḳ.) — And *A road*, or *way*. (TA, as from the Ḳ [in which I do not find it].)

قَرْيَةٌ عَتِيبَةٌ [*A town*, or *village*,] *in which is little of good*, or *of good things*. (O, Ḳ.)

عَتَّابٌ One *who reproves, blames*, or *censures, much*, or *frequently*, [*in an absolute sense*, (see 1,) or] *in anger*, or *displeasure*. (Mṣb.) [See also عِتْبَانٌ.] — أُمُّ عِتَابٍ: see عَتْبٌ.

أُعْتُوبَةٌ [like أُسْبُوبَةٌ &c.] *A thing* [meaning *speech*] *with which one is reproved, blamed*, or *censured*. (O, Ḳ.) See 6.

مَعْتَبَةٌ and مَعْتِبَةٌ: see 1, in three places.

مَعْتُوبٌ is for مَعْتُوبٌ عَلَيْهِ [i. e. *Reproved, blamed*, or *censured*; &c.]: Mṭr says, it is said to signify مُفْسَدٌ [*corrupting, rendering unsound, vitiating*, &c.]; but I am not sure of it. (Ḥar p. 77.)

مُعْتَتَبٌ [is used, agreeably with analogy, in the sense of the inf. n. of اِعْتَتَبَ]. El-Kumeyt says,

• فَاعْتَتَبَ ▼ الشَّوْقُ مِنْ فُؤَادِى وَالشِّـ •
• ـعْرُ إِلَى مَنْ إِلَيْهِ مُعْتَتَبُ •

[*And desire turned away from my heart*, and my *poetry unto him unto whom was its turning*]. (Ṣ, O.)

مُسْتَعْتَبٌ is used in the sense of [the inf. n. of اِسْتَعْتَبَ, meaning] اِسْتِرْضَاءٌ: thus in the saying, وَلَا بَعْدَ المَوْتِ مِنْ مُسْتَعْتَبٍ [*And after death there is no asking, petitioning*, or *soliciting, favour* of God]: for after death is the abode of retribution, not that of works. (TA from a trad.)

عتد

1. عَتُدَ, [aor. ـُ,] (O, L, Mṣb, Ḳ,) inf. n. عَتَادٌ (O, Mṣb, Ḳ) and عَتَادَةٌ, (O, L, Ḳ,) *It* (a thing, L, Mṣb) *was*, or *became, ready, at hand*, or *prepared*. (O, L, Mṣb, Ḳ.) — And عَتُدَ, inf. n. عَتَادٌ (L, TA) and عَتَادَةٌ, (TA,) *It* (a thing) *was*, or *became, great, big*, or *bulky*. (L, TA.)

2: see the next paragraph.

4. اعتدهُ, (Ṣ, O, Mṣb, Ḳ,) inf. n. إِعْتَادٌ; (Ṣ;) and ▼ عتّدهُ, (Ṣ, Mṣb, Ḳ,) inf. n. تَعْتِيدٌ; (Ṣ, Ḳ;) *He made it ready, or prepared it*, (Ṣ, O, Mṣb, Ḳ,) *for a* [*future*] *day*. (Ṣ, O.) The former verb occurs in the Ḳur xii. 31. (Ṣ, O, Mṣb.) Yaạḳoob says that the [former] ت in أَعْتَدْتُهُ is a substitute for the [former] د in أَعْدَدْتُهُ: and some say that أَعَدَّ is originally أَعْتَدَ; but others deny this. (L.)

5. تعتّد فِى صَنْعَتِهِ *He was nice*, or *scrupulously nice and exact, in his work, art*, or *craft*. (O, Ḳ.)

عَتَدٌ: see عَتِيدٌ. — [Hence,] فَرَسٌ عَتَدٌ, as also ▼ عَتِدٌ, *A horse made ready*, or *prepared, for running*; (Ṣ, O, L, Ḳ;) *of strong make; quick in leaping*, or *springing; not incongruous, unsound, faulty*, or *weak, in make; nor lax*, or *uncompact*: (L:) or *strong, and perfect in make*: (ISk, Ṣ, O, Ḳ:) or *that performs run after run*: (O:) or *made ready*, or *prepared, for riding*: and applied alike to a male and to a female. (L.)

عَتِدٌ: see the next preceding paragraph.

عُتْدَةٌ and عَتَدَةٌ: see what next follows.

عَتَادٌ (Ṣ, A, O, L, Mṣb, Ḳ) and ▼ عُتْدَةٌ, (L, Ḳ,) or ▼ عَتَدَةٌ, (so in the O,) *Apparatus*; syn. عُدَّةٌ [q. v.]; (Ṣ, A, O, L, Ḳ;) which is said by some to be formed from عُدَّةٌ, but others deny this; (L;) *implements*, or *instruments*, or *the like*; (Ṣ, O;) or *weapons, beasts, and instruments*, or *equipage, of war*: (L, Mṣb:) pl. أَعْتُدٌ (O, L, Mṣb, Ḳ) and أَعْتِدَةٌ (L, Mṣb) [both pls. of pauc.] and عُتُدٌ. (L.) One says, أَخَذَ لِلْأَمْرِ عَتَادَهُ *He took his apparatus*, or *implements*, or *instruments*, or *the like*, [or *he prepared*, or *provided, himself*,] *for the affair*: (Ṣ, O:) or *he took, for the affair, what he had prepared of weapons, and beasts, and instruments*, or *equipage, of war*. (Mṣb.) — And sometimes, (Ṣ, O,) عَتَادٌ signifies also *A large drinking-cup* or *bowl*: (Ṣ, O, Ḳ:) *i. q.* عُسٌّ and صَحْنٌ: (IAạr, L:) or *a large drinking-cup* or *bowl* (عُسٌّ) *of* [*wood of the tree called*] أَثْلٌ. (AḤn, TA.)

عَتُودٌ *A yearling goat*; (Mṣb, Ḳ;) *a young goat that pastures, and is strong, and has become a year old*: (Ṣ, O, L:) or *a kid that has begun to pasture*: (L:) or *that pastures, and has become strong*; (Mgh, TA;) as also عَرِيضٌ: or *that has become a* جَذَعٌ [*a year old, in the second year*]; and such is called عَرِيضٌ also; both of which appellations are applied to the *male* and the *female*; or such is only termed عَرِيضٌ; عتود signifying one *that has become a* ثَنِىّ [app. meaning *in the third year*]: (TA:) or *that has attained the fit age for procreation*: (L:) pl. [of pauc.] أَعْتِدَةٌ and [of mult.] عِدَّانٌ the latter originally عِتْدَانٌ, (Ṣ, O, L, Mṣb, Ḳ,) the use of which last form is also allowable. (Mṣb.) — Also [*A tree of the species called*] *a* سِدْرَة: or *a* طَلْحَة. (O, L, Ḳ.)

عَتِيدٌ A thing (Ṣ, O, L) *ready, at hand*, or *prepared*; (Ṣ, A, O, L, Ḳ;) as also ▼ عَتَدٌ [q. v.]: pl. [of pauc.] of the latter أَعْتَادٌ and [of mult.] عُتُدٌ: (Mṣb:) the former occurs in the Ḳur l. 22, (O, L,) in this sense: or as meaning *near*: (L:) or as meaning ▼ مُعْتَدٌ, (O,) i. e. *made ready*, or *prepared*. (Ḳ.)

عَتِيدَةٌ *A receptacle for perfume* (A, Mṣb) *and unguent* (A) or *unguents*: (Mṣb:) *a kind of wooden tray* (طَبْلَة), or *a small round box* (حُقَّة), *in which are the perfume of a man*, (O, Ḳ,) or his unguent, (O,) *and the perfume of the bride,* (O, Ḳ,) *prepared* (أُعْتِدَتْ) *for what she requires of perfume, and substance for fumigation, and a comb, and other things;* [formed from عَتِيدٌ;] the ة being affixed to it as being a subst.: (O:) or *a* طَبْل [or *small round basket covered with leather*] *prepared for the perfume,* (Az, Mgh, L,) *and utensils, and substance for fumigation,* (Az, L,) *and comb,* (Az, Mgh, L,) *and mirror,* (Mgh,) *and other things, required by a bride:* (Az, Mgh, L:) or *a thing like a casket,* or *small chest, in which a woman puts such of her goods,* or *utensils, as she values.* (L.)

مُعْتَدٌ : see عَتِيدٌ.

عتر

1. عَتَرَ, aor. ـِ , inf. n. عَتْرٌ [and تَعْتَارٌ (mentioned below in this paragraph), a form denoting repetition, or frequency, of the action, or its application to several objects, or it may be an inf. n. of which the verb is ▼عتّر], *He slaughtered* [or *sacrificed*] (Ṣ, O, Ḳ, TA) *an* عَتِيرَة, (Ṣ, O,) [i. e.] a sheep or goat, or a gazelle or the like. (TA.) Sometimes a man, (Ṣ, O,) of the people of the Time of Ignorance, (Ṣ,) made a vow that, if he should see what he loved, he would slaughter such and such of his sheep or goats; and when the performance of the vow became obligatory, he would be unwilling to do so, and would slaughter gazelles instead of the sheep or goats: (Ṣ, O:) sometimes he would say, "If my camels amount to a hundred, I will slaughter for them an عَتِيرَة;" but when they amounted to a hundred, he would be niggardly of the sheep or goat, and would hunt a gazelle, and slaughter it. (TA.) One says, هٰذِهِ أَيَّامُ تَرْجِيبٍ and تَعْتَارٍ [*These are days of the sacrificing of the* عَتِيرَة]. (Ṣ, O.)

2: see above, first sentence.

عِتْرٌ *Origin,* or *original state* or *condition;* (Ṣ, O, Ḳ;) and *natural disposition;* like عِكْرٌ. (O.) One says, هُوَ كَرِيمُ العِتْرِ *He is of generous origin.* (TḲ.) And it is said in a prov., عَادَتْ إِلَى عِتْرِهَا لَمِيسُ *Lemees* [a proper name of a woman] *returned to her original state* or *condition* (Ṣ, O) and *natural disposition:* (O:) applied to him who has returned to a natural disposition which he had relinquished. (Ṣ, O.) [See also عِكْرٌ.] — Also *A certain plant,* (Ṣ, O, Ḳ,) *used medicinally, like the* مَرْزَنْجُوش [or *marjoram*]; (Ṣ;) *growing like this latter plant, in a straggling manner; and when it has grown tall, and its stem is cut, there comes forth from it what resembles milk:* (TA:) accord. to Aboo-Ziyád, it is *a plant of those termed* أَحْرَار [pl. of حُرٌّ], *having a small round fruit* (جُرَىٌّ [dim. of جِرْو]), *which is sweet,* or *pleasant in taste, eaten by men; and it grows like as does the poppy, but is smaller:* (AḤn, O:) or *certain small trees* [or *plants*], (Ṣ, Ḳ, TA,) *having round fruits* (جِرَآء [pl. of جِرْو]), *like those of the poppy:* (TA as on the authority of AḤn:) AḤn says, (O,) some assert it to mean the مَرْزَنْجُوش; (O, TA;) but, he adds, this I have not found to be known: (O:) and some say that it is the عَرْفَج: (TA:) the n. un. is عِتْرَةٌ: (Ṣ, O:) AḤn says, a desert-Arab of Rabee'ah told me that this is *a small tree* [or *plant*], *that rises to the height of a cubit, having many branches, and green, round leaves, like the* تَنُّوم, *and round fruits* (جِرَآء), *which are in pairs, near together, hanging down towards the ground, and sweet,* or *pleasant in taste, their taste being like that of small cucumbers: it seldom,* or *never, grows singly, but is found in pairs,* or *in fours, in one place:* and some assert that *it abounds with milk:* (O:) it is also said to be *a tree* [or *plant*] *that grows by the burrow of the* [*lizard called*] ضَبّ, which mumbles it so that it does not increase; whence the saying هُوَ أَذَلُّ مِنْ عِتْرَةِ الضَّبِّ [*He is more vile than the* عترة *of the* ضبّ]: and it is also said, in the Ḳ, to signify the مَرْزَنْجُوش, mentioned above as being said to be a signification of عِتْر: (TA:) also, the *caper.* (Ḳ,* TA.) It is said in a trad. that there is no harm in a man's treating himself medically with senna and عِتْر while in a state of إِحْرَام: (Ṣ, O:) which, some say, means that there is no harm in taking these from the sacred territory for such treatment. (O.) — Also *An idol,* (O, Ḳ,) *such as had victims* (عَتَائِر) *sacrificed to it.* (O.) — See also عَتِيرَةٌ.

عِتْرَةٌ The *stem,* or *stock,* of a tree: on the authority of Aboo-Sa'eed and IAạr: (TA:) and the *branches* of a tree. (A, TA.) — [And hence,] † The *people,* or *tribe,* of a man, *consisting of his nearer relations,* (A'Obeyd, ISk, Ṣ, A, O, Mṣb, Ḳ,) *both* the *dead and* the *living:* (Ṣ, Ḳ:) or his *relations:* (Mṣb:) or his *relations consisting of* his *offspring and* his *paternal uncle's sons:* (A:) or his *relations consisting of* his *offspring and of others:* (TA:) or the *more distinguished of* one's *relations:* (IAth, TA:) or the *people of a man's house,* the *more near and more distant:* (O, TA:) and a man's *offspring,* or *progeny;* (IAạr, Th, Az, Ṣ, O, Mṣb, Ḳ;) which is said to be the only meaning of the word known to the Arabs; (Mṣb;) or imagined by the vulgar to be its meaning peculiarly. (TA.) عِتْرَةُ النَّبِىِّ means [*The nearer portion of the tribe of the Prophet, consisting of*] *the sons of 'Abd-El-Muttalib:* (Aboo-Sa'eed, O:) or *'Abd-El-Muttalib and his sons:* (TA:) or *the offspring of Fátimeh:* (IAạr, TA:) or *the nearer members of the house of the Prophet, consisting of his own offspring and of 'Alee and his offspring:* or *the nearer and the more distant in relationship of the house of the Prophet:* or, as is commonly held, *the people of the house of the Prophet;* who are those from whom it is forbidden to exact the poor-rate, and those to whom is assigned the fifth of the fifth mentioned in the Soorat el-Anfál [the eighth chapter of the Ḳur-án, verse 42]. (TA.) — Also n. un. of عِتْر [q. v.]. (Ṣ, O.)

عَتِيرَةٌ *A sheep, or goat, which they used to slaughter,* (Ṣ, O, Mṣb, Ḳ,) *in* [*the month of*] *Rejeb,* (Ṣ, O, Mṣb,) *to their gods,* (Ṣ, O, Ḳ,) or *to their idols;* (Mṣb;) i. q. رَجَبِيَّةٌ, (A'Obeyd, TA,) i. e. *a victim which was sacrificed in Rejeb, as a propitiation, in the Time of Ignorance,* (A'Obeyd, Mgh, TA,) *and also by the Muslims in the beginning of El-Islám;* (Mgh;) but the custom was afterwards abolished; (A'Obeyd, Mgh, O;) as also ▼عِتْرٌ; (Ṣ, O, Ḳ;) which likewise signifies *any slaughtered animal;* (Ḳ;) and so does ▼عَاتِرَةٌ; this being like رَاضِيَةٌ, in the phrase عِيشَةٌ رَاضِيَةٌ, for مَرْضِيَّةٌ; (Lth, TA;) or it may be a possessive epithet [meaning ذَاتُ عَتْرٍ]: (TA:) the pl. of عَتِيرَةٌ is عَتَائِرُ. (Mṣb.)

عَاتِرَةٌ : see the next preceding paragraph.

عتق

1. عَتَقَتِ الفَرَسُ, aor. ـِ , inf. n. عِتْقٌ; (Ṣ, O;) or عَتُقَ الفَرَسُ, aor. ـُ; and عَتَقَ; *The mare,* (Ṣ, O,) or *horse,* (Ḳ,) *preceded, and became safe,* or *secure:* (Ṣ, O, Ḳ:) [or,] accord. to IDrd, عَتُقَ الفَرَسُ, with ḍamm, signifies *the horse became such as is termed* عَتِيقٌ [q. v.]. (O.) The meaning of The *state,* or *act, of preceding,* or *having precedence,* [assigned to the inf. n. عِتْقٌ,] is said to be the turning-point of the art.: and hence, عَتَقَ الخَيْلَ, said of a horse, means *He preceded the other horses, and became safe,* or *secure, from them.* (Mgh.) And عَتَقْتُ الشَّىْءَ, aor. ـِ , *I preceded the thing.* (Mṣb.) — عَتَقَ العَبْدُ, (Ṣ, Mgh, O, Mṣb, Ḳ,) aor. ـِ , (Ṣ, O, Mṣb, Ḳ,) inf. n. عِتْقٌ (Ṣ, Mgh, O, Ḳ) and عَتْقٌ, (Ḳ,) or the former is a simple subst. and the latter is an inf. n., (Mṣb, Ḳ,) as also عَتَاقٌ (Ṣ, Mgh, O, Mṣb, Ḳ) and عَتَاقَةٌ, (Ṣ, O, Mṣb, Ḳ,) *The slave became free;* (Ṣ, O;) *the slave passed forth from the state of slavery.* (Mgh, Ḳ.) And sometimes عِتْقٌ is used in the place of إِعْتَاقٌ; (Mgh;) and so is عَتَاقٌ, in the saying حَلَفَ بِالعَتَاقِ [*He swore by emancipation*]: (TA:) but see 4. [Hence,] one says, فُلَانٌ مَوْلَى عَتَاقَةٍ [*Such a one is a freed slave*]. (Ṣ, O, Ḳ. [See also عَتِيقٌ.]) — عَتَقَتْ مِنَ الصِّبَا is said of a girl when she has attained to the marriageable state [meaning *She has passed forth from the state of childhood*]. (O, TA.) And عَتَقَتْ, aor. ـِ , *She* (a girl) *attained to the commencement of the state of puberty:* and as some say, *had not married:* (Ḳ,* TA:) [or] *she* (a woman) *passed forth from the state,* or *condition, of serving her father and mother, and from being possessed by a husband.* (Mṣb.) — عَتَقَ بَعْدَ اسْتِغْلَاجٍ, aor. ـُ , *He* (a man, Ṣ, O) *became thin,* or *fine,* or *delicate, in his external skin, after having been coarse and rough;* (Ṣ, O, Ḳ;) as also عَتُقَ. (Ḳ.) — عَتُقَ, said of anything, *It attained its utmost point, reach,* or *degree.* (TA.) — عَتَقَتِ البَكْرَةُ *The young she-camel became free from* القُرْحَة [or *purulent pustules in the mouth*] and العُرَّة [i. e. *mange,* or *scab*]: until this is the case, she is not reckoned a بَكْرَة: so said an Arab of the desert. (TA.) — عَتَقَ, (Mṣb,) or عَتُقَ المَالُ,

(Ṣ, O, Ḳ,) aor. ـُ, (Ḳ,) inf. n. عِتْقٌ; (Fr, Ṣ, O;) and عَتَاقٌ; (Ḳ;) *It*, (Mṣb,) or *the property*, or *cattle*, (Fr, Ṣ, O, Ḳ,) *became in a good, right*, or *proper, state*. (Fr, Ṣ, O, Mṣb, Ḳ.) — See also 4. — عَتُقَ الشَّىْءُ, (Ṣ, Mgh, O, Ḳ,) inf. n. عَتَاقَةٌ; (Ṣ, Mgh, O;) and عَتَقَ, aor. ـِ (Ṣ, O, Ḳ) and ـُ; (Ḳ;) *The thing became old*. (Ṣ, Mgh, O, Ḳ.) Both of these verbs, in this sense, are said of clarified butter. (TA.) And you say, عَتُقَتِ الخَمْرُ; (Ṣ, Mṣb, Ḳ;) and عَتَقَتْ, (Mṣb, Ḳ,) aor. ـُ, inf. n. عِتْقٌ and عُتْقٌ; (Mṣb;) *The wine became old* (Mṣb, Ḳ) *and good*. (Ḳ.) — عَتَقَتْ عَلَيْهِ يَمِينٌ, (Ṣ, O, Ḳ,) aor. ـِ; (Ṣ, Ḳ; in one of my copies of the Ṣ ـُ;) and عَتُقَتْ; (Ṣ, O, Ḳ;) *The oath was binding on him*: (Ḳ:) or *was old, and binding on him*; as though he kept it [long], not violating it. (Ṣ, O.) = عَتَقَهُ بِفِيهِ, inf. n. عَتْقٌ, *He bit it*: (Ḳ:) or بِفِيهِ ▼عَتَّقَ *he bit with his front teeth*: and [simply] *he bit*: (So in the O:) [both are app. correct; for it is said that] تَعْتِيقٌ signifies the act of *biting*. (L, Ḳ.)

2: see 4. — عَتَّقْتُ الشَّىْءَ, (Ṣ, O,) inf. n. تَعْتِيقٌ, (Ṣ, Ḳ,) *I made the thing old*. (Ṣ, O, Ḳ.*) عُتِّقَتْ زَمَانًا is said of wine (الخَمْرُ) [as meaning *It was kept long, so that it became old*]. (Ṣ, O.) — See also 1, last sentence.

4. اعتق فَرَسَهُ *He made his mare to hasten*, or *be quick*, [*and to precede*, (see 1, first sentence,)] *and become safe*, or *secure*. (Ṣ, O, Ḳ.) — اعتق العَبْدَ *He emancipated the slave; freed him from slavery*: (Ṣ, Mgh, O, Mṣb,* Ḳ:) ▼عَتَقَهُ in this sense is not known, (TA,) and should not be said, therefore it is said in the Bári' that one should not say عَتَقَ العَبْدَ, nor should one say أُعْتِقَ العَبْدُ with the verb in the active form [and making العبد the agent]. (Mṣb.) — اعتق المَالَ *He put the cattle*, or *property, into a good, right*, or *proper, state*; (Fr, Ṣ, O, Ḳ;) as also ▼عَتَّقَهُ, inf. n. تَعْتِيقٌ; (O;) and ▼عَتَقَهُ, (Mṣb,* Ḳ, TA,) aor. ـُ, inf. n. عِتْقٌ. (TA.) — اعتق قَلِيبَهُ *He dug his well, and cased it* [*with stones* or *bricks*], (AA, O, Ḳ,) *and made it good*. (AA, O.) — اعتق مَوْضِعَهُ *He took for himself his place* (حَازَهُ), *so that it became his property*. (O, Ḳ.) — اعتق دِيوَانَهُ [is expl. by the words] إِذَا اسْتَقَامَ لَهُ وَأَخَذَ مِنْهُ شَيْئًا [app. as meaning *He took something from his register*, or *his account* or *reckoning, when it had become in a right*, or *correct, state for him*]. (O, TA.) — اعتق يَمِينَهُ *He made his oath to be inexpiable*. (L, TA.)

عَتْقٌ: see the next paragraph.

عِتْقٌ [mentioned above as an inf. n. and also as a simple subst. (see 1)] *i. q.* نَجَابَةٌ [app. as a quality of a horse and the like, meaning *Generousness, excellence*, or *swiftness*: see 1, first and second sentences]. (Ḳ.) — And *i. q.* كَرَمٌ [*Generousness, generosity*, or *nobility*]; (Ṣ, Mgh, O, Ḳ;) as in the saying, مَا أَبْيَنَ العِتْقَ فِى وَجْهِ فُلَانٍ [*How manifest is generousness, &c., in the face of such a one!*]. (Ṣ, O.) — And *i. q.* شَرَفٌ [*Highness*, or *eminence, of rank* or *condition*]. (Ḳ.) — Also *Beauty*, or *comeliness*. (Ṣ, O, Ḳ.) — And The *state*, or *condition, of freedom*; *contr. of slavery*. (Ṣ, O, Ḳ.) — [And *Oldness*: in which sense,] accord. to some, عِتْقٌ and ▼عَتْقٌ relate to inanimate things, as wine and dates; and قِدَمٌ relates to inanimate things and also to animals. (L, Ḳ.) = Also, and ▼عُتُقٌ, *A species of trees from which Arabian bows are made*: (AḤn, Ḳ:*) the name being meant to imply the excellence of the bow [made therefrom]. (AḤn.)

عُتُقٌ: see what next precedes.

عُتَاقٌ: see the next paragraph, last quarter.

عَتِيقٌ A horse *that precedes, outstrips*, or *outgoes*; as also ▼عَاتِقٌ; or this signifies a horse *that precedes, and becomes safe*, or *secure*; (TA; [see 1, first and second sentences;]) or *that precedes, outstrips*, or *outgoes, the* [*other*] *horses*: (Mṣb:) and the former, a *generous*, or an *excellent*, horse: (Mṣb, TA:) or a horse *swift and excellent*; or *that excites admiration by his generousness* or *excellence*; syn. رَائِعٌ: (Ṣ, Mgh, O, TA:) pl. عِتَاقٌ: (Ṣ, O, Mṣb:) عَتِيقَةٌ applied to a young she-camel means *generous, excellent*, or *swift*: (TA:) and عِتَاقٌ has this meaning applied to camels, (TA,) or to such as are termed أَرْحَبِيَّات, (Ṣ, O, TA,) and to horses; (Ḳ, TA;) or the عِتَاق of horses are the *generous*, or *excellent*, thereof; and so of birds; (Mgh;) [the *noble* thereof, in a sense wider that that in which this epithet is applied in English falconry;] or of birds, *such as prey*; (Ṣ, O, Ḳ, TA;) عَتِيقٌ being applied to one of them: (TA:) عِتَاقُ الطَّيْرِ is also applied [particularly] to *eagles*: (IAạr, TA voce عُقَابٌ:) and عَتِيقُ الطَّيْرِ, to *the hawk*, or *falcon*: (O, TA:) and عَتِيقٌ signifies anything *generous*, or *excellent*; (Ṣ;) and anything *choice*, or *best*; (Ṣ, O, Ḳ;) thus applied to a hawk, and dates, and water, and fat: (Ṣ:) or العَتِيقُ means *dates* [themselves], (AḤn, O, Ḳ,) as in a verse of 'Antarah (or of Khuzaz-Ibn-Lowdhán, Ṣ, TA) cited voce كَذَبَ, (O,) as a proper name thereof; (Ḳ;) or, as some say, the *dates termed* شِهْرِيز; and its pl. is عُتُقٌ: (TA:) and *water* [itself]: (Ḳ:) and *fat* [itself]: and accord. to IAạr, anything *that has attained the utmost degree in goodness* or *badness* or *beauty* or *ugliness* is termed عَتِيقٌ; pl. عُتُقٌ. (TA.) — Also *Beautiful*, or *comely*: so in the saying, فُلَانٌ عَتِيقُ الوَجْهِ [*Such a one is beautiful*, or *comely, in respect of the face*]. (O, TA.) And اِمْرَأَةٌ عَتِيقَةٌ means *A woman beautiful*, or *comely*; *generous*, or *noble*. (TA.) — And (applied to a man, Ṣ, O) *Thin*, or *fine*, or *delicate, in his external skin*, after having been coarse and rough. (Ṣ, O, Ḳ.) — And, applied to a slave, signifying *Freed from slavery*, or *emancipated*; (Ṣ, Mgh, O, Mṣb,* Ḳ;) as also ▼عَاتِقٌ, and ▼مُعْتَقٌ; (Ṣ, O, Mṣb, Ḳ;) and some of the relaters of traditions say ▼مَعْتُوقٌ, (TA,) but this is not allowable: (Mṣb, TA:) عَتِيقَةٌ is applied to a female, (Ṣ, O, Mṣb, Ḳ,) and عَتِيقٌ also: (Mṣb:) the pl. of عَتِيقٌ is عُتَقَاءُ, (Ṣ, Mgh, O, Mṣb, Ḳ,) and عِتَاقٌ also sometimes occurs, like كِرَامٌ as a pl. of كَرِيمٌ; (Mṣb;) and the pl. of عَتِيقَةٌ is عَتَائِقُ. (Ṣ, O, Mṣb.) العَتِيقُ is an appellation applied to Eṣ-Ṣiddeeḳ, (Ṣ, Ḳ,) i. e. (Ṣ) to Aboo-Bekr, (Ṣ, O, Ḳ,) as a surname, (Ḳ,) because he was said by the Prophet to be freed (عَتِيق) from the fire [of Hell]: or because of his beauty, or comeliness: (Ṣ, O, Ḳ:) or he was so named by his mother. (O, Ḳ.) — And *Old*; (Ṣ, Mgh, O, L, Mṣb, Ḳ;) as also ▼عَاتِقٌ: (Ṣ, O:) the former is applied in this sense to anything, even to a man: (Ṣ, L:) and the pl. is عِتَاقٌ, which occurs in a trad. applied to the earlier verses of the Ḳur-án that were revealed at Mekkeh, (L, TA,) and عُتْقٌ, (Ṣ, Ḳ,*) or عُتُقٌ, with two ḍammehs, (Mgh, Mṣb,) like بُرُدٌ pl. of بَرِيدٌ, (Mṣb,) applied to دَرَاهِم, (Mgh, Mṣb,) عُتْقٌ being [probably] a contraction of عُتُقٌ (like as بُرْدٌ is of بُرُدٌ) and in like manner applied to دَنَانِير, (Ṣ,) [and عُتَّقٌ occurs in the TA in art. سهر, agreeably with general analogy if pl. of عَاتِقٌ,] but عُتُّقٌ, with two ḍammehs and teshdeed, is a mistake. (Mgh.) البَيْتُ العَتِيقُ is an appellation of *The Kaabeh*, (Ṣ, O, Ḳ,) given to it in the Ḳur-án [xxii. 30 and 34, as meaning *the Old House*], (O,) because it was the first house founded upon the earth, (O, Ḳ,) as is said in the Ḳur [iii. 90]: (O:) or [as meaning † *the Freed House*,] because it was freed from submersion (O, Ḳ) in the days of the Deluge, (O,) being taken up; (TA;) or from the imperious, overbearing, or tyrannical, of mankind; or from the Abyssinians; or because not possessed by any one; (O, Ḳ;) and [thus expl.] it is tropical. (TA.) You say قَنْطَرَةٌ عَتِيقَةٌ [*An old bridge*], (Ṣ, O, Ḳ,) with ة, (Ṣ, O,) and قَنْطَرَةٌ جَدِيدٌ [meaning the contr.], (Ṣ, O, Ḳ,) without ة, (Ṣ, O,) because عَتِيقَةٌ has the meaning of the measure فَاعِلَة, (Ṣ, O, Ḳ,) but جَدِيدٌ has the meaning of the measure مَفْعُولَة. (Ṣ, O.) And رَاحٌ عَتِيقٌ, (O, Ḳ,) without ة, (O,) and عَتِيقَةٌ and ▼عَاتِقٌ [app. meaning *Old wine*]: (Ḳ:) and خَمْرٌ ▼عَاتِقٌ and عَتِيقٌ and ▼عُتَاقٌ *good and old wine*: (Ḳ, in a later portion of the art.:) or ▼عَاتِقٌ means *old* wine: (Ṣ, O, TA:) or *long kept in its receptacle*: (L, TA:) or *of which no one has broken the seal* [*upon the mouth of its jar*]: (Ṣ, O, TA:) or *that has just attained to maturity*: (Z, TA:) Ḥassán says, [using it as an epithet in which the quality of a subst. predominates,]

كَالمِسْكِ تَخْلِطُهُ بِمَآءِ سَحَابَةٍ
أَوْ عَاتِقٍ كَدَمِ الذَّبِيحِ مُدَامِ

[*Like musk which thou mixest with the water of a cloud, or old wine* (&c.) *like the blood of the slaughtered animal, made to continue long in its unopened jar*]. (Ṣ, O, TA: but the last, for تَخْلِطُهُ, has مُخْتَلِطُهُ.) — And العَتِيقُ signifies *Wine* [itself]. (Ḳ.) And [*What is termed*] الطِّلَآء [app. as meaning *expressed juice of grapes boiled until the quantity thereof is reduced to one third* or *half*]. (Ḳ.) — And *Milk*. (Ḳ.) —

And A [sort of] male palm-tree, (Ḳ, TA,) well known, (TA,) of which the female palm-tree will not shake off, or drop, its fruit (لَا تَنْفُضُ نَخْلَتُهُ) (Ḳ, TA.) — And ثَوْبٌ عَتِيقٌ means جَيِّدُ الحبكة [app. a mistranscription, for جَيِّدُ الحَبْكِ, i. e. A garment, or piece of cloth, well woven]. (TA.)

عَاتِقٌ: see the next preceding paragraph, in six places. — Also A young bird (Ṣ, O, Ḳ, TA) above the stage of that which is termed نَاهِض, (Ṣ, O, TA,) i. e. of that of which the first feathers have fallen off and strong feathers have grown; (TA;) when it has flown and become independent; (Ḳ, TA;) thought by A'Obeyd to be from the meaning of "outgoing," or "outstripping," كَأَنَّهُ يَعْتِقُ أَىْ يَسْبِقُ [as though it outwent, or outstripped]: (Ṣ, O, TA:) or of the young of the sand-grouse (القَطَا), or of the pigeon, while not yet firm, or strong, (Ḳ, TA,) not advanced in age: (TA:) pl., in this and the following senses, عَوَاتِقُ. (Ḳ.) — And A girl that has attained to the commencement of the state of puberty, (Ṣ, O, Ḳ,) and become kept behind the curtain in the tent, or house, of her family, (Ṣ, O,) and not been separated to a husband: (Ṣ, O, Ḳ:) said by IAạr to be so called because she has passed forth from the state of childhood, and attained to being marriageable; (O;) or because she has passed forth from the state, or condition, of serving her father and mother, and has not yet been possessed by a husband; but AAF says that this is not valid: or that has attained to the wearing of the garment called دِرْع, and has passed forth from the state of childhood and of being required to help in the service of her family: (TA:) or such as is between the stages of puberty and middle age: (Ḳ:) or a woman who has passed forth from the state, or condition, of serving her father and mother, and from being possessed by a husband: (Mṣb:) pl. as above, and عُتَّقٌ also; the latter occurring in a trad. (TA.) — And A زِقّ [or wine-skin], (T, Ṣ, &c.,) of which the wine is good: (T, TA:) or of which the odour is pleasant, because of its oldness: (Ṣ:) or wide, (Ibn-'Abbád, O, L, Ḳ,) and good: or wide as applied to a [leathern water-bag such as is called] مَزَادَة. (TA.) — And A bow (قَوْس) that has become altered in colour; as also عَاتِكٌ: (IF, O:) or عَاتِقَةٌ (Ṣ, O, Ḳ) and عَاتِقٌ (Ḳ) a bow that has become old and red; (Ṣ, O, Ḳ;) as also عَاتِكَةٌ. (Ṣ, O.) — العَاتِقُ also signifies The part, of the مَنْكِب [or shoulder], which is the place of the [garment called] رِدَآء: (Ṣ, O, Ḳ:) or the part between the مَنْكِب and the neck; (Mgh, Mṣb, Ḳ:) which is the place of the رِدَآء: (Mṣb:) or the part, of the كَتِف [properly the shoulder-blade, but app. here meaning, as in some other instances, the shoulder itself], which is the place of the suspensory-cord of the sword: (Ḥam p. 556:) it is [said to be] masc. and fem.; (Ṣ, O, Mṣb;) sometimes fem.; (Ḳ;) but this is not of established authority: a verse which is cited by IB [and in the O] as an instance of its being fem. is asserted by some to be forged: (TA:) the pl. is عَوَاتِقُ (Mṣb, Ḳ, and Ḥam ubi suprà,) and عُتُقٌ. (Ḳ.) One says رَجُلٌ أَمْيَلُ العَاتِقِ A man bent, or bending, [or sloping,] in [the part which is] the place of the رِدَآء. (Ṣ, O.) حَبْلُ العَاتِقِ see in art. حبل. — And [the pl.] العَوَاتِقُ signifies also النَّوَاحِى [The sides; or lateral, or outward, or adjacent, parts or portions; &c.: see the sing., نَاحِيَةٌ]. (Ibn-'Abbád, O.)

مُعْتِقٌ: see عَتِيقٌ, in the former half.

مُعَتَّقَةٌ, applied to wine (خَمْر), Old, (Ṣ, O, Ḳ,) having been kept (عُتِّقَتْ) long. (Ṣ, O.) — And المُعَتَّقَةُ [as a subst.] A certain perfume, or odoriferous substance; syn. عِطْرٌ; (Ḳ;) a sort of عِطْر. (L.)

رَجُلٌ مِعْتَاقُ الوَسِيقَةِ A man who, when he drives away a number of camels that he has captured, renders them secure (Ṣ, O) from being overtaken, (O,) and outstrips with them: (Ṣ:) from أَعْتَقَ العَبْدَ: (O:) you should not say مِعْتَاق. (Ṣ.)

مَعْتُوقٌ: see عَتِيقٌ, in the former half.

عتك

1. عَتَكَ بِهِ الطِّيبُ, (Ṣ, O,) aor. ِ, inf. n. عَتْكٌ, (O,) The perfume stuck to him, or it. (Ṣ, O.) — And عَتَكَ البَوْلُ عَلَى فَخِذِ النَّاقَةِ The urine dried upon the thigh of the she-camel: (Ṣ, O, Ḳ:) but as some relate a verse cited as an ex. of the verb in this sense, it is عَبَكَ. (O.) — And عَتَكَ بِهِ, inf. n. as above, He, or it, clave to him, or it. (TA.) — عَتَكَتْ بِالطِّيبِ She (a woman) daubed, or smeared, herself with perfume. (IDrd, O.) — عَتَكَتِ القَوْسُ, aor. ِ, inf. n. عَتْكٌ and عُتُوكٌ, The bow became red (IDrd, O, Ḳ) in its wood (IDrd, O) by reason of oldness. (IDrd, O, Ḳ.) — عَتَكَتْ said of a woman, She was, or became, high, or exalted, in rank, condition, or estimation; high-born, or noble. (Ibn-'Abbád, O, Ḳ.)

قَطِيفَةٌ عَتِكَةٌ [A nappy, or villous, cloth or outer garment,] coherent [in its nap], or matted [therein]: and in like manner, نَعْجَةٌ عَتِكَةُ الصُّوفِ [A ewe having the wool coherent, or matted]. (Ibn-'Abbád, O.)

عَاتِكٌ, (Ḳ,) or عَاتِكَةٌ, (Ṣ,) or both, (IDrd, O,) applied to a bow (قَوْس), Red (IDrd, Ṣ, O, Ḳ) in its wood (IDrd, O) by reason of oldness: (IDrd, Ṣ, O, Ḳ:) as also عَاتِقٌ (Ḳ in art. عتق) and عَاتِقَةٌ: (Ṣ and O and Ḳ in that art.:) [or] عَاتِكَةٌ, so applied, signifies of a pure, or clear, yellow colour. (Skr, TA.) أَحْمَرُ عَاتِكٌ signifies Intensely red. (Lḥ, O, TA.) And عَاتِكٌ, alone, Yellow. (TA. [App. applied therein, in this sense, to a vein or a root (عرق, thus without any vowel-sign)].) And Pure, or unmixed; applied to a colour (Ḳ, TA) of any kind, and to a thing of any kind. (TA.) And Clear; applied to [the beverage called] نَبِيذ: (IDrd, O, Ḳ, TA:) or, so applied, old; accord. to Lth with ن, but correctly with ت. (TA in art. عنك.) And i. q. كَرِيمٌ [as meaning Highly esteemed, or excellent, or the like]; (Ḳ, TA;) applied to anything. (TA.) — عَاتِكَةٌ applied to a woman means Being, or becoming, red (مُحْمَرَّةٌ [in the CḲ مُحْمَرَةٌ]) by reason of perfume; (Ḳ, TA;) from عَتَكَتِ القَوْسُ [expl. above]: (IKt, TA:) or having a stain of perfume: (TA:) or being, or becoming, yellow from saffron: (R, TA:) or having clearness and redness: or, accord. to Ibn-Saad, lean, or light of flesh; slender and lean; or lean, and lank in the belly: (TA:) or high, or exalted, in rank, condition, or estimation; high-born, or noble: (O, TA:) or, accord. to IAạr, from عَتَكَتْ عَلَى بَعْلِهَا, [said of a woman,] meaning نَشَزَتْ; but this is said by Th to be correctly عَنَكَتْ, the ت being a mistranscription. (TA.)

عَاتِكِىٌّ A certain kind of cloth or garment, red and yellow, brought from Syria: a rel. n. from [a place called] مَشْهَدُ عَاتِكَةَ. (TA.)

عتل

1. عَتَلَهُ, aor. ُ and ِ, (Ṣ, O, Ḳ, TA,) as in the Ḳur xliv. 47 accord. to different readers, inf. n. عَتْلٌ, (TA,) He drew him along, or dragged him, roughly, or violently, (Ṣ, O, Ḳ,) namely, a man, and likewise a horse, (Ṣ, O,) and carried him off or away: (Ḳ:) he pushed him, or thrust him, and urged him, driving him along roughly, or violently: (TA:) accord. to ISk, عَتَلَهُ and عَتَنَهُ signify the same; (Ṣ, O, TA;) i. e. he pushed him, or thrust him, roughly, or violently, to the prison: or العَتْلُ signifies the laying hold upon the clothes at the bosom of a man, and drawing him, or dragging him to thee, and taking him away to prison, or to trial, or affliction. (TA.) And عَتَلَ النَّاقَةَ He led the she-camel (Ḳ, TA) roughly, or violently, taking hold of her nose-rein. (TA.) — عَتِلَ إِلَى الشَّرِّ, aor. َ, (Ḳ,) inf. n. عَتَلٌ, (Ṣ, O, TA,) He (a man, Ṣ, O) hastened, or was quick, to do evil, or mischief. (Ṣ,* O,* Ḳ.)

2. تَعْتِيلٌ [app. The making one to quit his place]: see 7.

3. مُعَاتَلَةٌ The act of pushing, or thrusting, one another [app. roughly, or violently]. (TA.)

5: see the next paragraph, in two places.

7. انعتل He was, or became, drawn along, or dragged, roughly, or violently: (Ḳ:) or i. q. اِنْقَادَ [he suffered himself to be led, &c.]. (Ibn-'Abbád, O, TA.) — And لَا أَنْعَتِلُ مَعَكَ; (so in copies of the Ṣ and Ḳ and in the TA;) or لا أَتَعَتَّلُ ↓ مَعَكَ, (so in the O and in one of my copies of the Ṣ,) from ↓ التَّعْتِيلُ; (O;) I will not quit my place with thee; (Ṣ, O, Ḳ, TA;) and will not come with thee. (TA.) And لَا أَنْعَتِلُ مَعَكَ شِبْرًا, thus in the handwriting of J in one of the copies [of the Ṣ, or ↓ أَتَعَتَّلُ may be the correct word], I will not come with thee [a span]. (TA.)

عَتَلٌ: see [its n. un.] عَتَلَةٌ, in two places.

عَتِلٌ A man (Ṣ, O) *who hastens*, or *is quick, to do evil*, or *mischief*. (Ṣ, O, Ḳ.)

عَتَلَةٌ The بَيْرَم [i. e. *auger, wimble*, or *gimlet*,] *of the carpenter*. (Ṣ, O, Ḳ.) — And The مِجْثَاث [or *iron implement with which young palm-trees*, or *shoots of palm-trees, are pulled up* or *off*, as expl. in art. جث, and in the Ḥam p. 102]: (Ṣ, Ḳ: [in one copy of the Ṣ, المِحثات is erroneously put for المِجْثَاث; and in another of the Ṣ, and in some copies of the Ḳ, and in the O, المُجْتَاب:]) pl. [or rather coll. gen. n.] ▼ عَتَلٌ. (TA.) *An iron implement with which young palm-trees*, or *shoots of palm-trees, and the branches*, or *shoots, of grape-vines, are cut*, or *lopped*. (TA.) — And *An iron thing resembling the head of a* [*hoe*, or *the like, such as is called*] فَأْس, (Ḳ, TA,) *broad, and having in its lower part a piece of wood; with which earth and walls are dug*, or *excavated; not curved like the* فأس, *but even with the piece of wood*: (TA:) or [in the CḲ "and"] *a large*, or *thick, rod of iron, having a wide head*, (Ḳ, TA,) *like the* قَبِيعَة [or *pommel*] *of the sword, used by the builder*, (TA,) *with which the wall is demolished*. (Ḳ, TA.) — And *A thick staff* (Ṣ, O, Ḳ, TA) *of wood*. (TA.) [Now commonly applied to *A shoulder-pole by means of which burdens are carried by two men*.] — And ▼ عَتَلٌ signifies *Persian bows*; one of which is termed عَتَلَةٌ: (Ṣ, O, Ḳ:) or *strong bows*. (KL.) ═ Also, i. e. عَتَلَةٌ, *A large clod of clay*, or *cohesive earth, that is plucked from the ground* (ISh, O, Ḳ) *when it is ploughed*, or *turned over*. (ISh, O.) ═ And *A she-camel that does not conceive*, (Ṣ, O, Ḳ,) *and is therefore always strong*. (Ṣ, O.) ═ [It is also a pl. of عَاتِلٌ, q. v., voce عَتِيلٌ.]

عُتُلٌّ *A great eater, who denies*, or *refuses to give*, (Er-Rághib, L, Ḳ,* TA, [المَنِيعُ in the Ḳ, as is said in the TA, being a mistake for المَنُوعُ,]) *and draws*, or *drags*, [*to him*] *a thing roughly*, or *violently*; (Er-Rághib, TA;) *gross, coarse, rough*, or *rude*: (Ṣ, O, Ḳ:) occurring in the Ḳur lxviii. 13: (Ṣ, O:) or one *who recoils from admonition*: (Fr, Towsheeḥ, TA:) or *vehement in altercation; gross, coarse, rough*, or *rude; low, ignoble*, or *mean, in natural disposition*: or, accord. to Ibn-'Arafeh, *unkind, churlish*, or *surly; gross, coarse, rough*, or *rude; who will not suffer himself to be led to a thing that is good*: (O:) or *gross, coarse, rough*, or *rude, and strong*; applied to a man and to any beast, and, some say, to anything. (TA.) — Also *A thick spear*. (Ṣ, O, Ḳ.) — And *A hard mountain*. (TA.)

عَتِيلٌ *A hired man*, or *hireling*; (Ṣ, O, Ḳ;) so in the dial. of Jedeeleh of Ṭeiyi; (Ṣ, O;) as also ▼ عَاتِلٌ: (TA:) pl. of the former عُتَلَاءُ (Ṣ, O, Ḳ) and عُتُلٌ also; and of the latter عَتَلَةٌ: (TA:) which last pl. also signifies a man's *aiders*, or *assistants*: (TA in art. امل:) and some say that عَتِيلٌ signifies *a servant*. (O.) — Also *A violent*, or *severe, disease*, or *malady*. (O, Ḳ.)

عَتَّالٌ *A porter*, or *carrier of burdens, for hire* [*by means of the* عَتَلَة, or *shoulder-pole*]. (TA.)

عَاتِلٌ: see عَتِيلٌ. — Also *An aid*, or *officer, of the prefect of the police*: pl. عُتَّلٌ. (TA.)

مِعْتَلٌ *Strong to draw along*, or *drag, roughly*, or *violently*. (Ṣ,* Ḳ, TA.)

عتم

1. The primary signification of the inf. n. عَتْمٌ in the [genuine] language of the Arabs is that of *Tarrying* [or *delaying*]: and of *withholding*, or *restricting*, or *limiting, oneself*. (TA.) See 2, in three places. [Hence,] one says, غَرَسْتُ الوَدِىَّ فَمَا عَتَمَ مِنْهَا شَىْءٌ i. e. [*I planted the shoots of palm-trees*,] *and not any of them was slow* or *tardy* [*in its growth*]. (Ṣ.) And عَتَمَتْ حَاجَتُهُ *The object of his want was*, or *became, slow* or *tardy* [*of accomplishment*]; as also ▼ أَعْتَمَتْ. (TA.) — عَتَمَ اللَّيْلُ, (Ṣ, Ḳ,) aor. ـِ, (Ṣ, TA,) inf. n. عَتْمٌ, (TA,) *The night was*, or *became, dark, in the period termed* عَتَمَة: (Ṣ:) or *a portion of the night passed*; as also ▼ اعتم: (Ḳ:) the latter mentioned by IAạr. (TA.) — And عَتَمَتِ الإِبِلُ, aor. ـِ and ـُ, *The camels were milked at nightfall* [i.e. *at the commencement of the* عَتَمَة]; as also ▼ أَعْتَمَتْ and ▼ استعتمت. (Ḳ.) — See also 4.

2. تَعْتِيمٌ and ▼ عَتْمٌ signify The *being slow*, or *tardy*. (Ṣ.) You say, عتّم قِرَاهُ and ▼ عَتَمَ *His entertainment for his guest*, or *guests, was*, or *became, slow*, or *tardy*; syn. أَبْطَأَ [not أَبْطَأَ بِهِ]: (Ṣ, Ḳ:) and *he delayed it*: (TA: [but this, though virtually a correct rendering, is app. not so literally:]) and ▼ اعتم likewise has the former meaning: (Ḳ:) or اعتم قِرَى الضَّيْفِ signifies *he delayed the entertainment of the guest*. (Ṣ.) And مَا عَتَّمَ أَنْ فَعَلَ كَذَا *He delayed not*, or *was not slow, to do*, or *in doing, such a thing*. (Ṣ, Ḳ.*) And ▼ اعتم حَاجَتَهُ *He delayed* [*the accomplishment of*] *the object of his want*. (TA.) — And عتّم عَنْهُ *He refrained, forbore, abstained*, or *desisted, from it*, (Ṣ, Ḳ,) namely, an affair, (Ṣ,) *after having made progress therein*; as also ▼ اعتم; and ▼ عَتَمَ, aor. ـِ, (Ḳ, TA,) inf. n. عَتْمٌ: (TA:) or this last signifies *he withheld himself from doing it*, meaning, a thing that he desired: (Ḳ:) and ▼ اعتم signifies *he delayed* to do it. (TA.) And [hence] one says, ضَرَبَهُ فَمَا عَتَّمَ, (Ṣ,) and حَمَلَ عَلَيْهِ فَمَا عَتَّمَ, (Ṣ, Ḳ,) i. e. [*He beat him*, and *he attacked him*,] *and did not withhold*, or *restrict*, or *limit, himself, in beating him*, [and *in attacking him*,] (Ṣ,) or *and did not recede*, or *draw back*, or *desist*: (Ḳ, TA:) the vulgar say, ضَرَبَهُ فَمَا عَتَّبَ. (Ṣ.) — See also 4.

4: see 2, in five places: and see also 1, in three places. — اعتم (Ṣ, Mṣb) from العَتَمَةُ (Ṣ) is like أَصْبَحَ from الصُّبْحُ; (Ṣ, Mṣb;*) i. e. it signifies *He entered upon the period termed* عَتَمَة; (Mṣb;) as also ▼ عَتَّمَ, inf. n. ▼ تَعْتِيمٌ: (TA:) or *he journeyed in that period*; (Ḳ, TA;) and so ▼ عتّم: (Ṣ, Ḳ, TA:) or both signify *he became in that period*: (TA:) or *he brought* [*his camels*] *to the watering-place and* [in the CḲ "or"] *he brought* [*them*] *back therefrom in that period*; (Ḳ, TA;) and *did any kind of work* or *action* [*therein*]. (TA.)

8. [اِعْتَتَمَتِ الإِبِلُ, accord. to Golius, (whom Freytag has followed in this instance,) signifies the same as اِسْتَعْتَمَتْ, as on the authority of the Ḳ, in which I do not find it. He probably found the former verb thus written erroneously for أَعْتَمَت in this sense, which he has not mentioned.]

10. استعتمهُ *He deemed him*, or *reckoned him, slow*, or *tardy*. (Z, TA.) — اِسْتَعْتِمُوا نَعَمَكُمْ حَتَّى تُفِيقَ means *Delay ye the milking of your camels*, or *cattle, until the milk shall have collected*: (Ḳ, TA:) for they used to bring back their camels a little after sunset to their nightly resting-place, and make them to lie down there a while, until, when their milk had collected, after a portion of the night had passed, they roused them and milked them. (TA.) ═ استعتمت الإِبِلُ: see 1.

عُتْمٌ and ▼ عُتُمٌ (Ṣ, Ḳ, but only the former in some copies of the Ṣ,) The *wild olive-tree*: (Ṣ, Ḳ, TA:) or *such as does not bear anything*: or *such as grows in the mountains*: written by IAth ▼ عَتَمٌ, and expl. by him as the *olive-tree*: or *a species of tree resembling it, growing in the Sarāh* (السَّرَاة). (TA.)

عَتْمٌ: see عَتَمَةٌ, first sentence: ═ and see also عُتْمٌ.

عُتُمٌ: see عُتْمٌ.

عَتَمَةٌ *Slowness*, or *tardiness*: (IB, TA:) hence the saying of a rájiz,

• طَيْفُ أَلَمَّ • بِذِى سَلَمْ •

• يَسْرِى عَتَمْ • بَيْنَ الخِيَمْ •

meaning يَسْرِى بَطِيئًا, [i. e. *A phantom visited* (أَلَمَّ being for أَلَمَّ) *in Dhoo-Selem, journeying by night slowly amid the tents*,] the ة of عَتَمَة [i. e. عَتَمَةً] being elided. (TA. [But عَتْمٌ is also mentioned in the TA, in the beginning of this art., not as being originally عَتَمَة, but simply as a subst. in the sense expl. above.]) ═ [Also, in its most usual sense,] The *first third of the night, after the disappearance of the* شَفَق [or *redness that is seen in the sky after sunset*]; (Kh, Ṣ, Mṣb, Ḳ;) the *first part* of the night, *after the setting of the light of the* شَفَق: (Mṣb:) or the *time of the prayer of nightfall*: (Ṣ, Ḳ:) but the calling of that prayer the prayer of the عَتَمَة, as the Arabs of the desert called it, instead of calling it the prayer of the عِشَاء, is said to be forbidden in a trad. (TA.) — عَتَمَةُ رُبَعٍ [*The* عتمة *of a young camel brought forth in the* رِبْع, *which is the beginning of the breeding-time*], (Ṣ, Ḳ,) meaning *the space during which it* (i. e. *the* رُبَع) *is confined at its evening-feed*, (Ḳ,) is applied to *the moonlight of the night when the moon is four nights old*. (Ṣ, Ḳ.) AZ says, The Arabs say in relation to the moon when it is one night old,

عَتَمَةُ سُخَيْلَةٍ حَلَّ أَهْلُهَا بِرُمَيْلَةٍ [*The* عتمة *of a little lamb* or *kid, the owners of which have alighted in a small tract of sand*]; meaning that it does not long continue; like the lamb, or kid, that sucks its mother and soon returns to the sucking: and when it is two nights old, حَدِيثُ أَمَتَيْنِ بِكَذِبٍ وَمَيْنٍ [*The discourse of two female slaves, with lying and falsehood*]; because their discourse is not long, by reason of their being busied with the serving of their owners: and when it is three nights old, حَدِيثُ فَتَيَاتٍ غَيْرِ مُؤْتَلِفَاتٍ [*The discourse of young women not united by affection*]: and when it is four nights old, عَتَمَةُ رُبَعٍ غَيْرِ جَائِعٍ وَلَا مُرْضَعٍ [*The* عتمة *of a* ربع (expl. above) *not hungry nor suckled*]; meaning that it is limited to the space of the فُوَاق [or time between two suckings] of this ربع or of the فواق [or time between two milkings] of its mother; or, as IAar says, عَتَمَةُ أُمِّ الرُّبَعِ [*The* عتمة *of the mother of the* ربع]: and when it is five nights old, حَدِيثٌ وَأُنْسٌ وَبَقَاءُ عَشَآءِ خَلِفَاتٍ قُعْسٍ [*Discourse and sociableness, and the continuance of the evening-feed of pregnant camels having their heads and necks inclining towards their backs*: see also art. قعس]: and when it is six nights old, يُسْرٌ وَبَتٌّ [app. A twisting and a grinding by *a turning towards the left and from the left*; as though meaning that it is a time fit for active employment]: and when it is seven nights old, دُلْجَةُ الضَّبُعِ [*The night-journeying of the hyena*]: and when it is eight nights old, قَمَرٌ إِضْحِيَانٌ [*A bright moon*]: and when it is nine nights old, يُلْقَطُ فِيهِ الْجَزْعُ [*The onyx is picked up in it*, being distinguishable by the light of the moon]: and when it is ten nights old, مُخَنِّقُ الْفَجْرِ [lit. *The choker of the dawn*; as though its light were about to overtake, and grapple with, that of daybreak]. (TA.) [It should be observed that every one of these ten sayings is fancifully framed so as to rhyme, perfectly or imperfectly, with words preceding it: the first being preceded by اِبْنُ لَيْلَةٍ; the second, by اِبْنُ لَيْلَتَيْنِ; the third, by اِبْنُ ثَلَاثٍ; the fourth, by اِبْنُ أَرْبَعٍ; and so on.] — عَتَمَةٌ signifies also The *darkness* of the night: (Ṣ, Ḳ, TA:) or the *darkness of the first part of the night*, [*after nightfall*, i. e.] *after the setting of the light of the* شَفَق [or *redness that is seen in the sky after sunset*]: and the vulgar [sometimes] pronounce it عَتْمَة. (TA.) — And The *remains of the milk that has collected in the udders of the camels, or of the camels and other cattle, at the period thus termed*. (Ṣ, ISd, Ḳ.) One says, حَلَبْنَا عَتَمَةً [*We milked some remains of what had collected in the udders* &c.]. (Ṣ, TA.) And حُلِبَتْ عَتَمَتُهَا *The milk that was obtained from them at the period termed the* عَتَمَة *was drawn.* (TA, from the trad. of Aboo-Dharr.) And قَعَدَ عِنْدَنَا فُلَانٌ قَدْرَ عَتَمَةِ الحَلَائِبِ i. e. [*Such a one sat with us*, or *at our abode*,] *as long as the space during which the milch camels are confined for the purpose of the collecting of the milk in their udders*. (TA.) — And The *return of the camels from the place of pasturing after their entering upon evening*. (ISd, Ḳ.)

عَتُومٌ A she-camel *that does not yield her milk copiously except in the period termed* عَتَمَة: (Ṣ, Ḳ:) or a she-camel *abounding in milk, the milking of which is deferred to the latter*, or *last, part of the night*: thus accord. to Az: and *that is retarded in the milking*; as also ▾ عَاتِمٌ; pl. عَوَاتِمُ: and عَتُومَةٌ, as mentioned by IB, on the authority of Th, a she-camel *that yields a copious supply of milk*. (TA.)

عَاتِمٌ *Tardy*, or *late*; *entering upon*, or *coming in, the evening*; applied to a guest; (Ṣ, Ḳ;) and to the entertainment for a guest, or guests: (Ṣ:) and ▾ مُعْتِمٌ, applied to a guest, signifies [the same, or] *entering upon*, or *coming in, the evening*; or, as some say, *remaining, staying, dwelling*, or *abiding*. (TA.) And one says, فُلَانٌ عَاتِمُ القِرَى *Such a one is slow*, or *tardy, in respect of the entertainment for the guest*, or *guests*: (TA:) and in like manner, [but in an intensive sense,] ▾ مِعْتَامُ القِرَى. (Ḥar p. 579.) See also عَتُومٌ. — النُّجُومُ العَاتِمَاتُ means *The stars that are dark by reason of a dusty hue in the air*: (Ḳ:) such is the case in drought; for the stars of winter are more bright because of the clearness of the sky: but El-Aạshà applies it to the stars of winter. (TA.)

عَيْتُومٌ A camel *slow in journeying*. (Ḳ,* TA.) And A man *bulky, big-bodied*: (Ḳ,* TA:) but J mentions, on the authority of Aṣ, جَمَلٌ عَيْثُومٌ, [as meaning *a great camel*,] with ث. (TA.)

مُعْتِمٌ: } see عَاتِمٌ.
مِعْتَامٌ: }

عته

1. عُتِهَ, (Mgh, Mṣb, Ḳ, and so accord. to copies of the Ṣ,) inf. n. عَتَاهَةٌ and عَتَاهِيَةٌ, (Mgh, Mṣb,) [but see the former of these below,] and عُتْه [app. عُتْهٌ], (Mgh,) or عَتْهٌ and عُتْهٌ and عُتَاهٌ; (Ḳ;) and (Mṣb, TA) عَتِهَ, (Mṣb, TA, and so in one of my copies of the Ṣ in the place of عُتِهَ, and said in the TA to be mentioned by J,) on the authority of Akh, and also mentioned by IḲṭṭ, (TA,) inf. n. عَتَهٌ, (Mṣb, TA,) which is mentioned by A'Obeyd as of the inf. ns. from which no verbs are derived, (so in my copies of the Ṣ, in some copies of which this remark applies to التَّعَتُّهُ,) and عَتَاهٌ, with fet-ḥ; (Mṣb;) *He* (a man, TA) *was idiotic*, or *an idiot*, i. e. *deficient*, or *wanting, in intellect*; (Ṣ, Mgh, Mṣb, Ḳ;) or *one who had lost his intellect*; (Ḳ;) or *bereft of his intellect*, or *so in consequence of shame* or *fear* &c., syn. دُهِشَ; (Mgh, Mṣb, Ḳ;) *without diabolical possession*, or *madness*: (Mgh, Mṣb:) or, accord. to IAar, عُتِهَ signifies *he* (a man) *was*, or *became, possessed*, or *mad*. (Ḥam p. 680.) [See also العَتَهُ, below.] — عُتِهَ فِى العِلْمِ *He was*, or *became, addicted, attached*, or *devoted, to knowledge*, or *science, and vehemently desirous thereof*. (Ḳ.) — And عُتِهَ فِى فُلَانٍ *He was*, or *became, addicted to annoying such a one, and mimicking his speech*. (Ḳ.)

5. تَعَتُّهٌ signifies The *being*, or *becoming*, or the *feigning oneself, possessed*, or *mad*; syn. تَجَنُّنٌ: and the *being*, or *becoming, foolish, stupid, unsound in intellect*, or *deficient therein*, and *lax*, or *languid*; syn. رُعُونَةٌ. (Ṣ, Ḳ.) [تَعَتَّهَ بِجَارِيَةٍ, occurring in this art. in the TA, app. means *He was*, or *became, infatuated by* love of *a girl*, or *young woman*.] — Also The *feigning ignorance*. (Ḳ.) — And The *feigning oneself unmindful*, or *heedless*. (Ḳ.) One says, هُوَ يَتَعَتَّهُ لَكَ عَنْ كَثِيرٍ مِمَّا تَأْتِيهِ i. e. *He feigns himself unmindful*, or *heedless*, [*to thee, of much that thou dost*, or] *of thee, in much that thou dost*. (TA.) — And The *affecting cleanliness*, (Ḳ, TA,) and *nicety*, or *refinement*: (TA:) and the *exceeding the usual bounds in dress and eating*. (Ḳ, TA.) One says, تَعَتَّهَ فِى كَذَا *He affected nicety*, or *refinement, and exceeded the usual bounds, in such a thing*. (TA.)

عَتَهٌ [see 1, first sentence, where it is mentioned as an inf. n.]. العَتَهُ is *An evil affection, of essential origin, necessarily occasioning unsoundness in the intellect; so that the person affected therewith becomes confused in intellect; and therefore some of his speech resembles that of the intelligent; and some, that of the possessed*, or *mad*: it differs from السَّفَهُ; for this does not resemble possession, or madness. (KT.)

عُتُهٌ and ▾ عُتْهِىٌّ (so in the TA as from the Ḳ [but not found by me in the latter]) and ▾ عُتَّهٌ and ▾ عُتَّهِىٌّ (so too in the TA, but not as from the Ḳ, [though I find these two words without the two preceding in the copies of the Ḳ that I have been able to consult,]) A man *who greatly exceeds the usual bounds in an affair*. (Ḳ, TA.)

عُتْهِىٌّ: see what next precedes. — It is also a subst. from التَّعَتُّهُ, of the measure فُعْلِىٌّ: thus in the saying of Ru-beh [which is cited in the Ḥam p. 680],

فِى عُتْهِىِّ اللِّبْسِ وَالتَّتَقُّنِ •

[*In affecting cleanliness*, or *nicety*, or *refinement*, or *in exceeding the usual bounds, in dress; and in self-adornment*]. (TA.)

عُتَهِىٌّ: see عَاتِهٌ.

عَتَاهَةٌ a subst. from عُتِهَ [app. in all its senses; i. e., meaning *Idiocy*; &c.; though it might be supposed, from the manner in which it is mentioned, to be a subst. from عُتِهَ in the last only of the senses above assigned to it]; (Ḳ, TA;) as also ▾ عَتَاهِيَةٌ: (TA:) or each is an inf. n. of that verb [q. v.]. (Mgh, Mṣb.) — See also the next paragraph.

عَتَاهِيَةٌ: see عَتَاهَةٌ. — Also *Foolish*, or *stupid*: and so ▾ عَتَاهِيَةٌ; (Akh, Ṣ, Ḳ, TA;) applied to a man. (TA.) — And, in a pl. sense, The *erring* of mankind; and so ▾ عَتَاهَةٌ; (Ḳ, TA;) which latter signifies also, in a pl. sense, *foolish*, or *stupid*. (TA.)

عُتَاهِيَةٌ: see the next preceding paragraph.

عَاتِهٌ A man *addicted to annoying another, and mimicking his speech*; (Ḳ, TA;) as also ▾ عَتِيهٌ: (TA:) pl. [accord. to analogy, of the latter, but mentioned in the Ḳ as of the former,] عُتَهَاءُ. (Ḳ, TA.)

عُتْهُهٌ and } see عُتُهٌ.
عُتُهُّوتٌ: }

مُعَتَّهٌ *Intelligent, and symmetrical in make*: and also *possessed*, or *mad, and incongruous in make*: thus having two contr. significations. (Ḳ, TA.)

مَعْتُوهٌ *Idiotic*, or *an idiot*, i. e. *deficient*, or *wanting, in intellect*; (Ṣ, Mgh, Mṣb, Ḳ;) or one *who has lost his intellect*; (Ḳ;) or *bereft of his intellect*, or *so in consequence of shame* or *fear* &c.; (Mgh, Mṣb, Ḳ;) *without diabolical possession*, or *madness*: (Mgh, Mṣb:) also expl. as signifying *possessed*, or *mad*; *smitten*, or *afflicted, in his intellect*. (TA.)

عتى and عتو

1. عَتَا, aor. يَعْتُو, inf. n. عُتُوٌّ (Ṣ, Mṣb, Ḳ) and عُتِيٌّ and عِتِيٌّ, (Ṣ, Ḳ,) of which عُتُوٌّ is the original form, one [i. e. the second] of the two dammehs being changed into a kesreh and therefore the و into ى, and then the other dammeh being assimilated to the kesreh, (Ṣ, TA,) *He behaved proudly*, (Mṣb, Ḳ,) *and was immoderate, inordinate*, or *exorbitant*: (Ḳ:) *he was excessively, immoderately*, or *inordinately, proud* or *corrupt* or *unbelieving*: (AO, TA; and so in a copy of the Ṣ as on the authority of A'Obeyd:) or *he revolted, recoiled*, or *was averse, from obedience*: (Er-Rághib, TA:) and ▾ تَعَتَّيْتُ signifies the same as عَتَوْتُ; (Ṣ, Ḳ;) or *I* [*disobeyed*, or] *did not obey*; (TA;) and so does عَتَيْتُ; (Ḳ, accord. to some copies; but in some, عَتِيتُ;) or, accord. to J and others, one should not say عَتَيْتُ. (TA.) It is said in the Ḳur [li. 44], فَعَتَوْا عَنْ أَمْرِ رَبِّهِمْ (TA) i. e. *But they turned with disdain from* obeying *the command of their Lord*. (Bḍ, Jel.) — [Hence,] عَتَتِ ٱلرِّيحُ † *The wind blew immoderately*. (IḲṭṭ, TA.) — And عَتَا said of an old man, (Ṣ, Mṣb, Ḳ, [but in my copy of the Mṣb الشى is put for الشيخ,]) aor. يَعْتُو, (Ṣ, Mṣb,) inf. n. عُتُوٌّ (Ṣ, Mṣb) and عُتِيٌّ, (Ṣ,) or عِتِيٌّ and عَتِيٌّ, with ḍamm and also with fet-ḥ, (Ḳ,) *He became advanced in age*, and *in a declining state*: (Ṣ, Mṣb,* Ḳ:) [or *he became dried up*; as is shown by what here follows.] It is said in the Ḳur [xix. 9], accord. to one reading, وَقَدْ بَلَغْتُ مِنَ ٱلْكِبَرِ عُتِيًّا, (TA,) from عَتَا *It became dried up*; (Ksh,* Jel;) said of wood, or a branch; as also عَسَا: (Ksh:) the meaning here being, [*And I have reached*] *the extreme degree of old age*: (Jel:) or *dryness, and hardness*, or *rigidness, in the joints and the bones; like the dry wood* or *branch*. (Ksh.)

5: see the preceding paragraph.

عُتِيٌّ: see عَاتٍ.

عَتِّيٌّ a dial. var. of حَتَّى, (Ṣ, Ḳ,) of the dial. of Hudheyl and Thakeef. (Ṣ.)

عَاتٍ part. n. of 1; (Ṣ, Mṣb, Ḳ;) *Proud*, (Mṣb, Ḳ,) *and immoderate, inordinate*, or *exorbitant*: (Ḳ:) *excessively, immoderately*, or *inordinately, proud* (Mgh) [or *corrupt* or *unbelieving*: or *revolting, recoiling*, or *averse, from obedience*: (see 1:)] i. q. جَبَّارٌ: (Mgh, TA:) and ▾ عَتِيٌّ signifies the same: (Ḳ:) pl. عُتِيٌّ, (Ṣ, Mṣb, Ḳ,) originally [عُتُوٌّ,] of the measure فُعُولٌ, (Mṣb,) the [former] و being changed into ى, agreeably with a rule which, Moḥammad Ibn-Es-Seree says, should be observed in a word of this [class and] measure when it is a pl., though not [generally] when it is an inf. n., (Ṣ, TA,) or this is pl. of عَتِيٌّ, and the pl. of عَاتٍ is عُتَاةٌ. (TA.) [See also أَعْتَاءٌ, below.] — Also *Advanced* [*and declining*] *in age*: [or *dried up*: (see 1, last sentence but one:)] pl. عُتِيٌّ. (Mṣb.) — And لَيْلٌ عاتى [a mistranscription, the latter word being correctly عَاتٍ,] *A night intensely dark*. (TA.)

أَعْتَى *Most* [and *more*] *excessive, immoderate*, or *inordinate, in pride* [&c.: see عَاتٍ]. (Mgh.)

أَعْتَاءٌ [a pl., app. of عَاتٍ, like as أَصْحَابٌ is of صَاحِبٌ,] applied to men as meaning دُعَّارٌ [i. e. *Who act corruptly*, or *vitiously*; *who transgress the command of God*; or *who commit adultery* or *fornication*; &c.]. (ISd, Ḳ, TA.)

عث

1. عَثَّهُ, (Ṣ, Ḳ,) aor. ـُ, (Ṣ, Mṣb,) inf. n. عَثٌّ, said of the عُثَّة [or moth-worm], *It ate it*, or *fretted it*, namely, wool, (Ṣ, Mṣb, Ḳ, TA,) and a garment [&c.]. (TA.) And عُثَّ, said of wool [&c.], *It was eaten*, or *fretted, by the* عُثّ [or *moth-worm*, or *moth-worms*]. (TA.) — Also, (O, TA,) aor. as above, (TA,) and so the inf. n., (Ḳ, TA,) said of a serpent (حَيَّة), *It bit him*. (O, Ḳ, TA.) And *It* (a serpent) *blew upon him, without biting him, and his hair in consequence fell off*. (TA.) — And عَثَّنِى, (O,) inf. n. as above, (Ḳ,) *He importuned me* (O, Ḳ*) by asking. (TA.) [And عَثَّثَنِى signifies the same.]

2: see the next paragraph, in two places.

3. عَاثَّ, (O,) inf. n. مُعَاثَّةٌ and عِثَاثٌ; (O, Ḳ;) and ▾ عَثَّثَ, (O,) inf. n. تَعْثِيثٌ; (Ḳ;) *He raised his voice with singing*: (O:) or *he trilled*, or *quavered, in singing*: (Ḳ:) or *he raised his voice with singing, and trilled*, or *quavered*: (L:) and عَاثَّ فِى غِنَائِهِ, inf. n. as above; and ▾ عَثَّثَ; *he trilled*, or *quavered, in his singing*. (TA.) And عِثَاثٌ is also used to signify The *sounding* [or *ringing*] of a bow when its string has been pulled to try its strength: some say that it is *like the* تَرَنُّم [or *ringing*] *of a basin when it has been struck*. (O, TA.)

عَثٌ: see عُثَّةٌ.

عُثٌّ i. q. سُوسٌ [i. e. The *moth-worm that eats*, or *frets, wool*, or *woollen cloths*]: (Mṣb:) [and the *book-worm*, or *species of moth-worm that eats books*: applied to both of these in the present day: and,] accord. to IAạr, *an insect* [*of the same kind*] *that clings to skin*, or *leather, and eats it*: (TA:) [and the *weevil*; i. e.] the *kind of worm*, or *grub, that eats corn*; also called سُوسٌ: (M in art. سوس:) one thereof is termed ▾ عُثَّةٌ: (Mṣb:) [i. e.] عُثَّةٌ signifies *a* سُوسَة [or *moth-worm*] *that eats*, or *frets, wool*: (Ṣ, A, O, Ḳ:) or *a worm*, or *grub, that attacks wool and cloths* (Mgh and Mṣb in art. سوس) *and wheat* or *other food*; (Mgh in that art.;) also called سُوسَةٌ: (Mgh and Mṣb in that art.:) and it is said to be the أَرَضَة, [generally signifying the *wood-fretter*, but here meaning] *a certain insect that eats wool, and skin*, or *leather*: (Mṣb:) the pl. of عُثَّةٌ is عُثَثٌ, (O,) or عُثٌّ, (Ḳ,) or both, (Ṣ,) or [rather] عُثٌّ, which is expl. by IDrd as a pl., is a gen. n., having a pl. meaning though it is a sing: (TA:) the pl. of عُثٌّ is عِثَاثٌ. (Mṣb.) An Arab of the desert, being asked respecting his son, said, أُعْطِيهِ كُلَّ يَوْمٍ مِنْ مَالِى دَانِقًا وَإِنَّهُ فِيهِ لَأَسْرَعُ مِنَ العُثِّ فِى الصُّوفِ فِى الصَّيْفِ [*I give him, every day, of my property, a dánik* (a small silver coin), *and verily he is quicker in* consuming *it than the moth-worm in wool in the summer*]. (TA.) And one says, فُلَانٌ عُثُّ مَالٍ, (Ṣ, O,) meaning † *Such a one is a consumer of property*; (PṢ;) like as one says إِزَآءُ مَالٍ, (Ṣ, O,) meaning "a manager of property." (PṢ.) [See also عُثَّةٌ below: and عُثَيْثَةٌ.] — أَطْعَمَنِى سَوِيقًا حُثًّا عُثًّا means [*He fed me with meal of parched barley* or *wheat*] *not moistened and beaten up with anything greasy* [*such as clarified butter* &c.]. (O: in the TA حُثًّا وَعُثًّا.)

عَثَّةٌ: see the paragraph here following.

عُثَّةٌ: see عُثٌّ. — It is also an appellation of ‡ *An old woman*: (Ṣ, O, Ḳ:) as though, by reason of her corrupt state or conduct, and want of skill or understanding, she were a سُوسَة. (TA.) — Also, (O, Ḳ, TA,) and ▾ عَثَّةٌ, (TA,) *A woman foul*, or *obscene, in tongue*; (O, Ḳ, TA;) *despised*; *obscure*, or *reputeless*: (TA:) and *a foolish*, or *stupid, woman*: (O, Ḳ:) or, the former signifies, accord. to AZ, *a woman obscure*, or *reputeless*; whether she be, or be not, lean, or emaciated: and the latter, accord. to IDrd, *a woman lean*, or *spare, in body*: and in like manner ▾ عَثٌ applied to a man: (O:) the pl. of عُثَّةٌ is عِثَاثٌ. (TA.)

عِثَاثٌ *Vipers that eat one another in a time of*

drought. (O, Ḳ.) —— Also pl. of عُثَّةٌ: (Mṣb:) —— and of عُثَّةٌ or عَثَّةٌ. (TA.)

عُثَيْثَةٌ dim. of عُثَّةٌ [n. un. of عُثٌّ, q. v.]. (L.) It is said in a prov.,

• عُثَيْثَةٌ تَقْرِمُ جِلْدًا أَمْلَسَا •

[*A little moth-worm gnawing a smooth skin*]: applied to a man endeavouring to make an impression, or produce an effect, upon a thing, and unable to do so: (Ṣ, O, L, Ḳ:*) and said in contempt of a man and of what the latter says in finding fault with one who is free from faults. (O.)

عَثَّاثٌ The *serpent.* (O, Ḳ.)

عثر

1. عَثَرَ, aor. ـُ (Ṣ, A, Mgh, O, Mṣb, Ḳ) and ـِ; (A, Mṣb, Ḳ;) and عَثِرَ, aor. ـَ; and عَثُرَ, aor. ـُ; (A, Ḳ;) inf. n. عِثَارٌ (Ṣ, Mgh, O, Mṣb, Ḳ) and عَثْرٌ and عُثُورٌ; (Ḳ;) said of a man and of a horse, (Ṣ, Mṣb,) *He stumbled,* or *tripped;* [the most usual meaning;] or *he fell upon his face;* syn. كَبَا [which has both of these meanings]; as also ▼تعثّر: (A, Ḳ:) or [simply] *he fell;* syn. سَقَطَ: (Mgh:) or one says of a man, (Mṣb on the authority of the Mukhtaṣar el-'Eyn, and TA on the authority of the T,) عَثَرَ, (Mṣb, TA,) inf. n. عُثُورٌ, (Mṣb,) or عَثْرَةٌ; (TA; [perhaps a mistranscription for عَثْرٌ;]) and of a horse, عَثَرَ, inf. n. عِثَارٌ; (Mṣb, TA;) فِعَالٌ being a measure of inf. ns. of verbs signifying various faults of horses and the like. (TA.) You say, عَثَرَ فِى ثَوْبِهِ [*He stumbled,* or *tripped, upon his garment*]. (Ṣ, O, Mṣb.) And خَرَجَ يَتَعَثَّرُ▼ فِى أَذْيَالِهِ [*He went forth stumbling,* or *tripping, upon his skirts*]. (A.) And عَثَرَ بِهِ فَرَسُهُ فَسَقَطَ [*His horse stumbled,* or *tripped, with him, and he fell*]. (Ṣ, O.) And it is said in a prov., الجَوَادُ قَدْ يَعْثُرُ [*The swift and excellent horse sometimes stumbles,* or *trips*]: applied to a person by whom a slip that is not of his nature is seen to have been committed. (O.) —— [Hence,] ‡ عَثَرَ فِى كَلَامِهِ and ▼تعثّر [*He stumbled,* or *tripped, in his speech*]. (A.) And ▼تعثّر لِسَانُهُ ‡ *His tongue halted, faltered,* or *hesitated.* (Ṣ, O, TA.) —— And [hence, app.,] عَثَرَ, (Kr, Ḳ, TA,) inf. n. عَثْرٌ, (Kr, O, TA,) † *He lied.* (Kr, O, Ḳ, TA.) One says, فُلَانٌ فِى العَثْرِ وَالبَاطِلِ, meaning † [*Such a one is occupied*] *in truth and falsehood* [or rather *in falsehood and truth*]. (O, TA.) —— And عَثَرَ عَلَيْهِ, (Ṣ, A, Mgh, O, Mṣb,) aor. ـُ (Ṣ, O, Mṣb) and ـِ, (TA,) inf. n. عَثْرٌ and عُثُورٌ, (O, Mṣb, Ḳ, [the latter erroneously written in the CḲ عُثُور,]) ‡ [*He stumbled on it; lighted on it by chance;*] *he got,* or *obtained, knowledge of it;* or *sight and knowledge of it; became acquainted with it; knew it;* or *saw it;* (Ṣ, A, Mgh, O, Mṣb, Ḳ,* TA;) *accidentally,* or *without seeking;* (TA;) [and so عَثَرَ بِهِ; (see an ex. voce أَشْوَسُ;)] and ▼أَعْثَرَ signifies the same; but accord. to the usage of the Ḳur-án, you say أَعْثَرْتُ غَيْرِى: so in the Kitáb el-Abniyeh of IḲṭṭ. (TA. [See 4.]) You say, عَثَرَ عَلَى سِرِّ الرَّجُلِ ‡ *He obtained knowledge of,* or *became acquainted with, the secret of the man* [*accidentally*]. (TA.) [Hence,] فَإِنْ عُثِرَ عَلَى أَنَّهُمَا ٱسْتَحَقَّا إِثْمًا, in the Ḳur [v. 106], means ‡ *But if it become known,* or *seen,* (Ksh, Mgh, O, Bḍ, Jel,) *that they two have done what has necessitated sin,* (Ksh, Bḍ, Jel,) and *deserved its being said of them that they were sinners.* (Ksh.) And عَثَرَ, aor. ـُ, inf. n. عُثُورٌ, as expl. by Lth, means † *He* (a man) *entered suddenly,* or *unexpectedly, upon an affair upon which another had not so entered.* (TA.) —— عَثَرَ جَدُّهُ, (Ḳ, TA,) aor. ـُ and ـِ, (TA,) means ‡ *His fortune,* or *good fortune, fell;* syn. تَعَسَ; (Ḳ, TA;) as being likened to one who has stumbled, or tripped, or fallen upon his face. (TA.) —— عَثَرَ العِرْقُ, (Lḥ, Ḳ,) inf. n. عَثْرٌ, (Lḥ, TA,) *The vein pulsed.* (Lḥ, Ḳ, TA.) —— عَثَرَ بِهِ: see 4. —— [Hence,] عَثَرَ بِهِمُ الزَّمَانُ ‡ *Time,* or *fortune, destroyed them:* (TA:) or *caused them to be overcome.* (O.)

2: see the next paragraph, in three places.

4. اعثرهُ *He caused him to stumble,* or *trip;* or *to fall upon his face;* [or simply, *to fall;*] as also ▼عثّرهُ; (Ḳ, TA;) [and so ▼عَثَرَ بِهِ; (see 1, last sentence, and see also عَاثُورٌ, first sentence;)] said of God. (TA.) IAạr cites as an ex.,

• فَخَرَجْتُ أُعْثَرُ فِى مَقَادِمِ جُبَّتِى •
• لَوْلَا الحَيَآءُ أَطَرْتُهُ إِحْضَارَا •

[*And I went forth, made to stumble,* or *trip, upon the fore parts of my jubbeh: but for the sense of shame, I had made it to fly, in running*]: accord. to one relation, however, the verb in question, in this verse, is أَعْثُرُ. (TA.) And اعثرهُ ٱللّٰهُ is syn. with أَتْعَسَهُ [of which see various explanations in art. تعس]. (TA.) —— [Hence,] اعثر بِهِ عِنْدَ السُّلْطَانِ, (Ḳ,) or ▼عثّرهُ عِنْدَهُ, (A,) ‡ *He impugned his character to the Sultán,* (A, O, Ḳ,) *and sought to make him fall into destruction by means of the latter.* (A.) —— And اعثرهُ عَلَيْهِ ‡ [*He made him to stumble upon it,* or *to light on it by chance;* or] *he made him to get,* or *obtain, knowledge of it,* or *sight and knowledge of it; to become acquainted with it; to know it;* or *to see it;* (Ṣ, A, O, Mṣb, Ḳ;*) *accidentally,* or *without seeking.* (B, TA.) Hence the phrase in the Ḳur [xviii. 20] أَعْثَرْنَا عَلَيْهِمْ; (Ṣ, TA;) in which غَيْرَهُمْ, the objective complement, is suppressed. (TA.) And اعثرهُ عَلَى أَصْحَابِهِ ‡ *He guided him,* or *showed him the way, to his companions.* (A.) —— اعثر جَدَّهُ, and ▼عثّرهُ, † *He* [i. e. God] *made his fortune,* or *good fortune, to fall.* (Ḳ. [See عَثَرَ جَدُّهُ.]) ══ See also 1, latter half.

5: see 1, in four places.

Q. Q. 1. عَثْيَرَ القَوْمُ [from عِثْيَرٌ] *The people,* or *party, raised the dust,* or *earth,* or *bits of dry clay* or *compact earth,* (termed عِثْيَر,) *with the extremities of their toes, in walking.* (Kh, Ḥar p. 488.) ══ عَيْثَرَ الطَّيْرَ [from عَيْثَرٌ] *He saw,* or *beheld, the birds:* or *he saw that the birds ran:* (O:) or *he saw the birds running, and augured from them* (فَزَجَرَهَا). (Ḳ. [But this addition, فزجرها, is evidently taken from an explanation of the words here following.]) A poet says,

• لَقَدْ عَيْثَرْتَ طَيْرَكَ لَوْ تَعِيفُ •

[i. e. *Thou sawest,* or *beheldest, thy birds;* &c.: *would that thou wouldst augur from them,* and take warning]. (O.) And you say, عَيْثَرْتُ الشَّىْءَ *I saw,* or *beheld, the thing;* (L, TA;) and *individuated it.* (TA.)

عُثْرَى: see عَثْرٌ.

عَثْرٌ *A lie;* or *falsehood;* (Ḳ;) as also ▼عَثَرٌ. (IAạr, Ḳ.) ══ Also The *Eagle:* (Ḳ:) a meaning also assigned in the Ḳ, in art. عبر, but erroneously, to عَبْرٌ. (TA.)

عَثَرٌ: see the next preceding paragraph.

عَثْرَةٌ *A stumble,* or *trip,* (Mṣb, TA,) *in walking,* or *going along:* pl. عَثَرَاتٌ. (TA.) —— And [hence,] ‡ *A slip, lapse, fault, wrong action,* or *mistake;* (Ṣ, O, Mṣb, TA;) so called as being *a fall into sin* or *crime.* (Mṣb.) One says, أَقَالَ ٱللّٰهُ عَثْرَتَكَ ‡ [*May God cancel thy slip, lapse, fault,* &c.]. (A.) And it is said in a trad., لَا حَلِيمَ إِلَّا ذُو عَثْرَةٍ i. e. ‡ *There is no one* to be characterized as *of a forbearing disposition except* he be *one who has committed a slip,* and becomes admonished thereby, distinguishing the occasions of error so as to avoid them [and to make allowance for others who have done the like]. (TA.) —— And † *War,* or *fight, against unbelievers* or *others;* because war, or fight, is an occasion of frequent stumbling, or tripping: so in a trad., in which it is said, لَا تَبْدَءُوهُمْ بِالعَثْرَةِ † [*Begin not ye with them by war*]; meaning invite ye them first to El-Islám or to the payment of the poll-tax; and if they assent not, then have recourse to war. (TA.)

عَثْرَةٌ Land (أَرْضٌ) *without herbage, being high, and overspread with* عِثْيَر, i. e. *dust:* (O, TA:) and said to occur in a trad. as the name of a particular land. (O, Ḳ,* TA.)

عَثَرِىٌّ i. q. عِذْىٌ, (Az, Ṣ, O, Mṣb, TA,) as some say; (Mṣb;) i. e., (Az, Ṣ, O, TA,) *Such as is watered by the rain* (Az, Ṣ, Ḳ, TA) *alone,* (Ṣ,) of palm-trees, (Az, O, TA,) or of seed-produce: (Ṣ:) or *such as is watered by water running upon the surface of the ground,* (O, Mṣb,) of palm-trees: (Mṣb:) or seed-produce *that is watered by torrents and by rain, the water being made to flow thereto in channels:* (TA:) and ▼عَثْرٌ signifies the same: (Ḳ, TA:) or, accord. to IAth, palm-trees (نَخِيل) *that imbibe with their roots of the rain-water that collects in a part hollowed out in the ground:* (TA:) the former term is said to be thus applied because what is so called is as though it stumbled upon water without any labour of its owner; regarding it as an irregular rel. n. from العَثْرُ: (O,* TA:) but Abu-l-'Abbás [i. e. Th] says that, thus applied, it is with teshdeed to the ث [i. e. عَثَّرِىٌّ], though not in the sense here following. (TA.) — Also ‡ A man *who does not occupy himself in seeking the things of the present world nor those of the world to come*: (O, Ḳ, TA:) occurring in a trad., in which such is said to be the most hateful of mankind to God: (O, TA:) in this sense, sometimes written with teshdeed to the ث, (Ḳ, TA,) and thus it is accord. to Sh (O, TA) and IAạr; (TA;) but correctly without teshdeed: (Th, Ḳ, TA:) and said by some to be from عَثَّرِىٌّ applied to palm-trees. (O,* TA.) One says also, جَآءَ فُلَانٌ عَثَرِيًّا, meaning ‡ *Such a one came unoccupied.* (O, TA.)

عَثَارٌ or عِثَارٌ: see عَاثُورٌ, in six places: — and for عِثَارٌ see also عِثْيَرٌ.

عَثُورٌ [*Having a habit of stumbling* or *tripping*, or *of falling*:] *that stumbles*, or *trips*, and *falls*, *much* or *often*. (Ḥar p. 296.)

عِثْيَرٌ, (Ṣ, O, Ḳ,) not عَثْيَرٌ, for there is not in the language any word of the measure فَعْيَلٌ, with fet-ḥ to the ف, except ضَهْيَدٌ, meaning "hardy, strong, or robust," and this is [said to be] forged, (Ṣ, O, [but see ضهيد,]) *Dust*, (MA, O, Ḳ,) syn. غُبَارٌ, (O,) or عَجَاجٌ, and تُرَابٌ, (Ḳ,) and thus ▼ عِثْيَرَاتٌ is expl. by Sb; (TA;) or *dust rising* or *spreading*; (Ṣ, MA;*) as also ▼ عِثْيَرَةٌ; (TA;) and ▼ عِثَارٌ signifies the same. (MA.) — And *Clay*, or *earth*, (Ḳ, TA,) or *dust*, or *bits of clay* or *compact earth*, (TA,) *which one turns over* (Ḳ, TA) *with the extremities of the feet* (Ḳ) or *of the toes, in walking*, or *going along, no other mark of the foot being seen*: (TA:) and *an obscure trace* or *mark*, (Ḳ, TA,) said to be *more obscure than such as is termed* أَثَرٌ: (TA:) and so ▼ عَيْثَرٌ, with the ى put before [the ث] and with fet-ḥ to the ع in both [of these senses: misunderstood by SM as meaning "and with fet-ḥ to the ع in both words," i. e. in عيثر and عيثر]: (Ḳ:) or ▼ عَيْثَرٌ signifies *an obscure trace* or *mark*: (Ṣ:) and Yaạḳoob mentions the saying مَا رَأَيْتُ لَهُ أَثَرًا وَلَا عَيْثَرًا ▼ and وَلَا عِثْيَرًا [app. meaning *I saw not any trace of him nor any obscure trace*]: (Ṣ, O:) or ولا عِثْيَرًا means, *nor clay*, or *earth*, &c., *turned over by the extremities of his feet*: (TA:) and it is said that ▼ ولا عَيْثَرًا means, *nor bodily form.* (O.) And [it is said that] مَا لَهُ أَثَرٌ وَلَا عِثْيَرٌ and ▼ ولا عَيْثَرٌ means *He is not known to be a pedestrian by the appearing of his foot-mark, nor to be a horseman by his horse's raising the dust.* (TA.) [See also Ḥar p. 488.]

عِثْيَرَةٌ, and its pl. عِثْيَرَاتٌ: see عِثْيَرٌ. — One says also أَرْضٌ عِثْيَرَةٌ, meaning *A land in which is much dust.* (TA.)

عَاثِرٌ [*Stumbling*, or *tripping*; &c. — And] † *A liar.* (TA.) — And one says also جَدٌّ عَاثِرٌ † [*Fortune*, or *good fortune*, *in a falling state*: (see 1, near the end:)] pl. عَوَاثِرُ: (TA:) — or this may be pl of عَاثِرٌ signifying The *snare of a sportsman*: — or it may be pl. of ▼ عَاثِرَةٌ signifying † *An accident that destroys*, or *causes to be overcome, him whom it befalls*: (O:) — or it may be pl. of عَاثُورٌ [q. v.], the ى being suppressed, (O, TA,) by poetic license, in a verse in which it occurs. (TA.)

عَيْثَرٌ The *substance* of a thing; its *bodily*, or *corporeal, form*; syn. عَيْنٌ and شَخْصٌ. (T, O, L, Ḳ, TA. [In this sense, it is said in the TA to be erroneously written in all the copies of the Ḳ عِثْيَرٌ, with the ث before the ى; but I find it written عَيْثَرٌ in my MS. copy of the Ḳ and also in the CḲ.]) See also عِثْيَرٌ, in five places.

عَاثِرَةٌ: see عَاثِرٌ.

عَاثُورٌ *A pit dug for a lion or other* [*animal*], (Ṣ, A, O,) *that he may fall into it*, (A,) *in order that he may be taken*: (Ṣ, O:) this is the primary signification: (A:) or *a thing that is prepared for one to fall into it*: (Ḳ:) or, as also عثار [i. e. ▼ عَثَارٌ or ▼ عِثَارٌ (see what follows)], *a thing by which one is made to stumble and fall*; expl. by مَا عُثِرَ بِهِ ▼: (TA:) the pl. is عَوَاثِيرُ; whence, perhaps, عَوَاثِرُ, by suppression of the ى. (O, TA. [See عَاثِرٌ.]) — [Hence,] † *A place of perdition*: (TA voce حَاجُورٌ:) or ‡ *a cause*, or *place, of perdition* or *of death*: (A, Ḳ:) applied to a land. (Ḳ.) You say, وَقَعَ فِى عَاثُورٍ ‡ *He fell into a cause*, or *place, of perdition* or *of death.* (A, TA.) And فُلَانٌ يَقِى صَاحِبَهُ العَوَاثِرَ ‡ [*Such a one preserves his companion from the causes*, or *places, of perdition* or *of death*]. (A.) And it is said in a trad., إِنَّ قُرَيْشًا أَهْلُ أَمَانَةٍ مَنْ بَغَاهَا العَوَاثِيرَ كَبَّهُ ٱللّٰهُ لِمَنْخِرَيْهِ ‡ [*Verily the tribe of Ḳureysh are people of fidelity: whoso seeks for them the causes*, or *places, of perdition* or *of death, may God lay him prostrate upon his nostrils*]: or, accord. to one relation, عَوَاثِرَ. (O, TA.) — And [hence,] ‡ *Difficulty*, or *distress*; as also عَاثُورُ شَرٍّ: (Ṣ, O:) and *evil*; (Ḳ, TA;) like عَاذُورٌ, which is a dial. var. thereof, or an instance of mispronunciation; (Ṣ and O in art. عذر;) as also ▼ عَثَارٌ, (accord. to some copies of the Ḳ,) or ▼ عِثَارٌ: (thus in other copies of the Ḳ and in the TA [in the latter of which it is said to be with kesr; and this I think to be the more probably correct; originally an inf. n.]:) and عِثَارُ شَرٍّ ▼ is said by Fr to signify the same as عَاثُورُ شَرٍّ. (TA.) You say, لَقِيتُ مِنْهُ عَاثُورًا, (Aṣ, Ṣ, O, TA,) and ▼ عِثَارًا, (TA,) ‡ *I experienced from him, or it, difficulty*, or *distress.* (Aṣ, Ṣ, O, TA.) And وَقَعُوا فِى عَاثُورِ شَرٍّ, (Aṣ, Ṣ, O, TA,) and عَافُورِ شَرٍّ, (Ṣ, O,) ‡ *They fell into difficulty*, or *distress*: (Aṣ, Ṣ, O:) or *into a confusion of evil and difficulty* or *distress.* (TA.) It is the opinion of Yaạḳoob that the ف in عافور is a substitute for the ث in عاثور: but Az observes that this is not necessarily the case, as the meaning of difficulty is implied in the root عفر. (TA.) — It is said to signify also *A kind of snare* (مِصْيَدَة) *made of bark.* (O.) — And *A channel that is dug for the purpose of irrigating thereby a palm-tree such as is termed* بَعْل. (O.) — And *A well.* (Ḳ.) ═ And it may also be used as an epithet [app. meaning *Perilous*, or *destructive*]. (ISd, TA.)

عثكل

Q. 1. عَثْكَلَ الهَوْدَجَ, (Ḳ, TA,) inf. n. عَثْكَلَةٌ, (TḲ,) *He adorned the* هودج [or *women's camel-vehicle*] *with the kind of pendant termed* عُثْكُولَة. (Ḳ,* TA.) And عُثْكِلَ الهَوْدَجُ *The* هودج *was* [so] *adorned.* (Ṣ.) ═ And [the inf. n.] عَثْكَلَةٌ signifies *A heavy kind of running.* (Ḳ.) One says, هُوَ يُعَثْكِلُ *He runs heavily.* (TḲ.)

Q. 2. تَعَثْكَلَ العِذْقُ *The* عذق [or *raceme of a palm-tree* or *of dates*] *had many* شَمَارِيخ [or *fruit-stalks*, also called عَثَاكِيل, whence the verb]. (Ṣ, TA.)

عِثْكَالٌ and ▼ عُثْكُولٌ (Ṣ, Mgh, O, Mṣb, Ḳ) and ▼ عُثْكُولَةٌ (Ḳ) *i. q.* شِمْرَاخٌ (Ṣ, O, Mṣb, Ḳ) and شُمْرُوخٌ, (Mṣb,) i. e. [*A fruit-stalk of the raceme of a palm-tree*; or] *a stalk, of a* كِبَاسَة, *upon which are the ripening dates*: (Ṣ, O:) or [so in some copies of the Ḳ and in the TA, but in other copies of the Ḳ "and,"] *i. q.* عِذْقٌ [i. e. *a raceme of a palm-tree* or *of dates*]; (Ḳ;) [i. e.] *an* عُنْقُود *of a palm-tree*, of which the شِمْرَاخ is a single branching stalk: (Mgh:) [agreeably with this last explanation and the latter of the two here given from the Ḳ, it is said,] and *it is, in relation to the palm-tree, like the* عُنْقُود *in relation to the grape-vine*: (Ṣ, O:) and in one dial., the ع is changed into ء, so that one says إِثْكَالٌ [and أُثْكُولٌ]: the pl. is عَثَاكِيلُ. (Mṣb.) It is said in a trad., خُذُوا عِثْكَالًا فِيهِ مِائَةُ شِمْرَاخٍ فَاضْرِبُوهُ بِهَا ضَرْبَةً [i. e. *Take ye a raceme of a palm-tree in which are a hundred fruit-stalks, and strike him therewith a single stroke*]. (O.)

عُثْكُولٌ: see the next preceding paragraph: — and that here following.

عُثْكُولَةٌ: see عِثْكَالٌ. — Also, (Ḳ,) and ▼ عُثْكُولٌ, (TA,) † *A kind of pendant, of* عِهْن [i. e. *wool*, or *dyed wool*], or *some* [*other*] *ornament*, (Ḳ, TA,) *suspended to a* هودج [or *women's camel-vehicle*], (TA,) *so as to dangle in the air*: (Ḳ, TA:) pl. عَثَاكِل occurring in a verse [by poetic license for عَثَاكِيل]. (TA.)

عِذْقٌ مُعَثْكَلٌ [*A raceme of a palm-tree* or *of dates*] *having many* شَمَارِيخ [or *fruit-stalks*]. (TA.) [See also the following paragraph.] — And, by way of comparison [thereto], هَوْدَجٌ مُعَثْكَلٌ † *A* هودج [or *women's camel-vehicle*] *having much wool* [*in the form of pendants, suspended to it*]. (TA.)

عِذْقٌ مُتَعَثْكِلٌ and مُتَعَثْكَلٌ [*A raceme of a palm-*

tree or *of dates*] *having* عَثَاكِيل [i. e. *fruit-stalks*]. (Ḳ.) [See also the next preceding paragraph.]

عثم

1. عَثَمَ, said of a broken bone, (Ṣ, Ḳ,) or it is peculiarly said of the arm, (Ḳ, [i. e. one says عَثَمَتِ اليَدُ,]) aor. ـُ, (PṢ,) inf. n. عَثْمٌ, (TA,) *It became set unevenly*, (Ṣ, Ḳ, TA,) i. e. [*forming a node*, or *protuberance, like a swelling, not so hard as bone*, (see عَثْمٌ, below,) or] *so as to have an unevenness remaining in it*: (TA:) or, said of a broken bone, *it approached to a state of consolidation, but was not as yet consolidated*; and in like manner, a wound: (ISh, TA:) or *it was*, or *became, in a bad state, and wanting in its former strength*, or *in its form*. (TA.) And عَثِمَ, aor. ـَ, inf. n. عَثَمٌ, said of a [broken] bone, signifies [the same, or] *It was badly set, so that there remained in it an unevenness.* (TA.) And sometimes it is used metaphorically in relation to the sword: so says IJ. (TA. [In a verse there cited as an ex., the verb app. relates to a sword in its scabbard or its case cut in pieces by another sword.]) — عَثَمَ said of a wound means as expl. above: (ISh, TA:) or *It became callous, and covered with a skin, but not as yet healed.* (Ḳ.) — عَثَمْتُهُ *I set it unevenly*, [*so as to form a node*, or *protuberance, like a swelling, not so hard as bone*, (see the first sentence above,)] namely, a broken bone; (Ṣ, Ḳ;) the verb being trans. as well as intrans., (Ṣ, TA,) like رَجَعَ and وَقَفَ. (TA.) — And عَثَمَتِ المَزَادَةَ, (Ṣ, Ḳ,) inf. n. عَثْمٌ, (TA,) *She sewed the* مزادة [or *leathern water-bag*] *not strongly*, or *not firmly*; (Ṣ, Ḳ;) as also ↓ اِعْتَثَمَتْهَا; (Ṣ, TA;) in the Ḳ, erroneously, ↓ أَعْثَمَتْهَا. (TA.)

2. عَثَّمَهُ, inf. n. تَعْثِيمٌ, *He set it*; namely, a [broken] bone. (TA.)

4: see 1, last sentence.

8: see 1, last sentence. — [Hence,] it is said in a prov., إِلَّا أَكُنْ صَنَعًا فَإِنِّى أَعْتَثِمُ, meaning † *If I be not skilful, verily I do according to the degree of my knowledge.* (Ṣ, Meyd.) — اعتثم به *He sought help by means of it*; (Ṣ, Ḳ;) and *profited by it*, or *made use of it*. (Ḳ.) One says, خُذْ هٰذَا فَاعْتَثِمْ بِهِ *Take thou this, and seek help by means of it* [or *profit by it*]. (Ṣ.) — And اعتثم بِيَدِهِ *He extended*, or *stretched forth, his arm*, or *hand*; syn. أَهْوَى بِهَا. (Ḳ.)

عَثْمٌ inf. n. of 1 [q. v.]. (TA.) — جُبِرَتْ يَدُهُ عَلَى عَثْمٍ means عَلَى عُقْدَةٍ, (Ṣ and O in art. عقد,) [i. e. *His arm was set and joined unevenly*,] *so as to form a node*, or *protuberance, like a swelling, not so hard as bone.* (ISk, L in art. اجر.)

عَثِمٌ, applied to a [broken] bone, *Badly set, so as to have an unevenness remaining in it.* (TA.) [And ↓ عَثْمَآءُ signifies the same, applied to an arm (يَدٌ); expl. by Golius as applied to a hand, and meaning *Distortedly consolidated*, on the authority of Meyd.]

عَثْمَآءُ: see the next preceding paragraph.

عُثْمَانٌ The *young one of the* [*species of bustard called*] حُبَارَى. (Ṣ, Ḳ.) — And The *young one of the* [*serpent called*] ثُعْبَان. (AA, Ḳ.) And, (Ḳ,) some say, (TA,) The *serpent*, (AA, Ḳ,) *of whatever species it be*: (AA:) or the *young one thereof.* (AA, Mgh, Ḳ.) And أَبُو عُثْمَانَ is a surname of *The serpent*; (Ḳ, TA;) mentioned by 'Alee Ibn-Ḥamzeh. (TA.)

عَيْثَمٌ, applied to a camel, *Big*, or *bulky, tall, and thick.* (TA.) — See also عَيْثَامٌ.

عَيْثَمِىٌّ The *wild ass*; (Ḳ, TA;) so called because of his bigness, or bulkiness, and strength. (TA.)

عَيْثَامٌ (in the T, voce دُلْبٌ, written ↓ عَيْثَمٌ,) *A species of tree*; (Ṣ, Ḳ, TA;) said to be the *same as the* دُلْب [q. v.]; it is *a white tree, that grows very tall*: n. un. with ة. (TA.) — Also *A certain sort of food, in which locusts are cooked*; (Ḳ, TA;) *of the food of the people of the desert.* (TA.)

عَيْثُومٌ *A great* camel. (Aṣ, Ṣ. [See also عَيْثُومٌ.]) And Anything *big*, or *bulky, and strong.* (TA.) — And The *female elephant*: (El-Ghanawee, Ṣ:) or the *elephant, male* and *female*: (Ḳ:) pl. عَيَاثِمُ. (TA.) — And The ضَبُع [i. e. *hyena*, or *female hyena*]. (A'Obeyd, Ṣ, Ḳ.)

عَثَمْثَمٌ *Strong*; applied to a camel; (AA, Ṣ;) and to a mule; and likewise to a shoulder: (IAạr, TA:) or, applied to a camel, *strong and tall*: (Ḳ, TA:) or *tall and thick*: or *big*, or *bulky*: (TA:) fem. with ة: (AA, Ṣ, Ḳ, TA:) pl. عَثَمْثَمَاتٌ. (TA.) — And The *lion*: (AA, Ṣ, Ḳ:) so called because of the heaviness of his tread. (AA, Ṣ.)

عثن

1. عَثَنَتِ النَّارُ, (Ṣ, Ḳ,) aor. ـِ, (Ṣ,) inf. n. عَثْنٌ and عُثُونٌ and عُثَانٌ, (Ḳ,) *The fire smoked*, or *sent up smoke*; (Ṣ, Ḳ;) as also ↓ عثّنت. (Ḳ.) — And عَثَنَ فِى الجَبَلِ, (Ḳ,) aor. ـِ, inf. n. عُثُونٌ, (TA,) *He ascended the mountain*: (Ḳ, TA:) like عَفَنَ: mentioned by Kr. (TA.) — عَثِنَ, aor. ـَ, (Ḳ,) inf. n. عَثَنٌ, (TḲ,) said of a garment, *It became perfumed with the odour of incense, or some substance for fumigation.* (Ḳ,* TA.)

2. عَثَّنْتُ الثَّوْبَ *I fumigated the garment*: (Mgh:) or عَثَّنَتِ الثَّوْبَ بِالطِّيبِ *She fumigated the garment over the perfume so that it* [the perfume] *clung to it*: (TA:) or عَثَّنْتُ ثَوْبِى بِالبَخُورِ, (Ṣ,) inf. n. تَعْثِينٌ, (Ṣ, Ḳ,) *I perfumed my garment with incense, or some substance for fumigation.* (Ḳ.*) — And عَثَّنَتِ المَرْأَةُ بِدُخْنَتِهَا *The woman perfumed herself with her incense*, or *substance for fumigation.* (TA.) — See also 1. — One says also عَثَّنَ عَلَيْنَا فُلَانٌ meaning † *Such a one caused confusion*, or *disorder*, or *disturbance*, *to happen between us*, or *among us*; from عُثَان signifying "smoke:" (A, TA:) [or *caused confusion, &c., and excited evil, or corrupt, conduct, between us*, or *among us*: for] التَّعْثِينُ signifies *the causing confusion*, or *disorder*, or *disturbance, and exciting evil, or corrupt, conduct.* (Ḳ.)

4. لَا تُعْثِنْ عَلَيْنَا [*Do not thou raise a smothering smoke upon us*] is said when one kindles a fire with bad, smoking, wood. (TA.)

عِثْنٌ *A species of* خُوصَة [q. v.] *upon which camels*, or *the like, feed*, (Ḳ, TA,) *when it is succulent; but when it becomes dry, it is useless.* (TA.) — And [hence, perhaps,] *A good tender and manager, of camels*, or *the like*. (Ḳ.) — And *i. q.* عِهْنٌ [i. e. *Wool*; or *wool dyed of various colours*]: (Ḳ:) a dial. var. thereof. (TA.)

عَثَنٌ: see عُثَانٌ. — Also *A small idol*: pl. أَعْثَانٌ: (Ḳ:) [it is said that] وَثَنٌ signifies "a large idol." (TA.)

عَثِينٌ Food *infected with smoke*; as also ↓ مَعْثُونٌ. (Ḳ.)

عُثَانٌ *Smoke*; (Ṣ, Mgh, Mṣb, Ḳ;) as also ↓ عَثَنٌ: (Ṣ, Ḳ: [in one of my copies of the Ṣ, written with the ث quiescent:]) mostly used in relation to a substance with which one fumigates: (Mgh, Mṣb:) and also expl. as signifying *smoke without fire*: (TA:) pl. عَوَاثِنُ, (Ṣ, Ḳ, TA,) deviating from rule, (TA,) like دَوَاخِنُ pl. of دُخَانٌ, the only other instance of the kind. (Ṣ, TA.) — And ‡ *Dust* (Az, Ṣ, Mgh, Ḳ) is sometimes thus called, (Ṣ, Mgh,) metaphorically, (Mgh,) as being likened to smoke, which is the primary meaning: so says A'Obeyd, and Aboo-'Amr Ibn-El-'Alà says the like. (Az.)

عُثْنُونٌ *Small long hairs under the part beneath the lower jaw of the camel*: (Ṣ, Ḳ:) [pl. عَثَانِينُ:] one says بَعِيرٌ ذُو عَثَانِينَ [*a camel having such small long hairs*], like as they said, for the مَفْرِق of the head, مَفَارِق. (Ṣ.) And The *beard*: or the *portion thereof that extends beyond the two sides of the cheeks*: or the *portion that grows upon the chin and beneath it, downwards*: or *length of the beard*: (Ḳ:) or the *portion of the beard that depends from the chin*: (Ḥam p. 820:) and عُثْنُونُ اللِّحْيَةِ signifies *the extremity of the beard.* (TA.) And *Certain small hairs at the part in which the he-goat is slaughtered.* (TA.) And The رَعْثَة [or *wattle*] of the cock. (Ṣ and Ḳ in art. رعث, q. v.) — Also The *first* of wind and of rain; (Ṣ, Ḳ;) so says [the Imám] Aboo-Ḥaneefeh: (TA:) or *rain generally*: or *rain while it is between the heaven and the earth*: pl. عَثَانِينُ: (Ḳ:) AZ says that العَثَانِينُ signifies *the rain that is between the clouds and the earth*; like السَّبَلُ: sing. عُثْنُونٌ: (Ṣ, TA:) and عُثْنُونُ السَّحَابِ signifies *the clouds that have fallen upon the earth*: and عَثَانِينُ السَّحَابِ *the pendent skirts of the clouds*: and عُثْنُونُ الرِّيحِ *the trail of the wind when it comes drawing along the dust*: pl. as above. (TA.) And The *first* of anything. (Ḥam p. 820.)

عَوَاثِنُ A lion *having much hair.* (Ḳ.)

مُعَثَّنٌ (Ḳ, TA) A man (TA) *large in the* عُثْنُون. (Ḳ, TA.)

مُعَثْنُونٌ : see عَثِنٌ.

عثو and عثى

1. عَثَا, aor. يَعْثُو, (Ṣ, Mṣb, Ḳ,) inf. n. عُثُوٌّ, (Ḳ, TA,) [accord. to the CḲ عُثْوٌ, but] like سُمُوٌّ; (TA;) and عَثِىَ, aor. يَعْثَى, (Ṣ, Mṣb, Ḳ,) which is of the dial. of El-Ḥijáz, and of which the inf. n. is عُثًا; (TA;) and عَثَى, aor. يَعْثَى and يَعْثِى; inf. n. عُثِىٌّ and عِثِىٌّ and عَثَيَانٌ; (Ḳ, TA;) *He acted corruptly; or made,* or *did, mischief:* (Ṣ, Mṣb, Ḳ:) or *did so in the utmost degree:* (TA:) فِى الأَرْضِ [*in the earth*]: (Ṣ, TA:) the aor. of one of the dial. vars. occurs in the Ḳur ii. 57; &c.: some say that عثا, aor. يعثا, [or عَثِىَ, aor. يَعْثَى,] is formed by transposition from عَاثَ, aor. يَعِيثُ: (TA:) accord. to Er-Rághib, عَيْثٌ and عُثِىٌّ, or عِثِىٌّ, and عُثُوٌّ are nearly alike; but عَيْثٌ is mostly used in relation to that which is perceived by sense; and عثىّ and عثوّ, in relation to that which is perceived by the [mind or] judgment: some say that عثوّ [as also عثىّ] is the *acting wrongfully, injuriously,* or *unjustly;* and sometimes does not involve the acting corruptly: (MF and TA in art. عيث:) Lḥ says that عَثِىَ is of the dial. of El-Ḥijáz, and is the [more] approved form; and عاث is of the dial. of the Benoo-Temeem. (TA in that art.) — And عَثِىَ, aor. يَعْثَى, inf. n. عَثًا, said of the hair of the head, *It was,* or *became, dry and matted, and was long left uncombed.* (TA.)

عُثًى *Hair:* this is its primary signification. (TA.) [See the next paragraph.] — And, metaphorically, ‡ *Such as is straggling, of plants,* or *herbage; as the* نَصِىّ*, and the* نَبِىّ*, and the* صِلِّيَان. (TA.) And [hence] one says, شَابَ عُثَى الأَرْضِ † *The plants,* or *herbage, of the earth, dried up,* or *became yellow:* (Ḳ:) so in the Tekmileh, and so says ISk. (TA.)

عُثْوَةٌ *A long* لِمَّة [or *quantity of hair descending below the ear* or *to the shoulder*]: (Ḳ:) pl. عُثًى, like رُبًى; (so in some copies of the Ḳ;) or عُثِىٌّ, like رُبِىٌّ; (so in other copies;) or عِثِىٌّ; like رِبِىٌّ; (so in my MS. copy of the Ḳ; [app. taken from the TA; the first of which (i. e. عُثًى) I hold to be the right; (see the paragraph next preceding this;) though SM says what here follows;]) it is correctly عِثًى, like إِلًى; agreeably with what is said in the M, i. e. that اللِّمَمُ الطِّوَالُ signifies العِثَى. (TA.)

عُثْوَةٌ The *state of the hair of the head when it has become dry and matted, and has been long left uncombed.* (TA.)

عِثْيَانٌ : see أَعْثَى.

عَاثٍ *Acting corruptly;* or *making,* or *doing, mischief.* (Mṣb. [See 1.])

أَعْثَى *Having much hair;* (Ṣ, Ḳ;) sometimes applied in this sense to a man. (Ṣ.) And *Having a thick beard.* (TA.) — And The *male hyena;* (Ṣ, Ḳ;) as also ↓ عِثْيَانٌ: (Ṣ:) and [the fem.] عَثْوَآءُ the *female hyena;* (Ṣ, Ḳ;) because of the abundance of her hair: (Ṣ:) and [the pl.] عُثْوٌ, and عُثْىٌ, *a number of hyenas together.* (TA.) — [The fem.] عَثْوَآءُ is also an appellation applied to *An old woman.* (Ṣ, TA.) — And the masc. signifies also *Thick, gross,* or *coarse, in size.* (TA.) — And *Foolish,* or *stupid,* (Ṣ, Ḳ,) *heavy,* or *dull.* (Ṣ.) — And One *whose colour inclines to blackness.* (Ḳ.) — And *A colour* [itself] *that inclines to blackness:* (Ḳ, TA:) or, accord. to the M, العثى [perhaps a mistranscription] signifies *a colour inclining to blackness, with abundance of hair.* (TA.)

عج

1. عَجَّ, (Ṣ, A, Mgh, O, &c.,) aor. ـِ, (Ṣ, Mgh, Mṣb, Ḳ,) or ـُ; (so in the O; [but this is at variance with a general rule;]) and عَجِجَ with kesr to the medial radical [in the first and second persons, عَجِجْتُ and عَجِجْتَ], (TA,) aor. ـَ; (Ḳ;) inf. n. عَجٌّ and عَجِيجٌ; (Ṣ, A, Mgh, O, Mṣb, Ḳ;) *He cried out,* or *vociferated;* (Ḳ, TA;) like ضَجَّ; accord. to Az, *supplicating,* and *begging aid,* or *succour;* (TA;) and (Ḳ) *he raised his voice;* (Ṣ, A, O, Ḳ;) as also ↓ عَجْعَجَ; (Ḳ;) or this signifies *he cried out, vociferated,* or *raised his voice, repeatedly;* (Ṣ, O, TA;) and عَجَّ, *he raised his voice with the* تَلْبِيَة [or *saying* لَبَّيْكَ]: it is said in a trad., أَفْضَلُ الحَجِّ العَجُّ وَالثَّجُّ (Ṣ, Mgh, O, Mṣb) i. e. *The most excellent of the actions of the pilgrimage are* (Mgh) *the raising of the voice with the* تلبية (Mgh, O, and Mṣb in art. ثج) *and the shedding of the blood of the victims brought for sacrifice to the sacred territory:* (Mgh, and Mṣb in art. ثج:) and عَجِيجٌ signifies the *crying out,* or *vociferating, and clamouring,* of a people, or party. (TA.) — And عَجَّ, aor. ـِ, inf. ns. as above, said of a camel, *He made a* [*loud*] *noise in his braying:* and ↓ عَجْعَجَ *he repeated,* or *reiterated,* [*such*] *a noise:* and عَجَّ, aor. ـِ, inf. n. عَجِيجٌ, said of water, *it made a sound;* and so [or as meaning *it made a reiterated sound*] ↓ عَجْعَجَ: and in the same sense the former verb is used in relation to a bow: and also in relation to the [piece of stick or wood called] زَنْد on the occasion of its producing fire: (TA:) and ↓ عَجْعَجَ said of a camel, when beaten, or heavily laden, *he uttered a grumbling cry;* syn. رَغَا. (O, Ḳ.) — عَجَّتِ الرِّيحُ, and ↓ اعجّت, *The wind was,* or *became, violent, and raised the dust,* (Ṣ, O, Ḳ, TA,) *and drove it along.* (TA.) [See also 2.] — And عَجَّتِ الرَّائِحَةُ ‡ [*The odour diffused itself strongly,* or *powerfully*]. (A, TA.) — And عَجَّ ثَدْيَاهَا, (A,) or ثَدْيَاهَا, (TA,) said of a girl, ‡ *Her breast,* or *breasts, began to swell,* or *become protuberant.* (A, TA.) — عَجَّ القَوْمُ and ↓ اعجّوا, (Ḳ, TA,) and هَجُّوا and اهجّوا, and ضَجُّوا and اضجّوا [?], as is said in the "Nawádir," (TA,) mean أَكْثَرُوا فِى فُنُونِهِمُ الرُّكُوبَ (Ḳ, TA,) in one copy فى فُنُونِهِ: (TA:) [Ibr. D thinks that both of these readings are mistranscribed, for أَكْثَرُوا مِنْ فُنُونِ الرُّكُوبِ, meaning *The people,* or *party, practised many modes,* or *manners, of riding;* agreeably with an explanation in the TḲ: but the case is very perplexing; and is rendered the more so by the facts that this is not in the O, and that what here follows is not in the Ḳ nor in the TA, and that I do not find in art. هج nor in any other art. anything that throws light upon it:] عَجَّ القَوْمُ فِى الوَادِى and ↓ اعجّوا, and هَجُّوا and اهجّوا, and ضَجُّوا and اضجّوا [?], mean *The people,* or *party, descended into the valley, and trod it much.* (O.) — عَجَّ النَّاقَةَ: see R. Q. 1.

2. عَجَّجَتِ الرِّيحُ الغُبَارَ, inf. n. تَعْجِيجٌ, *The wind raised the dust.* (TA.) [See also 1.] — And عَجَّجْتُ البَيْتَ دُخَانًا, (Ṣ, O, and so in a copy of the Ḳ,) or مِنَ الدُّخَانِ, (so in other copies of the Ḳ,) inf. n. as above, (Ḳ,) *I filled the house,* or *tent, with smoke.* (Ḳ, TA.)

4: see 1, latter half, in three places.

5. تعجّج, said of a house, or tent, (Ṣ, Ḳ,) *It was,* or *became, filled with smoke.* (Ḳ.)

R. Q. 1. عَجْعَجَ: see 1, in four places. — عَجْعَجَ بِالنَّاقَةِ, (Ṣ, O, L,) or ↓ عَجَّ النَّاقَةَ, *He chid the she-camel,* (Ṣ, O, L, Ḳ,) *saying* عَاجِ عَاجِ, (Ṣ, Ḳ,) or عَاجٍ: (L:) or the former signifies *he turned the she-camel to a thing, saying* عَاجِ عَاجِ. (TA.) — And [the inf. n.] عَجْعَجَةٌ signifies The *changing of* ى *into* ج *when occurring with* ع [*immediately preceding it*]: a practice that obtained among the tribe of Ḳuḍá'ah; (Ṣ, O;) and accord. to Fr, among the tribe of Ṭeiyi, and some of the tribe of Asad; (TA in art. ج, q. v.;) like as عَنْعَنَة did among that of Temeem: (TA in the present art.:) they used to say, هٰذَا رَاعِجٌ خَرَجَ مَعِجْ for رَاعٍ خَرَجَ مَعِى [*This is a pastor who went forth with me*]. (Ṣ, O.)

عَجَّةٌ *A crying out,* or *vociferating,* and *clamour,* or *confusion of cries* or *noises,* of a people, or party. (TA.) وَحَّدَ ٱللّٰهَ فِى عَجَّتِهِ means [*He declared the unity of God*] *aloud.* (TA, from a trad.)

عُجَّةٌ [*An egg-fritter,* or *omelet:* so in the present day:] *a certain food made of eggs:* (Ṣ, O, Ḳ:) or *flour kneaded with clarified butter,* (AA, TA,) *and then fried,* or *roasted:* IDrd says, it is *a sort of food;* but what sort I know not: accord. to IKh, it is *any food compounded;* as *dates* and [*the preparation of curd called*] أَقِط: (TA:) it is a post-classical word: (Ḳ:) [J says,] I think it to be post-classical: (Ṣ:) it is of the dial. of Syria. (TA.)

عَجَاجٌ *Dust:* (Ṣ, A, O, Ḳ:) or *dust raised by the wind:* (TA:) and *smoke:* (Ṣ, A, O, Ḳ:) ▼ عَجَاجَةٌ is a more special term [signifying *a portion,* or *cloud, of dust:* and *of smoke*]: (Ṣ, O:) and this latter signifies [also] *a dust that buries in it everything;* as also عَجَاجَةٌ. (TA.) —— Also *Low, vile, base, mean,* or *ignoble, people;* (Sh, O, Ḳ, TA;) *lacking intellect,* or *understanding;* (Sh, O;) *in whom is no good:* [a coll. gen. n.; for] ▼ عَجَاجَةٌ signifies *one of such persons* [as is indicated in the O]. (TA.) And, applied to a single person, *Foolish; stupid; unsound,* or *deficient, in intellect,* or *understanding.* (Ḳ.)

عَجَاجَةٌ: see the next preceding paragraph, first sentence. [Hence,] one says, فُلَانٌ يَلُفُّ عَجَاجَتَهُ عَلَى بَنِى فُلَانٍ [*Such a one folds his cloud of dust*], meaning, *makes a hostile,* or *predatory, incursion,* or *attack, upon the sons of such a one.* (Ṣ, O, Ḳ.*) And لَبَّدَ عَجَاجَتَهُ (O, Ḳ) *He laid,* or *allayed, his* عجاجة [or *cloud of dust*], (O,) meaning *he desisted from that in which he was engaged.* (O, Ḳ.) —— Also *Many great camels:* (Ṣ, O, Ḳ:) so accord. to Fr, (Ṣ, O,) as mentioned by A'Obeyd: (Ṣ:) but Sh says, I know not the word in this sense. (TA.) —— See also the next preceding paragraph, second sentence.

عَجَّاجٌ *Vociferous, clamorous, sounding much,* or *noisy;* an epithet applied to anything that has a voice, or sound, or noise, (Ṣ, O, Ḳ,) as a bow and the wind [&c.]; (Ṣ, O;) as also ▼ عَجْعَاجٌ, (Ḳ,) this latter mentioned by Lḥ as applied in this sense to a man: (Ṣ:) and the former, applied to a stallion [camel], *vociferous,* or *noisy,* in his braying: and, applied to a river, *sounding:* (Ṣ, O:) or, thus applied, *containing much water;* as though it vociferated by reason of the abundance thereof and of the sound of its copious pouring. (IDrd, TA.) [See a tropical ex. of it voce ثَجَّاجٌ.] —— يَوْمٌ عَجَّاجٌ and ▼ مُعِجٌّ *A day of violent wind that raises the dust.* (Ṣ, O, Ḳ.)

عَاجِ, (Ṣ, Ḳ,) or عَاجٍ, (L,) *A cry by which a she-camel is chidden.* (Ṣ, L, Ḳ.) [But the former belongs to art. عوج, q. v.]

عَاجٌّ [part. n. of 1], applied to a road, [app. because a crowded road is usually noisy,] means *Full.* (Ṣ, O, Ḳ.) [Compare عَجَّاجٌ applied to a river.]

عَجْعَاجٌ: see عَجَّاجٌ. —— Also, applied to a horse, *Generous,* or *excellent, and advanced in age:* (O, Ḳ:) or, accord. to IF, *that runs vehemently.* (O.)

مُعِجٌّ: see عَجَّاجٌ, last sentence.

رِيحٌ مِعْجَاجٌ *A wind that raises the dust:* (IAạr, TA:) [the pl.] رِيَاحٌ مَعَاجِيجُ (Ṣ, O, Ḳ) signifies the *contr. of* مَهَاوِينُ. (Ṣ, O.)

عجب

1. عَجِبَ مِنْهُ, (Ṣ, O, Mṣb, Ḳ,) [and لَهُ, as shown by what follows,] aor. ـَ, inf. n. عَجَبٌ; (Mṣb, TA;) and ▼ تعجّب منه, and ▼ استعجب منه, (Ṣ, O, Mṣb, Ḳ,) which two are syn. each with the other, (Ṣ, O, Ḳ,) and with the first also; (Ṣ, Ḳ;) all signify *He wondered at it;* i. e. *he deemed it strange, extraordinary,* or *improbable,* said of a thing occurring, or presenting itself, to him; (Ḳ, TA;) *on account of his being little accustomed to it:* (TA:) or the first signifies [as above, i. e.] *he deemed it strange, extraordinary,* or *improbable:* and ▼ تَعَجُّبٌ is of two kinds; one is [the *wondering*] at a thing which one commends, and it means the *accounting* (a thing) *good* or *goodly,* or *approving* [it], *and expressing one's approval* of a thing; and the other is at a thing that one dislikes, and it means the *deeming* [a thing] *strange, extraordinary,* or *improbable, and discommending* [it]: (Mṣb:) or, accord. to some of the grammarians, it signifies the *mind's becoming affected,* or *acted upon, by some excessive quality* in the thing by which it is so affected; [so that it may be rendered the *becoming affected with wonder;*] as when one says مَا أَشْجَعَهُ [" how courageous is he!"] and أَسْمِعْ بِهِمْ وَأَبْصِرْ [" how clearly shall they hear! and how clearly shall they see!"]: (Mṣb, MF, TA:) or it is [the *wondering*] at a thing of which the cause, or reason, is hidden, and not known: or it is when one sees a thing that pleases him, and thinks that he has not seen the like of it: (L, TA:) [therefore تَعَجَّبَ مِنْهُ may be rendered *he wondered at it,* and *he admired it:*] accord. to some, it peculiarly relates to what is deemed good or goodly, or approved; [though this is inconsistent with the application of the grammatical term فِعْلُ التَّعَجُّبِ *the verb of wonder;*] and the subst. derived from it is ▼ عُجْبٌ: and ▼ استعجب relates to what is good or goodly or approved, and to what is otherwise; and the subst. is ▼ عَجَبٌ [which is also the inf. n. of عَجِبَ]: or accord. to the A and L, ▼ استعجب signifies *he wondered* at a thing *intensely;* or *became affected with intense wonder.* (TA.) —— [عَجَبًا لِهٰذَا, a phrase of common occurrence, (mentioned in the Ḳ voce وَيْبٌ, &c.,) is for أَعْجَبُ عَجَبًا لِهٰذَا *I wonder greatly,* lit. *with wondering, at this.* See also an ex. voce عَجَبٌ, last sentence but two.] —— Of the words in the Ḳur xxxvii. 12, there are two readings, بَلْ عَجِبْتَ ويسخرون and بَلْ عَجِبْتُ وَيَسْخَرُونَ: accord. to the former, the meaning is, *Nay, thou wonderest* at their conduct, or *deemest it extraordinary,* [O Mohammad,] *and they mock:* respecting the latter reading, [which may be rendered *Nay, I wonder,* &c.,] it is observed that عَجِبَ when attributed to God has a meaning different from that which it has when attributed to men; IAth says that, when attributed to God, it is used in a tropical manner, as the causes of things are not hidden from Him: or, accord. to IAmb, the verb here means *I have recompensed* them *for* their *wondering* at the truth, or their *deeming* it *strange* or *improbable:* and in like manner it is said [in the Ḳur viii. 30], يَمْكُرُونَ وَيَمْكُرُ ٱللّٰهُ [lit. " They plot and God plotteth"], meaning, " God recompenseth them for their plotting." (L, TA.) —— It is also said that عَجِبَ when attributed to God [sometimes] means *The being well pleased, content,* or *satisfied.* (Ḳ, TA.) The saying, in a trad., عَجِبَ رَبُّكَ مِنْ قَوْمٍ يُقَادُونَ إِلَى الجَنَّةِ فِى السَّلَاسِلِ means *Thy Lord wonders at a people who will be led to Paradise in chains* [because of their deeming themselves unworthy thereof]; the verb عجب being here used in a tropical sense: or the meaning is, *thy Lord is well pleased with,* and will reward, *a people* &c.: and there are other trads. of the same kind. (L, TA.) —— عَجِبَ إِلَيْهِ means *He loved,* or *liked, him,* or *it.* (L, TA.) [See a verse cited voce عَجِيبٌ; from which it seems to signify lit. *He,* or *it, was an object of love to him.*] —— عَجِبَتْ, inf. n. عَجَبٌ; and عَجُبَتْ; said of a she-camel, *She was,* or *became, such as is termed* عَجْبَآء. (TA.)

2. عَجَّبَهُ, inf. n. تَعْجِيبٌ, *He caused him to wonder,* (Ṣ, O, Ḳ, TA,) بِالشَّىْءِ [*by the thing*]. (TA. [See also 4.])

4. اعجبهُ *It* (a thing, or an affair, or event, TA) *induced,* or *excited, him to wonder.* (Ḳ, TA. [See also 2.]) In the following saying of Ibn-Ḳeys-er-Ruḳeiyát,

• رَأَتْ فِى الرَّأْسِ مِنِّى شَيْبَةً لَسْتُ أُغَيِّبُهَا •
• فَقَالَتْ لِى ٱبْنُ قَيْسٍ ذَا وَبَعْضُ الشَّيْبِ يُعْجِبُهَا •

the meaning is, [*She saw upon my head some hoariness, which I did not hide; and she said to me, " Is this Ibn-Ḳeys?" somewhat of hoariness*] *causing her to have wonder.* (TA.) —— And *It* (a thing, or an affair, or event, TA) *induced in him wonder,* or *admiration, and pleasure,* or *joy:* (Ḳ:) or *it excited his admiration,* or *approval:* (Mṣb:) or *it pleased,* or *rejoiced, him.* (TA.) You say, أَعْجَبَنِى هٰذَا الشَّىْءُ لِحُسْنِهِ [*This thing has excited my admiration,* or *approval,* or *has pleased me, for its goodness,* or *goodliness,* or *beauty*]. (Ṣ, O.) And أَعْجَبَنِى حُسْنُهُ [*Its goodness,* or *goodliness,* or *beauty, excited my admiration,* &c.]. (Mṣb.) —— And أُعْجِبَ بِهِ *He was excited to wonder,* or *admiration, and pleasure,* or *joy, by it; he admired it, and was pleased with it,* or *rejoiced by it.* (Ḳ.) You say, أُعْجِبَ بِنَفْسِهِ, (Ṣ, O, Mṣb,) inf. n. إِعْجَابٌ, [which is often used as syn. with عُجْبٌ, the corresponding subst.,] (O,) [*He admired himself,* (lit. *was excited to admiration by himself,*) *was pleased with himself,* or *was self-conceited,* or *vain;* or] *he exalted,* and *magnified, himself; was haughty,* and *proud.* (Mṣb.) —— [مَا أَعْجَبَهُ generally signifies *How wonderful is it!*] —— مَا أَعْجَبَهُ بِرَأْيِهِ [*How greatly does he admire his opinion* or *judgment!* or *how greatly is he pleased with it!* or *how conceited,* or *vain,* or *proud, is he of it!*] is anomalous [in two respects], (Ṣ, O, Ḳ,) not to be taken as an example to be imitated; (Ṣ, O;)

for the verb here is formed from a passive [and augmented] verb [أُعْجِبَ], like as is the case in مَا أَشْغَلَهُ; whereas it is the primary rule with respect to the verb of wonder that it shall not be formed from any but an active [and unaugmented] verb. (TA.)

5: see 1, in two places. — One says also, تعجّب فِى مِشْيَتِهِ [app. meaning *He showed* عُجْب, i. e. *self-admiration*, &c., *in his gait*]. (TA voce تَفَتَّكَ.) = تَعَجَّبَنِى signifies تَصَبَّانِى [*He excited my desire, and invited me*, or *made me to incline, to ignorant*, or *foolish*, or *silly, and youthful, conduct, so that I yearned towards him*: or *he deceived me*, or *beguiled me, and captivated my heart*]; (O, Ḳ, TA;) said of a man: (O, TA:) and تَقَتَّنَنِى [in the O تَقَتَّنِى, which I think a mistranscription, though I do not find تَقَتَّنَ elsewhere in the sense here assigned to it,] signifies the same. (TA.)

10: see 1, in three places.

عَجْبٌ: see عَجَبٌ, in two places: = and see also عُجْبٌ. = Also The *root*, or *base*, *of the tail*: (Ṣ, O, Ḳ:) or the *part of the root*, or *base*, *of the tail*, of any beast, *which the haunch encloses*, (Mṣb, TA,) *and which is inserted in the hinder part of the rump*: (TA:) or the *root*, or *base, and bone, of the tail*: (Lḥ, TA:) also called the عُصْعُص [q. v.]: (Mṣb, TA:) or it is the *head of the* عصعص: (TA:) or the *upper part of the* عصعص: or the *external extremity of the spine*; and the عصعص is its internal extremity: (Az, L voce فَنْفَخ:) it is said in a trad., that every part of a man will become consumed, except the عَجْب, (TA,) or the عَجْب of the tail, (O, TA,) accord. to different relations; (TA;) from which [as a rudiment] he was created, and upon which he will [at the resurrection] be put together: (O:) i. e. the *bone at the lower*, or *lowest, part of the spine, at the rump*; which is the عَسِيب of beasts: it is said to be *like a grain of mustard-seed*: or, as Z says in the "Fáïḳ," it is the *bone that is between the buttocks*: it is also pronounced ▼ عُجْبٌ; and accord. to MF, ▼ عِجْبٌ, but no one else says this: and, as El-Khafájee says, it is also called عَجْمٌ and عُجْمٌ and عِجْمٌ, in this case with the three vowel-sounds. (TA.) — Also ‡ The *hinder part* (Ṣ, O, Ḳ, TA) of a tract of sand, (Ṣ, O,) or of anything: (Ḳ, TA:) and hence, عَجْبُ كَثِيبٍ i. e. *the thin hinder portion* [*of a sand-hill*, or *of an extended and gibbous sand-hill*, or *of a collection of sand that has poured down*]: (TA:) pl. عُجُوبٌ, (Ṣ, O,) and perhaps أَعْجَابٌ also in the former sense [and therefore in this likewise]. (TA.)

عُجْبٌ: see عَجْبٌ. — Also a subst. from the phrase أُعْجِبَ بِنَفْسِهِ, (Ṣ,) or from الإِعْجَابُ; (O;) [i. e. it signifies *Self-admiration*; or *self-conceitedness*; or] *vanity*; and *pride*: (Ḳ:) it is said to be [a result, or an offspring, of stupidity, or folly; or] a redundance of stupidity, or folly, which one has turned to what is thus termed. (TA.) [Er-Rághib makes a distinction between عُجْب and تِيه; as will be seen below, voce مُعْجَب.] = Also, and ▼ عِجْبٌ, and ▼ عَجُبٌ, *A man who is pleased to sit with women*, (O, Ḳ,) *and to converse with them, without his doing what induces doubt*, or *suspicion*, or *evil opinion*: (O:) or *with whom women are pleased*: (Ḳ, TA:) the pl. is perhaps أَعْجَابٌ. (TA.) = See also عَجَبٌ.

عِجْبٌ: see عُجْبٌ: = and see also عَجَبٌ.

عَجَبٌ [originally an inf. n.] (Ṣ, O, Ḳ) and ▼ عُجْبٌ, (accord. to the Ḳ,) or ▼ عَجْبٌ, (accord. to the TA,) *Wonder*; i. e. *a deeming strange, extraordinary*, or *improbable, what occurs*, or *presents itself, to one*, (Ḳ, TA,) *on account of being little accustomed to it*; (TA;) or [the *effect, upon the mind, of*] *the consideration of a thing with which one is not familiar, and to which one is not accustomed*: (IAar, TA:) for a distinction between عَجَب and ▼ عُجْب, see 1, in the middle of the paragraph: the pl. of عَجَب [in this sense] is [said to be] أَعْجَابٌ; (Ḳ;) or it has no pl.: (Ṣ, O, Ḳ:) [this statement correctly applies to عَجَب as an epithet; for as such it is app. used as sing. and pl., being originally an inf. n.:] but El-'Ajjáj has pluralized it, [regarding it in the sense expl. above,] saying,

• ذَكَّرْنَ أَشْجَانًا لِمَنْ تَشَجَّبَا •
• وَهِجْنَ أَعْجَابًا لِمَنْ تَعَجَّبَا •

[*They mentioned griefs to him who grieved, and they excited wonder to him who wondered*]. (O.) يَا لَلْعَجَبِ [may be rendered *O case of wonder!* but properly] means *O wonder come, for this is thy time*: and يَا لِلْعَجَبِ [may also be rendered *O case of wonder!* but properly] means *O* [people, or the like, come] *to wonder*; the noun signifying the invoked being suppressed. (Ḥar p. 27.) = It is also an epithet applied to a thing, an affair, an event, or a case; one says أَمْرٌ عَجَبٌ [*A wonderful thing* or *affair* &c.]; and so ▼ عَجِيبٌ [which is more common in this sense], and ▼ عُجَابٌ, and ▼ عُجَّابٌ: or ▼ عَجِيبٌ is *syn. with* عَجَبٌ; but ▼ عُجَابٌ signifies *more than* عَجَبٌ: (Ḳ:) or ▼ عُجَابٌ is *syn. with* ▼ عَجِيبٌ, (Ṣ, O,) which signifies a thing, (Ṣ, O, Mṣb,) or an affair, or event, or a case, (Ṣ, O,) *wondered at*; (Ṣ, O, Mṣb, TA;) or *inducing wonder*, or *admiration, and pleasure*, or *joy*; or *pleasing*, or *rejoicing*; syn. ▼ مُعْجِبٌ; (TA;) and ▼ عُجَّابٌ signifies *more than* عَجَبٌ: (Ṣ, O, TA:) [it is said that] عَجَبٌ has no pl.; [app. meaning when it is used as an epithet, as observed above;] nor has ▼ عَجِيبٌ; (Ṣ, O, Ḳ;) or the pl. of this is عَجَائِبُ [respecting which see عَجِيبَةٌ]; (Ṣ, O, Ḳ;) like as أَفَائِلُ is pl. of أَفِيلٌ; and تَبَائِعُ, of تَبِيعٌ. (Ṣ, O.) [Being originally an inf. n., it is used alike as masc. and fem.:] one says قِصَّةٌ عَجَبٌ [meaning *A wonderful story*: and for the same reason, it may, as an epithet, be also used alike as sing. and pl.: like عَدْلٌ &c.]. (O.) — [It is also used as a subst. in a pl. sense, signifying *Wonders*, as meaning *wonderful things*; like the pl. عَجَائِبُ, &c.; and it may be similarly used in a sing. sense for شَىْءٌ عَجَبٌ or أَمْرٌ عَجَبٌ: but when used as a subst. in the pl. sense expl. above, it seems to be regarded by some as a coll. gen. n., of which ▼ عَجَبَةٌ is the n. un.; for] one says, مَا فُلَانٌ إِلَّا عَجَبَةٌ مِنَ العَجَبِ [*Such a one is none other than a wonder of wonders*]. (A, TA.) [Hence, also,] أَبُو العَجَبِ [lit. *The father of wonders*] is a surname of *Fortune*. (TA.) And it signifies also *The practiser of legerdemain*, or *sleight-of-hand*; syn. الشَّعْوَذِىُّ, (A, TA,) or المُشَعْوِذُ: (Eth-Tha'álibee, TA in art. شعذ:) and *any one who does wonderful things*. (A, TA.) And a poet says,

• يَا عَجَبًا لِلدَّهْرِ ذِى الأَعْجَابِ •

[for يَا أَعْجَبُ عَجَبًا O, *I wonder greatly*, lit. *with wondering, at fortune that is ever attended with wonders*]. (TA.) [See also عَجِيبَةٌ.] = Also The *quality*, in a she-camel, *that is denoted by the epithet* عَجْبَآءُ [fem. of أَعْجَبُ, q. v.]; and so ▼ عُجْبَةٌ. (O.)

عُجْبَةٌ: see the last preceding sentence.

عَجَبَةٌ: see عَجَبٌ, last quarter.

عُجَابٌ: see عَجَبٌ, in three places, near the middle of the paragraph: — and see also عُجَّابٌ.

عَجِيبٌ: see عَجَبٌ, in four places, near the middle of the paragraph. — Also *Loved, beloved*, or *an object of love*: so in the following verse, cited by Th:

• وَمَا البُخْلُ يَنْهَانِى وَلَا الجُودُ قَادَنِى •
• وَلٰكِنَّهَا ضَرْبٌ إِلَىَّ عَجِيبُ •

[*And neither does niggardliness forbid me nor liberality lead me; but she is a sort* of person, *to me, an object of love*]: by قَادَنِى, the poet means يَقُودُنِى. (L, TA.)

عَجِيبَةٌ (Ḳ) and ▼ أُعْجُوبَةٌ (Ṣ, O, Ḳ) *A wonderful thing; a thing at which one wonders*: (Ṣ, O, Ḳ:*) [the pl. of the former, accord. to modern usage, is عَجَائِبُ, mentioned above as pl. of عَجِيبٌ: and] أَعَاجِيبُ seems to be pl. of أُعْجُوبَةٌ, like as أَحَادِيثُ is pl. of أُحْدُوثَةٌ: (Ṣ, O:) and ▼ تَعَاجِيبُ signifies *wonderful things*; syn. عَجَائِبُ; (Ṣ, O, Ḳ;) and is a word [of a rare form, (see تَبَاشِيرُ,)] having no proper sing., (Ṣ, O,) like تَعَاشِيبُ; (O;) erroneously thought by the author of the "Námoos" [on the Ḳámoos] to be most probably a mistake for أَعَاجِيبُ: (TA:) a poet says,

• وَمِنْ تَعَاجِيبِ خَلْقِ اللّٰهِ غَاطِيَةٌ •
• يُعْصَرُ مِنْهَا مُلَاحِىٌّ وَغِرْبِيبُ •

[*And of the wonderful things of God's creation is a grape-vine covering the ground* (so غَاطِيَةٌ is expl. by IB), *whereof* grapes of the kinds called مُلَاحِىّ

and طريب *are pressed* for making wine]. (Ṣ, O.)

عُجَابٌ : see عَجَبٌ, near the middle of the paragraph, in two places.

عَجَبٌ عَاجِبٌ [meaning *Very wonderful* or *admirable* or *pleasing*] (Ṣ, O, Ḳ) is like لَيْلٌ لَائِلٌ, the latter word being a corroborative of the former; (Ṣ, O;) and one says also [in like manner] ▾ عَجَبٌ عُجَابٌ. (Ḳ.)

أَعْجَبُ [*More*, and *most*, *wonderful* or *admirable* or *pleasing*]. — [And the fem.] عَجْبَآءُ signifies A female *wondered at for her beauty*: and also, *for her ugliness*. (O, Ḳ.) ═ Also, i. e. the former, A *thick*, or *big*, or *coarse*, camel. (O, Ḳ.*) And so the fem. applied to a she-camel: (O, Ḳ:) or, so applied, *thick in the* عَجْب [or *root*, &c.,] *of the tail*: (TA:) or *whereof the hinder part*, (O, Ḳ,) or *the upper portion of that part*, (L, TA,) *is narrow, and whereof the* جَاعِرَتَانِ [q. v.] *are prominent*: (O, L, Ḳ, TA:) the kind of make thus particularized is ugly. (TA.)

أُعْجُوبَةٌ : see عَجِيبَةٌ.

رَجُلٌ تِعْجَابَةٌ *A man of* (lit. *having*, *possessing*, or *endowed with*,) *wonders*, or *wonderful things*. (O, Ḳ, TA.)

تَعَاجِيبُ, a pl. without a sing.: see عَجِيبَةٌ.

مُعْجَبٌ بِنَفْسِهِ, and بِرَأْيِهِ, [*Admiring himself*, (lit. *excited to admiration by himself*,) or *pleased with himself*, and *his opinion*, or *judgment*; *self-conceited*, and *conceited of his opinion* or *judgment*,] (Ṣ, O, TA,) [or] *vain*, or *proud*, [*thereof*; for] مُعْجَب signifies a man *vain*, or *proud*, *of what proceeds from him, whether good* or *bad*, and *of himself*, or *of a thing* [*belonging to him*, such as his dress or wealth &c.]: but Er-Rághib makes a distinction between مُعْجَب and تَائِهٌ; saying that the معجب believes himself with respect to the opinion or judgment that he forms of himself indecisively from evidence outweighed in probability; [so that it rather denotes conceit than vanity;] whereas the تائه believes himself decisively. (MF, TA.)

مُعْجِبٌ [*Inducing wonder*, or *admiration*, &c.]: see عَجَبٌ, in the middle of the paragraph: [or] a thing that is *very good* or *goodly* or *beautiful*. (TA.)

عجر

1. عَجَرَ عُنُقَهُ, aor. ـِ, inf. n. عَجْرٌ, *He bent his neck*, (ISk, Ṣ, O, Ḳ, TA,) and *twisted it*: said of one who desires not to comply with a command to do a thing: or عَجَرَ عُنُقَهُ إِلَى كَذَا وَكَذَا [*he bent*, and *twisted*, *his neck*, *turning towards such and such things*,] is said of one who is going in a particular direction, and returns from it to a thing behind him which he is forbidden: so in the Nawádir el-Aaráb. (TA.) — And one says, عَجَرَ بِهِ بَعِيرُهُ as though meaning *His camel returned with him towards his usual associates and his family when he was desiring to ride him in a particular direction*; as also عَكَرَ بِهِ. (ISk, Ṣ, O.) [See also the latter verb.] — And عَجَرَ الفَرَسُ, (Ṣ, O,) aor. ـِ, inf. n. عَجْرٌ and عَجَرَانٌ, (O,) *The horse extended* [or, accord. to an explanation of the act. part. n. in the L, *raised*] *his tail towards his* عَجُز [or *croup*] *in running*. (Ṣ, O.) — And hence, (Ṣ,) مَرَّ الفَرَسُ يَعْجِرُ (Ṣ, O, Ḳ*) and يَعْجُرُ, (so in one of my copies of the Ṣ, and accord. to the TA,) inf. n. عَجْرٌ (Ṣ, Ḳ) and عَجَرَانٌ, (Ḳ,) *The horse went along swiftly*, (Ṣ, O, Ḳ,*) by reason of briskness, liveliness, or sprightliness, (O,) or from fear and the like: and ▾ مُعَاجَرَةٌ is syn. with the inf. ns. of يَعْجِرُ used in this sense: (Ḳ:) [so that one says in like manner ▾ مَرَّ يُعَاجِرُ:] and one says also, ▾ عَاجَرَ الرَّجُلُ الرَّجُلَ, meaning *The man ran before the man, fleeing*. (O, TA.) — عَجَرَ, aor. ـِ, inf. n. عَجْرٌ, said of an ass, is *syn. with* قَمَصَ [app. as meaning *He raised his fore legs together and put them down together, and beat the ground with his hind legs*]: (Ḳ, TA:) and a similar action is signified by the phrase يَعْجِرُ بِرِجْلَيْهِ, inf. n. عَجَرَانٌ, [app. meaning *He beats the ground with his hind legs, rearing while doing so*], said of a horse. (TA.) ═ عَجَرَهُ بِالعَجْرَآءِ *He beat him*, or *struck him, with the knotted staff* or *stick, so that the place struck became swollen*; as also بَجَرَهُ. (O.) — And عَجَرْتُ الشَّىْءَ *I clave*, or *split*, *the thing*. (IḲṭṭ, TA.) — And عَجَرَ عَلَيْهِ بِالسَّيْفِ, (Ṣ, O, Ḳ,*) aor. ـِ, inf. n. عَجْرٌ, (Ḳ,) *He made an assault*, or *attack*, *upon him with the sword*. (Ṣ, O, Ḳ.*) — عَجَرْتُ عَلَيْهِ, (Sh, O, Ḳ,*) aor. ـِ, inf. n. عَجْرٌ, (Ḳ,) is also *syn. with* حَجَرْتُ عَلَيْهِ [meaning *I prohibited him from using*, or *disposing of*, *his property according to his own free will*]. (Sh, O, Ḳ.*) — And عَجَرَ is also *syn. with* إِلْحَاحٌ; in which sense, as in others, its aor. is said in the Ḳ to be يَعْجِرُ; but this is not the case, for the verb is used only in the pass. form: you say, عُجِرَ عَلَى الرَّجُلِ, meaning *The man was importuned for his property*, or *was asked for it by many persons, so that it became little*. (TA.) One says رَجُلٌ ▾ مَعْجُورٌ عَلَيْهِ meaning *A man importuned by begging so that all his property has been taken from him*. (Ḳ,* TA.) ═ One says also, عَجَرَ الرَّجُلُ بِثَوْبِهِ عَلَى رَأْسِهِ [app. meaning *The man wound his garment upon his head*: see 8]. (TA.) — And hence, عَجَرَ الرِّيقُ عَلَى أَنْيَابِهِ ‡ *The saliva became dry upon his canine teeth, and stuck*. (TA.) ═ عَجِرَ, (Ṣ, O, Ḳ,) aor. ـَ, inf. n. عَجَرٌ, (Ṣ,) *He* (a man, Ṣ) *was*, or *became*, *thick and fat*. (Ṣ, O, Ḳ.) And عَجِرَ, (Ḳ,) inf. n. عَجَرٌ, (Ṣ, O,) *He* (a man, Ṣ, O) *was*, or *became*, *big-bellied*. (Ṣ, O, Ḳ.) — Also *He* (a horse) *was*, or *became*, *hard* (Ḳ, TA) *in his flesh*. (TA.) And عَجِرَ, inf. n. عَجَرٌ and عُجْرَةٌ, *It* (a solid hoof, and the belly,) *was*, or *became*, *hard*. (IḲṭṭ, TA.) [See also عَجِرٌ below.]

3. عَاجَرَ, inf. n. مُعَاجَرَةٌ: see 1, in three places.

5. تَعَجَّرَ said of the belly (Ṣ, O) of a man, (Ṣ,) *It became wrinkled by reason of fatness*. (Ṣ, O.)

8. اعتجرت *She* (a woman) *bound a* مِعْجَر [q.v.] *upon her head*; (Ṣ;) *she attired herself with the* مِعْجَر: (O, Mṣb:) or *with a* خِمَار: (Mgh:) اِعْتِجَارٌ is *a mode of attiring peculiar to a woman*, (Ḳ, TA,) *resembling that termed* اِلْتِحَافٌ. (TA.) — And اعتجر *He wound a turban round his head*: (IF, Ṣ, Mgh, O, Mṣb:) and *he wound a turban* (or *a piece of cloth*, TA) *upon his head without turning* [*a portion of*] *it beneath his lower jaw*; (Az, El-Ghooree, Mgh, Ḳ,* TA;) as also اِقْتَعَطَ: the winding it in which manner [and so wearing it] in prayer, is forbidden: but another explanation, which is, *he wound the turban upon his head so as to show the* هَامَة [or *crown of the head*], is more probable; as it is from مِعْجَر, meaning "a piece of a cloth, like a fillet, wound upon the round of a woman's head." (Mgh.) One says, ▾ هُوَ حَسَنُ المُعْتَجَرِ *He is comely in respect of the manner of winding the turban upon the head*. (A.) [See also عِجْرَةٌ: and see مُعْتَجَرٌ.] — One says also اعتجرت بِغُلَامٍ, or بِجَارِيَةٍ, meaning ‡ *She brought forth a boy*, or *a girl*, *after she had despaired of her giving birth to a child*. (O, Ḳ, TA.)

عَجْرٌ inf. n. of عَجَرَ [q. v.]. (Ṣ.) — Also *Projection*, *protrusion*, *prominence*, or *protuberance*, and *elevation*. (Ṣ, O, TA.) — And *Strength, with greatness of body*. (TA.)

عَجَرٌ : see what next follows.

عَجِرٌ and ▾ عَجَرٌ, applied to a وَظِيف [or shank of a beast], (Ṣ, O, Ḳ,) *Thick*; (Ṣ, O;) as also ▾ أَعْجَرُ: (O:) or *hard*, (Ḳ,* TA,) *and strong*; and in like manner applied to a solid hoof, and to a pastern. (TA.) — And for another meaning of the first of the words, see أَعْجَرُ.

عُجْرَةٌ *A place of projection, protrusion, prominence*, or *protuberance*, and *elevation*. (A,* Ḳ* TA.) — [*A protuberance*; *a knob*; *a lump*.] — *A knot in wood*, (Ṣ, Mgh, O, Ḳ,) *and the like*, (Ḳ,) or *in other things*: (Mgh:) or *in the veins of the body*: (Ṣ:) or *a knotted vein in the body*; and بُجْرَةٌ, with which it is coupled, "a knotted vein in the belly," particularly: (A'Obeyd, TA:) or the former, *a thing that collects in the body, like a ganglion* (سِلْعَة); (Aṣ, O, TA;) and the latter signifies the like: (Aṣ, TA:) or, as some say, عُجَرٌ, which is the pl., signifies the *vertebræ of the back*: (IAth, TA:) or عُجْرَةٌ signifies *a tumour*, or *swelling*, or *an inflation*, *in the back*; and بُجْرَةٌ, the like in the navel. (TA.) [See also بُجْرَةٌ.] — Hence, one says, ذَكَرَ عُجَرَهُ وَبُجَرَهُ ‡ *He mentioned his vices*, or *faults, which no one knew save he who tried him*, or *tested him*: (TA:) or *his external and internal conditions*; *what he showed and what he concealed*. (IAth, TA.) And أَفْضَيْتُ إِلَيْهِ بِعُجَرِى وَبُجَرِى ‡ *I revealed to him my vices*, or *faults*, by reason of my confidence in him: (A'Obeyd, O, TA:) or *I acquainted him with my whole state*, or *case*; *not concealing from him anything thereof*. (Aṣ, TA.) And أُحَدِّثُهُ بِعُجَرِى وَبُجَرِى ‡ *I relate to* him my vices, or *faults*. (TA.) And يَشْكُو عُجَرَهُ وَبُجَرَهُ ‡ *He complains of his vices*, or *faults*, or the like: and *of his sorrows*: and *of what is apparent and what is concealed*. (Ḳ,* TA. [In the CḲ, أَبْدَرُ is put by mistake for أَبْدَى.]) One says also, جَآءَ فُلَانٌ بِالعُجَرِ وَالبُجَرِ † i. e. [*Such a one uttered*] *falsehood*: or *a great*, or *terrible, thing*. (Fr, TA.) [See, again, بُجْرَةٌ.] — عُجْرَةٌ also signifies The *mark made upon the waist by the running string of the drawers*. (A, TA.) To this a poet likens the mark made by a blunt sword. (Aboo-Sa'eed, TA.) — And one says, السَّيْفُ فِى فِرِنْدِهِ عُجَرٌ [*The sword has, in its diversified wavy marks, what resemble knots*]. (TA.)

عِجْرَةٌ *A mode of winding the turban upon the head*. (Ṣ, O.) One says, فُلَانٌ حَسَنُ العِجْرَةِ [*Such a one is comely in respect of the mode of winding the turban upon the head*]. (O. [See also 8.])

عِجَارٌ: see مِعْجَرٌ.

عَجُورٌ [*A species of melon*: accord. to Forskål, (Flora Aegypt. Arab., pp. lxxvi. and 168,) this name and عبدلاوى are both applied to the *cucumis chate*: but accord. to Delile, (Floræ Aegypt. Illustr., no. 922,) the latter name is thus applied; and عجور (written by him as though it were عَجُّور, but it is without teshdeed,) is the name of the *fruit of this species of cucumis while immature*; so too says 'Abd-El-Lateef: (see De Sacy's Transl. and Notes, pp. 35 and 127; and p. 54 of the Ar. Text edited by White:) I have, however, found the name عَجُور to be commonly applied to *a species different from the* عَبْدَلَاوِى, (which is also called عَبْدَلِى, see art. عبد,) as Sonnini asserts it to be, (in his Travels in Upper and Lower Egypt, pp. 574 and 636 of the Engl. Transl., 4to., London, 1800,) *and differing therefrom in shape, being*, as he describes it, *in some instances round, in some instances oval, and in others much elongated*: the name is probably derived from the Greek ἀγγούριον (in modern Greek ἀγγοῦρι), signifying the "water-melon"]: it is said in the Mṣb that قِثَّآءٌ is a name of what the [common] people call خِيَار and عَجُور and فَقُّوس: but it is said [by some, not by the author of the Mṣb,] that عَجُور signifies *large* قِثَّآء [q. v.]. (TA in art. قثا.)

أَعْجَرُ, applied to a man, (Ṣ, O,) *Thick and fat*: (Ḳ:) *big-bellied*: (Ṣ, O, Ḳ:) a stallion *big*, or *bulky*: (Ṣ, O:) and a belly, (TA,) and a purse, (Ṣ, O,) *full*: (Ṣ, O, TA:) pl. عُجْرٌ. (TA.) See also عَجِرٌ. — Anything *having knots*: (TA:) and so ▼ عَجِرٌ applied to a string, or thread: (Ham p. 815:) and the former, *knotty*, or *having many knots*. (TA.) [Hence,] عَجْرَآءُ [for عَصًا عَجْرَآءُ] *A staff*, or *stick, knotted*, or *having knots*. (A, O, Ḳ.) One says, ضَرَبَهُ بِعَجْرَآءَ مِنْ سَلَمٍ [*He beat him, or struck him, with a knotted staff*, or *stick, of wood of the* سَلَم]. (TA.) — It is also applied to a sword [as meaning *Having, in its diversified wavy marks, what resemble knots*: see عُجْرَةٌ, and see also the paragraph next following this]. (TA.) — Also *Hump-backed*. (Fr, O, TA.)

سَيْفٌ ذُو مَعْجَرٍ فِى مَتْنِهِ *A sword having what resemble knots* [in the diversified wavy marks of *the broad side of its blade*: see also the next preceding paragraph]. (TA.)

مِعْجَرٌ (Ṣ, A, Mgh, O, Mṣb, Ḳ) and ▼ عِجَارٌ (Ṣ, Mṣb, TA, in the O [erroneously] written مُعْجَار,) *A piece of cloth* (Mṣb, Ḳ, TA) *which is bound upon the head*, (Ḳ, TA,) *smaller than the* رِدَآء, (Mṣb, TA,) *and larger than the* مِقْنَعَة, (TA,) *worn by a woman*: (Mṣb:) *a thing which a woman binds upon her head*: (Ṣ:) *a piece of cloth*, (Lth, Mgh, O, Mṣb, L,) *like a fillet*, (Mgh, Mṣb,) *which a woman winds upon the round of her head*, (Lth, Mgh, O, Mṣb, L,) *after which she puts on, over it, her* [*garment*, or *covering*, *called*] جِلْبَاب; (Lth, O, L:) [it is also said that] مِعْجَرٌ signifies *a turban*: or *a turban* [*wound*] *upon the head without a turning* [*of a portion thereof*] *beneath the jaw*: (Ḥam p. 709:) its pl. is مَعَاجِرُ: whence الاِعْتِجَار. (L, TA.) — And مِعْجَرٌ signifies also *A kind of garment*, or *cloth*, *of the fabric of El-Yemen*, (Lth, Ḳ, TA,) *used as the* لِحَاف *or* مِلْحَفَة *and the* رِدَآء: pl. as above. (TA.) — And *A thing woven of* [*the fibres of the palm-tree called*] لِيف, *like the* جَوَالِق: (Ḳ:) pl. as above. (TA.)

مُعْجَرٌ, applied to a rope, or to a bow-string: see مُجْرَع and مُحْرَدٌ, with which it is syn.

مَعْجُورٌ عَلَيْهِ: see 1, last quarter.

مُعْتَجَرٌ: see 8, of which it is an inf. n.

مُعْتَجِرٌ is expl. as meaning A man *wearing his turban as a* نِقَاب [q. v.], *so that* [*a portion of*] *it covers his nose* [*and the lower part of his face*]. (Mgh.) [See also its verb, 8.]

عجرف

Q. 2. تَعَجْرَفَ *He* (a camel) *took what was not the right course, being refractory*, or *untractable*: (Ḥam p. 618:) [or *he went obliquely, by reason of briskness, liveliness*, or *sprightliness*: or *he was as though he were rough, ungentle*, or *awkward, in going, when tired, and wanting in due care, by reason of speed*; and likewise said of a man:] see عَجْرَفِيَّةٌ. — Also *He* (a man, O) *magnified himself* (O, Ḳ) عَلَيْنَا *against us*. (O.) And رَجُلٌ فِيهِ تَعَجْرُفٌ [*A man in whom is self-magnification*]. (TA.) — And فُلَانٌ يَتَعَجْرَفُ عَلَىَّ, (Ṣ, O,) or عَلَيْهِمْ, (Ḳ,) *Such a one does to me*, (Ṣ, O,) or *to them*, (Ḳ,) *what I*, (Ṣ, O,) or *they*, (Ḳ,) *dislike*, or *hate, he not fearing*, or *dreading, anything*. (Ṣ, O, Ḳ.) — And تَعَجْرَفَ الأَمْرَ *He ventured upon*, or *undertook, the affair, not having knowledge in it*. (TA.)

عَجْرَفَةٌ: see عَجْرَفِيَّةٌ [which is probably syn. with it in all the senses of the former]. — Also *Coarseness, roughness*, or *rudeness, in speech*: and *roughness, ungentleness*, or *awkwardness, in work*. (Lth, Ḳ, TA.) — And *Audaciousness, with* هَوَج [i. e. *foolishness*, or *tallness combined with foolishness or with foolishness and ficklenes and hastiness*]. (IDrd, Ḳ.) And The *venturing upon*, or *undertaking, an affair without having knowledge in it*. (TA.)

عَجْرَفِىُّ المَشْىِ [in the CḲ عَجْرَفِى المَشْى] A camel *in whose manner of going is what is termed* تَعَجْرُف *and* عَجْرَفَة *and* عَجْرَفِيَّة, [see the next paragraph,] (Az, Ḳ, TA,) *by reason of his speed*: (Az, TA:) and عَجْرَفِىٌّ alone, a camel *that does not go in the right direction, by reason of his briskness, liveliness*, or *sprightliness*: fem. with ة. (TA.)

فِيهِ عَجْرَفِيَّةٌ and ▼ عَجْرَفَةٌ and ▼ تَعَجْرُفٌ, said of a camel, *He is as though there were in him roughness, ungentleness*, or *awkwardness*, (Ṣ, TA,) *and want of due care, by reason of his speed*: (Ṣ, Ḳ, TA:) or عَجْرَفِيَّةٌ is a camel's *taking to the going with roughness, ungentleness*, or *awkwardness, when fatigued*: (M, TA:) or a camel's *going obliquely, by reason of briskness, liveliness*, or *sprightliness*. (Az, TA.) And عَجْرَفِيَّةٌ is also in a man. (AZ, Ṣ, O, and Ḳ, voce عُرْضِيَّةٌ.) [See also عَجْرَفَةٌ.] عَجْرَفِيَّةُ ضَبَّةَ is thought by ISd to mean [*The tribe of*] *Dabbeh's guttural speech* (تَقَعُّرُهُمْ فِى الكَلَامِ). (TA.)

عُجْرُوفٌ *A certain small creeping thing*, (Lth, Ṣ, Ḳ,) *having long legs*; (Lth, TA;) said to be the *long-legged* نَمْلَة [or *ant*]: (Ṣ:) or the نَمْل [or *ant*], (Az, TA,) or *long* نَمْل, (Ḳ,) *the legs of which raise it from the ground*: (Az, Ḳ, TA:) or it is *larger than the* نَمْل. (ISd, TA.) — And A *light*, or an *agile*, she-camel. (Ibn-'Abbád, Ḳ.) — And *An old woman*; as also with ة. (El-'Ozeyzee, Ḳ.)

عَجَارِفُ الدَّهْرِ (Ṣ, Ḳ*) and ▼ عَجَارِيفُهُ *The accidents of time*, or *fortune*. (Ṣ, Ḳ.) — And عَجَارِفُ المَطَرِ and ▼ عَجَارِيفُهُ *The vehemence of rain* (IDrd, Ḳ) *at its coming*: (IDrd:) or عَجَارِفُ الغَيْثِ *The rain's coming with thunder and wind*. (Ḥam p. 750.) — ذُو عَجَارِفَ and ▼ عَجَارِيفَ A camel *having briskness, liveliness*, or *sprightliness*. (TA.)

عَجَارِيفُ: see the next preceding paragraph, in three places.

عجز

1. The primary signification of عَجْزٌ [an inf. n. of عَجَزَ] is The *being*, or *becoming, behind*, or *behindhand*, or *backward*, with respect to a thing; or *holding back, hanging back*, or *abstaining*, from it: and its *happening at the latter*, or *last, part*, or *at the end, of an affair*: and hence, in common conventional language, it has the signification shown by the explanation here next following. (Er-Rághib, B, &c., and TA.) — عَجَزَ, aor. ـِ, inf. n. عَجْزٌ and مَعْجِزَةٌ and مَعْجَزَةٌ (Ṣ, Mgh, O, Mṣb, Ḳ) and مَعْجَزٌ, (Ṣ, O, Mṣb, Ḳ,) which is

agreeable with rule, (Ṣ,) and مَعْجِزٌ, (Ṣ, O, Mṣb, Ḳ,) which is extr., (Sb, TA,) and عَجَزَانٌ and عُجُوزٌ; (O, Ḳ;) and عَجِزَ, aor. ـَ, (O, Mṣb, Ḳ,) inf. n. عَجَزٌ, (Mṣb,) said by IḲṭṭ to be mentioned by Fr, as of the dial. of some of the tribe of Ḳeys, but by others [and among them Ṣgh in the O] said to be a bad form, (TA,) or mentioned by AZ, as of the dial. of some of the tribe of Ḳeys-'Eylán, but not known to them, and said by IF to be disallowed by IAạr in the sense here immediately following; (Mṣb;) *He lacked strength,* or *power,* or *ability; he was,* or *became, powerless, impotent,* or *unable.* (Ṣ,* Mṣb,* Ḳ, TA.) You say, عَجَزَ عَنْ كَذَا, (Ṣ, A, O, Mṣb, TA,) and accord. to some, as shown above, عَجِزَ عَنْهُ, (Mṣb, TA,) *He lacked strength,* or *power,* or *ability, for,* or *to do, effect, accomplish, achieve, attain,* or *compass, such a thing; he was unable to do it:* (Ṣ,* O,* Mṣb,* TA:) or ‡ *he was too old to do it.* (A, TA.) And it is said in a trad., (Ṣ,* Mgh,) of 'Omar, (TA,) لَا تُلِثُّوا بِدَارِ مَعْجَزَةٍ, meaning *Remain ye not in a country,* or *district,* or *town, where ye are unable to gain your livelihood.* (Ṣ, A, Mgh,* TA.) You say also, لَا يَسْعُنِى شَىْءٌ وَيَعْجِزُ عَنْكَ ‡ [app. *A thing will not suffice me when it cannot thee*]. (A, TA.) And جَآءُوا بِجَيْشٍ تَعْجِزُ الأَرْضُ عَنْهُ ‡ [*They came with an army which the earth had not strength to bear,* or *scarce sufficed to contain*]. (A, TA.) — [And عَجَزَ عَنْ كَذَا also signifies *He,* or *it, lacked such a thing:* see an ex. voce عُرْقٌ.] — [Hence,] عَجَزَتْ, (Ṣ, O, Mṣb, Ḳ,) aor. ـِ, (Ṣ, O, Ḳ,) or ـُ, (Mṣb,) inf. n. عُجُوزٌ (Ṣ, O, Ḳ) and عَجْزٌ, (TA,) *She* (a woman, Ṣ, O, Mṣb) *became aged;* (Ṣ, O, Mṣb, Ḳ;) [because the aged lacks strength;] as also عَجُزَتْ, aor. ـُ; (O, Ḳ;) and ↓ عَجَّزَتْ, inf. n. تَعْجِيزٌ. (Ṣ, O, Ḳ.) = عَجِزَتْ, aor. ـَ, (Ṣ, O, Ḳ,) inf. n. عَجَزٌ and عُجْزٌ, (Ṣ, Ḳ,) [or the latter is a simple subst.,] or عُجْزٌ and عُجْزَانٌ, (O,) *She* (a woman, Ṣ) *became large in the hinder parts,* or *posteriors;* (Ṣ, O, Ḳ;) as also ↓ عَجَّزَتْ, inf. n. تَعْجِيزٌ: (Yoo, O, Ḳ:) and عَجِزَ, inf. n. عَجَزٌ, *he* (a man) *became large therein:* (Mṣb:) accord. to IAạr, as related by Th, one does not say thus of a man except in this sense. (Ṣ, O.) — [Hence,] عَجِزَتِ الرَّمْلَةُ † *The piece of sand became high.* (IḲṭṭ, TA.) = عُجِزَ *He* (a man) *was importuned for his property:* part. n. ↓ مَعْجُوزٌ. (O.) = عَاجَزْتُهُ فَعَجَزْتُهُ: see 3.

2. عَجَّزَهُ, (Mṣb,) inf. n. تَعْجِيزٌ, (Ṣ, O, Mṣb, Ḳ,) *He attributed,* or *imputed, to him lack of strength* or *power* or *ability;* i. e., *inability,* or *impotence:* (Ṣ,* O,* Ḳ,* TA:) *he asserted him to be,* or *called him,* or *made him,* (جَعَلَهُ,) *unable,* or *impotent.* (Mṣb.) [Compare 4, in a sense given below from the B.] You say also, عَجَّزَ فُلَانٌ رَأْىَ فُلَانٍ *Such a one attributed,* or *imputed, the opinion of such a one to littleness of good judgment,* or *of prudence;* as though he attributed it to inability. (TA.) — Also *He withheld him,* or *kept him back,* or *diverted him,* (Ṣ, Ḳ,) from (عَنْ) a person or thing: (TA:) [as though he made him unable to attain his object: compare 4.] = عَجَّزَتْ, said of a woman: see 1, latter part. = عَجَّزَتْ, said of a woman: see 1, latter part. — عَجَّزَ دَابَّتَهُ *He put the* حَقِيبَة [q. v.] *upon his beast.* (Ṣgh, TA.) — عَجَّزَ الشَّاعِرُ *The poet uttered,* or *wrote, the* عَجُز, or *last foot, of the verse.* (TA.)

3. عاجزه: see ↓ أَعْجَزَهُ. = عَاجَزْتُهُ فَعَجَزْتُهُ, (A, Ḳ,) aor. of the latter ـُ, (TA,) *I contended with him in a race, and I outstripped him.* (A, O, Ḳ.) — And عاجز (inf. n. مُعَاجَزَةٌ, TA) *He outstripped, and was not reached;* as also ↓ اعجز: (A:) or *he went away, and was not reached:* (Ṣ, O, Ḳ:) or *he fled, and could not be caught.* (Mṣb.) = عاجز إِلَى ثِقَةٍ *He inclined to a trusty person,* (Ṣ, A, O, Ḳ,) *and had recourse to him for refuge.* (A.) [Hence,] فُلَانٌ يُعَاجِزُ عَنِ الحَقِّ إِلَى البَاطِلِ *Such a one declines from the truth to falsehood, and has recourse to the latter for protection.* (A, TA.) — And عاجز القَوْمُ *The people,* or *company of men, left a thing and began another.* (TA.)

4. اعجزهُ *He found him to be without strength,* or *power,* or *ability; to be unable,* or *impotent.* (Ṣ, O, Mṣb, Ḳ.) — *He,* or *it, made him to be* (جَعَلَهُ) *without strength* or *power* or *ability, to be unable,* or *impotent; disabled him;* or *incapacitated him;* as also ↓ عاجزهُ. (B, TA.) [For an illustration of the latter verb, see its act. part. n., below: and compare 2, in a sense given above from the Mṣb. You say, اعجزهُ عَنِ الأَمْرِ *He,* or *it, rendered him unable to do, effect, accomplish, achieve, attain,* or *compass, the affair.*] — *He,* or *it, rendered him* (صَيَّرَهُ) *unable* (TṢ, Ḳ, TA) *to attain,* or *overtake, him:* (TṢ, TA:) — and [thus, by an inversion, it also signifies] *he was unable to reach,* or *overtake, him.* (Lth, TA.) — [*It frustrated his power* or *ability,* or *his skill,* or *endeavours.*] — *It escaped him, so that he was unable to attain it,* or *to do it,* or *to accomplish it:* (Ṣ, O, Mṣb, Ḳ:) and simply, *he was unable to attain it,* or *to do it,* or *to accomplish it.* (TA.) — See also 3.

5. تعجّز البَعِيرَ *He rode upon the hinder part,* or *rump, of the camel.* (Yaạḳoob, Ṣ, A, O, Ḳ.)

عَجْزٌ: see عَجُزٌ. — Also, [said in the TA to be written by Ṣgh عَجَزٌ, but it is written عُجْزٌ in the O, and is thus accord. to the Ḳ,] *A disease in the hinder part of a horse* or *the like, rendering him heavy.* (O, Ḳ.)

عِجْزٌ *Old age* of a woman: a simple subst. (TA.) You say, اِتَّقِى اللّٰهَ فِى شَبِيبَتِكِ وَعِجْزِكِ *Fear thou God in thy youth and* [*thine old age,* or] *when thou becomest an old woman.* (TA. [But اتّقى is there put for اِتَّقِى: and in the explanation, تصير for تَصِيرِينَ. See عَجَزَتْ.]) = See also عَجُزٌ. — [And see عَجِزَتْ.]

عُجْزٌ: see the next paragraph.

عَجُزٌ (Ṣ, A, O, L, Mṣb, Ḳ) and ↓ عُجْزٌ (O, L, Mṣb, Ḳ) and ↓ عُجُزٌ (L, Mṣb) and ↓ عَجْزٌ (O, L, Mṣb, Ḳ) and ↓ عَجِزٌ (O, L, Ḳ) and ↓ عِجْزٌ, (Ḳ,) but the first form is the most chaste, (Mṣb,) fem. and masc., (Ṣ, O, Mṣb, Ḳ,) in the first of the following senses, i. e., in the general application; and in the second, or restricted application, fem., but made masc. by the Benoo-Temeem, (Mṣb,) or, accord. to El-Heythemee, fem. only, (TA,) The *hinder part* of a thing; (Ṣ, A, O, L, Mṣb, Ḳ;) i. e., of anything: (Mṣb:) and particularly the *hinder parts, posteriors, buttock,* or *buttocks, rump,* or *croup,* (Ṣ,* O,*) or *what is between the two hips,* (Mgh, Mṣb,) or *what is after the back,* (TA,) of a man, and of a woman; (Ṣ, Mgh, O, Mṣb, TA;) [and of a camel, &c.;] and ↓ عَجِيزَةٌ signifies the same, but of a woman only, (Ṣ, O, Mṣb, Ḳ,) in its proper application, though sometimes of a man also by way of comparison: (IAth, Mgh, TA:) pl. of عَجُزٌ, (Ṣ, Mṣb, Ḳ,) and of its variants, (Mṣb, Ḳ,) أَعْجَازٌ, (Ṣ, Mṣb, Ḳ,) the only pl. form: (TA:) and of ↓ عَجِيزَةٌ, عَجِيزَاتٌ: they do not say عَجَائِزُ, [the regular form of pl. of عجيزة,] for fear of confusion [as it is pl. of عَجُوزٌ or of عَجُوزَةٌ]. (TA.) One says also, إِنَّهَا لَعَظِيمَةُ الأَعْجَازِ *Verily she is large in the hinder parts:* as though the term عَجُزٌ were applicable to every portion thereof. (Lḥ, TA.) And رَكِبَ فِى الطَّلَبِ أَعْجَازَ الإِبِلِ *He exposed himself, in seeking* [a thing], *to abasement and difficulty and patient endurance, and exerted unsparingly his power* or *ability,* (Ḳ, TA,) *not caring for undergoing long night-journeying.* (TA.) Thus expl. in a saying of 'Alee: لَنَا حَقٌّ إِنْ نُعْطَهُ نَأْخُذْهُ وَإِنْ نُمْنَعْهُ نَرْكَبْ أَعْجَازَ الإِبِلِ وَإِنْ طَالَ السُّرَى [*There is a right belonging to us: if we be given it, we take it: and if we be refused it, we expose ourselves to abasement, &c., though the night-journeying be long*]: (O,* TA:) or, accord. to Az, he does not mean this, but alludes to others' having precedence in respect of his right, and his being himself kept back from it. (TA.) One also says, بَنُو فُلَانٍ يَرْكَبُونَ أَعْجَازَ الإِبِلِ *The sons of such a one are in a state of abasement, dependents of others:* or *experience difficulties;* because the rump, or croup, of the camel is a difficult place to ride upon. (A.) And it is said by one of the wise, (Aktham Ibn-Ṣeyfee, T, in TA, art. دبر,) لَا تَدَبَّرُوا أَعْجَازَ أُمُورٍ قَدْ وَلَّتْ صُدُورُهَا, (TA, in this art., and O,) or لَا تَتَدَبَّرُوا, (T, in TA, art. دبر,) ‡ [*Think ye not upon the ends of things whereof the beginnings have passed:*] meaning, when a thing has passed, make not your minds, or desires, to follow after it, regretting what has passed, but be consoled for it, placing your reliance upon God: (O, TA:) and, as IAth says, it is intended to incite to the consideration of the results, or issues, of affairs before the entering upon them. (TA.) [See also دُبُرٌ.] — أَعْجَازُ نَخْلٍ The *trunks of palm-trees.* (Ṣ, O, Ḳ.) [See Ḳur liv. 20 and lxix. 7.) And أَعْجَازُ الصِّلِّيَانِ [*The stems of the* صِلِّيَان]. (AḤn, M in art. صل.) — عَجُزٌ also signifies The *last foot* of a verse; contr. of صَدْرٌ. (TA.) And The *latter hemistich* of a verse: the former hemistich is termed صَدْرٌ. (O.) [And The *last word* of a clause of rhyming prose. And the *latter part* of a word.] — See also عَاجِزٌ. — أَيَّامُ العَجُزِ : see عَجُوزٌ.

عُجْزٌ : see عَجُزٌ : — and see also عَاجِزٌ.

عُجُزٌ : see عَجُزٌ.

عُجْزَةٌ : see the next paragraph.

عِجْزَةٌ The *last* of the children of a man; (Ṣ, O, Ḳ;) as also ▼ عُجْزَةٌ. (IAạr, O, Ḳ.) You say, فُلَانٌ عِجْزَةُ وَلَدِ أَبَوَيْهِ *Such a one is the last of the children of his parents;* and in like manner you say of a female, and of a plural number: (Ṣ, O, TA:) and so, [accord. to some,] كِبْرَةُ وَلَدِ أَبَوَيْهِ. (TA.) You say also, وُلِدَ لِعِجْزَةٍ *He was born after his parents had become old:* and such you term ٱبْنُ العِجْزَةِ. (O, TA.)

عَجُوزٌ i. q. عَاجِزٌ, q. v. (Ḳ.) — *An old,* or *aged, woman:* (Ṣ, O, Mṣb, Ḳ:) *a woman extremely old;* or *old and weak:* so called because of her inability to do many things: (TA:) [this is the most common signification of the word:] accord. to ISk, (Ṣ, O, Mṣb,) you should not say ▼ عَجُوزَةٌ; (Ṣ, O, Mṣb, Ḳ;) or this is bad; (Ḳ;) and is said by the vulgar; (Ṣ, O;) but IAạr authorizes it; (O;) and IAmb allows it, to demonstrate its being fem.; and Yoo is related to have heard it from the Arabs: (Mṣb:) pl. عَجَائِزُ, (Ṣ, O, Mṣb, Ḳ,) or this is pl. of عَجُوزَةٌ; (R, TA;) and عُجُزٌ, (Ṣ, O, Mṣb, Ḳ,) and عُجْزٌ, a contraction of عُجُزٌ, occurring in traditions. (TA.) — *A man's wife,* whether old or young: (Az, O, Ḳ,* TA:) and in like manner, the husband, though young, is called شَيْخٌ. (Az, O, TA.) — *An old,* or *aged, man:* (O, TA:) *a man extremely old;* or *old and weak.* (TA.) — ‡ *Wine;* (Ṣ, O, Ḳ;) because of its oldness: (Ṣ, O:) or *old wine.* (A, TA.) — *A certain nail in the hilt of a sword,* (IAạr, O, Ḳ,) *with which is another nail called* الكَلْبُ. (IAạr, O, TA.) Az approves of this explanation. (O.) — *A sword-blade.* (Lth, Ṣ, O, Ḳ.) — *A sword.* (O, TA.) — [It has a great variety of other significations; but these are of very rare occurrence, and are therefore to be mentioned (ان شآء الله) in Book II.] — أَيَّامُ العَجُوزِ; (Ṣ, O, Ḳ;) also called ▼ أَيَّامُ العَجُزِ, because they come in the latter part (عَجُز) of winter; but the former is the correct appellation; (MF;) accord. to the usage of the Arabs, *Five days, the names of which are* صِنٌّ *and* صِنَّبْرٌ *and* وَبْرٌ *and* مُطْفِئُ الجَمْرِ *and* مُكْفِئُ الظُّعْنِ; *said by Ibn-Kunáseh to be of the* نَوْء *of* الصَّرْفَة [by which is meant the auroral setting of the Twelfth Mansion of the Moon, which, in Central Arabia, about the commencement of the era of the Flight, happened on the 9th of March O. S.: in the modern Egyptian Almanacs, the ايام العجوز are said to commence now on the 9th of March N. S., which is now the 26th of February O. S.]: (Ṣ, O, TA:) or, accord. to Abu-l-Ghowth, (Ṣ,) they are *seven days,* (Ṣ, Ḳ,) *named* صِنٌّ *and* صِنَّبْرٌ *and* وَبْرٌ *and* الآمِرُ *and* المُؤْتَمِرُ *and* المُعَلِّلُ *and* مُطْفِئُ الجَمْرِ, or مُكْفِئُ الظُّعْنِ: (Ḳ:) *and some reckon* مكفئ الظعن *an eighth:* but most authors hold these names to be post-classical: (MF:) accord. to Esh-Shereeshee, they are *seven days; four of the last* [*days*] *of February, and three of the first* [*days*] *of March:* (Ḥar p. 295:) during these days blew the wind by which the tribe of 'Ád was destroyed: and they are thus called because they are [in] the latter part (عَجُز) of winter; or because an old woman (عَجُوز) of 'Ád concealed herself in a subterranean excavation, from which the wind dragged her forth on the eighth day, and destroyed her: (Bḍ in lxix. 7:) or آمِرٌ and مُؤْتَمِرٌ are the names of the last two days; (Ḳ in art. امر;) the former being the sixth, and the latter the seventh. (M in that art.) Ibn-Aḥmar says, (Ṣ,) or, accord. to IB, not Ibn-Aḥmar, but Aboo-Shibl 'Aṣim Ibn-el-Aạrábee, as Th says, on the authority of IAạr, (TA,) or Aboo-Shibl 'Oṣm Ibn-Wahb Et-Temeemee, (O,)

كُسِعَ الشِّتَآءُ بِسَبْعَةٍ غُبْرِ
أَيَّامِ شَهْلَتِنَا مِنَ الشَّهْرِ
فَإِذَا ٱنْقَضَتْ أَيَّامُهَا وَمَضَتْ
صِنٌّ وَصِنَّبْرٌ مَعَ الوَبْرِ
وَبِآمِرٍ وَأُخَيِّهِ مُؤْتَمِرٍ
وَمُعَلِّلٍ وَبِمُطْفِئِ الجَمْرِ
ذَهَبَ الشِّتَآءُ مُوَلِّيًا عَجِلًا
وَأَتَتْكَ وَاقِدَةٌ مِنَ النَّجْرِ

[*The winter is driven away,* or *is closed, by seven dusty (days), our old woman's days of the month; and when her days come to an end, and Ṣinn and Ṣinnabr, with El-Webr, and with Ámir and his little brother Mu-temir, and Mo'allil, and with Muṭfi-el-Jemr, pass, the winter goes away, retiring quickly, and a burning wind* (رِيحٌ being understood) *comes to thee from the first day of the ensuing month,* or, accord. to a reading which I find in one copy of the Ṣ, *from the sea,* مِنَ البَحْرِ]. (Ṣ, O, TA.)

عِجْزٌ One *who does not come to women* [*by reason of impotence*]: (Ṣ, Ḳ:) and so عِجِيزٌ, (Ṣ, TA,) and عِجِّيسٌ. (TA.) And A *stallion impotent to cover:* as also عَجِيسٌ. (IDrd, O, TA.)

عِجَازَةٌ: see إِعْجَازَةٌ. — Also The دَابِرَة [in the CḲ (erroneously) دائرة], (O, Ḳ, TA,) i. e. *back-toe,* (O, TA,) of a bird. (O, Ḳ, TA.)

عَجُوزَةٌ: see عَجُوزٌ.

عُجَيْزَةٌ: see عَجُزٌ, in two places.

عَاجِزٌ *Lacking strength,* or *power,* or *ability; powerless, unable,* or *impotent;* (Ḳ,* TA;) as also ▼ عَجُوزٌ, (Ḳ,) and ▼ عَجِزٌ and ▼ عَجُزٌ: (TA:) pl. of the first [عَاجِزُونَ, and] عَجَزٌ, [or rather this a quasi-pl. n.,] like as خَدَمٌ is of خَادِمٌ, (TA,) and عَوَاجِزُ, (O, Ḳ,) but this is only in the dial. of Hudheyl, and, applied to men, is anomalous. (O, TA.) You say also, ٱمْرَأَةٌ عَاجِزٌ *A woman lacking strength,* or *power,* or *ability, to do a thing; unable to do a thing.* (IAạr, TA.) And it is said in a trad., respecting Paradise, لَا يَدْخُلُنِى إِلَّا سَقَطُ النَّاسِ وَعَجَزُهُمْ [*There shall not enter me save the mean of mankind, and*] *those lacking in intelligence and in power with respect to worldly things.* (TA.) — ثَوْبٌ عَاجِزٌ ‡ *A garment that is* [*too*] *short:* (A, O, TA:) or *narrow,* or *scanty.* (O.)

أَعْجَزُ: fem. عَجْزَآءُ. — The latter signifies A woman *large in the hinder parts,* or *posteriors;* (Ṣ, O, Mṣb, Ḳ;) as also ▼ مُعَجَّزَةٌ; (TA;) [unless this be a mistake for ▼ مُعَجِّزَةٌ, from عَجَّزَتْ:] or *wide in the belly, heavy in the flesh upon the hips, and consequently large in the hinder parts.* (TA.) — And each, *Having the disease termed* عَجَزٌ [q. v.]. (O, TA.) — And the fem., An eagle (عُقَابٌ) *short in the tail,* (Ṣ, O, Ḳ, TA,) *and deficient therein:* (TA:) and (some say, O) *having in its tail a white feather,* (O, Ḳ,) or *two* [*white*] *feathers:* (O:) or *having a whiteness,* or *a colour differing* [*from the rest*], *in its hinder part:* (TA:) and (some say, O) *strong in the* دَابِرَة (O, Ḳ, TA, in the CḲ [erroneously] دائرة,) *of the* كَفّ, (Ḳ, TA,) i. e. *in the back-toe:* (TA:) so says IDrd. (O.) — رَمْلَةٌ عَجْزَآءُ † *A high piece of sand:* (Ṣ, O, Ḳ:) or *an oblong piece of sand producing plants* or *herbage:* (M, TA:) or *a high oblong piece of sand, as though it were hard ground, not sand heaped up, but fertile:* pl. عُجْزٌ, because it is an epithet. (T, TA.)

إِعْجَازَةٌ *A thing* (Ṣ, O, Ḳ, TA) *resembling a pillow,* (O, TA,) *with which a woman enlarges* [*in appearance*] *her hinder part,* (Ṣ, O, Ḳ, TA,) *binding it upon that part,* (O, TA,) *in order that she may be thought to be large in her hinder part,* (O, Ḳ, TA,) *when she is not so;* (TA;) as also ▼ عِجَازَةٌ. (O, Ḳ.)

مُعْجِزٌ [act. part. n. of 4, q. v.]. — The words of the Ḳur [xxix. 21] وَمَا أَنْتُمْ بِمُعْجِزِينَ فِى الأَرْضِ وَلَا فِى السَّمَآءِ signify, accord. to Fr, *And ye shall not escape in the earth, nor shall those in the heaven escape:* or, accord. to Aboo-Is-ḥáḳ, *and ye shall not escape in the earth, nor should ye if ye were in the heaven:* or, accord. to Akh, *and ye shall not escape* by fleeing *in the earth nor in the heaven:* but Az says that the explanation of Fr is the best known. (L.) — ▼ مُعْجِزَةٌ [*A miracle performed by a prophet;* distinguished from كَرَامَةٌ, which signifies one performed by a saint, or righteous man, not claiming to be a prophet;] *that by which a prophet disables the opponent in a contest;* the ة implying intensiveness; (Ḳ;) as defined by the Muslim theologians, *an event at variance with the usual course* [*of nature*], *produced by means of one who lays claim to the office of a prophet, in contending with those who disacknowledge* [*his claim*], *in such a manner as renders them unable to produce the like thereof;* (O;) or *an event breaking through,* or *infringing, the usual course* [*of nature*] (أَمْرٌ خَارِقٌ لِلْعَادَةِ), *inviting to good and happiness, coupled with a claim to the prophetic office, and intended to manifest the veracity of him who claims to be an apostle of God:* (KT:) pl. مُعْجِزَاتٌ. (Ṣ, O, TA.)

مُعْجِزَةٌ: see مُعْجِزٌ: — and see also أَعْجَزُ.

مَعْجَزَةٌ *A* [*zone, or waist-belt, such as is termed*] مِنْطَقَةٌ: so called because it is next to the عَجُز of the person wearing it. (TA.)

مِعْجَازٌ *Always lacking strength,* or *power,* or *ability; always unable,* or *impotent.* (TA.) — Also *A road.* (O, Ḳ. [In the TA, المعاجز كَمُحَارِب is erroneously put for المِعْجَاز كَمِحْرَاب.])

مَعْجُوزٌ *Outstripped.* (Z, TA.) — And *Importuned by begging.* (IAạr, Ḳ, TA.) See also 1, last sentence but one.

مُعْجَزَةٌ: see أَعْجَزُ.

مُعَجِّزٌ [act. part. n. of 2]: see مُعَاجِزٌ. — Also, (TA,) or مُعَجِّزَةٌ, (Yoo, TA,) *A woman becoming aged:* (TA:) or *become aged.* (Yoo, TA.)

مُعَاجِزٌ act. part. n. of 3 [q. v.]. — In the Ḳur xxii. 50 and xxxiv. 5, مُعَاجِزِينَ signifies *Fighting and contesting* with the prophets and their friends, *to render* them *unable* to perform the command of God: (Ibn-'Arafeh, O, Ḳ:) or *opposing:* or *striving to outstrip,* or *gain precedence:* (TA:) or *opposing,* (Ḳ,) [and] *striving to outstrip* or *gain precedence:* (O, Ḳ:) or *imagining that they will render us unable to attain them,* or *that they will escape us;* (Zj, Ḳ;) for they imagined that they were not to be raised from the dead, and that there was no Paradise nor Hell: (Zj, O, TA:) but some read ▾ مُعَجِّزِينَ, meaning, *withholding,* or *keeping back,* or *diverting,* the followers of the Prophet from him and from belief in the signs or miracles: or *attributing impotence* to the followers of the Prophet. (TA.)

عجس

1. عَجَسَهُ, (Ḳ,) [aor. ـِ,] inf. n. عَجْسٌ, (Ṣ, O,) *He grasped it;* (Ṣ, O, Ḳ;) namely, a thing [such, for ex., as a bow]: (Ṣ:) [and *he grasped it hard;* for] عَجْسٌ signifies also the *grasping* a thing *hard.* (TA.) — And عَجَسَهُ عَنْ حَاجَتِهِ, aor. as above, (O, Ḳ,) and so the inf. n., (O,) *He,* or *it, withheld him from the object of his want;* (O, Ḳ;) as also ▾ تَعَجَّسَهُ: (TA:) and ▾ تَعَجَّسَهُ is likewise said of a radical, or hereditary, evil quality, meaning *It withheld him from generous actions;* (Sh, O, Ḳ;) as also تَعَقَّلَهُ and تَثَقَّلَهُ. (Sh, O.) And عَجَسَنِى عَنْكَ *It* (an affair, or event,) *withheld me from thee.* (AO, O.) And ▾ تَعَجَّسَ بِهِمْ *He withheld them;* and *he held them back,* or *made them slow* or *tardy:* (Sh, O, Ḳ:*) and one says, ▾ تَعَجَّسَتْ بِى الرَّاحِلَةُ *The riding-camel kept me back,* or *made me slow* or *tardy.* (TA.) — عَجَسَ and ▾ تَعَجَّسَ alone signify *He was,* or *became, slow, tardy, late,* or *backward:* (TA:) and the latter signifies [likewise] *he was,* or *became, behind,* or *backward;* or *he remained behind,* or *held back.* (O, TA.) — And one says of a she-camel, عَجَسَتْ بِهِ, (O, Ḳ,) aor. as above, (Ḳ,) and so the inf. n., (TA,) meaning *She turned aside,* or *away, with him from the road, by reason of her briskness, liveliness,* or *sprightliness;* (O, Ḳ, TA;) and so ▾ تَعَجَّسَتْ; and, as written by El-Urmawee, ▾ عَجَّسَتْ. (TA.)

2: see what next precedes.

5: see 1, in six places. — تَعَجَّسَهُ also signifies *He reckoned,* or *esteemed, his judgment,* or *opinion, weak.* (Sh, O,* TA.) — And *He upbraided him,* or *reproached him, for a thing,* or *an affair,* (IDrd, Ḳ, TA,) *which he had commanded him to do.* (IDrd, TA.) — And تَعَجَّسَ أَمْرَهُ *He searched repeatedly after the knowledge of his* (i. e. another's, Ṣ, O) *affair,* or *case.* (Ṣ, O, Ḳ.) Hence, in a trad., فَيَتَعَجَّسُكُمْ فِى قُرَيْشٍ *And he seeks repeatedly after you among Ḳureysh.* (TA.) — And تَعَجَّسَتِ الأَرْضَ غُيُوثٌ *Rains fell, one after another, upon the earth,* or *land,* (Ṣ, O, Ḳ, TA,) *and bore heavily upon it.* (TA.) — تَعَجَّسَ الرَّجُلُ *The man went forth in a last portion, before daybreak,* (▾ بِعُجْسَةٍ, O, or ▾ بِعَجْسَةٍ, Ḳ, [but see what follows,]) *of the night:* (O, Ḳ:) El-Marrár Ibn-Sa'eed El-Faḳ'asee says, describing his travelling-companions,

* وَإِذَا هُمُ ارْتَحَلُوا بِلَيْلٍ حَابِسٍ *
* أُخْرَى النُّجُومِ بِعُجْسَةِ ▾ المُتَعَجِّسِ *

[*And when they departed in an impeding night, in the last period* of the appearance *of the stars, in a last portion of the night of him who goes forth at that time*]. (O: in which بعجسة is thus written, with fet-ḥ and ḍamm, and with معًا above them.) [It is also said in the O (immediately after this verse), and likewise in the Ḳ and TA (in neither of which is the verse cited), in all of them probably from one and the same source, that ▾ المُتَعَجِّسُ means المُتَشَمِّرُ; and it is added in the TA that this has been mentioned in its place: but it is not mentioned in its proper art. in the O nor in the Ḳ nor in the TA; and it is evidently a mistranscription, for المُسْتَحِرُ, part. n. of اِسْتَحَرَ (q. v. voce أَسْحَرَ), and therefore I have rendered المُتَعَجِّس as above.]

عَجْسٌ and ▾ عُجْسٌ and ▾ عِجْسٌ The *handle,* or *part that is grasped by the hand,* of a bow; (Ṣ, O, Ḳ, TA;) which is the *part,* thereof, *that is the place of the arrow;* as AḤn says, the *thickest place* therein; (TA;) as also ▾ مَعْجِسٌ [lit. the *place of grasping*]. (Ṣ, O, Ḳ.) — And, (Ḳ,) or the first of these words, (Ṣ, O,) *A portion of the middle* of the night; (Ṣ, O, Ḳ;) as though from the عَجْس of the bow; [whence] one says, مَضَى عَجْسٌ مِنَ اللَّيْلِ [*A portion of the middle of the night passed*]: (Ṣ, O:) or the *last part* of the night: (Lth, O, Ḳ:) or the *blackness* of the night &c. (TA.) [See also عُجْسَةٌ.] — And see أَعْجَسُ.

عُجْسٌ: see the next preceding paragraph.

عِجْسٌ: see عَجْسٌ. [It is of the dial. of Hudheyl. (Freytag, from the Deewán of the Hudhalees).] — Also The *part,* of an arrow, *that is below,* or *exclusive of, the feathers.* (TA.)

عَجْسَةٌ: see 5, last sentence but one.

عُجْسَةٌ, with ḍamm, *A period* (سَاعَةٌ) of the night. (O, Ḳ, TA.) And The *blackness* of night. (IAạr, TA. [See also عَجْسٌ.]) And see 5, last sentence but one, in two places.

عَجَسَةٌ: see 5, last sentence but one.

عَجُوسٌ *Pouring* rain, (Ṣ, O, Ḳ, TA,) *that does not clear away.* (TA.) And Clouds (سَحَابٌ) *heavy* [*with rain*], (O, Ḳ,) *not passing away.* (O.)

عَجِيسٌ, applied to a stallion, (Ṣ, Ḳ, TA,) *Impotent to cover;* (TA;) *that will not impregnate:* (Ṣ, Ḳ, TA:) as also عَجِيزٌ. (Ṣ.) And both signify also A man *who does not come to women* [*by reason of impotence*]. (TA in art. عجز.) — See also what next follows.

لَا آتِيكَ سَجِيسَ عُجَيْسٍ, (Ṣ, O,) and ▾ سَجِيسَ عَجِيسٍ and ▾ سَجِيسَ عَجِيسَ عَجِيسٍ, (O,) both of which words are written in the Ḳ in this art. like أَمِير, with a reference to art. سجس, but the latter of them is correctly عُجَيْس, in the dim. form, (TA,) mean *I will not come to thee ever;* (Ṣ, O;) or *while time lasts.* (TA.) And one says also, لَا آتِيكَ عُجَيْسَ الدَّهْرِ *I will not come to thee to the end of time.* (TA.)

أَعْجَسُ *Strong in the* ▾ عَجْس, i. e. the *middle.* (O, Ḳ.) [To what this epithet is applied is not said.]

مَعْجِسٌ: see عَجْسٌ.

مُتَعَجِّسٌ see 5, last two sentences.

عجف

1. عَجِفَ, (Fr, Ṣ, O, Mṣb, Ḳ,) aor. ـَ, inf. n. عَجَفٌ; (Ṣ,* O,* Mṣb, Ḳ;*) and عَجُفَ; (Fr, Ṣ, O, Mṣb, Ḳ;) *He,* i. e. [a beast, or] a horse, (Mṣb,) or *they,* i. e. cattle, (مَالٌ, Fr, Ṣ, O,) *became lean, meagre,* or *emaciated;* (Ṣ;) *lost his,* or *their, fatness* or *plumpness:* (O, Ḳ:) or *became weak.* (Mṣb.) [See also عَجَفٌ, below.] — عَجَفَ نَفْسَهُ, or عَجَفَ الدَّابَّةَ, see 4. — عَجَفَ عَنِ الطَّعَامِ, aor. ـِ, inf. n. عَجْفٌ and عُجُوفٌ, *He withheld himself from the food, though desiring it, preferring that one who was hungry should have it;* (O, Ḳ;) or (Ḳ) *he left the food, though desiring it,* (O,) *in order that he who was eating with him might become satisfied in stomach;* (O, Ḳ;) as also ▾ عَجَّفَ, inf n. تَعْجِيفٌ. (Ḳ.) And عَجَفَ نَفْسَهُ عَلَى فُلَانٍ [*He restrained himself for such a one*] means *he chose that such a one should have the food in preference to himself.* (Ṣ.) عُجُوفٌ also signifies The *leaving,* or *relinquishing, food,* (IAạr, O, Ḳ, TA,) *with desire for it.* (TA.) And [hence, app.,] The *withholding*

oneself from evil acts or *dispositions*. (TA.) — And عَجَفَ نَفْسَهُ, (L, Ḳ,) aor. ِ, inf. n. عَجْفٌ, (L, TA,) *He constrained himself to be forbearing.* (L, Ḳ, TA.) You say, عَجَفَ نَفْسَهُ عَلَى فُلَانٍ, (O, Ḳ,) aor. ِ, inf. n. عَجْفٌ [and app. عُجُوفٌ also], (O,) *He bore,* or *endured, what proceeded from such a one, and did not punish him.* (O, Ḳ.) And عَجَفَ نَفْسَهُ عَلَى المَرِيضِ, (O, Ḳ,) aor. and inf. n. as above, (O,) *He constrained himself to exercise patience toward the sick man in tending him in his sickness;* as also ▼ أَعْجَفَ بِنَفْسِهِ عَلَيْهِ. (O, Ḳ.) — And عَجَفَ عَنْ فُلَانٍ [نَفْسَهُ being app. understood] *He withdrew himself,* or *became aloof, from such a one.* (Ḳ.)

2: see 1. — التَّعْجِيفُ also signifies *The eating less than what would satisfy the stomach.* (Ṣ, O, Ḳ.) — And One's *transferring his food to another before satisfying his stomach, by reason of drought,* or *dearth.* (IAạr, TA.) — And *The feeding on bad food, and being lean, meagre,* or *emaciated.* (TA.)

4. اعجفهُ, (Ṣ, O, Mṣb,) or اعجف الدَّابَّةَ; (O, Ḳ;) and ▼ عَجَّفَهُ, (O, Mṣb,) or عَجَّفَ الدَّابَّةَ, (O, Ḳ,) aor. ُ (O, Mṣb, Ḳ) and ِ, (O, Ḳ,) inf. n. عَجْفٌ; (O, Mṣb;) *He rendered him,* (Ṣ, O, Mṣb,) i. e. a horse, (Mṣb,) or *he rendered the beast,* (O, Ḳ,) *lean, meagre,* or *emaciated,* (Ṣ, O, Ḳ,) or *weak.* (Mṣb.) — اعجفوا *They became in the state,* or *condition, of having their cattle lean, meagre,* or *emaciated.* (O, Ḳ.) And *They confined their cattle, by reason of hardness and straitness* [*of circumstances*]. (TA.) — See also 1, last sentence but one.

5. تَعَجَّفَ *The being in a difficult and hard state* or *condition.* (TA.)

عَجَفٌ *Leanness, meagreness,* or *emaciation;* (Ṣ;) *loss of fatness* or *plumpness:* (O, Ḳ:) and *thickness,* or *roughness, and leanness* (عَرَآء), *of the bones.* (TA.) [See 1, first sentence.]

عَجِفٌ: see أَعْجَفُ, in three places.

عُجَافٌ, like غُرَابٌ, *A sort of dates:* (L, Ḳ:) or so ▼ عِجَافٌ, accord. to Lth. (O.)

عِجَافٌ pl. of أَعْجَفُ [q. v.], (Ṣ, O, Mṣb, Ḳ,) and of its syn. عَجِفٌ. (TA.) ═ Also *The colocynth:* (Ḳ:) or the *grains of the colocynth.* (Ibn-'Abbád, O, TA.) — And حَبٌّ عِجَافٌ *Grain,* or *grains, not increasing.* (A, TA.) — See also عُجَافٌ. ═ And العِجَافُ is one of the names of *Time,* or *fortune.* (Ibn-'Abbád, O, Ḳ.*)

عَجِيفٌ: see أَعْجَفُ, in two places.

عَنْجَفٌ, like جَنْدَلٌ, (Ḳ in the present art.,) or عُنْجُفٌ, (AA, O and Ḳ in art. عنجف,) like قُنْفُذٌ, (Ḳ in the latter art.,) and ▼ عُنْجُوفٌ, *Dry,* or *tough, by reason of leanness, meagreness,* or *emaciation,* (AA, Ḳ in this art., and O and Ḳ in art. عنجف,) or *of disease:* thus expl. by AA, and mentioned by IDrd and Az among quadriliteral-radical words. (TA.) And *Short, and compact,* or *contracted* [*in make* or *body*]: and sometimes applied as an epithet to an old woman: (Ḳ:) thus the latter word is expl. by IDrd. (TA.)

عُنْجُوفٌ: see the next preceding paragraph.

أَعْجَفُ *Lean, meagre,* or *emaciated;* (Ṣ;) *having lost his fatness* or *plumpness:* (O, Ḳ:) or *weak:* (Mṣb:) and ▼ عَجِفٌ signifies the same, applied to a man and to a woman: and ▼ عَجِيفٌ also signifies *lean, meagre, or emaciated:* (TA:) and ▼ مَعْجُوفٌ [likewise] is *syn. with* أَعْجَفُ, applied to a camel; (O, Ḳ;) as also ▼ مُنْعَجِفٌ, (Ḳ, TA,) in some copies of the Ḳ erroneously written مُتَعَجِّفٌ: (TA:) the fem. of أَعْجَفُ is عَجْفَآءُ: and the pl. is عِجَافٌ, which is irreg., having this form to assimilate it to سِمَانٌ, (Ṣ, O, Mṣb, Ḳ,) or to its like ضِعَافٌ, (Mṣb,) and which is applied to males and to females: (O, TA:) the pl. of ▼ عَجِفٌ, also, is عِجَافٌ: (TA:) and the pl. of ▼ عَجِيفٌ, if this be of established authority, may be عَجْفَى, agreeably with analogy. (MF, TA.) [Hence,] وَجْهٌ أَعْجَفُ and ▼ عَجِفٌ *A face having little flesh.* (TA.) And لِثَةٌ عَجْفَآءُ *A gum having little flesh.* (TA.) And شَفَتَانِ عَجْفَاوَانِ *Two thin lips.* (Ks, O, Ḳ.) — And نَصْلٌ أَعْجَفُ *A thin,* or *slender, arrow-head:* (Ṣ, O, Ḳ:) pl. نِصَالٌ عِجَافٌ. (O, Ḳ.) — And أَرْضٌ عَجْفَآءُ *Land in which is no good.* (O, Ḳ.) And أَرَضُونَ عِجَافٌ *Lands not rained upon.* (O.) And عِجَافٌ is sometimes used [alone] as signifying *Lands affected by drought:* a poet says, describing clouds (سَحَاب),

* لَقِحَ العِجَافُ لَهُ لِسَابِعِ سَبْعَةٍ *

meaning *The lands affected by drought produced herbage by reason thereof at a period of seven days* after the rain. (L, TA.)

مَعْجُوفٌ: see أَعْجَفُ. — Also *A rusty, unpolished,* sword; or one *sullied by remaining long unpolished.* (O, Ḳ.)

مُنْعَجِفٌ: see أَعْجَفُ.

عجل

1. عَجِلَ, [aor. َ,] (Ṣ, Mgh, O, Mṣb, Ḳ,) inf. n. عَجَلٌ and عَجَلَةٌ, (Ṣ,* Mgh, O,* Mṣb, Ḳ,*) *He hasted, hastened, made haste,* or *sped; he was,* or *became, hasty, speedy, quick,* or *expeditious;* (Ṣ, Mgh, O, Mṣb, Ḳ;) as also ▼ تعجّل; (Mgh, Mṣb, Ḳ;) and ▼ عجّل, [app. for عجّل نَفْسَهُ,] inf. n. تَعْجِيلٌ; (Ḳ;) and ▼ استعجل; (Mgh, Mṣb;) or this last signifies *he required himself to haste, &c., constraining,* or *tasking, himself to do so.* (Sb, Ḳ.) [See also عَجَلٌ below.] One says, عَجِلْتُ لَهُ [*I hasted, &c., to him,* or *it*]. (O.) And عَجِلْتُ بِهِ [*I was quick,* or *beforehand, with him*]: see 4. (Mgh.) And عَجِلْتُ إِلَى الشَّىْءِ *I preceded, outwent,* or *got first, to the thing.* (Mṣb.) — Also *i. q.* حَضَرَ [meaning *It was,* or *became, present,* or *ready;* said of a price, hire, payment, or the like; *contr. of* أَجِلَ]. (Mṣb.) — And عَجِلَ مِنْهُ *He turned aside from him,* or *it.* (TA.) ═ [It is also trans., as having, or implying, the meaning of سَبَقَ:] see 4.

2. عجّلهُ, inf. n. تَعْجِيلٌ: see 4, in two places. — [It generally relates to some inanimate object.] It is said in the Ḳur [xxxviii. 15], رَبَّنَا عَجِّلْ لَنَا قِطَّنَا قَبْلَ يَوْمِ الحِسَابِ [*O our Lord hasten to us our portion before the day of reckoning*]: (TA:) accord. to some, *our portion of punishment:* but accord. to Sa'eed Ibn-Jubeyr, it means, *of Paradise.* (TA in art. قط.) And you say, عَجَّلْتُ إِلَيْهِ المَالَ *I brought,* or *conveyed, hastily,* or *speedily, to him the property;* or *hastened its coming to him.* (Mṣb.) And عَجَّلْتُ لَهُ مِنَ الثَّمَنِ كَذَا *I paid him in advance, of the price, such a sum.* (Ṣ, O.) And عَجَّلَهُ مِنَ الكِرَآءِ كَذَا *He gave him in ready money,* [or *promptly,* or *quickly,* or *in advance,*] *of the hire, such a sum.* (Mgh.) And عَجَّلَ لَهُ الثَّمَنَ *He gave to him* [*in ready money,* or *promptly,* or *quickly,* or *in advance, the price*]. (Mgh.) And عجّل نَقْدَهُ [*He paid it in ready money, promptly,* or *quickly*]. (ISk, Ṣ and Ḳ in art. زكأ.) And بِعْتُهُ تَعْجِيلًا بِتَعْجِيلٍ [*I sold it,* or *I sold to him, present,* or *ready,* merchandise, *for present,* or *ready,* money]. (Ṣ voce نَاجِز, q. v.) And عَجَّلْتُ اللَّحْمَ, (Ṣ, O,) inf. n. as above, (TA,) *I cooked the flesh-meat in haste.* (Ṣ, O.) And ▼ لَوْ عَجَّلْتَ بِأَيِّمِكَ العَجُولَ, a prov., [which, app., is properly rendered *Would that thou didst hasten, with thy husbandless woman, the early portion of food called* عَجُول, or the right reading may be العُجُولَ,] meaning عَجِّلْ بِهَا الزَّوَاجَ [† *hasten thou, with her, i. e. with thy husbandless woman, marriage*]. (TA.) One says also عَجَّلْتُمْ like as one says لَهَّنْتُمْ [i. e. *Ye supplied,* or *fed, with the early portion of food called* لُهْنَة; which is also called عَجُول, or عُجُول, &c.]. (Ṣ, TA. [For لَهَّنْتُمْ, Golius appears to have read لَهَيَّتُمْ, which is evidently wrong.]) — عجّل أَقِطَهُ, inf. n. as above; and ▼ تعجّلهُ; *He made his* [*preparation of dried curd called*] اقط *into what are termed* عَجَاجِيل, (Ḳ, TA,) pl. of عُجَّالٌ: (TA:) or you say, عَجَّلْتُ أَقِطِى عَجَاجِيلَ [*I made my* اقط *into* عجاجيل]. (O.) ═ See also 1, first sentence.

3. عاجلهُ [inf. n. مُعَاجَلَةٌ] *i. q.* بَادَرَهُ [*He hastened,* or *made haste,* or *strove to be first* or *beforehand, in doing,* or *attaining,* or *obtaining, it*]; (M and Ḳ in art. بدر;) namely, a thing. (M ibid.) And عاجل غَيْرَهُ إِلَيْهِ *i. q.* بَادَرَهُ اليه, (M and Ḳ in art. بدر,) like بَادَرَهُ اليه [*He hastened with another,* or *vied* or *strove with him in hastening, to it,* or *to do,* or *attain,* or *obtain, it*]. (M ibid.) — [Also *He dealt hastily with him.*] And عاجلهُ بِذَنْبِهِ *He punished him for his sin,* or *crime,* or *offence,* (أَخَذَهُ بِهِ,) *not granting him any delay,*

(Ṣ, TA. [For بِدَنِيهِ, Golius appears to have read بِدَنِيهِ.])

4. اعجلهُ, (Ṣ, Mgh, Mṣb, TA,) inf. n. إِعْجَالٌ; (TA;) and ▼ عجّلهُ, inf. n. تَعْجِيلٌ; (Ṣ, O, TA;) and ▼ تعجّلهُ (Ṣ;) and ▼ استعجلهُ; (Ḳ, TA;) *He incited, excited, urged, instigated, induced,* or *made, him to haste, hasten, make haste, speed,* or *be quick;* (Ṣ, Mgh, Mṣb, Ḳ, TA;) and *commanded,* or *bade, him, to haste,* &c. (Ḳ.) One says, أَعْجَلَنِى فَعَجِلْتُ لَهُ [*He incited me,* &c., *to haste,* &c., *and I hasted,* &c., *to him*]. (O, TA.) And it is said in the Ḳur [xiii. 7], ▼ وَيَسْتَعْجِلُونَكَ بِٱلسَّيِّئَةِ قَبْلَ ٱلْحَسَنَةِ [*And they incite thee to haste with that which is evil before that which is good*]: and [in xxii. 46 and xxix. 53,] ▼ وَيَسْتَعْجِلُونَكَ بِٱلْعَذَابِ [*And they incite thee to haste with the punishment*]: (TA:) and ▼ استعجل بِنَفْسِهِ signifies *He hastened himself.* (MA.) — اعجلهُ signifies also [*He incited him to haste,* &c., *by going before him:* and hence it is expl. as meaning also] سَبَقَهُ [i. e. *he preceded him,* or *it; he had, got,* or *took, precedence of him,* or *it; he was,* or *became, beforehand with him,* or *it;* or *he anticipated him,* or *it*]; as also ▼ عجّلهُ; and ▼ استعجلهُ: (Ḳ:) or ▼ اِسْتَعْجَلْتُهُ signifies *I went before him,* or *preceded him,* (Ṣ, O, TA,) *and so incited him to haste:* (TA:) and أَعَجِلْتُمْ ▼ أَمْرَ رَبِّكُمْ, in the Ḳur [vii. 149], means أَسَبَقْتُمْ [i. e. *Have ye anticipated the command of your Lord?*]: (Ṣ, O:) or *have ye left* [*the fulfilment of*] *the command of your Lord incomplete?* (Ksh, Bḍ;) عَجِلَ being made to imply, (Ksh,) or as though it were made to imply, (Bḍ,) the meaning of سَبَقَ, wherefore it is made trans. like this latter verb; (Ksh, Bḍ;) the phrase meaning أَعَجِلْتُمْ عَنْ أَمْرِ رَبِّكُمْ. (Ksh.) وَمَا أَعْجَلَكَ عَنْ قَوْمِكَ, in the Ḳur [xx. 85, lit. *And what caused thee to hasten from thy party?*], means [virtually] كَيْفَ سَبَقْتَهُمْ [i. e. *how is it that thou camest before thy party?*]. (O.) — One says also, اعجل الشَّىْءَ عَنْ وَقْتِهِ [*He did the thing hastily,* or *hurriedly, before its time*]. (O and Ḳ in art. غرض.) And اعجلهُ عَنْ إِدْرَاكِهِ [*He made it,* or *did it, hastily,* or *hurriedly,* or *he hurried it, before,* or *so as to prevent, its becoming mature*]. (Ṣ and Ḳ* in art. فطر.) And أَعْجَلْتُهُ عَنِ ٱسْتِلَالِ سَيْفِهِ i. e. ▼ عَجِلْتُ بِهِ [*I was quick,* or *beforehand, with him, and*] *I flurried him, so that he could not draw his sword:* whence the saying, رَأَى صَيْدًا فَرَكِبَ فَرَسَهُ وَأُعْجِلَ عَنْ حَرْبَتِهِ أَوْ سَوْطِهِ [*He saw an animal of the chase, and he mounted his horse,* or *mare, and was incited by haste so as to be prevented from taking his dart or his whip*]: and the saying, هَلَاكُ ٱلْمَالِ أَعْجَلَهُ عَنْ أَدَائِهَا, meaning مَنَعَهُ [i. e. *The perishing of the cattle,* or *property, prevented,* or *precluded, him from paying it*], namely, the زَكَاة [or *poor-rate*]; which is an instance of the extension of the signification. (Mgh.) — أَعْجَلَتْ said of the pregnant, (O,) or of a she-camel, (Ḳ,) [as though for اعجلت وَلَدَهَا,] *She brought forth,* (O,) or *cast,* (Ḳ,) *her offspring before its maturity.* (O, Ḳ.) — And اعجل said of palm-trees, (نَخْل,) *They had ripe fruit before its full time.* (Mgh.) — And, said of a camel, *He leaped* [*up*] *when the rider had mounted him and had not yet become firmly seated upon him.* (TA.) [See مُعْجِل.]

5, as intrans.: see 1, first sentence. — Hence, تعجّل الحَرُّ *The heat came speedily,* or *quickly.* (Mgh.) And تعجّل الثَّمَنُ [*The price was,* or *became, given in ready money,* or *promptly,* or *quickly,* or *in advance*]. (Mṣb in art. نض.) — And تعجّل الشَّىْءُ *The thing came before its time.* (W p. 83.) — تعجّل مِنَ الكِرَاءِ كَذَا (Ṣ, Mgh, O) *He took,* or *received, in ready money,* or *promptly,* or *quickly,* [or *in advance,*] *of the hire, such a sum.* (Mgh.) And تعجّل المَالَ *He took,* or *received, promptly,* or *quickly,* [or *in advance,*] *the property.* (Mṣb.) — تَعَجَّلْتُ الشَّىْءَ *I constrained myself to do the thing in haste.* (Ḥam p. 28.) — And تَعَجَّلْتُ خَرَاجَهُ *I constrained him to hasten* [*the payment of*] *his* [*tax called*] خراج. (TA.) — See also 4, first sentence. — And see 2, near the end.

10, as intrans.: see 1, first sentence. — اِسْتَعْجَلْتُهُ *I desired,* or *required,* or *demanded, his hasting,* or *speeding,* or *being quick.* (Ṣ, O.) And استعجل الشَّىْءَ *He desired,* or *required,* or *demanded, the thing's being speedy,* or *quick, not waiting patiently until its time,* or *full time.* (Ḥam p. 665.) See also 4, in six places.

عُجَالَةٌ: see عُجَالٌ.

عِجْلٌ *A calf* the *young one of the* بَقَرَة, (Aboo-Kheyreh, Ṣ, Mgh, O, Mṣb, Ḳ,) [both *domestic* and *wild,* which latter is a bovine antelope,] *from the time when his mother brings him forth* (Aboo-Kheyreh, Mgh, TA) *until a month old;* (Aboo-Kheyreh, Mgh, Mṣb, TA;) after which [accord. to some] he is called بُرْغُز, when about two months old; and then he is called فُرْقُدٌ: (Aboo-Kheyreh, TA:) or he is thus called while *in the first year,* then تَبِيعٌ, (Ṣ and Ṣgh and Ḳ in art. سلغ,) or, correctly, accord. to IB, he is called while in the first year عِجْلٌ and تَبِيعٌ, (TA in that art.,) then جَذَعٌ, then ثَنِىٌّ, then رَبَاعٍ, then سَدِيسٌ, then سَالِغٌ سَنَةٍ and سَالِغُ سَنَتَيْنِ and so on: (Ṣ and Ṣgh and Ḳ ibid.:) the fem. is with ة: (Abu-l-Jarráḥ, Ṣ, O, Mṣb:) pl. of the masc. عِجَلَةٌ (Mgh, Mṣb) and عُجُولٌ (Mṣb, TA) and, of pauc., أَعْجِلَةٌ and أَعْجَالٌ; (IB, TA;) [and of the fem. عِجَلٌ;] but as to عِجَالٌ as a pl., [Mṭr says,] I have not heard it: (Mgh:) and ▼ عِجَّوْلٌ signifies the same as عِجْلٌ; (Ṣ, Mgh, O, Ḳ;) fem. with ة; (TA;) and pl. عَجَاجِيلُ. (Ṣ, Mgh, O, Ḳ.)

عَجَلٌ and ▼ عَجَلَةٌ, both inf. ns. of عَجِلَ [q. v.], (Mgh, Mṣb,) are *Syn. with* سُرْعَةٌ; (Ḳ;) *contr. of* بُطْءٌ: (Ṣ, O:) the latter is expl. by Th as signifying the *seeking,* and *pursuing,* or *endeavouring after, a thing before its proper time,* or *season;* and as proceeding from the desire of the soul; wherefore it is generally discommended in the Ḳur-án, so that it is said to be from the Devil. (TA.) It is said in the Ḳur [xxi. 38], خُلِقَ ٱلْإِنْسَانُ مِنْ عَجَلٍ, meaning, it is said, *Man is composed of haste;* (O;) so says Fr, and in like manner says Aboo-Is-ḥáḳ; (T, TA;) to denote the excess of this attribute in him: (T, O, TA:) or, accord. to Th, (TA,) the phrase is inverted, the meaning being, *haste is created from man;* (Mṣb, TA;) but IJ disapproves this explanation, and also another which will be mentioned in what follows. (TA.) — عَجَلٌ signifies also *Food that is hastily prepared, and brought, before the* [*meal called*] غَدَاء *has become matured.* (TA.) [See also عُجَالٌ.] — Also *Clay,* or *earth;* syn. طِينٌ: (IAạr, O, Ḳ:) or *black mud,* or *black fetid mud;* syn. حَمْأَةٌ: and ▼ عَجَلَةٌ has both of these meanings, i. e. طِين and حَمْأَة: (O,* Ḳ:) the former of these two significations of عَجَلٌ is said by AO to be of the dial. of Ḥimyer; and IAạr says that it is what is meant in the phrase in the Ḳur [xxi. 38] cited above; but Ibn-'Arafeh disapproves this; (O, TA;) and so does Az; and Er-Rághib says that some expl. it as meaning in this instance *stinking black mud,* but that their saying is nought. (TA.) — See also عَجَلَةٌ, in four places.

عَجُلٌ: see the next paragraph, in two places.

عَجِلٌ (Ṣ, O, Mṣb, Ḳ) and ▼ عَاجِلٌ (Mṣb, Ḳ) and ▼ عَجُلٌ (Ṣ, O, Ḳ) and ▼ عَجُولٌ (Ṣ, O) and ▼ عَجِيلٌ (Ḳ) and ▼ عَجْلَانُ (Ṣ, Mgh, O, Mṣb, Ḳ) *Hasting, hastening, making haste,* or *speeding;* [thus more properly the first and second, and often the last; the rest generally signifying] *hasty, speedy, quick,* or *expeditious:* (Ṣ, Mgh, O, Mṣb,* Ḳ:) pls., (Ḳ, TA,) all of عَجْلَانُ, (TA,) عَجَالَى and عُجَالَى and عِجَالٌ; (Ḳ, TA;) the first and last of which pls., as pls. of عَجْلَى [fem. of عَجْلَانُ], are applied to women (Ṣ, O, TA) also: (TA:) عَجِلٌ has no broken pl., nor has ▼ عَجُلٌ: (Sb, TA:) ISk says that, for the dim. of عَجِلٌ, they use ▼ عُجَيْلَانُ, as formed from عَجْلَانُ; though they also form it regularly, saying ▼ عُجَيْلٌ; but the former is the better. (O, TA.)

عُجْلَةٌ: see عُجَالَةٌ.

عِجْلَةٌ fem. of عِجْلٌ [q. v.]. (Abu-l-Jarráḥ, Ṣ, O, Mṣb.) — Also *A water-skin,* or *skin for water and for milk;* syn. سِقَآءٌ: (Ṣ, O, Ḳ:) pl. عِجَلٌ and عِجَالٌ. (Ṣ, O.) — And *A* [*water-wheel such as is called*] دُولَاب: (IAạr, O, Ḳ: [see also عَجَلَةٌ:]) pls. as above. (Ḳ.) — And *A species of plant,* (Ṣ, O, Ḳ, TA,) *which extends along the ground,* (TA,) *also called* وَشِيج [q. v.]: (O, TA:) AḤn says of the وشيج, on the authority of Aboo-Ziyád, *it grows, at first, from one root, then branches forth upon the surface of the earth, in innumerable branches, every branch having a knot,* or *joint,* (كَعْب,) *from which knot,* or *joint, grow other branches; it cleaves to the ground, not rising high; its leaves are like those of wheat; and while green, it is called* عِجْلَة; (O;) *and it is the best of pasture, and is not* [*what is termed*] *a* بَقْل: (O, TA:) and it is said to be *a tree having leaves and joints,* or *knots,* (كُعُوب,) *and pliant canes,* [for قضب in my original, I read قَصَب, (see وَشِيج,)] *long,* or *elongated, with a fruit like the foot of the domestic fowl, contracted, which, when it dries up, opens; and not having any blossom.* (TA.) See also عِجَالَة.

عَجَلَة: see عَجَل, first sentence. — Also [*A cart,* or *wheeled carriage of any kind;*] the *thing,* (Ṣ, O,) or آلة [meaning آلَةُ حَمْلٍ i. e. *instrument of carriage*], (Ḳ,) *that is drawn along by the bull:* (Ṣ, O, Ḳ:) said by Er-Rághib to be so called because of the quickness of its passing along: (TA:) pl. ▼عَجَل [or rather this is a coll. gen. n.] and [pl. of pauc.] أَعْجَال (Ṣ, O, Ḳ) and [of mult.] عِجَال. (Ḳ.) — And *Pieces of wood constructed,* (Ḳ,) or *a piece of wood,* (Mṣb,) or *a thing that is constructed like the* [*women's camel-vehicle called*] مِحَفَّة, (Mgh,) *upon which burdens are carried:* (Mgh, Mṣb,* Ḳ:) pl. [or coll. gen. n.] ▼عَجَل. (Mgh, Mṣb.) — And *A* [*water-wheel such as is called*] مَنْجَنُون (Ṣ, O) or دُولَاب (Ḳ) *upon which water is drawn:* (Ṣ, O: [see also عَجَلَة:]) or *a* مَحَالَة [app. meaning *a great sheave of a pulley by means of which camels draw water*]: (Ḳ:) pl. [or coll. gen. n.] ▼عَجَل. (Ṣ, O.) — And *A piece of wood lying transversely,* or *horizontally, upon the* نَعَامَة [or rather نَعَامَتَان or *two posts*] *of the well, to which the large bucket is suspended:* (El-Kilábee, Ṣ, O, Ḳ: [see زُرْنُوق:]) pl. [or coll. gen. n.] ▼عَجَل. (TA.) — And *A kind of ladder made from a palm-tree, like the* نَقِير, (O, Ḳ,) *which is the trunk of a palm-tree hollowed, and having the like of steps made in it:* mentioned in a trad. as the means of ascending to an upper chamber. (O.) — And *A small* [*leathern vessel for water such as is called an*] إِدَاوَة: and some say, *a* [*leathern water-bag such as is called*] مَزَادَة. (TA.) — And i. q. كَارَةُ ثَوْبٍ [app. *A garment made up into a bundle*]: pl. عِجَال and أَعْجَال, by the rejection of the augmentative [ة in the sing.]. (TA.) — And *A rock* [*that is as though*] *growing forth by itself upon rugged, elevated, hard ground.* (AA, O.) — See also عَجَل, latter half.

عَجْلَان: see عَجِل, in two places. — [Hence,] قَوْسٌ عَجْلَى *A bow of which the arrow is quick* [*in its flight*]. (AḤn, Ḳ.) — And أُمُّ عَجْلَان *A certain bird,* (Ṣ, O, Ḳ,) *black, but white in the base of the tail, that moves about its tail much,* or *often; also called* الفَتَّاح. (O.) — And العَجْلَان is [a name of *The month*] شَعْبَان: so called because of the quickness of its passing away and coming to an end; (L, Ḳ; [in the latter of which, in some copies, وَنَفَاده is erroneously put for وَنَفَادِهِ;]) i. e. because of its seeming short on account of the fast that follows it. (L.)

عَجُول: see عَجِل. — Also *A she camel distracted,* or *confounded,* or *perplexed, having lost her young one;* (Ṣ, O, Ḳ;*) because of her quickness in her motions, (Ḳ, TA,) i. e. in her coming and going, (TA,) by reason of impatience: (Ḳ, TA:) and a woman *bereft of her child:* pl. عُجُل, (O, Ḳ,) and, accord. to the Ḳ, عَجَائِل, but correctly ▼مَعَاجِيل, as in the L, an anomalous pl. (TA.) — And العَجُول signifies *Death,* or *the decree of death;* syn. المَنِيَّة: (AA, Ḳ, TA:) because it [often] hurries him whom it befalls so as to prevent him from reaching his family. (TA.) — See also عُجَّال: and see a phrase in the latter half of the second paragraph of this art.

عَجِيل: see عَجِل.

عُجَيْل a dim. of عِجْل, q. v. (O, TA.) — See also عُجَّال.

عُجَالَة (Ṣ, O, Ḳ) and ▼عِجَالَة (O, Ḳ) and ▼عُجْل and ▼عُجْلَة (Ibn-'Abbád, O, Ḳ) *A thing that one takes hastily,* or *quickly:* (Ṣ, O, Ḳ:) and the first, [or all,] the rider's *provision of food whereof the eating does not fatigue, as dates, and meal of parched barley;* (Meyd, TA;) because he desires its readiness, for the journeying hurries him so as to prevent his having food prepared with pains: (TA:) and *hasty provision for a guest.* (Ḥar p. 84.) One says, التَّمْرُ عُجَالَةُ الرَّاكِبِ [*Dates are the hastily-taken food of the rider*]: (Ṣ, O:) and so, الثَّيِّبُ [q. v.]; (Ṣ, O;) which is a prov., (Ṣ,) said by A'Obeyd to be used in urging one to be content with a little of what is wanted when much thereof is unattainable. (Meyd.) — Also, the same four words, The *milk which the* مُعَجِّل [q. v.] *draws;* and so ▼إِعْجَالَة: (Ḳ:) or this last signifies the *milk* (Ṣ, O, TA) *of his camels* (TA) *which the pastor hastens to bring* (Ṣ, O, TA) *to his family before the* [*fresh*] *milking,* (Ṣ, O,) or *when his camels return from the water;* and its pl. is إِعْجَالَات: (TA:) and عُجَالَة signifies the *milk which the pastor carries from the place of pasture to the owners of the sheep or goats before the sheep or goats return;* this being done only when there is abundance of milk. (IAth, O, TA.)

عِجَالَة: see the next preceding paragraph. — Also *A certain plant:* (Ḳ, TA:) said to be the ▼عِجْلَة mentioned above. (TA.)

عُجَيْلَة: see what next follows.

عُجَيْلَى *A certain quick pace;* (Aṣ, O, Ḳ;) as also ▼عُجَيْلَة, (Ḳ,) and ▼عُجَّيْلَى, mentioned, and thus written, by Ibn-Wellád, like سُمَّيْهَى. (TA.)

عُجَيْلَان an anomalous dim. of عَجْلَان, q. v. (O, TA.)

عُجَّال and ▼عِجَّوْل *A thing with which one hastes* [i. e. *an early portion of food that one eats*] *before the* [*morning-meal called*] غَدَاء; i. q. لُهْنَة; (Th, TA;) and (TA) so ▼عَجُول; (Ḳ, TA;) or, some say, it is [correctly] عِجَّوْل, as above; (TA;) so too ▼عُجَيْل: (Ḳ:) or this last signifies *food that is presented to a party before a preparation has been made for them.* (IDrd, O, Ḳ.) [See also عَجَل.] — Also (i. e. عُجَّال and ▼عِجَّوْل) *A* كُفَّة [or *cake of the length and thickness of the hand*] *of* حَيْس [or *dates mixed and kneaded with clarified butter and with the preparation of dried curd called* أَقِط, &c.], (Ḳ, TA, accord. to several copies of the Ḳ جُمَّاعُ كَفٍّ [which means the same],) or *of dates* [*alone*], *which is eaten in haste:* (Ḳ:) or (Ḳ, TA, in some copies of the Ḳ "and") *a handful of dates kneaded with* سَوِيق [or *meal of parched barley or wheat*], (ISh, O, Ḳ, the last in two places,) or *with* أَقِط: (ISh, O:) pl. عَجَاجِيل: (TA:) which signifies [also] *certain things of* أَقِط, *made in a long form, of the thickness of the hand,* (ISh, O, Ḳ,) *and of the length thereof, like the* عَجَاجِيل *of dates and* حَيْس; one of which is called عُجَّال. (ISh, O.)

عِجَّوْل: see the next preceding paragraph, in two places. — And see also عِجْل.

عُجَّيْلَى: see عُجَيْلَى.

عَاجِل: see عَجِل. [Also *Fleeting; quickly transitory.*] — And *Present; ready;* (Mṣb;) *not delayed;* (PṢ;) [applied to a price, hire, payment, or the like;] *contr. of* آجِل; (Ṣ, O, Ḳ;) as applied to anything. (Ḳ.) عَاجِلٌ بِعَاجِلٍ [*Ready* merchandise *with ready* money] is like نَاجِزٌ بِنَاجِزٍ, and يَدٌ بِيَدٍ. (TA in art. نجز.) — And hence, [or because fleeting, or quickly transitory,] العَاجِلَةُ signifies *The present hour* or *time:* (Mṣb:) and *the present dwelling, abode, world, life,* or *state of existence:* (TA:) *contr. of* الآجِلَة, (Ṣ, O, TA,) in relation to anything. (TA.)

أَعْجَل [*More,* and *most, hasty, speedy, quick,* or *expeditious:* and *more,* and *most, fleeting,* or *short-lived*]. They say, in relation to the affecting of hardiness, or strength, and endurance, and to soundness of body, لَيْتَنِى وَفُلَانًا يُفْعَلُ بِنَا كَذَا حَتَّى يَمُوتَ الأَعْجَلُ [*Would that such a thing might be done to me and such a one until the more short-lived die*]. (O.)

إِعْجَالَة: see عُجَالَة, last sentence.

أَعَاجِل [mentioned by Freytag, on the authority of the Deewán of the Hudhalees, as a pl. derived by some from عِجْل, and signifying *Little ones* ("*parvi*")].

مُعْجِل *A young camel brought forth before the completion of the year, and living.* (Ḳ.)

مُعْجِل and ▼مُعَجِّل and ▼مِعْجَال *A she-camel that brings forth before the completion of the year, and whose young one lives:* (Ḳ:) or مُعْجِلَة and ▼مِعْجَال signify the pregnant *that brings forth her young before its full time:* (O:) or مُعْجِلَة signifies a she-camel *that casts her young prematurely:* (TA:) and مُعْجِل applied to a بَقَرَة [meaning a cow, either domestic or wild, the latter being a bovine antelope], (Ṣ, O, Mṣb, Ḳ,) *having a calf,* (Ṣ, Mṣb, Ḳ,) or *having her calf with her.* (O.) — Also [i. e. the three epithets first mentioned], A she-camel *that leaps* [*up*] *when the foot is put in her stirrup;* as also مُعْجِلَةٌ: (Ḳ:) or thus this last word: (O:) or مِعْجَالٌ ▼ is so applied, like مُعْجِلَةٌ; and is in like manner applied to a he-camel; meaning *that rises and leaps* &c. as above. (TA.) — Also, (Ḳ,) or مِعْجَالٌ ▼ [only], (TA,) A palm-tree *that matures its fruit on the first occasion of its bearing.* (Ḳ, TA.)

مُعَجِّلٌ: see the next preceding paragraph. — Also One *who brings to his family the* إِعْجَالَة (Ṣ, O) or عُجَالَة [q. v.]; (Ḳ;) as also مُتَعَجِّلٌ ▼: (Ṣ, O, Ḳ:) or one *who brings the* إِعْجَالَة *from the camels pasturing at a distance from their owners.* (TA.) — And The pastor *who milks the camels once while they are in the pasture.* (Ḳ.)

مِعْجَالٌ: see مُعْجِلٌ, in four places. — Also sing. of مَعَاجِيلُ (A, TA) which means, The مُخْتَصَرَات [i. e. *nearer,* or *nearest,* (in art. خصر erroneously written مُخْتَصِرَات,)] of the roads, or ways. (A, O, Ḳ, TA.) One says also, أَخَذْتُ مُسْتَعْجِلَةً ▼ مِنَ الطَّرِيقِ (O, Ḳ, in the CḲ مُسْتَعْجِلَةٌ,) [*I took a short cut,*] and هٰذِهِ مُسْتَعْجِلَاتُ ▼ الطَّرِيقِ [*These are the short cuts*]: both denote nearness and shortness. (O, Ḳ.)

مَعَاجِيلُ an anomalous pl. of عَجُولٌ, q. v. (L, TA.)

مُعَجَّلٌ: see مُتَعَجِّلٌ.

المُسْتَعْجِلَةُ — مِعْجَالٌ and its pl.: see مُسْتَعْجِلَةٌ is a name of *A certain plant that fattens women; also called* العُرُوقُ البِيضُ. (Ḳ in art. عرق.)

عجم

1. عَجَمَهُ, (Ṣ, Mṣb, Ḳ,) aor. ـُ, (Ṣ, Mṣb,) inf. n. عَجْمٌ (Ṣ, Mṣb, Ḳ) and عُجُومٌ, (Ḳ,) *He bit it:* (Mṣb, Ḳ:) and *he chewed it:* (Mṣb:) or *he chewed it for the purpose of eating* or *of trial:* (Ḳ:) or *he bit it with the lateral teeth, not with the central incisors:* (TA:) or *he bit it,* namely, a piece of wood, or a stick, or rod, or the like, *in order to know whether it were hard or fragile:* (Ṣ:) or *he tried it with his lateral teeth in order that he might know,* or *prove, its hardness:* and *he bit it,* namely, a gaming-arrow known for winning, *between two lateral teeth, in order to make upon it a mark by which he might know it.* (TA.) — Hence, (TA,) ‡ *He tried, tested,* or *proved, him.* (Ḳ, TA.) And عَجَمْتُ عُودَهُ † *I tried, tested, or proved his case, and knew his state,* or *condition.* (Ṣ, TA.) And عَجَمَتْهُ الأُمُورُ † *Affairs exercised him so as to render him strong for them,* and *habituated,* or *inured, to them.* (TA.) And Ḳabeeṣah Ibn-Jábir says,

وَعَاجَمْتُ ▼ الأُمُورَ وَعَاجَمَتْنِى • كَأَنِّى كُنْتُ فِى الأُمَمِ الخَوَالِى

[† *And I have tried affairs, and they have tried me, as though I were of the generations that have passed away*]; meaning, as though I were one of the long-lived, by reason of my many trials. (Ḥam p. 340.) — [Hence also,] one says, الثَّوْرُ يَعْجُمُ قَرْنَهُ † *The bull smites the tree with his horn to try, or test, it.* (Ṣ, Ḳ.) — And عَجَمَ السَّيْفَ, (Ṣ, Ḳ,) inf. n. عَجْمٌ, (TA,) † *He shook the sword to try, or test, it.* (Ṣ, Ḳ.) — مَا عَجَمَتْكَ عَيْنِى مُنْذُ كَذَا means † *My eye has not seen thee since such a time;* (Ṣ, Ḳ, TA;) and is said by a man to one with whom his [last] meeting was long past. (TA.) An Arab of the desert is related to have said, تَعْجُمُكَ عَيْنِى, meaning † [*My eye seems to know thee;* or] *it seems to me that I have seen thee.* (TA.) And one says, رَأَيْتُ فُلَانًا فَجَعَلَتْ عَيْنِى تَعْجُمُهُ i. e. † [*I saw such a one,*] *and my eye seemed to know him,* (Lḥ, Ṣ, Ḳ, TA,) *not knowing him perfectly, as though not certain of him.* (TA.) And عَجَمُونِى † *They knew me.* (TA.) — And [hence, app.,] one says, نَظَرْتُ فِى الكِتَابِ فَعَجَمْتُ, meaning † [*I looked into the book, or writing, and*] *I did not know surely its letters.* (TA.) — See also 4. — عَجُمَ, [aor. ـُ,] inf. n. عُجْمَةٌ, *He had an impotence,* or *an impediment,* or *a difficulty, in his speech,* or *utterance;* and [*a barbarousness,* or *vitiousness, therein,* especially *in speaking Arabic;* (see عُجْمَةٌ below;) i. e.] *a want of clearness, perspicuousness, distinctness, chasteness,* or *correctness, therein.* (Mṣb.)

2: see 4.

3: see the verse cited in the first paragraph.

4. اعجمهُ *He made it* (i. e. speech, or language, Ṣ, Ḳ, or a thing, TA) *to want,* or *be without,* or *to have a quality the contrary of, clearness, perspicuousness,* or *distinctness;* (Ṣ, Mṣb, Ḳ,* TA;) or [*to be barbarous,* or *vitious,* i. e.] *to want,* or *be without, chasteness,* or *correctness.* (Ḳ,* TA.) Ru-beh says, [in some verses very differently cited in different copies of the Ṣ,] of him who attempts poetry without having knowledge thereof,

• يُرِيدُ أَنْ يُعْرِبَهُ فَيُعْجِمُهُ •

[*He desires to make it clear,* &c., *and he makes it to want clearness,* &c.]. (Ṣ.) — And *He dotted it,* or *pointed it,* (Ṣ, Ḳ,) namely, a letter, (Ṣ,) or a writing; (Ḳ;) *he removed its* عُجْمَة [or *want of clearness,* &c.,] *by means of dots,* or [*diacritical*] *points,* (Nh, Mṣb, TA,) *and* [*the signs called*] شَكْل, [but see شكل,] *which distinguished it,* namely, a letter, *from other letters;* the ا denoting privation; (Mṣb;) as ISd holds to be the case; (TA;) and so عَجَّمَهُ ▼, (Ṣ,* Ḳ,) inf. n. تَعْجِيمٌ; (Ṣ;) and عَجَمَهُ ▼, (Ḳ,) inf. n. عَجْمٌ; (Ṣ;) for J's assertion [in the Ṣ] that one should not say عَجَمْتُ is a mistake: (Ḳ:) this last verb, however, which J thus disallows, is disallowed also by Th, in his Fṣ, and by most of the expositors thereof; and J confined himself to the correct and chaste. (TA.) — And *He locked it;* namely, a door. (Mṣb.) — نَهَانَا النَّبِىُّ أَنْ نُعْجِمَ النَّوَى طَبْخًا [*The Prophet forbade us to make the date-stones to become as though they were chewed and bitten*], (Ḳ,* TA,) occurring in a trad., means that when dates are cooked for دِبْس, (Ḳ, TA,) i. e. for taking their sweetness, (TA,) they should be cooked gently, so that the cooking shall not extend to the stones, (Ḳ, TA,) nor produce upon them such an effect as that of their being chewed and bitten, (TA,) and thus spoil the taste of the حَلَاوَة, (Ḳ, TA,) so in the copies of the Ḳ, but correctly, as in the Nh, the سُلَافَة [here meaning the sweet decocture]; (TA;) or because they [the date-stones] are food for the home-fed animals, and therefore they should not be thoroughly cooked, that their taste, (Ḳ, TA,) in the Nh their strength, (TA,) may not go away: (Ḳ, TA:) or the meaning is, [that he forbade] the cooking the date-stones immoderately, so that they would crumble, and their strength, with which they would be good for the sheep, or goats, would be spoiled. (TA.)

7: see the next paragraph.

10. استعجم *He was unable to speak:* (TA:) *he was silent, mute,* or *speechless;* (Ḳ, TA;) said of a man. (TA.) And اِسْتَعْجَمَتِ الدَّارُ عَنْ جَوَابِ سَائِلِهَا [*The dwelling kept silence from replying to its interrogator*]: and Imra-el-Ḳeys says,

• صَمَّ صَدَاهَا وَعَفَا رَسْمُهَا • وَٱسْتَعْجَمَتْ عَنْ مَنْطِقِ السَّائِلِ •

[*Its echo has become dumb, and its trace has become effaced, and it has become in the state of keeping silence from answering the speech of the interrogator*]: he makes استعجمت trans. by means of عن because it is used in the sense of سَكَتَتْ. (TA.) — One says also, استعجم عَلَيْهِ الكَلَامُ, (Ṣ,) or عَلَيْنَا, (Mṣb,) meaning *Speech was as though it were closed against him,* or *us;* or *he,* or *we, became impeded in speech, unable to speak,* or *tongue-tied;* syn. اِسْتَبْهَمَ: (Ṣ, Mṣb:) and انعجم ▼ عليه الكلام; [which means the same;] syn. اِنْغَلَقَ and اِنْطَبَقَ. (Ḳ* and TA in art. طبق.) And accord. to the Ḳ, one says, استعجم القِرَآءَةَ, meaning *He was unable to perform* [or *continue*] *the recitation,* or *reading, by reason of the overcoming of drowsiness:* but what is said in the Nh and other works is اِسْتَعْجَمَتْ عَلَيْهِ قِرَآءَتُهُ i. e. *His recitation,* or *reading, was cut short, and he was unable to perform* [or *continue*] *it, by reason of drowsiness:* and it is also expl. as meaning *he was,* or *became, impeded in his recitation,* or *reading, and unable to perform* [or *continue*] *it, as though he became one in whom was* عُجْمَة. (TA.) — And استعجم الخَبَرُ means *The information,* or *narration, was dubious, confused, vague,* or *difficult to be understood* or *expressed;* or *was not to be understood* or *expressed; as though it were closed* [*against the hearer* or *speaker*]; syn. اِسْتَبْهَمَ, and اِسْتَغْلَقَ. (Mṣb in art. بهم.)

عَجْمٌ The *young of camels;* (Ṣ, Mṣb, Ḳ, TA;) *such as the* بَنَات لَبُون *and* حِقَاق *and* جِذَاع: (IAạr, Ṣ,* Mṣb,* TA:) thus far: (Ṣ, Mṣb:) when they have entered upon the state of إِثْنَآء, they are of the جِلَّة thereof: (IAạr, TA:) applied to the *male* and to the *female*: (Ṣ, Mṣb, Ḳ:) pl. عَجُومٌ [app. meaning *young camels of different ages not exceeding the age of the* جَذَع]. (Ṣ, Ḳ.) ― And The *root*, or *base*, *of the tail*; (Ṣ, Mṣb, Ḳ;) which is the عُصْعُص; (Ṣ, Mṣb;) as also ▼ عُجْمٌ; (Ḳ;) like عَجْبٌ [and عُجْبٌ]; (Ṣ, Mṣb;) [each] a dial. var. of عجب; (Mṣb;) or, accord. to Lḥ, the م is a substitute for the ب of عجب. (TA.) ― See also عَجَمٌ. ― [Golius and Freytag have assigned to this word a meaning belonging to عَجْمِىٌّ.]

عُجْمٌ: see the next preceding paragraph: ― and that here following.

عَجَمٌ [*Foreigners, as meaning*] *others than Arabs; such as are not Arabs;* [often used as implying disparagement, like *barbarians;* and often especially meaning *Persians;*] (Ṣ, Mgh, Mṣb, Ḳ;) as also ▼ عُجْمٌ, [of which see an ex. in a verse of Lebeed cited voce رَازِقِىٌّ,] (Ṣ, Mṣb, Ḳ,) or this latter may be a pl. of the former: (TA:) ▼ عَجَمِىٌّ (of which أَعْجَامٌ is pl., TA) signifies *one thereof;* (Ṣ, Mgh, Mṣb, Ḳ;) *one who is of the race of the* عَجَم; (Ḳ;) *though he may be chaste*, or *correct, in* [*the Arabic*] *speech;* (Mgh, Ḳ;) the ى denoting unity; but it is also the relative ى, and thus one may apply to an Arab the appellation ▼ عَجَمِىٌّ as meaning called thus in relation to the عَجَم: (Mṣb:) and one says also ▼ رَجُلٌ أَعْجَمُ [*a man not of the Arabs*]: and ▼ قَوْمٌ أَعْجَمُ [*a people*, or *party, not of the Arabs*]. (Ḳ.) ― Also The *stones* of dates (Ṣ, Mgh, Mṣb, Ḳ) and of the drupes of the lote-tree (Mṣb) and of grapes (Mgh, Mṣb) and of raisins and of pomegranates and the like, (Mgh,) or also of other things, (Mṣb,) or the similar stones of anything, (Ḳ,) or also *whatever is in the interior of a thing that is eaten such as the raisin and the like;* (Ṣ;) and ▼ عُجَامٌ signifies the same: (Ḳ:) the vulgar say ▼ عَجْمٌ: (Yaạḳoob, Ṣ:) [see also ضِيضٌ, in an explanation of which عَجَمٌ is evidently, I think, used as meaning the *heart* (commonly termed جُمَّار q. v.) *of the palm-tree:*] the n. un. is عَجَمَةٌ, (Ṣ, Mgh, Mṣb,) which is incorrectly expl. by AḤn as meaning *a grape-stone when it germinates.* (ISd, TA.) ― Also Camels *that bite, or chew, the* [*trees called*] عِضَاه *and the tragacanths and* [*other*] *thorny trees, and satisfy themselves therewith so as to be in no need of the* [*plants called*] حَمْض. (Ṣ.)

عَجْمَةٌ sing. of عَجَمَاتٌ, (Ḳ, TA,) which signifies *Hard rocks* (Ṣ, Ḳ, TA) *protruding* (lit. *growing forth*) *in a valley.* (TA.) ― See also عُجْمَةٌ.

عُجْمَةٌ (Ṣ, Mgh, Mṣb, Ḳ, TA) *An impotence*, or *an impediment*, or *a difficulty*, (Mṣb, TA,*) *in speech*, or *utterance;* (Ṣ, Mṣb, Ḳ, TA;) and [*a barbarousness*, or *vitiousness, therein;* i. e.] *a want of clearness, perspicuousness, distinctness, chasteness*, or *correctness, therein*, (Mgh, Mṣb,) meaning, *in speaking Arabic.* (Mgh, Mṣb.*) [See also 1, last sentence, where it is mentioned as an inf. n.] ― Also, (Ṣ, Ḳ,) and ▼ عِجْمَةٌ, (Ḳ,) *Such as is accumulated*, or *congested, of sand:* or *abundance thereof:* (Ḳ, TA:) or *sand rising above what is around it:* (TA:) or the *last portion* of sand. (Ṣ in explanation of the former.)

عِجْمَةٌ: see the next preceding paragraph.

عَجَمَةٌ, (Ṣ, TA,) thus in the L, and thus correctly, (TA,) i. e. بِالتَّحْرِيك, (Ṣ, TA,) but in the Ḳ ▼ عَجْمَةٌ, (TA,) [app. from the same word as signifying "a date-stone," n. un. of عَجَمٌ,] *A palm-tree growing from a date-stone.* (Ṣ, Ḳ, TA.)

عَجْمِىٌّ, with the ج quiescent, *Intelligent and discriminating;* (Ḳ, TA;) applied to a man. (TA.)

عَجَمِىٌّ; pl. أَعْجَامٌ: see عَجَمٌ, first sentence. [The sing. is applied to anything as meaning *Of*, or *belonging to, the* عَجَم.]

عَجَمِيَّةٌ [*A speech*, or *language, foreign to the Arabs*]. (TA in art. رطن.)

عُجَامٌ: see عَجَمٌ, latter half.

عَجُومٌ: see عَجَمْجَمَةٌ.

عُجَامَةٌ *A thing that one has bitten*, or *chewed* [like مُضَاغَةٌ]. (TA. [The explanation there given is ما عجمه: correctly مَا عَجَمْتَ.])

عَجُومَةٌ: see عَجَمْجَمَةٌ.

عَجَّامٌ The *large* خُفَّاش [or *bat*]; and the وَطْوَاط [which accord. to some signifies the same as خُفَّاش; but accord. to others, the *large* خُفَّاش; or the *swallow;* or *a species of the swallows of the mountains*]. (Ḳ.)

عَاجِمَةٌ: and عَاجِمَاتٌ: see what next follows.

عَوَاجِمُ [a pl. of which the sing. ▼ عَاجِمَةٌ (a subst. formed from the act. part. n. عَاجِمٌ) I do not find mentioned] The *teeth.* (Ṣ, Ḳ.) ― And *Camels;* because they bite, or chew, bones; and so ▼ عَاجِمَاتٌ. (TA.)

عَجَمْجَمَةٌ applied to a she-camel, (AA, Ṣ, Ḳ,) *Strong;* like عَثَمْثَمَةٌ: (AA, Ṣ:) or *strong to journey;* as also ▼ عَجُومَةٌ (Ḳ, TA) and ▼ عَجُومٌ: (TA:) pl. of the first عَجَمْجَمَاتٌ. (AA, Ṣ.)

أَعْجَمُ One *having an impotence*, or *an impediment*, or *a difficulty, in speech*, or *utterance*, (Ṣ, Mṣb,) though he may be clear, perspicuous, distinct, chaste, or correct, in speaking a foreign language; (Ṣ;) and [*barbarous*, or *vitious therein;* i. e.] *not clear, perspicuous, distinct, chaste*, or *correct, therein;* (Ṣ, Mgh, Mṣb, Ḳ;) meaning, *in speaking Arabic*, (Ṣ, Mgh, Mṣb,* Ḳ,*) though he may be an Arab; (Ṣ, Mgh, Mṣb;) and ▼ أَعْجَمِىٌّ signifies the same, (Mgh, Mṣb, Ḳ,) and therefore, if applied to an Arab, it does not imply reproach; (Mṣb; [but it is said in the Mgh that this demands consideration;]) or this latter epithet is applied to a tongue, or speech, and to a book, or writing, but not to a man unless it be syn. with the former epithet: (Ṣ:) the fem. of the former is عَجْمَآءُ: (Ṣ, Mgh, Mṣb:) and the dual masc. أَعْجَمَانِ (Ṣ) and fem. عَجْمَاوَانِ; (Ḥar p. 226;) and the pl. masc. أَعْجَمُونَ (Ṣ, Mṣb, TA) and أَعَاجِمُ (Ṣ, TA) and عُجْمَانٌ: (TA:) and the pl. of ▼ أَعْجَمِىٌّ is أَعْجَمِيُّونَ. (Mṣb.) See also عَجَمٌ, first sentence, in two places. ― Also *Dumb; speechless; destitute of the faculty of speech;* (Ḳ, TA;) *unable to speak;* and so ▼ مُسْتَعْجِمٌ: (Ṣ, TA:) fem. of the former as above. (TA.) ― Hence, (Ṣ,) by predominance of its application, (Mgh,) عَجْمَآءُ signifies *A beast*, or *brute;* syn. بَهِيمَةٌ; (Ṣ, Mgh, Ḳ;) and so ▼ مُسْتَعْجِمٌ [or the fem. of this]: (TA:) pl. of the former in this sense, as a subst., عَجْمَاوَاتٌ: (Ḥar p. 13:) [and] عَجْمَآءُ is applied [also] as an epithet to a beast, or brute, (بهيمة,) for the like reason. (Mṣb.) It is said in a trad., جُرْحُ العَجْمَآءِ جُبَارٌ [expl. in art. جبر]. (Ṣ, Mgh.) ― [Hence also] فَحْلٌ أَعْجَمُ signifies *A stallion* [*camel*] *that brays in a* شِقْشِقَة [or *faucial bag*] *to which there is no perforation, so that the sound does not issue from it:* and they approve of the sending such among the شَوْل [or she-camels that have passed seven or eight months since the period of their bringing forth] because he usually begets females. (TA.) ― ‡ The *prayer of the daytime* is termed عَجْمَآءُ because the reciting [of the Ḳur-án] therein is inaudible; (Ṣ, Mgh, Mṣb, Ḳ, TA;) i. e. the *prayer of noon* and *of afternoon;* (TA;) and these two together are termed العَجْمَاوَانِ. (Ḥar p. 226.) ― مَوْجٌ أَعْجَمُ means ‡ *Waves that do not sprinkle their water, and of which no sound is heard.* (Ṣ, Ḳ.) ― And عَجْمَآءُ [or رَمْلَةٌ عَجْمَآءُ?] † *A tract of sand in which are no trees.* (IAạr, Ḳ.)

أَعْجَمِىٌّ: see the next preceding paragraph, first sentence, in two places. [It is often improperly used for عَجَمِىٌّ.]

أَعْجَمِيَّةٌ [*A barbarous*, or *vitious, speech* or *language*]. (TA in art. رطن.)

صُلْبُ المَعْجَمِ [lit. *Hard in respect of the place of biting*, or *of chewing.* And hence,] applied to a man, (Ṣ, Ḳ, TA,) as also ▼ صُلْبُ المَعْجَمَةِ, (TA,) ‡ *Mighty, strong, resisting*, or *indomitable, in respect of spirit;* (Ṣ, Ḳ, TA;) *such as, when tried by affairs*, or *events, is found to be mighty, strong*, or *resisting*, and *hard*, or *hardy.* (TA.) And ▼ نَاقَةٌ ذَاتُ مَعْجَمَةٍ ‡ *A she-camel having strength*, or *power, and fatness, and endurance of journeying:* (Ṣ, Ḳ, TA:) or *having patience, and soundness, and strength for treading* the way *with vehemence:* [for الدعك the last word of this explanation in my original, (evidently, I think, a mistranscription,) I read الدَّعْق:] Sh disapproves of the saying *having fatness:* accord. to IB, the phrase signifies *a she-camel such as, when tried, is found to have strength for traversing the desert*, or *waterless desert;* and he says that it does not mean *in which is fatness.* (TA.)

مُعْجَمٌ [pass. part. n. of 4: and also an inf. n. of that verb]. حُرُوفُ المُعْجَمِ, an appellation of *The letters of the alphabet* (الحُرُوفُ المُقَطَّعَةُ) [*of the language of the Arabs*], most of which are distinguished by being dotted from the letters of other peoples, means حُرُوفُ الخَطِّ المُعْجَمِ [*the letters of the dotted character*]: (Ṣ:) or by المُعْجَم is meant الإِعْجَامُ, it being an inf. n., like المُدْخَل (Ṣ, Ḳ) and المُخْرَج, (Ṣ,) so that the meaning of حُرُوفُ المُعْجَمِ is [*the letters*] *of which a property is the being dotted:* (Ṣ, Ḳ:) of which explanations, the latter is held by Mbr and IB and others to be the more correct. (L, TA.) — Also, applied to a door, *Locked.* (Ṣ, Ḳ.)

مُعْجَمَةٌ: see مُعْجَمٌ, in two places.

مُعَجَّمٌ [applied to a plant, or herbage, *Much bitten;* or] *eaten* [or *depastured*] *until but little thereof has remained.* (IAạr, TA.)

مُسْتَعْجِمٌ: see أَعْجَمُ, in two places.

عجن

1. عَجَنَهُ, aor. ـُ and ـِ, [inf. n. عَجْنٌ,] *He kneaded it;* i. e. *he bore upon it with his fist,* or *clinched hand, pressing it;* as also ▾ اعتجنهُ: (Ḳ:) or عَجَنَتْ, (Ṣ, TA,) or عَجَنَتْ عَجِينًا, (Mṣb,) aor. ـِ, (Mṣb, TA, and so in copies of the Ṣ,) or ـُ, (so in a copy of the Ṣ,) inf. n. عَجْنٌ, *she* (a woman) *made,* or *prepared,* [or *kneaded,*] عَجِين [i. e. *dough*]; (Ṣ, Mṣb, TA;) as also ▾ اعتجنت, (Ṣ, TA,) or اعتجنت ▾ عَجِينًا. (Mṣb.) إِنَّ فُلَانًا لَيَعْجِنُ بِمِرْفَقَيْهِ حُمْقًا [*Verily such a one kneads with his two elbows by reason of stupidity*] is a saying mentioned by Lth. (TA.) — And عَجَنَ, said of a man, *He rose bearing upon the ground* (IF, Ṣ, Mṣb, Ḳ, TA) *with his fist,* or *clinched hand,* (TA,) *as though he were kneading* (كَأَنَّهُ يَعْجِنُ), (IF, Mṣb,) by reason of age (IF, Ṣ, Mṣb, Ḳ, TA) or fatness. (TA.) It is said in a trad., of Ibn-'Omar, كَانَ يَعْجِنُ فِى الصَّلٰوةِ i. e. *He used to bear upon his two hands when he rose in prayer, like as does he who kneads dough:* and he said that he had seen the Apostle of God do so. (TA.) And one says of an old man, عَجَنَ وَخَبَزَ, which is expl. in the A as meaning † *He became old,* or *aged;* because such, when he desires to rise, bears upon the outer sides of the fingers of his two hands like the kneader, and upon his two palms like the maker of bread. (TA.) [See also 4, first sentence.] — And عَجَنَ عَلَى العَصَا, aor. ـِ, inf. n. عَجْنٌ, *He* (a man) *bore,* or *stayed himself, upon the staff.* (Mṣb.) — And عَجَنَتْ, (Ṣ, Ḳ,) aor. and inf. n. as above, (TA,) *She* (a camel) *beat the ground with her fore feet in her going along.* (Ṣ, Ḳ.) And one says of a horse or other animal, يَعْجِنُ بِرِجْلَيْهِ [*He beats the ground with his hind feet*]. (Ṣ and Ḳ in art. قمص.) ═ عَجَنَهُ, (Ḳ,) inf. n. as above, (TA,) also signifies *He struck his* عِجَان, [q. v.]. (Ḳ.) ═ عَجِنَتْ, aor. ـَ, (Ṣ, Ḳ, TA,) inf. n. عَجَنٌ, (Ṣ, TA,) said of a she-camel, (Ṣ, Ḳ, TA,) [app. signifies *She was,* or *became, such as is termed* عَجِنَةٌ *or* عَجْنَآءُ *in any of the senses assigned to these epithets:* or] *she was,* or *became, fat:* (Ṣ:) or *she had much flesh in the udder, with little milk:* (TA:) or *she had in her vulva a tumour* (Ḳ, TA) *like a wart, and resembling what is termed* عَفَل, (TA,) *preventing conception,* (Ḳ, TA,) *and sometimes reaching to the anus.* (TA.) [See also the next paragraph.]

4. اعجن *He* (A man) *was,* or *became, advanced in age.* (TA.) [See also عَجَنَ وَخَبَزَ, above.] ═ And *He rode a fat she-camel.* (Ḳ,* TA.) ═ And *He had a tumour in his* عِجَان [q. v.]. (Ḳ.) [See also 1, last signification.] ═ And *He begot a stupid child, such as is termed* عَجِينَة. (TA.)

[7. انعجن *It* (dough) *became kneaded:* so accord. to Freytag; but he has not named any authority for this.]

8: see 1, first sentence, in three places.

عَجَنٌ *A tumour incident to a she-camel, between her vulva and her anus, which sometimes in consequence thereof become conjoined.* (Ṣ.) [See also عَجِنَتْ (of which it is the inf. n.), last signification.]

عَجِنٌ (Ṣ, Ḳ) and ▾ مُتَعَجِّنٌ (Ḳ) A camel *compact,* or *firm, by reason of fatness;* (Ṣ, Ḳ, TA;) *as though consisting of flesh without bone.* (TA.) — For the fem. of the former, with ة, see أَعْجَنُ, in two places.

عِجَانٌ [The *perinæum;* i. e.] *what is between the anus and the scrotum:* (Ṣ, Mṣb:) or the [*portion of the*] قَضِيب [or *virga*] *that is extended from the scrotum to the anus;* (Ḳ;) or *the hinder portion of the penis, extended within the skin:* and that of a woman is the وَتَرَة [or *intervening part,* perhaps so called as being likened to the partition between the nostrils,] *that is between the vulva and the anus:* (TA:) and the اِسْت [or *anus* itself]: (Ḳ:) [see also عَضْرَطٌ:] pl. [of pauc.] أَعْجِنَة and [of mult.] عُجُنٌ. (TA.) اِبْنُ حَمْرَآءِ العِجَانِ is an appellation used in reviling, applied to one who is not an Arab; (TA in this art.;) or meaning *Son of the female slave.* (TA in art. حمر.) — Also The *neck,* (Ḳ, TA,) in the dial. of El-Yemen: or, as in the "Nawádir" of El-Ḳálee, the *part beneath the chin.* (Ḳ.)

عَجِينٌ *Kneaded;* i. e. *borne upon with the fist,* or *clinched hand, and so pressed;* as also ▾ مَعْجُونٌ. (Ḳ.) — [Also, as a subst. mentioned in the Ṣ and Mṣb &c. as well known,] *Dough; flour kneaded with water.* (MA, KL, &c.) — And *A catamite;* as also ▾ عَجِينَة: (IAạr, Ḳ:*) pl. عُجُنٌ: or this means *soft,* or *yielding, persons, of men* and *of women:* (IAạr, Ḳ:) and عَجِينٌ and ▾ عَجِينَة are both applied to a man, but only the latter is applied to a woman: applied to a man, meaning *weak in his body and in his intellect:* (IAạr, TA:) and ▾ عَجِينَة as a masculine epithet signifies, (Ḳ, TA,) accord. to Lth, (TA,) *stupid,* or *foolish;* (Ḳ, TA;) as also ▾ عَجَّانٌ. (Lth, Ṣ, Ḳ.)

عَجِينَةٌ: see the next preceding paragraph, in three places. ═ Also *A company, an assembly,* or *an assemblage;* syn. جَمَاعَةٌ; as also ▾ مُتَعَجِّنَةٌ [written by Freytag تَعْجِنَة]: or *such as is numerous.* (Ḳ.) ═ أُمُّ عَجِينَةَ is an appellation of *The* رَخَمَة [or *female of the vultur percnopterus*]. (Ḳ, TA.)

عَاجِنٌ [act. part. n. of عَجَنَ: as such signifying *Kneading.* — And hence, as such, signifying also] *Bearing with his hands upon the ground when rising,* by reason of age [or fatness: see 1]: (Ṣ, Mṣb:) pl. عُجُنٌ, with two ḍammehs: so in the T. (Mṣb.) — And, [without ة,] applied to a she-camel, [and in a similar sense applied to a horse or other animal, (see 1,)] *Beating the ground with her fore feet in her going along.* (Ṣ, TA.) — And also, applied to a she-camel, *In whose womb the young will not rest,* or *remain.* (Ḳ.)

عَاجِنَةٌ The *middle* of a place. (Ḳ.)

عَجَّانٌ: see عَجِينٌ.

أَعْجَنُ, applied to an udder, The *most scant of udders in milk and the goodliest thereof in appearance.* (TA.) — And [the fem.] عَجْنَآءُ, applied to a she-camel, (Ṣ,) *Fat;* (Ṣ, Ḳ;) as also ▾ عَجِنَةٌ: (Ṣ:) and, so applied, *that has attained the utmost degree in fatness;* and so ▾ مُتَعَجِّنَةٌ: and one *having little milk:* (Ḳ, TA:) or *having much flesh in the udder, with paucity of milk:* and sometimes, one *having much milk:* (TA:) and one *whose udder is pendulous,* (Ḳ, TA,) *by reason of the abundance of the flesh,* (TA,) *and whose teats cohere, and rise into the upper parts of the udder.* (Ḳ, TA.) — Also, i. e. عَجْنَآءُ, (Ṣ, Ḳ, TA,) and ▾ عَجِنَةٌ, (Ḳ, TA,) applied to a she-camel, (Ṣ, Ḳ, TA,) *Having a tumour between her vulva and her anus, which sometimes in consequence thereof become conjoined:* (Ṣ:) or *having in her vulva a tumour,* (Ḳ, TA,) *like a wart, and resembling what is termed* عَفَل, (TA,) *preventing conception,* (Ḳ, TA,) *and sometimes reaching to the anus:* and likewise applied to a ewe and to a cow. (TA.)

مِعْجَنٌ A [*bowl of the kind called*] جَفْنَة [*probably used for kneading dough therein*]. (Fr and IAạr, in TA, voce قَعْر.)

مَعْجُونٌ: see عَجِينٌ. — [Also, as a subst., *An electuary; any drug,* or *drugs, mixed up with honey* or *inspissated juice* or *sirup;* generally applied to *such as contains opium,* or *some other intoxicating ingredient:* pl. مَعَاجِينُ.]

مُتَعَجِّنٌ: see عَجِنٌ: and أَعْجَنُ: ═ and see also عَجِينَةٌ.

عجو and عجى

عَجْوَةٌ (Ṣ, Ḳ, &c.) and ▾ عَجَاوَةٌ and ▾ عَجَايَةٌ, or ▾ عُجَاوَةٌ and ▾ عُجَايَةٌ, (accord. to different copies of the Ḳ, [but in the TA these two words are expl. only as in another paragraph which will be found below,]) *A sort of dates in El-Medeeneh,* (Ṣ, Ḳ,) *of the best kind, the palm-tree of which is called* لِينَةٌ; (Ṣ; [or, accord. to Fr and Akh, cited in the TA in art. لون, the term لِينَةٌ is applied to a palm-tree but not to that of the عَجْوَة;]) *said to be from what was planted by the hand of the Prophet;* accord. to IAth, they are *larger than the* صَيْحَانِىّ [q. v.], *inclining to blackness;* but accord. to Az, *the* عَجْوَة *in El-Medeeneh are the* صَيْحَانِيَّة, *and there are sorts of the* عجوة *there that have not the sweetness nor the odour nor the fulness of the* صيحانيّة: (TA:) or the *best of dates:* (Mgh:) and, *in El-Ḥijáz,* the *dates that are stuffed* (مُحْشَى) [or *pressed into a compact mass, while moist, in the receptacle of palm-leaves* or *skin,* as are the dates called عَجْوَة in the present day]; (Ḳ, TA;) they are *termed* أُمُّ التَّمْرِ [lit. *the mother of dates,* app. because many persons keep a stock thereof], *to which recourse is had, like the* [*dates called*] شِهْرِيز *in El-Baṣrah.* (TA.)

عُجَاوَةٌ, or عُجَاوَةٌ, and عَجَايَةٌ: see the preceding paragraph: — and for the second, see also the paragraph here following, in two places.

العُجَايَةُ and ▼ العُجَاوَةُ are two dial. vars., each signifying *A piece of the size of a gobbet of flesh, conjoined with a sinew* (عَصَبَة) *which descends from the knee of the camel to the foot:* (Aṣ, Ṣ, TA:) or the عُجَايَتَانِ are *two sinews* (عَصَبَتَانِ) *in the interior of the fore legs of the horse, in the lower parts of which are things resembling nails* (أَظْفَار), *called* السُّعْدَانَات: and عُجَايَةٌ is a term applied to *all sinews* (عَصَب) *that conjoin with the solid hoof:* (Ṣ, TA:) or it signifies *certain sinews* (عَصَب) *in which are set ossicles resembling the gems that are set in signet-rings, at the pastern of the horse, or similar beast;* (Ḳ, TA;) when one is hungry, he bruises them between two stones, and eats them; and ▼ عُجَاوَةٌ is a dial. var. thereof: (TA:) or *any sinew* (عَصَبَة) *in a fore leg* (يَد) or *in a hind leg* (رِجْل): or *a sinew* (عَصَبَة) *in the interior of the shank* (وَظِيف) *of the horse* and *of the bull:* (Ḳ, TA:) or, *in a horse,* the *sinew* (عَقَبَة) *extending lengthwise from the shank and ending at each of the pasterns; and in it is what is termed* الحطر [a mistranscription, correctly السَّطَر, which means a certain disease in the leg]: and *in a she-camel, a sinew* (عَقَبَة) *in the interior of her fore leg:* and also *in a horse, a piece of flesh like a small gobbet:* accord. to IAth, العُجَايَات signifies *the sinews* (أَعْصَاب) *of the legs of camels* and *of horses:* (TA:) pl. عُجِىٌّ (Ṣ, Ḳ) and عِجِىٌّ and عَجَايَا (Ḳ) and عُجَايَا and عُجَايَات. (TA.) — See also the first paragraph.

عد

1. عَدَّهُ, (Ṣ, A, O, Mṣb, &c.,) aor. ـُ, (O, Mṣb,) inf. n. عَدٌّ (Ṣ, O, Mṣb, Ḳ) and عِدَّةٌ and تَعْدَادٌ [which last has an intensive signification, and may also be regarded as an inf. n. of the verb next following]; and ▼ عَدَّدَهُ; (TA;) or this latter has an intensive signification; (Mṣb;) *He numbered, counted, reckoned,* or *computed, it:* (Ṣ, A, O, Mṣb, Ḳ:) [and ▼ اِعْتَدَّهُ sometimes signifies the same, as is shown by what here follows:] فَمَا لَكُمْ عَلَيْهِنَّ مِنْ عِدَّةٍ تَعْتَدُّونَهَا, in the Ḳur xxxiii. 48, means [*Then there shall not be for you, as incumbent on them, any* عِدَّة (q. v.)] *of which ye shall count the number* [of the days]: (Bḍ, Jel:) or the meaning is, *of which ye shall exact the accomplishment of the number* [of the days]: (Ksh, Bḍ:) and Lḥ has mentioned, as heard from the Arabs, عَدَدْتُ الدَّرَاهِمَ أَفْرَادًا and وِحَادًا [*I counted the dirhems by single pieces*], and ▼ أَعْدَدْتُ, also, followed by the same words; then adding, "I know not whether it [i. e. the latter] be from العَدَدُ or from العُدَّةُ" [i. e. whether the meaning be *I counted* or *I prepared* or *provided,* the latter of which is a well-known meaning]: his doubt indicates that أَعْدَدْتُ is a dial. var. of عَدَدْتُ; but [SM says] "I know it not." (TA.) عَدَّ is doubly trans.: you say عَدَدْتُ لَكَ المَالَ as well as عَدَدْتُكَ المَالَ [both meaning *I numbered, counted, reckoned,* or *computed, to thee the articles of property*]. (TA.) And you say, عُدَّ فِى قَوْمٍ *He was numbered,* or *reckoned, among a people,* or *party.* (Ṣ, Ḳ.) [And عَدَّ مَحَاسِنَهُ, and ▼ عَدَّدَهَا, inf. n. of the former عَدٌّ, and of either تَعْدَادٌ, *He enumerated,* or *recounted, his good qualities* or *actions:* a phrase of frequent occurrence.] — [Also *He counted,* or *reckoned,* as meaning *he accounted,* or *esteemed, him,* or *it,* good or bad &c.:] one says عَدَّهُ حَسَنًا *He counted, accounted, reckoned,* or *esteemed, him,* or *it, good,* or *goodly;* syn. اِسْتَحْسَنَهُ: (Ṣ in art. حسن, &c.:) and ▼ اعتدّ signifies the same as عَدَّ [in this sense]; whence the saying,

وَيَعْتَدُّهُ قَوْمٌ كَثِيرٌ تِجَارَةً

[*And many people count it,* or *reckon it, as merchandise*]. (Ḥar p. 127.)

2: see above, in two places. — عدّدهُ also signifies *He made it a provision against the casualties of fortune:* (Ṣ, O, Ḳ: see also 4:) so, accord. to Akh, in the Ḳur civ. 2: or, as some say, *he made it numerous:* (Ṣ, O:) or it may mean *he reckoned it* (Bḍ and Jel in civ. 2) *time after time.* (Bḍ.)

3. [عَادَّ بَعْضُهُمْ بَعْضًا, inf. n. مُعَادَّةٌ and عِدَادٌ, app. signifies *They enumerated,* or *recounted, their good qualities* or *actions, one to another:* for] يَوْمُ العِدَادِ is expl. by Sh as meaning يَوْمُ الفَخَارِ وَمُعَادَّةِ بَعْضِهِمْ بَعْضًا [i. e. *The day of vying,* or *contending for superiority, in glory,* or *excellence,* &c., and app. *of persons enumerating,* or *recounting, their good qualities* or *actions, one to another*]. (TA.) [See also عِدَادٌ.] — عَادَّهُمُ الشَّىْءَ *He shared with them equally in the thing:* and عَادَّ بَعْضُهُمْ بَعْضًا فِى الشَّىْءِ *They shared one with another in the thing;* i. e., in anything. (TA.) [Hence,] one says, عَادَّهُ فِى المِيرَاثِ [*He shared with him in the inheritance*]. (Ṣ.) — [The inf. n.] عِدَادٌ also signifies The *contributing equally,* or *clubbing, for the purchase of corn,* or *food, to eat:* and a people's *having money,* or *property, divided into lots,* or *portions, and distributed in shares among them:* syn. بِدَادٌ; (T and L in art. بد from IAạr, and O in the present art.;) and مُبَادَّةٌ. (T and L in art. بد from IAạr, and O and Ḳ in the present art.) [You say, عَادَّ القَوْمَ: see بَادَّ.] — عَادَّهُ, inf. n. مُعَادَّةٌ and عِدَادٌ, said of a malady, and of the pain of a venomous sting or bite, and of insanity, *It intermitted, and returned to him.* (TA.) It is said in a trad., (Ṣ, O,) مَا زَالَتْ أُكْلَةُ خَيْبَرَ تُعَادُّنِى (Ṣ, O, Ḳ) *The pain of the poison of the food of Kheyber which I ate has not ceased to return to me at certain periods.* (TA.) And one says, عَادَّتْهُ اللَّسْعَةُ *The pain of the venomous sting,* or *bite, returned to him with vehemence at the expiration of a year.* (Ṣ, O, Ḳ.)

4. أَعَدَّهُ, (Mṣb,) inf. n. إِعْدَادٌ, (Mṣb, TA,) with which ▼ اِعْتِدَادٌ and ▼ اِسْتِعْدَادٌ and ▼ تَعْدَادٌ [as inf. n. of 2] are syn., (TA,) *I made it ready, prepared it,* or *provided it.* (Mṣb, TA.*) One says, اعدّهُ لِأَمْرٍ كَذَا *He made it ready, prepared it,* or *provided it, for such an affair.* (Ṣ, O, K.*) And أَعْدَدْتُ لِلْأَمْرِ عُدَّتَهُ [*I made ready, prepared,* or *provided, for the affair, its proper apparatus*]. (TA.) Some say that أَعَدَّ is originally أَعْتَدَ; but others deny this. (L in art. عتد.) See also 1, former half. — أَعَدَّ is also intrans.: [but when it is used as such, نَفْسَهُ may be considered as understood after it:] see 10.

5. [تعدّد *It was,* or *became, numerous:* often used in this sense. — Hence, one says,] هُمْ يَتَعَدَّدُونَ عَلَى عَشَرَةِ آلَافٍ *They exceed in number ten thousand;* and ▼ يَتَعَادُّونَ signifies the same; (Ṣ, O, Ḳ;*) or the latter means *they participate, one with another,* in such generous qualities as may be shared. (TA.) — See also 10.

6. تعادّوا *They shared, one with another,* in a thing. (TA.) See also 5. [And see 3.]

7. انعدّ: see what next follows.

8. اعتدّ *It was,* or *became, numbered, counted, reckoned,* or *computed.* (Ṣ, O.) Many of the learned say that ▼ انعدّ should not be [thus] used as a quasi-pass. of عَدَّهُ: it is said to be vulgar, or bad. (MF.) — اعتدّهُ: see 1, first and last sentences. — One says also اعتدّ بِهِ (Ṣ, O, Mṣb) meaning *He included it in a numbering,* or *reckoning.* (Mṣb.) [And hence, *He made account of it; accounted it a matter of importance.* And لَا يُعْتَدُّ بِهِ *No account is made of it,* or *him; it,* or *he, is not reckoned,* or *esteemed, as of any account,* or *importance:* a phrase of frequent occurrence.] — [*He made it ready, prepared it,* or *provided it:*] see 4. — See also

8. إِعْتَدَّتْ, said of a woman, *She observed,* or *kept, the period of her* عِدَّة [q. v.]. (Ṣ, O.)

10. استعدّ, (Ṣ, O, Mṣb, Ḳ,) as also ↓ اعدّ and ↓ اعتدّ and ↓ تعدّد, the last, as well as the first, mentioned by Th, (TA,) *He made himself ready, prepared himself,* or *became in a state of preparation,* (Ṣ, O, Ḳ, TA,) لِلْأَمْرِ *for the affair;* (Ṣ, O, Ḳ,* TA;*) *he prepared,* or *provided, himself with proper,* or *necessary, apparatus,* or *implements,* or *the like.* (A'Obeyd, Mṣb, &c.) — All except the last are also trans.: see 4.

R. Q. 1. عَدْعَدَ, (IAạr, O, TA,) inf. n. عَدْعَدَةٌ, (IAạr, O, Ḳ, TA,) *He was quick,* (IAạr, TA,) or *he hastened,* and *was quick,* (O, Ḳ,) in walking, or going along, (IAạr, O, Ḳ, TA,) &c. (IAạr, TA.) — [And app. said of the sand-grouse (القَطَا) meaning *It uttered its cry:* see عَدْعَدَةٌ below.]

Q. Q. 2. تَمَعْدَدَ, in which, accord. to Sb, the م is a radical letter, because of the rarity of the measure تَفَعْلَلَ, but others contradict him, (Ṣ, Ḳ,*) *He assumed the dress, garb, habit,* or *external appearance, of the sons of Ma'add,* who was the son of 'Adnán, and who is called the Father of the Arabs [because through him all the descendants of Ismá'eel, or Ishmael, trace their ancestry], (Ṣ, O, Ḳ,) *imitating them in their coarseness therein:* (Ḳ:) or *he asserted himself to be related to them:* (Ṣ, O, Ḳ:) or *he spoke their language:* (TA:) or *he affected,* or *constrained himself, to endure with patience their mode of life:* (Ṣ, O, Ḳ:) or *he imitated their mode of life, which was coarse and rude; abstaining from ease and luxury, and from the garb of the foreigners:* (Ṣ, O:) and *he* (a boy) *attained to the prime of manhood, and became thick,* or *coarse.* (Ṣ, O, Ḳ.) 'Omar said, (Ṣ, O,) or not 'Omar, but the Prophet, (Ḳ,) اِخْشَوْشِنُوا وَتَمَعْدَدُوا, (Ṣ, O,* Ḳ,*) i. e. [*Lead ye a rough,* or *coarse, life, and*] *imitate the mode of life of the sons of Ma'add,* &c. (TA.) [See also art. معد.] — It is also used by the poet Maạn Ibn-Ows for تَبَاعَدَ [*He went,* or *withdrew himself, far away*]: (Ṣ, O:) it means thus, and *he went away into the country,* or *in the land.* (TA.)

عَدْ عَدْ *A cry by which the mule is chidden;* (AZ, O, Ḳ;) like عَدَسْ. (AZ, O.)

عُدٌّ and ↓ عُدَّةٌ *Pustules in the face:* (IJ, TA:) or *pustules that come forth in the faces of beautiful,* or *goodly, persons:* (O, Ḳ:) pl. of the former [and app. of the latter also, which is probably a n. un.,] أَعْدَادٌ. (Marg. note in a copy of the Ṣ.)

عِدٌّ *Multitude, muchness,* or *abundance,* (Ṣ, O, Ḳ,) in a thing. (Ḳ.) One says, إِنَّهُمْ لَذَوُو عِدٍّ وَقِبْصٍ (in one of my copies of the Ṣ and in the O لَذَوُو, and in the other of my copies of the Ṣ and in the O قِبْصٍ,) [*Verily they are many,* or *numerous*]. — [It is also an epithet, signifying] Water *having a continual increase;* (Ṣ, O, Ḳ;) *that does not cease;* as the water of a spring; (Ṣ, O, Mṣb, Ḳ;) and of a well: (Ṣ, O, Mṣb:) or *copious* water *of the earth:* or *spring*-water; rain-water being called كَرَعٌ: (TA:) or *old* water, *that does not become exhausted:* (IDrd, TA:) or an *old* well; (M, O, Ḳ;) said in the M [and O] to be from حَسَبٌ عِدٌّ: (TA: [but see this in what follows:]) or in the dial. of Temeem, *much* water; but in the dial. of Bekr Ibn-Wáïl, *little* water: (AO, TA:) or *well*-water, *whether little or much;* so accord. to a woman of Kiláb; opposed to that of the rain: accord. to Lth, *a place which men make,* or *prepare, wherein much water collects;* but Az says that this is a mistake: (TA:) pl. أَعْدَادٌ. (Ṣ, A, O.) — And حَسَبٌ عِدٌّ ‡ *Old nobility* or *the like:* (M, A, O:) accord. to IDrd, from عِدٌّ applied to old water that does not become exhausted. (TA. [This derivation is probably correct: but see above.]) — See also عَدِيدٌ. — And see the paragraph here following.

عُدَّةٌ *Apparatus, equipments* or *equipage, accoutrements, furniture, gear, tackle* or *tackling,* (Ṣ, O, L, Mṣb,) *that one has prepared for the casualties of fortune,* (Ṣ, O, L,) *consisting of property and weapons,* (Ṣ, O,) or *of property,* or *weapons,* or *other things,* (Mṣb,) or *of implements, instruments, tools,* or *the like, and of beasts:* (L:) accord. to some, formed from عَتَدَةٌ [q. v.]; but others deny this: (L in art. عتد:) pl. عُدَدٌ. (Mṣb.) One says, أَخَذَ لِلْأَمْرِ عُدَّتَهُ and عَتَادَهُ [*He took, for the affair, his apparatus,* &c.; or *he prepared,* or *provided, himself for the affair*]: both signify the same. (Ṣ, O.) — Also, (Ṣ, O,) and ↓ عُدٌّ, this latter of the dial. of Temeem, (A'Obeyd, Mṣb,) *A state of preparation.* (A'Obeyd, Ṣ, O, Mṣb.) One says, كُونُوا عَلَى عُدَّةٍ *Be ye in a state of preparation.* (Ṣ, O.) — See also عُدٌّ.

عِدَّةٌ an inf. n. of 1 [q. v.]. (TA.) — And *A number collected together; a number collectively.* (TA.) You say, رَأَيْتُ عِدَّةَ رِجَالٍ *I saw a number of men collected together.* (TA.) And أَنْفَذْتُ عِدَّةَ كُتُبٍ *I transmitted a number of letters together.* (Ṣ, Ḳ,* TA.) — عِدَّةُ المَرْأَةِ *The days of the menstruation of the woman,* (Ṣ, O, Mṣb, Ḳ, TA,) *which she numbers, when she has been divorced,* or *when her husband has died;* [*until the expiration of which she may not marry again;* the period being, in the case of a divorced woman, not pregnant, that of three menstruations]; or [in the case of a pregnant woman] *the days of her pregnancy;* or [in the case of a widow not pregnant] *four months and ten nights:* (TA:) or *the woman's waiting the prescribed time after divorce,* or *after the death of her husband, until she may marry again:* (Mṣb:) and *the days of the woman's mourning for a husband, and of abstaining from the wearing of ornaments &c.;* (Ḳ, TA;) whether it be a period of months or of menstruations, or the period completed by her giving birth to offspring in her womb, which she has conceived by her husband: (TA:) pl. عِدَدٌ. (Mṣb.) One says, اِنْقَضَتْ عِدَّتُهَا *Her* عِدَّة *ended,* (Ṣ, TA,) from the period of the death of her husband, or of his divorcing her. (TA.) — اِنْقَضَتْ عِدَّةُ الرَّجُلِ means *The man's term of life ended:* pl. عِدَدٌ. (TA.) — And one says, فُلَانٌ إِنَّمَا يَأْتِى أَهْلَهُ العِدَّةَ *Such a one comes to his wife,* or *family, only once in the month,* or *in the two months.* (O, L.) See also عِدَادٌ, in two places.

عَدَدٌ a subst. from عَدَّهُ "he numbered it;" as also ↓ عَدِيدٌ: (Ṣ, O, Ḳ:) [originally] What is *numbered, counted, reckoned,* or *computed:* (O, Mṣb, Ḳ: [in the CḲ, a و is inadvertently omitted after the explanation of this meaning:]) [and hence,] *a number;* (Mṣb;) and ↓ عَدِيدٌ is syn. therewith [in this sense, as will be seen in what follows]; (A;) *a quantity composed of units;* and therefore not [properly] applicable to one; but accord. to the grammarians, one belongs to the predicament of العَدَدُ because it is the root thereof, and because it implies quantity, for when it is said "How many hast thou?" it is as proper to answer "One" as it is to answer "Three" &c.: (Mṣb:) pl. أَعْدَادٌ. (TA.) ↓ مَا أَكْثَرَ عَدِيدَهُمْ means عَدَدَهُمْ [i. e. *How great is their number!*]. (A.) Zj says that عَدَدٌ is sometimes used in the sense of an inf. n.; as in the phrase in the Ḳur [xviii. 10], سِنِينَ عَدَدًا: but many say that it is in this instance used in its proper sense, meaning مَعْدُودَةً [i. e. *numbered*], and is made masc. because سِنِين is syn. with أَعْوَام. (Mṣb.) In the phrase وَأَحْصَى كُلَّ شَىْءٍ عَدَدًا, in the Ḳur [lxxii. last verse], it is used in its proper sense of مَعْدُودًا, and is put in the accus. case as a denotative of state; or it is used in this case as an inf. n. (IAth, O.) — It signifies also The *years of* a man's *life, which one numbers,* or *counts.* (IAạr, O, Ḳ. [In the CḲ, after the words وَالعَدَدُ المَعْدُودُ, a و should be inserted.]) Hence the phrase رَقَّ عَدَدُهُ *The years of his life, which he numbered, became few, the greater part having passed.* (IAạr, O.)

عُدَدٌ: see the next paragraph.

عِدَادٌ an inf. n. of 3 [q. v.]. (TA.) — يَوْمُ العِدَادِ [as expl. by Sh: see 3, first sentence. — Also] *The day of giving:* (Ṣ, O:) العَطَآءُ signifies العِدَادُ (Ṣ, O, Ḳ) in this phrase. (Ṣ, O.) — And *i. q.* يَوْمُ العَرْضِ [which generally means *The day of the last judgment*]. (TA.) — And one says, أَتَيْتُ فُلَانًا فِى يَوْمِ عِدَادٍ meaning *I came to such a one on a Friday* (يوم جُمُعَة), or *on a Minor Festival* (يوم فطر), or *on a Great Festival* (يوم أَضْحَى). (O, Ḳ,* TA.) — And لَقِيتُ فُلَانًا عِدَادَ الثُّرَيَّا القَمَرَ, (Ṣ, O, Ḳ,) or فِى عِدَادِ الثُّرَيَّا القَمَرَ, and ↓ عِدَّةِ نُزُولِ القَمَرِ الثُّرَيَّا, (TA,) meaning *I met such a one once in the month:* (Ṣ, O, Ḳ:) because the moon makes its abode in الثُّرَيَّا [the Pleiades, its third Mansion,] once in every month: (Ṣ, O:) IB [understood the meaning to be, *once in the year;* for he] asserts that, correctly, J should have said, because the moon is in conjunction with الثُّرَيَّا once in every year, and that is on the fifth day of [the Syrian month] Ádhár [corresponding to March O. S.], agreeably with what is said in a verse of Ibn-Ḥoláhil which will be found cited in what follows: but [this verse evidently relates to what was the case in its author's time; for it is well known that] the moon traverses the firmament once in every month, and is every night in a [different], Mansion, and it is therefore in [the Mansion of] الثُّرَيَّا once in every month. (L, TA.) [Accord. to some,] one says, لَا آتِيكَ إِلَّا عِدَادَ القَمَرِ الثُّرَيَّا, meaning *I will not come to thee save once in the year:* because the moon makes its abode in الثريّا but once in the year: (A:) and مَا يَأْتِينَا فُلَانٌ إِلَّا عِدَادَ الثُّرَيَّا القَمَرَ, and إِلَّا قِرَانَ القَمَرِ الثُّرَيَّا, meaning *Such a one comes not to us save once in the year:* and مَا أَلْقَاهُ إِلَّا عِدَادَ الثُّرَيَّا القَمَرَ, and عِدَّةَ ▾ الثُّرَيَّا القَمَرَ, and الَّا عِدَادَ الثُّرَيَّا مِنَ القَمَرِ, meaning *I do not meet him save once in the year:* (TA:) [but these explanations are probably founded upon a want of due consideration of a statement which here follows:] after citing this verse of Aseed, or Useyd, or Useiyid, [written in the TA اسيد;] Ibn-Ḥoláḥil, or Ibn-El-Ḥoláḥil, [thus differently written in different places,]

• إِذَا مَا قَارَنَ القَمَرُ الثُّرَيَّا •
• لِثَالِثَةٍ فَقَدْ ذَهَبَ الشِّتَآءُ •

[*When the moon is in conjunction with the Pleiades in a third* night, *then winter has departed*], AHeyth said, [as though what was the case at a particular period of a cycle were the case generally,] the moon is in conjunction with الثريّا only in a third night from the new moon, [meaning only once in the year in the third night,] and that is in the beginning of spring and the end of winter. (TA.) — And عِدَادٌ and ▾ عِدَدٌ, (Ṣ, O, Ḳ,) the latter a contraction of the former, used by poetic license, (Ṣ, O,) signify *A paroxysm of pain which a person stung or bitten by a venomous reptile suffers on the completion of a year from the day on which he was stung or bitten:* (Ṣ, O, Ḳ:*) *a paroxysm of pain occurring at a certain period:* (A:) *a paroxysm such as that of a tertian, or quartan, fever;* and *the pain of poison which kills at a certain period:* and the *regular period of the return* of a fever is called its عِدَاد. (TA.) One says, أَتَتْهُ اللَّسْعَةُ لِعِدَادٍ *The pain of the venomous sting, or bite, returned to him with vehemence at the expiration of a year.* (Ṣ, O,* Ḳ.) And بِهِ مَرَضٌ عِدَادٌ *He has a malady that intermits and returns.* (A.) And عِدَادُ السَّلِيمِ is said to signify *A period of seven days from that on which the person has received a venomous sting* or *bite:* when it has expired, his recovery is hoped for: as long as it has not expired, one says, هُوَ فِى عِدَادِهِ. (A, TA.) [See also 3.] — عِدَادٌ signifies also *The time of death.* (O, Ḳ.) — And *A day,* or *night, when the family of a person deceased assemble together to wail for him.* (ISk, TA.) — And *A touch of insanity* or *diabolical possession:* (Ṣ, O, Ḳ:) or *an affection resembling insanity* or *diabolical possession, that takes a man at certain times.* (As, TA.) One says, بِالرَّجُلِ عِدَادٌ *In the man is a touch of insanity* [&c.]. (Ṣ, O.) — And The *twanging* of a bow; (Ṣ, O, Ḳ;*) and so ▾ عَدِيدٌ. (O, Ḳ.) — See also the next paragraph, in five places: — and see عَدِيدَةٌ.

عَدِيدٌ: see عَدَدٌ, in three places. — Also *A man who introduces himself into a tribe, to be numbered,* or *reckoned, as belonging to it, but has no kindred in it:* (Mṣb:) or عَدِيدُ قَوْمٍ signifies *one who is numbered,* or *reckoned, among a people,* (Ḳ, TA,) *but is not with them* (معهم [app. a mistranscription for مِنْهُمْ *of them*]); as also ▾ عِدَادٌ. (TA.) One says, فُلَانٌ عَدِيدُ بَنِى فُلَانٍ, (Ṣ, Mgh, O, Mṣb,) and ▾ مِنْ عِدَادِهِمْ, (Mṣb,) *Such a one is numbered,* or *reckoned, among the sons of such a one.* (Ṣ, Mgh, O, Mṣb.) And عِدَادُهُ ▾ فِى بَنِى فُلَانٍ *He is numbered among the sons of such a one in the* دِيوَان [or *register of soldiers* or *pensioners*]. (Ṣ, O, Ḳ.) And فُلَانٌ فِى عِدَادِ ▾ أَهْلِ الخَيْرِ *Such a one is numbered,* or *reckoned, among the people of goodness,* or *of wealth.* (Ṣ, O.) — And *A like,* or *an equal;* [originally, *in number;*] (A, O, Ḳ;) as also ▾ عِدٌّ and ▾ عِدَادٌ: (IAạr, O, Ḳ:) pl. of the first عَدَائِدُ; and of the second and third أَعْدَادٌ. (TA.) One says, هٰذِهِ الدَّرَاهِمُ عَدِيدُ هٰذِهِ *These dirhems are equal to these.* (A,* TA.) And هُمْ عَدِيدُ الحَصَى وَالثَّرَى *They are equal in multitude,* or *quantity, to the pebbles and the moist earth;* (Ṣ,* O,* TA;) i. e. *they are innumerable.* (TA.) The saying of Aboo-Duwád, describing a mare,

• وَطِمِرَّةٍ كَهِرَاوَةِ الأَعْزَابِ لَيْسَ لَهَا عَدَائِدُ •

Th explains by saying that he likens her to the staff of the wayfarer, because of her being smooth, as though عدائد here meant *knots:* [so that, accord. to him, we should render the verse thus: *And compact in make,* or *swift and excellent, like the staff of those who go far away with their camels to pasture, having no knots:*] but Az says that the meaning is, [*like Hirâwet-el-Aạzáb* (a celebrated mare)], *having no equals.* (TA.) ═ See also عِدَادٌ, last sentence but one.

عَدِيدَةٌ *A lot, portion,* or *share:* (IAạr, O, Ḳ:) like غَدِيدَةٌ: (IAạr, O:) pl. عَدَائِدُ; (IAạr, O, TA;) with which ▾ عِدَادٌ is syn.: and عَدَائِدُ signifies also *property divided into shares;* and *an inheritance* [*so divided*]. (TA.) Lebeed says,

• تَطِيرُ عَدَائِدُ الأَشْرَاكِ شَفْعًا •
• وَوِتْرًا وَالزَّعَامَةُ لِلْغُلَامِ •

The portions of property and inheritance *of the sharers fly away* in the course of time, *two together and singly; but the lordship,* or *mastery, is still remaining for the boy:* (IAạr, TA:) or the poet means *those who share with him* [i. e. with the boy] (مَنْ يُعَادُّهُ) in the inheritance: or it (عدائد) is from عُدَّةُ المَالِ [i. e. what one prepares for a future time, of property]: (Ṣ, O:) for عدائد, in this verse, some read غَدَائِدُ. (L in art. غد [q. v.]) [See also زَعَامَةٌ.]

عِدَّانٌ and عَدَّانٌ The *time,* or *period,* of a thing; (IAạr, Ḳ, TA;) as in the phrase أَنَا عَلَى عَدَّانِ ذٰلِكَ *I was at the time,* or *period, of that;* (IAạr, TA;) and in the saying جِئْتُ عَلَى عَدَّانِ تَفْعَلُ ذٰلِكَ *I came at the time of thy doing that;* (TA;) and thus in the saying كَانَ ذٰلِكَ عَلَى عَدَّانِ فُلَانٍ *That was in the time of such a one:* (Ṣ, O:) or the *first, and best,* or *most excellent, part,* (Ḳ, TA,) and the *most,* (TA,) of a thing; (Ḳ, TA;) accord. to Az, from أَعَدَّهُ "he prepared it;" and so in the saying كَانَ ذٰلِكَ فِى عَدَّانِ شَبَابِهِ and مُلْكِهِ [*That was in the first and best and chief part of his young manhood* and *of his dominion*]. (TA.) [See also art. عدن.] ═ عِدَّانٌ as a contraction of عِتْدَانٌ: see عَتُودٌ, of which it is a pl.

عَدْعَدَةٌ inf. n. of عَدْعَدَ [q. v.]. (IAạr, O.) ═ And The *cry,* or *crying, of the sand-grouse* (القَطَا): (A'Obeyd, O, Ḳ:) app. onomatopoetic. (A'Obeyd, O.)

جَيْشٌ أَعَدُّ *An army in the most complete state of preparation,* or *equipment.* (TA, from a trad.)

مَعَدٌّ The *side* (ISd, TA) of a man and of a horse &c.: (L in art. معد [in which it is fully explained]:) المَعَدَّانِ signifies the *places of the two boards of the saddle* (Ṣ,* O,* A, Ḳ,* TA) *upon the two sides* of the horse. (A, TA.) One says, عَرِقَ مَعَدَّاهُ [*The parts of his sides beneath the two boards of the saddle sweated*]. (A, TA.)

اللِّبْسَةُ المَعَدِّيَّةُ *The mode of dress of the sons of Ma'add, which was coarse and rude.* (Ṣ, from a trad. [See Q. Q. 2.])

مَعْدُودٌ [meaning *Numbered, counted, reckoned,* or *computed,*] is applied to any number, little or large; but مَعْدُودَاتٌ more particularly denotes few; and so does every pl. formed by the addition of ا and ت, as دُرَيْهِمَاتٌ and حَمَامَاتٌ; though it is allowable to use such a pl. to denote muchness. (Zj, TA.) الأَيَّامُ المَعْدُودَاتُ signifies *The days called* أَيَّامُ التَّشْرِيقِ; (Ṣ, Mgh, O, Mṣb, Ḳ;) *the three days next after the day of the sacrifice* [which is the tenth of Dhu-l-Ḥijjeh]; thus called because they are few. (TA.) And one also says دَرَاهِمُ مَعْدُودَةٌ [lit. *Numbered,* or *counted, dirhems*] as meaning *a few dirhems.* (TA.)

المُعَيْدِىُّ is the dim. of المَعَدِّىُّ, (Ṣ, O, Ḳ,) meaning *He whose origin is referred to Ma'add,* (Ṣ, O, TA,) and is originally المُعَيْدِدِىُّ, then المُعَيْدِّىُّ, and then المُعَيْدِىُّ, (IDrst, TA,) thus pronounced without the teshdeed of the د because the double teshdeed, (IDrst, Ṣ, O, Ḳ, TA,) that of the د with that of the ى after it, (IDrst, TA,) is found difficult of pronunciation, (IDrst, Ṣ, O, Ḳ, TA,) combined with the ى that denotes the dim.: (Ṣ, O, Ḳ:) it is thus pronounced in the prov., أَنْ تَسْمَعَ بِالْمُعَيْدِىِّ خَيْرٌ مِنْ أَنْ تَرَاهُ [*Thy hearing of the Mo'eydee is better than thy seeing him*]: (Ks, Ṣ, O:) or تَسْمَعُ بالمعيدىّ خير من ان تراه, (Ḳ, TA,) which means the same, the ع

in تسمع being pronounced with ḍamm because أَنْ is suppressed before it; but some pronounce it with naṣb, regarding أَنْ as understood, though this is anomalous: (TA:) or تَسْمَعُ بِالْمُعَيْدِيِّ لَا أَنْ تَرَاهُ; as though meaning *hear thou of the Mo'eydee, but do not see him:* (ISk, Ṣ, O, Ḳ:) of which three variants, the second is that which is best known: so says A'Obeyd: (TA:) the prov. is applied to him who is of good repute, but whose outward appearance is contemned. (Ṣ, O, Ḳ, TA. [See also Freytag's Arab. Prov. i. 223.])

مُعْتَدٌّ بِهِ A thing *included in a numbering,* or *reckoning.* (Mṣb.) [And hence, A thing *of which account is made; that is accounted a matter of importance.* See the verb.]

مُسْتَعِدَّاتٌ is used in a verse of Ibn-Muḳbil as meaning The *legs* of a she-camel. (AA, TA voce أَطَامِيمُ, q. v.)

عدس

1. عَدَسَ فِى الأَرْضِ, (AA, Ṣ, O, Ḳ,) aor. ـِ, inf. n. عَدْسٌ (AA, O, Ḳ) and عَدَسَانٌ and عِدَاسٌ (Ibn-'Abbád, O, Ḳ) and عُدُوسٌ, (O, Ḳ,) *He went away* [or *journeyed*] *into,* or *in,* or *through, the country,* or *land.* (AA, Ṣ, O, Ḳ.) One says, عَدَسَتْ بِهِ الْمَنِيَّةُ (Ṣ, O) i. e. [*Death*] *took him away.* (O.) And El-Kumeyt says,

• أُكَلِّفُهَا هَوْلَ الظَّلَامِ وَلَمْ أَزَلْ •
• أَخَا اللَّيْلِ مَعْدُوسًا ♦ إِلَىَّ وَعَادِسَا ♦ •

or عَلَىَّ, as some relate it, (O, [and thus, instead of إِلَىَّ, in one of my copies of the Ṣ,]) meaning [*I constrain them* (referring to camels mentioned in a preceding verse) *to bear the terror of the darkness, and I cease not to be, as a nightfarer,*] *journeyed to* by night [*and journeying*]. (Ṣ, O.) [It is added in the Ṣ, as though to indicate another meaning, وَعَدَسَ لُغَةٌ فِى حَدَسَ; and in the O and Ḳ, وَالعَدْسُ الحَدْسُ; (in the O with أَيْضًا between these two inf. ns.;) but accord. to the TA, the meaning intended by this is, *The going away* into, or in, the country, or land: see, however, what here follows.] — العَدْسُ also signifies *The treading hard,* or *vehemently,* (شِدَّةُ الوَطْءِ, Ṣ, O, Ḳ, TA,) *upon the ground;* and so الحَدْسُ. (TA.) — And i. q. الكَدْحُ [app. as meaning *The working,* or *labouring;* or *toiling,* or *labouring hard*]; (Ṣ, O, Ḳ, TA;) as also الحَدْسُ. (TA.) — And, accord. to IḲṭṭ, عَدَسَ, said of a man, signifies قَوِىَ عَلَى الشَّرِّ [*He was strong to do evil,* or *mischief:* but I think it probable that the right explanation is, على السَّيْرِ or على السُّرَى, i. e. *to journey,* or *to journey by night:* see عَدُوسٌ]. (TA.) ═ عَدَسَ, aor. ـِ, (AA, O, Ḳ,) inf. n. عَدْسٌ, (TA,) also signifies *He served* [another]; syn. خَدَمَ. (AA, O, Ḳ.) — And عَدَسَ المَالَ, inf. n. عَدْسٌ, *He pastured the cattle,* or *camels* &c. (Ibn-'Abbád, O, Ḳ, TA.) And هُوَ يَعْدِسُ عَلَيْهِ *He pastures for him.* (Ibn-'Abbád, O.) ═ عَدَسَ بِهِ, (O, Ḳ,) and عَدَّسَهُ, (IḲṭṭ,* O,) *He said to him* (i. e. to a mule, O) عَدَسْ [q. v.]. (IḲṭṭ, O, Ḳ.) ═ عُدِسَ, *He had an eruption of the small pustule called* عَدَسَة [q. v.]. (Ḳ,* O,* TA.)

[3. عادس *He journeyed continually.* (Freytag, from the Deewán of Jereer.)]

عَدَسْ *A cry by which one chides a mule,* (IDrd, Ṣ, IḲṭṭ,* O, Ḳ,) *to urge him:* (IḲṭṭ:) sometimes, by poetic license, it is made decl.: (L, TA:) the vulgar say عد [app. عَدْ]. (TA.) — Hence, (TA,) sometimes, (Ṣ, O,) it is also used as a name for *The mule;* (Ṣ, O, Ḳ;) like as the ass is [sometimes] called سَأْ سَأْ, which is [originally] a cry whereby one chides an ass; and there are other instances of the same kind. (TA.)

عَدَسٌ [*Lentils;*] *a well-known grain;* (Ṣ, O, Ḳ;) also called عَلَسٌ and بُلْسُنٌ: (TA:) n. un. with ة. (O, Ḳ.) — عَدَسُ المَآءِ *A certain plant* [of which I have not found any description]. (See art. سادج, last sentence.)

عَدَسَةٌ *A small pustule,* (Lth, Ṣ,* O,* Ḳ,) *resembling the* عَدَسَة [commonly so called, i. e. the *single grain of lentil*], (Lth, TA,) *which comes forth* (Lth, O, Ḳ) *in the body* (Lth, Ḳ) *in a man,* (Ṣ, O,) *dispersedly, like the* طَاعُون [or *plague*], (Lth, TA,) *of which it is said to be a kind,* (Lth, O, TA,) *and kills,* (Lth, O, Ḳ,) or *sometimes kills,* (Ṣ,) or *generally kills,* (Lth, TA,) *few recovering from it:* (Lth, O:) it was feared by the tribe of Ḳureysh, as being transitive. (O.)

[عَدَسِيَّةٌ *A soup made by boiling yellow lentils in water, till nearly dissolved, and then adding red vinegar, coriander, and salt.* (Ibn-Jezleh, quoted, from Channing, by Greenhill, in his Transl. of Er-Rázee on Small-pox and Measles.) ═ It is now applied also to *Bats' dung;* which is used in medicine, administered internally; and also applied externally, mixed with vinegar, to tumours: so says Forskål in his Descr. Animalium, p. iii.: but he there states عدسيه to be an appellation of the *bat* itself.]

عَدُوسٌ, applied to a female, [and app. to a male also,] *Bold,* or *daring;* (Ibn-'Abbád, O, Ḳ, TA;) *strong to journey.* (TA.) And عَدُوسُ السُّرَى *Strong to journey* (Ṣ, O, Ḳ) *by night;* as a masc. epithet; (O, Ḳ;) and as a fem. epithet applied to the hyena: (Ṣ, O:) or عَدُوسُ اللَّيْلِ, as meaning *strong to journey by night,* is applied to a man and to a woman and to a camel. (TA.)

عَادِسٌ: see the verse cited in the first paragraph.

مَعْدُوسٌ: see the verse above mentioned. ═ Also *Having an eruption of the small pustule termed* عَدَسَة. (Ḳ,* O,* TA.)

عدف

1. عَدَفَ, aor. ـِ, inf. n. عَدْفٌ, *He ate.* (Ṣ, O, Ḳ.) In the dial. of Rabee'ah with ذ. (Ṣ, O, Ḳ,* in art. عذف.)

5. مَا تَعَدَّفْتُ اليَوْمَ *I have not tasted a little today, far less much.* (El-'Ozeyzee, O, Ḳ.) [See also 5 in art. عذف.]

عَدْفٌ: see عَدُوفٌ. — Also *A small quantity of fodder,* or *provender.* (L, Ḳ.) — And *A small gift.* (IF, O, Ḳ.) One says, أَصَبْنَا مِنْ مَالِهِ عَدْفًا [in the TA فِى مَالِهِ] i. e. [*We obtained from his property*] *a small gift.* (IF, O.)

عَدَفٌ: } see the paragraph here following.
عُدَافٌ: }

عَدُوفٌ *Anything that is tasted:* (Ṣ, O, Ḳ:) or the *least of what is eaten* and *of what is drunk:* (Ḥam p. 448:) pl. عُدُفٌ. (Ḳ, TA.) One says, مَا ذُقْنَا عَدُوفًا, (Ṣ, O,) or مَا ذُقْتُ عَدُوفًا, (Ḳ,) i. e. [*I,* or *we, have not tasted,* or *did not taste,*] *anything;* (Ṣ, O, Ḳ;) as also ♦ عَدُوفَةً, (O, Ḳ,) and ♦ عُدَافًا, and ♦ عَدْفًا, (Ṣ, O, Ḳ,) and ♦ عَدَفًا. (Ḳ.) And بَاتَتِ الدَّابَّةُ عَلَى غَيْرِ عَدُوفٍ i. e. [*The beast passed the night*] *without fodder,* or *provender.* (Ṣ, O, Ḳ.*) Of the dial. of Muḍar: (Ṣ:) or pronounced by Rabee'ah with ذ; and by the rest of the Arabs with د. (AA, O.)

عَدُوفَةٌ: see the next preceding paragraph.

عدل

1. عَدَلَ, (Ṣ, O, Mṣb, Ḳ,) aor. ـِ, (Mṣb, Ḳ,) inf. n. عَدْلٌ (Ṣ,* O,* Mṣb, Ḳ,* TA) and مَعْدِلَةٌ (Ṣ,* O,* Mṣb, Ḳ*) and مَعْدَلَةٌ (Ṣ,* Mṣb, Ḳ*) and عَدَالَةٌ and عُدُولَةٌ, (Ḳ,* TḲ,) *He acted equitably, justly,* or *rightly.* (Ṣ, O, Mṣb, Ḳ.) So in the phrase عَدَلَ فِى أَمْرِهِ, [*He acted equitably,* &c., *in his affair,*] inf. n. عَدْلٌ. (Mṣb.) And so in the phrase عَدَلَ عَلَيْهِ فِى القَضِيَّةِ [*He acted equitably,* &c., *towards him in the judgment*]: (Ṣ, O:) and عَدَلَ عَلَى القَوْمِ, [*he acted equitably,* &c., *towards the people,* or *party,*] inf. n. عَدْلٌ and مَعْدِلَةٌ and مَعْدَلَةٌ. (Mṣb.) وَلَنْ تَسْتَطِيعُوا أَنْ تَعْدِلُوا بَيْنَ النِّسَآءِ, [*Ye will not be able to act with* perfect *equity between women*], in the Ḳur [iv. 128], is said to mean, in respect of love, and of جِمَاع. (TA.) [See also عَدْلٌ below.] — وَإِنْ تَعْدِلْ كُلَّ عَدْلٍ, in the Ḳur [vi. 69], means *And if it would ransom with every* [degree of] *ransoming:* (T, Ṣ, O, Mṣb, TA:) AO used to say, *and if it would act equitably with every* [degree of] *equitable acting;* but Az says that this is a blunder. (TA.) [See, again, عَدْلٌ below.] — عَدَلَ [signifies also *He declined, deviated,* or *turned aside* or *away;* and particularly from the right course: thus having a meaning nearly agreeing with that assigned to عَدَلَ in the last sentence of this paragraph.] بَلْ هُمْ قَوْمٌ يَعْدِلُونَ, in the Ḳur [xxvii. 61], means [*Nay but they are a people*] *who decline,* or *deviate,* from the truth, and from the right course; i.e., who disbelieve. (O.) And one says, عَدَلَ عَنْهُ, aor. ـِ, inf. n. عَدْلٌ and [more com-

monly] عُدُولٌ, *He declined, deviated,* or *turned aside* or *away, from him,* or *it.* (Ḳ.) And عَدَلَ عَنِ الطَّرِيقِ, (Ṣ, O, Mṣb,) inf. n. عُدُولٌ, (Mṣb,) *He declined,* &c., *from the road,* or *way;* (Ṣ, O, Mṣb;) as also عَنْهُ ↓ انعدل. (Ṣ, O, Ḳ.*) And عَدَلَ الطَّرِيقُ *The road declined,* or *deflected.* (Ḳ.) And عَدَلَ الفَحْلُ عَنِ الإِبِلِ (Ṣ, O, Ḳ) (Ṣ, O) *The stallion left, left off,* or *desisted from, covering the she-camels;* (Ṣ, O, Ḳ;*) and so عَنِ الضِّرَابِ ↓ انعدل. (TA.) [عَدَلَ الفَحْلَ see in what follows.] And عَدَلَ إِلَيْهِ, inf. n. عُدُولٌ, *He returned to him,* or *it.* (Ḳ.) ═ عَدَّلَهُ: see 2, in two places. — عَدَلَ فُلَانًا بِفُلَانٍ *He made such a one to be equal,* or *like, to such a one;* (Ḳ;) [and] so به ↓ عادله: (Ṣ:) or, accord. to some, العَدْلُ signifies *the rating* a thing *as equal* to a thing of another kind *so as to make* it *like* the latter. (TA.) One says, عَدَلْتُ هٰذَا بِهٰذَا *I made this to be like* and *to stand in the stead of, this.* (Mṣb.) And عَدَلَ بِرَبِّهِ, (El-Aḥmar, TA,) aor. ـِ, (Ṣ, O, TA,) inf. n. عَدْلٌ and عُدُولٌ, [غَيْرَهُ being understood,] *He made another to be equal with his Lord, and worshipped him.* (El-Aḥmar, TA.) بِرَبِّهِمْ يَعْدِلُونَ, in the Ḳur [vi. 151, and accord. to some in vi. 1], means *Attributing a copartner,* or *copartners, to their Lord.* (O. [And the like is said in the Ṣ and Mṣb and TA.]) — عَدَلْتُ أَمْتِعَةَ البَيْتِ *I made the goods,* or *furniture, of the house,* or *tent, into equal loads,* [*so as to counterbalance one another,*] on the day of departure, or removal. (TA.) And بَيْنَ الشَّيْئَيْنِ ↓ عَادَلَ (Ṣ, O, TA) *He made an equiponderance to subsist between the two things.* (TA.) — فُلَانٌ يَعْدِلُ فُلَانًا *Such a one is equal to such a one.* (TA.) And يَعْدِلُهُ *He,* or *it, is like him,* or *it.* (Fr, Ṣ, O.) [Hence] one says, مَا يَعْدِلُكَ عِنْدَنَا شَيْءٌ *Nothing stands with us in thy stead.* (TA.) And عَدَلَهُ, aor. ـِ, (Ḳ,) inf. n. عَدْلٌ, (TA,) *It was,* or *became, equiponderant to it;* as also ↓ عادلهُ, (Ḳ,) inf. n. مُعَادَلَةٌ. (TA.) And [hence] عَدَلَهُ فِى المَحْمِلِ, (Ḳ,) and ↓ عادلهُ, (TA,) *He rode with him in the* [*vehicle called*] محمل [*so as to counterbalance him*]. (Ḳ, TA.) — And عَدَلَ, aor. ـِ, inf. n. عَدْلٌ, signifies also *He turned* a thing from its course, direction, or manner of being. (TA.) You say, عَدَلْتُ فُلَانًا عَنْ طَرِيقِهِ *I turned such a one from his road,* or *way.* (TA.) And لَا تُعْدَلُ سَارِحَتُكُمْ *Your pasturing cattle shall not be turned away, nor prevented, from pasturing.* (TA, from a trad.) And عَدَلَ الفَحْلَ عَنِ الضِّرَابِ (Ḳ, TA) (TA) *He removed the stallion,* or *made him to withdraw* [or *desist*], *from covering.* (Ḳ, TA.) And عَدَلْتُ الدَّابَّةَ إِلَى مَوْضِعِ كَذَا *I turned the beast to such a place.* (TA.) [See also two meanings assigned to this verb in the next paragraph, third sentence.] ═ عَدُلَ, [aor. ـُ,] inf. n. عَدَالَةٌ (Ṣ, O, Mṣb) and عُدُولَةٌ, (Mṣb,) *He* (a man, Ṣ, O, i. e. a witness, Mṣb) *was,* or *became, such as is termed* عَدْلٌ [q. v.]. (Ṣ, O, Mṣb.) ═ عَدَلَ, aor. ـِ, inf. n. عَدْلٌ, *He acted wrongfully, unjustly, injuriously,* or *tyrannically.* (Mṣb.)

2. عدّلهُ, inf. n. تَعْدِيلٌ, i. q. أَقَامَهُ, (Ḳ,) meaning *He made it to be conformable with that which is right;* (TḲ;) namely, a judgment, or judicial decision. (Ḳ, TḲ.) — *He made it straight,* or *even;* namely, a thing; as, for instance, an arrow; (TA;) *right,* or *in a right condition; direct,* or *rightly directed;* (Ṣ, O, Mṣb, Ḳ, TA;) and so ↓ عَدَلَهُ. (O, Ḳ.) Hence, فَعَدَّلَكَ and ↓ فَعَدَلَكَ, accord. to different readers, in the Ḳur [lxxxii. 7, which I would rather render *And hath made thee symmetrical*]: (O:) or the latter means *and hath turned thee from unbelief to belief;* (IAạr, O, TA;) or, accord. to Fr, *and hath turned thee to whatever form He pleased,* beautiful or ugly, tall or short: but Az says that the former reading was the more pleasing to Fr, and is the better. (TA.) — *He made it equal;* (Mgh, Mṣb, Ḳ, TA;) namely, a pair of scales, or a weight, (Ḳ, TA,) and a measure, &c. (TA.) Hence, قِسْمَةُ التَّعْدِيلِ i. e. *The division* of a thing [*in an equal manner*] *with regard to the value and utility, not with regard to the quantity, so that the smaller portion may be equal to the larger portion in value and utility.* (Mṣb.) You say, عَدَلَ القَسَّامُ الأَنْصِبَآءَ لِلْقَسْمِ بَيْنَ الشُّرَكَآءِ i. e. [*The divider of inheritances*] *made equal the shares* [*for distribution among the participators*]. (TA.) — عدّل الشِّعْرَ *He made the poetry,* or *verse, to be right in measure.* (TA.) — تَعْدِيلُ أَرْكَانِ الصَّلَاةِ means *The making the limbs,* or *members, to be still, in the bowing of the head and body, and in the prostration, and in the standing between these two acts, and in the sitting between the two prostrations.* (Mgh.) — عدّلهُ signifies also *He attributed to him* (i. e. a witness, Mṣb) *what is termed* عَدَالَة [inf. n. of عَدُلَ]; (O, Mṣb;) *described him as possessing that quality;* (Mṣb;) *pronounced him to be veracious,* and *good,* or *righteous;* (Ḳ;) *pronounced him to be such as is termed* عَدْل [q. v.]: (TA:) تَعْدِيلُ الشُّهُودِ is *the pronouncing the witnesses to be* عُدُول [pl. of عَدْل]. (Ṣ.) — عدّل أَمْرَهُ: and عَدَّلْتُ بَيْنَهُمَا: see 3. — شَرِبَ حَتَّى عَدَّلَ *He drank until he became full:* (Aboo-'Adnán, O, TA:) or *until his belly became like the* [*load called*] عِدْل. (Ḳ.)

3: see 1, in four places. One says, يُعَادِلُ فِى الوَزْنِ [*It is equal in weight; is equiponderant*]. (IF, Mṣb.) And يُعَادِلُكَ فِى الوَزْنِ وَالقَدْرِ [*He is equal to thee in weight and in size:* as one who rides with thee in a مَحْمِل]. (Ṣ.) يُعَادِلُهُ فِى القِيمَةِ وَالمَنْفَعَةِ [*It is equal to it in value and utility*]. (Mṣb.) — And عَادَلَهُمَا عَلَى نَاضِحٍ *He bound them two upon the two sides of a camel* [or *of a camel used for carrying water for irrigation, so that they counterbalanced each other*] *like the* [*two loads called*] عِدْلَانِ. (TA.) — And فُلَانٌ يُعَادِلُ أَمْرَهُ, and يُقَسِّمُهُ, (O, and so accord. to a copy of the Ṣ,) or يُقْسِمُهُ, (so in another copy of the Ṣ,) inf. n. عِدَالٌ, *Such a one wavers,* or *vacillates,* [*in his case*] *between two affairs, hesitating which of them he shall do.* (Ṣ, O.) And هُوَ يُعَادِلُ هٰذَا الأَمْرَ *He is in a state of entanglement in this affair, and does not execute it:* (Ḳ:) *he is in doubt respecting it.* (TA.) And عادل أَمْرَهُ *He paused* [*in his case*], *hesitating between two affairs, which he should do;* as also ↓ عدّلهُ inf. n. تَعْدِيلٌ: and hence, in the trad. of the مِعْرَاج [or ladder by which Moḥammad is related to have ascended from Jerusalem to Heaven], ↓ فَعَدَّلْتُ بَيْنَهُمَا [*And I paused in hesitation between them two*]; meaning that they were equal in his estimation, and he could not make choice of either of them. (TA.) And عَادَلْتُ بَيْنَ أَمْرَيْنِ أَيَّهُمَا آتِى *I wavered,* or *vacillated, between two affairs, hesitating which of them I should do.* (TA.) المُعَادَلَةُ is *The doubting* respecting two affairs: and one says, أَنَا فِى عِدَالٍ مِنْ هٰذَا الأَمْرِ *I am in doubt respecting this affair, whether I should do it or leave it undone:* (TA:) or العِدَالُ is *the considering deliberately respecting the case of two affairs that have occurred to one, when one knows not to which of them he should betake himself.* (IAạr, Ḳ.) And *The case of one person's saying "There is in it something remaining" and another's saying "There is not in it anything remaining."* (Ṣ, O.) And one says, when he wavers, or vacillates, between two affairs, hesitating which of them he shall do, and then a right opinion occurs to him, and he determines upon that which is the more fit in his estimation, قَطَعْتُ العِدَالَ فِى أَمْرِى وَمَضَيْتُ عَلَى عَزْمِى [*I cut short wavering in my affair, and executed my determination*]. (TA.) — And عادل signifies also *It became crooked,* or *bent.* (Ḳ.)

5. تعدّل *It became,* or *was rendered, straight,* or *even;* syn. تَقَوَّمَ. (Mṣb in art. قوم.) — And تَعَدَّلَتْ قِيمَةُ المَتَاعِ بِكَذَا *The value of the commodity was equal to such a thing;* syn. قَامَ المَتَاعُ بِكَذَا. (Mṣb in art. قوم.)

6. تَعَادُلٌ The *being,* or *becoming, equal.* (Mṣb.) You say, تَعَادَلَا [*They two became equal*]. (M and Ḳ voce تَبَاوَآ, q. v., in art. بوأ.) — [Also The *being,* or *becoming, intermediate in quality.*]

7: see 1, former half, in two places.

8. اعتدل *It was,* or *became, right,* or *in a right condition; direct,* or *rightly directed; straight,* or *even;* (Ṣ, O, Mṣb, TA;) *equal;* (as a pair of scales, or a weight, and a measure, &c.; TA;) *equable,* or *uniform;* (Mṣb, TA;) [*symmetrical, proportionate,*] *suitable in itself* [or *in its parts*]. (Ḳ.) The saying, cited by Sh,

* وَاعْتَدَلَتْ ذَاتُ السَّنَامِ الأَمْيَلِ *

means *And she that had an inclining hump became straight* [*and erect*] *in her hump* by reason of fatness. (TA.) And one says جَارِيَةٌ حَسَنَةُ الاِعْتِدَالِ *A girl,* or *young woman, goodly in respect of stature* [or *proportion*]. (A, TA.) And اعتدل الشِّعْرُ *The poetry,* or *verse, was,* or *became, measured, and right in its feet.* (TA.) — Also *It was,* or *became, of a middling sort, in quantity,* or *quality;* (Ḳ, TA;) as a body between tallness and shortness, and water between the hot and the cold; and [*moderate*, or *temperate*,] as a day of which the air is pleasant. (TA.)

عَدْلٌ *Equity, justice,* or *rectitude; contr. of* جَوْرٌ; (Ṣ, O, Mṣb, Ḳ, TA;) i. e. *i. q.* قَصْدٌ, in affairs; (Mṣb;) and قِسْطٌ; (Ṣ, M, Mgh, &c., in art. قسط;) and سَوِيَّةٌ; (O, Ḳ;) and اِسْتِقَامَةٌ; (IAạr, Ḳ;) and *a thing that is established in the minds as being right;* (Ḳ, TA;) as also ▼ مَعْدِلَةٌ (Ṣ, O, Mṣb, Ḳ) and ▼ مَعْدَلَةٌ (Ṣ, Mṣb, Ḳ) and ▼ عَدَالَةٌ and ▼ عُدُولَةٌ: (Ḳ:) or, as some say, it is the *mean between excess and falling short:* and Er-Rághib says, it is of two sorts: one is *absolute, such that reason requires the inference of its goodness;* and this will not at any time be abrogated, nor described as a mode of transgression; as the doing good to him who does good to thee, and the abstaining from harming him who abstains from harming thee: and the other is *such as is known to be* عَدْل *by the law;* and this may be abrogated sometimes; as retaliation, and fines for wounds and maimings, and the taking the property of the apostate; and this is what is meant by the saying in the Ḳur [xvi. 92], إِنَّ ٱللّٰهَ يَأْمُرُ بِٱلْعَدْلِ وَٱلْإِحْسَانِ i. e. [*Verily God commandeth*] *equality in recompensing, if good, with good, and if evil, with evil, and the requiting of good with more good, and of evil with less evil:* [see also 4 in art. حسن:] and he says of عَدَالَةٌ and ▼ مَعْدِلَةٌ, that each is a term requiring the inference of equality, and is used with a regard to correlation. (TA.) One says, بَسَطَ الوَالِى عَدْلَهُ and ▼ مَعْدِلَتَهُ (Ṣ, O) and ▼ مَعْدَلَتَهُ (Ṣ) [*The governor,* or *ruler, largely extended his equity,* or *justice*]. And ▼ فُلَانٌ مِنْ أَهْلِ المَعْدَلَةِ, (Ṣ,) or ▼ المَعْدِلَةِ, (O,) i. e. من اهل العَدْلِ [*Such a one is of the people of equity, &c.*]. (Ṣ, O.) وَأَشْهِدُوا ذَوَىْ عَدْلٍ مِنْكُمْ, in the Ḳur [lxv. 2], is said by Sa'eed Ibn-El-Museiyib to mean ذَوَىْ عَقْلٍ [i. e. *And make ye to be witnesses two persons of intelligence from among you:* but this rendering I think questionable]. (TA.) —— Also *Repayment, requital, compensation,* or *recompense.* (Ḳ.) —— And *Ransom,* (Ṣ, O, Mṣb, Ḳ, TA,) *when regard is had therein to the meaning of equality,* or *equivalence.* (TA.) This is [said to be] the meaning in the phrase of the Ḳur [v. 96], أَوْ عَدْلُ ذٰلِكَ صِيَامًا [*Or the ransom thereof by fasting:* but this is generally expl. as meaning *or the like thereof of fasting;* (see عِدْلٌ;) i. e., in lieu of feeding a number of poor men, one shall fast the like number of days]. (Ṣ, O.) And so [accord. to some] in the saying, occurring in a trad., لَا يُقْبَلُ مِنْهُ صَرْفٌ وَلَا عَدْلٌ [of which see various explanations (including three renderings here following) in art. صرف]. (O, Mṣb.) —— And *Measure;* syn. كَيْلٌ. (Ḳ.) So in the phrase أَعْطَاهُ بِالعَدْلِ [*He gave him by measure*]. (TḲ.) —— And *An obligatory act* or *divine ordinance.* (En-Naḍr, O, Ḳ.) —— And *A supererogatory act.* (O, Ḳ.) ═ Also One *who acts equitably, justly,* or *rightly;* and so ▼ عَادِلٌ: (Ḳ, TA:) or the latter signifies thus: (Ṣ, O:) and the former [particularly] signifies a man *approved and satisfactory in testimony;* originally an inf. n.; (Ṣ, O, TA;) *whose testimony is approved and available;* (Mṣb;) a man *whose testimony is allowable,* or *legally admissible,* as also ▼ عَادِلٌ; a man *whose saying, and whose judgment,* or *judicial decision, are approved;* and, accord. to Ibráheem, one *from whom a thing occasioning doubt,* or *suspicion,* or *evil opinion, has not appeared:* being originally an inf. n., it means ذُو عَدْلٍ: or, accord. to IJ, it is an intensive epithet, as though meaning *possessing every kind of* عَدْل: (TA:) one says رَجُلٌ عَدْلٌ, (Ṣ, O, Mṣb,* Ḳ,) and اِمْرَأَةٌ عَدْلٌ and عَدْلَةٌ, (Mṣb, Ḳ,) the latter mentioned by IJ, (TA,) and رَجُلَانِ عَدْلٌ and عَدْلَانِ, (Mṣb,* TA,) and نِسْوَةٌ عَدْلٌ (TA) and قَوْمٌ عَدْلٌ (Ṣ, O, Mṣb,* Ḳ) and قَوْمٌ عُدُولٌ, (Ṣ, O, Mṣb,* Ḳ,) عُدُولٌ being pl. of عَدْلٌ, (Ṣ, O, Mṣb,) or of عَادِلٌ, (Ḳ,) and عَدْلٌ used in a pl. sense being a quasi-pl. n. of عَادِلٌ, (M, Ḳ,) like تَجْرٌ [of تَاجِرٌ] and شَرْبٌ [of شَارِبٌ]; (M, TA;) or رِجَالٌ عَدْلٌ and نِسْوَةٌ عَدْلٌ mean رِجَالٌ ذَوُو عَدْلٍ and نِسْوَانٌ ذَوَاتُ عَدْلٍ. (TA.) —— العَدْلُ as one of the names of God means *He whom desire does not cause to incline,* or *decline, so that he should deviate from the right course in judgment.* (TA.) —— And one says, هٰذَا عَدْلٌ بَيْنَهُمَا, meaning *This is intermediate in quality between them two, not in the utmost degree of goodness nor in the extreme degree of badness.* (Mgh.) And مَكَانٌ عَدْلٌ بَيْنَ فَرِيقَيْنِ [*A place equidistant,* or *midway, between two parties*]. (Ṣ in art. سوى.) —— See also عِدْلٌ, throughout the greater part of the paragraph. ═ عَدْلٌ is also the name of a certain chief of the [body of armed men called] شُرَط, (Ṣ, O,) or شُرْطَة, (Ḳ,) of a تُبَّع [or King of El-Yemen], who, when he desired the slaughter of a man, delivered him to this person; (Ṣ, O, Ḳ;) whereupon the people said, وُضِعَ عَلَى يَدَىْ عَدْلٍ [*He has been consigned to the hands of 'Adl*]; (Ṣ, O;) and this was afterwards said of anything of which one despaired. (Ṣ, O, Ḳ.) [Meyd mentions عَلَى يَدَىْ عَدْلٍ, as a prov., without وُضِعَ: see Freytag's Arab. Prov. ii. 80.]

عِدْلٌ The *like* (IAạr, Zj, O, Ḳ) of a thing; (IAạr, O;) as also ▼ عَدْلٌ; syn. مِثْلٌ; (IAạr, Zj, O, Ḳ;) and نَظِيرٌ [which signifies the same, or the *equal*]; and so ▼ عَدِيلٌ: (Ḳ:) or, accord. to Er-Rághib, ▼ عَدْلٌ and عِدْلٌ are nearly the same; but the former is used in relation to what is perceived mentally, as in the phrase of the Ḳur [v. 96], أَوْ عَدْلُ ذٰلِكَ صِيَامًا [mentioned voce عَدْلٌ]; and عِدْلٌ and ▼ عَدِيلٌ, in relation to what is perceived by the sense, as things weighed and things numbered and things measured: Ibn-'Ámir, however, read او عِدْلُ ذلك; and Ks and the people of El-Medeeneh, with fet-ḥ [i. e. عَدْلُ]: (TA:) or عِدْلُ الشَّىْءِ, with kesr, signifies *the like of the thing in kind,* (Mgh, Mṣb,) or *in quantity,* or *measure,* or *the like,* (Mṣb,) or also *in quantity,* or *measure,* or *the like,* (Mgh,) and IF says, *in weight;* (Mṣb;) and ▼ عَدْلُهُ, with fet-ḥ, (Mgh, Mṣb,) *its like,* (Mgh,) or *what will stand in its stead,* (Mṣb,) *of a thing different in kind,* (Mgh, Mṣb;) whence the phrase of the Ḳur أَوْ عَدْلُ ذٰلِكَ صِيَامًا [mentioned above]; عَدْل being originally an inf. n.: (Mṣb:) Akh says, العِدْلُ, with kesr, signifies المِثْلُ; and ▼ العَدْلُ, with fet-ḥ, is originally an inf. n., but is made a subst. to denote المِثْلُ in order to distinguish it from the عِدْل of goods or commodities [which will be expl. in what follows]: Fr says, العِدْلُ, with kesr, is *the like* (المِثْلُ), as in the saying عِنْدِى عِدْلُ غُلَامِكَ [*I have the like of thy boy* or *young man*] and عِدْلُ شَاتِكَ [*the like of thy sheep* or *goat*]; but you say ▼ العَدْلُ, with naṣb [i. e. fet-ḥ] to the ع, when you mean *the* [*equal in*] *value, of what is different in kind;* though sometimes it is pronounced with kesr by some of the Arabs, app. by an error on their part: (Ṣ, O:) or some allow one's saying عِنْدِى عِدْلُ غُلَامِكَ as meaning *I have the like of thy boy* or *young man,* [and app. ▼ عَدْلُهُ also,] and عَدْلُهُ with fet-ḥ only as meaning *his value:* (TA:) but Zj says that العَدْلُ and العِدْلُ both signify *the like,* whether it be *of the same kind* or *of a different kind;* and if one make a mistake, he should not say that some of the Arabs have erred: (O:) the pl. (Ṣ, O, Ḳ) of عِدْلٌ, by common consent, (Ṣ, O,) is أَعْدَالٌ, (Ṣ, O, Ḳ,) and [that of ▼ عَدِيلٌ is] عُدَلَآءُ. (Ḳ.) —— Also The *half of a load,* (Ḳ, TA,) *such as is on either of the two sides of the camel;* (TA;) or *a burden* [*borne on one side of a beast, counterbalancing another on the other side,* or] *made equiponderant to another burden:* (Az, TA:) pl. [of pauc.] أَعْدَالٌ and [of mult.] عُدُولٌ: (Sb, Ḳ:) and ▼ عَدِيلٌ signifies the *equal* of a person *in weight and measure* or *size* or *the like* (Ṣ, Ḳ,* TA) in the [vehicle called] مَحْمِل: (TA:) Sb says that it signifies *a human being that is the equal of another* [*in weight*]; distinguishing it from عِدْلٌ, which, he says, is applied only to goods, or commodities: (IB, TA:) [but] ▼ عَدِيلَتَانِ signifies *two sacks* (غِرَارَتَانِ); because each counterbalances, or is equiponderant to, the other. (TA.) Hence one says of the عُدُول of an evil judicial decision, مَا هُمْ عُدُولٌ وَلٰكِنْ عُدُولٌ [meaning *They are not witnesses whose testimony is approvable, but equalized loads of merchandise*]. (TA.) And [hence also] one says, وَقَعَ المُصْطَرِعَانِ عِدْلَىْ بَعِيرٍ, meaning *The two* [*men wrestling*] *fell together, neither of them having thrown down the other.* (TA. [See also عِكْمٌ.])

عَدَلٌ The *equalizing of the* [*two burdens,* or *half-loads, called*] عِدْلَانِ. (IAạr, O, Ḳ.)

عَدَلَةٌ: see what next follows, in two places.

عُدَلَةٌ Men *who pronounce witnesses to be veracious,* and *good,* or *righteous;* (AZ, IAạr, O, Ḳ,* TA;) as also ▼ عَدَلَةٌ; (Ḳ;) and the former is also applied to a man *who does so:* (AZ, O, TA:*) or the former is applied to a single person, and ▼ عَدَلَةٌ is applied to a pl. number. (AA, Ḳ, TA.)

عَدِيلٌ : see عِدْلٌ, in four places.

عَدَالَةٌ : see عَدْلٌ, in two places. It is an inf. n. of عَدُلَ (Ṣ, O, Mṣb) said of a witness; like ▼ عُدُولَةٌ: and signifies The *quality of a witness such as is termed* عَدْلٌ [q. v.]: it is expl. as being *a quality the regard of which necessitates the guarding against what falls short of the requirements of manly virtue* or *moral goodness, habitually and evidently; which evident falling short thereof is not effected by small instances of lapses* or *falls into wrongdoing, and by perversion of speech, because mistake and forgetfulness are supposable* [*as the causes thereof*], *and interpretation not according to the obvious meaning; but it is when such is the known and repeated practice of the person: regard is to be had to the goodness,* or *honesty, of every individual, and his usual practice in respect of his apparel, and his dealing in selling and buying, and the conveyance of goods, and other things; and when he does that which is not suitable to him, without necessity, his testimony is impugned; otherwise it is not.* (Mṣb.)

عُدُولَةٌ : see عَدْلٌ, first sentence: and عَدَالَةٌ.

عَدِيلَتَانِ : see عِدْلٌ, last quarter.

عَدَوْلِىٌّ *An old, tall tree*: (Ḳ:) or ▼ شَجَرٌ عَدَوْلِىٌّ signifies *old trees*; one of which is termed عَدَوْلِيَّةٌ: or, accord. to AḤn, ▼ عَدَوْلِىٌّ signifies anything *old*. (TA.) — See also the next following paragraph.

عَدَوْلِىٌّ : see the next preceding paragraph, in two places. — Also, thus correctly, as in the Ṣ, (TA, [and thus, app., accord. to the Ḳ, though this is thought by SM, and not altogether without reason, to require by its context the reading of ▼ عَدَوْلِىٌّ, as does, app., the O,]) *A seaman,* or *mariner.* (Ṣ, O, Ḳ, TA.) — And pl. [app. a mistake for n. un.] of عَدَوْلِيَّةٌ, (Ḳ,) which latter means *Certain ships* or *boats,* (O, Ḳ, TA,) or *a* [*sort of*] *ship* or *boat,* (Ṣ,) or it is an epithet applied to certain ships or boats, (EM p. 58,) so called as being *of* عَدَوْلَى, (Ṣ, O,* Ḳ, TA,) meaning *a city of El-Baḥreyn,* (Ṣ, O,* TA,) not meaning, as would be imagined from the context in the Ḳ, the tree [said to be] thus called; (TA;) mentioned in the poetry of Ṭarafeh, (Ṣ, O, TA,) in the fourth verse of his Mo'allaḳah, (O, TA,) and thus expl. by Aṣ: (TA:) or meaning *old*; or *large*: (O, TA:) or so called as being *of a place named* عَدَوْلَاةٌ, of the measure فَعَوْلَاةٌ: (TA:) or *of* عَدَوْلٌ, *a man who used to construct ships* or *boats*: or *of a people who used to alight and abide in Hejer.* (O, Ḳ.)

عَادِلٌ : see عَدْلٌ, latter half, in two places. — Also *An attributer of a copartner,* or *of copartners, to God.* (Ṣ, TA.) A woman is related to have said to El-Ḥajjáj, يَا قَاسِطُ يَا عَادِلُ; [by which she meant *O deviater from the right course; O attributer of a copartner,* or *of copartners, to God*;] (Ṣ,* O;) whereupon, the people thinking that she was commending him, he said that by her saying يا قاسط, she referred to the words of the Ḳur [lxxii. 15] أَمَّا ٱلْقَاسِطُونَ فَكَانُوا لِجَهَنَّمَ حَطَبًا [expl. voce قاسط; and by her saying يا عادل, to the words in the same [vi. 151] وَهُمْ بِرَبِّهِمْ يَعْدِلُونَ [expl. above, see 1]. (O.)

مَعْدِلٌ *A place of turning away* or *back*; as also ▼ مَعْدُولٌ: so in the saying, مَا لَهُ مَعْدِلٌ and ▼ مَعْدُولٌ [*There is for him no place of turning away* or *back*]: (Ḳ:) pl. مَعَادِلُ: Aboo-Khirásh says,

تَضِيقُ عَلَىَّ الأَرْضُ ذَاتُ المَعَادِلِ •

meaning [*The earth having those ways in which one may turn in various directions becomes strait to me*; or] *having such amplitude that by reason thereof one may turn in it to the right and left.* (TA.) — And *A way, course, mode,* or *manner, of acting* or *conduct* or *the like*: thus in the saying أَخَذَ فِى مَعْدِلِ الحَقِّ [*He took to the right way of acting*], and مَعْدِلُ البَاطِلِ [*the false,* or *wrong, way of acting*]: and in like manner one says, أُنْظُرُوا إِلَى سُوْءِ مَعَادِلِهِ *Look ye at his evil ways of acting*: and هُوَ سَدِيدُ المَعَادِلِ [*He is one who takes a right direction in respect of the ways of acting*]. (TA.)

مُعَدَّلَةٌ : see عَدْلٌ, former half, in seven places.

مُعَدَّلٌ Anything *straightened,* or *made even*: (Ṣ, O, Ḳ:) [&c.: see its verb.] — الكُرُّ المُعَدَّلُ see in art. كر.

مُعَدَّلَاتٌ The *angles,* or *corners, of a house* or *chamber.* (IAạr, O, Ḳ.)

مَعْدُولٌ : see مَعْدِلٌ, in two places.

مُعْتَدِلٌ [*Right,* or *having a right direction; straight,* or *even; equal; equable,* or *uniform; symmetrical, proportionate; suitable in itself* or *in its parts*: see its verb]. مُعْتَدِلَةٌ applied to a she-camel means *Whose limbs,* or *members, are rendered even, one with another,* (Lth, Az, TA,) *including her hump and other parts*; as is the case when she becomes fat: erroneously said by Sh, on the authority of Moḥárib, to be مُعْتَدِلَةٌ, belonging to art. عندل. (Az, TA.) — And *Of a middling sort, in quantity,* or *quality*; as a body between tallness and shortness, and water between the hot and the cold; and [*moderate,* or *temperate,*] as a day of which the air is pleasant; contr. of مُعْتَذِلٌ, with the pointed ذ. (TA.) فَرَسٌ مُعْتَدِلُ الفرقِ [app. الفَرْقِ] means *A horse whose* غُرَّة [or *blaze*] *occupies the middle of his forehead, not reaching to one of the eyes nor inclining upon one of the cheeks.* (AO, TA.) أَيَّامٌ مُعْتَدِلَاتٌ signifies [*Days moderate in temperature*; or] *pleasant, not hot, days.* (TA.) And المُعْتَدِلَاتُ is applied to *Forty nights of varying,* or *alternating, heat and cold, commencing from the* [*auroral*] *rising of Suheyl* [or *Canopus,* which, in Central Arabia, at the commencement of the era of the Flight, was about the 4th of August, O. S.]: (AZ, TA in art. صفر: see صَفَرِىٌّ:) or *the days of heat known by the appellation of* وَقَدَاتُ سُهَيْلٍ [*the most vehement heats of Canopus*]; as also المُعْتَذِلَاتُ [q. v.]. (El-Ḥareeree's Durrat-el-Ghowwáṣ, in De Sacy's Anthol. Gramm. Arabe, p. 37 of the Arabic text.)

عدم

1. عَدِمَهُ, with kesr to the د, (Ṣ, MA, Mṣb, Ḳ, &c.,) aor. ـَ, (Ṣ,) inf. n. عَدَمٌ, (Ṣ, MA, Mṣb, Ḳ,) which is anomalous [as the verb is trans.], (Ṣ,) and عُدْمٌ, (Ṣ, MA, Ḳ,) or the latter is a simple subst., (Mṣb,) *He had it not, was destitute of it, was without it, lacked it, wanted it, found it not,* or *lost it*; (Ṣ,* MA, Mṣb,* Ḳ;*) syn. فَقَدَهُ; (Ṣ, Mṣb, Ḳ;*) or لَمْ يَجِدْهُ; so says Ibn-El-Kemál in the Exposition of the Hidáyeh. (TA.) And عَدِمْتُ فُلَانًا [*I wanted,* or *lost, such a one*]. (TA.) And عَدِمَ, [inf. n. عَدَمٌ,] *It lacked, wanted, was wanting, was not found, did not exist,* or *was lost*; syn. فُقِدَ. (AḤát, Mṣb.) [See also عَدَمٌ below.] — لَا يَعْدِمُنِى هٰذَا الأَمْرُ means مَا يَعْدُونِى [i. e. *This thing,* or *affair, does not pass from me*]. (Ṣ, Ḳ, TA. [In the CḲ, erroneously, مَا يُعْدِمُنِى.]) — عَدِمَ as intrans.: see the next paragraph, last sentence. — عَدُمَ, (Ḳ, TA,) inf. n. عَدَامَةٌ, (TA,) *He was,* or *became, foolish,* or *stupid*; (Ḳ, TA;) being *destitute of intellect,* or *understanding.* (TA.)

4. اعدمهُ is *syn. with* أَفْقَدَهُ [meaning *He made him to lack, want,* or *lose, it,* or *him*]: (AḤát, Mṣb:) and has a second objective complement: one says, لَا أَعْدَمَنِى ٱللّٰهُ فَضْلَهُ [*May God not make me to lack, want,* or *lose, his bounty*]: (Mṣb:) or لَا أَعْدَمَنِى فَضْلَكَ *May He* (i. e. God) *not make thy bounty to depart from me*: and اعدمنى اللّٰه فلانًا [*God made me to lack, want,* or *lose, such a one*]. (TA.) — And *He denied him,* or *refused him,* (Az, MA, Ḳ, TA,) what he sought, (Az, TA,) or a thing. (MA.) — And *He rendered him poor, needy,* or *destitute*: (Ṣ,* Ḳ,* TA: [in the Ṣ, this meaning seems to be indicated by the context; but in the Ḳ, the context seems rather to indicate the first of the meanings expl. in this paragraph:]) in this sense, said of God. (Ṣ, Ḳ, TA) — أَعْدَمَنِى الشَّىْءُ means [app. *The thing excited my want,* or *made me to want it*; and hence, *the thing was not found by me*; or] *I did not find the thing.* (Ḳ.) — [And اعدمهُ signifies also *He made it to have no existence; to be non-existent*; or *he annihilated it*; or *did away with it*; agreeably with explanations of the inf. n. (إِعْدَامٌ) in the KL and PṢ &c., and with present usage.] — اعدم as intrans., (Kr, Ṣ, Mṣb, Ḳ,) inf. n. إِعْدَامٌ and ▼ عُدْمٌ, (Kr, Ḳ, TA,) like إِيسَارٌ and يُسْرٌ as inf. ns. of أَيْسَرَ, and إِعْسَارٌ and عُسْرٌ as of أَعْسَرَ, and إِفْحَاشٌ and فُحْشٌ as of أَفْحَشَ, or rather the latter in every one of these instances is a simple subst., as ISd says, (TA,) signifies *He* (a man, Ṣ) *was,* or *became,*

poor, needy, or *destitute;* (Kr, Ṣ, Mṣb, Ḳ;) as also ↑عَدِيمٌ. (TA.)

7. انعدم in the phrase of the Muslim theologians وُجِدَ الشَّىْءُ فَٱنْعَدَمَ [meaning *The thing existed, and became non-existent,*] is a barbarism. (Ḳ,* TA.)

عُدْمٌ: see the next paragraph.

عَدَمٌ and ↑عُدْمٌ are inf. ns. of the trans. verb عَدِمَ, (Ṣ, M, Ḳ,) or the latter is a simple subst., (Mṣb,) and each signifies, as also ↑عُدُمٌ, *Lack,* or *want,* as meaning *non-possession;* or *loss;* [of a thing, and of a quality, or faculty, &c.;] and by predominance of application, *lack,* &c., *of property* or *wealth;* (Ḳ, TA;) and *departure thereof;* and *paucity thereof;* (TA;) or *poverty, neediness,* or *destitution.* (Ṣ in explanation of the first and second; respecting the latter of which, see 4, last sentence.) [Also *Non-performance* of an act; and *non-observance* of a duty &c. And *Lack,* or *want,* as meaning *non-existence;* and *absence;* or the *state of being lost.*]

عَدِمٌ: see عَدِيمٌ.

عُدُمٌ: see عَدَمٌ.

أَرْضٌ عَدْمَآءُ *Land such as is termed* بَيْضَآءُ; (Ḳ, TA;) i. e., *without,* as though [meaning] *lacking, plants,* or *herbage.* (TA.) — And شَاةٌ عَدْمَآءُ *A sheep,* or *goat, of which the head is white and the rest differing therefrom.* (Ḳ.)

عَدَامٌ: see عُدَامٌ.

عَدِيمٌ *Not having, being without, lacking, wanting, not finding,* or *having lost:* one says, هُوَ عَدِيمُ النَّظِيرِ *He is one not having, without, lacking,* &c., *the likes* [or *like*]; and عَدِيمُ المَعْرُوفِ [*destitute of goodness, gentleness, beneficence,* &c.]: and هِىَ عَدِيمَةُ المَعْرُوفِ [*She is destitute of goodness,* &c.]. (TA.) — And *Poor, needy,* or *destitute;* (Ṣ, Mṣb, Ḳ;) as also ↑عَدِمٌ, (Ḳ,) and ↑مُعْدِمٌ, (Ṣ,) and ↑مَعْدُومٌ, (Mṣb, TA,) which last occurs in a trad. as meaning *the poor who has become, by reason of the pressure of his want, as though himself were not existing,* or *lost:* عَدِيمٌ signifies *having no property;* as also ↑مُعْدِمٌ: and *having nothing:* it is of the measure فَعِيلٌ in the sense of the measure فَاعِلٌ: and its pl. is عُدَمَآءُ; erroneously said in the Ḳ to be pl. of عَدَمٌ. (TA.) — Also *Stupid; foolish;* (Ḳ, TA;) *destitute of intellect,* or *understanding.* (TA.) And *Insane; demented.* (IAạr, Az, Ḳ,* TA.)

عُدَامٌ, (Ḳ, and so in copies of the Ṣ,) or ↑عَدَامٌ, (so accord. to other copies of the Ṣ,) *A sort of fresh ripe dates found in El-Medeeneh,* (Ṣ, Ḳ,) *that are late* [*in ripening*], (Ḳ,) or *that come the last of fresh ripe dates.* (Ṣ.)

مُعْدِمٌ: see عَدِيمٌ, in two places.

مَعْدُومٌ [*Lacking, wanting, not found, not existing,* or *lost:* see عَدِمَ, of which it is the part. n.]. — يَكْسِبُ المَعْدُومَ means *He is fortunate,* or *possessed of good fortune;* [properly,] *he attains what others are denied.* (Ḳ.) It is said in a trad., إِنَّكَ تَكْسِبُ المَعْدُومَ وَتُطْعِمُ المَأْدُومَ. (M and TA in art. ادم: expl. voce أَدِيمٌ.) — See also عَدِيمٌ.

عدن

1. عَدَنَ بِهِ, (Mgh, Mṣb, Ḳ,) aor. ـُ and ـِ, inf. n. عَدْنٌ and عُدُونٌ, (Mṣb, Ḳ,) *He remained, stayed, dwelt,* or *abode, in it,* (Mgh, Mṣb, Ḳ,) namely, a place, (Mgh, Mṣb,) or a country, or town. (Ḳ.) Whence, (Mṣb, Ḳ,) or from عَدَنَتْ said of camels as expl. in what follows, (Ṣ,) جَنَّاتُ عَدْنٍ, (Ṣ, Mṣb, Ḳ,) [applied to Paradise,] meaning *Gardens of abode,* (Ṣ, Mṣb,) or *gardens of perpetual abode.* (TA.) And عَدَنْتُ البَلَدَ means *I took for myself the country,* or *town, as a home,* or *settled place of abode.* (Ṣ.) — And عَدَنَتِ الإِبِلُ بِمَكَانِ كَذَا, (Ṣ, Mṣb TA) (Ṣ, TA,) aors. as above, (Mṣb, TA,) and so the inf. ns., (TA,) *The camels kept to such a place, not quitting it:* (Ṣ:) or *remained,* or *stayed,* (Mṣb, TA,) *in such a place, in the pasturage,* (TA,) or *pasturing upon the* [*plants,* or *trees, called*] حَمْض: (Mṣb, TA:) or عَدَنَتِ الإِبِلُ فِى الحَمْضِ *the camels found the* حمض *to be wholesome* (اِسْتَمْرَتْهُ [for اِسْتَمْرَأَتْهُ]), *and increased,* or *fattened, thereon, and kept thereto:* (Ḳ, TA:) accord. to AZ, the verb is used of camels only in relation to the حمض: or, as some say, it is in relation to anything: (TA:) and the epithet ↑عَادِنٌ, (Ṣ, Ḳ,) without ة, (TA,) is applied to a she-camel of which this verb is used; (Ṣ, Ḳ;) and its pl. is عَوَادِنُ. (TA.) — عَدَنَ الأَرْضَ, aor. ـِ, (Ḳ,) inf. n. عَدْنٌ, (TA,) *He dunged,* or *manured, the land;* as also ↑عَدَّنَهَا. (Ḳ.) — And عَدَنَ الشَّجَرَةَ, (Ḳ,) inf. n. عَدْنٌ, (TA,) *He marred the tree with an axe or the like.* (Ḳ.) — عَدَنَ الحَجَرَ, (Ḳ,) inf. n. عَدْنٌ, (TA,) *He pulled out the stone* (Ḳ, TA) *with the* فَأْس [meaning *hoe*]. (TA.) — See also Q. Q. 1.

2. عدّن الأَرْضَ: see 1, near the end. — Also, inf. n. تَعْدِينٌ, *He smote the ground* بِالمِعْدَنِ, i. e. *with the* صَاقُور [or *pickaxe*], (Ḳ, TA,) *to put it in a good state* [app. *for cultivation, by breaking it up*]. (TA.) — عدّن الغَرْبَ *He added a piece, called* عَدِينَة, *in one side of the hide of which the* غرب [or *large leathern bucket*] *was made, to render it of full dimensions, it being* [*too*] *small.* (ISh, TA.) [And probably, *He added to the* غرب *an* عَدِينَة (q. v.) *of any kind.*] — And عدّن said of a drinker, *He became full.* (Ḳ.)

Q. Q. 1. عَيْدَنَتِ النَّخْلَةُ, (Ḳ accord. to the TA, and so in the TA in art. عود, as on the authority of Az,) or ↑عَدَّنَتْ, (so in the CḲ and in my MS. copy of the Ḳ,) *The palm-tree became such as is termed* عَيْدَانَة (Ḳ, TA) i. e. *tall* [&c., n. un. of عَيْدَان, mentioned in art. عود]. (TA.)

عَدَنِىٌّ *Of,* or *belonging to,* [*the place called*] عَدَن [*in El-Yemen*]: — hence, عَدَنِيَّاتٌ meaning *Highly-prized garments:* and an epithet applied to رِيَاط [pl. of رَيْطَة] worn by young women, or girls: — and hence likewise عَدَنِىٌّ is an epithet applied to a man as meaning *Generous in natural dispositions:* (TA:) [or this may be from what next follows:] — عَدَنِىٌّ signifies also *One who weaves* [*the garments called*] الثِّيَاب العَدَنِيَّة *in Neysáboor* [app. from سِكَّة عَدَنِى, which, as is said in the TA, is in Neysáboor]. (TA.)

عَدَانٌ *A place of* عُدُون [i. e. of *remaining, staying, dwelling,* or *abiding,* of men in a place, or of camels in the pasturage &c.: see 1]. (TA.) — Also The *shore* of the *sea:* (Ṣ, Ḳ:) but in the phrase بِعَدَانِ السِّيفِ in a verse of Lebeed, it is said that he meant عَدَن [of El-Yemen], adding the ا by poetic license; or some other place: (Ṣ:) Sh says that it there means a place on the shore of the sea: and AHeyth related it with kesr to the ع. (TA.) And (Ḳ, TA) accord. to IAạr (TA) it signifies The *side* of a river. (Ḳ, TA.) — And *A period of seven years:* one says, مَكَثُوا عَدَانًا [*They tarried during a period of seven years*], (Ḳ, TA,) and عَدَانَيْنِ i. e. *fourteen years.* (TA.)

عَدَانَةٌ *A company* (AA, Ḳ, TA) *of men:* (AA, TA:) pl. عَدَانَاتٌ: (AA, Ḳ, TA:) or this latter signifies *parties,* or *distinct bodies, of men:* (Ṣ, TA:) and accord. to IAạr رِجَالٌ عَدَانَاتٌ means *men remaining, staying, dwelling,* or *abiding.* (TA.) — See also what next follows.

عَدِينَةٌ *A piece,* or *patch, in the bottom,* or *lower part, of a leathern bucket;* (Ṣ, Ḳ;) as also ↑عَدَانَةٌ: (Ḳ:) or *at the extremities of the loops of the* [*leathern water-bag called*] مَزَادَة: (AA, TA:) or *any piece that is added in the* [*large leathern bucket called*] غَرْب, *like the* بَنِيقَة *in the shirt:* (ISh, TA:) pl. عَدَائِنُ. (Ṣ, Ḳ.)

عِدَّانٌ, signifying *A time,* [as also عَدَّانٌ,] is said by some to be of the measure فِعْلَال [a mistranscription for فِعَّال] from عَدَنَ; but Fr held it to be more probably of the measure فِعْلَان from العَدّ and العِدَاد, in the place of which [i. e. in art. عد] it has been mentioned. (TA.)

عَدَوْدَنِىٌّ *Swift;* (Ḳ, TA;) applied to a camel: (TA:) or *strong, robust,* or *hardy;* (Ḳ, TA;) so applied: (TA:) or *whose origin is referred to a certain stallion,* (Ḳ, TA,) *named* عَدَوْدَن; (TA;) or *to a certain land,* (Ḳ, TA,) *so named.* (TA.)

عَادِنٌ [act. part. n. of 1:] as an epithet applied to a she-camel; pl. عَوَادِنُ: see 1, latter half.

عَيْدَانٌ (Ṣ, Ḳ) meaning *Tall palm-trees* (Ṣ) [or the *tallest of palm-trees* &c. (see art. عود)] has been mentioned in the portion appropriated to words of which the last radical letter is د, (Ṣ, Ḳ,) as being of the measure فَيْعَلَان: (TA:) or they are so called because of their long remaining;

the word being of the measure فَيْعَالٌ from عَدَنَ بِالمَكَانِ: (Ḥam p. 712:) [it is a coll. gen. n.:] n. un. with ة. (Ṣ, O, Ḳ, all in art. عود.)

مَعْدِنٌ, (Ṣ, Mgh, Mṣb, Ḳ, &c.,) and accord. to some مَعْدَنٌ also, but this is not of established authority, (TA,) *A mine*; i. e. *a place of the origination of the* جَوَاهِر [meaning *native ores*] *of gold and the like*: (Ḳ:) the *place of the origination of anything*, (Lth, Mṣb, Ḳ, TA,) as *of gold*, and *of silver*, and *of other things*: (Lth, TA:) or the *gold*, and *silver*, [and *any other metal* or *mineral, such as is of value*,] *created by God in the earth*: (Mgh:) so called because the people thereof remain there (Ṣ, Mgh, Mṣb, Ḳ) always, (Ḳ,) summer and winter; (Ṣ, Mgh, Mṣb;) or because the native ore created therein by God has remained fixed in it; (Mṣb; [and the like is said in the Mgh and Ḳ;]) or, as some say, from عَدَنْتُ الحَجَرَ meaning "I pulled out the stone:" (Ḥam p. 81:) the pl. is مَعَادِنُ. (TA.) It signifies also *A place of fixedness of anything*. (Ṣ, TA.) And مَعَادِنُ signifies also *Origins*, or *sources*. (TA.) [Hence the saying,] هَجَرُ مَعْدِنُ التَّمْرِ † [*Hejer is* famous as *the place of production of dates*]. (Ṣ in art. بضع.) And [hence] one says, هُوَ مَعْدِنٌ لِلْخَيْرِ وَالكَرَمِ ‡ [*He is a natural source of goodness and generosity*], meaning that he was created with a disposition thereto. (TA.) [And هُمْ كِرَامُ المَعَادِنِ † *They are generous in respect of* their *origins*: see a verse cited voce إِنْ, p. 107.]

صَاقُورٌ مِعْدَنٌ *A* صاقور [or *pickaxe*], (Ḳ, TA,) *resembling a* فَأْس. (TA.)

غَرْبٌ مُعَدَّنٌ [*A large leathern bucket*] *having a piece*, or *patch, called* عُدَيْنَة, *sewed upon its bottom*, or *lower part*, (Ṣ, Ḳ,) *in consequence of its having been rent in that part*. (Ṣ. [See also 2.]) And خُفٌّ مُعَدَّنٌ *A boot having a piece added at the end of the shank, so as to widen it.* (TA.)

مُعَدِّنٌ One *who extracts the masses of stone from a mine, seeking to find in them gold* and *the like*, (Ḳ, TA,) *after having then broken them in pieces*. (TA.)

[مَعْدِنِيٌّ, also pronounced مَعْدَنِيٌّ, *Of*, or *belonging to, a mine; mineral*; and *metallic*. — And *A mineral*; and *a metal*: pl. مَعْدِنِيَّاتٌ.]

عدو

1. عَدَاهُ, (Mgh, Ḳ,) first pers. عَدَوْتُهُ, (Mṣb,) aor. يَعْدُو, (Mgh, Mṣb,) [inf. n. عَدْوٌ,] *He passed from it*, (Mgh, Mṣb, Ḳ,) namely, a thing, or an affair, (Ḳ,) to another, (Mgh, Mṣb,) *and left it*; (Ḳ;) and عَدَا عَنْهُ signifies the same; (Ḳ;) as also ▾ تَعَدَّاهُ; (Ṣ,* Ḳ;) and in like manner one says, ▾ عَدَّيْتُهُ, inf. n. تَعْدِيَةٌ; (Mṣb;) [but I do not find this elsewhere, and think that correctly one should say, عَدَّيْتُ ▾ عَنْهُ; agreeably with what here follows:] the saying عَدِّ ▾ عَنْ هٰذَا means *Leave thou this*, and *turn from it to another*; and is app. from the phrase عَدِّ ▾ هَمَّكَ إِلَى غَيْرِهِ [*Turn thy anxiety to other than him*, or *it*]; the objective complement being altogether left out, so that the verb becomes as though it were intrans.; and there are many instances similar to this in the language: (Ḥar p. 478:) one says, عَدَّيْتُ ▾ عَنِّي الهَمَّ *I turned away from me anxiety*: and [hence] you say to him who has pursued you, عَدِّ ▾ عَنِّي إِلَى غَيْرِي, meaning *Turn thou* the beast upon which thou art riding *towards other than me*: (TA:) and عَدِّ ▾ عَمَّا تَرَى, meaning *Turn thou* thine eye *from what thou seest*. (Ṣ.) [See an ex. of the first of these verbs in the Ḥam p. 125.] One says also, عَدَاهُ الأَمْرُ, and ▾ تعدّاهُ *The thing*, or *affair, passed from him*. (TA. [See an ex. in the first paragraph of art. عدم.]) And the Arabs say, إِنَّ الجَرَبَ لَيَعْدُو, meaning *Verily the mange*, or *scab, passes* from him that has it to him that is near to him so that the latter becomes mangy, or scabby. (Mṣb.) And مَا عَدَا فُلَانٌ أَنْ صَنَعَ [app. meaning *Such a one did not leave*, or, accord. to an explanation of the verb in a similar phrase in Ḥar p. 333, *did not delay, his doing* such a thing]. (Ṣ.) Accord. to Er-Rághib, العَدْوُ primarily signifies *Transition*; [whence what here precedes;] or *the going*, or *passing, beyond*, or *the exceeding*, a limit, or the usual limit: and *incompatibility to coalesce*. (TA.) — And [hence,] عَدَاهُ, aor. as above, [inf. n. عَدْوٌ,] *He went*, or *passed, beyond it; exceeded it*; or *transgressed it*. (Ṣ, TA.*) So in the saying عَدَا طَوْرَهُ [*He went*, or *passed, beyond his proper limit; exceeded it*; or *transgressed it*]: and in like manner, تعدّى ▾ الحَقَّ and ▾ اعتداهُ signify *He went*, or *passed, beyond*, &c., *what was true*, or *right*; and so فَوْقَ الحَقِّ, and عَنِ الحَقِّ. (TA.) أَمَا عَدَا مَنْ بَدَا, a saying in which the vulgar erroneously omit the interrogative أ, means *Does not he transgress that which is right who begins* by acting injuriously? (TA.) And it is said عَدَا القَارِصُ فَحَزَرَ ‡ *What was biting to the tongue attained to an excessive degree, so that it became acid*: meaning that the affair, or case, became distressing. (Ṣ in art. قرص.) — And عَدَا عَلَيْهِ, inf. n. عَدْوٌ and عَدَآءٌ (Ṣ, Mgh, Mṣb, Ḳ) and عُدُوٌّ (Ṣ, Mṣb, Ḳ) and عُدْوَانٌ (ISd, Mṣb, Ḳ) and عِدْوَانٌ (ISd, Ḳ) and عُدْوَى; (Ḳ;) and ▾ تعدّى, and ▾ اعتدى; (Ṣ, Mṣb, Ḳ;) *He acted wrongfully, unjustly, injuriously*, or *tyrannically, against him*; (Ṣ, Mṣb, Ḳ;) and *transgressed against him*, or *exceeded the proper limit against him*: (Ṣ, Mṣb:) [and *he acted aggressively against him*; agreeably with an explanation of the inf. n. of the last of these verbs in what follows: (see an ex. in a verse cited voce ربح:)] or *he acted with excessive wrongfulness*, &c., *against him*: (Mgh:) and ▾ اعدى signifies the same as the other verbs here mentioned; (Ḳ, TA;) whence (TA) one says, أَعْدَيْتَ ▾ فِي مَنْطِقِكَ *Thou hast deviated from that which is right in thy speech*: (Ṣ, TA:) ▾ الاِعْتِدَآءُ is *the exceeding what is right*; and it is sometimes *in the way of aggression*; and sometimes *in the way of requital*; and instances of the usage of its verb in both of these manners occur in the Ḳur ii. 190: (Er-Rághib, TA:) the first and third of the inf. ns. of عَدَا, mentioned above, occur in the Ḳur vi. 108 accord. to different readings: (Ṣ, TA:) and [it is said that] العُدْوَانُ signifies *sheer*, or *unmixed, wrongful* or *unjust* or *injurious* or *tyrannical conduct*: (Ṣ:) or, as some say, *the worst of* [*such conduct*, i. e., *of*] الاِعْتِدَآء, *in strength*, or *deed*, or *state* or *condition*. (TA.) — And عَدَا عَلَيْهِ *He acted corruptly towards him*. (TA.) — And عُدِىَ عَلَيْهِ *He had his property stolen, and was wronged*. (TA.) And عَدَا عَلَى القُمَاشِ, inf. n. عَدَآءٌ [said in the TA to be like سَحَاب, but in the CḲ عَدًا,] and عُدْوَانٌ and عَدَوَانٌ, (Ḳ, TA,) but in the M written with ḍamm and fet-ḥ [i. e. عُدَوَان and عُدْوَان], (TA,) said of a thief, *He stole the* قماش [meaning *goods*, or *utensils and furniture*]. (Ḳ, TA.) And عَدَا فِى ظَهْرِهِ *He stole what was behind him*: (A in art. ظهر:) [or *he acted wrongfully in respect of what was behind him*: for] لِصٌّ عَادِى ظَهْرٍ is expl. by the words عَدَا فِى ظَهْرٍ فَسَرَقَهُ [so that it app. means *A thief who has acted wrongfully in respect of what was behind one, and stolen it*]. (O and Ḳ in that art.) — And عَدَا عَلَيْهِ, (Ḳ, TA,) inf. n. عَدْوٌ, (TA,) signifies also *He leaped upon him*, or *it*. (Ḳ, TA.) — And عَدَا, (Ḳ,) or عَدَا فِى مَشْيِهِ, (Mṣb,) aor. يَعْدُو, (Mṣb, Ḳ,) inf. n. عَدْوٌ (Ṣ, Mgh, Mṣb, Ḳ) and عُدُوٌّ and عَدًا and عَدَوَانٌ and تَعْدَآءٌ, (Ḳ,) signifies أَحْضَرَ [i. e. *He ran*; or *rose in his running*]; (Ṣ,* Ḳ, TA;) said of a man and of a horse: (TA:) or *he went a pace nearly the same as that termed* هَرْوَلَة, (Mṣb, TA,) *not so quick*, (TA,) or *which is not so quick*, (Mṣb,) *as that termed* جَرْى: (Mṣb, TA:) or *he went a pace less quick than* شَدّ *and more so than* مَشْى: (TA in art. سعى:) or [*he went quickly*, or *swiftly*; for] العَدْوُ signifies السُّرْعَةُ: (Mgh:) [or rather *he ran*, whether *gently* or *moderately* or *vehemently*: that it often signifies *he ran vehemently* is shown by the prov. أَعْدَى ▾ مِنْ سُلَيْكٍ *More vehement in running than Suleyk*, who is said to have outstripped fleet horses; and by numerous exs.:] and ▾ عدّى signifies the same as عَدَا, denoting a quick pace. (TA in art. هبص.) — And [hence, perhaps,] عَدَا المَآءُ, aor. يَعْدُو, † *The water ran*. (TA.) — عَدَاهُ عَنِ الأَمْرِ, inf. n. عَدْوٌ and عُدْوَانٌ; as also ▾ عدّاهُ; (Ṣ, Ḳ;) signifies *He*, or *it, diverted him*; or *turned him away*, or *back*; (Ṣ, Ḳ;) and *occupied him so as to divert him*; (Ḳ;) *from the thing*, or *affair*. (Ṣ, Ḳ.) You say, عَدَتْ عَوَادٍ. (Ṣ, TA. See عَادِيَةٌ, voce عُدَوَآءُ: and see also the last sentence of the first paragraph of art. عود.) — عَدَانِى مِنْهُ شَرٌّ means بَلَغَنِى [i. e., app., *Evil*, or *mischief, reached me from him*, or *it*]. (TA. [See a signi-

fication of 4.]) — عَدِيتُ لَهُ signifies *I hated him,* or *it.* (ISd, Ḳ.) — عَدَا is also a verb by which one makes an exception, with مَا [preceding it] and without مَا: (Ṣ, Ḳ:) you say, جَآءَنِى القَوْمُ مَا عَدَا زَيْدًا [*The people,* or *party, came to me, except Zeyd*]; and جَآؤُونِى عَدَا زَيْدًا [which means the like]; putting what follows it in the accus. case; the agent being implied in it: (Ṣ: [see this expl. in what has been said of خَلَا as used in the same manner:]) accord. to MF, it is a verb when what follows it is put in the accus. case; and when what follows it is put in the gen. case, it is a particle, by common consent: (TA: [and the like is said in the Mughnee; i. e., that it is similar to خَلَا in respect of the explanations there given of the different usages of this latter; but that Sb did not know it to have been used otherwise than as having the quality of a verb:]) one says, رَأَيْتُهُمْ عَدَا أَخَاكَ and مَا عَدَاهُ, meaning مَا خَلَا [i. e. *I saw them, except thy brother*]: and sometimes it governs the gen. case without ما: thus in the M: Az says, [as though regarding it as only a particle,] when you suppress [ما], you make it to govern the accus. case as meaning إِلَّا and you make it to govern the gen. case as meaning سِوَى. (TA.

2. عدّاهُ, (Ṣ, Ḳ,) inf. n. تَعْدِيَةٌ, (Ḳ,) *He made him,* or *it, to pass* [from a thing, or an affair, to another: see 1, first sentence]: (Ṣ, Ḳ:) and *he made it to pass through, and go beyond;* syn. أَنْفَذَهُ. (Ḳ.) — Hence تَعْدِيَةُ الفِعْلِ, a phrase of the grammarians, [generally meaning † *The making the verb transitive,*] as in خَرَجَ زَيْدٌ فَأَخْرَجْتُهُ [*Zeyd went forth and I made him to go forth*]. (TA.) — See also 1, first quarter, in seven places: — and again, in the latter half, in two places.

3. عاداهُ, (Ḳ, TA,) inf. n. مُعَادَاةٌ, (Ṣ, Ḳ, TA,) [*He treated him,* or *regarded him, with enmity,* or *hostility:*] the verb in this phrase is that of which the epithet is عَدُوٌّ, and the subst. is عَدَاوَةٌ. (Ḳ, TA.) [It is perhaps from one of the three phrases next following]. — عادى الشَّىْءَ signifies *He was,* or *became, distant,* or *aloof, from the thing;* or *he made the thing to be,* or *become, distant,* or *aloof;* syn. بَاعَدَهُ. (TA.) And you say, فُلَانٌ لَا يُعَادِينِى وَلَا يُوَادِينِى, meaning لَا يُجَافِينِى وَلَا يُوَاتِينِى [app. *Such a one will not make me to be,* or *become, remote,* or *aloof, from him, nor will he comply with me:* but لَا يُوَادِينِى properly signifies *he will not take from me the* دِيَة, or *bloodwit*]. (TA.) And عَادِ رِجْلَكَ عَنِ الأَرْضِ *Draw away thy leg,* or *foot, from the ground.* (TA.) And عَادَى الأَدَاةَ عَنِ البَعِيرِ *He raised* [*partially*] *the furniture* (*consisting of the saddle and saddle-cloth*) *from contact with the camel* [*so as to render it bearable by him*]. (ISh, TA in art. خلق.) — عادى شَعْرَهُ *He took* [*somewhat*] *from his hair:* or *he raised it,* (Ḳ, TA,) *in washing it:* or *he neglected it, and did not oil it,* or *anoint it:* or *he subjected it time after time to the purification termed* وُضُوء, *and to washing.* (TA.) — عادى الوِسَادَةَ *He folded the pillow.* (TA.) — عادى القِدْرَ *He lowered one of the three stones upon which the cooking-pot rested, in order that it* (the pot) *might incline upon the fire.* (TA.) — عادى بَيْنَ الصَّيْدَيْنِ, (Ṣ,* Ḳ,) inf. n. عِدَآءٌ (Ṣ, Ḳ) and مُعَادَاةٌ, (Ḳ,) *He made a succession, of one to the other, between the two animals of the chase,* (Ṣ, Ḳ,) *by throwing down one of them immediately after the other,* (Ṣ,) *in one* طَلَق [or *heat*]. (Ṣ, Ḳ.) Imra-el-Ḳeys says, [describing a horse,]

فَعَادَى عِدَآءً بَيْنَ ثَوْرٍ وَنَعْجَةٍ ◦ دِرَاكًا وَلَمْ يَنْضَحْ بِمَآءٍ فَيُغْسَلِ

[*And he made a succession, of one to the other, between a wild bull and a wild cow, by running down one after the other in a single heat, overtaking uninterruptedly, and not breaking out with water* (i. e. *sweat*) *so as to become suffused therewith*]. (Ṣ. [See EM p. 49.]) In like manner also المُعَادَاةُ بَيْنَ رَجُلَيْنِ means *The piercing,* or *thrusting, two men, one after the other, uninterruptedly.* (TA.) — And عَادَيْتُهُ [sometimes] signifies *I vied,* or *contended, with him in running;* i. q. حَاضَرْتُهُ, from الحُضْرُ. (A in art. حضر.)

4. اعدى الأَمْرَ *He passed from,* or *beyond, another, to the thing,* or *affair:* so in the Ḳ. (TA.) But in the M it is said, اعداهُ الدَّآءُ signifies *The disease passed from another to him.* (TA.) And one says, أَعْدَى فُلَانٌ فُلَانًا مِنْ خُلُقِهِ, or مِنْ عِلَّةٍ بِهِ, or جَرَبٍ, (Ṣ, TA,) i. e. *Such a one made somewhat of his natural disposition,* or *of a disease,* or *malady, that was in him,* or *of mange,* or *scab, to pass* [*from him*] *to such a one;* [or *infected him therewith;* (see two exs., in a verse and a hemistich, cited in the first paragraph of art. جنى;)] and اعداهُ بِهِ signifies the same: and اعدى صَاحِبَهُ *He made his companion to acquire the like of what was in him.* (TA.) And يُعْدِى is said of the mange, or scab, &c., meaning *It passes from him that has it to another;* (Ṣ, Ḳ;) and in like manner one says of a disease, يتعدّى ♦: (Nh, TA:) but it is said in an explanation of a trad., لَا يُعْدِى شَىْءٌ شَيْئًا [i. e. *A thing* (meaning disease) *does not pass* by its own agency *to a thing*]. (Ṣ, TA.) [Therefore] one says, of the mange, or scab, [or the like,] اعداهُ ٱللّٰهُ *God made it to pass from him that had it to one that was near to him, so that he became affected therewith.* (Mṣb.) — One says also, of a man, قَدْ أَعْدَى النَّاسَ بِشَرٍّ *He has made evil,* or *mischief, to cleave to men.* (TA.) — See also 1, near the middle, in two places. — اعداهُ عَلَيْهِ *He aided,* or *assisted, him,* (Ṣ, Mgh, Mṣb, Ḳ,) *and strengthened him,* (Ḳ,) *against him;* (Ṣ, Mgh, Mṣb, Ḳ;) *and avenged him of him;* (Ṣ, Mṣb;) namely, one who had wronged him. (Ṣ, Mgh, Mṣb.) And اعداهُ *He* (a judge) *heard his accusation against another, and commanded to bring his adversary.* (Mgh.) — اعداهُ, namely, a horse, (Ṣ, TA,) and also a man, (TA,) [*He made him to run,* whether *gently* or *moderately* or *vehemently:* or, as sometimes used,] *he made him,* (Ḳ, TA,) or *desired him,* (Ṣ,) *to go the pace termed* حُضْر: (Ṣ, Ḳ, TA:) or *he made him to go a pace nearly the same as that termed* هَرْوَلَة, (Mṣb, TA,) *not so quick,* (TA,) or *which is not so quick,* (Mṣb,) *as that termed* جَرْى: (Mṣb, TA: [see 1, latter half:]) and استعداهُ ♦ signifies the same. (Ṣ.)

5: see 1, first quarter, in two places: and see 4. — [Hence تعدّى said of a verb, *It was,* or *became, transitive.*] — تعدّى الحَقَّ: and تعدّى عَلَيْهِ: see 1, second quarter, in two places. — تَعَدَّوْا *They found milk,* (Ḳ, TA,) *which they drank,* (TA,) *and it rendered them in no need of wine:* (Ḳ, TA:) so in the copies of the Ḳ; but correctly, *of flesh-meat,* as in the M. (TA.) — And *They found pasturage for their cattle, and it rendered them in no need of purchasing fodder.* (Ḳ,* TA.) — And تعدّى مَهْرَ فُلَانَةَ *He took,* or *received, the dowry,* or *bridal gift, of such a woman.* (Ḳ.)

6. تعادى القَوْمُ *The people,* or *party, became affected,* [or *infected,*] or *smitten,* (Ṣ, TA,) *one with the disease of another,* or *one with the like of the disease of another:* (Ṣ:) or *died, one after another,* (Ṣ, TA,) *in one month,* and *in one year.* (TA.) And تعادت الإِبِلُ *The camels died in great numbers.* (TA.) — And تعادى القَوْمُ عَلَىَّ بِنَصْرِهِمْ *The people,* or *party, came upon me consecutively with their aid,* or *assistance.* (TA.) — One says also, تعادى القَوْمُ (Ṣ, Ḳ) from العَدَاوَةُ (Ṣ) meaning *The people,* or *party, treated,* or *regarded, one another with enmity,* or *hostility.* (Ḳ.) — And تعادى مَا بَيْنَهُمْ (Ṣ, Ḳ) *The case,* or *affair, that was between them became in a bad,* or *corrupt, state,* (Ṣ,) or *complicated, intricate,* or *confused, so as to be a subject of disagreement,* or *difference, between them.* (Ḳ.) — And تعادى المَكَانُ *The place was,* or *became, dissimilar in its several parts;* and *uneven.* (TA.) And [hence] one says, بِعُنُقِى وَجَعٌ مِنْ تَعَادِى الوِسَادِ مِنَ المَكَانِ المُتَعَادِى i. e. [*In my neck is a pain from the unevenness of the pillow from*] *the uneven place.* (TA.) — And تعادى *He,* or *it, was,* or *became, distant, remote, far off,* or *aloof,* (Ṣ,* Ḳ,* TA,) عَنْهُ *from him,* or *it.* (Ṣ, TA.) — تعادوا *They vied, competed,* or *contended for superiority, in going the pace termed* العَدْو [meaning *in running*]. (Ḳ, TA.)

8: see 1, second quarter, in three places. — الاِعْتِدَآءُ in supplication [to God] is *The exceeding the limits of the* [*Prophet's*] *rule,* or *usage, that has been transmitted from generation to generation.* (TA.)

10. الاِسْتِعْدَآءُ signifies *The asking,* or *demanding, of aid,* or *assistance,* (Mgh, Mṣb,) and *of vengeance,* or *avengement,* (Mgh,) and *of strengthening:* (Mṣb:) and also *the act of aiding,* or *assisting.* (Mgh.) You say, استعداهُ *He asked,* or *demanded, of him* (i. e. the prince, or governor, or commander, Ṣ, Mgh, Mṣb) *aid,* or *assistance,* (Ṣ, Mgh, Mṣb, Ḳ,) عَلَيْهِ *against him,* (Ṣ, Mgh, Mṣb,) namely, one who wronged him:

(Mgh, Mṣb:) [or,] accord. to El-Khuwárezmee (who derives it from العَدْوُ signifying الرَّجَّالَةُ (الَّذِينَ يَعْدُونَ,) [استعدى القَاضِىَ [or استعدى means *he asked*, or *demanded, of the judge, that he should make his foot-messengers to run in quest of his antagonist and to bring him, for the purpose of exacting from him his right*, or *due*. (De Sacy's Chrest. Arabe, sec. ed., iii. 100. [And an explanation similar to this, but not a similar derivation, is indicated in the Mgh by an explanation of أَعْدَاهُ, q. v.]) — See also 4, last sentence.

عَدَا, as a verb, or a preposition, or both, denoting an exception: see 1, last sentence.

عَدْوٌ an inf. n. of 1 [q. v.]. — فَعَلَ كَذَا عَدْوًا بَدْوًا means *He did thus openly*, or *publicly*. (TA.)

عُدْوٌ: see عِدًى: — and see also عَدَآءٌ.

عَدًى [or عَدًا]: see عُدْوَةٌ, in two places: and عَادٍ, last sentence.

عُدًى: see the next paragraph. ═ [It is also a pl. of عَدُوٌّ, q. v.]

عِدًى The *stones of a grave*; as also ▼ عُدًى: (KL:) [i. e.] the *broad stones with which the* [*oblong excavation called*] لَحْد *is covered over*: (AA, TA:) or *a thin stone with which a thing is concealed*, or *covered over*; as also ▼ عِدَآءٌ; (Ḳ, TA;) the latter written in [a copy of] the M ▼ عَدَآءٌ, like سَحَابٌ; but [the former explanation seems to be the more correct, for] it is added in the Ḳ that one thereof is termed ▼ عِدْوٌ; and accord. to this, the word expl. above [or each of the two words expl. above] is a pl. (TA. [See also عُدْوَةٌ.]) — And *Any piece of wood that is put between two* [*other*] *pieces of wood*. (Ḳ,* TA.) ═ See also عُدْوَةٌ, in two places: and عَادٍ, last sentence: — and عُدَوَآءُ: — and عَدَآءٌ. ═ [It is also a pl. of عَدُوٌّ, which see in two places. ═] And عِدًى is used as a prefixed n. for عِدَةٌ as syn. with وَعْدٌ. (Fr; Ṣ and L in art. وعد, q. v.)

عَدْوَةٌ [inf. n. un. of عَدَا: pl. عَدَوَاتٌ. — Hence the saying, السُّلْطَانُ ذُو عَدَوَاتٍ وَذُو بَدَوَاتٍ, expl. voce بَدَآءٌ, in art. بدو. See another reading of this saying voce عَدْوَانٌ.]. — [Hence also,] one says, لَهُ عَدْوَةٌ شَدِيدَةٌ *He has a vehement run of the kind termed* عَدْو, inf. n. of عَدَا. (Mṣb) — عَدْوَةُ الأَمَدِ means *The extent of the eyesight*. (TA.) And one says, هُوَ مِنِّى عَدْوَةَ القَوْسِ [app. meaning *He*, or *it, is at the distance of a bow-shot from me*]. (TA.) ═ See also عُدْوَةٌ. — عَدَايَا is used in poetry as a pl. of عدوة [app. عَدْوَةٌ, but in what sense is not shown]. (TA.)

عُدْوَةٌ and ▼ عِدْوَةٌ, (Ṣ, Mṣb, Ḳ,) the former of the dial. of Ḳureysh and the latter of the dial. of Ḳeys, (Mṣb,) and ▼ عَدْوَةٌ, (Ḳ,) all mentioned by ISd, (TA,) The *side of a valley*; (Ṣ, Mṣb, Ḳ;) as also ▼ عِدًى; (Ḳ;) which last likewise signifies [absolutely] *a side*, or *lateral part* or *portion*; and so ▼ عَدًى; (Ḳ, TA; [see both voce عَادٍ, last sentence;]) thus in the M; (TA;) and the pl. is أَعْدَآءٌ; (Ḳ, TA;) or this last signifies [particularly] the *sides* of a valley, and so do ▼ عِدًى and ▼ عَدًى: (TA:) the pl. of عُدْوَةٌ and ▼ عِدْوَةٌ is عِدَآءٌ and [of عُدْوَةٌ] عُدَيَاتٌ also. (Ṣ.) — And عُدْوَةٌ signifies also *An elevated place*; and so ▼ عِدْوَةٌ: (AA, Ṣ, Ḳ:) pl. [as above, i. e. of both] عِدَآءٌ and [of the former] عُدَيَاتٌ [also]. (Ḳ. [In some copies of the Ḳ, the latter pl. is written عَدَيَاتٌ; in the CḲ عُدْيَاتٌ; but it is correctly عُدَيَاتٌ, as above, thus in my copies of the Ṣ; and perhaps عِدَيَاتٌ may also be a pl., i. e. of عِدْوَةٌ, being thus written accord. to the TA in copies of the Ṣ.]) — And *A place far extending*: (Ḳ, TA:) mentioned by ISd. (TA.) — See also عَدَآءٌ. — [Reiske, as stated by Freytag, has expl. عُدْوَةٌ as signifying "Atrium, impluvium domus:" but this the former has app. done from his having found عدوة erroneously written for عُذْرَةٌ.] ═ عُدْوَةٌ signifies also The *kind of plants*, or *herbage, termed* خُلَّة; i. e., *in which is sweetness*. (TA.)

عِدْوَةٌ: see عُدْوَةٌ, in three places: — and see also عَدَآءٌ. — [Freytag states, as from the Deewán of the Hudhalees, that, accord. to some, it signifies *A stone with which a grave*, or *a well, is covered*: and that the pl. is ▼ عِدَآءٌ: this latter, if correct, is a quasi-pl. n.: but perhaps it is correctly عِدَآءٌ: see عِدًى, first sentence.] ═ أُمُورٌ عِدْوَةٌ [app. أُمُورٌ عُدْوَةٌ, or perhaps أُمُورٌ عِدْوَةٌ,] signifies *Remote affairs*. (TA.)

عَدْوَى *Mange*, or *scab*, or *other disease, that passes*, or *is transitive, from one to another*; (Ṣ, Ḳ, TA;) *a transitive disease*; and such is said to be the جَرَب, and the بَرَص, and the رَمَد, and the حَصْبَة, and the جُذَام, and the وَبَآء, and the جُدَرِىّ. (Kull p. 259.) You say, لَا تُقَرِّبْهُ مِنْهُ فَإِنَّ بِهِ عَدْوَى *Do not thou bring him near to him, for in him is a disease such as the mange, or scab, that is transitive from one to another*. (TḲ.) — And The *transition of the mange, or scab, or other disease, from him that has it to another*: (Ṣ, Ḳ, TA, TḲ:) the subst. from يُعْدِو said of the mange, or scab, expl. above, as meaning "it passes" &c. (Mṣb. [See 1, first quarter.]) It is said in a trad., لَا عَدْوَى, i. e. لَا يُعْدِى شَىْءٌ شَيْئًا [*A thing* (meaning disease) *does not pass* by its own agency *to a thing*]; (Ṣ;) or [lit.] *there is no transition of the mange, or scab, or other disease, from him that has it to another*. (TḲ.) — And *i. q.* فَسَادٌ [i. e. *Badness, corruptness, unsoundness*, &c.]. (Ḳ, TA. [In the CḲ erroneously written in this sense عُدْوِى; which, however, being an inf. n. of عَدَا in the phrase عَدَا عَلَيْهِ, q. v., may be correctly used as having the same, or nearly the same, meaning.]) So in the saying, بِهِ عَدْوَى [*In him, or it, is badness*, &c.]. (TḲ.) ═ Also *A demand that one makes upon a prefect*, or *governor*, [or *judge*,] *to aid*, or *assist, him against him who has wronged him*, i. e. *to inflict penal retribution on him*, (IF, Ṣ, Mṣb,) *for his wrongdoing to him*. (IF, Mṣb.) — And *Aid*, or *assistance, against a wrongdoer*, (Ṣ, Mgh, TA,) *required of a judge, for the bringing into his presence the antagonist*: and also applied to *a signet*, or *a* [*sealed*] *piece of clay, given by the judge as a token to denote the summoning of him whose presence is required*. (Mgh.)

عُدَوَآءُ (Ṣ, Ḳ) and ▼ عَادِيَةٌ and ▼ عَدَآءٌ (Ḳ) *Distance*, or *remoteness*, (Ṣ, Ḳ, TA,) as also ▼ عِدًى, (Ḥam p. 377,) [or particularly] of a house, or an abode, or a dwelling. (Ṣ, TA.) [Hence,] one says, طَالَتْ عُدَوَاؤُهُمْ *Their distance, or remoteness, one from another*, and *their separation, was*, or *became, long*. (TA.) — Also (i. e. the first and ▼ second and ▼ third words) *Occupation*, or *business, that turns one away*, or *back, from a thing*: (Ḳ, TA:) or عُدَوَآءُ signifies *a custom*, or *habit, of occupation* or *business*: (TA:) and عُدَوَآءُ الشُّغْلِ, *the hindrances*, or *impediments, of occupation* or *business*: (Ṣ, TA:) and one says, جِئْتَنِى وَأَنَا فِى عُدَوَآءَ عَنْكَ i. e. [*Thou camest to me when I was* engaged] *in an occupation that diverted* [*me from thee*]: (so in one of my copies of the Ṣ:) the pl. of ▼ عَادِيَةٌ is عَوَادٍ: (TA:) عَوَادِى الدَّهْرِ means *the accidents*, or *casualties, of time* or *fortune, that divert* [or *intervene as obstacles*] *by occupying* or *busying*: (Ṣ:) and you say, عَدَتْ ▼ عَوَادٍ, [lit.] meaning *Things*, or *events, turning away*, or *back, turned*, or *have turned, away*, or *back*; [but this phrase, when followed by بَيْنَ or دُونَ, I would rather render, simply, *obstacles occurred*, or *have occurred*;] (Ṣ, TA;) thus in the latter of two verses cited voce حَبَّ. (Ṣ.) — عُدَوَآءُ الدَّهْرِ means *The shifting, and varying, of time* or *fortune*. (TA.) — And عُدَوَآءُ الشَّوْقِ *What has severely affected, distressed*, or *afflicted, its sufferer, of the yearning*, or *longing, of the soul*, or *of longing desire*. (TA.) — And عُدَوَآءُ signifies also *A* مَرْكَب [i. e. *beast*, or *saddle*, or *thing on which one rides*,] *that is not easy*: (Ḳ:) or, accord. to Aṣ, *a place where he who sits thereon is not in a state of ease*: and one says, جِئْتُ عَلَى مَرْكَبٍ ذِى عُدَوَآءَ i. e. [*I came upon a beast, or saddle*, &c.,] *that was not easy*: (Ṣ:) and جِئْتُكَ عَلَى فَرَسٍ ذِى عُدَوَآءَ, the last word imperfectly decl., i. e. [*I came to thee upon a horse*] *that was not easy*: (TA:) and جَلَسَ عَلَى عُدَوَآءَ *He sat upon an uneven thing* or *place*; (M, TA;) the last word imperfectly decl., as is said by ISd. (TA.) — Also *Dry, hard, land*; (Ḳ, TA;) *sometimes occurring in a well when it is dug*; *and sometimes it is stone, from which the digger turns aside*: and one says, أَرْضٌ ذَاتُ عُدَوَآءَ, meaning *land that is not even*, or *plain*; *not easy to walk* or *ride* or *lie upon*: or, as some say, it means *a rough, rugged, place*: or *an elevated place upon which the camel lies down and then reclines thereon upon his side, having by his side a depressed place, which causes him to tend downwards, in consequence whereof he becomes in the state termed* تَوْهِين, [*weak, or languid, and unable to rise,*] i. e. *in the condition of extending his body towards the low place while his legs are upon the* عُدْوَاء, *which is the elevated, so that he is unable to rise, and dies.* (TA.) ═ And [it is said that] العُدَوَآءُ also signifies اناخة قليلة [app. إِنَاخَةٌ قَلِيلَةٌ, meaning *A little,* or *brief, making* of a camel *to lie down upon the breast,* as is done on the occasions of mounting and dismounting &c.]. (TA.)

عُدَوِىٌّ and عَدَوِىٌّ [are rel. ns. of which only the fem. forms are mentioned, in what here follows]. عُدْوِيَّةٌ and عَدَوِيَّةٌ are rel. ns. of عُدْوَةٌ as meaning "the kind of plants, or herbage, termed خُلَّة," the former reg. and the latter irreg.; and عَوَادٍ [pl. of ▼ عَادٍ or of عَادِيَةٌ] is a possessive epithet [from the same], without the relative ى: [all are app. applied to camels, as meaning *Having for their pasture the plants,* or *herbage, called* عُدْوَة, *above mentioned:* but it is immediately added,] and عُدَوِيَّةٌ and عُدْوِيَّةٌ applied to camels signify *that pasture upon the* [*plants called*] حَمْض: (TA:) and ▼ عَادِيَةٌ and [the pl.] عَوَادٍ, so applied, have this latter meaning accord. to the M and Ḳ: but accord. to the Ṣ, they are applied to camels as meaning *abiding among the* [*trees called*] عِضَاه, *not quitting them, and not pasturing upon the* حَمْض; and so is [the pl.] عَادِيَاتٌ. (TA in another portion of this art.) [See also عَادِيَةٌ, in art. عذو.]

عِدَوِىٌّ, being a rel. n. of عِدَةٌ, see in art. وعد.

عَدَوِيَّةٌ The *herbage of the* صَيْف [q. v., here app. meaning *spring*], *after the departure of the* رَبِيع [q. v., here app. meaning *winter*]: (Ṣ, Ḳ:) it is applied to the *young trees which then become green and are depastured by the camels:* (Ṣ:) or, as some say, the [*plants, or herbage, called*] رَبْل [q. v.]. (TA.) — And The *young ones of sheep* or *goats.* (Ḳ.) — And *Female infants* [*of the age*] *of forty days;* (Ḳ, TA; [in the CḲ, نَبات is erroneously put for بَنَات;]) *but when their* [*hair termed*] عَقِيقَة *has been cut off, this appellation is no longer applied to them:* so says Lth; but Az pronounces him to have erred: (TA:) or it is with غ (Ḳ, TA) and ذ, both dotted, or only the former of them dotted, and one of them is called غَذِىٌّ [or غَذَوِىٌّ, or غَدِىٌّ or غَدَوِىٌّ]: thus in the M, and thus accord. to Az. (TA.)

عُدْوَانٌ [expl. in the Ṣ as signifying *Sheer* or *unmixed, wrongful* or *unjust* or *injurious* or *tyrannical conduct,*] is an inf. n. of عَدَا in the phrase عَدَا عَلَيْهِ [q. v.]; (ISd, Mṣb, Ḳ;) as also عِدْوَانٌ. (ISd, Ḳ.)

عَدَوَانٌ, applied to a wolf, (Ṣ, Ḳ,) means يَعْدُو عَلَى النَّاسِ [i. e. *That acts aggressively against men*]; (Ṣ, TA;) *i. q.* ▼ عَادٍ [app. in this sense], (Ḳ, TA,) which occurs in a trad. applied to a beast of prey, (TA,) an epithet applied to a beast of prey by the Prophet: (Mgh:) one says سَبُعٌ عَادٍ and سِبَاعٌ عَادِيَةٌ. (Mṣb.) [In the Ṣ, immediately after the words يَعْدُو عَلَى النَّاسِ, it is added, and hence their saying, السُّلْطَانُ ذُو عَدَوَانٍ وَذُو بَدَوَانٍ; and thus I find the saying cited as from the Ṣ in arts. عدو and بدو of the PṢ: but I think that عَدَوَانٍ and بَدَوَانٍ, here, are mistranscriptions for عَدَوَاتٍ and بَدَوَاتٍ, as I find them written in my copies of the Ṣ and TA in the arts. above mentioned: see عَدْوَةٌ, above; and see بَدَآءٌ in art. بدو, where it seems to be clearly shown that بَدَوَاتٌ is correct, as pl. of بَدَآءٌ.] — Also, (Ṣ, Ḳ, and Ḥam p. 81,) and ▼ عَدَّآءٌ, (Mgh, Mṣb, Ḳ, and Ḥam ubi suprà,) *That runs vehemently,* or *much;* (Ṣ, Mgh, Mṣb, Ḳ;*) *i. q.* كَثِيرُ العَدْوِ, (Ṣ, TA,) or شَدِيدُ العَدْوِ; (Ḥam;) applied to a horse: (Mgh, and Ḥam:) [and to a man:] الشَّدِيدَةُ, in the Ḳ, is a mistake for الشَّدِيدُ العَدْوِ, meaning الشَّدِيدُهُ. (TA.)

عَدَآءٌ an inf. n. of عَدَا in the phrase عَدَا عَلَيْهِ [q. v.]. (Ṣ, Mgh, Mṣb, Ḳ.) — And, as also ▼ عِدَآءٌ, *A single* طَلَق [or *heat;* i. e., *a single run, at once, to a goal,* or *limit*]; (Ḳ, TA;) of a horse. (TA.) ═ And عَدَآءُ كُلِّ شَيْءٍ, (Ṣ, Ḳ,) as also ▼ عِدَاؤُهُ, (Ḳ, TA,) [the latter written in the CḲ عِدَاؤُهُ, but] the former is with the lengthened ا and the latter with the shortened ا, (TA,) and ▼ عَدْوَتُهُ and ▼ عِدْوَتُهُ and ▼ عُدْوَتُهُ, (Ḳ,) signify طَوَارُهُ, (Ṣ, Ḳ,) i. e. [*The equal, of anything, in breadth and length;* or] *what is coextensive with anything in its breadth and its length.* (Ṣ, TA.) One says, لَزِمْتُ عَدَآءَ الطَّرِيقِ, or النَّهْرِ, or الجَبَلِ, meaning طَوَارَهُ [i. e. *I kept to the tract coextensive in its breadth and its length with the road,* or *the river,* or *the mountain*]. (TA.) ═ See also عُدَوَآءُ, first and third sentences. ═ And see عِدْوَةٌ, and عِدًى.

عِدَآءٌ: see the next preceding paragraph: ═ and see also عِدًى.

عَدُوٌّ *An enemy, contr. of* وَلِىٌّ, (Ṣ,) or *of* صَدِيقٌ, (Ḳ,) or *of* صَدِيقٌ مُوَالٍ; (Mṣb;) an epithet, but resembling a subst.: (Ṣ:) [and (like our word "enemy" in military parlance) *a hostile party:* for] it is used alike as sing. and pl. and masc. and fem.; (Mṣb, Ḳ;) as is said in the "Mukhtaṣar el-'Eyn:" (Mṣb:) but sometimes it is dualized and pluralized and feminized: (Ḳ:) the pl. is أَعْدَآءٌ; (Ṣ, Mṣb, Ḳ;) and the pl. of أَعْدَآءٌ is أَعَادٍ; (Mṣb, Ḳ;*) and عُدًى and عِدًى are also pls. of عَدُوٌّ; (Ṣ, Mṣb, Ḳ; [each improperly termed in the Ḳ اِسْمُ جَمْعٍ; for فِعَلٌ and فُعَلٌ are measures of pls., not of quasi-pl. ns.;]) the former said by ISk to be the only pl. of this measure among epithets; (Ṣ, Mṣb;*) and عُدَاةٌ, with ḍamm and with ة, is another pl.; (Th, Ṣ, Mṣb;) and is pl. of ▼ عَادٍ, (Ḳ, TA,) which is *syn. with* عَدُوٌّ; (Ṣ, Ḳ, TA;) as in the saying of a woman of the Arabs, أَشْمَتَ رَبُّ العَالَمِينَ عَادِيَكَ [*May the Lord of the beings of the universe make thy enemy to rejoice at thy affliction*]: (Ṣ, TA:) the fem. form of عَدُوٌّ is عَدُوَّةٌ, (Ṣ, Mṣb,) which is said by Az to be used when the meaning of an epithet is intended: (Mṣb:) it is said by ISk, (Ṣ, TA,) and in the "Bari'," (Mṣb,) that there is no instance of the measure فَعُولٌ in the sense of فَاعِلٌ but its fem. is without ة, except عَدُوَّةٌ, (Ṣ, Mṣb, Ḳ,) in the phrase هٰذِهِ عَدُوَّةُ ٱللّٰهِ [*This woman is the enemy of God*]: accord. to Fr, عَدُوَّةٌ has the affix ة to assimilate it to صَدِيقَةٌ; for a word is sometimes formed to accord with its contr.: (Ṣ, TA:) AZ says that he heard certain of the tribe of 'Okeyl say, [of some women,] هُنَّ وَلِيَّاتُ ٱللّٰهِ and عَدُوَّاتُ ٱللّٰهِ and أَوْلِيَاؤُهُ and أَعْدَاؤُهُ [i. e. *They are the friends of God* and *the enemies of God*]. (Mṣb.) [The pl.] عِدًى signifies also *Persons distant,* or *remote, one from another:* (ISd, Ḳ, TA:) and (Ḳ) *strangers,* or *foreigners:* (ISk, Ṣ, Ḳ, TA:) and *such as are distant,* or *remote, in respect of relationship;* or *not relations:* (TA:) as well as *enemies:* (M, TA:) كَالأَعْدَآءِ, which is added in the Ḳ after وَالغُرَبَآءِ, should be وَالأَعْدَآءِ. (TA.)

عُدَىٌّ is a pl. [or rather a quasi-pl. n.] of عَادٍ, q. v. (Ṣ, TA.)

عَدَاوَةٌ *Enmity,* or *hostility;* (Ṣ, Ḳ, TA;) like مُعَادَاةٌ [inf. n. of 3, q. v.]. (TA.)

عَدَّآءٌ: see عَدَوَانٌ, last sentence.

عَادٍ [act. part. n. of عَدَا, q. v. — As such particularly signifying] *Acting wrongfully, unjustly, injuriously,* or *tyrannically; transgressing,* or *exceeding the proper limit:* (Mṣb, TA:) pl. عَادُونَ. (Mṣb.) Hence the saying, لَا أَشْمَتَ ٱللّٰهُ بِكَ عَادِيَكَ i. e. [*May God not make to rejoice at thy affliction*] *him who acts wrongfully to thee.* (TA.) [And hence the phrase لِصٌّ عَادِى ظَهْرٍ, expl. in art. ظهر.] See also عَدَوَانٌ. And see عَدُوٌّ, with which it is syn. — Also *Seizing,* or *carrying off, by force;* or *snatching at unawares.* (TA.) And العَادِى signifies [particularly] *The lion;* (Ḳ, TA;) because of his injuriousness, and his seizing men and making them his prey. (TA.) — ▼ عُدًى is a pl. of عَادٍ, [or rather a quasi-pl. n.,] like as غُزًّى is of غَازٍ; as such signifying *Runners upon their feet:* (Ṣ, TA:) or *a company of men,* (Ḳ, TA,) in the dial. of Hudheyl, (TA,) *that run to the fight* (Ḳ, TA) and *the like:* (TA:) or the *first, of the footmen,* [or *foot-soldiers,*] *that charge,* or *assault;* (Ḳ, TA;) because they run quickly: (TA:) like عَادِيَةٌ, (Ḳ, TA,) of which the pl. is عَوَادٍ, (TA,) in both senses: or this signifies the *horsemen;* (Ḳ, TA;) i. e. the *first, of the horsemen, that charge,* or *assault, in a hostile,* or *predatory, incursion,* especially; (TA;) or *horses making a hostile,* or *predatory, incursion;* and hence [the pl.] العَادِيَات in the Ḳur c. 1. (TA in the supplement to this art.) And accord. to El-Khuwárezmee, عُدَىٌّ particularly signifies The *foot-messengers of the sovereign*, and *of the judge, who are made to run in quest of one against whom an accusation has been made, and to bring him, for the purpose of exacting from him the right, or due, of his accuser.* (De Sacy's Chrest. Arabe, sec. ed., iii. 100.) ═ عَادِى العَوَادِى, a phrase used by a poet, is expl. by IAar as meaning *The hardest*, or *most pressing*, or *most severe, of occupations that turn one away*, or *back, from a thing.* (TA.) ═ See also عَادٍ and its fem. عَادِيَةٌ voce عُدْوَةٌ. ═ عَادِيَا اللَّوْحِ signifies طَرَفَاهُ [*The two extremities*, or *two sides, of the tablet* or *the like*]; (K, TA;) each of them being called عادى [i. e. عَادِى اللَّوحِ, or a mistranscription for عَادٍ], like عِدى [i. e. ▾ عِدًى or ▾ عُدًى, both mentioned above, voce عُدْوَةٌ, as meaning, absolutely, *a side*, or *lateral part* or *portion*]. (TA.)

عَادِيَةٌ [fem. of. عَادٍ, q. v. ═ As a subst., it signifies] *Wrongdoing, injustice, injuriousness*, or *tyranny*; and *evil*, or *mischief*; (S, TA;) as in the saying دَفَعْتُ عَنْكَ عَادِيَةَ فُلَانٍ [*I repelled*, or *have repelled, from thee the wrongdoing* &c., and *the evil*, or *mischief, of such a one*]: (S:) it is an inf. n. [or rather a quasi-inf. n.] like عَافِيَةٌ: and signifies also *sharpness*, or *hastiness, of temper*; and *anger.* (TA.) Also The *harm*, or *hurt*, of poison. (Har p. 304.) ═ See also عُدَوَآءُ, in three places. ═ عَوَادِى الكَرْمِ, (K, TA,) of which عَادِيَةٌ is the sing., (TA,) signifies *The grape-vines that are planted at the feet*, or *roots, of great trees.* (K, TA.)

أَعْدَى [a noun denoting the comparative and superlative degrees, and having several different significations]. أَعْدَى مِنَ الجَرَبِ *More transitive*, or *wont to pass from one to another, than the mange*, or *scab*, is a prov. (Meyd.) And أَعْدَى مِنَ الثُّوَبَآءِ is another prov., having a similar meaning [i. e. *More wont to pass from one to another*, or, as we commonly say, *more catching, than yawning*]; (Meyd;) for when a man yawns in the presence of others, they become affected as he is. (TA in art. ثأب.) — أَعْدَى مِنَ الذِّئْبِ is also a prov., and may mean *More wrongful*, or *more inimical*, or *more vehement in running, than the wolf.* (Meyd.) أَعْدَى مِنْ سُلَيْكٍ, another prov., (expl. in the latter half of the first paragraph,) is from العَدْوُ. (Meyd.) — هُوَ أَعْدَى شَىْءٍ [app. meaning *It is the most effectual thing to aid*, or *assist*, or *to avenge*; أَعْدَى in this case being irregularly formed from the augmented verb in the phrase أَعْدَاهُ عَلَيْهِ]. (TA in art. ادو: see آدَى in that art.)

تَعَادٍ *Uneven places*, (K, TA,) *dissimilar in their several parts*: occurring in this sense in a trad. (TA.) As mentions the saying نِمْتُ عَلَى ▾ مَكَانٍ مُتَعَادٍ, meaning [*I slept upon*] *a place dissimilar in its several parts*; *uneven*: and هٰذِهِ ▾ أَرْضٌ مُتَعَادِيَةٌ *This is land having in it burrows*, and [*trenches*, or *channels, such as are termed*] نَفَاقِيق. (S, TA.)

مَا لِى عَنْ فُلَانٍ مَعْدًى means *There is not for me any going beyond such a one to another, nor any stopping short of him.* (S.)

مَعْدُوٌّ: see what next follows.

فُلَانٌ مَعْدِىٌّ عَلَيْهِ and ▾ مَعْدُوٌّ (S, K*) mean [*Such a one is*] *treated wrongfully, unjustly, injuriously*, or *tyrannically*: (K:) the ى in مَعْدِىٌّ is substituted for و because the latter [in this case] is deemed difficult of utterance. (S.)

مُتَعَادٍ; and its fem., with ة: see تَعَادٍ.

عذب

1. عَذُبَ, (S, O, Msb, K, TA,) aor. ـُ, (TA,) inf. n. عُذُوبَةٌ, said of water, (S, O, Msb, K, TA,) [and app. of wine or other beverage, and of food, (see عَذْبٌ,)] *It was*, or *became, sweet*: (S, O,* TA:) or *it was*, or *became, easy and agreeable to be drunk* or *swallowed.* (Msb.) [See also 12. — Freytag has also assigned to it a meaning belonging to أَعْذَبَ, q. v.] ═ عَذَبَ: see 4, in two places. ═ And see also 2, last sentence. ═ [عَذِبَ, inf. n. عَذَبٌ, is mentioned by Golius as signifying "*Quisquiliis* aut *lente palustri obducta fuit*," and in a similar manner by Freytag; by both as said of water, and as on the authority of the K: but I find, in the K, no ground for this, except an explanation of عَذِبٌ, q. v., of which ISd knew not a verb.]

2. عَذَّبَهُ, inf. n. تَعْذِيبٌ, *He punished, castigated*, or *chastised, him*: (S, O, Msb, K:) [and *he*, or *it, tormented*, or *tortured, him*:] originally, *he beat him*: then, *he punished him in any painful manner.* (Msb.) It is said in a trad., إِنَّ المَيِّتَ يُعَذَّبُ بِبُكَآءِ أَهْلِهِ عَلَيْهِ [*Verily the dead will be punished for his family's weeping for him*]: the reason of which is probably this; that the Arabs used to charge their families to weep and wail for them; therefore the dead is obnoxious to punishment for his having done this. (IAth, TA.) And the verb is used metaphorically in relation to that which has not sensation: a poet says,

* لَيْسَتْ بِسَوْدَآءَ مِنْ مَيْثَآءِ مُظْلِمَةٍ *
* وَلَمْ تُعَذَّبْ بِإِدْنَآءٍ مِنَ النَّارِ *

[*It* (app. wine) *is not black, from Meythà, dark-coloured; nor has it been mulled* (such seems to be here the meaning of the verb) *by being put near to fire*, or by being boiled]. (L, TA. [See also مُعَذَّبَةٌ.]) — See also 4, in two places. ═ عَذَّبَ سَوْطَهُ, and هَذَّبَهُ, [perhaps a mistranscription for ▾ عَذَبَهُ, for accord. to Golius, this last and the first here mentioned are expl. by Z in the sense here following,] *He put an* عِلَاقَة [i. e. *an* عَذَبَة] *to his whip*: so in the A. (TA.)

4. اعذب القَوْمُ *The people*, or *party, became in the condition of having sweet water.* (K, TA. [Freytag has erroneously assigned this meaning to عَذُبَ.]) ═ And اعذب, (O, TA,) inf. n. إِعْذَابٌ, (K, TA,) *He abstained*, or *desisted*, (O, K,* TA,) عَنْ شَىْءٍ *from a thing*; (TA;) and, (K, TA,) in like manner followed by عَنْ, (TA,) *he left, quitted*, or *relinquished*, (K, TA,) a thing: (TA:) and ▾ استعذب, (K, TA,) likewise followed by عَنْ, (TA,) signifies the same: (K, TA:) and عَذْبٌ, (K, TA,) as inf. n. of ▾ عَذَبَ, (MF, TA,) signifies the *abstaining*, &c., (K, MF, TA,) from a thing: and [particularly] the *abstaining* (of a man, and of an ass, and of a horse, TA) *from eating, by reason of intense thirst*; (K, TA;) *being neither fasting nor breaking fast*; (TA;) and so عُذُوبٌ as inf. n. of the same verb. (MF, TA.) ═ And اعذبهُ, (S, O,) inf. n. إِعْذَابٌ; (K;) and ▾ عذّبهُ, (O,) inf. n. تَعْذِيبٌ; (K;) and ▾ عَذَبَهُ, (O,) inf. n. عَذْبٌ; (K;) *He prevented, hindered, withheld, restrained*, or *forbade, him*, (S, O, K,*) عَنِ الأَمْرِ *from* [doing] *the thing*, or *affair.* (S, O.) One says, أَعْذِبْ نَفْسَكَ عَنْ كَذَا *Withhold*, or *restrain, thyself from such a thing.* (S, O.) ═ اعذبهُ [*He deprived it of its* عَذَب; i. e.] *he removed from it*, (S, O, K,) namely, water, (K,) or a watering-trough, or tank, (S, O,) *the floating particles that were upon it*, (S, O,) or *its* [*green substance termed*] طُحْلُب, (K,) or *both of these*: (TA:) and ▾ تَعْذِيبٌ [in like manner] signifies the *removing of what is termed* عَذَب. (Bd in ii. 6.)

8. اعتذب *He made* [*the*] *two ends* (عَذَبَتَيْنِ) *of his turban to hang down behind.* (O, K, TA.)

10. استعذب المَآءَ *He reckoned*, or *esteemed, the water sweet.* (O, Msb, TA.) — And *He sought sweet water*: you say, استعذب لِأَهْلِهِ *he sought sweet water for his family.* (TA.) — And *He drank the water sweet.* (TA.) — And *He drew sweet water.* (S, O, K.*) One says, يُسْتَعْذَبُ لِفُلَانٍ مِنْ بِئْرِ كَذَا i. e. [*Sweet water*] *is drawn for such a one from such a well.* (S, O.) — And استعذب لَهُ المَآءَ *He brought to him sweet water.* (TA.) ═ See also 4.

12. اعذوذب, like اِحْلَوْلَى, said of water, *It was*, or *became, sweet*, [like عَذُبَ,] or *very sweet.* (Lb, TA.)

عَذْبٌ *Sweet water*: (S, O:) or water, (Msb,) or wine, or beverage, and food, (K,) *that is easy and agreeable to be drunk* or *swallowed*: (Msb, K:) pl. عِذَابٌ (O, Msb, TA) and عُذُوبٌ. (TA.) You say رَكِيَّةٌ عَذْبَةٌ [*A well of sweet water*]: and مَآءٌ عَذْبٌ [*sweet water*]: and also مَآءَةٌ عَذْبَةٌ [*a sweet water*]: and مَآءٌ عِذَابٌ [*sweet water* or *waters*], using a pl. epithet in this last case because مَآءٌ is a coll. gen. n., of which مَآءَةٌ is the n. un. (TA.) And Aboo-Heiyeh En-Nemeree says, describing water,

* لَهُ غَلَلٌ بَيْنَ الإِجَامِ عُذُوبُ *

[*Having sweet water permeating amid the reed-beds*, or *the thickets*]: he uses غَلَلٌ as a coll. gen. n., and therefore pluralizes the epithet. (L,

TA.) — One says also نِسَآءٌ عِذَابُ الثَّنَايَا †[*Women sweet in respect of the front teeth*]. (A.) — And إِنَّهُ لَعَذْبُ اللِّسَانِ †[*Verily he is sweet in respect of the tongue*]; likening his tongue to the water that is termed عَذْب. (Lḥ, TA.) ═ Also *A sort of trees;* (Ḳ, TA;) the same that is called عَذَبٌ [q. v.]. (TA.)

عَذَبٌ, (Ṣ, O, Ḳ,) [a coll. gen. n.] of which, in all its senses, the n. un. is ▼ عَذَبَةٌ, (Ḳ, TA,) *Motes, or particles of rubbish or the like,* (Ṣ, O, Ḳ, TA,) *floating upon water.* (TA.) [In this sense, it is said in the Ṣ and O that عَذَبَةٌ is its sing. or n. un.] One says مَآءٌ ذُو عَذَبٍ *Water abounding with such motes or particles.* (Ṣ, O. See also عَذِبٌ.) And ▼ عَذِبَةٌ has the same meaning as the n. un. of عَذَبٌ in this sense: (Ḳ:) and signifies likewise, as also ▼ عَذَبَةٌ and ▼ عُذْبَةٌ, (L, Ḳ,) this last mentioned by IAạr, (L,) [the *green substance called*] طُحْلُب (L, Ḳ, TA) *and* عَرْمَض *and the like,* (L, TA,) or طُحْلُب *and dung* (دِمْن), *floating upon water.* (TA.) — And *What comes forth next after the fœtus from the womb.* (O, Ḳ.) ═ Also *A sort of trees,* (AḤn, O, Ḳ,) *of the shrub-kind:* (AḤn, O:) the same that is called عَذْبٌ. (TA.) ═ And The *pieces of rag that women hold when wailing for the dead;* as also مَعَاذِبُ, (O, Ḳ,) pl. of ▼ مَعْذَبَةٌ [or probably مِعْذَبَةٌ, like its syn. مِثْلَاةٌ, originally مِثْلَوَةٌ], or, accord. to AA, an anomalous pl. of [the n. un. of عَذَبٌ, i. e.] عَذَبَةٌ: (O:) one of such pieces of rag is also called مِعْوَز, as well as عَذَبَةٌ. (TA.) — And *Straps,* or *thongs:* (Ṣ, O:) or the *extremities thereof;* as also ▼ عَذَبَاتٌ. (TA.) So in the saying of Dhu-r-Rummeh, (Ṣ, O, TA,) describing dogs of the chase, (O,)

• غُضْفٌ مُهَرَّتَةُ الأَشْدَاقِ ضَارِيَةٌ •
• مِثْلُ السَّرَاحِينِ فِى أَعْنَاقِهَا العَذَبُ •

[*Having pendulous ears, wide in the sides of the mouth, habituated to the chase, resembling wolves, with straps, or thongs, or the extremities thereof, upon their necks*]. (Ṣ, O, TA.) — Also, (Ḳ,) or ▼ عَذَبَةٌ, in this and other senses following, (Ṣ, O, Mṣb, &c.,) [the former evidently wrong, the latter (as is said in the Ḳ) being its n. un. in all its senses,] The *string with which a balance, or pair of scales, is raised.* (Ṣ, O, Mṣb, Ḳ.) — And The *end,* or *extremity,* of a whip; (Mgh in art. ثمر, and Mṣb;) its *tail;* also called its ثَمَرَة: (Mgh ubi suprà:) or its عِلَاقَة, (TA in the present art.,) which means the [*suspensory*] *thong in the handle* thereof: (TA in art. علق:) or [it may have both of these significations, for it is said that it is] *one of the* عَذَبَتَانِ of a whip. (Ṣ, O.) — The *end,* or *extremity* of anything. (A, Ḳ.) — The *extremity* of the tongue; (Ṣ, O, Mṣb;) its [*tip* or] *narrow extremity:* (TA:) pl. ▼ عَذَبَاتٌ. (Mṣb.) One says, الحَقُّ عَلَى عَذَبَاتِ ▼ أَلْسِنَتِهِمْ [*Truth is on the tips of their tongues*]. (A, TA.) — The *extremity of the penis* of a camel: (ISd, Ḳ, TA:) or the *extremity of a camel's penis thin in the fore part.* (TA.) — The *part that hangs down* of the [thong called] شِرَاك [q. v.] of a sandal. (O, TA. [See also ذُؤَابَةٌ.]) — *A piece of skin which is hung behind the hinder part* (مُؤْخِرَة, O, Ḳ, or مُؤَخَّرَة, CḲ) *of the* [*camel's saddle called*] رَحْل, (O, Ḳ,) *from its upper portion;* (O;) also termed ذُؤَابَةٌ. (TA in art. ذأب.) — And عَذَبٌ [accord. to the TA, but correctly ▼ عَذَبَةٌ, (see 8,)] The *portion* [i. e. *end*] of a turban, *that is made to hang down between the shoulders.* (TA.) — And the same, [correctly ▼ عَذَبَةٌ, as is shown by what follows,] *A piece of rag* [or *strip of linen or the like,* called in French *cravate,*] *that is bound upon the head of a spear.* (TA.) One says, خَفَقَتْ عَلَى رَأْسِهِ العَذَبُ (A, TA) i. e. خِرَقُ الأَلْوِيَةِ [*The cravates fluttered over his head*]. (A.) — And ▼ عَذَبَةٌ signifies also *A branch* of a tree; (Ṣ, O, Mṣb;) and so ▼ عُذْبَةٌ. (TA.)

عَذِبٌ (Ḳ, TA) and ▼ ذُو عَذَبٍ (TA) Water *overspread by* [*the green substance termed*] طُحْلُب: (Ḳ, TA:) or *abounding therewith, and with motes, or particles of rubbish or the like:* (TA:) [or the latter signifies as expl. before: see عَذَبٌ, third sentence:] عَذِبٌ is thought by ISd to be a possessive epithet, [meaning ذُو عَذَبٍ,] because he found no verb belonging to it. (TA.) ═ عَذِبٌ is also syn. with عَطِبٌ meaning A man *alighting, or abiding, in places of dried-up herbage, and in a waterless desert.* (TA in art. عطب.)

عُذْبَةٌ: see عَذَبٌ. ═ Also *A certain tree, that kills camels,* (O, Ḳ, TA,) *if they eat thereof.* (TA.) — And *A well-known medicine.* (Ḳ, TA. [In some copies of the Ḳ, دَآءٌ, or "disease," is put for دَوَآءٌ, accord. to the TḲ, as observed by Freytag.])

عَذَبَةٌ, and its pl. عَذَبَاتٌ: see عَذَبٌ, in nine places. — The pl. above mentioned signifies also The *legs* of a she-camel. (TA.)

عَذِبَةٌ: see عَذَبٌ, fourth and last sentences. ═ Also *What is taken forth from* طَعَام [i. e. *wheat,* or *corn* in general,] *and thrown away;* (Lḥ, Ḳ, TA;) being the *worst thereof;* also termed عِذْرَةٌ. (Lḥ, TA in art. عذر.) ═ And *Pasturage,* or *herbage:* so in the phrase مَآءٌ مَا بِهِ عَذِبَةٌ, (O,) or مَآءٌ لَا عَذِبَةَ فِيهِ [*Water where is no pasturage,* or *herbage*]. (TA.) — It is also expl. in copies of the Ḳ as signifying, with the article, مَا أَحَاطَ مِنَ الدِّرَّةِ: but the right explanation is مَا أَحَاطَ بِالدَّبْرَةِ [app. meaning *The ridge of earth that surrounds a sown piece of ground to retain the water for irrigation* (see دَبْرٌ)], as in the M and L &c. (TA.)

عُذَبِىٌّ, (thus in my copies of the Ṣ,) or عُذَبِىٌّ, (O, Ḳ, TA,) with the pointed ذ, accord. to AA, mentioned in the T in art. عدب, as written with the unpointed د, and here said in the Ḳ to be *syn. with* عُذَبِىٌّ, (TA,) *Generous in natural dispositions.* (AA, Ṣ, O, TA.)

أَصَابَهُ عَذَابٌ عِذَبِينَ, (O, Ḳ, TA,) with kesr to the ع and fet-ḥ to the ذ, (O, TA,) like بِلَغِينَ, (Ḳ, TA, in the CḲ عُذَبِينَ like بُلَغِينَ,) and أَصَابَهُ العِذَبُونَ, (O, TA,) [*May the punishment that will not be remitted befall him,* or] *may his punishment not be remitted:* (O, Ḳ, TA:) so says Ibn-Buzurj. (O, TA.)

عَذَابٌ *Punishment, castigation,* or *chastisement,* [or] *such as serves to give warning to others than the sufferer,* or *to restrain the offender from repeating the offence;* syn. عُقُوبَةٌ, (Ṣ, O,) or نَكَالٌ: (Ḳ, and Ksh and Bḍ in ii. 6:) so termed from عَذَبَ "he prevented" &c.; because it prevents the person punished from returning to the like of his offence, and prevents others from doing the like of that which he has done: (MF, TA:) [it generally signifies *any corporal punishment:*] and, by an extension of the original signification, *any* [*infliction of*] *pain that disgraces,* or *puts to shame:* (Ksh and Bḍ ubi suprà:) originally, *beating:* afterwards used to signify *any painful punishment:* [*torture;* or *torment:*] and metaphorically applied to ‡ *an affair,* or *event, that is difficult, distressing, afflicting,* or *troublesome;* whence the saying, السَّفَرُ قِطْعَةٌ مِنَ العَذَابِ [*Travel is a portion of that which is difficult,* &c.; or *of torment*]: (Mṣb:) in the Ḳur xxiii. 78, it means *hunger,* or *famine:* (Zj, O, TA:) the pl. is أَعْذِبَةٌ: (Zj, Ḳ, TA:) the author of the Ḳ says in art. نهر [voce نَهَارٌ] that it has no pl.: [and it seems to be doubted whether it have a pl. because it is properly an inf. n. though its verb in the unaugmented form is not used:] but MF observes that if it be a name for that whereby one is prevented [from repeating an offence], as hunger, or famine, agreeably with what Zj says, there is no reason why it should not have this pl. (TA.)

عَذُوبٌ: see عَاذِبٌ, in seven places.

عَذَابَةٌ The *womb;* thus mentioned by Az, on the authority of El-Mundhiree and AHeyth, with the pointed ذ; (O, TA;) *i. q.* عَدَابَةٌ. (Ḳ, TA.)

عَاذِبٌ and ▼ عَذُوبٌ, applied to a horse or the like, &c., (Ṣ, O,) *Such as is standing still,* or *stopping from fatigue,* (قَائِمٌ, Ṣ,) *that will not eat nor drink:* (Ṣ, O:) or *abstaining,* or *that abstains, from eating, by reason of intense thirst;* (Ḳ, TA;) applied to a man, and an ass, and a horse: but Az says that the assertion respecting these two epithets that they signify [a horse, &c.] *that neither eats nor drinks* is more correct than the assertion respecting ▼ عَذُوبٌ that it signifies [one] *that abstains from eating by reason of his thirst:* also, that عَاذِبٌ signifies any animal, but generally a horse and a camel, *that will not eat anything:* accord. to Th, this and ▼ عَذُوبٌ signify a horse or the like *standing still, or stopping from fatigue,* (قَائِمٌ,) *that raises his head, and will not eat nor drink;* and the former, *that passes a night without eating anything:* (TA:) the pl. of عَاذِبٌ is عُذُوبٌ, like as سُجُودٌ is a pl. of سَاجِدٌ: and the pl. of ▼ عَذُوبٌ is عُذُبٌ, and, accord. to

A'Obeyd, عُذُوبٌ [like as هُجُودٌ is pl. of هَجُودٌ]: Az says that this is a mistake, for a word of the measure فَعُولٌ does not form a pl. of the measure فُعُولٌ; but [SM says] this is an extr. instance; and he who preserves an authority in his mind is an evidence against him who does not. (TA.) One says, بَاتَ عَذُوبًا ↓, meaning *He passed the night without eating or drinking anything;* because abstaining therefrom. (O.) — عَاذِبٌ signifies also [*Unsheltered;*] *having no covering between him and the sky;* (O, Ḳ;) and so ↓ عَذُوبٌ. (Ḳ, TA.) El-Jaadee says, describing a wild bull (ثَوْر وَحْشِىّ [a species of bovine antelope]) that had passed the night alone, tasting nothing,

* فَبَاتَ عَذُوبًا ↓ لِلسَّمَآءِ كَأَنَّهُ *
* سُهَيْلٌ إِذَا مَا أَفْرَدَتْهُ الكَوَاكِبُ *

[*And he passed the night exposed without shelter to the sky, as though he were Canopus when the other stars have left him solitary*]. (TA.)

الأَعْذَبَانِ [*The two most sweet things;*] *saliva* (الرِّيق, Ṣ, O, Ḳ, or الرُّضَاب, A) *and wine:* (Ṣ, A, O, Ḳ: [for, in the amorous language of the Arab, the sweetness of the saliva of his beloved is often praised:]) or *food and coïtus.* (Ḳ.)

لِجَامٌ مُعْذِبٌ *A bridle that withholds from going away in a headlong manner.* (O.)

مَعْذَبَةٌ [or مِعْذَبَةٌ?]: see عَذَبٌ.

مُعَذَّبَةٌ [for خَمْرٌ مُعَذَّبَةٌ] *Wine mixed* [*with water, or with some other thing or things*]. (A, TA.) — And معذب [app. مُعَذَّب] is applied by the vulgar to Fresh ripe dates *soaked with water.* (TA voce مَنْقُوش.) — سَوْطٌ مُعَذَّبٌ *A whip having an* عِلَاقَة [or عَذَبَة] *attached to it.* (TA.)

اِمْرَأَةٌ مِعْذَابُ الرِّيقِ *A woman whose saliva is pleasant to be swallowed, and sweet.* (TA.)

عذر

1. عَذَرَهُ, aor. ِ, inf. n. عُذْرٌ (Ṣ, O, Mṣb, Ḳ) and عُذُرٌ (Ṣ, O, Ḳ) and عُذْرَى (O, Ḳ) and مَعْذِرَةٌ and مَعْذُرَةٌ (Ḳ) [all of which are also used as simple substs.]; and ↓ اعذرهُ; (Ṣ, O, Mṣb, Ḳ;) *He excused him; freed, cleared, or exempted, him from blame; exculpated him:* (Mṣb:) or *he accepted his excuse:* properly, عَذَرْتُ signifies *I cancelled evil conduct.* (TA.) [See also عُذْرٌ below.] You say, عَذَرْتُهُ فِيمَا صَنَعَ (Ṣ, O, Mṣb) *I excused, or exculpated, him for what he did.* (Mṣb.) And in a trad. of El-Mikdád it is said, لَقَدْ أَعْذَرَ ↓ اللّٰهُ إِلَيْكَ i. e. *Verily God hath excused thee,* and exempted thee from the obligation to fight against the unbelievers; for he had become extremely fat, and unable to fight. (TA.) And you say [also], عَذَرَهُ عَنِ الشَّىْءِ, *He excused him for, or from, the thing.* (MA.) [And accord. to Golius, عَذَرَهُ عَلَى الشَّىْءِ, as well as فِى الشَّىْءِ: but he has not mentioned his authority: see an explanation of عَذِيرٌ, from which the former phrase was perhaps derived by him.] And عَذَرْتُهُ مِنْ فُلَانٍ [*I excused him, or held him excusable, for his conduct to such a one*]; meaning, I did not blame him, but I blamed such a one. (Ṣ,* TA.) And مَنْ يَعْذِرُنِى مِنْهُ *Who will excuse me, or make my excuse, if I requite him* (Mṣb, TA) *for his action,* (Mṣb,) or *for his evil action,* (TA,) *and will not blame me* (Mṣb, TA) *for it?* (Mṣb:) or *who will excuse me with respect to his case, and will not blame me for it?* (Mṣb.) [And a similar ex. is mentioned in the TA with فِى in the place of مِنْ.] — [Hence,] عَذَرَ, (Az, Ṣ, IḲṭṭ, O, Mṣb, Ḳ,) aor. ِ; (O, TA;) and ↓ اعذر, (Ṣ, IḲṭṭ, Mṣb, Ḳ,) inf. n. إِعْذَارٌ; (TA;) *He was vitious, or faulty, and corrupt:* (Mṣb:) or *he was guilty of many crimes, sins, faults, offences, or acts of disobedience,* (Ṣ, O, Mṣb, Ḳ,) *so as to render him excusable who punished him.* (TA.) It is said in a trad., لَنْ يَهْلِكَ النَّاسُ حَتَّى يَعْذِرُوا مِنْ أَنْفُسِهِمْ, (O, and so in some copies of the Ṣ and Ḳ,) or ↓ يُعْذِرُوا, (so in other copies of the Ṣ and Ḳ,) both of which readings are the same in meaning, (TA,) i. e. [*Men will not perish, or die,*] *until they are guilty of many crimes, or sins, &c.;* (Ṣ, O, Mṣb, Ḳ;) meaning, (accord. to A'Obeyd, Ṣ, O,) *until they deserve punishment, so as to render excusable him who punishes them.* (Ṣ, A, O, TA.) And you say, اعذر ↓ مِنْ نَفْسِهِ, meaning *He placed himself within the power of another.* (TA.) — And عَذَرْتُهُ *I aided him, or assisted him, against an enemy.* (Mṣb.) — عَذَرَ, inf. n. عَذْرٌ, *He cut, or cut off.* (TA: but only the inf. n. of the verb in this sense is there mentioned.) — And [hence, probably, as is implied in a passage in the TA, (see عُذْرَةٌ,)] عَذَرَ, aor. ِ, (Ṣ, O,* Mṣb, Ḳ,) inf. n. عَذْرٌ; (Ṣ, Mṣb;) and ↓ اعذر; (Ṣ, O, Mṣb, Ḳ;) both as expl. by A'Obeyd; (Ṣ;) ‡ *He circumcised* a boy, (Ṣ, O, Mṣb, Ḳ,) and in like manner a girl; (Ṣ, O, Mṣb;) but when a girl is the object, خَفَضَ is more common. (Ṣ, O.) — عَذَرَ الفَرَسَ بِالعِذَارِ, aor. ِ and ُ; and ↓ اعذرهُ; *He fastened, or bound, the horse's* عِذَار [q. v.]: (Ṣ, O, Ḳ:) and ↓ اعذر الفَرَسَ *he bridled the horse;* syn. أَلْجَمَهُ; (Ḳ, TA;) as also عَذَرَهُ, and ↓ عذّرهُ: (TA:) or ↓ اعذرهُ, (Ḳ,) or ↓ عذّرهُ, (thus in the TA,) *he put to him* [or *upon him*] *an* عِذَار; (Ḳ, TA;) and so عَذَرَهُ, aor. ِ and ُ, inf. n. عَذْرٌ: (Mṣb:) and اعذر ↓ *he put to the* لِجَام [i. e. *bridle or bit*] *an* عِذَار. (TA.) — And it is said in the Tahdheeb of IḲṭṭ that عَذَرْتُ الفَرَسَ, inf. n. عَذْرٌ, signifies *I cauterized the horse in the place of the* عِذَار: — and also حملت على عذاره [an explanation in which there seems to be a mistranscription or an omission, or both; perhaps correctly جَعَلْتُ عَلَى الفَرَسِ عِذَارَهُ *I put upon the horse his* عِذَار; a meaning given above]; and ↓ أَعْذَرْتُهُ is a dial. var. thereof. (TA.) — عُذِرَ said of a camel means *He was branded with the mark called* عِذَار. (TA.) — [Hence, app., the phrase عَذَرَهُ بِاللَّوْمِ † *He branded him with blame;* like خَطَمَهُ بِاللَّوْمِ, q. v.] — عَذَرَهُ, from العُذْرَةُ, *He* (God, Ṣ) *caused him* (i. e. a child, TA) *to be affected with the pain, in the fauces, termed* عُذْرَة: and عُذِرَ *He was, or became, affected therewith:* (Ṣ, Ḳ,* TA:) inf. n. عَذْرٌ and عُذْرَةٌ. (IḲṭṭ, TA.)

2. عذّر, inf. n. تَعْذِيرٌ, *He was without excuse;* (Ḳ,* TA;) as also ↓ عاذر, (Ḳ, TA,) inf. n. مُعَاذَرَةٌ: (TA:) *he affected to excuse himself, but had no excuse: he excused himself, but did not adduce an excuse* [*that was valid*]. (TA.) [See also 8.] — And *He was remiss, wanting, deficient, or defective,* (Ṣ, O, Mṣb, TA,) in an affair, (Ṣ, Mṣb,) *setting up an excuse* [*for being so*]; (O;) *fell short, or did less than was incumbent on him,* (Ṣ, O, Mṣb, TA,) in it; (Ṣ, Mṣb;) *did not exert himself, or act vigorously,* in it; (Mṣb, TA;) *causing it to be imagined that he had an excuse when he had none.* (Bḍ in ix. 91.) You say, قَامَ فُلَانٌ قِيَامَ تَعْذِيرٍ *Such a one acted remissly, falling short, or doing less than was incumbent on him.* (TA.) And it is said in a story of the Children of Israel, نَهَاهُمْ أَحْبَارُهُمْ تَعْذِيرًا *Their learned men forbade them remissly:* the inf. n. being here put in the place of the act. part. n. as a denotative of state; as it is in جَآءَ مَشْيًا. (O, TA.) [See also 4.] — Also ‡ *He made, or prepared, a feast,* (O, Ḳ,) *such as is termed* إِعْذَار [q. v.] (O) or عِذَار: (Ḳ:) and *he invited to a feast such as is thus termed.* (Ḳ. [Accord. to the TA, these are two distinct significations of the verb. See, again, 4.]) — عذّر الفَرَسَ: see 1, latter half, in two places. — عَذِّرْ عَنِّى بَعِيرَكَ, (Ṣ, O,) and ↓ أَعْذِرْهُ عَنِّى, (O,) *Brand thy camel with a brand different from that of mine, in order that our camels may be known, one from the other.* (Ṣ, O.) — عذّر الغُلَامُ *The hair of the boy's* عِذَار (Ḳ, TA) i. e. of his *cheek* (TA) *grew.* (Ḳ, TA.) — عذّر الدَّارَ (inf. n. as above, TA) *He effaced the traces of the house, or dwelling.* (Ḳ, TA.) — عذّرهُ, (Ṣ, O, Ḳ,) inf. n. as above, (Ṣ, O,) *He defiled, or besmeared, it* (a thing, Ḳ) *with* عَذِرَة [or *human dung*]. (Ṣ, O, Ḳ.)

3: see 2, first sentence. [And see also the last clause of the last paragraph of this art.]

4. اعذر: see 1, in five places from the commencement. — Also *He had an excuse;* [or *he was, or became, excusable;*] (Ṣ, O, Ḳ;) and so ↓ اعتذر. (Ṣ, O, Ḳ.) It is said in a prov., أَعْذَرَ مَنْ أَنْذَرَ [*He has an excuse, or is excusable, who warns*]. (Ṣ. [See also below: and see art. نذر. It is held by some in the present day that the ا in اعذر, in this phrase, has a privative effect, and that the meaning is, *He deprives of excuse who warns:* but for this I have not found any authority.]) And Lebeed says, (Ṣ, O, TA,) addressing his two daughters, (O, TA,) and telling them to wail and weep a year for him after his death, (TA,)

* إِلَى الحَوْلِ ثُمَّ ٱسْمُ السَّلَامِ عَلَيْكُمَا *
* وَمَنْ يَبْكِ حَوْلًا كَامِلًا فَقَدِ ٱعْتَذَرْ ↓ *

[*Until the end of the year: then the name of peace be on you both: for such as weeps a whole* year has become excusable]. (Ṣ, O.) You say also, أَعْذَرْتُ عِنْدَ السُّلْطَانِ *I got excuse of the Sulṭán* [or *ruling power*]. (TA.) —— And *He manifested an excuse:* (Ḳ, TA:) in which sense, عُذْرٌ is said to be its inf. n., as well as إِعْذَارٌ; but the former is correctly a simple subst. (TA.) And *He pleaded that by which he should be excused.* (TA.) [See also 8.] —— *He did that by which he should be excused.* (TA.) —— *He did that in which he should be excused:* hence the saying of Zuheyr,

سَتَمْنَعُكُمْ أَرْمَاحُنَا أَوْ سَنُعْذِرُ

[*Our spears shall prevent you,* or *shall defend you,*] *or we will do that in which we shall be excused.* (Ṣ, O: but in the latter, وَتَمْنَعُكُمْ.) —— And *He exceeded the usual bounds,* (A, Mgh, O,) or *went to the utmost point,* (TA,) *in excuse,* (A, Mgh, O, TA,) i. e. *in being excused.* (A.) So in the saying أَعْذَرَ مَنْ أَنْذَرَ [*He exceeds the usual bounds in rendering himself excused who warns*]. (A, Mgh, O. [See also above, third sentence.]) And it is said in a trad., لَقَدْ أَعْذَرَ ٱللّٰهُ إِلَى مَنْ بَلَغَ مِنَ العُمُرِ سِتِّينَ سَنَةً [app. meaning *Verily God hath freed himself from the imputation of injustice to an extraordinary degree,* or *to the utmost point, to him who hath attained sixty years of age:*] i. e. He hath left him no plea for excuse [for his sins], since He hath granted him respite for all this length of time and he hath not excused himself. (TA. [As اعذر is here followed by إِلَى, I do not think that this explanation is meant to show that the ا has a privative effect, and that the verb signifies "he deprived of excuse."]) —— [Hence,] *He exerted himself, acted vigorously, took extraordinary pains,* or *exceeded the usual bounds,* [*so as to render himself excused,*] (Ṣ, O, Mṣb, Ḳ, TA,) فِى الأَمْرِ *in the affair;* (Ṣ, O, Mṣb;) as, for instance, in eating, in relation to which it occurs in a trad., wherein one is enjoined to do so when eating with others, [app. meaning with guests and with a host,] such having been the custom of the Prophet; for, when he ate with others, he was the last in eating. (TA.) [Hence also,] أَعْذَرْتُ إِلَيْكَ *I took extraordinary pains,* or *exceeded the usual bounds, in exhortation and precept to thee.* (TA.) —— And *He was remiss, wanting, deficient,* or *defective; he fell short,* or *did less than was incumbent on him; feigning* (يُرِى [in the CḲ, erroneously, يُرَى]) *that he was doing the contrary:* as though the verb bore two contrary significations. (Ḳ.) [See also 2.] ═ Also *I. q.* أَنْصَفَ: (O, Ḳ:) you say, أَعْذِرْنِى مِنْ هٰذَا i. e. أَنْصِفْنِى مِنْهُ [*Give thou me,* or *obtain for me, my right,* or *due, from this person*]: and hence the saying of the Prophet to Aboo-Bekr, respecting 'Áisheh, أَعْذِرْنِى مِنْهَا إِنْ أَدَّبْتُهَا [*Obtain thou for me my right,* or *due, from her if I discipline her,* or *chastise her*]: (O:) or this means *undertake thou to excuse me* [*for my conduct to her* &c.]: (TA:) and the Arabs say, أَعْذَرَ فُلَانٌ مِنْ نَفْسِهِ [*Such a one became bound to render an excuse for his conduct to himself;* (see عَذِيرٌ;)] meaning *such a one was destroyed by himself.* (Yoo, TA.) ═ As signifying *He circumcised:* see 1, latter half. It is said in a trad., كُنَّا إِعْذَارَ يَوْمٍ وَاحِدٍ, meaning *We were circumcised in one day.* (TA.) —— Also ‡ *He made a feast on the occasion of a circumcision,* (AZ, Mṣb, Ḳ, TA,) لِلْقَوْمِ *for the people,* or *party:* (Ḳ:) *he prepared such a feast:* from the same verb signifying "he circumcised." (TA.) [See also 2: and see إِعْذَارٌ as a subst.] ═ اعذر الفَرَسَ and اللِّجَامَ: see 1, latter half, in five places. —— And أَعْذِرْ عَنِّى بَعِيرَكَ: see 2, near the end. —— أَعْذِرْ عَلَى نَصِيبِكَ *Make a mark upon thy share.* (O.) —— اعذر فِى ظَهْرِهِ *He beat him* (O, Ḳ) with whips (O) *so as to make a mark,* or *marks, upon his back.* (O, Ḳ.) And ضَرَبَهُ حَتَّى أَعْذَرَ مَتْنَهُ *He beat him so that he made the beating heavy upon his back and obtained from him relief from his anger.* (TA.) And ضُرِبَ فَأُعْذِرَ, (Ṣ, O, Ḳ,) in the Tahdheeb of IḲṭṭ فَأَعْذَرَ, (TA,) *He* (a man) *was beaten so that he was at the point of death.* (Ṣ, O, Ḳ, TA.) And أُعْذِرَ مِنْهُ *He had wounds inflicted upon him so that fear was excited for him in consequence thereof.* (O.) And أَعْذَرَ بِهِ *He,* or *it, left a scar upon him.* (O,* TA.) —— And أَعْذَرْتُ الدَّارَ and فِى الدَّارِ *I made a mark,* or *marks, in,* or *upon, the house,* or *dwelling.* (O.) ═ اعذر also signifies *He* (a man, TA) *voided his ordure.* (O, Ḳ.) —— And اعذرت الدَّارُ *The house,* or *dwelling, had in it much* عَذِرَة [or *human ordure*]. (Ṣ, O.)

5. تعذّر: see 8, in three places. —— Also *He went backwards; drew back; remained behind;* or *held back:* (Ḳ:) or *he held back,* or *withheld himself, for a cause rendering him excused.* (TA voce تَعْذَرٌ, q. v.) —— And *He fled.* (Ḳ.) You say, تعذّروا عَلَيْهِ *They fled from him, and abstained from aiding,* or *assisting, him,* or *held back from him.* (O.) —— And *He resisted,* and *was difficult:* it is said in a trad., [respecting Mohammad,] كَانَ يَتَعَذَّرُ فِى مَرَضِهِ *He used to resist, and be difficult, in his malady.* (TA.) —— And تعذّر الأَمْرُ (O, Ḳ, TA) *The affair was not direct in its tendency;* (Ḳ, TA;) i. e. (TA) *it was,* or *became, difficult:* one says, تعذّر عَلَيْهِ الأَمْرُ *The affair was,* or *became, difficult to him.* (O, Mṣb, TA.) [And *The affair was,* or *became, impracticable,* or *impossible.*] ═ تعذّر الرَّسْمُ *The* رسم [i. e. *trace,* or *relic, of an abode,* or *of a place of sojourning,* &c.,] *became effaced;* (Ṣ, O, Ḳ;) as also ▼ اعتذر: (Ṣ,* O,* Ḳ:) or *became altered and effaced:* and اعتذرت ▼ المَنَازِلُ *the places of alighting,* or *abode, had their traces,* or *remains, effaced.* (TA.) ═ And تعذّر (from العَذِرَةُ, Ṣ, O) *He,* or *it, became defiled,* or *besmeared,* (Ṣ, O, Ḳ,) *with* عَذِرَة [or *human ordure*]. (Ḳ.)

8. اعتذر, (Ṣ, O, Mṣb, &c.,) inf. n. إِعْتِذَارٌ, (Ṣ, O, TA,) and [quasi-inf. ns.] ▼ مَعْذِرَةٌ and ▼ عِذْرَةٌ; (TA;) and for اعتذر one says also إِعَذَّرَ, aor. يَعَذِّرُ, inf. n. إِعِذَّارٌ; and it is allowable to say اِعِذَّرَ, aor. يَعِذِّرُ; but the former of these two variations is the more approved; (AHeyth, TA;) [in the former case, the original being changed to اِعْتَذَرَ, then to اِعْذَذَرَ, then to اِعَذَّرَ; and in the latter case, to اِعْتَذَرَ, then to اِعْتِذَرَ, then to اِعِذْذَرَ, then to اِعْذَّرَ, and then to اِعِذَّرَ;] *He excused himself; he adduced,* or *urged, an excuse,* or *a plea, for himself;* (Fr, Ṣ,* O,* TA;) as also ▼ تعذّر. (Ṣ, O, Ḳ.) [See عُذْرٌ.] You say, اعتذر إِلَىَّ [*He excused himself to me;*] *he begged me to accept his excuse;* (Mṣb;) and AZ says, I have heard two Arabs of the desert, one of the tribe of Temeem and one of the tribe of Ḳeys, say, تَعَذَّرْتُ ▼ إِلَى الرَّجُلِ in the sense of اِعْتَذَرْتُ [i. e. *I excused myself to the man*]. (TA.) And اعتذر مِنْ ذَنْبِهِ (Ṣ,* O,* TA) and ▼ تعذّر (TA) [*He excused himself,* or *urged an excuse, for his crime, sin,* or *misdeed:* or] *he asserted himself to be clear of his crime, sin,* or *misdeed.* (TA.) And اعتذر عَنْ فِعْلِهِ [or مِنْ فعله] *He showed,* or *manifested, his excuse for his deed.* (Mṣb.) [It is said that] the primary meaning of الاِعْتِذَارُ is *The cutting a man off from the object of his want, and from that to which he clings in his heart.* (TA.) [Hence, perhaps, one says اعتذر meaning *He excused himself for not complying with a claim,* or *request.*] —— See also 4, in two places, near the beginning. —— Also *He did not adduce an excuse.* (Fr, TA.) [Thus it has two contr. significations. See also 2.] ═ Also *He complained,* (O, Mṣb, Ḳ,) مِنْهُ *of him,* or *it.* (Mṣb.) ═ And اعتذرت المِيَاهُ *The waters stopped, ceased,* or *became cut off.* (O, Ḳ.) —— See also 5, last sentence but one, in two places. ═ And اعتذر العِمَامَةَ *He made the turban to have two portions* [*its two ends*] *hanging down behind.* (O, Ḳ.) ═ And الاِعْتِذَارُ signifies also *The act of devirginating.* (Ṣ, O. [See عُذْرَةٌ.])

10. استعذر مِنْ فُلَانٍ *He asked,* or *desired, to be excused if he should lay violent hands upon such a one* [or *requite him for an evil action*]; *he said,* مَنْ عَذِيرِى مِنْ فُلَانٍ. (A, TA.) It is said in a trad. of the Prophet, اِسْتَعْذَرَ أَبَا بَكْرٍ مِنْ عَائِشَةَ i. e. *He said to Aboo-Bekr, Undertake thou to excuse me for my conduct to 'Áisheh* if I discipline her, or chastise her. (O,* TA.) —— And one says to him who has neglected the giving information of a thing, (A, TA,) or to him who reproves thee for a thing before giving thee any command, or order, or injunction, respecting it, (O, TA,) وَٱللّٰهِ مَا ٱسْتَعْذَرْتَ إِلَىَّ وَلَا ٱسْتَنْذَرْتَ *By God, thou didst not offer to me excuse, nor didst thou offer warning.* (A, O, TA.)

عِذْرَةٌ (Mṣb, Ḳ) and ▼ عُذْرٌ (Mṣb) and ▼ عُذُرٌ (Ṣ, O, Ḳ) and ▼ مَعْذِرَةٌ (Ṣ, Mṣb) and ▼ عُذْرَى (Ṣ, O, Mṣb, Ḳ) and ▼ مَعْذُرَةٌ and ▼ مَعْذَرَةٌ (Ḳ) [all as simple substs., but all except the third and the last mentioned also as inf. ns.,] *An excuse; an apology; a plea whereby one excuses himself* [or *another*]: accord. to the B, عُذْرٌ [as a subst. from اِعْتَذَرَ or from أَعْذَرَ] is of three kinds;

the saying "I did it not;" and the saying "I did it for such a cause," mentioning what might exempt him from being culpable; and the saying "I did it, but will not do it again," or the like; which third kind is the same as تَوْبَةٌ: (TA:) the pl. of عُذْرَةٌ is أَعْذَارٌ; (Mṣb, Ḳ;) and that of ♦ عِذْرَةٌ is عِذَرٌ; (O;) and that of ♦ معذرة is [مَعَاذِرُ, and, irregularly,] مَعَاذِيرُ: (TA:) and ♦ عَذِيرٌ, of which عُذُرٌ, (Ksh,) or ♦ عُذُرٌ, (Bḍ,) may be pl., is syn. with [عُذْرٌ and] معذرة; (Ksh and Bḍ in lxxvii. 6;) and ♦ مِعْذَارٌ is [likewise] syn. with عُذْرٌ. (Bḍ in lxxv. 15.) It is said in a prov., ♦ المَعَاذِرُ مَكَاذِبُ [*Excuses are lies*]. (TA.) And it was said by Ibráheem En-Nakha'ee, إِنَّ ♦ المَعَاذِيرَ يَشُوبُهَا الكَذِبُ [*Verily excuses, lying mixes therewith*]. (Ṣ, O.) — عُذْرًا أَوْ نُذْرًا, in the Ḳur [lxxvii. 6], or ♦ عُذُرًا أَوْ نُذُرًا, (Bḍ,) means *For excusing or terrifying*; the two ns. being inf. ns.: or *for excuses or warnings*; the two ns. being pls., of ♦ عَذِيرٌ in the sense of معذرة and of نَذِيرٌ in the sense إِنْذَارٌ: or *such as excuse and such as warn*; the two ns. being pls. of ♦ عَاذِرٌ and مُنْذِرٌ: (Ksh, Bḍ:) or, accord. to Th, both mean the same. (TA.) [See also نُذْرٌ.] — And the Arabs say, ♦ عُذْرَاكَ لَا نُذْرَاكَ i. e. أَعْذِرْ وَلَا تُنْذِرْ [app. meaning *Do that for which thou wilt be excused*, by inflicting punishment when it is deserved, *and do not* merely *warn, and put in fear*]. (TA in art. نذر.) ═ عُذْرٌ also signifies *Success*; or the *attainment*, or *accomplishment*, *of one's wants*, or *of a thing*: (IAạr, O, Ḳ:) and *victory*, or *success in a contest*. (O, Ḳ.) One says, with respect to a war or a battle, لِمَنِ العُذْرُ *Whose is the success*, or *victory?* (O.) ═ See also عُذْرَةٌ, in five places: and see عِذَارٌ, last quarter.

عَذِرٌ [an epithet of which I find only the fem., with ة, mentioned]. دَارٌ عَذِرَةٌ means *A house*, or *dwelling*, *of which there are many traces*, or *relics*. (O.) — And أَرْضٌ عَذِرَةٌ *Land that does not yield herbage freely, and if it give growth to anything, this soon becomes blighted*. (O and TA in art. عثر.)

عُذُرٌ: see عُذْرٌ, in three places. ═ Also pl. of عِذَارٌ [q. v.]. (Ṣ, O, Mṣb, Ḳ.)

عُذْرَةٌ The *virginity*, *maidenhead*, or *hymen*; syn. بَكَارَةٌ, (Ṣ, Mgh, Mṣb, Ḳ,) or قِضَّةٌ; so called from عَذْرٌ signifying the "act of cutting," because a girl's hymen (خَاتَمُ عُذْرَتِهَا) is rent when she is devirginated; (Lḥ, Az, TA;) العُذْرَةُ being *that whereby a girl is a virgin*: (Lḥ, TA:) [and ♦ عُذْرٌ perhaps signifies the same: (see an ex. voce أَدِيمٌ; and see also the next sentence here following:)] pl. عُذَرٌ. (Mṣb.) — And *Devirgination* of a girl [or woman]: (Lḥ, Ḳ:) [and ♦ عُذْرٌ is used in the same sense:] one says, فُلَانٌ أَبُو عُذْرِهَا (Ṣ, A, O, Ḳ) and ابو عُذْرَتِهَا (TA) ‡ [lit. *Such a one is the father*, i. e. *the author*, *of her devirgination*]; meaning *such a one is he who devirginated her*. (Ṣ, A, O, Ḳ, TA.) And [hence] one says also, هُوَ أَبُو عُذْرِ ♦ هٰذَا الكَلَامِ ‡ [*He was the first utterer of this speech*]. (A.) And مَا أَنْتَ بِذِى عُذْرِ ♦ هٰذَا الكَلَامِ ‡ *Thou art not the first utterer of this speech*. (Ṣ, O, TA. [But see an assertion of Sb cited voce شَغْرٌ.]) — And The [*part in the external organs of generation of a girl or woman termed*] بَظْر [q. v.]; (Ḳ;) the *place of a girl where the operation of circumcision is performed*: so called from عَذْرٌ signifying the "act of cutting." (Lḥ, Az, TA.) [See also العَاذُورُ.] — And The *prepuce* of a boy: (O, Ḳ:) so accord. to Lḥ, who does not say whether it be so called before or after it has been cut off: said by others to be the *portion of skin which the circumciser cuts off*. (TA.) — And *Circumcision*; syn. خِتَانٌ. (Ḳ.) One says, دَنَا وَقْتُ عُذْرَةِ الصَّبِىِّ *The time of the circumcision of the boy drew near*. (TḲ.) — And *A sign*, or *mark*; syn. عَلَامَةٌ; (O, Ḳ, TA;) as also ♦ عُذْرٌ. (TA.) See also عِذَارٌ, last quarter. — And The *hair upon the withers* of a horse: (Ṣ, O, Ḳ:) and, (Ḳ,) accord. to Aṣ, (Ṣ, O,) *a lock, or small quantity, of hair*: (Ṣ, O, Ḳ:) and the نَاصِيَة [or *forelock* of a horse]; (Ḳ;) the *hair of the* نَاصِيَة of a horse: (A:) or, accord. to some, the *mane* of a horse: (TA:) pl. عُذَرٌ: (Ṣ, O, TA:) which is said by some to mean *hairs* [*extending*] *from the back of the head to the middle of the neck*: (TA:) and, as pl. of عُذْرَةٌ, *a sign, mark, or token, that is tied to the forelock of a horse that outstrips*, [*as a preservative*] *from the* [*evil*] *eye*. (Ḥam p. 795.) — And العُذْرَةُ is the appellation of *Five stars at the extremity of the Milky Way*: (Ṣ, O, Ḳ:) or, as some say, *below Sirius, and also called* ♦ العَذَارَى, [app. *the star* ε *of Canis Major* (which is called by our astronomers "adara," often written "adard,") *with four other neighbouring stars*,] *which rise* [*aurorally*] *in the midst of the heat*: (TA:) and, (O, Ḳ, TA,) as some say, (O, TA,) العُذْرَةُ is *a star at the time of the* [*auroral*] *rising of which the heat becomes intense*; (O, Ḳ, TA;) [app. *the star* η *of Canis Major* (which is called by our astronomers "aludra");] *it rises* [*aurorally, in Central Arabia, in the latter part of July O.S.*,] *after Sirius and before Canopus, and is accompanied with intense heat, without wind, taking away the breath*. (O, TA.) — Also (i. e. العُذْرَةُ) *Pain in the fauces*, (Mgh, Ḳ,) [*arising*] *from the blood*; (Mgh;) as also ♦ العَاذُورُ, (Ḳ, accord. to the TA,) or ♦ العَاذُورَاءُ; (thus in some copies of the Ḳ, and thus accord. to the CḲ;) or *pain of the fauces*, (Ṣ, O, Ḳ,) *in a part near the uvula*, (Ṣ, O,) [*arising*] *from the blood*: (Ṣ, O, Ḳ:) it is said to be *a small swelling*, or *pustule*, *that comes forth in the* خَوْم [app. meaning the *uvula*, as being a *projection* from the soft palate,] *which is between the fauces and the nose*: *it is incident to children, at the time of the* [*auroral*] *rising of* العُذْرَة, i. e. *the star that rises after Sirius, mentioned above*; *and on the occasion thereof, a woman has recourse to a piece of rag, which she twists tightly, and inserts into the nose so as to pierce that place, whereupon there issues from it black blood, and sometimes it becomes ulcerated*; and this piercing is called الدَّغْرُ: then they suspended to the child some such thing as the [amulet termed] عُوذَة. (TA. [See 1 in art. دغر.]) — It also signifies *The place of the pain above mentioned*, (Ṣ, O, Ḳ,) *which is near the uvula*. (Ṣ, O.)

عِذْرَةٌ: see عُذْرٌ, in two places: and see also 8. [Accord. to analogy, it signifies *A mode*, or *manner*, *of excusing*.]

عَذِرَةٌ *Human dung* or *ordure*; (Ṣ,* O,* Mṣb, Ḳ, TA;) as also ♦ عَاذِرٌ (IAạr, IDrd, O, L, Ḳ, TA) and ♦ عَاذِرَةٌ: (O, Ḳ:) pl. of the first [which is the most common] عَذِرَاتٌ, (Mṣb,) and of ♦ the second عُذَّرٌ. (IAạr, TA.) — And hence, (Ṣ, O, Mṣb,) ‡ The *court*, or *yard*, (فِنَآء,) *of a house*: (Ṣ, O, Mṣb, Ḳ, TA:) so called because the human ordure (العذرة) used to be cast in it: (Ṣ, O, Mṣb:) or, accord. to Aṣ, this is the primary signification; what is before mentioned being so termed because cast in the فناء; like as it is termed غائط because cast in the غائط, which means "a depressed piece of ground;" (Ḥar p. 403;) [and] thus says A'Obeyd: pl. as above: (O, TA:) and مَعَاذِرُ [pl. of ♦ مَعْذَرٌ which lit. signifies *a place of human dung* or *ordure*] is *syn. with* عَذِرَاتٌ as meaning أَفْنِيَةٌ [pl. of فِنَآء]. (Ḥam p. 677, q. v.) It is related of 'Alee that he reproved some persons, and said, مَا لَكُمْ لَا تُنَظِّفُونَ عَذِرَاتِكُمْ (A,* O, TA) i. e. ‡ [*What aileth you that ye will not cleanse*] *the courts*, or *yards*, *of your houses?* (TA.) And in a trad. (O, TA) of the Prophet (O) it is said, اليَهُودُ أَنْتَنُ خَلْقِ ٱللّٰهِ عَذِرَةً, (A, O, TA,) which may mean ‡ [*The Jews are the most stinking of God's creatures*] *in respect of the court*, or *yard*, *of the house*: or *in respect of ordure*. (TA.) And it is said in a prov., إِنَّهُ لَبَرِىْءُ العَذِرَةِ, a phrase like بَرِىْءُ السَّاحَةِ ‡ [lit. *Verily he is clear in respect of the court*, or *yard*, *of the house*; app. meaning, *clear of disgrace*]. (TA.) — Also † *A place where people sit* (Ḳ, TA) *in the court*, or *yard*, *of the house*. (TA.) — And † The *worst of what comes forth from wheat or corn* (طَعَام), (Lḥ, O, Ḳ, TA,) *and is thrown away*, (Lḥ, TA,) *when it is cleared*; (O;) as also عَذِبَةٌ. (Lḥ, TA.)

عُذْرَى: see عُذْرٌ, in two places.

عَذْرَآءُ *A virgin*: (Ṣ, O, Ḳ:) used as an epithet: you say جَارِيَةٌ عَذْرَآءُ *a virgin girl*: (TA:) and اِمْرَأَةٌ عَذْرَآءُ, meaning ذَاتُ عُذْرَةٍ: (Mṣb:) accord. to IAạr alone, so called لِضِيقِهَا, from تَعَذَّرَ عَلَيْهِ الأَمْرُ: (TA:) pl. عَذَارَى and عَذَارٍ [with the art. العَذَارِى, and thus written in the Ṣ and O and Ḳ] (Ṣ, O, Ḳ, TA) and عَذْرَاوَاتٌ, (Ṣ, O, Ḳ,) like صَحَارَى [&c.]. (Ṣ, O.) — [Hence,] العَذْرَآءُ † [*The sign Virgo*;] *the sign* السُّنْبُلَة: or الجَوْزَآءُ [which is an evident mistake]. (Ḳ.) — And العَذَارَى † *Certain stars, described above*: see عُذْرَةٌ, latter half. — And أَصَابِعُ العَذَارَى † *A sort of grapes, black and long, like acorns*; likened to the dyed fingers of virgins. (TA.) — And دُرَّةٌ عَذْرَآءُ ‡ *A pearl not bored.* (A, O, Ḳ,* TA.) —— And رَمْلَةٌ عَذْرَآءُ ‡ *A sand upon which one has not trodden* (A, O, Ḳ,* TA) *nor ridden, because of its height.* (TA.) —— And العَذْرَآءُ † *A kind of collar by means of which the hands, or arms, are confined together with the neck:* (T, O, TA:) or *such as is put upon the throat of a man and has not been put upon the neck of any one before:* (TA:) or *a thing of iron by means of which a man is tortured in order to make him confess an affair, or the like;* (Ḳ, TA;) as, for instance, *for the purpose of extorting property &c.*: pl. عَذَارَى. (TA.) [Compare the term "maiden" applied to an instrument for beheading.] —— Also a name of [*El-Medeeneh,*] *the City of the Prophet:* (Ḳ, TA:) because of its not having been abased. (TA.)

عِذَارٌ *A certain appertenance of a horse* or *the like;* (Ṣ, O;) i. e. the *part,* (T, M, Mgh,) or *strap,* (Mṣb,) *of the bridle,* (T, M, Mgh, Mṣb,) *that lies,* (T,) or *extends down,* (M, Ḳ,) *upon the cheek,* (M, Mgh, Mṣb, Ḳ,) or *two cheeks,* (T,) of the horse (T, M, Mgh, Mṣb, Ḳ) or the like: (T, Mgh, Mṣb:) the عِذَارَانِ are the *two straps upon the two cheeks* of the horse, *on the right and left:* (IDrd in his Book on the Saddle and Bridle:) or, as some say, the عذار is the *two straps* of the bridle *that meet at the back of the neck:* (TA:) [thus it signifies *either of the two cheek-straps,* or, accord. to some, the *two cheek-straps together, that compose the headstall:*] some say that it is called by the name of its place; but the converse is the case accord. to others: (TA:) [and عِذَارُ الرَّسَنِ signifies *the appertance, of the halter, corresponding to the cheek-strap,* or *cheek-straps, of the bridle* or *headstall:* (see a verse of Ibn-Muḳbil cited voce رَسَنٌ:)] pl. عُذُرٌ, (Ṣ, O, Mṣb, Ḳ, [in the CḲ عُذْرٌ,]) like as كُتُبٌ is pl. of كِتَابٌ. (Mṣb, TA.) It is said in a trad., لَلْفَقْرُ أَزْيَنُ لِلْمُؤْمِنِ مِنْ عِذَارٍ حَسَنٍ عَلَى خَدِّ فَرَسٍ [*Verily poverty is more ornamental to the believer than a beautiful cheek-strap,* or *headstall, upon the cheek of a horse*]. (TA.) فَرَسٌ قَصِيرُ العِذَارِ [*A horse short in the cheek-strap,* or *headstall,*] implies commendation, as denoting width of the lip. (TA, voce عِنَانٌ.) And عِذَارٌ signifies also The *thing that connects the leading-rope* (حَبْلُ الخِطَامِ) *to the head of the he-camel* (Ḳ, TA) *and of the she-camel.* (TA.) And *A halter;* syn. رَسَنٌ: (Mṣb:) and ✝ مُعَذَّرٌ signifies *a halter* (رَسَن) *having a double* عذار (ذُو عِذَارَيْنِ). (TA.) One says, فُلَانٌ شَدِيدُ العِذَارِ † *Such a one is strong in respect of determination.* (A, TA.) And فُلَانٌ خَلِيعُ العِذَارِ † *Such a one is weak in respect of determination;* [or *is a person who has thrown off restraint;*] like a horse that has no bridle upon him, and that therefore falls upon his face. (TA. [See also art. خلع.]) And خَلَعَ عِذَارَهُ † [*He threw off restraint;* or] *he persisted in error:* (Ṣ, O:) or *he departed from obedience, and persisted in error:* (TA:) or *he broke off from his family, or disagreed with them, and wearied them by his wickedness;* syn. تَشَاطَرَ; as also ✝ خلع مُعَذَّرَهُ: (A:) or the latter means *he did not obey a director in the right course:* (Aṣ, TA:) or, in the former phrase, (TA,) عِذَار means † *shame;* (Ḳ, TA;) خَلَعَ عِذَارَهُ meaning *he divested himself of shame;* like as a horse casts off his عِذَار, and becomes refractory, overcoming his rider and running away with him. (TA. [See, again, art. خلع.]) And لَوَى عَنْهُ عِذَارَهُ † *He disobeyed him.* (A, TA.) —— Also † The *two sides of the beard:* (Ḳ:) or *either side* thereof; (Mgh, TA;) the two sides thereof being called عِذَارَا اللِّحْيَةِ, (Mgh,) or العِذَارَانِ, (TA,) because they are in the place [corresponding to that] of the عذار of the horse or the like: (Mgh,* TA:) or the *hair,* of a boy, *that grows evenly in the place of the* عِذَار: (Ṣ:) or the *hair,* of the beard, *that descends upon the two jaws:* (Mṣb:) or a man's *hair that grows in the place of the* عِذَار: (O, TA:) the *line of the beard:* (TA:) or the *hair,* of a man, *that is in front of the ear, and between which and the ear is a whiteness:* (Ḥar pp. 208-9:) and the *part,* of the face, *upon which grows the hair in a lengthened form in front of the lobula of the ear* [*extending*] *to the base of the jaw.* (Ḥar p. 495.) —— And † The *cheek;* as also ✝ مُعَذَّرٌ: (Ḳ:) which latter [properly] signifies the *place of the* عِذَار, (A, TA,) or the *place of the* عِذَارَانِ. (Ṣ, O.) You say, فُلَانٌ طَوِيلُ المُعَذَّرِ ✝ † *Such a one is long in the place of the* عِذَار. (A, TA.) —— And † *A mark made* [on a camel (see مَعْذُورٌ)] *with a hot iron in the place of the* عِذَار; (Ṣ, O, Ḳ;) as also ✝ عُذْرَةٌ: (Ḳ:) or *on the back of the neck, extending to the temples:* so in the Tedhkireh of Aboo-'Alee; but the former explanation is the better known: El-Aḥmar mentions ✝ عُذْرٌ as meaning *one kind of the marks made with a hot iron.* (TA.) —— Also ‡ The *two sharp sides* or *edges,* (Ḳ,) or [rather] *either of these,* for both together are called the عِذَارَانِ, (TA,) of a نَصْل [i. e. of the iron head of an arrow or of a spear &c.]. (Ḳ, TA.) —— And ‡ *Either side* of a road, (A,) and of a valley, (A, TA,) and of a wall. (TA.) —— And ‡ *A row* of trees, (TA,) or of palm-trees. (A.) —— And ‡ *An elongated tract of sand.* (A.) The dual as used in a verse of Dhu-r-Rummeh means † *Two elongated tracts* [in the CḲ جَبْلَانِ] حَبْلَانِ) *of sand:* (Ṣ, O, Ḳ, TA:) or the *two sides thereof:* (TA:) or *two roads* (طَرِيقَانِ). (Ṣ, O, Ḳ, TA.) —— And ‡ *A rugged tract of ground,* (O, Ḳ, TA,) and [*a tract*] *of sand,* (TA,) *lying across in a wide plain:* (O, Ḳ, TA:) pl. عُذُرٌ. (TA.) —— See also إِعْذَارٌ. —— It also signifies *Resistance,* or *refusal;* from التَّعَذُّر. (TA.)

عَاذِرٌ✝ : see عُذْرٌ, in two places. —— Also *i. q.* عَذِيرٌ [act. part. n. of 1, *Excusing; an excuser;* &c.]. (Ḳ.) You say, مَنْ عَذِيرِى مِنْ فُلَانٍ *Who will excuse me, or make my excuse,* or *be my excuser, if I requite such a one* (Mṣb, TA) *for his action,* (Mṣb,) or *for his evil action,* (TA,) *and will not blame me* (Mṣb, TA) *for it?* or *who will excuse me with respect to the case of such a one, and not blame me for it?* (Mṣb: [see عَذَرْتُهُ مِنْ فُلَانٍ: and see also 10:]) or *who will aid me,* or *assist me, against such a one,* or *to defend myself from him?* (Mṣb;) *who will be my aider,* or *assistant, against such a one?* (TA:) for عَذِيرٌ is also said to signify *an aider,* or *assister, against an enemy.* (Mṣb, Ḳ, TA.) The Prophet said thus with respect to 'Abd-Allah Ibn-Ubei, demanding of the people that they should excuse him for laying violent hands upon him. (TA.) [It is a phrase by which one asks for permission to retaliate, or punish, &c.] And one says also, عَذِيرَكَ مِنْ فُلَانٍ, meaning *Bring him who will excuse thee* [*for what thou hast done,* or *doest,* or *wilt do, to such a one*]; (Ṣ, O, TA;) i. e. *bring him who will blame him and will not blame thee.* (Ṣ, O.) And عَذِيرَكَ إِيَّاىَ مِنْهُ *Bring thine excuse of me* [*for what I have done,* &c., *to him*]. (TA.) A poet (Dhu-l-Iṣba' El-'Adwánee, O, TA) says,

عَذِيرَ الحَىِّ مِنْ عَدْوَا
نَ كَانُوا حَيَّةَ الأَرْضِ
بَغَى بَعْضٌ عَلَى بَعْضٍ
فَلَمْ يَرْعَوْا عَلَى بَعْضٍ
فَقَدْ أَضْحَوْا أَحَادِيثَ
بِرَفْعِ القَوْلِ وَالخَفْضِ

(Ṣ,* O,* L, TA) [Bring *an excuse for the tribe, for what they have done to 'Adwán,* i. e., one to another; for the tribe of 'Adwán were rent by intestine wars, in which Dhu-l-Iṣba' took a prominent part; (see the Essai sur l'Histoire des Arabes by Caussin de Perceval, vol. ii. p. 202;) therefore we may render the phrase, bring *an excuse for the tribe, 'Adwán,* regarding مِنْ as redundant in this instance, like as it is in فَاجْتَنِبُوا الرِّجْسَ مِنَ الأَوْثَانِ, in the Ḳur xxii. 31; and then proceed thus: *they were the serpent of the earth* (meaning *cunning, guileful, malignant,* or *mischievous, and strong, not neglecting to take blood-revenge,* as expl. in art. حى in the TA): but *some acted wrongfully against some, and were not regardful* of the rights *of some: so they became subjects of talk* uttered *by the raising of speech and the lowering* thereof]: he means, bring an excuse for what some of them have done to some by mutual hatred and slaughter, some of them being not regardful of some; after their having been the serpent of the earth, which every one fears. (L, TA.) —— Also *A state,* or *condition,* (حَال,) *which one desires,* or *seeks after, for which,* or *on account of which, he is to be excused* (يُعْذَرُ عَلَيْهَا): (Ṣ, O, Ḳ, TA:) [and in one of my copies of the Ṣ is added, إِذَا فَعَلَهَا, as though by حال were here meant *an action:*] pl. عُذُرٌ, sometimes, in poetry, contracted into عُذْرٌ. (Ṣ, O.) El-'Ajjáj said, (Ṣ, O, TA,) in reply to his wife, who, seeing him repairing the saddle of his she-camel for a journey which he had determined to make, asked him, "What is this that thou repairest?" (TA,)

جَارِىَ لَا تَسْتَنْكِرِى عَذِيرِى
سَعْيِى وَإِشْفَاقِى عَلَى بَعِيرِى

(Ṣ, O,) or, as some relate it, سَيْرِى واشفاقى, (O,)

[i. e. *O girl, inquire not as disapproving it respecting my desired state for which I shall be excusable* (or rather *my excusable purpose*), *my work* (or *my journeying*), *and my benevolent care for my camel;*] meaning يَا جَارِيَةُ, [and suppressing يا] and apocopating [جارية]. (Ṣ, O. [In the TA, البَعِيرِ is put for بَعِيرِى.]) ═ See also عَاذِرٌ: ═ and إِعْذَارٌ.

عَذِيرَةٌ [*A disposition to excuse*]. One says, مَا عِنْدَهُمْ عَذِيرَةٌ, meaning [*They have not a disposition to excuse; or*] *they do not excuse.* (O.) [See also غَفِيرَةٌ.] ═ See also عَاذِرٌ: ═ and إِعْذَارٌ. — Also *I. q.* غَذِيرَةٌ [app. as *syn. with* وَغِيدَةٌ]. (O, TA.)

عَذُورٌ ‡ *Evil in disposition;* (Ṣ, O, Ḳ, TA, and Ḥam p. 417;) as though needing to excuse himself for his evildoing; (Ḥam ibid.;) *vehement in commanding and forbidding,* (Ḥam p. 469,) and *in spirit.* (Ḳ.) [*Clamorous.* (Freytag, from the Deewán of Jereer.)] — Applied to an ass, *Wide in the* جَوْف [i. e. *belly,* or *chest*], (Ṣ, O, Ḳ,) and فَحَّاش [app. meaning *very lewd*]. (Ḳ.) — And, applied to dominion, (مُلْك, O, TA, in the copies of the Ḳ erroneously written مَلِك, TA, [in which and in the O exs. are cited showing the former to be right,]) *Wide,* or *ample:* (O:) or *strong,* (Ḳ, TA,) *and wide,* or *ample.* (TA.) — [Also, accord. to Golius, from the Destoor el Loghah, *An agile animal.* — And Freytag adds, from the Deewán of Jereer, عَذَوَّرٌ as signifying *Brisk* ("alacris").]

عَاذِرٌ: see عَذِيرٌ; and عُذْرٌ, latter half. — عَاذِرَةٌ, [fem. of عَاذِرٌ] as an epithet applied to a woman: see the fem. of مَعْذُورٌ. ═ Also *A scar,* or *mark of a wound;* (Ṣ, O, Ḳ;) and so ↓ عَذِيرَةٌ, (O, and thus in copies of the Ṣ,) or ↓ عَذِيرٌ. (TA, and so in a copy of the Ṣ.) One says, تَرَكَ بِهِ عَاذِرًا *He,* or *it, left upon him a scar,* or *mark of a wound.* (TA.) And the same is said of rain, meaning, *It left upon him,* or *it, a mark.* (TA.) ═ See also عَذِرَةٌ, in two places. ═ And العَاذِرُ signifies *The vein whence flows the blood of what is termed* الاِسْتِحَاضَة: [see 10 in art. حيض:] (Ṣ,* O,* Mṣb, Ḳ:*) a dial. var. of العَاذِلُ, or an instance of mispronunciation: (Ṣ, O:) or it may be so called because it serves as an excuse for the woman. (TA.)

عَاذِرَةٌ, as a subst.: see عَذِرَةٌ.

عَاذُورٌ *A brand,* or *mark made with a hot iron, like a line:* pl. عَوَاذِيرُ. (Ṣ, O.) ═ And لَقِيتُ مِنْهُ عَاذُورًا is a saying mentioned by Aṣ, as meaning *I experienced, from him,* or *it, evil:* عَاذُورٌ being a dial. var. of عَاثُورٌ, or an instance of mispronunciation. (Ṣ, O.) ═ العَاذُورُ also signifies *What is cut off from the place of circumcision of a girl* [which place is termed her عُذْرَة]. (O, TA.) ═ See also عُذْرَةٌ, last quarter.

عَاذُورَآءُ: see عُذْرَةٌ, last quarter.

إِعْذَارٌ, (AZ, Ṣ, A, O, Mṣb, Ḳ,) originally an inf. n., (Ṣ, O, Mṣb,) and ↓ عَذِيرَةٌ (Ṣ, A, O, Ḳ) and ↓ عَذِيرٌ (A, Ḳ) and ↓ عِذَارٌ, (Ḳ,) *A repast,* or *food, prepared on the occasion of a circumcision;* (AZ, Ṣ, A, O, Mṣb, Ḳ;) or *on some joyful occasion:* (Mṣb:) and the last of these words likewise signifies *a repast,* or *food, prepared on the occasion* [*of the completion*] *of a building:* and also *a repast,* or *food, which one prepares, and to which he invites his brethren, on the occasion of the acquisition of something new:* (O, Ḳ:) and accord. to the Ḳ, all the other words mentioned above also have, app., the former, or perhaps the latter, of these two meanings, as well as the meaning first mentioned above, which is the most common. (TA.)

مَعْذَرٌ; pl. مَعَاذِرُ: see عَذِرَةٌ, second sentence.

مُعْذِرٌ: see مُعْتَذِرٌ, in two places.

مَعْذِرَةٌ and مَعْذُرَةٌ and مَعْذَرَةٌ; and the pl. مَعَاذِرُ: see عُذْرٌ, in five places: and for the first, see also 8.

مُعَذَّرٌ [properly signifying The *place of the* عِذَار or *of the* عِذَارَانِ]: see عِذَارٌ, in four places.

مُعَذِّرٌ and مُعِذِّرٌ and مُعُذِّرٌ: see مُعْتَذِرٌ, in six places.

مِعْذَارٌ sing. of مَعَاذِيرُ, (O, Ḳ,) which signifies [*Excuses,* or *apologies;*] *pleas, allegations,* or *arguments:* (Ḳ, TA: see عُذْرٌ, in two places:) — and also, (Ḳ, TA,) in the dial. of El-Yemen, (TA,) *Veils, curtains,* or *coverings.* (O, Ḳ, TA.) The saying in the Ḳur [lxxv. 14 and 15], بَلِ الإِنْسَانُ عَلَى نَفْسِهِ بَصِيرَةٌ وَلَوْ أَلْقَى مَعَاذِيرَهُ is expl. as meaning [*Nay, the man* shall be *witness against himself, though he throw*] *his veils* or *coverings* [over his offences]: (TA:) or (accord. to Mujáhid, Ṣ, O), [*though he offer his excuses;* or] *though he dispute respecting it* (Ṣ, O, TA) *with every plea by which he may excuse himself.* (TA.)

مَعْذُورٌ *Excused; freed, cleared,* or *exempted, from blame; exculpated.* (Mṣb.) — And [hence, perhaps,] مَعْذُورَةٌ applied to a woman signifies مُسْتَحَاضَة [q. v. in art. حيض]: and sometimes one says ↓ عَاذِرَةٌ; as meaning *having an excuse:* (Mṣb:) the latter is said to be used in the sense of مُسْتَحَاضَة; but it requires consideration; (O, TA;) as though it were of the measure فَاعِلَةٌ in the sense of مَفْعُولَةٌ, [i. e. in the sense of مَعْذُورَةٌ as meaning *excused,*] from إِقَامَةُ العُذْرِ. (TA.) — [Golius assigns to مَعْذُورٌ the meaning of "*Voti impos;*" as on the authority of the KL; in which, however, I do not find it.] ═ Also ‡ *Circumcised.* (Ṣ, A, O, Mṣb.) ═ And A camel *branded with the mark called* عِذَار. (TA.) ═ And [A child] *affected with the pain, of the fauces, termed* عُذْرَة. (Ṣ, O, Ḳ.)

مُعَاذِرٌ: see its pl. in the last clause of the following paragraph.

مُعْتَذِرٌ *One excusing himself, whether he have, or have not, an excuse:* (TA:) the person to whom this epithet is applied may be a speaker of truth, and he may be not a speaker of truth: (Mṣb, TA:) and so ↓ مُعَذِّرٌ, which, as applied to a speaker of truth, signifies *having an excuse,* like مُعْتَذِرٌ, (Ṣ, O, Ḳ,) [of which it is a variation,] for the ت is changed into ذ, and this is incorporated [into the radical ذ], and its vowel is transferred to the ع, like as is the case in يَخِصِّمُونَ; (Ṣ, O;) and ↓ مُعِذِّرٌ is also allowable, (Ṣ, O, TA,) and also ↓ مُعُذِّرٌ; (Ṣ, O;) but [it is said that] ↓ مُعَذِّرٌ applied to him who does not speak truth, (Ṣ, O, Ḳ,) being [originally] of the measure مُفَعِّلٌ, [not a variation of مُعْتَذِرٌ,] (Ṣ, O,) means *falling short,* or *doing less than is incumbent on him,* (Ṣ, O, Ḳ,) *excusing himself* (Ṣ, O) *without having any* [*real* or *valid*] *excuse.* (Ṣ, O, Ḳ.) In the Ḳur ix. 91, I'Ab read ↓ المُعْذِرُونَ [instead of the more usual reading ↓ المُعَذِّرُونَ], (Ṣ, O, Ḳ,) and so did Yaḳoob El-Ḥadramee, (Az, TA,) from أَعْذَرَ; the former asserting that it was so revealed; app. considering ↓ مُعَذِّرٌ, with teshdeed, to apply to one not speaking truth, (Ṣ, O, Ḳ,) meaning *pretending to excuse himself, without having any real excuse;* (Ṣ, O;) and ↓ مُعْذِرٌ to mean *having an excuse:* (Ṣ, O, Ḳ:) Ibn-Abee-Leylà and Ṭá-oos read ↓ المُعَاذِرُونَ, as meaning *those striving,* or *labouring, in seeking excuse.* (O.)

عذط

1. عَذِطَ: see what here follows.

Q. Q. 1. عَذْيَطَ, (O, Mṣb, Ḳ,) inf. n. عَذْيَطَةٌ, (Ṣ, Mṣb,) *Alvum ejecit, ventumve per anum emisit, in coïtu:* (Ṣ, O, Mṣb, Ḳ:) or *semen emisit ante congressum:* (Ḳ:) or *semen in coïtu non emisit:* (TA:) and ↓ عَذِطَ, aor. ـَ, inf. n. عَذَطٌ, signifies the same: (Mṣb:) or there is no verb derived from عِذْيَوْطٌ, because it denotes a natural quality: (O, Ḳ:) so says El-Mufaḍḍal Ibn-Selemeh, in his book on the errors in the 'Eyn: but the rule is only one which applies in most instances, of which this is not one; for the former of these words is of established authority, mentioned by Ibn-Málik and others of the leading lexicologists. (TA.)

عَذْطٌ the subst. [or abstract n.] from عَذْيَطَ. (Lth, Ḳ.)

عِذْوَطٌ: see what follows.

عِذْيَوْطٌ (Ṣ, O, Mṣb, Ḳ) and عُذْيُوطٌ (Th, L, Ḳ) and ↓ عِذْوَطٌ (Ibn-'Abbád, O, Ḳ) *Qui alvum ejicit, ventumve per anum emittit, in coïtu:* (Ṣ, O, Mṣb, Ḳ:) or *qui semen emittit ante congressum:* (Ḳ:) or *qui semen in coïtu non emittit:* (TA:) and so with ة applied to a woman: (Ṣ, O, Mṣb:) pl. عِذْيَوْطُونَ [masc.] and عَذَايِطُ and عَذَاوِيطُ; (Lth, O, Ḳ;) the last contr. to rule. (TA.)

عذف

1. عَذَفَ, (Ṣ, Ḳ) aor. ـِ, (Ḳ,) inf. n. عَذْفٌ, (IDrd, Ṣ, O,) *He ate:* (Ṣ, O, Ḳ:) as also with

د: (IDrd, O:) the former of the dial. of Rabee'ah. (Ṣ, O.)

5. ♦ تَعَذَّفْتُ عَذُوفَةً I tasted a portion the least in quantity of what is eaten and of what is drunk. (Ḥam p. 448.) [See also 5 in art. عدف.]

عَذْفٌ: see عَذُوفٌ.

سَمٌّ عُذَافٌ Deadly poison: (O, Ḳ:) formed by transposition from ذُعَافٌ: (O:) mentioned by Yaạḳoob and Lḥ. (TA.)

عَذُوفٌ and عَدُوفٌ are syn.; (IDrd, O, Ḳ;) signifying Food of man and of beast; (IDrd, O;) [or food and drink; (see عدوف;)] and in like manner the dial. vars.: with ذ in the dial. of Rabee'ah, and with د in the dials. of the rest of the Arabs. (Ḳ.) — One says, مَا ذُقْتُ عَذُوفًا, and ♦ عَذْفًا [&c.] i. e. [I have not tasted, or did not taste,] anything. (Ṣ, O.) And بَاتَتِ الدَّابَّةُ عَلَى غَيْرِ عَذُوفٍ [like عَدُوفٍ, q. v.]. (Ṣ, O.)

عَذُوفَةٌ [i. q. عَدُوفَةٌ &c.]: see 5 [and see also عَذُوفٌ and عَدُوفٌ].

عَاذِفٌ [as act. part. n. of عَذَفَ should signify Eating: but see what here follows]. Ibn-'Abbád says, (O,) مَا زِلْتُ عَاذِفًا مُنْذُ اليَوْمِ means I have not tasted anything [to-day]. (O, Ḳ.)

عذق

1. عَذَقَ الشَّاةَ, (Ṣ, O, Ḳ,) aor. ِ, inf. n. عَذْقٌ, (Ṣ, O,) He appended to the sheep, or goat, a sign whereby the latter might be known, termed ♦ عَذَقَةٌ (Ṣ, O, Ḳ) and ♦ عِذْقَةٌ, (Ḳ,) being a flock of wool, (Ṣ, O,) differing in colour from the animal: (Ṣ, O, Ḳ:) some particularize the animal to which this is done as being a goat: (TA:) and ♦ اعذقها signifies the same. (Ṣ, Ḳ.) — Hence the saying, مَنْ عُذِقَتْ بِهِ الأَعْمَالُ أُعْلِقَتْ بِهِ الآمَالُ † [The person to whom offices of administration are assigned, to him hopes are made to cling]. (Ḥar p. 489.) — Hence also, (O, TA,) عَذَقَ الرَّجُلَ, (Ṣ, O,) or عَذَقَهُ بِشَرٍّ or بِقَبِيحٍ, (Ḳ,) ‡ He reproached him, or upbraided him, with a thing that was bad, evil, abominable, or foul, (Ṣ, O, Ḳ, TA,) and stigmatized him with it, (Ṣ, O, TA,) so that he became known thereby. (TA.) — And عَذَقَهُ إِلَى كَذَا i. e. نَسَبَهُ إِلَيْهِ [commonly meaning نَسَبَ إِلَيْهِ كَذَا † He attributed, or imputed, to him such a thing]. (Ibn-'Abbád, O, Ḳ.) ═ عَذَقْتُ النَّخْلَةَ I cut off the branches of the palm-tree: (Ṣ, O:) and [in like manner one says] ♦ عَذَّقْتُ, with teshdeed to denote muchness [of the action] or multiplicity [of the objects]. (Ṣ.) ═ عَذَقَ said of the [species of sweet rush called] إِذْخِر, It put forth its fruit; as also ♦ أَعْذَقَ: (Ṣ, O, Ḳ:) or the latter, accord. to IAth, it had عُذُوق [pl. of عِذْقٌ] and شُعَب [pl. of شُعْبَة, i. e. bunches, or sprigs]: or, as some say, it blossomed. (TA.) And, said of the [species of tree, or plant, called] سَخْبَر, It grew tall. (IAạr, O, TA.) ═ عَذَقَ الفَحْلُ عَنِ الإِبِلِ, (O, Ḳ,) aor. ُ, (Ḳ,) inf. n. عَذْقٌ, (TA,) The stallion [camel] repelled from the [she-] camels, and drew them together. (O, Ḳ.) ═ And عَذَقَ البَعِيرُ The camel voided his dung in a thin state. (Ibn-'Abbád, O, Ḳ.)

2: see the preceding paragraph.

4. اعذق: see 1, first sentence. ═ Also He (a man) had many عُذُوق, i. e. palm-trees, pl. of عَذْقٌ. (O.) — And اعذقت النَّخْلَةُ The palm-tree had many أَعْذَاق, i. e. racemes, or bunches of dates, pl. of عِذْقٌ. (O.) — See also 1, latter half.

8. اعتذق بَكْرَةً مِنْ إِبِلِهِ He made a mark, or sign, upon a young female of his camels, for his riding her before she had been trained: (O, Ḳ:*) [the Ḳ has لِيَقْبِضَهَا in the place of لِيَقْتَضِبَهَا, which latter is the reading in the O, and is evidently the right:]) the mark, or sign, is termed ♦ عَذَقَةٌ, as mentioned by Az. (TA.) — And اعتذقهُ بِكَذَا means اِخْتَصَّهُ بِهِ [i. e. He distinguished him particularly, peculiarly, or specially, by such a thing; or he particularized him, or particularly or peculiarly or specially characterized him, thereby]; (O, Ḳ;) namely, a man. (Ḳ.) — And اعتذق He made [the] two ends of his turban to hang down behind; (IAạr, O, Ḳ;) like اعتذب. (TA.)

عَذْقٌ A palm-tree with its fruit: (Ṣ, O, Ḳ:) so called by the people of El-Ḥijáz: (TA:) or [simply] a palm-tree: (Mgh, Mṣb:) pl. [of pauc.] أَعْذُقٌ and [of mult.] عِذَاقٌ (Ḳ, TA) [the latter erroneously written in the CḲ عُذَّق] and عُذُوقٌ. (O: in which no other is mentioned.) [The dim. is ♦ عُذَيْقٌ:] hence the saying, أَنَا عُذَيْقُهَا المُرَجَّبُ [expl. in art. رجب]. (Ṣ, O.) — And Certain dates of El-Medeeneh. (CḲ.) It it is applied to several sorts of dates; of which are those called عَذْقُ ابْنِ الحُبَيْقِ, (Mṣb,) or عَذْقُ ابْنِ حُبَيْقٍ, (Mgh,) and عَذْقُ ابْنِ طَابٍ and عَذْقُ زَيْدٍ [mentioned in art. طوب]: so says AḤát: (Mṣb:) or عَذْقُ ابْنِ طَابٍ is the name of a sort of palm-trees in El-Medeeneh. (Ḳ in art. طوب.)

عِذْقٌ A raceme of a palm-tree, or of dates; (Ṣ, Mgh, O, Mṣb, Ḳ, TA;) i. e. the base thereof, (TA,) together with the fruit-stalks [and fruit]; (Mṣb, TA;) when ripe: (TA:) pl. أَعْذَاقٌ (O, Mṣb, Ḳ) and عُذُوقٌ. (Ḳ.) — Hence, (TA,) ‡ Might; or high, or elevated, rank or condition; syn. عِزٌّ. (O, Ḳ, TA.) So in the saying, فِى بَنِى فُلَانٍ عِذْقٌ خَصْلٌ ‡ In the sons of such a one is might, &c., that has attained its utmost point; and so عذق يَانِعٌ. (O, TA.) — Also A bunch of grapes: (Lth, O, Ḳ:) or when what was upon it has been eaten. (Ibn-'Abbád, O, Ḳ.) — And A branching portion of a plant: (Lth, O:) and any branch having branchlets. (Lth, O, Ḳ.)

عَذِقٌ, applied to a man, i. q. لَبِقٌ: (O, Ḳ:) so in the phrase عَذِقٌ بِالقُلُوبِ [app. meaning Congenial with hearts]. (O, TA.) — Applied to perfume, Fragrant. (O, Ḳ.) — نَعْجَةٌ عَذِقَةٌ A ewe having goodly wool: one should not say عَنْزٌ عَذِقَةٌ. (Ibn-'Abbád, O.)

عَذَقَةٌ and عِذْقَةٌ: see 1, first sentence: and for the former, see also 8.

عَذَقَةٌ The fruit of the [species of tree, or plant, called] سَخْبَر. (IAạr, O.)

عُذَيْقٌ dim. of عَذْقٌ, q. v.

عَاذِقٌ One who undertakes the affairs of palm-trees, the fecundating of them, and the adjusting of their racemes of fruit, and disposing them properly for the cutting off. (TA.)

هُوَ مَعْذُوقٌ بِالشَّرِّ ‡ He is stigmatized with evil. (TA.)

عذل

1. عَذَلَهُ, (Ṣ, Mṣb,) aor. ُ (Ṣ, O, Mṣb) and ِ, (Mṣb,) inf. n. عَذْلٌ, (Ṣ, O, Mṣb, Ḳ,) He blamed him, or censured him; (Ṣ, O, Mṣb, Ḳ;*) [and ♦ عذّلهُ he did so much; for] تَعْذِيلٌ is like عَذْلٌ, signifying مَلَامَةٌ, (Ḳ, TA,) [and تَعْذَالٌ is a dial. var. thereof, occurring in the Mo'allaḳah of Imra-el-Ḳeys, (see EM p. 33,)] but its verb has teshdeed to denote muchness. (TA.) سَبَقَ السَّيْفُ العَذْلَ [The sword preceded the censure] is a prov. [expl. voce شَجْنٌ]. (TA.) Accord. to IAạr, [عَذَلَهُ may signify as above; or he afflicted, annoyed, or hurt, him; for he says,] العَذْلُ signifies الإِحْرَاقُ; [perhaps meaning الإِحْرَاقُ بِاللِّسَانِ; for SM adds,] as though the censurer burned (يُحْرِقُ) by his عَذْل the object thereof: (TA:) [or it may mean also he burned him; for Ṣgh says,] and العَذْلُ signifies also الإِحْرَاقُ. (O.)

2: see the preceding paragraph.

5: see 8, in two places.

6. [تعاذلوا They blamed, or censured, one another]. See the last sentence in this art.

8. اعتذل He blamed, or censured, himself: (Ṣ, O, Mṣb:) or i. q. قَبِلَ المَلَامَةَ [he admitted, or accepted, blame, or censure]; as also ♦ تعذّل: (Ḳ:) [or, accord. to SM,] one says, اعتذل الرَّجُلَ and ♦ تعذّل as meaning قَبِلَ مِنْهُ المَلَامَةَ وَأَعْتَبَ [i. e. he admitted, or accepted, blame, or censure, from the man, and reverted; but I think that the right reading is الرَّجُلُ, and that منه should be erased]. (TA.) — Also He shot, or cast, a second time; (ISk, O, Ḳ;) having shot, or cast, and missed: (ISk, O:) or, accord. to the A, he blamed himself for having missed, and therefore shot, or cast, a second time, and hit. (TA.) — And i. q. اِعْتَزَمَ [perhaps said of a man, and meaning He kept to the course, or right course, in running, or walking, &c.: but more probably, I think, said of a horse, meaning he went along overcoming his rider, in his running, not complying with his desire when he pulled him in]: (Ḳ:) accord. to AA, said of a horse as meaning he went quickly, after slowness, and strove, or exerted himself. (O.) — And اعتذل يَوْمُنَا † Our day became intensely hot; as though it had been remiss, and made amends for its remissness by excess, blaming itself for what had proceeded from it. (A, TA.)

عَذَلٌ *Blame*, or *censure*: a subst., as distinguished from the inf. n. عَذْلٌ. (O, Ḳ.)

أَيَّامٌ عُذَلٌ: see مُعْتَذِلَاتٌ, in two places.

عُذَلَةٌ One *who blames*, or *censures*, *others much* or *often*; (Ṣ, O, Ḳ;) an epithet like ضُحَكَةٌ and هُزَأَةٌ; (Ṣ;) [and ▼ عَذُولٌ is used in the same sense, agreeably with analogy, but is perhaps post-classical;] as also ▼ عَذَّالٌ; (Ḳ;) and this last with ة is applied in this sense to a woman. (TA.) Hence the prov., أَنَا عُذَلَةٌ وَأَخِى خُذَلَةٌ وَكِلَانَا لَيْسَ بِٱبْنِ أَمَةٍ [lit. *I am one who blames others much, and my brother is one who constantly abstains from rendering aid, and neither of us is a son of a female slave*; but expl. as] meaning *I blame my brother, and he abstains from aiding me*. (TA.)

عَذُولٌ: } see the next preceding paragraph.
عَذَّالٌ: }

عَذَّالَةٌ A man *who blames*, or *censures*, [*very*] *much* or *often*: the ة is added to render it [more] *intensive*. (O, TA.) — [Also fem. of عَذَّالٌ, q. v.] — And العَذَّالَةُ is an appellation of *The* اِسْت [i. e. the *podex*, or the *anus*]. (O, Ḳ.)

عَاذِلٌ *Blaming*, or *censuring*; or *a blamer*, or *censurer*: (TA:) pl. عَذَلَةٌ and عُذَّالٌ and عُذَّلٌ; (Ḳ, TA;) all pls. of عَاذِلٌ: the fem., applied to a woman, is عَاذِلَةٌ; and the pl. of this is عَوَاذِلُ, and عَاذِلَاتٌ is allowable. (TA.) — And العَاذِلُ signifies † *The vein from which flows the blood called that of* الاِسْتِحَاضَة [inf. n. of أُسْتُحِيضَتْ, q. v., in art. حيض]; (Ṣ, O, Mṣb, Ḳ, TA;) as though it were so called because the woman becomes liable to be blamed by her husband; the blaming being attributed to the vein by reason of its being the cause thereof: (O:) and sometimes it is called العَاذِرُ [q. v.]: (Mṣb, TA:*) the pl. is عُذُلٌ, like شُرُفٌ pl. of شَارِفٌ. (TA.) — عَاذِلٌ was *The name of* [*the month*] شَعْبَانُ *in the Time of Ignorance*: (Ḳ,* TA:) or of شَوَّالٌ; (Ḳ, TA;) but the former has been pronounced to be the right: (TA:) [see شَهْرٌ:] the pl. is عَوَاذِلُ. (Ḳ, TA.)

مُعَذَّلٌ A man *much blamed*, or *censured*, *for his excessive munificence*. (Ṣ, O, Ḳ.*)

أَيَّامٌ مُعْتَذِلَاتٌ ‡ *Intensely hot days*; (Ṣ, O, Ḳ, TA;) as also ▼ عُذَلٌ; (Ḳ;) as though they blamed one another; one saying to another, "I am hotter than thou, and why is not thy heat like my heat?" (TA:) or, accord. to IAạr, ▼ العُذَلُ signifies *the hot days*. (O.) And مُعْتَذِلَاتُ سُهَيْلٍ ‡ *Certain intensely hot days that come before the* [*auroral*] *rising of Suheyl* [i. e. *Canopus*], or *after it*; so called as [though] meaning that they blame one another (▼ يَتَعَاذَلْنَ), and bid one another to be intensely hot or to desist from heat: and also called مُعْتَدِلَاتٌ [q. v.], with the unpointed د, as being equal in intensity of heat. (TA.)

عذو

1. عَذَا البَلَدُ, aor. يَعْذُو, *The country*, or *town*, *was good*, or *pleasant*, *in respect of its air*. (IAạr, Ḳ, TA.) — And you say, عَذُوَتِ الأَرْضُ (AZ, Ḳ, TA) and عَذِيَتْ (Ḳ) أَحْسَنَ العَذَاةِ or العَذَاءَةِ. (So accord. to different copies of the Ḳ [in which what immediately precedes app. indicates that the meaning is, *The land was such as is termed* عَذَاة, *in the best degree*; so that العَذَاة or العَذَاءَة, the former of which is the reading in the T, is the inf. n.: but accord. to the TḲ, عَذُوَتِ الأَرْضُ, having for its inf. n. عَذَاوَةٌ, and عَذِيَتْ, having for its inf. n. عَذًى, mean, without any addition, كَانَتْ أَحْسَنَ العَذَاةِ i. e. *the land was the best of what is termed* عَذَاة].)

10. اِسْتَعْذَيْتُ المَكَانَ [*I found that*] *the place was suitable to me* (Ḳ, TA) *in its air*, (TA,) *and I deemed it good*, or *pleasant*. (Ḳ, TA. [Mentioned in art. عذى; but more properly belonging to the present art.; though both of these arts. are intimately connected, each with the other.])

عَذًى [or عَذًا]: see the next paragraph.

عَذَاةٌ and ▼ عَذِيَةٌ, (Ṣ, Ḳ, TA,) the latter written in [some copies of] the Ḳ, erroneously, عَذِيَّةٌ, (TA,) Land *good* (Ṣ, Ḳ) *in its soil*, (Ṣ,) *remote from water and from tainted air*: (Ḳ:) or land *good in its soil, and fertile*: or *remote from men*: or *remote from water and from tainted air and from pestilence*: or *remote from the* [*sunken waters*, or *the watery beds of sand* or *earth, called*] أَحْسَآء, *and from the waters that ooze from the ground*: or *not having in it* [*plants of the kind called*] حَمْض, *nor near to a region thereof*: (TA: [see also عِذْىٌ, in art. عذى:]) pl. of the former عَذَوَاتٌ (Ṣ, Ḳ) and [coll. gen. n. of the same, app. when used as a subst., which may generally be the case,] ▼ عَذًى [or عَذًا]. (TA.) [See also عِذْىٌ, again, in art. عذى.] — And عَذَاةٌ signifies also *A* خَامَة [or *portion that grows forth upon a single stalk*, or *fresh* or *juicy bunch or plant*, &c., (see art. خيم,)] *of seed-produce*. (TA in art. عذى.)

عَذِيَةٌ: see the next preceding paragraph.

عَذَوَانٌ *Brisk, lively*, or *sprightly*; *light*, or *active*; *not having great forbearance nor* أَصَالَة [app. as meaning *firmness*, or *soundness*, *of judgment*]: fem. with ة: or, as some say, it is with غ. (TA.)

عَذَوِيَّةٌ: see عَاذِيَةٌ, below.

عَذَآءٌ the subst. from عَذَاةٌ [app. signifying The *quality*, or *condition*, *of land that is termed* عَذَاة]. (TA in art. عذى.)

عَاذِيَةٌ and ▼ عَذَوِيَّةٌ, and عَوَاذٍ [the pl. of the first], applied to camels, *Being in a place of pasture that has not in it* [*plants of the kind called*] حَمْض. (Ḳ and TA in art. عذى.) [See also عَاذِيَةٌ, voce عِذْوِىٌّ, in art. عدو.]

عذى

1. عَذِىَ, aor. يَعْذَى, [inf. n. عَذًى,] *It was*, or *became*, *such as is termed* عِذْىٌ, said of seed-produce, and of herbage, and of palm-trees. (Mṣb.) See also 1, in art. عذو.

10: see art. عذو [with which the present art. is intimately connected].

عَذْىٌ: see the next paragraph, in two places.

عِذْىٌ (Ṣ, Mṣb, Ḳ) and ▼ عَذْىٌ (IAạr, Mṣb, Ḳ) *Such as is not watered but by the rain*, of seed-produce, (Ṣ, Mṣb, Ḳ, TA,) and of herbage, (Mṣb,) and of palm-trees: (Mṣb, TA:) [app. used as epithets and as substs.: see also عَثَرِىٌّ: and see بَعْلٌ:] and ▼ عَذٍ and ▼ عَذِىٌّ, the latter of the measure فَعِيلٌ, are applied as epithets to the same in the same sense: the pl. of عِذْىٌ is أَعْذَآءٌ. (Mṣb.) — And عِذْىُ الكَلَإِ *Herbage*, or *pasturage*, *that is remote from the* رِيف [or *land of sown fields and of seed produce* &c.], *and that grows from the rain*. (TA.) — And عِذْىٌ signifies also *A place that gives growth to plants*, or *herbage*, *in winter and summer, without the welling forth of water*. (Lth, TA.) — And *Any place not having in it* [*plants of the kind called*] حَمْض (Ḳ, TA) *nor land that exudes water and produces salt*; (TA;) as also ▼ عَذْىٌ. (Ḳ.) — And *i. q.* عَذَاةٌ: [perhaps in the sense last expl. above: (see the latter in art. عذو:)] pl. أَعْذَآءٌ. (TA.)

عَذٍ: } see the next preceding paragraph.
عَذِىٌّ: }

عر

1. عَرَّتِ الإِبِلُ, aor. ـِ (Ṣ, O, Ḳ) and ـُ, (Ḳ,) inf. n. عَرٌّ; (Ṣ;) *The camels were*, or *became*, *mangy*, or *scabby*, or *affected with the mange or scab*; (Ṣ, O, Ḳ;*) as also ▼ تَعَرْعَرَتْ; (O, Ḳ;*) and عُرَّتْ: (Ḳ:*) or this last verb signifies *they* (the camels) *had purulent pustules, like the* [*cutaneous eruption called*] قُوَبَاء [q. v.], *coming forth dispersedly in their lips* (Ṣ, O) *and their legs*, (Ṣ,) *and discharging a fluid resembling yellow water*; *in consequence of which the healthy camels are cauterized, in order that the diseased may not communicate to them the malady*: (Ṣ, O:) or the same verb signifies, (IKṭṭ, Ḳ,* TA,) and so the first, and ▼ the second, (Ḳ,*) said of young, or unweaned, camels, *they had purulent pustules in their necks*: (IKṭṭ, Ḳ,* TA:) and all the three verbs, said of camels, signify *they had a disease which caused their fur to fall off*, (Ḳ, TA,) *so that the skin appeared and shone*. (TA.) — عَرَّ البَدَنَ, said of the mange, or scab, signifies اِعْتَرَضَهُ [app. meaning *It attached the body*]. (B, TA.) — عَرَّ, aor. ـُ, inf. n. عَرَّةٌ, said of a bird, *It muted*, or *dunged*. (Ṣ, O.) — عَرَّ, (Ṣ, Mgh, TA,) aor. ـُ, (Ṣ, TA,) inf. n. عَرٌّ; (O;) and ▼ عَرَّرَ, inf. n. تَعْرِيرٌ; (Ṣ, O;) *He manured* land: *he dunged* it: (Mgh, TA:) *he manured it with*

human ordure. (TA.) — And [hence] عَرَّهُ, (Mgh, Mṣb,) aor. ُ, (Mṣb,) *He defiled*, or *besmeared, him*, or *it*, (Mgh, Mṣb,) *with* عُرَّة, i. e. *dung such as is called* سِرْقِين, (Mgh,) or with a thing. (Mṣb.) — And عَرَّهُ بِشَرٍّ † *He sullied*, or *bespattered, him with evil, by charging him therewith; aspersed him;* or *charged*, or *upbraided, him with evil:* (Ṣ, O, Ḳ, TA:) from عَرٌّ signifying "he dunged" land; or, accord. to A'Obeyd, it may be from عَرٌّ signifying "mange," or "scab:" and † *he wronged him*, or *treated him unjustly* or *injuriously; and reviled him;* and *took his property*. (TA.) — And [in like manner] هُوَ يَعُرُّ قَوْمَهُ † *He brings against his people*, or *party, an abominable*, or *evil, charge*, (يُدْخِلُ عَلَيْهِمْ مَكْرُوهًا,) *aspersing them with it*. (Ṣ, O.) † *He disgraces*, or *dishonours, his people*, or *party*. (TA.) — And عَرَّهُ, aor. ُ, † *He applied to him a surname*, or *nickname, that disgraced him*, or *dishonoured him:* and عُرَّ † *He received*, or *became called by, such a surname* or *nickname*. (TA.) — And عَرَّهُ, (Ṣ, O, Ḳ,) aor. ُ, (TA,) inf. n. عَرٌّ, (Ḳ,) † *He did to him an abominable*, or *evil, thing:* (Ḳ:) *he displeased him; grieved*, or *vexed, him; did to him what he disliked*, or *hated; did evil to him*. (Ṣ, O, Ḳ.) — And عَرَّهُ also signifies *It* (a thing that he disliked, or hated, and that distressed him,) *befell him;* syn. عَرَاهُ, meaning دَهَاهُ. (Ksh in xlviii. 25. [In Bḍ, اعراه; app. a mistranscription for عَرَاهُ.]) — Also, (O, Mṣb, Ḳ,) aor. ُ, (O, TA,) inf. n. عَرٌّ; (O, Ḳ;) and ▼ اعترّهُ, (Mṣb, Ḳ,) and اعترّ بِهِ; (Ḳ;) and عَرَاهُ and اعتراهُ likewise; (Mṣb, TA; [see art. عرو;]) *He addressed*, or *applied, himself to obtain favour*, or *bounty, of him, without asking;* (Mṣb, Ḳ;) *he came to him, and sought his favour*, or *bounty;* or *seeking his favour*, or *bounty:* (O, TA:) or *he went round about him, seeking to obtain what he had*, whether *asking him* or *not asking him*. (TA, as implied in an explanation of مُعْتَرٌّ.) — And عَرَّهُ *He alighted at his abode as a visiter and guest*. (IḲṭṭ, TA.) — See also 3.

2: see the preceding paragraph, former half.

3. عارّ, (Ṣ, O, Ḳ,) aor. يُعَارُّ, (Ṣ,) inf. n. عِرَارٌ (Ṣ, O, Ḳ) and مُعَارَّةٌ; (Ḳ;) and, (Ṣ, O, Ḳ,) as some say, (Ṣ, O,) ▼ عَرَّ, aor. ِ, (Ṣ, O, Ḳ,) or ُ, (thus in the L,) inf. n. عِرَارٌ, (Ṣ, O, Ḳ,) with kesr; (Ḳ; [in one of my copies of the Ṣ عُرَارٌ; but عِرَارٌ, which would be agreeable with analogy, I do not find;]) *He* (an ostrich [said of the male only]) *cried; uttered a cry* or *cries:* (Ṣ, O, Ḳ:) like as they say of a female ostrich زَمَرَتْ: (Ṣ, O:*) IḲṭṭ cites an assertion that it is عَارَ, aor. يَعُورُ. (TA.)

4. اعرّت الدَّارُ *The house had in it* عُرَّة [i. e. *dung*, or *human ordure*], (Ṣ,* O, Ḳ,*) or *much thereof;* like أَعْذَرَتْ. (TA.)

6. تعارّ *He awoke from his sleep*, (Ṣ, A, O,) *in the night, with a sound*, or *cry*, (Ṣ, O,) or *speaking*, or *talking:* (A:) *he was sleepless, and turned over upon the bed, by night, speaking*, or *talking*, (A, Ḳ,) *and with a sound*, or *cry, and*, as some say, *stretching*. (TA.) A'Obeyd says that some derive it [as Z does] from عِرَار, signifying the "crying" of a male ostrich; but that he knows not whether it be so or not. (TA.)

8: see 1, near the end of the paragraph.

10. اِسْتَعَرَّهُمُ الجَرَبُ *The mange*, or *scab, appeared and spread among them*. (Ṣ, O,* Ḳ.) [See also 8 in art. سعر.]

R. Q. 2. تَعَرْعَرَتْ: see 1, first quarter, in two places.

عَرٌّ The *mange*, or *scab;* (Ṣ, A, Mgh, O, Ḳ;) as also ▼ عُرٌّ (Ḳ) and ▼ عُرَّةٌ (IF, Mṣb, Ḳ) and ▼ عَرَّةٌ: (IF, Mṣb, and so in a copy of the A:) see also عُرُورٌ: or عَرٌّ has this signification; but ▼ عُرٌّ, with ḍamm, signifies *purulent pustules in the necks of young*, or *unweaned, camels:* and a *certain disease, in consequence of which the fur of the camel falls off*, (Ḳ, TA,) *so that the skin appears and shines;* as some say: (TA:) or *purulent pustules, like the* [*cutaneous eruption called*] قُوبَاء [q. v.], *which comes forth in camels, dispersedly, in their lips* (Ṣ, O) *and their legs*, (Ṣ,) *discharging a fluid which resembles yellow water; in consequence of which the healthy camels are cauterized, in order that the diseased may not communicate to them the malady*. (Ṣ, O.) En-Nábighah says, (addressing En-Noamán Ibn-El-Mundhir, O,)

فَحَمَّلْتَنِى ذَنْبَ ٱمْرِئٍ وَتَرَكْتَهُ
كَذِى العُرِّ ▼ يُكْوَى غَيْرُهُ وَهْوَ رَاتِعُ

[*And thou hast charged me with the crime*, or *offence, of a man* other than myself, *and left him like that which has the disease called* عُرّ, *another than which is cauterized while he is pasturing at pleasure*]: he who says العَرّ, in relating this verse, errs; for cauterization is not practised as a preservative from the mange, or scab. (IDrd, Ṣ, O.) — [Hence, app.,] † *A vice*, or *fault*, or *the like*. (Ḥar p. 366.) [See also عُرَّة.] — And † *Evil*, or *mischief*. (Ḥar ibid.) One says, لَقِيتُ مِنْهُ شَرًّا وَعُرًّا † [*I experienced from him, or it, evil and mischief:* the two nouns being synonymous: and the latter of them also an inf. n. of عَرَّهُ, q. v.]. (TA: but written without any syll. signs.) [See also an instance of the use of the phrase شَرٌّ وَعُرٌّ voce دَفِينٌ.] — See also عَارٌّ.

عُرٌّ: see عَرٌّ, in three places: — and see عُرَّة.

عَرَّةٌ: see عَرٌّ.

عُرَّةٌ: see عَرٌّ. — Also *Madness*, or *such as is caused by diabolical possession, affecting a man:* you say, بِهِ عُرَّةٌ *In him is madness*, &c. (Ṣ, O.) — *Dung, such as is called* بَعَر, *and* سِرْجِين, (Ṣ, O,) or سِرْقِين, (Mgh,) [i. e. *dung of horses* or *other solid-hoofed animals*, and *of camels, sheep and goats, wild oxen*, and *the like*,] and *that of birds;* (Ṣ, O, Ḳ;) as also ▼ عُرٌّ: (O, Ḳ:) and *human ordure*. (O, Ḳ.) It is said in a trad., لَعَنَ ٱللّٰهُ بَائِعَ العُرَّةِ وَمُشْتَرِيَهَا i. e. [*God has cursed*, or *may God curse, the seller of*] سرقين [or perhaps the meaning may be *human ordure, and the buyer thereof*]. (Mgh.) — *Dirt*, or *filth*. (Mṣb.) — † *Filthiness in the natural dispositions*. (O.) — ‡ *A thing that exposes its author to disgrace; a vice*, or *fault*, or *the like*. (O, Mṣb, TA.) See also مَعَرَّة. [And see عُرٌّ, voce عَرٌّ. Hence,] عُرَّةُ النِّسَآءِ ‡ *That which disgraces women; their evil conversation or behaviour, with others*. (TA.) — As an epithet applied to a man, (Ṣ, O, Mṣb,) † *Dirty*, or *filthy;* as also ▼ عَارُورٌ and ▼ عَارُورَةٌ: (Ṣ, O:) [or] having an intensive signification [as though meaning "dirt," or "filth," itself]: (Mṣb:) † a man *who is the disgrace of the people* [*to whom he belongs*]: (Ḳ:) a man *sullied*, or *bespattered, with evil*. (IDrd, O.) And one says, فُلَانٌ عُرَّةُ أَهْلِهِ meaning † *Such a one is the worst of his family*. (TA.) — Also † The *act of doing an abominable*, or *evil, thing, to another*. (Ḳ.)

عُرُرٌ and ▼ عُرُورٌ *Manginess*, or *scabbiness:* (Ḳ:) or, accord. to some, *mange*, or *scab*, itself; like ▼ عَرٌّ. (TA.)

عَرَارٌ *A certain plant, of sweet odour*, (Ṣ, O,) *intensely yellow and wide in the blossom;* (O;) i. q. بَهَارُ البَرِّ [q. v., i. e. *buphthalmum*, or *ox-eye;* which is called by both of these names in the present day]: (Ṣ, O, Ḳ:) accord. to IB, the *wild narcissus* (النَّرْجِسُ البَرِّيُّ): (TA:) and said by some to be *a sort of tree* [or *plant*] *to which the complexion of a woman is likened:* (Ḥam p. 548:) n. un. with ة: (Ṣ, O, Ḳ:) IAar says that the عَرَارَة *is like the* بَهَار; *having wood*, [or *arborescent*, app. meaning that it is the *buphthalmum arborescens*, the flower of which is intensely yellow, agreeably with what is said of it in the O,] *having a sweet odour, and growing only in plain land*. (O.) — Also, i. e. like سَحَاب [in measure], *Retaliation of slaughter* or *of wounding* or *of mutilation;* syn. قَوَدٌ: and *anything that is slain in retaliation for another* (كُلُّ شَىْءٍ بَآءَ بِشَىْءٍ): (Ḳ, TA:) of any such thing one says, هُوَ لَهُ عَرَارٌ [*It is one slain in retaliation for it*]. (TA.) [This latter meaning is app. taken from the prov. بَآءَتْ عَرَارِ بِكَحْلٍ, relating to two cows; mentioned in art. بوأ.]

عُرُورٌ: see عُرُرٌ.

عَرِيرٌ *A stranger* (Az, Ṣ, Z, O, Ḳ) *among a people:* (O, Ḳ:) occurring, in the accus. case, in a trad., in which some read غَرِيرًا, with the pointed غ; and some say that the right reading is غَرِيًّا, i. e. مُلْصَقًا [here meaning "an adherent"]: but Hr and IAth agree with Az [and the Ṣ] and Z and the [O and] Ḳ. (TA.)

عَرْعَرٌ The tree called سَرْو [which is the common,

or *evergreen, cypress*; but the former name is generally applied in the present day to the *juniper-tree*]; (Ṣ, O, Ḳ;) a Pers. word: (Ḳ:) it is *a kind of great tree, of the trees of the mountains*: (O:) some say that it is the [*tree called*] سَاسَم, *and also* [*said to be*] *called* شِيزَى: others, that it is *a great kind of mountain-tree, evergreen, called by the Persians* سَرْو: (TA:) AḤn says that he had been informed by an Arab of the desert, of the people of the Sarāh (السَّرَاة), who are possessors of the عَرْعَر, that it is the أَبْهَل [q. v., a name now applied to the *juniper-tree*, like عَرْعَر; and particularly to the species thereof called the *savin*]; and he adds that he knew it in his own country, and afterwards saw it in the province of Ḳazween, cut for firewood from the mountains thereof, in the borders of Ed-Deylem; whence he knew that his informant was well acquainted with it, for those mountains are places of growth of the ابهل: (O:) he says that *it has a fruit like the* نَبِق [or *fruit of the lote-tree called* سِدْر], *first green, then becoming white, then becoming black until it is like* حُمَم [or *charcoal, &c.*], *and sweet, when it is eaten*: (TA:) n. un. with ة. (O, TA.)

عَرْعَار: see وَعْوَاعٌ, in art. وع.

عَارٌّ A camel *having the mange*, or *scab*; as also ↓ أَعَرُّ; (A'Obeyd, Ṣ, O;) which latter [in some of the copies of the Ḳ written ↓ أَعَرّ] is applied in this sense to a man; and ↓ مَعْرُورٌ to a camel: (Ḳ:) or this last signifies *having*, or *affected with, the disease called* عُرّ. (Ṣ, O, Ḳ.) — See also مُعْتَرٌّ.

عَارُورٌ and عَارُورَةٌ: see عُرَّةٌ.

أَعَرُّ: see عَارٌّ. — One says also, أَنْتَ شَرٌّ مِنْهُ وَأَعَرُّ [meaning † *Thou art worse than he, and more evil*: the two nouns being synonymous, like شَرٌّ and عَرٌّ]. (TA.)

مَعَرَّةٌ *A place of* عَرّ, i. e. *mange*, or *scab*: this is the primary signification. (TA.) — Hence, المَعَرَّةُ *The region of the sky that is beyond the Milky Way* (المَجَرَّة) *in the direction of the North Pole*; so called because of the multitude of the stars therein; (O,* TA;) like as the sky is called الجَرْبَآءُ because of its numerous stars; these being compared to scabs on the body of a man: (TA:) and to this and the مَجَرَّة a man alluded, when, being asked respecting the place where he alighted and abode, he informed the inquirer that he alighted and abode between two tribes, (O, TA,) great and numerous; (O;) saying, نَزَلْتُ بَيْنَ المَعَرَّةِ وَالمَجَرَّةِ [*I have alighted between the* مَعَرَّة *and the* مَجَرَّة]: (O, TA:) or, as some say, (O,) المَعَرَّةُ is the name of *a certain star*, or *asterism*, [*which is*] *below the* مَجَرَّة [or *Milky Way*, app. meaning *when the latter, as viewed from Arabia, is seen stretching across the sky above the North Pole*]. (O, Ḳ.) — [Hence likewise, app.,] مَعَرَّةٌ signifies also † *A cause of reviling*, or *of being reviled*; syn. مَسَبَّةٌ: (TA:) *a crime*, or *sin*; syn. إِثْمٌ; (Ṣ, O, Mṣb, Ḳ;) and جِنَايَةٌ; (TṢ, L, TA; in the copies of the Ḳ خِيَانَةٌ; [and thus in the O;] but this is a mistake; TA;) and جُرْمٌ; (TA;) as also ↓ عُرَّةٌ: (Ḳ:) or *a crime*, or *sin*, [*that is noxious*] *like the mange*, or *scab*: (L, TA:) *a foul*, or *an abominable, thing*: (O, TA:) *a cause of grief* or *vexation*: (Mgh, Mṣb:) *annoyance*, or *hurt*; or *a thing by which one is annoyed* or *hurt*; syn. أَذًى; (Sh, Mgh, Ḳ;) or أَذِيَّةٌ: (O:) *displeasing, grieving*, or *vexing, conduct*: (Mgh, Mṣb:) and *i. q.* شِدَّةٌ [app. as meaning *violence*, or *the like*]. (O: there mentioned between the significations of إِثْمٌ and أَذِيَّةٌ.) Also † The *slaying unexpectedly*, (Ṣ,) or the *fighting*, (O, Ḳ,) of an army, *without the permission of the commander*: (Ṣ, O, Ḳ: [omitted in one of my copies of the Ṣ:]) or the *alighting* of an army *among a people, and eating of the produce of their fields without knowledge* (Sh, O, TA) *of the commander*: (O:) or an army's *oppressing*, or *assaulting, those by whom they pass*, whether *Muslims*, or *unbelievers with whom terms of peace have been made, and afflicting them in respect of their women under covert and their possessions by conduct not permitted to them*. (TA.) — And † *A debt, fine*, or *mulct, which one is obliged to pay*: and *a fine for homicide*: (Ḳ, TA:) thus expl. by Mohammad Ibn-Is-ḥáḳ Ibn-Yesár: (TA:) or *a thing that one dislikes*, or *hates, relating to fines for homicide*; of the measure مَفْعَلَةٌ from عُرٌّ signifying "mange," or "scab." (Th, TA.) — And † The *changing of the face in colour by reason of anger*: (O, Ḳ, TA:) Az says that it is thus mentioned by Abu-l-'Abbás with teshdeed to the ر: but if it be from تَمَعَّرَ وَجْهُهُ, not from العَرّ, it is without teshdeed. (O, TA.)

مَعْرُورٌ: see عَارٌّ. — Also, with ة, applied to a palm-tree (نَخْلَةٌ), [and to land (أَرْض),] *Dunged with* عُرَّة [q. v.]. (TA.) — And, without ة, † A man *sullied*, or *bespattered, with evil*; or *aspersed*: (Ṣ, Mṣb:) and *wronged*, or *treated unjustly* or *injuriously*; *and reviled*; and *deprived of his property*. (TA.)

مُعْتَرٌّ One *who addresses*, or *applies, himself to obtain favour*, or *bounty, without asking*; (I'Ab, Ṣ, O,* Mṣb, Ḳ;) one *who comes to another, and seeks his favour*, or *bounty*; or *seeking his favour*, or *bounty*; as also ↓ عَارٌّ: or one *who goes round about another, seeking to obtain what the latter has*, whether *asking him* or *not asking*. (TA.) And *A guest visiting*. (Mṣb.) And *A poor man*. (Ḳ, TA.) It occurs in the Ḳur xxii. 37: accord. to some, having the last of these meanings: accord. to others, the first thereof. (TA.)

عرب

1. عَرُبَ لِسَانُهُ, [aor. ـُ,] inf. n. عُرُوبَةٌ, *His tongue* [or *speech*] *was*, or *became, Arabic*, (Ṣ, O,) or *chaste Arabic*. (Mṣb.) — See also 4, first sentence, in three places. = عَرِبَ, aor. ـَ, inf. n. عَرَبٌ, *He* (a man) *became disordered in the stomach by indigestion*. (TA.) And عَرِبَتْ مَعِدَتُهُ, inf. n. as above, *His stomach became in a corrupt*, or *disordered, state*, (Ṣ, O, Mṣb, Ḳ,) *from being burdened*. (TA.) — Also, (O, Ḳ,) inf. n. as above, (TA,) said of a camel's hump, (O, TA,) *It became swollen and purulent*. (O, Ḳ, TA.) — And, said of a wound, (Ṣ, O, Ḳ, TA,) *It became corrupt*: (TA:) or *it broke open again*; or *became recrudescent*: (Ṣ, O:) or *it had a scar remaining after it had healed*. (Ḳ.) — Said of a river, *It abounded with water*. (Ḳ.) And عَرِبَتِ البِئْرُ *The well contained much water*; or *its water became abundant*. (Ḳ.) — And, (Ḳ, TA,) inf. n. عَرَبٌ (O,* Ḳ,* TA) and عَرَابَةٌ, said of a man, (TA,) *He was*, or *became, brisk, lively*, or *sprightly*. (Ḳ, TA.) = عَرَبَ, (O, Ḳ,) aor. ـِ, (Ḳ,) inf. n. عَرْبٌ, (TḲ,) *He ate* (O, Ḳ) food. (TḲ.)

2. عرّب, (Ṣ, O,) inf. n. تَعْرِيبٌ, (Ṣ,) *He* (an Arab) *arabicized* a foreign word; *spoke it*, or *pronounced it, agreeably with the ways of Arabic speech*; (Ṣ;) as also ↓ اعرب, (Ṣ, O,*) inf. n. إِعْرَابٌ. (TA.) — And *He taught* another *the Arabic language*. (TA, from a trad.) — See also 4, in fourteen places. — The inf. n. signifies also The *showing*, or *declaring, one's saying*, (Ḳ, TA,) and *one's deed*, (TA,) *to be bad, evil, abominable*, or *foul*. (Ḳ, TA.) One says, عرّب عَلَيْهِ *He showed him*, or *declared to him, that his saying*, and *his deed, was bad, &c.*; and *upbraided him for it*. (TA.) And فَعَلْتُ كَذَا وَكَذَا فَمَا عَرَّبَ عَلَىَّ أَحَدٌ *I did so and so, and no one upbraided me*; or *charged me with having acted disgracefully*. (AZ, TA.) And عرّب عَلَيْهِ فِعْلَهُ, (Ṣ, O,) and قَوْلَهُ, (TA,) *He showed him*, or *declared to him, that his deed was bad, evil, abominable*, or *foul*, (Ṣ, O,) and so *his saying*. (TA.) تَعْرِيبٌ is The *saying to a man who has uttered what is foul*, or *erroneous*, "*It is not so, but so*;" *telling him what is more correct*. (Sh, TA.) And The *replying against a speaker*; (Ḳ, TA;) and so ↓ إِعْرَابٌ. (TA.) One says, عرّب عَلَيْهِ *He replied against him, denying* or *disallowing* or *disapproving what he said*: (Ṣ:) or *he prevented, hindered*, or *forbade, him*: or *he did so, and denied* or *disallowed* or *disapproved* [*what he said* or *did*]. (TA.) [See what next follows.] — Also The *treating medically, to remove his disease, one whose stomach is in a corrupt*, or *disordered, state*. (O, Ḳ. [In both, التَّعْرِيبُ is expl. as meaning تَمْرِيضُ العَرِبِ i. e. الذَّرِبِ المَعِدَةِ. Freytag has strangely rendered the verb as signifying "ægrotum reddidit aliquem stomachi corruptio."]) Az says that التَّعْرِيبُ followed by عَلَى and having for its object him who says what is disapproved may be from this. (TA.) — Also The *lopping a palm-tree*; or *pruning it by cutting off some of its branches*. (Ṣ, O, Ḳ.*) — And The *scarifying* a horse or similar beast *in the parts of the skin next the hoofs and then cauterizing those parts*: (Ḳ, TA:) or the *cauterizing* a horse *in several places in those parts, and then gently scarifying them without producing any effect upon the sinews*, or *tendons*, (Az, O, TA,) *in order to strengthen the*

parts, (Az, TA,) or *in order that the hair may become strong:* (O:) or عَرَّبَ الفَرَسَ signifies *he made an incision in the bottom of the horse's hoof;* and the verb implies that, by this operation, what was concealed becomes apparent to the eye, so that one knows the state of the hoof, whether it be hard or soft, sound or diseased. (L, TA. See also 1 in art. بزغ.) — Also, the inf. n., The *getting,* or *procuring for oneself, an Arabian horse.* (TA. [See also 4, near the end.]) — And The *taking,* or *making, for oneself, an Arabian bow.* (O, Ḳ.) — Also the *drinking much clear,* or *limpid, water,* (O, Ḳ,) which is termed عَرِبٌ. (O.) — عَرَّبَ البَقَرَةَ, (Ḳ,) or ↑ أَعْرَبَهَا, (O,) *He rendered the cow desirous* [*of copulation*]; said of a bull. (O, Ḳ.) — And عَرَّبَ, (Fr, Mgh, O,) inf. n. تَعْرِيبٌ; (Fr, O, Ḳ;) and ↑ اعرب, (Fr, Mgh, O, Mṣb,) inf. n. إِعْرَابٌ; (Fr, Mgh, Ḳ;) and ↑ عَرْبَنَ; (O, and Ṣ and Ḳ in art. عربن;) *He gave what is termed an* عُرْبُون (O, Mṣb, Ḳ) or عُرْبَان (Fr, Mgh) [i. e. an *earnest*], فِى كَذَا [*in the case of such a thing*], (O,) or فِى بَيْعِهِ [*in the case of his purchase*]. (Mṣb.) One says, ↑ أَعْرَبُوا فِى الدَّارِ أَرْبَعَمِائَةٍ *They paid in advance, as an earnest, in the case of the house, four hundred* [dirhems]. (L, TA.) It is related in a trad. that ↑ الإِعْرَاب in buying and selling is forbidden: (Mgh, O, TA:) this is said by Sh to mean A man's *saying to another, If I do not purchase this for so much, thou shalt have such and such of my property.* (O, TA.)

3. [The following ex. is given of the inf. n. of this verb.] One says, مَا أُوتِىَ أَحَدٌ مِنْ مُعَارَبَةِ النِّسَآءِ مَا أُوتِىَ فُلَانٌ, (O,) or مَا أُوتِيتُهُ أَنَا, (TA,) meaning, (O, TA,) app., (TA,) [*No one has been given what such a one has been given,* or *what I have been given, of*] *the means of coïtus* [*with women*]. (O, TA.)

4. اعرب, (AZ, Mṣb, TA,) [for اعرب الكَلَامَ, like افصح for افصح الكَلَامَ,] inf. n. إِعْرَابٌ, (A, Ḳ,) *He spoke clearly, plainly, distinctly,* or *intelligibly,* (AZ, A, Mṣb, Ḳ,* TA,) *in Arabic;* (Mṣb;) as also ↑ تعرّب, and ↑ استعرب; said of a foreigner, or one [previously] not clear, plain, distinct, or intelligible, in speech: (AZ, Mṣb, TA:) and ↑ عَرُبَ, aor. ـُ, inf. n. عُرْبٌ and عُرُوبٌ and عُرْبَةٌ and عَرَابَةٌ [which accord. to general analogy would be عَرَابَةٌ] and عُرُوبِيَّةٌ; (TA;) or ↑ عَرِبَ, aor. ـَ; (Mṣb;) [likewise] signifies *he spoke clearly, plainly,* or *distinctly, after being barbarous,* or *vitious, in speech:* (Mṣb, TA:) and ↑ عَرُبَ *he spoke without incorrectness;* (Mṣb;) and [so* اعرب, for] إِعْرَابٌ signifies the *committing no error in speech:* (Ḳ, TA:) and the *expressing of meanings clearly, plainly, distinctly,* or *perspicuously, by words.* (TA.) [↑ عرّب, also, has a similar meaning:] it is said in a trad., كَانُوا يَسْتَحِبُّونَ أَنْ يُلَقِّنُوا الصَّبِىَّ حِينَ يُعَرِّبُ ↑ أَنْ يَقُولَ لَا إِلٰهَ إِلَّا اللّٰهُ سَبْعَ مَرَّاتٍ (O, TA) i. e. [*They used to like teaching the boy,*] *when he spoke distinctly,* or *articulately,* [*to say "There is no deity but God" seven times.*] (TA.) And one says, اعرب الكَلَامَ, and اعرب بِهِ, meaning *He made the speech* [that he spoke] *clear, plain, distinct,* or *perspicuous.* (TA.) And اعرب بِحُجَّتِهِ *He declared,* or *spoke out clearly* or *plainly, his argument, plea, allegation,* or *the like, without fearing any one.* (Ṣ, O.) And أَعْرَبْتُ الشَّىْءَ and اعربت عَنْهُ, and ↑ عَرَّبْتُهُ and عَرَّبْتُ عَنْهُ, which last, accord. to Fr, is better than عرّبتهُ and اعربتهُ, *I made the thing clear, plain, distinct,* or *manifest.* (Mṣb.) And اعرب عَمَّا فِى ضَمِيرِهِ *He declared,* or *spoke out clearly* or *plainly, what was in his mind.* (TA.) And اعرب عَنْهُ لِسَانُهُ, and ↑ عرّب عنه, *His tongue made clear,* or *plain,* or *spoke clearly,* or *plainly, for him:* and يُعَرِّبُ ↑ عَمَّا فِى قَلْبِهِ لِسَانُهُ *His tongue tells plainly,* or *declares, what is in his heart.* (Az, TA.) It is said in a trad., الثَّيِّبُ تُعْرِبُ عَنْ نَفْسِهَا, (Ṣ,) or الأَيِّمُ, and ↑ تُعَرِّبُ, accord. to different relaters, but some say the former only, (Mṣb,) i. e. [*She who has become a widow,* or *been divorced,* &c., or *she who has no husband, whether she be a virgin* or *not,* or *not being a virgin,*] *shall speak out plainly for herself* [when demanded in marriage]: (Ṣ, Mṣb:) or الثَّيِّبُ يُعْرِبُ عَنْهَا لِسَانُهَا, so accord. to IḲt, (O,) or ↑ يُعَرِّبُ عنها, (Mgh, O,) so accord. to A'Obeyd, but, as IAmb says, both are dial. vars. of which neither is preferable to the other; and the meaning is [*she who has become a widow,* &c., *her tongue*] *shall declare for her.* (O.) One says also, اعرب عَنِ الرَّجُلِ *He spoke out,* or *explained, for the man.* (TA.) And ↑ عَرَّبْتُ عَنِ القَوْمِ *I spoke for the people,* or *party;* (Fr, Ṣ, Mgh,* O, Ḳ;) *and pleaded for them;* (Fr, Mgh,* TA;) as also أَعْرَبْتُ; but the former in this sense is better known. (Mgh.) And اعرب عَنْهُ, and ↑ عرّب عنه, *He pleaded his cause.* (TA.) And ↑ عرّب عَنْ حَاجَتِهِ *He spoke and pleaded for the object of his want.* (A.) — اعرب also signifies *He was,* or *became, chaste, uncorrupt,* or *free from barbarousness, in speech;* although not an Arab. (Mṣb.) And عَرَّبْتُ لَهُ الكَلَامَ, inf. n. تَعْرِيبٌ; as also أَعْرَبْتُ له, inf. n. إِعْرَابٌ; *I made the speech* [that I spoke] *clear,* or *plain, to him, so that there was in it no barbarousness.* (TA.) And ↑ عرّب مَنْطِقَهُ, (Ṣ, O,) inf. n. تَعْرِيبٌ, (Ḳ,) *He made his speech free from error,* or *incorrectness.* (Ṣ, O, Ḳ.) And أَعْرَبْتُ الحَرْفَ *I made the* حرف [i. e. *word*] *clear,* or *plain:* or the ا in this case denotes privation, and the meaning is † *I removed its* عرب, [app. ↑ عَرَب, from this word as inf. n. of عَرِبَ used in relation to the stomach &c.,] i. e. *vagueness.* (Mṣb.) And اعرب كَلَامَهُ *He made his speech free from error,* or *incorrectness, in* [*what is termed*] الإِعْرَاب [here meaning what grammarians generally intend thereby, namely, *desinential syntax,* or *the science of the various inflections of words, literal* or *virtual, by reason of the various governing words*]. (Ṣ, O.) [اعرب is also used by grammarians as meaning *He declined* a word; and أُعْرِبَ as meaning *It was declined,* or *declinable;* in these senses opposed to بَنَى and بُنِىَ, inf. n. بِنَآءٌ: and the former also as meaning *He analyzed grammatically,* or *parsed,* a sentence: and the inf. n. of the verb (act. and pass.) in these senses is إِعْرَابٌ.] — See also 2, first sentence: — and again in the first third part of the paragraph. — إِعْرَابٌ also signifies The *making* [a person] *to revert from,* or *relinquish, foul speech;* (Ḳ, TA;) and so ↑ تَعْرِيبٌ. (TA.) — And The *speaking foul,* or *obscene, language;* as also ↑ تَعْرِيبٌ, and ↑ اِسْتِعْرَابٌ: (O, Ḳ:) thus it bears two contr. significations. (Ḳ, TA.) One says of a man, اعرب [&c.], (Ṣ, O,) or اعرب فِى كَلَامِهِ, (Mṣb,) *He spoke foul,* or *obscene, language.* (Ṣ, O, Mṣb.) [Golius and Freytag have assigned this meaning to ↑ تعرّب also: the latter of them as from the Ṣ and Ḳ; in neither of which do I find it.] — And The *act of copulating:* or the *speaking of that act in an oblique,* or *indirect, manner.* (Ḳ.) — And اعرب, (Ṣ, O,) inf. n. إِعْرَابٌ, (Ḳ,) *He had a child born to him of Arabian complexion,* or *colour.* (Ṣ, O, Ḳ.) — And *He possessed,* or *acquired,* or *sought to acquire, horses,* or *camels, of pure Arabian race.* (TA. [See also 2, in the middle of the latter half; and see مُعْرِبٌ.]) — And إِعْرَابٌ signifies One's *knowing* a horse *of pure Arabian race from one of mean race by his neighing.* (Ḳ.) And A horse's *being known by his neighing to be of pure Arabian race, free from any admixture of other than Arabian blood:* (Ḳ, TA:) [or his *making himself to be known as such by his neighing;* for] اعرب means *he* (a horse) *neighed, and was consequently known to be of Arabian race.* (A.) — And The *making* a horse *to run.* (Ḳ.) Accord. to Fr, one says, اعرب عَلَى فَرَسِهِ, meaning *He made his horse to run:* but he adds that some say اغرب. (O.) — And إِعْرَابٌ signifies The *taking as one's wife a woman such as is termed* عَرُوبٌ [q. v.]. (Ḳ.) — اعرب سَقْىُ القَوْمِ means *The people's watering* [*of their camels*], *having been at one time on alternate days, and another time on the fourth day after that of the next preceding watering, then became, and continued to be, of one uniform way.* (Ṣ, O.) — See also 2, last four sentences.

5. تعرّب *He assimilated himself to the Arabs.* (Ṣ.) *He* (a man not of genuine Arabian descent) *introduced himself among the Arabs, and spoke their language, and imitated their manner* or *appearance;* [*he became a naturalized,* or *an insititious, Arab;* (see العَرَبُ;)] as also ↑ استعرب. (Az, TA.) — *He became an Arab of the desert;* (Ṣ, Mgh;) *he returned to the desert,* (Az, Mgh, TA,) *after he had been dwelling in a region of cities or towns or villages and of cultivated land, and joined himself to the Arabs of the desert.* (Az, TA.) Hence, تعرّب بَعْدَ هِجْرَتِهِ *He became an Arab of the desert* [*after his flight,* or *emigration,* for the sake of El-Islám], (Ṣ, Mgh,) *returning to the desert.* (Mgh.) — *He dwelt,* or *abode, in the desert.* (O, Ḳ.) — See also 4, first sentence. — تَعَرَّبَتْ لِزَوْجِهَا *She acted in an amorous manner,* or *with amorous dalliance, and mani-*

fested love, to her husband. (A, TA.) — Respecting a meaning assigned to تعرّب by Golius and Freytag, see 4, latter half.

10. استعرب: see 5: — see also 4, first sentence: — and the same again in the latter half of the paragraph. ═ استعرب جَرَبًا, said of a camel, *He was affected with mange,* or *scab, which began in his armpits and groins* or *similar parts, and his lips, and appeared upon the general extent of his skin.* (O.) — And استعربت, said of a cow, *She desired the bull.* (O, Ḳ.)

Q. Q. 1. عَرْبَنَ: see 2, near the end.

عَرْبٌ is *syn. with* إِعْرَابٌ in the sense of إِفْصَاحٌ [but app. as a subst. (not an inf. n.) meaning *Clear, plain,* or *distinct, speech*]. (TA.) — And *syn. with* عِرَابَةٌ, q. v. (TA.) — And *syn. with* عَرَبٌ *as* [inf. n. of عَرِبَ, and] *meaning* نَشَاطٌ [i. e. *Briskness, liveliness,* or *sprightliness*]. (O, Ḳ.)

العُرْبُ: see العَرَبُ, first sentence.

عَرِبٌ *Such as is dried up, of the* [*species of barley-grass called*] بُهْمَى: (Ṣ, O, Ḳ:) or *of any herb,* or *leguminous plant:* n. un. with ة: or عَرِبُ البُهْمَى signifies *the prickles of the* بُهْمَى. (TA.)

العَرَبُ, (Ṣ, A, Mgh, O, Mṣb, Ḳ, &c.,) as also ▾ العُرْبُ, (Ṣ, O, Mṣb, Ḳ,) *A certain people,* or *nation;* [*the Arabs,* or *Arabians;*] (Ṣ, O;) *the contr. of* العَجَمُ (A, Mṣb, Ḳ, TA) and العُجْمُ; (TA;) *the inhabitants of the cities,* or *large towns,* (Ṣ, A, O, Ḳ,) or *of the Arabian cities and towns or villages:* (Mgh:) [but now, on the contrary, generally applied to those who dwell in the desert:] or *those who have alighted and made their abode in the cultivated regions, and have taken as their homes the Arabian cities and towns or villages, and others also that are related to them:* (Az, Mṣb:) or [accord. to general usage] *an appellation of common application* [*to the whole nation*]: (T, Ḳ:) [and in the lexicons and lexicological works applied to *the desert Arabs of pure speech:*] it is of the fem. gender: (Mṣb, Ḳ:) and العَرَبُ has two pls., namely, العُرُبُ, with two ḍammehs, and الأَعْرُبُ [which is a pl. of pauc.]: (Mṣb:) the rel. n. [which serves as a sing.] is ▾ عَرَبِىٌّ: (Ṣ, O, Ḳ: [عَرَبٌ عَرَبِىٌّ in the CḲ is a mistake:]) accord. to Az, (TA,) this appellation is applied to a man *of established Arab lineage, even if he be not chaste,* or *correct, in speech.* (Mṣb, TA.) The dim. of العَرَبُ is ▾ العُرَيْبُ, (Ṣ, O,) without ة, (O, TA,) an extr. word [with respect to analogy, as the undiminished noun is fem.]: (TA:) a poet (Abu-l-Hindee, whose name was 'Abd-El-Mu-min, son of 'Abd-El-Ḳuddoos, O, TA) says,

• وَمَكْنُ الضِّبَابِ طَعَامُ العُرَيْبِ •

• وَلَا تَشْتَهِيهِ نُفُوسُ العَجَمْ •

[*And the eggs of ḍabbs are food of the little Arabs; but the souls of the Foreigners do not desire them*]: in which he uses the dim. form to imply respect, or honour, like as it is used in the saying أَنَا جُذَيْلُهَا المُحَكَّكُ وَعُذَيْقُهَا المُرَجَّبُ [expl. in art. جذل]. (Ṣ, O.) — ▾ العَرَبُ العَارِبَةُ (in which the latter word is used as a corroborative of the former as in لَيْلٌ لَائِلٌ, Ṣ, O) and ▾ العَرَبُ العَرْبَآءُ (Ṣ, A, O, Mṣb, Ḳ) and ▾ العَرَبُ العَرِبَةُ (O) and ▾ العَرَبُ العَرِبَاتُ (Ḳ) and ▾ العَرَبُ العَرِبَةُ (CḲ [but this I do not find in any other copy of the Ḳ]) are appellations of *The pure,* or *genuine Arabs:* (Ṣ, A, O, Ḳ:) or *those who spoke the language of Yaạrub Ibn-Ḳaḥṭán;* which is the ancient language: (Mṣb:) and ▾ العَرَبُ المُسْتَعْرِبَةُ, (Ṣ, O, Mṣb, Ḳ,) as also ▾ العَرَبُ المُتَعَرِّبَةُ, (Ṣ, O, Ḳ,) is an appellation of *The insititious* [or *naturalized Arabs*]; (Ḳ;) *those who are not pure,* or *genuine, Arabs:* (Ṣ, O:) or *those who spoke the language of Ismá'eel* [or *Ishmael*] *the son of Ibráheem* [or *Abraham*], i. e., *the dialects of El-Ḥijáz and the parts adjacent thereto:* (Mṣb:) and the appellation of ▾ مُسْتَعْرِبَةٌ is thought by Az to apply [also] to *people not of pure Arabian descent, who have introduced themselves among the Arabs, and speak their language, and imitate their manner* or *appearance.* (TA.) [The former division is most reasonably considered as consisting of the extinct tribes ('Ád, Thamood, and others mentioned in what follows); or of these together with the unmixed descendants of Ḳaḥṭán, whose claims to the appellation of genuine Arabs are held by many to be equally valid: and the latter division, as consisting of those whose origin is referred, through Ma'add and 'Adnán, to Ismá'eel (or Ishmael), whose wife was descended from Ḳaḥṭán. What I find in the TA, on this subject, is as follows.] The former of these two divisions consisted of nine tribes, descendants of Irem [or Aram] the son of Sám [or Shem] the son of Nooḥ [or Noah]; namely, 'Ád, Thamood, Umeiyim, 'Abeel, Ṭasm, Jedees, 'Imleeḳ [or Amalek], Jurhum, and Webári; and from them Ismá'eel [or Ishmael is said to have] learned the Arabic language: and the ▾ مُتَعَرِّبَة are [said to be] the descendants of Ismá'eel, the descendants of Ma'add the son of 'Adnán the son of Udd: so says Abu-l-Khaṭṭáb Ibn-Diḥyeh, surnamed Dhu-n-Nesebeyn: or the former division consisted of seven tribes, namely, 'Ád, Thamood, 'Imleeḳ, Ṭasm, Jedees, Umeiyim, and Jásim; the main portion of whom has become extinct, some remains of them, only, being scattered among the [existing] tribes: so says IDrd: and the appellation of ▾ العَرَبُ العَارِبَةُ is also given to the descendants of Yaạrub the son of Ḳaḥṭán [only]. (TA.) [It should be observed, however, that the appellation of ▾ المُتَعَرِّبَة is, by those who hold the extinct tribes above mentioned as the only genuine Arabs, applied to the unmixed descendants of Ḳaḥṭán; and ▾ المُسْتَعْرِبَة, to those who are held to be the descendants of Ismá'eel: thus in the Mz, 1st نوع. Also, it should be observed that the appellation of ▾ العَرَبُ العَارِبَةُ, in the conventional language of Arabic lexicology, is often applied to the Arabs of the classical ages, and the later Arabs of the desert who retained the pure language of their ancestors, indiscriminately: it is thus applied by writers quoted in the Mz (1st نوع) to all the descendants of Ḳaḥṭán, and those of Ma'add the son of 'Adnán (through whom all the descendants of Ismá'eel trace their ancestry) who lived before the corruption, among them, of the Arabic language.] — ▾ الأَعْرَابُ is the appellation given to *Those* [*Arabs*] *who dwell in the desert;* (Ṣ, Mgh, O, Mṣb, Ḳ;) *such as go about in search of herbage and water;* and Az adds, *whether of the Arabs or of their freedmen:* he says that it is applied to *those who alight and abide in the desert, and are neighbours of the dwellers in the desert, and journey,* or *migrate, with them, to seek after herbage and water:* (Mṣb:) it is not a pl. of العَرَبُ, not being like الأَنْبَاطُ, which is pl. of النَّبَطُ; (Ṣ, O;) but is a [coll.] gen. n.: (Ṣ:) الأَعَارِيبُ occurs as its pl. (Ṣ, O, Ḳ) in chaste poetry: (Ṣ:) it has no sing. [properly so termed]: (Ḳ:) the rel. n. is ▾ أَعْرَابِىٌّ, (Ṣ, O,) which is applied to a single person; (Mṣb;) as also بَدَوِىٌّ: (TA:) Az says, if one say to an أَعْرَابِىٌّ, يَا عَرَبِىُّ, he is pleased; and if one say to an عَرَبِىٌّ, يَا أَعْرَابِىُّ, he is angry. (TA.) — Authors differ as to the cause why the عَرَب were thus called: some say, because of the perspicuity of their speech, from إِعْرَابٌ: others, that they were so called from Yaạrub the son of Ḳaḥṭán, who is said to have been the first that spoke the Arabic language; his original language having been, as asserted by IDrd, [what the Arabs term] Syriac; though some say that Ismá'eel was the first that spoke the Arabic language; and some, that Yaạrub was the first that spoke Arabic, and that Ismá'eel was the first that spoke the pure Arabic of El-Ḥijáz, in which the Ḳur-án was revealed: others say that the عَرَب were so called from العَرَبَة, the name of a tract near El-Medeeneh, or a name of Mekkeh and the adjacent region, where Ismá'eel settled, or the same as Tihámeh [as is said in the Mgh, in which this is pronounced to be the most correct derivation], or the general name of the peninsula of Arabia, which is also called العَرَبَاتُ [as is said in the Mṣb]: but some say that they were so called in like manner as were the فُرْس and the رُوم and the تُرْك and others, not after the name of a land or other than a land, but by the coining of the name, not a term expressive of a quality or a state or condition &c. (TA.) [If the country were called العَرَبَة, an inhabitant thereof might be called, agreeably with analogy, عَرَبِىٌّ; and then, the people collectively, العَرَبُ: but I think that the most probable derivation is from the old Hebrew word עֲרָב, meaning "a mixed people," which the Arabs assert themselves to have been, almost from the first; and in favour of this derivation it may be reasonably urged that the old Ḥimyeritic language agrees more in its vocabulary with the Hebrew and Phœnician than it does with the classical and modern Arabic.] ═ See also عَرَبَة. ═ And see عَرِبٌ. ═ [It also app. signifies † *Vagueness* (considered as an unsoundness) in a word; from the same as inf. n. of عَرِبَ used in relation to the stomach &c.:] see 4, latter half.

عَرِبٌ [part. n. of عَرِبَ, q. v.: as such signifying]

Having the stomach in a bad, or corrupt, state. (O, Ḳ.) And مَعِدَةٌ عَرِبَةٌ *A stomach in a bad, or corrupt, state,* (Ṣ, O, TA,) *from being burdened.* (TA.) — Also, and ‡ عَرِبٌ, (O, Ḳ,) the former of which is the more common, (TA,) and ‡ عُرُبٌ, (O, Ḳ,) *Abundant* water, (O, Ḳ,) *such as is clear,* or *limpid.* (Ḳ.) And نَهْرٌ عَرِبٌ (TA) and ‡ عَارِبٌ and ‡ عَارِبَةٌ (Ḳ) *A river containing abundance of water.* (Ḳ, TA.) And بِئْرٌ عَرِبَةٌ *A well containing much water.* (Ḳ.) — عَرِبَةٌ applied to a woman: see عَرُوبٌ, in four places. — العَرِبَةُ and العَرِبَاتُ: see العَرَبُ, first quarter.

عُرْبَةٌ: see عِرَابَةٌ.

عَرِبَةٌ *A river that flows with a vehement,* or *strong, current.* (Ṣ, O, Ḳ.) ═ And *i. q.* نَفْسٌ [The *soul, mind,* or *self*]. (Ṣ, O, Ḳ.) [It is thought to occur in a pl. sense, without ة, as a coll. gen. n., in the following sense, quoted in the Ṣ immediately after the explanation above.] A poet says, (Ṣ,) namely, Ibn-Meiyádeh, (O,)

لَمَّا أَتَيْتُكَ أَرْجُو فَضْلَ نَائِلِكُمْ
نَفَحْتَنِى نَفْحَةً طَابَتْ لَهَا العَرَبُ ‡

[*When I came to thee, hoping for the redundance of your bounty, thou gavest me a gift with which the souls were pleased*]: (Ṣ, O:) thus related by some, and expl. as meaning طَابَتْ لَهَا النُّفُوسُ: but the [approved] relation is, طَارَتْ بِهَا العَرَبُ [† *which the Arabs made to fly* upon the wings of fame], i. e. حَدَّثَتِ العَرَبُ النَّاسَ بِهَا [meaning † *of which the Arabs talked to the people*]. (O.) ═ Also sing. of عَرِبَاتٌ (TA) which is the name of *Certain stationary vessels that used to be in the Tigris.* (Ḳ, TA.) — [As meaning *A wheel-carriage of any kind* (which is commonly called in Egypt عَرَبِيَّة) it is post-classical.]

العَرَبُ العَرْبَاءُ: see العَرَبُ, first quarter: and see عَرْبَانُ.

عُرُبٌ: see عَرُوبٌ.

عَرَبِىٌّ; and العَرَبُ العَرَبِيَّةُ: see العَرَبُ, first quarter. — لَا تَنْقُشُوا فِى خَوَاتِيمِكُمْ عَرَبِيًّا, (Mgh, O, Ḳ, TA,) in a trad., or, as some relate it, ‡ العَرَبِيَّةَ, (TA,) means *Engrave not on your signets* مُحَمَّدٌ رَسُولُ ٱللّٰهِ; (Mgh, O, Ḳ, TA;) because this was engraved on the Prophet's own signet: (O, TA:) as though he had said, نَبِيًّا عَرَبِيًّا [*an Arabian prophet*]; meaning himself. (O, Ḳ, TA.) Omar said, ‡ لَا تَنْقُشُوا فِى خَوَاتِيمِكُمُ العَرَبِيَّةَ [*Engrave not on your signets Arabic*]: and Ibn-'Omar disapproved of engraving on a signet words from the Ḳur-án. (Mgh,* O, TA.) [عَرَبِىُّ الوَجْهِ often occurs in post-classical works as meaning *Having an Arab face*; i.e. *long-faced*; opposed to تُرْكِىُّ الوَجْهِ.] — See also عِرَابٌ, in two places. ═ Also *A white barley, the ears of which are bifurcate* [so I render, agreeably with the TḲ, سُنْبُلَةٌ حَرْفَانِ]: (Ḳ, TA:) *it is wide, and its grain is large, larger than the grain of the barley of El-'Irák, and it is the best of barley.* (TA.)

العَرَبِيَّةُ *The Arabic language*; (Ṣ, TA;) *the language of the Ḳur-án.* (Mṣb.) Ḳatádeh says that the tribe of Ḳureysh used to cull, or select, what was most excellent in the dialects of the Arabs, [in the doing of which they were aided by the confluence of pilgrims from all parts of the country,] so that their dialect became the most excellent of all, and the Ḳur-án was therefore revealed in that dialect. (TA.) See also عَرَبِىٌّ, in two places. — And see عَرُوبَةٌ.

عَرْبَانُ [written in the TA without any syll. signs, but it is app. thus, fem. عَرْبَى (like حَيْرَى fem. of حَيْرَانُ), whence, probably, the appellation ‡ العَرَبُ العَرْبَاءُ,] A man *chaste, uncorrupt,* or *free from barbarousness, in speech*: so in the Towsheeḥ. (TA.) [See also عَرِيبٌ.]

عُرْبَانٌ and عَرَبَانٌ: see what next follows.

عُرْبُونٌ and عَرَبُونٌ and ‡ عُرْبَانٌ (Mgh,* O, Mṣb, Ḳ) and ‡ عَرَبَانٌ, mentioned on the authority of Ibn-Es-Seed, as of the dial. of El-Ḥijáz, and عَرْبُونٌ, mentioned by AḤei, but this last is a vulgar word, and is disallowed by Lb; (TA;) as also أُرْبَانٌ and أُرْبُونٌ and أَرَبُونٌ; (Mgh,* Mṣb, Ḳ;) [*An earnest,* or *earnest-money*;] *a portion of the price, whereby a bargain is ratified*; (Ḳ, TA;) *a thing that is paid by the purchaser of a commodity,* (Mgh, O, Mṣb,) or *by the hirer of a thing,* (Mṣb,) *on the condition that if the sale* (Mgh, O, Mṣb) or *hire* (Mṣb) *have effect, it shall be reckoned as part of the price, and otherwise shall not be reclaimed*; (Mgh, O, Mṣb;) called by the vulgar رَبُونٌ: (O:) it is forbidden in a trad., (Mgh, O, TA,) and by most of the lawyers, but allowed by some: (TA:) عربون is said by Aṣ to be a foreign word arabicized, (Mṣb,) and so say many authors; though it is said by some of the expositors of the Fṣ to be from التَّعْرِيبُ signifying "the making clear, plain," &c.; اربون being also derived from أُرْبَةٌ signifying "a knot:" (TA:) and [it is said that] the ن in عربون and عربان may be augmentative or radical, because one says أَعْرَبَ فِى كَذَا and عَرْبَنَ. (O.) — [Hence,] أَلْقَى عَرْبُونَهُ † *He ejected his excrement,* or *ordure.* (O, Ḳ, TA.)

عَرْبَاءُ: see عَرُوبَاءُ.

عُرَابٌ The *fruit of the species of tree called* حَزَم [q. v.], *of the bark of which* [*tree*] *ropes are made*: (O, Ḳ, TA:) [*beads which are used in prayer are made thereof,* (Freytag, from the Deewán of the Hudhalees,) i. e., *of the berries thus called, and*] *it* [the fruit] *is eaten by the apes,* or *monkeys, and sometimes, in a case of hunger, by men*: n. un. with ة. (O, TA.)

خَيْلٌ عِرَابٌ *Horses of pure Arabian race*; (Mgh, Ḳ;) *opposed to* بَرَاذِينُ; (Ṣ, O, Mṣb;) also termed ‡ أَعْرُبٌ and ‡ مُعْرِبَةٌ, (Ḳ,) which last [erroneously written in the CḲ مُعْرَبَةٌ] is fem. of مُعْرِبٌ, signifying a horse *having no strain of admixture of other than Arabian blood*: (Ks, Ṣ, O:) one of such horses is [also] termed ‡ عَرَبِىٌّ: (Mgh, Mṣb:) by the pl. عِرَابٌ, they distinguish beasts from human beings. (Mgh.) — And إِبِلٌ عِرَابٌ (Ṣ, O, Mṣb, Ḳ) and ‡ أَعْرُبٌ (TA) *Camels of pure Arabian race*; (Ḳ;) opposed to بَخَاتِىُّ. (Ṣ, O, Mṣb.) — And بَقَرٌ عِرَابٌ *A goodly sort of oxen, of generous race, with short and fine hair, smooth,* or *sleek,* (Mṣb,) *having even backs, and thick hoofs and hides*: one of which is termed ‡ عَرَبِىٌّ. (TA voce دَرْبَانِيَّةٌ.)

عَرُوبٌ A woman *who manifests love to her husband*; (IAạr, Ṣ, O, Ḳ, TA;) *and is obedient to him*; (IAạr, TA;) as also ‡ عَرُوبَةٌ: (TA:) and (so in the O and TA, but in the CḲ "or") a woman *disobedient to her husband*; (IAạr, O, Ḳ, TA;) *unfaithful to him by unchastity*; *corrupt in her mind*: (IAạr, O, TA:) as though having two contr. meanings; [the latter meaning] from عَرْبٌ [a mistranscription for عَرَبٌ] signifying "corruptness" of the stomach: (O:) or *who loves him passionately,* or *excessively*: or *who manifests love to him, evincing passionate,* or *excessive, desire*: [lit., *evincing that*; meaning what is expressed by the words immediately preceding it; for otherwise this last explanation would be the same as the first; and as I have rendered it, it is nearly the same as an explanation in the Expos. of the Jel (lvi. 36), *manifesting love to her husband, by reason of passionate,* or *excessive, desire*:] (Ḳ:) and (so in the TA, but in the CḲ "or") a woman *who is a great laugher*: and ‡ عَرُوبَةٌ and ‡ عَرِبَةٌ signify the same: (Ḳ:) the pl. of the first is عُرُبٌ (Ṣ, O, Ḳ) and عُرْبٌ; (TA;) and the pl. of ‡ عَرِبَةٌ is عَرِبَاتٌ: (Ḳ:) IAth says that ‡ عَرِبَةٌ signifies a woman *who is eager for play,* or *sport*: and عُرُبٌ, he adds, is pl. of ‡ عَرِيبٌ, which signifies a woman *of goodly person, who manifests love to her husband*: and it is also said that عُرُبٌ signifies women *who use amorous gesture or behaviour, and coquettish boldness, with feigned coyness or opposition*: or *who make a show of,* or *act with, lasciviousness*: or *passionately loving*: and ‡ عَرِبَةٌ and عَرُوبٌ, accord. to Lḥ, signify a woman *passionately loving, and lascivious.* (TA.)

عَرِيبٌ *i. q.* ‡ مُعْرِبٌ, which means, accord. to Az, A man *chaste, uncorrupt,* or *free from barbarousness, in speech.* (TA.) — [Hence,] مَا بِالدَّارِ عَرِيبٌ (Ṣ, O, Ḳ) and ‡ مُعْرِبٌ (Ḳ) † *There is not in the house any one*: (Ṣ, O, Ḳ:) used [in this sense] as applying to either sex, but only in a negative phrase. (TA.) — See also عَرُوبٌ, latter half.

العُرَيْبُ: see العَرَبُ (of which it is the dim.), second sentence.

عِرَابَةٌ: see عِرَابَةٌ. — Also *Coïtus.* (TA.) ═ And *A bag with which the udder of a sheep,* or *goat, is covered*: pl. عَرَابَاتٌ. (IAạr, O, Ḳ.)

عِرَابَةٌ (Ṣ, O, Ḳ) and ↑ عُرَابَةٌ (O, TA) and ↑ عُرْبَةٌ (O) or ↑ عُرْبٌ (TA) *Foul,* or *obscene, speech* or *talk;* (Ṣ,O, Ḳ,TA;) like إِعْرَابٌ and تَعْرِيبٌ. (Ḳ.)

عَرُوبَةٌ: see عَرُوبٌ, in two places. — عَرُوبَةُ (O, Ḳ) and العَرُوبَةُ (Ḳ) and (O) يَوْمُ العَرُوبَةِ (Ṣ, O) *Friday;* (Ṣ, O, Ḳ;) an ancient name of that day (Ṣ, O, TA) in the Time of Ignorance: (TA:) accord. to some, it is most chastely without the article; (TA;) thus it occurs in old poetry of the Time of Ignorance; (O;) and it is thought to be not Arabic; (TA;) and said to be arabicized from the Nabathæan أَرُبَا: (Ḥar p. 340, q. v.:) accord. to others, the article is inseparable from it; and its meaning, accord. to Ibn-En-Naḥḥás is *the manifest and magnified,* from أَعْرَبَ "he made clear, plain," &c.; or accord. to an authority cited in the R, its meaning is *mercy.* (TA.) [See art. ابجد.]

عُرُوبَةٌ (Ṣ, Ḳ) and ↑ عُرُوبِيَّةٌ (Ḳ) The *quality of being Arabian:* (Ṣ, Ḳ, TA:) each [said to be] an inf. n. having no verb. (TA. [But see عَرُبَ at the commencement of this art. and under أَعْرَبَ.]) And ↑ عَرَبِيَّةٌ is used [in the same sense] as denoting the quality of a horse such as is termed عَرَبِىٌّ. (TA.)

عَرُوبَآءُ a name of *The seventh heaven:* (IAth, Ḳ, TA:) or, accord. to Suh, it is ↑ عَرِيبَآءُ, corresponding to جَرِيبَآءُ, which is a name of "the seventh earth;" (TA in this art.;) or these two words are with the article ال. (TA in art. جرب.)

عُرُوبِيَّةٌ: see عُرُوبَةٌ.

عَرَّابٌ *One who makes* عَرَابَات (pl. of عَرَابَةٌ) i. e. *bags to cover the udders of sheep or goats.* (IAạr, O, Ḳ.)

عَرْبَرْبٌ *i. q.* سُمَّاقٌ [i. e. *Sumach*]. (O, TA.)

سُمَّاقِيَّةٌ *i. q.* قِدْرٌ عَرْبَرِبِيَّةٌ [app. meaning *A cooking-pot in which food prepared with sumach is cooked*]. (O.)

عَارِبٌ and عَارِبَةٌ: see عَرَبٌ. — العَرَبُ العَارِبَةُ: see العَرَبُ, in two places.

أَعْرَبُ *More,* or *most, distinct* or *plain* [&c.]. (TA.)

الأَعْرُبُ is a pl. of العَرَبُ [q. v.]. (Mṣb.) — See also عِرَابٌ, in two places.

الأَعْرَابُ: and أَعْرَابِىٌّ: } see العَرَبُ, latter half.

مُعْرِبٌ: see عَرِيبٌ, in two places: — and see عِرَابٌ. — Also One *who has horses of pure Arabian race:* (Ṣ, O:) one *who has with him a horse of such race:* and one *who possesses,* or *acquires,* or *seeks to acquire, horses,* or *camels, of such race.* (TA.)

اِسْمٌ مُعْرَبٌ [*An arabicized noun;*] *a noun received by the Arabs from foreigners, indeterminate,* [i. e. *significant of a meaning,* (as is said in the Mz, 19th نوع,)], *such as* إِبْرَيْسَمٌ [meaning "silk"], *and, if possible, accorded to some one of the forms of Arabic words; otherwise, spoken by them as they received it; and sometimes they derived from it:* but if they received it as a proper name, it is not termed مُعْرَبٌ, but أَعْجَمِىٌّ, like إِبْرَاهِيمُ and إِسْحَاقُ. (Mṣb.) [مُعْرَبٌ alone is also used in this sense, as a subst.: and as such its pl. is مُعْرَبَاتٌ: thus in the Mz, ubi suprà; and often in lexicons &c.]

العَرَبُ المُتَعَرِّبَةُ and العَرَبُ المُسْتَعْرِبَةُ: } see العَرَبُ, each in three places.

عربد

Q. 1. عَرْبَدَ, inf. n. عَرْبَدَةٌ, *He showed illnature, or an evil disposition, and behaved unsociably, towards his cup-companion.* (TḲ.) One says, هُوَ يُعَرْبِدُ عَلَى أَصْحَابِهِ عَرْبَدَةَ السَّكْرَانِ *He behaves in an annoying manner towards his companions as does the drunken.* (A.) Accord. to some, this verb is from عِرْبِدٌ as signifying "a red and malignant, or noxious, serpent." (TA.)

عَرْبَدٌ: see عِرْبِدٌ: — and مُعَرْبِدٌ. — Also *Rough ground.* (Ḳ.)

عَرْبَدَةٌ *Illnature,* or *evil disposition.* (Ṣ, A, O, Ḳ. [See the verb of which it is the inf. n., above.])

عِرْبَدٌ, (Ṣ, O, Ḳ,) quasi-coordinate to جِرْدَحْلٌ, (Ṣ, O,) and عِرْبِدٌ, (Ḳ,) *A serpent that blows but does not hurt;* (Ṣ, O, Ḳ;) accord. to Aboo-Kheyreh and ISh, (TA,) or Sh, (O,) *a serpent of a red colour with dusky and black specks,* (O, TA,) *always appearing among us,* (O,) *that does not hurt,* (TA,) or *that seldom injures small or great,* (O,) *unless it be hurt:* (O, TA:) or *a red and malignant,* or *noxious, serpent;* (O, Ḳ;) for a man, in some verses cited by IAạr, likens himself, in his treatment of his enemies, to this serpent; and how should he describe himself as a serpent that blows at the enemies and does not hurt them? (TA:) and, (Ḳ,) or the former word, accord. to Sh, (O,) the *male viper:* (O, Ḳ:) and the former, accord. to Th, *a light,* or *an active, serpent:* (L:) or so ↑ عِرْبِيدٌ: (TA:) or this last signifies the *serpent* [absolutely]. (IAạr, O, Ḳ.) — Also the former word, (O, Ḳ,) and the latter, (Ḳ,) *i. q.* شَدِيدٌ [app. as meaning *Vehement,* or the like], applied to anything: (O, Ḳ:) accord. to Ibn-'Abbád, the latter is applied in this sense to anger. (O.) — Also both words, (Ḳ,) or, accord. to Ibn-'Abbád, the latter, (O,) *Custom, habit,* or *wont:* (O, Ḳ:) but app. mistranscribed for عَرِيدٌ. (TA.) — And one says, رَكِبْتُ عِرْبَدِّى, (Ḳ, TA,) or عِرْبِدَّى, (Ibn-'Abbád, O,) meaning *I went without pausing,* or *waiting, for anything:* (Ibn-'Abbád, O, Ḳ, TA:) or *I followed my own opinion.* (TA in art. عصد.)

عِرْبِيدٌ: see what follows, in two places.

مُعَرْبِدٌ (IDrd, Ṣ, A, O, Ḳ) and ↑ عِرْبِيدٌ (IDrd, O, Ḳ) One *who behaves in an annoying manner* (Ṣ, A, Ḳ) *towards his cup-companion,* (Ṣ, Ḳ,) or *towards his companions,* (A,) *in his intoxication;* (Ṣ, A, Ḳ;) as also ↑ عِرْبِدٌ: and the first and second, a man *who behaves in an evil,* or *a mischievous, manner, towards another* or *others:* (TA:) or ↑ the second signifies *having much evilness of disposition,* or *manners, in intoxication.* (Ḥar p. 453.)

عربن

Q. 1. عَرْبَنَهُ *He gave him what is termed an* عُرْبُون or عَرَبُون &c. [i. e. an *earnest,* or *earnest-money*]. (Ṣ, TA: mentioned as a quadriliteral-radical word, and also in art. عرب, q. v.)

عُرْبَانٌ and عُرْبُونٌ: and عَرَبُونٌ and عُرْبُونٌ: } see art. عرب.

عرتب

العَرْتَبَةُ a dial. var. of العَرْتَمَةُ; (Ṣ, O;) *The nose:* or *the soft,* or *pliable, part thereof:* or *the* [*depression termed*] دَائِرَة *beneath the nose, in* [or *above*] *the middle of the lip,* (Ḳ, TA,) i. e., *of the upper lip, next the nose:* (TA:) or *the extremity of the partition between the nostrils:* (Ḳ:) [J says,] I asked an Arab of the desert, of the tribe of Asad, whereupon he put his finger upon the extremity of the partition between his nostrils. (Ṣ.)

عرتن

Q. 1. عَرْتَنَ *He tanned* a hide *with* [*the plant,* or *tree, called*] عَرْتَن or عَرَتُن &c. (TA.)

عَرْتَنٌ, (Ṣ, Ḳ,*) [in the Ḳ it is not clear whether this be thus or عَرَتْنٌ,]) and عَرَتُنٌ, (Ṣ, Ḳ,) and عَرَتَنٌ, [thus accord. to copies of the Ḳ,] with تَحْرِيك, (Ḳ, TA,) and with kesr to the ت, (TA, [which may mean that it is عَرَتِنٌ and عَرْتِنٌ or only the latter, but what is meant in the Ḳ is evidently عَرَتِنٌ,]) originally ↑ عَرَنْتُنٌ, like قَرَنْفُلٌ, (Kh, Ṣ, Ḳ,) and ↑ عَرَنْتَنٌ, or both and ↑ عَرَنْتِنٌ, as also ↑ عَرَتُونٌ, (Ḳ,) *A species of plant,* (Ṣ,) or *tree,* (Ḳ,) *rough, resembling the* عَوْسَج [or *box-thorn*], *except that it is bigger, full and luxuriant in the branch, and not having tall stems,* (TA, [see also عِرْنَةٌ, of which the same is said,]) *with which,* (Ṣ, Ḳ, TA,) *it being* [*first*] *cooked,* (TA,) *one tans,* (Ṣ, Ḳ, TA,) *and the hide tanned therewith becomes red.* (TA.)

عَرَتُونٌ: and عَرَنْتُنٌ: } see the next preceding paragraph.

مُعَرْتَنٌ *A hide tanned with* عَرْتَن or عَرَتُن &c. (Ṣ, Ḳ.)

عرج

1. عَرَجَ, (Ṣ, A, O, Ḳ,) aor. ـُ, (Ṣ,) inf. n. عُرُوجٌ (Ṣ, O, Ḳ) and مَعْرَجٌ, (O, Ḳ,) *He ascended,* or

mounted. (Ṣ, A, O, Ḳ.) So in the saying عَرَجَ فِى السُّلَّمِ and فِى الدَّرَجَةِ [*He ascended*, or *mounted, the stair*, or *the series of steps*, and *the ladder*]. (Ṣ, O.) And عَرَجَ فِى الشَّىْءِ, and عَلَيْهِ, aor. ُ and ِ, inf. n. عُرُوجٌ, *He ascended*, or *mounted, upon the thing.* (TA.) And عُرِجَ بِهِ means *He was taken up to a high place*; as, for instance, إِلَى عَنَانِ السَّمَآءِ [*to the clouds of Heaven*]. (Ḥam p. 87.) — And عَرَجَ الشَّىْءُ *The thing became high*, or *elevated.* (TA.) ═ عَـرِجَ, (Ṣ, O, Mṣb, Ḳ,) with fet-ḥ to the ر, (O,) aor. َ, inf. n. عَرَجٌ; (Mṣb; [accord. to the O عَرْجٌ;]) or عَرَجَ and عَرِجَ and عَرُجَ; (Ḳ;) *He limped*, or *had a slight lameness*, (Ṣ, O, Mṣb, Ḳ,) *and walked like the lame*, (Ṣ, O,) *by reason of some accident that had befallen him* (Ṣ, O, Mṣb, Ḳ) *in his leg or foot*, (Ṣ, O, Ḳ,) *not naturally*, (Ṣ, Ḳ,) or *not by reason of a chronic ailment:* (Mṣb:) or عَرَجَ, aor. ُ; and عَرِجَ and عَرُجَ; inf. n. عَرَجَانٌ; *he walked like the lame, with a limping gait, by reason of some accident.* (L.) — And عَرِجَ, (Ṣ, O, Mṣb, Ḳ,) aor. َ, (Mṣb, Ḳ,) inf. n. عَرَجٌ (Ṣ,* O,* Mṣb, Ḳ,* TA) and عُرْجَةٌ, (TA,) *He was lame, walked lamely*, or *limped*, (Ṣ, O, Mṣb, Ḳ,) *naturally*, (Ṣ, O, Ḳ,) or *by reason of a chronic ailment:* (Mṣb:) or *he became lame.* (TA.) [See also عَرَجٌ below.] — عَرْجٌ also signifies The *setting* of the sun: or its *inclining towards the place of setting:* (Ṣ, O, Ḳ:) inf. n. of عَرَجَتْ. (TḲ.) — And عَرَجَ, inf. n. عَرْجٌ, *He* (a camel) *emitted his urine indirectly:* said of the male only, when the hind girth is bound upon him [so as to press upon his sheath]: like حَقِبَ. (TA.)

2. عَرَّجَ, inf. n. تَعْرِيجٌ, *He made* (a building, or structure, Ṣ, O, and a river, or rivulet, TA) *to incline.* (Ṣ, O, Ḳ, TA.) ═ عَرَّجْتُ عَنْهُ *I turned from it, and left it*, or *forsook it*; as also ▼ انعرجت عنه. (Mṣb.) — And عرّج عَلَيْهِ *He bent*, or *inclined, to*, or *towards, him*, or *it.* (TA.) You say, مَرَّ بِهِ فَمَا عَرَّجَ عَلَيْهِ [*He passed by him*, or *it*,] *and did not bend*, or *incline, to him*, or *it.* (A.) [But this may be otherwise rendered, as is shown by what follows.] — عرّج also signifies *He remained, stayed, abode*, or *dwelt*; (Ḳ, TA;) as also ▼ تعرّج. (T, TA.) You say, عرّج بِالمَكَانِ *He remained, stayed*, &c., *in the place.* (TA.) And عرّج عَلَى الشَّىْءِ, (O,) inf. n. as above, (Ṣ, A,) *He remained, stayed*, or *abode, intent upon the thing*; (Ṣ, A, O;) as also ▼ تعرّج عليه. (O.) See also عُرْجَةٌ, in two places: and see 2 in art. عوج. And مَا عَرَّجْتُ عَلَى الشَّىْءِ means *I did not pause, or stop, at the thing:* (Mṣb: [and the like is said in the Mgh:]) or *I did not care for it*, or *regard it.* (TA in art. دبر.) And عرّج عَلَى المَنْزِلِ, (Ṣ, O, Ḳ,) and ▼ تعرّج, (Ṣ, Ḳ,) *He confined his camel that he rode at the place of alighting* or *abode*, (Ṣ, O, Ḳ,) *and remained*, or *stayed:* (Ṣ, O:) or تَعْرِيجٌ signifies the *confining the camel that one rides, remaining*, or *staying, for one's travelling-companions* or *for some object of want:* and عرّج النَّاقَةَ means *he confined the she-camel.* (TA.) ═ See also 4.

4. اعرجهُ *He* (God) *rendered him lame.* (Ṣ, O,* Ḳ.) ═ And *He gave him a herd of camels such as is termed* عَرْجٌ. (Ṣ, Ḳ.) ═ And اعرج *He had*, or *possessed, a herd of camels such as is termed* عَرْجٌ: (O, TA:) thus in the L and other lexicons: in the Ḳ, إِبِلٌ عُرْجٌ is erroneously put for عَرْجٌ مِنَ الإِبِلِ. (TA.) [This signification is erroneously assigned by Freytag to 2: and so is that next preceding it by him and by Golius.] ═ Also *He entered upon the time of the setting of the sun*; and so ▼ عرّج, (O, Ḳ,) inf. n. تَعْرِيجٌ. (O.)

5. تعرّج *It* (a building, or structure,) *inclined.* (Ṣ, O.) — See also 2, in three places: and see عُرْجَةٌ, in two places.

6. تعارج [*He pretended to be lame*;] *he imitated the gait of a lame person.* (TA.)

7. انعرج *It* (a thing, Ṣ, Mṣb) *bent* or *inclined*; (Ṣ, O, Mṣb, TA;) and so a road: (TA:) and *it was*, or *became, curved*, or *crooked.* (Mgh.) You say, انعرج بِنَا الطَّرِيقُ [*The road bent*, or *inclined, with us*]. (A.) And انعرج عَنِ الطَّرِيقِ *He declined from the road:* (Mgh:) and انعرج الرَّكْبُ عَنْ طَرِيقِهِمْ [*The company of riders declined from their road*]. (A.) See also 2, second sentence.

R. Q. 3. اِعْرَنْجَجَ فِى أَمْرِهِ *He strove*, or *exerted himself, in his affair.* (O, Ḳ.*)

عَرْجٌ and ▼ عِرْجٌ *A herd of camels consisting of about eighty:* (Ṣ, O, Ḳ:) or *from seventy to eighty:* (TA:) or *from eighty to ninety:* (Ḳ:) or *a hundred and fifty and a little above that number:* (AO, Ṣ, O, Ḳ:) or *from five hundred to a thousand:* (Aṣ, Ṣ, O, Ḳ:) or *more than two hundred, and near a thousand:* (AḤát, TA:) or *a thousand:* (TA:) or *many camels:* (AZ, TA:) pl. أَعْرَاجٌ [a pl. of pauc.] (Ṣ, O, Ḳ) and عُرُوجٌ. (Ḳ.)

عُرْجٌ: see أَعْرَجُ, in two places.

عِرْجٌ: see عَرْجٌ.

عَرَجٌ inf. n. of عَرِجَ: (Mṣb, TA:) [as a simple subst.,] *Natural lameness*; (Ṣ, O, Ḳ;) as also ▼ عُرْجَةٌ, which is likewise an inf. n. of عَرِجَ. (TA.) One says, مَا أَشَدَّ عَرَجَهُ [*How great is his natural lameness!*]: not مَا أَعْرَجَهُ; for from that which signifies a colour, or a quality in the body, one does not derive the form مَا أَفْعَلَهُ. (Ṣ, O.) ═ Also *A river*, or *rivulet:* and *a valley:* because of their bending, or inclining. (TA.)

عَرِجٌ A camel *that emits his urine indirectly:* (O, Ḳ, TA:) an epithet applied to the male only. (TA. [See 1, last sentence.])

عُرَجَةٌ: see the next paragraph, in two places.

عُرْجَةٌ: see عَرَجٌ. — Also, (TA in this art.,) or ▼ عُرَجَةٌ, like جُدَعَةٌ and قُطَعَةٌ, (TA in art. جدع,) The *place*, or *seat, of lameness, in the leg*, or *foot.* (TA.) — And you say, مَا لِى عِنْدَكَ عُرْجَةٌ, and ▼ عَرْجَةٌ, and ▼ عِرْجَةٌ, and ▼ عُرَجَةٌ, and ▼ تَعْرِيجٌ, and ▼ تَعَرُّجٌ, *There is not for me any remaining, staying, abiding*, or *dwelling*, or, as some say, *any confining*, or *place of confinement*, [*of my beast*,] *with thee, or at thy abode.* (L, TA.) And مَا لِى عَلَيْهِ عُرْجَةٌ, and ▼ عَرْجَةٌ, (Ṣ, O,) and ▼ عِرْجَةٌ, and ▼ عُرَجَةٌ, (so in a copy of the Ṣ,) and ▼ تَعْرِيجٌ, and ▼ تَعَرُّجٌ, (Ṣ, O,) [i. e., as is implied in the Ṣ, *There is not for me any confining of my camel that I ride, and remaining*, or *staying, at it:* or] *there is not for me any bending*, or *inclining, to*, or *towards, him*, or *it.* (O.)

عَرْجَةٌ: see the next preceding paragraph, in two places.

عِرْجَةٌ: see عُرْجَةٌ.

عُرَجَةٌ: see عُرْجَةٌ, in two places.

عَرَجَانٌ [mentioned in the L as an inf. n.,] The *gait of him who is naturally lame.* (Ṣ, Ḳ.)

عُرْجُونٌ, mentioned in the A and Mgh and Mṣb in this art.: see art. عرجن.

عُرْجَانٌ: see أَعْرَجُ, in two places.

عَرِيجٌ *High*, or *elevated.* (TA.) ═ And An affair *not firmly, solidly*, or *soundly, executed.* (Ṣ, O, Ḳ.)

العُرَيْجَآءُ [dim. of العَرْجَآءُ fem. of الأَعْرَجُ; and therefore, if without the article ال, imperfectly decl.;] *The* هَاجِرَة [or *midday*; or *midday in summer*, or *when the heat is vehement*; &c.]. (O, Ḳ.) — And *The coming*, of camels, *to water one day at noon, and one day in the morning between daybreak and sunrise:* (Aṣ, Ṣ, O, Ḳ:) or *their coming to water in the morning between daybreak and sunrise, then returning from the water and remaining the rest of the day in the pasturage, and the next night and day, and coming to the water again at night, then returning from the water, and remaining the rest of the night in the pasturage, and the next day and night, then coming to the water in the morning between daybreak and sunrise:* this is one of the descriptions of رِفْه: or, as some say, their *coming to water thrice every day*; but this is strange. (TA.) — Also A man's *eating but once every day.* (Ḳ.) One says, فُلَانٌ يَأْكُلُ العُرَيْجَآءَ *Such a one eats but once every day.* (O, TA.)

عَارِجٌ *Limping*, or *having a slight lameness, not by reason of a chronic ailment, but in consequence of some accident that has befallen him.* (Mṣb.) ═ Also i. q. غَائِبٌ [i. e. *Absent*, &c.]: (O, Ḳ:)

thus written, with the pointed غ; but [SM says, though without adducing any ex. to confirm his assertion, that] it is correctly عَائِب, with the unpointed ع, [i. e. *being*, or *becoming, faulty*, &c.; or *making*, or *causing, to be faulty*, &c.; or *blaming*, &c.;] as in the L. (TA.)

أَعْرَجُ *Lame,* (Ṣ, Mṣb, Ḳ,) *by nature,* (Ṣ, Ḳ,) *or by reason of a chronic ailment*: fem. عَرْجَآءُ: (Mṣb:) pl. عُرْجٌ and عُرْجَانٌ. (Ṣ, Ḳ.) — الأَعْرَجُ is an appellation of *The crow;* (O, Ḳ;) [and] so الأَعْوَرُ الأَعْرَجُ: because of its hopping, or leaping in going, as though shackled. (A, TA.) — And العَرْجَآءُ is an appellation of *The female hyena:* (Ṣ, O, Ḳ:) pl. عُرْجٌ: the male is not called أَعْرَجُ. (TA.) And ▼ عُرْجُ, determinate, and imperfectly decl., means *The female hyenas*, so called as though they were a قَبِيلَة [or tribe]; (Sh, O, Ḳ;) and so ▼ عُرَاجُ, likewise determinate, and imperfectly decl.: (Ḳ:) or, accord. to IAạr, in the phrase ▼ أَبْنَآءُ عُرْجَ in a verse of Aboo-Muk'it El-Asadee, the poet makes the latter word, which is a pl., imperfectly decl. because he means التَّوْحِيدَ وَالعَرْجَة; as though he regarded it as a sing. [proper] name: (L: [i. e., accord. to Ibr D, because he uses عُرْج as a sing. proper name, curtailed by poetic license from العَرْجَة: if so, this last word seems here to signify a personification of lameness:]) and accord. to him (i. e. IAạr), one says ▼ هٰذِهِ عُرَاجُ, meaning *This is the female hyena* [not hyenas]; the latter word imperfectly decl. (O.) — الأَعْرَجُ is also an appellation of *A certain deaf, malignant serpent.* (TA.) [See also the next paragraph.] — And العُرْجُ signifies *Three nights of the first part of the lunar month:* [perhaps in allusion to the curved aspect of the moon; though on this ground it might also be applied to three nights of the last part:] mentioned on the authority of Th. (TA.)

الأُعَيْرِجُ [dim. of الأَعْرَجُ] *A certain deaf serpent,* (O, Ḳ, TA,) *of the most malignant of serpents,* (TA,) *that will not admit of being charmed, and that leaps up like the viper:* (O, Ḳ:) accord. to ISh, *a certain broad serpent, having a single broad leg; like the* [*serpent called*] أَصَلَة: IAạr says, *it springs upon the horseman so as to become with him on his saddle:* (O:) the word has no fem. form: (Lth, O, Ḳ:) [but] the pl. is الأُعَيْرِجَاتُ. (O, Ḳ.)

مَعْرَجٌ: see مِعْرَاجٌ, in two places.

مِعْرَجٌ: see the next paragraph.

مِعْرَاجٌ (Ṣ, A, O, Ḳ) and ▼ مِعْرَجٌ and ▼ مَعْرَجٌ, (Ṣ, O, Ḳ,) the second and third allowable accord. to Akh, like مِرْقَاةٌ and مَرْقَاةٌ, (Ṣ, O,) *A ladder, or series of steps* or *stairs:* (Ṣ, A, O, Ḳ:) or, with the article ال, [but most commonly the first of these with ال,] *a thing resembling a* دَرَجَة [i. e. *ladder*, or *series of steps* or *stairs*], *upon which the souls ascend when they are taken* [*from their bodies*]: it is said that there is nothing more beautiful than it; so that when the soul sees it, it cannot refrain from making its exit [from the body]: (TA:) hence لَيْلَةُ المِعْرَاجِ [*the Night of the Ladder;* in which Moḥammad is related to have ascended from Jerusalem to Heaven, after having been conveyed to the former from Mekkeh upon the beast named البُرَاق]: pl. مَعَارِيجُ and مَعَارِجُ, like مَفَاتِيحُ and مَفَاتِحُ. (Ṣ, O.) Also, (Ḳ,) or [properly the last only, i. e.] ▼ مَعْرَجٌ, (L, Mṣb, TA,) *A place of ascent:* (L, Mṣb, Ḳ, TA:) and the *way whereby the angels ascend:* (TA:) pl. مَعَارِجُ, (Mṣb, TA,) [in both senses, i. e.] this signifies *places of ascent:* (Ṣ, A, O:) and in the Ḳur lxx. 3, the *places of ascent of the angels:* or it there means *benefits*, or *favours:* (O:) and مِعْرَاجٌ is [said to be] like مَعْرَجٌ [in meaning, though this is a loose explanation]. (Mṣb.)

مُعَرَّجٌ A garment, or piece of cloth, *having upon it curving stripes* or *lines.* (O, Ḳ.)

مُعَرْجَنٌ: see art. عرجن.

مُنْعَرَجٌ, (Ṣ, O, Ḳ, TA,) or ▼ مُنْعَرِجٌ, (Mṣb,) or the latter is wrong, (TA,) *A place of bending*, or *inclining*, (Ṣ, O, Mṣb, Ḳ,) of a valley, *to the right* and *to the left.* (Ṣ, O, Mṣb.)

مُنْعَرِجٌ: see what next precedes.

عرجن

Q. 1. عَرْجَنَهُ *He struck him*, or *beat him, with an* عُرْجُون [q. v.]. (Ṣ, Ḳ.) And عَرْجَنَهُ بِالعَصَا *He struck him*, or *beat him, with the staff*, or *stick.* (TA.) — And *He figured it* (i. e. a garment, or piece of cloth,) *with the forms of* عَرَاجِين, pl. of عُرْجُون. (Ḳ.) — And *He smeared*, or *rubbed over, him*, or *it, with blood*, or *with saffron*, or *with* خِضَاب [i. e. *ḥinnà*, or *the like*]. (Ḳ.)

عُرْجُونٌ *A raceme of a palm-tree*, or *of dates;* syn. عِذْق: or, *when it has become dry and curved:* (Ḳ:) or the *base*, or *lower part*, (أَصْل, Ṣ, Ḳ, and also A and Mgh and Mṣb in art. عرج [because the ن is therein regarded as augmentative],) *of the* عِذْق (Ṣ, Ḳ) or كِبَاسَة [which signifies the same as عِذْق], (A, Mgh, Mṣb,) *which curves, and from which the fruit-stalks are cut off, and which then remains upon the palm-tree, dry:* (Ṣ:) or the عُود [meaning *main stem*] *of the* كِبَاسَة: (Th, Ḳ:) Az says, it is yellow and broad: [but it is the contrary of broad in comparison with its length:] and in the Ḳur xxxvi. 39, the moon when it has become slender [in appearance, towards the end of the lunar month,] is likened to the old عُرْجُون, in respect, as ISd says, of its slenderness and curvature: (TA:) [in the TA voce شُبَاطَة, the pl. عَرَاجِين is strangely used as meaning the *fruit-stalks* of the raceme of a palm-tree:] بَنَاتُ عُرْجُونٍ signifies *the fruit-stalks of a raceme of dates:* (T in art. بنى:) [it is said that] the ن of عُرْجُون, though this word imports the meaning of اِنْعِرَاج [or "a state of bending"], is shown to be radical by the word مُعَرْجَن, occurring in a verse of Ru-beh, and also by the fact that there is no verb of the measure فُعْلَنَ. (TA. [But عَشْوَنَ and سَبْعَنَ, though these are said to be post-classical, and, accord. to some, عَلْوَنَ, may be mentioned, and perhaps some others, as being of this measure.]) — Also *A certain plant*, (Ḳ, TA,) *white*, accord. to Th, (TA,) *like the* فُطْر [or *toadstool*], *resembling the* فَقْع [*a white and soft sort of* كَمْء], (Ḳ, TA,) *which dries, having a round form:* or *a species of the* كَمْأَة, *of the measure of a span*, or *a little less than that; good*, or *pleasant, while fresh:* (TA:) pl. عَرَاجِين. (Ḳ.)

مُعَرْجَنٌ, occurring in a verse of Ru-beh, (TA,) *A garment, or piece of cloth, in which are* [*figured*] *the forms of* عَرَاجِين [pl. of عُرْجُون]. (A and TA in art. عرج.)

عرد

1. عَرَدَ, (AḤn, Ṣ, O, Ḳ,) aor. ـُ, inf. n. عُرُودٌ, (AḤn, Ṣ, O,) *It* (a plant, and a canine tooth, &c.,) *came forth, and became high*, or *tall:* (Ṣ, O, Ḳ:) or *it* (a plant) *came forth, and became high*, or *tall, and hard:* (AḤn, TA:) and *it* (a canine tooth, and a plant,) *came forth altogether, and became hard and erect:* *it* (a camel's tush) *became thick and strong:* and *it* (a tree) *came forth:* or *became crooked:* or *became thick and great;* as also ▼ اعرد. (TA.) — عَرَدَ الحَجَرَ, (Ḳ,) aor. ـُ, inf. n. عَرْدٌ, (TA,) *He threw the stone far.* (Ḳ, TA.) — عرد بِحَاجَتِنَا [app. عَرَّدَ] *He did not accomplish our want.* (TA.) — عَرِدَ: see the next paragraph, in two places.

2. عَرَّدَ, inf. n. تَعْرِيدٌ, *He* (a man, Ṣ) *fled;* (IAạr, Ṣ, O, Ḳ;) as also ▼ عَرِدَ, aor. ـَ. (IAạr, O, Ḳ.) *He drew back*, or *drew back in fear*, عَنْ قِرْنِهِ *from his adversary:* or *he went away quickly, being put to flight.* (TA.) *He* (a man) *quitted the road:* (O, Ḳ:) or *he quitted the right direction of the road, and turned aside from it.* (TA.) And عرّد عَنْهُ *He turned aside, and went to a distance*, or *far away, from him*, or *it.* (A.) — *It* (a star) *rose high:* and also *it inclined to set after it had culminated:* (O, Ḳ:) [or] *it set.* (A.) *It* (water) *rose high.* (A.) — And *He*, or *it, descended*, or *alighted.* (MF.) — عرّد السَّهْمُ فِي الرَّمِيَّةِ *The arrow penetrated into the inside of the animal at which it was shot and its extremity went forth from the other side.* (Aboo-Naṣr, O, Ḳ.) — And عرّد, inf. n. تَعْرِيدٌ; (TA;) or ▼ عَرِدَ; (thus in the O, as on the authority of IAạr;) *He* (a man, TA) *became strong in body after disease.* (IAạr, O, TA.)

4: see 1.

[5. تعرّد *He was put to flight:* (Freytag, from the "Fákihet el-Khulafà," p. 93, l. 27:) probably post-classical.]

عَرْدٌ A thing, (Ṣ, O,) or anything, (TA,) *hard:* (Ṣ, O:) or *strong, hard, and erect:* (Lth, O, Ḳ:) or *thick;* (Aṣ, AḤn, O;) as also ▼ عَارِدٌ and عُرُدٌ [correctly ▼ عُرُدٌّ] and عُرُنْدٌ [evidently a mistranscription for ▼ عُرُنْدٌ] and ▼ عَرِدٌ: (AḤn, O:) and ▼ عَرَنْدَدٌ, (Ṣ, O, Ḳ,) quasi-coordinate to سَفَرْجَلٌ, (Ṣ, O,) and ▼ عُرُنْدٌ, (Ḳ, TA,) with two dammehs, (TA, in the CḲ عَرَنْدٌ,) the ن being a substitute for د, (TA,) and ▼ عُرُدٌّ (O, Ḳ) and ▼ عُرُدٌّ, (Ḳ,) signify *hard,* (Ṣ, O, Ḳ,) or *hard and strong,* applied to anything: (TA:) and ▼ عُرُدٌّ, applied to a spear, and a bow-string, signifies *strong:* (Fr, TA:) and ▼ عُرُنْدٌ, in measure like تُرُنْجٌ, applied to a bow-string, (Sb, Ṣ, O,) *thick;* (Sb, Ṣ;) or *strong and thick;* as also ▼ عُرُدٌ; and thus both signify applied to a rope, or well-rope, and any other thing. (O.) One says, إِنَّهُ لَعَرْدُ مَغْرِزِ العُنُقِ [*Verily he is hard,* or *strong,* or *thick, in respect of the base of the neck*]. (Lth, O, TA.) — [Hence,] The *penis:* or *a hard and strong penis:* (TA:) or *a penis distended and erect* (O, Ḳ, TA) and *hard:* pl. أَعْرَادٌ. (TA.) — And The *ass:* (O, Ḳ:) so called because of the thickness of his neck. (TA.) — And [it is said to signify] The *base of the neck.* (Ḳ. [But this I think doubtful: see a saying mentioned above (in this paragraph), from a mistranscription of which it may have originated.])

عَرِدٌ : see عَرْدٌ, in two places. In the phrase عَرَادٌ عَرِدٌ, the latter word may be added to give intensiveness to the signification, or it may be used by poetic license for عَارِدٌ. (TA.)

عُرُدٌّ : see عَرْدٌ, in four places.

عِرْدَادٌ The *elephant:* (O, Ḳ:) because of his thickness and bulkiness. (TA.) — And *Courageous, and hard,* or *sturdy;* (O, Ḳ;) applied to a man. (TA.) — And *A staff by means of which the horse and the camel are tied.* (O, Ḳ.)

عَرَادٌ, applied to a plant, *Thick and hard.* (AḤn, O, Ḳ.) — And *A certain plant,* (Ṣ, O, Ḳ,) *of the kind termed* حَمْض, (Ṣ,) *hard and erect:* (TA:) or *a certain herb, said to be* [*of the kind termed*] حَمْض, *eaten by the camels, growing in sands and sand-plains:* or, as some say, it is [*a sort*] *of the* نَجِيل [q. v.] *that grows in good and salubrious land, remote from water:* n. un. with ة: Az says, I have seen the عَرَادَة in the desert, [*a plant*] *having hard wood, spreading branches, and no scent.* (L.) — See also عَرَادَةٌ.

عَرِيدٌ *Distant,* or *remote:* (Ḳ:) of the dial. of El-Yemen. (TA.) ═ And *Custom, habit,* or *wont.* (Lḥ, Ḳ.) One says, مَا زَالَ ذٰلِكَ عَرِيدَهُ *That ceased not to be his custom, habit,* or *wont.* (Lḥ, TA.) [See also عِرْبَدٌ.]

عَرَادَةٌ *A single locust:* (Ḳ: [if so, ▼ عَرَادٌ probably signifies *locusts;* as a coll. gen. n.:]) or *a female locust.* (Ṣ, O.) ═ And *A state,* or *condition.* (Ṣ, O, Ḳ.) You say, فُلَانٌ فِي عَرَادَةِ خَيْرٍ *Such a one is in a good state,* or *condition.* (Ṣ, O.)

عَرَّادَةٌ *A certain thing, smaller than the* مَنْجَنِيق, (Ṣ, O, Ḳ, TA,) *but resembling it;* (TA;) [i. e. *an engine of war,* app. *similar to that called by the Romans onager;*] *that casts a stone to a long distance:* (Ḥam p. 307:) pl. عَرَّادَاتٌ. (TA.)

عُرُنْدٌ : see عَرْدٌ, in three places.

عَرَنْدَدٌ : see عَرْدٌ.

عَارِدٌ : see عَرْدٌ. — Also *Separate;* syn. مُتَنَبِّذٌ. (Ḳ.) In the saying (Ṣ, O, Ḳ) of a rájiz, (Ṣ,) of a man of the Benoo-Asad, (O,) or of Ḥajl, (Aṣ, O, Ḳ, TA, in the CḲ Ḥajal,) a freedman of the Benoo-Fezárah, describing a male camel, [and the sutures of his skull,] (Aṣ, O, Ḳ,) or it is of Aboo-Moḥammad El-Fak'asee, (IB, TA,)

* تَرَى شُؤُونَ رَأْسِهِ العَوَارِدَا *

(IB, O, Ḳ) not رَأْسِهَا, as in the Ṣ, (IB, Ḳ,) the last word [pl. of عَارِدٌ] means *separate* (مُتَنَبِّذَة) *one from another:* or *rugged* (غَلِيظَة): (Ḳ:) or *rising high,* or *elevated.* (Ṣ, O.)

مُعَرَّدٌ, applied to a bow-string, [like مُعَجَّرٌ,] i. q. مُجَرَّعٌ [q. v.] and مُعَجَّرٌ. (ISh, TA in art. جرع.)

نِيقٌ مُعَرَّدٌ *A high mountain-top.* (O, TA.)

عرس

1. عَرِسَ بِهِ, (Ṣ, O, Mṣb, Ḳ,) aor. ـَ, (Mṣb, Ḳ,) inf. n. عَرَسٌ, (TA,) *He kept,* or *clave, to him* or *it;* (Ṣ, O, Mṣb, Ḳ;) as also ▼ أَعْرَسَهُ. (O, Ḳ.) From this, and from another signification of the same verb, which see below, عَرُوسٌ is said [by some] to be derived. (Mṣb.) You say, عَرِسَ الرَّجُلُ بِقِرْنِهِ *The man kept,* or *clave, to his opponent* or *adversary,* in fight. (Mgh.) And عَرِسَ الصَّبِىُّ بِأُمِّهِ, (TA,) or أُمَّهُ, (Mgh,) *The child kept to his mother.* (Mgh, TA.) And عَرِسَ الشَّرُّ بَيْنَهُمْ *Evil clung,* or *stuck fast, to them, and continued.* (TA.) — [Hence, perhaps,] عَرِسَ الشَّىْءُ [or, perhaps, الشَّرُّ,] inf. n. as above, *The thing* [or *evil* or *mischief*] *became vehement,* or *severe,* or *distressful.* (TA.) ═ عَرِسَ, aor. ـَ, inf. n. عَرَسٌ, *He* (a man) *was,* or *became, fatigued:* (TA:) or عَرِسَ, (IḲṭṭ,) or عَرِسَ عَنِ الجِمَاعِ, (Mṣb,) *he* (a man) *was,* or *became, fatigued,* or *weak, and so disabled,* or *incapacitated, from copulation;* syn. كَلَّ, (Mṣb,) and أَعْيَا, (IḲṭṭ, Mṣb,) عن الجماع. (IḲṭṭ.) From this, and from another signification of the same verb, mentioned above, عَرُوسٌ is said [by some] to be derived. (Mṣb.) — Also *He was,* or *became, confounded* or *perplexed, and unable to see his right course;* syn. دَهِشَ: (Ṣ, O, Ḳ:) and so عَرِشَ. (TA.) — And عَرِسَ عَنْهُ *He held back,* or *refrained, from him,* or *it, through cowardice.* (TA.) — And عَرِسَ عَلَىَّ مَا عِنْدَهُ i. q. اِمْتَنَعَ [i. e. *What he had was unattainable,* or *difficult of attainment, to me*]. (IAạr, O, Ḳ. [In the CḲ, على is put for عَلَىَّ.]) ═ عَرَسَ البَعِيرَ, (Ṣ, O, Ḳ,) aor. ـُ (Ṣ, O, TA) and ـِ, (TA,) inf. n. عَرْسٌ, (Ṣ, O,) *He bound the camel's fore shank to his neck,* (Ṣ, O, Ḳ,) *while he was lying down,* (Ṣ, O,) *with the rope called* ▼ عِرَاس: (Ṣ, O, Ḳ:) or, as some say, *he bound the neck of the camel to both of his fore legs.* (TA.)

2. عَرَّسُوا, (Mṣb, Ḳ,) inf. n. تَعْرِيسٌ; (Ṣ, Mgh, O, Mṣb;) and ▼ اعرسوا; (Ṣ, O, Ḳ;) but the former is the more common; (Ḳ;) the latter, rare; (Ṣ, O;) *They alighted* (Ṣ, Mgh, O, Mṣb, Ḳ) *during a journey,* (Ṣ, Mgh, O, Mṣb,) *in the last part of the night,* (Ṣ, Mgh, O, Ḳ,) *for a rest,* (Ṣ, O, Mṣb, Ḳ,) *and made their camels lie down, and took a nap,* or *slight sleep,* (TA,) *and then departed,* (Ṣ, Mṣb,) *and continued their journey, at daybreak:* (TA:) [see also 2 in art. عوه:] or *they journeyed all the day, and alighted in the first part of the night:* (TA:) or *they alighted* (AZ, Mṣb, TA) *in a usual place of resort* (TA) *at any time of the night or day.* (AZ, Mṣb, TA.) [Hence,] لَيْلَةُ التَّعْرِيسِ *The night in which the Apostle of God slept:* (O, Ḳ:) the story of which is well known, in the biographies of him and in the traditions. (TA.) [It was when he was returning from the siege and capture of Kheyber: he halted in the latter part of the night, and unintentionally slept until the time of the prayer of daybreak had passed. See "Mishcát ul-Masábíh," vol. i., p. 146.] ═ See also 4. ═ عَرَّسَ, inf. n. as above, *It* (a chamber) *had an* عَرْس [q. v.] *made to it.* (TA.)

4. اعرس *He made,* or *prepared, a marriage-feast.* (Ṣ, O, Mṣb, Ḳ, TA.) — [*He became a bridegroom.*] And اعرس بِأَهْلِهِ, (Ṣ, O, Ḳ,) or بِامْرَأَتِهِ, (Mgh,* Mṣb,) *He had his wife conducted to him on the occasion of the marriage;* syn. بَنَى بِهَا, (T, Ṣ,) or بَنَى عَلَيْهَا; (Mgh, O, Ḳ;) as also ▼ عَرَّسَ بِهَا; (TA;) or this latter is only used by the vulgar; (Ṣ, O, TA;) or is a mistake: (Mgh, Mṣb:) and *he abode with his wife during the days of and after that event:* (TA:) [and] *he went in to his wife* (IAth, Mṣb) [a signification which may be meant to be included in the explanation بنى عليها or بنى بها] *on the occasion of that event;* meaning, *he compressed her;* وَطْئًا being thus called إِعْرَاس because it is a consequence of إِعْرَاس [properly so termed]: (IAth:) the phrase also signifies [simply] *he compressed his wife.* (Ṣ, TA.) ═ See also 2: ═ and see عَرِسَ بِهِ.

5. تعرّس لِامْرَأَتِهِ *He manifested,* or *showed, love,* or *affection, to his wife,* (A, Ibn-'Abbád, O, Ḳ,) *and kept to her.* (TA.) [App. originally signifying *He behaved like a bridegroom* (عَرُوس) *to his wife.*]

عَرْسٌ *A wall which is placed between the two* [*main lateral*] *walls of the winter-chamber, not reaching to the further end thereof,* (Ṣ, O, Ḳ, TA,) *then the beam is laid from the inner extremity of that wall to the further end of the chamber*, (TA,) *and it is roofed over*, (Ṣ, O, Ḳ, TA,) i. e. *the whole chamber is roofed over: what is between the two walls* [*above mentioned*] *is* [*called*] *a* سَهْوَة [q. v.], *and what is beneath the beam* [app. *with what is screened by the middle wall from the portion* (*of the chamber*) *in which is the entrance*] *is the* مُخْدَع: (TA:) *this is done for the sake of more warmth, and only in cold countries:* (Ṣ, O, Ḳ, TA:) *and it is called in Pers.* ابجه [correctly بيچه]: (Ṣ, TA:) and عَرْص is [said to be] a dial. var. thereof. (TA.)

عُرْسٌ (Az, Ṣ, Mṣb, Ḳ) and ▼ عُرُسٌ (Az, Ṣ, Ḳ) substs. from أَعْرَسَ as signifying "he had his wife conducted to him on the occasion of his marriage," and "he went in to her:" (Az, TA:) The *ceremony of conducting a bride to her husband:* (Mṣb:) or the *ministration*, or *performance, of a marriage, and of the ceremony of conducting the bride to her husband:* (TA:) or [simply] *marriage:* or *coitus:* syn. نِكَاحٌ: (Ḳ, TA:) because this is the real thing intended by الإِعْرَاس: (TA:) in the first of these senses, it is masc. and fem.; or, accord. to some, fem. only: as masc., its pl. is أَعْرَاسٌ; and as fem., its pl. is عُرُسَاتٌ. (Mṣb.) Hence [the trad.], إِذَا دُعِىَ أَحَدُكُمْ إِلَى وَلِيمَةِ عُرْسٍ فَلْيُجِبْ *When any one of you is invited to a marriage-feast, or a feast given on the occasion of the conducting of a bride to her husband, let him consent.* (Mgh.) — And hence, (Az, TA,) *A marriage-feast:* (A'Obeyd, Az, Ṣ, O, Ḳ:) or *a feast made on the occasion of conducting a bride to her husband:* (Mṣb:) in this sense it is masc.: (Mṣb:) or masc. and fem.: (Ṣ, O:) or fem., and sometimes masc. (Az, TA.) A rájiz says,

* إِنَّا وَجَدْنَا عُرُسَ الحَنَّاطِ *
* لَئِيمَةً مَذْمُومَةَ الحُوَّاطِ *

[*Verily we found the marriage-feast of the wheat-seller to be mean, discommended for the managers:* see also حُوَاطَةٌ]. (Az, Ṣ, O, TA.) Pl. as above, i. e., أَعْرَاسٌ and عُرُسَاتٌ. (Ṣ, O, Ḳ.) [See an ex. voce خُرْسٌ.] — [And hence,] *A state of rejoicing.* (IB, voce مَأْتَمٌ, q. v.) — The dim. is [عُرَيْسٌ,] without ة; which is extr., [accord. to those who hold it to be fem. only,] for [accord. to them] it should have ة, being a fem. n. of three letters. (TA.)

عِرْسٌ A man's *wife:* (Ṣ, Mgh, O, Mṣb, Ḳ:) and a woman's *husband:* (O, Mṣb, Ḳ:) pl. (in both senses, TA) أَعْرَاسٌ: (Ṣ, O, Mṣb, Ḳ, TA:) the dual, عِرْسَانِ, is sometimes applied to the *male and female*, (Ṣ, O,) or *husband and wife:* (TA:) and to *a male and female ostrich:* (IB:) and the sing., to the *mate* of the lion: (Ṣ, A, O, Ḳ:) and the pl. is applied, metaphorically, by Málik Ibn-Khuweylid El-Hudhalee, to *lions.* (TA.) — اِبْنُ عِرْسٍ [*The weasel; and a weasel;*] *a certain small animal*, (Lth, Ṣ, O, Mṣb, Ḳ,) *well known*, (TA,) *resembling the rat* (الفَأْرَة), (Mṣb,) *smaller than the cat*, (Lth, O, TA,) *having the lower lip cleft* (أَشْتَر), *and very short ears, as though they were amputated*, (Lth, O, Ḳ,) *and having a canine tooth;* (TA;) *called in Persian* رَاسُو: (Ṣ, Mgh:) the name is determinate and indeterminate: (TA:) pl. بَنَاتُ عِرْسٍ, (Ṣ, Mṣb, Ḳ,) applied to the males and the females; (O, Ḳ;) like as you say اِبْنُ آوَى and اِبْنُ مَخَاضٍ and اِبْنُ لَبُونٍ and اِبْنُ مَآءٍ, and in the pl. بَنَاتُ آوَى and بَنَاتُ مَخَاضٍ and بَنَاتُ لَبُونٍ and بَنَاتُ مَآءٍ; or, accord. to Akh, you say بَنَاتُ عِرْسٍ and بَنُو عِرْسٍ, like بَنَاتُ نَعْشٍ and بَنُو نَعْشٍ. (Ṣ, O.)

عَرِسٌ One *who quits not the place of conflict, by reason of courage.* (TA.) — العَرِسُ *The lion:* (O, Ḳ:) because he keeps to the preying upon men; or because he keeps to his covert, or retreat. (O,* TA.) — Also *Confounded*, or *perplexed, and unable to see his right course;* syn. دَهِشٌ. (Ṣ, O, Ḳ.)

عُرُسٌ: see عُرْسٌ.

عِرْسِىٌّ *A certain dye;* (Ḳ;) *a certain colour of dye, likened to the colour of the* اِبْن عِرْس [or *weasel*]. (Ṣ, O.)

عِرَاسٌ: see 1, last sentence.

عَرُوسٌ *A bridegroom:* and *a bride:* i. e., *a man*, and *a woman, during the period of their* أَعْرَاس or إِعْرَاس [thus differently written in different MSS.]; (Ṣ, A, O, Mṣb, Ḳ;) or *when the one goes in to the other:* (IAth:) you say رَجُلٌ عَرُوسٌ [*a bridegroom*, vulgarly, in the present day, ▼ عَرِيس,] and اِمْرَأَةٌ عَرُوسٌ [*a bride*, vulgarly, in the present day, ▼ عَرُوسَة]: (Ṣ:) and عُرُوسٌ is a dial. var. of the same: (IAar, TA:) pl. masc. عُرُسٌ (Ṣ, O, Mṣb, Ḳ) and أَعْرَاسٌ; (TA;) and pl. fem. عَرَائِسُ. (Ṣ, O, Mṣb, Ḳ.) [See عُرْسٌ, in two places.] It is said in a prov., كَادَ العَرُوسُ يَكُونُ أَمِيرًا [*The bridegroom was near to being a prince*]. (Ṣ: in the O, مَلِكًا.) The dim. is عُرَيِّسٌ, without the addition of ة to distinguish the fem., because of the fourth letter. (TA.) — [Hence,] أَبْيَاتٌ عَرَائِسُ ‡ *Verses of which the words are marked with diacritical points:* for, as Esh-Shereeshee says, the Arabs used to adorn the bride by speckling her cheeks with saffron: opposed to أَبْيَاتٌ عَوَاطِلُ. (Ḥar p. 610.) — [Hence also,] عَرَائِسُ الإِبِلِ † *The high-bred of camels.* (A.)

عَرِيسٌ, عَرُوسَةٌ: see the next preceding paragraph.

عِرِّيسٌ and عِرِّيسَةٌ, [the latter the more common,] *A thicket:* (L:) the *covert*, or *retreat, of the lion*, (Ṣ, O, Ḳ, TA,) *in a thicket.* (TA.) [It is said in a prov.,]

* كَمُبْتَغِى الصَّيْدِ فِى عِرِّيسَةِ الأَسَدِ *

[*Like the seeker of game in the covert of the lion*]: from a verse of Eṭ-Ṭirimmáḥ. (Z, O. [See Freytag's Arab. Prov., ii. 360.] (TA.) — Also the former, The *place of growth* [or *origin*] *of the stock of a man, among his people.* (TA.)

عِرِّيسَةٌ: see the next preceding paragraph.

مُعْرَسٌ: see what next follows.

مُعَرَّسٌ (Ṣ, O, Ḳ) and ▼ مُعْرَسٌ, (O, Ḳ,) [the former of which is the more common,] *A place where people alight* (Ṣ, O, Ḳ) *during a journey*, (Ṣ,) *in the last part of the night, for a rest*, (Ṣ, O, Ḳ,) *and make their camels lie down, and take a nap, or slight sleep*, (TA,) *after which they depart*, (Ṣ,) *and continue their journey, at daybreak:* (TA:) or *a place where people alight in the first part of the night, after journeying all the day:* or *a usual place of resort where people alight at any time of the night or day.* (TA.) — Also the former, A chamber (بَيْت) *having an* عَرْس [q. v.] *made to it.* (Ṣ, O, Ḳ.)

عرش

1. عَرَشَ, aor. ـِ and ـُ, (Ṣ, O, Ḳ,) inf. n. عَرْشٌ, (Ṣ, O,) *He constructed*, or *built, what is called an* عَرِيش; (Ḳ;) as also ▼ اعرش; (Zj, Ḳ;) and ▼ عرّش, (Ḳ,) inf. n. تَعْرِيشٌ: (TA:) or *he built a building of wood.* (Ṣ, O.) — عَرَشَ البَيْتَ, (Ḳ,) aor. ـِ and ـُ, inf. n. عَرْشٌ and عُرُوشٌ, (TA,) *He built the house*, or *the like.* (Ḳ.) — عَرَشَ الكَرْمَ: see 2. — عَرَشَ البِئْرَ, (A, Ḳ,) aor. ـِ and ـُ, (Ḳ,) inf. n. عَرْشٌ, (Ṣ, A, O,) *He cased the well with stones to the height of the stature of a man in the lowest part, and the rest of it with wood:* (Ḳ:) or *he cased the well with wood, after having cased the lowest part thereof with stones to the height of the stature of a man.* (Ṣ, O.) — عَرَشَ فُلَانًا, (Ḳ, TA,) aor. ـُ, inf. n. عَرْشٌ, (TA,) *He struck such a one in the* عُرْش, (Ḳ, TA,) i. e. *base*, (TA,) *of his neck.* (Ḳ, TA.)

2. عرّش, inf. n. تَعْرِيشٌ: see 1. — Also † *He* (a bird) *rose, and shaded with his wings him who was beneath him.* (TA.) — عرّش العَرْشَ *He made the* عَرْش [q. v.: or perhaps we should read العَرِيشَ]. (TA.) — عرّش البَيْتَ, (O, Ḳ,) inf. n. as above, (TA,) *He roofed the house, or the like;* (O, Ḳ, TA;) *and raised the building thereof.* (TA.) — عرّش الكَرْمَ, (Ṣ, O, Mṣb, Ḳ,) inf. n. as above, (Ṣ, O, TA,) *He made an* عَرِيش *for the grape-vine:* (Mṣb:) or *he raised the shoots of the grape-vine upon the pieces of wood* [*made to support them*]; as also ▼ عَرَشَهُ, (Zj, O, Ḳ,) aor. ـِ and ـُ, inf. n. عَرْشٌ and عُرُوشٌ; (Ḳ;) or both signify *he made an* عَرْش *for the grape-vine, and raised its shoots upon the pieces of wood;* (TA;) and ▼ اعرشهُ signifies the same as عرّشهُ: (Zj, O, TA:) or عرّشهُ signifies *he bent the pieces of wood upon which its branches, or shoots, were trained.* (TA.)

4. اعرش: see 1. — اعرش الكَرْمَ: see 2.

5. تَعَرَّشْنَا *We pitched our tent*, or *tents.* (A, TA.) — تعرّش بِالبَلَدِ *He became fixed, settled*, or *established, in the country*, or *town.* (AZ, O, Ḳ.)

8. اعترش *He made, or took, for himself an* عَرِيش. (O, Ḳ.) — اعترش العِنَبُ *The grapes mounted* (Ṣ, O, Ḳ) *upon the* عَرِيش, (O, Ḳ,) or,

as in the Mufradát, *upon their* عريش, (TA,) or *upon the* عِرَاش [which may be a pl. of عَرِيش, like عَرَائِش, or perhaps it is a mistranscription for this last word]: (Ṣ: so in two copies:) and in like manner, اعترش العِنَبُ العَرِيشَ: (L, TA: [expl. by عَلَاهُ عَلَى العِرَاشِ, which seems to be a mistake for عَلَا عَلَى العَرِيشِ:]) and اعترشت القُضْبَانُ عَلَى العَرِيشِ *The branches*, or *shoots, mounted upon the* عريش. (A, TA.)

عَرْشٌ *A booth*, or *shed*, or *thing constructed for shade*, (مِظَلَّةٌ,) *mostly made of canes*, or *reeds*; (Ḳ;) and sometimes, (TA,) *made of palm-sticks, over which is thrown* ثُمَام [*a species of panic grass*]; (Mgh, TA;) as described by Az, on the authority of the Arabs; (TA;) and such is meant by the عَرْش of Moses: (Mgh:) *a thing resembling a house*, or *tent, made of palm-sticks, over which is put* ثُمَام; as also ♦ عَرِيشٌ: (Mṣb:) *a booth*, or *shed*, syn. خَيْمَةٌ, (Ḳ, TA,) *made of wood and* ثُمَام; (TA;) as also ♦ عَرِيشٌ; (Ṣ, A,* O, Ḳ;) and such is meant by the ♦ عريش of Moses; (A;) and sometimes the ♦ عَرِيش was *made of palm-sticks, with* ثُمَام *thrown over them*: (TA:) both signify *a thing*, (Ṣ, O,) or *a house*, or *the like*, (Ḳ,) *used for shade*: (Ṣ, O, Ḳ:) pl. of the former, عُرُوشٌ (ISd, Mgh, Mṣb, Ḳ) and أَعْرَاشٌ [which is a pl. of pauc.] and عُرْشٌ: (Ḳ:) or عُرُشٌ is pl. of ♦ عَرِيشٌ, (Ṣ, ISd, O, Mṣb,) not of عَرْشٌ: (ISd:) or it is also pl. of ♦ عَرِيشٌ: (Ḳ:) and عُرُوشٌ is also a pl. of ♦ عُرُشٌ, which is a pl. of ♦ عَرِيشٌ. (L.) Hence *The houses of Mekkeh*, (Ṣ, A, Mgh, O, Mṣb,) *in which the needy of its inhabitants dwelt*, (Mgh,) or *its ancient houses*, (Ḳ,) were called العُرُوشُ, (Ṣ, A, Mgh, O, Mṣb, Ḳ,) and العُرُشُ, (Ṣ, Mṣb,) and ♦ العُرْشُ; (O, Ḳ;) because they were of poles, or sticks, set up, and shaded over: (Ṣ, O, Mṣb:) or *Mekkeh* itself was called ♦ العُرْشُ: (Az, O, L, Ḳ:) or it was called العَرْشُ, with fet-ḥ, and ♦ العَرِيشُ: (Az, L, Ḳ:) and *its houses* were called ♦ العُرُشُ, and العُرُوشُ. (Ḳ.) And hence, (Ṣ, O, Mṣb,) the saying in a trad., (Ṣ, O,) i. e., the saying of Saad, (Ḳ, TA,) when he heard that Mo'áwiyeh forbade the performing conjointly the greater and minor pilgrimages, (TA,) تَمَتَّعْنَا مَعَ رَسُولِ ٱللّٰهِ صَلَّى ٱللّٰهُ عَلَيْهِ وَسَلَّمَ وَفُلَانٌ كَافِرٌ بِالعُرُشِ, (Ṣ, O, Ḳ,*) or بِالعُرُوشِ, (Ṣ, TA,) i. e., [*We performed conjointly the greater and minor pilgrimages with the Apostle of God,* (*God bless and save him,*)] *when such a one*, meaning Mo'áwiyeh, *was abiding* (O, L, Ḳ) *in his state of unbelief*, (L,) *in Mekkeh*; (L, Ḳ;) i. e. *in the houses thereof*: (O, L:) or, as some say, *was hiding himself in the houses of Mekkeh*. (L.) — *A house* [*in an absolute sense*]; *a dwelling*, or *place of abode*: (Kr, TA:) pl. عُرُوشٌ (TA) [and عُرُوش]. — *A* [*building of the kind called*] قَصْر. (Ḳ.) — *The wood upon which stands the drawer of water*: (Ḳ:) or *a structure of wood built at the head of the well, forming a shade*: [pl. عُرُوش:] when the props are pulled away, the عُرُوش fall down. (TA.) [عَرْش in relation to a well has also another meaning; which see below.] — The *wooden thing* [or *trellis*] *which serves for the propping* of a grape-vine. (TA.) [But this is more commonly called عَرِيش, q. v.] — The *roof* of a house or the like: (Ṣ, Mgh, O, Mṣb, Ḳ:) pl. عُرُوشٌ. (A.) So in a trad., where a lamp is mentioned as suspended to the عَرْش: (O, TA:) and in another, in which a man relates that he used, when upon his عرش, to hear the Prophet's reciting [of the Ḳur-án]. (TA.) And so it has been expl. as occurring in the phrase of the Ḳur [ii. 261 and xxii. 44], خَاوِيَةٌ عَلَى عُرُوشِهَا *Having fallen down upon its roofs*: meaning that its walls were standing when their roofs had become demolished and had fallen to the foundations, and the walls fell down upon the roofs demolished before them: (O, TA:) but some consider على as here meaning عَنْ [from]. (TA.) — [Hence, app.,] العَرْشُ is applied to *The* عَرْش *of God, which is not definable*: (A, Ḳ:) I'Ab is related to have said that the كُرْسِىّ is the place of the feet and the عَرْش is immeasurable: and it is said in the Mufradát of Er-Rághib that the عَرْش of God is *one of the things which mankind know not in reality, but only by name*; and it is not as the imaginations of the vulgar hold it to be; [namely, *the throne of God*;] for were it so, it would be a support to Him; not supported; whereas God saith [in the Ḳur., xxxv. 39], "Verily God holdeth the heavens and the earth, lest they should move from their place; and if they should move from their place, no one would hold them after Him:" or, as some say, it is *the highest sphere*; [or *the empyrean*;] and the كرسىّ is the sphere of the stars: and they adduce as an indication thereof the saying of Moḥammad, that the seven heavens and earths, by the side of the كرسىّ, are nought but as a ring thrown down in a desert land; and such is the كرسىّ with respect to the عَرْش: and this assertion is mentioned in the B, but without approval: (TA:) [it appears, however, to be most commonly accepted:] or *a red sapphire, which glistens with the light of the Supreme*. (A, Ḳ.) [Hence the saying,] مِنَ العَرْشِ إِلَى الفَرْشِ meaning, [*From the highest sphere*, or *the empyrean, to*] *the earth*. (A.) — Also *The* سَرِير [or *throne*] (Ṣ, A, O, Mṣb, Ḳ) *of a king*; (Ṣ, A, O, Ḳ;) the *seat of a sulṭán*; [perhaps as being likened to the عرش of God; or, more probably, from its being generally surmounted by a canopy; or] because of its height. (Er-Rághib.) [Hence,] the phrase اِسْتَوَى عَلَى عَرْشِهِ means *He reigned as king*. (A, TA.) — And [hence, also,] *Certain stars in advance of* السِّمَاكُ الأَعْزَلُ [which is *Spica Virginis*]; (TA;) [app. those meant by what here follows;] عَرْشُ السِّمَاكِ signifies *four small stars* [app. γ, δ, ε, and η, *of Virgo*, regarded as *the seat of Bootes*, the principal star of which is called السِّمَاكُ الرَّامِحُ, being described as] *beneath* العَوَّآء [which is a name of Bootes and also of the four stars mentioned above], *and also called* عَجُزُ الأَسَدِ [*the rump of Leo*, the figure of which was extended by the Arabs far beyond the limits which we assign to it]. (Ṣ, O, Ḳ.) — And عَرْشُ الجَوْزَآءِ [*The seat of Orion*; applied by our astronomers to α *of Lepus*; but described as] *four stars, of which two are on the fore legs and two on the hind legs, of Lepus*. (Ḳzw.) — And عَرْشُ الثُّرَيَّا *Certain stars near* الثُّرَيَّا [or *the Pleiades*]. (T, TA.) — عَرْشٌ also signifies The جَنَازَة; (O, Ḳ, TA;) i. e., the *bier of a corpse*. (O, TA.) And hence, as some say, the expression in a trad., اِهْتَزَّ العَرْشُ لِمَوْتِ سَعْدِ بْنِ مُعَاذٍ, meaning *The bier rejoiced* [lit. *shook*] *at the death of Saad Ibn-Mo'ádh*; i. e., at carrying him upon it to his place of burial: (O, Ḳ,* TA:) but there are other explanations, for which see art. هز. (TA.) — The *wood with which a well is cased after it has been cased with stones* (Ṣ, O, Ḳ) *in its lowest part* (Ṣ, O) *to the height of the stature of a man*: (Ṣ, O, Ḳ:) pl. عُرُوشٌ. (Ṣ, O.) [Another meaning of the same word in relation to a well has been mentioned before.] — † The *nest* of a bird, *such as is built in a tree*, (Ḳ,) [app. as being likened to a booth.] — The *angle*, or *corner*, or *strongest side*, syn. رُكْن, (Ks, Zj, Ḳ,) of a house, (Ks, Zj,) or [other] thing: (Ḳ:) pl. عُرُوشٌ. (Ks, Zj.) Accord. to some, the phrase in the Ḳur [ii. 261, mentioned above], خَاوِيَةٌ عَلَى عُرُوشِهَا, means *Empty, and fallen to ruin upon its* أَرْكَان [or *angles*, &c.]. (Ks, Zj, O.) — [Hence,] ‡ The *head*, or *chief, who is the manager* or *regulator of the affairs*, of a people, or company of men: (Ḳ:) likened to the عَرْش of a house. (TA.) — [Hence also,] † The *means of support of a thing*, or *an affair*. (A, O, Ḳ.) Hence the saying, ثُلَّ عَرْشُهُ, (O, Ḳ,) meaning ‡ *His means of support became taken away*: (TA:) or *he perished*: (A:) or *he was slain*; as also ♦ ثُلَّ عُرْشُهُ: (IDrd, in M, art. ثل:) or *his might*, or *power, departed*: (TA:) or *his affairs*, or *state, became weak, and his might*, or *power, departed*. (Ṣ, O. [See also art. ثل.] [For عَرْش also signifies] — ‡ *Might*, or *power*: (Er-Rághib, Ḳ:) *regal power*; *sovereignty*; *dominion*: (IAṭr, Er-Rághib, Ḳ:) from the same word as signifying the throne, or seat, of a king. (Er-Rághib.) — And The *protuberant part* (Ṣ, O, Ḳ) in, (Ṣ, O,) or *of*, (Ḳ,) *the upper surface* of the foot, (Ṣ, O, Ḳ,) *in which are the toes*; (Ṣ, O, TA;) as also ♦ عُرْشٌ: pl. [of pauc.] أَعْرَاشٌ and [of mult.] عِرَشَةٌ: (O, TA:) and the *part between the* عَيْر [or *prominent bone*] *and the toes, of the upper surface* of the foot; as also ♦ عُرْشٌ: (Ibn-'Abbád, O, Ḳ:) pls. the same as last mentioned above: (Ḳ:) or ♦ عُرْشٌ signifies the *upper surface* of the foot; and its lower surface is called the أَخْمَص. (IAṭr.)

عُرْشٌ, both as a sing. and as a pl.: see عَرْشٌ, last sentence, in three places: — and the same paragraph, first and second sentences, in four places: and see ثُلَّ عَرْشُهُ in the latter part of the same paragraph. — العُرْشَانِ signifies *Two oblong portions of flesh in the two sides of the neck*, [app.

the two sterno-mastoid muscles,] (Ṣ, A, O, Ḳ, TA,) between which are the vertebræ [of the neck]: (TA:) or in the base of the neck: (Ḳ:) or the base [itself] of the neck: so in the phrase ثَلَّ عُرْشَيْهِ: (IDrd and M in art. ثل, q. v.:) or the أَخْدَعَانِ [or two branches of the occipital artery], (TA, as from the Ḳ, [in which I do not find it,]) which are (TA) [in] the two places of the cupping-vessels: (Ḳ, TA:) or the أَخْدَعَانِ are in the عُرْشَانِ: (Ibn-'Abbád, O:) or the عُرْش is a vein in the base of the neck: (Th, O:) or the عُرْشَانِ are [app. the two greater cornua of the os hyoides, which forms a support to the tongue; two bones in the لَهَاة [meaning furthest part of the mouth], which erect the tongue. (Ibn-'Abbád, O, Ḳ.) It is related in a trad., respecting the slaying of Aboo-Jahl, that he said to Ibn-Mes'ood, خُذْ سَيْفِى فَاحْتَزَّ بِهِ رَأْسِى مِنْ عُرْشَىَّ [Take thou my sword, and cut with it my head from my عُرْشَانِ]. (O, TA.) — And † The ear: (Ḳ:) or † the two ears: because near to the عُرْشَانِ [properly so called]: hence the saying, نَفَثَ فِى عُرْشَيْهِ † He spoke secretly to him, or with him. (Aṣ, A, O.) — And The extremity of the hair of the mane of a horse: (IDrd, O, Ḳ:) or so العُرْش. (TA.) — Also, (Ḳ,) or العُرْش, (TA [and thus accord. to a verse there cited],) The bulky she-camel; as though her chest were cased like a well. (Ḳ, TA. [See 1.])

عَرِيشٌ: see عَرْشٌ, first and second sentences, in several places. — Also, (Ḳ,) or عَرِيشُ كَرْمٍ, (Ṣ, Mgh, Mṣb,) [The trellis of a grape-vine;] the structure made for a grape-vine, of sticks, or pieces of wood, in the form of a roof, upon which are put the branches, or shoots, of the vine; (Ḳ,* TA;) [also, but less commonly, called عَرْشٌ;] the structure made for a grape-vine to rise upon it; (Mgh;) the elevated structure upon which a grape-vine spreads itself: (Mṣb:) pl. عَرَائِشُ, (Mgh, Mṣb,) [and perhaps عِرَاشٌ also: see 8.] — Also, عَرِيشٌ, A thing resembling a هَوْدَج, (Ṣ, O, Ḳ,) but not [exactly the same as] it, made for a woman, who sits in it upon her camel: (Ṣ, O:) so called as being likened in form to the عريش of a vine: (Er-Rághib:) or ↓ عَرِيشَةٌ, with ة, is the same as هودج; and its pl. is عَرَائِشُ, (Mṣb,) which signifies the same as هَوَادِجُ. (ISh, A.) — And An enclosure of the kind called حَظِيرَة, made for beasts, to protect them from the cold. (TA.)

عَرِيشَةٌ: see the next preceding paragraph.

عُرُوشَاتٌ Grape-vines. (TA.)

كُرُومٌ مَعْرُوشَاتٌ [Grape-vines furnished with, or trained upon, عَرَائِش, or trellises, pl. of عَرِيش]. (Ṣ.) — بِئْرٌ مَعْرُوشَةٌ [A well cased with what is termed an عَرْش]. (Ṣ.) — Hence, (O,) مَعْرُوشُ الجَنْبَيْنِ A camel large in the sides. (O, Ḳ.)

عرص

1. عَرِصَ, [aor. ـَ,] (Fr, Th, Ṣ, O,) inf. n. عَرَصٌ, (Ṣ, A, O, Ḳ,) He (a man, Fr, Ṣ, O, and a cat, Th,) was, or became, brisk, lively, or sprightly; (Fr, Th, Ṣ, A, O, Ḳ;) as also ↓ اعترص, (Fr, Th,) said of a man, (Fr,) and of a cat. (Th.) — He (a man) leaped, jumped, sprang, or bounded; as also ↓ اعترص. (Lḥ.) — عَرِصَ القَوْمُ The company of men played, or sported, and advanced and retired, urging, or pushing, [one another] from behind: (TA:) and ↓ اعترص he (a child, T, Mṣb) played, or sported, and was very joyful, or glad, and very brisk, lively, or sprightly. (T, O, Mṣb, Ḳ.) — عَرِصَ البَرْقُ, (IDrd, A, O, Ḳ,) aor. ـَ, inf. n. عَرَصٌ and عَرْصٌ, (IDrd, O, TA,) The lightning gleamed, or glistened, much: (A:) or was, or became, in a state of commotion, or agitation; quivered; flickered; (IDrd, O, Ḳ;) as also ↓ اعترص: (TA:) and in like manner, عَرِصَ السَّيْفُ, inf. n. as above, The sword vibrated, or quivered: (TA:) and جِلْدُهُ ↓ اعترص His skin quivered, or quaked; (Ḳ, TA;) as also ارتعص. (TA.) — Also عَرَصَ, aor. ـُ, said of a camel, (O, Ḳ, TA,) or other [animal], (O, TA,) He struggled, or quivered, (اِضْطَرَبَ, O, Ḳ, TA,) with his hind legs; (O, TA;) as also ↓ اعرص. (O, Ḳ.) — And عَرَصَتِ السَّمَآءُ, (AZ, Ṣ, O, Ḳ,) or السَّحَابَةُ, as in some copies of the Ṣ, (TA,) aor. ـِ, (AZ, Ṣ, O, Ḳ,) inf. n. عَرْصٌ, (AZ, Ṣ, O, TA,) or عَرَصٌ, (as in one copy of the Ṣ,) The sky, or cloud, lightened continually. (AZ, Ṣ, O, Ḳ.) = عَرِصَ, (Ṣ, O,) inf. n. عَرَصٌ, (Ṣ, O, Ḳ,) said of a tent or house, (بَيْت, Ṣ, O, Ḳ,) and of a plant, (نَبْت, O, Ḳ,) Its odour became foul, (Ṣ, O,) and stinking, (TA,) or altered, (Ḳ,) from the dew (النَّدَا). (Ṣ, O, Ḳ.)

4: see 1, last sentence but two.

5. تعرّص He remained, stayed, dwelt, or abode. (Ḳ.) The imperative of the verb in this sense is mentioned by IAạr. (O.)

8: see 1, in five places.

عَرْصٌ I. q. عَرْشٌ (O, Ḳ, TA) meaning as expl. in art. عرس: (TA:) or a piece of wood which is laid across a chamber when they desire to roof it: then they lay upon it the ends of the short pieces of wood: (A'Obeyd, O, TA:) occurring in a trad., mispronounced by the relaters عَرْض. (O,* Ḳ, TA.) = See also عَرَّاصٌ, in two places.

عَرِصٌ: see عَرَّاصٌ, in two places.

عَرْصَةٌ The court, or open area, (سَاحَة,) of a house; (T, Mṣb;) i. e., a spacious vacant part, or portion, thereof, in which is no building; (Mṣb;) so called because the children play, or sport, &c., (يَعْتَرِصُونَ,) therein: (T, Mṣb:) or any spacious piece of ground between houses, in which is no building: (Ṣ, O, Ḳ:) or any distinct piece of ground in which is no building; accord. to Eth-Tha'álibee, in his book entitled "Fiḳh el-Loghah:" (Mṣb:) or any open space in which is no building: (Aṣ, TA:) or the ground of a house, where it is built; and any chamber of a house, in which one sits, not in the upper part: (A:) pl. أَعْرَاصٌ (Ḳ) and عِرَاصٌ and عَرَصَاتٌ. (Ṣ, A, O, Mṣb, Ḳ.)

عَرُوصٌ A she-camel having a pleasant odour when she sweats. (IAạr, O, Ḳ.)

عَرَّاصٌ Clouds (سَحَابٌ) having thunder and lightning: (Ṣ, O, Ḳ:) or having thunder and lightning, without which they are not thus called, in which the lightning is in commotion, or flickering, and which overshadow and approach so as to become like a roof: (O, TA:) or of which the lightning does not cease: (Lḥ, TA:) and (Ḳ) that gleam, or glisten, much, (A, Ḳ,) with lightning: (A:) or that lighten at one time, and become concealed at another: (TA:) or which the wind carries to and fro. (O, TA.) — Lightning in a state of commotion, or agitation; quivering; flickering; as also ↓ عَرِصٌ and ↓ عَرْصٌ: (Ḳ:) or vehemently so, (IDrd, O, TA,) and vehement in its thunder: (TA:) or that gleams, or glistens, much: or that lightens at one time, and becomes unapparent at another; as also ↓ عَرِصٌ and ↓ عَرْصٌ. (Ibn-'Abbád, O.) — A pliant spear, (AA, Ṣ, O, Ḳ, TA,) that vibrates, or quivers, when shaken: (Ṣ,* O,* TA:) and so applied to a sword: (AA, Ṣ, O, Ḳ:) or, applied to a spear, it signifies of which, when it is shaken, the head glistens; from عَرِصَ البَرْقُ. (Ibn-'Abbád, O, TA.)

مُعَرَّصٌ Flesh-meat laid in the عَرْصَة [q. v.] to dry: (Ṣ, O, Ḳ:) or cut in pieces: (Fr, O, Ḳ:) or laid in, or upon, the live coals, so that it becomes mixed with the ashes and not well and thoroughly cooked: (Lth, O, Ḳ, TA:) Az says that this last explanation, the like of which has also been given on the authority of ISk, is more pleasing to him than that of Fr. (O, TA.) [See also مُعَرَّضٌ, with ض.] = Also A camel whose back has become submissive, but not his head: (Ibn-Ḥabeeb, O, Ḳ:) because they used [sometimes] to ride without bridling. (TA.)

المِعْرَاصُ The هِلَال [or new moon, or moon when near the change]. (Ibn-'Abbád, O, Ḳ.)

عرصف

Q. 1. عَرْصَفَهُ He pulled it, (Lth, O, L, Ḳ,) namely, a thing, (O,) so that he slit it, or divided it lengthwise. (Lth, O, Ḳ.)

عُرْصُفٌ A certain plant, called in ancient Greek كَمَافِيطُوس [i. e. χαμαίπιτυς, the chamæpitys, or ground-pine], (Ḳ, TA,) by which name it is commonly known to the physicians, who say, (TA,) when a mixture of some of its leaves with hydromel is drunk for forty days, it cures the sciatica; and when for seven days, it cures the jaundice. (Ḳ, TA.)

عُرْصَافٌ One of the عَرَاصِيف of the [camel's saddle called] رَحْل [or قَتَب], (Ṣ, O,) which are four pegs, or pins of wood, that unite, or conjoin, the heads of [the curved pieces of wood called] the أَحْنَآء of the قَتَب; in the head of each حِنْو are two pegs, or pins of wood, bound with [the sinews called] عَقَب, (Ṣ, O, Ḳ,) or with [pieces of] the skins of camels; and in it [or appertaining to the same part] are the عَلِقَات; (Ṣ, O;) and they are also called the عَصَافِير, which is formed from عراصيف by transposition: (Ṣ and O in art. عصفر:) or, (Ḳ,) accord. to Aṣ, (O,) they are the *two pieces of wood* (O, Ḳ) *that bind,* (O,) or *are bound,* (Ḳ,) *between* [*the upright piece of wood called*] *the* وَاسِط [*in the fore part*] *of the* رَحْل *and its* آخِرَة [*which is in its hinder part*]; *on the right and left.* (O, Ḳ.) —— The عِرْصَاف of the [kind of saddle called] إِكَاف, also called its ▼ عُرْصُوف and its عُصْفُور, is *A piece of wood bound between* [or *conjoining*] *the anterior* [*curved pieces called*] حِنْوَان. (Ṣ, O, Ḳ.) —— And, [so in the O, but in the Ḳ "or,"] accord. to Az, (O,) عِرْصَاف signifies *A whip made of* [*the sinews called*] عَقَب; (O, Ḳ;) as also عِرْفَاص. (O.) And, (O, Ḳ,) accord. to Lth, (O,) *Elongated* عَقَب; (O, Ḳ;) mostly applied to the عَقَب *of the two sides and of the two elongated portions of flesh between which is the backbone:* (O:) or, (Ḳ,) accord. to IDrd, as also عِرْفَاص, (O, TA,) *a fascicle* (خُصْلَة) *of* عَقَب *and of thongs,* (O, TA,) *upon a* قُبَّة [q. v.], *with which the* [*women's camel-vehicle called*] هَوْدَج *is bound,* or *made fast.* (TA.)

عُرْصُوف: see عِرْصَاف. —— العُرْصُوفَانِ signifies *Two sticks* (عُودَانِ) *inserted in the* دُجْرَان *of the plough,* (Ibn-'Abbád, O, Ḳ,) *forking;* the دُجْر being the piece of wood upon which is bound the iron [or share] of the plough. (Ibn-'Abbád, O.) —— The عَرَاصِيف of the hump of the camel are The *extremities of the* سَنَاسِن [pl. of سِنْسِن, q. v.,] *of his back;* (Ibn-'Abbád, O, Ḳ;) sing. عُرْصُوف: (Ibn-'Abbád, O:) or *what are upon the* سَنَاسِن; and also called the عَصَافِير; and ISd says, I think that العَرَافِيص is a dial. var. thereof. (L, TA.) ═ The عَرَاصِيف of the خُرْطُوم [or nose, or fore part of the nose, &c.,] are *Certain bending bones in the* [*part called*] خَيْشُوم [q. v.]. (Ibn-'Abbád, O, Ḳ.)

عرض

1. عَرُضَ, aor. ـُ, inf. n. عِرَضٌ, [instead of which, as a simple subst., عَرْض is generally used,] and عَرَاضَة, *It was,* or *became, broad,* or *wide;* (Ṣ, O,* Mṣb, Ḳ, TA;) as also ▼ اعرض, (A, TA,) which occurs in this sense in two exs. following. (TA.) [And in like manner, ▼ استعرض *It grew,* or *spread, wide;* said of a tree; opposed to طَالَ; occurring in the TA in art. بهل.] It is said in a prov., أَعْرَضَتِ ▼ القِرْفَةُ (Ṣ, O,* TA [but in two copies of the Ṣ, I find the verb in this instance written اعرضتْ, and in the O اعرضتْ, and I do not know that the reading in the TA, which seems to be the common one, is found in any copy of the Ṣ,]) *Suspicion became,* or *has become, wide;* syn. اِتَّسَعَت: (TA:) used when it is said to a man, "Whom dost thou suspect?" and he answers, "The sons of such a one," referring to the whole tribe. (Ṣ, O, TA.) [See Freytag's Arab. Prov. ii. 112, where another reading is mentioned, which, by what he says, is shown to be أَعْرَضْتَ القِرْفَةَ *Thou hast made suspicion wide.*] In another prov. it is said, أَعْرَضَ ▼ ثَوْبُ المُلْبَسِ (IAạr, A, TA, and Ḳ in art. لبس,) and المِلْبَسِ and المُلْتَبِس (IAạr, and Ḳ in art. لبس,) and المُلْبِس (TA in art. لبس,) i. e. صَارَ ذَا عَرْضٍ, (A, TA,) and عَرُضَ, and اِتَّسَعَ; (Sh;) [meaning the same as the prov. before mentioned;] used with reference to him whose suspicion has become wide; (IAạr, and TA in art. لبس;) i. e. with reference to him who suspects many persons (IAạr, Az, and Ḳ in art. لبس,) of a theft; (IAạr, Az, and TA in that art.;) or of saying a thing: (TṢ, and TA in that art.:) or when thou askest a person respecting a thing and he does not explain it to thee. (TA in that art.) [See, again, Freytag's Arab. Prov. ii. 100, where it is said that أَعْرَضَ ثَوْبُ المُلْبِسِ app. means *The garment of the suspected appeared,* or *has appeared:* but that another reading is عَرُضَ, meaning *became,* or *has become, wide.*] ═ عَرَضَ, aor. ـِ, (Fr, Ṣ, O, Mṣb, Ḳ,) inf. n. عَرْضٌ; (TA;) and عَرِضَ, (Aṣ, TṢ, Ḳ,) aor. ـَ, (Fr, Ḳ,) or ـِ, like حَسِبَ, aor. ـِ, deviating from the general rule; (Aṣ, TṢ;) *It* (a thing) *appeared,* or *became apparent,* لَهُ *to him;* (Ṣ, O, Mṣb, Ḳ; [but in some copies of the Ḳ, instead of the explanation ظَهَرَ وَبَدَا, we find ظَهَرَ عَلَيْهِ وَبَدَا, which is a mistake;]) as also ▼ اعرض, (Fr, Ṣ, O, Mṣb, Ḳ,) which is a deviation from a general rule, being quasi-pass. of عَرَضَهُ, which see below; (Ṣ,* O,* Mṣb, Ḳ;) [lit.] *it showed its breadth,* or *width.* (O,* TA.) You say, اعرض ▼ لَكَ الشَّىْءُ مِنْ بَعِيدٍ *The thing appeared to thee from afar.* (TA.) And عَرَضَتْ لَهُ الغُولُ, and عَرِضَتْ, (AZ, Ṣ, O, Ḳ,) *The ghool appeared to him.* (Ḳ.) The Arabs say, of a thing, عَرَضَ and ▼ اعرض and ▼ تعرّض and ▼ اعترض, using these verbs as syn.; (Sh;) [app. as meaning *It showed, presented,* or *offered, itself,* (lit. *its breadth,* or *width,* or *its side,* see 5,) to a person: the first and last also often signify, and the others sometimes, *he obtruded himself* in an affair; *interfered* therein:] IḲt disallows ▼ اعرض in the sense of اعترض, as not having been found by him: (TA:) [but] an instance of the former of these two verbs used in the sense of the latter of them occurs in the phrase إِذَا أَعْرَضَتْ ▼ لِلنَّاظِرِينَ [app. meaning *When she shows,* or *presents, herself to the lookers*], in a poem by one of the tribe of Ṭeiyi. (Sh.) —— عَرَضَ لَكَ الخَيْرُ, [in one place in the TA الخَبَرُ, and الخبر in a copy of the Mṣb,] inf. n. عُرُوضٌ; (TA; [in one place in the TA عُرُوض there referring to الخَبَر, which is app. a mistranscription;]) and ▼ اعرض; (Ṣ, O, Ḳ, TA;) *Good* [i. e. *the doing of good*] *hath become within thy power,* or *practicable to thee,* or *easy to thee.* (Ṣ, O, Ḳ, TA.) And اعرض ▼ لَكَ الظَّبْىُ *The gazelle hath exposed to thee its side;* (TA;) or *hath put its side in thy power,* (Ṣ, O, Ḳ, TA,) *by turning it towards thee:* (O, TA:) said to incite one to shoot it, or cast at it. (Ṣ, O.) Or اعرض ▼ لَكَ, said of an animal of the chase, or other thing, signifies *It hath put in thy power,* [or *exposed to thee,*] *its breadth,* or *width:* (A:) or اعرض ▼ لَهُ signifies *it* (a thing) *became within his power,* or *practicable to him,* or *easy to him;* lit., *it showed its side* [*to him*]. (Mgh.) [In the TA, I find أَعْرَضَ فِى الشَّىْءِ expl. as signifying *He had the width of the thing in his power:* but فى, here, seems to be a mistake for لَهُ.] A poet, also, says أَعْرِضِى ▼ addressing a woman; meaning أَمْكِنِى [*Empower thou;* i. e. *grant thou access*]. (Ṣ.) —— عَرَضَ لَهُ, aor. ـِ; (Aṣ, Ṣ, Ḳ, TA;) and عَرِضَ, aor. ـَ; (TA;) are also said of an event, (Aṣ, TA,) or of a disease, and the like, (Ṣ, Ḳ, TA,) such as disquietude of mind, and a state of distraction of the mind or attention; (TA;) [meaning *It happened to him; it befell him; it occurred to him; was incident to him;*] and also of doubt, and the like. (TA.) [So, too, is ▼ اعترض.] You also say, عَرَضَهُ عَارِضٌ مِنَ الحُمَّى وَنَحْوِهَا [*An occurrence of fever, and the like, happened to him,* or *befell him*]. (Ṣ.) And اعترض ▼ البَدَنَ [*It befell the body*] is said of [a disease, as, for instance,] the mange, or scab. (B, in TA in art. عر.) —— عَرَضَ لَهُ, aor. ـِ; (Mṣb, TA;) and عَرِضَ له, aor. ـَ; (Mṣb;) *He intervened as an obstacle to him, preventing him from attaining his desire,* (Mṣb, TA,*) or *from seeking to attain his desire,* and *from going his way;* (TA;) as also ▼ اعترض له. (Mṣb.) You say also, عَرَضَ لَهُ أَشَدَّ العَرْضِ, and ▼ اعترض, *He opposed himself to him* (قَابَلَهُ بِنَفْسِهِ) *with the most vehement opposition of himself.* (TA.) See also 5, second sentence. One should not say, عرّضتُ لَهُ, with teshdeed, in the sense of اِعْتَرَضْتُ. (Mṣb.) You also say, عَرَضَ عَارِضٌ, meaning [*An obstacle intervened,* or *prevented;* lit.] *an intervening thing intervened; a preventing thing prevented.* (TA.) And سِرْتُ فَعَرَضَ لِى فِى الطَّرِيقِ عَارِضٌ مِنْ جَبَلٍ وَنَحْوِهِ *I journeyed, and there opposed itself to me, so as to prevent my going on, an obstacle consisting in a mountain, and the like;* as also ▼ اعترض: whence the اِعْتِرَاضَات [or *objections*] of the lawyers; because they prevent one's laying hold upon the evidence. (Mṣb.) And عَرَضَ لَهُ الشَّىْءُ فِى الطَّرِيقِ *The thing intervened as an obstacle to him in the way, preventing him from going on.* (TA.) And عَرَضَ الشَّىْءُ *The thing stood up and prevented;* [or *stood in the way,* or *presented itself as an obstacle;* or *opposed itself;*] as also ▼ اعترض. (TA.) [And *The thing lay,* or *extended, breadthwise,* or *across,* or *athwart;* like اعترض, q. v.] And اعترض ▼ الشَّىْءُ دُونَ الشَّىْءِ *The thing intervened as an obstacle in the way to the thing;* syn. حَالَ. (Ṣ, O.) —— مَا عَرَضْتُ لَهُ بِسُوْءٍ, aor. ـِ; and مَا عَرِضْتُ, aor. ـَ; signify مَا تَعَرَّضْتُ: see 5: or, as some say, *I did not,* or *have not, become exposed to his reviling,* or *evil-speaking, by reviling,* or *speaking evil, of him.* (Mṣb.) [See also عَرَضَ عَرْضَهُ, below.] —— عَرَضَ لَهُ also signifies *He went towards him;* (TA in art. نحو;) and عَرَضَ عَرْضَهُ and عُرْضَهُ [the same, i. e.] نَحَا نَحْوَهُ; (Ḳ;) as also ▼ اعترض عرضه. (TA.) —— In the saying of El-Kumeyt,

فَأَبْلِغْ يَزِيدَ إِنْ عَرَضْتَ وَمُنْذِرًا

he means [*And convey thou to Yezeed,*] *if thou*

pass by him, [*and to Mundhir:* or perhaps, *if thou go* to him: or *if thou present thyself* to him.] (Ṣ.) — عَرَضَ الفَرَسُ, (L, Ḳ,) aor. ـِ, inf. n. عَرْضٌ, (L, TA,) *The horse went along inclining towards one side:* (Ḳ, TA:) or *ran inclining his breast and head:* (L, TA:) and *ran inclining his head and neck;* (Ḳ; [in which only the inf. n. of the verb in this last sense is mentioned;]) the doing of which is approved in horses, but disapproved in camels. (TA.) [See also 3, and 5.] — عَرَضَ البَعِيرُ, (Ḳ,) inf. n. عَرْضٌ, (TA,) *The camel ate of the* أَعْرَاض, i. e. of the *upper parts of the trees* [or *shrubs*]. (Ḳ.) — عَرَضَتْ, said of a she-camel, *A fracture,* (Ṣ, O, Ḳ,) or *some injurious accident,* (Ṣ, O,) *befell her;* (Ṣ, O, Ḳ;) as also عَرِضَتْ; (O, Ḳ;) but the former is the more approved: (TA:) and عَرَضَ لَهَا *a disease,* or *a fracture, befell her.* (TA, from a trad.) Also, said of a sheep, or goat, (شَاة,) *It died by disease.* (Ḳ.) And عَرِضَ الشَّآءُ *The sheep,* or *goats, burst,* or *became rent, from abundance of herbage.* (Ḳ.) And عَرَضَ, (IḲṭṭ,) inf. n. عَرْضٌ, (Ḳ,) *He* (an animal, IḲṭṭ, or a man, Ḳ, [but it is said in the TA that there is no reason for this restriction,]) *died without disease.* (IḲṭṭ, Ḳ.) — عَرَضَ بِسِلْعَتِهِ *i. q.* عَارَضَ بِهَا. (Ḳ.) See 3, in two places. [And under the same, see a similar phrase.] — عَرَضَ *He* (a man, Ṣ, O) *came to* العَرُوض, i. e. *Mekkeh* and *El-Medeeneh,* (Ṣ, O, Ḳ, TA,) and *El-Yemen,* (TA,) *and what is around them.* (Ṣ, O, Ḳ, TA.) = عَرَضَ الشَّىْءَ, (Ṣ, Mṣb, Ḳ,) aor. ـِ, inf. n. عَرْضٌ, (Mṣb,) *He made the thing apparent; showed it; exhibited it; manifested it; exposed it to view; presented it;* (Ṣ, O, Mṣb, Ḳ;) *unfolded it; laid it open:* and also *he mentioned it:* (Mṣb:) [lit. *he showed its breadth,* or *width,* or *its side:* and hence it also signifies *he made the thing to stand as an obstacle,* دُونَ شَىْءٍ *in the way to,* or *of, a thing.*] You say, عَرَضَ لَهُ الشَّىْءَ *He made apparent, showed, exhibited, manifested,* or *exposed to view, to him the thing;* (Ṣ, O, Ḳ;) *unfolded it,* or *laid it open, to him.* (Ṣ, TA.) And عَرَضَ عَلَيْهِ أَمْرَ كَذَا (Ṣ, O, Ḳ*) *He showed, propounded,* or *proposed, to him, such a thing,* or *such a case:* (Ḳ,* TA:) [and *he asked,* or *required, of him, with gentleness, the doing of such a thing;* for] العَرْضُ signifies طَلَبٌ بِلِينٍ, (Mughnee and Ḳ, voce أَلَا,) or طَلَبٌ بِلِينٍ وَتَأَدُّبٍ. (Mughnee voce لَوْلَا.) And عَرَضْتُ المَتَاعَ لِلْبَيْعِ [*I showed, exposed, presented,* or *offered, the commodity for sale;* or] *I showed the commodity to those desirous of purchasing it.* (Mṣb.) The phrase عَرَضَ عَلَيْهِ المَتَاعَ [*He showed,* or *offered, to him the commodity*] is used because the person shows to the other the length and breadth of the thing (طُولَهُ وَعَرْضَهُ), or because he shows him one of its sides (عُرْضًا مِنْ أَعْرَاضِهِ). (Mgh.) [Hence,] it is said in a trad. of Ḥodheyfeh, تُعْرَضُ الفِتَنُ عَلَى القُلُوبِ عَرْضَ الحَصِيرِ, which means, accord. to some, that فِتَن [*Temptations,* &c.,] *will be* [*displayed and*] *embellished to the hearts* of men *like* [*as*] *the ornamented and variegated garment called* حصير [*is displayed and embellished*]: (B, TA in art. حصر:) or the meaning is, that they *will be laid and spread upon the hearts like the* حصير: (IAth, TA in the present art.:) and some say that by this last word is here meant a certain vein extending across upon the side of a beast, towards the belly. (TA in art. حصر.) [Hence also,] عَرْضٌ سَابِرِىٌّ [*A slight exhibition:* (see art. سبر:)] so in the proverbs by A'Obeyd, in the handwriting of Ibn-El-Jawáleeḳee: (TA:) or عَرْضٌ سَابِرِيٌّ: (TA, and so in a copy of the Ṣ in this art.:) or عَرْضٌ سَابِرِيٌّ. (O, TA, and so in a copy of the Ṣ in this art.) With this agrees in meaning the saying, عَرَضَ عَلَيَّ سَوْمَ عَالَّةٍ [*He offered to me in the manner of offering* water *to camels taking a second draught:* see also arts. سوم and عل; and see Freytag's Arab. Prov. ii. 84]. (TA.) You say also, عَرَضْتُ الجَارِيَةَ عَلَى البَيْعِ [*I showed,* or *displayed,* or *exposed,* or *offered, the girl for sale*]: (Ṣ, O, TA:) and in like manner المَتَاعَ [*the commodity*]. (TA.) And عَرَضْتُ لَهُ ثَوْبًا مَكَانَ حَقِّهِ; (Ṣ, O;) and عَرَضْتُ لَهُ مِنْ حَقِّهِ ثَوْبًا, (Ṣ, O, Ḳ,) or مَتَاعًا, (TA,) this meaning, [as also the former phrase,] *I gave to him a garment,* or *piece of cloth,* [or *a commodity,*] *in place of his due:* (Ṣ, O, Ḳ:) and in like manner, عرضت بِهِ. (El-Umawee, TA.) And عَرَضْتُ البَعِيرَ عَلَى الحَوْضِ, which is an instance of inversion, meaning عَرَضْتُ الحَوْضَ عَلَى البَعِيرِ [*I showed the watering-trough to the camel*]: (Ṣ, O, Mṣb:) [or it agrees in meaning with the phrase] عَرَضَ النَّاقَةَ عَلَى الحَوْضِ, and ↓ أَعْرَضَهَا, [as rendered] *He offered to the she-camel to drink* [*at the watering-trough*]. (L, TA.) And عَرَضَهُمْ عَلَى السَّيْفِ [lit. *He exposed them to the sword;* (see also 2;) meaning] *he slew them* (Ṣ, A, O, Mṣb, Ḳ) *with the sword.* (Mṣb.) And عَرَضَهُمْ عَلَى السَّوْطِ *He beat them with the whip; he flogged them.* (Ḳ,* TA.) And عَرَضَهُمْ عَلَى النَّارِ *He burned them.* (A, TA.) And عَرَضْتُ العَسَلَ عَلَى النَّارِ *I cooked the honey* [*upon the fire*] to separate it from the wax. (Mṣb.) [And عَرَضَ نَفْسَهُ لِلْهَلَاكِ *He exposed himself to destruction.*] — عَرْضٌ also signifies The *bringing* a man *before a judge, and accusing* him. (IAạr, in TA, art. عقب.) [And The *presenting,* or *addressing,* a petition, &c., with عَلَى or لِ before the word signifying the person to whom it is presented or addressed.] — One says also, مَا يَعْرِضُكَ لِفُلَانٍ, (Ṣ, [so in two copies,] and O,) or مَا يَعْرُضُكَ, (L, TA,) with fet-ḥ to the ى and ḍamm to the ر, (L,) the verb being coordinate to نَصَرَ: (TA:) [app. meaning *What causeth thee to present thyself to such a one?*]: Yaạḳoob disallows one's saying ↓ مَا يُعَرِّضُكَ لِفُلَانٍ, with teshdeed. (Ṣ, O, TA.) [But the latter of these two verbs has a signification nearly allied to that which is here assigned to the former, and exactly agreeing with one mentioned before. See 2.] — عَرَضَ الجُنْدَ, (Ṣ, Mṣb,) and عَرَضَ العَيْنِ, (Ṣ, O,) or عَرْضَ عَيْنٍ, (A, Ḳ, B, except that in the A and B we find الجَيْشَ instead of الجند,) aor. ـِ, (Mṣb,) inf. n. عَرْضٌ, (Yoo, Ṣ,) *He made the army,* or *body of soldiers, to pass by him, and examined their state,* (Ṣ, O, Ḳ,) *what it was:* (Ṣ, O:) [i. e. *he reviewed them:*] or *he made them to pass before him in review, that he might know who was absent and who was present:* (A, B:) or *he caused them to come forth, and examined them, that he might know them:* (Mṣb:) and you say also, ↓ اعترضهم, (Ṣ, O, Ḳ,) meaning [the same, or] *he made them to pass by him, or before him, and examined them, one by one,* (Ḳ, TA,) *to see who were absent from those who were present.* (TA.) You say also, ↓ اعترض المَتَاعَ وَنَحْوَهُ and اعترضهُ ↓ عَلَى عَيْنِهِ [*He examined the commodity, and the like thereof, having it displayed before his eye*]. (Th.) [See also عَرْضٌ.] — عَرَضْتُ الكِتَابَ, (Ṣ, O, Mṣb,) aor. ـِ, inf. n. عَرْضٌ, (Mṣb,) *I read,* or *recited, the writing,* or *book:* (O, TA: [in the Ṣ it is unexplained, but immediately followed by عَرَضْتُ الجُنْدَ عَرْضَ العَيْنِ:]) or *I recited it by heart,* or *memory.* (Mṣb.) = عَرَضَ عِرْضَهُ, aor. ـِ; (TA;) and ↓ اعترضهُ; (A, TA;) [perhaps originally signified *He examined his grounds of pretension to respect,* or *the like:* and then became used to express a frequent consequence of doing so; i. e.] *he spoke evil of him; reviled him; detracted from his reputation:* (A, TA:) or *he corresponded to him,* or *equalled him, in grounds of pretension to respect:* (TA:) [the former seems to be the more probable of the two meanings; for it is said that] ↓ اعترض فُلَانًا signifies *he spoke evil of such a one; reviled him; detracted from his reputation;* (Lth, Ṣ, O, Ḳ;) *and annoyed him.* (Lth, TA.) = عَرَضَ الشَّىْءَ, (Ḳ,) aor. ـِ, inf. n. عَرْضٌ, (TA,) *He hit the side* (عُرْض) *of the thing.* (Ḳ.) = عَرَضَ العُودَ عَلَى الإِنَآءِ, (Ṣ, O, Mṣb, Ḳ,) and السَّيْفَ عَلَى فَخِذِهِ, (Ṣ, O, Ḳ,) aor. ـُ and ـِ, (Ṣ, O, Mṣb, Ḳ,) in both phrases, (O, Ḳ,) [J says, in the Ṣ, app. referring, not, as SM thinks, to the latter of the two phrases, but to the meaning, "this, only, with ḍamm,"] *He put the stick breadthwise, across, athwart,* or *crosswise,* (مَعْرُوضًا, TA, or بِالعَرْضِ, Mṣb, TA, both meaning the same, TA,) *upon the vessel,* (Mṣb, TA,) [and so *the sword upon his thigh:* and ↓ عرّضهُ signifies the same.] — عَرَضَ الرُّمْحَ, aor. ـِ, [and probably ـُ also,] inf. n. عَرْضٌ; and ↓ عرّضهُ, inf. n. تَعْرِيضٌ; (TA;) *He turned,* or *placed, the spear sideways; contr. of* سَدَّدَهُ. (Ṣ, in art. سد, relating to the former verb; and L, in the same art., relating to the latter verb.) — عَرَضَ الرَّامِى القَوْسَ, inf. n. عَرْضٌ, *The archer laid the bow upon its side on the ground,* and then shot with it. (TA.) — The saying of Aboo-Kebeer El-Hudhalee, cited, but not expl., by Th,

فَعَرَضْتُهُ فِى سَاقِ أَسْمَنِهَا

is thought by ISd to mean *And I made its* (the sword's) *breadth to become concealed in the thigh of the fattest of them.* (TA.) = عَرَضَهُ *He fed him:* (Fr, TA:) [or *he offered,* or *presented, to him food:* for] عُرِضُوا signifies *They were fed:* and *they had food offered,* or *presented, to them.* (L, TA.) [See also 2, in the last quarter.] —

عَرَّضَ الحَوْضَ and القِرْبَةَ *He filled the watering-trough* and *the water-skin.* (Ḳ.) — عَرَّضَ الشَّوْكَ: see 8, near the end. — عَرَضَ بَعِيرَهُ, inf. n. عَرْضٌ, *He branded his camel with the mark called* عِرَاض; (Ṣ;) and so ▾ عَرَّضَهُ: (Ṣ, TA:) and عُرِضَ البَعِيرُ, inf. n. as above, *The camel was branded with that mark.* (Ḳ.) — عَرَضْتُهُ, (Ḳ,) aor. ـِ, (TA,) inf. n. عَرْضٌ, (Ḳ, TA,) *I defrauded,* or *deceived, him* in selling. (Ḳ.) — عُرِضَ, (Ḳ,) or عُرِضَ لَهُ, (A, TA,) inf. n. عَرْضٌ, (Ḳ,) *He was,* or *became, mad,* or *insane,* or *possessed by jinn* or *by a jinnee:* (A, Ḳ:) or *he was,* or *became, affected, by a touch,* or *stroke, from the jinn.* (TA.)

2. عرّضهُ, inf. n. تَعْرِيضٌ, *He made it* (a thing) *broad,* or *wide;* (Ṣ, Ḳ;) as also ▾ اعرضهُ, (Lth, Ṣ, Ḳ,) inf. n. إِعْرَاضٌ. (TA.) — See also 1, near the end, in three places. — تَعْرِيضٌ also signifies *The speaking obliquely, indirectly, obscurely, ambiguously,* or *equivocally; contr. of* تَصْرِيحٌ; (Ṣ, Mgh, Mṣb, Ḳ;) *as when thou askest a man, "Hast thou seen such a one?" and he, having seen him, and disliking to lie, answers, "Verily such a one is seen:"* (Mṣb:) or the *making a phrase,* or *the like, to convey an allusion,* or *an indication not expressly mentioned therein; as when you say "How foul is niggardliness!" alluding to such a one's being a niggard* (تُعَرِّضُ بِأَنَّهُ بَخِيلٌ): differing from كِنَايَةٌ, which is the mentioning of the consequence and meaning that of which it is the consequence; as when you say "Such a one has a long suspensory cord to his sword, and has many ashes of the cooking-pot;" meaning that he is tall of stature, and one who entertains many guests: (Mgh:) [but many hold these two words to be identical in meaning.] You say, عَرَّضْتُ لِفُلَانٍ and بِفُلَانٍ, i. e. *I said something* [*in the manner explained above*], *meaning such a one.* (Ṣ, Mṣb.) [See also an ex. voce حَفَلَ.] 'Omar defined [or rather explained] التَّعْرِيضُ بِالفَاحِشَةِ [*The making an allusion to that which is foul,* or *obscene*] by the instance of a man saying to another "My father is not an adulterer, nor is my mother an adulteress." (O, TA.) Or, accord. to the early authorities, عرّض signifies *He used a phrase susceptible of different meanings,* or *an equivocal phrase, by which the hearer understood a meaning different from that which he* (*the speaker*) *intended:* or, accord. to the later authorities, as Et-Teftezánee, *he mentioned a thing by a proper or tropical or metonymical expression, to signify some other thing, which he did not mention;* as when one says, "I heard him whom thou hatest praying for thee, and making good mention of thee;" meaning in his praying for the Muslims in general. (El-Munáwee, in explaining the trad. إِنَّ فِى المَعَارِيضِ الخ, which see below, voce مِعْرَاضٌ.) تعريض with respect to the demanding of a woman in marriage in [the period of] her عِدَّة, [during which she may not contract a new marriage,] is the using language which resembles a demand of her in marriage, but does not plainly express it; as the saying to her "Verily thou art beautiful," or "Verily there is a desire for thee," or "Verily women are of the things that I need:" and تعريض is sometimes made by the quoting of proverbs, and by the introducing of enigmas in one's speech. (TA.) [When followed by عَلَى, it signifies The *making an indirect objection* against a person or saying &c.] — Also عرّض, (Ṣ, O,) inf. n. as above, (Ḳ,) *He wrote indistinctly;* (Ṣ, O, Ḳ;) *not making the letters distinct, nor the handwriting rightly formed* or *disposed.* (TA.) — تَعْرِيضٌ also signifies The *making* a thing *to be exposed* [or *liable*] to another thing. (Ḳ. [It is there expl., with the article ال prefixed to it, by the words أَنْ يَجْعَلَ الشَّىْءَ عَرْضًا ▾, or عُرْضًا ▾ لِلشَّىْءِ, accord. to different copies; the latter (which see, last sentence but one,) app. the right reading; meaning مَعْرُوضًا, whichever be the right; for an inf. n. may be used in the sense of a pass. part. n.; and many a word of the measure فُعْلٌ is used in that sense, as, for instance, خُبْطٌ and نُفْضٌ and هُدْمٌ. That I have rightly rendered the above-mentioned explanation in the Ḳ is indicated by what here immediately follows.]) Hence the trad. مَا عَظُمَتْ نِعْمَةُ اللّٰهِ عَلَى عَبْدٍ إِلَّا عَظُمَتْ مَؤُونَةُ النَّاسِ عَلَيْهِ فَمَنْ لَمْ يَحْتَمِلْ تِلْكَ المَؤُونَةَ فَقَدْ عَرَّضَ تِلْكَ النِّعْمَةَ لِلزَّوَالِ [*The blessing of God upon a servant,* or *man, hath not become great but the burden of* other *men upon him hath become great; and he who doth not take upon himself that burden causeth that blessing to be exposed to cessation*]. (O, TA.) You also say, عَرَّضْتُ فُلَانًا لِكَذَا فَتَعَرَّضَ ▾ هُوَ لَهُ [*I caused such a one to expose himself,* or *I exposed him, to such a thing, and he exposed himself,* or *became exposed, to it*], (Ṣ, O,*) i. e. جَعَلْتُهُ عَرَضًا ▾ لِكَذَا. (O.) See also 1, last quarter. — Also The *giving a thing in exchange for, as an equivalent for,* or *in the place of, another thing.* (TA.) — And The *act of bartering,* or *selling, a commodity for a like commodity.* (Ḳ,* TA.) See 3, in two places. — And The *giving what is termed an* عُرَاضَة: (TA:) and the *feeding with what is so termed:* (Ḳ:) or the *giving food of what is so termed.* (Ṣ.) [See also 1, near the end.] It is said in a trad., respecting a company of travelling merchants making presents to Moḥammad and Aboo-Bekr, عَرَّضُوهُمَا ثِيَابًا بِيضًا *They gave to both of them white garments,* or *pieces of cloth.* (L.) And you say, عَرَّضُوهُمْ مَحْضًا *They gave them to drink* [*unmixed*] *milk.* (TA.) And عَرِّضُونَا *Give ye to us food of your* عُرَاضَة; *your wheat,* or *corn, which ye have brought.* (Ṣ, TA.) — عرّض المَاشِيَةَ, inf. n. تَعْرِيضٌ, *He made the cattle to have such pasturage as rendered them in no need of being fed with fodder.* (TA.) — عرّض, (IAạr, O,) inf. n. تَعْرِيضٌ (Ḳ,) also signifies *He became possessed of* عَارِضَة [i. e. *courage,* or *courage and energy*], (IAạr, O, Ḳ,) *and strength,* or *power,* (IAạr, O,) *and a faculty of speech,* (IAạr, O, Ḳ,) or, as in the Tekmileh, *and power of speech.* (TA.) — And *He kept continually to the eating of* عِرْضَان, (O,* Ḳ, TA, [in the O عِرَاض,]) pl. of عَرِيضٌ. (TA.) — See also 4, last sentence.

3. [عارضهُ has two contr. significations, which are unequivocally expressed by saying عارضهُ بِالوِفَاقِ and بِالخِلَافِ. (See عَانَدَهُ.) Thus one says,] عارضهُ, (Mṣb,) inf. n. مُعَارَضَةٌ, (TA,) *He opposed him* [*being opposed by him*]. (Kull p. 342.) — And [*He vied, competed,* or *contended for superiority, with him; emulated, rivalled,* or *imitated, him;*] *he did like as he* (the latter) *did.* (Mṣb, TA.) You say also, عَارَضْتُهُ بِمِثْلِ مَا صَنَعَ, (Ṣ, O,) or بِمِثْلِ صَنِيعِهِ, (Ḳ,) *I did to him like as he did:* (Ṣ, O, Ḳ:) whence المُعَارَضَة [in trafficking, as will be seen below]: as though the breadth (عَرْض) of the action of the one were like the breadth of the action of the other. (O, Ḳ.) And عارضهُ بِمَا صَنَعَهُ *He requited him for that which he did.* (L.) — [Hence] مُعَارَضَةٌ also signifies The *selling a commodity for another commodity; exchanging it for another;* as also عَرْضٌ: (TA:) and [in like manner] ▾ تَعْرِيضٌ, the *act of bartering,* or *selling a commodity for a like commodity.* (Ḳ,* TA.) You say, عارض بِسِلْعَتِهِ; and ▾ عَرَّضَ بِهَا, (Ḳ, TA,) aor. ـِ, inf. n. عَرْضٌ; (TA;) *He exchanged his commodity; giving one commodity and taking another:* (TA:) and ▾ عَرَضَ مَتَاعَهُ *he sold his commodity for another commodity.* (TḲ.) Also عارضهُ بِالبَيْعِ (M and L in art. بدل) and بَاعَهُ مُعَارَضَةً (Ṣ and Ḳ in that art.) [*He bartered,* or *exchanged commodities, with him*]. And ▾ أَخَذْتُ هٰذِهِ السِّلْعَةَ عَرْضًا *I took this commodity giving another in exchange for it.* (TA.) And when persons demand blood of other persons, and they [the latter] do not retaliate for them, they [the latter] say, نَحْنُ نُعَرِّضُ مِنْهُ [*We will give a compensation for it*]: and they [the former] accept (اعترضوا) the bloodwit. (L.) — You say also, عَارَضْتُهُ فِى البَيْعِ فَعَرَضْتُهُ [*I vied with him in endeavouring to defraud,* or *deceive, in selling,* or *buying,*] *and I defrauded,* or *deceived, him therein.* (Ḳ,* TA.) And عارضهُ بِالمَجْدِ [*He vied,* or *competed,* or *contended, with him,* or *emulated him,* or *rivalled him, in glory,* or *honour,* &c.]: (L and Ḳ in art. مجد:) and in like manner عارضهُ بِالفَخْرِ. (Ḳ in art. فخر.) See 6. — عارضهُ, (O, Ḳ,) or عارضهُ فِى المَسِيرِ (Ṣ,) or فِى السَّيْرِ, (A,) *He went along over against him;* or *on the opposite side to him;* (Ṣ, A, O, Ḳ;) *in a corresponding manner;* (TA;) [*each taking the side opposite to the other.*] — [Hence, عارضهُ as signifying *It* (a tract &c.) *lay over against him.* Also as *syn. with* اعرض عَنْهُ.] See 4. — [Hence also,] عارض, (Ṣ, O, Ḳ,) inf. n. مُعَارَضَةٌ, (TA,) *He took to one side* (Ṣ, O, Ḳ*) *of the way,* or *ways,* (accord. to different copies of the Ḳ,) *while another took to another way, so that they both met.* (TA. [See 3 in arts. خزم and زور.]) El-Ba'eeth says,

مَدَحْنَا لَهَا رَوْقَ الشَّبَابِ فَعَارَضَتْ
جَنَابَ الصِّبَا فِى كَاتِمِ السِّرِّ أَعْجَمَا

[cited in the Ṣ, voce رَيِّق, but with رَيِّقَ, in the place of رَوْقَ, and there ascribed to Lebeed,] meaning, accord. to ISk, [*We praised to her the first part of youth, and thereupon*] *she took to the side of* الصبا [or *youthful foolishness, and amorous dalliance*], or, as another says, *she entered with us into it, in a manner not open, but making it appear to us that she was entering with us;* جناب الصبا meaning جَنْبَهُ. (TA.) — عارض الجِنَازَةَ *He came to the bier, or the bier conveying the corpse, intermediately* (مُعْتَرِضًا), *in a part of the way, not following it from the abode of the deceased:* (O, Ḳ, TA:) said of Mohammad, in a trad. respecting the funeral of Aboo-Tálib. (O, TA.) — عارض المَرْأَةَ, inf. n. مُعَارَضَةٌ and عِرَاضٌ, *He came in to the woman* [*indirectly,* or] *unlawfully;* (Sgh, Ḳ, TA;) i. e. *without marriage and without possession* [*of her as his slave*]. (Sgh, TA.) Hence the saying, جَآءَتْ بِوَلَدٍ عَنْ عِرَاضٍ and مُعَارَضَةٍ *She brought forth a child in consequence of a man's having so come in to her:* (Ḳ:) or *a child whose father was unknown.* (A, O, TA.) [Hence also,] اِبْنُ مُعَارَضَةٍ i. q. سَفِيحٌ; (O, Ḳ;) i. e. *A son the offspring of fornication.* (O, TA.) — الجَوْزَآءُ تَمُرُّ عَلَى جَنْبٍ وَتُعَارِضُ النُّجُومَ, inf. n. مُعَارَضَةٌ, [*Orion passes along towards one side, and is oblique in its course with respect to the* other *stars;*] i. e. it is not direct [in the disposition of its stars, particularly of the three conspicuous stars of the belt, with respect to its course] in the sky. (Aṣ, Ṣ, O.) [See also 5.] — عارض الرِّيحَ, said of a camel, (TA,) [*He turned his side to the wind;*] *he did not face the wind nor turn his back to it.* (A, TA.) — نَظَرَ إِلَيْهِ مُعَارَضَةً *He looked at him, or towards him, sideways,* or *obliquely.* (A, TA.) You say also, نَظَرَ عَنْ مُعَارَضَةٍ [*He looked sideways,* or *obliquely*]. (TA in art. خزر.) And you say of a she-camel, تَمْشِى مُعَارَضَةً لِلنَّشَاطِ [*She goes obliquely by reason of briskness, liveliness, or sprightliness*]. (Ṣ, Ḳ.*) [See again 5, latter half.]) — عارض الشَّىْءَ بِالشَّىْءِ *He compared the thing with the thing.* (Mṣb.) You say, عارض الكِتَابَ, (Ṣ, O, Ḳ,) inf. n. مُعَارَضَةٌ and عِرَاضٌ, (TA,) *He compared,* or *collated, the writing,* or *book,* (Ṣ, O, Ḳ,) بِكِتَابٍ آخَرَ *with another writing, or book.* (Ṣ,* O,* TA.) And كَتَبَ كِتَابًا عَنْ مُعَارَضَةٍ [*He copied,* or *transcribed, the writing, or book*]. (Ḳ in art. نسخ.) — And المُعَارَضَةُ is *syn. with* المُدَارَسَةُ [probably as meaning *The reading,* or *studying, with another*]. (TA.) = ضَرَبَ النَّاقَةَ عِرَاضًا [*He covered the she-camel agreeably with her desire*] is said when the stallion is offered to her, and if she desire he covers her, but otherwise he does not: (Ṣ, O, TA:) in the Ḳ it is said, if he desire her; which is wrong: (TA:) this is because of her generous quality. (Ṣ, O, TA.) — And لَقِحَتْ عِرَاضًا *She* (a camel) *conceived by a stallion, she not being of the camels among which he was sent.* (AO, TA.) — See also 3, near the end.

4. اعرض: see 1, first sentence; and in thirteen places after that, as far as the break after the words "grant thou access." — Also *He went wide* (Ṣ, O, Mṣb, Ḳ) *and long;* (Ṣ, O, Ḳ;) فِى الشَّىْءِ [*in the thing*]; (Mṣb;) and فِى المَكَارِمِ † [*in generous actions*]. (TA.) — اعرض عَنْهُ, (Ṣ,* O,* Mṣb, Ḳ,) inf. n. إِعْرَاضٌ, (Ṣ, O,) *He turned away from, avoided, shunned, and left, it;* (Ṣ, O, Mṣb, Ḳ;) lit. *he took a side* (عُرْضًا i. e. جَانِبًا) *other than the side in which it was:* (Mṣb:) or *he turned his back upon it:* (IAth, TA:) and [in like manner] ↓ عارضهُ *he turned aside,* or *away, from him; avoided him; shunned him;* (Ṣ, O, Ḳ;) lit. *he became aside with respect to him.* (TA.) = اعرضهُ: see 2, first signification. — أَعْرَضَتْ بِوُلْدِهَا *She* (a woman) *brought forth her children broad* [*in make*]; expl. by the words وَلَدَتْهُمْ عِرَاضًا; (Ṣ, O, Ḳ;) [not meaning عَنْ عِرَاضٍ, (see 3,) as Freytag, deviating from Golius, has understood it; unless SM be in error; for he says that] the last word in this explanation is pl. of عَرِيضٌ. (TA.) — اعرض المَسْأَلَةَ *He put,* or *expressed, the question broadly;* (Mgh;) *widely;* (Mgh, TA;) *largely.* (TA.) — اعرض النَّاقَةَ عَلَى الحَوْضِ: see عَرَضَ, latter half. — اعرض العِرْضَانَ *He put for sale the* عرضان [pl. of عَرِيضٌ, q. v.]. (O.) — And (O) *He castrated the* عرضان. (Ṣ, IḲṭṭ, O.) — [And app. *He circumcized* a boy: or so ↓ عرّض: see مُعَرَّضٌ.]

5. تعرّض: see عَرَضَ, near the beginning, where these two verbs, and اعرض and اعترض, are said to be used as syn.; [app. as meaning *It showed, presented,* or *offered, itself,* to a person; lit. *it showed,* or *presented, its breadth,* or *width;* or, as تعرّض is expl. in the EM p. 19, *it showed its* عُرْض, i. e. *side:* this, or *it,* or *he, presented,* or *offered,* or *exposed, its,* or *his, side,* seems to be the primary signification of تعرّض, and of اعترض, as well as of عَرَضَ; and is of frequent occurrence: and all (as mentioned voce عَرَضَ) signify also *he obtruded himself* in an affair; *interfered* therein.] — [Hence,] تعرّض لَهُ *He opposed himself to him; he offered opposition to him;* or *he attacked him;* said of a man, and of a beast of prey, or noxious reptile, and the like; as also ↓ عَرَضَ and ↓ اعترض: this signification also is of frequent occurrence. (The lexicons passim.) — [Hence also,] *He addressed,* or *applied,* or *directed, himself,* or *his regard,* or *attention,* or *mind, to him,* or *it;* [as though he set himself over against the object to which the verb relates;] syn. تَصَدَّى. (Lth, Lḥ, Ṣ, O, Mṣb, Ḳ.) So in the saying, تعرّض لِمَعْرُوفِهِمْ and مَعْرُوفَهُمْ [*He addressed himself, &c., presented himself, betook himself, advanced, came forward,* or *went forward,* or *attempted, to obtain their favour,* or *bounty*]: and تعرّض لِلْمَعْرُوفِ and المَعْرُوفَ [*He addressed himself, &c., to obtain favour,* or *bounty;* and] *he sought,* or *demanded, it:* (Aẑ, Mṣb:) and [so] ↓ اعترض للمعروف. (Mṣb in art. عو. [See also اعترض لَهُ.]) So too in the saying, تَعَرَّضُوا لِنَفَحَاتِ رَحْمَةِ ٱللّٰهِ [*Address ye yourselves, &c., to become objects of the effusions of the mercy of God*]; (O, Ḳ, TA;) occurring in a trad. (TA.) And hence the saying, تعرّض فِى شَهَادَتِهِ لِكَذَا *He addressed himself, &c.,* (تَصَدَّى,) *in his testimony, to the mention of such a thing.* (Mṣb.) It is likewise syn. with تَصَدَّى in the saying, تعرّض لِى فُلَانٌ بِمَكْرُوهٍ [*Such a one addressed himself, &c.,* or *attempted, to do me an abominable,* or *evil, action;* or *opposed himself to me with an abominable,* or *evil, action*]. (Lth.) [In like manner also you say,] يَتَعَرَّضُ لِلنَّاسِ بِالشَّرِّ [*He addresses himself, &c., to do to men evil;* or *he opposes himself to men with evil* or *mischief*]. (Ṣ, Ḳ.) And مَا تَعَرَّضْتُ لَهُ بِسُوْءٍ [*I did not address myself,* or *have not addressed myself, &c., to do to him evil*]: and ↓ مَا عَرَضْتُ and ↓ مَا عَرَضْتُ are said to signify the same. (Mṣb.) [See 1.] You say also, تَعَرَّضْتُ أَسْأَلُهُمْ [*I addressed myself, &c., to ask them*]. (Ṣ, O.*) And جَآءَ فُلَانٌ يَتَعَرَّضُ, and يَتَضَرَّعُ, *Such a one came asking,* or *petitioning,* to another, *for a thing that he wanted.* (Fr, in Ṣ, art. ضرع.) — And تعرّض الرِّفَاقَ *He asked the companies of travellers for what are termed* عُرَاضَات [pl. of عُرَاضَةٌ, q. v.]. (TA.) — تعرّض لِكَذَا [also signifies *He exposed himself,* or *became exposed, to such a thing*]. (Ṣ.) See 2, latter portion. — Also تعرّض, [from عُرْضٌ,] *He,* or *it, turned aside; turned from the right course* or *direction;* syn. تَعَوَّجَ; (Ṣ, Ḳ, TA;) and زَاغَ: (TA:) *his,* or *its, course,* or *march, was,* or *became, indirect,* or *oblique.* (L, TA.) You say, تعرّض الجَمَلُ فِى الجَبَلِ *The camel went to the right and left,* [*in,* or *upon, the mountain,*] on account of the difficulty of the road, or way. (Ṣ, O, Ḳ.) And تَعَرَّضَتِ الإِبِلُ المَدَارِجَ *The camels went along the routes* (فِى المَدَارِجِ) [المدارج being in the accus. case because فى is understood, not that the verb is trans.] *to the right and left;* (A;) i. e., *alternately to the right and left.* (T in art. ثنى.) [See a verse cited voce تَصَدَّفَ, and its explanation.] Dhu-l-Bijádeyn, being guide to the Apostle, addressing his she-camel, said,

تَعَرَّضِى مَدَارِجًا وَسُومِى
تَعَرُّضَ الجَوْزَآءِ لِلنُّجُومِ
هٰذَا أَبُو القَاسِمِ فَاسْتَقِيمِى

(Ṣ, O) *Go thou along routes to the right and left, avoiding the rugged acclivities,* [*and continue thy course,* or as expl. in the TA, art. سوم, *pass along quickly,*] (TA,) *like as* الجوزاء [*Orion*] *passes along* in the sky *obliquely,* or *indirectly,* in the disposition of its stars [*with respect to the* other *stars:* (see 3, towards the end:) *this is Abu-l-Kásim; therefore go thou right*]. (IAth, TA.) — تعرّض الفَرَسُ فِى رَسَنِهِ i. q. اعترض, q. v. (TA.) — You say also, of a camel, ↓ يَعْتَرِضُ فِى سَيْرِهِ [*He inclines towards one side, in his march,* or *course;* or *goes obliquely,* or *inclining towards one side*]. (Ḳ: and so in one copy of the Ṣ: in another copy of the Ṣ, يَتَعَرَّضُ. [See also 3, last quarter.]) — تعرّض also signifies *It* (a thing) *became infected, vitiated,* or *corrupted;* and in this sense it is said of love: (TA:) [as though it turned from the right course, or direction; a signification mentioned before; and thus it is expl. in the Ṣ, as occurring in the phrase تعرّض وَصْلُهُ, in the Mo'allakah of Lebeed; or, thus used, it signifies] *it* (a person's attachment to another) *became altered*, so as to cease. (EM p. 149.)

6. تعارضوا *They opposed each other.* (Ibn-Maaroof, in Golius. [The verb is very often used in this sense.]) — *They fought*, or *combated, each other.* (MA.) — *They did each like as the other did; they imitated each other: they vied, competed*, or *contended, each with the other; they emulated*, or *rivalled, each other:* (TA in art. برى:) syn. تَبَارَيَا. (Ḳ in that art.)

8. اعترض: see عَرَضَ, near the beginning, where these two verbs and اعرض and تعرّض, are said to be used as syn., app. in the senses expl. there and in the beginning of 5. — [Hence,] اعترض عَلَيْهِ *He opposed, resisted*, or *withstood, him*, or *it*; syn. اِمْتَنَعَ. (MA.) [See 1 in art. شنف, in two places.] — See also 5, second sentence. — And see from عَرَضَ لَهُ as signifying "it happened to him" as far as the end of the sentence explaining اعترض الشَّىْءُ دُونَ الشَّىْءِ. اعترض signifies [*It lay*, or *extended, breadthwise, across, transversely, athwart, sideways, obliquely*, or *horizontally:* or *so as to present an obstacle:* or *so intervened in any manner*; as shown in the part last referred to, above: or rather it has both of these meanings; and in the former sense it is used, in the TA, art. حر, in describing the direction of an asterism, opposed to اِنْتَصَبَ: or, in other words,] *it* (a thing, Ṣ) *became*, (Ḳ,) or *became an obstacle*, (صَارَ عَارِضًا, Ṣ, O,) *like a piece of wood lying across*, or *athwart*, or *obliquely*, (مُعْتَرِضَة,) *in a channel of running water*, (Ṣ, O, Ḳ,) or *a road*, (O, L,) and *the like, preventing persons from passing along it.* (L.) It is also said [of a collection of clouds appearing, or presenting itself, or extending sideways, or stretching along in the horizon like a mountain; see عَارِضٌ: and] of a building, or other thing, such as a trunk of a palm-tree, or a mountain, lying in a road: and as this prevents the passengers from passing along the road, it is used as signifying *He*, or *it, prevented*, or *hindered:* (O, Ḳ:) it is quasi-pass. of عَرَضَهُ. (Ḳ,* TA.) [And hence,] أُعْتُرِضَ عَنْ اَمْرَأَتِهِ, (O, TA,) not اِعْتَرَضَ, as the Ḳ seems to indicate, (TA,) *He was prevented from going in to his wife, by an obstacle that befell him, arising from the jinn*, or *genii*, or *from disease:* (O, Ḳ, TA:) occurring in a trad. (TA.) — [Hence,] اِعْتِرَاضٌ which is forbidden in a trad. [respecting horse-racing] signifies A man's *coming intermediately with his horse, in a part of the course, and so entering among the* [*other*] *horses.* (O, L, Ḳ.) [See also عَارِضُ الجِنَازَةِ.] — [And hence,] اعترض الشَّهْرَ *He commenced* [the observances of] *the month not from the beginning thereof.* (Ṣ, O, Ḳ.) — [اعترضت الجُمْلَةُ *The clause intervened parenthetically.*] — اعترض عَلَيْهِ *He interposed* in an argument, or the like; *objecting against him* something, by way of confutation]. And اعترض عَلَى أَحَدٍ مِنْ قَوْلٍ أَوْ فِعْلٍ *He attributed to any one an error in respect of a saying or an action.* (Ḥar p. 687.) — اعترض الفَرَسُ فِي رَسَنِهِ *The horse was perverse, untoward*, or *intractable*, [*in his halter*,] *to his leader;* (Ṣ, A, O, Ḳ;) as also ▼ تعرّض. (TA. [See مُعْتَرِضٌ.]) And اِعْتِرَاضٌ in a man is The *appearing and engaging in what is vain*, or *false, and refusing to obey the truth.* (TA.) — اعترضهُ *He faced him, and advanced towards him:* (Ḥar p. 420:) and اعترض عَرْضَهُ and عَرْضَهُ [has nearly, if not exactly, the same signification]: see عَرَضَ. And اعتراض also signifies The *coming in upon any one:* or *entering upon an affair.* (Ḥar p. 687.) — اعترض لَهُ often means *He presented himself*, or *advanced*, or *came forward, to him:* and *he addressed* or *betook himself*, or *advanced*, or *went forward, to it;* namely, an action; like تعرّض له: see its syns. اِنْبَرَى and تَبَرَّى. — See also 5, second sentence. — اعترض لَهُ بِسَهْمٍ *He advanced towards him with an arrow, and shot at him, and slew him.* (Ṣ, O, Ḳ.) — اعترض لِلْمَعْرُوفِ: see 5. — يَعْتَرِضُ فِي سَيْرِهِ: see 5, near the end. — اعترض *He rode while reviewing the army*, or *body of soldiers*, or *making them to pass by him and examining their state*, (Ṣ, O, Ḳ,) عَلَى الدَّابَّةِ *upon the beast.* (Ṣ, O.) — اعترض الجُنْدُ *The army*, or *body of soldiers, was reviewed:* (Mgh, L:) quasi-pass. of عَرَضَ الجُنْدَ [which signifies the same as the phrase next following]. (O, L, TA.) — اعترض الجُنْدَ: and المَتَاعَ وَنَحْوَهُ and اعترضهُ عَلَى عَيْنِهِ: see عَرَضَ, last quarter. — اعترض عِرْضَهُ: and اعترض فُلَانًا: see عَرَضَ, last quarter. — اعترض البَعِيرَ *He rode the camel while refractory*, or *untractable*, (Ṣ, O, Ḳ,) *as yet.* (Ḳ.) And اعترض العَرُوضَ *He took the untrained she-camel in her untrained state.* (TA. [In the original of this explanation is a mistranscription, which I have rectified in the translation; اخذها for أَخَذَهَا.]) — [Hence, app.,] اعترض فُلَانٌ الشَّىْءَ *Such a one undertook the thing*, or *constrained himself to do it, it being difficult*, or *troublesome*, or *inconvenient.* (IAth.) — اعترض الشَّوْكَ (Ḳ, TA) *He ate the thorns:* and ▼ عَرَضَ الشَّوْكَ, aor. ـِ, inf. n. عَرْضٌ, *he took and ate of the thorns:* both said of a sheep or goat, or rather of a camel: (TA:) and [in like manner] one says of a camel, ▼ عَارِضٌ الشَّجَرَ ذَا الشَّوْكِ بِفِيهِ: and the camel that does so is said to be ذُو عِرَاضٍ. (Ṣ, O, Ḳ.) — See also 10, in five places. — اعترض مِنْهُ [*He accepted an equivalent*, or *a substitute*, or *compensation, for it*]. You say, كَانَ عَلَى فُلَانٍ نَقْدٌ فَأَعْسَرْتُهُ فَاعْتَرَضْتُ مِنْهُ [*Such a one owed a debt of money, and I demanded it of him when it was difficult for him to pay it, and I accepted an equivalent*, &c., *for it*]: and اعترضوا مِنْهُ, referring to blood, when retaliation has been refused, means *they accepted* [قَبِلُوا, for which اقبلوا has been substituted by the copyists in the L and TA,] *the bloodwit* [*as a compensation for it*]. (L.)

10. استعرض: see عَرَضَ; second sentence. — قُذِفَتْ استعرضت النَّاقَةُ بِاللَّحْمِ is like the phrase بِاللَّحْمِ, (O, Ḳ, TA,) meaning *The she-camel became fat and plump.* (TA.) — استعرضهُ *He asked him to show*, or *exhibit, to him what he had.* (Ṣ, TA.) — استعرض الجَارِيَةَ *He asked to show*, or *display, to him the girl* on the occasion of sale. (Mṭr, in Ḥar p. 557.) — استعرضها *He came to her from the direction of her side.* (TA.) — [Hence, استعرضهُ also signifies, and so ▼ اعترضهُ, *He betook himself to him* or *it*, or *he took him* or *it*, or *he acted with respect to him* or *it, without any direct aim, at random*, or *indiscriminately:* and hence the phrases here following.] استعرض النَّاسَ الخَوَارِجُ and ▼ اِعْتَرَضُوهُمْ *The people went forth against the Khárijees not caring whom they slew.* (Mgh.) And لَا بَأْسَ بِأَنْ يَعْتَرِضُوا ▼ مَنْ لَقُوا فَيَقْتُلُوا [*There will be no harm to them*] *in their taking without distinguishing who and whence he is him whom they find, and slaying.* (Mgh.) And يَسْتَعْرِضُ الخَارِجِىُّ النَّاسَ *The Khárijee slays men* (Ṣ, O, Ḳ,* TA) *in any possible manner, and destroys whomsoever he can*, (TA,) *without inquiring respecting the condition of any one*, (Ṣ,* O, Ḳ, TA,) *Muslim or other*, (Ṣ, O, TA,) *and without caring whom he slays.* (TA.) And اِعْتَرِضْهُ ▼ وَاشْتَرِهِ مِمَّنْ وَجَدْتَهُ وَلَا تَسْأَلْ عَمَّنْ عَمِلَهُ [*Take thou it at random*, or *indiscriminately, and buy it of him whom thou findest, and ask not respecting him who made it*]. (Ṣ, Ḳ.) And اِسْتَعْرَضَ يُعْطِى مَنْ أَقْبَلَ وَمَنْ أَدْبَرَ [*He acted indiscriminately, giving to him who advanced and to him who retired*]. (Ṣ.) And اِسْتَعْرِضِ العَرَبَ *Ask thou whom thou wilt of the Arabs* respecting such and such things. (Ṣ.) You say also, of land (أَرْض) in which is herbage, ▼ يَعْتَرِضُهَا and يَسْتَعْرِضُهَا المَالُ [*The camels*, or *the like*,] *depasture it* [app. *at random*] *when traversing it.* (Ḳ.)

عَرْضٌ *Breadth; width; contr. of* طُولٌ; (Ṣ, Mgh, O, Mṣb, Ḳ;) and *i. q.* سَعَةٌ; (Ḳ;) the *mutual distance of the edges* or *sides of a thing:* (Mṣb:) primarily relating to corporeal things, but afterwards used in relation to other things: [see عَرِيضٌ:] (TA:) this word as signifying the contr. of طول is the common source of derivation of the other words of this art., notwithstanding their multitude: (O:) pl. [of pauc.] أَعْرَاضٌ (IAar, TA) and of mult. عُرُوضٌ and عِرَاضٌ. (TA.) It is said in the Ḳur [lvii. 21,] وَجَنَّةٍ عَرْضُهَا كَعَرْضِ السَّمَآءِ وَالأَرْضِ *And a paradise whereof the breadth*, or *width, is like the breadth*, or *width, of the heaven and the earth:* and in iii. 127, [عَرْضُهَا السَّمٰوَاتُ وَالأَرْضُ [*the breadth*, or *width, whereof is as the heavens and the earth*]: and Ibn-'Arafeh observes that when the عَرْض is described as being much, it indicates that the طُول is much, for the latter is more than the former. (O, TA.) You say also, عَرَضَ عَرْضَهُ, and ▼ عُرْضَهُ, *He went towards him:* [lit. *towards his breadth*, and *his side*.] (Ḳ.) And ذَهَبَ عَرْضًا وَطُولًا [*He went wide and long*]; (Ṣ, Mṣb,* Ḳ;) فِى الشَّىْءِ [*in the thing*]; (Mṣb;) and فِى المَكَارِمِ [*in generous actions*]. (TA.) And قَطَعَهُ عَرْضًا [*He* *cut it breadthwise*, or *across*, or *crosswise*]. (Ṣ in art. قط, &c.) And قَطَعَ الوَادِىَ عَرْضًا [*He crossed the valley*]; (Ṣ and Ḳ in art. جزع &c.;) and in like manner, الأَرْضَ [*the land*]. (Ḳ in that art.) And وَضَعَ العُودَ عَلَى الإِنَآءِ بِالعَرْضِ [*He put the stick upon the vessel breadthwise*, or *across*, or *crosswise*]; (Mṣb;) *i. q.* مَعْرُوضًا. (TA.) — [In geography, The *latitude* of a place.] — The *middle*, or *midst*, of a thing: or عُرْضُ الشَّىْءِ signifies *the thing itself*. (TA.) See also عُرْض, former half, and in three places towards the end. ═ *A mountain*; (Ṣ, Ḳ;) as also ▼ عَارِض: (Ṣ, O, Ḳ:) or the former, the *lowest part*, or *base*, (سَفْح,) *thereof*; (Ṣ, Ḳ;) as also ▼ عُرْض: (O, Ḳ:) and (so in the Ṣ, but in the Ḳ "or") the *side thereof*; (Ṣ, Ḳ;) as also ▼ عُرْض: (TA:) or the *place whence*, or *whereby*, (مِنْهُ,) *a mountain is ascended*: (Ḳ:) and ▼ عَارِض, *a lofty mountain*: (TA:) pl. of the first, أَعْرَاض and عُرُوض. (Ṣ, TA.) ═ *A collection of clouds*: (Ḳ:) or *a collection of clouds that obstructs the horizon*: (Ṣ, Ḳ:) [see also عِرْض and عَارِض:] pl. عُروض. (TA.) ═ † *An army*: (O, Ḳ:) or *a great army*: (Ṣ, TA:) and ▼ عِرْض also has the former signification: (Ḳ:) or the latter: (TA:) so called as being likened to a mountain; or to the clouds that obstruct the horizon: (Ṣ, TA:) pl. أَعْرَاض. (TA.) — جَرَادٌ عَرْضٌ † *Numerous locusts*; (Ṣ, O, Ḳ;*) likened to the clouds that obstruct the horizon; (TA;) as also ▼ عِرْض: (Ḳ:) pl. of the former, عُرُوض: (TA:) and ▼ عَارِض also signifies *a multitude of locusts*; (Ṣ, O, TA;) and *of bees*: (TA:) as in the saying, مَرَّ بِنَا عَارِضٌ قَدْ مَلَأَ الأُفُقَ [*There passed by us a multitude of locusts*, or *of bees, which had filled the horizon*]: (Ṣ, O, TA:) so says Aboo-Naṣr Aḥmad Ibn-Ḥátim. (Ṣ, O.) ═ *A valley*. (IDrd, Ḳ.) See also عِرْض. ═ [As inf. n. of عَرُضَ, it occurs in the phrases عَرْضُ الجُنْدِ: see عَرْضَ العَيْنِ and عَرْضَ عَيْنٍ.] You say also, نَظَرَ إِلَيْهِ عَرْضَ عَيْنٍ (Th, A) *He looked at*, or *examined, him*, or *it, having him*, or *it, before his eye*; *i. q.* اعْتَرَضَهُ عَلَى عَيْنِه. (TA.) And رَأَيْتُهُ عَرْضَ عَيْنٍ *I saw him*, or *it*, *obviously*; *nearly*. (TA.) [See also an ex. voce عَيْن.] — [يَوْمُ العَرْضِ is an appellation of *The day of the last judgment*.] ═ *A compensation*; *a substitute*; *a thing that is given or received or put instead* of another thing: so, accord. to some, in the Ḳur iii. 127, quoted above: [but this is strange:] and so in the phrase عَرْضُ هٰذَا الثَّوْبِ كَذَا وَكَذَا [*The compensation*, or *substitute, for this garment*, or *piece of cloth, is such a thing, and such a thing*: but not necessarily; for عرض in this phrase may have the meaning first assigned to it above]. (TA.) See also what next follows. — *A commodity*; or *commodities*, or *goods*; syn. مَتَاع; (Ṣ, O, Mṣb, Ḳ;) as also ▼ عَرَض; accord. to Ḳz; (Ḳ;) which is the *contr.* of عَيْن: (Mgh:) and the former, *anything except silver and gold money*, or *dirhems and deenárs*, (Ṣ, Mṣb, Ḳ,) which are termed عَيْن: (Ṣ, Mṣb:) or *any worldly goods or commodities except silver and gold money*: (Mgh,* O, TA:) but ▼ عَرَض, which see below, has a more comprehensive signification; everything that is termed عَرْض being included in عَرَض, whereas everything that is termed عَرَض is not عَرْض: (TA:) the pl. of عَرْض is عُرُوض, (Mṣb,) which A'Obeyd explains as signifying the *commodities*, or *goods, whereof none are meted in a measure nor weighed, and which are not animals, and do not consist in* عَقَار [or *immoveable property*]. (Ṣ, O, Mṣb.) You say, اشْتَرَيْتُ المَتَاعَ بِعَرْضٍ *I bought the commodity for a commodity like it*. (Ṣ, O.) ═ جَعَلَ الشَّىْءَ عَرْضًا لِلشَّىْءِ, or عُرْضًا, accord. to different copies of the Ḳ: see 2, in the latter half of the paragraph. ═ سَأَلْتُهُ عَرْضَ مَالٍ: see عُرَاضَة. ═ عَرْض also signifies *Madness*; *insanity*; or *possession by jinn*, or *by a jinnee*. (Ḳ, TA.) [See 1, last sentence.] ═ مَضَى عَرْضٌ مِنَ اللَّيْلِ *An hour*, or *a portion, of the night passed*; syn. سَاعَةٌ. (Ḳ,* TA.) ═ See also عَرْض, with the unpointed ص.

عُرْض *A side*; *a lateral*, or *an outward, part*, or *portion*; syn. جَانِبٌ, (Ṣ, Mgh, O, Mṣb, Ḳ,) and نَاحِيَةٌ, (Ṣ, O, Mṣb, Ḳ,) *from whatever direction one comes to it*, (Ṣ, O,) and شِقٌّ: (Ṣ, Mgh:) and so ▼ عِرْض; syn. نَاحِيَة; of anything: (TA:) and ▼ عَارِضَة, or ▼ عَارِض, (accord. to different copies of the Ḳ,) or both; (TA;) syn. نَاحِيَة: (Ḳ, TA:) and ▼ عَرُوض; syn. نَاحِيَة: (Ṣ, A, O, Ḳ:) and ▼ عِرَاض; syn. نَاحِيَة, and شِقٌّ: (Ṣ, O, Ḳ:) [or] this last is pl. of عُرْض; (Ṣgh, Ḳ;) or, accord. to the M, of عَرْض as signifying the contr. of طُول: and أَعْرَاض is pl. [or is another pl.] of عُرْض; and is also pl. of عِرْض in the sense expl. above. (TA.) You say, عُرْضُ السَّيْفِ *The side*, or *flat*, (صَفْح,) *of the sword*. (Ḳ.) And عُرْضَا العُنُقِ *The two sides of the neck*: (Ḳ:) or *each side of the neck*. (TA.) [See also عَارِض.] And عُرْضَا أَنْفِ البَعِيرِ *The beginning of the part of the bone of the camel's nose which slopes downwards, in both its edges*. (Az, TA.) And نَظَرَ إِلَيْهِ بِعُرْضِ وَجْهِهِ *He looked at him with the side of his face* [*turned towards him*]. (Ṣ, O.) And نَظَرَ إِلَيْهِ عَنْ عُرْضٍ and ▼ عُرُضٍ *He looked at him from one side*. (Ṣ, O, Ḳ.*) And خَرَجُوا يَضْرِبُونَ عَنْ عُرْضٍ (Ṣ, O, Ḳ*) *They went forth smiting the people from one side, in whatever manner suited*, (Ṣ, O,) *not caring whom they smote*. (Ṣ, O, Ḳ.) And اضْرِبْ بِهِ عُرْضَ الحَائِطِ *Strike thou with it indiscriminately any part that thou findest of the wall*: (Ṣ, O, Mṣb, TA:) or *the side thereof*. (TA.) And أَلْقِهِ فِى أَىِّ أَعْرَاضِ الدَّارِ شِئْتَ *Throw thou it in any side*, or *quarter, of the house which thou wilt*. (TA.) And خُذْهُ مِنْ عُرْضِ النَّاسِ, and ▼ عُرُضِهِمْ, *Take thou him from any side of the people which thou wilt*. (TA.) And أَوْصَى أَنْ يُنْفَقَ عَلَيْهِ مِنْ عُرْضِ مَالِهِ *He enjoined that he should expend upon him, or it, of any part of his property indiscriminately*. (Mgh.) And فُلَانٌ مِنْ عُرْضِ العَشِيرَةِ *Such a one is of the collateral class of the kinsfolk*, or *tribe*; *not of the main stock thereof*. (Mgh.) And عَرَضَ عُرْضَهُ, *He went towards him*: [lit. *towards his side*.] (Ḳ.) See also عَرْض, near the beginning. And أَخَذَ فِى عَرُوضٍ ▼ مِنَ الطَّرِيقِ (Ṣ,* Ḳ) *He took to one side of the way*. (Ṣ,* TA.) And خُذْ فِى عَرُوضٍ ▼ سِوَى هٰذِهِ *Take thou to a side other than this*. (A.) And أَخَذَ فُلَانٌ فِى عَرُوضٍ ▼ مَا تُعْجِبُنِى (Ṣ, A) *Such a one took to a way and side not pleasing to me*. (Ṣ.) [عَرُوض, it will be observed, is fem.] And سِرْتُ ▼ فِى عِرَاضِهِ *I went along over against him*. (A.) And سِرْنَا فِى عِرَاضِ ▼ القَوْمِ *We went along not facing the people*, or *company of men, but coming to them from their side*. (TA.) And Aboo-Dhueyb says,

أَمِنْكِ بَرْقٌ أَبِيتُ اللَّيْلَ أَرْقُبُهُ
كَأَنَّهُ فِى عِرَاضِ ▼ الشَّامِ مِصْبَاحُ

(Ṣ,* TA,) i. e. [*Is there lightning* proceeding *from thee, which I pass the night watching, as though it were a lamp*] *in the side*, or *region, of Syria?* (Ṣ.) — See also عَرْض, as signifying the "lowest part, or base, of a mountain;" and the "side thereof." [And see شُقّ, last sentence but one.] — The *middle*, or *midst*, of a river or rivulet or the like, (O, Ḳ,) and of the sea, (Ḳ,) and of men or people, and of a story or tradition; and ▼ عَرْض signifies the same, of men or people, &c.: (TA:) and the former, the *main part* of men or people; as also ▼ the latter; and of a story or tradition; (Ḳ;) as also ▼ عِرَاض, (TA, and so in some copies of the Ḳ,) and ▼ عُرَاض. (TA, and so in some copies of the Ḳ.) You say, رَأَيْتُهُ فِى عُرْضِ النَّاسِ *I saw him among the people*: (Ṣ, O:) and some of the Arabs say, رَأَيْتُهُ فِى عَرْضِ ▼ النَّاسِ, meaning فِى عُرْضِ; (Yoo, Ṣ, O, TA;) or meaning *I saw him in the midst of the people*; (TA;) or, as also فِى عُرُضِ ▼ النَّاسِ, *in the middle portions of the people*; or, as some say, *in the surrounding portions of the people*. (Mṣb.) And فُلَانٌ مِنْ عُرْضِ النَّاسِ *Such a one is of the common people*, or *vulgar*. (Ṣ, Ḳ.*) — كُلِ الجُبْنَ عُرْضًا [*Eat thou cheese indiscriminately*; or] *take thou cheese at random*, or *indiscriminately, and buy it of him whom thou findest, not asking respecting him who made it*, (Aṣ, Ṣ, O, Ḳ,) *whether it be of the making of the people of the Scriptures*, or *of the making of the Magians*. (Aṣ, Ṣ, O.) ═ نَاقَةٌ عُرْضُ أَسْفَارٍ: and عُرْضَة: see عُرْضُ هٰذَا البَعِيرِ السَّفَرُ وَالحَجَرُ, last two sentences but one. ═ أَعْرَاضُ الكَلَامِ: see مَعَارِض. [But whether اعراض in this phrase be pl. of عُرْض, or whether it have any sing., I know not.] — See also عَرْض.

عِرْض: see عُرْض, first signification. — Also The *side of a valley*, and *of a* بَلَد [i. e. *country* or *the like*, or *town* or *the like*]: (Ḳ: [in the CḲ, بلد is in the nom. case, which I think a mistake:]) or (as some say, TA) *a part, region, quarter*, or *tract*, (Ḳ, TA,) and the *low ground or land*, (TA,) *of, or pertaining to, either of these:* (Ḳ, TA:) pl. أَعْرَاض. (TA.) — *A valley in which are towns,* or *villages, and waters:* (O, Ḳ:) or *in which are palm-trees:* (Ḳ:) or *a valley containing many palms and other trees:* (TA:) or *any valley in which are trees:* (Ṣ, O:) [see also عُرْض, explained as applied to a valley:] pl. as above, (Ṣ,) and عُرْضَانٌ. (TA.) — أَعْرَاضُ الحِجَازِ *The towns,* or *villages, of El-Ḥijáz:* (Ḳ:) or these, (TA,) or the أَعْرَاض, (Ṣ, O,) are *certain towns,* or *villages,* [*with their territories; i. e. certain provinces,* or *districts;*] *between El-Ḥijáz and El-Yemen:* (Ṣ, O, TA:) and some say that أَعْرَاضُ المَدِينَةِ is applied to *the towns,* or *villages, that are in the valleys of El-Medeeneh:* (TA:) or *the low lands of its towns,* or *villages, where are seed-produce and palm-trees:* so says Sh: (O, TA:) the sing. is عِرْض. (Ḳ.) — And عِرْض, (Ṣ, O,) or أَعْرَاض, (Ḳ,) which is its pl., (TA,) signifies [The *trees called*] أَرَاك (Ṣ, O, Ḳ) *and* أَثْل (Ṣ, O) *and* حَمْض. (Ṣ, O, Ḳ.) = Also *A great cloud,* (Ḳ, TA,) *appearing,* or *presenting itself,* or *intervening,* (يَعْتَرِضُ,) *in the horizon.* (TA.) [See عَرْض and عَارِض, which signify nearly the same.] = *I. q.* عَرْض, q. v., as signifying † *An army:* (Ḳ:) or *a great army:* (TA:) — and as signifying † *Numerous locusts.* (Ḳ.) = *One's self;* syn. نَفْس; (Ṣ, O, Mṣb, Ḳ;) i. e. نَفْسُ رَجُلٍ. (IḲt.) You say, أَكْرَمْتُ عَنْهُ عِرْضِى *I preserved myself from it.* (Ṣ, O.) And فُلَانٌ نَقِىُّ العِرْضِ *Such a one is* [*pure in respect of himself;* or] *free from reproach;* (Ṣ, O;) or *from fault,* or *vice,* or *the like.* (Ṣ, Mṣb.) And in the same sense it occurs in the saying of Abu-d-Dardà, أَقْرِضْ مِنْ عِرْضِكَ لِيَوْمِ فَقْرِكَ [*Lend thou from thyself for the day of thy poverty:* but see art. قرض]: and in other instances. (TA.) — *The body;* syn. جَسَدٌ, (IAạr, Ṣ, O, Ḳ,) or بَدَنٌ: (IḲt, Az:) pl. أَعْرَاضٌ. (Az, Ṣ.) So in the description of the people of Paradise, (Az, Ṣ,) in a trad., (Az,) إِنَّمَا هُوَ عَرَقٌ يَجْرِى مِنْ أَعْرَاضِهِمْ [*It is only sweat which flows from their bodies*]. (Az, Ṣ, O.) — *The skin.* (Ibráheem El-Ḥarbee, O, Ḳ.) — *Any place of the body that sweats:* (O, Ḳ:) so in the trad. cited above: (TA:) or *any part of the body such as the arm-pit and the groin and the like.* (A'Obeyd.) — *The odour of the body,* (Ṣ, O, Ḳ,) and *of other things,* (Ṣ, O,) *whether sweet or foul.* (Ṣ, O, Ḳ.) You say, فُلَانٌ طَيِّبُ العِرْضِ [*Such a one is sweet in respect of odour*], and مُنْتِنُ العِرْضِ [*foul in respect of odour*]; and سِقَآءٌ خَبِيثُ العِرْضِ *a stinking water-skin,* or *milk-skin;* from A'Obeyd. (Ṣ, O.) — *A man's honour,* or *reputation,* (جَانِبُهُ,) *which he preserves from impairment and blame, both as it relates to himself and to his* حَسَب [or *grounds of pretension to respect on account of the honourable deeds or qualities of his ancestors, &c.*]: (IAth, O, Ḳ:) or *whether it relate to himself or to his ancestors or to those of whose affairs the management is incumbent on him:* (Ḳ:) or *a subject of praise,* and *of blame, of a man,* (Abu-l-'Abbás, IAth, O, Ḳ,) *whether it be in himself or in his ancestors or in those of whose affairs the management is incumbent on him:* (IAth:) or *those things by the mention whereof with praise or dispraise a man rises or falls; which may be things whereby he is characterized exclusively of his ancestors; and it may be that his ancestors are mentioned in such a manner that imperfection shall attach to him by reason of the blaming of them:* respecting this there is no disagreement among the lexicologists, except IḲt [whose objection see in what follows]: (Abu-l-'Abbás, O:) or (accord. to some, Ṣ) *grounds of pretension to respect on account of the honourable deeds or qualities of one's ancestors, &c.,* (حَسَبٌ, Ṣ, Mṣb, Ḳ,) *and eminence,* or *nobility,* (شَرَفٌ,) *in which one glories.* (Ḳ.) You say, فُلَانٌ كَرِيمُ العِرْضِ *Such a one is generous,* or *noble, in respect of* حَسَب: and هُوَ ذُو عِرْضٍ *he is a possessor of* حَسَب; and *of* شَرَف. (TA.) — Sometimes, *Ancestors* are meant by it. (A'Obeyd, Ḳ.) Thus you say, شَتَمَ فُلَانٌ عِرْضَ فُلَانٍ, meaning *Such a one spoke evil of the ancestors of such a one.* (A'Obeyd.) And فُلَانٌ جَرِبُ العِرْضِ *Such a one is base,* or *ignoble, in respect of ancestry.* (TA.) IḲt disallows this signification, asserting عِرْض to have no other signification than those of a man's نَفْس and his بَدَن: (O,* TA:) but IAmb says that this is an error; as is shown by the saying of Aboo-Miskeen Ed-Dárimee,

رُبَّ مَهْزُولٍ سَمِينٍ عِرْضُهُ
وَسَمِينِ الجِسْمِ مَهْزُولُ الحَسَبْ

in which عِرْض cannot be syn. with بَدَن and جِسْم, for, were it so, it would involve a contradiction; the meaning being only *Many a person meagre* in respect of his body *is noble* [or *great*] *in respect of his ancestry;* [*and fat in respect of the body, meagre in respect of grounds of pretension to honour on account of the honourable deeds or qualities of his ancestors, &c.:*] and by Moḥammad's using the expression دَمُهُ وَعِرْضُهُ; for if عِرْض were [here] syn. with نَفْس, it had sufficed to say دمه without عرضه. (O, TA.) — Also *A natural disposition that is commended.* (IAth, Ḳ.) — And *A good action.* (TA.) = Also One *who speaks evil of men* (يَعْتَرِضُهُمْ) *falsely;* (O, Ḳ;) applied to a man: and so with ة applied to a woman: (O, Ḳ:*) so too ▼ عِرْضِنٌ applied to a man, and with ة to a woman. (TA.)

عَرَضٌ *A thing that happens to, befalls,* or *occurs to, a man; such as disease, and the like;* (Ṣ, O, Ḳ;) *as disquietude of mind, and a state of distraction of the mind* or *attention:* or *a misfortune, such as death, and disease, and the like:* (TA:) or *an event that happens to a man, whereby he is tried:* (Aṣ:) or *a thing that happens to a man, whereby he is impeded; such as disease,* or *a theft:* (Lḥ:) or *a bane,* or *cause of mischief, that occurs in a thing;* as also ▼ عَارِضٌ: (TA:) [both signify also *an accident of any kind:*] pl. أَعْرَاضٌ. (TA.) — *A thing's befalling,* or *hitting, unexpectedly.* (O, Ḳ. [I follow the reading of the O, which is that of the Ḳ as given in the TA, and of my MS. copy of the Ḳ, أَنْ يُصِيبَ الشَّىْءُ عَلَى غِرَّةٍ; in preference to that in the CḲ, أَنْ تُصِيبَ الشَّىْءَ عَلَى غِرَّةٍ.]) You say, أَصَابَهُ سَهْمُ عَرَضٍ (Ṣ, A, O, Ḳ*) and سَهْمٌ عَرَضٌ, (A, TA,) and حَجَرُ عَرَضٍ (Ṣ, O) and حَجَرٌ عَرَضٌ, (TA,) [*A random arrow, and a random stone,* or] *an arrow,* and *a stone, aimed at another, hit him:* (Ṣ, O, Ḳ:) such as hits, or falls upon, a man without any one's shooting it, or casting it, is not thus termed. (L.) And مَا جَآءَكَ مِنَ الرَّأْىِ عَرَضًا خَيْرٌ مِمَّا جَآءَكَ مُسْتَكْرَهًا, i. e. [*The opinion*] *that comes to thee without consideration,* or *thought,* [*is better than that which comes to thee forced.*] (TA.) And عَلِقْتُهَا عَرَضًا *I became attached to her* (Ṣ, O, Ḳ) *accidentally,* or *unintentionally,* (Ṣ, O,) *in consequence of her presenting herself to me* (ISk, Ṣ, O, Ḳ) *as a thing occurring without my seeking it.* (ISk.) [See an ex., in a verse of 'Antarah, cited in the first paragraph of art. زعم; and another, in a verse of El-Aạshà, cited in the first paragraph of art. علق.] — *A thing that is not permanent:* (Mgh, O, B, Ḳ:) so in the conventional language of the Muslim theologians: (Mgh:) opposed to جَوْهَرٌ: (TA:) or hence metaphorically applied by the Muslim theologians to ‡ *a thing that has not permanence unless in,* or *by, the substance;* [i. e., in the language of old logicians, *an accident; an essential,* and *an accidental* (as meaning *a non-essential*), *property,* or *quality;* or what modern logicians call *a mode;* whether it be, in their language, *an essential mode* or *an accidental mode;* which latter only they term "an accident;"] *as colour, and taste:* (B:) or, in the conventional language of the Muslim theologians (المُتَكَلِّمُون) [expl. in the TA as signifying "the philosophers," from whom, however, they are generally distinguished]), *a thing that subsists in,* or *by, another thing;* (O, Ḳ;) *as colours, and tastes, and smells, and sounds, and powers, and wills:* (O: [and the like is said in the Mṣb:]) or, in philosophy, *a thing that exists in its subject,* or *substance, and ceases therefrom without the latter's becoming impaired or annihilated;* and also *such as does not cease therefrom: the former kind being such as tawniness occasioned by an altered state of the body, and yellowness of complexion, and motion of a thing moving; and the latter kind, such as the blackness of pitch, and of* [*the beads called*] سَبَج, *and of the crow.* (L.) — [Hence, *An appertenance of any kind.* — Hence also,] The *frail goods* (حُطَام) *of the present world* or *state;* (Aṣ, O, Ḳ;) and *what a man acquires thereof:* (Aṣ, O:) [so called as being not permanent:] or *worldly goods* or *commodities,* (AO, Mṣb,) *of whatever kind,* are thus called, with fet-ḥ to the ر: (AO:) and *any property* or *wealth, little or much,* (Ṣ, O, Ḳ,) is thus called, (Ḳ,) or is called عَرَضُ الدُّنْيَا. (Ṣ, O.) See also عَرْض, expl. as signifying "a commodity," or "commodities" or "goods." One says, الدُّنْيَا عَرَضٌ حَاضِرٌ يَأْكُلُ مِنْهَا البَرُّ وَالفَاجِرُ [*The world is a present frail good: the righteous and the unrighteous eat thereof*]: (Ṣ, O, TA:) i. e. it has no permanence: a trad. related by Sheddád Ibn-Ows. (TA.) And in another trad. related by the same, it is said, لَيْسَ الغِنَى عَنْ كَثْرَةِ العَرَضِ إِنَّمَا الغِنَى غِنَى النَّفْسِ [*Richness is not from the abundance of worldly goods: richness is only richness of the soul*]. (O, TA.) One says also, قَدْ فَاتَهُ العَرَضُ, (Yoo, Ṣ, L,) and ▾ العَرْضُ, but the former is the more approved, (L,) [*The property*, &c., (but see another meaning below,) *had escaped him*], which is from عَرَضُ الجُنْدِ, [see قَدْ أَلْقَاهُ] like as one says قَبَضَ قَبْضًا and عَرَضًا, [فِى القَبَضِ: (Yoo, Ṣ:) [which seems to indicate that عَرَضٌ properly signifies مَعْرُوضٌ, like as قَبَضٌ signifies مَقْبُوضٌ.] — *Booty; spoil.* (O, Ḳ.) So in the Ḳur ix. 42: (O:) or it there signifies — *i. q.* مَطْلَبٌ [app. meaning *A thing sought*, or *desired; an object of desire*; rather than *a place where a thing is sought*]. (TA.) — *I. q.* طَمَعٌ [app. meaning *A thing that is eagerly desired*, or *coveted*: and also *eager desire*; or *covetousness*]. (AO, O, Ḳ.) So explained by some as occurring in the saying قَدْ فَاتَهُ العَرَضُ, mentioned above. (TA.) And the following verse is also cited as an ex.,

• مَنْ كَانَ يَرْجُو بَقَآءً لَا نَفَادَ لَهُ •
• فَلَا يَكُنْ عَرَضُ الدُّنْيَا لَهُ شَجَنَا •

[*Whoso hopeth for continuance without cessation, let not the eager desire of worldly goods be to him a cause of anxiety*]. (O, TA.) — *A gift.* (TA.) See also عُرَاضَةٌ. — هُوَ عَلَى عَرَضِ الوُجُودِ signifies عَلَى إِمْكَانِهِ [app. meaning *It is in the condition of possibility of existence*; for على seems to be here used in the sense of فِى, as in some other instances]; from أَعْرَضَ لَهُ meaning "it became within his power," &c. (Mgh.) And one says, هُوَ بِعَرَضِ أَنْ يَضِيعَ [*He is exposed*, or *liable, to perish*]. (Mgh voce ضَيَاعٌ.) — جَعَلَ الشَّىْءَ عَرَضًا لِلشَّىْءِ, or عُرْضًا, accord. to different copies of the Ḳ: see 2, in the latter half of the paragraph, in two places.

عُرُضٌ, (L, TA,) in the Ḳ, erroneously, ▾ عُرْضٌ, (TA,) *A certain manner of going along*, (Ḳ, TA,) *towards one side*, (TA,) *approved in horses, but disapproved in camels.* (Ḳ, TA.) — نَظَرَ إِلَيْهِ عَنْ عُرُضٍ: see عُرْضٌ: — and رَأَيْتُهُ فِى عُرُضِ النَّاسِ: see عُرْضٌ.

عُرْضَةٌ is of the measure فُعْلَةٌ in the sense of the measure مَفْعُولٌ, like قُبْضَةٌ; (Bḍ, ii. 224;) and is applied to *A thing that is set as an obstacle in the way of a thing*: (Bḍ, TA:) and also to *a thing that is exposed to a thing*: (Bḍ:) or *that is set as a butt, like the butt of archers.* (TA.) You say, جَعَلْتُ فُلَانًا عُرْضَةً لِكَذَا, meaning نَصَبْتُهُ لَهُ; (Ṣ, O, Ḳ;*) i. e. *I set such a one as an obstacle to such a thing*: or *as a butt for such a thing.* (TA.) And هُوَ لَهُ دُونَهُ عُرْضَةٌ *He is an obstacle to him intervening in the way of it.* (Ṣ, O.) And فُلَانٌ عُرْضَةٌ لِلنَّاسِ *Such a one is* [*a butt to men*; i. e.] *a person whom men cease not to revile*: (Ṣ, O, Mṣb, Ḳ:) or *a person to whom men address themselves to do evil, and whom they revile.* (Az, TA.) And هُمْ ضُعَفَآءُ عُرْضَةٌ لِكُلِّ مُتَنَاوِلٍ *They are weak persons; persons who offer themselves as a prey to any one who would take them.* (TA.) And it is said in the Ḳur [ii. 224], وَلَا تَجْعَلُوا ٱللّٰهَ عُرْضَةً لِأَيْمَانِكُمْ أَنْ تَبَرُّوا وَتَتَّقُوا وَتُصْلِحُوا بَيْنَ ٱلنَّاسِ, (Ṣ,* &c.,) meaning نَصْبًا; (Ṣ, TA;) admitting the two significations of *an obstacle* and *a butt*: (TA:) i. e. *And make not God an obstacle* between you and that which may bring you near unto God, &c.: (O, Ḳ:) or *make not God an obstacle to the performance of your oaths to be pious* (O, Bḍ) *and to fear God and to make reconciliation between men*: or *make not God an obstacle, because of your oaths, to your being pious* &c.: (Bḍ:) or *make not the swearing by God an obstacle to your being pious* [&c.]: (Fr:) and Zj says the like of this: (L:) or عُرْضَةٌ signifies *intervention* with respect to good and evil; (Abu-l-'Abbás, O, Ḳ;) and the meaning is, *do not intervene by swearing by God every little while so as not to be pious* &c.: (O, Ḳ,* TA:) or *make not God an object of your oaths, by ordinary and frequent swearing by Him*, (Bḍ,) or *a butt for your oaths, like the butt of archers*, (TA,) *in order that ye may be pious* &c.; for the habitual swearer emboldens himself against God, and is not pious &c.: (Bḍ:) or, as some say, the meaning is *make not the mention of God a means of strengthening your oaths.* (TA.) You say also, هٰذَا عُرْضَةٌ لَكَ as meaning *This is a thing prepared for thy common*, or *ordinary, use.* (O, TA.) — *A purpose; an intention*; or *an object of desire*, or *of endeavour*; [as though it were a butt;] syn. هِمَّةٌ. (Ṣ, O, Ḳ.) Ḥassán says, (Ṣ, O,) i. e. Ibn-Thábit, (O, TA,)

• وَقَالَ ٱللّٰهُ قَدْ يَسَّرْتُ جُنْدًا •
• هُمُ ٱلْأَنْصَارُ عُرْضَتُهَا ٱللِّقَآءُ •

[*And God said I have prepared an army: they are the Anṣár; whose purpose*, or *the object of whose desire, is conflict* with the unbelievers]. (Ṣ, O, TA. [In one copy of the Ṣ, in the place of يَسَّرْتُ, I find أَعْدَدْتُ, which signifies the same.]) — *A pretext; an excuse.* (MA.) — One says also, فُلَانٌ عُرْضَةٌ لِذَاكَ, (Ṣ, O,) or عُرْضَةُ ذَاكَ, (Ṣ, O, Ḳ,) *Such a one is possessed of the requisite ability and strength for that*: (Ṣ, O, Ḳ:) and عُرْضَةٌ لِلشَّرِّ *possessed of strength to do evil, or mischief*: and in like manner عُرْضَةٌ is applied to two things, and to more. (TA.) And فُلَانَةُ عُرْضَةٌ لِلزَّوْجِ (Ṣ, O, Ḳ) *Such a female is possessed of sufficient strength for the husband*; [i. e., to be married;] (TA;) or لِلنِّكَاحِ *for marriage.* (A.) And نَاقَةٌ عُرْضَةٌ لِلْحِجَارَةِ *A she-camel having strength enough for* [going upon] *the stones.* (Ṣ, O, Ḳ.) And [in like manner] نَاقَةٌ عُرْضٌ ▾ أَسْفَارٍ *A she-camel having strength sufficient for journeys.* (Ṣ, O, Ḳ.*) And ▾ هٰذَا البَعِيرُ عُرْضٌ لِلسَّفَرِ وَالحَجَرِ (Ṣ, O, Ḳ) *The strength of this camel is sufficient for journeying and for going over stone.* (IB.) — عُرْضَةٌ also signifies *A kind of trick*, or *artifice, in wrestling*, (Ṣ, O, Ḳ,) by which one throws down men. (Ṣ, O.)

عُرْضِىٌّ [in the CḲ عَرْضِىٌّ] *A kind of cloths* or *garments.* (Ṣ, O, Ḳ.) — And *Certain of the appertenances* (مَرَافِق, O, Ḳ) *and chambers* (O) *of the house*: a word of the dial. of El-'Irák: (O, Ḳ:) unknown to the Arabs. (O.)

عُرْضِىٌّ *A camel that goes obliquely*, or *inclining towards one side, because not yet completely trained*: (Ṣ, O, Ḳ:) or *submissive in the middle part* [or body, *so as to be easy to ride, but*] *difficult of management*: and *perverse, untoward*, or *intractable*: and with ة, a she-camel *not completely trained*: (TA:) or *difficult to manage; refractory.* (Ṣ, O, Ḳ.) See also عَرُوضٌ. — One *who does not sit steadily*, or *firmly, upon the saddle*; (IAạr, O, Ḳ;) *inclining at one time this way, and at another time that way.* (IAạr, O.)

يَمْشِى بِالعُرْضِيَّةِ, and ▾ بِالعُرْضِيَّةِ, the latter from Lḥ, *He goes sideways.* (TA.)

عُرْضِيَّةٌ: see what next precedes. *Refractoriness, and a random* or *heedless manner of going, by reason of pride*: in a horse, the *going sideways*: and in a she-camel, the *state of being untrained*: (TA:) and in a man, [so expressly shown in the Ṣ and TA; but in the CḲ, قِيلَ is erroneously put for فِيكَ;] *what resembles roughness, ungentleness*, or *awkwardness; want of due care, by reason of haste*; (syn. عَجْرَفِيَّةٌ;) and *pride*; and *refractoriness.* (AZ, Ṣ, O, Ḳ.) — [See also عُرْضِىٌّ.]

عِرَضْنٌ, with fet-ḥ to the ر; (O;) or عِرِضْنٌ, like زِمِكَّى; (Ḳ;) *Briskness, liveliness*, or *sprightliness.* (IAạr, O, Ḳ. [See also عِرَضْنَةٌ.]) — And [app. for ذُو عِرَضْنٍ] meaning also *Brisk, lively*, or *sprightly.* (TA. [See, again, عِرَضْنَةٌ.])

عِرَضْنٌ; fem. with ة: see عُرُضٌ, last sentence.

عِرَضْنَةٌ *An oblique course* or *motion*: (A'Obeyd, L, TA:) and *briskness, liveliness, sprightliness*: and عِرِضْنَةٌ signifies the same. (TA. [See also العِرَضْنَى.]) One says, يَمْشِى العِرَضْنَةَ and ▾ العِرَضْنَى *He goes along with a proud gait*, (Ṣ, O, Ḳ,) *inclining towards one side*, (Ṣ, O,) *by reason of his briskness, liveliness*, or *sprightliness.* (Ṣ, O, Ḳ.) And ▾ تَعْدُو العِرَضْنَى and العِرَضْنَةَ and العِرَضْنَاةَ [perhaps correctly العِرَضْنَاتِ] *She* (a mare) *runs in a sidelong manner, one time in one direction and another time in another.* (O, TA.) And يَعْدُو العِرَضْنَةَ *He* (a man) *runs so that he outstrips.* (L, TA.) And نَظَرْتُ إِلَى فُلَانٍ عِرَضْنَةً *I looked towards such a one from the outer angle of my eye.* (Ṣ, O, Ḳ.*) The dim. of ▾ عِرَضْنَى is ▾ عُرَيْضِنٌ; the ن being retained because it is a letter of quasi-coordination, and the ى suppressed because it is not such. (Ṣ, O.) — Also, [app. for ذَاتُ عِرَضْنَةٍ,] A she-camel *that goes along obliquely*, (Ṣ, O, Ḳ,) *by reason of briskness, liveliness*, or *sprightliness*: pl. عِرَضْنَاتٌ. (Ṣ, O. [See, again, عُرْضِىٌّ.] But A'Obeyd disallows the application of this epithet to a she-camel. (TA in art. عرضن.) —— And A woman *that has become broad by reason of her fatness and plumpness.* (TA.)

عِرَضْنَى : see the next preceding paragraph, in three places.

عُرَاضٌ : see عَرِيضٌ, in four places: ═ see also عُرُوضٌ, in the latter half of the paragraph.

عِرَاضٌ : see عُرْضٌ, in the first sentence, and again, in four places, in the latter half of the paragraph. —— أَخَذَ فِى عِرَاضِ كَلَامِهِ *He began to say the like of that which he* [another] *had said:* or, as in the O, *he matched him, and equalled him, by saying the like of what he had said.* (TA.) [See also عَرُوضٌ.] —— Also *A certain brand;* (Ṣ, O, Ḳ;) or, (Ḳ,) accord. to Yaạkoob, (Ṣ, O,) *a line upon the thigh of a camel, crosswise;* (Ṣ, O, Ḳ;) or *upon the neck, crosswise.* (Ibn-Er-Rummánee, TA.) —— And *An iron with which the feet of a camel are marked in order that his foot-prints may be known.* (O, Ḳ.)

عَرُوضٌ : see عُرْضٌ, first sentence, and three of the examples which follow it, near the middle of the paragraph: —— see also عَارِضٌ, in the sentence commencing with "The side of the cheek." —— Also *A road in a mountain:* (Ṣ:) or *in the side,* or *lowest part,* (عُرْض,) *of a mountain,* (O, Ḳ,) or, as some say, *a part thereof lying across,* or *obliquely,* (مَا اعْتَرَضَ مِنْهُ, TA,) *in a narrow place:* (O, Ḳ:) and *a road down a descent,* or *declivity:* (TA:) or [simply] *a road:* (Ḥam p. 346:) pl. عُرُضٌ (TA) and أَعَارِيضُ. (Ḥam ubi suprà.) Hence the phrase in a trad. of Aboo-Hureyreh, فَأَخَذَ فِى عَرُوضٍ آخَرَ † *And he took another way of speech.* (TA.) —— *The place that is over against one, or on the opposite side to one, as he goes along.* (Ṣ, O, Ḳ.) ═ A she-camel *that takes to a side, or tract, different from that which her rider would traverse;* for which reason this epithet is applied to her: (O:) or *that goes to the right and left, and does not keep to the road:* (IAth:) or *that has not been trained:* (Ṣ, O, Ḳ:) or *that has received some training, but is not thoroughly trained:* (ISk:) or *such as is termed* ↓ عُرُضْنَةٌ, *stubborn in the head, but submissive in her middle part; that is loaded; and then the other loaded camels are driven on; and if a man ride her, she goes straight forward, and her rider has not the power of exercising his own free will* [*in managing her*]. (Sh.) To such a camel, 'Omar likened a class of his subjects. (TA.) And 'Amr Ibn-Aḥmar El-Báhilee says,

* أُخِبُّ ذَلُولًا أَوْ عَرُوضًا أَرُوضُهَا *

[*I make a submissive one to go the pace termed* خَبَب, *or an untrained one I train*]; meaning that he recites two poems; one of which he has made easy, and the other whereof is difficult: J gives a different reading, أُسِيرُ عَسِيرًا, meaning أُسَيِّرُ; with the same explanation that is given above, of the former reading. (IB, O.) —— A camel, (Ṣ, O, TA,) in the Ḳ, erroneously, a sheep or goat, (TA,) *that eats the thorns* (Ṣ, O, Ḳ, TA) *when herbage is unattainable by him.* (Ṣ, O.) —— And *i. q.* عَتُودٌ [*A yearling goat,* &c.]. (TA. [See also عَرِيضٌ.]) ═ Also *i. q.* كَثِيرٌ, (Ibn-'Abbád, O, Ḳ,) [as meaning *A large quantity* or *number*] of a thing [or of things], (Ḳ,) [or *large in number,*] as in the phrase حَىٌّ عَرُوضٌ [*A tribe large in number*]. (Ibn-'Abbád, O.) ═ And *Clouds;* syn. سَحَابٌ; (Ibn-'Abbád, O, Ḳ;) and عَرُوضٌ *Food.* (Fr, O, Ḳ.) ═ عَرُوضُ كَلَامٍ *The meaning,* or *intended sense, of speech;* syn. فَحْوَاهُ, (ISk, Ṣ, O, Ḳ,) and مَعْنَاهُ: (ISk, Ṣ, O:) as also ↓ مِعْرَاضُ كَلَامٍ, (Ḳ,) of which the pl. is مَعَارِيضُ and مَعَارِضُ. (TA.) One says عَرَفْتُ ذٰلِكَ فِى عَرُوضِ كَلَامِهِ [*I knew that in the intended sense of his speech*]; (ISk, Ṣ, O;) and فِى ↓ مِعْرَاضِ كَلَامِهِ; (A, O;) and in like manner, عَرَفْتُهُ فِى مَعَارِضِ كَلَامِهِ: (L, TA:) and فِى لَحْنِ كلامه and ↓ مِعْرَاضِ كَلَامِهِ and نَحْوِ كلامه signify the same. (Mṣb.) [See also مِعْرَاضٌ.] ═ هٰذِهِ المَسْأَلَةُ عَرُوضُ هٰذِهِ *This question is the like of this.* (TA.) [See also عِرَاضٌ.] ═ عَرُوضٌ also signifies The *transverse pole* or *piece of wood* (عَارِضَة) *which is in the middle of a tent, and which is its main support.* (Aboo-Is-ḥáḳ.) —— And hence, (Aboo-Is-ḥáḳ,) The *middle portion* [or *foot*] *of a verse;* (Aboo-Is-ḥáḳ, O;) for the بَيْت of poetry is constructed after the manner of the بَيْت inhabited by the Arabs, which is of pieces of cloth; and as the عروض of the latter is the strongest part, so should that of the former be; and accordingly we see that a deficiency in the ضَرْب is more frequent than it is in the عروض: (Aboo-Is-ḥáḳ:) the *last foot of the first half* or *hemistich* (Ṣ, Ḳ) *of a verse;* (Ṣ;) *whether perfect or altered:* (Ḳ:) some make it to be the طَرَائِق of poetry, and its عَمُود: (TA:) [i. e. they liken it to these parts of the tents:] it is fem.: (Ḳ:) or sometimes masc.: (L:) the pl. is أَعَارِيضُ; (Ṣ, O, Ḳ;) contr. to rule, as though pl. of إِعْرِيضٌ; and one may use as its pl. أَعَارِضُ. (Ṣ, O.) —— Also [The *science of prosody, or versification;*] the *science of the rules whereby the perfect measures of Arabic verse are known from those which are broken;* (Mṣb;) the *standard whereby verse is measured:* (Ṣ, O, Ḳ:) because it is compared (يُعَارَضُ) therewith: (Ṣ, O:) or because what is correct in measure is thereby distinguished from what is broken: (Ḳ: [in which some other reasons are added, too futile, in my opinion, to deserve mention: I think it more probable that عروض is used by a synecdoche for شِعْر, as being the most essential part thereof; and then, elliptically, for عِلْمُ العَرُوضِ, which is the more common term for the science:]) it is fem.; and has no pl., because it is a gen. n. (Ṣ, O.) ═ See also عَارِضَةٌ; second and two following sentences. ═ العَرُوضُ is a name of *Mekkeh and El-Medeeneh,* (Ṣ, O, Mṣb, Ḳ, TA,) and *El-Yemen,* (Mṣb, TA,) *with what is around them.* (Ṣ, O, Ḳ, TA.)

عُرُوضٌ [thus app., but written without any vowel-sign to the ع,] The *quality,* in a she-camel, *of being untrained.* (L, TA. [See عَرُوضٌ, near the beginning.])

عَرِيضٌ *Broad,* or *wide;* (Ṣ, Mgh, O, Mṣb, Ḳ;*) as also ↓ عُرَاضٌ; (Ṣ, O, Ḳ;) like as one says كَبِيرٌ and كُبَارٌ: (Ṣ, O:) fem. of the former, (Ṣ, Mṣb,) and of the latter, (Ṣ, Ḳ,) with ة: (Ṣ, Mṣb, Ḳ:) the pl. of عَرِيضٌ is عِرَاضٌ, like as كِرَامٌ is pl. of كَرِيمٌ. (Mṣb.) You say, قَوْسٌ عَرِيضَةٌ and ↓ عُرَاضَةٌ [*A broad, or wide, bow*]. (Ṣ.) And ↓ عُرَاضَاتٌ, (TA,) or ↓ عُرَاضَاتٌ أُثْرًا, in which the latter word is in the accus. case as a specificative, (Ṣ, O, TA,) meaning Camels *whose foot-marks are broad.* (Ṣ, O, TA.) And فُلَانٌ عَرِيضُ البِطَانِ † *Such a one is rich;* or *in a state of competence:* (A, TA:) or *possessed of much property.* (Ṣ,* O, Ḳ,* TA. [See also art. بطن.]) And عَرِيضُ القَفَا ‡ *Fat:* (TA:) or † *stupid.* (Mgh.) And عَرِيضُ الوِسَادِ ‡ *Sleepy:* (TA:) or † *stupid, dull,* or *wanting in intelligence.* (Mṣb in art. وسد.) دُعَآءٌ عَرِيضٌ, occurring in the Ḳur [xli. 51], means † *Large,* or *much, prayer,* or *supplication:* (Ḳ,* TA:) or in this instance we may say *long.* (L.) ═ Also A goat (Aṣ, O, Ḳ) *that is a year old,* (Ḳ,) or *about a year old,* (Aṣ, O,) *and that takes* [or *crops*] *of the herbage* (Aṣ, O, Ḳ) *and trees* [or *shrubs*] (Aṣ, O) *with the side of his mouth:* (Ḳ:) or (O, Ḳ) *such as is termed* عَتُود [q. v.], (Ṣ, O,) *when he rattles, and desires copulation:* (Ṣ, O, Ḳ:) or a [*young*] goat *above such as is weaned and below such as is termed* جَذَع [q. v.]: or *such as has pastured and become strong:* or *such as is termed* جَذَع: or a *young* goat *when he leaps the female:* it is applied only to *a male;* the female is termed عَرِيضَةٌ: with the people of El-Ḥijáz it means peculiarly *such as is gelded:* it is also applied to a gazelle *that has nearly become a* ثَنِىّ [q. v.]: (TA:) pl. عِرْضَانٌ and عُرْضَانٌ. (Ṣ, O, Ḳ.)

عُرَاضَةٌ *A present: what is brought to one's family:* (Ṣ, O, Ḳ:) called in Persian رَاه آوَرْد: (Ṣ:) *a present which a man gives when he returns from his journey:* (TA:) *such as a man gives to his children when he returns from a journey:* (Ṣgh, TA:) and *what is given as food by the bringer,* or *purveyor, of wheat,* or *corn, of the said wheat,* or *corn:* (Ṣ, O, Ḳ:) *what a person riding gives as food to any one of the owners of waters who asks him for food.* (Aṣ.) You say, اِشْتَرِ عُرَاضَةً لِأَهْلِكَ *Purchase thou a present to take to thy family.* (Ṣ, O.) And سَأَلْتُهُ عُرَاضَةً and ↓ عَرْضَ مَالٍ and ↓ عَرَضَ مَالٍ [*I asked him for a present of property*] فَلَمْ يُعْطِنِيهِ [*and he did not give it to me*]. (L.) [See also Ḥam p. 103, l. 8.]

[عَرُوضِىٌّ *Of,* or *relating to, prosody,* or *the art of versification. A prosodist.*]

عُرَيْضِنٌ dim. of عِرَضْنَى, q. v., voce عِرَضْنَةٌ. (Ṣ, O.)

عَرُوضَاوَاتٌ *Places in which grow* أَعْرَاض [pl. of

عَرُوض] i. e. the [trees called] أَثْل and أَرَاك and حَمْض. (TA.)

عِرِّيض Forward; officious; meddling; a busy-body: (TA in art. قمح:) one who addresses himself to do evil to men. (Ṣ, O, Ḳ.)

عَارِض [Showing its breadth, or width; (see عَرَضَ, first signification;) or] having its side apparent: (TA:) and [in like manner] ▼ مُعْتَرِض, q. v., anything showing its breadth, or width: [or its side:] (TA:) [and hence, both signify appearing. (See again عَرَضَ.)] — A collection of clouds appearing, or presenting itself, or extending sideways, (▼ مُعْتَرِض,) in the horizon; (Ṣ, O, Ḳ;) overpeering: (TA:) or a collection of clouds which one sees in a side of the sky, like that which is termed جُلْب, except that the former is white, whereas the latter inclines to blackness, and is narrower than the former, and more distant: (AZ:) or a collection of clouds that comes over against one (مُعَارِضًا) in the sky, unexpectedly: (El-Báhilee, O:) or a collection of clouds that appears, or presents itself, or extends sideways, (يَعْتَرِضُ,) in the sky, like as does a mountain, before it covers the sky, is called سَحَابٌ عَارِضٌ, and also حَبِيٌّ: (Aṣ, O:) pl. عَوَارِضُ. (TA.) [See also عَرْضٌ and عِرْضٌ.] In the phrase عَارِضٌ مُمْطِرُنَا, in the Ḳur [xlvi. 23], ممطرنا means مُمْطِرٌ لَنَا; for as being determinate it cannot be an epithet to عَارِض, which is indeterminate: and the like of this the Arabs do only in the instances of nouns derived from verbs; so that you may not say هٰذَا رَجُلٌ غُلَامُنَا. (Ṣ, O.) — See also عَرْضٌ, in the sentence commencing with "A mountain," in two places: — and again, shortly after. — A gift appearing (Aṣ, Ṣ, O, Ḳ) from a person. (Aṣ, Ṣ, O.) [See an ex. voce عَائِضٌ.] — [Happening; befalling; occurring: an occurrence; as a fever, and the like. (See عَرَضَ لَهُ.)] A bane, or cause of mischief, that occurs in a thing; as also ▼ عَرَضٌ, q. v. (TA.) And ▼ شُبْهَةٌ عَارِضَةٌ A doubt, or dubiousness, occurring, or intervening, in the mind. (TA.) In the saying of 'Alee, يَنْقَدِحُ الشَّكُّ فِى قَلْبِهِ بِأَوَّلِ عَارِضَةٍ ▼ مِنْ شُبْهَةٍ, the word عارضة may perhaps be an inf. n., [or a quasi-inf. n.,] like عَاقِبَةٌ and عَافِيَةٌ: (TA:) [so that the meaning may be Doubt makes an impression upon his heart at the first occurrence of dubiousness.] — Whatever faces one, of a thing: (TA, and so in some copies of the Ḳ: in other copies of the Ḳ, this signification is given to ▼ عَارِضَةٌ:) or anything facing one. (O.) — Intervening; preventing: an intervening, or a preventing, thing; an obstacle: (TA:) a thing that prevents one's going on; such as a mountain and the like. (Mṣb.) [Its application to a cloud, and some other applications to which reference has been made above, may be derived from this signification, or from that next preceding, or from the first.] — I. q. عَرُوضٌ, in the first of the senses assigned to this latter above; as also ▼ عَارِضَةٌ. (The former accord. to some copies of the Ḳ: the latter accord. to others: but both accord. to the TA.) — What appears, of the face, (Ḳ,) or of the mouth, accord. to the L, (TA,) when one laughs. (L, Ḳ, TA: but in some copies of the Ḳ, and in the O, this signification is given to ▼ عَارِضَةٌ.) — The side of the cheek (Ḳ, TA) of a man; (TA;) as also ▼ عَارِضَةٌ; (O, L, Ḳ;) the two sides of the two cheeks of a man being called the عَارِضَانِ, (Mṣb, TA,) or the ▼ عَارِضَتَانِ: (Ṣ:) the two sides of the face: (Lḥ, O, Ḳ:) or the side of the face; as also ▼ عَرُوضٌ; the two together being called the عَارِضَانِ: (Lḥ, TA:) or this last signifies the two sides of the mouth: or the two sides of the beard: pl. عَوَارِضُ. (TA.) خَفِيفُ العَارِضَيْنِ means Light, or scanty, in the hair of the two sides of the cheeks, (Ṣ, O, Mṣb,) and of the beard; (O;) being elliptical. (Mṣb.) But in a certain trad., in which a happy quality of a man is said to be خِفَّةُ عَارِضَيْهِ, the meaning is said to be ‡ His activity in praising and glorifying God; i. e. his not ceasing to move the sides of his cheeks by praising and glorifying God. (IAth, on the authority of El-Khaṭṭábee; and O.) — The side of the neck; (Ḳ;) the two sides thereof being called the عَارِضَانِ: (IDrd, O:) pl. as above. (TA.) [See also عُرْضٌ, near the beginning.] — The tooth that is in the side of the mouth: (TA; and Ḳ, as in some copies of the latter; but in other copies, this signification is given to ▼ عَارِضَةٌ:) pl. as above: (Ḳ:) or the side of the mouth; (Ṣ;) and so, as some say, عَوَارِضُ; (TA;) [meaning the teeth in the side of the mouth; for] you say اِمْرَأَةٌ نَقِيَّةُ العَارِضِ (Ṣ,) and العَوَارِضِ, (TA,) a woman clean in the side of the mouth: (Ṣ, TA:) and Jereer describes a woman as polishing her عَارِضَانِ with a branch of a beshámeh, [a tree of which the twigs are used for cleaning the teeth,] meaning, as Aboo-Naṣr says, the teeth that are after the central incisors, which latter are not of the عوارض: or, accord. to ISk, عَارِضٌ signifies the canine tooth and the ضِرْس [or bicuspid] next thereto: or, as some say, what are between the central incisor and the [first] ضرس [which is a bicuspid]: (Ṣ, O:) some say that the عوارض are the central incisors, as being [each] in the side of the mouth: others, that they are the teeth next to the sides of the mouth: others, that they are four teeth next to the canine teeth, and followed by the أَضْرَاس: Lḥ says that they are of the اضراس: others, that they are the teeth that are between the central incisors and the اضراس: and others, that they are eight teeth in each side; four above, and four below. (TA [from the O &c.].) — عَارِضٌ as applied to a she-camel, or a sheep or goat: see the paragraph next following. — Giving a thing, or the giver of a thing, in exchange, for (مِنْ) another thing. (TA.) — A reviewer of an army, or of a body of soldiers, who makes them to pass by him, and examines their state. (Ṣ.) — See also the next paragraph; last three sentences.

عَارِضَةٌ: see عَارِضٌ, in eight places, from the sentence commencing with شُبْهَةٌ عَارِضَةٌ. — A want; an object of need: (Ṣ:) and [in like manner] ▼ عَرُوضٌ a want, or an object of need, that has occurred to one: (Ṣ, O, Ḳ:) pl. of the former عَوَارِضُ. (Ṣ.) ▼ عَرُوضٌ has the signification above assigned to it in the saying, فُلَانٌ رَكُوضٌ بِلَا عَرُوضٍ [Such a one is running without any want that has occurred to him]. (Ṣ, O. [In the Ḳ, in the place of ركوض, we find رَبُوضٌ, which I think a mistake.]) [In Freytag's Arab. Prov. i. 555, we find ▼ رَكُوضٌ فِى كُلِّ عَرُوضٍ, which is expl. as meaning Running swiftly in every region; and said to be applied to him who disseminates evil, or mischief, among men.] — A she-camel having a fracture or a disease, (Ṣ, O, Ḳ,) for which reason it is slaughtered; (Ṣ;) as also ▼ عَارِضٌ: (O, Ḳ:) and in like manner, a sheep or goat: (TA:) pl. عَوَارِضُ. (Ṣ.) It is opposed to عَبِيطَةٌ, which is one that is slaughtered without its having any malady. (Ṣ, O.) One says, بَنُو فُلَانٍ لَا يَأْكُلُونَ إِلَّا العَوَارِضَ [The sons of such a one do not eat any but camels such as are slaughtered on account of disease]; reproaching them for not slaughtering camels except on account of disease befalling them. (Ṣ, O.) — عَوَارِضُ, applied to camels, also signifies That eat the [trees called] عِضَاه, (Ṣ, L,) wherever they find them. (L.) — [A thing lying, or extending, across, or athwart; any cross piece of wood &c.: so in the present day.] — The [lintel, or] piece of wood which holds the عِضَادَتَانِ [or two side-posts], above, of a door; corresponding to the أُسْكُفَّة [or threshold]; (Ṣ, L;) the upper piece of wood in which the door turns. (O, Ḳ. [In some copies of the latter, this signification is erroneously given to عَارِضٌ.]) The عَارِضَتَانِ of a door are also [said to be] the same as the عِضَادَتَانِ. (TA, voce عَتَبَةٌ.) — A [rafter, or] single one of the عَوَارِض of a roof: (Ṣ, O, Ḳ: [but in some copies of the last, and in the TA, this signification is erroneously given to عَارِضٌ:]) the عوارض of a house are the pieces of wood of its roof, which are laid across; one of which is called عَارِضَةٌ: and عَارِضٌ [a mistranscription for عَوَارِضُ] also signifies the سَقَائِف [or pieces of wood which form the roof] of a [vehicle of the kind called] مَحْمِل. (L.) — Also, (Ṣ, and so in some copies of the Ḳ,) or ▼ عَارِضٌ, (as in other copies of the Ḳ,) or both, (TA,) Hardiness: (Ṣ, Ḳ, TA:) and this is what is meant by its being said, in [some copies of] the Ḳ, that عَارِضٌ is also syn. with عَارِضَةٌ; (TA;) [for in some copies of the Ḳ, after several explanations of العَارِضُ, we find وَالعَارِضَةُ وَالسِّنُّ الَّتِى فِى عُرْضِ الفَمِ; whereas, in other copies, the و before السِّنُّ is omitted:] courage; or courage and energy: (Ṣ, Ḳ, TA:) power of speech: (Ṣ:) perspicuity, or chasteness, of speech; and eloquence: (Ḳ, TA:) or the former signifies intuitive knowledge (بَدِيهَة): or determination, resolution, or decision: (A:) and the trimming of speech or language, and the removal of its faults: and good judgment. (TA.) You say, فُلَانٌ ذُو عَارِضَةٍ (AZ, IDrd, Ṣ, O, TA) Such a one is possessed of hardiness; (Ṣ, TA;) as also ▼ ذُو عَارِضٍ; (TA;) and of courage, or courage and energy; and of power of speech: (Ṣ:) or of eloquence,

(AZ, IDrd, O,) *and perspicuity*, or *chasteness, of speech*. (IDrd, O.) And فُلَانٌ شَدِيدُ العَارِضَةِ *Such a one is hardy*; (Kh, O, TA;) as also ▾ شَدِيدُ العَارِضِ; (TA;) and *courageous*, or *courageous and energetic*. (Kh, TA.)

أَعْرَاضٌ is pl. of مِعْرَاضٌ: see أَعْرَاضُ الكَلَامِ —— and of عُرْضٌ and of عِرْضٌ and of عَرَضٌ. —— أَعْرَاضُ الشَّجَرِ means *The upper parts of the trees* [or *shrubs*]. (Ḳ.)

مَعْرِضٌ The *place of the appearance*, [or *occurrence*,] and *of the showing*, or *exhibiting*, or *manifesting*, and *of the mentioning*, and *of the intending*, or *purposing*, of a thing. (Mṣb.) You say, قَتَلْتُهُ فِى مَعْرِضِ كَذَا *I slew him in the place of the appearance* [or *occurrence* &c.] *of such a thing*. (Mṣb.) And ذِكْرُ ٱللّٰهِ إِنَّمَا يَكُونُ فِى مَعْرِضِ التَّعْظِيمِ *The praise and glorification of God is only in the place* [or *case*] *of the appearance*, [or *of the manifesting*,] and *of the intending*, or *purposing*, *of magnifying*. (Mṣb.) [And hence, فِى مَعْرِضِ كَذَا also signifies *In the time*, or *case*, or *on the occasion*, *of the appearance*, &c., *of such a thing*. And *In the state*, or *condition*, or *manner*, *which is indicative of such a thing*: thus virtually agreeing with the phrase فِى مَعْرِضِ كَذَا, q. v. infrà.] —— Also *A place for the sale of slaves* or *beasts*. (MA.) —— And *Pasturage that renders the cattle in no need of their being fed with fodder*. (TA.)

مُعْرِضٌ Anything *showing its breadth*, or *width*; [or *its side*; as also ▾ عَارِضٌ.] (TA. See the latter word.) [And hence, *Appearing*, as also the latter.] And *i. q.* مُعْتَرِضٌ [app. as signifying *Presenting itself*; or *occurring*]. (Sh.) And Anything *putting its breadth*, or *width*, [or *side*, (as is shown by an explanation of أَعْرِضْ,)] *in one's power*. (TA.) You say, الشَّىْءُ مُعْرِضٌ لَكَ, meaning *The thing is in thy power*; *apparent to thee*; *not offering resistance to thee*. (IAth, O.*) —— And طَأْ مُعْرِضًا حَيْثُ شِئْتَ [*Tread thou* or] *put thy feet where thou wilt, fearing nothing, for it is in thy power to do so*. (Ṣ, O.) —— ادّان مُعْرِضًا (occurring in a saying of 'Omar, Ḳ, or, as some relate it, دَانَ مُعْرِضًا, Ḳ in art. دين,) means *He bought upon credit*, or *borrowed*, or *sought* or *demanded a loan*, [*doing so* (TA)] *of whomsoever he could*, (AZ, Ṣ, A, Mgh, O,) *not caring what might be the consequence*: (Ṣ, O:) or *addressing himself to any one who came in his way*: (Sh, Ḳ:) or *turning away from such as said Thou shalt not buy on credit, or borrow*: (IAth:) or *avoiding payment*: (TA:) or *from any quarter that was easy and practicable to him, without caring*, (O, Ḳ,) *and without being perplexed*: (O:) or *he incurred the debt without caring for not paying it*, or *for what might be the consequence*: (Aṣ:) or *he contracted a debt with every one who presented himself to him*: (Ḳ in art. دين;) Sh says that the making معرضا to signify مُمْكِنًا is improbable; because it is in the accus. case as a denotative of state with respect to [the agent implied in the verb] ادّان; and if you explain it as meaning he took it from him who enabled him, then معرضا applies to him whom he accosts, for he is the ممكن; [he suggests also, that the meaning may be *he bought upon credit*, or *borrowed*, *largely*; for] he adds that معرضا may be from عَرْضٌ, signifying اتَّسَعَ and أَعْرَضَ ثَوْبُ المَلْبَسِ. (TA.) —— أَرْضٌ مُعْرِضَةٌ, or مُعْرَضَةٌ, (Ḳ, TA, [the former only in the CḲ,]) means *Land wherein is herbage which the camels*, or *the like, depasture* [app. *at random*] *when traversing it*. (O, Ḳ.) —— See also مُعَرِّضٌ, last sentence.

مِعْرَضٌ *Garments in which girls are displayed*: (Ṣ:) or *a garment in which a girl is displayed*: (O, Ḳ:) or *a garment in which girls are displayed on the wedding-night*; *which is the goodliest of their apparel*, or *of the goodliest thereof*: (Mṣb:) and *a garment in which a girl is shown*, or *displayed, to the purchaser*: (TA:) or the *shirt in which a male slave, and a girl, is shown, displayed, exposed*, or *offered, for sale*. (Ḥar p. 129.) [And hence, فِى مِعْرَضِ كَذَا † *In the guise of such a thing*, used tropically, virtually agreeing with the phrase فِى مَعْرِضِ كَذَا in a sense expl. above.] See also مِعْرَاضٌ, last sentence but one.

مُعَرَّضٌ [pass. part. n. of 2, q. v.] Camels (نَعَمٌ) *branded with the mark called* عِرَاض. (Ṣ, O, Ḳ.) —— Also Flesh-meat *not well and thoroughly cooked*: (ISk, Ṣ, O, Ḳ:) occurring in a verse (Ṣ, O) of Es-Suleyk Ibn-Es-Sulakeh, (O,) as some relate it; but accord. to others it is with ص; (Ṣ, O;) and this latter is the more correct. (O.) —— مُعَرَّضَةٌ *A virgin before she is veiled*, or *concealed*: for she is once exhibited to the people of the tribe in order that some one or more may become desirous of her, and then they veil her, or conceal her. (TA.)

مُعَرِّضٌ [act. part. n. of 2, q. v.]. A poet describes a she-camel carrying dates, and having outgone the other camels, so that the crows, or ravens, alighted upon her, and ate the dates, as being مِنْ مُعَرِّضَاتِ الغِرْبَانِ, as though she were *of those feeding the crows*, or *ravens*, *of what is termed* عُرَاضَة, q. v. (Ṣ.) —— Also the *circumciser* of a boy: (Ḳ:) [or] so ▾ مُعْرِضٌ. (O.)

مِعْرَاضٌ *An arrow having no feathers* (Aṣ, Ṣ, Mgh, O, Mṣb, Ḳ) *nor head*, (Aṣ,) *slender at the two extremities, and thick in the middle*, (O, Ḳ,) *being in form like the wooden implement wherewith cotton is separated from its seeds*, or *is separated and loosened* [*by striking therewith the string of a bow*], (O, TA,) *which goes sideways*, (Mgh, [in the O and TA, مُسْتَوِيًا, app. a mistranscription, for مُسْتَعْرِضًا,]) *striking with its* عَرْض [or *middle part*, unless this be a mistake for عُرْض, or *side*], (Mgh, [in my copy of which, عرض is without any vowel-sign,] and Ḳ,) *not with its extremity*: (Mgh, Ḳ:) *sometimes, it strikes with its thick middle part in such a manner that it breaks and crushes what it strikes so that it is like the thing that is beaten to death*; *and if the object of the chase be near to it, it strikes it with the place of the head thereof*: if it make a hole, the game smitten with it may be eaten; but not if it strike with a middle part (بِعَرْضٍ). (O, TA.) —— *An oblique, indirect, obscure, ambiguous*, or *equivocal, mode of speech*; *as when thou askest a man, "Hast thou seen such a one?" and he, having seen him, and disliking to lie, answers, "Verily such a one is seen:"* (Mṣb:) from عَرَّضَ [q. v.]: (Mṣb, El-Munáwee: the latter in explaining a trad., q. v. infrà:) *i. q.* تَوْرِيَةٌ [signifying as above; or the *pretending one thing and meaning another*; or the *using a word, an expression*, or *a phrase, which has an obvious meaning, and intending thereby another meaning to which it applies but which is contrary to the obvious one*]; the original meaning of which is *concealment*: (Mṣb:) or *language whereof one part resembles another in the meanings*: (O, TA: [in the TA immediately follows the exemplification cited above, from the Mṣb; whence it seems that this explanation is itself somewhat of a معراض, meaning what it does not clearly express:]) or المَعَارِيضُ فِى الكَلَامِ [thus, with the pl. form, in two copies of the Ṣ, and in the TA,] signifies التَّوْرِيَةُ بِالشَّىْءِ عَنِ الشَّىْءِ [the *pretending*, or *making believe, a thing instead of another thing*]: (Ṣ:) and مَعَارِضُ الكَلَامِ and ▾ أَعْرَاضُهُ signify the same as مَعَارِيضُهُ. (TA.) [مَعَارِضُ is a contraction of مَعَارِيضُ, like as مِعْرَضٌ is said to be of مِعْرَاضٌ when syn. therewith.] It is said in a prov., (Ṣ,) a trad., (TA,) إِنَّ فِى المَعَارِيضِ لَمَنْدُوحَةً عَنِ الكَذِبِ [*Verily, in oblique, indirect, obscure, ambiguous*, or *equivocal, modes of speech is ample scope, freedom*, or *liberty*, (سَعَةٌ, Ṣ,) *to avoid lying*; or, as is said in the L in art. ندح, *that which renders one in no need of lying*]. (Ṣ, Mṣb.) One says also, عَرَفْتُهُ فِى مِعْرَاضِ كَلَامِهِ, expl. voce عَرُوضٌ which see in three places, and ▾ فِى مِعْرَضِ كَلَامِهِ, rejecting the ا: this latter is said by some of the learned to be a metaphorical expression, from مِعْرَضٌ signifying the "garment in which girls are displayed," as though the meaning were ‡ [*I knew it*] *in the form*, or *manner*, and *guise*, and *mould, of his speech*; but this does not obtain in all kinds of speech; for it may not be said in cases of reviling; indeed it would be bad, in these cases, to use as a metaphor the garment of adornment; therefore the proper way is to say that مِعْرَضٌ is a contraction of مِعْرَاضٌ. (Mṣb.) One also says الأَلْفَاظُ مَعَارِيضُ المَعَانِى ‡ [*Words are the robes of meanings*]: and this phrase also is [said to be] taken from مِعْرَضٌ signifying the "garment in which a girl is displayed;" because words adorn meanings. (TA.)

مُعَارِضٌ A camel *that does not go straightly in the file*, or *series*, *but takes to the right and left*: (A:) or a she camel *such as is termed* عَلُوق; *that makes a show of affection with her nose* [*by smelling her young one*], (تَرْأَمُ بِأَنْفِهَا,) *and refuses to yield her milk*. (AA, O, Ḳ.)

سَحَابٌ مُعْتَرِضٌ فِى الأُفُقِ: *i. q.* عَارِضٌ, q. v. —— فُلَانٌ [جُمْلَةٌ مُعْتَرِضَةٌ *A parenthetic clause*.]

مُعْتَرِضٌ فِى خُلُقِهِ [*Such a one is habitually cross, or perverse, in his disposition, in every case,*] is said of a man when everything of his affairs displeases thee. (TA.) —— هَوًى مُعْتَرِضٌ *Love that befalls at first sight, and captivates the heart at once unless it quit it quickly as it seized it quickly.* (Ḥam p. 551.)

عرضن

عِرَضْنَى : ═ and عِرَضْنَةٌ and عِرِضْنَةٌ : and عِرَضْنٌ ; and its dim. عُرَيْضِنٌ : see art. عرض.

عرطب

عَرْطَبَةٌ The *lute:* (Ṣ, O,* Ḳ:*) or the [*kind of mandoline called*] طُنْبُور : (O, Ḳ:) or the [*Persian lute, called*] بَرْبَط : (O:) or the *drum:* (Ṣ, Ḳ:) or the *drum that is contracted in the middle:* (O:) or the *Abyssinian drum:* (Ḳ:) also pronounced with ḍamm [i. e. عُرْطُبَةٌ] (Ḳ, TA) in the first two senses. (TA.)

عرف

1. عَرَفَهُ, (Ṣ, O, Mṣb, Ḳ, &c.,) aor. ـِ, (O, Ḳ,) inf. n. مَعْرِفَةٌ (Ṣ, O, Ḳ) and عِرْفَانٌ (Ṣ, O, Mṣb, Ḳ) and عِرِفَّانٌ (Ḳ) and عِرْفَةٌ, (Mṣb, Ḳ,) or مَعْرِفَةٌ is a simple subst., (Mṣb,) *He knew it; he had cognition of it;* or *he was,* or *became, acquainted with it;* syn. عَلِمَهُ : (Ḳ:) or *he knew it* (عَلِمَهُ) *by means of any of the five senses;* (Mṣb;) [and also, *by mental perception:*] Er-Rághib says, المَعْرِفَةُ is *the perceiving* a thing *by reflection,* and *by consideration of the effect* thereof [*upon the mind* or *sense*], so that it has a more special meaning than العِلْمُ, and its contr. is الإِنْكَارُ ; and one says, فُلَانٌ يَعْرِفُ ٱللّٰهَ وَرَسُولَهُ [*Such a one knows God and his apostle*], but one does not say يَعْلَمُ ٱللّٰهَ, making the verb [thus] to have a single objective complement, since man's مَعْرِفَة [or knowledge] of God is [the result of] the consideration of his effects, without the perception of his essence; and one says, ٱللّٰهُ يَعْلَمُ كَذَا, but not يَعْرِفُ كَذَا, since المَعْرِفَةُ is used in relation to عِلْم [or knowledge] which is defective, to which one attains by reflection: it is from عَرَفْتُهُ meaning *I found,* or *experienced, its* عَرْف i. e. *odour;* or as meaning *I attained its* عُرْف i. e. *limit:* (TA:) it is said in the B that المَعْرِفَةُ differs from العِلْمُ, in meaning, in several ways: the former concerns the thing itself [which is its object;] whereas the latter concerns the states, or conditions, or qualities, thereof: also the former generally denotes *the perceiving* a thing *as a thing that has been absent from the mind,* thus differing from the latter; therefore the contr. of the former is الإِنْكَارُ, and the contr. of the latter is الجَهْلُ ; and the former is *the knowing* a thing itself *as distinguished from other things;* whereas the latter concerns a thing collectively with other things: (TA in art. علم:) and sometimes they put ↓ اعترف in the place of عَرَفَ ; (Ṣ, O;) [i. e.] اعترف الشَّىْءَ signifies عَرَفَهُ : (Mgh, Ḳ:) and so, sometimes, does ↓ استعرفهُ. (Ḥar p. 486.) —— And عَرَفَ is also used in the place of اعترف [in the first of the senses assigned to the latter below]. (Ṣ, O.) See the latter verb, in four places. —— عَرَفَهُ also signifies *He requited him.* (O, Ḳ.) Ks read, (O, Ḳ,) and so five others, (Az, TA,) in the Ḳur [lxvi. 3], (O,) عَرَفَ بَعْضَهُ, meaning *He requited* her, namely, Ḥafṣah, *for part* [*thereof,* i. e.] of what she had done: (Fr, O, Ḳ:) and he did so indeed by divorcing her: (Fr, TA:) or it means *he acknowledged part thereof:* (Ḳ:) but others read ↓ عَرَّفَ بَعْضَهُ, which, likewise, has the former of the two meanings expl. above: (Bḍ:) or this means *he told* Ḥafṣah *part thereof.* (Fr, O, Bḍ,* TA. [See also 2.]) As first expl. above, this phrase is like the saying to him who does good or who does evil, أَنَا أَعْرِفُ لِأَهْلِ الإِحْسَانِ وَأَعْرِفُ لِأَهْلِ الإِسَآءَةِ, (O,) or لِلْمُحْسِنِ وَالمُسِىْءِ, (Ḳ,) [*I know how to requite the doer of good and the doer of evil,*] i. e. the case of the doer of good and that of the doer of evil are not hidden from me nor is the suitable requital of him. (O, Ḳ.) لَأَعْرِفَنَّكَهَا عِنْدَ رَسُولِ ٱللّٰهِ occurs in a trad., meaning *I will assuredly requite thee for it in the presence of the Apostle of God so that he shall know thy evil-doing:* and is used in threatening. (TA.) ═ عَرَفَ الفَرَسَ, (Ṣ, O, Ḳ,) aor. ـِ, (O,) inf. n. عَرْفٌ, (O, Ḳ,) *He clipped the* عُرْف [i. e. *mane*] *of the horse.* (Ṣ, O, Ḳ.) ═ عَرَفْتُ عَلَى القَوْمِ, aor. ـُ, inf. n. عِرَافَةٌ, *I was,* or *became,* عَرِيف *over the people,* or *party;* i. e., *manager,* or *orderer, of their affairs;* as also عَرُفْتُ عَلَيْهِمْ : (Mṣb:) or عَرُفَ, inf. n. عَرَافَةٌ, signifies *he was,* or *became, an* عَرِيف ; (Ṣ, O, Ḳ;) as also عَرَفَ, aor. ـِ ; (Ḳ;) i. e., *a* نَقِيب : (Ṣ, O:) and when you mean that he acted as an عَرِيف, you say, عَرَفَ عَلَيْنَا سِنِينَ, aor. ـُ, inf. n. عِرَافَةٌ, [*he acted over us as an* عريف *during some years,*] like كَتَبَ, aor. يَكْتُبُ, inf. n. كِتَابَةٌ. (Ṣ, O, Ḳ.*) ═ عَرَفَ لِلْأَمْرِ, aor. ـِ, *He was patient in relation to the affair,* or *event;* (Ḳ;) as also ↓ اعترف, (O, Ḳ,) as some say. (O.) And عَرَفَ عِنْدَ المُصِيبَةِ *He was patient on the occasion of the affliction,* or *misfortune.* (TA.) —— And عَرَفَ *He was,* or *became, submissive,* or *tractable;* (Ibn-'Abbád, O, TA;) and so ↓ اعترف, (IAạr, O, Ḳ,) said of a man, (IAạr, O,) and of a beast that one rides. (O.) ═ عَرُفَ, inf. n. عَرَافَةٌ, *He* (a man) *was,* or *became, pleasant,* or *sweet, in his odour.* (TA.) And ↓ اعرف, said of food, *It was sweet in its* عَرْف, i. e. *odour.* (TA.) —— عَرِفَ *He* (a man, TA) *made much use of perfume.* (IAạr, O, Ḳ.) —— And *He relinquished,* or *abstained from, perfume.* (IAạr, O.) ═ عُرِفَ, (Ṣ, O, Ḳ,) inf. n. عَرْفٌ, (Ḳ, TA,) accord. to one or more of the copies of the Ḳ عِرْفَانٌ, (TA,) *He* (a man, Ṣ, O) *had a purulent pustule, termed* عُرْفَة, *come forth in the whiteness* [or palm] *of his hand.* (Ṣ, O, Ḳ.)

2. تَعْرِيفٌ signifies The *making to know;* syn. إِعْلَامٌ : (Ṣ, O, Ḳ, TA:) [or rather it has a more restricted signification than the latter word, as is indicated in the preceding paragraph:] and in this sense its verb may have two objective complements: one says, عَرَّفَهُ الأَمْرَ *He made him to know the affair,* or *case;* syn. أَعْلَمَهُ إِيَّاهُ : [or *he acquainted him with it;* or *told him of it:*] and عَرَّفَهُ بَيْتَهُ *He made him to know,* or *acquainted him with, the place of his house,* or *tent;* syn. أَعْلَمَهُ بِمَكَانِهِ : (TA:) [and] one says عَرَّفْتُهُ بِهِ, meaning *I made him to know it by means of any of the five senses* [or *by mental perception;* as also عَرَّفْتُهُ إِيَّاهُ]. (Mṣb.) See also 1, former half. And see 4. —— Also The *making known;* contr. of تَنْكِيرٌ. (O, Ḳ.) عَرَّفَ بَعْضَهُ, in the Ḳur [lxvi. 3], has been expl. as meaning *He made known part thereof.* (TA. [For other explanations, see 1.]) And عَرَّفْتُهُ بِزَيْدٍ means *I made him known by the name of Zeyd;* like the phrase سَمَّيْتُهُ بِزَيْدٍ. (Sb, TA.) —— [Hence, The *explaining* a term: and *an explanation* thereof: thus used, its pl. is تَعْرِيفَاتٌ : it has a less restricted meaning than حَدٌّ, which signifies the "defining," and "a definition." —— And The *making* a noun, or a nominal proposition, *determinate.* —— Hence also,] The *crying* a stray-beast, or a beast or some other thing that has been lost; (Ṣ, TA;) the *mentioning* it [*and describing* it] *and seeking to find him who had knowledge of* it. (TA.) —— And [hence likewise,] عَرَّفَهُ بِذَنْبِهِ *He branded him,* or *stigmatized him, with his misdeed.* (TA.) ═ Also The *rendering* [a thing] *fragrant;* (Ṣ, O,* Ḳ,* TA;) from العَرْفُ : (Ṣ:) and the *adorning* [it], *decorating* [it], or *embellishing* [it]. (TA.) عَرَّفَهَا لَهُمْ, in the Ḳur [xlvii. 7], is said to mean *He hath rendered it fragrant* [i. e. Paradise (الجَنَّة)] *for them:* (Ṣ, O:) or it means *He hath described it to them so that, when they enter it, they shall know it by that description,* or *so that they shall know their places of abode therein:* (O:) or *He hath described it to them, and made them desirous of it:* (Er-Rághib, TA:) [and the like is said by Bḍ:] or *He hath defined it for them so that there shall be for every one a distinct paradise.* (Bḍ.) —— One says also, عَرَّفَ رَأْسَهُ بِالدُّهْنِ *He moistened the hair of his head abundantly with oil,* or *with the oil;* syn. رَوَّاهُ. (TA.) —— And عَرَّفَ طَعَامَهُ *He made his food to have much seasoning,* or *condiment.* (TA.) ═ Also The *halting* [of the pilgrims] *at 'Arafát.* (Ṣ, O, Ḳ.) You say, عَرَّفُوا, (Ṣ, Mgh, O, Mṣb,) inf. n. as above, *They halted at 'Arafát;* (Mgh, Mṣb;) or *they were present at 'Arafát.* (Ṣ, O.) And [hence], in a post-classical sense, *They imitated the people of 'Arafát, in some other place, by going forth to the desert and there praying, and humbling themselves,* or *offering earnest supplication;* (Mgh;) or *by assembling in their mosques to pray and to beg forgiveness:* (Ḥar p. 672:) the first who did this was Ibn-'Abbás, at El-Baṣrah. (Mgh, and Ḥar ubi suprà.) And عَرَّفَ بِالهَدْىِ *He brought the animal for sacrifice to 'Arafát.* (Mgh.) ═ عَرَّفَ الشَّرَّ بَيْنَهُمْ *He excited evil,* or *mischief, between them,* or *among them:* the verb in this phrase being formed by permutation from أَرَّثَ. (Yaḳoob, TA.)

4. اعرف فُلَانًا *He told such a one of his misdeed, then forgave him;* and so ▼ عرّفهُ. (TA.) ═ اعرف (said of a horse, Ṣ, O) *He had a long* عُرْف [or *mane*]. (Ṣ, O, Ḳ.) ═ See also 1, near the end.

5. تعرّف *It was,* or *became, known.* (Ḥar p. 6.) — And تعرّف إِلَيْهِ *He made himself known to him;* (TA;) [and so ▼ استعرف; for] you say, أَتَيْتُ مُتَنَكِّرًا ثُمَّ ٱسْتَعْرَفْتُ i. e. [*I came disguising myself,* or *assuming an unknown appearance, then*] *I made known who I was:* (L:) and اِئْتِ فُلَانًا فَٱسْتَعْرِفْ إِلَيْهِ حَتَّى يَعْرِفَكَ [*Come thou to such a one and make thyself known to him, that he may know thee*]. (Ṣ, O, Ḳ.*) [See also 8.] — [Hence,] one says, تعرّف إِلَى ٱللّٰهِ بِالعِبَادَاتِ وَالأَدْعِيَةِ [*He made himself known to God by religious services and prayers*]. (Er-Rághib, TA.) And تَعَرَّفْ إِلَى ٱللّٰهِ فِي الرَّخَآءِ يَعْرِفْكَ فِي الشِّدَّةِ, occurring in a saying of the Prophet to Ibn-'Abbás, [may be rendered *Make thyself known to God* by obedience *in ampleness of circumstances,* then *He will acknowledge thee in straitness:* or] means *render thou obedience to God* [&c., then] *He will requite thee* [&c.]. (O.) ═ تعرّفهُ [*He acquainted himself,* or *made himself acquainted, with it,* or *him; informed himself of it; learned it;* and *discovered it:* often used in these senses: for an instance of the last, see تَفَرَّسَ: it is similar to تَعَلَّمَهُ, but more restricted in meaning. — And] *He sought the knowledge of it:* (Ḥar p. 6:) [or *he did so leisurely,* or *repeatedly, and effectually:*] you say, تَعَرَّفْتُ مَا عِنْدَ فُلَانٍ *I sought leisurely,* or *repeatedly, after the knowledge of what such a one possessed until I knew it.* (Ṣ, O, Ḳ.*) — And تعرّفهُ المَكَانَ, and فِي المَكَانِ, *He looked at it, endeavouring to obtain a clear knowledge thereof, in the place;* syn. تَأَمَّلَهُ بِهِ. (TA.) ═ [تَعَرُّفٌ is also expl. in the KL by the Pers. words بعرف كارى كردن, app. meaning *The acting with* عُرْف i. e. *goodness,* &c.: but Golius has hence rendered the verb "convenienter opus fecit."]

6. تعارفوا *They knew,* or *were acquainted with, one another.* (Ṣ, O, Ḳ.) — And *i. q.* تَفَاخَرُوا [i. e. *They vied, competed,* or *contended for superiority, in glorying,* or *boasting,* or *in glory,* &c.; or simply *they vied, one with another*]: it occurs in a trad., or, as some relate it, with ز; and both are expl. as having this meaning. (TA.)

8. اعترف بِهِ *He acknowledged it,* or *confessed it,* (Ṣ, Mgh, O, Mṣb, Ḳ,) namely, a misdeed, (Ṣ, O,) or a thing; (Mgh, Mṣb;) and so ▼ عَرَفَ بِهِ and لَهُ, namely, his misdeed [&c.]; (Ḳ;) [for] sometimes they put عَرَفَ in the place of اعترف; (O;) and so ▼ عَرَفَهُ: (Ksh and Bḍ and Jel in xvi. 85:) ▼ عِرْفَانُ ▼ الإِحْسَانِ (occurring in the Ḳ voce شُكْر &c.) means *The acknowledgment,* or *confession, of beneficence; thankfulness,* or *gratitude:*] and one says, مَا أَعْرِفُ ▼ لِأَحَدٍ يَصْرَعُنِى (Ṣ, O, TA) i. e. مَا أَعْتَرِفُ, (Ṣ, O,) meaning *I do not acknowledge* [*any one that will throw me down*]; this was said by an Arab of the desert. (TA.) — اعترف إِلَىَّ *He acquainted me with his name and condition.* (Ḳ.) And اعترف لَهُ *He described himself to him in such a manner as that he would certify himself of him thereby.* (TA.) [See also 5.] — اعترف also signifies *He described* a thing that had been picked up, and a stray-beast, *in such a manner as that he would be known to be its owner.* (TA.) — And you say, اِعْتَرَفْتُ القَوْمَ, (Ṣ, O,) or فُلَانًا, (Ḳ,) *I asked the people,* or *party,* (Ṣ, O,) or *such a one,* (Ḳ,) *respecting a subject of information, in order that I might know it.* (Ṣ, O, Ḳ.) — See also 1, former half. ═ And see 1, last quarter, in two places.

10. استعرف [*He sought,* or *desired, knowledge;* or *asked if any had knowledge;* of a person or thing: a meaning clearly shown in the M by an explanation of a verse cited in art. بلو, conj. 8, q. v.]. — استعرف إِلَيْهِ: see 5. Also *He mentioned his relationship, lineage,* or *genealogy, to him.* (TA.) — استعرفهُ: see 1, former half.

12. اِعْرَوْرَفَ *He* (a horse, TA) *had a mane* (عُرْف). (Ṣ, O, TA.) — اعرورف الفَرَسَ *He* (a man, O) *mounted upon the mane* (عُرْف) *of the horse.* (O, Ḳ. [In the CḲ, وَالفَرَسَ عَلَا عُرْفَهُ is erroneously put for وَالفَرَسَ عَلَا عَلَى عُرْفِهِ.]) — And اعرورف (said of a man, Ḳ) † *He rose upon the* أَعْرَاف [pl. of عُرْف, and app. here meaning the wall between Paradise and Hell: (see the Ḳur vii. 44:) probably used in this sense in a trad.]. (Ibn-'Abbád, O, Ḳ.) — Said of the sea, ‡ *Its waves became high,* (Ṣ, O, Ḳ, TA,) *like the* عُرْف [or *mane*]: and in like manner said of the torrent, ‡ *It became heapy and high.* (TA.) — Said of blood, † *It had froth* (O, Ḳ) *like the* عُرْف [or *mane*]. (O.) — Said of palm-trees (نَخْل), ‡ *They became dense, and luxuriant,* or *abundant,* or *thickly intermixed, like the* عُرْف [or *mane*] *of the hyena.* (O, Ḳ, TA.) — And, said of a man, ‡ *He prepared himself for evil,* or *mischief,* (Ṣ, O, Ḳ, TA,) *and raised his head,* or *stretched forth his neck, for that purpose.* (TA.) [See also 12 in art. عزف.]

عَرْفٌ *An odour,* whether *fragrant* or *fetid,* (Ṣ, O, Ḳ, TA,) in most instances the former, (Ḳ, TA,) as when it is used in relation to Paradise: (TA:) and ▼ عَرْفَةٌ signifies [the same, i. e.] رِيحٌ (Ḳ, TḲ) and رَائِحَةٌ. (TḲ.) One says, مَا أَطْيَبَ عَرْفَهُ [*How fragrant is its odour!*]. (Ṣ, O.) And لَا يَعْجِزُ مَسْكُ السَّوْءِ عَنْ عَرْفِ السَّوْءِ [*The bad hide will not lack the fetid odour*]; (Ṣ, O, Ḳ;) a prov.; (Ṣ, O;) applied to the low, ignoble, mean, or sordid, who will not cease from his evil doing; he being likened to the hide that is not fit for being tanned; (O, Ḳ;) wherefore it is cast aside, and becomes fetid. (O.) And some read, in the Ḳur [lxxvii. 1], وَالْمُرْسَلَاتِ عَرْفًا, [as meaning *By the winds that are sent forth with fragrance,*] instead of عُرْفًا. (TA.) ═ Also *A certain plant:* or the ثُمَام [or *panic grass*]: (Ḳ:) or *a certain plant, not of the* [*kind called*] حَمْض, *nor of the* [*kind called*] عِضَاه; (Ibn-'Abbád, O, L, Ḳ;) *of the* [*kind called*] ثُمَام. (Ibn-'Abbád, O, L.)

عُرْفٌ [*Acknowledgment,* or *confession;*] a subst. from الإِعْتِرَافُ, (Ṣ, O, Ḳ, TA,) as meaning الإِقْرَارُ. (TA.) Hence, (Ṣ, O,) you say, (Ḳ,) لَهُ عَلَىَّ أَلْفٌ عُرْفًا, meaning اِعْتِرَافًا [i. e. *A thousand is due to him on my part by acknowledgment,* or *confession*]; (Ṣ, O,* Ḳ;) the last word being a corroborative. (Ṣ, O.) — Also *i. q.* ▼ مَعْرُوفٌ; (Ṣ, O, Mṣb, Ḳ;) as also ▼ عَارِفَةٌ, (Ṣ, O, Ḳ,) of which the pl. is عَوَارِفُ; (O, Ḳ;) عُرْف being contr. of نُكْر, (Ṣ, O, Ḳ,) and ▼ مَعْرُوف being contr. of مُنْكَر [as syn. with نُكْر]; (Ṣ, Mgh, O, Ḳ;) i. e. *Goodness,* or *a good quality* or *action;* and *gentleness,* or *lenity;* and *beneficence,* [*favour, kindness,* or *bounty,*] or *a benefit, a benefaction,* or *an act of beneficence* [or *favour* or *kindness*]: (Mṣb:) عُرْف is also expl. as signifying *liberality,* or *bounty;* (Ḳ, TA;) and so ▼ عُرُف, which is a dial. var. thereof: (TA:) and *a thing liberally,* or *freely, bestowed;* or *given:* (Ḳ:) and ▼ مَعْرُوف is expl. as signifying *liberality,* or *bounty,* when it is *with moderation,* or *with a right and just aim:* [and sometimes it means simply *moderation:*] and *sincere,* or *honest, advice or counsel or action:* and *good fellowship with one's family and with others of mankind:* it is an epithet in which the quality of a subst. predominates: (TA:) and signifies *any action,* or *deed, of which the goodness is known by reason and by the law;* and مُنْكَر signifies the contr. thereof. (Er-Rághib, TA.) It is said in the Ḳur [vii. 198], وَأْمُرْ بِالْعُرْفِ, (O,) meaning [*And enjoin thou goodness,* &c., or] *what is deemed good,* or *approved, of actions.* (Bḍ.) And you say, أَوْلَاهُ عُرْفًا, (Ṣ, O,) or ▼ عَارِفَةً, (TA,) meaning ▼ مَعْرُوفًا [i. e. *He did to him,* or *conferred upon him, a benefit,* &c.]. (Ṣ, O, TA.) وَلِلْمُطَلَّقَاتِ مَتَاعٌ بِٱلْمَعْرُوفِ ▼ [in the Ḳur ii. 242] means [*And for the divorced women* there shall be *a provision of necessaries*] *with moderation,* or *right and just aim, and beneficence.* (TA.) And ▼ قَوْلٌ مَعْرُوفٌ وَمَغْفِرَةٌ خَيْرٌ مِنْ صَدَقَةٍ يَتْبَعُهَا أَذًى [in the same, ii. 265,] means Refusal with *pleasing* [or *gracious*] *speech,* (Bḍ, Jel, TA,) *and prayer* [expressed to the beggar, that God may sustain him,] (TA,) *and forgiveness* granted to the beggar for his importunity (Bḍ, Jel) or obtained by such refusal from God or from the beggar, (Bḍ,) *are better than an alms which annoyance follows* (TA) by reproach for a benefit conferred and for begging. (Jel.) And مَنْ كَانَ فَقِيرًا فَلْيَأْكُلْ ▼ بِٱلْمَعْرُوفِ [in the same, iv. 6,] means [*And such as is poor, let him take for himself* (lit. *eat*)] *according to what is approved by reason and by the law,* (TA,) or *according to his need* (Bḍ) and *the recompense of his labour.* (Bḍ, Jel.) — العُرْفُ, in lexicology, signifies *The commonly-known, commonly-received,* or *common conventional, language; common parlance,* or *common usage:* mostly meaning that of a whole people; in which case, the epithet العَامُّ is sometimes added: but often meaning that of a particular class; as, for instance, of the lawyers. Hence the terms حَقِيقَةٌ عُرْفًا and مَجَازٌ عُرْفًا, expl. in arts. حق and جوز. See also مُتَعَارَفٌ: and see عَادَةٌ. ═ Also The عُرْف of the horse; (Ṣ, O;) [i. e. the *mane;*] the *hair*

(Mgh, Mṣb, Ḳ) *that grows on the ridge* (Mṣb) *of the neck* of the horse (Mgh, Mṣb, Ḳ) or similar beast; (Mṣb;) as also ↑ عُرُفٌ: (Ḳ:) [see also مَعْرَفَةٌ:] or the *part, of the neck, which is the place of growth of the hair:* [see again مَعْرَفَةٌ:] and the *part, of the neck* [of a bird], *which is the place of growth of the feathers:* (TA:) [or the *feathers* themselves *of the neck;* used in this sense in the Ḳ and TA in art. بول, as is shown by the context therein:] and the [*comb* or] *elongated piece of flesh on the upper part of the head* of a cock; to which the بَظْر of a girl is likened: (Mṣb:) pl. أَعْرَافٌ [properly a pl. of pauc.] (O, TA) and عُرُوفٌ. (TA.) Aṣ used it in relation to a man, explaining the phrase جَآءَ فُلَانٌ مُبْرَئِلًّا لِلشَّرِّ as meaning نَافِشًا عُرْفَهُ [i. e. † *Such a one came as though ruffling the feathers of his neck to do evil,* or *mischief*]. (TA.) And [hence] it is said in a trad., جَاؤُوا كَأَنَّهُمْ عُرْفٌ † [*They came as though they were a mane*], meaning, *following one another.* (TA.) And one says, جَآءَ القَوْمُ عُرْفًا عُرْفًا † [*The people, or party, came*] *one after another:* like the saying, طَارَ القَطَا عُرْفًا † [*The sand-grouse flew*] *one after another.* (Ḳ.) And hence, وَالْمُرْسَلَاتِ عُرْفًا, (Ṣ, O, Ḳ,) in the Ḳur [lxxvii. 1], a metaphorical phrase, from the عُرْف of the horse, meaning ‡ [*By the angels,* or *the winds, that are sent forth*] *consecutively, like* [*the several portions of*] *the* عُرْف [or *mane*] *of the horse:* (Ṣ, O:) or the meaning is, *sent forth* بِالْمَعْرُوفِ, (Ṣ, O, Ḳ, TA,) i. e. *with beneficence,* or *benefit:* (TA:) [for further explanations, see the expositions of Z and Bḍ or others: and see also art. رسل:] some read عُرُفًا [expl. in the next preceding paragraph]. (TA.) —— [Hence also,] ‡ The *waves of the sea.* (Ḳ, TA.) —— And † *Elevated sand;* as also ↑ عُرُفٌ and ↑ عُرْفَةٌ: pl. (of the last, TA) عُرَفٌ and (of the first, TA) أَعْرَافٌ: (Ṣ, O, Ḳ:) and all signify likewise † *an elevated place:* (Ḳ:) and the first, † the *elevated,* or *overtopping, back* of a portion of sand, (Ḳ, TA,) and of a mountain, and of anything high: and † *an elevated portion* of the earth or ground: and [the pl.] أَعْرَافٌ † the حَرْث [meaning *land ploughed,* or *prepared, for sowing*] *that is upon the* [*channels for irrigation that are called*] فُلْجَان [pl. of فَلْجٌ] and قَوَائِد [pl. of قَائِدٌ]. (TA.) —— [The pl.] الأَعْرَافُ, (Ṣ, O, Ḳ,) mentioned in the Ḳur [vii. 44 and 46], (Ṣ, O,) is applied to † *A wall between Paradise and Hell:* (Ṣ, O, Ḳ:) so it is said: (Ṣ, O:) or *the upper parts of the wall:* or by عَلَى الأَعْرَافِ may be there meant عَلَى مَعْرِفَةِ أَهْلِ الجَنَّةِ وَأَهْلِ النَّارِ [i. e., app., *and possessing knowledge of the people of Paradise and of the people of Hell:* for it seems that مُسْتَوُونَ, or the like, is to be understood before على]. (Zj, TA.) [And hence it is the name of *The Seventh Chapter of the Ḳur-án.*] By أَصْحَابُ الأَعْرَافِ [*The occupants of the* اعراف], there mentioned, are said to be meant persons whose good and evil works have been equal, so that they shall not have merited Paradise by the former nor Hell by the latter: or prophets: or angels. (Zj, TA.) —— See also عُرُوفٌ. —— [The pl.] أَعْرَافٌ also signifies ‡ The *higher,* or *highest,* (Ḳ, TA,) and *first,* or *foremost,* (TA,) of winds; (Ḳ, TA;) and likewise of clouds, and of mists. (TA.) —— And عُرْفٌ signifies also, (Aṣ, O, Ḳ,) in the speech of the people of El-Baḥreyn, (Aṣ, O,) *A species* [or *variety*] *of palm-trees;* (Aṣ, O, Ḳ;) and so [the pl.] أَعْرَافٌ (O, Ḳ) is expl. by IDrd: (O:) or *when they first yield fruit,* or *edible fruit,* or *ripe fruit;* (Ḳ, TA;) or *when they attain to doing so:* (TA:) or *a* [*sort of*] *palm-tree in El-Baḥreyn, also called* بُرْشُوم; (Ḳ, TA;) but this is what is meant by Aṣ and IDrd. (TA.) —— And The *tree of the* أُتْرُجّ [i. e. *citrus medica,* or *citron*]. (Ḳ.) ==== Also pl. of عَرُوفٌ: —— and of عُرْفَةٌ and أَعْرَفُ. (Ḳ.)

عِرْفٌ, with kesr, is from the saying, مَا عَرَفَ عِرْفِي إِلَّا بِأَخَرَةٍ, (Ṣ, O,) which means *He did not know me save at the last,* or *lastly,* or *latterly.* (Ṣ, O, Ḳ.) ==== And it signifies *Patience.* (IAạr, O, Ḳ.) A poet says, (namely Aboo-Dahbal El-Jumaḥee, TA,)

قُلْ لِٱبْنِ قَيْسٍ أَخِي الرُّقَيَّاتِ *
مَا أَحْسَنَ العِرْفَ فِي المُصِيبَاتِ *

[*Say thou to the son of Ḳeys, the brother of Er-Ruḳeiyat, How good is patience in afflictions!*]. (IAạr, O, TA.)

عُرُفٌ: see عُرْفٌ, in three places.

عُرْفَةٌ *A question,* or *questioning, respecting a subject of information, in order to know it;* (Ḳ,* TA;) as also ↑ عِرْفَةٌ. (Ḳ, TA.) ==== See also عُرْفٌ. ==== Also *A purulent pustule that comes forth in the whiteness* [or *palm*] *of the hand.* (ISk, Ṣ, O, Ḳ.)

عُرْفَةٌ: see عُرْفٌ, latter half. —— Also *An open, elongated, tract of land, producing plants,* or *herbage.* (O, Ḳ.) —— Also, (O, Ḳ,) and ↑ عُرْفٌ, (TA,) *A limit* (O, Ḳ, TA) between two things: (Ḳ:) [like أُرْفَةٌ:] pl. of the former عُرَفٌ. (O, Ḳ, TA.)

عِرْفَةٌ [an inf. n.] *I. q.* مَعْرِفَةٌ. (O, Ḳ. [See 1, first sentence. In the O, it seems to be regarded as a simple subst.]) —— See also عُرْفَةٌ.

يَوْمُ عَرَفَةَ *The ninth day of* [*the month*] ذُو الحِجَّةِ [*when the pilgrims halt at* عَرَفَات]: (Ṣ, Mgh, O, Mṣb, Ḳ:) the latter word being without tenween, (Ṣ, O,) imperfectly decl., because it is of the fem. gender and a proper name, (Mṣb,) and not admitting the art. ال. (Ṣ, O, Mṣb.) —— See also the next paragraph.

عَرَفَاتٌ *The place* [or *mountain*] *where the pilgrims halt* (Mgh, O, Mṣb, Ḳ) *on the day of* عَرَفَة [above mentioned], (O, Ḳ,) [described by Burckhardt as a granite hill, about a mile, or a mile and a half, in circuit, with sloping sides, rising nearly two hundred feet above the level of the adjacent plain,] *said to be nine miles,* (Mṣb,) or *twelve miles,* (Ḳ,) *from Mekkeh;* (Mṣb, Ḳ;) said by J to be *a place in,* or *at, Minè,* but incorrectly, (Ḳ, TA,) unless thereby be meant *near Minè;* (TA;) also called by some ↑ عَرَفَةُ; (Mgh, Mṣb;) but the saying نَزَلْنَا عَرَفَةَ, (Ṣ, O, Ḳ,) or نَزَلْتُ بِعَرَفَةَ, (Mṣb,) [*We,* or *I, alighted at* عَرَفَة,] is like a post-classical phrase, (Ṣ, O, Ḳ,) and (Ṣ, O) it is said to be (Mṣb) not genuine Arabic: (Ṣ, O, Mṣb:) عَرَفَاتٌ is a [proper] name in the pl. form, and therefore is not itself pluralized: (Ṣ, O, Ḳ:) it is as though the term عَرَفَة applied to every distinct portion thereof: (TA:) as Fr says, it has, correctly, no sing.; (Ṣ, O;) and it is determinate as denoting a particular place; (Sb, Ṣ, O, Ḳ, TA;) and therefore not admitting the article ال; (Sb, TA;) differing from الزَّيْدُونَ [because this is a proper name common to a number of persons]: you say, هٰؤُلَاءِ عَرَفَاتٌ حَسَنَةً [lit. *These are 'Arafát, in a good state*], putting the epithet in the accus. case because it is indeterminate [as a denotative of state, like مُصَدِّقًا in the saying وَهُوَ الحَقُّ مُصَدِّقًا لِمَا مَعَهُمْ, in the Ḳur ii. 85]: (Ṣ, O:) it is decl. (مَصْرُوفَةٌ [more properly مُعْرَبَةٌ]) because the ت is equivalent to the ى and و in مُسْلِمِينَ and مُسْلِمُونَ, (Ṣ, O, Ḳ,) the tenween becoming equivalent to the ن, therefore, being used as a proper name, it is left in its original state, like as is مُسْلِمُونَ when used as a proper name: (Akh, Ṣ, O, Ḳ:) [i. e.,] it is decl. in the manner of مُسْلِمَاتٌ and مُؤْمِنَاتٌ, the tenween being like that which corresponds to the masc. pl. termination ن, not the tenween of perfect declinability, because it is a proper name and of the fem. gender, wherefore it does not admit the article ال. (Mṣb.) عَرَفَاتٌ was thus named because Adam and Eve knew each other (تَعَارَفَا) there (IF, O, Ḳ, TA) after their descent from Paradise: (TA:) or because Gabriel, when he taught Abraham the rites and ceremonies of the pilgrimage, said to him "Hast thou known?" (أَعَرَفْتَ), (O, Ḳ,) and he replied "I have known" (عَرَفْتُ): (Ḳ:) or because it is a place sanctified and magnified, as though it were rendered fragrant (عُرِّفَ i. e. طُيِّبَ): (O, Ḳ:) or because the people know one another (يَتَعَارَفُونَ) there: or, accord. to Er-Rághib, because of men's making themselves known (لِتَعَرُّفِ العِبَادِ) there by religious services and prayers. (TA.)

[عُرْفِيٌّ *Of, or relating to,* العُرْف as meaning *the commonly-known* or *commonly-received* or *conventional language,* or *common parlance,* or *common usage.* Hence حَقِيقَةٌ عُرْفِيَّةٌ and مَجَازٌ عُرْفِيٌّ, expl. in arts. حق and جوز.]

عَرَفِيٌّ *Of, or relating to,* عَرَفَات. (O, Ḳ.)

عِرِفَّانٌ, (O, Ḳ,) accord. to Th, A man (O) *who acknowledges,* or *confesses, a thing, and directs to it,* or *indicates it;* (O, Ḳ;) thus expl. as an epithet, though Sb mentions his not knowing it as an epithet; (O;) occurring in a poem of Er-Rá'ee, and expl. by some as the name of a companion of his: (O, Ḳ:*) and عُرُفَّانٌ signifies the same; (Ḳ;) but this is said by Sb to be a word transferred from the category of proper names. (O.) ═ Also the latter, (O,) or both, (Ḳ,) *A small creeping thing that is found in the sands of 'Álij and of Ed-Dahnà*: (O, Ḳ:) or *a large* [*sort of locust, or the like, such as is termed*] جُنْدَب, *resembling the* جَرَادَة, (AḤn, Ḳ, TA,) *having a crest* (لَهُ عُرْفٌ), (AḤn, TA,) *not found save upon* [*one or the other of two species of plants, i. e.*] *a* رِمْثَة *or an* عُنْظُوَانَة: (AḤn, Ḳ, TA:) but AḤn mentions only the latter form of the word, عُرُفَان. (TA.)

عَرُوفٌ: see عَارِفٌ, in two places.

عَرِيفٌ: see عَارِفٌ, first sentence. — [Hence,] *One who knows his companions*: pl. عُرَفَآءُ. (O, Ḳ.) The *chief*, or *head*, (Mgh, Ḳ, TA,) of a people, or party; (Ḳ, TA;) because he knows the states, or conditions, of those over whom he acts as such; (Mgh;) or because he is known as such [so that it is from the same word in the last of the senses assigned to it in this paragraph]; (Ḳ;) or because of his acquaintance with the ordering, or management, of them: (TA:) or the نَقِيب [or *intendant, superintendent, overseer,* or *inspector, who takes cognizance of, and is responsible for, the actions* of a people], who is below the رَئِيس: (Ṣ, O, Ḳ:) or the *manager and superintendent of the affairs, who acquaints himself with the circumstances,* of a tribe, or of a company of men; of the measure فَعِيل in the sense of the measure فَاعِل: (IAth, TA:) or the *orderer*, or *manager, of the affairs* of a people, or party; as also ↓ عَارِفٌ: (Mṣb:) pl. as above: (Ṣ, IAth, Mṣb:) it is said that he is *over a few persons*, and the مَنْكِب is over five عُرَفَآء, then the أَمِير is over these. (Mṣb.) It is said in a trad. that the عُرَفَآء are in Hell, as a caution against undertaking the office of chief, or head, on account of the trial that is therein; for when one does not perform the duty thereof, he sins, and deserves punishment. (TA.) — [It is now used as meaning *A monitor in a school, who hears the lessons of the other scholars.*] ═ See also مَعْرُوفٌ, with which it is syn.

عِرَافَةٌ The *holding*, and the *exercising, of the office of* عَرِيف. (Ṣ, Mgh,* O, Mṣb,* Ḳ. [An inf. n.: see 1, in the middle of the latter half.])

عَرُوفَةٌ: see عَارِفٌ, in two places.

عَرَّافٌ *A* كَاهِن [or *diviner*]: (Ṣ, O, Mṣb, Ḳ:) or the former is *one who informs of the past*, and the latter is one who informs of the past and of the future: (Mṣb:) or, accord. to Er-Rághib, [but the converse of his explanation seems to be that which is correct,] the former is *one who informs of future events*, and the latter is one who informs of past events. (TA.) Hence the saying of the Prophet, that whoso comes to an عَرَّاف and asks him respecting a thing, prayer of forty nights will not be accepted from him. (O.) — And (Mṣb) *An astrologer*, (IAth, Mgh, Mṣb,) *who lays claim to the knowledge of hidden*, or *invisible, things*, (IAth, Mgh,) *which God has made to belong exclusively to Himself*: (IAth:) and this is [said to be] meant in the trad. above mentioned. (Mgh.) — And *A physician*. (Ṣ, O, Ḳ.) — And *One who smells* [for يسمر I read يَشَمُّ] *the ground, and thus knows the places of water, and knows in what country*, or *district, he is*. (ISh, in TA, art. حزى.)

عَارِفٌ and ↓ عَرِيفٌ are syn., (Ṣ, O, Ḳ,) like عَالِمٌ and عَلِيمٌ, (Ṣ, O,) signifying *Knowing*; [&c., agreeably with the explanations of the verb in the first quarter of the first paragraph of this art.;] as also ↓ عَرُوفَةٌ, (Ṣ, O, Ḳ,) but in an intensive sense, which is denoted by the ة, (Ṣ, O, TA,) meaning [*knowing, &c., much*, or *well*; or] *knowing*, or *acquainted with, affairs*, and *not failing to know* [or *recognise*] *one that has been seen once*; (TA;) as in the phrase, رَجُلٌ عَرُوفَةٌ ↓ بِالْأُمُورِ [*A man much*, or *well, acquainted with affairs*]. (Ṣ, O.) — For the first, see also عَرِيفٌ. — It also signifies particularly [*Skilled in divine things*;] *possessing knowledge of God, and of his kingdom, and of the way of dealing well with Him*. (TA.) — See also مَعْرُوفٌ. ═ Also, the first, [*Patient*; or] *very patient*, or *having much patience*; syn. صَبُورٌ; (AO, Ṣ, O, Ḳ;) and so ↓ عَرُوفٌ; (Ṣ, O, Ḳ;) of which latter the pl. is عُرُفٌ. (Ḳ.) One says, أُصِيبَ فُلَانٌ فَوُجِدَ عَارِفًا [*Such a one was smitten, or afflicted, and was found to be patient*]. (Ṣ, O.) And حَبَسْتُ نَفْسًا عَارِفَةً, meaning صَابِرَةً [i. e. *I restrained a patient soul*, or *mind*]: (O, TA:) like the phrase صَبَرْتُ عَارِفَةً in a verse of 'Antarah [cited in the first paragraph of art. صبر]. (Ṣ,* O.) And ↓ نَفْسٌ عَرُوفٌ means [*A soul*, or *mind*,] *enduring; very patient; that endures an event*, or *a case, when made to experience it*. (TA.) عَوَارِفُ [is pl. of عَارِفَةٌ, and] means *Patient* she-camels. (IB, TA.)

عَارِفَةٌ as a subst.; pl. عَوَارِفُ: see عُرْفٌ, first quarter, in two places.

عُوَيْرِفٌ [dim. of عَارِفٌ, i. e. signifying One *possessing little knowledge* &c.]. One says of him in whom is a sin, or crime, مَا هُوَ إِلَّا عُوَيْرِفٌ [*He is none other than one possessing little knowledge*]. (TA.)

أَعْرَفُ is mentioned in "the Book" of Sb as used in the phrase هٰذَا أَعْرَفُ مِنْ هٰذَا [meaning *This is more known than this*]: irregularly formed from مَعْرُوفٌ, not from عَارِفٌ. (ISd, TA.) ═ Also A thing *having what is termed* عُرْف [i. e. *a mane*, or *the like*]: (Ṣ, O, Ḳ:) fem. عَرْفَآءُ: pl., masc. and fem., عُرْفٌ. (Ḳ.) It is applied to a horse, (Mgh, Ḳ, TA,) meaning *Having a full mane*, or *much hair of the mane*. (Mgh, TA.) And to a serpent (O, Ḳ) such as is termed شَيْطَان [which is described as having an عُرْف]. (O.) And the fem. is applied to a she-camel, (Ḳ, TA,) meaning *High in the hump*: or *resembling the male*: or *long in her* عُرْف [or *mane*]: (TA:) or *having what resembles the* عُرْف *by reason of her fatness*: or *having, upon her neck, fur like the* عُرْف. (Ḥam p. 611.) — The fem. is also used as meaning The ضَبُع [i. e. *hyena*, or *female hyena*], because of the abundance of its hair (Ṣ, O, Ḳ, TA) of the neck, (O, Ḳ, TA,) or because of the length of its عُرْف. (TA.) — And one says سَنَامٌ أَعْرَفُ *A long*, or *tall, camel's hump, having an* عُرْف. (TA.) And جَبَلٌ أَعْرَفُ † *A mountain having what resembles the* عُرْف. (TA.) And قُلَّةٌ عَرْفَآءُ ‡ *A high mountain-top*. (TA.) And حَزْنٌ أَعْرَفُ † *High rugged ground*. (TA.)

مَعْرَفٌ (Ṣ, O, Ḳ [in one of my copies of the Ṣ written مُعَرَّف]) and مَعْرِفٌ also (Ḥam p. 47) sing. of مَعَارِفُ, which means The *face* [and *faces*], and *any part thereof that appears*; as in the saying اِمْرَأَةٌ حَسَنَةُ المَعَارِفِ [*A woman beautiful in the face*, or *in the parts thereof that appear*]; (Ṣ, O, Ḳ;) because the person is known thereby: (TA:) or, as some say, no sing. of it is known: (Ḥar p. 146:) and some say that it signifies the *beauties*, or *beautiful parts, of the face*. (TA.) Er-Rá'ee says,

* مُتَلَفِّفِينَ عَلَى مَعَارِفِنَا *
* نَثْنِى لَهُنَّ حَوَاشِىَ العَصْبِ *

[*Muffling our faces*, or *the parts thereof that appeared, we fold*, or *folding, to them the selvages of the* عَصْب (a sort of garment).] (Ṣ, O: but the latter has مُتَلَثِّمِينَ.) And one says, حَيَّا اللّٰهُ المَعَارِفَ, meaning [*May God preserve*] *the faces*. (O, Ḳ.) And قَدْ هَاجَتْ مَعَارِفُ فُلَانٍ *The features of such a one, whereby he was known to me, have withered*, like as the plant withers: said of a man who has turned away, from the speaker, his love, or affection. (TA.) And هُوَ مِنَ المَعَارِفِ *He is of those who are known*; [or *of those who are acquaintances*;] (O, Ḳ;) as though meaning مِنْ ذَوِى المَعَارِفِ, i. e. *of those having faces* [*whereby they are known*]: (O:) or مَعَارِفُ الرَّجُلِ means *Those who are entitled to the man's love*, or *affection*, and *with whom he has acquaintance*; [and simply *the acquaintances of the man*;] and is pl. of ↓ مَعْرِفَةٌ. (Ḥar p. 146.) مَعَارِفُ الأَرْضِ means *The faces*, and *known parts, of the land*. (TA.)

مَعْرَفَةٌ The *place* [or *part*] *upon which grows the* عُرْف [or *mane*]; (Ṣ, Mgh;) the *place of the* عُرْف *of the horse*, (O, Ḳ, TA,) *from the forelock to the withers*: or the *flesh upon which grows the* عُرْف. (TA.) But the phrase الأَخْذُ مِنْ مَعْرَفَةِ الدَّابَّةِ means *The cutting* [or *taking*] of somewhat *from the* عُرْف *of the beast*. (Mgh.)

مَعْرِفَةٌ a subst. [signifying *Knowledge, cognition, cognizance*, or *acquaintance*; &c.: as such having for its pl. مَعَارِفُ, meaning *sorts of knowledge*:] from عَرَفَهُ signifying as expl. in the beginning of this art.: (Mṣb:) or an inf. n. therefrom. (Ṣ, O, Ḳ.) — See also مَعْرَفٌ, last sentence but one. — [In grammar, *A determinate noun*; opposed to نَكِرَة.]

مُعَرَّفٌ [pass. part. n. of 2, q. v. ═] Food *rendered fragrant*. (TA.) ═ And Food *put part upon part* [app. *so that the uppermost portion resembles a mane* or *the like* (عُرْف)]. (TA.) [Golius, as on the authority of J, and hence Freytag, assign to it a meaning belonging to مُعَرَّق.] ═ Also The *place of halting* [of the pilgrims] *at* عَرَفَات. (Ṣ, O, Ḳ.) — And in a trad. of I'Ab, the phrase بَعْدَ المُعَرَّفِ occurs as meaning *After the halting at* عَرَفَة [or rather عَرَفَات]. (TA.)

مَعْرُوفٌ [*Known*: and particularly *well*, or *commonly, known*]. أَمْرٌ مَعْرُوفٌ and ▼ عَارِفٌ, (O, Mṣb, Ḳ, TA,) accord. to Lth, but the latter is disapproved by Az, having not been heard by him on any other authority than that of Lth, (O, TA,) [though there are other similar instances well known, (see أَمْرٌ, and دَافِقٌ,)] signify the same [i. e. *A known affair* or *event* &c.]; (O, Mṣb, Ḳ, TA;) as also ▼ عَرِيفٌ. (Mṣb, TA.) — [Hence, in grammar, The *active voice*; opposed to مَجْهُولٌ.] — See also عُرْفٌ, former half, in seven places. ═ أَرْضٌ مَعْرُوفَةٌ *Land having a fragrant* عَرْف [or odour]. (TA.) ═ رَجُلٌ مَعْرُوفٌ *A man having a purulent pustule, termed* عَرْفَة, *come forth in the whiteness* [or *palm*] *of his hand*. (Ṣ.)

مُعْتَرِفٌ [part. n. of 8, q. v.]. 'Omar is related to have said, أَطْرُدُوا المُعْتَرِفِينَ, meaning [*Drive ye away*] *those who inform against themselves* [or *confess* or *acknowledge* the commission] of something for which castigation is due to them; as though he disliked their doing so, and desired that people should protect them. (TA.)

مُتَعَارَفٌ [applied to language, or a phrase, or word, means *Known by common conventional usage*]. One says, هُوَ مُتَعَارَفٌ بَيْنَهُمْ *It is known* [*by common conventional usage*] *among them*. (MA. See also عُرْفٌ.])

عرفج

عَرْفَجٌ *A certain plant*, (Ṣ,) or *a sort of trees* [or *shrubs*], (Ḳ,) *growing in plain*, or *soft, land*: n. un. with ة: (Ṣ, Ḳ:) it is said to be *of the trees* [or *shrubs*] *of the* صَيْف [meaning either *spring* or *summer*], *soft*, or *pliable*, *dust-coloured, and having a rough produce like the* حَسَك [or *prickly heads of thistles and similar plants*]: (TA:) Aboo-Ziyád says, (O, TA,) as related by AḤn, (O,) that *it is of sweet*, or *pleasant, odour, dust-coloured, inclining to greenness, having a yellow blossom*; (O, TA;) and when it becomes aggregated and abundant in a place, that place is called حَوْمَانٌ: (O:) *it has no grains nor thorns*: (O, TA:) *it and the* ثُمَام *and the* ضَعَة *grow in plain*, or *soft, land, and on the mountain; and none of these has thorns: its firewood is the best of firewood in odour, and the quickest in taking fire and in blazing*: (O:) AḤn [also] says, certain of the Arabs of the desert informed me that *its root is wide, occupying a* [*considerable*] *piece of ground; and it sends forth many shoots, proportionate to the root, without leaves*, [but see خُوص,] *being only slender shoots, at the extremities whereof are* [*buds, or the like, such as are termed*] زَمَع, *at the heads of which appears a yellow substance like hair*: and he says that, accord. to the ancient Arabs of the desert, *it occupies a space like that of a man sitting, becomes white when it dries up, has a yellow produce, is eaten in the fresh and dry state by the camels and sheep* or *goats, and its flame is intensely red*, whence one says, كَأَنَّ لِحْيَتَهُ ضِرَامُ عَرْفَجَةٍ or عَرْفَجٍ [*As though his beard were the blazing*, or *flaming, of an 'arfajeh* or *of 'arfaj*]. (TA.) The fire of the عرفج is called نَارُ الزَّحْفَتَيْنِ [The fire of the two walks]; because he who kindles it walks to it, and when it burns up he walks from it: (T, TA:) or because it quickly blazes and quickly subsides; so when it blazes they walk from it, and when it subsides they walk to it. (O. [See also art. زحف.]) When the greenness of plants appears in it, it is termed عَرْفَجَةٌ خَاضِبَةٌ. (Aboo-'Obeyd El-Bekree, TA.) When it has been rained upon, and its stalk has become soft, one says ثَقَّبَ عُودُ العَرْفَجِ: when it has become somewhat black, قِيلَ: when a little more so, أَرْقَاطٌ: when more so, أَدْبَى: and when its خُوص are perfect, أَخْوَصَ. (AA, TA.) — كَمَنِّ الغَيْثِ عَلَى العَرْفَجَةِ [*Like the benefit conferred by the rain upon the 'arfajeh*], meaning its falling upon it when dry, and causing it to become green, is a prov., said, accord. to AZ, to him upon whom thou hast conferred a benefit and who says to thee, Dost thou confer a benefit upon me? (TA.) — لَيُّ العَرْفَجَةِ signifies *A certain mode of coïtus*. (O, Ḳ.)

عَرَافِجُ *Sands in which is no road*. (O, Ḳ. [In the latter it is expl. as though it were a proper name.])

عرفط

عُرْفُطٌ [*A species of mimosa*; called by Forskål *mimosa örfota*; (see his Flora Ægypt. Arab., pp. cxxiii. and 177;)] *a sort of trees of the* [*description termed*] عِضَاه, (Ṣ, O, Ḳ,) *which exudes* [*the gum called*] مُغْفُور, *and of which the fruit* (بَرَمَة) *is white and round*: (Ṣ:) *it has a gum of disagreeable odour; and when bees eat it, somewhat of its odour is found in their honey*: (TA:) AḤn says that, accord. to Aboo-Ziyád, *it is of the* عضاه, *and spreads upon the ground, not rising towards the sky, and has a broad leaf, and a sharp, curved thorn; it is of those trees of which the bark is stripped off and made into well-ropes*; (O, TA;) *and there comes forth from its fruit* (بَرَم) *what is termed* عُلَّفَة, [i. e. *a pod*,] *resembling a bean*, (O,* TA,) *which is eaten by the camels and the sheep* or *goats*: (O:) it is said by another, or others, that *its fruit* (بَرَمَة) *is called* فَتْلَة, *and is white, as though fringed with cotton*; (O, TA;) *like the button of the shirt*, or *somewhat larger*: (O:) Aboo-Ziyád [further] says, (TA,) *it is compact in its branches; has no wood that is useful like other wood; and has abundance of gum, which sometimes drops upon the ground until there are, beneath the trees, what resemble great mill-stones*: Sh says that *it is a short tree, the branches of which are near together, having many thorns; its height is like that of a camel lying down; it has a small, diminutive leaf; grows upon the mountains; and the camels eat it, particularly desiring the upper extremities of its branches*: (O, TA:) [the word is a coll. gen. n.:] the n. un. is with ة. (O, Ḳ.)

إِبِلٌ عُرْفُطِيَّةٌ *Camels that eat the* [*kind of trees called*] عُرْفُط. (TA.)

عرق

1. عَرَقَ العَظْمَ, (Ṣ, O, Mṣb, Ḳ,) aor. ـُ, (Ṣ, O, Mṣb,) inf. n. عَرْقٌ (Ṣ, O, Mṣb, Ḳ) and مَعْرَقٌ; (Ṣ, O, Ḳ; [see an ex. of the last voce عَارِقٌ;]) and ▼ تَعَرَّقَهُ; (Ṣ, O, Ḳ;) *He ate off the flesh from the bone*, (Ṣ, O, Mṣb, Ḳ, TA,) *taking it with his fore teeth*: (TA:) and one says also تَعَرَّقَ ▼ اللَّحْمَ [meaning as above]: (Lḥ, TA in art. نهس:) and اِعْتَرَقَ ▼ العَظْمَ is likewise said to signify as above. (TA.) — عَرَقْتُ مَا عَلَى العُرَاقِ مِنَ اللَّحْمِ *I pared off what was on the bone, of flesh*, with a مِعْرَق, i. e. a large, or broad, knife or blade. (TA.) — And [hence,] عَرَقَتْهُ السِّنُونَ, aor. as above, i. e. [*The years*, or *droughts*, or *years of drought*,] *took from him* [*his flesh*, or *rendered him lean*]; namely, a man. (TA.) تَعَرَّقَتْهُ ▼ الخُطُوبُ, also, signifies the like, i. e. [*Afflictions*, or *calamities*,] *took from him* [*his flesh*, &c.]. (TA.)

• أَيَّامَ أَعْرَقَ ▼ بِي عَامُ المَعَاصِمِ •

cited by Th, he expl. as meaning *In the days when the year of the* مَعَاصِم *took away my flesh*: i. e., when the dirt, consequent upon drought, reached my مَعَاصِم [or wrists]; المَعَاصِمِ being here used by poetic license for المَعَاصِمِ: but ISd says, "I know not what this explanation is." (L.) And عَرُقَ, inf. n. عُرْقٌ, signifies *He* (a man) *was*, or *became, emaciated*, or *lean*. (Ḳ.) ▼ التَّعَرُّقُ is also used in relation to other than material objects; as the strength and patience of camels, which are meant by جِلَالَهُنَّ [" their properties " or " qualities," جِلَال in this case being pl. of جُلَّة,] in the phrase يَتَعَرَّقُونَ جِلَالَهُنَّ [*They exhaust*, or *wear out, their properties*, or *qualities*, of strength and patience], in a verse cited by IAạr, describing camels and a company of riders. (TA.) — [Hence, app.,] طَرِيقٌ يَعْرُقُهُ النَّاسُ (Ḳ, TA) *A road which men travel* [as though they pared it]. (TA.) ═ عَرَقَ فِي الأَرْضِ, (Ṣ, O, Ḳ,) aor. ـِ, (Ṣ, O, TA,) not ـُ, as seems to be required by the method of the Ḳ, (TA,) inf. n. عُرُوقٌ (Ṣ, O, TA) and عَرْقٌ, (TA,) *He* (a man, Ṣ, O, TA) *went away into the country*, or *in the land*; syn. ذَهَبَ [which, followed by فى الارض, often means *he went into the open country*, or *out of doors*, *to satisfy a want of nature*]. (Ṣ, O, Ḳ, TA.) ═ عَرَقَ المَزَادَةَ, (Ḳ, TA,) and السُّفْرَةَ, aor. ـِ, inf. n. عَرْقٌ, (TA,) *He made to the* مَزَادَة [or *leathern water-bag*], (Ḳ, TA,) and *to the* سُفْرَة [*or round piece of skin in which food is put and upon which one eats*], (TA,) *what is termed an* عِرَاق [q. v.]. (Ḳ, TA.) ═ عَرِقَ, (Ṣ, O, Mṣb, Ḳ,) aor. ـَ , inf. n. عَرَقٌ, (Mṣb,) *He sweated.* (Ṣ, O, Ḳ.) —— And [hence, app.,] عَرِقَ, inf. n. عَرَقٌ, said of a wall, *It became moist:* [or *it exuded moisture:*] and in like manner one says of earth, or land, when the dew, or rain, has percolated in it (نَتَحَ فِيهَا) so that it has met the moisture thereof. (TA.) —— [It is also said in the TA, in the supplement to this art., that عرقت اليه بخير means ندبت: but I think that the phrase is correctly عَرَقْتُ إِلَيْهِ بِخَيْرٍ; and the explanation, نَدَيْتُ: meaning *I did to him good:* see art. ندو and ندى.] —— And عَرِقَ, (O, Ḳ,) inf. n. عَرَقٌ, (TA,) signifies also *He was, or became, heavy, sluggish, lazy,* or *indolent.* (O, Ḳ.) ═ عَرُقَ, inf. n. عَرَاقَةٌ, *It had root:* and *he was of generous origin.* (MA.) [See also 4, latter half.]

2: see 4, third sentence. —— عَرَّقَ الشَّرَابَ, (Ṣ, O, Ḳ,) inf. n. تَعْرِيقٌ, (Ṣ, O,) *He mixed the wine,* [*with water,*] *not doing so immoderately:* (Ṣ, O:) or *he put a little water into it;* as also ▼ اعرقهُ; (Ḳ;) or the latter signifies *he put into it some water, not much:* (Ṣ:) [but] accord. to Lḥ, أَعْرَقْتُ ▼ الكَأْسَ signifies *I filled the cup of wine:* or, accord. to IAạr, عَرَّقْتُ الكَأْسَ signifies *I put little water to the cup of wine;* and so ▼ أَعْرَقْتُهَا: but the former of these two phrases is also expl. as meaning *I mixed the cup of wine;* whether with little or much water not being specified: (TA:) and تَعَرَّقْتُ ▼ الخَمْرَةَ signifies *I mixed* [*with water the wine,* or *portion of wine*]. (Ḥam p. 561.) —— عرّق فِى الدَّلْوِ, (Ṣ, O, Ḳ, TA,) inf. n. as above; (O, Ḳ;) and اعرق ▼ فِيهَا; (O, Ḳ, TA;) *He put into the bucket less water than what would fill it,* (Ṣ, O, Ḳ,) *on the occasion of drawing:* (Ṣ, O:) or *he put little water into the bucket;* and so فِى السِّقَآءِ [*into the skin*]: (TA:) and عَرِّقْ فِى الإِنَآءِ *Put thou less than what would fill it into the vessel.* (Ṣ.) —— بَرَّقْتَ وَعَرَّقْتَ *Thou madest a sign with a thing, that had nothing to verify it,* [or *madest a false display,* or *a vain promise,*] *and didst little.* (IAạr, TA in this art and in art. برق.) ═ عرّق الفَرَسَ, (O, TA,) inf. n. as above; and ▼ اعرقهُ; (TA;) *He made the horse* [*to sweat,* or] *to run in order that he might sweat, and become lean, and lose his flabbiness of flesh.* (O,* TA.) ═ See also 4, again, in three places.

4: see 1, former half. ═ اعرقهُ عَرْقًا *He gave him a bone with flesh upon it,* or *of which the flesh had been eaten.* (TA.) —— And [hence, app.,] مَا عَرَّقْتُهُ ▼ and مَا أَعْرَقْتُهُ شَيْئًا *I gave him not anything.* (O, TA.) —— And اعرقهُ *He gave him to drink pure,* or *unmixed, wine;* or *wine with a little mixture* [*of water*]. (Ḥam p. 561.) —— See also 2, in four places. ═ اعرق الفَرَسَ: see 2, last sentence but one. ═ اعرق الشَّجَرُ, (Ṣ, O, Ḳ,) and النَّبَاتُ, (Ṣ,) *The trees,* (Ṣ, O, Ḳ,) and *the plants,* (Ṣ,) *extended their roots into the earth;* (Ṣ, O, Ḳ,* TA;) in the Ḳ, اشْتَدَّتْ is erroneously put for امْتَدَّتْ, and so [in one place] in the O; (TA;) as also ▼ تعرّق, said of trees, (M, O, TA,) and ▼ عرّق, (M, TA,) and in like manner, ▼ اعترق, and ▼ استعرق, said of trees, i. e., *struck their roots into the earth,* as in the A: (TA:) [but accord. to Mṭr,] in the phrase رَجُلٌ لَهُ شَجَرَةٌ تَعَرَّقَتْ ▼ فِى مِلْكِ غَيْرِهِ, meaning [*A man of whom a tree*] *whereof the root crept along beneath the ground* [*into the property of another*], in [one of the books of which each is entitled] "the Wáḳi'át," تعرّقت should correctly be ▼ عَرَّقَتْ. (Mgh.) —— [Hence,] one says, أَعْرَقَ فِيهِ أَعْمَامُهُ وَأَخْوَالُهُ [*His paternal uncles and his maternal uncles implanted,* or *engendered, in him, by natural transmission, a quality,* or *qualities, possessed by them,* or *what is termed a strain*]; (Ṣ, O, TA; [in which the meaning is indicated by the context;]) and so ▼ عرّق. (L, TA.) [See also the saying ضَرَبَتْ فِيهِ فُلَانَةُ بِعِرْقٍ ذِى أَشَبٍ in the second quarter of the first paragraph of art. ضرب.] And أَعْرَقَ, (Ṣ, O, [agreeably with the context in both, in like manner as it is with explanations of phrases here preceding,]) or أُعْرِقَ, (Ḳ, [but I know nothing that is in favour of this latter except a questionable explanation of مُعْرِقٌ which will be mentioned below, voce عَرِيقٌ,]) said of a man, and likewise of a horse, (Ṣ, O,) *He was,* or *became, rooted* (عَرِيقًا), (Ṣ, O, Ḳ,) i. e. *one having a radical,* or *hereditary, share* (لَهُ عِرْقٌ), in generousness or nobleness [of origin, which, accord. to the Ṣ and O, and common usage, seems to be implied by the verb when used absolutely], (Ṣ, O, Ḳ,) and also in meanness or ignobleness [thereof; meaning *he had a strain* of, i. e. *an inborn disposition* to, generousness or nobleness, and also meanness or ignobleness]. (Ṣ,* O,* Ḳ.) [See an ex. in a verse cited voce طَابَ, in art. طيب. And see also the last form of 1 (عَرُقَ) in the present art.] ═ أَعْرَقَ also signifies *He* (a man, Ṣ, O) *went,* or *came,* (صَارَ, Ṣ, or أَتَى, Ḳ,) or *journeyed,* (سَارَ, O,) *to El-'Irák:* (Ṣ, O, Ḳ:) and ▼ اعترقوا *They entered upon,* or *took their way in* or *into, the country of El-'Irák.* (Th, TA.)

5: see 1, former half, in four places: ═ and 2, former half: ═ and 4, former half, in two places. ═ تَعَرَّقْ فِى ظِلِّ نَاقَتِى *Walk thou in the shade of my she-camel, and profit by it, little and little.* (TA.) ═ صَارَعَهُ فَتَعَرَّقَهُ *He wrestled with him, and took his head beneath his armpit and threw him down.* (Ḳ.)

8: see 1, first sentence: ═ and 4, former half: ═ and the same, last sentence. ═ اعترق النَّاقَةَ *He took the she-camel and tied the cord called* عِرَاق *to her* خِطَام [or *halter,* or *the like*]. (TA.)

10. استعرق *He exposed himself to the heat in order that he might sweat:* (IF, O, Ḳ:) *he stood in a place on which the sun shone, and covered himself with his clothes* [*for that purpose*]. (Z, TA.) ═ See also 4, former half. ═ استعرقت الإِبِلُ *The camels pastured near to the sea* or *a great river,* i. e., *in a place of pasture such as is termed* عِرَاق: so says AZ: or, as AḤn says, *the camels came to a piece,* or *tract, of land, such as is termed* عِرْق, i. e., *one exuding water and producing salt and giving growth to trees.* (TA.)

Q. Q. 1. عَرْقَيْتُ الدَّلْوَ, inf. n. عَرْقَاةٌ, *I bound,* or *tied, upon the leathern bucket the two cross-pieces of wood called the* عَرْقُوَتَانِ. (Ṣ.)

عَرْقٌ (Ṣ, O, Mṣb, Ḳ) and ▼ عُرَاقٌ (Ḳ) [the latter also a pl.] *A bone of which the flesh has been taken:* (Ṣ, O:) or *a bone of which the flesh has been eaten:* (Mṣb, Ḳ:) or *a bone of which most of the flesh has been taken, some thin and savoury portions of flesh remaining upon it:* (TA:) or the former signifies *a bone upon which is flesh:* and *one upon which is no flesh:* or, as some say, *whereof most of that which was upon it has been taken, some little remaining upon it:* (Mgh:) or, as some say, *a piece of flesh-meat;* as also ▼ عَرْقَةٌ: (TA:) or عَرْقٌ signifies *a bone with its flesh:* and ▼ عُرَاقٌ, *a bone of which the flesh has been eaten:* (Ḳ:) thus they are correctly expl. accord. to Ez-Zejjájee; and the like is said by AZ respecting ▼ عُرَاقٌ: (TA:) but accord. to A'Obeyd, this signifies *a piece of flesh-meat;* and IAmb says that this is the right explanation, because the Arabs say أَكَلْتُ العُرَاقَ, and they do not say أَكَلْتُ العَظْمَ: (Ḥar p. 26:) [or, app., the *flesh-meat* of a bone: and likewise the *portions,* of trees, *that are cropped* by camels: (see عُرَامٌ:)] the pl. (of عَرْقٌ, Ṣ, Mgh, O) is ▼ عُرَاقٌ, (Ṣ, Mgh, O, Ḳ,) which is extr., (IAth, Ḳ,) a pl. of a measure of which, as that of a pl., there are few instances, (ISk, Ṣ, O,) [see an ex. voce جَنَاحٌ,] and عِرَاقٌ, also, (IAạr, Ḳ,) which is more agreeable with analogy. (IAạr, TA.) —— Also *A road which men travel* [as though they pared it] *so that it becomes plainly apparent:* (Ḳ,* TA:) an inf. n. used as a subst. [properly so termed]. (TA.) —— See also عِرْقٌ, near the end.

عِرْقٌ *A certain appertenance of a tree;* (Ṣ, Mgh, O, Mṣb, Ḳ;) the *root* thereof; or the *part* thereof *that is beneath the ground;* (MA;) or its *branching roots* [*collectively*]: (TA:) pl. [of mult.] عُرُوقٌ (Ṣ, O, Mṣb, Ḳ) and عِرَاقٌ and [of pauc.] أَعْرَاقٌ. (Ḳ.) —— It is said in a trad., لَيْسَ لِعِرْقٍ ظَالِمٍ حَقٌّ, (Ṣ, Mgh, O, Mṣb,) i. e. لِذِى عِرْقٍ ظَالِمٍ, (Mgh, O, Mṣb,) meaning ‡ [*There is no right pertaining*] *to him who plants,* (Ṣ, Mgh, O, Mṣb,) or *sows,* (Ṣ,) *in land,* (Mgh, Mṣb,) or *in land which another has brought into cultivation* (Ṣ, O, Mṣb) *after it has been waste,* (Ṣ, O, Mṣb,*) *wrongfully, in order that he may have a claim to that land:* (Ṣ, Mgh, O, Mṣb:) the epithet being tropically applied to the عِرْق, (Mgh, Mṣb,) as it properly applies to the owner thereof: (Mgh:) but some, in relating this trad., say لِعِرْقِ ظَالِمٍ, making the former noun to be a prefix to the latter, governing it in the gen. case. (O.) —— The roots of the أَرْطَى (عُرُوقُ الأَرْطَى) are long, red, penetrating into the moist earth, succulent, compact, and dripping with water: and to them, in a trad., certain camels are likened in respect of their redness and plumpness and the compactness of their flesh and fat. (TA.) — العُرُوقُ also signifies *A certain plant with which one dyes*: (Ṣ, O:) or العُرُوقُ الصُّفْرُ, *a certain plant used by the dyers, called in Pers.* زَرْدْچُوبَة [or زَرْدْ چُوبْ], (Ḳ, TA,) i. e. *yellow wood*: (TA:) or i. q. الهُرْدُ: or المَامِيرَانُ الصِّينِىُّ, (Ḳ,) or المَامِيرَانُ: (TA:) or الكُرْكُمُ الصَّغِيرُ: (Ḳ:) all which are nearly alike. (TA. [See also بَقْلَةُ الخَطَاطِيفِ, voce بقل.]) — And العُرُوقُ الحُمْرُ *Madder*, (الفُوَّةُ, Ḳ, TA,) *with which one dyes.* (TA.) — And العُرُوقُ البِيضُ *A certain plant that fattens women; also called* المُسْتَعْجِلَةُ. (Ḳ.) — [عُرُوقٌ seems sometimes to signify *Straggling plants* or *stalks, spreading like roots*: see جَنْبَةٌ.] — And it signifies also *Sprouts from the roots* of trees: see عُسْلُوجٌ.] — And عِرْقٌ signifies also The *root, origin*, or *source, of anything*: (Ḳ, TA:) and the *basis* thereof. (TA.) [And particularly The *origin* of a man, considered as the root from which he springs: hence عِرْقُ الثَّرَى is said to be applied by Imra-el-Ḳeys to *Adam*, as the root, or source, of mankind; or to *Ishmael*, as, accord. to some, the root, or source, of all the Arabs: (see "Le Diwan d'Amro'l-kais," p. 33 of the Ar. text, and p. 103 of the Notes:) and the pl.] أَعْرَاقٌ signifies the *ancestors* of a man. (Ḥar p. 634.) [And *A quality*, or *disposition, possessed by a parent* or *by an ancestor* or *by a collateral of such person*, considered as the source of that quality or disposition in a descendant or in a collateral of a descendant: and *such a quality*, or *disposition, when transmitted*; *a strain*; i. e. *a radical, a hereditary, an inborn*, or *a natural, disposition*: and *a radical*, or *hereditary, share* in some quality or the like: pl. أَعْرَاقٌ.] One says, تَدَارَكَهُ أَعْرَاقُ خَيْرٍ [*Good qualities or dispositions possessed by a parent or by an ancestor or by a collateral of such a person*, or *strains of a good kind, extended to him*]; and أَعْرَاقُ شَرٍّ or سُوْءٍ [*evil qualities or dispositions* &c., or *strains of an evil kind*]. (TA.) And العِرْقُ دَسَّاسٌ [*The natural disposition is wont to enter*; i. e., to be transmitted to succeeding generations]. (TA in art. دس, q. v.) And عرقت فِيهِمْ عِرْقَ سَوْءٍ [i. e. عَرَقَتْ, or, accord. to more common usage, أَعْرَقَتْ, meaning *She implanted*, or *engendered, in them*, or *among them, an evil strain*, or *radical* or *hereditary disposition*]. (TA in art. ضرب.) And لَهُ عِرْقٌ فِى الكَرَمِ [*He has a radical*, or *hereditary, share in generousness* or *nobleness of origin*]: (Ṣ, O:) and in like manner one says of a person between whom and Adam is no living ancestor, لَهُ عِرْقٌ فِى المَوْتِ [*He has a radical*, or *heriditary, share in death*]; meaning that he will inevitably die. (O. [See also عُرَيْقٌ.]) — [Hence, app., *A little*, or *modicum*, or *small quantity* or *admixture*, of something]. One says, فِيهِ عِرْقٌ مِنْ حُمُوضَةٍ, and مُلُوحَةٍ, i. e. *In it is a little*, or *a modicum, of acidity*, and *of saltness*. (TA.) And فِى الشَّرَابِ عِرْقٌ مِنَ المَآءِ *In the wine is a small quantity* [or *admixture*] *of water*. (Ṣ, O, Ḳ.) — Also *A certain appertenance* of the body; (O, Mṣb, K, TA;) i. e. the *hollow* [*canal*] *in which is the blood*; (TA;) [*a blood-vessel*; *a vein*, and *an artery*: also any *duct*, or *canal*, in an animal body: and sometimes, though improperly, *a nerve*: or *any one of the appertenances* of the body *that resemble roots*:] pl. [of mult.] عُرُوقٌ (O, Mṣb, Ḳ) and عِرَاقٌ (Ḳ) and [of pauc.] أَعْرَاقٌ. (Mṣb, Ḳ.) [Hence it may be applied to *A spermatic duct*: and hence, app.,] it is said in a trad., عَلَيْكُمْ بِالصَّوْمِ فَإِنَّهُ مَحْسَمَةٌ لِلْعِرْقِ, meaning † [*Keep ye to fasting, for it is*] *a cause*, or *means, of stopping venereal intercourse*: or *an impediment to venery, and a cause of diminishing the seminal fluid, and of stopping venereal intercourse* or *passion*. (T* and TA in art. حسم.) — عُرُوقُ الأَرْضِ means *The pores through which exudes the moisture of the earth*. (TA.) — And (i. e. عروق الارض) i. q. شَحْمَةُ الأَرْضِ [the significations of which see in art. شحم]. (TA.) — عِرْقٌ also signifies The *body*. (Ḳ, TA.) Thus in the saying, إِنَّهُ لَخَبِيثُ العِرْقِ [*Verily he is corrupt*, or *impure, in respect of the body*]. (TA.) — And *Milk*. (Ḳ.) One says, نَاقَتُكَ دَائِمَةُ العِرْقِ, meaning *Thy she-camel has a constant flow*, or *abundance, of milk*: or *has constant milk*. (TA.) [See also عَرَقٌ, first quarter.] — And *Numerous offspring*: (IAạr, Ḳ:) or *milk and offspring*; as in the saying, مَا أَكْثَرَ عِرْقَ إِبِلِكَ وَغَنَمِكَ [*How abundant are the milk and offspring of thy camels and thy sheep* or *goats!*]. (TA.) [See, again, عَرَقٌ, first quarter.] — Also *Salt land that gives growth to nothing*. (Ḳ.) — And (Ḳ) *A piece*, or *tract, of land exuding water and producing salt*, (AḤn, Ḳ,) *that gives growth to trees*, (AḤn, TA,) or *that gives growth to the* [*species of tamarisk called*] طَرْفَآء: (Ḳ:) a signification the contr. of that in the next preceding sentence. (TA.) — And *A mountain that is travelled, or traversed*: (TA:) or *a mountain that is rugged, and extending upon the earth*, (Ḳ,* TA,) *debarring one by reason of its height*, (TA,) *and not to be ascended, because of its difficult nature*, (Ḳ, TA,) *but not long*. (TA.) And *A small mountain* (Ḳ, TA) *apart from others*. (TA.) Thus it has two contr. significations. (Ḳ.) — And *A thin* حَبْل [or *elongated and elevated tract* (not جَبَل as in the CḲ)] *of sand extending along the ground*: (Ḳ, TA:) or *an elevated place*: pl. عُرُوقٌ. (Ḳ.) — See also عِرَاقٌ, latter half, in two places. — عِلْقٌ مَضَنَّةٌ and عِرْقٌ مَضِنَّةٌ (the latter of which is that commonly known, TA) signify *A thing of which one is tenacious*; (O;) *a thing held in high estimation, of which one is tenacious*, (Ṣ and Ḳ and TA in art. ضن,) *and for which people vie in desire*: (TA in that art.:) but [said to be] used only in a case of negation: one says, مَا هُوَ عِنْدِى بِعِرْقِ مَضَنَّةٍ, meaning *It is not, in my estimation, a thing of any value*, or *worth*. (TA.)

عَرَقٌ *Sweat*; i. e. the *moisture*, or *fluid, that exudes* (Ṣ,* O,* Ḳ, TA) *from the skin* of an animal; (Ḳ, TA;) or the *water of the skin, that runs from the roots of the hair*: a gen. n.; having no pl.; (TA;) or no pl. of it has been heard: (Mṣb:) Lth says, I have not heard a pl. of العَرَقُ; but if it be pluralized, it should be, accord. to analogy, أَعْرَاقٌ. (O, TA.) — It is metaphorically used [in a similar sense] in relation to other things than animals. (Ḳ.) [Thus] it signifies The [*exuded*] *moisture* of a well: (Ḳ:) and in like manner of earth, or land, when the dew, or rain, has percolated in it (تَتَبَّعَ فِيهَا) so that it has met the moisture thereof. (TA.) — And The دِبْس [or *honey*] of dates; (Ḳ;) because it flows, or exudes, from them. (TA.) — And *Milk*; because it flows in the ducts (عُرُوق) [thereof] until it comes at the last to the udder: (Ḳ:) or *milk at the time of bringing forth*; as in the saying, مَا أَكْثَرَ عَرَقَ غَنَمِكَ *How abundant is the milk of thy sheep*, or *goats, at the time of their bringing forth!* (AZ, O.) [See also عِرْقٌ, latter half.] — And (Ḳ) The *offspring* of camels: (Ṣ, O, Ḳ:) so in the saying, مَا أَكْثَرَ عَرَقَ إِبِلِهِ [*How numerous are the offspring of his camels!*]. (Ṣ, O.) [See, again, عِرْقٌ, latter half.] — And *Advantage, profit, utility*, or *benefit*: (O, Ḳ, TA; in [several of] the copies of the second of which, النَّقْعُ is erroneously put for النَّفْعُ: TA:) and *a recompense*, or *reward*: (Ḳ, TA; in some copies of the former of which, الثَّوَابُ is erroneously put for الثَّوَابُ: TA:) or *a little thereof*; (Ḳ, TA;) likened to عَرَق [as meaning "sweat"]. (TA.) عَرَقُ الخِلَالِ means *A thing that one gives*, or *yields, for friendship*: (Ṣ, O, TA:) or *a reward for friendship*. (TA.) A poet says, namely El-Ḥárith Ibn-Zuheyr, describing a sword named النُّونُ, (O, TA,) belonging to Málik Ibn-Zuheyr, which Ḥamal Ibn-Bedr took from him on the day when he slew him, and which El-Ḥárith took from Ḥamal when he slew him, (TA,)

* وَيُخْبِرُهُمْ مَكَانَ النُّونِ مِنِّى *
* وَمَا أُعْطِيتُهُ عَرَقَ الخِلَالِ *

[*And he shall tell them the place of En-Noon, from me, and that I was not given it as a reward for friendship*]; meaning, that I took this sword by force. (O, TA. [In the Ṣ, the former hemistich of this verse is given differently, and, as is said in the TA, erroneously.]) — لَقِيتُ مِنْ فُلَانٍ عَرَقَ القِرْبَةِ (which is a prov., TA) means [*I experienced from such a one*] *hardship*, as expl. by Aṣ, who says that he knew not the origin thereof, (Ṣ, O,) or *difficulty*, or *distress*, as expl. by IDrd: (O:) and it is said that the عَرَق [or sweat] is of the man, not of the قِرْبَة [or water-skin]; and the origin of the saying is, that water-skins (قِرَب) are [generally] carried only by female slaves that bear burdens, and by him who has no assistant; but sometimes a man of generous origin becomes poor, and in need of carrying them himself, and he sweats by reason of the trouble that comes upon him, and of shame; (Ṣ, O;) wherefore one says, تَجَشَّمْتُ لَكَ عَرَقَ القِرْبَةِ [expl. in art. جشم], (Ṣ,) or جَشِمْتُ إِلَيْكَ عَرَقَ القِرْبَةِ [likewise expl. in art. جشم]: accord. to Ks, the meaning is, *I have suffered fatigue, and imposed upon myself difficulty, for thee,* [or *in coming to thee,*] *so that I have sweated like the sweating of the water-skin:* or, accord. to A'Obeyd, *I have imposed upon myself, in coming to thee, what no one has attained, and what will not be;* because the قربة does not sweat: (O:) عَرَقُ القِرْبَةِ is a metonymical expression for *hardship,* and *difficulty,* or *distress;* because, when the قربة sweats, its odour becomes foul: or because it has no sweat; therefore it is as though one imposed upon himself an impossible thing: or it means *the benefit of the* قربة; (which is *the flowing of its water,* TA;) as though one imposed upon himself such a task that he became in need of the water of the قربة, i. e. of journeying to it; or it means *a* سَفِيفَة [or *plaited suspensory*] *which the carrier of the* قربة *puts over his chest* [*when carrying the* قربة *on his back*]: (K:) accord. to IAar, it signifies *the suspensory* (مِعْلَاق) *by means of which the* قربة *is carried;* as also عَلَقُهَا; (O, TA;) the ر being substituted for ل: (TA: see art. ر:]) but he says also that عَرَقُ القِرْبَةِ means *one's sweating with the* قربة by reason of the difficulty, or trouble, of carrying it; and عَلَقُهَا, that by which it is tied, or bound, and then suspended: (L, TA:) the former is also said to signify *the* ▼ عِرَاق [q. v.] *of the* قربة, *that is sewed around it:* (TA:) or it means that one has imposed upon himself *difficulty,* or *trouble,* or *fatigue, like that of the carrier of the* قربة, who sweats beneath it by reason of its heaviness. (K.) — عَرَقٌ also signifies *A heat;* i. e. *a single run,* or *a run at once, to a goal,* or *limit.* (S, O, K.) One says, جَرَى الفَرَسُ عَرَقًا or عَرَقَيْنِ *The horse ran a heat* or *two heats.* (S, O.) — Also *A row of horses,* and *of birds,* (S, O, Msb, K,) and *the like;* (S, Msb;) and *any things disposed in a row;* (S, O, K, TA;) as also ▼ عَرَقَةٌ; (TA;) or this latter is the n. un. [app. signifying *one of such as compose a row*]: (S:) pl. أَعْرَاقٌ and عَرَقَاتٌ. (Msb.) [See an ex. in a verse of Tufeyl cited in art. صدر, conj. 5; also cited in the present art. in the S and O.] — And *Any row of bricks, crude and baked, in a wall:* one says, بَنَى البَانِى عَرَقًا وَعَرَقَيْنِ and ▼ عَرَقَةً وَعَرَقَتَيْنِ [*The builder built a row of bricks and two rows thereof*]: (K, TA:) pl. أَعْرَاقٌ. (TA.) — And *Roads in mountains;* as also ▼ عَرْقَةٌ, (K, TA,) with fet-h and then sukoon. (TA.) — And *Foot-marks of camels following one another:* (K, TA:) n. un. ▼ عَرَقَةٌ. (TA.) [See an ex. of the latter voce طَرَقٌ.] A poet says,

• وَقَدْ نَسَجْنَ بِالفَلَاةِ عَرَقَا •

[*And they had woven in the desert,* or *waterless desert, foot-marks in their following one another*]. (TA.) — And *A plait of palm-leaves* (S, O, Msb, K) &c. (S, O) *before a* زَبِيل [so in the S and O] or زِنْبِيل [so in the K, both meaning the same, i. e. a *basket,*] *is made therewith:* (S, O, K:) or *a* زنبيل *itself:* (K:) or hence (S, O) it signifies also (S, O, Msb) *a* زَبِيل (S, O) or [*what is called*] *a* مِكْتَل (Mgh, Msb) and زِنْبِيل, (Msb,) *of large size, woven of palm-leaves,* (Mgh,) *capable of containing fifteen times as much as the measure termed* صَاع, as some say, (Mgh, Msb,) or *thirty times as much as that measure:* (Mgh:) also pronounced ▼ عَرْقٌ. (K.) — [And *A suspensory* of a زَبِيل: see حَتِىٌّ, in art. حتى. (A similar meaning has been mentioned above, in this paragraph.)] — See also عَرَقَةٌ. — And *Raisins.* (K. [But this is said in the TA to be extr.: and I think it to have been probably taken from some copy of a lexicon in which زَبِيب has been erroneously written for زَبِيل.])

لَبَنٌ عَرِقٌ *Milk of which the flavour is corrupted by the sweat of the camel upon which it is borne;* (S, O, K;) *the skin containing it being bound upon him without any preservative between it and his side.* (S, O.)

عُرَقٌ: see عُرَقَةٌ.

عُرُقٌ a pl. of عِرَاقٌ [q. v.]. (Lth, AZ, S, &c.) — It is also expl. by IAar as meaning *People of soundness in religion.* (TA.)

عَرْقَةٌ: see عَرَقٌ: — and see also عِرْقٌ, last quarter.

عِرْقَةٌ: see عِرْقَاةٌ, in four places.

عَرَقَةٌ: see عَرَقٌ, last quarter, in three places. — Also *The piece of wood,* or *timber, that intervenes between the* [or *any*] *two rows of bricks of a wall.* (S, O, K, TA. [ساقى, in this explanation in the CK, is a mistake for سَافَى, with ف.]) — And The *border* (طُرَّة) *that is woven in the sides of the* [*tent called*] فُسْطَاط. (S, O.) See also عِرْقَاةٌ, last sentence. — And The دِرَّة [or *whip*], *with which one beats,* or *flogs.* (K.) — And The *plaited thong with which a captive is bound:* pl. عَرَقَاتٌ and [coll. gen. n.] ▼ عَرَقٌ: (K:) or عَرَقَاتٌ signifies [simply] *plaited thongs* (نُسُوع). (S, O.)

عُرَقَةٌ, (S, O, K,) which is agreeable with general analogy, and ▼ عُرَقٌ, (K, TA,) which is not so, but which is used by some in the same sense as the former, (TA,) A man *who sweats much.* (S, O, K, TA.)

عَرْقٍ, originally عَرْقُوٌ: see عَرْقُوَةٌ, of which it is a coll. gen. n.

[عرقى, said by Reiske to signify The *inner and thin skin in the egg of an ostrich,* is evidently a mistake for غِرْقِئٌ.]

عَرْقَاةٌ: see عَرْقُوَةٌ: — and the paragraph here following, in two places: — and see also عِرَاقٌ.

عِرْقَاةٌ (O, K) and ▼ عَرْقَاةٌ and ▼ عِرْقَةٌ (K) *A root, race, stock,* or *source;* syn. أَصْلٌ: (O, K:) or *a source of wealth* or *property:* or the *main portion of the root of a tree, from which the* عُرُوق [or *minor roots*] *branch off:* (K:) or, as some say, عِرْقَاةٌ has this last meaning; or, as others say, ▼ عِرْقَةٌ. (Lth:, O.) They said, اِسْتَأْصَلَ اللّٰهُ عِرْقَاتِهِمْ and ▼ عَرْقَاتَهُمْ; if they pronounced the first letter with fet-h, they so pronounced the last letter [before the pronoun]; and if they pronounced the former with kesr, they thus pronounced the latter, regarding the word as pl. of ▼ عِرْقَةٌ: (K:) or, accord. to Lth, the Arabs are related to have said, اِسْتَأْصَلَ اللّٰهُ عِرْقَاتَهُمْ, meaning شَأْفَتَهُمْ [i. e. *May God utterly destroy their race, stock,* or *family*], pronouncing the ت with nasb because regarding the word as [a sing.] like سِعْلَاةٌ; or holding it to be pl. of ▼ عِرْقَةٌ, but pronouncing the ت thus like as they do in saying رَأَيْتُ بَنَاتَكَ: it is said, however, that this is a mistake; that only he should pronounce it thus who makes the word to be a sing. like سِعْلَاةٌ. (O.) [The saying is a prov., mentioned by Meyd, who adds another reading, namely, عَرْقَاتِهِمْ, holding this to be from ▼ العَرَقَةُ meaning "the طُرَّة that is woven around the فُسْطَاط:" and Freytag, in his Lexicon, adds also عِرْقَاتَهُ, with nasb, as on the authority of Meyd; in whose "Proverbs" I do not find it.]

عَرْقَانُ [accord. to general analogy without tenween and having for its fem. عَرْقَى, or accord. to the dial. of the Benoo-Asad with tenween and having for its fem. عَرْقَانَةٌ,] *Sweating.* (Msb.)

عَرْقُوَةُ الدَّلْوِ is thus, (S, O, K,) with fet-h to the ع, (S, O,) like تَرْقُوَةٌ, (K,) and should not be pronounced with damm to the first letter; (S, O, K;) and ▼ عَرْقَاتُهَا signifies the same; (K, TA; [in the CK, erroneously, عَرْقَاتُها; but expressly stated in the TA to be with fet-h and then sukoon;]) i. e. *The piece of wood that is put across the* دلو [or *leathern bucket, from one part of the brim to the opposite part*]: (TA:) the عَرْقُوَتَانِ being the *two pieces of wood that are put athwart the* دلو [*to keep it from collapsing and for the purpose of attaching thereto the well-rope*], *like a cross:* (As, S, O, K:) pl. عَرَاقٍ; (S, O, K;) and if you pluralize it by suppressing the ة [of the sing., or rather if you form from it a coll. gen. n.], you say ▼ عَرْقٍ, originally عَرْقُوٌ, (S, O, L,) then عَرْقِىٌ, and then عَرْقٍ. (L.) — العَرْقُوَتَانِ also signifies *The two pieces of wood that connect the* وَاسِط [or *fore part*] *of the* [*camel's saddle called*] رَحْل *and the* مُؤَخَّرَة [or *hinder part thereof*]: (S, O, K:) or, accord. to Lth, *two pieces of wood which are upon the* عَضُدَانِ [q. v.], *on the two sides of the* [*camel's saddle called*] قَتَب. (O.) — ذَاتُ العَرَاقِى means † *Calamity,* or *misfortune:* (S, O, K, TA:) for it is [properly] the دَلْو [or *leathern bucket*]; and الدَّلْوُ is one of the names for calamity: one says, لَقِيتُ مِنْهُ ذَاتَ العَرَاقِى [*I experienced from it,* or *him, calamity*]: (TA:) or, as some say, it is from what here follows. (S, O, TA.) — عَرَاقِى الإِكَامِ signifies *Such* [*eminences of the kind called* إِكَام (pl. of أَكَمَةٌ or of أُكُمٌ)] *as are very rugged, not to be ascended unless with difficulty,* or *trouble:* (S, O, TA:) or عَرْقُوَةٌ signifies *any* أَكَمَة *extending upon the earth,* [*in form*] *as though it were the heap over a grave,* (Lth, O, K,) *elongated:* (Lth,

O:) an أَكَمَة *that extends, not high, but overtopping what is around it, near to the ground* or *not near, and varying in different parts so that one place thereof is soft and another place thereof rugged;* being only *a level portion of the earth overtopping what is around it:* (ISh, TA:) and العَرَاقِى is also said to signify *continuous,* or *connected,* إِكَام, *that have become as though they were one long* جُرْف [or *abrupt, water-worn bank* or *ridge*] *upon the face of the earth.* (TA.) — العَرَاقِى signifies also *The collar-bones* (التَّرَاقِى), in the dial. of El-Yemen. (L, TA.)

عَرَقِيَّة, meaning *A thing* [i. e. *a close-fitting cap, generally of cotton, to imbibe the sweat,*] *which is worn beneath the turban and the* [cap called] قَلَنْسُوَة, is a post-classical word. (TA.)

عُرَاق: see عَرَقٌ, in four places. — Also, and ↓ عُرَاقَة, *i. q.* نُطْفَةٌ مِنَ المَآءِ (O, Ḳ) [app. meaning *Clear water,* whether *much* or *little;* or *a little water remaining in a bucket* or *skin*]: (Ḳ:) or, accord. to the L, the former word is pl. [or rather a coll. gen. n.] of the latter in this sense: (TA:) and ↓ عُرَقَاة signifies the same. (Ḳ.) — And *A copious rain:* (Ḳ:) or so ↓ عُرَاقَة [only]. (TA.) — And عُرَاقُ الغَيْثِ *The herbage that has come forth after the rain.* (Ibn-'Abbád, A, O, Ḳ.)

عِرَاقٌ The *double suture that is in the lower part* of the [leathern water-bag called] مَزَادَة and رَاوِيَة; (Lth, O, Ḳ;) and this is of the firmest kinds of suture therein: (Lth, O:) or the *suture that is in the middle* of the قِرْبَة [or water-skin]: (TA:) or the *piece* [or *strip*] *of skin that is put upon the place where the two extremities,* or *edges, of the* [main] *skin meet when it is sewed in,* or *upon, the lower part* of the مزادة: (Ḳ:) or the *appertenance* of the قربة, and of the مزادة, &c., *which is* [*a strip of skin*] *doubled and then sewed* [*thereon thus*] *doubled:* (Mṣb:) or, accord. to AZ, the [*piece of*] *skin that is doubled, and then sewed upon the lower part* of the [water-skin or milk-skin called] سِقَآء: (Ṣ:) and, (Ḳ,) accord. to Aṣ, (Ṣ, O,) *i. q.* طِبَابَة; (Ṣ, O, Ḳ;) i. e. the *piece of skin with which the punctures of the seams are covered:* (Ṣ, O: see also عَرَقٌ, latter half: [and see طِبَابَة:]) pl. عُرُقٌ (Lth, AZ, Ṣ, O, Ḳ, TA) and عُرْقٌ (TA) and أَعْرِقَة; (Lth, O, TA;) the last a pl. of pauc. (Lth, O.) And عِرَاقُ السُّفْرَةِ signifies *The suture surrounding the* [*round piece of skin called*] سُفْرَة [q. v.]. (Ḳ.) — Also *Nearness, together, of the stitch-holes* in a skin or hide: [so I render تَقَارُبُ الخُرَزِ; reading الخُرَز: and it seems to mean also *uniformity thereof:* for it is added,] hence the prov., لِأَمْرِهِ عِرَاقٌ, meaning † *His affair is uniform, right,* or *rightly disposed.* (TA.) — Also The *side,* or *shore,* (Lth, O, Ḳ,) of water, (Ḳ,) or of a sea, or great river, *along the whole length* thereof. (Lth, O, Ḳ.* [It is said in the Ḳ that عُرُقٌ is pl. of عِرَاقٌ in this sense: but afterwards, that the pl. of the latter in all its senses is أَعْرِقَة also; to which the TA adds عُرْقٌ.]) And accord. to AZ, *Any pasturage adjacent to a great river or a sea.* (TA.) And عِرَاقُ النَّهْرِ, (Ḳ,) or الرَّكِيبِ, (TA,) *The border of the rivulet* [*for irrigation*] (Ḳ, TA) *by which the water enters a* حَائِط [i. e. *garden,* or *garden of palm-trees surrounded by a wall*], (TA,) *from its nearest to its furthest extremity.* (Ḳ, TA.) — Also The قُطْر [app. meaning *side* (but see this word)] *of a mountain, by itself;* [or so, perhaps, عِرَاقُ جَبَلٍ;] and so ↓ عِرْقٌ [or عِرْقُ جَبَلٍ]. (Ibn-'Abbád, O, Ḳ.) — And, as also ↓ عِرْقٌ, *Remains of the* [*plants,* or *trees, called*] حَمْض. (Ḳ.) — عِرَاقُ الدَّارِ *The court,* or *yard, in front,* or *extending from the sides, of the house.* (IB, Ḳ.) — عِرَاقُ الأُذُنِ *The circuit,* or *surrounding edge, of the ear.* (Ḳ.) — عِرَاقُ الظُّفُرِ *The flesh surrounding the nail.* (Ḳ,* TA.) — عِرَاقُ الحَشَا *The intestines that are above the navel, lying breadthwise,* or *across, in the belly.* (Ḳ.) — And عِرَاقٌ signifies also The *inside of feathers.* (AA, Ḳ.) — The عِرَاقَانِ of the horse's saddle are The *two edges of the* دَفَّتَانِ, *at the fore part of the saddle and its hinder part.* (IDrd, TA voce قَرَبُوس, q. v.) = [Also *A pace,* or *rate of going.*] One says in relation to a horse, on the occasion of drawing forth the sweat, and of careful tending, and fattening, احْمِلْهُ عَلَى العِرَاقِ الأَعْلَى وَالعِرَاقِ الأَسْفَلِ, meaning [*Urge,* or *make, thou him to go*] *the vehement pace and the inferior pace.* (Ibn-'Abbád, O, TA.) = العِرَاقُ is the name of *A certain country,* (Ṣ, O, Mṣb, Ḳ,) *well known,* (Mṣb, Ḳ,) *extending from 'Abbádán to El-Mowṣil in length and from El-Ḳádiseeyeh to Ḥulwán in breadth;* (Ḳ;) masc. and fem.: (Ṣ, O, Mṣb, Ḳ:) said to be so named because upon the عِرَاق, i. e. "side," or "shore," of the Tigris and Euphrates: (O,* Ḳ: [in which, and in other works, several other supposed derivations are mentioned, but such as I think too fanciful to deserve notice:]) accord. to some, it is arabicized, (Ṣ, O, Mṣb, Ḳ,) from a Pers. appellation, (Ṣ, O,) i. e. from إِيرَان شَهْر, (Aṣ, O,* Ḳ, TA,) of which the meaning is [said to be] "having many palm-trees and [other] trees;" (Ḳ;) but [SM justly says,] in my opinion the meaning requires consideration. (TA.) — العِرَاقَانِ is an appellation of *El-Baṣrah and El-Koofeh.* (Ṣ, O, Ḳ.)

عَرِيقٌ, (Ṣ, O, Ḳ,) applied to a man and to a horse, means [*Rooted,* i. e.] *having a radical,* or *hereditary, share,* (لَهُ عِرْقٌ, Ṣ, O,) in generousness or nobleness [of origin, which, accord. to the Ṣ and O, and common usage, seems to be implied by the epithet when used absolutely], (Ṣ, O, Ḳ,) and also in meanness or ignobleness [thereof; or *having a strain* of, i. e. *an inborn disposition* to, generousness or nobleness, and also meanness or ignobleness]. (Ṣ,* O,* Ḳ.) And you say also فُلَانٌ مُعْرِقٌ ↓ فِى الكَرَمِ and فِى اللُّؤْمِ [*Such a one is rooted,* &c., *in generousness* or *nobleness* and *in meanness* or *ignobleness*]; and إِنَّهُ لَمُعْرَقٌ ↓ لَهُ فِى الكَرَمِ, إِنَّهُ لَمَعْرُوقٌ ↓ لَهُ فِى الكَرَمِ; (Ṣ, O;) and [the part. n. being formed] on the supposition of the suppression of the augmentative letter [in its verb, which is أُعْرِقَ]: (TA:) and in like manner, (Ṣ, O, TA,) in a trad., (O, TA,) a man of whom there is no living ancestor between him and Adam is said to be مُعْرَقٌ ↓ لَهُ فِى المَوْتِ (Ṣ, O, TA) i. e. *Made to have a radical,* or *hereditary, share* (عِرْق) *in death;* (O, TA;) meaning that he will inevitably die. (Ṣ, O, TA.) [In the Ḥam p. 438, مُعْرِقٌ ↓ is expl. as syn. with عَرِيقٌ: but in the verse to which this explanation relates it is evidently employed in the sense of the act. part. n. of أَعْرَقَ as used in the phrase أَعْرَقَ فِيهِ أَعْمَامُهُ وَأَخْوَالُهُ, q. v.] — غُلَامٌ عَرِيقٌ means [*A boy,* or *young man,*] *slender,* or *spare, and light of spirit.* (TA.)

عُرَاقَة: see عُرَاقٌ, in two places.

عِرَاقِىٌّ *Of,* or *belonging to, the country called* العِرَاق. (Mṣb.) — إِبِلٌ عِرَاقِيَّةٌ means *Camels that pasture upon what are termed* عِرَاق, i. e. *remains of the* [*plants,* or *trees, called*] حَمْض: (Ḳ,* TA:) or, app., accord. to Az, *camels of,* or *belonging to,* العراق as meaning *the waters of Benoo-Saad-Ibn-Málik and Benoo-Mázin:* or, as some say, *of,* or *belonging to, the* عِرَاق as meaning the *side,* or *shore, of water:* and it is also said that the epithet in this phrase is a rel. n. from العرق [thus in my original, without any syll. sign and without explanation]. (TA.)

عَرَّاقَة, with teshdeed [to the ر], *A thing* [app. *a cloth for imbibing the sweat*] *that is put beneath the* تكلة [app. meaning *pad*] *of the* سَرْج [or *horse's saddle*] *and the* بَرْذَعَة [q. v.]. (TA. [The word تكلة, which I have not found anywhere except in this instance, I can only suppose to be an arabicized word from the Pers. or Turkish تَكَلْتُو, which is commonly pronounced by the Turks تَكَلْتِى, with ك and ى, and which means *a pad,* or *a piece of felt, put beneath the saddle to prevent its galling the beast's back.*])

عَارِقٌ [act. part. n. of عَرَقَ]. A poet says,

* أَكُفُّ لِسَانِى عَنْ صَدِيقِى فَإِنْ أُجَأْ *
* إِلَيْهِ فَإِنِّى عَارِقٌ كُلَّ مَعْرَقِ *

[*I restrain my tongue from my friend; but if I be compelled to have recourse to him in a case of need, I am one who gnaws to the utmost:* مَعْرَق being here an inf. n.]. (Ṣ, O: mentioned in both immediately after the explanation of عَرَقْتُ العَظْمَ.) — And [the pl.] العَوَارِقُ signifies *The* أَضْرَاس [i. e. *teeth,* or *lateral teeth,* &c.]: (Ḳ:) an epithet in which the quality of a subst. predominates. (TA.) — And *The* سِنُون [i. e. *years,* or *droughts,* or *years of drought*]; so called لِأَنَّهَا تَعْرُقُ الإِنْسَانَ, (Ḳ, TA, in some copies of the Ḳ الأَسْنَانَ,) i. e. because they take from the man [his flesh, or render him lean]. (TA.)

أَعْرَقُ لَيْلَةٍ فِى السَّنَةِ, *The night, in the year, most abundant in milk.* (O.) = [أَعْرَقُ is also a comparative and superlative epithet signifying *More,* and *most, rooted* in a quality or faculty: regularly formed from عَرَقَ, or irregularly from أَعْرَقَ: but perhaps post-classical. (See De Sacy's "Anthol. Gram. Arabe," p. 183, lines 1 and 3, of the Ar. text; and p. 441 of the Notes, in which he has expressed his opinion that it signifies "qui a jeté de plus profondes racines.")]

مَعْرَقٌ an inf. n. of 1 in the sense first expl. in this art. (Ṣ, O, Ḳ.) ═ [And a noun of place, signifying *A place of sweat* or *of sweating* of an animal; such as the armpit and the groin: pl. مَعَارِقُ. — Hence,] مَعَارِقُ الرَّمْلِ *i. q.* آبَاطُهُ [i. e. † *The places where the main body of the sand ends, and where it is thin, not deep*]: likened to the مَعَارِق of the animal. (TA.) — And معرق [thus in my original; perhaps مَعْرَقٌ, as denoting "a place of sweat," like مَمْطَرٌ from المَطَرُ; or ↓ مِعْرَقٌ, as being likened to a utensil, like مِمْطَرٌ, and as being in form agreeable with many words denoting articles of dress;] signifies *An innermost garment for imbibing the sweat, lest it should reach to the garments of pride* [i. e. *the outer garments*]. (TA.)

مُعْرَقٌ Wine (شَرَاب) *having a little water put into it;* (Ṣ, Ḳ;) and so ↓ مُعَرَّقٌ, (Ṣ, O, Ḳ,) applied to طِلَآء [which likewise signifies wine, or thick wine, &c.]; (Ṣ, O;) and ↓ مَعْرُوقٌ, (Ḳ,) of which last no verb has been mentioned: (TA:) or مُعْرَقَةٌ signifies wine (خَمْر) *pure,* or *unmixed:* or *having a little mixture* [*of water*]. (Ḥam p. 561.) ═ See also عَرِيقٌ, in three places.

مُعْرِقٌ: see عَرِيقٌ. ═ [Accord. to Reiske, as mentioned by Freytag, it signifies *Rain that appears to the people of El-Yemen from the region of El-'Irák.*] ═ تَرَكْتَ الحَقَّ مُعْرِقًا means *Thou hast left the truth apparent,* or *manifest, between us.* (TA.)

مِعْرَقٌ *An iron implement,* or *a knife,* or *broad knife,* or *broad blade, with which one pares a bone with some flesh upon it, removing the flesh.* (TA.) ═ See also مَعْرَقٌ.

مُعَرَّقٌ: see مَعْرُوقٌ, in four places: ═ and see مُعْرَقٌ.

مَعْرُوقٌ A bone *of which the flesh has been* [*eaten or*] *thrown from it.* (TA.) — And A man *having little flesh;* (Ḳ;) and so مَعْرُوقُ العِظَامِ; (Ṣ, O, Ḳ;) and ↓ مُعْتَرَقٌ, (Ṣ, O, TA, [and probably in correct copies of the Ḳ, but in my MS. copy of it and in the CḲ ↓ مُعْتَرِقٌ, which does not accord with any of the explanations of its verb,]) and مُعْتَرَقُ ↓ العِظَامِ; (TA;) and ↓ مُعَرَّقٌ, and مُعَرَّقُ العِظَامِ. (Ḳ.) And A horse *having no flesh upon his* قَصَب [meaning *bones of the legs*]; as also ↓ مُعْتَرَقٌ. (TA.) And مَعْرُوقُ الخَدَّيْنِ, applied to a horse, in which the quality denoted thereby is approved, *Having no flesh in the cheeks:* (TA:) and مُعَرَّقُ ↓ الخَدَّيْنِ a man *having little flesh in the cheeks:* (Ṣ, O:) and مُعَرَّقُ ↓ القَدَمَيْنِ, (Ḳ and TA in art. نهس,) and الكَعْبَيْنِ, a man *having little flesh upon the feet,* and *upon the ankle-bones:* (TA in that art.:) and ↓ مُعَرَّقٌ applied to a horse signifies مُضَمَّرٌ [i. e. *rendered lean,* or *light of flesh,* probably *by being made to sweat,* agreeably with an explanation of the latter epithet, and thus radically differing from مَعْرُوقٌ and مُعْتَرَقٌ]. (TA.) ═ See also مُعْرَقٌ. ═ And see عَرِيقٌ.

مُعْتَرَقٌ and مُعْتَرِقٌ: see مَعْرُوقٌ; the former in two places.

عرقب

Q. 1. عَرْقَبَ الدَّابَّةَ *He hocked, houghed, hamstrung,* or *cut the hock-tendon of, the beast.* (Ṣ, A, O, Ḳ.*) — And عَرْقَبَهُ *He raised his hocks,* (namely, a camel's, O,) *in order that he might stand up:* (O, Ḳ:) *he assisted him* (i. e. a camel) *to stand up, by raising* [*his hocks*]. (TA.) Thus the verb has two contr. meanings. (Ḳ.) — And عَرْقَبَ † *He practised artifice, craft,* or *cunning.* (O, Ḳ.) One says, إِذَا أَعْيَاكَ غَرِيمُكَ فَعَرْقِبْ † [*When thy debtor wearies thee,*] *practise artifice,* &c. (AA, O, TA.)

Q. 2. تَعَرْقَبَ *He mounted* a beast *from behind.* (O, TA.) — And † *He took his course along the narrow roads,* or *ways, of the mountain, which are called* عَرَاقِيب. (Ṣ, O, Ḳ.) — And تعرقب لِخَصْمِهِ † *He pursued a way hidden from his adversary:* said when one adopts another and easier course of speech. (TA.) — And تعرقب عَنِ الأَمْرِ † *He turned away,* or *declined, from the affair.* (Ḳ.) — إِذَا مَطَلَ تَعَقْرَبَ وَإِذَا وَعَدَ تَعَرْقَبَ † [*When he puts off the fulfilment of his promise, he acts like 'Akrab* (a man notorious for putting off the fulfilment of his promises); *and when he promises, he acts like 'Orkoob*] (A, TA) is a prov. (TA. [See the following paragraph, last sentence but one.])

عُرْقُوبٌ [The *tendo Achillis,* or *heel-tendon;*] *a certain tense,* (T, A, Mgh, Mṣb,) or *thick,* (Ḳ,) or *thick and tense,* (Ṣ, O,) *tendon,* (T, Ṣ, A, Mgh, O, Mṣb, Ḳ,) *behind the two ankle-bones,* (T, A, Mgh, Mṣb,) *above the heel;* (Ṣ, O, Ḳ;) the *thing that conjoins the shank and the foot;* (Aṣ, TA;) in a human being: (Ṣ, O, Ḳ:) pl. عَرَاقِيبُ. (TA, &c.) The saying of the Prophet, وَيْلٌ لِلْعَرَاقِيبِ مِنَ النَّارِ [*Woe to the heel-tendons from the fire* of Hell] means, to him who neglects the washing of them (Mgh, Mṣb) in the [ablution termed] وُضُوء. (Mṣb.) — [In a beast, it is in some instances applied to The *hock,* or *hough;* i. e.] the عُرْقُوب of a beast is *that which, in its hind leg, corresponds to the* رُكْبَة [or *knee*] *in its fore leg:* (Ṣ, O, Ḳ:) [in other instances, it is applied to the *tendon of the hock,* or *hough;* i. e., to the *hamstring;* for, as] Aṣ says, in every quadruped, the عُرْقُوبَانِ are in the hind legs, and the رُكْبَتَانِ in the fore legs; (Ṣ, O, TA;) and the عُرْقُوب of the horse is the *tendon that conjoins the part wherein meet the* وَظِيف [here meaning the *metatarsus*] *and the* سَاق [here meaning the *tibia*]: (TA: [he says "of the horse," instead of using a more comprehensive term, app. because he is describing that animal:]) it is, in a quadruped, the *tendon that* [*corresponds to that which in a human being*] *is behind the two ankle-bones, between the joint of the foot and the shank:* in a human being it is a little above the heel. (TA, from an explanation of a trad. [This last explanation evidently employs terms according to their applications in the comparative anatomy of quadrupeds and human beings, and therefore requires the words which I have supplied. That عُرْقُوب, in relation to a beast, signifies the *hock-tendon* is well known: and that it also signifies the *hock* itself is shown by a usage of the verb عَرْقَبَ (for it is by raising the hocks that a man assists a camel to stand up), and by an explanation voce رُكْبَة.]) شَرٌّ مَا أَجَاءَكَ إِلَى مُخَّةِ عُرْقُوبٍ [*It is an evil thing that has compelled thee to have recourse to the marrow of a hock*] (Ḳ, TA) is a prov. (TA) applied to him who seeks to obtain a thing from a mean, or sordid, person; (Ḳ, TA;) for the عرقوب has no marrow. (TA.) And one says, فُلَانٌ يَضْرِبُ العَرَاقِيبَ وَيَقْرَعُ الظَّنَابِيبَ [*Such a one smites the hock-tendons* of camels to slaughter them, *and strikes the shins* of camels to make them lie down that he may mount them in haste]; meaning that he entertains guests and gives aid, or succour. (A.) — عُرْقُوبُ الأَسَدِ is a name of *The Thirteenth Mansion of the Moon.* (Ḳzw: see العَوَّآءُ, in art. عو.) — طَيْرُ عُرْقُوبٍ is an appellation given to *Any bird from which one augurs evil to camels, because it wounds them in the hocks* or *hock-tendons* (يُعَرْقِبُهَا). (Meyd, TA.) The Arabs say that when the bird called أَخْيَل [q. v.] lights upon a camel, its hocks, or hock-tendons, will assuredly be laid bare: and accord. to the [O and] Ḳ, طَيْرُ العَرَاقِيبِ is an appellation of *The* [*bird called*] شِقِرَّاق [which is said in the Ṣ &c. to be the same as the أَخْيَل]; and [Ṣgh and SM add that] they regard it as of evil omen. (TA.) — عُرْقُوبُ القَطَا means *The* سَاق [or *shank*] *of the* قطا [or *sand-grouse*]. (Ṣ, O, Ḳ.) To this a thing is hyperbolically likened to denote its shortness: one says يَوْمٌ أَقْصَرُ مِنْ عُرْقُوبِ القَطَا [*A day shorter than the shank of the kaṭà*]: (L, TA:) and a poet says, (Ṣ, &c.,) namely, El-Find Ez-Zimmánee, (O, L, TA,) or, accord. to Seer, Imra-el-Keys Ibn-'Ábis, (IB, L, TA,)

* وَنَبْلِي وَفُقَاهَا كَعَرَاقِيبِ قَطًا طُحْلِ *

[*And my arrows, with their notches, like the shanks of ash-coloured sand-grouse*]. (Ṣ, O, L, TA.) — عُرْقُوبٌ also signifies † *A turning,* or *bending, part of a valley:* (Ḳ:) or *a part of a valley in which is a great turning* or *bending.* (Ṣ, O.) And *A road in a mountain:* (Ḳ:) or *a narrow road in a mountain:* or *a road in a deep valley, in which only one can walk.* (TA.) And [the pl.] عَرَاقِيبُ, ‡ The *prominences,* or *projecting parts,* of mountains: (O, Ḳ, TA:) and the *most distant,* or *far-extending, roads,* or *ways,* thereof: (Aboo-Kheyreh, O, TA:) for [in travelling mountains,] you follow the most easy way, wherever it be: (Aboo-Kheyreh, TA:) or the *narrow roads* or *ways, in the hard and elevated parts,* of mountains. (Ṣ, O, Ḳ.) And [hence, app.,] عَرَاقِيبُ الأُمُورِ † *Great and difficult affairs:* (Ṣ, O, Ḳ:) as also عَرَاقِيلُهَا. (Ṣ, O.) — And *A mountain always crowned with clouds, not rained upon.* (TA.) — Also † *Artifice, craft,* or *cunning;* or *a stratagem,* or *trick.* (O, Ḳ. [See Q. 1, last signification.]) — And † *Knowledge* (عِرْفَان) *of an argument, a plea, an allegation,* or *a proof.* (O, Ḳ.) = Also the name of a certain man of the Amalekites, (Ṣ, O, Ḳ, TA,) or, (so says Ibn-El-Kelbee, O,) of the Benoo-Abd-Shems-Ibn-Saad, (Jm, O, TA,) but this is said to be of no authority, (O,) or of El-Ows, (Jm, TA,) the greatest liar of his time, (Ḳ,) proverbial for breach of promises: (Ṣ, O:) El-Ashja'ee (whose name was Jubeyhà, O, Ḳ) says,

وَعَدْتَ وَكَانَ الخُلْفُ مِنْكَ سَجِيَّةً

مَوَاعِيدَ عُرْقُوبٍ أَخَاهُ بِيَتْرَبِ

(Ṣ, O, Ḳ, TA) i. e. ‡ *Thou promisedst, but breach of promise was an inherent quality of thee, like the promises of 'Orkoob to his brother in Yetreb;* which is in El-Yemámeh; or, as some relate it, بِيَثْرِبِ, i. e. El-Medeeneh, or, as some say, the land of the Benoo-Saad; but the former is the more correct. (TA. [See also Ḥar p. 160.]) And one says, هُوَ أَكْذَبُ مِنْ عُرْقُوبِ يَتْرَبَ ‡ [*He is more mendacious than 'Orkoob of Yetreb*]. (A, TA.)

عرك

1. عَرَكَهُ, (Ṣ, O, Ḳ,) aor. ـُ, (Ṣ,) inf. n. عَرْكٌ, (Ṣ, O,) *He rubbed it,* or *rubbed and pressed it,* or *did so well;* syn. دَلَكَهُ; namely, a thing; (Ṣ, O;) such as a skin or hide, or a tanned skin or hide, and the like. (TA.) — And [*He wore it away by scraping,* &c.;] *he scraped, rubbed, chafed,* or *fretted, it, until he erased,* or *effaced, it.* (Ḳ.) — Hence, عَرَكَ بِجَنْبِهِ مَا كَانَ مِنْ صَاحِبِهِ, aor. and inf. n. as above, meaning † [*He acted*] *as though he scraped,* &c., [*with his side,*] *what had proceeded from his companion, until he erased,* or *effaced, it:* (TA;) [like as a camel allays an itching by rubbing with his side the trunk of a tree: i. e. *he bore,* or *endured, what proceeded from his companion:* for] يَعْرُكُ الأَذَى بِجَنْبِهِ means يَحْتَمِلُهُ [i. e. † *He bears,* or *endures, annoyance,* or *molestation;* or *forgives it,* and *feigns himself neglectful of it*]. (O and Ḳ in explanation of عَرَكَهُ.) — And عَرَكْتُ القَوْمَ فِى الحَرْبِ, inf. n. as above, † [*I fretted,* or *ground,* or *crushed, the party in the war,* or *battle.*] (Ṣ, O.) And دَارَتْ عَلَيْهِمْ i. q. عَرَكَتْهُمُ الحَرْبُ ‡ [i. e., lit., *The war,* or *battle, revolved upon them* like the mill or mill-stone; meaning *fretted,* or *ground,* or *crushed, them*]. (TA.) Zuheyr says,

فَتَعْرُكْكُمْ عَرْكَ الرَّحَى بِثِفَالِهَا

وَتَلْقَحْ كِشَافًا ثُمَّ تُنْتَجْ فَتُتْئِمِ

(O) meaning ‡ *And it,* i. e. war, *will fret* [or *grind* or *crush*] *you, as the mill with its skin put beneath it, upon which the flour falls, frets* [or *grinds*] *the grain;* and *it,* i. e. war, *will conceive two years, one after the other; then bring forth, and give birth to twins:* he makes war's destruction of them to be like the mill's grinding of the grain, and the various evils that are engendered from war to be like children. (EM pp. 123-4.) — عَرَكَ أُذُنَهُ, (MA,) inf. n. عَرْكٌ, (MA, KL,) *He rubbed,* or *rubbed and pressed,* [or generally, as now used, *he wrung,* or *twisted,*] *his ear.* (MA, KL.) — عَرَكَ ظَهْرَهَا, aor. and inf. n. as above, *He felt her back,* namely, that of a she-camel, &c., *doing so much* or *often, to know her state of fatness:* (TA:) and عَرَكَ السَّنَامَ *He felt the hump, to know if there were in it fatness or not.* (Ṣ, O, TA.) — عَرَكَ البَعِيرُ جَنْبَهُ بِمِرْفَقِهِ, (Ṣ, Ḳ,*) inf. n. as above, (TA,) *The camel made an incision,* or *a cut, in his side with his elbow,* (Ḳ, TA,) *and rubbed it,* or *rubbed and pressed it,* (TA,) *so as to reach to the flesh,* (Ḳ, TA,) *cutting through the skin:* (TA:) in which case the epithets ▾ عَارِكٌ and ▾ عَرَكْرَكٌ are applied to the camel. (Ḳ.) [See also عَرْكٌ below, which indicates another meaning.] — عَرَكَهُ, (Lḥ, Ḳ, TA,) aor. and inf. n. as above, (Lḥ, TA,) also signifies † *He put upon him evil* (Lḥ, Ḳ, TA) *and misfortune:* (Ḳ, TA: [the CḲ has حَمَلَ عليه الشرُّ والدَّهْرُ, meaning *evil and misfortune assailed him,* instead of حَمَلَ عَلَيْهِ الشَّرَّ وَالدَّهْرَ, as in other copies of the Ḳ and in the TA:]) and, as some say, عَرَكَهُ بِشَرٍّ signifies *he did evil to him,* or *brought evil upon him, repeatedly.* (TA.) — عَرَكَ الدَّهْرُ فُلَانًا ‡ *Time,* or *fortune, rendered such a one experienced;* or *trained,* or *disciplined, and reformed,* or *improved, him.* (Ḳ, TA.) — عَرَكَ الإِبِلَ فِى الحَمْضِ *He left the camels amid the plants termed* حَمْض, *to obtain thereof what they wanted.* (Lḥ, Ḳ.) — عَرَكَتِ المَاشِيَةُ النَّبَاتَ *The cattle ate the plants,* or *herbage.* (Ḳ.) — عَرَكَتْ said of a woman, (Ṣ, O, Ḳ,) or of a girl, or young woman, (Lḥ, TA,) aor. ـُ, (Ṣ, O,) inf. n. عُرُوكٌ (Ṣ, O, Ḳ) and عِرَاكٌ (O,* Ḳ) and عَرْكٌ, (Ḳ,) *She menstruated;* (Ṣ, O, Ḳ;) as also ▾ اعركت. (Ḳ.) = عَرِكَ, (Ḳ,) [aor. ـَ,] inf. n. عَرَكٌ, (TA,) *He was,* or *became, such as is termed* عَرِكٌ [q. v.]; *strong,* or *vehement, in striving, contending,* or *conflicting,* (Ḳ, TA,) and *in might, courage, valour,* or *prowess,* (TA,) *in war,* or *battle,* (Ḳ, TA,) and *in altercation.* (TA.)

3. عَارَكَهُ, (TA,) inf. n. مُعَارَكَةٌ (Ṣ, O, Ḳ, TA) and عِرَاكٌ, (TA,) *He fought him; contended with him in fight,* or *battle:* (Ṣ,* O,* Ḳ,* TA:) مُعَارَكَةٌ signifies the act of *fighting;* and *thrusting at and wounding, one another, in fight,* or *battle.* (KL.) — And عِرَاكٌ signifies also, in relation to camels, The *pressing,* or *crowding, one another, at,* or *to get to, the water.* (TA.) [See also this word below. And see 8.]

4: see 1, last sentence but one.

6: see the next paragraph.

8. اعتركوا, (Ṣ, O,) or اعتركوا فِى المَعْرَكَةِ, (Ḳ, TA,) [and ▾ تعاركوا, mentioned by Freytag, and agreeable with analogy, but I do not find any authority for it,] *They pressed, straitened,* or *crowded, one another,* (Ṣ, O, TA,) and *rubbed,* or *rubbed and pressed, one another,* (TA,) or *strove together,* and *fought one another,* (Ḳ, TA,) *in the place of fight,* or *battle;* (Ṣ, O, Ḳ, TA;) and فِى الخُصُومَةِ [*in altercation*]. (TA.) — And اعتركت الإِبِلُ فِى الوِرْدِ *The camels pressed,* or *crowded, one another, in the coming to water.* (Ḳ.) [See also 3.] — اعتركت مُعْتَرَكَةً, (Ibn-'Abbád, O,) or بِمُعْتَرَكَةٍ, (Ḳ,) said of a woman [menstruating] *She stuffed her vulva with a piece of rag.* (Ibn-'Abbád, O, Ḳ.)

عَرْكٌ, [originally an inf. n.,] accord. to El-'Adebbes El-Kinánee, i. q. حَازٌّ, i. e. *An incision,* or *a cut, made by the elbow* [*of a camel*], *in the arm,* [probably a mistake for *in the side,* (see 1, near the middle of the paragraph,)] *so as to reach to the flesh, cutting through the skin, by the side of the callous protuberance upon the breast.* (O.) [See also حَازٌّ, in art. حز.] — [Hence, app.,] ذُو عَرْكَيْنِ, as used by a poet, [the dual, it seems, being put for the sing. for the sake of the rhyme, as it ends a verse,] is a metaphorical term for The *vulva* of a woman; the عَرْك in its primary sense being in the camel. (TA.) = Also The *dung* of beasts or birds of prey. (O, Ḳ.) = And Herbage *trodden and eaten.* (TA.)

عَرَكٌ *Fishermen;* (AA, Ṣ, MA, O, Ḳ;) as also ▾ عَرَكَةٌ; (MA; [but this I do not find elsewhere;]) and عُرُوكٌ: (O, Ḳ:) one of whom is called ▾ عَرَكِىٌّ, (AA, Ṣ, MA, O, Ḳ,) meaning *a fisherman who holds in his hand an iron implement having five prongs:* (MA:) عَرَكٌ and ▾ عَرَكِىٌّ being like عَرَبٌ and عَرَبِىٌّ: (AA, Ṣ, O:) [i. e. عَرَكِىٌّ is the n. un.:] accord. to the Ḳ, عَرَكٌ and عُرُوكٌ are pls. of عَرَكِىٌّ; but IAth says that عُرُوكٌ is pl. of عَرَكٌ: (TA:) hence عَرَكٌ is used as meaning *sailors,* or *mariners,* (AA, Ṣ, O, Ḳ,) because they fish, not as being [properly] a name for them: (AA, Ṣ, O:) Zuheyr says,

تَغْشَى الحُدَاةُ بِهِمْ حُرَّ الكَثِيبِ كَمَا

يُغْشِى السَّفَائِنَ مَوْجَ اللُّجَّةِ العَرَكُ

[*The camel-drivers cover with them the middle of the elevated expanse of sand like as the seamen cause the waves of the deep to cover the ships*]: but AO related this verse otherwise, saying مَوْجُ, in the nom. case, and making العَرَكُ to be an epithet applied to the موج as signifying المُتَلَاطِمُ [as though the meaning were, *like as the colliding waves of the deep cover the ships* with their surf]. (Ṣ, O.) = Also i. q. صَوْتٌ [*A sound, noise, voice,* &c.]; and so ▾ عَرَكٌ. (Ṣ, O, Ḳ.) = It is also the subst. denoted by the phrase عَرَكَ الإِبِلَ فِى الحَمْضِ [q. v., app. as meaning The *act of leaving camels amid the pasturage termed* حَمْض, *to obtain thereof what they want;* a meaning given in the O as an explanation of ▾ عَرَكْرَكٌ, which is perhaps in this instance a mistranscription]. (Ḳ.)

عَرِكٌ A man *who throws down*, or *prostrates*, *his antagonists much*, or *often*; syn. صَرِيعٌ; (Ṣ, O;) in the Ḳ and in some of the copies of the Ṣ صَرِيع, like أَمِير; [which is app. a mistranscription;] (TA;) *strong*, or *vehement*, (Ṣ,* O,* Ḳ, TA,) *in striving, contending*, or *conflicting*, (Ḳ, TA,) and *in might, courage, valour*, or *prowess*, (TA,) *in war*, or *battle*, (Ḳ, TA,) and *in altercation*; (TA;) as also ▼ مُعَارِكٌ: (Ḳ, TA:) pl. of the former عَرِكُونَ. (Ṣ, O, Ḳ, TA: in the CḲ عَرِكُوا.) = رَمْلٌ عَرِكٌ and ▼ مَعْرَوْرِكٌ *Sand*, or *sands, intermingling*; (IDrd, O, Ḳ;) as also ▼ عَرِيكٌ, (L, TA,) which last epithet is erroneously applied in the Ḳ to the word رَجُلٌ instead of رَمْلٌ, as is also in one instance ▼ مَعْرَوْرِكٌ [in the CḲ in this latter instance written مُعْرَوْرِك]. (TA.) = See also عَرُوكٌ.

عَرْكَةٌ as meaning *A war*, or *battle*, is post-classical. (TA.) — لَقِيتُهُ عَرْكَةً, (Ṣ, O, Ḳ,) and عَرْكَةً بَعْدَ عَرْكَةٍ, and عَرْكَتَيْنِ, (TA,) and عَرَكَاتٍ, (Ṣ, O, Ḳ,) mean *I met him once*, (Ṣ, O, Ḳ,) and *time after time*, and *twice*, (TA,) and *several times*: (Ṣ, O, Ḳ:) the noun not being used otherwise than adverbially. (TA.)

عُرْكَةٌ: see عَرِكٌ.

عُرَكَةٌ, (O, Ḳ,) and عُرَكَةٌ لِلْأَذَاةِ بِجَنْبِهِ, a phrase used by 'Áïsheh in describing her father, (O,) † One *who bears*, or *endures, annoyance*, or *molestation*; or *who forgives it, and feigns himself neglectful of it*. (O, Ḳ. [See 1, third sentence.])

عَرَكِيٌّ: see عَرِكٌ, in two places. = عَرَكِيَّةٌ A *vitious*, or an *immoral*, or *unrighteous*, woman; or *an adulteress*, or *a fornicatress*. (O, Ḳ.) — And A *thick, gross, coarse*, or *rude*, woman; as also ▼ عَرَكَانِيَّةٌ. (Ḳ, TA. [The latter thus expl. in the O, and, as is said in the TA, on the authority of Ibn-'Abbád: in my MS. copy of the Ḳ written عَرَكَانِيَّةٌ; and in the CḲ, عَرَنِيَّةٌ.])

عَرَكَانِيَّةٌ: see the next preceding paragraph.

عِرَاكٌ an inf. n. of 3 [q. v.]. (TA.) [Hence,] one says, أَوْرَدَ إِبِلَهُ العِرَاكَ, (Ṣ, O, Ḳ,) or, as in the "Book" of Sb, أَرْسَلَهَا العِرَاكَ, (TA,) *He made his camels to come*, or *go, to the water together*; (Ṣ, O, Ḳ;) the last word being in the accus. case after the manner of inf. ns.; (Ṣ, O;) originally عِرَاكًا; then they prefixed ال, which does not change it from its proper state of an inf. n.: (Ṣ, O, Ḳ:) it is like the phrases مَرَرْتُ بِهِمُ الجَمَّآءَ الغَفِيرَ and الحَمْدُ لِلّٰهِ: (Ṣ, O:) IB says that العِرَاكَ and الجَمَّآءَ الغَفِيرَ are in the accus. case as denotatives of state; and الحَمْدُ لِلّٰهِ as the inf. n.: but Sb says that they prefix ال to the inf. n. that is in the place of the denotative of state. (TA.) [See also a similar phrase voce حَقٌّ: and see a verse cited voce رِفْقٌ.]

عَرُوكٌ, applied to a she-camel, (Ṣ, O, Ḳ,) *i. q.* شَكُوكٌ; (Ṣ, O, TA;) i. e. (TA) *Whose fatness is not known unless by feeling her hump*: or *of whose hump one doubts whether there be in it fat* or *not*: pl. عُرُكٌ. (Ḳ.)

عَرِيكٌ: see عَرِكٌ.

عُرَاكَةٌ *What is drawn from the udder before the first* فِيقَة [or *milk that collects in the udder between two milkings*], (Ḳ,) *and before the second* فِيقَة *collects*: also termed عُلَاكَةٌ [perhaps a mistranscription for عُلَالَة] and دُلَاكَةٌ. (TA.)

عَرِيكَةٌ *A camel's hump*: or the *remainder thereof*: (Ḳ:) or عَرِيكَةُ السَّنَامِ signifies *what remains of the hump*: (ISk, Ṣ, O:) so called because the purchaser feels that part (يَعْرُكُهُ) to know the fatness and strength [of the animal]: (TA:) pl. عَرَائِكُ; which is said by some to signify the *humps with the backs*. (O.) — [Hence, in phrases here following,] † *Nature*; *natural, native*, or *innate, disposition* or *temper* or *the like*; (Ṣ, O, Ḳ;) and *soul, spirit*, or *mind*. (Ḳ.) One says, فُلَانٌ لَيِّنُ العَرِيكَةِ † *Such a one is easy*, or *gentle*, (Ṣ, O, Ḳ, TA,) *in natural disposition*, (Ḳ, TA,) *submissive, tractable*; (Ṣ,* O,* TA;) *one whose pride*, or *haughtiness, has been broken*, or *subdued*; (Ḳ, TA;) *having little contrariness and aversion*: and شَدِيدُ العَرِيكَةِ *strong in spirit, incompliant*, or *resisting*: (TA:) and لَانَتْ عَرِيكَتُهُ *His pride*, or *haughtiness, became broken*, or *subdued*: (Ṣ, O:) originally relating to the camel; for they used to betake themselves to the camel when he had the disposition of refusing to be ridden or mounted, and incompliance, and cut [a part] in his hump, it being high, difficult to ride upon; and when this was done, he became quiet, and was rendered inclinable, and the part of him that was the place of riding became easy to sit upon; so one said, قَدْ لَانَتْ عَرِيكَتُهُ. (Ḥar pp. 566-7.) One says also رَجُلٌ مَيْمُونُ العَرِيكَةِ, meaning [*A man fortunate, happy*, or *blest, in natural disposition*, or] *in mind*. (TA.)

عَرَكْرَكٌ: see 1, latter half. — Also A *thick, strong* camel. (Ṣ, O, Ḳ.) See also مَعْرُوكٌ. — And the fem., with ة, A *fat* she-camel: pl. عَرَكْرَكَاتٌ. (TA.) — And † A *bulky, corpulent* woman: (Ṣ, O:) or a woman *ugly*, or *unseemly*, (وَسْخَآءُ,) *fleshy*, (Ḳ, TA,) *bulky*, or *corpulent*, (TA,) *and foul*; (Ḳ, TA;) as being likened to the camel. (TA.) — And the masc., applied to a رَكَب [or pubes] (T, O, Ḳ) of a woman, (T, TA,) *Large*, or *big*. (T, O, Ḳ.) = See also عَرِكٌ, last sentence.

عَارِكٌ: see 1, latter half. — Also (without ة) A woman *menstruating*; (Ṣ, O, Ḳ;) and so ▼ مُعْتَرِكٌ: (Ḳ:) pl. of the former عَوَارِكُ. (O.)

مَعْرَكٌ and ▼ مَعْرَكَةٌ and ▼ مَعْرُكَةٌ and ▼ مُعْتَرَكٌ *A place* [or *scene*] *of battle*, or *fight*: (Ṣ, O, Ḳ:) pl. [of the first and second and third] مَعَارِكُ. (TA.) It is said in a trad., ذَمَّ السُّوقَ فَإِنَّهَا ▼ مَعْرَكَةُ الشَّيْطَانِ وَبِهَا تُنْصَبُ رَايَتُهُ [*Discommend thou the market; for it is the battle-ground of the Devil, and in it is set up his banner*]: meaning that it is the dwelling of the Devil, and his place of alighting to which he repairs and which he frequents, because of the unlawful doings and the lying and the usury and the violence that occur therein. (IAth, TA.) And it is said in another trad., ▼ مُعْتَرَكُ المَنَايَا مَا بَيْنَ السِّتِّينَ إِلَى السَّبْعِينَ † [*The space of the conflict of the decrees of death is that between* the ages of *sixty and seventy*]. (O, TA.*)

مَعْرُكٌ: see عَارِكٌ.

مَعْرَكَةٌ and مَعْرُكَةٌ: see مَعْرَكٌ, in three places.

مِعْرَكَةٌ *A piece of rag with which a woman stuffs her vulva* (O, Ḳ) *when menstruating*. (O.)

مَعْرُوكٌ [*Much rubbed*, or *much rubbed and pressed*: &c.: see 1].

• أَصْبَرُ مِنْ ذِى ضَاغِطٍ مَعْرُوكٍ •

[*More patient than* a camel, *such as has a* ضاغط *much rubbed*, or *much rubbed and pressed*]: or, as some relate it, ▼ عَرَكْرَكٍ, meaning a camel *strong and thick*: the ضاغط *is a tumour in the armpit of a camel, like a bag, straitening him*: the saying is a proverb. (Meyd. [See also Freytag's Arab. Prov. i. 737—9.])

مَآءٌ مَعْرُوكٌ *Water to which there is a pressing* or *crowding together* [*of camels*]. (Ṣ, O, Ḳ.) — أَرْضٌ مَعْرُوكَةٌ *Land which the cattle* (Ṣ, O, Ḳ) *pasturing at their pleasure* (Ṣ, O) *have rubbed and pressed* [*with their feet*] (عَرَكَتْهَا) *so that it has become barren*. (Ṣ, O, Ḳ.) — And رَجُلٌ مَعْرُوكٌ ‡ *A man pressed with petitions*. (TA.)

مَعْرَوْرِكٌ: } see عَرِكٌ; the former in two places.
مُعَارِكٌ: }

مُعْتَرَكٌ: see مَعْرَكٌ, in two places.

عرم

1. عَرَمَ, aor. ـُ and ـِ, (Ṣ, Mṣb, Ḳ,) inf. n. عَرَامَةٌ (Ṣ, Ḳ) and عُرَامٌ (Ṣ,* Mṣb,* Ḳ) and عَرْمٌ; (CḲ;) and عَرُمَ, aor. ـُ, (Mṣb, Ḳ,) inf. n. عَرْمٌ; (Mṣb;) and عَرِمَ; (Ḳ; [in which the inf. ns. mentioned above follow this last form of the verb;] and so in a copy of the Ṣ in the place of عَرَمَ, with يَعْرُمُ only for the aor.;) *He was*, or *became, evil in disposition*, or *illnatured, and very perverse* or *cross* or *repugnant*; (Ṣ, Mṣb, Ḳ;*) and *sharp*: (Mṣb:) or *vehement*, or *strong*: (Ḳ:) said of a boy, or child: (Ṣ:) or of a man: and, said of a boy, or child, (or so [particularly] عَرَمَ, inf. n. عَرَامَةٌ and عُرَامٌ, TA,) *he behaved insolently and unthankfully*, or *ungratefully*; syn. أَشِرَ, or مَرِحَ, or بَطِرَ; [all of which signify the same;] or *he was*, or *became, bad, corrupt*, or *wicked*; عَلَيْنَا [*to us*]. (Ḳ, TA.) And accord. to IAạr, عَرِمَ, aor. ـَ, signifies *He was*, or *became, ignorant*; as also عَرُمَ, and عَرَمَ. (TA.) [See also عُرَام, below.] — عَرَمَ said of a bone, [app. when burnt,] aor. ـُ, (Ḳ, TA,)

inf. n. عَرْمٌ, accord. to the copies of the Ḳ i. q. قَتَرٌ, but correctly قَتَّرَ [i. e. *It exhaled its scent, smell, or odour*]. (TA.) ═ عَرَمَ فُلَانًا, (Ḳ, TA,) inf. n. عَرَامَةٌ, (TA,) *He treated such a one with illnature, and exceeding perverseness* or *crossness* or *repugnance.* (Ḳ,* TA.) — عَرَمَ العَظْمَ, (Ṣ, Ḳ,) aor. ـُ and ـِ, inf. n. عَرْمٌ; (Ṣ;) and ▼ تعرّمهُ; (Ṣ, Ḳ;) are like عَرَقَهُ and تعرّقهُ; (Ṣ;) [i. e.] both signify *He stripped off the flesh from the bone* [*with his fore teeth, eating it*]. (Ḳ.) — And in like manner, (Ṣ,) عَرَمَتِ الإِبِلُ الشَّجَرَ *The camels* [*cropped the trees; or*] *obtained* [*pasture*] *from the trees.* (Ṣ, Ḳ.) — And عَرَمَ أُمَّهُ, (Ḳ, TA,) inf. n. عَرْمٌ, (TA,) *He* (a child) *sucked the breast of his mother*; (Ḳ, TA;) and so ▼ اعترم ثَدْىَ أُمِّهِ. (TA.)

2. تَعْرِيمٌ The act of *mixing.* (Ḳ.) One says, عرّمهُ بِهِ *He mixed it with it.* (TḲ.)

3. مُعَارَمَةٌ The *contending in an altercation, disputing,* or *litigating*; and *occasioning* فِتْنَة (i. e. *conflict,* or *discord,* or *the like,*) *with another*; syn. مُخَاصَمَةٌ; and مُفَاتَنَةٌ. (TA.)

4. اعرمهُ *He brought upon him,* meaning *he induced him to do,* a deed [of an evil nature] that he had not committed. (Ḥam p. 707.)

5. تعرّم العَظْمَ: see 1, latter half.

8. اِعْتِرَامُ الفِتَنِ *The being,* or *becoming, hard to be borne, severe,* or *distressing,* said of فِتَن [i. e. *trials,* or *conflicts and factions,* &c.]. (TA.) — اِعْتَرَمَتْ, said of a mare, *She went at random, heedlessly,* or *in a headlong manner, not obeying guidance*; and *deviated from the right course.* (Ḥam p. 277.) — And, said of a mother, *She sought one who would suck her breast: or she sucked the milk from her own breasts and spirted it forth from her*: a poet says,

لَا تَلْغَبَنَّ كَأُمِّ الغُلَا

مِ إِلَّا تَجِدْ عَارِمًا ▼ تَعْتَرِمْ

[in my original لا تلغبنّ; for which I have substituted what I think to be the right reading: i. e. *Do not thou become wearied like the mother of the boy if she find not a sucker of her breast, seeking for such*: or] he means, if she finds not one who will suck her, she contrives, and milks her own breasts, and sometimes she sucks it [i. e. the milk] and spirts it forth from her mouth: accord. to IAạr, this is said to him who imposes upon himself the task of doing that which is no part of his business: or, accord. to Az, the meaning is, be not thou like him who censures, or satirizes, himself, when he finds not whom he may censure, or satirize. (TA.) — See also 1, last sentence.

عَرْمٌ *Grease,* or *gravy*; i. e. the *dripping that exudes from flesh-meat and from fat.* (Ḳ.) And The *remains of the cooking-pot*: (Ḳ, TA:) or the *dirt of the cooking-pot*; as also ▼ عُرَامٌ. (TA.)

عَرَمٌ The *quality,* in anything, *of being of two colours*: a leopard has this quality: (Th, TA:) or, as also ▼ عُرْمَةٌ, *blackness mixed with whiteness,* in anything: or the *quality of being speckled with blackness and whiteness, without largeness of every speckle*: and *a whiteness in the lip of the sheep* or *goat*: (Ḳ:) or thus the latter word: (Ṣ, TA:) and likewise the *quality of being speckled with black, in the ear thereof.* (TA.) Also (i. e. عَرَمٌ) The *quality,* in a collection of small cattle, *of consisting of sheep and goats.* (Ṣ.) ═ See also عَرَمَةٌ.

عَرِمٌ: see عَارِمٌ, in two places. ═ Also *A dam*; syn. مُسَنَّاةٌ: (Ṣ, TA:) [or rather *dams,* agreeably with what here follows:] a pl. [or coll. gen. n.] (Ḳ) having no sing. [or n. un.]: (Ṣ, Ḳ:) or its sing. [or n. un.] is ▼ عَرِمَةٌ, (Ṣ, Mṣb, Ḳ,) which signifies, (Kr, Ḳ, TA,) as also ▼ عَرَمَةٌ, (Kr, TA,) *a dam* (مُسَنَّاةٌ, Kr, or سُدٌّ, Ḳ) *that is raised across a valley,* or *torrent-bed*: (Ḳ:) or عَرِمٌ signifies [*dams such as are termed*] أَحْبَاس [pl. of حِبْس] *constructed in valleys,* or *torrent-beds,* (AḤn, Ḳ, TA,) *in the middle parts of these*: (AḤn, TA:) in each of which senses it is said to be used in the Ḳur xxxiv. 15: (TA:) or it there signifies *a torrent of which the rush is not to be withstood*: (Mṣb:) and *a violent rain,* (Ḳ, TA,) *that is not to be endured*: thus, accord. to some, in the Ḳur: (TA:) and the *male of the* [*species of rat called*] جُرَذ, (Ḳ, TA,) *which is the* خُلْد, so, Az says, is there meant accord. to some: (TA:) and, (Ḳ, TA,) as some say, in that instance, (TA,) it is the name of *a certain valley* (Ḳ, TA) *in El-Yemen*: so says Az. (TA.)

عُرْمَةٌ: see عَرَمٌ: ═ and see also عَرَمَةٌ. ═ Also *A helmet of iron.* (TA.)

عَرَمَةٌ *A quantity of reaped corn* or *grain, collected together,* (Ṣ, Mṣb, Ḳ,) *trodden out,* (Ṣ, Ḳ,) *to be winnowed,* (Ṣ,) *not yet winnowed,* (Ḳ,) or *that is trodden out, then winnowed*: (Mṣb:) said by some to called only عَرْمَةٌ; but correctly عَرَمَةٌ, as is shown by its having for its pl. [or rather coll. gen. n.] ▼ عَرَمٌ, as in an ex. cited by J [in the Ṣ]; حَلَقَةٌ and حَلَقٌ being anomalous: (IB, TA:) and ▼ عُرْمَةٌ, of which the pl. is عُرَمٌ, signifies the same; (Mṣb;) or عُرْمَةٌ signifies *heaps of reaped wheat and of barley.* (TA.) — And *A place in which sand is collected*: (Ṣ, Ḳ:) pl. عَرَمَاتٌ. (IB, TA.) — And it is said to signify جُثْوَةٌ مِنْ دَمَالٍ [app. meaning *A heap of dung such as is termed* دَمَال, q. v.]. (TA.) — See also عَرِمٌ. ═ Also *Flesh-meat.* (Fr, Ḳ, TA: omitted in the CḲ.) One says, إِنَّ جَزُورَكُمْ لَطَيِّبُ العَرَمَةِ *Verily your slaughtered camel is savoury in respect of the meat.* (Fr, TA.) — And The *odour of cooked flesh-meat.* (Ḳ.) ═ Also a pl. of عَارِمٌ [q. v.]. (TA.)

عَرِمَةٌ: see عَرِمٌ. — [It is also said, by Golius, on the authority of Meyd, to signify *A vineyard.*]

عَرَمِى وَٱللّٰهِ is a dial. var. of أَمَا وَٱللّٰهِ, (IAạr, Ḳ, TA,) as also [غُرَمِى وٱللّٰه, and] حَرَمِى وَٱللّٰهِ: one says, عَرَمِى وَٱللّٰهِ لَأَفْعَلَنَّ كَذَا [*Verily,* or *now surely, by God, I will indeed do such a thing*]. (IAạr, TA.)

عُرَامٌ, [mentioned in the first sentence of this art. as an inf. n.,] (Ṣ, Mgh, Mṣb, Ḳ,) when used as [a simple subst.] denoting a quality of a boy, or child, (Ṣ, Mgh,) or of a man, (Ḳ,) signifies *Evilness of disposition,* or *illnature, and exceeding perverseness* or *crossness* or *repugnance*; (Ṣ, Mṣb, Ḳ;) and *vehemence,* and *strength*; (Mgh,* TA;) and *sharpness*; (Mṣb;) and *annoyance,* or *molestation*: (Ḳ:) [and] the *quality of quitting the right course,* and *exorbitance.* (Ḥam p. 277.) — Hence, in a trad. of 'Omar, metaphorically used as meaning † *Sharpness and strength* of [the beverage termed] نَبِيذ made of raisins. (Mgh.) — And *Numerousness* of an army, (Ṣ, Ḳ,) and *sharpness,* and *vehemence,* thereof. (Ḳ.) — Also *Ignorance.* (Fr, TA.) ═ And The عُرَاق [app. meaning *flesh-meat*] of a bone: and likewise [i. e., app., *portions that are cropped* by camels] of trees. (Ṣ, Ḳ. [See عُرَاق, voce عَرْق.]) One says ▼ أَعْرَمُ مِنْ كَلْبٍ عَلَى عُرَامٍ [*More evil in disposition than a dog over a piece of flesh-meat of a bone*]. (TA.) Or, accord. to Az, العُرَامُ signifies, (TA,) or it signifies also, (Ḳ,) *What falls of the bark of the* [*thorn-tree called*] عَوْسَج: (Ḳ, TA:) but others explain it in a general manner, saying that عُرَامُ الشَّجَرَةِ signifies *the bark of the tree.* (TA.) — See also عَرْمٌ.

عَرِيمٌ *A calamity,* or *misfortune*: (Ḳ, TA:) because of its hardness, or pressure. (TA.) ═ See also أَعْرَمُ, last two sentences.

عُرَامِىٌّ is [app. a rel. n. signifying *Of,* or *relating to, ignorance*; being] said by Fr to be from عُرَامٌ signifying "ignorance." (TA.)

عَارِمٌ and ▼ عَرِمٌ, (Ṣ, Mṣb, Ḳ,) applied to a boy, or child, (Ṣ,) or to a man, (Ḳ,) *Evil in disposition,* or *illnatured, and very perverse* or *cross* or *repugnant*; (Ṣ, Mṣb, Ḳ;*) and *sharp*: (Mṣb:) or *vehement,* or *strong*: (Ḳ:) and, applied to a boy, or child, *insolent and unthankful,* or *ungrateful*: or *bad, corrupt,* or *wicked*: the former epithet, applied to a man, signifies also *abominable,* or *evil*: (TA:) and so its fem. pl. عَارِمَات, (Ṣ, TA,) applied by a rájiz as an epithet to creeping [ticks, or similar insects, such as are termed] أَنْبَار [pl. of نِبْر]: (Ṣ:) and ▼ عَرِمٌ is said (Mṣb, TA) by IAạr (TA) to signify *ignorant*: (Mṣb, TA:) عَرَمَةٌ is pl. of عَارِمٌ, and is applied as an epithet to boys, like عَقَقَةٌ [pl. of عَاقٌّ]. (TA.) — [Hence,] لِسَانٌ عَارِمٌ *A vehement tongue.* (TA. [See an ex. voce شَكِىٌّ.]) — And يَوْمٌ عَارِمٌ *A day vehemently cold*: (TA:) or *a day cold in the utmost degree*: (Ḳ, TA:) and in like manner لَيْلٌ عَارِمٌ [*a night vehemently cold*: &c.]: and [the pl. in this sense is عُرَّمٌ:] اللَّيَالِى العُرَّمُ signifies *the vehemently-cold nights.* (TA.) ═ Also [*Sucking the breast*; or] *a sucker of the breast*: so in a verse cited above: see 8. (TA.) ═ مَا هُوَ بِعَارِمِ عَقْلٍ see expl. voce حَارِمٌ.

عَرَمْرَمٌ *Hard, strong,* or *vehement*; (Ḳ, TA;) applied to anything. (TA.) — And *Numerous*; applied to an army; (Ṣ, Ḳ, TA;) or, as some say, to anything. (TA.) — And, applied to a man, *Having a strong degree of* عُجْمَة [i. e. *impotence*, or *difficulty, in speech*, or *utterance*; or *barbarousness*, or *vitiousness, therein*; or *in speaking Arabic*].

أَعْرَمُ [*More*, and *most, evil in disposition*, or *illnatured*, &c.]: see an ex. voce عُرَامٌ. — Also [*Having the quality termed* عَرَمٌ *and* عُرْمَةٌ: fem. عَرْمَآءُ: and pl. عُرْمٌ: i. e.] *having in it blackness and whiteness:* [&c.:] (Ṣ, Ḳ:*) the eggs of the sand-grouse are عُرْمٌ; (Ṣ, Ḳ,* TA;) they are meant by this word in a verse of Aboo-Wejzeh Es-Saadee: (TA:) and عَرْمَآءُ is applied to a serpent; (Ṣ;) and means *a serpent speckled with black and white;* (Ḳ, TA;) pl. عُرْمٌ. (TA.) And *i. q.* أَبْرَشُ: (Ḳ, TA:) and, some say, أَبْرَصُ: [the former meaning *Speckled:* and the latter, and sometimes the former also, *leprous:*] fem. عَرْمَآءُ. (TA.) Applied to a sheep or goat, *Having a whiteness in the lip:* fem. as above: (Ḳ:) [but] it occurs in a trad., applied to a ram, as meaning *white, with black specks.* (TA.) And *Coloured* (Ḳ, TA) *with two colours.* (TA.) Hence دَهْرٌ أَعْرَمُ † [*Time*, or *fortune, of two sorts*]. (TA.) — [Hence also,] applied to a collection of small cattle, *Consisting of sheep and goats.* (Ṣ, Ḳ.) — And *Uncircumcized:* pl. عُرْمَانٌ, and pl. pl. عَرَامِينُ, (Ḳ, TA,) which is mentioned by AA as an epithet applied to men, syn. with قُلْفَانٌ [a pl. of أَقْلَفُ]. (TA.) — Also a sing. of عُرْمَانٌ signifying *Tillers*, or *cultivators, of land*, syn. أَكَرَةٌ, [in the CḲ أُكْرَةٌ (which is a sing.),] (Az, Ḳ, TA,) and so is ▼ عَرِيمٌ, in the copies of the Ḳ, erroneously written عوم [in some of them عُوْمٌ and in others عَوَمٌ]. (TA.) — And أَعْرُمٌ and ▼ عُرُمٌ, the latter more agreeably with analogy, are likewise pls. of عُرْمَانٌ signifying *Places of seed-produce.* (TA.)

عرمض

Q. 1. عَرْمَضَ, inf. n. عَرْمَضَةٌ and عِرْمَاضٌ, (Lḥ, O, Ḳ,) *It* (water) *became overspread with* عرمض [q. v.]; (Lḥ, O;) *i. q.* طَحْلَبَ. (Ḳ.)

عَرْمَضٌ (Lth, Ṣ, O, Ḳ) and ▼ عِرْمَاضٌ (IDrd, Ḳ, TA, written in the O (عُرْمَاضٌ) *i. q.* طُحْلُبٌ; (Ṣ, O, Ḳ;) i. e. The *green substance that comes forth from the bottom of water, so as to overspread it;* (Ṣ, O, L;) *also called* ثَوْرُ المَآءِ; [O; in the L, and in one copy of the Ṣ, ثَوْبُ المَآءِ, which is a mistake;] accord. to AZ; (Ṣ, O;) the *green substance like* خِطْمِىّ [or *marsh-mallow*], *which is upon water;* (Lḥ;) *a soft green substance, like loosened and separated wool, upon stale water;* so says Lth, and he adds his opinion that it is vegetative: (TA:) n. un. with ة. (Ḳ.) — Also the former, (O, Ḳ,) and ▼ عِرْمِضٌ, (El-Hejeree, Ḳ,) *A sort of trees, of those called* عِضَاه, (Lth, O, Ḳ,) *having thorns like the beaks of birds; the hardest thereof in the wood:* (Lth, O:) or the former, (O, Ḳ,) as some assert, (AḤn, O,) the *small of the* أَرَاك (AḤn, O, Ḳ) *and of the* سِدْر *and of all trees that never become great:* (Ḳ:) or *small trees of those called* سِدْر, *that do not become large nor tall, of which the thorns are like the beaks of birds; the hardest thereof in the wood, and the best for bows:* (IAạr, O:) or *certain small trees:* or the *small of the* عِضَاه: or the *small of all trees:* n. un. with ة. (O.)

عِرْمِضٌ: see the next preceding paragraph.

عِرْمَاضٌ inf. n. of 1: — and *i. q.* عَرْمَضٌ, q. v.

مَآءٌ مُعَرْمِضٌ [so in the TA, agreeably with the verb; but in my two copies of the Ṣ, مُعَرْمَضٌ;] *Water overspread*, or *becoming overspread, with* عَرْمَض. (Ṣ, TA.)

عرن

1. عَرَنَ البَعِيرَ, aor. ـُ (Ṣ, Ḳ) and ـِ, (Ḳ,) inf. n. عَرْنٌ, (Ṣ, TA,) *He put the wooden thing called* عِرَان [q. v.] *into the nose of the camel.* (Ṣ, Ḳ.) — And عَرِنَ, like عَنِىَ, *He* (a camel, TA) *had a complaint of his nose arising from the* عِرَان [above mentioned]. (Ḳ.) — عَرَنَ السَّهْمَ, (Ḳ,) [aor. ـُ,] inf. n. عَرْنٌ, (TA,) *He bound*, or *wound, a sinew upon the socket of the head of the arrow.* (Ḳ.) — And عَرَنَ, (Ḳ,) aor. ـُ, (TḲ,) inf. n. عُرُونٌ, (TA,) is *syn. with* مَرَنَ, (Ḳ,) inf. n. مُرُونٌ, (TA,) i. e. *He became accustomed*, or *habituated;* as in the phrase عَرَنَ عَلَى الشَّىْءِ [*he became accustomed*, or *habituated, to the thing*]. (TḲ.) — عَرِنَتِ الدَّارُ, (so in copies of the Ḳ,) or عَرُنَت, (so accord. to the TḲ,) inf. n. عِرَانٌ, *The house*, or *dwelling*, or *abode, was*, or *became, distant*, or *remote*, (Ḳ, TA,) *and in a quarter*, or *direction, that he who loved it did not desire.* (TA.) — عَرِنَتْ, (Ṣ, Ḳ,) aor. ـَ, inf. n. عَرَنٌ, (TA,) said of the hind leg of a horse, or similar beast, (Ṣ,) or said of such a beast itself, (TḲ, [and this is plainly indicated in the Ḳ,]) *It had the disease termed* عَرَن (Ṣ, Ḳ) *and* عَرْنَة *and* عِرَان. (Ḳ.) — And عَرَنَ, aor. ـُ, inf. n. عَرْنٌ, is said of a camel as meaning *He had the disease termed* عَرَن expl. below on the authority of ISk. (Ṣ.)

[2. عرّن الرُّمْحَ is app. said, as meaning *He nailed its head to the shaft of the spear:* see the pass. part. n., مُعَرَّنٌ, below.]

4. اعرن *He* (a man) *continually ate what is termed* عَرَن, meaning *cooked flesh-meat.* (IAạr, Ḳ,* TA.) — And *He had the shanks of his young weaned camels much cracked* or *chapped.* (Ḳ.) — And *He had the* حِكَّة, [i. e. *mange*, or *scab*, or *dry mange* or *scab*], (Ḳ, TA,) or, as ISk says, *purulent pustules* (قُرُوح) *that arise in the neck and occasion a scratching* or *scraping*, (TA, [see عَرَنٌ,]) *among his camels.* (Ḳ, TA.)

عِرْنٌ: see the next paragraph, latter half: — and see also عِرْنَةٌ, last sentence but one.

عَرَنٌ *A callousness in the hind leg of a horse* or *similar beast, above the pastern, in the hinder part thereof;* and it is *what is called* شُقَاق [q. v.]: and, as ISk says, *purulent pustules* (قُرُوح) *that arise in the neck of a camel, in consequence of which he scratches*, or *scrapes, himself, and sometimes he lies down against the stem of a tree and scratches*, or *scrapes, himself therewith; and its cure*, he says, *is the burning of fat upon him:* (Ṣ:) and *an eruption like pustules*, or *purulent pustules, in the necks of young weaned camels, in consequence of which they scratch*, or *scrape, themselves:* (IB, TA:) or, as also ▼ عُرْنَةٌ and ▼ عِرَانٌ, *a certain disease in the hinder part of the hind leg of a horse* or *similar beast*, (Ḳ, TA,) *like an abrasion in the skin*, (TA,) *causing the hair to fall off:* or *a cracking*, or *chapping*, (Ḳ, TA,) *incident to horses*, (TA,) *in their fore legs and their hind legs:* or *a callousness that arises in the pastern of a horse* (Ḳ, TA) or *similar beast, and in the place of its fetlock, in the hinder part, and a* شُقَاق [q. v.] *that betides it from the kicking against a mountain or stone.* (TA.) — Also The *foul smell*, or *foulness* [of the hands] *with the smell, of flesh-meat and its grease;* syn. غَمَرٌ: (Ḳ:) so in the saying, أَجِدُ رَائِحَةَ عَرَنٍ بِيَدَيْكَ [*I perceive the odour of the foulness of thy hands with the smell of flesh-meat and its grease*]: (IAạr, TA:) or عَرَنٌ signifies the *odour of flesh-meat that has* عُرَام [i. e. *grease*, or *gravy*]: and also *i. q.* عُرَام [*itself*, q. v.]. (TA.) And The *odour of cooked flesh-meat;* (Kr, Ḳ;) as also ▼ عِرْنٌ. (Ḳ.) And *A mark*, or *relic*, [or *soil*,] *of broth upon the hand of the eater.* (El-Hejeree, TA.) And *Cooked flesh-meat:* (IAạr, Ḳ:) or, as some say, *flesh*, or *flesh-meat*, in an absolute sense. (TA.) — And *Smoke.* (Ḳ.) — Also *A species of tree, with which one tans.* (Ḳ.) Dioscorides asserts the عرن to be *A plant having leaves resembling those of the small lentil, except that they are longer than they, and having a stem about a span tall, and a red flower, and a small root; growing in neglected*, or *uncultivated, places: a poultice of its leaves with olive-oil is sudorific; its bruised leaves applied as a poultice act as a discutient to wounds and inflamed pustules; and taken in a beverage*, or *sirup, they cure the dribbling of the urine.* (Avicenna, i. e. Ibn-Seenà, book ii. p. 235.)

عَرِنٌ the masc. epithet applied to a horse, or similar beast, signifying *Having the disease termed* عَرَن [q. v.]: (TA:) the fem. epithet having this meaning is عَرِنَةٌ; with which ▼ عَرُونٌ is syn. (Ḳ, TA.) — Also One *who keeps close to the* يَاسِر [or *slaughterer*, or *superintendent of the slaughtering and of the division, of the camel for the game called* المَيْسِر], *in order that he may eat of the slaughtered camel.* (Ḳ.)

عُرْنَةٌ: see عَرَنٌ, former half. — عُرْنَتَانِ signifies *Two specks*, or *spots, above the eye of a dog:* so in a trad. in which men are commanded to kill every dog that is entirely black having عرنتان. (TA.)

عِرْنَةٌ One *who prostrates*, or *throws down, his antagonists much*, or *often; with whom one cannot cope:* (Ṣ, Ḳ, TA: [in the CḲ, الصَّرِيع is erroneously put for الصَّرِيعُ:]) accord. to IB, as signifying صِرِّيعٌ, it is used in commendation: Fr says that when a man is *one who prostrates*, or *throws down, his antagonists much*, or *often, abominable, wicked*, or *crafty*, [*with whom one cannot cope*,] it is said that he is عِرْنَةٌ لَا يُطَاقُ. (TA.) — Also A man *coarse, rough*, or *rude, and niggardly*. (TA.) — And One *who serves houses*, or *tents*. (TA.) — Also The *roots of the* عَرْتَن, (AA, Ṣ, TA, in the Ḳ, erroneously, of the عِرْنِين, TA,) *which is a plant used for tanning*. (Ṣ in art. عرتن.) — And The *wood of the* ظَلْمَخ, (Ṣ, Ḳ,) *a species of tree*, (Ṣ, TA,) *having the form of the* دُلْب [or *plane-tree*], (TA,) *with which skins for water or milk are tanned*, (Ṣ, Ḳ,) *and from which is cut the wood of the beaters and washers and whiteners of clothes, which is buried*: accord. to ISk, [but the same is also said of the عَرْتَن,] it is *a species of tree resembling the* عَوْسَج [or *box-thorn*], *except that it is bigger than it, full and luxuriant in the branch, and not having tall stems*: (TA:) or it is called ▼ عِرْنٌ, [which is a coll. gen. n.,] and عِرْنَةٌ is the n. un. (AA, T in art. ظلمخ.) And [it is also expl. as signifying] The *piece of wood of the beaters and washers and whiteners of clothes upon which the beating is performed with that which is called the* مِيجَنَة. (IKh, TA.)

عِرْنِينٌ The *first part* or *portion* of anything. (Ṣ, Mṣb, Ḳ.) — And hence, (Mṣb,) [particularly,] the *first* [or *upper*] *part* [i. e. the *bridge*] of the nose, *beneath the place where the eyebrows come together*; the *place of what is termed* الشَّمَمُ: (Ṣ, Mṣb, TA:) or the *head* of the nose: (TA:) or the *hard part of the bone* of the nose: (Ḳ:) or it signifies, (Ḳ,) or is sometimes applied to, (Mṣb,) the *nose*, (Mṣb, Ḳ,) *altogether*: (Ḳ:) pl. عَرَانِينُ. (TA.) One says, هُمْ شُمُّ العَرَانِينِ [*They are high in respect of the noses*, or *of the bridges thereof*; often meaning † *they are haughty*, or *disdainful*]. (Ṣ, Mṣb.) And one of the learned has used it metaphorically, saying,

* وَأَصْبَحَ الدَّهْرُ ذُو العِرْنِينِ قَدْ جُدِعَا *

[lit. *And nosed fortune became mutilated in the nose*; by *nosed* being app. meant † *haughty*, or *disdainful*; and by *mutilated in the nose*, † *marred*, or *abased*]. (TA.) Hence also, عَرَانِينُ السَّحَابِ *The first of the rains of the clouds*. (TA.) — And ‡ *A noble chief*: (Ḳ, TA:) عَرَانِينُ signifies ‡ the *chiefs*, (Ṣ, TA,) and *nobles*, (TA,) of a people, or party, (Ṣ,) or of the people, or of men. (TA.)

عِرَانٌ *A piece of wood*, or *stick, which is inserted in the partition between the nostrils of a camel* (Ṣ, Ḳ) *of the species called* بُخْتِىّ. (Ṣ. [See also خِشَاش.]) — And (hence, as being likened thereto, TA) The *wooden thing* [app. meaning the *pin*, or *axis*,] *of the sheave of a pulley*, (Ṣ, Ḳ, TA,) *by which the* خُطَّاف [or *iron thing in which is the pin whereon the sheave turns*] *is made firm*: (Ṣ, TA:) pl. أَعْرِنَةٌ. (TA.) — And *A nail*; (Ṣ, Ḳ, TA;) accord. to El-Hejeree, *that conjoins the spear-head and the shaft*. (TA.) And *A horn*. (Ḳ.) — Also *Trees occupying an extended*, or *oblong, tract*. (TA.) — And *Roads*: in this sense a pl. having no singular. (TA.) — See also عَرِينٌ. — And see عَرْنٌ, former half. — Also *Distance*, or *remoteness*, (Ṣ, Ḳ,) of a house, or dwelling, or abode. (Ṣ.) — And [hence,] دَارٌ عِرَانٌ (TA) and ▼ دَارٌ عَارِنَةٌ (Ṣ) *A distant*, or *remote, house* or *dwelling* or *abode*; (Ṣ, TA;) and دِيَارٌ عِرَانٌ and ▼ دِيَارٌ عَارِنَةٌ *distant*, or *remote, houses* &c.; (Ḳ, TA;) عِرَانٌ being an inf. n. used as an epithet [and therefore applicable to a pl. and to a fem. as well as a masc. sing.]: ISd says, it is not in my opinion a pl., as the lexicologists hold it to be. (TA.) — Also *Fight*, or *conflict*. (Ḳ.)

عُرُونٌ: see عِرْنٌ.

عَرِينٌ *A collection of trees*, (Ṣ, Mṣb, Ḳ, TA,) *tangled*, or *luxuriant*, or *abundant and dense*; *a thicket, wood*, or *forest*: (TA:) this is the primary signification; (Ṣ, Mṣb, TA;) whether there be in it a lion or not. (TA.) And [particularly] *A collection of thorn-trees*, (Ḳ, TA,) and *of such as are called* عِضَاه; whether there be a lion therein or not. (TA.) — And [hence], as also ▼ عَرِينَةٌ, The *covert*, or *place of resort, of the lion*, (Ṣ, Mṣb, Ḳ,) and *of the hyena*, as also ▼ عِرَانٌ, and *of the wolf*, and *of the serpent*: and the former signifies also the *burrow of the* [*lizard called*] ضَبّ: pl. عُرُنٌ. (Ḳ, TA.) — And (hence, TA) عَرِينٌ signifies also ‡ *An open*, or *a wide, space, in front*, or *extending from the sides, of a house*, [in this case meaning *a yard*,] and *of a town*, as, for instance, in this latter case, of Mekkeh, occurring in this sense in a trad., likened to the place of resort of the lion, because of its resistibility. (TA.) — And (hence also, TA) ‡ *Eminence*, or *nobility*; and *might, strength*, or *resistibility*. (Ḳ, TA.) — Also *Such as is dry and broken of the* [*trees called*] عِضَاه. (Ḳ.) — And *Flesh*: (Ṣ, Ḳ:) so it is said to signify. (Ṣ.) — And The *prey of the lion*, or *the like*. (Ḳ.) — And The *cry of the* [*dove called*] فَاخِتَة: (Ḳ, TA:) so in the T in art. عزهل. (TA.)

عَرِينَةٌ: see the next preceding paragraph.

عُرَانِيَةٌ The *crests*, or *upper parts, of waves, rising high*; as in the phrase, مَآءٌ ذُو عُرَانِيَةٍ, (Ṣ, TA,) meaning *water having many and high waves* or *billows* or *surges*; (TA;) used by 'Adee Ibn-Zeyd in describing the flood of Noah: (Ṣ:) or the *middle, and main body*, or *deepest part, of the sea*: and the *flow*, or *extending, of a torrent*. (Ḳ.)

عَرَّانٌ *A seller of the wood called* عِرْنَة. (TA.)

عَارِنٌ: see its fem., with ة, voce عِرَانٌ, last sentence but one, in two places. — العَارِنُ *The lion*: (Ḳ:) [app. a possessive epithet, meaning ذُو العَرِينِ: but he is said to be thus called] because of his abominable nature, and his strength. (TA.)

مُعَرَّنٌ A spear *having its head nailed* [*to the shaft*] *with the nail called* عِرَان. (Ṣ, Ḳ.) — See also the following paragraph.

مَعْرُونٌ A camel *having the wooden thing called* عِرَان [q. v.] *put into his nose*. (TA.) — Also, applied to a سِقَآء [or skin for water or milk], *Tanned with the wood called* عِرْنَة; (Ṣ, Ḳ, TA;) and so ▼ مُعَرَّنٌ. (TA.) And, so applied, *Tanned with the tree called* عَرْن. (TA.)

عرو

1. عَرَاهُ, (Ṣ, Mgh, Mṣb, Ḳ,) aor. يَعْرُوهُ, (Ṣ, Mṣb, Ḳ,) inf. n. عَرْوٌ; (Ṣ, Mṣb;) and ▼ اعتراهُ; (Mṣb, Ḳ;) *He came to him*, (Ṣ, Mgh, Ḳ,) syn. أَتَاهُ, (Ṣ, Mgh,) and أَلَمَّ بِهِ, (Ṣ,) or غَشِيَهُ, (Ḳ,) or *he repaired to him*, syn. قَصَدَهُ, (Mṣb,) *seeking* (Ṣ, Mgh, Ḳ) *his beneficence*, or *bounty*, (Mgh, Ḳ,) or *for the purpose of seeking his gift*, or *aid*: (Mṣb:) or both signify [simply] *he*, or *it, came to him*; syn. جَآءَهُ: (Ḥam pp. 24 and 109:) or عَرَوْتُهُ, also, signifies [simply] *I came to him*; syn. غَشِيتُهُ; and so عَرَيْتُهُ: (Ḳ in art. عرى:) and one says, عَرَى الرجل عرية شَدِيدَةً and عروةً شديدةً [app. *He came to the man*, or upon *him, with a vehement coming*; for it seems that الرَّجُلَ is meant, and that عَرْيَة and عَرْوَة are inf. ns. of un.]: (TA, immediately after what here next precedes:) and عَرَا, aor. يَعْرُو, also signifies [simply] *he sought* [&c.]: and hence the saying of Lebeed in a verse cited in art. ثأر [q. v., conj. 8]: (Ṣ,* TA:) the pass. part. n. is ▼ مَعْرُوٌّ. (Ṣ, Mṣb.) One says also, فُلَانٌ تَعْرُوهُ الأَضْيَافُ and ▼ تَعْتَرِيهِ i. e. *Such a one, guests come to him*; syn. تَغْشَاهُ. (Ṣ, TA.) And عَرَانِى هٰذَا الأَمْرُ and ▼ اِعْتَرَانِى *This affair*, or *event, came upon me*; syn. غَشِيَنِى. (Ṣ.) And عَرَاهُ الأَمْرُ, (Mṣb, TA,) aor. يَعْرُوهُ, *The affair*, or *event, came upon him* (غَشِيَهُ), (TA,) and *befell him*; (Mṣb, TA;) as also ▼ اعتراهُ. (Mṣb.) And عَرَاهُ المُهِمُّ and ▼ اعتراهُ *The hard*, or *difficult, affair*, or *event, befell him*. (Mgh.) And عَرَّهُ signifies the same. (Ksh in xlviii. 25.) [And in like manner ▼ اعتراهُ said of a malady, and of diabolical possession, &c., *It befell*, or *betided, him*; *attached him*; or *occurred*, or *was incident* or *incidental, to him*.] And عَرَاهُ البَرْدُ *The cold smote him*. (TA.) — See also 2. — عُرِىَ *He* (a man, Ṣ) *was*, or *became, affected with what is termed the* عُرَوَآء [q. v.] *of fever*: (Ṣ, Ḳ, TA:) and El-Fárábee has mentioned, in the "Deewán el-Adab," among verbs of the class of فَعَلَ, aor. يَفْعُلُ, عَرَا, from العُرَوَآء: (Ḥar p. 406:) ISd says that the verb mostly used is the former, and its part. n. is ▼ مَعْرُوٌّ: but some say that the verb [i. e. عُرِيَتْ, imperfectly written in my copy of the TA, but cleared from doubt by its being there added that the part. n. is مَعْرُوَّة,] is said of a fever, as meaning *it came with a shivering,*

or *trembling*. (TA.) — Also, *He* (a man) *was*, or *became, affected with the tremour of fear*. (TA.) — One says also, عُرِىَ إِلَى الشَّىْءِ, meaning ‡ *He felt a want of the thing* (اِسْتَوْحَشَ إِلَيْهِ) *after having sold it*. (Ḳ, TA.) And عُرِيتُ إِلَى مَالٍ لِى أَشَدَّ العُرَوَاءِ ♦, meaning † *My soul followed* [*most vehemently*, or *I felt a most vehement yearning towards*,] *property that belonged to me after having sold it*. (TA.) And عَرِىَ هَوَاهُ إِلَى كَذَا † *He yearned towards*, or *longed for, such a thing*. (TA.)

2. عرّى القَمِيصَ *He put button-loops* (عُرًى [pl. of عُرْوَةٌ]) *to the shirt*; as also ♦ اعراه. (TA.) — And عرّى المَزَادَةَ, thus, with teshdeed, in copies of the Ḳ, agreeably with the Tekmileh, or ♦ عَرَى [or عَرَا], without teshdeed, as in the M, (TA,) *He put a loop-shaped handle* (عُرْوَة) *to the* مزادة [or *leathern water-bag*]. (Ḳ, TA.)

4. اعراهُ نَخْلَةً (Ṣ, Ḳ) *He assigned to him* (i. e. a man in need, Ṣ) *a palm-tree as an* عَرِيَّة [q. v.; accord. to some, belonging to art. عرى], (Ṣ, Mṣb,) *for him to eat its fruit*: (Mṣb:) [i. e.] *he gave to him the fruit of a palm-tree during a year*. (Ṣ; and Ḳ in art. عرى.) — اعراهُ صَدِيقُهُ *His friend went*, or *removed, far away from him, and did not aid him*. (Ṣ.) And أَعْرَوْا صَاحِبَهُمْ *They left their companion* (Ḳ, TA) *in his place*; and *went away from him*. (TA.) [But these two significations seem rather to belong to art. عرى.] — See also 2. — اعرى, intrans., *He* (a man) *was*, or *became, fevered*, or *affected with fever*. (TA. [From عُرَوَآءٌ.]) — And أَعْرَيْنَا *We were*, or *became, affected by a cold night* [*such as is termed* لَيْلَةٌ عَرِيَّةٌ]: or *we came to experience the cold of evening*. (TA.) One says, أَهْلَكَ فَقَدْ أَعْرَيْتَ i. e. [Betake thyself to *thy family, for thou hast reached the time when*] *the sun has set and the evening has become cold*. (Ṣ.)

8. اعتراهُ: see 1, in six places. — Also *i. q.* قَصَدَ عَرَاهُ i. e. نَاحِيَتَهُ [app. as meaning *He repaired to his region*, or *quarter*; or *his vicinage*]. (TA.) — And *i. q.* خَبَلَهُ [*He*, or *it, rendered him possessed*, or *insane*; or *unsound in his intellect*, or *in a limb* or *member*]. (TA.)

10. استعرى النَّاسُ *The people ate the fresh ripe dates* (Ṣ, Ḳ, the latter in art. عرى,) فِى كُلِّ وَجْهٍ [*in every direction*]: from العَرِيَّةُ. (Ṣ.)

عَرًا, (T, Ṣ, Ḳ, TA,) mentioned in the Ḳ in art. عرى, but accord. to Az, thus written with ا, as belonging to the present art., (TA,) *i. q.* نَاحِيَةٌ [as meaning *A region*, or *quarter*; or *a vicinage*]; (Ḳ in art. عرى;) and so ♦ عِرْوٌ, (Ḳ in art. عرو,) of which the pl. is أَعْرَآءٌ; (TA;) and جَنَابٌ [which likewise signifies *a vicinage*; and *a place of alighting* or *abode*; &c.; and also has the two meanings here following]; as also ♦ عَرَاةٌ; (Ḳ in art. عرى;) this last and عَرًا both signify *a yard*, syn. فِنَآءٌ; (Ṣ;) and *a court*, syn. سَاحَةٌ; (T, Ṣ;) as also ♦ عَرْوَةٌ. (T, TA.) One says, نَزَلَ فِى عَرَاهُ [or بِعَرَاهُ and بِحَرَاهُ (Ṣ in art. حرى)] meaning نَاحِيَتِهِ [i. e. *He alighted*, or *descended and abode, in his region*, or *quarter*, or *his vicinage*]: (TA:) or نَزَلَ بِعَرَاهُ and ♦ عروته i. e. [*he alighted, &c.,*] *in his court*. (Az, TA.)

عَرْوٌ: see عُرْوَةٌ.

عِرْوٌ: see عَرًا: — and see also عُرْوَةٌ. — Also One *who is not disquieted*, or *rendered anxious*, or *grieved, by an affair*: (Ḳ:) [or] أَنَا عِرْوٌ مِنْهُ means *I am free*, or *free in mind*, (خِلْوٌ,) *from it*: (Ṣ:) but it is held by ISd to belong to art. عرى: (TA:) the pl. is أَعْرَآءٌ; (Ḳ, TA;) which is said in the Tekmileh to signify persons *who are not disquieted*, or *rendered anxious*, or *grieved, by that which disquiets, &c., their companions*. (TA.) — And *A company* of men: [pl. as above:] one says, بِهَا أَعْرَآءٌ مِنَ النَّاسِ [*In it are companies of men*]. (TA.)

عَرَاةٌ: see عَرًا. — Also *Vehemence*, or *intenseness, of cold*: (Ṣ, Ḳ; mentioned in the latter in art. عرى:) originally عَرْوَةٌ. (TA.)

عَرْوَةٌ: see عَرًا, in two places.

عُرْوَةٌ primarily signifies *A thing by means of which another thing is rendered fast*, or *firm, and upon which reliance is placed*: (TA:) or it is metaphorically applied in this sense; from the same word as signifying an appertenance of a shirt, and of a mug, and of a leathern bucket. (Mgh, Mṣb.*) — The عُرْوَة of a shirt, (Ṣ, M, Mṣb,) or of a garment, (Ḳ,) is well known; (Ṣ, Mṣb;) i. e. [*A button-loop*, or *loop into which a button is inserted and by means of which it is rendered fast*;] the *thing into which the* زِرّ [or *button*] *thereof enters*; (M, TA;) the *sister of the* زِرّ *thereof*; (Ḳ;) as also عُرًى, accord. to the copies of the Ḳ, or عُرَىٌ, accord. to some of them; and with kesr; but correctly with ḍamm and with the ر quiescent [i. e. ♦ عُرْوٌ] as in the Tekmileh; and also with kesr [i. e. ♦ عِرْوٌ]; as though these two were pls. [or rather coll. gen. ns.] of عروة [i. e. عُرْوَة and عِرْوَة]: (TA:) the pl. is عُرًى: (Mṣb:) عراوى [i. e. عَرَاوَى] as pl. of عُرْوَة is vulgar. (TA.) — [The pl.] عُرًى also signifies [in like manner] *Certain* [*well-known*] *appertenances* [i. e. *loops*] of loads, or burdens, and of the camels that bear saddles or burdens: whence the trad. لَا تُشَدُّ العُرَى إِلَّا إِلَى ثَلَاثَةِ مَسَاجِدَ [*The loops* of loads *shall not be made fast* for the purpose of journeying *save to three mosques*; that of Mekkeh, that of El-Medeeneh, and that of El-Aḳṣà at Jerusalem: see also similar trads. in art. ضرب (first paragraph, sec. col.,) and in art. عمل (conj. 4)]. (TA.) — The عُرْوَة of the leathern bucket is likewise well known, (TA,) and so is that of the mug: (Ṣ, TA:) each is The [*loop-shaped*] *handle*: (Ḳ, TA:) [so too is that of the leathern water-bag: (see 2:)] that of the mug is [also called] its أُذُن. (Mṣb.) — The عُرْوَة of the فَرْج [or vulva of a woman] is The *flesh of its exterior*, (Ḳ, TA,) or *an external flesh*, (so in some copies of the Ḳ,) *which is*, or *becomes, thin, and turns to the right and left, with* [or *at*] *the lower part of the* بَظْر [here meaning the *clitoris*]; (Ḳ, TA;) *each of what are termed* عُرْوَتَانِ [i. e. the *nymphæ*]. (TA.) — And عُرْوَةٌ signifies also *A collection of* [*the trees called*] عِضَاه *and of* [*those called*] حَمْض *that are depastured in the case of drought*: (Ḳ:) or especially *a collection of* عِضَاه *upon which men pasture* [*their beasts or cattle*] *when they experience drought*: or *such as remain of* عِضَاه *and of* حَمْض *and are depastured in the case of drought*; and it is not applied to any trees but these, unless to *any trees that have remained in the* صَيْف [here app. meaning *spring*, having survived the winter]: (TA:) also *tangled*, or *luxuriant*, or *abundant and dense, trees, among which the camels pass the winter, and whereof they eat*: (Ḳ:) and (as some say, TA) *trees of which the leaves fall not in the winter*, (Ḳ, TA,) *such as the* أَرَاك *and the* سِدْر: (TA:) or *trees that remain incessantly in the earth, not going*: (Ṣ:) or *such as suffice the camels*, or *cattle, throughout the year*: (TA:) or *shrubs of which the lower portions remain in the earth, such as the* عَرْفَج *and the* نَصِىّ *and the several kinds of* خُلَّة *and* حَمْض; *so that when men experience drought, the cattle gain the means of subsistence*; thus accord. to Az: or *pasture that remains after the* [*other*] *herbage has dried up*; because the cattle cling thereto, or eat thereof in the winter, (تَتَعَلَّقُ بِهَا,) and are preserved thereby; wherefore they are also called عُلْقَة: (Mgh: [but for عَلَقَة in my copy of that work, I have substituted عُلْقَة as being evidently the right word:]) [see also عُقْدَةٌ, in the last quarter of the paragraph, in two places:] the pl. is عُرًى. (Ṣ, TA.) — Also The *environs* of a town [*where people pasture their cattle*]. (Ḳ, TA.) One says, رَعَيْنَا عُرْوَةَ مَكَّةَ i. e. [*We pastured* our cattle] *in the environs of Mekkeh*. (TA.) — And the pl., عُرًى, signifies ‡ *A company*, or *party, of men by whom one benefits*, or *profits*; as being likened to the trees [so called] that remain [throughout the winter]: (TA:) or a company, or party, of men is likened to the trees thus called. (Ṣ.) — And the sing., ‡ *Such as is held in high estimation*, or *in much request, of camels*, or *cattle*, or *other property*; as *an excellent horse*; (Ḳ, TA;) and *the like*. (TA.) — عُرْوَةُ الصَّعَالِيكِ means † *The stay*, or *support, of the* صعاليك [i. e. *poor*, or *needy*]: and [hence] is the name [or a surname] of a well-known man. (TA. [See صُعْلُوكٌ.]) — العُرْوَةُ الوُثْقَى signifies *The firmest thing upon which one lays hold*: (Bḍ in xxxi. 21: [see also ii. 257, where the same phrase occurs:]) and is [said to be] the saying "There is no deity but God:" from العُرْوَةُ [in the first of the senses assigned to it above, as is indicated in the Mṣb in relation to a similar phrase here following; or] as signifying "the trees that have a lower portion remaining in the earth, as the نَصِىّ and the عَرْفَج &c.;" as expl.

above. (TA.) And أَوْثَقُ عُرَى [*The firmest of things upon which one lays hold*], occurring in a saying of the Prophet, is expl. as being [religious] belief, or faith. (Mṣb.) —— And العُرْوَةُ is a name of *The lion*. (Ṣ, Mgh, Ḳ.)

عُرَوَآءُ *A tremour*, or *shivering*: (Mz, 40th نوع:) or the *access of a fever, on the occasion of the first tremour*, or *shivering, thereof*. (Ṣ, Ḳ.) —— [And accord. to Freytag, it occurs in the Deewán of the Hudhalees as meaning The *coming of a hero, and the tremour thence arising in others*. —— And *A feeling of yearning*, or *longing*:] see 1, last sentence but one. —— And The *low voice* (syn. حِسّ) of the lion. (Ḳ.) —— And The *interval from the sun's becoming yellow to the night, when cold wind springs up*, (M,* Ḳ, TA,) i. e., the *north*, or *northerly, wind*. (TA.)

عَرِىٌّ an epithet applied to a palm-tree such as is termed عَرِيَّةٌ [q. v.]: one says نَخْلَةٌ عَرِىٌّ, (Ṣ, Mṣb,) the latter word without ة; like as one says اِمْرَأَةٌ قَتِيلٌ. (Mṣb.) ═ And رِيحٌ عَرِيَّةٌ (Ṣ, Ḳ) and عَرِىٌّ (Ḳ) *A cold wind*. (Ṣ, Ḳ: mentioned in the Ḳ in this art. and also in art. عرى.) And one says also, إِنَّ عَشِيَّتَنَا هٰذِهِ لَعَرِيَّةٌ [*Verily this our evening is cold*]. (El-Kilábee, Ṣ.) And لَيْلَةٌ عَرِيَّةٌ *A cold night*. (TA.)

عَرِيَّةٌ [as a subst.] *A palm-tree which its owner assigns to another*, (Ṣ, Mgh, Mṣb, Ḳ,*) *who is in need*, (Ṣ, Mgh,) *for him to eat its fruit* (Ṣ, Mgh, Mṣb, Ḳ*) *during a year*: (Ṣ, Mgh, Ḳ:) and *of which what was upon it has been eaten*: (Ḳ:) so some say: or *that does not retain its fruit, this becoming scattered from it*: (TA:) and *one that has been excluded from the bargaining on the occasion of the selling of palm-trees*: (Ḳ:) so some say: (TA:) the pl. is عَرَايَا: (Ṣ, Mgh, Mṣb:) it is said that on the occasion of the prohibition of المُزَابَنَة, which is the selling of the fruit upon the heads of palm-trees for dried dates, license was conceded in respect of the عَرَايَا, because a needy man, attaining to the season of fresh ripe dates, and having no money with which to buy them for his household, nor any palm-trees to feed them therefrom, but having some dried dates remaining of his food, would come to the owner of palm-trees, and say to him, "Sell to me the fruit of a palm-tree," or "of two palm-trees," and would give him those remaining dried dates for that fruit: therefore license was conceded in respect of that fruit when less than five أَوْسُق [pl. of pauc. of وَسْق, q. v.]: (Nh, TA: [and the like is said, but much less fully, in the Mgh; and somewhat thereof in the Ṣ:]) the word is of the measure فَعِيلَةٌ in the sense of the measure مَفْعُولَةٌ, because the person to whom it is assigned repairs to it (Ṣ, Nh,* Mgh, Mṣb, TA) to gather its fruit: (Mgh:) or the tree is so called because it is freed from prohibition, (Nh, Mgh, TA,) from عَرِىَ, aor. يَعْرَى, (Nh, TA,) in which case the word is of the measure فَعِيلَةٌ in the sense of the measure فَاعِلَةٌ; or because it is as though it were divested of its fruit: (Mgh:) the ة is affixed because the word is reckoned among substs., like نَطِيحَةٌ and أَكِيلَةٌ. (Ṣ, Mṣb.) [It is mentioned in the Ḳ in art. عرى. See also عَرِىٌّ, above.] —— Also *A* مِكْتَل [or *kind of basket, made of palm-leaves, in which dates &c. are carried*]. (Ḳ and TA in art. عرى. [In the CḲ, المَكِيلِ is erroneously put for المِكْتَلُ.])

[عَرَاوَةٌ, expl. by Freytag as signifying "oleris species" &c., is a manifest mistake for عَرَارَةٌ, n. un. of عَرَار, q. v.]

عَارٍ act. part. n. of عَرَاهُ in the first [and in others also] of the senses assigned to it above. (Mṣb.) En-Nábighah says,

* أَتَيْتُكَ عَارِيًا خَلَقًا ثِيَابِى *
* عَلَى خَوْفٍ يُظَنُّ بِىَ الظُّنُونُ *

meaning *I came to thee*, or *have come to thee, as a guest* [or *seeking thy beneficence, with my clothes old and worn out, in fear*, various *thoughts being thought of me*]. (Ṣ; one of my copies of which has تُظَنُّ instead of يُظَنُّ.)

أُعْرُوَانٌ (so in copies of the Ḳ and accord. to the TA, in the CḲ عُروان,) *A certain plant*: (Ḳ, TA:) or *one of which the leaves fall not in the winter*. (CḲ.)

مُعَرًّى An epithet applied to a فَرْج as meaning *Having what is termed* عُرْوَةٌ [q. v.] (Ḳ, TA) or *what are termed* عُرْوَتَانِ. (TA.)

مَعْرُوٌّ pass. part. n. of عَرَا, q. v. (Ṣ, Mṣb.) —— And part. n. of عُرِىَ, q. v. (ISd, TA.)

عرى

1. عَرِىَ (Ṣ, MA, Mgh, Mṣb, Ḳ) مِنْ ثِيَابِهِ, (Ṣ, MA, Mgh, Mṣb,) aor. يَعْرَى, (Ṣ, Mṣb,) inf. n. عُرْىٌ (Mgh, Mṣb, Ḳ, and so in some copies of the Ṣ, accord. to other copies of which it is عُرْيَةٌ, and also with kesr to the ع, as stated in the TA, [العُرْىُ commencing the art. in the CḲ is a mistake for العُرْىُ,]) and عُرْيَةٌ, (Mṣb, Ḳ,) *He* (a man, Mṣb, TA) *was*, or *became, naked, nude, bare*, or *without clothing*; (Ḳ, TA;) or *bare of his clothes*: (MA:) and ▼ تعرّى signifies the same: (MA, Ḳ:) [or rather] the latter is quasi-pass. of عرّاه [and therefore is more correctly rendered *he was made naked*, &c.; or *made bare of his clothes*, or *denuded thereof*, or *divested*; or *he made himself naked*, &c.; or *denuded himself of his clothes*]. (Ṣ.) [And sometimes it means *He was*, or *became, bare of clothing*, or *of his clothes, except one*, or *more, of his inner garments*: and in like manner, ▼ تعرّى, *he was made*, or *he made himself, bare of clothing*, or *of his clothes, except one*, or *more, of his inner garments*.] —— And [hence] one says also, عَرِىَ البَدَنُ مِنَ اللَّحْمِ [*The body was*, or *became, bare of flesh*, or *lean*]. (TA.) —— And عَرِىَ مِنَ العَيْبِ, aor. as above, † *He*, or *it, was*, or *became, free from fault, defect*, or *blemish*: part. n. ▼ عَرٍ [if not a mistranscription for عَارٍ]. (Mṣb.) And عَرِىَ مِنَ الأَمْرِ † *He was*, or *became, free from the affair*: and مَا يَعْرَى مِنْ هٰذَا الأَمْرِ † *He is not*, or *does not become, free from this affair*: and hence, لَا يَعْرَى مِنَ المَوْتِ أَحَدٌ † [*No one will be exempt from death*]. (TA.) ═ عَرِيتُهُ *I came to him*; syn. غَشِيتُهُ; like عَرَوْتُهُ [q. v.]. (Ḳ.)

2: see 4. —— [Hence,] one says also, عَرَّاهُ مِنَ الأَمْرِ † *He freed him from the affair*. (TA.) —— And عَرَّيْتُهُ † *I left it*; or *let it alone*; i. e., anything. (TA.)

3. نَحْنُ نُعَارِى *We ride the horses not saddled*. (Ḳ, TA.) [See also 12.]

4. اعراهُ (Ṣ, MA, Mṣb, Ḳ) مِنْ ثِيَابِهِ, (Mṣb,) or مِنَ الثَّوْبِ and مِنَ الثِّيَابِ, (MA,) or الثَّوْبَ; (Ḳ;) and ▼ عرّاهُ, (Ṣ, MA, Mṣb, Ḳ,) inf. n. تَعْرِيَةٌ; (Ṣ, Ḳ;) *He denuded him, made him bare*, or *divested him*, (Ṣ,* MA, Mṣb,* Ḳ,) *of his clothes*, (Mṣb,) or *of the clothes*, (MA,) or *of the garment*. (Ḳ.) —— And اعراهُ signifies also *He plucked out the hair of his* (a horse's) *tail*; like أَعَارَهُ: mentioned by IḲṭṭ and others. (TA in art. عير.) —— See also three other significations (two of which seem to belong to this art.) in art. عرو. ═ اعرى as intrans. *He* (a man, TA) *journeyed in* [*a bare and wide tract*, or] *what is termed* عَرَآءٌ [q. v.]: and *he remained, stayed, dwelt*, or *abode, therein*. (Ḳ, TA.) And *He remained, stayed, dwelt*, or *abode, in the lateral*, or *adjacent, part* or *tract* (بِالنَّاحِيَةِ). (TA.) And أَعْرَيْتُ signifies also اِجْتَنَبْتُ [app. as meaning *I was*, or *became, distant, remote, far off*, or *aloof*; or *I went*, or *removed*, or *retired*, or *withdrew myself, to a distance*, or *far away*; though I do not know اجتنبت used otherwise than as trans.]; as also ▼ اِسْتَعْرَيْتُ, and ▼ اِعْتَرَيْتُ: mentioned by Ṣgh. (TA.)

5: see the first paragraph, in two places.

8: see 4, last sentence.

10: see 4, last sentence: ═ and see 10 in art. عرو.

12. اعروري الفَرَسَ, (Ṣ, Ḳ,) or الدَّابَّةَ, (Mgh, Mṣb,) *He rode the horse*, or *the beast, without a saddle*, (Ṣ, Mgh, Mṣb, Ḳ,* and Ḥam p. 42,) *and having nothing beneath him*: (Ḥam:) the verb being of the measure اِفْعَوْعَلَ, (Ṣ, TA,) a measure of which there is no other trans. v. except اِحْلَوْلَى. (TA.) —— Hence the usage of the verb in the saying of Taäbbaṭa-Sharrà,

* يَظَلُّ بِمَوْمَاةٍ وَيُمْسِى بِغَيْرِهَا *
* جَحِيشًا وَيَعْرَوْرِى ظُهُورَ المَهَالِكِ *

† *He passes the day in a waterless desert, and enters upon the evening in another than it, alone, and he ventures upon* [*the surfaces of*] *the places of perdition without anything to protect him from them*. (Ḥam ubi suprà.) [See also an ex. of the

act. part. n. in a verse cited in the second paragraph of art. دوم.] — And اعرورى السَّرَابُ الآكَامَ means رَكِبَهَا [i. e. † *The mirage surmounted the hills,* or *mounds*]. (TA.) — And اعرورى أَمْرًا قَبِيحًا † *He ventured upon,* or *did, an evil,* or *a foul, thing;* (Ṣ, Ḳ;*) syn. رَكِبَهُ, (Ṣ,) or أَتَاهُ, (Ḳ,) or both. (TA.) — And اعرورى signifies also † *He journeyed by himself, alone, in the earth,* or *land.* (Ḳ.)

عَرًى *A hard and elevated,* or *an elevated and plain, part,* or *tract,* of the earth, *that is apparent,* or *open:* pl. أَعْرَآءٌ. (TA.) [عَرَآءٌ, also, (q. v.,) has a similar meaning, and the same pl.] — And i. q. حَائِطٌ [*A wall; or a wall of enclosure;* or *one that surrounds a garden:* or *a garden,* in general; or *a garden of palm-trees, surrounded by a wall*]. (TA.) — See also عَرًا in art. عرو: and in the same paragraph see its syn. عَرَآءٌ.

عَرٍ: see 1, last quarter.

عُرْىٌ A horse *not having a saddle upon him;* (Ṣ, Mṣb, Ḳ;) and so ▼ مُعْرَوْرًى and ▼ مُعْرَوْرٍ: (TA:) or *not having upon him a saddle nor a saddle-cloth,* or *housing;* as also ▼ مُعْرَوْرًى; but ▼ مُعْرَوْرٍ signifies *riding without a saddle and without a saddle-cloth,* or *housing:* (Mgh:) or عُرْىٌ [as also ▼ مُعْرَوْرًى] signifies *not having upon him a saddle nor any furniture:* (TA:) ▼ عُرْيَانٌ is not applied as an epithet to a horse, nor is عُرْىٌ to a man: (Mgh, Mṣb, TA:) the latter is an inf. n. used as an epithet, and then made a subst., having a pl., (Mṣb, TA,) which is أَعْرَآءٌ. (Ṣ, Mgh, Mṣb, TA.)

جَارِيَةٌ حَسَنَةُ العِرْيَةِ, and ▼ العِرْيَةِ, and ▼ المَعْرَى, and ▼ المَعْرَاةِ, (Ḳ, TA,) or, as in the M, ▼ المُعْرَى, and ▼ المُعْرَاةِ, and in like manner in the A, ▼ المُعْرَى and العُرْيَةِ being [there] said to be like المُجَرَّد and الجُرْدَة in measure and in meaning, (TA,) signify حَسَنَةُ المُجَرَّدِ, (Ḳ, TA,) i. e. [*A girl,* or *young woman, beautiful in respect of what is unclad* of her person; or] *beautiful when she is unclad:* (TA: [see also جُرْدَةٌ: the CḲ, for والمُعْرَى والمُعْرَاةِ, has والمَعْرَى وَالمَعْرَاةِ أَيِ المُجَرَّدِ, أَيِ المُجَرَّدُ:]) and ▼ المَعَارِى (of which the sing. is مَعْرًى, TA) signifies *the hands* or *arms, and the feet* or *legs, and the face,* (Ṣ, Ḳ, TA,) as being *the parts that are seen,* (Ḳ, TA,) of a woman: (Ṣ, TA:) so in the saying, مَا أَحْسَنَ مَعَارِىَ هٰذِهِ المَرْأَةِ [*How beautiful are the hands* or *arms,* &c., *of this woman!*]: (Ṣ, TA:) or, as some say, *the parts where the bones appear* [*as distinct*] *from the flesh:* or, some say, *what are necessarily made to appear,* of a woman: and, some say, *the* عَوْرَة [or *pudenda* of a woman]: and the فَرْج [or *vulva*]. (TA.)

العِرْيَةُ: see the next preceding paragraph.

عُرْيَانٌ and ▼ عَارٍ *Naked, nude, bare,* or *without clothing;* (Ṣ,* MA, Mgh,* Mṣb,* Ḳ, TA;) applied to a man: (Mṣb, TA:) fem. عُرْيَانَةٌ (Ṣ, MA, Mgh, &c.) and ▼ عَارِيَةٌ, (MA, Mgh, Mṣb, &c.,) applied to a woman: (Ṣ, Mṣb:) the pl. of عُرْيَانٌ is عُرْيَانُونَ; (Ḳ;) and the pl. of ▼ عَارٍ is عُرَاةٌ, (Mṣb, Ḳ,) and that of عَارِيَةٌ is عَارِيَاتٌ. (Mṣb.) [Also, sometimes, *Bare of clothing,* or *of his clothes, except one,* or *more, of his inner garments.*] See also عُرْىٌ. — عُرْيَانٌ applied to sand, † *An extended and gibbous tract* (نَقًا), or *such as is accumulated and congested* (عَقَدٌ, in the CḲ (عَقْدٌ), of sand, *having no trees upon it.* (ISd, Ḳ, TA.) — Applied to a plant, or to herbage, † *Such as has become apparent.* (TA.) — عُرْيَانُ الشَّجِىِّ is an appellation applied to † *A wife:* but in the A it is implied that it is used as denoting anyone *who will not conceal a secret.* (TA.) — عُرْيَانٌ applied to a horse signifies † *Light,* or *active, and quick; tall; and long in the legs.* (Ḳ, TA. [Expl. in the Ḳ and TA by the words مُقْلَّص طَوِيل; to which is added in the TA القَوَائِمِ: the first of these words I find written, in copies of the Ḳ, only مُقَلَّص; but it is correctly مُقْلِص.])

عُرَآءٌ [is app. a subst. signifying *Nakedness,* or *bareness,* or *the like:* for عُرَآءُ العِظَامِ مِنَ اللَّحْمِ occurs in the TA, in art. عجف, evidently as meaning *Leanness of the bones.* — Also] *A wide,* or *spacious, place* or *tract of land,* (Ṣ, M, Mṣb, Ḳ,) *in which is nothing that hides,* or *conceals,* (Ṣ, Mṣb,) or *in which nothing will be hidden,* (M, TA,) or *in which one will not be hidden by anything;* (Ḳ;) occurring in the Ḳur xxxvii. 145 [and lxviii. 49]: (Ṣ:) or the *vacant surface of the earth* or *land,* or *of a wide space of land:* (TA in this art.:) or *a tract such as is termed* جَهْرَآءٌ [q. v.]: (TA in art. جهر:) pl. أَعْرَآءٌ. (Ḳ.) [In the TA in art. جهر the pl. is said to be أَعْرِيَةٌ. See also عَرًى.]

عَارٍ; and its fem., with ة: see عُرْيَانٌ, in three places. — [Hence,] عَارِى الأَشَاجِعِ: see أَشْجَعُ. — عَارِى الثَّنْدُوَتَيْنِ means *Having no flesh on the* ثَنْدُوَتَانِ [or *two paps*]. (TA.) — And [hence] one says, الحَقُّ عَارٍ † *The truth is* [*naked,* i. e.] *manifest.* (TA in art. عجز.)

طَرِيقٌ اعرورى [thus I find the latter word, like the verb (12), and without any syll. signs, perhaps a mistranscription, and, if so, it may be correctly عَرَوْرًى, of the measure فَعَوْعَلٌ, like شَجَوْجًى &c.,] *A rugged road.* (TA.)

المَعْرَى; and its pl., المَعَارِى: see العُرْيَةُ. — [The pl.] مَعَارٍ [with the article المَعَارِى] signifies also † *Places that do not give growth to plants,* or *herbage.* (Ḳ.) — And † *Beds, or the like;* syn. فُرُشٌ, (Ḳ, TA,) pl. of فِرَاشٌ. (TA.) And in this sense, (TA,) مَعَارِى occurs for مَعَارٍ, by poetic license. (Ṣ, TA.)

المَعْرَاةُ: see العُرْيَةُ.

المُعْرَى and المُعْرَاةُ: see العُرْيَةُ, in three places.

— The former signifies also *That* [camel or beast] *which is left to pasture by itself, and upon which no burden is put.* (TA.)

مُعْرَوْرًى: see عُرْىٌ, in three places.

مُعْرَوْرٍ: see عُرْىٌ, in two places.

عز

1. عَزَّ, aor. ـِ, inf. n. عِزٌّ (AZ, Ṣ, A, O, Mṣb, Ḳ) and عِزَّةٌ, (AZ, Ṣ, Ḳ,) or the latter is a simple subst., (Mṣb,) and عَزَازَةٌ, (Ṣ, Ḳ,) *He was,* or *became, mighty, potent, powerful,* or *strong;* (TA, in explanation of عِزٌّ;) and so ▼ تعزّز; or the latter signifies *he made himself so; he strengthened himself;* syn. تَقَوَّى: (Mṣb:) and the former, *he became so after being low,* or *mean, in condition;* (AZ, Ṣ, A, Ḳ;) as also عَزُّ, sec. pers. عَزُزْتَ, aor. ـَ: (Mṣb:) *he was,* or *became, high,* or *elevated, in rank,* or *condition,* or *state; noble, honourable, glorious,* or *illustrious;* (Ṣ,* A,* Ḳ,* TḲ; and TA in explanation of عِزٌّ;) as also ▼ تعزّز. (Ṣ,* Ḳ,* TḲ.) [عَزَّ وَجَلَّ, referring to the name of God expressed or understood, is a phrase of frequent occurrence, meaning, *To Him,* or *to Whom, belong might and majesty,* or *glory and greatness.*] — You also say, عَزَزْتُ عَلَيْهِ, (Ṣ, O, Ḳ,) aor. ـُ, (O, Ḳ,) meaning, كَرُمْتُ عَلَيْهِ, (Ṣ, O, Ḳ,*) i. e., *I exceeded him in nobleness,* or *generosity.* (TḲ.) — And عَزَّ, [aor. ـِ, inf. n. عِزٌّ and عِزَّةٌ and app. عَزَازَةٌ also,] *He magnified,* or *exalted, himself:* (TA:) ‡ *he was disdainful, scornful,* or *indignant, in a blamable manner.* (TA, in explanation of عِزَّةٌ; q. v. infrà.) [See also 5.] — *He resisted,* or *withstood:* (TA, in explanation of عِزٌّ:) *he was indomitable, invincible; not to be overcome.* (B and TA, in explanation of عِزَّةٌ, q. v. infrà.) And عَزَّ الشَّىْءُ, aor. ـِ, *The thing was,* or *became,* [*difficult,* or *hard;* as also ▼ اعتزّ, (occurring in the TA, coupled with تَعَسَّرَ, in an explanation of مَنُعَ, in art. منع,) and ▼ تعزّز: and] *impossible, insuperable,* or *unattainable:* or so, as Es-Saraḳustee says, ▼ تعزّز. (Mṣb.) — And عَزَّ, (Ṣ, O, Ḳ,) aor. ـِ, inf. n. عِزٌّ and عِزَّةٌ and عَزَازَةٌ, (Ṣ, O,) *It* (a thing, Ṣ, O, Ḳ, meaning anything, TA) *was,* or *became, rare, scarce, hardly to be found.* (Ṣ, O, Ḳ.) — [And hence, *He,* or *it, was,* or *became, dear, highly esteemed,* or *greatly valued.*] — عَزَّ عَلَىَّ أَنْ تَفْعَلَ كَذَا, (Ṣ, Mgh, O, Mṣb, Ḳ,) aor. ـِ (Mgh, O, Mṣb, Ḳ) and ـَ (Fr, Mgh, O, Ḳ,) [the second pers. of the pret. being عَزَزْتَ and عَزِزْتَ,] the latter aor. the more chaste, (O,) means *Thy doing so distressed,* or *hath distressed,* or *afflicted, me;* or, emphatically, *distresses,* or *afflicts, me;* syn. اشْتَدَّ, (Ṣ, Mgh, O, Mṣb, Ḳ, TA,) and حَقَّ, (Ṣ, O, Ḳ, TA,) and شَقَّ: (TA:) a phrase [often, but not always,] alluding to a loathing of the action, or indignation thereat. (Mṣb.) In like manner also you say, عَزَّ عَلَىَّ كَذَا *Such a thing*

distressed, or afflicted, me. (Ṣ.) And عَزَّ عَلَىَّ أَنْ أَسُوْءَكَ It distressed, or afflicted, me to displease thee. (A.) And عَزَّ مَا أَنَّكَ ذَاهِبٌ, like حَقَّ أَنَّكَ ذَاهِبٌ [or حَقَّ مَا أَنَّكَ ذاهب, meaning It is distressing that thou art going away]. (TA.) And one says to a man, Dost thou love me? and he replies, لَعَزَّ مَا, i. e., لَشَدَّ مَا, (A, O, Ḳ,) and لَحَقَّ مَا, (A, TA,) meaning It distresses me, what thou sayest; or it has distressed me. (TḲ.) You say also, أُعْزِزْتُ ▼ بِمَا أَصَابَكَ I was, or am, distressed by what befell, or hath befallen, thee. (Ṣ, O, Ḳ.) And أَعْزِزْ ▼ عَلَىَّ بِمَا أُصِبْتَ بِهِ That by which thou hast been afflicted distresses me: (Ṣ, O:) [or how doth it distress me!] so in a trad. of 'Alee; when he beheld Talḥah slain, he said, أَعْزِزْ ▼ عَلَىَّ أَبَا مُحَمَّدٍ أَنْ أَرَاكَ مُجَدَّلًا تَحْتَ نُجُومِ السَّمَآءِ [It distresses me, or how doth it distress me! O Aboo-Mohammad, that I see thee prostrated upon the ground beneath the stars of heaven]. (TA.) [A similar ex. is given in the A; without ب prefixed to أَنْ.] ═ عَزَّ also signifies He was, or became, weak: thus having two contr. meanings. (Mṣb.) ═ عَزَّهُ, aor. ـُ, (Ṣ, A, O, Ḳ,) inf. n. عَزٌّ, (Ṣ, O, TA,) He overcame him, or conquered him: (Ṣ, A, O:) he overcame him in argumentative contest; (Ḳ,* TA;) as also ▼ عَزْعَزَهُ, (Ḳ,) inf. n. عَزْعَزَةٌ; (TA;) and so عَزَّهُ فِى الخِطَابِ: (Jel in xxxviii. 22, and TA:) or this last signifies he became stronger than he therein; (TA;) or he strove with him to overcome therein; as also ▼ عَازَّهُ فيه, (Ṣ, Ḳ,) inf. n. مُعَازَّةٌ: (O, TA:) in the Ḳur xxxviii. 22, some read عَزَّنِى; and others, ▼ عَازَّنِى: and you say, عَازَّنِى ▼ فَعَزَزْتُهُ, meaning, he strove with me to overcome, and I overcame him: and مُعَازَّةٌ signifies the contending together in argument: (TA:) you say also of a horse, اعتزّ ▼ فَارِسَهُ [he overcame his rider, or gained the mastery over him]. (Ṣ and Ḳ in art. جمح.) It is said in a prov., (Ṣ,) مَنْ عَزَّ بَزَّ He who overcomes takes the spoil. (Ṣ, A, O, Ḳ.) And in another prov., (Ṣ,) إِذَا عَزَّ أَخُوكَ فَهُنْ (Th, Ṣ, O, Ḳ) When thy brother overcomes thee, and thou art not equal to him (لَمْ تُقَاوِمْهُ) be thou gentle to him: (Az, O, Ḳ, TA:) or when thy brother magnifies and exalts himself against thee, abase thyself: (Th, TA:) or, accord. to Aboo-Is-ḥáḳ, what Th says is a mistake; the right reading being فَهِنْ, with kesr, and the meaning, when thy brother is hard, or severe, to thee, treat thou him with gentleness, or blandishment; not فَهُنْ, with ḍamm, which is from الهَوَانُ: but ISd approves and justifies the reading given by Th. (TA.) [See also 10.] ═ عَزَّهُ, aor. ـُ, inf. n. عَزٌّ, also signifies the same as عَزَّزَهُ (Mṣb, TA*) and أَعَزَّهُ, (TA,) in a sense pointed out below: see 2, in two places. (Mṣb, TA.) — [And hence,] with the same aor. and inf. n., He aided, or helped, him. (IḲṭṭ, TA.) ═ عَزَّ المَآءُ, (O, Ḳ,) aor. ـِ, (O,) The water flowed. (O, Ḳ.) — And عَزَّتِ القَرْحَةُ, (O, Ḳ,) aor. ـِ, (O,) The قرحة [i. e. wound, or pustule,] discharged what was in it. (O, Ḳ.) ═ عَزَّتْ, aor. ـُ, inf. n. عُزُوزٌ and عِزَازٌ; (Ṣ, O, Ḳ;) and, (Ḳ,) accord. to IAạr, (O,) عَزُزَتْ, (O, Ḳ,) inf. n. عُزُوزٌ; (O, TA;) She (a camel, IAạr, Ṣ, O, Ḳ, and a ewe or goat, IAạr, O) was narrow in the orifices of the teats; (Ṣ, O,* Ḳ;) as also ▼ اعزّت, (Ṣ, O, Ḳ,) and ▼ تعزّزت: (Ṣ, Ḳ:) or عَزُزَتْ, [which is of a very uncommon form, (see دَمَّ, last sentence,)] she (a ewe, or goat,) became scant in her milk. (IKh, TA in art. لب.)

2. عَزَّزَهُ, (inf. n. تَعْزِيزٌ, TA,) He rendered him mighty, potent, powerful, or strong; he strengthened him; (Ṣ, Mṣb, TA;) بِآخَرَ by, or by means of, another; (Mṣb;) as also ▼ عَزَّهُ, (Ṣ, Mṣb, TA,) aor. ـُ, inf. n. عَزٌّ; (Mṣb;) and ▼ اعزّه: (O, TA:) the agent is God, (Ṣ, TA,) and a man: (Mṣb, TA:) He (God, Ṣ, TA) rendered him mighty, potent, powerful, or strong, after he had been low, or mean, in condition; (Ḳ, TA;) as also ▼ اعزّه [which is the more common in this sense, and as signifying He rendered him high, or elevated, in rank or condition or state, or noble, honourable, glorious, or illustrious]. (Ṣ, Ḳ, TA.) In the Ḳur [xxxvi. 13], some read, فَعَزَزْنَا بِثَالِثٍ; (Ṣ, TA;) and others, فَعَزَّزْنَا ▼ بثالث; meaning And then we strengthened [them] by a third. (Ṣ, O, TA.) [See also an explanation of a verse cited voce عَزَاةٌ in art. عزى.] — عَزَّزَ المَطَرُ الأَرْضَ, (Ṣ, O, Ḳ,) and عَزَّزَ مِنْهَا, (O, Ḳ,) inf. n. تَعْزِيزٌ, (Ḳ,) The rain made the earth compact, or coherent, (Ṣ, O, Ḳ, TA,) and hard, so that the feet did not sink into it. (TA.) — عَزَّزَ بِهِمْ, (inf. n. as above, TA,) He treated them with hardness, severity, or rigour; not with indulgence. (A, TA.)

3. عَازَّهُ, inf. n. مُعَازَّةٌ: see عَزَّهُ, in three places.

4. اعزّهُ: see 2, in two places. — Also He loved him: (AZ, O, Ḳ:) but Sh reckons this weak. (O.) ═ أُعْزِزْتُ: and the verb of wonder أَعْزِزْ: see عَزَّ, in three places. ═ اعزّت said of a camel and of a ewe: see 1, last sentence. — Also She (a cow) had difficult gestation, (Ṣ, O, Ḳ,) or, accord. to IḲṭṭ, bad gestation. (TA.) — And She (a goat, and a ewe,) manifested her pregnancy, and became large in her udder: (AZ, O, Ḳ:) or, as some say, i. q. أَضْرَعَتْ [q. v.]. (O.) ═ And اعزّ He became, (Ṣ, O, Ḳ,) and journeyed, (TA,) in ground such as is termed عَزَاز [q. v.]. (Ṣ, O, Ḳ, TA.)

5. تعزّز: see 1, first quarter, in four places. [It is sometimes changed to تعزّى.] It is said in a trad., مَنْ لَمْ يَتَعَزَّ بِعِزِّ ٱللّٰهِ فَلَيْسَ مِنَّا [Such as does not strengthen himself by the strength of God, he is not of us]; expl. by Th as meaning he who does not refer his affair to God is not of us. (TA. [See another reading voce تَعَزَّى, in art. عزى.]) You say also, تَعَزَّيْتُ عَنْهُ, meaning I constrained myself to endure the loss, or want, of him, or it, with patience; originally تَعَزَّزْتُ, meaning, I exerted my strength or energy [to divert myself from him, or it]; like تَظَنَّيْتُ for تَظَنَّنْتُ. (TA.) [But see art. عزى.] — He magnified and hardened himself; he behaved in a proud and hard manner, towards others. (TA.) — تعزّز بِهِ He gloried, or prided himself, in, or by reason of, him [or it]; (TA;) as also ▼ اعتزّ به; (O, TA;) [and ▼ استعزّ به.] — تعزّز لَحْمُ النَّاقَةِ The flesh of the she-camel became hard, or tough. (Ṣ,* A, O,* L, Ḳ.*) — تعزّزت said of a camel and of a ewe: see 1, last sentence.

8. اعتزّ به He reckoned himself strong, or mighty, &c., (عَزِيز,) by means of him; (Ṣ,* Ḳ;) [as also ▼ استعزّ به.] — See also 5. ═ And see 1, in two places.

10: see 8, and 5. — استعزّ فُلَانٌ بِحَقِّى Such a one overcame me. (Ṣ, TA.) And استعزّ بِهِ المَرَضُ, (A, O,) or استعزّ عَلَيْهِ, (O, Ḳ,) The disease became violent, or severe, to him, and overcame him. (O, Ḳ.) And أُسْتُعِزَّ بِهِ He was overcome by disease or any other thing: (Ṣ, O:) or, accord. to AA, he (a sick man) became in a state of violent, or severe, pain, and his reason was overcome. (Ṣ.) You say also اسْتَعَزَّ ٱللّٰهُ بِهِ God caused him to die. (O, Ḳ.) And أُسْتُعِزَّ بِهِ He died. (O, TA.) — استعزّ said of sand, (Ṣ, A, O, Ḳ,) and of other things, (Ṣ,) also signifies It held together, or cohered, (Ṣ, A, O, Ḳ,) and did not pour down. (Ṣ, O, Ḳ.)

R. Q. 1. عَزْعَزَهُ: see 1, latter half.

عَزٌّ: see عَزِيزٌ. ═ جِئَ بِهِ عَزًّا بَزًّا He was brought without any means of avoiding it; (A, O, Ḳ;) willingly or against his will: (TA:) [as though originally signifying by being overcome and despoiled.]

عِزٌّ Might, potency, power, or strength; (TA;) as also ▼ عِزَّةٌ: (Ṣ, O, TA:) and especially after lowness, or meanness, of condition; as also ▼ the latter word: (AZ, Ṣ, A,* Mṣb, and Ḳ, in explanation of عِزٌّ:) high, or elevated, rank or condition or state; nobility, honourableness, gloriousness, or illustriousness; syn. رِفْعَةٌ; (TA;) contr. of ذُلٌّ; (Ṣ, A, O;) [as also ▼ the latter word: see عِزٌّ.] بِعِزِّى لَقَدْ كَانَ كَذَا وَكَذَا, and بِعِزِّكَ, [By my might, &c., and by thy might, &c., such and such things have happened,] like لَعَمْرِى and لَعَمْرُكَ, are bad phrases of the people of Esh-Shiḥr. (TA.) — [Self-magnification; self-exaltation: see عِزٌّ:] and ▼ عِزَّةٌ [or عِزَّةُ النَّفْسِ signifies the same: and also,] ‡ disdainfulness; scornfulness; indignation; (O, TA;) of a blameable kind; as in the Ḳur ii. 202. (TA.) — The quality, or power, of resisting, or withstanding; resistibility: (TA:) and ▼ عِزَّةٌ [signifies the same: and] the quality, in a man, of being invincible, or not to be overcome: (B, TA:) and both signify [difficulty, or hardness: and] impossibility, insuperableness, or unattainableness, of a thing. (Mṣb.) — [Rareness; scarceness; as also ▼ عِزَّةٌ: see عِزٌّ.] — The act of overcoming; conquest; superior power or force;

(TA;) as also ↑ عِزَّةٌ: (Ṣ, O, TA:) and the latter has this signification especially *in relation to an argumentative contest.* (Ḳ.) ═ مَطَرٌ عِزٌّ *Vehement rain:* (Ṣ, Ḳ:) or *copious rain:* (IAạr, AḤn, O, TA:) or *mighty, great, rain, that causes the plain and the mountain to flow.* (TA.) And سَيْلٌ عِزٌّ *An overpowering torrent.* (A, TA.)

عَزَّةٌ The *female young one of a gazelle.* (Ṣ, O, Ḳ.)

عِزَّةٌ: see عِزٌّ, throughout.

عَزَزٌ: see عَزَازٌ. ═ Also The *state of being narrow in the orifices of the teats;* and so ↑ عَزَازٌ. (TA. [See 1, last sentence.])

عَزَازٌ *Hard ground:* (Ṣ, O, Ḳ:) or *hard, rugged ground,* but only *in the borders of a tract of land:* (TA:) or *a hard place, that quickly flows* [*with rain*]; (Ḳzz, TA;) as also ↑ عَزَزٌ: (TA:) or, accord. to ISh, *rugged ground, upon which the rain quickly flows, in plains, and* [*particularly*] *such as are bare* or *barren, and the acclivities of mountains and* [*hills* or *eminences such as are termed*] آكَام*, and the elevated parts* (ظُهُور) *of* [*the high grounds termed*] قِفَاف. (TA.) ═ See also عَزَزٌ.

عَزُوزٌ *Narrow in the orifices of the teats;* (Ṣ, A, O, Ḳ;) applied to a she-camel, (Ṣ, O, Ḳ,) and to a ewe, (O,) and to a she-goat. (TA.) One says of a niggardly man possessing much property, † فُلَانٌ عَنْزٌ عَزُوزٌ لَهَا دَرٌّ جَمٌّ [*Such a one is like a she-goat narrow in the orifices of the teats, that has much milk*]. (TA.)

عَزِيزٌ *Mighty, potent, powerful,* or *strong,* [in an absolute sense; as also ↑ عَزٌّ, accord. to the Mṣb; and especially,] *after lowness,* or *meanness, of condition:* (Ṣ, A, Mṣb:) [*high,* or *elevated, in rank* or *condition* or *state; noble, honourable, glorious,* or *illustrious:* see عِزٌّ:] *rough in manners* or *behaviour:* (TA: [see ذَلِيلٌ, which signifies, sometimes, the contr. of this:]) [*proud: disdainful; scornful; indignant:* see عِزٌّ:] *resisting; withstanding; indomitable; invincible; not to be overcome;* applied to a man: (TA:) [*difficult,* or *hard:* and *impossible, insuperable,* or *unattainable:* see عِزٌّ:] *rare; scarce; hardly to be found:* (Ṣ, Ḳ:) [and hence, *dear, highly esteemed,* or *greatly valued:* hence, also, applied to a word or phrase, *rare,* or *extraordinary, in respect of usage* or *analogy* or *both:*] and ↑ أَعَزُّ also signifies the same as عَزِيزٌ [mostly in the first of the senses expl. above, or in a similar sense]: (Ṣ, O, Ḳ:) and ↑ عُزَّى the same as عَزِيزَةٌ [app. as meaning *noble,* or *the like*], (O, Ḳ, TA,) applied to a woman: (TA:) the pl. of عَزِيزٌ is عِزَازٌ (Ṣ, O, Ḳ) and أَعِزَّةٌ (Ṣ, Mṣb, Ḳ) and أَعِزَّآءُ; (Ṣ, Ḳ;) but one does not say أَعْزِزَآءُ, on account of the reduplication, which is disliked. (TA.) — مَلِكٌ أَعَزُّ ↑ signifies the same as عَزِيزٌ [*A mighty, potent, powerful,* or *strong, King;* or *a glorious King*]. (TA.) And El-Farezdaḳ says,

إِنَّ ٱلَّذِى سَمَكَ ٱلسَّمَآءَ بَنَى لَنَا
بَيْتًا دَعَائِمُهُ أَعَزُّ وَأَطْوَلُ

[*Verily He who raised the heaven built for us a tent of which the props are strong and tall*]: meaning, عَزِيزَةٌ طَوِيلَةٌ: like the phrase in the Ḳur [xxx. 26], وَهُوَ أَهْوَنُ عَلَيْهِ [meaning هَيِّنٌ]: not implying excess, accord. to ISd, because أَلْ and مِنْ supply each other's places [and one or the other of these, or a noun in the gen. case expressed or understood after the epithet, is necessary to denote excess: see أَكْبَرُ]. (TA.) — العَزِيزُ, as a name of God, signifies *The Mighty,* (TA,) *who overcomes* (O, TA) *everything:* (TA:) or *He who resists,* or *withstands, so that nothing overcomes Him:* (Zj, TA:) or *The Incomparable,* or *Unparalleled.* (TA.) — It also signifies *The King;* because he has the mastery over the people of his dominions: (O, Ḳ:) and especially *the ruler of Miṣr together with Alexandria;* (Ḳ, TA;) a surname; like النَّجَاشِىُّ applied to the King of the Abyssinians, and قَيْصَرُ to the King of the Romans. (TA.) — وَإِنَّهُ لَكِتَابٌ عَزِيزٌ, [said of the Ḳur, in that book, xli. 41, means *And verily it is a mighty book:* meaning, *inimitable:* or] *defended,* or *protected,* (Bḍ, Jel,) *from being rendered void and from being corrupted:* (Bḍ:) or *of great utility; unequalled.* (Bḍ.) [الكِتَابُ العَزِيزُ, *The mighty book,* is an appellation often given to the Ḳur-án.] — عِزٌّ عَزِيزٌ signifies *Great might,* or *the like:* or *might,* or *the like, that is a cause of the same* to a person. (TA.) — It is said in the Ḳur [v. 59], فَسَوْفَ يَأْتِى ٱللّٰهُ بِقَوْمٍ يُحِبُّهُمْ وَيُحِبُّونَهُ أَذِلَّةٍ عَلَى ٱلْمُؤْمِنِينَ أَعِزَّةٍ عَلَى ٱلْكَافِرِينَ, meaning, [*God will bring a people whom He will love and who will love Him,*] *gentle to the believers, rough in manners,* or *behaviour, to the unbelievers:* (TA:) or *submissive to the believers,* though they be [themselves] mighty, or noble, *proud to the unbelievers,* though they be [themselves] inferior to them in highness of rank and in grounds of pretension to respect. (Az, TA.) — [And one says, هُوَ العَزِيزُ أَنْ يُضَامَ: expl. voce أَلْ (p. 75). And هُوَ عَزِيزٌ:] ... اِمْرَأَةٌ عَزِيزَةٌ عِنْدَ نَفْسِهَا: see صُلْبٌ. And عَزِيزُ النَّفْسِ see ظَلِفٌ. — عَزِيزٌ also signifies *Severe, difficult, distressing,* or *grievous;* (see an ex. voce عَنِتَ;) and so ↑ أَعَزُّ, fem. عَزَّآءُ:] you say, سَنَةٌ عَزَّآءُ *A severe year:* (Ṣ, O, Ḳ:) and مَنْ حَسُنَ مِنْهُ العَزَآءُ هَانَتْ عَلَيْهِ العَزَّآءُ [*He whose patient endurance of a loss is of a good description, what is difficult,* or *distressing, becomes easy to him*]. (A.) ═ حَبُّ العَزِيزِ [*The small tubercles that compose the root of the cyperus esculentus, which have a sweet and pleasant taste, and which women eat with the view of acquiring fatness thereby:* and also *that plant itself:* both are thus called in the present day]. (TA voce سُقَيْطٌ, &c.)

عَزَازَةٌ *A small water-course of a valley, shorter than a* مِذْنَب [q. v.]. (AA, TA.) — See also مَعْزُوزَةٌ.

عَزِيزَةٌ [fem. of عَزِيزٌ, q. v. — Also] *An eagle:* so in a verse of Aboo-Kebeer El-Hudhalee: but as some relate that verse, it is عَزِيبَةٌ, (Ḳ, TA,) i. e. "that has gone far from the seeker:" (TA:) or غَرِيبَةٌ, (TA, and thus in the CḲ,) expl. by Skr as meaning "black" (سَوْدَآء) [as though for غِرْبِيبَةٌ, fem. of غِرْبِيبٌ: but the word سَوْدَآء immediately follows it in that verse]. (TA.)

عُزَيْزَى and عُزَيْزَآءُ The *extremity of the hip,* or *haunch,* of a horse: (Ṣ, O, Ḳ, TA:) or the *part between the root of the tail and the* جَاعِرَة [q. v.]: (TA as from the Ḳ [in which I do not find it]): or the former, *a sinew inserted in the rectum, extending to the hip,* or *haunch:* (Aboo-Málik, TA:) dual of the former عُزَيْزَيَانِ, and of the latter عُزَيْزَاوَانِ. (Ṣ, O, TA.)

عُزَّى: see أَعَزُّ, in four places: and عَزِيزٌ.

عَزَّآءُ [fem. of أَعَزُّ, q. v., last sentence: — and] *i. q.* مَعْزُوزَةٌ, q. v. (TA.)

أَعَزُّ [*More,* and *most, mighty, potent, powerful,* or *strong:* &c.: see عَزِيزٌ, of which it is the comparative and superlative form: and see an ex. voce أَلْ (p. 75): and another in a verse cited in art. صب, conj. 8]. It is related in a trad. of Aboo-Bekr, that he said to 'Áïsheh, إِنَّ أَحَبَّ النَّاسِ إِلَىَّ غِنًى أَنْتِ وَأَعَزَّهُمْ فَقْرًا أَنْتِ, meaning, *Verily the one of mankind whose richness is most pleasing to me art thou; and the one of them whose poverty is most distressing to me art thou.* (Mgh.) The fem. of أَعَزُّ [as a noun of excess] is ↑ عُزَّى: (Ṣ, ISd, O, Ḳ;) like as فُضْلَى is of أَفْضَلُ. (ISd.) [But see what follows.] — ↑ العُزَّى was the name of *A certain idol,* (Ṣ, O, Ḳ,) *belonging to Ḳureysh and Benoo-Kinááneh:* (Ṣ, O, TA:) or *a certain gum-acacia-tree,* (سَمُرَة,) *which the tribe of Ghaṭafán* (Ṣ, O, Ḳ) *the son of Saad the son of Ḳeys-'Eilán* (TA) *used to worship;* (Ṣ, O, Ḳ;) *the first who took it as an object of worship was Ḍhálim the son of As'ad; above Dhát-'Irḳ, nine miles towards El-Bustán,* (O, Ḳ, TA,) *at* [*the valley called*] *En-Nakhleh Esh-Shámeeyeh,* (O, TA,) *near Mekkeh; or, as some say, at Eṭ-Ṭáif:* (TA:) he, (Ḳ,) Ḍhálim, (O,) or they, (Ṣ,) built over it a house, (Ṣ, O, Ḳ,) and named it بُسّ, (O, Ḳ,) accord. to Ibn-El-Kelbee; or, accord. to others, بُسَّآء; (TA;) and they appointed to it ministers, (Ṣ, TA,) like those of the Kaabeh; (TA;) and they used to hear in it a voice: (O, Ḳ, TA:) but Moḥammad sent to it Khálid Ibn-El-Weleed, (Ṣ, O, Ḳ,) in the year of the conquest [of Mekkeh], (O, TA,) and he demolished the house, (Ṣ, Ḳ,) and slew the [chief] minister, (TA,) and burned the gum-acacia-tree: (Ṣ, O, Ḳ:) or, as is related on the authority of I'Ab, *a certain she-devil,* who used to come to three gum-acacia-trees (سَمُرَات) in Baṭn-Nakhleh, against whom Moḥammad, when he conquered Mekkeh, sent Khálid Ibn-El-Weleed; and he cut down the trees, and slew her and her minister. (TA.) A poet says,

أَمَا وَدِمَآءٍ مَائِرَاتٍ تَخَالُهَا
عَلَى قُنَّةِ العُزَّى وَبِالنَّسْرِ عَنْدَمَا

[*Verily, or now surely, by bloods flowing, and running hither and thither, which thou wouldst think to be dragon's-blood, upon the mountain-top of El-'Ozzà, and by En-Nesr*]. (Ṣ.) ISd says, I hold ▼ العُزَّى to be fem. of الأَعَزّ; and if so, the ال in the former is not redundant, but is like the ال in الحَارِثُ and العَبَّاسُ: but properly it should be redundant, because we have not heard العُزَّى as an epithet [of excess] like as we have heard الكُبْرَى and الصُّغْرَى. (L, TA.) — ▼ عُزَّى is [however] used in the sense of عَزِيزَةٌ: (Ḳ, TA:) and أَعَزُّ [fem. عَزَّآءُ] is also syn. with عَزِيزٌ, which see in four places. (Ṣ, Ḳ.)

المُعِزُّ, as a name of God, *He who giveth* عِزّ [or *might*, &c.] *to whomsoever He will, of his servants.* (TA.)

مَعَزَّةٌ [accord. to analogy signifies *A cause*, or *means*, *of* عِزّ i. e. *might*, &c.]: see ظَفَارِ.

إِنَّكُمْ مَعَزُوزٌ بِكُمْ *Verily ye are treated with hardness, severity*, or *rigour; not with indulgence.* (Ṣ, O, TA.) From a trad. of Ibn-'Omar. (O, TA.)

فُلَانٌ مِعْزَازُ المَرَضِ *Such a one is in a severe state of disease.* (Ṣ, O, Ḳ.)

مَعْزُوزَةٌ, applied to land, or ground, (أَرْضٌ, Ṣ, O,) *Hard*, or *firm*; syn. شَدِيدَةٌ. (Ṣ, O, Ḳ.) — And, so applied, *Rained upon* (O, Ḳ, TA) *by rain such as is termed* عَزّ, *and rendered compact*, or *coherent, and hard*; as also ▼ عَزَازَةٌ and ▼ عَزَّآءُ. (TA.)

مُعْتَزٌّ is syn. with مُسْتَعِزٌّ. (TA.) You say, أَنَا مُعْتَزٌّ بِبَنِى فُلَانٍ and ▼ مُسْتَعِزٌّ بِهِمْ [*I reckon myself strong by means of the sons of such a one*]. (A.) — فَرَسٌ مُعْتَزَّةٌ *A mare having thick and strong flesh.* (TA.)

مُسْتَعِزٌّ: see the next preceding paragraph.

عزب

1. عَزَبَ, aor. ـُ (Ṣ, O, Mṣb) and ـِ, (Ṣ, O,) inf. n. عُزُوبٌ, (Ṣ, Mṣb,) *He*, (a man, Ṣ, O,) or *it*, (a thing, Mṣb,) *was*, or *became*, *distant*, or *remote*; (Ṣ, O, Mṣb;) and *absent*; عَنِّى *from me*: (Ṣ, O:) or ▼ اعزب has the former meaning: (Ḳ:) and عَزَبَ, aor. ـُ and ـِ, (Mṣb, Ḳ,) inf. n. as above, (Ḳ,) signifies *he*, or *it*, *was*, or *became*, *absent*, (Mṣb, Ḳ,) and *concealed*: (Mṣb:) and *went away*, or *departed*. (Ḳ, TA.) You say, عَزَبَ بِهَا, referring to sheep or goats, *He went to a distance*, or *far off*, *with them*: so in a trad.: or, as some relate it, ▼ عَزَّبَ بِهَا, meaning *he went with them to a remote pasturage:* and *he pastured them* (namely, camels,) *at a distance from the place of abode of the tribe, not repairing*, or *returning, to them* [*in the evening*]: and ▼ تعزّب, and thus the verb is written in copies of the Ḳ in a place where some copies have يَعْزُبُ, occurs in the phrase تعزّب عَنْ أَهْلِهِ وَمَالِهِ [*He went away to a distance from his family and his cattle*, or *camels* &c.]. (TA.) And عَزَبَتِ الإِبِلُ *The camels went away to a distance in the pasturage, not returning in the evening:* (Ṣ, O:) and in like manner one says of sheep or goats. (O.) And لَا يَعْزُبُ عَنْ عِلْمِهِ شَىْءٌ *Nothing is absent from his* (God's) *knowledge.* (TA. [See Ḳur x. 62 and xxxiv. 3.]) And عَزَبَ طُهْرُ المَرْأَةِ [*The woman's state of pureness from the menstrual discharge was a remote thing*] means † *the woman's husband was absent from her:* (Ḳ:) or [rather] is said of the woman when her husband is absent from her. (Ṣ, O.) And عَزَبَ عَنْ فُلَانٍ حِلْمُهُ [*Such a one's forbearance quitted him*]; (Ṣ, O;) as also ▼ اعزب. (O.) — Also, aor. ـُ, (Mṣb, Ḳ,) inf. n. عُزْبَةٌ and عُزُوبَةٌ, (Mṣb, MF, TA,) or these are simple substs., (Ṣ, Ḳ,) † *He was without a wife;* or *in a state of celibacy.* (Mṣb, Ḳ.) [And app. عَزَبَتْ is said in like manner of a woman, meaning † *She was without a husband.* See also 5.] — And عَزَبَتِ الأَرْضُ † *The land*, whether fruitful or unfruitful, *was*, or *became*, *destitute of inhabitants; had in it no one.* (Ṣ, O, Ḳ.)

2. عَزَّبَ بِهَا: see 1, second sentence. عَزَّبَ بِهِ عَنِ الدَّارِ is said of a herd of pasturing camels [meaning *It was taken to pasture at a distance from the place of abode*]. (Ṣ, O, Ḳ.*) — It is said in a trad. (Ṣ, O) of the Prophet, (O,) مَنْ قَرَأَ القُرْآنَ فِى أَرْبَعِينَ لَيْلَةً فَقَدْ عَزَّبَ, meaning ‡ [*He who reads, or recites, the Ḳur-án in forty nights*] *goes to a remote period of time from his commencement;* (Ṣ, O, TA;) or *makes the time of the commencement thereof to be remote;* (A;) and is *tardy in doing so.* (TA.) — عزّب إِبِلَهُ: see 4. — لَيْسَ لِفُلَانٍ ٱمْرَأَةٌ تُعَزِّبُهُ, meaning † *There is not for such a one a woman to put an end to his celibacy by marriage*, is like the saying هِىَ تُمَرِّضُهُ "she takes care of him in his sickness." (O, TA.) — And one says, فُلَانٌ يُعَزِّبُ فُلَانًا وَيُرَبِّضُهُ † [*Such a one undertakes*, or *manages*, *the affairs of such a one, and his expenses*]; i. e., *acts for him like a treasurer.* (TA, from the Nawádir el-Aạráb. [In art. ربض in the TA, عزّبه is said to signify, agreeably with the explanation above, قَامَ عَلَيْهِ.])

4. اعزب *He made to be distant*, or *remote;* or *to go far away.* (Ḳ,* TA.) You say, اعزبهُ ٱللّٰهُ *God made him*, or *may God make him*, *to go away*, or *far away.* (Ṣ, TA.) — اعزب الإِبِلَ *He drove the camels to a distance in the pasturage, not to return in the evening.* (TA.) And اعزب إِبِلَهُ and ▼ عزّبها *He made his camels to pass the night in the pasturage, not bringing them back in the evening.* (TA.) And اعزب جَمَلَهُ is like أَضَلَّهُ [*He made his camel to go astray*]. (A.) — [Hence,] اعزب ٱللّٰهُ عَنْهُ حِلْمَهُ † *God made his forbearance to become remote from him.* (O.) — And أَعْزَبْنَا الكَلَأَ, (O,) or أَعْزَبْنَا alone, (Ṣ,) *We lighted upon remote herbage.* (Ṣ, O.) — As intrans.: see 1, first sentence: and the same in the latter half. — [Hence,] اعزب القَوْمُ *The people's camels went away to a distance in the pasturage, not to return in the evening.* (Ṣ,* O,* Ḳ,* TA.)

5. تعزّب: see 1, second sentence. — Also *He passed the night with his camels in the pasturage, not returning in the evening.* (TA.) — And † *He abstained from marriage:* (Ḳ, TA:) and in like manner تعزّبت is said of a woman. (TA.) One says, تعزّب زَمَانًا ثُمَّ تَأَهَّلَ (Ṣ, O) † *He was without a wife* [*a long time*, or *he abstained from marriage a long time; then he took a wife*]. (O.) [See also 1, near the end.]

عَزَبٌ [correctly thus, but in the sense here following written in the TA without any syll. signs, and in the O written عَزِبٌ,] A man *who goes away to a distance into the country*, or *in the land.* (O, TA.) [And One *who goes far away with his camels to pasture:* pl. أَعْزَابٌ. (See also عَازِبٌ and مُعْزِبٌ and مِعْزَابَةٌ and عَزِيبٌ.)] هِرَاوَةُ الأَعْزَابِ means *The staff of those who go far away with their camels to pasture;* and a horse is likened thereto, (Ṣ, O, TA,) on account of its compactness and smoothness; so in a marginal note in the L: (TA:) [Ṣgh, however, says,] thus in some of the lexicons, but in my opinion, (O,) it was the name of a mare which was not to be outstripped, and which was thus called because her owner gave her gratuitously for the use of those of his people who had no wives, who made predatory attacks upon her, and when one of them acquired for himself property and a wife, he resigned her to another of his people: (O, Ḳ:*) whence the prov.

أَعَزُّ مِنْ هِرَاوَةِ الأَعْزَابِ

[*More highly esteemed than Hiráwet-el-Aạzáb*]. (O.) See an ex. in a verse cited voce عَدِيدٌ. — See also عَازِبٌ. — Also Whatever is *alone, solitary*, or *apart from others.* (TA.) — And † A man *having no wife;* (Ks, Ṣ, Mgh, O, Mṣb, Ḳ;) as also ▼ عَازِبٌ, (Mṣb,* TA,) which is the original; (Mṣb;) and ▼ عَزِيبٌ, and ▼ مِعْزَابَةٌ [which see below]; (Ḳ;) but not ▼ أَعْزَبُ, (Mgh, O, Mṣb, Ḳ,) this being disallowed by AḤát, (O, Mṣb,) and others; (TA;) or it is rare; (Ḳ;) but it occurs in a trad.; (Mgh, O;) and some allow it: (O, Mṣb:) the pl. of the first is أَعْزَابٌ, (O, Ḳ,) or عُزَّابٌ, (Ṣ,* Mṣb,) which is thus because the original form of the sing. is considered as being ▼ عَازِبٌ, this pl. being like كُفَّارٌ as pl. of كَافِرٌ, (Mṣb,) or عَزَبٌ has both of these pls., (O,) or عُزَّابٌ is pl. of ▼ عَازِبٌ, (TA,) and is applied to men and to † women as meaning *having no spouses:* (Ṣ, TA:) عَزَبَةٌ is applied to † a woman [as meaning *having no husband*], (Ks, Ṣ, O, Mṣb, Ḳ,) and (O, Mṣb, Ḳ) so عَزَبٌ; (Zj, Ḳz, Mgh,

O, Mṣb, Ḳ;) and if أَعْزَبُ be applied to a man, ↑ عَزْبَآءُ, may by rule be applied to a woman; and the pl. of عَزَبَةٌ is عَزَبَاتٌ: (Mṣb:) or, accord. to Zj, عَزَبَةٌ is a mistake of Abu-l-'Abbás [i. e. Th], and عَزَبٌ is used as an epithet of a man and of a woman, like as is خَصْمٌ, and does not assume a dual form nor a pl. nor a fem. form, because it is originally an inf. n.; MF, however, denies that we have any authority for calling عَزَبٌ an inf. n.: he considers it to be a simple epithet, like حَسَنٌ &c.; and if used in the fem. sense without the termination ة otherwise than by poetic license, to be an anomalous epithet, like عَانِسٌ, which is applied alike to a man and to a woman: the phrase رَجُلَانِ عَزَبَانِ is also mentioned: and the saying إِنَّهُ لَعَزَبٌ لَزَبٌ [in which the latter epithet is merely an imitative sequent corroborative of the former], and إِنَّهَا لَعَزَبَةٌ لَزَبَةٌ; and عَزَبٌ is said to be [also] a quasi-pl. n. [of عَازِبٌ], like as خَدَمٌ is of خَادِمٌ. (TA.)

عُزْبَةٌ and ↑ عُزُوبَةٌ The *state of having no wife* or *husband; celibacy.* (Ṣ, Ḳ. [Each said in the Ṣ and Ḳ to be a simple subst.: but see 1, near the end.])

عَزِيبٌ A man *who has gone away to a distance* (تَعَزَّبَ, as in some copies of the Ḳ), or *who goes away to a distance* (يَعْزُبُ, as in other copies of the Ḳ), *from his family and his cattle,* or *camels &c.* (Ḳ, TA.) — And Cattle, or camels &c., *at a distance from the tribe:* heard by Az in this sense from the Arabs: (TA:) or a herd of camels, and the like of sheep or goats, *that go away to a distance from their owners in the pasturage:* (Ḳ, TA:) and إِبِلٌ عَزِيبٌ *camels that do not return in the evening to the tribe:* عَزِيبٌ thus used is pl. (or a quasi-pl. n., TA) of ↑ عَازِبٌ, like as غَزِىٌّ is of غَازٍ. (Ṣ, Ḳ, TA.) — See also عَازِبٌ. — And see عَزَبٌ, near the middle.

عَزُوبَةٌ A land *in which one has to go far for pasturage;* (O, Ḳ;) *in which the pasturage is little:* (TA:) the ة is to render the signification intensive. (O.)

عُزُوبَةٌ: see عُزْبَةٌ.

عَازِبٌ *Distant,* or *remote:* (Mṣb, TA:) applied in this sense to herbage: (Ṣ, Ḳ:) or, applied to herbage, *such as has not been depastured at all, nor trodden:* and, accord. to the A, only *such as is in a desert in which is no seed-produce:* (TA:) and it is likewise applied to meadows (رَوْضٌ) [app. as meaning *distant,* or *remote*]; as also ↑ عَزِيبٌ. (A, TA.) In the following saying,

* وَصَدْرٍ أَرَاحَ اللَّيْلُ عَازِبَ هَمِّهِ *

* تَضَاعَفَ فِيهِ الحُزْنُ مِنْ كُلِّ جَانِبِ *

‡ [*In many a bosom whose remote* (or *long-past*) *anxiety night has brought back, grief has multiplied from every quarter*], it is used metaphorically. (A.) And [in like manner,] in a trad. of 'Átikeh,

* فَهُنَّ هَوَآءٌ وَالحُلُومُ عَوَازِبُ *

means † *And they are devoid of reason, the intellects* [being] *far away:* عَوَازِبُ here being pl. of عَازِبٌ. (L, TA.) And [in a similar manner,] عَوَازِبُ الأَطْهَارِ [in which عَوَازِبُ is pl. of عَازِبَةٌ] is applied as an epithet to women whose husbands are absent: (Ṣ and O and TA, from a verse of En-Nábighah Edh-Dhubyánee: [for the lit. meaning, see 1, latter half:]) — [for] عَازِبٌ signifies also *Absent;* and *concealed.* (Mṣb.) — It is also applied to sheep or goats, (شَآءٌ, O, TA, and غَنَمٌ, O,) and to camels, (إِبِلٌ, O,) meaning *Remote in the pasturage,* (O, TA,) *that do not return in the evening,* (O,) or *that do not repair to the place of alighting and abode* [*of their owners*] *in the night:* (TA:) and [in like manner] ↑ عَزَبٌ is applied to cattle, or camels &c., (مَالٌ, A, O, TA,) meaning *that go away to a distance from their owners.* (O.) See also عَزِيبٌ [which, thus applied, is a quasi-pl. n. of عَازِبٌ]. And عَازِبَةٌ is likewise applied to camels (O, Ḳ) as meaning *That go far away to pasture:* (O, Ḳ:*) so in the prov. إِنَّمَا اشْتَرَيْتُ الغَنَمَ حِذَارَ العَازِبَةِ [*I only bought the sheep,* or *goats, in fear of* loosing *those that go far away to pasture*]: said by a man who had camels, and sold them, and bought sheep, or goats, lest they [the camels] should go far away to pasture; and his sheep, or goats, did so: (O, Ḳ:) it is applied to the case of him who acts with gentleness [or precaution] in the easiest of affairs, and has unexpected difficulty, or trouble, inseparable from him. (O.) — See also عَزَبٌ, in three places. — And see مِعْزَابَةٌ.

عَوْزَبٌ *An old woman:* (O, Ḳ:) so called because of the long period that has elapsed since her marriage. (TA.)

أَعْزَبُ; and the fem. عَزْبَآءُ: see عَزَبٌ.

مُعْزِبٌ One *who goes away from his family with his camels.* (Az, TA.) [See also عَزَبٌ and عَزِيبٌ &c.] — And *Seeking distant herbage, such as is termed* عَازِبٌ. (TA.) — And One *whose camels go away to a distance in the pasturage, not to return in the evening.* (Ṣ, TA.)

مِعْزَبَةٌ *A female slave:* (O, Ḳ:) or, accord. to Th, applied only to a woman *that has not a husband:* (TA:) pl. مَعَازِبُ, for which مَعَازِيبُ occurs in a verse of Aboo-Khirásh El-Hudhalee. (O.) — See also مَعْزَبَةٌ.

مُعَزَّبٌ A herd of pasturing camels *taken to pasture at a distance* (عُزِّبَ بِهِ) *from the place of abode.* (Ṣ, O, Ḳ.*)

مَعْزَبَةٌ (A, O, Ḳ) and ↑ مِعْزَبَةٌ and ↑ عَازِبَةٌ (Ḳ) ‡ *A man's wife,* (A, O, Ḳ,) *to whom he resorts, and who undertakes the preparing of his food and the taking care of his implements, utensils, accoutrements,* or *furniture.* (O.)

مِعْزَابٌ: see what follows, in two places.

مِعْزَابَةٌ A man *who goes away to a distance with his cattle,* or *camels &c.,* (Ṣ, A, O, Ḳ,) *from others, in the pasturage;* (Ṣ, O;) as also ↑ مِعْزَابٌ: (A, O, Ḳ:) accord. to Az, the former is the only epithet of the measure مِفْعَالَةٌ, except مِجْذَامَةٌ, which is sometimes used; [but in the TA, مِطْرَابَةٌ and مِطْوَاعَةٌ and مِقْدَامَةٌ also are mentioned;] the ة in مِعْزَابَةٌ, he says, is added to give intensiveness to the signification, and to imply praise; the meaning being, in his opinion, a man *who frequently betakes himself, with his cattle,* or *camels &c., pasturing at a distance from others, to the places where rain has fallen, and to the uncropped herbage produced thereby;* and he adds that the ة is affixed to a masc. epithet to imply praise or blame when intensiveness is meant. (TA.) The two epithets above are also expl. as applied to a man *who pastures his camels at a distance from the abode of the tribe, not repairing to them to rest.* (TA.) [See also عَزَبٌ &c.] — Also, (Ṣ, O, Ḳ, TA,) or ↑ مِعْزَابٌ, (A, TA,) ‡ A man *who has been long without a wife,* (Ṣ, A, O, Ḳ, TA,) *so that he has no need of one.* (TA.) — See also عَزَبٌ.

عزر

1. عَزَرَهُ, aor. ـِ, inf. n. عَزْرٌ, *He prevented, hindered, withheld,* or *forbade, him;* (Mgh,* O, Ḳ,* TA;) and *turned him away,* or *back;* (Mgh,* O, TA;) عَنِ الشَّىْءِ *from the thing:* this is the primary signification, from which others, mentioned in the next paragraph, are derived. (TA.) See 2, in eight places. — And عَزَرْتُ البَعِيرَ, inf. n. عَزْرٌ, *I tied a cord upon the* خَيَاشِيم [app. meaning the *upper parts of the nostrils*] *of the camel, and then put medicine into his mouth.* (O, TA.) — And عَزَرَ المَرْأَةَ, (TA,) inf. n. as above, (Ḳ,) *He compressed the woman.* (Ḳ,* TA.)

2. عَزَّرَهُ, (O, TA,) inf. n. تَعْزِيرٌ, (Ṣ, O, Ḳ, TA,) *He disciplined, chastised, corrected,* or *punished, him;* (Ṣ, O, TA;) meaning *he did to him that which should turn him away,* or *back, from evil,* or *foul, conduct.* (Ibráheem Es-Seree, O,* TA.) — And hence, (Ṣ,) *He inflicted upon him a beating,* or *flogging, less than that prescribed by the law;* (Ṣ, M, Mgh,* O, Mṣb,* Ḳ;) as also ↑ عَزَرَهُ, inf. n. عَزْرٌ: (TA: but only the inf. n. of the latter verb in this sense is there mentioned:) because it prevents the criminal from returning to disobedience: but whether this meaning belong only to the conventional language of the law or be implied in the proper signification, is disputed: (TA:) or *he beat,* or *flogged, him with the utmost vehemence:* (M, Ḳ:) or تَعْزِيرٌ signifies [simply] the act of *beating.* (A.) And one says, ضَرَبَهُ تَعْزِيرًا, meaning *He beat him moderately; not exceeding the ordinary bounds.* (TA in art. حل.) — Also *He constrained him against his will,* عَلَى الأَمْرِ *to do the thing,* (O, Ḳ,*) *and taught him by forbidding him to return to the doing of that which was at variance therewith;* and so ↑ عَزَرَهُ: (IAạr, O:) and *he taught him the* فَرَائِض and أَحْكَام [or *obligatory statutes* or *ordinances of God*]; (O;)

or التَّعْزِيرُ, (Az, L,) or ↓ العَزْرُ, (K,) signifies *the teaching* [one] (Az, L, K) *religion*, (Az, L,) or بَابُ الدِّينِ [i. e. *the declaration of belief in the unity of God and in the mission of Mohammad*] and the فَرَائِض and أَحْكَام. (L, K.) — And *He blamed, censured*, or *reproved, him*; as also ↓ عَزَرَهُ, aor. ـِ, inf. n. عَزْرٌ. (K.) — And *He aided*, or *assisted, him*; as also ↓ عَزَرَهُ, inf. n. as above: (K,* TA:) and *he strengthened him*; (K,* TA;) and so ↓ عَزَرَهُ, inf. n. as above. (TA.) *He aided him against his enemy*, or *enemies, by repelling the latter*; (O, TA;) as also ↓ عَزَرَهُ, aor. ـِ and ـُ, but the former is the more chaste, inf. n. as above: (O:) or *he did so time after time*: or *with the sword*. (O, TA.) — And *He treated him with reverence, veneration, respect*, or *honour*; (S, A, O, Msb, K;) and so ↓ عَزَرَهُ, aor. ـِ and ـُ, inf. n. as above. (O.) — Also *He abased him; rendered him abject, vile, despicable*, or *ignominious*: thus it has two contr. significations. (B, TA.) — And *He loaded him*, namely, an ass. (S.)

عَزْرَائِيلُ, as some write it, or, as others, عِزْرَائِيلُ, [*The Angel of Death*;] *a certain angel, well known*. (MF.)

عَيْزَارٌ *A species of trees*. (S, O, L, K.) = أَبُو العَيْزَارِ the surname of *A certain long-necked bird, which one always sees in shallow water*, (S, O, K,*) *called the* سَبَيْطَر: (S, O:) or it is *the* كُرْكِيّ [or *Numidian crane*]. (K.)

عزف

1. عَزَفَ عَنِ الشَّىْءِ, aor. ـِ and ـُ; inf. n. عَزْفٌ and عَزِيفٌ [or عُزُوفٌ?], *He turned away*, or *back, from the thing*: (Msb:) [or] عَزَفَتْ نَفْسِى عَنْهُ, aor. ـِ, (S, O, K) and ـُ, (S, O,) inf. n. عُزُوفٌ (S, O, K) and عَزْفٌ, and عُزْفٌ, which is a contraction of عُزُوفٌ, (TA, the last from a verse of Umeiyeh Ibn-Abee-'Áidh,) *My soul abstained from it, relinquished it*, or *forsook it*, (S, O, K, TA,) *after having been pleased with it*; (TA;) and *turned away*, or *back, from it*; (S, O, K, TA;) namely, a thing: (S, O:) or *became averse from it*. (IDrd, O, K,* TA.) = And عَزَفَ نَفْسَهُ عَنْ كَذَا *He withheld*, or *restrained, himself from such a thing*. (TA.) = عَزَفَ, (S, O, Msb,) aor. ـِ, (Msb,) inf. n. عَزْفٌ (S, O, Msb) and عَزِيفٌ, (Msb,) *He played with*, or *upon, the musical instruments called* مَعَازِف: (S, O, Msb:) and *he sang*: (S, O:) and عَزْفٌ signifies [particularly] the *beating* of tambourines; whence the saying in a trad., of 'Omar, مَرَّ بِعَزْفِ دُفٍّ [*He passed by the beating of a tambourine*], whereupon he said, "What is this?" and they said "A circumcision," and he was silent: and it signifies also *any playing*. (TA.) — And عَزَفَتِ الجِنُّ, (S,) aor. ـِ, (S, O, K,) inf. n. عَزِيفٌ (S) and عَزْفٌ, (TA,) *The jinn*, or *genii, uttered*, or *made, the sound termed* عَزِيف, expl. below. (S, O,* K.*) = And عَزَفَتِ القَوْسُ, inf. n. عَزْفٌ and عَزِيفٌ, *The bow* [*twanged*, or] *made a sound*. (AHn, TA.) = عَـزَفَ, aor. ـِ, (IAar, O, K,) inf. n. عَـزْفٌ, (TA,) *He* (a man, IAar, O) *continued occupied in eating and drinking*. (IAar, O, K.) = عَزَفَ said of a camel, *The head of his windpipe heaved* (نَزَتْ حَنْجَرَتُهُ) *on the occasion of death*: (Ibn-'Abbád, O, K:) app. a dial. var. of عَسَفَ [q. v.]. (TA.)

4. اعزف *He heard the* عَزِيف *of the sands*, (IAar, O, K, TA,) and *of the winds*, expl. below, voce عَزِيفٌ. (TA.)

6. تعازفوا *They recited, one to another, poems of the metre termed* رَجَز, [which are usually chanted,] *and satirized one another*: or *they vied, competed*, or *contended for superiority, one with another, in glorying*, or *boasting*, or *in glory*, or *excellence*. (TA.)

12. اِعْزَوْزَفَ لِلشَّرِّ *He prepared himself for evil*, or *mischief*. (Lh, TA.) [Perhaps a mistranscription; for اِعْزَوْرَفَ, q. v.]

عَزْفٌ: see عَزِيفٌ, in two places. — See also مَعَازِفُ. = [Freytag explains it as meaning also *A person from whom we are averse; whom we do not love*: from the Deewán of the Hudhalees.]

عَزْفٌ The *pigeons called* طُورَانِيَّة, (O, K,) i. e. *wild pigeons*; (S and TA in art. طور;) *which have a cooing cry*. (TA in the present art.)

عَزُوفٌ عَنْ أَمْرٍ *Abstaining from an affair*, (O, K,*) *relinquishing it*, or *forsaking it*, and *turning away*, or *back, from it*: or *averse from it*: (K:) [i. e.] عَزُوفٌ is syn. with ↓ عَازِفٌ, as also ↓ عَزُوفَةٌ [but in an intensive sense because of the affix ة], and ↓ عَزِيفٌ; all as epithets applied to a man. (Ham p. 675.) You say رَجُلٌ عَزُوفٌ عَنِ اللَّهْوِ *A man not desirous of play*, or *sport*. (TA.) And عَزُوفٌ عَنِ النِّسَآءِ *Not desirous of women*. (TA.) And عَزُوفٌ, alone, signifies One *hardly*, or *not at all, constant in true friendship*. (TA.)

عَزِيفٌ [mentioned above as an inf. n.] *A sounding*, or *an emission of sound*: (Msb:) [and particularly] the *low*, or *faint*, or *humming, sound of the jinn*, or *genii, that is heard by night in the deserts*; as also ↓ عَزْفٌ [which is likewise mentioned above as an inf. n.]: (O, K:) or *a sound heard in the night, like drumming*: or the *sound of the winds in the atmosphere, imagined by the people of the desert to be the sound of the jinn*. (TA.) ↓ عَزْفُ الرِّيَاحِ means *The sounds of the winds*; (S, O, K;) and عَزِيفُ الرِّيَاحِ means [the same; or both mean] *the confused and continued sound* [or *the rustling* or *murmuring*] *of the winds*. (TA.) And one says also عَزِيفُ الرَّعْدِ (S, O, K) *The confused and continued sound* [or *the rumbling*] *of the thunder*. (S.) And عَزِيفُ الرِّمَالِ (IAar, O, K) *The sound of the sands; a certain sound therein; but what it is* [or *what is its cause*] *is not known*: it is said to be [*the sound of*] *the falling of portions thereof, one upon another*. (TA.) = See also عَزُوفٌ.

عَزُوفَةٌ: see عَزُوفٌ.

عَزَّافٌ Clouds (سَحَابٌ) *in which is heard the* عَزِيف (i. e. *confused and continued sound* [or *rumbling*], S) *of thunder*. (S, O, K.*) And Rain *sounding*, or *sounding vehemently*; syn. مُجَلْجِلٌ. (TA.) And Sand *causing a sound* [*such as is termed* عَزِيف (q. v.)] *to be heard*; as also ↓ عَازِفٌ. (TA.)

عَازِفٌ: see عَزُوفٌ. = Also *Playing with*, or *upon, the musical instruments called* مَعَازِف: and *singing*. (S, O, K.) — [And, applied to a jinnee, *Uttering*, or *making, the sound termed* عَزِيف: pl., masc. and fem., عَوَازِفُ.] A poet says, in relation to the sound of the jinn,

* وَإِنِّى لَأَجْتَابُ الفَلَاةَ وَبَيْنَهَا *

* عَوَازِفُ جِنَّانٍ وَهَامٌ صَوَاخِدُ *

[*And verily I cross the waterless desert when amid it are nightly hummers of the jinn, and hooting owls*]. (TA.) — See also عَزَّافٌ.

مِعْزَفٌ and مِعْزَفَةٌ: see what follows.

مَعَازِفُ *Musical instruments*; (S, O, K;) *pulsatile instruments of music*; (Mgh, Msb;*) accord. to some of the lexicologists, (O,) *such as the lute and* [*mandoline called*] طُنْبُور (O, K, TA) *and the like of these* (O) *and the tambourine &c.*: (TA:) sing. ↓ عَزْفٌ, (Lth, Az, Mgh, O, Msb, K,) as is transmitted from the Arabs; (Lth, Az, Mgh, O, Msb;) the pl. being irreg., (Msb, TA,) like مَشَابِهُ and مَلَامِحُ, pls. of شَبَهٌ and لَمْحَةٌ; (TA;) or the sing. is ↓ مِعْزَفٌ and ↓ مِعْزَفَةٌ, (K,) which are applied to *a sort of musical instrument having many strings*; (Lth, O;) or the former of these signifies *a sort of* طُنْبُور *made by the people of El-Yemen*, (Mgh, Msb, TA,) *now called* قبوس; (TA;) or the *lute*. (Msb, TA.)

عزق

1. عَزَقَ الأَرْضَ, aor. ـِ, (S, O, Msb, K,) inf. n. عَزْقٌ, (S, O, Msb,) *He clave*, or *furrowed, the earth*, or *land, with the implement called* مِعْزَقَة (S, O, Msb, K) *and* مِعْزَق. (S, O, K.) — And *He dug the earth until the water came forth from it*. (TA.) — The verb is [said to be] used only in relation to the earth, or land. (S, O, Msb, K.) [But] لَا تَعْزِقُوا occurs in a trad. as meaning *Cut not ye* (لَا تَقْطَعُو). (TA.) — العَزْقُ metonymically used as meaning *The act of eating* is post-classical. (TA.)

2. عَزَّقْتُ القَوْمَ, inf. n. تَعْزِيقٌ, *I routed*, or *defeated, and slew, the people*, or *party*. (TA.)

4. اعزق *He worked with the* مِعْزَقَة [q. v.]. (TA.)

عَزْقٌ: see the next paragraph.

عُزُقٌ *Winnowers of wheat* (مُذَرُّوا حِنْطَةٍ) [originally مُفَرْبُوا, in the CK̇ (مُدْرُوا)]. (O, K̇, TA.) [See also what here follows.] —— And Men *evil in dispositions:* (O, K̇, TA:) sing. [app. in the former sense as well as in this] ▼ عَزِقٌ: (TA:) or this latter signifies, (K̇,) or signifies also, (TA,) like ▼ مُتَعَزِّقٌ, *difficult in disposition:* (K̇, TA:) or *hard, and niggardly, and difficult in disposition.* (Lth, TA.)

مِعْزَقٌ: see the next paragraph. —— Accord. to IAạr, The مَرّ, i. e. *handle, of the* [*implement called*] مِسْحَاة [q. v.]. (L, voce سِخِّينٌ.)

مِعْزَقَةٌ The *implement with which the earth,* or *land, is cloven,* or *furrowed;* (Ṣ, O, Mṣb, K̇;) [*a kind of hoe,*] *resembling the* قَدُوم, or *larger than this;* as also ▼ مِعْزَقٌ: (Ṣ, O, K̇:) accord. to IDrd, the *implement with which the earth,* or *land, is cloven,* or *furrowed;* whether it be *a* فَأْس [meaning *hoe*], or *a* مِسْحَاة [i. e. *spade*], or *a* سِكَّة [i. e. *ploughshare*]: and he says, it is *a* بِيلَة [from the Pers. بِيلَه meaning a *kind of mattock* or *hoe*] *which is curved* [*in its blade*]: and some say that it is [particularly] *a* فَأْس [i. e. *hoe*] *with two extremities to its* [*iron*] *head:* (TA:) [it is applied in the present day to *a kind of hoe with a broad blade:*] pl. مَعَازِقُ. (O, TA.) —— And, (K̇,) accord. to IAạr, (O,) The *forked,* or *pronged, implement with which wheat is winnowed.* (O, K̇; and L and TA voce حِفْرَاة.)

أَرْضٌ مَعْزُوقَةٌ *Land cloven,* or *furrowed,* (Ṣ, TA,) *with the* مِعْزَقَة, (Ṣ,) *for sowing,* or *cultivating.* (TA.)

مُتَعَزِّقٌ: see عَزِقٌ.

IF says that there is no word with ع and ز and ق that is of well-founded authority. (O.)

عزل

1. عَزَلَهُ, (Ṣ, O, Mṣb, K̇,) aor. ـِ, (Mṣb, K̇,) inf. n. عَزْلٌ, (Mṣb, TA,) *He put it,* or *set it, apart, away,* or *aside; removed it;* or *separated it;* (Ṣ, O, Mṣb, K̇;) i. e., a thing; عَنْ غَيْرِهِ [*from another thing,* or *from other things*]. (Mṣb.) —— And hence, *He removed, deposed,* or *displaced, him,* namely, an agent, or a deputy, *from his office,* or *exercise of authority.* (Mṣb.) Or عَزَلَهُ عَنِ العَمَلِ *He removed, deposed,* or *displaced, him* [*from the agency,* or *administration,* or *government*]. (Ṣ, O, TA.) And ▼ عَزَّلَهُ, (K̇, TA,) inf. n. تَعْزِيلٌ, (TA,) signifies the same as عَزَلَهُ. (K̇, TA.) [In like manner also اعزل is said by Freytag to signify *Semovit,* followed by عن, as on the authority of the K̇; in which I do not find it.] And عُزِلَ *He was,* or *became, removed, deposed,* or *displaced,* [from his office, &c.,] (Ṣ, O, Mṣb,) used as quasi-pass. of عَزَلَهُ; in which sense ▼ انعزل is [said to be] not used, because in it [i. e. عَزَلَهُ] no labour, or exertion, is implied. (Mṣb.) —— عَزَلَ said of the مُجَامِع means *Paulò ante emissionem,* [*penem suum*] *extraxit, et extra vulvam semen emisit.* (Az,* Mṣb, TA.*) You say, عَزَلَ عَنْهَا, (Ṣ, O, K̇,) the pronoun referring to the man's female slave, (Ṣ, O,) inf. n. عَزْلٌ, (Az, Mgh, O, TA,) [vaguely expl. as] meaning *He did not desire her* [*having*] *offspring;* as also ▼ اِعْتَزَلَهَا: (K̇:) the motive being that the woman might not conceive. (Az, TA.) —— عَزِلَ, aor. ـَ, (TA,) inf. n. عَزَلٌ, (Mgh,* TA,) *He* (a horse) *had his tail inclining to one side,* (Mgh, TA,) *by habit, not naturally:* (TA:) when it inclines to the right side, the Arabs deem it unlucky. (Z, TA.) [See also عَزَلٌ below.]

2: see the preceding paragraph.

5: see 8, in four places.

6. تعازلوا *They went apart, away,* or *aside; removed;* or *separated themselves; each from other,* or *one party from another.* (K̇, TA.)

7: see 1: and see also the paragraph here following, in two places.

8. اعتزلهُ and ▼ تعزّلهُ both signify the same, (Ṣ, O, TA,) i. e. *He went apart, away,* or *aside; removed;* or *separated himself; from him,* or *it:* (O, TA:) and so اعتزل عَنْهُ and ▼ تعزّل عنه: (TA:) or اِعْتَزَلْتُ النَّاسَ and ▼ تَعَزَّلْتُهُمْ *I went apart, away,* or *aside; removed;* or *separated myself; from men,* or *the people;* [*withdrew from association,* or *communion, with them; seceded from them;*] and *left, forsook,* or *quitted, them:* and both verbs are sometimes used intransitively: (Mṣb:) [i. e.] اعتزل and ▼ تعزّل [used alone sometimes] signify *he went apart, away,* or *aside;* &c.; as also ▼ انعزل: (K̇, TA: [the last omitted in this place in the CK̇; but mentioned afterwards, voce تعازلوا:]) and they said, انعزل ▼ عَنِ النَّاسِ meaning *he went apart,* or *aside, from men,* or *the people:* (Mṣb:) and one says, of a pastor, يَعْتَزِلُ بِمَاشِيَتِهِ وَيَرْعَاهَا بِمَعْزِلٍ ▼ مِنَ النَّاسِ [*He goes apart,* or *aside, with his cattle, and pastures them in a place remote,* or *separate, from men,* or *the people*]. (Ṣ, O.) وَإِنْ لَمْ تُؤْمِنُوا لِى فَاعْتَزِلُونِ, in the Ḳur [xliv. 20], means, accord. to Ibn-'Arafeh, [*And if ye believe me not,*] *leave me on equal terms, not being against me nor for me.* (O.) [And you say, اعتزلهُ إِلَى غَيْرِهِ *He withdrew himself from him to another:* see Ḥar p. 245.] And اِعْتَزَلَهَا, expl. above, as syn. with عَزَلَ عَنْهَا: see 1. And يَعْتَزِلُ الحَرْبَ [*He withholds himself,* or *keeps aloof, from war,* or *battle*]: said of him who has no weapon. (TA.)

عَزْلٌ *What is brought to the treasury of the state in advance, not weighed, nor picked so as to have the bad put forth from it, to the time of the falling-due of the instalment:* (O, K̇, TA:) [for the second of the last three words of the explanation, which are correctly إِلَى مَحِلِّ النَّجْمِ, the O has مَحَلّ; the CK̇, مَحَلّ; and my MS. copy of the K̇, محل, without any vowel-sign and without the sheddeh:] from Ibn-'Abbád; (O;) and thus in the L. (TA.)

عُزْلٌ: see the next paragraph.

عَزَلٌ inf. n. of عَزِلَ [q. v.]. (TA.) —— Also The *state,* or *condition, of not having with one any weapon;* and so ▼ عُزْلٌ: (K̇, TA: [the latter, by reason of an ambiguity in the K̇, misunderstood by Freytag as syn. with عَزَالٌ in the sense in which this is expl. in the CK̇:]) they are two dial. vars., like شَغَلٌ and شُغْلٌ, and بَخَلٌ and بُخْلٌ. (TA.) —— And *A deficiency in one of the* حَرْقَفَتَانِ [app. meaning, *in the crest of one of the two hip-bones*]. (IAạr, O, K̇.) —— And The *hinder part* of an ass: so in the saying, اِقْرَعْ عَزَلَ حِمَارِكَ [*Strike thou the hinder part of thy ass*]: (O, K̇:) said to the driver of the ass. (O.)

عُزُلٌ: see أَعْزَلُ, in three places.

عُزْلَةٌ a subst. (Ṣ, Mṣb) signifying *A going apart, away,* or *aside; removal,* or *separation of oneself;* (Ṣ,* L, Mṣb,* K̇;) [*a withdrawing of oneself from association* or *communion;* or *secession:* and it seems to be sometimes used in a sense similar to that of اِعْتِكَاف; for] one says, العُزْلَةُ عِبَادَةٌ [app. meaning *Retirement,* or *self-seclusion, is a mode of religious service*]. (Ṣ, L, TA.)

العَزْلَةُ *The* حَرْقَفَة [app. meaning the *crest of the hip-bone*]. (K̇.)

عَزْلَآءُ [originally fem. of أَعْزَلُ; a subst. signifying] The *lower mouth* [or *spout* or *outlet*] *of the* [*leathern water-bag called*] مَزَادَة; (Ṣ, Mgh, O, Mṣb;) the *part where the water pours forth from the* رَاوِيَة [a word here, as in many other instances, used as syn. with مَزَادَة,] *and the like of this,* (K̇, TA,) *such* [*for instance*] *as the* قِرْبَة, *in the bottom thereof, where the water contained in it is drawn forth:* Kh says that *to every* مزادة *there are* عَزْلَاوَانِ [dual of عَزْلَآءُ], *in the bottom thereof:* but it is said in the M that *the* عزلاء *is thus called because it is in one of the* خُصْمَانِ [meaning the *two lower corners*] *of the* مزادة; not in its middle; nor is it like its mouth, in which it receives the water: (TA:) [the mouth, by means of which this kind of water-bag is filled, is in the middle of the upper edge; and the عزلاء, in every instance that I remember to have seen, is in the hinder of the two lower corners, and is tied round with a thong: (see مَزَادَة in art. زيد:)] the pl. is عَزَالٍ (Ṣ, Mgh, O, Mṣb, K̇,* written with the article العَزَالِى, and in the K̇ [improperly] عَزَالِى without the article,) and عَزَالَى also (Ṣ, O, Mṣb, K̇) is allowable; (Ṣ, O;) and ▼ العَزَائِلُ occurs in a trad. for العَزَالِى; these two words being like الشَّاكِى and الشَّائِكُ. (TA.) —— [Hence,] El-Kumeyt says, [describing clouds (سَحَاب),]

• مَرَتْهُ الجَنُوبُ فَلَمَّا اكْفَهَرّ •
• رَ حَلَّتْ عَزَالِيَهُ الشَّمْأَلُ •

† [*The south wind drew them forth; and when they became black and dense and accumulated, the north wind loosed their spouts;* i. e. caused the rain to pour forth]. (Ṣ, O.) And one says of a cloud (سَحَابَة), (Mgh, TA,) when it discharges

its pouring [rain], (Mgh,) or when it pours forth copious rain, (TA,) أَرْخَتْ عَزَالِيَهَا ‡ [*It loosed its spouts*], (Mgh,) or قَدْ حَلَّتْ عَزَالِيَهَا [*it has loosed its spouts*], and أَرْسَلَتْ عَزَالِيَهَا, (TA,) which [means the same and] is said [also] of the sky (السَّمَآء) by way of indicating the vehement falling of the rain, this being likened to its descent from the mouths [meaning spouts] of the مَزَادَة [or rather of the مَزَاد or مَزَايِد]. (Mṣb.) — And [hence also,] العَزْلَآءُ signifies † *The* اِسْت [i. e. the *anus;* as being an outlet; and as being closed by means of a sphincter, like as the عزلآء properly thus termed is closed by means of a thong tied round it]. (O, Ḳ.)

عُزْلَانٌ is a word used by the vulgar in the sense of عَزْلٌ [app. as inf. n. of عَزَلَهُ, q. v.]. (TA.)

عِزَالٌ *Weakness;* syn. ضَعْفٌ. (L, Ḳ, TA: in the CḲ ضَعِيف.) ═ It is also a vulgar term for The *goods,* or *furniture and utensils, of the house* or *tent.* (TA.)

العَزَالَانِ [a dual of which the sing. is not mentioned] *The two feathers that are at the extremity of the tail of the eagle:* (Ibn-'Abbád, O, Ḳ:) pl. أَعْزِلَةٌ. (Ibn-'Abbád, O.)

العَزَالِى, for العَزَالِى: see عَزْلَآء.

المُعْتَزِلَةُ: see العَزَّالُ.

أَعْزَلُ Sand (رَمْل) *separate,* or *cut off,* (IAạr, O, Ḳ,) *from other sands.* (IAạr, O.) — Also A man *not having with him any weapon;* (Ṣ, O, Ḳ;) as also ↓ عُزُلٌ, (O, Ḳ,) occurring in a trad.; (O;) and ↓ مِعْزَالٌ, (Ḳ,) or this signifies *not having with him a spear;* (Ṣ,* Ḳ;) and the first is sometimes expl. as having this particular meaning: (TA:) pl. of the first, (Ṣ, O, Ḳ,) and of ↓ عُزُلٌ, (Ḳ, TA,) عُزْلٌ and عُزْلَانٌ and عُزَّلٌ, (Ṣ, O, Ḳ,) which is anomalous, but made to accord with حُسَّرٌ, pl. of the epithet حَاسِرٌ, because nearly like it in meaning, (R, MF,) and أَعْزَالٌ, (Ḳ,) or or this is pl. of ↓ عُزُلٌ, (O, TA,) and مَعَازِيلُ, (IJ, Ḳ,) which is anomalous, (TA,) and this is pl. of ↓ مِعْزَالٌ (Ṣ, O, Ḳ) also. (Ḳ.) Hence, the epithet الأَعْزَلُ is applied to one of the سِمَاكَانِ, (Ṣ, O, Ḳ, TA,) i. e., to one of the two stars of which each is called السِّمَاكُ [q. v.]; (TA;) because, unlike [the other سماك, i. e.] الرَّامِح, it has no star [near] before it that is regarded as its weapon; (Ṣ,* O,* Ḳ,* TA;) or because in the days of its rising [aurorally] there is no cold nor wind. (O, Ḳ.) — And A bird *that cannot fly.* (MF, TA.) — And Clouds (سَحَاب) *in which is no rain.* (Ṣ, O, Ḳ.) — And A horse *having his tail inclining to one side,* (Ṣ, Mgh, O, Ḳ,) *by habit,* (Ṣ, O, Ḳ,) *not naturally.* (Ṣ, O.) [See عَزِلَ.] Hence the saying, أَعُوذُ بِٱللّٰهِ مِنَ الأَعْزَلِ عَلَى الأَعْزَلِ i. e. [*I seek protection by God*] *from a* [or *the*] *man having with him no weapon, upon a* [or *the*] *horse of which the* عَسِيب [or *bone of the tail,* or *part of the tail where the hair grows,*] *is crooked.* (TA.) — And [app. as an epithet applied to an ass or the like,] *Deficient in one of the* حَرْقَفَتَانِ [which seems here to mean, *in the crest of one of the two hip-bones*]. (IAạr, O, Ḳ.) — And The *share,* of flesh-meat, *of an absent man:* (IAạr, O, Ḳ:*) pl. عُزْلٌ. (IAạr, O.)

مَعْزِلٌ *A place of removal,* or *separation of oneself:* so in the saying, كُنْتُ بِمَعْزِلٍ عَنْ كَذَا وَكَذَا [*I was in a place,* and hence *in a state, of removal,* or *separation, of myself, from such and such things; I was aloof therefrom*]. (TA.) See 8. وَكَانَ فِى مَعْزِلٍ, in the Ḳur [xi. 44], means *And he was aloof* from the ship [i. e. the ark], or from the religion of his father. (O, TA.) And one says, أَنَا عَنْ هٰذَا الأَمْرِ بِمَعْزِلٍ [*I am aloof from this affair*]. (Ṣ, O.) And فُلَانٌ عَنِ الحَقِّ بِمَعْزِلٍ *Such a one is aloof from the truth.* (Mṣb.)

مِعْزَالٌ A pastor *who goes apart,* or *aside, with his cattle, and pastures them in a place remote,* or *separate, from men,* or *the people:* (Ṣ, O:) or a pastor *apart from others* (Ḳ, TA) *with his camels depasturing the herbage not previously pastured upon and seeking successively the places where rain had fallen:* in this sense not an epithet of discommendation, for the doing thus is an act of the courageous and valiant of men: (TA:) pl. مَعَازِيلُ. (Ṣ.) — And One *who alights apart,* or *aloof, from the company of travellers;* (Ḳ, TA; [مِنَ السَّفْرِ in the CḲ should be من السَّفْرِ;]) *who alights by himself;* in which sense it is an epithet of discommendation. (TA.) — And One *who separates himself from the players at the game called* المَيْسِر, *by reason of meanness.* (Ṣ, O, Ḳ.) — And One *who is alone in his opinion, having no one to share with him in it.* (TA.) — See also أَعْزَلُ in two places. — Also *Weak and stupid.* (Ṣ, O, Ḳ.)

مَعْزُولٌ [pass. part. n. of عَزَلَهُ; *Put,* or *set, apart, away,* or *aside;* &c.]. إِنَّهُمْ عَنِ السَّمْعِ لَمَعْزُولُونَ, in the Ḳur [xxvi. 212], means *Verily they are debarred,* or *precluded, from hearing* [the speech of the angels]. (TA.)

المُعْتَزِلَةُ *A sect of the* قَدَرِيَّة [q. v.], *who asserted that they seceded from what were in their estimation the two parties of error, the people of the* سُنَّة *and* خَوَارِج: (O, Ḳ:) [*therefore they were thus called,* i. e. *the Seceders:*] or *they were thus called by El-Ḥasan* (Ḳ, TA) *Ibn-Yesár El-Baṣree* (TA) *when Wáṣil Ibn-'Aṭà and his companions withdrew from him to one of the columns of the mosque,* [agreeably with a common practice of lecturers in a mosque, each of them seating himself on the ground at the foot of a column, while his hearers, with him, seated also on the ground, form a ring,] *and he* (i. e. Wáṣil, TA) *began to establish the dictum of the condition between the two conditions, that the committer of a great sin is not a believer absolutely* (Ḳ, TA) *nor an unbeliever absolutely* (Ḳ, TA, but not in the CḲ,) *but between the two conditions:* (Ḳ, TA:) and they are also called ↓ العَزَّالُ. (TA.)

عزم

1. عَزَمَ عَلَيْهِ, (Ṣ, Mṣb, Ḳ,) aor. ـِ, (Mṣb, Ḳ,) inf. n. عَزْمٌ (Ṣ, Mṣb, Ḳ) and عُزْمٌ (Ṣ, Ḳ) and عَزْمَةٌ (TA) and عُزْمَانٌ (Ḳ) and عَزِيمَةٌ and عَزِيمٌ (Ṣ, Ḳ) and مَعْزَمٌ and مَعْزِمٌ; (Ḳ;) and عَزْمَةٌ; (Mṣb, Ḳ;) both signify the same; (IB, TA;) and ↓ اعتزم عَلَيْهِ, (Ṣ, Ḳ,) and ↓ اعتزمهُ; and ↓ تعزّم [app. تعزّم عليه, but accord. to the TḲ تعزّمهُ]; (Ḳ;) [*He determined, resolved,* or *decided, upon it,* or *upon doing it,* namely, an affair;] *he desired to do it, and decided,* or *determined, upon it;* (Ṣ, Ḳ;) *he settled,* or *determined, his heart,* or *mind, firmly* (عَقَدَ ضَمِيرَهُ) *upon doing it:* (Mṣb:) or *he strove, laboured,* or *toiled, in it,* namely, an affair; or *exerted himself* or *his power* or *efforts* or *endeavours* or *ability therein:* (Ḳ:) or so عَزَمَ: (TA:) or عَزَمَ, inf. n. عَزِيمَةٌ and عَزْمَةٌ, signifies also *he strove,* &c., *in his affair:* (Mṣb:) and عَزَمَ الأَمْرَ signifies *he made the affair to have,* or *take, effect;* and *settled it firmly:* (Ḥar p. 3:) or, accord. to Ḳṭr, *he so settled it,* and *confirmed it.* (Id. p. 105.) [See also عَزْمٌ and عَزِيمَةٌ, below.] وَلَمْ نَجِدْ لَهُ عَزْمًا, in the Ḳur [xx. 114], means [*And we found him not to have*] *a quality of deciding an affair.* (Ṣ.) [قَدْ أَحْزِمُ لَوْ أَعْزِمُ, a prov.: see expl. in art. حزم.] — One says also, عَزَمَ الأَمْرُ, meaning عُزِمَ عَلَيْهِ: (Ḳ, TA:) and hence, in the Ḳur [xlvii. 23], فَإِذَا عَزَمَ الأَمْرُ [*And when the affair is determined upon*]: or the meaning may be, فَإِذَا عَزَمَ أَرْبَابُ الأَمْرِ [*and when the disposers of the affair determine* upon it]: but accord. to Zj, the meaning is, *and when the affair is serious,* or *earnest,* and the command to engage in fight becomes obligatory. (TA.) — عَزَمَ عَلَى الرَّجُلِ means *He conjured the man:* (Ṣ,* Ḳ, TA:) or *he commanded him,* or *enjoined him, earnestly:* لَيَفْعَلَنَّ كَذَا [*that he should surely do such a thing*]: (TA:) or عَزَمْتُ عَلَيْكَ means *I make thy informing me to be a decided thing in which there shall be no exception:* and one says also, عَزَمْتُ عَلَيْكَ إِلَّا فَعَلْتَ and لَمَّا فَعَلْتَ [virtually meaning *I conjure thee to do* such a thing]; as though one said, By Allah, *I demand not of thee* [aught] *save* [*thy doing*] this: so says Mṭr, referring to "the Book" of Sb. (Ḥar pp. 21 and 22. [But لَا is there, inadvertently, put for إِلَّا.]) — And one says, عَزَمَ الرَّاقِى *The charmer recited* عَزَائِم, meaning *charms,* or *spells,* [for the cure of a disease, &c.;] (Ḳ, TA;) as though he conjured the disease [&c.]: and in like manner, عَزَمَ الحَوَّآءُ [*The serpent-charmer recited charms,* or *spells,*] is said when he draws forth the serpent; as though he conjured it. (TA.) [See an ex. voce دَادَ, in art. دود.] — Hence, عَزَمَ is used in the present day as meaning *He invited to an entertainment.* — And Freytag mentions its occurring often in the book entitled بغية المستفيد فى مدينة زبيد as signifying *He went,* or *tended,*

to, or towards, (إِلَى,) some place: but this signification is probably post-classical: it is correctly expressed by 8, q. v.]

5: see the preceding paragraph, first sentence.

8: see 1, first sentence, in two places. — اعتزم signifies also *He* (a man, Ḳ) *kept to the course,* or *right course,* (القَصْد,) (Ṣ, Ḳ,) in a thing, (Ṣ,) in running, and walking, &c. (Ḳ.) And اعتزم الطَّرِيقَ *He went along upon the road without turning aside.* (TA.) — Also *He tended, repaired,* or *betook himself,* to, or towards, him, or it, either *in a direct course,* or *indirectly.* (IJ; M and L in art. قصد.) — And اعتزم, (Ḳ, TA,) or اعتزم فِى عِنَانِهِ, (Ḥar p. 3,) said of a horse, *He went along overcoming his rider,* (Ḳ, TA, Ḥar,) *in his running, not complying with the desire of his rider when he pulled him in,* (TA,) [and] *not turning aside.* (Ḥar.) — And اعتزم لَهُ *He bore it, and endured it with patience;* or *he bore,* and *was patient, with him.* (TA.)

عَزْمٌ an inf. n. of 1. (Ṣ, Mṣb, Ḳ, &c.) [Hence,] أُولُو العَزْمِ مِنَ الرُّسُلِ, (Ḳ, &c.,) mentioned in the Ḳur [xlvi. 34], (TA,) *Those, of the apostles, who determined upon doing what God had enjoined them:* or they were *Noah and Abraham and Moses and Moḥammad;* (Ḳ, TA;) to which several add *and Jesus:* (TA:) or *those, of the apostles, who were endowed with earnestness and constancy and patience:* (Ksh, Ḳ, TA:) عَزْمٌ in the dial. of Hudheyl meaning *patience;* as in their saying, مَا لِى عَنْكَ عَزْمٌ [*I have not patience of separation from thee*]: (TA:) or, (Ḳ,) it is said, (Ksh,) they were *Noah and Abraham and Isaac and Jacob and Joseph and Job and Moses and David and Jesus:* (Ksh, Ḳ:) or *Noah and Hood and Abraham and Moḥammad:* thus accord. to Aboo-Is-ḥáḳ. (Yoo, R, TA.) — See also عَزِيمَةٌ, in three places. — عَزْمٌ is expl. by Lth as meaning *An affair upon the doing of which one's heart, or mind, is firmly settled* or *determined.* (TA.) = Also The *dregs of pressed raisins:* pl. عُزُمٌ. (Ḳ.)

أُمُّ العِزْمِ, (Ḳ,) or أُمُّ عِزْمٍ, (T in art. ام,) and ▼ عِزْمَةٌ, and ▼ أُمُّ عِزْمَةَ, (Ḳ,) and ▼ العَزُومُ, (TA,) *The* اِسْت [i. e. *anus,* or *podex,* app. the former]. (Ḳ, TA.)

عَزْمَةٌ is an inf. n. of 1, meaning *A striving, labouring,* or *toiling, in an affair;* (Mṣb, TA;) and *strength.* (TA.) — And one says, مَا لَهُ عَزْمَةٌ وَلَا عَزِيمَةٌ ▼, meaning *He has not* [*determination,* or *resolution,* or] *a deliberate way of acting* or *proceeding, nor patience, in that upon which he determines,* or *resolves,* or *decides:* (Ḥam p. 31:) or مَا لِفُلَانٍ عَزِيمَةٌ ▼ means *Such a one will not keep constantly, firmly,* or *steadily,* [or rather *has not the quality of keeping constantly,* &c.], *to an affair upon which he determines.* (TA.) — See also عَزِيمَةٌ. — عَزْمَةٌ مِنْ عَزَمَاتِ ٱللّٰهِ, (Ḳ, TA,) such, in a trad., the poor-rate is said to be, (TA,) means *A due of the dues of God;* i. e. [in the CḲ "or"] *a thing that is obligatory, of the things that God has made obligatory.* (Ḳ, TA.)

عِزْمَةٌ A man's أُسْرَة [or *near kinsmen;* or his *near kinsmen on the father's side*]: and his قَبِيلَة [or *tribe*]: pl. عِزَمٌ. (Ḳ.)

عِزْمَةٌ, and أُمُّ عِزْمَةَ: see أُمُّ العِزْمِ, above.

عَزَمَةٌ a pl. of عَازِمٌ [q. v.]. (TA.)

عَزْمِىٌّ A man *who fulfils his promise;* (Ḳ, TA;) *who, when he promises a thing, performs it,* and *fulfils it.* (TA.) = And *A seller of* عُزْم, meaning *dregs of pressed raisins.* (Ḳ.)

عَزُومٌ [*Determined,* or *resolute;*] *one who perseveres in his determination until he attains that which he seeks,* or *desires.* (Ḥam p. 532.) — See also عَوْزَمٌ, in two places. — And see أُمُّ العِزْمِ.

عَزِيمٌ *A vehement running.* (Ḳ, TA. [In the CḲ, العَدُوُّ is erroneously put for العَدْوُ.]) Rabeeạ Ibn-Maḳroom Ed-Ḍabbee says,

لَوْلَا أُكَفْكِفُهُ لَكَادَ إِذَا جَرَى
مِنْهُ العَزِيمُ يَدُقُّ فَأْسَ المِسْحَلِ

[*If I did not restrain him, when he runs, his vehement running would almost break the piece of iron that stands up in the mouth from the middle of the bit-mouth:* see مِسْحَل.] (TA.)

عَزِيمَةٌ an inf. n. of عَزَمَ in the sense first expl. above. (Ṣ, Ḳ.) [As a simple subst., it signifies *Determination, resolution, decision,* or *fixed purpose of the mind;* as also ▼ عَزْمٌ and ▼ عَزْمَةٌ: or] the *disposition and subjection of the mind to the wish,* or *thing desired:* (Ḥam p. 336:) or it is a subst. [signifying the *making an affair to have,* or *take, effect;* and *settling it firmly;*] from عَزَمَ الأَمْرَ meaning أَمْضَاهُ and أَحْكَمَهُ: or, as in the Mj, the *settling,* or *determining, the heart,* or *mind, firmly upon the thing that one desires to do;* as also ▼ عَزْمٌ: or, accord. to El-Ghooree, ▼ عَزْمٌ signifies the *preceding desire to dispose and subject the mind to the act.* (Ḥar p. 3.) [The pl., in all the senses, is عَزَائِمُ. Hence,] اِشْتَدَّتِ العَزَائِمُ means *The determinations* (عَزَمَات) *of the commanders in the hostile and plundering expedition to distant parts, and their taking to them, became strong.* (TA. [Probably from a trad.]) — See also عَزْمَةٌ, in two places. — عَزَائِمُ ٱللّٰهِ means *The obligatory statutes* or *ordinances of God:* (Mgh, Mṣb, Ḳ, TA:) sing. عَزِيمَةٌ. (Mṣb.) — And, accord. to Er-Rághib, عَزِيمَةٌ signifies *A charming;* syn. تَعْوِيذٌ; as though thou imaginedst thy having imposed an obligation [thereby] upon the devil, lest [for اى in my original I read أَنْ as meaning لِئَلَّا] he should execute his desire upon thee: pl. عَزَائِمُ: (TA:) or عَزَائِمُ signifies *charms,* or *spells,* (Ṣ, Ḳ,) *that are recited* [*for the cure of diseases,* &c.]: or *certain verses of the Ḳur-án that are recited over persons affected with diseases,* or *the like, in the hope of cure:* (Ḳ, TA:) these are termed عَزَائِمُ القُرْآنِ: but عَزَائِمُ الرُّقَى are *those* [*charms,* or *spells,*] *by which one conjures the jinn,* or *genii, and spirits.* (TA.) — عَزَائِمُ السُّجُودِ is an appellation of *Certain portions of the Ḳur-án,* which are الٓمٓ تَنْزِيلُ [*chap.* xxxii.] *and* حٰمٓ السَّجْدَةُ [*chap.* xli.] *and* النَّجْمُ [*chap.* liii.] *and* اِقْرَأْ بِاسْمِ رَبِّكَ [*chap.* xcvi.]; (Mgh;) [thus called because] they are *those in* [*the reciting of*] *which one is commanded to prostrate himself.* (Mṣb.)

العَزَّامُ *The lion;* as also ▼ المُعْتَزِمُ. (Ḳ.)

عَازِمٌ sing. of عَزَمَةٌ, (TA,) which signifies [*Such as act with determination, resolution,* or *decision.* And particularly] *Such as are sound,* or *true, in love,* or *affection.* (Ḳ, TA.) — [And sing. of عَوَازِمُ applied to affairs.] خَيْرُ الأُمُورِ عَوَازِمُهَا means *The best of affairs are those in which is determination, resolution,* or *decision:* or *upon which one has confirmed his determination, and in which one has fulfilled what God has enjoined.* (TA.)

عَوْزَمٌ A she-camel *advanced in age,* (Aṣ, Ṣ, Ḳ, TA,) and so عَوْزَمَةٌ as expl. by IAạr, (TA,) *but having somewhat remaining of youthful vigour;* (Aṣ, Ṣ, Ḳ, TA;) as also ▼ عَزُومٌ; (Ḳ, TA;) of which the pl. is عُزُمٌ: (TA:) or one *whose teeth have been eroded by old age:* or one *extremely aged, such as is termed* دِلْقِمٌ: [but see دَلُوقٌ:] the pl. is عَوَازِمُ. (TA.) — And † *An old woman;* (Ṣ, Ḳ;) as also ▼ عَزُومٌ. (Ḳ.) — And *Short,* as an epithet applied to a woman. (Ḳ,* TA.)

مُعَزِّمٌ *Charming,* or *a charmer,* (Ḳ, TA,) *by means of spells.* (TA.)

المُعْتَزِمُ: see العَزَّامُ.

عزو

1. عَزَاهُ إِلَى أَبِيهِ, (Ṣ,* Mṣb,* Ḳ,) first pers. عَزَوْتُهُ, (Ṣ, Mṣb,) aor. ـُ, (Ṣ, Mṣb, and Ḳ in art. عزى,) inf. n. عَزْوٌ, (TA,) *He asserted his relationship* [*of son*] *to his father:* (Ṣ, Mṣb, Ḳ:) [you say, عَزَاهُ إِلَى فُلَانٍ *He asserted his* (another's) *relationship as son to such a one:*] and so عَزَاهُ إِلَيْهِ, (Ṣ,* Mṣb, O,* and Ḳ in art. عزى,) first pers. عَزَيْتُهُ, (Ṣ, Mṣb,) aor. ـِ, (Ṣ, Mṣb, Ḳ,) inf. n. عَزْىٌ; (TḲ;) this latter verb being a dial. var. of the former. (Ṣ, Mṣb.) [And the latter verb has a similar signification expl. in art. عزى.] — And عَزَا إِلَى أَبِيهِ and لَهُ, intrans.: see 8. = See also the first sentence in art. عزى.

5: see the next paragraph, in two places.

8. اعتزى إِلَيْهِ (Ṣ, Mgh,* Mṣb, Ḳ) and لَهُ (Ḳ) *He asserted his* [*own*] *relationship* [*of son*] *to him:* (Ṣ, Mgh,* Mṣb, Ḳ:) [you say, اعتزى إِلَى فُلَانٍ and لِفُلَانٍ *He asserted his relationship of son to such a one:*] and so ▼ تعزّى, (Ṣ, Mgh, Mṣb, Ḳ,) and ▼ عَزَا. (Ḳ.) It is said in a trad., ▼ مَنْ تَعَزَّى بِعَزَآءِ ▼ الجَاهِلِيَّةِ فَأَعِضُّوهُ بِهَنِ أَبِيهِ وَلَا تَكْنُوا [expl. in art. عض: see 4 in that art.]. (Ṣ, Mgh, Mṣb.) See also art. عزى.

عِزَةٌ *A party of men* (Ṣ, Mṣb, Ḳ) *such as is termed* عُصْبَةٌ [i. e., as expl. in the O in art. عصب, *who league together to defend one another*], (Ḳ, TA,) *above*, or *exceeding*, [*such as compose*] *a* حَلْقَة: (TA:) or, accord. to Er-Rághib, *a company of men who assert their relationship, one to another*, either *by birth* or *by the leaguing together for mutual aid:* (TA:) [for] the ة is a substitute for the final radical letter which is و: (Mṣb:) or, as some say, it is from عَزَى signifying "he was, or became, patient;" as though they were a company who took patience by one another's example: (TA:) [for, accord. to J,] the ة is a substitute for ى: (Ṣ:) the pl. is عِزُونَ (Ṣ, Mṣb, Ḳ) and عُزُونَ and عِزًى, but they did not say عِزَاتٌ: (Ṣ:) hence عِزِينَ in the Ḳur lxx. 37, (Ṣ, TA,) [expl. as] meaning *companies in a state of dispersion:* (TA:) or *separate*, or *sundry, parties:* pl. of عِزَةٌ, which is [said to be] originally عِزْوَةٌ, from [the inf. n.] العَزْوُ: as though each party asserted their relationship [as sons] to other than those to whom the other party asserted their relationship: (Ksh, Bḍ:) عِزُونَ is expl. by Eṭ-Ṭarasoosee as meaning *companies coming in a state of dispersion*. (Mṣb.) One says, فِى الدَّارِ عِزُونَ, meaning [*In the house*, or *abode, are*] *several sorts of men*. (Aṣ, Ṣ.)

عِزْوَةٌ: see عَزَآءٌ, below, in two places: —— and also in art. عزى.

عَزْوَى, which is of the dial. of the tribe of Mahrah Ibn-Ḥeydán, but disapproved, (IDrd, TA,) is a word expressive of desire for one's becoming favourably inclined; [as though meaning *Mercy on me!* or *I cry mercy;*] and so ↓ تَعْزَى: (Ḳ, TA:) or a word expressive of the being, or becoming, favourably inclined; [as though meaning *Mercy on thee!*] and so ↓ يَعْزَى, (IDrd, TA,) which is of the dial. of the people of Esh-Shiḥr, a bad word: (TA in art. عزى:) يَعْزَى ↓ مَا كَانَ كَذَا, (Ḳ and TA in that art., in the CḲ يُعْزَى,) a saying of that people, (TA,) [app. meaning *Mercy on thee!* (or the like) *it was not thus*, or *such a thing was not*,] is like the saying لَعَمْرِى لَقَدْ كَانَ كَذَا ["By my life," or "by my religion," &c.]. (Ḳ, TA.)

بَنُو عَزْوَانَ *A certain tribe of the Jinn*, or *Genii*. (ISd, Ḳ, TA.)

عَزَآءٌ a subst. [signifying The *assertion of relationship of son* to a particular person] from اِعْتَزَى or تَعَزَّى; (Ṣ, Mgh, TA; see an ex. above, voce اعتزى;) and so ↓ عِزْوَةٌ: (TA:) one says, إِنَّهُ لَحَسَنُ العِزْوَةِ ↓ and العِزْيَةِ also, meaning [*Verily he is good in respect of*] *the assertion of relationship* [*of son;* i. e. he asserts his relationship to a good father]. (Ḳ, TA.) —— See also art. عزى.

عزى

1. عَزِىَ, (Mṣb, Ḳ, and Ḥam p. 369,) aor. يَعْزَى, (Mṣb,) inf. n. عَزَآءٌ; (Ḳ;) and عَزَى, (Ḥam ubi suprà,) or عَزَا, inf. n. as above; (Ḥam p. 125;) *He was*, or *became, patient*, or *enduring*, (Mṣb, Ḳ, and Ḥam,) or *commendably so*, (Ḳ,) *of that which befell him*. (Mṣb.) —— عَزَاهُ إِلَى أَبِيهِ, first pers. عَزَيْتُهُ, aor. يَعْزِى, inf. n. عَزْىٌ: see 1 in art. عزو. —— [Hence,] عَزَيْتُ الحَدِيثَ, aor. أَعْزِيهِ, *I traced up*, or *ascribed*, or *attributed, the tradition* [إِلَى قَائِلِهِ *to the original relater thereof*]; syn. أَسْنَدْتُهُ. (Mṣb, TA.*)

2. عَزَّاهُ, inf. n. تَعْزِيَةٌ (Ṣ, Mṣb, Ḳ, TA) and تَعْزَآءٌ, (TA,) *He enjoined* [or *exhorted*] *him to be patient*, or *enduring*, (Ṣ,* Ḳ,* TA,) or *to have comely patience;* (Ḳ, TA;) i. q. أَسَّاهُ [q. v.]: (Ṣ, M, Ḳ, TA, all in art. اسو:) [and hence, *he consoled him;* often used in this sense:] or *he said to him*, أَحْسَنَ اللّٰهُ عَزَآءَكَ, meaning *May God grant thee comely patience*. (Mṣb.) [You say, عَزَّاهُ عَنْهُ *He enjoined*, or *exhorted, him to endure with patience the death of him;* or *the loss*, or *want, of it:* and hence, *he consoled him for the death of him;* in which sense, عَزَّاهُ فِيهِ is also now used.] —— See also عَزَآءٌ, below.

5. تعزّى *He took patience;* or *constrained himself to be patient*, or *enduring;* syn. تَصَبَّرَ, (Ṣ, Mṣb, TA,) and تَأَسَّى [q. v.]; (TA;) the sign of doing which is the saying, إِنَّا لِلّٰهِ وَإِنَّا إِلَيْهِ رَاجِعُونَ [Verily to God we belong, and verily unto Him we return]. (Mṣb.) It is said in a trad., [as some relate it,] مَنْ لَمْ يَتَعَزَّ بِعَزَآءِ اللّٰهِ فَلَيْسَ مِنَّا, expl. by some as meaning *Such as does not constrain himself to be patient* [*with the patience of God, he is not of us*]. (TA. [See another reading voce تَعَزَّزَ.]) And you say, تَعَزَّيْتُ عَنْهُ, meaning *I constrained myself to endure with patience the loss*, or *want, of him*, or *it:* [and hence, *I consoled myself for the loss*, or *want, of him*, or *it:* held by some to be] originally تَعَزَّزْتُ, meaning *I exerted my strength* or *energy* [*to divert myself from him, or it*]; like تَظَنَّيْتُ for تَظَنَّنْتُ. (TA in art. عز.) You say also تَعَزَّى بِهِ, meaning تَأَسَّى بِهِ [i. e. *He took patience*, or *constrained himself to be patient, by reflecting upon him*, or *it;* or *he took example by him*, or *became consoled by his example*, meaning the example of a person who had suffered in like manner and had been patient]. (Ṣ in art. اسو.)

6. تَعَازَوْا *They enjoined* [or *exhorted*] *one another to be patient*, or *enduring*, or *to have comely patience*. (Ḳ, TA.) [And hence, *They consoled one another*.]

8: see art. عزو; to which, as well as to the present art., this verb belongs. الاِعْتِزَآءُ [often] signifies الاِدِّعَآءُ وَالشِّعَارُ فِى الحَرْبِ [i. e. *The asserting one's relationship by saying "I am such a one the son of such a one;"* and *the call*, or *cry, by means of which to know one another; in war:* see 8 (last sentence but one) in art. دعو; and see also شِعَارٌ]. (Ḳ in this art.)

عَزٍ *Patient*, or *enduring;* or *having comely patience*. (Ḳ.)

عِزَةٌ, held by some to belong to this art.: see art. عزو.

عِزْيَةٌ: see عَزَآءٌ in art. عزو.

عَزَآءٌ *Patience*, or *endurance;* (Ṣ, Ḳ;) and عِزْوَةٌ signifies the same, as in the saying هُوَ حَسَنُ العِزْوَةِ [*He is comely in respect of patience or endurance*]: (Ḥam p. 369:) or *patient endurance of the loss of anything:* (TA:) or *comely patience* or *endurance;* (Ḳ, TA;) as also تَعْزُوَةٌ accord. to the copies of the Ḳ, but correctly ↓ تَعْزِيَةٌ [inf. n. of 2, as though for تَعْزِيَةُ النَّفْسِ i. e. *self-enjoinment*, or *self-exhortation, to be patient* or *enduring*, as is indicated by what follows]: an Arab of the desert, whose brother had slain a son of his, is cited by the author of the Ḥamáseh as saying, [on his brother's being brought to him that he might retaliate upon him, (see Ḥam p. 100,)]

* أَقُولُ لِلنَّفْسِ تَأْسَآءً وَتَعْزِيَةً *
* إِحْدَى يَدَىَّ أَصَابَتْنِى وَلَمْ تُرِدِ *

[*I say to the soul*, i. e. to myself, *enjoining patience and enjoining endurance, One of my two hands has smitten me, not desiring*, or *not meaning*, to do so]: (TA:) تَأْسَآءً is [syn. with تَأْسِيَةً, inf. n. of أَسَّى,] from الإِسْوَةُ: and التَّعْزِيَةُ [signifies as rendered above; or] is derived from العَزَازُ, i. e. "the hard ground," and means *the strengthening of the heart:* or it is from عَزَوْتُهُ إِلَى أَبِيهِ; because the afflicted remembers his ancestors who have gone before him; and he means, I enjoin the soul to endure his loss with patience, becoming consoled by the example of others whose sons have been slain. (Ḥam ubi suprà.) —— عَزَآءٌ is also a quasi-inf. n.; like عَطَآءٌ, meaning إِعْطَآءٌ, from أَعْطَى: (TA:) or a subst. [signifying *Enjoinment*, or *exhortation, to be patient:* and hence, *consolation:* and, as often used in the present day, the *state*, or *ceremony, of mourning, when relations and friends come to console the bereaved:*] from عَزَّيْتُهُ; like سَلَامٌ from سَلَّمَ, and كَلَامٌ from كَلَّمَ. (Mṣb.) —— See also art. عزو.

عَزِىٌّ *Very patient* or *enduring*. (Ḥam p. 125.)

تَعْزَى: see عَزْوَى, in art. عزو.

مَعْزًى [*A place of consoling;* and hence *a place of wailing for a dead person*, because relations and friends go thither to console the bereaved]. (A. [There used as an explicative adjunct to مَنَاحَة.])

يَعْزَى: see عَزْوَى (in art. عزو) in two places.

عس

1. عَسَّ, (Ṣ, A, O, Mṣb, Ḳ,) aor. يَعُسُّ, (Ṣ, A, O, Mṣb,) inf. n. عَسٌّ (Ṣ, O, Mṣb, Ḳ) and عَسَسٌ; (Ṣ, O, Ḳ;) and ↓ اعتسّ; (Ṣ, O, Ḳ;) *He went round-about, patrolled*, or *went the rounds, by night*, (Ṣ, A, O, Ḳ,) *to guard the people:* (TA:) *he made search by night after suspicious persons*, or *persons to be suspected*, (Ṣ, A, O, Mṣb, Ḳ,) *and investi-*

gated, or discovered, their opinions, or sentiments: (TA:) *he went to and fro;* syn. اِخْتَلَفَ. (Ḥam p. 320.) It is said in a prov., كَلْبٌ عَسَّ خَيْرٌ مِنْ كَلْبٍ رَبَضَ, (Ṣ, O,) or ↑ اِعْتَسَّ; (O, Ḳ;) or, as some relate it, عَاسٌّ, and رَابِضٍ; (TA;) [*A dog that has gone the rounds by night is better than a dog that has lain down; or a dog going the rounds* &c.;] said for the purpose of urging to make gain: meaning that he who occupies himself in business is better than he who lacks power or ability: (TA:) or, as some relate it, كَلْبٌ عَسَّ خَيْرٌ مِنْ أَسَدٍ اَنْدَسَّ [*a dog that has gone the rounds by night is better than a lion that has hidden himself*]; alluding to the superiority of the weak who occupies himself in making gain over the strong who holds back. (O, TA.) You also say of a wolf, (Ṣ, O, Ḳ,) and of any beast of prey, (TA,) ↑ عَسْعَسَ, meaning, *He went roundabout by night,* (Ṣ, O, Ḳ, TA,) *seeking for prey:* (TA:) and ↑ تَعَسْعَسَ *he* (a wolf, TA) *sought for prey* (Ṣ, O, Ḳ, TA) *by night:* (Ṣ, TA:) and ↑ اعتسّ *he* [a man] *sought, sought after,* or *sought to gain, sustenance:* (Ṣ, O, Ḳ:) and ↑ تَعَسْعَسَ *he* (a wolf, AA, Ṣ) *smelt* [app. *to find prey*]. (AA, Ṣ, O, Ḳ.*) — عَسَّ خَبَرُهُ, (Ṣ, L, Ḳ,) aor. ـُ, inf. n. عَسٌّ, (L, TA,) *His tidings were slow,* or *tardy.* (Ṣ, L, Ḳ, TA. [In the O, خَبِرُهُ.]) — عَسَّتْ, aor. ـُ, *She* (a camel) *yielded little milk, though her milk had collected in her udder since the next previous milking.* (TA.) — And عَسَّتْ, aor. ـُ, inf. n. عِسَاسٌ, *She* (a camel) *grumbled much on being milked.* (TA.) Hence, دَرَّتْ عِسَاسًا *She yielded her milk unwillingly.* (IDrd, O, Ḳ, TA.) — And عَسَّتْ, (Ṣ, O, Ḳ,) aor. ـُ, (Ṣ, O, TA,) inf. n. عَسٌّ, (TA,) *She* (a camel) *pastured alone.* (Ṣ, O, Ḳ.) — And عَسَّ عَلَىَّ بِخَيْرِهِ *He was parsimonious to me with his wealth.* (AA, TA.) — عَسَّهُ, (A,) aor. ـُ, (Ṣ, A,) inf. n. عَسٌّ; (A;) and ↑ اعتسّهُ; (Ṣ,* Ḳ,* TA;) *He sought,* or *sought for* or *after, him* [or *it*]: (Ṣ,* A, Ḳ:*) or the latter, *he sought,* or *sought for* or *after, it* (a thing) *by night.* (TA.) You say, ذَهَبَ يَعُسُّ صَاحِبَهُ *He went away seeking his companion.* (A.) And اِعْتَسَسْنَا ↑ الإِبِلَ فَمَا وَجَدْنَا عِسَاسًا ↑ وَلَا قِسَاسًا *We sought for the camels,* or *sought for them by night, and found not any trace.* (TA.) And فُلَانٌ يَعْتَسُّ ↑ الآثَارَ *Such a one traces footsteps.* (A.) And يعتسّ ↑ الفُجُورَ *He follows vice, immorality,* or *unrighteousness.* (A.) — عَسَّ القَوْمَ, (O, Ḳ,) aor. ـُ, inf. n. عَسٌّ, (TA,) *He fed the people,* or *party, with somewhat little in quantity.* (O, Ḳ, TA.)

8: see عَسَّ, in three places: — and عَسَّهُ, in four places. — You say also, اعتسّ بَلَدَ كَذَا *He trod such a country, and knew its tidings.* (TA.) — And اعتسّ النَّاقَةَ *He sought to obtain the she-camel's milk.* (TA.) — And اعتسّ الإِبِلَ *He entered into the midst of the camels, and stroked their udders in order that they might yield their milk.* (O, Ḳ.*)

R. Q. 1. عَسْعَسَ: see عَسَّ. — عَسْعَسَ اللَّيْلُ *The night came on:* (AO, IAạr, Mṣb:) or *came on with its darkness;* (TA;) *its darkness came on:* (IDrd, Ṣ, O, Ḳ:) or *departed:* (IDrd, O, Ḳ:) or it has this last meaning also; (AO, IAạr, Mṣb;) bearing two contr. significations: (Ḳṭr, AḤát, Mṣb:) or *was dark;* meaning, all the night: (IAạr:) Fr says that, in the Ḳur [lxxxi. 17], وَاللَّيْلِ إِذَا عَسْعَسَ, accord. to all the expositors, signifies *and by the night when it departeth:* but that some of his companions asserted the meaning to be *when its commencement approacheth, and it becometh dark:* like as you say عَسْعَسَ السَّحَابُ, (Ṣ, O,) which signifies *the clouds approached the earth:* (Fr, Ṣ, O, Ḳ:) or this is only said when it is *in the night, with darkness and lightning.* (Lth, O, TA.)

R. Q. 2. تَعَسْعَسَ: see عَسَّ, in two places.

جِئْ بِالمَالِ مِنْ عَسِّكَ وَبَسِّكَ (Ṣ, O, Ḳ) [*Bring thou the property*] *from where it is and where it is not:* (TA:) i. q. مِنْ حَسِّكَ وَبَسِّكَ: (Ṣ, O, Ḳ, TA:) which means thus: (TA in art. حس:) or *whence thou wilt:* (Ṣ, O, Ḳ, TA, ibid.:) or *from any,* or *every, quarter.* (TA ibid.)

عُسٌّ *A* [*drinking-cup* or *bowl, of the kind called*] قَدَح: (TA:) or *a large* قَدَح, (Ṣ, A, Mgh, O, L, Mṣb, Ḳ,) *from which two or three or more* [*men*] *may satisfy their thirst;* (L, TA;) *larger than the* غُمَر; (L, voce رِفْد;) though this is greater in height; (TA;) *and larger than the* قَعْب; (IAạr, in TA, voce قَعْب;) *but not so large as the* رِفْد: (Ṣ, O:) pl. عِسَاسٌ (Ṣ, A, Mgh, O, Mṣb, Ḳ) and عِسَسَةٌ (TA) and [pl. of pauc.] أَعْسَاسٌ. (IAth, Mṣb.) — Hence, one says, هُوَ لَكَ عَلَى ظَهْرِ العُسِّ, meaning † *It is apparent, manifest,* or *conspicuous, to thee.* (O in art. ظهر.) — And *The penis.* (O, Ḳ.)

عَسَسٌ: see عَاسٌّ.

عُسْعُسٌ *Slowness,* or *tardiness.* (TA.) — Also, [in the CḲ, erroneously, عُسْعَسٌ,] *Covetous merchants* or *traders:* (IAạr, O, Ḳ,* TA:) accord. to [some of] the copies of the Ḳ, it signifies حُرَصَاءُ and تُجَّارٌ; but the conjunction should be omitted. (TA.) — And *Large vessels.* (IAạr, O, Ḳ.)

عِسَاسٌ *A trace, footstep, vestige,* or *the like:* see 1, latter part. (TA.)

عَسُوسٌ *A seeker:* (TA:) [see عَاسٌّ:] or *a seeker,* or *pursuer, of prey,* or *game,* (Ṣ, O, Ḳ, TA,) *by night,* or *at any time;* applied to a wolf, or to any beast of prey: (TA:) or a wolf, or, as some say, any beast of prey, *that seeks much for prey by night;* as also ↑ عَسَّاسٌ and ↑ عَسْعَسٌ and ↑ عَسْعَاسٌ: (TA:) and hence, (Ṣ,) ↑ each of the last three, (Ṣ, O, Ḳ,) as well as the first, (Ḳ,) *a wolf:* (Ṣ, O, Ḳ:) and the first (عسوس), *a dog that pursues much, and will not eat.* (TA.) — Also *A she-camel that yields little milk:* (Ibn-'Abbád, O, Ḳ:) or *that will not yield her milk until she becomes remote from men:* (O, Ḳ:) and one *that, when she is roused to be milked, goes along awhile, then goes roundabout, and then yields her milk:* (O,* Ḳ,* TA:) and one *evil in disposition when milked,* (O, Ḳ, TA,) *that grumbles much,* (O, TA,) *and goes aside from the other camels:* (TA:) and one *that kicks the milker, and spills the milk:* (TA:) and one *whose udder is stroked to try if she have milk* or not. (O, Ḳ.) Also A she-camel *that pastures alone;* (AZ, Ṣ, O, Ḳ;) like قَسُوسٌ. (AZ, Ṣ, O.) And A she-camel *that seeks after bones, and eats the flesh upon them* تَرْتَمُّهَا [in the TḲ erroneously ترويها]. (Ibn-'Abbád, O, Ḳ.) — Also A woman *who does not care for,* or *mind, her approaching men:* (O, Ḳ:) or, accord. to Er-Rághib, *who ventures upon that which occasions suspicion,* or *evil opinion.* (TA.) — And A man *in whom is little,* or *no, good* or *goodness;* or *who does little good.* (O, Ḳ.) — And One who is *slow,* or *tardy.* (TA.)

عَسِيسٌ: see عَاسٌّ.

عَسَّاسٌ: } see عَسُوسٌ; each in two places.
عَسْعَسٌ: }

عَسْعَاسٌ: see عَسُوسٌ, in two places. — Also The سَرَاب [or *mirage*]. (O, Ḳ.)

عَسَاعِسُ *Hedge-hogs:* because of their often going to and fro by night. (Ṣ, O, Ḳ.)

عَاسٌّ *One who patrols,* or *goes the rounds, by night,* (Ṣ, A, O, Mṣb, Ḳ,) *for the Sultán,* (Mṣb,) *to guard the people:* (TA:) *who makes search by night after suspicious persons,* or *persons to be suspected,* (Ṣ, A, O, Ḳ,) *and investigates,* or *discovers, their opinions,* or *sentiments:* (TA:) and *any seeker* of a thing: (A:) used as a sing. and pl.: or it is a quasi-pl. n. also; being, without idghám, [i. e., in its original form, عَاسِسٌ,] like بَاقِرٌ and جَامِلٌ: (TA:) or the pl. is ↑ عَسَسٌ, (Ṣ,* A; O, Mṣb,* Ḳ,) or this is a quasi-pl. n., (TA,) and ↑ عَسِيسٌ, like حَجِيجٌ, (O, Ḳ,) [or this is also a quasi-pl. n.,] and عُسَّاسٌ and عَسَسَةٌ. (TA.) [See طَائِفٌ.]

مَعَسٌّ *A place where a thing is sought,* or *to be sought;* syn. مَطْلَبٌ. (Ṣ, O, Ḳ.) ISd cites, as an ex., from El-Akhṭal,

• مُعَفَّرَةٌ لَا يُنْكِهُ السَّيْفُ وَسْطَهَا •
• إِذَا لَمْ يَكُنْ فِيهَا مَعَسٌّ وَطَالِبُ •

[*Defiled with dust, the sword will not reach the middle of it if there be not in it a place where something is to be sought and a seeker*]. (TA.) You say also, هُوَ قَرِيبُ المَعَسِّ [*He, or it, is near as to the place where he, or it, is to be sought*]. (TḲ.)

عسب

1. عَسَبَ النَّاقَةَ, aor. ـِ, inf. n. عَسْبٌ, *He* (the stallion) *covered,* or *compressed, the she-camel.* (Mgh, Mṣb, TA.) [See also عَسْبٌ below.] — And one says, الكَلْبُ يَعْسِبُ *The dog chases the bitches with the desire of coupling.* (TA.) — And عَسَبَهُ فَحْلَهُ, aor. and inf. n. as above, *He let him*

his stallion to cover for hire. (Ṣ.) [See also 4.] —— And عَسَبَ, aor. and inf. n. as above, *He gave hire for a stallion's covering.* (A,* Ḳ.) You say, عَسَبْتُ الرَّجُلَ, inf. n. as above, *I gave the man hire for a stallion's covering.* (Mṣb.)

4. اعسبهُ جَمَلَهُ *He lent him his he-camel* [app. *for covering*]. (Lḥ, TA.) [See also 1.] ══ اعسب said of a wolf, *He ran,* and *fled.* (O, Ḳ.)

10. استعسبهُ جَمَلَهُ *He asked,* or *demanded,* or *desired, of him, the loan of his he-camel* [app. *for covering*]. (TA.) —— استعسبت *She* (a mare) *desired the stallion.* (Ṣ.) And استعسب *He* (a dog) *became excited by lust:* you say, فُلَانٌ يَسْتَعْسِبُ ٱسْتِعْسَابَ الكَلْبِ *Such a one becomes excited by lust like as does the dog.* (TA.) ══ And استعسبت نَفْسِى مِنْهُ *My soul disliked,* or *hated, him,* or *it.* (O, Ḳ.*)

عَسْبٌ A stallion's *covering,* or *compressing:* (Ṣ, A, Mgh, O, Ḳ:) [in this sense an inf. n.: (see 1:)] also used, metaphorically, as relating to a man: (TA:) or (so in the A and Ḳ; but in the Ṣ, "and, it is said,") his *sperma;* (Ṣ, A, Ḳ, TA;) that of a horse or of a camel; in which sense it has no verb: (TA:) or his *progeny:* and *offspring;* syn. وَلَدٌ; (A, O, Ḳ;) [app. of human beings; for it is added by SM that,] in this sense, it is, accord. to some, tropical. (TA.) One says, قَطَعَ ٱللّٰهُ عَسْبَهُ, (A, TA,) meaning [*God cut short,* or *may God cut short,*] *his progeny,* (A,) or *his sperma* and *his progeny.* (TA.) And Kutheiyir says, describing mares that had cast abortively their offspring,

* يُغَادِرْنَ عَسْبَ الوَالِقِىِّ وَنَاصِحٍ *
* تَخُصُّ بِهِ أُمُّ الطَّرِيقِ عِيَالَهَا *

[*They leave behind them the offspring of El-Wálikee and Náṣiḥ: the hyena appropriates them to her dependants for maintenance*]: (O, TA:) الوالقىّ and ناصح were two horses; (O;) two stallions; and امّ الطريق is the hyena. (TA.) —— Also The *hire of covering,* for كِرَآءُ عَسْبٍ; (Mgh, Mṣb, TA;) the *hire that is taken for a stallion's covering:* (Ṣ, O, TA:) so in a trad. in which it is said that عَسْبُ الفَحْلِ is forbidden. (Ṣ, Mgh, O, Mṣb, TA.)

رَأْسٌ عَسِبٌ *A head that has remained long without being combed and anointed.* (O,* Ḳ,* TA.)

عَسْبَةٌ: see عَسِيبٌ, last sentence.

عَسُوبٌ: see يَعْسُوبٌ.

عَسِيبٌ *A palm-branch from which the leaves have been removed:* (T, Mṣb, TA:) or *a straight and slender palm-branch from which the leaves have been stripped off:* and *one upon which leaves have not grown:* (Ḳ:) or *the part, of a palm-branch, a little above the* كَرَب [or *lower, thick,* and *broad, portions,*] *upon which no leaves have grown;* that [or those parts] upon which leaves have grown being termed سَعَف: (Ṣ, O:) pl. [of mult.] عُسُبٌ, (O, Mṣb, TA,) with two ḍammehs, (TA,) and عُسْبَانٌ (Mṣb, TA) and عِسْبَانٌ and عُسُوبٌ and [of pauc.] أَعْسِبَةٌ. (TA.) It is said of the Prophet, in a trad., قُبِضَ وَالقُرْآنُ فِى العُسُبِ وَالقُضُمِ وَالكَرَانِيفِ [*He was taken,* i. e. *he died, while the Ḳur-án was* written only *upon leafless palm-branches, and skins,* or *white skins, and stumps of palm-branches*]. (O, TA.*) —— Also The *bone of the tail;* and so ↓ عَسِيبَةٌ: (Ḳ:) or the *slender part thereof:* (TA:) or the *part where grows the hair thereof,* (Ḳ, TA,) i. e. *of the tail:* (TA:) or عَسِيبُ الذَّنَبِ signifies the *part, of the skin and bone of the tail, where the hair grows.* (Ṣ, O, TA.) —— And The *outer* [here meaning *upper*] *part of the human foot:* and *likewise* [i. e. the *shorter side,* or app., accord. to some, the *shaft* (see ظَهْرٌ as used in relation to a feather),] *of a feather, lengthwise.* (Ḳ.) —— And *A cleft,* or *fissure, in a mountain;* as also ↓ عَسْبَةٌ. (Ḳ.)

عَسِيبَةٌ: see the next preceding paragraph.

يَعْسُوبٌ The *king of the bees:* (Ṣ, O, Ḳ:*) the *male bee.* (A, O,* Ḳ.) —— And hence, (Ṣ, O,) ‡ The *lord,* or *chief,* of his people: (Ṣ, A, O:) or *a great chief;* as also ↓ عَسُوبٌ; (Ḳ;) or this signifies [simply] *a lord,* or *chief,* like يَعْسُوبٌ: (O:) pl. يَعَاسِيبُ. (TA.) It is said in a trad. of 'Alee, When such and such things shall happen (mentioning factions, or seditions), ضَرَبَ يَعْسُوبُ الدِّينِ بِذَنَبِهِ; (A, O, TA;) in which, accord. to Aṣ, يعسوب الدين means *the chief of men in respect of religion* at that time; (TA;) or it means *the leader of the religion:* (T and TA in art. ضرب:) and it is said that ضرب بذنبه here means *shall quit the faction,* or *sedition, and its party, with his partisans in religion;* by ذنبه being meant *his followers;* and by ضرب, *shall go away through the land, journeying,* or *warring in the cause of the religion:* or, as Z says, ضرب بذنبه means ‡ *shall remain, and be firm, together with his religious followers;* and accord. to Aboo-Sa'eed, the same is said of the locust, when it lays its eggs, thrusting its tail into the ground; and the meaning here is, † *shall remain firm* until the people shall return to him, and the religion become manifest, and spread abroad. (TA. [See also ضَرَبَ and ذَنَبٌ.]) —— Also ‡ *Gold;* so called because it is that by means of which an affair is managed, or ordered: and [in a larger sense] *a thing to which one has recourse for protection* or *the like;* as in a saying of 'Alee, in which wealth is termed the يعسوب of the unbelievers or of the hypocrites. (TA.) —— And *A certain flying thing, smaller than the locust;* (Aṣ, A'Obeyd, Ḳ;) or *larger;* (Ḳ;) *and having a long tail:* (TA:) or *a certain flying thing, longer than the locust, that does not contract its wings when it alights;* to which a horse is likened for the slenderness of its body: (Ṣ, O:) or *a kind of moth, or the like,* (فَرَاشَةٌ,) *of a greenish colour, that flies in the* [*season called*] رَبِيع. (IAth, TA.) [Golius explains it as "*Insectum oblongum, quaternis pennis volucre, mordella Gazæ, seu orsodacna Aristot.*"] —— And *A species of* حَجَل [or *partridge*]. (O, Ḳ, TA.) —— And *A blaze,* or *white mark, on a horse's face,* (Ḳ, TA,) *of a long shape, terminating before it extends as far as the upper parts of the nostrils;* or *extending upwards along the bone of the nose, wide and straight, until it reaches the lower part of the even portion of the forehead, whether it be little or much, if it do not reach as far as the eyes:* (TA:) or *a white line,* or *stripe, of the blaze, extending downwards until it touches the fore part of the nose and mouth.* (En-Naḍr, A'Obeyd, Az, O.) —— And (accord. to Lth, O) *A* دَائِرَة [or what we term a *feather*] *in the part of the flank of a horse where the rider strikes it with his foot:* (O, Ḳ, TA:) but Az says that this is a mistake, and that the correct meaning is that given above on the authority of A'Obeyd. (TA.) —— The ى in يَعْسُوبٌ is augmentative; because there is no Arabic word of the measure فَعْلُولٌ except صَعْفُوقٌ. (Ṣ, O.)

عسج

1. عَسَجَ, (Ḳ,) aor. ـِ, (L, TA,) inf. n. عَسْجٌ (L, TA, and so in some copies of the Ṣ, in other copies of the Ṣ and in the O عَسَجٌ [which is wrong],) and عَسِيجٌ and عَسَجَانٌ, (O, L, TA,) *He* [a camel] *stretched out his neck in going along* [*quickly:* or *went a pace quicker than that termed* الذَّمِيل, *but not so quick as that termed* الوَسْج: see وَسَجَ]. (Ṣ, O, L, Ḳ, TA.) —— And عَسَجَ, aor. ـُ, inf. n. عَسَجَانٌ, *He* (a beast) *limped, halted,* or *was slightly lame:* so in the M. (TA.) ══ An Arab of the desert said, when the lion was desiring to devour him, and he [the lion] therefore betook himself to a tree [or shrub] of the species termed عَوْسَج,

* يَعْسِجُنِى بِالعَوْتَلَهْ * يُبْصِرُنِى لَا أُحْسِبُهْ *

meaning يَخْتِلُنِى بِالعَوْسَجَةِ يَحْسَبُنِى لَا أُبْصِرُهُ [*He conceals himself, to seize me, by means of the 'owsajeh: thinking that I shall not see him:* the transpositions in the verse being app. meant to be understood as occasioned by the terror of the man; for the words of the explanation may be read so as to have the same metre as those of the verse]. (TA.) ══ عَسِجَ المَالُ, [aor. ـَ,] *The camels became diseased from pasturing upon the* [*shrubs called*] عَوْسَج. (O, Ḳ, TA.)

9. اعسجّ, inf. n. اعْسِجَاجٌ, *He* (an old man) *went away bent by reason of age.* (O, Ḳ.)

عَسْجٌ *A certain pace,* or *manner of going, of* camels. (TA.) [See 1, first sentence.]

عُسْجَةٌ *A portion of the night.* (O.)

عَاسِجٌ [part. n. of عَسَجَ]. Dhu-r-Rummeh says, describing his she-camel,

* وَالعِيسُ مِنْ عَاسِجٍ أَوْ وَاسِجٍ خَبَبًا *
* يُنْحَزْنَ مِنْ جَانِبَيْهَا وَهْىَ تَنْسَلِبُ *

[*And the reddish,* or *yellowish,* or *dingy, white camels, of a sort that goes the pace termed* عَسْج, or *of a sort that goes the pace termed* وَسْج, *with a quick running, are struck with the feet on their sides, but she outstrips*]: he means, the camels go swiftly, struck with the feet in their course, but do not overtake my she-camel. (Ṣ, O.)

عَوْسَجٌ [The *lycium*, or *box-thorn; of several species;* but now particularly applied to the *lycium Europæum* of Linn.: accord. to Sprengel (Hist. rei herb. p. 252, as stated by Freytag), applied to the *zizyphus spina Christi*, which is the *rhamnus spina Christi* of Linn.; but this is the سِدْر:] *a species of thorn:* (Ṣ, O, Ḳ:*) *certain trees of the thorn-kind,* (L,) *having a round red fruit* [or *berry*] *like the carnelian-bead,* (O, L,) *which is sweet, and is eaten:* (O:) or *a species of thorn-trees having a bitter red fruit in which is acidity, called* مُصَعٌ: (Mṣb:) or *certain trees having many thorns, and of several species, whereof is one that produces a red fruit, called* مُصَعٌ, *in which is acidity:* (T:) *when it grows large, it is called* غَرْقَدٌ: (O, Mṣb:) *and because of the softness of its wood, the women of the Arabs of the desert make of it spindles for spinning wool:* (O:) the n. un. is with ة: (Ṣ, O, Mṣb: [in the Ḳ, عَوْسَجٌ is termed the pl. of عَوْسَجَةٌ:]) and it is said that the pl. of the n. un. is عَوَاسِجُ: (TA:) ISd says, *the genuine* عَوْسَج *is short between the knots, hard in the wood, small in the leaves, and does not grow large, and this is the best sort:* thus says AḤn: (L:) some say that it is the عُلَّيْق [i. e. عُلَّيْق, q. v.]: Dioscorides says, *it is a tree that grows in tracts that exude water and produce salt, having erect thorny branches, and leaves somewhat long, overspread with a moist viscous substance: and there is another species, whiter than this: and another species, of which the leaves are blacker than those of the former, and wider, inclining a little to redness, and its branches are long, their length being about five cubits, and having more numerous thorns, and weaker, and less sharp, and its fruit is wide and thin, as though it were in sheaths: and the* عوسج *has a fruit like the* توت [or *mulberry*], *which is eaten: it grows mostly in cold, or cool, countries.* (Avicenna [Ibn-Seenà], book ii. p. 232. [In this extract from Dioscorides, in the original, are some unimportant words which I have passed over, including two imperfectly printed, and unintelligible: and what is said in it respecting the fruit I think doubtful, as being inapplicable to the fruit of the box-thorn.])

مِعْسَاجٌ an epithet applied to a camel [app. meaning *That stretches out his neck much in going along:* or *that goes the pace termed* عَسْج *much* or *well*]. (Ṣ, O, Ḳ.)

عسجد

عَسْجَدٌ, an instance of a quadriliteral-radical word without any letter of the kind termed ذَوْلَقِيَّة; (Ṣ, O, TA;) the letters of this kind being six; three pronounced with the tip of the tongue, namely, ر and ل and ن; and three labial, namely, ب and ف and م; (TA;) *Gold:* (Ṣ, O, Ḳ:) and (as some say, O, TA) *any gems, such as pearls and* يَاقُوت [or *sapphires*]. (O, Ḳ.) — Also *A large,* or *bulky,* camel: (O, Ḳ:) a small one is called لَطِيمٌ. (TA.) — And, accord. to AZ, *A certain stallion-camel.* (O.) See also the following paragraph.

عَسْجَدِيَّةٌ *Large* weaned camels: (O, Ḳ:) small ones are called لَطِيمَةٌ. (TA.) — And, (O, Ḳ,) accord. to El-Mufaḍḍal, (TA,) Camels *on which kings ride;* [and particularly] certain camels *which were decked,* or *adorned, for En-Noạmán* (Ṣ, O, Ḳ, TA) *Ibn-El-Mundhir;* or, accord. to AO, camels *on which kings ride, which bear* [*fine housings* or *the like, of the kind of stuff called*] دِقّ [q. v. voce دَقِيق] *of great price:* (TA:) and, (O, Ḳ, TA,) by El-Mázinee, (TA,) it is said to signify (O, TA) camels *that carry gold;* (O, Ḳ, TA;) but IAạr rejected this assertion: (O:) it is said (O, TA) by Naṣr, on the authority of Aṣ, (TA,) to be a [fem.] rel. n. from the name of a certain market in which is عَسْجَد, i. e. gold: (O, TA:) IAạr relates, on the authority of El-Mufaḍḍal, that it is a rel. n. from the name of a certain stallion of generous race, called ▼عَسْجَدٌ; and he is said to have been called العَسْجَدِىُّ also: (TA:) in the T, (TA,) or by AO, (O,) it is said that العَسْجَدِيَّةُ, (O, TA,) or العَسْجَدِىُّ, (O,) was a horse or mare (فَرَس) of the offspring of Ed-Deenáree (O, TA) Abu-l-Humeys Ibn-Zád-er-Rákib: (TA:) in the Ḳ, العَسْجَدِيَّةُ is said to have been [the name of] a mare (فَرَس) of the offspring of Ed-Deenáree. (TA.)

عسر

1. عَسُرَ, aor. ـُ, inf. n. عُسْرٌ (Ṣ, A, O, Mṣb, Ḳ) and عُسُرٌ (Ṣ, A, Ḳ) and عَسَارَةٌ (Mṣb, Ḳ) [and عُسْرَى and مَعْسَرَةٌ and عُسْرَةٌ and مَعْسُورٌ (see عُسْرٌ below)]; and عَسِرَ, aor. ـَ, inf. n. عَسَرٌ; (Ṣ, O, Mṣb, Ḳ;) and ▼تعسّر, (A, O, Mṣb, Ḳ,) and ▼تعاسر, (Ḳ,) and ▼استعسر; (A, O, Mṣb, Ḳ;) *It* (an affair, or a thing, Ṣ, A, O, Mṣb) *was,* or *became, difficult, hard, strait,* or *intricate.* (Ṣ, A, O, Mṣb, Ḳ,* TA.) You say, عَسُرَ عَلَيْهِ, (TA,) and عَسِرَ, (Ṣ, O,) and ▼تعسّر, and ▼تعاسر, and ▼استعسر, (Ḳ,) *It was,* or *became, difficult, hard, strait,* or *intricate, to him.* (Ṣ,* O,* Ḳ.) — عَسَرَ مَا فِى البَطْنِ, (as in the CḲ and a MS. copy of the Ḳ,) or عَسُرَ, (accord. to the TA,) *What was in the belly would not come forth.* (Ḳ.) You say عَسَرَ عَلَيْهِ مَا فِى البَطْنِ *What was in his belly would not come forth.* (TA.) — See also 4. — عَسُرَ, (Mṣb,) or عَسَرَ, (IḲṭṭ, TA,) or عَسِرَ, (TḲ,) inf. n. عُسْرٌ and عَسَارَةٌ (Mṣb, IḲṭṭ, TA) and عَسَرٌ, (IḲṭṭ, Ḳ,) *He* (a man) *had little gentleness,* (Mṣb, IḲṭṭ,) فِى الأُمُورِ [*in the execution of affairs*]; (Mṣb;) *and was narrow,* or *niggardly, in disposition:* (IḲṭṭ:) or *he was hard in disposition;* or *illnatured.* (Ḳ,* TḲ.) — عَسَرَ عَلَيْهِ, (A, and so in the CḲ and a MS. copy of the Ḳ,) or عَسَرَ, (as in the TA,) inf. n. عُسْرٌ, (TA,) *He acted contrarily,* or *adversely, to him; opposed him;* (A, Ḳ;) as also ▼عسّر, (Ḳ,) inf. n. تَعْسِيرٌ: (TA:) and ▼عسّر عليه also signifies *he straitened him.* (Sb, O,* TA.) — عَسَرَ الزَّمَانُ, (so in the CḲ and in a MS. copy of the Ḳ,) or عَسِرَ, (so in the TA,) *Time,* or *fortune, became severe, rigorous, afflictive,* or *adverse,* (Ḳ,) عَلَيْنَا *to us.* (TA.) — عَسَرَتِ النَّاقَةُ and عَسِرَت *The she-camel was untrained.* (O.) — And عَسَرَتْ, (Ḳ, TA,) and عَسَرَتْ بِذَنَبِهَا, (Ṣ, O, TA,) aor. ـِ, inf. n. عَسَرَانٌ (Ṣ, O, Ḳ, TA) and عَسْرٌ, (O, Ḳ, TA,) *She* (a camel) *raised her tail, after conception, to show the stallion that she was pregnant:* (Ṣ,* O, TA:) and [as also, app., ▼عسّرت, or عسّرت ذَنَبَهَا, inf. n. تَعْسِيرٌ, (see نَاقَة عَسِيرٌ, voce عَسِيرٌ,)] *she* (a camel) *raised her tail in her running.* (Ḳ, TA.) [In the former case, the action denotes repugnance to the stallion: in the latter, a degree of refractoriness: in both, difficulty.] — عَسَرَ الغَرِيمَ, aor. ـُ and ـِ, (Ṣ, O, Mṣb, Ḳ,) inf. n. عَسْرٌ; (Ṣ, O;) and ▼أَعْسَرَهُ; (O, Mṣb, Ḳ;) *He demanded the debt of the debtor, it being difficult to him to pay it:* (Ṣ, O, Mṣb, Ḳ:*) and *he took it of him, it being difficult to him to pay it, and was not lenient towards him until he was in easy circumstances.* (TA.) — عَسَرَهُ, (Aṣ, TA,) and ▼اعتسرهُ, (Ṣ, TA,) *He forced,* or *compelled, him, against his wish;* [عَلَى الأَمْرِ *to do the thing;*] i. q. قَسَرَهُ, (Aṣ, TA,) and اقتسرهُ. (Ṣ, O, TA.) — عَسِرَ, and عَسِرَتْ, (TḲ,) or عَسَرَتْ, (Ḳ, TA,) aor. ـَ, (TḲ,) inf. n. عَسَرٌ, (Ṣ, Mgh, O, Mṣb, Ḳ,) *He,* (a man, TḲ,) and *she,* (a woman, TḲ,) *was left-handed.* (Ṣ, Mgh, O, Mṣb, Ḳ.) — عَسَرَنِى, (O, L, and Ḳ, and so in a copy of the Ṣ,) aor. ـُ, (L,) or ـِ, (TA,) inf. n. عَسْرٌ; (L, TA;) and ▼عَسَّرَنِى, (Ḳ,) or عَسِرَنِى, (L and TA, and so in a copy of the Ṣ,) aor. ـَ; (TA;) *He came on my right side.* (Ṣ, O, L, Ḳ, TA.)

2: see 1, in four places: and see 4.

3. عاسرهُ, (Ḳ,) inf. n. مُعَاسَرَةٌ, (Ṣ, O,) *He treated him,* or *behaved towards him, with hardness, harshness,* or *ill-nature;* (Ṣ,* O,* Ḳ;) مُعَاسَرَةٌ is the contr. of مُيَاسَرَةٌ. (Ṣ, O.)

4. اعسر, (Ṣ, Ḳ, &c.,) inf. n. إِعْسَارٌ, (Kr, Mgh, &c.,) and, accord. to Kr, عُسْرٌ; but correctly, the former is an inf. n., and عُسْرَةٌ is a simple subst.; [as is also عُسْرٌ;] (TA;) *He was,* or *became, in a state of difficulty; possessing little power* or *wealth:* (TA:) *he became poor:* (Mgh, Mṣb, Ḳ:) *he lost his property.* (Ṣ, O.) عَسَارٌ in the sense of إِعْسَارٌ is a pure mistake. (Mgh.) — اعسرت *She* (a woman) *had,* or *experienced, difficulty in bringing forth;* (Lth, Ṣ, O, Ḳ;) as also ▼عَسَّرَتْ. (O, TA.) You say, in praying for a woman in labour, أَيْسَرَتْ وَأَذْكَرَتْ (Lth, A) *May she have an easy birth, and may she bring forth a male child:* (Lth, O:) and in the contr. case you say, أَعْسَرَتْ وَآنَثَتْ [*May she have a difficult birth, and may she bring forth a female child*]. (Lth, A, O, TA.) — And in like manner, *She* (a

camel) *had difficulty in bringing forth, her young one sticking fast at the time of the birth.* (O, TA.) — And *She* (a camel) *did not conceive during her year* [*after she had been covered*]; (Ḳ,* TA;) as also ▼ عُسِرَتْ, in the pass. form. (TA.) ═ اعسر الغريمَ: see عَسَّرَ.

5. تعسّر: see 1, in two places. — *It* (spun thread, غَزْلٌ, in the Ḳ قَوْلٌ [speech], but this is a mistake, TA) *became entangled, so that it could not be unravelled;* as also تغسّر, with the pointed غ: so accord. to Lth, as related by Az, who confirms it as of the language of the Arabs: but Ṣgh, in the TṢ [and O], says, You say of a thing, when it has become difficult, استعسر and تعسّر; but of spun thread, when it has become entangled, so that it cannot be unravelled, تغسّر, with the pointed غ; not with the unpointed ع, unless using a forced, or constrained, mode of speech. (TA.)

6. تَعَاسَرَا [*They were difficult,* or *hard, each with the other; they treated,* or *behaved towards, each other with hardness, harshness,* or *illnature;*] *they disagreed, each with the other;* said of a buyer and seller, and of a husband and wife; (TA;) تَعَاسُرٌ is the *contr. of* تَيَاسُرٌ: (Ṣ, O:) see Ḳur lxv. 6. (TA.) — See also 1, in two places.

8. اعتسرهُ in the sense of اقسرهُ: see عَسَرَهُ. — اعتسر النَّاقَةَ *He rode the she-camel before she was trained,* (Ṣ, A, O,) *while she was difficult to manage:* (A:) or *he took her in the first stage of her training, while yet difficult to manage, and attached her rein to her nose, and rode her.* (Ḳ.) — Hence, اعتسر الكَلَامَ ‡ *He uttered the speech without premeditation; without measuring and preparing it in his mind.* (Az, A.) — اعتسر مِنْ مَالِ وَلَدِهِ *He took of the property of his son,* or *child,* or *children, against the wish of the latter:* (Ṣ, O, Ḳ:) so occurring in a trad., with س; from الاعتسار signifying "the act of forcing, or compelling:" but accord. to one relation of that trad., it is with ص. (TA.)

10: see 1, in two places. ═ استعسرهُ *He sought,* or *desired,* or *demanded, that in which he experienced,* or *would experience, difficulty.* (O, Ḳ.)

عَسْرٌ, or العَسْرُ: see عِسْرٌ, in two places.

عُسْرٌ and ▼ عُسُرٌ (Ṣ, A, O, Ḳ) and ▼ عَسَرٌ (Ṣ, A, Ḳ) and ▼ مَعْسُورٌ [respecting which, as well as some other words here mentioned, see below, in this paragraph, and see what is said of its contr. مَيْسُورٌ, voce يُسْرٌ,] and ▼ عُسْرَةٌ and ▼ مَعْسَرَةٌ and ▼ مَعْسُرَةٌ and ▼ عُسْرَى [all of which are app. inf. ns., of 1, q. v.,] (Ḳ) *Difficulty; hardness; straitness; intricacy; contr. of* يُسْرٌ. (Ṣ, A, O, Ḳ.) — 'Eesà Ibn-'Omar observes that every noun of three letters of which the first is with damm and the second quiescent is pronounced by some of the Arabs with the second movent like the first; as عُسْرٌ and عُسُرٌ, and رُحْمٌ and رُحُمٌ, and حُلْمٌ and حُلُمٌ. (Ṣ, O.) — It is said in the Ḳur [lxv. 7], سَيَجْعَلُ اللّٰهُ بَعْدَ عُسْرٍ يُسْرًا [*God will give, after difficulty, ease*]. (O, TA.) And again, [xciv. 5 and 6,] فَإِنَّ مَعَ الْعُسْرِ يُسْرًا إِنَّ مَعَ الْعُسْرِ يُسْرًا [*And verily with difficulty shall be ease: verily with difficulty shall be ease*]: on reciting which, Ibn-Mes'ood said, لَنْ يَغْلِبَ عُسْرٌ يُسْرَيْنِ [*A difficulty will not predominate over twofold ease*], which, says Abu-l-'Abbás, is meant as an explanation of the words of the Ḳur immediately preceding it, agreeably with a rule mentioned by Fr [and applying to most cases, but not to all]: for العسر being mentioned, and then repeated with ال, the latter is known to be the same as the former; and يسرا being mentioned, and repeated without ال, the latter is known to be different from the former. (O,* TA.) — It is also said, لَوْ دَخَلَ العُسْرُ جُحْرًا لَدَخَلَ اليُسْرُ عَلَيْهِ [*If difficulty were to enter a burrow in the ground, ease would enter upon it*]. (TA.) — As to ▼ مَعْسُورٌ, it is the *contr. of* مَيْسُورٌ, and both are inf. ns.: (Ṣ, O:) or they are put in the places of عُسْرٌ and يُسْرٌ: (TA:) or accord. to Sb, they both are epithets; for he holds that there is no inf. n. of the measure مَفْعُولٌ; and the saying دَعْهُ إِلَى مَيْسُورِهِ وَإِلَى مَعْسُورِهِ is expl. as signifying *Leave thou him to a thing in which he experiences ease, and to a thing in which he experiences difficulty:* and مَعْقُولٌ is also expl. in like manner. (Ṣ, O.) [In like manner also,] بَلَغْتُ مَعْسُورَ ▼ فُلَانٍ [may be expl. as signifying *I effected a thing in which such a one experienced difficulty;* meaning *I treated such a one with hardness, harshness,* or *illnature;* being] said when thou hast not treated the person of whom thou speakest with gentleness, graciousness, courtesy, or civility. (O, TA.) You also say, [using معسور and its contr. ميسور as epithets,] ▼ خُذْ مَيْسُورَهُ وَدَعْ مَعْسُورَهُ [*Take thou what is easy thereof, and leave thou what is difficult thereof*]. (A.) — عُسْرٌ also signifies *Poverty:* (Mṣb:) and ▼ عُسْرَةٌ, [*the same:* or] *littleness of possessions,* of *property,* of *wealth,* or *of power:* (Ṣ, TA:) and ▼ مَعْسَرَةٌ and ▼ مَعْسُرَةٌ, [*the same:* or] *difficulty, and poverty;* contr. of مَيْسَرَةٌ: (O, TA:) both inf. ns.: (O:) and ▼ عُسْرَى, [*the same:* or] *difficult things, affairs,* or *circumstances;* (TA;) *contr. of* يُسْرَى: (Ṣ, O, TA:) and fem. of أَعْسَرُ, applied to a thing, or an affair, or a circumstance. (TA.) — ▼ جَيْشُ العُسْرَةِ [*The army of difficulty*] is an appellation given to the army of Tabook; because they were summoned to go thither during the intense heat of summer, (O, Ḳ,) and in the season of the ripening of the fruit, (O, TA,) so that it was hard to them; (O, Ḳ;) and because the Prophet never warred before with so numerous an army, amounting to thirty thousand. (O, TA.) — ▼ فَسَنُيَسِّرُهُ لِلْعُسْرَى, in the Ḳur [xcii. 10], signifies, as some say, [*We will smooth his way*] *to punishment, and a difficult case.* (O, TA.)

عِسْرٌ, (Ṣ,) or العِسْرُ, (O, Ḳ,) *A certain tribe of the Jinn, or Genii;* (Ṣ, O, Ḳ;) as also ▼ عَسْرٌ, (Ṣ,) or العَسْرُ: (O, Ḳ:) or the first, (Ṣ, O,) or second and ▼ last, (Ḳ,) *a land inhabited by Jinn.* (Ṣ, O, Ḳ.)

عُسُرٌ: see عُسْرٌ.

عَسِرٌ *Difficult, hard, hard to be done* or *accomplished, hard to be borne* or *endured, distressing, strait,* or *intricate;* (Ṣ, O, Mṣb, Ḳ;*) applied to an affair, or a thing; (Ṣ, O, Mṣb;) as also ▼ عَسِيرٌ. (Ṣ, A, O, Mṣb, Ḳ.) — حَاجَةٌ عَسِرٌ, and ▼ عَسِيرٌ, (Ḳ,) or عَسِيرٌ and ▼ عَسِيرَةٌ, (L,) *A want difficult of attainment.* (L, Ḳ.) — يَوْمٌ عَسِرٌ, (Ḳ,) and ▼ عَسِيرٌ, (Ṣ, Ḳ,) and ▼ أَعْسَرُ, (Ḳ,) *A difficult day; a day of difficulty;* (Ṣ;) *a hard, distressful,* or *calamitous, day:* or *an unfortunate,* or *unlucky, day.* (Ḳ.) — رَجُلٌ عَسِرٌ *A man having little gentleness in* [*the execution of*] *affairs:* (Mṣb:) or *hard in disposition;* or *illnatured.* (Ḳ.) [See 1.] — نَاقَةٌ ▼ عَسِيرٌ, (Ṣ, A, O,) or ▼ عَسِيرَةٌ, (as in one copy of the Ṣ,) *A she-camel not trained:* (Ṣ, A, O:) or نَاقَةٌ ▼ عَسِيرٌ and ▼ عَوْسَرَانَةٌ and ▼ عَيْسَرَانَةٌ [and app. ▼ عَيْسُرَانَةٌ] (Ḳ) or ▼ عَوْسَرَانِيَّةٌ (Lth, Az, Ṣ, O, L) and ▼ عَيْسَرَانِيَّةٌ (Lth, Az, TṢ, O, L) and ▼ عَيْسُرَانِيَّةٌ, (Lth, Az, TṢ, O,) but what Lth says is not agreeable with the usage of the Arabs, (Az, TṢ, O,) *a she-camel that is ridden,* (Lth, Az, Ṣ, O, TA,) or *laden,* (TA,) *before she has been trained:* (Lth, Az, Ṣ, O, TA:) or *that has been taken in the first stage of her training, while yet difficult to manage, and had her nose-rein attached, and been ridden:* (Ḳ:) and the epithet applied to a he-camel is ▼ عَسِيرٌ, (Ḳ, TA,) or عَسِرٌ, (CḲ,) and ▼ عَيْسَرَانٌ (Lth, Az, and so in some copies of the Ḳ,) and ▼ عَيْسُرَانٌ (Lth, Az, TA, and so, in the place of the form immediately preceding, in some copies of the Ḳ,) and ▼ عَيْسَرَانِىٌّ (TA) and ▼ عَيْسُرَانِىٌّ (Ḳ, TA) and ▼ عَوْسَرَانِىٌّ. (Ṣ, O.) — Also نَاقَةٌ ▼ عَسِيرٌ *A she-camel that raises her tail in her running;* as also ▼ عَاسِرٌ: (Ḳ:) or the latter, *raising her tail after conception:* (TA:) [see 1:] and [its pl.] ▼ عَوَاسِرُ, applied to wolves, *that are agitated in their running, and shake the head, and contort* (تَكْسِرُ) *their tails,* (Ṣ, TA,) *by reason of briskness.* (TA.) And نَاقَةٌ ▼ عَوْسَرَانِيَّةٌ *A she-camel that is wont to raise her tail when she runs,* (TṢ, O, Ḳ,) *by reason of sprightliness.* (O, TA.) In the L, instead of تَكْسِرُ, preceding, we find تَكْسِرُ ذَنَبَهَا. (TA.) — Also, نَاقَةٌ ▼ عَسِيرٌ, (Lth, O, Ḳ,) or ▼ عَسِيرَةٌ, (Ṣ,) accord. to Lth, (TA,) *A she-camel not conceiving during her year* [*after having been covered*]: (Lth, Ṣ, O, Ḳ:) but Az says that this explanation by Lth is not correct, and that ناقة عسير signifies, as expl. above, "a she-camel that is ridden before she has been trained;" and so Aṣ explains it; and ISk says the same. (TA.)

عُسُرٌ: see عُسْرٌ.

عُسْرَةٌ: see عُسْرٌ, in three places.

عُسْرَةٌ: see أَعْسَرُ, last sentence.

عُسْرَى: see عُسْرٌ, in three places: and see also أَعْسَرُ.

عَسِيرٌ and عَسِيرَةٌ: see عَسِرٌ, throughout.

عَاسِرٌ; and [its pl.] عَوَاسِرُ : see عَسِرٌ, latter half.

عُوسَرَانَةٌ and عُوسَرَانِىٌّ and عُوسَرَانِيَّةٌ : see عَسِرٌ; the last in two places.

عَيْسَرَانَةٌ and عَيْسُرَانٌ and عَيْسَرَانٌ and عَيْسُرَانَةٌ and عَيْسَرَانِىٌّ and عَيْسُرَانِىٌّ and عَيْسَرَانِيَّةٌ and عَيْسُرَانِيَّةٌ : see عَسِرٌ.

أَعْسَرُ [*More*, and *most*, *difficult*, *hard*, *strait*, or *intricate*; *contr. of* أَيْسَرُ;] applied to a thing, or an affair, or a circumstance: fem. ▼ عُسْرَى. (TA.) — Applied to a day, *i. q.* عَسِرٌ, q. v.; (Ḳ;) *unfortunate*, or *unlucky*. (O.) ═ A *left-handed* man; one *who works with his left hand*; (Ṣ, O, Mṣb, Ḳ;) one *whose strength is in his left hand or arm, and who does with that what others do with the right*: (TA:) fem. عَسْرَآءُ: (Ḳ:) and pl. عُسْرَانٌ, (O, TA,) like as سُودَانٌ is a pl. of أَسْوَدُ, (TA,) and عُسْرٌ. (O.) None is stronger in casting or shooting than the أَعْسَرُ. (TA.) — أَعْسَرُ يَسَرٌ A man *who uses both his hands* [*alike*]; *ambidextrous*; *an ambidexter*: (Ṣ, O, Ḳ:) fem. عَسْرَآءُ يَسَرَةٌ: (TA:) you should not say [of a man that he is] أَعْسَرُ أَيْسَرُ; (Ṣ, TA;) nor of a woman that she is عَسْرَآءُ يَسْرَآءُ. (TA.) — العَسْرَآءُ, fem. of الأَعْسَرُ, *The left hand* or *arm*. (TA.) — حَمَامٌ أَعْسَرُ *A pigeon*, or *pigeons*, *having a whiteness in the left wing*. (Ṣ, O.) And عُقَابٌ عَسْرَآءُ *An eagle whose feathers on the left side are more numerous than those on the right*: (Ṣ, O, Ḳ:*) and (Ṣ, O, Ḳ) some say (Ṣ, O) *having, in its wing, white primary feathers*. (O, Ḳ.) And عَسْرَآءُ *A white primary feather*; (O, Ḳ;) and so ▼ عُسْرَةٌ. (Ṣ, O, Ḳ; in one of my copies of the Ṣ written عِسْرَةٌ.)

مُعْسِرٌ A man *who presses his debtor, and straitens him*, or *puts him in difficulty*. (T, TṢ, O, Ḳ.) [See 1, latter half].

مَعْسَرَةٌ and مَعْسُرَةٌ : see عُسْرٌ; each in two places.

مَعْسُورٌ : see عُسْرٌ, in four places.

عسف

1. عَسَفَ فِى الأَمْرِ, (Mṣb,) [aor. ِ ,] inf. n. عَسْفٌ, (TA,) *He did the affair* [or *he acted in it*] *without consideration*; (Mṣb, TA;*) and ▼ تعسّف and ▼ اعتسف have the like meaning: (Mṣb,* TA:) whence what next follows. (Mṣb.) — عَسَفَ الطَّرِيقَ *He travelled the road not following a right direction*: (Mṣb:) [or you say,] عَسَفَ عَنِ الطَّرِيقِ, (O, Ḳ,) aor. ِ , (Ḳ,) inf. n. عَسْفٌ; (TA;) and ▼ اعتسف, and ▼ تعسّف; (O, Ḳ;) *he declined from the road*, (O, Ḳ, TA,) *and journeyed without direction and without pursuing a right course*: (TA:) or عَسَفَ الطَّرِيقَ (Ḳ,* TA) *he travelled the road*, (Ḳ, TA,) *seeking an object of want*, (TA,) *without direction*; (Ḳ, TA:) and ▼ اعتسفهُ, and ▼ تعسّفهُ, *he travelled it without aiming at and hitting upon a right course*: (TA:) and عَسَفَ الفَلَاةَ, (Mgh,) or المَفَازَةَ, inf. n. as above, (TA,) *he traversed*, or *crossed*, *the desert*, or *waterless desert, without direction*, (Mgh, TA,) *and without any travelled road*; as also ▼ اعتسفها: (Mgh:) or عَسْفٌ signifies the *taking a course not along the road*, (Ṣ, IAth, O, TA,) *and without knowledge*: (IAth, TA:) this is said by IAth to be the primary meaning: (TA:) or, accord. to IDrd, the primary meaning is the *travelling the road without direction*: (O:) and ▼ الإِعْتِسَافُ signifies the *taking a course at random, without direction and without knowledge*. (Ḥam p. 613.) And one says, بَاتَ يَعْسِفُ اللَّيْلَ, inf. n. as above, *He passed the night journeying therein without direction, seeking a thing*. (Mṣb.) And عَسْفٌ [alone] signifies The *going round about by night seeking an object of quest*, or *desire*. (O, Ḳ.) [See also 2, and 4.] — Hence, i. e. from the frequent usage of the verb in its primary sense, عَسَفَ فُلَانٌ فُلَانًا, meaning *Such a one treated*, or *used*, *such a one wrongfully*, *unjustly*, *injuriously*, or *tyrannically*; (O;) as also ▼ تعسّفهُ: (O,* Ḳ:) and عَسَفَ السُّلْطَانُ (O, Ḳ) i. e. [*The Sulṭán*, or *ruling power*,] *acted wrongfully*, *unjustly*, &c.: (Ḳ:) inf. n. as above. (IAth, Mgh, TA.) — And [hence,] عَسَفَ فُلَانَةً *He violated such a woman*. (TA.) — And الدَّمْعُ يَعْسِفُ الجُفُونَ † *The tears are copious so that they flow in other than their* [*proper*] *channels*. (A, TA.) — And عَسَفَهُ, aor. and inf. n. as above, *He took him*, or *it*, *with strength*, or *force*. (Mṣb.) — And عَسَفَهُ *He took him as a servant*, (O, Ḳ, TA,) or *an* عَسِيف; (TA;) as also ▼ اعتسفهُ. (O, Ḳ, TA.) — عَسَفَ عَلَيْهِ and لَهُ *He worked*, or *wrought*, *for him* [*as a hired servant*]. (Ḳ.) One says, كَمْ أَعْسِفُ عَلَيْكَ (O) or لَكَ (TA) i. e. [*How long shall I*] *work for thee*, (O, TA,) *and earn*, or *gain*, *for thee, going repeatedly to and fro for thee like him who goes round about in the night seeking an object of quest*, or *desire?* (TA.) — And عَسَفَ ضَيْعَتَهُمْ, (Ḳ,) aor. as above, (O,) *He kept*, *minded*, or *managed*, *their estate, and ordered its affairs in their stead*, (O, Ḳ, TA,) *and went to and fro occupied in that which should put it* [or *keep it*] *in a good*, or *right*, *state*. (TA.) ═ عَسْفٌ signifies also The *breathing of death*. (O, Ḳ.) And عَسَفَ, (O, Ḳ,) aor. ِ , inf. n. عَسْفٌ (O, TA) and عُسُوفٌ, (TA,) said of a camel, (O, Ḳ,) *He was at the point of death, and had* [*the affection*, or *disease, termed*] عُسَافٌ: or, as some say, *he had the affection*, or *disease, termed* غُدَّةٌ [q. v.]: (O:) or *he was at the point of death by reason of the* [*affection*, or *disease, termed*] غُدَّة, *and began to breathe* [or *pant*] *so that his* حَنْجَرَة [or *head of the windpipe*] *became convulsed*. (Ḳ.) [See also عَزَفَ.]

2. تَعْسِيفٌ The *journeying without any sign of the way and without track*; (TA;) and so ▼ تَعَسُّفٌ. (TA in art. سمت : see a verse cited in the first paragraph of that art.) [See also 1, and 4.] ═ عسّفهُ, inf. n. as above, *He fatigued*, or *jaded*, *him*, (O, Ḳ, TA,) namely, his camel, (O, TA,) *by journeying*. (TA.)

4. اعسف *He journeyed by night*, [*going at random, in a headstrong and reckless manner*,] *like the weak-sighted she-camel that beats the ground with her fore feet as she goes along, not guarding herself from anything*. (IAạr, O, Ḳ, TA.) [See also 1, and 2.] — And *He punished his young man with hard work*. (IAạr, O, Ḳ.) ═ Also *He* (a man, O) *had his camel taken with the breathing of death*, (IAạr, O, Ḳ,) *termed* العَسْف. (IAạr, O.) ═ And *He kept to drinking from the large cup* or *bowl* [*termed* عَسْف]. (IAạr, O, Ḳ.)

5: see 1, first quarter, in three places: and see 2. — تَعَسُّفٌ in language is from عَسَفَ الفَلَاةَ, [and the like,] expl. above: (Mgh:) it signifies [in its general application The *using*, or *use of*, *a discommendable license in language*: and particularly *vague*, or *vagueness of*, *expression*; or] the *making language to accord with* [or *to bear*] *a meaning which it does not plainly indicate*. (KT.) — See also 1, third quarter. — [Hence,] one says, وَقَعَ عَلَيْهِ السَّيْفُ فَتَعَسَّفَهُ i. e. [*The sword fell upon him, and*] *hit the bone that was the main stay of the limb, falling short of the joint*. (TA.)

7. انعسف *It bent*, or *inclined*; syn. انعطف. (O, Ḳ.) Hence, (TA,) Aboo-Wejzeh says,

* وَٱسْتَيْقَنَتْ أَنَّ الصَّلِيفَ مُنْعَسِفْ ▼ *

meaning [*And she knew*, or *became sure, that*] *the side of the neck* [*was bending*, or *inclining*]. (O, TA.)

8: see 1, in six places.

عَسْفٌ [inf. n. of 1, q. v. passim. ═ Also] *A large drinking-cup* or *bowl*; (Ṣ, O, Ḳ, TA;) like عُسٌّ: pl. عُسُوفٌ. (TA.)

عَسَفَاتٌ : see what next follows.

عُسَافٌ, in a camel, as expl. by Aṣ on the authority of an Arab of the desert, is [The *suffering experienced*] *when the* حَنْجَرَة [or *head of the windpipe*] *is convulsed* (تَرْجُفُ, O, or تَقَمَّصُ, i. e. تَرْجُفُ, Ṣ) *by the breathing* (Ṣ, O) *at death*: (O:) they say that it is to camels *like* نِزَاعٌ *to man*. (TA.) One says of a she-camel, بِهَا عُسَافٌ (O, Ḳ) and ▼ عَسَفَاتٌ, (Ḳ,) meaning *In her is the suffering expl. above*: (O:) or *the* [*affection*, or *disease, termed*] غُدَّةٌ (O, Ḳ) *occasioning her to be at the point of death and to breathe* [or *pant*] *so that her* حَنْجَرَة *is convulsed*. (Ḳ.)

عَسُوفٌ *Travelling without following a right direction*; [as also ▼ عَاسِفٌ; and, app., in like manner, ▼ عَسِيفٌ, but in an intensive sense, occurring in a verse of Esh-Shenfarà, (see De Sacy's Chrest. Ar., sec. ed., ii. 359-60,) but not found by me in any of the lexicons:] pl. عُسُفٌ, like as رُسُلٌ is pl. of رَسُولٌ. (Mṣb.) Applied to a she-camel as meaning *That goes along at random, heedlessly*, or *in a headlong manner, not obeying a guide to the right course, and that is not turned by anything*. (TA.) — And [hence,] *Acting wrongfully*, *unjustly*, *injuriously*, or *tyrannically*; syn. جَائِرٌ: (TA:) or one *who acts wrongfully*, &c., *much*, or *often*; syn. ظَلُومٌ: (Ṣ, Mgh, O,* Ḳ, TA:) and ▼ عَسَّافٌ also has the former [or rather the latter] meaning. (TA.) —— And One *who takes with strength*, or *force*; and so, but in an intensive sense, ▼ عَسَّافٌ. (Mṣb.)

عَسِيفٌ *A hired man; a hireling*: (Ṣ, Mgh, O, Mṣb, Ḳ:) or *a slave who is held in light*, or *mean, estimation*, or *in contempt*: (O, L, TA:) in the Ḳ, المُسْتَعَانُ بِهِ is erroneously put for المُسْتَهَانُ بِهِ, the reading in the O and L: (TA:) a poet says, (O,) namely, Nubeyh Ibn-El-Ḥajjáj, (TA,)

أَطَعْتُ النَّفْسَ فِى الشَّهَوَاتِ حَتَّى
أَعَادَتْنِى عَسِيفًا عَبْدَ عَبْدِ

[*I obeyed the soul in respect of appetites until it rendered me a despised bondman, a slave of a slave*]: (O, TA:) it is of the measure فَعِيلٌ in the sense of the measure فَاعِلٌ, from عَسَفَ لَهُ meaning "he worked for him;" or in the sense of the measure مَفْعُولٌ, from عَسَفَهُ meaning "he took him as a servant:" (Ḳ: [and the like is said in the O:]) pl. عُسَفَآءُ (Ṣ, Mgh, O, Mṣb) and عِسَفَةٌ, which latter is anomalous. (TA.)

عَسَّافٌ : see عَسُوفٌ, last two sentences.

عَيْسَفٌ : see عَسُوفٌ, first sentence.

عَاسِفٌ : see عَسُوفٌ. ═ Also, applied to a she-camel, (Aboo-Yoosuf, Ṣ, O, Ḳ,) without ة, (O,) as well as to a he-camel, (TA,) *At the point of death, and having* [*the affection, or disease, termed*] عُسَاف : or, as some say, *having the affection*, or *disease, termed* غُدَّة [q. v.]: (O:) or *at the point of death by reason of the* غُدَّة, *and beginning to breathe* [or *pant*] (Aboo-Yoosuf, Ṣ, Ḳ) *so that the* حَنْجَرَة [or *head of the windpipe*] *becomes convulsed*. (Ḳ.)

هُوَ رَاكِبُ التَّعَاسِيفِ means *He is one who has no known place of aim*, or *pursuit*: (Mṣb in art. ركب:) the last word is app. pl. of تَعْسَافٌ, which is of a form common to triliteral-radical verbs, in general. (Mṣb in the present art.)

مَعْسِفٌ *A place in which one travels without direction*: (O, TA:) [*in which is no sign of the way nor any track*: pl. مَعَاسِفُ:] one says, أَخَذُوا فِى مَعَاسِفِ البِيدِ [*They took their way in the tracts of the deserts*, or *of the waterless deserts, in which one travels without direction*]. (TA.)

مَعْسُوفَةٌ, applied to a woman, *Violated*. (TA.)

مُنْعَسِفٌ part. n. of 7, q. v. (O, TA.)

عسكر

Q. 1. عَسْكَرَ الرَّجُلُ [*The man collected an army*]. (Ṣ.) —— عَسْكَرْتُ الشَّىْءَ *I collected the thing*. (Mṣb.) —— عَسْكَرَ القَوْمُ *The people collected themselves together*, (Ḳ,) بِالْمَكَانِ *in the place*: (TA:) or *the people fell into difficulty, distress, or adversity*: (Ḳ:) or *into dearth, scarcity, or drought*. (TA.) —— عَسْكَرَ اللَّيْلُ *The night became densely dark*. (O, Ḳ.)

عَسْكَرٌ, a Pers. word arabicised, (Ibn-El-Jawáleekee, Mgh, Mṣb, Ḳ,*) from لَشْكَرْ, (Mgh, TA,) *An army*: (Ṣ, A, O, Mṣb:) pl. عَسَاكِرُ. (A, O.) You say, العَسْكَرُ مُقْبِلٌ, and مُقْبِلُونَ, *The army is coming*, and *are coming*. (Th, TA.) —— *A collection*. (A, Ḳ.) —— *A large number*, or *quantity*, of anything: (A, Ḳ:) as, of men, and of camels or other property, and of horses, and of dogs. (TA.) —— The *camels* or *sheep* or *goats* of a man, *collectively*. (Az, O, TA.) You say, إِنَّهُ لَقَلِيلُ العَسْكَرِ *Verily he has few beasts*. (TṢ, O, TA.) —— † The *darkness* of night. (TA.) —— عَسَاكِرُ الهَمِّ † *Anxieties, coming one upon another, consecutively*. (O, TA.) —— See also مُعَسْكَرٌ. —— [Hence,] العَسْكَرَانِ *'Arafeh and Minè* (عَرَفَةُ وَمِنًى): (Ṣ, A, O, Mṣb, Ḳ:) because places of assembling. (Mṣb.)

عَسْكَرَةٌ *Difficulty, distress*, or *adversity*: (Ṣ, O, Ḳ:) and *dearth, scarcity*, or *drought*. (Ḳ.) Ṭarafeh says,

ظَلَّ فِى عَسْكَرَةٍ مِنْ حُبِّهَا

i. e., *He became in a state of difficulty*, or *distress, by reason of love of her*. (Ṣ, O.)

مُعَسْكَرٌ *Collected together*. (Mṣb.) ═ And The *place where an army collects itself*; (Ṣ,* Mṣb;) as also ▼ عَسْكَرٌ. (TA.)

مُعَسْكِرٌ *Collecting an army*; or *a collector of an army*. (Ṣ,* Mṣb.)

عسل

1. عَسَلَ الطَّعَامَ, aor. ِ and ُ, (Ṣ, O, Ḳ,) inf. n. عَسْلٌ, (TA,) *He made*, or *prepared, the food with* عَسَل [i. e. *honey*]: (Ṣ, O:) or, as also ▼ عَسَّلَهُ, (Ḳ, TA,) inf. n. تَعْسِيلٌ, (TA,) *he mixed the food with honey*, (Ḳ, TA,) *and made it pleasant and sweet*. (TA.) —— [Hence,] عَسَلَهُ ‡ *He made him an object of eulogy*. (IAạr, Ḳ, TA.) And ‡ *He* (i. e. God) *made him an object of love to men*. (Ḳ, TA.) Accord. to an explanation by the Prophet, of a saying of his in which it occurs, ‡ *He* (i. e. God) *granted him*, or *permitted him*, (O, TA,) i. e. *disposed him*, (TA,) *to do a good deed, before his death, so that those around him were pleased with him, and eulogized him*; the good deed being likened to honey. (O, TA.) —— And *He fed him with honey*. (TA.) See also 2. —— The inf. n. عَسْلٌ also signifies The *extracting honey from a bee-hive*. (KL.) —— And عَسَلَ المَرْأَةَ, aor. ُ, (Ḳ, TA,) inf. n. عَسْلٌ, (TA,) ‡ *He compressed the woman*: (Ḳ, TA:) the verb in this sense may be derived from a phrase mentioned voce عُسَيْلَةٌ, or it may be a word independently coined: ISd says, "In my opinion it is derived." (TA.) —— عَسَلَ مِنْ طَعَامِهِ, inf. n. عَسْلٌ, [in form] like حَلَبَ, inf. n. حَلَبٌ, *He tasted his food*. (AA, O, Ḳ.) ═ عَسَلَ, said of a spear, aor. ِ, inf. n. عَسَلَانٌ (Ṣ, O, Ḳ) and عَسْلٌ [correctly عَسَلٌ] and عُسُولٌ, (Ḳ,) *It quivered*: (Ṣ, Ḳ:) or *quivered much*. (Ḳ. [In the CḲ, عَسْلًا and عَسْلَانًا are put for عَسَلًا and عَسَلَانًا.]) —— And عَسَلَ said of water, inf. n. عَسْلٌ and عَسَلَانٌ, (Ḳ, TA,) both with fet-ḥ to the س, (TA, [but the former in the CḲ is with the س quiescent,]) *It became agitated* (Ḳ, TA) *and rippled*, (TA,) *being put in a state of commotion by the wind*. (Ḳ, TA.) —— And عَسَلَ said of a wolf, (Ṣ, O, Ḳ,) or of a horse, (Ḳ,) or of a fox, (TA,) inf. n. عَسَلٌ and عَسَلَانٌ, (Ṣ, O, Ḳ, TA, [but both in the CḲ with the س quiescent,]) *He went the pace termed* عَنَق, or خَبَب, [i. e., *with wide steps*,] *and quickly*: and in like manner said of a man: (Ṣ, O:) or *he was in a state of agitation in his running, and shook his head*, (Ḳ, TA,) *going along quickly*: (TA:) or عَسَلَانٌ signifies the *shaking of the limbs in running*; and is mostly used in relation to the wolf: (Er-Rághib, TA:) and, as some say, عَسَلُ الفَرَسِ and عَسَلَانُهُ signify *the horse's being vehement*, or *ardent*, (أَنْ يَضْطَرِمَ,) *in his running, bending down his head, and having his back even*: and عَسَلَ الطَّرِيقَ, said of a fox, occurs in a verse of Sá'ideh Ibn-Ju-eiyeh, for عَسَلَ عَنِ الطَّرِيقِ [app. a mistranscription for عسل فى الطريق], like the phrase دَخَلْتُ البَيْتَ [for دخلت فِى البَيْتِ]. (TA. [See what next follows.]) One says also, of a guide, عَسَلَ بِالْمَفَازَةِ, (Ḳ, TA,) or فِى الطَّرِيقِ, (Ḥam p. 353,) *He went quickly*, (Ḳ,) or *went with wide steps, like the wolf*, (TA,) [*in the desert*, or *waterless desert*, or *in the way*]. كَذَبَ عَلَيْكَ العَسَلُ (Ṣ, Ḳ) and العَسَلَ, (Ḳ,) occurring in a trad., means *Keep thou to going along quickly*; (Ṣ, Ḳ, TA;) from العَسَلَانُ signifying *the going along* of the wolf and *the quivering* of the spear: or, as some say, by العَسَل is here meant عَسَلُ النَّحْلِ [*the honey of bees*]. (TA. See also art. كذب.) ═ عَسِلَ بِالشَّىْءِ, (O, TA,) with kesr [to the س], (O,) like عَلِمَ, (TA,) or عَسَلَ بالشىء, (so in two copies of the Ṣ, [in one of my copies of the Ṣ omitted,]) inf. n. عَسَلٌ, with fet-ḥ to the س, (O,) or عُسُولٌ (Ṣ, TA) and عَسْلٌ, (TA,) *He kept*, or *clave, to the thing*. (Ṣ, O, TA.)

2. عَسَّلَ الطَّعَامَ, inf. n. تَعْسِيلٌ: see 1, first sentence. —— عَسَّلْتُهُمْ, (Ṣ, O, Ḳ,) inf. n. as above, (Ṣ, O,) *I furnished them with* عَسَل [i. e. *honey*] *for travelling-provision*; (Ṣ, O, Ḳ;) as also ▼ عَسَلْتُهُمْ. (Ḳ.) —— And عَسَّلَ الرَّجُلَ, inf. n. as above, *He made the man's condiment to be* عَسَل [or *honey*]. (TA.) —— And the Arabs say, عَسِّلُوا ضَيْفَكُمْ, meaning *Divert ye your guest with something* [*whereby to allay the craving of his stomach*] *before the* [*morning-meal called*] غَدَآء; like لَبِّجُوهُ and لَهِّنُوهُ &c. (El-Umawee, TA in art. لبج.) —— And عَسَّلَتِ النَّحْلُ *The bees made honey*. (TA.) —— [And, accord. to Freytag, عسّل signifies *He collected honey*: but for this he names no authority.]

10. اِسْتَعْسَلُوا *They sought*, or *demanded*, or *asked for*, عَسَل [i. e. *honey*], (Ṣ, O, Ḳ,) *as a gift*. (Ḳ.)

عَسَلٌ : see عَنْسَلٌ, below. ═ عَسْلًا لَهُ means

تَعْسًا لَهُ [i. e. *May he stumble and fall;* &c.; (see art. تعس;) عَسْلًا being app. an inf. n., of which, in this sense, the verb is not mentioned]: (O, Ḳ:) [or *may he be reviled;* for] it is said that العَسْلُ signifies *the reviling in blaming.* (TA.)

عِسْلُ مَالٍ (O, Ḳ) and ▼ عَسِيلُ مَالٍ (O) *i. q.* إِزَاؤُهُ, (O, Ḳ, TA,) i. e. *A good manager and pastor of cattle,* or *camels &c.:* the pl. of عِسْلٌ is أَعْسَالٌ. (TA.) — And هٰذَا عِسْلُ هٰذَا means *This is the like of this:* and so عِسْنُهُ. (O.)

عَسَلٌ [*Honey;*] the *fluid that is discharged from the mouths of bees,* (Ḳ, TA,) *when they have eaten, of the flowers and the leaves, what fills their bellies, these substances being then converted by God, within their bellies, into* عَسَل, *which they eject from their mouths:* (TA: [in which, and in the Ḳ, several other explanations are added, too fanciful to deserve notice:]) the word is masc. and fem.; (Ṣ, O, Mṣb, Ḳ;) in most instances fem.: (Ṣ, O, Mṣb:) عَسَلَةٌ signifies *a portion,* or *somewhat, thereof;* (Ṣ, Mgh, O, TA;) being the n. un.: (TA:) the dim. is ▼ عُسَيْلَةٌ, with ة, because عَسَل is mostly fem., or as meaning عَسَلَةٌ; (Ṣ, O, Mṣb;) or it is the dim. of عَسَلَةٌ: (Mgh:) the pl. of عَسَل is أَعْسَالٌ [a pl. of pauc.] and عُسُلٌ and عُسْلٌ and عُسُولٌ and عُسْلَانٌ; (AḤn, Ḳ;) and these pls. are used when one means *sorts of* عَسَل. (AḤn, TA.) — [It is also used tropically for نَوْرٌ, i. e. † *Flowers,* or *blossoms;* because honey is made therefrom. (See جَرَسَ.) — And it is applied also to † The *sweet, thick, inspissated,* or *melligenous, juice* of fruit:] and it signifies [particularly] † the *juice that flows from fresh ripe dates;* (O, Ḳ,* TA;) because of its sweetness. (O.) [See also دِبْسٌ.] — Also † The *gum of the* [*species of mimosa called*] عُرْفُط [q. v.]; (O, Ḳ;) because of its sweetness. (O.) And عَسَلُ اللُّبْنَى is † *The gum that flows from the species of tree called* اللُّبْنَى, *having no sweetness;* (O;) *a thing* [or *substance*], (M, TA,) or *a certain odoriferous substance,* (Ḳ,) *that exudes from the species of tree above mentioned,* (M, Ḳ,* TA,) i. e. المَيْعَةُ [generally applied to *storax,* or *styrax*], (TA in art. لبن,) *used for fumigation, and called by the vulgar* حَصَى لُبَانٍ. (Ḳ. [See art. حصو and حصى.]) And عَسَلُ الرِّمْثِ is *A white thing* [or *substance, a species of manna,*] *that comes forth from the* [*shrub called*] رِمْث [q. v.], *resembling* جُمَان [i. e. *pearls,* or *silver beads like pearls*]. (Ḳ,* TA.) — Also † *A good,* or *righteous, deed, the eulogy for which is deemed sweet.* (AZ, O.) See عَاسِل. — And The حَبَاب [app. as meaning *ripples*] *of running water,* (IAạr, O, Ḳ,) [*arising*] *from the blowing of the wind.* (IAạr, O.) — [In one place in the CḲ, العَسَلُ is erroneously put for العَسْلُ: see عَنْسَل, below.]

عَسِلٌ, (Ṣ, O, TA,) in the Ḳ erroneously said to be like أَمِيرٌ, i. e. ▼ عَسِيلٌ, (TA,) applied to a man, (Ḳ,) *Vehement in beating,* (Ṣ, O, Ḳ,) *quick in the raising,* (سَرِيعُ رَفْعٍ, O, and so in copies of the Ṣ,) or *in the falling,* (وَقْعٍ, so in a copy of the Ṣ,) or *in the returning,* (رَجْعٍ, so in the Ḳ,) *of the hand,* or *arm,* (Ṣ, O, Ḳ,) *with the beating.* (TA.)

أَبُو عِسْلَةَ: see عَاسِلٌ.

عَسَلَةٌ n. un. of عَسَلٌ [q. v.]. — [مَضْرِبُ عَسَلَةٍ is a euphemism for † *The place of injection of sperma:* and hence it means † *the source from which one springs; origin; ancestry,* or *parentage;* &c.] One says, مَا لِفُلَانٍ مَضْرِبُ عَسَلَةٍ i. e. † [*Such a one has no source*] *of kindred* (نَسَب), (Ṣ, O,) *nor of cattle* or *property* (مَال). (Ṣ in art. ضرب.) And مَا أَعْرِفُ لَهُ مَضْرِبَ عَسَلَةٍ meaning أَعْرَاقَهُ [i. e. † *I know not the sources* (or *the source*) *from which he has sprung;* or *his ancestry,* or *parentage*]: (Ṣ, O,* Ḳ:) or ‡ *his origin,* and *any wife from whom he has sprung.* (A, TA.) And مَا تَرَكَ لَهُ مَضْرِبَ عَسَلَةٍ ‡ *He reviled him so that he demolished his parentage, and denied his origin,* or *rank* or *quality.* (Z, TA.) And كُلُّ ضَرْبَةٍ لَهَا مِنْ عَسَلَةٍ, said respecting his mother by an Arab of the desert, meaning ‡ *Every child that she has brought forth is from a manly sire.* (A, TA.) And عَلِمَ فُلَانٌ عَسَلَةَ بَنِي فُلَانٍ † *Such a one knew the whole company, and case,* or *condition,* [or *origin,*] *of the sons of such a one.* (O.)

عَسَلِيٌّ A thing *of the colour of* عَسَل [i. e. *honey*]. (TA.) — [Hence,] عَسَلِيُّ اليَهُودِ *The distinctive mark,* or *sign,* [which has sometimes been *a honey-coloured turban,* at other times *a girdle,* or *some other article of attire, of the same colour,*] *of the Jews.* (Ṣ, Mgh, O, Ḳ.)

عَسُولٌ: see عَاسِلٌ: — and see also عَسَّالٌ.

عَسِيلٌ The *broom,* or *implement for sweeping, of the seller of perfumes,* (Ṣ, O, Ḳ,* TA, مِكْنَسَة in the Ḳ being a mistake for مِكْنَسَةُ, TA,) *with which he gathers together the perfume;* (Ṣ, O, TA;) it is a *hair-broom, with which he sweeps up the perfume from his paved floor:* (TA:) or *a feather with which* [*the compound of perfumes called*] غَالِيَة *is detached,* or *displaced:* (Fr, IAạr, O, Ḳ:) pl. عُسُلٌ. (TA.) A poet says,

فَرِشْنِي بِخَيْرٍ لَا أَكُونَنْ وَمِدْحَتِي
كَنَاحِتِ يَوْمًا صَخْرَةٍ بِعَسِيلِ

[*Then amend thou my condition by means of wealth: I will assuredly not be, with my mode of praising, like a hewer, one day, of a rock with a hair-broom,* or *a feather, of a seller of perfumes*]: he means, كَنَاحِتِ صَخْرَةٍ يَوْمًا, this last word intervening between the prefixed noun and its complement because the noun of time is held by them to be like what is redundant. (Ṣ, O, TA. [One of my copies of the Ṣ has أَكُونَنَّ; the O, أَكُونَا: and each of my copies of the Ṣ has صَخْرَةً; and one of them, يَوْمٍ.]) — And The *pizzle of an elephant,* (Ṣ, O, Ḳ,) and *of a camel:* pl. as above. (Ḳ.) — See also عِسْلُ مَالٍ. — And see عَسِلٌ.

عُسَيْلَةٌ dim. of عَسَلٌ, q. v.: or of its n. un. — [Hence,] ‡ *i. q.* نُطْفَةٌ [i. e. The *sperma of a man* and *of a woman*]: or the مَآء [meaning *sperma*] of a man. (Ḳ, TA.) — And ‡ The *deliciousness,* (Ṣ, Mgh, O, Mṣb, TA,) or *sweetness,* (Mgh, Ḳ, TA,) *of* جِمَاع; as being likened to عَسَل [i. e. honey]. (Ṣ, O, Mṣb, Ḳ, TA.) Thus, (Mgh, O, Mṣb, TA,) or as expl. in the next preceding sentence, (TA,) in the saying of the Prophet to a woman who desired to be divorced from a husband in order that she might return to a former husband, لَا حَتَّى تَذُوقِي عُسَيْلَتَهُ وَيَذُوقَ عُسَيْلَتَكِ. (Mgh, O, Mṣb, TA. [See 1 in art. ذوق.]) — And العُسَيْلَتَانِ signifies العُضْوَانِ [meaning *The male and female genital organs*]; because means of experiencing delight. (Z, TA.)

عَسَّالٌ: see عَاسِلٌ. — Also, (Ṣ, O, Mṣb, Ḳ,) and ▼ عَاسِلٌ, (Mṣb, Ḳ,) and ▼ عَسُولٌ, (Ḳ,) A spear *that quivers,* (Ṣ, O, Mṣb,) by reason of pliableness: (Mṣb:) or [so the second, but the first and last,] a spear *that quivers much.* (Ḳ.) And رِمَاحٌ عَسَّالَةٌ [*Spears that quiver much*]. (A in art. زعب.) — See, again, عَاسِلٌ.

عَسَّالَةٌ [as a subst.] *Bees.* (Ṣ, O, Ḳ.) — And The شُورَة *of bees;* (Ḳ, TA;) i. e. the *thing, such as a* رَاقُود [q. v.] *&c., in which bees make honey.* (TA.) [See also مُعَسَّلَةٌ.]

عَاسِلٌ *A gatherer of honey* (Ṣ, O, Ḳ) *from the hive* (Ṣ, O) or *from its place;* as also ▼ عَسَّالٌ. (Ḳ.) [And نَحْلٌ عَوَاسِلُ *Bees occupied in gathering honey:* see a verse of Aboo-Dhu-eyb cited in art. خلف, conj. 3.] — Also, as a possessive epithet, A place *in which is honey.* (TA.) One says خَلِيَّةٌ عَاسِلَةٌ (Ṣ, O, TA) *A hive containing honey.* (TA.) — Also an epithet applied to a man, (O, Ḳ,) said by Az to be as though it were for ▼ ذُو عَسَلٍ, (O,) meaning † *Having a good,* or *righteous, deed attributable to him, for which the eulogy of him is deemed sweet:* (Az, O, Ḳ:) and (O, Ḳ) accord. to IAạr, (O,) a *good,* or *righteous,* man; as also ▼ عَسُولٌ; (O, Ḳ;) the former said by him to be an instance of the measure فَاعِلٌ in the sense of مَفْعُولٌ بِهِ [as meaning † *made an object of eulogy:* see 1, second sentence]: (O:) pl. of both عُسُلٌ, (O, Ḳ,) accord. to him. (O.) — See also العَاسِلُ. — عَسَّالٌ also signifies *The wolf;* [because of his manner of running; (see 1, latter half;)] (Ṣ, O, Ḳ;) and so ▼ العَسَّالُ; (TA;) and ▼ أَبُو عِسْلَةَ (O, Ḳ) and ابو غِسْلَة, with ع and غ: (O:) pl. of the first عُسُلٌ and عَوَاسِلُ (Ṣ, O, Ḳ) [and عَاسِلَاتٌ is mentioned by Freytag as signifying *wolves* from the Deewán of the Hudhalees].

عَنْسَلٌ A *swift* she-camel; (Ṣ, Ḳ;) as also ▼ عَسْلٌ: (Ḳ, TA: [العَسَلُ in the CḲ, as syn. with العَنْسَلُ, is a mistranscription:]) the ن in the former is augmentative; (IJ, Ṣ, TA;) for, as Sb says, the word is of the measure فَنْعَلٌ from [the inf. n.] العَسَلَانُ; not, as Mohammad Ibn-

Ḥabeeb asserts it to be, syn. with عَنْسٌ, and of the measure فُعْلَلٌ, with the ل augmentative. (IJ, TA.)

أَعْسَالٌ *i. q.* [آسَالٌ and] آسَانٌ: so in the saying هُوَ عَلَى أَعْسَالٍ مِنْ أَبِيهِ [*He is of a semblance and of characteristics and natural dispositions which are those of his father*]. (O, Ḳ.)

تَعْسِيلَةٌ *A light sleep:* but this is a vulgar [post-classical] word. (TA.)

مَعْسَلَةٌ *i. q.* خَلِيَّةٌ [q. v., i. e. The *habitation of bees,* whether it be *a manufactured hive* or *a hollow in the trunk of a tree* or *in a rock, in which they deposit their honey*]. (Ḳ.) [See also عَسَّالَةٌ.]

مُعَسَّلٌ *Made* [or *preserved*] *with* عَسَل [i. e. *honey*]: applied as an epithet in this sense to زَنْجَبِيل [or ginger]. (Ṣ, TA.)

حَدِيثٌ مَعْسُولٌ † *Sweet* [or (as we say) *honeyed*] *talk* or *discourse.* (TA.) And جَارِيَةٌ مَعْسُولَةُ الكَلَامِ † *A girl,* or *young woman, sweet in speech, beautiful in expression, pleasing in the modulation of the voice.* (TA.) And مَعْسُولُ المَوَاعِيدِ † *Veracious,* or *faithful, in promises.* (TA.)

عسلج

Q. 1. عَسْلَجَتِ الشَّجَرَةُ *The tree put forth its* عَسَالِيج, or *soft and green rods* or *twigs* or *shoots* [&c.: see عُسْلُوجٌ]. (Ṣ, Ḳ.)

عُسْلُجٌ: see عُسْلُوجٌ, in four places.

عَسَلَّجٌ, applied to food (طَعَام), *i. q.* رَقِيقٌ [app. meaning *Thin,* or *unsubstantial*], (Ibn-'Abbád, O, Ḳ,) i. e. *in which are flour and water:* (Ibn-'Abbád, O:) or *good, sweet,* or *pleasant.* (O, Ḳ.)

عِسْلَاجٌ: see the following paragraph.

عُسْلُوجٌ *A branch,* or *twig,* or *shoot:* (Mṣb:) or *a branch,* or *twig,* or *shoot, that is a year old:* (Lth, O:) or *a rod,* or *twig,* or *shoot, of recent growth:* (TA:) or *any plant that comes forth green, twisting,* or *wreathing, and soft, before it assumes other colours:* (AḤn, O:) or, as also ↓ عُسْلُجٌ, (Ṣ, O, Ḳ,) and ↓ عِسْلَاجٌ, (O,) *a soft and green rod* or *twig* or *shoot* (Ṣ, O, Ḳ) *of a tree, and of a grape-vine, when it first grows forth:* (Ṣ, O:) or all signify *a branch,* or *twig,* or *shoot, until a year old:* (M, TA:) or ↓ عُسْلُجٌ signifies *a soft,* or *tender, branch* or *twig* or *shoot:* (TA:) the pl. of عُسْلُوجٌ is عَسَالِيجُ: (Mṣb:) and this is said to signify *a certain* [*sort of*] *white thing, that comes forth in the* صَيْف [meaning either *spring* or *summer*], *and stretches along like the* خَيْزُرَان [or *kind of cane called rattan*], *soft,* or *supple, and bending:* (O:) it is [also] said to signify the عُرُوق of trees, i. e. the نُجُوم thereof [meaning the *sprouts from the roots* (see art. نجم)] *that shoot forth in the year:* and *certain things that spread upon the surface of the earth, like* عُرُوق [or *roots*], *and are green:* or *a certain plant upon the banks of rivers, bending and inclining by reason of softness,* or *tenderness,* or *luxuriance:* and, as used by the vulgar, *rods,* or *twigs,* or *shoots, of recent growth.* (L.) — Also † A boy, or young man, *hot-headed, and light,* or *active, in spirit.* (IAạr, O.) And جَارِيَةٌ عُسْلُوجَةُ النَّبَاتِ (O, Ḳ) and القَوَامِ (O) † *A soft,* or *tender, girl* or *young woman.* (O, Ḳ, TA.) And ↓ قَوَامٌ عُسْلُجٌ † *A soft,* or *tender, figure,* or *person:* (O, Ḳ:) the latter word, used in this sense by El-'Ajjáj, said to be a contraction of عُسْلُوجٌ. (TA.) And ↓ شَبَابٌ عُسْلُجٌ † *A perfect state of youthfulness.* (TA.)

عسم

1. عَسِمَ, aor. ـَ, (Mṣb, Ḳ,) inf. n. عَسَمٌ, (Ṣ,* Mṣb, Ḳ,*) *It* (a man's hand, and his foot,) *was,* or *became, distorted,* (Ṣ,* Mṣb, Ḳ,) [or, accord. to the Ḳ, app. said of a man, meaning *he was,* or *became, distorted in his hand,* and *his foot,* and thus in the TḲ,] *in consequence of rigidity in the wrist,* and *ankle.* (Ṣ,* Mṣb, Ḳ.* [See also عَسَمٌ below.]) — عَسَمَ, aor. ـِ, (Ṣ, Mṣb, Ḳ,) inf. n. عَسْمٌ, (Ṣ, Mṣb,) *He coveted.* (Ṣ, Mṣb, Ḳ.) [It is trans. by means of فِى.] One says, لَا يَعْسِمُ فِيهِ [*He will not covet it*]. (Ṣ.) And أَمْرٌ لَا يُعْسَمُ فِيهِ *A thing,* or *an affair, the contending with which for the mastery, and the mastering of which, will not be coveted.* (Ṣ, Ḳ.) — Also, inf. n. عَسْمٌ and عُسُومٌ, *He gained,* or *earned;* or *he sought sustenance;* syn. كَسَبَ; (Ḳ, TA;) *for himself;* or *for his family,* or *household:* (TA:) accord. to Fr, الاِكْتِسَابُ signifies العَسْمُ [i. e. *the gaining,* or *earning;* or *the seeking sustenance*]; (Ṣ;) [and] so signifies ↓ الاِعْتِسَامُ. (TA.) — عَسَمَ فِى الأَمْرِ, (Ṣ, Ḳ,) aor. ـِ, (Ṣ,) *He strove, laboured,* or *toiled;* or *he exerted himself,* or *put himself to labour;* in *the affair.* (Ṣ, Ḳ.*) — And عَسَمَ, (Ḳ,) or عَسَمَ وَسْطَ القَوْمِ بِنَفْسِهِ, (Ṣ,) *He plunged into the midst of the people,* or *party, so that he mixed with them, not caring whether it were in battle or not:* (Ṣ, Ḳ, TA:) or, accord. to some, it is peculiarly in war, or battle; one says, عَسَمَ, aor. ـِ, inf. n. عَسْمٌ, meaning *he went at random, heedlessly,* or *in a headlong manner, without consideration, into war,* or *battle, and threw himself into the midst of it, not caring.* (TA.) — عَسَمَتْ عَيْنُهُ *His eye shed tears* (ذَرَفَتْ [in the CḲ ذَرِفَتْ]): and (some say, TA) *had foul matter in its inner angle* (غَمِصَتْ [in the CḲ غَمَضَتْ]); as also ↓ أَعْسَمَتْ: or *had its lids closed, one upon the other.* (Ḳ, TA.)

4. اعسم يَدَهُ *He,* or *it, rendered his hand rigid* [*and* app. *distorted:* see 1, first sentence]. (Ḳ.) — اعسمهُ *He gave to him.* (TA.) — See also 1, last sentence.

8. اِعْتَسَمْتُهُ *I gave him what he coveted from me.* (Ṣ, TA.) — And الاِعْتِسَامُ signifies الاِكْتِسَابُ [expl. above]: see 1. (TA.) — Also *The sheep's,* or *goats', bringing forth, and the pastor's coming and putting to every one of them her young one.* (Ṣ, Ḳ.) [Accord. to the TḲ, one says, اِعْتَسَمَتِ الشَّاةُ, (using الشاة, as is sometimes done, in the sense of the coll. gen. n. الشَّآء, or the former may be a misprint for the latter,) meaning *The sheep,* or *goats, brought forth,* &c.] — And *The taking and wearing an old and worn-out sandal,* or *boot.* (Ḳ.) [Accord. to the TḲ, one says, اعتسم النَّعْلَ, or الخُفَّ, meaning *He took the sandal,* or *the boot, in an old and worn-out state, and wore it.*]

عَسَمٌ [mentioned above as an inf. n.] signifies *A rigidity in the wrist,* and *ankle; in consequence of which the hand,* and *foot, become distorted:* (Ṣ, Ḳ:) or, as some say, *a rigidity in a man's wrist:* (TA:) or *a distortion in the hand,* or *arm, in consequence of a rigidity in the wrist,* or *in the elbows.* (Mgh.) — See also مَعْسِمٌ.

عَسِمِىٌّ One *who gains,* or *earns, much for his family,* or *household.* (TA.)

عَسُومٌ One *who toils,* or *works laboriously,* or *who seeks gain* or *the means of subsistence, for his family,* or *household;* as also ↓ عَاسِمٌ: pl. [of the former, and perhaps of the latter also,] عُسُمٌ. (Ḳ.) — And A she-camel *that has many young ones.* (Ḳ.)

عَاسِمٌ: see the next preceding paragraph.

أَعْسَمُ *Having a distortion of the hand,* and *of the foot, in consequence of rigidity in the wrist,* and *ankle;* applied to a man: and so عَسْمَآءُ applied to a woman. (Ṣ, Mṣb, Ḳ. [See also عَسَمٌ.]) — And An ass *slender in the legs.* (TA.)

مَعْسِمٌ *A thing that is,* or *that is to be, coveted;* syn. مَطْمَعٌ; (Ṣ, TA;) as also ↓ عَسَمٌ; or this latter signifies *coveting,* or *covetousness;* and مَعْشَمٌ, with ش, is a dial. var. of it. (TA in this art. and in art. عشم.) So the former signifies in the saying مَا لَكَ فِى بَنِى فُلَانٍ مَعْسِمٌ [*There is not for thee, in the sons of such a one, anything that is,* or *is to be, coveted*]. (Ṣ.) [Freytag has written this word مَعْسَمٌ, as from the Ḳ, in which I do not find it; and has expl. it as signifying *desire.*]

عسو

1. عَسَا العُودُ, aor. يَعْسُو, inf. n. عُسُوٌّ and عَسَآءٌ, *The wood,* or *stick, was,* or *became, dry and hard:* (Aṣ, Ṣ:) and عَسَا النَّبَاتُ, (Kh, Ṣ, Ḳ,) inf. ns. as above, (Ḳ, TA,) *the plant was,* or *became, thick,* or *coarse,* or *rough,* (Kh, Ṣ, Ḳ,) *and dry,* (Ḳ,) *and hard;* (TA;) as also عَسِىَ, (Kh, Ṣ, TA, [in the CḲ, in art. عسى, erroneously written عَسَى,]) a dial. var. of the former, (Kh, Ṣ,) inf. n. عَسًا. (TA.) — And عَسَتْ يَدُهُ, aor. تَعْسُو, inf. n. عُسُوٌّ (El-Aḥmar, Ṣ, Mṣb, TA) and عَسِىَ, (Mṣb,) *His hand became thick,* or *coarse,* or *rough, from work.* (El-Aḥmar, Ṣ, Mṣb, TA.) — عَسَا said of an old man, aor. يَعْسُو, (Aṣ, Ṣ, Mṣb, Ḳ,) inf. n. عُسِىٌّ, (Aṣ, Ṣ,) or عُسُوٌّ, (Mṣb,) or both, and عَسَآءٌ and عُسُوٌّ; (Ḳ;) and عَسِىَ, (Kh, Ṣ, Ḳ,) inf. n. عَسًا; (Ḳ;) *He became aged,* or *ad-*

vanced in age, (Mṣb, Ḳ,) and (Mṣb) *in a declining state* (Ṣ, Mṣb) *by reason of age:* like عَتَا. (Ṣ.) [See also an explanation of عَتَا more agreeable with the first and second of the significations mentioned in this paragraph.] —— And عَسَا اللَّيْلُ *The night became intensely dark:* (Ḳ:) but غَسَا is more known [in this sense]. (TA.)

عَسْوٌ i. q. شَمْعٌ [*Wax, or wax-candles*]. (Ḳ.)

عَسًا *Dates while green and small:* (Ṣ:) said in the Ḳ, in art. عسى, and [before] by Hr as is stated in the handwriting of Aboo-Zekereeyà, to be correctly with غ; but mentioned by Sb in the "Book of Palm-trees," and by AḤn in the "Book of Plants," as being with ع and غ. (TA.) —— [Also, as stated by Freytag on the authority of Dmr, The *female locust.*]

عِسْوَةٌ *Age; old age.* (TA. [See 1.])

عَاسٍ [part. n. of 1;] *Thick, coarse,* or *rough.* (TA.) ═ And The *fruit-stalk of the raceme of a palm-tree:* (A'Obeyd, Ṣ, and TA in art. عسى:) of the dial. of Belḥárith Ibn-Kaab. (TA.) —— And (TA) *Palm-trees* (نَخْلٌ). (Ḳ, TA, both in art. عسى.)

أَعْسَآءٌ [a pl. of which the sing. is not mentioned;] *Hard* [*hollows, or cavities, in stone,* or *in rugged ground, that retain the water of the rain, such as are termed*] أَرْزَانٌ. (TA.)

عسى

1. عَسَى is [said by some to be] one of the verbs of appropinquation, implying eager desire, or hope, and fear, and not perfectly inflected, for it is applied in the form of the preterite to that which occurs in the present: one says عَسَى زَيْدٌ أَنْ يَخْرُجَ [meaning, accord. to what has been said above, *Zeyd is near to going forth,* though generally otherwise expl., as will be shown in what follows], and عَسَتْ فُلَانَةُ أَنْ تَخْرُجَ [*Such a woman is near to going forth*]; زَيْدٌ being the agent of عَسَى, and أَنْ يَخْرُجَ being its objective complement and meaning الخُرُوجَ: and one says also, عَسَيْتُ أَنْ أَفْعَلَ ذَاكَ [as meaning, accord. to what here precedes, *I am near to doing that*], and عَسِيتُ, with kesr, agreeably with readings [in the Ḳur xlvii. 24], فَهَلْ عَسِيتُمْ and عَسَيْتُمْ, with kesr and fet-ḥ; and one says to a woman, عَسَيْتِ أَنْ تَفْعَلِى ذَاكَ; and [to women,] عَسَيْتُنَّ; but one does not use the form يَفْعَلُ thereof, nor the form فَاعِلٌ; (Ṣ;) both of which [however] are mentioned [as used] by the author of the "Inṣáf:" (I'Aḳ p. 88:) [or, accord. to Fei,] عَسَى is a preterite verb, [used in the sense of the present,] aplastic, not perfectly inflected, of the verbs of appropinquation, implying hope, and eager desire, and sometimes opinion, and certainty; and it is incomplete [i. e. non-attributive], and complete [i. e. attributive]: the incomplete has for its predicate an aor. manṣoob by means of أَنْ, as in the saying, عَسَى زَيْدٌ أَنْ يَقُومَ, meaning قَارَبَ زَيْدٌ القِيَامَ [*Zeyd is near to standing*], the predicate being an objective complement or having the meaning of an objective complement: or, as some say, the meaning is لَعَلَّ زَيْدًا أَنْ يَقُومَ, i.e. [virtually, but not literally,] *I eagerly desire,* or *I hope, that Zeyd may be performing the act of standing:* [but see عَلَّ and لَعَلَّ in art. علّ, as well as what follows in this paragraph after the explanation of the next ex.:] the complete is such as occurs in the saying, عَسَى أَنْ يَقُومَ زَيْدٌ [meaning, accord. to what is said above, *Zeyd's standing is near to being a fact*]; the agent being literally a phrase composed of a subject and an attribute because أَنْ is here what is termed مَصْدَرِيَّة [so that أَنْ يَقُومَ زَيْدٌ is equivalent to قِيَامُ زَيْدٍ]: (Mṣb:) —— [in the MA and PṢ and TḲ &c., عَسَى is expl. as meaning *It may be that;* and this, or simply *may-be,* or *may-hap,* or *perhaps,* I regard as the preferable rendering; as being virtually the meaning in all cases: for عَسَى زَيْدٌ أَنْ يَقُومَ, in which it is used as an incomplete verb, however it may be rendered, virtually means *It may be that Zeyd is,* or *will be, standing;* or *may-be Zeyd* &c.: and عَسَى أَنْ يَقُومَ زَيْدٌ, in which it is used as a complete verb, virtually means the same, though more properly rendered *Zeyd's standing may be a fact:* its usages are various, and have occasioned much dispute respecting its grammatical character and its meaning or meanings; as will be shown by what here follows:] —— it is [said to be] a verb unrestrictedly, or a particle unrestrictedly: (Ḳ:) [but this statement seems to have originated from a mistranscription: IHsh says,] it is a verb unrestrictedly: not a particle unrestrictedly, contrary to the opinion of Ibn-Es-Sarráj and Th; nor when it has an affixed pronoun, as in عَسَاكَ, contrary to an opinion of Sb, ascribed to him by Seer: (Mughnee:) it denotes hope in the case of that which is liked, and fear in the case of that which is disliked; as in the saying in the Ḳur [ii. 213], وَعَسَى أَنْ تَكْرَهُوا شَيْئًا وَهُوَ خَيْرٌ لَكُمْ وَعَسَى أَنْ تُحِبُّوا شَيْئًا وَهُوَ شَرٌّ لَكُمْ [*But it may be that ye dislike a thing when it is good for you, and it may be that ye like a thing when it is evil for you*]: (Mughnee, Ḳ:*) —— it is used in various ways; one of which is the saying, عَسَى زَيْدٌ أَنْ يَقُومَ [mentioned above], respecting the analysis of which there are different opinions: that of the generality is, that it is like كَانَ زَيْدٌ يَقُومُ [inasmuch as عسى is here an incomplete verb]; but this is deemed dubious, because the predicate [أَنْ يَقُومَ] is rendered by an inf. n., and the subject [زَيْدٌ] is a substance; to which several replies have been made; one being that a prefixed noun is meant to be understood, either before the subject, so that the meaning is, عَسَى أَمْرُ زَيْدٍ القِيَامُ [*It may be that the case of Zeyd is,* or *will be, the performing of the act of standing*], or before the predicate, so that the meaning is عَسَى زَيْدٌ صَاحِبَ القِيَامِ [*It may be that Zeyd is,* or *will be, the performer of the act of standing*]; and another reply is, that it is of the class of زَيْدٌ عَدْلٌ and صَوْمٌ [meaning عَادِلٌ and صَائِمٌ, for أَنْ يَقُومَ is equivalent to an inf. n., and an inf. n. may be used in the sense of an act. part. n.]; and another is, that أَنْ is here redundant, which reply is [said to be] nought, because ان has rendered the aor. manṣoob, and because it seldom falls out [from the phrase, though it should be remarked that لَعَلَّ, which is said in the Mughnee to be like عَسَى in meaning, is generally followed by a simple aor. and sometimes by أَنْ and an aor.]: another opinion respecting the analysis of the phrase is, that عَسَى is a trans. verb, like قَارَبَ in meaning and in government, [agreeably with the explanations mentioned above from the Ṣ and Mṣb,] or intrans. like قَرُبَ مِنْ with the preposition suppressed; and this is the opinion of Sb and Mbr: the opinion of the generality is, that it is an incomplete verb [like كَانَ in the phrase كَانَ زَيْدٌ يَقُومُ, mentioned above], and that أَنْ and the verb following it compose a substitute of implication supplying what is wanting in the two preceding portions of the sentence: —— the second way of using it is, the making it to have أَنْ and the verb following this for its object, [as in عَسَى أَنْ يَقُومَ زَيْدٌ, mentioned above], so that it is a complete verb: —— the third and fourth and fifth are when it is followed by a simple aor., [being in this case likened to كَادَ, (Ṣ, Ḳ,* TA,)] or an aor. with س prefixed, or a single noun; as in عَسَى زَيْدٌ يَقُومُ [*It may be that Zeyd stands,* or *will stand*] and عَسَى زَيْدٌ سَيَقُومُ [*It may be that Zeyd will stand*] and عَسَى زَيْدٌ قَائِمٌ [*It may be that Zeyd is standing*]; the first whereof is one of which there are few exs., such as the saying,

• عَسَى الكَرْبُ الَّذِى أَمْسَيْتَ فِيهِ •
• يَكُونُ وَرَآءَهُ فَرَجٌ قَرِيبُ •

[*It may be that the state of anxiety in which thou hast become* (or, as some relate it, أَمْسَيْتُ i. e. *I have become,*) *is such that after it will be a near removal thereof*]; and the third is one of which there are fewer exs., [and which is said in the Ṣ to be not allowable,] such as the saying,

• أَكْثَرْتَ فِى العَذْلِ مُلِحًّا دَائِمَا •
• لَا تُكْثِرَنْ إِنِّى عَسِيتُ صَائِمَا •

[or, as some relate it, عَسَيْتُ, which is more common, i. e. *Thou hast been profuse in censuring, persisting constantly: be not thou profuse: verily it may be that I am,* or *shall be, abstaining*]; and as to the prov., عَسَى الغُوَيْرُ أَبْؤُسًا [expl. in art. بأس, and of which it is said in the Ḳ that the verb therein is used in the manner of كَانَ, and in the Ṣ that the phrase is extr., that ابؤسا is there put in the place of the predicate, and that there sometimes occurs in provs. what does not occur elsewhere], the right opinion is that يَكُونُ is suppressed before ابؤسا; and [in the latter of the two verses cited above] أَكُونُ is suppressed before صائما; because thus the primary usage is preserved, and because what is hoped is the person's being an abstainer, not the abstainer himself; and as to the second of the three modes of using عَسَى last mentioned above, with س prefixed to the aor., it is very extr.: — the sixth way of using it is the saying عَسَانِى and عَسَاكَ and عَسَاهُ, which is rare: in this case, accord. to Sb, it is used in the manner of لَعَلَّ, as governing the subject in the accus. case, and the predicate in the nom.; the predicate being sometimes expressed, in the nom. case, as in the saying,

• فَقُلْتُ عَسَاهَا نَارُ كَأْسٍ وَعَلَّهَا •
• تَشَكَّى فَآتِى نَحْوَهَا فَأَعُودُهَا •

[*And I said, May-be it is the fire of Ka-s*, (for I suppose that كأس is here a proper name, that of a woman, daughter of El-Kelhabeh El-'Oranee,) *and perhaps she has a complaint*, (تَشَكَّى being for تَتَشَكَّى,) *so I will come towards her, and visit her*]: — the seventh way is the saying, عَسَى زَيْدٌ قَائِمٌ, mentioned by Th; which is to be explained on the ground that عسى is here an incomplete verb, and that its subject is the ضَمِيرُ الشَّأْنِ [i. e. إِنَّهُ] is suppressed, the meaning being, *It may be that* the case is this, *Zeyd is standing*], the nominal proposition being the predicate. (Mughnee. [Several other statements in that work, respecting عَسَى, I have omitted, as being refuted therein, or as being of little or no importance.]) — It also denotes opinion, (Mṣb,) or doubt, (Ḳ, TA,) and certainty: (Mṣb, Ḳ, TA:) the last is meant in the saying of Ibn-Muḳbil,

• ظَنِّى بِهِمْ كَعَسَى وَهُمْ بِتَنُوفَةٍ •
• يَتَنَازَعُونَ جَوَائِزَ الْأَمْثَالِ •

[*My opinion of them is like an expression of certainty while they, in a desert*, or *in a desert destitute of water* or *of herbage and water*, &c., *are contending in reciting current proverbs* instead of attending to the wants of themselves and their camels]. (Ṣ, TA.) — As uttered by God, it is expressive of an event of necessary occurrence, (Ṣ, Ḳ,) in the whole of the Ḳur-án, except the saying, [in lxvi. 5,] عَسَى رَبُّهُ إِنْ طَلَّقَكُنَّ أَنْ يُبْدِلَهُ أَزْوَاجًا خَيْرًا مِنْكُنَّ [*It may be that his Lord, if he divorce you, will give him in exchange wives better than you*]. (Ṣ.) — هَلْ عَسَيْتُمْ with what follows it, in the Ḳur [ii. 247], means [virtually] *Are ye near to fleeing?* (Ḳ:) some read thus; and some, عَسِيتُمْ. (TA.) — عَسِىَ النَّبَاتُ [erroneously written in the CḲ عَسَى]: see the first sentence in art. عسو.

4. أَعْسِ بِهِ means *How well adapted* or *disposed*, or *how apt, meet, suited, suitable, fitted, fit, competent*, or *proper*, or *how worthy, is he!* (Lḥ, Ḳ, TA.)

بِالْعَسَى أَنْ تَفْعَلَ means بِالْحَرَى [i. e. *It is suitable, fit*, or *proper, that thou shouldst do* such a thing]. (Ḳ. [In the CḲ, and likewise in the TḲ, erroneously, بِالعَسِىِّ and بِالحَرِىِّ.]) — عَسًا: see art. عسو.

هُوَ عَسٍ بِهِ: see what next follows.

هُوَ عَسِىٌّ بِهِ *He is adapted* or *disposed by nature, apt, meet, suited, suitable, fitted, fit, competent, proper*, or *worthy, for it* or *of it*; as also ▼ عَسٍ بِهِ: (Ḳ, TA:) but one should not say عَسًى. (TA.) [See also مَعْسَاةٌ.]

عَاسٍ: see art. عسو.

مَعْسَآءٌ A girl *thought to have attained puberty*: (Lḥ, TA:) or a girl *near to attaining puberty*. (Ḳ.)

مَعْسَاةٌ is from عَسَى, like مَئِنَّةٌ from إِنَّ: you say, هُوَ مَعْسَاةٌ لِلْخَيْرِ, meaning *He is a person* (مَحَلٌّ) [*fit*, or *proper*,] *for one's saying of him*, عَسَى أَنْ يَفْعَلَ خَيْرًا [*It may be that he will do good*]: (A and TA in art. ان:) and إِنَّهُ لَمَعْسَاةٌ بِكَذَا, meaning مَخْلَقَةٌ [i. e. *Verily he is adapted* or *disposed by nature, apt, meet, suited*, &c., *for such a thing*]: (Ḳ, TA:) and in like manner, without variation, it is used in speaking of a female, and of two persons, and of a pl. number. (TA.)

مُعْسِيَةٌ A she-camel *of which one doubts whether there be in her milk or not*: (IAạr, Ḳ, TA:) or *whose milk has stopped and it is hoped that it will return*. (Er-Rághib, TA.)

عش

1. عَشَّ, (TḲ,) inf. n. عُشٌّ, (Ḳ,) *He* (a bird) *kept to his* عُشّ [or *nest in a tree*]. (Ḳ, TḲ.)

2. عشّش, inf. n. تَعْشِيشٌ, *He* (a bird) *made for himself a nest in a tree*; (Ṣ, O, Ḳ;) as also ▼ اعتشّ, (A, Ḳ,) or اعتشّ عُشَّهُ, (O,) inf. n. اِعْتِشَاشٌ. (TA.) — It is said in a trad., (A, Ḳ,) in the story of Umm-Zarạ, (O, TA,) لَا تَمْلَأُ بَيْتَنَا تَعْشِيشًا, meaning *She will not be unfaithful with respect to our food*, or *wheat, by hiding somewhat in every corner*, (A, O, Ḳ,) *like birds that make their nests in sundry places*, (O,) *so that it becomes like the nest of the bird in a tree*, (A, O,) or *so that it becomes like the place where the birds make their nests in a tree*. (Ḳ.) [See another reading in the first paragraph of art. غش.] — You say also, of a person greatly erring, and obstinately persevering in evil, عشّش الشَّيْطَانُ فِى قَلْبِهِ † [*The devil hath made a nest in his heart*]. (TA in art. فحص.) — عشّش الخُبْزُ *The bread became mouldy*, or *spoiled and overspread with greenness*, (Ṣ, A, O, Ḳ,) *and dried up*. (Ṣ.) — عشّش الخُبْزَ *He left the bread until it became mouldy*, or *spoiled and overspread with greenness* [*and dried up*]. (A.)

8: see the next preceding paragraph.

عَشٌّ: see the paragraph here following.

عُشٌّ The *nest of a bird, formed of what it collects together*, (Ṣ, A, Mgh, O, Mṣb, Ḳ,) *of slender pieces of sticks*, (Ṣ, A, O, Ḳ,) &c., (Ṣ, O,) or *of fragments of sticks*, (Mgh, Mṣb,) *in which it lays its eggs*, (Mgh,) *in a tree*, (Ṣ, A, Mgh, O, Mṣb, Ḳ,) *in the branches thereof*; (Ṣ, A, O, Ḳ;) as also ▼ عَشٌّ: (A, Ḳ:) but if in a mountain, (Ṣ, O, Mṣb,) or a building, (Mṣb,) or a wall or the like, (Ṣ, O,) it is called وَكْرٌ, and وَكْنٌ; and if in the ground, أُفْحُوصٌ, (Ṣ, O, Mṣb,) and أُدْحِىٌّ: (Ṣ, O:) or the *nest of a raven* or *other bird, upon a tree, when it is dense*, or *compact, and large*: (Lth, T:) pl. [of pauc.] أَعْشَاشٌ (Ṣ, Mṣb) and [of mult.] عُشُوشٌ and عِشَشَةٌ (Ṣ, Mgh, Mṣb) and عِشَاشٌ. (TA.) [See also عُشْعُشٌ.] It is said in a prov., quoted in a خُطْبَة of El-Ḥajjáj, (O, TA,) لَيْسَ هٰذَا بِعُشِّكَ فَادْرُجِى [† *This is not thy nest*, or] *thou hast no right in this; therefore go thy way*: (A, O, Ḳ:*) addressed to him who alights in a place of abode not befitting him: (A, TA:) or to him who raises himself above his rank: and to him who applies himself to a thing not of his business to do: and to him who is at ease in an improper time; wherefore he is thus ordered to be diligent and in motion. (TA.) And in another prov., (TA,) تَلَمَّسْ أَعْشَاشَكَ † *Seek thou*, or *seek thou repeatedly, after pretexts, and* [*causes for*] *false accusation, in thy family* (O, L, Ḳ, TA) *and those belonging to thee*: (TA:) [not in others: (see Freytag's Arab. Prov., i. 235:)] nearly like the former proverb. (TA.) [In the CḲ, تَلَمَّسْ is erroneously put for تَلَمَّسْ.]

عُشَيْشَةٌ and عُشَيْشِيَةٌ: } see art. عشو.
عُشَيْشَانٌ and عُشَيْشِيَانٌ: }

عُشْعُشٌ, (IAạr, Ṣ,) or عَشْعَشٌ, as written by Ṣgh, (TA,) or both, (O, Ḳ,) *A nest such as is called* عُشّ, *when heaped up, one part upon another*. (IAạr, Ṣ, O, Ḳ.)

مَوْضِعُ كَذَا مُعَشَّشُ الطُّيُورِ [*Such a place is the place where the birds make their nests in the branches of trees*]. (Ṣ, O, Ḳ.*)

عشب

1. عَشِبَتِ الْأَرْضُ and عَشِبَ الْمَوْضِعُ: see 4. — عَشِبَ said of bread, (Yaạḳoob, TA,) *It was*, or *became, dry*. (Yaạḳoob, Ḳ, TA.) — And عشب, [so in the TA, app. عَشُبَ,] inf. n. عَشَابَةٌ and عُشُوبَةٌ, said of a man, *He became dry*, or *tough, by reason of leanness*. (Yaạḳoob, TA.)

2: see what next follows.

4. اعشب المَوْضِعُ; and ▼ عَشَبَ, aor. ـِ, inf. n. عُشْبٌ; *The place produced its* [*herbs*, or *herbage, of the kind termed*] عُشْب: (Mṣb:) and in like manner, (Mṣb,) اعشبت الأَرْضُ, (Ṣ, O, Mṣb, Ḳ,) and ▼ عَشِبَتْ, (Mṣb,) and thus in a copy of the Ḳ, [and in my MS. copy,] but in another copy, [and in the CḲ,] ▼ عشّبت, (TA,) *The land produced* عُشْب. (Ṣ, O, Ḳ.) [See also 12. After the mention of بَلَدٌ عَاشِبٌ in the Ṣ and O, it is said in the former that for the verb one does not say otherwise than اعشبت الأَرْضُ, and in the latter that one does not say عَشَبَ البَلَدُ.] — And اعشب القَوْمُ *The people*, or *party, lighted on*, or *found*, عُشْب; (Ṣ, O, Ḳ;) as also ▼ اِعْشَوْشَبَ القَوْمُ [but

probably in an intensive sense]. (K.) One says to him who is sent to seek for herbage, أَعْشَبْتَ فَٱنْزِلْ [*Thou hast found fresh herbage: alight*]. (O.) — See also 5. = سَأَلْتُهُ فَأَعْشَبَنِى [*I asked him and*] *he gave me an old she-camel*, (Ṣ, O, Ḳ, TA,) i. e. *what is termed* عَشَبَةٌ. (TA.)

5. تعشّبت الإِبِلُ *The camels fed upon* [*herbs*, or *herbage, of the kind termed*] عُشْب; and [accord. to the TA as a distinct meaning] *became fat* (Ḳ, TA) *therefrom*; (TA;) as also ▼ أَعْشَبَتْ accord. to the Ḳ, but this latter is wrong, being correctly ▼ اعتشبت, as in the parent-lexicons. (TA.)

8: see what next precedes.

12. اِعْشَوْشَبَتِ الأَرْضُ *The land produced abundance*, or *much, of* [*herbs*, or *herbage, of the kind termed*] عُشْب; this verb having an intensive signification, like اخشوشن [q. v.]. (Ṣ, O, TA.) [It is erroneously mentioned in the Ḳ as syn. with أَعْشَبَتْ.] — See also 4.

عُشْبٌ [a coll. gen. n.], n. un. with ة; (TA;) *Fresh, green, juicy, soft*, or *tender, herbs* or *herbage*, (Ṣ, A, O, Mṣb, Ḳ,) *in the first part of the* [*season called*] رَبِيع [i. e. رَبِيعُ الكَلَإِ, which begins in January and ends in March, O.S.]: (Mṣb:) not termed حَشِيش until drying up: (Ṣ, O:) or, in the opinion of the generality of the lexicologists, عُشْب is applied to *such as is fresh* and to *such as is dry*: (ISd, TA voce حَشِيش:) or the *first*, or *earliest, of herbage*, (سَرَعَانُ الكَلَإِ,) *in the* رَبِيع, *that* [*afterwards*] *dries up, and does not remain*; the term كَلَأٌ being applied by the Arabs to عُشْب and to other kinds: and عُشْب is applied to *fresh, green, juicy, soft*, or *tender, herbs* or *leguminous plants, of the desert, that come forth in the* رَبِيع: and under this term are included *those that are hard and thick*, which are termed the ذُكُور thereof; as well as to *those that are slender and soft*, which are termed the أَحْرَار thereof: or, accord. to AḤn, *whatever is destroyed by winter, and grows again from the stocks*, or *roots, thereof*, or *the seed*: he says also that it is applied to *such* [*herbage*] *as is uninterrupted*; as opposed to تَعَاشِيب: or, accord. to Th, it is applied to the *mature*; as so opposed. (TA.) — عُشْبَةُ الدَّارِ [*The green herb of the dwelling*] means *that which grows in the* دِمْنَة [or *patch of ground which people have blackened by their cooking and where their cattle have staled and dunged*] *of the dwelling, surrounded by fresh*, or *green, herbs, in a white* [or *clean*] *part of the ground, and good soil*: and hence, ‡ *The* هَجِينَة [or *woman whose father is a free man*, or *an Arab, and her mother a slave*]; an appellation like خَضْرَآءُ الوَضَرِ [app. lit. meaning "The green herb that grows in the place where the water with which skins have been washed, or the like, is poured out:" but IbrD thinks that it may be a mistranscription for خَضْرَآءُ الدِّمَنِ]. (TA.) — عُشْبُ الذِّئْبِ [is *Eyptian toad-flax; antirrhinum Aegyptiacum*; the name of which is written by Forskål (Flora Aegypt. Arab., pp. lxviii. and 112,) عشب الديب and *Asjib ed dîb* and *Aeschib ed dib*.]

عِيَالٌ عَشَبٌ *A family*, or *household, among whom is none little*, or *young*. (Ṣ, O, Ḳ.) — See also عَشَبَةٌ.

عَشِبٌ; fem. with ة: for the latter see عَاشِبٌ.

عَشَبَةٌ An *old* she-camel (نَابٌ كَبِيرَةٌ) [mistranslated by Golius and Freytag "dens exertus magnus"]; (Ṣ, O, Ḳ; [see 4;]) as also عَشَمَةٌ. (Ṣ, O.) And An *old ewe, advanced in age*. (Ḳ.) Also An old man *bent with age*. (Ḳ.) A man, and an old woman, *bent, and slender, and advanced in age*: (Lḥ, L, TA:) or a *decrepit* old man and old woman. (Ṣ, O.) A *short* man; (O, Ḳ;) as also ▼ عَشِيبٌ. (Ḳ.) And A woman *short, and ugly*, or *despicable*; (O, Ḳ, TA;) and so applied to a man; (TA;) or so ▼ عَشَبٌ applied to a man. (O.) And A man *dry*, or *tough, by reason of leanness*. (Yaạḳoob, TA.)

عَشِيبٌ; and its fem., with ة: see عَاشِبٌ, in three places. = And see also عَشَبَةٌ.

عَشَابَةٌ The *state of having*, or *producing*, [*herbs*, or *herbage, of the kind termed*] عُشْب, (Ṣ, O,) or *much thereof*. (Ḳ.)

بَلَدٌ عَاشِبٌ (Ṣ, A, O) and ▼ مُعْشِبٌ, (A,) and مَكَانٌ عَشِيبٌ ▼ (Mṣb) and مَوْضِعٌ عَاشِبٌ, (Ṣ, O,) and رَوْضٌ عَاشِبٌ and ▼ مُعْشِبٌ, (TA,) and أَرْضٌ عَاشِبَةٌ (Mṣb, Ḳ) and ▼ عَشِيبَةٌ (Ṣ, O, Mṣb, Ḳ) and ▼ عَشِبَةٌ (Mṣb, Ḳ) and ▼ مُعْشِبَةٌ, (Ṣ, Mṣb,) but some do not say ▼ عَشِيبٌ, (Mṣb,) [*A country*, and *a place*, and *meadows*, and *land*,] *having*, or *producing*, [*herbs*, or *herbage, of the kind termed*] عُشْب, (Ṣ, A, O, Mṣb,) or *much thereof*. (Ḳ. [See also مِعْشَابٌ.]) — And بَعِيرٌ عَاشِبٌ *A camel feeding upon* عُشْب. (Ṣ, O.)

تَعَاشِيبُ *Scanty, and scattered*, or *disunited*, [*herbs*, or *herbage, of the kind termed*] عُشْب: a word [of an extr. form (see تَبَاشِير) and] having no sing.: (Ṣ, O:) or *scattered*, or *disunited, portions thereof*: (AḤn, Ḳ, TA:) or *different kinds of herbage*: in the saying of a seeker of herbage, عُشْبٌ وَتَعَاشِيبُ وَكَمْأَةٌ شِيبٌ تُثِيرُهَا بِأَخْفَافِهَا النِّيبُ, it means *scattered*, or *disunited*, عُشْب: (AḤn, TA:) or عُشْب *not yet mature*. (Th, TA.) [See عُشْب as opposed thereto.]

مُعْشِبٌ and its fem.: see عَاشِبٌ, in three places.

أَرْضٌ مِعْشَابٌ, and أَرَضُونَ مَعَاشِيبُ, [*Land*, and *lands*,] *having*, or *producing, much herbage* [*of the kind termed* عُشْب]: (Ḳ,* TA:) معاشيب is pl. of مِعْشَاب, or it has no proper sing. (TA.) [See also عَاشِبٌ.]

عشر

1. عَشَرَ, (Ḳ,) aor. ِ, as is expressly stated by the expositors of the Fṣ and by others, but F, confounding two usages of the verb, says ُ, (TA,) inf. n. عَشْرٌ, (TA,) *He took one from ten*. (Ḳ.) — And عَشَرَهُمْ *He took one from among them, they being ten*. (Mṣb.) — And عَشَرَهُمْ, (Ṣ, Ḳ,) aor. ُ, (Ṣ, O, TA,) accord. to the Ḳ ِ, but this is at variance with other authorities, as mentioned above, (TA,) inf. n. عَشْرٌ, (Ḳ,) or عُشْرٌ, with ḍamm, (Ṣ, O,) the former correct, but the latter is preferred by MF, who quotes it from the Expositions of the Fṣ, (TA,) and عُشُورٌ; (Ḳ;) and ▼ عشّرهم, (O, Ḳ,) inf. n. تَعْشِيرٌ; (TA;) *He took from them the* عُشْر [i. e. the *tenth*, or, by extension of the term in the Muslim law, the *half of the tenth*, or the *quarter of the tenth*,] *of their several kinds of property*. (Ṣ, O, Ḳ.) And in like manner you say, (TA,) عَشَرَ المَالَ, (Mṣb, TA,) aor. ُ, inf. n. عَشْرٌ and عُشُورٌ; (Mṣb;) and ▼ عشّره; (TA;) *He took the* عُشْر *of the property*. (Mṣb, TA.) It is said in a trad., respecting women, لَا يُعْشَرْنَ, meaning, *They shall not have the tenth of the value of their ornaments taken*. (TA.) — عَشَرَ, aor. ِ, *He added one to nine*. (L, Ḳ.) [In the TA and CḲ, this signification is connected with the first mentioned above, at the commencement of this art., by أَوْ, instead of وَ, which latter is evidently the right reading.] — And عَشَرَهُمْ, aor. ِ, (Ṣ, O, Mṣb, Ḳ,) inf. n. عَشْرٌ, (Ṣ, O, Mṣb,) *He became the tenth of them*: (Ṣ, O, Mṣb, Ḳ:) or *he made them ten by* [*adding to their number*] *himself*. (TA.) [See also 2: and see Q. Q. 1.]

2: see 1, in two places. — عشّرهم, (O, Mṣb, TA,) inf. n. تَعْشِيرٌ, (TA,) also signifies *He made them ten, by adding one to nine*. (O, Mṣb, TA. [See وَحَّدَهُ.]) And اعشر ▼ العَدَدَ *He made the number ten*. (TA.) — عشّر المُصْحَفَ, inf. n. تَعْشِيرٌ, *He put, in the copy of the Ḳur-án*, [*the marks called*] *the* عَوَاشِر [pl. of عَاشِرَةٌ]. (Ṣ, O, Ḳ.*) — اَللّٰهُمَّ عَشِّرْ خُطَاىَ *O God, write down ten good deeds for every one of my steps*. (Lḥ, TA.) — عشّر لِٱمْرَأَتِهِ, or عِنْدَهَا, *He remained ten nights with his wife*: and in like manner the verb is used in relation to any saying or action. (TA voce سَبَّعَ.) — عشّرت, (Ṣ, Mṣb, Ḳ, [in the CḲ عَشَرَت,]) inf. n. تَعْشِيرٌ; (Ṣ;) and ▼ اعشرت; (Ḳ;) *She* (a camel) *became what is termed* عُشَرَآء; (Ṣ, Ḳ;) *she completed the tenth month of her pregnancy*. (Mṣb.) — And عشّروا *Their camels became such as are termed* عِشَار [pl. of عُشَرَآء]. (O.) — See also 4. — عشّر القَدَحَ *He broke the* قدح [or *drinking-bowl*] *into ten pieces*. (O, TA.) — And [hence, app.,] عشّر الحُبُّ قَلْبَهُ † *Love emaciated him* [as though it broke his heart into ten pieces]. (TA.) — And عشّر, (A, Ḳ,) inf. n. تَعْشِيرٌ, (Ṣ, O, Ḳ,) *He* (an ass) *brayed with ten uninterrupted reciprocations of the sound*. (Ṣ, A, O, Ḳ.*) They assert that, when a man arrived at a country of pestilence, he put his hand behind his ear, and brayed in this manner, like an ass, and then entered it, and was secure from the pestilence: (Ṣ,* O, TA:) or he so brayed at the gate of a city where he feared pestilence, and consequently it did not hurt him. (A.) — Also *He* (a hyena) *cried,* or *howled, in the same manner.* (A.) And *He* (a raven) *croaked in the same manner.* (Ḳ.)

3. عَاشَرَهُ, (Ḳ,) inf. n. مُعَاشَرَةٌ, (Ṣ, O, Mṣb, Ḳ,) *He mixed with him; consorted with him; held social* or *familiar intercourse,* or *fellowship, with him; conversed with him;* or *became intimate with him;* syn. خَالَطَهُ. (Ṣ, O, Mṣb, Ḳ.) [See also 6.]

4. اعشر العَدَدَ : see 2. — اعشروا *They became ten.* (Ṣ, O.) — اعشرت, said of a she-camel: see 2. — Also *She* (a camel) *completed ten months from the time of her bringing forth.* (TA.) — Also, or ↓ عشّرت, *She brought forth her tenth offspring.* (TA in art. بكر.) — And the former, said of camels, *They came to water on the tenth day, counting the day of the next preceding watering as the first.* (O.) — And اعشر *He was,* or *became, one whose camels came to water on the tenth day, counting the day of the next preceding watering as the first;* expl. by the words وَرَدَتْ إِبِلُهُ عِشْرًا, (Ṣ, TA,) or العِشْرَ. (TA.) — And *He came to be within* [*the period of*] *the* [*first*] *ten* [*nights*] *of Dhu-l-Ḥijjeh* (فِى عَشْرِ ذِى الحِجَّةِ). (T, TA.) — And أَعْشَرْنَا مُنْذُ لَمْ نَلْتَقِ *We have had ten nights pass over us since we met.* (L, TA.)

6. تَعَاشَرُوا *They mixed; consorted;* or *held social* or *familiar intercourse,* or *fellowship; one with another; conversed together;* or *became intimate, one with another;* syn. تَخَالَطُوا; (Ṣ, O, Mṣb, Ḳ;) as also ↓ اعتشروا. (TA.)

8: see what next precedes.

Q. Q. 1. عَشْرَنَهُ *He made it twenty:* an extr. word [with respect to formation, and post-classical, like سَبْعَنَ, q. v.]. (Ḳ, TA.) [In the CḲ, عَشْرَنْتُهُ, and expl. there as signifying *I made it twenty:* but this is evidently a mistranscription.]

عَشْرٌ fem. of عَشَرَةٌ [q. v.].

عُشْرٌ (Ṣ, O, Mṣb, Ḳ) and ↓ عُشُرٌ (TA) *A tenth; a tenth part; one part of ten parts;* as also ↓ عَشِيرٌ and ↓ مِعْشَارٌ; (Ṣ, O, Mṣb, Ḳ;) which last is [of a form] not used [to denote a fractional part] except as applied to the tenth part (Ṣ, O) and [in the instance of مِرْبَاعٌ applied to] the fourth part: (O:) or, as some say, مِعْشَارٌ is the *tenth of the tenth* [i. e. *a hundredth part*]: and as some say, مِعْشَارٌ is the *tenth of the* ↓ عَشِير, which latter is the *tenth of the* عُشْر; so that, accord. to this, the معشار is *one of a thousand;* for it is the *tenth of the tenth of the tenth:* (Mṣb:) [in the TA, "and as some say, معشار is pl. of عشير, which latter is pl. of عُشْر:" but this is evidently a mistake:] the pl. of عُشْرٌ is أَعْشَارٌ (Mṣb, Ḳ) and عُشُورٌ; (Ḳ;) and that of عَشِيرٌ is أَعْشِرَاءُ: (Ṣ, O, Mṣb:) it is said in a trad., تِسْعَةُ أَعْشِرَاءِ الرِّزْقِ فِى التِّجَارَةِ وَجُزْءٌ مِنْهَا فِى السَّابِيَاءِ, i. e. [*Nine tenths of the means of subsistence consist in merchandise, and one part of them consists in*] *the increase of animals.* (Ṣ, A,* O.*) — أَخَذَ عُشْرَ أَمْوَالِهِمْ [means *He took the tenth,* or *tithe,* or by extension of the term in the Muslim law, *the half of the tenth,* or *the quarter of the tenth, of their several kinds of property*]. (Ṣ, Ḳ.) [See 1, and see عَشَّارٌ.] — عُشْرٌ [as a pl. of which the sing. is not mentioned], applied to she-camels, *That excern into the udder* (تُنْزِلُ) *a scanty* دِرَّة [or *quantity of milk* (in the CḲ دَرَّة)] *without its collecting* [*and increasing*]. (O, Ḳ.)

عِشْرٌ *A period of eight days between* [*camels'*] *twice coming to water;* for they come to water on the tenth day [counting the day of the next preceding watering as the first]; and in like manner, the term for every one of the periods between two waterings is with kesr: [see ثِلْثٌ:] (Ṣ, O:) or *camels' coming to water on the tenth day* [*after the next preceding period of abstinence,* i. e., *counting the day of the next preceding watering as the first*]: or *on the ninth day* [*not counting the day of the next preceding watering;* for it is evident that these two explanations are virtually one and the same]; (Ḳ;) as in the Shems el-'Uloom, on the authority of Kh, where it is added that they keep them from the water nine nights and eight days, and then bring them to water on the ninth day, which is the tenth from [by which is meant including] the former [day of] watering: (TA:) after the عِشْر, there is no name for a period between the two waterings until the twentieth [day]; (Ṣ, O;) but you say, هِىَ تَرِدُ عِشْرًا وَغِبًّا, and عِشْرًا وَرِبْعًا, [and so on,] to the twentieth [day counting the day of the next preceding watering as the first]; (Aṣ;) and then you say, that their period between two waterings is عِشْرَانِ, (Aṣ, Ṣ, O,) i. e., *eighteen days;* (Ṣ, O;) and when they exceed this, they are termed جَوَازِئُ [meaning "that satisfy themselves with green pasture so as not to need water"]. (Aṣ, Ṣ, O.) — Also The *eighth young one,* or *offspring.* (A in art. ثلث.) — And *A piece that is broken off* from a cooking-pot, (Ḳ, TA,) or from a drinking-cup or bowl, (TA,) and from anything; (Ḳ, TA;) as though it were one of ten pieces; (TA;) as also ↓ عُشَارَةٌ, (Ḳ, TA,) which signifies *a piece* of anything: (O, TA:) pl. of the former, أَعْشَارٌ [and pl. pl. أَعَاشِيرُ]; (TA;) and of ↓ the latter, عُشَارَاتٌ. (O, TA.) — [Hence, app.,] بُرْمَةٌ أَعْشَارٌ *A cooking-pot,* or *one of stone, broken in pieces:* thus [we find the latter word] occurring in the pl. form [and used as an epithet]. (Ṣ, O.) And قِدْرٌ أَعْشَارٌ *A cooking-pot broken into ten pieces:* (Ḳ:) or *a large cooking-pot, of ten pieces joined together by reason of its largeness:* (A:) or *a cooking-pot so large that it is carried by ten men,* (Ḳ,) or *by ten women:* (TA:) or [simply] *a cooking-pot broken in pieces;* not derived from anything: (TA:) pl. قُدُورٌ أَعْشَارٌ, (A,) and أَعَاشِيرُ. (A, Ḳ.) And جَفْنٌ أَعْشَارٌ [*A scabbard of a sword,* or *a sword-case,*] *broken in pieces.* (O.) And قَلْبٌ أَعْشَارٌ [† *A broken heart.*] (Ṣ, Ḳ.) And أَعْشَارُ جَزُورٍ *The portions of a slaughtered camel* [for which players at the game called المَيْسِر contend, and which are ten in number; not seven, as is said in one place in the TA. In Ḥar p. 579, اعشار in this case is said to be pl. of عُشْر; but I think that we have better reason for regarding it as a pl. of عِشْر]. (Az, Ṣ, O, Ḳ.) Imra-el-Ḳeys says,

وَمَا ذَرَفَتْ عَيْنَاكِ إِلَّا لِتَضْرِبِى
بِسَهْمَيْكِ فِى أَعْشَارِ قَلْبٍ مُقَتَّلِ

[*And thine eyes did not shed tears but that thou mightest play with thy two arrows for the portions of a heart subdued and killed by the passion of love*]: he means, by the two arrows, the two called المُعَلَّى and الرَّقِيب; to the former of which are assigned seven portions, and to the latter, three; so that both together gain all the portions; for the slaughtered camel is divided into ten portions: therefore he means that she has played for his heart with her two arrows, [alluding to the glances shot from her eyes,] and gained possession of it altogether: (Az, Ṣ,* O:* [see also a verse cited voce رَقِيبٌ:]) or accord. to some, he means that his heart had been broken, and then repaired like as cooking-pots are repaired: but Az says that the former explanation, which is mentioned by Th, pleases him more. (TA.) Hence the saying, ضَرَبَ فِى أَعْشَارِهِ وَلَمْ يَرْضَ بِمِعْشَارِهِ [*He played for all the portions of it, and was not content with the fifth of it*]; meaning he took the whole of it. (A.) — And أَعْشَارٌ alone means *Cooking-pots that boil the ten portions* [*of a* جَزُور]. (Ḥar. p. 579.) — أَعْشَارٌ also signifies The *primary feathers of the wing of a bird;* (Ṣ, O, TA;) and so ↓ عَوَاشِرُ. (TA.)

عُشَرٌ *Three nights of the* [*lunar*] *month,* [the *tenth, eleventh, and twelfth,*] *after the* تُسَع [q. v.]. (Ṣ, O.) — Also [The *asclepias gigantea* of Linnæus; or *gigantic swallow-wort;*] *a species of tree* [or *shrub*] *in which is a substance answering the purpose of tinder,* (Ḳ,) *like cotton,* (TA,) *than which there is nothing better wherein to strike fire, and with which cushions are stuffed,* (Ḳ,) *on account of its softness:* (TA:) [see زَنَّ, in art. روا:] accord. to AḤn, (TA,) *a large species of tree* [or *shrub*], *of the kind called* عِضَاه, *having a sweet gum,* (AḤn, Ṣ, O,*) *and milk,* (O,) *and broad leaves, growing up high,* (AḤn,) *from the flowers and shoots of which,* (AḤn, Ḳ,) or *from the joints of the branches and from the places of the flowers whereof,* (O,) *there comes forth a well-known kind of sugar,* (AḤn, O,* Ḳ,) *in which is somewhat of bitterness,* (O, Ḳ,) *called* سُكَّرُ العُشَرِ; (AḤn, TA;) [or *this is a kind of red sugar, which falls like dew upon this tree;* (Golius, from Ibn-Maaroof and the Mj;)] *it produces also bladders, resembling the* شَقَاشِق [or *faucial bags*] *of camels, in which they bray,* [blowing them out from their mouths, with a gurgling sound,] (AḤn, TA,) [*and*] *like the bladder of the smaller* قَتَاد [q. v.]; (Ṣ, O;) *and it has a blossom like that of the* دِفْلَى, *tinged,* [but with what hue is not said,] *and shining, and beautiful in appearance, as well as a fruit:* (AḤn, TA:) n. un. with ة: and pl. [of this latter] عُشْرٌ [or rather this is a coll. gen. n.] and عُشْرَاتٌ. (Ṣ, O.) [See also سَلَعٌ.]

عُشْرٌ: see عُشْرٌ.

عِشْرَةٌ *Social*, or *familar*, *intercourse; fellowship; i. q.* مُخَالَطَةٌ; (O,* Ḳ;) or a subst. from the latter word. (Ṣ, Mṣb.) Sometimes it governs as a verb, [like the inf. n.,] accord. to some grammarians, as in the following ex.:

بِعِشْرَتِكَ الكِرَامَ تُعَدُّ مِنْهُمْ

[*By thine associating with the generous thou wilt be reckoned* as one *of them*]. (I'Aḳ p. 211.)

عَشَرَةٌ [*Ten;*] the *first of the* عُقُود; (A, Ḳ;) with ة, (Mṣb,) and with fet-ḥ to the ش, (TA,) for the masc.; (Mṣb, TA;) and عَشْرٌ, without ة, (Mṣb, TA,) and with one fet-ḥah, (TA,) for the fem. (Mṣb, TA.) You say, عَشَرَةُ رِجَالٍ [*Ten men*]: and عَشْرُ نِسْوَةٍ [*ten women*]. (Ṣ, O, Mṣb, TA.) [In De Sacy's Arabic Grammar, for the former is inadvertently put عَشْرَةٌ; and for the latter, عَشَرُ: and in Freytag's lexicon we find عشر instead of عَشْرٌ.] عَشَرَاتٌ [is the pl. of عَشَرَةٌ: and also] signifies *Decimal numbers.* (M in art. ست.) The vulgar make عَشْر masc., as meaning a number of days, saying العَشْرُ الأَوَّلُ, and العَشْرُ الأَخِيرُ; but this is wrong [unless thereby they mean to speak of nights with their days, as will be shown by what follows]: the month consists of three عَشَرَاتٌ; namely, العَشْرُ الأُوَلُ [*The first ten* nights, with their days], pl. of أُولَى; and العَشْرُ الوُسَطُ [*The middle ten* nights, with their days], pl. of وُسْطَى; and العَشْرُ الأُخَرُ [*The last*, lit. *the other, ten* nights, with their days], pl. of أُخْرَى; or العَشْرُ الأَوَاخِرُ [*The last ten* nights, with their days], pl. of آخِرَةٌ. (Mṣb.) [العَشْرُ الأَوَاخِرُ is also especially applied to *The last ten* nights of Ramaḍán, with their days: and عَشْرُ ذِى الحِجَّةِ to *The first ten* nights *of Dhu-l-Ḥijjeh*, with their days: and العَشْرُ, alone, to *The first ten* nights of El-Moḥarram, with their days.] The Arabs also said, سِرْنَا عَشْرًا, meaning *We journeyed ten* nights, with their days; making the fem. [لَيَالٍ] to predominate over the masc. [أَيَّام]; as is the case in the Ḳur ii. 234. (Mṣb.) And أَيَّامُ العَشْرِ is used for أَيَّامُ اللَّيَالِى العَشْرِ [*The days of the ten nights*]. (Mgh.) [See some other observations applying to the syntax of عَشَرَةٌ and عَشْرٌ, voce خَمْسَةٌ. And respecting a peculiar pronunciation of the people of El-Ḥijáz, and a case in which عَشَرَة is imperfectly decl., see ثَلَاثَةٌ.] —— [عُشْرٌ is also applied to *A portion*, or *paragraph*, *of the Ḳur-án properly consisting of ten verses;* but it is often applied to *somewhat more*, or *less*, *than what is considered by some*, or *by all*, *as ten verses*, either because there is much disagreement as to the divisions of the verses or for the sake of beginning and ending with a break in the tenour of the text: (see عَاشِرَةٌ:) pl. أَعْشَارٌ. These divisions have no mark to distinguish them in some MSS.: in others, each is marked by a round ornament at the end; or by the word عشر, or the letter ع, over, or over against, the commencement.] —— When you have passed the number ten, you make the masc. fem., and the fem. masc. [to nineteen inclusively]: in the masc., you reject the ة in عَشَرَة; and from thirteen to nineteen [inclusively], you add ة to the former of the two nouns; and [in every case] you pronounce the ش with fet-ḥ; and you make the two nouns one noun, [and, as such,] indecl., with fet-ḥ for the termination: (TA:) you say, أَحَدَ عَشَرَ [*Eleven*], (Ṣ, O, Mṣb,) [and اِثْنَا عَشَرَ *Twelve*,] and ثَلَاثَةَ عَشَرَ [*Thirteen*], and so on; (Mṣb, TA;) with fet-ḥ to the ش; and in one dial. with sukoon [أَحَدَ عْشَرَ, &c.]; (Mṣb;) or the former only: (Ṣ, O:) and, as ISk says, some of the Arabs make the ع quiescent, [as many do in the present day,] saying أَحَدَ عْشَرَ, and so on to تِسْعَةَ عْشَرَ [inclusively] except in the instance of اِثْنَا عَشَرَ and اِثْنَىْ عَشَرَ, because of the quiescence of the ا and ى; and Akh says that they make the ع quiescent because the noun is long and its vowels are many: (Ṣ, O:) in the fem., you add ة to the latter of the two nouns, and reject the ة in the former of them, and make the ش in عشرة quiescent: you say إِحْدَى عَشْرَةَ, (TA,) [and اِثْنَتَا عَشْرَةَ,] and so on to تِسْعَ عَشْرَةَ [inclusively]: and if you choose, you say إِحْدَى عَشِرَةَ, [&c.,] with kesr to the ش: the former is of the dial. of the people of El-Ḥijáz, [and is the more common,] and the latter is of the dial. of the people of Nejd: (Ṣ, O, TA:) but fet-ḥ to the ش in this case is unknown to the grammarians and lexicologists, as Az says, though an instance has been adduced in an unusual reading of the Ḳur ii. 57, and another in vii. 160. (TA.) Every noun of number, from eleven to nineteen [inclusively], is manṣoob, [or more properly speaking, each of the two nouns of which it is composed is indecl., with fet-ḥ,] in the cases of rafa and naṣb and khafḍ, except that of twelve; for اِثْنَا and اِثْنَتَا are decl. [i. e. you say, in a case of naṣb or khafḍ, اِثْنَىْ عَشَرَ and اِثْنَتَىْ عَشْرَةَ]. (TA.) —— [In the same manner also عَشَرَ and عَشْرَةَ are used in the ordinal compounds.]

عُشَرَآءُ A she-camel *that has been ten months pregnant*, (Ṣ, Mgh, O, Mṣb, Ḳ,) *from the day of her having been covered by the stallion:* she then ceases to be [of those] called مَخَاض, and she is called عشراء *until she brings forth*, and also *after she has brought forth*, (Ṣ, O,) or *when she has brought forth, at the completion of a year:* or when she has brought forth she is termed عَائِذٌ: (TA:) or *that has been eight months pregnant:* or, applied to a she-camel, *i. q.* نُفَسَآءُ *applied to a woman:* (Ḳ:) it is applied also to any female that is pregnant, but mostly to the female of the horse and camel: (IAth:) it is the only sing. word of this measure, which is a pl. measure, except نُفَسَآءُ: (MF:) the dual is عُشَرَاوَانِ: (Ṣ, O, TA; in one copy of the Ṣ عُشْرَاوَانِ:) and pl. عُشَرَاوَاتٌ; (Ṣ, O, Ḳ, TA; in one copy of the Ṣ, and in the CḲ عُشْراوات;) but some disallow this; (MF;) and عِشَارٌ; (Ṣ, O, Mṣb, Ḳ;) like as نِفَاسٌ is pl. of نُفَسَآءُ; (Mṣb;) and عُشَارٌ: (Ḳ in art. نفس:) or عِشَارٌ is applied to she-camels *until some of them have brought forth and others are expected to bring forth.* (Ḳ.) Some say that عِشَار have no milk; though El-Farezdaḳ applies this term to camels that are milked, because of their having recently brought forth; and it is said that camels are most precious to their owners when they are عشار. (TA.) عَشَائِرُ, as pl. of عِشَارٌ, which is pl. of عُشَرَآءُ, signifies Gazelles *that have recently brought forth.* (O.)

لَبَنٌ عُشَرِىٌّ *Milk of camels that feed upon the* عُشَر, q. v. (TA.)

عِشْرُونَ *Twenty; twice ten:* (Ḳ:) applied alike to a masc. and a fem.: (Mṣb:) you say عِشْرُونَ رَجُلًا [*Twenty men*], and عِشْرُونَ ٱمْرَأَةً [*Twenty women:* the noun following it being in the accus. case as a specificative]: (TA:) it is decl. with و and ى [like a pl. formed by the addition of و and ن]; (Mṣb;) and when you prefix it to another noun, making it to govern the latter in the gen. case, you drop the ن, (Ṣ, Mṣb,) and say, عِشْرُو زَيْدٍ [*The twenty of Zeyd*], (Mṣb,) and عِشْرُوكَ [*Thy twenty*], (Ṣ, O, Mṣb,) and عِشْرِىَّ [*My twenty*], changing the و into ى [in this last case], because of the letter following it, and then incorporating: (Ṣ, O:) so says Ks; but most disallow this mode of prefixing in the case of a decimal number [of this kind]. (Mṣb.) [It signifies also *Twentieth.*] It is not a pl. of عَشَرَة, (so in a copy of the Ṣ and in the O and in the TA,) or عَشْرٌ, (so in another copy of the Ṣ,) [or perhaps the right reading is عِشْرٌ, as may be inferred from what will be presently added: but first it should be observed that if it were pl. of عَشَرَة, or of عَشْرٌ, it would signify at least three times ten:] some hold it to be a pl. of عِشْرٌ, saying, (TA,) as عِشْرٌ signifies camels' coming to water on the ninth day, they do not say عِشْرَانِ [for twenty], but they say عِشْرُونَ, (in the Ḳ, لَمْ يَقُلْ عِشْرَيْنِ وَقَالُوا عِشْرِينَ: but the correct reading seems to be لَمْ يَقُولُوا: TA: [in the CḲ it is more incorrect, لم يقل عِشْرِينَ وقالوا عِشْرَيْنِ:]) making eighteen days to be عِشْرَانِ, and the nineteenth and twentieth a portion of the third عِشْر; and so, [regarding the portion as a whole,] forming the pl. عِشْرُونَ; (Ḳ,* TA;) agreeably with a well-known license, which allows the calling two and a part of the third a pl.: (TA:) this is the opinion of Kh and IDrd and some others: but J and most of the lexicologists hold that عِشْرُونَ is not a pl. of عَشَرَة nor of عِشْر nor of any other word, and their opinion I hold to be correct, applying as it does to the other similar nouns of number. (MF.)

عُشَارَ *Ten and ten;* [or *ten and ten together;* or *ten at a time and ten at a time;*] (MF;) changed from عَشَرَةً عَشَرَةً, (Ṣ,) or rather عَشَرَةً عَشَرَةً; as also مَعْشَرَ; (MF;) [for which reason, and its having the quality of an epithet, each is imperfectly decl.] You say, جَاؤُوا عُشَارَ عُشَارَ, (Ṣ, M, O, L, Ḳ,) and ▼مَعْشَرَ مَعْشَرَ, (M, O, L, Ḳ,) and عُشَارَ once, and ▼مَعْشَرَ once, (M, L, TA,) *They came ten* [*and*] *ten*. (Ṣ, M, O, L, Ḳ.) MF says that the repetition is manifestly wrong; but it is allowed by the M and L, as well as the Ḳ; [and is for the purpose of corroboration;] and مَعْشَرَ ▼مَعْشَرَ is also authorized by the TṢ. (TA.) A'Obeyd says that more than أُحَادَ and ثُنَاءَ and عُشَارَ and رُبَاعَ and ثُلَاثَ has not been heard, except occurring in a verse of El-Kumeyt. (O, TA.) [But خُمَاسَ is mentioned in the Ḳ.]

عَشِيرٌ: see عُشْرٌ, in three places. — Also *A certain measure of land, a tenth of the* قَفِيز, (O, Mṣb, Ḳ,) *which is the tenth of the* جَرِيب [q. v.]: (O, TA:) pl. أَعْشِرَآءُ. (TA in art. جرب.) ═ And *An associate; i. q.* مُعَاشِرٌ. (Ṣ, O, Mṣb, Ḳ.) — And *A husband;* (Ṣ, O, Mṣb, Ḳ;) because he and his wife are associates, each of the other. (Ṣ, O.) يَكْفُرْنَ العَشِيرَ means *They are ungrateful to the husband*. (Mṣb.) — And *A wife*. (Mṣb.) — And *A relation*. (Ḳ.) — And *A friend*. (Ḳ.) Pl. عُشَرَآءُ. (Ḳ.) — See also عَشِيرَةٌ. ═ Also The *cry of the* ضَبُع [or *hyena*, or *female hyena*]: (Ḳ:) in this sense, a word not derived. (TA.)

عُشَارَةٌ; and its pl.: see عِشْرٌ.

عُشَارِىٌّ A garment, or piece of cloth, (A, Ḳ,) *ten cubits long*. (Ṣ, A, Mgh, O, Ḳ.) — And A boy *ten years old*: fem. with ة. (TA.)

عَشُورَى and عَشُورَآءُ: see عَاشُورَآءُ.

عَشِيرَةٌ A man's *kinsfolk*: (Bḍ and Jel in ix. 24:) or his *nearer* or *nearest relations*, or *next of kin, by descent from the same father* or *ancestor*: (Ḳ:) or *a small sub-tribe; a small portion*, or the *smallest subdivision, of a tribe, less than a* فَصِيلَة: (TA voce شَعْبٌ, q. v.:) or *a tribe;* syn قَبِيلَةٌ; (Ṣ, O, Mṣb;) a man's قَبِيلَة; (Ḳ;) as also ▼عَشِيرٌ, without ة: (TA:) or *a community, such as the Benoo-Temeem*, and *the Benoo-'Amr-Ibn-Temeem*: (ISh:) a word having no proper sing.: (Mṣb:) accord. to some, from عِشْرَةٌ: accord. to others, from عَشَرَةٌ, the number so called: (Bḍ ubi suprà, and MF:) pl. عَشَائِرُ (Mṣb, Ḳ) and عَشِيرَاتٌ. (Mṣb.) [See also مَعْشَرٌ.] ═ عَشَائِرُ is also a pl. pl. of عُشَرَآءُ [q. v., last sentence]. (O.)

عَشَّارٌ (Ṣ, O, Mṣb, Ḳ) and ▼عَاشِرٌ (O, Mṣb, Ḳ) and ▼مُعَشِّرٌ (TA) *One who takes*, or *receives, the* عُشْر [q. v.] *of property*. (Ṣ, Mṣb, Ḳ.) Where the punishment of the عَشَّار, or عَاشِر, is mentioned in traditions, as where it is said that the عَاشِر is to be put to death, the meaning is, he who takes the tenth as the people in the Time of Ignorance used to do: such is to be put to death because of his unbelief; or because, being a Muslim, he holds this practice to be lawful: but such as performed the like office for the Prophet and for the Khaleefehs after him may be thus called because of the relation of what he takes to the tenth, as the quarter of the tenth, and the half of the tenth, and as he takes the tenth wholly of the produce that is watered [only] by the rain, and the tenth of the property in merchandise [of foreigners, and half the tenth of that] of non-Muslim subjects. (TA.) [There is either a mistake or an omission in the last part of the statement above, in the TA, which I have rectified by inserting "of foreigners" &c.]

عَاشِرٌ: see عَشَّارٌ. — One says also, صَارَ عَاشِرَهُمْ [meaning *He became the tenth of them*]. (Ṣ, Mṣb, Ḳ.)

عَاشِرَةٌ The *circular sign which marks a division of an 'ashr* (عُشْر) *in a copy of the Ḳur-án*: (O, L, Ḳ:) a post-classical term: (O, L:) pl. عَوَاشِرُ. (Ṣ, Ḳ.) — And عَوَاشِرُ القُرْآنِ means The *verses that complete an* عُشْر *of the Ḳur-án*. (Ḳ.) — And إِبِلٌ عَوَاشِرُ *Camels coming to water after an interval of eight days;* (Ṣ, O;) *on the tenth day* [*counting the day of the next preceding watering as the first*]: or *on the ninth day* [*not counting the day of the next preceding watering*: see عِشْرٌ]. (Ḳ.) ═ For another signification of the pl., عَوَاشِرُ, see عُشْرٌ, last sentence. ═ عَاشِرَةُ is a proper name of *The* ضَبُع [i. e. *hyena*, or *female hyena*]; a determinate noun: [but it has for] pl. عَاشِرَاتٌ. (O.)

عَاشُورٌ: see what next follows.

عَاشُورَآءُ and ▼عَشُورَآءُ (Mṣb, Ḳ) and عَاشُورَى (Mṣb, Ḳ) and ▼عَشُورَى (Ḳ) and ▼عَاشُورٌ, (Mṣb, Ḳ,) or يَوْمُ عَاشُورَآءَ (Ṣ, O, and Ḳ in art. تسع, &c.) or يَوْمُ العَاشُورَآءِ (Ṣ in that art., &c.) and يَوْمُ عَشُورَآءَ, (Ṣ, O,) *The tenth day of the month El-Moḥarram*: (Ṣ, Mṣb, Ḳ:) or *the ninth thereof*, (Ḳ,) accord. to some; but most of the learned, of old and late times, agree that it is the former; (Mṣb in art. تسع;) and AZ says that by the ninth may be meant the tenth; after the same manner as the term عِشْرٌ, relating to camels' coming to water, is [said to be] applied to a period of nine days, [but means the coming to water on the tenth day, counting the day of the next preceding watering as the first,] as Lth says, on the authority of Kh. (TA.) Few nouns of the measure فَاعُولَآءُ have been heard. (Az, TA.)

مَعْشَرٌ *A company*, or *collective body*, (Az, Ṣ, O, Mṣb, Ḳ,) *of people*, (Ṣ,) *consisting of men, exclusive of women;* like نَفَرٌ and قَوْمٌ and رَهْطٌ; (Az, Mṣb;) having no proper sing.: (Az:) or *any company*, or *collective body, whose state of circumstances is one; a community;* as the معشر of the Muslims and that of the Polytheists: (Lth:) or *a great company*, or *collective body;* so called [from عَشَرَةٌ,] because they are many; for عشرة is that large and perfect number after which there is no number but what is composed of the units comprised in it: (MF:) or the *family* of a man: or *jinn* (i. e. *genii*) *and mankind*: (Ḳ: [or the author of the Ḳ may mean, or *jinn*: and also *mankind*:]) in the Ḳur [vi. 130, and lv. 33], we find the expression يَا مَعْشَرَ الْجِنِّ وَالْإِنْسِ; but this means *O* معشر *consisting of the jinn and of mankind*: and [vi. 128], يَا مَعْشَرَ الجِنِّ, without the mention of الانس: (MF:) pl. مَعَاشِرُ. (Ṣ, Mṣb.) [See also عَشِيرَةٌ.] ═ مَعْشَرَ: see عُشَارَ, in four places.

مُعْشِرٌ ‡ A woman *who has completed her full time of pregnancy*. (TA.)

[مُعَشَّرٌ pass. part. n. of 2, q. v. See also مُثَلَّثٌ.]

مُعَشِّرٌ: see عَشَّارٌ. ═ Also One *whose camels have brought forth*: and one *whose camels have become* عِشَار [pl. of عُشَرَآء]. (O, Ḳ.)

مِعْشَارٌ: see عُشْرٌ. ═ Also A she-camel *whose milk is abundant* (Ḳ, TA) *in the nights of her bringing forth*. (TA.)

عشرق

Q. 1. عَشْرَقَ, said of a plant, or of herbage, and [عَشْرَقَتْ] said of land, *It became green*. (Ibn-'Abbád, O, Ḳ.)

عِشْرِقٌ *A certain plant*, (Ṣ, Ḳ,) *of the* [*kind of plants called*] أَغْلَاث, *the grain of which is good for the piles, and for generating milk, and blackens the hair*, (Ḳ,) or *the leaves whereof, which are like those of the* عِظْلِم, *intensely green, blacken the hair when it is dressed therewith, and cause it to grow*: (TA:) n. un. with ة: (Ḳ:) Aboo-Ziyád says, it is *of the* [*kind of plants called*] أَغْلَاث, and is *a tree* [or *plant*] *that spreads upon the ground, having thick* [in the TA *wide*] *leaves, and not having thorns, and is scarcely*, or *never, eaten by anything but the goats, which take some little thereof, except its grain, for this is eaten: some of the Arabs call it* فَنًا; *and when a grain thereof falls upon the ground and dries, it becomes red as though it were a bit of red wool: sometimes*, he says, *the women use its leaves in combing and dressing their hair, which it blackens, and causes to grow*: he says also, an Arab of the desert, of Rabee'ah, informed me that *the* عِشْرِقَة *rises upon a short stem, then spreads into many branches, and bears numerous fruits, which are long, broad pods, in every one of which pods are two rows of grains exactly like the stones of raisins, and these are eaten while fresh, and are cooked, and are pleasant in taste; and when the wind blows, those pods become in a state of commotion, being suspended by slender stalks, so that they make a rustling sound, and you hear, in the valley in which they are found, a low and confused sound, which frightens the camels; and the serpents do not make their abode in that valley, fleeing from the sound: its leaves are like those of the* عِظْلِم, *intensely green; and its grain is white, pleasant to the taste, easily broken, unctuous, and hot; good for the piles*: Aboo-Ziyád also says that *the* عِشْرِق and سَنًا [i. e. *senna*] *are like each other, except that the leaves of the latter are thin;* also, that an Arab of the desert, of the Benoo-Asad, told him that *the blossom of the* عشرق *inclines to whiteness*; and that *the places of its growth were said by some to be the rugged tracts*: (O:) Az says that it is *a herb of which the leaves and produce are like those of the* غار [or bay], *except in being larger*: IAạr, that it is *a red plant, of sweet odour, used by the brides*: and IB, from Aṣ, that it is *a cubit in height, having small grains, and, when dry, producing a sound by reason of the passage of the wind*: (TA:) [Forskål (in his Flora Aegypt. Arab. pp. cxi. and 86) mentions it as *a species of cassia*:] عَشَارِقُ is pl. of عِشْرِقَةٌ, or of the gen. n. عِشْرِقٌ. (TA.)

Quasi عشرن

Q. Q. 1. عَشْرَنَهُ: see art. عشر.

عشق

1. عَشِقَ, aor. ـَ, (Ṣ, O, Mṣb, Ḳ, [accord. to the TA, said in the Mṣb to be like ضَرَبَ, but in my copy of the Mṣb it is correctly said to be of the class of تَعِبَ,]) inf. n. عِشْقٌ and عَشَقٌ, (Ṣ, O, Ḳ,) the latter mentioned by Fr, and said by Ibn-Es-Sarráj to be thus by poetic license, and with two fet-ḥahs because two kesrehs are rare in nouns, (Ṣ, O,) or the former is a simple subst., and the latter is the inf. n., (Mṣb,) [and app. مَعْشَقٌ also,] *He loved* (another, Ṣ, O, Ḳ) *excessively*; (IF, Ṣ, O, Mṣb, Ḳ;) [or *passionately*; or *with amorous desire*; or, agreeably with explanations of عِشْق below, *admiringly*; or *with blindness to defects in the object of his love*; or *with a disease of the nature of melancholia*;] and ▾ تعشّق as trans. is *syn. with* عَشِقَ as such. (TA.) [See also عَاشِقٌ.] —— And عَشِقَتْ said of a she-camel, *She was*, or *became, vehemently desirous of the stallion*. (AA, TA.) —— And عَشِقَ بِهِ *He*, or *it, stuck to him*, or *it*; (O, Ḳ;) as also عَسِقَ بِهِ. (O.)

[2. عشّقهُ is used in the present day as meaning *He made him to be affected with* عِشْق; but is probably post-classical.]

5. تعشّق *He affected* عِشْق: (Ṣ, O, Ḳ:* [in the Ḳ, تعشّقهُ, in which the pronoun app. refers to العِشْق, is erroneously put for تعشّق:]) or *he showed*, or *exhibited*, عِشْق. (KL.) And *He was*, or *became*, عَاشِق. (KL.) ═ See also 1.

عِشْقٌ (IF, Ṣ, O, Mṣb, Ḳ) [generally held to be an inf. n.] and ▾ مَعْشَقٌ [likewise app. an inf. n.] (O, Ḳ) *Excessive love*; (IF, Ṣ, O, Mṣb, Ḳ;) [or *passionate love*; or *amorous desire*:] or *attachment to women*: (IF, Mṣb:) or the lover's *admiration* (عُجْب [for عَجَب in the CḲ is a mistranscription for عُجْب]) *of the beloved*; and it may be in chasteness and in immorality; (Ḳ;) or عِشْق may be in chasteness and حُبّ may be in immorality: (TA:) or *blindness of the sense to the faults*, or *defects, of the beloved*: or *a disease of the nature of melancholia* (مَرَضٌ وَسْوَاسِىّ), *which one procures to himself by making his thought to exercise absolute power over the approval of certain forms*: (Ḳ:) Th, being asked respecting الحُبّ and العِشْق, which of them is the more commendable, said, الحُبّ, because in العِشْق is excess: (TA:) [see also حُبّ:] Ibn-Seenà, [whom we commonly call Avicenna,] in a treatise on العِشْق, [regarding it as meaning *natural propension*,] says that it is not peculiar to the human species, but pervades all existing things of the celestial and the elemental and the vegetable and the mineral and the animal, and that its meaning is not perceived nor known, and is rendered more obscure by explanation thereof: (MF, TA:) it is said in the A that العِشْق is derived from العَشَقَةُ, which means the [plant commonly called] لَبْلَاب, because it twines upon trees, and cleaves to them. (TA.)

عَشَقٌ The لَبْلَاب [*a species of dolichos*, the *dolichos lablab* of Linn.]; one of which is called عَشَقَةٌ: IDrd says, the [common] people assert that the عَشَقَة is the لَبْلَابَة: (O:) accord. to Zj, (TA,) عَشَقَةٌ signifies *a certain tree* [or *plant*] *that becomes green, and then becomes slender and yellow*: (Ḳ, TA:) and عَشَقٌ is its pl. [or rather the coll. gen. n.]: (Ḳ:) and Kr says that with the post-classical authors it is the لَبْلَاب. (TA.) —— Also The [*tree called*] أَرَاك. (TA.)

عُشُقٌ, with two dammehs, A camel *that keeps to the female which he covers and which desires none but him*. (IAạr, TA.) ═ And Men *who trim*, or *dress*, or *put into a good* or *right state, the sets* [so I render غُرُوس, as pl. accord. to general analogy of غَرْس,] *of sweet-smelling plants*. (IAạr, O, Ḳ.)

عَشِيقٌ *i. q.* عَاشِقٌ, q. v. (TA.) —— عَشِيقُ العُلَى is a metaphorical expression like خَدِينُ العُلَى [meaning *Excessive lover of eminence*]. (TA in art. خدن.) ═ Also *i. q.* ▾ مَعْشُوقٌ [*Loved excessively*, &c.]. (TA.)

عِشِّيقٌ *Affected with much* عِشْق; (ISk, Ṣ, O, Ḳ;) applied to a man. (ISk, Ṣ, O.)

عَاشِقٌ *Loving excessively*; [or *passionately*;] &c.; (Mṣb, Ḳ;) [or *an excessive*, or *a passionate, lover*;] as also ▾ عَشِيقٌ: (TA:) the former applied to a man and to a woman, (Mṣb, Ḳ,) and عَاشِقَةٌ also is applied to a woman: (Ḳ:) they said اِمْرَأَةٌ عَاشِقٌ لِزَوْجِهَا [*A woman excessively*, or *passionately, loving to her husband*]; (Fr, Ṣ, O;) and sometimes they said عَاشِقَةٌ: (O:) pl. عُشَّاقٌ (TA) [and عُشُقٌ, mentioned in the O as an epithet applied to eyes (عُيُون), by Ru-beh]: it is asserted that the عَاشِق is thus called from العَشَقَةُ meaning the لَبْلَابَة, because of his becoming dried up: (O, TA:) or from عَشِقَ بِهِ, because of his cleaving to the object of his love. (TA.) —— [Hence,] عَاشِقُ الأَبْكَارِ an appellation of *The insect called* حُرْقُوص [q. v.]; because of its entering into the فَرْج of the virgin girl. (IB, TA voce حرقوص.)

مَعْشَقٌ: see عِشْق.

مَعْشُوقٌ: see عَشِيقٌ.

عشو

1. عَشَا, (TA, and so accord. to some copies of the Ḳ,) first pers. عَشَوْتُ, (Ṣ,) aor. يَعْشُو, (TA,) inf. n. عَشْوٌ and عُشُوٌّ; (KL;) as also عَشِىَ, like رَضِىَ [i. e. having for its aor. يَعْشَى, but the inf. n. is app. عَشًا, as in the similar sense expl. in the next sentence]; (TA, and so in my MS. copy of the Ḳ;) *i. q.* ▾ تعشّى, (Ṣ, Ḳ, TA,) [which is more commonly used than either of preceding verbs, and] which signifies *He ate the* [*evening-meal*, or *evening-repast*, or *supper*, i. e. *what is called the*] عَشَآء. (Mṣb, Ḳ, TA.) And عَشِيَتِ الإِبِلُ, (ISk, Ṣ, Ḳ, TA,) aor. تَعْشَى, inf. n. عَشًا, (ISk, Ṣ, TA,) *i. q.* ▾ تَعَشَّتْ [i. e. *The camels ate the evening-pasture*, or *evening-feed, called the* عَشَآء]. (ISk, Ṣ, Ḳ, TA.) —— And عَشَاهُ, (Ḳ,) first pers. عَشَوْتُهُ, (Ṣ, Mṣb,) aor. يَعْشُوهُ, (Ṣ, TA,) inf. n. عَشْوٌ; (Ḳ, TA;) and inf. n. عُشُوٌّ also, (TA, and thus in some copies of the Ḳ,) thus correctly, as in the M, عشيانا in [some of] the copies of the Ḳ being a mistake for عَشْيًا, the aor. being also يَعْشِيهِ; (TA;) *i. q.* ▾ عشّاهُ, (Ṣ, Mṣb, Ḳ, TA,) [which is more commonly used than either of the preceding verbs,] inf. n. تَعْشِيَةٌ, (Ṣ,) i. e. *He fed him* (namely, a man, Mṣb, or a horse, or a camel, Ṣ) *with the* [*evening-meal*, or *supper*, or *the evening-pasture* or *evening-feed*, i. e. *what is called the*] عَشَآء; (Ṣ, Mṣb, Ḳ;) as also ▾ اعشاهُ: (Ḳ:) and عَشَا الإِبِلَ, (Ḳ, TA,) like دَعَا [i. e. having for its aor. يَعْشُو]; (TA;) and ▾ عشّاها; *He pastured the camels by night*. (Ḳ, TA.) ═ عَشَوْتُهُ also signifies *I repaired*, or *betook myself, to*, or *towards, him*, or *it, by night*: and hence ▾ عَاشٍ is applied to any one *repairing*, or *betaking himself, to* or *towards* [an object]. (Ṣ.) —— And عَشَوْتُ إِلَى النَّارِ, aor. أَعْشُو, inf. n. عَشْوٌ, *I sought to be directed*, or *guided*, or *I directed*, or *guided, myself, by weak eyesight, to the fire*: (Ṣ:) or *I looked at the fire*, or *endeavoured to see it, and repaired*, or *betook myself, to it*, or *towards it*; and *I saw it*, or *looked towards it trying whether I could see it, and sought to be directed*, or *guided, to it by its light*: (Ḥar p. 535:) El-Ḥoṭei-ah says,

* مَتَى تَأْتِهِ تَعْشُو إِلَى ضَوْءِ نَارِهِ *
* تَجِدْ خَيْرَ نَارٍ عِنْدَهَا خَيْرُ مُوقِدِ *

[*When thou comest to him, looking with blinking eyes towards the light of his fire and seeking to be guided by it thereto, thou findest the best fire*, and *at it is the best kindler*]; meaning مَتَى تَأْتِهِ عَاشِيًا; using the marfooạ verb between two verbs whereof each is mejzoom because the verb in the future tense when it occurs in the place of a denotative of state is marfooạ: (Ṣ:) or عَشَا النَّارَ and إِلَى النَّارِ, inf. n. عَشْوٌ and عُشُوٌّ; as also ▾ اعتشى النَّارَ and بِالنَّارِ; signifies *he saw the fire by night from* afar, and repaired, or betook himself, to it, or towards it, seeking to light himself thereby, (Ḳ, TA,) and hoping to obtain thereby guidance and good. (TA.) —— And عَشَا عَنِ النَّارِ *He turned away and went from the light of the fire.* (TA.) —— And عَشَوْتُ عَنْهُ *I went,* or *turned, from him,* or *it, to another:* whence, it is said, the saying in the Ḳur [xliii. 35], وَمَنْ يَعْشُ عَنْ ذِكْرِ ٱلرَّحْمٰنِ [*And such as turns from the admonition of the Compassionate*]. (Ṣ. See another explanation of this saying in what follows.) [This and other meanings expl. below are app. from what here next follows.] —— عَشِىَ, aor. يَعْشَى, (Ṣ, Mṣb, Ḳ,) dual يَعْشَيَانِ, not يَعْشَوَانِ, (Ṣ,) inf. n. عَشًا, (Ṣ, Mṣb, Ḳ,) *He was,* or *became, weak-sighted:* (Mṣb:) or *he did not see by night, but saw by day:* (Ṣ:) or *he had bad sight by night and by day:* or *he was,* or *became, blind:* [said of a man, and of a beast of the equine kind, and of a camel, and of a bird: (see عَشًا, below:)] and عَشَا, aor. يَعْشُو, signifies the same: (Ḳ:) or the two verbs differ in meaning; so as that وَمَنْ يَعْشَ عَنْ ذِكْرِ ٱلرَّحْمٰنِ, in the Ḳur xliii. 35, thus read by some, means † *And such as is blind to the admonition of the Compassionate,* i. e., to the Ḳur-án; but مَنْ يَعْشُ, as others read, † *such as feigns himself blind:* (Ksh and Bḍ:*) [see also 6: and see another explanation of the latter reading, above: or] عَشَا signifies also *he* (a man, TA) *did as does the* أَعْشَى [q. v.]. (Ḳ, TA.) One says also, عشى مِنَ الشَّىْءِ, aor. يعشو, [thus in my original, but the pret. is app. عَشِىَ, and the aor. يَعْشَى,] meaning *He lacked strength of sight to perceive the thing.* (TA.) And عَشِىَ عَنْ حَقِّهِ like عَمِىَ in measure and in meaning [i. e. † *He was,* or *became, blind to his right,* or *due*]. (TA.) And لَا يَعْشَى إِلَّا بَعْدَ مَا يَعْشُو is one of their sayings, meaning [app. *He will not become weak-sighted except*] *after his eating the* [*evening-meal called the*] عَشَآء: (TA:) [for it is said that] the eating of food in the night occasions weakness of sight more than [do] other things. (Ḥar p. 52. [العَشَا is there written in one instance for العشآء.]) —— عَشِىَ عَلَيْهِ, inf. n. عَشًا, means *He wronged him; treated him wrongfully, injuriously, unjustly,* or *tyrannically:* (Ḳ, TA:) mentioned by ISd. (TA.)

2: see 1, former half, in two places. One says, عَشِّ إِبِلَكَ وَلَا تَغْتَرَّ, (Meyd, TA,) or عَشِّ وَلَا تَغْتَرَّ [a prov., meaning *Pasture thy camels by night, and be not negligent,* or *be not made to desire what is vain,* or *false*]. (Ṣ. [See Freytag's Arab. Prov., ii. 92.]) And عَشَّيْتُ الإِبِلَ عَنِ الوِرْدِ *I pastured the camels with the* [*evening-pasture called*] عَشَآء, *so that they might come to the water having satisfied themselves with food:* and in like manner one says, ضَحَّيْتُهَا عَنْهُ. (A and TA in art. ضحو and ضحى.) And عَشِّ رُوَيْدًا *Pasture thou the camels in the evening* (عَشِيًّا) *gently:* and in like manner one says, ضَحِّ رُوَيْدًا. (A, TA.) And hence, عشّى عَنِ الأَمْرِ (inf. n. تَعْشِيَةٌ, Ḳ) ‡ *He acted gently,* or *deliberately, in the affair:* (A and TA in art. ضحو and ضحى, and Ṣ* and Ḳ* in the present art.:) and in like manner, ضَحَّى عَنْهُ. (A and TA in the former art., and Ṣ* in the present art.) ==== See also the next paragraph. [Hence,] عَشَّى الطَّيْرَ, inf. n. تَعْشِيَةٌ, *He kindled a fire for the birds in order that they might become dim-sighted* (لِتَعْشَى) *and consequently be captured.* (M, Ḳ.)

4: see 1, former half. —— [Hence, app.,] اعشى also signifies † *He gave.* (Ḳ.) ==== And اعشاه *He* (God) *rendered him* أَعْشَى [i. e. *weak-sighted,* &c.: and in like manner one says ▼ عَشَّاهُ: see 2, last sentence; and see also Ḥar p. 52].

5: see 1, first quarter, in two places. One says also, تعشّى بِهِ *He fed himself with it* [*in the evening,* or] *in the time called the* عَشَآء: and [in like manner] تَتَعَشَّاهُ is said of camels [as meaning *they feed themselves with it,* or *pasture upon it, in the evening*]. (TA.) And when one says to thee, تَعَشَّ [*Eat thou the evening-meal*], thou sayest, مَا بِى تَعَشٍّ, (Ṣ,) or مَا بِى مِنْ تَعَشٍّ, (TA,) [*I have no* desire for *eating the evening-meal;* see 5 in art. غدو;] and not مَا بِى عَشَآءٌ, (Ṣ,) or not ما بِى مِنْ عَشَآءٍ. (TA.) ==== See also 6. ==== And تعشّاهُ signifies also *He gave him an* عَشْوَة [or عُشْوَة, i. e. *a firebrand*]. (TA.)

6. تعاشى *He feigned himself* أَعْشَى [i. e. *weak-sighted,* &c.; and so ▼ تعشّى as used by Bḍ in xliii. 35]. (Ṣ, TA.) —— And [hence] ‡ *He feigned himself ignorant,* (Ḳ, TA,) عَنْ كَذَا [*of such a thing*], *as though he did not see it;* like تَعَامَى. (TA.)

8. اعتشى *He journeyed in the time of the* عَشَآء [or *nightfall*]: (Ḳ, TA:) like اهتجر meaning "he journeyed in the time of the هَاجِرَة." (TA.) ==== See also 1, latter half.

10. استعشاهُ *He found him to be deviating from the right course,* or *acting wrongfully, injuriously, unjustly,* or *tyrannically,* (وَجَدَهُ جَائِرًا, Ḳ, TA, in some copies of the Ḳ حَائِرًا,) فِى حَقِّ أَصْحَابِهِ [*in respect of the right,* or *due, of his companions*]. (TA.) ==== And استعشى نَارًا *He guided himself by means of a fire.* (Ḳ.)

عَشْوٌ *A bowl* (قَدَحٌ) *of milk which is drunk at the time when the sheep,* or *goats, return from the pasture in the evening* or *afternoon,* or *after that time.* (Ḳ.)

عِشْىٌ: see عَشَآءٌ.

عَشًا inf. n. of عَشِىَ: (Ṣ, Mṣb, Ḳ:) [used as a simple subst., *Weakness of sight:* or *sightlessness by night with ability to see by day:* or] *badness of sight by night and by day;* as also ▼ عَشَاوَةٌ: (Ḳ:) it is in human beings, and beasts of the equine kind (دَوَابّ), and camels, and birds; as is said in the M: (TA:) or it is *darkness that happens to the eye:* (Er-Rághib, TA:) or *blindness;* (Ḳ, TA;) i. e. *absolute destitution of sight.* (TA.)

عَشٍ applied to a he-camel, and عَشِيَةٌ applied to a she-camel, *That exceeds the other camels in the* [*evening-pasture,* or *evening-feed, called*] عَشَآء; each after the manner of the possessive epithet, having no verb. (TA. [And عَشِىٌّ is said to have a similar meaning.]) ==== See also أَعْشَى.

عَشْوَةٌ *Darkness,* (Ḳ, TA,) in [any part of] the night and in the سَحَر [or period a little before daybreak]; (TA;) as also ▼ عَشْوَآءُ: (Ḳ:) or *the first of the darkness* of the night: (Az, TA:) or the *period between the beginning and* [*the end of*] *the* [*first*] *quarter* of the night: (AZ, Ṣ, Ḳ:) thus in the saying, مَضَى مِنَ اللَّيْلِ عَشْوَةٌ [*A period between the beginning* &c. *of the night passed*]: and one says also, أَخَذْتُ عَلَيْهِمْ بِالعَشْوَةِ, meaning [*I laid hold upon them*] *in the blackness of night:* (AZ, Ṣ:) the dim. is ▼ عُشَيَّةٌ. (Az, TA.) In the saying جَآءَ عَشْوَةً, meaning عِشَآءً [i. e. *He came at nightfall*], it [is an adv. n. which] may not be used otherwise than thus: you may not say, مَضَتْ عَشْوَةٌ. (TA.) —— العشوة [app. العَشْوَةُ] as meaning العَشَآء, like الغدوة [app. الغَدْوَةُ] as meaning الغَدَآء, is vulgar. (TA.) ==== Also *The venturing upon,* or *embarking in, an affair that is not clear;* as also ▼ عُشْوَةٌ and ▼ عِشْوَةٌ: (Ṣ, Ḳ:) one says, أَوْطَأْتَنِى عَشْوَةً and عُشْوَةً and عِشْوَةً, meaning [*Thou hast made me to venture upon,* or *embark in,*] *a confused and dubious affair:* this is when you tell him of a thing by means of which you have made him to fall into perplexity or trial. (Ṣ.) —— خَبَّاطُ عَشَوَاتٍ, occurring in a trad., see expl. in art. خبط.

عُشْوَةٌ: see عَشْوَةٌ. ==== Also, (Ṣ, Ḳ, TA,) and ▼ عِشْوَةٌ, (Ḳ, TA,) *A fire which one sees by night from afar, and to which,* or *towards which, he repairs,* or *betakes himself, seeking to light himself thereby:* (Ḳ, TA:) or (TA) *a firebrand* (شُعْلَةٌ مِنْ نَارٍ). (Ṣ, TA.)

عِشْوَةٌ: see عَشْوَةٌ: ==== and see also عُشْوَةٌ.

عَشْوَى *A state of perplexity, and of having little guidance:* so in the saying, إِنَّهُمْ لَفِى عَشْوَى أَمْرِهِمْ [or, perhaps, مِنْ أَمْرِهِمْ, i. e. *Verily they are in a state of perplexity,* &c., *in respect of their case,* or *affair*]. (TA.)

عَشَوِىٌّ *Of,* or *relating to, the* [*time called*] عَشِيَّةٌ [or عَشِىٌّ, q. v.]. (Ṣ.)

عُشْوَانٌ *A species of dates:* (IDrd, Ḳ, TA:) or *of palm-trees,* (Ḳ, TA,) *of such as are late in bearing.* (TA.)

عَشْيَانُ, (Ṣ, Ḳ, TA,) originally عَشْوَانُ, like غَدْيَانُ [q. v.] which is originally غَدْوَانُ, (TA,) A man (Ṣ) *eating the* [*evening-meal,* or *evening-repast,* i. e. *what is called the*] عَشَآء; (Ṣ, Ḳ, TA;) as also ▼ عَاشٍ. (TA.)

عَشَآءٌ The *meal,* or *repast,* (Ṣ, Mṣb, Ḳ,) *of the* عِشَآء [or *nightfall*], (Ṣ,* Mṣb,) or *of the* عَشِىّ [or *late part of the evening,* &c.]; (Ṣ,* Ḳ, TA;) [i. e. *supper,* in a general sense;] opposed to غَدَآء; (Ṣ;) as also ▼ عِشْىٌ: (Ḳ: [in the CK,

العشى is erroneously put for العِشْىُ:]) and in like manner both are used in relation to camels [as meaning their *evening-pasture*, or *evening-feed*: see an ex. voce عَتَمَةٌ, and another voce أَقْعَسُ]: (Ṣ, TA:) pl. of the former أَعْشِيَةٌ; (Ḳ, TA;) to which is added, in [some of] the copies of the Ḳ, and عُشِىٌّ; but this is correctly عَشِىَ, [or عَشَا, as in some copies,] and commences another sentence. (TA.)

عِشَآءٌ [The time of *nightfall*; i. e.] the *first*, or *beginning*, *of the darkness* (Mṣb, Ḳ) *of night*: (Mṣb:) [this is the sense in which it is generally used, and always when it is used as applied to *one of the five times of the divinely-appointed acts of prayer*; صَلَاةُ العِشَآءِ, and elliptically العِشَآء alone, meaning *the prayer of nightfall*:] or it is [the *time*] *when the sun has disappeared*: (Az, TA:) or [the *time*] *from sunset* (Ḳ) [i. e.] *from the prayer of sunset* (Mṣb, TA) *to the* عَتَمَة [or *darkness after nightfall*]; (Mṣb, Ḳ, TA;) [and this is what is meant by its being said that it is] *syn. with* عَشِىٌّ: (Ṣ:) or [the *time*] *from the* زَوَال [meaning the *declining of the sun from the meridian*] *to the rising of the dawn*: (Ṣ, Ḳ:) so some assert, and they cite, as an ex.,

غَدَوْنَا غُدْوَةً سَحَرًا بِلَيْلٍ * عِشَآءً بَعْدَ مَا آنْتَصَفَ النَّهَارُ

[*We went early in the morning, a little before daybreak, in a period between the declining of the sun from the meridian and the rising of the dawn, after the daytime had become halved*]: (Ṣ, TA:) [sometimes] the Arabs said, أَقْبَلَتِ العِشَآءُ, meaning العِشَآء; and هٰذَا العَشِيَّةُ, meaning العَشِيَّةُ. (Mṣb voce صَوْتٌ.) العِشَآءَانِ means *The time of sunset and the* عَتَمَة [or *darkness after nightfall*]: (IF, Ṣ, Mṣb, Ḳ: [compare הָעַרְבָּיִם in Exodus xii. 6 and xvi. 12:]) this is accord. to the saying that the عِشَآء is from the prayer of sunset to the عَتَمَة. (TA.)

عَشَاوَةٌ: see عَشًا.

عَشِىٌّ [The *late part of the evening*: or the *evening*: or the *afternoon*: i. e.] the *last*, or the *latter*, *part of the day*; (Mgh, Mṣb, Ḳ, TA;) as also ↓ عَشِيَّةٌ: (Ḳ, TA:) this is the meaning commonly known: (Mgh:) or [the *time*] *from the prayer of sunset to the* عَتَمَة [or *darkness after nightfall*]; (Ṣ, Mṣb, TA;) like عِشَآءٌ; (Mṣb;) and so ↓ عَشِيَّةٌ: you say, أَتَيْتُهُ عَشِىَّ أَمْسِ and عَشِيَّةَ ↓ أَمْسِ [*I came to him late in the evening*, or *in the time between sunset and nightfall*, &c., *of yesterday*]: (Ṣ, TA:) or عَشِىٌّ has the meaning expl. in the Ḳ [and mentioned above]; but ↓ عَشِيَّةٌ relates to one day: and one says, جِئْتُهُ عَشِيَّةً [*I came to him late in an evening*, &c.] and عَشِيَّةً [*late this evening*, &c.], and أَتَيْتُهُ العَشِيَّةَ *I came to him in the* عشيّة [or *late part of the evening*, &c.,] *of this day*; and آتِيهِ عَشِىَّ غَدٍ [*I will come to him in the late part of the evening*, &c., *of to-morrow* (in my original اتيته, an obvious mistranscription,)] without ة when relating to the future; and أَتَيْتُكَ عَشِيًّا [*I came to thee in the late part of an evening*, &c.]; and أَتَيْتُهُ بِالغَدَاةِ وَالعَشِىِّ i. e. [*I came to him early in the morning and late in the evening*, &c., meaning,] *every* عَشِيَّة [or عَشِىّ] *and* غَدَاة: (TA:) or, as some say, ↓ عَشِيَّةٌ is a sing. [or n. un.] and عَشِىٌّ is its pl. [or a coll. gen. n.]: and, as IAmb says, sometimes the Arabs make ↓ عَشِيَّةٌ masc., as meaning عَشِىٌّ: (Mṣb:) or عَشِىٌّ signifies the *time between the declining of the sun* [*from the meridian*] *and sunset*: (Az, Mgh, Mṣb, TA:) or [the *time*] *from the declining of the sun* [*from the meridian*] *to the* صَبَاح [app. here, as generally, meaning *morning*]: (Er-Rághib, Mṣb, TA:) and sometimes it means the *night*: (TA:) the pl. is عَشَايَا and عَشِيَّاتٌ, (Ḳ, TA,) the former of which [is pl. of ↓ عَشِيَّةٌ, like the latter, or perhaps of عَشِىٌّ also, and] is originally عَشَايِوُ, then عَشَايِىُ, then عَشَائِىُ, then عَشَاءَى, and then عَشَايَا: (TA:) the dim. of عَشِىٌّ is ↓ عُشَيَّانٌ, irreg., as though formed from عَشْيَانٌ, and its pl. is عُشَيَّانَاتٌ; and another form of its dim. is ↓ عُشَيْشِيَانٌ, pl. عُشَيْشِيَانَاتٌ: and the dim. of ↓ عَشِيَّةٌ is ↓ عُشَيْشِيَةٌ, pl. عُشَيْشِيَاتٌ: (Ṣ, TA:) one says, ↓ لَقِيتُهُ عُشَيْشِيَةً [another form of dim., properly meaning *I met him in a short period of a late part of an evening*, &c.], and [in like manner] ↓ عُشَيَّانًا, and ↓ عُشَيْشَانًا [in some copies of the Ḳ عشانا], and ↓ عُشَيْشِيَةً [accord. to the Mgh meaning عِشَآءً], and عُشَيْشَاتٍ, and عُشَيْشِيَانَاتٍ. (Ḳ.) صَلَاتَا العَشِىِّ [*The two prayers of the afternoon*] means *the two prayers of the* ظُهْر *and the* عَصْر; (Az, Mgh, Mṣb, Ḳ;) because they are in the latter part of the day (فِى آخِرِ النَّهَارِ), after the زَوَال [or declining of the sun from the meridian]. (TA.) In the phrase عَشِيَّةً ↓ أَوْ ضُحَاهَا [i. e. *A late part of an evening*, &c., *or its early portion of the forenoon*, meaning *or an early portion of the forenoon of the same civil day*], in the Ḳur lxxix. last verse, the ضحى is prefixed to [the pronoun referring to] the عشيّة because the ضحى and the عشيّة belong to the same [civil] day, [for this day is reckoned as the period from sunset to sunset,] (Ksh Bḍ, Jel,*) and also [by a kind of poetic license, for the sake of the rhyme, i. e.] because ضحاها occurs as a فَاصِلَة [q. v.]. (Jel.) — عَشِىٌّ also signifies, (Ḳ, TA,) and so does ↓ عَشِيَّةٌ, (Ḳ,) *Clouds* (Ḳ, TA) *coming late in the evening* or *at eventide* (عَشِيًّا). (TA.) — And the former, as an epithet applied to a camel, *That continues long eating the* عَشَآء [i. e. *evening-pasture*, or *evening-feed*]: fem. with ة. (Ḳ. [See also عَشٍ.])

عَشِيَّةٌ: see عَشِىٌّ, in ten places.

عُشَيَّةٌ dim. of عَشْوَةٌ, q. v.

عُشَيَّانٌ, pl. عُشَيَّانَاتٌ: see عَشِىٌّ, in two places.

عُشَيْشِيَةٌ and عُشَيْشِيَةٌ, pls. عُشَيْشَاتٌ and عُشَيْشِيَاتٌ: see عَشِىٌّ; the latter in two places.

عُشَيْشَانٌ and عُشَيْشِيَانٌ, pl., of the latter عُشَيْشِيَانَاتٌ: see عَشِىٌّ.

عَاشٍ: see عَشْيَانُ. The fem., عَاشِيَةٌ, applied to camels, means *Eating the* [*evening-pasture*, or *evening-feed*, *called the*] عَشَآء. (ISk, Ṣ, Ḳ.) It is said in a prov., العَاشِيَةُ تَهِيجُ الآبِيَةَ [*Such as are eating the* عشآء *excite such as desire not*, or *refuse*; or *she that is eating* &c.]: i. e., when the camels that desire not, or refuse, the عشآء see those that are eating it, they follow them, and eat it with them. (Ṣ. [See also Freytag's Arab. Prov. ii. 83.]) And [the pl.] العَوَاشِى, (Ṣ, Ḳ, TA,) [when indeterminate, عَوَاشٍ,] as an epithet in which the quality of a subst. predominates, (TA,) signifies *Those* (Ṣ, Ḳ, TA) *camels*, and *sheep* or *goats*, (Ḳ, TA,) *that are pasturing by night*. (Ṣ, Ḳ, TA.) — See also 1, former half. — [Hence,] عَاشِيَةٌ signifies also *Anything* [meaning *any man* or *animal*] *looking and repairing*, *by night*, *towards the fire of a person who entertains guests*. (TA.)

أَعْشَى *Weak-sighted*: (Mṣb:) or *sightless by night*, *but seeing by day*: (Ṣ:) or *having bad sight by night and by day*: and so ↓ عَشٍ: (Ḳ:) fem. عَشْوَآءُ, (Ṣ, Mṣb, Ḳ,) applied to a woman; (Ṣ, Mṣb;) [the masc. being applied to a man, and either masc. or fem. to a beast of the equine kind, and a camel, and a bird, (see عَشًا,)] and dual masc. أَعْشَيَانِ (TA) and fem. عَشْوَاوَانِ: (Ṣ, TA:) [and pl. عُشْىٌ.] — The fem. عَشْوَآءُ also particularly signifies, A she-camel *that sees not before her*, (Ṣ, Ḳ, TA,) [or *that has weak sight*,] *and therefore strikes everything with her fore feet*, (Ṣ, TA,) *not paying attention to the places of her feet* [*on the ground*]. (TA.) [Hence] one says, رَكِبَ فُلَانٌ العَشْوَآءَ, meaning ‡ *Such a one prosecuted his affair without mental perception*, or *without certainty*. (Ṣ, TA.) And خَبَطَهُ خَبْطَ عَشْوَآءَ (Ḳ, TA) ‡ *He did it* [*at random*, or] *without aim*; thus accord. to the M: (TA:) or *he ventured upon it without mental perception*, and *without certainty*: (Ḳ,* TA:) or, as some say, *he took it upon himself without his endeavouring to ascertain the right course*; the doing of which is sometimes, or often, attended with error: it is a prov., applied to him who goes at random and does not care for the result of his conduct. (TA. [See also 1 in art. خبط.]) — And عُقَابٌ عَشْوَآءُ *An eagle that cares not how it beats the ground, and where it strikes with its talons*. (TA.) — See also the fem. voce عَشْوَةٌ.

[مُتَعَشًّى *A place in which one eats the evening-meal*, or *supper*.]

Quasi عشى

عَشِىٌّ: and عَشِىٌّ, &c.: see in art. عشو.

عص

عُصْعُصٌ and عُصْعُصٌ : see عُصْعُصٌ.

عُصُوصٌ : see what next follows.

عُصْعُصٌ (Ṣ, Mgh, O, Mṣb, Ḳ) and عُصْعَصٌ (O, Mṣb) and عَصْعَصٌ (IAạr, Mgh, O, Ḳ) and عُصْعِصٌ (IAạr, Ḳ, TA) and ↓ عُصُصٌ and ↓ عُصُصٌ and ↓ عُصْعُوصٌ (IAạr, O, Ḳ) and ↓ عُصُوصٌ (L, TA) The [*caudal bone called the*] عَجْب [q. v.] *of the tail*; (Zj in his "Khalḳ el-Insán," Ṣ, Mgh, O, Mṣb, Ḳ;) *which is felt by him who feels for it*; (Zj ubi suprà;) i. e., the [*os coccygis*, or] *tail-bone*; (Ṣ;) the *small bone between the two buttocks*: (Mgh:) or *that of which the upper part is the* عَجْب, *and its lower part the* ذَنَب: or the *internal extremity of the spine*; and the عَجْب is its external extremity: (Az, in L, voce قُحْقُحٌ:) it is said to be the first part that is created, and the last that wastes away: (Ṣ, O:) or *i. q.* قُحْقُحٌ [q. v.]: (IAạr, O voce عُكْدَةٌ:) pl. عَصَاعِصُ. (Mṣb, TA.) — Also عُصْعُصٌ (Mgh, IAth) and عُصْعُصٌ (Mgh) *What is in the middle of the* أَلْيَة [*or tail, or fat of the tail,*] *of the sheep*; (Mgh;) [i.e.,] *flesh-meat in the interior of that part*: (IAth, TA:) this is what the doctors of practical law mean by this word in speaking of sales: (Mgh:) pl. as above. (IAth, TA.) — Also عُصْعُصٌ † A man (IF, O) *compact and strong in make*. (IF, O, Ḳ.) — Also, (Ibn-'Abbád, Ḳ,) or ضَيِّقُ العُصْعُصِ, (O, L, TA,) † A man (Ibn-'Abbád, L,) *unpropitious*, or *mean*, or *hard*, (L, Ḳ, TA,) *having little*, or *no*, *good*, or *goodness*. (Ibn-'Abbád, O, L, Ḳ, TA.)

عُصْعُصَةٌ *Pain of the* عُصْعُص. (O, Ḳ.)

عُصْعُوصٌ : see عُصْعُصٌ.

عصب

1. عَصَبَ, aor. ـِ, (Ḳ,) inf. n. عَصْبٌ, (Ṣ, A, Mgh, O, Ḳ,) *He twisted* [a thing], or *wound* [it] *round*: (A, Ḳ, TA:) this is the primary signification: (TA:) and *he folded* [it]; (A, Ḳ;) or *he folded* [it] *tightly*: (Ṣ, O, TA:) and *he bound* [it], or *tied* [it]: (A, Mgh, Ḳ, TA:) عَصْبٌ denotes the *binding*, or *tying*, a thing with another thing, *lengthwise*, or [more commonly] *around*. (O.) See also 2, first sentence. [And see مَعْصُوبٌ.] — *He twisted*, or *spun*, thread. (Ḳ,* TA.) And *He put together* thread, *and bound* it, previously to dyeing it. (TA.) — عَصَبَ الكَبْشَ, (Ṣ, O, Mṣb, Ḳ,*) aor. as above, (Ḳ,) and so the inf. n., (Ṣ, Mṣb, Ḳ,) *He bound*, or *tied*, (*tightly*, TA) *the testicles of the ram, in order that they might fall, without his extracting them*: (Ṣ, O, Mṣb, Ḳ:) and in like manner one says of a goat, (Ḳ,) and of other beasts. (TA.) — عَصَبَ النَّاقَةَ, (O, Mṣb, Ḳ,*) aor. as above, (Ḳ,) and so the inf. n., (Mṣb, Ḳ, TA,) and عِصَابٌ also; (TA;) and ↓ اعتصبها; (O, Ḳ;) *He bound the thighs of the she-camel*, (Mṣb, Ḳ, TA,) or *the lower parts of her nostrils*, (TA,) *with a cord*, (Mṣb, TA,) in order that she might yield her milk copiously: (Mṣb, Ḳ, TA:) and (O) عَصَبَ فَخِذَ النَّاقَةِ [*He bound the thigh of the she-camel*] for that purpose. (Ṣ, O.) [See عَصُوبٌ.] Hence one says, أَعْطَى عَلَى العَصْبِ ‡ *He gave by means of force*. (TA.) And مِثْلِى لَا يُدِرُّ بِالعِصَابِ † *Such a one as I am will not give by means of force*. (A, TA.) — عَصَبَتْ فَرْجَهَا *She* (a woman) *bound her vulva with a bandage*. (Mṣb.) — عَصَبَ الشَّجَرَةَ, (Ṣ, O, Ḳ,) aor. ـِ, inf. n. عَصْبٌ, (Ḳ,) *He drew together the branches of the tree* (Ṣ, O, Ḳ, TA) *that were straggling*, (Ḳ, TA,) *by means of a rope*, (TA,) *and then beat it*, (Ṣ, O, Ḳ, TA,) in order that its leaves might fall. (Ṣ, O, TA.) [Golius assigns this signification also to عَصَّبَ, as on the authority of the Ṣ, in which I do not find it.] El-Ḥajjáj said, (Ṣ, TA,) when preaching to the people at El-Koofeh, (TA,) لَأَعْصِبَنَّكُمْ عَصْبَ السَّلَمِ (Ṣ) or السَّلَمَةِ (TA) [*I will assuredly draw you together and beat you as one does the selem* or *the selemeh*]. The سَلَمَة is a tree of the kind called عِضَاه, having thorns, and its leaves are the قَرَظ with which hides are tanned: [but see قَرَظٌ:] the removal of the leaves with the hand being difficult on account of the many thorns, its branches are drawn together and bound tightly with a rope; then the beater pulls them towards him, and beats them with his staff; whereupon the leaves become scattered for the cattle and for him who desires to gather them. (TA.) Or this is done, (Ṣ, O, TA,) accord. to A'Obeyd, (Ṣ, O,) only (TA) when they desire to cut down the selemeh, that they may get at the stock. (Ṣ, O, TA.) [Hence,] one says, فُلَانٌ لَا تُعْصَبُ سَلَمَاتُهُ [*Such a one will not have his selemehs bound round with a rope, and beaten*]: a prov., applied to a strong, mighty man, not to be subdued nor abased. (A,* TA.) And one says also of winds, تَعْصِبُ الشَّجَرَ عِنْدَ ذُرُوجِهَا فِيهِ † [*They compress the branches of the trees, as though they bound them round, in their passage among them*]: and such winds are termed ↓ عَصَائِبُ. (O.) And عَصَبَ القَوْمَ, aor. ـِ, inf. n. عَصْبٌ, † *It* (an affair, or event,) *drew the people together, and became severe to them*. (Az, TA.) — عَصَبَ صَدْعَ الزُّجَاجَةِ بِضَبَّةٍ مِنْ فِضَّةٍ *He* (a smith) *repaired the crack of the glass vessel by putting round it a band of silver*. (O, TA.) — عَصَبَ بِرَأْسِ قَوْمِهِ العَارَ † *He made disgrace to befall his people* [*as though he bound it upon the head of their chief or upon the head of each of them*]. (O.) It is related in a trad. respecting the battle of Bedr, that 'Otbeh the son of Rabee'ah said, ارْجِعُوا وَلَا تُقَاتِلُوا وَاعْصِبُوهَا بِرَأْسِى † [*Return ye, and fight not; and bind it upon my head*]; meaning attach and attribute to me the disgrace that will befall you for relinquishing the battle and inclining to peace. (IAth, TA.) And it is said in another trad., قُومُوا بِمَا عَصَبَكُمْ بِهِ † *Fulfil ye the obligations with which He* (meaning God) *has bound you*; or *which He has imposed upon you and attached to you*; by his commands and prohibitions. (TA.) — عَصَبَ الشَّىْءَ and عَلَى الشَّىْءِ, aor. ـِ, inf. n. عَصْبٌ and عِصَابٌ, *He grasped the thing with his hand*. (Ḳ,* TA.) A poet, cited by IAạr, says,

• وَكُنَّا يَا قُرَيْشُ إِذَا عَصَبْنَا •
• يَجِىءُ عِصَابُنَا بِدَمٍ عَبِيطِ •

[*And we were, O Ḳureysh, when we grasped* our opponents, *such that our grasping brought fresh blood*]; عِصَابُنَا meaning *our grasping* those whom we opposed with the swords. (TA.) — And عَصَبَ, aor. ـِ, inf. n. عَصْبٌ, *He clung*, or *kept*, *to* a thing. (Ḳ.) One says, عَصَبَ المَآءَ *He kept to*, or *by*, *the water*. (IAạr, TA.) And عَصَبَ الرَّجُلُ بَيْتَهُ *The man remained*, or *stayed*, *in his house*, or *tent*, *not quitting it*. (O, TA.) — And *He went round*, *encompassed*, or *surrounded*, a thing. (Ḳ.) It is said in a trad., of the angel Gabriel, on the day of Bedr, قَدْ عَصَبَ رَأْسَهُ الغُبَارُ *The dust had overspread*, [or *surrounded*,] *and clung to*, *his head*: or, as some relate it, قَدْ عَصَمَ ثَنِيَّتَيْهِ الغُبَارُ; and if this be not a mistake, the latter verb is syn. with the former: ب and م being often interchangeable: (L, TA:) the latter phrase means, as also with عَصَبَ, *the dust had stuck to his two central incisors*. (TA in art. عصم.) And Ibn Aḥmar says,

• إِذْ عَصَبَ النَّاسَ شَمَالٌ وَقُرْ •

[وَقُرْ being for وَقُرٌّ] i. e. *When north wind and cold environ me*. (L, TA.) And one says also, عَصَبَ الغُبَارُ بِالجَبَلِ *The dust encompassed*, or *surrounded*, *the mountain*. (L, TA.) And عَصَبُوا بِهِ *They encompassed*, or *surrounded*, *him*: (Ṣ, A, Mgh, O, TA:) and *they encompassed*, or *surrounded*, *him*, *looking at him*: (Ṣ, O:) and, (Mṣb, Ḳ,) as also عَصِبُوا, (Ḳ,) aor. of the former ـِ, (Mṣb, Ḳ,) and inf. n. عَصْبٌ, (Mṣb,) and aor. of the latter ـَ, (Ḳ,) *they assembled around him* (Mṣb, Ḳ) *for fight* or *defence*. (Mṣb. For another explanation of عَصَبَ and عَصِبَ, see 12.) And عَصَبَ القَوْمُ بِالنَّسَبِ *i. q.* أَحَاطُوا بِهِ [app. meaning *The people*, or *party*, *included*, or *comprehended*, *the relations*, or *kinsmen*; for النَّسَب is often used for ذَوُو النَّسَبِ]. (Mṣb.) And عَصَبَتِ الإِبِلُ بِالمَآءِ *The camels surrounded*, or *encircled*, *the water*. (Ṣ, O.) — عَصَبَ الرِّيقُ بِفِيهِ, (Ṣ, O, Ḳ,* TA,) aor. ـِ, inf. n. عَصْبٌ; (Ḳ, TA;) and عَصِبَ, aor. ـَ; (TA;) *The saliva became dry in his mouth*. (Ṣ, O, Ḳ,* TA.) And عَصَبَ الرِّيقُ فَاهُ (Ṣ, O, TA) *The saliva* by its drying *made his mouth dry*: and *the saliva adhered to his mouth*. (TA.) Aboo-Moḥammad El-Faḳ'asee says,

• يَعْصِبُ فَاهُ الرِّيقُ أَىَّ عَصْبِ •
• عَصْبَ الجُبَابِ بِشِفَاهِ الوَطْبِ •

[*The saliva makes his mouth dry, with what a drying! as the drying of the spume of camels' milk on the lips of the skin*]. (Ṣ, O.) And عَصَبَ فُوهُ, aor. ـِ, inf. n. عَصْبٌ, *His mouth, with* *his saliva, became dry.* (O.) And عَصَبَ الفَمُ, (Ḳ,* TA,) aor. ـِ, inf. n. عَصْبٌ and عُصُوبٌ, meaning [*The mouth*, or *teeth*, (the latter accord. to the explanation in the Ḳ,)] *became foul*, or *dirty, from dust and the like*, (Ḳ, TA,) as *from vehement thirst*, or *fear*. (TA.) — عَصَبَ, aor. ـِ, inf. n. عُصُوبٌ, *He was*, or *became*, [*hungry*; or] *very hungry*; or *his bowels were almost dried up with hunger*: because it is said of the practice of a hungry man's binding round his belly, as expl. voce مَعْصُوبٌ [q. v.]. (TA.) — عَصَبَ الأُفُقُ *The horizon became red.* (Ṣ, O. [In Freytag's Lex. عَصِبَ, as from the Ḳ, in which I do not find it. See عَصْبٌ.]) = عَصِبَ, (Ṣ, O, Ḳ,) with kesr, (Ṣ, O,) like فَرِحَ, (Ḳ,) said of flesh, or flesh-meat, *It had many* عَصَب [i. e. *sinews*, or *tendons*]. (Ṣ, O, Ḳ.) — And عَصِبَ, aor. ـَ, inf. n. عَصَبٌ, [so in the TA, and so in a verse there cited, not عَصْبٌ,] *He was*, or *became, firm and compact in flesh.* (TA.) — [Other meanings of this verb have been mentioned above.]

2. عَصَّبَ, (Ṣ, A, O, &c.,) inf. n. تَعْصِيبٌ, (Ṣ, A, O,) [*He bound*, or *wound round*, a thing *with several circumvolutions*:] *he bound* [or *wound round*] a man's head with a turban, fillet, bandage, or the like; (Ṣ,* O,* Mṣb, Ḳ,* TA;) as also ↓ عَصَبَ, inf. n. عَصْبٌ: (MA:) and *he bound* a broken limb, or a wound, with a piece of rag or a bandage. (L, TA.) *He turbaned* a man; *attired* him *with a turban*. (A, TA.) — Hence, (A, O,) تَعْصِيبٌ signifies ‡ [The *crowning* a man: (see the pass. part. n.:)] the *making* a man *a chief*: (A, O, Ḳ, TA:) for turbans are the crowns of the Arabs: (O:) when a man's people made him a chief, they bound his head with a turban: (A, TA:) as kings wore crowns, so the chiefs of the Arabs wore red turbans: (L, TA:) there were brought to the desert, from Haráh (هَرَاة), red turbans, which the nobles among the Arabs wore. (Az, TA.) — [Hence also,] عَصَّبَهُ بِالسَّيْفِ i. q. عَمَّمَهُ بِهِ † [*He cut*, or *wounded, him in the place of the turban, with the sword*]. (A, TA.) — And عَصَّبَهُ, inf. n. as above, *He*, or *it*, [*caused him to bind his waist by reason of hunger*: (see the pass. part. n.:) and hence,] *made him to hunger*: (Ḳ:) and عَصَّبَتْهُمُ السِّنُونَ *The years of drought*, or *sterility, made them to hunger*: (TA:) or عَصَّبَتْهُ السِّنُونَ *The years of drought*, or *sterility, ate up his property*, or *cattle*. (A'Obeyd, Ṣ, O.) And *It* [i. e. drought or the like] *destroyed him*: (Ḳ:) and عَصَّبَ الدَّهْرُ مَالَهُ *Adverse fortune destroyed his cattle*, or *camels &c.* (TA.) — And *He called him* مُعَصَّب [meaning *poor*]: so says IAạr; and he cites as an ex.,

* يُدْعَى المُعَصَّبَ مَنْ قَلَّتْ حَلُوبَتُهُ *
* وَهَلْ يُعَصَّبُ مَاضِى الهَمِّ مِقْدَامُ *

[*He is called the poor, whose milch-cattle have become few: but should one whose purpose is effectual, one of great boldness, be called poor?*]. (TA.) — الذَّكَرُ يُعَصِّبُ الأُنْثَى means *The male makes the female to be such as is termed* عَصَبَة [by his being consociated with her as such]. (Mgh.)

4: see 12. — [Golius explains this v. as meaning "*Firmiter religavit*:" or, as a trans. v. governing an accus., "*constringi jussit*:" as on the authority of the Ṣ, in which I do not find it in any sense.]

5. تعصّب i. q. شَدَّ العِصَابَةَ [i. e. *He bound the turban*, or *fillet, round his* (own) *head*; a meaning well known, whence that explained in the next sentence: (see also 8:) and *he bound a bandage of some kind round his* (own) *body*, by reason of hunger: see مُعَصَّب]. (Ṣ, O, Mṣb,* Ḳ.) — And † *He was made a chief*; quasi-pass. of 2 [q. v.]. (L, TA.) — And it has also another signification, from العَصَبِيَّة; (Ṣ, O;) [i. e.] it signifies also أَتَى بِالعَصَبِيَّةِ; (Ḳ, TA;) which means [*He aided his people*, or *party, against hostile conduct*: or *he was angry*, or *zealous, for the sake of his party, and defended them*: (see عَصَبِىّ and عَصَبِيَّة:) or] *he invited*, or *summoned, others to the aid of his party, and to combine*, or *league, with them against those who acted towards them with hostility, whether they were wrongdoers or wronged*. (TA.) And you say, تَعَصَّبُوا عَلَيْهِمْ *They leagued*, or *collected themselves, together against them*: and تَعَصَّبْنَا لَهُ, and مَعَهُ, *We* [*leagued together for him, and with him, and*] *defended him*. (TA.) [See also De Sacy's Chrest. Ar., sec. ed., i. 445-6; where it is shown that التَّعَصُّب in religion means *The being zealous*, or *a zealot*: and see Ḥar pp. 423 and 573.] — And تعصّب بِالشَّىْءِ *He was*, or *became, content with the thing*; as also ↓ اعتصب بِهِ. (Ḳ.)

7. انعصب i. q. اِشْتَدَّ [app. meaning, as seems to be indicated by the context (both before and after) in the Ṣ, *It was*, or *became, hard, firm*, or *strong*]. (Ṣ, O, Ḳ.)

8. اعتصب بِالعِمَامَةِ [*He attired himself*, or *surrounded his head, with the turban*], and بِالتَّاجِ [*with the crown*]. (Ṣ, O.) And اعتصب التَّاجَ عَلَى رَأْسِهِ *He encircled his* [own] *head with the crown*. (Az, TA.) — اعتصب النَّاقَةَ: see 1, in the middle of the first quarter. — اعتصبوا *They became formed*, or *collected, into companies such as those whereof one is called* عُصْبَة: (Ḳ:) or, *into one of such companies*. (M, L, TA.) [See also 12.] — اعتصب بِهِ: see 5, last sentence.

12. اِعْصَوْصَبَ القَوْمُ *The people*, or *party, collected themselves together*: (TA:) or *did so, and became companies such as are called* عَصَائِب, (Ṣ, O, TA,) and *became one of such companies*: [see also 8; and see عُصْبَة:] and in like manner, [*did so, and*] *strove*, or *exerted themselves, in journeying*, or *pace*. (TA.) And اعصوصبت الإِبِلُ *The camels strove*, or *exerted themselves, in journeying*, or *pace*; as also ↓ اعصبت: and *collected themselves together*; (Ḳ;) [and] so ↓ عَصَبَتْ and ↓ عَصِبَتْ: (Fr, Ṣ, O:) or *collected themselves together so as to become one* عِصَابَة, *and strove*, or *exerted themselves, in journeying*, or *pace*. (TA.) — اعصوصب is also said of a day, [app. in relation to heat,] meaning *It was*, or *became, vehement*, or *severe*: (Ṣ, O:) and of evil, meaning *it was*, or *became, vehement*, or *severe*, (Ḳ, TA,) *and concentrated*. (TA.)

عَصْبٌ: see عِصَابَة, in two places. — And see also عَصَبٌ. — Also *A particular sort of the garments called* بُرُود, (Ṣ, A, Mgh, O, Ḳ,) *of the fabric of El-Yemen*; (Ṣ, Mgh, O;) *a* بُرْد *of which the yarn is dyed, and then woven*; (Mṣb;) or *of which the yarn is put together and bound, then dyed, and then woven*; (A, Mgh, TA;*) not of the sort called بُرُودُ الرَّقْمِ: (TA:) it has no pl., (Nh, Mṣb, TA,) nor dual: (Mṣb:) you say بُرْدُ عَصْبٍ (Nh, Mgh, TA) and بُرُودُ عَصْبٍ (Nh, Mgh, Mṣb, TA) and بُرْدَا عَصْبٍ, (Mṣb,) and also ثَوْبُ عَصْبٍ and بُرُودٌ عَصْبٌ, (Nh, TA,) and عَصْبٌ, (Mṣb,) and أَرْدِيَةُ العَصْبِ; (A, TA;) and sometimes they say عَصْب alone, the بُرْد being known by this name: (TA:) or *garments of the kind called* بُرُود, *of the fabric of El-Yemen, the yarn of which is put together and bound, and then dyed, and woven, so that they become party-coloured, because what has been bound thereof remains white, the dye not having taken it*; and such garments a woman in the period termed عِدَّة [q. v.] is allowed to wear, but not garments that are [wholly] dyed: or *striped garments of the kind called* بُرُود; and what is forbidden in that case is a garment that has been dyed after it has been woven; or what are forbidden are the عَصْب of El-Yemen, which are said to have been dyed with urine: so in the L &c.: (TA:) or, accord. to Suh, *garments of the kind called* بُرُود *of the fabric of El-Yemen*; so called because they are dyed with عَصْب, which grows only in El-Yemen; [he says that العَصْبُ is *a certain dye that does not grow but in El-Yemen*; (Mṣb;)] but in this he opposes the generality of authorities; for they agree in stating that the garments in question are thus called from العَصْبُ, "the act of binding," because the yarn is bound in order that the dye may not pervade the whole of the بُرْد. (MF, TA.) — Hence, † *Clouds like such as are termed* لَطْخ [q. v.]: (Ṣ, O:) or *red clouds* or *mist* (Ḳ, TA) *seen in the western horizon* (TA) *in a time of drought*, or *sterility*; as also ↓ عِصَابَة, (Ḳ, TA,) pl. عَصَائِب. (TA.) = In a trad., mention occurs of a necklace made of عَصْب: El-Khaṭṭábee says, if it do not mean the garments of El-Yemen, I know not what it is; yet I see not how a necklace can be made of these: Aboo-Moosà thinks it may be عَصَب, meaning the tendons of joints, as they may have taken the tendons of certain clean animals, and cut them in pieces, and made them like beads, and, when dry, made necklaces of them; but he adds his having been told by some of the people of El-Yemen that عَصْب is the name of *A certain beast of the sea*, or *of the great river*, called also فَرَسُ فِرْعَوْنَ [i. e. *Pharaoh's horse*, perhaps meaning the *hippopotamus*], *of which* [meaning *of the teeth* or *bones of which*] *beads and other things, as the handles of knives &c., are made, and which is white*. (L, TA.) =

And *Saliva that sticks and dries in the mouth*: whence the saying, لَفَظَ فُلَانٌ عَصَبَهُ, meaning † *Such a one died.* (T and TA in art. لفظ.) —— And A *light*, or *an active, and sharp-headed*, boy, or young man; (IAar, TA;) [and] so عَضْب. (IAar, TA in art. عضب.)

عُصْبٌ and ‌† عَصْبٌ and ‌† عَصَبٌ (K, TA) *Certain trees that twine round other trees, having weak leaves*; (TA;) the *kind of tree called* لُبْلَاب [*dolichos lablab* of Linn.]; (K;) said by Sh to be *a kind of plant that twines round trees, i. q.* لُبْلَابٌ: [coll. gen. ns.:] the ns. un. are عُصْبَةٌ and عَصْبَةٌ and عَصَبَةٌ: (TA:) accord. to Abu-l-Jarráh, (O, TA,) عُصْبَةٌ signifies *a certain thing* [app. meaning *plant*] *that twines about a* قَتَادَة [or *tragacanth*], (O, K, TA,) thus, correctly, in many copies of the K, but in some قَتَاة, and in some قَنَاة, both of which are wrong, though some assert the latter to be correct, (TA,) *not to be pulled off from it but with an effort*: (O, K, TA:) [see عَلِقَةٌ:] one says of a man strong in struggling for the mastery, قَتَادَةٌ لُوِيَتْ بِعُصْبَةٍ † [*A tragacanth twined about by a lebláb*; the strong man being app. likened to a tragacanth, and his antagonist to a lebláb]: (TA:) and in a trad. of Ez-Zubeyr Ibn-El-'Owwám, he is related to have said,

* عَلِقْتُهُمْ إِنِّى خُلِقْتُ عُصْبَهْ *
* قَتَادَةً تَعَلَّقَتْ بِنُشْبَهْ *

(O, TA:) he puts عصبه for علقة, [evidently, I think, a mistranscription for عَلِقًا, (see نُشْبَةٌ, in its proper art., for a confirmation,)] the meaning being خلقت علقة لخصومى [in which for علقة I read عَلِقًا]; then he likens himself to a tragacanth in respect of his excessive tenaciousness; for بنشبه means "by the help of a thing of great tenaciousness:" [or نشبه may be here an inf. n., i. e. of نَشِبَ: the meaning of the verse may therefore be, *I clung to them: verily I have been created a grasper*, and *a tragacanth that has clung by means of a strong holdfast*, or *that has clung with great tenaciousness*:] (TA:) Sh explains عُصْبَة (O, TA) with damm on the authority of Ed-Deenawaree [i. e. AHn], and عَصْبَة with fet-h on the authority of AA, (O,) as meaning *a certain plant that twines about a tree, and is called* لُبْلَاب; and نُشْبَة as meaning a man who, when he sports with a thing (عَبِثَ بِشَىْءٍ) [but probably the right reading is نَشِبَتْ or شَبِثَ بشىء, i. e. clings to a thing]), hardly, or never, quits it. (O, TA.)

عَصَبٌ [The *sinews*, or *tendons*; though the following explanation seems rather to denote the *ligaments*;] the أَطْنَاب *of the joints*, (S, O, Msb, K, TA,) *which connect and bind together the structure thereof*, in man and in others, such as the ox-kind, and sheep or goats, and gazelles, and ostriches; so says AHn; (TA;) *i. q.* عَقَبٌ: (S and K &c. in art. عقب:) or *such as are yellow of the* اطناب (Mgh, Msb) *of the joints*; the عَقَب being the white: (Mgh:) [it is also used as meaning *ligaments*: (see an ex. of its n. un. in an explanation of الصَّدَفَتَانِ, voce صَدَفٌ:) and sometimes it means *nerves*: (see a usage of its pl. voce صَرَعٌ:) it is a coll. gen. n.:] the n. un. is with ة: (S, O, TA:) and the pl. is أَعْصَابٌ. (S, Mgh, O, Msb.) —— And † The *best* (in a pl. sense) *of a people* or *party*. (K.) —— See also عُصْبٌ.

عَصِبٌ Flesh, or flesh-meat, *having many* عَصَب [i. e. *sinews*, or *tendons*]. (TA.)

عَصْبَةٌ n. un. of عَصْبٌ as syn. with عُصْبٌ [q. v.]. (TA.)

عُصْبَةٌ n. un. of عُصْبٌ [q. v.]. (TA.) —— And *A party*, or *company*, *of men* (AZ, S, O, Msb) *who league together to defend one another*; (O; [See also عَصَبَةٌ;]) *in number from ten to forty*; (AZ, S, O, Msb;) or, *about ten*: (IF, Msb:) or accord. to Akh, *a company* [*of men*]; as also ‌† عِصَابَةٌ; having no sing.: (O:) or ‌† the latter, (S, O, Msb,) or each, (K,) signifies *a company*, or an *assemblage*, of men, and of horses, (S, O, Msb, K,) or of horses with their riders, (TA,) and of birds, (S, O, Msb, K,) and of other things, (TA,) *in number from ten to forty*, (K, TA,) or the former *from three to ten*, or *consisting of forty*, or *of seventy*, but said to be originally applied to an unlimited number: its pl. is عُصَبٌ: (IAth, Msb, TA:) and the pl. of ‌† عِصَابَةٌ is عَصَائِبُ. (S, O, Msb, TA.) It is said in a trad. of 'Alee that the أَبْدَال are in Syria; and the نُجَبَآء, in Egypt; and the ‌† عَصَائِب, in El-'Irák; meaning, by the last, *Companies assembled for wars*: or a *company of devotees*, because coupled with the ابدال and the نجباء. (TA.)

عِصْبَةٌ *A mode*, or *manner*, *of binding*, or *winding round, one's head* with a turban or the like. (L, TA.)

عَصَبَةٌ n. un. of عَصَبٌ. (S, &c. [See the latter word in the paragraph headed by it and also voce عُصْبٌ.]) —— Also A man's *people*, or *party*, *who league together for his defence*: (K, TA: [see also عُصْبَةٌ:]) thus accord. to the leading lexicologists. (TA.) —— And The *heirs of a man who has left neither parent nor offspring*: and [particularly], with respect to the [portions of inheritances termed] فَرَائِض [pl. of فَرِيضَةٌ q. v.], *all such as have not a* فَرِيضَة *named, and who receive if there remain anything after* [*the distribution of*] *the* فَرَائِض: (K, TA:) thus accord. to those who treat of the فرائض, and accord. to the [other] lawyers: (TA:) or the *relations by the side of the males*: this is the meaning of what is said by the leading lexicologists: (Msb:) or, as is said by Az, a man's *heirs consisting of male relations*: (Msb, TA:) or his *sons, and relations on the father's side*: (S:) so called because they encompass him; the father being a طَرَف [i. e. an extremity in the right line], and so the son, and the paternal uncle being a جَانِب [i. e. a collateral relation], and so the brother: (Az, S, TA:) or a man's *relations on the father's side*; (Mgh, TA;) because they encompass him and he is strengthened by them: (TA:) afterwards it became applied to a single person as well as to a pl. number, and both a male and a female: (Mgh:) or the lawyers apply it to a single person when there is no other than he, because he stands in the place of the collective number in receiving the whole of the property; and in the language of the law it is applied to a female in certain cases relating to emancipation and inheritances, but not otherwise either in the proper language or in the language of the law: (Msb:) and ‌† عُصُوبَةٌ is used as its inf. n. [meaning the *state of being persons*, or *a person, to whom the term* عَصَبَة *is applied*]: (Mgh:) it is said [by Az] in the T, "I have not heard any sing. of عَصَبَة: accord. to analogy it should be عَاصِب, like as طَالِب is sing. of طَلَبَة:" (TA: [and the like is also said in the Mgh: in the Msb it is said that عَصَبَة is pl. of عَاصِب, like as كَفَرَة is pl. of كَافِر:]) the pl. is عَصَبَات. (Az, S, TA.)

عَصَبِىٌّ *One who aids his people*, or *party*, *against hostile conduct*: or *who is angry* [or *zealous*] *for the sake of his party, and defends them*: [or *one who invites others to the aid of his party*, or *to combine*, or *league, with them against those who act towards them with hostility, whether they be wrongdoers or wronged*: or *one who leagues with others*: or *one who defends others*: or *a partisan*; *a person of party-spirit*; or *one zealous in the cause of a party*: (see 5, and see the paragraph next following this:)] occurring in a trad. (TA.)

عَصَبِيَّةٌ [The *quality of him who is termed* عَصَبِىٌّ: i. e., *of him who aids his people*, or *party*, *against hostile conduct*: or *of him who is angry*, or *zealous, for the sake of his party, and defends them*: or *of him who invites others to the aid of his party*, and *to combine*, or *league, with them against those who act towards them with hostility, whether they be wrongdoers* or *wronged*: or *of him who leagues with others*: or *of him who defends others*: or *partisanship*; *party-spirit*; or *zeal in the cause of a party*: or (as expl. by De Sacy, Chrest. Ar., sec. ed., i. 411,) *a strong attachment, which holds several persons closely united by the same interest or the same opinion*: see 5, and see the paragraph next preceding this]. (S, K, TA.)

عِصَابٌ *A cord with which the thigh of a she-camel is bound in order that she may yield her milk copiously.* (S.) —— See also عِصَابَةٌ, in two places.

عَصُوبٌ A she-camel *that will not yield her milk copiously unless her thigh*, (S, O,) or *thighs*, (A, K,) *be bound with a cord*: (S, A, O, K:) or *unless the lower parts of her nostrils be bound with a cord, and she be then urged to rise, and not loosed until she is milked.* (AZ, TA.) —— And A woman *having little flesh in her posteriors and thighs*: or *light in the hips*, or *haunches*. (Kr, K.)

عَصِيبٌ *Lights* [of an animal] *bound round with guts, and then roasted*, or *broiled*: (S, O, K:) pl. [of pauc.] أَعْصِبَةٌ (K) and [of mult.] عُصُبٌ. (S, O, K.) And *Such as are twisted*, of the guts of a sheep or goat. (TA.) And its pl. عُصُبٌ, *Guts* of a sheep or goat, folded, and put together, and then put into one of the winding guts of the belly. (L, TA.) —— Also, and ▼ عَصَبْصَبٌ A vehement, or severe, day: (Fr, Ṣ, O, Ḳ:) or a vehemently-hot day: (Fr, Ḳ:) and the former is in like manner applied to a night (لَيْلَة), without ة: (TA:) and ▼ the latter signifies also a cold, and very cloudy, day, in which nothing is seen of the sky. (Abu-l-'Alà, L, TA.)

عِصَابَةٌ A thing with which another thing is bound, or wound round; as also ▼ عِصَابٌ (Ḳ, TA) and ▼ عَصْبٌ: (L, TA:) or a thing with which the head is bound, or wound round; (Ṣ, A, Mgh, O, TA;) and ▼ عِصَابٌ signifies a thing with which a thing other than the head is bound, or wound round; (A, TA;) anything, such as a piece of rag, or a fillet, or bandage, with which a broken limb, or a wound, is bound, is termed thus, i. e. عِصَابٌ: (L, TA:) and عِصَابَةٌ signifies also a turban; syn. عِمَامَةٌ: (A, Mgh, Mṣb, Ḳ, TA:) or this [in the TA by mistake written عمامة] signifies a small thing that serves as a covering for the head, [such as a kerchief or a fillet,] being wound round it; and what is larger is termed عِمَامَةٌ: ('Ináyeh of Esh-Shiháb, MF, TA:) or whatever is bound, or wound, round the head, whether it be a turban or a kerchief or a piece of rag: (TA, from an explanation of a trad.:) and ▼ عَصْبٌ [likewise] signifies a turban, and anything with which the head is bound, or wound round: (Ṣ, O:) the pl. of عِصَابَةٌ is عَصَائِبُ. (Mgh, TA.) El-Farezdaḳ says,

وَرَكْبٍ كَأَنَّ الرِّيحَ تَطْلُبُ مِنْهُمُ

لَهَا سَلَبًا مِنْ جَذْبِهَا بِالعَصَائِبِ

[And a company of riders in such a state that it seemed as though the wind desired to take for itself spoil from them, by its dragging away the turbans]: he means that the wind untwisted their turbans by its violence, as though it despoiled them thereof. (TA.) —— And [hence] † A crown. (A, TA.) —— See also عَصْبٌ, latter half. —— And see عُصْبَةٌ, in four places. —— And for the pl. applied to winds, see 1, former half.

عُصُوبَةٌ: see عُصْبَةٌ, near the end.

عَصَبْصَبٌ: see عَصِيبٌ, in two places.

عَصَّابٌ A vender, or spinner, of thread, or yarn; syn. غَزَّالٌ. (AA, Ṣ, O.)

فُوهُ عَاصِبٌ His mouth is dry from the drying up of the saliva: and رَجُلٌ عَاصِبٌ A man in whose mouth the saliva has dried up. (TA.)

مُعَصَّبٌ, (Ṣ, O, TA,) accord. to the author of the Ḳ ▼ مُعْصَبٌ, like مُحْدَثٌ, in all its senses there explained, but accord. to others like مُعَظَّمٌ, (TA,) One having his waist bound round in consequence of hunger; (Ṣ, O;) one who binds round his body (يَتَعَصَّبُ) with pieces of a garment or of cloth, by reason of hunger; (Ḳ, TA;) one who, in consequence of leanness occasioned by hunger, binds round his belly with a stone [placed under the bandage: see مَعْصُوبٌ]; (TA:) or, accord. to A'Obeyd, one whose property, or cattle, years of drought, or sterility, have eaten up: (Ṣ, O:) [or] it signifies also a poor man. (Ḳ, TA.) —— And Turbaned; attired with a turban; (O, L, TA;) [as also ▼ مُعْتَصِبٌ.] —— And [hence] † A chief; (Ḳ;) one made a chief. (Az, L, TA. [See 2.]) —— And [hence] † Crowned: (O:) or a crowned king; as also ▼ مُعْتَصِبٌ: (A, TA:) because the crown encircles the head like a turban. (Az, TA.)

مُعْصَبٌ: see the next preceding paragraph.

مَعْصُوبٌ [Twisted, or wound round: and folded, or folded tightly: and bound, or tied: see 1, first sentence. —— And hence,] † Firm, or strong, in the compacture of the flesh. (Ṣ, O.) You say رَجُلٌ مَعْصُوبُ الخَلْقِ † [A man firm, or compact, in respect of make]; (Ṣ, A, O;) strongly, or firmly, knit, or compacted; not flabby in flesh. (TA.) And جَارِيَةٌ مَعْصُوبَةٌ, meaning حَسَنَةُ العَصْبِ i. e. مَجْدُولَةُ الخَلْقِ † [A girl, or young woman, goodly in respect of compacture; well compacted in respect of make]. (Ṣ, O.) —— And † A slender, or an elegant, sword. (Ḳ.) —— And † Hungry, having his belly bound round: (A:) or [simply] hungry; in the dial. of Hudheyl: (Ṣ, O:) or very hungry: (Ḳ:) or one whose bowels are almost dried up by hunger: an epithet said to be applied to a hungry man because he binds round his belly with a stone [within the bandage] on account of his hunger: it is said to have been the custom of any hungry man, among the Arabs, to bind his belly with a bandage, under which he sometimes put a stone. (TA.) —— And † A letter (كِتَابٌ); thus called because bound round with a thread, or string: so in the saying, وَرَدَ عَلَىَّ مَعْصُوبٌ [A letter came to me]. (A, TA.)

مُعْتَصِبٌ: see مُعَصَّبٌ, in two places.

رَجُلٌ يَعْصُوبٌ A strong, or sturdy, man. (TA.)

عصد

1. عَصَدَهُ, (Ṣ, O, Ḳ,) aor. ـِ, (O, Ḳ,) inf. n. عَصْدٌ, (Ṣ, O,) He twisted it; turned, or wreathed, it round or about; contorted it; wound it; or bent it; (Ṣ, O, Ḳ;) as also ▼ اعصدهُ. (Ḳ.) —— [Hence,] عَصَدَ العَصِيدَةَ, aor. ـِ, (Ṣ, O, L, Mṣb,) inf. n. as above; (Mṣb;) and ▼ اعصدها; (O, L, Mṣb;) He stirred about and turned over the عصيدة with a مِعْصَد, or مِعْصَدَة; (O,* L, Mṣb;*) he made, or prepared, the عَصِيدَة. (L.) —— And عَصَدَ عُنُقَهُ, [and app. عَصَدَ alone, (see عَاصِدٌ,)] aor. ـِ, inf. n. عُصُودٌ, He (a camel) bent his neck towards his withers in dying. (TA.) —— عَصَدْتُهُ عَلَى الأَمْرِ, (O, Ḳ,*) inf. n. عَصْدٌ, (O,) I made him to do the thing against his will. (O, Ḳ.*) —— عَصَدَتْهُمُ العَصَاوِيدُ Clamours such as are raised in trial, or affliction, assailed them. (Lth, L.) —— عَصَدَ said of an arrow, It wound, or turned, in its course, not going directly towards the butt. (L.) —— And عَصَدَ, (Ṣ, O, Ḳ,) aor. ـِ, (Ḳ,) inf. n. عُصُودٌ; (Ṣ, O, Ḳ;) as also عَصِدَ, aor. ـَ; (Ḳ;) said of a man, (TA,) He died. (Ṣ, O, Ḳ.)

4: see above, first and second sentences.

Q. Q. 1. عَصْوَدُوا, (O, Ḳ,) inf. n. عَصْوَدَةٌ; (TA;) and ▼ تَعَصْوَدُوا; (O, Ḳ;) They cried out, (O, Ḳ,) and fought one another: (Ḳ:) and ▼ the latter, they raised a clamour, and became in a state of confusion. (TA.)

Q. Q. 2. تَعَصْوَدُوا: see Q. Q. 1, in two places.

عَصِيدٌ Twisted; turned, or wreathed, round or about; contorted; wound; or bent; as also ▼ مَعْصُودٌ. (TA.)

عَصِيدَةٌ is well known; (Ḳ;) [as being A sort of thick gruel, consisting of] wheat-flour moistened and stirred about with clarified butter, and cooked; (L;) one stirs it about, and turns it over, with a مِسْوَاط, [i. e. stick, or the like,] (also called ▼ مِعْصَدٌ and ▼ مِعْصَدَةٌ, L,) so that no part of it that has not been turned over remains in the vessel; (IF,* Ṣ, O, Mṣb;*) and hence it is thus called: (IF, Mṣb:) [it is also commonly made with boiling water, flour, clarified butter, and honey:] accord. to El-Mufaddal, it is properly thus called when it is so thick that it may be chewed. (TA voce حَرِيرَةٌ [q. v.: see also وَطِيئَةٌ.]

عَصْوَدٌ A long day: (IAạr, Ḳ:) and so عَطْوَدٌ and عَطْرَدٌ. (L in arts. عطد and عطرد.) —— And all signify A high mountain. (L in arts. عطد and عطرد.)

عَصْوَادٌ: see the next paragraph, in two places.

عَصَوَادٌ Evil, or mischief, arising from slaughter; or mutual reviling; or clamour; so in the phrase, تَرَكْتُهُمْ فِى عَصَوَادٍ [I left them in a state of evil, &c.]: (TA:) or clamour and confusion in war or altercation; as also ▼ عَصْوَادٌ: (M, TA:) or clamour in trial or affliction: (Lth, TA:) or a formidable, or terrible, case; (Ṣ, Ḳ;) so in the phrase, وَقَعُوا فِى عَصَوَادٍ [They fell into a formidable, or terrible, case]: (Ṣ:) and هُمْ فِى عَصَوَادٍ [They are in a formidable, or terrible, case]: (Ḳ:) or you say, هُمْ فِى عَصَوَادٍ بَيْنَهُمْ They are in trials, or afflictions, and altercations. (TA.) —— Also, and ▼ عَصْوَادٌ, A man, and a woman, difficult, or stubborn, hard, and evil, or mischievous: (O, Ḳ:) applied to a woman, evil, or mischievous; (O;) or very evil or mischievous. (TA.) [Pl. عَصَاوِيدُ.] You say, قَوْمٌ عَصَاوِيدُ فِى الحَرْبِ A people who cleave to their adversaries in war, (O, Ḳ,) and will not quit them. (O.) —— And عَصَاوِيدُ الكَلَامِ Distorted language; (O, Ḳ;) [as though] heaped together, one part upon another. (TA.) And عَصَاوِيدُ الظَّلَامِ Confused (O,* TA) and dense darkness. (O,* Ḳ, TA.) And in like manner عصاويد is used in relation to camels: (Ḳ:) one says, جَآءَتِ الإِبِلُ عَصَاوِيدَ The camels came pressing, or crowding, one upon another: (Ṣ, O:) and accord. to Ibn-'Abbád, came in a state of dis-

persion. (O.) —— عَصَاوِيدُ signifies also *Thirsty,* (ISh, O, Ḳ,) applied to camels. (ISh, O.) —— And عَصْوَادٌ signifies A *fatiguing* approach, (O, Ḳ,) or night-journey, (O,) to water. (O, Ḳ.)

عَاصِدٌ A camel *bending his neck towards his withers in dying.* (Ṣ, O, Ḳ.)

عَصِيدَةٌ and مِعْصَدَةٌ : see مِعْصَدٌ.

مَعْصُودٌ : see عَصِيدٌ.

عصر

1. عَصَرَهُ, (Ṣ, Mṣb, Ḳ,) aor. ـِ, (O, Mṣb, Ḳ,) inf. n. عَصْرٌ; (Ṣ, Mṣb;) and ↓ اعتصره; (Ṣ, O, Mṣb, Ḳ;) [*He pressed it,* or *squeezed it, so as to force out,* i. e. *he expressed, its juice, sirup, honey, oil, water, or moisture;*] *he extracted,* or *fetched out by labour* or *art* [i. e. *by pressure* or *wringing*], (Mṣb, Ḳ,) *its water,* or *juice,* or *the like,* (Mṣb,) or *what was in it,* (Ḳ,) namely, what was in grapes, (Ṣ, Mṣb, Ḳ,) and the like, (Mṣb, Ḳ,) of things having oil, or sirup, or honey: (TA:) or عَصَرَهُ signifies *he performed that act himself;* (Ḳ;) as also ↓ عصّره, inf. n. تَعْصِيرٌ: (Sgh, TA:) or the latter, *he superintended the pressing thereof,* i. e., of grapes: (O:) and ↓ اعتصره, *he had it done for him:* (Ḳ:) or this last, *he did it for another,* or *others:* (Mgh, as implied by an explanation of مُعْتَصِرٌ:) and ↓ اعتصر عَصِيرًا *he prepared expressed juice or the like.* (Ṣ, O.) [See also 8 below.] عَصْرَ is used as a contraction of عَصَرَ. (Ṣ, O.) —— [Hence,] عَصَرَ الثَّوْبَ, inf. n. as above, *He wrung out the water of the garment,* or *piece of cloth; he forced out its water by wringing it.* (Mṣb.) —— And عَصَرَ الدُّمَّلَ لِتَخْرُجَ مِدَّتُهُ [*He squeezed,* or *pressed, the pustule in order that its thick purulent matter might come forth*]. (Mṣb.) —— And عَصَرَ حَلْقَهُ [*He squeezed his throat*]. (Mgh and Mṣb in art. خنق.) —— And عَصَرَ, aor. ـِ, † *He took,* or *collected, the produce of the earth:* from the same verb in the first of the senses expl. above: and hence, accord. to Abu-l-Ghowth, in the Ḳur [xii. 49], وَفِيهِ يَعْصِرُونَ † *And in it they shall take,* or *collect, the produce of the earth:* (Ṣ:) or the meaning is, *and in it they shall press grapes,* or *olives,* or *the like:* or *they shall milk the udders.* (Bḍ.) [And there are other explanations, which see below.] —— عُصِرُوا, (Ṣ, IḲṭṭ, O,) or ↓ أُعْصِرُوا, (O, Ḳ,) *They were rained upon; they had rain;* syn. مُطِرُوا, (Ṣ, O,) or أُمْطِرُوا [which is less correct]. (IḲṭṭ, Ḳ.) Hence, in the Ḳur [ubi suprà], accord. to one reading, وَفِيهِ يُعْصَرُونَ [*And in it they shall have rain*]. (Ṣ, O.) [See also above, and below.] —— عَصَرَهُ also signifies *He saved him; preserved him:* and hence, in the Ḳur [ubi suprà], accord. to one reading, وَفِيهِ يُعْصَرُونَ [*And in it they shall be saved,* or *preserved*]. (Bḍ.) —— Hence also, perhaps, the other reading, وَفِيهِ يَعْصِرُونَ *And in it they shall aid, or succour, one another.* (Bḍ.) —— See also 8, last quarter, in two places. —— Also, عَصَرَهُ, (O, TA,) inf. n. عَصْرٌ, (O, Ḳ, TA,) *It* [or *he*] *withheld, hindered,* or *prevented, him:* (O, Ḳ,* TA:) one says, مَا عَصَرَكَ *What withheld, hindered, or prevented, thee?* (O, TA.) And *He refused,* and *withheld, it;* (Ḳ,* TA;) namely, anything. (TA.) [See also 8, which signifies the same.] —— And عَصَرَهُ, (Ḳ,) aor. ـِ, inf. n. عَصْرٌ, *He gave* (O, Ḳ, TA) *to him.* (Ḳ, TA.) Thus it has two contr. significations. (IḲṭṭ, TA.) Ṭarafeh says,

* لَوْ كَانَ فِى أَمْلَاكِنَا أَحَدٌ *

* يَعْصِرُ فِينَا كَالَّذِى تَعْصِرُ *

(Ṣ, O, TA, but in the Ṣ with مَلِكٌ in the place of أَحَدٌ,) i. e. [*If there were,* or *would that there were, among our kings one*] *giving to us the like of what thou givest:* (TA:) and another reading is, مِثْلَ مَا تَعْصِرُ; (O;) and it is expl. (by A'Obeyd, TA) as meaning, *doing to us benefits* (O, TA) *like as thou dost:* (O:) but Aboo-Sa'eed relates it thus;

* يُعْصَرُ فِينَا كَالَّذِى تُعْصَرُ *

i. e. يُصَابُ مِنْهُ [app. from عَصَرَ signifying "he pressed" grapes and the like; and thus meaning, † *from whom is gotten, among us, like what is gotten from thee;* or, as it may be less freely rendered, *who has his bounty drawn forth, among us, like as thou hast thine drawn forth*]; and he disallowed the reading [يَعْصِرُ and] تَعْصِرُ. (TA.) See also 8, first quarter. —— See also 4, second sentence: —— and last two sentences. —— And see the paragraph here following.

2: see 1: —— and see also 4, second sentence. —— عصّر الزَّرْعُ, inf. n. تَعْصِيرٌ; (Ḳ, TA;) but in the Tekmileh written عَصَرَ الزَّرْعُ, without teshdeed; (TA;) *The corn put forth its glumes:* (Ḳ, TA:) app. from عَصَرٌ meaning "a place of protection:" i. e. [*the rudiments of its ears*] *became protected in its glumes.* (TA.)

3. عاصر فُلَانًا, inf. n. مُعَاصَرَةٌ and عِصَارٌ, *He was contemporary with such a one:* or *he attained to,* or *reached, the time of such a one.* (O, TA.) Hence the saying, المُعَاصَرَةُ مُعَاسَرَةٌ وَالمُعَاصِرُ لَا يُنَاصِرُ [*The being contemporary is an occasion of hard,* or *harsh, treatment; and the contemporary will not render reciprocal aid* to his fellow]. (TA. [But I have substituted معاسرة for معاصرة, which latter seems to have been written by mistake for the former.]) —— See also 8, last quarter.

4. اعصر *He* (a man, TA) *entered upon the time called* العَصْر: (Ḳ, TA:) and also *he entered upon the evening, or last part of the day;* like اقصر. (TA.) —— And اعصرت, (Ṣ, Mṣb, Ḳ,) and ↓ عَصَّرَتْ, (Ḳ,) so in all the copies of the Ḳ, but in a copy of the Tahdheeb of IḲṭṭ ↓ عَصَرَتْ, without teshdeed, (TA,) ‡ *She* (a girl, Ṣ, Mṣb, or woman, Ḳ) *attained the* عَصْر *of her youth,* (TA,) or [simply] *attained the period of her youth,* (Ḳ,) *and arrived at the age of puberty:* (Ḳ, TA:) or *entered upon the time of puberty, and began to have the menstrual discharge;* (Ṣ, O;) because of her womb's being pressed; (O;) or as though she entered upon the عَصْر of her youth: (Ṣ, O, TA:) or *she attained the age of puberty:* (Ṣ, IḲṭṭ:) or *she had the menstrual discharge:* (Mṣb:) or *she entered upon the time of that discharge:* (Ḳ:) or *she approached that time;* for, said of a girl, it is like رَاهَقَ said of a boy; accord. to Abu-l-Ghowth el-Aạrábee: (Ṣ:) or *she approached the age of twenty:* (Ḳ:) or *she became confined in the house,* (Ḳ,) *and had a retreat* (عَصَرٌ) *appointed for her,* (TA,) *at the time of her having the menstrual discharge:* (Ḳ:) or *she brought forth;* (Ḳ;) in which sense it is of the dial. of Asd. (TA.) The woman, or girl, is termed ↓ مُعْصِرٌ (Ṣ, O, Mṣb, Ḳ) and ↓ مُعْصِرَةٌ, with ة: (IDrd, O, TA:) pl. مَعَاصِرُ (Ṣ, Ḳ) and مَعَاصِيرُ. (Ḳ.) —— أَعْصَرَتِ السَّحَائِبُ † *The clouds were at the point of having rain pressed forth from them by the winds.* (O, and Bḍ in lxxviii. 14. [But see مُعْصِرٌ.]) —— أُعْصِرُوا: see 1. —— اعصرت الرِّيحُ, (O, TA,) and ↓ عَصَّرَتْ, (TA,) *The wind brought what is termed* إِعْصَار [q. v. infrà]. (O, TA.) And you say also, عَصَّرَتِ الرِّيحُ بِالتُّرَابِ فِى الهَوَآءِ [*The wind raised the dust into the air in the form of a pillar*]. (TA.)

5. تعصّر: see 7: —— and 8, latter half. —— *I. q.* تَعَسَّرَ [*it was, or became, difficult, strait,* or *intricate*]. (TA.) —— ‡ *He wept.* (A.)

7. انعصر quasi-pass. of 1 in the first of the senses expl. above; [*It became pressed,* or *squeezed, so that its juice, sirup, honey, oil, water,* or *moisture, was forced out; its juice,* or *the like, became extracted,* or *fetched out by labour or art,* i. e. *by pressure* or *wringing;*] (Ṣ, O, Mṣb, Ḳ;) as also ↓ تعصّر. (Ṣ, O, Ḳ.) —— You say also, انعصر الخِنَاقُ فِى حَلْقِهِ [*The strangling-rope,* or *the like, became compressed upon his throat*]. (TA in art. خنق.)

8. اعتصرهُ: see عَصَرَهُ, in three places. —— [Hence, app.,] اعتصر ‡ *He voided his ordure.* (O, Ḳ,* TA.) [See the act. part. n., below.] —— And اعتصر بالمَآءِ † *He swallowed the water by little and little in order that some food by which he was choked might be made to descend easily in his throat.* (Ṣ, O, Ḳ.) —— And اعتصر مَالَهُ ‡ *He extracted,* or *extorted, his property from his hand,* or *possession:* (Ṣ, Mṣb, TA:) from the same verb as syn. with عَصَرَ with expl. in the beginning of this art.: (Mṣb:) *he took forth his property for a debt or for some other reason:* (Ḳ,* TA:) and اعتصر, † *he took;* (Ḳ;) as also ↓ عَصَرَ, aor. ـِ: (TA:) † *he took* of, or from, a thing: (TA:) † *he got, and took,* of, or from, a thing: (Ṣ, as implied in an explanation of the act. part. n.:) † *he got* a thing from a person: (L:) or, accord. to El-'Itreefee, † *he took* the property of his son *for himself;* or *he suffered* the property of his son *to remain in his* (the latter's) *possession:* you do not say اعتصر فُلَانٌ مَالَ فُلَانٍ [*such a one took for himself the property of such a one*] unless he be a relation to him: [you say so of a father:] and of a boy you say, اعتصر مَالَ أَبِيهِ, meaning, † *he*

took the property of his father. (TA.) [See اعتسر.] And اعتصر العَصَّارُ ▼ بِالمَالِ [or المَالَ?] i. e. ‡ *The extorter*, or *exacter, extorted*, or, *exacted the property*]. (A, TA.) — Also اعتصر, ‡ *He took back* a gift: (A, Mgh, L, TA:) in the Ḳ, the inf. n. is expl. by إِنْتِجَاعُ العَطِيَّةِ; but in the L, the verb is expl. by إِرْتَجَعَ العَطِيَّةَ, [and in like manner in the A and Mgh,] and رَجَعَ فِيهَا: (TA:) † *he revoked, recalled*, or *retracted*, the gift; syn. إِرْتَجَعَ, (Mgh, O,) and اِسْتَرَدَّ. (Mgh.) Hence the trad. of 'Omar, الوَالِدُ يَعْتَصِرُ وَلَدَهُ فِيمَا أَعْطَاهُ وَلَيْسَ لِلْوَلَدِ أَنْ يَعْتَصِرَ مِنْ وَالِدِهِ, i. e., ‡ *The father may take from his child what he has given him; [but it is not for the child to take from his father what he has given him.]* (Mgh, O.) But as to the trad. of Esh-Shaabee, يَعْتَصِرُ الوَالِدُ عَلَى وَلَدِهِ فِى مَالِهِ [‡ *The father may take back what he has given to his child*], the verb is made trans. by means of على because it implies the meaning of يَعُودُ عَلَيْهِ and يَرْجِعُ عَلَيْهِ: (IAth, Mgh, O:*) or this latter trad. means, *the father may forbid his child his property, and withhold it from him*: (Ṣ:) and [in like manner] the former trad., *the father may withhold his child from giving his property, and forbid it to him*: (TA:) for اعتصر also signifies *he prevented, hindered, withheld*, or *refused*; syn. مَنَعَ. (Ḳ, TA.) Hence, اِعْتِصَارُ الصَّدَقَةِ [*The withholding*, or *refusing, the poor-rate*]. (TA.) [See also 1.] — اعتصر also signifies † *He was niggardly*, or *avaricious*, (Ḳ, TA,) عَلَيْهِ *towards him.* (TA.) ═ اعتصر بِهِ; (Ṣ, A, Ḳ;) and ▼ تعصّر بِهِ, (Ṣ, Ḳ,) or إِلَيْهِ; (O;) and ▼ عَصَرَ بِهِ, inf. n. عَصْرٌ; (TA;) and ▼ عاصرهُ; (A;) ‡ *He had recourse to him for refuge, protection*, or *preservation*; (Ṣ, A, Ḳ;) *and sought, desired*, or *asked, aid*, or *succour, of him.* (A.) In the Ḳur [xii. 49], ▼ وَفِيهِ تُعْصَرُونَ [sic], which is one reading, is expl. by Lth as signifying *And in it ye shall have recourse for refuge*, or *protection*; but Az disapproves of this: (TA:) [the common reading] وفيه يَعْصِرُونَ, accord. to AO, (so in one copy of the Ṣ,) or A'Obeyd, (as in another copy of the Ṣ,) signifies *and in it they shall be safe*; from عُصْرَةٌ signifying "a cause, or means, of safety:" (Ṣ:) or *they shall be safe from trial*, or *affliction, and shall preserve themselves by plenty*, or *fruitfulness.* (TA.)

عَصْرٌ [which is the most common form] and ▼ عُصُرٌ (Ṣ, A, O, Mṣb, Ḳ) and ▼ عُصْرٌ (Ṣ, A, O, Ḳ) and ▼ عَصُرٌ (A, O, Ḳ) *i. q.* دَهْرٌ [as meaning *Time*; or *a time*; or *a space* or *period of time*]; (Ṣ, A, O, Mṣb, Ḳ;) or *any unlimited extent of time, during which peoples pass away and become extinct*; (Esh-Shihâb, in the "Sharḥ esh-Shifà;") [*a succession of ages*:] such is said by Fr to be its meaning in the Ḳur ciii. 1: (TA:) pl. (of pauc., O) أَعْصُرٌ (O, Ḳ) and أَعْصَارٌ; (Ḳ;) and [of mult.] عُصُورٌ (Ṣ, O, Ḳ) and عُصُرٌ. (Ḳ.) You say, مَا فَعَلْتُهُ عَصْرًا, and بِعَصْرٍ, *I did it not in its time.* (A.) And جَآءَ لٰكِنْ لَمْ يَجِئْ ▼ لِعُصْرٍ *He came, but he came not at the* [*proper*] *time of coming.* (AZ, O, Ḳ: but AZ relates it without لكن. TA.) And ▼ نَامَ وَمَا نَامَ لِعُصْرٍ, (Ḳ,) or, accord. to AZ and Ṣgh and the author of the L and others, ما نام ▼ عُصْرًا, (TA,) *He slept, but hardly*, or *scarcely, slept.* (AZ, Ḳ, &c.) And نَامَ فُلَانٌ وَلَمْ يَنَمْ عَصْرًا, and بِعَصْرٍ, *Such a one slept, but slept not during a* [*considerable period of*] *time*, or *day*; (A;) agreeably with other significations, here following. (TA.) — عَصْرٌ also signifies *An hour*, or *a time*, (سَاعَةٌ,) *of the day.* (Ḳatádeh, O.) — *A day*: (Ḳ:) [or *day, as opposed to night*:] and *a night*: (Ḳ:) [or *night, as opposed to day*:] also the *morning, before*, or *after, sunrise*; syn. غَدَاةٌ: and the *afternoon*; or *evening*; or *last part of the day; until the sun becomes red*; as also ▼ عَصَرٌ, (IDrd, Ḳ.) Hence, العَصْرَانِ *The night and the day*: (O, TA:) or *night and day*: (Mṣb:) and *the morning, before*, or *after, sunrise, and the afternoon* or *evening*; or *the first part of the day and the last part thereof*; الغَدَاةُ وَالعَشِىُّ. (ISk, Ṣ, O, Mṣb.) [See also الأَبْرَدَانِ.] A poet says,

وَأَمْطُلُهُ العَصْرَيْنِ حَتَّى يَمَلَّنِى • • وَيَرْضَى بِنِصْفِ الدَّيْنِ وَالأَنْفُ رَاغِمُ

[*And I put him off, delaying the payment of his debt, morning and evening*, or *from morning to evening, so that he loathes me, and is content with half of the debt, though unwilling*]: meaning, when he comes to me in the first part of the day, I promise to pay him in the last part of it: (ISk, Ṣ:) or, accord. to Ṣgh, the right reading (instead of والانف راغم) is فِى غَيْرِ نَائِلٍ [*without liberality*]: and the verse is by 'Abd-Allah Ibn-Ez-Zubeyr El-Asadee. (TA.) — Hence also (Ṣ, O) صَلَاةُ العَصْرِ, (Ṣ, O, Mṣb,) and ▼ صلاة العَصَرِ, (O, TA,) fem. only, and simply العَصْرُ, [and ▼ العَصَرُ,] masc. and fem., (Mṣb,) [*The prayer of afternoon*; the time of which commences about mid-time between noon and nightfall; or accord. to the Sháfi'ees, Málikees, and Ḥambelees, when the shade of an object, cast by the sun, is equal to the length of that object, added to the length of the shade which the same object casts at noon; and accord. to the Ḥanafees, when the shadow is equal to twice the length of the object added to the length of its mid-day shadow: its end being sunset, or the time when the sun becomes red:] so called because performed in one of the عَصْرَانِ, i. e., in the last portion of the day: (O:) also called الصَّلَاةُ الوُسْطَى [accord. to some], because it is between the two prayers of the day [that of day-break and that of noon] and the two prayers of the night [that of sunset and that of nightfall]: (Abu-l-'Abbás:) pl. [of pauc.] أَعْصُرٌ; and [of mult.] عُصُورٌ. (Mṣb.) [And hence likewise,] العَصْرَانِ is applied in a trad. to *The prayer of day-break and that of the* عَصْر; one being made predominant over the other; (Mṣb, TA;) as is the case in القَمَرَانِ applied to the sun and the moon; (TA;) or they are so called because they are performed at the two extremities of the عَصْرَانِ, meaning the night and the day; (Mṣb, TA;) but the former is the more likely. (TA.) [See an ex. of the dim., العُصَيْرُ, voce مُرْهَقَةٌ, in art. رهق.] — You say also, جَآءَ فُلَانٌ عَصْرًا, meaning *Such a one came late.* (Ks, Ṣ, O.) ═ See also عَصِيرٌ. — عَصْرٌ also signifies † *Rain from the* [*clouds called*] مُعْصِرَات. (Ḳ.) ═ Also A man's [*near kinsfolk such as are termed his*] رَهْط and عَشِيرَة: (O, Ḳ,* TA:) or his عَصَبَة [q. v.]. (TA.)

عُصُرٌ: see عَصْرٌ, in four places. ═ And see also عُصْرٌ.

عَصَرٌ: see عَصْرٌ.

عُصْرٌ: see عَصْرٌ, in three places. ═ Also *A place to which one has recourse for refuge, protection, preservation, concealment, covert*, or *lodging; a place of refuge; an asylum; a refuge*: (Ṣ, O, Ḳ:) and *a cause*, or *means, of safety*; syn. مَنْجَاةٌ: (Ṣ, Ḳ:) as also ▼ عُصُرٌ (Ḳ) and ▼ عُصْرَةٌ (Ṣ, O, TA) and ▼ مُعْتَصَرٌ (O, Ḳ) and ▼ مُعْتَصَرٌ (TA) and ▼ عَصَرٌ, from which عُصْرٌ is said to be contracted, (TA,) [and ▼ عُصَيْرَةٌ.] You say, ▼ زَيْدٌ عُصْرَتِى and ▼ عُصَيْرَتِى and ▼ مُعْتَصَرِى ‡ [*Zeyd is my refuge*]. (A.) ═ Also *Dust*; or *dust raised and spreading*; syn. غُبَار: (Ṣ, O, Ḳ:) or *vehement dust*; (TA;) which latter is also the signification of ▼ عِصَار and ▼ عَصَرَةٌ: (O, Ḳ, TA:) or this last, or, accord. to some, ▼ عُصْرَةٌ, has the former signification. (L.) It is said in a trad., مَرَّتْ اِمْرَأَةٌ مُتَطَيِّبَةٌ لِذَيْلِهَا عَصَرٌ, (Ṣ, O,) or ▼ عُصْرَةٌ, or, as some relate it, ▼ عَصَرَةٌ, (L,) *A perfumed woman passed by, her skirt having a dust proceeding from it*, (Ṣ, A, L,) occasioned by her dragging it along [upon the ground], (L,) or occasioned by the abundance of the perfume: (A:) or ▼ عَصَرَةٌ may mean ‡ *an exhalation of perfume*: (L, TA:*) [for] it has this meaning also: (IDrd, O:) but accord. to one relation, it is إِعْصَارٌ, (L,) which also signifies *dust raised by wind.* (TA.)

عُصْرٌ: see عَصْرٌ: ═ and see عَصَرٌ.

عُصْرَةٌ [app., *A thing from which water* or *the like may*, or *may almost, be expressed*, or *wrung out*]. You say, بَلَّ المَطَرُ ثِيَابَهُ حَتَّى صَارَتْ عُصْرَةً *The rain wetted his clothes so that their water was almost wrung out.* (TA.) ═ See also عُصْرٌ, in four places. ═ Also *i. q.* دِنْيَةٌ: one says, هٰؤُلَآءِ مَوَالِينَا عُصْرَةً i. e. دِنْيَةً [*These are sons of our paternal uncle*, or *the like, closely related*], *exclusively of others*: (Ṣ, O:) and so قُصْرَةً. (TA.)

عَصَرَةٌ: see عُصْرٌ, in three places.

عُصَارٌ: see عُصَارَةٌ.

إِعْصَارٌ: see عُصْرٌ, and إِعْصَار.

عُصُورٌ: see عَاصِرٌ.

عَصِيرٌ *i. q.* ▼ مَعْصُورٌ [*Pressed*, or *squeezed*, or *wrung, so that its juice, sirup, honey, oil, water*, or *moisture, is forced out*]; (Ḳ;) as also ▼ عَصْرٌ. (TA.) See also عُصَارَةٌ, in two places.

عُصَارَةٌ *Expressed juice* or *the like; what flows*

(Ṣ, O, Mṣb, Ḳ) from grapes and the like, (Mṣb, Ḳ,) of things having oil or sirup or honey, (TA,) *on pressure* or *squeezing* or *wringing*; (IDrd, Ṣ, O, Mṣb, TA;) [*an extract*; but properly, *such as is expressed*;] as also ▼عَصِيرٌ (Mgh, Mṣb, Ḳ) and ▼عُصَارٌ; (Ḳ;) or, as some say, عُصَارٌ is a pl. of [or rather a coll. gen. n. of which the n. un. is] عُصَارَةٌ. (TA.) — Also *What remains of dregs, after pressing to force out the juice* or *the like*. (Ṣ, O, TA.) — Also The *choice part*, or the *refuse*, (نُقَايَةٌ [which has these two contr. significations]) of a thing. (TA.) — Also ‡ The *produce* (IF, A, O) of a land. (A.) — وَلَدُ فُلَانٍ عُصَارَةُ كَرَمٍ and مِنْ عُصَارَاتِ الكَرَمِ [means ‡ *The children of such a one are of generous race*, or *of generous disposition*]. (A.) — رَجُلٌ كَرِيمُ العُصَارَةِ, (Ḳ,) and ▼المَعْصَرِ, (Ṣ, O, Ḳ,) and ▼المُعْتَصَرِ, (Ḳ,) ‡ *A man generous*, or *liberal, when asked*. (Ṣ, O, Ḳ.) And ▼مَنِيعُ المُعْتَصَرِ ‡ One *with whom one cannot take refuge*, or *whose protection is unobtainable*. (TA.) And ▼كَرِيمُ العَصِيرِ, (O, L,) or كَثِيرُ العَصِيرِ, not كَرِيمُ العَصْرِ as in the [O and] Ḳ, (TA,) ‡ *Of generous race*. (O, L, Ḳ.) [See also عُنْصُرٌ.]

عَصِيرَةٌ: see عَصْرٌ, in two places.

عَصَّارٌ *A presser* of [grapes or] oil [and the like]. (MA, KL.) — [And hence, ‡ *An extorter*, or *exacter*.] See 8, former half.

عَاصِرٌ act. part. n. of 1. — لَا أَفْعَلُهُ مَا دَامَ لِلزَّيْتِ عَاصِرٌ [*I will not do it as long as there is an expresser of the oil of the olive*]; i. e., *ever*. (Ṣ, O.) — ▼عَوَاصِرُ [as though pl. of عَاصِرٌ or of عَاصِرَةٌ] *Three stones with which grapes are pressed so as to force out the juice*, (Ḳ,) *being placed one upon another*. (TA.) — عَاصِرٌ and ▼عَصُورٌ ‡ One *who takes of the property of his child without the latter's permission*. (TA.) — فُلَانٌ عَاصِرٌ ‡ *Such a one is tenacious*, or *avaricious*. (TA.)

عُنْصُرٌ (Ṣ, O, Mṣb, Ḳ) and عُنْصَرٌ, (Ṣ, O, Ḳ,) the former of which is the more commonly known, but the latter [accord. to my copy of the Mṣb عَنْصَرٌ, but this I regard as a mistake of the copyist,] is the more chaste, (TA,) *Origin*; syn. أَصْلٌ: (Ṣ, O, Mṣb, Ḳ:) *race, lineage*, or *family*: (Mṣb:) *rank* or *quality, nobility* or *eminence, reputation* or *note* or *consideration, derived from ancestors*, or *from one's own deeds* or *qualities*; syn. حَسَبٌ: (Ṣ, O, Ḳ:) pl. عَنَاصِرُ. (Mṣb.) You say فُلَانٌ كَرِيمُ العُنْصُرِ [*Such a one is of generous origin*, or *race*, &c.,] like as you say كَرِيمُ العَصِيرِ. (L.) — *An element* (أَصْلٌ) [*of those*] *whereof are composed the material substances of different natures*; [*an element considered as that from which composition commences*:] *it is of four kinds*; namely, *fire, air, earth*, and *water*. (KT.) [But this application belongs to the conventional language of philosophy. See also مَادَّةٌ, and جِسْمٌ.]

عَاصِرٌ: see عَوَاصِرُ.

إِعْصَارٌ *A whirlwind of dust* [or *sand*], *resembling a pillar*; *a wind that raises dust* [or *sand*] *between the sky and the earth, and revolves, resembling a pillar*; *called also by the Arabs a* زَوْبَعَةٌ; of the masc. gender; (Mṣb;) *a wind that raises the dust* [or *sand*], *and rises towards the sky, as though it were a pillar*; (Ṣ, O;) *a wind that blows from the ground*, (Ḳ, TA,) *and raises the dust* [or *sand*], *and rises* (TA) *like a pillar towards the sky*; (Ḳ, TA;) *called by the people a* زَوْبَعَةٌ: (TA:) unless it blow in this manner, with vehemence, it is not thus called: (Zj, TA:) [see عَمُودٌ:] *a wind that rises into the sky*: (AZ:) or *a wind that raises the clouds*, (Ṣ, O, Ḳ,) *with thunder and lightning*: (Ṣ, O:) or *in which is fire*: (Ḳ:) mentioned in the Ḳur ii. 268: (Ṣ, O:) or *in which is* ▼عِصَارٌ, which signifies *vehement dust*, (Ḳ,) or this latter word signifies *dust raised into the air, by the wind, in the form of a pillar* (مَا عَصَرَتْ بِهِ الرِّيحُ مِنَ التُّرَابِ فِى الهَوَآءِ): (TA:) [see also عَصْرٌ:] pl. أَعَاصِيرُ, (Mṣb, TA,) and أَعَاصِرُ [occurring in poetry]. (Ḥam p. 678.) — إِنْ كُنْتَ رِيحًا فَقَدْ لَاقَيْتَ إِعْصَارًا [*If thou be a wind, thou hast met with a whirlwind of dust like a pillar*] is a prov. of the Arabs, (O, TA,) relating to a man in whom is somewhat of power and who meets with one superior to him, (O,) or to a man who meets his adversary with courage. (TA.) — And one says, وَعْدُهُ إِعْصَارٌ [*His promising is unprofitable like a whirlwind of dust*]. (A, TA.)

عُصَارَةٌ: see كَرِيمُ المَعْصَرِ.

مَعْصَرٌ and مَعْصَرَةٌ: see 4, near the end. — مُعْصِرَاتٌ signifies † *Clouds*; (Az, Ḳ;) so called because they press forth water: (Aboo-Is-ḥáḳ, TA:) this explanation is most agreeable with what is said in the Ḳur lxxviii. 14, because the winds called أَعَاصِيرُ [pl. of إِعْصَارٌ] are not of the winds of rain: (Az, TA:) or *clouds at the point of having rain pressed forth from them by the winds*: (Bḍ in lxxviii. 14; and TA:*) or *clouds ready to pour forth rain*: (TA:) or *clouds pressing forth rain*: (Ṣ, O:) or *clouds that flow with* [or *ooze forth*] *rain but have not yet collected together*; like as مُعْصِرٌ is applied to a girl who has almost had the menstrual discharge but has not yet had it: (Fr, TA:) or *winds ready to press forth the rain from the clouds*: (Bḍ, ubi suprà:) or *winds having* أَعَاصِير; (Bḍ, ubi suprà; and TA;) i. e., *dust*. (TA.)

مَعْصَرٌ (Ḳ, TA) and مَعْصَرَةٌ (Ṣ, O, TA) The *thing in which grapes* (Ṣ, O, Ḳ) *and olives* (Ṣ) *are pressed, to force out their juice* (Ṣ, O, Ḳ) *and oil*. (Ṣ.) [See also مِعْصَارٌ.]

مَعْصَرَةٌ *A place in which grapes and the like are pressed, to force out their juice* or *the like*. (Ḳ,* TA.)

مُعْصَرٌ: see عَصْرٌ.

مِعْصَارٌ *That in which a thing is put and pressed, in order that its water, or the like, may flow* [or *ooze*] *out*. (Ḳ,* TA.) [See also مَعْصَرٌ.]

مَعْصُورٌ: see عَصِيرٌ. — Also ‡ A tongue *dry* (O, TA) *by reason of thirst*. (TA.)

مُعْتَصَرٌ: see عَصْرٌ, in two places: — and see عُصَارَةٌ, in two places.

مُعْتَصِرٌ: One *who expresses* the juice of grapes, to make wine, *for another* or *others*. (Mgh.) [But see 1.] — ‡ *Voiding ordure*: (Mgh, Ḳ,* TA:) from عَصْرٌ, or from عَصَرٌ signifying "a place of refuge or concealment." (TA.) — And ‡ One *who gets*, and *takes*, of, or from, a thing. (Ṣ, O.)

عصف

1. عَصَفَتِ الرِّيحُ, aor. ـِ, (Ṣ, O, Mṣb, Ḳ,) inf. n. عَصْفٌ and عُصُوفٌ, (O, Mṣb, Ḳ,) *The wind blew violently*, or *vehemently*; as also ▼أَعْصَفَت; (Ṣ, O, Mṣb, Ḳ;) the latter of the dial. of Benoo-Asad. (Ṣ, O.) — Hence, (TA,) عَصْفٌ signifies also ‡ The *being quick*, or *swift*; (Lth, O, TA;) and so [▼إِعْصَافٌ and] ▼تَعَصُّفٌ: (TA:) and is used in relation to anything: (Lth, O:) عَصَفَ signifying † *He*, or *it, was quick*, or *swift*. (Ḳ.) One says, of a she-camel, تَعْصِفُ بِرَاكِبِهَا ‡ *She goes quickly*, or *swiftly, with her rider*; (Sh, Ṣ, Z, O, TA;) likening her to the wind in the swiftness of her course. (Z, TA.) And ▼أَعْصَفَت فِى السَّيْرِ † *She* (a camel) *was*, or *became, quick*, or *swift, in going along*: (TA:) and ▼أَعْصَفَ said of a horse, *he went*, or *passed, along quickly*, or *swiftly*; (Ṣ, O, Ḳ;) like أَحْصَفَ, (O,) of which it is [said to be] a dial. var. (Ṣ.) — [Hence, also,] عَصَفَتِ الحَرْبُ بِالقَوْمِ, (O, Ḳ,* TA,) aor. تَعْصِفُ بِهِمْ, (Ṣ, O, TA,) ‡ *War*, or *the war, carried off*, and *destroyed, the people*, or *party*; (Ṣ, O, Ḳ, TA;) as also ▼أَعْصَفَت بِهِمْ, (O, Ḳ,) which is [said to be] the more correct. (O, TA.) — And عَصَفَ signifies † *It* (a thing) *inclined*, or *declined*. (Ḳ.) [See عَاصِفٌ, last sentence.] — عَصَفَ عِيَالَهُ, (Ibn-'Abbád, O, Ḳ, TA,) and لِعِيَالِهِ, (Ibn-'Abbád, O,) aor. ـِ, (Ḳ,) inf. n. عَصْفٌ, (Ṣ, O,) *He gained*, or *earned*, or *he sought sustenance*, (Ibn-Abbád, Ṣ, O, Ḳ, TA,) *for his household*, or *family*; (Ibn-'Abbád, O, Ḳ, TA;) and so ▼اِعْتَصَفَ لِعِيَالِهِ; (Lḥ, Ṣ,* O,* TA;) like as one says صَرَفَ and اِصْطَرَفَ: and some add, in explaining عَصَفَ عِيَالَهُ, *and he sought for his household*, or *family*; and *exercised for them art*, or *skill, in the management of affairs*. (TA.) — عَصَفَ الزَّرْعَ, (Ṣ, O, Ḳ, TA,) aor. ـِ, inf. n. عَصْفٌ, (TA,) *He cut*, or *clipped, the corn before its attaining to maturity*; (Ṣ, O, Ḳ, TA;) i. e. *he cut off its leaves that were inclining in its lower part, in order to lighten it*; for if he did not thus, it would lean: or *he cut it from its stalks*. (TA.)

4: see 1, in five places. — أَعْصَفَ (said of a man, Ṣ, O) *He died*, or *perished*. (Ṣ, O, Ḳ.) — And *He* (a man) *deviated, declined*, or *wandered, from the road*, or *way*. (TA.) — أَعْصَفَتِ الإِبِلُ *The camels went round about the well, eager for the water, raising the the dust*, (En-Naḍr, O, Ḳ,) and spreading it, around. (En-Naḍr, O.) ═══ اعصف الزَّرْعُ *The corn, or seed-produce, put forth* its عَصْف [q. v.]: (Ṣ,* O, Ḳ:) or *its* عَصْف *became long:* or *it attained to the time for its being cut,* or *clipped.* (TA. [See 1, last sentence.])

5: see 1, second sentence.

8: see 1, last sentence but one.

10. استعصف الزَّرْعُ *The corn, or seed-produce: produced its culm,* or *jointed stalk.* (TA.)

عَصْفٌ The *herb* (بَقْل) *of corn,* or *seed-produce:* (Fr, Ṣ, O, Ḳ:) and (TA) the *leaves,* or *blades, of corn,* or *seed-produce;* (MA,* Mgh, TA;) as also عُصُوفٌ; each a pl. of ▾ عَصْفَةٌ: (MA: [or rather عَصْف is a coll. gen. n. of which عُصُوف is the pl. and ▾ عَصْفَةٌ is the n. un.:]) or *the leaves,* or *blades, that are upon the stalk of corn,* or *seed-produce, and that dry up and crumble;* as also ▾ عَصْفَةٌ and ▾ عَصِيفَةٌ and ▾ عُصَافَةٌ: or the *leaves, and what is not eaten, thereof:* in these three different senses it is expl. as used in the Ḳur lv. 11: (TA:) or it there means the *stalk,* or *stem,* of corn: (Fr, Ṣ voce رَيْحَانٌ:) or *straw;* (Jel, TA;) and so ▾ عَصِيفُ الزَّرْعِ; (M voce تِبْنٌ;) or ▾ عَصِيفَةُ الزَّرْعِ: (so in copies of the Ḳ voce تِبْنٌ:) and عُصُوفٌ signifies *straws:* (IAạr, TA:) or عَصْفٌ signifies *dry leaves, like straw:* (Bḍ in lv. 11:) or *corn,* or *seed-produce,* or *barley, cut while green, for fodder;* syn. قَصِيلٌ: (En-Naḍr, TA:) or *leaves of corn,* or *seed-produce, that are cut, and eaten while fresh:* or the *leaves of the ears of corn;* as also ▾ عَصِيفَةٌ: or *what are cut thereof;* as also ▾ عَصِيفٌ: or both signify the *leaves, of corn, that incline in its lower part, and which one cuts off, in order that it may become lightened:* or the former signifies the *ears,* themselves, *of corn:* and the pl. is عُصُوفٌ. (TA.) كَعَصْفٍ مَأْكُولٍ, in the Ḳur [cv. last verse], means *Like corn of which the grain has been eaten and the straw thereof remains:* (El-Ḥasan El-Baṣree, Ṣ, O, Ḳ:) or *like leaves of which the contents have been taken and which remain without any grain therein:* (O, Ḳ:) or *like* عَصْف, (O,) or *leaves,* (Ḳ,) *which the beasts have eaten:* (O, Ḳ:) or, as Sa'eed Ibn-Jubeyr is related to have said, *like barley growing* or *growing forth* [*that has been eaten*]. (TA.) —— And IAạr says, (O, TA,) [the pl.] عُصُوفٌ, (O, Ḳ, TA,) with ḍamm to the ع, (TA,) [in the CḲ, erroneously, عَصُوف,] signifies *Handfuls of reaped corn;* syn. كَدَرٌ [a coll. gen. n. of which the n. un. is كَدَرَةٌ]: (O, TA:) in the copies of the Ḳ, كُدْرَةٌ; and in the L, كدر. (TA.) ═══ And accord. to IAạr, (O,) عُصُوفٌ signifies also *Wines;* syn. خُمُورٌ. (O, L, Ḳ. [In the CḲ خَمْرَةٌ; and in the TA, as from the Ḳ, خمر.])

عَصْفَةٌ [as an inf. n. un. of 1 signifies *A gust,* or *strong puff,* of wind. —— And hence,] † The *odour,* (Ḳ,) or *fragrance* (نَفْحَة) *of odour,* (Z, TA,) or *exhaled odour,* (IF, O,) of wine: (IF, Z, O, Ḳ, TA:) likened to the عَصْفَة of wind. (Z, TA.) ═══ See also عَصْفٌ, in three places.

عَصَّافٌ *A seller of* تِبْن [i. e. *straw,* or *straw that has been trodden,* or *thrashed, and cut*]. (IAạr, O, TA.)

عَصُوفٌ: see عَاصِفٌ. —— Hence, (Z, TA,) ‡ *Swift;* applied to a she-ostrich, and to a she-camel (Ṣ, O, Ḳ, TA) *that goes swiftly with her rider;* (Ṣ, O, TA;) likened to the wind in the swiftness of her course: (Z, TA:) pl. عُصُفٌ: (TA:) and ▾ عَاصِفٌ is applied in like manner to a she-camel as meaning *swift;* (Sh, TA;) and so too is ▾ مُعْصِفَةٌ. (TA.)

عَصِيفٌ: see عَاصِفٌ: ═══ and see also عَصْفٌ, in two places.

عُصَافَةٌ *What has fallen from the ears of corn,* [app. *when they are trodden,* or *thrashed, consisting*] *of the straw,* (Ṣ, O, Ḳ, [but in the CḲ, التِّبْن is put in the place of التَّبْن,]) *and the like.* (Ṣ.) See also عَصْفٌ. Also *What the wind has carried away.* (TA.)

عَصِيفَةٌ The *combined leaves in which are the ears of corn:* (Ṣ, O, Ḳ, TA:) or the *leaves that open from around the fruit:* or the *heads of the ears of wheat.* (TA.) See also عَصْفٌ, in three places.

رِيحٌ عَاصِفٌ (Ṣ, O, Mṣb, Ḳ) and عَاصِفَةٌ (O, Mṣb, Ḳ) and ▾ عَصُوفٌ [but this app. has a more intensive meaning] (Ṣ, O, Ḳ) [and ▾ عَصِيفٌ as used in "Fákihet el-Khulafà" p. 196 line 18 but not found by me in this sense in any lexicon] and ▾ مُعْصِفٌ (Ṣ, O, Ḳ) and ▾ مُعْصِفَةٌ (Ṣ, O, Mṣb, Ḳ) *Wind blowing violently,* or *vehemently:* (Ṣ, O, Mṣb, Ḳ:) pl. of the first عَوَاصِفُ, and of the second عَاصِفَاتٌ; (Mṣb;) and of the last two ▾ مَعَاصِفُ and ▾ مَعَاصِيفُ; and ▾ مُعْصِفَاتٌ [pl. of مُعْصِفَةٌ] which signifies winds *that raise the clouds and the winds.* (TA.) —— One says also يَوْمٌ عَاصِفٌ, (Fr, Ṣ, O, Mṣb,) because of the violent blowing of the wind therein, (Fr, O, Mṣb,) عَاصِف in this case being an instance of فَاعِل in the sense of مَفْعُولٌ فِيهِ, (Ṣ, O,) like as one says يَوْمٌ بَارِدٌ, (Fr, O,) or like لَيْلٌ نَائِمٌ; the meaning being, *A day in which the wind blows violently,* or *vehemently:* (Ṣ, O:) this is the meaning in the phrase فِى يَوْمٍ عَاصِفٍ (Fr, O, Ḳ) in the Ḳur [xiv. 21]: or this phrase may mean فِى يَوْمٍ عَاصِفِ الرِّيحِ [*in a day violent,* or *vehement, in respect of the wind*], because the wind is mentioned in the former part of the sentence. (Fr, O.) —— See also عَصُوفٌ. —— عَاصِفٌ also signifies ‡ An arrow *turning aside,* or *declining, from the butt;* (El-Mufaḍḍal, O, Ḳ, TA;) pl. عُصُفٌ; a tropical meaning: (TA:) and anything *inclining,* or *declining.* (El-Mufaḍḍal, O, Ḳ.)

مُعْصِفٌ, and the fem., and pls.: see عَاصِفٌ, in five places: —— and for the fem., see also عَصُوفٌ. ═══ مَكَانٌ مُعْصِفٌ *A place abounding with corn,* or *seed-produce:* (Lḥ, Ṣ, L:) or *with straw.* (Lḥ, L.)

عصفر

Q. 1. عَصْفَرَ *He dyed* a garment, or piece of cloth, *with* عُصْفُر. (Ṣ, O, Mṣb, Ḳ.)

Q. 2. تَعَصْفَرَ *It* (a garment, or piece of cloth,) *became dyed with* عُصْفُر. (Ṣ, O, Ḳ.)

عُصْفُرٌ [*Safflower,* or *bastard saffron;* i. e., *cnicus,* or *carthamus tinctorius;*] *a certain dye,* (Ṣ, O,) or *plant,* (Mṣb, Ḳ,) *well known,* (O, Mṣb,) *with which one dyes,* (M,) *the first juice* (سُلَافَة) *of which is called* جِرْيَال, (TA,) *and one of the properties of which is that it causes tough meat to become thoroughly cooked, so as to fall off from the bone,* (Ḳ,* TA,) *when somewhat thereof is thrown into it:* (TA:) *its seed is called* قُرْطُم: (Ḳ:) *there are two kinds of it; one of the cultivated land, and one of the desert; and both grow in the country of the Arabs:* (M, TA:) it is an Arabicized word. (Az, TA.)

عُصْفُورٌ (Ṣ, O, Mṣb, Ḳ, &c.) and عَصْفُورٌ, (Ibn-Rasheeḳ, MF,) but the latter is not an approved form, because there is no chaste word of the measure فَعْلُول, (MF, TA,) [The *sparrow;*] *a certain bird,* (Ṣ, O, Ḳ,) *well known;* (Mṣb:) accord. to AḤát, the *same that is called the* نُغَّار; *the male black in the head and neck, the rest of it inclining to ash-colour, with a redness in the wings; the female inclining to yellowness and whiteness:* (O:) the word is masc.: (TA:) fem. with ة: (Ṣ, O, Ḳ:) pl. عَصَافِيرُ. (Mṣb.) Accord. to Ḥamzeh, it is so called because it was disobedient, and fled, عَصَى وَفَرَّ. (MF, TA.) [This, I believe, is said to have been the case when the beasts and birds &c. were summoned before Adam, to be named by him. See the Ḳur ii. 29—31.] —— [It is also applied to *Any passerine bird.* And hence,] عُصْفُورُ الجَنَّةِ [*The passerine bird of Paradise;* meaning] *the swallow;* syn. الخُطَّافُ. (ISd in TA art. خطف, and IB in TA art. وط.) —— [Also, sometimes, *Any small bird.*] —— طَارَتْ عَصَافِيرُ رَأْسِهِ [lit., *The sparrows of his head flew;*] is a prov., meaning ‡ *he became frightened;* as though there were sparrows upon his head when he was still, and they flew away when he was frightened: (Meyd:) [or *he became light,* or *inconstant:* or *he became angry:* like طَارَ طَائِرُهُ: (see طَائِرٌ:)] or *he became aged.* (TA.) —— نَقَّتْ عَصَافِيرُ بَطْنِهِ [lit. *The sparrows of his belly cried*], (Ḳ,) like نَقَّتْ ضَفَادِعُ بَطْنِهِ, alluding to the intestines, is also a prov., (TA,) meaning ‡ *he was,* or *became, hungry.* (Ḳ, TA.) In like manner also one says, لَا تَأْكُلْ حَتَّى تَطِيرَ عَصَافِيرُ بَطْنِكَ, meaning ‡ *Eat thou not until thou be hungry.* (TA.) ═══ أَصَافِيرُ المُنْذِرِ is an appellation of † *Certain excellent camels, that belonged to kings:* (Ṣ, O, Ḳ:) or *certain excellent camels that belonged to En-Noamán Ibn-El-Mundhir* were called أَصَافِيرُ النُّعْمَانِ. (T, TA.) ═══ العُصْفُورُ also signifies *The male locust.* (O, Ḳ.) — And *The chief,* or *lord.* (IAạr, O, Ḳ.) — And *The king.* (Ḳ.) — Also *A portion,* (Ṣ, O,) or *small portion,* (Ḳ,) *of the brain,* (Ṣ, O, Ḳ,) *beneath the* قَرْع *of the brain,* (TA,) *as though separated therefrom:* (Ṣ, O, TA:) *between the two is a pellicle.* (Ṣ, O, Ḳ.) — And *A certain vein in the heart.* (IF, O.) — And *A prominent bone in the temple of the horse,* (Ṣ, O, Ḳ,) *on the right* and *on the left;* both being called عُصْفُورَانِ. (Ṣ, O.) — And *The place whence grows the forelock* [app. *of the horse*]. (M, Ḳ.) — And *A narrow blaze extending downwards from the blaze on the forehead of the horse, not reaching to the muzzle.* (O, Ḳ.) — The عَصَافِير of a camel's hump see expl. voce عُرْصُوف. — And عُصْفُور signifies also *A piece of wood in the* [*kind of camel-vehicle called*] هَوْدَج, *uniting the extremities of certain* [*other*] *pieces of wood therein;* [perhaps what unites the outer extremities of two long pieces of wood which project horizontally from the lower part of the هودج, from the two extremities of either side;] (Ḳ;) *having the form of the* [*kind of saddle called*] إِكَاف: (L:) or the *pieces of wood which are in the* [*kind of camel's saddle called*] رَحْل, *by which the heads of the* [*curved pieces of wood called the*] أَحْنَآء *are fastened* [*together*]: (Ḳ:) and the *wood by which are fastened the heads of the* [*kind of saddle called*] قَتَب: (Ḳ:) the pl. is عَصَافِيرُ: or the عصافير of the قتب are its عَرَاصِيف, from which عصافير is formed by transposition; and they are *four pins of wood which are put between* [or rather *which unite* or *conjoin*] *the heads of the* احناء *of the* قتب; *in each* حِنْو *are two of these pins, fastened with sinews or with camel's skin; and in it* [or *appertaining to the same part*] *are the* ظَلِفَات: (Ṣ, O:) or the *nails which unite the head of the* قتب: (IDrd:) or the عُصْفُور of the [kind of saddle called] إِكَاف is its عُرْصُوف, from which latter word the former is formed by transposition; and it is *a piece of wood fastened between* [or rather *uniting* or *conjoining*] *the anterior* حِنْوَانِ. (Ṣ, O.) In a trad. it is said that it it is unlawful to cut or shake off aught from the trees of El-Medeeneh, except for the عصفور of a قتب, or to supply a sheave of a pulley, or for the handle of an iron implement. (Ṣ.) — Also *A nail of a ship.* (O, Ḳ.)

عصل

1. عَصَلَ العُودَ, (Ḳ, TA,) aor. ِ, inf. n. عَصْلٌ, (TA,) *He made the* عود [or *piece of wood,* or *branch,* or *the like,*] *crooked:* — and عَصِلَ, aor. َ, [inf. n. عَصَلٌ, q. v.,] *It was crooked naturally* [or *originally*]: thus in the Ḳ: or, as in some copies, [and among them my MS. copy, and the CḲ,] the latter verb has this meaning: and it is added, فَإِنْ كَانَ ٱعْوِجَاجُهُ بِهِ قُلْتَ عَصَّلَ ✝ تَعْصِيلًا [app. meaning that this last verb signifies *it became crooked of itself,* i.e., *by some accident of its growth*]. (TA.) And عَصِلَ, aor. َ, [inf. n. عَصَلٌ,] signifies also *It was crooked, with hardness:* (Ḳ, TA:) and *it was crooked and strong* or *hard;* said of the canine tooth of a camel; as is the case only when he has become advanced in age: and, said of the same, [simply,] *it became strong* or *hard;* as also ✝ اعْصَلَّ. (TA.) Also, said of a horse, *He had that twisting of the tail which is signified by the term* عَصَلٌ expl. below. (Ḳ,* TḲ.) — عَصَلَ, (Ḳ, TA,) aor. ِ, inf. n. عَصْلٌ, (TḲ,) said of a man, and of other than man, (TA, [in the TḲ said of a boy,]) also signifies *He urined; made water:* (Ḳ, TA: [in the CḲ, مالَ is erroneously put for بَالَ:]) it occurs in a trad. as said of a fox that made water upon the head of an idol. (TA.)

2. عَصَّلَ: see 1. — Also, inf. n. تَعْصِيلٌ, *It* (an arrow) *twisted when shot.* (TA. [But see مُعَصَّلٌ.]) — Also, (AA, O,) inf. n. as above, (AA, O, Ḳ,) said of a man, (AA, O,) *He was,* or *became, slow, dilatory, late,* or *backward.* (AA, O, Ḳ.)

4: see 1.

Q. Q. 4. اعْصَالَّ *He grasped,* or *laid hold upon, his staff.* (IKh, O, Ḳ.)

عِصْلٌ: see the next paragraph.

عَصَلٌ [inf. n. of عَصِلَ, q. v.:] *A twisting in the* عَسِيب [or *bone,* or *slender part,* or *part where the hair grows,*] *of the tail* (Ṣ, O, Ḳ) *of the horse,* (Ḳ,) *so that a portion of the inner side upon which is no hair appears,* (Ṣ, O,) or *so that it hits* [*the flesh of the part of the thigh that is called*] *his* عَكْوَة *and* [*the flesh upon the socket of the hip,* or *the vein in the thigh, that is called*] *his* فَائِل. (Ḳ, TA. [In the CḲ, فَالَّهُ is erroneously put for فَائِلَهُ.]) And *Crookedness with hardness:* (Ḳ:) or *crookedness and strength* or *hardness* of a canine tooth. (Ṣ, O.) — Also sing. of أَعْصَالٌ signifying The *intestines into which the food passes from the stomach;* (Aṣ, Ṣ, O, Ḳ;) and it (the sing.) is also pronounced ✝ عِصْلٌ. (Ḳ.) — And *Wreathed,* or *twisting, and curved, sands:* occurring in this sense in a trad. (TA.) — And *Certain trees which, when the camel eats thereof, cause him to void thin dung:* (Ṣ, O:) or the *trees called* دِفْلَى [q. v.]: (Ḳ:) or *certain trees resembling the* دِفْلَى, *which the camels eat, and after which they drink water every day:* or, as some say, [*trees of the kind called*] حَمْض *that grow upon,* or *at, the waters:* (TA:) a single tree thereof is called عَصَلَةٌ. (Ṣ, O, Ḳ. [See also عَصَلَةٌ, in art. عضل.]) [Accord. to Forskål (Flora Aegypt. Arab. pp. cxiv. and 110) now applied to a species of *Ocymum* which he terms *serpyllifolium.*]

عَصِلٌ: see أَعْصَلُ, in three places. — Also An *arrow crooked* in [the portion called] its مَتْن [q. v.]. (TA.) — And شَجَرَةٌ عَصِلَةٌ *A crooked tree,* (Ṣ, O, TA,) *that cannot be straightened by reason of its hardness.* (TA.)

عَاصِلٌ, applied to an arrow, *Strong,* or *hard.* (Ḳ,* TA.)

العُنْصُلُ and العُنْصَلُ, and ✝ العُنْصُلَآءُ and العُنْصَلَآءُ, (Ṣ, O, Ḳ, [in the O, and a second time in the Ḳ, mentioned in art. عنصل,]) *What is called* (Ṣ, O, Ḳ) *by the physicians* (Ṣ, O) الإِسْقَالُ, (Ṣ, O, Ḳ,) pronounced with إِمَالَة [i. e. *el-iskeel,* notwithstanding the ق, which is generally an obstacle to امالة], *and in some of the books of the physicians written with* ى, [i. e. الإِسْقِيلُ,] (O,) or *only known to them as thus pronounced;* (TA;) [i. e. *scilla,* or *squill;* particularly *the officinal squill;*] i. q. البَصَلُ البَرِّىُّ; (O, Ḳ;) *also called* بَصَلُ الفَأْرِ; (Ḳ;) [see art. بصل;] *and a vinegar is prepared from it:* (Ṣ, TA:) IAạr says that it is *a certain plant in the deserts, of which they assert that longing pregnant women desire it and eat it, and that it is what is called* البَصَلُ البَرِّىُّ: AḤn says, *it consists of leaves like the leek, appearing extended and lank:* and in one place he says, *it is a certain tree* [or *plant*] *of the plain,* or *soft, tracts, growing in places of water and moisture, in like manner as does the* مَوْزَة [?], *and it has a blossom like that of the white* سُوْسَن [or *lily*], *of which the bees eat, and make honey; and the oxen, in cases of drought, eat its leaves, which are mixed for them in the fodder:* (TA:) *it is good for the alopecia, and hemiplegia* (الفَالِج), *and sciatica; and the vinegar thereof, for chronic cough, and asthma, and the rattles; and strengthens the weak body:* (Ḳ:) the pl. is عَنَاصِلُ. (Ṣ, O.) — أَخَذَ طَرِيقَ العُنْصُلِ, (Ṣ, O) and فِى طَرِيقِ العُنْصُلَيْنِ, (Ṣ,) [*He entered upon,* or *took to, the road of* العنصل and العنصلين,] a road from El-Yemámeh to El-Baṣrah, is said of a man as meaning † *he went astray:* (Ṣ, O:) but AḤát says that he asked Aṣ respecting طريق العنصلين, and he pronounced the latter word with fet-ḥ to the ص; adding that it should not be pronounced with ḍamm; and that the saying originated from El-Farezdaḳ's mentioning, in his poetry, a man who went astray in this road. (O.) One says also, سَلَكَ طَرِيقَ العنصلين, meaning † *He pursued that which was false, vain,* or *futile.* (TA.)

العُنْصُلَآءُ and العُنْصَلَآءُ: see the next preceding paragraph.

أَعْصَلُ, applied to a horse, *Having a twisting of the* عَسِيب [*of the tail, such as is termed* عَصَلٌ, expl. above]: pl. عُصْلٌ, (Ḳ,* TA,) which is extr.; or, in the opinion of ISd, this is pl. of ✝ عَصِلٌ. (TA.) And *Crooked, with hardness;* as also ✝ عَصِلٌ; (Ḳ, TA;) both applied to anything: (TA:) pl. as above. (Ḳ, TA.) And [simply] *Crooked;* applied in this sense to a canine tooth; and to an arrow: pl. عُصْلٌ: (Ḳ, TA: [in the CḲ and in my MS. copy of the Ḳ, وَكَكِتَابٍ وَلِلنَّابِ الأَعْوَجِ وَالسَّهْمِ المُعْوَجِّ is erroneously put for الأَعْوَجِ وَالسَّهْمِ المُعْوَجِّ:]) or [the pl.] عُصْلٌ is أَعْصَلُ applied in this sense to arrows: and أَعْصَلُ applied to a canine tooth signifies *crooked and strong* or *hard;* (Ṣ, O, TA;) and ✝ عَصِلٌ likewise signifies *crooked and strong* or *hard, and old;* applied to the canine tooth of a camel, because it is thus only when the camel has become advanced in age: and the former, applied to an arrow, signifies also *scanty in the feathers.* (TA.) — Also *Crooked in the shank,* (Ṣ, O, Ḳ, TA,) *dry,* or *tough, in the body:* (TA:) pl. عُصْلٌ: (Ḳ:) and the sing., applied to a man, [simply,] *dry,* or *tough, in the body;* and so [the fem.] عَصْلَآءُ applied to a woman: (TA:) or this, thus applied, signifies *having no flesh upon her,* (Ḳ, TA,) *and dry,* or *tough:* (TA:) and [the pl.] عُصْلٌ is applied to camels as meaning *lank in their bellies.* (O.) — Also (Ḳ, TA, in the CḲ "or") *Keeping,* or *clinging, to a thing, and favourably inclined to it.* (Ḳ, TA.) — And أَمْرٌ أَعْصَلُ † *An affair,* or *a case, that is hard, troublesome,* or *distressing.* (TA.)

مِعْصَلٌ One who is *hard upon his debtor.* (O, Ḳ.)

مُعَصَّلٌ An arrow *that twists when it is shot:* (Ṣ, O, Ḳ:) or, accord. to 'Alee Ibn-Ḥamzeh, it is correctly مُعَضَّلٌ, with the pointed ض; from عَضَّلَتْ meaning "the egg twisted, or became difficult [to be excluded], in her inside." (TA.)

مِعْصَالٌ *A stick,* or *staff, with a crooked,* or *bent, head, with which one reaches,* or *takes hold of,* [or *draws towards him,*] *the branches of a tree.* (IDrd, O, Ḳ.) And The [*kind of goff-stick called*] صَوْلَجَان [q. v.]; as also † مِعْصِيلٌ. (O, Ḳ.)

مِعْصِيلٌ: see what next precedes.

عصم

1. عَصَمَ, aor. ِ, (Ḳ, TA,) inf. n. عَصْمٌ, (TA,) i. q. مَنَعَ [as meaning *He,* or *it, prevented,* or *hindered:* or, as is generally the case, *defended,* or *protected*]: (Ḳ, TA:) this is [said to be] the primary signification: (TA: [but see عِصْمَةٌ:]) and *he,* or *it, preserved,* or *kept;* syn. وَقَى: (Ḳ, TA:) and *it withheld* (أَمْسَكَ) a thing. (TA.) One says, عَصَمَهُ الطَّعَامُ [for عَصَمَهُ مِنَ الجُوعِ] *The food prevented him,* or *defended him,* (مَنَعَهُ,) *from being hungry.* (Ṣ, Ḳ.) And عَصَمَهُ اللّٰهُ, (Mgh, Mṣb, TA,) aor. as above, (Mṣb, TA,) inf. n. عِصْمَةٌ, (Mgh,) or this is a simple subst., (Mṣb,) and the inf. n. is عَصْمٌ, (TA,) *God defended,* or *protected, him;* (TA;) or *preserved him;* (Mgh, Mṣb, TA;) مِنَ السُّوْءِ [*from evil*], (Mgh,) or مِنَ المَكْرُوهِ [*from what was disliked,* or *hated*]. (Mṣb.) And عَصَمْتُهُ *I* [*defended,* or *protected, him;* or] *preserved him.* (Ṣ.) — And [hence,] عَصَمَ القِرْبَةَ, (Ḳ, TA,) aor. ِ, inf. n. عَصْمٌ, (TA,) *He put,* or *made, to the water-skin, an* عِصَام; (Ḳ, TA;) as also † أَعْصَمَهَا: (ISk, Ṣ, Ḳ, TA:) or the latter signifies, (TA,) or signifies also, (Ḳ,) *he bound it with the* عِصَام, (Ḳ, TA,) i. e. the [*tie called*] وِكَآء [*which is bound round its head to confine the contents*]. (TA.) — عَصَمَ إِلَيْهِ: see 8. — عَصَمَ, aor. ِ, (Ṣ, Ḳ,) inf. n. عَصْمٌ, (Ṣ,) signifies also اِكْتَسَبَ [i. e. *he gained,* or *earned;* or *he sought means of subsistence*]. (Ṣ, Ḳ.) — عَصَمَ ثَنِيَّتَهُ الغُبَارُ means *The dust stuck to his central incisor;* like عَصَبَ [q. v.]. (TA.) — عَصِمَ, aor. َ, (Ḳ, TA,) inf. n. عَصَمٌ, (Ṣ,* TA,) said of a gazelle, and of a mountain-goat, [and app. of a horse,] *He was such as is termed* أَعْصَم. (Ḳ, TA.)

4. اعصم *He exerted his strength, and laid hold,* or *fast hold, upon a thing,* or *clung to it,* lest his horse, or his camel, should throw him down; [or rather اعصم بِشَىْءٍ has this meaning, or *he laid hold,* or *fast hold, upon a thing,* or *clung to it;*] and in like manner one says † اعتصم به, and † استعصم به; (Ṣ;) † اعتصم به is said by Er-Rághib, to signify thus; whence, in the Ḳur [iii. 98], وَٱعْتَصِمُوا † بِحَبْلِ ٱللّٰهِ [expl. in art. حبل]: (TA:) and [hence, likewise,] اعصم بِحَبْلِهِ signifies تَمَسَّكَ بِهِ [meaning *He held fast by his covenant*]. (Mgh.) One says also, اعصم بِالبَعِيرِ *He laid hold upon one of the cords,* or *ropes, of the camel,* (Ḳ, TA,) lest the camel should throw him down. (TA.) And اعصم بِالفَرَسِ *He laid hold upon the mane of the horse,* (Ḳ, TA,) lest his horse should throw him down. (TA.) And اعصم بِفُلَانٍ *He laid upon such a one:* (Ḳ:) or اعصم بِصَاحِبِهِ *He clung to his companion.* (Ṣ.) — And [hence,] *He took refuge,* and *defended,* or *protected, himself,* مِنَ الشَّرِّ *from evil;* as also † اعتصم, and † استعصم. (Ḥam p. 810.) — Also *He was not firm* [*in his seat*] *upon the back of the horse.* (Ḳ.) — اعصم فُلَانًا *He prepared for such a one,* (Ṣ, Ḳ,) *in the camel's saddle,* and *in the horse's saddle,* (Ṣ,) *a thing upon which he might lay hold,* (Ṣ, Ḳ,) *lest he should fall.* (Ṣ.) — اعصم القِرْبَةَ: see 1, latter half.

7. انعصم *He became* [*defended,* or *protected,* or] *preserved;* quasi-pass. of عَصَمْتُهُ. (Ṣ.)

8: see 4, first sentence, in three places. [Hence,] اعتصم بِٱللّٰهِ *He held fast,* or *clung, unto God:* (Jel in iii. 96:) or, *to his religion:* or *he had recourse to God for protection, in,* or *in respect of, the concurrences,* or *combinations, of his affairs:* (Bḍ ibid:) *he confided in,* or *relied upon, God,* (Bḍ and Jel in xxii. last verse,) *in,* or *in respect of, the concurrences,* or *combinations, of his affairs, not seeking aid from any but Him:* (Bḍ ibid.:) or *he defended,* or *preserved, himself,* or *he refrained,* or *abstained,* (اِمْتَنَعَ,) *by the grace of God,* (Ṣ, Mṣb,* Ḳ,) *from disobedience.* (Ṣ, Ḳ. [See also 10.]) And † عَصَمَ إِلَيْهِ signifies the same as اعتصم به. (Ḳ.) See also 4, latter half. — اِعْتَصَمَتْ, said of a girl, or young woman, [from عِصَام,] *She applied collyrium to her eyes.* (El-Muärrij, TA.)

10. استعصم: see 4, in two places. — Also *He defended,* or *preserved, himself,* or *he refrained,* or *abstained;* syn. اِمْتَنَعَ. (TA. [See also 8.])

عُصْمٌ (Ṣ, Ḳ) and † عُصُمٌ (Ḳ) and † عَصِيمٌ (Ṣ, Ḳ) *A relic,* and *a trace,* of anything, (Ṣ, Ḳ,) such as tar [with which camels are smeared when mangy], (Ṣ,) and خِضَاب [i. e. ḥinnà (حِنَّآء) and the like, with which one dyes, or tinges, the hair &c.], and the like: (Ṣ, Ḳ:) and عُصْمٌ is also expl. as signifying *a trace* of anything such as وَرْس [q. v.] or saffron or the like. (TA.) Aṣ says, I heard an Arab woman of the desert say to her fellow-wife, أَعْطِينِى عُصْمَ حِنَّائِكِ, meaning [*Give me*] *what thou hast wiped off and cast away of thy* حِنَّآء (Ṣ, TA*) *after thy dyeing of thy hands with it.* (TA.) — عُصْمٌ is also a pl. of عِصَام [q. v.]. (TA.)

عُصُمٌ: see عِصْمَةٌ.

عُصُمٌ: see عُصْمٌ. — Also a pl. of عِصَام [q. v.]. (Mṣb.)

عُصْمَةٌ A قِلَادَة [meaning *collar for a dog*]; (Ṣ, Ḳ;) as also † عِصْمَةٌ; (Kr, Ḳ, &c.;) *resembling a bracelet:* (Er-Rághib, TA:) pl. (of the latter, TA) عِصَمٌ, and pl. pl. أَعْصُمٌ and عِصَمَةٌ [in the CḲ عِصَمَةٌ, but, as is said in the TA, with kesr and then fet-ḥ], and pl. pl. pl. أَعْصَامٌ; (Ḳ;) or this last, which is said in the Ṣ to be pl. of عِصْمَةٌ, and thought by ISd to be formed from عِصْمَةٌ after rejecting the augmentative letter [ة], and said by some to be a pl. of which the sing. is † عِصْمٌ, like as أَعْدَالٌ is of عِدْلٌ, is correctly pl. of عِصَمٌ, which is pl. of عِصْمَةٌ, (IB, TA,) of which أَعْصِمَةٌ is also a pl. [of pauc.]. (TA.) And أَعْصَامٌ signifies also The *straps* (عَذَبَات) *that are upon the necks* of dogs: and the sing. is عِصْمَةٌ, and, (Ḳ, TA,) some say, (TA,) † عِصَامٌ, (Ḳ, TA,) with kesr, [in the CḲ عُصَامٌ,] mentioned by Lth. (TA.) [Hence,] one says, دَفَعْتُهُ إِلَيْهِ بِعُصْمَتِهِ and † بِعِصَامِهِ [i. e. *I gave it to him altogether*]; like as one says, بِرُمَّتِهِ [q. v.]. (TA.) — Also The *quality denoted by the epithet* أَعْصَم [q. v.]: (Ṣ, Ḳ:) ISh says, it is *in the arm of the gazelle* and *of the mountain-goat:* and IAạr says, it is *in cloven-hoofed animals in the fore legs;* and *in the crow, in the shanks;* and sometimes, he says, it is *in horses.* (TA.)

عِصْمَةٌ [mentioned in the Mgh as an inf. n., but said in the Mṣb to be a simple subst.,] primarily (TA) signifies مَنْعٌ [as meaning *Prevention,* or *hindrance:* or, as seems to be indicated by most of its subordinate applications, *defence,* or *protection*]: (Ṣ, Ḳ, TA:) or, as some say, its primary signification is the *act of tying,* or *binding;* and hence the meaning of مَنْع: or, accord. to Zj, it primarily signifies حَبْل [i. e. *a rope,* or *cord*]; and accord. to Moḥammad Ibn-Neshwán El-Ḥimyeree, سَبَب and حَبْل [which mean the same]. (TA.) *Defence,* or *protection,* (TA,) or *preservation,* (Ṣ, Mṣb, Ḳ,) [in an absolute sense, and] as an act of God, (Mṣb, TA,) *from that which would cause destruction* of a man. (TA.) عِصْمَةُ الأَنْبِيَآءِ signifies God's *preservation of the prophets;*

first, by the peculiar endowment of them with essential purity of constitution; then, by the conferring of large and highly-esteemed excellences; then, by aid against opponents, and rendering their feet firm; then, by sending down upon them tranquillity (السَّكِينَة, q. v.), [see the Ḳur ix. 26, &c.,] *and the preservation of their hearts,* or *minds, and adaptation to that which is right.* (Er-Rághib, TA.) — Also [*A defence* as meaning] *a defender from a state of perdition* and *from want:* so in a saying of Aboo-Tálib, in praise of the Prophet, cited voce ثِمَال. (TA.) — And *A faculty of avoiding,* or *shunning, acts of disobedience,* [or *of self-preservation therefrom,*] *with possession of power to commit them:* (El-Munáwee, TA:) [or,] as used by the Muslim theologians, *inability to disobey:* or *a disposition that prevents* [*disobedience*], *not such as constrains* [*to act*]. (MF, TA.) — عِصْمَةُ النِّكَاحِ means *The tie,* or *bond, of marriage:* [also called, in the present day, عِصْمَةُ المَرْأَةِ i. e. *the woman's matrimonial tie* or *bond, which is in her husband's hand,* or *power:* a term used by the lawyers:] one says, بِيَدِهِ عِصْمَةُ النِّكَاحِ i. e. [*In his hand,* or *power, is*] *the tie,* or *bond, of marriage:* pl. عِصَمٌ: whence, in the Ḳur [lx. 10], وَلَا تُمْسِكُوا بِعِصَمِ الكَوَافِرِ [*And hold ye not to the matrimonial ties,* or *bonds, of the unbelieving women;* meaning divorce ye such women: but the common reading is وَلَا تُمَسِّكُوا, which signifies the same]. (TA.) — See also عُصْمَةٌ.

عِصَامٌ The *tie of a* قِرْبَة [or water-skin]; (Ṣ, Mṣb;) [i. e.] its [*tie called*] وِكَاء [*which is bound round the head to confine the contents*]: (TA:) and the *strap that is used for the carrying* thereof: (Ṣ, Mṣb:) or *a cord that is used for the tying,* or *binding,* of the leathern bucket and of the water-skin and of the [leathern vessel for water called] إِدَاوَة: and the *loop-shaped handle that serves for the suspending* of the [bag, or other receptacle, for travelling-provisions or for goods or utensils &c. called] وِعَاء: (Ḳ:) and *anything that serves for the protection,* or *preservation,* of a thing: (TA:) pl. [of pauc.] أَعْصِمَةٌ and [of mult.] عُصُمٌ, (Ḳ, TA,) or عُصْمٌ, (Mṣb, and so in some copies of the Ḳ,) and عِصَامٌ, like the sing., of the class of دِلَاصٌ: (AZ, Ḳ:) but Az states, as what had been heard [app. by him] from the Arabs, respecting the عُصُم of [the leathern water-bags called] مَزَاد, that they are the *cords that are fixed in the loops of the pairs of water-bags, and with which they are tied when they are bound upon the back of the camel; after which the* [rope called] رِوَآء *is bound over them:* they are erroneously said by Lth to be the طَرَائِق [app. meaning *borders*] *of the extremity of the* مَزَادَة [or *leathern water-bag*], *at the place of the* كُلْيَة [or *kidney-shaped piece of leather to which a loop is sewed*]. (TA. [See also عُصُمٌ.]) Mention is made, in a trad., of a place where a camel was shackled with عُصُم, as meaning that its abundance of herbage confined him so that he would not go away in search of pasturage. (TA.) — Also The *cord,* or *bond,* of the [vehicle called] مَحْمِل, (Ḳ,* TA,) *which is bound at the extremity of* [*each of the transverse pieces of wood called*] *the* عَارِضَانِ [correctly عَارِضَتَانِ], *in the upper part of each of these:* [for,] as Lth says, *there are two of such cords,* or *bonds:* and Az says that *the* عِصَامَانِ *of the* مَحْمِل *are like those of the* [*pair of leathern water-bags called*] مَزَادَتَانِ. (TA.) — And The *slender part of the end of the tail;* (M, Ḳ;) and عِصَامٌ is a dial. var. thereof: (TA: [but see the latter:]) or the *tail with its hair and its* عَسِيب [q. v.]: (ISh, TA:) pl. أَعْصِمَةٌ. (Ḳ.) — See also عُصْمَةٌ, in two places. — Also *Collyrium:* (Ḳ, TA:) mentioned on the authority of El-Muärrij: so called because it defends and strengthens the eye. (TA.)

عَصُومٌ *Edacious; voracious;* (Ḳ, TA;) applied to a she-camel; (TA;) and † عَيْصُومٌ signifies the same, (Ḳ, TA,) applied to a human being, male and female; (TA;) the latter occurring in the saying of a rájiz, applied to an old woman, (Ṣ, TA,) and said to have this meaning, (Ṣ,) but as some relate it, the word is there with ض; (Ṣ, TA;) and عَيْضُومٌ signifies thus accord. to Kr, applied to a woman: عَيْصُومٌ, however, is of higher authority: (TA in art. عضم:) † عَيْصَامٌ also signifies the same, applied to a man. (TA.) — Also A female *whose family,* or *household, have become numerous.* (Az, TA.)

عَصِيمٌ: see عُصُمٌ. — Also *Sweat:* (Ḳ:) or, accord. to Lth, *rust* [*that is an effect*] *of sweat.* (TA.) — And *Dirt, and urine that dries, upon the thighs of camels,* (Ḳ, TA,) *so as to become like the road, in thickness.* (TA.) — And *Black hair that grows beneath the fur of the camel when it falls off* (إِذَا أَنْسَلَ) [perhaps a mistranscription for إِذَا أَنْسَلَ]. (Ḳ.) — And The *leaves of trees.* (IB, TA.)

عِصَامِيٌّ [a rel. n. used as meaning *Of the class of 'Iṣám;* and hence, *self-ennobled*]. عِصَامٌ is the name of a chamberlain of En-Noamán Ibn-El-Mundhir: and [in relation to him] it is said in a prov., كُنْ عِصَامِيًّا وَلَا تَكُنْ عِظَامِيًّا, (Ṣ, Ḳ, TA,) [the former clause meaning *Be thou of the class of 'Iṣám,* i. e. *be thou self-ennobled,* and] the latter clause meaning *and be not of those who glory in old and wasted and crumbling bones,* [i. e. *in their ancestors,*] (TA,) alluding to his saying, [so in the Ṣ and Ḳ and TA, but correctly the saying of En-Nábighah, (see Ḥar p. 297,)]

نَفْسُ عِصَامٍ سَوَّدَتْ عِصَامَا
وَعَلَّمَتْهُ الكَرَّ وَالإِقْدَامَا

[*The soul of 'Iṣám ennobled 'Iṣám, and taught him the art of attack, and boldness*]. (Ṣ, Ḳ, TA.) And [hence] one says also, فُلَانٌ عِصَامِيٌّ وَعِظَامِيٌّ i. e. *Such a one is noble in respect of soul,* or *self, and of origin.* (A, TA.)

عَاصِمٌ [act. part. n. of عَصَمَ, signifying] *Defending* [&c.], or *a defender* [&c.]. (TA.) لَا عَاصِمَ اليَوْمَ مِنْ أَمْرِ ٱللّٰهِ, in the Ḳur [xi. 45], may mean *There is no defender* [*this day from the decree of God*]: (TA:) or the meaning may be, *no* [*person*] *defended:* or *no possessor of defence:* (Ṣ, TA:) so that عاصم may be an instance of فَاعِل in the sense of مَفْعُول: (Ṣ:) or it may thus be a possessive epithet. (TA. [See also دَافِقٌ.]) — [Hence,] العَاصِمَةُ is a name of *El-Medeeneh.* (Ḳ.) — أَبُو عَاصِمٍ is an appellation of *The meal of parched barley or the like* (السَّوِيق). (Ṣ, Ḳ.) And also *The food called* سِكْبَاج [q. v.]. (Ḳ.)

عَيْصَامٌ: see عَصُومٌ.

عَيْصُومٌ: see عَصُومٌ. — Also A woman *who sleeps long, and speaks angrily when she is roused.* (TA.)

أَعْصَمُ A gazelle, and a mountain-goat, *having in his arms,* (Aṣ, T, Ṣ, Ḳ,) or *in one of them,* (AO, Ṣ, M, Ḳ,) *a whiteness,* (Ṣ, Ḳ,) *the rest of him being red* or *black:* (Ḳ:) or a goat *white in the fore legs,* or *in the fore leg:* (Az, TA:) fem. عَصْمَآءُ: (Ṣ, Ḳ:) and pl. عُصْمٌ. (Ṣ.) — And A horse *white in the fore leg:* (Aṣ, TA:) or *having a whiteness in one of his fore legs, above the pastern:* (ISh, TA:) or *having a whiteness in his fore shanks:* (Ḥam p. 18:) or *having a whiteness in one of his fore legs,* (Ṣ, TA,) *but not in his hind legs,* (TA,) *little* or *much;* in which case he is termed أَعْصَمُ اليُمْنَى or اليُسْرَى [*white in respect of the right* fore leg or *of the left*]: when the whiteness is in both of his fore legs, he is termed أَعْصَمُ اليَدَيْنِ [*white in respect of the two fore legs*]; unless having a blaze in his face, in which case he is termed مُحَجَّل, not أَعْصَم; (Ṣ, TA;) though a blaze in his face does not cause him to be termed مُحَجَّل when the whiteness is in one fore leg. (Ṣ.) — And A crow *having a white feather in its wing;* (Ṣ, Ḳ; [in some copies of the Ḳ, *in its two wings;*]) i. e., *in one of its wings:* (TA:) because the wing of the bird corresponds to the fore leg [of the beast]: (Ṣ, TA:) or *white in the wings:* (ISh, IAth, TA:) or *white in the legs:* (TA:) or *red* (أَحْمَر) *in the legs and beak;* (Az, Ḳ, TA;) and this is said by Az to be the correct explanation; [but] he adds that the Arabs term بَيَاض [i. e. whiteness] حُمْرَة [which properly signifies redness], saying of a woman of white complexion that she is حَمْرَآء: [so that by the last of the foregoing explanations of أَعْصَم applied to a crow is app. meant *white in the legs and beak:*] the Prophet is said to have explained this epithet, thus applied, as meaning *of which one of the legs is white:* (TA:) some say that الغُرَابُ الأَعْصَمُ is like بَيْضُ الأَنُوقِ and الأَبْلَقُ العَقُوقُ, applied to anything that is rarely found: (Ṣ, TA:) it occurs in a number of trads.; and a righteous woman is likened thereto. (TA.)

مِعْصَمٌ The *part, of the fore arm, which is the place of the bracelet;* (Ṣ, Mṣb, Ḳ;) [the *wrist:*] pl. مَعَاصِمُ: in a citation from a poet (voce عَرَقٌ), المَعَاصِم is used by poetic license for المَعَاصِيم. (L in art. عرق.) — And The يَد [meaning *arm*];

(K, TA;) used in this sense in a verse of El-Aạshà. (TA.) ═ Also, thus without the article ال, a name for *The she-goat;* which is called to be milked by one's saying مِعْصَرْ مِعْصَرْ, with the last letter quiescent. (K.)

مُعْتَصَرٌ *A place of defence, protection,* or *preservation.* (Ksh and Bḍ in xi. 45.)

عصو

1. عَصَاهُ, (K, TA,) aor. يَعْصُوهُ, (TA,) inf. n. عَصْوٌ, (TK,) *He struck him,* or *beat him, with the staff* or *stick* or *rod* (بِالعَصَا): (K, TA:) or عَصَوْتُهُ بالعصا *I struck him,* or *beat him, with the staff* &c. (Ṣ.) — And عَصِىَ بِهَا *He took it,* i. e. the staff &c.: and عَصِىَ بِسَيْفِهِ *he took his sword as one takes the staff:* or *he struck,* or *beat, with it as one does with the staff;* as also عَصَا, aor. ـُ, inf. n. عَصًا: or you say عَصَوْتُ بِالسَّيْفِ and عَصِيتُ بالعصا [in the CK عَصَيْتُ]: or the reverse of this: or each of these verbs followed by بالسيف and بالعصا: (K, TA:) all these phrases are mentioned by the leading lexicologists and by ISd in the M: (TA:) or you say عَصِىَ بِالسَّيْفِ, aor. ـَ, inf. n. عَصًا, meaning *he struck with the sword.* (Ṣ.) [See also 5.] — عَاصَانِى فَعَصَوْتُهُ: see 3. — [See also 2.] ═ عَصَوْتُ القَوْمَ, (K, TA,) aor. أَعْصُوهُمْ, (TA,) *I collected together the people,* or *party, for good* or *for evil.* (K, TA.) [This seems to be regarded by some as the primary signification; (see عَصًا;) but, I think, without good reason.] — And عَصَوْتُ الجُرْحَ, (Ṣ, K,) inf. n. عَصْوٌ, *I bound the wound.* (Ṣ, K.) ═ عَصَا, inf. n. عَصْوٌ, also signifies *It was,* or *became, hard:* as though for عَسَا; the س being changed into ص. (TA.) ═ And عَصَا, aor. يَعْصُو, said of a bird, *It flew.* (TA.)

2. عَصَّاهُ العَصَا, inf. n. تَعْصِيَةٌ, *He gave him the* عصا [or *staff,* &c.]. (K. [Accord. to Golius, عَصَّاهُ; evidently a mistake, for عصّاه is not mentioned by him.])

3. عَاصَانِى فَعَصَوْتُهُ *He contended with me in striking,* or *beating,* (K, TA,) or, as in the M, *he acted roughly towards me,* and *opposed me,* or *contended with me,* (TA,) *with the* عَصَا [or *staff,* &c.], *and I overcame him* [*therein*]. (K, TA.)

4. اعصى *It* (a grape-vine) *put forth its* عِيدَان (Ṣ, K, TA) or عُصِىّ [i. e. *rods*]. (TA.)

5. تعصّى *He struck,* or *beat, with the* عَصَا [or *staff,* &c.]. (Mgh.) And تعصّى بِالعَصَا *He made use of the* عصا [or *staff,* &c.]: and *he struck,* or *beat, with it.* (Mgh.)

8. اعتصى عَلَى العَصَا *He leaned,* or *he supported,* or *stayed, himself, upon the* عَصَا [or *staff,* &c.]. (Ṣ, Mgh.) — And يَعْتَصِى بِالسَّيْفِ He *makes use of the sword as a staff.* (Ṣ, and TA in this art. and in art. عصى.) — And اعتصى الشَّجَرَةَ *He cut a staff,* or *stick,* or *rod,* (عَصًا,) *from the tree.* (K.)

عَصًا i. q. عُودٌ [as meaning *A staff,* or *stick,* or *rod*]: (K:) originally عَصَوٌ, and accordingly its dual is as below: said to be thus called because the fingers and hand are put together upon it [to grasp it], from the saying عَصَوْتُ القَوْمَ "I collected together the people, or party;" as related by Aṣ from some one or more of the Baṣrees: (TA:) of the fem. gender: (Ṣ, Mṣb, K:) it is said in a prov., العَصَا مِنَ العُصَيَّةِ [lit. *The staff is from the little staff;* the dim. having the affix ة because it is the dim. of a fem. n.]; (Ṣ;) [or] العصا in this prov. is the name of a mare of Jedheemeh [mentioned voce ضَلَّ], and العُصَيَّة is that of her dam; meaning that part of the thing, or affair, is from part; (Ṣ, K, TA;) and said when one is likened to his father; or meaning that the big thing is in its commencement small: (TA: [see also Freytag's Arab. Prov. i. 17:]) it is not allowable to say عَصَاة; nor to affix ة: (Aṣ, TA:) one says, هٰذِهِ عَصَاىَ أَتَوَكَّأُ عَلَيْهَا [*This is my staff; I support,* or *stay, myself upon it*]: Fr says that the first incorrect speech heard in El-'Irák was the saying, هٰذِهِ عَصَاتِى: (Ṣ:) the dual is عَصَوَانِ: (Ṣ, Mṣb:) and the pl. [of mult.] is عُصِىٌّ, (Ṣ, Mṣb, K,) [originally عُصُوٌّ,] of the measure فُعُولٌ, (Ṣ, Mṣb,) and عِصِىٌّ, (Ṣ, K,) in which the ع is with kesr because of the kesrah following it, and [of pauc.] أَعْصٍ (Ṣ, Mṣb, K) and أَعْصَآءٌ, (K,) or this last is agreeable with analogy, but has not been transmitted, (ISk, Mṣb,) and is disallowed by Sb, who says that عُصِىّ was used in its stead. (TA.) — [Hence various sayings, here following.] — أَلْقَى عَصَاهُ [lit. *He threw down his staff;*] meaning ‡ *he stayed,* (Ṣ, Mṣb, K, TA,) and *rested,* (Mṣb,) and *ceased from journeys,* (Ṣ,) *having reached his place:* (K, TA:) a prov.; (Ṣ, TA;) applied to him to whom an affair has become suitable and who has therefore kept to it: (TA:) or *he made firm his tent-pegs, and pitched his tent,* or *stayed;* (K, TA;) like him who has returned from his journey. (TA.) And رَفَعَ عَصَاهُ [*He took up his staff*] means † *he ceased from staying* [*in a place at which he had alighted; he departed*]. (Ḥar p. 454.) — لَا تَرْفَعْ عَصَاكَ عَنْ أَهْلِكَ [*Put not thou away thy staff,* or *stick, from thy family,* or *thy wife,*] denotes [the practice of] discipline. (Ṣ. [See art. رفع, p. 1122, col. 3.]) — هُمْ عَبِيدُ العَصَا [*They are the slaves of the staff*] means † *they are* [*persons*] *beaten with the staff.* (K, TA.) It is said in the A, النَّاسُ عَبِيدُ العَصَا [*Mankind are the slaves of the staff*], meaning that they are dreaded by reason of their doing harm [and are therefore to be kept in awe]. (TA.) — And مَا هُمْ إِلَّا عَبِيدُ العَصَا [*They are none other than the slaves of the staff*] is said of persons regarded as low, base, or vile. (TA.) — إِنَّهُ لَيِّنُ العَصَا [*Verily he is one whose staff is supple*] means ‡ *he is gentle, a good manager of that whereof he has the charge:* (Ṣ, K:*) accord. to ISd, alluding to the beating little with the عصا. (TA.) And إِنَّهُ ضَعِيفُ العَصَا [*Verily he is one whose staff is weak*], meaning تَرْعِيَّةٌ [i. e., † *one who performs well the act of keeping* or *tending,* or *of pasturing* or *feeding, camels*]: (Ṣ:) or *one who beats the camels little* (K, TA) *with the* عصا: and such is commended. (TA.) And صَلِيبُ العَصَا and صُلْبُهَا [*One whose staff is hard*], i. e. † *one who is ungentle with the camels, beating them with the* عصا: and such is discommended. (TA.) See an ex. in a verse of Er-Rá'ee cited voce صُلْبٌ. — قَرَعَهُ بِعَصَا المَلَامَةِ [*He struck him with the staff of censure*] means † *he exceeded the usual bounds in censuring him.* (TA.) — See also 1 in art. قرع. — فُلَانٌ يُصَلِّى عَصَا فُلَانٍ [*Such a one straightens the staff of such a one by turning it round over the fire*] means † *such a one manages, orders,* or *regulates, the affairs of such a one.* (TA.) — لَا تَدْخُلْ بَيْنَ العَصَا وَلِحَائِهَا [*Enter not thou between the staff and its peel*] means [† *intermeddle not thou between two close friends;* (see Freytag's Arab. Prov. i. 153;) or] *enter not thou into that which does not concern thee.* (TA.) And قَشَرْتُ لَهُ العَصَا [*I peeled for him the staff*] means † *I discovered to him what was in my mind.* (TA.) — شَقُّ العَصَا [lit. *The splitting of the staff*] means † *the contravening of the collective body* [or *the community*] *of El-Islám* [i. e. *of the Muslims*]: (K, TA:) and also † *the disuniting of the collective body of the tribe:* (TA:) or شَقَّ العَصَا means ‡ *He separated himself from, and he contravened, the collective body* [or *the community*]: (Mṣb:) and [it is said that] the primary signification of العَصَا is *the state of combination and union:* (TA:) this is the meaning in the saying, respecting the خَوَارِج [see خَارِجِىّ], قَدْ شَقُّوا عَصَا المُسْلِمِينَ † *They have made a schism in the state of combination and union,* or *in the communion, of the Muslims*]. (Ṣ, TA.) [Hence,] their saying إِيَّاكَ وَقَتِيلَ العَصَا means † *Beware thou of slaying or being slain in making a schism in the communion of the Muslims* (فِى شَقِّ عَصَا المُسْلِمِينَ). (TA.) And one says, انْشَقَّتِ العَصَا (Ṣ, TA) [*The staff became split*], meaning, † *disagreement,* or *discord, befell.* (TA.) And طَارَتْ عَصَا بَنِى فُلَانٍ شِقَقًا [lit. *The staff of the sons of such a one flew in splinters*], a prov., meaning † *the sons of such a one became scattered in various directions.* (Meyd.) — عَصَا العَبْدِ [*The stick of the slave*] is *the thing with which one stirs the* مَلَّة [or *hot ashes wherein bread is baked*]. (TA.) — العَصَا signifies also ‡ *The bone of the shank;* (K, TA;) as being likened to the عصا [properly so called]. (TA.) And [the pl.] العِصِىُّ, † *The bones that are in the wing.* (Ṣ.) And [the same, or] العُصِىُّ, † *Certain stars, having the form of the* عَصَا [or rather of عِصِىّ]. (TA. [But what stars these are, I have not been able to determine.]) — Also, (i. e. العَصَا,) *The tongue.* (K.) [Perhaps as being likened to a staff because used in chiding.] — And *The woman's* [*muffler,* or *head-covering, called*] خِمَار. (K.) — عَصَا الرَّاعِى [*The pastor's rod;* an appellation of *knot-grass; a species of polygonum, p. aviculare;*] *the* بطباط

[i. e. بَطْبَاط, but the former name is the better known]; *male and female, the former of which is the more potent:* asserted by Dioscorides to be *diuretic, and a remedy for him who suffers suppression of the urine.* (Ibn-Seenà, whom we call Avicenna, book ii. p. 229.)

عُصَيَّةٌ dim. of عَصًا, q. v.

العَاصِى : see عَاصٍ in art. عصى.

عصى

1. عَصَاهُ, aor. يَعْصِيهِ, inf. n. عَصْىٌ and مَعْصِيَةٌ (Ṣ, Mṣb, Ḳ, TA) and عِصْيَانٌ, (TA, and so in some copies of the Ṣ,) or this last is a simple subst., (Mṣb,) *He* ([for instance] a slave, Mṣb, TA) *disobeyed him,* or *rebelled against him,* (Ṣ, Ḳ, TA,) i. e., his master; (Mṣb, TA;) as also ↓ عَاصَاهُ, (Ṣ, Mṣb, Ḳ, TA,) inf. n. مُعَاصَاةٌ; (TA;) and ↓ اِسْتَعْصَى عَلَيْهِ, (Ṣ,) meaning *he opposed him,* or *resisted him,* and *did not obey him,* [or *he rebelled against him,*] namely, his prince, or commander. (TA.) [See also an ex. of the first in a verse cited voce زَجَّ.] فُلَانٌ يَعْصِى الرِّيحَ means † *Such a one faces the quarter from which the wind blows, not opposing his side to the wind.* (TA.)

3: see the preceding paragraph.

5. تعصّى *It* (an affair) *was,* or *became, difficult;* syn. اِعْتَاصَ: (Ḳ, TA:) said by some to be originally تَعَصَّصَ; like تَقَضَّى and تَظَنَّى. (TA.)

6. تعاصى [occurs in the Ṣ and TA, voce تَحَمَّسَ, as meaning *He feigned disobedience,* or *rebellion:* and in the A and TA, voce تَشَاغَبَ, as meaning *he manifested incompliance*].

8. اِعْتَصَتِ النَّوَاةُ *The date-stone was,* or *became, hard.* (Ṣ, Ḳ.)

10: see the first paragraph.

عِصْيَانٌ [mentioned above as an inf. n., but accord. to the Mṣb a simple subst.,] *Disobedience,* or *rebellion; contr. of* طَاعَةٌ. (Ṣ, Ḳ.)

عَصِىٌّ : see what follows, in two places.

عَاصٍ and ↓ عَصِىٌّ *Disobeying,* or *rebelling;* or *disobedient,* or *rebellious:* (Ṣ, Ḳ:) [both are mentioned in the Ṣ and Ḳ as though syn.: but] ↓ the latter is an intensive epithet [and therefore has the latter signification, or means *very disobedient* or *rebellious*]: the pl. of the former is عُصَاةٌ. (Mṣb.) — العَاصِى is an appellation of *The young camel when it disobeys its mother, and does not follow her.* (TA.) — And it signifies also ‡ *The vein that will not cease bleeding:* (Ṣ, Ḳ, TA:) belonging to this art. and to art. عصو: (TA: mentioned in art. عصو in the Ḳ:) pl. العَوَاصِى. (Ṣ.)

عض

1. عَضِضْتُهُ, and عَضِضْتُ عَلَيْهِ, (Ṣ, O, Mṣb, Ḳ,) and بِهِ, (Ṣ, O, Mṣb,) third pers. عَضَّ, (Ṣ,) aor. َ, (Ṣ, Mṣb, Ḳ,) i. e. يَعَضُّ, (ISk, Ṣ, O,) imp. عَضَّ [i. e. عَضَّ and عَضِّ] and اِعْضَضْ, (TA,) inf. n. عَضٌّ (Mgh, O, Mṣb, Ḳ) and عَضِيضٌ (O, Ḳ) and عُضَاضٌ, (TA, [see also عِضَاضٌ, below,]) [*I bit it;* or] *I seized it,* or *took hold of it, with my teeth,* (A, Mgh, Mṣb, Ḳ,) *and pressed it therewith;* (TA;) namely, a thing, (A,) or a morsel of food: (Ṣ, Mṣb:) or *with my tongue;* (A, Ḳ;) as, for instance, a serpent does; but not a scorpion; for this latter stings: (TA:) accord. to the Book of Verbs by IḲṭṭ, one also says عَضَضْتُ, aor. ُ: (Mṣb:) and [it has been asserted that] one says, (Mṣb, Ḳ,) though rarely, (Mṣb,) عَضَضْتُ, aor. ِ: (Mṣb, Ḳ:) it is said in the Ṣ [and O] that ISk cites AO as asserting that عَضَضْتُ, with fet-ḥ [to the first ض] is a dial. var. [which obtained] among [the tribes of] Er-Ribáb: but, IB says, this is a mistranscription; for what ISk says, in the book entitled "El-Iṣláḥ," is, غَصِصْتُ بِاللُّقْمَةِ فَأَنَا أَغَصُّ بِهَا غَصَصًا قَالَ أَبُو عُبَيْدَةَ وَغَصَصْتُ لُغَةٌ فِى الرِّبَابِ, with [the pointed غ and] the unpointed ص: to which [says SM] I add, that thus it is found in the handwriting of Aboo-Zekereeyà and of Ibn-El-Jawáleeḳee, in the "Iṣláḥ" of ISk, and they expressly assert that what is in the Ṣ is a mistranscription. (TA.) — عَضَّ الفَرَسُ عَلَى لِجَامِهِ [*The horse champed his bit*]. (Mṣb.) — It is said in the Ḳur [iii. 115], وَإِذَا خَلَوْا عَضُّوا عَلَيْكُمُ الأَنَامِلَ مِنَ الغَيْظِ † [*And when they are alone, they bite the ends of the fingers by reason of wrath,* or *rage, against you*]: meaning that, by reason of the vehemence of their hatred of the believers, they eat [or rather bite] their hands in wrath, or rage. (O, TA.) You say also, عَضَّ عَلَى يَدِهِ غَيْظًا ‡ [*He bit his hand in wrath,* or *rage*], when a man is inordinate in his enmity. (TA.) In like manner, it is said in the Ḳur [xxv. 29], وَيَوْمَ يَعَضُّ الظَّالِمُ عَلَى يَدَيْهِ ‡ [*And the day when the wrong-doer shall bite his hands*]; meaning, in repentance and regret. (O, TA.) And it is said in a prov., عَضَّ عَلَى شِبْدِعِهِ, i. e. لِسَانِهِ † [*He bit his tongue*]: applied to the clement, or forbearing. (O, TA.) One says also, عَضَّ بِالْخَمْسِ, meaning *He bit the fingers.* (Ḥam p. 790.) — عَضَّ فِى العِلْمِ بِنَاجِذِهِ ‡ *He confirmed his knowledge; made it sound.* (Mgh.) — Mohammad said, عَلَيْكُمْ بِسُنَّتِى وَسُنَّةِ الخُلَفَآءِ الرَّاشِدِينَ مِنْ بَعْدِى عَضُّوا عَلَيْهَا بِالنَّوَاجِذِ, meaning † [*Keep ye to my course of conduct, and the course of conduct of the orthodox Khaleefehs after me:*] *cleave ye,* or *hold ye fast, thereto.* (Mgh,* Mṣb.) And you say, of a man, عَضَّ بِصَاحِبِهِ, (Ṣ, O, Ḳ,) aor. َ, (Ṣ,) inf. n. عَضِيضٌ (Ṣ, O, Ḳ) and عَضٌّ, (TA,) † *He kept,* or *clave, to his companion;* (Ṣ, O, Ḳ;) *he stuck to him:* (TA:) and عَضَّهُ has the same, which is said to be the primary, signification; (TA;) or this signifies *he seized him with his teeth,* because the doing so is a means of cleaving. (IAth, TA.) You say also عضضت بمالى, [so in the TA, without any vowel-signs to the verb,] inf. n. عَضَاضَةٌ and عُضُوضَةٌ, [to agree with which, the pret. by rule should be عَضُضْتُ,] † *I clave,* or *held fast, to my property.* (TA.) And عَضَّ فُلَانٌ بِالشَّرِّ ‡ *Such a one kept,* or *clave, to evil,* or *mischief, and did not leave it.* (A, TA.) — عَضَّهُ, (Aboo-'Is-ḥáḳ, TA in art. همز,) or عَضَّهُ بِلِسَانِهِ, (A, TA,*) inf. n. عَضٌّ, (TA,) ‡ *He defamed him; spoke evil of him;* or *backbit him.* (Aboo-Is-ḥáḳ, ubi suprà; A, TA.) — عَضَّ الثِّقَافُ بِأَنَابِيبِ الرُّمْحِ, and عَضَّ عَلَيْهَا, inf. n. عَضٌّ, ‡ *The straightening-instrument held fast to* [or *pinched*] *the internodal portions of the spear.* (TA.) — عَضَّهُ القَتَبُ, inf. n. عَضٌّ, ‡ [*The camel's saddle hurt him*] *as though it bit him.* (IB.) — عَضَّهُمُ السِّلَاحُ ‡ [*The weapon,* or *weapons, wounded them*]. (O, TA.) — عَضَّهُ الأَمْرُ ‡ *The thing,* or *affair, was,* or *became, severe,* or *distressing,* or *afflictive, to him.* (A, TA.) And you say also, عَضَّتْهُ الحَرْبُ (A, O) and عَضَّتْ بِهِ ‡ *War,* or *the war, was,* or *became, severe to him.* (Ḥam p. 628. See an ex. voce رَجِيمٌ.) عَضُّ الزَّمَانِ and الحَرْبِ signify ‡ *The severity,* or *rigour, of time,* or *fortune,* and *of war:* or in these two cases, the former word is with ظ: (Ḳ:) or, accord. to IḲṭṭ and others, عَضٌّ and عَظٌّ are two dial. vars. (TA.) And عَضَّ, aor. َ, inf. n. عَضِيضٌ, signifies also † *He,* or *it, was,* or *became, strong,* or *hard;* syn. اِشْتَدَّ and صَلُبَ: (IḲṭṭ, TA:) app. said of a man: (TA:) [or, thus used, it has a more comprehensive meaning; for] it is said in the Ṣ that عَضِضْتُ, addressed to a man, signifies ‡ *thou becamest,* or *hast become, such as is termed* عِضٌّ [q. v.]; and the like is said in the A; and Ṣgh adds [in the O] that its inf. n. is عَضَاضَةٌ. (TA.) — عَضَّتْهُ الأَسْفَارُ ‡ *Travels rendered him experienced,* or *expert.* (A, TA.) And one says, عَضَّتْهُ الأُمُورُ بِأَضْرَاسِهَا وَأَحْكَمَتْهُ حَتَّى عَرَّفَتْهُ ‡ [*The management of affairs rendered him experienced so that they taught him*]. (A in art. جرس.)

2. عضّضهُ, inf. n. تَعْضِيضٌ, [*He bit him,* or *it, much,* or *frequently,*] a word of the dial. of Temeem. (TA.) You say, فُلَانٌ يُعَضِّضُ شَفَتَيْهِ *Such a one bites* (يَعَضُّ) *his lips much,* or *often,* by reason of anger. (Ṣ.) And, of an ass, عَضَّضَتْهُ الحُمُرُ *The asses bit him much,* (O, Ḳ,) *and lacerated him with their teeth.* (O.) — [And hence,] عضّض *He jested with his girl,* or *young woman.* (IAạr, O, Ḳ.) ═ Also عضّض, (inf. n. as above, IAạr,) † *He drew water from a well such as is termed* عَضُوضٌ. (IAạr, O, Ḳ.) ═ And *He fed his camels with* [*the provender termed*] عُضٌّ. (IAạr, O, Ḳ.)

3. عَاضَّتِ الدَّوَابُّ, (Ḳ,* TA,) inf. n. عِضَاضٌ (Ṣ, Ḳ) and مُعَاضَّةٌ, (Ṣ,) *The beasts bit one another.* (Ṣ,* Ḳ,* TA.) And in like manner you say, هُمَا ↓ يَتَعَاضَّانِ *They two bite each other.* (Ṣ.) —

[Hence the saying,] عَاضَ القَوْمُ العَيْشَ مُنْذُ العَامِ فَاشْتَدَّ عِضَاضُهُمْ i. e. عَيْشُهُمْ [app. meaning *The people, or company of men, have grappled with life during this year, and their life has been strait, or difficult, or hard*]. (Ṣ.) [See عِضَاضُ عَيْشٍ.]

4. أَعْضَضْتُهُ الشَّىْءَ *I made him to bite the thing; or to seize it, or take hold of it, with his teeth*. (Ṣ,* O, Ḳ.) —— It is said in a trad., مَنْ تَعَزَّى بِعَزَآءِ الجَاهِلِيَّةِ فَأَعِضُّوهُ بِهَنِ أَبِيهِ وَلَا تَكْنُوا (Ṣ,* Mgh, Mṣb, Ḳ) i. e. *Whoso asserteth his relationship* [*of son*] *in the manner of the people of the Time of Ignorance*, meaning by saying, in crying out for aid or succour, يَا لَفُلَانٍ, (Mgh and Mṣb in art. عزو,) and exclaiming, أَنَا فُلَانُ بْنُ فُلَانٍ, (Mṣb,) *say ye to him* اِعْضَضْ بِأَيْرِ أَبِيكَ, (Mgh, O, L, Mṣb,) or اعضض أَيْرَ أَبِيكَ, (Ḳ,) [*Bite thou the* اير *of thy father*,] *and use not a metonymical term* for it, by saying هن for اير. (Mgh, O, L, Ḳ.) —— أَعْضَضْتُهُ سَيْفِى † [*I made my sword to wound him;*] *I smote him with my sword*. (Ṣ, O, Ḳ.) And أَعَضَّ السَّيْفَ بِسَاقِ البَعِيرِ ‡ [*He made the sword to wound the thigh*, or *shank, of the camel*]. (A, TA.) And أَعَضَّ المَحَاجِمَ قَفَاهُ (Lḥ, A, O*) ‡ *He made the cupping-instruments to cleave to the back of his neck*. (Lḥ.) = أَعَضَّتِ البِئْرُ † *The well became such as is termed* عَضُوض. (Ṣ, O, Ḳ.) = أَعَضُّوا *Their camels ate* [*the provender called*] عُضّ: (Ṣ, O, Ḳ:) and *their camels pastured upon* [*the trees called*] عِضّ, (Ṣ, O,) or عِضَاض. (L.) —— And اعضّت الأَرْضُ *The land abounded with* عِضّ, (Ṣ, O,) or عُضّ, (Ḳ,) or both. (TA.)

6: see 3.

عُضٌّ *The provender*, or *fodder, of the people of the cities* or *towns; such as the dregs of sesame-grain from which the oil has been expressed, and crushed date-stones:* (Ṣ, O, TA:) or *dough with which camels are fed:* (AḤn, O, Ḳ:) and [the *trefoil called*] قَتّ, (AḤn, O, Ḳ,) i. e. فِصْفِصَة: (AḤn, O:) and *barley and wheat, not mixed with any other thing:* (AA, O, Ḳ:) or *date-stones* (Ḳ, TA) *crushed*, (TA,) *and* قَتّ, (Ḳ, TA,) *with which camels are fed:* (TA:) and *thick*, or *coarse, trees* [or *shrubs*] *remaining in the earth;* (AA, O, Ḳ;) as also ▼ عُضَاض: (AA, O:) or *date-stones* (Ḳ, TA) *crushed*, (TA,) *and dough:* (Ḳ, TA:) and *barley* (Ḳ, TA) *with one of those two things;* (TA;) but 'Alee Ibn-Ḥamzeh disallows its application to date-stones: (IB, TA:) or *thick, large firewood, collected:* (Ḳ, TA:) and *dry herbage* (Ḳ, TA) *with which beasts are fed*. (TA.) [See an ex. in a verse cited in art. صلب, conj. 2.] —— See also the next paragraph, last sentence, in two places.

عِضٌّ [is of the measure فِعْلٌ, in the sense of the measure فَاعِلٌ in some cases, and in the sense of the measure مَفْعُولٌ in other cases; but appears to have only tropical significations]. —— ‡ A lock *that will scarcely open;* or *that is not near to opening;* expl. by لَا يَكَادُ يَنْفَتِحُ: (Ṣ, A, O, Ḳ;) or *that will not open*. (TA.) —— ‡ One *who keeps close to his property:* (TA:) a man *who improves his means of subsistence and his property, attends closely to it, and manages it well:* (L:) or a *manager of property:* (Ḳ:) or عِضُّ مَالٍ signifies one *who manages property well:* (A:) or *who manages property vigorously*. (Ṣ, O.) —— ‡ *Niggardly, tenacious*, or *avaricious:* (Ḳ, TA:) for a man's keeping close to his property generally causes him to fall into niggardliness: or such a person is likened to a lock that will not open. (TA.) —— ‡ *Evil in disposition;* (Lth, O, Ḳ, TA;) *bad, wicked*, or *malignant*. (TA.) —— ‡ A *strong* man; (IAạr, T, A, Ḳ;) as also ▼ عِضْعِضٌ. (IAạr, T, TA.) It is said in the A that العِضْعِضُ and العِضُّ signify الشَّدِيدُ: and in one place in the Ḳ, that العِضْعِضُ signifies العِضُّ الشَّدِيدُ: and by Ṣgh, in his two books, [the O and TṢ,] as on the authority of IAạr, that العِضْعِضُ signifies العِضُّ الشَّدِيدُ: but the correct reading is that which is given in the T, with which other lexicons agree. (TA.) —— ‡ *Having strength*, or *power, sufficient for a thing*. (Ḳ.) You say, هُوَ عِضُّ سَفَرٍ ‡ *He has strength*, or *power, sufficient for travel:* (Ṣ, A, O:) *he is rendered experienced*, or *expert, by travels:* of the measure فِعْلٌ in the sense of the measure مَفْعُولٌ. (A, TA.) And عِضُّ قِتَالٍ ‡ *Having strength*, or *power, sufficient for fight*. (TA.) —— † *An equal in courage*, or *generally;* or *an opponent*, or *adversary;* syn. قِرْنٌ: (O, Ḳ:) of another; (TA;) as also ▼ عَضِيضٌ. (TA.) [See the latter, below.] —— ‡ *Cunning*, or *intelligent*, or *skilful and knowing, and contentious;* in the sense of the measure فَاعِلٌ, because such a person defames, or speaks evil of, or backbites, others: (A, TA:) ‡ *understanding and knowing obscure*, or *abstruse, things:* (A, TA:) † *eloquent, and cunning* or *intelligent* or *skilful and knowing:* (Ṣ, O, Ḳ:) and [simply] † *cunning;* syn. دَاهٍ; applied to a man: (Ṣ, O:) or † *very cunning;* syn. دَاهِيَةٌ: (Ḳ:) pl. [of mult.] عُضُوضٌ (O, Ḳ) and [of pauc.] أَعْضَاضٌ. (TA.) = Also *i. q.* شِرْسٌ, i. e. (AZ, Ṣ, O) *Such as are small, of thorny trees*, (AZ, Ṣ, O, Ḳ,) *as the* شُبْرُم *and* حَاج *and* شِبْرِق *and* لَصَف *and* عِتْر *and the smaller* قَتَاد (AZ, Ṣ, O) *and* نُغْر *and* عَقَلَة [app. a mistranscription]; (AZ, TA;) as also ▼ عُضّ, (Ḳ, TA,) accord. to AḤn: (TA:) or the طَلْح *and* عَوْسَج *and* سَلَم *and* سَيَال *and* شَبَهَان *and* سَمُر *and* عُرْفُط *and* سَرْح *and* كَنَهْبَل; (Ḳ, TA;) as also ▼ عُضّ: (CḲ:) or the كنهبل and سيال and عرفط and سمر and عوسج are of the trees called عِضَاه [q. v.]. (AZ, TA.)

عَضَّةٌ [*A bite*]. (A and TA voce ضَمْزٌ, q. v.)

عَضَاضٌ (Ibn-Buzurj, Ṣ, A, O, Ḳ) and ▼ عَضُوضٌ (Ibn-Buzurj, Ṣ, O, Ḳ) and ▼ مَعْضُوضٌ (Ibn-Buzurj) *A thing to be bitten* (Ibn-Buzurj, Ṣ, A, O, Ḳ) *and eaten*. (Ṣ, O, Ḳ.) You say, مَا أَتَانَا مِنْ عَضَاضٍ, and ▼ عَضُوضٍ, and ▼ مَعْضُوضٍ, *He brought not to us anything that we might bite*. (Ibn-Buzurj.) And مَا عِنْدَنَا عَضُوضٌ ▼ and عَضَاضٌ, *We have not what is to be bitten and eaten*. (Ṣ, O.) And مَا ذُقْتُ عَضَاضًا *I have not tasted a thing to be bitten*. (A.) —— Also عَضَاضٌ, *Trees* [or *shrubs*] *that have become thick*, or *coarse:* (Ḳ:) or *plants that have become thick*, or *coarse, and dry*, or *tough, and hard*. (TA.) See also عُضّ. = See also the next paragraph, in two places.

عِضَاضٌ, (ISk, Ṣ, Mṣb, Ḳ,) with kesr, (Ṣ, Mṣb,) like كِتَابٌ, (Ḳ,) or ▼ عَضَاضٌ, (Sb, A,) like سَحَابٌ, (A,) a subst., like سِبَابٌ, not an inf. n., (Sb,) and ▼ عَضِيضٌ, (ISk, Ṣ, Mṣb,) The *act*, or *fault, of biting*, (Ṣ,* Mṣb,* Ḳ,* TA,) in a beast, (ISk, A, TA,) or a horse. (Mṣb, Ḳ.) You say (Yaạḳoob, Ṣ, TA) to the purchaser of a beast, when selling it, (TA,) بَرِئْتُ إِلَيْكَ مِنَ العِضَاضِ, and ▼ العَضِيضِ, (Yaạḳoob, Ṣ, O, TA,) i. e. [*I am irresponsible to thee for*] its *biting* men; (TA;) or مِنْ عَضَاضِ ▼ هٰذِهِ الدَّابَّةِ [*for the biting of this beast*]. (A.) And دَابَّةٌ ذَاتُ عَضِيضٍ ▼ and عِضَاضٍ [*A beast having a fault of biting*]. (TA.) = فُلَانٌ عِضَاضُ عَيْشٍ † *Such a one endures distress, or affliction, with patience*. (Ṣ, O, Ḳ.)

عَضُوضٌ A horse *that bites;* (Ṣ, O, Mṣb;) [i. e. *that has a habit of biting;* or *that bites much;* as the form of the word indicates;] and a camel; as also ▼ عَضَّاضٌ. (TA.) —— ‡ A bow *having its string cleaving*, or *sticking, to its* عَجْس [or *handle*]. (A, O, Ḳ. [Omitted in the TA.]) —— ‡ A woman *narrow in the* فَرْج, (O,* Ḳ, TA,) *so that the* ذَكَر *will not penetrate into it;* (TA;) as also ▼ تَعْضُوضَةٌ: (Ḳ:) the latter is thought by Az to have this signification. (O, TA.) —— ‡ A well *that is deep*, or *having its bottom distant*, (Ṣ, A, O, L, Ḳ,) *and narrow*, (Ṣ, O,) *from which one draws by means of the* سَانِيَة; (Ṣ, O, L;) as though it bit the water-drawer by the distress which it occasions him; (A;) and in like manner a water; (L;) and waters; as also ▼ عَضِيضٌ: ("Nawádir" of AA:) or a well *distressing to the water-drawer:* (TA:) or a well *having much water:* (O, Ḳ:) pl. عُضُضٌ, (as in some copies of the Ṣ and Ḳ, and in the O and TA,) or عُضُضٌ, (as in other copies of the Ṣ and Ḳ,) and عِضَاضٌ. (Ḳ.) —— ‡ *Severe; grievous; distressing; afflictive:* applied to time, or fortune; (Ṣ, A, O, Ḳ;) and to war. (TA.) —— ‡ *Unjust*, or *tyrannical*, rule, or dominion; (A, O, Ḳ, TA;) as though the subjects thereof were bitten; (O, TA;) an intensive epithet. (TA.) —— ‡ *A calamity; a misfortune*. (O, L, Ḳ, TA.) = See also عَضَاضٌ, in three places.

عَضِيضٌ: see عِضَاضٌ, in three places. = † *An associate; a companion:* or *an equal in age:* syn. قَرِينٌ: (O, Ḳ:) of another. (O, TA.) See also عِضٌّ. —— Applied to waters, *i. q.* عَضُوضٌ, q. v. ("Nawádir" of AA.) —— In the A and Ḳ, written by mistake for عِضْعِضٌ, as mentioned above, voce عِضٌّ. (TA.)

عَضَّاضٌ : see عَضُوضٌ, first signification.

عَضْعَضٌ : see عِضٌّ.

عَاضٌّ A camel *that feeds upon the trees called* عِضّ. (ISk, Ṣ, O.)

تَعْضُوضٌ *A sort of black dates,* (Ṣ, O, Ḳ,) *sweet,* (Ḳ,) *very sweet, the place of origin of which is Hejer:* (Ṣ, O:) n. un. with ة: (Ṣ, O, Ḳ:) which latter is said by AḤn to be *a date of a colour like that of the spleen, large, succulent, melliferous, luscious:* and [also *a tree producing such dates;* for] he mentions his having been told that the تَعْضُوضَة bears, in Hejer, a thousand pounds, of the weight of the pound of El-'Irák. (O.)

تَعْضُوضَةٌ n. un. of تَعْضُوضٌ [q. v.]. — See also عَضُوضٌ, third signification.

مَعَضٌّ [lit. *A place in which to bite.* — And hence,] *i. q.* مُسْتَمْسَكٌ ‡ [*A place in which,* or *on which, to lay hold:* and *a thing on which to lay hold*]. (Ṣ, A, O, Mṣb.) So in the saying مَا لَنَا فِى الأَرْضِ مَعَضٌّ ‡ [*There is not for us, in the earth, any place in which,* or *on which, to lay hold;* meaning, *in which to settle*]. (A, TA.) And in the saying مَا لَنَا فِى هٰذَا الأَمْرِ مَعَضٌّ ‡ [*There is not for us, in this affair, anything on which to lay hold*]. (Ṣ, O, Mṣb,* TA.)

مُعِضٌّ One *whose camels feed upon* [*the trees called*] عِضّ (Ṣ, O) [and *upon* عُضّ also: see the verb]. — And أَرْضٌ مُعِضَّةٌ *Land abounding with* [*the trees called*] عِضّ (Ṣ) [and *with* عُضّ].

حِمَارٌ مُعَضَّضٌ *An ass bitten much by other asses,* (O, Ḳ,) *and lacerated with their teeth.* (O.)

مَعْضُوضٌ [pass. part. n. of 1; *Bitten:* &c.] — See also عَضَّاضٌ, in two places.

عضب

1. عَضَبَهُ, (Ṣ, O, Mṣb, Ḳ,) aor. ـِ, (Mṣb, Ḳ,) inf. n. عَضْبٌ, (Ṣ, A, O, &c.,) *He cut,* or *cut off, him,* or *it.* (Ṣ, A,* Mgh,* O, Mṣb, Ḳ.) مَا لَهُ عَضَبَهُ اللّٰهُ, meaning [*What aileth him?*] *may God cut off* (O, TA) *his arm and his leg,* or *his hand and his foot,* (O,) or *his arms and his legs,* or *his hands and his feet,* is a form of imprecation used by the Arabs. (TA.) And hence, (O,) one says, إِنَّ الحَاجَةَ لَيَعْضِبُهَا طَلَبُهَا قَبْلَ وَقْتِهَا † *Verily the seeking of the object of want before its time assuredly cuts it off,* or *precludes it, and mars it:* a prov. (O, TA.) And إِنَّكَ لَتَعْضِبُنِى عَنْ حَاجَتِى † *Verily thou cuttest me off from* [*the attainment of*] *the object of my want.* (TA.) — And [hence] † *He reviled him;* (A,* Ḳ;) and (A) so عَضَبَهُ بِلِسَانِهِ. (Ṣ, A, O.) — And *He beat him,* or *struck him,* (O, Ḳ,) with a staff, or stick. (O.) — And *He thrust him,* or *pierced him,* (Ḳ,) with a spear. (TḲ.) [But in the O and TA, عَضَبَهُ بِالرُّمْحِ is expl. by the words هُوَ أَنْ تَشْغَلَهُ عَنْهُ; and the meaning app. is, *I occupied him so as to divert him with the spear;* though this meaning would be expressed more agreeably with usage by saying هو ان يشغله عنه; or rather هو ان تَشْغَلَهُ عَنْكَ, which, I think, is the right reading.] — And *It* (disease, O) *rendered him weak,* or *infirm:* (Ṣ, O:) and (O) *deprived him of the power of motion.* (A,* O, Ḳ.) You say, عَضَبَتْهُ الزَّمَانَةُ, aor. as above, (O, TA,) and so the inf. n., (TA,) meaning [*Disease of long continuance,* or *want of some one or more of the limbs,*] *deprived him of the power of motion:* and AHeyth says, it [in the O هُوَ (so that it does not refer to الزمانة), and in the TA العضب,] is الخَبَلُ and الشَّلَلُ and العَرَجُ [*a state of privation of the power of motion,* and *unsoundness,* and *lameness;* app. meaning that these are the effects denoted by the phrase عضبته الزمانة]. (O, TA.) — See also 4. — عَضَبَ, (O, Ḳ,) aor. and inf. n. as above, (Ḳ,) signifies also *He returned* (O, Ḳ) عَلَيْهِ [*against him*]. (O.) — عَضِبَ, said of a ram, (Ḳ,) or عَضِبَتْ, said of a شَاة [i. e. sheep or goat, male or female], (Ṣ, O, Mṣb,) aor. ـَ, (Mṣb, Ḳ,) inf. n. عَضَبٌ, (Ṣ, O, Mṣb,) *He,* or *she, had the inner* [*part of the*] *horn broken:* (Ṣ, O, Mṣb, Ḳ:) or *had one of the horns broken.* (Ṣ, O, Mṣb.) — العَضَبُ is mostly used in relation to the horn: but sometimes, in relation to the ear: (A'Obeyd, TA:) one says of a شَاة [expl. above], and of a she-camel, عَضِبَتْ, inf. n. عَضَبٌ, meaning *He,* or *she, had her ear slit,* or *had a slit ear:* (Mṣb:) [or *had half,* or *a third, of the ear cut off;* for] accord. to IAạr, العَضَبُ in relation to the ear is when half, or a third, thereof has gone. (O.) — عَضُبَ, aor. ـُ, inf. n. عُضُوبَةٌ (Ṣ, O, Ḳ) and عُضُوبٌ, (O, Ḳ,) said of a man's tongue, ‡ *It was,* or *became, sharp in speech;* (Ṣ, O,* Ḳ, TA;) being likened to a sharp sword. (O.)

3. عاضبهُ *i. q.* رَادَّهُ [*He endeavoured to turn him* from, or to, a thing]. (O, Ḳ.)

4. اعضب, (Fr, Ṣ, O, Mṣb, Ḳ,*) inf. n. إِعْضَابٌ; (Ḳ;) and ▼ عَضَبَ, (Fr, O, Ḳ,) aor. ـِ, inf. n. عَضْبٌ; (Ḳ;) *He rendered* a شَاة [i. e. sheep or goat, male or female], (Fr, Ṣ, O, Mṣb, Ḳ,) and a she-camel, (Mṣb, Ḳ,) *such as is termed* عَضْبَآء. (Fr, Ṣ, O, Mṣb, Ḳ.)

7. انعضب *It* (a horn) *became cut,* or *broken, off.* (TA.)

عَضْبٌ *A sharp sword;* (Ṣ, O, Mṣb;) an inf. n. (Mṣb, TA) used as a subst. [properly so termed], (Mṣb,) or as an epithet (TA) applied to a sword as meaning *sharp:* (TA:) or it signifies *a sword.* (Ḳ.) — And † A tongue *sharp in speech;* (Ṣ, TA;) likened to a sharp sword: (TA:) and so applied to a man; (Ḳ;) or so عَضْبُ اللِّسَانِ. (O.) — And, applied to a boy, or young man, (O, Ḳ, TA,) † *Light-headed:* (Ḳ:) or *light,* or *active, sharp-headed, light in body;* (IAạr, O, TA;*) as also عَضُبٌ. (IAạr, TA.) — And † The offspring of the cow *when his horn comes forth,* (Aṣ, O, Ḳ, TA,) which is *after he is a year old:* (Aṣ, O, TA:) or, accord. to Eṭ-Ṭáïfee, *when his horn is* [or *can be*] *laid hold upon:* fem. with ة: after that, he is termed جَذَعٌ; then, ثَنِىٌّ; then, رَبَاعٌ; then, سَدَسٌ; then, تَمَّمٌ; and when all his teeth are grown, عَمَمٌ. (O, L, TA.)

عَضَبٌ inf. n. of عَضِبَ [q. v.]. (Ṣ, &c.) — Also *A fracture* in a spear. (TA.)

عَضَّابٌ † A man *who reviles much.* (Ṣ, A, O.)

أَعْضَبُ applied to a ram, and the fem. عَضْبَآءُ applied to a شَاة [i. e. sheep or goat, male or female], *Having the inner* [*part of the*] *horn* (*which is called the* مُشَاش, AZ, Ṣ, O) *broken:* (AZ, Ṣ, O, Mṣb, Ḳ; and so in the Mgh as applied to a شَاة:) or *having one of the horns broken.* (Ṣ, O, Mṣb.) — And the masc. applied to a camel, (Mṣb, TA,) and the fem. applied to a she-camel (Ṣ, O, Mṣb, Ḳ) and to a شَاة [expl. above], (Ṣ, Mgh, Mṣb, Ḳ,) *Having a slit ear.* (Ṣ, Mgh, O, Mṣb, Ḳ.) The she-camel of the Prophet, called العَضْبَآء, was not slit-eared; this being only her surname: (Ṣ, IAth, Mgh, O, Mṣb, Ḳ:) or, accord. to some, the fewer number, she was slit-eared: (IAth, TA:) or her name was taken from the epithet عضباء applied to a she-camel as meaning "short in the fore leg." (Z, TA.) — And the fem. is applied to a horse's ear as meaning *Of which more than a fourth part has been cut off.* (Ḳ.) — And, applied to she-camel, *Short in the fore-leg;* as mentioned above: (Z, TA:) and the masc., (O, Ḳ,) applied to a man, (O,) *short in the arm.* (O, Ḳ.) — Also the masc., applied to a man, † *Who has no aider against an enemy,* (Ṣ, O, Ḳ,) *nor brethren:* (O:) and one *whose brother has died:* or *who has no brother, nor any one* [*beside*]. (Ḳ.)

مَعْضُوبٌ *Weak,* or *infirm.* (Ṣ, O, Ḳ.) And *Crippled,* or *deprived of the power of motion, by disease,* or *by a protracted disease.* (A, Mgh, O, Mṣb, Ḳ.) — And مَعْضُوبُ اللِّسَانِ *Impotent in tongue; having an impediment in his speech.* (TA.)

عضد

1. عَضَدَهُ, aor. ـُ, (Ṣ, O, Mṣb, Ḳ,) inf. n. عَضْدٌ, (Mṣb,) *He hit,* or *hurt, his* عَضُد [or *upper arm, between the elbow and the shoulder-blade*]; (Ṣ, O, Mṣb, Ḳ;) i. e., a man's. (Mṣb.) — And, aor. as above, (Ṣ, A, &c.,) and so the inf. n., (Mṣb,) ‡ *He aided,* or *assisted, him;* (Ṣ, A, O, Mṣb, Ḳ;) *he was,* or *became, an* عَضُد i. e. *aider,* or *assistant, to him:* (Mṣb:) thus used, it is doubly tropical; for عَضُد primarily [and properly] relates to the arm, then it was metaphorically applied to signify an aider, or assistant, then they formed the verb in this meaning, and it obtained so extensively as to become a حَقِيقَة عُرْفِيَّة [i. e. a word so much used in this tropical sense as to be, in the said sense, conventionally regarded as proper]; therefore it is not mentioned by Z [in the A] as tropical; (TA;) and ▼ عاضدهُ, (Ḳ,* TA,) inf. n. مُعَاضَدَةٌ, (Ṣ, A, O, TA,) likewise signifies *he aided him* against another. (Ṣ,* Ḳ,* TA.) — Also, عَضَدَهُ, *He* (a camel) *took him* (another camel) *by his* عَضُد [i. e. *arm*], *and threw him down.* (L.) — عَضَدَهُ فِى العَضُدِ [*He bound it,* or

attached it, upon the عضد (or *upper arm*)]; namely, a thong, or the like; (O, Ḳ, TA;) such, for instance, as an amulet. (TA.) —— عَضَدَ الدَّابَّةَ, aor. ـُ, [thus I find it in this instance,] inf. n. عُضُودٌ [in the TA عضد,] *He walked by the side* [as though *by the* عَضُد (or *arm*)] *of the beast,* (L, Mṣb,) *on the right* or *left,* (Mṣb,) or *sometimes on its right and sometimes on its left, not quitting it.* (L.) —— عَضَدَ الرَّكَائِبَ, (L, Ḳ,) aor. ـِ, inf. n. عَضْدٌ, (L,) *He came to the camels,* or *other beasts, used for riding, from the tracts,* or *parts, surrounding them, and gathered them together.* (L, Ḳ.*) —— See also 4. —— عَضَدَ الشَّجَرَ, aor. ـِ, (Ṣ, Mgh, O, &c.,) inf. n. عَضْدٌ, (Mgh, Mṣb,) ‡ *He cut,* or *lopped, the trees* (Ṣ, Mgh, O, Mṣb, Ḳ*) *with a* مِعْضَد; (Ṣ;) as also ↓ اِسْتَعْضَدَهُ. (Hr, O, Ḳ.*) —— And عَضَدَ الشَّجَرَةَ ‡ *He scattered the leaves from the tree for his camels.* (Th, TA.) —— عَضَدَهُ القَتَبُ, (O, Ḳ,) inf. n. عَضْدٌ, (TA,) *The saddle galled and wounded him;* namely, a camel. (O, Ḳ.) ═ عُضِدَ, (L, Ḳ,) a verb like عُنِىَ, (Ḳ,) *He had a complaint of his* عضد [or *upper arm*]. (L, Ḳ.) And in like manner are formed verbs relating to all other members, or parts of the body. (L.) ═ عَضِدَ *He* (a camel) *had the disease termed* عَضَدٌ [q. v.]. (Ṣ, O, Ḳ.)

2: see 4, in two places.

3: see 1, second sentence.

4. اعضد المَطَرُ, and ↓ عضّد, *The moisture of the rain reached* [or *penetrated*] *to the* [*measure of the*] عَضُد [or *upper arm*]. (L.) —— رَمَى فَأَعْضَدَ, as also ↓ عضّد, inf. n. تَعْضِيدٌ; [and app. ↓ عَضَدَ likewise, said of an arrow; (see its part. n. عَاضِدٌ;)] ‡ *He shot,* or *cast, and it* [i. e. the arrow or other missile] *went to the right and left* (O, Ḳ) [or *fell on the right,* or *left, of the butt:* see عَاضِدٌ].

5: see 8.

6. تعاضدوا ‡ *They aided,* or *assisted, one another.* (O, Mṣb, Ḳ.)

8. اعتضدهُ *He put it,* or *placed it,* (i. e. a thing, Ṣ,) *upon* (فِى) *his* عَضُد [or *upper arm*]: (Ṣ, O, Ḳ:) [or] *he placed it under his arm;* as also ↓ تعضّدهُ; syn. اِحْتَضَنَهُ. (A.) ═ اعتضد ‡ *He became strong; or he strengthened himself.* (TA.) —— اعتضد بهِ † *He asked, begged,* or *desired, aid,* or *assistance, of him.* (Ṣ, A, O, Ḳ.)

10. استعضدهُ: see 1, last quarter. —— Also *He gathered it;* namely, fruit; (O, Ḳ;) *he cut it off and gathered it from a tree, to eat it.* (Hr, O.*)

عَضْدٌ: see عَضُدٌ, first sentence: —— and عِضَادٌ.

عُضْدٌ: / عِضْدٌ: } see عَضُدٌ, first sentence.

عَضَدٌ *A certain disease in the* أَعْضَاد [or *arms* (pl. of عَضُدٌ)] *of camels,* (Ṣ, O, Ḳ,) *on account of which they are slit* [*in those parts*]. (Ṣ, O.) ═ And ‡ What is *cut,* or *lopped,* of trees; (Ṣ, O, Ḳ;) as also ↓ عَضِيدٌ (TA) and ↓ مَعْضُودٌ: (Ṣ, O:) or العَضَدُ signifies *what is cut,* or *lopped, from trees;* or *the leaves that are made to fall by beating trees, and used as food for camels;* as also ↓ عَضِيدٌ: (TA:) or *the leaves scattered off from a tree for camels.* (Th, TA.) ═ See also عَضُدٌ, first sentence: —— and again, near the middle, in two places.

عَضُدٌ, (Ṣ, O, Mṣb, Ḳ,) which is the most common form of the word, (TA,) and ↓ عَضِدٌ, (Ṣ, O, Mṣb, Ḳ,) of the dial. of Asad, (O, Mṣb,) and ↓ عُضُدٌ, (AZ, O, Mṣb, Ḳ,) of the dial. of Tihámeh, (AZ, TA,) or of El-Ḥijáz, (Mṣb,) and ↓ عَضَدٌ, (Th, TA,) and ↓ عَضْدٌ, (Ṣ, O, Mṣb, Ḳ,) of the dials. of Temeem and Bekr, (O, Mṣb,) and ↓ عُضْدٌ, (Ṣ, O, Mṣb, Ḳ,) and ↓ عِضْدٌ, (Ḳ,) the last three of which are said to be contractions of the first or second, or variants thereof formed to assimilate them to other words preceding them; (TA;) all masc. and fem.; (L;) or fem. only; (Lḥ, TA;) or masc. in the dial. of Tihámeh; (AZ, L;) or fem. in the dial. of Tihámeh, and masc. in the dial. of Temeem; (AZ, Mṣb;) *i. q.* سَاعِدٌ, (Ṣ, L,) i. e. [The *upper arm,* or *upper half of the arm,*] *from the elbow to the shoulder-blade,* (Ṣ,) or the *part between the elbow and the shoulder-blade,* (L, O, Mṣb, Ḳ,) of a human being: (L:) [and in a beast, the *arm;* (see أَبْضَةٌ &c.;) in this case like ذِرَاعٌ:] pl. أَعْضُدٌ and أَعْضَادٌ, (Mṣb,) or only the latter, (L,) which is used in a poem of Sá'ideh Ibn-Ju-eiyeh as meaning the *legs* of bees. (TA.) مَلَأَ مِنْ شَحْمٍ عَضُدِى, in the story of Umm-Zarạ, means † *He filled with fat,* not peculiarly *my* عَضُد, but *my whole body;* for when the عَضُد becomes fat, the whole body becomes so. (O, L.) —— [Hence,] عَضُدٌ [in the CḲ العُضُدُ is erroneously put for العَضُدُ] signifies also ‡ *An aider,* or *assistant;* (L, Ḳ, TA;) and so [app. any of its variants mentioned above, and] ↓ عَاضِدٌ (TA) and ↓ عِضَادَةٌ. (L, TA.) And it is also used for [its pl.] أَعْضَادٌ; as in the Ḳur xviii. 49, in which the sing. form is said to be employed for the sake of agreement with the other verses [preceding and following], that they may all end with singulars: (TA:) but one also says, هُمْ أَعْضَادِى and عَضُدِى ‡ [*They are my aiders,* or *assistants*]. (O, Ḳ, TA.) And one says, فُلَانٌ عَضُدِى, meaning † *Such a one is my support,* or *stay.* (Mṣb.) And فَتَّ فِى عَضُدِهِ † *He broke some of the intentions, purposes,* or *designs, of his aiders,* or *assistants,* (or *of the people of his house,* TA,) *and separated,* or *dispersed, them from him:* (O, Ḳ:) or *he sought to injure him by diminishing,* or *impairing,* [*in number* or *power,*] *the people of his house;* (T and O in art. فت;) and in like manner, فَتَّ فِى أَعْضَادِهِ. (TA in the present art.) And فَتَّ فِى عَضُدِى وَهَدَّ رُكْنِى † *He broke my strength, and dispersed,* or *separated, my aiders,* or *assistants:* (TA in art. فت:) [for] عَضُدٌ signifies also ‡ *Strength,* because the part so called, of a man, is a mean of strength to him. (L.) سَنَشُدُّ عَضُدَكَ بِأَخِيكَ, in the Ḳur [xxviii. 35], means, accord. to Zj, ‡ *We will aid thee,* or *assist thee, by thy brother.* (L.) —— Also † The *side* of the armpit; and so ↓ عَضْدٌ. (L.) And † *A side* of a road; (O, L; [in this sense written in the TA عَضَدٌ;]) as also ↓ عِضَادَةٌ. (L.) † *The side,* or *quarter,* from which the wind blows. (L.) † *A side;* or *a lateral,* or *an outward,* or *adjacent, part,* or *portion; a quarter, region,* or *tract;* (O, L, Ḳ;) of a house, and of anything: pl. أَعْضَادٌ. (L.) [Hence,] عَضُدُ الرَّكَائِبِ † *The tract,* or *part, surrounding the camels,* or *other beasts, used for riding.* (L.) One says, اِمْلِكْ أَعْضَادَ الإِبِلِ ‡ [lit. *Have thou possession of the tracts adjacent to the camels*], meaning *direct thou aright the course of the camels, so that they may not wander away to the right and left.* (A.) —— Also, and ↓ عَضْدٌ, (L,) and أَعْضَادٌ, (Ṣ, L, Ḳ,) which last is a pl. of the two preceding words, as is also عُضُودٌ, (L,) ‡ *A raised enclosing border,* or *such borders, of built work,* (Ṣ, O, L, Ḳ,) *&c.,* (Ṣ, L,) of a watering-trough or tank, and of a road, &c., (Ḳ,) or of anything, (Ṣ, O,) such as the أَعْضَاد of a watering-trough or tank, which are *stones,* (Ṣ,) or *broad and thin stones,* (L,) *set up around the brink;* (Ṣ, L;) also called عَضُدٌ; *extending from the place whence the water flows into it, to its hinder part:* (L:) or عَضُدٌ signifies the *two sides* of a watering-trough or tank: (IAạr, L:) or its *side:* (O, TA:) and its أَعْضَاد are its *sides:* and the أَعْضَاد of a portion of sown land that is separated from the parts adjacent to it by ridges of earth, for irrigation, are its *raised borders that confine the water;* (A;) أَعْضَادُ المَزَارِعِ signifying *the* [*raised*] *boundaries between the portions of sown land.* (En-Naḍr, L.) —— عَضُدٌ (O, Ḳ, in the CḲ عَضُد,) is also syn. with ↓ عَضِيدٌ, (Ḳ,) or ↓ عَضِيدَةٌ, (O,) as signifying † *A row* of palm-trees: (O, Ḳ:) the first of these words is mentioned by Hr as occurring in a trad., and is thus expl.: but others say that it is ↓ عَضِيدٌ, (TA,) which, accord. to Aṣ, signifies a palm-tree *having such a* [*low*] *trunk that one can reach from it* [*the fruit* or *branches*]; (Ṣ, TA;) and the pl. is عِضْدَانٌ: (Ṣ, Ḳ:) he adds that when it exceeds the reach of the hand it is called جَبَّارَةٌ. (Ṣ, TA.) عَضُدَا شِرَاكِ النَّعْلِ [and ↓ عِضَادَتَاهَا and عَضُدَا النَّعْلِ] signifies † *The two branches of the* شِرَاك *of the sandal,* described voce أُذُنٌ, q. v.;] *the two appertenances, of the sandal, that lie upon the foot.* (L.) —— عَضُدَا الرَّحْلِ † *The two pieces of wood that are attached to the fore part of the camel's saddle,* (L,) or *to the lower portions of its fore part* (the وَاسِط): (Lth, O, L:) or, accord. to AZ, *the upper portions of the* ظَلِفَتَانِ [a mistake for *the* حِنْوَانِ] *of the camel's saddle, next* [*the pieces of wood called*] *the* عَرَاقِى; *below them being the* ظَلِفَتَانِ, *which are the lower parts of the* مُؤْخِرَة *of the* وَاسِط *and of the* حِنْوَان. (O, L. [See ظَلِفَةٌ. In a similar manner, also, the term عَضُدَانِ is used in relation to a horse's saddle: see قَرَبُوسٌ.]) —— See also عِضَادٌ.

عَضِدٌ *Having a complaint of his* عَضُد [or upper arm]. (O, Ḳ.) — A camel *having the disease termed* عَضَد. (TA.) — One *that has drawn near*, or *approached, to the* عَضُدَانِ [i. e. the *two sides*] (O, TA) *of the watering-trough*, or *tank*. (O, Ḳ.) — A male [wild] ass *that has drawn together the she-asses* (الأُتُن) *from their several quarters* (مِنْ جَوَانِبِهَا); as also ↑ عَاضِدٌ: (O, Ḳ:) the former occurs in a verse of El-Akhṭal, describing a sportsman shooting at [wild] asses. (O.) — يَدٌ عَضِدَةٌ *An arm of which the* عَضُد [or *portion between the elbow and the shoulder-blade*] *is short*. (ISk, Ṣ, O, Ḳ.) And عَضُدٌ عَضِدَةٌ *A short upper arm*. (TA.) ═ See also عَضُدٌ, first sentence. — And see عِضَادٌ.

عُضُدٌ: see عَضُدٌ, first sentence.

عُضَادٌ and عِضَادٌ A woman *thick and ugly in the* عَضُد [or *upper arm*]: (Fr, O,* Ḳ:) or, as some say, *short*. (TA.) And the former, applied to a man and to a woman, signifies *Short*: (O, Ḳ:) or this epithet is applied to a woman, and ↑ عَضُدٌ and ↑ عَضِدٌ and ↑ عُضُدٌ are applied in this sense to a man. (L.) And عُضَادٌ, [in the CḲ and my MS. copy of the Ḳ عِضَادٌ, but it is] like رُبَاعٍ, applied to a boy, or young man, *Short, compact, of moderate dimensions*, (O, Ḳ, TA,) *firm in make*. (TA.) — نَاقَةٌ عُضَادٌ *A she-camel that does not come to the watering-trough*, or *tank, to drink, until it is left to her unoccupied; that cuts herself off from the other camels*: (O, L:) such is also termed قَذُورٌ. (L.)

عِضَادٌ: see مِعْضَدٌ, in three places. — Also *A mark made with a hot iron upon the* عَضُد [or *arm*] *of a camel*, (Ibn-Ḥabeeb, Ṣ, O, TA,) *crosswise*. (Ibn-Ḥabeeb, TA.)

عَضِيدٌ: see عَضُدٌ, in two places: ═ and see عَضُدٌ, latter half, likewise in two places.

عِضَادَةٌ: see عَضُدٌ, in three places. — عِضَادَتَانِ also signifies ‡ The *two sides*, (L,) or *wooden side-posts, of a door*, (Ṣ, O, L,) *which are on the right and left of a person entering it*. (L.) One says, وَقَفَا كَأَنَّهُمَا عِضَادَتَانِ ‡ *They two stood still as though they were two side-posts of a door*. (A.) And فُلَانٌ عِضَادَةُ فُلَانٍ ‡ *Such a one is the close attendant of such a one; not quitting him*. (A.) [See also عَنْمَةُ الوَدَجِ, in art. عنم.] — Also The *two sides* of a buckle and the like: each of them is called عِضَادَةٌ. (L.) — And The *two sides* [or *branches*] of a bit. (Az, TA voce قَيْقَبٌ.) — And *Two pieces of wood in the yoke that is upon the neck of a bull that draws a cart* or *the like*: the piece that is in the middle is called الوَاسِطُ. (O, L.)

عَضِيدَةٌ: see عَضُدٌ, latter half.

عُضَادِيٌّ (Ṣ, O, Mṣb, Ḳ) and عِضَادِيٌّ (O, Mṣb, Ḳ) and عَضَادِيٌّ (O, Ḳ) A man *large in the* عَضُد [or *upper arm*]. (Ṣ, O, Mṣb, Ḳ.)

عَاضِدٌ: see عَضِدٌ, former half: — and see also عَضُدٌ. — Also A he-camel *that takes the* عَضُد [or *arm*] *of a she-camel, and makes her lie down that he may cover her*. (Ṣ, O, Ḳ.) — And One *who walks by the side of a beast*, (O, Ḳ,) *on the right* or *left thereof*. (O.) — And † An arrow *that falls on the right* or *left of the butt*: pl. عَوَاضِدُ. (Mṣb.) — عَاضِدَانِ † *Two rows of palm-trees upon* [*the two sides of*] *a river*, or *rivulet*: and [the pl.] عَوَاضِدُ *palm-trees growing upon the sides of a river*. (L.) ═ And *A cutter*, or *lopper, of trees*. (TA.)

أَعْضَدُ A man (Ṣ) *slender in the* عَضُد [or *upper arm*]. (Ṣ, O, Ḳ.) And *Having one* عَضُد *shorter than the other*; (O;) *short in one of his* عَضُدَانِ. (Ḳ.)

مِعْضَدٌ *An amulet that is bound upon the* عَضُد [or *upper arm*]; as also ↑ عِضَادٌ: (TA:) and ↑ مِعْضَادٌ signifies *a thong*, or *the like*, (O, Ḳ,) *such as an amulet*, (TA,) *which thou bindest*, or *attachest*, (تُعَضِّدُهُ,) *upon the* عَضُد; (O, Ḳ;) *called in Pers.* بَازُوبَنْد. (TA.) Also, (O, Ḳ,) ↑ عِضَادٌ (Ṣ, O, Mṣb, Ḳ) and ↑ مِعْضَادٌ and ↑ مِعْضَدٌ (O, Ḳ) *An armlet, or bracelet for the arm*; syn. دُمْلُجٌ; (Lḥ, Ṣ, O, Mṣb, Ḳ;) which is thus called because it is [*worn*] *upon the* عَضُد, like a مِعْضَدَة: (Lḥ, TA:) pl. of the first مَعَاضِدُ. (A.) — And *An instrument with which trees are cut*, or *lopped*; (O, Ḳ;) as also ↑ مِعْضَادٌ: (TA:) *anything with which this is done*: described by an Arab of the desert as *a heavy iron instrument in the form of a reaping-hook, with which trees are cut*, or *lopped*: (AḤn, TA:) ↑ مِعْضَادٌ also, (TA,) or ↑ عِضَادٌ, (O, Ḳ,) signifies *an iron instrument like a reaping-hook*, (O, Ḳ, TA,) *without teeth, having its handle bound to a staff* or *cane*, (TA,) *with which the pastor draws down the branches of trees to his camels*, (O, Ḳ, TA,) or *his sheep* or *goats*: (TA:) and مِعْضَدٌ, *a sword which is commonly*, or *usually, employed for cutting*, or *lopping*, trees; (Ṣ, Mgh, O, Mṣb, Ḳ;) and so ↑ مِعْضَادٌ; (Ṣ, O, Ḳ;) which also signifies *a sword wherewith a butcher cuts bones*. (O, Ḳ.)

مِعْضَدَةٌ *A purse for money*; (O, Ḳ;) *the thing that the traveller binds upon his* عَضُد [or *upper arm*], *and wherein he puts the money for his expenses*. (Lḥ, TA.)

مُعَضَّدٌ ‡ A garment *having some figured*, or *embroidered, work on the place of the* عَضُد [or *upper arm*] (Ṣ, O, Ḳ) *of its wearer*: (Ṣ, O:) or *marked with stripes in the form of the* عَضُد: (TA:) or *of which its figured work is in its sides*: (Lḥ, TA:) or i. q. مُضَلَّعٌ [q. v.]. (A, TA.) — إِبِلٌ مُعَضَّدَةٌ *Camels branded upon the* عَضُد [or *arm*] *with the mark called* عِضَاد. (Ṣ, O, L.) — In a description of the Prophet, as related by Yaḥyà Ibn-Ma'een, the epithet مُعَضَّدٌ is applied to him, meaning *Firmly made*: but accord. to the relation commonly retained in the memory, it is مُقَصَّد [q. v.]. (TA.)

بُسْرٌ مُعَضِّدٌ † *Dates beginning to ripen on one side*. (Ṣ, O, Ḳ.)

مِعْضَادٌ: see مِعْضَدٌ, in five places.

مَعْضُودٌ: see عَضِدٌ.

يَعْضِيدٌ [a word of a very rare measure (see يَقْطِينٌ)] *A certain herb*, or *leguminous plant*; (Ṣ, O, Ḳ;) *also called* طَرْخَشْقُوق, (Ṣ, O, TA, [and hence supposed by Golius to be the *taraxicon*, with which the description has little agreement,] in the T تَرْخَجْقُوق, TA,) this being an Arabicized word from [the Pers.] تَلْخ چُكُوك: accord. to Aboo-Ziyád, it is *a herb*, or *leguminous plant, of those termed* أَحْرَار, *bitter, and having a yellow blossom, desired by the camels and the sheep* or *goats, and liked also by the horses, which thrive upon it; and it has a viscous milk*: (O:) it is *a herb*, or *leguminous plant, of which the blossom is more intensely yellow than the* وَرْس [q. v.]: or, as some say, it is *of the class of trees* (مِنَ الشَّجَرِ) [but this term شجر is often applied to small plants]): and some say that it is *of the herbs*, or *leguminous plants, of* [*the season called*] *the* رَبِيع, *having in it a bitterness*: thus in the M. (TA.)

عضرط

عِضْرِطٌ (A'Obeyd, Ṣ, O, Ḳ) and ↑ عُضْرُطٌ (Ḳ) The عِجَان, (A'Obeyd, Ibn-'Abbád, Ṣ, O, Ḳ,) which is [*the perinæum*, i. e.] *what is between the anus and the genitals*; (A'Obeyd, Ṣ, TA;) so in the dial. of Hudheyl; also called ↑ عُضَارِطِيٌّ: (Ibn-'Abbád, O:) and, (O, Ḳ,) some say, (O,) the اِسْت [or *anus itself*]; (O, Ḳ;) as also ↑ عُضَارِطِيٌّ: (Ḳ:) and, (O, Ḳ,) accord. to IAạr, (O,) the [*caudal bone called*] عُصْعُص: (O, Ḳ:) or [the meaning is that first expl. above, i. e.] the *line* [or *seam*] *that extends from the penis to the anus*; (Ḳ;) as in the M. (TA.) One says, فُلَانٌ أَهْلَبُ العُضْرُطِ *Such a one is a person having much hair* (Ṣ, O) *of the part between the anus and the genitals*, (Ṣ,) [or *of the anus*,] or *of the body*. (O.)

عِضْرِطٌ and ↑ عُضْرُوطٌ and ↑ عُضَارِطٌ *One who acts as a servant for the food of his belly*: and *a hired man*: pl. عَضَارِطُ and عَضَارِيطُ and عَضَارِطَةٌ: (Ḳ:) or عُضْرُوطٌ has the former of these significations; and the pl. is عَضَارِيطُ and عَضَارِطَةٌ: (Lth, O:) and the former, (Ṣ,) or each, (O,) of these two pls. signifies *followers*, (Ṣ, O,) and the *like of them*; (Ṣ;) and the sing. is عُضْرُطٌ and عُضْرُوطٌ: (Ṣ, O:) and accord. to Aṣ, عَضَارِيطُ signifies *hired men*; as also عَضَارِطُ; of which latter the sing. is عُضْرُطٌ. (O.) Also, [i. e. the three sings. above mentioned,] (Ḳ,) or ↑ عِضْرِطٌ, (Lth, O, TA,) with kesr, (TA,) The *base, low, ignoble, mean*, or *sordid*, (Lth, O, Ḳ, TA,) of men. (Lth, O, TA.) And قَوْمٌ عَضَارِيطُ means صَعَالِيكُ [i. e. *Poor*, or *needy, persons*: or *thieves*, or *robbers*]. (TA.)

عُضْرُوطٌ : see عَضْرَطٌ : — and see also عِضْرَطٌ.

عُضْرُوطٌ ; pl. عَضَارِيطُ and عَضَارِطَةٌ : see عُضْرُطٌ. — Also The œsophagus, or gullet, (مَرِىْءُ الحَلْقِ,) which is the head of the stomach, adherent to the حُلْقُوم, red, oblong, and white in its interior. (Ibn-'Abbád, O, Ḳ.) — And العَضَارِيطُ signifies [app. The axillary artery with its branches;] the veins that are in the arm-pit, between the two portions of flesh. (Ibn-'Abbád, O, Ḳ.)

عُضَارِطٌ : see عُضْرُطٌ.

عُضَارِطِىٌّ : see عَضْرَطٌ, in two places. — Also A flabby vulva. (Ḳ, TA.)

عضرفط

عَضْرَفُوطٌ The عُنْفُوط, (Ḳ,) [i. e.] a small creeping thing called عِسْوَدٌ, white, soft, or smooth, to which the fingers of girls are likened, found in the sands, and called by some عُضْفُوطٌ and عُنْفُوطٌ, of which the pls. are عَضَافِيطُ and عَنَافِيطُ : (Lth, O:) or the male of the [species of lizard called] عَظَآءَة ; (Ṣ, O, Ḳ;) and it is (O, Ḳ) said to be (O) one of the animals ridden by the jinn, or genii: (O, Ḳ:) pl. عَضَارِفُ and عَضْرَفُوطَاتٌ : (Lth, O, Ḳ:) dim. عُضَيْرِفٌ and عُضَيْرِيفٌ. (Ṣ.)

عضل

1. عَضَلَهَا, (Aṣ, Ṣ, O, Mṣb, Ḳ,) aor. ـُ and ـِ ; (Aṣ, Ṣ, O, Mṣb;) or it is مُثَلَّثَة, (Ḳ,) i. e. the aor. is ـُ and ـَ and ـِ, the first of which is the most chaste and most known, and the second is mentioned by such as IḲṭṭ and ISd, whereas the last is unknown and there is no reason for it; (MF;) or the author of the Ḳ may mean by this that the verb is like نَصَرَ and ضَرَبَ and عَلِمَ, not as one might understand it to mean at first sight; (TA; [but I do not find that any one has mentioned عَضِلَهَا ;]) inf. n. عَضْلٌ (Aṣ, Ṣ, O, Mṣb, Ḳ) and عِضْلٌ and عِضْلَانٌ ; (Fr, O, Ḳ;) and عضّلها ♦, (Ḳ, TA,) inf. n. تَعْضِيلٌ ; (TA;) He prevented, withheld, or debarred, her from marrying, (Aṣ, Ṣ, O, Mṣb, Ḳ, [الزَّوْجُ in the CḲ being a mistake for الزَّوْجَ,]) wrongfully; (Ḳ;) i. e., a woman, (Ḳ,) or his husbandless woman, (Ṣ, O,) or a woman highly esteemed by him. (Mṣb.) The primary signification of العَضْلُ is The act of straitening; (O;) or preventing, withholding, or debarring; and straitening. (Ḥam p. 466.) — عَضَلَ عَلَيْهِ : see 2. — عَضَلَ بِهِ : see 4. — عَضَلْتُهُ, inf. n. عَضْلٌ, I struck his عَضَلَة [i. e. muscle]. (TA.) — عَضِلَ, (Ṣ, O, Ḳ,) aor. ـَ, (Ḳ,) inf. n. عَضَلٌ, said of a man, (Ṣ, O,) [He was, or became, muscular, musculous, or brawny;] he had many عَضَلَات (Ṣ) or عَضَل (O, Ḳ) [i. e. muscles]: or he was large in the عَضَلَة [or muscle] of his shank. (Ḳ.)

2 : see 1, first sentence. — عضّل عَلَيْهِ, inf. n. تَعْضِيلٌ ; (Ṣ, O, TA;) or عَضَلَ ♦ عليه, (Ḳ, TA,) inf. n. عَضْلٌ ; (TA;) He straitened him (Ṣ, O, Ḳ, TA) in his affair, (Ṣ, O,) and intervened as an obstacle between him and that which he desired. (Ṣ, O, TA.) — عضّل الشَّىْءُ The thing was, or became, strait. (TA.) — عَضَّلَتْ, (Ṣ, O,) or عَضَّلَتْ بِوَلَدِهَا, (Ḳ,) inf. n. تَعْضِيلٌ ; (Ṣ;) and أَعْضَلَتْ ♦ ; (Ḳ;) said of a woman, (Ṣ, O, Ḳ,) and of a ewe or goat, (Ṣ, O,) She had her child, or young one, sticking fast [in her vagina], (Ṣ, O, TA,) and not coming forth easily, (Ṣ, O,) or so that part of it came forth and part did not, thus remaining: (TA:) or she had difficulty in bringing forth her child, or young one; (Ḳ,* TA:) and in like manner one says of a hen (Ḳ, TA) بِبَيْضِهَا, (TA,) and of others: (Ḳ, TA:) عضّلت [said of any bird] meaning the egg twisted, or became difficult [to be excluded] in her inside: (TA in art. عصل:) or عضّلت بولدها, said of a woman, means her child became choked in her vulva, and did not come forth nor go in [or back]: (Aboo-Málik, TA:) and عَضَّلَهَا وَلَدُهَا, occurring in a trad., said of a gazelle, means Her young one made her to be such as is termed مُعَضِّلَة, by sticking fast in her belly, not coming forth. (IAth, TA.) — And [hence,] عَضَّلَتِ الأَرْضُ بِأَهْلِهَا ‡ The land became choked with its people, (Ṣ, O, Ḳ, TA,) by reason of their multitude. (TA.) And عضّل المَكَانُ ‡ The place became strait, (Ḳ, TA,) بِهِمْ with them. (TA.) — See also 4. — عَضَّلَتِ النَّاقَةُ The she-camel became fatigued in consequence of travelling, and being ridden, and from any work. (TA.)

4. اعضل It (an affair) was, or became, hard, strait, or difficult, syn. اِشْتَدَّ ; (Ṣ, O, Mṣb;) and as though it were closed against one, syn. اِسْتَغْلَقَ. (Ṣ, O.) You say, اعضل بِهِ الأَمْرُ, (Ḳ, TA,) and عَضَلَ ♦ به, (IDrd, O, Ḳ,) and عَضَّلَ ♦ به, (TA, and Ḥam p. 258,) and اعضلهُ, (Ḳ, TA,) The affair was, or became, hard, strait, or difficult, to him, syn. اشتدّ ; (IDrd, O, Ḳ, TA, and Ḥam ubi suprà;) and as though it were closed against him, syn. استغلق. (TA.) — And أَعْضَلَنِى فُلَانٌ, (Ṣ,) or اعضل بِى, (O,) Such a one's affair, or case, wearied me. (Ṣ, O.) Hence the phrase, in a trad. of 'Omar, أَعْضَلَ بِى أَهْلُ الكُوفَةِ, (O,) i. e. [The people of El-Koofeh have caused that] the means of effecting my object in their affair, or case, have become strait to me, (O, TA,) and the treating them with gentleness has become difficult to me: (TA:) from عُضَالٌ, (O, TA,) as applied to a disease, (O,) or as meaning a "hard," or "difficult," affair, "which one will not undertake," or "[be able to] manage." (TA.) One says of a disease [such as is termed عُضَال,] اعضل الأَطِبَّآءَ, and تَعَضَّلَهُمْ ♦, It overcame the physicians, (Ḳ, TA,) and wearied them. (TA.) — See also 2.

5 : see the next preceding paragraph.

Q. Q. 4. اِعْضَأَلَّتِ الشَّجَرَةُ The tree had many branches, and was tangled, or luxuriant, or dense. (Ṣ, Ḳ.) But [its part. n.] مُعْضَئِلَّة, applied to branches, in a verse cited by J [in the Ṣ], is said by Az to be correctly مُعْطَئِلَّة, meaning نائمة [app. a mistranscription for نَاعِمَة i. e. soft, &c.]. (TA.) See Q. Q. 4 in arts. عطل and عظل.

عَضِلٌ, applied to a man, Very cunning; or possessing much intelligence or sagacity, or much intelligence mixed with craft and forecast. (IAạr, Ḳ,* TA.) — And Very bad, evil, foul, or unseemly; as also مُعْضِلٌ ♦ ; (IAạr, Ḳ, TA;) applied to a thing. (IAạr, TA.)

عَضَلٌ : see عَضَلَة. — Also, (O, Ḳ, TA,) accord. to the context in the Ṣ, (Ḳ, TA,) and as written in all the copies, (TA,) with ḍamm to the ع, but it is only with fet-ḥ to that letter and to the ض, (Ḳ, TA,) and thus it is written by IAạr and other leading lexicologists, (TA,) The [large species of rat called] جُرَذ : (Ṣ, O, Ḳ:) or, accord. to IAạr, the male of the فَأْر [or rat]: (TA, and T in art. فار:) pl. عِضْلَانٌ. (Aboo-Naṣr, Ṣ, O, Ḳ.) [See also عَضِلٌ.]

عَضِلٌ, (Ṣ, O, Ḳ,) and accord. to the Ḳ عَضْلٌ, but correctly عُضُلٌ ♦, (TA,) applied to a man, (Ṣ, O,) [Muscular, musculous, or brawny;] having many عَضَلَات (Ṣ) or عَضَل (O, Ḳ) [i. e. muscles]: or large in the عَضَلَة [or muscle] of his shank. (Ḳ) — And عَضِلَةٌ, applied to a woman, Compact in flesh, and unseemly, or devoid of beauty. (TA.) — See also عُضَالٌ.

عُضْلَةٌ A calamity, or misfortune: pl. عُضَلٌ (Ṣ, O, Ḳ) and عُضْلٌ [which latter may be a coll. gen. n.]. (Ḳ.) One says, إِنَّهُ لَعُضْلَةٌ مِنَ العُضَلِ Verily it is a calamity of the calamities [meaning a great calamity]. (Ṣ, O.)

عَضَلَةٌ (Ṣ, O, Ḳ) and عَضِيلَةٌ ♦ (Ḳ) [A muscle; or any of what are termed the voluntary muscles; i. e.] any tendon, or sinew, with which is thick flesh; (Ḳ;) or any collected and compact flesh upon a tendon or sinew: and particularly of the shank: (Ṣ, O:) pl. عَضَلٌ ♦, (Ṣ, O, Ḳ,*) [or rather this is a coll. gen. n.,] and [the pl. properly so termed is] عَضَلَاتٌ. (Ṣ.) — Also the former, accord. to AA, A certain tree resembling the دِفْلَى, which the camels eat, after which they drink water every day: but Az says that he thinks it be عَضَلَة, [n. un. of عَضَل, q. v.,] with the unpointed ص ; and what he says is correct. (O.)

عَضِيلٌ : see عَضِلٌ.

عُضَالٌ, applied to a disease, (Ṣ, O, Mṣb, Ḳ,) Severe, or distressing, (Ṣ, O, Mṣb,) that wearies the physicians; (Ṣ, O;) as also عَضِلٌ ♦ and عَضِيلٌ ♦ : (O:) or wearing and overcoming: (Ḳ:) or, so applied, hateful, that attacks suddenly, and is not slow to kill; the treatment of which wearies the physicians: (Sh, TA:) or that frustrates the ability of the physicians, there being no cure for it. (IAth, TA.) And in like manner it is applied to an affair [as meaning That wearies him who would perform it]: (Ṣ, O:) or meaning hard, or difficult, which one will not undertake, or [be able to] manage; and in like manner

▼ مُعْضِلٌ [or ▼ مُعْضَلٌ]: or, as some say, the affair [that is hard, or difficult,] is termed عُضَالٌ *in its first state;* and معضل [i. e. ▼ مُعْضِلٌ or ▼ مُعْضَلٌ] *when it is obligatory.* (TA.) And حَلْفَةٌ عُضَالٌ means *A hard,* or *severe, oath, in which is no exception:* (Ḳ:) or, accord. to IAạr, in the phrase حَلَفْتُ عُضَالًا, the latter word signifies *a wonderful calamity;* and the phrase means *I swore an oath that was a severe calamity.* (TA.)

عَضِيلٌ: see the next preceding paragraph.

عَضِيلَةٌ: see عَضَلَةٌ.

عِضْيَلٌ *Base, ignoble,* or *mean; narrow* [or *illiberal*] *in disposition.* (O, Ḳ.)

مُعْضِلٌ, applied to an affair, [*Hard, strait,* or *difficult;* (see its verb, 4, first sentence;)] *such that one cannot find the way to perform it.* (Ṣ, O.) See also عُضَالٌ, in two places. — And see مُعَضِّلٌ: — and عِضْلٌ.

مُعْضِلَةٌ [as a subst.] sing. of مُعْضِلَاتٌ (TA) which signifies *Hard,* or *distressing, events:* (Ṣ, O, Ḳ, TA:) and معضلة [app. accord. to the context ▼ مُعَضِّلَةٌ] *a hard,* or *difficult,* or *strait, calamity.* (Ḥam p. 258.) Also, and ▼ مُعَضِّلَةٌ, *An affair,* or *a case, that is strait in respect of the ways of getting out therefrom.* (TA.) [Hence,] أَعُوذُ بِاللّٰهِ مِنْ كُلِّ مُعْضِلَةٍ لَيْسَ لَهَا أَبُو حَسَنٍ, (O, TA,) or, as some relate it, ▼ مُعَضِّلَةٍ, (TA,) is a saying of 'Omar, (so in the O, but in the TA "in the trad. of Ibn-'Omar,") who meant thereby [*I seek protection by God from*] *every difficult question* or *case* [*for which there is no Aboo-Ḥasan;* meaning, no one such as 'Alee the son of Aboo-Ṭálib, who was surnamed أَبُو الحَسَنِ, and was celebrated for his answers to what are termed المَسَائِلُ المُعْضِلَاتُ, as is related by En-Nawawee, in his Biographical Dictionary (p. 437)]: (O, TA:) ابو حسن, though determinate, is put in the place of that which is indeterminate. (IAth, TA.)

مُعَضَّلٌ [from عَضَلَةٌ "a muscle"] *Rendered firm, strong,* or *compact, in make:* such, it is said, was the Prophet. (TA.)

مُعَضِّلٌ (Ṣ, O, Ḳ) and مُعَضِّلَةٌ (Ṣ, O) and ▼ مُعْضِلٌ (Ḳ) are epithets applied to a woman (Ṣ, O, Ḳ) and to a sheep or goat (Ṣ, O) and in like manner to a hen and to others; (Ḳ;) meaning *Having her child,* or *young one, sticking fast* [*in her vagina*], *and not coming forth easily:* (Ṣ, O:) or *having difficulty in bringing forth her child,* or *young one:* (Ḳ:) [&c.: see 2:] accord. to Lḥ, مُعَضِّلَةٌ signifies *whose child,* or *young one, will not come forth, so that she dies:* and Lth says that مُعَضِّلٌ is applied to a قَطَاة as meaning *whose eggs stick fast* [*in her*]; but Az says that the epithet applied by the Arabs to a قطاة is مُطَرِّقٌ: (TA:) the pl. applied to sheep or goats is ▼ مَعَاضِيلُ [irreg.]. (O.) — See also عُضَالٌ, in two places. — مُعَضِّلٌ applied to an arrow: see مُعَضَّلٌ.

مُعَضِّلَةٌ [as a subst.] see مُعْضِلَةٌ, in three places.

مَعَاضِيلُ: see مُعَضِّلٌ.

عضم

عَضْمٌ *A winnowing-fork;* i. e. the *wooden implement* (Ṣ, ISd, Ḳ) *with prongs* (ISd, Ḳ) *with which wheat is winnowed:* (Ṣ, ISd, Ḳ:) and عَظْمٌ is a dial. var. thereof: (AḤn, TA:) pl. أَعْضِمَةٌ and عُضْمٌ, [the former of pauc. and the latter of mult.,] (Ḳ, TA,) both anomalous; the true state of the case being that they formed from عَضْمٌ the pl. عِضَامٌ; and from this, أَعْضِمَةٌ and عُضُمٌ, [of which latter, عُضْمٌ is app. a contraction,] like أَمْثِلَةٌ and مُثُلٌ pls. of مِثَالٌ. (TA.) — And *The board,* (Ṣ, Ḳ,) i. e. the *broad board,* (TA,) *of the plough, at the head of which is the iron* [or *share*] (Ṣ, Ḳ, TA) *that cleaves the earth:* and so عَظْمٌ, accord. to AḤn. (TA.) — And The *handle,* or *part that is grasped by the hand, of a bow:* (Ṣ, Ḳ:) and عَظْمٌ is a dial. var. thereof: (AḤn, TA:) pl. عِضَامٌ. (Ḳ.) — And The [*part of the tail called*] عَسِيب [q. v.], (Ṣ, Ḳ, TA,) or the عُكْوَة [or *root of the tail where it is bare of hair,* Ṣ in art. عكو], (TA,) of the camel, (Ṣ, TA,) or of the horse, (ISd, TA,) or of both: (Ḳ:) as also ▼ عِضَامٌ, (Ḳ,) of which عِصَامٌ is a dial. var.: (TA: [but see the latter:]) pl. أَعْضِمَةٌ (Ṣ, TA) and عُضُمٌ, [both, accord. to analogy, of the latter sing.,] the former of pauc. and the latter of mult. (TA.) — And *A line,* or *streak, in a mountain, differing from the rest in colour.* (Ḳ, TA.) = Also *Mountain goats.* (Ḳ.)

عِضَامٌ: see the preceding paragraph.

عُضْمُومٌ, applied to a she-camel, *Hard,* or *robust,* (Ḳ, TA,) *in her body; strong to journey.* (TA.)

عَيْضُومٌ *Edacious; voracious;* (Kr, Ḳ;) applied to a woman: (Kr, TA:) but عَيْصُومٌ is of higher authority [in this sense]. (TA.) — And *Having a habit of biting;* syn. عَضُوضٌ. (Ḳ.)

عضه

1. عَضَهَ, said of a camel, (Mṣb, Ḳ,) or عَضِهَتْ, (Ṣ, TA,) said of camels, (Ṣ,) or of a she-camel, (TA,) aor. ـَ, (Ṣ, Mṣb, Ḳ, TA,) inf. n. عَضَهٌ, (Ṣ, Mṣb, TA,) *He,* or *they,* or *she, depastured the trees called* عِضَاه: (Ṣ, Mṣb, Ḳ, TA:) or *had a complaint of the belly from the eating thereof:* and عَضَهَ, aor. ـَ, inf. n. عَضْهٌ, *he* (a camel) *ate the* عِضَاه. (Ḳ.) — And عَضَهَ العِضَاهَ; as also عَضَهَهَا; (so accord. to the copies of the Ḳ;) or عَضَهَ العِضَاهَ, like مَنَعَ [in form], inf. n. عَضْهٌ; as also ▼ عَضَّهَهَا, inf. n. تَعْضِيهٌ; (so accord. to the TA;) *He cut the trees called* عِضَاه: (Ḳ, TA:) accord. to AḤn, (TA,) ▼ التَّعْضِيهُ signifies *the cutting of the* عِضَاه, (Ṣ, TA,) and *the collecting firewood thereof.* (TA.) = عَضَهَ, aor. ـِ, inf. n. عَضْهٌ and عَضَهٌ and عَضِيهَةٌ and عِضْهَةٌ, *He lied.* (Ḳ.) And *He excited discord,* or *dissension, and made known discourse in a mischievous manner,* or *embellished speech with falsehood;* or *he calumniated;* syn. نَمَّ; (Ḳ, TA;) or بَهَتَ: (TA:) whence the saying, in a trad., أَتَدْرُونَ مَا العَضْهُ (TA) i. e. [*Know ye what is*] *the reporting of conversation,* or *of what has been said, from one person to another, to make mischief between them?* (El-Jámi' eṣ-Ṣagheer:) [or,] accord. to IAth, *the calumnious speech between men?* or, accord. to Aṣ, *the evil,* or *foul, speaking?* (TA.) And the same verb, (so accord. to my MS. copy of the Ḳ,) or عَضَهَ, (so accord. to other copies and the TA,) *He uttered falsehood and calumny;* as also ▼ اعضه: (Ḳ, TA:) [whence] one says, قَدْ ▼ أَعْضَهْتَ يَا رَجُلُ *Thou hast uttered calumny, O man.* (Ṣ, TA.) — And عَضَهَ فُلَانًا, (Ṣ,* Ḳ, TA,) [in some copies of the Ḳ عَضَهَ, but it is] like مَنَعَ, [in form], (TA,) inf. n. عَضْهٌ (Ṣ, TA) and عَضِيهَةٌ, (TA,) *He calumniated such a one,* (Ṣ, Ḳ, TA,) *and said that there was in him what was not.* (Ḳ, TA.) — And عَضَهَهُ, inf. n. عَضْهٌ, *He reviled him,* or *vilified him, plainly* [or *in coarse language,* as is shown by an explanation of it in the R]. (TA.) — And عَضَهَ, inf. n. عَضْهٌ and عَضَهٌ and عَضِيهَةٌ and عِضْهَةٌ, *He enchanted:* (Ḳ, TA:) because enchantment is a lying, and a causing to imagine that which has no reality: and *he divined.* (TA.)

2: see 1, former half, in two places.

4. أَعْضَهَتِ الأَرْضُ *The land abounded with the trees called* عِضَاه. (Ḳ.) — And اعضه القَوْمُ *The people,* or *party, had their camels depasturing the* عِضَاه. (Ṣ, Ḳ.) = See also 1, latter half, in two places.

عَضِهَةٌ : see عَاضِهَةٌ, in three places. — أَرْضٌ عَضِهَةٌ and ▼ عَضِيهَةٌ (Ḳ, TA) and ▼ مُعْضِهَةٌ (Ṣ, Ḳ, TA) *A land having trees such as are called* عِضَاه: (TA:) or *abounding with such trees.* (Ṣ, Ḳ, TA.)

عَضَهٌ [also pronounced ▼ عِضَةٌ] *A lie,* or *falsehood; and a calumny;* (Ks, Ṣ, Ḳ, TA;) as also ▼ عَضِيهَةٌ: (Ṣ, TA:*) the former said by Eṭ-Ṭoosee to be a mistranscription for عَضْهٌ; but it is not so: (IB, TA:) and it signifies also *enchantment,* (Ṣ, Ḳ, TA,) and *divination:* (Ṣ, TA:) and its pl., (Ṣ, Ḳ,) or [rather] the pl. of ▼ عِضَةٌ, (thus accord. to the TA and one of my copies of the Ṣ,) is عِضُونَ, like as عِزُونَ is of عِزَةٌ: (Ṣ, Ḳ, TA:) whence the saying in the Ḳur [xv. 91], الَّذِينَ جَعَلُوا القُرْآنَ عِضِينَ [*Those who pronounced the Ḳur-án to be lies,* or *enchantments*]: (Ṣ, TA:) accord. to Fr, [the sing.] ▼ عِضَةٌ is originally عِضْهَةٌ, the deficient [radical] letter being ه; (Ṣ,* TA;) for عِضَةٌ and عِضُونَ in the dial. of Ḳureysh signify *enchantment* [and *enchantments*], and they term the enchanter عَاضِهٌ: (Ṣ:) or, as some say, the deficient [radical] letter is و, (Ṣ, TA,) from عِضْوَةٌ meaning فِرْقَةٌ, (Ṣ,) or from عَضَّيْتُ الشَّىْءَ

meaning فَرَّقَتْهُ ; (TA;) because they divided their sayings respecting the Ḳur-án, pronouncing it to be falsehood, or enchantment, or divination, or poetry. (Ṣ, TA.) And one says, ▼ يَا لِلْعَضِيهَةِ, with kesr to the ل, [*O the lie!*] denoting a calling to aid; (Ṣ;) or said on an occasion of wondering at a great lie; and with fet-ḥ to the ل [i. e. يَا لَلْعَضِيهَةِ] denoting a calling for aid. (TA.)

عِضَةٌ, originally عِضَهَةٌ : see عِضَاهٌ, in two places. —— And see also عِضَةٌ, in three places: and art. عضو.

عِضَاهٌ : see عِضَهٌ.

عِضَهِىٌّ, applied to a camel, *That depastures the trees called* عِضَاه ; as also ▼ عِضَاهِىٌّ so applied; (Ṣ, Ḳ;) and in like manner, applied to camels, ▼ عِضَاهِيَّةٌ ; (Ṣ;) the second and third being rel. ns. from عِضَةٌ, and therefore irregularly formed, or from عِضَاهَةٌ, not from عِضَاهٌ because this is a pl. or has the meaning of a pl.: (TA:) so too عَضَوِىٌّ applied to a camel, (Ṣ, Ḳ,) and عَضَوِيَّةٌ applied to camels, both with fet-ḥ, irregular. (Ṣ.) [See also عَاضِهٌ.]

عِضَاهٌ *Any great trees having thorns; these being of two sorts, genuine* (خَالِص) and *not genuine* (غَيْرُ خَالِصٍ): *the former sort are the* غَرْف, *the* عُرْفُط, *the* طَلْح, *the* سَلَم, *the* سِدْر, *the* سَيَال, *the* سَمُر, *the* يَنْبُوت, *the greater* قَتَاد, *the* كَنَهْبَل, *the* غَرَب, *and the* عَوْسَج: *the other sort are the* شَوْحَط, *the* نَبْع, *the* شِرْيَان, *the* سَرَآء, *the* نَشَم, *the* عُجْرُم, *and the* تَأْلَب; *and these are called the* عِضَاه *of bows* (عِضَاهُ القِيَاسِ [i. e. القِسِيّ pl. of قَوْس]): the small thorny trees are called عِضّ [q. v.]: and such as are neither عِضّ nor عِضَاه, of thorny trees, are the شُكَاعَى, the حُلَاوَى, the حَاذ, the كُبّ, and the سُلَّج: (Ṣ:) or, as AZ says in the beginning of his book of herbage and trees, عِضَاهٌ is the general name of *certain thorny trees which have different particular names: the genuine* عِضَاه (العِضَاهُ الخَالِصُ) *are those which are large and have strong thorns:* such as are small, of thorny trees, are called عِضّ and شِرْس [q. v.]: *of the* عِضَاه *are the* قَرَظ, *the* سَيَال, *the* عُرْفُط, *the* سَمُر, *the* سِدْر, *the* عَوْسَج, *the* كَنَهْبَل, *the greater* قَتَاد, *the* غَاف, *and the* غَرَب: these are the genuine عِضَاه : and *of the* عِضَاه *of bows* (عِضَاهُ القِيَاسِ i. e. القِسِيّ) *are the* شَوْحَط, *the* نَبْع, *the* شِرْيَان, and the سَرَآء : (TA voce عِضّ :) or عِضَاهٌ signifies *any trees having thorns; as the* طَلْح *and the* عَوْسَج : or, accord. to some, *except the* قَتَاد *and the* سِدْر : (Mṣb:) or the *greatest of trees:* or the خَمْط [q. v., for it is variously explained]: or *any having thorns:* or *such as are great and tall, of these:* (Ḳ:) [حُبْلَةٌ and سِنْفَةٌ are terms applied to the fruit, or produce, of trees of the kind called عِضَاه : see the former of those words:] a single tree thereof is called عِضَاهَةٌ (Ṣ, Ḳ) and ▼ عِضَهَةٌ and ▼ عِضَةٌ, (Ṣ, Mṣb, Ḳ, [but in the copies of the Ḳ the last of these is erroneously written عِضَه,]) the radical ه being rejected in the last, as it is in شَفَةٌ ; or, accord. to some, the rejected radical letter is و ; (AAF, Ṣ, Mṣb;*) opinions differing on this point because of the different forms of the pl.; (AAF, Ṣ, TA;) the pl. being عِضَاهٌ and (of pauc., TA) عِضَهَاتٌ (AAF, Ṣ, Ḳ, TA, in the CḲ عِضَوَاتٌ,) and عِضُونَ ; (Ḳ;) [the second and third of which are pls. of ▼ عِضَةٌ ;] or, accord. to ISd, عِضَاهٌ may be an instance of the kind of pl. that differs from its sing. [only] in respect of the ة, like قَتَادٌ, of which the sing. is قَتَادَةٌ, [i. e., what is more properly termed a coll. gen. n.,] or it may be a broken pl., as though its sing. were عِضَهَةٌ : (TA:) the dim. [of عِضَهَةٌ] is ▼ عُضَيْهَةٌ. (Ṣ, TA.) [Hence,] one says, فُلَانٌ يَنْتَجِبُ غَيْرَ عِضَاهِهِ [lit. *Such a one takes the bark of other than his own* عِضَاه, to tan therewith]; meaning † such a one arrogates to himself the poetry of another. (Ṣ. See a verse cited in art. نجب.) [See also 1, first sentence.]

عِضَهَةٌ : see عِضَةٌ. —— And see also عِضَةٌ, in two places.

عُضَيْهَةٌ [dim. of عِضَهَةٌ]: see عِضَاهٌ.

عِضَاهِىٌّ ; and its fem., with ة: see عِضَهِىٌّ.

عَاضِهٌ applied to a he-camel, as also ▼ عَضِهٌ, (Ṣ,) and عَاضِهَةٌ applied to a she-camel, (Ṣ, Ḳ,) and thus also عَاضِهٌ, (Ḳ,) *Depasturing the trees called* عِضَاه ; (Ṣ, Ḳ, TA;) and the pl. [of عَاضِهٌ and عَاضِهَةٌ] in this sense, applied to camels, is عَوَاضِهُ : (Ṣ, TA:) or, accord. to 'Alee Ibn-Ḥamzeh, (IB, TA,) ▼ عَضِهٌ has this meaning; (IB, Mṣb, TA;) but عَاضِهٌ signifies *having a complaint from eating the* عِضَاه : (IB, TA:) or ▼ عَضِهٌ has the latter meaning, or the former meaning: or, accord. to AḤn, عَاضِهَةٌ applied to a she-camel signifies *breaking the branches,* or *twigs, of the* عِضَاه. (TA.) [See also عِضَهِىٌّ.] —— Also *Enchanting,* or *an enchanter;* (Aṣ, Ṣ, Ḳ, TA;) in the dial. of Ḳureysh. (Aṣ, Ṣ, TA.) See also the last paragraph of this art. A poet says,

أَعُوذُ بِرَبِّى مِنَ النَّافِثَا

تِ فِى عُقَدِ العَاضِهِ المُعْضِهِ ▼

[*I seek protection by my Lord from the women sputtering upon the knots of the lying enchanter:* see art. نفث, and the Ḳur-án cxiii. 4]: (Ṣ, TA:) or, as some relate it, فِى عِضَهٍ [*upon the enchantment*]. (TA.) —— And حَيَّةٌ عَاضِهَةٌ and عَاضِهَةٌ *A serpent that kills instantly* (AO, Ṣ, Ḳ) *when it bites.* (AO, Ṣ.)

مُعْضِهٌ : see its fem. voce عَضِهٌ : —— and see the verse cited voce عَاضِهٌ.

مُسْتَعْضِهَةٌ A woman *seeking,* or *demanding, enchantment:* hence the trad., لَعَنَ ٱللّٰهُ العَاضِهَةَ ▼ وَالمُسْتَعْضِهَةَ [*May God curse her who enchants and her who seeks,* or *demands, enchantment*]. (TA.)

عضو

1. عَضَا, aor. يَعْضُو, inf. n. عَضْوٌ : see 2, in three places. —— العَضْوُ in the language of the Arabs signifies [also] السِّحْرُ [i. e. عَضْوٌ is the inf. n. of عَضَا signifying *He enchanted;* like عَضْهٌ an inf. n. of عَضَهَ : see the last sentence of the first paragraph of art. عضه]. (TA.) —— And كَانَ يَعْضُو الجِرَاحَ occurs in the "Aghánee" of Abu-l-Faraj, in the biographical notice of Eṭ-Ṭufeyl: [it means *He used to understand,* or *have skill in, wounds:* for it is added] ▼ العَاضِى means *He who understands,* or *is skilled in, wounds.* (TA.)

2. تَعْضِيَةٌ signifies The act of *dividing* [a thing] *into parts,* or *portions:* and the act of *distributing:* as also ▼ عَضْوٌ [in both of these senses]. (Ḳ, TA.) You say, عَضَّيْتُ الشَّاةَ, (Ṣ,) or الذَّبِيحَةَ, (Mṣb,) inf. n. تَعْضِيَةٌ, (Ṣ,) *I divided the sheep,* or *goat,* (Ṣ,) or *the slaughtered animal,* (Mṣb,) *into* أَعْضَآء [i. e. *limbs,* or *members,* &c.; *I limbed it,* or *dismembered it*]: (Ṣ, Mṣb:) and ▼ عَضَا الشَّاةَ, aor. يَعْضُوهَا, inf. n. عَضْوٌ, *he divided the sheep,* or *goat, into parts,* or *portions.* (TḲ.) And عَضَّيْتُ الشَّىْءَ, inf. n. as above, *I distributed the thing:* (Ṣ:) and ▼ عَضَاهُ, aor. يَعْضُوهُ, inf. n. عَضْوٌ, *he distributed it.* (TA.) It is said in a trad., لَا تَعْضِيَةَ فِى مِيرَاثٍ إِلَّا فِيمَا ٱحْتَمَلَ القَسْمَ [*There shall be no distributing in an inheritance, except in the case of that which is susceptible of division*]; i. e., what is not susceptible of division, such as the bead of precious stone, and the like, shall not be distributed, even though one or more of the inheritors demand its division, because therein would be injury to them or to one or more of them; but it shall be sold, and its price shall be divided among them. (Ṣ.)

عُضْوٌ and عِضْوٌ, (Ṣ, Mṣb, Ḳ, &c.,) the former of which is the more commonly known, (Mṣb, TA,) [*A limb, a member,* and *an organ,* of the body;] *any bone with the flesh entire,* or *with much flesh;* (M, TA;) *any entire bone of the body;* thus in the Abridgment of the 'Eyn; (Mṣb;) *any flesh that is entire,* or *much in quantity, with its bone;* (Ḳ, TA;) *a* [*distinct*] *portion of the body;* (ḲL;) *a part of an animal, such as the head,* (Mṣb in art. رأس,) or the *heart,* and the *brain,* and the *liver,* and the *testicles:* (Mgh and Ḳ in that art.:) and † of a bow: (Ḳ in art. تبع :) pl. أَعْضَآءٌ. (Ṣ, Mṣb, TA.) One says عُضْوٌ مِنَ اللَّحْمِ [*A portion of flesh forming a distinct limb* or *member*]. (Ḳ voce عُضْلَةٌ.) [And العُضْوَانِ is used as meaning *The male and female genital organs;* which are also called العُسَيْلَتَانِ : see عُسَيْلَةٌ, last sentence.]

عِضَةٌ *A piece, part,* or *portion,* (Mṣb, Ḳ,) of a thing: originally عِضْوَةٌ : pl. عِضُونَ, irreg., like

سُنُونَ. (Mṣb.) — And *A party, sect,* or *class,* (Ḳ, TA,) of people: (TA:) [pl. as above:] one says, فِى الدَّارِ عِضُونَ مِنَ النَّاسِ *In the house,* or *place of abode, are* [*several*] *parties, sects,* or *classes, of people:* (Ṣ, TA:) so says Aṣ, (Ṣ,) or Ks. (TA.) = Also *A lie,* or *falsehood:* pl. عِضُونَ. (Ḳ.) In this sense, (TA,) as sing. of the last word in the saying in the Ḳur [xv. 91], اَلَّذِينَ جَعَلُوا ٱلْقُرْآنَ عِضِينَ, its deficient [radical] letter is و or ه, as has been mentioned in art. عضه [q. v.]: (Ṣ, TA:) those who say that it is و regard as an evidence its having for a pl. عِضَوَاتٌ; and those who say that it is ه regard as an evidence their saying عُضَيْهَةٌ. (TA.) — العِضُونَ as meaning السِّحْرُ [i. e. *Enchantment,* in the CḲ (erroneously) الشِّعْرُ,] is [said to be] pl. of عِضَةٌ [in the CḲ عِضَةٌ], with ه. (Ḳ. [But see عِضَةٌ, in art. عضه.])

عُضْوٌ The *state of possessing sufficient clothing and food.* (ISd, Ḳ.)

عَضَوِىٌّ applied to a camel, and عَضَوِيَّةٌ applied to camels: see عِضَهِىٌّ, in art. عضه.

عَاضٍ A man *possessing sufficient clothing and food.* (ISd, Ḳ.) = See also 1, last sentence.

عط

1. عَطَّ الثَّوْبَ, (Ṣ, O, Ḳ,) aor. ـُ, inf. n. عَطٌّ, (Ṣ, O,) *He slit,* or *rent, the garment,* or *piece of cloth, lengthwise,* (Lth, Ṣ, O, Ḳ,) or *breadthwise, without separation,* (Lth, O, Ḳ,) but not heard by Mṭr as meaning breadthwise in chaste language; (Ḥar p. 636;) like ▼عَطَّطَهُ; (Ḳ;) or this, of which the inf. n. is تَعْطِيطٌ (Ṣ, O, TA) and تِعْطَاطٌ also, (TA,) is with teshdeed to denote muchness [of the action], or multiplicity [of the objects]: (Ṣ, O,* TA:) and ▼اعتطّ الثَّوْبَ signifies [the same, or simply] *he slit,* or *rent, the garment,* or *piece of cloth.* (TA.) El-Mufaḍḍal is related to have said that he had read in a copy of the Ḳur-án, [in xii. 28,] فَلَمَّا رَأَى قَمِيصَهُ عُطَّ مِنْ دُبُرٍ [*And when he saw that his shirt was rent in the hinder part*]. (O, Ḳ.*)

2: see the preceding paragraph.

5: see what next follows.

7. انعطّ *It* (a garment, or piece of cloth,) *became slit,* or *rent,* (Ṣ, O, Ḳ,) *lengthwise,* or [accord. to some] *breadthwise, without separation;* as also ▼تعطّط: (Ḳ:) or the latter signifies تَشَقَّقَ [as meaning *it became slit,* or *rent,* &c., *much,* or *in several,* or *many, places;* or is like the former verb but said of several, or many, garments, &c.]. (O.) — Also, said of a stick, or branch, or the like, *It bent without breaking so as to part asunder.* (AZ, O, Ḳ.)

8: see 1. — [Hence,] one says, اعتطّ أَوَائِلَ القَوْمِ ‡ *He clave the foremost persons of the people,* or *party.* (TA.)

عُطُطٌ [*Wrappers of the kind called*] مَلَاحِف [pl. of مِلْحَفَةٌ] *slit,* or *rent;* or *slit,* or *rent, much,* or *in many places.* (IAạr, O, Ḳ.)

عَطِيطٌ A garment, or piece of cloth, *slit,* or *rent,* [*lengthwise,* or, accord. to some, *breadthwise, without separation;*] as also ▼مَعْطُوطٌ. (TA.)

مَعَطٌّ [*A place of slitting* or *rending* &c.]. One says شَقٌّ وَاسِعُ المَعَطِّ [*A rent of which the place of slitting is wide*]. (TA.)

مَعْطُوطٌ: see عَطِيطٌ.

عطب

1. عَطِبَ, (Ṣ, A, Mgh, O, Mṣb, Ḳ,) aor. ـَ, (A, Mgh, Mṣb, Ḳ,) inf. n. عَطَبٌ, (Ṣ,* Mgh,* O,* Mṣb,) and مَعْطَبٌ also may be an inf. n. of the same, (Ḥar p. 196,) *He perished,* or *died:* (Ṣ, A, Mgh, O, Mṣb, Ḳ:) [Freytag mentions عَطَبَ also in the same sense, as from the Ḳ, in which I do not find it:] it is said of a man, and of other than man: in a trad. it is said of seed-produce. (TA.) — And *He* (a camel, and a horse,) *flagged,* or *became powerless:* (Ḳ, TA:) or *stopped with his master* [or *rider*] *from fatigue.* (TA.) — And عَطِبَ عَلَيْهِ *He was,* or *became, violently,* (O,) or *most violently,* (Ḳ,) *angry with him.* (O, Ḳ.) = العَطَبُ signifies لِينُ القُطْنِ (O,* Ḳ) and الصُّوفِ, (O,) and نُعُومَتُهُ: (Ḳ:) you say, عَطِبَ, aor. ـَ, (A, O, Ḳ,) inf. n. عَطَبٌ and عُطُوبٌ, (O,) *It* [i. e. cotton, and wool,] *was,* or *became, soft.* (A, O,* Ḳ. [See also عُطْبٌ, below.])

2. تَعْطِيبٌ, (O, Ḳ,) inf. n. of عطّب, (TA,) signifies The *brewing* (عِلَاج) of beverage, or wine, *in order that its odour may become good:* (O, Ḳ:) so says Aboo-Sa'eed. (O.) The phrase رَحِيق مُعَطَّب occurs in a poem of Lebeed, as some relate it; but as others relate it, it is مُقَطَّب, which means "mixed:" (O, TA:) so says Az; and he adds, "I know not what مُعَطَّب is." (TA.) = Also, in a grape-vine, The *appearing of the knots,* or *gems, in the places whence grow the bunches of grapes.* (Ḳ.)

4. اعطبهُ *He* (a man, Mṣb), or *it* (calamity, A), *destroyed him,* or *caused him to perish.* (Ṣ, A, O, Mṣb, Ḳ.)

8. اعتطب النَّارَ *He took fire in a portion of cotton:* (A:) or اعتطب بِعُطْبَةٍ *he took fire in a piece of rag* (O, Ḳ) or *a portion of cotton.* (O.)

عُطْبٌ and ▼عُطُبٌ *Cotton:* (IAạr, Ṣ, O, Ḳ:) and ▼عُطْبَةٌ signifies *a portion thereof,* (Ṣ, A, O, TA,) or *of wool.* (TA.) [SM says,] In the T, العطب is said to mean لِينُ القُطْنِ وَالصُّوفِ, [and so in the O, where it is written العَطَبُ, and said to be with fet-ḥ,] and its n. un. is عطبة; but I have found it written with ḍamm [to the ع]; therefore by لين seems to be meant لَيِّن [i. e. *Such as is soft* of cotton and of wool: which I think to be evidently a mistake: see 1]. (TA.)

عَطِبٌ [*Perishing,* or *dying*]: see an ex., from a poet, voce رُبَّ.

عُطُبٌ: see عُطْبٌ.

عُطْبَةٌ: see عُطْبٌ. — Also *A portion of rag by means of which fire is taken:* (Ḳ:) or *a portion of burning cotton* (Ṣ, A, O) or *rag:* (Ṣ, O:) so in the saying, أَجِدُ رِيحَ عُطْبَةٍ [*I perceive the odour of a portion of burning cotton or rag*]. (Ṣ, A, O.)

عَوْطَبٌ *A calamity,* or *misfortune:* (Aṣ, O, Ḳ:) from العَطَبُ [inf. n. of عَطِبَ]. (Aṣ, TA.) — And The *main part,* or *fathomless deep, of the sea:* (Aṣ, Ḳ:) likewise from العَطَبُ: (Aṣ, TA:) and so عَوْبَطٌ, (Ḳ in art. عبط,) formed by transposition: (TA ibid.:) or the *deepest place in the sea:* (IAạr, O:) or *a depressed part between two waves.* (IAạr, O, Ḳ.)

أَعْطَبُ *More* [and *most*] *soft:* so in the saying, هٰذَا الكَبْشُ أَعْطَبُ مِنْ هٰذَا [*This ram is more soft* in his wool *than this*]. (O.)

مَعْطَبٌ *A place of perdition* or *destruction:* pl. مَعَاطِبُ. (Ṣ, O, Mṣb.) [See also 1, first sentence.]

مُعْطِبٌ One *who scants his household;* syn. مُقْتِرٌ. (O, Ḳ.)

عطد

عَطْدٌ *Hardness, severity, rigour,* or *difficulty.* (IDrd,* O,* L.)

عَطْوَدٌ *Hard, severe, rigorous,* or *difficult:* (IDrd, O, L, Ḳ:) applied in this sense to anything: and particularly to a journey: or in this case meaning *distant.* (L.) — *A quick* pace, or rate of going: (Ṣ, O, L, Ḳ:) and so عَطَرَّدٌ [q. v.]. (L.) — A *high* mountain: (O, L, Ḳ, TA: [in the CḲ, مِنَ الحِبالِ is erroneously put for مِنَ الجِبالِ:]) as also عَصْوَدٌ and عَطَوَّدٌ. (L.) — A *long* day: (O, Ḳ:) a *complete* day (L) or year: (Ibn-'Abbád, O, Ḳ:) a *whole* day. (T, O, L, Ḳ.) One says, ذَهَبَ عَطْوَدًا *He went away a whole day.* (O, Ḳ.) — *A conspicuous, clear, open, road, along which one goes whithersoever he will.* (ISh, O, L, Ḳ.) — *A generous, noble, liberal,* man. (Ibn-'Abbád, O, Ḳ.) — *A sharpened* spear-head. (Ibn-'Abbád, O, Ḳ.) — Accord. to [IDrd and] Az [and J], this word is quasi-coordinate to the quinqueliteral-radical class. (TA.)

عطر

1. عَطِرَتْ, (Ṣ, A, O, Mṣb,) aor. ـَ, inf. n. عَطَرٌ, (Ṣ, O, Mṣb,) said of a woman, (Ṣ, A, Mṣb,) *She perfumed herself;* (TA;) and ▼تعطّرت, (A, O, Mṣb,) inf. n. تَعَطُّرٌ; (Ṣ;) and ▼استعطرت; (A;) [signify the same: also عَطِرَ *he* (a man) *was sweet in the odour of his body;* and عَطِرَتْ, said of a woman, signifies the same: see the part. n. عَطِرٌ:] and ▼استعطرت signifies *she* (a woman) *made use of perfume.* (TA.) [See also 5.]

2. عطّر *He perfumed* a woman [&c.; and so, app., ▼اعطر]. (Mṣb.) — بَطْنِى عَطِّرِى, (Ḳ,) but in other lexicons than the Ḳ we find ▼أَعْطِرِى, (TA,) [occurring in a prov.,] see in art. سأر [voce سَائِر]. (Ḳ.)

4: see 2, in two places.

5: see 1. — It is said in a trad., of Moḥammad, كَانَ يَكْرَهُ تَعَطُّرَ النِّسَآءِ وَتَشَبُّهَهُنَّ بِالرِّجَالِ, (O, Ḳ, TA,) meaning *He used to dislike women's perfuming themselves with perfume of which the odour was perceived like that of men* [*and their affecting to be like men*]: (TA:) or *their being without ornaments* (O, Ḳ, TA) *and dye on the hands &c.* [*and their affecting to be like men*]; (TA;) the ر in this case being substituted for ل: (O, Ḳ,* TA:) or تعطّر, here, is from what follows: (TA:) — تعطّرت *She* (a woman, O, TA) *remained in the house,* or *tent, of,* (O, Ḳ,) or *with,* (L,) *her father and mother, and did not marry.* (O, L, Ḳ, TA.)

10: see 1, in two places.

عِطْرٌ *Perfume; an odoriferous,* or *a fragrant, substance;* syn. طِيبٌ: (Ṣ, A, O, Ḳ:) pl. [of pauc.] أَعْطَارٌ (A) and [of mult.] عُطُورٌ. (A, O, Ḳ.) [And ▼عِطَارَةٌ, as used in the present day, and in medical books, signifies *Perfumes and drugs:* see an ex. voce صَيْدَلَةٌ.] — [عِطْرُ الأَمَةِ *A certain herb:* see ذَفِرٌ.]

عَطِرٌ, applied to a man, (Ḳ, TA,) and عَطِرَةٌ, applied to a woman, (Ṣ, A, O, Mṣb, Ḳ,) *Having perfume upon,* or *using perfume for,* or *perfuming,* [*himself,* and] *herself;* (Ṣ, O;) and ▼مُتَعَطِّرَةٌ, applied to a woman, (Ṣ, Ḳ,) signifies the same. (Ṣ.) [See also عَاطِرٌ, and مُعَطَّرَةٌ, and مِعْطِيرٌ.] — Also عَطِرٌ, *Sweet in the odour of his body;* and in like manner عَطِرَةٌ applied to a woman. (TA.) اِمْرَأَةٌ عَطِرَةٌ مَطِرَةٌ means *A woman who perfumes and cleanses and washes herself much:* (O:) [or *is sweet in the odour of her body, and often uses the tooth-stick;* for] مَطِرَةٌ signifies here كَثِيرَةُ السِّوَاكِ. (TA.) — عَطِرَةٌ A she-camel *easy of sale in the market;* (O, Ḳ;) *that sells herself by her goodliness;* (TA;) as also ▼عَطَّارَةٌ (O, Ḳ) and ▼مِعْطَارَةٌ: (TA:) or a she-camel *of generous race,* or *excellent;* (Ṣ, O, Ḳ;) as also ▼مِعْطَارٌ (Ṣ, O, TA) and ▼مِعْطَارَةٌ and ▼مُعْطِرَةٌ [or مُعْطَرَةٌ?]; (Ḳ, TA;) or ▼مِعْطَرَةٌ: (O:) and عَطِرَاتٌ and ▼مَعَاطِرُ she-camels *goodly, and of generous race,* or *excellent.* (A.)

عِطْرِيَّةٌ [*Fragrance*]. (TA in art. ورد.)

عِطَارَةٌ The *trade of a seller of perfumes.* (Ḳ.) — See also عِطْرٌ.

عَطَّارٌ *A seller of perfumes;* (O, Ḳ;) and ▼مِعْطِيرٌ signifies the same in the saying of El-'Ajjáj, describing the [wild] he-ass and the she-asses,

* يَتْبَعْنَ جَأْبًا كَمُدُقِّ المِعْطِيرْ *

[*They* (the she-asses) *follow a bulky male like the stone with which the seller of perfumes pounds,* or *pulverizes, his perfume*]. (Ṣ, O.)

عَطَّارَةٌ: see عَطِرٌ.

عَاطِرٌ One *who loves perfume:* (IAạr, O, Ḳ:) or *i. q.* عَطِرٌ [q. v.]: (TA:) pl. عُطْرٌ. (O, Ḳ.)

أَعْطَرُ العَرَبِ *The most sweet, in perfume, of the Arabs.* (TA, from a trad.)

مُعْطِرٌ [or مُعْطَرٌ is the correct form, pass. part. n. of أَعْطَرَ, and agreeable with the pl. in two copies of the Ṣ,] (Ḳ, TA) *A beautiful* she-camel, as though there were a dye upon her fur by reason of her beauty: (TA; and so the pl. is explained in the Ṣ:) or *strong and beautiful;* as also ▼مِعْطَارٌ: (Ḳ, TA:) pl. of the former مُعْطِرَاتٌ, (TA,) or مُعْطَرَاتٌ, (Ṣ, O,) meaning *fat:* or *red,* as though dyed. (O.) — مُعْطِرَةٌ [or مُعْطَرَةٌ] *A red* she-goat. (El-Báhilee, as cited in the TA.) — See also عَطِرٌ.

مِعْطَرَةٌ: see عَطِرٌ, last sentence.

مُعَطَّرَةٌ, applied to a woman [*Perfumed:* see 2]. (Ḳ.)

مِعْطَارٌ and مِعْطَارَةٌ: see مِعْطِيرٌ; each in two places. — and see مُعْطِرٌ; and عَطِرٌ, in three places.

مِعْطِيرٌ, applied to a woman, (Mṣb,) or to a man and a woman, (Ṣ, Ḳ,) and ▼مِعْطَارٌ, applied to a woman, (Ṣ, Mṣb,) or to a man and a woman, (Ḳ,) and ▼مِعْطَارَةٌ, (Ḳ,) One *who perfumes himself, and herself, much;* (Ṣ, Mṣb;) and *who frequently does so:* and ▼مِعْطَارٌ and ▼مِعْطَارَةٌ a woman *who is accustomed to do so:* pl. مَعَاطِيرُ. (TA.) Lḥ says that an epithet of the measure مِفْعَالٌ is masc. and fem. without ة, except in some extraordinary instances, in which the fem. is with ة. (TA.) — Also مِعْطِيرٌ, A she-camel *red, and whose sweat has a sweet odour.* (L, and so in the CḲ.) In [some of] the copies of the Ḳ, طَيِّبَةُ العَرْفِ is put by mistake for طَيِّبَةُ العَرَقِ. (TA.) — See also عَطَّارٌ.

مَعَاطِرُ: see عَطِرٌ, last sentence.

مُتَعَطِّرَةٌ: see عَطِرٌ, first sentence.

عطرد

Q. 1. عَطْرِدْهُ لَنَا *Make thou it to be to us,* (O, Ḳ,) *with thee,* or *in thy estimation,* (O,) *like the promise,* (كَالعِدَةِ, Ḳ, TA, inf. n. of وَعَدَ, and this is the only explanation given by the leading authorities on strange words, TA, [in the O, كَالعُدَّةِ,]) or *like the apparatus that is prepared for the casualties of fortune;* (كَالعُدَّةِ and العَتَادِ; Ibn-'Abbád, O, Ḳ;) and ▼اِجْعَلْهُ لَنَا عُطْرُودًا signifies the same. (O, Ḳ.)

عَطَرَّدٌ *i. q.* عَطْرُودٌ in its several meanings: (Ḳ:) signifying *High,* applied to a mountain: — and *Tall,* applied to a man or camel: (L:) — and *Long,* applied to a day; and to a limit, term, reach, or goal, or to a heat, or single run to a goal or limit; (Ṣ, O, L;) and to a road: (L:) — and *Generous, noble,* or *liberal,* applied to a man: (O:) — and *Quick,* applied to a pace, or rate of going: (L:) — and *Sharpened,* applied to a spear-head. (O.)

اِجْعَلْهُ لَنَا عُطْرُودًا: see the first paragraph.

عُطَارِدٌ or عُطَارِدُ, (accord. to different copies of the Ṣ,) or both, being perfectly and imperfectly decl., (Ḳ,) but what is the cause of its being imperfectly decl., with the quality of a proper name, requires consideration, (MF,) [*The planet Mercury;*] *the star of the scribes;* (Az, TA;) *one of the stars called* الخُنَّس; (Ṣ, O, Ḳ;) accord. to the Ḳ [and O], *in the sixth heaven* [or *sphere*]; but the sheykh 'Alee El-Maḳdisee says that this is a mistake, for it is well known to be *in the second.* (TA.)

عطس

1. عَطَسَ, aor. ـِ (Ṣ, A, O, Mṣb, Ḳ) and ـُ, (Ṣ, O, Mṣb, Ḳ,) the former of which is the more approved, and therefore it alone is mentioned in some copies [of the Ḳ], (TA,) inf. n. عَطْسٌ, (Mṣb,) or عُطَاسٌ, (Ṣ,* A,) or both, (O, Ḳ,) or the latter is a simple subst., (TA,) *He sneezed;* expl. by أَتَتْهُ العَطْسَةُ: (A, Ḳ:) [properly] said only of a man. (MF, from the "Iḳtiráḥ.") It is said in a trad., كَانَ يُحِبُّ العُطَاسَ وَيَكْرَهُ التَّثَاؤُبَ [*He* (Moḥammad) *used to like sneezing, and dislike yawning*]: (O, TA:) because the former is accompanied by lightness of the body, and openness of the pores, and facilitation of movements; whereas, in yawning, the contrary is the case; and these properties are caused by taking light nourishment and little food and drink: (TA:) but the Arabs used to augur evil from sneezing; (A, O;) so that if a man were journeying and heard a sneeze, it prevented him from going on. (A.) — عَطَسَ الصُّبْحُ, (Ṣ, O, Ḳ,) inf. n. عَطْسٌ, (TA,) ‡ *The dawn broke:* (Ṣ, Ḳ:) or *shone forth.* (A, Mṣb.) — عَطَسَتْ بِهِ اللُّجُمُ, (A, O, Ḳ,) and اللُّجْمُ, (A,) *Evil omens brought ill luck upon him:* (A, O:*) لُجْمٌ and لُجُمٌ are pls. of لُجْمَةٌ and لِجَامٌ, which are syn. with طِيَرَةٌ, because the طيرة refrains one from a thing that he wants: for they used to augur evil from sneezing [as remarked above]: (A:) or *he died;* (A, O, Ḳ;) as also عَطَسَ, alone. (Ḳ.) [See also غَطَسَ.]

2. عَطَّسَهُ, inf. n. تَعْطِيسٌ, *He* [or *it*] *made him to sneeze.* (Ḳ.)

عَطْسَةٌ (Ṣ, A, O, Ḳ) and ▼عُطَاسٌ (Mṣb, TA) [*A sneeze,* or *a sneezing:* or, accord. to the A and O and Ḳ, the latter is an inf. n.: see 1]. It is said, خُلِقَ السِّنَّوْرُ مِنْ عَطْسَةِ الأَسَدِ [*The cat was created from the sneeze of the lion*]: (A:) [app. because it resembles the lion in make and disposition: for] one says also, فُلَانٌ عَطْسَةُ فُلَانٍ,

meaning *Such a one resembles such a one in make and disposition;* (A, O, Ḳ, TA;) and [in the same sense] they say, كَأَنَّهُ عَطْسَةُ مِنْ أَنْفِهِ. (TA.)

عُطَاس : see عَطْسَةٌ. — العُطَاسُ ‡ *The dawn,* or *daybreak;* (Lth, Az, A, O, Ḳ;) as also ▼ العَاطِسُ. (Ḳ.) You say, جَآءَ فُلَانٌ قَبْلَ طُلُوعِ العُطَاسِ and هُبُوبِ العُطَاسِ ‡ [*Such a one came before the rising of the dawn*]. (A.) And a poet says,

وَقَدْ أَغْتَدِى قَبْلَ العُطَاسِ بِسَابِحٍ *

† [*And sometimes I go early in the morning, before dawn, with a horse that runs stretching out his fore legs gracefully as if swimming*]: but Aṣ relates that the meaning is said to be, *before I hear the sneeze of a sneezer* and augur evil from it; and that he had not heard any authority worthy of reliance for the meaning assigned by Lth. (TA.)

عَطُوس is [said to be] applied to a man as meaning *Bold in wars and rigours,* (TA in this art.,) [and to be] thus correctly, as written by Az and others, but in the O and Ḳ with غ. (TA in art. غطس.) — And one says, أَصَابَتْهُ اللُّجَمُ العَطُوسُ, (A, O,* Ḳ,*) and ▼ العَاطِسُ, (A, TA,) and اللُّجَمُ, (TA,) [accord. to the A, app. meaning *A portentous event bringing ill luck befell him:* (see 1, last sentence:) or] meaning *death* [*befell him*]: (O, Ḳ:) اللُّجَمُ being here made sing.; (A, TA;) and so اللُّجَمُ. (TA.)

عَطُوس : see عَاطِس : — and see also عُطَاس. — Also A gazelle *coming towards one from before his face;* (A, O, Ḳ;) *i. q.* نَاطِحٌ : because one augurs evil from it. (A, TA.)

عَاطُوس *A thing by which one is made to sneeze.* (Seer, Ḳ.) — *A certain beast, from which one augurs evil:* (IAạr, O, Ḳ:) or *a certain fish in the sea, from which the Arabs augur evil.* (IKh.)

المَعْطِس (Ṣ, O, Mṣb, Ḳ) and المَعْطَس, (Lth, Ṣ, O, Ḳ,) the latter being sometimes used, (Ṣ,) or only the former, (Az,) *The nose:* (Lth, Ṣ, O, Mṣb, Ḳ:) pl. مَعَاطِس. (TA.)

مُعَطِّس *Abased.* (Ibn-'Abbád, A, O, Ḳ.) You say, رَدَدْتُهُ مُعَطَّسًا *I repelled him abased.* (A.)

عطش

1. عَطِشَ, aor. ـَ, inf. n. عَطَشٌ, (Ṣ, O, Mṣb, Ḳ,) and sometimes مَعْطَشٌ, (TA,) *He thirsted; was thirsty: was in want of drink;* and *it was in want of irrigation:* عَطَش being the *contr.* of رِىّ. (Ṣ, O, TA.) — عَطِشَ إِلَى لِقَائِهِ ‡ *He longed,* or *desired,* [lit. *thirsted,*] *to meet with him:* like as they say ظَمِئَ. (IDrd, O.) And أَنَا شَدِيدُ العَطَشِ إِلَى لِقَائِكَ ‡ [*I am vehemently longing,* or *desiring, to meet with thee*]. (A.) [See also the first paragraph of art. عمى.] — عَاطَشَهُ فَعَطَشَهُ : see 3.

2 : see 4.

3. عَاطَشَهُ فَعَطَشَهُ [aor. of the latter, accord. to general rule, ـُ,] *He vied with him in endeavouring to satisfy,* (see 6,) or *in bearing, thirst, and surpassed him therein*]. (O, Ḳ, TA. [But whether sanctioned by usage, seems to be doubtful.])

4. اعطش *His camels,* or *cattle, thirsted.* (T, Ṣ, M, O, Ḳ.) — اعطش فُلَانًا *He made such a one to thirst.* (O,* Ḳ,* TA.) — اعطش الإِبِلَ *He increased the intervals between the two drinkings,* or *waterings, of the camels, and withheld them from coming to the water,* (O, Ḳ,) or *from the water on the day of their coming thereto:* (TA:) and ▼ عَطَّشَهَا, [in like manner,] *he increased their thirsting:* (A:) or the latter, of which the inf. n. is تَعْطِيش, has a more intensive signification than the former verb: (O, Ḳ, TA:) or it signifies *he kept them thirsty;* i. e., *did not water them at all;* or, *watered them little, so that they were not satisfied:* (TA, voce ثَأْثَأَ:) when a man has been accustomed to bring his camels to water on the third day, or the fourth, and waters them one day beyond that, you say أَعْطَشَهَا. (TA.)

5. تعطّش *He constrained himself to thirst;* syn. تَكَلَّفَ العَطَشَ. (O, Ḳ.)

6. تَعَاطَشَا [app. *They vied, each with the other, in endeavouring to satisfy their thirst,* (see Ḳ, voce تَجَاشَعَا,) or *in bearing thirst*].

عَطَشٌ; fem. with ة : see the next paragraph, in three places.

عَطِشٌ (Mgh, O, Mṣb, Ḳ) and ▼ عَطُشٌ (Ḳ) and ▼ عَطْشَانُ [without and with tenween, as is shown by the two forms of its fem., which see in what follows,] (Ṣ, Mgh, O, Mṣb) and ▼ عَاطِشٌ (TA) *Thirsting;* or *thirsty:* (Ṣ, TA:) or *needing water:* (Mgh:) or you say, هُوَ عَطْشَانُ ▼ آلْآنَ [*He is thirsting,* or *thirsty, now*]; (Lḥ, Ḳ;) and هُوَ ▼ عَاطِشٌ غَدًا [*He will be thirsting,* or *thirsty, to-morrow*]; (Lḥ, O, Ḳ;) and مَا هُوَ بِعَاطِشٍ ▼ بَعْدَ هٰذَا اليَوْمِ [*He will not be thirsting,* or *thirsty, after this day*]: (Lḥ, TA:) fem. [of the first] عَطِشَةٌ (O, Mṣb, Ḳ) and [of the second] ▼ عَطُشَةٌ (TA) and [of the third] ▼ عَطْشَى, (Ṣ, O, Mṣb, Ḳ,) which is also used as a pl., (Ṣ, Ḳ,) and ▼ عَطْشَانَةٌ : (Lth, O, Ḳ:) pl. masc. [of the first and third and fourth, and perhaps of the second also,] عِطَاشٌ (Ṣ, O, Mṣb, Ḳ) and عُطَّاشٌ [which is irregular] and عَطِشُونَ and [of the second] عَطُشُونَ (TA) and [of the third] عَطَاشَى : (Ṣ, O, Ḳ:) pl. fem. عِطَاشٌ, like the masc., (Ṣ, O, Ḳ,) and [of the first] عَطِشَاتٌ, (Lth, O, Ḳ,) but this was ignored by Aboo-Leylà, (O,) and [of the second] عَطُشَاتٌ (TA) and [of the third] عَطْشَانَاتٌ. (Lth, O, Ḳ.) Accord. to Mohammad Ibn-Es-Seree, ▼ عَطْشَانُ is originally عَطْشَآءُ, like صَحْرَآءُ, the ن being substituted for the fem. ا, as is shown by its plural's being عَطَاشَى like صَحَارَى : (Ṣ, O:) [but there are many similar pls. of epithets of the measure فَعْلَان; as سَكَارَى and غَيَارَى and كَسَالَى &c.] You say also عَطْشَانُ نَدَامَى and نَطْشَانُ; the latter being an imitative sequent to the former, not used alone. (Ṣ, O.) And إِنَّكَ إِلَى الدَّمِ عَطْشَانُ ▼ كَأَنَّكَ عَطْشَانُ [*Verily thou art thirsting for blood, as though thou wert 'Atshán*]: (A:) this being the name of a sword of 'Abd-El-Muttalib Ibn-Háshim. (A, O, Ḳ.) The dim. of عَطِشٌ is ▼ عُطَيْشَانُ, as though from عَطْشَان; and ▼ عُطَيْشٌ also; but the former is the better. (ISk, O.) — [Hence,] ▼ عَطْشَانُ also signifies ‡ *Longing;* or *desiring.* (Ḳ.) You say, إِنِّى إِلَيْكَ ▼ لَعَطْشَانُ ‡ [*Verily I am longing for seeing thee*]. (IAạr, O.) — مَكَانٌ عَطِشٌ (Ṣ, O, Mṣb) and ▼ عَطْشٌ (Ṣ, O) *A place in which is little water:* (Ṣ, O, Mṣb:) or *in which is no water.* (Mṣb.) عَطِشَةُ الوِشَاحِ or (A) فُلَانَةُ عَطْشَى ▼ الوِشَاحِ — (TA) ‡ [*Such a woman is slender in the waist;* or *in the belly and flanks;* like غَرْثَى الوِشَاحِ].

عَطْشَانُ : fem. عَطْشَى and عَطْشَانَةٌ : see عَطِش, throughout.

عُطَاش [*Insatiable thirst;*] *a certain disease,* (Ṣ, O, Ḳ, TA,) *that attacks a man,* (Ṣ, O, TA,) or *a child,* (TA,) *the sufferer from which drinks water and cannot satisfy his thirst:* (Ṣ, O, Ḳ,* TA:) or *intense thirst:* the sufferer thereof is permitted to break his fast. (TA.)

عُطَيْش : } dims. of عَطِش, q. v. (ISk, O.)
عُطَيْشَان : }

عَاطِش : see عَطِش, in three places.

مَعْطَش [The *space in which one becomes thirsty:* see an ex. voce مَجَاع. And] sing. of مَعَاطِش, (O, Ḳ,) which signifies The *appointed times* (مَوَاقِيت, Ṣ, A, O, Ḳ) *of thirst,* or *of the restraining of camels from water,* (Ṣ, A, O,) or *of thirsts,* or *of the restrainings of camels from water.* (Ḳ.)

مُعْطِش A man *whose camels have become thirsty.* (TA.) [See also مِعْطَاش.] — See also مَعْطَشَة.

مُعَطَّش A man *who has not had drink given to him.* (TA.)

مَعْطَشَةٌ *A land in which is no water;* (O, Ḳ;) as also ▼ أَرْضٌ مُعْطِشَةٌ : (TA:) pl. of the former مَعَاطِش. (O, Ḳ.) — *A cause of thirst.* (TA in art. بخل.)

مُعَطَّش *Confined,* or *withheld,* (O, Ḳ, TA,) *from water, purposely.* (TA.)

مِعْطَاش *Very thirsty;* or *often thirsty:* applied to a man and to a woman. (Lḥ) — *Having thirsty camels:* applied to a man and to a woman. (O, Ḳ.) [See also مُعْطِش.]

عطف

1. عَطَفَ, (Ṣ, Mgh, O, Mṣb, Ḳ,) aor. ـِ, (O, Ḳ,) inf. n. عُطُوفٌ, (Mgh, Mṣb,) or عَطْفٌ, (O, TA,) *He,* or *it,* (a man, Ṣ, O, or a thing, Mṣb,) *inclined;* (Ṣ, Mgh, O, Mṣb, Ḳ;) or *bent:* (MF, TA:) and ▼ انعطف also has the former meaning, (Mgh, Mṣb,* TA,) as in the saying انعطف نَحْوَهُ i. e. *he,* or *it, inclined towards him,* or *it;* (TA;)

[or the latter meaning;] or *it became inclined,* (Mṣb,) or *became bent,* (Ṣ,* O, Mṣb, Ḳ,) or *both,* (TA,) as quasi-pass. of عَطَفَهُ; (Ṣ, O, Mṣb, TA;) and ▼ تعطّف likewise has both of these meanings, as quasi-pass. of عطّفهُ, or [signifies *it became much inclined* and *bent,* for] عطّف is with teshdeed to denote muchness. (TA.) — Hence, (MF, TA,) عَطَفَ عَلَيْهِ, (Ṣ, Mgh, MA, O, Ḳ,) [aor. as above,] inf. n. عَطْفٌ; (MA, MF, TA;) and ▼ تعطّف عليه; (Ṣ, MA, O, Ḳ;) [and ▼ انعطف عليه;] ‡ *He was,* or *became, favourably inclined towards him;* or *affectionate,* or *kind, to him;* (MA, PṢ;) *he regarded him,* or *treated him, with mercy* or *pity* or *compassion;* (MA, Mgh;) because in mercy, or pity, or compassion, is an inclining towards its object; (Mgh;) i. q. أَشْفَقَ عَلَيْهِ; (Ṣ, O, Ḳ;) and وَصَلَهُ, and بَرَّهُ. (TA in explanation of the second.) And عَطَفَتْ عَلَى وَلَدِهَا, aor. as above, inf. n. عَطْفٌ, said of a she-camel, † *She became favourably inclined,* or *compassionate, towards her young one, and yielded her milk;* (Mṣb;) and ▼ تعطّفت عَلَيْهِ [signifies the same, or *she was made to incline to him,* or *to affect him*]. (M in art. رأم, &c.) — عَطَفَ عَلَيْهِ also signifies *He turned,* or *returned, against him:* (Ṣ:) or *he charged,* or *made an assault* or *attack, upon him,* [in battle,] *and turned,* or *returned, against him:* (O, Ḳ:) or *he returned against him with that which he disliked,* or *hated:* and *to him with that which he desired.* (L, referring to a verse of Aboo-Wejzeh Es-Saadee cited in art. حين, q. v.) — And عَطَفَ, aor. as above, (TA,) inf. n. عُطُوفٌ, (Ḳ, TA,) signifies also *He turned away,* or *back.* (Ḳ,* TA.) — And [hence,] عَطَفَ عَنْهُ signifies ‡ *the contr. of* عَطَفَ عَلَيْهِ in the first of the senses assigned to this latter above [i. e. it signifies ‡ *He was,* or *became, averse from him;* or *disaffected,* or *unkind, to him;* or *unmerciful, unpitying,* or *uncompassionate, to him*]. (MF, TA.) — عُطُوفٌ and عَطْفٌ [as intrans. inf. ns.] also signify A sheep's, or goat's, *bending the neck, not by reason of an ailment.* (TA.) — And عَطْفٌ [app. likewise as an intrans. inf. n.] also signifies The *folding of the extremities of the skirt, of the facing,* or *outer side, upon,* or *against, the lining,* or *inner side.* (TA.) = عَطَفَهُ, (Mgh, Mṣb, TA,) [aor. as above,] inf. n. عَطْفٌ, (Mgh, Mṣb,) *He inclined it;* (Mgh, Mṣb, TA;) namely, a thing; (Mṣb, TA;) as also ▼ استعطفهُ: (Mgh:) or *he bent it,* or *doubled it,* or *folded it:* (Mṣb:) or it signifies also *he bent it:* and ▼ عطّفهُ likewise, inf. n. تَعْطِيفٌ, has both of these meanings: (TA:) or this latter verb is with teshdeed to denote muchness [of the action], or multiplicity [of the objects]: (Ṣ, O, TA:) you say, عَطَفْتُ العُودَ (Ṣ) *I bent* [or *inclined*] *the stick,* or *piece of wood:* (MA, PṢ:) and ▼ عَطَّفْتُ العِيدَانَ [*I bent,* or *inclined, the sticks,* or *pieces of wood*]: (Ṣ, O:) and ▼ عَطَّفْتُ رَأْسَ الخَشَبَةِ [*I bent,* or *inclined, much, the head of the piece of wood*]. (TA.) One says of a she-gazelle, تَعْطِفُ جِيدَهَا إِذَا رَبَضَتْ [*She inclines,* or *bends, her neck when she lies down on her breast*]. (O, Ḳ.) And one says, عَطَفَ رَأْسَ بَعِيرِهِ إِلَيْهِ *He inclined,* or *bent,* or *turned aside, the head of his camel towards him;* inf. n. عَطْفٌ: (TA:) and ▼ استعطف نَاقَتَهُ *He turned aside his she-camel* (عَطَفَهَا) *by pulling her nose-rein in order that she should incline her head.* (Mgh.) And عَطَفَ الوِسَادَةَ, (Ṣ, O, Ḳ,) aor. and inf. n. as above; (O;) and ▼ عَطَّفَهَا; (Ḳ;) *He bent,* or *doubled,* or *folded, the pillow,* or *cushion,* (Ṣ, O, Ḳ,) *when leaning with his elbow upon it.* (O.) — And [hence] one says, عَطَفَ ٱللّٰهُ بِقَلْبِ السُّلْطَانِ عَلَى رَعِيَّتِهِ † *God made the heart of the Sultán,* or *ruling power, to be favourably inclined towards his subjects; to regard them,* or *treat them, with mercy.* (TA.) And عَطَفَتْكَ عَلَيْهِمُ الرَّحِمُ † [*The feeling of relationship,* or *consanguinity,* or *the sympathy of blood, caused,* or *hath caused, thee to be favourably inclined towards them;* &c.]. (Ḥam p. 765.) And عَطَفَ النَّاقَةَ عَلَى وَلَدِهَا † [*He made the she-camel to incline to,* or *affect, her young one*]. (M in art. رأم; &c.: see also لِقَاحٌ مُعَطَّفَةٌ in this art.) And تُعْطَفُ عَلَى البَوِّ † [*She* (a camel) *is made to incline to,* or *affect, the stuffed skin of a young unweaned camel* in order that she may yield her milk, when her young one has died]. (Ṣ, O. [See عَطُوفٌ.]) — And عَطَفْتُهُ عَنْ حَاجَتِهِ † *I turned him away,* or *back, from his object of want.* (Mṣb.) — And عَطْفُ المُدْمَجِ i. e. القِدْحِ means *The turning round about,* or *shuffling, of the gaming-arrow.* (Ṣ voce مُدْمَجٌ: see a verse there cited.)

2: see 1, latter half, in four places. = عَطَّفْتُهُ ثَوْبِي, inf. n. تَعْطِيفٌ, *I made my garment to be to him an* عِطَاف, (O, Ḳ, TA,) i. e. *a* رِدَآء, [*by putting it*] *upon his shoulders,* as men do in the [season of] heat. (TA.)

5: see 1, former half, in three places. — [تعطّف also signifies *He* (a man) *affected a bending of his body;* like تَثَنَّى, with which it is coupled in the Ṣ and O and Ḳ in art. غوج.] = تعطّف بِالعِطَافِ *He clad himself* (Ṣ, O, Ḳ*) *with the* عطاف (O) [i. e.] *with the* رِدَآء; (Ṣ;) as also ▼ اعتطف بِهِ. (Ibn-'Abbád, O, Ḳ.*) — Hence, in a trad., (TA,) in a prayer of the Prophet, (O,) سُبْحَانَ مَنْ تَعَطَّفَ بِالعِزِّ وَقَالَ بِهِ, (O, TA,) meaning ‡ [*I declare,* or *celebrate,* or *extol, the absolute perfection*] *of Him who hath clad Himself with might as with a* رِدَآء [*and* (as expl. in the Ḳ in art. قول and by Ṣgh) *hath predominated thereby*]. (IAth, TA.)

6. تعاطفوا means عَطَفَ بَعْضُهُمْ عَلَى بَعْضٍ [i. e. † *They were,* or *became, favourably inclined, one towards another;* or *affectionate,* or *kind, one to another;* &c.: see 1]. (Ṣ, O, Ḳ.) — And تعاطف فِي مِشْيَتِهِ *He* (a man, Lth, O) *shook,* or *moved about, his head, in his gait:* (Lth, O, Ḳ:) or *he inclined from side to side, therein:* or *he walked with an elegant and a proud and self-conceited gait.* (O,* Ḳ.)

7: see 1, first quarter, in two places.

8: see 5. — [Hence,] اعتطف القَوْسَ *He hung upon himself the bow, putting its suspensory belt or cord upon his neck or shoulder;* (IAạr, TA;) and so السَّيْفَ *the sword.* (TA.)

10. استعطفهُ, (O, Ḳ,) or استعطفهُ عَلَيْهِ, (Ṣ, [in which the meaning is indicated by the addition of فَعَطَفَ,]) signifies سَأَلَهُ أَنْ يَعْطِفَ عَلَيْهِ [*He asked him to become favourably inclined towards him; to be affectionate,* or *kind, to him;* or *to regard him,* or *treat him, with mercy* or *pity* or *compassion*]: (O, Ḳ:) [or *he sought,* or *endeavoured, to conciliate to him his affection,* or *good will:*] or سَأَلْتُهُ أَنْ يَنْعَطِفَ signifies [*I asked him to incline,* or *bend:* but perhaps ينعطف is a mistranscription for يَعْطِفَ]. (Mṣb.) — See also 1, latter half, in two places.

عَطْفٌ: see the next paragraph, last sentence, in two places. — [It is used in grammar as meaning *Adjunction* to an antecedent: this is of two kinds; عَطْفُ البَيَانِ *the explicative adjunction,* as in جَآءَ أَخُوكَ زَيْدٌ; and عَطْفُ النَّسَقِ *the ordinal adjunction,* as in جَآءَ زَيْدٌ وَعَمْرٌو: (in each of which instances the latter noun is termed ▼ مَعْطُوفٌ; and the former noun ▼ مَعْطُوفٌ عَلَيْهِ:) and hence, حَرْفُ عَطْفٍ, meaning *a particle of adjunction;* or what we commonly call *a conjunction;* (as وَ, and ثُمَّ, &c.;) also termed ▼ حَرْفٌ عَاطِفٌ *an adjunctive particle.*]

عِطْفٌ The *side* of a human being, *from the head to the hip,* or *to the foot:* (Mgh:) and the *side* of a thing: (Mṣb:) or the dual signifies the *two sides* of a man, *from the part next the head to the hips:* (Ṣ, O:) and the *two sides of the neck* of a man: (TA:) and the *two sides* of anything: (Ṣ, O, Ḳ:) as relating to a man, (TA,) or a thing, (Mṣb,) the pl. is أَعْطَافٌ, [properly a pl. of pauc.,] (Mṣb, TA,) and, as relating to a man, عِطَافٌ also, and عُطُوفٌ. (TA.) Hence the phrase, هُمْ أَلْيَنُ عِطْفًا [*They are more pliant,* or *pliable;* properly as meaning *flexible, supple, lithe,* or *limber;* but app. here used tropically, as meaning *compliant:* compare لَيِّنُ الجَانِبِ]. (Mgh.) And لَيِّنُ الأَعْطَافِ [*Pliant,* or *pliable,* &c.], applied to a horse: (En-Naḍr, TA voce غَوْجٌ: [see also عَاجٍ, in art. عوج:]) and ▼ سَهْلُ المُعْطِفِ [and ▼ المَعَاطِفِ and الأَعْطَافِ, which signify the same,] so applied. (Ṣ and O and TA voce غَوْجٌ.) And [hence, also,] one says, ثَنَى عَنِّي عِطْفَهُ [lit. *He bent from me his side*], meaning *he turned away from me.* (Ṣ, O, Ḳ.) And جَآءَ ثَانِىَ عِطْفِهِ *He came in an unstraitened,* or *an easy,* or *a pleasant and plentiful, state,* or *condition:* (O, Ḳ:) or (Ḳ) ثَانِىَ عِطْفِهِ in the Ḳur [xxii. 9] means (O) *twisting,* or *bending, his neck:* (O, Ḳ:) or (Ḳ) *magnifying himself,* or *behaving proudly, and turning away* (O, Ḳ) *from El-Islám.* (O.) And فُلَانٌ يَنْظُرُ فِي عِطْفَيْهِ [lit. *Such a one looks at his sides*], meaning, *is self-conceited.* (IDrd, O, Ḳ.*) —

Also The *armpit* (Az, O, Ḳ, TA) of a man: and his *shoulder*: pl. عُطُوفٌ. (Az, TA.) —— And The *curved part of each of the two extremities* of the bow; (O, Ḳ, TA;) the two being called its عِطْفَانِ. (TA.) One says, تَعَوَّجَ القَوْسُ فِى عِطْفَيْهِ, (O, TA,) in the copies of the Ḳ, تَعَرَّجَ القَوْسُ فِى عِطْفَيْهِ, but the former is the right, (TA,) meaning [*The bow*] *bent to the right and left* [*in the two curved parts of its extremities*]. (O, Ḳ, TA.) —— One says also, تَنَحَّ عَنْ عِطْفِ الطَّرِيقِ [i. e. *Go thou aside from*] *the beaten track of the road*; as also ▼ عَطْفِه: (IAạr, O, Ḳ:) or ▼ عَطْفٌ signifies *a bending* (Mgh, Mṣb) in a street (Mgh) or road, (Mṣb,) being an inf. n. used as a simple subst.; but the عطف in a street [or road] is [*a bent part*, being] of the measure فِعْلٌ in the sense of the measure مَفْعُولٌ. (Mgh. [See similar instances voce ذِبْحٌ.])

عَطَفٌ: see عَطْفَةٌ. —— Also *Length of the edges of the eyelids*, (O, Ḳ, TA,) *and a bending* [app. *upwards*] *thereof*: (TA:) occurring in a trad.: or the word, as some relate it, is غَطَفٌ [q. v.]; (O, TA;) which is of higher authority. (TA.)

عَطْفَةٌ [as an inf. n. un.] *An inclining*: hence, in a trad., كَأَنَّ عَطْفَتَهُمْ حِينَ سَمِعُوا صَوْتِى عَطْفَةُ البَقَرِ عَلَى أَوْلَادِهَا [*As though their inclining, when they heard my voice, were the inclining of the cows* (app. meaning wild cows) *towards their young ones*]. (O, TA.) —— And *A certain bead by means of which women captivate men*; (Ṣ, O, Ḳ;) as also ▼ عَطَفَةٌ. (Ḳ.) —— Also, (Ḳ,) or ▼ عَطَفَةٌ, for which عَطْفَةٌ is used by poetic license, (ISh and O, [referring to a verse which will be found at the close of this paragraph, in which verse, however, it is certainly not used as applied to what here immediately follows,]) *A tree to which the* حَبَلَة [i. e. *grape-vine*, or *branch of a grape-vine*,] *clings*; (ISh, O, Ḳ;) and so ▼ عِطْفَةٌ, (Ḳ,) or thus as written in the "Book of Plants" by AḤn, who says that it is thus called because of its bending and twining upon trees: (O: [but this remark seems evidently to show that he means thereby one of the plants mentioned below voce عَطَفَةٌ or voce عُطْفَةٌ, or perhaps what here follows:]) IB says that the عَطْفَة is the لَبْلَاب [*dolichos lablab* of Linn.]; so called because of its twining upon trees: (TA:) [and this, or what will be found mentioned voce عَطَفَةٌ below, may be meant in the following verse:] a poet says,

تَلَبَّسَ حُبُّهَا بِدَمِى وَلَحْمِى
تَلَبُّسَ عَطْفَةٍ بِفُرُوعِ ضَالِ

[*The love of her mingled with, and clung to, my blood and my flesh, like the mingling and clinging of an* عطفة *with, and to, the branches of a wild lote-tree*]. (ISh, O, TA.)

عِطْفَةٌ: see عَطْفَةٌ, in two places. —— Also The *extremities* [or *tendrils*] *of the vine, that hang therefrom*. (Ḳ.) —— And The *tree* [or *plant*] *called* عَضْبَة [n. un. of عَضْبٌ, q. v., said by some to signify the لَبْلَاب, mentioned in the next preceding paragraph]. (Ḳ.)

عَطَفَةٌ *A certain plant which twines upon trees and has no leaves nor branches, fed upon by the oxen* [app. meaning the wild oxen,] (Ḳ, TA,) *but injurious to them*: (TA:) some of its عُرُوق [app. here meaning root-like stalks] are taken, and twisted, and charmed [by some invocation or otherwise], and cast upon the woman that hates her husband, and she consequently loves him: (Ḳ, TA:) so they assert: (TA:) accord. to AA, ▼ عَطَفٌ signifies *one of the strange kinds of trees of the desert*: (O, TA:) عَطَفَةٌ is the n. un. thereof. (TA.) See also عَطْفَةٌ.

قَوْسٌ عَطْفَى: see مَعْطُوفٌ.

عَطْفَآءُ [as an epithet applied to a شَاة, i. e. sheep or goat,] *Having the horn twisted*; like عَقْصَآءُ: occurring in a trad. relating to the poor-rate. (TA. [The masc., أَعْطَفُ, I do not find mentioned.])

عِطَافٌ and ▼ مِعْطَفٌ [*A garment of either of the kinds called*] *a* رِدَآء, (Ṣ, O, Ḳ) and *a* طَيْلَسَان, and *any garment that is worn like as is the* رِدَآء, (TA,) and the former also signifies *an* إِزَار: (Ḳ:) the two words are like إِزَارٌ and مِئْزَرٌ, &c.: and the رِدَآء is said to be called عطاف because it falls against the two sides of the man's neck, which are termed his عِطْفَانِ: the pl. [of pauc.] of عِطَافٌ is أَعْطِفَةٌ and [of mult.] عُطُفٌ and عُطُوفٌ; (TA;) and عُطُفٌ [also] is a pl. of عِطَافٌ as meaning an إِزَار: (Ḳ, TA:) the pl. of ▼ مِعْطَفٌ is مَعَاطِفُ; but Aṣ says that he had not heard any sing. of this pl. (O, TA.) —— Hence, (Ṣ, O, TA,) عِطَافٌ signifies also *A sword*; (Ṣ, O, Ḳ, TA;) because the Arabs called it [in like manner] رِدَآء [q. v.]; (TA;) and so ▼ مِعْطَفٌ. (Ḳ.) —— And one says, السَّيْفُ عِطَافِى وَإِبَاطِى, meaning *I put*, or *place, the sword upon my side, and beneath my armpit*. (TA in art. ابط.)

عَطُوفٌ, applied to a bow: see مَعْطُوفَةٌ. —— Applied to a gaming-arrow, (O, Ḳ,) of those used in the game called المَيْسِر, (O,) as also ▼ عَطَّافٌ, *That inclines towards*, or *upon, the other arrows* [*in the receptacle called the* رِبَابَة], *and comes forth winning*, or *before the others*: [app. because it is the first upon which the hand falls:] (O, Ḳ:) an ex. of the former occurs in a verse of Ṣakhr-el-Ghei cited in art. عض: (O, TA:) [in the TA, in art. عوض, it is expl. as meaning, in that verse, a *borrowed* arrow, in the luck of which one has confidence:] or the former, accord. to El-Ḳutabee, (O,) or each, (Ḳ,) signifies the arrow *to which is assigned no fine and no gain*; (O, Ḳ;) it is *one of the three* أَغْفَال; and is called عطوف because it returns into every رِبَابَة with which one plays; and El-Ḳutabee says that قِدْحًا عَطُوفًا in the verse of Ṣakhr is a sing. in a pl. sense: (O:) or, (O, Ḳ,) accord. to Skr, (O,) عَطُوفٌ signifies *that comes* [*forth*] يَرِدُ, so in the O, in the copies of the Ḳ يَرِدُ, [which would make this explanation virtually the same as the one immediately following it,]) *time after time*: or *that is repeated*, [i. e. *repeatedly put into the* رِبَابَة *and drawn forth from it*,] *time after time*: and ▼ عَطَّافٌ signifies a gaming arrow *that turns aside from the places whence the* [*other*] *arrows are taken* (عَنْ مَآخِذِ القِدَاحِ [for which the CḲ has على مَآخِذِ القِداحِ]), *and becomes alone, by itself*. (O, Ḳ.) —— Also عَطُوفٌ, † One *much inclined to favour*; or *to be affectionate*, or *kind*; *and to show mercy* or *pity* or *compassion*. (O.) † *A bestower of favour*, or *bounty*; *good in disposition*; as also ▼ عَاطِفٌ; (TA;) of both of which عُطُفٌ is pl.; (Ḳ, TA;) and ▼ عَطَّافٌ also has this meaning, applied to a man: (Lth, TA:) and also this last, and عَطُوفٌ, † a man *who protects*, or *defends, those who are defeated*, or *put to flight*. (TA.) And † *A woman loving to her husband, affectionate to her child* or *children*. (TA.) And † *A she-camel that is made to incline to*, or *affect*, (Ṣ, O,) or *that inclines to*, or *affects*, (so in the copies of the Ḳ,) *the stuffed skin of a young unweaned camel*, [when her young one has died,] *and that keeps*, or *cleaves, to it*: (Ṣ, O, Ḳ:) pl. عُطُفٌ. (TA. [See 1, near the end.]) —— Also, and ▼ عَاطُوفٌ, A مِصْيَدَة [or *snare, trap, gin*, or *net*], (O, Ḳ, TA,) so called because (O, TA) *having in it a piece of wood that bends*, or *inclines*, (O, Ḳ, TA,) *in its head*: (TA:) also called غَاطُوفٌ. (TA in art. غطف.)

عَطِيفٌ † A woman *having no pride*; *gentle*; *very submissive* or *obedient*. (AZ, O, Ḳ.)

عَطَافَةٌ: see مُنْعَطَفٌ: —— and see what here follows.

عَطِيفَةٌ and ▼ عِطَافَةٌ *A bow*: pl. عَطَائِفُ. (TA.)

عَطَّافٌ: see عَطُوفٌ, in three places. —— العَطَّافُونَ is like العَكَّارُونَ, meaning † *They who return to the fight* [after fleeing, or wheeling away]. (TA in art. عكر.)

عَاطِفٌ A she-gazelle (ظَبْيَةٌ) *inclining*, or *bending, her neck when she lies down on her breast*. (Ṣ, O, Ḳ.) And عَاطِفَةٌ A sheep or goat (شَاة) *bending its neck, not by reason of an ailment*. (TA.) —— See also عَطُوفٌ, latter half. —— And see the explanations of the verse of Aboo-Wejzeh Es-Saạdee cited in art. حين. —— العَاطِفُ is applied to *The sixth* [*in arriving at the goal*] *of the horses that are started together for a race*; (MA, TA, and Ḥam p. 46;) related as on the authority of El-Muärrij; but Az did not find that those who related this as from him were trustworthy persons, though he was himself trustworthy: (TA:) or *the fourth thereof*. (Ḥar p. 270.) —— See also عَطْفٌ.

عَاطِفَةٌ [† *A bias*, or *cause of inclining*: pl. عَوَاطِفُ]. One says, مَا يَثْنِينِى عَلَيْكَ عَاطِفَةٌ مِنْ قَرَابَةٍ وَرَحِمٍ [† *A bias of relationship does not incline me towards thee*; or *no bias of relationship inclines me towards thee*]. (Ṣ, O, TA.) —— [And hence, as being a cause of inclining,] العَاطِفَةُ signifies [also] *Relationship* [itself]; or *the tie*, or *ties, thereof*; syn. الرَّحِمُ: an epithet in which the quality of a substantive predominates. (TA.) — [And] † *Affection*, or *kindness; mercy, pity*, or *compassion*. (MA.)

عَاطُوفٌ: see عَطُوفٌ, last sentence.

مُنْعَطَفٌ; and its pl. مَعَاطِفُ: see مُنْعَطَفٌ. [*A place of inclining*, or *bending*, of the body; whence,] سَيْلُ المَعْطِفِ and المَعَاطِفِ: see عِطْفٌ: [and *a place of flexure*, or *creasing*, of the skin; whence it is said that the pl.] مَعَاطِفُ signifies the *places*, of the body, *that sweat*. (TA in art. عرض.) [And *A place of doubling*, or *folding*; or *a duplicature*, or *fold*, of a garment, or piece of cloth.]

مِعْطَفٌ: see عِطَافٌ, in three places.

مُعَطَّفَةٌ, applied to bows (قِسِىٌّ), is with teshdeed to denote muchness or multiplicity; (Ṣ, O, Ḳ, TA;) [so that it may signify either *Much bent*, or, as applied to a number of bows, simply *bent*: but it is said that] the meaning is, *having one of the curved extremities bent towards the other*; and so applied to a single bow (قَوْسٌ); as also † عَطُوفٌ. (TA.) — And in like manner applied to milch camels (لِقَاحٌ); [meaning ‡ *Made to incline to*, or *affect, a young one*: for] sometimes, or often, they made a number of she-camels to incline to, or affect, a single young one, (عَطَفُوا † عِدَّةَ ذَوْدٍ عَلَى فَصِيلٍ وَاحِدٍ,) and drew their milk while they were in the condition of doing thus, in order that they might yield it copiously. (Ṣ, O, Ḳ, TA.)

مَعْطُوفٌ [*Inclined*, or *bent*: &c.]. — قَوْسٌ مَعْطُوفَةٌ *An Arabian bow*, (IDrd, Ṣ, O, Ḳ,*) *of which the curved extremity is much bent towards it, and which is used for* [*shooting at*] *the butts*: (IDrd, O, Ḳ:) and † قَوْسٌ عَطْفَى signifies the same. (TA.) — See also عَطْفٌ, in two places.

مُنْعَطَفٌ *A place of inclining*, or *bending*; (Ṣ, O, Mṣb, Ḳ;) [as also † مَعْطِفٌ, pl. مَعَاطِفُ;] and so † مَعَاطَفَةٌ: (TA:) you say مُنْعَطَفُ الوَادِى *the place of inclining*, or *bending, of the valley*: (Ṣ, O, Mṣb, Ḳ:) and مَعَاطِفُ † الأَوْدِيَةِ [*the places of inclining*, or *bending, of the valleys*]. (Ḳ voce كُسُورٌ.)

عطل

1. عَطِلَتْ, [in my copy of the Mṣb said to be of the class of قتل, perhaps a mistranscription for قَبِلَ, but see what is said below of عَطَلَ as syn. with بَطَلَ, from which it may be inferred that عَطَلَتْ is correct in the sense here following as well as عَطِلَتْ,] said of a woman, [aor. ـَ,] inf. n. عَطَلٌ (Ṣ, O, Ḳ) and عُطُولٌ; (O, Ḳ;) and † تعطّلت; (Ṣ, O, Ḳ;) *She had not upon her any women's ornaments*; (Ḳ, TA;) and *wore not any ornature, or decoration*: (TA:) or *her neck was destitute of necklaces or the like*; (Ṣ, O;) as also † استعطلت: (Ḥar p. 268:) accord. to Er-Rághib, العَطَلُ signifies *the being destitute of ornature*, or *decoration*. (TA.) — And sometimes العَطَلُ is used [for العَطَلُ مِنْ شَىْءٍ] as meaning *The being destitute* of a thing; though primarily relating to women's ornaments. (Ṣ, O.) One says, عَطِلَ مِنَ المَالِ *He* (a man, O) *was*, or *became, destitute* [*of property*], and مِنَ الأَدَبِ [*of discipline*, or *good qualities and attributes, of the mind*, &c.]. (O, Ḳ.) — And it signifies also *The being destitute of occupation*. (Er-Rághib, TA.) One says, عَطَلَ الأَجِيرُ, aor. ـُ, like بَطَلَ, aor. ـُ, in measure and in meaning [i. e. *The hired man was without occupation*; though it seems that in this sense also, accord. to general usage, the verb is عَطِلَ, aor. ـَ]. (Mṣb. [See also 5.]) And عطلت الإِبِلُ *The camels were without a pastor to tend them*. (Mṣb. [The context there app. indicates that the verb in this case, likewise, is with fet-ḥ to the ط; but I believe it to be more correctly عَطِلَتْ.]) — And عَطِلَ, (O, Ḳ,) with kesr [to the ط], (O,) [i. e.] like فَرِحَ, (Ḳ,) signifies also *He was*, or *became, large in the body*. (O, Ḳ.)

2. عطّل الشَّىْءَ and † اعطله signify the same [app. in all the senses assigned to the former]. (O.) — 'Áïsheh is related, in a trad., to have said respecting a woman who had died, عَطِّلُوهَا, meaning *Divest ye her of her ornaments*. (Ṣ, O.) — [Hence,] عطّل القَوْسَ, inf. n. تَعْطِيلٌ, *He divested the bow of its string*. (TA.) — [Hence likewise, the inf. n.] التَّعْطِيلُ signifies [also] *The rendering vacant, void*, or *unoccupied*, (Ḳ, TA,) a place of abode, and the like. (TA.) And *The leaving* a thing *untended, unminded*, or *neglected*. (Ḳ, TA. [ضِيَاعًا in the CḲ is a mistake for ضَيَاعًا.]) One says of the frontier of a hostile country, عُطِّلَ, meaning *It was left without any to defend it*. (TA.) And of subjects one says, عُطِّلُوا, meaning *They were left without any one to govern them*. (TA.) One says also, عَطَّلْتُ الإِبِلَ, inf. n. as above, *I left the camels without a pastor to tend them*. (Mṣb.) وَإِذَا العِشَارُ عُطِّلَتْ, in the Ḳur lxxxi. 4, means *And when the pregnant camels* [*ten months gone with young*] *shall be left without a pastor*, or *without being milked* [?]; (Jel;) by reason of the terrors of the hour; (O;) i. e. by men's having their minds occupied by the terrors of the day of resurrection. (TA.) And عُطِّلَتْ is said of lands of seed-produce as meaning *They were left uncultivated*. (TA.) — التَّعْطِيلُ signifies also التَّفْرِيغُ [as meaning *The making*, or *leaving, vacant* from any work, occupation, employment, or use; *free* therefrom; *unoccupied*; or *unemployed*]. (Ṣ, O, Ḳ.) One says, عَطَّلْتُ الأَجِيرَ *I made the hired man to be unoccupied*. (Mṣb.) And عطّل الخَيْلَ مِنَ الغَزْوِ (Ṣ and Ḳ in art. ابو) [*He freed the horses from service in warfare*;] *he did not go to war upon the horses*. (TA in that art.) — [Also *The assertion of the tenet*, or *tenets, of the* مُعَطِّل, q. v.] — And تَعْطِيلُ الحُدُودِ means *The not inflicting the* [*punishments termed*] حدود *upon him to whom they are due*. (TA.)

4: see 2, first sentence.

5: see 1, first sentence. — تعطّل, said of a man, (Ṣ, O,) *He remained* [or *became*] *without work*, or *occupation*. (Ṣ, O, Ḳ.) [Said of a man, &c., *He*, or *it, was*, or *became, inactive*, or *inert*. (See غُشِىَ عَلَيْهِ.)] — [تَعَطَّلَتْ مِنَ الإِسْتِقَآءِ بِهَا is said of a دَلْو [or leathern bucket, meaning *It was exempted from*, i. e. *unused for, the drawing of water therewith*]. (TA.) — And تعطّل is said of a tent [as meaning *It became vacant*]. (TA in art. ابو.)

10: see 1, first sentence.

Q. Q. 4. اِعْطَأَلَّتِ الشَّجَرَةُ *The tree had many branches, and was much tangled*, or *very luxuriant* or *dense*: so accord. to Az. (TA.) See also Q. Q. 4 in arts. عضل and عظل.

عُطْلٌ: see عَطَلٌ, last sentence.

عَطَلٌ inf. n. of 1 [q. v.]. (Ṣ, O, Ḳ.) = Also *The denuded*, or *unclad, part*, or *parts, of the body*; syn. جُرْدَةٌ: so in the saying اِمْرَأَةٌ حَسَنَةُ العَطَلِ [*A woman beautiful in respect of the denuded*, or *unclad, part*, or *parts, of the body*]. (TA.) — And The *body*, or *person*; syn. شَخْصٌ; (Ṣ, O, Ḳ, TA;) particularly, as some say, of a human being; (TA;) like عَلَلٌ: (Ṣ, O, TA:) pl. أَعْطَالٌ. (Ḳ.) And one says, مَا أَحْسَنَ عَطَلَهُ, meaning [*How beautiful is*] *his tallness*, or *justness of stature, and his perfectness* [*of make*]! (Ṣ, O.) — And The *neck*. (Ḳ.) — And *Beauty of body*. (TA.) = Also *A stalk of a raceme of a palm-tree*; (Ṣ, O;) as also † عُطْبُولٌ, accord. to IDrd: (O:) or the former, (TA,) and † the latter, accord. to IDrd, and accord. to Az, who says that he heard it from the cultivators of palm-trees (مِنَ النَّخْلِيِّينَ) in El-Aḥsà, (O,) the *stalk of a raceme of a male palm-tree*, (O, TA,) to which Az adds, *with which the female palm-tree is fecundated*: (O:) or † عُطْبُولٌ and † عُنْطُلٌ signify *a stalk of a* طَلْع [or *spadix*] *of a male palm-tree* [*with the flowers upon it*]. (Ḳ, TA.)

[عَطِلٌ is an epithet of which only the fem. (with ة) is mentioned.] — عَطِلَةٌ is applied to a she-camel as meaning *Goodly*, or *beautiful*: pl. عَطِلَاتٌ: (Ṣ, O:) which is expl. by A'Obeyd in this sense, and not derived by him: held by ISd to be a possessive epithet: (TA:) or the sing., thus applied, *goodly*, or *beautiful, in body*: (Ḳ:) or thus as applied to a woman: and, applied to a she-camel, *perfect in body and tallness*. (TA.) — Also, applied to a she-camel, *i. q.* صَفِىٌّ [i. e. *Abounding in milk*; or *whose milk lasts throughout the year*]. (Ḳ.) And, applied to a ewe or she-goat, *Abounding much in milk*: (Ḳ:) or, accord. to Lth, *that is known in* [*the appearance of*] *her neck to be one abounding in milk*. (O.) = And, applied to A دَلْو [or leathern bucket], *Having its* [*thongs called*] وَذَم *broken*, (O, Ḳ, TA,) *so that it has become exempted from* (تَعَطَّلَتْ

مِن [i. e. *unused for*]) *the drawing of water therewith:* (TA:) or *that has been left for a time unused, and of which the thongs above mentioned, and the loop-shaped handles, have been broken.* (IAth, TA.) Hence the saying of 'Áïsheh, describing her father, رَأَبَ الثَّأْىَ وَأَوْذَمَ العَطِلَةَ [*He repaired the rending, and put* وَذَم *to that bucket of which the* وَذَم *were broken*]; meaning that he restored the affairs to their state of order, and strengthened the condition of El-Islám after the apostatizing of men. (O, TA.)

عُطُلٌ and ▼ عَاطِلٌ, applied to a woman, (Ṣ, O, Mṣb, Ḳ,) *Having no women's ornaments upon her;* (Mṣb, Ḳ;) [and] so ▼ عَطْلَآءُ: (IDrd, O:) or *whose neck is destitute of necklaces or the like;* as also ▼ مِعْطَالٌ: (Ṣ, O:) or ▼ this last signifies *usually having no women's ornaments upon her:* (Ḳ:) the pl. (of عُطُلٌ, TA) is أَعْطَالٌ and (of ▼ عَاطِلٌ, TA) عَوَاطِلُ and عُطَّلٌ. (Ḳ, TA.) — [Hence,] أَعْطَالٌ applied to camels, (Ṣ, O, Ḳ,) *Having no halters upon them:* (Ṣ, O:) or *having no collars upon them, nor halters;* and so as applied to horses: (Ḳ:) and, (Th, Ḳ,) applied to camels, (Th, TA,) *having upon them no brands:* (Th, Ḳ:) sing. عُطُلٌ. (Ḳ.) [See also غُفْلٌ.] — And, applied to men, *Having no weapons with them:* (Ṣ, O, Ḳ:) in this sense, also, pl. of عُطُلٌ. (Ḳ.) — عُطُلٌ applied to a bow, *Having no string upon it:* (Ṣ, O, Mṣb, Ḳ:) pl. أَعْطَالٌ. (TA.) — And عُطُلٌ and ▼ عُطْلٌ [or عطل مِنَ المَالِ and مِنَ الأَدَبِ] (see 1)] signify, applied to a man, *Destitute of property* and *of discipline,* or *good qualities and attributes, of the mind,* &c. (Ṣ, O, Ḳ.)

عُطْلَةٌ The *state of being,* or *remaining, without work,* or *occupation;* (Ṣ, MA, O, Ḳ;) a subst. from تَعَطَّلَ. (Ṣ, O, Ḳ.) One says, هُوَ يَشْكُو العُطْلَةَ [*He complains of being without work, or occupation*]. (TA.) — And هُوَ ذُو عُطْلَةٍ means *He is one who has no estate upon which to labour,* or *work.* (TA.)

عَطْلَآءُ: see عُطُلٌ, first sentence.

عَطِيلٌ: see عُطُلٌ, latter half, in three places.

عَاطِلٌ: see عُطُلٌ, first sentence, in two places. — [Hence,] أَبْيَاتٌ عَوَاطِلُ ‡ *Verses of which the words are without diacritical points:* opposed to أَبْيَاتٌ عَرَائِسُ. (Ḥar pp. 608-10.)

عَيْطَلٌ *Long* (Ḳ, TA) *in the* عَطَل, i. e., (TA,) *in the neck, with beauty of body;* (Ḳ, TA;) applied to a woman: (TA:) or *long,* or *tall,* in an absolute sense; and thus as applied to a she-camel and to a horse: (TA:) or *long in the neck;* (Ṣ, O, Ḳ, TA;) applied in this sense to a woman, and to a she-camel, (Ṣ, O,) and to a horse, (Ṣ,) or to any animal: (Ḳ, TA:) or *tall, with beauty of aspect and fatness;* thus as applied to a she-camel: the ى is augmentative. (TA.) It is also a proper name of a certain she-camel. (Ṣ, O.) — Also *Tall,* as applied to a [hill, or mountain, such as is termed] هَضْبَة. (O.) — And شَجَرٌ عَيْطَلٌ *Soft,* or *tender, trees.* (TA.) — See also عَطَلٌ, last sentence.

مُعْطَلٌ: see the next paragraph, in two places.

مُعَطَّلٌ [pass. part. n. of 2 (which see for some of its significations)] is applied to Anything *left untended, unminded,* or *neglected;* as also ▼ مُعْطَلٌ. (TA.) [Thus] مُعَطَّلُونَ signifies People, or subjects, *left without any one to govern them.* (TA.) And إِبِلٌ مُعَطَّلَةٌ *Camels* [*left*] *without a pastor.* (Ṣ, O, Ḳ.) And المُعَطَّلُ *What has no owner, of which no use is made, and from which no advantage is derived,* of land. (Ṣ, O, Ḳ.) And بِئْرٌ مُعَطَّلَةٌ, (Ṣ, O, TA,) and ▼ مُعْطَلَةٌ accord. to one reading [in the Ḳur xxii. 44], (O, TA,) *A well from which water is not drawn, and of the water of which no use is made:* (TA:) or it is thus called because [it is *one of which*] *its owners have perished:* (Ṣ, O, TA:) *neglected by reason of the death of its owners.* (Jel.)

مُعَطِّلٌ One *who asserts that the universe is devoid of an artificer who constructed it skilfully and adorned it:* (Er-Rághib, TA:) [but] the مُعَطِّلَة of the Arabs were of different sorts: *one sort of them disacknowledged the Creator, and the raising and restoring to life, and asserted that nature is that which brings to life and time is that which brings to nought: another sort of them acknowledged the Creator, and the beginning of creation, but disacknowledged the raising and restoring to life:* and *another sort of them acknowledged the Creator, and the beginning of creation, and a mode of restoration to life, but disacknowledged the apostles, and worshipped idols, and asserted them to be their intercessors with God in the life to come, and performed pilgrimage to them, and sacrificed victims to them, and offered offerings, and sought to advance themselves in their favour by means of religious rites and ceremonies, and legalized* [*certain things*] *and prohibited* [*others*]; and these were the generality of the Arabs, except a small portion of them. (Esh-Shahristánee.)

مِعْطَالٌ: see عُطُلٌ, first sentence, in two places.

مَعَاطِلُ [a pl. of which the sing. is not mentioned] The *parts which are the places of the ornaments* of a woman. (IDrd, O, Ḳ.)

[مُعْطَئِلٌّ part. n. of اِعْطَأَلَّ, q. v.: see also Q. Q. 4 in arts. عضل and عطل.]

عطن

1. عَطَنَتِ الإِبِلُ (Ṣ, Mṣb, Ḳ) or عَطَنَتِ الإِبِلُ عَلَى المَآءِ, (TA,) aor. ـِ and ـُ, inf. n. عُطُونٌ, (Ṣ, Mṣb, Ḳ,) *The camels lay down* [*at the water*] *after having satisfied their thirst;* (Ṣ, Mṣb,* Ḳ;) as also ▼ عَطَّنَتْ: (Ḳ:) and العُطُونُ, (Ḳ, TA,) it is said, (TA,) signifies *the resting,* or *the driving back to the nightly resting-place,* a she-camel *after her drinking:* (Ḳ, TA:) or *the bringing* her *back to the* عَطَن [q. v.], *waiting in expectation with her, because she did not drink the first time,* (so in the Ḳ accord. to the TA, but in the CḲ, agreeably with the Ṣ, this last meaning is made to relate to 4, q. v.,) *then offering* her *the water a second time:* (Ḳ, TA:) or it signifies [agreeably with the first explanation above] her *satisfying her thirst, then lying down:* (Ḳ,* TA:) in which explanation, in [some of the copies of] the Ḳ, ثم تبرك is erroneously put for ثُمَّ تَبْرُكَ. (TA.) قَدْ عَطَنُوا مَوَاشِيَهُمْ occurs in a trad. as meaning *They had rested,* or *had driven back to the nightly resting-place, their cattle.* (TA.) ═ عَطَنَ الجِلْدَ, aor. ـِ (Ṣ, Ḳ) and ـُ, (Ḳ,) inf. n. عَطْنٌ, (Ṣ,) *He took* عَلْقَى, *which is a certain plant,* (Ṣ,) so says J, but, as 'Alee Ibn-Ḥamzeh says, it is the غَلْقَة, a well-known plant, not the عَلْقَى, that is used for this purpose, (IB, TA,) [or perhaps عَلْقَى is a mistranscription for غَلْقَى, which is said in the Ḳ in art. غلق to be a syn. of غَلْقَة,] or فَرْث [i. e. *the fæces thus termed*], or *salt, and threw the skin into it, and covered it over, in order that its wool might become dissundered and loose;* after which it is thrown into the tan: (Ṣ:) or, as also ▼ عَطَّنَهُ, *he put the skin into the tan, and left it so that it became corrupt and stinking:* (Ḳ:) or *he sprinkled water upon it,* (Ḳ, TA,) *and folded it,* (TA,) *and buried it* (Ḳ, TA) *for a day and a night,* (TA,) *so that its hair* (Ḳ, TA) or *its wool,* (TA,) *became loose;* in order that it might be plucked off; (Ḳ, TA;) and that it [the skin] might be then thrown into the tan, it being then stinking in the utmost degree: (TA:) or العَطْنُ signifies *the putting* [a skin] *into the tan.* (Az, TA.) ═ عَطِنَ, aor. ـَ, (Ṣ, Ḳ,) inf. n. عَطَنٌ, (Ṣ,) said of a hide, *It became stinking, and its wool fell off, in the process termed* عطن [expl. above]: (AZ, Ṣ, TA:) or *it was put into the tan, and left so that it became corrupt and stinking:* (Ḳ:) or *water was sprinkled upon it,* (Ḳ, TA,) *and it was folded,* (TA,) *and buried* (Ḳ, TA) *for a day and a night,* (TA,) *so that its hair* (Ḳ, TA) or *its wool* (TA) *became loose;* in order that it might be plucked off; (Ḳ, TA;) and that it [the skin] might be then thrown into the tan, it being then stinking in the utmost degree: (TA:) and ▼ انعطن signifies the same: (Ṣ, Ḳ:) or this signifies *it* (a skin) *became loose in its wool without becoming corrupt.* (AḤn, TA.)

2. عطّن, inf. n. تَعْطِينٌ, *He made for himself an* عَطَن [q. v.]: (Ḳ, TA:) like as one says of a bird عَشَّشَ, meaning "he made for himself an عُشّ" [i. e. "a nest"]. (TA.) — عطّنت الإِبِلُ: see 1, first sentence. ═ عطّن الجِلْدَ: see 1, near the middle.

4. اعطن القَوْمُ means عَطَنَتْ إِبِلُهُمْ [*The people, or party, had their camels lying down at the water after having satisfied their thirst:* see 1, first sentence]. (Ṣ, Ḳ.) ═ اعطن الإِبِلَ *He watered the camels and then made them to lie down* [*at the water*]: (Ṣ, TA:) or *he confined the camels at the water, and they lay down, after having come to it* [*and drunk*], (Ḳ, TA,) *in order that they might drink again:* (TA:) this the Arabs do only in the intense heats of summer; not when the season becomes cool: (Mṣb:) or they do this only when the asterism of the Pleiades (الثُّرَيَّا) rises [auro-

rally, i. e. about the middle of May, O. S.], and men return from the seeking after herbage to the places of waters, or of constant sources of water: they do so only on the day of the camels' coming to the water; and they cease not to do thus [when necessary] until the time of the [auroral] rising of Canopus (سُهَيْل [i. e. early in August, O. S.]), in the خَرِيف, [app. here meaning the period of the rain so called, (see the latter of the two tables in page 1254,)] after which they do it not, but the camels come to the water and drink their draught and return from the water: (Az, TA:) or اعطن الإِبِلَ signifies *he brought back the camels to the* عَطَن [q. v.], *waiting in expectation with them, because they did not drink the first time.* (So in the CK [agreeably with what here follows; but see 1, first sentence].) And one says, اعطن الرَّجُلُ بَعِيرَهُ *The man brought back his camel to the* عَطَن, *waiting in expectation with him, he not having drunk.* (S.)

7: see 1, last sentence.

عَطَنٌ and ↓ مَعْطِنٌ (ISk, S, Mgh, Msb, K) or مَعْطَنٌ (TA [but this I find not elsewhere]) The *usual abiding-place of camels:* (K:) and also, (K, TA,) by predominance of usage, (TA,) or only, (Az, Msb, TA,) the *place of camels, where they lie down,* (Az, S, Mgh, Msb, TA,) *at the water,* (Az, S, TA,) or *around the water,* (Mgh, Msb,) or *around the watering-trough,* (K, TA,) *in order that they may drink a second time, after the first draught, and then be sent back to the places of pasture to remain there during the intervals between the waterings;* (S;) and likewise the *places of sheep or goats, where they lie down around the water:* (ISk, S, Msb, K, TA:) pl. of the former أَعْطَانٌ; and of the latter ↓ مَعَاطِنُ; (Az, S, Mgh, Msb, K;) which latter pl. is used by the lawyers as meaning [generally] the *places of lying down of camels.* (Msb.) The [space called] حَرِيم [q. v.] of the well of the عَطَن is said to be forty cubits. (Mgh.) Prayer in the أَعْطَان of camels is forbidden, because the person praying is not secure from being hurt by them, and diverted from his prayer, and defiled by the sprinkling of their urine. (IAth, TA.) ضَرَبَتِ الإِبِلُ بِعَطَنٍ [in which الأَرْضَ is understood after الابل] means *The camels lay down* [*in a place by the water*]: (S:) or *satisfied themselves with drinking and then lay down around the water* or *by the watering-troughs, to be brought again to drink another time.* (IAth, TA.) And one says, ضَرَبَتِ النَّاقَةُ بِعَطَنٍ *The she-camel lay down* [&c.]. (TA.) And ضَرَبَ النَّاسُ بِعَطَنٍ † *The people's camels satisfied themselves with drinking until they lay down and remained in their place* [*at the water*]; occurring in a trad.: (TA in art. ضرب:) or *the people satisfied their thirst and then abode at the water.* (K and TA in the present art.) —— [Hence] one says, فُلَانٌ وَاسِعُ العَطَنِ وَالبَلَدِ, (S,) or رَحْبُ العَطَنِ, (K, TA,) ‡ *Such a one is a person possessing much wealth; having an ample dwelling or place of abode;* (K, TA;) *endowed with extensive power or strength or might;* or *liberal, munificent,* or *generous.* (S, K, TA.) ═ And العَطَنُ signifies العِرْضُ [app. as meaning *Odour,* from the same word as inf. n. of عَطِنَ said of a hide]: so in the saying of 'Adee Ibn-Zeyd, cited by Sh,

* طَاهِرُ الأَثْوَابِ يَحْمِى عِرْضَهُ *
* مِنْ خَنَا الذِّمَّةِ أَوْ طَمْثِ العَطَنْ *

[*Pure in conduct,* or *actions; he guards his honour,* or *reputation, from unseemliness in respect of that which should be held sacred,* or *inviolable, or filthiness of odour*]. (TA.)

عَطِنٌ part. n. of عَطِنَ [q. v.] said of a hide. (S, TA.) [Hence,] أُهُبٌ عَطِنَةٌ *Stinking hides.* (TA.)

عَطَنَةٌ a subst. from أَعْطَنَ الإِبِلَ [q. v., as such signifying The *watering of camels and then making them to lie down at the water:* or the *confining of camels at the water, where they lie down, after having come to it and drunk*]. (K.) ═ Also The *place of* [*the operation termed*] العَطْن [inf. n. of عَطَنَ in the phrase عَطَنَ الجِلْدَ, q. v.]. (AZ, TA.)

عِطَانٌ *Feces such as are termed* فَرْث, or *salt, which one puts in,* or *upon, a hide,* [*in preparing it for tanning,*] *in order that it may not stink.* (K.)

عَطِينٌ *i. q.* مَعْطُونٌ, q. v., applied to a skin. (K.) —— And (hence, TA), as also ↓ عَطِينَةٌ, applied to a man, *Stinking* (K, TA) *in the exterior of the skin:* or the latter, *blamed in respect of some foul affair.* (TA.)

عَطِينَةٌ: see what next precedes.

عَاطِنَةٌ, (S, K,) applied to a she-camel, (K,) or to camels, (S, Msb,) as also [the pls.] عَوَاطِنُ (S, Msb, K) and عُطُونٌ, (K,) but not عُطَّانٌ thus applied, (TA,) *Lying down* [*at the water*] *after having satisfied her,* or *their, thirst.* (S, Msb,* K.) —— And عُطَّانٌ and عُطُونٌ and عَطَنَةٌ (K, TA) and عَاطِنُونَ (TA) [all pls. of عَاطِنٌ] Men *who have alighted,* or *descended and abode, in* مَعَاطِن [pl. of مَعْطِن]. (K, TA.)

مَعْطِنٌ; and its pl. مَعَاطِنُ: see عَطَنٌ.

مَعْطُونٌ A skin *prepared for tanning in the manner signified by the phrase* عَطَنَ الجِلْدَ, expl. above; (S, K;) as also ↓ عَطِينٌ. (K.)

عطو

1. عَطَا, [aor. يَعْطُو,] inf. n. عَطْوٌ: see 6, first quarter, in five places. —— [Hence] one says طَوِيلٌ لَا تَعْطُوهُ الأَيَادِى [*High,* so that *the hands will not reach it*]. (TA.) —— And عَطْوٌ signifies also The act of *raising the head and the hands* (K, TA) *to take a thing.* (TA.) See also an ex. in a verse cited voce أَنْ, p. 106, first col. [And see عَطْوٌ, and عَاطٍ.] ═ تَعَاطَيْنَا فَعَطَوْتُهُ: see 6.

2. هُوَ يُعَطِّينِى, (S, K, TA,) with teshdeed, (S, TA,) thus in the M, as well as the S, erroneously written in [some of] the copies of the K يُعْطِينِى, (TA,) *He serves me, does service for me,* or *ministers to me;* as also ↓ يُعَاطِينِى. (S, K, TA.) You say, مَنْ يُعَطِّيكَ i. e. *Who has the office of serving thee?* (TA.) ═ And عَطَّيْتُهُ *I incited him,* or *made him, to hasten,* or *be quick.* (Sgh, K.)

3: see 4, in two places: —— and see also 2. —— عَاطَى الصَّبِىُّ أَهْلَهُ means *The boy wrought for his family, and gave them,* or *handed to them, what they desired.* (ISd, Z, K, TA.) —— And المُعَاطَاةُ signifies A man's *meeting, face to face, a man having with him a sword, and saying, "Bring near thy sword," and he gives it, and thereupon each acts with the other awhile in a manner resembling the slaying with the edge of the sword* [see غَرَّ فُلَانٌ فُلَانًا بِغُرُوهِ]; they being in a market-place or a mosque: the doing of which is forbidden. (TA.) —— عَاطَيْتُ الأَرْطَالَ means [*I joined in mutually,* or *reciprocally, giving,* or *presenting, the pints* of wine; i. e.] أَعْطَيْتُ النَّدَامَى وَأَعْطَوْنِى أَرْطَالَ الخَمْرِ [*I gave,* or *presented to, the cup-companions, and they gave,* or *presented to, me, the pints of wine*]. (Har p. 650.)

4. إِعْطَآءٌ, (K, MF, TA,) and ↓ مُعَاطَاةٌ (S, Msb, K) and عَطَآءٌ, (K,) The act of *giving, presenting,* or *offering;* or *giving with the hand in the way of presenting* or *offering;* syn. مُنَاوَلَةٌ (S, Msb, K, MF, TA) عَلَى جِهَةِ التَّقْرِيبِ; and إِعْطَآءٌ has been expl. as *syn. with* إِيتَآءٌ; but several authors make a distinction between these two words, saying that the latter is sometimes obligatory and sometimes by way of favour, whereas the former is never but by way of sheer favour; as El-Fakhr Er-Rázee says; though most of the leading lexicologists know not this distinction. (MF, TA.) One says, أَعْطَاهُ الشَّىْءَ; and ↓ عَاطَاهُ إِيَّاهُ, inf. n. مُعَاطَاةٌ and عِطَآءٌ; *He gave him,* &c., *the thing.* (TA.) And اعطاهُ مَالًا [*He gave him,* &c., *property*]. (S.) And أَعْطَيْتُهُ دِرْهَمًا *I gave him,* &c., *a dirhem.* (Msb.) And as the signification of this verb does not depend upon the condition of taking, or receiving, but only upon giving, or delivering, one may say, أَعْطَيْتُهُ فَمَا أَخَذَ [*I gave,* or *delivered,* &c., *to him, and he did not take,* or *receive*]. (Msb.) [See also a verse cited in the first paragraph of art. رأم, in which this verb has a single objective complement with ب redundantly prefixed to it.] —— اعطى, (S,) inf. n. as above, (K,) signifies also ‡ *He was,* or *became, tractable, manageable,* or *submissive;* (S, K, TA;) said of a camel: (S:) and اعطى بِيَدِهِ [lit. *he gave his hand,* said of a man,] signifies the same: accord. to Er-Rághib, اعطى, said of a camel, primarily signifies *he gave his head, and did not resist.* (TA.) [Hence,] one says to a tractable camel, when his haltering becomes loosed (lit. opened) from his muzzle, أَعْطِ [meaning *Give thy head*]; whereupon he bends his head towards his rider, and he renews his haltering. (TA.) ——

مَا أَعْطَاهُ لِلْمَالِ [*How large a giver is he of property!*] is like the phrase مَا أَوْلَاهُ لِلْمَعْرُوفِ, and مَا أَكْرَمَهُ لِى; anomalous, because the verb of wonder is not formed from the measure أَفْعَلَ, and only what has been heard, of this kind, from the Arabs, is allowable. (Ṣ, TA.)

5. تعطّى: see 10. — And see also 6, last quarter, in two places. — Also *He hastened*, or *made haste*. (Ṣgh, Ḳ.)

6. تَعَاطٍ The act of *taking* [a thing that is given, presented, or offered, or that is as though it presented, or offered, itself], or *taking with the hand*; as also ▼عَطْوٌ; syn. of both تَنَاوُلٌ. (Ḳ.) One says, تعاطاهُ *He took it*, or *took it with his hand*; syn. تَنَاوَلَهُ: (Ṣ:) and هُوَ يَتَعَاطَى كَذَا *He takes*, or *takes with his hand, such a thing*; [as, for instance, food, and beverage;] syn. يَتَنَاوَلُهُ: (TA:) and زَيْدٌ دِرْهَمًا ▼عَطَا *Zeyd took*, or *took with his hand, a dirhem*; syn. تَنَاوَلَهُ: (Mṣb:) and ▼عَطَوْتُ الشَّىْءَ *I took the thing with the hand*; syn. تَنَاوَلْتُهُ بِالْيَدِ: (Ṣ:) or ▼عَطَا الشَّىْءَ, and إِلَيْهِ [i. e. إِلَى الشَّىْءِ], inf. n. عَطْوٌ, *He took the thing*, or *took it with his hand*; syn. تَنَاوَلَهُ: and ▼عَطَا بِيَدِهِ إِلَى الإِنَآءِ *He took the vessel*, or *took it with his hand*, (تَنَاوَلَهُ,) *before its being put upon the ground*. (TA.) — And The *taking with the hand* (تَنَاوُل) *what is not right*, or *just*, or *due*. (Ḳ.) — And The *contending in taking*. (Ḳ.) One says, تَعَاطَوُا الشَّىْءَ *They took the thing*, or *took it with the hand, one from another*, and *contended together in doing it*. (TA.) — [And The *contending in giving, presenting, or offering*.] One says also, ▼تَعَاطَيْنَا فَعَطَوْتُهُ, (Ṣ, Ḳ, TA,) aor. أَعْطُوهُ, (TA,) i. e. [*We contended in giving*, and it may also mean *in taking, and*] *I overcame*, or *surpassed, him* [*therein*]. (Ṣ, Ḳ, TA.) — [And simply The *giving, presenting*, or *offering, mutually, reciprocally*, or *by one to another*. See an ex. voce شَبْرٌ. — And hence, The *reciting, one with another*, or the *vying, one with another, in reciting*, verses, or poetry.] One says تَعَاطَوُا الرَّجَزَ بَيْنَهُمْ (TA and TḲ in art. رجز) † *They recited, one with another*, [or *they vied, one with another, in reciting*,] *verses*, or *poetry, of the metre termed* رَجَز; as also تَنَازَعُوهُ. (TḲ in that art.) — And The *standing upon the extremities of the toes, with raising the hands* to a thing. (Ḳ.) And hence, (Ḳ, TA,) as some say, (TA,) فَتَعَاطَى فَعَقَرَ, (Ḳ, TA,) in the Ḳur [liv. 29]: (TA:) for this is said to mean *And he stood upon the extremities of his toes, then raised his hands, and smote her*: (Ṣ, TA:) or this means *and he took* the sword, (Ksh, Bḍ, Jel,) or the she-camel, (Ksh,) *and slew* her: (Ksh, Bḍ, Jel:) or *and he emboldened himself* &c.: (Ksh, Bḍ:) [for] — تَعَاطٍ signifies also The *being bold, daring*, or *courageous, so as to attempt*, or *venture upon, a thing without consideration or hesitation*: (TA:) or, as also ▼تَعَطٍّ, the *venturing upon*, or *embarking in*, or *doing*, (Ḳ, TA,) a thing, or an affair, (Ḳ,) or a bad, or foul, thing or affair: (TA:) or the former is used in relation to that which is noble, or honourable; and ▼the latter, in relation to that which is bad, or foul. (Ḳ, TA.) And one says, فُلَانٌ يَتَعَاطَى كَذَا (Ṣ, Mṣb) i. e. *Such a one enters into such a thing*: (Ṣ:) or *ventures boldly, daringly*, or *courageously, upon such a thing, and does it*. (Mṣb.) [And *Such a one takes*, or *applies himself, to such a thing*; as wine, or the drinking thereof; and gaming: you say, تعاطى الخَمْرَ; and المَيْسِرَ: see Ksh and Bḍ and Jel in ii. 216.] And تَعَاطَى قَوْلَ الشِّعْرِ *He affected to be a poet but was not*. (TA in art. شعر.) And تَعَاطَى البَلَاغَةَ وَلَيْسَ مِنْ أَهْلِهَا [*He affected*, or *attempted, eloquence, not being of those endowed therewith*]. (TA in art. بلغ.)

10. استعطى *He asked for a gift*; as also ▼تعطّى. (Ṣ, Ḳ.) And استعطى النَّاسَ بِكَفِّهِ and فِى كَفِّهِ *He sought, demanded*, or *asked*, [*a gift*] *of men* or *of the people* [*with his hand* and *in his hand*]. (M, TA.)

عَطًا: see عَطَآءٌ.

عَطْوٌ and عُطُوٌّ and عِطْوٌ, applied to a gazelle, (Ḳ, TA,) and to a kid, accord. to Kr, who mentions only the first, as though an inf. n. used as an epithet, (ISd, TA,) *Stretching itself up towards the trees, to take therefrom*; as also ▼عَطُوٌّ. (Ḳ.) [See also عَاطٍ.]

قَوْسٌ عَطْوَى † *A bow that is easy* (Ṣ, Ḳ) and *yielding*. (Ṣ.) [See also مُعْطٍ.]

أَلْقَى فُلَانٌ عَطَوِيًّا *Such a one voided thin ordure* [*as an 'Atawee*, meaning] *much in quantity*: originating from the fact that a man of the Benoo-'Ateeyeh voided thin excrement on his being flogged. (Z, TA.) — العَطَوِيَّةُ is the appellation of *A sect of the* خَوَارِج, so called in relation to 'Ateeyeh Ibn-El-Aswad El-Yemámee El-Ḥanafee. (TA.)

عَطَآءٌ and ▼عَطًا *A gift*, as meaning *an act of giving* [in an absolute sense, or] *of such as is liberal, bountiful, munificent*, or *generous*: (Ḳ:) [as signifying the act of *giving*,] عَطَآءٌ is a subst. [i. e. a quasi-inf. n.] from أَعْطَى; (Ṣ, Mṣb;) and is originally عَطَاوٌ: and when they affixed to it ة, to denote unity, some said ▼عَطَآءَةٌ, and some said ▼عَطَاوَةٌ: and in forming the dual, they said عَطَاوَانِ and عَطَآءَانِ: (Ṣ, TA:) it is used as a quasi-inf. n. in the saying,

أَكُفْرًا بَعْدَ رَدِّ المَوْتِ عَنِّى
وَبَعْدَ عَطَائِكَ المِائَةَ الرِّتَاعَا

[Shall I show *ingratitude after the repelling of death from me and after thy giving* as a bloodwit for me *the hundred* camels *pasturing at large amid abundant herbage?*], المِائَة being governed in the accus. case by عطائك: (IAḲ p. 211:) the dim. of عَطَآءٌ is ▼عُطَىٌّ. (Ṣ, TA. [See مُحَيٌّ, in art. حى.]) — Also [i. e. عَطَآءٌ and عَطًا] *A gift* as meaning *a thing that is given*; (Ḳ;) or so عَطَآءٌ; (Mgh;) and (Mgh, Ḳ) so ▼عَطِيَّةٌ: (Ṣ, Mgh, Mṣb, Ḳ:) or, as some say, عَطَآءٌ is a coll. n.; and when the sing. is meant, one says ▼عَطِيَّةٌ: (TA:) the pl. of عَطَآءٌ is أَعْطِيَةٌ [a pl. of pauc.] and أَعْطِيَاتٌ (Mgh, Ḳ) which latter is a pl. pl.: (Ḳ:) and the pl. of ▼عَطِيَّةٌ is عَطَايَا: (Ṣ, Mgh, Mṣb:) and عَطَآءٌ has also for a pl. ▼مَعَاطِىُّ, anomalously. (TA.) عَطَآءٌ also signifies [*A soldier's stipend*, or *pay*; or *his allowance*; and so ▼عَطِيَّةٌ:] *what is given out to the soldier from the government-treasury once a year*, or *twice*; and رِزْقٌ, what is given out to him every month: or the former, *every year*, or *month*; and the latter, day by day: or the former, and ▼عَطِيَّةٌ, *what is assigned to those who fight*: and رِزْقٌ and ▼عَطِيَّةٌ, *what is assigned to the poor Muslims when they are not fighting*. (Mgh. [See also رِزْقٌ.])

عُطُوٌّ: see عَطْوٌ.

عُطَىٌّ dim. of عَطَآءٌ, q. v. (Ṣ, TA.)

عَطَآءَةٌ and عَطَاوَةٌ: see عَطَآءٌ, first sentence.

عَطِيَّةٌ: see عَطَآءٌ, latter half, in six places. — [Hence] أُمُّ عَطِيَّةَ *The mill*, or *hand-mill*; syn. الرَّحَا. (T in art. ام.)

عَاطٍ A gazelle *raising his head to take the leaves* [*of a tree*]. (TA.) [See also عَطْوٌ.] Hence, (TA,) عَاطٍ بِغَيْرِ أَنْوَاطٍ (Ṣ, Meyd, TA) *Taking* [or *reaching to take*] *without* there being aught of *things suspended*, (Meyd,) a prov.; (Ṣ, Meyd, TA;) applied to him who arrogates to himself that which he does not possess; (Meyd;) or to him who arrogates to himself knowledge that does not regulate him; (TA;) or meaning, taking [or reaching to take] that which is not to be hoped for (Ṣ, TA) nor to be taken. (Ṣ. [See also art. نوط.]) [And عَاطِيَةٌ is applied to a mare as meaning *Raising her head*: see شَبَاةٌ (last sentence) in art. شبو.]

أَعْطَى [signifying *More*, and *most, excellent in giving* is anomalous, being formed from the augmented verb أَعْطَى]: see أَجْوَبُ.

مُعْطٍ [*Giving*, &c.]. When thou desirest Zeyd [i. e. any person] to give thee a thing, thou sayest, هَلْ أَنْتَ مُعْطِيَّهُ [lit. *Art thou my giver of it?*], with fet-ḥ and teshdeed to the ى: and in like manner thou sayest to a pl. number, هَلْ أَنْتُمْ مُعْطِيَّهُ, because the ن [of the word مُعْطُونَ] falls out by reason of the word's becoming a prefixed noun, and the و is changed into ى and incorporated [into the pronominal ى], and the ى is pronounced with fet-ḥ because [originally] preceded by a quiescent letter [i. e. the و which is changed into ى]: and to two persons thou sayest, هَلْ أَنْتُمَا مُعْطِيَايَهُ, with fet-ḥ to the ى: and thus you do in similar cases. (Ṣ, TA.) — [Hence,] قَوْسٌ مُعْطِيَةٌ † *A pliable bow, not rigid nor resisting to him who pulls the string*: or, as some say, *that has been bent and not been broken*. (TA.) [See also عَطْوَى.]

مِعْطَآءٌ A man, and a woman, *who gives much*, or *often*: pl. مَعَاطِىُّ and مَعَاطٍ. (Akh, Ṣ, Ḳ.)

مَعَاطِىُّ [a pl. of مِعْطَآءٌ and] an anomalous pl. of عَطَآءٌ, q. v. (TA.)

عظل

1. عَظِلَتِ الكِلَابُ, aor. ـَ; and عَظَلَت, aor. ـِ; (Ḳ, TA;) inf. n. عَظْلٌ; (TA;) *The dogs mounted, one upon another,* (Ḳ, TA,) *in coitu.* (TA. [See also 3.])

2. عظّلوا عَلَيْهِ: see 5.

3. عَاظَلَتْ, (Ṣ, TA,) or عاظلت فِى السِّفَادِ, (O,) inf. n. مُعَاظَلَةٌ and عِظَالٌ, (Ṣ, Ḳ,) said of dogs, (Ṣ, O, Ḳ,) and of beasts of prey, (TA,) and of locusts, (Ṣ, Ḳ,) and of whatever stick fast (Ṣ, O, Ḳ, TA) in coitu; (TA;) as also ▾ تعاظلت, (Ṣ, O, Ḳ,*) and ▾ اعتظلت, (O, Ḳ,*) said of locusts (O) &c.; (Ḳ;) [and so ▾ تعظّلت; (see 5 below;)] *Cohæserunt in coitu.* (Ṣ, O, Ḳ, TA.) —— And عاظلهُ is said of anything as meaning *It mounted upon it,* or *overlay it.* (El-Ámidee, TA.) —— التَّضْمِينُ العِظَالُ فِى القَوَافِى signifies [i. e. *The introducing into verses a hemistich,* or *a verse,* or *more, of another poet;* &c.: see more in art. ضمن]. (Ṣ, O.) One says, عاظل فِى القَافِيَةِ, inf. n. عِظَالٌ, meaning ضَمَّنَ [i. e. *He introduced into the ode a hemistich,* &c.]. (Ḳ.) And فُلَانٌ لَا يُعَاظِلُ فِى القَوَافِى [*Such a one does not,* or *will not, introduce into verses* &c.]. (Ṣ.) 'Omar said, of the best of poets, لَا يُعَاظِلُ الكَلَامَ, meaning *He does not make one part of the language to accord in meaning with another,* [so I render لَمْ يَحْمِلْ بَعْضَهُ عَلَى بَعْضٍ, (see art. حمل,) i. e. *he does not make use of tautology,*] *nor does he utter that which is a repetition,* or *that which is disapproved,* (الرَّجِيع مِنَ القَوْلِ,) *nor reiterate an expression:* or, accord. to El-Ámidee, *he does not make the language obscure, nor crowd one part of it upon another:* (TA:) or he said, لَمْ يُعَاظِلْ بَيْنَ القَوْلِ, referring to Zuheyr, and meaning *he rendered the saying distinct and plain, and did not make it obscure.* (O, TA.*) —— عاظلهُ also signifies *He said to him, "I am like thee," or "better than thou," the latter saying the same.* (Marg. note in an autographical copy of the TA.)

5. التَّعَظُّلُ is a dial. var. of التَّعَاظُلُ. (Marg. note in an autographical copy of the TA. See 3, first sentence.) —— تعظّلوا عَلَيْهِ *They collected themselves together against him;* (Ṣ, O, Ḳ;) as also ▾ عظّلوا, inf. n. تَعْظِيلٌ: (Ḳ:) or *they bore,* or *pressed,* or *crowded, as though mounting one another, upon him, to beat him.* (TA.) —— And one says, ظَلَّ يَتَعَظَّلُ فِى أَثَرِهِ مُنْذُ اليَوْمِ *He passed the time pursuing hard after it during the day;* meaning a thing that had escaped him. (O, TA.)

6: see 3, first sentence. —— تعاظلوا عَلَى المَآءِ *They became numerous at the water, and pressed,* or *crowded, upon it.* (Marg. note in an autographical copy of the TA.)

8: see 3, first sentence.

Q. Q. 4. اِعْظَأَلَّ الشَّجَرُ *The trees had many branches.* (IKh, O.) See also Q. Q. 4 in arts. عضل and عطل.

عُظْلٌ: see عُظَّلٌ.

عَظَلٌ and عُظَلٌ *A large* فَأْرَة [or *rat*]: also mentioned as with ض: on the authority of Aboo-Sahl. (Marg. note in an autographical copy of the TA.) [See also عَضَلٌ.]

عُظَّلٌ [a pl. of which the sing. is not mentioned] *i. q.* مَأْبُونُونَ [of which see the sing., مَأْبُونٌ]; (IAạr, O, Ḳ;) as also ▾ عُظْلٌ. (Marg. note in an autographical copy of the TA.)

هُوَ عَظِيلُهُ *He is the person who says to him, "I am like thee," or "better than thou," and to whom the latter says the same.* (Marg. note in an autographical copy of the TA.)

عَاظِلٌ and [its pls.] عَظْلَى (Ṣ, O, Ḳ) and عِظَالٌ (marg. note in an autographical copy of the TA) and عُظَالَى, (ISh, TA,) applied to locusts (جَرَادٌ), *Cohærentes in coitu.* (Ṣ, O, Ḳ, TA.) —— [Hence,] يَوْمُ العُظَالَى *A certain day* (i. e. *conflict*) *of the Arabs, well known;* (Ṣ, O, Ḳ;) said in the A to be *that of Benoo-Temeem, when they went to fight against Bekr Ibn-Wáïl:* (TA:) so called because the people bore, or pressed, or crowded, as though mounting, one upon another, (رَكِبَ بَعْضُهُمْ بَعْضًا,) (Ṣ, O, Ḳ,) therein, (Ṣ, O,) when they were routed: (TA:) or because they congregated therein as though they were mounting, one upon another: (AḤei, TA:) or because two and three of them rode upon one beast (Ṣ, O, Ḳ, TA) in the rout: thus says Aṣ: or because Bisṭám Ibn-Ḳeys and Háni Ibn-Ḳabeeṣah and Mafrooḳ Ibn-'Amr and El-Ḥowfazán combined therein for the command. (TA.)

مُعْظِلٌ and ▾ مُعْظَئِلٌّ A place *abounding in trees.* (Kr, Ḳ.)

مُعْظَئِلٌّ: see what next precedes. [And see its verb, Q. Q. 4.]

عظلم

Q. 2. تَعَظْلَمَ, [from عِظْلِمٌ as signifying a certain plant or dye,] said of the night, *It was,* or *became, dark, and very black;* (Ḳ, TA;) i. e. *it became like the* عِظْلِم. (TA.)

عِظْلِمٌ, (Ṣ, Mṣb, Ḳ,) of which عَظْلَمٌ is a dial. var., (MF, TA,) The *expressed juice of a species of tree or plant,* (Az, Ḳ, TA,) *the colour of which is like* نِيل [or *indigo*], *green* (أَخْضَر) *inclining to duskiness:* (Az, TA:) or *a certain plant,* (Ṣ, Ḳ,) or *thing,* (Mṣb,) *with which one dyes,* (Ṣ, Mṣb, Ḳ,) *said to be* (Mṣb) *called in Pers.* نيل [i. e. the *indigo-plant*]: (Mṣb, and so in some copies of the Ṣ; other copies of which, for نيل, have تفل:) or *i. q.* وَسْمَةٌ [an appellation now applied to *woad;* as is also عِظْلِم]: (Ṣ, Mṣb, Ḳ:) AḤn says, one of the Arabs of the desert told me that the عظلم is the *male* وَسْمَة: he also says that it is *a small tree* or *plant,* (شُجَيْرَة), *of the* [*class called*] رِبَّة, *that grows in a late season, and the greenness of which is lasting:* and in one place he says, an Arab of the desert, of the Saráh (السَّرَاة), told me that the عِظْلِمَة [which is the n. un.] is *a tree* or *plant* (شَجَرَة) *that rises upon a stem about a cubit* [*in height*] *and has branches at the extremities of which are what resemble the blossoms of the* كُزْبَرَة [or *coriander*], *and it* (the tree or plant) *is dust-coloured:* (TA:) some say that it is the بَقَّم [or *Brazil-wood*]: (Mṣb:) MF says, it is the خِطْمِىّ [or *marsh-mallow*]: (TA:) thus says El-Ḥareeree; but El-'Okbaree says that it is not that: (Ḥar p. 625:) and some say that it is *a certain red dye.* (TA.) Hence the prov.,

* بَيْضَآءُ لَا يُدْجِى سَنَاهَا العِظْلِمُ *

i. e. [*A white,* or *fair, female,*] *whose whiteness* [or *brightness*] عظلم *will not blacken* [or *darken*]: applied to that which is notable, which nothing will conceal. (Meyd, TA.) —— Hence, as being likened thereto, (Ṣ,) it signifies also The *dark night:* (Ṣ, Ḳ:) one says لَيْلٌ عِظْلِمٌ. (TA.)

عَظْلَمَةٌ *Darkness.* (Ḳ.)

عِظْلَامٌ *Dust;* syn. قَتَرَةٌ and غَبَرَةٌ. (Ḳ.)

عظم

1. عَظُمَ, [aor. ـُ,] inf. n. عِظَمٌ (Ṣ, Mṣb, Ḳ) and عَظَامَةٌ, (Mṣb, Ḳ,) accord. to El-Iṣbahánee, primarily signifies *He was,* or *became, great in his bone:* then metaphorically said of anything كَبِير [or great], whether an object of sense or of intellect, a substance or an accident: (TA:) *i. q.* كَبُرَ, (Ṣ, TA,) said of a thing [as meaning *it was,* or *became, great, big,* or *large*], (Ṣ, Mṣb, TA,) *in length* and *breadth* and *thickness:* (TA:) [and in like manner, metaphorically, said of an object of intellect; meaning *it was,* or *became, great in estimation* or *rank* or *dignity;* and thus also said of a man: or it imports more than كَبُرَ; signifying *it was,* or *became, great in comparison with other things of its kind; huge, enormous,* or *vast;* and in a similar sense it is said of a man; and in an incomparably higher sense, of God: (see عَظِيمٌ, below:)] and ▾ اعظم said of an affair, or event, signifies [like عَظُمَ] *it became* عَظِيم. (TA.) عَظُمَ is the *contr.* of صَغُرَ. (Ḳ.) —— عَظُمَ عَلَيْهِ: see 6, in three places: and see also 4. And مَا يَعْظُمُنِى [which is similar in meaning to ما يَعْظُمُ عَلَىَّ if not a mistranscription for ما يُعْظِمُنِى]: see 4. —— In the case of expressing wonder, one says, عُظْمَ البَطْنُ بَطْنُكَ [*How great is the belly, thy belly!*], contracting عَظُمَ, and transferring the vowel of its middle letter to [the place of] its first; and thus one does in the case of that which denotes praise or blame, and of whatever [verb] may be well used in the manner

of نِعْمَ, and بِئْسَ: but what may not be thus used does not admit of the transferring, though it may be contracted; so that you may say, حَسُنَ الوَجْهُ حُسْنَ الوَجْهُ and حَسُنَ الوَجْهُ وَجْهُكَ and وَجْهُكَ, but not قَدْ حُسْنَ الوَجْهُ وَجْهُكَ. (Ṣ.) — عَظَمَ الكَلْبَ, inf. n. عَظْمٌ, *He gave the dog a bone to eat*; as also ▼ اعظمه. (Ḳ.) — And عَظَمَ فُلَانًا, inf. n. عَظْمَةٌ (Ḳ, TA) and عَظْمٌ, (TA,) *He struck such a one upon his bones.* (Ḳ, TA.)

2. عَظَّمَهُ, inf. n. تَعْظِيمٌ; and ▼ اعظمهُ; [*He made it great, big,* or *large*: see إِعْظَامَةٌ. — And hence,] *He magnified, honoured,* or *treated with respect* or *reverence* or *veneration, him,* [generally meaning thus, i. e. a person,] or *it,* (Ṣ, Mṣb, Ḳ,) i. e. an affair. (Ṣ.) [One says, فَعَلْتُ هٰذَا تَعْظِيمًا لَهُ *I did thus for the purpose of rendering honour &c. to him, or it.*] — عظّم المَطَرُ, inf. n. as above, *The rain moistened to the measure of the* عَظَمَة [or *thick part*] *of the arm.* (TA voce أَسَلَّ [q. v.].) — عظّم الشَّاةَ, inf. n. as above, *He cut up the sheep,* or *goat, bone by bone.* (Ḳ.)

4. اعظم as intrans.: see 1, former half. — اعظمهُ: see 2: — and 10, in two places. — One says also, أَعْظَمَنِى مَا قُلْتَ هَالَنِى وَعَظُمَ ▼, meaning عَلَىَّ [i. e. *What thou saidst frightened me,* or *terrified me, and was grievous,* or *distressing, in its effect upon me* (like كَبُرَ عَلَىَّ)]: and ▼ مَا يُعْظِمُنِى أَنْ أَفْعَلَ ذٰلِكَ [if not a mistranscription for مَا يُعْظِمُنِى], meaning مَا يَهُولُنِى [*My doing that will not frighten me,* or *terrify me*]. (TA.) — اعظم الكَلْبَ: see 1, last sentence but one.

5. تعظّم [*He made himself to appear great, big,* or *large*: as is indicated by an explanation of the word رُفَاعَةٌ in the Ṣ, in art. رفع. — And hence,] *He magnified himself*; or *behaved proudly, haughtily,* or *insolently*; as also ▼ استعظم; (Ṣ, Mṣb, Ḳ;) [and so ▼ تعاظم:] — whence one says, تعظّم عَنْهُ and ▼ تعاظم عنه, both of which occur in the Ḳ, the former in art. ابه in explanation of تَأَبَّهَ عَنْ كَذَا, and the latter in art. جل in explanation of تَجَالَّ عَنْهُ; both meaning *He held himself above it, disdained it,* or *was disdainful of it.*] — [تَعَظَّمَ اللّٰهُ and ▼ تَعَاظَمَ may be best rendered *Incomparable in greatness,* or *majesty, is God.*] — See also 10.

6. تعاظم as intrans.: see 5, in three places: — and see عَظَمَةٌ. — [تعاظمهُ signifies *It was,* or *became,* عَظِيم i. e. *great, &c., in comparison with it.*] One says, سَيْلٌ لَا يَتَعَاظَمُهُ شَىْءٌ, meaning [*A torrent*] *in comparison with which nothing will be great.* (TA.) And أَصَابَنَا مَطَرٌ لَا يَتَعَاظَمُهُ شَىْءٌ i. e. ▼ لَا يَعْظُمُ عِنْدَهُ [meaning, in like manner, *Rain in comparison with which* (lit. *in juxtaposition to which*) *nothing will be great fell upon us*]. (Ṣ, TA.) And هٰذَا أَمْرٌ لَا يَتَعَاظَمُهُ شَىْءٌ (Ḳ,* TA) [*This is an affair*] *in comparison with which nothing will be great.* (Ḳ, TA.) — تعاظمهُ said of an affair, or event, (أَمْر, Ṣ, Mṣb, TA,) signifies (Mṣb, Ḳ, TA) also (Ḳ, TA) ▼ عَظُمَ عَلَيْهِ [i. e. *It was,* or *became, of great magnitude,* or *moment,* or *importance*; or *of great gravity*; or (like كَبُرَ عَلَيْهِ) *difficult, hard, severe, grievous, distressing, afflictive, troublesome,* or *burdensome; in its effect upon him*]. (Mṣb, Ḳ, TA.) In a trad., God is related to have said, لَا يَتَعَاظَمُنِى ذَنْبٌ أَنْ أَغْفِرَهُ, meaning لَا يَعْظُمُ عَلَىَّ and عِنْدِى [i. e. *A sin is not difficult, &c., to me to forgive it*; like as one says, لَا يَكْبُرُ عَلَىَّ and عِنْدِى]. (TA.)

10. استعظم as intrans.: see 5. — استعظمهُ *He reckoned it,* (Ṣ,) or *he saw it,* or *judged it, to be,* (Mgh, Mṣb, Ḳ,) عَظِيم [i. e. *great, &c.*]; (Ṣ, Mgh, Mṣb, Ḳ;) as also ▼ اعظمهُ, (Mgh, Ḳ,) which latter is mentioned by ISd, but disapproved by him: one says, ▼ سَمِعْتُ خَبَرًا فَأَعْظَمْتُهُ [*I heard a narration and I judged it to be of great moment, &c.*]: (TA:) and ▼ تعظّم is thought by ISd to mean *he looked upon* [a thing] *as* عَظِيم. (TA in art. شرف.) — Also, *He took the greater,* or *main, part of it,* (Ḳ, TA,) namely, a thing. (TA.)

عَظْمٌ The قَصَب [here meaning *bone,* but properly applied to the bones of the hands and feet, or of the arms and legs,] *of an animal, upon which is the flesh*: (Ḳ:) [dim. ▼ عُظَيْمٌ:] pl. [of mult.] عِظَامٌ (Ṣ, Mṣb, Ḳ) and عِظَامَةٌ, with ة as characteristic of the fem. gender, (Ḳ,) and [of pauc.] أَعْظُمٌ. (Mṣb, Ḳ.) — [And app. *A portion of a camel slaughtered for distribution in the game called* المَيْسِر:] Freytag explains it as signifying, in the Deewán of the Hudhalees, "portio animalis mactati in ludo alearum:" and having for its pl. أَعْظُمٌ.] — عَظْمُ وَضَّاحٍ, or ▼ عُظَيْمُ وَضَّاحٍ, is the name of *A certain game of the Arabs,* (Ḳ, TA,) *of the children of the Arabs of the desert,* (L in art. وضح,) *in which they throw in the night a piece of bone,* (TA,) or *a white bone,* (L in art. وضح,) *and he who lights upon it overcomes his companions: when one of the two parties overcame, he, or they, used to ride those of the other party from the place in which they found it to the place from which they threw it, saying,* عُظَيْمٌ وَضَّاحٌ ضِحَنَّ اللَّيْلَهْ وَلَا تَضِحَنَّ بَعْدَهَا مِنْ لَيْلَهْ [*O little bone of a thing very apparent, do thou appear to-night, and do not thou appear any night after it*]. (TA.) — عَظْمُ الرَّحْلِ *The wood of the* [*camel's saddle called*] رَحْل, *without* أَنْسَاع [i. e. *the broad, plaited, leathern bands with which it is bound*], *and without any gear.* (Ṣ, Ḳ.) — عَظْمُ الفَدَّانِ *The broad board of the plough,* (Ḳ, TA,) *at the head of which is the iron* [or *share*] *whereby the earth is cloven*: and عَضْم is a dial. var. thereof. (TA.) — عَظْمٌ is also a dial. var. of عَضْمٌ signifying *A winnowing-fork.* (AḤn, TA in art. عضم, q. v.) — And a dial. var. of عَضْمٌ as signifying The *handle,* or *part that is grasped by the hand, of a bow.* (AḤn, TA in art. عضم.) — See also مُعْظَمٌ.

عِظَمٌ: see عَظَمَةٌ: — and see مُعْظَمٌ, in three places.

عِظَمُ الطَّرِيقِ *The main part,* or *middle,* or *beaten track, of the road.* (Ḳ.)

عُظْمَةٌ: see إِعْظَامَةٌ.

عَظَمَةٌ *Self-magnification, pride, haughtiness,* or *insolence*; (Ṣ, Mṣb, Ḳ;) as also ▼ عِظَمٌ (Ṣ, Ḳ) and ▼ عَظَامَةٌ and ▼ عَظَمُوتٌ: (Ḳ:) as an attribute of a human being, it is [generally] blamable: (Az, Ḳ, TA:) [but] one says, لِفُلَانٍ عَظَمَةٌ عِنْدَ النَّاسِ meaning *To such a one belongs a title to honour,* or *respect, in the estimation of men*; and ▼ إِنَّهُ لَعَظِيمُ المَعَاظِمِ likewise: and ▼ لَهُ تَعَاظُمٌ i. e. *Verily he is great in respect of the title that he has to honour, and of the rights that are held in high account; one to whom it is incumbent* [on others] *to pay regard,* or *consideration.* (TA.) — As an attribute of God, it is not to be ascribed to a human being; (Az, Ḳ, TA;) for, in relation to Him [it means *Incomparable greatness* or *majesty,* and] it is not to be specified by the ascription of its quality, nor defined, nor likened to anything. (TA.) — Also The *thick part* of the fore arm; (Ṣ;) the *half next the elbow,* of the fore arm, *in which is the* [*main*] *muscle*; the half next the hand being called the أَسَلَة. (Lḥ, Ḳ.) — And The *thick part* of the tongue, (Ḳ, TA,) *above the* عَكَدَة, which is the root thereof. (TA.) — عَظَمَاتُ القَوْمِ *The chiefs,* and *nobles, of the people,* or *party.* (Ḳ,* TA.) — See also إِعْظَامَةٌ.

عَظِمَةٌ A female *that desires great* أُيُور [pl. of أَيْر, q. v.]; as also ▼ مَعْظُومَةٌ. (Ḳ.)

عُظْمِىٌّ [in the CḲ عَظْمِىٌّ, but it is a rel. n.,] A pigeon *inclining to whiteness*; (Ḳ, TA;) app. so called in relation to the bone (العَظْم), by reason of its whiteness. (TA.)

عَظَمُوتٌ: see عَظَمَةٌ, first sentence.

عُظَامٌ: see the next paragraph.

عَظِيمٌ *Having the quality denoted by the verb* عَظُمَ; [i. e. *great, big,* or *large*; &c.;] (Ṣ, Mṣb, Ḳ;) as also ▼ عُظَامٌ (Ṣ, Ḳ, TA) in an intensive sense [i. e. signifying *very great* &c.], (TA,) and ▼ عُظَّامٌ (Ḳ, TA) in a more intensive sense than عُظَامٌ [i. e. signifying *very very great* &c.]: (TA:) or عَظِيمٌ signifies *esteemed great &c. by another* or *others*; differing from كَبِير, which signifies "great &c. in itself:" (El-Fakhr Er-Rázee, TA:) or the former is the *contr. of* حَقِير; [i. e. it signifies *of great account* or *estimation*;] and as حَقِير is inferior to صَغِير, so عَظِيم is superior to كَبِير; (Ksh and Bḍ in ii. 6;) and signifies *great, or the like, in comparison with other things of its kind*: (Bḍ ibid:) [it may therefore often be rendered *huge, enormous,* or *vast*: used metaphorically, as applied to an object of the intellect, it means *great in estimation* or *rank* or *dignity*; and thus as applied to a man: also *of great magnitude* or *moment* or *importance*: *of great gravity*: *difficult, hard, severe, grievous, distressing, afflictive, troublesome,* or *burdensome*: (see 6:)] and *formidable,* or *terrible.* (Bḍ in

xxii. 1.) Hence one says, رَجُلٌ عَظِيمٌ فِي المَجْدِ وَالرَّأْيِ † [*A man great in respect of glory, honour, dignity,* or *nobility, and of judgment,* or *opinion*]. (TA.) And رَمَاهُ بِعَظِيمٍ and ▼ بِمُعْظَمٍ † [*He reproached him,* or *upbraided him, with,* or *he accused him of, a thing,* or *an act, of great gravity; or an enormity*]: both mean the same. (TA.) [The pl. of عَظِيمٌ is عِظَامٌ and, applied to rational beings, عُظَمَآءُ.] — العَظِيمُ as an epithet applied to God is *syn. with* الكَبِيرُ [signifying *The Incomparably-great*]. (TA.)

عُظَامٌ : and عُظَامٌ وُضَاحٌ : see عَظِيمٌ.

عِظَامَةٌ : see إِعْظَامَةٌ.

عَظِيمَةٌ *A severe calamity* or *misfortune;* as also ▼ مُعْظَمَةٌ; (Ṣ, Ḳ;) [and so ▼ مُعْظَمٌ, thus in a verse cited in the Ṣ in art. ولب:] pl. of the first عَظَائِمُ; and of the second مَعَاظِمُ. (TA.) — [And *A great crime* or *the like;* a meaning well known: so I have rendered it voce صَعٌّ: in art. طمو in the O and TA, its pl., عَظَائِمُ, is rendered by ذُنُوب : see مُعْظَمٌ.] — See also إِعْظَامَةٌ.

عِظَامِيٌّ [a rel. n. from عِظَامٌ, pl. of عَظْمٌ]: see عِصَامِيٌّ, in art. عصم, in two places.

عُظَّامٌ : see عَظِيمٌ.

عُظَّامَةٌ : see عَظِيمَةٌ : — and see also what here follows.

عُظْمَةٌ and إِعْظَامَةٌ and ▼ عِظَامَةٌ and ▼ عُظَّامَةٌ and ▼ عَظْمَةٌ (Ṣ, Ḳ, TA) [the last written in one of my copies of the Ṣ عُظْمَةٌ] and ▼ عَظِيمَةٌ (TA) [and ▼ عَظَمَةٌ (Freytag from the Deewán of Jereer)] *A thing like a pillow* (Fr, Ṣ) *&c.,* (Fr,) or *a garment,* or *piece of cloth,* (Ḳ,) *with which a woman makes her posteriors* [*to appear*] *large.* (Fr, Ṣ, Ḳ.)

مُعْظَمٌ The *greater, main,* [*principal, chief,*] or *most, part* or *portion,* [or *body,* or *aggregate,*] (Ṣ, Mṣb, Ḳ,) of a thing [or of things], (Ṣ, Mṣb,) or of an affair, or event; (Ḳ;) [the *main, gross, mass,* or *bulk,* of a thing or of things;] as also ▼ عُظْمٌ (Ṣ, Mgh, Mṣb, Ḳ) and ▼ عَظْمٌ: (Lḥ, Ḳ:) or ▼ عُظْمٌ, it is said, [as also مُعْظَمٌ in many cases,] signifies the *middle,* or *midst,* of a thing. (TA.) It is said in a trad. of Ibn-Seereen, جَلَسْتُ إِلَى مَجْلِسٍ فِيهِ عُظْمٌ ▼ مِنَ الأَنْصَارِ, meaning [*I sat by an assembly in which was*] *a numerous company of the Ansár.* (TA.) [مُعْظَمُ الحَرْبِ, and المَوْتِ, signify *The thick,* or *thickest,* or *the main stress* or *struggle, of the fight* or battle, and *of death* in battle: see رَحًى (near the end of the paragraph) in art. رحو and رحى.] — [And accord. to Freytag, it occurs in the Deewan of the Hudhalees as signifying The *harder parts of the body,* as the *neck,* the *thigh, &c.*] — See also عَظِيمٌ: — and عَظِيمَةٌ.

مُعْظَمَةٌ; and its pl., مَعَاظِمُ: see عَظِيمَةٌ. — And for مَعَاظِمُ as a pl. of which the sing. is not mentioned, see عَظْمَةٌ.

مَعْظُومٌ A young weaned camel *having a bone in his tongue broken, in order that he may not suck.* (Ḳ.) — مَعْظُومَةٌ : see عَظِيمَةٌ.

عظى or عظو

عَظَآءٌ, in the CḲ عِظَآءٌ: see what follows.

عَظَآءَةٌ, (Ṣ, Mṣb, TA,) which is of the dial. of the people of El-'Áliyeh, (Mṣb, TA,) and عَظَايَةٌ, (Ṣ, Mṣb, Ḳ, TA,) which is of the dial. of Temeem, (Mṣb, TA,) [in the CḲ عِظَايَةٌ,] *A certain reptile,* or *small creeping thing,* (Ṣ, Ḳ, TA,) *larger than the* وَزَغَة, (Ṣ,) *like the* [*lizard called*] سَامّ أَبْرَص (Mṣb, Ḳ, TA) *in form,* or *make,* (Mṣb,) *but somewhat larger:* (TA:) or *a* غنده [or غُنْدَه, a Pers. word said to signify a *species of spider*]: (MA:) [or] *a species of lizard;* (MA, PṢ;) *a certain reptile,* or *creeping thing,* (دَابَّة,) *larger than the* وزغة; *a species of large lizard:* (MA:) [see also عَضْرَفُوطٌ:] pl. ▼ عَظَآءٌ, (Ṣ, Mṣb, Ḳ, TA, in the CḲ عِظَآءٌ,]) i. e. pl. of عَظَآءَةٌ, (Ṣ, Mṣb,) [or rather عَظَآءٌ is a coll. gen. n. of which عَظَآءَةٌ is the n. un.,] and عَظَايَا, (TA,) and also عَظَايَاتٌ, which last is pl. of عَظَايَةٌ. (Mṣb.) A woman of the desert, whom her lord (مَوْلَاهَا) had beaten, said, رَمَاكَ اللّٰهُ بِدَآءٍ لَا دَوَآءَ لَهُ إِلَّا أَبْوَالُ العَظَآءِ [*May God smite thee with a disease for which there is no remedy but the urine* (lit. *urines*) *of the* عظاء], which is a thing hard to be found. (TA.)

عف

1. عَفَّ, (Ṣ, O, Mṣb, Ḳ, &c.,) aor. ـِ, (Ṣ, O, Mṣb,) inf. n. عِفَّةٌ and عَفَافٌ (Ṣ, O, Mṣb, Ḳ) and عَفٌّ and عَفَافَةٌ, (Ṣ, O, Ḳ,) *He abstained* (Ṣ, O, Mṣb, Ḳ) from (عَنْ) what was unlawful, (Ṣ, O,) or from what was not lawful nor comely or decorous, (M, Ḳ,) or from things that should be sacred or inviolable, and base, or carnal, objects of inordinate desire, (TA,) or from a thing: (Mṣb:) [but it is implied in the Ḳ that the verb is used without the expression of the object, or objects; and it is very often so used, as meaning *he was abstinent, continent, chaste, virtuous, modest, decent,* or *decorous:*] and ▼ استعفّ signifies the same; (Ḳ;) as also ▼ تعفّف: (Mṣb, Ḳ:) or this last signifies, (Ṣ, O,) or signifies also, (Ḳ,) *he affected,* or *constrained himself, to abstain from what was unlawful:* (Ṣ, O, Ḳ:) or *he was patient, and kept himself remote,* or *aloof, from a thing* [*that was unlawful* or *the like*]: (TA:) and ▼ استعفّ عَنِ المَسْأَلَةِ means *he abstained* (عَفَّ) *from begging:* (Ṣ, O:) whence the trad. of the Prophet اِسْتَعْفِفْ عَنِ السُّؤَالِ مَا اسْتَطَعْتَ [*Abstain thou from begging, as much as thou art able*]: (O:) or, as some say, الاِسْتِعْفَافُ signifies *the seeking to abstain from what is unlawful,* and *from begging of men:* and one says also, ▼ اعفّ عَنِ القَبِيحِ [*he abstained from that which was evil,* or *foul*]; this being [likewise] from العِفَّةُ. (TA.) — عَفَّ said of milk, aor. ـِ, (IDrd, O, Ḳ,) inf. n. عَفٌّ, (IDrd, O,) *It collected in the udder:* (IDrd, O, Ḳ:) or *it remained in the udder;* (Ḳ;) or thus عَفَّ فِي الضَّرْعِ. (Ibn-'Abbád, O.)

2. عَفَّفْتُهُ, inf. n. تَعْفِيفٌ, *I gave him to drink what is termed* عُفَافَة [q. v.]. (IDrd, O, Ḳ.)

4. اعفّهُ اللّٰهُ *God made him to be* عَفِيف [i. e. *abstinent,* &c.]. (Ṣ, O, Mṣb, Ḳ.) — أَعَفَّتْ, [in the CḲ, erroneously, أُعِفَّتْ,] said of a ewe, or she-goat, is from العُفَافَةُ [and therefore signifies *She had milk collected in her udder:* or *she had some milk remaining in her udder after most of it had been sucked*]. (IDrd, O, Ḳ.)

5. تعفّف: see 1. — Also *He* (a man, Ṣ, O) *drank what is termed* عُفَافَة [q. v.]. (Ṣ, O, Ḳ.)

6. تَعَافَّ نَاقَتَكَ *Milk thou thy camel after the first milking.* (Ṣ, O, L, Ḳ.) — And تعافّ said to a sick man, *Treat thyself medically.* (Ḳ.) One says, بِأَيِّ شَىْءٍ نَتَعَافُّ *With what thing shall we treat ourselves medically?* (AA, O, TA.)

8: see 1. — اعتفّت الإِبِلُ اليَبِيسَ *The camels took with the tongue* [or *licked up*] *the dry herbage above the earth* or *dust, taking the best,* or *choice, thereof;* as also ▼ استعفّت. (O, Ḳ.)

10: see 1, in two places: — and see also 8.

عَفٌّ; and its fem.: see عَفِيفٌ.

عُفَّةٌ: see عُفَافَةٌ. — Also *An old woman:* (Ibn-El-Faraj, O, Ḳ, TA:) like عُقَّةٌ: being formed [from the latter] by substitution. (TA.) — And *A certain fish, smooth, white, and small; when cooked, having a taste like that of rice.* (Ibn-El-Faraj, O, Ḳ.)

عَفَافٌ *A medicine,* or *remedy.* (AA, O, Ḳ.)

عَفِيفٌ and ▼ عَفٌّ epithets from عَفَّ, as such signifying *Abstaining* (Ṣ, O, Mṣb, Ḳ) from what is unlawful, (Ṣ, O,) or from what is not lawful nor comely or decorous, (Ḳ,) or from things that should be sacred or inviolable, and base, or carnal, objects of inordinate desire, (TA,) or from a thing: (Mṣb:) [and very often used as meaning *abstinent, continent, chaste, virtuous, modest, decent,* or *decorous:*] fem. of the former with ة; (Ṣ, O, Ḳ;) and so of ▼ the latter, (Ṣ, O, Mṣb, Ḳ,) which has no broken pl.: (TA:) the pl. masc. (of عَفِيفٌ, Mṣb, TA) is أَعِفَّآءُ (O, Mṣb, Ḳ, TA) and أَعِفَّةٌ: (Mṣb, TA:) عَفِيفَةٌ, applied to a woman, signifies *excellent,* or *high-born, good, righteous,* or *virtuous;* and [more commonly] *continent,* or *chaste;* (TA;) and the pl. of this is عَفَائِفُ and عَفِيفَاتٌ. (O, Ḳ.)

عُفَافَةٌ is the subst. from عَفَّ said of milk: (O, Ḳ:) so says IDrd: (O:) [accord. to him, it app. signifies *Milk that has collected in the udder:*] and it signifies (Ṣ, O, Ḳ) accord. to another or others, (O,) as also ▼ عُفَّةٌ, *somewhat of milk remaining in the udder* (Ṣ, O, Ḳ) *after most of it has been sucked.* (O, Ḳ.) — And F explains العُفَافَةُ, with ḍamm, by the words أَنْ تَأْخُذَ الشَّىْءَ

بَعْدَ الشَّىْءِ فَأَنْتَ تَعْتَفُّهُ [as though signifying *The taking thing after thing, by licking it up, or otherwise, from the ground, choosing the best thereof:* but this mode of explanation is often used in lexicons to denote the thing, or things, mentioned therein; not the act: and I think that what is here meant is *the thing,* or *things, thus taken:* this, moreover, is agreeable with the general analogy of words of the measure فُعَالَةٌ; as is shown by many exs. in the Mz, 40th نوع]. (TA.)

جَآءَ عَلَى عِفَّانِ ذٰلِكَ *He* (a man, Ṣ, O) *came at the time of that:* (Ṣ, O, Ḳ:*) a dial. var. of إِفَّانٌ: (Ṣ, O:) or, accord. to IF, formed [from the latter] by substitution. (O.)

عفج

1. عَفَجَ, [aor. ـِ,] inf. n. عَفْجٌ, *He* [a man, or a beast other than a ruminant,] *was,* or *became, fat in his* أَعْفَاج [pl. of عَفَجٌ, q. v.]. (L.)

عَفْجٌ and عِفْجٌ: see the next paragraph.

عَفَجٌ and ▼ عِفَجٌ and ▼ عَفِجٌ (Ṣ, O, Ḳ) and ▼ عَفْجٌ (L, and some copies of the Ḳ) sings. of which the pl. is أَعْفَاجٌ (Ṣ, O, Ḳ) and عِفَجَةٌ: (TA:) the أَعْفَاج are The أَمْعَآء [or *intestines into which the food passes from the stomach*]: (TA, and Ḥam p. 641:) or the *lower* أَمْعَآء: (TA, and Zj in his "Khalḳ el-Insán:") or *in human beings, and in solid-hoofed animals, and in beasts of prey,* (Ṣ, O,) *that* [*portion of the intestines*] *to which the food passes from the stomach;* (Ṣ, O, Ḳ;) *which is like the* [*intestines called*] مَصَارِين *in camels and in cloven-hoofed animals, to which the stomach transmits what it has concocted,* lit. *what it has tanned* (مَا دَبَغَتْهُ): (Ṣ, O: in some copies of the former, مَا دَفَعَتْهُ:) or the عفج is *what is in the place of the* كَرِش *to that which has no* كرش: or, accord. to Lth, it is, *to any animal that does not ruminate, such of the* أَمْعَآء [or *lower intestines*] *of the belly as is like the* مَمْرَقَة *to the sheep* or *goat.* (TA.) ═ عَفْجٌ is also the inf. n. of عَفِجَ [q. v.]. (L.)

عَفِجٌ: see the next preceding paragraph. ═ Also A man [and app. a solid-hoofed animal and a beast of prey] *fat in his* أَعْفَاج [pl. of عَفَجٌ, q. v.].

أَعْفَجُ *Large in the* أَعْفَاج. (Ḳ, TA.)

عفر

1. عَفَرَهُ, aor. ـِ, (Ṣ, O, Mṣb, Ḳ,) inf. n. عَفْرٌ, (Ṣ, O, Mṣb,) *He rubbed it* (namely a vessel) *with dust:* and ▼ عَفَّرَهُ *he rubbed it much with dust:* (Mṣb:) or the latter, *he defiled,* or *soiled, it with dust:* (Mgh:) and the former, and ▼ latter, (Ṣ, O, Ḳ,) of which the inf. n. is تَعْفِيرٌ, (Ṣ, O,) *he rolled,* or *turned over, him,* or *it,* فِى التُّرَابِ *in the dust:* (Ṣ, O, Ḳ:) or *he hid* (دَسَّ) *him,* or *it,* therein. (Ḳ.) It is is said in a trad. of Aboo-Jahl, هَلْ يُعَفِّرُ ▼ مُحَمَّدٌ وَجْهَهُ بَيْنَ أَظْهُرِكُمْ [*Doth,* or *shall, Moḥammad defile his face with dust,* or *rub his face in the dust, in the midst of you?*], meaning his prostrating himself in the dust: and at the end he says, لَأَطَأَنَّ عَلَى رَقَبَتِهِ أَوْ لَأُعَفِّرَنَّ ▼ وَجْهَهُ فِى التُّرَابِ [*I will assuredly trample upon his neck,* or *I will defile,* or *roll, his face in the dust*]; meaning that he would abase him, or render him abject. (TA.) — *He dragged him,* being about to roll him in the dust: and you say اِعْتَفَرَ ▼ ثَوْبَهُ فِى التُّرَابِ [*He dragged his garment in the dust*]. (Aboo-Naṣr, L, TA.) — And عَفَرَهُ, (Ḳ,) inf. n. عَفْرٌ, (TA,) *He cast him upon the ground;* as also ▼ اعتفره. (Ḳ.) You say, ▼ اعتفره الأَسَدُ *The lion cast him upon the ground:* (A:) or *the lion seized him, and broke his neck,* (Ṣ, O, TA,) *and cast him upon the ground, and shook him about.* (TA.) And ▼ اعتفره *He leaped,* or *sprang, upon him,* or *at him,* (سَاوَرَهُ, O, Ḳ, for which شاوره is erroneously put in some copies of the Ḳ, TA,) *and dragged him, and cast him upon the ground.* (TA.) [See also 2.] ═ عَفِرَ, aor. ـَ, (Mṣb, Ḳ,) inf. n. عَفَرٌ, (Mṣb,) *He, or it, was of the colour termed* عُفْرَة: (Mṣb, Ḳ:) or *of a colour resembling that.* (Mṣb.)

2: see 1, in four places. — عفّر قِرْنَهُ, and عافره ▼ فَأَلْزَقَهُ بِالعَفَرِ, *He wrestled with his adversary, and made him cleave to the dust.* (A.) ═ عفّر, inf. n. تَعْفِيرٌ, *He mixed his black sheep* or *goats with others of the colour termed* عُفْرَة: (O, Ḳ, TA:) or *he took white sheep* or *goats in exchange for black;* because the former have more increase. (Ṣ, O, TA.) — And *He made,* or *rendered, white.* (Ṣ, O.)

3: see the next preceding paragraph.

5: see 7, in three places. — تعفّر الوَحْشُ ‡ *The wild animals became fat.* (O, Ḳ, TA.)

6. تعافر said of [food of the kind called] ثَرِيد, *It was made white.* (Ḳ. [See أَعْفَرُ, latter half.])

7. انعفر and ▼ اعتفر *It* (a vessel) *became rubbed with dust:* and ▼ تعفّر *it became much rubbed with dust:* (Mṣb:) or the first and ▼ second, (Ṣ, O,) and ▼ the last also, (O,) *it* (a thing) *became defiled with dust:* (Ṣ, O:) or the first and ▼ last, *he,* or *it, became rolled,* or *turned over,* فِى التُّرَابِ *in the dust:* or *became hidden* therein. (Ḳ.) — And one says, دَخَلْتُ المَآءَ فَمَا ٱنْعَفَرَتْ قَدَمَاىَ *I entered the water, and my feet did not reach the ground.* (A, TA.)

8: see 1, in four places. ═ See also 7, in two places.

Q. Q. 2. تَعَفْرَتَ *He became,* or *acted like, an* عِفْرِيت; (Ḳ, TA;) from which latter word this verb is derived, the [final] augmentative letter being preserved in it, with the radical letters, to convey the full meaning, and to indicate the original. (TA.)

عَفْرٌ: see عَفَرٌ, in four places.

عُفْرٌ: see عِفْرٌ. ═ Also pl. of أَعْفَرُ [q. v.]. (Ṣ, &c.)

عِفْرٌ *A boar;* (Ṣ, O, Ḳ;) as also ▼ عُفْرٌ: or *a swine,* as a common term: or the *young one of a sow.* (Ḳ.) ═ عِفْرٌ (Ṣ, A, O, Ḳ) and ▼ عَفِرٌ (Ṣgh in TA in art. نفر) and ▼ عِفْرِيَةٌ, (A, O, Ḳ,) in which the ى is to render the word quasi-coordinate to شِرْذِمَةٌ, [I substitute this word for شِرْذِوَةٌ, in the L, and شُرْذُوَةٌ in the TA,] and the ة to give intensiveness, (L, TA,) and ▼ عِفْرِيت, (A, O, Ḳ,) in which the ت is to render the word quasi-coordinate to قِنْدِيلٌ, (TA,) [or to render it a contraction of عِفْرِيَةٌ,] and ▼ عِفْرِيتٌ, which occurs in one reading of the Ḳur, [xxvii. 39, and is agreeable with modern vulgar pronunciation,] (O, CḲ,) and ▼ عِفْرَاتٌ, (CḲ,) and ▼ عُفَارِيَةٌ, (A, O, L, Ḳ,) in which the ى is to render the word quasi-coordinate to عُذَافِرَةٌ, and the ة is to give intensiveness, (TA,) and ▼ عِفِرٌّ, (O, Ḳ,) and ▼ عِفْرِىٌّ, (Ṣgh, Ḳ,) and ▼ عِفْرِنَّةٌ, (Ṣgh, Ḳ,) and ▼ عِفْرِينٌ, and ▼ عِفِرِّينٌ, (Lḥ, TA,) and ▼ عَفَرْنًى, (Lth, TA,) [respecting which last, see the latter portion of this paragraph,] applied to a man, (Ṣ, O, Ḳ,) and to a jinnee, or genie, (Ḳur, ubi suprà,) *Wicked,* or *malignant;* (Ṣ, O, Ḳ;) *crafty,* or *cunning;* (Ṣ, O;) *abominable, foul,* or *evil;* (Ḳ;) *abounding in evil;* (TA;) *strong,* or *powerful;* (A;) *insolent and audacious in pride and in acts of rebellion* or *disobedience;* (A, TA;) *who rolls his adversary in the dust:* (A:) and the epithet applied to a woman is عِفْرَةٌ, (Ṣ, O,) and ▼ عِفْرِيتَةٌ, (Lḥ, Ḳ,) and ▼ عِفِرَّةٌ: (Sh, O:) or ▼ عِفْرِيتٌ signifies anything *that exceeds the ordinary bounds;* and ▼ عُفَارِيَةٌ is syn. with it: (AO, Ṣ, O:) and ▼ عِفْرِيتٌ and ▼ عِفْرِينٌ and ▼ عِفِرِّينٌ (Zj, Ḳ) applied to a man, and as applied in the Ḳur, ubi suprà, [to a jinnee,] (Zj,) *sharp, vigorous, and effective, in an affair, exceeding the ordinary bounds therein, with craftiness,* or *cunning,* (Zj, O, Ḳ,) *and wickedness,* or *malignity:* (Zj:) or ▼ عِفْرِيتٌ is properly applied to a jinnee, and signifies *evil in disposition, and wicked* or *malignant;* and is metaphorically applied to a man, like as is شَيْطَانٌ: (B:) it is applied to *an evil jinnee that is powerful, but inferior to such as is termed* مَارِدٌ: (Mir-át ez-Zemán:) ▼ عِفْرِيَةٌ also signifies i. q. دَاهِيَةٌ [app. meaning *very crafty* or *cunning,* rather than *a calamity*]: (Ṣ, O:) ▼ عِفْرِيَةٌ and ▼ عِفْرِيتٌ are also applied as epithets to a شَيْطَان [or devil]: (Kh, Ṣ:) the pl. of the former of these two epithets is عَفَارِيَةٌ, (Kh, Ṣ, O,) or عَفَارِى; (Fr;) and that of ▼ عفريت is عَفَارِيتُ; (Kh, Fr, Ṣ, O;) and that of ▼ عفر is عِفْرُونَ; (Sh;) and that of عفرّ is أَعْفَارٌ. (TA in art. جشر.) You say, فُلَانٌ عِفْرِيَةٌ ▼ نِفْرِيَةٌ, and عِفْرِيتٌ ▼ نِفْرِيتٌ; [*Such a one is wicked,* or *malignant;* &c.;] the latter of these two words being an imitative sequent. (AO, Ṣ, O.) And in a trad. it is said, إِنَّ ٱللّٰهَ يُبْغِضُ

العِفْرِيَةَ ▼ النِّفْرِيَةَ الَّذِى لَا يُرْزَأُ فِى أَهْلٍ وَلَا مَالٍ (AO, Ṣ) [*Verily God hates*] *the crafty* or *cunning, the wicked* or *malignant, the abounding in evil;* or *him who collects much and refuses to give;* or *him who acts very wrongfully* or *unjustly* or *tyrannically;* [*who will not suffer loss in his family nor in his property.*] (TA.) — أَسَدٌ عِفْرٌ, and ▼ عِفْرِيَةٌ, and ▼ عِفْرِيتٌ, and ▼ عُفَارِيَةٌ, (Ḳ,) and ▼ عِفِرٌّ, (TA,) and ▼ عَفَرْنًى, (Ḳ, [respecting which see what follows: in the CḲ عَفَرْنَى, which is wrong in two respects:]) *A strong,* (Ḳ,) *powerful, great,* (TA,) *lion:* (Ḳ, TA:) or العَفَرْنَى *the lion;* so called because of his strength: (Ṣ, O:) and لَبُؤَةٌ عَفَرْنًى, (Ṣ, O, TA,) like the masc., (TA, [or it may be in this case with the fem. ى, i. e. without tenween,]) or ▼ عَفَرْنَاةٌ, (Ḳ, TA,) *a strong lioness:* (Ṣ, O, Ḳ:) or the epithet, of either gender, signifies *bold:* from عَفَرٌ signifying "dust," or from عَفْرٌ in the sense of اِعْتِفَارٌ, or from the strength and hardiness of the animal: (TA:) and نَاقَةٌ عَفَرْنَاةٌ *a strong she-camel;* pl. عَفَرْنَيَاتٌ: (Ṣ, O:) but you do not say جَمَلٌ عَفَرْنًى: (Az:) the alif [which is in this case written ى] and ن in عَفَرْنًى are to render it quasi-coordinate to سَفَرْجَلٌ [which shows that it is with tenween]. (Ṣ.)

عَفَرٌ (IDrd, Ṣ, A, O, Mṣb, Ḳ) and ▼ عَفْرٌ (IDrd, A, O, Ḳ) *Dust:* (IDrd, Ṣ, O, Mṣb:) [like عَفَارٌ *the dust of the earth:* (Freytag, from Meyd:)] or *the exterior of the dust* or *earth:* (A, Ḳ:) and *the surface of the earth;* (Mṣb;) as also عَفَرُ الأَرْضِ: (TA:) pl. أَعْفَارٌ. (Ḳ.) You say مَا عَلَى عَفَرِ ▼ الأَرْضِ مِثْلُهُ *There is not upon the face of the earth the like of him,* or *it.* (O, TA.) And لَا عَفَرَ لَهُ, (Ḳ,) or كَلَامٌ لَا عَفَرَ فِيهِ, (TṢ, TA,) [lit., *Language in which is no dust;* or *which has no dust;* like the saying كَلَامٌ لَا غُبَارَ عَلَيْهِ "language on which is no dust;" meaning] † *language in which is nothing difficult to be understood.* (Ḳ.) And IAạr mentions, but without explaining it, the saying, عَلَيْهِ العَفَارُ ▼ وَالدَّبَارُ وَسُوْءُ الدَّارِ [app. meaning, *May the dust, and perdition, and evil of the dwelling, be his lot.* See دَبَارٌ]. (O, TA.)

عَفِرٌ [part. n. of عَفِرَ]. أَرْضٌ عَفِرَةٌ *Land of the colour termed* عُفْرَةٌ [q. v.]. (O and TA in art. عشر.) — See also عِفِرٌّ.

عُفْرٌ, and the fem., with ة: see عِفْرٌ, in four places.

عُفْرَةٌ *A dust-colour inclining to whiteness; a whitish dust-colour:* (TA:) or *whiteness that is not clear:* (Mgh, Mṣb:) or *whiteness that is not very clear,* (AZ, Aṣ,) *like the colour of the surface of the earth:* (AZ, Aṣ, Mgh:) or *whiteness with a tinge of redness over it:* (A:) *the colour of an antelope such as is termed* أَعْفَرُ. (Ḳ.) — See also عِفْرِيَةٌ, in three places.

عِفْرِيَةٌ, or عِفْرَى: see عِفْرِيَةٌ.

عِفْرِىٌّ: see عِفْرٌ, first quarter.

عِفْرَاةٌ: see عِفْرِيَةٌ.

عِفْرَاتٌ: see عِفْرٌ, first quarter: — and see the next paragraph, in three places.

عِفْرِيَةٌ: see عِفْرٌ, in six places. — The *hair,* and the *feathers, of the back of the neck,* of the lion, and of the cock, &c., *which it turns back towards the top of its head when exasperated;* as also ▼ عُفْرَةٌ (Ṣ, O) and ▼ عِفْرَاتٌ, (Ṣ,) or ▼ عِفْرَاةٌ: (O, TA:) and ▼ عُفْرَةٌ, the *feathers around the neck* of a cock and of a bustard (حُبَارَى) &c.: (Ṣ in art. برل:) or عِفْرِيَةٌ and ▼ عِفْرَى, or عَفْرَى, [whether without or with tenween is not shown, but I think it is more probably without,] of a cock, the *feathers of the neck;* (Ḳ;) as also ▼ عُفْرَةٌ: (TA:) and of a man, the *hair of the back of the neck:* (Ḳ:) or the *hair of the part over the forehead:* (TA:) and of a beast, the *hair of the fore-lock:* (Ḳ:) or the *hair of the back of the neck:* (TA:) and [of a man,] the *hairs that grow in the middle of the head,* (Ḳ,) *that stand up on an occasion of fright;* (TA;) as also ▼ عِفْرَاتٌ and ▼ عُفْرُنِيَةٌ. (Ḳ.) You say جَآءَ فُلَانٌ نَافِشًا عِفْرِيَتَهُ, meaning *Such a one came in a state of anger.* (Ṣ, O.) And جَآءَ نَاشِرًا عِفْرِيَتَهُ, and ▼ عِفْرَاتَهُ, *He came spreading his hair, by reason of covetousness, and inordinate desire.* (ISd, TA.)

عِفْرِيتٌ; and عَفَرِيتٌ; and the fem., عِفْرِيتَةٌ: see عِفْرٌ, in ten places.

عِفْرِينٌ: see عِفْرٌ, in two places.

عِفِرِّينٌ: see عِفْرٌ, in two places. — لَيْثُ عِفِرِّينَ *The lion.* (AA, Ḳ.) So in the prov., إِنَّهُ لَأَشْجَعُ مِنْ لَيْثِ عِفِرِّينَ [*Verily he is more courageous than the lion*]. (AA, TA.) عِفِرِّينُ is the name of a certain place in which are lions, or abounding with lions: (Ṣ, O, Ḳ:) or the name of a certain country or town. (Aṣ, AA, Ṣ, M.) — *A certain insect, whose retreat is the soft dust at the bases of walls;* (O, Ḳ;) *that rolls a ball, and then hides itself within it; and when it is roused, throws up dust:* (O, TA:) the word [عفرّين] is of one of those forms not found by Sb: (TA:) or *a certain creeping animal* (دَابَّة), *like the chameleon, that opposes itself to the rider* [*upon a camel or horse*], *and that strikes with its tail.* (O, Ḳ.) [See also طُحَنٌ: and see Ḥam p. 131.] — Also ‡ *A complete man;* [i. e., *complete with respect to bodily vigour, having attained the usual term thereof;*] (O, Ḳ, TA;) *fifty years old.* (O, TA.) — And ‡ *Resolute,* or *firm-minded; strong,* or *powerful.* (Ṣ, O, Ḳ, TA.)

عَفَرْنًى and عَفَرْنَاةٌ: see عِفْرٌ, in three places. — The latter also signifies The [*kind of goblin,* or *demon, called*] غُولٌ. (O, Ḳ.)

عُفْرُنِيَةٌ: see عِفْرٌ; first quarter. — and see عِفْرِيَةٌ.

عَفَارٌ: see عَفَرٌ. — Also *A certain kind of tree,* (Ṣ, O, Ḳ,) *by means of which fire is produced;* (Ṣ, O;) زِنَادٌ [or *pieces of wood,* or *stick, used for that purpose,*] *being made of its branches:* (Ḳ,* TA:) accord. to information given to AḤn by certain of the desert-Arabs of the Saráh (السَّرَاة), *it resembles the kind of tree called the* غُبَيْرَاء, *by reason of its smallness, so that when one sees it from afar he doubts not its being the latter kind of tree; its blossom, also, is like that of the latter tree; and it is a kind of tree that emits much fire, so that the* زناد *made of it are excellent:* (TA:) pl. of عَفَارَةٌ; (Ḳ;) or, more properly, [a coll. gen. n., and] its n. un. is with ة: (O, TA:) *it and the* مَرْخ *contain fire that is not in any other kind of tree:* Az says, I have seen them both in the desert, and the Arabs make them the subject of a prov., relating to high nobility: (TA:) they say فِى كُلِّ شَجَرٍ نَارٌ وَٱسْتَمْجَدَ المَرْخُ وَالعَفَارُ (Ṣ, O, TA) *In all trees is fire; but the markh and 'afár yield much fire,* more than all other trees. (O,* TA.) [See also مَرْخٌ, and استمجد.] It is also said, in another prov., اِقْدَحْ بِعَفَارٍ أَوْ مَرْخٍ ثُمَّ اشْدُدْ إِنْ شِئْتَ أَوْ أَرْخِ [*Produce thou fire with markh or with 'afár: then tighten, if thou please,* or *loosen*]. (TA.) — See also عَافُور.

عَفَارَةٌ The *quality,* or *disposition, of him who is termed* عِفْرٌ *and* عِفْرِيَةٌ *and* عِفْرِيتٌ *&c.;* i. e., *wickedness,* or *malignity, &c.* (Ḳ,* TA.)

عُفَارِيَةٌ: see عِفْرٌ, in three places.

عَافِرٌ and ▼ مُنْعَفِرٌ and ▼ مَعْفُورٌ and ▼ مُعَفَّرٌ *Defiled with dust:* hence, العَافِرُ الوَجْهِ *He whose face is defiled with dust:* and هُوَ مُنْعَفِرُ ▼ الوَجْهِ فِى التُّرَابِ, and ▼ مُعَفَّرُهُ, *He has the face defiled in the dust.* (TA.)

وَقَعُوا فِى عَافُورِ شَرٍّ, (Ṣ, Ḳ,) and ▼ فِى عَفَارِ شَرٍّ, (TA,) *i. q.* فِى عَاثُورِ شَرٍّ, (Fr, Ṣ, Ḳ,) i. e., *They fell into difficulty,* or *distress.* (Ṣ.) Some say that the ف is substituted for ث. (TA.) [But see عاثور.]

أَعْفَرُ *Dust-coloured inclining to white; of a whitish dust-colour:* (TA:) or *white, but not of a clear hue:* (Mṣb:) or, applied to a buck-antelope, *white, but not of a very clear white,* (AZ, Aṣ, Ṣ, O, Ḳ,) *being like the colour of the surface of the earth:* (AZ, Aṣ, Mgh:) or a buck-antelope *having a tinge of red over his whiteness,* (AA, Ṣ, A, Ḳ,) *with a short neck;* and such is the weakest of antelopes in running: (AA, Ṣ, O:) or *having a redness in his back, with white flanks:* (Ḳ:) [in the CḲ, after the words thus rendered, is an omission, of the words أَوِ الأَبْيَضُ وَ:] or *such as inhabits elevated, rugged, stony tracts, and hard grounds; and such is red:* (AZ:) or *having white horns:* (A:) fem. عَفْرَآءُ: (Ṣ, Ḳ, &c.:) also applied to a she-goat, meaning *of a clear white colour:* (TA:) pl. عُفْرٌ. (Ṣ, A, O.) — El-Kumeyt says,

• وَكُنَّا إِذَا جَبَّارُ قَوْمٍ أَرَادَنَا •
• بِكَيْدٍ حَمَلْنَاهُ عَلَى قَرْنِ أَعْفَرَا •

[*And we used, when an insolent tyrant of a people desired to execute against us a plot, to carry him upon the horn of an antelope of a whitish dust-colour, or white but not of a clear hue, &c.*]; meaning, we used to slay him, and to carry his head upon the spear-head; for the spear-heads, in time past, were of horns. (Ṣ, O.) — Hence the saying رَمَانِى بِدَاهِيَةٍ *i. q.* رَمَانِى عَنْ قَرْنِ أَعْفَرَ ‡ [*He sent upon me a calamity; or he made a very crafty man to be my assailant*]: for the same reason, also, قَرْنُ أَعْفَرَ is proverbially used to signify ‡ *A difficulty, or distress, that befalls one:* and one says to a man who has passed the night in disquieting distress, كُنْتَ عَلَى قَرْنِ أَعْفَرَ ‡ [*Thou wast pierced by grief*]. (TA.) One says also, of him who is frightened and disquieted, كَأَنَّهُ عَلَى قَرْنِ أَعْفَرَ [*He is as though he were upon the horn of an antelope of a whitish dust-colour, &c.: meaning, upon the head of a spear*]: the like of this phrase is used by Imra-el-Ḳeys. (A.) — Also عَفْرَآءُ, A ewe *of a colour inclining to whiteness.* (O.) — And أَعْفَرُ, *Red sand.* (Ṣ, O.) — [Food of the kind called] ثَرِيدٌ *made white:* (Ḳ, TA:) from عُفْرَةٌ signifying the "colour of the earth." (TA.) — عَفْرَآءُ *White.* (Ḳ.) — أَرْضٌ عَفْرَآءُ *Untrodden land.* (Ḳ, TA.) — العَفْرَآءُ *The thirteenth night* [*of the lunar month*]: (Ṣ, O:) or *the night of blackness:* (A:) but accord. to IAạr, اللَّيَالِى العُفْرُ signifies *the white nights;* (A;) and so says Th, without particularizing: (TA:) or the nights thus called are *the seventh and eighth and ninth nights of the lunar month;* (Ḳ;) because of the whiteness of the moon [therein]. (TA.) It is said in a trad. لَيْسَ عُفْرُ اللَّيَالِى كَالدَّآدِى *The moon-lit nights are not like the black nights:* some say that this is a proverb. (TA.)

مُعْفَرٌ: see عَافِرٌ, in two places.

مُعْفِرٌ One *whose sheep or goats are of the colour termed* عُفْرَةٌ: there is no tribe among the Arabs to whom this appellation applies, except Hudheyl. (A, TA.) [Accord. to analogy, this should rather be written مُعْفِرٌ; and perhaps it is thus in correct copies of the A.]

مَعْفُورٌ: see عَافِرٌ. — أَرْضٌ مَعْفُورَةٌ *Land of which the herbage has been eaten.* (Ṣ, O.)

مَعَافِرُ: see مَعَافِرِىٌّ, in three places.

مُعَافِرٌ ‡ One *who walks with companies of travellers,* (Ṣ, O, Ḳ, TA,) and so, accord. to the L, ▼ مُعَافِرِىٌّ, (TA,) *and obtains of their superabundance* [*of provisions*]. (Ṣ, O, TA.)

ثَوْبٌ مَعَافِرِىٌّ, (Ṣ, Mgh, O, Mṣb,) pl. ثِيَابٌ مَعَافِرِيَّةٌ, (Ṣ, O, Ḳ,) and بُرْدٌ مَعَافِرِىٌّ, (Az,) and hence, simply, ▼ مَعَافِرُ, (Az, Mgh,) as a subst., (Az,) without the relative ى, (Az, Mgh,) accord. to Aẓ, (Mgh,) *A kind of garment, or piece of cloth,* (Ṣ, Mgh, O, Mṣb,) and *a garment of the kind called* بُرْدٌ, (Az,) *so called in relation to* ▼ مَعَافِرُ, (Ṣ, O, Ḳ, &c.,) a word imperf. decl., (Ṣ, O, Ḳ,) because of its being of the form of an imperf. decl. pl., (Ṣ, O,) as the name of a tribe of Hemdán; (Ṣ, O;) or as being the name of a son of Murr, (Sb, Mgh, Mṣb,) brother of Temeem the son of Murr, (Sb, Mgh,) and father of the tribe above mentioned, (Mṣb, Ḳ,) which was a tribe of El-Yemen; (Mṣb;) or as being the name of a place, (IDrd, O,) or a town, or district, (Ḳ, TA,) of El-Yemen, (IDrd, O, TA,) in which Ma'áfir Ibn-Udd took up his abode, accord. to Z: (TA:) معافرىّ is perfectly decl. because the relative ى is added to it: (Ṣ:) and it is thus formed because مَعَافِرُ is sing. in its application; whereas, in a rel. n. from a pl. used as a pl., the formation is from the sing., as in the instance of مَسْجِدِىٌّ as a rel. n. from مَسَاجِدُ: (TA:) ▼ معافر should not be pronounced with ḍamm to the م: (Mṣb, Ḳ:) and it is wrong to call the kind of garment above mentioned مُعَافِرِىٌّ, with ḍamm, and مَعَافِرِىٌّ, without tenween, and مَعَافِيرُ. (Mgh.)

مُعَافِرِىٌّ: see مُعَافِرٌ.

مُنْعَفِرٌ: see عَافِرٌ, in two places.

يَعْفُورٌ The *dust-coloured gazelle:* (Ḳ:) or the *gazelle, as a general term:* (Ḳ,* TA:) as also ▼ يُعْفُورٌ: (Ḳ:) and the [*young gazelle such as is called*] خِشْفٌ: (Ṣ, O, Ḳ:) or the *buck-gazelle:* (Ṣ, Mgh, O:) and (Ṣ, IAth, O, in the Mgh "or") the *young one of the wild cow:* (Ṣ, IAth, Mgh, O:) n. un. with ة: (TA:) pl. يَعَافِيرُ. (Ṣ, O.) — Also *A light,* or *an active, ass.* (IAạr.) — And it is said to mean † *The form of a man, seen from a distance, resembling a* يعفور [in one of the senses expl. above]. (L, TA.) — And *One of the divisions of the night,* (Ḳ, TA,) *which are five, called* سُدْفَةٌ *and* شُعْفَةٌ *and* هَجْمَةٌ *and* يَعْفُورٌ *and* خُدْرَةٌ. (TA.)

عفص

1. عَفَصَ الشَّىْءَ, aor. ـِ, (Ḳ,) inf. n. عَفْصٌ, (TḲ,) *He doubled, folded, or bent, the thing.* (Ḳ.) Hence عِفَاصُ القَارُورَةِ. (TA.) — عَفَصَ القَارُورَةَ, (Fr, Ṣ, A, O, Mṣb, Ḳ,) aor. ـِ, (Mṣb, Ḳ,) inf. n. عَفْصٌ, (Mṣb,) *He tied, or bound, the* عفاص (q. v.) *upon the flask, or bottle;* (Ṣ, A,* O, Ḳ;) as also ▼ اعفصها: (Ḳ:) or *he put the* عفاص *upon the head of the bottle;* and so, accord. to some, ▼ the latter also: (Mṣb:) or ▼ the latter signifies *he made for it, or put to it,* (جَعَلَ لَهَا,) *an* عفاص; (Fr, Ṣ, O, Mṣb;) and so, (Fr, O, Mṣb,) accord. to some, (Mṣb,) the former also; (Fr, O, Mṣb;) each having two meanings: (Mṣb:) and the former, also, *he stopped the bottle with a stopper.* (A) — عَفَصَهُ, aor. ـِ, *He pulled it out or forth.* (Ḳ.) And عَفَصْتُ أُذُنَيْهِ *I pulled towards me its ears;* namely, the ears of a head that I was eating. (Ibn-'Abbád, O.) And IAạr allows this verb with س as well as with ص. (TA.) — See also 8. — عَفَصَ يَدَهُ *He twisted his arm, or hand.* (O, Ḳ.) — عَفَصَهُ, (O, Ḳ,) aor. ـِ, inf. n. عَفْصٌ, (TA,) *He weakened, or enervated, him,* (أَضْعَفَهُ,) *in wrestling.* (O, Ḳ.) — And عَفَصَهَا *He compressed her,* (Ibn-'Abbád, O, Ḳ,) namely, a woman, (Ibn-'Abbád, O,) or his young woman. (Ḳ.)

2. [عفّص الثَّوْبَ *He dyed the garment, or piece of cloth, with* عَفْص, or *galls.* See the pass. part. n., below.]

4. اعفص القَارُورَةَ: see 1, in three places. — اعفص الحِبْرَ *He put* عَفْص [or *galls*] *into the ink.* (TA.)

8. اعتفص مِنْهُ حَقَّهُ *He took from him his right, or due;* (Ibn-'Abbád, O, Ḳ;) as also ▼ عَفَصَ. (O, Ḳ.*)

عَفْصٌ [*Galls:* and the *trees which bear them:*] *a certain thing well known,* (Mṣb, Ḳ,) *of which ink is made,* (Ṣ, O, TA,) *and with which one tans;* (Mṣb;) the *produce of the tree called* بَلُّوط [or *oak*]: (L, TA:) or applied to the *trees* [*which bear it*] and to the *fruit* [*thereof*]: (Ḳ:) or *a certain tree of the kind called* بلّوط, *which* [*is also the name of a produce of that tree,* i. e., of the acorn, (both of which applications are agreeable with modern usage,) *like as* عَفْص *is also the name of another produce thereof,* i. e., the *gall,* or *gall-nut; for it is said that this tree*] *bears one year* بَلُّوط, *and another year* عَفْص, (Lth, O, Ḳ,) *of which ink is made:* (CḲ:) *it is not of the growth of the land of the Arabs:* (IB, TA:) *it is astringent; drying; having the quality of repelling effluent matters; and strengthening flaccid and weak members;* (Ḳ, TA;) *and especially the teeth;* (TA;) *and when steeped in vinegar, it blackens the hair:* (Ḳ:) the word is post-classical; (Ṣ, O, Ḳ;) not of the language of the people of the desert: (Ṣ, IF, O, Mṣb:) or it is Arabic; (AḤn, O, Ḳ;) and from it is derived ▼ عُفُوصَةٌ, signifying "a taste in which is astringency and bitterness;" as also the epithet ▼ عَفِصٌ, applied to a taste. (AḤn, O.)

عَفَصٌ *A twisting in the nose:* (O, Ḳ:) so they say. (O.)

عَفِصٌ A taste (AḤn, Ṣ, O, Mṣb) *having an astringent quality,* (AḤn, Ṣ, O, Mṣb, Ḳ,) *and bitterness,* (AḤn, O, Ḳ,) *which render swallowing difficult;* (TA;) *disagreeable and choking;* or *disagreeable, with dryness and bitterness;* or *rough;* syn. بَشِعٌ. (TA.) See عَفْص.

عَفْصِىٌّ [app. *A seller of* عَفْص, or *galls.* Five relaters of traditions of whom each bore this appellation are mentioned in the TA.]

عِفَاصٌ The *receptacle in which is put money or the like that one expends,* (A'Obeyd, Az, A, Mgh, O, Mṣb, Ḳ,) or, as some say, *in which is the pastor's money or the like that he expends,* (TA,) *made of skin, or of a piece of rag, or other material.* (A'Obeyd, Az, A,* Mgh, O, Mṣb, Ḳ.*) — And hence, (A'Obeyd, O, Az, &c.,) The *skin with* which the head of a flask, or bottle, is covered: (A'Obeyd, Az, Ṣ, A, Mgh, O, Mṣb, Ḳ:) it is said to be its صِمَام [or stopper]; (Az, Mgh, O, Mṣb;) by Lth; (Az, O, Mṣb;) but the right explanation is that given by A'Obeyd: (Az, Mṣb:) that which enters into its mouth is the صِمَام: (Ṣ:) or it has this latter signification also: (A:) or it signifies accord. to El-Ghooree, (Mgh,) or signifies also, (A, Ḳ,) the *case* (غِلَاف [which has app. been misunderstood as meaning the skin cover of the head of a flask or bottle, before mentioned,]) *of a flask*, or *bottle:* (A, Mgh, O, Ḳ:) but the first is the explanation that is preferred. (Mgh.) [See 1, first signification.]

عُفُوصَةٌ in taste, (Ṣ,) *Astringency* (Ṣ, Ḳ) *and bitterness,* (Ḳ,) *which render swallowing difficult:* (TA:) *a taste in which is astringency and bitterness:* derived from عَفْص, q. v. (AḤn, O.) [See also عَفِص.]

مُعَفَّصٌ A garment, or piece of cloth, *dyed with* عَفْص [or *galls*]. (O, Ḳ.)

مِعْفَاصٌ A young woman *extremely evil in disposition:* but the مِعْقَاص (with ق) is more evil than she. (IAạr, O, Ḳ.)

عفل

1. عَفِلَتْ, aor. ـَ, (Mṣb, Ḳ,) inf. n. عَفَلٌ, (Mṣb,) said of a woman, (Mṣb, Ḳ,) and of a she-camel, (Ḳ,) or of any female, (Mṣb,) *She had a certain thing,* (Mṣb, Ḳ,) *called* عَفَلٌ *and* عَفَلَةٌ, (Ḳ,) *come forth in her vulva, resembling the* أُدْرَة [or *scrotal hernia*] *of a man.* (Mṣb, Ḳ.) — عَفَلَهُ *He felt his* (i. e. a ram's) عَفْل [q. v.] *in order to see what was his state of fatness.* (TA.)

2. عَفَّلْتُهَا, (O,) inf. n. تَعْفِيلٌ, (O, Ḳ,) *I attributed to her the having what is termed* عَفَل. (O, Ḳ.*) — And تَعْفِيلٌ signifies also The *curing what is termed* عَفَل. (Ibn-'Abbád, O, Ḳ.) One says, عَفَّلَ المَرْأَةَ *He cured the woman's* [عَفَل or] عَفَلَة. (TḲ.)

عَفْلٌ [in the CḲ (erroneously) عَفَلٌ] The *part* of a sheep or goat, (Ks, Ṣ, O,) or of a ram, (Ḳ,) *which is the place where it is felt,* (Ks, Ṣ, O,) *between its hind legs,* (Ks, Ṣ,) *to know whether it be fat or lean.* (Ks, Ṣ, O, Ḳ.*) — And The *fat of the testicles* of a ram, *with what is around it.* (IF, Ḳ.) — And *Abundance of the fat of what is between the hind legs* of the he-goat and of the bull; seldom or never used except in relation to the gelded (Ḳ, TA) of these two; and not used in relation to the female. (TA.) — And The *perinæum;* or *line between the anus and the penis.* (Ḳ.)

عَفَلٌ *A certain thing that comes forth in the vulva of a woman* and *of a camel, resembling the* أُدْرَة [or *scrotal hernia* (in the TA the أُدْرَة in the خُصْيَة)] *of men;* as also ▼ عَفَلَةٌ: (Ṣ, O, Ḳ: [the latter word is said in the Mṣb to be the subst. from عَفِلَتْ, q. v.:]) accord. to IAạr, *a certain excrescence of flesh in the vulva of a woman;* also called قَرَنٌ: [but see this word;] (Az, Mṣb, TA;) they say that *it is not in the virgin, but only in the woman after childbirth:* (Mṣb:) so says Aboo-'Amr Esh-Sheybánee: (TA:) and it is said to be *a swelling between the* مَسْلَكَانِ [or *vagina and rectum*] *of a woman, by reason whereof her vulva is contracted so as to prevent initus:* (Mṣb:) accord. to IDrd, it is, *in men, a thickness that arises in the anus;* and *in women, a thickness in the* رَحِم [here meaning *vulva*], and so *in beasts.* (TA.)

عَفَلَةٌ: see عَفَلٌ. — Also The بُظَارَة [q. v.] *of a woman:* so accord. to IAạr. (TA.)

عَفَالِ, [indecl.,] like قَطَامِ, an expression of reproach, (O, Ḳ,) addressed to a woman: (Ḳ:) one says to a female slave, يَا عَفَالِ [as though meaning *O thou that hast what is termed* عَفَل or عَفَلَة]. (O.)

عَافِلٌ One *who wears short clothes over such as are long.* (IAạr, O, Ḳ.)

أَعْفَلُ A ram *having much fat of the* خُصْيَة [i. e. *testicle,* or *scrotum*], *by reason of plumpness.* (TA.) — And [the fem.] عَفْلَاءُ A woman *having what is termed* عَفَلَة (Ṣ, O, Mṣb, Ḳ) or عَفَل. (Ṣ, O, Ḳ.) It is said in a trad. of I'Ab, that the selling, and giving in marriage, of such is not allowable. (TA.) — And شَفَةٌ عَفْلَاءُ [in the CḲ (erroneously) عَفْلَاة] *A lip that becomes inverted on the occasion of laughing.* (O, Ḳ.)

عفن

1. عَفِنَ, aor. ـَ, inf. n. عَفَنٌ (Ṣ, Mgh, Mṣb, Ḳ, TA, in the CḲ [erroneously] عَفْن,) and عُفُونَةٌ, (Ḳ,) *It* (a thing) *was,* or *became, putrid,* or *rotten;* i. e. *it became decayed,* (Mgh,) or *in a corrupt,* or *an unsound, state,* (Mṣb,) *by the effect of moisture upon it,* (Mgh,* Mṣb,) *so as to become dissundered when felt:* (Mṣb:) said of a rope, (Ṣ, Ḳ,) *it became decayed,* (Ṣ,) or *in a corrupt,* or *an unsound, state,* (Ḳ,) *from the effect of water,* (Ṣ,) or *from moisture,* or *some other cause,* (TA,) *so as to crumble on its being felt;* as also ▼ تعفّن. (Ḳ.) And عَفِنَ اللَّحْمُ *The flesh,* or *flesh-meat, became* [*stinking,* or] *altered* [*for the worse*] *in odour;* and so ▼ تعفّن. (Mṣb.) — عَفَنَ اللَّحْمَ, (Mṣb, Ḳ,) aor. ـِ, (Mṣb,) inf. n. عَفْنٌ, (TA,) *He made the flesh,* or *flesh-meat, to become* [*stinking,* or] *altered* [*for the worse*] (Mṣb, Ḳ) *in odour;* (Mṣb;) and ▼ عفّنه signifies the same. (Ḳ.) — عَفَنَ فِى الجَبَلِ, (Kr, Ḳ,) inf. n. عَفْنٌ, (TA,) *He ascended the mountain;* (Kr, Ḳ;) as also عَثَنَ. (Kr, TA.)

2: see the preceding paragraph.

4. اعفن *He* (a man) *had his skin,* or *hide,* or *tanned skin* or *hide, pierced with holes.* (Ḳ.) — And اعفن اللَّحْمَ *He found the flesh,* or *flesh-meat, to be* [*stinking,* or] *altered* [*for the worse*] *in odour.* (Mṣb.)

5: see the first paragraph, in two places.

عَفِنٌ A thing, (Az, Ṣ,) or a rope, (Ḳ,) *putrid,* or *rotten;* i. e. *decayed,* (Ṣ,) or *in a corrupt,* or *an unsound, state,* (Az, Ḳ,) *from moisture,* (Az, Ṣ,* TA,) or *some other cause,* (TA,) *and from being kept in a close place,* (Az, TA,) *so as to crumble on its being felt.* (Ḳ.) And Flesh, or flesh-meat, (Mṣb, Ḳ,) [*stinking,* or] *altered* [*for the worse*] *in odour;* (Mṣb;) or *rendered so;* as also ▼ مَعْفُونٌ. (Ḳ.)

عُفُونَةٌ [mentioned above (see 1) as an inf. n.] *Putridity,* or *rottenness;* i. e. *a state of decay from moisture* &c. (Ṣ.) And [*A stinking,* or] *alteration* [*for the worse*] *in odour,* of flesh, or flesh-meat. (Mṣb.)

مَعْفُونٌ: see عَفِنٌ.

عفو

1. عَفَا, aor. يَعْفُو, (Ṣ, Mṣb,) inf. n. عَفَآءٌ (Ṣ, Mṣb, Ḳ) and عُفُوٌّ and عَفْوٌ, (Mṣb, Ḳ,) *It was,* or *became, effaced, erased, rased,* or *obliterated;* (Ṣ, Mṣb, Ḳ;) as also ▼ تعفّى: (Ḳ:) and *it,* or *he, perished, came to nought* or *to an end,* or *died.* (Ṣ, TA.) One says, عَفَا الأَثَرُ *The trace, vestige,* or *footprint, was,* or *became, effaced,* &c. (TA.) And [hence,] عَفَا أَثَرُهُ, inf. n. عَفَآءٌ, *He perished,* or *died.* (Ḳ.) And عَفَا المَنْزِلُ, aor. as above, (Ṣ, Mṣb,) and so the inf. ns. as in the first sentence, (Mṣb,) *The place of alighting,* or *abode, was,* or *became, effaced,* &c.: (Ṣ, Mṣb:) and عَفَتِ الدَّارُ, aor. تَعْفُو, inf. n. عَفَآءٌ and عُفُوٌّ [and عَفْوٌ]; (TA;) and ▼ تَعَفَّتْ, (Ṣ, TA,) and ▼ عَفَّتْ also; (TA;) *The house,* or *dwelling,* or *abode, was,* or *became, effaced,* &c. (Ṣ, TA.) A'Obeyd cites, as an ex. of العَفَآء signifying *the being,* or *becoming, effaced,* &c., and *the perishing,* &c., the saying of Zuheyr, (Ṣ, TA,) mentioning a dwelling, or an abode, (TA,)

* تَحَمَّلَ أَهْلُهَا عَنْهَا فَبَانُوا *
* عَلَى آثَارِ مَا ذَهَبَ العَفَآءُ *

[*Its occupants departed from it, and separated themselves,* or *removed far away: may the state of that which is effaced,* &c., *be,* or *rest, upon the traces of what has gone away:* or the meaning may be, *dust is upon the traces* &c.: (see عَفَآءٌ as a subst., below:) but it is not thus accord. to A'Obeyd; for] he says, This is like their saying عَلَيْهِ الدَّبَارُ as an imprecation against one, expressing a prayer that he may go away and not return. (Ṣ, TA.) MF says that عَفَا is one of those verbs that have contr. significations: for it signifies *It was,* or *became, unapparent,* or *imperceptible:* and also *It was,* or *became, apparent,* or *perceptible:* and it has two other contr. significations, which will be mentioned in what follows. (TA.) — And عَفْوٌ signifies also The *act of effacing, erasing, rasing,* or *obliterating.* (Ḳ, TA.) One says, عَفَتِ الرِّيحُ الأَثَرَ, (TA,) or المَنْزِلَ, (Ṣ, Mṣb,) and الدَّارَ, (TA,) *The wind effaced,* &c., (Ṣ, Mṣb, TA,) *the trace, vestige,* or *footprint,* (TA,) or *the place of alighting,* or *abode,* (Ṣ, Mṣb,) and *the house,* or *dwelling,* or *abode*: (TA:) and in like manner, عَفَّتِ ↓ الرِّيحُ الدَّارَ, (Ṣ, TA,) inf. n. تَعْفِيَةٌ, (TA,) in which the verb is with teshdeed to denote intensiveness [of the signification, i. e. *the wind effaced*, &c., *mightily*, or *utterly*, *the house*, or *dwelling*, or *abode*]: (Ṣ, TA:) and عَفَّى ↓ عَلَى أَثَرِهِ *It*, or *he*, *effaced its*, or *his*, *traces*, *vestige*, or *footprint*. (MA.) — Hence, as some say, عَفَا ٱللّٰهُ عَنْكَ i. e. *May God efface* [*from thee* thy sin, &c.; meaning *may God absolve thee*]; (TA;) or *may God efface thy sins*: (Mṣb:) [and عُفِىَ عَنْهُ *May he be absolved*, or *forgiven*, or *pardoned*:] and hence the saying in a trad., سَلُوا ٱللّٰهَ العَفْوَ i. e. [*Ask ye of God*] *the effacement of sin*; [or *ask ye of God absolution*, or *forgiveness*, or *pardon*;] and ↓ المُعَافَاةَ, and ↓ العَافِيَةَ [which have a similar meaning: see 3]: (TA:) and one says, عَفَوْتُ عَنْ ذَنْبِهِ, meaning *I left him, and did not punish him*: (Ṣ:) or عَفَوْتُ عَنْ ذَنْبِهِ and عَفَوْتُ عَنْهُ and عَفَوْتُ لَهُ عَنْ ذَنْبِهِ i. e. *I turned away from him*, or *from his crime, sin, fault*, or *offence*; syn. صَفَحْتُ عَنْهُ; and *I turned away* (أَعْرَضْتُ) *from punishing him*: (Mgh:) or العَفْوُ signifies *the turning away* (الصَّفْحُ, Ḳ, TA) from the committer of a crime or the like; (TA;) and *the relinquishing the punishment of the deserving* [*thereof*]: and one says, عَفَا عَنْهُ and عَفَا لَهُ ذَنْبَهُ and عَنْ ذَنْبِهِ [*he turned away from him*, or *from his crime*, &c.; and *relinquished the infliction of his merited punishment*, i. e. *forgave him*, or *pardoned him*]: (Ḳ, TA:) or عَنْ ذَنْبِهِ and عَفَا لَهُ ذَنْبَهُ and عَفَا عَنْهُ ذَنْبَهُ: (so accord. to the CḲ:) accord. to MF, the primary signification of العَفْوُ is التَّرْكُ: but this is not the case: and الصَّفْحُ [by which it is expl. in the Ḳ] is [or rather implies] the relinquishing of blame, or reproof, or of severe, or angry, blame or reproof; and this is more than [is signified by] العَفْوُ, for the latter is sometimes without the former: the primary signification of العَفْوُ [when trans.] is [said to be] *the purposing to take* a thing; and Er-Rághib says that عَفَوْتُ عَنْكَ is as though it meant *I have purposed to remove* [or *to take away*] *thy crime* or *the like*: (TA:) [but I think that the primary signification of العَفْوُ when its object is a crime or the like is that of *effacement*: and hence likewise what next follows:] — العَفْوُ is also metaphorically used as meaning ‡ *The withdrawing* from a right, or due, and from seeking, or demanding, it: and thus the verb is used in the Ḳur ii. 238 [q. v.]: and in the saying of the Prophet, عَفَوْنَا لَكُمْ عَنْ صَدَقَةِ الخَيْلِ وَالرَّقِيقِ [i. e. ‡ *We have remitted to you the poor-rate of horses and of the slave* or *slaves*]: (Mgh:) [and hence] عَفَوْتُ عَنِ الحَقِّ means † *I have annulled* [or *remitted*] *the right*, or *due*; as though I erased it from [the account of] him who owed it: (Mṣb:) and عَفَوْتُ لَهُ عَنْ مَا لِى عَلَيْهِ † *I have relinquished* [or *remitted*] *to him what was due to me on his part*. (TA.) ═ عَفَا signifies also *It was*, or *became, much in quantity*, or *many in number*: (Mṣb, MF, TA:) and also the contr., i. e. *It was*, or *became, little in quantity*, or *few in number*. (MF, TA.) It is said in the former sense of hair, and of herbage, &c.: (Ṣ:) or, said of hair, *It was*, or *became, long, and much in quantity*; (TA;) and said of the hair of a camel, (Ḳ,) or of the hair of a camel's back, (TA,) *it became abundant and long, and covered his rump*; (Ḳ, TA;) and said of herbage, *it was*, or *became, much in quantity, and tall*. (TA.) And عَفَوْا in the Ḳur vii. 93 means *They became many*, or *numerous*. (Ṣ, Mṣb.) And عَفَتِ الأَرْضُ *The land became covered with herbage*. (Ḳ and TḲ. [In the CḲ, والارض is erroneously put for وَالأَرْضُ.]) — And عَفَوْتُهُ *I made it to become much in quantity*, or *many in number*; as also ↓ أَعْفَيْتُهُ; (Ṣ,* Mṣb, TA;*) and so ↓ عَفَّيْتُهُ. (TA.) Accord. to Es-Saraḳusṭee, one says, عَفَوْتُ الشَّعَرَ, aor. أَعْفُوهُ, inf. n. عَفْوٌ; and عَفَيْتُهُ, aor. أَعْفِيهِ, inf. n. عَفْىٌ; meaning *I left the hair to become abundant and long*. (Mṣb.) And one says, اعفى ↓ اللِّحْيَةَ *He left the beard to become abundant and long*, (Mgh, Ḳ, TA,) *having ceased from cutting it*: (Mgh:) whence, (TA,) it is said in a trad., أَمَرَ أَنْ تُحْفَى الشَّوَارِبُ وَتُعْفَى اللِّحَى [*He commanded that the mustaches should be clipped closely*, or *much, and that the beards should be left to become abundant and long*]: (Ṣ, TA:) or أَحْفُوا الشَّوَارِبَ وَأَعْفُوا اللِّحَى [*Clip ye* &c.], and one may also use the unaugmented verb [saying وَٱعْفُوا, from عَفَا]. (Mṣb, TA.) And أَعْفَيْتُ ↓ شَعَرَ البَعِيرِ, (Ḳ,) or شَعَرَ ظَهْرِ البَعِيرِ, (TA,) *I left the hair of the camel*, or *the hair of the back of the camel, to become abundant and long*; as also ↓ عَفَّيْتُهُ; (Ḳ, TA;) this latter with teshdeed. (TA. [In the CḲ, عَفَيْتُهُ.]) عَفَا الصُّوفَ, expl. in the Ḳ as signifying *He shore*, or *sheared, the wool*, signifies *he left the wool to become abundant and long, then shore*, or *sheared, it*. (TA.) ═ Also, inf. n. عَفْوٌ, i. q. فَضَلَ [*It exceeded; it was*, or *became, redundant*, or *superfluous*; or *it remained over and above*]. (Mṣb.) You say, خُذْ مَا صَفَا وَعَفَا, [correctly, مَا عَفَا وَصَفَا,] meaning فَضَلَ وَتَسَهَّلَ [i. e. *Take thou what has exceeded*, or *become redundant, and has become facilitated*]. (Mgh.) — [And *He exceeded*.] You say, عَفَا عَلَيْهِ فِى العِلْمِ *He exceeded him in knowledge*; syn. زَادَ. (Ḳ.) And هُوَ يَعْفُو عَلَى مُنْيَةِ المُتَمَنِّى وَسُؤَالِ السَّائِلِ *He exceeds, in giving, the wish of the wisher and the petition of the petitioner*. (TA.) And عَفَوْتُ لَهُ بِمَالِى *I exceeded to him* [*what was incumbent on me*] *with my property, and gave him*. (TA.) — And عَفَا, aor. يَعْفُو, signifies also [simply] *He gave*. (TA.) And ↓ اعفاه *He gave to him*, namely, one seeking, or demanding, his beneficence. (Ham pp. 377 and 723.) And ↓ اعفاه بِحَقِّهِ *He gave to him fully*, or *wholly, his right*, or *due*. (Ḥar p. 117.) — And عَفَوْتُ لَهُ مِنَ المَرَقِ *I laded out for him first, and gave to him in preference, some of the broth*. (Ṣ. [See عِفَاوَةٌ.]) — And عَفَوْتُ القِدْرَ *I left in the bottom of the cooking-pot* [*as a gratuity for the lender thereof*] *the last of the broth, which is termed the* عُفَاوَة. (Ṣ.) ═ And عَفَوْتُ الرَّجُلَ *I asked*, or *petitioned, the man*. (Mṣb.) And عَفَوْتُهُ and ↓ اعْتَفَيْتُهُ *I came to him seeking*, or *demanding, his beneficence*: you say, فُلَانٌ تَعْفُوهُ الأَضْيَافُ and ↓ تَعْتَفِيهِ [*Such a one, guests come to him seeking*, or *demanding, his hospitality*]. (Ṣ.) — And عَفَتِ الإِبِلُ المَرْعَى, (Ḳ, TA,) aor. تَعْفُوهُ, inf. n. عَفْوٌ, (TA,) *The camels took* [or *cropped*] *the pasture near by*. (Ḳ, TA.) ═ عَفَا المَآءُ *The water was untrodden by what would render it turbid*. (Ṣ, Ḳ.)

2. عَفَّتِ الرِّيحُ الدَّارَ: and — عَفَّى عَلَى أَثَرِهِ: see 1, former half, in three places. [Hence] one says, عَفَّى عَلَيْهِمُ الخَبَالُ, inf. n. تَعْفِيَةٌ, [*Perdition*, or *destruction*, &c., *effaced them*,] meaning ‡ *they died*. (Z, Ḳ, TA.) And عَفَّى عَلَى مَا كَانَ مِنْهُ [*He effaced what had proceeded from him*], meaning † *he acted well*, or *rightly, after acting ill*, or *wrongly*. (Ṣ.) ═ See also 1, latter half, in two places. — [Hence] one says, عَفُّوا ظَهْرَ هٰذَا الجَمَلِ, meaning *Leave ye this camel* [lit. *the back of this camel*] *so that he may become fat*. (TA.)

3. عَافَاهُ ٱللّٰهُ, (Ṣ, Mṣb, Ḳ,) مِنَ المَكْرُوهِ, inf. n. مُعَافَاةٌ (Ḳ) and عِفَآءٌ (TA as from the Ḳ) and ↓ عَافِيَةٌ, (Ḳ,) or this is a subst. (Ṣ, Mṣb) put in the place of an inf. n., (Ṣ,) or also an inf. n.; (Mṣb;) and ↓ اعفاه; (Ṣ, Ḳ;) *God granted him* [*health*, or *soundness, and safety*, or *security*, i. e.] *defence* (Ṣ, Ḳ) *from diseases and from trial*: (Ḳ:) or [*restored him to health*, or *soundness, and to security from punishment*, i. e.] *effaced from him diseases, and sins*. (Mṣb. See also 1, former half.) And عُوفِىَ and ↓ اعفى [the latter perhaps أَعْفَى, but more probably, I think, أُعْفِىَ, agreeably with what here precedes,] are both used in the same sense, said of a sick person [as meaning *He was restored to health*, or *soundness*]. (TA.) — And مُعَافَاةٌ signifies also God's *defending thee from men and defending them from thee*: (Ḳ, TA:) IAth says that it signifies his *rendering thee independent*, or *in no need, of them, and rendering them independent*, or *in no need, of thee, and averting their harm from thee and thy harm from them*: and some say that it signifies one's *forgiving*, or *pardoning, men, and their forgiving*, or *pardoning, him*. (TA. [See also 6.])

4. اعفاه مِنَ الأَمْرِ *He made him to be free*, or *exempted him, from the affair*. (Ḳ.) You say, أَعْفِ عَنِّى مِنْهُ and أَعْفِنِى مِنْ هٰذَا الأَمْرِ [*Make thou me to be free*, or *exempt thou me, from this affair*]. (TA.) And أَعْفِنِى مِنَ الخُرُوجِ مَعَكَ *Exempt thou me*, or *excuse me, from going forth with thee*. (Ṣ, Mgh, Mṣb.*) — See also 3, in two places: — and 1, latter half, in three places: — and the same paragraph, last quarter, in two places. ═ اعفى also signifies *He expended the* عَفْو *of his property*; (Ḳ, TA;) i. e., *the clear portion thereof*; or *the redundant portion of it*. (TA.) ═ And *He was*, or *became, a possessor of*

much property; and *independent,* or *in no need.* (TA.)

5: see 1, first and fourth sentences.

6. التَّعَافِى signifies [*The forgiving,* or *pardoning, one another,* or] *the turning away from punishing one another:* and تَعَافَوْا الحُدُودَ فِيمَا بَيْنَكُمْ, originally تَعَافَوْا عَنِ الحُدُودِ, [i. e. *Relinquish ye the prescribed punishments in respect of what occurs between you,*] means *let every one of you turn away from* [or *relinquish*] *punishing his fellow;* the phrase being elliptical, or the verb being made to imply the meaning of التَّرْك, and therefore being made trans. in the same manner as التَرك: [hence,] لَوْ تَعَافَيْتُهَا is used by El-Ḥareeree as meaning *If I relinquished them:* (Ḥar p. 60:) [and hence it is said that التَّعَافِى signifies التَّجَاوُزُ [app. when each is followed by عَنْ, and thus meaning *The passing by,* or *over,* another, or one another, *without punishing*]. (TA.) ═ And it signifies also *The finding, experiencing,* or *obtaining, health,* or *soundness.* (KL.)

8: see 1, last sentence but two, in two places: — and see also the paragraph here following.

10. الاِسْتِعْفَآءُ is *Thy seeking,* or *demanding, of him who imposes upon thee an affair that is difficult,* or *troublesome,* or *inconvenient, his exempting,* or *excusing, thee from doing it.* (Ḳ.) You say, اِسْتَعْفَاهُ مِنَ الخُرُوجِ مَعَهُ *He asked,* or *petitioned, him to exempt,* or *excuse, him from going forth with him.* (Ṣ, Mṣb,* TA.) — اِسْتَعْفَتِ الإِبِلُ اليَبِيسَ and ♦ اِعْتَفَتْهُ mean *The camels took with their lips the dry herbage* (Ḳ, TA) *from above the dust,* (TA,) *picking out the clear,* or *best.* (Ḳ, TA.)

عَفًا: see عَفْوٌ, second and last sentences.

عِفًا: see the next paragraph, last sentence.

عَفْوٌ [an inf. n.; for which see 1, throughout. ═ And also] *A land in which is no sign of the way nor trace of habitation* or *cultivation; untrodden, and not having in it any traces,* or *vestiges,* or *footprints:* (Ṣ:) or *a country,* or *portion of the earth* or *of land, in which is no trace of its being possessed by any one:* and so ♦ عَفًا. (Ḳ.) — And *A redundant portion,* (Ṣ, Mgh, Ḳ,) being such as is left, (Mgh,) of property, *remaining over and above what is expended.* (Ṣ.) A poet says, [app. addressing his wife,]

خُذِى العَفْوَ مِنِّى تَسْتَدِيمِى مَوَدَّتِى
وَلَا تَنْطِقِى فِى سَوْرَتِى حِينَ أَغْضَبُ

[*Take thou what is redundant from me, seeking the continuance of my affection; and speak not in my fit of irritation, when I am angry*]. (Ṣ.) قُلِ العَفْوَ, in the Ḳur [ii. 217], means *Say thou, Expend ye what is redundant and abundant.* (TA.) And خُذِ العَفْوَ, in the same [vii. 198], means [*Take thou,* or *accept thou,*] *what is redundant:* or *accept thou what is easily obtained from the dispositions of men;* and oppose them not, for in that case they would oppose thee, and thence would be engendered hatred and enmity. (TA.) And you say, أَعْطَيْتُهُ عَفْوَ المَالِ i. e. [*I gave him, of the property, that for which he did not ask;* or *spontaneously;*] *without being asked.* (Ṣ.) And أَعْطَيْتُهُ عَفْوًا [*I gave him spontaneously;*] *without being asked:* (Ḳ, TA:) or *without constraint.* (TA.) And أَدْرَكَ الأَمْرَ عَفْوًا صَفْوًا *He attained the thing easily.* (TA.) And أَتَانِى ذٰلِكَ عَفْوًا [*That came to me easily*]. (A and Ḳ in art. غمض.) — Also The *portion* of water *that remains over and above what is required by the* شَارِبَة [which may mean either the *people that dwell thereby and to whom it belongs* or the *drinkers*], (Ḳ, TA,) *and is taken without constraint and without crowding* or *pressing.* (TA.) — And The *most lawful,* (أَحَلُّ,) so in the copies of the Ḳ, but in the M أَجْمَلُ [*most beautiful,* or *goodly*], (TA,) *and most pleasant,* of wealth, or property: (M, Ḳ, TA:) and the *clear portion* thereof. (TA.) — And The *choice, and best,* or *most excellent, portion* of a thing, (Ḳ, TA,) and *such as is not attended with fatigue,* or *weariness.* (TA.) — And *Goodness,* or *beneficence;* or *a benefit,* or *benefaction:* syn. مَعْرُوف. (Ḳ.) — And *A first run:* one says of a courser, هُوَ ذُو عَفْوٍ وَعَقْبٍ *He has a first run, and a subsequent, and more vehement, run.* (A in art. عقب.) ═ Also, and ♦ عُفُوٌّ, and ♦ عِفْوٌ, *A young ass;* and so ♦ عَفًا; (Ṣ, Ḳ;) or, accord. to ISk, ♦ عِفًا: (Ṣ:) and the female is called عَفْوَةٌ (Ṣ, TA) and ♦ عِفَاوَةٌ: (TA:) pl. [of mult.], accord. to the copies of the Ḳ, عُفُوَّةٌ, but correctly عِفَوَةٌ, said by ISd to be the only instance of a word with و as a final radical movent after a fet-ḥah, (TA,) and عِفَآءٌ, (ISd, Ḳ, TA,) and [of pauc.] أَعْفَآءٌ: (ISd, TA:) and [hence] أَبُو العِفَآءِ means *The ass;* (Ḳ, TA;) [lit. *the father of the young asses;*] العِفَآء being pl. of عَفْوٌ signifying the *young ass.* (TA.)

عُفُوٌّ and عِفْوٌ: see the next preceding sentence.

عَفْوَةٌ *A bloodwit:* (Ḳ, TA:) because by means of it pardon is obtained from the heirs of the slain man. (TA.) ═ عَفْوَةُ القِدْرِ and ♦ عِفْوَتُهَا and ♦ عُفْوَتُهَا, as also ♦ عُفَاوَتُهَا, and ♦ عِفَاوَتُهَا and ♦ عَفَاوَتُهَا, signify *The froth,* or *foam, of the cooking-pot;* (Ḳ, TA;) and *the best,* or *choice, portion thereof,* i. e., [*of the contents*] *of the cooking-pot:* (TA:) or ♦ العُفَاوَةُ signifies *the broth that is first taken up out of the cooking-pot, and with which he who is honoured is peculiarly favoured:* or, as some say, *the first and best of the broth:* and ♦ العِفَاوَةُ, *the last of the broth, which the borrower of the cooking-pot returns with the cooking-pot.* (Ṣ, TA. [See also عَافٍ.]) — عَفْوَةٌ is *What has not been depastured,* of المَرْعَى *herbage, and is therefore abundant.* (TA.) — And عَفْوَةُ المَآءِ is *The supply of water that has collected before the drawing from it.* (TA.) — See also عِفْوَةٌ.

عُفْوَةٌ: see the next preceding paragraph: — and also the next following, in two places.

عِفْوَةٌ: see عَفْوَةٌ. — Also, (Ṣ, TA,) and ♦ عُفْوَةٌ, (TA,) The *best,* or *choice,* (Ṣ, TA,) and *abundant,* (TA,) of a thing, (Ṣ,) or of property, (TA,) and of food, and of beverage. (Ṣ, TA.) One says, ذَهَبَتْ عِفْوَةُ هٰذَا النَّبْتِ *The soft,* or *tender, and best, of this herbage, has gone:* (Ṣ, TA:) and accord. to the M, ♦ عُفْوَةٌ, with ḍamm, signifies *such as is soft,* or *tender,* of any herbage, and *such as has not in it anything troublesome,* or *burdensome, to the pasturing cattle.* (M, TA.) — And عِفْوَةٌ and ♦ عُفْوَةٌ signify The *hair of the head* of a man. (TA.)

عَفَآءٌ [an inf. n.: used as a subst., signifying The *state of being effaced, erased, rased,* or *obliterated:* and *of perishing,* or *dying.* ═ Also] *Dust.* (Ṣ, Ḳ.) One says, in reviling, بِفِيهِ العَفَآءُ وَعَلَيْهِ العَفَآءُ [*In his mouth be dust, and may the state of that which is effaced, &c., be,* or *rest, upon him:* see also the verse cited near the beginning of this art.]. (TA.) — And *Rain:* (Ḳ:) because it effaces the traces of the places of alighting. (TA.) — And *A whiteness upon the black of the eye.* (Ḳ.)

عِفَآءٌ *Such as is abundant of the plumage of the ostrich,* (Ṣ, Ḳ,) and *of the fur,* or *soft hair, of the camel,* (Ṣ, and so in the Ḳ accord. to the TA,) and *long and abundant hair:* (Ḳ:) [see an ex. of the last meaning in a verse cited in art. صب, conj. 6:] the n. of un. is with ة; but it is said that a single feather is not termed عِفَآءَةٌ unless it be [one of feathers that are] dense and abundant. (TA.) One says نَاقَةٌ ذَاتُ عِفَآءٍ [*A she-camel having abundant fur*]. (Ṣ.) — عِفَآءُ السَّحَابِ means † *What resembles nap,* or *pile, in the surface of the clouds, which* [*when they have this*] *scarcely ever,* or *never, break their promise of yielding rain.* (TA.)

عَفُوٌّ عَنِ الذَّنْبِ A man *forgiving* [or *who forgives*] *the crime,* or *misdeed:* (Ḳ:) [or rather] العَفُوُّ signifies *he who forgives much:* (Ṣ:) and [as meaning thus, or *the Very Forgiving,*] it is one of the names of God. (TA.)

عُفَاوَةٌ: see عَفْوَةٌ.

عِفَاوَةٌ: see عَفْوَةٌ, in two places.

عَفَاوَةٌ: see عَفْوَةٌ, in two places: ═ and see also عَفْوٌ, last sentence.

عَافٍ *Being,* or *becoming, effaced, erased, rased,* or *obliterated:* [&c.: see 1, of which it is a part. n.:] pl. عُفِىٌّ. (Ṣ, TA.) ═ *Having long hair.* (Ṣ, Ḳ.) — *A fleshy, plump,* boy. (TA.) And نَاقَةٌ عَافِيَةُ اللَّحْمِ A she-camel *having much flesh:* pl. عَافِيَاتٌ. (Ḳ.) — And أَرْضٌ عَافِيَةٌ *A land of which the herbage, not having been depastured, has become abundant.* (TA.) ═ *Some broth that is returned in the cooking-pot when it has been borrowed;* (Ḳ:) or عَافِى القِدْرِ means *what is left in the cooking-pot* (Aṣ, Ṣ, M) *by the borrower, for the lender.* (M, TA.) [See also عَفْوَةٌ.] ═ *A guest:* (Ṣ,* Ḳ:) and *any seeker,* or *demander, of a favour* or *bounty,* (Ṣ, Ḳ,) or *of means of subsistence:* as also ♦ مُعْتَفٍ: (Ḳ:) pl. عُفَاةٌ (Ṣ, TA) and عُفًى, (Ṣ,* Ḳ,) both signifying *guests*, &c., (TA,) as also عَافِيَةٌ; (Ṣ,* TA;) which last signifies also beasts, and birds, (Ṣ, TA,) as well as men, (Ṣ,) *seekers of*, or *seeking, the means of subsistence*; (Ṣ, TA;) and its pl. is عَوَافٍ. (TA.) One says, هُوَ كَثِيرُ العُفَاةِ and العَافِيَةِ and العُفَى [*He is one who has many guests*, &c.]. (Ṣ, TA.) — And *A seeker of herbage*. (Ḳ,* TA. [In the CḲ, الزَّائِدُ is erroneously put for الرَّائِدُ.]) — And *A comer to water*: (Ḳ,* TA:) and عَافِيَةُ المَآءِ *the comers to the water*. (Ṣ, TA.)

عَافِيَةٌ a subst. from عَافَاهُ ٱللّٰهُ, q. v., (Ṣ, Mṣb,) and from الإِعْفَآءُ [inf. n. of 4, q. v.], (TA,) signifying *Health*, or *soundness, and safety*, or *security*: (TḲ:) [or, as it may be best rendered, *health and safety*, considered as proceeding from God; i. e.] *God's defence* of a man (Ṣ, Ḳ) *from diseases and from trial*: (Ḳ:) or *freedom from evil*. (KL.) See also 1, former half. ═ [Also fem. of عَافٍ (q. v.), and used as a pl.]

أَعْفَى a word occurring in the saying of 'Omar Ibn-'Abd-El-'Azeez, لَعَمْرِى مَا ٱلْبَرَاذِينُ بِأَعْفَى مِنَ ٱلْفَرَسِ فِيمَا كَانَ مِنْ مَؤُونَةٍ وَحَرْسٍ i. e. [*By my life*, or *by my religion, the hackneys*] *are not more easy in respect of sustenance* [*and guardianship than the horse*, or *mare, of good breed*: see فَرَسٌ]. (Mgh.)

مُعْفٍ, thus correctly, like مُكْرِمٌ, as in the M, in the Ḳ said to be like مُحَدِّثٌ, (TA,) *One who associates with another without seeking to obtain his bounty*. (Ḳ, TA.) You say, اِصْطَحَبْنَا وَكِلَانَا مُعْفٍ [*We associated, each of us doing so without seeking to obtain the other's bounty*]: and hence the saying of Ibn-Muḳbil,

* فَإِنَّكَ لَا تَبْلُو ٱمْرَأً دُونَ صُحْبَةٍ *
* وَحَتَّى تَعِيشَا مُعْفِيَيْنِ وَتَجْهَدَا *

[*For verily thou wilt not test a man before companionship, and until ye live associating without either's seeking to obtain the other's bounty, and toil* in so living]. (TA.)

مُعْفًى. A camel *left unridden*. (Ḳ and TA in art. سنو.)

مُعْتَفٍ: see عَافٍ.

عفى

1. عَفَيْتُ ٱلشَّعَرَ, aor. أَعْفِيهِ, inf. n. عَفْىٌ: see 1 (latter half) in art. عفو.

عق

1. عَقَّ, (Mṣb, Ḳ, TA,) aor. ـُ, (TA,) inf. n. عَقٌّ, (Mgh, O, Mṣb, TA,) *He clave, split, slit, ripped*, or *rent*; (Mgh, O, Mṣb, Ḳ, TA;) and *he cut*. (Mgh, O, TA.) You say, عَقَّ ثَوْبَهُ *He slit, ripped*, or *rent, his garment*. (Mṣb.) And عُقَّتْ تَمِيمَتُهُ فِى بَنِى فُلَانٍ [*His amulet was cut off among the sons of such a one*]; said of a boy when he has attained to the prime of manhood, and become strong, with a tribe; originating from the fact that as long as the boy was an infant, his mother hung upon him amulets to preserve him from the evil eye; and when he became full-grown, they were cut off from him: whence the saying of a poet,

* بِلَادٌ بِهَا عَقَّ ٱلشَّبَابُ تَمِيمَتِى *
* وَأَوَّلُ أَرْضٍ مَسَّ جِلْدِى تُرَابُهَا *

[*A country in which the attaining to the prime of manhood cut off my amulet, and the first land of which the dust touched my skin*]. (TA.) — And [hence,] عَقَّتِ ٱلرِّيحُ ٱلْمُزْنَ, aor. and inf. n. as above, *The wind drew forth a shower of fine rain from the* مزن [or *clouds containing water*]; as though it rent them. (TA.) And عَقَّتِ ٱلسَّحَابَةُ *The cloud poured forth its water*; [as though it were rent;] and ▼ اِنْعَقَّتْ [means the same]; (TA;) and ▼ اِعْتَقَّتْ [likewise]. (O.) — And عَقَّ عَنْ وَلَدِهِ, (Ṣ, Mṣb,) or عَنِ ٱلْمَوْلُودِ, (Ḳ,) aor. ـُ (Ṣ, Mṣb, TA) and ـِ, (TA,) inf. n. عَقٌّ, (Ṣ, Mṣb,) *He slaughtered as a sacrifice* (Ṣ, Mṣb, Ḳ, TA) *for his child*, (Ṣ, Mṣb,) or *for the new-born child*, (Ḳ,) *a sheep or goat*, (T, Mṣb, TA,) [*generally the latter*,] *on the seventh day after the birth*. (T, Ṣ, Mṣb, TA.) And *He shaved the* [*hair termed*] عَقِيقَة [q. v.] (Ṣ, TA) *of his child*, (Ṣ,) or *of the new-born child*. (TA.) — And عَقَّ بِٱلسَّهْمِ *He shot the arrow towards the sky*; and that arrow was called عَقِيقَةٌ; (Ṣ, O, Ḳ;) and it was the arrow of self-excuse: they used to do thus in the Time of Ignorance [on the occasion of a demand for blood-revenge]; and if the arrow returned smeared with blood, they were not content save with the retaliation of slaughter; but if it returned clean, they stroked their beards, and made reconciliation on the condition of the bloodwit; the stroking of the beards being a sign of reconciliation: the arrow, however, as IAạr says, did not [ever] return otherwise than clean: (Ṣ, O:) the origin was this: a man of the tribe was slain, and the slayer was prosecuted for his blood; whereupon a company of the chief men [of the family of the slayer] collected themselves together to the heirs [who claimed satisfaction for the blood] of the slain, and offered the bloodwit, asking forgiveness for the blood; and if the heir [who claimed satisfaction and who acted for himself and his coheirs] was a strong man, impatient of injury, he refused to take the bloodwit; but if weak, he consulted the people of his tribe, and then said to the petitioners, "We have, between us and our Creator, a sign denoting command and prohibition: we take an arrow, and set it on a bow, and shoot it towards the sky; and if it return to us smeared with blood, we are forbidden to take the bloodwit, and are not content save with the retaliation of slaughter; but if it return clean, as it went up, we are commanded to take the bloodwit:" so they made reconciliation; for this arrow never returned otherwise than clean; and thus they had an excuse in the opinion of the ignorant of them. (L, TA.) A poet (Ṣ, O, TA) of the family of the slain, said by some to be of Hudheyl, by IB to be El-As'ar El-Joafee, who was absent from this reconciliation, (TA,) says,

* عَقُّوا بِسَهْمٍ ثُمَّ قَالُوا صَالِحُوا *
* يَا لَيْتَنِى فِى ٱلْقَوْمِ إِذْ مَسَحُوا ٱللِّحَى *

[*They shot an arrow towards the sky; then they said, "Make ye reconciliation:" would that I were among the party when they stroked the beards*]: (Ṣ, O, TA:) or, as some relate it, the first word is عَقَوْا, with fet-ḥ to the ق; which belongs to the class of unsound verbs [i. e. to art. عقى]. (Ṣ, O.) — One says also, عَقَّ وَالِدَهُ, (Ṣ, O, Ḳ,) or أَبَاهُ, (Mṣb,) aor. ـُ, (Ṣ, O, Mṣb,) inf. n. عُقُوقٌ (Ṣ, O, Mṣb, Ḳ) and مَعَقَّةٌ (Ṣ, O, Ḳ) and عَقٌّ, (TA,) *He was undutiful, disobedient, refractory*, or *ill-mannered, to his parent*, or *father*; *contr. of* بَرَّهُ; (Ḳ;) *he broke his compact of obedience to his parent*, or *father*; (TA;) *he disobeyed his father*; and *failed*, or *neglected, to behave to him in a good*, or *comely, manner*. (Mṣb.) And عَقَّ ٱلرَّحِمَ, (TA, and Ḥam p. 93,) like قَطَعَهَا [i. e. *He severed the tie*, or *ties, of relationship, by unkind behaviour to his kindred*]. (Ḥam ib.) And عَقَّ [alone], aor. ـُ, inf. n. عُقُوقٌ, [*He was undutiful*, &c.; or *he acted undutifully*, &c.; or] *he contravened*, or *opposed, him whom he was under an obligation to obey*. (Ḥar p. 158.) عُقُوقُ ٱلْوَالِدَيْنِ [*Undutiful treatment*, &c., *of the two parents*] is said in a trad. to be one of the great sins. (O.) And it is said in a prov., العُقُوقُ أَحَدُ ٱلثُّكْلَيْنِ [*Undutiful treatment of a parent is one of the two sorts of being bereft of a child*]: or, as some relate it, العُقُوقُ ثُكْلُ مَنْ لَمْ يَثْكَلْ [*Undutiful treatment of a parent is* (like) *the bereavement of him who is not* (really) *bereft of his child*]: i. e. he whom his children have treated undutifully (مَنْ عَقَّهُ وَلَدُهُ) is as though he were bereft of his children although they are living. (O.) [See also 3: and 4.] — Hence, from عُقُوقُ ٱلْوَالِدَيْنِ, the verb is metaphorically used in the saying, in a trad., مَثَلُكُمْ وَمَثَلُ عَائِشَةَ مَثَلُ ٱلْعَيْنِ فِى ٱلرَّأْسِ تُؤْذِى صَاحِبَهَا وَلَا يَسْتَطِيعُ أَنْ يَعُقَّهَا إِلَّا بِٱلَّذِى هُوَ خَيْرٌ لَهَا [*The similitude of you and of 'Áïsheh is that of the eye in the head, when it hurts its owner, and he cannot treat it severely save with that which is good for it*: app. meaning that her severity was for the good of the objects thereof]. (TA.) ═ عَقَّ, intrans., said of lightning: see 7. ═ عَقَّتْ said of a mare, and of an ass: see 4. ═ عَقَّتِ ٱلدَّلْوُ, inf. n. عَقٌّ, means *The bucket came up full from the well*; and some of the Arabs say عَقَّتْ as having تَعْقِيَةٌ for its inf. n.; but it is [said to be] originally ▼ عَقَّقَتْ, the third ق being changed into ى, [which is then in this case suppressed,] like as they said تَظَنَّيْتُ from الظَّنُّ: [it is, however, mentioned in the TA in art. عقو also, and there expl. as meaning *it rose in the well turning round*: and from what here follows, it appears to mean *it rose swiftly, cleaving the air*:] a poet, cited by IAạr, says, of a bucket,

• عَقَّتْ عَقَّا عَقَّتْ دَلْوُ العِقْبَانْ •

meaning *It clave* [the air of] the well, *rising swiftly, like the hastening of the swift eagle* in its flight towards the prey. (TA in the present art.)

2: see above, last sentence.

3. عَاقَقْتُ فُلَانًا, aor. أُعَاقُّهُ, inf. n. عِقَاقٌ, *I contravened,* or *opposed, such a one.* (TA.) [See also عَقَّ وَالِدَهُ, in the latter half of the first paragraph.]

4. اعقّ فُلَانٌ i. q. جَآءَ بِالعُقُوقِ [i. e. *Such a one did that which was an act of undutifulness, disobedience, refractoriness,* or *ill manners, to his father* or *the like*]. (Ṣ, TA.) [See also عَقَّ وَالِدَهُ, in the latter half of the first paragraph.] — And you say, مَا أَعَقَّهُ لِوَالِدِهِ [*How undutiful, disobedient, refractory,* or *ill-mannered, is he to his father!*]. (TA.) = اعقّت *She* (a mare, Ṣ, O, Ḳ, and an ass, TA) *conceived,* or *became pregnant;* (Ṣ, O, Ḳ;) or *she did not conceive,* or *become pregnant, after having been covered by the stallion,* or *during a year* or *two years* or *some years;* (Ḳ;) and ▼ عَقَّتْ, aor. ـِ, (O, Ḳ, TA,) the verb being of the class of ضَرَبَ, (TA,) inf. n. عَقَاقٌ and عَقَقٌ (O, Ḳ, TA) and عُقُوقٌ, (CḲ, but not in other copies,) signifies the same, (O,* Ḳ, TA,) said of a mare, (O, Ḳ,) and of an ass; (O;) or عَقَاقٌ signifies *pregnancy itself,* as also عِقَاقٌ, (Ḳ,) and عَقَقٌ; (Ṣ, O;) or عَقَّتْ signifies *she became pregnant;* and اعقّت, *the* [*hair called*] عَقِيقَة *grew in her belly upon the young one that she bore.* (TA.) — Also *It* (a palm-tree, and a grape-vine) *put forth what are termed* عِقَّان [q. v.]. (Ṣ, O, Ḳ.) = اعقّهُ *He made it bitter;* (Ṣ, O, Ḳ;) namely, water; said of God; like اقعّهُ. (Ṣ, O.) And اعقّت الأَرْضُ المَآءَ *The earth made the water bitter.* (TA.)

7. انعقّ *It became cloven, split, slit, ripped,* or *rent;* or *it clave, split,* &c.; said of anything; (Ṣ, O, Ḳ, TA;) mentioned by Th as said of a garment. (TA.) — انعقّت السَّحَابَةُ *The cloud became rent with the water.* (Ṣ, O, Ḳ.) See also 1, first quarter. [And see 8.] — انعقّ البَرْقُ and ▼ عَقَّ [of which latter the aor. is probably يَعِقُّ, and the inf. n. عَقِيقٌ, said in the Ḳ to mean انشقّ,] signify تَشَقَّقَ and انشقّ [as though meaning *The lightning became cloven*]; (TA;) [but] the former is expl. as signifying *the lightning was,* or *became, in a state of commotion* (تَضَرَّبَ) *in the clouds.* (Ṣ, O.) [Another meaning is suggested by an explanation of عَقِيقَةٌ (q. v.) in relation to lightning.] — انعقّ الغُبَارُ i. q. سَطَعَ [app. as meaning *The dust spread,* or *diffused itself*]: (IF, O, Ḳ:) or انشقّ وَسَطَعَ [*became cleft, and diffused itself*]. (TA.) — انعقّ الوَادِى *The valley was,* or *became, deep.* (TA.) = انعقّت العُقْدَةُ *The knot became strongly,* or *firmly, tied.* (O,* Ḳ,* TA.)

8. اعتقّ السَّحَابُ *The clouds became rent,* (Ḳ, TA,) *and their water poured forth.* (TA.) See also 1, first quarter. [And see 7.] = اعتقّ السَّيْفَ *He drew the sword* (O, Ḳ) from its scabbard. (O.) = And اعتقّ [probably from عَقَّ بِالسَّهْمِ, q. v.,] *He exceeded the due bounds,* or *was immoderate, in excusing himself.* (TA.)

R. Q. 1. عَقْعَقَ بِصَوْتِهِ, (O, TA,) inf. n. عَقْعَقَةٌ, (Ṣ, O,) said of the عَقْعَق [or magpie], *It uttered a* [*kind of chattering*] *cry,* (Ṣ,* O, TA,) *resembling the sound of* ع *and* ق [or *the repeated sound of* عَقّ]; (O, TA;) whence its name: and said of a bird [that utters a cry of this kind] when it comes and goes. (TA.) — And عَقْعَقَةٌ signifies also The *shaking,* or *being in a state of commotion,* [*so as to produce a kind of crackling,* or *rustling, sound,*] of paper, and of a new garment; like قَعْقَعَةٌ [q. v.]. (TA.)

عَقٌّ *Any cleft,* or *furrow,* and *any hole,* in sand &c. (Ṣ, TA.) See also عَقِيقَةٌ. = Also i. q. عَاقٌّ, q. v. (O, Ḳ.) = مَآءٌ عَقٌّ: see عُقٌّ.

مَآءٌ عُقٌّ, with ḍamm, (Ḳ, TA,) or ▼ عَقٌّ, (thus written in my copies of the Ṣ and in the O,) and ▼ عُقَاقٌ, (O, Ḳ, TA,) *Bitter water:* (Ṣ, O, Ḳ:) or *intensely bitter water:* used alike as sing. and pl.: (TA:) like قُعٌّ, (TA,) or قَعٌّ, (Ṣ, O,) and قُعَاعٌ. (O, TA.)

عِقٌّ: see what next follows.

عَقَّةٌ *A deep excavation, hollow, cavity, trench,* or *the like, in the ground;* (Ḳ, TA;) as also ▼ عِقٌّ, accord. to the Ḳ, there said to be with kesr, but correctly ▼ عَقٌّ, with fet-ḥ, [q. v.,] which signifies *an elongated excavation in the ground,* and is originally an inf. n.: thus in the L. (TA.) — And *A blaze of lightning extending in an elongated form in the sky,* (IDrd, O, Ḳ,) or *in the side of the clouds,* (A, TA,) and said to be *as though it were a drawn sword.* (TA.) [See also عَقِيقَةٌ.]

عُقَّةٌ *A certain thing with which boys play.* (L, Ḳ, TA.)

عِقَّةٌ: see عَقِيقَةٌ, in the former half.

عَقَقٌ: see عَقَاقٌ. — It is said in the Ḳ to be syn. with عَاقٌّ; but in this sense the correct word is عُقَقٌ. (TA.)

عُقَقٌ: see عَقِيقَةٌ, latter half: = and see also عَاقٌّ, in two places.

عُقُقٌ, as a sing. and as a pl.: see عَاقٌّ.

عَقَاقٌ is an inf. n. of عَقَّتْ said of a mare (O, Ḳ) and of an ass: (O:) or it signifies *Pregnancy* (AA, Ṣ, Ḳ) *itself;* (Ḳ;) as also ▼ عِقَاقٌ, (Ḳ,) and ▼ عَقَقٌ [which is likewise said to be an inf. n. of عَقَّتْ]. (Ṣ.) You say, أَظْهَرَتِ الأَتَانُ عَقَاقًا *The she-ass manifested pregnancy.* (AA, Ṣ, O.) — And, accord. to Esh-Shafi'ee, *An embryo;* or *a fœtus.* (TA.) = عَقَاقِ, like قَطَامِ, [indecl.,] is a [proper] name for العُقُوقُ [*Undutifulness, disobedience, refractoriness,* or *ill manners, to a parent,* or *the like*]: (Ḳ, TA:) mentioned by IB, and in the O. (TA.)

عُقَاقٌ, applied to water: see عُقٌّ.

عِقَاقٌ: see عَقَاقٌ.

عَقُوقٌ, applied to a mare, (Ṣ, O, Ḳ, TA,) and to an ass, (TA,) *Pregnant:* (Ṣ, O, Ḳ:) or *not pregnant after having been covered by the stallion,* or *during a year* or *two years* or *some years;* (Ḳ;) or it signifies thus also; (O;) having two contr. meanings; (Ḳ;) or it is applied to one in the latter state as implying a presage of good; (O, Ḳ;) so says AḤát; (O, TA;) i. e., as though they meant that she would become pregnant: (TA:) it is extr.; [as being from أَعَقَّتْ;] and one should not say ▼ مُعِقٌّ; or this is a bad dial. var.; (Ṣ, O, Ḳ;) or, accord. to AA, it is from اعقّت, and عَقُوقٌ is from عَقَّتْ: (TA:) the pl. is عُقُقٌ, and عِقَاقٌ is a pl. pl., (Ṣ, O, Ḳ,) i. e. pl. of عُقُقٌ. (Ṣ, O.) It is said in a prov., طَلَبَ الأَبْلَقَ العَقُوقَ, meaning *He sought an impossible thing;* because ابلق is applied to a male, and عقوق means pregnant: (Ṣ, O, and Ḳ in art. بلق:) or الابلق العقوق means *the dawn,* because it breaks, lit. cleaves. (O, and Ḳ in art. بلق.) — نَوَى العَقُوقِ means *Date-stones that are easily broken,* (Lth, Ṣ, O, Ḳ,) *soft to be chewed;* (Lth, O, Ḳ;) which are given as provender to camels, (Ṣ,) or to the pregnant thereof, in consideration of her state, wherefore they are thus called; and which are eaten, or chewed, by the old woman: but this is of the speech of the people of El-Baṣrah, and not known by the Arabs in their desert: (Lth, O:) and sometimes they called *a single date-stone of this sort* ▼ عَقِيقَةٌ. (Ṣ.) = See also عَاقٌّ.

عَقِيقٌ *Cleft, split, slit, ripped,* or *rent;* and *cut;* as also ▼ مَعْقُوقٌ. (TA.) — And [hence] *Any channel which the water of a torrent has cloven* (Ṣ, O, Mṣb,* Ḳ) *of old* (Mṣb) *and made wide:* (Ṣ, O:) and *a valley:* (O, Ḳ:) pl. أَعِقَّةٌ (Ṣ, O, Mṣb, Ḳ, TA) and عَقَائِقُ. (TA.) And عَقَائِقُ signifies also *Pools of water in cleft furrows:* (AḤn, TA:) and some say, *red sands.* (TA.) — See also عَقِيقَةٌ, in two places. = Also [*Carnelian;*] *a species of* فُصُوص [or *stones that are set in rings*]; (Ṣ;) *a sort of stone,* (Mṣb,) or *red* خَرَز [meaning *precious stones*], (O, Ḳ,) *of which* فُصُوص *are made;* (O, Mṣb;) *existing in El-Yemen,* (Ḳ, TA,) *near to Esh-Shiḥr, said by Et-Teefáshee to be brought from mines thereof at Ṣan'á,* (TA,) *and on the shores of the Sea of Roomeeyeh; one kind thereof is of a turbid appearance, like water running from salted flesh-meat, and having in it faint white lines,* (Ḳ, TA,) *and this, Et-Teefáshee says, is what is known by the appellation* الرطبى [so in my original]; *the best kind is the red; then, the yellow; then, the white; and the other kinds are bad:* or, *as some* *say, the streaked* (الْمُشَطَّب) *is the best*: (TA:) [I omit some absurd assertions in the Ḳ and TA respecting various virtues supposed to be possessed by this stone:] the n. un. is with ة: and the pl. is عَقَائِقُ. (O, Ḳ.) [العَقِيقُ اليَمَانِىُّ is an appellation applied by some to *The agate*.]

عَقِيقَةٌ [a subst. from عَقِيقٌ, made so by the affix ة. Hence, because cleft, or furrowed, in the earth,] *A river*, or *rivulet*. (IAạr, O, Ḳ.) — And *A fillet*, or *bandage*, (عِصَابَةٌ,) *at the time of its being rent from a garment*, or *piece of cloth*. (IAạr, O, Ḳ.) — And The *prepuce of a boy* (AO, IAạr, O, Ḳ) *when he is circumcised*. (TA.) — And [app. because made of cut pieces of skin,] *A* [*leathern water-bag such as is commonly called*] مَزَادَة. (IAạr, O, Ḳ.) — Also The *wool of a* جَذَع [or *sheep in or before its second year*]: (Ṣ, O, Ḳ, TA:) that of a ثَنِىّ [or sheep in its third year] is called جَنِيبَة: (TA:) and the *hair of a young one recently born*, (Ṣ, Mgh, O, Mṣb, Ḳ, TA,) *that comes forth upon his head in his mother's belly*, (TA,) *of human beings*, (Ṣ, Mgh, O, Mṣb, Ḳ, TA,) because it is cut off on his seventh day, (Mgh,) *and of others*, (Mṣb,) [i. e.] *of beasts likewise*; (Ṣ, O, Ḳ, TA;) as also ▼ عَقِيقٌ and ▼ عِقَّةٌ; (Ṣ, O, Mṣb, Ḳ;) but A'Obeyd says that he had not heard this last except in relation to human beings and asses: (Ṣ, O, Ḳ:*) its pl. (i. e. the pl. of عِقَّةٌ) is عِقَقٌ: (O, Ḳ:) [the pl. of عَقِيقَةٌ and عَقِيقٌ is عَقَائِقُ:] a law of the Sunneh requires that the عَقِيقَة of an infant should be weighed, and its weight in silver be given to the poor: (and Herodotus, in ii. 65, mentions a similar custom as obtaining among the Ancient Egyptians:)] when the hair has once fallen from the young [by its being cut], the term عَقِيقَةٌ ceases to be applied to it: so says Lth: (O, TA:) but it occurs in a trad. applied to *hair* as being likened to the hair of a recently-born infant. (TA.) — Hence, (Ṣ, O,) it is applied also to The *sheep*, or *goat*, [*generally the latter*,] *that is slaughtered* (Ṣ, Mgh, O, Mṣb, Ḳ) *as a sacrifice for the recently-born infant* (Ṣ, Mgh, Mṣb) *on the occasion of the shaving of the infant's hair* (O, Ḳ) *on the seventh day after his birth*, (Ṣ, Mṣb,) *and of which the limbs are divided, and cooked with water and salt, and given as food to the poor*: (Lth, TA:) Z holds it to be thus called from the same word as applied to the hair: but it is said [by some] to be so called because it is slaughtered by cutting the windpipe and gullet and the two external jugular veins: (TA:) the Prophet disallowed this appellation, (Mgh, Mṣb,) as being of evil omen, (Mgh,) or as though he saw them to regard it as of evil omen, (Mṣb,) and desired them to use نَسِيكَةٌ in its stead; (Mgh, Mṣb, TA;) saying I like not العُقُوق. (TA.) — عَقِيقَةُ البَرْقِ signifies *What remains* [*for an instant*] *in the clouds, of the rays*, or *beams, of lightning*; (Lth, O, Ḳ;) as also ▼ العَقَقُ; (Ḳ;) which, as well as العَقِيقَةُ, is also expl. as meaning *lightning which one sees in the midst of the clouds, resembling a drawn sword*: (TA:) or عَقِيقَةُ البَرْقِ signifies *lightning in a state of commotion in the clouds*: (Ṣ, O:) or *lightning extending in an elongated form in the side*, or *breadth, of the clouds*: (TA:) or *lightning that cleaves the clouds, and extends high, into the midst of the sky, without going to the right and left*: (Ṣ in art. عقو:) or, as expl. by Aboo-Sa'eed, *a flash of lightning that has spread in the horizon*: (O, voce شَقِيقَةٌ:) a sword is likened thereto: (Ṣ, O, Ḳ:) and [the pl.] عَقَائِقُ is a name for *swords*: (O, Ḳ:) ▼ عَقِيقٌ, also, signifies *lightning*. (TA.) — And عَقِيقَةٌ signifies also *An arrow shot towards the sky*; (Ṣ, O, Ḳ;) the *arrow of self-excuse*; which was used in the manner described in the explanation of the phrase عَقَّ بِالسَّهْمِ [q. v.]. (Ṣ, O.) — See also عُقُوقٌ, last signification.

سَحَابَةٌ عَقَّاقَةٌ *A cloud pouring forth its water*: (TA:) or *a cloud much rent by water*. (T, TA voce هَيْدَبٌ.)

عُقَّانٌ *Shoots that come forth from the* أُصُول [meaning *trunks*, or *stems*,] of palm-trees and of grape-vines; (Ṣ, O, Ḳ;) *and which, if not cut off, cause the* اصول *to become vitiated*, or *unsound*. (Ṣ, O.) [See also صُنْبُورٌ: and see عَوَاقٌّ, below.]

عَقْعَقٌ [The *magpie, corvus pica*; so called in the present day;] *a certain bird*, (Ṣ, O, Mṣb, Ḳ,) *well known*, (Ṣ, O,) *of the size of the pigeon*, (Mṣb,) *party-coloured, black and white*, (O, Mṣb, Ḳ,) *having a long tail*, (O, Mṣb,) said by Is-ḥáḳ El-Mowsilee to be the *same that is called* شَجَجَى, (Th, IB, TA,) *a species of crow*, (IAth, Mṣb, TA,) wherefore it is said in a trad. that the man in the state of إِحْرَام may kill it; (IAth, TA;) *its cry resembles the sound of* ع *and* ق [or *the repeated sound of* عَقْ]; (O, Ḳ;) *and the Arabs regard it as an evil omen*. (Mṣb.) [See also صُرَدٌ.]

عَاقٌّ *Undutiful, disobedient, refractory*, or *ill-mannered, to his parent*, or *father*; (Ṣ,* O,* Ḳ;) *breaking*, or one *who breaks, his compact of obedience to his parent*, or *father*; (TA;) *disobeying*, or *disobedient to, his father*; and *failing*, or *neglecting, to behave to him in a good*, or *comely, manner*; (Mṣb;) [and *severing*, or one *who severs, the tie*, or *ties, of relationship, by unkind behaviour to his kindred*; (see its verb;)] and ▼ عَقٌّ signifies the same; (O, Ḳ;) as also ▼ عُقَقٌ, (Ṣ, O, TA,) but in an intensive sense, altered from عَاقٌّ, like غُدَرٌ and فُسَقٌ from غَادِرٌ and فَاسِقٌ, in the Ḳ erroneously said to be عَقَقٌ; (TA;) and ▼ عُقُقٌ; (L, and TA as from the Ḳ, but not in my MS. copy of the Ḳ nor in the CḲ;) which last signifies also [as a pl.] men *severing*, or *who sever, the ties of relationship, by unkind behaviour to their kindred*; and also *remote*, or *distant, enemies*: (TA:) [and ▼ عَقُوقٌ is app. used (as Freytag asserts it to be) in the sense of عَاقٌّ in the Fákihet el-Khulafà, p. 55, l. 7 from the bottom:] the pl. of عَاقٌّ is عَقَقَةٌ, (Ṣ, O, Mṣb, Ḳ,) like كَفَرَةٌ, (Ṣ,) and عُقَّقٌ, like رُكَّعٌ, a form used by Ru-beh, (O,) and أَعِقَّةٌ, which is an extr. [meaning anomalous] pl. (Ḥam p. 93.) ▼ ذُقْ عُقَقُ, (Ṣ, O,) in a trad., (Ṣ,) said by Aboo-Sufyán to Ḥamzah on the day of Ohod, when he passed by him slain, (Ṣ,* O,) means ذُقْ جَزَآءَ فِعْلِكَ [*Taste thou the recompense of thy deed*], (Ṣ,) or ذُقِ القَتْلَ [*taste thou slaughter*], (O,) يَا عَاقُّ [*O undutiful*, &c.; or, accord. to the explanation in the TA mentioned above, عُقَقُ, for يَا عُقَقُ, means *O very undutiful*, &c.]. (Ṣ, O.)

عَوَاقُّ النَّخْلِ *The shoots*, or *offsets, of the palm-trees, that grow forth therewith*. (O, Ḳ.) [See also عُقَّانٌ.]

أَعَقُّ مِنْ ضَبٍّ [*More undutiful*, &c., *to kindred, than a* lizard of the species called ضَبّ] is a prov. [mentioned, but not expl., in the O]: IAạr says, the female [of the ضَبّ] is meant; and its عُقُوق consists in its eating its young ones. (TA.) [See also Freytag's Arab. Prov. ii. 152-3. And see an ex. of أَعَقُّ in a verse cited in art. زهد, conj. 2.]

مُعِقٌّ: see عَقُوقٌ.

مَعْقُوقٌ: see عَقِيقٌ, first sentence.

عقب

1. عَقَبَهُ, (Ṣ, Ḳ,) aor. ـُ, (TA,) inf. n. عَقْبٌ, (TḲ,) *He struck his* عَقِب [or *heel*]. (Ṣ, Ḳ, TA.) — And عَقَبَهُ, (Ṣ, Mgh, Mṣb, Ḳ, TA,) aor. ـُ, (Mgh, Mṣb, TA,) inf. n. عَقْبٌ and عُقُوبٌ, (Mṣb, TA,) *He came after him*; [as though *at his heel*; and hence, properly, *close after him*; but often meaning *near after him*;] (Ṣ, Mgh, Mṣb, Ḳ, TA;) *followed him; succeeded him*; (Ṣ, Mgh, Ḳ, TA;) *came in*, or *took, his place*; as also ▼ اعقبه: (Ṣ, Ḳ, TA:) and in like manner both are said of anything, (TA,) as also ▼ عَقَّبَهُ, (Mṣb, Ḳ, TA,) inf. n. تَعْقِيبٌ; (Ṣ, Mṣb, Ḳ;) and ▼ عاقبه; (Ṣ, Mṣb, Ḳ;) and ▼ اعتقبه; (TA;) meaning *it came after*; (Ṣ,* Mṣb, Ḳ,* TA;) &c., as above: (TA:) and ▼ تعقّبه is used in this sense, but not rightly. (Mgh.) [All primarily denote proximate sequence.] You say, عَقَبُونَا and عَقَبُوا مِنْ خَلْفِنَا *They came after us*. (TA.) And ▼ عَقَّبُونَا and عَقَبُونَا مِنْ خَلْفِنَا *They succeeded us, in alighting*, or *taking up their abode, after our departure*. (TA.) And العِدَّةُ تَعْقُبُ الطَّلَاقَ *The* عِدَّة [q. v.] *follows divorce*. (Mgh, Mṣb.) And ذَهَبَ فُلَانٌ فَأَعْقَبَهُ ▼ ابْنُهُ, as also عَقَبَهُ, *Such a one went away, and his son succeeded him*, or *took his place*. (Ṣ, O.) And ▼ اعقب هٰذَا هٰذَا [*This succeeded this*] is said when the latter is gone, and there remains nothing of it, and the former has taken its place. (TA.) And one says, عَقَبَ فُلَانٌ مَكَانَ أَبِيهِ, (Ṣ, O, TA,) aor. ـُ, inf. n. عَقْبٌ, (TA,) and quasi-inf. n. ▼ عَاقِبَةٌ, this being a subst. used in the sense of an inf. n., like as كَاذِبَةٌ is [said to be] in the Ḳur lvi. 2, (Ṣ, O,) or it is an inf. n. syn. with عَقْبٌ, (Mṣb in art. عقو,) *Such a one succeeded*, or *took the place of, his father*; (Ṣ,

O, TA;) as also ▼ عقّب. (TA.) [Hence also several phrases here following.] — It is said in a trad., كُلُّ غَازِيَةٍ غَزَتْ يَعْقُبُ بَعْضُهَا بَعْضًا i. e. [*Every party that goes forth on a warring, or warring and plundering, expedition*] *shall take its turn, one after another:*] when one company has gone forth and returned, it shall not be constrained to go forth again until another has taken its turn after it. (TA.) — عَقَبْتُ الرَّجُلَ فِى أَهْلِهِ means بَغَيْتُهُ بِشَرٍّ وَخَلَفْتُهُ [i. e. *I sought to do evil to the man, and took his place* (see art. خلف), *with respect to his wife;* i. e. *I committed adultery with his wife*]: (Ṣ, O:) or عَقَبَهُ signifies [simply] بَغَاهُ بِشَرٍّ [*he sought to do evil to him*]: (Ḳ: [in which وَخَلَفَهُ seems to have been inadvertently omitted: but SM immediately adds what here follows:]) and one says also, عَقَبَ فِى إِثْرِ الرَّجُلِ بِمَا يُكْرَهُ, aor. ـُ, inf. n. عَقْبٌ, meaning *He accused the man* [app. *behind his back*] *of a thing disliked,* or *hated; he* [*so*] *defamed him,* or *charged him with a vice* or *fault* or *the like.* (TA.) — عَقَبَ فُلَانٌ عَلَى فُلَانَةَ [like خَلَفَ عَلَيْهَا] *Such a man married such a woman after her first husband.* (TA.) — عَقَبَ الشَّيْبُ, aor. ـِ and ـُ, inf. n. عُقُوبٌ, *Whiteness of the hair,* or *hoariness, came after* [or *took the place of*] *blackness;* as also ▼ عقّب. (TA.) — عَقَبَ said of a horse, aor. ـِ [or ـُ?], inf. n. عَقْبٌ, [which see below,] *He performed a run after another run.* (L, TA.) — عَقَبَتِ الإِبِلُ مِنْ مَكَانٍ إِلَى مَكَانٍ, aor. ـُ, inf. n. عَقْبٌ; and ▼ اعتقبت; *The camels removed from place to place, pasturing.* (IAạr, TA.) — مَا عَقَبَ فِيهَا فَعَلَيْكَ مِنْ مَالِكَ, (TA,) or ▼ مَا عَقَّبَ, (so in the O, [in which فِى مالك is put in the place of من مالك,]) *Whatever evil consequence happen* to me, *with respect to it,* (referring to merchandise,) *the responsibility* for it *will be on thee* [and compensation shall be made *from thy property*]: and [تَعْقِبَةٌ (thus in the O) appears, from what follows, to be an inf. n. of the latter verb in this sense; or it may perhaps be from the former verb, like تَهْلِكَةٌ from هَلَكَ; for] one says, بَاعَنِى سِلْعَةً وَعَلَيْهِ تَعْقِبَةٌ إِنْ كَانَتْ فِيهَا [*He sold me an article of merchandise, and was responsible for an evil consequence,* (or for damage afterwards found in it,) *should there be any in it*]. (ISh, O, TA.*) — عَقَبَهُ and ▼ عقّبه and ▼ اعقبه signify also *He took,* or *received, from him something in exchange, an exchange, a substitute,* or *an equivalent, for another thing:* it is said in a trad., إِنْ لَمْ يَقْرُوهُ فَلَهُ أَنْ يَعْقُبَهُمْ بِمِثْلِ قِرَاهُ *If they entertain him not, he shall have a right to take from them as a substitute the likes of his entertainment* which they denied him: and one says also ▼ استعقب مِنْهُ خَيْرًا, or شَرًّا, *He took,* or *received, from him in exchange good,* or *evil:* (TA:) and عَقَبَ الرَّجُلَ, aor. ـُ, *He took from the man's property the like of what he* (the latter) *had taken from him.* (O,* TA.) After the words in the Ḳur lx. 11, وَإِنْ فَاتَكُمْ شَىْءٌ مِنْ أَزْوَاجِكُمْ إِلَى الكُفَّارِ, there are three different readings, ▼ فَعَاقَبْتُمْ, and ▼ فَعَقَّبْتُمْ, and فَعَقَبْتُمْ: (TA:) the first means *and ye take,* or *carry off, spoil:* (Masrooḳ Ibn-El-Ajdaʼ, Ṣ, TA:) or the second has this meaning; and the first means *and ye punish them so that ye take,* or *carry off, spoil:* and the third means *and ye have a requital:* the second is the best; and the third is also good; but the second has a more intensive meaning: (Aboo-Is-ḥáḳ the Grammarian, L, TA:) accord. to Fr, the first and second signify the same: (L, TA:) and Aṣ says that عَقْبٌ [inf. n. of عَقَبَ] is syn. with عِقَابٌ [inf. n. of عَاقَبَ; but whether with reference to this case, I do not find]. (TA.) — And عَقَبَ, aor. ـُ, inf. n. عَقْبٌ, also signifies *He sought,* or *sought after, wealth,* or *some other thing.* (TA.) = عَقَبَ, (Ṣ, O, Ḳ,) aor. ـِ and ـُ, (TA,) inf. n. عَقْبٌ, (Ṣ, O,) *He bound* a thing *with* [*the kind of sinew,* or *tendon, called*] عَقَب; as also ▼ عقّب [inf. n. تَعْقِيبٌ, of which see an ex. in a verse cited voce مُضَنَّعٌ]: *he bound therewith* a خَوْق, i. e. the ring of an ear-drop, fearing lest it should incline on one side: or *he bound* an earring *with a thread called* عُقَاب: (TA:) *and he wound round* a bow, (Ṣ, O, Ḳ,) and an arrow, (Ṣ, O,) *with* [*the kind of sinew,* or *tendon, called*] عَقَب, (O,) or *with somewhat thereof:* (Ṣ, Ḳ:) or عَقَبَهُ بِالعَقَبِ *he bound it,* namely, the [arrow termed] قِدْح, *with the* عَقَب, in consequence of its having broken. (IB, L, TA.) = عَقَبْنَا الرَّكِيَّةَ [thus I find it written without teshdeed, but perhaps it should be ▼ عَقَّبْنَا, from أَعْقَابُ الطَّىِّ, (see عَقْبٌ,)] *We lined the well with stones behind* [*the other*] *stones.* (TA. [See also 4.]) = [The inf. n.] العَقْبُ also signifies الرَّجْعُ, [which generally means *The making,* or *causing, to return,* or *go back;* but this may perhaps be a mistake for الرُّجُوعُ, for it is immediately added,] Dhu-r-Rummeh says,

كَأَنَّ صِيَاحَ الكُدْرِ يَنْظُرْنَ عَقْبَنَا
تَرَاطُنُ أَنْبَاطٍ عَلَيْهِ طَغَامِ

meaning [*As though the crying of the dusky* she-camels] *looking,* or *waiting, for our returning* from watering that they might go to the water after us [*were the barbarous talk of low,* or *ignoble, Nabathæans, over it,* i. e. over the water]. (TA.) = عَقَبَ النَّبْتُ, [aor. ـُ,] inf. n. عَقْبٌ, *The branches of the plant,* or *herbage, became slender, and the leaves thereof turned yellow.* (IAạr, TA. [See also 2.])

2: see 1, first three quarters, in seven places. — The inf. n., تَعْقِيبٌ, signifies also The *doing a thing and then returning to doing it:* (IAth, TA:) the *performing an act of prayer,* or *another act, and then returning to doing it in the same day:* (Sh, TA:) and [particularly] the *making a warring,* or *warring and plundering, expedition, and then another in the same year.* (Ṣ, O, Ḳ.) [See also مُعَقِّبٌ.] You say, عقّب بِصَلَاةٍ بَعْدَ صَلَاةٍ, and بِغَزَاةٍ بَعْدَ غَزَاةٍ, *He followed up one prayer with another,* and *one warring,* or *warring and plundering, expedition with another.* (TA.) And صَلَّى مِنَ اللَّيْلِ ثُمَّ عَقَّبَ *He prayed in the night and then repeated the prayer.* (IAạr, TA.) And عُقِّبَ الغَازِيَةُ بِأَمْثَالِهَا, and ▼ أُعْقِبَ, *The warring,* or *warring and plundering, party was made to be followed by another, consisting of the likes of it, sent in its place.* (TA.) And it is said in a trad. of 'Omar, كَانَ كُلَّ عَامٍ يُعَقِّبُ الجُيُوشَ *He used, every year, to call back one party of the forces and to send another to take its turn after the former.* (O, TA.) — Also The *performing of prayer* (IAth, O, Ḳ, TA) *as a supererogatory act* (TA) *after the* [*prayers called*] تَرَاوِيح: (IAth, O, Ḳ, TA:) such prayer is to be performed in the house, at home, (IAth, O, TA,) not in the mosque. (IAth, TA.) — And The *waiting* (Ḳ, TA) in prayer; or *remaining in one's place* in prayer *waiting for another prayer.* (TA.) And you say, عقّب فِى الصَّلَاةِ, (Ṣ, O,) inf. n. as above, (Ṣ, A, O, Mṣb, Ḳ,) *He sat after the performing of the* [ordinary] *prayer for the purpose of a supplication* (Ṣ, A, O, Mṣb, Ḳ) or *a petition.* (Ṣ, O, Mṣb.) وَلَّى مُدْبِرًا وَلَمْ يُعَقِّبْ, in the Ḳur [xxvii. 10 and xxviii. 31], means [*He did did not turn back retreating*] *and did not wait;* (O, TA;) properly, *did not make advancing to follow his retreating:* (O:) or *and did not turn aside* (Ṣ, Mṣb) *nor wait in expectation:* (Ṣ:) or *and did not turn aside nor return:* (O:) or *and did not look aside:* (Ḳ,* TA:) or *and did not return;* from عقّب said of a combatant, meaning *He returned after fleeing:* (Bḍ in xxvii. 10:) you say, عقّب عَلَيْهِ *He returned against him;* syn. كَرَّ, and رَجَعَ: and تَعْقِيبٌ signifies also The *turning back,* or *receding, from a thing that one had desired to do.* (TA.) — عَقَّبَ فِى الشَّيْبِ بِأَخْلَاقٍ حَسَنَةٍ [app. means *He had latterly, in the time of hoariness, good dispositions*]. (O. [The meaning that I have assigned to this phrase seems to be there indicated by the context: but I incline to think that the right reading is عُقِّبَ, † lit. *He was made to be followed, in hoariness, by good dispositions;* agreeably with what next follows.]) — أَتَى فُلَانٌ إِلَىَّ خَيْرًا فَعَقَّبَ بِخَيْرٍ مِنْهُ [means *Such a one caused good to betide me, and it was made to be followed by what was better than it*]. (A, TA. [In the former it is followed by the words وَأَرْدَفَ بِخَيْرٍ مِنْهُ, evidently for the purpose of explanation.]) — [Hence,] one says, تَصَدَّقَ بِصَدَقَةٍ لَيْسَ فِيهَا تَعْقِيبٌ, meaning اِسْتِثْنَآءٌ [i.e. *He gave an alms in which was no making an exception* by following it up with a condition]. (Ṣ, A, O, Mṣb.*) — عقّبنى حَقِّى *He delayed,* or *deferred, the giving,* or *paying, to me my due.* (Ṣ.) — عقّب الأَمْرَ *He looked to the consequence, end, issue,* or *result, of the affair, event,* or *case.* (TA. [See also 5.]) — And عقّب فِى الأَمْرِ *He went repeatedly to and fro,* or *made repeated efforts, in seeking to accomplish the affair, striving,* or *exerting himself.* (Ṣ, O, L, TA.) In the Ḳ, التَّعْقِيبُ [the inf. n.] is expl. as signifying التَّرَدُّدُ

فِى طَلَبِ المَجْدِ: but the right reading is فِى طَلَبِ مَجْدًا. (TA.) [See also مُعَقِّبٌ.] — عقّب said of the [plant called] عَرْفَج, (Ṣ, O,) inf. n. تَعْقِيبٌ, (Ḳ,) *It became yellow in its fruit,* (Ṣ, O, Ḳ,) *and attained to the season of its drying up:* (Ṣ, O:) from عَقِبَ said of a plant or herbage. (TA.) — عقّب عُقَابًا, inf. n. as above, *He planed off a stone of the kind called* عُقَاب, *in a well.* (TA. [See also مُعَقِّبٌ.]) — See also 1, last quarter, in two places.

3. عاقبهُ: see 1, second sentence. — Also عاقب الرَّجُلَ, (Mgh,* TA,) inf. n. مُعَاقَبَةٌ and عِقَابٌ, (Mgh,) *He did a thing with the man alternately, each taking his turn;* (Mgh, TA;) and so ↓ اعقبهُ. (TA.) And [particularly], (TA,) inf. n. مُعَاقَبَةٌ, (Ṣ, O,) *He rode in his turn after the man, each riding in his turn;* (Ṣ, O, TA;) as also ↓ اعقبهُ, (Ṣ, O, Ḳ,) and ↓ اعتقبهُ. (TA.) And عَاقَبْتُ الرَّجُلَ فِى الرَّاحِلَةِ *I rode in my turn after the man, upon the camel, he riding in his turn after me.* (Ṣ, O.) And in like manner you say, ↓ اعْتَقَبُوهُ, and ↓ تَعَاقَبُوهُ *They rode by turns with him, taking their turns after him.* (TA.) — And عاقب بَيْنَ الشَّيْئَيْنِ [*He made an interchange,* or *alternation between the two things; he made the two things interchangeable,* or *commutable;*] *he brought,* or *did, the two things interchangeably,* or *alternately,* i. e. *one of them one time and the other of them another time.* (TA.) [Thus, for instance,] العَرَبُ تُعَاقِبُ بَيْنَ الفَآءِ وَالثَّآءِ [*The Arabs make an interchange between* ف *and* ث; *make* ف *and* ث *interchangeable,* or *commutable;* i. e. *put* ف *in the place of* ث, *and* ث *in the place of* ف]; as in جَدَثٌ and جَدَفٌ; and ↓ تُعْقِبُ signifies the same. (Ṣ, O.) — And عاقب signifies also *He stood upon one of his legs one time and upon the other another time;* or *moved his legs alternately.* (TA.) — [عاقبهُ as denoting consequence, and retaliation, or retribution, also signifies *He punished him.*] You say, عاقبهُ بِذَنْبِهِ, (Ṣ, Mṣb,* TA,) inf. n. عِقَابٌ (Ṣ, Mṣb, TA) and مُعَاقَبَةٌ, (Mṣb, TA,) *He punished him for his crime, sin, fault,* or *offence:* (Ṣ,* Mṣb,* TA:) and [in like manner] ↓ تعقّبهُ *He punished him* (i. e. a man, Ṣ, O) *for a crime, a sin, a fault,* or *an offence, that he had committed.* (Ṣ, O, Ḳ.) In the saying in the Ḳur [xvi. last verse but one], وَإِنْ عَاقَبْتُمْ فَعَاقِبُوا بِمِثْلِ مَا عُوقِبْتُمْ بِهِ [*And if ye punish, then punish ye with the like of that with which ye have been afflicted,* lit. *punished*], the verb first denotes punishment, and is afterwards used for the purpose of assimilation: and similar to this is the saying in the same [xxii. 59], وَمَنْ عَاقَبَ بِمِثْلِ مَا عُوقِبَ بِهِ [*And whoso punisheth with the like of that with which he hath been afflicted,* lit. *punished*]. (O.) For another ex., from the Ḳur lx. 11, [where it implies retaliation or retribution,] see 1, latter half. [In like manner,] it is said in a trad., أَبْطَلَ النَّفْحَ إِلَّا أَنْ يُضْرَبَ فَيُعَاقِبَ [*He made the kicking* of a beast *with the hind leg to be of no account unless it were beaten* by its master, or rider, *and retaliated* by kicking another person]; meaning, he made nothing to be incumbent on the master of the beast unless the latter made the kicking to be a consequence of that [i. e. unless the beast kicked in consequence of its being beaten by the master, or rider]. (TA.) [See also 4, which has a similar meaning, that of requital.] — عُوقِبَتْ said of a mare means *She was required to perform run after run.* (Ḥam p. 277.)

4. اعقبهُ: see 1, first quarter, in three places: — and see 3, in three places. — [Also *He made him to take his place.* And hence,] *He descended from his beast in order that he* (another) *might ride in his turn:* and one says also أَعْقِبْ meaning *Descend thou in order that I may ride in my turn:* and in like manner with respect to any kind of action: thus, when the office of Khaleefeh became transferred from the sons of Umeiyeh to the Háshimees, Sudeyf, the poet of the 'Abbásees, said,

* أَعْقِبِى آلَ هَاشِمٍ يَا مَيَّا *

meaning *Descend* from the station of the Khaleefehs *that the family of Háshim may mount, O Meiyà* [for O sons of Umeiyeh]. (TA.) — [And *It made* a thing *to follow as a consequence to him:* the verb in this sense being doubly trans.] One says, اعقبهُ نَدَمًا *It occasioned him as its consequence repentance,* (Mgh, Mṣb, TA,) and هَمًّا *anxiety.* (TA.) And أَكَلَ أَكْلَةً أَعْقَبَتْهُ سَقَمًا *He ate a repast that occasioned him as its consequence a sickness.* (Ṣ, O.) And [hence] أُعْقِبَ عِزُّهُ ذُلًّا *His might was exchanged for,* or *changed into,* [lit. *made to be followed by,*] *abasement.* (TA.) See also 2, first quarter, for another ex. [Hence, likewise,] فَأَعْقَبَهُمْ نِفَاقًا, in the Ḳur [ix. 78], means [*Therefore He caused hypocrisy to follow as a consequence to them;* or] *He caused them to err,* because of their evil deed, *as a punishment to them.* (O.) And [in like manner] one says, أَعْقَبَهُ ٱللّٰهُ بِإِحْسَانِهِ خَيْرًا [*God gave him,* or *may God give him, as a recompense,* or *requital, for his beneficence, good,* or *prosperity*]. (TA.) And اعقبهُ بِطَاعَتِهِ *He recompensed,* or *requited, him for his obedience,* (Ṣ, O, Ḳ,*) and عَلَى مَا صَنَعَ *for what he did.* (TA. [See also 3, which has a similar meaning, that of retribution.]) اعقبهُ خَيْرًا means also *He gave him in exchange good.* (TA.) See also 1, latter half, where the verb is expl. in the contr. sense, that of taking, or receiving, in exchange. — اعقبهُ الطَّائِفُ *The diabolical visitation,* or *insanity, returned to him at times.* (Ṣ, O.) — اعقب عَلَى البِئْرِ بِحِجَارَةٍ مِنْ وَرَائِهَا [is app. from أَعْقَابُ الطَّىِّ (see عَقِبٌ), and] means *He laid stones compactly together at the back* [*behind the regular casing*] *of the well.* (TA. [See also 1, near the end.]) — اعقب as intrans., *He* (a man) *died, and left offspring.* (Ṣ, O, Ḳ.) One says, أَعْقَبَ مِنْهُمْ رَجُلَانِ وَدَرَجَ وَاحِدٌ [*Two men of them died and left offspring, and one died and left no offspring*]: and Ṭufeyl El-Ghanawee says,

* كَرِيمَةُ حُرِّ الوَجْهِ لَمْ تَدْعُ هَالِكًا *
* مِنَ القَوْمِ هُلْكًا فِى غَدٍ غَيْرَ مُعْقِبِ *

[*A female noble of countenance,* (or whose nobility was manifest in what appeared of her countenance,) *she did not invoke one of the people dead, on a morrow* after an engagement, *as having perished without leaving a successor,* or *one to fill his place:*] i. e. when a chief of her people died, another chief came; so that she did not bewail a chief who had not his equal. (TA.) — *He* (a borrower of a cooking-pot) *returned a cooking-pot with the remains termed* عُقْبَة *in it.* (Ṣ, O, Ḳ.) — *He* (a man) *returned from evil to good.* (TA.) — اعقب عَلَيْهِ يَضْرِبُهُ *He set upon him beating him.* (O.) — أَعْقَبَتْ رَاحِلَتُكَ *Thy riding-camel became,* or *has become, jaded,* or *fatigued.* (O.)

5. تعقّب *He looked to the consequence, end, issue,* or *result:* and *he considered a second time.* (TA. [See also 2, last quarter.]) — تعقّب مِنْ أَمْرِهِ *He repented of his affair.* (TA.) — تعقّب عَنِ الخَبَرِ *He doubted of the information,* or *questioned it, and asked again respecting it.* (Ṣ, O, Ḳ, TA. [In my copies of the Ṣ, and in the O, الخَبَرَ: but see what follows; in which مُتَعَقَّب is used as a noun of place of the verb in this sense.]) Ṭufeyl says,

* وَلَمْ يَكُ عَمَّا خَبَّرُوا مُتَعَقَّبُ *

[*And there was no place of,* or *ground for, doubting, and asking again, respecting what they told*]. (Ṣ, O, TA.) And one says, لَمْ أَجِدْ عَنْ قَوْلِكَ ↓ مُتَعَقَّبًا, (A, TA,) i. e. [*I found not*] *any place of,* or *ground for, inquiring into,* or *investigating, thy saying;* syn. مُتَفَحَّصًا; (A, TA;) [or *questioning it;* or *returning to examine it;*] meaning, thy saying was right and true, so that it did not require التَّعَقُّب; (A;) or I did not allow myself to doubt, and ask again, respecting it, that I might see whether I should do what thou saidst or abstain from it. (TA.) — [And the verb is used transitively in a similar sense.] You say, تعقّب الخَبَرَ *He searched after the information repeatedly,* or *time after time;* (Mgh,* TA;) syn. تَتَبَّعَ: (Mgh, TA:) and ↓ اعتقب has a like meaning. (Ḥam p. 287.) And *He asked respecting the information another person than the one whom he asked the first time.* (A, TA.) — And تَعَقَّبْتُ الرَّجُلَ *I sought to discover in the man that which he would be ashamed to expose;* or *the slip,* or *fault, that he had committed:* and ↓ اِسْتَعْقَبْتُهُ signifies the same. (O, Ḳ.*) [In critical observations and the like, تعقّبهُ is often used as meaning *He found fault with him; animadverted upon him;* or *impugned his judgment* or *assertion;* بِقَوْلِهِ كَذَا وَكَذَا *by his saying so and so.* And تعقّب عَلَيْهِ seems to be similarly used as meaning *He animadverted upon his saying:* (compare اِعْتَرَضَ عَلَيْهِ:) but more commonly as meaning *he animadverted upon it,* i. e. a saying, and the like.] — See also 3, near the middle of the paragraph. — تعقّب الأَمْرَ *He thought repeatedly upon the affair*, or *case*. (TA in art. روا.) — تعقّب رَأْيَهُ *He found his opinion to have a good issue*, or *result*. (Ṣ, O. [See a somewhat similar signification of 8 and 10, under the former.]) — See also 1, second sentence. — [The saying of Aboo-Thumámeh,

* وَإِنْ مَنْطِقٌ زَلَّ عَنْ صَاحِبِى *
* تَعَقَّبْتُ آخَرَ ذَا مُعْتَقَبْ *

may be rendered, nearly in accordance with an explanation by Et-Tebreezee, *And if a speech slip by mistake from my companion, I substitute another having superiority*: or تعقّبت may here mean *I search out*: but see the Ḥam p. 287; where are some remarks, on this verse, that appear to me to be fanciful and far-fetched.]

6. يَتَعَاقَبَانِ (T, Ṣ, O, Mṣb, TA) *They follow each other* [*by turns*]; or *alternate*; (T, Mṣb, TA;) *one coming and the other going*; (TA;) said of the night and the day; (T, Mṣb;) or as the night and the day; (Ṣ, O, TA;) as also ↓ يَعْتَقِبَانِ. (TA.) You say, تَعَاقَبَ المُسَافِرَانِ عَلَى الدَّابَّةِ *The two travellers rode upon the beast, each of them in his turn*. (TA: and the like is said in the Mṣb.) And تعاقبا عَمَلًا *They two did a work*, or *deed, by turns*, or *alternately*; syn. تَرَاوَحَاهُ, (Ḳ and TA in art. روح,) and اِرْتَوَحَاهُ. (TA in that art.) And تعاقبا *They helped each other by turns*. (TA.) And يَعْتَقِبَانِهِ ↓ بِالضَّرْبِ *They two ply him by turns with beating*. (A.) See also 3, near the beginning. التَّعَاقُبُ also signifies *The coming to water* [*by turns*, or] *time after time*. (TA.)

8: see 1, former half, in two places: — and see 3, near the beginning, in two places; and 6, also in two places. — [اعتقبهُ signifies also *He took it*, or *had it*, *subsequently*. Thus one of the meanings of العُقْبَةُ is expl. in the A and TA by the words مَا يَعْتَقِبُونَهُ بَعْدَ الطَّعَامِ مِنَ الحَلَاوَةِ i. e. *What they have*, or *take*, *after* the main portion of *the meal*, consisting *of sweetmeat*. — And *He had it*, or *experienced it*, *as a consequence* of an act &c.: and that it may have ↓ مُعْتَقَبٌ for an inf. n. in this sense (as well as in other senses agreeably with analogy) seems to be meant by its being said (in the Ḥam p. 287) that المُعْتَقَبُ signifies آخِرُهُ i. e. أَخْذُ عُقْبَةِ الشَّىْءِ. See also a somewhat similar signification of 5.] One says, فَعَلْتُ كَذَا فَٱعْتَقَبْتُ مِنْهُ نَدَامَةً i. e. [*I did such a thing and*] *I found*, or *experienced*, *in consequence thereof repentance*; (Ṣ, O;) as also ↓ اِسْتَعْقَبْتُ. (A, O.) And استعقب ↓ مِنْ كَذَا خَيْرًا *He found*, or *experienced*, *in consequence of such a thing*, or *after such a thing*, *good*. (T, Mṣb.) And hence, perhaps, the saying of the lawyers, يَصِحُّ الشِّرَآءُ إِذَا ٱسْتَعْقَبَ ↓ عِتْقًا [as meaning *The sale*, or *purchase*, *is valid when it has emancipation as an after-event*]: but this does not agree with the former phrase unless by a far-fetched interpretation; and therefore one should say, إِذَا عَقَبَهُ العِتْقُ i. e. *when emancipation follows it*. (Mṣb.) — اعتقب also signifies *He withheld*, or *detained*, a thing *in his possession*. (TA.) And [particularly] *He* (a seller) *withheld*, or *detained*, an article of merchandise *from the purchaser until he should receive the price*: (Ṣ, A, O, Ḳ:) for the doing of which he is said in a trad. to be responsible; meaning, if it perish in his keeping. (Ṣ, A, O.) And *He detained*, *confined*, or *imprisoned*, a man. (Ṣ, O.) — See also 5.

10: see the next preceding paragraph, in three places: — and see also 1, latter half: — and 5. — [Accord. to Reiske, as mentioned by Freytag, استعقبهُ signifies also *He followed his footsteps*.]

عَقْبٌ: see عَقِبٌ, in eight places.

عُقْبٌ: see عَقِبٌ, in seven places.

عَقَبٌ The عَصَب [meaning *sinews*, or *tendons*,] *of which* أَوْتَار [i. e. *strings for bows or the like*] *are made*: (Ṣ, O, Ḳ: [see also 1, last quarter:]) n. un. with ة: (Ṣ, O:) or *such as are white of the* أَطْنَاب *of the joints*; (Mgh, Mṣb; [see عَصَبٌ;]) the عَصَب being such as are yellow: (Mgh and Mṣb in art. عصب:) accord. to IAth, the عَصَب [or *sinews*, or *tendons*,] *of the two portions of flesh next the back-bone on either side, and of the* سَاقَانِ and وَظِيفَانِ [meaning the *hind and fore shanks*], *that are intermingled with the flesh, of any animal; the half of one whereof, divided lengthwise from the other half, is extended*, or *drawn out, and trimmed, and cleansed of the flesh, and the* وَتَر [or *string for the bow or the like*] *is made thereof; and they are sometimes in the two sides of the camel*; but [*properly speaking*] *there is a difference between the* عَصَب *and the* عَقَب; *the former being such as incline to yellow, whereas the latter incline to white, and are the harder, and firmer*, or *stronger*, *of the two*: AHn says, on the authority of Aboo-Ziyád, that the عَقَب are [the *sinews*, or *tendons*,] *of the two portions of flesh next the back-bone on either side, of the sheep or goat, and of the camel, and of the ox or cow*. (TA.) [See also عِلْبَآءٌ.]

عَقِبٌ (Ṣ, Mgh, O, Mṣb, Ḳ, &c.) and ↓ عَقْبٌ, (Mṣb, TA,) the latter being a contraction of the former, (Mṣb,) [The *heel* of a human being;] the *hinder part of the foot* of a human being: (Ṣ, Mgh, O, Mṣb, Ḳ:) of the fem. gender: (Ṣ, O, Mṣb:) pl. [of pauc.] أَعْقُبٌ (TA) and [of mult. as well as of pauc.] أَعْقَابٌ: (Mṣb, TA:) and ↓ عُقَيْبٌ is said to signify the same; but MF cites an assertion that this is a word of a bad dialect. (TA.) وَيْلٌ لِلْأَعْقَابِ مِنَ النَّارِ [*Wo to the heels from the fire* of Hell], (O, Mṣb, TA,) and ويل لِلْعَقِبِ من النار [*Wo to the heel* &c.], (TA,) occurring in a trad., means wo to him who neglects the washing of the heels in the ablution preparatory to prayer. (O,* Mṣb, TA.*) عَقِبُ الشَّيْطَانِ, (O, Mṣb, TA,) or, as some say, ↓ عُقْبَةُ الشيطان, (Mṣb, TA,) with ḍamm, (TA,) which is forbidden in prayer, is expl. as meaning *The placing the buttocks upon the heels between the two prostrations*; which is what some term الإِقْعَآء: (Mgh,* O, Mṣb, TA:) so says A'Obeyd: (Mṣb:) or, accord. to some, this means *the leaving the heels unwashed in the ablution preparatory to prayer*. (O.) وَطِئَ النَّاسُ عَقِبَ فُلَانٍ [lit. *The people trod upon the heel of such a one*] means *the people walked after*, or *near after, such a one*: and in like manner, هُوَ مُوَطَّأُ العَقِبِ [lit. *He is one whose heel is trodden upon*]: (O, TA:*) because of his having command over people, and their being submissive to him: (O:) the latter phrase means *he is one who has many followers*: (A, TA: [see also art. وطأ:]) جَآءَ زَيْدٌ يَطَأُ عَقِبَ عَمْرٍو primarily signifies *Zeyd came putting his foot in the place of the foot* [or *heel*] *of 'Amr every time that the latter raised his foot*. (Mṣb.) And one says, مِنْ أَيْنَ عَقِبُكَ, (A, O,) or مِنْ أَيْنَ كَانَ عَقِبُكَ, (TA,) meaning *Whence camest thou?* or *Whence hast thou come?* (A, O, TA.) And رَجَعَ فُلَانٌ عَلَى عَقِبِهِ *Such a one returned by the way of his heel*; i. e., *by the way that was behind him, and whence he had come; quickly*. (Mṣb.) And عَلَى عَقِبَيْهِ, and وَلَّى عَلَى عَقِبِهِ, *He turned back*, or *receded, from a thing to which he had betaken himself*. (TA.) لَا تَرُدَّهُمْ عَلَى أَعْقَابِهِمْ, occurring in a trad., means *Turn not thou them back to their former condition* of not emigrating [for the sake of religion]: and مَا زَالُوا مُرْتَدِّينَ عَلَى أَعْقَابِهِمْ, in another trad., means *They ceased not to return to infidelity*; as though they went backwards. (TA.) — The عَقِب of the نَعْل [or sandal] is The *part* [or *wide strap*] *that embraces the heel*. (AO, in an anom. MS. in my possession.) — [And عَقِبُ البَابِ means *The pivot* (generally of wood) *at the bottom of the door, turning in a socket in the threshold*.] — And عُقْبٌ and ↓ عَقْبٌ (TA) and ↓ عُقُبٌ and عَقِبٌ (Ṣ, O, Mṣb, Ḳ, TA) and ↓ عُقْبَةٌ and ↓ عُقْبَى and ↓ عُقْبَانٌ and ↓ عِقْبَانٌ and ↓ عَاقِبٌ (TA) are syn. with ↓ عَاقِبَةٌ, (Ṣ, O, Mṣb, Ḳ, TA,) which signifies, (Ṣ, O, Mṣb, Ḳ,) i. e. as signifying, (TA,) The *end*; or the *last*, or *latter, part* or *state*; [but generally as explanatory of this last word, and often as explanatory of عُقْبٌ and عُقُبٌ and عُقْبَى, as meaning the *consequence*, or *result*, or *issue*;] of anything: (Ṣ, O, Mṣb, Ḳ, TA:) [and the same words, app. with the exception of عُقْبَى and عَاقِبَةٌ, signify also *a time*, or *state, of subsequence*:] the pl. [of the first four words is أَعْقَابٌ, and] of the last عَوَاقِبُ. (TA.) Hence, (Ṣ,) it is said in the Ḳur [xviii. 42], هُوَ خَيْرٌ ثَوَابًا وَخَيْرٌ عُقْبًا [or ↓ عُقُبًا or ↓ عُقْبَى, accord. to different readings, i. e. *He is the best in respect of recompense*, or *reward, and the best in respect of consequence*, or *result*, or *issue*; i. e., the consequence of the actions &c. of believers]. (Ṣ, O.) And in the same [xci. last verse], وَلَا يَخَافُ ↓ عُقْبَاهَا i. e. *And He feareth not the consequence thereof*. (Th, TA.) And they said, العَاقِبَةُ ↓ لَكَ فِى الخَيْرِ meaning العُقْبَى [i. e.

May the end to thee be in that which is good; or may thy case end in good]. (TA.) And it is said in a trad., سَافَرَ فِى عَقِبِ رَمَضَانَ, (T, O, Mṣb,) meaning *He journeyed in the end,* or *the last,* or *latter, part, of Ramaḍán:* (T, Mṣb:) or, *when Ramaḍán had almost ended.* (O.) One says, جِئْتُ فِى عَقِبِ رَمَضَانَ, (ISk, Ṣ, O,* Mṣb,*) with kesr to the ق, (ISk, Ṣ,) meaning [*I came*] *when there was somewhat remaining of Ramaḍán.* (ISk, Ṣ, O,* Mṣb.) And جِئْتُكَ فِى عَقِبِ الشَّهْرِ, and ▼ فِى عُقْبِهِ, and عَلَى عَقِبِهِ, *I came to thee in the latter part of the month, when ten days of it, or less, remained.* (L.) هُوَ فِى عَقِبِ المَرَضِ *He is in the state of convalescence in which somewhat remains of the disease:* (Mṣb:) and فِى أَعْقَابِ المَرَضِ *in the* [*state in which there are some*] *remains of the disease.* (TA.) One says also, جَآءَ فِى عَقِبِهِ and ▼ عُقْبِهِ, meaning *He came after him;* or *near after him;* [as though *at his heel;* and hence, properly, *close after him;*] and جَآءَ عَقِبَهُ; from the phrase جَآءَ زَيْدٌ يَطَأُ عَقِبَ عَمْرٍو, meaning as expl. above. (Mṣb.) And بَنُو فُلَانٍ سَقْىُ إِبِلِهِمْ عَقِبَ بَنِى فُلَانٍ i. e. [*The sons of such a one, the watering of their camels is*] *after* [*that of*] *the sons of such a one;* a saying mentioned by ISk. (Mṣb.) And صَلَّيْنَا أَعْقَابَ الفَرِيضَةِ تَطَوُّعًا i. e. [*We performed prayer*] *after the obligatory* [*by way of supererogation*]. (Lḥ, IF, Mṣb, TA.) And جِئْتُ فِى عَقِبِ الشَّهْرِ i. e. *I came after the month had passed.* (El-Fárábee, Mṣb.) And خَلَفَ فُلَانٌ بِعَقِبِى *Such a one remained,* or *stayed, after me.* (Mṣb.) Er-Rázee says, in the Mukhtár eṣ-Ṣiḥáḥ, that he had found no authority in the T nor in the Ṣ for the phrase جَآءَ فُلَانٌ عقب فُلَانٍ [app. عَقِبَ], meaning *Such a one came after such a one,* except a similar saying of ISk, cited by Az, in which عقب is expl. as signifying *after.* (TA.) [But if the word in question be عَقِبَ, sufficient authorities for its use in this sense have been cited above: though it seems from what here follows that عُقْبَ or عُقُبَ in this sense is preferable.] One says, جِئْتُ فِى عُقْبِ ▼ شَهْرِ رَمَضَانَ, (Ṣ,) or ▼ عَلَى عُقْبِهِ, (O,) and ▼ عُقُبِهِ and ▼ فِى عُقْبَانِهِ, (L,) and ▼ عُقْبِهِ, (Ṣ, O,) meaning *I came when the whole of the month of Ramaḍán had passed:* (Ṣ, O, L:) and ▼ جِئْتُكَ عُقْبَ رَمَضَانَ *I came to thee at the end of Ramaḍán:* and ▼ جِئْتُ فُلَانًا عَلَى عُقْبِ مَرِّهِ and ▼ عُقْبِهِ and ▼ عُقْبَانِهِ and عَقِبِهِ *I came to such a one after he had gone:* and أَتَيْتُكَ عَلَى عُقْبِ ▼ ذَاكَ and ▼ عُقْبِ ذَاكَ and ▼ عُقْبَانِ ذَاكَ *I came to thee after that:* and ▼ جِئْتُهُ عُقْبَ قُدُومِهِ *I came to him after his arrival.* (Lḥ, TA.) One says also, فُلَانٌ يَسْتَقِى عَلَى عُقْبَةِ ▼ آلِ فُلَانٍ *Such a one draws water after the family of such a one.* (TA.) And MF mentions ▼ جِئْتُكَ عَلَى عَاقِبِهِ [app. meaning *I came to thee after him, or it*]: and Aboo-Mis-ḥal mentions [app. in this sense] ▼ عُقْبَانَهُ, with kesr. (TA.) —— عَقِبٌ (Ṣ, A, Mgh, O, Mṣb, Ḳ) and ▼ عَقْبٌ (Ṣ, O, Mṣb, Ḳ) also signify *The child,* or *children,* (Ṣ, A, O, Mṣb, Ḳ,) of a man; (Ṣ, O;) as also ▼ عَاقِبَةٌ: (Ṣ, O, Ḳ:) and the *child,* or *children, of the child* or *children,* (Ṣ, A, O, Mṣb, Ḳ,) of a man: (Ṣ, O:) applied to *such as remain after the father:* (TA:) or a man's *offspring;* (Mgh;) and so ▼ عَاقِبَةٌ: (Mṣb:) or his *male children:* and, accord. to some of the lawyers, the *children of the daughters* [of a man, also]: (Mgh:) of the fem. gender, on the authority of Akh: (Ṣ, O:) pl. أَعْقَابٌ. (TA.) The Arabs say, لَا عَقِبَ لَهُ, meaning *There is,* or *are, no male offspring remaining to him:* (TA:) and ▼ لَيْسَتْ لِفُلَانٍ عَاقِبَةٌ *There is,* or *are, to such a one, no* [*remaining*] *child,* or *children.* (Ṣ, O, Mṣb.) —— ▼ عَقْبٌ شَىْءٍ [or عَقْبُ شَىْءٍ] signifies *A thing,* whatever it be, *that follows, succeeds, comes after,* or *takes the place of, a thing;* as the water of a well, and the blowing of the wind, and the flying of the sand-grouse (القَطَا), and the running of a horse. (TA. [See also عَاقِبٌ.]) —— And عَقِبٌ, (IAạr, IF, A, Mṣb,) or ▼ عَقْبٌ, (Ṣ, Ḳ,) or, as Aṣ says, each of these, some of the Arabs using the latter form, by way of contraction, (Mṣb,) *A run after another run,* (Aṣ, IF, Ṣ, Mṣb, Ḳ,) of a horse: (Aṣ, IF, Ṣ, Mṣb:) or the *last,* or *latter, run,* of a horse: (IAạr, Mṣb:) or one says of a courser, هُوَ ذُو عَلْوٍ وَعَقِبٍ meaning *He has a first run, and a subsequent, and more vehement, run:* (A:) and ▼ عِقَابٌ is said in the L to have the first of these meanings: (TA:) or it is pl. of عَقْبٌ [or عَقِبٌ] as having that meaning: (Ḥam p. 358:) an ex. of it occurs in the following verse, (Ḥam, TA,) cited by IAạr: (TA:)

* يَمْلَأُ عَيْنَيْكَ بِالفِنَآءِ وَيُرْ *
* ضِيكَ عِقَابًا إِنْ شِئْتَ أَوْ نَزَقَا *

[*That would satisfy thine eye by his beauty, in the area before the dwelling, and content thee by run after run,* or *by runs after runs, if thou wilt,* or *by lightness,* or *agility*]: (Ḥam, TA:) [or it may be here an inf. n., (of 3,) meaning *on an occasion of being required to perform run after run:* (see 3, last sentence:)] or, accord. to IAạr, the meaning in this instance is, *by his owner's making, upon him, warring,* or *warring and plundering, expeditions time after time:* (TA:) accord. to Kh, لَهُ عِقَابٌ, said of a horse, means *he has a recovering of strength* (جمام [i. e. جَمَامٌ]) *after ceasing to run.* (Ḥam ubi suprà.) —— Hence, *A reply:* so in the saying, relating to him who stops, or breaks off, in speech, لَوْ كَانَ لَهُ عَقِبٌ تَكَلَّمَ [*If he had a reply, assuredly he would have spoken*]. (A, TA.) —— See also عُقْبَةٌ.

عُقُبٌ: see the next preceding paragraph, in six places.

عَقْبَةُ القَمَرِ i. q. عِقْبَةُ القَمَرِ, q. v. (L.) —— And عَقْبَةٌ and ▼ عِقْبَةٌ signify *Variegated,* or *figured, cloth:* (TA:) or *one of the sorts of variegated,* or *figured, cloths* [*that serve for the covering*] *of the* [*women's camel-vehicle called*] هَوْدَج: (O, Ḳ, TA:) as also عَقْمَةٌ: (O, TA:) accord. to Yaạḳoob, the ب is a substitute for م. (TA.)

عُقْبَةٌ: see عَقِبٌ, in three places. —— Also *The last that remains:* so in the saying, فُلَانٌ عُقْبَةُ بَنِى فُلَانٍ [*Such a one is the last that remains of the sons of such a one*]. (L.) —— And *A turn;* or *time at which,* or *during which, anything is,* or *is to be, done,* or *had, in succession:* (Ṣ, Mgh, O, Mṣb, Ḳ:) pl. عُقَبٌ. (Mṣb.) One says, تَمَّتْ عُقْبَتُكَ *Thy turn is completed.* (Ṣ, O.) And دَارَتْ عُقْبَةُ فُلَانٍ *The turn of such a one came round.* (TA.) And رَكِبَ عُقْبَةً *He rode one turn:* and رَكِبَ عُقْبَتَهُ *He rode his turn,* or *in his turn.* (TA.) And it is said in a trad., مَنْ مَشَى عَنْ دَابَّتِهِ عُقْبَةً فَلَهُ كَذَا *Whoso walks a turn to a certain point, instead of his beast, to him shall be given such a thing.* (TA.) عُقْبَةُ الأَجِيرِ means *The hired-man's turn to ride; when the hirer dismounts,* for example in the morning, *and he* (*the former*) *rides.* (Mgh.) And [the pl.] عُقَبٌ means [particularly] The *turns of camels, when they are being watered:* the watering of a number of camels together after another number is termed their عُقْبَة. (TA.) [See also عُقْبَى.] —— And [it is said that] it means also *Camels which a man pastures and waters in his turn;* and IAạr cites as an ex.

* إِنَّ عَلَىَّ عُقْبَةً أَقْضِيهَا *
* لَسْتُ بِنَاسِيهَا وَلَا مُنْسِيهَا *

[but this I would rather render, *Verily I have incumbent on me a turn* to pasture and water camels; *and I perform it; I am not a neglecter thereof nor a delayer of it*]; meaning I drive the camels which I pasture and water in my turn, and I tend them well: مُنْسِيهَا is for مُنْسِئُهَا, for the sake of the rhyme. (TA.) —— Also The *place in which one mounts a beast to ride* [app. *in his turn*]. (TA.) —— And The *distance,* or *space, of two leagues;* i. e. *twice the distance termed* فَرْسَخ: and the *distance to which one journeys* [app. *from one halting-place to the next;* i. e. *a stage of a journey*]: pl. as above: a poet says,

* خَوْدًا ضِنَاكًا لَا تَسِيرُ العُقَبَا *

[*Soft,* or *tender, heavy in the hinder part, that will not perform men's marches*]; meaning that she will not [or cannot] journey with men, because she will not endure the doing so on account of her soft and delicate life. (TA.) —— And The *distance,* or *space, between the ascending and descending* of a bird. (Ṣ, O, Ḳ.) —— And The *night* and the *day;* because they follow each other. (Ḳ.) —— And *A substitute;* or *thing that is given,* or *taken, in exchange for another thing;* (Ṣ, O, L, Ḳ;) as also ▼ عُقْبَى. (L, TA.) One says, أَخَذْتُ مِنْ أَسِيرِى عُقْبَةً *I took,* or *received, for my captive, a substitute,* or *something in exchange.* (Ṣ, O.) And ▼ سَأُعْطِيكَ مِنْهَا عُقْبَى occurs in a trad., meaning *I will give thee something in exchange* [*for her,* i. e.] for sparing her life, and liberating her. (L, TA.) — And *Pasture,* or *food,* of an ostrich, *that is eaten after other pasture* or *food:* [and likewise of camels: and of men:] pl. as above. (AA, Ṣ, O.) One says of camels, رَعَتْ عُقْبَتَهَا i. e. *They pastured upon the* [*kind of plants termed*] حَمْض *after the* [*kind termed*] خُلَّة; (A, L;) or *upon the* خُلَّة *after the* حَمْض: (L:) and of men one says, أَكَلُوا عُقْبَتَهُمْ *They ate their repast of sweetmeat after the other food.* (A, TA. [See 8, near the beginning.]) — And The *remains of the contents of a* cooking-pot, *adhering to the bottom.* (TA.) And *Somewhat of broth which the borrower of a cooking-pot returns when he returns the pot.* (Ṣ, O, Ḳ.) — [Hence,] أُمُّ عُقْبَةَ is an appellation of *The cooking-pot.* (T in art. امر.) أَبُو عُقْبَةَ is a surname of *The hog.* (Ḥar p. 663. [But the origin of this I know not.]) — One says also, لَقِيتُ مِنْهُ عُقْبَةَ الضَّبُعِ, meaning *I experienced from him,* or *it, difficulty:* [as though lit. signifying, *the result of the deed* that I had done:] and [simply] لَقِىَ مِنْهُ عُقْبَةً *He experienced from him,* or *it, difficulty.* (TA. [But in a copy of the A, and in my opinion correctly, the last word in this phrase is written ↓ عَقَبَةً: see عَقَبَةٌ, below.]) — And كُنْتُ مَرَّةً نُشْبَةً وَأَنَا اليَوْمَ عُقْبَةٌ, expl. by IAạr as meaning *I was such that, when I clung to a man, he experienced evil from me; but now I have reverted from being such, through weakness.* (TA. [It is a prov., somewhat differently related in art. نشب, q. v.]) — See also the next paragraph, in four places.

عِقْبَةٌ (Lḥ, Ṣ, O, Ḳ) and ↓ عُقْبَةٌ, (Lḥ, O, Ḳ,) but the former is the more approved, (Lḥ, TA,) and عقب, (so in the TA, [app., if not a mistranscription, ↓ عَقِبٌ,]) *A mark, sign, trace, impress, characteristic,* or *outward indication.* (Lḥ, Ṣ, O, Ḳ.) One says, عَلَيْهِ عِقْبَةُ السَّرْوِ, (Ṣ, O,) and ↓ عُقْبَتُهُ, (O,) and الجَمَالِ, (Ṣ, O,) i. e. *Upon him is the mark* &c. [*of generosity and manliness,* and *of beauty*]. (Ṣ, O, Ḳ.) — عِقْبَةُ القَمَرِ and ↓ عُقْبَةُ القَمَرِ mean *The return of the moon, when it has set,* or *disappeared, and then risen:* (L:) [or *the return of the moon after the change;* for] one says, مَا يَفْعَلُ ذٰلِكَ إِلَّا عِقْبَةَ القَمَرِ, (Ṣ,) or ↓ عُقْبَةَ القَمَرِ, (so in the O,) meaning *He does not that save once in each month:* (Ṣ, O:) but, accord. to IAạr, ↓ عُقْبَةُ القَمَرِ, with ḍamm, is *a certain star,* or *asterism, which is in conjunction with the moon once in the year;* and عُقْبَةَ القَمَرِ means *once in the year:* so in the following verse, of one of the Benoo-'Ámir:

• لَا يُطْعِمُ المِسْكَ وَالكَافُورَ لِمَّتَهُ •
• وَلَا الذَّرِيرَةَ إِلَّا عُقْبَةَ القَمَرِ •

[*He will not apply to his hair that descends below the ear musk and camphor, nor the perfume called* ذريرة, *save once in the year*]: or, as Lḥ relates it, عِقْبَةَ القمر: thus in the L; in which it is added that this saying of IAạr requires consideration, because the moon cuts [a meridian of] the celestial spheres once in every month: but MF replies that it may be in conjunction with the said star only once in the year, as the moon's path varies in each successive month. (TA. [See also عُقْبَةٌ.]) — See also عُقْبَةٌ.

عَقَبَةٌ [*A mountain-road;*] *a road in* [or *upon*] *a mountain:* (Bḍ in xc. 11:) or *a road in the upper part of a mountain:* (Ḥam p. 287:) or *a difficult place of ascent of the mountains:* (Ḳ:) or it is *in a mountain* and *the like thereof:* (Mṣb:) or [it sometimes signifies] *a long mountain that lies across the way, and over which the way therefore leads; long,* or *high, and very difficult; so called, too, when it is further impassable after it is ascended; rising high towards the sky, ascending and descending; most difficult of ascent; but sometimes its height is one* [or *uniform*]; *and its acclivity is in appearance like a wall:* (TA:) [generally it means *a road over,* or *up,* or *down,* or *over some part of, a mountain:*] pl. عِقَابٌ. (Ṣ, O, Mṣb, Ḳ.) اِقْتَحَمَ العَقَبَةَ [properly signifying *He attempted the mountain-road*] is metaphorically used as meaning *He entered upon a hard,* or *difficult, affair.* (Bḍ in xc. 11.) See also عُقْبَةٌ, near the end. — It is also n. un. of عَقَبٌ [q. v.]. (Ṣ, O.)

عُقْبَى: see عَقِبٌ, second quarter, in four places. — It occurs in a trad. respecting the prayer of fear; in which it is said of that prayer, كَانَتْ عُقْبَى [*It was an affair of turns*]; meaning that it was performed by one company after another; several companies performing it successively, by turns. (TA. [Compare عُقْبَةٌ as expl. in the third sentence of the paragraph on that word.]) — Also i. q. مرجع [app. مَرْجِعٌ i. e. *A returning,* &c.]. (TA.) — And The *requital,* or *recompence,* of an affair, or action. (Ṣ, O, Ḳ.) — See also عُقْبَةٌ, latter half, in two places.

عُقْبِىُّ الكَلَامِ i. q. عُقْمِىُّ الكَلَامِ, [the ب being app. a substitute for م,] i. e. *Obscure speech* or *language, which men do not know.* (TA in art. عقم.)

عُقْبَانٌ: see عَقِبٌ, in four places.

عِقْبَانٌ: see عَقِبٌ, in two places.

رَجُلٌ عِقِبَّانٌ *A rough, coarse,* or *rude, man;* syn. غَلِيظٌ: pl. عقبان [so in the TA, either عِقْبَانٌ or عُقْبَانٌ]: mentioned by Kr: but Az doubted its correctness. (TA.)

عُقَابٌ [The *eagle;*] *a certain bird,* (Ṣ, O, Ḳ,) *of those that prey,* (Mṣb,) *well known:* (Ḳ:) of the fem. gender: (Ṣ, O, Mṣb:) [though] applied to the *male* and the *female;* but with this distinction, that you say of the male, هٰذَا عُقَابٌ ذَكَرٌ [*This is a male eagle*]: or it is only *female;* and a bird of another kind couples with it; whence Ibn-'Oneyn says, satirizing a person named Ibn-Seyyideh, Say thou to Ibn-Seyyideh,

• مَا أَنْتَ إِلَّا كَالعُقَابِ فَأُمُّهُ •
• مَعْرُوفَةٌ وَلَهُ أَبٌ مَجْهُولُ •

[*"Thou art not other than the like of the eagle;" for his mother is known, but he has a father unknown*]: (MF, TA:) the pl. (of pauc., Ṣ, O) is أَعْقُبٌ, (Ṣ, O, Ḳ,) because it is of the fem. gender and the measure أَفْعُلٌ specially belongs to pls. of fem. nouns [though not to such exclusively], (Ṣ, O,) and أَعْقِبَةٌ, (Kr, TA,) and (of mult., Ṣ, O) عِقْبَانٌ (Ṣ, O, Ḳ) and عَقَابِيبُ accord. to AḤei, but Ed-Demámeenee thinks this to be strange; and pl. pl. عَقَابِينُ. (TA.) عِقْبَانُ الجِرْذَانِ [*The eagles that prey upon the large field-rats*] are not black, but of the colour termed كُهْبَة; and no use is made of their feathers, except that boys feather with them round-topped pointless arrows. (AḤn, TA.) — [Hence,] العُقَابُ is the name of † *One of the northern constellations,* [i. e. Aquila,] *the stars of which are nine within the figure, and six without, of the former of which are three well known, called* النَّسْرُ الطَّائِرُ [q. v.]. (Ḳzw.) — [Hence also,] † *The* عُقَاب *of the banner,* or *standard;* (Ṣ, O;) [app. meaning *the flag attached to a lance;*] *what is bound* [*to a lance*] *for a prefect,* or *governor;* likened to the bird so called; and of the fem. gender. (L, TA.) It is also the name of † *The banner,* or *standard, of the Prophet.* (O, Ḳ.) And عُقَابٌ also means † *A large banner* or *standard.* (TA.) And † i. q. غَايَةٌ: so in the saying of Aboo-Dhu-eyb, describing wine,

• لَهَا غَايَةٌ تَهْدِى الكِرَامَ عُقَابُهَا •

[meaning *It has a banner, which guides the generous;* like as the military banner guides and attracts warriors: for غَايَةٌ sometimes signifies a sign which the vintner used to set up to attract customers]: the repetition is approvable because of the difference of the two words in themselves: pl. عِقْبَانٌ. (TA.) — عُقَابٌ also signifies † *A black she-camel;* as being likened to the bird [so called]. (AA, O.) — And *A stone* (or *piece of rock,* L) *protruding in the inside of a well, which lacerates the* [*leathern*] *bucket;* (Ṣ, O, Ḳ, TA;) *sometimes it is before* [i. e. *above*] *the casing* [*of stones* or *bricks*]: *it is when a mass of stone becomes displaced; and sometimes the water-drawer stands upon it:* it is of the fem. gender: pl. as above. (TA.) And The *stone upon which the waterer stands,* (O, Ḳ,) [accord. to SM,] *projecting beyond the casing in a well,* the same that is meant in the next preceding sentence, (TA,) [but this I think doubtful, for Ṣgh adds,] *between two stones which support it.* (O.) Accord. to IAạr, the قَبِيلَة is a mass of stone, or rock, at the mouth of a well; and the عُقَابَانِ are [*two masses of stone*] *at the two sides of the* قبيلة, *supporting it.* (TA.) And *A rock,* or *mass of stone, projecting in the side of a mountain, like a stair,* or *series of steps:* (Ṣ, O, Ḳ:) or *an ascent, like stairs, in the side of a mountain.* (TA.) — Also *A hill;* syn. رَابِيَةٌ. (O, Ḳ.) And *Anything elevated, that is not very long* or *tall.* (O, Ḳ.*) — *A channel by which water flows to a trough,* or *tank.* (O, Ḳ.) — *A thing resembling an almond, that comes forth in one of the legs of a beast.* (O, Ḳ.) — *A small thread that enters into* [or *passes through*] *the two bores of the ring of the* قُرْط [or *ear-drop*], (O, Ḳ,*) *with which the* *latter is bound*, or *fastened:* (O:) or, accord. to Az, the *thread that binds the two extremities of the ring of the* قُرْط. (TA.) — Accord. to Th, it signifies also *Garments of the kind called* أَبْرَاد [pl. of بُرْد, q. v.]. (TA voce خُدَارِيَّةٌ.) — And accord. to Kr, [in the Munjid,] *i. q.* حَرْثٌ [app. meaning *A ploughshare*]. (TA.) — See also أَعْقَابٌ. — And العُقَابَانِ signifies *Two pieces of wood between which a man is extended to be flogged:* (L, TA:) or *two pieces of wood which are set up, stuck in the ground, between which he who is beaten, or he who is* [*to be*] *crucified, is extended.* (Mgh.)

عِقَابٌ: see عَقِبٌ, last quarter. — It is also pl. of عُقْبَةٌ [q. v.]. (Ṣ, &c.) — See also أَعْقَابٌ.

عُقُوبٌ: see عَاقِبٌ, near the end.

عَقِيبٌ *Anything that is a sequent*, of, or to, another thing; [*in an absolute sense,*] (Ṣ, Mṣb, TA,) *as when you say,* السَّلَامُ عَقِيبُ التَّشَهُّدِ [*The salutation is a sequent to the* تشهّد (q. v.)], and العِدَّةُ عَقِيبُ الطَّلَاقِ [*The* عدّة (q. v.) *is a sequent to divorcement*], i. e., one follows the other; (Mṣb;) and [*by alternation,*] *as when one says of the night and the day,* كُلُّ وَاحِدٍ مِنْهُمَا عَقِيبُ صَاحِبِهِ [*Each of them is the alternating sequent of its correlative*]: (Az, Mṣb, TA:) you say of the night and the day, هُمَا عَقِيبَانِ [*They are two alternating sequents*]; and عَقِيبُكَ signifies *He who does a deed, or work, with thee by turn, he doing it one time and thou another:* (A,* TA:) and ▼ مُعَاقِبٌ signifies the same, (Ṣ, Mṣb,) as also [▼ مُعْقِبٌ and ▼ مُعْتَقِبٌ and] ▼ مُعَقِّبٌ. (Mṣb.) As for the saying of the lawyers, يَفْعَلُ ذٰلِكَ عَقِيبَ الصَّلَاةِ [meaning *He does that after the prayer*], and the like thereof, there is no reason to be given but a suppression; the meaning being, فِى وَقْتٍ عَقِيبِ وَقْتِ الصَّلَاةِ [*in a time following that of prayer*], عقيب being an epithet qualifying وقت: (Mṣb:) and Er-Rázee says, in the Mukhtár eṣ-Ṣiḥáḥ, that he had found no authority in the T nor in the Ṣ for the phrase جَآءَ عَقِيبَهُ meaning *He came after him.* (TA.) See also عَقِبٌ, first sentence. [And compare عَاقِبٌ.]

عُقُوبَةٌ *Punishment;* (Ṣ,* MA, Mṣb,* KL;) *i. q.* نَكَالٌ. (MA.) — And *Detention, confinement*, or *imprisonment:* so in the trad., لَىُّ الوَاجِدِ يُحِلُّ عُقُوبَتَهُ وَعِرْضَهُ i. e. [*The solvent man's putting off the payment of his debt with promises repeated time after time renders allowable*] *the imprisoning of him and the accusing of him.* (IAạr, TA. [Accord. to one relation, mentioned in the TA in art. عرض, this trad. ends with وَعَرْضَهُ, there said to mean وَنَفْسَهُ.])

عُقَّيْبٌ, with teshdeed of the ى, (O,) or عُقَيْبٌ, like قُبَيْطٌ, (Ḳ,) *A certain bird,* (O, Ḳ,) *well known.* (O.) [If the name be correctly as in the O, the bird meant is probably *an eaglet*, or *a small species of eagle.*]

عُقَابٌ عَقَنْبَاةٌ, and عَبَنْقَاةٌ, and بَعَنْقَاةٌ, (Ṣ, O, Ḳ,) and قَعَنْبَاةٌ, (O,) and عَبَنْقَاةٌ, (Ḳ in art عبق,) the vars. of the first being formed by transposition, (O,) *An* عُقَاب [or *eagle*] *having sharp talons:* (Ṣ, O, Ḳ:) or *having abominable*, or *hideous, talons:* (T, TA:) or *quick in seizing, and abominable*, or *hideous:* accord. to IAạr, the epithet denotes intensiveness of quality, as in the cases of كَلْبٌ كَلِبٌ and أَسَدٌ أَسِدٌ: accord. to Lth, عَقَنْبَاةٌ applied to an عُقَاب signifies *cunning:* and the pl. is عَقَنْبَيَاتٌ. (TA.) [See also art. عبق.]

عَاقِبٌ [act. part. n. of عَقَبَ;] *Coming after* [&c.]. (Mṣb.) عَاقِبُ شَىْءٍ means *Any person* [or *thing*] *that comes after*, or *succeeds*, or *comes in the place of, a thing.* (Ṣ, O, TA.) العَاقِبُ is an appellation applied to the Prophet (Ṣ, O, Mṣb) by himself (Ṣ, O) because he came after other prophets, (Mṣb,) meaning *The last of the prophets,* (Ṣ, O.) And عَاقِبٌ لِٱمْرَأَةٍ means *One who is the last of the husbands of a woman.* (TA.) — [Hence,] عَاقِبَةٌ مِنْ طَيْرٍ *Birds succeeding one another, this alighting and flying, and then another alighting in the place where the former alighted.* (TA.) And إِبِلٌ عَاقِبَةٌ *Camels that betake themselves to plentiful pasture where they feed freely, after eating of the* [*kind of plants called*] حَمْض: [or] they are not so called unless they be *camels that, in a severe year, eat of trees, and then of the* حمض; not when they pasture upon fresh, juicy, or tender, herbage. (IAạr, TA.) And إِبِلٌ عَوَاقِبُ *Camels that drink water, and then return to the place where they lie down by the water, and then go to the water again.* (IAạr, Ṣ, O, Ḳ.) — And عَاقِبٌ signifies also *A successor* of another *in goodness*, or *beneficence;* and so ▼ عُقُوبٌ. (O, Ḳ.) — And *A chief*, or *lord:* or *one who is below the chief* or *lord:* (TA:) or the *successor of the chief* or *lord.* (Ṣ, Ḳ.) — See also عَقِبٌ, in two places.

عَاقِبَةٌ a quasi-inf. n.: see 1, first quarter. — See also عَقِبٌ, in four places.

أَعْقَابٌ pl. of عَقِبٌ [q. v.]. (Mṣb, TA.) — And [hence] *Streaks, one behind another;* as streaks of fat so disposed. (TA.) — And *Pottery* [or *potsherds*] *put between the bricks in the casing of a well, in order that it may become strong;* said by Kr to have no sing.: (TA:) [or,] accord. to IAạr, ▼ عِقَابٌ, i. e. like كِتَابٌ, (TA,) or ▼ عُقَابٌ, (thus written in the O,) signifies *pottery* [or *potsherds*] *between the rows*, or *courses, of bricks,* (O,* TA,) *in the casing of a well.* (O.) [IAạr cites an ex., in a verse, in which اعقاب would not be admissible.] And أَعْقَابُ الطَّىِّ signifies *What surround the casing of a well;* i. e. *what are behind it.* (TA. [See 4, latter half.])

[تَعْقِيبَةٌ a modern word signifying *A catchword at the bottom of a page:* pl. تَعَاقِيبُ.]

مُعْقَبٌ [appears, from what here follows, to be used for مُعْقَبٌ حَالُهُ i. e. *One whose state is changed*]. IAạr cites as an ex. of this word,

* كُلُّ حَيٍّ مُعْقَبٌ عُقَبَا *

meaning [*Every living being*] *comes to a state different from that in which he was* [*by turns*, or *time after time*]. (TA.)

مُعْقِبٌ [accord. to the O, مُعْقَبٌ, but this I think a mistranscription,] *A star that succeeds,* i. e. *rises after, another star,* (Ṣ, Ḳ, TA,) *and on the rising of which, he who rides in his turn, after another, mounts the beast:* (TA:) *a star at the appearance of which two persons who ride by turns during a journey take each the other's place; when one star sets and another rises, he who was walking mounts the beast.* (AO.) See عَقِيبٌ. — See also 4, latter half; where an ex. occurs in a verse.

مُعَقَّبٌ He *who is brought up for the office of Khaleefeh after the* [*actual*] *Imám* [or *Khaleefeh*]. (O, Ḳ.) — And *A skilful driver.* (O, Ḳ.) — And A camel *that is ridden by different persons in turns.* (O,* TA.) — And *A woman's* خِمَار [i. e. *muffler*, or *head-covering*]; (IAạr, O,* Ḳ, TA;) so called because it takes the place of the مُلَآءَة. (O, TA.) — And *An ear-drop;* syn. قُرْطٌ. (O, Ḳ.)

مُعَقِّبٌ One *who is made to go forth,* (so in the CḲ,) or *who goes forth,* (O, and so in my MS. copy of the Ḳ,) *from the shop of the vintner when a greater man than he enters.* (O, Ḳ.) — جَآءَ مُعَقِّبًا *He came at the end*, or *close, of the day.* (TA.) — قِدْحٌ مُعَقِّبٌ *An arrow which* [*in the game called* المَيْسِر] *is returned into the* رِبَابَة [q. v.] *time after time;* the prize allotted to which is hoped for. (TA.) — جَزُورٌ سَحُوفُ المُعَقِّبِ *A fat slaughtered camel.* (TA.) — نَعْلٌ مُعَقَّبَةٌ *A sandal having an* عَقِب [q. v.]. (O, TA.)

مُعَقِّبٌ *Coming after*, or *near after, another thing.* (O.) See عَقِيبٌ. — It is said that it is applied as an epithet to an angel; that one says مَلَكٌ مُعَقِّبٌ [meaning *An angel that follows another*]; and مَلَائِكَةٌ مُعَقِّبَةٌ; and that مُعَقِّبَاتٌ is a pl. pl. (O.) المُعَقِّبَاتُ means *The angels of the night and the day;* (Ṣ, O, Ḳ;) because they succeed one another by turns; and the fem. form is used because of the frequency of their doing so, in like manner as it is in the words نَسَّابَةٌ and عَلَّامَةٌ: (Ṣ, O:) *the angels called* الحَفَظَةُ [pl. of حَافِظٌ, q. v.]: so in the Ḳur xiii. 12: in which some of the Arabs of the desert read مَعَاقِيبُ: (TA:) this [may be an anomalous pl. of عَقِيبٌ, like as مَهَاجِينُ is of هَجِينٌ, or it] is pl. of مُعَقِّبٌ or of مُعَقِّبَةٌ, the ى being to compensate for the suppression of one of the two قs. (Bḍ.) — المُعَقِّبَاتُ also signifies *The she-camels that stand behind those that are pressing towards the watering-trough, or tank; so that when one she-camel goes away, another comes in her place.* (Ṣ, O, Ḳ.) — And *The ejaculations of* سُبْحَانَ ٱللّٰهِ, *which follow one another*, (O, Ḳ,) *repeated at the end of the ordinary prayer, thirty-three in number, and which are followed by* اَلْحَمْدُ لِلّٰهِ *thirty-three times, and* اللّٰهُ أَكْبَرُ *thirty-four times.* (O.) — And مُعَقِّبٌ signifies also One *who makes repeatedly warring*, or *warring and plundering, expeditions*; and *who journeys repeatedly, and does not stay with his family after his return.* (TA.) — And One *who seeks after a thing repeatedly, striving*, or *exerting himself*: (Ṣ, O:) one *who follows after a thing that is his due, demanding restitution of it*: or one *who follows close after a man, for something that is his due*: one *who seeks to recover his right*, or *due*: and one *who, being despoiled of all his property in a hostile attack, makes a hostile attack upon him from whom he has thus suffered, and endeavours to recover his property.* (TA.) Lebeed says, describing a [wild] he-ass and his female,

حَتَّى تَهَجَّرَ بِالرَّوَاحِ وَهَاجَهَا
طَلَبَ المُعَقِّبِ حَقَّهُ المَظْلُومُ

(Ṣ, O, but in the latter فِى الرَّوَاحِ,) i. e. [*Until he went along in the midday heat,* (بالرواح or فى الرواح being redundant,)] *and drove her on* [by a pursuit] *like the seeking of him who is making repeated efforts, having been wronged, to obtain his due*: (O:) المظلوم is an epithet qualifying المعقّب, and is in the nom. case agreeably with the meaning, (Ṣ, O,) because it is put after its proper place; (O;) and المعقّب is literally in the gen. case, but as to the meaning is an agent: (Ṣ, O:*) or, accord. to some, المعقّب [here] signifies *the debtor who puts off the payment of his debt*; so that المظلوم is an agent and المعقّب is an objective complement: (Ṣ:) or, as some say, المعقّب signifies *he who demands the payment of a debt and repeats his demand thereof.* (TA.) — Also Any one *returning* [app. to the doing of a thing]. (O.) — See also مُعَاقِبٌ. — لَا مُعَقِّبَ لِحُكْمِهِ, in the Ḳur [xiii. 41], means *There is no repeller of his decree.* (TA.) — Also A man *who descends into a well to raise a stone of the kind called* عُقَاب. (TA.) [See also the verb.]

مِعْقَابٌ A woman *who usually brings forth a male after a female.* (Ṣ, O, Ḳ.) — And *A chamber* (بَيْت) *in which raisins are put.* (Ḳ.)

مُعَاقِبٌ: see عَقِيبٌ, with which it is syn. — [Hence,] إِبِلٌ مُعَاقِبَةٌ *Camels that eat one time*, or *turn, of the* [*kind of plants called*] حَمْض, *and another of the* [*kind called*] خُلَّة. (Ṣ, O, Ḳ.) — And نَخْلَةٌ مُعَاقِبَةٌ *A palm-tree that bears fruit one year, and fails to do so another.* (TA.) — And مُعَاقِبٌ also signifies *A revenger of blood*: a poet, cited by IAạr, says,

وَنَحْنُ قَتَلْنَا بِالمَخَارِقِ فَارِسًا
جَزَآءَ العُطَاسِ لَا يَمُوتُ المُعَاقِبُ

meaning [*And we slew, in El-Makhárik*, (app. the name of a place,) *a horseman*,] taking our blood-revenge quickly, *in the time that elapses between a sneeze and the prayer for the sneezer* [which is usually "God have mercy on thee"]: the memory of *the blood-revenger shall not die.* (TA. [It is there also said that العقب (app. a mistranscription for ▼المُعْقِب, as may be conjectured from the fact that the م after the article is often indistinctly written, and inferred on other grounds,) is syn. with المُعَاقِب as here explained.])

مُعْتَقِبٌ: see 8: = and see also 5, last sentence.

مُعْتَقَبٌ: see عَقِيبٌ.

مُتَعَقِّبٌ: see 5, former half, in two places.

يَعْقُوبُ, perfectly decl., because it is an Arabic word, not altered, and, although having an augmentative letter at the beginning, not of the measure of a verb; whereas يعقوب as a proper name of foreign origin is imperfectly decl.; (Ṣ, O;) The حَجَل [or *partridge*]: (Ḳ:) or the *male of the* حَجَل; (Ṣ, O, Mṣb;) or *of the* قَبْج; (Lḥ, Mgh;) but ISd says, I know not whether Lḥ mean by this the حَجَل or the قَطَا or the كَرَوَان, nor do I know that the قبج is the same as the حَجَل: (TA:) and the *male of the* قَطَا [or *sand-grouse*]: (TA:) pl. يَعَاقِيبُ. (Ṣ, Mgh, O, Mṣb.) كَأَنَّكُمْ يَعَاقِيبُ الحَجَلِ, occurring in a trad., means [*As though ye were the males of partridges*] in your haste, and your flying into destruction: for they are such that, when they see the female in the possession of the fowler, they throw themselves upon him, so as to fall into his hand. (Z, TA in art. ركب.) — And accord. to some, (TA,) the pl. also signifies *Horses*: they being thus termed as being likened to the يعاقيب of the حَجَل, (O, TA,) because of their swiftness: (TA:) so in the phrase رَكْضُ اليَعَاقِيبِ [*As the running of the horses*, or *of the swift horses*]; in a verse of Selámeh Ibn-Jendel: (O, TA:) but others say that the meaning [here] is, *the males of the* حَجَل. (TA.) It is said in the L that فَرَسٌ يَعْقُوبٌ means *A horse that has a run after another run* [or *the power of repeating his running*] (ذُو عَقِبٍ [or عَقِبٍ]). (TA.) — J has cited [in the Ṣ] the words of a poet,

عَالٍ يُقَصِّرُ دُونَهُ اليَعْقُوبُ

[*High*, so that *the* يعقوب *falls short of reaching it*] as an ex. of the last word meaning *the male of the* حَجَل: but IB says that it appears to mean in this case *the male of the* عُقَاب [or *eagle*]; like as اليُرْخُومُ means the male of the رَخَم; and اليَخْبُورُ, the male of the حُبَارَى; for the حَجَل is not known to have so high a flight: and El-Farezdaḳ describes يَعَاقِيب as congregating with vultures over the slain. (TA.)

اليَعْقُوبِيَّةُ [a coll. gen. n., n. un. يَعْقُوبِىٌّ,] the name of *A sect of the* خَوَارِج, *followers of Yaạḳoob Ibn-'Alee El-Koofee.* (TA.) — And *A sect of the Christians; the followers of Yaạḳoob El-Barádi'ee* [or *Jacobus Baradæus*], *who assert the unity of the divine and human natures* [*in the person of Christ*], *and who are the most unbelieving and stubborn of the Christians*: so says El-Maḳreezee, in one of his tracts. (TA.)

عقد

1\. عَقَدَ الحَبْلَ, (Ṣ, Mgh, L, Mṣb, Ḳ, &c.,) aor. ـِ, (L, Mṣb, Ḳ,) inf. n. عَقْدٌ (Mgh, L, Mṣb) and تَعْقَادٌ [of which see an ex. in a verse cited voce وَتَرٌ, and which is properly an intensive or a frequentative form]; and ▼عقّدهُ [which is also intensive or frequentative, inf. n. تَعْقِيدٌ]; and ▼اعتقدهُ; (L;) *He tied the cord*, or *rope*; *knit it*; *complicated it so as to form a knot* or *knots*; *tied it in a knot* or *knots*; *tied it firmly, fast*, or *strongly*; *contr. of* حَلَّهُ; (L;) syn. شَدَّهُ: (Ḳ:) the etymologists assert that the primary signification of عَقْدٌ is the contr. of حَلٌّ: that it was afterwards used in relation to sales, or bargains, contracts, &c.: and then, in relation to a firm determination of the mind. (MF.) [عَقَدَ لَهُ لِوَآءً *He tied for him a banner*, to a spear, is said of a man on appointing him to a command.] And one says, عَقَدَ حَبْلَهُ meaning † *He exerted and prepared himself for action &c.*: and لَا يَعْقِدُ الحَبْلَ † *He is incompetent*, or *lacks power* or *ability, to do a thing, by reason of his abject state.* (L.) — عَقَدَ البَيْعَ, and العَهْدَ, (Ṣ, L, Mṣb,* Ḳ, &c.,) and اليَمِينَ, (L, Mṣb,) aor. as above, (L, Ḳ,) inf. n. عَقْدٌ; (L;) and ▼عقّد العَهْدَ, (L,) and اليَمِينَ, (L, Mṣb,) which latter form of the verb has a more energetic signification; (Mṣb;) *He concluded, settled, confirmed*, or *ratified, the sale*, or *bargain*, and *the contract, compact, covenant, agreement*, or *league*, (L, Mṣb, Ḳ,) and *the oath.* (L, Mṣb.) In the phrase وَالَّذِينَ عَقَدَتْ, or ▼عَقَّدَتْ, or ▼عَاقَدَتْ, أَيْمَانُكُمْ, accord. to different readings, in the Ḳur [iv. 37], by the verb is meant ratification; and by ايمانكم, your oaths, or your right hands: (L:) [i. e., accord. to the first and second readings, the meaning is, *And those* whose contracts, or the like, (عُهُودُهُمْ being understood,) *your oaths*, or *your right hands, have ratified*: and accord. to the third reading, *and those* with whom (هُمْ being understood) *your oaths*, or *your right hands have ratified* a contract, or the like.] One says also, عَقَدَ عَلَيْهِمْ عُقُودًا *He imposed upon them obligations.* (L.) And عَقَدَ الجِزْيَةَ فِى عُنُقِهِ *He imposed upon himself the obligation to pay the* [*tax called*] جِزْيَة. (L, from a trad.) And عَقَدْتُ عَلَيْهِ فِى كَذَا, and ▼عَاقَدْتُهُ فى كذا, *I obliged him to do such a thing, by taking*, or *exacting, from him an engagement*, or *a security.* (L.) عَقَدَ قَلْبَهُ عَلَى الشَّىْءِ [*He settled*, or *determined, his heart*, or *mind, firmly upon the thing*; (see the first sentence of this art.; and see also عَزَمَ;)] *he held, adhered*, or *clave, to the thing* [*with his heart*, or *mind; he knit his heart to it*]. (L.) See also 8. — عَقَدَتْ بِذَنَبِهَا, said of a she-camel, (Ṣ, O, L,) *She twisted her tail, as though tying it in a knot*: (L:) this she does to make it known that she has conceived. (Ṣ, O, L.) — عَقَدَ لِحْيَتَهُ *He dressed his beard* *so as to make it knotted, and crisp,* or *curly:* this they used to do in wars, and their doing so was forbidden by the Prophet: (O, L:) they did it from a motive of pride and self-conceit. (L.) —— عَقَدَ نَاصِيَتَهُ [lit. *He knotted his forelock*] means † *he was angry, and prepared himself to do evil,* or *mischief.* (A, O, L.) [See 2.] —— عَقَدَ عُنُقَهُ إِلَيْهِ † *He had recourse, betook himself,* or *repaired, to him, for refuge,* or *protection;* (O, L, Ḳ;*) heard by Is-ḥáḳ Ibn-Faraj from an Arab of the desert: (L:) and so عَكَدَهَا. (O.) —— عَقَدَ, (Ḳ,) or عَقَدَ بِأَصَابِعِهِ, (O,) or عَقَدَ الحِسَابَ, (MA,) aor. ِ, (O, TA,) inf. n. عَقْدٌ, (TA,) *He numbered, counted,* or *reckoned,* (M, A, O, Ḳ,) *with his fingers* [*by bending their tips down upon the palm, one after another, commencing with the little finger, and then by extending them in like manner*]. (MA, O.) —— عَقَدَ فَمُ الفَرْجِ عَلَى المَآءِ [*The mouth of the vulva closed upon the sperma* of the male]. (O.) —— عُقِدَتِ السِّبَاعُ † *The beasts,* or *birds, of prey were restrained from injuring the cattle,* and *the like, by means of charms* and *talismans.* (L, from a trad.) —— عَقَدَ التَّاجَ فَوْقَ رَأْسِهِ, and ↓ اعتقدهُ, *He put the crown upon his head.* (L.) —— عَقَدَ البِنَآءَ, (A, L,) [aor. ِ,] inf. n. عَقْدٌ; (L;) and ↓ عقّدهُ, (A, O, L, Ḳ,) inf. n. تَعْقِيدٌ; (L;) *He arched* [or *vaulted*] *the building,* or *structure.* (A, O, L, Ḳ.) —— And عَقَدَ البِنَآءَ بِالجِصِّ, aor. ِ, inf. n. عَقْدٌ, *He cemented the building,* or *structure, with gypsum.* (L.) —— عَقَدَ ثَمَرَهُ, said of a plant, (M in art. ثمر,) or ↓ عقّدهُ, (Ḳ in that art., [in the CḲ عَقَدَ ثَمَرَهُ,]) and عَقَدَ alone, (A, O, Ḳ, in art. حبل, [see 4 in that art. and also in art. علف,]) [*It organized and compacted,* or *compactly organized, its fruit;* and in like manner each verb is said of a fruit in relation to a fruit-stone, such as that of a date, and of a peach, &c.]. —— لَا تَعْقِدُ عَلَيْهِ السَّائِمَةُ شَحْمًا وَلَا لَحْمًا [*The pasturing cattle will not make upon it fat nor flesh*], said of a pasturage. (O in art. ضرع.) —— عَقَدَ الشَّحْمُ *The fat became formed and compacted, and became apparent.* (L.) —— عَقَدَ, (Ṣ, M, A, L, [in the O عَقُدَ, which is app. a mistranscription,]) aor. ِ, (M, L,) inf. n. عُقُودٌ; (A;) and ↓ تعقّد; (Ks, Ṣ, O, L, Ḳ;) and ↓ انعقد; (M, A, L;) said of rob, (Ks, Ṣ, O, M, A,) and of tar, (Ks, Ṣ, O,) and of honey, (M, A, O,) and of expressed juice of fresh ripe dates, (Ḳ,) and the like, (Ks, Ṣ, M, O,) [generally meaning when boiled,] *It thickened; became thick,* or *inspissated.* (Ks, Ṣ, M, A, O, L, Ḳ.) —— [Hence, app.,] عَقَدَ بَطْنُهُ [*His belly became constipated*]. (M voce ضَرِبَ, q. v.) —— عَقِدَتْ, said of a bitch, (TḲ,) [aor. َ,] inf. n. عَقَدٌ, (O, L, Ḳ,) *Her vulva clung fast to the head of the* قَضِيب *of the dog.* (O, L, Ḳ, TḲ.) —— عَقِدَ, said of the tongue, (Ṣ, O, Ḳ,*) aor. َ, (Ṣ, [in the O ِ, an evident mistake,]) inf. n. عَقَدٌ, (Ṣ, O,) *It had in it an impediment.* (Ṣ,* O,* L, Ḳ.*) And, said of a man, *He had an impediment in his tongue; was unable to speak freely; was tongue-tied.* (TA.) —— Also, said of sand, *It became moistened in consequence of much rain* [*so as to cohere*]. (L.)

2: see 1, first sentence. [Hence,] عَقَّدُوا النَّوَاصِىَ [*They tied the forelocks* of their horses *in knots*] on an occasion of war, or battle; it being customary on such an occasion to do thus to the hair of the mane and that of the tail. (W p. 140.) —— See again 1, former half, in two places: —— and latter half also in two places. —— See also 4. —— عقّد كَلَامَهُ *He rendered his speech,* or *language, obscure.* (A, L.) And فِى كَلَامِهِ تَعْقِيدٌ *In his speech,* or *language, is obscurity.* (A.)

3. عَاقَدْتُهُ عَلَى كَذَا, (Mṣb,) inf. n. مُعَاقَدَةٌ, (Ṣ, O, L,) *I united with him in a contract, a compact, a covenant, an agreement, a league, a treaty,* or *an engagement,* or *I covenanted with him, respecting,* or *to do, such a thing.* (Ṣ,* O,* L,* Mṣb.) —— See also 1, former half, in two places.

4. اعقدهُ; (Ks, Ṣ, M, A, O, Ḳ;) and ↓ عقّدهُ, (Ṣ, O, L, Ḳ,) inf. n. تَعْقِيدٌ; (Ṣ, O, Ḳ;) but the former is the more approved, (L,) *He thickened it; caused it to become thick,* or *inspissated;* (Ks, Ṣ, M, A, O, Ḳ;) *by boiling it;* (O, Ḳ;) namely, rob, (Ks, Ṣ, O, M, L,) and tar, (Ks, Ṣ, O,) and honey, (M, A, O,) and the like. (Ks, Ṣ, M, O.)

5. تعقّد: see 7, first sentence. —— See also 8, last quarter. —— تَعَقَّدَتْ قَوْسُ قُزَحَ *The rainbow became like a constructed arch* (O, L, Ḳ) in the sky. (O, L.) And in like manner تعقّد is said of a collection of clouds (سَحَاب). (A, L.) —— تَعَقُّدٌ in a well is The *projecting of the lower part of the interior casing of stone, and the receding of the upper part thereof as far as the* اِتِّسَاع *of the well,* (O, L, Ḳ,) *which is its* جِرَاب [app. here meaning *the main portion of the well, from the water,* or *a little above this, to the mouth;* this portion, it seems, being without casing]: (O, L:) thus expl. by El-Aḥmar. (O.) —— تعقّد said of sand, [as also ↓ انعقد, (Ṣ and O and Ḳ voce سَلَاسِلُ,)] *It became accumulated,* or *congested.* (Ṣ, Ḳ.*) And the former said of moist earth, *It became contracted, and compacted in lumps.* (L.) —— And تَعَقَّدَتِ القَرْحَةُ [*The wound,* or *ulcer, formed itself into a knot,* or *lump*]. (Ḳ in art. جرد: see 1 in that art.) —— تعقّد said of rob, and of tar, and the like: see 1, last quarter.

6. تعاقدوا *They united in a contract, a compact, a covenant, an agreement, a league, a treaty,* or *an engagement,* (Ṣ, O, Ḳ,) فِيمَا بَيْنَهُمْ [*respecting the matter between them*]. (Ṣ, O.) —— تَعَاقَدَتِ الكِلَابُ *The dogs stuck fast together in coupling.* (Ṣ, O, Ḳ.)

7. انعقد, said of a cord, or rope, (Ṣ, O, L, Mṣb,) as also ↓ تعقّد, (Ṣ,* O,* L,) [but the latter has an intensive or a frequentative signification,] *It became tied, knit, complicated so as to form a knot* or *knots, tied in a knot* or *knots, tied firmly* or *fast* or *strongly.* (L.) —— And the former, said of a sale or bargain, and of a contract or compact or the like, (Ṣ, O, L,) *It was,* or *became, concluded, settled, confirmed,* or *ratified.* (L.) One says, انعقد النِّكَاحُ بَيْنَ الزَّوْجَيْنِ *The marriage was,* or *became, concluded, settled,* &c., *between the husband and wife.* (L.) —— Said of an animal's tail, *It became twisted* [*as though tied in a knot*]. (L.) —— And said of hair, *It became knotted, and crisp,* or *curly.* (L.) —— Said of the date [and other fruit, *It became organized and compact,* or *compactly organized*]. (Ḳ in art. بسر, &c.) See also 8, latter half. —— Said of sand: see 5. —— And said of rob, and of tar, and the like: see 1, last quarter.

8. اعتقدهُ: see 1, first sentence: —— and see also 1 in the latter half. —— اعتقد كَذَا, (Mṣb,) or اعتقد كَذَا بِقَلْبِهِ, (Ṣ, O,) *He settled,* or *determined, his heart,* or *mind, firmly upon such a thing;* or *he held, adhered,* or *clave, to such a thing with the heart,* or *mind;* i. q. عَقَدَ ↓ عَلَيْهِ القَلْبَ وَالضَّمِيرَ; (Mṣb;) [*he believed,* or *believed firmly,* or *was firmly persuaded of, such a thing;* this is its most usual meaning;] *he was,* or *became, certain,* or *sure, of such a thing.* (PṢ.) [It is mostly used in relation to matters of religion, to religious dogmas and the like.] See also عَقِيدَةٌ. —— اعتقد also signifies *He acquired,* (Ṣ, Mgh, O, L, Ḳ,) or *bought,* (A,) an estate consisting of land, or of land and a house, &c., (Ṣ, A, O, L, Ḳ,) or other property: (Ṣ, A, Mgh, O, L, Ḳ:) *he collected* property. (Mgh,* Mṣb.) Also, [without any objective complement expressed,] *He bought what is termed* عُقْدَةٌ, i. e. *an estate,* or *a property, consisting in land* or *houses.* (L.) —— And اعتقد أَخًا فِى ٱللّٰهِ *He adopted a brother in God.* (A.) —— اعتقد الدُّرَّ, and الخَرَزَ, *He made the pearls,* and *the beads, into a necklace;* and in like manner, other things. (L.) —— اعتقد said of a date-stone, (A,) or other thing, (Ṣ, O, L,) [as also ↓ انعقد, which frequently occurs in the lexicons &c. in the sense here following,] *It became hard.* (Ṣ, A, O, L.) —— And hence, [so in the A,] اعتقد بَيْنَهُمَا الإِخَآءُ *Fraternity became true,* or *sincere, and firmly established, between them two:* (A:) and [in like manner] ↓ تعقّد *it* (i. e. fraternity) *became firmly established.* (L.) —— And accord. to Ibn-Buzurj, اعتقد signifies *He* (a man) *closed,* or *locked, a door upon himself, when in want, that he might die:* (O:) thus Sh found in the Book of Ibn-Buzurj, i. e. اعتقد, with ق: (TA in art. عفد:) but others say that it is اعتفد, with ف: (O:) [or] اعتقد and اعتفد signify the same. (Ḳ.)

10. استعقدت *She* (a sow) *desired the male.* (O, Ḳ.)

عَقْدٌ [as an inf. n.: see 1. —— See also أُعْقُدَةٌ, which is syn. with the inf. n. تَأْكِيدٌ. —— As a simple subst.,] see عُقْدَةٌ, third sentence. —— Also *A contract, a compact, a covenant, an agreement, a league, a treaty,* or *an engagement:* (Mgh, O, L, Ḳ:) pl. عُقُودٌ. (O, L.) Agreeably with this explanation, the pl. is used in the Ḳur v. 1, as meaning *Contracts,* &c.: or it there means the *obligatory statutes,* or *ordinances, of God:* or, accord. to Zj, *the covenants imposed by God,* and *those imposed mutually by men agreeably with the requirements of religion.* (L.) And ▼ مُعَاقِدُ is used in the sense of عُقُودٌ: thus one says, بَيْنَهُمْ مَعَاقِدُ [*Between them are contracts, compacts,* &c.]. (A.) — Also *Responsibility, accountableness,* or *suretiship*; syn. ضَمَانٌ. (Ibn-'Arafeh, O, Ḳ.) — See also مَعْقُودٌ. — Also *An arch*; [and *a vault*;] *a structure that is curved in like manner as are* [*in many instances*] *doorways*: (A,* O, L,* Ḳ:) pl. عُقُودٌ (A, O, L, Ḳ) and أَعْقَادٌ [a pl. of pauc.]. (L.) [Hence,] أَعْقَادُ السَّحَابِ *The arches of the clouds*: sing. عَقْدٌ. (L.) — Applied to a he-camel, it means *Having the back firmly compacted*: (Ṣ, O, Ḳ:) and so ▼ مَعْقُودَةُ القَرَا applied to a she-camel. (Ṣ, A, O.) — [And *A decimal number*; of those numbers of which the first is ten and the last is ninety: (I have not found any satisfactory authority for the orthography of the word in this sense; and have therefore followed the general usage, in mentioning it as عَقْدٌ: in the MA, it is written عِقْدٌ, as from only one MS.; and Freytag has mentioned its pl. under عِقْدٌ; which I hold to be wrong:) the pl. is عُقُودٌ: thus in the A and Ḳ in art. عشر, it is said that العَشَرَةُ is the first of the عُقُود.]

عِقْدٌ *A necklace*; (Ṣ, O, Mṣb, Ḳ;) *a string upon which beads are strung*: (L, TA:) pl. عُقُودٌ: (O, L, Mṣb, Ḳ:) and ▼ مِعْقَادٌ signifies *a string upon which beads are strung and which is hung upon the neck of a boy*; (O, L, Ḳ;) as does عِقْدٌ also: (TA:) and ▼ عُقْدَةٌ, likewise, signifies *a kind of necklace.* (L.)

عَقَدٌ [as an inf. n.: see 1, last four sentences. — Also] *A twisting in the tail* of a sheep or goat, *as though it were knotted,* or *tied in a knot.* (L.) And *A twisting,* or *a knottiness, in the horn* of a he-goat. (L.) — And *A canker, corrosion, rottenness,* or *blackness,* (syn. قَادِحٌ,) in teeth. (L.) — See also the next paragraph. — And see عَقَدَانٌ.

عَقِدٌ: see أَعْقَدُ. — Also, applied to moist earth (ثَرًى), *Contracted, and compacted in lumps*: [said to be] in this sense a possessive epithet [as distinguished from a part. n.: but see 1, last sentence]. (L.) — And [as an epithet in which the quality of a subst. predominates, i. e. used as a subst.,] *Sand accumulated,* or *congested*; as also ▼ عَقَدٌ; (Ṣ, O, L, Ḳ;) the latter accord. to AA: (Ṣ, O:) n. un. of each with ة: (Ṣ, O, L, Ḳ:) pl. أَعْقَادٌ. (L.) See also عَقِصٌ, in two places. — رَوْضَةٌ عَقِدَةٌ *A meadow of which the herbage is continuous,* or *uninterrupted.* (O.) — عَقِدٌ applied to a camel, *Short, and patient in endurance of labour*: (IAạr, O, Ḳ:) or, so applied, *strong.* (TA.) — And *A kind of tree, the leaves of which consolidate wounds.* (Ḳ.)

عُقْدَةٌ *A knot*; *a tie*; (L, Mṣb;) pl. عُقَدٌ. (L.) [Hence النَّفَّاثَاتُ فِى العُقَدِ: see art. نفث. And العُقْدَةُ meaning † *The star α Piscium*; as being in the place of the knot of the two strings: the same, app., that is called ▼ عُقَدُ الخَيْطَيْنِ, mentioned by Freytag under عَقْدٌ. Hence also] one says, تَحَلَّلَتْ عُقْدَتُهُ [lit. *His knots became loosed,* or *untied*], meaning † *his anger became appeased.* (Ṣ, A, O, Ḳ.) And فِى عُقْدَتِهِ ضَعْفٌ † *In his judgment and his consideration of his own affairs is a weakness.* (TA.) And حَصِيفُ العُقْدَةِ, occurring in a letter of 'Omar, means † [*Firm*] *in judgment, and in the management, conducting, ordering,* or *regulating, of affairs.* (TA in art. حصف.) And فِى لِسَانِهِ عُقْدَةٌ (Ṣ, O, L, Ḳ*) † *In his tongue is an impediment* [*as though it were tied*], or *a distortion.* (L. [See عَقَدٌ.]) — The *knot, tie,* or *bond,* (L,) or the *obligation,* (O, Ḳ,) of marriage, (O, L, Ḳ,) and of anything, (O, Ḳ,) as a sale and the like: (TA:) and the *ratification* (O, L, Mṣb) of marriage (O, Mṣb) &c., (Mṣb,) or of anything. (L.) It is said in a trad. relating to prayer, لَكَ مِنْ قُلُوبِنَا عُقْدَةُ النَّدَمِ, meaning [We offer *to Thee, from our hearts,*] *the ratification of the resolution to repent.* (L.) — *A promise of obedience,* or *vow of allegiance, ratified to persons in acknowlegment of their being prefects,* or *governors*: (O, L, Ḳ,* TA:) from عُقْدَةُ الحَبْلِ [*the knot,* or *tie, of the cord* or *rope*]: (O:) thus in the saying, in a trad. of Ubei, هَلَكَ أَهْلُ العُقْدَةِ [*Those who have received the promise of obedience* &c. *have perished*; virtually meaning the same as the saying in the sentence here following]. (L.) And [hence also] The *prefecture over,* or *government of, a town, country, province,* or *the like*: pl. عُقَدٌ: (L, Ḳ, TA:) thus in the saying of 'Omar, هَلَكَ أَهْلُ العُقَدِ [*The possessors of the prefectures* &c. *have perished*]. (L.) — Also *A place where a knot,* or *node, is formed*: and [particularly] *an uneven juncture* (عَثْمٌ) [of a bone] in the arm: (Ṣ, O, Ḳ:) thus in the saying, جُبِرَتْ يَدُهُ عَلَى عُقْدَةٍ [*His arm was set and joined unevenly, so that a node,* or *protuberance, was produced in the bone*]: (Ṣ, O:) and in like manner one says, جَبَرَ عَظْمَهُ عَلَى عُقْدَةٍ *He set and joined his bone unevenly.* (L.) — [Hence also *A joint,* i. e. *an articulation,* of the fingers: and *a bone* of a finger, i. e. *any one of the phalanges*: it is used in both of these senses in the present day: and العُقْدَةُ مِنَ الأَصَابِعِ occurs in the Mṣb, in art. نمل, in explanation of الأَنْمُلَةُ; which is generally expl. as meaning "the head of the finger," or "the portion in which is the nail." (See also مَعْقِدٌ.) — *A knot,* or *joint,* of a cane and the like. And what is termed *A knot* in the horn of a mountain-goat (as in the Ṣ and Ḳ in art. حيد) and the like. — *A knot* in a tree. — *A node,* of a plant, *whence a leaf shoots forth*: *a bud,* or *gem,* of a plant: and *any fruit,* or *produce,* of a plant, *forming a compact and roundish head*; by some termed حَسَكَةٌ, n. un. of حَسَكٌ, q. v. — العُقْدَتَانِ signifies *The nodes of a planet.* (See تِنِّينٌ.) — And عُقْدَةٌ signifies also *Any small nodous lump*; *such as the substance of a ganglion*; see غُدَّةٌ: and *a gland,* or *glandular body*; see غُدَّةٌ. And *A knob* in a general sense. — And hence,] The *penis of a dog* (IAạr, A, O, L, Ḳ) *compressus in coitu, et extremitate turgens*: otherwise it is not thus called: (IAạr, O, L:) and when this is the case, the epithet ▼ أَعْقَدُ is applied to the dog. (IAạr, O.) — Also *An estate consisting of land,* or *of land and a house,* or *of a house* or *land yielding a revenue,* or *of a house and palm-trees,* or *the like,* syn. ضَيْعَةٌ, (Ṣ, A, O, L, Ḳ,) and عَقَارٌ, *which a person has acquired* (اِعْتَقَدَهُ) *as a possession.* (O, L, Ḳ.) — *Any land abounding with herbage* (Ḳ, TA) *and with trees.* (TA.) *A place abounding with trees* or *palm-trees*; (Ṣ;) or *with trees and palm-trees*; (O, L, Ḳ;) or *with trees of the kinds called* رِمْث *and* عُرْفُط, or, accord. to some, *not of the latter kind,* (L, TA,) *serving for pasturage*: (TA:) or *a garden of many palm-trees, surrounded by a wall*: and *a town,* or *village, abounding with palm-trees,* the crows of which are not made to fly away: (Ibn-Ḥabeeb, L:) [whence] it is said in a prov., آلَفُ مِنْ غُرَابِ عُقْدَةٍ [*More familiar than the crow of a place abounding with trees* or *palm-trees*]; because its crow is not made to fly away, (Ṣ, O, L, Ḳ, [or, as in some copies of the Ṣ and Ḳ, does not fly away,]) on account of the abundance of its trees; (Ḳ;) [or مِنْ غُرَابِ عُقْدَةَ *than the crow of 'Okdeh*; for] عُقْدَة is perfectly decl. as a name for any fruitful land, and is imperfectly decl. as a proper name of a particular land (O, Ḳ) abounding with palm-trees. (O.) Also *Herbage,* or *pasturage, sufficient for camels*: (O, Ḳ:) or *a place abounding with herbage,* or *pasturage, sufficient for cattle.* (TA.) And *Pasturage such as is termed* جَنْبَةٌ, (O, L, Ḳ, [in the CḲ جُنْبَة, and in my MS. copy of the Ḳ جُنْبَة,]) *remaining from the next preceding year*; also termed عُرْوَةٌ: (O, L:) or *remains of pasturage*: (L:) pl. عُقَدٌ (O, L) and عِقَادٌ. (L.) And accord. to the copies of the Ḳ, it signifies also *Camels,* or *cattle, that are constrained to feed upon trees*: but [this is evidently a mistake; for] it is said in the L, [as also in the O,] sometimes camels, or cattle, are constrained to feed upon trees, and these [*trees*] are termed عُقْدَةٌ and عُرْوَةٌ; but while the جَنْبَة exists, the trees are not termed عُقْدَةٌ nor عُرْوَةٌ. (TA.) — Also *Anything whereby a man feels himself to be well established, and whereon he relies*; from the same word signifying "a garden of many palm-trees, surrounded by a wall;" because, when a man has this, he considers his condition to be well established: (L, TA:) or *a thing,* (Ḳ, TA,) or *an estate consisting of land* or *of land and a house* &c., (عَقَار, O,) *in which is a sufficiency for a man*: (O, Ḳ, TA:) pl. عُقَدٌ. (TA.) — See also عِقْدٌ.

عُقْدَةٌ The *root* of the tongue; (O, Ḳ;) as also عُكْدَةٌ [q. v.]; (O;) i. e. the *thick part* thereof. (TA.) — Also n. un. of عَقَدٌ as applied to sand. (Ṣ, O, L, Ḳ. [See عَقِدٌ.])

عَقِدَةٌ n. un. of عَقِدٌ [q. v.] as applied to sand. (Ṣ, O, L, Ḳ.)

عَقَدَانٌ *A species,* or *sort, of dates*; (O, L, Ḳ;*) as also ▼ عَقَدٌ. (L.)

عَقِيدٌ i. q. ▼ مُعَاقِدٌ, (Ṣ, O, Ḳ,) *One who unites,*

or *joins, in a contract, a compact, a covenant, an agreement, a league, a treaty, or an engagement*: (Ḳ, TA:) *a confederate*. (TA.) One says, هُوَ عَقِيدُ الكَرَمِ and اللُّؤْمِ [*He is bound by nature to generosity* and *to meanness*]: (Ṣ, O, Ḳ:) the former is said of him who is by nature generous; and the latter, of him who is by nature mean. (TḲ.) —— Also, (Ṣ, M, A, O,) and ↑ مُعْقَدٌ, (M,) and ↑ مُعَقَّدٌ, (A,) applied to rob, (Ṣ, M, A,) and honey, (M, A, O,) and the like, (Ṣ, M, A,) *Thick*, or *thickened*, or *inspissated*. (Ṣ, M, A, O.*)

عَقِيدَةٌ [*A doctrine*, or *the like, upon which one's mind is firmly settled* or *determined*; or *to which one holds, adheres*, or *cleaves, with the heart*, or *mind*; *a belief*, or *firm belief* or *persuasion*; *a creed*; *an article of belief*; *a religious tenet*; i. e.] مَا يَدِينُ الإِنْسَانُ بِهِ: (Mṣb:) [see اِعْتَقَدَ عَقْدًا, in connection with which it is mentioned in the Mṣb: pl. عَقَائِدُ: and ↑ مُعْتَقَدٌ signifies the same as عَقِيدَةٌ; pl. مُعْتَقَدَاتٌ: so too does ↑ اِعْتِقَادٌ, an inf. n. used in the sense of a pass. part. n.; pl. اِعْتِقَادَاتٌ.] One says, لَهُ عَقِيدَةٌ حَسَنَةٌ [*He has a good belief*]; meaning *he has an* عقيدة *free from doubt*. (Mṣb.) [See also مَعْقُودٌ.]

عَاقِدٌ A she-camel *that has confessed herself to have conceived*; (Ṣ, O, Ḳ;) or *that has closed her vulva upon the sperma of the stallion*; (L;) *for she then twists her tail as if tying it in a knot, and it is thereby known that she has conceived*: (Ṣ, O, L:) and a she-camel *twisting her tail as if tying it in a knot*, (L,) or *that has so twisted her tail*, (O,) *on the occasion of her conceiving*; (O, L;) *in order that it may be known that she has conceived*: (O:) pl. عَوَاقِدُ. (L.) —— And A she-gazelle *having the end of her tail twisted* [*as if tied in a knot*]: or *bending her neck in lying down*: or *raising her head in fear for herself and her young one*. (L.) And A gazelle *putting his neck upon his rump*, (O, L,) *having bent it to sleep*: (L:) or *having bent his neck* (O, Ḳ, TA) *to sleep*: (TA:) or *having put his neck upon his rump*: (Ḳ:) pl. as above. (O, L.) —— And one says, جَآءَ عَاقِدًا عُنُقَهُ, meaning *He came twisting his neck by reason of pride*. (A, O, L.) —— عَاقِدٌ is also applied as an epithet to أَقِطٌ [q. v.] meaning That *of which the water has gone, and which is thoroughly cooked*. (AḤát, TA voce عَكَشَةٌ.) ═ Also The [*space called the*] حَرِيم [q. v.] *of a well*; (Ṣ, M, O, Ḳ;) and *what is around it*, (مَا حَوْلَهُ, Ṣ, M, TA,) i. e. *what is around the* حريم: in the Ḳ [and O], مَا حَوْلَهَا, i. e. *what is around the well*; but the former is the right. (TA.)

عِنْقَادٌ: see what next follows.

عُنْقُودٌ and ↑ عِنْقَادٌ (Ṣ, O, L, Mṣb, Ḳ, &c.) *A raceme*, or *bunch*, (Mgh voce عِثْكَالٌ,) of grapes, (Ṣ, O, L, Mṣb, Ḳ,) and the like, (Mṣb,) as of dates, (Mgh ubi suprà, and ISh in art. شمرخ of the TA,) and of [the fruit of] the أَرَاك, and بُطْم, (O, Ḳ,) and the like: (Ḳ:) pl. عَنَاقِيدُ. (Ṣ, O, L, &c.)

أَعْقَدُ A wolf, (O, L, Ḳ,) and a dog, and a ram, and any other animal, (L.) *having a twisted tail* [*as though it were tied in a knot*]: (O, L, Ḳ:) and [the fem.] عَقْدَآءُ, a sheep or goat (شَاةٌ) *having a twisted tail as though it were knotted* or *tied in a knot*. (Ṣ,* L, Ḳ.*) And الأَعْقَدُ signifies *The dog*; (Ṣ, O, L, Ḳ;) a well-known name thereof; (Ṣ, O, L;) because of his tail's being twisted as though it were tied in a knot. (Ṣ, L.) —— And A *crooked* tail. (L.) —— And A stallion [app. of the camels] *that raises his tail*; which he does by reason of sprightliness. (L.) —— And A he-goat *having a twist*, or *a knot, in his horn*. (L.) —— For one of its meanings as an epithet applied to a dog, see عُقْدَةٌ, latter half. —— Also, and ↑ عَقِدٌ, A man *having an impediment in his tongue*; *unable to speak freely*; *tongue-tied*. (Ṣ,* O,* L, Ḳ.*) —— And تَيْسٌ أَعْقَدُ A *mean* man, *of difficult*, or *stubborn, disposition*. (ISk, O, L.) —— And [the fem.] عَقْدَآءُ signifies *A female slave*. (AA, O, Ḳ.)

مَعْقِدٌ The *place of the* عَقْد [or *tying*, &c.,] of a thing: (Mṣb:) pl. مَعَاقِدُ. (Ṣ, O: in which this is similarly explained.) مَعْقِدُ حَبْلٍ signifies *The place of a cord*, or *rope, where it is tied, knit*, or *tied in a knot* or *knots*. (L.) [Hence,] one says, هُوَ مِنِّى مَعْقِدَ الإِزَارِ [lit. *He is, in respect of me, in the place of the tying of the waist-wrapper*], meaning *he is near to me in station, standing*, or *grade*: (Ṣ, O, L, Ḳ:) and in like manner, مَعْقِدَ القَابِلَةِ: (TA:) مَعْقِدَ الإِزَارِ being an adverbial phrase having a special application, but used as one not having such an application. (L.) —— And *A joint, an articulation*, or *a place of juncture between two bones*. (L. [See also عُقْدَةٌ, in the latter part of the former half.]) —— أَسْأَلُكَ بِمَعَاقِدِ العِزِّ مِنْ عَرْشِكَ i. e. *I ask Thee by the properties wherein consists the title of thy throne to glory*, or *by the places wherein those properties are* [*as it were*] *knit together*, properly meaning *by the glory of thy throne*, is a phrase used in prayer, of which, IAth says, the party of Aboo-Ḥaneefeh disapprove. (L.) —— For another meaning of the pl., مَعَاقِدُ, see عَقْدٌ.

مُعْقَدٌ: see عَقِيدٌ.

مُعَقَّدٌ [*Tied in many knots*]. One says خُيُوطٌ مُعَقَّدَةٌ [*Threads*, or *strings, tied in many knots*]: the latter word being with teshdeed to denote muchness, or multiplicity. (Ṣ, O, L.) —— And [hence] applied to language, (Ṣ, O, L, Ḳ,) as meaning *Rendered obscure*: (Ṣ, O, L:) or [simply] *obscure*. (Ḳ.) —— See also مَعْقُودٌ. —— And see عَقِيدٌ. —— It also occurs in a trad. as meaning *A sort of* بُرُود, *of the manufacture of Hejer*. (L.)

مُعَقِّدٌ [*Tying a number of knots* or *many knots*: as enchanters used to do. (See نَفَثَ.) —— And hence,] *An enchanter*. (A, O, Ḳ.)

مِعْقَادٌ: see عِقْدٌ.

مَعْقُودٌ A cord, or rope, *tied, knit, complicated into a knot* or *knots*, or *tied firmly, fast*, or *strongly*. (L.) الخَيْلُ مَعْقُودٌ فِى نَوَاصِيهَا الخَيْرُ, a saying occurring in a trad., means *Good fortune cleaves to the forelocks of horses* as though it were tied to them. (L.) —— Also A sale, or bargain, and a contract, a compact, or the like, *concluded, settled, confirmed*, or *ratified*. (L.) —— لَيْسَ لَهُ ↑ مَعْقُودُ رَأْيٍ means لَيْسَ لَهُ عَقْدُ رَأْيٍ [i. e. *He has not any settled*, or *determined, opinion* or *judgment*]. (Ṣ, O, Ḳ.) —— بِنَآءٌ مَعْقُودٌ *A building*, or *structure*, [*arched*, or *vaulted*, or] *having arches, like those of* [*many*] *doorways*; (A, O, Ḳ;) as also ↑ مُعَقَّدٌ. (A.) —— مَعْقُودَةُ القَرَا: see عَقْدٌ.

مُعَاقِدٌ: see عَقِيدٌ.

مُعْتَقَدٌ: see عَقِيدَةٌ.

يَمِينٌ مُنْعَقِدَةٌ *An oath to do, or to abstain from doing, a thing in the future*. (KT.)

يَعْقِيدٌ, asserted by some to be the only word in the language of the measure يَفْعِيلٌ except يَعْضِيدٌ, (O,) *Honey thickened*, or *inspissated*, (O, L, Ḳ,) *by means of fire*: (O, Ḳ:) and (as some say, L) *food*, or *wheat*, (طَعَام,) *made thick with honey*. (O, L, Ḳ.)

عقر

1. عَقَرَهُ, (Ṣ, Mgh, O, &c.,) aor. ـِ, (Mgh, O, Mṣb, Ḳ,) inf. n. عَقْرٌ, (Ṣ,* Mgh, O, Mṣb, Ḳ,) *He wounded him*; (Ṣ, Mgh, O, Mṣb, Ḳ;) [and so, app., accord. to the Ḳ, ↑ عَقَّرَهُ, inf. n. تَعْقِيرٌ; or the latter signifies *he wounded him much*; for it is said that] تَعْقِيرٌ signifies more than عَقْرٌ: (Ṣ, O:) you say of a lion, and of a lynx, and of a leopard, and of a wolf, يَعْقِرُ النَّاسَ [*He wounds men*]. (Az, Mṣb.) —— And عَقَرَهُ, (Ṣ, O, Mṣb, Ḳ, &c.,) and عَقَرَهَا, (L, Mgh, &c.,) aor. ـِ, (Ḳ,) inf. n. عَقْرٌ; (Mgh, &c.;) and ↑ عَقَّرَهُ, (Ḳ,) and عَقَّرَهَا, (L,) inf. n. تَعْقِيرٌ; (TA;) [or the latter has an intensive signification, or applies to many objects; see above;] *He hocked, houghed*, or *hamstrung*, (عَرْقَبَ,) *him*, or *her*, namely, a beast; (TA;) *he laid bare his* [or *her*] (namely, a camel's) عُرْقُوب [or *hock-tendon*]; such being the meaning of عقر with the Arabs; (Az, TA;) *he struck*, (Ṣ, IAth, Mgh, Mṣb,) or *cut*, (TA,) *his*, (a camel's, Ṣ, IAth, O, Mṣb, or a horse's, Ṣ, O, or a sheep's or goat's, IAth,) or *her*, (a camel's, L, Mgh,) *legs*, بِالسَّيْفِ, *with the sword*, (Ṣ, IAth, Mgh, O, Mṣb, TA,) *while the beast was standing*; (IAth;) *he cut one of his*, or *her*, (a camel's,) *legs*, previously to stabbing the animal, that it might not run away when being stabbed, but might fall down, and so be within his power; *he mowed* [*his* or] *her* (a camel's) *legs with the sword*; (IḲṭṭ, TA;) *he made a mark*, or *wound, like a notch, in his*, or *her*, (a horse's, or a camel's,) *legs*. (Ḳ.) [See عَقْرٌ, below.] —— Hence, (Az, TA,) عَقَرَهُ, aor. and inf. n. as above, *He stabbed him*, namely, a camel; *slaughtered him by stabbing*: (Az, Mṣb, TA:) because the slaughterer of the camel first lays bare its عُرْقُوب [or hock-tendon; or hocks it; or strikes or cuts its legs,

or one of its legs, with a sword: see above]. (Az, TA.) So in the saying of Imra-el-Ḳeys,

* وَيَوْمَ عَقَرْتُ لِلْعَذَارَى مَطِيَّتِى *

[*And the day when I slaughtered for the virgins my riding-camel*]. (TA.) And so in the trad. لَا عَقْرَ فِى الإِسْلَامِ [*There shall be no slaughtering of camels* at the grave *in the time of El-Islám*]: for they used to slaughter camels at the graves of the dead, saying, The occupant of the grave used to slaughter camels for guests in the days of his life; so we recompense him by doing the like after his death. (IAth, TA.) — Hence also, *He slew him; he destroyed him:* of this signification we have an ex. in the story of Umm-Zara: وَعَقْرُ جَارَتِهَا *And* [a cause of] *the destruction of her fellow-wife* through [the latter's] envy [of her] and rage [against her]. (TA.) — عَقْرَى ✝ حَلْقَى, (Mgh, O, Mṣb, Ḳ, &c.,) said of a woman, (TA,) occurring in a trad. of Ṣafeeyeh, (Mgh, Mṣb, TA,) in which Moḥammad is related to have used this expression, on the day of the return of the pilgrims from Minè, when he was told that she had her menstrual flux, to which he added, "I see her not to be aught but a hinderer of us;" thus accord. to the relaters of traditions, each word being an inf. n., like دَعْوَى; (O,* TA;) of the measure فَعْلَى; or, as some say, the ى is to mark a pause; (Mgh;) and عَقْرًا حَلْقًا, (O, Ḳ,) which are also inf. ns.; (TA;) and this is accord. to the usage of the Arabs; (Az, TA;) being a form of imprecation, though not meant to express a desire for its having effect, (Az, Mṣb, TA,) for what is meant by it is only blame; (Mṣb;) expl. by عَقَرَهَا اللّٰهُ تَعَالَى وَحَلَقَهَا, (Ḳ,) i. e., [*May God (exalted be He) wound her, &c., and*] *shave her hair,* or *afflict her with a pain in her throat:* (TA:) or *may her body be wounded* (عُقِرَ), *and may she be afflicted with a disease in her throat:* (Mgh, O:*) so accord. to A'Obeyd: or *may her leg and her throat be cut:* or *may her leg be cut and her head shaven:* (Mgh:) [or *may she be destroyed, and may her throat be cut:*] or the two words عقرى and حلقى are epithets, applied to a woman of ill luck; and the meaning is, (Z, O, TA,) *she is one who extirpates* [or *destroys, and cuts the throats of,*] *her people, by the effect of her ill luck upon them;* (Z, O, Ḳ,* TA;) being virtually in the nom. case, as enunciatives; i. e., هِىَ عَقْرَى ✝ وَحَلْقَى. (Z, TA.) Lḥ mentions the phrase, لَا تَفْعَلْ ذٰلِكَ أُمُّكَ عَقْرَى ✝ [app. meaning, *Do thou not that: may thy mother be childless:* (see عَقُرَتْ:)] without explaining it: but he mentions it with the phrases أُمُّكَ ثَاكِلٌ and أُمُّكَ هَابِلٌ. (TA.) Or ✝ عَقْرَى signifies *Having the menstrual flux.* (Ḳ.) One says also, imprecating a curse upon a man, جَدْعًا لَهُ وَعَقْرًا وَحَلْقًا, meaning, *May God* [*maim him, and*] *wound* (عَقَرَ) *his body, and afflict him with a pain in his throat:* and sometimes, عَقْرَى ✝ حَلْقَى, without tenween. (Ṣ.) [See also 1 in art. حلق.] — عَقَرَ بِهِ *He killed the beast which he was riding, and made him to go on foot: he hocked, houghed,* or *hamstrung, his beast.* (TA.) — Hence, عَقَرْتَ بِى *Thou hast long detained me,* or *restrained me;* as though thou hadst hocked (عَقَرْتَ) my camel and I were therefore unable to journey: ISk cites as an ex.

* قَدْ عَقَرَتْ بِالْقَوْمِ أُمُّ خَزْرَجِ *

[*Umm-Khazraj has long detained the party,* or *people*]. (Ṣ, O, TA.) And in the A it is said that عَقَرَتْ فُلَانَةُ بِالرَّكْبِ means *Such a woman,* or *girl, came forth to the riders on camels, and they staid long in her presence;* as though she hocked (عَقَرَتْ) the camels upon which they rode. (TA.) One says also قَدْ كَانَتْ لِى حَاجَةٌ فَعَقَرَنِى عَنْهَا *I had a want, and he withheld me from it, and hindered me.* (Ibn-Buzurj, L.) Hence, عَقْرُ النَّوَى, (Az, TA,) meaning صَرْفُهَا حَالًا بَعْدَ حَالٍ [i. e. *The shifting about of the course of a journey by successive changes:* see صَرْفٌ, third sentence]. (O, TA.) — And عَقَرَ بِالصَّيْدِ i. q. وَقَعَ بِهِ [app. meaning *He made much slaughter among the objects of the chase*]. (O, Ḳ.) — And عَقَرَتْ بِهِمْ *She* (a woman) *smote their souls, and wounded their hearts.* (O.) — عَقَرَ النَّخْلَةَ, (inf. n. عَقْرٌ, TA, and subst. [or quasi-inf. n., like جَدَادٌ and صَرَامٌ and قَطَافٌ &c.,] ✝ عَقَارٌ, T, Ṣ, O, TA,) *He cut off the head of the palm-tree,* (T, Ṣ, O, Ḳ,) *altogether, with the heart* (الجُمَّار), (T, Ṣ, O,) *so that it dried up,* (Ḳ,) *and nothing came forth from its trunk.* (IḲṭṭ.) — لَا تَعْقِرَنَّ شَجَرًا *Thou shalt by no means cut down trees.* (Mgh.) — عَقَرَ المَرْعَى *He cut down the trees of the pasture-land: he cut down the herbage,* or *pasture, and spoiled it.* (TA.) — عَقَرَ الكَلَأَ *He ate the herbage,* or *pasture.* (O, Ḳ.) And *He had the herbage for pasturage.* (O.) — You say of wine, يَعْقِرُ العَقْلَ [*It disables the intellect;* like as a man disables a beast by hocking him]. (IAar.) — عَقَرَهُ, (Ṣ, O, TA,) aor. ِ, (TA,) inf. n. عَقْرٌ, (Ṣ, O, TA,) *He* (a man) *galled his* (a camel's) *back:* (TA:) *he galled it;* namely, a camel's back: (Ṣ, O:) *it* (a camel's saddle, TA, and a horse's saddle, Ṣ, O, TA) *galled his* (the beast's) *back.* (Ṣ, O, TA.) — And عُقِرَتْ رَكِيَّتُهُمْ *Their well was demolished.* (O.) ═ عَقِرَ, (Ṣ, Ḳ,) aor. َ, (Ḳ,) inf. n. عَقَرٌ, (Ṣ, O,) *His* (a man's) *legs betrayed him, so that he was unable to fight, by reason of fright and stupefaction:* (Ṣ, O:) *he became stupified,* or *deprived of his reason:* (Ṣ, Ḳ:) or *he was taken by sudden fright,* (Ḳ, TA,) *and stupified,* or *deprived of his reason,* (TA,) *so that he could not advance nor retire.* (Ḳ, TA.) عَقِرْتُ حَتَّى خَرَرْتُ إِلَى الأَرْضِ [*My legs betrayed me, &c., so that I fell to the earth*] was said by 'Omar. (Ṣ.) And one says, عَقِرْتُ حَتَّى مَا أَقْدِرُ عَلَى الكَلَامِ [*I am stupified,* or *taken by sudden fright, &c., so that I am not able to talk*]. (M, TA.) [And عَقِرَ alone means *He became unable to speak.* In one place in the L, this verb is written عُقِرَ; but this is probably a mistake.] ═ عَقُرَتْ, aor. ُ; (Ṣ, IJ, M, IḲṭṭ, L, Mṣb;) in the Ḳ, عُقِرَتْ, of the class of عُنِىَ; but the authorities indicated above show that عَقُرَتْ is the correct form; (TA;) and عَقَرَتْ, aor. ِ; (M, IḲṭṭ, L, Mṣb, Ḳ;) and عَقِرَتْ, aor. َ; (M, IḲṭṭ, L;) inf. n. عُقْرٌ, (Ṣ, M, IḲṭṭ, L, Mṣb, Ḳ,) of the first, (Ṣ, Mṣb, like as حُسْنٌ is inf. n. of حَسُنَتْ,) (Ṣ,) or of the second, (M, L, Ḳ,) and عَقَارَةٌ (M, L, Ḳ) and عُقَارَةٌ, (Ḳ,) or عِقَارَةٌ, (M and L, as in the TA,) which are of the first, (M, L, Ḳ,) and عَقْرٌ, (M, IḲṭṭ, L, Mṣb, Ḳ,) which is of the second, (M, L, Mṣb, Ḳ,) and عُقَارٌ, or عِقَارٌ, (accord. to different copies of the Ḳ,) or عِقَارٌ, (M and L, as in the TA,) also of the second, (Ḳ,) or of the third; (M, L;) *She* (a woman [and a camel &c.]) *was,* or *became, barren:* (Ḳ, TA:) or *did not conceive:* (Ṣ:) or *ceased to conceive.* (IḲṭṭ, Mṣb.) — عَقُرَ, aor. ُ; and عَقِرَ, aor. َ; *He* (a man [and a beast]) *was barren; did not generate.* (TA.) — عَقُرَ, aor. ُ, inf. n. عُقْرٌ, † *It* (an affair) *did not produce any issue, or result.* (Ḳ.) ═ عَقَرَهَا *He* (God) *made her* [*to be barren,* or] *to cease to conceive.* (Mṣb.)

2. عَقَّرَهُ: see 1, first and second sentences. — جَدَّعْتُهُ وَعَقَّرْتُهُ *I said to him* جَدْعًا لَكَ وَعَقْرًا. (Ṣb.) [See 1.]

3. عاقره *He contended with him for superior glory* (Ḳ, TA) *and generosity and excellence* (TA) *in the hocking,* or *slaughtering,* (عَقْر [see 1],) *of camels.* (Ḳ, TA.) It was customary for two men thus to contend for superior munificence, [giving away the flesh of the victims,] but they did so for the sake of display and vain glory; wherefore the eating of the flesh of camels slaughtered on an occasion of this kind is forbidden in a trad., and they are likened to animals sacrificed to that which is not God. (TA.) — And عَاقَرَهُ, (TḲ,) inf. n. مُعَاقَرَةٌ, (Ṣ, Ḳ,) *He held a dialogue* or *colloquy,* or *a disputation* or *debate, with him,* (Ṣ, Ḳ,) *and encountered him with mutual reviling and satire* (Ṣ, TA) *and cursing.* (TA.) ═ Also عَاقَرَهُ, (Ḳ,) inf. n. مُعَاقَرَةٌ, (Ṣ, O, Ḳ,) *He,* or *it, kept, confined himself* or *itself, clave, clung,* or *held fast, to him,* or *it:* (Ṣ, O, Ḳ:*) *he kept,* or *applied himself, constantly,* or *perseveringly, to him,* or *it.* (TA.) You say عَاقَرَ الخَمْرَ, (Ṣ,* TA,) and simply عَاقَرَ, (TA,) *He kept,* or *applied himself, constantly,* or *perseveringly, to the drinking of wine:* (Ṣ, TA:) or مُعَاقَرَةُ الشَّرَابِ signifies *the contending with wine for superiority;* as when a man says, I have more, or most, strength for drinking, and so contending with it for superiority, and being overcome thereby. (Aboo-Sa'eed, TA.) You say also, عَاقَرَتِ الخَمْرُ الدَّنَّ *The wine remained long confined to the* [*jar called*] دَنّ; syn. لَازَمَتْهُ. (Ṣ, Ḳ.) And عاقرت الخَمْرُ العَقْلَ [app., *The wine took hold upon the intellect: or contended with it for superiority*]. (Ṣ.)

4. اعقره *He stupified him* [*so that his legs betrayed him and he was unable to fight or to advance or retire:* see عَقِرَ]. (Ṣ, O.) ═ اعقر اللّٰهُ رَحِمَهَا *God rendered her womb barren;* (O, TA;) *God affected her womb with a disease* (Ḳ, TA) *so that she did not conceive.* (TA.) ═ اعقر فُلَانًا *He assigned to such a one a grant of land;* syn. أَطْعَمَهُ عُقْرَةً i. e. طُعْمَةً. (Ḳ.) — And one says, أَعْقَرْتُكَ كَلَأَ مَوْضِعِ كَذَا *I have given thee permission to pasture thy beasts upon the herbage of such a place.* (O.) ═ And اعقر *He*

became possessed of much property such as is termed عَقَار. (Ṣ, IḲṭṭ, O.)

6. تَعَاقَرَا, (Ḳ,) or تعاقرا إِبِلَيْهِمَا, (Ṣ, O,) *They two hocked, or hamstrung, their camels,* (عَرْقَبَا إِبِلَيْهِمَا, Ṣ, O, or عَقَرَاهَا, Ḳ,) *vying, each with the other, therein,* (Ṣ, O,) *that it might be seen which of them should do so most.* (Ḳ.) [See 3.]

7. انعقر *He* (a camel, and a horse, [&c.,]) [*became hocked, houghed,* or *hamstrung; had his hock-tendon laid bare;*] *had his legs struck* [or *cut*] *with a sword.* (Ṣ.) [See 1.] — *It* (a camel's or a horse's back) *became galled by the saddle;* as also ▼ اعتقر. (Ṣ, Ḳ.)

8: see what next precedes.

عَقْرٌ The *act of wounding;* &c.: [see 1:] *a mark,* or *wound,* (أَثَرٌ,) *like a notch,* (كَالحَزِّ, Ḳ, TA, [in the CḲ, كَالحَزِّ,]) *in the legs of a horse,* and *of a camel.* (Ḳ.) [Hence, عَقْرًا حَلْقًا, and عَقْرَى حَلْقَى: see 1.] — See also عُقْرٌ, first sentence: — and again in the last quarter. — Also *What is,* or *constitutes, the most essential part,* of anything; or the *prime,* or the *principal part,* thereof; syn. أَصْلٌ: [such appears to me to be the meaning of اصل as here used, from what follows.] (Ṣ, IF, Mṣb.) — The *principal part* (أَصْل) of a دَار [i. e., a country]; (Aṣ, Ṣ, Mṣb, Ḳ;) which is the *place where the people dwell,* or *abide;* (Aṣ, Ṣ;) as also ▼ عُقْرٌ: (Aṣ, Ṣ, Mṣb, Ḳ:) the former of the dial. of Nejd; (Aṣ, TA;) and the latter of the dial. of the people of El-Medeeneh, (Aṣ, Ṣ,) or of the dial. of El-Ḥijáz; (TA;) or both of the dial. of the people of El-Ḥijáz; and the latter, in the dial. of others, signifies the *chief,* or *main, part* of a دار; (Mṣb;) and the latter also signifies the *middle* [or *heart*] of a دار: (Ḳ:) or عَقْرُ الدَّارِ and ▼ عُقْرُهَا both signify *the principal part* (اصل) *of the place of abode of a people, upon which they rest their confidence.* (Mgh, O.) This last signification is exemplified by the trad. of 'Alee, مَا غُزِىَ قَوْمٌ فِى عَقْرِ دَارِهِمْ إِلَّا ذَلُّوا [*No people have had war waged against them in the principal part of their country, upon which they rest their confidence, but they have become abased,* or *brought into subjection*]: (Mgh, O:) or the meaning here is, *in the midst* [or *heart*] *of their country,* &c.; i. e., *in the place where they abide,* or *lodge.* (L.) It is said in another trad., عَقْرُ دَارِ ٱلْإِسْلَامِ ٱلشَّأْمُ, meaning, *The principal part* (اصل), *and the place, of the country of El-Islám is Syria:* apparently pointing to a time of conflicts and factions, or seditions, when Syria should be free from them, and the Muslims should there be more secure. (TA.) Lth has confounded in explaining what is the عقر of a دار and what is the عقر of a tank or trough for watering beasts &c. (Az.)

عُقْرٌ (Ṣ, M, &c.) and ▼ عَقْرٌ, (M,) or ▼ عَقَارَةٌ and ▼ عُقْرَةٌ, (A, Ḳ,) *Barrenness,* in a woman, (Ṣ, Ḳ, &c.,) and in a man. (Ṣ, TA.) You say also لَقِحَتِ النَّاقَةُ عَنْ عُقْرٍ [*The she-camel conceived after having been barren*]. (Ṣ, O.) And لَقِحَ لِقَاؤُكَ عَنْ عُقْرٍ [app., † *The meeting thee hath been productive of good after barrenness thereof*]. (A, TA.) And لَقِحْنَ إِلَى عُقْرٍ, a phrase used by Dhu-r-Rummeh, referring to wars; i. e. † *They returned to stillness.* (TA.) And رَجَعَتِ الحَرْبُ إِلَى عُقْرٍ † *The war became languid.* (A, TA.) — عُقْرٌ in a palm-tree means [*Barrenness,* or *a drying up, and perishing, occasioned by*] *having the* [*fibrous substance called*] لِيف *stripped off* (O, Ḳ, TA) *from the heart,* (O, TA,) *and the heart itself taken away;* (O, Ḳ, TA;) which being done, it dries up and perishes. (Az, O, TA.) — Also, or ▼ عَقْرٌ, or the latter is used only by poetic license, *Anything which a man drinks, and in consequence thereof has no offspring born to him.* (O, TA.) — Also, عُقْرٌ, *A kind of dowry,* (Ṣ,) or *compensation,* (IAth,) *which is given to a woman when connection has been had with her in consequence of dubiousness, or a likeness* [*on her part to the man's wife*]: (إِذَا وُطِئَتْ عَنْ شُبْهَةٍ, Ṣ; or بِشُبْهَةٍ, Mgh; or عَلَى وَطْءِ الشُّبْهَةِ, IAth:) or *a recompense which is given to a woman for connection with her:* (AO:) or *a mulct,* or *fine, which is paid to a woman for ravishing her:* (Lth, Mṣb, Ḳ:) or *what is given to a female slave who has been ravished, like a dowry in the like case to a free woman:* (Aḥmad Ibn-Ḥambal:) so called because devirgination wounds the object of it: pl. أَعْقَارٌ. (IAth, TA.) — Hence, in consequence of frequency of usage, (Mṣb,) A woman's *dowry;* (Mṣb, Ḳ;) *i. q.* بُضْعٌ. (O.) — Also The *exploration of a woman to see if she be a virgin or not:* (Kh, O, Ḳ, TA:) but Az says that this is unknown. (TA.) [Perhaps it is a meaning inferred from what here follows.] — بَيْضَةُ العُقْرِ is *That* [*egg*] *with which a woman is tested on the occasion of devirgination:* (Ḳ: [but what is meant by this, I have not been able to learn:]) or *the first egg of the hen;* (Ḳ, TA;) because it wounds her: (TA:) or *the last egg of the hen;* (O, Ḳ, TA;) *when she is old and weak:* (TA:) or *the egg of the cock, which* [*they say*] *he lays once in the year,* (O, Ḳ,) [or *once in his life,* for] they assert that it is *the egg of the cock, because he lays, in his life, one egg, somewhat inclining to length; so called because the virginity of the girl,* or *young woman, is tested with it:* hence, they say of a thing given one time [only], كَانَتْ بَيْضَةَ العُقْرِ: or, as some say, it is like the phrases بَيْضُ الأَنُوقِ and الأَبْلَقُ العَقُوقُ; so that it is a phrase proverbially used as applied to a thing that never is: (Ṣ, O:) accord. to A'Obeyd, when a niggard gives once, and not again, one says [of the gift], كَانَتْ بَيْضَةَ الدِّيكِ; and when he gives a thing, and then stops doing so, one says of the last time [of his giving], كَانَتْ بَيْضَةَ العُقْرِ. (TA.) One says also, كَانَ ذٰلِكَ بَيْضَةَ العُقْرِ, meaning † *That happened once, not a second time.* (TA.) And بَيْضَةُ العُقْرِ means also ‡ *He who has no offspring.* (Ḳ, TA. [See also عَاقِرٌ.]) And † *He who stands another in no stead.* (TA.) — Also *A grant of land;* syn. طُعْمَةٌ; (O, Ḳ;) and so ▼ عُقْرَةٌ. (Ḳ. [See 4.]) — And *A place where people alight* (مَحَلَّةُ قَوْمٍ, Ḳ, TA) *between the house,* or *abode, and the trough,* or *tank, for watering beasts* &c.; (TA;) as also ▼ عَقْرٌ: (Ḳ, TA:) or (TA, but in the Ḳ "and") the *hinder part* of a trough, or tank, for watering beasts &c., (Ṣ, Ḳ, TA,) *where the camels stand when they come to water;* as also ▼ عُقُرٌ: (Ṣ:) or the *station of the drinker;* (Ḳ;) as in all the copies of the Ḳ; but accord. to the T and Nh, the *station of the animals drinking:* (TA:) or the *place where the bucket is emptied, at the hinder part* of the trough, or tank; the place at the fore part being called its إِزَآءٌ: (IAạr:) pl. أَعْقَارٌ. (Ṣ, O.) It is said in a prov., إِنَّمَا يُهْدَمُ الحَوْضُ مِنْ عُقْرِهِ [lit., *The trough,* or *tank, for watering beasts* &c. *is demolished only* by commencing *from its hinder part*]; meaning, *an affair is performed only by setting about it in the proper way.* (TA.) — Also The *part* of a well *where the fore feet of the animals watering stand when they drink.* (TA.) — See also عَقْرٌ, in two places.

عَقِرٌ: fem. عَقِرَةٌ: see the latter voce عَقُورٌ: — and see عَاقِرٌ. — نَاقَةٌ عَقِرَةٌ, accord. to the Ḳ, *A she-camel that will not drink save from fear:* but accord. to IAạr [and the Ṣ and O], *that will not drink save from the* عُقْر *of the trough,* or *tank;* and أَزِيَةٌ signifies one "that will not drink save from its إِزَآء," i. e. "from its fore part." (TA.)

عُقُرٌ: see مُعَقَّرٌ, in two places.

عُقُرٌ: see عُقْرٌ, in two places.

عَقْرَةٌ: see عُقْرٌ, first sentence.

عُقْرَةٌ: see عُقْرٌ, first sentence: — and again in the last quarter.

عُقَرَةٌ: see مُعَقَّرٌ, in two places; and عَقُورٌ. — Also *A kind of bead* (خَرَزَةٌ, Ṣ, O, Ḳ) *which a woman binds upon her flanks, in order that she may not conceive;* (T, Ṣ, O;) or *which a woman bears,* or *carries, in order that she may not bear offspring:* (Ḳ:) accord. to IAạr, *a kind of bead which is hung upon her who is barren, in order that she may bear offspring;* but this is strange. (TA.) Hence the saying, عُقَرَةُ العِلْمِ النِّسْيَانُ [*That which renders knowledge barren is forgetfulness*]. (Ṣ, O.) — See also عَاقِرٌ, in two places.

عَقْرَى: see 1, in five places.

عُقْرَى: see the paragraph here following.

عَقَارٌ: see عَقْرُ النَّخْلَةِ. — Also *Real,* or *immoveable, property,* (كُلُّ مَالٍ لَهُ أَصْلٌ, Mgh, or مِلْكٌ ثَابِتٌ لَهُ أَصْلٌ, Mṣb, or مَا لَهُ أَصْلٌ وَقَرَارٌ, KT,) [*an estate*] *consisting of a house or land yielding a revenue;* (Mgh;) or *such as land and a house;* (KT;) or *such as a house and palm-trees:* (Mṣb:) or simply, *land yielding a revenue;* syn. ضَيْعَةٌ; (Mgh, Ḳ:) as also ▼ عُقْرَى: (Ṣgh, Ḳ:) or *land;* or *lands yielding revenues* (syn. ضِيَاعٌ); and *palm-trees;* (Ṣ, O, TA;) and *the like:* (TA:) and *palm-trees* (L, Ḳ) *in particular:* (L:) pl. عَقَائِرُ.

(Mṣb.) You say مَا لَهُ دَارٌ وَلَا عَقَارٌ *He has not a house nor land, or lands yielding revenues, or palm-trees.* (Ṣ, O.) —— Also (sometimes, Mṣb) *Household goods, or furniture and utensils,* (Ṣ, O, Mṣb,* Ḳ, TA,) *which are not used except on the occasions of festivals,* (Ḳ, TA,) *and necessary affairs of great importance,* (TA,) *and the like:* (Ḳ, TA:) thus, with fet-ḥ, accord. to AZ and IAạr; (TA;) and sometimes with ḍamm [↓عُقَارٌ], (Ḳ,) thus accord. to Aṣ; (O, TA;) but in saying so, he differs from the generality of authorities: (TA:) or the *best* of furniture and the like, because none but the best is spread on the occasions of festivals: (TA:) and the *best* of anything. (O, TA.) One says فِى البَيْتِ عَقَارٌ حَسَنٌ *In the house, or tent, are goodly furniture and utensils.* (Ṣ, O.)

عُقَارٌ *Wine:* (Ṣ, O, Ḳ:) or *wine that does not delay to intoxicate:* (TA:) so called because of its taking hold upon the intellect, or contending with it for superiority, (لِأَنَّهَا عَاقَرَتِ العَقْلَ,) accord. to Aboo-Naṣr; (Ṣ;) or because of its remaining long confined to the [jar called] دَنّ, (Ṣ, O, Ḳ,) accord. to AA; (Ṣ, O;) [see 3;] or because the drinker keeps closely to it; (TA;) or because it prevents the drinker from walking; (Ḳ;) or because it disables (يَعْقِرُ) the intellect. (IAạr.) ═══ See also عَقَارٌ.

عَقُورٌ, applied to a dog, (Ṣ, O, Mṣb, Ḳ,) and to any animal of prey, as a lion, and a lynx, and a leopard, and a wolf, (Az, IAth, Mṣb,) and the like, (IAth,) each of these being called كَلْبٌ عَقُورٌ, (Az, IAth, Mṣb,) because of the same rapacious nature as the dog, (IAth,) meaning, *That wounds,* (Az,* IAth, O, Mṣb,) *and kills, and seizes its prey and breaks its neck:* (IAth:) [or *that wounds, &c., much;* for] it is an intensive epithet: (TA:) only applied to an animal; (Ṣ, Ḳ; [in the latter of which, the words thus rendered are preceded by "or;" the epithet in what precedes being restricted to a dog, but not explained;]) ↓عَقُورَةٌ being applied to an inanimate thing: (Ḳ:) pl. عُقُرٌ, (Mṣb, and so in some copies of the Ḳ,) or عُقْرٌ. (So in some copies of the Ḳ, and in the TA.)

عَقِيرٌ *i. q.* ↓مَعْقُورٌ; (IF, O, Ḳ;) applied to a man, *Wounded:* (Ṣ, O:) pl. عَقْرَى. (Ṣ, Mgh, O, Ḳ.) —— Applied to a camel, (Ṣ, Mgh, O,) both to a male and to a female, (TA,) and to a horse [or mare, &c.], (Ṣ, O,) [*Hocked, houghed,* or *hamstrung;*] *having the* [hock-tendon or] *two hock-tendons laid bare, so as to be unable to run;* applied to a horse; (TA;) *struck* [or *cut*] *in the legs* with a sword; (Ṣ, Mgh, O;) [a camel *having one of the legs cut,* previously to being stabbed; *having a mark,* or *wound, like a notch, made in his,* or *her,* (a camel's or a horse's) *legs:* see 1:] pl. as above. (Ṣ, Mgh.) [See also عَقِيرَةٌ.] —— [Hence,] applied to a camel, (male, Mṣb, and female, L,) *Stabbed; slaughtered by stabbing:* (L, Mṣb, TA:) pl. as above. (Mṣb.) —— Applied to a palm-tree (نَخْلَةٌ), as also ↓مَعْقُورَةٌ, (Az, TA,) and, accord. to the copies of the Ḳ, ↓عَقِيرَةٌ, but correctly ↓عَقِرَةٌ, as in the M, (TA,) *Having its head cut off,* (Az, Ḳ, TA,) *altogether, with the heart,* (Az, TA,) *and having in consequence dried up,* (Ḳ, TA,) *so that nothing comes forth from its trunk.* (IḲṭṭ, TA.) ═══ A man *unable to walk,* or *to fight, by reason of fright and stupefaction;* (TA;) *taken by sudden fright, so as to be unable to advance or retire:* or *stupified:* (Ḳ:) in which last sense it is applied to an antelope. (TA.) ═══ See also عَاقِرٌ.

عَقِيرَةٌ signifies مَا عُقِرَ [*What is wounded,* or *hocked,* or *struck* or *cut in the legs,*] of wild animals that are snared or hunted or chased, and the like; (Ḳ;) of the measure فَعِيلَةٌ in the sense of the measure مَفْعُولَةٌ. (TA.) See عَقِيرٌ. —— *A man of high rank who is slain.* (Ṣ, Ḳ.) So in the saying, مَا رَأَيْتُ كَالْيَوْمِ عَقِيرَةً وَسْطَ قَوْمٍ [*I have not before seen, as on this day, a man of high rank who is slain in the midst of a people*]. (Ṣ.) —— *A leg,* or *shank, cut.* (Ṣ, O, Ḳ.) —— Hence, The *voice,* or *a cry;* (Ṣ;) the *voice of a singer* (Ḳ, TA) *singing;* (TA;) the *voice of a weeper* (Ḳ, TA) *weeping;* (TA;) the *voice of a reciter* or *reader* (Ḳ, TA) *reciting* or *reading;* (TA;) the *utmost extent of the voice* or *of a cry.* (TA.) You say رَفَعَ فُلَانٌ عَقِيرَتَهُ *Such a one raised his voice:* the origin of the saying was this: a man had one of his legs cut, or cut off, and he raised it, and put it upon the other, and cried out with his loudest voice: so this was afterwards said of any one who raised his voice: (Ṣ, O:) or it is expl. thus: a man had one of his limbs wounded, and he had camels which were accustomed to his singing in driving them, and which had become dispersed from him; so he raised his voice, crying, by reason of the wound; and his camels, hearing, and thinking that he was singing to drive them, came together to him: and hence this was afterwards said of any one who raised his voice, singing. (Az, TA.)

عُقَيْرَى a dim. n., of the occurrence of which the only instance known to Ḳt is in a trad. cited and expl. voce أَصْحَرُ: said by IAth to be derived from عُقْرٌ in the phrase عُقْرُ الدَّارِ. (TA.)

عَقَّارٌ [*A simple; a drug;*] *any of the elements* (أُصُول) *of medicines;* (Ṣ, O;) *what is used medicinally, of plants* and *of their roots* (أُصُول) and *of trees:* (Ḳ, TA:) [accord. to the CḲ, *what is used medicinally, of plants,* or *of their roots:* and *trees:* the last word being in the nom. case:] as also ↓عَقِيرٌ: (Ḳ:) or *what is used medicinally, of plants* and *trees:* (L, TA:) or *a medicine that is used for moving the bowels:* (Az, TA:) or *any curative plant;* as also its pl., (AHeyth,) which is عَقَاقِيرُ: (AHeyth, Ṣ:) nothing thus termed is called قُوَّة. (AHeyth.) —— [Hence,] حَدِيدٌ جَيِّدُ العَقَاقِيرِ † *Iron of excellent manufacture.* (O, Ḳ.)

عَقِيرٌ: see the next preceding paragraph.

عَاقِرٌ; see مُعْقِرٌ. ═══ Also, applied to a woman, *Barren:* (O, Ḳ, TA:) *that does not conceive:* (Ṣ, O:) or *that has ceased to conceive:* (Mṣb:) as being from عَقُرَتْ, it is an instance of the confusion of dialects; [being properly from عَقِرَتْ;] or it is a possessive epithet [meaning *having the quality of barrenness*]: (IJ:) pl. عُقَّرٌ, (Ḳ, TA,) which is applied to women and to she-camels, (TA,) or عَوَاقِرُ and عَاقِرَاتٌ: (Mṣb:) and ↓عَقِرَةٌ is in like manner applied to a woman, signifying, *having a disease in her womb,* (O, Ḳ, TA,) *in consequence of which she does not conceive.* (TA.) —— Applied to a man, *Barren; that has no offspring born to him;* (Ṣ, O, Mṣb, Ḳ;) as also ↓عَقِيرٌ: (Ḳ:) the former anomalous; [if regarded as from عَقُرَ, not from عَقِرَ; but عَقِرَ said of a man, I do not find;] the latter regular; [if from عَقِرَ;] and the latter has not been heard applied to a woman: (TA:) pl. عُقَّرٌ: (Mṣb, TA:) and ↓عُقَرَةٌ is also applied to a man, and signifies, one *who comes to women, and feels them, and indulges himself with them in mutual embracing,* or *pressing to the bosom,* (يُحَاضِنُهُنَّ,) *but has no offspring born to him.* (IAạr, TA.) —— ‡ A tree (شَجَرَةٌ) *that does not bear; barren:* and in like manner ↓عَقِرَةٌ, occurring in a trad., as the name of a certain tract of land (أَرْض), which name Moḥammad changed to خَضِرَةٌ; or this may be from the same epithet applied to a palm-tree. (TA.) [See also عَقِيرٌ.] —— Applied to a tract of sand (رَمْلَةٌ), ‡ *That produces no plants or herbage;* (O, Ḳ, TA;) likened to a [barren] woman: (TA:) or *of which the sides produce plants* or *herbage, but the middle does not produce:* (TA:) or such as is *large:* (Ḳ:) or *large and producing no plants* or *herbage.* (Ṣ.)

عَاقُورٌ: see مِعْقَرٌ.

أَعْقَرُ مِنْ بَغْلَةٍ [*More barren than a she-mule*]. (TA in art. بغل.)

مُعْقِرٌ A man *having much property such as is termed* عَقَار. (Ṣ, Ḳ.) ═══ See also the next paragraph.

مِعْقَرٌ (Ṣ, O, Ḳ) and ↓مِعْقَارٌ and ↓مُعْقِرٌ (Ḳ) and ↓عُقَرٌ (AZ, Ṣ, O, Ḳ) and ↓عُقَرَةٌ (Ṣ, O, Ḳ) and ↓عَاقُورٌ, (O, Ḳ,) applied to the saddle of a horse (Ṣ, Ḳ) and that of a camel, (TA,) *That galls the back;* (Ṣ,* O,* Ḳ;) i. e., *that usually galls the back:* if it galls it but once it is only termed ↓عَاقِرٌ. (A'Obeyd.) —— Also مِعْقَرٌ and ↓عُقَرٌ and ↓عُقَرَةٌ A man *who galls the backs of camels by fatiguing them with labour,* or *by urging them much in a journey.* (L, Ḳ.)

مُعْقَرَةٌ *Having her womb rendered barren* by God. (TA.)

مِعْقَارٌ: see مِعْقَرٌ.

مَعْقُورٌ and مَعْقُورَةٌ: see عَقِيرٌ.

مُعْتَقَرٌ *A place of* عَقْر [or اِعْتِقَار, i. e. *of galling,* or *being galled,* upon the back of a camel or the like]. (TA in art. أرى.)

عقرب

Q. 1. عَقْرَبَ *He twisted, wreathed, curled, curved,* or *bent,* a thing. (MA.) ═ [And, accord. to Freytag, *He imitated the scorpion in acting:* but for this he names no authority; and I doubt its correctness: see the next paragraph.]

Q. 2. تَعَقْرَبَ [*It was crisp and curved;* said of a lock of hair hanging down upon the temple: so accord. to Reiske, as mentioned by Freytag. — And *He acted like 'Akrab;* a man notorious for putting off the fulfilment of his promises; as is said in the TA in the present art.]. (A and TA in art. عرقب: see Q. 2 in that art.)

عَقْرَبٌ [The *scorpion;*] *a certain venomous reptile,* (TA,) *well known:* (Ḳ, TA:) the word is masc. (TA) and it is fem., (Ṣ, O, Ḳ, TA,) generally the latter; (T, Mṣb, TA;) but is applied to the *male* and the *female:* (Lth, T, O, Mṣb, TA:) and the *male* is called ↓ عُقْرُبَانٌ, (T, Ṣ, O, Mṣb, Ḳ, TA,) accord. to some, (O,) when one desires to denote it in a corroborative manner, (Mṣb, TA,) and ↓ عُقْرُبَّانٌ also; (Ḳ;) or these two words are syn. with عَقْرَبٌ: (Ḳ:) and the *female* is called ↓ عَقْرَبَةٌ, (T, Ṣ, O, Mṣb, Ḳ,) sometimes, (T, Mṣb,) and ↓ عَقْرَبَاءُ, which is imperfectly decl.; (Ṣ, O, Ḳ;) or these two words and عَقْرَبٌ, accord. to the "Taḥreer et-Tembeeh," all denote the *female,* and the *male* is called ↓ عُقْرُبَانٌ: (TA:) or, as some say, the *male* and the *female* are called only عَقْرَبٌ: (Mṣb, TA:) and of ↓ عُقْرُبَانٌ it is said by IB, on the authority of AḤát, that it does not signify the male of عَقَارِب, but [as expl. below] "a certain creeping thing, having long legs:" (TA:) IJ says that you may drop the ا and ن in عُقْرُبَان, and say ↓ عُقْرُبٌ: (L, TA:) and an instance occurs of ↓ عَقْرَابٌ, as a coll. gen. n., in the following verse:

أَعُوذُ بِٱللّٰهِ مِنَ العَقْرَابِ
ٱلشَّائِلَاتِ عُقَدَ ٱلْأَذْنَابِ

[*I seek protection by God from the scorpions raising the joints of the tails*]: but the ا here is said to be inserted for the purpose of what is termed الإِشْبَاع: (MF, from the "Mukhtaṣar el-Bayán:") and الشائلات is applied as an epithet to a sing. n. because this is used as a coll. gen. n.: (M voce سَبْسَبٌ:) the pl. of عَقْرَبٌ is عَقَارِبُ. (Ṣ, O.) — And [hence] العَقْرَبُ is the name of † *A certain sign of the Zodiac,* (T, Ṣ, O, Ḳ,) [i. e. *Scorpio,*] to which belong the Mansions of the Moon called الشَّوْلَةُ and القَلْبُ [and الإِكْلِيلُ] and الزُّبَانَيَانِ. (T, TA. [See these words, and see also شِيَانٌ, and مَنَازِلُ القَمَرِ in art. نزل. It should also be observed that the Arabs extended the figure of this constellation (as they did that of Leo) far beyond the limits that we assign to it.]) — [Hence, likewise,] عَقْرَبٌ signifies † *A thong,* or *strap,* of a sandal, (O, Ḳ, TA,) *in the form of the reptile of this name.* (TA.) [See also عَقْرَبَةٌ.] — And † *A thong,* or *strap,* (O, Ḳ,) *plaited, and having a buckle at its extremity,* (O,) *by which the crupper of a horse,* or *the like, is bound to the saddle.* (O, Ḳ.) — And the pl. عَقَارِبُ signifies also ‡ *Malicious and mischievous misrepresentations, calumnies,* or *slanders.* (O, Ḳ, TA.) One says, إِنَّهُ تَدِبُّ عَقَارِبُهُ ‡ *Verily his malicious and mischievous misrepresentations,* &c., *creep along:* (TA:) or *he traduces,* or *defames, people behind their backs,* or *otherwise.* (O, Ḳ.) And the phrase دَبَّتْ عَقَارِبُهُ is sometimes used to signify ‡ *His downy hair crept* [along his cheeks]. (MF.) — And ‡ *Reproaches for benefits conferred:* so in the saying of En-Nábighah,

عَلَىَّ لِعَمْرٍو نِعْمَةٌ بَعْدَ نِعْمَةٍ
لِوَالِدِهِ لَيْسَتْ بِذَاتِ عَقَارِبِ

‡ [*I owe unto 'Amr favour after favour, for his father, not accompanied by reproaches for benefits conferred*]. (TA.) — And † *Hardships, severities, difficulties, troubles,* or *distresses.* (Ḳ.) عَقَارِبُ الشِّتَآءِ means † *The hardships, severities,* &c., *of winter:* (TA:) or *the intense cold thereof:* (O, Ḳ:) and عَقْرَبُ الشِّتَآءِ, accord. to IB, *the assault, and intense cold, of winter.* (TA.) And عَيْشٌ ذُو عَقَارِبَ means † *An uneasy life:* or *a life in which is evil and roughness.* (TA.) — See also the next paragraph.

عَقْرَبَةٌ: see عَقْرَبٌ, first sentence. — Also † *An iron thing like the* كُلَّاب [or *flesh-hook*], *which is suspended,* or *attached, to the horse's saddle.* (O, Ḳ.) — And, of a sandal, † The *knots of the* [*thong,* or *strap, called*] شِرَاك [q. v.]. (TA.) — And, (O, Ḳ,) thus in all the copies of the Ḳ, and in the handwriting of Ibn-Mektoom, but in the L ↓ عَقْرَب, (TA,) † *An intelligent female slave, who does much service,* or *work.* (O, L, Ḳ, TA.)

عَقْرَبَاءُ: see عَقْرَبٌ, first sentence.

عُقْرُبَانٌ: see عَقْرَبٌ, first sentence, in three places. — Also, [or it has this meaning only, as stated above, voce عَقْرَبٌ,] *A certain creeping thing, having long legs, and the tail of which is not like that of the* عَقْرَب [or *scorpion*]: (Ṣ, IB, O, TA:) or *a small creeping thing that enters the ear; long, yellow, and having many legs:* (TA:) *i. q.* دَخَّالُ الأُذُنِ [an appellation now applied to the *earwig*]; (Az, Ḳ;) and (Ḳ) so ↓ عُقْرُبَّانٌ. (O, Ḳ.)

عُقْرُبَانَةٌ: see مُعَقْرَبٌ.

عُقْرُبٌ: see عَقْرَبٌ, first sentence.

عُقْرُبَّانٌ: see عَقْرَبٌ, first sentence: — and عُقْرُبَانٌ.

عَقْرَابٌ: see عَقْرَبٌ, first sentence.

مُعَقْرَبٌ [*Twisted, wreathed, curled,*] *curved,* or *bent.* (Ḳ.) A صُدْغٌ [or lock of hair hanging down upon the temple *curled,* or] *curved,* or *having one part turned upon another.* (Ṣ, O.) — And *Strong and compact in make:* (Ḳ:) or مُعَقْرَبُ الخَلْقِ, applied to a wild ass, *compact and strong in make.* (O.) — Also, and ↓ ذُو عُقْرُبَانَةٍ, One *who aids,* or *assists, much,* or *well,* (O,* Ḳ,* TA,) *and resists attack:* (Ḳ:) or *an aider who resists attack with energy.* (MF.)

مَكَانٌ مُعَقْرِبٌ *A place having in it scorpions* (عَقَارِب). (Ṣ, O.) And أَرْضٌ مُعَقْرِبَةٌ (Ṣ, O, Mṣb, Ḳ) and مَعْقَرَةٌ, (Ṣ, O,* Ḳ,) the latter as though formed from عَقْرَبٌ after reducing it to three letters, (Ṣ,) *A land in which are scorpions:* (Ṣ, O, Mṣb:) or *a land abounding with scorpions.* (Ḳ.)

عقص

1. عَقَصَتْ شَعَرَهَا, aor. ـِ, (Mṣb,) inf. n. عَقْصٌ, (Lth, Ṣ, Mgh, IAth, Mṣb,) *She* (a woman, Lth, Mṣb) *twisted her hair, and inserted the ends thereof into the parts next the roots:* (Mgh, IAth, Mṣb:) this is the primary signification: (IAth:) or *she took each lock of her hair, and twisted it, then tied it, so that there remained in it a twisting, and then let it hang down;* (Lth, O;*) each of the said locks is termed عَقِيصَةٌ: (Lth:) and *she tied her hair upon the back of her neck:* (TA:) and *she plaited her hair:* (Mṣb:) or عَقْصُ الشَّعَرِ signifies *the gathering of the hair together upon the head:* (Mgh:) or *the plaiting of the hair:* and *the twisting it upon the head:* (Ṣ:) and you say, عَقَصَ شَعَرَهُ, aor. as above, (and so the inf. n., O,) meaning, *he plaited his hair:* and *he twisted it.* (A, O, Ḳ.) ═ عَقِصَ, (Ṣ, TA,) aor. ـَ, (TA,) inf. n. عَقَصٌ, [q. v.], (Ṣ, O, TA,) ‡ *He was,* or *became, niggardly,* or *close-handed,* (Ṣ, O,* TA,) *and evil in disposition.* (Ṣ.) — And عَقِصَتْ عَلَىَّ الدَّابَّةُ [as also عَكِصَتْ] ‡ *The beast became restive,* or *refractory, to me, and stopped.* (TA.)

2. عقّص أَمْرَهُ ‡ *He rendered his affair difficult,* or *intricate, and involved in confusion,* or *doubt.* (TA.)

3. أَخَذْتُهُ مُعَاقَصَةً † *I took it striving to overcome;* (O, Ḳ;*) as also مُقَاصَعَةً. (O.)

عَقْصٌ [app. an inf. n. of which the verb is عَقِصَ] *A twisting,* or *contortion,* in the horn of a sheep or goat: (A:) or *a twisting,* or *contortion, of the horns of a goat, upon his ears, backwards.* (Ṣ.)

عَقَصٌ *Sand accumulated,* or *congested, in which there is no way:* (Ṣ, O, Ḳ:) said to be syn. with عَقَدٌ: and ↓ عَقَصَةٌ signifies *sand like such as is termed* سِلْسِلَةٌ [q. v.]; or عَقَصَةٌ and ↓ عَقِصَةٌ, as expl. by Aboo-'Alee, signify *sand contorted, one part upon another, and extended;* like عَقَدَةٌ and عَقِدَةٌ. (TA.) — And The *neck of the* كَرِش [or *stomach of a ruminant animal*]. (IF, O, Ḳ. [In the CḲ, for وَعُنُقُ الكَرِشِ is erroneously put وعُنُقُ الكرش; after which a و should have been inserted.]) — Also, (Ṣ, O, Ḳ,) and ↓ عَقِيصٌ, (O, Ḳ,) and ↓ عُقَيْصٌ, (IDrd, O, Ḳ,) and ↓ أَعْقَصُ, (TA,) ‡ *Niggardly, stingy,* or *close-handed,* (Ṣ, O, Ḳ, TA,) and *evil in disposition:* (Ṣ:) and عقيص [app. ↓ عَقِيصٌ, or perhaps ↓ عُقَيْصٌ,] signifies *evil and perverse in disposition.* (TA.)

عُقْصَةٌ *A knot* of a horn: (O, Ḳ:) pl. عُقَصٌ. (O.)

عُقْصَةٌ: see عَقِيصَةٌ, in two places.

عَقَصَةٌ and عِقْصَةٌ: see عَقْصٌ.

عِقَاصٌ *A string with which the ends of the* ذَوَائِب [or *locks of hair hanging down loosely from the middle of the head to the back*] *are tied*: (O, Mṣb, Ḳ:) or *a thong with which the hair is gathered together*: (Mgh:) pl. عُقُصٌ: (Mṣb:) or, as some say, عُقُصٌ, (Mgh,) or عُقُوصٌ, (TA,) signifies *black strings*, (Mgh,) or *strings of twisted wool, dyed black*, (TA,) *which a woman joins to her hair*: (Mgh, TA:) of the dial. of El-Yemen: (TA:) [in Egypt, in the present day, the term عُقُوص is applied to *red silk strings, each with a tassel at the end, worn by women of the lower orders, who divide their hair behind into two tresses, and plait, with each tress, three of these strings, which reach more than half-way towards the ground, so that they are usually obliged to draw aside the tassels before they sit down*:] MF says that, accord. to some, عِقَاصٌ signifies *a thorn*, or *the like, with which a woman arranges*, or *puts in order, her hair*: which is strange: (TA:) and IAạr says that it signifies مَدَارِى [i. e. *horns with which people scratch their heads; or things like packing-needles, with which the female hair-dresser arranges*, or *puts in order, the locks of women's hair*]; and this meaning he assigns to it in explaining a verse of Imra-el-Ḳeys [which see below, voce عَقِيصَةٌ, of which word, as well as of عِقْصَةٌ, the word عِقَاصٌ is also a pl.]. (O,* TA.)

عُقُوصٌ: see the next preceding paragraph.

عَقِيصٌ: see عَقْصٌ, last sentence.

عَقِيصَةٌ *A portion of a woman's hair which is twisted, and of which the ends are inserted into the parts next the roots*; (IAth,* Mṣb;) as also ▼ عِقْصَةٌ: (Mṣb:) or *a lock of a woman's hair which she twists, then ties, so that there remains in it a twisting, and then lets hang down*: (Lth, A:) [i. e., *a twisted lock of a woman's hair, which* either *has its end inserted into the part next the roots*, or *is tied, and left to hang down*:] or *i. q.* ضَفِيرَةٌ; as also ▼ عِقْصَةٌ; (Ṣ, O, Ḳ;) the latter on the authority of A'Obeyd: (Ṣ:) pl. (of the former, Ṣ, A, Mṣb, TA) عَقَائِصُ, (Ṣ, A, Mṣb, Ḳ,) and (of the latter, Ṣ, Mṣb) عِقَصٌ, (Ṣ, O, Mṣb, Ḳ,) and (of the former also, Ṣ, Mṣb, and of the latter also, Ṣ, TA) عِقَاصٌ, (Ṣ, O, Mṣb, Ḳ,) of which A'Obeyd cites the following ex. in a verse of Imra-el-Ḳeys:

• غَدَائِرُهُ مُسْتَشْزِرَاتٌ إِلَى العُلَى •
• تَضِلُّ العِقَاصُ فِى مُثَنًّى وَمُرْسَلِ •

[*Its pendent locks being twisted upwards, the twists becoming concealed among* hair *doubled and* hair *made to hang down*]: or, as some say, it [عقاص] signifies *what a woman makes, of her hair, like a pomegranate; each lock of which is termed* عَقِيصَةٌ; the pl. being عِقَاصٌ and عَقَائِصُ. (Ṣ, O.) [See also عِقَاصٌ as expl. by IAạr, above.] عِقَاصٌ is also used in the sense of ذَوَائِبُ [or *Locks of hair hanging down loosely from the middle of the head to the back*]. (Mgh. [But this is said in relation to an instance of its occurrence in which it may with propriety be regarded as pl. of عَقِيصَةٌ or عِقْصَةٌ in any of the senses before explained.])

عِقِّيصٌ: see عَقْصٌ, last sentence, in two places.

عَيْقَصٌ: see عَقْصٌ, last sentence.

أَعْقَصُ A goat (Ṣ, O, Mṣb, Ḳ) or sheep (Mṣb) *whose horns are twisted*, or *contorted, upon his ears*, (Ṣ, O, Mṣb, Ḳ,) *backwards*: (Ṣ, O, Ḳ:) fem. عَقْصَآءُ: (Mṣb:) or عَقْصَآءُ القَرْنِ signifies a شَاة [i. e. sheep or goat] *having a twisting*, or *contortion, in the horn*: (A:) and ▼ مِعْقَاصٌ, a sheep or goat *crooked in the horn*. (Ḳ.) — Also *Having the fingers twisting, one upon another*. (Ibn-'Abbád, O, Ḳ.) — And *Whose central incisors enter into his mouth*, (O, Ḳ, TA,) *and are twisted*. (TA.) — See also عَقْصٌ, last sentence.

مِعْقَصٌ *A crooked arrow*: (Ṣ, O, Ḳ:) and, (Ḳ,) or accord. to Aṣ, (TA,) *an arrow of which the head breaks, and its tongue*, or *tang, remaining therein, is extracted, and beaten until it becomes long, and then restored in its place*; (Ḳ, TA;) but it does not perfectly serve in its stead: (TA:) pl. مَعَاقِصُ. (Ṣ.)

مِعْقَاصٌ: see أَعْقَصُ. — See also مِعْقَاصٌ.

عقف

1. عَقَفَهُ, (Ṣ, O, Mṣb, Ḳ,) aor. ـِ, (O, Mṣb, Ḳ,) inf. n. عَقْفٌ, (Ṣ, O, Mṣb, KL,) *He bent it*; (Ṣ, O, Mṣb, Ḳ, KL;) *crooked it*; *made it hooked*; or *doubled it*: (KL:) and ▼ عقّفهُ, (Mṣb,) inf. n. تَعْقِيفٌ, (Ṣ, KL,) signifies [the same, or] *he bent it*, or *crooked it*: (Ṣ, Mṣb, KL:) [or *he did so much*:] and تَعْقِيفٌ signifies also *the making crook-backed*. (KL.) — عقفت, [app. عَقَفَتْ, the part. n. being عَاقِفٌ, or this may be a possessive epithet, and, if so, the verb may be عَقِفَتْ or عُقِفَتْ,] said of a sheep or goat (شَاة), and likewise, sometimes, of any beast (دَابَّة), *It had the disease termed* عُقَاف [q. v.]. (TA.)

2: see the preceding paragraph.

5: see the next following paragraph.

7. انعقف *It became bent*, (Ṣ, O, Mṣb, Ḳ,) or *crooked*; (Ḳ;) as also in either sense, ▼ تعقّف. (O, Ḳ.)

عَقْفٌ *The fox*. (IF, Ṣ, O, Ḳ.) So in the following verse, (ascribed by IF and IB to Ḥomeyd El-Arḳaṭ, and by J to Ḥomeyd Ibn-Thowr, but said by Ṣgh to be of neither of the Ḥomeyds, TA,)

• كَأَنَّهُ عَقْفٌ تَوَلَّى يَهْرُبُ •
• مِنْ أَكْلُبٍ يَتْبَعْنَ أَكْلُبُ •

[*As though he were a fox that had turned away fleeing from dogs which* (other) *dogs were following*]. (Ṣ, O, TA.)

عُقَافٌ *A disease that attacks the sheep* or *goat*, (Ṣ, O, Ḳ,) *and sometimes any beast*, (O,) *in its legs, so that they become bent*, or *crooked, in consequence of it*. (Ṣ, O, Ḳ.)

عَقُوفٌ A cow's udder *of which the stream of milk comes forth contrarily, on the occasion of milking*. (AḤát, O, Ḳ.)

شَوْكَةٌ عَقِيفَةٌ *A thorn bent like the crooked piece of iron in the head of the spindle*. (TA.)

عُقَّافَةٌ *A piece of wood* [or *a stick*] *crooked* [or *hooked*] *at the head thereof, with which a thing is extended*, (يُمَدُّ, so in the O and L and copies of the Ḳ,) or *drawn*, or *pulled, towards one*, (يُحْجَنُ, so in the CḲ,) *like the* مِحْجَن [q. v.]: (O, L, Ḳ:) or it is [*a part*, app. the *crooked*, or *hooked, head*,] *of the* مِحْجَن: (Mṣb:) and some say that it is *a* صَوْلَجَان [q. v.]. (TA.) [In the present day it is applied to *A hook*, or *a small hook*.]

عَاقِفٌ, applied to a sheep or goat (شَاة, O, Ḳ), and sometimes to any beast (دَابَّة, O), *Having the disease termed* عُقَاف; as also ▼ مَعْقُوفَةُ الرِّجْلِ. (O, Ḳ.)

أَعْقَفُ Anything (IDrd, O) *bent, curved, crooked*, [*hooked*,] *contorted*, or *distorted*. (IDrd, O, Ḳ.) And *Bending*. (O, Ḳ.) — A gazelle *having the horns bent*. (TA.) And [the fem.] عَقْفَآءُ A sheep or goat (شَاة) *of which the horns are contorted* [or *bent down*] *upon its ears*. (TA.) — Also † *Coarse, rough, rude*, or *churlish*; as an epithet applied to an Arab of the desert. (Ṣ, O, Ḳ.) — And † *Poor*; *needy*: (Lth, O, Ḳ:) pl. عُقْفَانٌ. (TA.) — And [the fem.] عَقْفَآءُ signifies [*An iron hook*;] *a piece of iron of which the extremity has been contorted, and in which is a bending*. (O, Ḳ.)

شَعَرٌ مُعَقَّفٌ [*Hair that is recurvate at the extremities*; as though ending with hooks]: (M and TA voce أَحْجَنُ:) and ▼ شَعَرٌ مَعْقُوفٌ [signifies the same]. (TA in art. سدل.) [See also مُعَكَّفٌ, and مَعْكُوفٌ.]

مَعْقُوفٌ applied to an old man, *Bent by reason of great age*. (TA.) — See also عَاقِفٌ: — and مُعَقَّفٌ.

عقفر

Q. 1. عَقْفَرَتْهُ الدَّوَاهِى, (Ṣ, O, Ḳ,) and عقفرت عَلَيْهِ, (Ḳ,) and ▼ اِعْقَنْفَرَتْ عليه, (Lth, O, Ḳ,) *Calamities destroyed him*: (Lth, Ṣ, O:) or *prostrated and destroyed him*. (Ḳ.)

Q. 2. تَعَقْفَرَ *He* (a man) *perished*: (Lth, O:) or *became prostrated and destroyed*, (Ḳ,) by calamities. (Lth, O, Ḳ.)

Q. 3: see 1.

عَقْفَرَةٌ [inf. n. of 1. — Also] *Craftiness*, or *cunning*, of a [demon of the kind called] غُول. (O, TA.)

عَنْقَفِيرٌ *A calamity* (Ṣ, O, Ḳ, TA) *of fortune:* (TA:) like عَنْقَاءُ; from which it is said by IF to be formed, by additional letters: (O:) pl. عَقَافِيرُ. (O, TA.) — *A crafty,* or *cunning,* [demon of the kind called] غُول. (O, TA.) — *A clamorous and foul-tongued* woman, (Ḳ, TA,) *that overcomes with evil.* (TA.) — *A scorpion.* (O, Ḳ.) — A she-camel *so old that the back of her neck almost touches her shoulder* (Ḳ, O, TA) *by reason of her extreme old age.* (TA.)

عقل

1. [The inf. n.] عَقْلٌ signifies The act of *withholding,* or *restraining;* syn. مَنْعٌ. (TA.) [This is app. the primary signification, or it may be from what next follows.] — عَقَلَ البَعِيرَ, (Ṣ, Mgh, O, Mṣb, Ḳ,) aor. ـِ, (Ṣ, O, Mṣb,) inf. n. عَقْلٌ, (Ṣ, Mgh, O, Mṣb,) *He bound the camel with the* [rope *called*] عِقَال; (Mgh;) meaning *he bound the camel's fore shank to his arm;* (Ḳ;) i. e. *he folded together the camel's fore shank and his arm and bound them both in the middle of the arm with the rope called* عِقَال; (Ṣ, O, Mṣb;) and ▼ اعتقلهُ signifies the same; as also ▼ عَقَّلَهُ; (Ḳ;) or you say, عَقَّلْتُ الإِبِلَ, from العِقَال, (Ṣ, O,) inf. n. تَعْقِيلٌ, (O,) [i. e. *I bound the camels in the manner expl. above,*] this verb being with teshdeed because of its application to a number of objects: (Ṣ, O:) and sometimes the hocks were bound with the عِقَال. (TA.) The she-camel, also, was bound with the عِقَال on the occasion of her being covered: — and hence العَقْلُ is metonymically used as meaning الجِمَاعُ [i. e. † *The act of compressing* a woman]. (TA.) — عَقَلْتُ القَتِيلَ, (Ṣ, Mgh, Mṣb, Ḳ,*) or المَقْتُولَ, (Ṣ, O,) aor. as above, (TA,) and so the inf. n., (Mṣb, TA,) means *I gave,* or *paid, the bloodwit to the heir,* or *next of kin, of the slain person:* (Ṣ, Mgh, O, Mṣb, Ḳ:*) for the camels [that constituted the bloodwit] used to be bound with the عِقَال in the yard of the abode of the heir, or next of kin, of the slain person; and in consequence of frequency of usage, the phrase became employed to mean thus when the bloodwit was given in dirhems or deenárs. (Aṣ, Ṣ, O, Mṣb.* [See a verse cited in the first paragraph of art. عيف.]) And [hence] one says also, عَقَلْتُ عَنْهُ, (inf. n. as above, TA,) meaning *I paid for him,* (the slayer, Mgh,) i. e., *in his stead,* (Ṣ, Mgh, O, Mṣb, Ḳ,*) *the bloodwit that was obligatory upon him,* (Ṣ, Mgh, O, Ḳ,*) or *what was obligatory upon him of the bloodwit.* (Mṣb.) And عَقَلْتُ لَهُ دَمَ فُلَانٍ *I relinquished in his favour retaliation of the blood of such a one for the bloodwit.* (Ṣ, O, Mṣb, Ḳ.*) لَا تَعْقِلُ العَاقِلَةُ عَمْدًا وَلَا عَبْدًا, (Ṣ, Mgh, O, Mṣb, Ḳ,) in a trad. (Ṣ, O, Mṣb) of Esh-Shaabee, (O,) or a saying of Esh-Shaabee, (Mgh,* Ḳ,) not a trad., (Ḳ,) but the like occurs in a trad. related on the authority of I'Ab, (TA,) [meaning, accord. to an expl. of the verb when trans. without a particle, mentioned above, *Those who are responsible for the payment of a bloodwit* in certain cases *shall not pay it for an intentional act* of slaying or the like, *nor for* the slaying or the like of *a slave,*] applies, accord. to Aboo-Ḥaneefeh, to the case of a slave's committing a crime against a free person: (Ṣ, O, Mṣb, Ḳ: [and thus as expl. in the Mgh:]) but, (Ṣ, O, Mṣb, Ḳ,) accord. to Ibn-Abee-Leylà, (Ṣ, O, Mṣb,) it applies to the case of a free person's committing a crime against a slave; for if the meaning were as Aboo-Ḥaneefeh says, the phrase would be لَا تَعْقِلُ العَاقِلَةُ عَنْ عَبْدٍ; (Ṣ, O, Mṣb, Ḳ;) and Aṣ pronounced this to be correct: (Ṣ, O, Mṣb:*) Akmal-ed-Deen, however, in the Exposition of the Hidáyeh, says that عَقَلْتُهُ is used in the sense of عَقَلْتُ عَنْهُ, and that the context of the trad. indicates this meaning, which MF also defends. (TA.) [See also the saying لَا أَعْقِلُ الكَلْبَ الهَرَّارَ in art. هر.] — عَقَلَهُ, inf. n. as above, also means *He set him up* [app. a man] *on one of his legs;* [app. from عَقَلَ البَعِيرَ;] as also عَكَلَهُ: and every عَقْل is *a raising.* (TA.) — Also, [agreeably with the explanation of the inf. n. in the first sentence of this art.,] and ▼ عقّلهُ, and ▼ تعقّلهُ, (TA, [see also the first paragraph of art. عجس,]) and ▼ اعتقلهُ, (Mṣb, TA,) *He withheld him,* or *restrained him,* (Mṣb, TA,) عَنْ حَاجَتِهِ *from the object of his want.* (TA.) — And [hence,] عَقَلَ الدَّوَآءُ بَطْنَهُ, (Ṣ, O, Mṣb, Ḳ,) aor. ـِ (Ṣ, Ḳ) and ـُ, (Ḳ,) inf. n. عَقْلٌ, (TA,) *The medicine bound,* or *confined, his belly* [or *bowels*]; syn. أَمْسَكَهُ: (Ṣ, O, Mṣb, Ḳ:) accord. to some, particularly *after looseness:* and ▼ اعتقل بَطْنَهُ signifies the same. (TA.) And يَعْقِلُ الطَّبْعَ is said of a medicine [as meaning, in like manner, *It binds the bowels; is astringent*]. (TA in art. حمض; &c.) And عقل البَطْنُ [app. عَقَلَ] *The belly* [or *bowels*] *became bound,* or *confined;* syn. اسْتَمْسَكَ. (TA.) — عَقَلَ عَلَى القَوْمِ, [aor. ـِ,] inf. n. عِقَالٌ, means *He collected,* or *exacted, the poor-rates of the people,* or *party;* [app. from عَقَلَ البَعِيرَ; as though he bound with the rope called عِقَال the camels that he collected;] on the authority of IKṭṭ. (TA.) 'Omar, when he had deferred [collecting] the poor-rate in the year [of drought called] عَامُ الرَّمَادَةِ, sent Ibn-Abee-Dhubáb, and said, اِعْقِلْ عَلَيْهِمْ عِقَالَيْنِ فَاقْسِمْ فِيهِمْ عِقَالًا وَأْتِنِى بِالآخَرِ [*Collect thou from them two years' poor-rate; then divide among them one year's poor-rate, and bring to me the other*]. (O.) One says of the collector of the poor-rate, يَعْقِلُ الصَّدَقَةَ [*He collects,* or *exacts, the poor-rate*]. (Ṣ, O.) — عَقَلَ فُلَانًا and ▼ اعتقلهُ signify *He threw down such a one* [*in wrestling*] *by twisting his leg upon the latter's leg:* (Ḳ,* TA:) [or] you say, صَارَعَهُ فَاعْتَقَلَهُ ▼ الشُّغْزُبِيَّةَ *He wrestled with him and twisted his leg upon the leg of the latter:* (Ṣ, O:) and one says of a wrestler, لِفُلَانٍ ▼ عُقْلَةٌ يَعْقِلُ بِهَا النَّاسَ, (Ṣ, O,) or يَعْتَقِلُ بِهَا النَّاسَ, i. e. [*Such a one has*] *a* [*mode of*] *twisting his leg with another's* [*whereby he wrestles with men*]. (TA.) — عَقَلَتْ شَعْرَهَا, (inf. n. عَقْلٌ, TA,) said of a woman, *She combed her hair:* (Ṣ, O:) or *combed it in a certain manner;* as also ▼ عَقَّلَتْهُ. (TA.) = عَقَلَ, aor. ـِ, inf. n. عَقْلٌ and ▼ مَعْقُولٌ, (Ṣ, O, Ḳ,) or the latter, accord. to Sb, is an epithet, [or a pass. part. n.,] for he used to say that no inf. n. has the measure مَفْعُولٌ, (Ṣ, O,) *He was,* or *became,* عَاقِل [i. e. *intelligent,* &c.; and so ▼ تعقّل; as though he were withheld, or restrained, from doing that which is not suitable, or befitting: see عَقْلٌ below]: and ▼ عقّل, (Ḳ, TA,) inf. n. تَعْقِيلٌ, (TA,) signifies the same, (Ḳ,) or [*he possessed much intelligence,* for] it is with teshdeed to denote muchness: (TA:) and عَقُلَ, aor. ـُ, is a dial. var. of عَقَلَ, aor. ـِ, signifying *he became* عَاقِل. (IKṭṭ, TA.) — And عَقَلَ الشَّىْءَ, (Mṣb, Ḳ, TA,) aor. ـِ, inf. n. عَقْلٌ, (Mṣb, TA,) *He understood,* or *knew, the thing;* syn. فَهِمَهُ: (Ḳ, TA:) or *i. q.* تَدَبَّرَهُ [app. as meaning *he looked into, considered, examined,* or *studied, the thing repeatedly, until he knew it*]; and عَقُلَ, aor. ـُ, is a dial. var. thereof. (Mṣb.) See also 5. — مَا أَعْقِلُهُ عَنْكَ شَيْئًا, (Ṣ, and so in the Ḳ accord. to my copy of the TA, but in the CḲ and in my MS. copy of the Ḳ ▼ أَعْقَلَهُ,) meaning دَعْ عَنْكَ الشَّكَّ [*Dismiss from thee doubt*], is [said to be] mentioned by Sb; as though the speaker said, مَا أَعْلَمُ شَيْئًا مِمَّا تَقُولُ فَدَعْ عَنْكَ الشَّكَّ [*I know not aught of what thou sayest, so dismiss from thee doubt*]; and [to be] like the phrases حُلْ عَنْكَ and بِرْ عَنْكَ: Bekr El-Mázinee says, "I asked AZ and Aṣ and Aboo-Málik and Akh respecting this phrase, and they all said, 'We know not what it is:'" (so in the Ṣ:) [but] it is a mistake, for مَا أَغْفَلَهُ; (Ḳ, TA;) and thus it is mentioned by Sb and others, with غ and ف. (TA.) نَخْلَةٌ لَا تَعْقِلُ الإِبَارَ ‡ *A palm-tree that will not receive fecundation* is a tropical phrase [perhaps from عَقَلَ meaning "he understood" a thing]. (A, TA.) — عَاقَلْتُهُ فَعَقَلْتُهُ: see 3. — عَقَلَ, aor. ـِ, inf. n. عُقُولٌ (Ṣ, O, Ḳ) and عَقْلٌ, (Ḳ,) *He* (a mountain-goat, Ṣ, O) *became,* or *made himself, inaccessible in a high mountain:* (Ṣ: in the O unexplained:) or *he* (a gazelle) *ascended* [*a mountain*]. (Ḳ.) Accord. to Az, العُقُولُ signifies *The protecting oneself in a mountain.* (TA.) And one says, عَقَلَ إِلَيْهِ, aor. ـِ, inf. n. عَقْلٌ and عُقُولٌ, *He betook himself to him,* or *it, for refuge, protection, covert,* or *lodging.* (Ḳ.) — عَقَلَ الظِّلُّ, (Ṣ, O, Ḳ,) aor. ـِ, (Ḳ,) inf. n. عَقْلٌ (Ḳ) [and probably عُقُولٌ also], *The shade declined, and contracted,* or *shrank, at midday;* (Ṣ, O;) *the sun became high, and the shade almost disappeared.* (Ṣ, O, Ḳ.) = عَقَلَ, (O, Ḳ,) aor. ـِ, (Ḳ,) inf. n. عَقْلٌ, (TA,) said of a camel, *He pastured upon the plant called* عَاقُول. (O, Ḳ.) = عَقِلَ, aor. ـَ, (Ḳ,) inf. n. عَقَلٌ, (Ṣ, O, Ḳ,) *He* (a camel) *had a twisting in the hind leg,* (Ṣ, O, Ḳ,) *and much width* [*between the hind legs*]: (Ṣ, O:) or *had an excessive wideness,* or *spreading, of the hind legs, so that the hocks knocked together:* (ISk, Ṣ, O:) or *had a knocking together of the knees.* (Ḳ.) [See also رَوَحٌ.]

2: see 1, in four places. = عقّلهُ, inf. n. تَعْقِيلٌ,

also signifies *He, or it, rendered him* عَاقِل [i. e. *intelligent, &c.*]. (O, Ḳ.) — And عَقَّلَ said of a grape-vine, (O, Ḳ,) inf. n. as above, (TA,) *It put forth its* عُقَّيْلَى, or *grapes in their first, sour, state.* (O, Ḳ.)

3. المَرْأَةُ تُعَاقِلُ الرَّجُلَ إِلَى ثُلُثِ دِيَتِهَا (Ṣ, Mgh, O, Ḳ) means *The woman is on a par with the man to the third part of her bloodwit;* (Ṣ, Mgh, O;) she receives like as the man receives [up to that point]: (Mgh:) i. e., [for instance,] his مُوضِحَة [or wound of the head for which the mulct is five camels] and her مُوضِحَة are equal; (Ḳ;) but when the portion reaches to the third of the bloodwit, her [portion of the] bloodwit is the half of that of the man: (Ṣ, O, Ḳ:) thus, for one of her fingers, ten camels are due to her, as in the case of the finger of the man; for two of her fingers, twenty camels; and for three of her fingers, thirty; but for four of her fingers, only twenty, because they exceed the third, therefore the portion is reduced to the half of what is due to the man: so accord. to Ibn-El-Museiyab: but Esh-Sháfi'ee and the people of El-Koofeh assign for the finger of the woman five camels, and for two of her fingers ten; and regard not the third part. (TA.) — ▾ عَاقَلْتُهُ فَعَقَلْتُهُ, (Ṣ, O, Ḳ,*) inf. n. of the former مُعَاقَلَةٌ, (TA,) and aor. of the latter ـُ, (Ṣ, O, Ḳ,) and inf. n. عَقْلٌ, (TA,) means *I vied,* or *contended, with him for superiority in* عَقْل [or *intelligence*], (O, TA,) *and I surpassed him therein.* (Ṣ, O, Ḳ,* TA.)

4. اعقل *He* (a man) *owed what is termed* عِقَال, (O, Ḳ, TA,) i. e. *a year's poor-rate.* (TA.) — اعقل القَوْمُ *The people,* or *party, became in the condition of finding the shade to have declined, and contracted,* or *shrunk, with them, at midday.* (Ṣ, O.) — اعقلهُ *He found him to be* عَاقِل [i. e. *intelligent, &c.*]: (Ḳ:) it is similar to أَحْمَدَهُ and أَبْخَلَهُ. (TA.) — See also 1, last quarter.

5. تعقّلهُ: see 1, near the middle: — and see 8, in four places. — تَعَقَّلْ لِى بِكَفَّيْكَ حَتَّى أَرْكَبَ بَعِيرِى, (O, Ḳ,*) a saying heard by Az from an Arab of the desert, (O,) means *Put thy two hands together for me, and intersert thy fingers together, in order that I may put my foot upon them,* i. e. upon thy hands, *and mount my camel;* for the camel was standing; (O, Ḳ;*) and was laden; and if he had made him to lie down, would not rise with him and his load. (O.) — [It is used in philosophical works as meaning *He conceived it in his mind, abstractedly,* and *otherwise;* and so, sometimes, ▾ عَقَلَهُ, aor. ـِ, inf. n. عَقْلٌ. Hence one says, هٰذَا شَىْءٌ لَا يُتَعَقَّلُ *This is a thing that is not conceivable.*] — تعقّل as intrans.: see 1, latter half. — [Hence, *He recovered his intellect,* or *understanding.* — And] *He affected,* or *endeavoured to acquire,* عَقْل [i. e. *intelligence, &c.*]: like as one says تَحَلَّمَ and تَكَيَّسَ. (Ṣ, O.) [See also 6.] — Said of an animal of the chase, as meaning *It stuck fast,* and *became caught,* in a net or the like, it is a coined word, not heard [from the Arabs of chaste speech]. (Mgh.)

6. تعاقلوا دَمَ فُلَانٍ *They paid among themselves,* or *conjointly, the mulct for the blood of such a one.* (Ḳ.) It is said in a trad., إِنَّا لَا نَتَعَاقَلُ المُضَغَ *Verily we will not pay among ourselves,* or *conjointly, the mulcts for slight wounds of the head,* [lit. *the stroke with a sword,*] but will oblige him who commits the offence to pay the mulct for it: i. e. the people of the towns or villages shall not pay the mulcts for the people of the desert; nor the people of the desert, for the people of the towns or villages; in the like of the case of the [wound termed] مُوضِحَة. (TA.) And in another it is said, يَتَعَاقَلُونَ بَيْنَهُمْ مَعَاقِلَهُمُ الأُولَى [*They shall take and give among themselves,* or *conjointly, their former bloodwits*]: i. e. they shall be as they were in respect of the taking and giving of bloodwits. (TA.) And one says, القَوْمُ عَلَى مَا كَانُوا يَتَعَاقَلُونَ عَلَيْهِ [*The people,* or *party, are* acting *in conformity with that* usage *in accordance with which they used to pay and receive among themselves bloodwits*]. (Ṣ, O.) — تعاقل also signifies *He affected,* or *made a show of possessing,* عَقْل [i. e. *intelligence, &c.*], *without having it.* (Ṣ, O.) [See also 5.]

8: see 1, former half, in three places. — اِعْتَقَلَ said of a man, *He was withheld, restrained,* or *confined.* (Ṣ, O.) — And اُعْتُقِلَ لِسَانُهُ, (Ṣ, Mgh, O, Mṣb, Ḳ,) and اِعْتَقَلَ, also, (Mṣb,) *His tongue was withheld,* or *restrained,* (Mgh, Mṣb, TA,) *from speaking;* (Mgh, Mṣb;) *he was unable to speak.* (Ṣ, Mgh, O, Mṣb, Ḳ.) — [Hence,] اعتقل الشَّاةَ *He put the hind legs of the ewe,* or *she-goat, between his shank and his thigh,* (Ṣ, O, Ḳ,) *to milk her,* (Ṣ, O,) or *and so milked her.* (Ḳ.) And اعتقل رُمْحَهُ *He put his spear between his shank and his stirrup* [or *stirrup-leather*]: (Ṣ, O, Ḳ:) or *he* (a man riding) *put his spear beneath his thigh, and dragged the end of it upon the ground behind him.* (IAth, TA.) And اعتقل الرَّحْلَ, and ▾ تعقّلهُ; (O;) or اعتقل الرِّجْلَ, (O, Ḳ,) accord. to one relation of a verse of Dhu-r-Rummeh, (O,) and ▾ تعقّلها; (Ḳ;) *He* [a man riding upon a camel] *folded his leg, and put it upon the* مَوْرِك: (O, Ḳ,* TA:) in the Ḳ, الوَرِك is erroneously put for المَوْرِك: (TA:) the مَوْرِك is before the وَاسِطَة [or upright piece of wood in the fore part] of the camel's saddle: (AO, in TA art. ورك:) and one says also, اعتقل قَادِمَةَ رَحْلِهِ and ▾ تعقّلها; both meaning the same [as above]: (TA:) and اعتقلهُ and ▾ تعقّل السَّرْجَ *He folded his leg upon the fore part of the* سرج [or *saddle of the horse or the like*]. (Mgh.) — See also 1, latter half, in three places. — الاِعْتِقَالُ also signifies *The inserting a* سَيْر [or *narrow strip of skin or leather*], *when sewing a skin, beneath a* سَيْر, *in order that it may become strong, and that the water may not issue from it.* (AA, O.) — And one says, اعتقل مِنْ دَمِ فُلَانٍ, (O, Ḳ,) and مِنْ طَائِلَتِهِ, (O,) meaning *He took,* or *received, the* عَقْل, (O, Ḳ, TA,) i. e. the *mulct for the blood of such a one.* (TA.)

10. [استعقلهُ *He counted, accounted,* or *esteemed, him* عَاقِل, i. e. *intelligent, &c.*: for] you say of a man, يُسْتَعْقَلُ [from العَقْلُ], like as you say يُسْتَحْمَقُ [from الحُمْقُ], and يُسْتَرَاىُ from الرَّأْى. (AA, Ṣ in art. رأى.)

عَقْلٌ an inf. n. used as a subst. [properly so termed], (Mṣb,) *A bloodwit,* or *mulct for bloodshed;* syn. دِيَةٌ; (Aṣ, Ṣ, Mgh, O, Mṣb, Ḳ;) so called for a reason mentioned in the first paragraph in the explanation of the phrase عَقَلْتُ القَتِيلَ; (Aṣ, Ṣ, Mgh,* O, Mṣb;) as also ▾ مَعْقُلَةٌ, (Ṣ, Mgh, O, Ḳ,) of which ▾ مَعْقَلَةٌ, with fet-ḥ to the ق, is a dial. var., mentioned in the R; (TA;) and of which the pl. is مَعَاقِلُ: (Ṣ, O, Ḳ:) one says, ▾ لَنَا عِنْدَ فُلَانٍ ضَمَدٌ مِنْ مَعْقُلَةٍ i. e. *We have a remainder of a bloodwit owed to us by such a one.* (Ṣ, O.) And ▾ هُمْ عَلَى مَعَاقِلِهِمِ الأُولَى *They are* [acting] *in conformity with* [the usages relating to] *the bloodwits that were in the Time of Ignorance;* (Ḳ, TA;) or meaning عَلَى مَا كَانُوا يَتَعَاقَلُونَ عَلَيْهِ [expl. above (see 6)]: (Ṣ, O:) or *they are* [acting] *in conformity with the conditions of their fathers;* (Ḳ, TA;) but the former is the primary meaning: (TA:) and [hence] صَارَ دَمُ فُلَانٍ مَعْقُلَةً ▾ عَلَى قَوْمِهِ *The blood of such a one became* [*the occasion of*] *a debt incumbent on his people,* or *party,* (Ṣ, O, Ḳ,*) *to be paid by them from their possessions.* (Ṣ, O.) — And as being originally the inf. n. of عَقَلَ in the phrase عَقَلَ الشَّىْءَ meaning فَهِمَهُ [or] تَدَبَّرَهُ; (Mṣb;) or as originally meaning المَنْعُ, because it withholds, or restrains, its possessor from doing that which is not suitable; or from المَعْقِلُ as meaning "the place to which one has recourse for protection &c.," because its possessor has recourse to it; (TA;) العَقْلُ signifies also *Intelligence, understanding, intellect, mind, reason,* or *knowledge;* syn. الحِجْرُ, (Ṣ, O,) and النُّهَى, (Ṣ,) or النُّهْيَةُ, (O,) or الحِجَا, and اللُّبُّ, (Mṣb,) or العِلْمُ, (Ḳ,) or *the contr. of* الحُمْقُ; (M, TA;) or *the knowledge of the qualities of things, of their goodness and their badness, and their perfectness and their defectiveness;* or *the knowledge of the better of two good things, and of the worse of two bad things,* or *of affairs absolutely;* or *a faculty whereby is the discrimination between the bad and the good;* (Ḳ, TA;) but these and other explanations of العَقْل in the Ḳ are all in treatises of intellectual things, and not mentioned by the leading lexicologists; (TA; [in which are added several more explanations of a similar kind that have no proper place in this work;]) some say that it is *an innate property by which man is prepared to understand speech;* (Mṣb;) the truth is, that it is *a spiritual light,* (Ḳ, TA,) *shed into the heart and the brain,* (TA,) *whereby the soul acquires the instinctive and speculative kinds of knowledge, and the commencement of its existence is on the occasion of the young's becoming in the fœtal state,* [or *rather of its quickening,*] *after which it continues to increase until it becomes complete on the attainment of puberty,*

(Ḳ, TA,) or *until the attainment of forty years:* (TA:) the pl. is عُقُولٌ: (Ḳ:) Sb mentions عَقْلٌ as an instance of an inf. n. having a pl., namely, عُقُولٌ; like شُغْلٌ and مَرَضٌ: (TA in art. مرض:) IAạr says, (O,) العَقْلُ is [*syn. with*] القَلْبُ, and القَلْبُ is [*syn. with*] العَقْلُ: (O, Ḳ:) and ▼ المَعْقُولُ is [said to be] a subst., or name, for العَقْلُ, like المَيْسُورُ and المَجْلُودُ for اليُسْرُ and الجَلَادَةُ: (Ḥar p. 12:) it is said in a prov., ▼ مَا لَهُ جُولٌ وَلَا مَعْقُولٌ, (Meyd, and Ḥar ubi suprà,) meaning *He has not strong purpose of mind,* [to withhold, or protect, him,] like the جول [or casing] of the well of the collapsing whereof one is free from fear because of its firmness, *nor intellect,* or *intelligence,* (عَقْل,) to withhold him from doing that which is not suitable to the likes of him. (Meyd. [But see مَعْقُولٌ below.]) [Hence, أَسْنَانُ العَقْلِ (see 1 in art. حنك) and أَضْرَاسُ العَقْلِ (see ضِرْسٌ), both meaning *The wisdom-teeth.*] ═ [It is said that] عَقْلٌ also signifies *A fortress;* syn. حِصْنٌ. (Ḳ.) [But this seems to be doubtful.] See مَعْقِلٌ. ═ And *A sort of red cloth* (Ṣ, O, Ḳ) *with which the* [*women's camel-vehicle called*] هَوْدَج *is covered:* (Ḳ:) or *a sort of what are called* بُرُود [pl. of بُرْدٌ, q. v.] or *a sort of figured cloth,* (Ḳ,) or, as in the M, *of red figured cloth:* (TA:) or *such as is figured with long forms.* (Ḥar p. 416.)

عُقْلَةٌ *A bond like the* عِقَال [q. v.]: or *a shackle.* (Ḥar p. 199.) — [Hence it seems to signify *An impediment* of any kind.] One says, بِهِ عُقْلَةٌ مِنَ السِّحْرِ وَقَدْ عُمِلَتْ لَهُ نُشْرَةٌ [app. meaning *In him is an impediment arising from enchantment, and a charm,* or *an amulet, has been made for him*]. (Ṣ, O.) — And *A* [*mode of*] *twisting one's leg with another's in wrestling.* (TA.) See 1, latter half. — And *A twisting of the tongue when one desires to speak.* (Mbr, TA in art. حبس.) — And, in the conventional language of the geomancers, (O, Ḳ,) it consists of *A unit and a pair and a unit,* (O,) the *sign* ⁞: (Ḳ, TA:) also called ثِقَافٌ. (O, TA.)

[عَقْلِيٌّ *Intellectual,* as meaning *of,* or *relating to, the intellect.*]

عِقَالٌ *A rope with which a camel's fore shank is bound to his arm, both being folded together and bound in the middle of the arm:* pl. عُقُلٌ. (Ṣ, O, Mṣb.) [See also شِكَالٌ.] — And The *poor-rate* (Ṣ, Mgh, O, Mṣb, Ḳ) *of a year,* (Ṣ, Mgh, O, Ḳ,) *consisting of camels* and *of sheep* or *goats.* (Ḳ.) [See a verse cited in the first paragraph of art. سعى and سعو.] One says, عَلَى بَنِى فُلَانٍ عِقَالَانِ *On the sons of such a one lies a poor-rate of two years.* (Ṣ, O.) And hence the saying of Aboo-Bekr, لَوْ مَنَعُونِى عِقَالًا (Mgh, O, Mṣb) *If they refused me a year's poor-rate:* (Mgh, O:) and it is said that the phrase أَخَذَ عِقَالًا was used when the collector of the poor-rate took the camels themselves, not their price: (TA:) or Aboo-Bekr meant *a rope of the kind above mentioned;* (Mgh, O, Mṣb;) for when one gave the poor-rate of his camels, he gave with them their عُقُل: (O, Mṣb:) or (Mgh, TA) he meant thereby a paltry thing, (Mgh, Mṣb, TA,) of the value of the [rope called] عِقَال: (TA:) or he said عَنَاقًا ["a she-kid"]; (Mgh, TA;) so accord. to Bkh, (Mgh,) and most others: (TA:) or جُدَيًّا ["a little kid"]. (Mgh, TA.) — Also *A young* [*she-camel such as is called*] قَلُوص. (Ḳ.) — عِقَالُ المِئِينَ means *The man of high rank who, when he has been made a prisoner, is ransomed with hundreds of camels.* (Ḳ.)

عَقُولٌ A medicine *that binds, confines,* or *astringes, the belly* [or *bowels*]; (Ṣ, O, Mṣb;) as also ▼ عَاقُولٌ; *contr. of* حَادُورٌ. (A in art. حدر.) ═ See also عَاقِلٌ, latter half, in two places.

عَقِيلَةٌ A woman *of generous race,* (Ṣ, O, Ḳ,) *modest,* or *bashful,* (Ṣ, O,) *that is kept behind the curtain,* (Ḳ,) *held in high estimation:* (TA:) the *excellent* of camels, (Az, Ṣ, O, Ḳ,) and of other things: (Az, TA:) or the *most excellent* of every kind of thing: (Ṣ, O, Ḳ:) and the *chief* of a people: (Ḳ:) the first is the primary signification: then it became used as meaning the *excellent* of any kind of things, substantial, and also ideal, as speech, or language: pl. عَقَائِلُ. (TA.) And العَقِيلَةُ, (Ḳ,) or عَقِيلَةُ البَحْرِ, (Ṣ, O, TA,) signifies *The pearl,* or *large pearl:* (Ṣ, O, Ḳ,* TA:*) or *the large and clear pearl:* or, accord. to IB, *the pearl,* or *large pearl, in its shell.* (TA.)

إِبِلٌ عُقَيْلِيَّةٌ *Certain hardy, excellent, highly esteemed, camels, of Nejd.* (Mṣb.)

عُقَّالٌ *A limping,* or *slight lameness,* syn. ظَلَعٌ, (so in copies of the Ṣ,) or ضَلَعٌ [which is said to signify the same, or correctly to signify *a natural crookedness*], (so in other copies of the Ṣ and in the O,) *which occurs in the legs of a beast:* (Ṣ, O:) or *a certain disease in the hind leg of a beast, such that, when he goes along, he limps,* or *is slightly lame, for a while, after which he stretches forth;* (Ḳ, TA;) accord. to A'Obeyd, (TA,) *peculiar to the horse;* (Ḳ, TA;) but *it mostly occurs in sheep* or *goats.* (TA.) — دَآءٌ ذُو عُقَّالٍ *A disease of which one will not be cured.* (TA.) ═ عُقَّالُ الكَلَإِ *Three herbs that remain after having been cut,* which are the سَعْدَانَة and the حُلَّب and the قُطْبَة. (TA.) ═ And عَقَاقِيلُ, [a pl.] of which the sing. is not mentioned, [perhaps pl. of عُقَّالٌ, but in two senses a pl. of عَقَنْقَلٌ,] signifies The *portions* of a grape-vine *that are raised and supported upon a trellis* or *the like.* (TA.)

عُقَيْلَى *Grapes in their first, sour, state.* (O, Ḳ.)

أَخَذَهُ العُقَيْلَى *i. q.* شَغْزَبَةٌ and شَغْرَبَةٌ. (AZ, TA in art. شغزب.)

عَاقِلٌ [act. part. n. of عَقَلَ: and as such,] The *payer of a bloodwit:* pl. [or rather coll. gen. n.] ▼ عَاقِلَةٌ: (Mṣb:) the latter is an epithet in which the quality of a subst. predominates; (TA;) and signifies a man's *party* (Ṣ, Mgh, O, Ḳ, TA) *who league together to defend one another,* (Ṣ, O, Ḳ, TA,) *consisting of the relations on the father's side,* (Ṣ, Mgh,* O, TA,) *who pay the bloodwit* (Ṣ, Mgh, O, TA) [app. *in conjunction with the slayer*] *for him who has been slain unintentionally:* (Ṣ, O, TA:) it was decided by the Prophet that it was to be paid in three years, to the heirs of the person slain: (TA:) they look to the offender's brothers on the father's side, who, if they take it upon them, pay it in three years: if they do not take it upon them, the debt is transferred to the sons [meaning all the male descendants] of his grandfather; and in default of their doing so, to those of his father's grandfather; and in default of their doing so, to those of his grandfather's grandfather; and so on: it is not transferred from any one of these classes unless they are unable [to pay it]: and such as are enrolled in a register [of soldiers or pensioners or any corporation] are alike in respect of the bloodwit: (IAth, TA:) or, accord. to the people of El-'Irák, it means the *persons enrolled in the registers* [*of soldiers* or *of others*]: (Ṣ, O:) or it is applied to the *persons of the register which was that of the slayer; who derive their subsistence-money,* or *allowances, from the revenues of a particular register:* (Mgh:) Aḥmad Ibn-Ḥambal is related to have said to Is-ḥáḳ Ibn-Manṣoor, it is applied to the *tribe* (قَبِيلَة) [of the slayer]; but that they bear responsibility [only] in proportion to their ability; and that if there is no عَاقِلَة, it [i. e. the bloodwit] is not to be from the property of the offender; but Is-ḥáḳ says that in this case it is to be from the treasury of the state, the bloodwit not being [in any case] made a thing of no account: (TA:) the pl. of عَاقِلَةٌ thus applied is عَوَاقِلُ. (Mṣb.) ═ عَاقِلٌ also signifies *Having,* or *possessing,* عَقْل [i. e. *intelligence, understanding,* &c.; or *intelligent,* &c.; a *rational* being]; (Ṣ, O, Mṣb, Ḳ;) and so ▼ عَقُولٌ, (Ṣ, O, Ḳ,) or this latter has an intensive signification [i. e. *having much intelligence* &c.]: (TA: [see an ex. in a saying cited voce أَبْلَهُ, in art. بله:]) the former is expl. by some as applied to a man *who withholds,* or *restrains, and turns back, his soul from its inclinations,* or *blamable inclinations:* (TA:) and it is likewise applied to a woman, as also عَاقِلَةٌ: (Mṣb:) the pl. masc. is عُقَّالٌ and عُقَلَآءُ, (Mṣb, Ḳ,) this latter pl. sometimes used; and the pl. fem. is عَوَاقِلُ and عَاقِلَاتٌ. (Mṣb.) — عَاقِلٌ is also applied to a mountain-goat, as an epithet, signifying *That protects himself in his mountain from the hunter:* (TA:) [and in like manner ▼ عَقُولٌ is said by Freytag to be used in the Deewán of Jereer.] And it is [also] a name for *A mountain-goat,* (Ṣ, O,) or *a gazelle;* (Ḳ;) because it renders itself inaccessible in a high mountain. (Ṣ, O, Ḳ.*) — And عَاقِلَةٌ signifies *A female comber* of the hair. (Ṣ, O.)

عَاقِلَةٌ, as a coll. gen. n.: see عَاقِلٌ; of which it is also fem.

عَاقُولٌ: see عَقُولٌ. ═ Also *A bent portion,* (Ṣ,

O,) or *place of bending*, (Ḳ,) of a river, and of a valley, (Ṣ, O, Ḳ,) and of sand: (Ṣ, O:) pl. عَوَاقِيلُ: or the عَوَاقِيل of valleys are the *angles, in the places of bending,* thereof; and the sing. is عَاقُولٌ. (TA.) — And The *main of the sea*: or the *waves thereof.* (Ḳ.) — And *A land in which* (so in copies of the Ḳ, but in some of them *to which,*) *one will not find the right way,* (Ḳ, TA,) *because of its many places of winding.* (TA.) — [Hence,] عَوَاقِيلُ الأُمُورِ *What are confused and dubious of affairs.* (Ṣ, O, Ḳ.*) — And [hence] one says, إِنَّهُ لَذُو عَوَاقِيلَ, meaning *Verily he is an author,* or *a doer, of evil.* (TA.) — Also *A certain plant,* (O, Ḳ,) *well known,* (Ḳ,) not mentioned by AḤn (O, TA) in the Book of Plants; (TA;) [the *prickly hedysarum; hedysarum alhagi* of Linn.; common in Egypt, and there called by this name; fully described by Forskål in his Flora Aegypt. Arab., p. 136;] *it has thorns; camels pasture upon it; and* [*hence*] *it is called* شَوْكُ الجِمَالِ; *it grows upon the dykes and the* تُرَع [or *canals for irrigation*]; *and has a violet-coloured flower.* (TA.) [See also تَرَنْجَبِينٌ; and see حَاجٌ, in art. حوج.]

عَنْقَلٌ: see the next paragraph.

عَقَنْقَلٌ *A great* كَثِيب [i. e. *hill,* or *heap,* or *oblong* or *extended gibbous hill,*] *of intermingled sands:* (Ṣ, O:) or *a* كثيب *that is accumulated* (Ḳ, TA) *and intermingled:* or *a* حَبْل [or *long and elevated tract*] *of sand, having winding portions, and* حِرَف [app. meaning *ridges*], *and compacted:* (TA:) accord. to El-Aḥmar, it is the *largest quantity of sand; larger than the* كثيب: (Ṣ voce لَبَبٌ:) pl. عَقَاقِلُ (Ṣ, O) and عَقَاقِيلُ (O) and عَقَنْقَلَاتٌ. (TA.) — And *A great, wide, valley:* (Ḳ:) pl. عَقَاقِلُ and عَقَاقِيلُ. (TA.) — Also, (Ṣ, O, Ḳ,) sometimes, (Ṣ, O,) and ↓ عَنْقَلٌ, (O, Ḳ,) The مَصَارِين [or *intestines into which the food passes from the stomach*], (Ṣ, O,) or قَانِصَة [which here probably signifies the same], (Ḳ,) of a [lizard of the species called] ضَبّ: (Ṣ, O, Ḳ:) or the [*portion of fat termed*] كُشْيَة of the ضبّ. (TA.) أَطْعِمْ أَخَاكَ مِنْ عَقَنْقَلِ الضَّبِّ [*Give thy brother to eat of the intestines, &c., of the ḍabb:* or, as some relate it, مِنْ كُشْيَةِ الضَّبِّ:] is a prov., said in urging a man to make another to share in the means of subsistence; or, accord. to some, denoting derision. (TA.) — Also *A* [*drinking-cup, or bowl, of the kind called*] قَدَح. (Ibn-'Abbád, O, Ḳ.) — And *A sword.* (Ibn-'Abbád, O, Ḳ.)

أَعْقَلُ, applied to a camel, *Having what is termed* عَقَلٌ, i. e. *a twisting in the hind leg,* &c.: (Ṣ, O, Ḳ: [see the last portion of the first paragraph:]) fem. عَقْلَآءُ, applied to a she-camel. (Ṣ, Ḳ.) — [Also *More,* and *most,* عَاقِل, or *intelligent,* &c.]

مَعْقِلٌ *A place to which one betakes himself for refuge, protection, preservation, covert,* or *lodging;* syn. مَلْجَأٌ; (Ṣ, Mgh, O, Mṣb, Ḳ;) as also ↓ عَقْلٌ, (Ṣ, O, Ḳ,) of which the pl. is عُقُولٌ: (Ṣ, O:) but Az says that he had not heard عقل in this sense on any authority except that of Lth; and held العُقُول, which is cited as an ex. of its pl., to signify "the protecting oneself in a mountain:" (TA:) and مَعْقِلٌ signifies also *a fortress;* [like as عَقْلٌ is said to do;] syn. حِصْنٌ: (Mgh:) the pl. is مَعَاقِلُ. (TA.) Hence one says, using it metaphorically, هُوَ مَعْقِلُ قَوْمِهِ ‡ *He is the refuge of his people:* and the kings of Ḥimyer are termed in a trad. مَعَاقِلُ الأَرْضِ, meaning *The fortresses* [or *refuges*] *of the land.* (TA.) — [It is perhaps primarily used in relation to camels; for] مَعَاقِلُ الإِبِلِ means *The places in which the camels are bound with the rope called* عِقَال. (TA.)

مَعْقُلَةٌ and مَعْقَلَةٌ; and the pl.: see عَقْلٌ, first quarter, in five places. — [It seems to be implied in the Ṣ and O that the former signifies also *Places that retain the rain-water.*]

تَمْرٌ مَعْقِلِيٌّ, (Mgh, Mṣb,) or رُطَبٌ مَعْقِلِيٌّ, (Ṣ,) *A certain sort of dates,* (Mgh,* Mṣb,) [or *fresh ripe dates,*] *of El-Baṣrah:* (Mṣb:) so called in relation to Maḳil Ibn-Yesár. (Ṣ, Mgh, Mṣb.)

مُعَقَّلَةٌ is applied to camels (إِبِل) as meaning *Bound with the rope called* عِقَال. (O, TA.) And also to a she-camel bound therewith on the occasion of her being covered: and hence the epithet مُعَقَّلَاتٌ is applied by a poet, metonymically, to women, in a similar sense. (TA.)

مَعْقُولٌ [pass. part. n. of عَقَلَ in all its senses as a trans. verb. — Hence it signifies *Intellectual,* as meaning *perceived by the intellect;* and *excogitated:* thus applied as an epithet to any branch of knowledge that is not necessarily مَنْقُول, which means "desumed," such as the science of the fundamentals of religion, and the like. — Hence also, *Intelligible.* — And *Approved by the intellect;* or *reasonable.* — It is also said to be an inf. n.]: see 1, latter half. — And see عَقْلٌ, latter half, in two places.

[مَعْقُولَاتٌ *Intellectual things,* meaning *things perceived by the intellect:* generally used in this sense in scientific treatises. — And hence, *Intelligible things.* — And *Things approved by the intellect;* or *reasonable.*]

عقم

1. عَقِمَتْ مَفَاصِلُهُ *His joints* (Ṣ, Ḳ) of the arms and legs (Ṣ) *became dry.* (Ṣ, Ḳ.) [See عُقْمٌ, below.] Hence, (TA,) it is said in a trad. (Ṣ, TA) of Ibn-Mes'ood, relating to the resurrection, تُعْقَمُ أَصْلَابُ المُنَافِقِينَ وَالمُشْرِكِينَ وَلَا يَسْجُدُونَ (TA.) (Ṣ,* TA) i. e. *The joints* [*of the backbones of the hypocrites and of the believers in a plurality of gods*] *shall become dry, and bound, so that their backbones shall be* [*as*] *one vertebra, impacted together in their constituent parts,* [*and they shall not* be able to *prostrate themselves.*] (TA.) — And عُقِمَتْ; (Ṣ;) or عَقَمَتْ; (Mṣb;) or both; and عَقِمَتْ, aor. ـَ; and عَقُمَتْ; (Ḳ;) inf. n. عَقْمٌ and عُقْمٌ (Ṣ, Ḳ) and عَقَمٌ, (Ḳ,) or the second of these is a simple subst., and the last is the inf. n. of the second verb; (Mṣb;) said of the womb (الرَّحِم, Ṣ, Mṣb, Ḳ, TA), *It was,* or *became, barren,* (Mṣb,) or *incapable of receiving offspring,* (Ṣ, Ḳ,) *in consequence of a* هَزْمَة *therein.* (Ḳ. [See عُقْمٌ, below.]) And عُقِمَتْ and عَقِمَتْ and عَقُمَتْ are said of a woman [as meaning *She was,* or *became, barren*]. (IB, TA.) — [Hence,] عَقُمَ خُلُقُهُ, said of a man, ‡ *His disposition was,* or *became, bad,* or *evil.* (TA.) — And عَقِمَ, (Ḳ, TA,) inf. n. عَقْمٌ, (TA,) † *He* (a man, TA) *was,* or *became, silent.* (Ḳ, TA.) — عَقَمَ اللّٰهُ رَحِمَهَا, (IB, Mṣb, Ḳ, TA,) aor. ـِ, (Mṣb, Ḳ, TA, [in the CḲ عَقَمَهَا and تَعْقِمُهَا are erroneously put for عَقَمَهَا and يَعْقِمُهَا,]) inf. n. عَقْمٌ; (IB, Mṣb, TA;) and (IB, Ḳ) ↓ أَعْقَمَهَا; (Ṣ, IB, Ḳ;) the former used by those who say عُقِمَتْ, and the chaste form; the latter, by those who say عَقِمَتْ and عَقُمَتْ; the two being like حَزَنْتُهُ and أَحْزَنْتُهُ; (IB, TA;) *God made her womb to be barren,* (Mṣb,) or *incapable of receiving offspring.* (Ṣ, Ḳ.) — [Hence,] one says, اليَمِينُ الفَاجِرَةُ تَعْقِمُ الرَّحِمَ i. e. † [*The false oath*] *severs communion and kindness between men.* (TA.)

2. عَقَّمَهُمْ, inf. n. تَعْقِيمٌ, † *He silenced them.* (Ḳ.)

3. عَاقَمَهُ, (Ṣ, Ḳ,) inf. n. مُعَاقَمَةٌ and عِقَامٌ, (TA,) ‡ *He contended with him in an altercation, disputed with him,* or *litigated with him:* (Ṣ, Ḳ, TA:) and *vied with him, contended with him for superiority,* or *strove to surpass him, in strength, power,* or *force.* (TA.)

4: see 1, last sentence but one.

5. In the saying of a poet, (Ṣ,) namely, Rabee'ah Ibn-Maḳroom Ed-Ḍabbee, (TA,)

* وَمَآءٍ آجِنِ الجَمَّاتِ قَفْرٍ *
* تَعَقَّمُ فِى جَوَانِبِهِ السِّبَاعُ *

the meaning is تَحْتَفِرُ [i. e. the verse means *Many a water,* or *and a water, of which the supplies are altered for the worse,* and which is *deserted, by the sides of which the beasts of prey dig* hollows in the ground, app. to obtain water that has become purified by filtration]: or, as some say, the meaning is تَرَدَّدُ [i. e. *go to and fro*]. (Ṣ, TA.)

6. التَّعَاقُمُ is *syn. with* التَّعَاقُبُ, (Ḳ, TA,) *The coming to water* [*by turns,* or] *time after time;* and some say that the م of the former is a substitute for the ب of the latter. (TA.)

8. الاِعْتِقَامُ signifies *The digging a well, and, when one has nearly reached the water, digging a small well,* (Ṣ, Ḳ, TA,) *in the middle of the former,* (TA,) *of sufficient dimensions for one's finding the flavour of the water; when, if it be sweet, the rest of it is dug,* (Ṣ, Ḳ, TA,) *and made wide; otherwise it is abandoned.* (TA.) — Also

The entering into, or *upon, an affair.* (TA.) — And *The overcoming* [another] *in a game of hazard;* syn. القَمْرُ. (TA.)

عَقْمٌ and ▼ عَقْمَةٌ and ▼ عِقْمَةٌ *A red* [*garment of the sort called*] مِرْط [q. v.]: or *any red garment:* and the last signifies *a variegated,* or *figured, cloth* or *garment;* syn. وَشْىٌ: (K:) [see an ex. of this last in a verse cited voce جِرْمَةٌ:] or all signify *a certain sort of* وَشْى: (S:) or, accord. to Lh, the last signifies *one of the sorts of variegated,* or *figured, cloths* [*that serve for the coverings*] *of the* [*women's camel-vehicles called*] هَوَادِج; (TA;) as also the second; and so عُقْبَةٌ: (O and TA in art. عقب:) but some, Lh adds, say that it signifies *sorts of* لَبن [evidently, I think, a mistranscription for لِبْس i. e. *clothing*], *white* and *red.* (TA.)

عُقْمٌ [accord. to the S and K an inf. n., but accord. to the Msb a simple subst.,] *Dryness that prevents the receiving of an impression:* this is the primary signification accord. to Er-Rághib. (TA.) — [And] *Barrenness* of the womb: (Msb:) or *a* هَزْمَة [generally and properly signifying *a depression,* or *dint,* but here app. meaning *a stricture,* (see عَقِيمٌ,)] *that takes place in the womb, in consequence of which it is incapable of receiving offspring:* (K, TA:) so in the M. (TA.)

[عِقْمٌ accord. to the TK signifies the same as عَقْمٌ as syn. with عَقْمَةٌ and عِقْمَةٌ: but this I do not find in the K.]

عَقْمَةٌ: see عَقْمٌ. — عَقْمَةُ القَمَرِ [in the CK عَقْمَةُ القَمَرِ] *The return of the moon.* (K, TA, TK.) [See عَقَبَةُ القَمَرِ and عُقْبَةُ القَمَرِ, of the latter of which it is app. a dial. var.]

عِقْمَةٌ: see عَقْمٌ.

عِقْمِىٌّ: see the paragraph here following.

عُقْمِىٌّ A man *of old* [or *hereditary*] *nobility and generosity.* (K, TA. [For وَالكَرِيمِ in the CK, I read وَالكَرَمِ, as in other copies of the K and in the TA.]) — Also, and ▼ عِقْمِىٌّ, [as rel. ns. from عُقْمٌ and its syn. عُقْمٌ, both inf. ns. accord. to the S and K,] (so in copies of the S,) or عُقْمِىٌّ and ▼ عِقْمِىٌّ, with damm and with kesr, (K,) applied to speech, or language, (كَلَامٌ,) ‡ *Obscure, recondite,* or *abstruse,* (S, K, TA,) *which men do not know; like what are termed* نَوَادِر; and so عُقْمِىٌّ: or *such as is termed* ▼ عَقِيمٌ [lit. *barren*], *from which no verb is derived:* accord. to the A, *strange,* or *difficult to understand; the mode,* or *manner, of which is not known:* expl. to AA by a man of Hudheyl as meaning *of the Time of Ignorance, not now known:* accord. to Th, *old and obsolete.* (TA.) [Hence,] ▼ فُلَانٌ ذُو عَقْمِيَّات [i. e. عِقْمِيَّات or عُقْمِيَّات, app. meaning *Such a one has obscure modes of expression*], mentioned by IAar as said of a man اذا كان يلوى بخصمه [which I can only conjecture to mean "when he turns his adversary in a dispute from the right point:" the difficulty in the phrase lies in the verb, which I think to be more probably يَلْوِى than يُلْوِى: (see أَلْوَى:) what follows it is evidently بِخَصْمِهِ]. (TA.)

عِقْمِىٌّ: see the next preceding paragraph.

عُقْمِيَّات or عِقْمِيَّات: see عُقْمِىٌّ, last sentence.

عُقَامٌ: see عَقِيمٌ, in two places. — Also ‡ A *vehement* war or battle, (S, K, TA,) and so ▼ عَقَامٌ and ▼ عَقِيمٌ, (K, TA,) all meaning one *in which no one pauses nor waits for another, in which is much slaughter, and women become husbandless.* (TA.) — And ‡ A man *of evil disposition;* (S, K, TA;) as also ▼ عَقَامٌ; (CK, but not in other copies of the K nor in the TA;) and a woman likewise. (TA.) — And † An *incurable* disease; (S, K;) as also ▼ عَقَامٌ, which is the more chaste; (K;) or the latter is that which is accord. to analogy, but the former is that which has been heard: (S:) or *of which one will not hope to be cured.* (A, TA.) — And A *strong* she-camel *such as is termed* بَازِل [i. e. *in her ninth,* or *eighth, year*]. (K.) — And *A species of fish.* (K.) — And (K) it is said to be (TA) *A serpent inhabiting the sea;* (K, TA;) respecting which they say, (TA,) the أَسْوَد (i. e. the serpent so called, TA) comes from the land, and whistles upon the shore, whereupon the عقام comes forth to it, and they twist together (يَتَلَاوَيَانِ); then they separate, and each goes away to its abode. (K, TA.)

عَقَامٌ: see the next preceding paragraph, in three places. — Also, (K, TA,) and ▼ عَقِيمٌ, (TA,) A *hard, distressing,* or *distressful,* day: (K, TA:) accord. to Er-Rághib, one *in which is no joy.* (TA.)

عَقِيمٌ, (K,) with which ▼ عُقَامٌ is syn., (S,) is applied to a womb, meaning [*Barren;* or] *incapable of receiving offspring, in consequence of a* هَزْمَة *therein;* [see عُقْمٌ;] as also عَقِيمَةٌ, and ▼ مَعْقُومَةٌ; (K;) the last of which is expl. by Ks as signifying, thus applied, *bound,* or *constricted;* (مَشْدُودَةٌ;) so in some copies of the S, and in the TA;) or *obstructed;* (مَسْدُودَةٌ; so in other copies of the S;) *that will not bring forth offspring.* (S, TA.) It is also applied to a woman, (IAar, S, Msb, K,) as meaning *Barren; that will not bring forth offspring:* (IAar, Msb, TA:) so in a trad. cited voce أَسْوأ, in art. سوأ: (TA:) pl. عَقَائِمُ and عُقُمٌ, (S, Msb,) and sometimes عُقْمٌ, (S, and so in some copies of the K instead of عُقُمٌ,) a contraction of عُقُمٌ. (S.) And it is also applied to a man, meaning *To whom no child is born;* (S, Msb, K;) and so ▼ عُقَامٌ: (K:) pl. عُقَمَاءُ and عِقَامٌ (Msb, K) and عَقْمَى. (K.) — [Hence,] applied to a wind, ‡ *Such as does not fecundate,* or *fructify;* (K, TA;) *that does not cause clouds to produce rain, nor trees to produce fruit;* (S;) i. e. *that does not bring rain, but is destructive:* or *that does not fructify the trees, nor raise clouds, nor bear rain.* (TA.) And الرِّيحُ العَقِيمُ [mentioned in the Kur li. 41] means † *The west,* or *westerly, wind, by means of which* [*the tribe of*] *'Ád were destroyed.* (TA.) — Applied to intellect (عَقْل), it means † [*Barren,* or] *unprofitable to him who possesses it:* (Msb:) or *unfruitful of good.* (TA.) — As applied to speech, or language, see عُقْمِىٌّ. كَلِمَاتٌ عُقْمٌ means † [*Words,* or *expressions,* or *sentences,*] *strange,* or *difficult to understand.* (TA.) — It is applied to a day as meaning † *Without air* [or *wind*], *and therefore* [*sultry,* or] *intensely hot.* (Msb.) — See also عُقَامٌ. — And see عَقَامٌ. — The day of resurrection is termed يَوْمٌ عَقِيمٌ because [it is † *A day*] *having no day after it.* (S, TA.) Accord. to some, it is thus termed in the Kur xxii. 54. (Bd &c.) — الدُّنْيَا عَقِيمٌ means † [*The present world*] *does not render good to him who is of the people thereof.* (TA.) — And one says, المُلْكُ عَقِيمٌ meaning ‡ *Dominion is a condition in which,* (A, K, TA,) or *in the seeking of which,* (Msb,) *relationship profits not,* (A, Msb, K, TA,) *nor friendship:* (Msb:) for a man will slay his son, (S, Msb,) if he fear him, (S,) and his father, (Msb,) for dominion; (S, Msb;) or because, in seeking it, the father will be slain, and the son, and the brother, and the paternal uncle; (Th, K;) or because, in it, the ties of relationship are severed by slaughter and by undutiful conduct. (TA.)

مَعْقِمٌ *A joint* of a horse; (S, K;) *such as* [*that of*] *the pastern, next the hoof, and the knee, and the hock:* (S:) pl. مَعَاقِمُ: (S, K:) the pl. signifies *certain vertebræ between* [*the one called*] *the* قَرِيدَة [q. v.] *and the* عَجْب [i. e. the *root,* or *base, of the tail*], *in the hinder part of the backbone,* (K, TA,) of the horse. (TA.) One says of a horse, هُوَ شَدِيدُ المَعَاقِمِ, meaning *He is strong in respect of the vertebræ above mentioned:* and likewise, *in the joints of the pasterns.* (TA.) — Also *A joint,* or *knot, in straw.* (S, TA.)

مَعْقُومَةٌ: see عَقِيمٌ, first sentence.

عقو

1. عَقَا الأَمْرَ, aor. يَعْقُو, and [عَقِىَ, aor.] يَعْقَى, *He disliked,* or *hated, the thing,* or *affair.* (K.) — And عَقَاهُ, aor. يَعْقُوهُ, is syn. with عَاقَهُ [meaning *He,* or *it, hindered, prevented, impeded,* or *withheld, him*], being formed from the latter by transposition; (S, TA;) *i. q.* حَبَسَهُ; as also ▼ اعتقاهُ; (TA;) [and this is app. meant by its being said that] الاِعْتِقَاءُ is syn. with الاِحْتِبَاسُ, and is formed by transposition from الاِعْتِيَاقُ. (S, TA.)

8: see the preceding paragraph.

عَقًا and [its n. un.] عَقَاةٌ: see the next paragraph; the latter in two places.

عَقْوَةٌ (S, K) and ▼ عَقَاةٌ (S) The *environs of a house:* (S, K:) and the سَاحَة [i. e. *court,* or *open area,*] *of a house:* (Ṣ:) and the former, the *environs of a* مَحَلَّة [or *place of alighting*, or *of descending and stopping*, &c.]: (ISd, Ḳ, TA: [والمَحَلَّةُ in the CḲ should be والمَحَلَّة:]) as also ▼ عَقَاة: (Ḳ, TA:) the pl. (of عَقْوَة TA) is عِقَاء, (Ḳ, TA,) and the pl. [or rather coll. gen. n.] of عَقَاة is ▼ عَقًا, like as حَصًى is of حَصَاة. (TA.) One says, مَا يَطُورُ بِعَقْوَتِهِ أَحَدٌ [*No one approaches the environs of his house*]. (Ṣ, TA.) And اِذْهَبْ فَلَا أَرَيَنَّكَ بِعَقْوَتِى [*Depart thou, and I will assuredly not see thee in the environs of my house*]. (TA.)

مُعَقٍّ, mentioned here in the Ḳ: see the next art.

عقى

1. عَقَى الأَمْرَ, aor. يَعْقِى: see 1 in art. عقو. ═ عَقَى, aor. as above, inf. n. عَقْىٌ, said of an infant, (Ṣ, Ḳ,) *He voided his* عِقْى; (Ḳ;) [i. e.] *he voided his ordure for the first time, and, after that, while he was a youngling.* (Ṣ.) It is said in a trad. of I'Ab, that when a child once suckled by a woman voids his عِقْى, she and her children become, to him, within the prohibited degrees of marriage, because it is known thereby that the milk has entered his belly. (TA.) ═ مَا أَدْرِى مِنْ أَيْنَ عَقَيْتَ and ▼ اعْتَقَيْتَ mean *I know not whence thou camest*, or *hast come.* (Ḳ,* TA.)

2. عقّى *He* (a bird) *rose high in his flight.* (Ṣ, Ḳ.) — And عَقَّتِ الدَّلْوُ *The bucket rose* in the well *turning round.* (TA in art. عقو.) [See also 1, (last sentence,) in art. عق.] — And عقّى بِسَهْمِهِ, (Ṣ, Ḳ,) inf. n. تَعْقِيَةٌ, (Ḳ,) *He shot his arrow* [*up*] *into the air*; (Ṣ, Ḳ;) a dial. var. of عَقَّهُ [or rather of عَقَّ بِهِ]. (Ṣ.) The Hudhalee, (Ṣ,) El-Mutanakhkhil, (TA,) or Aboo-Dhu-eyb, (L in art. وضح,) says,

عَقَّوْا بِسَهْمٍ فَلَمْ يَشْعُرْ بِهِ أَحَدٌ

ثُمَّ ٱسْتَفَاؤُوا وَقَالُوا حَبَّذَا الوَضَحُ

[*They shot an arrow towards the sky, and no one knew of it: then they returned, and said, An excellent thing is milk*]; (Ṣ, TA;) meaning, "we would rather have milk than the blood of him who killed our companion;" preferring that camels should be given them as a compensation: (L in art. وضح:) it is related [thus] with fet-ḥ to the doubled ق, so that its place is here; and also with ḍamm thereto, so that its place is art. عق, in which it has been mentioned. (TA. [See a similar verse cited voce عَقِيقَة, and the explanation thereof, there preceding that verse.]) ═ And عقّاهُ, inf. n. as above, *He gave him to drink* [or *to swallow*] *what would cause his* عِقْى [q. v.] *to pass forth,* (Ḳ, TA,) or *honey in order that it might have that effect.* (TA.)

4. اعقى *It was, or became, bitter,* (Ḳ,) or *intensely bitter.* (Ṣ, Ḳ.) — And اعقاهُ *He removed it from his mouth because of its bitterness:* (Ṣ, Ḳ:) like as one says أَشْكَيْتُهُ meaning "I removed him from that of which he complained," (Ṣ, TA,) [or "I removed from him that of which he complained,"] the hemzeh having a privative effect. (TA.) It is said in a prov., لَا تَكُنْ حُلْوًا فَتُسْتَرَطَ وَلَا مُرًّا فَتُعْقِى, (Ṣ, TA,) or فَتُعْقَى, accord. to different relaters. (TA. [See 1 in art. سرط, where both these readings are expl., and where the reading فَتُسْتَرَطَ is given instead of فَتُسْتَرَطَ.])

8: see 1, last sentence.

عِقْىٌ *What comes forth from the belly of the child* (Ṣ, Mṣb, Ḳ) *before he eats,* (Ṣ,) or *when he is born,* (Mṣb, Ḳ,) *black and viscous as though it were glue;* (Mṣb;) and likewise *from the mare's foal, and the young ass, and the young camel, and the kid;* (ISd, TA;) or what comes forth from the lamb or kid, and the mare's foal, is called رَدَجٌ: (Ṣ, TA:) and Az states that it is said to be *what comes forth from the belly of the fœtus, inclosed in the* [*membrane called*] حُوَلَآء [q. v.]; *a thing* [or *substance*] *that comes forth from its anus while it is in the belly of its mother, part of it black and part of it yellow:* (TA:) pl. أَعْقَآءٌ. (Az, Ḳ, TA.) أَحْرَصُ مِنْ كَلْبٍ عَلَى عِقْىِ صَبِىٍّ is a prov. [meaning *More eager than a dog for the feces of a young child*]. (Ṣ.) — Also *A youngling,* or *young infant:* whence the saying of Z, ▼ فُلَانٌ لَهُ عِقْيَانِ وَلَيْسَ عِنْدَهُ العِقْيَانُ i. e. *Such a one has two younglings,* or *young infants, but gold is not in his possession.* (TA.)

عِقْيَانٌ *Gold:* (KL:) or *pure gold:* (Ṣ, TA:) or *gold that grows,* [meaning *native gold,*] (Ṣ, Ḳ, TA,) *not such as is produced from the stones,* (Ṣ, TA,) or, as in the M and A, *not such as is educed, by melting, from the stones:* the ا and ن are augmentative. (TA.) See an ex. in the latter sentence of the next preceding paragraph.

أَعْقَى [*More,* and *most, intensely,* or *nauseously, bitter*]. (AḤn, TA voce شَيْلَمٌ.)

مُعَقٍّ *Circling over a thing, aloft, like the eagle.* (Ḳ, TA: mentioned in the former in art. عقو.)

علك

1. عَلَكَ, aor. ـَ, (Ṣ, O, Ḳ,) inf. n. عَلَكٌ, (Ḳ,) *It* (a day) *was, or became,* [*sultry;* i. e.] *vehemently hot,* (Ṣ, O, Ḳ,) *with moisture, and without wind.* (Ḳ.) — And عَلَكَ *He* (a man) *remained, stayed, or abode, and confined himself.* (IAạr, TA.) ═ عَلَكَتْهُ الحُمَّى, (Ṣ, O,) [aor., app., ـُ,] inf. n. عَلْكٌ, (TA,) *The fever clave to him, and heated him,* or *made him vehemently hot,* (Ṣ, O, TA,) *so that it emaciated him,* or *oppressed him.* (TA.) — And عُلِكَ *He* (a man) *was, or became, fevered.* (TA.) — And *It boiled,* or *estuated,* or *fermented, by reason of the heat.* (TA.) ═ عَلَكَهُ, (Ṣ, O,) aor. ـُ, (TA,) inf. n. عَلْكٌ, (O, TA,) *He hindered, prevented, impeded,* or *withheld, him, from the object of his want:* (Ṣ, O:) or عَلَكَهُ عَنْ حَاجَتِهِ signifies thus; and *he turned him back,* or *away, therefrom.* (Ḳ.) — And also, i. e. عَلَكَهُ, (Ṣ, O, Ḳ,) aor. ـُ, inf. n. عَلْكٌ, (TA,) *He deferred with him, delayed with him,* or *put him off, in the matter of his due, by promising time after time to render it to him.* (Ṣ, O, Ḳ.) — And *He asked him to repeat to him* [*by relating it*] *twice,* or *three times, a narration,* or *story, that he had related to him:* (Ḳ:) or عَلَكْتُهُ الحَدِيثَ, aor. ـُ, inf. n. عَلْكٌ, *I asked him to repeat the narration,* or *story, until he repeated it* [*by relating it*] *twice.* (AZ, Ṣ, O.) — And عَلَكَ الكَلَامَ *He interpreted,* or *explained, the speech,* or *language.* (Ḳ.) It is related of IAạr that, being asked respecting a thing, he said, سَوْفَ أَعُكُّهُ لَكَ *I will interpret it,* or *explain it, to thee.* (TA.) — [And app. *He rejected the speech,* or *saying:* for] العَلْكُ signifies also *the rejecting* a man's speech, or saying, and *not accepting it.* (O.) — And عَكَّهُ بِالقَوْلِ *He repeated to him the speech,* or *saying,* (رَدَّهُ عَلَيْهِ,) *occasioning annoyance,* or *molestation.* (L, TA.) [This might be rendered agreeably with the next preceding explanation: but] one says, مَا زِلْتُ أَعُكُّهُ بِالقَوْلِ حَتَّى غَضِبَ *I ceased not to reiterate to him* (أُرَدِّدُ عَلَيْهِ) *the speech,* or *saying, until he was angry.* (El-Jurjánee, TA.) And in like manner, عَكَّنِى بِالأَمْرِ, inf. n. عَكٌّ, *He reiterated to me* (رَدَّدَ عَلَىَّ) *the thing, affair, case,* or *action, until he fatigued me:* (L, TA:) or عَكَّهُ بالامر *he repeated to him* (رَدَّ عَلَيْهِ) *the thing,* &c., *until he fatigued him.* (Ḳ.) And عَكَّهُ بِشَرٍّ *He repeated,* or *reiterated, evil,* or *wrongdoing, to him;* syn. كَرَّرَهُ عَلَيْهِ. (Lḥ, Ḳ.) — [Hence, perhaps, because the act is generally reiterated,] عَكَّهُ بِالسَّوْطِ *He struck him* [or *flogged him*] *with the whip.* (Ṣ, O, Ḳ.) — And عَكَّهُ بِالحُجَّةِ, (IDrd, O, Ḳ,) aor. ـُ, inf. n. عَكٌّ, (IDrd, O,) *He overcame him by, or with, the argument,* or *plea.* (IDrd, O, Ḳ.) — And العَكُّ signifies also الدَّقُّ [*The breaking, crushing, bruising,* &c., *of a thing*]. (O.)

4. أَعَكَّتْ, said of a she-camel [when she has conceived (see عُكَّة)], (Ṣ, Ḳ,) or of such as is termed عُشَرَآء [q. v.], (TA,) *She assumed an altered colour.* (Ṣ, Ḳ, TA.)

يَوْمٌ عَكٌّ, and ▼ عَكِيكٌ, (Ṣ, O, Ḳ,) and ▼ ذُو عَكِيكٍ, (TA,) [*A sultry day;* i. e.] *a day vehemently hot,* (Ṣ, O, Ḳ,) *with moisture, and without wind:* (Ḳ:) thus يَوْمٌ عَكٌّ أَكٌّ is expl. by Th, among instances of imitative sequents; meaning, perhaps, that أَكٌّ is an imitative sequent, or that it signifies "vehemently hot:" (TA:) or *a day vehemently hot and dense* [*in the air*]. (El-Jurjánee, TA.) And لَيْلَةٌ عَكَّةٌ [*A sultry night;* i. e.] *a night vehemently hot,* &c. (Ḳ.) And أَرْضٌ عَكَّةٌ, and ▼ أَرْضٌ عَكِيكَةٌ, *A hot* [or *sultry*] *land;* (Ṣ, O, Ḳ:) mentioned by Fr. (Ṣ, O.) And ▼ حَرٌّ عَكِيكٌ *Vehement* [or *sultry] heat.* (TA.) —— عَكٌّ applied to a man, (Ṣ, O,) *Tough, strong,* (AZ, Ṣ, O, TA,) *and compact.* (AZ, TA.) ═ اِتَّزَرَ إِزْرَةً عَكَّ وَلَكَّ, (Ṣ, O, Ḳ,) and ▾ إِزْرَةً عُكَّى, (Ṣ,) or عُكَّى وَلُكَّى, (O, Ḳ,) *He wore a waist-wrapper so that he made its two ends to hang down and drew together the rest of it [round his waist].* (Ṣ, O, Ḳ.)

عَكَّةٌ (Lth, Ṣ, O, Ḳ) and ▾ عُكَّةٌ (Lth, Ṣ, Ḳ) and ▾ عِكَّةٌ and ▾ عَكَاكٌ (Ḳ) and ▾ عَكِيكٌ and ▾ عِكَاكٌ, (Ṣ, O, Ḳ,) which last is also a pl., (Ḳ,) said to be pl. of عَكَّةٌ, (O,) [*Sultriness;* i. e.] *vehemence of heat* (Lth, Ṣ, O, Ḳ) *in summer* (Lth) [*with moisture* (see the first sentence of this art.) *and*] *with stillness of the wind:* (Ḳ:) *it may be with the south* or *southerly wind* (الجَنُوب) *and the east* or *easterly wind* (الصَّبَا). (TA.) Hence the saying of the rhyming-proser, إِذَا طَلَعَ السِّمَاكُ ذَهَبَ العِكَاكُ ▾ وَقَلَّ اللِّكَاكُ [*When* السماك *rises* aurorally, *the sultriness goes,* or rather *has gone,* (see السِّمَاكُ, and another ex. of العكاك there cited,) *and the pressing,* or *crowding, at,* or *to, the water becomes little*]. (O.) —— See also عَكٌّ. —— And see عُكَّةٌ, in two places.

عُكَّةٌ : see عَكَّةٌ. —— Also *A sand heated by the sun;* (T, Ṣ, O, Ḳ;) and so ▾ عَكَّةٌ : (Ḳ:) pl. of the former عِكَاكٌ. (TA.) —— And The *access of a fever, on the occasion of the first tremour,* or *shivering, thereof;* as also ▾ عَكَّةٌ. (Ḳ.) —— And العُكَّةُ, (Ḳ,) or عُكَّةُ العِشَارِ, (Ṣ, O,) *A colour that overspreads she-camels when they have conceived,* (Ṣ, O, Ḳ,) *like the* كَلَف *of the woman.* (Ḳ.) ═ And The *receptacles,* (Ṣ, Ḳ,) or [correctly] *one of the receptacles,* (O,) *for clarified butter,* (Ṣ, O, Ḳ,) *smaller than the* قِرْبَة ; (Ḳ;) said by ISk to be *like the* شَكْوَة, [i. e. it is *a skin of a sucking kid,* (see شَكْوَةٌ, and وَطْبٌ,)] *in which clarified butter is put:* (Ṣ, O:) or, accord. to IAth, *a round receptacle of skins, for clarified butter and honey, but more particularly for clarified butter:* (TA:) pl. عُكَكٌ and عِكَاكٌ. (Ṣ, O, Ḳ.) One says of a woman, سَمِنَتْ حَتَّى صَارَتْ كَالعُكَّةِ [*She became fat so that she was like the skin of clarified butter*]. (El-Jurjánee, TA.)

عِكَّةٌ : see عَكَّةٌ.

عُكًّى : see عَكٌّ, last sentence.

عُكًّى The سَوِيق [or *meal of what has been parched,* or perhaps *of what has been dried in the sun,*] *of the* مُقْل [or *fruit of the Theban palm*]. (O, Ḳ.)

عَكَاكٌ : see عَكَّةٌ.

عِكَاكٌ : see عَكَّةٌ, in two places.

عَكِيكٌ : see عَكٌّ, in three places: and also عَكَّةٌ.

عُكَوَّكٌ, inadvertently said by J [and in the O] to be of the measure فُعَلَّعٌ, whereas it is of the measure فُعَوَّلٌ, like عُطَوَّدٌ, (IB, TA,) *Fat and short, with toughness:* (Ṣ, O:) or *short, compact and strong,* (Ḳ, TA,) *of middling make:* (TA:) or *fat:* (Ḳ, TA:) or *tough and strong.* (TA.) —— And A place *rugged and hard:* (Ṣ, O:) or [simply] *hard:* or *soft,* or *plain.* (Ḳ.)

عُكَوْكَانٌ *Plump, fat, and short.* (Ibn-'Abbád, O.)

مِعَكٌّ A horse *that runs a little and then requires to be struck* (Ṣ, O, Ḳ, TA) *with the whip.* (TA.) —— And A man *contentious, disputatious,* or *litigious;* (O, Ḳ;) *difficult to be managed.* (O.)

إِبِلٌ مُعَكْوَكَةٌ *Camels confined,* or *kept within bounds.* (Ṣ, O.)

عكب

عُكُبٌ and عِكَابٌ and أَعْكُبٌ quasi-pl. ns. of عَنْكَبُوتٌ, which is mentioned under this head by J and IM and others. (TA.) See art. عنكب.

عكد

1\. عَكَدَنِى, (O, Ḳ,) aor. ـُ, (Ḳ,) inf. n. عَكْدٌ [q. v. infrà], (TḲ,) *It* (an affair) *was,* or *became, possible,* or *practicable, to me.* (O, Ḳ.) —— عَكَدَ إِلَيْهِ *He had recourse, betook himself,* or *repaired, to him for refuge,* or *protection;* (O, Ḳ;) as also ▾ اعكد اليه ; (O, Ḳ; omitted in the TA;) and عَكَدَ عُنُقَهُ إِلَيْهِ, (O, TA,) and عَقَدَ likewise; (TA;) so too عَكَدَ بِهِ ; (TA;) which last signifies (O, Ḳ) also (TA) *he stuck to him,* or *it.* (O, Ḳ, TA.) See also 8. [And see 10.] ═ عَكِدَ, (Ṣ, O, L, Ḳ,) aor. ـَ, (L, Ḳ,) inf. n. عَكَدٌ ; (L;) said of a [lizard of the species termed] ضَبّ ; (Ṣ, O, L, Ḳ;) and in like manner said of a camel; as also ▾ استعكد ; (Ḳ;) or in like manner [عَكِدَتْ] said of a she-camel; and ▾ استعكد said of a boy; (O;) *He became fat,* (Ṣ, O, L, Ḳ,) *and hard in his flesh.* (L.)

4: see the preceding paragraph.

8\. اعتكدهُ *He* (a man, O) *kept,* or *clave, to it,* (O, Ḳ,) namely, a thing; (O;) like ▾ عَكَدَهُ. (TA.)

10\. استعكد *He* (a bird) *drew close,* or *betook himself, to a thing, in fear of the birds of prey.* (O, Ḳ.) And استعكد بِحَجَرٍ, or بِشَجَرٍ, *He* (a [lizard of the species termed] ضَبّ) *betook himself,* or *repaired, for refuge,* or *protection, to a stone,* or *to trees, in fear of the eagle or the hawk.* (T, M, O, TA.) —— And, said of water, *It collected.* (TA.) —— See also 1, in two places.

عَكْدٌ : see مَعْكُودٌ : ═ and see also what here follows.

عَكَدٌ, (so accord. to the O and my MS. copy of the Ḳ,) or ▾ عَكْدٌ, (so accord. to the L and the copy of the Ḳ followed in the TA,) [in the CḲ عُكْد,] The *middle* of a thing. (O, L, Ḳ.) —— See also عَكَدَةٌ.

عَكِدٌ *Fat,* (Ṣ, O, L, Ḳ,) *and hard in his flesh;* (L;) applied to a [lizard of the species termed] ضَبّ, (Ṣ, O, L, Ḳ,) and to a camel: (Ḳ:) fem. with ة, (Ṣ, O, L, Ḳ,) applied to a she-camel. (Ṣ, O, L.)

عَكَدَةٌ The [*rump-bone called*] عُصْعُص (IAar, O, Ḳ) *and* قُحْقُح ; both of which signify the same thing. (IAar, O. [But they are differently expl. by different authors.]) See also عَكَدَةٌ, in two places. The pl. is عَكَدٌ. (L.) ═ And The *hole,* or *burrow,* of the [lizard called] ضَبّ. (O, Ḳ.*) ═ And *Power,* or *strength.* (O, Ḳ.)

عَكَدَةٌ The *root* of the tongue; (Ṣ, O, L, Ḳ;) as also ▾ عُكْدَةٌ and عَقَدَةٌ ; (L;) i. e. the *thick part* thereof: (TA in art. عقد:) or the *main part* thereof: or the *middle* thereof. (L.) —— And The *root* of the tail; (O, L;) as also ▾ عُكْدَةٌ [q. v.]. (L.) The pl. is ▾ عَكَدٌ [or rather this is a coll. gen. n. of which عَكَدَةٌ is the n. un.]. (L.) —— Also The *base* of the heart, (O, L, Ḳ, TA,) *between the two lungs.* (L, TA.) ═ And *A feather with which bread is marked with points, like dots.* (O, Ḳ.)

مَعْكَدٌ *A place to which one has recourse,* or *betakes himself, for refuge,* or *protection.* (O, Ḳ.)

مَعْكُودٌ *Possible,* or *practicable.* (Ḳ. [Omitted in the O and in the TA, except in as far as it is implied by what here follows.]) One says, أَمْرٌ مَعْكُودُكَ أَنْ تَفْعَلَ كَذَا, (O, TA,) and مَعْكُودُكَ, (O,) meaning *The utmost that is possible,* or *practicable, to thee is thy doing such a thing:* (O, TA:) and ▾ عَكْدُكَ هٰذَا الأَمْرُ *The utmost that is possible,* or *practicable, to thee is this affair.* (TA.) ═ Also *Remaining, staying, dwelling,* or *abiding, and keeping close.* (O, Ḳ.) And *Imprisoned,* or *confined.* (Yaạkoob, O, Ḳ.) —— And, applied to food, *Unfailing, constant,* or *permanent;* (O, Ḳ, TA;) and *prepared.* (TA.)

مُسْتَعْكَدُ مَآءٍ [*A place in which water collects:* see 10]. (TA.)

عكر

1\. عَكَرَ, aor. ـِ (Ṣ, O, Mṣb) and ـُ, (Mgh, Mṣb,) inf. n. عَكْرٌ (Ṣ, O) and عُكُورٌ (O) [and مَعْكَرٌ, occurring in the Ḥam p. 200], *He,* or *it,* (a thing, Mṣb,) *turned,* or *inclined;* (Ṣ, O, Mṣb;) *turned back; returned:* (Mgh, Mṣb:) and ▾ انعكر [likewise] signifies *he,* or *it, turned* or *inclined;* or *became turned* or *inclined.* (O.) —— عَكَرَ بِهِ بَعِيرُهُ *His camel turned with him towards his family, and overcame him;* like عَجَرَ بِهِ [q. v.]; (Ṣ, O;) *overcame him, and turned back.* (Mṣb.) —— عَكَرَ عَلَى الشَّىْءِ, aor. ـِ, inf. n. عَكْرٌ and عُكُورٌ ; and ▾ اعتكر ; *He turned back,* or *returned, against the thing.* (Ḳ.) You say فَرَّ مِنْ قِرْنِهِ ثُمَّ عَكَرَ عَلَيْهِ بِالرُّمْحِ [*He fled from his adversary,* or *wheeled about widely from him, then*] *turned back against him with the spear:* (A, TA:) and ▾ اعتكر [likewise] signifies *he turned back* [against his adversary] *after fleeing,* or *wheeling about widely* [from him]. (IDrd, O.) [Hence, عَكَرَ عَلَيْهِ † *It* (a saying) *contradicted it,* namely, another saying; *it was contradictory,* or *repugnant, to it.* See an ex. voce سَنَعَ.] —— [And He returned to the thing. See an ex. voce قَرَدٌ.] You say also عَكَرَ الزَّمَانُ عَلَيْهِ بِخَيْرٍ *Fortune turned towards him with good.* (IḲṭṭ.) ═ [And عَكَرَ is also trans. as signifying *He made* his soul *to turn,* &c., against another in fight: see Ḥam p. 200.] ═ See also 4. ═ عَكِرَ, aor. ـَ, (Ṣ, O, Mṣb, Ḳ,) inf. n. عَكَرٌ, (Ṣ, Mṣb,) *It* (water, Ṣ, O, Ḳ, and wine, Ṣ, O, and beverage of the kind called نَبِيذ, Ḳ, and oil, Ṣ, O) *became dreggy,* or *feculent,* (Ṣ, O, Ḳ,) *thick,* (Ṣ, O,) or *turbid.* (Mṣb.) —— عَكِرَتِ المِسْرَجَةُ *The lamp had dregs collected in it.* (Ṣ, O.)

2: see the next paragraph in two places.

4. اعكرهُ; (Ṣ, O, Mṣb, Ḳ;) and ↓ عكّرهُ, (Ṣ, Mṣb, Ḳ,) inf. n. تَعْكِيرٌ; (Ṣ, O, Ḳ;) *He rendered it* (namely, a fluid, O, or water, and beverage of the kind called نَبِيذ, [&c.,] Ḳ) *dreggy,* or *feculent,* (Ḳ,) or *turbid:* (O, Mṣb:) or ↓ the latter verb signifies, (Ṣ, O,) or signifies also, (Ḳ,) and so the former, (Ṣ, Ḳ,) *He put into it* (namely water, Ḳ, and wine, Ṣ, and نَبِيذ, Ḳ, and oil, Ṣ) *dregs,* (Ṣ, O, Ḳ,) or *earth,* or *dust* (تربة [but this is perhaps a mistake of a copyist]); as also ↓ عَكَرَهُ, inf. n. عَكْرٌ. (IḲṭṭ, TA.) ═ See also 8.

6: see 8, in three places.

7: see 1, first sentence.

8. اعتكر: see 1, in two places. —— Also *It* (darkness) *became confused;* (Ṣ, Mṣb;) as though one part thereof turned back upon another, from the slowness of its clearing away: (Ṣ, O:) *it* (night) *became intense in its blackness, and confused;* (Ḳ;) as also ↓ اعكر: (O, Ḳ;) or *it became dense in its darkness, and confused.* (A.) —— اعتكروا *They* (people) *became confused;* (Ṣ;) as also ↓ تعاكروا: (Ṣ, O:) *they became confused,* or *mixed together, in war,* or *fight;* (Ḳ;) as also ↓ تعاكروا: (TA:) *they became embroiled together in contention;* (TA;) as also ↓ تعاكروا. (Ḳ.) [Hence,] اِعْتِكَارُ الضَّرَائِرِ [lit., *The wrangling of fellow-wives;* meaning,] † *confusion of discordant affairs.* (TA.) —— اعتكر العَسْكَرُ *One part of the army returned upon another, so that it could not be numbered.* (O, Ḳ.) —— اعتكر المَطَرُ *The rain became vehement:* (Ḳ:) or *copious and vehement.* (Ṣ, TA.) —— اعتكرت الرِّيَاحُ, (Ṣ, O,) or الرِّيحُ, (Ḳ,) *The winds,* (Ṣ, O,) or *wind,* (Ḳ,) *brought dust,* (Ṣ, O, Ḳ,) *and removed the fruit of the trees.* (O.) —— اعتكر الشَّبَابُ *Youthfulness continued* (O, Ḳ) *until its term was ended.* (O.)

عِكْرٌ i. q. أَصْلٌ [*Origin;* and *original state* or *condition,* and *natural disposition*]; (Ṣ, O, Ḳ;) as also عِتْرٌ. (Ṣ, O.) You say هُوَ كَرِيمُ العِكْرِ *He is of generous origin.* (TḲ.) And بَاعَ فُلَانٌ عِكْرَهُ, (Ṣ, O, TA,) or ↓ عِكْرَةَ أَرْضِهِ, (TA,) *Such a one sold the* أَصْل [meaning the *fundamental property,* i. e. *the property itself,*] *of his land.* (Ṣ, O, TA.) And رَجَعَ فُلَانٌ إِلَى عِكْرِهِ [*Such a one returned to his original state* or *condition,* or *natural disposition:* see عِتْرٌ]. (Ṣ, O.) —— Also *Custom; habit:* so in the prov., عَادَتْ لِعِكْرِهَا لَمِيسُ *Lemees* [a proper name of a woman] *returned to her custom,* or *habit.* (O, L.) [See also عِتْرٌ.] And it is said in a trad., that when the words اِقْتَرَبَ لِلنَّاسِ حِسَابُهُمْ [in the Ḳur xxi. 1] were revealed, those who were in error refrained a little from what was forbidden, and then عَادُوا إِلَى عِكْرِهِمْ, i. e., *they returned to their original bad way of acting* or *of opinion, and to their evil deeds:* (Ṣ, O, TA:) or, accord. to one relation of the trad., ↓ الى عَكَرِهِمْ, *to their filthiness,* from عَكَرٌ relating to oil: (O, TA:) but the former is the more proper. (TA.)

عَكَرٌ The *dregs, feces, lees,* or *sediment,* or *what remains at the bottom,* (Ṣ, Mgh, O, Ḳ,) of oil, (Ṣ, Mgh, O,) &c., (Ṣ, O,) and of the beverage called نَبِيذ, (Mgh,) or of anything; (Ḳ;) *what is thick, and subsides,* of oil and the like; (Mṣb;) the *last and thick part* of water and of wine and of oil: (Ṣ, O:) *earth,* or *dust;* syn. تربة. (IḲṭṭ [but see 4].) —— *Rust* of a sword (IAạr, Ṣ, O, Ḳ) &c. (IAạr, Ṣ.) —— See also عِكْرٌ.

عَكِرٌ *Dreggy,* or *feculent,* wine [&c.]. (Ṣ, O.)

عَكْرَةٌ *A return to the fight,* or *charge, after fleeing* or *wheeling away.* (Ṣ, O, TA.)

عِكْرَةٌ: see عِكْرٌ.

عَكَّارٌ One *who returns to the fight after fleeing* or *wheeling away.* (Ṣ,* Mgh, O,* Ḳ.) It is said in a trad., أَنْتُمُ العَكَّارُونَ لَا الفَرَّارُونَ (Ṣ, Mgh,* O, TA) *Ye are they who return to the fight; not they who flee.* (Mgh,* TA.) And عَطَّافُونَ signifies the like. (TA.)

طَعَامٌ مُعْتَكِرٌ *Much food* or *wheat.* (ISh, O.)

عكز

1. عَكَزَ عَلَى عُكَّازَتِهِ, (Ḳ,) and عَلَى عَصَاهُ, aor. ـُ, (A, O,) inf. n. عَكْزٌ and عَكَزَانٌ, (O,) *He leaned,* or *stayed himself,* (A, O, Ḳ,) *upon his* عُكَّازَة, (Ḳ,) and *upon his staff;* (A, O;) as also ↓ تعكّز: (O,* Ḳ:) or this verb signifies *he bent himself* upon the عُكَّازَة. (O.) —— عَكَزَ بِالشَّيْءِ, (IḲṭṭ, Ḳ,) inf. n. عَكْزٌ, (O,) *He used the thing as a leader,* or *guide;* (IḲṭṭ;) *he guided himself with the thing.* (O,* Ḳ.) —— And *He grasped the thing with his fingers.* (IḲṭṭ.) —— عَكَزَ الرُّمْحَ *He stuck the spear into the ground.* (O, Ḳ.) —— And عَكَزَهُ *He struck him with the* عُكَّازَة. (O.)

2. عكّزه, inf. n. تَعْكِيزٌ, *He fixed the* عُكَّاز [or *pointed iron foot*] *upon it;* (O, Ḳ;) namely, the spear. (O, Ḳ.)

5. تعكّز: see 1. —— تعكّز قَوْسَهُ *He made use of his bow as an* عُكَّازَة. (A.)

عَكُوزٌ, or عُكُوزٌ: see the next paragraph.

عَكُوزٌ, (Ḳ,) or ↓ عَكُّوزٌ, like صَبُّورٌ as written by Ṣgh, (TA,) or ↓ عُكُّوزٌ, (thus accord. to the O,) [or more probably, I think, ↓ عُكُوزٌ,] *A thing like the* جُبَّة [or *socket of a spear-head*], *of iron, into which the* أَجْذَم [app. meaning the *person afflicted with elephantiasis*] *puts his leg,* or *foot.* (Ibn-'Abbád, O, Ḳ.) —— See also عُكَّازَة.

عُكَّاز: see عُكَّازَة. —— Also *A* زُجّ [or *pointed iron foot* of a spear or the like]; as also ↓ عُكُوز [or ↓ عُكُّوز ?]. (O.)

عُكُوز: see عُكَّازَة: —— and عَكُوز: —— and عُكَّاز.

عُكُّوز: see عُكَّاز.

عُكَّازَةٌ (Ṣ, A, O, Mṣb, Ḳ*) and ↓ عُكَّازٌ, (A, Ḳ,) or this is a pl., (O,) [or a coll. gen. n.,] and accord. to the Ḳ ↓ عَكُّوزٌ, but correctly ↓ عُكُّوزٌ, as written by Ṣgh, (TA,) *A staff having a* زُجّ [i. e. *a pointed iron foot*] (Ṣ, A, O, Ḳ) *at the lower extremity,* (O,) *upon which a man leans,* or *stays himself:* (TA:) or *i. q.* عَنَزَة [q. v.]: (Mṣb:) pl. عَكَاكِيزُ (Ṣ, O, Mṣb) and عُكَّازَاتٌ. (O, Mṣb.) —— The first of these words is also used metonymically for مَنْصِب [‡ *A post, an office, a function,* or *a magistracy*]: hence the saying فُلَانٌ مِنْ أَرْبَابِ العَكَاكِيزِ [‡ *Such a one is of the functionaries,* or *magistrates:* because officers of rank made use of walking-sticks]. (TA.)

عكس

1. عَكَسَهُ, aor. ـِ, (A,* Mṣb, Ḳ,*) inf. n. عَكْسٌ, (Ṣ, A, O, Mṣb, Ḳ,) *He reversed it; made the last part of it to be first, and the first to be last;* or *turned it hind part before, and fore part behind.* (Ṣ, A, O, Mṣb, Ḳ.) [Hence,] عَكَسَ الكَلَامَ وَنَحْوَهُ, (A, O, Ḳ,) aor. and inf. n. as above, (O,) *He inverted, reversed, converted,* or *transposed, the language* or *sentence, and the like;* [as, for instance, a word;] *he changed its order by inversion* or *transposition:* (A, O, Ḳ:) sometimes a word, when this is done, remains as at first; as in the instances of بَابٌ and خَوْخٌ and عَكَوْكَعٌ: (TA:) or *he perverted its order:* (TA) [or *its meaning:* see مَعْكُوس]. [Hence the phrase بِالعَكْسِ *Vice versâ.*] One says to him who speaks wrongly, لَا تَعْكِسْ [*Pervert not thou*]. (A.) And ↓ مُعَاكَسَةٌ with respect to language and the like is like عَكْسٌ. (TA.) —— [Hence, said of a mirror and the like, *It reflected it;* namely, an object before it; because the object seen in it is reversed.] —— From the first of the significations mentioned above is derived the expression [used by the Arabs in the "Time of Ignorance"], عَكْسُ البَلِيَّةِ عِنْدَ القَبْرِ [*The tying, with her head turned backwards, of the she-camel that is left to die at the grave in which her master is buried*]; because they used to tie her with her head turned backwards towards the part next her breast and belly, or, as some say, towards her hinder part next the back, and to leave her in that state until she died. (Ṣ, O.) And [hence, app.,] العَكْسُ also signifies *The confining* a beast (دَابَّة) *without fodder.* (TA.) You say also, عَكَسَ رَأْسَ البَعِيرِ, aor. ـِ, *He turned the head of the camel* [app. meaning *backwards*].

(TA.) And عَكَسَ البَعِيرَ, (IKṭṭ, O, L, Mṣb,) aor. ـِ, (Mṣb, [in the L, ـُ, which is evidently a mistranscription,]) inf. n. عَكْسٌ (Ṣ, IKṭṭ, O, L, Ḳ) and عِكَاسٌ, (IKṭṭ, L,) *He tied the camel's neck to one of his fore legs while he was lying down:* (IKṭṭ, L, Mṣb:) or *he tied the camel's fore shank to his* (the camel's) *arm with a rope, and then turned back the rope beneath his belly and tied it to his flank:* (IDrd, O:) or *he tied a cord in the fore part of the nose, or mouth, of the camel,* (Ṣ, O, Ḳ,) [*attaching it*] *to his fore legs,* (Ḳ,) or *to the pastern of* [*each of*] *his fore legs,* (Ṣ, O,) *to render him submissive,* or *tractable:* (Ṣ, Ḳ:) or *he put a halter* (خِطَام) *upon the head of the camel, and then tied it in a knot upon his knee, to prevent his being impetuous:* (El-Jaádee:) or, accord. to an Arab of the desert, *he pulled the rein* (جَرِير) *of the camel, and kept fast hold of his head, so that he went an easy and a quick pace:* and عَكَسَ الدَّابَّةَ is said to signify *he pulled the head of the beast towards him, to make him go backwards.* (TA.) — عَكَسْتُ عَلَيْهِ أَمْرَهُ i. q. رَدَدْتُهُ عَلَيْهِ [*I reversed to him his affair,* or *case; I made his affair,* or *case, to become the contrary of what it was to him*]. (Mṣb.) — عَكَسْتُهُ عَنْ أَمْرِهِ *I prevented him from executing his affair.* (Mṣb.) It is said in a trad. of Er-Rabeeạ Ibn-Kheythem, اعْكِسُوا أَنْفُسَكُمْ عَكْسَ الخَيْلِ بِاللُّجُمِ (TA,) *Rein in,* or *refrain,* (TA,) or *turn back,* (A, TA,) *yourselves* [*as one reins in, &c., horses by means of the bits and bridles*]. (TA.) — And عَكَسَ الشَّىْءَ *He pulled the thing towards the ground, and pressed it,* or *squeezed it, hard, then smote the ground with it.* (TA.) = One says also, عَكَسْتُ, aor. ـِ, inf. n. عَكْسٌ, [app. meaning *I poured milk upon broth;* for it is said to be] from عَكِيسٌ in the first of the senses assigned to it below: (O:) or العَكْسُ signifies *the pouring* عَكِيس, meaning as first expl. below, *upon* طَعَام [or *food*]: (Ḳ:) and اعْتَكَسَ ↓ اللَّبَنَ signifies the same as عَكَسَ: (TA:) [or both of these verbs are intrans.;] عَكَسَ and اعتكس from عَكِيس signify the same [app. without اللَّبَنَ]. (JM.)

2. عكّس, inf. n. تَعْكِيسٌ, [*He said the contrary of what he meant; spoke ironically.*] (A and Mgh in art. حرس. [In the former, تعكيس is coupled with تَهَكُّم, which signifies the same.])

3. عَاكَسَ, مُعَاكَسَةٌ and عِكَاسٌ [are inf. ns. of عَاكَسَ]: for the former see 1, near the beginning. — دُونَ ذٰلِكَ الأَمْرِ عِكَاسٌ وَمِكَاسٌ (Ṣ, A,* O, Ḳ) means [*In the way to the accomplishment of that affair is*] *a striving to turn* [*therefrom*]: (A, TA:) or *a mutual seizing of the forelock:* (A, O, Ḳ, TA:) [مِكَاس and عِكَاس may signify alike:] or مكاس is an imitative sequent. (O,* Ḳ,* TḲ.)

5. تعكّس فِى مِشْيَتِهِ [*He moved along like the viper in his gait;*] *he went along like the viper,* (Lth, O, Ḳ, TA,) *as though his veins had become dry,* or *stiff:* said of a man: sometimes a drunken man goes along thus. (Lth, O, TA.)

7. انعكس, said of a thing, i. q. ↓ اعتكس; (O, Ḳ;) each is quasi-pass. of عَكَسَهُ [and signifies, therefore, *It became reversed; the last part of it became first, and the first last;* or *it became turned hind part before, and fore part behind:* it (language) *became inverted, reversed, converted,* or *transposed:* or *its order,* or *meaning, became perverted*]. (TA.) You say, الحَدُّ يَطَّرِدُ وَيَنْعَكِسُ [*The definition is of uniform,* or *general, application, and may become inverted,* or *converted:* for instance, you may say, "a man is a rational animal," and "a rational animal is a man"]. (A, TA. [See also العَكْسُ in Kull p. 255.]) You say also, انعكس الحَالُ *The state,* or *condition, became reversed.* (TA.)

8: see 7: = and see also 1, last sentence.

[عَكْسٌ, an inf. n. used as an epithet in which the quality of a subst. predominates; The *reverse* either *in respect of order* or *of sense,* i. e. the *converse* or the *contrary,* of a proposition &c. You say, هٰذَا عَكْسُ هٰذَا *This is the reverse, &c., of this.*]

عِكَاسٌ The *cord which is tied in the fore part of the nose,* or *mouth, of a camel,* (Ṣ, O, Ḳ,) [*and attached*] *to his fore legs,* (Ḳ,) or *to the pastern of* [*each of*] *his fore legs,* (Ṣ, O,) *to render him submissive,* or *tractable:* (Ṣ, Ḳ:) the *cord mentioned in explanations of* عَكَسَ البَعِيرَ [q. v.]. (Ṣ, O, Ḳ.)

عَكِيسٌ *Milk poured upon broth,* (O, Ḳ,) *in whatever state it* [*the former*] *be.* (O.) And (O, Ḳ) *Fresh milk with* إِهَالَة [or *melted fat,* &c.,] *poured upon it, after which it is drunk:* (Ṣ, O, Ḳ:) or *flour upon which it is poured, and which is then drunk.* (A'Obeyd, TA.) = Also *A shoot of a grape-vine that is reversed* (يُعْكَسُ) *under the ground to* [*come forth at*] *another place.* (Ṣ, O, Ḳ.) — لَيْلَةٌ عَكِيسَةٌ *A dark night.* (O, Ḳ.) — إِبِلٌ عَكِيسَةٌ *Many camels.* (O, Ḳ.)

كَلَامٌ مَعْكُوسٌ *Language,* or *a sentence, inverted, reversed, converted,* or *transposed:* (A:) or *perverted in order,* or *in meaning.* (Mṣb.)

عكف

1. عَكَفَ عَلَيْهِ, aor. ـُ and ـِ, [the former, only, mentioned in the Mgh, and only the latter in the CḲ,] inf. n. عُكُوفٌ (Ṣ, O, Mṣb, Ḳ) and عَكْفٌ, (Mṣb, TA,) or the latter is of the trans. verb, (T, TA,) *He kept,* or *clave, to it constantly,* or *perseveringly;* (Ṣ, Mgh,* O, Mṣb, Ḳ, TA;) namely, a thing; (Ṣ, O, Mṣb;) *not turning his face from it:* or, as some say, *he continued intent upon it:* (TA:) and, accord. to Er-Rázee, ↓ اعتكف عَلَيْهِ would be agreeable with analogy, in the sense of عَكَفَ عليه, but has not been heard. (Ḥar p. 682.) Hence, in the Ḳur [vii. 134], يَعْكُفُونَ عَلَى أَصْنَامٍ لَهُمْ, (Ṣ,* O, TA,) or يَعْكِفُونَ, accord. to different readers, (O, TA,) i. e. A people *keeping,* or *cleaving, constantly,* or *perseveringly, to* the worship of *idols belonging to them;* (Ksh;) or *continuing intent upon* the worship of *idols belonging to them.* (Bḍ, Jel.) — And عُكُوفٌ [or عُكُوفٌ فِى مَكَانٍ] signifies The *keeping,* or *cleaving, to a place.* (TA.) See also 8. — And أَقْبَلَتْ عَلَيْهِ meaning عَكَفَتِ الخَيْلُ بِقَائِدِهَا [i. e. *The horses,* or *horsemen,* (for the latter may be meant notwithstanding the fem. pronoun, agreeably with an ex. in De Sacy's Gram., sec. ed., ii. 265,) *advanced,* or *approached, towards their leader;* or *kept,* or *clave, to him*]. (TA.) — And عَكَفُوا حَوْلَهُ *They went round it;* (Ṣ, O, Ḳ;) namely, a thing. (Ṣ, O.) El-'Ajjáj says,

* عَكْفَ النَّبِيطِ يَلْعَبُونَ الفَنْزَجَا *

[*Like the going round of the Nabathæans playing the* game called فَنْزَج: in which عَكْف is probably used by poetic license for عُكُوف]. (Ṣ, O.) And in like manner one says, عَكَفَتِ الطَّيْرُ عَلَى القَتِيلِ, (O,) or حَوْلَ القَتِيلِ, (Ḳ,) [*The birds went round the slain person*], inf. n. عُكُوفٌ. (TA.) And عَكَفَ الجَوْهَرُ فِى النَّظْمِ (Ṣ, O, Ḳ) i. e. [*The gems*] *went round* [*among the strung beads*]. (O, Ḳ.) — And عَكَفَ signifies also تَأَخَّرَ [*He went back* or *backwards,* &c.; or *became,* or *remained, behind;* &c.]. (O, Ḳ.) = عَكَفَهُ, aor. ـُ and ـِ, [the former, only, mentioned in the Mgh, and only the latter in the CḲ,] inf. n. عَكْفٌ, (Ṣ, O, Mṣb, Ḳ,) *He,* or *it, made him,* or *it, still,* or *motionless:* (Ṣ, O:) and *he,* or *it, detained, withheld,* or *debarred, him,* or *it;* (Ṣ, Mgh, O, Mṣb, Ḳ;) as also ↓ عَكَّفَهُ, (O,* TA,) inf. n. تَعْكِيفٌ; (TA;) and so عَكَفَ بِهِ. (Ḥar p. 293.) One says, عَكَفْتُهُ عَنْ حَاجَتِهِ, (Mṣb,) aor. and inf. n. as above, (TA,) *I withheld him from the object of his want:* (Mṣb:) or *I turned him away,* or *back, therefrom.* (TA.) And مَا عَكَفَكَ عَنْ كَذَا [*What has withheld thee,* or *turned thee away* or *back, from such a thing?*]. (Ṣ, O.) — See also 2. — عَكَفَ, (O, Ḳ,) inf. n. عَكْفٌ, (O,) also signifies رَعَى [app. as trans., meaning *He tended,* or *pastured,* cattle; &c.]. (O, Ḳ.) — And i. q. أَصْلَحَ [*He put into a good, sound, right,* or *proper, state;* &c.]. (O, Ḳ.)

2: see 1, last quarter. — One says, عكّف السِّلْكُ السُّمُوطَ i. e. [*The thread of the necklace*] *kept from becoming scattered* [*the things suspended therefrom*]. (O, from a verse of El-Aạshà.) — And عكّف النَّظْمُ, inf. n. تَعْكِيفٌ, *The strung beads had gems disposed in regular order* (نُضِّدَ, Lth, O, or نُظِمَ, Ḳ) *among them.* (Lth, O, Ḳ.) — And عُكِّفَ الشَّعَرُ *The hair was crisped, curled,* or *twisted, and contracted.* (O, Ḳ.) And عكّفت شَعَرَهَا *She* (a woman) *made her hair to cleave together, one part to another, and disposed it in plaits;* as also ↓ عَكَفَتْهُ; (Ḥam p. 267;) but, accord. to Lth, they seldom said عَكَّفَ in relation to hair that is termed مُعَكَّفٌ, i. e. "combed and plaited," though, if this were said, it would be correct. (O.)

[3. عاكف, accord. to Reiske, as mentioned by Freytag, (app. followed by an accus.,) signifies *He clave continually to the side of any one.*]

5. تعكّف *He confined, restrained, withheld,* or

debarred, himself; (O, Ḳ;) as also ▼ اعتكف: one should not say ▼ انعكف. (Ḳ.)

7: see what next precedes.

8: see 1, first sentence: and see also 5. — اعتكف, (Mgh, O, Mṣb, Ḳ,*) or اعتكف فِى ٱلْمَسْجِدِ, (Ṣ, O,* Ḳ,*) and ▼ عَكَفَ فِيهِ, signify the same, (O, Ḳ,) i. e. *He secluded himself,* (Ṣ, O, TA,) or *remained,* (Mgh, TA,) *in the mosque,* or *place of worship,* (Ṣ, Mgh, O, TA,) *performing a particular sort of religious service, with the observance of certain conditions,* (Mgh,) [*during a period of days and nights, or at least during one whole day, fasting from daybreak to sunset, and occupying himself in prayer and religious meditation, without any interruption by affairs distracting the mind from devotion and not pressing,*] *not going forth therefrom except for human necessity:* (TA:) اِعْتِكَافٌ is thus termed because it is the *withholding oneself from the customary exercises of freedom of action in the disposal,* or *management, of affairs.* (Mṣb.)

عَكَفٌ *Crisp, curly,* or *twisted, and contracted,* hair. (Ibn-'Abbád, O, Ḳ.)

عَاكِفٌ *Keeping,* or *cleaving, constantly,* or *perseveringly,* [عَلَى شَىْءٍ *to a thing,* and فِى مَكَانٍ *in a place:*] (Ṣ, O:*) or *continuing intent* [upon a thing]: and *remaining, staying, dwelling,* or *abiding,* in a place: (O:) pl. عَاكِفُونَ and عُكُوفٌ (O, Ḳ, TA) and عُكَّفٌ. (TA.) One says, فُلَانٌ عَاكِفٌ عَلَى فَرْجٍ حَرَامٍ [*Such a one is keeping,* or *cleaving, constantly,* or *perseveringly, to an unlawful* فَرْج]. (Ṣ, O.)

مُعَكَّفٌ *Bent, crooked, contorted,* or *distorted.* (TA.) [See also مُعَقَّفٌ.]

مَعْكُوفٌ *Made still,* or *motionless:* and *detained, withheld,* or *debarred.* (Ṣ, O.) Hence مَعْكُوفًا in the Ḳur [xlviii. 25], (Ṣ, O,) meaning *Being detained,* or *withheld;* (Mgh, TA;) as expl. by Mujáhid and 'Aṭà. (TA.) — And Hair *combed and plaited.* (O, Ḳ.) [See also مَعْقُوفٌ, voce مُعَقَّفٌ.]

مُعْتَكَفٌ A man's *place of* اِعْتِكَاف [or *self-seclusion in a mosque or the like:* see 8]. (TA.)

عكم

1. عَكَمَ ٱلْمَتَاعَ, (Ṣ, Ḳ,) aor. ـِ, (Ḳ,) inf. n. عَكْمٌ, (TA,) *He bound* [or *tied up*] *the goods,* (Ṣ, Ḳ,) *with a string,* (Ṣ,) or *rope,* (TA,) *in a garment,* or *piece of cloth,* (Ḳ,* TA,) [*so as to form a bundle,* or *the like,*] *by spreading the garment,* or *piece of cloth, and putting the goods in it, and binding it:* the goods thus bound being then called ▼ عِكْمٌ. (TA.) — And عَكَمَ ٱلْبَعِيرَ *He bound, upon the camel,* [or, app., *upon each side of the camel,*] *the* عِكْم. (Ṣ.) — And عَكَمْتُ ٱلرَّجُلَ *I bound, for the man, the* عِكْم. (Ṣ.) See also 4. — عَكَمَ ٱلْبَعِيرَ, inf. n. عَكْمٌ, signifies also [*He muzzled the camel;*] *he bound the mouth of the camel.* (TA.) [In this sense it is probably formed by transposition from كَعَمَ; for the latter is better known.]) = عَكَمَهُ عَنْ زِيَارَتِهِ, inf. n. عَكْمٌ, *He turned him away,* or *back, from visiting him.* (TA.) And عَكَمَ عَنَّا, (Ṣ,) or عَنْهُ, (Ḳ,) inf. n. as above, (Ṣ,) *He was turned away,* or *back, from visiting us,* or *him.* (Ṣ, Ḳ.) = عَكَمَ لِأَرْضِ كَذَا, (Ḳ, [thus in my MS. copy, in the CḲ الارض كذا,]) inf. n. as above, (TA,) *He repaired,* or *betook himself,* [as though properly meaning *he bound his goods upon his camel* or *camels, for the purpose of repairing,*] *to such a land.* (Ḳ.) — And عَكَمَ, (Ḳ,) aor. and inf. n. as above, (Ṣ, TA,) *He expected,* or *waited.* (Ṣ, Ḳ.) — And *He returned,* or *turned back,* syn. كَرَّ, (Ṣ, Ḳ, TA,) عَلَيْهِ [*against him*], (Ḳ, TA,) after fleeing. (Ṣ, TA.) — And مَا عَكَمَ عَنْ شَتْمِهِ *He did not hold back from reviling him.* (Ḳ,* TA.) = عَكَمَتِ ٱلْإِبِلُ: see what next follows.

2. عَكَّمَتِ ٱلْإِبِلُ, (Ṣ, Ḳ,) inf. n. تَعْكِيمٌ, (Ṣ,) *The camels became fat, and laden with fat upon fat;* (Ṣ, Ḳ;) as also ▼ عَكَمَت, (Ḳ,) inf. n. عَكْمٌ. (TA.)

3. ٱلْمُعَاكَمَةُ, relating to two men, or two women, *The being together in a state of nudity, without anything intervening between their two bodies:* which is forbidden: thus expl. by Eṭ-Ṭaháwee. (TA.)

4. اعكمهُ *He assisted him to perform what is termed* العَكْم [i. e. *the binding,* or *tying up, of his goods,* or *the binding them upon a camel*]; (Ṣ, Ḳ;) [and so ▼ عَكَمَهُ; for] a man says to his companion, اِعْكِمْنِى and أَعْكِمْنِى, meaning *Assist thou me to perform* العَكْم; like as one says أَحْلِبْنِى [and اُحْلُبْنِى], meaning "Assist thou me to milk." (Fr, TA.)

8. اعتكموا *They equalized the* أَعْدَال [i. e. the *burdens called* أَعْكَام, pl. of عِكْم], *in order to their taking them up and carrying them,* (Ḳ, TA,) *and binding them upon the camel,* or *camels, that was,* or *were, to bear them:* Az says, I have heard the Arabs say thus to their servants on the day of departure. (TA.) — And اعتكم ٱلشَّىْءُ *The thing was,* or *became, heaped up, one part upon another:* (Ḳ:) or *mixed.* (TA.)

عَكْمٌ A [*thing such as is called*] نَمَط [q. v.]. (TA. [See also the next paragraph, near the end.]) — And hence, as being likened thereto, (TA,) The *interior of the side:* (Ḳ, TA:) occurring in a trad. (TA.)

عِكْمٌ *A burden that is borne on one side of a camel or other beast, made equiponderant to another burden;* syn. عِدْلٌ; (Ṣ, Mgh, Ḳ;) i. e. *one of two such burdens:* (Ṣ:) so called as long as *containing goods:* two such burdens are bound upon the two sides of the [women's camel-vehicle called] هَوْدَج: or, accord. to A'Obeyd, *a burden,* and *a burden such as is described above, containing receptacles of various sorts of food, and goods:* (TA:) pl. أَعْكَامٌ; (Az, M, Ḳ;) accord. to the M, the only pl.; but accord. to Az, عُكُومٌ also. (TA.) كَعِكْمَىِ ٱلْعَيْرِ [*Like the two equiponderant burdens of the ass*] is a prov. applied to two men who are equals in eminence or nobility. (TA.) And one says, وَقَعَ ٱلْمُصْطَرِعَانِ عِكْمَىْ عَيْرٍ, and كَعِكْمَىْ عَيْرٍ, meaning *The two* [*men wrestling*] *fell together, neither of them having thrown down the other.* (TA. [See also عِدْلٌ, last sentence.]) — Also *A bundle* (كَارَة, Ḳ, TA) *of clothes* [&c., *put in one piece of cloth and tied up*]: (TA:) pl. عُكُومٌ. (Ḳ.) See also 1, first sentence. — And *A* نَمَط [q. v.] *in which a woman puts what she lays up for a time of need* (ذَخِيرَتَهَا). (Ṣ, Ḳ. [See also عَكْمٌ.]) — See also عِكَامٌ. — Also The بَكَرَة [i. e. *pulley,* or *sheave of the pulley,*] *of a well.* (Ḳ.)

عُكْمَةٌ *A corner* of the belly: (Ḳ:) pl. عُكُومٌ. (TA.) Some restrict it to negative phrases: they say, مَا بَقِىَ فِى بَطْنِ ٱلدَّابَّةِ هَزْمَةٌ وَلَا عُكْمَةٌ إِلَّا ٱمْتَلَأَتْ [*There remained not in the belly of the beast a depression nor a corner but it became full*]. (TA.)

عِكَامٌ (Ṣ, Ḳ, TA) and ▼ عِكْمٌ (Ḳ, TA) *The thing,* (Ḳ, TA,) i. e. *rope,* (TA,) or *string,* (Ṣ, TA,) *with which one binds goods:* (Ṣ, Ḳ, TA:) and the former, if not a mere repetition in the Ḳ, may signify also the *thing* [or *muzzle,* more commonly called كِعَام,] *with which the mouth of a camel is bound:* (TA:) the pl. of the former is عُكُمٌ, (so in copies of the Ḳ,) or عُكْمٌ. (So in the TA.)

عَكُومٌ: see مَعْكَمٌ. = Also A woman *who usually brings forth a male after a female.* (Ḳ.)

عَكَّامٌ *One who binds the burdens upon the camels that are to bear them:* (TA:) [thus applied in the present day: and also to *one who has the charge of the baggage and tents:* coll. gen. n. with ة.]

مَعْكَمٌ *A place of turning away or back;* (Ṣ, TA;) and (TA) so ▼ عُكُومٌ, (Ḳ, TA,) as in the saying مَا عِنْدَهُ عُكُومٌ [*He has not a place of turning away or back*]. (TA.)

مُعْكَمٌ *Compact,* or *hard, in flesh;* (Ṣ, Ḳ;) applied to a man. (Ṣ.) [See also what next follows.]

مُعَكَّمٌ † A man *hard in the flesh, and* كَثِيرُ ٱلْمَفَاصِلِ [app. a mistranscription for كَبِيرُ ٱلْمَفَاصِلِ *large in the joints*]; likened to the عِكْم: and, accord. to IAạr, a boy, or young man, *plump and pampered.* (TA.)

مُعَاكِمٌ [app. *A man asking another to assist him in the binding of the burdens upon his camel*]. (Ḥam p. 233 l. 21.)

عكن

5. تعكّن, said of the belly (Ṣ, Mṣb, Ḳ) of a girl, or young woman, (Ḳ,) *It had creases,* or *wrinkles, originating from fatness.* (Ṣ, Mṣb, Ḳ.) — And *It* (a thing) *was,* or *became, heaped up, one part upon another, and folded.* (TA.)

عُكْنَةٌ *A crease, or wrinkle, in the belly, originating from fatness:* pl. عُكَنٌ (Ṣ, Mgh, Mṣb, Ḳ) and (Ṣ, Mṣb) sometimes they said (Mṣb) أَعْكَانٌ [which is a pl. of pauc.]. (Ṣ, Mṣb, TA.) — عُكَنُ الدِّرْعِ means *The folds of the coat of mail:* so in a verse cited voce أَخْنَسُ: one says دِرْعٌ ذَاتُ عُكَنٍ [*A coat of mail having folds*] when it is wide, folding upon the wearer by reason of its width. (TA.)

عَكْنَآءُ A girl, or young woman, *having creases, or wrinkles, in her belly, originating from fatness;* as also ↓ مُعَكَّنَةٌ. (Ḳ.) — And A she-camel *thick in the teats* (Ḳ, TA) *and in the flesh of the udder;* and in like manner a ewe or goat. (TA.)

نَعَمٌ عُكْنَانٌ, and sometimes pronounced عُكَنَانٌ [app. by poetic license], (Ṣ,) or إِبِلٌ عُكْنَانٌ and عُكَنَانٌ, (Ḳ,) *Numerous camels:* (Ṣ, Ḳ:) or *numerous great camels.* (TA.)

عُكَانٌ The *neck:* (Ḳ:) app. a dial. var. of عِجَانٌ, of the dial. of El-Yemen. (TA.)

مُعَكَّنَةٌ: see عَكْنَآءُ.

عل

1. عَلَّهُ, aor. عَلُ (Ṣ, O, Mṣb, Ḳ) and عَلِ, (Ṣ, O, Ḳ,) inf. n. عَلَلٌ (Mṣb, Ḳ) and عَلٌّ, (Ḳ,) *He gave him to drink the second time;* (Ṣ, O, Mṣb, Ḳ;) and so ↓ اعلّهُ, (Ḳ, TA,) inf. n. إِعْلَالٌ. (TA.) [See also 2 and 4.] — [Hence, † *He dyed it a second time;* namely, a hide: see a verse cited voce مُخْلِفٌ.] — Hence [also], (TA,) عَلَّ الضَّارِبُ المَضْرُوبَ ‡ *The beater plied the beaten with a continued beating;* (Ṣ, O, Ḳ, TA;) and so عَلَّهُ ضَرْبًا. (TA.) — And عَطَآءُ ٱللّٰهِ مُضَاعَفٌ يَعُلُّ بِهِ عِبَادَهُ مَرَّةً بَعْدَ أُخْرَى † [*The gift of God is redoubled; He bestows it upon his servants one time after another*]. (TA.) ═ And عَلَّ, (Mṣb, Ḳ,) or عَلَّ بِنَفْسِهِ, the verb being also intrans., (Ṣ, O,) aor. عَلِ (IAṭr, Mṣb, Ḳ) and عَلُ, (IAṭr, Ḳ,) inf. ns. as above, (TḲ,) *He drank* (IAṭr,* Ṣ, O, Mṣb, Ḳ) *the second draught:* (IAṭr,* Ṣ, O, Ḳ:) or *drank after drinking, uninterruptedly:* (Ḳ:) and عَلَّتِ الإِبِلُ, aor. عَلِ and عَلُ, *The camels drank the second draught.* (TA.) ═ And هٰذَا طَعَامٌ قَدْ عُلَّ مِنْهُ *This is food of which some has been eaten.* (Kr, Ḳ.*) ═ عَلَّ, aor. عَلِ, (IAṭr, Mṣb, Ḳ,) inf. n. عَلٌّ, (TA,) *He* (a man, IAṭr, Mṣb) *was, or became, diseased, sick, or ill;* (IAṭr, Mṣb, Ḳ;) and (Mṣb, Ḳ) so ↓ اعتلّ, (Ṣ, O, Mṣb, Ḳ,) inf. n. إِعْتِلَالٌ; (Ḳ;) and so عُلَّ, in the pass. form: ═ and the trans. verb is عَلَّهُ, [syn. with أَعَلَّهُ,] aor. in this case عَلُ. (Mṣb. See 4.) ═ [عُلَّ الشَّىْءُ is mentioned in the Ṣ, with the addition ↓ فَهُوَ مَعْلُولٌ, but without any explanation; perhaps as meaning *The thing was caused;* from عِلَّةٌ "a cause," of which مَعْلُولٌ (q. v.) is the correlative: but the context seems to indicate that it means *the thing was used for the purpose of diverting from some want:* Golius appears to have read عُلِّلَ, and to have been led by what next precedes it in the Ṣ to render it *loco alterius rei fuit lactavitve res.*]

2. تَعْلِيلٌ signifies The *giving to drink after giving to drink.* (Ṣ.) See 4. [And see also 1, first sentence.] — And The *plucking fruit one time after another.* (Ṣ.) — And عَلَّلَهُ بِهِ, (Ṣ, O, Ḳ,) inf. n. as above (Ḳ) [and تَعِلَّةٌ, q. v.], *He diverted, or occupied, him* [*so as to render him contented*] *with it;* (Ṣ, O, Ḳ;) namely, a thing, (Ṣ, O,) or food, &c., (Ḳ, TA,) as, for instance, discourse, and the like; (TA;) *like as the child is diverted, or occupied, with somewhat of food, by which he is rendered contented to be restrained from milk.* (Ṣ, O, TA.*) One says, فُلَانٌ يُعَلِّلُ نَفْسَهُ بِتَعِلَّةٍ [*Such a one diverts, or occupies, himself, so as to render himself contented, with something diverting*]. (Ṣ, O.) [See also مُعَلَّلٌ. And see 5.] ═ Also The *assigning a cause:* and the *asserting a cause.* (KL.) [One says, عَلَّلَهُ بِكَذَا *He accounted for it by assigning as the cause such a thing:* and *he asserted it to be caused by such a thing.*]

3. عَالَلْتُ النَّاقَةَ *I milked the she-camel in the morning and the evening and the middle of the day:* (Lḥ, O, TA:) in the Ḳ, erroneously, عَالَّتِ النَّاقَةُ [as meaning *the she-camel was milked at those times*]: (TA:) and the subst. is ↓ عِلَالٌ: (Ḳ: [but there is no reason why this should not be regarded as a reg. inf. n.:]) Lḥ cites this verse, (O,) of an Arab of the desert, (TA,)

> • اَلْعَنْزُ تَعْلَمُ أَنِّى لَا أُكَرِّمُهَا •
> • عَنِ العِلَالِ وَلَا عَنْ قِدْرِ أَضْيَافِى •

[*The she-goat knows that I will not preserve her from the milking in the morning and the evening and the middle of the day nor from the cooking-pot of my guests*]: (O:) or, accord. to Az, عِلَالٌ signifies the *milking after milking, before the udder requires it by the abundance of the milk.* (TA.) [See also 6.]

4. أَعْلَلْتُ الإِبِلَ *I brought,* or *sent, back the camels from the water* (Ṣ, O, Ḳ) *after they had satisfied their thirst,* (O,) or *before they had satisfied their thirst:* (Ṣ, Ḳ:) or, (Ṣ, O, Ḳ,) [if the latter is meant,] accord. to some of the etymologists, (Ṣ, O,) it is with غ; (Ṣ, O, Ḳ; [see 4 in art. غل;]) as though it were from the meaning of "thirsting;" but the former is what has been heard; (Ṣ, O;) and it means *I gave the camels to drink the second draught,* or *watered them the second time, and then brought them,* or *sent them, back from the water, having their thirst satisfied;* and thus, too, means ↓ عَلَّلْتُ الإِبِلَ; *the contr. of* أَغْلَلْتُهَا. (TA.) See also 1, first sentence. — And اعلّ القَوْمُ *The people,* or *party, were,* or *became, persons whose camels had drunk the second time.* (Ṣ, O, Ḳ.*) ═ اعلّهُ ٱللّٰهُ *God caused him to be diseased, sick, or ill;* (Mṣb, Ḳ;) as also ↓ عَلَّهُ, aor. عَلُ. (Mṣb.) One says, لَا أَعَلَّكَ ٱللّٰهُ, meaning *May God not smite thee with a disease, a sickness,* or *an illness.* (Ṣ, O.) — And اعلّهُ signifies also *He made him,* or *pronounced him, to have an excuse* (جَعَلَهُ ذَا عِلَّةٍ): whence إِعْلَالَاتُ الفُقَهَآءِ [*The excusings of the lawyers*]. (Mṣb.)

5. تعلّل بِهِ *He diverted himself,* (Ṣ,) or *occupied himself so as to divert himself,* (Ḳ,) *and* (Ṣ, in the Ḳ "or") *contented,* or *satisfied, himself,* or *he was,* or *became diverted, &c., with it;* (Ṣ, Ḳ;) as also ↓ اعتلّ: (Ḳ:) as, for instance, with a portion of food, [*so that the craving of his stomach became allayed,*] before the [morning-meal called] غَدَآء; (M voce سُلْفَةٌ, and Ḳ voce لُمْجَةٌ, &c.;) and as a beast does with the cud: (TA:) *he occupied himself so as to divert himself,* and *fed* [or *sustained*] *himself, with it:* (Ḥar p. 23:) and *he whiled away his time with it.* (W p. 55.) And تعلّل بِالْمَرْأَةِ *He diverted himself with the woman.* (Ḳ.) — And تعلّل signifies also *He occupied himself vainly.* (Ṣ and TA in art. جدب: see a verse cited voce جَادِبٌ.) — And *He made an excuse.* (KL. [See also 8.]) — And تَعَلَّلَتْ مِنْ نِفَاسِهَا, and ↓ تَعَالَّتْ, (Ḳ, TA,) as also تَعَالَتْ, without teshdeed, (TA, [see 5 in art. علو,]) *She passed forth from her state of impurity consequent upon childbirth,* (Ḳ,* TA,) *and became lawful to her husband.* (TA.)

6. هُوَ يَتَعَالُّ نَاقَتَهُ means *He milks the* عُلَالَة [q. v.] *of his she-camel.* (TA. [See also 3.]) And الصَّبِىُّ يَتَعَالُّ بِثَدْىِ أُمِّهِ [perhaps correctly ثَدْىَ أُمِّهِ], and app. meaning *The child exhausts the* عُلَالَة, or *remains of milk, in the breast of his mother*]. (TA.) — And تَعَالَلْتُ النَّاقَةَ † *I elicited from the she-camel what power she had* [*remaining*] *of going on.* (Ṣ, O.) — And تَعَالَلْتُ نَفْسِى signifies the same as تَلَوَّمْتُهَا [app. meaning *I waited for myself* to accomplish a want, or an object of desire, *so that I might avoid blame:* for تَلَوَّمَ as signifying اِنْتَظَرَ and تَنَظَّرَ is trans. as well as intrans.; and seems to be originally similar to تَأَثَّمَ and تَحَنَّثَ and &c.]. (TA.) — See also 5, last sentence.

8. اعتلّ: see 1, latter half. — [Hence, اعتلّت الرِّيحُ † *The wind became faint,* or *feeble.*] ═ See also 5, first sentence. — Also *He excused himself;* or *adduced,* or *urged, an excuse,* or *a plea;* (MA, Ḳ,* TA;*) or *he laid hold upon a plea,* or *an allegation.* (El-Fárábee, Mṣb.) You say, اعتلّ عَلَيْهِ بِعِلَّةٍ (Ṣ, MA, O) *He adduced,* or *urged, an excuse,* or *a plea,* or *pretext, for it.* (MA.) And hence, اِعْتِلَالَاتُ الفُقَهَآءِ [*The pleas,* or *allegations, of the lawyers, which they adduce,* or *upon which they lay hold*]. (Mṣb.) ═ اعتلّهُ *He hindered, prevented, impeded,* or *withheld, him; turned him back* or *away; retarded him;* or *diverted him by occupying him otherwise; from an affair.* (Ṣ, O.) — And (Ṣ, O, in the Ḳ "or") *He accused him of a crime, an offence,* or *an injurious action, that he had not committed.* (Ṣ, O, Ḳ.)

R. Q. 2. تَعَلْعَلَ *He,* or *it, was,* or *became, unsteady,* or *shaky, and lax,* or *uncompact.* (Ḳ.)

عَلَّ and لَعَلَّ and عَلَّكَ and لَعَلَّكَ : see عَلَّ, below. ═ عَلْ عَلْ (Ḳ, TA, in the O written as one word,) *A cry by which one chides sheep* or *goats* (Yaạḳoob, O, Ḳ) and *camels*. (O.)

عَلُ : see art. علو.

عَلَّ and لَعَلَّ (Ṣ, O, Mughnee, Ḳ) are dial. vars.; or the former is the original, the ل being augmentative, (Ṣ, O, Mughnee,) prefixed for the purpose of corroboration: the meaning is expectation of a thing hoped for or feared; (Ṣ, O;) importing hope, or eager desire, and fear, or caution: (Ṣ, O, Ḳ:) each is a particle, like إِنَّ and لَيْتَ and لٰكِنَّ and كَأَنَّ : (Ṣ, O:) and like عَسَى [q. v.] in meaning; but like إِنَّ in government; (Mughnee;) governing the subject in the accus. case, and the predicate in the nom.: one says, عَلَّكَ تَفْعَلُ [*May-be, or perhaps, thou wilt do* such a thing], and لَعَلِّى أَفْعَلُ [*May-be I shall do*], and عَلِّى أَفْعَلُ; and sometimes they said, عَلَّنِى and لَعَلَّنِى ; (Ṣ, O;) and one says also ▼ عَلْ and ▼ لَعَلْ, with the ل quiescent, and ▼ عَلَّكَ and ▼ لَعَلَّكَ : (O:) [and accord. to general usage, one says, لَعَلَّ زَيْدًا قَائِمٌ *May-be Zeyd is standing*:] and the tribe of 'Okeyl made each to govern the subject in the gen. case, (Ṣ, O, Mughnee,) saying, لَعَلَّ زَيْدٍ قَائِمٌ ; (Ṣ, O;) and allowed the pronouncing عَلِّ and لَعَلِّ : (Mughnee:) sometimes its subject is suppressed, as in عَلَّ أَنْ أَتَقَدَّمَ, meaning لَعَلِّى أَنْ أَتَقَدَّمَ [*May-be I shall precede*]: (Ḥam p. 517:) the Koofees allow the manṣoob aor. [immediately] after, on the authority of the reading of Ḥafṣ, [in the Ḳur xl. 38,] لَعَلِّى أَبْلُغَ الأَسْبَابَ [*May-be I may reach the places of ascent*, or *the regions*, or *tracts*, of the heavens]. (Mughnee.) Other dial. vars. of عَلَّ are mentioned in art. لعل [q. v.]. (Ḳ.)

عَلُّ : see عَلَلٌ, in two places. ═ Also [in the CḲ erroneously with ḍamm to the ع in all the senses here following that are expl. in the Ḳ] *An emaciated tick*: (Ṣ, O:) or *a big-bodied tick*: or *a small-bodied one*: (Ḳ, TA:) pl. عِلَالٌ. (TA.) — And *A man advanced in age*, (Ṣ, O, Ḳ,) *small in body*, (Ṣ, O,) or *slender*, or *spare*; (Ḳ;) as being likened to the tick. (Ṣ, O.) And anything *slender* (دَقِيق, for رَقِيق in the Ḳ is a mistranscription, TA) *in body, advanced in age*. (M, Ḳ,* TA.) And A man *whose skin is contracted by disease*. (IDrd, O, Ḳ.) — Also *One in whom is no good*: Esh-Shenfarà says, وَلَسْتُ بِعَلٍّ [And *I am not one in whom is no good*: but the context seems rather to require one of the other meanings mentioned above: and another reading (بِغُلٍّ) is mentioned by De Sacy, in his Chrest. Ar., 2nd ed., ii. 359]. (O, TA.) — Also A man *who visits women much*, or *often*, (Ḳ, TA,) *and diverts himself with them*. (TA.) — And A *big-bodied, large* he-goat. (Ḳ.)

عَلٌّ and عِلٌّ : see عُلْعُلٌ.

عَلَّةٌ *A* [*single*] *second draught*. (Mgh.) — And hence, (Mgh,) A woman's *fellow-wife*; *her husband's wife*: (Mgh, Mṣb,* Ḳ:) or, as some say, *a step-mother*: but the former is the more correct meaning: (Mgh:) pl. عَلَّاتٌ. (Mṣb.) Whence, بَنُو العَلَّاتِ *The sons of one father by different mothers*: as though, when he added by marriage a second wife to the first, he took a second draught. (Ṣ,* Mgh, O,* Mṣb,* Ḳ.*) أَوْلَادُ الأَخْيَافِ means the contr. of this: and أَوْلَادُ الأَعْيَانِ, the sons of the same father and mother. (Mṣb.) Accord. to IB, one says, هُمَا أَخَوَانِ مِنْ ضَرَّتَيْنِ [They two are brothers from two fellow-wives]; but they did not say, مِنْ ضَرَّةٍ : and accord. to ISh, one says, أَوْلَادُ عَلَّةٍ and هُمْ بَنُو عَلَّةٍ. (TA.) And it is said in a trad., الأَنْبِيَآءُ بَنُو عَلَّاتٍ, (Mgh,) or أَوْلَادُ عَلَّاتٍ, (TA,) meaning *The prophets are of different mothers, but of one religion*: (T, Mgh, TA:) or *of one faith, but of different religious laws* or *ordinances*. (Nh, TA.) ═ See also عُلَالَةٌ.

عِلَّةٌ *An accident that befalls an object and causes its state*, or *condition*, *to become altered*. (TA.) — And hence, (TA,) *A disease, sickness*, or *malady*; (Ṣ, O, Ḳ, TA;) because, by its befalling, the state becomes altered from strength to weakness; so says El-Munáwee in the "Towḳeef:" (TA:) or *a disease that diverts* [*from the ordinary occupations*; app. regarded as being from what next follows]: pl. عِلَلٌ (Mṣb) [and عِلَّاتٌ]. — Also *An accident*, or *event*, *that diverts the person to whom it occurs from his course*, (Ṣ, O, Ḳ,) or *from the object of his want*: (M:) as though it became a second occupation hindering him from his former occupation. (Ṣ, O.) — And [hence,] *an excuse*; *an apology*; *a plea whereby one excuses himself*. (TA.) Hence, (Ḳ,* TA,) لَاتَعْدَمُ خَرْقَاءُ عِلَّةً [expl. in art. خرق]. (Ḳ, TA.) [See also another ex. in art. سأل, conj. 3.] — And *A cause*: [and particularly *an efficient cause*:] (M, Ḳ:) one says, هٰذَا عِلَّةٌ لِهٰذَا *This is a cause of this*: (M:) and هٰذِهِ عِلَّتُهُ *This is its cause*: (Ḳ:) [and عِلَّةٌ وَمَعْلُولٌ ▼ *Cause and effect*; a phrase of frequent occurrence in theological and other works:] and [sometimes عِلَّةٌ signifies *a pretext*, or *pretence*:] it is said in a trad. of 'Áïsheh, فَكَانَ عَبْدُ الرَّحْمٰنِ يَضْرِبُ رِجْلِى بِعِلَّةِ الرَّاحِلَةِ, meaning *And 'Abd-Er-Raḥmán was beating my leg with the pretence*, or *pretext*, *of his beating the side of the camel* with his leg. (TA.) — The phrase عَلَى عِلَّاتِهِ means *In every case*. (Ṣ, O, Ḳ.) Zuheyr says,

* إِنَّ البَخِيلَ مَلُومٌ حَيْثُ كَانَ وَلَا *
* كِنَّ الجَوَادَ عَلَى عِلَّاتِهِ هَرِمُ *

[*Verily the niggard is blamed wherever he be; but the liberal in all his circumstances is Herim*]: (Ṣ, O:) meaning his companion Herim Ibn-Sinán El-Murree. (Ṣ in art. هرم.)

عَلَلٌ and ▼ عَلٌّ [both mentioned in the first paragraph as inf. ns.] The *second draught*: or *a drinking after drinking, uninterruptedly*: (Ḳ:) or the former signifies *a second drinking*; one says عَلَلٌ بَعْدَ نَهَلٍ [*a second drinking after a first drinking*]: (Ṣ, O:) or *a drinking after drinking*: (Mṣb:) and the *second watering* of camels; the first being termed the نَهَل : (Aṣ, TA:) these two terms are also similarly used in relation to suckling: and one of the unknown poets says,

* ثُمَّ انْثَنَى مِنْ بَعْدِ ذَا فَصَلَّى *
* عَلَى النَّبِىِّ نَهَلًا وَعَلَّا ▼ *

[*Then he turned*, or *turned away* or *back*, *after that, and blessed the Prophet a first time and a second time*]. (TA.) — Also, the former, Food *that has been eaten*. (Kr, TA.) [See also نَهَلٌ.]

عُلُلٌ : see عُلْعُلٌ.

عِلَالٌ : see 3; of which it is said in the Ḳ to be the subst., though app. the inf. n.

عَلُولٌ *Some light food with which the sick person is diverted* or *occupied* [*so as to be rendered contented*]: pl. عُلُلٌ. (TA.)

عَلِيلٌ *Diseased, sick*, or *ill*; (Ṣ, Mṣb;) and so with ة applied to a woman: (Mgh:) or, the former, *rendered diseased* &c. by God; [being used as the pass. part. n. of أَعَلَّهُ in the phrase أَعَلَّهُ اللّٰهُ ;] (Ḳ;) as also ▼ مُعَلٌّ, (Mṣb, Ḳ,) agreeably with rule, but this is seldom used; (Mṣb;) and ▼ مَعْلُولٌ, from عَلَّهُ اللّٰهُ ; (Mṣb;) or this last should not be said, for, though the theologians say it, it is not of established authority. (Ḳ,* TA.) ═ عَلِيلَةٌ also signifies A woman *perfumed repeatedly*: (AA, O, Ḳ, TA:) and accord. to AA, ▼ مُعَلَّلٌ, as used in a verse of Imra-el-Ḳeys, signifies *perfumed time after time*. (O.) [See also مُعَلَّلٌ.]

عُلَالَةٌ (Ṣ, Ḳ) and ▼ تَعِلَّةٌ (Ṣ,* Ḳ) and ▼ عَلَّةٌ, (Ḳ, TA,) with fet-ḥ, (TA, [in the CḲ العِلَّةُ is put for العَلَّةُ,]) *A thing with which a person*, (Ṣ, Ḳ,) or *a child*, (TA,) *is diverted*, or *occupied so as to be diverted, and contented*, or *satisfied*, (Ṣ, Ḳ, TA,) *such as talk, and singing, and food, &c.*, (Ḥar p. 308,) [or *such as a small quantity of food by which the craving of his stomach is allayed*,] *in order that he may be quiet*. (TA.) It is said in a trad., accord. to different relations thereof, that dates are the ▼ تَعِلَّة of the child or of the guest. (TA.) — Also, the first, accord. to the copies of the Ḳ, *What is drawn from the udder after the first* فِيقَة : but accord. to IAar, *what is drawn from the udder before the first* فِيقَة [*or milk that collects in the udder between two milkings*], *and before the second* فِيقَة *collects*: also termed عُرَاكَةٌ and دُلَاكَةٌ : (TA:) [or] the *milking that is between two milkings*: (Ṣ, O:) [or] it signifies also *the middle milking of the camel that is milked in the first part and the middle and the last part of the day*: (Ḳ:) or, as some say, the *milk that she excerns* [*into her udder*] *after the milking of the copious flow thereof*. (TA.) — And *A remaining portion of milk* (Ṣ, O, Ḳ, TA) *in the udder*: (TA:) and † *of other things*: [for instance,] ‡ *of the course* [*of a beast*]: (Ḳ:) ‡ *of the running of a horse*; (Ṣ, O, TA;) the former portion whereof is termed بُدَاهَةٌ: (TA:) and † *of anything*: (Ṣ, Ḳ:) as ‡ *of the flesh* of a sheep or goat: and ‡ *of the strength* of an old man. (TA.)

عُلِّىٌّ: see the next paragraph, in three places.

عِلِّيَّةٌ (Ṣ, O, Ḳ) and عُلِّيَّةٌ (O, Ḳ) *An upper chamber*; syn. غُرْفَةٌ: pl. عَلَالِىُّ. (Ṣ, O, Ḳ.) [It is mentioned also in art. علو, q. v.] — هُوَ مِنْ عِلِّيَّةِ قَوْمِهِ and عُلِّيِّهِمْ, [both mistranscribed in the CḲ,] and عِلْيَتِهِمْ, without teshdeed, [which belongs to art. علو,] and † عُلِّيِّهِمْ and † عِلِّيِّهِمْ, [which are also mistranscribed in the CḲ,] mean † *He is of the exalted*, or *elevated*, *of his people*. (Ḳ, TA.) — † عِلِّيُّونَ mentioned in the Ḳur [lxxxiii. 18 and 19] is [said to be] a pl. of which the sing. is † عِلِّىٌّ, or عِلِّيَّةٌ or عُلِّيَّةٌ, or a pl. having no sing., (Ḳ, TA,) [or rather it is from the Hebr. עֶלְיוֹן signifying "high," or "higher,"] and is said to be *A place in the Seventh Heaven, to which ascend the souls of the believers*: or *the most elevated of the Paradises*; like as سِجِّينٌ is the most elevated of the places of the fires [of Hell]: or rather it is properly a name of *the inhabitants thereof*; for this [sort of] pl. is peculiar to rational beings: (TA:) it is mentioned again in art. علو [in which see other explanations]. (Ḳ, TA.)

عَلَّانٌ *Ignorant*: (O, Ḳ:) so in the saying, أَنَا عَلَّانٌ بِأَرْضِ كَذَا وَكَذَا [*I am ignorant of such and such a land*]: (O:) and so, with ة, applied to a woman: (O, Ḳ:) mentioned by Aboo-Sa'eed, as being well known: but said by Az to be unknown to him. (O.)

هُوَ فُلَانُ بْنُ عِلَّانٍ means *He is a person unknown*. (TA.)

عِلِّيُّونَ: see عِلِّيَّةٌ.

عُلْعُلٌ (Ṣ, O, Ḳ) and عَلْعَلٌ (Kr, IF, O, Ḳ) The رَهَابَة [or *ensiform cartilage*, or *lower extremity of the sternum*], *which is the portion of the bone that impends over the belly, resembling a tongue*: (Ṣ, O, Ḳ:) or the *head of the* رَهَابَة *of the horse*: or the *extremity of the rib that impends over the* رَهَابَة, *which is the extremity of the stomach*: pl. علل [so in my original, perhaps † عُلَلٌ,] and † عُلٌّ and † عِلٌّ [all of which are anomalous]. (TA.) — And The *male of the* قُنَابِر, (Ṣ, O,) the *male* قُنْبُر [or *lark*]; as also † عَلْعَالٌ. (Ḳ.) In some one or more of the copies of the Ṣ, الذَّكَرُ مِنَ القَنَافِذِ is erroneously put for الذكر من القنابر. (TA.) — And The *membrum virile*, (Ṣ, O,) or the *penis*, (Ḳ,) or the جُرْدَان, (IKh, TA,) *when in a state of distention*: (IKh, TA, and so in a copy of the Ṣ:) or *such as, when in a state of distention, does not become hard*, or *strong*. (Ḳ.)

عَلْعَلَانٌ *A species of large trees*, (O, Ḳ,) *the leaves of which are like those of the* قُرْم. (O.)

عَلْعَالٌ: see عُلْعُلٌ, second sentence.

عَلْعُولٌ *Continual evil* or *mischief*; and *commotion*, or *tumult*; and *fight*, or *conflict*. (Ḳ.) One says, إِنَّهُ لَفِى عَلْعُولِ شَرٍّ and زُلْزُولِ شَرٍّ, meaning *Verily he is in a state of fighting*, or *conflict*, *and commotion*, or *tumult*. (Fr, O.) [See also زُلْزُولٌ.]

عَالَّةٌ and [its pls.] عَوَالُّ and عُلًّى epithets applied to camels [as meaning *Taking*, or *having taken, a second draught*; and so the first applied to a single she-camel]. (TA.) It is said in a prov., عَرْضَ عَلَىَّ سَوْمَ عَالَّةٍ [*He offered to me in the manner of offering* water *to those* (camels) *taking*, or *having taken, a second draught*]; (Ṣ, O, Ḳ, TA; in the CḲ, عُرِضَ and سَوْمُ;) applied to one who offers food to him who does not need it; like the saying of the vulgar, عَرْضٌ سَابِرِىٌّ; (TA;) i. e., without energy; for one does not offer drink to the عَالَّة with energy, as one does to the نَاهِلَة [or those taking, or having taken, the first draught]. (Ṣ, O, Ḳ, TA. [See also Freytag's Arab. Prov. ii. 84.])

تَعِلَّةٌ an inf. n. of 2 [q. v.]. (Ḥam p. 91.) — See also عُلَالَةٌ, in two places.

مُعَلٌّ: see عَلِيلٌ.

مُعَلَّلٌ: see عَلِيلٌ. [And see also the paragraph here following.]

مُعَلِّلٌ *Giving to drink time after time*. (Ḳ.) — And [hence,] *That diverts with the saliva him who sucks it in* [*when kissing*]; thus in a verse of Imra-el-Keys, accord. to one relation thereof; (O, and Ḥar p. 566;) as expl. by Az; and thus, with ة, applied to a female: (Ḥar:) but accord. to IAạr, *that aids with kindness after kindness* (بِالْبِرِّ بَعْدَ البِرِّ [in Ḥar على البره بعد البره]): another reading of the word in that verse, المُعَلَّل, has been expl. above, voce عَلِيلٌ, on the authority of AA. (O.) — Also *Plucking fruit time after time*. (Ḳ.) — And One *who repels the collector of the* [*tax called*] خَرَاج *with excuses*. (IAạr, M, O, Ḳ.) — Also, (TA,) or المُعَلِّلُ, (Ṣ, O, Ḳ,) *One of the days called* أَيَّامُ العَجُوزِ; [respecting which see art. عجز;] (Ṣ, O, Ḳ, TA;) because it diverts men by somewhat of an alleviation of the cold: (Ṣ, O, TA:) or, accord. to some, it is called مُحَلِّلٌ. (TA.)

مَعْلُولٌ: see عَلِيلٌ: ═ and see عِلَّةٌ: and also 1, last sentence.

يَعْلُولٌ *A pool of water left by a torrent, white, and flowing in a regular*, or *continuous, course, one portion following another*: (Aṣ, O, Ḳ, TA:) or, accord. to Suh, in the R, [simply] *a pool of water left by a torrent*; so called because it waters the ground a second time (يَعُلُّ الأَرْضَ بِمَائِهِ [after its having been watered by the rain]): pl. يَعَالِيلُ. (TA.) — And A dye (صِبْغ) *that is imbibed* (عُلَّ) *one time after another*: (O, Ḳ:) or, accord. to 'Abd-El-Lateef El-Baghdádee, a garment, or piece of cloth, *dyed, and dyed again*. (TA.) — Accord. to AA, [app. as applied to camels,] يَعَالِيلُ signifies *That have drunk one time after another*; and has no sing.: but it is said on other authority to signify *that go away at random to pasture* (الَّتِى تَنْبَعِى) *one time after another*; and to have for its sing. يَعْلُولٌ: and some say that it signifies *such as are excessive in respect of whiteness*. (TA.) — Also, the sing., *Rain after rain*: (AO, O, Ḳ:) pl. as above. (TA.) — And the pl., (Ṣ, M, O, TA,) [accord. to the context in the Ḳ the sing., which is clearly wrong,] *Bubbles* (حَبَاب, M, Ḳ, TA, [in the CḲ حُبَاب,] and نُفَّاخَات, Ṣ, O, Ḳ, [both, I think, evidently meaning thus,]) *upon water*; (Ṣ, M, O, Ḳ;) said to be *from the falling of rain*; and to be used in a verse of Kaạb Ibn-Zuheyr for ذَاتُ يَعَالِيل as meaning *having bubbles*: (TA:) sing. as above. (O.) — And *Clouds disposed one above another*; (Ṣ, O;) sing. as above: (Ṣ:) or [simply] *clouds*; so in the R; to which ISd adds *containing rain*: (TA:) or *white clouds*; (Ḳ, TA; a meaning assigned in the Ḳ to the sing.;) but this is said by Nifṭaweyh in explanation of the phrase بِيضٌ يَعَالِيلُ in a verse of Kaạb Ibn-Zuheyr to which reference has been made above: (TA:) or [the sing. signifies] *a white portion of clouds*. (M, Ḳ.) — The pl. is also said to signify *Lofty mountains*; and Suh adds, *from the upper parts of which water descends*. (TA.) ═ Also, the sing., A camel *having two humps*. (IAạr, O, Ḳ.) — And A camel *such as is termed* أَفْيَل [q.v.]. (O.)

علب

1. عَلَبَهُ, aor. ـُ, (Ṣ, O, TA,) inf. n. عَلْبٌ (Ḳ,* TA) and عُلُوبٌ, (TA,) *He made a mark*, or *an impression, upon it*, (Ṣ, O, Ḳ,* TA,) accord. to Az, *like the mark termed* عِلَاب [q. v.]; (TA;) and *he marked him*, or *it, with a hot iron*; or *scratched him*, or *it, so as to cause bleeding* or *not so*: (Ṣ, O, TA;) and تَعْلِيبٌ [inf. n. of † علّب] likewise signifies the *doing thus* [i. e. the *making a mark* &c.]: (Ṣ, TA:*) and, as also عَلْبٌ [inf. n. of عَلَبَ], the *cutting* [a thing], syn. حَزٌّ; (so in the CḲ and in my MS. copy of the Ḳ;) or *inciding* [it], or *notching* [it]; syn. حَزٌّ. (Ḳ accord. to the TA.) لَا تَعْلُبْ صُورَتَكَ i. e. *Make not thou a mark upon thy* صُورة [here meaning *face*, as in some other instances,] occurs in a trad., as said to a man upon whose nose was seen a mark [of dust, or an impression,] made by pressing hard upon it in prostration. (O, TA.) ═ عَلَبَ السَّيْفَ, aor. ـُ (Ṣ, O, Ḳ) and ـِ, (Ḳ,) inf. n. عَلْبٌ; (Ṣ, O, Ḳ;) and † عَلَّبَهُ, (O,) inf. n. تَعْلِيبٌ; (O, Ḳ;) *He bound round the hilt of the sword with the* عِلْبَآء [q. v.] *of a camel*: (Ṣ, O, Ḳ:) and in like manner one says of things similar to a sword, (Ḳ, TA,) as a knife, and a spear. (TA.) — [And عُلِبَ seems to signify sometimes *It was tied* with, or by, a sinew, or tendon: see a usage of its part. n. voce مَتْنٌ.] ═ عَلِبَ, [aor. ـَ,] (TA,) inf. n. عَلَبٌ, (Ḳ, TA,) *It* (a sword) *became broken in its edge*. (Ḳ,* TA.) ═ And عَلِبَ, [aor. ـَ,] (Ṣ, O, TA,) inf. n. عَلَبٌ, (TA,) said of a camel,

He was, or became, affected by a disease in the two sides of his neck; (Ṣ, O;) *by what is termed* ▼عَلَبٌ, (TA,) which is *a disease attacking in the* عِلْبَاوَانِ, (Ḳ, TA,) dual of عِلْبَآءٌ [q. v.], *in consequence of which the neck swells, and becomes bent.* (TA.) ═ And عَلِبَ, aor. ـَ, inf. n. عَلَبٌ; and عَلُبَ, aor. ـُ, inf. n. عُلُوبٌ; *It was,* or *became, hard,* or *firm;* (O, Ḳ;) and *hard, tough,* or *coarse:* (Ḳ:) each, said of flesh, or flesh-meat, and of a plant, has the former meaning: (O:) or the latter verb, said of flesh, or flesh-meat, has that meaning; and the former verb, said of a plant, has the latter meaning: (Ṣ:) or the former verb, said of flesh, or flesh-meat, means *it was,* or *became, hard,* or *firm, and thick,* or *coarse;* and the latter verb also, *it was,* or *became, thick,* or *coarse, and hard, not soft,* or *tender.* (Suh, TA.) And عَلِبَتْ يَدُهُ *His hand was,* or *became, thick, coarse,* or *rough.* (TA.) [See also 10.] — And عَلِبَ, aor. ـَ, inf. n. عَلَبٌ; and عَلَبَ, aor. ـُ; and ▼استعلب; said of flesh-meat, *It became altered in odour* [*for the worse*], *after having been hard,* or *firm.* (Ḳ.)

2: see 1, former half, in two places.

10. استعلب, said of flesh, or flesh-meat, *It was,* or *became, thick,* or *coarse; not soft,* or *tender:* (O:) or *it was,* or *became, hard,* or *firm, and thick,* or *coarse;* and likewise said of skin. (L.) [And عَلِبَ and عَلُبَ are similarly explained.] — See also 1, last sentence. ═ استعلب البَقْلَ *He found the herbs,* or *leguminous plants, to be hard, tough,* or *coarse.* (TA.) And (TA) استعلبت البَقْلَ, said of cattle, *They loathed the herbs,* or *leguminous plants, and found them,* or *deemed them, thick,* or *coarse,* (O, Ḳ, TA,) *being withered.* (O, TA.)

Q. Q. 1. عَلْبَى, said of a man, *His* عَلَابِىّ [or rather عِلْبَاوَانِ, the former being pl., and the latter dual, of عِلْبَآء, q. v.,] *became apparent, by reason of old age:* (O, Ḳ:) or accord. to the T, *his* عِلْبَآء *became depressed.* (TA.) ═ عَلْبَاهُ *He cut his* عِلْبَآء [q. v.], (O, Ḳ, TA,) i. e., his slave's علباء: (Ḳ, TA:) or *he perforated his* (i. e. his slave's) علباء, (Ḳ, TA,) *and put into it a string,* or *thread.* (TA.)

Q. Q. 3. اِعْلَنْبَى, inf. n. اِعْلِنْبَآءٌ, *He* (a man) *raised himself;* or *drew,* or *stretched, himself up; like as is done on the occasion of altercation,* (Ṣ, O, Ḳ,) *and of reviling.* (Ṣ, O.) — And hence, (Ḳ,) it is said also of a cock, and of a dog, (Ṣ, O,) and other than these, (Ṣ, O, TA,) as a cat, meaning *He prepared himself for evil,* or *mischief,* (Ḳ, TA,) *and fighting:* (TA:) [or *ruffled his feathers,*] or *bristled up his hair:* it is from the عِلْبَآء of the neck, and quasi-coordinate to اِفْعَنْلَلَ, with ى [for the final ل]: (Ṣ, O, TA:) and sometimes it is with ء [in the place of the ى]. (TA.) — And one says also, اِعْلَنْبَا بِالحِمْلِ *He rose,* or *raised himself, with the burden.* (TA.)

عَلْبٌ *A mark, an impression,* or *a scar,* (Ṣ, O, Ḳ, TA,) of beating, and of burning with a hot iron, &c.; (TA;) or *such as is mangled and bleeding:* (Ḳ in art. حبط:) [an inf. n. used as a subst. properly so termed:] pl. عُلُوبٌ. (Ṣ, O.) Ṭufeyl El-Ghanawee has used لَعْب for عَلْب in this sense. (IAạr, TA.) — And *A rugged place;* (Ṣ, O, Ḳ, TA;) as also ▼عِلْبٌ: (Ḳ, TA:) and ▼ the latter, (O,) or *each,* (Ḳ, TA,) *a place,* (Ḳ,) or *a rugged* (O, TA) *and hard* (TA) *place* of the earth, (O, TA,) *which, if rained upon for a long time, will not give growth* (O, Ḳ, TA) *to any green thing:* (O, TA:) and ▼ the latter signifies also *any rough and hard place* of the earth. (O.) — And A *hard* thing; as also ▼عَلِبٌ; (Ḳ;) each applied in this sense to flesh, or flesh-meat; the former being an inf. n. used as an epithet. (O.)

عُلُبٌ: see عَلِبٌ: — and عُلْبَةٌ, last sentence.

عِلْبٌ: see عَلْبٌ, in three places. — Also *A place where the* سِدْر [*rhamnus nabeca,* or *rhamnus spina Christi, a species of lote-tree,*] *grows:* pl. عُلُوبٌ. (AZ, O, Ḳ.) [Accord. to Forskål, (Flora Aegypt. Arab., p. cvi.,) علب (thus written by him, and also "œlb," app. for عِلْب,) is an appellation applied by some in El-Yemen to the tree which he calls *Rhamnus nabeca rectus.*] — And A man *such that one should not covet,* or *hope to get, what he has,* (O, Ḳ,) whether *of words* or *of other than words.* (O.) — And one says, إِنَّهُ لَعِلْبُ شَرٍّ *Verily he is strong to do evil,* or *mischief.* (TA.)

عَلَبٌ *A certain disease of camels,* expl. above: see 1, latter half.

عَلِبٌ: see عَلْبٌ, last sentence. — Also, applied to a he-goat, and to a [lizard of the species called] ضَبّ, *Advanced in age, and hard, tough,* or *coarse:* (Ṣ, O:) and applied to a mountain-goat, (O, Ḳ, TA,) in this sense; (TA;) or as meaning *advanced in age;* (O;) or *large,* or *bulky,* (Ḳ, TA,) *advanced in age;* because of his strength; (TA;) and [in the same sense applied to] a ضَبّ, as also ▼عُلَّبٌ: (Ḳ:) and applied to a man, as meaning *thick, coarse, rough,* or *rude.* (TA.) And A *hard, tough,* or *coarse,* plant. (TA.) ═ And A camel *having the disease termed* عَلَبٌ [q. v.]; as also ▼أَعْلَبُ. (TA.)

عُلْبَةٌ *A milking-vessel of skin,* (Ṣ, O, TA,) or *of wood, like a large* قَدَح [or *bowl*]: (TA:) or *a large* قَدَح *of camel's skin, or of wood, into which one milks:* (Ḳ:) or *a bowl into which the she-camel is milked:* or *a* قَدَح *of wood,* or *of skin and wood:* or *a vessel of skin, in the form of a bowl, with a wooden hoop:* Az says, it is *a piece of skin taken from the side of a camel's hide while it is fresh; it is made round, and filled with soft sand; then its edges are drawn together, and perforated with a wooden skewer, and it is bound so as to be closed,* [*thus*] *contracted, by a cord* [*passed through the holes made with the skewer*], *and left until it becomes dry and tough; then its upper part is cut off, and it stands by reason of its dryness, resembling a round bowl, as though it were carved out,* or *fashioned by the turner; the pastor and the rider suspend it, and milk into it, and drink out of it; and it is convenient to the man of the desert by its lightness, and its not breaking when the camel shakes it about* or *when it falls to the ground:* (TA:) IAạr says that this word and جَنْبَةٌ and دَسْمَآءُ and سَمْرَآءُ all signify the same: (O:) the pl. is عُلَبٌ (Ṣ, O, Mṣb, Ḳ) and عِلَابٌ. (Ṣ, Mṣb, Ḳ.) ═ Also *A tall palm-tree:* (O, Ḳ:) [see ▼عُلْبٌ (voce سَاجِدٌ), a coll. gen. n. used as a pl.; or a pl., and, if so, app. a contraction of عُلُبٌ, by poetic license: Ṣgh, however, adds,] but some say that it is ▼عَلَبَةٌ [i. e.] بِالتَّحْرِيكِ. (O.)

عِلْبَةٌ *A thick knot of wood,* (IAạr, O, Ḳ, TA,) otherwise expl. as *a great branch of a tree,* (TA,) *whereof is made the* مِقْطَرَة, (IAạr, O, Ḳ, TA,) *which is a wooden thing having in it holes adapted to the size of the legs of the persons confined* [*by it,* i. e. *a kind of stocks*]: (TA:) pl. عِلَبٌ. (IAạr, O, TA.) A poet says,

* فِى رِجْلِهِ عِلْبَةٌ خَشْنَآءُ مِنْ قَرَظِ *

[*Upon his leg was a rough kind of stocks of the* wood of the tree called *ḳaraḍh*]. (O, TA.)

عَلَبَةٌ: see عُلْبَةٌ, last sentence.

عِلْبَآءٌ [perfectly decl., because the ء is a letter of quasi-coordination, i. e., added to render the word quasi-coordinate to the class of قِرْطَاسٌ and the like,] The عَصَب *of the neck;* [app. meaning the *upper, cervical, tendinous portion of the trapezius muscle;*] (Ṣ, O, Ḳ; [in all of which, mention is made of the علباء of the camel, to which it seems to be most commonly applied, and also to that of a man;]) it is *one of a pair, and between one* علباء *and the other is the place of growth of the mane;* (Ṣ, O;) Az explains it as specially applied to the *thick* عَصَب; and IAth, as the عَصَب *in the neck, extending to the* كَاهِل [or *part between the two shoulder-blades*]: ISd says that it is *syn. with* عَقَبٌ [q. v.]: (TA:) [it is also said that] it signifies the عَصَبَة [i. e. *tendon,* or *sinew,*] *that extends in the neck:* (Mṣb:) or the *yellow* عَصَبَة *in the side* (صَفْحَة) *of the neck; one of a pair:* (A:) and the عِلْبَاوَانِ in a man are [said to be] the *two yellow tendons* or *sinews* (العَصَبَتَانِ) (الصَّفْرَاوَانِ) *in the* مَتْن [or *part next the spine, on either side,*] *of the neck:* (Zj in his "Khalḳ el-Insán:") [but of all the meanings thus assigned to it, the first seems to be the most proper, or at least the most usual: see Q. Q. 1:] the Arabs used to bind therewith, in the fresh, or moist, state, the أَجْفَان [or sheaths] of their swords, and also their spears when cracked, and it dried upon them, and became strong: (IAth, TA:) the word is masc., (Lḥ, TA,) or [it is masc. and fem., but] the making it fem. is preferred [though this is contr. to analogy]: (Mṣb:) the dual is عِلْبَاوَانِ (Ṣ, A, O, Mṣb) and عِلْبَاآنِ; (Ṣ, O, Mṣb, Ḳ;) [the former app. the more common, but the latter the more proper;] for the ء [in the sing.] is a letter of quasi-coordination [and therefore properly with tenween]; but if you will, you may liken it to the fem. ء that is in حَمْرَآءُ [of which the dual is more properly حَمْرَاوَانِ], or to the radical ا [or rather the ء that is substituted for the last radical letter] in كِسَآءٌ [of which the dual is more properly [عِكَنَانٌ]: (Ṣ, O:) and the pl. is عَلَابِىُّ. (Ṣ, O, Ḳ.) You say of a man when he has become advanced in age, تَشَنَّجَ عِلْبَاءُ الرَّجُلِ [*The* علباء *of the man has become contracted*]. (Ṣ, O.) — The pl. عَلَابِىُّ is expl. in the Ḳ as signifying also *Lead:* and in the Ṣ as signifying *lead*, or *a kind thereof:* (TA:) El-Ḳutabee says, "I have been told that العَلَابِىُّ signifies *lead;* but I am not sure of it:" and Az says, "I know not any one who has said it, and it is not true;" (O, TA;) and this is the case: (O:) MF observes that its explanation as signifying *lead* requires it to be a sing. of a pl. form, or a pl. that has no sing., like عَبَادِيدُ and أَبَابِيلُ: (TA:) in a trad., mention is made of swords of which the ornaments were الآنُكُ and العلابىّ; (O, TA;) and the coupling of these two words together has led to the supposition that the former means lead; but there is no evading the fact that it is the pl. of علباء meaning the عَصَب of the camel. (TA.)

عُلْبُوبَةُ القَوْمِ *The best persons of the people,* or *party.* (Sh, O, Ḳ.)

عِلَابٌ *A mark made with a hot iron along the length of the neck* [*of a camel*], (Ṣ, O, Ḳ,) *upon,* or *over, the* عِلْبَاء. (TA.)

عَلَابِىُّ pl. of عِلْبَاءٌ [q. v.].

أَعْلَبُ: see عَلِبٌ, last sentence.

مُعْلِبَةٌ: see the next paragraph.

مُعَلَّبٌ A sword *having its hilt bound* (A, O) *with the* عِلْبَاء *of a camel;* (O;) as also ↓ مَعْلُوبٌ. (A.) — And مُعَلَّبَةٌ A she-camel (Ṣ, Ḳ) *marked with the mark called* عِلَاب; (Ṣ, O, Ḳ;) as also ↓ مُعْلِبَةٌ. (Ḳ.)

مُعَلِّبٌ One *who makes the kind of vessel called* عُلْبَة. (Ṣ, O.)

مُعَلْبَاةٌ One *who has a perforation made in her* عِلْبَاوَانِ [dual of عِلْبَاء] *with the instrument called* مِثْرَى [q. v.]. (O.)

مَعْلُوبٌ A *conspicuous* road (Ṣ, O, Ḳ, TA) *that is marked in its two sides; or marked with the traces of travellers.* (TA.) — And A sword *broken in its edge.* (O.) — See also مُعَلَّبٌ.

علث

1. عَلَثَهُ, aor. ـِ, (Ḳ,) inf. n. عَلْثٌ, (Ṣ, O,) to which غَلْثٌ is like in its meanings (Ḳ and TA in art. غلث) for the most part, (TA in that art.,) *He mixed it;* (Ṣ,* O,* Ḳ, TA;) as also ↓ علّثه, inf. n. تَعْلِيثٌ; and ↓ اعتلثه. (TA.) You say, عَلَثْتُ البُرَّ بِالشَّعِيرِ, aor. as above, *I mixed the wheat with the barley.* (Ṣ, O.) — Also, (Ḳ, TA,) aor. as above, (TA,) and so the inf. n., (O, TA,) *He collected it together,* (O,* Ḳ, TA,) *from different places.* (TA.) — عَلَثَ السِّقَآءَ *He tanned the* [*skin called*] سقاء *with the* أَرْطَى [q. v.], (Ḳ,) or *with any of the trees of the kind called* عَلَث [q. v.]: accord. to AḤn, it is with غ [i. e. غَلَثَ]. (TA.) [But مَغْلُوثٌ, with غ, is expl. on the authority of ISk, as meaning, applied to a سقاء, "Tanned with dry, or with unripe, dates."] — عَلَثَ, (Ṣ, O, Ḳ, TA,) [or, perhaps, عَلِثَ, like غَلِثَ,] as also ↓ اعتلث, (TA,) said of a زَنْد [or piece of stick, or wood, for producing fire], *It failed to produce fire,* (Ṣ, O, Ḳ, TA,) and *was difficult to use:* and the subst. is ↓ عُلَاثٌ [app. meaning The *quality of failing to produce fire,* &c.]. (L, TA.) — عَلْثٌ The *fighting vehemently, and cleaving to fight:* (Ṣ, O, Ḳ:) and so غَلْثٌ. (Ṣ, O.) One says, عَلَثَ القَوْمُ, aor. ـِ, inf. n. عَلْثٌ, *The people,* or *party, fought one another* [or *did so vehemently and perseveringly*]: and عَلَثَ بَعْضُ القَوْمِ بِبَعْضٍ [*One portion of the people,* or *party, fought another portion vehemently and perseveringly*]. (TA.) And عَلَثَ الذِّئْبُ بِالغَنَمِ *The wolf kept to worrying the sheep* or *goats.* (L. [And so غَلَثَ.])

2: see 1, first sentence. — [The inf. n.] تَعْلِيثٌ also signifies *Confusion of mind:* or, as some say, the *beginning of pain.* (TA. [See also 2 in art. غلث; and see مُغَلِّثٌ, with غ.])

4: see 8.

5. تعلّث *He,* or *it, clung, clave,* or *held fast,* (O, Ḳ, TA,) به *to it* [or *him*]. (TḲ. [See also 5 in art. غلث.]) — Also *He made,* or *did,* [a thing] *faultily,* or *unsoundly.* (O, Ḳ.) [Accord. to the TḲ, one says, تعلّث السَّهْمَ, meaning *He made the arrow faultily,* or *unsoundly:* but this is perhaps a mistake: see 8.] — And i. q. تَمَحَّلَ: (Ḳ:) Fr says, تَعَلَّثْتُ لَهُ الذُّنُوبَ is like تَمَحَّلْتُ [app. meaning *I laboured, and exercised art* or *management, in seeking to do to him misdeeds:* see art. محل]. (O.)

8: see 1, first sentence. You say, اعتلث العُلَاثَةَ *He* (a man) *mixed the* [*mess called*] عُلَاثَة [q. v.]. (Aṣ, O.) — And اعتلث زَنْدًا *He took a* زَنْد [or *piece of stick, or wood, for producing fire*] from trees, *without knowing whether or not it would produce fire:* (Ṣ, O, Ḳ:) or *he acted unskilfully in selecting a* زند: (A:) or *he took,* or *made, for himself a* زند *from any tree that he found in his way:* and so اغتلث, with غ. (AḤn, TA.) And one says, فُلَانٌ يَعْتَلِثُ الزِّنَادَ meaning † *Such a one does not select his* مَنْكِح [or *wife*]: (Ṣ, A,* O, Ḳ:*) in which sense also يغتلث is a dial. var.: (TA:) and in like manner one says اعتلث [alone], and ↓ أَعْلَثَ. (So in a copy of the A. [But I doubt the correctness of the latter verb; and the more so as it is not quite clear whether it be meant to be expl. as having this meaning, or as meaning *It* (a زَنْد) *failed to produce fire,* and therefore, perhaps, a mistranscription for عَلَثَ.]) — And اعتلث السَّهْمَ *He took* [or *made*] *the arrow from any of the trees that were before him.* (L.) And *He made the arrow faultily,* or *unsoundly.* (L, TA. [See also 5.]) — See also 1, latter half.

عَلْثٌ [originally an inf. n.] *A mixture;* as also ↓ عُلَاثَةٌ. (TA.)

عَلَثٌ *What is mixed with wheat &c., of those things that are taken forth and thrown away.* (TA. [It is used in this sense in the present day; as also غَلَثٌ.]) — See also عَلِيثٌ. — Also a term applied to The [*trees,* or *plants, called*] طَرْفَاء *and* أَثْل [or أَسْل (see غَلَث)] *and* حَاج *and* عَكْرِش *and* يَنْبُوت: pl. أَعْلَاثٌ. (TA. [See also أَعْلَاثٌ, which is somewhat similarly explained.]) — And *A* زَنْد [or *piece of stick,* or *wood, for producing fire*] *that has not produced fire.* (A.) And الأَعْلَاثُ [or أَعْلَاثُ الشَّجَرِ] signifies [also] *The promiscuous pieces of trees that one uses for producing fire, of the* [*trees called*] مَرْخ, *and of such as are dried up.* (Ṣ, O, Ḳ.) — And أَعْلَاثُ الزَّادِ *Such things as are eaten without being selected, of travelling-provisions.* (O, Ḳ.)

عَلِثٌ One *whose origin is referred to a person who is not his father* [or *forefather*], (O, Ḳ, TA,) his lineage being confused; (TA;) as also ↓ مُعْتَلِثٌ. (O, Ḳ.) — Also *Firm,* or *constant, in fight.* (TA.) [رَجُلٌ عَلِثٌ is expl. in the O by the words مُلَازِمٌ لِمَنْ يُطَالِبُ, and in like manner العَلِثُ is expl. in the Ḳ; app. meaning *A man cleaving,* or *holding fast,* applied to *such as is seeking,* or *demanding,* blood-revenge, or a debt or the like; agreeably with what here immediately precedes, and with the explanation in the L, which is, مُلَازِمٌ أَىْ طَالِبٌ فِى قِتَالٍ أَوْ غَيْرِهِ *cleaving,* or *holding fast, i. e. seeking,* or *demanding, in fight or in some other case.* See عَلِثَ, of which عَلِثٌ is the part. n.: and see also غَلِثٌ.]

عُلْثَةٌ, with ḍamm, (Ḳ, but written in the O عَلْثَة,) *i. q.* عُلْقَةٌ [most probably, I think, in the sense in which this is used in the phrase لِى فِى هٰذَا المَالِ عُلْقَةٌ (q. v.), from تَعَلَّثَ in the first of the senses assigned to it above, syn. with تَعَلَّقَ]. (O, Ḳ.)

عَلْثِىٌّ *Food having poison mixed with it, by which vultures are killed:* mentioned by Kr: and غَلْثِىٌّ is a dial. var. thereof. (TA.)

عُلَاثٌ: see عُلَاثَةٌ: — and see also 1, latter half.

عَلِيثٌ *Bread made of barley and wheat:* (Ṣ, O, Ḳ:) and so غَلِيثٌ. (Ṣ, O.) And خُبْزٌ عَلِيثٌ *Bread made of barley and* [*the grain called*] سُلْت. (TA, from a trad.) — And *Wheat mixed with barley;* (AZ, TA;) as also ↓ عَلَثٌ and ↓ عَلِيثَةٌ: or, accord. to Abu-l-Jarráḥ, *barley and wheat mixed together for sowing and then reaped together.* (TA.)

عُلَاثَةٌ *Clarified butter,* (Ṣ, O, Ḳ, TA,) or *olive-oil,* (TA,) *and* [*the preparation of curd called*] أَقِط, *mixed together:* (Ṣ, O, Ḳ, TA:) and *any two things mixed together:* (Ṣ, O, Ḳ:) pl. [or rather coll. gen. n.] ▼ عُلَاثٌ. (O.) See also عَلْثٌ. — Also *A man who collects from various places.* (O, Ḳ.)

عَلِيثٌ : see عَلِيثَةٌ.

مُعْتَلِثُ الزِّنَادِ [evidently, I think, a mistranscription, correctly ▼ مُعْتَلَث,] A man *whose* زِنَاد [pl. of زَنْدٌ] *fail to produce fire.* (L.) — See also the following paragraph.

مُعْتَلَثٌ : see عَلِثٌ : — and see the next preceding paragraph. — Also, (O,* L, [thus in the latter, with kesr to the ل, but in the former without any vowel-sign to that letter, perhaps from اعْتَلَثَ الزَّنْدَ, but more probably ▼ مُعْتَلَثٌ, from اعتلث السَّهْمَ,]) An arrow *in which is no good.* (O, L.)

علج

1. عَلَجَهُ : see 3. — عَلَجَتْ, (TA,) inf. n. عَلَجَانٌ, (O, Ḳ, TA,) *She* (a camel) *was,* or *became, in a state of commotion.* (O,* Ḳ,* TA.) — عَلِجَ, aor. ـَ, inf. n. عَلَجٌ, *He* (a man) *was,* or *became, strong, robust,* or *sturdy.* (Mṣb.)

2. علّج الإِبلَ *He fed the camels with the fodder of the* [*shrub called*] عَلَجَان. (TA.)

3. عالجهُ, inf. n. عِلَاجٌ (Ṣ, A, O, Ḳ) and مُعَالَجَةٌ, (Ṣ, O, Ḳ,) *He laboured, exerted himself, strove, struggled, contended,* or *conflicted, with it,* (namely, a thing, Ṣ, O,) *to prevail, overcome,* or *gain the mastery* or *possession,* or *to effect an object; he worked,* or *laboured, at it,* or *upon it, to do, execute, perform, effect,* or *accomplish, it,* or *to manage,* or *treat, it;* syn. زَاوَلَهُ; (Ṣ, A, O, Ḳ;) and مَارَسَهُ. (TA.) [And *He exercised his skill upon it; worked,* or *wrought, it; worked it together; mingled, mixed up,* or *compounded, it, with some degree of labour; mashed it; kneaded it; manipulated it; brewed it; treated it* with some admixture; *dressed it,* or *prepared it for use;* namely, some substance, composition, food, medicine, or the like.] مِنْ كَسْبِهِ وَعِلَاجِهِ is a phrase occurring in a trad., meaning *From his gain,* or *earning, and his work,* or *labour.* (L.) And one says, عالج الحَدِيدَ *He worked,* or *wrought, iron.* (L in art. حد, &c.) And عالج فُرُشًا وَوَسَائِدَ [*He manufactured beds, or the like, and pillows*]. (Ḳ in art. نجد.) And عالج الشَّرَابَ بِالنَّارِ [*He brewed,* or *prepared with pains, the beverage,* or *wine, by means of fire;* or *boiled it well*]. (Ḳ voce مُصَعْفَدٌ.) And عالج السِّحْرَ [*He wrought enchantment*]. (Ḳ in art. تول.) And عَالَجْنَا غَيْبَ السَّمَآءِ [*We laboured,* or *strove, after the secrets of heaven*]. (Ḳ in art. لمس.) — Also *He laboured,* or *strove, with him, to prevail,* or *overcome;* syn. زَاوَلَهُ. (L.) One says, عَالَجَهُ ▼ فَعَلَجَهُ, (Ṣ, O,* L, Ḳ,*) [aor. of the latter ـُ,] inf. n. عَلْجٌ, (Ṣ,) *He laboured,* or *strove, with him, to prevail,* or *overcome,* (L,) *and he overcame him* (Ṣ, O, L, Ḳ) *in so doing;* (O, Ḳ;) namely, another man. (Ṣ, O.) It is said in a trad., عَالَجْتُ آمْرَأَةً فَأَصَبْتُ مِنْهَا [*I strove with a woman, and obtained what I desired of her*]. (L.) And لَمْ يُعَالِجْ, in another trad., is said to mean *He did not strive,* or *contend, with the confusion of intellect* [*usually*] *attendant upon death,* which would be an expiation for [some of] his sins: or *he did not strive,* or *contend, with the severity of long-continued sickness, nor suffer the perturbation* [*usually*] *attending death:* or, as some relate it, the phrase is لَمْ يُعَالَجْ, meaning *he was not tended,* or *treated medically, in his sickness.* (L.) In another trad. occurs the saying, إِنِّى صَاحِبُ ظَهْرٍ أُعَالِجُهُ, meaning *Verily I am the owner of a camel for riding or carriage, which I ply,* or *work,* (أُمَارِسُهُ,) *and employ to carry for hire.* (L.) And it is related in another trad. that 'Alee sent two men in a certain direction, and said, إِنَّكُمَا عِلْجَانِ فَعَالِجَا عَنْ دِينِكُمَا, meaning *Verily ye are two strong, bulky men, therefore labour ye* [*in defence of your religion*] in the affair to the performance of which I have called and incited you. (L.) — [And *He plied it;* i. e. *kept it at work,* or *in action;* namely, a thing. See an ex. voce ذَنَبٌ.] — Also, (O, Ḳ,) inf. ns. as above, [but generally عِلَاجٌ,] (Ḳ,) *He treated him* (i. e. a person either sick or wounded, or a beast, O) *medically, curatively,* or *therapeutically:* (O, Ḳ:) *he tended him,* or *took care of him, in his sickness:* (L:) [*he endeavoured to cure him* (i. e. a sick person), or *it* (i. e. a diseased part of the body):] and عالجهُ مِنَ الدَّآءِ, inf. n. عِلَاجٌ, *he treated him medically to cure him of the disease.* (MA.) [And *He dressed it,* namely, a wound or the like.] And one says, عُولِجَتِ السِّبَاعُ بِأُخَذٍ, meaning *The beasts,* or *birds, of prey were wrought upon,* or *operated on, by charms,* so as to prevent their injuring cattle and the like. (L in art. عقى.)

5. تعلّج الرَّمْلُ, and ▼ اعتلج, *The sand became collected together.* (TA.) — ▼ مَا تَعَلَّجْتُ بِعَلُوجٍ and ما تَأَلَّكْتُ بِأَلُوكٍ signify the same, (O, Ḳ,) i. e. [*I have not occupied myself in chewing with anything that is chewed;* or] *I have not tasted anything;* and so مَا تَعَلَّكْتُ بِعَلُوكٍ. (O.) — تعلّجت الإِبِلُ *The camels obtained,* or *took, of the* [*shrub called*] عَلَجَان. (TA.)

6. تعالجوا *They laboured, exerted themselves, strove, struggled, contended,* or *conflicted, one with another, to prevail, overcome,* or *gain the mastery* or *possession,* or *to effect an object;* syn. تَزَاوَلُوا. (Ṣ and Ḳ in art. زول. [See also 8.]) One says, تَعَالَجَا الشَّرَّ بَيْنَهُمَا [*They two laboured,* or *strove, each with the other, to do evil,* or *mischief*]. (Ṣ in art. كوح.)

8. اعتلجوا *They wrestled together, striving to throw one another down;* and *fought one another.* (A, O, Ḳ.) And اعْتَلَجَتِ الوَحْشُ *The wild animals contended in smiting one another, and strove,* or *struggled, together for the mastery.* (TA.) [See also 6.] — [Hence,] اعتلجت الأَمْوَاجُ (Ṣ, A, O, Ḳ) ‡ *The waves conflicted,* or *dashed together.* (Ṣ, O, Ḳ.) — And اعتلج الهَمُّ فِى صَدْرِهِ ‡ *Anxiety conflicted in his bosom.* (TA.) — And اعتلجت الأَرْضُ † *The land produced,* or *had, tall plants,* or *herbage.* (Ṣ, O, Ḳ.) — See also 5.

10. استعلج is said of a man's make [as meaning *It was,* or *became, strong,* or *sturdy, and big,* or *bulky*]: (A:) [or] *it was,* or *became, thick, big,* or *coarse.* (Kh, O.) And said of a man, *His beard grew forth,* (AZ, L, Mṣb,) *and he became thick, big,* or *coarse, and strong,* or *sturdy, and bulky in his body:* and it is also said of a boy, or young man, meaning خَرَجَ وَجْهُهُ [for خَرَجَ نَبَاتُ وَجْهِهِ *the hair of his face grew forth*]. (L.) And said of the skin (Ṣ, O, Ḳ) of a man, (Ṣ, O,) *It was,* or *became, thick, coarse,* or *rough.* (Ṣ, O, Ḳ.) — It is also said of a lock (مِغْلَاق), [app. as meaning *It required labour, exertion,* or *effort, to open it,*] from العِلَاجُ. (O. [I suppose it to be like اِسْتَكَدَّ, from الكَدُّ; &c.])

عِلْجٌ *A strong,* or *sturdy, man:* (Mṣb:) or *a strong,* or *sturdy, and thick, big,* or *coarse, man:* (L:) or *any man having a beard;* (AZ, L, Mṣb;) not applied to the beardless: (AZ, Mṣb:) and *any* [*man* or *beast*] *that is hardy, strong,* or *sturdy:* (L:) and *an ass,* (Ṣ, Ḳ, TA,) in an absolute sense: (TA:) and, (Ḳ,) or as some say, (TA,) *a fat and strong wild ass:* (Ḳ, TA:) or *a fat and thick, big,* or *coarse, wild ass:* (O:) and *a man,* (Ṣ, A, O, L, Ḳ,) or *a big,* or *bulky, man,* (Mgh, Mṣb,) or *a strong and big,* or *bulky, man,* (TA,) *of the unbelievers of the* عَجَم [i. e. *Persians* or other *foreigners*], (Ṣ, A, Mgh, O, L, Mṣb, Ḳ, TA,) and *of others;* (L;) so called because of the thickness, bigness, or coarseness, of his make: (O:) or *a strong and big,* or *bulky, unbeliever:* (L:) or simply *an unbeliever;* (L, Mṣb;) thus accord. to some of the Arabs, in an absolute sense: (Mṣb:) fem. with ة: (L:) pl. [of pauc.] أَعْلَاجٌ and [of mult.] عُلُوجٌ (Ṣ, O, Mṣb, Ḳ) and عِلَجَةٌ and [quasi-pl. n.] ▼ مَعْلُوجَآءُ, (Ṣ, O, Ḳ,) like مَشْيُوخَآءُ [q. v.], (TA,) and ▼ مَعْلُوجَى (O, L, CḲ) and ▼ مَعْلَجَةٌ. (Sb, R, TA.) El-Ḥasan applied the epithet عُلُوجٌ, contemptuously, to certain men who neglected the supererogatory prayers before daybreak, performing only [afterwards] the prescribed prayers. (Mgh.) — فُلَانٌ عِلْجُ مَالٍ is like إِزَآءُ مَالٍ [meaning *Such a one is a manager, tender,* or *superintendent,* or *a good pastor, of cattle,* or *camels &c.*]. (Ṣ, O, Ḳ.) — And عِلْجٌ signifies also *A cake of bread:* (Abu-l-'Omeythil, TA:) or *a cake of bread that is thick* (O, Ḳ, TA) *in the edges* (O) or *in the edge.* (Ḳ, TA.)

عَلَجٌ The *small ones,* or *young ones,* of palm-trees. (AḤn, Ṣ, O, Ḳ.) — See also عَلَجَانٌ, in two places.

عَلِجٌ (Ṣ, O, Ḳ) and ▼ عَلْجٌ and ▼ عُلَّجٌ, (O, Ḳ,) applied to a man, *Strong*, or *sturdy*, (Ṣ, O, Ḳ,) in labouring, or striving, to prevail, (TA,) *who throws down his antagonists much* or *often*, (صِرِّيعٌ, [in the CḲ, erroneously, صَرِيعٌ,]) *and who labours*, or *exerts himself, in performing, accomplishing*, or *managing, affairs:* (O, Ḳ:) or ▼ عُلَّجٌ signifies a man *strong*, or *sturdy, in fighting, and in contending like the ram.* (L.) — And عَلِجَةٌ, applied to a she-camel, *Strong*, or *sturdy:* (O:) or, so applied, *having much flesh:* (TA:) pl. عَلِجَاتٌ. (O, TA.)

عَلْجٌ and عُلَّجٌ: see عَلِجٌ; the latter in two places.

عَلْجَنٌ A she-camel *compact and firm in flesh:* (Ṣ, O, Ḳ:) or *strong;* (Az and TA in art. علجن;) as also ▼ عُلْجُومٌ: (Ḳ in that art.:) or *thick, big*, or *coarse:* (Aboo-Málik, TA in that art.:) [but] the ن is augmentative. (O.) — And A woman *who cares not for what she does nor for what is said to her.* (T, Ḳ; and Ṣ in art. علجن.)

عُلْجَانٌ *A collection of* [*thorny trees of the kind called*] عِضَاه. (O, Ḳ.)

عَلَجَانٌ (Ṣ, O, L, Ḳ) and ▼ عَلَجٌ (L, TA) *A certain sort of plant;* (Ṣ, O, Ḳ;) *growing in the sand:* n. un. with ة: (O:) AḤn says, on the authority of certain of the Arabs of the desert, that *it grows in the form of slender strings, intensely green, of a greenness like that of herbs, or leguminous plants, inclining to yellowness, bare, having no leaves:* (O:) he says [also] that the عَلَج [or عَلَجَان, as will be shown by what follows,] is, with the people of Nejd, *a sort of trees* [or *shrubs*] *having no leaves, consisting only of bare strings, of a dusty green colour:* (L, TA:) *the asses eat it, and their teeth become yellow in consequence of their eating it;* wherefore one says of him who has yellow teeth, كَأَنَّ فَاهُ فُو حِمَارٍ أَكَلَ عَلَجَانًا [*As though his mouth were the mouth of an ass that had eaten 'alaján;* by the *mouth* being meant the *teeth*, as is often the case]: (O, L, TA:) and he says that *it sometimes grows, not in the sand, but in soft*, or *plain, tracts;* and accord. to some, (O,) the عَلَجَان is *a sort of trees of a dark green colour, not having leaves, consisting only of twigs, one of such trees occupying the space of a man sitting;* (O, L, TA;*) *growing in plain*, or *soft, land, and not eaten by the camels unless of necessity:* Az says that the عَلَجَان is *a sort of trees resembling that called* عَلَنْدَى, which he had seen in the desert: and its pl. [or rather the pl. of the n. un. (عَلَجَةٌ) of its syn. ▼ عَلَجٌ] is عَلَجَاتٌ. (L, TA.)

عَلَجَانَةٌ n. un. of عَلَجَانٌ [q. v.]. — Also *Dust which the wind collects at the foot of a tree.* (O, Ḳ.)

عُلْجُومٌ: see عَلْجَنٌ.

عِلَاجٌ an inf. n. of 3 [q. v.]. (Ṣ, A, O, Ḳ.) — And [*A medicine*, or *remedy;* often used in this sense;] *a thing with which one treats a patient medically*, or *curatively.* (TA.)

عَلُوجٌ i. q. أَلُوكٌ (O, Ḳ) and عَلُوكٌ, meaning *A thing that is eaten* [or *chewed*]: (O:) so in the phrase هٰذَا عَلُوجٌ صِدْقٍ [*This is an excellent thing that is chewed*]. (O, Ḳ.) See also 5.

عَالِجٌ A camel *pasturing*, or *that pastures, upon the* [*shrub called*] عَلَجَان. (Ṣ, O, Ḳ.) — *A quantity of sand that has become accumulated and intermixed:* pl. عَوَالِجُ. (TA, from a trad.)

مَعْلَجَةٌ: }
مَعْلُوجَى: } [quasi-pl. ns.] see عِلْجٌ.
مَعْلُوجَاءُ: }

مُعَلْهَجٌ [mentioned in the O and Ḳ in art. علهج] One *whose father is free*, or *an Arab, and whose mother is a slave;* syn. هَجِينٌ: (Ṣ, Ḳ:) or one *who claims as his father a person who is not his father;* or *who is claimed as a son by a person who is not his father:* and one *born of two different races:* (Lth, O:) or one *born of a slave the daughter of a female slave:* (Ibn-'Abbád, O:) or, accord. to ISd, one *who is not of pure race:* (TA:) a *low*, a *vile*, or an *ignoble*, man; *foolish*, or *stupid*, or *deficient in intellect;* (Lth, O, Ḳ;) *a frivolous babbler.* (Lth, O.) F charges J with error in asserting the ه to be augmentative; but all the authorities on inflection assert the same thing. (MF.)

مَعَالَجٌ *A place of* عِلَاج [i. e. *medical*, or *curative, treatment*]. (TA in art. اوى.)

مُعَالِجٌ One *who treats patients, whether sick or wounded, or beasts, medically*, or *curatively.* (TA.)

أَرْضٌ مُعْتَلِجَةٌ *Land of which the herbage has become strong*, or *tall, and tangled*, or *luxuriant, and abundant.* (TA.)

مُسْتَعْلِجُ الخَلْقِ A man [*strong*, or *sturdy, and big*, or *bulky*, or] *thick, big*, or *coarse, in make.* (Ṣ, O. [See the verb.])

Quasi علجن

عَلْجَنٌ &c. see in art. علج.

علد

1. عَلِدَ, aor. ـَ, (O, L, Ḳ,) inf. n. عَلَدٌ (O, L, Ḳ*) and عُلُودٌ, (O,) said of a man, (O,) or of anything, (L,) *He*, or *it, was*, or *became, strong and hard.* (O, L, Ḳ. [See also Q. Q. 3.]) — And *He stood fast, and refused to be led*, or *to turn.* (L. [See also Q. Q. 1.])

12. اِعْلَوَّدَ: see Q. Q. 3: — and Q. Q. 1. — Also *He* (a man) *was*, or *became, grave, staid, steady, sedate*, or *calm.* (O, Ḳ.)

Q. Q. 1. عَلْوَدَ *He*, or *it, kept*, or *clave, to his*, or *its, place, and could not be moved by any one;* (L, Ḳ;) as also ▼ اِعْلَوَّدَ. (L. [See also 1.])

Q. Q. 3. اِعْلَنْدَى *He* (a camel) *was*, or *became, thick, big*, or *coarse, and strong;* (Abu-s-Semeyda', Ṣ, O, L, Ḳ;) as also اِعْلَنْدَى: (Abu-s-Semeyda', Ṣ, L:) and so ▼ اِعْلَوَّدَ said of a man. (O, L,* Ḳ. [See also 1.])

عَلْدٌ *Hardness and strength.* (Ḳ. [See 1.]) — And A thing, (Ṣ,) or anything, (TA,) *hard*, (Ṣ, Ḳ,) *and strong:* (Ḳ:) or, accord. to Kh, anything *thick, big*, or *coarse, and strong.* (Ḥam p. 81.) — And *Standing fast, and refusing to be led*, or *to turn.* (L.) — Also, (Ṣ, Ḳ,) or أَعْلَادٌ, (IAạr, TA,) which is the pl., (TA,) The *sinews* عَصَب *of the neck.* (IAạr, Ṣ, Ḳ.)

عَلَنْدٌ: see مُعْلَنْدَدٌ.

عِلْوَدٌ: see what next follows.

عِلْوَدٌ (Ṣ, O, L, Ḳ) and عَلْوَدٌ (Ibn-Ḥabeeb, MF) and ▼ عِلْوَدٌ as written in some copies of the "Book" [of Sb] and said by Seer to be a dial. var., (TA,) *Great*, or *old* or *full-grown;* syn. كَبِيرٌ: (El-Umawee, Ṣ, Ḳ:) or *great*, or *old* or *full-grown*, (كَبِيرٌ,) *advanced in age, and strong:* (so in a copy of the Ṣ:) or *advanced in age, and strong;* applied to a man and to a camel; as also ▼ عِلْوَدٌ: or *thick, big*, or *coarse;* as also ▼ عِلْوَدٌ: and *old* (كَبِيرٌ) *and decrepit:* (L:) applied to a man: (TA:) and with ة, *decrepit*, applied to a she-camel: (Ḳ:) also, without ة, *big*, or *bulky;* applied to a [lizard of the species termed] ضَبّ: and applied by El-Farezdaḳ to the بَظْر [q. v.] of a woman, as meaning *large and hard:* (L:) and a *thick-necked* man: (AA, TA:) and applied [app. as meaning *thick*] as an epithet to a neck: (AO, Ṣ, O:) and the *neck* itself, of a she-camel: also *strong, and having hardness;* applied to a man; and likewise, with ة, to a woman: (L:) and applied to a lord, or chief, as meaning *grave, staid, steady, sedate*, or *calm*, (O, L, Ḳ,) *and of firm judgment:* (L:) and, with ة, A mare that is *stubborn, and not to be led unless driven;* (Ḳ;) *that extends her legs, and pulls vehemently the person who leads, with her neck, so that he can seldom lead her unless she be urged on from behind.* (ISh, O,* L.)

عِلْوَدٌ: see the next preceding paragraph, in two places.

عُلَادِيٌّ: }
عَلَنْدَى: } see the next paragraph.
عَلَنْدَدٌ: }

عَلَنْدَى Anything *thick, big*, or *coarse;* (Ṣ, O,* Ḳ;) as also عُلَنْدَى: (O, Ḳ:) and *bulky, strong, and tall;* applied to a camel and to a horse: (TA:) and sometimes they applied the epithet عُلَنْدَى to a camel: (Ṣ:) this and ▼ عُلَادِيٌّ signify *strong*, so applied, (O, Ḳ,) as does also ▼ عَلَنْدَدٌ applied to a horse; (L;) or *bulky and tall*, applied to a camel and to a horse: or, accord. to En-Naḍr, one says نَاقَةٌ عَلَنْدَاةٌ, meaning *a great and tall she-camel;* but not جَمَلٌ عَلَنْدَى;

like as one says نَاقَةٌ عَفَرْنَاةٌ; but not جَمَلٌ عَفَرْنًى: (TA:) and علندى occurs in old poetry as an epithet applied to a she-camel [app. in this instance with what is termed the fem. alif, i. e. without teshdeed]: (Ḥam p. 82:) the pl. of عَلَنْدًى is عَلَادِدُ (Ṣ, O) and عَلَادَى: and Sb mentions [app. as a dial. var. of the sing.] ▼ عَلَنْدَى. (L.) —— Also *A species of tree,* (O, Ḳ, TA, and so in a copy of the Ṣ,) *of the kind called* عِضَاه, *having thorns:* (O, Ḳ:) [a coll. gen. n.:] n. un. عَلَنْدَاةٌ; (AḤn, O, Ḳ:*) it is *of the trees of the sands, not such as is termed* حَمْض, (O, TA,) *and yields an intense smoke:* (TA:) accord. to Lth, the علنداة is *a tall tree, having no thorns, of the kind termed* عِضَاه: but he is incorrect in so saying: it is *a tree having hard branches, for which the cattle,* or *camels and other beasts, have no desire, and not of the kind termed* عِضَاه; and indeed how can it be of the kind thus termed having no thorns? *nor is it tall, the tallest being of the height of a man sitting; but, with its shortness, it is dense and compact in its branches.* (Az, TA.)

مَا لِى عَنْهُ مُعْلَنْدَدٌ, (Lḥ, L, and Ḳ in art. عند,) and مُعْلَنْدَدٌ, (Ḳ in that art.,) and مُعْلَنْدَدٌ, (Lḥ, L,) or ما لى مِنْهُ مُعْلَنْدَدٌ, (AZ, and Ṣ and O in art. عند,) and ▼ عَلَنْدٌ, (L,) as also عُنْدُدٌ and عُنْدَدٌ, (AZ, O and Ḳ in art. عند,) *I have no way of avoiding it, or escaping it:* (Lḥ, L, and O and Ḳ in art. عند, q. v.:) or مَا لِى عَنْهُ مُعْلَنْدَدٌ, *I have, in the way to it, no place in which to make my camel lie down, nor any in which to take a noontide-sleep, but only a direct course to it.* (L in art. علند.) And مَا لِى إِلَيْهِ مُعْلَنْدَدٌ, (Lḥ, L, and O* and Ḳ in art. عند,) and مُعْلَنْدَدٌ, (Lḥ, O in that art.,) *I have no way of attaining to it.* (Lḥ, L, and O and Ḳ in art. عند.) ═══ مُعْلَنْدَدٌ also signifies A country, (O in art. عند, on the authority of Ibn-'Abbád,) or a land, (Ḳ in that art.,) *containing neither water nor pasture.* (O and Ḳ in that art.)

علس

عَلَسٌ *A certain kind of wheat, having two grains in one husk,* (Ṣ, O, Mṣb, Ḳ,) *and sometimes one grain,* or *three grains;* (Mṣb;) *it is found in the region of El-Yemen;* (TA;) *and is the wheat of Ṣan'à:* (Ṣ, O, Ḳ:) or *a sort of wheat, of good quality, but difficult to cleanse, growing in the parts of El-Yemen:* (AḤn, O:) or [*a kind of grain*] *like wheat, but difficult to cleanse,* (Mgh, Mṣb,) *having two grains in one envelope, and it is the corn of Ṣan'à:* (Mgh:) or *a certain black grain, which people eat in times of dearth,* or *drought,* (Mgh, Mṣb,) *after grinding it:* (Mgh:) or, (Mṣb, in the Ḳ "and,") accord. to IAạr, (O,) *i. q.* عَدَسٌ [or *lentils*]. (O, Mṣb, Ḳ.)

علط

1. عَلَطَهُ, aor. ـُ (Ṣ, O, Ḳ,) and ـِ, (O, Ḳ,) inf. n. عَلْطٌ, (O,) *He branded* (Ṣ, O, Ḳ) his camel, (Ṣ, O,) or a she-camel, (Ḳ,) *with the mark called* عِلَاط; (Ṣ, Ḳ;) as also ▼ علّط, (Ḳ,) inf. n. تَعْلِيطٌ: (TA;) or the latter verb is with teshdeed to denote muchness [of the action], or multiplicity [of the objects]; (Ṣ, M, TA;) you say, علّط إِبِلَهُ [*he branded his camels with that mark*]. (Ṣ.) —— [Hence,] one says, لَأَعْلُطَنَّكَ عَلْطَ البَعِيرِ, (TA,) or عَلْطَ سَوْءٍ, (O,) † *I will assuredly brand thee* [*with the branding of the camel,* or *with an evil branding,* meaning,] *with a branding that shall remain upon thee.* (O, TA.) And عَلَطَهُ بِشَرٍّ, (Ṣ, O, Ḳ, TA,) and بِسُوْءٍ, inf. n. عَلْطٌ and عُلُوطٌ, (TA,) ‡ *He mentioned him,* (Ṣ, O, Ḳ, TA,) and *aspersed him,* (TA,) [or *branded,* or *stigmatized, him,*] *with evil.* (Ṣ, O, Ḳ, TA.) And عَلَطَهُ بِالقَوْلِ, inf. n. عَلْطٌ, ‡ *He branded,* or *stigmatized, him with a mark* [*of reproach*] *whereby he should be known.* (TA.) —— And عَلَطَهُ بِسَهْمٍ † *He hit him with an arrow;* (Ṣ, O;) inf. n. عَلْطٌ. (Ṣ.)

2: see above, first sentence. —— علّط البَعِيرَ, inf. n. تَعْلِيطٌ, *He pulled off the cord called* عِلَاط *from the neck of the camel.* (A'Obeyd, Ṣ, O,* Ḳ.)

4. مَا أَعْلَطَهُ, said of a poet, means مَا أَنْكَرَهُ [*How great is his intelligence,* or *skill, and knowledge!* &c.]. (AA, O, Ḳ.)

5. تعلّط القَوْسَ *He hung upon himself the bow.* (TA.)

8. اعتلطهُ and اعتلط بِهِ *He contended with him in an altercation; disputed,* or *litigated, with him; and treated him with enmity,* or *hostility;* or *did evil to him, obliging him to do the like in return.* (O, Ḳ.)

12. اِعْلَوَّطَ البَعِيرَ *He clung to the neck of the camel, and mounted him:* (Ṣ, O, Ḳ:) or it signifies, (Ḳ,) or signifies also, (O,) *he rode the camel without a* [*cord such as is termed*] خِطَام [q. v.]: (Ibn-'Abbád, O, Ḳ:) or *he rode the camel bare, without saddle:* (Ḳ:) and اعلوّط الفَرَسَ *he rode the mare without bridle.* (TA.) —— And اعلوّط النَّاقَةَ, said of a camel, (O, Ḳ, TA,) *He got upon the neck of the she-camel, and mounted upon her in a headlong,* or *heedless, manner:* (TA:) or *he mounted the she-camel to cover her.* (O, Ḳ, TA.) —— [Hence,] اعلوّط رَأْسَهُ, (O, TA,) and اعلوّط أَمْرًا, (Ḳ, TA,) ‡ *He pursued a headlong,* or *heedless, course, and plunged,* or *rushed, into an affair without consideration.* (O, Ḳ, TA.) —— And اعلوّطهُ *He took him and confined him.* (Lth,* O,* Ḳ.) —— And *He clave to him,* (IAạr, Ṣ, O, Ḳ,) *like as the* [*cord called*] عِلَاط *cleaves to the neck of the camel.* (IAạr, TA.) —— And *He clung to him, and drew him to him;* (Ibn-'Abbád, O;) and so ▼ تَعَلْوَطَهُ. (Ibn-'Abbád, O, Ḳ.)

Q. Q. 2. تَعَلْوَطَهُ: see what next precedes.

عَلْطٌ *A brand upon the side of the cheek of a camel:* (IDrd, O: [see also عِلَاطٌ:]) or *the scar of the branding upon the side of the fore part of the neck of a camel:* app. an inf. n. used as a subst. (TA.) —— See also عُلْطَةٌ.

عُلُطٌ, applied to a she-camel, (Ṣ, O, Ḳ,) and to a he-camel, (O,) accord. to Aṣ, (Ṣ,) *Without a* [*cord such as is called*] خِطَام [q. v.]: (Ṣ, O, Ḳ:) and, (Ḳ,) accord. to El-Aḥmar, (Ṣ, O,) *without a brand:* (Ṣ, O, Ḳ: [see عِلَاطٌ:]) like عُطُلٌ: (TA:) pl. أَعْلَاطٌ. (Ṣ, O, Ḳ.) —— Hence, (O,) أَعْلَاطُ الكَوَاكِبِ † *The shining,* or *brightly-shining, stars,* (الدَّرَارِىُّ, Ḳ, TA, [in the O الدَّرَارِىُّ, an evident mistranscription,]) *that have no names:* (O, Ḳ:) or *the named, known stars;* as though they were مَعْلُوطَة, i. e. marked with brands. (O.) [See also عِلَاطٌ.] —— And عُلُطٌ signifies *Tall she-camels:* —— and *short asses.* (IAạr, O, Ḳ.)

عُلْطَةٌ *A necklace,* or *collar,* or *the like;* syn. قِلَادَةٌ: (Ṣ, O, Ḳ:) pl. عُلَطٌ. (O, TA.) —— Also *A black mark which a woman makes upon her face for adornment;* (IDrd, O, Ḳ, TA;) like نُعْطَةٌ; (TA;) and so ▼ عَلْطٌ. (IDrd, O, Ḳ.) —— And *A* سُفْعَة [or *blackness tinged with redness*] *in the face* of a hawk; as also نُعْطَةٌ. (TA.) —— See also عُلْطَاةٌ. —— العُلْطَتَانِ *The* رَقْمَتَانِ [app. meaning *two ringstreaks*] *upon the necks of the* [*collared doves called*] قَمَارِىّ, *and the like thereof of birds;* as also ▼ العِلَاطَانِ: (TA:) or this latter signifies *the black* طَوْق [or *ring*] *on the two sides of the neck* of the dove: (Az, O, TA:) or so العِلَاطُ: (Ḳ:) and العُلْطَتَانِ signifies, accord. to Th, a طَوْق [or *neckring*]: and some say, *a* سِمَة [or *brand*]; but ISd says, "I know not how this is:" it is mentioned, however, by Suh, in the R. (TA.) —— Also *Two cowries* (وَدَعَتَانِ) *which are upon the necks of boys.* (TA.) —— And عُلْطَتَا المَرْأَةِ ‡ *The anterior and posterior pudenda of the woman.* (TA.)

عُلْطَاةٌ A ewe *having in the side of her neck a black* [*mark termed*] ▼ عُلْطَة, *the rest of her being white.* (TA.)

عِلَاطٌ The *side of the neck:* (Ḳ:) the عِلَاطَانِ are the *two sides of the neck* (Ṣ, O, Ḳ) of anything [i. e. of any creature]. (O.) —— And *A brand* (Ṣ, O, Ḳ) *on the neck of a camel,* (Ṣ, O,) *breadthwise,* (Ṣ,) *on the side* (عُرْض [in the CK عَرْض]) *of his neck:* (Ḳ, TA:) this is [said to be] its primary meaning: or, accord. to IDrd, *a brand on the side of the cheek of a camel:* (O:) or, accord. to the R, *on the base of the neck:* in the book of Ibn-Ḥabeeb, said to be *on the neck breadthwise; sometimes a single line, sometimes two lines,* and *sometimes several lines, on each side:* (TA:) and ▼ إِعْلِيطٌ signifies the same: the pl. (of عِلَاطٌ, TA) is أَعْلِطَةٌ [a pl. of pauc.] and عُلُطٌ. (Ḳ, TA.) —— See also عُلْطَةٌ. —— Also *A rope which is put upon the neck of a camel.* (Ṣ, O, Ḳ.) —— And ‡ The *thread* of the needle. (Lth, O, TA.) —— And [hence] العِلَاطُ, (Ḳ, TA,) or عِلَاطُ الشَّمْسِ, (Lth, O,) ‡ *What is, when one looks at it, as though it were thread* [*proceeding from the sun,* app. *when its light enters through an aperture in a wall or the like into a dark,* or *shady, place*]. (Lth, O,

Ḳ,* TA.* [In the Ḳ expl. as meaning خَيْطُ الشَّمْسِ. See also خَيْطُ البَاطِلِ, in art. خيط.]) — And عِلَاطُ النُّجُومِ ‡ *What is suspended to the stars:* [as though meaning *the rays proceeding from the stars:*] pl. أَعْلَاطٌ [which is also pl. of عُلُطٌ, q. v.]. (TA.) [But this is app. a conjectural explanation, suggested by a verse of Umeiyeh Ibn-Abi-ṣ-Ṣalt, incorrectly cited by Lth, and after him by Az, in which what are termed أَعْلَاطُ النُّجُومِ, or أَعْلَاطُ الكَوَاكِبِ, (see عُلُطٌ,) are described as being كَحَبْلِ القَرْقِ, i. e. "like the cord of flax," thus expl. by Az; whereas the right reading, as is stated in the O and TA, is كَخَيْلِ القَرْقِ; by القرق being meant the game thus called, and also called السُّدَّرُ; to which is added in the TA, that the خَيْل thereof are the stones used therein.] — Also ‡ *Contention, altercation, dispute,* or *litigation;* and *evil,* or *mischief;* (Ḳ, TA;) and *inimical,* or *hostile, treatment;* or *evildoing that obliges one to return evil:* (TA:) or the *branding,* or *stigmatizing, with evil.* (Ṣ,* O.)

عِلْيَطٌ *A species of trees,* (Ḳ, TA,) *in the Sarāh* (السَّرَاة), *from which bows are made.* (TA.)

شَاعِرٌ عَالِطٌ [*A poet possessing intelligence,* or *skill, and knowledge;* or *great intelligence* &c.]: of such one says, مَا أَعْلَطَهُ [q. v.]. (AA, O, Ḳ.*)

إِعْلِيطٌ The *pericarp of the* مَرْخ, which is like the shale of the bean, (O, Ḳ,) and to which the ear of the horse is likened: (O, TA:) said by certain of the lexicographers, (O,) as expl. by J, (TA,) to mean the *leaves of the* مَرْخ; but this is incorrect; for the مرخ has no leaves, its branches being bare and slender twigs: (O, TA:*) n. un. with ة. (TA.) — And *A branch,* and *a twig, of which the leaves have fallen.* (Ḳ.) — See also عِلَاطٌ.

مُعَلَّطٌ The *place of the brand called* عِلَاط *on the neck of the camel:* (O, Ḳ, TA:) and so, accord. to the Ḳ, ▼ مُعْلُوطٌ; but this latter means the *place of the neck of the camel to which one clings* [*to mount him:* see 13]. (TA.)

مُعَلَّطٌ A camel *whose cord called* عِلَاط *has been pulled off from his neck.* (TA.)

مَعْلُوطٌ A camel *branded with the mark called* عِلَاط. (O, TA.)

مُعْلُوطٌ: see مُعَلَّطٌ.

علف

1. عَلَفَ الدَّابَّةَ, (Ṣ, Mgh, O, Mṣb,) aor. ـِ, (O, Mṣb, TA,) inf. n. عَلْفٌ; (Ṣ, Mgh, O, Mṣb, Ḳ;) and ▼ اعلفها, (Mgh, Mṣb,) inf. n. إِعْلَافٌ; (Ḳ;) *He fed the beast* (Ṣ,* Mgh, O,* Mṣb,* Ḳ) *with* عَلَف [i. e. *fodder,* or *provender*], (Ṣ,* Mgh, O,* Mṣb,) [i. e. *he foddered the beast,*] in the مَعْلَف [or *manger*]: (Mgh:) or ▼ the latter signifies *he repaired to it often, putting* عَلَف *for it.* (TA.) Fr cites the following verse:

* عَلَفْتُهَا تِبْنًا وَمَاءً بَارِدًا *
* حَتَّى شَتَتْ هَمَّالَةً عَيْنَاهَا *

[meaning *I fed her with straw, and* gave her to drink *cool water, so that she passed the winter with her eyes flowing abundantly with tears*]: (Ṣ, O:) i. e. وَسَقَيْتُهَا مَآءً. (Ṣ.) — And عَلْفٌ signifies also The *drinking much.* (AA, O, Ḳ.) [Accord. to the TḲ, one says, عَلَفَهُ, aor. ـِ, inf. n. عَلْفٌ, meaning *He drank it much.*]

2: see the next paragraph, in two places. — [Accord. to Golius, علّف signifies *He fed well with fodder:* but for this he mentions no authority.]

4: see 1, in two places. — اعلف الطَّلْحُ *The* [trees called] طلح *put forth their* عُلَّف [q. v.]; (Ṣ, O, Ḳ;) as also ▼ علّف; but this is extr., for a verb of this meaning is [regularly] of the measure أَفْعَلَ only: (Ibn-'Abbád, O, Ḳ:) accord. to AA, as AḤn states in mentioning the حَبَلَة, (O, TA,) ▼ علّف, (O, Ḳ,) inf. n. تَعْلِيفٌ, (Ḳ,) signifies *they scattered their blossoms, and organized and compacted their fruit* [i. e. *their pods with the seeds therein*]; expl. by تَنَاثَرَ وَرْدُهُ وَعَقَّدَ [meaning عَقَّدَ الثَّمَرَ]; (O, Ḳ;) like أَحْبَلَ. (O.)

5. تعلّف *He sought* عَلَف [i. e. *fodder,* or *provender,*] *repeatedly,* or *leisurely, in the places in which it was thought,* or *known, usually to be.* (Mgh.)

8. تَعْتَلِفُ, said of a beast, (دَابَّة, O,) *It eats* (O, TA) [fodder, or provender, or] green herbage. (TA in art. ربع.) — And اِعْتَلَفَ [perhaps a mistranscription for اِعْتَلَقَ] ‡ *He was a great eater.* (TA.)

10. استعلفت الدَّابَّةُ *The beast* [meaning horse] *sought,* or *demanded,* عَلَف [i. e. *fodder,* or *provender,*] *by neighing.* (O, Ḳ.)

عَلْفٌ *A great eater;* one *who eats much;* (AA, O, Ḳ;) as also ▼ مُعْتَلِفٌ [perhaps a mistranscription for ▼ مُعْتَلِقٌ, but see 8]. (TA.) — Also *A certain tree,* or *plant,* (شَجَرَة,) *of El-Yemen, the leaves of which are like* [*those of*] *the grape* [*-vine*]: *they are pressed* [app. *in the nose-bags of horses,* the TA here inserting فى المخالى, for which I read فِي المَخَالِي, and it is there added وَيُسَوَّى, app. as meaning *and made into a flat mass,*] *and dried, and flesh-meat is cooked therewith instead of with vinegar;* (Ḳ;) *and they* [i. e. the leaves] *are used as a* ضِمَاد [or *dressing for wounds*] (وَيُضَمَّدُ بِهِ). (Ḳ accord. to the TA. [But in the place of these words, the CḲ and my MS. copy of the Ḳ have وَيُضَمَّرُ, as relating to a form of the pl. of عَلُوفَة, there mentioned in the next sentence.])

عَلَفٌ is for beasts, or horses and the like; (Ṣ, O;) a word of well-known meaning; (Ḳ;) i. e. *Fodder,* or *provender for beasts;* (KL;) *food of cattle,* or *of animals,* (TA,) or *of quadrupeds;* (MA;) *food with which the beast is fed* (Mgh, Mṣb*) *in the* مَعْلَف [or *manger*]: (Mgh:) accord. to ISh, applied to *herbs,* or *leguminous plants,* both *fresh* and *dry:* (TA voce حَشِيش:) said by ISd to be the قَضِيم [generally meaning *barley*] *of the beast:* (TA in the present art.:) [see also عَلُوفَة:] pl. [of mult.] عِلَافٌ (Ṣ, O, Mṣb, Ḳ) and عُلُوفَة (Mgh, O, Ḳ) and [of pauc.] أَعْلَافٌ. (O, Ḳ.) See also عَلَفَة. — [Hence,] one says, هُمْ عَلَفُ السِّلَاحِ وَجَزَرُ السِّبَاعِ † [*They are the provender of the weapons, and the flesh that is food of the beasts,* or *birds, of prey*]. (TA.)

عَلَفَةٌ The *food,* or *victuals, of soldiers;* as also ▼ عَلُوفَةٌ [which is a pl. of ▼ عَلَفٌ, or perhaps it is correctly ▼ عُلُوفَة, which is expl. by Golius as meaning *a stipend,* peculiarly *of a soldier*]. (KL.)

العَلَفِى, from عَلَفٌ, *What a man assigns, on the occasion of the reaping of his barley, to a guardian* [*thereof*] *from the birds, or to a friend.* (El-Hejeree, TA.)

عَلِيفٌ, (Ḳ, TA,) applied to a sheep or goat (شَاة), (TA,) i. q. ▼ مَعْلُوفَةٌ [i. e. *Fed with fodder,* or *provender; foddered*]: (Ḳ, TA:) accord. to AZ, applied to a ram; and having for its pl. عَلَائِفُ: and expl. by Lḥ as meaning *tied up, and fed with fodder,* or *provender; not sent forth to pasture where it pleases, nor led to pasture.* (TA.) [See also عَلُوفَةٌ.]

عِلَافَةٌ The *seeking,* and *buying,* and *bringing, of* عَلَف [i. e. *fodder,* or *provender for beasts*]. (Mgh.)

عَلُوفَةٌ A sheep or goat and other animal, and sheep or goats and other animals, *fed with fodder,* or *provender:* (Mgh, Mṣb:) or, as also ▼ عَلِيفَةٌ, a sheep or goat (شَاة), and a she-camel, *fed with fodder,* or *provender, and not sent forth to pasture;* (Ṣ, O, Ḳ, TA;) in order that it may become fat, (TA,) by means of the fodder collected: (Az, TA:) the pl. of each is عَلَائِفُ, accord. to Lḥ: or the pl. of the former is عُلُفٌ and عَلَائِفُ: (TA:) accord. to Lth, they said عَلُوفَةُ الدَّوَابِّ, as though the former word were a pl.; and it is more properly to be regarded as a pl. (O.) [See also عَلِيفٌ.] — Also The *food of the beast:* pl. عُلُفٌ (Ḳ, TA) [and accord. to the CḲ and my MS. copy of the Ḳ عَلَفٌ also; but see what is said above, voce عَلْفٌ, respecting this latter]. [See also عَلَفٌ.] And see عَلَفَةٌ.

عُلُوفَةٌ: see عَلَفَةٌ.

عَلِيفَةٌ: see عَلُوفَةٌ.

عِلَافِىٌّ [for رَحْلٌ عِلَافِىٌّ], (Ṣ, O,) and رِحَالٌ عِلَافِيَّةٌ, (Ṣ, O, Ḳ,) *A camel's saddle,* (Ṣ, O,) and *camels' saddles,* [*of a particular sort,*] *so called in relation to* عِلَافٌ (Ṣ, O, Ḳ) *the son of* حُلْوَان, (O, TA,) in the Ḳ, erroneously, طُوَار, (TA,) *a man of Ḳuḍá'ah,* (Ṣ, O,) *because he was the first* maker thereof; (O, Ḳ;) or, (Ḳ,) accord. to Lth, (O,) the *largest of* رِحَال *in the* [*hinder part and the fore part which are called*] آخِرَة [in the CḲ آخِرَة] *and* وَاسِط: in a verse of Ḥomeyd Ibn-Thowr, ▾ العُلَيْفِىّ occurs as an abbreviated dim. [of العِلَافِىّ]: (O, Ḳ:) the pl. of عِلَافِيَّة is عِلَافِيَّاتٌ. (O.)

العُلَيْفِىّ: see what next precedes.

عُلَّفٌ The *fruit of the* [*trees called*] طَلْح, *which resembles the fresh bean,* (Ṣ, O, Ḳ,) *and upon which, when they come forth, the camels pasture:* (Ṣ, O:) or the *pods,* or *receptacles of the fruit, thereof:* (TA:) [i. e.] the *fruit of the* طلح *when it succeeds the* بَرَمَة; *resembling the* [*kidney-bean called*] لُوبِيَآء: (IAạr, TA:) the n. un. is عُلَّفَةٌ: (Ṣ, O, Ḳ:) AḤn says that *this is like the great Syrian carob* (خَرُّوبَة [n. un. of خَرُّوب q. v.]), *except that it is bigger, and in it are grains like lupines, of a tawny colour, upon which the cattle pasturing at their pleasure feed, but which men eat not save in case of necessity:* and the *like thereof in size, of the fruit of the* عِضَاه, is also termed عُلَّفٌ: what is smaller than it, like the fruit of the سَلَم and of the سَمُر and of the عُرْفُط, is [properly] termed حُبْلَة: the عُلَّف are *long, and expanded,* or *extended:* (O:) [it is also said that] عُلَّفٌ signifies the *fruit of the* أَرَاك. (Ḥam p. 196.)

عَلَّافٌ *A seller of* عَلَف [i. e. *fodder,* or *provender for beasts*]: (O, Ḳ:) and ▾ عَلَّافَةٌ [as a coll. gen. n.] signifies [*sellers thereof:* or] *possessors of* عَلَف: and *seekers thereof.* (Mgh.)

شَيْخٌ عِلَّوْفٌ *An old man very aged.* (Lth, O, Ḳ.)

عَلَّافَةٌ: see عَلَّافٌ. — Also *A place in which* عَلَف [i. e. *fodder*] *is produced:* like مَلَّاحَةٌ signifying "a place in which salt is generated." (Mgh.)

عُلْفُوفٌ (applied to a man, Ṣ, O) *Coarse, rough, rude,* or *churlish, and advanced in age:* (Yaạḳoob, Ṣ, O, Ḳ:) and in this sense also applied to a woman: (TA:) or, thus applied, it signifies *old,* or *aged.* (Ibn-'Abbád, O, Ḳ, TA.) And An *old man, fleshy, and having much hair:* (Ḳ, TA: [in the CḲ, الشُّعْرَانِىّ is put for المُشْعَرَانِىّ:]) or, accord. to Az, شَيْخٌ عُلْفُوفٌ signifies *an old man having much flesh and hair.* (O.) And it is also expl. as signifying A man *in whom is negligence.* (TA.) — Also, applied to a horse, *Generous,* or *high-bred,* or *a male,* or *a stallion, large, big,* or *bulky;* syn. حِصَانٌ ضَخْمٌ. (Ibn-'Abbád, O, Ḳ.*) — And, applied to a goat, *Having much hair.* (TA.) — And نَاقَةٌ عُلْفُوفُ السَّنَامِ *A she-camel having the hump much enveloped with fur* [so I render مُلَفَّفَتُهُ (see art. لف)], *as though wrapped with a* كِسَآء. (Ibn-'Abbád, O, Ḳ.)

مُعْلَفٌ: see what next follows.

مِعْلَفٌ, (Ṣ, Mgh, O,) with kesr (Ṣ, Mgh) to the م; (Mgh;) or ▾ مَعْلَفٌ, like مَقْعَدٌ; (Ḳ;) [*A manger;* thus called in the present day; i. e.] *a place of* عَلَف [i. e. *fodder,* or *provender for beasts*]: (Ṣ, Mgh, O, Ḳ:) [pl. مَعَالِفُ.] — [Hence,] المِعْلَفُ, (Ibn-'Abbád, O,) or المَعْلَفُ, (Ḳ,) is the name of *Certain stars, disposed in a round form,* [*but*] *separate;* (Ibn-'Abbád, O, Ḳ;) also called الخِبَآءُ: (Ibn-'Abbád, O:) [the latter appellation is app. wrongly identified in the TA in art. خبى with الأُخْبِيَةُ: what is here meant seems to be *the group of stars called by our astronomers Præsepe;* agreeably with the former appellation, and with the following statement:] in the مجسطى, [i. e. المِجِسْطِى, (thus the Arabs term the great work of Ptolemy, which we, imitating them, commonly call "Almagest,")] النَّثْرَة (in Cancer) is mentioned by the name of المعلف: (Ḳzw, descr. of Cancer:) [but it is also said that] the Arabs thus call *the seven stars that compose the constellation* البَاطِيَة [i. e. *Crater*]. (Ḳzw, descr. of Crater.) — [Accord. to Golius, مِعْلَفٌ signifies also *A bag for fodder, which, with fodder, is hung on the neck of a beast.*]

مُعَلَّفَةٌ *Fattened;* applied to a شَاة [i. e. sheep or goat]; (Lth, O, Ḳ;) with teshdeed because of its owner's frequent and continual attention to it. (Lth, O.)

مَعْلُوفَةٌ: see عَلِيفٌ.

مُعْتَلَفٌ: see عَلَفٌ.

مُعْتَلِفٌ: see عَلَفٌ. — المُعْتَلِفَةُ is a metaphorical appellation applied to *The midwife.* (Ibn-'Abbád, O, Ḳ.)

علق

1\. عَلِقَ بِهِ, (Ṣ, Mgh, O, Mṣb, TA,) aor. ـَ, (Mṣb,) inf. n. عَلَقٌ (Ṣ, O, Mṣb, KL, TA) and عَلَقَةٌ (L, TA) [and app. عُلُوقٌ also, as will be seen from what follows]; and ▾ تعلّق, (Ṣ, MA, Mgh, O, Mṣb,) and ▾ اعتلق; (O, Mṣb, KL;) *It hung to it; it was,* or *became, suspended to it:* (so the first and last accord. to the KL, and the second accord. to the MA and common usage: [in the Ṣ and Mgh and O, it is merely said that the first and second signify the same:]) [and] *it clung, caught, clave, adhered, held,* or *stuck fast, to it;* (Mṣb in explanation of all, and TA* in explanation of the first;) and so ▾ تعلّقهُ. (Ṣ,* O,* TA.) It is said in a prov., (Ṣ, O, TA,) asserted in the Ḳ to have been mentioned before, which is not found to be the case, (TA,)

• عَلِقَتْ مَعَالِقَهَا ▾ وَصَرَّ الجُنْدَبُ •

(Ṣ, O, Ḳ, [in the CḲ, erroneously, مُعالِقَها,]) [*It* (the bucket, الدَّلْوُ, Z, TA) *has become suspended in its places of suspension, and the* جندب (accord. to the Ṣ and Ḳ a species of locust) *has creaked*]: originating from the fact that a man went to a well, and suspended his well-rope to the rope thereof, and then went to the owner of the well, and claimed to be his neighbour [and therefore to have a right to the use of the well]; but the owner refused his assent, and ordered him to depart; whereupon he uttered these words, meaning The heat has come, [see صَرَّ الجُنْدَبُ in art. جدب,] and I am not able to depart. (Ṣ, O. [See more in Freytag's Arab. Prov. ii. 91.]) And one says, عَلِقَ الشَّوْكُ بِالثَّوْبِ, aor. ـَ, inf. n. عَلَقٌ; and ▾ تعلّق بِهِ; meaning *The thorns clung, caught,* &c., *to the garment.* (Mṣb.) And اعتلق ▾ ظُفْرِى بِالشَّىْءِ *My nail clung, caught,* &c., *to the thing.* (Mṣb.) And عَلِقَ الظَّبْىُ فِى الحِبَالَةِ, (Ṣ, O,) or عَلِقَ الصَّيْدُ; (Ḳ;) or عَلِقَ الوَحْشُ بِالحِبَالَةِ, inf. n. عُلُوقٌ, (Mṣb,) [*The gazelle,* or *the animal of the chase, became caught,* or *stuck fast, in the snare;* or *the wild animal became caught,* or *held fast, thereby,* or] *became withheld from getting loose* [*thereby*]: whence the saying, عَلِقَ الخَصْمُ بِخَصْمِهِ and ▾ تعلّق بِهِ [*The antagonist became held fast,* or *withheld from getting loose, by his antagonist;* and also *the antagonist clung,* or *held fast, to his antagonist*]. (Mṣb.) [— The primary significations are those mentioned above in the first sentence: and hence several other significations here following.] — ▾ تعلّق عَلَيْهِ and عَلِقَ عَلَى كَذَا *It depended upon such a thing, as a condition.* — ▾ تعلّق and عَلِقَ بِهِ *It pertained to him,* or *it: it concerned him,* or *it.* And *He had a hold upon it: he had a concern in it.*] — عَلِقَهَا, (Ṣ, O,) or عَلِقَ بِهَا, (Ṣ, O,) or بِهِ, (Ḳ,) inf. n. عَلَقٌ, عَلَقَهُ (Ṣ, O, Ḳ) and عُلُوقٌ (Ḳ [and mentioned also in the Ṣ and O but app. as a simple subst.]) and عِلَاقَةٌ, [but see this below voce عَلَقٌ] and عَلَاقَةٌ, (Ḳ,) [*He became attached by love to her,* or *to him;*] *he loved* (Ṣ, O, Ḳ) *her,* (Ṣ, O,) or *him;* (Ḳ;) and so عَلِقَ حُبُّهَا بِقَلْبِهِ; (Ṣ, O;) and ▾ تعلّقها, and تعلّق بِهَا; [the former of these two phrases being used for the latter, agreeably with a saying of IAmb cited in the TA in art. ارى, that تَعَلَّقْتُ فُلَانًا is for تعلّقت بِفُلَانٍ;] like ▾ اعتلقها [i. e. اعتلق بها], (Ḳ,) or اعتلقهُ, (Ṣ,) or اعتلق بِهِ; (TA;) and ▾ عُلِّقَهَا, (Ṣ,* O,* Ḳ, TA,) from عَلَاقَةٌ, الحُبّ, (Ṣ, O, TA,) and ▾ عُلِّقَ بِهَا, (TA,) [but this last verb is more commonly trans. by itself, for ex.,] El-Aạshà says,

• عُلِّقْتُهَا عَرَضًا وَعُلِّقَتْ رَجُلًا •
• غَيْرِى وَعُلِّقَ أُخْرَى غَيْرَهَا الرَّجُلُ •

[*I became attached to her accidentally, and she became attached to a man other than me, and the man became attached to another female, other than her*]. (Ṣ, O. [See also another ex., in a verse of 'Antarah, cited voce زَعَمَ.]) [See also عَلِقَ, below.] — عَلِقَتْ مِنْهُ كُلَّ مَعْلَقٍ [which may be rendered *She captivated him wholly*] occurs in a trad. as [virtually] meaning *he loved her, and was vehemently desirous of her.* (TA.) — عَلِقَتْ نَفْسُهُ الشَّىْءَ *His soul,* or *mind, clung to the thing persistently.* (L, TA.) — قَدْ عَلِقَ الكِبَرُ مَعَالِقَهُ ▾ [app. meaning *Old age has taken hold in its holding places,* or, agreeably with what is said in the next sentence, *has had its effects*], in which معالق is pl. of مُعْلَق, is said to an old man. (TA.) And of everything that has had its effect [so I here render وَقَعَ مَوْقِعَهُ, but see art. وقع], one says, عَلِقَ ♦ مُعَالَقَهُ. (TA, and Ḥam p. 172.) — عَلِقَتْ مَرَاسِيهَا بِذِى رَمْرَامٍ [*Their anchors have clung to a place having the species of herbage called* رمرام], meaning *they are abiding therein*, (see مُرْسَاةٌ, in art. رسو,) is said of camels when they are at rest, or at ease, and their eyes are refreshed by the pasturage; and is a prov., applied to persons in the like condition by reason of their means of subsistence. (TA.) — عَلِقَ بِهِ, inf. n. عَلَقٌ, *He contended with him in an altercation* [as though clinging to him]; *disputed with him*; or *litigated with him*. (TA.) — لَا يَعْلَقُ بِكَ means لا يَلِيقُ بك [*It will not be suitable to thee; it will not befit thee*]. (Ṣ and Ḳ in art. ليق.) — عَلِقَ يَفْعَلُ كَذَا *He set about, began*, or *betook himself to, doing such a thing*. (Ṣ, O, Ḳ.) فَعَلِقُوا وَجْهَهُ ضَرْبًا occurs in a trad., meaning *They set about*, or *betook themselves to, smiting his face*. (TA.) And a rájiz says,

* عَلِقَ حَوْضِى نُغَرٌ مُكِبُّ *

[*Nughar* (a species of birds) *bending down their heads*] *betook themselves to coming for the purpose of drinking to my* حوض [or *watering-trough*]: or, as some say, *liked it, and frequented it*. (Ṣ, O.) — And مَا عَلِقْتُ أَقُولُهُ means *I did not cease saying it*; like مَا نَشِبْتُ. (A in art. نشب.) [Thus عَلِقَ has two contr. meanings.] — عَلِقَتِ الإِبِلُ العِضَاهَ, (Ṣ, O, Ḳ,) aor. ـَ; (Ḳ;) and عَلَقَت likewise, aor. ـُ; (Ṣ, O, Ḳ;) inf. n. عَلْقٌ; (Ṣ, O, Ḳ;*) *The camels fed upon the upper*, or *uppermost, portions of the* [*trees called*] عضاه, (Ṣ, O, Ḳ,) *reaching them with their mouths*: (Ṣ and O in explanation of the latter verb:) and يَعْلُقُ العِضَاهَ, said of a camel, *he plucks from the* عضاه, [as though] hanging from it, by reason of his tallness: (Ṣ: in one of my copies of the Ṣ, and in the TA, يَعْلَقُ:) or one says, of camels, عَلَقَتْ مِنَ الشَّجَرِ, aor. ـُ, inf. n. عَلْقٌ and عُلُوقٌ, meaning *they ate of the trees with their mouths*: and عَلَقَتْ فِى الوَادِى, aor. ـُ, *they pastured*, or *pastured where they pleased, in the valley*: (Mṣb:) accord. to Lḥ, عَلَقَتْ, aor. ـُ, inf. n. عَلْقٌ, said of beasts, means *they ate* the leaves of the trees: and accord. to Aṣ, عَلَقَتْ, aor. ـُ, inf. n. عُلُوقٌ, means *they reached and took with their mouths*. (TA.) Hence, (TA,) it is said in a trad., أَرْوَاحُ الشُّهَدَآءِ فِى حَوَاصِلِ طَيْرٍ خُضْرٍ تَعْلُقُ مِنْ وَرَقِ الجَنَّةِ, (Ṣ, Mṣb,*) or مِنْ ثِمَارِ الجَنَّةِ, (TA,) and, as some relate it, تَعْلَقُ, (Mṣb, TA,) [both as meaning *The souls of the martyrs are in the crops of green birds that eat of the leaves*, or *fruits, of Paradise*,] but the former relation is that which should be followed, because the latter requires that one should say فِى ثمار الجنّة [or فى ورق الجنّة], though the latter is said to be the more common. (Mṣb.) One says also, عَلَقَتِ الإِبِلُ, aor. ـُ, inf. n. عَلْقٌ, meaning *The camels ate of the* عُلْقَة *of the trees*, i. e., *of the trees that remain in the winter and of which the camels are fed until they attain to the* رَبِيع [meaning *spring*, or *spring-herbage*]; as also ♦ تعلّقت. (TA.) And عَلَقَ, inf. n. عَلَاقٌ and عُلُوقٌ, *He ate*. (TA.) And الصَّبِىُّ يَعْلُقُ *The child sucks his fingers*. (TA.) — عَلَقَهُ بِلِسَانِهِ [inf. n. عَلْقٌ] *He blamed*, or *censured, him*; *he said to him that which he disliked*, or *hated*. (Lḥ, Ḳ,* TA.) — عَلِقَ أَمْرَهُ *He knew his affair*. (Ḳ.) — عَلِقَتِ المَرْأَةُ, (Ṣ, Mgh, O, Ḳ,) inf. n. عُلُوقٌ, (Mgh,) or عَلَقٌ, (TA,) *The woman conceived*, or *became pregnant*. (Ṣ, Mgh, O, Ḳ.) Hence the saying, الغِرَاسُ تَبَدَّلُ بِالعُلُوقِ ‡ [*The set*, or *shoot that is planted, becomes changed by pullulating*]; a metaphorical phrase; meaning that what is planted becomes changed because it increases and rises when it clings to the earth and germinates. (Mgh.) — عَلِقَتِ الدَّابَّةُ *The beast drank water and the leech* (العَلَقَةُ) *clave to it*: (Ṣ, O, Ḳ:) or, accord. to an explanation of [the part. n.] مَعْلُوقٌ by Lth, one says عُلِقَتْ, of the form of that whereof the agent is not named, meaning *it had leeches* (عَلَق) *that had taken hold upon its fauces when it drank*: (O:) or عُلِقَ, also, like عُنِىَ, is used in this sense, (Ḳ,* TA,) said of a man and of a beast. (TA.) — عَالَقْتُ فُلَانًا فَعَلَقْتُهُ: see 3.

2. عَلَّقَهُ, (Ṣ, O, Mṣb, Ḳ,) i. e. الشَّىْءَ, (Ṣ, O, Mṣb,) inf. n. تَعْلِيقٌ; (Ṣ, O, Ḳ;) and ♦ اعلقهُ, (Ṣ,* O,* Mṣb,) and ♦ تعلّقهُ; (Ṣ, O, Ḳ;) signify the same. (Ṣ, O, Mṣb, Ḳ.) You say, علّق الشَّىْءَ بِالشَّىْءِ, (Mgh, Mṣb, Ḳ,) inf. n. as above, *He hung*, or *suspended, the thing to the thing*; and so مِنَ الشَّىْءِ, and عَلَيْهِ: (TA:) [and] *he made the thing to cling, catch, cleave, adhere, hold*, or *stick fast, to the thing*; as also ♦ اعلقهُ بِهِ. (Mṣb.) [For ex.,] one says, عَلَّقْتُ رِشَائِى بِرِشَائِكَ [*I have suspended my well-rope to thy well-rope*]: and أَعْلَقَ ♦ رِشَآءَهُ بِرِشَآءِ البِئْرِ [*He suspended his well-rope to the rope of the well*]. (Ṣ, O.) [See also an ex. of the latter verb in a verse cited voce رَافِضٌ.] And عَلَّقَهُ عَلَى الوَتِدِ [*He hung it on the peg*]: and in like manner, علّق الشَّىْءَ خَلْفَهُ [*He hung the thing behind him*]; as, for instance, a حَقِيبَة, &c., behind the camel's saddle. (TA.) And تعلّق ♦ مَعَاذَةً *He hung* (عَلَّقَ) *upon himself an amulet*. (Ṣ, O.) And اعلق ♦ بِالغَرْبِ بَعِيرَيْنِ *He coupled two camels to the end of the well-rope* [*to the other end of which was attached the large bucket*]. (IF, Ḳ.) [And in like manner they say in the present day, علّق الخَيْلَ فِى العَرَبَةِ *He harnessed*, or *attached, the horses to the carriage*.] And اعلق ♦ أَظْفَارَهُ فِى الشَّىْءِ *He made his nails to cling, catch*, or *cleave, to the thing*. (Ṣ, TA.) And [in like manner,] علّق يَدَهُ and ♦ اعلقها [*He made his hands to cling*, &c.], followed by فى before the object: both signify the same. (TA.) And علّق الدَّابَّةَ, meaning عَلَّقَ عَلَيْهَا [for علّق عليها المِخْلَاةَ, agreeably with modern usage, i. e. *He hung upon the beast the nose-bag* containing barley, or the like; or *he supplied the beast with* عَلِيق, which means *barley*, or *the like, that is hung upon the beast*]. (TA.) [And, hence, as is indicated in the T and TA, علّق signifies, by a metaphor, ‡ *He supplied with* عَلِيق as meaning *wine*.] And علّق رَاحِلَتَهُ *He loosed the halter*, or *leading-rope, from the muzzle of his riding-camel and threw it* [or *hung it*] *upon her shoulders, to give her ease*. (TA.) — [The primary significations are those mentioned in the second sentence of this paragraph: and hence several other significations here following. — علّى كَذَا, and علّقهُ بِكَذَا, *He made it to depend upon such a thing, as a condition*.] You say, عَلَّقْتُ عِتْقَ عَبْدِى بِمَوْتِى [*I made the freedom of my slave to depend upon my death*]. (TA in art. دبر.) — إِنْ أَنْطِقْ أُطَلَّقْ وَإِنْ أَسْكُتْ أُعَلَّقْ, in the story of Umm-Zarạ, means [*If I speak, I am divorced; and if I be silent, I am left in suspense*, i. e.,] he leaves me like that which is suspended, (O, TA,) neither retained nor divorced. (TA.) [And similar to this is the phrase تَعْلِيقُ أَفْعَالِ القُلُوبِ *The suspending of the verbs significant of operations of the mind from government, as to the letter but not as to the meaning*:] see مُعَلَّقٌ. — [علّق البِنَآءَ *He made the building*, or *structure, pensile*, i. e. *supported above the ground*, or *above a stage* or *floor, by pillars* or *piers* or *otherwise*. Hence,] the saying نَقَبُوا الحَائِطَ وَعَلَّقُوهُ means *They dug beneath the wall* [or *made a hole through it*] *and left it* [or *rendered it*] مُعَلَّقًا [i. e. *pensile*, or *supported above the ground*, being partially hollowed beneath]. (Mgh.) — [علّق فِى حَاشِيَةِ كِتَابٍ *He appended a note in the margin of a book* or *writing*.] — علّق بَابًا *He set up, and fixed, a door*, (Mgh, TA,) عَلَى دَارِهِ [*upon*, or *to, his house*]. (Mgh.) — And (TA) *He closed*, or *made fast, a door, with a kind of latch*, or *sliding bolt*; syn. أَزْلَجَهُ, (O, TA,) or أَرْتَجَهُ; (Ḳ;) as also ♦ اعلقهُ. (TA.) [See مِعْلَاقٌ.] — عَلَّقَهَا, and عَلَّقَ بِهَا, in which the pronoun denoting the object relates to a woman: see 1, former half. — عَلَّقَ فُلَانٌ دَمَ فُلَانٍ [app. meaning *Such a one attached to himself responsibility for the blood of such a one*] is said when the former is the slayer of the latter. (TA. [Thus I find the phrase there written: but perhaps the right reading is عَلِقَ.]) — عَلَّقَهُ also signifies *He joined him, and overtook him*. (TA.) — And *He learned it, and took it or received it* [from another]. (TA.) — عَلِّقُوا رَمَقَهُ بِشَىْءٍ *Give ye to him something that shall stay*, or *arrest, what remains in him of life*. (Z, TA.) — عَلَّقْتُ مَعَ فُلَانٍ عَلِيقَةً, (Ṣ, TA,) and مَعَ القَوْمِ, (TA,) *I sent with such a one*, (Ṣ, TA,) *and with the people*, or *party*, (TA,) *a camel for the purpose of bringing corn for me upon it*. (Ṣ, TA. [See عَلِيقَةٌ.])

* أَرْضَى مِنَ المَرْكَبِ بِالتَّعْلِيقِ *

is a prov., said to a man who is thereby enjoined to be content with a part of that which he wants, instead of the whole thereof; like him who rides the camel termed عَلِيقَة one time after another time: [so that it means *Be thou content, instead of the riding* constantly, or *instead of the beast that is ridden* only, *with the sending a camel to bring corn*, upon which thou mayest ride occasionally:] (TA:) or the meaning may be, *be thou content, instead of* thy *riding, with the hanging* of thy goods upon the beast: or the meaning may be, *be thou content, in respect of the beast that is ridden, with the hanging* [thy goods] upon him in thy turn. (Meyd.) — And one says, عَلِّقْ نَاقَتَكَ, meaning *Go thou from thy she-camel* (اِمْشِ عَنْهَا). (O.)

3. ▼ عَالَقْتُ فُلَانًا فَعَلَقْتُهُ *I vied with such a one*, or *contended with him for superiority, in precious things* (أَعْلَاق, pl. of عِلْق), *and I surpassed him*, or *was better than he, in respect of a precious thing*. (TA.) And عَالَقْتُهُ بِعِلْقِى وَعِلْقِهِ *I laid a bet, or wager, with him with precious articles of property* [or, *I with my precious thing and he with his precious thing*]. (Ḥam p. 101, but without the vowel-signs.)

4: see 2, former half, in six places: and again, in the latter half. — اعلق القَوْسَ *He put a suspensory* (عِلَاقَة) *to the bow*. (Ṣ, O, Ḳ.) — اعلق said of one practising the capturing of game, or animals of the chase, *He had the game*, or *animal of the chase, caught*, or *stuck fast, in his snare*. (Ṣ, O, Ḳ.) = اعلق also signifies *He sent*, or *let go*, [or *applied*,] *leeches* (عَلَق), (Ṣ, O, Ḳ,) *upon a place*, (Ṣ, O, TA,) *to suck* (Ṣ, O, Ḳ) *the blood*. (O, TA.) = And *He found, lighted on*, or *met with, a precious article*, (عِلْقًا, Ḳ, TA, [in the CḲ عَلْقًا] i. e. نَفِيسًا, TA,) *of property*: (Ḳ, TA:) mentioned by Ibn-'Abbád. (TA.) = And *He brought to pass that which was a calamity*. (Ḳ.) You say to a man, أَعْلَقْتَ وَأَفْلَقْتَ, i. e. جِئْتَ بِعُلَقَ فُلَقَ, meaning [*Thou hast brought to pass*] *that which is a calamity*. (Ṣ, O.) — And أَعْلَقْتُ عَنْهُ *I removed from him* العَلُوق, meaning *that which was a calamity*. (O, TA.*) — Hence, الإِعْلَاق as meaning A woman's *pressing with the finger the* نَغَانِغ, which are *certain portions of flesh by the uvula, of a child, thereby endeavouring to cure his* عُذْرَة, (O, TA,*) which means a *pain and swelling in the fauces*; (TA;) i. q. الدَّغْر. (Ṣ, TA. [See 1 in art. دغر.]) You say of a woman, أَعْلَقَتْ وَلَدَهَا مِنَ العُذْرَةِ, (Ṣ,) or أَعْلَقَتْ عَلَيْهِ, (O, TA,) *She raised* (دَفَعَتْ [or دَغَرَتْ i. e. *thrust*]) *her child's* [*swelling termed*] عُذْرَة *with her hand*: (Ṣ:) or *she pressed that part with her finger, and thrust it*. (TA.) — And hence, (TA,) one says also, أَعْلَقْتُ عَلَىَّ, meaning *I put my hand into my fauces to constrain myself to vomit*. (O, TA.) = اعلقت البِلَادُ *The countries were*, or *became, distant*, or *remote*; like اعنقت. (TA in art. عنق, from the Nawádir el-Aạráb.)

5: see 1, former half, in seven places: — and see the same paragraph again, in the last quarter: = and see also 2, first quarter, in two places.

8: see 1, former half, in three places.

عَلْقٌ *A hole in a garment*, (Ḳ, TA,) *caused by one's passing by a tree or a thorn that has caught to it*; (TA;) as also ▼ عَلَقٌ: (Ḳ, TA:) or *a thing that has caught*, or *clung, to a garment, and pulled it* [and, app., *frayed*, or *rent, it*]. (Ṣ. [See also عَلْقَةٌ.]) = And The *act of reviling*. (Ḳ.) [See also عَلَقَهُ بِلِسَانِهِ, (of which it is the inf. n.,) near the end of the first paragraph.] = And *A species of trees used for tanning*. (Ḳ.) = See also the next paragraph, in two places.

عِلْقٌ *A precious thing*, or *thing held in high estimation, of any kind*, (Lḥ, Ṣ, O, Ḳ, TA,) *except of animate beings*; (Lḥ, TA;) as also ▼ عَلْقٌ: (Ḳ:) one says, هٰذَا عِلْقُ مَضِنَّةٍ *This is a precious thing*, or *thing held in high estimation, of which one is tenacious*; (Ṣ,* O;) as also عِرْقُ مَضِنَّةٍ [q. v.]: (O and TA in art. عرق:) pl. [of pauc.] أَعْلَاقٌ (Ṣ, Ḳ) and [of mult.] عُلُوقٌ, (Ḳ,) and, as some say, عِلْقَاتٌ. (O.) And [particularly] *A garment held in high estimation*: [see also عِلْقَةٌ:] or *a shield*: [see again عِلْقَةٌ:] or *a sword*: (Lḥ, Ḳ, TA:) and *property held in high estimation*. (TA.) — And *Wine*; (Ṣ, O, Ḳ;) because held in high estimation: (Ṣ, O:) or *old wine*. (Ḳ, TA.) — And one says, فُلَانٌ عِلْقُ عِلْمٍ *Such a one is a lover and pursuer of knowledge*: (O, Ḳ:*) and in like manner, عِلْقُ شَرٍّ [*a lover and pursuer of evil*]: (Ḳ:) and عِلْقُ خَيْرٍ [*a lover and pursuer of good*]. (TA.) = Also *A* جِرَاب [or *bag for travelling-provisions &c.*]; and so ▼ عَلْقٌ: (Ibn-'Abbád, O, Ḳ:) [pl. أَعْلَاقٌ, of which see an ex. in a verse cited voce رَائِحٌ, in art. روح.] = See also عِلْقَةٌ: — and see عَلَاقَةٌ, first quarter.

عَلَقٌ *Anything hung*, or *suspended*. (Ḳ.) — The *suspensory* [*cord*] *of the* بَكَرَة [or *pulley of a well*]; (Ḳ;) the *apparatus of the* بَكَرَة, *by which it is suspended*: (Ṣ, O:) and the بَكَرَة [or *pulley*] *itself*; (Ḳ, TA;) as some say; and the pl. is أَعْلَاقٌ: (TA:) or [in the CḲ "and"] the *well-rope and the large bucket and the* مِحْوَر [or *pin on which the sheave of the pulley turns*] (Ḳ, TA) *and the pulley*, (TA,) *all together*; (Ḳ, TA;) so says Lḥ: (TA:) or *all the apparatus for drawing water by means of the pulley; comprising the two pieces of wood at the head of the well, the two upper extremities of which are connected by a rope and then fastened to the ground by means of another rope, the two ends of this being extended to two pegs fixed in the ground; the pulley is suspended to the upper parts of the two pieces of wood, and the water is drawn by means of it with two buckets by two drawers*: it signifies only the سَانِيَة [here meaning the *large bucket with its apparatus*] *and all the apparatus consisting of the* خُطَّاف [or *bent piece of iron which is on each side of the sheave of the pulley and in which is the pin whereon the sheave turns*] *and the* مِحْوَر [or *pin itself*] *and the sheave and the* نَعَامَتَان [app. here meaning the *two pieces of wood mentioned above*, agreeably with an explanation mentioned voce زُرْنُوق,] *and the ropes thereof*: so says Aṣ, on the authority of Arabs: (TA:) or the *rope that is suspended to the pulley*: (Ḳ:) or, as some say, the *rope that is at the upper part of the pulley*. (TA.) — And The *suspensory of a* قِرْبَة [or water-skin]; i. e. عَلَقُ القِرْبَةِ signifies *the strap by which the* قِرْبَة *is suspended*; (TA;) i. q. عَرْقُوَة: (Ṣ, O, Ḳ, TA:) or *the thing with which it is tied and then suspended*: or *what has remained in it of the grease with which it is greased*. (TA.) One says, جَشِمْتُ إِلَيْكَ عَلَقَ القِرْبَةِ [expl. in arts. جشم and عرق]. (Ṣ, O.) — Also [*Leeches*;] *certain worms*, (Ṣ,) or *certain things resembling worms*, (Mgh, Mṣb,) or *certain small creeping things*, (O,) or a [*species of*] *small creeping thing*, (Ḳ,) *black*, (Mgh, Mṣb,) or *red*, (TA,) *found in water*, (Ṣ, O, Mṣb, Ḳ,) *and having the property of sucking blood*, (Ṣ, O, Ḳ, TA,) *and employed to suck the blood from the throat and from sanguineous tumours*: (TA:) *they cling* (Mgh, Mṣb) *to the* حَنَك [q. v.] (Mgh) or *to the fauces* (Mṣb) *of the beast when he drinks*, (Mgh, Mṣb,) *and suck the blood*: (Mṣb:) one thereof is termed عَلَقَةٌ. (Ṣ, O, Mṣb.) — And *Clay that clings to the hand*. (Ḳ.) — And *Blood*, in a general sense: or *intensely red blood*: (Ḳ:) or *thick blood*: (Ṣ, O, Ḳ:) or *clotted blood*, (Ḳ, TA,) *before it becomes dry*: (TA:) or *clotted, thick, blood*; because of its clinging together: (Mgh:) and عَلَقَةٌ signifies *a portion thereof*: (Ṣ, Mgh, O, Ḳ:) or this signifies *a little portion of thick blood*: (Jel in xcvi. 2:) or *a portion* [or *lump*] *of clotted blood*: (TA:) or the *seminal fluid, after its appearance, when it becomes thick, clotted, blood*; after which it passes to another stage, becoming flesh, and is what is termed مُضْغَة. (Mṣb. [See Ḳur xxiii. 14.]) = Also [*Attachment*, as meaning] *tenacious love*: (Ḳ:) and [simply] *love*, or *desirous love*, (Lḥ, Ṣ, O, Ḳ, TA,) *of a man for a woman*: (Lḥ, TA:) or *love cleaving to the heart*; (TA;) and so ▼ عَلَاقَة and ▼ عِلَاقَة; or the former of these two relates to love and the like and the latter relates to a whip and the like [as will be expl. below under the two words]. (Ḳ.) [In this sense it is originally an inf. n., of which the verb is عَلِقَ.] One says, إِنَّهُ لَذُو عَلَقٍ فِى فُلَانَةَ *Verily he is one having love*, or *desirous love, for such a woman*: (Lḥ, TA:) thus made trans. by means of فى. (TA.) And نَظْرَةٌ مِنْ ذِى عَلَقٍ *A look from one having love*, or *desirous love*: (Ṣ, O, TA:) a prov. (TA.) — See also عَلَاقَة, first quarter. — Also *Pertinacious contention in an altercation*; or *such disputation or litigation*. (Ḳ. [In this sense it is originally an inf. n., of which the verb is عَلِقَ. And عَلَاقَة, q. v., has a similar signification.]) — See also عَلْقَة, second sentence. = And see عَلْقٌ. = Also The *main* [or *middle*] *part* [or *beaten track*] *of a road*. (Ibn-'Abbád, O, Ḳ.) [See an ex. of the pl. (أَعْلَاق) in a verse cited voce عَمِيق.]

عَلِقٌ [part. n. of عَلِقَ: as such signifying *Hanging*, or *being suspended:* and *clinging*, &c.: — and] *pertinacious; adhering to affairs, and minding them.* (TA in art. دمر.) [See also عَلَاقِيَةٌ.] — [Also, as such, applied to a woman, *Pregnant:* a meaning assigned by Golius to عَلِقٌ.]

عُلَقَ and فُلَقَ in the saying جِئْتَ بِعُلَقَ فُلَقَ, [expl. above, see 4,] (Ṣ,) or جَآءَ بِعُلَقَ فُلَقَ [*He brought to pass*] *that which was a calamity,* (Ḳ,) are imperfectly decl., (Ṣ, Ḳ,) like عُمَرُ. (Ṣ.) — And عُلَقٌ [perfectly decl.] signifies *A numerous company,* or *collection* [*of men*]: (Ḳ:) thus it is said to mean: (Ṣ:) and this is meant in the saying above mentioned, as some explain it. (TA.) — And عُلَقٌ accord. to Ḳ, but correctly عُلُقٌ, with two dammehs, pl. of ↓ عَلُوقٌ, (TA,) signifies *Deaths,* or the *decrees of death;* syn. مَنَايَا: (Ḳ, TA:) and *calamities:* (TA:) and *businesses, occupations,* or *employments:* or *such as divert one* from other things: or *occurrences that cause one to forget,* or *neglect,* or *be unmindful:* syn. أَشْغَالٌ. (Ḳ, TA.)

عُلْقَةٌ *A* جَذْبَة [meaning *fray,* as being a kind of strain,] *that is occasioned in a garment* (Ḳ, TA) *and other* [*similar*] *thing when one passes by a thorn or a tree.* (TA. [See also عَلَقٌ.])

عُلْقَةٌ: see عَلَاقَةٌ, former half, in two places. — Also The *quantity that suffices the cattle,* (Ṣ, O, Mṣb, Ḳ,) *of what they obtain from the trees* [*or plants*]; (Ṣ, Ḳ;) as also ↓ عَلَقٌ; (Ṣ, O, Ḳ;) and so ↓ عَلَاقٌ, and ↓ عَلَاقَةٌ: (Ḳ:) and *a sufficiency of the means of subsistence,* (Ṣ, O, Ḳ,) *whatever it be;* (Ṣ;) as also ↓ عَلَاقٌ, (O,) or ↓ عَلَاقَةٌ: (Ṣ, Ḳ:) or it signifies also *food sufficient to retain life;* (Mṣb, TA;*) as also ↓ مُتَعَلَّقٌ; (TA;) and so ↓ عَلَاقٌ, as in a verse cited voce رَجِيعٌ: (Ṣ in art. رجع:) and, (O, Ḳ, TA,) accord. to AḤn, (O, TA,) the *trees that remain in the winter* (O, Ḳ, TA) *and of which the camels are fed,* (O, Ḳ,) or *with which the camels suffice themselves,* (TA,) *until they attain to the* رَبِيع [meaning *spring,* or *spring-herbage*]: (O, Ḳ, TA: [see also عُرْوَةٌ:]) and it is also expl. as signifying *herbage that does not stay:* (TA:) and *food that suffices until the time of the* [*morning-meal called*] غَدَآء; (Ḳ,* TA;) as also ↓ عَلَاقٌ: (Ḳ, TA:) and accord. to Az, *food,* and likewise *a beast for riding, such as suffices one, though it be not free from deficiency,* or *defect:* (TA:) the pl. of عُلْقَةٌ is عُلَقٌ. (Mṣb.) One says, لِى فِى هٰذَا المَالِ عُلْقَةٌ and ↓ عِلْقٌ and ↓ عَلُوقٌ and ↓ عَلَاقَةٌ and ↓ مُتَعَلَّقٌ, all meaning the same, (Ḳ, TA,) i. e. [*There is for me,* or *I have, in this property,*] *a sufficiency of the means of subsistence.* (TA.) And مَا يَأْكُلُ فُلَانٌ إِلَّا عُلْقَةً [*Such a one eats not save a bare sufficiency of the means of subsistence*]. (O, TA.) And ↓ مَا ذُقْتُ عَلَاقًا [*I have not tasted a sufficiency of the means of subsistence, or food sufficient to retain life*]. (TA.) And مَا فِى الأَرْضِ عَلَاقٌ ↓ وَلَا لَبَاقٌ *There is not in the land a sufficiency of the means of subsistence:* or *pasturage:* (TA:) or ↓ مَا بِهَا مِنْ عَلَاقٍ *there is not in it pasturage.* (Ṣ.) And لَمْ يَتْرُكِ الحَالِبُ بِالنَّاقَةِ ↓ عَلَاقًا *The milker did not leave in the she-camel's udder anything.* (Ṣ, O. [See also عَلُوقٌ.]) And لَمْ يَبْقَ لِى عِنْدَهُ عُلْقَةٌ [*There remained not with him*] *anything* [*belonging to me*]. (Ṣ, O,* Ḳ.*) And هٰذَا الكَلَامُ لَنَا فِيهِ عُلْقَةٌ [*In this speech is*] *a sufficiency* [*for us*]. (TA.) And عِنْدَهُمْ عُلْقَةٌ مِنْ مَتَاعِهِمْ [*With them is*] *somewhat remaining* [*of their goods*]. (TA.)

عِلْقَةٌ *A small garment,* (Ṣ, O,) the *first garment that is made for a boy:* (Ṣ, O, Ḳ:) or *a shirt without sleeves:* or *a garment in which is cut an opening for the head to be put through it,* [*so that nearly one half of it falls down before the wearer and the corresponding portion behind,*] *not having its two sides sewn* [*together*]; *it is worn by a girl;* (Ḳ, TA;) *like the* صُدْرَة; *she uses it for service and work;* (TA;) *and it extends to the place of the waist-band:* (Ḳ, TA: [see also إِتْبٌ:]) or *a garment held in high estimation;* (Ḳ, TA;) like عِلْقٌ [mentioned before]; *worn by a man:* one says of him who has not upon him costly garments, مَا عَلَيْهِ عِلْقَةٌ [*He has not upon him costly attire*]. (TA.) — And *A shield.* (Ibn-'Abbád, O, TA. [This last meaning is also assigned to عِلْقٌ, as mentioned before.]) — And *A certain tree, used for tanning.* (Ḳ.) — إِبِلٌ لَيْسَ بِهَا عِلْقَةٌ is a phrase mentioned by Ibn-'Abbád, (O, TA,) as meaning [app.] اصرة. (TA. [This word, in the TA, is blurred: and in the O, the place that it occupied has perished: I think that it is most probably أَصِرَّةٌ, pl. of صِرَارٌ; and therefore that the phrase means *Camels not having upon them strings,* or *pieces of rag, bound upon their udders* or *teats, to prevent their young ones from sucking:* for one says صَرَّ بِالنَّاقَةِ as well as صَرَّ النَّاقَةَ; and in like manner, I suppose, one may say لَيْسَ بِهَا أَصِرَّةٌ: and hence, perhaps, it may mean *not having milk:* see the phrase مَا بِالنَّاقَةِ عَلُوقٌ.]) — [For the phrase اِسْتَأْصَلَ اللّٰهُ عِلْقَاتِهِمْ, see the next paragraph but one.]

عَلْقَى, (Ṣ, O, Ḳ,) like سَكْرَى, (Ḳ,) *A certain plant:* (Ṣ, O, Ḳ:) accord. to Sb, (Ṣ, O,) it is used as sing. and pl.; (Ṣ, O, Ḳ;) and its alif [written ى] is to denote the fem. gender, therefore it is without tenween: but others say that its alif is to render it quasi-coordinate [to the quadriliteral-radical class], and is with tenween, the n. un. being عَلْقَاةٌ: (Ṣ, O:) IJ says that the alif in عَلْقَاةٌ is not to denote the fem. gender, because it is followed by ة; but when they elide the ة, they say عَلْقَى, without tenween: (L, TA: [in both of which, more is added, but with some mistranscription or omission rendering it inconsistent:]) *its twigs are slender, difficult to be broken, and brooms are made of it:* (Ḳ: [but this is taken from what here follows:]) Aboo-Naṣr says, the علقى is *a tree* [or *plant*] *of which the greenness continues during the hot season, and its places of growth are the sands, and the plain,* or *soft, tracts:* and he says, an Arab of the desert showed me a plant which he asserted to be the علقى; *having long and slender twigs, and delicate leaves; called in Pers.* خُلْوَام [?]; *those who collect* [*the dung used for fuel called*] جِلَّة *make of it brooms for that purpose:* to which he adds, and it is said, on the authority of the early Arabs, that the علقاة is *a certain tree* [or *plant*] *which is found in the sands, green, having leaves, but in which is no good:* (O:) [it is said, however, that] *the decoction thereof is drunk for the dropsy.* (Ḳ.)

عِلْقَاتِهِمْ, (O, Ḳ,) like سِعْلَاتِهِمْ, (O,) in the saying اِسْتَأْصَلَ اللّٰهُ عِلْقَاتِهِمْ, (O, Ḳ,* [in the CḲ عَلْقَاتِهِمْ,]) is a dial. var. of عِرْقَاتِهِمْ, (Ḳ, [in the CḲ عَرْقَاتِهِمْ,]) [and] is said by Ibn-'Abbád to mean أَصْلَهُمْ [i. e. *May God utterly destroy their race, stock,* or *family*]: but some say that it is a pl. of العِلْقُ signifying "that which is precious, or held in high estimation:" and in one dial. it is [عِلْقَاتِهِمْ,] with kesr to the ت. (O.)

عِلْقِنَةٌ: see عَلَاقِيَةٌ.

عَلَاقٌ: see عُلْقَةٌ, in eight places.

عَلَاقِ [an imperative verbal noun], like نَزَالِ &c., (IDrd, O, Ḳ,*) means تَعَلَّقْ, (Ḳ,) or تَعَلَّقْ بِهِ [i. e. *Cling thou, cleave thou,* or *stick thou fast, to him,* or *it*]. (IDrd, O.)

عِلَاقٌ *A thing that is hung,* or *suspended,* like the عُوذَة [or amulet]. (TA voce مَعْذُورٌ as an epithet applied to a child affected with the pain of the fauces, termed عُذْرَة.)

عَلُوقٌ *A thing that clings, cleaves,* or *sticks fast,* (يَعْلَقُ, [in the CḲ تَعَلَّقُ,]) *to a man.* (Ṣ, O, Ḳ.) — And [hence,] *Death,* or the *decree of death;* syn. مَنِيَّةٌ; (Ṣ, O, Ḳ;) as also ↓ عَلَّاقَةٌ, (Ṣ, TA,) accord. to the Ḳ, erroneously, عَلَاقَة [without teshdeed]: in a verse in which it occurs, some explain العَلَّاقَة as meaning thus; and some, as meaning *the serpent,* because of its clinging. (TA.) El-Mufaḍḍal En-Nukree says,

وَقَدْ عَلِقَتْ بِثَعْلَبَةَ العَلُوقُ

[*When death, or the decree of death, had clung to Thaalebeh*]. (Ṣ, O.) The pl. of عَلُوقٌ, in this sense, and in the sense next following, as mentioned before, in the paragraph commencing with the word عُلَقٌ, is عُلُقٌ, with two dammehs. (TA. See that paragraph.) — And [hence, likewise,] *A calamity,* or *misfortune.* (O, Ḳ.) It occurs in a trad. in this sense, applied to what is termed عُذْرَة, or to the operation performed upon it. (O, TA. [See 4.]) — See also عَوْلَقٌ. — Also *Pasture upon which camels feed.* (Ṣ, O, Ḳ.) And *Trees that are eaten by the camels that have been ten months pregnant,* (O, Ḳ,) *in consequence of which they assume a red hue.* (O.) El-Aashà speaks of it [in a verse of which I find four different readings] as occasioning a redness in she-camels: but some say that he means thereby The *young in the bellies*; and by the redness, the beauty of their colour on the occasion of conceiving. (Ṣ, O.) And some say that, as used by El-Aạshà, it means The *sperma of the stallion*; a signification mentioned by AHeyth; because the she-camels become altered in colours, and red, when they conceive. (TA.) — مَا بِالنَّاقَةِ عَلُوقٌ means *There is not in the she-camel aught of milk.* (Ṣ. [And عَلَاقٌ signifies the same: see an ex. voce عُلْقَةٌ.]) = Also A she-camel *that is made to incline* (تُعْطَفُ [in the CK تَعْطِفُ]) *to a young one not her own, and will not keep to it, but only smells it with her nose, and refuses to yield her milk*; (Ṣ, O, Ḳ; [see an ex. in a verse cited in the first paragraph of art. رأم;]) as also ▼ مُعَالِقٌ: (Ṣ:) or a she-camel *that inclines to her young one, and feels it, until it becomes familiar with her, but when it desires to suck the milk from her, strikes it, and drives it away.* (Ḥam p. 206.) [Hence,] one says of him who speaks a speech with which is no deed, عَامَلَنَا مُعَامَلَةَ العَلُوقِ [*He dealt with us with the dealing of the* علوق]. (O, Ḳ.) — And A she-camel *that does not become familiar with the stallion nor affect the young one*: (Lth, O, Ḳ:) as implying a presage of good [i. e. that she will cling to both]. (TA.) — And A woman *that does not love other than her husband*: (Lth, O, Ḳ:) likewise as implying a presage of good. (TA.) — And A woman *that suckles the child of another.* (Lth, O, Ḳ.) — See also عَلِيقَةٌ. = Also *i. q.* ثُؤَبَاءُ [generally meaning *A yawning*]. (Ibn-'Abbád, O, TA.)

عُلُوقٌ [originally an inf. n.]: see عُلْقَةٌ. — One says also, لِى فِى الأَمْرِ عُلُوقٌ *There is something made obligatory to me, or in my favour, in the affair, or case*; and so ▼ مُتَعَلَّقٌ. (TA.)

عَلِيقٌ *i. q.* قَضِيمٌ, (Ṣ, MA, Ḳ, TA,) i. e. *Barley for a horse or similar beast,* (MA,) [in which sense and also as meaning *provender of beans and the like,* the former word is now used, properly, or originally,] *that is hung upon the beast* [*in a* مِخْلَاة, or *nose-bag*]: (TA:) pl. عَلَائِقُ. (MA.) — And hence, as being likened thereto, ‡ *Wine.* (TA.)

عَلَاقَةٌ [is originally an inf. n.: and as a simple subst. signifies *An attachment, a tie,* or *a connection*; as also ▼ عُلْقَةٌ, mentioned in the TA, in art. ربط, together with وُصْلَةٌ, as syn. with رَابِطَةٌ:] a word relating to things conceived in the mind; as love, and contention in an altercation: ▼ عِلَاقَةٌ relating to things extrinsic to the mind; as a bow, and a whip: (Kull p. 262:) see عَلَقٌ, last quarter. — [Hence, as denoting an attachment, or a tie,] *Love,* and *friendship*; or *such as is true,* or *sincere*; syn. حُبٌّ, and صَدَاقَةٌ: (Ḳ, TA:) [or as expl. voce عَلَقٌ, last quarter:] or it means عَلَاقَةُ حُبٍّ [*an attachment,* or *a tie,* or *a clinging, of love*]: (Ṣ, O:) Lḥ mentions, on the authority of Ks, and as known to Aṣ, the saying لَهَا فِى قَلْبِى عَلَاقَةُ حُبٍّ [i. e. *There is to her, in my heart, an attachment,* or *a tie,* or *a clinging, of love*]; and likewise, on the authority of the former, but as unknown to Aṣ, عِلَاقَةُ ▼ حُبٍّ and عِلْقُ ▼ حُبٍّ, though Aṣ knew the phrase عَلَقُ ▼ حُبٍّ: (TA:) or عَلَاقَةُ حُبٍّ means *love to which one clings.* (Mṣb.) — And *A contention in an altercation; a dispute*; or *a litigation*: (Ḳ: [see also عَلَقٌ, near the end of the paragraph:]) or it means عَلَاقَةُ خُصُومَةٍ [app. one's *connection in such a contention*]: (Ṣ, O:) or عَلَاقَةُ خُصُومَةٍ means *the proportion* [or *share*] *that one holds* [*in such a contention*; or *what pertains to one thereof*; or *one's concern therein*]: (Mṣb:) [for] — عَلَاقَةٌ also signifies *A thing upon which one has,* or *retains, a hold*; like ▼ عُلْقَةٌ in the saying كُلُّ بَيْعٍ أَبْقَى عُلْقَةً فَهُوَ بَاطِلٌ i. e. [*Every sale that leaves remaining*] *a thing upon which the seller retains a hold* [*is null*]. (Mṣb.) And one says, مَا بَيْنَهُمَا عَلَاقَةٌ, with fet-ḥ, meaning *There is not between them two anything upon which either of them has a hold against the other*: and the pl. is عَلَائِقُ. (TA.) And لِفُلَانٍ فِى هٰذَا الدَّارِ عَلَاقَةٌ [or rather هٰذِهِ الدار,] with fet-ḥ, i. e. [*There belongs to such a one, in this house, something upon which he has a hold,* or *in which he has a concern,* or] *a remaining portion of a share.* (TA.) العَلَاقَةُ مِنَ المَهْرِ means *That* [*portion,* or *amount, of the dowry,* or *nuptial gift,*] *upon which they have a hold against him who takes a woman in marriage*: (Sh, Ḳ, TA:) pl. عَلَائِقُ [as above]: (Ḳ, TA:) whence the saying, in a trad., أَدُّوا العَلَائِقَ i. e., as expl. by the Prophet, [*Pay ye*] *what their families have agreed upon*; meaning, *what attach each one of them* [*by an obligation*] *to his companion,* or *fellow, like as a thing is attached to another thing.* (TA.) And [the pl.] عَلَائِقُ likewise signifies [*Obligations of bloodwits*; or] *bloodwits that are attached to a man.* (TA.) [See also another explanation in the fourth of the sentences here following.] — Also *A work, craft, trade,* and *any other thing* [or *occupation*], *to which a man has attached himself*: (Ḳ:) or *a work* or *craft* &c. as above, or *property* and *a wife* and *a child,* or *love,* or *a contention in an altercation, pertaining to a man* (يَتَعَلَّقُ بِإِنْسَانٍ): pl. as above. (Ḥar p. 372.) — See also عُلْقَةٌ, in three places. — [The pl.] عَلَائِقُ is also expl. by Lḥ as meaning *Articles of merchandise.* (TA.) — And العَلَاقَةُ is said by Sh to signify التَّبْلُ [evidently, I think, a mistranscription for التَّبْلُ, i. e. *Blood-revenge*; or *the seeking for blood-revenge,* or *the like*; though it seems to be better rendered *the obligation of blood-revenge*; or *the obligation of a bloodwit, attaching to a man,* agreeably with an explanation given above]: and by Aboo-Naṣr to signify التَّبَاعُدُ [which I think to be a mistranscription for التَّنَاقُدُ, signifying *contention, disputation,* or *litigation,* a meaning mentioned in the former half of this paragraph]: and both of these significations are assigned to it in the saying of Imra-el-Ḳeys,

• بِأَيِّ عَلَاقَتِنَا تَرْغَبُو •
• نَ عَنْ دَمِ عَمْرٍو عَلَى مَرْثَدِ •

[as though meaning *By reason of what blood-revenge, &c., of ours do ye relinquish the claim for the blood of 'Amr resting as a debt upon Marthad?* or *What is our contention, &c.? Do ye relinquish &c.*]: the ب [in بِأَيِّ] accord. to the latter explanation being redundant. (TA. [See also De Slane's "Diwan d'Amro'lkais," p. 48, line 4, of the Ar. text. (in which the former hemistich ends with ترغبون and the latter commences with أَعَنْ); and see his translation; and a gloss in the notes, p. 126.]) = See also عَلِيقَةٌ.

عِلَاقَةٌ: see عَلَقٌ, last quarter; and عَلَاقَةٌ, first and second sentences. It signifies *The suspensory thong* or *the like,* of the knife and of other things; (Mṣb;) it is of the bow, (Ṣ, O, [see also مُعَلَّقٌ,]) and of the whip (Ṣ, Mgh, Ḳ) and the like, (Ḳ, TA,) as the sword, and the shield, and the drinking-cup or bowl, and of the book, or copy of the Ḳur-án, &c., (TA,) and of the water-skin; (M voce شِنَاقٌ;) that of the whip being the *thong that is in the handle* thereof. (TA.) See also مِعْلَاقٌ. [Also The *suspensory stalk* of a fruit.] — And *A surname,* or *by-name*; because it is attached to a man; as also ▼ عِلَاقِيَةٌ, of which the pl. is عَلَاقِى: the pl. of عِلَاقَةٌ is عَلَائِقُ. (Ḳ.)

عَلِيقَةٌ (IAạr, Ṣ, O, Ḳ) and ▼ عَلَاقَةٌ (IAạr, O, Ḳ) and ▼ عَلُوقٌ (TA) *A camel,* (IAạr, Ṣ, O, Ḳ,) or *two camels,* (IAạr, TA,) *sent by a man with a people,* or *party, in order that they may bring corn for him,* (IAạr, Ṣ, O, Ḳ,) *thereon,* (Ṣ, O, Ḳ,) *he giving them money for that purpose*: pl. عَلَائِقُ, (Ṣ, O,) which may be of the first and of the second; (O;) and (Ṣ, O) of the first, (Ṣ,) عَلِيقَاتٌ. (Ṣ, O.) [See also جَنِيبَةٌ.] — [And in the present day عَلِيقَةٌ is applied to *A nose-bag, such as is called* مِخْلَاة; i. e. *a bag that is hung to the head of a horse or the like, in which he eats barley or other fodder.*]

عِلَاقِيَةٌ A man *who, when he clings to a thing, will not quit it.* (Ṣ, O, Ḳ.) [See also عَلِقٌ.] — And نَفْسٌ عِلَاقِيَةٌ and ▼ عَلِقَةٌ *A devoted,* or *an attached, soul*; *one that clings to a thing persistently.* (L, TA.) — See also عِلَاقَةٌ.

عُلَّاقٌ *A certain plant.* (Ibn-'Abbád, Ḳ.)

عُلَّيْقٌ and ▼ عُلَّيْقَى *A certain plant that clings to trees*; (Ṣ, O, Ḳ;) sometimes called by the latter name; (Ṣ;) *in Pers. called* سَرَنْد (Ṣ, O) or سِرِنْد: (Ṣ; in one of my copies of which it is written سَرِنْد:) [agreeably with this description, the former appellation is now applied to the *convolvulus arvensis* of Linn., or *field-bindweed*: (so in Delile's Flor. Aegypt. Illustr., no. 222:) and to *a species of dolichos; dolichos nilotica; dolichos sinensis* of Forskål: and *any climbing plant*: (no. 669 in the same:) but it is also said to be applied to the *rubus fruticosus,* or *common bramble*: (Forskål's

Flor. Aegypt. Arab., p. cxiii. :) and, agreeably with what here follows, it is now often applied to the *rubus Idæus*, or *raspberry* :] accord. to AḤn, both of these appellations signify *a thorny tree* [or *shrub*], *that does not grow large, such that when a thing catches to it, it can hardly become free, by reason of the numerousness of its thorns, which are curved and sharp; and it has a fruit resembling the* فِرْصَاد [or *mulberry*], (O, TA,) *which, when it becomes ripe, blackens, and is eaten*; (O;) [see also تُوتٌ;] and it is *called in Pers.* دَرْهَمَه [?]; (O, TA;) *they assert that it is the tree in which Moses beheld the fire*; (O;) *and the places of its growth are thickets, and tracts abounding with trees*: (O, TA:) *the chewing it hardens*, or *strengthens, the gum, and cures the* [*disease in the mouth called*] قُلَاع; *and a dressing*, or *poultice, thereof cures whiteness of the eye, and the swelling*, or *protrusion, thereof, and the piles; and its root*, or *stem*, (أَصْلُهُ,) *crumbles stones in the kidney*. (Ḳ.) عُلَّيْقُ الجَبَلِ [in the CḲ النَّخْلِ] is *A certain plant*: and عُلَّيْقُ الكَلْبِ [one of the appellations now applied to The *eglantine*, or *sweet brier*, more commonly called the نِسْرِين,] is *another plant*. (Ḳ.)

عُلَّاقَةٌ: see عَلُوقٌ, second sentence.

عُلَّيْقَى: see عُلَّيْقٌ.

عَالِقٌ *Clinging, catching, cleaving, adhering, holding*, or *sticking fast*: so in the phrase هُوَ عَالِقٌ بِهِ [*He*, or *it, is clinging*, &c., *to him*, or *it*]. (TA.) —— Also A camel *plucking from the* [*tree called*] عِضَاه; (Ṣ, O;) so termed because he is [as though he were] hanging from it, (Ṣ, O, Ḳ,*) by reason of his tallness: pl. عَوَالِقُ; which is also applied to goats. (Ṣ.) And A camel *pasturing upon the plant called* عَلْقَى. (Ṣ, O, Ḳ.)

عَوْلَقٌ The [*kind of goblin, demon, devil*, or *jinnee, called*] غُول; (Ṣ, O, Ḳ;) as also ▼ عَلُوقٌ. (Ḳ.) —— And A bitch *vehemently desirous* [*of the male*]. (Ṣ, Ḳ.) —— And The *wolf*. (Ḳ. [But what here follows suggests that الذِّئْبُ in the copies of the Ḳ may be a mistranscription for الذَّنَبُ.]) —— The saying هٰذَا حَدِيثٌ طَوِيلُ العَوْلَقِ means [lit. *This narrative*, or *story, is*] *long in the tail*. (Ṣ.) Kr mentions the phrase إِنَّهُ لَطَوِيلُ العَوْلَقِ without particularizing a narrative or story, or any other thing. (TA.) —— Also ‡ *Hunger*: (Ḳ, TA:) like عَوْلَقٌ. (O in art. عوق.)

أَعَالِيقُ a pl. having no sing.: see مِعْلَاقٌ.

[تَعَلُّقَاتٌ and ▼ مُتَعَلَّقَاتٌ are post-classical terms often used as meaning *Dependencies*, or *appertenances*, of a thing or person: *circumstances* of a case: and *concerns* of a man.]

تَعْلِيقٌ: see the next paragraph.

[تَعْلِيقَةٌ a post-classical term, sing. of تَعَالِيقُ signifying *Coins*, and *the like, suspended to women's ornaments*. See also مِعْلَاقٌ. —— Also *An appendix* to a book or writing: and hence, *a tract*, or *treatise*; properly *such as is intended by its author to serve as a supplement to what has been written by another or others on the same subject*; as also ▼ تَعْلِيقٌ: and, more commonly, *a marginal note*: pl. تَعَالِيقُ and تَعْلِيقَاتٌ.]

مَعْلَقٌ, and its pl. (مَعَالِقُ): see 1, in four places.

مُعْلَقٌ *A small* عُلْبَة [or *milking-vessel*]: (Ṣ, O, TA:) next is the جَنْبَة, larger than it: then, the حَوْبَة, the largest of these: the مُعْلَق is the best of these, and is *a drinking-cup*, or *bowl, which the rider upon a camel hangs with him* [*upon his saddle*]: (TA:) pl. مَعَالِقُ. (Ṣ, O, TA.) [See an ex. voce شَرْبَةٌ.]

رَجُلٌ ذُو مَعْلَقَةٍ *A man who attacks and plunders*, (O,) *who clings to everything that he finds*, or *attains*, or *obtains*. (O, Ḳ.)

مِعْلَقَةٌ *One of the implements*, or *utensils, of the pastor* [probably *a thing upon which he hangs his provision-bag* &c.]. (Lḥ, TA.)

مُعَلَّقٌ [pass. part. n. of 2, *Hung*, or *suspended*, &c.: see its verb. —— Hence, السَّبْعُ or المُعَلَّقَاتُ السَّبْعُ المُعَلَّقَاتُ *The seven suspended* odes; accord. to several writers: two reasons for their being thus called are mentioned in the Mz (49th نوع); one, that "they were selected from all the poetry, and written upon قَبَاطِيّ (pieces of fine white cloth of Egypt) with water-gold, and suspended upon the Kaạbeh;" the other, that "when an ode was deemed excellent, the King used to say, 'Suspend ye for us this,' that it might be in his repository:" that these odes were selected from all the poetry, and that any copies of them were suspended collectively upon the Kaạbeh, has been sufficiently confuted in Nöldeke's "Beiträge zur Kenntniss der Poesie der alten Araber," pp. xvii.—xxiii.: it is not so unreasonable to suppose that they may have been suspended upon the Kaạbeh singly, at different times, by their own authors or by admiring friends, and suffered to remain thus placarded for some days, perhaps during the period when the city was most thronged by pilgrims; but the latter of the two assertions in the Mz seems to be more probable. —— Hence also مُعَلَّقُ القَوْسِ *The appendage of the bow, by which it is suspended*: see نِيَاطٌ and وَتَرٌ: and see also عِلَاقَةٌ.] —— مُعَلَّقَةٌ applied to a woman means One *whose husband has been lost* [*to her*]: (Ṣ, TA:) or [*left in suspense*;] *neither husbandless nor having a husband*; (O;) [i. e.] *whose husband does not act equitably with her nor release her, so that she is neither husbandless nor having a husband*; (Az, TA;) or *neither having a husband nor divorced*. (Mṣb.) It occurs in the Ḳur iv. 128. (Ṣ, TA.) —— And one says of a man when he does not decide, or determine upon, his affair, nor relinquish it, أَمْرُهُ مُعَلَّقٌ [*His affair is left in suspense*]. (Z, TA.)

مِعْلَاقٌ The *thing by means of which flesh-meat*, (Ṣ, Mgh, O, Mṣb,) and *other things*, (Mgh, Mṣb,) or *grapes*, and *the like*, (Ṣ, O,) *are suspended*; (Ṣ, Mgh, O, Mṣb;) as also ▼ مُعْلُوقٌ: (Ṣ, O:) and *anything by means of which a thing is suspended* (Ṣ, O, Ḳ) is called its مِعْلَاق, (Ṣ, O,) or is called مِعْلَاق and ▼ مُعْلُوق, (Ḳ,) which latter is a word of a rare form: (TA:) and ▼ عِلَاقَةٌ likewise signifies the مِعْلَاق *by means of which a vessel is suspended*: (TA:) pl. of the first [and of the second] مَعَالِيقُ. (Mgh, Mṣb.) Also *A stirrup-leather*: pl. as above. (MA.) And المِعْلَاقَانِ signifies مِعْلَاقَا الدَّلْوِ وَشِبْهِهَا [app. meaning *The two suspensory cords of the leathern bucket and of the like thereof*]. (IDrd, O, Ḳ: but the CḲ, for مِعْلَاقَا, has مِعْلَاق: and the O has وَمَا أَشْبَهَهَا in the place of وَشِبْهِهَا [which means the same].) —— Also *A thing suspended to a beast of burden*; *such as the* قِرْبَة *and the* مِطْهَرَة *and the* قُمْقُمَة: pl. as above. (Mgh, Mṣb: but in the former, only the pl. of معلاق in this sense is mentioned.) —— [And *A pendant* of a necklace and of an ear-ring and the like; in which sense its pl. is expl. as follows:] the مَعَالِيق of necklaces (O, TA) and of [the ear-rings or ear-drops called] شُنُوف (TA) are *what are put therein* or *thereto*, [meaning *suspended thereto*,] *of anything that is beautiful*; (O,* TA;) and ▼ الأَعَالِيقُ, which has no sing., is like المَعَالِيقُ, each of them signifying *what are suspended*. (TA.) [See also شَنْفٌ.] —— مِعْلَاقُ البَابِ [means *A kind of latch*, or *sliding bolt*;] *a thing that is suspended*, or *attached, to the door, and is then pushed, whereupon it* [i. e. *the door*] *opens*; different from the مِغْلَاق, with the pointed غ. (TA.) One says, مَا لِبَابِهِ مِغْلَاقٌ وَلَا مِعْلَاقٌ i. e. [*There is not to his door*] *a thing that is opened with a key nor* [*a thing that is opened*] *without it*. (A, TA.) —— مِعْلَاقٌ also signifies The *tongue* (O, Ḳ) of a man: (O:) or *an eloquent tongue*. (TA.) —— And رَجُلٌ ذُو مِعْلَاقٍ *A man whose antagonist, when he clings to him, will not* [*be able to*] *free himself from him*: (Mbr, Z, TA:) or *a man vehement in altercation* or *dispute* or *litigation*, (IDrd, Ṣ, O, Ḳ,) *who clings to arguments*, or *pleas*, (IDrd, O, Ḳ,) *and supplies them*; (IDrd, O;) and رَجُلٌ مِعْلَاقٌ signifies the same. (IDrd, O, Ḳ.) —— And [the pl.] مَعَالِيقُ signifies *A sort* [or *variety*] *of palm-trees*. (IDrd, O, Ḳ.)

مَعْلُوقٌ One *to whose fauces leeches have clung* (Lth, O, Ḳ) *on the occasion of his drinking water*; (Lth, O;) applied to a man and to a beast. (TA.) —— And *A suspended cluster*, or *bunch, of grapes* or *dates*. (MA.)

مُعْلُوقٌ: see مِعْلَاقٌ, first sentence, in two places.

مُعَالِقٌ: see عَلُوقٌ, latter half.

مُتَعَلِّقٌ: see عُلْقَةٌ, in two places: —— and see also عَلُوقٌ.

مُتَعَلَّقَاتٌ: see تَعَلُّقَاتٌ. —— لَيْسَ المُتَعَلِّقُ كَالمُتَأَنِّقِ means *He who is content with what is little is not like him who seeks, pursues*, or *desires, the most pleasing of things*, or *who is dainty*, (مَنْ

يَتَأَنَّقُ,) *and eats what he pleases.* (Ṣ, O, Ḳ.) [See also مُتَأَنِّق.]

علقم

Q. 1. عَلْقَمَ, [inf. n. عَلْقَمَةٌ,] said of the colocynth, *It attained its utmost degree of bitterness.* (Ḥam p. 166.) —— عَلْقَمَ طَعَامَهُ, (TA,) inf. n. as above, (Ḳ, TA,) *He made his food bitter;* (TA;) or *put something bitter into it.* (Ḳ.)

عَلْقَمٌ *A species of bitter tree or plant.* (Ṣ, TA.) — And it is applied to, (Ṣ,) or is said to be, (Mṣb, TA,) *The colocynth:* (Ṣ, Mṣb, Ḳ, TA:) or *the pulp of the colocynth:* (Az, TA:) or *the colocynth when intensely bitter:* (Ḥam p. 509:) or, as some say, قِثَّآءُ الحِمَارِ [a name now applied to the *elaterium;* the *wild,* or *squirting, cucumber*]. (Mṣb.) Hence one says of anything in which is intense bitterness, كَأَنَّهُ العَلْقَمُ [*As though it were colocynth,* or *the pulp of colocynth,* &c.]. (Az, TA.) — And *Anything bitter.* (Ṣ, Mṣb, Ḳ.) — Also *A bitter* نَبِقَة [or *drupe of the species of lote-tree called* سِدْر]: (Ḳ:) or so † عَلْقَمَةٌ: mentioned by IAạr. (TA.) — And The *bitterest of water:* (Ḳ:) or so † عَلْقَمَةٌ: mentioned by IAạr. (TA.)

عَلْقَمَةٌ *Bitterness.* (Ḳ. [Originally an inf. n.: see Q. 1.]) — And *A mixed and turbid state of water.* (IDrd, TA.) — See also عَلْقَمٌ, last two sentences.

علك

1. عَلَكَهُ, (Ṣ, Mṣb, Ḳ,) aor. ُ (Mṣb, Ḳ) and ِ, (Ḳ,) inf. n. عَلْكٌ, (Mṣb,) *He chewed it;* (Ṣ, Mṣb, Ḳ;) and *moved it backwards and forwards in his mouth, to chew it.* (Ḳ.) —— عَلَكَ اللِّجَامَ, (Ṣ, O, Mṣb, Ḳ,) aor. ُ, (Ṣ,) or ِ, (O,) *He* (a horse) *chewed,* or *champed, the bit,* (Ṣ, O, Mṣb,) or *moved it about,* (Ḳ,) *in his mouth;* (Ṣ, O, Ḳ;) like أَلَكَهُ. (ISd and Ḳ in art. الك.) — And عَلَكَ نَابَيْهِ *He ground,* or *grated, his canine teeth, one with the other, so that a sound was produced.* (Ḳ.) — عَلَكَتْ عَجِينَتَهَا *She kneaded well her dough.* (TA.)

2. عَلَّكَ القِرْبَةَ, (Ḳ,) inf. n. تَعْلِيكٌ, (O, Ḳ,) *He tanned well the water-skin:* (O, Ḳ:) mentioned by AḤn (TA) and Ibn-'Abbád (O, TA) and Z. (TA.) — عَلَّكَ مَالَهُ *He tended,* or *managed, well, his cattle,* or *property.* (O, Ḳ, TA.) — And عَلَّكَ يَدَيْهِ عَلَى مَالِهِ *He tightened his hands upon his property, from niggardliness,* (Ḳ, TA,) *not entertaining a guest nor giving to a petitioner or beggar.* (TA.)

5. مَا تَعَلَّكْتُ بِعَلُوكٍ [*I have not occupied myself in chewing with anything that is chewed;* or] *I have not tasted anything;* and so مَا تَأَلَّكْتُ بِأَلُوكٍ and مَا تَعَلَّجْتُ بِعَلُوجٍ. (O in art. علج.)

R. Q. 3. اِعْلَنْكَكَ الشَّعْرُ *The hair was,* or *became, intensely black,* (اِحْلَنْكَكَ, Ṣ,) or *abundant,* (Ḳ,) *and collected together.* (Ṣ, Ḳ.)

عِلْكٌ [*Resin;*] *a certain thing that is chewed;* (Ṣ, O;) the صَمْغ [meaning *resin*] *of the* صَنَوْبَر and *of the* أَرْزَة and *of the* فُسْتُق and *of the* سَرْو and *of the* يَنْبُوت and *of the* بُطْم; the last of which is the best of these; (Ḳ, TA;) *like* لُبَان [or *frankincense*], *which is chewed and is not thereby liquefied;* (TA;) *heating, diuretic, and strengthening to the venereal faculty;* (Ḳ, TA;) *any* صَمْغ [or *resin*] *that is chewed, consisting of frankincense* (لُبَان) and *of other sorts, and that does not flow* [*in consequence of its being chewed*]: (Mṣb:) pl. [of mult.] عُلُوكٌ (Mṣb, Ḳ) and [of pauc.] أَعْلَاكٌ. (Mṣb, TA.)

عَلَكٌ and † عَلَاكٌ (O, Ḳ) and † عُلَاكٌ (accord. to some copies of the Ḳ, but not in the O nor in the TA,) *A tree of El-Ḥijáz:* (Ḳ:) or *a species of trees growing in the region of El-Ḥijáz:* AḤn says, the عَلَك are certain trees, of the characteristics of which I have not heard a description. (O.)

عَلِكٌ Food *tough,* or *hard to chew;* (O, Ḳ;) as also † عَالِكٌ. (Ḳ.) [And] *A viscous, glutinous, cohesive, sticky, ropy,* or *slimy,* thing. (Ṣ.) — طِينَةٌ عَلِكَةٌ *A piece,* or *portion, of clay* or *earth, green,* or *of a dark* or *an ashy dust-colour,* (خَضْرَآءُ,) *and soft,* (O, TA,) *in which is no sand.* (TA.) — And أَرْضٌ عَلِكَةٌ *Land near to water.* (O, Ḳ.)

عَلِكَةٌ *A fat and goodly she-camel.* (Ḳ.)

عَلَكَةٌ The شِقْشِقَة [or *faucial bag*] *of the camel, when he brays:* (O, Ḳ:) pl. عَلَكَاتٌ. (O.) — And the latter, (عَلَكَاتٌ,) *Strong canine teeth:* (Ḳ:) this is said by some to be its meaning in a verse of Ru-beh. (O.)

عَلَاكٌ: see عُلَاكٌ: —— and see also عَلَكٌ.

عُلَاكٌ *A thing that is chewed;* as also † عَلَاكٌ [and † عَلُوكٌ (see 5)]: so in the saying مَا ذَاقَ عُلَاكًا and عَلَاكًا [and عَلُوكًا, i. e. *He tasted not a thing that is chewed;* meaning, *anything*]. (Ḳ, TA.) —— See also عَلَكٌ.

عَلُوكٌ: see the next preceding paragraph: and see also أَلُوكٌ.

عُلَاكِمَةٌ i. q. عُرَاكِمَةٌ [q. v.]. (TA in art. عرك.)

عَلَّاكٌ *A seller of* عِلْك [or *resin*]. (Ḳ.)

عَالِكٌ [act. part. n. of 1; *Chewing;* &c.]. — [The pl.] عَوَالِكُ is applied by Ru-beh to bitted mares [as meaning *Chewing,* or *champing the bits*]. (O.) — See also عَلِكٌ.

عَوْلَكٌ *A stammering,* or *stuttering,* (لَجْلَجَةٌ,) *in the tongue:* (Ḳ:) [or, app., *an action, in the tongue, like chewing:* for it is said that] فِى لِسَانِهِ عَوْلَكٌ means يَعْلُكُهُ and يَمْضُغُهُ [i. e., app., *He chews his tongue* in speaking]. (O, from Ibn-'Abbád.) —— Also *A certain vein* (Ṣ, O, Ḳ) *in the* رَحِم [app. here meaning, as in many other instances, the *vulva*]; accord. to El-'Adebbes El-Kinánee, (Ṣ, O,) *in mares* and *she-asses* and *ewes* or *she-goats, in the* بُظَارَة [q. v.], *unapparent,* (Ṣ, O, Ḳ,) *in the interior thereof:* (Ṣ, O:) the بظارة is between the two sides of the vulva: (TA:) pl. عَوَالِكُ. (Ṣ, O.) Accord. to Ibn-Abbád, i. q. بَظْرٌ [q. v.]. (O.)

مِعْلَاكٌ *A thing like an arrow, which is shot.* (IB, TA.)

علم

1. عَلِمَهُ, aor. َ, inf. n. عِلْمٌ, *He knew it;* or *he was,* or *became, acquainted with it;* syn. عَرَفَهُ: (Ṣ, Ḳ:) or *he knew it* (عَرَفَهُ) *truly,* or *certainly:* (B, TA:) by what is said above, and by what is afterwards said in the Ḳ, العِلْمُ and المَعْرِفَةُ and الشُّعُورُ are made to have one meaning; and this is nearly what is said by most of the lexicologists: but most of the critics discriminate every one of these from the others; and العِلْمُ, accord. to them, denotes the highest quality, because it is that which they allow to be an attribute of God; whereas they did not say [that He is] عَارِفٌ, in the most correct language, nor شَاعِرٌ: (TA:) [respecting other differences between العلم and المعرفة, the former of which is more general in signification than the latter, see the first paragraph of art. عرف: much might be added to what is there stated on that subject, and in explanation of العلم, from the TA, but not without controversy:] or عَلِمَ signifies تَيَقَّنَ [i. e. *he knew* a thing, *intuitively,* and *inferentially,* as expl. in the Mṣb in art. يقن]; العِلْمُ being syn. with اليَقِينُ; but it occurs with the meaning of المَعْرِفَةُ, like as المَعْرِفَةُ occurs with the meaning of العِلْمُ, each being made to import the meaning of the other because each is preceded by ignorance [when not attributed to God]: Zuheyr says, [in his Mo'allaḳah,]

* وَأَعْلَمُ عِلْمَ اليَوْمِ وَالأَمْسِ قَبْلَهُ *

* وَلٰكِنَّنِى عَنْ عِلْمِ مَا فِى غَدٍ عَمِ *

meaning وَأَعْرِفُ [i. e. *And I know the knowledge of the present day, and of yesterday before it; but to the knowledge of what will be to-morrow I am blind*]: and it is said in the Ḳur [viii. 62], لَا تَعْلَمُونَهُمُ اللّٰهُ يَعْلَمُهُمْ, meaning لَا تَعْرِفُونَهُمُ اللّٰهُ يَعْرِفُهُمْ [i. e. *Ye know them not,* but *God knoweth them*]; المَعْرِفَةُ being attributed to God because it is one of the two kinds of عِلْم, [the intuitive and the inferential,] and the discrimination between them is conventional, on account of their different dependencies, though He is declared to be free from the imputation of antecedent ignorance and from acquisition [of knowledge], for He knows what has been and what will be and how that which will not be would be if it were, his عِلْم being an eternal and essential attribute: when عَلِمَ denotes اليَقِين, it [sometimes] has two objective complements; but as syn. with عَرَفَ, it has a single objective complement: (Mṣb:) it has two objective complements in the saying, in the Ḳur [lx. 10], فَإِنْ عَلِمْتُمُوهُنَّ مُؤْمِنَاتٍ [*And if ye know them to be believers*]; and [in like manner] they allowed one's saying عَلِمْتُنِى [meaning *I knew myself to be*], like as they said رَأَيْتُنِى and حَسِبْتُنِى &c.: (TA:) and sometimes it imports the meaning of شَعَرَ, and is therefore followed by بِ: (Mṣb:) [thus] عَلِمَ بِهِ signifies شَعَرَ or شَعُرَ (accord. to different copies of the Ḳ) [i. e. *He knew it*; as meaning *he knew*, or *had knowledge, of it*; *was cognizant of it*; or *understood it*: or *he knew the minute particulars of it*: or *he perceived it by means of any of the senses*: and sometimes this means *he became informed*, or *apprised, of it*: and sometimes, *he was*, or *became, knowing in it*]: or in this case, [as meaning شَعَرْتُ بِهِ,] you say, عَلِمْتُ بِهِ and عَلِمْتُهُ [*I knew it*; &c.]: (Mṣb:) and one says, مَا عَلِمْتُ بِخَبَرِ قُدُومِهِ, meaning مَا شَعَرْتُ [*I knew not*, &c., *the tidings of his coming*, or *arrival*]. (TA.) ▼ اعتلمهُ, also, signifies عَلِمَهُ [*He knew it*; &c.]. (Ḳ.) And one says ▼ تَعَلَّمْ in the place of اِعْلَمْ [*Know thou*; &c.]: ISk says, تَعَلَّمْتُ أَنَّ فُلَانًا خَارِجٌ is a phrase used in the place of عَلِمْتُ [as meaning *I know*, or, emphatically, *I know, that such a one was*, or *is, going forth*]; adding, [however,] when it is said to thee, اِعْلَمْ أَنَّ زَيْدًا خَارِجٌ [*Know thou that Zeyd is going forth*], thou sayest قَدْ عَلِمْتُ [lit. *I have known*, meaning *I do know*]; but when it is said, تَعَلَّمْ أَنَّ زَيْدًا خَارِجٌ, thou dost not say, قَدْ تَعَلَّمْتُ; (Ṣ:) accord. to IB, these two verbs are not used as syn. except in the imperative forms: (TA:) [or] عَلِمَ الأَمْرَ and ▼ تَعَلَّمَهُ are syn. as signifying أَتْقَنَهُ [app. meaning *he knew*, or *learned*, *the case*, or *affair*, *soundly*, *thoroughly*, or *well*: see art. تقن: but I think it not improbable, though I do not find it in any copy of the Ḳ, that the right reading may be أَيْقَنَهُ, which is syn. with تَيَقَّنَهُ; an explanation of عَلِمَ in the Mṣb, as mentioned above, being تَيَقَّنَ]. (Ḳ, TA.) And ▼ تعالمهُ الجَمِيعُ means عَلِمُوهُ [i. e. *All knew him*; &c.]. (Ṣ, Ḳ.) —— عَلِمْتُ عِلْمَهُ [lit. *I knew his knowledge*, or *what he knew*, app. meaning *I tried, proved*, or *tested, him, and so knew what he knew*; and hence *I knew his case or state or condition, or his qualities*;] is a phrase mentioned by Fr in explanation of رَبَأْتُ فِيهِ. (TA voce رَبَأَ, q. v. See also the explanation of لَأَخْبُرَنَّ خُبْرَكَ, in the first paragraph of art. خبر: and see خَبَنُوا خَبْرَهَا, in art. خبن.) —— عَلِمْتُ is also used in the manner of a verb signifying swearing, or asseveration, so as to have a similar complement; as in the saying,

* وَلَقَدْ عَلِمْتُ لَتَأْتِيَنَّ عَشِيَّةً *

[*And I certainly knew that thou wouldst*, or *that she would, assuredly come in the evening*]. (TA in art. شهد.) And يَعْلَمُ اللّٰهُ [*God knoweth*] is a form of asseveration. (IAth, TA voce قَيْرَوَان: see an ex. in art. قير.) —— عَلِمَ, agreeably with what is said in the M, which is عَلِمَ هُوَ نَفْسُهُ, accord. to the Ḳ عَلِمَ هُوَ فِى نَفْسِهِ, but the verb in this case is correctly like كَرُمَ, (TA,) *He was*, or *became, such as is termed* عَالِم and عَلِيم; (M,* Ḳ,* TA;) meaning *he possessed knowledge* (العِلْم) *as a faculty firmly rooted in his mind*: (IJ,* TA:) accord. to IB, *i. q.* ▼ تعلّم [q. v., as intrans.]: and *he was*, or *became, equal to the* عُلَمَآء [pl. of عَالِم and of عَلِيم]. (TA.) —— عَالَمَهُ فَعَلَمَهُ, aor. ـُ: see 3. —— عَلَمَهُ, aor. ـُ and ـِ, (Ḳ,) inf. n. عَلْمٌ, (TA,) signifies *He marked it*; syn. وَسَمَهُ. (Ḳ.) And one says, عَلَمْتُ عِمَّتِى, meaning *I wound my turban upon my head with a mark whereby its mode should be known*. (TA.) [See also 4.] —— عَلَمَ شَفَتَهُ, aor. ـِ, (Ṣ, Ḳ,) inf. n. عَلْمٌ, (Ṣ,) *He slit his* [upper] *lip*. (Ṣ, Ḳ.) —— عَلِمَ, aor. ـَ, (Ṣ, Mṣb, Ḳ,) inf. n. عَلَمٌ, (Ṣ, Mṣb,) *He* (a man, Ṣ) *had a fissure in his upper lip*: (Ṣ, Mṣb, Ḳ:) or *in one of its two sides*. (Ḳ.)

2. عَلَّمَهُ [*He*, or *it, made him to be such as is termed* عَالِم *and* عَلِيم; i. e., *made him to possess knowledge* (العِلْم) *as a faculty firmly rooted in his mind*: and hence, *he taught him*. And it generally has a second objective complement]. You say, عَلَّمْتُهُ الشَّىْءَ [*I made him to know*, or *taught him, the thing*], in which case the teshdeed is [said to be] not for the purpose of denoting muchness [of the action; but see what follows]; (Ṣ;) and عَلَّمْتُهُ الفَاتِحَةَ [*I taught him the Opening Chapter of the Ḳur-án*], and الصَّنْعَةَ [*the art*, or *craft*], &c.; inf. n. تَعْلِيمٌ; (Mṣb;) and عَلَّمَهُ العِلْمَ, inf. n. تَعْلِيمٌ and عِلَّامٌ, the latter like كِذَّابٌ; and ▼ اعلمهُ إِيَّاهُ; (Ḳ;) both, accord. to the Ḳ, signifying the same [i. e. *he taught him knowledge*, or *science*]; but Sb makes a distinction between them, saying that عَلَّمْتُ is like أَذَّنْتُ, and that ▼ أَعْلَمْتُ is like آذَنْتُ; and Er-Rághib says that ▼ الإِعْلَامُ is particularly applied to quick information; and التَّعْلِيمُ is particularly applied to that which is repeated and much, so that an impression is produced thereby upon the mind of the مُتَعَلِّم: and some say that the latter is *the exciting the attention of the mind to the conception of meanings*; and sometimes it is used in the sense of الإِعْلَام when there is in it muchness: (TA:) you say, ▼ أَعْلَمْتُهُ الخَبَرَ and بِالخَبَرِ [meaning *I made known*, or *notified*, or *announced, to him*, or *I told him*, or *I made him to know*, or *have knowledge of, the news*, or *piece of information*; *I acquainted him with it*; *told, informed, apprised, advertised*, or *certified, him of it*; *gave him information, intelligence, notice*, or *advice, of it*]: (Mṣb:) see also 10: [hence the inf. n. ▼ إِعْلَامٌ is often used, as a simple subst., to signify *a notification, a notice, an announcement*, or *an advertisement*:] and sometimes ▼ اعلم has three objective complements, like أَرَى; as in the saying, أَعْلَمْتُ زَيْدًا عَمْرًا مُنْطَلِقًا [*I made known*, &c., *to Zeyd that 'Amr was going away*]. (IAḳ p. 117.) —— See also 4, in three places.

3. ▼ عَالَمَهُ فَعَلَمَهُ, aor. of the latter ـُ, means [*I contended with him*, or *strove to surpass him, in* عِلْم,] *and I surpassed him in* عِلْم [i. e. *knowledge*, &c.]: (Ṣ, Ḳ:) [the measure يَفْعُلُ,] and in like manner the measure يَفْعِلُ, in every case of this kind, is changed into يَفْعُلُ: so says Az: [but see 3 in art. خصم:] and Lḥ mentions the phrase, مَا كُنْتُ أَرَانِى أَنْ أَعْلُمَهُ [*I did not think*, or *know, that I should surpass him in knowledge*]. (TA.)

4: see 2, in six places. —— One says also, اعلم الثَّوْبَ (Ṣ, Mgh, TA) *He* (i. e. a beater and washer and whitener of clothes, Ṣ, Mgh) *made the garment*, or *piece of cloth, to have a mark*; (Mgh;) or *he made upon it*, or *in it, a mark*. (TA.) [And, said of a weaver, or an embroiderer,] *He made to the garment*, or *piece of cloth, a border*, or *borders, of figured*, or *variegated*, or *embroidered, work*, or *the like*. (Mṣb.) —— And اعلم عَلَيْهِ *He made*, or *put*, or *set, a mark upon it*; namely, a writing, or book, &c.: (Mṣb:) [or] اعلم عَلَى مَوْضِعِ كَذَا مِنَ الكِتَابِ عَلَامَةً [*He made*, &c., *a mark upon such a place of the writing*, or *book*]. (TA.) —— اعلم الفَرَسَ *He suspended upon the horse some coloured wool*, (Ḳ, TA,) *red*, or *white*, (TA,) *in war*, or *battle*. (Ḳ, TA.) And اعلم نَفْسَهُ *He marked himself with the mark, sign, token*, or *badge, of war*; as also ▼ عَلَّمَهَا. (Ḳ.) [Or] اعلم الفَارِسُ *The horseman made*, or *appointed, for himself*, [or *distinguished himself by*,] *the mark, sign, token*, or *badge, of the men of courage*. (Ṣ.) And ▼ عَلَّمْتُ لَهُ عَلَامَةً *I appointed to him* (وَضَعْتُ لَهُ) *a mark, sign*, or *token, which he would*, or *should, know*. (Mṣb.) —— And ▼ عَلَّمَ القَبْرَ (Ḳ in art. وجر) *He put a tombstone* [*as a mark*] *to the grave*. (TḲ in that art.) —— اعلم said of a well-sinker, *He found the well that he was digging to be one having much water*. (TA.)

5. تعلّم is quasi-pass. of 2 [i. e. it signifies *He was*, or *became, made to know*, or *taught*; or *he learned*: and is trans. and intrans.]. (Ṣ, Mṣb, Ḳ,* TA.) You say, تعلّم العِلْمَ (MA, Ḳ) *He learned* [*knowledge*, or *science*]. (MA.) See also 1, latter half, in three places. [In the last of those places, تعلّم app. signifies, as it often does, *He possessed knowledge as a faculty firmly rooted in his mind*.] Accord. to some, التَّعَلُّمُ signifies *The mind's having its attention excited to the conception of meanings*, or *ideas*. (TA.)

6. تَعَالَمَهُ الجَمِيعُ: see 1, latter half.

8. اعتلمهُ: see 1, latter half. —— اعتلم said of water, *It flowed* (Ḳ, TA) *upon the ground*. (TA.) —— And said of lightning it means لَمَعَ فِى العلم [app. فِى العَلَمِ, and, if so, meaning *It shone, shone brightly*, or *gleamed, in*, or *upon, the long mountain*]: a poet says,

* بَلْ بُرَيْقًا بِتُّ أَرْقُبُهُ *
* لَا يُرَى إِلَّا إِذَا اعْتَلَمَا *

[*But a little lightning, in watching which I passed*

the night, not to be seen save when it shone, &c.]. (TA.)

10. استعلمهُ *He asked*, or *desired, him to tell him* [a thing; or *to make* it *known to him*]. (MA, KL.*) You say, استعلمنى الخَبَرَ فَأَعْلَمْتُهُ ▼ إِيَّاهُ [*He asked*, or *desired, me to tell him*, or *make known to him, the news*, or *piece of information, and I told him it*, or *made it known to him*]. (Ṣ.)

عَلْمٌ : see مَعْلَمٌ, in two places.

عِلْمٌ is an inf. n., (Ṣ, Ḳ, &c.,) and [as such] has no pl. [in the classical language]. (Sb, TA voce فِكْر.) [As a post-classical term, used as a simple subst., its pl. is عُلُومٌ, signifying The *sciences*, or *several species of knowledge*.] — Sometimes it is applied to *Predominant opinion*; [i. e. *preponderant belief*;] because it stands in stead of that which is عِلْم properly so termed. (Ḥam p. 632.) — And sometimes it is used in the sense of عَمَلٌ [*A doing*, &c.], as mentioned by Az, on the authority of Ibn-'Oyeyneh, agreeably with an explanation of عَالِمٌ as signifying one "who does according to his knowledge;" and it has been expl. as having this meaning in the Ḳur xii. 68 [where the primary meaning seems to be much more apposite]. (TA.) — لَقِيتُهُ أَدْنَى عِلْمٍ means [*I met him the first thing*, like لقيته أَدْنَى دَنِىٍّ and أَدْنَى دَنًا; or] *before everything* [*else*]. (TA.)

عَلَمٌ : see عَلَامَةٌ. — Also *An impression*, or *impress*; or *a footstep*, or *track*, or *trace*. (TA.) — And The عَلَم of a garment, or piece of cloth; (Ṣ;) [i. e. the *ornamental*, or *figured*, or *variegated, border* or *borders* thereof;] the *figured*, or *variegated*, or *embroidered, work* or *decoration*, (Mṣb, Ḳ, TA,) *in the borders*, (TA,) thereof: (Mṣb, Ḳ, TA:) pl. أَعْلَامٌ. (Mṣb.) — And [*A way-mark*; i. e.] *a thing set up*, or *erected, in the way*, (Ḳ, TA,) or, as in the M, *in the deserts*, or *waterless deserts*, (TA,) *for guidance*, (Ḳ, TA,) in the M, *for the guidance of those going astray*; (TA;) as also ▼ عَلَامَةٌ: (Ḳ:) the former is also applied to *a building raised in the beaten track of the road, of such as are places of alighting for travellers, whereby one is guided to the land* [*that is the object of a journey*]: pl. أَعْلَامٌ: and عَلَمٌ also signifies *a* مَنَارَة [app. a mistranscription for مَنَار, without ة: see these two words]. (TA. [See also مَعْلَمٌ.]) [Hence, أَعْلَامُ الكَوَاكِبِ *The stars*, or *asterisms, that are signs of the way to travellers*: see مِصْبَاحٌ.] — And *A separation between two lands*; [like مَنَارٌ;] as also ▼ عَلَامَةٌ. (Ḳ.) [Hence,] أَعْلَامُ الحَرَمِ *The limits that are set to the Sacred Territory.* (TA.) — And *A mountain*; (Ṣ, Ḳ;) as a general term: or *a long mountain*: (Ḳ:) [app. as forming a separation: or as being a known sign of the way:] pl. أَعْلَامٌ and عِلَامٌ: (Ḳ:) the former pl. occurring in the Ḳur [xlii. 31 and] lv. 24. (TA.) — And *A banner*, or *standard*, syn. رَايَةٌ, (Ṣ, Ḳ, TA,) *to which the soldiers congregate*: (TA:) and, (Ḳ,) some say, (TA,) the *thing* [i. e. *flag*, or *strip of cloth*,] *that is tied upon the spear*: (Ḳ, TA:) it occurs in a verse of Aboo-Ṣakhr El-Hudhalee with the second fet-ḥah lengthened by an alif after it [so that it becomes ▼ عَلَامٌ]. (IJ, TA.) — And ‡ The *chief of a people* or *party*: (Ḳ, TA:) from the same word as signifying "a mountain" or "a banner:" (TA:) pl. أَعْلَامٌ. (Ḳ.) — [In grammar, it signifies *A proper name* of a person or place &c. — And the pl. أَعْلَامٌ is applied to *Things pertaining to rites and ceremonies* of the pilgrimage or the like, *as being signs* thereof; such as the *places where such rites and ceremonies are performed*, the *beasts destined for sacrifice*, and the *various practices performed during the pilgrimage &c.*; as also مَعَالِمُ, pl. of ▼ مَعْلَمٌ: the former word is applied to such places in the Ksh and Bḍ and the Jel in ii. 153; and the latter, in the Ksh and Bḍ in ii. 194: the former is also applied to the beasts destined for sacrifice in the Ksh and Bḍ and the Jel in xxii. 37; and the latter, in the Ksh and Bḍ in xxii. 33: and both are applied to the practices above mentioned, the former in the TA and the latter in the Ḳ, in art. شعر: see شِعَارٌ.] — See also what next follows.

عَلْمَةٌ and ▼ عَلَمَةٌ and ▼ عَلَمٌ [the last of which is originally an inf. n., see 1, last sentence,] *A fissure in the upper lip*, or *in one of its two sides*. (Ḳ.)

عَلَمَةٌ : see what next precedes.

عَلْمَآءُ fem. of أَعْلَمُ [q. v.].

عَلْمَآءِ in the saying عَلْمَآءِ بَنُو فُلَانٍ [meaning *At the water are the sons of such a one*] is a contraction of عَلَى المَآءِ. (Ṣ.)

[عِلْمِىٌّ *Of*, or *relating to, knowledge* or *science*; *scientific*; *theoretical*; opposed to عَمَلِىٌّ.]

[عَلَمِيَّةٌ, in grammar, The *quality of a proper name*.]

عَلَامٌ : see عَلَامَةٌ: — and see also عَلَمٌ. — [عَلَامَ is for عَلَى مَ.]

عُلَامٌ : see عُلَّامٌ. — Also *i. q.* غُلَامٌ [q. v.]: an instance of the substitution of ع for غ. (MF and TA on the letter ع.)

عَلِيمٌ : see عَالِمٌ. — العَلِيمُ and ▼ العَالِمُ and ▼ العَلَّامُ, as epithets applied to God, signify [*The Omniscient*;] *He who knows what has been and what will be*; *who ever has known, and ever will know, what has been and what will be*; *from whom nothing is concealed in the earth nor in the heaven*; *whose knowledge comprehends all things, the covert thereof and the overt, the small thereof and the great, in the most complete manner.* (TA.)

عَلَامَةٌ *i. q.* سِمَةٌ [*A mark, sign*, or *token, by which a person* or *thing is known*; *a cognizance*, or *badge*; *a characteristic*; *an indication*; *a symptom*]; (Ḳ; [see also مَعْلَمٌ;]) and ▼ عَلَمٌ is syn. therewith [as meaning thus]; (Ṣ, Mṣb, TA;) and so ▼ أُعْلُومَةٌ, (Abu-l-'Omeythil El-Aạrábee, TA,) as in the saying ▼ بَيْنَ القَوْمِ أُعْلُومَةٌ [*Among the people*, or *party*, *is a mark, sign*, or *token*]; and the pl. of this last is أَعَالِيمُ: (TA:) the pl. of عَلَامَةٌ is عَلَامَاتٌ (Mṣb) and [the coll. gen. n.] ▼ عَلَامٌ, (Ḳ, TA,) differing from عَلَامَةٌ only by the apocopating of the ة. (TA.) — See also عَلَمٌ, in two places.

عُلَامِىٌّ *Light*, or *active*; *and sharp*, or *acute, in mind*; (Ḳ, TA;) applied to a man: it is without teshdeed, and with the relative ى; from عُلَامٌ [signifying "a hawk"]. (TA.)

عَلَّامٌ and ▼ عُلَّامٌ, (Ḳ, TA,) both mentioned by ISd, the latter [which is less used] from Lḥ, (TA,) and ▼ عَلَّامَةٌ (Ṣ, Ḳ) and ▼ تِعْلِمَةٌ and ▼ تِعْلَامَةٌ, (Ḳ,) *Very knowing* or *scientific* or *learned*: (Ṣ, Ḳ:) the ة in ▼ عَلَّامَةٌ is added to denote intensiveness; (Ṣ;) or [rather] to denote that the person to whom it is applied has attained the utmost degree of the quality signified thereby; [so that it means *knowing* &c. *in the utmost degree*; or it may be rendered *very very*, or *singularly, knowing* or *scientific* or *learned*;] and this epithet is applied also to a woman: (IJ, TA:) [▼ تِعْلَامَةٌ, likewise, is doubly intensive; and so, app., is ▼ تِعْلِمَةٌ:] the pl. of عَلَّامٌ is عَلَّامُونَ; and that of ▼ عُلَّامٌ is عُلَّامُونَ. (TA.) See also, for the first, عَلِيمٌ. — Also the same epithets, (Ḳ,) or عَلَّامٌ and ▼ عَلَّامَةٌ, (TA,) *i. q.* نَسَّابٌ; (Ḳ, TA;) [or rather عَلَّامٌ signifies نَسَّابَةٌ, i. e. *very skilful in genealogies*, or *a great genealogist*; and ▼ عَلَّامَةٌ signifies نَسَّابَةٌ, i. e. *possessing the utmost knowledge in genealogies*, or *a most skilful genealogist*;] from العِلْمُ. (TA.)

عُلَّامٌ : see the next preceding paragraph, in two places. — Also, and ▼ عُلَامٌ, The صَقْر [or *hawk*]; (Ḳ;) the latter on the authority of IAạr: (TA:) and [particularly] the بَاشَق [i. e. the *musket*, or *sparrow-hawk*]; (Ḳ;) as some say: (TA:) or so the former word, (T,* Ṣ, TA,) or the latter word accord. to Kr and IB. (TA.) — And the former word, The [*plant called*] حِنَّآء [i. e. *Lawsonia inermis*]: (IAạr, Ṣ, Ḳ, TA:) thus correctly, but mentioned by Kr as without teshdeed. (TA.) — And the same, i. e. with teshdeed, The *kernel of the stone of the* نَبِق [or *fruit*, i. e. *drupe, of the lote-tree called* سِدْر]. (TA.)

عَلَّامَةٌ : see عَلَّامٌ, in four places.

عَلَامَةٌ : see مَعْلَمٌ.

العَالَمُ, (Ṣ, Mṣb, Ḳ, &c.,) said by some to be also pronounced ▼ العَالِمُ, (MF, TA,) and pronounced by El-Ḥajjáj with hemz [i. e. العَأْلَمُ], is primarily a name for *That by means of which one knows* [a thing]; like as الخَاتَمُ is a name for "that by means of which one seals" [a thing]: accord. to some of the expositors of the Ḳur-án, its predominant application is to *that by means of which the Creator is known*: then to *the intelligent beings of mankind and of the jinn* or *genii*: or to *mankind and the jinn and the angels*: and *mankind* [alone]: Es-Seyyid Esh-Shereef [El-

Jurjánee] adopts the opinion that it is applied to *every kind* [of these, so that one says عَالَمُ الإِنْسِ (which may be rendered *the world of mankind*) and عَالَمُ الجِنِّ (*the world of the jinn* or *genii*) and عَالَمُ المَلَائِكَةِ (*the world of the angels*), all of which phrases are of frequent occurrence], and to *the kinds* [thereof] *collectively*: (TA:) or it signifies الخَلْقُ [i. e. *the creation*, as meaning *the beings*, or *things, that are created*], (Ṣ, Mṣb, Ḳ,) *altogether* [i. e. *all the created beings* or *things*, or *all creatures*]: (Ḳ:) or, as some say, peculiarly, *the intelligent creatures*: (Mṣb:) or *what the cavity* (lit. *belly*) *of the celestial sphere comprises*, (Ḳ, TA,) *of substances and accidents*: (TA:) [it may often be rendered *the world*, as meaning *the universe*; and as meaning *the earth with all its inhabitants and other appertenances*; and in more restricted senses, as instanced above: and one says عَالَمُ الحَيَوَانِ meaning *the animal kingdom*, and عَالَمُ النَّبَاتِ *the vegetable kingdom*, and عَالَمُ المَعَادِنِ *the mineral kingdom*:] Jaafar Eṣ-Ṣádiḳ says that the عَالَم is twofold: namely, العَالَمُ الكَبِيرُ, which is *the celestial sphere with what is within it*; and العَالَمُ الصَّغِيرُ, which is *man, as being* [*a microcosm*, i. e.] *an epitome of all that is in the* كَبِير: and Zj says that العَالَم has no literal sing., because it is [significant of] a plurality [of classes] of diverse things; and if made a sing. of one of them, it is [significant of] a plurality of congruous things: (TA:) the pl. is العَالَمُونَ (Ṣ, M, Mṣb, Ḳ, &c.) and العَوَالِمُ: (Ṣ, TA:) and the sing. is [said to be] the only instance of a word of the measure فَاعَلٌ having a pl. formed with و and ن, (ISd, Ḳ, TA,) except يَاسَمٌ: (Ḳ, TA:) [but see this latter word:] العَالَمُونَ signifies *the* [*several*] *sorts of created beings* or *things*: (Ṣ:) [or *all the sorts thereof*: or *the beings of the universe*, or *of the whole world*:] it has this form because it includes mankind: or because it denotes particularly *the sorts of created beings consisting of the angels and the jinn and mankind, exclusively of others*: IAb is related to have explained رَبُّ العَالَمِينَ as meaning *the Lord of the jinn, or genii, and of mankind*: Ḳatádeh says, *the Lord of all the created beings*: but accord. to Az, the correctness of the explanation of IAb is shown by the saying in the beginning of ch. xxv. of the Ḳur-án that the Prophet was to be a نَذِير [or warner] لِلْعَالَمِينَ; and he was not a نذير to the beasts, nor to the angels, though all of them are the creatures of God; but only to the jinn, or genii, and mankind. (TA.) —— عَالَمٌ is also *syn. with* قَرْنٌ [as meaning *A generation of mankind*; or the *people of one time*]. (O, voce طَبَقٌ, q. v.)

عَالِمٌ and ↓ عَلِيمٌ signify the same, (IJ, Mṣb, Ḳ,*) as epithets applied to a man; (Ḳ;) i. e. *Possessing the attribute of* عِلْم (IJ, Mṣb, TA) *as a faculty firmly rooted in the mind*; [or *learned*; or *versed in science and literature*;] the former being used in [what is more properly] the sense of the latter; (IJ, TA;) which is an intensive epithet: (TA:) the pl. is عُلَمَآءُ and عُلَّامٌ, (Ḳ,) the latter of which is pl. of عَالِمٌ; (IB, TA;) the former being [properly] pl. of عَلِيمٌ; and عَالِمُونَ is [a] pl. of عَالِمٌ; (Mṣb;) [but] عُلَمَآءُ is used as a pl. of both, (IJ, TA,) and by him who says only عَالِمٌ [as the sing.], (Sb, TA;) because عَالِمٌ is used in the sense of عَلِيمٌ: to him who is entering upon the study of العِلْم, the epithet ↓ مُتَعَلِّمٌ [which may generally be rendered *learning*, or *a learner*,] is applied; not عَالِمٌ. (IJ, TA.) عَالِمٌ is also expl. as signifying One *who does according to his knowledge*. (TA.) —— See also عَلِيمٌ: and أَعْلَمُ. —— And see العَالَمُ.

عَيْلَمٌ *A well having much water*: (Ṣ, Ḳ:) or *of which the water is salt*: (Ḳ:) and *a wide well*: and sometimes a man was reviled by the saying, يَا ٱبْنَ العَيْلَمِ, referring to the width of his mother [in respect of the فَرْج]: (TA:) pl. عَيَالِمُ or عَيَالِيمُ. (Ṣ, accord. to different copies: in the TA, in this instance, the latter.) —— And The *sea*: (Ṣ, Ḳ:) pl. عَيَالِمُ. (TA.) —— And The *water upon which is the earth*: (Ṣ, Ḳ:) or *water concealed*, or *covered, in the earth*; or *beneath layers*, or *strata, of earth*; mentioned by Kr: (TA:) [عَيْلَمُ المَآءِ occurs in the JK and TA in art. خسف, and is there plainly shown to mean *the water that is beneath a mountain*, or *stratum of rock*: (see also غَيْثٌ: and see غَيْلَمٌ:) and it is said that] المَآءُ العَيْلَمُ means *copious water*. (Ḥam p. 750.) —— And *A large cooking-pot*. (T, TA voce جِلْحَابٌ.) —— Also *Plump*, and *soft, tender*, or *delicate*. (Ṣ, Ḳ.) —— And The *frog*. (AAF, Ḳ. [This meaning is also assigned to غَيْلَمٌ.]) —— And *i. q.* ↓ عَيْلَامٌ; (Ḳ;) which signifies *A male hyena*; (Ṣ, Ḳ;) occurring in a trad. (خَبَر) respecting Abraham, relating that he will take up his father to pass with him the [bridge called] صِرَاط, and will look at him, and lo, he will be عَيْلَامٌ أَمْدَرُ [*a male hyena inflated in the sides, big in the belly*, or *having his sides defiled with earth* or *dust*]. (TA.)

عَيْلَامٌ: see the next preceding sentence.

أَعْلَمُ [*More*, and *most, knowing* or *learned*]. Applied to God, [it may often be rendered *Supreme in knowledge*: or *omniscient*: but often, in this case,] it means [simply] ↓ عَالِمٌ [in the sense of *knowing*, or *cognizant*]. (Jel in iii. 31, and IAḳ p. 240.) [Therefore أَللّٰهُ أَعْلَمُ virtually means, sometimes, *God knows best*; or *knows all things*: and sometimes, simply, *God knows*.] —— Also [*Harelipped*; i. e.] *having a fissure in his upper lip*: (Ṣ, Mgh, Mṣb, Ḳ:) or *in one of its two sides*: (Ḳ:) the camel is said to be اعلم because of the fissure in his upper lip: when the fissure is in the lower lip, the epithet أَفْلَحُ is used: and أَشْرَمُ is used in both of these, and also in other, similar, senses: (TA:) the fem. of أَعْلَمُ is عَلْمَآءُ: (Ṣ, Mṣb, TA:) which is likewise applied to a lip (شَفَةٌ). (TA.) —— العَلْمَآءُ signifies also *The coat of mail*: (Ḳ:) mentioned by Sh, in the book entitled كِتَابُ السِّلَاحِ; but as not heard by him except in a verse of Zuheyr Ibn-Khabbáb [?]. (TA.)

أُعْلُومَةٌ: see عَلَامَةٌ, in two places.

تِعْلَامَةٌ and تِعْلِمَةٌ: see عَلَّامٌ; each in two places.

مَعْلَمٌ i. q. مَظِنَّةٌ; مَعْلَمُ الشَّىْءِ signifying مَظِنَّتُهُ; (Ḳ, TA;) as meaning *The place in which is known the existence of the thing*: (Mṣb in art. ظن:) pl. مَعَالِمُ; (TA;) which is the *contr. of* مَجَاهِلُ, pl. of مَجْهَلٌ [q. v.] as applied to a land; meaning *in which are signs of the way*. (TA in art. جهل.) And hence, [*A person in whom is known the existence* of a quality &c.:] one says, هُوَ مَعْلَمٌ لِلْخَيْرِ [*He is one in whom good*, or *goodness, is known to be*]. (TA.) —— Also *A thing*, (Ḳ,) or *a mark, trace*, or *track*, (Ṣ, TA,) *by which one guides himself*, or *is guided*, (Ṣ, Ḳ, TA,) *to the road*, or *way*; (Ṣ, TA;) as also ↓ عَلَامَةٌ and ↓ عَلَمٌ: (Ḳ: [in several copies of which, in all as far as I know, وَالعَلَمُ is here put in the place of وَالعَلَمِ; whereby العَلَمُ is made to be syn. with العَالَمُ: but accord. to SM, it is syn. with المَعْلَمُ, as is shown by what here follows:]) and hence a reading in the Ḳur [xliii. 61], ↓ وَإِنَّهُ لَعَلَمٌ لِلسَّاعَةِ, meaning *And verily he*, i. e. Jesus, by his appearing, and descending to the earth, shall be *a sign* of the approach *of the hour* [of resurrection]: it is also said, in a trad., that on the day of resurrection there shall not be a مَعْلَمٌ for any one: and the pl. is مَعَالِمُ. (TA.) And مَعْلَمُ الطَّرِيقِ signifies *The indication*, or *indicator, of the road*, or *way*. (TA.) —— [And hence it signifies likewise *An indication*, or *a symptom*, of anything; like عَلَامَةٌ.] —— See also عَلَمٌ, last quarter.

مُعْلَمٌ pass. part. n. of أَعْلَمَ [q. v.] in the phrase اعلم الثَّوْبَ, and thus applied as an epithet to a garment, or piece of cloth: (Ṣ:) [and also in other senses: thus in a verse of 'Antarah cited voce مَشُوفٌ:] and applied to a قِدْح [or gaming-arrow] as meaning *Having a mark* [*made*] *upon it*. (TA.) —— [See also a verse of 'Antarah cited voce مِشَكٌّ.]

مُعْلِمٌ act. part. n. of أَعْلَمَ [q. v.] in the phrase اعلم الثَّوْبَ: [and in other senses:] —— thus also of the same verb in the phrase اعلم الفَارِسُ. (Ṣ.)

مُعَلَّمٌ [pass. part. n. of 2, in all its senses: —— and hence particularly signifying] *Directed by inspiration to that which is right and good*. (TA.)

مُعَلِّمٌ [act. part. n. of 2, in all its senses: and generally meaning] *A teacher*. (KL.) —— [It is now also a common title of address to a Christian and to a Jew.]

مَعْلُومٌ [*Known*; &c.]. الوَقْتُ المَعْلُومُ [mentioned in the Ḳur xv. 38 and xxxviii. 82] means [*The time of*] *the resurrection*. (TA.) And الأَيَّامُ المَعْلُومَاتُ [mentioned in the Ḳur xxii. 29] means

[*The first*] *ten days of Dhu-l-Hijjeh,* (Ṣ, Mgh, Mṣb, Ḳ,) *the last of which is the day of the sacrifice.* (TA.) — [In grammar, The *active voice.*]

مُتَعَلِّمٌ : see عَالِمٌ.

علن

1. عَلَنَ الأَمْرُ, aor. ـُ (Ṣ, Mṣb, Ḳ) and ـِ ; (Ḳ;) and عَلِنَ, aor. ـَ ; (Ḳ;) and عَلُنَ, aor. ـُ ; (ISk, Ṣ, Mṣb, Ḳ;) inf. n. عُلُونٌ, which is of the first; (Ṣ, Mṣb;) and عَلَنٌ, (ISk, Ṣ, Mṣb, Ḳ, TA, [app., accord. to the CḲ, عَلْنٌ, but this is wrong,]) which is of the last; (ISk, Ṣ, Mṣb, TA;) and عَلَانِيَةٌ, (Ḳ, TA,) which is of the three; (TA;) or this last is a simple subst.; (Mṣb;) *The affair, or case, or event, was, or became, overt, open, manifest, public,* (Ṣ,* Mṣb, Ḳ, TA,) *published, or spread;* (Mṣb, TA;) and ▼ اعتلن signifies the same; (Ḳ;) [and so ▼ استعلن, but for this I know not any authority except modern usage: and اعلن has a similar meaning, expl. below.] — [The CḲ has عَلَنْتُهُ where other copies of the Ḳ, and the TA, have عَلَّنْتُهُ, as syn. with أَعْلَنْتُهُ, q. v.]

2: see 4, first sentence.

3. مُعَالَنَةٌ and عِلَانٌ signify the same, (Ṣ, Ḳ,) i. e. *i. q.* مُجَاهَرَةٌ [meaning The *behaving,* or *acting, openly with another,* or *others*]; as also ▼ إِعْلَانٌ. (Ḳ.) You say, عَالَنْتُهُمْ بِالأَمْرِ *i. q.* جَاهَرْتُهُمْ بِهِ [i. e. *I was open,* or *I acted openly, with them in the affair,* or *case*]. (JK in art. جهر.) And عَالَنَ بِالعَدَاوَةِ *i. q.* جَاهَرَ [i. e. *He showed open enmity* or *hostility, with another*]. (TḲ.) — Or The *laying open,* or *manifesting, of each one to his fellow, what is in his mind.* (TA.) You say, عَالَنْتُ بِهِ, [or عَالَنْتُهُ,] inf. n. مُعَالَنَةٌ and عِلَانٌ, [*I laid open,* or *manifested, to him what was in my mind, he doing the same to me,*] i. e. *each of us laid open,* or *manifested, to the other, what was in his mind.* (Mṣb.) — See also the next paragraph.

4. أَعْلَنْتُهُ *I laid it open, manifested it, revealed it, made it public,* or *published it;* namely, an affair, a case, or an event; (Ṣ, Mṣb, Ḳ, TA;) as also اعلنت به; and ▼ عَلَّنْتُهُ, (Ḳ, TA,) [for which latter the CḲ has عَلَنْتُهُ, but it is] with teshdeed, (TA,) inf. n. تَعْلِينٌ; (TḲ;) [and ▼ عَالَنْتُهُ, for] عَالَنَهُ, (Ḳ,) or [rather] عالنهُ الأَمْرَ, (TḲ,) means اعلن إِلَيْهِ الأَمْرَ [*He laid open,* &c., *to him, the affair,* or *case,* or *event*]. (Ḳ.) — Hence, أَعْلَنَتْ, occurring in a trad., as said of a woman [accused of adultery], *She revealed* [or *confessed*] *the enormity,* or *act of adultery.* (TA.) — [And اعلن بِهِ app. signifies *He made him to be,* or *become, publicly known:* see 10; and see also أَظْهَرْتُ بِفُلَانٍ in art. ظهر.] — اعلن الأَمْرُ *The affair,* or *case,* or *event, was,* or *became, notorious;* or *commonly,* or *publicly, known;* syn. اِشْتَهَرَ. (TA. [Compare 1.]) — See also 3, first sentence.

8: see the first paragraph.

10. استعلن *i. q.* تَعَرَّضَ لِأَنْ يُعْلَنَ بِهِ [app. meaning *He addressed himself to being,* or *sought to be, made publicly known*]. (TA.) — [And] اِسْتِعْلَانٌ signifies [or is said to signify] The *seeking,* or *desiring, to lay open, manifest, reveal, make public,* or *publish.* (KL.) — [And] *i. q.* إِعْلَانٌ [inf. n. of 4, but in what sense is not shown; perhaps of 4 as signifying اِشْتَهَرَ, expl. above]. (JM.) — See also 1.

Q. Q. 1. عَلْوَنْتُ الكِتَابَ, (Ṣ,) inf. n. عَلْوَنَةٌ and عُلْوَانٌ, (Ḳ in art. علو,) *i. q.* عَنْوَنْتُهُ [i. e. *I put a title to the book,* or *writing*]: (Ṣ:) it may be of the measure فَعْوَلْتُ from العَلَانِيَةُ, or the former ن in عَنْوَنْتُ may be a substitute for the ل in عَلْوَنْتُ [or the ل for the ن]: Lth says that it is not a good word. (TA.) [It is also mentioned in art. علو.]

عَلِنٌ part. n. of عَلِنَ: see عَالِنٌ. (Mṣb.)

عُلَنَةٌ A man *who reveals his secret;* (Ṣ;) [or a *revealer of secrets;*] or one *who will not conceal a secret.* (Ḳ.)

عَلِينٌ [part. n. of عَلُنَ]: see عَالِنٌ.

عَلَانِيَةٌ an inf. n. of 1 [q. v.]: (Ḳ, TA:) or a simple subst. from 1; (Mṣb;) [as such] signifying *Openness,* or *publicity;* (Ṣ, Mṣb;) *contr. of* سِرٌّ. (Ṣ.) [Hence, عَلَانِيَةً meaning *Openly,* or *publicly;* and *aloud:* see Ḳur ii. 275; &c.] — Also One's *outward man;* syn. بَرَّانِيٌّ, q. v.: opposed to سَرِيرَةٌ and جَوَّانِيٌّ. (T in art. بر.) — [And it is also used as an epithet; app. by those who hold it to be originally an inf. n.; or rather its being thus used may be regarded as corroborating the assertion that it is originally an inf. n., like عَدْلٌ &c., though, as an epithet, it has a pl.:] one says رَجُلٌ عَلَانِيَةٌ, pl. عَلَانُونَ; as also ▼ عَلَانِيٌّ, pl. عَلَانِيُّونَ; *A man whose affair,* or *case, is open,* or *manifest;* (Ḳ, TA;) mentioned by Lḥ. (TA.)

عَلَانِيٌّ, and its pl.: see what next precedes.

عُلْوَانٌ The عُنْوَان [or *title*] of a book, or writing. (Ṣ, Ḳ.) — And an inf. n. of the verb عَلْوَنَ. (Ḳ in art. علو.)

عَالِنٌ part. n. of عَلَنَ; applied to an affair, a case, or an event, *Overt, open, manifest, public, published,* or *spread;* as also ▼ عَلِنٌ and ▼ عَلِينٌ. (Mṣb.)

علند

عَلَنْدٌ and عَلَنْدَدٌ and عَلَنْدَى &c.: see arts. علد and عند.

علو

1. عَلَا, (Mṣb, Ḳ,) aor. يَعْلُو, (Mṣb,) inf. n. عُلُوٌّ; (Mṣb, Ḳ;) and عَلِيَ; and ▼ تعلّى [which last see also below]; (Ḳ;) *It* (a thing, Mṣb) *was,* or *became, high, elevated,* or *lofty;* (Mṣb, Ḳ;*) syn. اِرْتَفَعَ; (Mṣb;) and so ▼ تعالى: (Ṣ, Ḳ:) or you say, عَلَا فِى المَكَانِ [*it was,* or *became, high,* or *elevated, in place*], aor. يَعْلُو, inf. n. عُلُوٌّ: (Ṣ:) and عَلِىَ فِى الشَّرَفِ [† *he was,* or *became, high,* or *elevated,* or *exalted, in dignity,* or *nobility*], (Ṣ, Mgh,) with kesr, (Ṣ,) aor. يَعْلَى, inf. n. عَلَآءٌ; (Ṣ, Mgh;) and also عَلَا, with fet-ḥ, aor. يَعْلَى: a poet says,

لَمَّا عَلَا كَعْبُكَ لِى عَلِيتُ

[† *When thy nobility became exalted to me, I became exalted*]; thus combining the two dial. vars.: (Ṣ:) or you say, عَلِىَ فِى المَكَارِمِ [† *he was,* or *became, eminent in generous,* or *honourable, actions* or *qualities*], inf. n. عَلَآءٌ [in some copies of the Ḳ عَلًا]; (Mṣb, Ḳ;) and عَلَا, inf. n. عُلُوٌّ; (Ḳ;) and thus the two verbs are used in the saying of the poet cited above: (TA:) and ▼ استعلى, said of a man, signifies the same as عَلَا. (Ṣ.) [Hence,] عَلَتِ الشَّمْسُ *The sun became high;* as also ▼ اِعْتَلَتْ: (Nawádir el-Aạráb, TA in art. دلك:) and [hence,] عَلَا النَّهَارُ *The day became advanced, the sun being somewhat high;* syn. اِرْتَفَعَ [q. v.]; as also ▼ اعتلى and ▼ استعلى. (Ḳ.) — عَلَا فِى المَكَانِ, inf. n. عُلُوٌّ, signifies [also] *He ascended the place,* or *upon the place;* syn. صَعِدَ: and عَلَوْتُ أَعْلَاهُ and عَلَوْتُ عَلَى الجَبَلِ are syn. [as meaning *I ascended the mountain,* or *upon the mountain,* or *upon the top,* or *highest part, thereof*]: and عَلَوْتُهُ and عَلَوْتُ فِيهِ signify *I ascended it;* syn. رَقِيتُ فِيهِ. (Mṣb.) عَلَاهُ (Ṣ, Mṣb, Ḳ, TA) and عَلَا بِهِ, (Ḳ, TA, [in the CḲ علاه وبه is put for عَلَاهُ وَبِهِ,]) and ▼ استعلاهُ, (Ṣ, Ḳ, TA,) and ▼ اعتلاهُ, (Ṣ,) and ▼ اِعْلَوْلَاهُ, and ▼ اعلاهُ, and ▼ علّاهُ, (Ḳ, TA,) this last [for which the CḲ has عالاهُ] being with teshdeed, (TA,) and ▼ عالاهُ and ▼ عالى بِهِ, (Ḳ, TA, [in the CḲ عَالَاهُ وبه,]) are syn., (Ṣ, Ḳ,) signifying *He ascended it,* or *upon it;* (Ḳ; [in the CḲ صَعَدَهُ, and so in my MS. copy of the Ḳ, but in other copies صَعِدَهُ, which is certainly the right reading;]) whether the object be a mountain or a beast: (TA:) [or] you say, عَلَا الدَّابَّةَ *He mounted the beast;* (Ḳ, TA;) and in like manner, anything: (TA:) and عَلَى السَّطْحِ, aor. يَعْلِيهِ; (Ḳ, TA;) but in the M عَلِىَ السَّطْحَ, i. e., like رَضِىَ; (TA;) inf. n. عَلْىٌ (Ḳ, TA) and عِلِىٌّ (TA, and so accord. to some copies of the Ḳ,) and عُلِىٌّ; (TA, and so accord. to other copies of the Ḳ instead of عِلِىٌّ;) *He ascended upon the flat house-top;* syn. صَعِدَهُ. (Ḳ, TA.) — [عَلَاهُ signifies also *He,* or *it, was,* or *became, upon it,* or *over it:* and *it came,* or *arose, upon it; overlay it; was,* or *became, superincumbent,* or *supernatant, upon it;* or *overspread it;* as scum, and rust, &c. And *It lay on him as a burden.* Hence,] one says, مَا سَأَلْتُكَ مَا يَعْلُوكَ ظَهْرًا i. e. [† *I did not ask,* or *demand, of thee, what would lie as a burden on thy back;* or] *what would be onerous, burdensome, oppressive,* or *troublesome, to thee.* (TA.) — And [hence also] عَلَاهُ *It over-*

topped it, rose above it, or *exceeded it in height.* (TA in art. دصر.) [And in like manner, ▼استعلى *It became elevated above it.*] — And عَلَوْتُهُمْ بِالْجَمَالِ وَالشَّرَفِ and [† *I was,* or *became, superior to them in nobility* and *in goodliness*]. (Ṣ in art. فرع.) — And عَلَاهُ [† *He had,* or *gained, ascendancy over him,* or *it;* as also عَلَا عَلَيْهِ and ▼استعلى عليه: and] † *he overcame him;* or *had,* or *gained, the mastery over him;* (Ṣ, Mṣb, TA;) and *subdued him;* (Mṣb;) namely, his opponent, or adversary; as also ▼استعلاهُ: and in like manner, عَلَا حَاجَتَهُ and ▼استعلاها † *he gained the mastery over the object of his want:* and ▼اعتلى الشَّىْءَ † *he prevailed against the thing,* or *had power over it, and overcame it;* and عَلَا لِلشَّىْءِ, aor. يَعْلُو, † *he was,* or *became, able to do,* or *accomplish,* or *to bear, the thing.* (TA.) عَلَا بِالْأَمْرِ means اِضْطَلَعَ بِهِ وَٱسْتَقَلَّ [i. e. † *He had strength,* or *power, sufficient for the affair, and had absolute control over it*]: (Ṣ: [so in one of my copies: the other has اِطَّلَعَ, which I find also in the PṢ and in my copy of the TA; and which is allowed by some, but disallowed by others, in the sense of اِضْطَلَعَ, as is shown voce مُضْطَلِعٌ:]) a poet says,

* فَٱعْمِدْ لِمَا تَعْلُو فَمَا لَكَ بِالَّذِى *
* لَا تَسْتَطِيعُ مِنَ الْأُمُورِ يَدَانِ *

[*Then aim thou at that for which thou hast sufficient strength,* or *power, and over which thou hast absolute control:* (به being understood after تعلو:) *for what object hast thou* in meddling *with that which a pair of hands cannot accomplish, of affairs?*]. (Ṣ.) [And hence, perhaps,] one says to him who possesses much property, اعل به i. e. اَبْقِ بَعْدَهُ [app. ابق بعده, and أَعْلِ بِهِ, as though meaning † *Have thou ability to consume it,* and so *survive thou it;* like as one says to him who puts on a new garment, أَبْلِ (see 4 in art. بلو)]: or [perhaps a mistake for "and"] it is [virtually] a prayer for his continuance in life. (TA.) — عَلَوْتُ عَلَى فُلَانٍ الرِّيحَ means *I was* [or *went*] *on the windward side of such a one:* and one says, لَا تَعْلُ الرِّيحَ عَلَى الصَّيْدِ فَيَرَاحَ رِيحَكَ وَيَنْفِرَ [i. e. *Go not thou on the windward side of the game, lest it scent thy odour, and take fright and flee*]. (TA.) — عَلَوْتُهُ بِالسَّيْفِ means *I smote him* [*with the sword;* or, more properly, *I set upon him therewith*]. (Ṣ, TA.) And [in like manner] one says, عَلَاهُ بِالشَّتْمِ وَالضَّرْبِ [† *He set upon him,* or *assailed him,* or *overcame him, with reviling and beating*]. (Ṣ and M in art. ثول, &c.) — عَلَا فِى الأَرْضِ, (Ṣ, TA,) inf. n. عُلُوٌّ, (Ṣ,) signifies † *He exalted,* or *magnified, himself,* [*in the earth,*] or *behaved proudly, insolently,* or *exorbitantly.* (Ṣ,* TA.) And [in like manner] لَا تَعْلُوا عَلَى ٱللّٰهِ, in the Ḳur xliv. 18, † *Exalt not,* or *magnify not, yourselves against God;* or *behave not proudly,* &c. (Bḍ, Jel.) — عَلَا عَنْهُ [lit. signifies *It rose from it:* and hence,] *it recoiled from it,* i. e., a thing from another thing; *it did not cleave to it:* and تَعْلُو عَنْهُ العَيْنُ means † *The eye recoils from him.* (TA.) — أَعْلُ عَنِّى : see 3. — عَلَا بِهِ as syn. with أَعْلَاهُ: see expl. with the latter below.

2. عَلَّاهُ : see 4. — [Hence,] one says, عَلَّيْتُ بِهِ عَلَى البَعِيرِ [*I raised it, and put it, upon the camel*]: (Ṣ:) [and so ▼عَالَيْتُهُ; as in a verse cited voce رَائِحٌ, in art. روح; in which, and in the present art., it is cited in the Ṣ and TA: and ▼عَالَيْتُ بِهِ; as in a verse cited voce إِلَى in the sense of مِنْ, in art. الو:] and ▼عَالِ عَلَىَّ means اِحْمِلْ [i. e. *Put thou upon me* such a thing *to be carried by me;* or *load thou me*]. (Ṣ, Ḳ.) — And عَلَّيْتُ الحَبْلَ, inf. n. تَعْلِيَةٌ, *I raised the cord to its proper place in respect of the channel of the sheave, and in respect of the* [*main*] *well-rope.* (Ṣ.) — And عَلَّى الدَّلْوَ, inf. n. as above, *He raised the bucket from a stone projecting in the lower part of the casing of a well* [*and impeding its ascent*]; *he having descended the well for that purpose:* [or simply *he raised the filled bucket;* for] some say that ▼المُعَلِّى signifies *he who raises the filled bucket;* i. e., *who draws water thereby.* (TA.) — And عَلَّى المَتَاعَ عَنِ الدَّابَّةِ *He put down the goods,* or *furniture and utensils, from the beast:* [app. because he who does so lifts them off the beast:] (Ḳ, TA:) أَعْلَاهُ in this sense is disapproved. (TA.) — See also 1, former half. — And see Q. Q. 1.

3. مُعَالَاةٌ signifies † The *vying, competing,* or *contending for superiority, in highness, loftiness, elevation,* or *eminence.* (KL.) You say, عَالَاهُ, meaning سَامَاهُ. (M in art. سمو. [See 3 in that art. in two places.]) — See 4, in two places. — عُولِىَ, said of clarified butter, and of the fat of anything having fatness, means *It was wrought* (صُنِعَ) [app. *over a fire*]) *until it rose in the operation.* (TA.) — عَالَوْا نَعْيَهُ † *They manifested the announcement of his death:* (Ḳ, TA:) [as though meaning *they raised the report of his death:*] one should not say أَعْلَوْهُ nor عَلَّوْهُ. (TA.) — See 2, in three places. — عَالَتِ البَيْقُورَ, occurring in a verse of Umeiyeh Ibn-Abi-ṣ-Ṣalt, is mentioned and explained in the Ṣ in this art. and in art. عول: see the latter art. [to which it seems more properly to belong]. — See 1, former half, in two places. — عَالِ عَنِّى *Remove thou,* or *go thou away* or *aside, from me;* as also ▼أَعْلِ عَنِّى; (Ṣ, TA;) for which latter, أَعْلِ عَنِّجْ occurs in a trad. respecting the slaughter of Abu-Jahl; and ▼أَعْلُ عَنِّى with the conjunctive ا is a dial. var. of أَعْلِ عَنِّى with the disjunctive ا, mentioned by Fr. (TA.) — [Hence,] one says, ▼أَعْلِ عَنَّا and عَالِ [i. e. and عَالِ عَنَّا], meaning † *Seek the object of thy want at the hands of other than us* (عِنْدَ غَيْرِنَا), *for we are not able to accomplish it.* (TA.) — And عالى and ▼اعلى signify *He came to the 'Áliyeh of Nejd,* i. e. *the region above Nejd, extending to the land of Tihámeh and the part behind Mekkeh,* (Ṣ, Ḳ,) i. e. [*to*] *El-Ḥijáz and what is next to it.* (Ṣ.)

4. اعلاهُ *He* (a man, Mṣb) *elevated it* (i. e. a thing, Mṣb); or *made it high,* or *lofty;* (Mṣb, Ḳ;) as also ▼عَلَّاهُ, (Ḳ,) with teshdeed, (TA,) and ▼عَلَا بِهِ [without teshdeed]: (Ḳ:) it is [also] said of God, meaning † *He elevated,* or *exalted, him;* and ▼عالاهُ is like it [in meaning]: (Ṣ:) and ▼عَالَيْتُ بِفُلَانٍ signifies the same as أَعْلَيْتُهُ [† *I elevated,* or *exalted, such a one;* as also, app., أَعْلَيْتُ بِفُلَانٍ (see 4 in art. ظهر)]. (Ḥam p. 175.) Hence one says, أَعْلَى ٱللّٰهُ كَعْبَهُ [‡ *God exalted,* or *may God exalt, his nobility*]. (TA.) — See also 1, former half. — أَعْلِ الوِسَادَةَ means *Sit thou upon the cushion.* (TA.) — And أَعْلِ عَنِ الوِسَادَةِ *Rise thou from the cushion;* syn. قُمْ: (TA in art. دلو:) or *descend thou from it.* (Ṣ* and TA in the present art.) And اعلى عَنِ الدَّابَّةِ *He alighted from the beast.* (Ḳ, TA.) — See also 3, latter half, in three places.

5. تعلّى : see 1, first sentence. — Also (Ḳ) *He,* or *it, was,* or *became, high, elevated,* or *lofty, gently,* or *leisurely.* (Ṣ, Ḳ.) — And *He came upon a party of men suddenly,* or *at unawares, without permission.* (TA.) — تَعَلَّتْ مِنْ نِفَاسِهَا † *She* (a woman) *became free,* (Ṣ, Mgh, Ḳ,) and *passed forth,* (Mgh,) *from her state of impurity consequent upon childbirth;* (Ṣ, Mgh, Ḳ;) as also ▼تَعَالَتْ; (Mgh; and TA in art. عل;) and so تَعَلَّلَتْ, as well as تَعَلَّتْ: (Ḳ and TA in that art.:) or مِنْ مَرَضِهَا *from her disease:* (Ḳ:) or you say of a woman, تعلّت من نفاسها meaning [as above or] *she became pure from the effects of her childbirth:* (TA:) and of a man you say, تَعَلَّى مِنْ عِلَّتِهِ (Ṣ, TA) *he recovered from his disease.* (TA.)

6. تعالى : see 1, first sentence. — Addressing a man, (Ṣ, Mṣb,) using the imperative form, you say, تَعَالَ, (Ṣ, Mṣb, Ḳ,) with fet-ḥ to the ل, (Ṣ, Ḳ,) originally meaning *Be thou elevated,* (Ṣ, Mṣb,) and said by a man in a high place in calling a man in a low place; (Mṣb;) then, by reason of frequency of usage, employed in the sense of هَلُمَّ [meaning *Come thou*], (Ṣ, Mṣb,) absolutely, whether the place of the person called be high or low or on the same level; so that it is originally applied to denote a particular meaning, and then used in a general meaning: (Mṣb:) and to a woman one says, تَعَالَىْ; (Ṣ, Ḳ;) and to two women, (Ṣ,) or two persons, (TA,) تَعَالَيَا; (Ṣ, TA;) and to a pl. number of men, تَعَالَوْا; (Mṣb, TA;) and to a pl. number of women, تَعَالَيْنَ; (Ṣ, Mṣb, TA;) and sometimes the ل is pronounced with ḍamm in the pl. masc., and with kesr in the fem.; whence El-Ḥasan El-Baṣree read, [in the Ḳur iii. 57,] قُلْ يَا أَهْلَ ٱلْكِتَابِ تَعَالُوا [*Say thou, O people of the Scriptures, come ye,* the usual reading being تَعَالَوْا], for the sake of congeniality with the و: (Mṣb, TA:) it is not allowable to say تَعَالَيْتُ [as meaning *I came*], nor to use the prohibitive form; (Ṣ;) but one

says, (thus accord. to several copies of the Ṣ,) or nor does one say, (thus accord. to one of my copies of the Ṣ, [and accord. to the TA, in which it is said that the verb is not used otherwise than in the imperative form,]) قَدْ تَعَالَيْتُ [as meaning *I have come*], and إِلَى أَيِّ شَيْءٍ أَتَعَالَى [as meaning *To what thing shall I come?* like as one says, إِلَامَ أَعْلَمُ]. (Ṣ.) — [تعالى signifies also † *He was*, or *became*, *exalted*, or *extolled*: and † *he exalted himself*: and in both of these senses it is often followed by عَنْ as syn. with عَلَى, denoting superiority: you say, تعالى فُلَانٌ عَنْ كَذَا, meaning † *Such a one was*, or *became*, *exalted above such a thing*; or simply, *was*, or *became*, *above it*, i. e. *too elevated in character for it*: and also, *exalted himself above such a thing*; or *held himself above it*.] Said of God, in the Ḳur xx. 113 [and in other instances therein], it means [† *Exalted*, or *supremely exalted*, *is He*] in his essence and his attributes, above the created beings. (Bḍ.) [But in common speech, it is generally used as an ejaculation of praise, meaning † *Exalted* or *extolled*, or *supremely exalted* or *extolled*, *be He*, or *his greatness* or *majesty* or *glory*, or *his name*; or *acknowledged be his absolute supremacy*. And the common expression (used in citing words of the Ḳur-án) قَالَ تَعَالَى means † *He saith*, or *hath said*, *exalted* or *extolled*, or *supremely exalted* or *extolled*, *be He*; &c.] — See also 5.

8: see 1, in two places as trans.: — and also in two places as intrans. = [It may also be used for, or in the sense of, اِئْتَلَى, as meaning *He fell short* in an affair: see its part. n.]

10: see 1, in seven places. [The inf. n. اِسْتِعْلَاءٌ, properly denotes *Superiority that is perceptible by sense*: and tropically, *such as is ideal*, or *perceived by the intellect*: see عَلَى, below.] — One says also, هٰذِهِ الكَلِمَةُ تَسْتَعْلِى لِسَانِى, meaning [† *This word*, or *sentence*,] *is often current upon my tongue*. (TA.) — And اِسْتَعْلَى عَلَى الغَايَةِ, said of a horse in the contending to outstrip in a race, means † *He reached the goal*. (TA.)

12. اِعْلَوْلَاهُ: see 1, former half.

Q. Q. 1. عَلْوَنَ الكِتَابَ, (Ṣ, Ḳ,) inf. n. عَلْوَنَةٌ and عُلْوَانٌ, (Ḳ,) i. q. عَنْوَنَهُ [*He put a superscription*, or *title*, *to the book*, or *writing*; or *he wrote the superscription*, or *title*, *thereof*]; (Ṣ, Ḳ;) as also † عَلَّى الكِتَابَ; (Ḳ;) which latter is the more agreeable with analogy. (TA.) [See also Q. Q. 1 in arts. عن and عنو.]

مِنْ عَلُ: see the next paragraph. It also signifies, simply, *Above him* or *it*; or *in the higher*, or *highest*, *part of him* or *it*: thus in a hemistich cited voce تَحْتَ. (Mughnee.) [In all cases,] عَلُ is determinate, and indecl., with ḍamm for its invariable termination: (Mughnee, TA:) [for it is regarded as a prefixed noun of which the complement is to be understood as to the meaning but not as to the letter:] in the saying of Ows,

• كَفِرْقِئِ بَيْضٍ كَنَّهُ القَيْضُ مِنْ عَلُو •

[*Like the thin pellicle of eggs, which the shell covers above*], the و [in عَلُو] is augmentative, being added to render the rhyme unrestricted: (Ṣ, TA:) and in the instance of مِنْ عَلُهُ, likewise ending a verse, the ه is that of pausation: for if عَلُ were [really] a prefixed noun, it would not be thus indecl. (Mughnee, TA.)

أَتَيْتُهُ مِنْ عَلِ, (Ṣ,* Ḳ,) whence the saying of Imra-el-Ḳeys cited in the first paragraph of art. حط, (Ṣ, Mughnee, TA,) and † مِنْ عَلُ, [respecting which see the next preceding paragraph,] and † مِنْ عَلَا, (Ṣ, Ḳ,) of which a verse cited voce نَاشَ in art. نوش is an ex., (Ṣ, TA,) and † مِنْ عَالٍ, signify the same, (Ṣ, Mughnee, Ḳ,) i. e. مِنْ فَوْقٍ; (Ḳ;) [which, with أَتَيْتُهُ preceding it, means *I came to him*, or *it*, *from above*; and † *I overcame*, or *subdued*, *him*, or *it*; for] اتاه من فوق and من علو [app. من عَلْوٍ (see عُلْوٌ below,) tropically used,] means قَهَرَهُ; (Ḥam p. 128;) [but the former is here meant in many, if not in all, instances, as is shown by what follows;] and [in like manner] one says, † أَتَيْتُهُ مِنْ مُعَالٍ; [whence] Dhu-r-Rummeh says,

• وَنَفْضَانُ الرَّحْلِ مِنْ مُعَالِ •

[*And the shaking of the camel's saddle in the upper part*]. (Ṣ, TA.) عَلِ in مِنْ عَلِ is indeterminate [in itself] and decl. [as being a prefixed noun of which the complement is to be understood as to the meaning and as to the letter; thus differing from عَلُ in مِنْ عَلُ: if the complement were not to be understood either as to the letter or as to the meaning, one would say مِنْ عَلٍ, originally مِنْ عَلْوٍ]. (TA.) One says also أَتَيْتُهُ مِنْ عَلِ الدَّارِ, [thus in several copies of the Ṣ, from which one of my copies deviates by erroneously substituting عَلَى for عَلِ,] with kesr to the ل, meaning مِنْ عَالِى الدَّارِ [or rather مِنْ عَالِ الدَّارِ, i. e. *I came to him*, or *it*, *from the high*, or *elevated*, *part of the house* or *abode*]: (Ṣ:) or the using عَلُ [thus] as a prefixed noun is a mistake. (Mughnee.) — And one says, أُزْجُرِ الفَزَّ عَلِ عَلِ and † عَلَا عَلَا [*Chide thou the young one of the wild cow*, saying عَلِ عَلِ and عَلَا عَلَا]. (TA.)

عَلَا [as a subst.]: see the next preceding paragraph, in two places. = See also عَلَاةٌ.

عَلْوٌ: see عُلْوٌ in five places. — Also *A high*, or *an elevated*, *state of the base*, or *foundation*, *of a building*. (TA.) — And you say, أَخَذَهُ عَلْوًا, meaning † *He took him*, or *it*, *by force*. (Ḳ, TA.) See also the next but one of the preceding paragraphs.

عُلْوٌ and † عِلْوٌ (Ṣ, Mṣb, Ḳ) and † عَلْوٌ (Ḳ) signify The *higher*, or *highest*, *part* (Ṣ, Mṣb, Ḳ) of a house, or an abode, (Ṣ, Mṣb,) or of a thing; (Ḳ;) as also † عِلْوَةٌ (Ḳ voce سُفْلٌ) and † عُلَاوَةٌ and † عَالِيَةٌ. (Ḳ in the present art.) You say, قَعَدْتُ فِى عُلْوِهِ and فِى عِلْوِهِ and † عِلْوَهُ and † عَلْوَةٌ [i. e. *I sat in the higher*, or *highest*, *part of it*]. (TA.) And Aạshà-Báhileh says,

• إِنِّى أَتَتْنِى لِسَانٌ لَا أُسَرُّ بِهَا •
• مِنْ عَلْوَ لَا عَجَبٌ مِنْهَا وَلَا سَخَرُ •

(Ṣ,) or, as in one of my copies of the Ṣ, أُسُرُّ and سُخُرٌ, i. e. *Verily information has come to me* [*by which I shall not be rejoiced* (or *by which I shall not rejoice* others, accord. to the latter reading mentioned above,)] *from the higher*, or *highest*, *parts of Nejd*, (مِنْ أَعْلَى نَجْدٍ, thus in some copies of the Ṣ and in the TA, but in other copies of the Ṣ the word نَجْد is omitted,) [*at which there is no wondering*, *as at a thing that is improbable*, *nor any scoffing*;] related [thus] with fet-ḥ to the و and with ḍamm thereto and with kesr thereto [i. e. عَلْوَ as above and also † عَلْوُ and † عَلْوِ]. (Ṣ, TA.) — One says also, هٰذَا شِعْرٌ عَلْوٌ [app. عُلْوٍ], meaning † *This is poetry of a high class*: or [the last word may be † عَلْوٍ or عُلْوٍ or عِلْوٍ, for it may mean], *of the higher*, or *highest*, *part of Nejd*. (TA.)

عِلْوٌ: see the next preceding paragraph, in three places.

عَلِىٌّ: see عَلْيَاءُ.

عَلِىٌّ: see عَلِىٌّ.

عَلَى is a particle and a noun (Mbr, Ṣ, Mughnee, Ḳ) and a verb; (Mbr, Ṣ;) though some assert that it is only a noun, and ascribe this assertion to Sb: (Mughnee:) its alif, (Sb, Ṣ, Mṣb,) [which, when it has no affix, is written ى, and] which is originally و, (Sb, Ṣ,) [like that of إِلَى, q. v.,] is changed into [what is properly] ى when it has a pronominal affix, (Sb, Ṣ, Mṣb,) as in عَلَيْكَ, (Sb, Ṣ,) and عَلَيْهِ; (Mṣb;) but some of the Arabs [in this case] leave it unchanged, as in the saying of a rájiz,

• طَارُوا عَلَاهُنَّ فَطِرْ عَلَاهَا •

[*They fled*, or *have fled*, *upon them*, (referring to camels,) *and flee thou upon her*]; this, it is said, being of the dial. of Belḥárith Ibn-Kaạb. (Sb, Ṣ.) — As a particle, it has nine [or more than nine] meanings. (Mughnee.) As such, (Mughnee,) or, accord. to Sb, as a noun, (Ḳ,) it denotes الاِسْتِعْلَاءُ [i. e. superiority] (Mṣb, Es-Subkee, Mughnee, Ḳ, TA) properly thus termed, (Mṣb,) such as is perceptible by sense; (Es-Subkee, TA;) either with respect to what is signified by the noun governed by it, and this is generally the case, (Mughnee,) as in the saying [in the Ḳur xxiii. 22 and xl. 80], وَعَلَيْهَا وَعَلَى الْفُلْكِ تُحْمَلُونَ [*And upon them* (referring to camels) *and upon the ship*, or *ships*, *ye are carried*]; (Mughnee, Ḳ;) or with respect to what is near thereto, as in the saying [in the Ḳur xx. 10], أَوْ أَجِدُ عَلَى النَّارِ هُدًى [*Or I shall find near upon the fire*, i. e. *at the fire*, *a right direction*]: (Mughnee:) and using it to denote الاِسْتِعْلَاءُ properly thus termed, you say, كُنْتُ عَلَى السَّطْحِ [*I was* upon the flat house-top]: (Mṣb:) [in like manner also,] as denoting الاستعلاء that is perceptible by sense, it occurs in the saying [in the Ḳur lv. 26], كُلُّ مَنْ عَلَيْهَا فَانٍ [*Every one that is upon it* (referring to the earth) *is transitory*]: (Es-Subkee, TA:) and you say, عَلَى زَيْدٍ ثَوْبٌ [*Upon Zeyd is, or was, a garment*], عَلَى being here a particle; and عَلَا زَيْدًا ثَوْبٌ [*A garment was upon Zeyd,*] عَلَا being here a verb. (Mbr, Ṣ.) And it denotes الاستعلاء, likewise, tropically thus termed, (Mṣb, TA,) such as is ideal, or perceived by the intellect; (Mṣb, Es-Subkee, Mughnee, TA;) as in the saying زَيْدٌ عَلَيْهِ دَيْنٌ ‡ [*Zeyd, a debt is lying upon him,* or *incumbent on him,* i. e. *he owes a debt,* لِفُلَانٍ *to such a one*], that which is ideal being thus likened to that which is corporeal; (Mṣb;) and in the phrases عَلَيْنَا أَمْرٌ and عَلَيْنَا مَالٌ, meaning ‡ *An affair,* or *a command, lies,* or *rests, upon us,* or *is incumbent on us,* and so *property,* [*as due from us,* i. e.] *the former as a duty* and *the latter as a debt,* i. e. يَثْبُتُ, like as the thing lies, or rests, (يَثْبُتُ,) upon the place; the latter phrase importing responsibility: and ثَبَتَ عَلَيْهِ مَالٌ is also said to mean كَثُرَ [i. e. † *property was,* or *became, much in quantity,* or *amount, upon him,* app. *as a burden imposing upon him responsibility*]. (TA.) And it [likewise] denotes ideal استعلاء in the phrase لَهُمْ عَلَىَّ ذَنْبٌ ‡ [*A crime,* or *an offence, committed upon* (or here, as in many other instances, it may be rendered *against*) *me is imputable to them*]: (Mughnee:) and so in the saying [in the Ḳur ii. 254 and xvii. 22], فَضَّلْنَا بَعْضَهُمْ عَلَى بَعْضٍ ‡ [*We have made some of them to have superiority over some*]. (Es-Subkee, Mughnee, TA.) [See also أَنْتَ عَلَى عَيْنِى, and أَنْتَ عَلَى رَأْسِى, voce عَيْنٌ, first quarter.] — It also denotes concomitance, like مَعَ; as in the saying [in the Ḳur ii. 172], وَآتَى ٱلْمَالَ عَلَى حُبِّهِ [*And giveth property with* (or *notwithstanding*) *the love of it*]; (Mughnee, Ḳ;) and so it is said to be used in the phrase, in a trad. respecting the alms of the breaking of the fast [of Ramaḍán], عَلَى كُلِّ حُرٍّ وَعَبْدٍ صَاعٌ [*With every free man and slave, a ṣáa*], because the alms-gift of the breaking of the fast is not incumbent on the slave, but only on his master; (IAth, TA;) and so it is used in the [common] phrase, عَلَى أَنِّى رَاضٍ [*With* (or *notwithstanding*) *my being pleased,* or *well pleased,* or *content*]. (Ḥar p. 13.) — It also denotes transition, (Mughnee, Ḳ,) like عَنْ; (Mughnee;) as in the saying (of El-Ḳoheyf El-'Okeylee, TA),

• إِذَا رَضِيَتْ عَلَىَّ بَنُو قُشَيْرٍ •
• لَعَمْرُ ٱللّٰهِ أَعْجَبَنِى رِضَاهَا •

[*When the sons of Ḳusheyr shall be pleased,* or *well pleased,* or *content, with me,* (or rather, if عَلَىَّ here denote transition, *with what will proceed from me,*) *by the everlasting existence of God, their being pleased, &c., will induce in me admiration,* or *pleasure*], (Mughnee, Ḳ,* TA,) i. e. عَنِّى; (Mughnee, TA;) or it may be that رَضِىَ is made to imply the meaning of عَطَفَ [which is trans. by means of عَلَى]; (Mughnee;) or, as Ks says, it is made to accord with its contr. سَخِطَ, (Mughnee, TA,) by its being made trans. by means of عَلَى: (TA:) and so in the saying,

• فِى لَيْلَةٍ لَا نَرَى بِهَا أَحَدًا •
• يَحْكِى عَلَيْنَا إِلَّا كَوَاكِبُهَا •

[*In a night in which we shall not see any one that shall report what will proceed from us, except its stars*], i. e., عَنَّا; or it may be said that يَحْكِى is [here] made to imply the meaning of يَنِمُّ. (Mughnee.) — It is also used to assign a cause, like لِ; as in the saying [in the Ḳur ii. 181], وَلِتُكَبِّرُوا ٱللّٰهَ عَلَى مَا هَدَاكُمْ, (Mughnee, Ḳ,) meaning لِهِدَايَتِهِ إِيَّاكُمْ [i. e. *And that ye should magnify God for,* or *on account of, his rightly directing you*]; (Mughnee;) [and in the same, vi. 90, &c., لَا أَسْأَلُكُمْ عَلَيْهِ أَجْرًا i. e. *I will not ask of you for it,* or *on account of it, a recompense;*] and as in the saying of Rabee'ah Ibn Maḳroom Eḍ-Ḍabbee,

• فَدَعَوْا نَزَالِ فَكُنْتُ أَوَّلَ نَازِلٍ •
• وَعَلَامَ أَرْكَبُهُ إِذَا لَمْ أَنْزِلِ •

i. e. [*And they called out, "Alight;" and I was the first of any alighting:*] *and for what* [or *wherefore*] *do I ride him if I do not alight* when called upon to do so? (Ḥam p. 29. [عَلَامَ is here, as usually, for عَلَى مَ.]) — It is also used in the sense of فِى [generally followed by a noun significant of time]; (Ṣ, Mughnee, Ḳ;*) as in the saying [in the Ḳur xxviii. 14], وَدَخَلَ ٱلْمَدِينَةَ عَلَى حِينِ غَفْلَةٍ [*And he entered the city in,* or *during, a time of inadvertence*]; (Mughnee, Ḳ;) and in the saying [in the same ii. 96], وَٱتَّبَعُوا مَا تَتْلُو ٱلشَّيَاطِينُ عَلَى مُلْكِ سُلَيْمَانَ, meaning, فِى زَمَنِ مُلْكِ سليمان [i. e. *And they followed what the devils related,* or *recited, in the time of,* or *during, the reign of Suleymán* (or *Solomon*)]; (Mughnee;) and in the phrase, كَانَ كَذَا عَلَى عَهْدِ فُلَانٍ, meaning, فِى عَهْدِهِ [i. e. *It was thus,* or *such a thing was, in the time of such a one*]: (Ṣ:) [and in like manner it is used in the saying in the Ḳur iii. 173, مَا كَانَ ٱللّٰهُ لِيَذَرَ ٱلْمُؤْمِنِينَ عَلَى مَا أَنْتُمْ عَلَيْهِ *God is not purposing to leave,* or *certainly will not leave, the believers in that* state *wherein ye are:* and in the phrase عَلَى سَفَرٍ, in ii. 180 &c. of the same, i. e. *In* (or, as we also say, *on*) *a journey:* in like manner also] لَقَدْ سَرَيْتُ عَلَى ٱلظَّلَامِ, in a verse of Aboo-Kebeer El-Hudhalee, means, فِى ٱلظَّلَامِ [i. e. *I have journeyed by night in the darkness*], فى الظلام holding the place of a noun in the accus. case as a ظَرْف [i. e. an adverbial noun of time or place]; or it may be in the place of a denotative of state, meaning وَأَنَا عَلَى ٱلظَّلَامِ i. e. رَاكِبٌ لَهُ [*riding upon the darkness*]: (Ḥam p. 37:) and you say of one who was desiring to rise and hasten, رَأَيْتُهُ عَلَى أَوْفَاضٍ [i. e. *I found him in a state of haste:* see وَفْضٌ]. (TA.) — [It also denotes conformity, accordance, adaptation, or agreement; as in the phrase, اِضْرِبْهُ عَلَى طَبْعِ هٰذَا i. e. *Make thou it, fashion it,* or *mould it, conformably,* or *according, to the model, make, fashion,* or *mould, of this;* (see طَبْعٌ;) and in طُبِعَ عَلَى الشَّىْءِ and جُبِلَ and فُطِرَ &c. i. e. *He* (a man) *was created conformably,* or *with an adaptation* or *a disposition, to the thing:* (see 1 in art. طبع:) so too in the phrase in the Ḳur xxiv. last verse, قَدْ يَعْلَمُ مَا أَنْتُمْ عَلَيْهِ *Certainly He knoweth that* state of conduct and mind *to which ye are conforming yourselves;* and in many other passages therein: thus also in the saying of Moḥammad, كُلُّ مَوْلُودٍ يُولَدُ عَلَى ٱلْفِطْرَةِ *Every infant is born in a state of conformity to the natural constitution with which he is created in his mother's womb in relation to the soul;* (see art. فطر;) and in the prov., mentioned by Meyd, ٱلنَّاسُ عَلَى دِينِ ٱلْمُلُوكِ *The people are in conformity to,* i. e. *are followers of,* or *follow, the religion of the kings;* and in the phrase, relating to a saying or an opinion, عَلَيْهِ أَكْثَرُ ٱلْعُلَمَآءِ *Upon it most of the learned are in agreement;* in which, as in other exs. of the same kind, a verb or a part. n., (in the last, for instance, مُجْمِعُونَ or the like,) is understood. — It also denotes a condition; as in the phrases, صَالَحَهُ عَلَى كَذَا *He made peace,* or *reconciliation,* or *a compromise, with him on the condition of such a thing,* and عَلَى أَنْ يَفْعَلَ كَذَا *on the condition of his doing such a thing.* — And there are various other usages of this prep. depending upon verbs or part. ns. expressed or obviously understood in connection with them, too numerous to be here collected. Many of these will be found among the explanations of words with which they occur.] — It is also used in the sense of مِنْ; as in the saying, إِذَا ٱكْتَالُوا عَلَى ٱلنَّاسِ يَسْتَوْفُونَ, (Ṣ, Mughnee, Ḳ,) in the Ḳur [lxxxiii. 2], meaning, مِنَ ٱلنَّاسِ [i. e. Who, *when they take by measure from men, take fully*], (Ṣ,) or, as in the T, عَنِ ٱلنَّاسِ [which signifies the same]. (TA.) — It is also used in the sense of بِ; (Ṣ, Mughnee, Ḳ;) as in the saying in the Ḳur [vii. 103], عَلَى أَنْ لَا أَقُولَ عَلَى ٱللّٰهِ إِلَّا ٱلْحَقَّ, (Mughnee, Ḳ,*) meaning بِأَنْ, (TA,) [i. e. *That I should not say of God* aught *save the truth,*] and Ubei read with ب [i. e. بِأَنْ]; (Bḍ, Mughnee;) like as they say, رَمَيْتُ عَلَى ٱلْقَوْسِ [meaning بِٱلْقَوْسِ, i. e. *I shot with the bow*], and جِئْتُ عَلَى حَالٍ حَسَنَةٍ [meaning بِحَالٍ حَسَنَةٍ, i. e. *I came in a good condition*]; (Bḍ; [in which, and also voce حَقِيقٌ, last sentence, see more;]) and they said also, اِرْكَبْ عَلَى ٱسْمِ ٱللّٰهِ [meaning, بِٱسْمِ ٱللّٰهِ, i. e. *Mount thou in the name of God*]: (Mughnee:) thus [too] it is used in the saying of Aboo-Dhu-eyb,

• يَسَرٌ يُفِيضُ عَلَى ٱلْقِدَاحِ وَيَصْدَعُ •

[expl. in art. فيض, conj. 4,] meaning بِٱلْقِدَاحِ:

(Ṣ:) [and in the phrase عَلَى يَدِهِ i. e. *By his hand*, or † *by his means*.] — It is also used to denote an emendation, (Mughnee, Ḳ,) and a digression, or transition, (Mughnee,) like لٰكِنَّ; (TA;) as in the saying, فُلَانٌ لَا يَدْخُلُ الجَنَّةَ لِسُوْءِ صَنِيعِهِ عَلَى أَنَّهُ, (Mughnee,) or فُلَانٌ جَهَنَّمِىٌّ, (Ḳ,) لَا يَيْأَسُ مِنْ رَحْمَةِ ٱللّٰهِ لٰكِنَّهُ, (Mughnee, Ḳ,) meaning [i. e. *Such a one will not enter Paradise, because of the evilness of his deed*, or *conduct*, or *such a one is hell-doomed; but*, or *yet, he will not despair of the mercy of God*]: (TA:) and thus it is used in the saying,

* بِكُلٍّ تَدَاوَيْنَا فَلَمْ يُشْفَ مَا بِنَا *
* عَلَى أَنَّ قُرْبَ الدَّارِ خَيْرٌ مِنَ البُعْدِ *
* عَلَى أَنَّ قُرْبَ الدَّارِ لَيْسَ بِنَافِعٍ *
* إِذَا كَانَ مَنْ تَهْوَاهُ لَيْسَ بِذِى وُدِّ *

[*With everything we treated*, or *have treated, ourselves curatively, and what was in us was not*, or *has not been, healed; but the nearness of the abode is better than the remoteness; but the nearness of the abode is not profitable when the person whom thou lovest is not endued with affection*]: the poet invalidates by the first عَلَى his saying فَلَمْ يُشْفَ مَا بِنَا; and then, by the second عَلَى, the clause immediately preceding it. (Mughnee.) — It is also redundant, for the purpose of compensation; as in the saying,

* إِنَّ الكَرِيمَ وَأَبِيكَ يَعْتَمِلْ *
* إِنْ لَمْ يَجِدْ يَوْمًا عَلَى مَنْ يَتَّكِلْ *

meaning مَنْ يَتَّكِلُ عَلَيْهِ [i. e. *Verily the generous, by thy father, will work for himself when he finds not, some day, him upon whom he may rely*]; عَلَى being added before مَنْ for the purpose of compensation [for its omission in its proper place]: (Mughnee, Ḳ:) Es-Subkee says, it may be redundant, as in the saying, لَا أَحْلِفُ عَلَى يَمِينٍ, meaning لا احلف يمينا [i. e. *I will not swear an oath*]. (TA.) ═ It is also a noun, having the meaning of فَوْقَ [i. e. The *location that is above*, or *over*], this being the case when it is immediately followed by مِنْ; (Ṣ, Mṣb, Mughnee, Ḳ;*) as in the saying (of Muzáḥim-El-'Okeylee, describing a قَطَاة [or sand-grouse, and, afterwards, its making a rumbling sound in its inside, from thirst], TA),

* غَدَتْ مِنْ عَلَيْهِ بَعْدَ مَا تَمَّ ظِمْؤُهَا *

[*It went away in the early morning from the location above it*, (or, as we say, *from above it*,) *after that her interval between two comings to water was complete*]: (Mṣb, Mughnee, Ḳ: [and a similar ex. is cited in the Ṣ:]) or, accord. to Aṣ, meaning مِنْ عِنْدِهِ [*from its vicinage*]: and, used in this sense, as a noun, it admits before it no other prep. than مِنْ. (Mṣb.) ═ عَلَيْكَ is also a verbal noun, used as an incentive: (TA:) you say, عَلَيْكَ زَيْدًا, (Ṣ, Ḳ, TA,) and بِزَيْدٍ, (TA,) meaning *Take thou Zeyd*; or *take thou hold of Zeyd*: (Ṣ, TA:) or *keep thou*, or *cleave thou, to Zeyd*: (Ḳ, TA:) and عَلَيْكَ بِكَذَا *keep thou to such a thing*: (El-Munáwee, TA in art. ب:) [thus] it is said in a trad., عَلَيْكَ بِالرِّفْقِ [*Keep thou to gentleness*]. (El-Jámi' eṣ-Ṣagheer.) — And [in like manner] you say, عَلَىَّ زَيْدًا, and بِزَيْدٍ, meaning *Give thou me*, or *present thou to me, Zeyd*: (Ṣ, TA:) [or, more commonly, *bring thou to me Zeyd*:] you say, عَلَىَّ بِكَذَا, meaning *bring thou to me such a thing*. (MA.)

عُلًى: see عَلَاةٌ. — [It is also pl. of عُلْيَا, fem. of أَعْلَى, q. v.]

عَلَاةٌ The سِنْدَان [or *anvil*], (Ṣ, Mgh, Ḳ, TA,) whether *of* شَجَر [app. meaning of *such as are made from trees*, or perhaps this is a mistranscription for صَخْر, i. e. *rock*], or of *iron*; or the زُبْرَة [i. e. *iron anvil*] *upon which the blacksmith beats iron*: (TA:) pl. [or rather coll. gen. n.] ↓ عَلًا. (Ṣ.) — Hence it is applied to a she-camel, as being likened thereto in respect of her hardness: you say نَاقَةٌ عَلَاةُ الخَلْقِ † [*A she-camel hard*, or *firm, in respect of make*]: (Ṣ:) or عَلَاةٌ thus applied signifies *tall*, or *overtopping*; as also ↓ عِلْيَانٌ, and ↓ عِلِيَانٌ: (Ḳ, TA:) or ↓ عِلْيَانٌ, (TA,) or ↓ عِلِيَانٌ, (Ṣ,) and ↓ عِلِّيَانٌ, (TA,) signify, thus applied, *tall and bulky*; (Ṣ, TA;) or, as some say, *outstripping in pace* or *journeying*; *never seen otherwise than before the other camels*. (TA.) — Also *A stone* [*placed upon two other stones called* حِمَارَانِ (q. v.)] *upon which is put* [*to dry the preparation of curd called*] أَقِط: (Ṣ, Ḳ, TA:) or, as some say, *a piece of rock upon which is made a circle of* أَخْثَاء [or *lumps of dung such as is called* خِثْى (q. v.)] *and bricks*, or *crude bricks*, (لَبِن,) *and ashes, and in*, or *upon*, *which* أَقِط *is then cooked*: pl. [or coll. gen. n.] as above. (TA.) — And *A thing like the* [*milking-vessel called*] عُلْبَة, *around which* [*dung such as is called*] خِثْى *is put, and which is used for milking therein*. (Ḳ.)

عِلْوَةٌ: see عُلْوٌ.

عِلْيَةٌ: see عَلِىٌّ [of which it is said to be pl.].

عَلْوَى, accord. to IAạr, [and so in my MS. copy of the Ḳ,] but accord. to [other copies of] the Ḳ ↓ عَلْوَاءُ, (TA,) i. q. قِصَّةٌ عَالِيَةٌ [app. *A story*, or *an affair, of a high quality*]. (Ḳ, TA. [See also عَلْيَاءُ.])

عَلْوَاءُ: see what next precedes.

عَلْيَاءُ *A high place*; (IAth, Ḳ, TA;) a subst. in this sense, not [an epithet syn. with عُلْيَا] fem. of أَعْلَى; for if it were this, it would [by rule] be necessarily determinate; (IAth, TA;) [though] it is sometimes used as syn. with عُلْيَا, see أَعْلَى: (Mṣb:) any *high*, or *overtopping, place*: (Ṣ, Mṣb:) this is its primary meaning: (Mṣb:) and [in like manner] ↓ عَلَايَةٌ signifies any *high*, or *lofty, place*; as also ↓ عَلِىٌّ. (Ḳ.) And Any *high thing*. (Ḳ.) The *head of a mountain*: (Ḳ, TA:) or the *head of any high*, or *overtopping, mountain*. (TA.) And العَلْيَاءُ signifies *The sky*: (Ḳ, TA:) a subst., not an epithet. (TA.) مَا زَالَ مِنْهَا بِعَلْيَاءَ means *He ceased not to be ennobled, and elevated in rank*, or *dignity, in consequence of it*; i. e., a deed that he had done. (Aṣ, TA in art. بعل.) — Also ‡ *A high*, or *an eminent, deed*. (Ḳ, TA.)

عُلْوِىٌّ: see عَالِىٌّ.

عُلْوَانٌ of a book or writing, The عُنْوَان thereof; (Ṣ, Mṣb, Ḳ,* TA;) i. e. its *superscription*, or *title*; syn. سِمَةٌ. (TA.) [See arts. عن and عنو.]

عُلْيَانٌ: see the next paragraph: and see also عَلَاةٌ.

عِلْيَانٌ, with kesr, (Ḳ, TA,) thus accord. to Az and ISd, but accord. to J, [in the Ṣ,] ↓ عِلِيَانٌ, like عِطِشَانٌ [in measure] *Tall and corpulent*, applied to a man, (Ṣ, TA,) and likewise to a woman: (TA:) or *bulky*: and *tall*: (Ḳ:) or *bulky and tall*, applied to a man and to a camel; fem. with ة: or, applied to a camel, *old and bulky*. (TA.) See also عَلَاةٌ, in two places. — Also, عِلْيَانٌ, The *male hyena*: (Ḳ, TA:) or *a tall hyena*. (TA.) — And *A high*, or *loud*, voice, as also ↓ عِلِّيَانٌ. (Ḳ.) ═ And *Household-goods*, or *furniture and utensils*; syn. مَتَاعٌ. (TA, as from the Ḳ; and TḲ; but not in my MS. copy of the Ḳ, nor in the CḲ.)

عَلَاءٌ inf. n. of عَلِىَ (Ṣ, Mgh, Mṣb) in the phrase فِى المَكَارِمِ (Ṣ, Mgh) or عَلِىَ فِى الشَّرَفِ: (Mṣb:) and [used as a simple subst.] it signifies *High*, or *elevated, rank* or *station*; or *eminence*, or *nobility*; (Ḳ;) as also ↓ عُلًى, and ↓ مَعْلَاةٌ; (Ṣ;) or this last signifies the *acquisition of high*, or *elevated, rank* or *station*, or *of eminence*, or *nobility*; (Ḳ;) [or, agreeably with analogy, *a cause*, or *means, of acquiring high*, or *elevated, rank* &c.; being originally مَعْلَوَةٌ, of the measure مَفْعَلَةٌ, like مَجْبَنَةٌ and مَبْخَلَةٌ &c.;] and its pl. is مَعَالٍ, (Ṣ, Mṣb,) whence مَعَالِى الأُمُورِ i. e. مكتسب الشرف [a strange explanation of a pl. by a sing., app. meaning (*the affairs*, or *actions, that are*) *the cause*, or *means, of acquiring high*, or *elevated, rank* &c.]. (Mṣb.) — أَبُو العَلَاءِ [is a name for *The kind of sweet food called*] الفَالُوذَج [and الفَالُوذ, q. v.]. (Ḥar pp. 228.)

عُلُوٌّ, like عَدُوٌّ [in measure], an epithet used in the phrase رَجُلٌ عُلُوٌّ لِلرِّجَالِ [app. meaning *A man wont to exalt himself to* other *men*]. (TA.)

عُلُوٌّ: [see 1, of which it is an inf. n., and] see عِلِّىٌّ.

عَلِىٌّ *High, elevated*, or *lofty*; (Ṣ, Ḳ;) applied to a thing; (Ḳ;) [and] so ↓ عَالٍ: (Mṣb:) so, too, the former, [and more commonly so,] *in respect of rank, condition*, or *state*; *eminent*, or *noble*: and ↓ عِلْيَةٌ is a pl. thereof in the latter sense; like as صِبْيَةٌ is of صَبِىٌّ; [or, as some hold a word of this form and class to be, a quasi-pl. n.;] as in the saying, فُلَانٌ مِنْ عِلْيَةِ النَّاسِ [*Such a one is of the high in rank, &c., of men*]; (Ṣ;) or عِلْيَةٌ, as also ▼ عِلِّىٌّ, [which latter is of a form proper to quasi-pl. ns. by common consent,] signifies the *great in respect of estimation, rank,* or *dignity,* of men, thus used in a pl. sense. (Ḳ.) —— It signifies also *Strong, robust,* or *powerful:* (Ḳ, TA:) and hence it is used as a proper name of a man; (Ḳ,* TA;) and it may be also from the meaning of highness of rank &c., eminence, or nobility. (TA.) —— العَلِىُّ as a name of God signifies [*The High:* or *the Most High,* like ▼ الأَعْلَى; i. e.] *He above whom is nothing.* (TA.) —— عَلِيُّونَ [is also a pl. of عَلِىٌّ, and] signifies Persons *alighting,* or *abiding, in the high parts of a country;* in this sense opposed to سُفْلِيُّونَ: —— and it signifies also Persons *having opulence,* and *eminence,* or *nobility;* in this sense likewise opposed to سُفْلِيُّونَ. (TA.) —— عَلِيَّةٌ applied to a she-camel means *Having strength to bear her burden;* as also ▼ مُعْتَلِيَةٌ and ▼ مُسْتَعْلِيَةٌ: and you say نَاقَةٌ حَلِيَّةٌ عَلِيَّةٌ, the former epithet meaning *pleasing in appearance and pace,* and عالية [an evident mistranscription for عَلِيَّةٌ] meaning *excelling.* (TA.) —— And one says, فُلَانٌ هَبِىٌّ عَلِىٌّ, meaning [*Such a one is a person of goodly form* or *aspect* or *the like,*] *one who acts effeminately to women.* (TA.)

عِلِىٌّ *i. q.* ▼ عُلُوٌّ [an inf. n. of 1, q. v.]. (Ḳ, TA.) Hence the reading of Ibn-Mes'ood [in the Ḳur xxvii. 14], ظُلْمًا وَعِلِيًّا [*By reason of wrongfulness and self-exaltation*]. (TA.)

عُلَاوَةٌ: see عُلْوٌ. —— عُلَاوَةُ الرِّيحِ means *The windward side; the side,* or *quarter, from which the wind blows;* with respect to the game, or object of the chase; (Ṣ, TA;) and with respect to a man: (TA:) opposed to سُفَالَتُهَا. (Ṣ, Mṣb,* TA.) [See 1, last quarter.]

عِلَاوَةٌ *Anything that one has raised and put,* (Ṣ,) or *a thing that one has hung, upon a camel, after the loading him* (Ṣ, Mgh, Mṣb) *completely, such as the water-skin and the* سَفُود [q. v.], (Ṣ,) or *such as the* [*small leathern water-bag called*] إِدَاوَة *and the* سُفْرَة [q. v.]: (Mgh, Mṣb:) or *a thing that is put between the two equiponderant burdens,* (Ḳ, TA,) *after the binding of them upon the camel* or *other animal:* (TA:) pl. عَلَاوَى, (Ṣ,) or عِلَاوَاتٌ. (Mṣb.) —— Also *A superaddition* of anything; as meaning *something added.* (Ḳ, TA.) One says, أَعْطَاهُ أَلْفَ دِينَارٍ وَدِينَارٍ عِلَاوَةً [as though the phrase were, وَدِينَارٌ عِلَاوَةٌ, but the right reading is app. وَدِينَارًا عِلَاوَةً, i. e. *He gave him a thousand deenárs, and a deenár as a superaddition,* or *over and above*]. (TA.) —— And † The *upper,* or *uppermost, part of the head,* or *of the neck:* (Ḳ:) or the *head* of a human being *as long as it remains upon the neck:* one says, ضَرَبَ عِلَاوَتَهُ i. e. رَأْسَهُ † [*He smote his head,* app. meaning *he beheaded him*]: (Ṣ:) or ضَرَبَ عِلَاوَةَ رَأْسِهِ, which is tropical: (Mgh:) and سَبَتَ عِلَاوَتَهُ † *he smote his neck* [*so as to decapitate him*]: (Ṣ and M in art. سبت:) and سُبِتَتْ عِلَاوَتُهُ ‡ *His head was cut off;* a tropical phrase. (A in that art.)

عَلَايَةٌ: see عَلْيَاءُ.

عِلْيَانٌ: see عَلَاةٌ, in two places: —— and عِلِّيَانٌ.

عِلِّيُّونَ: see عِلِّىٌّ.

عُلِّيَّةٌ, (Ṣ, Mṣb, Ḳ,) with ḍamm, (Mṣb, Ḳ,) the ل, which is meksoorah, being with teshdeed, as is also the ى, (TA,) of the measure فُعِّيلَةٌ, like مُرِّيقَةٌ [n. un. of مُرِّيقٌ], (Ṣ,) originally عُلِّيوَةٌ, (Ṣ, Mṣb,) from عَلَوْتُ; (Ṣ;) and عِلِّيَّةٌ, with kesr, (Ṣ, Mṣb, Ḳ,) of the measure فِعِّيلَةٌ; or, as some say, from a reduplicate root, and of the measure فُعْلِيَّةٌ; adding that there is no instance of فُعِّيلَةٌ in the language; (Ṣ;) [therefore it is also mentioned in art. عل;] *An upper chamber;* or *a chamber in the upper,* or *uppermost, story;* syn. غُرْفَةٌ: (Ṣ, Mṣb, Ḳ:) pl. عَلَالِىُّ. (Ṣ, Mṣb, Ḳ.) —— And عُلِّيَّةٌ, it is said, may signify also The *board upon which is placed the* مِعْيَار [or *assay-balance*]. (Ḥar p. 550.) —— See also the next paragraph.

عِلِّيُّونَ, [said to be] a pl. of which the sing. is ▼ عِلِّىٌّ, (Ḳ and TA in this art. and in art. عل,) or ▼ عِلِّيَّةٌ or عُلِّيَّةٌ, or a pl. having no sing., (Ḳ and TA in art. عل,) [or rather it is from a Hebr. word, as I have stated in art. عل,] *A place in the Seventh Heaven, to which ascend the souls of the believers:* (Ḳ, TA:) or *the highest of the places:* or *a certain thing above another thing;* [a word] of which the sing. is not known, nor the fem.: or *loftiness above loftiness:* or *the Seventh Heaven* [altogether]: or *the* دِيوَان [or *register,* or *place of reckoning,*] *of the guardian angels, to which are brought up the reports of the deeds of the righteous:* (TA:) or *Paradise:* or *the right leg* [or *pillar*] *of the* عَرْش [which is vulgarly held to mean the *throne of God*]: or [*the lote-tree called*] سِدْرَةُ المُنْتَهَى [respecting which see art. سدر]. (Ḥar p. 5.) [See also other explanations in art. عل.]

عَالٍ: see عَلِىٌّ. —— [Hence,] رَجُلٌ عَالِى الكَعْبِ † *A man who is elevated, exalted, eminent,* or *noble.* (Ḳ. [See also كَعْبٌ.]) It is said in a trad. respecting Ḳeyleh, لَا يَزَالُ كَعْبُكِ عَالِيًا, meaning *May thou not cease to be elevated,* or *noble; exalted above such as treats,* or *regards, thee with enmity.* (TA.) —— مِنْ عَالٍ signifies the same as مِنْ عَلٍ, q. v. (Ṣ, Ḳ.) —— عَالِيَةُ الدَّمِ, said of the حَائِض, means One *whose blood rises above the water.* (TA.) —— [عَالٍ applied to a word, or form of word, signifies † *Of high authority, approved,* or *chaste:* and hence, *usual,* or *common:* see أَعْلَى.] ━━ See also عَائِلٌ, in art. عول.

عَالِيَةٌ [a subst. from عَالٍ, rendered such by the affix ة]: see عُلْوٌ. —— Also [particularly] The *upper portion* of the spear-shaft; (Ḳ, TA;) سَافِلَة signifying the "lower portion" thereof: (TA:) or the *head* (رَأْس) thereof: or the *half that is next to the iron head:* (Ḳ, TA:) or the *part,* of the spear, *that is below the iron head:* (Er-Rághib, TA:) or the *portion,* of the spear, *that enters the iron head, extending to the third part thereof* [i. e. *of the shaft;* so that it signifies the *uppermost of the three equal portions of the shaft*]: (Ṣ, TA:) pl. عَوَالٍ, which some explain as meaning the *iron heads* of spears. (TA. [See an ex. of the pl. in a verse cited voce زَجٌّ.]) Also *A straight spear-shaft.* (TA.) —— And The [*upper*] *part,* of a valley, *whence the water thereof descends.* (TA.) —— العَالِيَةُ, also, is *The region above Nejd, extending to the land of Tihámeh,* (Ṣ, Mgh, Mṣb, Ḳ,) *and to the part behind Mekkeh,* (Ṣ, Ḳ,) i. e. [*to*] *El-Ḥijáz and what is next to it:* (Ṣ:) and it is said that the عَالِيَة of El-Ḥijáz is the *higher and more elevated part thereof, forming a wide extent of country.* (TA.) And [its pl.] العَوَالِى, (Ḳ, TA,) as also العَالِيَةُ, (TA,) is applied to *Certain towns,* or *villages, in the exterior of El-Medeeneh,* (Ḳ, TA,) *the nearest four miles distant from it, and the most distant, in the direction of Nejd, eight.* (TA.)

عَالِىٌّ *Of,* or *relating to, the region called* العَالِيَة; (Ṣ, Ḳ;) and so ▼ عُلْوِىٌّ, (Ṣ, Mṣb, Ḳ,) with ḍamm, (Mṣb, Ḳ,) which is anomalous. (Ṣ, Mṣb, Ḳ.)

أَعْلَى *Higher,* and *highest; contr. of* أَسْفَلُ: (M and Mṣb and Ḳ in art. سفل:) the fem. is عُلْيَا; (TA;) which is like دُنْيَا and قُصْيَا, with و changed into ى; (ISd, TA voce بُقْوَى;) and of which the pl. is عُلًى, like as كُبَرٌ is of كُبْرَى. (Mṣb, TA.) See عَلِىٌّ. —— One says شَفَةٌ عُلْيَا and ▼ عَلْيَاءُ, but the former is the more usual, meaning *An upper lip.* (IAmb, Mṣb, TA.) —— عُلْيَا مُضَرَ means *The higher* [app. *in respect of territory* (see a note in p. xi. of the preface to this work)] *of Muḍar;* (Ḳ, TA;) said to denote *Ḳureysh and Ḳeys;* the rest being called سُفْلَى مُضَرَ. (TA.) —— And one says, جَآءَ مِنْ أَعْلَى وَأَرْوَحَ, meaning *It came from the sky and the place whence the wind blows.* (TA.) —— أَعْلَى applied to a word, or form of word, means † [*Of higher authority, more approved,* or *more chaste;* and also, hence, as frequency of usage is a necessary condition of فَصَاحَة, q. v.,] *more usual* or *common.* (M and TA in art. فر.) —— One says also, هُمْ بِهِمْ أَعْلَى عَيْنًا i. e. † *They are most knowing respecting them, and most acquainted with their state,* or *condition.* (TA.) —— And هُوَ أَعْلَى بِكُمْ عَيْنًا i. e. † *He is in the highest degree a magnifier,* or *honourer, of you; ye being greatly esteemed by him.* (TA.) —— اليَدُ العُلْيَا † *The abstinent,* or *chaste, hand:* or *the expending,* or *disbursing, hand.* (TA.) ━━ أَعْلَى formed by transposition from أَعْوَلُ: see the latter, in art. عول.

مَعْلَاةٌ: see عَلَاةٌ.

ٱلْمُعَلَّى *The seventh of the arrows of the game called* ٱلْمَيْسِر; (Aṣ, A'Obeyd, Ṣ, M, Mgh, Ḳ;) *the most excellent of them; it has seven notches; and it obtains seven shares* [*of the slaughtered camel*] *when it wins, and occasions the imposition of seven fines when it does not win.* (M, TA.) [See an ex. in a verse cited voce رَقِيبٌ.]

ٱلْمُعَلِّى : see 2. — Also *He who comes to the milch beast* [meaning *the she-camel, when she is to be milked,*] *from the direction of her left side:* (Ṣ, Ḳ:) or the she-camel has two milkers; one of them holds the milking-vessel on the right side, and the other milks on the left side; and *the milker* [*thus standing on the left side*] is called ٱلْمُعَلِّى and ▼ ٱلْمُسْتَعْلِى; and the holder, ٱلْبَائِنُ: thus in the M: or ▼ ٱلْمُسْتَعْلِى is *he who stands on the left side of the milch beast: or he who takes the milking-vessel with his left hand and milks with his right hand: or he who milks from the left side.* (TA.)

أَرْضٌ مُعْلَوْلِيَةٌ : see مُعْلَوْلِيَةٌ, in art. غلو.

أَتَيْتُهُ مِنْ مُعَالٍ : see أَتَيْتُهُ مِنْ عَلٍ.

مُعْتَلٍ † *Having ability,* or *power;* as also ▼ مُسْتَعْلٍ. (TA.) — [Hence,] ٱلْمُعْتَلِى signifies † *The lion;* (Ḳ, TA;) because of his strength. (TA.) — See also عَلِىٌّ, last quarter. ═ هُوَ غَيْرُ مُعْتَلٍ فِى ٱلْأَمْرِ means *He is not one who falls short, or falls short of doing what is requisite,* or *who is remiss, in the affair;* like غَيْرُ مُؤْتَلٍ. (TA.)

ٱلْمُتَعَالِى, as a name of God, *He who is great,* or *supremely great, above the lie* [or *lying imputation*] *of the forgers of falsehood: or the High: and the Most high; who is higher than every* [*other*] *high one:* (TA:) or *He who has ascendency over everything by his power: or He who is great, and exalted,* or *supremely exalted, above* [*the ascription of*] *the attributes of the created beings.* (Ksh, Bḍ.)

مُسْتَعْلًى The *near,* i. e. *left, side of a she-camel:* you say, أَتَيْتُ ٱلنَّاقَةَ مِنْ قِبَلِ مُسْتَعْلَاهَا i. e. مِنْ قِبَلِ إِنْسِيِّهَا [*I came to the she-camel from the direction of her near,* or *left, side*]. (TA.)

مُسْتَعْلٍ : see مُعْتَلٍ; and عَلِىٌّ, last quarter: — and see also ٱلْمُعَلِّى, in two places. — ٱلْيَدُ ٱلْمُسْتَعْلِيَةُ means † *The hand of him who takes by force, and of the plunderer, and the like:* opposed to ٱلْيَدُ ٱلْمُسْتَخْفِيَةُ: the Sunneh ordains that the latter shall be cut off [except in certain cases] but not the former. (TA in art. خفى.) — ٱلْحُرُوفُ ٱلْمُسْتَعْلِيَةُ [*The high,* or *elevated, letters*] are خ, ص, ض, ط, ظ, غ, *and* ق; (Ḳ, TA;) in which is a rising [of the tongue] to the palate; with إِطْبَاق [of the tongue (see 4 in art. طبق)] except in خ and غ and ق: opposed to ٱلْمُنْخَفِضَةُ. (TA.)

علی

For words mentioned under this head in the Ḳ, see art. علو.

عم

1. عَمَّ, (Ṣ, Mṣb, Ḳ,) aor. ـُ, (Ṣ, Mṣb,) inf. n. عُمُومٌ, (Ṣ, Mṣb, Ḳ,) i. q. شَمِلَ ٱلْجَمَاعَةَ [i. e. *It was,* or *became, common,* or *general,* or *universal;* or *generally,* or *universally, comprehensive: it included the common,* or *general,* or *whole, aggregate, assemblage, bulk, mass,* or *extent, within its compass;* or *within the compass of its relation* or *relations, its effect* or *effects, its operation* or *operations, its influence,* or *the like*]: said of a thing: (Ṣ, Ḳ:) of rain, &c.: (Mṣb:) عُمُومٌ signifies the *including,* or *comprehending,* [*the generality,* or] *all:* (PṢ:) and the *happening,* or *occurring, to* [*the generality,* or] *all.* (KL.) عَمَّ ثُؤَبَاءُ ٱلنَّاعِسِ [*The yawning of the drowsy became common,* or *general,* or *universal,*] is a prov., applied to the case of an event that happens in a town, or country, and then extends from it to the other towns, or countries. (TA.) — It is also trans. [signifying *He,* or *it, included, comprehended,* or *embraced,* persons, or things, *in common, in general,* or *universally, within the compass of his action,* or *influence,* &c., or *within the compass of its relation* or *relations, its effect* or *effects, its operation* or *operations, its influence,* or *the like*]: and when trans., its inf. n. is عَمٌّ. (TḲ.) One says, عَمَّ ٱلْمَطَرُ ٱلْأَرْضَ [*The rain included the general,* or *the whole, extent of the land within the compass of its fall*]. (The Lexicons passim.) And عَمَّهُمْ بِٱلْعَطِيَّةِ [*He included them in common, in general,* or *universally, within the compass of the gift; or gave to them in common, in general,* or *universally*]. (Ṣ, Ḳ.) And عَمَّ فِى دُعَائِهِ وَخَصَّ [*He included,* or *comprehended,* persons or things *in common,* or *in general, in his prayer* or *supplication* &c., *and particularized,* or *specified,* some person or thing, or some persons or things]. (Ṣ voce خَلَّ.) And عَمَّهُمُ ٱلْمَرَضُ [*The disease was,* or *became, common,* or *general,* or *universal, among them*]. (The Lexicons passim.) ═ عَمَّ also signifies *He,* or *it, made long,* or *tall:* — and *He,* or *it, was,* or *became, long,* or *tall.* (IAạr, TA.) ═ [And *He became a paternal uncle* (صَارَ عَمًّا).] One says, مَا كُنْتُ عَمًّا وَلَقَدْ عَمِمْتُ [*I was not a paternal uncle, and now I have become a paternal uncle*]: (so in my copies of the Ṣ:) or عَمَمْتُ or مَا كُنْتُ عَمًّا وَلَقَدْ عَمَمْتُ [*Thou wast not* &c.]: (so accord. to different copies of the Ḳ: the former accord. to the TḲ [agreeably with my copies of the Ṣ; and this I believe to be the right reading, or at least preferable; like أَمِمْتَ]:) inf. n. عُمُومَةٌ; (Ṣ, Mṣb, Ḳ;) like خُؤُولَةٌ [and أُمُومَةٌ] and أُبُوَّةٌ. (TA.) And بَيْنِى وَبَيْنَ فُلَانٍ عُمُومَةٌ [*Between me and such a one is a relationship of paternal uncle*]. (Ṣ.) ═ عُمَّ : see the next paragraph.

2. تَعْمِيمٌ The *making* a thing *to be common, general,* or *universal; the generalizing it; contr. of* تَخْصِيصٌ. (Ḳ in art. خص.) ═ عَمَّمْتُهُ *I attired him with the* عِمَامَة [or *turban*]. (Ṣ.) And عُمِّمَ رَأْسُهُ *His head was wound round with the* عِمَامَة [or *turban*]; as also ▼ عُمَّ. (Ḳ.) — And [hence,] عُمِّمَ ‡ *He was made a chief* or *lord* [over others]: (Ṣ, Mṣb, Ḳ, TA:) because the turbans (ٱلْعَمَائِم) are the crowns of the Arabs: (Ṣ, TA:) and when they made a man a chief or lord, they attired him with a red turban. (TA.) [Hence likewise,] one says also, عَمَّمْنَاكَ أَمْرَنَا, meaning † *We have made thee to take upon thyself the management of our affair,* or *state,* or *case.* (TA.) — And عَمَّمْتُهُ سَيْفًا [*I attired him with a sword;* like كَسَوْتُهُ سَيْفًا]. (TA in art. غشو.) — And عَمَّمَهُ بِٱلسَّيْفِ † [*He cut,* or *wounded, him,* or *it* (i. e. his head), *in the place of the turban, with the sword*]: like عَصَبَهُ بِهِ, (A and TA in art. عصب,) and صَمَدَهُ. (A and L in art. صمد.) — And عَمَّمَ ٱللَّبَنُ, (Ṣ, Ḳ,) inf. n. تَعْمِيمٌ, (Ḳ,) ‡ *The milk frothed:* as though its froth were likened to the عِمَامَة [or *turban*]; (Ṣ, TA;) as also ▼ اِعْتَمَّ. (Ḳ.)

4. أُعِمَّ and أَعَمَّ, in the pass. and act. forms, [*He had many paternal uncles:* (see مُعَمٌّ:) or] *he had generous paternal uncles.* (Mṣb.)

5. تَعَمَّمْتُهُ *I called him a paternal uncle:* (AZ, Ṣ, Z:) or تَعَمَّمْنَهُ, said of women, *they called him a paternal uncle.* (Ḳ.) — تعمّم عَمًّا : see 10. ═ See also the next paragraph, in five places.

8. اعتمّ and ▼ تعمّم and ▼ استعمّ, (Ḳ,) or اعتمّ بِٱلْعِمَامَةِ and ▼ تعمّم بِهَا, (Ṣ,) *He attired himself with the turban:* (Ṣ, Ḳ:) and ▼ تعمّم is also expl. as meaning *he attired himself with the helmet:* or, *with the garments of war.* (TA.) — And [hence] one says, اِعْتَمَّتِ ٱلْآكَامُ بِٱلنَّبَاتِ and ▼ تَعَمَّمَتْ † [*The hills became crowned with plants,* or *herbage*]. (TA.) And تَعَمَّمَتْ ▼ بِهَا رُؤُوسُ ٱلْجِبَالِ † [*The heads of the mountains became crowned with its light*]: referring to the sun, when its light has fallen upon the heads of the mountains and become to them like the turban. (Mgh.) — And اعتمّ ٱللَّبَنُ : see 2, last sentence. — And اعتمّ ٱلنَّبْتُ ‡ *The plant,* or *herbage, became of its full height, and blossomed,* syn. اِكْتَهَلَ, (Ṣ, Ḳ, TA,) and طَالَ; and *became luxuriant,* or *abundant and dense:* (TA:) like اعتمّ. (TA in art. عمر.) — And اعتمّ ٱلشَّابُّ † *The youth,* or *young man, became tall.* (Ṣ.) — And اعتمّ is said of a beast of the bovine kind as meaning † *He had all his teeth grown.* (Aṣ, TA. [See عَمَمٌ and عَضْبٌ.])

10. اِسْتَعَمَّهُ, (Ḳ,) or اِسْتَعَمَّهُ عَمًّا, (Ṣ,) *I took him,* or *adopted him, as a paternal uncle:* (Ṣ, Ḳ:) and ▼ تعمّم عَمًّا *He took,* or *adopted, a paternal uncle.* (TA in art. خول.) ═ See also 8, first sentence.

R. Q. 1. عَمْعَمَ (inf. n. عَمْعَمَةٌ, TḲ) *He had a numerous army,* or *military force, after paucity* [*thereof*]. (Ḳ.)

عَمَّ, for عَمَّا, which is for أَمَّا: see this last, in art. اما.

عِمْ صَبَاحًا, and عِمُوا صَبَاحًا: see art. صبح.

عَمٌّ *A company of men:* (Ṣ:) or, as some say, *of a tribe:* (TA:) or *a numerous company;* as also ▼أَعَمٌّ; (Ḳ;) this latter mentioned by AAF, on the authority of AZ, and said by him to be the only instance of a word of the measure أَفْعَل denoting a plurality, unless it be a [coll.] gen. n., like أَرْوَى; and he cites as an ex. the phrase بَيْنَ الأَعَمِّ, occurring in a verse; but Fr is related to have read بَيْنَ الأُعُمِّ, with ḍamm to the ع, making it pl. of عَمٌّ, like as أَضُبٌّ is of ضَبٌّ. (TA.) — *A paternal uncle; a father's brother:* (Ṣ, Ḳ:) pl. أَعْمَامٌ (Ṣ, Mṣb, Ḳ) and عُمُومٌ (TA) and عُمُومَةٌ (Sb, Ṣ, Ḳ) and أَعِمَّةٌ (CḲ) and أَعُمٌّ, (Ḳ,) a pl. of pauc., mentioned by Fr and IAạr, (TA,) and pl. pl. أَعْمُمُونَ, (Ḳ, TA,) without idghám, by rule أَعُمُّونَ: (TA:) the female is termed ▼عَمَّةٌ [i. e. *a paternal aunt; a father's sister*]: (Ḳ:) and the pl. of this is عَمَّاتٌ. (Mṣb.) One says, يَا ٱبْنَ عَمِّى and يا ابن عَمِّ (Ṣ, L) and يا ابن عَمَّ (L) and يا ابن عَمِ, (Ṣ, L, [but in one copy of the Ṣ I find the first three and not the last,]) the last without teshdeed, (L,) dial. vars. [all meaning *O son of my paternal uncle*]: (Ṣ, L:) and Abu-n-Nejm uses the expression يَا ٱبْنَةَ عَمَّا [*O daughter of my paternal uncle*], meaning عَمَّاهْ, with the ه of lamentation. (Ṣ.) And one says, هُمَا ٱبْنَا عَمٍّ [meaning *Each of them two is a son of a paternal uncle of the other*]; (Ṣ, IB, Mṣb, Ḳ;) because each of them says to the other, يَا ٱبْنَ عَمِّى; (IB;) and in like manner, ٱبْنَا خَالَةٍ; (Ṣ, IB, Mṣb, Ḳ;) because each of them says to the other, يَا ٱبْنَ خَالَتِى: (IB:) but one may not say, ▼هُمَا ٱبْنَا عَمَّةٍ, nor ٱبْنَا خَالٍ; (Ṣ, IB, Mṣb, Ḳ;) because one of them says to the other, يَا ٱبْنَ عَمَّتِى, but the latter says to the former, يَا ٱبْنَ خَالِى. (IB.) And [عَمٌّ signifies also *A paternal great uncle, &c.:* therefore] one says, هُمَا ٱبْنَا عَمٍّ لَحًّا [*They two are cousins on the father's side, closely related*]; and in like manner, ٱبْنَا خَالَةٍ لَحًّا: but not ▼ٱبْنَا عَمَّةٍ لَحًّا, nor ٱبْنَا خَالٍ لَحًّا: (TA:) and هُوَ ٱبْنُ عَمِّهِ ظُهْرًا i. e. [*He is his cousin on the father's side,*] *distantly related.* (Aṣ, in A and O and TA, art. ظهر.) — It is said in a trad., أَكْرِمُوا ▼عَمَّتَكُمُ النَّخْلَةَ [*Honour ye your paternal aunt the palm-tree*]: i. e. [do ye so] because it was created of the redundant portion of the earth, or clay, of Adam. (TA.) — And عُمٌّ signifies also *Tall palm-trees,* (Ḳ, TA,) *of full tallness and abundance and density;* (TA;) and ▼عُمُمٌ signifies the same: (Ḳ, TA:) [or so عُمٌّ and نَخْلٌ عُمٌّ, which is perhaps meant in the Ḳ: for] عُمٌّ is an epithet applied to palm-trees, (Ṣ, Ḳ, TA,) and is pl. of عَمِيمَةٌ [fem. of عَمِيمٌ]. (Ṣ, Ḳ.) — And *All* [*herbs such as are termed*] عُشْب. (Th, Ḳ.)

عَمَّ in the phrase عَمَّ يَتَسَآءَلُونَ [*Respecting what do they ask one another?* in the Ḳur lxxviii. 1] is originally عَمَّا, [for عَنْ مَا,] the ا being elided in the interrogation [after the prep. عَنْ]. (Ṣ.)

عُمٌّ: see عَمٌّ, last sentence but one: — and see also عَمِيمٌ.

عَمَّةٌ fem. of عَمٌّ: see the latter, in four places.

عِمَّةٌ *A mode of attiring oneself with the turban:* so in the saying, هُوَ حَسَنُ العِمَّةِ [*He is comely in respect of the mode of attiring himself with the turban*]. (Ṣ, Ḳ.) — [And it is vulgarly used as meaning *A turban* itself, like عِمَامَةٌ; and is used in this sense in the TA in art. علم: see عَلَمْتُ عِمَّتِى near the end of the first paragraph of that art.]

عَمَمٌ The *state,* or *quality, of being collected together, and numerous,* or *abundant.* (Ḳ.) — And *Largeness,* or *bigness, of make,* in men and in others. (Ḳ.) — See also عُمُمٌ. — Also *Complete,* or *without deficiency;* applied to a body, and to a shoulder: (Ṣ:) or, applied to the latter, *long.* (TA.) [See also عَمِيمٌ.] — Applied to a beast of the bovine kind, *Having all his teeth grown.* (Aṣ, TA.) [See 8, last sentence; and see عَضْبٌ.] — And Any affair, or event, or case, *complete* [or *accomplished*], *and common* or *general* or *universal* [app. meaning *commonly* or *generally* or *universally known*]. (Ḳ.) — And quasi. pl. n. of عَامَّةٌ, q. v. (Ḳ.) — See also مُعَمٌّ.

عُمُمٌ *Completeness of body* [or *bodily growth*], *and of wealth, and of youthful vigour,* or *of the period of youthfulness:* so in the phrase ٱسْتَوَى عَلَى عُمُمِهِ, (Ṣ, Ḳ,) occurring in a trad. of 'Orweh Ibn-Ez-Zubeyr, on his mentioning Uḥeyḥah Ibn-El-Julạḥ and the saying of his maternal uncles respecting him, كُنَّا أَهْلَ ثُمِّهِ وَرُمِّهِ حَتَّى ٱسْتَوَى عَلَى عُمُمِهِ [i. e. *We were the masters of the meaner and the better articles of his property until he attained to man's estate, or to his completeness of bodily growth, &c.*]; (Ṣ;) [or] the meaning is, *his completeness of stature and of bones and of limbs:* (TA:) also pronounced with teshdeed [or idghám, i. e. ▼عُمِّهِ], for the sake of conformity [with ثُمِّهِ and رُمِّهِ]; (Ṣ, TA;) and by some, ▼عَمَمِهِ. (TA.) — It is also pl. of عَمِيمٌ [q. v.]. (Ṣ, Ḳ.)

عِمَامٌ: see عِمَامَةٌ, first sentence.

عَمِيمٌ A thing *complete,* or *without deficiency:* pl. عُمُمٌ. (Ṣ. [See also عَمَمٌ.]) — Anything *collected together, and abundant,* or *numerous:* pl. as above. (Ḳ.) — *Reaching to everything:* applied in this sense to perfume. (Ḥar p. 200.) — *Tall;* applied to a man, and to a plant: (TA:) and so عَمِيمَةٌ applied to a palm-tree (نَخْلَةٌ); (Ṣ, Ḳ;) and to a girl, or young woman; as also ▼عَمَّآءُ applied to both; of which last word the masc. is ▼أَعَمُّ: (Ḳ:) or عَمِيمَةٌ applied to a woman, (Ṣ,) or to a girl, or young woman, (TA,) signifies *complete,* or *perfect, in stature and make,* (Ṣ, TA,) *and tall:* (TA:) pl. عُمٌّ, (Ḳ,) which is applied to palm-trees (نَخِيل) as meaning *tall;* (Ṣ;) or, accord. to Lḥ, to a single palm-tree (نَخْلَة), and may be [thus, originally,] of the measure فُعْل, or of the measure فُعُل, originally عُمُمٌ: (TA:) ▼يَعْمُومٌ, also, signifies *tall,* applied to a plant, or herbage: (Ḳ:) and عَمِيمَةٌ applied to a بَقَرَة [or beast of the bovine kind] signifies *complete,* or *perfect, in make.* (TA.) — One says also, هُوَ مِنْ عَمِيمِهِمْ, meaning صَمِيمِهِمْ [i. e. *He is of the choice, best,* or *most excellent, of them;* or *of the main stock of them*]. (Ṣ, Ḳ.*) — Also *Such as is dry of* [*the species of barley-grass called*] نَصِىّ. (Ṣ, Ḳ.)

عِمَامَةٌ [*A turban;*] the *thing that one winds upon the head:* (Ḳ:) pl. عَمَائِمُ (Ṣ, Mṣb, Ḳ) and ▼عِمَامٌ, (Lḥ, Ḳ,) the latter either a broken pl. of عِمَامَةٌ or [a coll. gen. n., i. e.,] these two words are of the class of طَلْحٌ and طَلْحَةٌ. (TA.) [On the old Arab mode of disposing the turban, see عِمَارٌ.] The عَمَائِم were the crowns of the Arabs. (Ṣ, Mṣb.) أَرْخَى عِمَامَتَهُ [lit. *He slackened,* or *loosened, his turban,*] means † *he became,* or *felt, in a state of security,* or *safety, and at ease,* or *in easy circumstances;* (Ḳ, TA;) because a man does not slacken, or loosen, his turban but in easy circumstances. (TA.) — Also ‡ The مِغْفَر [q. v.]: and ‡ the *helmet:* (Ḳ, TA:) by some erroneously written with fet-ḥ [to the first letter]. (MF.) — And *Pieces of wood bound together, upon which one embarks on the sea, and upon which one crosses a river;* as also ▼عَامَّةٌ; or this is correctly عَامَةٌ, without teshdeed; (Ḳ, TA;) and thus it is rightly mentioned by IAạr. (TA.)

عَمِّىٌّ [*Of,* or *relating to, a paternal uncle;*] rel. n. of عَمٌّ; as though formed from عَمِّى, or عَمًّا. (Ṣ.)

[عَمَّا is for عَنْ مَا when not interrogative.]

عُمِّىٌّ, like قُبِّىٌّ, (Ḳ, TA,) with ḍamm, but in the M عمى, (TA, [in which this word is thus doubtfully written, and has been altered, perhaps from عُمِّىٌّ, for قُبِّىٌّ is a word which I do not find in any case other than this, and if any word of the measure فُعْلِىٌّ were meant, أُمِّىٌّ would be a much better instance of similarity of form,]) an epithet applied to a man, *i. q.* عَامٌّ [app. meaning *Of the common sort;* like عَامِّىٌّ]: (Ḳ, TA:) and قُصْرِىٌّ or قُصُرِىٌّ, (accord. to different copies of the Ḳ,) in the M قَصْرِىٌّ, (TA, [there thus written, only with a fet-ḥah to the ق and the sign of quiescence to the ص,]) signifies [the contr., i. e.] خَاصِّىٌّ. (Ḳ, TA.)

عُمِّيَّةٌ, (Ṣ, Ḳ,) like عُبِّيَّةٌ, (Ṣ,) and عِمِّيَّةٌ, (Ḳ,) [like عِبِّيَّةٌ,] *Pride*, or *haughtiness*. (Ṣ, Ḳ.)

عَمَاعِمُ [a pl. of which no sing. is mentioned] *Companies of men in a scattered*, or *dispersed, state*. (Ṣ, Ḳ.)

عَامٌّ part. n. of عَمَّ; applied to rain &c. [as meaning *Common*, or *general*, or *universal*; or *generally*, or *universally, comprehensive*: &c.: see 1, first sentence: *contr. of* خَاصٌّ]. (Mṣb.) — See also العَامَّةُ. — Also [*A general* word; i. e.] a word *applied by a single application to many things, not restricted, including everything to which it is applicable*: the words "by a single application" exclude the homonym, because this is by several applications; and the saying "to many things" excludes what is not applied to many things, as زَيْدٌ, and عَمْرٌو: and the words "not restricted" exclude the nouns of number, for المِائَةُ, for instance, is applied by a single application to many things and includes everything to which it is applicable, but the many things are restricted: and the words "including everything to which it is applicable" exclude the indeterminate plural, as in the phrase رَأَيْتُ رِجَالًا, all men not being seen: and the word is either عَامّ by its form and its meaning, as الرِّجَالُ, or عَامّ by its meaning only, as الرَّهْطُ and القَوْمُ. (KT. [The word in this sense is often used in the lexicons, but is expl. in few of them, as being conventional and post-classical.])

العَامَّةُ is *the contr. of* الخَاصَّةُ [i. e. the former signifies *The commonalty*, or *generality of people*; *the people in common* or *in general*; *the common people*; *the common sort*; or *the vulgar*]: (Ṣ, Mṣb, Ḳ:) the ة is a corroborative: (Mṣb:) and ▼ العَمَّةُ signifies the same as العَامَّةُ: (IAạr, TA voce سَامّ:) the pl. of عَامَّةٌ is عَوَامُّ, (Mṣb,) and ▼ عَمٌّ is quasi-pl. n. of عَامَّةٌ as contr. of خَاصَّةٌ. (Ḳ.) [And one says also ▼ الخَاصُّ وَالعَامُّ as well as الخَاصَّةُ وَالعَامَّةُ, meaning *The distinguished and the common people*; *the persons of distinction and the vulgar*. — عَامَّةً means *In common*, or *commonly, in general*, or *generally*; and *universally*. And one says, جَاؤُوا عَامَّةً meaning *They came generally*, or *universally*.] عَامَّةُ الشَّهْرِ means *The greater part of the month*. (TA in art. جلب.) And عَامَّةُ النَّهَارِ means *The whole of the day*. (TA in art. ادم.) — And العَامَّةُ signifies also *General*, or *universal, drought*. (TA.) — And *The resurrection*: because [it is believed that all beings living on the earth immediately before it shall die, so that] it will occasion universal [previous] death to mankind. (TA.) — See also عِمَامَةٌ.

عَامِّىٌّ *Of*, or *relating to, the* عَامَّة [or *common people*; *common*; or *vulgar*; often applied to a word, or phrase]. (Mṣb.)

أَعَمُّ [*More*, and *most, common* or *general*: applied to a word, *more*, and *most, general in signification*]. — As a simple epithet, with its fem. عَمَّآءُ: see عَمِيمٌ. — Also, the former, *Thick* (Ḳ, TA) *and complete* [or *of full size*]; applied in this sense to the middle of a she-camel, in a verse of El-Museiyab Ibn-'Alas. (TA.) — See also عَمٌّ, first sentence.

مُعَمٌّ مُخْوَلٌ *Having generous*, (T, L,) or *having many and generous*, (Ṣ,) *paternal and maternal uncles*; (T, Ṣ, L;) and both are sometimes pronounced with kesr [to the ع of the former and to the و of the latter, i. e. ▼ مُعِمٌّ مُخْوِلٌ: see مُخْوَلٌ in its proper art.]: (Ṣ:) or مُعَمٌّ and ▼ مِعَمٌّ, with damm to the [initial] م and with kesr to the same, [but the latter is app. a mistake, occasioned by a misunderstanding of what is said in the Ṣ,] signify *having many paternal uncles*: or *having generous paternal uncles*. (Ḳ.)

مُعِمٌّ: see the next preceding paragraph.

مِعَمٌّ, with kesr to the first letter, (Ḳ, TA, [in the CḲ, مِعَمٌّ خَيْرٌ بِكَسْرِ أَوَّلِهِ is erroneously put for مِعَمٌّ بِكَسْرِ أَوَّلِهِ خَيْرٌ,]) *One who is good*, or *very good*, (Ḳ, TA,) *who includes mankind in common, in general*, or *universally, within the compass of his goodness*, (Kr, T, Ḳ, TA,) *and his superabundant bounty*; (T, TA;) and ▼ عَمَمٌ signifies the same: (Ḳ:) [see also an ex. and explanation voce مِسَرٌّ, in art. سر:] مِعَمٌّ is almost the only instance of an epithet of the measure مِفْعَلٌ from a verb of the measure فَعَلَ, except مِلَرٌّ [and مِسَرٌّ, with both of which it is coupled]. (TA.) — See also مُعَمٌّ.

المَعَمَّةُ: see العَامَّةُ, first sentence.

مُعَمَّمٌ [*Attired with a turban*. — And hence, † *Made a chief* or *lord* over others; or] *a chief*, or *lord, who is invested with the office of ordering the affairs of a people and to whom the commonalty have recourse*. (TA.) — Applied to a horse, (Ṣ, Ḳ,) and other than a horse, (so in a copy of the Ṣ,) † *White in the ears and the place of growth of the forelock and what is around this, exclusively of other parts*: (Ṣ:) or *white in the* هَامَة [or *upper part of the head*], *exclusively of the neck*: or *white in the forelock so that the whiteness extends to the place of its growth*. (Ḳ.) And شَاةٌ مُعَمَّمَةٌ † *A sheep, or goat, having a whiteness in the* هَامَة. (Ṣ.)

رَوْضَةٌ مُعْتَمَّةٌ ‡ [*A meadow*] *having abundant and tall herbage*. (TA.)

يَعْمُومٌ: see عَمِيمٌ.

عمت

1. عَمَتَ, aor. ـِ, (T, Ḳ,) inf. n. عَمْتٌ; (T, Ṣ, O;) and ▼ عَمَّتَ, (O, Ḳ,) inf. n. تَعْمِيتٌ; (O;) *He wound* wool (Ṣ, O,* Ḳ) *in an oblong form*, (TA,) or *in a round form*, (Ṣ, O, Ḳ,) *like a ring*, (TA,) *for the purpose of its being put in the hand and spun* (Ṣ, O, Ḳ) *with the spindle*: (TA:) or *he wound* soft hair of the camel, and wool, *into the form of a ring, and spun it, putting it in his hand*: (T, TA:) the operation termed عَمْتٌ is performed after beating, and separating and loosening, the wool, and collecting it together, in order to wind it upon the hand, and spin it with the spindle. (AHeyth, TA.) An ex. of the former verb occurs in a verse cited voce رَاجِلَةٌ. (TA.) — And the former verb signifies also *He twisted* a rope of [the species of trefoil, or clover, called] قَتّ. (TA.) — And it is said in the Ḳ that عَمَتَ فُلَانًا means *He overcame*, or *subdued, such a one, and made him to refrain*, or *restrained him*; expl. by قَهَرَهُ وَكَفَّهُ: but [SM says that] the correct reading is probably وَلَفَّهُ; for in the L [and in the O, app. on the authority of Az, to whom the same is ascribed in the TA in art. لف] we find what here follows: فُلَانٌ يَعْمِتُ أَقْرَانَهُ means يَقْهَرُهُمْ وَيَلُفُّهُمْ [i. e. † *Such a one overcomes*, or *subdues, and throws into confusion, his antagonists*: and hence, app., what is said in the Ḳ; the author of which probably found يَكُفُّهُمْ erroneously written for يَلُفُّهُمْ in some lexicon, and therefore thought it allowable to make عَمَتَ in this case to have a sing. for its objective complement]: and it is added that this is said in relation to war, and excellence of judgment, and knowledge of the case of the enemy, and the subduing him with the infliction of many wounds. (TA.) — عَمَتَهُ also signifies *He beat him with a staff*, or *stick, not caring* [for any one]. (Ḳ.)

2: see the first sentence above.

عَمِيتٌ *A twisted* rope of [the species of trefoil, or clover, called] قَتّ; as also ▼ مَعْمُوتٌ. (TA.) — See also what next follows.

عَمِيتَةٌ *A portion* of wool, (Ṣ,* O,* Ḳ,) or of the soft hair of the camel, (Ṣ, O,) *wound in the manner described in the first sentence of this art.*; (Ṣ, O, Ḳ;) like a سَبِيخَة of cotton, and a فَلِيلَة of [goats'] hair, (Ṣ, O, TA,) or a قَلِيلَة of [goats'] hair: (ISd, TA:) the pl. [of pauc.] is أَعْمِتَةٌ and [of mult.] عُمُتٌ [and coll. gen. n., improperly called a pl.,] ▼ عَمِيتٌ; (Ḳ;) or, accord. to ISd, أَعْمِتَةٌ is pl. of عَمِيتٌ, which is pl. of عَمِيتَةٌ; (TA;) and عَمَائِتُ is a pl. of this last. (AHeyth, TA.)

عَمِيتٌ *A clever*, or *an intelligent, watcher*, or *guardian*: (Ṣ, O, Ḳ:) or *a knowing, intelligent, keeper*, or *preserver*, or *guardian*: (Az, TA:) and a *clever*, or an *intelligent*, and a *bold*, man. (TA.) — And (some say, Ṣ, O) *Ignorant and weak*. (Ṣ, O, Ḳ.) — And (some say, O) *Drunken*: (O, Ḳ:) and *who cannot go aright*, or *knows not the course*, or *way, that he would pursue*: (Ḳ:) which last explanation and that which immediately precedes it (i. e. "drunken") appear, from the L and other lexicons, to be one signification. (TA.) The pl. is عَمَامِيتُ. (Ṣ, O.)

مَعْمُوتٌ: see عَمِيتٌ.

عمج

1. عَمَجَ, aor. ـِ, *He hastened*, or *was quick*, or

swift, in his pace, or *course:* (Ṣ, O, Ḳ:) formed by transposition from مَعَجَ. (Ṣ, O.) —— And, (Ḳ,) or عَمَجَ فِى المَآءِ, (O,) *He swam in the water.* (O, Ḳ.) —— See also the next paragraph, in two places.

5. تعمّج; (Ṣ, O, Ḳ;) and ▼ عَمَجَ, (Ḳ,) inf. n. عَمْجٌ; (O;) *He wound,* or *bent,* (Ṣ, O, Ḳ,) *in going along,* (Ṣ, O,) or *in the road, to the right and left:* (Ḳ:) or عَمَجَ ▼ فِى سَيْرِهِ signifies *he proceeded in every direction, by reason of briskness, liveliness,* or *sprightliness.* (TA.) And تعمّجت الحَيَّةُ *The serpent wound about in its course.* (Ṣ, O.) And تعمّج السَّيْلُ فِى الوَادِى *The torrent wound in the valley to the right and left.* (O.)

عَمَجٌ (Ḳṭr, Ṣ, O, Ḳ) and ▼ عُمُجٌ (Ṣ, O, Ḳ) and ▼ عَوْمَجٌ (Kr, Ṣ, O, Ḳ) *A serpent:* (Ṣ, O, Ḳ, &c.:) so called because of its winding. (TA.)

عَمُوجَةٌ and عَمِيجَةٌ: see عَمُوجٌ.

عُمُجٌ: see عَمَجٌ.

عَمُوجٌ An arrow *that winds about in its course.* (Ṣ, O, Ḳ.) And A horse *that does not proceed in a straight,* or *direct, course:* and ▼ عَمُوجَةٌ and ▼ عَمِيجَةٌ a she-camel *that winds about.* (TA.) —— It is also used by Aboo-Dhu-eyb El-Hudhalee as meaning *Swimming.* (O.)

عَوْمَجٌ: see عَمَجٌ.

عمد

1. عَمَدَهُ, (Ṣ, A, O, L, Mṣb, Ḳ,) aor. ـِـ, (L,) inf. n. عَمْدٌ; (L, Mṣb;) and ▼ اعمدهُ; (Mṣb, Ḳ;) *He stayed it, propped it up, or supported it;* (Ṣ, A, O, L, Mṣb, Ḳ;) namely, a wall, (A, L, Mṣb,) or other thing; (Ṣ, O, L;) i. q. دَعَمَهُ: (A, L, Mṣb:) or ▼ اعمدهُ, [and app. sometimes عَمَدَهُ, (see مَعْمُودٌ,)] and in a similar manner ▼ عمّدهُ is expl. by Golius, as on the authority of J, whom I do not find to have anywhere mentioned it, but it is probably correct, (see its pass. part. n. in this art.,)] *he placed beneath it columns, pillars,* or *props.* (Ṣ, O. [See عَمُودٌ, &c.]) —— And عَمَدَهُ, (L, Ḳ,) aor. ـِـ, (L,) or ـُـ, (TA,) inf. n. عَمْدٌ, (L,) *He struck him,* or *beat him, with an* [*iron weapon such as is called*] عَمُود. (O, L, Ḳ.) —— And *He struck him,* or *beat him, upon the part called* عَمُود البَطْن. (O, L, Ḳ.) —— عَمَدَ لَهُ, (Ṣ, A, O, L, Mṣb,) and عَمَدَ إِلَيْهِ, (L, Mṣb,) and عَمَدَهُ, (L, Ḳ,) aor. ـِـ, [or ـِـ and ـُـ, (Ḥar p. 299,)] inf. n. عَمْدٌ (Ṣ, O, L, Mṣb) and عَمَدٌ and عِمَادٌ and عُمْدَةٌ (Mṭr, TA) and عَمُودٌ (Nawádir el-Aạráb, TA) and مَعْمَدٌ; (Ibn-'Arafeh, TA;) and ▼ تعمّدهُ, (L, Mṣb, Ḳ,) and ▼ تعمّد لَهُ; (Ṣ, L;) and ▼ اعتمدهُ; (L, TA;) *He intended it,* or *purposed it; did it intentionally,* or *purposely;* the inf. n. signifying the contr. of خَطَأٌ: (Az, Ṣ, L, TA:) *he directed himself,* or *his course or aim, to it,* or *towards it; made for it,* or *towards it; made it his object; aimed at it; sought,* or *endeavoured, after it;* or *tended, repaired,* or *betook himself, to it,* or *towards it;* syn. قَصَدَ لَهُ; (L, Ḳ;) or قَصَدَهُ, (Ṣ, A, O,) or إِلَيْهِ. (Mṣb.) You say, اعتمد ▼ الأَمْرَ *He intended,* or *purposed, the affair;* or *aimed at it;* &c.; syn. صَمَدَهُ; (A in art. صمد;) or صَمَدَ صَمْدَهُ, i. e. قَصَدَ قَصْدَهُ. (M in that art.) And تعمّد ▼ ذَنْبًا *He committed a sin,* or *the like, intentionally.* (TA in art. خطأ.) And تعمّد ▼ صَيْدًا [*He aimed at an object of the chase*]. (Ṣgh, in Mṣb.) And عَمَدَ لِرَأْسِهِ بِالعَصَا *He aimed at his head with the staff,* or *stick.* (M in art. صمد.) And عَمَدَهُ, [and عَمَدَ إِلَيْهِ,] aor. ـِـ; and ▼ اعتمدهُ; and ▼ تعمّدهُ; *He betook himself to him,* or *had recourse to him,* in a case of need. (A.) —— And [hence] one says, فَعَلْتُهُ عَمْدًا عَلَى عَيْنٍ, (Ṣ, O, Mṣb, Ḳ,) and عَمْدَ عَيْنٍ, (Ṣ, A, O, Mṣb, Ḳ,) *I did it seriously,* or *in earnest, and with certain knowledge,* or *assurance.* (Ṣ, A, O, Mṣb, Ḳ. [See also عَيْنٌ.]) When a man sees a bodily form and imagines it to be an object of the chase and therefore shoots at it, he cannot use this phrase, for he only aims at what is an object of the chase in his imagination: so says Ṣgh. (Mṣb.) —— عَمَدَهُ, (Ṣ, O, L, Ḳ,) aor. ـِـ, (L,) said of disease, (Ṣ, O, L,) *It pressed heavily upon him,* or *oppressed him;* (Ṣ, O, L, Ḳ;) on the authority of IAạr: (TA:) and so said of straitness, or confinement, or imprisonment, and captivity; (O;) and *it caused him to fall;* (O, Ḳ;) in this sense in like manner said of confinement, &c.: (O:) also, (O, Ḳ,) said of a disease, (O,) *it pained him.* (O, Ḳ.) And عَمَدَهُ, (Ḳ, TA,) aor., in this case, ـُـ, (TA, [but this, I think, requires confirmation,]) *It grieved him,* or *made him sorrowful.* (Ḳ, TA.) One says, مَا عَمَدَكَ *What has grieved thee,* or *made thee sorrowful?* (TA.) —— عَمِدَ, (Ṣ, O, L, Ḳ,) aor. ـَـ, inf. n. عَمَدٌ, (Ṣ, O,) said of earth, *It became moistened by rain so that when a portion of it was grasped in the hand it became compacted by reason of its moisture:* (Ṣ, O, L, Ḳ:) or *it became moistened by rain and compacted, layer upon layer.* (L.) And عَمِدَتِ الأَرْضُ, inf. n. as above, *The land became moistened by the rain's sinking into the earth so that when a portion of it was grasped in the hand it became compacted by reason of its moisture.* (AZ.) —— Also, (inf. n. as above, L,) said of a camel, *He had the inner part of his hump broken* [or *bruised*] *by being* [*much*] *ridden, while the outer part remained whole,* or *sound:* (Ṣ, O, L, Ḳ:) or *he had his hump swollen in consequence of the galling of the saddle and the cloth beneath it, and broken* [or *bruised*]: whence عَمِدٌ and مَعْمُودٌ as epithets applied to a man. (L.) And عَمِدَتْ أَلْيَتَاهُ مِنَ الرُّكُوبِ *His buttocks became swollen, and quivered,* or *throbbed, in consequence of* [*long and hard*] *riding.* (En-Naḍr, O, Ḳ.) And عَمِدَ, aor. and inf. n. as above, said of a pustule, *It became swollen in consequence of its having been squeezed before it had become ripe, and its egg* [or *white globule*] *did not come forth.* (L, TA.) —— Also *He suffered pain.* (L.) —— And, (T, O, L, Ḳ,) inf. n. as above, (T, L,) *He was,* or *became, angry:* (T, O, L, Ḳ:) like عَبِدَ (T, L) [and أَمِدَ and أَبِدَ]. One says, عَمِدَ عَلَيْهِ *He was angry with him.* (T, L.) —— [And *He wondered.*] One says, أَنَا أَعْمَدُ مِنْهُ *I wonder at him,* or *it:* (Ṣ, O, L, Ḳ:) or, as some say, *I am angry at him,* or *it:* and some say that it means *I lament at,* or *complain of, him,* or *it.* (L.) أَعْمَدُ مِنْ سَيِّدٍ قَتَلَهُ قَوْمُهُ (Ṣ, O, L) i. e. *Do I wonder at a chief whom his* [*own*] *people have slain?* (L) was said by Aboo-Jahl (Ṣ, O, L) when he lay prostrated at Bedr; meaning, hath anything more happened than the slaughter of a chief by his [own] people? this is not a disgrace [to him]: he meant thereby that the destruction that befell him was a light matter to him: (A'Obeyd, L:) the saying is interrogative; (Sh, L;) أَعْمَدُ being app. contracted from أَأَعْمَدُ, by the suppression of one of the two hemzehs. (Az, L.) And أَعْمَدُ مِنْ كَيْلٍ مُحِقٍّ, as related by A'Obeyd, [and thus in the O, in two copies of the Ṣ written مُحِقٍّ, and in a third copy omitted,] or مُحِقٍ, without teshdeed, as seen by Az written in an old book, [i. e. *Do I wonder at a measure incompletely filled?*] is a saying of the Arabs, expl. in the book above alluded to, and, Az thinks, correctly, as meaning is it anything more than a measure incompletely filled? [and in a similar manner, but not so fully, expl. in two copies of the Ṣ and in the O:] or, accord. to IB, is it anything more than the fact of my measure's being incompletely filled? (L:) thus expl. also by ISk: and in a similar manner the saying of Aboo-Jahl. (From a marginal note in one of my copies of the Ṣ.) —— عَمِدَ بِهِ means *He kept,* or *clave, to it;* (Ibn-Buzurj, O, Ḳ;) namely, a thing. (O.)

2. عمّد السَّيْلَ, inf. n. تَعْمِيدٌ, *He stopped,* or *obstructed, the course of the torrent, so as to make it collect in a place, by means of earth,* (O, Ḳ,) or *the like,* (Ḳ,) or *stones.* (O.) —— See also 1, first sentence. —— [عمّدهُ as used by the Christians, and held to be of Syriac origin, means *He baptized him:* see مَعْمُودِيَّةٌ.]

4: see 1, first sentence, in two places. —— أَعْمَدَتَاهُ رِجْلَاهُ occurs in a trad. as meaning *His legs rendered him* عَمِيد, i. e. *in such a state that he could not sit unless propped up by cushions placed at his sides:* (L:) it is of the dial. of Ṭeiyi, who say in like manner أَكَلُونِى البَرَاغِيثُ. (TA.)

5: see 1, former half, in five places.

7. انعمد *It became stayed, propped up,* or *supported;* (Ṣ, O, L, Ḳ;) said of a wall, (L,) or other thing. (Ṣ, O, L.)

8. اِعْتَمَدْتُ عَلَى الشَّىْءِ *I leaned, reclined, bore,* or *rested, upon the thing; stayed, propped,* or *supported, myself upon it.* (Ṣ, O, L, Mṣb.) —— And [hence] اعتمدت عَلَيْهِ فِى كَذَا † *I relied upon him in such a thing,* or *case;* (Ṣ, O, L;) as also اِعْتَمَدْتُهُ. (L.) And اعتمدت عَلَى الكِتَابِ [and اعتمدت الكِتَابَ, and perhaps بِالكِتَابِ (see De

Sacy's Chrest. Arabe, sec. ed., i. 315),] ‡ *I relied upon the book, and held to it:* a metaphorical phrase, from the first above. (Mṣb.) — [Hence also the phrase, used by grammarians, يَعْتَمِدُ عَلَى مَا قَبْلَهُ † *It is syntactically dependent upon what is before it;* as, for instance, an enunciative upon its inchoative, an epithet upon the subst. which it qualifies, and an objective complement of a verb upon its verb. — اعتمد المَطَرُ عَلَى الأَرْضِ, a phrase occurring in the Ḳ in art. نكح, app. means *The rain rested upon the ground so as to soak into it:* see عَمِدَ.] — اعتمد عَلَى السَّيْرِ *He went, or journeyed, gently; went a gentle pace.* (L in art. هود.) And اعتمد لَيْلَتَهُ *He rode on journeying during his night.* (A, O, Ḳ.) = See also 1, former half, in three places. — [اعتمدهُ بِكَذَا means قَصَدَهُ بِكَذَا i. e. *He brought to him such a thing;* lit. *he directed, or betook, himself to him with such a thing:* see two exs. in the first paragraph of art. بى.]

عَمَدٌ: see عَمُودٌ (of which it is a quasi-pl. n., as it is also of عِمَادٌ), in four places: and عُمْدَةٌ. = [It is also an inf. n. of عَمِدَ لَهُ, q. v.: = and the inf. n. of عَمِدَ, q. v.: — and hence it signifies] *A swelling, with galls, in the back of a camel.* (L.)

عَمِدٌ Earth *moistened by rain so that when a portion of it is grasped in the hand it becomes compacted by reason of its moisture:* (Ṣ, O, L:) or *moistened by rain and compacted, layer upon layer.* (L.) — [Hence] one says, هُوَ عَمِدُ الثَّرَى [*He is ab*]*undant in goodness, beneficence,* or *bounty.* (AZ, Sh, O, Ḳ.) — عَمِدٌ is also applied to a camel, meaning *Having the inner part of his hump broken* [or *bruised*] *by his being* [*much*] *ridden, while the outer part remains whole,* or *sound:* (Ṣ, O, L:) or *having his hump swollen in consequence of the galling of the saddle and of the cloth beneath it, and broken* [or *bruised*]: fem. with ة: and, with ة, a she-camel *broken,* or *subdued, by the weight of her burden.* (L.) Lebeed says, describing rain (Ṣ, O, L) that caused the valleys to flow, (Ṣ,)

• فَبَاتَ السَّيْلُ يَرْكَبُ جَانِبَيْهِ •
• مِنَ البَقَّارِ كَالعَمِدِ الثِّقَالِ •

[*And the torrent continued during the night, what resembled the heavy,* or *slow-paced, camel such as is termed* عَمِد *overlying its two sides, from* the valley of *El-Baḳḳár*]: Aṣ says, he means that a collection of clouds resembling the [camel termed] عَمِد overlay the two sides of the torrent; i. e., that clouds encompassed it with rain. (Ṣ, O, L.) — Also, applied to a pustule, *Swollen in consequence of its having been squeezed before it had become ripe, and retaining its egg* [or *white globule*]. (L.)

عُمْدَةٌ *A thing by which another thing is stayed, propped,* or *supported; a stay, prop,* or *support;* as also ▼ عِمَادٌ; of which latter the pl. [or rather quasi-pl. n.] is ▼ عَمَدٌ; (Mṣb;) as it is also of عَمُودٌ: (Ṣ, Mṣb, &c.:) *a thing upon which one leans, reclines,* or *bears; upon which one stays, props,* or *supports, himself: a thing upon which one relies:* (Ṣ,* O,* L,* Ḳ, TA:) and عِمَادُ ▼ أَمْرٍ (Ṣ and Ḳ voce قِوَامٌ) and ▼ عَمُودُهُ and ▼ عَمِيدُهُ (L) signify *the stay,* or *support, of a thing* or *an affair; that whereon it rests,* or *whereby it subsists; its efficient cause of subsistence; that without which it would not subsist:* (L, and Ṣ* and Ḳ* ubi suprà:) and ▼ مُعْتَمَدٌ, applied to a man, is syn. with سَنَدٌ [meaning *a person upon whom one leans, rests, stays himself,* or *relies;* a man's *stay, support,* or *object of reliance;* like عُمْدَةٌ and ▼ عِمَادٌ]: (Ṣ and Ḳ* in art. سند:) عُمْدَةٌ is used alike as masc. and fem. and as sing. and dual and pl.: (TA:) one says, أَنْتَ عُمْدَتُنَا *Thou art he to whom we betake ourselves,* or *have recourse, in our necessities;* (A;) or عُمْدَتُنَا فِى الشَّدَائِدِ *our stay,* or *support,* or *object of reliance, in difficulties:* (Mṣb:) and أَنْتُمْ (▼ مُعْتَمَدُنَا) عُمْدَتُنَا *Ye are they upon whom we stay ourselves,* or *rely:* (TA:) and one says also هُوَ عَمُودُ ▼ حَيِّهِ *He is the stay, or support, of his tribe:* (A:) and عِمَادُ ▼ القَوْمِ means *the stay, support,* or *object of reliance, of the people,* or *party;* syn. مُسْتَظْهَرٌ. (Ḥam p. 457.) See also عَمُودٌ, second quarter. — [Hence, as used by grammarians,] † *An indispensable member of a proposition;* as, for instance, the agent; contr. of فَضْلَةٌ. (I'Aḳ p. 143.) — Also *An intention, a purpose, an aim,* or *a course:* so in the phrase اِلْزَمْ عُمْدَتَكَ [*Keep to thy intention, &c.*]. (A.)

عُمْدَةٌ The *place that swells,* or *becomes inflated, in the hump and withers of a camel.* (L. [See عَمَدٌ and عَمِدَ.])

عُمْدَانٌ: see عَمُودٌ, second quarter.

عُمُدٌ and ▼ عُمُدَّانِىٌّ (O, L, Ḳ) and ▼ عُمُدَّانٌ and ▼ مُعْمَدٌّ (L) or ▼ مُعْمَدٌ (TA) *A youth,* or *young man, full of the sap,* or *vigour, of youth:* (O, L, Ḳ:) or *bulky,* or *corpulent, and tall:* (L:) the fem. (of every one of these, L) is with ة: (L, Ḳ:) and the pl. of the second is ▼ عُمُدَّانِيُّونَ: and ▼ عُمُدَّانِيَّةٌ signifies a *corpulent, bulky,* woman; (O, L;) as also ▼ عُمُدَّانَةٌ. (O.)

عُمُدَّانٌ (O, Ḳ, TA, in the CḲ عُمْدان) *Tall;* (O, Ḳ;) applied to a man; fem. with ة, applied to a woman: (O:) and ▼ مُعْمَدٌّ, (A, Ḳ,) like مُكْرَمٌ [in measure], (Ḳ,) or ▼ مُعَمَّدٌ, (O,) signifies the same, (A, O, Ḳ,) applied to a man; (A;) and so ▼ طَوِيلُ العِمَادِ. (Mbr, L.) — See also عُمُدٌ, in two places.

عُمُدَّانِىٌّ, and its pl.; and fem.: see عُمُدٌ.

عِمَادٌ: see عُمْدَةٌ, in four places: — and عَمُودٌ also, former half, in four places. — Also *Lofty buildings:* (Ṣ, O, L, Mṣb, Ḳ:) masc. and fem.: (Ṣ, O, L, Ḳ:) [being a coll. gen. n.:] one thereof is called عِمَادَةٌ. (Ṣ, O, L, Mṣb, Ḳ.) — إِرَمَ ذَاتِ العِمَادِ [mentioned in the Ḳur lxxxix. 6] means *Irem possessing lofty buildings supported by columns:* or *possessing tallness:* (L:) or *possessing tallness and lofty buildings:* (O:) or, accord. to Fr, *the possessors of tents;* i. e. who dwelt in tents, and were accustomed to remove to places of pasture and then to return to their usual places of abode. (O, L.) — طَوِيلُ العِمَادِ: see عُمُدَّانٌ. — Also (i. e. طويل العماد) † A man *whose abode is a place known for its visiters.* (Ṣ, O, L, Ḳ.) — And فُلَانٌ رَفِيعُ العِمَادِ means † [*Such a one is a person of exalted nobility;* lit.] *such a one has a high pole of the tent* of nobility. (A.)

عَمُودٌ a word of well-known meaning, (Mṣb, Ḳ,) The عَمُود of a بَيْت, (Ṣ, O,) or of a خَيْمَة; (Mgh;) [i. e.] *a pole* of a tent; as also ▼ عِمَادٌ: and *a column,* or *pillar,* of a house or the like: (L:) pl. (of pauc., Ṣ, O) أَعْمِدَةٌ, and (of mult., Ṣ, O) عُمُدٌ, and (quasi-pl. n., L) ▼ عَمَدٌ. (Ṣ, O, L, Mṣb, Ḳ.) [The former is the primary, and more common, meaning: and hence the phrase] أَهْلُ عَمُودٍ (Lth, A, Mṣb) and عُمُدٍ or ▼ عَمَدٍ, (Mṣb,) or this last is not said, (L,) and ▼ أَهْلُ عِمَادٍ, (Lth, A, Mṣb, Ḳ,) [*The people of the tent-pole* or *of the tent-poles;*] meaning *the people of,* or *who dwell in, tents:* (Lth, A, Mṣb, Ḳ:) or the last means *the people of lofty tents,* (Ḳ,) or *of lofty structures.* (TA.) خَلَقَ السَّمٰوَاتِ بِغَيْرِ عَمَدٍ ▼ تَرَوْنَهَا, in the Ḳur [xxxi. 9 (and see also xiii. 2)], (O, L,) accord. to Ibn-'Arafeh, (O,) or Fr, (L,) means either *He created the heavens without* عَمَد [or *pillars*] *as ye see them;* and with the sight ye need not information: or *He created the heavens with pillars* (عَمَد) *that ye see not;* [i. e., *with invisible pillars;*] (O,* L;) the pillars that are not seen being his power; or, accord. to Lth, Mount Ḳáf, which surrounds the world [or earth]; the sky being like a cupola, whereof the extremities rest on that mountain, which is of green chrysolite, whence, it is said, results the greenness of the sky. (L.) And ▼ عَمَدٍ and عُمُدٍ in the Ḳur [civ., last verse], accord. to different readings, are pls. [or rather the former is a quasi-pl. n.] of عَمُودٌ; (Fr, L;) or of ▼ عِمَادٌ; and mean [*pillars*] *of fire.* (Zj, L.) — Also *Any tent* (خِبَآء) *supported on poles:* or *any tent extending to a considerable length along the ground, supported on many poles.* (L.) — See also عُمْدَةٌ, in two places. — [Hence,] *A lord, master,* or *chief,* (Ṣ, O, Ḳ,) of a people, or party; (Ṣ, O;) as also ▼ عَمِيدٌ; (Ṣ, A, O, Ḳ;) both signify *a lord, master,* or *chief, upon whom persons stay themselves,* or *rely, in their affairs,* or *to whom they betake themselves,* or *have recourse;* and the pl. of the latter is عُمَدَاءُ. (TA.) And (accord. to IAar, O, L, TA) The رَئِيس [or *chief,* or *commander*], (so in the L, and in the copy of the Ḳ followed in the TA,) or رَسِيل [app. meaning, if correct, the *scout,* or *emissary,* or perhaps the *advanced guard*], (so in the O, and in the CḲ, and in my MS. copy of the Ḳ,) *of an army;* (O, L, Ḳ;) also called the زُوَيْر [which corroborates the former explanation, being syn. with رَئِيس]; (L, TA; [in the O written زَوِير;]) as also ▼ عِمَادٌ and ▼ عُمْدَةٌ and

♦ عُمْدَانٌ. (O, L, Ḳ.) — Also, [from the same word in the first of the senses expl. above,] *A staff*, or *stick*. (L.) — And *A weapon made of iron, with which one beats*, or *strikes*; (Mgh;) *a rod of iron*; (L;) [*a kind of mace*; app. *a rod of iron with a ball of the same metal at the head*: I have heard this appellation applied to the kind of weapon which I have mentioned in an explanation of طَوَارِقُ, pl. of طَارِقَةٌ, q. v.; and it is vulgarly said, in Egypt, to have been used by the فِدَاوِيَّة, the sect called in our histories of the Crusades "the Assassins:"] pl. [of pauc.] أَعْمِدَةٌ. (Mgh.) — [And *A bar of iron, or of any metal.* — And *A perpendicular.*] — And *A slender and lofty mountain*: so in the saying, العُقَابُ تَبِيضُ فِى رَأْسِ عَمُودٍ [*The eagle lays her eggs in the top of a slender and lofty mountain*]. (A.) — عَمُودَا البِئْرِ [*Each of*] *the two upright supports* (قَائِمَتَانِ [or قَامَتَانِ]) *upon which is* [*placed the horizontal cross-piece of wood whereto is suspended*] *the great pulley* (مَحَالَة) *of the well*: (O, Ḳ:) [both together being termed the عَمُودَانِ:] a poet says,

إِذَا ٱسْتَقَلَّتْ رَجَفَ العَمُودَانْ

[*When it* (the bucket, الدَّلْو,) *rises, the two upright supports of the piece of wood to which hangs the great pulley tremble*]. (O.) — عَمُودُ الظَّلِيمِ [*Each of*] *the two legs of the male ostrich*: (Ḳ:) his two legs are called his عَمُودَانِ. (O, L, TA.) — عَمُودُ الصَّلِيبِ [*The upright timber of the cross*] is an appellation applied by the vulgar to *the star* [ε] *upon the tail of the constellation Delphinus*. (Ḳzw.) — عَمُودُ المِيزَانِ *The* شَاهِين, (Ḳ voce شاهين,) i. e. *the beam of the balance*; *the same as the* مِنْجَمِ, *except that it* (the عَمُود) *is generally of the* قَبَّان, or *steelyard*. (MA.) — عَمُودُ السَّيْفِ *The* شَطِيبَة [or شُطْبَة, generally meaning a *ridge*, but sometimes a *channel*, or *depressed line*,] *that is in the* مَتْن [or *broad side*, or *middle of the broad side, of the blade*] *of the sword*, (En-Naḍr, O, Ḳ,) *in the middle of its* مَتْن, *extending to its lower part*: (En-Naḍr, O:) [the swords of the Arabs in the earlier ages being generally straight and two-edged:] and sometimes the sword had three أَعْمِدَة [pl. of pauc. of عَمُود] in its back, termed شُطَب and شَطَائِب. (En-Naḍr, O.) — And عَمُودُ السِّنَانِ *The ridge* (عَيْر, in the O and in copies of the Ḳ [erroneously] written غَيْر,) *rising along the middle of the spear-head, between its two cutting sides*. (ISh, O, L, Ḳ.*) — عَمُودُ البَطْنِ *The back*; (Ṣ, A, Mgh, O, L, Ḳ;) because it supports the belly: (Mgh, O, L:) or *a vein* (عِرْق), (Ḳ,) or *a thing resembling a vein*, (O, L,) *extending from the place of the* رَهَابَة [or *lower extremity of the sternum*] *to a little below the navel*, (O, L, Ḳ,) *in the middle whereof the belly of the sheep or goat is cut open*; so says Lth: (O, L:) or, accord. to Lth, *a vein extending from the* رهابة *to the navel*. (Mgh.) They said, حَمَلَهُ عَلَى عَمُودِ بَطْنِهِ, meaning *He carried it on his back*: (Ṣ, O, L:) or, in the opinion of A'Obeyd, ‡ *with difficulty*, or *trouble, and fatigue*; whether upon his back or not. (O, L.) — عَمُودُ الكَبِدِ *The rising thing* (المُشْرِفُ [app. meaning *the longitudinal ligament*]) *in the middle of the liver*: (Zj in his "Khalḳ el-Insán:") or *a certain vein that irrigates the liver*: (Lth, O, L, Ḳ:) or عَمُودَا الكَبِدِ signifies *two large veins, on the right and left of the navel*. (ISh, O, L.) One says, إِنَّ فُلَانًا لَخَارِجٌ عَمُودُ كَبِدِهِ مِنَ الجُوعِ [*Verily such a one has his* عمود *of his liver coming forth in consequence of hunger*]: (O:) or عَمُودُهُ مِنْ كَبِدِهِ [*his* عمود *from his liver*]; (L, TA;) and some say that by his عمود in this saying is meant what here next follows. (TA.) — وَتِينُ عَمُودِ السَّحْرِ *The* [app. meaning the *aorta*, as though it were considered as the support of the lungs]. (O, Ḳ.) — عَمُودُ الأُذُنِ *The main part, and support, of the ear*: (O, L, Ḳ, TA: [in the CḲ, قَوامُها is erroneously put for قِوَامُهَا:]) or *the round part which is above the lobe*. (L.) — عَمُودُ القَلْبِ *The middle of the heart*, (A, L,) *lengthwise*: or, as some say, *a certain vein that irrigates it*. (L.) One says, اِجْعَلْ ذٰلِكَ فِى عَمُودِ قَلْبِكَ *Put thou that in the middle of thy heart*. (A.) — عَمُودُ اللِّسَانِ *The middle of the tongue, lengthwise*. (L.) — عَمُودُ الكِتَابِ *The text of the book*: thus in the saying, هُوَ مَذْكُورٌ فِى عَمُودِ الكِتَابِ [*It is mentioned in the text of the book*]. (A, TA.) — عَمُودُ الصُّبْحِ *The bright gleam of dawn*; (L;) *the dawn that rises and spreads*, (A, L, Mṣb,*) *filling the horizon with its whiteness*: (Mṣb voce فَجْر:) [app. thus called as being likened to a tent, or long tent:] *it is the second*, or *true*, فَجْر, *and rises after the first*, or *false*, فجر *has disappeared*; *and with its rising, the day commences, and everything by which the fast would be broken becomes forbidden to the faster*. (Mṣb voce فَجْر.) One says, سَطَعَ عَمُودُ الصُّبْحِ, (Ṣ, O, L,) or ضَرَبَ الصُّبْحُ بِعَمُودِهِ (A,) or ضَرَبَ الفَجْرُ بِعَمُودِهِ, i. e. [*The bright gleam of dawn*] *rose and spread*. (Mṣb.) — عَمُودُ الإِعْصَارِ *That* [meaning *the dust*] *which rises into the sky*, or *extends along the surface of the earth, in consequence of the* [*wind called*] إِعْصَار [q. v.]. (O, L.) — عَمُودُ الحُسْنِ † *Tallness of stature*. (TA in art. مكر.) — عَمُودُ النَّوَى ‡ *The state of distance, from their friends, in which travellers continue*. (L.) — دَائِرَةُ العَمُودِ *The curl of the hair* [*which we term a feather*] *on a horse's neck, in the places of the collar*: it is approved by the Arabs. (L.) — اِسْتَقَامُوا عَلَى عَمُودِ رَأْيِهِمْ means *They continued in the course upon which they placed reliance*. (O, Ḳ.) — Also, i. e. عَمُودٌ, (accord. to the O and Ḳ,) or ♦ عَمِيدٌ, (accord. to the TA [agreeably with an explanation of the latter in the L],) *Affected with vehement*, or *intense, grief* or *sorrow*. (O, Ḳ, TA.)

عَمِيدٌ: see عُمْدَةٌ — and see also عَمُودٌ, first quarter. — Also A man *sick*, (L,) or *very sick*, (A,) *so that he cannot sit unless propped up by cushions placed at his sides*. (A,* L.) — Also, and ♦ مَعْمُودٌ, (Ṣ, O, L, Ḳ,) and ♦ مُعَمَّدٌ, (Ḳ,) A man *broken*, or *enervated, by the passion of love*; (Ṣ, O, Ḳ;) and in like manner all the three are applied to a heart: (O:) or the first and second signify a man *whose* عمود *of his heart is severed*: (A:) or a man *much distressed*, or *afflicted, by love*; likened to a camel's hump of which the interior is broken: (L. [See عَمِدَ:]) and ♦ مَعْمُودٌ signifies *diseased*, or *sick*. (L.) — See also عَمُودٌ, last sentence. — عَمِيدُ الوَجَعِ *The place of pain*. (L.)

عَامِدٌ applied to the latter part of the night, *Causing pain*. (IAạr, O.) And لَيْلَةٌ عَامِدَةٌ *A night causing pain*. (IAạr, Az, O.)

مُعْمَدٌ A *tall* [tent such as is called] طِرَاف. [So in a copy of the A. [Perhaps a mistranscription for مُعَمَّد, q. v.]) See also عُمْدَانٌ. — And see عُمُدٌ.

مُعَمَّدٌ, applied to a tent, *Set up with poles*: (O, Ḳ:) occurring in a verse of [the Mo'allaḳah of] Ṭarafeh [p. 88 in the EM]. (O. [See also مُعْمَد.]) — وَشْىٌ مُعَمَّدٌ (O, Ḳ, TA, in some copies of the Ḳ شَىْءٌ,) *A sort of* وَشْى [or *variegated cloth*] (O, Ḳ, TA) [*figured*] *with the form of* عِمَاد [app. meaning *lofty buildings*]. (TA.) — See also عُمْدَانٌ: — and عُمُدٌ: and عَمِيدٌ.

[مَعْمُودَانِىٌّ and مُعْمِدَانِىٌّ and مَعْمُودَانٌ epithets used by the Christian Arabs, meaning *A baptist*.]

مَعْمُودٌ applied to a thing that presses heavily, such as a roof, *Held* [*up*, or *supported*,] *by columns*: differing from مَدْعُوم [q. v.]. (TA in art. دعم.) — Also A person *resorted to* in cases of need. (A.) — See also عَمِيدٌ, in two places.

المَعْمُودِيَّةُ, thus correctly, as in the 'Ináyeh, without teshdeed to the ى, but in the copies of the Ḳ with teshdeed, [and so in the O; held by some to be of Arabic origin, but by others, of Syriac;] said by Eṣ-Ṣowlee to be an arabicized word, from مَعْمُودِيت, with the pointed ذ, signifying الطَّهَارَةُ [app. as meaning "ablution," or "purification"]; (TA;) [*Baptism*: and *baptismal water*; expl. as signifying] *a yellow water, pertaining to the Christians*, (O, Ḳ, TA,) *consecrated by what is recited over it from the Gospel*, (TA,) *in which they dip their children, believing that is is a purification to them, like circumcision to others*. (O, Ḳ, TA.) [See also صِبْغَةٌ.]

مُعْتَمَدٌ: see عُمْدَةٌ, in two places. — [Also *A ground of reliance*:] one says, مَا عَلَى فُلَانٍ مُعْتَمَدٌ [*There is not any ground of reliance upon such a one*]. (Ṣ voce مَحْمِل, q. v.)

عمر

1. عَمِرَ, aor. ـَ; (Ṣ, O, Mṣb, Ḳ;) and عَمَرَ, aor. ـُ (Ḳ) and ـِ; (Sb, Ḳ;) inf. n. عُمْر (Ṣ, O,

Mṣb, Ḳ) and عُمُرٌ, (Ṣ, O, Mṣb,) both anomalous, as inf. ns. of عَمِرَ, for by rule the inf. n. should be عَمَرٌ, (Ṣ,) but عَمَرٌ is also an inf. n., (TA,) and عُمْرٌ, which is the most chaste, (O,) and عَمَارَةٌ; (Ḳ;) *He lived,* (Ṣ, O,) or *continued in life* (بَقِىَ), (Ḳ,) *long,* or *a long time;* (Ṣ, O, Ḳ;*) *his life was,* or *became, long:* (Mṣb:) and عَمِرَ *he grew old.* (TA.) — عَمَرَ بِمَكَانٍ *He remained, continued, stayed, resided, dwelt,* or *abode, in a place.* (B, TA.) = عَمُرَ, aor. ـُ, inf. n. عُمْرٌ, (Mṣb,) or عِمَارَةٌ and عُمْرَانٌ, (MA,) *It* (a place of abode) *became inhabited;* (MA, Mṣb;) بِأَهْلِهِ [*by its people*]: (Mṣb:) [*it became peopled, well peopled, well stocked with people and the like, in a flourishing state, in a state the contrary of desolate* or *waste* or *ruined,* or *in a state of good repair:*] and in like manner you say, عَمُرَتِ الدَّارُ, aor. ـُ, inf. n. عُمْرٌ, *the house became inhabited* [&c.]. (MA.) — [You say also, عَمُرَتِ الأَرْضُ *The land became inhabited, peopled, well stocked with people and camels and the like, colonized, cultivated, well cultivated, in a flourishing state,* or *in a state the contrary of waste:* see its act. part. n., عَامِرٌ.] — And عَمُرَ المَالُ, aor. ـُ; and عَمِرَ, aor. ـَ; (Ḳ;) and عَمَرَ, aor. ـُ; (Sb, Ḳ;) inf. n. عِمَارَةٌ; (Ḳ; [so in most copies; in the TA, عَمَارَةٌ, and there said to be inf. n. of عَمُرَ; but, I think, erroneously;]) i. q. صَارَ عَامِرًا [*The property, consisting of camels* or *the like, became in a flourishing state*]; (Ḳ;) *the property became much; the camels,* or *the like, became many,* or *numerous.* (Ṣgh.) = عَمَرَهُ, (Mṣb, Ḳ,) aor. ـُ, (TA,) inf. n. عِمَارَةٌ (Ḳ [so in most copies, but in the TA, عَمَارَةٌ, with fet-ḥ, which I think erroneous;]) and عُمُورٌ (Ḳ) and عُمْرَانٌ, (TA,) *He inhabited it; remained, continued, stayed, resided, dwelt,* or *abode, in it;* namely, a place of abode: (Mṣb:) *he kept to it;* namely, his property, or his camels or the like, and his house, or tent: (Ḳ:) one should not say, of a man, أَعْمَرَ ▼ مَنْزِلَهُ, with ا. (Az, TA.) إِنَّمَا يَعْمُرُ مَسَاجِدَ اللّٰهِ, in the Ḳur [ix. 18], signifies *Only he shall abide in the mosques,* or *places of worship, of God:* or *shall visit them:* (TA:) see 8: but Z says, I know not عَمَرَ as occurring in the sense of اعتمر [*he visited*]: (TA:) or *shall enter them and sit in them:* (Jel:) or the verb in the above-cited phrase of the Ḳur has another signification, which see below. (TA.) = عَمَرَهُ is also syn. with عَمَّرَهُ, in the first of the senses expl. below: see 2. = عَمَرَ اللّٰهُ بِكَ مَنْزِلَكَ, (AZ, Ṣ, O, Ḳ,*) aor. ـُ, (TA,) inf. n. عِمَارَةٌ; (Ḳ;) and ▼ أَعْمَرَهُ; (AZ, Ṣ, O, Ḳ;) *May God make thy place of abode to become peopled,* [or *well peopled, well stocked with people and the like, in a flourishing state, in a state the contrary of ruined* or *waste* or *desolate,* or *in a state of good repair,*] *by thee* [or *by thy means*]: (Ḳ,* TA:) but AZ says that one should not say, of a man, أَعْمَرَ ▼ مَنْزِلَهُ, with ا. (Ṣ.) — عَمَرَ الخَرَابَ, aor. and inf. n. as above, [*He made the ruin,* or *waste,* or *the like, to become in a state of good repair, in a state the contrary of ruined* or *waste* or *desolate.*] (Ṣ, O, TA.) — [عَمَرَ الأَرْضَ, aor. and inf. n. as above, *He peopled the land; stocked it well with people and camels and the like; colonized it; cultivated it,* or *cultivated it well; rendered it in a flourishing state,* or *in a state the contrary of waste.*] — And عَمَرَ البِنَآءَ, aor. and inf. n. as above, *He kept the building in a good state;* syn. حَفِظَهُ. (TA.) So accord. to some, in the Ḳur, إِنَّمَا يَعْمُرُ مَسَاجِدَ اللّٰهِ, [quoted above,] *Only he shall keep in a good state* [or *in repair*] *the mosques,* or *places of worship, of God:* (TA:) among the significations of the verb as here used, are these; *he shall adorn them with carpets* or *the like, and light them with lamps, and continue the performance of religious worship and praise and the study of science in them, and guard them from* [*desecration by*] *that for which they are not built, such as worldly discourse.* (Bḍ.) — عَمَرَ الدَّارَ, aor. ـُ, inf. n. عُمْرٌ [and عِمَارَةٌ, (MA,) or this, accord. to the Mṣb, is a simple subst.], *He built the house.* (Mṣb.) [And] *He made the house to be inhabited; he peopled it;* (MA;) [or *made it to be well stocked with people and the like,* or *in a flourishing state,* or *in a state of good repair.*] — عَمَرَ الخَيْرَ, aor. ـُ, inf. n. عُمْرٌ and عِمَارَةٌ, [app., *He instituted what was good:* or perhaps, *he cultivated,* or *promoted, it:* or *he kept to it;* or *observed it;* or *regarded it.*] (Az, TA.) = عَمَرَ رَبَّهُ, (IAạr, Ḳ,) aor. ـُ, (IAạr, O,) [inf. n. عِمَارَةٌ,] *He served,* or *worshipped, his Lord;* (IAạr, Ḳ;) *he prayed and fasted.* (Ks, Lḥ, O, Ḳ.) You say تَرَكْتُ فُلَانًا يَعْمُرُ رَبَّهُ *I left such a one worshipping his Lord, praying and fasting.* (TA.)

2. عَمَّرَهُ اللّٰهُ, (Ṣ, O, Mṣb, Ḳ,) inf. n. تَعْمِيرٌ; (Ṣ, Mṣb;) and ▼ عَمَرَهُ, (Mṣb, Ḳ,) aor. ـُ, (Mṣb,) inf. n. عَمْرٌ; (TA;) *God lengthened,* or *prolonged, his life;* (Ṣ, O, Mṣb, TA;) *made him to continue in life; preserved him alive;* (Ḳ, TA;) as also ▼ اِسْتَعْمَرَهُ. (O and Bḍ in xi. 64.) It is said in the Ḳur [xxxv. 12], وَمَا يُعَمَّرُ مِنْ مُعَمَّرٍ وَلَا يُنْقَصُ إِلَّا فِى كِتَابٍ, i. e., *No one whose life is prolonged has life prolonged, nor is aught diminished of his,* meaning another's, *life, but it is recorded in a writing:* (I'Ab, Fr,* O:*) or the meaning is, *nor does aught pass of his,* i. e. the same person's, *life:* (Sa'eed Ibn-Jubeyr:) both these explanations are good; but the former seems more probably correct. (Az, TA.) — عَمَّرَ نَفْسَهُ *He determined for himself,* or *assigned to himself, a limited life.* (Ḳ.) — عَمَّرَ اللّٰهَ, inf. n. تَعْمِيرٌ, *He acknowledged the everlasting existence of God.* (Ṣ, TA.) — عَمَّرْتُكَ اللّٰهَ *I ask,* or *beg, God to prolong thy life:* (Ks, O, TA:) or *I remind thee of God.* (TA, app. on the authority of Mbr.) [It also seems to signify *I swear to thee by the everlasting existence of God.* See عَمْرَ اللّٰهِ.] — عَمَّرْتُكَ اللّٰهَ أَنْ تَفْعَلَ كَذَا *I adjure thee by God, and beg thee by the length of thy life, that thou do such a thing.* (Ḳ,* TA.) — See also 4. — عَمَّرَ خِبَآءً بِمَا اَحْتَاجَ إِلَيْهِ [*He furnished a tent with what he required*]. (Mṣb in art. بنى.)

3. عَامَرْتُهُ طُولَ حَيَاتِهِ [*I lived with him for the length of his life*]. (M in art. بلو.)

4: see 1, in three places. — اعمرهُ المَكَانَ, (Ḳ,) and ▼ اِسْتَعْمَرَهُ فِيهِ, (Ṣ, Ḳ,) i. q. جَعَلَهُ يَعْمُرُهُ (Ḳ) or جعله عَامِرَهُ (Ṣ) [*He made him to inhabit the place,* or *to people,* or *colonize,* or *cultivate, it*]. So the latter signifies in the Ḳur [xi. 64], وَاسْتَعْمَرَكُمْ ▼ فِيهَا (Ṣ) *And He hath made you to dwell therein:* (O, Jel:) or *hath required of you to inhabit it,* or *to people it,* &c.: (Z:) or *hath enabled and commanded you to do so:* (Bḍ:) or *hath permitted you to do so, and to fetch out by labour,* or *art, your food* [for قومكر in the L and TA, I read قُوتَكُمْ, and this is evidently the right,] *from it:* (TA:) or *hath given you your houses therein for your lives;* or *made you to dwell in them during your lives, and then to leave them to others:* (Bḍ:) or *hath prolonged your lives therein.* (Ibn-'Arafeh, O.) — أَعْمَرْتُهُ دَارًا, (Ṣ, Mgh, O, Mṣb, Ḳ,*) or أَرْضًا, or إِبِلًا, (Ṣ, O,) and ▼ عَمَرْتُهُ إِيَّاهَا, (Ḳ,*) *I assigned to him the house for his life,* (Mṣb, Ḳ,) or *for my life,* (Ḳ,) *to inhabit it for that period;* (Mṣb, TA;) *I said to him, of a house,* (Ṣ, Mgh, O,) or *of land,* or *of camels,* (Ṣ, O,) *It is thine,* (Ṣ, Mgh, O,) or *they are thine,* (Ṣ, O,) *for my life,* (Ṣ, Mgh, O,) or *for thy life, and when thou diest it returns,* or *they return, to me.* (Ṣ, O.) The doing so is forbidden. (Mgh, TA.) [See also عُمْرَى: and see أَرْقَبَ, and رُقْبَى.] — اعمر الأَرْضَ *He found the land to be* عَامِرَة, (Ṣ, O, Ḳ,) i. e., *peopled* [*and cultivated,* or *in a flourishing state*]. (TA.) — اعمر عَلَيْهِ *He rendered him rich; made him to be possessed of competence or sufficiency, to be without wants,* or *to have few wants.* (Ḳ.) = اعمرهُ *He aided him to perform the visit called* عُمْرَة; (Mgh, O, Ḳ;) [said to be] on the authority of analogy; not on that of hearsay; (Mgh;) but occurring in a trad.: (Mgh, TA:) or *he made him to perform that visit.* (IḲṭṭ, Mṣb.) = See also 8.

8. اعتمر *He visited.* (Mṣb, Ḳ: in some copies of the Ḳ اعتمرهُ.) You say, اعتمرهُ, (Ṣ, O,) and ▼ اعمرهُ, (ISk, Mṣb,) *He visited him,* or *it;* (Ṣ, O;) *he repaired,* or *betook himself, to him,* or *it;* (ISk, Ṣ, O, Mṣb;) as also ▼ عَمَرَهُ, accord. to one explanation of a passage in the Ḳur ix. 18, quoted above: [see 1:] but Z says, I know not عَمَرَ as occurring in the sense of اعتمر. (TA.) — *He performed the religious visit called* عُمْرَة. (O, TA.) You say اعتمر فِى الحَجِّ [*He performed the visit so called in the pilgrimage*]. (Ṣ.) — اعتمر أَمْرًا *He betook himself to a thing,* or *an affair;* as, for instance, a warring and plundering expedition; *aimed at it; purposed it.* (TA.) = Also *He attired his head* (i. e. his own head) *with an* عِمَارَة, i. e., *a turban,* &c. (Ṣ, Ḳ.)

10: see 2: — and also 4, in two places.

عُمْرٌ and ▼ عُمُرٌ are both inf. ns., signifying the same. (Ṣ, O.) [See 1. As such, the former is the more common.] And both of these words, (Mgh, Ḳ, &c.,) and ▼ عَمْرٌ, (Ḳ, &c.,) [used as simple substs., or abstract ns., in which case the second is more common than the first, except in forms of swearing, in which the former is used, and the third is more chaste than the second,] signify *Life*; (Mṣb, Ḳ;) [the *age to which the life extends*;] the *period during which the body is inhabited by life*: so that it denotes less than بَقَآء: wherefore the latter is [frequently] used as an attribute of God; but عمر is seldom used as such: (Er-Rághib, B:) pl. أَعْمَارٌ. (Ḳ.) You say ▼ أَطَالَ ٱللّٰهُ عُمْرَكَ and عَمْرَكَ [*May God prolong thy life*]. (Ṣ, O.) In a form of swearing, عمر only is used. (Ṣ.) [In a case of this kind, when ل is not prefixed to it, it is in the accus. case, as will be shown and expl. below: but when ل is prefixed to it, it is in the nom.] You say لَعَمْرُكَ لَأَفْعَلَنَّ, meaning *By thy life, I will assuredly do* [such a thing]. (Mṣb.) لَعَمْرُكَ occurs in the Ḳur xv. 72, and means *By thy life*: (IʼAb, Akh, Bḍ, Jel:) and ▼ لَعَمْرُكَ is a dial. var., mentioned by Yoo: (O:) or the former, accord. to the grammarians, means *by thy religion*: (AHeyth, O:) and [in like manner] لَعَمْرِى, and ▼ لَعَمْرِى, [*by my life*, or] *by my religion*. (Ḳ.) لَعَمْرُكَ is an inchoative, of which the enunciative, مَا أُقْسِمُ بِهِ, [*that by which I swear*, so that the entire phrase means *thy life is that by which I swear*,] is understood; therefore it is in the nom. case: (IJ, TA:) or the complete phrase is وَعَمْرُكَ فَلَعَمْرُكَ عَظِيمٌ [*by thy life*, &c.: *and thy life is of great account*]. (Fr, as related by AʼObeyd.) You say also لَعَمْرُ أَبِيكَ ٱلْخَيْرُ, and ٱلْخَيْرِ; the former meaning *By thy father's instituting*, or *promoting*, or *keeping to*, or *observing*, or *regarding, what is good*; الخير being the objective complement of عمر, from عَمَرَ ٱلْخَيْرَ, aor. ـُ, inf. n. عَمْرٌ and عِمَارَةٌ; [see 1;] but in the latter case, الخير is an epithet added to أَبِيكَ [so that the meaning is *by the life of thy good father*]. (AHeyth, Az, O, TA.) [See also art. خير.] You also say لَعَمْرُ ٱللّٰهِ, meaning *By the everlasting existence of God*; (Ṣ, O, Ḳ;) عمر being here in the nom. case as an inchoative, with ل prefixed to it as a corroborative of the inchoative state: the enunciative is understood; the complete phrase being لَعَمْرُ ٱللّٰهِ قَسَمِى or مَا أُقْسِمُ بِهِ [*the everlasting existence of God is my oath*, or *that by which I swear*]. (Ṣ, O.) This expression is forbidden in a trad., (Ḳ,) because عَمْرٌ [properly] means the life of the body: (TA:) [but] لَعَمْرُ إِلٰهِكَ, meaning *By the everlasting existence of thy God*, occurs in a trad. (TA.) When you do not prefix ل, you make it to be in the accus. case, as an inf. n.: thus you say, عَمْرَ ٱللّٰهِ مَا فَعَلْتُ كَذَا (Ṣ, O, Ḳ) *I swear by the everlasting existence of God, I did not so*: (Ṣ, O:) and عَمْرَكَ ٱللّٰهَ مَا فَعَلْتُ كَذَا (Ṣ, O, Ḳ, [in the CḲ اللّٰهُ, but this is a mistake,]) *By thine acknowledgment of the everlasting existence of God, I did not so*: (Ṣ, O:) or the original thereof is عَمَّرْتُكَ ٱللّٰهَ تَعْمِيرًا, (O, Ḳ,) i. e., *I ask*, or *beg, God to prolong thy life*: (Ks, O:) [and it is said in the Ṣ that عَمْرَكَ ٱللّٰهَ sometimes has this signification:] and in like manner عَمْرَكَ ٱللّٰهَ لَا أَفْعَلُ ذَاكَ means *I beg God to prolong thy life*: *I will not do that*: or it may be a form of oath without و [for وَعَمْرَكَ]: (Ks:) and you say عَمْرَكَ ٱللّٰهَ أَفْعَلُ كَذَا and إِلَّا فَعَلْتَ كَذَا and إِلَّا مَا فَعَلْتَ كَذَا [and, *By thine acknowledgment of the everlasting existence of God*, &c., *do thou so*]: (TA:) or عَمْرَكَ ٱللّٰهَ signifies *by thy worship of God*: (AHeyth:) or I remind thee, *reminding thee, of God*. (Ḳ.) Mbr says of this phrase, عمرك الله, that عمر may be in the accus. case on account of a verb understood; [such, for instance, as أُذَكِّرُكَ;] or by reason of وَ suppressed, the complete phrase being وَعَمْرِكَ ٱللّٰهَ; or as being for [the inf. n.] تَعْمِير. (TA.) It may also be [found written] عَمْرُ ٱللّٰهِ; but this is bad. (Ks.) Some of the Arabs, for لَعَمْرُكَ, said رَعَمْلُكَ. (Az.) — عَمْرًا وَشَبَابًا: see قُحَابٌ. — عُمْرٌ (AHeyth, Ḳ) and ▼ عَمْرٌ (Ḳ) signify *Religion*; (AHeyth, Ḳ;) as in the phrases لَعَمْرِى and ▼ لَعَمْرِى (Ḳ) and لَعَمْرُكَ (AHeyth) [mentioned above]. — Also عَمْرٌ (Ṣ, O, Mṣb, Ḳ) and ▼ عُمْرٌ (IAth, O, Ḳ) The *flesh that is between the teeth*: (Ṣ, O, Mṣb, Ḳ:) or the *pendent piece of flesh between the teeth*: (Az, Mṣb:) or the *flesh that is between the places in which the teeth are set*: (TA:) or the *flesh of the gum*: (Ḳ:) or the *flesh of the gum that runs between any two teeth*: (TA:) or *what appears of the gum*: (Kh, Mṣb:) or (so accord. to the TA, but in the Ḳ "and") *anything of an oblong shape between two teeth*: (Ḳ:) pl. عُمُورٌ: (Ṣ, O, Mṣb, Ḳ:) which some explain as signifying the *places whence the teeth grow*. (TA.) It is said in a trad., أَوْصَانِى جِبْرِيلُ بِالسِّوَاكِ حَتَّى خَشِيتُ عَلَى عُمُورِى [*Gabriel enjoined me to make use of the tooth-stick so that I feared for my* عمور]. (O, TA.) — أُمُّ عَمْرٍو: see عَامِرٌ.

عُمُرٌ: see عُمْرٌ, in two places.

عُمْرٌ: see عَمْرٌ, in four places.

عُمُرٌ: see عَمْرٌ, in two places.

عُمْرَةٌ: see عِمَارَةٌ. — أَبُو عَمْرَةَ means *Bankruptcy, insolvency*, or *the state of having no property remaining*; (Lth, O, Ḳ;) which is said to be thus called because it was the name of an envoy of El-Mukhtár the son of Aboo-ʼObeyd, on the occasion of whose alighting at the abode of a people, slaughter and war used to befall them: (Lth, O, Ḳ:*) — and (Ḳ) *hunger*. (IAạr, Ḳ.)

عُمْرَةٌ *A visit*, or *a visiting*: (Ṣ, Mṣb, Ḳ:) or *a visit in which is the cultivation* (عِمَارَة) *of love* or *affection*: (TA:) or *a repairing to an inhabited*, or *a peopled, place*: this is the primary signification. (Mgh.) — Hence the عُمْرَة in pilgrimage [and at any time]; (Ṣ, O;*) i. e. [*A religious visit to the sacred places at Mekkeh, with the performance of the ceremony of* الإِحْرَام,] *the circuiting round the Kaabeh, and the going to and fro between Eṣ-Ṣafà and El-Marweh*: الحَجّ [differs from it inasmuch as it is at a particular time of the year and] is not complete without the halting at ʼArafát on the day of ʼArafeh: (Zj, TA:) the عُمْرَة is the *minor pilgrimage* (الحَجُّ الأَصْغَرُ); (Mṣb, and Kull p. 168;) what is commonly termed الحَجّ being called sometimes the greater pilgrimage (الحَجُّ الأَكْبَرُ): (Kull:) pl. عُمَرٌ (Ṣ, O, Mṣb) and عُمُرَاتٌ or عُمْرَاتٌ or عُمَرَاتٌ. (Mṣb.) — Also A man's *going in to his* [*newly-married*] *wife in the abode of her family*: (IAạr, Ṣ, Ḳ:) if he removes her to his own family, the act is termed عُرْسٌ. (IAạr, Ṣ.)

عُمْرَى a subst., (إِسْمٌ) [strangely read by Golius أَسْمٌ,] (Ṣ, O,) or an inf. n., (TA,) [or rather a quasi-inf. n.,] from أَعْمَرَهُ دَارًا and the like; (Ṣ, O, TA;) A man's *assigning to another a house for the life of the latter*, or *for the life of the former*; (accord. to the explanation of the verb in the Ḳ;) a man's *saying to another, of a house*, or *of land*, or *of camels, It is thine*, or *they are thine, for my life*, or *for thy life, and when thou diest it returns*, or *they return, to me*; (accord. to the explanation of the verb in the Ṣ and Mgh and O;) a man's *giving to another a house, and saying to him, This is thine for thy life*, or *for my life*: (Th, in TA: [in which is added, "whichever of us dies," ايّنا مات, but this I consider a mistake for إِذَا مَاتَ, "when he dies,") "the house is given to his family:"]) so they used to do in the Time of Ignorance: (TA:) but some of the Muslim lawyers hold the gift to be absolute, and the condition to be null. (TA, &c.) — Also [The *property*, or *house*, &c., *so given*;] *what is assigned*, or *given, to another for the period of his life*, or *for that of the life of the giver*. (Ḳ.) [See also رُقْبَى.]

عُمْرِىٌّ, applied to trees (شَجَر), *Old*; (Ḳ;) a rel. n. from عُمْرٌ: (TA:) عُمْرِيَّةٌ, [the fem.,] applied to a tree (شَجَرَة), signifies *great and old, having had a long life*: (IAth, TA:) or the former, the [species of lote-tree called] سِدْر, *that grows upon the rivers* (O, Ḳ) *and imbibes the water*; as also عُبْرِىٌّ: (O:) or, accord. to Abu-l-ʼAmeythel [or ʼOmeythil] El-Aạrábee, the *old*, whether on a river or not; (O, TA;) and in like manner says Aṣ, the *old* of the سِدْر, whether on a river or not; and the ضَال is the recent thereof: some say that the م is a substitute for the ب in عُبْرِىّ [q. v.]. (TA.)

الفَرِيضَةُ العُمَرِيَّةُ: see المُشَرَّكَةُ.

عُمْرَانٌ [an inf. n. of عَمَرَ: — and of عَمُرَ: — then app. used as an epithet syn. with عَامِرٌ, q.v.: (of which it is also a pl.:) — and then as an epithet in which the quality of a subst. is predominant; meaning *A land*, or *house, inhabited, peopled, well peopled, well stocked with people and the like, in a flourishing state, in a state the contrary of desolate* or *waste* or *ruined*; *a land colo-*

nized, cultivated, or well cultivated; a house in a state of good repair: such seems to be meant in the JK and A and Ḳ, in art. خرب, where, as in the O in this art., it is said to be contr. of خَرَابٌ, q. v.] — It is also a subst. signifying بُنْيَانٌ [A building; a structure; an edifice: or perhaps the act of building]. (Mṣb.) [See also عِمَارَةٌ. — It is also a pl. of عَامِرٌ, q. v.]

عَمَارٌ: see عِمَارَةٌ, in three places.

عَمِيرٌ: see عَامِرٌ.

أَبُو عُمَيْرٍ The ذَكَر. (Ḳ; and TA voce شَامِر, q.v., in art. شمر.)

عِمَارَةٌ Anything (AO, Ṣ, O, Ḳ) which one puts, (Ṣ, O,) or which a chief puts, (TA,) upon his head, such as a turban, and a قَلَنْسُوَة, and a crown, &c., (AO, Ṣ, O, Ḳ,) as a sign of headship, and for keeping it in mind; (TA;) as also ▼ عَمْرَةٌ (Ḳ) and ▼ عَمَارٌ: (Ṣ, O,* TA:) which last [is app. a coll. gen. n., of which عَمَارَةٌ is the n. un., and] also signifies any sweet-smelling plant (رَيْحَان) which a chief puts upon his head for the same purpose: and hence, † any such plant, absolutely: (B:) or any such plant with which a drinking-chamber is adorned, (Ṣ, Ḳ,) called by the Persians مَيْوَرَان; when any one comes in to the people there assembled, they raise somewhat thereof with their hands, and salute him with it, wishing him a long life: so, accord. to some, in a verse of El-Aạshà, which see below: (Ṣ:) or it there signifies crowns of such plants, which they put upon their heads, as the foreigners (العَجَم) do; but ISd says, "I know not how this is:" or the myrtle; syn. آس: (TA:) and عَمَارَةٌ signifies a plant of that kind, with which one used to salute a king, saying, May God prolong thy life: or, as some say, a raising of the voice, saying so: (Az, TA:) a salutation; (Ḳ;) said to mean, may God prolong thy life; (TA;) as also ▼ عَمَارٌ (Ṣ, Ḳ) and ▼ عِمَارَةٌ; (L;) but Az says that this explanation is not valid. (TA.) El-Aạshà says,

فَلَمَّا أَتَانَا بُعَيْدَ الكَرَى
سَجَدْنَا لَهُ وَرَفَعْنَا العَمَارَا ▼

[And when he came to us, a little after slumber, we prostrated ourselves to him, and] we put the turbans from our heads, in honour of him: (Ṣ:) but IB says that, accord. to this explanation, the correct reading is وَضَعْنَا العَمَارَا: (TA:) or the former reading means, we raised our voices with prayer for him, and said, May God prolong thy life: or we raised the sweet-smelling plants: &c.: see above. (Ṣ, TA.) — Also عَمَارَةٌ, (Ḳ,) or ▼ عِمَارَةٌ, (O,) An ornamented piece of cloth which is sewed upon a مِظَلَّة, [by which is meant a kind of tent,] (O, Ḳ, TA,) i. e. sewed to the طَرِيقَة [q. v.], on each side of the tent-pole, (O,) as a sign of headship. (TA.) = See also عِمَارَةٌ.

عُمَارَةٌ Hire, pay, or wages, of, or for, عِمَارَةٌ as signifying مَا يُعْمَرُ بِهِ المَكَانُ [see below]. (Ḳ, TA.)

عِمَارَةٌ [is an inf. n.: and often signifies Habitation and cultivation; or a good state of habitation and cultivation: — and is also expl. as signifying] مَا يُعْمَرُ بِهِ المَكَانُ [That by which a place is rendered inhabited, peopled, well stocked with people and the like, colonized, cultivated, well cultivated, in a flourishing state, or in a state the contrary of desolate or waste or ruined; app. meaning, work, or labour, by which a place is rendered so; as it is immediately added in the Ḳ that عُمَارَةٌ signifies hire, pay, or wages, of it, or for it; and the explanation which I have here given is agreeable with ancient and modern usage; to which it may be further added, that the measure (فِعَالَةٌ) is common to words signifying arts, occupations, or employments, as زِرَاعَةٌ and فِلَاحَةٌ &c.]. (Ḳ, TA.) — Also a subst. from عَمَرَ الدَّارَ. (Mṣb.) [It has two significations, either of which may be meant in the Mṣb: The act, or art, of building a house: — and A building; a structure; an edifice: generally, accord. to modern usage, a public edifice: pl. عَمَائِرُ. See also عُمْرَانٌ.] = Also The breast of a man. (TA.) — Hence, (TA,) عِمَارَةٌ (Ṣ, O, Mṣb, Ḳ) and ▼ عَمَارَةٌ, (Mṣb, Ḳ,) the latter allowed by Kh, (O,) but the former is the more common, (Mṣb,) A great tribe, syn. قَبِيلَةٌ عَظِيمَةٌ, (Mṣb,) or حَىٌّ عَظِيمٌ, (O, Ḳ, TA,) that subsists by itself, migrating by itself, and abiding by itself, and seeking pasturage by itself: (O, TA:) or it is called by the former name because it peoples a land; and by the latter, because complex like a turban; (TA;) and ▼ عَمِيرَةٌ signifies the same; or, as some say, all signify a بَطْن: (Ḥam p. 682:) or i. q. قَبِيلَةٌ and عَشِيرَةٌ: (Ṣ, O:) or less than a قبيلة: (O, Ḳ:) or less than a قبيلة and more than a بَطْن: (IAth, TA:) [see also شَعْبٌ:] or a body of men by which a place is peopled: (B, TA:) pl. عَمَائِرُ. (TA.) = See also عِمَارَةٌ, in two places.

عَمِيرَةٌ: see the next preceding paragraph, near the end.

عَامِرٌ Living long. (Mṣb, TA.) — Remaining, continuing, staying, residing, dwelling, or abiding, in a place: (TA:) and thus, or remaining, &c., and congregated, in a pl. sense. (Muṣ'ab, O.) [Hence,] An inhabitant of a house: pl. عُمَّارٌ. (TA.) And عُمَّارُ البُيُوتِ The jinn, or genii, that inhabit houses. (Ṣ.) And عَوَامِرُ البُيُوتِ The serpents that are in houses: sing. عَامِرٌ and عَامِرَةٌ: accord. to some, they are so called because of the length of their lives. (TA.) — See also مُعْتَمِرٌ. = Also i. q. ▼ مَعْمُورٌ. (O, TA.) [See also عُمْرَانٌ.] You say أَرْضٌ عَامِرَةٌ A land peopled; [colonized; cultivated; &c.] (TA.) [See عَمَرَ.] And مَنْزِلٌ عَامِرٌ A place of abode inhabited [&c.]. (Mṣb.) And مَكَانٌ عَامِرٌ, and ▼ عَمِيرٌ, (Ṣ, O, TA,) i. e. ذُو عِمَارَةٍ [A place inhabited, peopled, well stocked with people and the like, in a flourishing state, in a state the contrary of desolate or waste or ruined]. (TA.) — It is applied also to that which has been a ruin or waste or the like [as meaning In a state of good repair; in a state the contrary of ruined or waste or desolate]; and so ▼ مَعْمُورٌ. (Ṣ, TA.) [Pl. عُمَّارٌ.] = إِنَّهُ لَعَامِرٌ لِرَبِّهِ Verily he is a server, or worshipper, of his Lord. (TA.) = أُمُّ عَامِرٍ, (Ṣ, O, Ḳ,) and ▼ أُمُّ عَمْرٍو, (Ḳ,) but the latter is extr., (TA,) The hyena; (Ṣ, O, Ḳ;) a metonymical surname, (Ṣ, O,) determinate, as applying to the species. (TA.) It is said in a prov., خَامِرِى أُمَّ عَامِرٍ أَبْشِرِى بِجَرَادٍ عَظْلَى وَكَمَرِ رِجَالٍ قَتْلَى [Hide thyself, O Umm-'Ámir: rejoice thou at the news of locusts cohering, and the glands of the penes of slain men: (in this prov., for كَمِّرٍ, in the TA, I have substituted كَمَرِ, which is the reading in variations of the prov.: see Freytag's Arab. Prov., i. 431:)] this being said by a man, [it is asserted that] the animal becomes obsequious to him, so that he muzzles it, and then drags it forth; for the hyena, says Az, is proverbial for its stupidity, and for its being beguiled with soft speech. (TA.) It is called أُمّ عامر, as though its young one were called عَامِر, and it is so called by a Hudhalee poet: (L:) or its whelp is called العَامِرُ: (Ḳ:) but it is not known with ال in the compound name with the prefixed noun [أُمّ, nor, app., without أُمّ]. (MF, from the Expos. of the دُرَّة.)

عَوْمَرَةٌ Clamour and confusion, (Ṣ, O,* Ḳ,) and evil, or mischief: (O:) or wearying contention or altercation. (TA in art. دقر.)

مَعْمَرٌ A place of abode peopled, or inhabited: (so in a copy of the Ṣ:) a place of abode spacious, (O, TA,) agreeable, peopled or inhabited, (TA,) abounding with water and herbage, (Ṣ, O,* Ḳ, TA,) where people stay. (TA.)

[مِعْمَارٌ and ▼ مِعْمَارِىٌّ, of which latter مِعْمَارِيَّةٌ is the coll. n., An architect: both app. post-classical.]

مَعْمُورٌ: see عَامِرٌ, in two places. — دَارٌ مَعْمُورَةٌ A house inhabited by jinn, or genii. (Lḥ.) — البَيْتُ المَعْمُورُ is [The edifice] in heaven, (Ḳ,) in the third heaven, or the sixth, or the seventh, (Jel, in lii. 4,) or in the fourth, (O, Bḍ,) over, or corresponding to, the Kaabeh, (O, Jel, Ḳ,) which seventy thousand angels visit every day, [or seventy thousand companies of which every one consists of seventy thousand angels, (see دِحْيَة,)] circuiting around it and praying, never returning to it: (O,* Jel:) or the Kaabeh: or the heart of the believer. (Bḍ.) = Also Served [or worshipped]. (TA.)

مِعْمَارِىٌّ: see مِعْمَارٌ.

مُعْتَمِرٌ Visiting; a visiter. (Ṣ, Ḳ.) — Performing the religious visit called عُمْرَة: (Kr, Ṣ:) having entered upon the state of إِحْرَام for the performance of that visit: (TA:) pl. مُعْتَمِرُونَ: and عُمَّارٌ [a pl. of ▼ عَامِرٌ] is syn. with مُعْتَمِرُونَ. (Kr.) — And Betaking himself to a thing; aiming at it;

purposing it. (Ḳ, TA.) — Also *Having his head attired with an* عَمَارَة, i. e. *a turban* [&c.]. (AO, Ṣ.)

مَا لَكَ مُعَمِّرًا بِالنَّاسِ عَلَى بَابِى means *Wherefore art thou congregating and detaining the people at my door?* (Ṣgh, TA.)

يَعْمُورٌ *A kid:* (IAạr, Ṣ, O, Ḳ:) and *a lamb:* pl. يَعَامِيرُ. (IAạr, Ṣ, O.)

عمرد

عَمَرَّدٌ *Long;* (Ṣ, O, Ḳ;) as also ▼ عُمْرُودٌ; (Ḳ;) applied to a road, (Ṣ, O,) as meaning *far extending,* (O,) and to a desert without water or herbage, (Ṣ, O,) and a limit, term, reach, or goal, or a heat, or single run to a goal or limit, (شَأْو,) (AA, Ṣ, O,) and a horse, (Ṣ, O,) or anything. (Ḳ.) — *Evil in disposition and very perverse, and strong;* (O, L, Ḳ;) applied to a horse. (L.) *Malignant,* or *noxious;* applied to a wolf. (L, Ḳ.) *Malignant,* or *noxious, and very cunning;* (O,* Ḳ;) and so عَمَرَّطٌ; applied to a wolf; and the latter sometimes applied in this sense to a man: pls. عَمَارِدُ and عَمَارِطُ. (O.) — An *excellent* camel, *used for riding.* (O, L, Ḳ.*) — A *quick, vehement* pace. (L.)

عُمْرُودٌ: see above, first sentence.

عمش

1. عَمِشَ, (Ṣ, TA,) aor. ـَ, (TA,) inf. n. عَمَشٌ, (Ṣ, A, O, Ḳ,) *He* (a man, Ṣ, TA) *was weak in sight,* (Ṣ, A, O, Ḳ,) *and generally,* or *at most times, shedding tears.* (Ṣ, O, Ḳ.) And عَمِشَتِ الْعَيْنُ, aor. and inf. n. as above, *The eye was generally,* or *at most times, shedding tears, and weak in sight.* (Mṣb.) — Hence, (A,) عَمِشَ فِيهِ, said of speech, † *It produced a good effect upon him.* (A, O, Ḳ.) And فُلَانٌ لَا تَعْمَشُ فِيهِ الْمَوْعِظَةُ † *Such a one, exhortation produces no good effect upon him.* (A, O.) Both of these are chaste phrases; for when exhortation produces an effect upon a man, it becomes as though it were weak-sighted, seeing nothing to amend in him. (A.)

2. تَعْمِيشٌ The *removing of* [*the weakness of sight termed*] عَمَش [inf. n. of عَمِشَ, q. v.]. (O, Ḳ.)

10. اِسْتَعْمَشَهُ *He deemed him foolish,* or *stupid,* (O, Ḳ, TA,) or, as in the Tekmileh, *ignorant:* (TA:) but this is post-classical. (O, TA.)

أَعْمَشُ A man *weak in sight, and generally,* or *at most times, shedding tears:* fem. عَمْشَآءُ: (Ṣ, Mṣb:) pl. عُمْشٌ; (Mṣb, TA;) which is also applied to camels: (TA:) or *disordered in the eye; whose eyes are dim,* or *watery;* and أَغْمَضُ signifies the like. (L, TA.)

عمق

1. عَمُقَ, (Ṣ, O, Ḳ,) or عَمُقَتْ, (Mṣb,) [aor. ـُ,] inf. n. عَمَاقَةٌ (Ṣ, O, Mṣb) and عُمْقٌ, (Mṣb,) said of a well (رَكِيّ, Ṣ, O, or بِئْر, Mṣb), *It was,* or *became, deep:* (Ṣ,* O,* Mṣb, Ḳ,* TA:) and so عَمِقَ. (TA.) One says, مَا أَبْعَدَ عَمَاقَةَ هٰذِهِ الرَّكِيَّةِ (O, Ḳ*) and ▼ مَا أَعْمَقَهَا (Ḳ) [*How great,* or *far-extending, is the depth of this well!*]: and so مَا أَمْعَقَهَا. (TA.) — And عَمُقَ and عَمِقَ, inf. n. (of the former, TA) عُمْقٌ and (of the latter, TA) عَمَاقَةٌ, said of a [road such as is termed] فَجّ, *It was,* or *became, far-extending:* or *long:* (Ḳ:) but accord. to a saying of IAạr, app. not used in the latter sense when said of a road. (TA.) And عَمُقَ said of a place, *It was,* or *became, distant, remote,* or *far off.* (Mṣb.)

2: see 4. — [Hence,] عَمَّقَ النَّظَرَ فِى الأُمُورِ, (Ṣ, O, Ḳ,) inf. n. تَعْمِيقٌ, (Ṣ,) *He exceeded the usual bounds* [*in looking,* or *examining,* or rather *he looked,* or *examined, deeply, into affairs,* or *the affairs*]. (Ḳ, TA.)

4. اعمق البِئْرَ, (Mṣb, Ḳ,) inf. n. إِعْمَاقٌ; (Ṣ, O;) and ▼ عَمَّقَهَا, (Mṣb, Ḳ,) inf. n. تَعْمِيقٌ; (Ṣ, O;) and ▼ اِعْتَمَقَهَا; (O, Ḳ;) *He made the well deep:* (Ṣ, O, Mṣb, Ḳ, TA:) and so امعقها. (TA.) — مَا أَعْمَقَهَا: see 1.

5. تعمّق فِى كَلَامِهِ *He went deeply,* or *far, in in his speech;* syn. تَنَطَّعَ. (Ṣ, O, Ḳ.) And تعمّق فِى الشَّىْءِ *He went,* or *dived, deeply,* or *far, in,* or *into, the thing.* (MA.) And تعمّق فِى الأَمْرِ *He was,* or *became, nice, exquisite, refined,* or *scrupulously nice and exact;* or *he chose what was excellent,* or *best to be done; and exceeded the usual bounds; in the affair.* (TA. [See also the part. n., below.])

8: see 4.

عَمْقٌ (Ṣ, O, Mṣb, Ḳ, TA) and ▼ عُمْقٌ, (Ṣ, O, Ḳ, TA,) or the latter is an inf. n., (Mṣb,) and ▼ عُمُقٌ, (Ḳ, TA,) The *bottom* (قَعْر) of a well (Ṣ, O, Ḳ, TA) and the like, (Ḳ, TA,) and of a [road such as is termed] فَجّ, and of a valley: (Ṣ, O, TA:) or the *depth* of a well (Mṣb, TA) and the like; [i. e.] the *distance to the bottom:* (TA:) [and عُمُوقٌ, which may be a pl. of the first or second, and perhaps of the third, signifies *deep places of the ground:* (see خَسْفٌ:) and ▼ عُمْقٌ signifies also *depth* of anything; or *distance between the two opposite surfaces* thereof:] but accord. to IAạr, ▼ عُمْقٌ as an attribute of a road signifies *distance:* and as an attribute of a well it is the *length of* its *cavity,* or *interior, from top to bottom.* (TA.) — And عَمْقٌ and ▼ عُمْقٌ signify also The *distant,* or *remote, extremity* of a desert, or waterless desert: pl. أَعْمَاقٌ: (Ṣ, O, Ḳ, TA:) which is also expl. as signifying *sides, regions,* or *tracts;* and *extremities;* without restriction: and *sides, regions,* or *tracts,* of the earth, or of a land. (TA.) Ru-beh says,

* فِى سَبْسَبٍ مُنْجَرِدِ الأَعْلَاقِ *

* غَيْرِ الفِجَاجِ عَيِقِ ▼ الأَعْمَاقِ *

[*In a desert,* or *waterless desert, bared of the beaten tracks, except the far-extending* (?), *remote in respect of the extremities*]. (O.) — And عُمَّقٌ *Full-grown unripe dates put in the sun to dry* (AḤn, Ḳ, TA) *and to ripen.* (AḤn, TA.) — [And accord. to Forskål, (Flora Aeg. Arab. p. cxii.,) The *Euphorbia officin. arborea;* mentioned by him as found at a place in Tihámeh, which suggests that its name may perhaps be correctly عِمْقَى, q. v.]

عُمُقٌ: see the next preceding paragraph, in four places.

عَمْقٌ *A right,* or *due.* (ISh, O, Ḳ.) So in the saying, فِى هٰذِهِ الدَّارِ عَمْقٌ [*In this house is a right,* or *due,* pertaining to some one]: (ISh, O:) and لَهُ فِيهِ عَمْقٌ [*There pertains to him, in it, a right,* or *due*]. (Ḳ.)

عَمِقٌ: see عَمِيقٌ, and the verse cited above.

عُمْقٌ: see عَمْقٌ, first sentence. — [And see عَمِيقٌ.]

عَمَقَةٌ *Feculence* (وَضَر) *of clarified butter,* [*adhering to the interior*] *in a skin:* (Lḥ, O, Ḳ:) the م is asserted by Lḥ to be a substitute for ب. (TA voce عَبَقَةٌ.)

عِمْقَى, (Ṣ, O, Ḳ,) said by Aboo-Naṣr to be of the fem. gender, (O,) *A species of trees,* (Ṣ,) or *a certain plant,* (O, Ḳ,) *in El-Ḥijáz and Tihámeh,* (Ṣ, [see عُمَّقٌ, last sentence,]) of which AḤn states his not having found any one who described its qualities, or attributes, (O,) and said by IB to be spoken of as *more bitter than the colocynth;* (TA;) also called ▼ عَمَاقِيَةٌ, (O, Ḳ,) which occurs in a verse of Sá'ideh Ibn-El-'Ajlán, or, as some relate it, the word there is عَبَاقِيَة [q. v.]. (O.)

عُمْقِىُّ الكَلَامِ A man *whose speech has depth.* (TA.)

عَمِيقٌ is of the dial. of the people of El-Ḥijáz: and the tribe of Temeem say مَعِيقٌ. (Fr, TA.) One says بِئْرٌ عَمِيقَةٌ (Ṣ, O, Mṣb, Ḳ) and مَعِيقَةٌ, formed by transposition, (O,) *A deep well:* (Ṣ,* O,* Mṣb, Ḳ,* TA:) pl. عَمَائِقُ and عُمُقٌ and عُمْقٌ and عِمَاقٌ. (Ḳ.) — Also, applied to a [road such as is termed] فَجّ, (O, Ḳ,) as in the Ḳur xxii. 28, (O,) *Remote,* or *far-extending;* (Mujáhid, O, Ḳ;) and so as applied to a place; (Mṣb;) [so too ▼ عَمِقٌ, applied to a desert, as in the verse cited above, voce عَمْقٌ;] and, applied to a road, عَمِيقٌ is more used than مَعِيقٌ: (Lth, TA:) or عَمِيقٌ applied to a فَجّ signifies *long;* (Ḳ;) or, app., accord. to IAạr, not thus when applied to a فَجّ as meaning a road. (TA. [See عُمْقٌ.])

عَمَاقِيَةٌ: see عِمْقَى.

بَعِيرٌ عَامِقٌ *A camel feeding upon the* [*trees,* or *plants, called*] عِمْقَى: (Ṣ, O, Ḳ;) and إِبِلٌ عَامِقَةٌ *camels so feeding.* (TA.)

أَعْمَقُ [*Deeper:* and *deepest*]. IAạr mentions his having heard one of the Arabs of chaste speech say, رَأَيْتُ خَلِيقَةً فَمَا رَأَيْتُ أَعْمَقَ مِنْهَا i. e.

[I saw] a recently-dug well [and I have not seen any deeper than it]. (O.)

مُتَعَمِّقٌ One *who exceeds the usual bounds in an affair; who acts with forced hardness, vigour,* or *hardiness, therein; seeking to accomplish the utmost thereof.* (TA.)

عمل

1. عَمِلَ, aor. ـَ, inf. n. عَمَلٌ, (Ṣ, O, Mṣb, Ḳ,) *He worked,* or *wrought; laboured; served,* or *did service: he did, acted,* or *performed:* (Ḳ, TA:) [generally, *he did, &c., with a sort of difficulty,* or *with intention;* but sometimes said of an inanimate thing: (see عَمَلٌ, below:)] *he did,* or *he made, wrought, manufactured,* or *constructed,* a thing. (Mṣb. [See, again, عَمَلٌ, below.]) Accord. to Az, عَمِلَ is the only trans. verb of its measure having the inf. n. of the measure فَعَلٌ, except هَبِلَتْ, said of a mother, inf. n. هَبَلٌ; other similar verbs having the inf. n. of the measure فَعْلٌ; as سَرِطْتُ اللُّقْمَةَ, inf. n. سَرْطٌ; and بَلِعْتُهُ, inf. n. بَلْعٌ. (TA. [But see arts. سرط and بلع; with respect to the former of which I must here state that, since it was printed, I have found an authority for سَرَطٌ as inf. n. of سَرِطَ in a copy of the Ṣ; though in the Ḳ it is said to be مُحَرَّكَة, and accord. to the Mṣb it is like تَعَبٌ.]) You say, عَمِلْتُ عَلَى الصَّدَقَةِ *I officiated in the collecting of the poor-rate.* (Mṣb.) [And عَمِلَ بِمَا فِى كِتَابِ ٱللّٰهِ *He did according to what is enjoined in the Book of God.*] And عَمِلَ فِى هَلَاكِهِ [*He laboured to destroy him,* or *to kill him*]. (Ḳ in art. شيط.) [And عَمِلَ فِيهِ *It acted upon him,* or *it:* and, said of a sword &c., *it had effect,* or *made an impression, upon him,* or *it.*] — [Hence,] عَمِلَ فِيهِ signifies [also † *It governed it syntactically;* or *caused* it to be مَرْفُوع or مَنْصُوب or مَجْرُور &c.; i. e.] *it produced in it a certain species of syntactical desinence.* (Ḳ.) — And عَمِلَ البَرْقُ *The lightning was continual.* (Ḳ.) And عَمِلَتْ بِأُذُنَيْهَا, said of a she-camel, (Ḳ,) and also, in a trad., of [the beast] البُرَاق, (O,* TA,) *She went quickly,* or *swiftly;* (O, Ḳ, TA;) because she that does thus puts her ears in motion by reason of the vehemence of the pace. (TA.) And عَمِلَتْ [alone] said of a she-camel, signifies [the same: or] *She was,* or *became, brisk, light, active,* or *quick.* (Ḳ.) — And [hence, app.,] لَمْ أَرَ النَّفَقَةَ تَعْمَلُ كَمَا تَعْمَلُ بِمَكَّةَ, a saying mentioned by Lḥ, is expl. by ISd as meaning تَنْفُقُ [i. e. *I have not seen the money that that one expends pass away as it passes away in Mekkeh*]. (TA.)

2. عَمَّلْتُ فُلَانًا عَلَى البَصْرَةِ, (Ṣ, O,) or عَلَى البَلَدِ, (Mṣb,) inf. n. تَعْمِيلٌ, (Ṣ, O,) *I made,* or *appointed, such a one governor* (Ṣ, O, Mṣb) *over El-Baṣrah,* (Ṣ, O,) or *over the province,* or *city,* &c. (Mṣb.) And عُمِّلَ فُلَانٌ عَلَيْهِمْ, inf. n. as above, *Such a one was made,* or *appointed, governor over them.* (Ḳ, TA.) And one says, مَنِ ٱلَّذِى عُمِّلَ عَلَيْكُمْ, *Who is he that has been set up as governor over you?* (TA.) And ↓ أُسْتُعْمِلَ فُلَانٌ [*Such a one was employed as governor* over a people: (see a saying of 'Omar in art. ضعف, conj. 2:) or] *such a one was appointed to one of the sovereign's offices of government.* (TA.) — And عَمَّلَهُ, (Mgh, O, Ḳ,) inf. n. as above, (Ḳ,) *He gave him his* عُمَالَة, or *pay,* or *salary, for work, service,* or *agency;* (Mgh, O, Ḳ;) as also ↓ اعملهُ. (TA.)

3. عاملهُ [*He worked, laboured, served, acted,* or *transacted business, with him.* Hence,] *He dealt with him in buying and selling,* (Mṣb, KL,) and *the like:* so in the language of the people of the cities. (Mṣb.) See also 6. [And hence the saying, عامله مُعَامَلَةَ اللَّيْثِ (mentioned in the Ṣ in art. ليث) *He did, acted,* or *dealt, with him in the manner of the lion.*] — And i. q. سَامَهُ بِعَمَلٍ [*He made to him an offer of working, mentioning the rate of payment;* or *bargained,* or *contracted, with him for work*]. (Ḳ.) Ṣgh says that المُعَامَلَةُ in the language of the people of El-'Irák is what is termed in the dial. of the people of El-Ḥijáz المُسَاقَاةُ, (Mṣb,) which is *The employing a man to take upon himself,* or *manage, the culture** [or *watering* &c.] *of palm-trees* or *grape-vines* [or *the like*] *on the condition of his having a certain share of their produce.* (Ṣ and TA in art. سقى.)

4. اعملهُ *He made him to work, labour, serve,* or *do service;* or *to do, act,* or *perform;* (Ṣ,* O,* Ḳ, TA;) as also ↓ استعملهُ: (Ṣ, Ḳ:) *he made him,* or *caused him, to do,* or *to make, manufacture,* or *construct,* a thing. (Mṣb.) And one says also, يُعْمِلُ نَفْسَهُ فِى الأَمْرِ [*He plies himself in the affair*]. (Ṣ in art. عسر.) — And [hence,] *He worked with it,* [i. e. *employed it,* or *used it,* or *plied it,*] namely, his judgment, or opinion, and [properly] his instrument, or implement, (Ḳ, TA,) and his tongue; (TA;) as also ↓ استعملهُ. (Ḳ, TA.) And أَعْمَلَ ذِهْنَهُ فِى كَذَا وَكَذَا [*He employed,* or *used, his intellect,* or *understanding, in such and such things;*] meaning *he considered,* or *forecast, the issues,* or *results, of such and such things with his intellect,* or *understanding.* (TA.) — And أَعْمَلْتُ النَّاقَةَ [*I hastened, and urged, the she-camel*]: whence the saying, in a trad., لَا تُعْمَلُ المَطِيُّ إِلَّا إِلَى ثَلَاثَةِ مَسَاجِدَ, meaning [*The camels that are used for riding*] *shall not be hastened nor urged* [or *plied, save to three mosques;* that of Mekkeh, that of El-Medeeneh, and that of El-Aḳṣà at Jerusalem: see also a variation of this saying in the first paragraph of art. ضرب; and another voce عُرْوَةٌ]: and in a trad. of Luḳmán, يُعْمِلُ النَّاقَةَ وَالسَّاقَ [*He hastens, and urges, the she-camel and the shank*], meaning *he is strong to journey, riding and walking.* (TA.) — See also 2, last sentence. ═ مَا أَعْمَلَهُمْ بِعَمَلِ أَهْلِ النَّارِ, a phrase occurring in art. صبر in the Ḳ, means *How much do they occupy themselves in doing the deed of the the people of the fire* of Hell! ═ أَعْمَلْتُ الرُّمْحَ means *I thrust,* or *pierced, with the* عَامِل [q. v.] *of the spear.* (Ḥar p. 77.) [Or one says, أَعْمَلْتُهُ بِالرُّمْحِ, meaning *I thrust him,* or *pierced him, with the* عَامِل *of the spear.* (See De Sacy's Chrest. Ar., sec. ed., iii. 191.)]

5. تعمّل *He suffered fatigue,* or *difficulty;* and *strove, laboured,* or *toiled;* syn. تَعَنَّى, (O, Ḳ, TA,) and اِجْتَهَدَ; (TA;) لِكَذَا [*for such a thing*]; (Ṣ, O;) and مِنْ أَجْلِهِ [*on his account,* or *for his sake*]; (Ḳ;) and فِى حَاجَتِهِ [*in the case of his object of want*]. (TA.)

6. تَعَامَلَ is syn. with ↓ مُعَامَلَةٌ [generally as meaning The *dealing together in buying and selling,* and *the like*]. (TA.) One says, تعامل النَّاسُ بِالدَّرَاهِمِ [*Men,* or *the people, dealt together in buying and selling with the dirhems;* i. e. *used the dirhems in buying and selling*]. (Mṣb in art. روج.) And يُتَعَامَلُ بِهِ [*The business of buying and selling is transacted with it;* i. e. *it is used in buying and selling*]; referring to the [coin called] فَلْس. (Mṣb in art. فلس.)

8. اعتمل signifies اِضْطَرَبَ فِى العَمَلِ [*He went to and fro occupied in work, labour,* or *service*]: (Ṣ, O, TA:) or *he worked, laboured,* or *did service, for himself;* like as one says اِخْتَدَمَ meaning خَدَمَ نَفْسَهُ: (T, TA:) or *he worked,* &c., *by himself:* (Ḳ, TA:) or *he worked,* &c., *for another:* (TA:) with an instrument, or tool, or the like; or with instruments, or tools, or the like. (M and Ḳ in art. اول.) ═ [It is also trans.] One says, اِعْتَمَلْتُ أَعْمَالًا, meaning اِكْتَسَبْتُ [*I laboured to earn,* or *gain, sustenance*]. (Mṣb.) And it is said in a trad., respecting Kheyber, دَفَعَ إِلَيْهِمْ أَرْضَهُمْ عَلَى أَنْ يَعْتَمِلُوهَا مِنْ أَمْوَالِهِمْ i. e. [*He gave to them their land*] *on the condition of their* [*bestowing labour upon it,* or] *doing what they required to be done* [*upon it*], *of cultivation, and sowing, and fecundating of the palm-trees, and guarding, and the like, from their own property.* (IAth, TA.) — [And اعتملهُ signifies also *He employed him,* or *used him, for work,* or *service;* like استعملهُ: but is perhaps post-classical.]

10. استعملهُ *He asked, required,* or *desired, him to work, labour, do service,* or *act,* (Ṣ, O, Mṣb,* TA,) *for him.* (TA.) [And استعمل, app. for استعمل نَفْسَهُ, *He desired to act:* see an ex. in art. روى, conj. 2.] — See also 4, in two places. — And see 2. One says also, أُسْتُعْمِلَ فُلَانٌ عَلَى الجِعَالَةِ [*Such a one was employed as collecter of the poll-tax*]. (Ṣ and Mṣb in art. جعل.) See also a similar ex. voce ضِبْعٌ. And اِسْتَعْمَلْتُ الثَّوْبَ *I made the garment to serve* [i. e. *made use of it*] *for clothing.* (Mṣb.) And اِسْتَعْمَلْتُ اللَّبِنَ [*I made use of the bricks*], meaning *I built with the bricks a building.* (Mṣb.) And استعمل البَلَهَ [*He feigned heedlessness,* &c.; or *made use of it as a mask,* or *pretext*]. (Ḳ in explanation of تَبَالَهَ and تَبَلَّهَ. See also a similar ex. voce تَحَلَّمَ.)

عَمَلٌ [mentioned in the beginning of this art. as an inf. n.] is *syn. with* مِهْنَةٌ and فِعْلٌ: (Ḳ:)

[accordingly, when used as a simple subst., it may be rendered *Work, labour,* or *service:* and *a deed,* or *an action:*] or it has a more particular meaning than فِعْلٌ; for it is *a* فِعْل [or *deed*] *with a sort of difficulty;* and therefore it is not attributed to God: or, accord. to Er-Rághib, it is *any* فِعْل [i. e. *deed* or *action*] *that proceeds from an animate being by his intention;* and thus it has a more particular meaning than فِعْلٌ; for the فعل is sometimes attributed to animate beings from which it proceeds without intention; and sometimes to inanimate things, to which the عَمَل is seldom attributed; and this is not used in relation to [irrational] animals except [as implied] in the phrases بَقَرٌ عَوَامِلُ and إِبِلٌ عَوَامِلُ: or, accord. to MF, the عَمَل is *a motion of the whole,* or *of a portion, of the body;* and sometimes, *of the mind;* so that it is *the utterance of a saying,* as well as *the doing a deed with the member,* or *limb, with which things are gained* or *earned;* though most readily understood as applied particularly to *the latter;* and some apply it particularly to *that which is not a saying:* it is also said that a saying is not termed عَمَل in the common conventional language: and the truth is said to be, that it is not included in the terms عَمَل and فِعْل otherwise than tropically: (TA:) [see also عِمْلَةٌ:] the pl. of عَمَل [used as a simple subst.] is أَعْمَالٌ. (Ḳ.) In the following saying, of a woman dandling her child, (Ṣ,) or of Ḳeys Ibn-'Áṣim, (O, TA,) dandling his child Ḥakeem, (TA,)

* أَشْبِهْ أَبَا أُمِّكَ أَوْ أَشْبِهْ عَمَلْ *

the last word is a proper name of a man: (Ṣ, O, TA:) or, accord. to Aboo-Zekereeyà, [the meaning is, *Share thou in the qualities of the father of thy mother,* or *share thou in the qualities of my course of action;* for he says that] by عَمَلْ is here meant عَمَلِى. (TA.) اِبْنُ عَمَلِى means *He who does my work,* or *the like of what I do.* (TA in art. بنى.) And [hence,] فُلَانٌ ٱبْنُ عَمَلٍ *Such a one is strong.* (TA.) And بَنُو عَمَلٍ *Those who journey on foot.* (O, Ḳ,* TA.) [And عَمَلُ النَّخْلِ, occurring in the T, voce ضَيْعَةٌ, means *The culture of palm-trees:* like as عَمَلُ الأَرْضِ means *agriculture*]. — And عَمَلٌ signifies also The *striving, labouring,* or *toiling, in work;* or the *holding on,* or *continuing, in work:* so in the saying of El-Ḳuṭámee

* فَقَدْ يَهُونُ عَلَى المُسْتَنْجِحِ العَمَلُ *

[*For verily the striving,* &c., *in work is a light matter to him who seeks success*]. (TA.) — [Also *An office of administration;* and particularly the *office of governor of a province;* and the *office of collector of the poor-rates,* and *the like:* and *an agency of any kind;* the *management of the affairs and property of another;* an *employment.* — Also *A province;* or *territory under a governor appointed by a sovereign.* Pl. in this and other senses as above.]

عَمِلٌ, as an epithet applied to a man, *i. q.* ذُو عَمَلٍ [*Having work, labour,* or *service*]; (Sb, Ḳ;) as also ↓ عَمُولٌ: (Ḳ:) or *adapted,* or *disposed, by nature, to work, labour,* or *service;* (Ṣ, O, Ḳ;) and so ↓ عَمُولٌ: (Ṣ,* O,* Ḳ:) or this latter signifies *that makes much gain.* (TA.) — And, applied to lightning, *Continuing,* or *continual.* (Ḳ.) — And عَمِلَةٌ, applied to a she-camel, *Brisk, light, active,* or *quick;* (Ḳ, TA;) like ↓ يَعْمَلَةٌ; (TA;) and so ↓ عَمَّالَةٌ. (A, TA.)

عَمْلَةٌ *Theft:* or *treachery, perfidy,* or *unfaithfulness:* (O, Ḳ:) it is not used otherwise than in relation to evil. (O.)

عُمْلَةٌ: see عُمَالَةٌ.

عِمْلَةٌ *A mode,* or *manner, of work, labour,* or *service;* or of *doing,* or *acting;* or *of making.* (Ḳ, TA.) One says رَجُلٌ خَبِيثُ العِمْلَةِ, meaning *A man bad,* or *corrupt, in respect of* [*the mode of*] *gain.* (TA.) — See also عَمِلَةٌ. — And see عُمَالَةٌ. = Also The *internal state,* or *condition, of a man, in relation to evil.* (Ḳ.)

عَمِلَةٌ, with kesr to the م, is *syn. with* عَمَلٌ [as signifying *A deed, or an action*]: (O, Ḳ:) so in the saying of a woman of the Arabs, مَا كَانَ لِى عَمِلَةٌ إِلَّا فَسَادُكُمْ [*There was no deed,* or *action, for me, except the corrupting of you*]. (O.) — And *A thing that is done,* or *performed;* or *that is made;* (مَا عُمِلَ;) as also ↓ عِمْلَةٌ. (Ḳ.)

عِمْلَى: see عُمَالَةٌ.

[عَمَلِىٌّ *Practical;* opposed to عِلْمِىٌّ: and *fabrile; factitious;* or *artificial.*]

عَمِلَ بِهِ العِمِلِّينَ, with two kesrehs and with the ل musheddedeh, (Ḳ, TA, but in the CḲ العِمِلِّينِ,) or العَمَلِينَ, or العُمَلِينَ, (Ḳ, TA,) or, accord. to ISd as on the authority of Th, العِمِلِّينَ and العُمَلِّينَ, [app. العَمَلِّينَ and العُمُلِّينَ,] (TA,) or العَمَلَيْنِ, [thus written without any vowel-sign to the م, and in the dual form,] (O as on the authority of Aboo-Zeyd,) and IAar adds العَمْلَيْنِ, with the م quiescent, (O,) [compare البُرَحِينَ and البُلَغِينَ, which suggest that the correct forms may be العُمَلِينَ and العِمَلِينَ,] *He exceeded the ordinary bounds,* (Ḳ,) or *went to the utmost point,* (O, Ḳ,) *in annoying him,* (Ḳ,) or *in reviling him and annoying him.* (O.)

عَمُولٌ: see عَمِلٌ, in two places.

عَمَالَةٌ *Briskness, lightness, activity,* or *quickness, of a she-camel.* (Ḳ.) — See also what next follows.

عُمَالَةٌ (T, Ṣ, Mgh, O, Mṣb, Ḳ) and ↓ عِمَالَةٌ (Lḥ, Mṣb, Ḳ) and ↓ عَمَالَةٌ (Ḳ) and ↓ عِمْلَةٌ and ↓ عُمْلَةٌ (Ḳ) or ↓ عُمَلَةٌ, with ḍamm, and ↓ عِمْلَى, like ذِكْرَى [in measure], this last on the authority of Fr, (O,) The *hire, pay,* or *recompense,* (T, Ṣ, Mgh, O, Mṣb, Ḳ,) *of him who works, labours,* or *serves,* (T, Ṣ, Mgh, O, Mṣb,) or *for work, labour,* or *service.* (Ḳ.) — And عُمَالَةٌ signifies also The *state,* or *condition, of being occupied;* or *having work, labour,* or *service, to perform;* *contr. of* بَطَالَةٌ as syn. with بِطَالَةٌ, inf. n. of بَطَلَ in the phrase بَطَلَ مِنَ العَمَلِ. (Mṣb in art. بطل.)

عِمَالَةٌ: } see the next preceding paragraph.
عَمَالَةٌ: }

عَمَّالٌ One *who does much work* or *labour* or *service:* or *who strives, labours,* or *toils, in work;* or *holds on,* or *continues, in work.* (TA.) — عَمَّالَةٌ, applied to a she-camel: see عَمِلٌ.

عَامِلٌ [*Working; labouring; serving,* or *doing service: doing, acting,* or *performing:* and *doing, making, working, manufacturing,* or *constructing,* a thing:] act. part. n. of عَمِلَ: (T, Mṣb, TA:) pl. عَامِلُونَ (Mṣb, Ḳ, TA) and عُمَّالٌ (Mṣb) and عَمَلَةٌ, (Ḳ, TA,) which last signifies [particularly] *workers with their hands,* (Mgh in art. فعل, Ḳ, TA,) *in various sorts of work,* (TA,) *in clay* (Mgh, TA) or *building* (Mgh) or *digging* (Mgh, TA) &c.; (TA;) like فَعَلَةٌ [a pl. of فَاعِلٌ]: (Mgh:) and عَوَامِلُ, (Ḳ, TA,) as pl. of [the fem.] عَامِلَةٌ, (TA,) [and likewise in this case of عَامِلٌ,] signifies oxen *that plough,* and *that tread the corn,* (Ḳ, TA,) and *upon which water is drawn,* and *that are employed in other labours;* and in like manner applied to camels: and it is said in a trad. that in the case of such animals no poor-rate is required. (TA.) — Also [*An administrator of public affairs;* and particularly *a governor of a province;* and] *a collector of the poor-rates* [and *the like*]: and *an agent who manages the affairs and property of another.* (TA.) = عَامِلُ الرُّمْحِ (Ṣ, O, Ḳ) and ↓ عَامِلَتُهُ (Ḳ) *The part, of the spear, that is next to the head, exclusive of the* ثَعْلَب [or *portion that enters into the head*]: (Ṣ, O:) or *the* صَدْر [or *fore part*] *of the spear,* (Ḳ, TA,) *exclusive of the head,* accord. to A'Obeyd *two cubits in length:* (TA:) or, as some say, *the spear-head itself* is called عَامِلٌ: (O, TA:) pl. عَوَامِلُ. (TA.) See also ذِرَاعٌ, last sentence.

عَامِلَةٌ [as a subst., rendered so by the affix ة,] sing. of عَوَامِلُ, (T, TA,) which signifies The *legs* (T, Ḳ, TA) of a beast or horse or the like. (T, TA.) — عَامِلَةُ الرُّمْحِ: see عَامِلٌ, near the end.

طَرِيقٌ مُعْمَلٌ *A conspicuous, travelled, road.* (Ṣ.)

مَعْمُولٌ [pass. part. n. of عَمِلَ, as such signifying *Done, made,* &c. — And] applied to beverage, or wine, (شَرَابٌ,) as meaning *In which are milk and honey* (Th, O, Ḳ) *and snow:* (Th, O:) occurring in a trad. of El-Shaabee. (O.) — [And An ass *whose testicles have been extracted.* (Freytag on the authority of Meyd.)]

مُسْتَعْمَلٌ as an epithet applied to a camel means *Employed in work, labour,* or *service.* (TA.)

يَعْمَلٌ *An excellent,* or *a strong, light, and swift, he-camel;* (O, Ḳ;) though disallowed by

Kh: (O:) and (O, Ḳ) يَعْمَلَةٌ *an excellent*, or *a strong, light, and swift, she-camel, adapted*, or *disposed, by nature, to work, labour*, or *service*: (Ṣ, O, Ḳ:*) or, accord. to Kr, the former signifies *a swift she-camel*; [but see what follows, as well as what precedes;] and is a subst. applied thereto, derived from العَمَلُ: and the pl. is يَعْمَلَاتٌ: (TA: see also عَمِلٌ:) neither of them is used as an epithet, each being only a subst., (M, Ḳ, TA,) accord. to Sb, for one does not say جَمَلٌ يَعْمَلٌ nor نَاقَةٌ يَعْمَلَةٌ, but only يَعْمَلٌ and يَعْمَلَةٌ as meaning a he-camel and a she-camel; and hence, he says, we know not يَفْعَلٌ occurring as [the measure of] an epithet: but some make يَعْمَلٌ to be an epithet. (M, TA.) يَوْمُ اليَعْمَلَةِ was one of the days [meaning days of conflict] of the Arabs. (O, Ḳ.)

عملق

عِمْلَاقٌ One *who deceives* (O, Ḳ) *men*, (O,) or *thee*, (Ḳ,) *with his eye* (بِطَرْفِهِ); (O, Ḳ, TA; in the TḲ بظرفه [i. e. بِظَرْفِهِ, meaning *with his excellence*, or *elegance, of mind, manners, and address* or *speech*; &c.]; in the CḲ بِطَرفِه;) so expl. by Ibn-'Abbád: (O:) or, accord. to the Nh, one *who deceives men, and beguiles them with his speech*. (TA.) — And *Tall*: pl. عَمَالِيقُ and عَمَالِقَةٌ and عَمَالِقُ, which last is extr. (TA.) == [And the pls.] العَمَالِقَةُ and العَمَالِيقُ [are appellations applied by the Arabs to *The Amalekites*;] *a people of the descendants of* عِمْلِيق, (Ṣ, O, Ḳ,) or عِمْلَاق [or *Amalek*]; (Ḳ;) who was *the son of* لَاوَذ [or *Lud*], *the son of* إِرَم [or *Aram*], *the son of* سَام [or *Shem*], *the son of* نُوح [or *Noah*]; (Ṣ, O, Ḳ;) or [rather, *who was the son of Lud, the son of Shem*, for,] accord. to the Mukaddameh Fádileeyeh, لَاوَذ was the brother of إِرَم: (TA:) *they dispersed themselves in the countries*, (Ṣ, O, Ḳ, TA,) *and most of them became extinct*: or, accord. to IAth, they were *of the remnant of the people of 'Ád* (عَاد): Suh says that *of them were the kings of Egypt, the Pharaohs, of whom were El-Weleed the son of Muṣ'ab, the consociate of Moses, and Er-Reiyán the son of El-Weleed, the consociate of Joseph*. (TA.)

عمن

1. عَمَنَ بِالمَكَانِ, (Ṣ, Mṣb, Ḳ,) aor. ـُ; and عَمِنَ, aor. ـَ; (Ḳ;) inf. n. عَمْنٌ; (TḲ;) *He remained, stayed, dwelt*, or *abode, in the place*. (Ṣ, Mṣb, Ḳ.)

2: see the next paragraph.

4. اعمن, (Ṣ, Ḳ,) and ▼ عمّن, (Ḳ,) *He* (a man, Ṣ) *betook himself*, or *repaired, to*, or *towards*, [*the region of*] *'Omán* (عُمَان): (Ṣ, Ḳ:* [accord. to the Ḳ, app., عَمَّان, a town of Syria; but correctly عُمَان, as is clearly shown by quotations from poets in the TA:]) or *he entered it*: (Ḳ:) and also, (Ḳ,) or the former verb, accord. to AA, (TA,) *he continued to remain, stay, dwell*, or *abide*, (Ḳ, TA,) *there*. (TA. [For دَامَ عَلَى المَقَامِ, in this last explanation, the CḲ has قَامَ على المَقَامِ.])

[عَمَّنْ a contraction of عَنْ مَنْ.]

عَمُونٌ and ▼ عَامِنٌ, (TA,) and the pl. عُمُنٌ, [pl. of عَمُونٌ accord. to analogy, like صُبُرٌ pl. of صَبُورٌ,] (IAṭr, Ḳ, TA,) *Residing, staying, dwelling*, or *abiding*, (IAṭr, Ḳ, TA,) in a place. (IAṭr, TA.)

عَمِينَةٌ *Plain*, or *soft, land*; (Ḳ, TA;) of the dial. of El-Yemen. (TA.)

عُمَانِيَّةٌ *A sort of palm-tree in El-Baṣrah, that ceases not to have upon it, during the year*, (Ḳ, TA,) i. e. *all the year*, (TA,) *new spadixes, and racemes putting forth fruit, and others bearing ripe dates*. (Ḳ, TA.)

عَامِنٌ [act. part. n. of 1]: see عَمُونٌ.

عمه

1. عَمِهَ, (Ṣ, Mṣb, Ḳ,) and عَمَهَ, aor. of each ـَ, (Ḳ,) inf. n. عَمَهٌ (Ṣ, Mṣb, Ḳ, TA, [عَمْهًا in the CḲ being a mistake for عَمَهًا,]) and عُمُوهٌ and عُمُوهَةٌ and عَمَهَانٌ, (Ḳ, TA,) [the first of the former verb, and the rest, app., of the latter verb,] *He was*, or *became, confounded*, or *perplexed, and unable to see his right course*; and *went repeatedly to and fro*: (Ṣ:) or *he went repeatedly to and fro*, (Mṣb, Ḳ,) *in confusion*, or *perplexity*, (Mṣb,) or *in error, and confusion*, or *perplexity*, (Ḳ,) *unable to see his right course*, (Mṣb, Ḳ,) in contending, disputing, or litigating; or in a way, or road: (Ḳ:) or *he knew not the* [*right*] *argument*, or *plea*, or *allegation*: (Th, Ḳ, TA:) and ▼ تعامه signifies the same: (Z, Ḳ, TA:) all are said when one turns aside, or away, from that which is right, or true: (TA:) or العَمَهُ is *the looking repeatedly, not knowing whither to go*: (Lḥ, TA:) or it is in the mental perception; and العَمَى is in the sight, or is common to both of these. (TA.) [Accord. to the Mṣb, عَمِهَ is from عَمْهَآءُ as an epithet applied to land, expl. below: but this requires consideration, as appears from what here follows.] — One says also, عَمِهَتِ الأَرْضُ ‡ *The land was destitute of signs of the way*: (Ḳ, TA:) a tropical phrase. (TA.)

2. عَمَّهْتَ فِى ظُلْمِهِ, inf. n. تَعْمِيهٌ, *Thou wrongedst him*, or *hast wronged him, without sure information*. (A, Ḳ.)

6: see the first paragraph.

عَمِهٌ (Ṣ, Mṣb, Ḳ) and ▼ عَامِهٌ (Ṣ, Ḳ) and ▼ أَعْمَهُ (Mṣb) *In a state of confusion*, or *perplexity, and unable to see his right course*; and *going repeatedly to and fro*: (Ṣ:) or *going repeatedly to and fro*, (Mṣb, Ḳ,) *in confusion*, or *perplexity*, (Mṣb,) or *in error, and confusion*, or *perplexity*, (Ḳ,) *unable to see his right course*: (Mṣb, Ḳ:) or *not knowing the* [*right*] *argument*, or *plea*, or *allegation*: (Ḳ:) [see 1:] pl. [of the first] عَمِهُونَ (Ḳ) and [of the second] عُمَّهٌ (Ṣ, Ḳ) [and of the third عُمْهٌ].

▼ العُمَّهَى and ذَهَبَتْ إِبِلُهُ العُمَّهَى *His camels went away, whither none knew*. (Ṣ, Ḳ.)

العُمَّهَى: see what next precedes.

عَامِهٌ: see عَمِهٌ.

أَعْمَهُ: see عَمِهٌ. — [Its fem.] عَمْهَآءُ, applied to a land (أَرْضٌ), signifies *Having in it no signs of the way* (Ṣ, Mṣb, Ḳ) *to guide to safety*. (Mṣb.) [Hence, accord. to the Mṣb, the verb عَمِهَ expl. above: but some hold it to be tropical: see 1, last sentence.]

عمى

1. عَمِىَ, [aor. يَعْمَى,] inf. n. عَمًى, *He was*, or *became, blind*, (Ṣ, Mṣb, Ḳ,) *of both eyes*; (Mṣb, Ḳ,* TA;) as also ▼ اِعْمَايَ, aor. يَعْمَايُ, inf. n. اِعْمِيَآءٌ; (Ḳ;) [said by SM to be like اِرْعَوَى, aor. يَرْعَوِى, inf. n. اِرْعِوَآءٌ; as though اِعْمَايَ were originally اِعْمَىَّ, like as اِرْعَوَى is originally اِرْعَوَّ, both being of the measure اِفْعَلَّ; but he adds, correctly, that,] accord. to Ṣgh, اِعْمَايَ is originally like اِدْهَامَّ, which becomes اِدْهَامَمَ, [i. e. it is originally اِعْمَايَىَ,] but the latter ى is changed into ا because of the fet-ḥah of the former, so that it becomes اِعْمَايَا, and the two, thus differing, do not easily admit of idghám; (TA;) and sometimes the ى of اِعْمَايَ is musheddedeh, (Ṣgh, Ḳ, TA,) so that it becomes [▼ اِعْمَايَّ, aor. يَعْمَايُّ, inf. n. اِعْمِيَايٌ,] like اِدْهَامَّ, aor. يَدْهَامُّ, inf. n. اِدْهِيمَامٌ; but this is by a straining of a point, and not in use: (Ṣgh, TA:) and ▼ تعمّى, likewise, signifies the same, (Ḳ, TA,) i. e., the same as عَمِىَ. (TA.) And you say also, عَمِيَتْ عَيْنَاهُ *His two eyes were*, or *became, blind*. (TA.) — Hence عَمًى is metaphorically used in relation to the mind, as meaning ‡ *An erring*; the connection between the two meanings being the *not finding*, or *not taking, the right way*: (Mṣb:) or the *being blind in respect of the mind*: and in this sense, the verb is as above, with the exception of the measure اِفْعَالَّ [and the abbreviated form of this]. (Ḳ,* TA. [اَفْعَالَّ in the CḲ in this passage is a mistranscription, for اِفْعَالَّ.]) You say, عَمِىَ عَنْ رُشْدِهِ, and حُجَّتِهِ, meaning لَمْ يَهْتَدِ † [*He did not*, or *could not, become guided to his right course*, and *his plea* or *the like*; i. e. *he was*, or *became, blind thereto*]. (TA.) And عَمِىَ عَنْ حَقِّهِ † [*He was*, or *became, blind to his right*, or *due*], like عَشِىَ عَنْهُ. (TA in art. عشو.) — One says also عَمِىَ عَلَيْهِ الخَبَرُ ‡ *The information was*, or *became, unapparent, obscure*, or *covert, to him*. (Mgh, Mṣb.*) And عَمِىَ عَلَيْهِ طَرِيقُهُ, (TA,) and الأَمْرُ, (Ṣ, TA,) and الشِّعْرُ, and الكَلَامُ, (Ḥar p. 190,) i. e. † [*His way*, or *road*, and *the affair*, and *the poetry*, or *verse*, and *the speech*, or *saying*,] *was*, or *became, obscure*, or *dubious, to him*; (Ṣ, TA, and Ḥar ubi suprà;) and so ▼ عُمِّىَ; (TA;) and ▼ تعمّى. (Ḥar ubi suprà.) Hence, accord. to different readings, in the Ḳur [xxviii. 66], فَعَمِيَتْ عَلَيْهِمُ الأَنْبَآءُ and ▼ فَعُمِّيَتْ † [*And the pleas shall*

be obscure, or dubious, to them]. (Ṣ, TA.) —— And عَمِيتُ إِلَى كَذَا † I betook myself to such a thing, not desiring any other; as also عَطِشْتُ. (TA. [Accord. to the TA, the inf. ns. of these two verbs, thus used, are عميان and عطشان: but they are correctly عَمًى and عَطَشٌ.]) —— عَمَى الْمَوْجُ, aor. يَعْمِى, (Ṣ, Ḳ,) inf. n. عَمْىٌ, (Ṣ,) The waves cast the particles of rubbish, or the like, (Ṣ, Ḳ, TA,) driving them to their upper, or uppermost, parts, (TA,) and the foam. (Ṣ, TA.) —— And عَمَى بِلُغَامِهِ, (Ḳ, TA,) aor. يَعْمِى, (TA,) He (a camel) brayed, and cast the foam of his mouth upon his head, or the upper part of his head, or anywhere: (Ḳ, TA:) mentioned by ISd. (TA.) —— And [hence] عَمَانِى بِكَذَا † He cast upon me a suspicion of such a thing. (TA.) —— عَمَى, aor. يَعْمِى, said of water, (Ḳ, TA,) and of other things, (TA,) also signifies It flowed; (Ḳ, TA;) and so هَمَى. (TA.) —— And عمى النَّبْتُ [app. عَمَى] and ↓ اعتمى and اعْتَمَّ are three syn. dial. vars., (TA in this art.,) meaning † The plant, or herbage, became of its full height, and blossomed; (Ṣ, Ḳ, TA, in explanation of the last, in art. عم;) and became luxuriant, or abundant and dense. (TA in that art.)

2. عَمَّاهُ, inf. n. تَعْمِيَةٌ, He rendered him blind, of both eyes: (Ḳ, TA:) and (TA) so ↓ اعماهُ, (Ṣ, Mṣb, TA,) said of God, (Ṣ, TA,) or of a man. (Mṣb.) Hence the saying of Sá'ideh Ibn-Ju-eiyeh,

وَعَمَّى عَلَيْهِ المَوْتُ بَابَىْ طَرِيقِهِ

[And death rendered blind, to him, the two doors of his way]; بابى طريقه meaning his two eyes. (TA.) —— And [hence] عَمَّيْتُ الخَبَرَ † I made the information unapparent, obscure, or covert. (Mṣb.) And عَمَّى مَعْنَى البَيْتِ, inf. n. as above, (Ṣ, Ḳ,) † He made the meaning of the verse unapparent, obscure, or covert. (Ḳ.) And عَمَّى مُرَادَهُ † He made his meaning enigmatical, or obscure, in his speech, or language. (Ṣ, A, Ḳ, in art. لغز.) And عَمَّى عَلَى إِنْسَانٍ شَيْئًا † He made a thing obscure, or dubious, to a man. (TA.) See also 1, latter half, in two places. [And see مُعَمًّى.]

4. اعماهُ: see 2, first sentence. —— Also He found him to be blind [app. meaning properly, and also † in mind]. (Ḳ, TA.) —— مَا أَعْمَاهُ means only مَا أَعْمَى قَلْبَهُ † [How blind is his mind!]: (Ṣ, Ḳ:) for the verb of wonder is not formed from that which is not significant of increase. (Ṣ.)

5. تعمّى [in its proper sense, and also in a tropical sense]: see 1, in two places.

6. تعامى He feigned himself أَعْمَى (Ṣ, Ḳ, TA) [i. e. blind], in respect of the eyes [as is implied in the Ṣ], —— and also † in respect of the mind [as is implied in the Ḳ]. (TA.) You say, تعامى عَنْ كَذَا † He feigned himself ignorant [of such a thing], as though he did not see it; like تَعَاشَى عَنْهُ. (TA in art. عشو.)

8. اعْتَمَاهُ He chose it, selected it, or preferred it; syn. اِخْتَارَهُ; (Ṣ, Ḳ, TA;) i. e., a thing; (Ṣ;) formed by transposition from اِعْتَامَهُ [mentioned in art. عيم]. (Ṣ, TA.) —— And i. q. قَصَدَهُ [i. e. He tended, betook himself, or directed himself or his course, or aim, to, or towards, him, or it; &c.]; (Ḳ, TA;) like اِعْتَامَهُ. (TA in art. عيم.) —— See also 1, last sentence.

11. اِعْمَايَّ, and its abbreviated form اِعْمَايَ: see 1, first quarter.

صَكَّةُ عُمَىٍّ: see عُمَىٌّ.

عَمَا in the phrase عَمَا وَٱللّٰهِ, i. q. أَمَا [expl. in art. اما]: (Ḳ, TA;) as also غَمَا, (Ḳ in art. غمى,) and هَمَا. (TA.)

عَمًى [sometimes written عَمَا] inf. n. of عَمِىَ [q. v.]. (Ṣ,* Mṣb, Ḳ.) [Hence the saying, لَا شَلَلًا وَلَا عَمًى: see 1 in art. شل. Hence also one says, رَكِبَ أَمْرًا عَلَى العَمَى, meaning He ventured upon, or embarked in, an affair blindly; like عَلَى غَيْرِ بَصِيرَةٍ.] —— See also أَعْمَآءٌ. —— And see عَمَآءٌ, in two places. —— Also Stature: and height. (Ḳ.) One says, مَا أَحْسَنَ عَمَى هٰذَا الرَّجُلِ i. e. [How goodly is] the height, or the stature, of this man! (TA.) —— And Dust; syn. غُبَارٌ. (Ḳ.) —— In the saying of a rájiz, describing a skin of milk, because of its whiteness,

يَحْسَبُهُ الجَاهِلُ مَا كَانَ عَمَا

شَيْخًا عَلَى كُرْسِيِّهِ مُعَمَّمَا

[The ignorant would think it, while there was remoteness, to be an old man upon his chair, turbaned,] the meaning is looking at it from afar; for العَمَا in this case signifies remoteness. (TA.)

عَمٍ, originally عَمِىٌ: see أَعْمَى, in four places.

عَمِيَةٌ, a contraction of عَمِيَةٌ fem. of عَمٍ: see أَعْمَى.

عِمْيَةٌ [in the CḲ erroneously عَمْيَةٌ] a subst. from اِعْتَمَاهُ in the sense of اِخْتَارَهُ [signifying A thing chosen, selected, or preferred; like خِيرَةٌ, a subst. from اِخْتَارَهُ]. (Ḳ, TA.)

عَمَوِىٌّ Of, or relating to, such as is termed عَمٍ [q. v. voce أَعْمَى]. (Ṣ, TA.)

عَمَآءٌ, (Ṣ, Ḳ, TA,) in some of the copies of the Ḳ ↓ عَمًى, and by some thus related in a trad. mentioned in what follows, (TA,) Clouds: or, accord. to AZ, [clouds] resembling smoke, surmounting the heads of mountains: (Ṣ, Mṣb:) or lofty clouds: or [in the CḲ "and"] dense: (Ḳ, TA:) or dense [clouds such as are termed] غَيْم: (TA:) or raining clouds: or thin clouds: or black: or white: or such as have poured forth their water; (Ḳ, TA;) but have not become dissundered like mountains: and ↓ عَمَآءَةٌ [is the n. un., and] signifies a dense, covering, cloud; as also ↓ عَمَايَةٌ: or a dense portion of cloud: but some disallow this, and make عَمَآءٌ to be [only] a coll. n. (TA.) It is related in a trad. that, in reply to the question "Where was our Lord (meaning the عَرْش [q. v.] of our Lord) before He created his creatures?" it was said, كَانَ فِى عَمَآءٍ تَحْتَهُ هَوَآءٌ وَفَوْقَهُ هَوَآءٌ [He (i. e. his عرش) was in clouds, or lofty clouds, &c., beneath which was a vacuity, and above which was a vacuity]: or, accord. to one relation, ↓ كَانَ فِى عَمًى [meaning He was in a vacuity] i. e. there was not with Him anything: or, as some say, it means anything that the intellectual faculties cannot perceive, and to the definition of which the describer cannot attain. (TA.) —— See also عَمَآءَةٌ.

لَقِيتُهُ صَكَّةَ عُمَىٍّ, اَتَيْتُهُ صَكَّةَ عُمَىٍّ, (Ṣ,) or ↓ عُمَىٍ, and ↓ عُمْىٍ, which occurs in poetry, (Ḳ, TA,) in a case in which the metre requires it, a verse of Ru-beh, who uses it for عُمَىٍّ, (TA, [which shows, by citing that verse, that عُمَى, the reading in the CḲ, is wrong,]) and ↓ أَعْمَى, (Ḳ,) i. e. [I came to him, or I met him,] in the time of midday when the heat was vehement, (Ṣ,) or in the most vehement heat of midday in summer (Ḳ, and Lḥ and O and TA in art. صك) when the heat almost blinded by its vehemence; (Lḥ and O and TA in that art.;) a time in which the divinely-appointed prayer [of midday] is forbidden: it is said only in the hot season; because when a man goes forth at that time, he cannot fill his eyes with the light of the sun; or, as ISd says, because the gazelle seeks the covert when the heat is vehement, and his eye becomes weak by reason of the whiteness of the sun, and the bright shining thereof, and he is dazzled, so that he knocks against his covert, not seeing it: (TA:) عُمَىٌّ being an abbreviated dim. of أَعْمَى: (Ṣ:) or it is a name for the heat, (Ḳ, TA,) itself: (TA:) or the name of a certain man, (Ḳ, TA,) of [the tribe of] 'Adwán, who used to press forward with the pilgrims when the heat was vehement, as is related in the Nh, or (TA) who used to decide cases judicially in, or concerning, the pilgrimage, and he came among a company journeying upon their camels, (Ḳ, TA,) performing the religious visit called عُمْرَة, (TA,) and they alighted at a station in a hot day, whereupon he said, "Upon whomsoever shall come this hour, or time, of tomorrow while he is حَرَام [i. e. in the condition of one performing the acts of the حَجّ or of the عُمْرَة], (Ḳ, TA,) not having accomplished his عُمْرَة, (TA,) he shall remain حَرَام until [this time] next year:" and they immediately sprang up, (Ḳ, TA,) hastening, (TA,) so that they arrived at the House [of God, at Mekkeh, in the time required,] from a distance of a journey of two nights, using exertion; (Ḳ, TA;) and this saying became a prov., as is related in the M: (TA:) or it was the name of a certain man, (Ṣ, Ḳ, TA,) of the Amalekites, (Ṣ, TA,) who made a sudden attack upon a people, and exterminated them; (Ṣ, Ḳ, TA;) and the time became called in relation to him. (Ṣ, TA.) [See also art. صك.]

عَمَايَةٌ, (Ḳ, TA,) or ↓ عَمَاءَةٌ, (CḲ, and so in my MS. copy of the Ḳ,) and ↓ عَمَايَةٌ, and ↓ عُمْيَةٌ, and ↓ عِمِّيَّةٌ, † Error: and † persistence; or contention, or *litigation*, or *wrangling*; or *persistence in contention* or *litigation* or *wrangling*; syn. لَجَاجٌ; (Ḳ, TA;) *in that which is false* or *vain* or *futile*: (TA:) [or the last but one, or the last, signifies † *ignorance*; for] فِيهِمْ ▼ عَمِيَّتُهُمْ or ▼ عُمِّيَّتُهُمْ (accord. to different copies of the Ṣ) means *In them is their ignorance*. (Ṣ.) [See also عَمِيَّةٌ, and عِمِّيَّا.] — For the first (عَمَايَةٌ), see also عَمَآءٌ.

عَمَايَةٌ *A remaining portion of the darkness of night.* (TA.) — [And *Dimness of the eyes from tears*: so, accord. to Freytag, in the Deewán of the Hudhalees.] — See also عَمَآءٌ. — And see عَمَايَةٌ.

عُمْيَةٌ: see عَمَايَةٌ, in two places. — Also *i. q.* دعوة عمياء [i. e., app., ▼ دَعْوَةٌ عَمْيَآءُ], meaning † *An obscure claim to relationship*]. (TA.)

عُمِّيَّةٌ: see عَمَايَةٌ, in two places.

عَمَّا is a compound of عَنْ and مَا.

تَرَكْنَاهُمْ فِى عُمًّى, or تَرَكْنَاهُمْ عُمًّى, (Ṣ, Ḳ,) or (so in some copies of the Ṣ, [thus in one of my copies,]) † *We left them at the point of death.* (Ṣ, Ḳ.) — See also أَعْمَآءٌ.

عِمِّيَّا, of the measure فِعِّيلَى, *i. q.* فِتْنَةٌ [i. e. † *Trial*, or *probation*; *punishment*; *slaughter*; *civil war*; *conflict and faction*, or *sedition*; &c.]. (Mz, 40th نوع.) [See also the next paragraph.] — [In the TA, عمياء, evidently a mistranscription for عِمِّيَّا, is expl. as having the second of the meanings assigned above to عَمَايَةٌ &c., i. e. † *Persistence*; or *contention*, &c.] — قُتِيلُ عِمِّيَّا, (Mz ubi suprà, and Ḳ,) [in the CḲ, erroneously, عَمِيًّا, and in the TA قُتِلَ عِمِّيًّا,] the latter word of the measure فِعِّيلَى, (Mz, TA,) like رِمِّيَّا, (Ḳ, TA, [in the CḲ like رَمْيًا,]) and عِصِّيصَى, (TA,) means † *A slain person whose slayer is not known.* (Mz, Ḳ, TA.) The predicament of him who has been so slain is like that of the slain unintentionally; the bloodwit being obligatory in his case [on his عَاقِلَة, q. v. voce عَاقِلٌ]. (TA.)

عُمِّيَّةٌ and عِمِّيَّةٌ, (Ḳ, TA,) of the measure فُعِّيلَةٌ from الْعَمَى, (TA,) *Pride*; or *self-magnification*: or *error*; or *deviation from that which is right*. (Ḳ, TA. [See also عَمَايَةٌ, and عِمِّيَّا.]) Hence, in a trad., مَنْ قُتِلَ تَحْتَ رَايَةٍ عُمِّيَّةٍ [*Whoso has been slain under a banner of pride*, &c.,] i. e. in فِتْنَةٌ [meaning conflict and faction, or the like], or error, as in the fighting in the case of partisanship, and of erroneous opinions. (TA.)

عَامٍ One *who does not see his road*, or *way*. (TA.) — عَامِيَةٌ, applied to a land (أَرْضٌ): see أَعْمَى. — Also, [thus applied,] *Of which the traces are becoming* [or *become*] *effaced*, or *obliterated*. (TA.) — See also أَعْمَآءٌ, in three places. — Applied to a woman, (TA,) عَامِيَةٌ signifies رَمَّآءَةٌ, (Ḳ, TA,) [a strange epithet,] meaning † *Having very little milk.* (TḲ.) — Applied to a man, عَامٍ signifies also رَامٍ [i. e. *Casting*, &c.]. (TA.)

أَعْمَى (Ṣ, Mṣb, Ḳ) and ▼ عَمٍ (Ḳ [but see what follows]) *Blind*, (Ṣ, Mṣb, Ḳ,) *of both eyes*: (Mṣb, Ḳ,* TA:) fem. of the former عَمْيَآءُ: (Mṣb, Ḳ, TA:) and pl. [masc.] عُمْيٌ (Ṣ, Mṣb, Ḳ, TA, but not in the CḲ) and عُمْيَانٌ (Mṣb, Ḳ, TA, but not in the CḲ) and عُمَاةٌ, as though this last were pl. of عَامٍ; (Ḳ, TA, but not in the CḲ;) and the dual of its fem. is عَمْيَاوَانِ; and its pl. is عَمْيَاوَاتٌ: (TA:) the fem. of ▼ عَمٍ is عَمِيَةٌ, (Ṣ, Ḳ, TA, [in the CḲ عَمِيَّةٌ, which is a mistranscription, for it is]) of the measure فَعِلَةٌ, (Ṣ,) like فَرِحَةٌ, (TA,) and ▼ عَمْيَةٌ, (Ḳ, TA, but not in the CḲ,) which is [a contraction] like فَخْذٌ for فَخِذٌ: (TA:) and the pl. masc. is عَمُونَ. (Ṣ, TA.) — And [hence,] † *Blind in respect of the mind*: (Ḳ, TA:) [but more commonly] one says, ▼ هُوَ عَمٍ as meaning ‡ *He is erring*, or *one who errs*; and أَعْمَى الْقَلْبِ [meaning the same, or *blind in respect of the mind*]: (Mṣb:) or ▼ رَجُلٌ عَمِى الْقَلْبِ i. e. † *An ignorant man* [or *a man blind in respect of the mind*]; and اِمْرَأَةٌ عَمِيَةٌ عَنِ الصَّوَابِ [*a woman ignorant of*, or *blind to, that which is right*], and عَمِيَةُ الْقَلْبِ [like عَمِى الْقَلْبِ as applied to a man]. (Ṣ.) In the saying in the Ḳur [xvii. 74], وَمَنْ كَانَ فِى هٰذِهِ أَعْمَى فَهُوَ فِى الْآخِرَةِ أَعْمَى, accord. to Er-Rághib, the former [اعمى] is a part. n. and the second is like it; (TA;) and the meaning is, *And whoso is in this* state of existence *blind in respect of the mind, not seeing his right course, he will be in the other blind with respect to the way of safety*: (Bḍ:) or, as some say, the second is what is termed أَفْعَلُ تَفْضِيلٍ, the complement of which is expressed by means of مِنْ, [meaning *more blind* &c.,] and therefore AA and Yaạḳoob did not pronounce it with الإِمَالَة, as not being like the first, (Bḍ, TA,*) which is subject to الامالة because its ا [written ى] becomes [really] ى in the dual: but Ḥamzeh and Ks and Aboo-Bekr pronounced both with الامالة. (Bḍ.) — الأَعْمَيَانِ means † *The torrent and the fire of a burning house* or *the like*; (Ḳ, TA;) because of the perplexity that befalls him whom they befall; or because, when they occur, they spare not a place, nor avoid anything; like the أَعْمَى [or blind], who knows not where he is travelling, so that he goes whither his leg conveys him: (TA:) or *the torrent and the night*: (Ḳ:) or *the torrent*, (Ṣ, Ḳ,) or *the tumultuous torrent*, (TA,) *and the camel excited by lust*. (Ṣ, Ḳ, TA.) — And الأَمْرُ الأَعْمَى † *The case* [*such as that*] *of partisanship* (الْعَصَبِيَّة) *whereof the manner of proceeding is not distinguishable*. (TA.) — And أَرْضٌ عَمْيَآءُ and ▼ عَامِيَةٌ, and مَكَانٌ أَعْمَى, † *A land*, and *a place, in which one will not*, or *cannot, be directed to his right course*. (TA.) — See also صَكَّةُ عُمَىٍّ: — and see عَمِيَةٌ.

أَعْمَآءٌ *Tracts* of land *in which is no sign of the way*, (Ṣ, Ḳ,) *nor any habitation* or *cultivation*, (Ḳ,) or *nor any trace of habitation* or *cultivation*; (Ṣ;) and ▼ مَعَامٍ signifies the same; (Ṣ, Ḳ;) this latter being a pl. of which the sing., said by ISd to be unknown to him, should by rule be معمية [app. مَعْمِيَةٌ], but it is ▼ عُمًّى, deviating from rule; (TA;) or it means مَجَاهِلُ, and its sing. is معماة [i. e. ▼ مَعْمَاةٌ] signifying *a place of erring*, or *wandering from the right way*: (Ḥar p. 85:) in the Ḳ, أَعْمَآءٌ is also expl. as signifying جُهَّالٌ [pl. of جَاهِلٌ], and is said to be [in this sense] pl. of أَعْمَى: but this is a double mistake, for it signifies مَجَاهِلُ, [like as مَعَامٍ is said to do above,] and its sing. is عمى [app. ▼ عُمًّى]. (TA.) In the phrase ▼ أَعْمَآءٌ عَامِيَةٌ, [in the CḲ, erroneously, عَامِيَةٌ,] the latter word is added to give intensiveness to the meaning; i. e., it signifies [*Tracts in which is no sign of the way*, &c.,] *in the utmost degree obscure* or *dubious*: thus it is in the following verse: (TA:) Ru-beh says,

• وَبَلَدٍ عَامِيَةٍ ▼ أَعْمَاؤُهُ •
• كَأَنَّ لَوْنَ أَرْضِهِ سَمَاؤُهُ •

[*And many a desert*, or *waterless desert, whereof the tracts in which is no sign of the way are in the utmost degree obscure* or *dubious, as though the colour of its ground were* like that *of its sky*]: (Ṣ, TA:) he means وَرُبَّ بَلَدٍ. (Ṣ.) — Also *Tall*; applied to men: (IAạr, Ḳ:) pl. of ▼ عَامٍ, like as أَنْصَارٌ is of نَاصِرٌ. (IAạr, TA.)

أَعْمَوِىٌّ *Of*, or *relating to, such as is termed* أَعْمَى [q. v.]. (Ṣ, TA.)

مَعْمَاةٌ; and the pl. مَعَامٍ: see أَعْمَآءٌ.

مُعَمًّى † A verse [or a saying] *of which the meaning is made unapparent, obscure*, or *covert*. (Ṣ, TA.)

الْمُعْتَمِى *The lion.* (Ḳ.)

عن

1. عَنَّ, aor. ـِ (Ṣ, Mgh, Mṣb, Ḳ) and ـُ, (Ṣ, Mṣb, Ḳ,) the former accord. to some relaters, and the latter accord. to others, occurring in a verse of a Hudhalee, (TA,) inf. n. عَنَنٌ (Ṣ, Mṣb, Ḳ) and عَنٌّ (Mṣb, Ḳ) and عُنُونٌ, the first of which is also [or is properly] a simple subst., (Ḳ, [and such, in one sense, it is said to be in the Mṣb, as will be shown in what follows,]) said of an affair, or event, (Mṣb,) or of a thing, (Ṣ,* Ḳ,) *It appeared before one*: (Ḳ:) [and] *i. q.* عَرَضَ (Ṣ, Mgh) and (Ṣ, Ḳ) اِعْتَرَضَ (Ṣ, Mṣb, Ḳ) [i. e. *it appeared; it showed, presented*, or *offered, itself*: *it occurred*: and *it presented itself*, or *intervened between a person and an object before him, as an obstacle*: *it opposed itself*]: and so ▼ اِعْتَنَّ. (Ṣ, Ḳ.) [See also عَنَنٌ, below.] Imra-el-Ḳeys says,

• فَعَنَّ لَنَا سِرْبٌ كَأَنَّ نِعَاجَهُ •
• عَذَارَى دَوَارٍ فِى مُلَآءٍ مُذَيَّلِ •

(Mgh, TA,*) meaning, عَرَضَ, (TA,) i. e. *And there appeared to us a herd* of wild oxen, *as though the females thereof were virgins* making the circuit *of Dawár*, or *Duwár*, *in long-skirted garments of the kind called* مُلَآء; Dawár, or Duwár, being the name of an idol around which the people of the Time of Ignorance used to curcuit. (Mgh,* and EM pp. 46 and 47.) And one says, لَا أَفْعَلُهُ مَا عَنَّ فِى السَّمَآءِ نَجْمٌ, meaning مَا عَرَضَ [i. e. *I will not do it as long as a star appears in the sky*]. (Ṣ.) — And عَنَّ, (Mṣb, TA,) aor. ـِ, (Mṣb,) inf. n. عَنَنٌ, (TA,) or this is a simple subst., (Mṣb, TA,) and the inf. n. is عَنٌّ, (TA,) *He opposed himself* (اِعْتَرَضَ, Mṣb, or تَعَرَّضَ, TA) *to another* (Mṣb) *from right and left*, (TA,) or *from either side of him*, (Mṣb,) *with an abominable*, or *evil, action*. (Mṣb, TA.) — And عَنَّ عَنِ الشَّىْءِ, aor. ـِ, [inf. n., app., عَنٌّ,] *He turned aside*, or *away, from the thing*. (Mṣb.) — Hence the saying of the lawyers, عَنَّ عَنِ ٱمْرَأَةٍ دُونَ أُخْرَى [*He turned away from one woman, not* from *another*]; meaning *he desired not one woman, but desired another*: thus in the active form: and one may also say عُنَّ i. e. in the passive form [from one or another of the following significations of the trans. verb]. (Mṣb.) For the latter of these, and its var. عُنِنَ, see 2. — عَنَنْتُ اللِّجَامَ: see 4. — عَنَّ دَابَّتَهُ *He put a rein* (عِنَان) *to his beast*. (TA.) And عَنَنْتُ الفَرَسَ, (Ṣ, Mṣb, Ḳ,) aor. ـُ; (Mṣb;) in the M [▼عَنَّنْتُ,] with teshdeed; (TA;) *I withheld the horse by means of his* عِنَان [or *rein*]; (Ṣ, Mṣb, Ḳ;) as also ▼أَعْنَنْتُهُ: (Ḳ:) or ▼أَعْنَنْتُ الفَرَسَ signifies *I put a rein to the horse*: (Mṣb:) and it is said in the T that ▼أَعَنَّ الفَارِسُ means *the horseman drew*, or *pulled, the rein of his beast, to turn him back*, or *away, from his course*. (TA.) — And عَنَنْتُهُ, (Mṣb,) and عُنَّ, (Mgh,) *I confined him*, (Mṣb,) and *he was confined*, (Mgh,) *in the* عُنَّة i. e. the *enclosure* (Mgh, Mṣb) *of the camels*. (Mgh.) — عَنَنْتُ فُلَانًا *I reviled such a one; vilified him*; or *gave a bad name to him*. (Ḳ.) — See also Q. Q. 1.

2. عَنَّنْتُ اللِّجَامَ: see 4. — عَنَّنْتُ الفَرَسَ: see 1, last quarter. — [Hence, perhaps,] عُنِّنَ عَنِ ٱمْرَأَتِهِ, (Ṣ, Mṣb, Ḳ,) inf. n. تَعْنِينٌ, (Mṣb,) which see also voce عُنَّةٌ, former half, in two places, *He was pronounced by the judge* (Ṣ, Mṣb, Ḳ) *to be incapacitated from going in to his wife*, (Mṣb, Ḳ,) or *to have no desire for his wife*: or *to be withheld from her by enchantment*, or *fascination*: (Ṣ, Mṣb, Ḳ:) and ▼أُعِنَّ signifies the same; as also ▼عُنَّ, (Ḳ, TA,) and ▼عُنِنَ; and ▼اُعْتُنَّ. (TA. [Thus in the supplement to this art. in the TA; but it seems that the last of these verbs may be a mistranscription for أُعِنَّ, as this verb is there omitted, though the other verbs are mentioned, and followed by the part. ns. مَعْنُونٌ and مُعَنٌّ and مُعَنَّنٌ, but not مُعْتَنٌّ.]) — التَّعْنِينُ also signifies *The confining in a deep* مُطْبَق [or *subterranean prison*]. (TA.) — And عَنَّنَتْ شَعَرَهَا, said of a woman, means شَكَلَتْ بَعْضَهُ بِبَعْضٍ [i. e. *She plaited together two locks of her hair, of the fore part of her head, on the right and left, and then bound them with her other pendent locks* or *plaits*]. (TA.) — See also Q. Q. 1.

3. المُعَانَّةُ and العِنَانُ signify المُعَارَضَةُ, (Ṣ, Mṣb, Ḳ, TA,) as inf. ns. of عَانَّهُ [meaning *He did like as he* (the latter) *did*: or *he opposed him, being opposed by him*]. (TA.) See, below, شِرْكَةُ العِنَانِ: and also عُنَانًا.

4. أَعَنَّ [i. q. تَعَرَّضَ]. One says, ▼أَعْنَنْتُ بِعُنَّةٍ مَا أَدْرِى مَا هِىَ, (Ṣ, Ḳ, but in the latter لا ادرى,) meaning *I addressed, applied*, or *directed, myself to a thing* (تَعَرَّضْتُ لِشَىْءٍ) *not knowing what it was*. (Ṣ, Ḳ.) — And أَعْنَنْتُهُ لِكَذَا *I exposed him*, or *caused him to become exposed*, (عَرَّضْتُهُ,) *to such a thing*; and *I turned him to it*, or *towards it*. (Ṣ.) — أَعْنَنْتُ اللِّجَامَ *I put a rein* (عِنَان) *to the bit*; (Ṣ, Ḳ;) as also ▼عَنَّنْتُهُ, (Ṣ,* Ḳ,) inf. n. تَعْنِينٌ; (Ṣ;) and ▼عَنَنْتُهُ. (Ḳ.) — See also 1, last quarter, in three places. — أُعِنَّ عَنِ ٱمْرَأَتِهِ: see 2.

5. تعنّن *He* (a man) *abstained from women without his being incapacitated from going in to them, because of blood-revenge that he sought*. (TA.)

8. اِعْتَنَّ: see 1, first sentence. — اِعْتَنَّ مَا عِنْدَهُمْ *He became acquainted with their state*, or *case*. (Ḳ.) — اُعْتُنَّ: see 2.

R. Q. 1. عَنْعَنَةٌ [an inf. n. of which the verb is عَنْعَنَ] The *substituting of* ع *for* ء; [for instance,] *saying* عَنْ *in the place of* أَنْ: a practice of [the tribe of] Temeem. (Ṣ, Ḳ:) or, accord. to Fr, it is of the dial. of Ḳureysh and of those in their neighbourhood, and of Temeem and Ḳeys and Asad and those in their neighbourhood: they change the أ of أَنَّ, with fet-ḥ, into ع; but not when it is with kesr. (TA.) [See two instances in art. عنف, conj. 8.] — Hence, عَنْعَنَةُ المُحَدِّثِينَ [i. e. *The saying of the relaters of traditions* فُلَانٌ عَنْ فُلَانٍ عَنْ فُلَانٍ, suppressing the word رَوَى or سَمِعَ or حَدَّثَ]: but this is said to be post-classical. (TA.)

Q. Q. 1. عَنْوَنَ الكِتَابَ *He put a superscription*, or *title*, (عُنْوَان,) *to the book*, or *writing*; (Ṣ,* Mṣb;) or *he wrote the* عُنْوَان *of the book*, or *writing*; (Ḳ;) like عَلْوَنَهُ; (TA;) and ▼عَنَّهُ, (Ṣ, Ḳ, TA,) aor. ـُ, inf. n. عَنٌّ, (TA,) signifies the same; as also ▼عَنَّنَهُ, (Ṣ, Ḳ, TA,) inf. n. تَعْنِينٌ, mentioned by Lḥ; (TA;) and عَنَّاهُ, (Ṣ, Ḳ, TA,) formed by changing one of the ن [of عَنَّنَ] into ى. (Ṣ, TA.) [See also Q. Q. 1 in art. عنو.]

عَنْ is used in three manners: — First, it is a prep.: and as such it has ten meanings. (Mughnee, Ḳ.) — (1) It denotes transition; (Mṣb, Mughnee, Ḳ;) either sensibly or virtually; (Mṣb;) and the Baṣrees have mentioned no other meaning than this: (Mughnee:) or, as Sb expresses it, (Mṣb,) it denotes what has passed [or rather it denotes passage] from the thing [that is mentioned immediately after it]: (Ṣ, Mṣb:) Er-Rághib says that it necessarily denotes transition from that to the mention of which it is prefixed: and the grammarians say that it is applied to denote what has passed and become remote from thee. (TA.) Thus in the saying, سَافَرْتُ عَنِ البَلَدِ [*I journeyed from the country*, or *town*]. (Mughnee, Ḳ.*) And in رَغِبْتُ عَنْ كَذَا [*I abstained from such a thing*; and hence, *I did not desire*, or *wish for, such a thing*]. (Mughnee.) And رَمَيْتُ عَنِ القَوْسِ [*I shot* an arrow, or arrows, *from the bow*]; (Ṣ, Mughnee;) because by means of the bow one projects his arrow from the bow, and makes it to pass therefrom: (Ṣ:) but another meaning of this will be mentioned in what follows. (Mughnee.) And أَطْعَمْتُهُ عَنْ جُوعٍ [*I fed him* so as to free him *from hunger*]; (Ṣ, Mṣb;) making hunger to be quitted, and passed from: (Ṣ,* Mṣb:) and in this case, مِنْ is used in its place, (Ṣ, TA,) as in the Ḳur cvi. 3; (TA;) or the meaning in this instance is, *because of hunger*. (Jel.) And جَلَسْتُ عَنْ يَمِينِهِ, [as though] meaning *I sat passing away from the place of his right side, in sitting, to another place* [*adjacent thereto*: but see another explanation near the end of the paragraph]. (Mṣb.) And تَنَحَّ عَنِّى and اِنْصَرِفْ عَنِّى [*Turn thou*, or *go thou, away*, or *aside, from me*]. (TA.) And أَخَذْتُ العِلْمَ عَنْهُ *I understood*, or *became acquainted with*, [or *acquired*,] *knowledge*, or *science, from him*; as though the understanding passed from him. (Mṣb.) [And similar to this is the phrase رَوَى عَنْ فُلَانٍ, for which عَنْ فُلَانٍ alone (the verb being understood) is often used, *He related* a tradition or traditions &c. as learned, or heard, or received, *from such a one*, or *on the authority of such a one*. In many other phrases also, some of which will be mentioned in treating of عَنْ as syn. with مِنْ, the former of these two prepositions is to be, or may be, expl. as denoting transition. For ex., one says, دَفَعَ عَنْهُ and دَافَعَ عَنْهُ *He repelled from him*; and hence, *he defended him*: (see art. دفع:) and رَمَى عَنْهُمْ *He shot in defence of them*: (see an ex. in a verse cited voce مَعْبُولٌ:) and عَنْهُ is sometimes used for دِفَاعًا عَنْهُ; as in the phrase قَاتَلْتُ عَنْهُ *I fought in defence of him*; i. e., *repelling from him*. But the instances of this and other usages of عَنْ, exclusive of those mentioned in this paragraph, depending upon verbs or part. ns. expressed or obviously understood, are far too numerous to be here collected: many of these will be found among the explanations of words with which they occur.] — (2) It denotes a compensation; or something given, or received, or put, or done, instead, or in lieu, of another thing. (Mughnee, Ḳ.) Thus in the saying [in the Ḳur ii. 45], وَٱتَّقُوا يَوْمًا لَا تَجْزِى نَفْسٌ عَنْ نَفْسٍ شَيْئًا [*And fear* *ye a day* wherein *a soul shall not give anything as a satisfaction for a soul*, i. e. *for another soul*: or *shall not make satisfaction for a soul at all*; accord. to the latter rendering, شيئا being put in the accus. case after the manner of an inf. n.]. (Mughnee, Ḳ.*) And in the saying in a trad., صُومِى عَنْ أُمِّكِ [*Fast thou for*, or *in lieu of, thy mother*]. (Mughnee.) —— (3) It denotes superiority (ٱلِٱسْتِعْلَآءُ) [as used tropically]); (Mughnee, Ḳ;) i. e. as *syn. with* عَلَى. (Mughnee.) Thus in the saying of Dhu-l-Iṣba' El-'Adwánee,

لَاهِ ٱبْنُ عَمِّكَ لَا أَفْضَلْتَ فِى حَسَبٍ
عَنِّى وَلَا أَنْتَ دَيَّانِى فَتَخْزُونِى

(Ṣ, Mughnee,) i. e. *To God be attributed the excellence of the son of thy paternal uncle* (the meaning being لِلّٰهِ دَرُّ ٱبْنِ عَمِّكَ), *thou hast not become possessed of superiority, in grounds of pretension to respect* or *honour, above me*, or *over me*, (عَلَىَّ,) *nor art thou my governor that thou shouldst rule me*; for the well-known mode is to say أَفْضَلْتُ عَلَيْهِ. (Mughnee.) [Thus too in the phrases تَعَاظَمَ عَنْهُ and تَعَظَّمَ عَنْهُ (expl. in art. عظم), and in the phrase تَجَالَّ عَنْهُ (expl. in art. جل), and the like.] And thus it has been said to be used in the phrase [in the Ḳur xxxviii. 31], إِنِّى أَحْبَبْتُ حُبَّ ٱلْخَيْرِ عَنْ ذِكْرِ رَبِّى, meaning قَدَّمْتُهُ عَلَيْهِ [i. e. *Verily I have preferred the love of good things above*, or *to, the remembrance*, or *praise, of my Lord*]: but it is also said that it is here used in its proper manner, as dependent upon a denotative of state suppressed; the meaning being, مُنْصَرِفًا عَنْ ذِكْرِ رَبِّى [i. e. *turning away from the remembrance*, &c.]: and AO is related to have said that أَحْبَبْتُ is from أَحَبَّ ٱلْبَعِيرُ, signifying "the camel lay down and did not become roused;" and that the meaning is, *I have become withheld by the love of good things from the remembrance*, &c. (Mughnee.) And it is [said to be] used as denoting superiority or the like in the saying [in the Ḳur xlvii. last verse], فَإِنَّمَا يَبْخَلُ عَنْ نَفْسِهِ [as though the meaning were *He is niggardly only to himself* (عَلَى نَفْسِهِ, for عَلَى is considered in this case as importing an ideal superiority); but the phrase may be better rendered, agreeably with the proper, or primary, signification of عَنْ, *he withholds, with niggardliness, only from himself*; as is indicated by Bḍ]. (Mughnee, Ḳ.) —— (4) It denotes a cause. (Mughnee, Ḳ.) Thus in the saying [in the Ḳur ix. 115], وَمَا كَانَ ٱسْتِغْفَارُ إِبْرٰهِيمَ لِأَبِيهِ إِلَّا عَنْ مَوْعِدَةٍ [*And Abraham's begging forgiveness for his father was not otherwise than because of a promise*]. (Mughnee, Ḳ.) And thus in the saying [in the Ḳur xi. 56], وَمَا نَحْنُ بِتَارِكِى آلِهَتِنَا عَنْ قَوْلِكَ [*And we are not*, or *will not be, relinquishers of our gods because of thy saying*]: or the meaning may be, *we do not*, or *will not, relinquish our gods, turning away* (صَادِرِينَ, as a denotative of state relating to the pronoun [implied] in تاركى,) *from thy saying*; and this is the opinion of Z. (Mughnee.) [See also an ex. voce دَنْدَنَ, last sentence.] —— (5) It is *syn. with* بَعْدَ. (Ṣ, Mughnee, Ḳ.) Thus in the saying [in the Ḳur xxiii. 42], عَمَّا قَلِيلٍ لَيُصْبِحُنَّ نَادِمِينَ, (Mughnee, Ḳ,) meaning بَعْدَ قَلِيلٍ [i. e. *After a little while, they will assuredly become repentant*]. (TA.) And in the phrase [in the Ḳur lxxxiv. 19], لَتَرْكَبُنَّ طَبَقًا عَنْ طَبَقٍ [expl. in art. طبق], meaning حَالَةً بَعْدَ حَالَةٍ. (Mughnee.) And in the saying,

وَمَنْهَلٍ وَرَدْتُهُ عَنْ مَنْهَلِ

[*And to many a watering-place have I come after a watering-place*]. (Mughnee.) And in the saying of El-Ḥárith Ibn-'Obád,

قَرِّبَا مَرْبِطَ ٱلنَّعَامَةِ مِنِّى
لَقِحَتْ حَرْبُ وَائِلٍ عَنْ حِيَالِ

(Ṣ,* TA,) meaning بَعْدَ حِيَالٍ [i. e. *Make ye two to be near to me the place of the tying of En-Na'ámeh* (the name of a horse of the poet): *the war of Wáïl has become pregnant after failing to be pregnant during a year*, or *years*]. (TA.) And in the saying of Eṭ-Ṭirimmáḥ,

سَيَعْلَمُ كُلُّهُمْ أَنِّى مُسِنٌّ
إِذَا دَفَعُوا عِنَانًا عَنْ عِنَانِ

i. e. [*All of them shall know that I am of full age, when they press forward*] *heat after heat*. (TA.) —— (6) It denotes the meaning of the preposition فِى. (Mughnee, Ḳ.) Thus in the saying,

وَلَا تَكُ عَنْ حَمْلِ ٱلرِّبَاعَةِ وَانِيَا

[*And be not thou remiss in bearing the responsibility of the obligation that thou takest upon thyself*]; as is shown by the phrase, [in the Ḳur xx. 44], وَلَا تَنِيَا فِى ذِكْرِى: (Mughnee, Ḳ:) so it is said; but it seems that the meaning of وَنَى عَنْ كَذَا is, "he passed from such a thing, not entering upon it;" and وَنَى فِيهِ, "he entered upon it but was remiss, or languid:" by ٱلرِّبَاعَة is meant *the payment of a bloodwit* or *the like*. (Mughnee.) —— (7) It is *syn. with* مِنْ. (Mughnee, Ḳ.) Thus in the saying [in the Ḳur xlii. 24], وَهُوَ ٱلَّذِى يَقْبَلُ ٱلتَّوْبَةَ عَنْ عِبَادِهِ [*And He is he who accepts repentance from his servants*]. (AO, Mughnee, Ḳ.) Az mentions among the cases in which there is a difference between مِنْ and عَنْ, that the former has adjoined to it a noun signifying what is near; and the latter, [one signifying] what is remote; as in one's saying سَمِعْتُ مِنْ فُلَانٍ حَدِيثًا [*I heard from such a one a narrative*], and حَدَّثَنِى عَنْ فُلَانٍ حَدِيثًا [*He related to me a narrative from such a one*, a phrase similar to رَوَى عَنْ فُلَانٍ, mentioned among exs. of the first meaning of عن]: accord. to Aṣ, one says, حَدَّثَنِى فُلَانٌ مِنْ فُلَانٍ, meaning عَنْهُ [i. e. *Such a one related to me from such a one*]; and لَهِيتُ مِنْ فُلَانٍ and عَنْهُ [*I became diverted from such a one so as to forget him*]: accord. to Ks, one says لَهِيتُ عَنْهُ only: and مِنْكَ جَآءَ هٰذَا as meaning عَنْكَ [i. e. *From thee came this*]. (TA.) —— (8) It is *syn. with* بِ. (Mughnee, Ḳ.) Thus [it is said to be used] in the phrase [in the Ḳur liii. 3], وَمَا يَنْطِقُ عَنِ ٱلْهَوَى [*Nor does he speak with the desire of self-gratification*]: (Mughnee, Ḳ:) but it seems that it is here used in its proper [or primary] sense; and that the meaning is, وَمَا يَصْدُرُ قَوْلُهُ عَنْ هَوًى [*nor does his speech proceed from desire of self-gratification*; so the phrase may be well rendered, *nor does he speak from the desire* &c.]. (Mughnee.) One says also, أَجَابُوا عَنْ بَوَآءٍ وَاحِدٍ, meaning بِجَوَابٍ وَاحِدٍ [i. e. *They replied with one reply*]. (Ṭ, Ṣ, Ó, Ḳ, all in art. بوأ.) And جَآؤُوا عَنْ آخِرِهِمْ [*They came with the last of them*; عَنْ being here syn. with بِ; meaning *they came all, without exception*]. (A in art. اخر.) [And in like manner, قَتَلُوهُمْ عَنْ آخِرِهِمْ *They slew them with the last of them*; meaning *they slew them all, without exception.*] —— (9) It denotes the using a thing as an aid or instrument. (Mughnee, Ḳ.) Thus in the saying, رَمَيْتُ عَنِ ٱلْقَوْسِ [*I shot with*, or *by means of, the bow*], accord. to Ibn-Málik; (Mughnee, Ḳ;) because one says also, رَمَيْتُ بِٱلْقَوْسِ; both mentioned by Fr. (Mughnee.) [Another explanation of this phrase has been mentioned before.] —— (10) It is redundant, to compensate for another [عن] suppressed (Mughnee, Ḳ.) Thus in the saying,

أَتَجْزَعُ إِنْ نَفْسٌ أَتَاهَا حِمَامُهَا
فَهَلَّا ٱلَّتِى عَنْ بَيْنَ جَنْبَيْكَ تَدْفَعُ

[*Art thou impatient if the decreed event of death befall a soul? but why wilt not thou repel from*, i. e. *defend, that which is between thy two sides?*]; (Mughnee, Ḳ;) the meaning being, تَدْفَعُ عَنِ ٱلَّتِى بَيْنَ جَنْبَيْكَ; (IJ, Mughnee;) عن being suppressed before the conjunct noun [التى], and added after it. (Mughnee, Ḳ.) And sometimes it is redundant without compensation, when conjoined with a pronoun: AZ says that the Arabs make عَنْكَ redundant in the phrase خُذْ ذَا عَنْكَ [meaning *Take thou*, or *receive thou, this*]: (TA:) [but خُذْ عَنْكَ is expl. in the Ṣ and L, in art. اخذ, as meaning خُذْ مَا أَقُولُ وَدَعْ عَنْكَ ٱلشَّكَّ وَٱلْمِرَآءَ: see 1 in art. اخذ:] and أَنْفُذْ عَنْكَ, occurring in a trad., is expl. as meaning دَعْهُ [i. e. *Leave thou it*]: (TA:) or this means *go thou from thy place; pass thou from it*. (L in art. نفذ.) [See also the last ex. in this paragraph.] ═ The second manner of using it is, as a particle of the kind called مَصْدَرِىٌّ, [combining with an aor. following it to form an equivalent to an inf. n.,] as is done by the tribe of Temeem, (Mughnee, Ḳ,*) in what is termed their عَنْعَنَة: (Ḳ: [see R. Q. 1:]) they use it in the place of أَنْ; (Ṣ, Mughnee;) saying, أَعْجَبَنِى عَنْ تَفْعَلَ, (Mughnee, Ḳ,) for أَنْ تَفْعَلَ [meaning *Thy doing* such a thing *pleased me*]. (Mughnee.) Dhu-r-Rummeh says,

أَعَنْ تَرَسَّمْتَ مِنْ خَرْقَآءَ مَنْزِلَةً
مَآءُ ٱلصَّبَابَةِ مِنْ عَيْنَيْكَ مَسْجُومُ

[*Is thy having looked upon the traces of a place of*

abiding of thy beloved *Kharkà* the cause that *the water of excessive love is shed from thine eyes?*]. (Ṣ, Mughnee.) And thus they do in the case of أَنَّ; saying, أَشْهَدُ عَنَّ ▼ مُحَمَّدًا رَسُولُ ٱللّٰهِ [*I acknowledge*, or *declare*, or *testify*, *that Mohammad is the apostle of God*]. (Mughnee.) ═ The third manner of using it is, as a noun, in the sense of جَانِب, (Mughnee, Ḳ,*) or نَاحِيَة: (Ṣ:) and this is said to be in three cases. (Mughnee.) — (1) It is when مِنْ is prefixed to it; and this is of frequent occurrence: (Mughnee:) as in the saying,

* وَلَقَدْ أَرَانِى لِلرِّمَاحِ دَرِيْئَةً *
* مِنْ عَنْ يَمِينِى مَرَّةً وَأَمَامِى *

[*And verily I see me to be like a ring for the spears to be aimed at, from the side of my right hand at one time, and from before me* at another time]: (Mughnee, Ḳ:*) and in the saying, جِئْتُ مِنْ عَنْ يَمِينِهِ *I came from the side of his right hand.* (Ṣ.) In the opinion of Ibn-Málik, مِنْ prefixed to عَنْ is redundant; but accord. to others, it is used [as expl. above,] to denote the beginning of a space between two limits: these say that قَعَدْتُ عَنْ يَمِينِهِ means فِى جَانِبِ يَمِينِهِ [i. e. *I sat in the side of his right hand*], either closely or otherwise; but if you say مِنْ [before عَنْ], the sitting is particularized as being close to the first part of the lateral space. (Mughnee.) — (2) It is also when عَلَى is prefixed to it: (Mughnee:) thus in the saying,

* عَلَى عَنْ يَمِينِى مَرَّتِ ٱلطَّيْرُ سُنَّحَا *

[*On*, or *over*, *the side of my right hand, the birds passed along turning the right side towards me*, or *turning the left side towards me*; the last word being a pl., accord. to analogy, of سَانِح, which is used in two opposite senses]: (Mughnee, Ḳ:) but this usage is extraordinary; no other instance of it than that here cited having been preserved. (Mughnee.) — (3) It is also when what is governed by it in the gen. case and the agent of the verb in connection with it are two pronouns having one application: so says Akh: as in the saying of Imra-el-Ḳeys,

* دَعْ عَنْكَ نَهْبًا صِيحَ فِى حَجَرَاتِهِ *

[or فَدَعْ عَنْكَ: see the entire verse cited and expl. in art. حجر]: but it is shown to be not a noun in such a case by this, that جَانِب may not take its place [unless used in a tropical sense]. (Mughnee. [See what has been said above, that عَنْكَ in a phrase of this kind is held to be redundant.])

عَنْ for أَنْ: see the next preceding paragraph, last quarter.

عَنٌّ: see أَعْنَانٌ. — إِنَّهُ يَأْخُذُ فِى كُلِّ عَنٍّ means the same as فِى كُلِّ فَنٍّ [i. e. *Verily he enters upon every mode*, or *manner*, *of speech or the like*]; and so فِى كُلِّ سَنٍّ. (TA.)

عُنَّةٌ: see what next follows.

عَنَّةٌ The *presenting*, or *opposing*, *oneself*, *with meddling*, or *impertinent*, *speech*; *with speech respecting that which does not concern him*; (Mṣb, TA;) as also ▼ عُنَّةٌ, with fet-ḥ, (Mṣb,) or ▼ عِنَّةٌ, with kesr. (TA.) — أَعْطَيْتُهُ عَنْ عُنَّةٍ, (Ṣ,) or عَيْنَ عُنَّةٍ, imperfectly decl., and sometimes عَيْنَ عُنَّةٍ, (Ḳ,) means *I gave to him distinguishing him particularly from among his companions*: (Ṣ, Ḳ:) from ٱلعَنُّ signifying "the presenting, or opposing, oneself." (TA.) And one says, رَأَيْتُهُ عَيْنَ عُنَّةٍ (Ṣ) or عُنَّةً (Ḳ) *I saw him just now*, (Ṣ, Ḳ, TA,) *presenting*, or *opposing*, *himself*, (TA,) *without my seeking him.* (Ṣ, TA.) And أَعْنَنْتُ بِعُنَّةٍ مَا أَدْرِى مَا هِىَ: see 4. (Ṣ, Ḳ.) ═ It is also the subst. from عُنِّنَ عَنِ ٱمْرَأَتِهِ [i. e. a subst. signifying The *state of being pronounced by the judge to be incapacitated from going in to his wife*, or *to have no desire for his wife*: or *of being withheld from her by enchantment*, or *fascination*]: (Ṣ, Mṣb,* Ḳ:) or *incapacity to go in to women*: (Mgh, Mṣb:) or *undesirousness of women*: (Mṣb:) a word used in this sense by the lawyers; (Mgh, Mṣb;) who say, بِهِ عُنَّةٌ: (Mṣb:) but it is declared to be a low word, not allowable; (Mgh, Mṣb;) instead of which one should say ▼ تَعْنِينٌ, (Mgh,) or, accord. to Th and others, ▼ عَنَنٌ, and ▼ عِنِينَةٌ, and accord. to the Bári', ▼ عَنَانَةٌ: (Mṣb:) [i. e.] ▼ عِنِّينَةٌ signifies *undesirousness of women*: (Ṣ:) or, as also ▼ عِنِينَةٌ, and ▼ عَنَانَةٌ, and ▼ تَعْنِينٌ, and ▼ تَعْنِينَةٌ, (Ḳ,) and ▼ عِنِّينِيَّةٌ, (TA,) it signifies thus, or *non-performance of the act of going in to women, by reason of impotence.* (Ḳ, TA.) ═ Also *An enclosure* (Ṣ, Mgh, Mṣb, Ḳ) *made of wood*, (Ṣ, Mṣb, Ḳ, TA,) or *of trees*, (TA,) *for camels*, (Ṣ, Mgh, Ḳ,*) or *for camels and horses*, (Mṣb,) or *for camels and sheep* or *goats, to be confined therein*: (TA:) or *an enclosure at the door of a man, in which are his camels and his sheep* or *goats*: (Th, TA:) pl. عُنَنٌ (Ṣ, Ḳ) and عِنَانٌ. (Ḳ.) لَا يَجْتَمِعُ ٱلثَّنَانِ فِى عُنَّةٍ [*Two* (app. meaning stallion-camels) *will not be together in an enclosure for camels*] is one of their sayings. (TA.) And one says, كَٱلْمُهَدِّرِ فِى ٱلْعُنَّةِ *Like the brayer* (meaning the braying stallion-camel) *in the enclosure of trees*, in which the stallion-camel is sometimes confined to prevent him from covering; such a stallion being hence termed ▼ مُعَنًّى, originally ▼ مُعَنَّنٌ: (Meyd:) it is a prov., applied to a man (Meyd, TA, and Ṣ and A and Ḳ in art. هدر) raising a cry and clamour, (Ṣ, Ḳ,) or threatening, (TA,) who does not make his saying, or action, to have effect; (Ṣ,* Meyd, Ḳ;) like the camel that is so confined, prevented from covering, and brays. (Ṣ, Ḳ.) — It is also said, by El-Bushtee and in the Ḳ, to signify *A rope*; and in a verse of El-Aạshà, in which he mentions flesh-meat as put upon the عُنَن, this last word has been expl. as meaning ropes which are stretched, and upon which is thrown the flesh-meat that is cut into strips, or oblong pieces, and dried in the sun: but Az says that the right meaning is, the enclosures for camels; that he had seen such enclosures in the desert, thus called because facing the direction whence blows the north wind, to protect the camels from the cold of that wind; and that he had seen the people spread the flesh-meat cut into strips, or oblong pieces, and dried in the sun, upon them: he thinks that the word was expl. as meaning ropes by one who had seen the poor of the sacred territory extending ropes in Minè, and putting upon them the flesh of the victims of sacrifice that had been given to them. (TA.) — Also *A booth by means of which one shades himself, made of panic grass* (ثُمَام) or [probably a mistake for *and*] *branches of trees.* (IB, TA.) — And *Reeds*, or *plants* or *herbage, which a man collects, to give, as fodder, to his sheep* or *goats*: one says, جَآءَ بِعُنَّةٍ عَظِيمَةٍ [*He came with*, or *brought*, *a great collection of reeds*, &c.]. (TA.) And one says, كُنَّا فِى عُنَّةٍ مِنَ ٱلكَلَإِ, and عَنَّةٍ, and عِنَّةٍ, i. e. *We were in abundant herbage.* (TA.) ═ Also The وِقْدَان (thus [correctly, as will be shown by an explanation in what follows, confirmed by an ex. from a poet,] in more than one of the copies of the Ḳ, in the CḲ وَدْقَان, in the copy of the Ḳ followed in the TA وقدان, and in the L رقدان,) *of the cooking-pot*: (Ḳ, TA:) MF read وقدان, and conjecturally, and from analogy, supposed it [to be وَقْدَان and] to mean غَلَيَان; but the word is arabicized from the Pers. ديكدان, [correctly ديگدان, pronounced *dégdán*,] a name for the *thing upon which the cooking-pot is set up*; and thus it [i. e. عُنَّة] is expl. in the M and other lexicons [among which may be mentioned the L]: hence the saying of a poet,

* عَفَتْ غَيْرَ أَنْآءٍ وَمَنْصَبِ عُنَّةٍ *
* وَأَوْرَقَ مِنْ تَحْتِ ٱلخَصَاصَةِ هَامِدِ *

[*It* (the دار, or place of abode,) *was effaced, save trenches dug around the tents to keep off the torrent, and the place of the setting-up of the support of the cooking-pot, and ashes beneath the space between the three stones that formed that support, in a state of extinction*]. (TA.)

عِنَّةٌ: see the next preceding paragraph, first sentence.

عَنَنٌ is a subst. [as well as an inf. n.] of عَنَّ; (Mṣb, Ḳ, TA;) [as such,] i. q. اِعْتِرَاضٌ [used as a simple subst., meaning *Opposition*]; (Ḳ,* TA;) as also ▼ عِنَانٌ: (Ḳ, TA:) or *opposition of oneself to another, from either side of him, with an abominable*, or *evil, action.* (Mṣb.) El-Ḥárith Ibn-Ḥillizeh says,

* عَنَنًا بَاطِلًا وَظُلْمًا كَمَا يُعْ *
* تَرُ عَنْ حَجْرَةِ ٱلرَّبِيضِ ٱلظِّبَآءُ *

(TA,) meaning *In wrong opposition*, (اِعْتِرَاضًا بَاطِلًا), [*and injurious conduct*], *like as when gazelles are sacrificed* [in fulfilment of a vow] *for what is due on the part of the flock of sheep*, or *herd of goats.* (EM p. 281.) And it is said in a trad., بَرِئْنَا إِلَيْكَ مِنَ ٱلوَثَنِ وَٱلعَنَنِ i. e. [*We are clear, to thee,*] *of the idol* (ٱلصَّنَم) *and opposition*

(الإِعْتِرَاض); as though saying, *of associating another with God and of wrongdoing*: or, as some say, the meaning [of the last word] in this case is *disagreement*, or *opposition*, or *contravention*, (الخِلَاف), and *that which is wrong* (البَاطِل). (TA.) And in another trad., دَهَمَتْهُ المَنِيَّةُ فِى عَنَنِ جِمَاحِهِ [*Death came upon him suddenly in the opposition of his heedless*, or *inconsiderate, course*]. (TA. [There expl. only by the words هُوَ مَا لَيْسَ بِقَصْدٍ.]) And one says, هُوَ لَكَ بَيْنَ الأَوْبِ وَالعَنَنِ, meaning [*He is to thee* in a state] *between obedience and disobedience*. (TA.) ▾ وَرْهَآءُ العِنَانِ, a phrase used by a poet, means [A woman *foolish in*] *opposing herself*, or *intervening, in every discourse*. (TA.) And العَنَنُ signifies also [particularly] *Death's opposing itself, and preceding*: (TA, JM:) occurring in a trad. of Sateeh [the Diviner]. (TA.) — See also عَنَانٌ, near the middle of the paragraph. — Also The *place in which a person*, or *thing, presents*, or *opposes, himself*, or *itself*. (TA.) — See also أَعْنَانٌ. = And see عُنَّةٌ, former half.

عَنَانٌ *Clouds*: (S, Msb, K:) or, accord. to some, *clouds appearing*, or *presenting themselves*, or *extending sideways, in the horizon*; as also ▾ سَحَابٌ عَانٌّ: (TA:) *such as retain the water*: (K:) one whereof is termed ▾ عَنَانَةٌ, (S, Msb, K,) and ▾ عَانَّةٌ. (S.) — And عَنَانُ السَّمَآءِ, (Mgh, MF, TA,) in the K said to be ▾ عِنَان, with kesr, but the former is the right, (MF, TA,) *The lofty region of the sky*: (Mgh:) or *what appears, of the sky, to one looking at it*. (K. [See also أَعْنَانٌ.]) — And عَنَانُ الدَّارِ, likewise with fet-h, accord. to the K ▾ عِنَان, with kesr, which is wrong, (TA,) *The side of the house*, (K, TA,) *that appears to one*. (TA.)

عِنَانٌ: see عَنَنٌ, in two places. — Also an inf. n. of 3 [q. v.]. (TA.) = And *A certain appertenance of a horse* or *the like*; (S, Msb;) [i. e. the *rein*;] the *strap of the bridle, by means of which the horse, or similar beast, is withheld*: (K:) [said to be] so called because it lies over against the mouth, not entering into it, (Msb,) or because its two straps lie over against the two sides of the neck of the beast, on the right and left: (TA:) pl. أَعِنَّةٌ (S, Msb, K) and عُنُنٌ, (K,) or, accord. to Sb, the former only. (TA.) [Sometimes it may be rendered The *bridle*; as in the first of the following phrases.] ثَنَّيْتُ عَلَى الفَرَسِ عِنَانَهُ *I put upon the horse his bridle*. (TA.) فَرَسٌ قَصِيرُ العِنَانِ [*A horse short in the rein*] implies discommendation, as denoting shortness of the neck: [but] هُوَ قَصِيرُ العِنَانِ [said of a man] means قَلِيلُ الخَيْرِ [i. e. † *He is one possessing little*, or *no, good*; or *few*, or *no, good things*; or *little*, or *no, goodness*]: and إِنَّهُ لَطَوِيلُ العِنَانِ [lit. *Verily he is one whose rein is long*] means, † *an exalted person*; *of great chiefdom*, or *eminence*. (TA.) رَجُلٌ طَرْفُ العِنَانِ (S,* K, TA, TK, in one of my copies of the S طَرِفٌ, and in the other طرف, and in copies of the K طَرْفٌ, [but correctly طَرِفٌ, q. v., like كَتِفٌ, as is said in the TK,]) means ‡ *A man light*, or *active*. (S, K, TA.) فُلَانٌ أَبِىُّ العِنَانِ † *Such a one is one who refuses the rein*. (TA.) ذُو العِنَانِ applied to the horse means † *The tractable*, or *submissive*. (TA.) And ذَلَّ عِنَانُ فُلَانٍ † *Such a one became submissive*. (TA.) ابغ مِنْ عِنَانِهِ [in which the first word is written in my original thus, but it has been altered by the copyist, and I doubt not that it is correctly أَرْخِ, the phrase, reading thus, being well known, i. e. *Slacken thou his rein*,] means † *ease thou him*, or *relieve him*. (TA.) اِثْنِ عَلَىَّ عِنَانَهُ means *Turn thou back* [or *bend thou*] *towards me his rein*. (TA.) جَآءَ ثَانِيًا فِى عِنَانِهِ [thus in my original, but correctly مِنْ عنانه, as in the S in art. ثنى, i. e. *He came bending* a part *of his rein*, turning from his course,] means † *he* [*came having*] *accomplished the object of his want*. (TA.) مَلَأَ عِنَانَ دَابَّتِهِ † *He made*, or *urged*, *his beast to run vehemently*. (TA.) And [hence, app.,] اِمْتَلَأَ عِنَانُهُ † *The utmost of his power*, or *ability*, *was accomplished*. (TA.) هُمَا يَجْرِيَانِ فِى عِنَانٍ † *They two are equal* in excellence or otherwise. (TA.) — Also † *A heat*; or *single run to a goal*, or *limit*: one says, جَرَى الفَرَسُ عِنَانًا † *The horse ran a heat*: and كَبَا فِى عِنَانِهِ † *He stumbled in his heat*. (TA.) See also an ex., in a verse of Et-Tirimmáh, voce عَنَّ, in the middle of the paragraph. And ▾ عَنَنٌ signifies the same, i. e. *A heat* of a beast: and also the *beginning of speech*: whence the prov.,

مُعْتَرِضٌ لِعَنَنٍ لَمْ يَعْنِهِ

meaning † *Addressing himself to that which is not of his business* (مَا لَيْسَ مِنْ شَأْنِهِ). (Meyd.) — And *A long rope* or *cord*. (TA.) — And العِنَانُ signifies حَبْلُ المَتْنِ [*The cord of the portion of the back along which extends the spine*; app. meaning *the spinal cord*, also called *medulla spinalis*, considered as a single cord]: (K:) [but this consists of two lateral cords, connected together: and therefore, app., it is said that] عِنَانَا المَتْنِ signifies حَبْلَاهُ [*the two cords of the* مَتْن]. (S.) = شِرْكَةُ العِنَانِ is *The copartnership of two persons in one particular thing*, (S, Mgh, Msb, K,) *exclusive of the rest of the articles of property of either*: (S, Msb,* K:) as though a thing presented itself to them (عَنَّ لَهُمَا, S, Mgh, Msb) and they bought it (S) and they then became copartners in it: (S, Mgh, Msb:) so says ISk: (Mgh:) or it is from the عِنَان of the horse, because each assigns to his companion the عنان of the free management of part of the property: (Mgh, Msb:) or because it is allowable for them to differ, like as does the عنان in the hand of the rider when pulled and when slackened: (Mgh:) or, accord. to As, it is *the case in which each of the two copartners produces deenárs or dirhems, which they mix together, and each gives permission to the other to traffic therewith*: and the lawyers differ not in respect of its being lawful; if they gain upon the two sums, the gain being between them; and if they lose, the loss being on the head of each of them [equally]: the partnership of two persons in everything that is in their possession is called شِرْكَةُ المُفَاوَضَةِ [q. v.]: (TA:) or it is *the case of one's competing with a man in the making of a purchase, and saying to him, "Make me to be a partner with thee;" this being before he* [the purchaser] *becomes entitled to* الغَلَق, or الغَلْق, or العلق, or العَلَق: (K: [the last word in this explanation, thus written in four different ways in different copies of the K, following the words قَبْلَ أَنْ يَسْتَوْجِبَ, I think to be most probably الغَلَق, and to mean *irredeemability* by the seller, from غَلِقَ الرَّهْنُ:]) or it is *the case of two persons' being equal in partnership*, (Z, Msb, K, TA,) *in respect of what they contribute of gold or silver*; and is from the عِنَان of the beast; (TA;) because the عنان of the beast consists of two equal single pieces: (Z, Msb, K, TA:) or it is from العِنَان as syn. with ▾ المُعَانَّة, meaning المُعَارَضَة; (Msb, TA;) because each of them does like as does the other in respect of his property [that he supplies] and in selling and buying. (TA.) See an ex. in a verse cited in art. شرك, conj. 3. — See also عَنَانٌ, in two places.

عَنُونٌ and ▾ عَانٌّ One *who presents*, or *opposes, himself, with meddling*, or *impertinent, speech*; *with speech respecting that which does not concern him*: pl. [of the former agreeably with analogy] عُنُنٌ. (TA.) — And the former, A beast (دَابَّة) *that precedes in journeying*, or *progress*; (S, K, TA;) *that vies with the* [*other*] *beasts in journeying*, or *progress, and precedes them*; and applied to a wild ass in this sense. (TA.)

عَنِينٌ One *unable to retain the wind of his belly*. (K.) — See also عِنِّينٌ.

عَنَانَةٌ: see عَنَانٌ: = and see also عُنَّةٌ, former half, in two places.

عِنِينَةٌ: see عُنَّةٌ, former half.

عَنَانَاكَ means *The utmost of thy power*, or *ability*, or *of thy case*: (S, K:) so in the saying, عَنَانَاكَ أَنْ تَفْعَلَ كَذَا [*The utmost of thy power*, &c., is, or *will be, thy doing such a thing*]: (S:) as though from ▾ المُعَانَّة; (S, TA;) the case being that thou desirest to do a thing, and an obstacle intervenes in the way to it, preventing thee and withholding thee from it: (TA:) but it is disputed whether it be correctly thus, or غُنَامَاكَ. (IB, TA.)

هُوَ عَنَّانٌ عَلَى آنُفِ القَوْمِ *He is wont to precede*, or *outstrip, the people*, or *party*. (TA.) — And هُوَ عَنَّانٌ عَنِ الخَيْرِ *He is* [*one who holds back from doing good*, or] *slow*, or *tardy, to do good*. (K.)

العَنُونُ, of the measure فَعُول, is an intensive

epithet applied to the present world (الدُّنْيَا) [as meaning *The offerer of much opposition*]; because it opposes itself to mankind. (TA.)

عِنِّينٌ, (Ṣ, Mgh, Mṣb,* Ḳ, TA,) of the measure فِعِّيلٌ in the sense of the measure مَفْعُولٌ, (Ṣ,) and ▼عِنِينٌ, [thus written in two places in the TA, and written without teshdeed in my copy of the Mṣb, but in the latter case app. from carelessness of the copyist, for otherwise the well-known form عِنِّينٌ is not there mentioned,] of which (i. e. of عِنِينٌ) عُنُنٌ is pl., [which seems to show that عِنِينٌ is not a mistranscription for عِنِّينٌ, for فُعُلٌ is a measure of a pl. of many epithets of the measure فَعِيلٌ, as جَدِيدٌ and نَذِيرٌ &c., but not, to my knowledge, of any word of the measure فِعِّيلٌ,] (TA,) A man *incapable of going in to women;* (Mgh, Mṣb;) one *who does not go in to women by reason of impotence:* (Ḳ:) or, as some say, one *who has connection with her who is not a virgin, but not with the virgin:* (TA:) or a man *who is not desirous of women:* (Ṣ, Ḳ:) and ▼مَعْنُونٌ and ▼مُعَنٌّ (Mṣb, TA) and ▼مُعَنَّنٌ (TA) signify the same. (Mṣb, TA.) And عِنِّينَةٌ signifies A woman *not desirous of men:* (Ṣ, Mṣb,* TA:) but there is disagreement in respect of the application of the epithet to a woman. (TA.)

عِنِّينَةٌ, as a subst.: see عُنَّةٌ, former half, in two places.

عُنْوَانٌ and عِنْوَانٌ (Ṣ, Mṣb, Ḳ) and ▼عُنْيَانٌ and عِنْيَانٌ, (Ṣ, Ḳ,) the first of which is the most chaste, (Ṣ,) originally عُنَّانٌ, (Ḳ,) of a book, or writing, (Ṣ, Mṣb,) The *superscription*, or *title*, thereof: (TḲ:) what these words denote is thus called because it occurs (يَعِنُّ, Ḳ, TA, i. e. يَعْرِضُ, TA) in a bordering part thereof: (Ḳ, TA:) and they also signify [sometimes, as indicating the nature of the contents,] the *preface* of a book, or writing. (TḲ.) And *Anything that serves as an indication* of another thing is called its عُنْوَان. (Mṣb, Ḳ.) One says, الظَّاهِرُ عُنْوَانُ البَاطِنِ, meaning *The outward* state of the man *is the indication of the inward* state. (TḲ.) And one says of a man who speaks obliquely, not plainly, جَعَلَ كَذَا عُنْوَانًا لِحَاجَتِهِ *He made such a thing to be an indication of his want.* (TA.) [See also art. عنو.]

عُنْيَانٌ and عِنْيَانٌ: see the next preceding paragraph.

عِنِّينِيَّةٌ: see عُنَّةٌ, former half.

عَانٌّ and عَانَّةٌ: see عَنَانٌ. — And for the former, see also عَنُونٌ. — Also, the former, *A long mountain* (جَبَلٌ), (Ḳ, TA, in some copies of the Ḳ حَبْلٌ [i. e. *rope*],) *that presents itself in the direction in which one is going, and interrupts his way.* (TA.)

أَعْنَانٌ The *sides, quarters, tracts,* or *regions,* of anything: (Yoo, TA:) this is the proper signification: (TA:) [hence,] أَعْنَانُ السَّمَآءِ [in one of my copies of the Ṣ السَّحَابِ, but altered from السَّمَآءِ,] means *The sides, quarters, tracts,* or *regions, of the sky:* (Ḳ:) or *the surfaces thereof,* and *what present themselves to view of the sides, quarters, tracts,* or *regions, thereof;* as though pl. of ▼عَنَنٌ, (Ṣ, TA,) or of ▼عَنٌّ: (TA:) the vulgar say عَنَانُ السَّمَآءِ. (Ṣ, TA.) — And [it is said that] أَعْنَانُ الشَّيَاطِينِ means *The natural dispositions of the devils.* (Ḳ.) It is said of camels, in a trad., خُلِقَتْ مِنْ أَعْنَانِ الشَّيَاطِينِ [as though meaning *They are created of the natural dispositions of the devils*]: and in another trad., أَعْنَانُ الشَّيَاطِينِ occurs as said [app. by Moḥammad] in answer to a question respecting camels: [but] accord. to IAth, the meaning seems to be, that, by reason of their many evil affections, they are as though they were from the tracts of the devil in respect of their natural dispositions. (TA.)

تَعْنِينَةٌ: see عُنَّةٌ, former half.

مُعَنٌّ: see عِنِّينٌ.

مِعَنٌّ One *who enters into that which does not concern him, and interferes in everything;* (Ḳ;) i. q. عِرِّيضٌ, (Ṣ,) or عِرِّيضٌ مِتْيَحٌ: (TA: [see these two words:]) fem. with ة. (Ṣ, Ḳ.) — And *An orator,* or *a preacher;* syn. خَطِيبٌ: (Ṣ, Ḳ:) or *an eloquent* خطيب. (TA.) = See also the next paragraph.

مُعَنَّنٌ: see عِنِّينٌ: — and see also مُعَنًّى, in art. عنو. = مُعَنَّنَةُ الخَلْقِ † A girl, or young woman, *compact in make;* (Ḳ, TA;) [*as though*] *compactly twisted like the* عِنَان [or *rein*]: (A, TA:) and ▼مُعَنَّةٌ † a woman *compact in make, not flabby in the belly.* (TA.) = See also عُنَّةٌ, near the middle.

مُعَنًّى: see عُنَّةٌ, near the middle.

مَعْنُونٌ [pass. part. n. of 1, q. v. = And] i. q. عِنِّينٌ; q. v. (Mṣb, TA.) — And *Possessed;* or *mad,* or *insane.* (Ḳ, TA.)

عنب

2. عَنَّبَ, (O, Ḳ,) inf. n. تَعْنِيبٌ, (Ḳ,) said of a grape-vine, [meaning *It produced grapes,*] (O, Ḳ,) is from العِنَبُ. (O.)

عِنَبٌ and ▼عِنَبَآءُ both signify the same, (Ṣ, O, Ḳ,) the latter said by Kr to be the only word of its measure except سِيَرَآءُ, but Kh mentions also خِيَلَآءُ, and Ibn-Ḳuteybeh adds to these حِوَلَآءُ, (TA,) [whence it seems to be, accord. to analogy, عِنَبَآءُ, imperfectly decl., with the fem. ء, but in a verse cited by F, and quoted in the O and TA, it is treated as masc., and in the TA it is treated as masc. in prose, and if so it is عِنَبَآءٌ, though it may be thus only by poetic license, and improperly in prose,] *Grapes,* the *fruit of the* كَرْم; (TA;) thus called only *while fresh;* when dry, called زَبِيب: (Mṣb:) عِنَبَةٌ signifies *a single berry thereof* [i. e. *a grape*]; (Ṣ, O, Mṣb, Ḳ;*) and is of a form generally belonging to a pl., rarely to a sing.: (Ṣ, O:) the pl. is أَعْنَابٌ, (Ṣ, O, Mṣb,) used in speaking of many; and the pl. of pauc. [i. e. pl. of عِنَبَةٌ] is عِنَبَاتٌ. (Ṣ, O.) — عِنَبٌ also signifies † The *grape-vine.* (MF [as from the Ḳ, in which I do not find it: but it is used in this sense in the Ḳur-án; pl. أَعْنَابٌ, expl. as meaning كُرُوم in xviii. 31 by Bḍ].) — And † *Wine:* (Ḳ:) so says AḤn, asserting it to be of the dial. of El-Yemen: like as خَمْرٌ signifies "grapes" in certain of the dials. [of El-Yemen: see خَمْرٌ]. (TA.) — [عِنَبُ الذِّئْبِ, and عِنَبُ الثَّعْلَبِ: see ثَعْلَبٌ; and see also عِنَبٌ.]

عِنَبَةٌ n. un. of عِنَبٌ [q. v.]. — Also *A small pustule that breaks forth in a human being,* (Ṣ, O, Ḳ, TA,) *emitting blood;* accord. to Az, *it swells, and fills* [*with blood* or *humour*], *and gives pain; and it attacks a human being in the eye and in the fauces.* (TA.)

عِنَبَآءُ: see عِنَبٌ.

[عِنَبِيٌّ *Of,* or *relating to, grapes.*]

عَنَبَانٌ, applied to a gazelle, (Ḳ,) to a male gazelle, (Ṣ, O,) *Brisk, lively,* or *sprightly:* (Ṣ, O, Ḳ:) having no corresponding verb: (Ṣ:) and, (Ḳ,) as some say, (TA,) so applied, *heavy,* or *sluggish:* thus having two contr. meanings: or one *advanced in age:* (Ḳ:) or, as some say, *a male gazelle:* pl. عُنْبَانٌ. (TA.) And A mountain-goat *long in the horn:* [in this sense also] having no corresponding verb. (O.) It is an epithet of a measure regularly belonging to inf. ns. (MF.)

عُنْبُبٌ, (O, and so accord. to copies of the Ḳ,) or عُنْبَبٌ, (accord. to some copies of the Ḳ,) The *foremost portion* of a torrent, (O, Ḳ,) and of a company of men. (O.) — And *Abundance of water.* (TA.) — [And accord. to Freytag, *A certain plant.*]

عُنَابٌ *Large in the nose;* (Ṣ, O, Ḳ;) applied to a man; (TA;) as also ▼أَعْنَبُ, (Ḳ,) or أَعْنَبُ الأَنْفِ: (O:) and it [app. عُنَاب] is also expl. as meaning *a big, ugly nose.* (TA.) — And i. q. عَفَلٌ: (Ṣ, O, Ḳ:) or i. q. بَظْرٌ: (Ḳ:) [see these two words:] or the *portion that is cut off of the* بظر. (TA.) — And *A small, black mountain:* (Lth, O, Ḳ:) or *a mountain small in circumference, black, and erect:* (TA:) and *a high, round mountain:* (Ḳ:) or *a high, isolated, sharp-headed hill, red,* and *black,* and *of any colour,* but *generally of a dusky yellowish hue, giving growth to nothing, and round:* (Sh, O:) pl. عُنُبٌ. (TA.)

عَنَّابٌ *A vender of* عِنَب [or *grapes*]. (O, Ḳ.)

عُنَّابٌ *A certain fruit* [and *tree*], (Ḳ,) *well known;* (Ṣ, O, Ḳ;) [the *jujube fruit* and *tree: rhamnus zizyphus* of Linn.;] called in Pers. سِنْجِد, or سِنْجِد جِيلَانِى, (MA,) or سنجد جيلان: (PṢ:) n. un. with ة. (Ṣ, O.) And, (Ḳ,) sometimes, (TA,) accord. to IDrd, (O,) The *fruit of the* أَرَاك [q. v.]. (O, Ḳ.) And The [*fruit, or tree, called*] غُبَيْرَآءُ [q. v.]. (TA.) Also, [as being likened to jujubes, because dyed red,] † The *fingers*, or *ends of the fingers*, of a woman. (A, voce تُفَّاحٌ, q. v.)

عُنَّابِىٌّ [*Of the colour of the* عُنَّاب, or *jujube*]. (TA, voce سِخْتِيَانٌ, q. v.) صَبَغَ الكِيسَ عُنَّابِى [lit. *He dyed the purse jujube-colour*] means *he became bankrupt*: but this, as Esh-Shiháb says, is a phrase of the Muwelleds [or rather of the vulgar, unless ending a verse, in which case it is allowable to say عُنَّابِى for عُنَّابِيًّا, as in a verse cited in the TA]. (MF, TA.)

عَانِبٌ A man *possessing* عِنَب [or *grapes*]: like لَابِنٌ and تَامِرٌ, (O, TA,) which mean "possessing milk" and "possessing dates." (TA.)

أَعْنَبُ: see عُنَّابٌ.

مُعْنَبٌ *Tall*; (O, Ḳ;) an epithet applied to a man. (O.) — And *Thick*; an epithet applied to tar. (O.)

عنبر

عَنْبَرٌ [*Ambergris*;] *a certain odoriferous substance*, (Ṣ, O, Mṣb, Ḳ,) *well known*; (O, Mṣb;) *an excrement found in the belly of a certain great fish*, [*the spermaceti-whale*,] *which is called by the same name*; (Towsheeḥ, TA;) or *an excrement of a certain marine beast*; (Ḳ;) or, accord. to Ks, *a vegetable* [*substance found*] *in the bottom of the sea and driven by the waves to the shores thereof, whence it is taken*; (O;) or, (O, Ḳ,) as the physicians say, (O,) *it issues from a source in the sea*; (O,* Ḳ;) [and there are other opinions respecting its origin, mentioned in the TA; but these I do not add, as it is well known to be an excrement of the spermaceti-whale;] *the best kind is the white*, and *the whitish*; *next, the blue* [or *gray*]; *and the worst, the black*: (TA:) the word is masc. and fem., (AA, IAmb, O, Mṣb,) like مِسْكٌ: (IAmb, TA voce ذَكِىٌّ:) MF says that most hold the ن to be augmentative, the measure being فَنْعَل, as it is said to be in the Mṣb. (TA.) — [As mentioned above, it signifies also The *spermaceti-whale*;] *a certain great fish*; (Mṣb in art. عبر;) *a certain marine fish*, (Az, O, Ḳ,) *the length of which reaches to fifty cubits, called in Pers.* بَالَه [app. a mistranscription for بَالٌ: see وَالٌ]: (Az, TA:) *shields are made of its skin*; (Mgh, O, TA;) *and the people of Juddeh have sandals*, or *shoes*, *made thereof*. (O, TA.) — And hence, (O,) *A shield* (Ṣ, O, Ḳ) *made of the skin of the fish above-mentioned*: (O, Ḳ:) and some say, *coats of defence* (دُرُوع). (O.) = Also *Saffron*. (Ḳ.) — And (as some say, TA) [The *plant called*] وَرْس. (Ḳ.) — [Accord. to Forskål (Flora Aegypt. Arab. p. lxiv.) now applied to *Gomphrena globosa*.] = See also the next paragraph, in two places.

عَنْبَرَةُ قَوْمٍ *The purity of the pedigree of a people*. (Ibn-'Abbád, O, Ḳ.) Hence the vulgar say of a thing that is pure, هٰذَا عَنْبَرٌ ♦. (TA.) — عَنْبَرَةُ القِدْرِ *The onion*: (Ḳ:) because it makes [the contents of] the قِدْر to become savoury. (TA.) — عَنْبَرَةُ الشِّتَآءِ, (Ks, O, Ḳ, TA,) or, accord. to Kr, it is عَنْبَرُ ♦ الشِّتَآءِ, (TA,) *The vehemence*, or *rigour*, *of winter*. (Ks, Kr, O, Ḳ.)

عَنْبَرِىٌّ *Of*, or *belonging to*, بَنُو العَنْبَرِ, (O, Ḳ,) or بَلْعَنْبَرِ, (O,) a tribe of تَمِيم, (O,) who were the most skilful people as guides: (O, Ḳ:) hence the proverbial saying, أَنْتَ عَنْبَرِىٌّ بِهٰذَا البَلَدِ [*Thou art an 'Amberee in this country*, or *district*]. (O, Ḳ.*)

عنبس

عَنْبَسٌ The *lion*; (O, Ḳ;) as also ♦ عُنَابِسٌ: (Ḳ: but in the O it is said, when you designate the lion, you say عَنْبَسٌ and عَنَابِسُ: [as though, by the latter, the pl. were meant: but it is probably a mistranscription for عُنَابِسٌ:]) or the *lion from whom other lions flee*: (TA in art. عبس:) when you particularize him by a [proper] name, you say ♦ عَنْبَسَةُ, [i. e. *The lion*,] making it imperfectly decl.; like as you say أُسَامَةُ. (O, Ḳ.) It is mentioned by Lth and Az among quadriliteral-radical words: Hishám says, I know not whether it be a subst. or an epithet: and A'Obeyd says, it is from العُبُوسُ; and if so, it is of the measure فَنْعَل: (O:) but 'Ikrimeh is related to have said that the lion is called ♦ عَنْبَسَةُ in the Abyssinian language. (TA voce قَسْوَرَةٌ.)

عَنْبَسَةُ : } see above; the former in two places.
عُنَابِسٌ : }

عنت

1. عَنِتَ, [aor. ـَ,] inf. n. عَنَتٌ, *He fell into a difficult, hard*, or *distressing, case*: (Ṣ, A,* O, TA:) or عَنَتٌ signifies the *meeting with difficulty, hardship*, or *distress*. (Ḳ.) [This is held by some to be the primary signification: see عَنَتٌ below; by the explanations of which it seems to be indicated that the verb has several significations that are not expressly assigned to it in the lexicons.] عَزِيزٌ عَلَيْهِ مَا عَنِتُّمْ, in the Ḳur [ix. last verse but one], means, accord. to Az [and most of the expositors], *Grievous unto him is your experiencing difficulty*, or *hardship*, or *distress*: or, as some say, the meaning is مَا أَعْنَتَكُمْ ♦, i. e., *what hath brought you into difficulty*, or *hardship*, or *distress*. (TA. [In the Ṣ and O, it seems to be indicated by the context that مَا عَنِتُّمْ means *your having sinned*.]) — عَنِتَتِ الدَّابَّةُ *The beast limped*, or *halted, in consequence of hard*, or *rough, treatment, such as it could not bear*. (TA.) It is said in a trad., أَنْعَلَ دَابَّتَهُ فَعَنِتَتْ *He shod his beast and it became lame*: thus as some relate it; as others relate it, فَعَنَتَتْ; but the former relation is preferred by Ḳt. (TA.) — عَنِتَتْ said of a bone, (Az, A, Ḳ, TA,) and عَنَتَتْ said of an arm or a leg, (Az, TA,) [aor. ـَ,] inf. n. عَنَتٌ, (TA,) *It broke* (Az, A, Ḳ, TA) *after its having been set and united*: (A, Ḳ:) [this is said in the Ksh and by Bḍ, in iv. 30, to be the primary signification:] and the former, said of a bone, *it became weak, and broke*. (Ḳ,* TA.) — عَنِتَ, (Ṣ, O, Mṣb, TA,) aor. ـَ, (Mṣb,) inf. n. عَنَتٌ, (Ṣ,* O,* Mṣb, Ḳ,* TA,) *He committed a sin, a crime*, or *an act of disobedience deserving punishment*: (Ṣ, O, Ḳ,* TA:*) or *he committed sins, crimes*, or *acts of disobedience deserving punishment*: (Ḳ,* TA:) or *he did wrong* [*intentionally* or *unintentionally*]. (Mṣb.) [And particularly *He committed fornication*, or *adultery*: see عَنَتٌ below.]

2. عَنَّتَهُ, inf. n. تَعْنِيتٌ, *He treated him with hardness, severity*, or *rigour, and constrained him to do that which was difficult to him to perform*; (IAmb, O, Ḳ, TA;) as also ♦ أَعْنَتَهُ: and afterwards it became applied to signify *he destroyed him*; or *caused him to perish*: (IAmb, TA:) [and ♦ اعنته has both of these significations: for it is said that] لَوْ شَآءَ ٱللّٰهُ لَأَعْنَتَكُمْ, in the Ḳur [ii. 219], means *If God had willed, He would assuredly have treated you with hardness*, &c., *and constrained you to do that which would be difficult to you to perform*: or it may mean, *would have destroyed you*: or, accord. to IAṭr, إِعْنَاتٌ signifies the *requiring to do that which is not in one's power*. (TA.) — See also 5.

4. اعنتهُ, (inf. n. إِعْنَاتٌ, Mgh,) *He caused him to fall into difficulty, hardship*, or *distress*; (Ṣ, Mgh, O, Mṣb, Ḳ, TA;) *into that which was difficult, hard*, or *distressing, to him to bear*. (Mgh, Mṣb.) See also 1, and 2. — *He* (the rider) *treated him* (i. e. a beast) *with hardness*, or *roughness, such as the latter could not bear, and so caused him to limp*, or *halt*. (TA.) — *He* (a physician) *treated him* (i. e. a sick man) *roughly*, or *without gentleness, and so harmed*, or *injured, him*. (A, O.*) — *He*, or *it, broke it* (i. e. a bone) *after it had been set and united*: (Az, Ṣ, A, O, Ḳ, TA:) or *he* (a bone-setter) *treated it* (i. e. a broken bone) *roughly*, or *ungently, so that the fracture became worse*. (TA.)

5. تعنّتهُ: see 2. Accord. to AHeyth, (TA,) *He brought upon him annoyance, molestation, harm*, or *hurt*: (Mṣb, TA:) or *he sought to occasion him difficulty, hardship*, or *distress*. (Mgh.) And hence, (Mgh,) *He asked him respecting a thing, desiring by doing so to involve him in confusion*, or *doubt*; (A, Mgh, TA;) *as when one says to a witness*, "*Where was this, and when was it, and what garment was upon him when thou tookest upon thyself to bear witness?*" and يَتَعَنَّتُ عَلَى الشُّهُودِ and يُعَنِّتُ ♦ الشُّهُودَ are also mentioned; but these require consideration. (Mgh.)

R. Q. 1. عَنْتَتَ, said of the horn of the عَتُود [or goat a year old], *It rose*, or *rose high*. (O, Ḳ.) — عنتت عَنْهُ *He turned away from, avoided*, or *shunned, him*, or *it*. (O, Ḳ.)

عَنَتٌ [inf. n. of 1, q. v.: and also expl. as having the following meanings:] *Difficulty, hardship*, or *distress*: (A, IAth, Mgh, Mṣb, TA:) this is [said to be] the primary signification: (Jel in iv. 30:) or *severe difficulty*, or *hardship*, or *distress*: (Zj,

TA:) or the *coming of difficulty* or *hardship* or *distress* upon a man. (Ḳ.) — *A state of perdition* or *destruction.* (A, IAth, Ḳ, TA.) — *A bad, an evil, or a corrupt, state:* or *bad, evil,* or *corrupt, conduct* or *doing:* syn. فَسَادٌ [which has both of these meanings; and may here have the former meaning as nearly agreeing with what precedes it, or the latter meaning as nearly agreeing with what follows it]. (A, IAth, Ḳ, TA.) — *A sin, a crime,* on *an act of disobedience deserving punishment;* (AHeyth, Ṣ, A, IAth, O, Ḳ, TA;) and so ↓ مَعْنَتَةٌ. (A.) — *A wrong action* [*intentional* or *unintentional*]; *an error; a mistake.* (IAth, Mṣb,* TA.) — *Fornication,* or *adultery:* (Ṣ, IAth, Mgh, O, Mṣb, Ḳ, TA:) but this is a conventional explanation of the lecturers of the colleges. (Mgh.) So in the Ḳur [iv. 30], where it is said, ذٰلِكَ لِمَنْ خَشِىَ ٱلْعَنَتَ مِنْكُمْ [*That is for him, among you, who fears the commission of fornication*]: (Ṣ, O, Mṣb, TA: [and the like is said in the Mgh:]) this, says Az, was revealed in relation to him who might not have the means of taking to wife a free woman; therefore it was allowed to him to take to wife a slave: (Mṣb, TA:) or the meaning of العنت here is *perdition:* or *perdition in* [or *by means of*] *fornication.* (TA.) — Also *Wrongful, unjust, injurious,* or *tyrannical, conduct:* and *annoyance, molestation, harm,* or *hurt.* (AHeyth, TA.) And *Distressing, grievous,* or *afflicting, harm, injury, hurt,* or *mischief.* (TA.) — And accord. to the 'Ináyeh, *Contention;* or *contention for superiority in greatness:* and *persistence in opposition,* or *in vain contention.* (TA.)

عَنِتٌ A bone *broken after its having been set and united;* as also ↓ مُعْنِتٌ. (Ṣ, O, Ḳ.)

عَنُوتٌ A hill (أَكَمَةٌ) *difficult of ascent;* (O, Mṣb,* Ḳ;) as also ↓ عُنْتُوتٌ: (O, Ḳ:) or *high, and difficult of ascent.* (A.)

عُنْتُوتٌ: see what next precedes. — With the article ال, *A mountain,* (O,) or *tapering mountain,* (Ḳ,) *in the* صَحْرَآء [or *desert*]: (O, Ḳ:) or, accord. to the L, *a small mountain tapering into* [or *towards*] *the sky* (جُبَيْلٌ مُسْتَدِقٌّ فِى السَّمَآءِ): and it is said to be دون الحرة [app. دُونَ الحَرَّةِ; but there seems to be here an omission or a mistranscription; for of the various meanings that may be assigned to this phrase, none seems to be apposite: I incline to think that العُنْتُوتُ thus expl. is the proper name of a particular mountain]. (TA.) — عُنْتُوتٌ signifies also The *notch in a bow:* accord. to Az, (TA,) the عُنْتُوت of the bow is the *notch into which enters the* غَانَةٌ, i. e. the *ring at the head of the string.* (O, TA.) — And The *first,* or *beginning,* or *commencement,* of anything. (O, Ḳ.) — And *Dry* حَلِىٌّ, (O, and so in the CḲ, [in my MS. copy of the Ḳ حَلَى, and thus accord. to the TA, but this is evidently a mistake,]) which is a certain plant. (TA.)

عَانِتٌ an epithet applied to a woman, *i. q.* عَانِسٌ [q. v.]: (O, Ḳ:) said to be formed [from the latter] by substitution, or a dial. var., or a word mispronounced. (MF, TA.)

مُعْنِتٌ: see عَنِتٌ.

مَعْنَتَةٌ: see عَنَتٌ. [Its primary signification seems to be *A cause of difficulty, hardship,* or *distress;* &c.]

جَآءَنِى فُلَانٌ مُتَعَنِّتًا *Such a one came to me seeking* [*to cause*] *my fall into a wrong action,* or *an error.* (Ṣ, O, Ḳ.*)

عنج

1. عَنَجَ, aor. ـُ, inf. n. عَنْجٌ, *He drew,* or *pulled,* anything; *drew* it, or *pulled* it, *to him,* or *towards him.* (L.) — عَنَجَ رَأْسَ البَعِيرِ, aor. ـُ and ـِ, inf. n. as above, *He* (the rider) *pulled up,* or *drew up, the camel's head by means of the* [*halter,* or *cord, called*] خِطَام. (TA.) And عَنَجَ البَعِيرَ, aor. ـُ, (Ṣ, O,) inf. n. عَنْجٌ as above; (Ṣ, O, Ḳ;) and ↓ اعنجه, (O,) inf. n. إِعْنَاجٌ; (Ḳ;) *He trained,* or *broke, the camel in a certain manner;* (Ṣ, O;) i. e. *he* (the rider) *pulled,* or *drew, the camel's* خطام (Ṣ, O, Ḳ, TA) *towards his head,* (TA,) *and forced him back upon his hind legs,* (Ṣ, O, Ḳ, TA,) *so that, sometimes, the prominent part behind his ears clave to the upright piece of wood that rises from the fore part of the saddle:* (TA:) and عَنَجَ الجَمَلَ *He pulled the nose-rein of the camel to make him stop:* and عَنَجَ النَّاقَةَ *He reined up the she-camel* on an occasion of her stumbling. (TA, from trads.) — عَنَجَ الدَّلْوَ, (IAṣr, Ṣ, O, L,) aor. ـُ, (L,) inf. n. as above; (Ṣ, O;) and ↓ اعنجها; (IAṣr, O;) *He put,* or *attached, to the leathern bucket, an appertenance called* عِنَاج [q. v.]. (IAṣr, Ṣ, O, L.) — And hence, عَنَجْتُ البَكْرَ, aor. ـُ, inf. n. as above, *I tied the young camel's* [*halter,* or *cord, called*] خِطَام *to his arm, and made it short:* thus one does to a young camel only when he is trained, or broken. (TA.) — عَنَجَهُ also signifies, *He bent it,* or *inclined it;* and occurs in this sense in a trad. of 'Alee, in which the pronoun relates to a sail. (TA.) And one says, عَنَجَ نَعْلَهُ *He bent* [app. *upwards*] *the head* [or *fore part*] *of his sandal.* (Ibn-'Abbád, O.)

4: see 1, in two places. — [Hence,] اعنج signifies also إِسْتَوْثَقَ مِنْ أُمُورِهِ [i. e. † *He secured himself against damage from his affairs;* virtually meaning *he ordered,* or *disposed, his affairs in a firm, solid, sound,* or *good, manner,* agreeably with an explanation in the TḲ as *syn. with* أَحْكَمَهَا]: (O, Ḳ, TA:) and it alludes to the fulfilment of covenants. (TA.) — And اعنجت, said of a she-camel, means *She withheld herself* or *refrained* [*from going on*]. (TA.) — Also *He had a complaint* (Ḳ, TA) *of his* ↓ عِنَاج, i. e., (TA,) *of his* صُلْب [meaning *back-bone,* or *loins,*] (Ḳ, TA) *and his joints.* (TA.)

عَنْجٌ a subst. from عَنَجَ البَعِيرَ; (Ṣ, O, Ḳ;*) [*A certain mode of training,* or *breaking, a camel;* (see the verb;)] whence the prov., عَوْدٌ يُعَلَّمُ العَنْجَ (Ṣ, O, TA) *An old camel that is trained,* or *broken, and forced back upon his hind legs:* (TA:) [or *that is taught the mode of training termed* عَنْج:] applied to him who takes to learning a thing after he has become old. (O,* TA.) — Also *An old man;* a dial. var. of عَنَعٌ: (Ḳ:) or *a man* in the dial. of Hudheyl; (O, TA; [in the former عَنَجٌ, app. a mistranscription;]) so says Ibn-'Abbád; but correctly عَنْعٌ: (O:) Az says, I have not heard it with ع from any one to whose knowledge reference is made, and I know not what is the truth thereof. (TA.) — Also *A company of men.* (TA.)

عَنْجَةُ الهَوْدَجِ The عِضَادَة [or *post,* perhaps meaning *each of two side-posts,*] *at the door of the* [*women's camel-vehicle called*] هودج, (O, Ḳ, TA,) *by means of which the door is strengthened* (يُشَدُّ بِهَا البَابُ). (TA. [In the O, تَشُدُّ البَابَ; app. a mistranscription for تُشَدُّ الباب.])

عِنَاجٌ *A rope,* or *cord,* (Ṣ, A, O, Ḳ,) or *girth,* (Ṣ, O,) or *strap,* (TA,) *that is tied to the lower part of the large* [*leathern bucket called*] دَلْو, (Ṣ, O, Ḳ,) or *that is put beneath the* دلو, (A,) *and then tied to the cross-pieces of wood* (العَرَاقِى), (Ṣ, A, O, Ḳ,) or *to the loops,* (TA,) *so that it serves as an aid to the cross-pieces of wood and to the* [*thongs called*] وَذَم [*which bind those cross-pieces to the loops of the bucket*]; *for when these* [*thongs*] *break, it holds fast the* دلو: (Ṣ, O:) and *when the* دلو *is light,* (Ṣ, O, Ḳ,) *it is a string,* (Ṣ, O,) or *a light string,* (Ḳ,) *that is tied from one of the loops to one of the cross-pieces of wood* (العراقى): (Ṣ, O, Ḳ:) or, as some say, *a loop in the lower part of the bucket, inside it, which is tied by a cord or the like to the upper part of the* [*rope called*] كَرَب [q. v.], *so that if the rope* [meaning the كرب, not the main rope,] *break, it keeps the bucket from falling in the well:* this is when the bucket is light: pl. [of pauc.] أَعْنِجَةٌ and [of mult.] عُنُجٌ. (TA.) One says, لَا بُدَّ لِلدَّآءِ مِنْ عِلَاجٍ وَلِلدِّلَآءِ مِنْ عِنَاجٍ [*It is absolutely necessary for the disease to have medical treatment, and for the buckets to have an* عناج]. (A, TA.) — [Hence,] El-Ḥoṭei-ah says, (Ṣ, O, TA,) praising a people, or party, who concluded a covenant with their neighbour and faithfully kept it, (TA,)

قَوْمٌ إِذَا عَقَدُوا عَقْدًا لِجَارِهِمُ
شَدُّوا العِنَاجَ وَشَدُّوا فَوْقَهُ الكَرَبَا

† [*A people who, when they conclude a covenant with their neighbour,* (lit. *tie a knot to their neighbour,*) *tie the* عناج, *and tie above it the* كرب: i. e., make it doubly sure]. (Ṣ, O, TA.) — [Hence also,] قَوْلٌ لَا عِنَاجَ لَهُ ‡ *A saying that is uttered without consideration of its result.* (Ṣ, O, Ḳ.) — And عِنَاجُ الأَمْرِ ‡ *The support,* or *foundation, of the affair; that upon which the affair rests,* or *whereby it subsists.* (A, O, L, TA. [In the Ḳ,

وَالأَمْرُ وَمِلَاطُهُ is erroneously put for وَمِنَ الأَمْرِ مِلَاطُهُ; as is said in the TA.]) Thus in the saying, † لَا أَدْرِى لِأَمْرِكَ عِنَاجًا [*I know not any foundation to thine affair*]. (O.) And عِنَاجُ الأَمْرِ إِلَى أَبِى سُفْيَانَ, occurring in a trad., means † *The management of the affair pertained to Aboo-Sufyán*; he being to his companions like the عناج that bears the weight of the bucket. (TA.) — عِنَاجٌ signifies also *A thing with which one draws*, or *pulls*. (TA.) — And The *nose-rein* (زِمَام) of a she-camel; because she is drawn, or pulled, by means of it. (A, TA.) — See also 4. — Also *Pain of the* صُلْب [meaning *back-bone*, or *loins*,] (O, Ḳ) *and of the joints*. (O.)

عَنَاجٍ and عَنَاجِى: see عُنْجُوجٌ.

أَعْلِ عَنِّجْ occurs in a trad. as a saying of Aboo-Jahl to Ibn-Mes'ood, when the latter put his foot upon the back of the former's neck; meaning أَعْلِ عَنِّى [*Rise thou from me*]; the ى being changed into ج. (TA. [See art. ج.])

عُنْجُجٌ, (O, Ḳ,) or, accord. to AḤn, عَنْجَجٌ, (O,) The ضَيْمُرَان [q. v.], (O, Ḳ,) *a species of sweet-smelling plants*; (O, TA;) said to be the شاه سفرم [or شَاهِسْفَرَم]: not heard by Aṣ on any other authority than that of Lth. (TA.)

عُنْجُوجٌ sing. of عَنَاجِيجُ, (A'Obeyd, Ṣ, O,) which signifies *Fleet*, or *swift, and excellent, horses* (A'Obeyd, Ṣ, O, Ḳ) and *camels*; (Ḳ;) sometimes applied to the latter: (Lth, TA:) or *horses that excite the admiration and approval of the beholder*: and ▼ عَنَاجٍ occurs in a verse cited by IAạr, as some relate it; and ▼ عَنَاجِى as others relate it; the former for عَنَاجِج, and the latter for عَنَاجِيج: (TA:) or *long-necked horses* (O, TA) and *camels*: (TA:) or *tall*, or *long, horses*. (Ḥam p. 445.) [See an ex. in a verse cited voce رَبٌّ.] — اِسْتَقَامَ عُنْجُوجُ القَوْمِ means *The way* or *course* (سَنَن) [*of the people*, or *party, was*, or *became, direct*, or *undeviating*]. (O.) — And عَنَاجِيجُ الشَّبَابِ signifies *The first part of youth*. (O, Ḳ.)

عَنْجَنْجٌ (in the Ḳ erroneously written عَنْجَجٌ, TA) *Great*, or *large*. (Ṣ, O, L, TA.)

مُعَنِّجٌ A man (O) *who addresses, applies*, or *directs, himself*, or *his regard*, or *attention*, or *mind, to affairs*. (O, TA.)

عنجف

عَنْجَفٌ, or عُنْجُفٌ, and عُنْجُوفٌ: see art. عجف.

عند

1. عَنَدَ عَنْهُ, aor. ـِ (Ṣ, O, L, Mṣb, Ḳ) and ـُ, (Fr, O, L,) inf. n. عُنُودٌ; (Ṣ, O, L, Mṣb, Ḳ;) and عَنِدَ, aor. ـَ, (L, Ḳ,) inf. n. عَنَدٌ; (L, TA;) and عَنُدَ, aor. ـُ; (Ḳ;) *He declined*, or *deviated, from it*, (Ṣ, O, L, Mṣb, Ḳ,) namely, the road, (Ṣ, O, L, Ḳ,) or the right course, (Mṣb,) and what was right or just or due, and from a thing; (L;) *he went aside from it*: (TA:) and *he went*, or *retired, to a distance*, or *far away, from it*. (L.) And عَنَدَ عَنْ أَصْحَابِهِ, aor. ـِ, inf. n. عُنُودٌ, *He left*, or *quitted, his companions, and passed beyond them*: and *he left*, or *quitted, his companions in a journey, and took a road different from that which they followed*, or *remained*, or *fell, behind them*: (ISh, L:) and *he removed to a distance from his companions*; as when a man leaves his people in El-Ḥijáz and goes to El-Baṣrah. (L.) — عَنَدَتْ and عَنِدَتْ and عَنُدَتْ *She* (a camel) *pastured alone*, (Ḳ, TA,) *disdaining to pasture with the other camels, and sought the best of the herbage*. (TA.) — عَنَدَ, (Ṣ, A, O, Ḳ,) aor. ـُ, (Ṣ, A, O,) or ـِ, (Ḳ,) inf. n. عُنُودٌ (Ṣ, O, L) and عَنْدٌ; (L;) and عَنِدَ, aor. ـَ; and عَنُدَ, aor. ـُ; (Ḳ;) and ▼ عاند, inf. n. مُعَانَدَةٌ and عِنَادٌ; (L;) *He opposed and rejected what was true*, or *just, knowing it to be so*; (Ṣ, A, O, L, Ḳ;) *he acted obstinately, knowing a thing and rejecting it*, or *declining from it*; as did Aboo-Ṭálib, who knew and acknowledged the truth, but scorned to have it said of him that he followed the son of his brother. (L.) — And عَنَدَ, aor. ـِ, inf. n. عُنُودٌ and عَنْدٌ, *He* (a man) *overstepped*, or *transgressed, the proper bound*, or *limit*; *acted exorbitantly*, or *immoderately*; and especially *in disobedience*, or *rebellion*. (L.) — And [hence (see عَانِدٌ)] عَنَدَ العِرْقُ, (Ṣ, O, L, Mṣb, Ḳ, [in the CḲ, erroneously, العَرَقُ,]) aor. ـِ, (Ḳ,) or ـُ, (Mṣb,) or both, the latter mentioned by Fr, (O,) inf. n. عُنُودٌ; (Mṣb;) and عَنِدَ, aor. ـَ; and عَنُدَ, aor. ـُ; (Ḳ;) as also ▼ اعند; (O,* Ḳ;) ‡ *The vein flowed with blood, and did not cease to flow*: (Ṣ, O, L, Ḳ, TA:) or *flowed, and hardly ceased*: (L:) or *flowed copiously*. (Mṣb.) And عَنَدَتِ الطَّعْنَةُ, aor. ـُ and ـِ, † *The spear-wound*, or *stab, poured forth blood to a distance*. (L.) And ▼ اعند أَنْفُهُ † *His nose bled copiously*. (L.) And عَنَدَ الدَّمُ † *The blood flowed on one side*. (L.) See also 10.

3. عاند, inf. n. عِنَادٌ [and مُعَانَدَةٌ], *He acted with opposition, disobedience*, or *rebellion*. (Mṣb.) — See also 1. — عانده, (L,) inf. n. مُعَانَدَةٌ, (Ḳ,) *He separated himself from him*; (L,* Ḳ;) *he went*, or *retired, to a distance*, or *to a place apart, from him*. (L, Ḳ. [See also 1, first and second sentences.]) — And عانده, (T, Ṣ, O, L, Mṣb,) inf. n. مُعَانَدَةٌ (T, Ṣ, L, Mṣb, Ḳ) and عِنَادٌ, (T, Ṣ, L, Ḳ,) *He opposed him, disagreeing with him*, or *doing the contrary of what he* (the other) *did*; (T, Ṣ, O, L, Mṣb, Ḳ;) as also ▼ اعنده; (O, L, Ḳ;) syn. عَارَضَهُ; (Ṣ, O, Mṣb, all in explanation of the former; [but it should be observed that عارضه bears the signification expressed above and also that given in the sentence next following;]) or عَارَضَهُ بِالخِلَافِ; (O in explanation of the latter, and Mṣb in explanation of the former, as on the authority of Az [in the T], and Ḳ in explanation of both;) or خَالَفَهُ: (MA in explanation of the former:) [this is the sense in which the former is most commonly known: or as meaning *he contended with him in an altercation*; or *did so vehemently*, or *obstinately*: (see 6:)] the author of the T, however, says, the common people expl. يُعَانِدُهُ as meaning *he does the contrary of what he* [another] *does*; but this I know not [as occurring in the genuine language of the Arabs], nor do I admit it as of established authority. (TA.) — And, sometimes, *He imitated him, doing the like of what he* (the other) *did*; (T, L, Mṣb;) [and] so ▼ اعنده; (O, L, Ḳ;) thus having two contr. significations; (Ḳ;) syn. عَارَضَهُ [respecting which see the sentence next preceding]; (Ṣ, O, Mṣb, all in explanation of the former;) or عَارَضَهُ بِالوِفَاقِ; (O and Ḳ in explanation of the latter;) and بَارَاهُ; (T and TA in explanation of the former;) مُعَارَضَةٌ بِغَيْرِ عِنَادٍ sometimes signifying خِلَافٍ, as is said by Aṣ, who derives it from عَنَدَ الحُبَارَى, making عَنَدَ in this phrase a subst. from عاند الحُبَارَى فَرْخَهُ *The bustard imitated the actions of his young one in flying*, on the first occasion of its rising, as though he would teach it to fly: and عاند البَعِيرُ خِطَامَهُ means *The camel conformed to* [and perhaps it may also mean *resisted*] *the motion of his halter*. (L.) — عانده, (O,) inf. n. مُعَانَدَةٌ, (Ḳ,) also signifies *He kept*, or *clave, to him*, or *it*: (O, Ḳ:) the contr. of the first signification assigned to it above. (TA.) — And مُعَانَدَةٌ means also The *disputing with another without knowledge of the truth or falsity of what he himself says and also of what his opponent says*. (Kull p. 342.)

4. اعند, as intrans.: see 1, last quarter, in two places. — [Hence,] اعند فِى قَيْئِهِ ‡ *He vomited with successive discharges*, (Ṣ, O, L, Ḳ, TA,) *and copiously*; (TA;) and اعند القَىْءَ signifies the same. (L, TA.) — [اعند is also said by Freytag, as on the authority of the Deewán of the Hudhalees, to signify *He*, and *it*, (namely, a man, and blood,) *went away*.] — اعنده: see 3, in two places.

6. تعاندا *They two* [*opposed each other*: (see 3:) or] *contended in an altercation*; or *did so vehemently*, or *obstinately*. (L.)

10. استعند رَأْيَهُ *He was*, or *became, alone in his opinion, having none to share it with him*. (O.) — اِسْتَعْنَدَنِى مِنْ بَيْنِ القَوْمِ *He directed his course towards me*, or *sought me*, [*singling me out*] *from among the people*, or *party*. (O, Ḳ.*) — استعند said of a camel, and of a horse, *He gained the mastery over the nose-rein*, and *over the halter*, or *leading-rope*, (Ḳ, TA,) *and resisted being led*: (TA:) or استعند البَعِيرُ الصَّبِىَّ *the camel overcame the boy by gaining the mastery over the nose-rein, and dragged it*, or *him, along*: and in like manner, استعند الفَرَسُ الرَّسَنَ [*the horse gained the mastery over the halter*, or *leading-rope*]. (O.) — استعنده said of vomit, (A, O, Ḳ,*) and of blood, (A,) *It overcame him*: (O, Ḳ:*) or *came forth from him copiously*: (A:) and ▼ عَنَدَهُ signifies the same. (TA.) — استعند عَصَاهُ *He struck*, or *smote, with his staff among the people*.

(O, Ḳ.) And [in like manner] اِسْتَعْنَدَ ذَكَرُهُ (O, Ḳ) i. e. زَنَى بِهِ فِيهِمْ (O) or زَنَى فِى ٱلنَّاسِ. (Ḳ.) —— And اِسْتَعْنَدَ السِّقَآءَ *He doubled the mouth of the water-skin*, or *milk-skin, outwards*, or *inside-out*, (O, Ḳ,) or *he inclined the water-skin*, or *milk-skin*, (TA,) *and drank from its mouth*. (O, Ḳ, TA.)

عَنْدٌ : and عَنْدَ : } see the next paragraph.
عُنْدٌ : and عُنْدَ : }

عِنْدٌ and ▼ عَنْدٌ and ▼ عُنْدٌ, (O, Ḳ,) accord. to Ibn-'Abbád, (O,) *i. q.* نَاحِيَةٌ [app. as meaning The *vicinage*, or the *quarter, tract, region*, or *place*, of a person or thing]: (O, Ḳ:) whence the saying, هُوَ عِنْدَ فُلَانٍ الآنَ [*He is in the vicinage*, or *the quarter*, &c., *of such a one, now*]. (O.) [See also عَنْدٌ, which has a similar meaning.] —— عِنْدَ and ▼ عَنْدَ and ▼ عُنْدَ signify the same, (Ṣ, O, Mṣb, Mughnee, Ḳ,) being dial. vars., (Ṣ, O, Mṣb,) the first of which is the most common, (Mughnee,) and the most chaste: (Mṣb:) each is an adv. n. of place, and also of time; (Ṣ, O, Mṣb, Mughnee, Ḳ;) [used in the manner of a prep., though properly a prefixed noun;] of place when prefixed to a noun signifying a place [or anything local]; (TA;) of time when prefixed to a noun signifying a time: (Mṣb, TA:) denoting presence, (Ṣ, O,) i. e. perceptible presence, and also ideal presence, or rather the place of presence; (Mughnee;) and nearness, (Ṣ, O, Mughnee,) or the place of nearness; (Mughnee;) or the utmost nearness, and therefore it has no dim.; (T, TA;) [i. e.] it is primarily used in relation to that which is present with a person [or thing], in any adjacent part or quarter with respect to that person [or thing]; or in relation to that which is near to a person [or thing]: (Mṣb:) [thus it signifies *At, near, nigh, by, near by*, or *close by*, a place, or thing; *with, present with*, or *in the presence of*, a person or persons, or a thing or things; *at the abode of* a person; *at the place of*, or *in the region of*, a thing; or *among*, or *amongst*, persons or things: and *at, near, nigh*, or *about*, a time; and *at*, or *on*, or *upon*, denoting *the occasion* of an event or an action:] —— using it as an adv. n. of place, you say عِنْدَ ٱلْبَيْتِ [*At, near, nigh, by, near by*, or *close by, the house* or *tent*]; (TA;) and عِنْدَ ٱلْحَائِطِ [*At, near, nigh*, &c., *the wall*]; (Ṣ, O;) [and عِنْدِى زَيْدٌ *With me, present with me, in my presence*, or *at my abode, is Zeyd*; and كُنْتُ عِنْدَ ٱلْقَوْمِ *I was with*, or *among, the people*, or *party*; and] فَلَمَّا رَآهُ مُسْتَقِرًّا عِنْدَهُ [*And when he saw it standing in his presence* (in the Ḳur xxvii. 40)] is an ex. of its use as denoting presence perceptible by sense: and it is used as denoting nearness in the phrase عِنْدَ سِدْرَةِ ٱلْمُنْتَهَى [*Nigh to the lote-tree of the ultimate point of access* (in the Ḳur liii. 14)]: (Mughnee:) you say also, عِنْدِى مَالٌ, meaning *With me*, or *by me*, i. e. *present with me, is property*; and meaning also *in my possession, and in my power and at my disposal, is property*, though absent from me; *I have*, or *possess, property*; (Mṣb, Mughnee;*) and لِى عِنْدَهُ مَالٌ [*I have property in his hands*, or *possession*; or *there is property due to me in his hands*, or *possession*; meaning, *owed to me by him*]; as also قِبَلَهُ: (TA in art. قبل:) hence it is used in relation to attributes; so that one says, عِنْدَهُ خَيْرٌ وَفَضْلٌ [*He has*, or *possesses, goodness and excellence*]; and مَا عِنْدَهُ شَرٌّ [*He has not evil*]: and hence the saying in the Ḳur [xxviii. 27], فَإِنْ أَتْمَمْتَ عَشْرًا فَمِنْ عِنْدِكَ i. e. [*And if thou complete ten* years, it will be] *of thy redundant bounty*; (Mṣb;) [or *of thine own freewill*; as is implied in the explanation by Bḍ, and agreeably with common usage:] and it is used as denoting ideal presence in the phrase قَالَ ٱلَّذِى عِنْدَهُ عِلْمٌ مِنَ ٱلْكِتَابِ [*He with whom was*, i. e. *who possessed, knowledge the of Scripture said* (in the Ḳur xxvii. 40)]: (Mughnee:) [hence also] one says, لِى عِنْدَ فُلَانٍ حَاجَةٌ [*I have an object of want to be sought*, or *required, at the hand of such a one*, or *a want to be supplied on the part of such a one*; meaning *I want a thing of such a one*; as also قِبَلَ فُلَانٍ]: (TA in art. حوج:) [and in like manner one says of a right or due (حَقٌّ): and طَلَبَ حَاجَةً عِنْدَ فُلَانٍ *He sought an object of want at the hand of such a one*: (see an ex. in art. علو, conj. 3:)] —— using it as an adv. n. of time, you say عِنْدَ ٱلصُّبْحِ [*At, near, nigh*, or *about, daybreak*]; (Mṣb, TA;) and عِنْدَ ٱللَّيْلِ [*At, near, nigh*, or *about, night*]; (Ṣ, O;) and جِئْتُكَ عِنْدَ طُلُوعِ ٱلشَّمْسِ [*I came to thee at, near*, &c., *the rising of the sun*]; (Mughnee;) [and عِنْدَ ذٰلِكَ *At, on, upon*, or *on the occasion of, that* event; *thereupon*; and عِنْدَمَا فَعَلَ كَذَا *At, on, upon*, or *on the occasion of, his doing such a thing*.] —— It admits before it the prep. مِنْ, (Ṣ, O, Mṣb, Mughnee, Ḳ,) but no other prep.; (Ṣ, O, Mṣb;) like as does لَدُنْ: (Ṣ, O:) as in the saying, جِئْتُ مِنْ عِنْدِهِ [*I came from his presence*, or *his vicinage*: or *I came from him*; for in this case it may be considered as redundant]: (Mṣb:) and in the saying آتَيْنَاهُ رَحْمَةً مِنْ عِنْدِنَا وَعَلَّمْنَاهُ مِنْ لَدُنَّا عِلْمًا [*Upon whom we had bestowed mercy from us, and whom we had taught, from us, knowledge* (in the Ḳur xviii. 64)]: (Mughnee:) [and in an ex. above, from the Ḳur xxviii. 27: and one says of a gift, هٰذَا مِنْ عِنْدِى, meaning *This is from*, or *of, my property*; or *from me*; or, by way of emphasis, *from myself*:] one should not say [as the vulgar do], مَضَيْتُ إِلَى عِنْدِكَ, nor إِلَى لَدُنْكَ. (Ṣ, O, Ḳ.*) —— Being a vague adv. n., (T, TA,) it may not be used otherwise than as an adv. n., (T, Ṣ, O, Ḳ, TA,) except in the following case: (T, O, TA:) one says of a thing without knowing it, هٰذَا عِنْدِى كَذَا [*This is in my judgment*, or *opinion, thus*]; and thereupon another says, أَوَلَكَ عِنْدٌ [*And hast thou a judgment*, or *an opinion?*]: (T, A,* O,* Ḳ,* TA:) and in like manner one says,

* وَمَنْ أَنْتُمْ حَتَّى يَكُونَ لَكُمْ عِنْدُ *

[*And who are ye, that ye should have a judgment*, or *an opinion?*]: (TA:) and thus in the saying, (Mughnee, TA,) of one of the Muwelleds, (Mughnee,)

* كُلُّ عِنْدٍ لَكَ عِنْدِى * لَا يُسَاوِى نِصْفَ عِنْدِ *

[*Every judgment*, or *opinion, of thine, in my judgment*, or *opinion, will not equal the half of a judgment*, or *an opinion*]: (Mughnee, TA:) they assert that عِنْد in this case means the *mind*, (T, O,* Ḳ,* TA,) i. e. ٱلْقَلْب, and ٱلْمَعْقُول, (O, Ḳ,) or ٱلْقَلْب and مَا فِيهِ مَعْقُولُ ٱللُّبِّ; (T, TA;) [as in the phrase بُرْ لِى مَا عِنْدَ فُلَانٍ, expl. in the Ṣ, in art. بور, as meaning *Try thou*, or *examine, and learn, for me, what is in the mind* (نَفْس) *of such a one*; and in many other instances:] but this assertion is not valid: (T, TA:) [in a case of this kind] it means *judgment* [or *opinion*]: thus one says, هٰذَا عِنْدِى أَفْضَلُ مِنْ هٰذَا i. e. [*This is*] *in my judgment* [*more excellent than this*]: (Mṣb:) and أَنْتَ عِنْدِى ذَاهِبٌ i. e. [*Thou art*] *in my opinion* [*going away*]: (Fr, Th, TA:) and هٰذَا ٱلْقَوْلُ عِنْدِى صَوَابٌ [*This saying is in my judgment*, or *opinion, right*, or *correct*]: (Mughnee:) [and in like manner, عِنْدَ ٱللّٰهِ is generally best rendered *In the estimation*, or *sight, of God*.] —— [Sometimes it denotes comparison: see an ex. voce تَعَاظَمَ.] —— It is also sometimes used to denote incitement, (Ṣ, O, Ḳ,) being in this case prefixed [to كَ or the like]; not alone: (MF:) you say, عِنْدَكَ زَيْدًا, meaning *Take thou Zeyd*. (Ṣ, O, Ḳ.) —— And in cautioning a person respecting a thing before him, one says, عِنْدَكَ, [meaning *Keep thou where thou art*; and it is still used in this sense;] in which case it is an intrans. verbal noun. (Sb, L, TA.)

عَنَدٌ The *side* [of a thing]; syn. جَانِبٌ. (Ṣ, A, O, L, Ḳ. [See also عِنْدٌ, first sentence.]) One says, يَمْشِى وَسَطًا لَا عَنَدًا [*He walks in the middle, not on*, or *at, one side*]. (Ṣ, O.) And عَنَدَهُ, [for عَنَدِهِ,] occurring at the end of a verse [of which I find several different readings, and which I have cited accord. to one of those readings voce حُبَارَى], means *by its side*: (O, L:) but Th says, in explaining that verse, as describing the حُبَارَى teaching its young one to fly, that ٱلعَنَدُ signifies ٱلِاعْتِرَاضُ: [so that عَنَدَهُ there, accord. to him, app. means اِعْتِرَاضًا لَهُ, which may be rendered *presenting itself before it*:] or, accord. to Aṣ, [عَنَدَهُ] there means *imitating its actions in flying*; for he says that] عَنَدٌ is a subst. from عَانَدَ ٱلْحُبَارَى فَرْخَهُ [expl. above: see 3]. (L.)

طَعْنٌ عَنَدٌ *A thrusting* [with a spear or the like] *to the right and left*. (Ṣ, O.) [See also عَانِدٌ.]

عُنْدُدٌ or عِنْدَدٌ, (accord. to different copies of the Ṣ,) or both, (O, L, Ḳ,) in which the radical letters are said to be عند because of the duplication of the د, and because ن when it occupies the second place in a word is not considered augmentative unless proved to be so, (L,) *An avoiding*, or *escaping*: (Ṣ, O, L, Ḳ:) and the former, *artifice.* (AZ, O, Ḳ.) One says, مَا لِى عَنْهُ عُنْدُدٌ and عُنْدَدٌ (Lḥ, L, Ḳ, and written, as on the authority of AZ, in both these ways in the O and in different copies of the Ṣ, but with مِنْهُ in the place of عَنْهُ,) and ▼ مُعْلَنْدَدٌ (Ṣ, O, L, Ḳ) and ▼ مُعْلَنْدِدٌ, (Ḳ,) meaning *I have no way of avoiding it, or escaping it.* (AZ, Lḥ, Ṣ, O, L, Ḳ.) And مَا وَجَدْتُ إِلَى ذٰلِكَ عُنْدُدًا and عُنْدَدًا (Lḥ, L) and ▼ مُعْلَنْدَدًا (Lḥ, Ṣ, O) and ▼ مُعْلَنْدِدًا (Lḥ, O) *I found no way of attaining to that:* (Lḥ, Ṣ, O, L:) and مَا لِى إِلَيْهِ ▼ مُعْلَنْدِدٌ (Lḥ, L in art. علد, and Ḳ) and ▼ مُعْلَنْدَدٌ (Lḥ, L) *I have no way of attaining to it.* (Lh, L, Ḳ.) [See also art. علد.] ══ عُنْدُدٌ also signifies *Old,* or *ancient.* (AA, O, Ḳ.)

[عِنْدِيَّةٌ *A saying* عِنْدِى, meaning *In my opinion; an assertion of mere opinion of one's own.* Hence the phrase, هٰذَا مِنْ عِنْدِيَّاتِهِ (occurring in the TA in art. جوب) *This is one of his assertions of mere opinion.*]

عِنْدَأْوٌ and عِنْدَأْوَةٌ: see art. عندأ.

عَنُودٌ One who *declines,* or *deviates, from the right way,* or *course;* (Ṣ, O, L;) as also ▼ عَنِيدٌ. (L.) See also عَانِدٌ as applied to a camel. —— A she-camel *that deviates from the road by reason of her sprightliness and strength:* pl. عُنُدٌ and عُنَّدٌ; or, as ISd thinks, this latter is pl. of ▼ عَانِدٌ, not of عَنُودٌ. (L.) —— A she-camel *that pastures aside;* (Ṣ, O;) *that does not mix with the other camels, but removes to a distance from them, and always pastures aside;* as also ▼ عَانِدٌ and عَانِدَةٌ, (L;) *that does not mix with the other camels, but is always apart from them;* (IAth;) *that is on one side of the other camels:* (IAạr and Aboo-Naṣr:) pl. of the first عُنُدٌ; (Ṣ, O, L;) and of the second and third, عُنَّدٌ and عَوَانِدُ. (L.) —— A she-camel *that continues to be opposite to the other camels,* [*or by their sides;*] *keeping pace with them:* one that precedes them, or leads them, is termed سَلُوفٌ: so says El-Ḳeysee: but accord. to ISd, عَنُودٌ is applied to a beast (دَابَّة), and to a wild ass, *that precedes others in her pace.* (L.) —— A man *who alights in a place by himself, and mixes not with other persons.* (A.) —— See also عَنِيدٌ. —— قِدْحٌ عَنُودٌ [*An arrow of those used in the game called* المَيْسِر] *that comes forth* [*from the* رِبَابَة] *successful, in a direction, or manner, different from that of the other arrows.* (O, L, Ḳ.) —— عَنُودُ المِرْفَقِ [A beast] *having the elbow far from the* زَوْر [or *breast*]. (Ṣ, O, L.) —— عَقَبَةٌ عَنُودٌ [*A mountain road*] *difficult of ascent.* (L.) —— سَحَابَةٌ عَنُودٌ ‡ *A cloud abounding with rain:* (O, L, Ḳ:) or *that hardly removes from its place:* (A:) pl. عُنُدٌ. (O, L.)

عَنِيدٌ: see عَنُودٌ, first sentence. —— A man *who deviates, or declines, from obedience to God.* (L.) One *who opposes and rejects what is true,* or *just, knowing it to be so;* [*who acts obstinately, knowing a thing and rejecting it, or declining from it;* (see 1;)] as also ▼ عَانِدٌ, (Ṣ, Mgh,* O, L, Ḳ,) and ▼ عَنُودٌ, (O, L, TA,) and ▼ مُعَانِدٌ. (A.) One *who oversteps,* or *transgresses, the proper bound,* or *limit; who acts exorbitantly,* or *immoderately;* and especially *in disobedience,* or *rebellion;* as also ▼ عَانِدٌ. (L.) The pl. of عَنِيدٌ is عُنُدٌ. (O.)

عَانِدٌ A camel *that deviates from the road,* (Ṣ, O, L, Ḳ,) *and from the right course;* (Ṣ, O, L;) as also ▼ عَنُودٌ: (O:) pl. of the former عُنَّدٌ. (Ṣ, O, Ḳ.) —— See also عَنُودٌ, in two places. —— And see عَنِيدٌ, likewise in two places. —— Also † Blood *flowing on one side.* (L.) —— And ‡ A vein *flowing with blood, and not ceasing to flow:* (Ṣ, Mgh, O, L:) or *flowing, and hardly ceasing:* (L:) or *flowing copiously:* (Mṣb:) likened to a man who exceeds the proper bound or limit, or acts exorbitantly; (A'Obeyd, L;) or to one who disallows, or rejects, what is true, or just, knowing it to be so. (Mgh.) —— And طَعْنَةٌ عَانِدَةٌ † *A spear-wound,* or *stab, pouring forth blood to a distance:* (L:) [or طَعْنٌ عَانِدٌ signifies the *lightest,* or *slightest, piercing* or *thrusting;* for] AA says that the lightest, or slightest, piercing or thrusting (أَخَفُّ الطَّعْنِ) is termed الوَلْقُ, and العَانِدُ signifies the like thereof. (Ṣ, O.)

عَانِدَةُ الطَّرِيقِ *The course that deviates from the* [*right*] *road.* (L.)

مُعَانِدٌ: see عَنِيدٌ. [And see also its verb.]

مُعْلَنْدَدٌ and مُعْلَنْدِدٌ: see عُنْدُدٌ, in six places. ══ The latter also signifies A country, (Ibn-'Abbád, O,) or land, (Ḳ,) *containing neither water nor pasture.* (Ibn-'Abbád, O, Ḳ.) It is mentioned in different places by the lexicographers; in arts. علد and علند and in the present art.

عندأ

عِنْدَأْوٌ *Bold,* or *daring,* (IDrd, O, Ḳ,) *to attempt,* or *undertake, things;* applied to a man; (IDrd, O;) as also ▼ عِنْدَأْوَةٌ: (Ḳ:) which latter is [also] applied to a she-camel, as meaning *bold,* or *fearless.* (IAạr, Sh.)

عِنْدَأْوَةٌ *Difficulty,* and *perverseness,* (Z, Ḳ, TA,) in a man: (Z, TA:) and *roughness,* or *hardness, of behaviour:* (Ḳ:) and *opposition,* and *wrongdoing:* (L, TA:) and *deceit,* or *guile:* (Ḳ, TA:) and pronounced by some without ء. (TA.) One says, تَحْتَ طِرِّيقَتِكَ لَعِنْدَأْوَةٌ *Beneath thy silence is deceit,* or *guile:* (Ḳ:) or *difficulty,* and *perverseness:* (Z, TA:) or *opposition,* and *wrongdoing.* (L, TA.) [See also طِرِّيقَةٌ.] —— And (accord. to Lḥ, TA) العِنْدَأْوَةُ signifies أَدْهَى الدَّوَاهِى [app. meaning *The greatest of calamities*]. (Ḳ, TA.) ══ See also the former paragraph.

[Accord. to some, the radical letters of عِنْدَأْوٌ and عِنْدَأْوَةٌ are عدأ: accord. to some, عدو: and accord. to some, عندأ.]

عندلب

عَنْدَلِيبٌ, of the measure فَعْلَلِيلٌ, as AḤei says, the ن being radical; though some say that it is of the measure فَنْعَلِيلٌ, making the ن augmentative; (MF, TA;) *A certain bird, called* هَزَار [q. v.]; (Ṣ, O, Mṣb, Ḳ;) or هَزَارْ دَسْتَان; (O;) or, as in the "Sifr es-Sa'ádeh," *a small passerine bird,* called هَزَار دَاسْتَان; (TA;) which is Pers., (O, TA,) meaning "a thousand notes" or "voices," (O,) or "a thousand tales;" (TA;) confirming a saying of Lth, accord. to whom, (O,) it is *a bird that utters various notes,* (O, Mṣb, Ḳ,) *of the passerine kind;* said by some to be the بُلْبُل [i. e. the *nightingale,* or *a certain melodious bird resembling the nightingale*]: (Mṣb:) said by Aṣ to be originally عَنْدَلِيلٌ: (O:) pl. عَنَادِلُ; (Ṣ, O, Mṣb, Ḳ;) because you reduce it to a quadriliteral, and then form from it the pl. and the dim. [which latter is عُنَيْدِلٌ]. (Ṣ, O.)

عندم

عَنْدَمٌ *Brazil-wood;* syn. بَقَّمٌ: or [the *red, resinous, inspissated juice called*] دَمُ الأَخَوَيْنِ: (Ṣ, Ḳ, the former in art. عدم:) mentioned in a verse cited voce أَعَزُّ: (Ṣ, TA:) and said to be *i. q.* أَيْدَعٌ [to which are assigned both of the meanings mentioned above, and others also]: or دَمُ الغَزَالِ [said to be the same as دَمُ الأَخَوَيْنِ, and said to be *a plant resembling the tarragon,*] *with bark of the* [*tree called*] أَرْطًى, *cooked together until the whole becomes thick, and then the girls,* or *young women, dye their hands with it:* Aṣ says that it is *a certain dye, with which, accord. to the assertion of the people of El-Baḥreyn, their girls,* or *young women, tinge their hands:* AA says that it is *a species of red trees.* (TA.)

عنز

1. عَنَزَ, (O, Ḳ,) inf. n. عَنْزٌ, (O,) or عُنُوزٌ, (TA,) *He turned away,* (O, Ḳ, TA,) and *declined,* (TA,) عَنْهُ [*from him, or it*]: (Ḳ, TA:) or *he removed, went away* or *aside,* or *retired to a distance;* (IKṭṭ, TA;) and thus اعتنز signifies; (Ṣ, O, Ḳ;) as also ▼ استعنز; (O, Ḳ;) or these two verbs, and ▼ تعنّز, signify *he removed, went away* or *aside,* or *retired to a distance, from the people,* or *from men;* (TA;) and ▼ اعتنز signifies also *he alighted in a place aside* or *apart* [*from others*]. (Ṣ. [See also مُعْتَنِزٌ.]) ══ عَنَزَهُ, (IKṭṭ, Ḳ,) or عَنَّزَهُ, (A,) inf. n. عَنْزٌ, (TA,) *He pierced him,* or *thrust him, with the* عَنَزَة, (IKṭṭ, Ḳ,) or *they pierced him,* or *thrust him;* from the word عَنَزَةٌ [q. v.]. (A.)

2. تَعْنِيزٌ is [the inf. n. of عَنَّزَ, and signifies The *having little flesh in the face;* being] from the phrase مُعَنَّزُ الوَجْهِ. (O.)

4. اعنزهُ, (Ḳ, TA,) or ▼ اعتنزهُ, (thus accord. to the O, [but the former is app. the right,]) *He,* or *it, made him to decline,* (O, Ḳ, TA,) and *to remove, go away* or *aside,* or *retire to a distance.* (TA.)

5: see 1.

8: see 1, in two places: ═ and see also 4.

10: see 1.

عَنْزٌ *A she-goat*; the *female of the common goat*: (Ṣ, O, Ḳ:) or *a she-goat a year old*; (Mṣb;) [and so ↓ عَنْزَةٌ: (Freytag, from the Kitáb el-Aḍdád:)] and the *female of the mountain-goat*; and *of the gazelle*: (Ṣ, O:) pl. [of pauc.] أَعْنُزٌ and [of mult.] عُنُوزٌ and عِنَازٌ, or, accord. to some, the last of these is pl. of عَنْزٌ in the last of the senses expl. above. (TA.) هُمَا كَرُكْبَتَيِ العَنْزِ [*They two are like the two knees of the she-goat*] is a prov. applied to two men vying with each other, (O, Ḳ,) or equalling each other, (TA,) because her two knees, when she desires to lie down, fall together. (O, Ḳ. [See Freytag's Arab. Prov. ii. 861: where, instead of العنز, we find البَعِير; and thus I find in a MS. copy of the Proverbs of Meyd.]) And it is said in another prov., to him who commits a crime that occasions his destruction, لَا تَكُ كَالْعَنْزِ تَبْحَثُ عَنِ المُدْيَةِ [*Be not thou like the she-goat that scrapes up the dust, or earth, from over the butcher's knife*]. (TA. [See also بَاحِثٌ.]) Hence the saying, يَوْمٌ كَيَوْمِ العَنْزِ [*A day like the day of the she-goat*]; mentioned by Th; alluding to its bringing death. (TA.) And لَقِىَ يَوْمَ العَنْزِ [*He met with the day of the she-goat*] is also a prov., (O, TA,) applied to him who meets with that which destroys him, (O, Ḳ,) or to him who labours for his own destruction. (A.) — العَنْزُ is a name of † *The star* [ε] *on the left* [or (as some figure the constellation) *the right*] *elbow of Auriga*: and العِنَازُ is a name of † *The two stars* [ζ and η] *on the left* [or *the right*] *wrist together with* العَيُوق [which is *Capella*]. (Ḳzw in his description of Auriga.) — Also *The female eagle*: (Ṣ, O, Ḳ: [see also عَنْس:]) pl. عُنُوزٌ. (TA.) And *The female vulture*: (IDrd, O, Ḳ:) pl. عُنُوزٌ. (IDrd, O.) And *The female of the* [*species of bustard called*] حُبَارَى (IDrd, O, Ḳ) is sometimes thus termed: (O:) and it is said to be also called ↓ العَنَزَةُ. (TA.) And *The female of the hawk*. (TA.) — Also *A species of aquatic bird*; (O, Ḳ;*) [by some, in the present day, applied to *a gray heron*;] *also called* عَنْزُ المَآءِ. (O.) — And *A species of fish*; *also called* عَنْزُ المَآءِ: (Az, O:) accord. to Ibn-'Abbád, (O,) *a certain great fish, which a mule can hardly, or in nowise, carry*: (O, Ḳ:) and the pl., he says, is أَعْنِزَةٌ. (O.) ═ عَنْزٌ also signifies *An* [*eminence, or a hill, such as is termed*] أَكَمَةٌ: (Ṣ:) or *a black* أَكَمَة. (O, Ḳ.) — And *A rock in the water*: pl. عُنُوزٌ. (TA.) — And *Land having in it ruggedness and sand and stones and* [*the species of tamarisk called*] أَثْل. (TA.) ═ And *I. q.* بَاطِلٌ [q. v.]. (TA.)

عَنَزٌ: see its n. un. عَنَزَةٌ.

عَنْزَةٌ: see عَنْزٌ, in two places.

عَنَزَةٌ *A short spear*; (A;) *a small spear, between a staff and a spear*, (O, Ḳ,) *longer than a staff and shorter than a spear*, (Ṣ,) *said to be of the measure of half a spear, or somewhat more, having a head like that of the spear*; (TA;) or *a staff shorter than a spear*; (Mṣb;) *and, as some say*, (TA,) *having a* زُجّ [i. e. *a pointed iron foot at the lower extremity*], (Ṣ, O, Mṣb, Ḳ, TA,) *like that of the spear*: (Ṣ, O, TA:) *the old man leans, or stays himself, upon it*; *and it is nearly like the* عُكَّازَة [q. v.]: (TA:) or *it is like the* عُكَّازَة, *which is a staff having a* زُجّ: (Mgh:) pl. ↓ عَنَزٌ, [or rather this is a coll. gen. n., of which عَنَزَةٌ is the n. un.,] and عَنَزَاتٌ. (Mṣb.) The Prophet is related to have prayed towards an عَنَزَة. (Mgh. [See سُتْرَةٌ.]) — Also The حَدّ [by which may be meant either the *edge* or *point*] of a فَأْس [which means a hoe and an adz and an axe, and also a pickaxe]: (O, Ḳ:) or the *long* حَدّ [or iron *point*] of the مِلْطَاس, which is a long double-headed pickaxe. (ISh, TA in art. لطس.) ═ Also *A certain beast*, (O, Ḳ,) *found in the desert, slender in the muzzle, smaller than the dog, of the beasts of prey*, (O,) *that seizes the camel in his rump*, (O, Ḳ,) *and is seldom seen*; *asserted by the Arabs to be a devil*: (O:) or, (Ḳ,) accord. to Aboo-Leyleh, (O,) *it is like the weasel* (O, Ḳ) *in size*: (O:) *it approaches the she-camel when she is lying down*, (O, Ḳ,) *then springs*, (O,) *and enters into her vulva, and conceals itself therein*, (O, Ḳ,) *until it reaches the womb*, (O,) *whereupon the she-camel* (O, Ḳ) *dies on the spot* (Ḳ) or *aborts and dies on the spot*. (O.)

عَنِيزٌ *Afflicted by a calamity*; as also ↓ مَعْنُوزٌ; (Ibn-'Abbád, O, Ḳ;) both applied to a man. (Ibn-'Abbád, O.)

مُعَنَّزٌ *Small in the head* (Ibn-'Abbád, O, Ḳ) *and ears*. (Ibn-'Abbád, O.) — مُعَنَّزُ الوَجْهِ A man (A, O) *having little flesh in his face*. (A, O, Ḳ.) — مُعَنَّزُ اللِّحْيَةِ *Whose beard is like* [*that of*] *the goat*: (Ḳ:) applied to a man as though his beard were like the beard of the goat: (O:) meaning, as expl. by Aboo-Dáwood, بُزْ رِيش in Pers. meaning the "goat" [and رِيش the "beard"]. (TA.)

مَعْنُوزٌ: see عَنِيزٌ.

مُعْتَنِزٌ is said to mean One *who does not dwell in the neighbourhood of* [*other*] *men lest something should be gotten from him*: and one says, نَزَلَ مُعْتَنِزًا meaning *He alighted and abode aside*, or *apart, from men*. (TA. [See its verb.])

عنس

1. عَنَسَتْ, (Ṣ, A, Mgh, O, Mṣb, Ḳ,) aor. ـُ (Ṣ, A, O, Mṣb, Ḳ) and ـِ; (A, O, Mṣb, Ḳ;) and عَنِسَتْ, aor. ـَ; (A, O, Ḳ;) inf. n. عُنُوسٌ (Ṣ, A, Mgh, O, Mṣb, Ḳ) and عِنَاسٌ, (Ṣ, A, O, Ḳ,) or the latter is a simple subst.; (Mṣb;) and ↓ أَعْنَسَتْ; (O, Ḳ;) and ↓ عَنَّسَتْ, (AZ, Ṣ, A, Mgh, O, Ḳ,) or this last has an intensive signification, (Mṣb,) inf. n. تَعْنِيسٌ; (AZ, Ṣ, Mgh, O;) and ↓ عُنِّسَتْ; (Ḳ;) or, accord. to Aṣ, (Ṣ, Mgh, O, Mṣb, TA,) you do not say عَنَسَتْ, (Mṣb,) or you do not say ↓ عَنَّسَتْ, (Ṣ, O,) or you do not say either of these two, (Mgh, TA,) but you say ↓ عُنِّسَتْ; (Ṣ, Mgh, O, TA;) or, accord. to some, you say عَنَسَتْ and ↓ عُنِّسَتْ, but not ↓ عَنَّسَتْ; (TA;) or what Aṣ says is, that you say ↓ عَنَّسَتْ, with fet-ḥ and teshdeed, and عَنَسَتْ, without teshdeed, contr. to what J says; (IB, TA;) *She* (a girl, Ṣ, A, Mgh, O, Ḳ, or woman, A, Mṣb) *became of middle age, remaining a virgin*, (A, Mgh,) *not having married*; (Mgh;) *she stayed long in the abode of her family after she had attained to puberty, until she ceased to be reckoned among virgins, and did not marry*: (Ṣ, A, O, Mṣb, Ḳ:) of one who has once married, you say not thus. (Ṣ, O, Mṣb.) Also عَنَسَ *He* (a man) *became advanced in age without having married*. (O,* Mṣb.)

2. عَنَّسَتْ and عُنِّسَتْ, inf. n. تَعْنِيسٌ: see 1, in seven places. ═ عَنَّسَهَا أَهْلُهَا, (inf. n. as above, Ḳ,) *Her family restrained her* (namely a girl or woman) *from marriage* (Lth, A, Mgh,* Mṣb) *until she was of middle age*; (A, Mgh;*) or *until she had passed the period of youthfulness but had not yet become aged*; (TA;) or *long after she had attained to puberty, until she had ceased to be reckoned among virgins*. (Ṣ, O, Mṣb, Ḳ.)

4. أَعْنَسَتْ: see 1. ═ اعنس *He nourished*, or *brought up, a girl who became of middle age remaining a virgin, not marrying*; expl. by رَبَّى عَانِسًا. (TA.) ═ اعنسهُ *He, or it, altered him*, or *it*. (Ḳ.) You say فُلَانٌ لَمْ تُعْنِسِ السِّنُّ وَجْهَهُ *Such a one, age did not alter his face*. (Ṣ, O.*) And اعنس الشَّيْبُ وَجْهَهُ, (O, Ḳ,) or رَأْسَهُ, (T, TA,) *Hoariness interspersed his face*, (O, Ḳ,) or *his head*. (TA.)

12. اِعْنَوْنَسَ, (Ṣ,) inf. n. اِعْنِيْنَاسٌ, (O, Ḳ,) *It* (the tail of a she-camel) *was, or became, full*, or *ample*, (Ṣ, O, Ḳ,) *and long, in its hair*. (O, Ḳ.)

عَنْسٌ *A rock*. (TA.) — And hence, as being likened thereto, (TA,) † *A she-camel that is hard*, or *firm*, (IAạr, Ṣ, O, Ḳ, TA,) or *strong*, (TA,) *such as is termed* بَازِل, *when she is of full age, and has become very strong, and full in her bones and her limbs*; not applied to any other [beast]: (IAạr, TA:) or *whose tail has become full*, or *ample*: (Ṣ:) pl. عِنَاسٌ and عُنُوسٌ. (IAạr, ISd, TA.) — And *An eagle*: (O, Ḳ;) because of its hardness: (TA:) and so عَنْز; (O;) or this signifies "a female eagle." (Ṣ, O, Ḳ, in art. عنز.)

عَانِسٌ A woman *who has become of middle age remaining a virgin*, (Lth, A, Mgh,) *not having married*; (Lth, Mgh;) or a woman *who has not married, but waits*, or *expects, to be married*; (Fr, TA;) or *who has stayed long in the abode of her family after having attained to puberty, until she has ceased to be reckoned among virgins, and has not married*; (Ṣ, O, Mṣb, Ḳ;) *beyond the age of her who is termed* مُعْصِر; (Ks, Ṣ, O;) and ↓ مُعَنَّسَةٌ signifies the same: (Fr, Mgh, TA:) pl. عُنُوسٌ and عُنَّسٌ and عُنْسٌ and عَوَانِسُ (Ṣ, O, Ḳ) and مَعَانِسُ: (O, Ḳ:) and the pl. of ↓ مُعَنَّسَةٌ is مَعَانِسُ and مُعَنَّسَاتٌ. (TA.) And عَانِسٌ is applied in like manner to a man, (Ṣ, O, Ḳ,) signifying One who is far advanced in age and has not married: (Mṣb, TA:) and its pl. is عَانِسُونَ. (Ṣ, O, TA.) —— Also † A camel fat, and complete, or perfect, in make: fem. with ة: (O, Ḳ, TA:) or [the pl.] عُنْسٌ applied to camels means such as are above the بِكَارَة [pl. of بَكْرٌ]; i. e. the young in a middling degree. (TA.)

مُعَنَّسَةٌ : see عَانِسٌ, in two places.

Quasi عنصر

عُنْصُرٌ and عُنْصَرٌ : see art. عصر.

Quasi عنصل

العُنْصُلُ and العُنْصُلَآءُ : see art. عصل.

عنف

1. عَنُفَ بِهِ (Ṣ, MA, Mgh, O, Mṣb, Ḳ) and عَلَيْهِ, (Ṣ, Mgh, O, Mṣb, Ḳ,) with damm, (Ṣ, O,) like قَرُبَ, (Mgh, Mṣb,) or like كَرُمَ, (Ḳ,) aor. ـُ, (MA, TA,) inf. n. عُنْفٌ (Ṣ,* MA, Mgh, O,* Mṣb, TA) and عَنَافَةٌ; (MA, Mgh, TA;) and عَنَفَ بِهِ, aor. ـِ; (MA;) [and عَنِفَ, inf. n. عَنَفٌ, is mentioned as syn. with عَنُفَ by Golius and Freytag, by the latter as on the authority of the Ṣ and Ḳ, in neither of which do I find it;] He was ungentle, rough, harsh, rigorous, severe, violent, or vehement, with him, or to him: (Ṣ, MA, Mgh, O, Mṣb, Ḳ, TA:) hence the phrase, عَنُفَ عَلَيْهِمْ فِى السَّوْقِ [He was ungentle, rough, &c., to them in driving]: (Mgh:) and ▼ عنّفهُ and عنّف عَلَيْهِ signify the same as عَنُفَ بِهِ: (MA:) you say عَنَّفْتُهُ, inf. n. تَعْنِيفٌ; and ▼ أَعْنَفْتُهُ; (Lth, O, Ḳ;) both meaning عَنُفْتُ عَلَيْهِ; (TḲ; [and the same is implied in the Ḳ;]) both from العُنْفُ: (Lth, O:) or ▼ التَّعْنِيفُ signifies the upbraiding, or reproaching; and blaming, reproving, or censuring: (Ṣ, O:) you say عنّفهُ, inf. n. تَعْنِيفٌ, (Mṣb, Ḳ, TA,) meaning he blamed, reproved, or censured, him; (Mṣb;) or did so with roughness or harshness, and vehemence; (Ḳ, TA;) omitted in some of the copies of the Ḳ; (TA;) or did so in anger or displeasure; (Mṣb;) upbraided, or reproached, him; blamed, reproved, or censured, him with reproach. (TA.)

2: see the preceding paragraph, in two places.

4: see 1. —— اعنف الشَّىْءَ He took the thing (أَخَذَهُ) [or this may mean he took to it, or set about it,]) with violence, or vehemence. (TA.) [See also 8, in two places. —— In Ḥar p. 386, اعنفت الشىء is expl. as meaning ائتنفته اذا استقبلته : but in the lexicons I find only اعتنفته in this sense.]

[5. تعنّف is expl. by Golius as signifying Incommodè et imperitè aggressus fuit rem, et incepit; on the authority of the Ṣ: but it is اعتنف that has this, or a similar, meaning.]

8. اِعْتَنَفْتُ الأَمْرَ I took to, or set about, the affair (أَخَذْتُهُ [for أَخَذْتُ أَفْعَلُهُ or أَخَذْتُ فِيهِ]) with ungentleness, roughness, violence, or vehemence. (Ṣ, O, Mṣb, Ḳ, TA. [See also 4.]) I entered into, engaged in, did, or performed, the affair, (أَتَيْتُهُ,) not having knowledge in it: (O, Ḳ, TA:) or (Ḳ) I was ignorant of the affair; (O, Ḳ, TA;) and found it troublesome, or difficult, and hard, to do; (TA;) whence the saying (O, TA) of Ru-beh, (TA,)

بِأَرْبَعٍ لَا يَعْتَنِفْنَ العَنَقَا

[With four legs not ignorant of the pace termed عَنَق]: (O, TA:) and [simply] I had no knowledge in the affair: (O:) and اعتنفت الشَّىْءَ I took to, or set about, the thing, (أَخَذْتُهُ [as above],) or I entered into, engaged in, did, or performed, the thing, (أَتَيْتُهُ,) not being skilled, nor having knowledge, in it. (TA. (See, again, 4.]) —— Also [simply] I began, or commenced, the affair: (O,* Ḳ:) some of the Benoo-Temeem use the phrase [thus] in the sense of ائْتَنَفْتُهُ: (Lth, O, TA:) an instance of العَنْعَنَة. (TA.) See also عُنُفَةٌ. —— And اِعْتَنَفْنَا المَرَاعِىَ We pastured [our cattle] upon the herbage that had not been pastured upon before, of the pasturages: (O, Ḳ: but the latter has اعتنف in the place of اعتنفنا:) an instance of the عَنْعَنَة of Temeem. (O.) —— And اعتنف المَجْلِسَ He removed from the sitting-place; (Ḳ, TA;) like ائْتَنَفَ: (TA:) Esh-Sháfi'ee, after recommending that a man when he is drowsy in the sitting-place [in the mosque] on Friday, and finds another sitting-place without his treading therein upon any one, should remove from it, says, وَاعْتِنَافُ المَجْلِسِ مَا يُذْعِرُ عَنْهُ النَّوْمَ [i. e. And the removing from the sitting-place is a cause of scaring from him sleep]: making الاِعْتِنَاف to be the putting himself in motion, and removing from place to place; which is like الاِئْتِنَاف [or the beginning, or commencing, anew]. (Az, O.) —— اِعْتَنَفْتُ الطَّعَامَ I disapproved, or disliked, the food that I had eaten; (El-Báhilee, O, Ḳ,* TA;) it disagreeing with me. (Az, TA.) And اِعْتَنَفْتُ الأَرْضَ I disliked the land, (Ṣ, O, Ḳ, TA,) and deemed it insalubrious. (TA.) And اِعْتَنَفَتْنِى البِلَادُ, (O,) or الأَرْضُ, (Ḳ,) The country, or the land, disagreed with me, or was unsuitable to me. (O, Ḳ.) —— اعتنف الطَّرِيقُ [perhaps أُعْتُنِفَ (see the part. n.)] The road swerved from the right course. (TA.)

عَنَفٌ : see the next paragraph. —— هُمْ يَخْرُجُونَ عَنَفًا عَنَفًا means [They go forth one after another, or] first and then first; as also ▼ عُنْفُوَانًا. (O, Ḳ.)

عُنْفٌ (Ṣ, Mgh, O, Ḳ, &c.) and ▼ عَنْفٌ and ▼ عِنْفٌ [the first of which is an inf. n.] Ungentleness, roughness, harshness, rigorousness, severity, violence, or vehemence; (TA;) contr. of رِفْقٌ (Ṣ, Mgh, O, Ḳ, TA.) It is said of God, in a trad., يُعْطِى عَلَى الرِّفْقِ مَا لَا يُعْطِى عَلَى العُنْفِ [He gives on account of gentleness in the petitioner, what He will not give on account of ungentleness]. (O.)

عِنْفٌ : see the next preceding paragraph.

عَنُفٌ : see عَنِيفٌ.

عُنُفٌ, with two dammehs, Roughness, and hardness: so expl. by Lḥ as used in the saying,

فَقَذَفَتْ بِبَيْضَةٍ فِيهَا عُنُفْ

[And she cast forth an egg in which were roughness and hardness]. (TA.)

كَانَ ذٰلِكَ مِنَّا عُنْفَةً, and ▼ عُنُفَةً, i. q. ▼ اِعْتِنَافًا, meaning اِئْتِنَافًا [i. e. That was, on our part, a beginning, or commencing]. (Ks, O, Ḳ.)

عَنَفَةٌ A thing [app. a wheel] which, being smitten [or put in motion] by water, turns a mill. (AA, O, Ḳ.) —— And The space between two lines of corn, or seed-produce. (AA, O, Ḳ.)

عُنُفَةٌ : see عُنْفَةٌ.

عَنِيفٌ Ungentle, [rough, harsh, rigorous, severe, violent, or vehement,] (Ṣ, Mgh, O, Mṣb, Ḳ, TA,) in his affair; as also ▼ عَنُفٌ and ▼ أَعْنَفُ and ▼ مُعْتَنِفٌ; (TA;) [thus] as applied to a driver; (Mgh;) [and particularly] in the riding of horses; (Ṣ, O, Ḳ;) or who does not ride well; or who is not acquainted with the riding of horses: (TA:) pl. عُنُفٌ. (Ṣ, O.) And Hard, severe, violent, or vehement, applied to a saying, (O, Ḳ,) and to journeying, or a pace. (Ḳ.)

عُنْفُوٌ : see عُنْفُوَانٌ.

عُنْفُوَةٌ Such as is dried up of the [plant called] نَصِىّ, (TA in this art.,) or of the حَلِىّ, when it has become black, and old and withered, or wasted. (TA in art. عنث.)

عُنْفُوَانٌ, (Ṣ, O, Mṣb, Ḳ,) of the measure فُعْلُوَانٌ from العُنْف, or it may be originally أُنْفُوَانٌ, having the أ then changed into ع, (TA,) or it is from اِعْتَنَفْتُ الشَّىْءَ meaning "I began, or commenced, the thing," (Ḥam p. 269,) and ▼ عُنْفُوٌ also, (Ibn-'Abbád, TA,) The first of a thing: (Ṣ, O, Mṣb, Ḳ:) or the first of the beauty and brightness thereof: (Lth, O, Ḳ:) and (Ṣ, O, TA) predominantly (TA) of youth, or youthfulness, and of plants, or herbage. (Ṣ, O, TA.) You say, هُوَ فِى عُنْفُوَانِ شَبَابِهِ [He is in the prime, spring, or bloom, of his youth]. (Ṣ, O, Mṣb.) —— See also عَنَفٌ. —— عُنْفُوَانٌ also signifies The juice that flows from grapes without their being pressed. (TA.) —— And The force, or strength, of wine. (TA.)

أَعْنَفُ : see عَنِيفٌ.

مُعْتَنَفٌ : see the next paragraph.

مُعْتَنِفٌ : see عَنِيفٌ. —— إِبِلٌ مُعْتَنِفَةٌ Camels in a district, or country, that disagrees with them, or is unsuitable to them. (Ṣ, O, Ḳ.*) —— And طَرِيقٌ مُعْتَنِفٌ, (Ḳ,) or ▼ مُعْتَنَفٌ, (so in the O,) A road swerving from the right course. (O, Ḳ.)

عنفق

عَنْفَقٌ Lightness, (IDrd, O, Ḳ,) and paucity,

(IDrd, O,) of a thing. (IDrd, Ḳ, TA. [In the O, المَشْىُ is erroneously put for الشَّىْءُ.]) Hence is derived the word here following. (O, Ḳ.)

عَنْفَقَةٌ *A few hairs between the lower lip and the chin:* (Lth, O, Ḳ:) or the *hairs of the fore part of the lower lip;* (T, TA;) the [*tuft of*] *hair of the lower lip;* (Mgh;) or the *hair that grows upon* [or *beneath*] *the lower lip:* or the *part between the lower lip and the chin;* because of the lightness of its hair: or the *part between the chin and the edge of the lower lip, whether there be on it hair or not:* pl. عَنَافِقُ. (TA.) بَادِى العَنْفَقَةِ means A man *bare of hair* (Mgh,* O, TA) *in the place,* (Mgh, TA,) or *in the two sides,* (O,) *of the* عنفقة. (Mgh, O, TA.)

عنق

1. عَنِقَ, aor. ـَ, inf. n. عَنَقٌ, *He* (a man, TḲ) *was,* or *became, long in the neck.* (TA, TḲ. [The verb in this sense is said in the TA to be like فَرِحَ: but in two instances in the same it is written عَنَقَ, with the same inf. n., and expl. as meaning *He was,* or *became, long and thick in the neck.*]) —— [Golius has assigned to عَنَّقَ (an unknown verb) two significations belonging to تعنّق.]

2. عنّق عَلَيْهِ, inf. n. تَعْنِيقٌ, *He went along and looked down upon it* or *came in sight of it;* expl. by مَشَى وَأَشْرَفَ. (O, Ḳ.) —— عنّقت السَّحَابَةُ *The cloud emerged from the main aggregate of the clouds, and was seen white by reason of the sun's shining upon it.* (TA.) —— عنّقت أَسْتُهُ *His posteriors,* or *his anus, protruded;* syn. خَرَجَتْ. (O, Ḳ.) —— عنّقت طَوَالِعُ النَّخْلِ *The spathes of the palm-trees became long,* (O, Ḳ,) *but had not split open.* (O.) —— عنّقت البُسْرَةُ *The date that had begun to colour ripened nearly as far as the* قِمَع [or *base*] *thereof,* (Ḳ, TA,) *so that there remained of it around that part what was like the finger-ring.* (TA.) ═ عنّقهُ *He took him by his neck, and squeezed his throat,* or *fauces.* (O,* L, Ḳ.*) It is related in a trad., that the Prophet said to Umm-Selemeh, when a sheep, or goat, of a neighbour of her's had come in and taken a cake of bread from beneath a jar belonging to her, and she had taken it from between its jaws, مَا كَانَ يَنْبَغِى لَكِ أَنْ تُعَنِّقِيهَا i. e. [*It did not behoove thee*] *that thou shouldst take hold of its neck and squeeze it:* or the meaning is, *that thou shouldst disappoint it;* (O, Ḳ;) from عنّقهُ signifying *he disappointed him;* (Ḳ;) which is from العَنَاقُ: (O:) or, as some relate it, he said ان تُعَنِّكِيهَا, (O, Ḳ,) i. e., *that thou shouldst distress it, and treat it roughly:* (O:) and تُعَنِّفِيهَا, with ف, would be approvable if agreeing with a relation. (O, Ḳ.*) And it is also related in a trad., that he said to the women of 'Othmán Ibn-Madh'oon, when he died, ابْكِينَ وَإِيَّاكُنَّ وَتَعَنُّقَ ▾ الشَّيْطَانِ, if correct, [meaning *Weep ye, but beware ye of the Devil's seizing by the neck, and squeezing the throat,*] from عنّقهُ as first expl. above: but it is by some related otherwise, i. e. وَنَعِيقَ الشيطان. (L.)

3. عَانَقَهُ, (Ṣ, TA,) and عَانَقَتِ المَرْأَةَ, (Mṣb,) inf. n. عِنَاقٌ (Ṣ, Mṣb, TA) and مُعَانَقَةٌ, *He embraced him, putting his arms upon his neck, and drawing,* or *pressing, him to himself,* (Ṣ, TA,) and *I so embraced the woman,* as also ▾ اعتنقتها; (Mṣb;) [and ▾ تعانقهُ, and ▾ تعنّقهُ: see the last of the verses cited voce بَيْنَ, and the remarks thereon: but see also what here follows:]. and ▾ تعانقنا *We so embraced each other* or *one another:* (Mṣb:) and ▾ تعانقا, and ▾ اعتنقا, [*They so embraced each other,*] both signifying the same; (Ṣ, O;) but (O) عانقا and ▾ تعانقا are said in a case of love, or affection, and ▾ اعتنقا is said in a case of war and the like; (O,* Ḳ;) or, accord. to Az, ▾ التَّعَانُقُ and ▾ الِاعْتِنَاقُ are both allowable in all cases: and [it is said that] when the act is predicated of one exclusively of the other, one says only عانقهُ, in both the cases above mentioned. (TA.) ═ See also the next paragraph.

4. اعنق الكَلْبَ *He put the collar upon the neck of the dog.* (Ṣ, O, Ḳ.) ═ اعنق, (Ṣ, Mṣb,) inf. n. إِعْنَاقٌ, (Mṣb,) said of a horse [and the like], (Ṣ,) *He went the pace termed* عَنَقٌ, (Ṣ, Mṣb,) i. e. *a stretching pace,* or *a hastening and stretching pace,* (Ṣ,) or *a quick pace with wide steps.* (Mṣb.) And *He hastened;* as also ▾ عانق. (TA.) اعنقوا إِلَيْهِ, meaning *They hastened to him,* or *it,* is from العَنَقُ signifying the pace thus termed. (Mgh.) In the phrase أَعْنَقَ لِيَمُوتَ, (Mgh,) occurring in a trad., (O,) the ل is used causatively: [i. e., the phrase signifies *He hastened that he might die:*] (Mgh:) [or] the meaning is, that the decree of death made him to hasten, and drove him on, to his place of slaughter. (O.) —— اعنقت البِلَادُ *The countries were,* or *became, distant,* or *remote;* and so اعلقت. (TA, from the Nawádir el-Aạráb.) —— اعنقت الثُّرَيَّا ‡ *The* ثريّا [or *Pleiades*] *set.* (O, Ḳ, TA.) And اعنقت النُّجُومُ † *The stars advanced to the place of setting.* (O.) —— اعنق الزَّرْعُ † *The corn became tall, and put forth its ears:* (O, Ḳ, TA:) as though it became such as had a neck. (TA.) —— اعنقت الرِّيحُ ‡ *The wind raised the dust,* or *carried it away, and dispersed it.* (O, Ḳ, TA. [See also 8.])

5: see 2, last sentence: —— and see also 3. —— تعنّق said of the jerboa, *It entered its hole called the* عَانِقَآء; (O, Ḳ;) or so تعنّق العَانِقَآءَ, and بِهَا: (TA:) and, said of the hare, *it hid,* or *inserted, its head and its neck in its burrow* [app. meaning *in the burrow of a jerboa:* but see عَانِقَآء]. (O, Ḳ.)

6: see 3, in five places.

8: see 3, in four places. —— [Hence, اِعْتِنَاقُ السَّلَاسِلِ, a phrase well known as meaning *The putting of chains upon one's* (own) *neck;* occurring in the Ḳ voce رَهْبَانِيَّةٌ. —— And] اعتنقت الأَمْرَ *I took to the affair with earnestness.* (Mṣb.) —— اعتنقت الدَّابَّةُ *The beast fell in the mire, and put forth its neck.* (TA.) ═ اعتنقت الرِّيحُ بِالتُّرَابِ [app. meaning, like اعنقت, (see 4, last significa-tion,) † *The wind raised the dust,* or *carried it away, and dispersed it,*] is from العَنَقُ, i. e. "the pace with wide steps" thus termed. (TA.)

عَنَقٌ: see عُنُقٌ, first sentence, in two places.

عَنَقٌ *Length of the neck.* (Ṣ, O, Ḳ. [See also 1.]) —— Also *A stretching pace,* or *a hastening and stretching pace,* of the horse or the like, and of camels: (Ṣ, O, Ḳ, TA:) or *a pace with wide steps:* (Mgh:) or *a certain quick pace, with wide steps:* a subst. from أَعْنَقَ: (Mṣb:) and ▾ عَنِيقٌ signifies the same. (O, TA.) [See also وَسَجَ, and نَصَبَ السَّيْرِ.] A rájiz (Abu-n-Nejm, TA) says,

يَا نَاقَ سِيرِى عَنَقًا فَسِيحَا ⁂ إِلَى سُلَيْمَانَ فَتَسْتَرِيحَا

[*O she-camel* (يا ناقَ being for يا نَاقَةُ) *go a stretching-pace, &c., with wide steps, to Suleymán, that thou mayest find rest*]. (Ṣ, O.)

عُنْقٌ: see what next follows.

عُنُقٌ and ▾ عُنْقٌ, (Ṣ, O, Mṣb, Ḳ, &c.,) the former of the dial. of El-Ḥijáz, and the latter of the dial. of Temeem, (Mṣb,) the latter said by Sb to be a contraction of the former, (TA,) [which is the more common,] and ▾ عَنِيقٌ and ▾ عَنَقٌ, (Ḳ, [in which it is implied that these two have all the significations assigned by its author to عُنُقٌ and عُنْقٌ,]) but [SM says] none of the leading lexicologists has mentioned these two, in what I have seen, (TA,) [adding that he had found in the O العَنِيقُ as meaning العَنَقُ, which he supposes the author of the Ḳ to have thought to be العُنُقُ,] *The neck;* i. e. the *part that forms a connexion between the head and the body;* (TA;) *i. q.* رَقَبَةٌ; (Mṣb;) or *i. q.* جِيدٌ: (Ḳ:) [but see these two words:] masc. and fem.; (Ṣ, O, Ḳ;) generally masc., (IB, Mṣb,* TA,) but in the dial. of El-Ḥijáz fem.; (Mṣb;) or, as some say, ▾ عُنْقٌ is masc., and عُنُقٌ is fem.: (TA:) the pl. (i. e. of the first and second, TA) is أَعْنَاقٌ, (Sb, Ṣ, O, Mṣb, Ḳ,) the only pl. form. (Sb, TA.) —— [Hence,] عُنُقُ الحَيَّةِ † *A star* [α] *in the neck of the constellation Serpens.* (Ḳzw.) [And عُنُقُ الشُّجَاعِ † *The star α in the hinder part of the neck of the constellation Hydra:* also called الفَرْدُ.] —— عُنُقُ الرَّحِمِ, [*The neck of the womb;*] *the slender part of the* رحم, *towards the* فَرْج. (TA.) —— عُنُقُ الكَرِشِ *The lowest portion of the stomach of a ruminant;* (AḤát, O, Ḳ;) *also called* القِبَةُ [q. v.]. (AḤát, O.) —— أَعْنَاقُ النَّخْلِ † [*The trunks of palm-trees*]. (Ṣ in art. قصر.) —— مَدَّ لِلْحَبِّ أَعْنَاقَهُ, said of seed-produce [or corn], means † *The internodal portions of its culms appeared.* (TA voce أُحْنَقَ, q. v.) —— أَعْنَاقُ الرِّيحِ ‡ *What have risen of the dust that is raised by the wind.* (O, Ḳ, TA.) [The phrase قد رأس اعناق الريح, mentioned by Freytag as from the Ḳ, is a strange mistake.] —— يَخْرُجُ عُنُقٌ مِنَ النَّارِ, occurring in a trad., means † *A portion* *will issue from the fire* [*of Hell*]. (TA.) — And خَرَجَ مِنَ النَّهْرِ عُنُقٌ † *A current of water issued from the river*, or *rivulet*. (ISh, TA.) — عُنُقُ الصَّيْفِ and الشِّتَآءِ *The first part* [*of summer* and *of winter*]: and in like manner عُنُقُ السِّنِّ [*The first part of the age* of a man as counted by years]: IAạr says, I said to an Arab of the desert, كَمْ أَتَى عَلَيْكَ [*How many years have passed over thee?*] and he answered, أَخَذْتُ بِعُنُقِ السِّتِّينَ i. e. [*I have entered upon*] *the first part of the* ستّين [or *sixtieth* year]: and the pl. is أَعْنَاقٌ. (L, TA.) And كَانَ ذٰلِكَ عَلَى عُنُقِ الدَّهْرِ (O, Ḳ, TA) and الإِسْلَامِ (TA) means *That was in the old* [or *early*] *period* [*of time*] (O, Ḳ, TA) [and *of El-Islám*]. (TA.) — [And عُنُقٌ app. signifies † The *upper portion* of an elevated and elongated tract of sand, or the like: see the pl. أَعْنَاق in the last sentence of this art.] — الكَلَامُ يَأْخُذُ بَعْضُهُ بِعُنُقِ بَعْضٍ and بِأَعْنَاقِ بَعْضٍ are tropical phrases [app. meaning ‡ *The speech*, or *language, is coherent*, or *compact*]. (TA.) — هُمْ عُنُقٌ إِلَيْكَ means † *They are inclining to thee*; and *expecting thee*: (Ṣ, O, Ḳ:) or, accord. to Az, *they have advanced towards thee with their company* [agreeably with what next follows]. (TA.) — عُنُقٌ signifies also ‡ *A company* of men: (O, Ḳ, TA:) or *a numerous company* of men: or *a preceding company* of men: and is masc.: (TA:) and the *heads*, or *chiefs*, (O, Ḳ, TA,) of men; (O, TA;) and the *great ones*, and *nobles*. (TA.) فَظَلَّتْ أَعْنَاقُهُمْ لَهَا خَاضِعِينَ, in the Ḳur [xxvi. 3], is expl. as meaning ‡ *And their great ones* and *their chiefs* [*shall continue submissive to it*]: or *their companies*: the pret. is here used in the sense of the future: (O, TA:) or, as some say, the meaning is, *their necks*. (TA. [See also art. خضع.]) One says also, جَآءَ فِى عُنُقٍ مِنَ النَّاسِ † *He came in a company of men*. (O.) And جَآءَ القَوْمُ عُنُقًا عُنُقًا † *The people came in* [*successive*] *parties*; as Az says, each, or every, company of them being termed عُنُق: or, as some say, *gradually, party by party*. (TA.) And هُمْ عُنُقٌ عَلَيْهِ † *They are a company*, or *party, combined against him*. (TA.) And it is said in a trad., لَا يَزَالُ النَّاسُ مُخْتَلِفَةً أَعْنَاقُهُمْ فِى طَلَبِ الدُّنْيَا i. e. † [*Mankind will not cease to have*] *their companies* [or *parties diverse in the seeking of worldly good*]: or, as some say, *their heads*, or *chiefs*, and *great ones*. (TA.) — Also † *A portion* of good; (IAạr, O, TA;) من الخير in the Ḳ being a mistake for مِنَ الخَيْرِ: (TA:) and of property: and of work, whether good or evil. (O.) One says, لِفُلَانٍ عُنُقٌ مِنَ الخَيْرِ † *To such a one pertains a portion of good*. (IAạr, O, TA.) And it is said in a trad., المُؤَذِّنُونَ أَطْوَلُ النَّاسِ أَعْنَاقًا يَوْمَ القِيَامَةِ, (IAạr, O, Ḳ,* TA,) meaning † [*The proclaimers of the times of prayer will be*] *the most abundant of men in* [*good*] *works* [*on the day of resurrection*]: (IAạr, O, Ḳ, TA:) or the meaning is, *chiefs*; because the Arabs describe such as being long-necked: but it is also related otherwise, i. e., إِعْنَاقًا, with kesr to the hemzeh, meaning, [*the most*] *hasting* [*of men*] to Paradise: (O, Ḳ, TA:) and there are other explanations: (Ḳ, TA:) one is, that they *shall be preceders* to Paradise; from the saying لَهُ عُنُقٌ فِى الخَيْرِ *he has precedence in that which is good*: so says Th: another, that they *shall be forgiven to the extent of the prolonging of their voice*: another, that they *shall be given an addition above other men*: another, that they *shall be in a state of happiness and sprightliness, raising the eyes and looking in expectation*; for permission will have been given to them to enter Paradise: and other explanations may be found in the Fáïḳ and the Nh and the Expositions of Bkh. (TA.) — عُنُقٌ is also a pl. of the next word. (TA.)

عَنَاقٌ *A she-kid*, (T, Ṣ, Mgh, O, Mṣb, Ḳ,) *when a year old*, (T, TA,) or *not yet a year old*: (IAth, Mṣb, TA:) and *a lamb* or *kid*, or *such as is just born*; syn. سَخْلَةٌ: (TA: [see مُعْنَاق, last sentence:]) pl. (of pauc., TA) أَعْنُقٌ and (of mult., TA) عُنُوقٌ (Ṣ, O, Mṣb, Ḳ, TA) and also عُنُقٌ, with two ḍammehs. (TA.) العُنُوقُ بَعْدَ النُّوقِ [*The she-kids after the she-camels*], (T, O, Ḳ, &c.,) meaning he has become a pastor of she-kids after having been a pastor of she-camels, (T,) is a prov., (T, O, Ḳ, &c.,) applied to him who has become lowered from a high station, (T,) or to a case of straitness after ampleness. (O, Ḳ.) — And العَنَاقُ, (Ṣ,) or عَنَاقُ الأَرْضِ, (T, Mgh, O, Mṣb, Ḳ, TA, &c.,) [which latter is now applied to *The badger*; *ursus meles*; if correctly, app. because it burrows in the earth; but this application does not well agree with the following descriptions;] *a certain beast*, (O, Mṣb, Ḳ, TA,) *of the beasts of the earth, like the* فَهْد [or *lynx*], (Ṣ,) *about the size of the dog, an animal of prey*, (Mṣb,) *that hunts*, (O, Mṣb, TA,) *smaller than the* فَهْد, *long in the back*, (TA,) *also called* التُّفَّةُ, (Mṣb, TA,) *or, by some*, التُّفَةُ, (O,* Mṣb,) with teshdeed to the ف and with the fem. ة, (Mṣb,) *and* الفُنْجُلُ, (O, TA,) *in Pers.* سياه گوش [or سِيَاه گُوش, i. e. "black ear," if meaning the badger, app. because of the black mark on each ear]; (Mgh, O, Ḳ, TA;) said by IAmb to be *a foul beast, that is not eaten, and that does not eat anything but flesh*; (Mṣb;) As says, *it is above the size of the Chinese dog, hunts like as does the* فَهْد, *eats flesh, and is of the beasts of prey; and is said to be the only beast that conceals its footmarks when it runs, except the hare*; and he says also, "I have seen it in the desert (البَادِيَة), and it was *black in the head, the rest of it being white*:" the pl. is عُنُوقٌ. (TA.) — العَنَاقُ is also the name of † *The middle star* [ζ] *of* [*the three stars called*] بَنَات نَعْشٍ الكُبْرَى [*in the tail of Ursa Major*]: (O,* Ḳ,* TA:) *by it is a small star called* السُّهَا, *by looking at which persons try their powers of sight*. (Ḳzw. [See also القَائِدُ, in art. قود.]) — [And the same, or عَنَاقُ الأَرْضِ, is the name of † *The star γ in what is figured by some as the right, and by others as the left, leg*, or *foot, of Andromeda*.] — And عَنَاقٌ signifies also *A calamity*, or *misfortune*: (Ṣ, O, Ḳ: [see also العَنْقَآء, voce أَعْنَقُ:]) and *a hard affair* or *event* or *case*: (Ḳ:) and one says, لَقِىَ مِنْهُ أُذُنَىْ عَنَاقٍ, (Ṣ, O, TA,*) and عَنَاقَ الأَرْضِ, (TA,) *He experienced, from him*, or *it, calamity*, or *misfortune*, and *a hard affair* &c. (Ṣ, O, TA.*) And جَآءَ بِأُذُنَىْ عَنَاقٍ means *He uttered an exorbitant lie*. (TA.) — Also *Disappointment*; (IAạr, Ṣ, O, Ḳ;) and so † عَنَاقَةٌ. (O, Ḳ.) Such is the meaning in the saying of a poet, أُبْتُمْ بِالعَنَاقِ [*Ye returned with disappointment*]: (Ṣ, O, TA:) or the meaning is بِالمُنْكَرِ [*with that which was disapproved*, or *abominable*, &c.]; agreeably with an explanation of العَنَاقُ by 'Alee Ibn-Ḥamzeh. (TA.) — And *A* [*stony tract such as is termed*] حَرَّة. (TA.) — And The *poor-rate of two years*: so in the saying of Aboo-Bekr (Ḳ, TA) to 'Omar, when he contended in war with the apostates, (TA,) لَوْ مَنَعُونِى عَنَاقًا [*If they refused me a poor-rate of two years*]: but it is also otherwise related, i. e. عِقَالًا, meaning *a poor-rate of a year*. (Ḳ, TA.)

عَنِيقٌ i. q. † مُعَانَقَةٌ [*Embracing by putting the arms around the neck* of another]. (Ṣ,* O, Ḳ.) A poet says,

* وَبَاتَ خَيَالُ طَيْفِكِ لِى عَنِيقًا *
* إِلَى أَنْ حَيْعَلَ الدَّاعِى الفَلَاحَا *

[*And the fancied image of thy form coming in sleep passed the night embracing my neck until the caller* to the prayer of daybreak *cried, Come to security* (حَىَّ عَلَى الفَلَاحِ)]. (Ṣ, O.) — See also مُعْنَاق: — and see عَنَق: — and عُنُق, first sentence.

ذوات العنيق [app. ذَوَاتُ العُنَيْقِ] *A sort* [app. *a bad sort*] *of dates*. (TA voce حُبَيْق.)

عَنَاقَةٌ: see عَنَاقٌ, last quarter.

يَوْمُ عَانِقٍ *One of the days* [or *conflicts*] *of the Arabs*, (O, TA,) *well known*. (Ḳ, TA.)

عَانِقَآءُ *One of the holes of the jerboa*, (IAạr, O, Ḳ,) *which it fills with earth or dust, and in which, when it fears, it conceals itself to its neck*: (IAạr, O:) and likewise, *of the hare* [?]. (TA. [See 5.]) The holes of the jerboa are this and the نَاعِقَآء and the نَافِقَآء and the قَاصِعَآء and the رَاهِطَآء and the دَامَّآء. (El-Mufaḍḍal, L.)

أَعْنَقُ *Long-necked*; (Ṣ, O, Ḳ;) as also † مُعْنِقٌ applied to a man, and † مُعْنِقَةٌ applied to a woman: (TA:) or أَعْنَقُ signifies *long and thick in the neck*: (TA:) fem. عَنْقَآءُ. (Ṣ.) — Applied to to a dog, *Having a whiteness in his neck*. (O, Ḳ.) — Also *A certain stallion, of the horses of the Arabs*, (O, Ḳ,) *well known*: (O:) whence بَنَاتُ أَعْنَقَ [*The progeny of Aạnak*], (O, Ḳ,) *certain fleet*, or *excellent, horses*, (TA in art. بنى,) *so called in relation to that stallion*. (O, Ḳ.) And also said to be the name of *A certain wealthy* دِهْقَان [or *headman*, or *chief, of a village* or *town*; or *proprietor thereof, in Khurásán and El-'Irák*; &c.]: (O, Ḳ:*) whence بَنَاتُ أَعْنَقَ

meaning *The daughters of* this *Aanak*: and it is said to have this or the former meaning in a verse of Ibn-Ahmar: (O, Ḳ:) accord. to Aṣ, *certain women that were in the first age, described as being beautiful*: accord. to Abu-l-'Abbás, *certain women that were in El-Ahwáz*; and mentioned by Jereer in satirizing El-Farezdaḳ. (O.) — العَنْقَآءُ signifies also *Calamity*, or *misfortune*: (Ṣ, O, Ḳ: [like العَنَاقُ:]) one says, حَلَّقَتْ بِهِ عَنْقَآءُ مُغْرِبٌ [for مُغْرِبَةٌ, meaning *A calamity carried him off* or *away*; lit., *soared with him*]; and [in like manner] طَارَتْ بِهِ العَنْقَآءُ: (Ṣ, O:) [see also art. غرب:] and (Ḳ) originally, (Ṣ,) العَنْقَآءُ signifies *a certain bird, of which the name is known, but the body is unknown*: (Ṣ, O, Ḳ:) [or it is *a fabulous bird*:] AHát says, in the Book of Birds, العَنْقَآءُ المُغْرِبَةُ means *calamity*; and not any of the birds that we know: IDrd says, عَنْقَآءُ مُغْرِبٌ is a phrase for which there is no foundation: it is said to mean *a great bird that is not seen save* [*once*] *in ages*; and by frequency of usage it became a name for *calamity*: (O:) it is also said to be called عنقآء because it has in its neck a whiteness like the neck-ring: Kr says that they assert it to be *a bird that is found at the place of the setting of the sun*: Zj, that it is *a bird that no one has seen*: some say that it is meant in the Ḳur cv. 3: and some, that it is *the eagle*: (TA:) it is *called in Pers.* سِيمُرْغ: (MA:) and it is mentioned also in art. غرب [q. v.]. (Ḳ.) [See also my translation of the Thousand and One Nights, chap. xx. note 22.] — Also, i. e. العَنْقَآءُ, (Ḳ,) or عَنْقَآءُ, (O,) *An* [*eminence of the kind called*] أَكَمَة, *above an overlooking mountain*: (O, Ḳ:) or العَنْقَآءُ المُغْرِبُ signifies *the summit of an* أَكَمَة *on the highest part of a tall*, or *long*, *mountain*: so says Aboo-Málik, who denies that it means a bird. (TA in art. غرب.) And عَنْقَآءُ applied to a [hill, or mountain, such as is termed] هَضْبَة signifies *High and long*. (TA. [And a meaning similar to this seems to be indicated in the Ṣ and O. See, again, art. غرب.])

تُعْنُوقٌ, with ḍamm, (Ḳ,) or تَعْنُوقٌ, (so in the O,) *A plain*, or *soft*, *tract of land*: pl. تَعَانِيقُ. (O, Ḳ.)

مُعْنِقٌ; and its fem., with ة: see أَعْنَقُ, first sentence. — Also, the former, *Hard and elevated land* or *ground*, *having around it such as is plain*, or *soft*, (O, Ḳ, TA,) *extending about a mile*, and *less*: pl. مَعَانِيقُ: and they have imagined it to be termed ▼ مِعْنَاقٌ, [partly on account of this pl., and partly] because of the many instances like مُذْكِرٌ and مِذْكَارٌ, and مُتْئِمٌ and مِتْآمٌ. (TA.) — And مَرْبَاةٌ مُعْنِقَةٌ *A lofty place of observation*. (O, Ḳ.) — See also مِعْنَاقٌ, in three places. — مُعْنِقٌ also occurs in a trad., applied as an epithet to a believer, meaning † *One who hastens in his obedience, and takes a wide range in his work*. (TA.) — And مُعْنِقَاتٌ, as applied by Dhu-r-Rummeh to [portions of sand such as are termed] أَدْعَاص [pl. of دِعْص] means *Lying in advance of others*. (TA.) — See also the next paragraph.

مُعْنِقَةٌ *A curved piece of rock*. (O, Ḳ.) — And بَلَدٌ مُعْنِقَةٌ *A country in which there is no abiding, by reason of the dryness and barrenness of the ground thereof*: (O, Ḳ:) thus says Ṣgh: but in the Nawádir el-Aaráb it is said that ▼ بِلَادٌ مُعْنِقَةٌ means *countries that are distant*, or *remote*. (TA. [See also 4.])

قِلَادَةٌ مُعْنِقَةٌ *A* قِلَادَة [meaning *collar*], (T, Ṣ, O, Ḳ, TA,) accord. to ISd, *that is put upon the neck of a dog*. (TA.) — Also *A small* [*elongated and elevated tract such as is termed*] حَبْل (ISh, O, Ḳ, TA, [الجَبَلُ in the CḲ being a mistake for الحَبْلُ,]) of sand, (ISh, O,) *in front of*, or *before*, *the* [*main portion of*] *sands*: by rule it should be مُعْنَاقَة, because they said in the pl. مَعَانِيقُ الرِّمَالِ: (ISh, O, Ḳ:) or one should say مَعَانِقُ الرَّمْلِ. (ISh, O.) — See also المُعَنَّقَةُ.

مُعْنِقِيٌّ, with kesr to the م, [app. مِعْنَقِيٌّ,] sing. of مَعَانِقُ applied to *Certain horses* (خُيُول) *of the Arabs*. (TA.)

المُعَنَّقَةُ, (thus in the O,) or ▼ المُعْنِقَةُ, like مُحَدِّثَة, thus in the copies of the Ḳ, but correctly with kesr to the م, [app. ▼ المِعْنَقَةُ,] pl. مَعَانِقُ, (TA,) *A certain small creeping thing*; (O, Ḳ, TA;) AHát says that المَعَانِقُ signifies [*the small creeping things called*] مُقَرِّضَاتُ الأَسَاقِى [*that gnaw holes in the skins used for water or milk*], *having neck-rings* (أَطْوَاق), [app. *white marks round the neck*, for it is added,] *with a whiteness in their necks*. (TA.)

مُعَنَّقَاتٌ, applied to mountains (جِبَال) accord. to the copies of the Ḳ, [and thus in the O,] but correctly حِبَال, with the unpointed ح, (TA,) [i. e. elongated and elevated tracts of sand,] signifies *Long*. (O, Ḳ, TA.) — See also المُعْنِقَةُ. = المُعَنَّقَةُ as signifying *Hectic fever* (حُمَّى الدِّقِّ) is post-classical. (TA.)

مِعْنَاقٌ, applied to a horse, signifies جَيِّدُ العَنَقِ [i. e. *Excellent*, or *good*, *in the pace called* عَنَق]; (Ṣ, O, Ḳ, TA; [in the CḲ, erroneously, العُنُقِ;]) as also ▼ مُعْنِقٌ (TA) and ▼ عَنِيقٌ: (O,* TA:) and the first is also applied to a she-camel, as meaning *that goes the pace called* عَنَق: (IB, TA:) the pl. is مَعَانِيقُ. (Ḳ.) And one says also رَجُلٌ ▼ مُعْنِقٌ [and مِعْنَاقٌ, meaning *A man hastening*]: and ▼ قَوْمٌ مُعْنِقُونَ and مَعَانِيقُ. (TA.) فَانْطَلَقْنَا مَعَانِيقَ إِلَى النَّاسِ occurs in a trad., meaning [*And we went away*] *hastening* [*to the people*]: (Sh, TA:) and in another, accord. to different relaters, ▼ فَانْطَلَقُوا مُعَانِقِينَ or مَعَانِيقَ i. e. [*And they went away*] *hastening*. (TA.) And مِعْنَاقُ الوَسِيقَةِ occurs in a verse of Abu-l-Muthellem El-Hudhalee, as some relate it, meaning *Hastening after*, or *near after, his* طَرِيدَة [app. as signifying *the camels driven away by him*]: but as others relate it, it is مِعْتَاقٌ, with ت, meaning as expl. in art. عتق. (O. [The former is said in the Ṣ, in art. عتق, to be not allowable.]) = It is also applied to a ewe or goat (شَاةٌ مِنْ غَنَمٍ) as meaning *That brings forth* [app., accord. to analogy, *that brings forth often*] عُنُوق [meaning *lambs* or *kids*, pl. of عَنَاقٌ]. (TA.) = See also مُعْنِقٌ.

مُعَانِقٌ: see عَنِيقٌ: — and see also مِعْنَاقٌ.

مُعَنَّقٌ *A place where the* أَعْنَاق [app. meaning *upper portions*] *of the* جِبَال [or *mountains*], accord. to the copies of the Ḳ, [and thus in the O,] but correctly حِبَال, with the unpointed ح, [i. e. *elongated and elevated tracts of sand*], (TA,) *emerge from the* سَرَاب [or *mirage*]: (O, Ḳ, TA:) used in this sense by Ru-beh. (O, TA.)

Quasi عنقد

عُنْقُودٌ and عِنْقَادٌ see in art. عقد; the ن being held to be augmentative.

عنكب

عَنْكَبٌ: see عَنْكَبُوتٌ, in two places.

عَنْكَبَاةٌ and عَنْكَبَآءُ: see the next paragraph.

عَنْكَبُوتٌ; (Ṣ, O, Ḳ;) generally fem., (Ṣ, O,) but sometimes masc.; (O, Ḳ;) also, fem., عَنْكَبَاةٌ, (Ṣ, O, Ḳ,) in the dial. of El-Yemen, with the ء put before the ن; (TA;) and ▼ عَنْكَبَاةٌ and عَنْكَبُوَةٌ (so in the O and TA, but in the CḲ and a MS. copy of the Ḳ عَنْكَبُوَةٌ); and ▼ عَنْكَبَآءُ; (O, Ḳ;) the last mentioned by Sb as shewing the ت in عنكبوت to be an augmentative letter; but it is doubtful whether this be a sing., or a quasi-pl. n.: (TA:) also, masc., ▼ عَنْكَبٌ; (IAạr, O, Ḳ;) fem., عَنْكَبَةٌ: (IAạr, Ḳ:) or the former of these two words is a coll. gen. n. [and the latter, its n. un.]: (TA:) [*The spider*;] the *thing that weaves*; (Ṣ, O;) *an insect that weaves a delicate web in the air and upon the upper part of a well*: (TA:) pl. عَنَاكِبُ (Ṣ, O, Ḳ) and عَنْكَبُوتَاتٌ (Ḳ) and عَنَاكِيبُ (Lḥ, TA) and عَنَاكِبِيتُ, (Aṣ, Ḳṭr, TA,) which last is anomalous, in its having four letters together after its ا: dim. ▼ عُنَيْكِبٌ and ▼ عُنَيْكِيبٌ and ▼ عُنَيْكِبِيتٌ; but this last is not approved: (TA:) quasi-pl. nouns أَعْكُبٌ and عُكُبٌ and عِكَابٌ [in the CḲ أَعْكَبٌ]. (Ḳ.) بَيْتُ العنكبوت [*The spider's web*] is also called عُكْدُبَة. (Fr, TA.) — Sá'ideh-Ibn-Ju-eiyeh says,

* مَقَتُّ نِسَآءً بِالحِجَازِ صَوَالِحًا *

* وَإِنَّا مَقَتْنَا كُلَّ سَوْدَآءَ عَنْكَبِ ▼ *

[meaning *I hated virtuous women in El-Ḥijáz; and verily we hated every black, short woman*: for] here عنكب signifies *short*: (Skr, L:) or it may be syn. with عَنْكَبُوتٌ, but be used as an epithet, though a subst., because it implies blackness and shortness. (IJ, L.) — زَهْرُ العَنْكَبُوتِ: see رُتَيْلَآءُ. — عنكبوت also signifies *A worm*, or *maggot*, *that is engendered in the honeycomb, and spoils the honey*. (AḤn, L.) — عنكبوت is mentioned in this art. agreeably with the rule of Sb;

when ن occupies the second place in a word, it is not to be pronounced augmentative without proof: but J and some others consider the ن augmentative, and mention the word in art. عكب. (TA.)

عُنَّيْكِبٌ and عُنَّيْكِيبٌ and عُنَّيْكِبِيتٌ: see the next preceding paragraph.

مُعَنْكَبُ القَرْنِ A he-goat *having a horn curved so as to resemble a ring.* (Az, TA.)

عنم

4. اعنم *He pastured upon, or depastured, the species of tree called* عَنَم. (AA, Ḳ,* TA.)

عَنَمٌ *A certain tree of El-Ḥijáz, having a red fruit, to which are likened the dyed fingers* or *ends of fingers:* (IAar, Ḳ:) in the "Nawádir" said to be *sappy,* or *tender, branches, that grow upon the trunks of the* [*trees called*] عِضَاه, *not resembling the other branches thereof, red in colour, the upper parts of the blossoms of which divide into four divisions, like a branch of an* أَرَاطَة [n. un. of أَرْطًى, q. v.]; *coming forth in winter and in summer:* (IDrd, TA:) or *a species of trees having tender branches, to which are likened the fingers,* or *the ends of the fingers, of girls,* or *young women:* (Ṣ:) in the "Book of Plants" [of AḤn] said to be *a small tree that grows in the midst,* or *interior part, of the* سَمُرَة [or *gum-acacia-tree*], *having a red fruit:* (TA:) or, accord. to AA, the [*fruit called*] زُعْرُور [q. v.]: (TA, and so in a copy of the Ṣ:) or, (Ṣ, Ḳ, TA,) as AO says, (Ṣ, TA,) the *extremities of the Syrian* خُرُوب [or *locust-tree*]: (Ṣ, Ḳ, TA:) and he says that a verse of En-Nábighah is recited thus:

بِمُخَضَّبٍ رَخْصٍ كَأَنَّ بَنَانَهُ
عَنَمٌ عَلَى أَغْصَانِهِ لَمْ يُعْقَدِ

[*With a dyed* member (عُضْو being understood, instead of كَفّ, because the latter is fem.,) *soft,* or *tender, as though its fingers,* or *its fingers' ends, were 'anam upon their branches, not yet compactly organized*]; which shows that it means a plant, not a worm: (Ṣ, TA:) [for] it is said to signify *a species of red worm, found in sand:* (Ḥam p. 288, in which are other explanations, nearly agreeing with some here:) or, as some say, the *fruit of the* عَوْسَج [or *box-thorn*], which is red, and then becomes black when thoroughly ripe; therefore En-Nábighah says لَمْ يُعْقَد, meaning *that had not yet become ripe:* (IB, TA; and also inserted in the text of a copy of the Ṣ:) and, (Ḳ, TA,) as AḤn says in one instance, (TA,) *threads* [or *tendrils*] *by means of which the vine clings to its trellises:* (Ḳ, TA:) and (accord. to Lth, TA) the *thorns of the* طَلْح [or *acacia gummifera*]; (Ḳ, TA;) but this is said by Az to be incorrect: (TA:) [see also a hemistich cited voce طَرَفٌ:] the n. un. is ↓ عَنَمَةٌ. (Ḳ.)

عَنَمَةٌ: see what immediately precedes. —— Also *A species of the* [*sort of lizard called*] وَزَغ; (Ḳ, TA;) accord. to Lth; but this is rejected, as incorrect, by Az: it is said to be *like the* عَظَايَة, *except that it is more white and more comely.* (TA.) —— Also, (accord. to copies of the Ḳ,) or عُنْمَةٌ, (accord. to the TA,) *A fissure in the lip of a human being.* (Ḳ.)

عَنَمِىٌّ A *beautiful red* face; (Ḳ, TA;) *tinged over with redness.* (TA.)

عَيْنُومٌ The *male frog.* (Ḳ.)

بَنَانٌ مُعَنَّمٌ [*Fingers,* or *fingers' ends,*] *dyed,* or *tinged* [with ḥinnà or the like]. (IJ, Ṣ, Ḳ.)

عنو

1. عَنَا, (Ṣ, Mgh, Mṣb,) first pers. عَنَوْتُ, (Ḳ,) aor. يَعْنُو, (Ṣ, Mṣb,) inf. n. عُنُوٌّ, (Ṣ, Mgh, Mṣb, Ḳ,*) and ↓ عَنْوَةٌ is the subst. thereof, (Mgh, Ḳ,* TA,) [and] so is ↓ عَنَآءٌ, (Mṣb,) or عَنْوَةٌ is its inf. n., (MA,) [and so, app., is عَنَآءٌ, in this sense as well as in another sense, accord. to the Ḳ,] *He was,* or *became, lowly, humble,* or *submissive;* (Ṣ, MA, Mgh, Mṣb, Ḳ,) and *obedient;* (MA, TA;) to the truth, &c. (TA.) You say, عَنَا لَهُ *He was,* or *became, lowly, humble,* or *submissive, to him;* or *obedient to him.* (MA.) And hence the saying in the Ḳur [xx. 110], وَعَنَتِ ٱلْوُجُوهُ لِلْحَىِّ ٱلْقَيُّومِ (Ṣ, TA) *And the countenances shall be lowly* &c. [*to the Deathless,* or *Ever-living, the Self-subsisting by Whom all things subsist:* or *shall be downcast;* like the Hebr. phrases ending verses 5 and 6 in Gen. iv.]: or *shall be submissive like captives:* or the meaning is [*shall be depressed by*] *the depressing of the forehead and the knee* [or rather *knees*] *and the hands in the lowering of the head and the prostrating oneself* [in prayer]: or [عَنَت is here from عَنِىَ, belonging to art. عنى, and الوجوه is used by a synecdoche for *the persons* (as being the most noble of all the parts thereof), and the meaning is] *shall suffer fatigue,* or *weariness,* and *shall toil.* (TA.) —— And عَنَا, inf. n. عُنُوٌّ (M, Mṣb, Ḳ, TA, accord. to some copies of the Ḳ [erroneously] عَنْوٌ) and عُنِىٌّ (TA) and عَنَآءٌ; (Ḳ;) and عَنِىَ; (M, Ḳ;) *He became a captive:* (Ḳ:) and the latter verb signifies also *he stuck fast in captivity:* (Ḳ in art. عنى:) or both of these verbs have this latter signification: (Mṣb:) [or] you say, عَنَا فِيهِمْ فُلَانٌ أَسِيرًا *Such a one remained among them a captive;* and *was in a state of confinement:* (Ṣ:) and عَنَآءٌ signifies also *confinement,* or *imprisonment, in hardship and humiliation.* (TA.) Hence the trad., الخَالُ وَارِثُ مَنْ لَا وَارِثَ لَهُ يَفُكُّ عُنْيَهُ i. e. أَسْرَهُ [*The maternal uncle is the heir of him who has* no more nearly-allied *heir: he shall loose his* (the latter's) *captivity*]: meaning [he shall acquit him of] what is incumbent on him, and clings to him, because of the actions that require punishment or retaliation, the way [or custom] of which is that the عَاقِلَة [q. v., of whom he is a member,] bear the responsibility for them. (Nh, TA.) And ↓ عَنْوَةٌ is the subst. of the verb in this sense also. (Ḳ,* TA.) —— And عَنَا, aor. يَعْنُو, inf. n. عَنْوَةٌ, *He took a thing by force:* — and also *he took it peaceably,* or *by surrender:* thus having two contr. significations. (Mṣb.) [But see below, where عَنْوَةٌ is expl. as though it were the subst. of the verb in these two senses.] —— عَنَوْتُ الشَّىْءَ *I put forth,* or *produced, the thing:* and *I made the thing apparent,* or *showed it:* (Ṣ:) or it has the latter signification; (Ḳ;) as also عَنَيْتُ الشَّىْءَ: (IḲṭṭ, TA in art. عنى:) and عَنَوْتُ بِالشَّىْءِ has the former signification. (Ḳ.) And ↓ عَنْوَةٌ is the subst. of the verb thus used, (Ḳ, TA,) i. e. in these two senses, as well as in others mentioned above. (TA.) And one says, عَنَتِ الأَرْضُ بِالنَّبَاتِ, (ISk, Ṣ, and Ḳ in this art. and in art. عنى,) aor. تَعْنُو, inf. n. عُنُوٌّ; (ISk, Ṣ;) and aor. تَعْنِى; (Ks, Ṣ;) *The land made apparent,* or *showed,* [or *put forth,* or *produced,*] *its plants,* or *herbage;* (Ṣ, Ḳ;) as also ↓ أَعْنَتْهُ. (Ḳ.) And لَمْ تَعْنُ بِلَادُنَا بِشَىْءٍ and لَمْ تُعْنِ *Our country did not give growth to anything.* (Ṣ.) And مَا أَعْنَتِ ↓ الأَرْضُ شَيْئًا *The land did not give growth,* or *has not given growth, to anything.* (Ṣ.) — And [hence, app.,] سَأَلْتُهُ فَلَمْ يَعْنُ لِى بِشَىْءٍ *I asked him, and he did not* (لَمْ يَنْدَ and لَمْ يَبِضَّ) *to me,* or *for me, anything.* (TA.) —— عَنَتْ بِهِ أُمُورٌ *Events befell him.* (Ṣ, Ḳ.) [See also 1 in art. عنى.] — And عَنَا الأَمْرُ عَلَيْهِ *The event,* or *affair, was difficult,* or *distressing, to him; distressed,* or *troubled, him.* (ISd, Ḳ, TA.) —— عَنَاهُ الأَمْرُ, aor. يَعْنُوهُ: see 1 in art. عنى, first sentence. — And عَنَا فِيهِ الأَكْلُ, aor. يَعْنُو, inf. n. عُنُوٌّ: see 1 in art. عنى. —— عَنَا الكَلْبُ الشَّىْءَ, (CḲ, [in the TA and in my MS. copy of the Ḳ, لِلشَّىْءِ, but see what follows,]) aor. يَعْنُوهُ, inf. n. عنو [app., supposing the verb to be trans. by itself, عَنْوٌ], (TA,) *The dog came to the thing and smelt it:* (Ḳ, TA:) and one says, هٰذَا يَعْنُو هٰذَا *This comes to this and smells it.* (TA.) —— عَنَتِ القِرْبَةُ بِمَآءٍ كَثِيرٍ, (Ḳ, TA,) aor. تَعْنُو, (TA,) *The water-skin did not keep,* or *retain, much water, so that it appeared* [*oozing from it*]: (Ḳ, TA:) or, as some say, عَنَتِ القِرْبَةُ signifies *the water-skin let flow its water.* (TA.) — And عَنَا, inf. n. عُنُوٌّ, said of blood, *It flowed.* (IḲṭṭ, TA.) —— And عَنَا, aor. يَعْنُو, inf. n. عُنُوٌّ, signifies also قَامَ [*He,* or *it, stood;* &c.]. (IḲṭṭ, TA.) —— See also Q. Q. 1.

2. عَنَّاهُ, (Ṣ, TA,) inf. n. تَعْنِيَةٌ, (Ṣ, Ḳ,) *He imprisoned him,* or *confined him,* (Ṣ, Ḳ, TA,) *long, straitening him.* (TA.) [See also 4.] — And تَعْنِيَةٌ is said to signify *Any long confining* or *restraining:* in a trad. of 'Alee, respecting the day of Ṣiffeen, he is related to have said, اِسْتَشْعِرُوا الخَشْيَةَ وَعَنُّوا بِالأَصْوَاتِ i. e. [*Make ye fear,* or *awe,* (app. of God,) *to be the thing next your hearts,*] *and restrain,* and *suppress, the voices;* as though he forbade their raising a confused and unintelligible clamour. (TA.) —— عَنَّيْتُ البَعِيرَ, (Ṣ,) inf. n. as above, (Ṣ, Ḳ,) *I smeared the camel*

with عَنِيَّة [q. v.]. (Ṣ, Ḳ.) [Hence تَعْنِيَةٌ as a subst., expl. below.] — See also Q. Q. 1.

4. اعناهُ *He rendered him lowly, humble,* or *submissive.* (Ṣ, TA.) — And (TA) *He made him* (Mṣb, Ḳ, TA) *to stick fast in captivity,* (Mṣb,) or *to be,* (Ḳ,) or *to remain,* or *continue,* (TA,) *a captive.* (Ḳ, TA.) — See also 1, in two places. — [Hence,] اعنى الوَلِيُّ الأَرْضَ *The* وَلِىّ, i. e. the *rain after the* وَسْمِىّ, *watered the land so that it gave growth to plants,* or *herbage.* (Ṣ,* IḲṭṭ, TA.) — And اعنى الرَّجُلُ *The man found,* or *lighted on, land that had produced herbage such as is termed* عُشْب, [for قد اعشرت (to which I cannot assign any apposite meaning) in my original, I read قَدْ أَعْشَبَتْ], *and of which the pasturage had become abundant.* (TA.) — See also Q. Q. 1.

5. تعنّى *He* [a camel] *was,* or *became, smeared with* عَنِيَّة [q. v.]: whence the saying of Esh-Shaabee, لَأَنْ أَتَعَنَّى بِعَنِيَّةٍ أَحَبُّ إِلَىَّ مِنْ أَنْ أَقُولَ فِى مَسْأَلَةٍ بِرَأْيِى [*Verily my being smeared with* عَنِيَّة *would be more approvable to me than my saying respecting a question according to my opinion*]. (TA.)

Q. Q. 1. عَنْوَنْتُ الكِتَابَ, (Ṣ, Ḳ, TA,) inf. n. عَنْوَنَةٌ and عِنْوَانٌ, (TA,) *i. q.* عَلْوَنْتُهُ, (Ṣ,) *I put an* عُنْوَان [i. e. *a superscription,* or *title,*] *to the book,* or *writing;* (Ḳ, TA;) syn. وَسَمْتُهُ: (TA:) and one says also, عَنَا ♦ الكِتَابَ, aor. يَعْنُوهُ, meaning عَنْوَنَهُ; (IḲṭṭ, TA;) and ♦ اعناهُ and ♦ عنّاهُ and عَنَّنَهُ [which is said to be the original of عَنَّاهُ], meaning the same; (Ḳ and TA in art. عنى;) and عَنَيْتُ الكِتَابَ, inf. n. عَنْىٌ, likewise signifies *I wrote the* عُنْيَان [or عُنْوَان] *of the book,* or *writing.* (IḲṭṭ, TA in art. عنى.)

عَنًا: see the paragraph next following.

عِنْوٌ sing. of أَعْنَآءٌ as signifying The *sides, regions, quarters,* or *tracts,* (Ṣ, Ḳ,) of a country, (Ṣ,) or of the sky; (Ḳ;) like أَحْنَآءٌ: (Ṣ in art. حنو and حنى:) or, accord. to IAạr, its sing., in this sense, is ♦ عَنًا: (Ṣ:) and the pl. signifies also the *sides* of the face. (TA.) — And sing. of أَعْنَآءٌ as signifying *A party* of men *of sundry,* or *different, tribes.* (Ṣ, Ḳ.)

عَنْوَةٌ *Force,* or *constraint:* (Mgh, Ḳ, TA:) or the *taking by force;* (Mṣb, TA;) as inf. n. of عَنَا [q. v.]. (Mṣb.) One says, فُتِحَتْ مَكَّةُ عَنْوَةً *Mekkeh was taken forcibly,* or *by force.* (Mgh.) And أَخَذَهُ عَنْوَةً *He took it by force.* (TA.) And فُتِحَتْ هٰذِهِ المَدِينَةُ عَنْوَةً i. e. [*This city was taken*] *by means of conflict; its occupants having been combated until they had it taken from them by superior power or force, and were powerless to keep it, so they left it without there having occurred between them and the Muslims* [or *invaders*] *a treaty of peace.* (TA.) — Also *Love,* or *affection:* (ISd, Ḳ, TA:) or *submission,* and *concession* or *a consequence of submission* and *concession, on the part of him from whom a thing is taken:* (TA:) or the *taking peaceably,* or *by surrender;* as inf. n. of عَنَا [q. v.]: (Mṣb:) thus it has two contr. significations. (Mṣb, Ḳ, TA.) A poet (cited by Fr, TA) says,

فَمَا أَخَذُوهَا عَنْوَةً عَنْ مَوَدَّةٍ
وَلٰكِنَّ ضَرْبَ المَشْرَفِيِّ ٱسْتَقَالَهَا

(Mṣb, TA;) which is said to mean, [*And they did not take it,* or *her,* or *them,*] *by concession,* and *obedience,* [*arising from love,* or *affection,*] without fighting: [*but the smiting of the Meshrafee* sword *demanded the renouncing thereof:*] 'Abd-El-Ḳádir Ibn-'Amr El-Baghdádee asserts the meaning of عَنْوَة to be *submission* and *concession;* adducing as evidence thereof this verse; attributing the contr. meaning to the vulgar: both, however, are correct; and that first mentioned occurs repeatedly in traditions: but the most learned Yáḳoot Er-Roomee, in his Moajam, says that the verse above-cited may be rendered as meaning *and they did not take it,* or *her,* or *them, by superior power attended by* [or *in consequence of*] *love,* or *affection:* but they did so by fighting: and that this may be regarded as indicated by the poet's saying اخذوها; for otherwise he would have said, فَمَا سَلَّمُوهَا: and he says, it is a matter of common consent that عَنْوَة signifies *force,* and *superior power.* (TA.) — It is also a subst. from عَنَا in the first of senses mentioned in this art.: [i. e. it signifies *Lowliness, humility,* or *submissiveness:*] (Mgh, TA:) [and] so is ♦ عَنَآءٌ: (Mṣb:) see 1, first sentence. — And it is also a subst. from عَنَا as meaning "he became a captive:" [i. e. it signifies also *A state of captivity:*] (TA:) see, again, 1. — And it is also a subst. from عَنَا in two other senses, as stated above: [i. e. it app. signifies also The *act of putting forth,* or *producing,* a thing: and *of making* it *apparent,* or *showing,* it:] (TA:) see, again, 1.

عُنْوَانٌ (Ṣ, Ḳ, TA) and عِنْوَانٌ (TA) The سِمَة [meaning *superscription,* or *title,*] of a book, or writing; (Ḳ, TA;) *i. q.* عُلْوَانٌ; (Ṣ;) and عُنْيَانٌ signifies the same; (Ḳ in art. عنى;) as also ♦ مَعْنَى: (Ḳ, TA: [in the CḲ, كَمَعْنَاهُ is put for كَمَعْنَاهُ:]) the *inscription on the back,* or *outside,* of a book, or writing: (Ḥar p. 163, in explanation of عُنْوَانٌ:) [and the *address* of a letter. And hence,] *Anything that serves as an indication* of another thing is called its عُنْوَان. (Mṣb and Ḳ in art. عن.) One says, فِى جَبْهَتِهِ عُنْوَانٌ مِنْ كَثْرَةِ السُّجُودِ i. e. [*On his forehead is*] *a mark* [*from much prostration* in prayer]. (TA.) [See more in art. عن.]

عَنَآءٌ: see 1, first sentence; and عَنْوَةٌ, near the end: — and see also art. عنى.

عَنِيَّةٌ, of the measure فَعِيلَةٌ, The *urine of the camel, inspissated in the sun, with which such as is affected with mange,* or *scab, is smeared;* on the authority of AA: (Ṣ:) or *certain mixtures of urine and dung of camels, with which the camel affected with mange,* or *scab, is smeared;* also termed ♦ تَعْنِيَةٌ: (Ḳ:) or the *urine of camels that are caused to void their urine* [in my original تُشْبَانُ is erroneously written for تُشْبَالُ] *in the* [*season called*] رَبِيع *when they are satisfied with fresh pasture so as to be in no need of water, cooked* [app. *by boiling*] *until it becomes thick, when some flowers of some sorts of herbs, and* حَبّ المَحْلَب [the *prunus mahaleb* of Linn.], *are thrown upon it, and it becomes inspissated thereby, then put into small* [*earthen vessels of the kind called*] بَسَاتِيق [pl. of بُسْتُوقَة]: or *urine* [app. *of camels*] *mixed with certain things, and kept close for some time:* or *any* هِنَآء [generally meaning *tar,* or *a kind thereof, with which camels are smeared, as a remedy for the mange,* or *scab*]. (TA.) It is said in a prov., العَنِيَّةُ تَشْفِى الجَرَبَ; (Ṣ, TA;) or عَنِيَّتُهُ تَشْفِى الجَرَبَ [for مِنَ الجَرَبِ, i. e. *His* عنيّة *cures the mange,* or *scab*]: applied to the man of good judgment [whose advice is like a remedy]. (TA.)

عَانٍ *Lowly, humble,* or *submissive.* (Mṣb, TA.) — And (Mṣb, TA) hence, app., (TA,) *A captive;* (Ṣ, Mgh, Mṣb, Ḳ, TA;) fem. عَانِيَةٌ: (Mgh, TA:) pl. masc. عُنَاةٌ; (Ṣ, Mgh, Mṣb, TA;) and pl. fem. عَوَانٍ. (Ṣ, Mgh, TA.) — And عَوَانٍ signifies † *Women;* (Mṣb, Ḳ;) sing. عَانِيَةٌ: (Mṣb:) because they are confined like captives in the abodes of their husbands; (Mṣb;) or because they are treated wrongfully and not defended against their wrongers. (Ḳ.) It occurs in a trad. as meaning Females *in the condition of captives:* (Mgh:) or women who are *captives;* or *like captives.* (IAth, TA.) — And it signifies also عَوَامِلُ [which, as pl. of عَامِلَةٌ, is used as meaning *Workers,* or *labourers;* and also, as a subst., as meaning the *legs* of a beast or horse or the like]: and it is said to be used by El-Jaạdee as an epithet applied to the limbs of camels, or other beasts, used for riding. (TA.) — And hence, perhaps, it is applied to The مَكَّاسُون [or *collectors of the impost termed* مَكْس, q. v.]; because they are workers, or labourers, for the oppressors. (TA.) — Also (the sing.) *Flowing,* applied to blood, (Ṣ, Ḳ, TA,) or to water. (TA.)

مَعْنَوِىٌّ: see art. عنى.

تَعْنِيَةٌ: [originally inf. n. of 2, q. v.: used as a subst.,] see عَنِيَّةٌ.

مُعَنًّى A stallion [camel] *of mean origin, which, when excited by lust, is confined in the* [*enclosure called*] عُنَّة, *because his exercise of the faculty of a stallion is avoided:* but it is said that it is originally مُعَنَّنٌ, from العُنَّةُ; one of the نs being changed into ى: (Ṣ, TA:*) or *of mean origin, of which the legs are bound with a rope, when he is excited by lust, for that reason.* (TA.) — And A camel *of which the people of the Time of Ignorance used to displace the* سَنَاسِن [pl. of سِنْسِن, q. v.] *of one of his vertebræ, and to wound his hump, in order that he might not be ridden, and that no use might be made of his back:* this was done when his owner possessed a hundred camels, he being the camel by which they became a hundred: and this act was termed الإِغْلَاقُ: it may be from عَنَآءٌ meaning "fatigue;" or from the signification of "confinement from freedom of action." (TA.) ═ See also عُنْوَانٌ.

عنى

1. عَنَاهُ الأَمْرُ, aor. يَعْنِيهِ and يَعْنُوهُ, inf. n. عِنَايَةٌ and عَنَايَةٌ (Ḳ, TA) and عُنِىٌّ, (TA, as from the Ḳ, but not in the CḲ nor in my MS. copy of the Ḳ,) *The affair,* or *event,* or *case, disquieted him;* syn. أَهَمَّهُ [more fully expl. by what here follows]: (Ḳ, TA:) [عَنَاهُ may be generally rendered *it concerned him;* agreeing with this in meaning *it made him uneasy in mind, anxious,* or *careful;* and in meaning *it affected his interest,* or *was of importance to him;* like أَهَمَّهُ: and also *it concerned him* meaning *it related,* or *belonged, to him;* or *was of his business;* as will be shown by what follows: and] عَنَانِى كَذَا, aor. يَعْنِينِى, means *such a thing occurred,* or *happened, to me, and occupied me* [or *my mind*]. (Mṣb.) The saying [in the Ḳur lxxx. 37], لِكُلِّ امْرِئٍ مِنْهُمْ يَوْمَئِذٍ شَأْنٌ يُغْنِيهِ, thus accord. to one reading, means يُهِمُّهُ [i. e. *To every man of them shall belong, on that day, a business that will disquiet him,* &c.]: (Ksh, Bḍ;) or *a business in conjunction with which no other will disquiet him:* and like this is the other reading, which is with غ; (TA;) i. e. يُغْنِيهِ, meaning *which will suffice him in respect of his being disquieted thereby;* (Ksh, Bḍ;) or the meaning of the latter reading is, [*a business such that*] *he will not be able, in conjunction with his being disquieted thereby, to be disquieted by any other;* (TA;) or *a state that will occupy him so as to divert him from the state of any other.* (Jel.) And it is said in a trad. respecting charming, بِسْمِ ٱللّٰهِ أَرْقِيكَ مِنْ كُلِّ دَآءٍ يَعْنِيكَ i. e. [*By the name of God I charm thee from,* or *against, any disease*] *that may disquiet thee,* &c., (يُهِمُّكَ,) *and occupy thee* [or *thy mind*]. (TA.) And in another trad. it is said, مِنْ حُسْنِ إِسْلَامِ ٱلْمَرْءِ تَرْكُهُ مَا لَا يَعْنِيهِ, meaning مَا لَا يُهِمُّهُ [i. e. A condition *of the goodness of the man's submitting himself to the requirements of God is his leaving,* or *relinquishing, that which does not disquiet him,* &c.]; (Ṣ, TA;) the exceptions therefrom being such things as necessary food and clothing. (So in a marginal note in a copy of the Jámi' eṣ-Ṣagheer of Es-Suyooṭee.) See also the prov.

مُعْتَرِضٌ لِعَنَنٍ لَمْ يَعْنِهِ

expl. voce عَنَنٌ. [It is like the common saying, يَتَكَلَّمُ فِيمَا لَا يَعْنِيهِ *He talks of that which does not concern him;* meaning *that which does not relate,* or *belong, to him;* or *that which is not of his business.*] — عُنِىَ in the phrase عُنِىَ بِالأَمْرِ is [said to be] one of a class of verbs used in the pass. form though having the sense of the act. form, like زُهِىَ: (Ṣ in art. زهو:) [but is expl. as though pass. of عَنَاهُ meaning as above, or quasi-pass.:] you say, عُنِىَ بِالأَمْرِ, with ḍamm, (Ḳ, TA,) i. e. in the pass. form, (TA,) inf. n. عِنَايَةٌ, (Ḳ, TA,) with kesr; (TA;) and عَنِىَ بِهِ, of the class of رَضِىَ, (Ḳ, TA,) mentioned by IDrst and others of the expositors of the Fṣ, and by Hr and Mṭr, (MF, TA,) and by IḲṭṭ on the authority of Eṭ-Ṭoosee, (TA,) but this is seldom used, (Ḳ, TA,) the former being that which is commonly known, and this alone being mentioned by Th in his Fṣ, and by J and others; (TA;) *i. q.* اِهْتَمَّ بِهِ [i. e. *He became disquieted by the affair,* or *case;* or *rendered uneasy in mind, anxious,* or *careful, by it;* and consequently, *he became occupied by it,* or *with it;* or *set about it, and managed it*]; as also ↓ اِعْتَنَى بِهِ: (Ḳ, TA:) or ↓ اِعْتَنَيْتُ بِأَمْرِهِ means *I became disquieted by his affair,* or *case;* or *rendered uneasy in mind, anxious,* or *careful, by it;* (اِهْتَمَمْتُ بِهِ;) *and minded it;* or *managed it well;* (اِحْتَفَلْتُ بِهِ;) and عَنَيْتُ بِهِ, of the class of رَمَى, inf. n. عِنَايَةٌ, signifies the same: and عُنِيتُ بِأَمْرِ فُلَانٍ, in the pass. form, inf. n. عِنَايَةٌ and عُنِىٌّ, signifies *I became occupied* [either *actually* or (as is shown by what follows) *in mind*] *by,* or *with, the affair,* or *case, of such a one;* and sometimes one said عَنَيْتُ بِأَمْرِهِ [in this sense as well as the similar sense expl. above], using the act. form: (Mṣb:) one says [also], عُنِيتُ بِحَاجَتِكَ, with ḍamm to the first letter, [which may be rendered *I became occupied by,* or *with, thy want,*] aor. أُعْنَى, inf. n. عِنَايَةٌ: (Ṣ:) and لِتُعْنَ بِحَاجَتِى, (Ṣ, Mṣb,) which is the imperative form, (Ṣ,) meaning [*Be thou occupied by,* or *with, my want;* or] *let my want occupy,* or *busy, thy mind:* (Mṣb:) and in interrogating, you say, كَيْفَ مَنْ تُعْنَى بِأَمْرِهِ [*How is he by,* or *with, whose affair,* or *case, thou art occupied,* or *disquieted,* &c.?]: you do not say, in this case, تَعْنَى [for تُعْنَى]. (Az, TA.) — عَنَى ٱللّٰهُ بِهِ, [inf. n. عِنَايَةٌ, as is implied in the TA,] means *God preserved him:* (Mṣb, TA:) and it is said that it may be from عَنِىَ بِحَاجَتِهِ [as syn. with عُنِىَ بِهَا]. (TA.) — And عَنِىَ, (Ṣ, Mṣb,) thus in the Tahdheeb of IḲṭṭ, (TA,) with kesr, (Ṣ, TA,) of the class of تَعِبَ, (Mṣb,) aor. يَعْنَى; (Ṣ, Mṣb;) or عَنَى, (Ḳ, TA,) with fet-ḥ, thus in the copies of the Ḳ, and likewise in the M; (TA;) inf. n. عَنَآءٌ, (Ṣ, Ḳ, TA,) or this is a simple subst., from عَنَاهُ, (Mgh, Mṣb,) and عُنْيَةٌ is syn. therewith; (ISd, Ḳ, TA;) *He suffered difficulty, distress,* or *trouble;* (Ṣ, Mṣb, Ḳ, TA;) or *fatigue,* or *weariness:* and ↓ تَعَنَّى, also, has the former or the latter meaning. (Ṣ, Ḳ, TA.) You say, عَنِيتُ فِى الأَمْرِ, meaning ↓ تَعَنَّيْتُ [i. e. *I suffered difficulty,* &c., *in the affair,* or *case*]: mentioned by Az. (TA.) — And عَنِىَ signifies [also] *He stuck fast in captivity;* (Ḳ in this art., and Mṣb in art. عنو;) as also عَنَا, inf. n. عُنُوٌّ: (Mṣb in art. عنو:) or both signify *he became a captive.* (Ḳ in art. عنو.) ═ عَنَى [as intrans.] said of an event, (Ḳ, TA,) inf. n. عُنِىٌّ, (TA,) *It befell,* or *betided,* (Ḳ, TA;) as also ↓ اعتنى: (TA:) and *it occurred,* or *happened:* (Ḳ:) عَنَى لَهُ الأَمْرُ is said to mean *The event occurred,* or *happened, to him.* (TA.) ═ عَنَى فِيهِ الأَكْلُ, (Ḳ, TA,) inf. n. عَنْىٌ and عُنِىٌّ and عَنًى, (TA,) signifies *The eating had an agreeable, a wholesome,* or *a beneficial, effect upon him,* (syn. نَجَعَ,) and [it is said that] the aor. is يَعْنِى, like يَرْضَى and يُرْضِى, (Ḳ, TA,) the latter mentioned by ISd, as being anomalous, but MF says that the latter has not been heard unless as having its pret. like رَضِىَ, [i. e. عَنِىَ, of which عَنًى is the inf. n. accord. to analogy,] and [SM adds that] thus it is accord. to IḲṭṭ, who mentions the verb as said also, in the same sense, of the drinking of milk; (TA in this art.;) and he states that عَنَا, aor. يَعْنُو, inf. n. عُنُوٌّ, is a dial. var. thereof. (TA in this art. and in art. عنو.) ═ عَنَى بِالْقَوْلِ كَذَا, (Ṣ, Ḳ, TA,) aor. يَعْنِى, (TA,) *He meant,* or *intended, by the saying, such a thing;* syn. أَرَادَ, (Ṣ, Ḳ, TA,) and قَصَدَ. (TA.) عَنَيْتُهُ, aor. أَعْنِيهِ, inf. n. عَنْىٌ, signifies قَصَدْتُهُ [as meaning *I intended it:* and app. in other senses expl. in art. قصد]. (Mṣb.) And you say, عَنَانِى أَمْرُكَ, meaning قَصَدَنِى [i. e., app., *Thy command,* or *thy affair, had me for its object*]. (TA.) — عَنَيْتُ الشَّىْءَ: and عَنَتِ الأَرْضُ بِالنَّبَاتِ: see 1 in art. عنو. ═ عَنَيْتُ الكِتَابَ: see Q. Q. 1 in art. عنو.

2. عَنَّاهُ, (Ṣ, Mgh, Mṣb, Ḳ,) inf. n. تَعْنِيَةٌ, (Ṣ, Mṣb,) *He caused him to suffer difficulty, distress,* or *trouble;* (Ṣ, Mgh,* Ḳ;) or *fatigue,* or *weariness;* (Ṣ, Ḳ;) as also ↓ تعنّاهُ, (Ṣ,) or as also ↓ اعناهُ: (Ḳ:) or *he imposed upon him that which was difficult, distressing,* or *troublesome, to him:* (Mṣb:) or *he annoyed, molested, harmed,* or *hurt, him;* and *caused him to grieve* or *mourn,* or *to be sorrowful* or *sad* or *unhappy.* (Ḥar p. 120.) — [See also 2 in art. عنو.] ═ عَنَّى الكِتَابَ, mentioned in the Ḳ in this art.: see Q. Q. 1 in art. عنو.

3. عَانَاهُ, (Ṣ, Ḳ,) inf. n. مُعَانَاةٌ, (Ṣ,) *He suffered,* or *endured,* or *he struggled* or *contended with* or *against, the difficulty* or *trouble* or *inconvenience that he experienced from it* or *him;* syn. قَاسَاهُ; as also ↓ تعنّاهُ: (Ṣ, Ḳ:) you say, هُوَ يُعَانِى كَذَا i. e. يُقَاسِيهِ [*He suffers,* &c., *the difficulty* &c. *that he experiences from such a thing*]. (TA.) — And *He contended, disputed,* or *litigated, with him;* syn. شَاجَرَهُ: (Ḳ:) you say, لَا تُعَانِ أَصْحَابَكَ i. e. لَا تُشَاجِرْهُمْ [*Do not thou contend,* &c., *with thy companions*]. (TA.) — And المُعَانَاةُ is also *syn. with* المُعَالَجَةُ [inf. n. of عَالَجَ, q. v.]. (Ḥar p. 7.) [Hence,] one says, عَانَى عَمَلَ الأَقْفَاصِ [*He plied the manufacture of cages,* or *coops*]. (TA in art. قفص.) And عُونِىَ بِأَدْوِيَةٍ [referring to hair] *It was treated* (دُووِىَ) *with remedies,* such as oils and the like. (M and TA in art. دوى.) And عَانَيْتُ المَرِيضَ *I treated the sick person;* syn. دَاوَيْتُهُ. (TA in art. دوى.) — It is also *syn. with* المُدَارَاةُ [*The treating with gentle-*

ness, or *blandishment*; &c.: see 3 in art. درى]. (TA.) —— And one says, هُمْ مَا يُعَانُونَ مَالَهُمْ *They do not tend, or take care of, their cattle, or camels, or* [other] *property* (Ṣ, Ḳ, TA) *well.* (TA.) —— And الهُمُومُ تُعَانِى فُلَانًا *Anxieties come to such a one.* (TA.) —— And شَاكِلْهُ i. e. خُذْ هٰذَا وَمَا عَانَاهُ [*Take thou this and what has become conformable, suitable, agreeable, or similar, to it*]. (TA.)

4: see 2. [See also 4 in art. عنو.] ═ ما اعنى شَيْئًا means مَا أَغْنَى [i. e. *It did not stand in any stead; or did not avail, or profit, at all*]. (TA.) See also أَغْنَى.

5. تعنّى, as intrans.: see 1, latter half, in two places. ═ تعنّاهُ: see 2: —— and see also 3, first sentence. [Hence the prov., جِبَابٌ فَلَا تَعَنَّ أَبْرًا, expl. voce جُبٌّ.] One says also, تعنّى العَنِيَّةَ, meaning تَجَشَّمَهَا [i. e. *He imposed upon himself the suffering of difficulty, distress, or trouble; or of fatigue, or weariness*]. (Ḳ.) —— تَتَعَنَّاهُ as meaning *It returns to him time after time* (تَتَعَهَّدُهُ) is said of fever (الحُمَّى); but not of aught else. (TA.) ═ And تَعَنَّيْتُ signifies also قَصَدْتُ [app. as intrans., meaning *I pursued a right, or direct, course; &c.*]. (TA.)

8: see 1, former half, in two places: —— and also in the last quarter of the paragraph.

عَنٍ is the part. n. from عَنِىَ بِالأَمْرِ as syn. with عُنِىَ [q. v.]: (Ḳ, TA:) you say, هُوَ بِالأَمْرِ عَنٍ (IAạr, Ḳ, TA) *He is disquieted* [&c.] *by the affair, or case*: (Ḳ, TA:) [and ▼ مَعْنِىٌّ signifies the same, as part. n. of عُنِىَ: or] أَنَا مَعْنِىٌّ ▼ بِهِ, from عَنَانِى هٰذَا [q. v.], means *I am occupied* [either *actually* or *in mind*] *by it*, or *with it*; i. e., a thing that has occurred, or happened, to me; and sometimes one says, أَنَا عَانٍ ▼, meaning the same, i. e., by the affair, or case, of another, from عُنِيتُ بِأَمْرِهِ [q. v.]: (Mṣb:) and one says [also], أَنَا مَعْنِىٌّ ▼ بِحَاجَتِكَ [*I am occupied by, or with, thy want*], from عُنِيتُ بِحَاجَتِكَ. (Ṣ.) —— [And] part. n. from عَنِيتُ فِى الأَمْرِ [q. v.]: you say, أَنَا عَنٍ [*I am suffering difficulty, distress, or trouble; or fatigue, or weariness; in an affair, or case*]: mentioned by Az. (TA.)

عَنِيَّةٌ: see عَنَآءٌ.

عُنْيَانٌ i. q. عُنْوَانٌ [expl. in art. عنو]. (Ḳ.)

عَنَآءٌ *Difficulty, distress, or trouble*; (Mgh, Mṣb;*) the subst. from عنّاهُ: (Mgh, Mṣb:) or the *suffering of difficulty, distress, or trouble; or of fatigue, or weariness*; inf. n. of عَنِىَ [or of عُنِىَ]; and ▼ عَنِيَّةٌ is syn. therewith. (Ḳ.) [See also art. عنو.] ═ It is also a subst. from عَنَى in the phrase عَنَى بِالقَوْلِ كَذَا [as such having the signification of the inf. n. of that verb, or perhaps as syn. with مَعْنًى]. (TA.)

عَانٍ: see عَنٍ. [See also art. عنو.] —— In the phrase عَنَآءٌ عَانٍ, it denotes intensiveness; [the meaning being *Severe difficulty, &c.*;] (Ḳ, TA;) like شَاعِرٌ and مَائِتٌ in the phrases شِعْرٌ شَاعِرٌ and مَوْتٌ مَائِتٌ: (TA:) as also ▼ مُعَنٍّ; (Ḳ, TA;) in the M like مُكْرَمٍ [i. e. ▼ مُعْنًى]. (TA.)

أَكْثَرُ عِنَايَةً means هُوَ بِهِ أَعْنَى [i. e. *He is more disquieted, uneasy in mind, anxious, or careful, by reason of it*]. (TA.)

مَعْنًى [signifying The *meaning*, or *intended sense*, of a word or saying,] is from عَنَى بِالقَوْلِ كَذَا [q. v.]; so says Z: (TA:) it is an inf. n. [of this verb] used in the sense of the pass. part. n.; or a contraction of the latter; i. e. of مَعْنِىٌّ: (Dict. of the Technical Terms used in the Sciences of the Musalmans:) or, accord. to Er-Rághib, it signifies the *import* of a word or an expression, from the phrase عَنَتِ الأَرْضُ بِالنَّبَاتِ meaning "the land made apparent, or showed, its plants, or herbage:" accord. to El-Munáwee, as he says in the Towḳeef, [and the like is said in the KT,] *an idea*, i. e. *a mental image, considered as having a word*, or *an expression, applied to denote it, and as being intended by that word* or *expression*: [the idea, or mental image,] considered as accruing, from the word or expression, in the mind, is termed مَفْهُومٌ: considered as what is said in reply to مَا هُوَ ["What is it?"], it is termed مَاهِيَّةٌ: considered as existing objectively, [as that by which a thing is what it is,] it is termed حَقِيقَةٌ: and considered as distinguished from others, it is termed هُوِيَّةٌ: (TA:) signifying [as expl. above, i. e.] the *opposite to* لَفْظٌ, it may be either *a substance*, or *thing that subsists by itself*, i. e. عَيْنٌ, or *an accident*, or *attribute*, i. e. عَرَضٌ: but it also signifies the *opposite to* عَيْنٌ, i. e. the *opposite to a thing that subsists by itself*: (Kull p. 238:) [hence اِسْمُ مَعْنًى, opposed to اِسْمُ عَيْنٍ; both of which are expl. voce اِسْمٌ, in art. سمو:] مَعْنَى الكَلَامِ and ▼ مَعْنَاتُهُ and ▼ مَعْنِيُّهُ (Ṣ, Ḳ, TA) and ▼ مَعْنِيَّتُهُ, (Ḳ, TA, [in the CḲ, erroneously, مَعْنِيَتُهُ, without the sign of teshdeed,]) the last mentioned by ISd, (TA,) are one [in signification], (Ṣ, Ḳ, TA,) as *syn. with* فَحْوَاهُ (TA, and so in some copies of the Ṣ,) and مَقْصَدُهُ [both of which are generally understood as signifying *the meaning*, or *intended sense, of the saying*]: (TA:) AḤát says, the vulgar say, لِأَىِّ مَعْنًى فَعَلْتَ [*For what intent didst thou* such a thing?]; but the Arabs know not المَعْنَى, and never say it: this is the case: but some of the Arabs say, مَا مَعْنِىُّ ▼ هٰذَا [i. e. *What is the meaning*, or *intent*, (lit. *the meant* or *intended* object,) *of this?*], with kesr to the ن and with the ى musheddedeh: and AZ says, هٰذَا فِى مَعْنَاةِ ▼ ذَاكَ and فِى مَعْنَاهُ سَوَآءٌ, i. e. *This is* [used] *in a manner the like of that in respect of indication* and *import* and *acceptation*: El-Fárábee, also, says, مَعْنَى الشَّىْءِ and ▼ مَعْنَاتُهُ are one [in signification]; and مَعْنَاهُ and فَحْوَاهُ and مُقْتَضَاهُ and مَضْمُونُهُ all signify *that which the word*, or *expression*, [termed before *the thing*,] *indicates*: and it is said in the T, on the authority of Th, that المَعْنَى and التَّفْسِيرُ and التَّأْوِيلُ, are one [in signification, as meaning *explanation*, or *interpretation*, or *the like*]: and people have used their phrase هٰذَا مَعْنَى كَلَامِهِ, and the like, meaning *this is the import*, and *the indication of the meaning, of his saying*; which is agreeable with what is said by AZ and El-Fárábee: the grammarians and lexicologists, moreover, have agreed respecting a mode of expression of which they have made frequent use, their saying هٰذَا بِمَعْنَى هٰذَا [*this is used with the meaning of this*], and هٰذَا وَهٰذَا فِى المَعْنَى وَاحِدٌ [*this and this are in meaning one*] and فِى المَعْنَى سَوَآءٌ [*in meaning alike*], and هٰذَا فِى مَعْنَى هٰذَا [*this is used in the sense of this*] i. e. *this is like this* [*in meaning*]: (Mṣb, TA:) the pl. of مَعْنًى is مَعَانٍ. (TA.) —— عِلْمُ المَعَانِى is expl. by El-Munáwee in the "Towḳeef" as *The science whereby one knows how to express clearly one meaning in various ways*: (TA:) [but this definition is applied in the "Talkheeṣ" (Talkheeṣ el-Miftáḥ), and Ḥájjee Khaleefeh uses the same words with only one unimportant variation, in explaining عِلْمُ البَيَانِ; and a similar explanation of the latter is given in the Kull: in a marginal note in a copy of the Ksh, cited by De Sacy in his Anthol. Gr. Ar. p. 305, علم المعانى is expl. as *the science whereby is known the manner of adapting language to the requirements of the case*; (and it is similarly expl. in the "Talkheeṣ" and other works;) and علم البيان, as the science that concerns comparisons and tropes and metonymies.] —— صُورَةٌ بِلَا مَعْنًى means *A form without any intrinsic quality.*] —— And المَعَانِى signifies also *The qualities that are commended*, or *approved*; [*the charms*, or *graces*;] *such as knowledge*, or *science*, and *piety*, and *generosity*, and *goodliness of make*, &c. (Ḥar p. 644.)

مُعْنًى: see عَانٍ.

مَعْنَاةٌ: see مَعْنًى, in three places.

مَعْنِىٌّ: see عَنٍ, in three places: ═ and see also مَعْنًى, in two places.

مَعْنِيَّةٌ: see مَعْنًى, in the former half.

مَعْنَوِىٌّ a rel. n. from مَعْنًى; signifying [*Of*, or *relating to, meaning*, or *intended sense*; opposed to لَفْظِىٌّ: —— and *Of*, or *relating to, idea, mind*, or *intellect*; *ideal, mental*, or *intellectual*; opposed to حِسِّىٌّ;] a thing *in which* [*neither*] *the tongue* [*nor any of the senses*] *has a share*; being *known only by the mind.* (TA.)

مُعَنًّى, mentioned in the TA in this art.: see art. عنو.

مُعَنٍّ: see عَانٍ.

عه

عَهْ عَهْ: see عَاهِ عَاهِ, in art. عوه.

عهج

عَوْهَجٌ *Long-necked;* applied to a gazelle, and to a she-camel, (Ṣ, O, Ḳ,) and to an ostrich, (O,) or a male ostrich. (Ṣ, Ḳ.) And A *young* she-camel: (O, Ḳ:) or one *perfect in make:* or only one *beautiful in colour, long in the neck:* and also applied to a gazelle, or young gazelle, in all these senses: and to a woman as meaning *perfect in make, and beautiful:* or *long-necked.* (TA.) And A *long-legged* ostrich: (O, Ḳ:) or it app. means thus: (L:) and [simply] *an ostrich.* (TA.) And A gazelle *having two black lines, or stripes, on its flanks:* (O, L, Ḳ:) or, accord. to Aṣ, *striped in the neck.* (O.) And *A serpent;* (O, Ḳ;) like عَوْمَجٌ and عَمَجٌ and عُمْجٌ: (O:) it is said to have this meaning by El-Bushtee; but Az says that it is a mistranscription; correctly عَوْمَجٌ, with م. (TA.) It is also the name of *A stallion of the camels, which belonged to [the tribe of] Mahrah,* (O, Ḳ, TA,) *characterized by the beauty of his make.* (TA.)

عهد

1. عَهِدَ إِلَيْهِ, (Ṣ, A, &c.,) aor. ـَ, (Mṣb,) inf. n. عَهْدٌ, (TA,) *He enjoined, charged, bade, ordered,* or *commanded, him;* (Ṣ, A, Mgh, O, Mṣb, Ḳ, TA;) as also ▼ استعهد مِنْهُ. (A.) One says, عَهِدْتُ إِلَيْهِ بِالأَمْرِ *I enjoined him,* or *charged him,* &c., *to do the thing.* (Mṣb.) And it is said in the Ḳur [xxxvi. 60], أَلَمْ أَعْهَدْ إِلَيْكُمْ يَا بَنِى آدَمَ أَنْ لَا تَعْبُدُوا الشَّيْطَانَ [*Did I not enjoin you,* or *charge you,* &c., *O sons of Adam, that ye should not serve the Devil?* or, saying, *Serve not ye the Devil?*]. (O, Mṣb.) [And in the same, ii. 119, وَعَهِدْنَا إِلَى إِبْرٰهِيمَ وَإِسْمٰعِيلَ أَنْ طَهِّرَا بَيْتِى *And we enjoined,* or *charged,* &c., *Abraham and Ishmael,* saying, *Purify ye my house.*] And one says also, عَهِدَ إِلَيْهِ فِيهِ, meaning تَقَدَّمَ [i. e. *He enjoined him,* or *charged him,* &c., *respecting it,* or *to do it*]. (TḲ.) And *He obliged him to do it.* (L in art. عقد.) — Also *He imposed a condition,* or *conditions, upon him;* (A;) and so ▼ استعهد مِنْهُ: (A, Ḳ:) which latter signifies (O, Ḳ) also (Ḳ) *he wrote a statement of a compact, covenant, confederacy,* or *league, as binding upon him.* (O, Ḳ.) — And *He made a compact, contract, covenant,* or *the like, with him;* or *a promise to him.* (MA.) [See also 3.] — And عَهِدَ إِلَىَّ فُلَانٌ فِى كَذَا *Such a one was,* or *became,* or *made himself, responsible, answerable, accountable, amenable, surety,* or *guarantee, to me, for,* or *in respect of, such a thing.* (TḲ.) ═ عَهِدَ وَعْدَهُ, inf. n. عَهْدٌ, *He fulfilled his promise.* (TḲ.) — And عَهِدَ الحُرْمَةَ, inf. n. as above, *He was mindful, regardful,* or *observant, of that which should be sacred,* or *inviolable;* or *of that which was entitled to reverence, respect, honour,* or *defence.* (TḲ.) ═ عَهِدَهُ, (Ṣ, Mgh, Mṣb,) inf. n. عَهْدٌ, (Mṣb, Ḳ,) *He met,* or *met with, him,* or *it,* (Ṣ, Mgh, Mṣb, Ḳ,*) بِمَكَانِ كَذَا *in such a place.* (Ṣ, Mgh, Mṣb.) [See also عَهْدٌ below.] — And *He knew,* or *was acquainted with, him,* or *it,* (Mṣb, Ḳ,* TA,) عَلَى حَالٍ *in a state,* or *condition,* or فِى مَكَانٍ *in a place.* (TA.) And عَهِدَ *He,* or *it, was known.* (Ṣ, O.) One says, الأَمْرُ كَمَا عَهِدْتَ *The affair,* or *case, was as thou knewest.* (Mṣb.) And the saying of Umm-Zarạ, وَلَا يَسْأَلُ عَمَّا عَهِدَ (O, TA,) means *Nor used he to ask respecting that which he saw,* (O,) or *that which he knew,* (TA,) in the tent, or house, by reason of his liberality. (O, TA.) [See, again, عَهْدٌ below.] ═ عُهِدَتِ الأَرْضُ, (Ṣ,) or الرَّوْضَةُ, (A,) *The land,* or *the meadow, was rained upon* (Ṣ, A) *by the rain called* عَهْدَةٌ [or عَهْد]: (A:) and عُهِدَ المَكَانُ [in the CḲ بِالمَكَانِ] *the place was rained upon by the rain called* عَهْد, i. e. *the first of the rain called* الوَسْمِىّ: (Ḳ:) or *was altogether rained upon.* (TA.)

3. مُعَاهَدَةٌ is between two persons; (O;) signifying The *uniting with another in a compact, a contract, a covenant, an agreement, a confederacy, a league, a treaty,* or *an engagement,* (Mṣb,) عَلَى كَذَا [*respecting,* or *to do, such a thing*]. (MA.) You say, يُعَاهِدُكَ وَتُعَاهِدُهُ [*He makes a compact,* &c., *with thee, and thou makest a compact,* &c., *with him*]. (Ṣ, O.) [See also عَهِدَ إِلَيْهِ.] — And عاهده *He swore to him.* (Ḳ in this art., and Mgh in art. وثق.) ═ See also 5.

4. أَنَا أُعْهِدُكَ مِنْ إِبَاقِهِ, (ISh, O, Ḳ,) inf. n. إِعْهَادٌ, (Ḳ,) *I hold thee clear of responsibility for his running away:* (ISh, O, Ḳ, TA:) said by one who has purchased a slave. (TA.) And in like manner, أَنَا أُعْهِدُكَ مِنْ هٰذَا الأَمْرِ *I hold thee,* or *make thee, secure from this thing.* (TA.) Hence the term ▼ عُهْدَةٌ. (TA.) And the latter phrase signifies [also] *I am responsible for thy security from this thing.* (ISh, O, Ḳ.)

5. تعهّدهُ *He renewed his acquaintance with it,* or *his knowledge of it;* (Ṣ, O, L, Mṣb, Ḳ;) this is the proper signification; (Mṣb;) as also ▼ اعتهدهُ; (O,* L, Ḳ;) and ▼ تعاهدهُ; (L, Ḳ;) and ▼ عاهدهُ, inf. n. مُعَاهَدَةٌ: (L:) and *he sought it,* or *sought for it* or *after it, it being absent from him;* syn. تَفَقَّدَهُ; as also ▼ تعاهدهُ, and ▼ اعتهده: (Ḳ:) or تعهّدهُ and تفقّدهُ are used, by some, each in the place of the other; but accord. to Er-Rághib and many others, the former signifies *he sought,* or *sought leisurely* or *repeatedly, to obtain knowledge of it, having known of it before;* and the latter, *he sought,* or *sought leisurely* or *repeatedly, to obtain knowledge of it, having lost it:* (MF in art. فقد:) or تعهّدهُ signifies *he renewed his acquaintance with it, or his knowledge of it, and sought,* or *sought leisurely* or *repeatedly, to find means of rectifying it, reforming it,* or *putting it into a good* or *right* or *proper state:* (IDrst, TA:) or *he came to it, and rectified it, reformed it,* or *put it into a good* or *right* or *proper state:* (Mgh:) or as first expl. above, and also *he returned to it time after time,* or *went frequently to it, and rectified it, reformed it,* or *put it into a good* or *right* or *proper state:* (Mṣb:) or, simply, [as also ▼ تعاهدهُ,] *he returned,* or *recurred, to it time after time,* [see an instance voce أَخْرَقُ,] or *went frequently to it:* (Et-Tedmuree, TA:) and also [i. e. both signify also *he paid repeated,* or *frequent, attention to it;* or] *he was careful,* or *mindful, of it;* or *attentive to it.* (Ṣ, O, Mṣb.*) One says also, تَعَهَّدْتُ فُلَانًا [*I renewed my acquaintance with such a one; repaired,* or *betook myself, to him frequently; paid frequent attention to him;* or simply *paid attention to him*]. (Ṣ, O.) And تَعَهَّدْتُ ضَيْعَتِى, (Ṣ, O, Mgh,) properly signifying *I renewed my acquaintance with,* or *my knowledge of, my estate,* is used as meaning *I came to my estate, and put it into a good* or *right* or *proper condition:* (Mgh:) [or *I paid repeated,* or *frequent,* or *much, attention to it, taking good and effectual care of it; I husbanded it well:*] or, accord. to IDrst, the verb here has the meaning given above on his authority: or, accord. to Ed-Tedmuree, the meaning is that given above as his explanation; and is from عَهْدٌ as signifying "rain that falls after other rain," or from the same word as signifying "a place of abode in which one has known a thing:" (TA:) and one may say also ▼ تَعَاهَدْتُ; (Fr, ISk, Mgh;) but تَعَهَّدْتُ is more chaste, (El-Fárábee, Ṣ, O, Mṣb,) because ▼ تَعَاهُدٌ is only between two [or more]: (Ṣ, O:) or تعاهدت is not allowable, (AZ, AḤát, Th, IF, Mṣb,) for the reason just mentioned: (IF, Mṣb:) AZ says that six Arabs of the desert, of chaste speech, being asked in the presence of himself and of Yoo, one after another, whether they said تعهّدت ضيعتى or ▼ تعاهدت, all answered, تعهّدت. (AḤát, TA.) One also says, of a man, يَتَعَهَّدُهُ صَرْعٌ [*Epilepsy befalls him repeatedly,* or *time after time*]. (Ṣ, O.)

6. تعاهدوا *They united in a compact, a contract, a covenant, an agreement, a confederacy, a league, a treaty,* or *an engagement,* [عَلَى كَذَا *respecting,* or *to do, such a thing;*] syn. تَعَاقَدُوا, (Ṣ and Ḳ in art. عقد,) and تَحَالَفُوا. (Ṣ and Ḳ in art. حلف.) ═ See also 5, in six places.

8: see 5, near the beginning, in two places.

10: see 1, former half, in two places. — One says also, اِسْتَعْهَدْتُهُ مِنْ نَفْسِهِ, meaning *I made him responsible for accidents* [*arising,* or *that might arise,*] *from himself.* (O, Ḳ.*)

عَهْدٌ [an inf. n. of 1, q. v.: used as a simple subst.,] *An injunction, a charge, a bidding, an order,* or *a command.* (Ṣ, A, Mgh, O, Mṣb, Ḳ, TA.) [Pl. in this and other senses عُهُودٌ.] عَهْدِى أَنْ لَا آخُذَ مِنْ رَاضِعٍ شَيْئًا, occurring in a trad., is a phrase tropically abridged, meaning ‡ *It is in the injunction,* or *charge, prescribed as obligatory on me* [*that I should not take anything from a suckling*]. (Mgh.) — *A compact, a contract, a covenant, an agreement, a confederacy, a league, a treaty, an engagement, a bond, an obligation,* or *a promise:* (Ṣ, A, Mgh, O, L, Mṣb, Ḳ, TA:) pl. عُهُودٌ: or, accord. to AHeyth, ▼ عُهْدَةٌ has this this meaning, and عَهْدٌ is its pl. [or rather a coll. gen. n.]. (TA.) Hence وَلِىُّ عَهْدٍ The suc-

cessor by virtue of a covenant of a Khaleefeh [or King]. (TA.) [And وِلَايَةُ عَهْدٍ The *succession by virtue of a covenant.*] — *Protection,* or *safeguard; a promise,* or *an assurance, of security* or *safety; responsibility,* or *suretiship;* syn. أَمَانٌ; and ذِمَّةٌ; (Sh, Ṣ, A, O, Mṣb, Ḳ;) and ضَمَانٌ; (O, Ḳ;) as also ↓ عُهْدَى [in the O ↓ عُهْدَى] and ↓ عِهْدَانٌ [which last is said in the Ṣ and O to be syn. with عَهْدٌ, but in what sense is not there specified]. (Ḳ.) Hence, ذُو عَهْدٍ, an appellation given to a Christian, and a Jew, [and a Sabian, who is a subject of a Muslim government,] meaning *One between whom and the Muslims a compact,* or *covenant, subsists, whereby the latter are responsible for his security* [*and freedom and toleration*] *as long as he acts agreeably to the compact* [*by living peaceably with them and paying a poll-tax*]; (Mgh,* Mṣb,* TA;) [i. e. *a free non-Muslim subject of a Muslim government;*] as also ↓ مُعَاهَدٌ and ↓ مُعَاهِدٌ, the act. and pass. forms being both applied to such a person because the compact is mutual; (Mṣb;) both syn. with ذِمِّىٌّ: (Ṣ:) persons of this description are called collectively أَهْلُ العَهْدِ. (TA.) — *An oath:* (Ṣ, A, O, Ḳ:) pl. عُهُودٌ: or, accord. to AHeyth, ↓ عَهْدَةٌ signifies *an oath whereby one secures himself against him with whom he makes a compact, contract, covenant,* or *the like,* and عَهْدٌ is its pl. [or rather a coll. gen. n.]. (TA.) [But it is generally used as a sing.: hence,] one says, عَلَىَّ عَهْدُ ٱللّٰهِ لَأَفْعَلَنَّ كَذَا [*The oath by attestation of God is binding on me that I will assuredly do such a thing*]. (Ṣ, O.) — *A writ,* or *diploma, of appointment to the office of a prefect* or *governor* or *the like:* (Ṣ, O, Ḳ:) pl. عُهُودٌ. (TA.) — *Defence of those persons,* or *things, that should be sacred,* or *inviolable,* or *that are entitled to reverence, respect, honour,* or *defence;* (Ṣ, A, O, Ḳ;) and *mindfulness, regard,* or *observance,* (Ṣ, Ḳ,) *of such things,* (Ḳ,) or *of love,* or *affection;* occurring in this sense in a trad., in which it is said that generosity therein is a point of religion. (Ṣ.) — *Fulfilment of a promise* or *the like.* (O, Ḳ.) So in the Ḳur vii. 100. (O.) — The *assertion of the unity of God:* whence, إِلَّا مَنِ ٱتَّخَذَ عِنْدَ ٱلرَّحْمٰنِ عَهْدًا [*Except such as hath made a covenant with the Compassionate to assert his unity*], (O, Ḳ,) in the Ḳur [xix. 90]: (O:) and the words of a trad. relating to prayer, أَنَا عَلَى عَهْدِكَ وَوَعْدِكَ مَا ٱسْتَطَعْتُ *I am persevering in the observance of my covenant and promise to Thee to believe in Thee and to assert thy unity incessantly* [*as far as I am able*]. (TA.) = Also *A time;* (Ṣ,* A, Ḳ;) and so ↓ عِهْدَانٌ. (A, TA.) One says, كَانَ عَلَى عَهْدِ فُلَانٍ and ↓ عِهْدَانِهِ *It was in the time of such a one.* (A.) And كَانَ ذٰلِكَ فِى عَهْدِ شَبَابِى *That was in the time of my youth,* or *young manhood.* (TḲ.) And أَتَى عَلَيْهَا عَهْدٌ طَوِيلٌ [*Over which a long time has passed*]. (Ṣ, in explanation of قَرْيَةٌ عَهِيدَةٌ meaning قَدِيمَةٌ.) — One says also, عَهْدِى بِهِ قَرِيبٌ i. e. *My meeting* [*with him, or it, was a short time ago*]. (Ṣ,* Mṣb.) And هُوَ قَرِيبُ العَهْدِ بِكَذَا *He knew,* or *was acquainted with, such a thing,* and *was in such a state,* or *condition, recently,* or *a short time ago.* (Mṣb. [And in like manner one says عَهْدِى بِهِ حَدِيثُ العَهْدِ and حَدِيثُ عَهْدٍ.]) And عَهِدْتُهُ بِمَوْضِعِ كَذَا, (Ḳ, TA,) and فِى حَالِ كَذَا, (TA,) *I met,* or *met with,* or *I knew,* [or *I saw,*] *him,* or *it, in such a place,* (Ḳ, TA,) and *in such a state,* or *condition.* (TA.) And مَا لِى عَهْدٌ بِهِ [*I have not any knowledge of,* or *acquaintance with, him,* or *it*]. (A.) And مَتَى عَهْدُكَ بِفُلَانٍ *When didst thou meet,* or *meet with, such a one?* (Mgh:) or *see such a one?* (TA.) And مَتَى عَهْدُكَ بِالخُفِّ *When didst thou wear the boots?* (Mgh.) And مَتَى عَهْدُكَ بِأَسْفَلِ فِيكَ [*When didst thou see the lower part of thy mouth?*]: a prov.; said in asking a person respecting an old affair of which he has no knowledge. (L.) The saying of the poet, (Aboo-Khirásh El-Hudhalee, TA, and so in a copy of the Ṣ,)

* فَلَيْسَ كَعَهْدِ الدَّارِ يَا أُمَّ مَالِكٍ *
* وَلٰكِنْ أَحَاطَتْ بِالرِّقَابِ السَّلَاسِلُ *

[*And it is not like the formerly-known state of the abode, O Umm-Málik; but chains have surrounded the necks;*] is expl. as meaning, the case is not as thou knewest it; but El-Islám has come, and has subverted that case. (Ṣ, TA.) [Hence, لِلْعَهْدِ and ↓ لِلْمَعْهُودِ, said of the article أَلْ; meaning *Used to distinguish a noun as known to the hearer, or reader, in a particular sense.*] = Also *A first rain;* the rain immediately following which is called وَلِىٌّ: (TA:) or the *first of the rain called* الوَسْمِىّ; (IAạr, M, Ḳ;) and so ↓ عَهْدَةٌ and ↓ عِهْدَةٌ and ↓ عِهَادَةٌ, (M, Ḳ, TA,) or, as in some copies of the Ḳ [and in the CḲ], ↓ عِهَادٌ, which is pl. of عَهْدٌ. (TA.) — And *Rain that falls after other rain,* (AḤn, Ṣ, Ḳ,) *while the moisture of the former yet remains;* (AḤn, Ḳ;) as also ↓ عَهْدَةٌ and ↓ عِهْدَةٌ: (TA:) pl. عِهَادٌ and عُهُودٌ: (Ṣ:) or عِهَادٌ, accord. to some, signifies *recent rains;* app. from the saying, أَصَابَتْنَا دِيمَةٌ بَعْدَ دِيمَةٍ عَلَى عِهَادٍ غَيْرِ قَدِيمَةٍ [*A continuous and still rain fell upon us after a continuous and still rain following upon rain not long anterior*]: (AḤn, TA:) or عِهَادٌ signifies *rains of the* [*season called*] رَبِيع [here meaning *autumn,* as is shown voce نَوْءٌ], *after the rain called* الوَسْمِىّ: (A:) or *weak, fine rain, of that which is called* وَسْمِىّ. (IAạr, TA.) — And عَامُ العُهُودِ means *The year of few rains.* (TA.) = See also عُهْدَةٌ, near the middle, in two places: = and see مَعْهَدٌ, in three places.

عَهِدٌ A man *who applies himself repeatedly to affairs,* and *to prefectures* or *governments* or *the like;* or *who applies himself repeatedly thereto, and to the reforming thereof;* expl. by the words يَتَعَاهَدُ الأُمُورَ وَالوِلَايَاتِ: (Ṣ, Ḳ:) or one *who loves prefectures* or *the like, and writs of appointment thereto;* expl. by مُحِبٌّ لِلْوِلَايَاتِ وَالعُهُودِ. (A.)

عَهْدَةٌ: see عَهْدٌ, former half, in two places: = and again, in the last quarter, in two places. = عهدة [thus written, without any syll. sign], in a verse cited by AHeyth, [the measure of which shows it to be ↓ عُهْدَةٌ or ↓ عَهْدَةٌ or ↓ عِهْدَةٌ, and in which it is applied to the depository of a secret,] is expl. as signifying [properly] *A place on which the sun does not come.* (TA.)

عُهْدَةٌ *A written statement of a purchase* or *sale:* (Ṣ, Mṣb, Ḳ:) so called because one recurs to it on an occasion of doubt. (Mṣb.) And *A written statement of a confederacy, league, compact,* or *covenant.* (Ḳ.) — Also *A return* [to claim an indemnification for a fault or the like in a thing purchased]; syn. رَجْعَةٌ: so in the saying, لَا عُهْدَةَ [*There shall be no return* to claim an indemnification]: (Ṣ, O, Ḳ:) one says, أَبِيعُكَ المَلَسَى لَا عُهْدَةَ i. e. [*I sell to thee on the condition that*] *thou shalt get thee away, and not return to me,* (Ṣ in this art., and Ṣ and Mṣb and Ḳ in art. ملس,) *nor have any claim upon me for indemnification:* (Mṣb in art. ملس:) عُهْدَةٌ with respect to an article of merchandise being when it is sold in a faulty state or subject to a claim on the part of its owner. (TA. [See more voce مَلَسَى.]) One says also, فِى عَلَيْكَ هٰذِهِ عُهْدَةٌ لَا تَتَفَصَّى مِنْهَا *Thou art subject to a claim for acting unjustly* [*in respect of this, from which thou wilt not liberate thyself*]. (A, TA.) And عُهْدَةُ الرَّقِيقِ ثَلَاثَةُ أَيَّامٍ *The claim for indemnification for a fault in a slave, from the property of the seller, if he have sold him without making it a condition that he is clear of responsibility for any fault, is during three days,* and the purchaser may return him without proof; but if he find a fault after three days, he may not return him without proof. (TA, from a trad.) And ↓ عُهْدٌ and عُهْدَةٌ signify the same: (TA:) you say, بَرِئْتُ إِلَيْكَ مِنْ عُهْدَةِ هٰذَا العَبْدِ [and ↓ مِنْ عُهْدِهِ], meaning *I am clear of responsibility to thee for any fault that thou mayest find in this slave known to exist in him while he was with me.* (AHeyth, Mgh, TA.) See 4. And you say also, عُهْدَتُهُ عَلَى فُلَانٍ *The responsibility for the rectification of any fault that may be found in him, or it, is upon such a one.* (Ṣ,* Mgh, Mṣb,* Ḳ,* TA.) And فِى الأَمْرِ عُهْدَةٌ *In the affair is an occasion for reverting to it for the purpose of its rectification;* (Mṣb;) i. e. *the affair is not yet performed soundly, thoroughly,* or *well,* (Ṣ, O, Mṣb,) *and the manager thereof has to revert to it in order to render it so.* (Mṣb.) And فِيهِ عُهْدَةٌ *In it is a fault, a defect,* or *an imperfection.* (TA.) And فِى عَقْلِهِ عُهْدَةٌ *In his intellect is a weakness.* (Ṣ, A, O, Ḳ.) And فِى خَطِّهِ عُهْدَةٌ *In his handwriting is a weakness:* (Ḳ:) or *badness:* (A:) or *faulty formation of the letters.* (O.) = See also عَهْدَةٌ.

عِهْدَةٌ: see عَهْدٌ, last quarter, in two places: = and see also عَهْدَةٌ.

عِهْدَانٌ: see عَهْدٌ, in three places.

عِهَادٌ: see عَهْدٌ, near the end of the paragraph.

—— Also *Parts of land upon which the rain called* الوَسْمِىّ *has fallen.* (TA.)

عَهِيدٌ *One who makes, and with whom is made, a compact, a contract, a covenant, an agreement, a confederacy, a league, a treaty,* or *an engagement;* [*a confederate;*] (Ṣ, O;) *i. q.* ▼ مُعَاهِدٌ [and ▼ مُعَاهَدٌ]. (A, Ḳ.) ══ Also *Old,* or *ancient.* (Ḳ.) قَرْيَةٌ عَهِيدَةٌ means *An old,* or *ancient, town* or *village.* (Ṣ, O.)

عِهَادَةٌ: see عَهْدٌ, last quarter.

عُهْدَى and عُهَيْدَى: see عَهْدٌ, first quarter.

مَعْهَدٌ *A place in which one used to know,* or *be acquainted with,* or *meet with, a thing;* (Ṣ, A, O;) *a place in which a thing is,* or *has been, known,* or *met with;* as also ▼ عَهْدٌ; (Ḳ;) the latter originally an inf. n.: (TA:) *an abode in which one used to know love,* or *desire:* (TA:) and, as also ▼ عَهْدٌ, *a place of abode to which people return:* (A:) or *a place of abode to which people, when they have gone far away from it, always return:* (Ṣ, O:) pl. of the former مَعَاهِدُ. (A.) One says, اِسْتَوْقَفَ الرَّكْبَ عَلَى عَهْدِ ▼ الأَحِبَّةِ and عَلَى مَعْهَدِهِمْ [*He asked the company of riders to stop at the place where he used to know, or meet, the objects of love;* or] *at the abode to which the objects of love used to return.* (A.)

أَرْضٌ مَعْهُودَةٌ *Land upon which a partial rain has fallen.* (AZ, O, Ḳ.*)

مَعْهُودٌ *Known.* (Ṣ, O.) مَعْهُودٌ وَمَشْهُودٌ وَمَوْعُودٌ, as meaning *Past and present and future,* are applied to denote the tenses of a verb. (Kh, L.) See also عَهْدٌ, last quarter. ══ Also, applied to a place, (Ḳ,) and, with ة, to a land, (أَرْضٌ, Ṣ,) and to a meadow, (رَوْضَةٌ, A,) *Rained upon by the rain called* عَهْدٌ (Ṣ,* Ḳ) or عَهْدَةٌ. (A.)

مُعَاهِدٌ and مُعَاهَدٌ: see عَهِيدٌ: and see also عَهْدٌ, former half. معاهد [i. e. either the act. or the pass. part. n.] is mostly applied in the trads. to *A person of the class called* أَهْلُ الذِّمَّةِ [or أَهْلُ العَهْدِ, expl. voce عَهْدٌ]: but sometimes it is applied also to *any other of the unbelievers with whom one is on terms of peace,* or *with whom peace has been made, for a definite time.* (L.)

عهر

1. عَهَرَ المَرْأَةَ, (Ḳ,) or عَهَرَ إِلَيْهَا, (M, Mgh, O,) aor. ـَ, (M, Mgh, O, Ḳ,) inf. n. عَهْرٌ and عَهَرٌ (Mgh, O, Ḳ) and عِهْرٌ, (Ḳ,) or this last is a simple subst., (Ṣ,) or a quasi-inf. n., (TA,) and عُهُورٌ (O, Ḳ) and عَهَرَانٌ (O) and عَهَارَةٌ and عُهُورَةٌ; (Ḳ;) and ▼ عَاهَرَهَا, inf. n. عِهَارٌ; (Ḳ;) *He came to the woman by night for the purpose of adultery* or *fornication:* (Mgh, O,* TA:) and hence the committing adultery or fornication, absolutely, has become the predominant signification: (TA:) or *he came to her by night for that purpose,* or *by day:* (Ḳ:) or *he committed adultery* or *fornication* (فُجُور) *with her at any time, in the night* or *in the day,* i. e., with a free woman or a slave: (TA:) or عَهَرَ بِهَا, inf. n. عَهْرٌ, *he committed adultery* or *fornication with her* (فَجَرَ بِهَا) *by night:* (IḲṭṭ, TA:) and عَهِرَ, (Ṣ, Mṣb, Ḳ,) aor. ـَ, (Ḳ, MṢ,) or ـِ, (Mṣb,) [but this I think a mistake,] inf. n. عَهَرٌ and عُهْرٌ, (Ṣ,) or عُهُورٌ, (Mṣb,) or all the forms mentioned above, (accord. to the Ḳ,) *he committed adultery* or *fornication;* syn. زَنَى, (Ṣ, Ḳ, TA,) or فَجَرَ; (Mṣb;) as also عَهَرَ, aor. ـَ, inf. n. عَهْرٌ; (Mṣb;) and ▼ عَاهَرَ; and ▼ تَعَيْهَرَ: (TA:) you say ▼ عَاهَرَ بِهَا *he committed adultery* or *fornication with her,* i. e., with a free woman or a slave: (TA, from a trad.:) or عَهَرَ signifies *he stole:* (Ḳ:) and *he followed evil,* (Ḳ, TA,) *whether by committing adultery* or *fornication,* or *by transgressing* [*in any other manner*], or *quitting the way of truth* or *justice,* or *forsaking the command of God:* (TA:) and ▼ تَعَيْهَرَ *he was,* or *became, an adulterer* or *a fornicator, following evil:* (Ṣ:) and ▼ عَيْهَرَتْ and ▼ تَعَيْهَرَتْ *she* (a woman) *committed adultery* or *fornication:* (TA:) or *she was,* or *became, light,* or *active, and volatile,* (Kr, Ḳ,) *not remaining fixed in her place,* (Kr,) *without continence.* (Ḳ, not added by Kr.)

3: see the preceding paragraph, in three places.

Q. Q. 1. عَيْهَرَتْ: see 1, near the end.

Q. Q. 2. تَعَيْهَرَ and تَعَيْهَرَتْ: see 1, in three places.

عَهْرٌ: see عَاهِرٌ.

عِهْرٌ *Adultery* or *fornication.* (Ṣ, O.) [See also 1.]

عَهَرَةٌ:
عَيْهَرَةٌ:
عُهَيْرَةٌ:
see the next paragraph.

عَاهِرٌ *An adulterer* or *a fornicator;* (Ṣ, O, Mṣb;) as also ▼ عَهْرٌ [originally an inf. n.]: and ▼ عُهَيْرَةٌ occurs in a trad. in the same sense, as a dim. of عَهْرٌ: or, accord. to ISh, on the authority of Ru-beh, عَاهِرٌ signifies one *who follows evil, whether by committing adultery or fornication,* or *by stealing:* (O, TA:) or, as in the L, *whether by committing adultery* or *fornication,* or *by transgressing* [*in any other manner*], or *quitting the way of truth* or *justice,* or *forsaking the command of God;* أَوْ فَاسِقًا being put in the L in the place of او سَارِقًا: (TA:) or any one *who does that which induces doubt,* or *suspicion* or *evil opinion,* or *doubt combined with suspicion* or *evil opinion:* (A, TA:) pl. عُهَّارٌ. (Ḥam p. 131.) It is said in a trad., الوَلَدُ لِلْفِرَاشِ وَلِلْعَاهِرِ الحَجَرُ, (Ṣ, Mgh, O, &c.,) i. e., *The child is for the master of the bed,* (Mgh, Mṣb, TA,) meaning, the husband (Mṣb, TA) of the child's mother, or, if she be a slave, her owner; (TA;) *and for the adulterer,* or *fornicator, disappointment;* (Mṣb;) meaning, he shall have no right of relationship, (A'Obeyd, Ṣ, Mgh, O, Mṣb,) nor any share in the child: (TA:) like the saying لَهُ التُّرَابُ, (A'Obeyd, Mgh, O, Mṣb,) which means "[he has, or shall have, or may he have,] disappointment," (Mṣb,) or "nothing:" (Mgh, O, TA:) for some of the Arabs used to establish relationship arising from adultery or fornication; therefore the law annulled this: (Mṣb:) some, however, explain it agreeably with the apparent [or literal] meaning, *and for the adulterer,* or *fornicator, stoning.* (Mgh.) [See also art. حجر.] —— Also عَاهِرَةٌ (AZ, Ṣ) and عَاهِرٌ, (Ḳ, TA,) if not a verbal epithet, [but a possessive epithet meaning properly ذَاتُ عِهْرٍ,] (TA,) A woman *who comes to a man by night for the purpose of* فُجُور [*adultery* or *fornication*], or *by day;* as also ▼ مُعَاهِرَةٌ (Ḳ) and ▼ مُعَاهِرٌ: (CḲ: [but this is app. a mistake:]) *an adulteress* or *a fornicatress;* as also ▼ مُعَاهِرَةٌ (AZ, Ṣ, O) and ▼ عَيْهَرَةٌ; (Ṣ;) which last is originally ▼ عَهَرَةٌ, like ثَمَرَةٌ, with an augmentative ى: (Th, Mbr:) or عَيْهَرَةٌ signifies a woman *light,* or *active, and volatile,* (Kr, O, Ḳ,) *who does not remain fixed in her place,* (Kr, O,) *without continence:* (Ḳ, not added by Kr:) and ▼ عَيْهَرَةٌ signifies the same as عَاهِرَةٌ, applied to a woman. (O, TA.)

عَيْهَرٌ A *strong* camel. (O, Ḳ.) —— عَيْهَرَةٌ: see عَاهِرٌ, near the end. —— Also The [*kind of goblin,* or *demon, called*] غُول. (O, Ḳ.)

عَيْهَرَانٌ The *male of the* عَيْهَرَة, i. e. غُول: pl. عَيَاهِيرُ. (O, Ḳ.)

مُعَاهِرٌ, and with ة: see عَاهِرٌ, near the end, in three places.

عهل

Q. Q. 1. عَيْهَلْتُ الإِبِلَ *I left the camels to pasture by themselves, without a pastor, by night and by day:* mentioned by IB, on the authority of A'Obeyd: and he cites as an ex.,

* عَيَاهِلُ ▼ عَيْهَلَهَا الذُّوَّادُ *

[app. meaning *Camels left to pasture by themselves, the drivers having left them to do so*]. (TA.)

عَاهِلٌ *A paramount sovereign, like a* خَلِيفَة. (Ṣ, O, Ḳ.) —— And A woman *having no husband:* [probably because of her independence:] (AO, Ṣ, O, Ḳ:) pl. عَوَاهِلُ. (O.)

عَيْهَلٌ A *swift* she-camel; as also عَيْهَلَةٌ; (Ṣ, O, Ḳ;) and so عَيْهُولٌ and ▼ عَيْهَالٌ: (IDrd,* O,* Ḳ:) or all signify an *excellent, strong,* she-camel: (Ḳ:) or عَيْهَلٌ signifies a *large, big,* she-camel; or a *tall* she-camel: (TA:) [see an ex. in a verse cited in the first paragraph of art. جهر:] and it is also applied to the male of camels, (Ḳ, TA,) as some say; (TA;) and عَيْهَلَةٌ to the female; (Ḳ, TA;) but, (TA,) accord. to AHát, one should not say جَمَلٌ عَيْهَلٌ; (Ṣ, O, TA;) and some say that one should apply to a she-camel the epithet عَيْهَلَةٌ only: (TA:) sometimes, by poetic license, they said عَيْهَلٌ. (Ṣ, O.) —— Also, applied to a man, and عَيْهَلَةٌ applied to a woman, (Ḳ,) or both applied to a woman, (Ṣ,) *That will not remain* *in one place, by reason of lightness*, or *unsteadiness*, or *lightwittedness*, (Ṣ, Ḳ, TA,) *going to and fro, forwards and backwards.* (TA.) —— And the former, A *tall* woman: (Ḳ, TA:) or a *strong* woman. (TA.) —— And عَيْهَلَةٌ An *old, aged,* woman. (O, Ḳ,* TA.) —— And رِيحٌ عَيْهَلٌ *A strong,* or *violent, wind.* (Ṣ, O, Ḳ.*) —— عَيَاهِلُ [a pl., of which the sing. is probably عَيْهَلٌ or عَيْهَلَةٌ,] see in the first paragraph.

عَيْهَالٌ : } see the next preceding paragraph.
عَيْهُولٌ :

عهن

1. عَهَنَ, (Ṣ, Ḳ,) aor. ـُ, (Ḳ,) inf. n. عُهُونٌ, (TḲ,) *He remained, stayed, dwelt,* or *abode,* (Ṣ, Ḳ,) بِالمَكَانِ [*in the place*]. (Ṣ.) —— And *He,* or *it, went forth:* thus the verb has two contr. significations. (Ḳ, TA.) One says, عَهَنَ مِنْهُ خَيْرٌ, aor. ـُ, inf. n. عُهُونٌ, *Good went forth* [or *proceeded*] *from him,* or *it.* (TA.) —— Also *It* (a thing) *continued, lasted,* or *endured.* (TA.) —— And *It was,* or *became, present,* or *ready;* syn. حَضَرَ. (TA.) —— And *He strove, laboured, exerted himself,* or *was diligent,* فِى العَمَلِ [*in the deed,* or *work*]. (Ḳ.) —— And i. q. عَهِدَ [probably in its most usual sense, meaning, with إِلَيْهِ following it, *He enjoined, charged,* or *bade, him;* or the like]. (Ḳ.) == عَهَنَ لَهُ مُرَادَهُ *He hastened to him what he wished,* or *desired.* (Ḳ.) == عَهِنَتِ السَّعَفَةُ, (AḤn, Ḳ, TA,) or عَهِنَتْ عَوَاهِنُ النَّخْلِ, (Ṣ,) aor. ـَ, with ḍamm, (AḤn, Ṣ, TA,) and ـَ, inf. n. عُهُونٌ, (AḤn, TA,) *The palm-branch,* (AḤn, Ḳ,) or *the palm-branches called* عَوَاهِن, (Ṣ,) *became dried up.* (AḤn, Ṣ, Ḳ, TA.) == عَهَنَ, aor. ـُ, (Ḳ,) inf. n. عَهْنٌ, (TḲ,) [and quasi-inf. n. عُهْنَةٌ, q. v.,] said of a branch, rod, or twig, *It bent:* or *it broke without becoming separated.* (Ḳ.)

عِهْنٌ *Wool,* (AO, Ṣ, Ḳ, TA,) in a general sense: (TA:) or *wool dyed of various colours;* (Ḳ, TA;) and it has been expl. as having this meaning in the Ḳur ci. 4: Er-Rághib says, it is peculiarly applied to *coloured wool;* referring to the Ḳur lv. 37: (TA:) and ↓ عِهْنَةٌ signifies *a portion* [or *flock* or *tuft*] *thereof:* the pl. of عِهْنٌ is عُهُونٌ [meaning *sorts of* عِهْن]. (Ṣ, Ḳ.) == هُوَ عِهْنُ مَالٍ means *He is a good manager,* or *tender, of property,* or *camels,* or *cattle.* (Ṣ, Ḳ.)

عُهْنَةٌ [as a quasi-inf. n.] The *bending* of a branch, rod, or twig: or its *breaking without becoming separated;* so that when one looks at it, he finds it to be whole; and when he shakes it, it bends. (TA. [See 1, last sentence.])

عِهْنَةٌ : see عِهْنٌ. == Also *A certain tree* (Ḳ, TA) *in the desert,* (TA,) *having a red* [*flower such as is termed*] وَرْدَةٌ; (Ḳ, TA;) mentioned by Az as having been seen by him: said by AḤn to be a بَقْلَة [i. e. *herb,* or *leguminous plant*]: and by IB to be *of the* بَقْل *termed* ذُكُور. (TA.) == And a dial. var. of إِحْنَةٌ; (Ḳ, TA;) meaning *Rancour, malevolence, malice,* or *spite:* and *anger.* (TA.)

عِهَانٌ The *base,* or *lower part, of a raceme of a palm-tree:* (IAạr, Ḳ:) like إِهَانٌ &c. (TA.)

عَاهِنٌ *Remaining, staying, dwelling,* or *abiding.* (Ṣ, Ḳ, TA.) —— And *Going forth;* thus having two contr. significations, (TA.) —— And *Continuing, lasting,* or *enduring.* (Ṣ, Ḳ, TA.) —— And *Present,* or *ready:* (Ṣ, Ḳ, TA:) applied in this sense to food, and to beverage; and to property, or camels, or cattle; as also ↓ آهِنٌ: one says, خُذْ مِنْ عَاهِنِ مَالِهِ and آهِنِهِ [*Take thou of what is present,* or *ready, of his property,* &c.]. (TA.) —— Also, applied to property, or camels, or cattle, *Long-possessed,* or *long-possessed and home-born,* or *inherited from parents.* (Ṣ, Ḳ.) So in the saying, أَعْطَاهُ مِنْ عَاهِنِ مَالِهِ [*He gave him of what had been long-possessed,* &c., *of his property,* &c.]. (Ṣ.) == Applied to a branch, rod, or twig, of a tree, *Broken without becoming separated, so that it remains suspended and lax:* this is said by Abu-l-'Abbás to be the primary signification [app. in relation to what here follows]. (TA.) —— And [hence,] † *Lax, and sluggish,* or *lazy.* (IAạr, Ḳ, TA.) —— And † *Poor;* syn. فَقِيرٌ: (Ḳ, TA:) because of his broken state. (TA.) —— Also sing. of عَوَاهِنُ, which signifies The *palm-branches that are next to the* قِلَبَة [which latter are the *branches that grow forth from the heart of the tree*]; (Ṣ, Ḳ, TA;) thus in the dial. of El-Ḥijáz; called by the people of Nejd الخَوَافِى: (Ṣ, TA:) or, accord. to Lḥ, the *branches below,* or *exclusive of, the* قِلَبَة; of the dial. of El-Medeeneh: one thereof is called عَاهِنٌ and ↓ عَاهِنَةٌ: or, accord. to IAth, it is pl. of ↓ عَاهِنَةٌ, and signifies the *branches that are next to the heart of the palm-tree:* and the heart is injured by the cutting of those that are near to it; therefore 'Omar, as is related in a trad., ordering a person to bring him a palm-branch stripped of the leaves, told him to avoid [cutting] the عواهن. (TA.) —— And hence, (Ṣ, TA,) as being likened to these palm-branches, (TA,) العَوَاهِنُ signifies also ‡ *The members,* or *limbs, of a human being, with which he works,* or *earns.* (Ṣ, Ḳ, TA.) —— And † *Certain veins of the she-camel, in her* رَحِم [which may here mean either *womb* or *vulva*]: (Ṣ, Ḳ:) or, accord. to IAạr, her عَوَاهِن are *in the place of her* رَحِم *internally, like the* عَوَاهِن *of palm-trees.* (TA.) —— رَمَى بِالكَلَامِ عَلَى, (Ḳ,) or رَمَى الكَلَامَ, (Ṣ,) عَوَاهِنِهِ (Ṣ, Ḳ) means *He adduced* [or *blurted out*] *the speech,* or *saying, without thought,* or *consideration;* like their saying أَوْرَدَ كَلَامَهُ غَيْرَ مُفَسَّرٍ: (TA:) or *he cared not whether he said right or wrong:* (Ṣ, Ḳ, TA:) or *he held it* [i. e. *his speech*] *in light estimation:* or *he said what was good and what was bad:* accord. to IAth, العَوَاهِنُ denotes one's taking what is not the right way in journeying or in speech; and is pl. of ↓ عَاهِنَةٌ. (TA.) And one says also, حَدَسَ الكَلَامَ عَلَى عَوَاهِنِهِ, meaning *He spoke without anything to guide him, and without caution.* (TA in art. حدس.)

عَاهِنَةٌ: see the next preceding paragraph, latter half, in three places.

عَيْهُونٌ *A certain good, pleasant,* or *sweet, plant.* (Ḳ.)

عو

1. عَوَى, aor. يَعْوِى, inf. n. عُوَآءٌ (Ṣ, Ḳ, TA) and عَىٌّ and عَوَّةٌ (Ḳ, TA) and عَوْيَةٌ, with fet-ḥ and then sukoon, thus in the M, but in the copies of the Ḳ عَوِيَةٌ, (TA,) said of a dog, (Ṣ, CḲ, TA,) and of a wolf, and of a jackal, (Ṣ, TA,) *He cried,* or *cried loudly:* (Ṣ:) [meaning *he howled:*] *he twisted his muzzle, then uttered a cry:* or *he prolonged his cry, not doing so with clearness:* and ↓ اعتوى signifies the same: (Ḳ, TA:) [in the Ḥam p. 693, the former is expl. as signifying صَاحَ and نَبَحَ; but] it is said that عَوَّةٌ signifies a prolonged crying; and is not the same as نَبْحٌ [which means "a barking"]. (TA.) It is said in a prov. لَوْ لَكَ أَعْوِى مَا عَوَيْتُ [*If to thee I were howling, I had not howled*]; (TA;) or لَوْ لَكَ عَوَيْتُ لَمْ أَعْوِهْ, in which the ه may be the ه of pausation, or it may be put by metonymy for the inf. n. so that the meaning is لَمْ أَعْوِ العُوَآءَ: (Meyd:) it originated from the fact that a man used, [and still uses, as I have had occasion to do,] when becoming benighted, in the desert, to howl, in order that the dogs, if any person by whose presence he might be cheered were near him, might hear, and reply to him, and he might be guided by their howling: so this man howled, and the wolf came to him, whereupon he said thus: it relates to the seeker of succour from him who will not succour him. (Meyd,* TA.) And it is said in a trad., كَأَنِّى أَسْمَعُ عُوَآءَ أَهْلِ النَّارِ i. e. † [*As though I heard*] *the crying* or *loud crying* [or *howling*] *of the people of the fire* [of Hell]: (TA:) [for] عَوَى is used metaphorically as meaning *he suffered distress, and complained;* from the عُوَآء of the dog: (Ḥar p. 634:) as IAth says, it is more especially used in relation to the wolf and the dog. (TA.) And one says of him who is esteemed, or found to be, weak, مَا يَعْوِى وَمَا يَنْبَحُ † [*He does not howl nor does he bark*]. (Ḥam p. 693.) —— And عَوَى إِلَى الفِتْنَةِ means † *He called* (Ḳ, TA) people, or a party, (TA,) [*to conflict and faction,* or *the like;*] عَوَى being used in this sense by way of likening the person who does so to a dog, or in contempt of him. (Ḥam p. 693.) [See also 10.] —— عُوَآءٌ signifies also The *grumbling cry* (رُغَآء) of a weak young camel: used in this sense by a poet. (TA.) —— عَوَى عَنِ الرَّجُلِ; and the phrase عُوَآءُ المُغْتَابِ; see in the next paragraph. == عَوَى, (Ṣ, Ḳ, TA,) inf. n. عَىٌّ, (Ṣ, TA,) *He bent* a thing; as also ↓ اعتوى; and likewise a bow; as also ↓ عَوَّى, (Ḳ, TA,) inf. n. تَعْوِيَةٌ: (TA:) and (TA) *he twisted* hair, and a rope; (Ṣ, TA;) as also ↓ عَوَّى, inf. n. تَعْوِيَةٌ. (Ṣ.) One says also عَوَى العِمَامَةَ

عَيَّةً *He twisted the turban with a single twisting.* (TA.) And عَوَيْتُ رَأْسَ النَّاقَةِ *I turned the head of the she-camel by means of the nose-rein.* (Ṣ, TA.) And عووها ↓ عوى القَوْمُ صُدُورَ رِكَابِهِمْ and *The party inclined the breasts of their camels that they were riding.* (TA.) And عَوَى البُرَةَ *He bent, or inclined, the nose-ring* of the she-camel. (Ḳ,* TA.) And النَّاقَةُ تَعْوِى بُرَتَهَا فِى سَيْرِهَا *The she-camel twists her nose-ring with her* خِطَام [or *halter*] *in her going.* (Ṣ, TA.) And عَوَاهُ عَنِ الشَّىْءِ *He turned him from the thing.* (TA.) And one says of the man who possesses prudence, or discretion, and precaution, or good judgment, and who is hardy, strong, or sturdy, ما ينهى ولا يعوى [i. e. مَا يُنْهَى وَلَا يُعْوَى *He is not forbidden nor is he turned*]. (TA.) — And عَوَى signifies also *He* (a man) *attained to the age of thirty years, so that his arm,* or *hand, became strong, and he twisted vehemently the arm,* or *hand, of another.* (ISd, Ḳ.)

2. عَوَّى عَنِ الرَّجُلِ, thus in the M, with teshdeed in the case of عوى and also in the case of كذّب in the explanation; but in the Ḳ, ↓ عَوَى [without teshdeed]; (TA;) † *He repelled from the man,* or *defended him;* syn. كَذَّبَ, and رَدَّ: (M, Ḳ, TA:) in the Ṣ is said the like of what is said in the M; عَوَّيْتُ عَنِ الرَّجُلِ being expl. in the Ṣ as meaning † *I repelled from,* or *defended, the man* (كذّبت عنه), *and replied against his backbiter* or *censurer* (رَدَدْتُ عَلَى مُغْتَابِهِ): and in the A, this phrase is said to be metaphorical, and expl. as meaning ‡ *I repelled from the man the clamouring* [or, as we say, *the barking*] *of the backbiter* or *the censurer* (رَدَدْتُ عَنْهُ عَوَّةَ ↓ المُغْتَابِ): thus all these three are express authorities for the teshdeed. (TA.) [Freytag has represented the phrase in the Ṣ as agreeing with the reading thereof in the Ḳ, and has strangely expl. the verb with عن following it as meaning "Mendacii arguit et refellit."] — See also 1, latter half, in three places.

3. عاوى الكِلَابَ *He cried,* or *cried loudly,* [meaning *he howled,*] *to the dogs, they doing so to him.* (Ṣ, TA.) And [hence] عَاوَاهُمْ, (Ḳ, TA,) inf. n. مُعَاوَاةٌ, (TA,) *He cried,* or *cried loudly, to them,* [i. e. to men,] *they doing so to him.* (Ḳ, TA.)

6. تعاوت الكِلَابُ *The dogs cried,* or *cried loudly,* [meaning *howled,*] *one to another.* (TA.) — And تَعَاوَوْا عَلَيْهِ, (Ḳ, TA,) and تَعَاوَوْا, (TA,) *They collected themselves together,* (Ḳ, TA,) or *aided one another,* (TA,) *against him.* (Ḳ, TA.)

7. انعوى *It became bent* [or *twisted*]. (Ṣ, Ḳ.)

8. اعتوى: see 1, first sentence: — and the same also in the latter half.

10. استعوى كَلْبًا [*He incited a dog to cry,* or *cry loudly,* or *to howl*]. (Esh-Sháfi'ee, TA in art. حمى.) — And اسْتَعْوَاهُمْ *He sought,* or *demanded, of them, aid,* or *succour:* (Ḳ, TA:) or, accord. to the Ṣ, it means نَعَقَ بِهِمْ إِلَى الفِتْنَةِ [*he urged them by clamour,* or *shouting, to conflict and faction,* or *the like*]: (TA: [in one of my copies of the Ṣ, for إِذَا نَعَقَ بِهِمْ, the reading followed in the JM and PṢ as well as in the TA, I find اذا يَعْوِيهِم, which is app. a mistranscription: see also عَوَى إِلَى الفِتْنَةِ:]) accord. to Z, it means *he desired,* or *demanded, of them, that they should cry,* or *cry loudly, behind him.* (TA.) — اِسْتَعْوَيْتُهُ *I desired,* or *demanded, of him, that he should twist* hair, or a rope. (Ṣ.)

R. Q. 1. عَاعَى, [mentioned in the Ḳ in this art., and also, but as unexplained, in art. عيع,] aor. يُعَاعِى, inf. n. مُعَاعَاةٌ (Ḳ, TA) and عَاعَاةٌ; (TA;) and عَوْعَى, [app. the original form,] aor. يُعَوْعِى, (Ḳ, TA,) inf. n. عَوْعَاةٌ; (TA;) and عَيْعَى, aor. يُعَيْعِى, inf. n. عَيْعَاةٌ and عِيعَآءٌ [in some copies of the Ḳ عَيْعَاءٌ]; *He chid sheep by the cry* عَا or عَوْ or عَاىْ (Ḳ, TA) or عَآءْ. (TA.)

عَوْ and عَا [in the CḲ عُو] and عَاىْ (Ḳ, TA) and عَآءْ (TA) are *Cries by which sheep are chidden.* (Ḳ, TA.)

عَوْ: see العَوَّآءُ, last sentence.

عَوَّةٌ [mentioned in the first sentence of this art. as an inf. n.] *A crying out, shouting,* or *clamouring;* like ضَوَّةٌ: one says, سَمِعْتُ عَوَّةَ القَوْمِ, i. e. [*I heard*] *the cries,* or *shouts,* or *clamour, of the people,* or *party:* so says AZ, and Aṣ says the like. (Ṣ.) — See also العَوَّآءُ, last sentence. — Also *A way-mark that is set up, composed of stones:* mentioned by IDrd, but incorrectly as being with ḍamm. (TA.)

عُوَّةٌ: see the next paragraph, last sentence.

العَوَّآءُ (Ṣ, Ḳ) and العَوَّا (Ḳ) *The dog* (Ṣ, Ḳ) *that howls* (يَعْوِى) *much.* (Ṣ.) Hence the saying, عَلَيْهِ العَفَآءُ وَالكَلْبُ العَوَّآءُ [*Upon him be the dust, and the howling dog*]: a form of imprecation. (TA.) — And the latter signifies also *The wolf.* (TA.) — Also, both, (Ṣ, Ḳ, TA,) but the latter is the more common, and its ا is to denote the fem. gender, like that of حُبْلَى [in which it is written ى], the word being fem., (TA,) ‡ *One of the Mansions of the Moon,* (Ṣ, Ḳ, TA,) namely, *the Thirteenth;* (Ḳzw in his Descr. of the Mansions of the Moon;) *consisting of five stars,* (Ṣ, Ḳ,) *said to be the haunch of the Lion* [of which the Arabs, or some of them, extended the figure (as they did also that of the Scorpion) far beyond the limits that we assign to it: see ذِرَاعٌ]: (Ṣ:) or *four stars* [γ, δ, ε, *and* η, *of Virgo*], (Ḳ, and Ḳzw ubi suprà,) *behind* الصَّرْفَة [q. v.], (Ḳzw ibid.,) *resembling an alif* (Ḳ, Ḳzw) *with the lower part turned back, in the Koofee handwriting* [in which it is nearly like the Roman L (see زَاوِيَةٌ, in art. زوى)]; (Ḳzw ibid;) *also called* عُرْقُوبُ الأَسَدِ; (TA, as from the Ṣ, in my copies of which I do not find this;) they regard it as dogs following the Lion; and *some say that it is the haunches of the Lion;* (Ḳzw ubi suprà;) accord. to the A, it is thus called because it rises [a mistake for sets, aurorally, (see مَنَازِلُ القَمَرِ, in art. نزل,)] in the tail, or latter part, of the cold, as though it were howling (كَأَنَّهُ يَعْوِى) after it, driving it away, wherefore they call it طَارِدَةُ البَرْدِ: (TA:) or it is an appellation applied by the Arabs to *the star that is on the edge of the left shoulder of Virgo, which is the Thirteenth Mansion of the Moon:* or, accord. to some, *the stars that are upon her belly and beneath her armpit;* as though they were dogs howling (تَعْوِى) behind the Lion; so called because of the vehemence of the cold; for when they rise or set [aurorally], they bring cold. (Ḳzw in his Descr. of Virgo.) And † [*The constellation Bootes;*] *a northern constellation, called also* الصَّيَّاحُ, *consisting of two and twenty stars within the figure, and one without it; the figure being that of a man having in his right hand a staff, between the stars of* الفَكَّة *and* بَنَاتُ نَعْشٍ: *the one that is without the figure is a red, bright star, between his thighs,* [i. e. *Arcturus,*] *called* السِّمَاكُ الرَّامِحُ, *and, by the Arabs,* حَارِسُ الشَّمَالِ and حَارِسُ السَّمَآءِ, *because it is always seen in the sky, not becoming concealed beneath the rays of the sun.* (Ḳzw in his Descr. of the Northern Constellations.) — Also, (Ḳ,) or the former word, (TA,) [*The aged she-camel;*] *the* نَاب *of camels;* (Ḳ, TA;) on the authority of AA. (TA.) — Also, both words, (Ḳ,) the former and sometimes the latter, (Ṣ,) the former said by Az to be the more common, but MF says that the latter is the more chaste, for the former was by AAF absolutely disallowed, (TA,) *The* سَافِلَة, (Ṣ,) or اِسْت, (Ḳ,) [each here app. meaning *anus,*] of a human being; (Ṣ;) app. from عَوَى, aor. يَعْوِى, signifying "he cried," or "cried loudly:" (TA:) as also ↓ عَوَّةٌ (IDrd, Ḳ, TA) and ↓ عُوَّةٌ, (Lth, Ḳ, TA,) of which last the pl. is ↓ عَوْ [or rather this is a coll. gen. n.] and [the pl. properly so termed is] عَوَّاتٌ: but IAạr is said to have expl. العَوَّآءُ as meaning الأَسْتَاهُ [pl. of سَتَهٌ which is the original of اِسْتٌ]. (TA.)

عَاوٍ [act. part. n. of عَوَى]. One says, مَا لَهُ عَاوٍ وَلَا نَابِحٌ i. e. *He has not belonging to him* [*a howler nor a barker,* meaning *sheep,* or *goats, among which the wolf howls and in the way to which the dog barks* [to defend them]. (TA.)

مُعَاوِيَةٌ *A bitch excited by lust,* (Lth, A, Ḳ, TA,) *that howls* (تَعْوِى) *to the dogs when she is in that state, and to which they howl.* (Lth, A,* TA.) — And *A fox's cub.* (Ḳ.) — And أَبُو مُعَاوِيَةَ is a surname of *The* فَهْد [or *lynx*]. (Ḳ, TA.) — The dim. of مُعَاوِيَةٌ is مُعَيَّةٌ; (Ṣ, Ḳ, TA;) thus say the people of El-Baṣrah; for when three ى occur together and the first of them is the characteristic of the dim., one of them is suppressed [by them]; (Ṣ, TA;) and مُعَيِّيَةٌ; (Ṣ, Ḳ, TA; [in the CḲ مُعَيِّيَةٌ;]) thus say the people of El-Koofeh, not suppressing anything, after the manner of those who say أُسَيِّدٌ; (Ṣ, TA;) and مُعَيْوِيَةٌ, (Ṣ,

Ḳ, TA, [in the CḲ مَعْيُوَةٌ,]) after the manner of those who say أَسْيُودٌ. (Ṣ, TA.)

عوج

1. عَوِجَ, (Ṣ, O, L, Mṣb, Ḳ,) aor. يَعْوَجُ, (TA,) inf. n. عَوَجٌ (Ṣ, O, L, Mṣb) and عِوَجٌ, (L,) or the latter is a simple subst.; (Ṣ, O, Ḳ;) and ▾ اِعْوَجَّ, [which is more common,] inf. n. اِعْوِجَاجٌ; (Ṣ, O, L, Mṣb, Ḳ;) and ▾ انعاج; and ▾ تعوّج; (L;) *It was, or became, crooked, curved, bent, winding, wry, contorted, distorted,* or *uneven:* (L:) or [عَوِجَ and] ▾ اعوجّ, *it was,* or *became, so of itself;* and [▾ انعاج and] ▾ تعوّج, *it was,* or *became, so by the operation of an external agent;* (L, Mṣb;) as is said by Az: (L:) ▾ انعاج is quasi-pass. of عُجْتُهُ; (L;) and ▾ تعوّج is quasi-pass. of عَوَّجْتُهُ: (Az, Ṣ, O, L, Mṣb, Ḳ:) and عَوِجَ and عَوَجَ are said to be used in relation to different things: (Ṣ, O, L, Mṣb, Ḳ, &c.:) [for instance,] one says, عَوِجَ العُودُ, inf. n. عَوَجٌ, *The wood,* or *stick, was,* or *became, crooked, curved, bent,* or *distorted:* and عَوِجَ الأَمْرُ, inf. n. عِوَجٌ, *The affair was,* or *became, difficult, arduous,* or *troublesome.* (MA.) [See عَوَجٌ below.] — لَا عِوَجَ لَهُ, in the Ḳur xx. 107, means *There shall be no evading it.* (Jel.) — عُجْتُ إِلَيْهِ, aor. أَعُوجُ, inf. n. عِيَاجٌ and عَوْجٌ, *I turned,* or *inclined, towards it;* namely, a place of abode. (L.) And ▾ انعاج عَلَيْهِ *He turned,* or *inclined, towards it,* or *him.* (Ṣ, O.) And ▾ انعاجت and ▾ تعوّجت, said of a she-camel, *She turned aside;* or *became turned aside;* the former quasi-pass. of عَاجَهَا; and the latter, of عَوَّجَهَا. (TA.) — عاج به *He inclined, and came to him,* or *came to him and alighted at his abode as a guest:* and *he passed by him.* (L.) And عُجْتُ بِالمَكَانِ, aor. أَعُوجُ, (Ṣ, O, Ḳ,*) inf. n. عَوْجٌ and مَعَاجٌ; (Ḳ;) and ▾ عوّجت; (TA;) *I remained, stayed, dwelt,* or *abode, in the place.* (Ṣ, O, Ḳ.*) And عاج عَلَيْهِ *He stopped,* or *paused, at it.* (Ṣ,* O,* Ḳ,* TA.) A poet says,

* عُجْنَا عَلَى رَبْعِ سَلْمَى أَيَّ تَعْرِيجِ *

[*We stopped at the abode of Selmà, with what a staying!*]: putting تعريج [in some copies of the Ṣ تعويج] in the place of عَوْج because their meaning is one. (Ṣ, O, TA.) — فُلَانٌ مَا يَعُوجُ عَنْ شَيْءٍ *Such a one does not revert from,* or *relinquish, anything.* (IAạr, Ṣ, O, Ḳ.*) — Accord. to AA, [the inf. n.] عِيَاجٌ signifies *The returning to that upon which one had been intent,* or *attent,* or *employed.* (O and TA in art. عيج.) ═ عُجْتُهُ: see 2. — عُجْتُ البَعِيرَ, (Ṣ, A,* O, Ḳ,*) and عُجْتُ رَأْسَ البَعِيرِ, (L,) aor. أَعُوجُهُ, inf. n. عَوْجٌ (Ṣ, O, L) and مَعَاجٌ, (Ṣ, O,) *I turned the camel's head by means of the nose-rein:* (Ṣ, A,* O, L, Ḳ:*) and in like manner one says of a horse: and عاج نَاقَتَهُ, and ▾ عوّجها, *He turned aside his she-camel.* (TA.) And عاج رَأْسَهُ إِلَى المَرْأَةِ (O and TA from a trad.) *He inclined his head towards the woman, and looked towards her.* (TA.) And المَرْأَةُ تَعُوجُ رَأْسَهَا إِلَى ضَجِيعِهَا [*The woman turns her head towards her bedfellow*]. (TA.) And عاج عُنُقَهُ, inf. n. عَوْجٌ, *He inclined,* or *bent, his neck.* (TA.) And عُجْ لِسَانَكَ عَنِّى وَلَا تُكْثِرْ [*Turn,* or *withhold, thy tongue from me, and do not multiply* words]. (A.) And عَوَّجَ بِهِ الطَّرِيقُ [*The road led him,* or *turned him, aside*]. (Ḳ in explanation of حَوَّجَ.) — مَا أَعُوجُ بِكَلَامِهِ *I do not pay regard,* or *attention, to his speech,* (ISk, Ṣ in art. عيج, A,* and O,) is a phrase of the Benoo-Asad, who take it from عُجْتُ النَّاقَةَ: (ISk, Ṣ, O:) others say مَا أَعِيجُ. (O.) And one says, مَا عُجْتُ بِحَدِيثِهِ [*I did not pay regard to his discourse*]. (A.) — عُجْتُهُ بِالمَكَانِ *I made him to remain, stay, dwell,* or *abide, in the place:* the verb being trans. as well as intrans. (Ṣ, O.)

2. عَوَّجْتُهُ, (T, Ṣ, O, Mṣb, Ḳ,) inf. n. تَعْوِيجٌ; (T, Ṣ, O, Mṣb;) *I crooked it, curved it, bent it, contorted it, distorted it,* or *rendered it uneven;* (T, Ṣ,* O,* Mṣb, Ḳ,* TA;) namely, a thing; (T, Ṣ, O, Mṣb, TA;) as also ▾ عُجْتُهُ, inf. n. عَوْجٌ and عِيَاجٌ. (TA.) — See also 1, latter half, in two places. — تَعْوِيجٌ [as an inf. n. of which the verb, if it have one in the following sense, is عَوَّجَ], in a horse, is *syn. with* تَجْنِيبٌ [app. as meaning *A bending,* or *curving, and tension of the sinews, in the hind leg*] which is a quality approved. (TA.) ═ See also 1, near the middle. [Hence] one says, مَا لَهُ عَلَى أَصْحَابِهِ تَعْوِيجٌ, meaning [*There is not for him any*] *remaining,* or *staying,* [*at the abode of his companions;*] as also تَعْرِيجٌ. (TA.) ═ عَوَّجَهُ, inf. n. as above, also signifies *He set it,* or *inlaid it, with* عَاج [which means *ivory,* and *tortoise-shell*]; (O, Ḳ, TA;) namely, a thing, (O,) or a vessel. (TA.)

5: see 1, former half, in four places.

7: see 1, former half, in five places.

9: see 1, first sentence, in two places.

عَاجٌ, as an epithet applied to a she-camel, *Pliable;* syn. لَيِّنَةُ الاِنْعِطَافِ, or لَيِّنَةُ الأَعْطَافِ, accord. to different copies of the Ḳ; and by the latter words is expl. (but not in the Ḳ) ▾ عَائِجَةٌ, as so applied: in the L, عَاجٌ is expl. as meaning *tractable, submissive,* or *manageable;* syn. مِذْعَانٌ: (TA:) or مِذْعَانُ السَّيْرِ لَيِّنَةُ الاِنْعِطَافِ: (thus in the O:) and it is said to be without a parallel in respect of the dropping of the [fem. termination] ة, whether its original measure be فَعِلٌ or فَاعِلٌ [?]. (TA.) ═ Also [*Ivory;*] *elephant's bones;* (Ṣ, O, Ḳ;) or [rather] only *elephant's tusk;* (Lth, Mṣb, TA;) thus say ISd and Ḳz: (TA:) n. un. with ة [signifying *a piece of ivory*]: (Ṣ, O:) of its properties are these: that if seed-produce or trees be fumigated with it, worms will not approach them; and the woman who drinks of it every day two drachms with water and honey, if compressed after seven days, conceives. (Ḳ.) — And *Tortoise-shell;* syn. ذَبْلٌ [q. v.]; (O, Ḳ;) i. e. (O) the *back* [or *shell*] *of the sea-tortoise* [or *turtle*]: (O, Mṣb:) *i. q.* مَسَكٌ: (Sh, L:) or *a thing that is made from the back of the sea-tortoise:* (L:) and it is said that the Arabs called *any* [*sort of*] *bone* by this name: n. un. with ة. (TA.) The Prophet is related to have had a comb of عاج, i. e. ذَبْل: (L:) and he is said to have ordered to purchase for Fáṭimeh a pair of bracelets of عاج, by which he meant not what is turned of elephants' tusks, for their tusks are مَيْتَة, [i. e. they are taken from an animal of which the flesh is unlawful food,] but ذبل: (O,* L, Mṣb:*) the عاج of the elephant is impure accord. to Esh-Sháfi'ee, but pure accord. to Aboo-Ḥaneefeh. (L.) — Also *Bracelets of* عاج, as distinguished from ذَبْل, [i. e. of *ivory:* and probably of *tortoise-shell* also:] (ISh:) n. un. with ة. (TA in art. جوح.) ═ عَاجِ, (Ṣ, O, L, Ḳ,) indecl., with kesr for its termination, (L, Ḳ,) as a determinate noun; and عَاجٍ, with tenween, as an indeterminate noun; (L;) *A cry by which a she-camel is chidden:* (Ṣ, O, L, Ḳ:) Az says, in chiding a she-camel, one says عَاجِ, without tenween; and if he please, عَاجْ, with jezm, as though a pause were imagined to be made after it: or, accord. to A'Obeyd, one says to her عَاجٍ, and جَاهٍ, with tenween: [but see art. جوه:] accord. to AHeyth, a word of this kind is originally mejzoom; but in the case of a rhyme, [and in any case of poetical necessity,] it may be makhfooḍ. (TA.) [See also art. عج.]

عَوَجٌ and ▾ عِوَجٌ [are inf. ns. of عَوِجَ, q. v., or the latter is a simple subst.; and both, used as simple substs.,] signify *Crookedness, curvity, a bending, a winding, wryness, contortion, distortion,* or *unevenness:* (L:) or the former is peculiar to objects of the sight, as bodies; and the latter, to what are not seen, as opinion, and a saying, and religion: or, as some say, the latter is used in both of these cases; but the distinction is more common: (IAth, TA:) AZ makes the same distinction; but adds that some of the Arabs used the latter word in relation to a road: (Mṣb:) accord. to ISk, (Ṣ, O,) the former is in anything erect, (Ṣ, O, Ḳ,) or in anything that was erect and has inclined, (TA,) as a wall, (Ṣ, O, Ḳ, TA,) and a stick, (Ṣ, O, Mṣb,) or a staff, (Ḳ, TA,) and a spear; (TA;) and the latter, in land, or ground, and in religion, (Ṣ, O, Mṣb, Ḳ, TA,) and in means of subsistence: (Ṣ, O:) in land, or ground, the latter means *unevenness;* thus in the Ḳur xx. 106: in a road, *deflection;* as also عَوَجٌ: in religion, and in natural disposition, *corruptness,* or *deviation from rectitude:* (TA:) and عَوَجٌ, (Ṣ, O, TA, [thus accord. to both of my copies of the Ṣ,]) or عِوَجٌ, (accord. to a copy of the A, [which

I incline to regard as the right, in consideration of its consistency with explanations here preceding, notwithstanding the apparent preponderance of authority in favour of عَوْج,]) in a man, signifies *evilness of natural disposition*: (Ṣ, A, O: [and so, app., عَوْج:]) or عَوَج, with fet-ḥ to the و, as an inf. n., signifies the *being evil in natural disposition*. (KL.)

عَوَج: see the next preceding paragraph.

العُوَيْجَآءُ [dim. of العَوْجَآءُ fem. of الأَعْوَجُ] *A species of* ذُرَة [or *millet*]. (TA.)

عَوَّاجٌ *A possessor of* عَاج [i. e. *ivory*, and app. *tortoise-shell* also]; (Ṣ, O, Ḳ;) accord. to Sb: (Ṣ, O:) and (O, Ḳ) accord. to another or others (O) *a seller thereof*. (O, Ḳ.)

عَائِجٌ: for its fem. (with ة) as an epithet applied to a she-camel, see عَاج, first sentence. — See also أَعْوَج, near the end. — Also *Stopping*, or *pausing*. (Ṣ, O.)

أَعْوَجُ *Crooked, curved, bent*, or *bending, winding, wry, contorted, distorted*, or *uneven*: (Ṣ,* O,* L, Mṣb:) and ▼ مُعْوَجٌّ, [or this and the former also,] *crooked, curved, &c., of itself*: fem. of the former عَوْجَآءُ: (L, Mṣb:) and pl. عُوجٌ. (L.) One says ▼ عَصًا مُعْوَجَّةٌ [*A crooked*, or *crooking, staff* or *stick*]; but not مِعْوَجَّةٌ, with kesr to the م: (Ṣ, O:) or, accord. to ISk, one says the former; but not ▼ مُعَوَّجَةٌ, with fet-ḥ to the ع and teshdeed to the و; though analogy does not forbid this, as it is allowable to say عَوَّجَهَا: accord. to Aṣ, one should not say ▼ مُعَوَّج, with teshdeed to the و, except in applying it to a stick, or in another sense expl. below: Az says that this word is allowable as signifying *rendered crooked* or *curved* &c. (Mṣb.) — [Hence,] العَوْجَآءُ signifies *The bow*. (Ṣ, A, Ḳ.) — And عَوْجَآءُ applied to a woman, *Inclining*, or *bending, towards her child, to suckle it*. (TA.) And, so applied, *That has become crooked by reason of leanness and hunger*. (Ḥam p. 744.) And, applied to a she-camel, *Lean, lank, light of flesh, slender*, or *lank in the belly*: (Ṣ, A, Ḳ:) or *emaciated so that her back has become crooked*, or *curved*. (TA.) — [And أَعْوَج applied to a هِلَال (or new moon), *Oblique*: see أَدْفَق.] — نَخِيلٌ عُوجٌ signifies *Palm-trees inclining*, or *leaning, and therefore crooked*, or *curved*: and accord. to some, the saying of Lebeed, describing a [wild] he-ass and his she-asses,

• وَأَوْرَدَهَا عَلَى عُوجٍ طِوَالِ

[the latter hemistich of a verse cited in the first paragraph of art. حوذ] means, *And he brought them to the watering-place at* [*tall*] *palm-trees growing over the water, inclining and curving* by reason of the abundance of their fruit: but others say that the meaning of عَلَى عوج is, *upon their crooked legs*. (TA.) — Hence, عُوجٌ signifies The *legs* of a horse or similar beast; (O, TA;) as ISd says, thus used as an epithet in which the quality of a subst. predominates [app. implying their *having that bending*, or *curving, and tension of the sinews, termed* تَجْنِيب, agreeably with what here follows]. (TA.) — And hence also, (TA,) خَيْلٌ عُوجٌ meaning *Horses that have, in their hind legs, the quality termed* تَجْنِيب. (A, TA.*) — أَعْوَجُ applied to a man means [*Crooked in temper*, or] *evil in natural disposition*. (Ṣ, A, O, Ḳ.) — المِلَّةُ العَوْجَآءُ [*The crooked*, or *perverted*, or *corrupted, religion*] is a phrase occurring in a trad., applied to the religion of Abraham as changed by the Arabs from its state of rectitude. (TA.) And one says خُطَّةٌ عَوْجَآءُ, and رَأْىٌ أَعْوَجُ, meaning [*An affair*, and *an opinion*,] *not of a right kind*. (A.) — الأَيَّامُ عُوجٌ رَوَاجِعُ [*The days are apt to decline from the right course, apt to return*,] is a prov., (Meyd, O, TA,) meaning fortune at one time declines from thee, and at another time returns to thee; (Meyd;) said by him at whose affliction one rejoices, or said on his part, and sometimes on an occasion of threatening: Az says that عُوج, here, may be pl. of أَعْوَج, or of ▼ عَائِج; or it may be pl. of عَوْجَآءُ, and originally عُوُج. (O, TA.) [Hence,] العُوجُ is used as signifying *The days* [in allusion to their variableness with respect to good and evil]. (TA.) — And أَعْوَجُ is a [proper] name of *A watering-trough*. (Th, TA.) — See also the next paragraph, in four places.

أَعْوَجِىٌّ the rel. n. of أَعْوَج: (Mṣb, TA:) and applied to *A* [single] *horse of those termed* الأَعْوَجِيَّاتُ, (TA,) an appellation of *certain horses so called in relation to one named* أَعْوَج, belonging to the Benoo-Hilál, (Ṣ, O, Ḳ,) a stallion than which there was none more celebrated among the Arabs, nor any that had a more numerous progeny: (Ṣ, O:) they were also called الخَيْلُ الأَعْوَجِيَّةُ, (L,) and ▼ بَنَاتُ أَعْوَج, (Ṣ, O,) and ▼ عُوج; and a poet says,

• أَحْوَى مِنَ العُوجِ ▼ وَقَاحُ الحَافِرِ

[*Brown*, or *a blackish bay, of the progeny of Aạwaj, hard in the hoof*]; meaning مِنْ وَلَدِ ▼ أَعْوَج; using that form of pl. because أَعْوَج is originally an epithet. (TA.)

مَعَاجٌ *A place to which one turns*; or *in which one remains, stays, dwells*, or *abides*. (Ḥar p. 325.) — Also an inf. n. of عَاجَ signifying "he remained" &c.: (Ḳ:) and of the verb in the phrase عُجْتُ البَعِيرَ. (Ṣ, O.)

مُعْوَجٌّ: see أَعْوَج, first and second sentences.

مُعَوَّجٌ: see أَعْوَج, second sentence, in two places. — Also A thing *set*, or *inlaid, with* عَاج [which means *ivory*, and *tortoise-shell*]: (Aṣ, Mṣb:) applied in this sense to a vessel. (TA.)

عود

1. عَادَ إِلَيْهِ, (Ṣ, A, O, TA,) and لَهُ, and فِيهِ, (TA,) aor. يَعُودُ, (Ṣ, O,) inf. n. عَوْدٌ and عَوْدَةٌ, (Ṣ, O, Ḳ, TA,) which latter is also an inf. n. of un., (TA,) and مَعَادٌ, (Ḳ, TA,) *He*, or *it, returned to it*, (Ṣ, A, O, Ḳ,* TA,) namely, a thing: (TA:) or, accord. to some, the verb is differently used with فِى and with other preps.: (MF, TA:) [with فى it seems generally to imply some degree of continuance, in addition to the simple meaning of the verb alone:] one says, عاد الكَلْبُ فِى قَيْئِهِ *The dog returned to his vomit*: (Mṣb in art. رجع:) and عاد لَهُ بَعْدَ مَا كَانَ أَعْرَضَ عَنْهُ [*He returned to it after he had turned away from it*]: (Ṣ, O:) and ▼ اِعْتَادَ, also, signifies *he returned*: (KL:) or عاد لَهُ, and عاد إِلَى كَذَا, inf. n. عَوْدٌ (Mgh, Mṣb) and عَوْدَةٌ, (Mṣb,) signifies *He*, or *it, came to such a thing* or *state* or *condition*; syn. صَارَ إِلَيْهِ; (Mgh,* Mṣb;) *at first*, or *for the first time*, or *originally*; and also, *a second time*, or *again*; and the verb is trans. by means of عَلَى and فِى as well as إِلَى and لِ, and also by itself: (Mgh:) لَتَعُودُنَّ فِى مِلَّتِنَا, in the Ḳur [vii. 86 and xiv. 16], means *Ye shall assuredly come to our religion*; for the words relate to the apostle: (O,* and Bḍ in xiv. 16:) or the words relate to the apostle and to those who believed with him, the latter being made to have a predominant influence upon the verb; (Bḍ in vii. 86 and xiv. 16, and Jel in vii. 86;) the meaning being *ye shall assuredly return to our religion*: (Bḍ* and Jel in vii. 86:) or the meaning is, *ye shall assuredly enter the communion of our religion*; the verb here signifying beginning: and the saying, of a poet,

• وَعَادَ الرَّأْسُ مِنِّى كَالثَّغَامِ

is cited as an ex. [i. e. as meaning *And my head began to be* white *like the* plant called ثغام]: or the meaning in this instance may be, *became like the* ثغام: (MF, TA:) you say also, عاد كَذَا *He*, or *it, became so*, or *in such a state* or *condition*: (Ḳ, TA:) and it is said in a trad., وَدِدْتُ أَنَّ هٰذَا اللَّبَنَ يَعُودُ قَطِرَانًا [*I wish that this milk would become tar*]. (O, TA.) عاد is also used as an incomplete [i. e. a non-attributive] verb in the sense of كَانَ [*He*, or *it, was*], requiring an enunciative [generally] on the condition of its being preceded by a conjunction, as in the saying of Ḥassán,

• وَلَقَدْ صَبَوْتُ بِهَا وَعَادَ شَبَابُهَا
• غَضًّا وَعَادَ زَمَانُهَا مُسْتَطْرَفَا

[*And I had inclined to silly and youthful conduct with her, when her youth was fresh and her time* of life *was deemed comely*]; the meaning being كَانَ زَمَانُهَا [and كَانَ شَبَابُهَا]. (MF, TA.) [See also an ex. in a verse cited voce مَطْمَعَةٌ. But the first of the significations mentioned in this art. is that which is most common. Hence several phrases mentioned below voce عَوْدٌ. And hence the phrase يَعُودُ عَلَى كَذَا, inf. n. عَوْدٌ, used by grammarians, *It refers*, or *relates, to such a thing*; as a pronoun to a preceding noun. Hence, likewise,] — عَادَهُ is also *syn. with* اِعْتَادَهُ, q. v. (Ṣ, O.) — [Hence, also,] عاد, (Az, TA,) inf. n. عَوْدٌ (Az, Ḳ, TA) and عِيَادٌ, (Ḳ,) *He repeated*, or *did a second time.* (Az, Ḳ,* TA.) One says, بَدَأَ ثُمَّ عَادَ *He began*, or *did a first time*, or *the first time: then repeated*, or *did a second time.* (Az, TA.) It is said in a prov., العَوْدُ أَحْمَدُ [*Repetition is more praiseworthy*: see art. حمد]. (Ṣ, O.) See also 4, in two places. — And عُدْتُهُ, (Ṣ, O, Mṣb, Ḳ,) aor. أَعُودُهُ, (Ṣ, O,) inf. n. عِيَادَةٌ (Ṣ, O, Mṣb, Ḳ) and عِيَادٌ and عَوْدٌ and عُوَادَةٌ (Ḳ) and عَيْدُودَةٌ [like كَيْنُونَةٌ], (MF,) [*I came to him time after time*: see its act. part. n., عَائِدٌ:] *I visited him*, (Mṣb, Ḳ, TA,) [commonly and especially (see again عَائِدٌ)] meaning a sick person. (Ṣ, O, Mṣb, Ḳ, TA.) — عَادَنِى الشَّىْءُ, (TA,) inf. n. عَوْدٌ; (Ḳ;) and ↓ اِعْتَادَنِى, (TA,) inf. n. اِعْتِيَادٌ; (Ḳ;) *The thing befell me, betided me*, or *happened to me.* (Ḳ,* TA.) One says, اعْتَادَنِى ↓ هَمٌّ وَحُزْنٌ [*Anxiety and grief betided me*]. (TA.) — عَادَ بِمَعْرُوفٍ, aor. يَعُودُ, inf. n. عَوْدٌ, *He conferred*, or *bestowed, favour*, or *a favour* or *benefit.* (Mṣb.) One says, عاد عَلَيْنَا فُلَانٌ بِمَعْرُوفِهِ [*Such a one conferred*, or *bestowed, his favour upon us*]. (A.) And عاد عَلَيْهِ بِصِلَةٍ [*He conferred*, or *bestowed, a free gift upon him*]. (TA.) And عاد عَلَيْهِ بِالعَائِدَةِ الصَّالِحَةِ, aor. يَعُودُ, [meaning *It brought him that which was a good return* or *profit*,] is said of a thing purchased with the price of another thing. (Ṣ and Ḳ in art. رجع.) — عاد عَلَيْهِمُ الدَّهْرُ *Fortune destroyed them.* (A.) And عَادَتِ الرِّيَاحُ وَالأَمْطَارُ عَلَى الدِّيَارِ حَتَّى دَرَسَتْ [*The winds and the rains assailed the dwellings so that they became effaced*]. (A.) — عَوْدٌ is also *syn. with* رَدٌّ: (Ḳ, TA:) one says عاد, inf. n. عَوْدٌ, meaning *He rejected* (رَدَّ) *and undid* (نَقَضَ) *what he had done* [as though he reverted from it]. (TA.) [Accord. to the TḲ, one says, عاد السَّائِلَ, meaning رَدَّهُ, i. e. *He turned back*, or *away, the beggar*, or *asker.*] — And *i. q.* صَرَفَ: (Ḳ:) one says, عَادَنِى أَنْ أَجِيْئَكَ, in which عادنى is [said to be] formed by transposition from عَدَانِى, meaning *He*, or *it, diverted me from coming to thee*: mentioned by Yaạḳoob. (TA.)

2. عَوَّدَهُ إِيَّاهُ *He accustomed*, or *habituated, him to it.* (Mṣb, Ḳ.) One says, عَوَّدَ كَلْبَهُ الصَّيْدَ *He accustomed*, or *habituated, his dog to the chase.* (Ṣ, O.) And هٰذَا أَمْرٌ يُعَوِّدُ النَّاسَ عَلَىَّ is a saying mentioned by Aboo-'Adnán as meaning *This is a thing that causes men to become accustomed*, or *addicted, to treating me wrongfully.* (O, TA.) = عَوَّدَ [from the subst. عُوَادَةٌ] *He* (a man, O) *ate what is termed* عُوَادَةٌ, (O, Ḳ,) i. e. *food brought again after its having been once eaten of.* (O.) = عَوَّدَ said of a camel, (Ṣ, O, Ḳ,) and of a sheep or goat, (IAth, TA,) inf. n. تَعْوِيدٌ, (Ḳ,) *He became such as is termed* عَوْدٌ [i. e. *old*, &c.]: (Ṣ, O, Ḳ:) or, said of a camel, *he exceeded the period of his* بُزُول [q. v.] *by three*, or *four, years*: one does not say of a she-camel عَوَّدَتْ. (T, TA.) And, said of a man, *He became advanced in age*, or *years.* (IAạr, TA.) = عَيَّدَ [from عِيدٌ, and therefore retaining the ى in the place of the original و], (Ṣ, Mṣb, Ḳ,) inf. n. تَعْيِيدٌ, (Mṣb,) *He was present on the occasion of the* عِيد [or *periodical festival*; or *at the prayers*, or other *observances, thereof*; or *he kept, observed*, or *solemnized, the festival*, or *a festival*]. (Ṣ, Mṣb, Ḳ.) One says, عَيَّدَ بِبَلَدِ كَذَا, meaning *He was, on the day of the* عيد, [or *he kept the* عيد or *an* عيد,] *in such a town*, or *country.* (O.)

3. مُعَاوَدَةٌ signifies *The returning to the first affair.* (Ṣ, O.) — And عاوده *He returned to it time after time.* (Mṣb.) — [Hence,] *i. q.* اِعْتَادَهُ, q. v., as syn. with تَعَوَّدَهُ. (Ḳ.) — عاوده الكَلَامَ, or عاوده alone, or each of these phrases, the latter being probably used for the former, like as رَاجَعَهُ is used for رَاجَعَهُ الكَلَامَ, app. signifies primarily *He returned time after time to talking with him*: and hence, *he talked with him alternately*; (compare a signification assigned to 6;) *he returned him answer for answer*, or *answers for answers*; *held a dialogue*, or *colloquy*, or *conference*, or *a disputation*, or *debate, with him*; *bandied words with him*: for it is said that رَاجَعَهُ الكَلَامَ is syn. with عَاوَدَهُ [app. meaning عاوده الكَلَامَ]; (Ṣ* and Ḳ in art. رجع;) [and that] رَاجَعْتُهُ is syn. with عَاوَدْتُهُ. (Mṣb in that art.) — And عاوده بِالمَسْأَلَةِ *He asked him the question repeatedly*, or *time after time.* (Ṣ, O.) — [Hence,] عاود مَا كَانَ فِيهِ *He persevered in that in which he was engaged.* (TA.) — And عَاوَدَتْهُ الحُمَّى (Ṣ, O, TA) [may signify *The fever returned to him time after time*: or] means *the fever clave perseveringly to him.* (TA.)

4. اعاده (O, Ḳ) *He returned it*, or *restored it*, (Ḳ,) إِلَى مَكَانِهِ [*to its place; he replaced it*]. (O, Ḳ.) — And *He did it a second time*: (Ṣ, Mṣb:) *he repeated it*, or *iterated it*; syn. كَرَّرَهُ; namely, speech; (Ḳ;) as also ↓ عَادَ لَهُ; *he said it a second time*; (Mgh;) and ↓ عاد إِلَيْهِ and عَلَيْهِ [likewise] signify the same as اعاده: (TA:) but Aboo-Hilál El-'Askeree says that كَرَّرَهُ signifies he repeated it once or more than once; whereas اعاده signifies only *he repeated it once*: (MF, TA:) اعاد الكَلَامَ means *he repeated the speech* [*saying it*] *a second time*; syn. رَدَّدَهُ ثَانِيًا. (O.) One says, اعاد الصَّلَاةَ *He said the prayer a second time.* (Mṣb.) And مَا يَتَكَلَّمُ بِبَادِئَةٍ وَلَا عَائِدَةٍ signifies مَا يُبْدِئُ وَمَا يُعِيدُ (Lth, A, O,) i. e. *He does not say anything for the first time*; *nor anything for the second time*; or *anything original, nor anything in the way of repetition*; بَادِئَةُ الكَلَامِ signifying *what is said for the first time*; and ↓ عَائِدَةُ الكَلَامِ, *what is said for the second time, afterwards*: (TA in art. بدأ:) or *he says not anything*: (A:) and *he has no art, artifice*, or *cunning.* (IAạr, TA; and A in art. بدأ; q. v.) — [Also *He returned it*, or *restored it, to a former state*: and hence, *he renewed it*: *he reproduced it.*] One says of God, يُبْدِئُ الخَلْقَ ثُمَّ يُعِيدُهُ, meaning [*He createth*, or *bringeth into existence, mankind*:] then *He returneth them, after life, to lifelessness*, in the present world; *and after lifelessness, to life*, on the day of resurrection. (TA.) — See also 8. — [اعاد also signifies *He*, or *it, rendered*; or *made to be*, or *become*; (like جَعَلَ;) in which sense it is doubly trans.: see an ex. in a verse cited voce ضَيْفٌ.]

5: see 8, in three places.

6. تعاودوا *They returned, each party of them to its chief*, or *leader*, in war or battle, (Ṣ, Ḳ,) &c. (Ṣ.) — And تَعَاوَدْنَا العَمَلَ وَالأَمْرَ بَيْنَنَا *We did the work, and the affair, by turns among us.* (T in art. دول. [But perhaps the right reading here is تَعَاوَرْنَا.])

8. اعتاد: see 1, near the beginning. = اعتاده *He frequented it*; or *came to it and returned to it*; namely, a place. (T in art. ارى.) — And *He looked at it time after time until he knew it.* (TA in art. بلد.) — And, as also ↓ تعوّده, (Ṣ, O, Mṣb, Ḳ,) and ↓ عَادَهُ; (Ṣ, O;) and so ↓ عاوده, inf. n. مُعَاوَدَةٌ and عِوَادٌ; and ↓ اعاده, (Ḳ,) and ↓ استعاده; (O, Ḳ;) *He became accustomed*, or *habituated, to it*; or *he accustomed*, or *habituated, himself to it*; or *made it his custom*, or *habit.* (Ṣ, O, Mṣb, Ḳ.) It is said in a trad., ↓ تَعَوَّدُوا الخَيْرَ فَإِنَّ الخَيْرَ عَادَةٌ وَالشَّرُّ لَجَاجَةٌ, meaning *Accustom yourselves to good*; *for good becomes a habit, and evil is persevered in.* (A.) And one says, ↓ تعوّد الكَلْبُ الصَّيْدَ *The dog became accustomed*, or *habituated, to the chase.* (Ṣ.) — See also 1, latter half, in two places.

10. استعاده *He asked him to return.* (O, Mṣb, Ḳ.) — And استعاده الشَّىْءَ *He asked him to repeat the thing*; *to do it a second time*: (Ṣ, O, Mṣb, Ḳ:) and استعاده مِنْهُ [*He asked for the repetition of it from him*]. (Ḥar p. 28.) — See also 8.

عَادٌ: see عَادَةٌ. = مَا أَدْرِى أَىُّ عَادَ هُوَ, (Ṣ, O, Ḳ,) عاد being in this case imperfectly decl., (Ṣ, O, [but in the CḲ and in my MS. copy of the Ḳ it is written عادٍ,]) means *I know not what one of mankind he is.* (Ṣ, O, Ḳ.) [Perhaps it is from عَادٌ the name of an ancient and extinct tribe of the Arabs.]

عَادِ, indecl., with kesr for its termination, is a particle in the sense of إِنَّ, governing an accus. case, on the condition of its being preceded by a verbal proposition and a conjunction; as in the saying, رَقَدْتُ وَعَادِ أَبَاكَ سَاهِرٌ [*I slept, and verily thy father was waking*, or *remaining awake, by night*]: — it is also an interrogative particle in the sense of هَلْ, indecl., with kesr for its termination, requiring an answer; as in the saying, عَادِ أَبُوكَ مُقِيمٌ [*Is thy father abiding?*]: — it also denotes an answer, in the sense of a proposition rendered negative by means of لم or of ما, only; indecl., with kesr for its termination; and this is when it is conjoined with a pronoun; as when an interrogator says, هَلْ صَلَّيْتَ [*Didst thou perform, or hast thou performed, the act of prayer?*], and thou answerest, عَادِنِى, meaning *Verily I* (إِنَّنِى) *did not perform, or have not performed, the act of prayer:* — and some of the people of El-Ḥijáz suppress the نِ in عَادِنِى: both the modes are chaste when عَادِ is used in the sense of إِنَّ: — sometimes, also, it is used by the interrogator and the answerer; the former saying, عَادِ خَرَجَ زَيْدٌ [*Did Zeyd go forth? or has Zeyd gone forth?*], and the latter saying, عَادِهِ, meaning *Verily he did not go forth, or has not gone forth:* — all this is unmentioned by the leading authors on the Arabic language, those of lengthy compositions as well as the epitomisers. (MF, TA.)

عَوْدٌ an inf. n. of 1, as also † عَوْدَةٌ, (Ṣ, O, Ḳ,) and † عُوَادَةٌ, and † مَعَادٌ. (K.) [Hence,] one says, لَكَ العَوْدُ and † العَوْدَةُ and † العُوَادَةُ *It is for thee to return* (Lḥ, Ḳ, TA) فِى هٰذَا الأَمْرِ *in this affair.* (TA.) And † اَللّٰهُمَّ ٱرْزُقْنَا إِلَى البَيْتِ مَعَادًا and † عَوْدَةً (A, TA) *O God, grant us a return to the House* [i. e. the Kaabeh, called "the House" as being "the House of God"]. (TA.) And رَجَعَ عَوْدَهُ عَلَى بَدْئِهِ, (Sb, Ḳ,) [expl. in the TA in art. غبر as meaning *He returned without his having obtained, or attained, anything,*] and عَوْدًا عَلَى بَدْءٍ: (Ḳ:) and رَجَعْتُ عَوْدِى عَلَى بَدْئِى: (Sb:) expl., with other similar phrases, in art. بدا, q. v. — See also عَائِدٌ. — Also A camel, (IAạr, Ṣ, O, Mṣb, Ḳ,) and a sheep or goat, (IAạr, O, Ḳ,) *old, or advanced in age:* (Ṣ, O, Mṣb, Ḳ:) applied to the former, *that has passed the ages at which he is termed* بَازِل and مُخْلِف: (Ṣ, O:) or *that has passed three years, or four, since the period of his* بُزُول: (Az, TA:) or a camel *old,* or *advanced in age, but retaining remains of strength:* (L:) or one *old,* or *advanced in age, and well trained, and accustomed to be ridden* or *the like:* (TA:) fem. with ة: you say نَاقَةٌ عَوْدَةٌ, (Aṣ, Ṣ, O,) and نَاقَتَانِ عَوْدَتَانِ, (Aṣ, TA,) and عَنْزٌ عَوْدَةٌ: (TA:) or one should not say نَاقَةٌ عَوْدَةٌ, nor نَعْجَةٌ عَوْدَةٌ; (Az, TA;) but one says شَاةٌ عَوْدَةٌ: (Az, IAth, O:) the pl. of عَوْدٌ is عِوَدَةٌ (Aṣ, Ṣ, O, Ḳ) and عِيَدَةٌ (O, Ḳ) as some say, but this is anomalous, (O,) of a particular dial., and bad; (Az, TA;) and the pl. of عَوْدَةٌ is عِوَدٌ. (Aṣ, O, TA.) It is said in a prov., إِنْ جَرْجَرَ العَوْدُ فَزِدْهُ وِقْرًا [*If the old camel make a grumbling sound in his throat, then increase thou his load*]. (Ṣ.) And in another, عَوْدٌ يُعَلَّمُ العَنَجَ [expl. in art. عنج]. (O.) — It is also applied to a man: (Ṣ, O:) one says, زَاحِمْ بِعَوْدٍ أَوْ دَعْ, (Ṣ, O, Ḳ,) † *Ask thou aid of a person of age,* (Ṣ, O,) *and experience in affairs,* (O,) *and knowledge,* (Ṣ, O,) *or let it alone;* (O;) for the judgment of the elder is better than the aspect, or outward appearance, (مَشْهَد,) of the youth, or young man: (Ṣ, O:) or *ask aid, in thy war, of perfect men advanced in age:* (Ḳ:) a proverb. (Ṣ, O.) [See also Freytag's Arab. Prov. i. 586.] — And ‡ *An old road:* (Ṣ, O, Ḳ:) from the same word as an epithet applied to a camel. (O.) A poet says, (Ṣ, O,) namely, Besheer Ibn-En-Nikth, (TA, and so in a copy of the Ṣ,)

* عَوْدٌ عَلَى عَوْدٍ لِأَقْوَامٍ أُوَلْ *
* يَمُوتُ بِالتَّرْكِ وَيَحْيَا بِالعَمَلْ *

(Ṣ,* O, TA) i. e. *An old camel upon an old road* [*belonging to prior peoples*], (Ṣ, O, TA,) a road *that dies away by being abandoned and revives by being travelled.* (TA.) And another says,

* عَوْدٌ عَلَى عَوْدٍ عَلَى عَوْدٍ خَلَقْ *

i. e. *An old man upon an old camel upon an old worn road.* (IB, TA.) [See also مُعِيدٌ.] — And سُودَدٌ عَوْدٌ means ‡ *Old* [*lordship,* or *glory* or *honour* or *dignity*]. (Ṣ, A, O, Ḳ, TA.) [See also عَادِىٌّ.] — And إِنَّكَ لَتَمُتُّ بِرَحِمٍ عَوْدَةٍ occurs in a trad., as said by Mo'áwiyeh, meaning [*Verily thou seekest to advance thyself in* my *favour*] *by an old and remote tie of relationship.* (TA.) — And عَوْدٌ is used by Abu-n-Nejm as meaning The *sun,* in the saying,

* وَتَبِعَ الأَحْمَرَ عَوْدٌ يَرْجُمُهُ *

[*And a sun followed the red dawn, driving it away*]: by الأَحْمَر he means الصُّبْح. (TA.)

عُودٌ *Wood; timber;* syn. خَشَبٌ: (Mgh, O, Ḳ:) *any slender piece of wood* or *timber:* (Lth, TA:) or *a piece of wood of any tree,* whether *slender* or *thick:* or *a part, of a tree, in which sap runs,* whether *fresh and moist* or *dry:* (TA:) *a staff; a stick; a rod:* and also *a sprig:* (the lexicons &c. passim:) *a branch;* or *twig;* properly, *that is cut off;* but also applied to one *not cut off:* (Ḥar p. 499:) [and the *stem* of the raceme of a palm-tree, and the like: (see فُحَّان, in art. فح:)] pl. [of mult.] عِيدَانٌ, (Ṣ, Mgh, O, Mṣb, Ḳ,) originally عِوْدَانٌ, (Mṣb,) and [of pauc.] أَعْوَادٌ. (Ṣ, O, Mṣb, Ḳ.) — [Hence,] رَكَّبَ ٱللّٰهُ عُودًا عَلَى عُودٍ, (A,) or عُودًا عُودًا, (TA,) *God caused the arrow to be put upon the bow,* for shooting; (A;) meaning that civil war, or conflict, or faction, or sedition, became excited. (A, TA.) — And سَبِيلُ ذِى الأَعْوَادِ † *Death:* الاعواد meaning *the pieces of wood upon which the dead is carried:* (El-Mufaḍḍal, Az, L:) for the Arabs of the desert, having no biers, put two pieces of wood together, and on them carry the dead to the grave. (Az, L.) — And العُودَانِ *The pulpit and the staff of the Prophet.* (Sh, O, Ḳ.) — And one says, هُوَ صُلْبُ العُودِ: ‡ see art. صلب. — And هُوَ مِنْ عُودٍ صِدْقٍ and سَوْءٍ ‡ [*He is of a good branch* and *of a bad branch*]. (TA.) — And it is said in a trad. of Shureyḥ, إِنَّمَا القَضَآءُ جَمْرٌ فَٱدْفَعِ الجَمْرَ عَنْكَ بِعُودَيْنِ [*Verily the exercise of the judicial office is* like the approaching *live coals; and repel thou the live coals from thee by means of two sticks*]: meaning, guard thyself well from the fire [of Hell] by means of two witnesses; like as he who warms himself by means of fire repels the live coals from his place with a stick or other thing that he may not be burned: or act firmly and deliberately in judging, and do thy utmost to repel from thee the fire [of Hell]. (L.) — عُودُ الصَّلِيبِ: see يَبْرُوحٌ. — العُودُ also signifies [*Aloes-wood;*] *a well-known odoriferous substance;* (Mṣb;) *that with which one fumigates himself;* (Ṣ, O, Ḳ;*) *a certain aromatized wood, with which one fumigates himself;* thus called because of its excellence: (L:) العُودُ الهِنْدِىُّ [which, like العُودُ القَمَارِىُّ and عُودُ النَّدِّ and عُودُ البَخُورِ and العُودُ القَاقُلِّىُّ, is a common, well-known, term for aloes-wood,] is said to be *the same as* القُسْطُ البَحْرِىُّ. (TA. [See art. قسط.]) — And *A certain musical instrument,* (Ṣ, O, L, Mṣb, Ḳ,) *well known;* (TA;) [*the lute;* which word, like the French "luth," &c., is derived from العُود: accord. to the L, *it has four chords;* but I have invariably found it to have *seven double chords:* it is figured and described in my work on the Modern Egyptians: in the present day it is generally played with a plectrum, formed of a slip of a vulture's feather; but in former times it seems to have been usually played upon with the tips of the fingers:] pl. as above, عِيدَانٌ and أَعْوَادٌ. (Mṣb.) — And *The bone* [*called os hyoides*] *at the root of the tongue;* (O, Ḳ;) also called عُودُ اللِّسَانِ. (O.) — And أُمُّ العُودِ signifies *The* [*portion,* or *appertenance, of the stomach of a ruminant animal, called*] قِبَة, (O,) or قِبَّة, (Ḳ,) i. e. *the* فَحِث: (TA:) pl. أُمَّهَاتُ العُودِ. (O.)

عِيدٌ, originally عِوْدٌ, the و being changed into ى because of the kesreh before it, (Az, TA,) *An occurrence that befalls,* or *betides, one,* or *that happens to one,* [or *returns to one,* of some former affection of the mind or body, i. e.] of anxiety, (Ṣ, O, Ḳ,) or of some other kind, (Ṣ, O,) of disease, or of grief, (O, Ḳ,) and the like, (Ḳ,) of affliction, and of desire: and accord. to Az, the *time of return* of joy and of grief. (TA.) — [And hence, *A festival;* or *periodical festival;*] *a feast-day;* (KL;) i. q. مَوْسِمٌ; (Mṣb;) *any day on which is an assembling,* or *a congregating;* (Ḳ;) [and particularly *an anniversary festival:*] so called because it returns every year with renewed joy: (IAạr, TA:) or, from عَادَ, because people return to it: or from عَادَةٌ, "a custom," because they are accustomed to it: (TA:) pl. أَعْيَادٌ; the ى being retained in the pl. because it is in the sing., or to distinguish it from أَعْوَادٌ the pl. of عُودٌ; (Ṣ, O, Mṣb;) for regularly its pl. would be أَعْوَادٌ, like as أَرْوَاحٌ is pl. of رِيحٌ. (TA.) [The two principal religious festivals of the Muslims are called عِيدُ الأَضْحَى *The festival of the victims* (see art. ضحو and ضحى) and عِيدُ الفِطْرِ *The festival of the breaking of the fast* after Ramaḍán.] The dim. of عِيدٌ is † عُيَيْدٌ; the ى being retained in it like as it is retained in the pl. (TA.) — See also عَادَةٌ, in two places. — Also, *A certain sort of mountain-tree,* (Ḳ, TA,) *that produces twigs about a cubit in length, dust-*

coloured, having no leaves nor blossoms, but having much peel, and having many knots: fresh wounds are dressed with its peel, and close up in consequence thereof. (TA.)

عَادَةٌ *A custom, manner, habit,* or *wont;* syn. دَأْبٌ, and وَتِيرَةٌ, (MA,) or دَيْدَنٌ: (Ḳ:) so called because one returns to it time after time: it respects more especially actions; and عُرْفٌ, sayings; as in indicated in the Telweeḥ &c.; or, accord. to some, عُرْفٌ and عَادَةٌ are syn.: (MF, TA:) and accord. to El-Mufaḍḍal, [▼عِيدٌ signifies the same as عَادَةٌ; for he says that] عَادَنِى عِيدِى means عَادَتِى [i. e. *My habit returned to me:* but see the next preceding paragraph, first sentence]: (L, TA:) the pl. of عَادَةٌ is عَادَاتٌ (Ṣ, O, Mṣb) and ▼عَادٌ, (Ṣ, O, Mṣb, Ḳ,) or rather this is a coll. gen. n., (TA,) and ▼عِيدٌ, (L, Ḳ, TA,) mentioned by Kr, but not of valid authority, (L, TA,) [app. a mistranscription for عِيَدٌ, like حِوَجٌ, a pl. of حَاجَةٌ,] and عَوَائِدُ, (Mṣb, TA,) like as حَوَائِجُ is pl. of حَاجَةٌ; but, accord. to Z and others, this last is pl. of عَائِدَةٌ, not of عَادَةٌ. (TA.)

عَوْدَةٌ: see عَوْدٌ, first three sentences.

عَادِىٌّ An *old,* or *ancient,* thing: (Ṣ, A, Mgh,* O, Mṣb,* Ḳ:) as though so called in relation to the [ancient and extinct] tribe of 'Ád (عاد). (Ṣ, A, O, Mṣb.) One says خَرِبٌ عَادِىٌّ *Old,* or *ancient, ruins.* (Mgh.) And بِئْرٌ عَادِيَّةٌ *An old,* or *ancient, well:* (O:) or *a well strongly cased with stone or brick, and abounding with water, the origin of which is referred to* [*the tribe of*] *'Ád.* (Mṣb.) And بِنَآءٌ عَادِىٌّ *A firm,* or *strong, building, the origin of which is referred to* [*the tribe of*] *'Ád.* (Mṣb.) And عَادِىُّ أَرْضٍ *Land possessed from ancient times.* (Mṣb.) And مُلْكٌ عَادِىٌّ *Dominion of old,* or *ancient, origin.* (Mṣb.) And مَجْدٌ عَادِىٌّ *Old,* or *ancient, glory.* (A.) [See also عَوْدٌ.]

عِيدِيَّةٌ an appellation given to *Certain excellent she-camels;* (Ṣ, O, Ḳ;) so called in relation to a stallion, (Ṣ, O, Ḳ,) well-known, (Ḳ,) that begat an excellent breed, (Ṣ, O,) named عِيدٌ: (O, Ḳ:) [so some say:] but ISd says that this is not of valid authority: (TA:) or so called in relation to El-'Eedee Ibn-En-Nadaghee Ibn-Mahrah-Ibn-Ḥeidán: (Ibn-El-Kelbee, O, Ḳ:) or in relation to 'Ád Ibn-'Ád: or 'Ádee Ibn-'Ád: (Ḳ:) but if from either of the last two, it is anomalous: (TA:) or in relation to the Benoo-'Eed-Ibn-El-'Ámiree: (O, Ḳ:) Az says that he knew not the origin of their name. (L.) — And accord. to Sh, [*A female lamb;*] *the female of the* بُرْقَانٌ [pl. of بَرَقٌ]; the male of which is called خَرُوفٌ until he is shorn: but this was unknown to Az. (L.)

عَيْدَانٌ *Tall palm-trees:* (Aṣ, Ṣ, O, Ḳ:) or *the tallest of palm-trees:* (Ḳ in art. عيد:) *but not so called unless the stumps of their branches have fallen off and they have become bare trunks from top to bottom:* (AḤn, M, TA in art. عيد:) or *i. q.* رَقْلَةٌ [q. v.]: (AO, TA in art. عيد:) [a coll. gen. n.:] n. un. with ة: (Ṣ, O, Ḳ:) which Aṣ explains as applied to *a hard, old tree, having roots penetrating to the water:* and he says, ومنه هيمان وعيلان [but what these words mean, I know not:] (TA:) the word belongs to this art. and to art. عيد: (Ḳ in art. عيد:) or it may belong to the present art., or to art. عدن [q. v.]. (Az, Ṣ, O.) The Prophet had a bowl [made of the wood] of an عَيْدَانَة, (Ḳ, TA,) or, accord. to some, it is preferably written with kesr [i. e. عِيدَانَة], (TA,) in which he voided his urine. (Ḳ, TA.)

عَوَادٌ: see عُوَادَةٌ. — عُدْ فَإِنَّ لَكَ عِنْدَنَا عَوَادًا حَسَنًا, (Ṣ, O, Ḳ,) as also عُوَادًا and عِوَادًا, (O, Ḳ,) these two only, not the first, mentioned by Fr, (O,) means [*Return thou, and thou shalt have with us*] *what thou wilt like:* (Ṣ, O, Ḳ:) or *kind treatment.* (TA.)

عَوَادِ, [an imperative verbal noun,] like نَزَالِ (Ṣ, O) and تَرَاكِ, (Ṣ,) means *Return thou;* syn. عُدْ. (Ṣ, O, Ḳ.)

عُيَيْدٌ dim. of عِيدٌ, q. v. (TA.)

عُوَادَةٌ: see عَوْدٌ, first and second sentences. — Also, (Ṣ, O, Ḳ,) and if you elide the ة you say ▼عُوَادٌ, like نُبَاطٌ and قُضَامٌ, (Az, TA,) [in the O عَوَادَةٌ and عُوَادَةٌ with ḍamm, (but the former is probably a mistranscription,)] *Food brought again after its having been once eaten of:* (Ṣ, O:) or *food brought again for a particular man after a party has finished eating.* (A, Ḳ.)

عَوَّادٌ *A player upon the* عُود [or *lute*]: (Ḳ:) or *one who makes,* (يَتَّخِذُ,) *the stringed* عُود [or *lute*]; (O;) or *a maker* (مُتَّخِذ) *of* عِيدَان [or *lutes*]. (TA.) [Fem. with ة.]

عَائِدٌ *A visiter* of one who is sick: (Mṣb, TA:) thus it more commonly and especially means: but it also signifies *any visiter* of another, *who comes time after time:* (TA:) pl. عُوَّادٌ (Mṣb, Ḳ) and ▼عُوْدٌ, (Ḳ,) or [rather] عُوْدٌ and عُوَّادٌ signify the same, like زُوْرٌ and زُوَّارٌ, (Fr, O, TA,) but عُوْدٌ is a quasi-pl. n. like as صَحْبٌ is of صَاحِبٌ: (TA:) the fem. is عَائِدَةٌ, of which the pl. is عُوْدٌ, (Az, Mṣb, TA,) incorrectly said in the Ḳ to be a pl. of عَائِدٌ; and عَوَائِدُ also is a pl. of the fem. (TA.)

عَائِدَةٌ fem. of عَائِدٌ [q. v.]. (Az, Mṣb, TA.) — عَائِدَةُ الكَلَامِ: see 4. — عَائِدَةٌ also signifies *Favour, kindness, pity, compassion,* or *mercy:* (Ṣ, O, Ḳ:) *a favour, a benefit, an act of beneficence* or *kindness: a gratuity,* or *free gift:* (Ḳ:) and [*a return,* i. e.] *advantage, profit,* or *utility;* or *a cause,* or *means, thereof:* (Ṣ, O, Ḳ:) a subst. from عَادَ بِمَعْرُوفٍ: (Mṣb:) pl. عَوَائِدُ. (A.) One says, فُلَانٌ ذُو صَفْحٍ وَعَائِدَةٍ *Such a one is a person of forgiving disposition, and of favour, kindness,* or *pity.* (Ṣ, A, O.) And إِنَّهُ لَكَثِيرُ العَوَائِدِ عَلَى قَوْمِهِ [*Verily he is one who confers,* or *bestows, many favours,* or *benefits, upon his people*]. (A.)

هٰذَا الشَّىْءُ أَعْوَدُ عَلَيْكَ مِنْ كَذَا means *This thing is more remunerative, advantageous,* or *profitable, to thee than such a thing:* (Ṣ, O, Ḳ:*) or *more easy,* or *convenient, to thee.* (A,* TA.)

مَعَادٌ, signifying *Return,* is originally مَعْوَدٌ. (IAth, TA.) See عَوْدٌ, first and third sentences. — Also *A place to which a person,* or *thing, returns: a place, state,* or *result, to which a person,* or *thing, eventually comes; a place of destination,* or *an ultimate state* or *condition:* syn. مَرْجِعٌ: and مَصِيرٌ. (Ṣ, A, O, Ḳ.) — [Hence,] المَعَادُ signifies [particularly] *The ultimate state of existence, in the world to come;* syn. الآخِرَةُ; (M, Ḳ, TA;) [and] so مَعَادُ الخَلْقِ: (Ṣ, O:) *the place to which one comes on the day of resurrection.* (TA.) And *Paradise.* (Ḳ.) And *Mekkeh:* (O, Ḳ:) the conquest of which was promised to the Prophet: (TA:) so called because the pilgrims return to it. (O.) لَرَادُّكَ إِلَى مَعَادٍ, in the Ḳur [xxviii. 85], is expl. as meaning *will assuredly return thee,* or *restore thee, to Mekkeh:* (O, Ḳ:) or معاد here means *Paradise:* (Ḳ:) or *thy fixed place in Paradise:* (I'Ab, TA:) or *the place of thy birth:* (Fr, TA:) or *thy home and town:* (Th, TA:) or *thy usual state in which thou wast born:* or *thy original condition among the sons of Háshim:* or, accord. to most of the expositors, the words mean *will assuredly raise thee from the dead.* (TA.) — And *The pilgrimage.* (Ḳ.) — And مَعَادٌ (Lth, TA) and ▼مَعَادَةٌ (Lth, A, TA) *A place of wailing for a dead person:* (Lth, A, TA:) so called because people return to it time after time: (Lth,* A:) pl. مَعَاوِدُ. (A.) [Hence,] one says, ▼لِآلِ فُلَانٍ مَعَادَةٌ, meaning *An affliction has happened to the family of such a one, the people coming to them in the places of wailing for the dead, or in other places, and the women talking of him.* (Lth, TA.)

مَعُودٌ and مَعْوُودٌ, (Ḳ,) the latter anomalous, (TA,) A sick person *visited.* (Ḳ.)

مُعِيدٌ A stallion-camel *that has covered repeatedly;* (Ṣ, M, O, Ḳ;) and *that does not require assistance in his doing so.* (Sh, O.) — And hence, (Sh, O,) applied to a man *Acquainted with affairs,* (Sh, O, Ḳ,) *not inexperienced therein,* (Sh, O,) *possessing skill and ability to do a thing.* (O, Ḳ.*) One says, فُلَانٌ مُعِيدٌ لِهٰذَا الأَمْرِ, meaning *Such a one is able to do this thing:* (Ṣ, O, Mṣb, Ḳ:*) because accustomed, or habituated, to it. (Mṣb.) — And hence, (O,) or because he returns to his prey time after time, (TA,) The *lion,* (O, Ḳ, TA.) — المُبْدِئُ المُعِيدُ applied to God: — and مُبْدِئٌ مُعِيدٌ applied to a man, and to a horse: see art. بدأ. — مُعِيدٌ also signifies A road *travelled and trodden time after time.* (TA.) [See also عَوْدٌ.]

مَعَادَةٌ: see مَعَادٌ, last two sentences.

مُعَاوِدٌ *Persevering;* (Lth, A, Ḳ;) applied to a man. (Lth, A.) — *A courageous* man; (Ṣ, O,

Ḳ;) because he does not become weary of conflict. (Ṣ, O.) —— And One *skilful in his work.* (A.)

عود

1. عَاذَ بِهِ, aor. يَعُوذُ, (Ṣ, A, O, L, Mṣb,) inf. n. عَوْذٌ (O, L, Ḳ) and عِيَاذٌ and مَعَاذٌ (O, L, Mṣb, Ḳ) and مَعَاذَةٌ; (O, Ḳ;) and ▼ تعوّذ به; (O, L, Mṣb, Ḳ;*) and ▼ استعاذ به; (Ṣ, A, O, L, Mṣb, Ḳ;*) *He sought protection,* or *preservation, by him; sought,* or *took, refuge in him; had recourse to him for protection, preservation,* or *refuge; sought his protection,* or *preservation; confided* or *trusted* or *put his trust in him,* or *relied upon him, for protection,* or *preservation;* (Ṣ, A, O, L, Mṣb, Ḳ;) namely, God, (Ṣ, A, O, L, Mṣb,) or a man; (Ṣ, O;) [and in like manner used in relation to a place; مِنْ كَذَا and عَنْهُ *from such a thing;* or followed by مِنْ أَنْ, or only أَنْ, and a manṣoob aorist.] ▼ إِنَّمَا قَالَهَا تَعَوُّذًا, occurring in a trad., means *He only said it* (referring to the profession of the faith) *to seek protection,* or *preservation,* thereby from slaughter; not being sincere in his profession of El-Islám. (L.) And one says, مَعَاذَ ٱللّٰهِ, (Ṣ, A, O, L, Ḳ,) and مَعَاذَةَ ٱللّٰهِ, (Ṣ, O, L, Ḳ,) and مَعَاذَ وَجْهِ ٱللّٰهِ, and (Ṣ, O, L,) and عِيَاذَ ٱللّٰهِ, (A,) meaning أَعُوذُ بِٱللّٰهِ مَعَاذًا [*I seek protection,* or *preservation, by God;* &c.; which is equivalent to the saying *may God protect me,* or *preserve me*]: (Ṣ, A, O, L, Ḳ:) مَعَاذًا [as also مَعَاذَةً] being here used instead of the verb because it is an inf. n., though [accord. to some] not employed as such [in other cases], like as is the case in the phrase سُبْحَانَ ٱللّٰهِ. (Ṣ, O, L.) [One says also, مَعَاذَ ٱللّٰهِ أَنْ أَفْعَلَ كَذَا, for مِنْ أَنْ أَفْعَلَ كَذَا, *I seek preservation by God,* &c., *from my doing such a thing;* as though meaning *may God preserve me from doing such a thing:* see an ex. in the Ḳur xii. 79: and] some reckon مَعَاذَ ٱللّٰهِ among the forms of oaths. (MF.) [In like manner also,] أَعُوذُ بِٱللّٰهِ مِنْكَ means عَوْذٌ بِٱللّٰهِ مِنْكَ [*I seek protection,* or *preservation, by God,* &c., *from thee*]. (Ṣ, O, L, Ḳ.*) [See also the phrase عَائِذًا بِٱللّٰهِ, voce عَائِذٌ.] —— عَاذَتْ بِوَلَدِهَا † *She* (a camel) *stayed with her young one, and attended to it affectionately, as long as it remained little,* is as though it were an inverted phrase, meaning عَاذَ بِهَا وَلَدُهَا [*her young sought protection by her:* or it may be from what next follows]. (TA.) —— عاذ بِالعَظْمِ ‡ *It* (flesh-meat) *clave to the bone:* (Ṣ, O, L, Ḳ:*) a tropical phrase. (A.) —— And عَاذَتْ, [aor. تَعُوذُ,] (L, Ḳ,) inf. n. عِيَاذٌ (Ṣ, O, L, Ḳ) and عُؤُوذٌ; (Ṣ, L; [in the O عُؤُوذَةٌ;]) and ▼ أَعَاذَتْ, and ▼ أَعْوَذَتْ; (L, Ḳ;) † *She* (a gazelle, Ṣ, O, L, Ḳ, and a camel, and a mare, Ṣ, O, L, and any female, L, Ḳ) *was in the state of such as is termed* عَائِذٌ [q. v.]; or *that of having recently brought forth.* (Ṣ, O, L, Ḳ.) One says, هِىَ فِى عِيَاذِهَا *She is in the early stage of the period after having brought forth.* (Ṣ, O, L.)

2. عَوَّذْتُ غَيْرِى بِفُلَانٍ, and ▼ أَعَذْتُهُ بِهِ, *I made another to seek protection,* or *preservation, by such a one; to seek,* or *take, refuge in him; to have recourse to him for protection, preservation,* or *refuge; to seek his protection,* or *preservation; to confide,* or *trust,* or *put his trust, in him,* or *to rely upon him, for protection,* or *preservation;* (Ṣ, O,* L;) [مِنْ كَذَا and عَنْهُ *from such a thing:* and in like manner, عَوَّذْتُهُ بِٱللّٰهِ, and ▼ أَعَذْتُهُ بِهِ, *I made him to seek protection,* or *preservation, by God;* &c.] —— And عَوَّذْتُهُ بِكَذَا *I prayed for his protection,* or *preservation, by such a thing* [i. e. by invoking God, or uttering some charm; مِنْ كَذَا *from such a thing;* and أَنْ يَفْعَلَ كَذَا *from his doing such a thing;* as also ▼ أَعَذْتُهُ بِهِ, of which see an ex. in art. يبس, conj. 2]. (Ḥar p. 49.) —— And عَوَّذَهُ [and ▼ أَعَاذَهُ] *He charmed him* [against such a thing (مِنْ كَذَا)]; or *fortified him by a charm,* or *an amulet.* (L.) And عَوَّذْتُهُ بِٱللّٰهِ and ▼ أَعَذْتُهُ بِهِ *I charmed him* (i. e. a child) [*by invoking God*]. (Mṣb. [Both mentioned in the present art. thereof, and the former said in art. رقى of the same to be syn. with رَقَيْتُهُ.]) And عَوَّذْتُ فُلَانًا بِٱللّٰهِ, and بِأَسْمَائِهِ, and بِالْمُعَوِّذَتَيْنِ, *I said to such a one, I charm thee* (▼ أُعِيذُكَ) *by* [*invoking*] *God, and by his names,* and *by the* مُعَوِّذَتَانِ [q. v.], against every evil person or thing, and every disease, and an envier, and destruction, or trial. (L.) It is said of the Prophet, كَانَ يُعَوِّذُ نَفْسَهُ بِالْمُعَوِّذَتَيْنِ [*He used to charm himself* against evil *by* reciting *the* مُعَوِّذَتَان]. (L.) And عَوَّذْتَاهُ, said of the مُعَوِّذَتَانِ, means *They preserved him* from any evil. (Mṣb.) —— عوّذه and ▼ اعاذه said of God mean *He granted him protection, preservation,* or *refuge; protected,* or *preserved, him.* (L.)

4: see 2, in seven places: —— and see also 1, last sentence but one, in two places.

5: see 1, in two places.

6. تعاوذوا *They sought protection, preservation,* or *refuge, one of another;* or *confided in,* or *relied upon, one another's protection,* or *preservation;* (A, O, L, Ḳ;*) فِى الحَرْبِ *in war.* (O, L.)

10: see 1, first sentence. فَٱسْتَعِذْ بِٱللّٰهِ in the Ḳur xvi. 100 means *Then say thou* أَعُوذُ بِٱللّٰهِ [*I seek protection,* or *preservation, by God;* &c.]. (L.)

عَوْذٌ: see مَعَاذٌ, in two places. —— Also *A tree,* or *some other thing, beneath which,* or *in which, one takes refuge,* or *shelter.* (L.) —— *A thing, such as a stone,* or *trunk of a tree, surrounded by things blown against it and around it by the wind.* (T, L.) —— *Fallen leaves;* (AḤn, L, Ḳ:) so called because they shelter themselves against any rising thing, such as a building or a sand-hill or a mountain. (AḤn, L.) —— *Vile,* or *ignoble, persons;* or *the worse* or *viler,* or *the worst* or *vilest, of mankind.* (IAạr, L, Ḳ.) —— أَفْلَتَ فُلَانٌ مِنْهُ عَوَذًا [*Such a one escaped from him without being beaten; or without being killed, though beaten;*] is said when one has frightened the other; but not beaten him; (Ṣ, O, L, Ḳ;*) or beaten him, desiring to kill him, but not killed him. (Ṣ, O, L.) —— And مَا تَرَكْتُهُ إِلَّا عَوَذًا مِنْهُ means *I left him not save from dislike,* or *hatred, of him;* as also ▼ عَوَاذًا منه. (Ṣ, O, L.)

عُوذَةٌ (Ṣ, A, O, L, Ḳ) and ▼ تَعْوِيذٌ (Ṣ, O, L, Ḳ) and ▼ مَعَاذَةٌ (Ṣ, A, L, Ḳ) are syn., (Ṣ, A, O, L, Ḳ,) signifying *A kind of amulet, phylactery,* or *charm, bearing an inscription, which is hung upon a man* [*or woman or child or horse &c.*], *to charm the wearer against the evil eye and against fright and diabolical possession,* and which is forbidden to be hung upon the person, (L,) unless inscribed with something from the Ḳur-án or with the names of God, for in this case there is no harm in it: (Ṣ and Mgh voce تَمِيمَةٌ:) accord. to some of the etymologists, originally signifying *an amulet, a phylactery,* or *a charm, upon which is* [*an inscription commencing with the word*] أَعُوذُ; and afterwards applied in a general manner [as meaning *any amulet*]; (MF;) i. q. رُقْيَةٌ, (Ḳ,) or تَمِيمَةٌ: (A:) or those who imagine that the ▼ مَعَاذَةٌ is the same as the تميمة are in error; for the latter is a bead: (Mgh in art. تم:) [in some instances] the ▼ تَعْوِيذ is *a thing made of silver, of a round shape like the moon, but partly hollowed out in the form of the horse-shoe, tied by a string to the neck of a child, as a preservative, and in some instances engraved with an inscription:* (Ḥar p. 49:) the pl. of عُوذَةٌ is عُوَذٌ; that of ▼ تَعْوِيذٌ is تَعَاوِيذُ; and that of ▼ مَعَاذَةٌ is مَعَاذَاتٌ. (L.)

عَوَاذٌ: see عَوَذٌ, last sentence.

عِيَاذٌ [originally an inf. n. of 1]: see عُوذٌ, in two places: —— and see also مَعَاذٌ, in two places.

عُوَّذٌ Birds *taking refuge in a mountain* or *in some other place;* as also ▼ عِيَاذٌ: [each app. a pl. of عَائِذٌ; like as نُوَّمٌ and نِيَامٌ are pls. of نَائِمٌ:] (L, Ḳ:) Bakhdaj says,

كَالطَّيْرِ يَنْجُونَ عِيَاذًا ▼ عُوَّذَا

[*Like birds saving themselves, taking refuge in a mountain* or *in some other place*]; repeating the epithet for the sake of emphasis: or عياذا may be here an inf. n. (L.) —— And ‡ *Herbage growing at the feet of thorn-trees,* or *in a rugged place,* (Ṣ, O, Ḳ,) *which the cattle can hardly reach,* (Ṣ, O,) or *which they cannot reach;* (Ṣ,* O,* Ḳ;) as also ▼ مَعُوذٌ and ▼ مُعْوِذٌ: (Ḳ:) or *herbage that has not risen so high as the branches* [*around it*], *and which the trees prevent the beasts from depasturing:* or *such as is in rugged ground and cannot be reached by the cattle:* or *trees growing at the foot of some rising thing, such as a building* or *a sand-hill* or *a mountain,* or *a tree,* or *a rock, that protects them;* as also ▼ مَعُوذٌ: or ▼ مُعْوِذٌ, with kesr, signifies *any herbage,* or *plant, at the foot of a tree or stone or other thing whereby it shelters,* or *protects, itself:* (L:) and ▼ مَعُوذٌ, (O, Ḳ,) with fet-ḥ to the و, (O,) *herbage upon which camels pasture around tents* or *houses:* (O, Ḳ:) or عُوَّذ

شَجَرٍ and ▾ مَعُوذَةٌ signify *herbage that shelters*, or *protects, itself by trees, and spreads beneath them.* (A.) [See also دُخَّلٌ.] — عُوذُ اللَّحْمِ ‡ *The parts of flesh-meat that cleave to the bone:* (Ṣ, A, O, L, Ḳ:*) such are the sweetest of flesh-meat. (Ṣ, A, O, L.)

عَائِذٌ [part. n. of 1]. عَائِذٌ بِاللّٰهِ occurs in a trad. as meaning أَنَا عَائِذٌ [i. e. *I am seeking protection*, or *preservation, by God; &c.*]. (L.) And one says, اَللّٰهُمَّ عَائِذًا بِكَ مِنْ كُلِّ سُوْءٍ, meaning, accord. to Az, أَعُوذُ بِكَ عَائِذًا [lit. *O God, I seek protection*, or *preservation, by Thee, &c., seeking, &c., from every evil*]: but accord. to Sb, in the phrase عَائِذًا بِاللّٰهِ مِنْ شَرِّهَا, the word عائذا is put in the place of the inf. n. [as an absolute complement of أَعُوذُ understood; so that the meaning is, *I seek protection*, or *preservation, by God, with* earnest *seeking* &c., *from her*, or *its, evil*, or *mischief*]. (L.) — Also A female gazelle, (Ṣ, O, L, Ḳ,) and a she-camel, and a mare, (Ṣ, O, L,) and any female, (L, Ḳ,) *that has recently brought forth;* (Ṣ, O, L, Ḳ;) as also ▾ مُعْوِذٌ (O, Ḳ) and ▾ مُعِيذٌ: (L, Ḳ:) or any female *that has brought forth within seven days:* because her young one has recourse to her for protection; so that it is of the measure فَاعِلٌ in the sense of the measure مَفْعُولٌ; or, as some say, it is a possessive epithet, meaning ذَاتُ عَوْذٍ: or, accord. to Az, a she-camel *that has brought forth some days before;* accord. to some, *seven days:* (L:) or a female gazelle, and a she-camel, and a mare, *that has brought forth within ten days*, or *fifteen days*, (Ṣ, O, L,) or *thereabout;* (L;) after which she is called مُطْفِلٌ: (Ṣ, O, L:) pl. عُوذٌ and عُوذَانٌ, (Ṣ, O, L, Ḳ,) like as حُولٌ is pl. of حَائِلٌ, and رُعْيَانٌ of رَاعٍ; (Ṣ, O, L;) [and عَوَائِذُ;] and from عُوذٌ is formed the pl. عُوذَاتٌ. (L.) [It is said that the phrase] وَمَعَهُمُ العُوذُ المَطَافِيلُ, occurring in a trad., means † *And with them the women and children.* (L. [See another rendering voce مُطْفِلٌ.]) — العَوَائِذُ is the name of † *Four stars*, (O, Ḳ,) *of the northern stars*, (O,) *forming an irregular quadrilateral figure, in the midst of which is a star* [for كَوَاكِبُ, in the O and Ḳ, I read كَوْكَبٌ,] *called* الرُّبَعُ; (O, Ḳ;) *the four stars in the head of* التِّنِّين, [or *Draco*, which, app., like some other constellations, the Arabs figured somewhat differently from our astronomers,] *in the midst of which is a very small star called by the Arabs* الرُّبَعُ: they are *between* النَّسْرُ الوَاقِعُ [q. v. voce ذِئْبٌ] *and* الذِّئْبَانِ. (Ḳzw.)

تَعْوِيذٌ [originally inf. n. of 2]: see عُوذَةٌ, in three places.

مَعَاذٌ *A refuge;* (A, O, L, Ḳ;) as also ▾ عِيَاذٌ (Ṣ, O, L, Ḳ) and ▾ عَوْذٌ (O, Ḳ, in both of which it is said to be بِالتَّحْرِيكِ, but written in the L عَوْذ,) [and ▾ مُسْتَعَاذٌ]; meaning *a place to which one has recourse for protection* or *preservation:* and it also means *a time at which one does so:* and is also an inf. n. (L.) [Hence,] one says, هُوَ مَعَاذِى, (O,) and ▾ عِيَاذِى, (Ṣ, O,) and ▾ عَوْذِى, (O,) *He is my refuge:* (Ṣ, O:) and ▾ اَللّٰهُ مُسْتَعَاذِى [*God is my refuge*]. (A.)

مُعْوِذٌ and مُعِيذٌ: see عَائِذٌ. The pl. مُعْوِذَاتٌ is expl. by Skr as meaning She-camels *having their young ones with them.* (L.)

مَعَاذَةٌ an inf. n. of 1. (O, Ḳ.) — And i. q. عُوذَةٌ. (Ṣ, A, L, Ḳ.) See the latter, in three places.

مَعُوذٌ The *place of the collar* (Ṣ, O, L, Ḳ) of a horse. (Ṣ, O, L.) [App. so called because it is a place where charms, or amulets, are often suspended.] And المَعُوذُ, (A'Obeyd, L,) or دَائِرَةُ المَعُوذِ, (Ṣ, O, L,) *The feather*, or *curling portion of the coat of a horse, that is in the place of the collar:* (A'Obeyd, L:) it is a دائرة approved. (A'Obeyd, Ṣ, O, L.) — Also, (accord. to the Ḳ,) or ▾ مُعَوَّذٌ, (accord. to the O,) A she-camel *that does not cease to remain in one place.* (O, Ḳ.) [SM says that the word thus expl. in the Ḳ is a mistranscription for معوّد; by which he means مُعَوَّدٌ, part. n. of عَوَّدَ said of a camel; but this I doubt; for مُعَوَّدٌ has not the meaning here assigned to معوّد.] — See also عُوذٌ, in four places.

مُعَوَّذٌ: see عُوذٌ, in two places: — and see also مَعُوذٌ. — المُعَوِّذَتَانِ, with kesr to the و, (Ṣ, O, L, Ḳ,) erroneously said to be with fet-ḥ, (TA,) an appellation of *Two chapters of the Ḳur-án;* (Ṣ, Ḳ;) *the last two chapters;* i. e. *the Soorat el-Falaḳ and that which follows it:* (O, L, Mṣb:) so called because each of them begins with the words قُلْ أَعُوذُ; (L;) or because they preserved their publisher from every evil. (Mṣb.) And المُعَوِّذَاتُ is sometimes used to denote *The two chapters above mentioned together with that which next precedes them.* (MF.)

مُسْتَعَاذٌ: see مَعَاذٌ, in two places.

عور

1. عَوِرَ, (O, Ḳ,) said of a man, (O,) aor. يَعْوَرُ, inf. n. عَوَرٌ, (Ṣ, O, Ḳ,) *He was*, or *became, blind of one eye:* (Ḳ:) [or *he became one-eyed; wanting one eye:* or *one of his eyes sank in its socket:* or *one of his eyes dried up:* see what next follows:] as also عَارَ, aor. يَعَارُ; and ▾ اعورّ; (Ḳ;) and ▾ اعوارّ. (Ṣgh, Ḳ.) And عَوِرَتْ عَيْنُهُ, (Az, Ṣ, IḲṭṭ, O, Mṣb,) aor. تَعْوَرُ, (Az, Mṣb,) inf. n. عَوَرٌ; (IḲṭṭ, Mṣb;) and عَارَتْ, aor. تَعَارُ (Az, Ṣ, IḲṭṭ, O) and تَعَارُ; (IḲṭṭ, TA;) and ▾ اعورّت; (Az, Ṣ, IḲṭṭ, O;) and ▾ اعوارّت; (Az, O, TA;) *His eye became blind:* (TA:) or *became wanting:* or *sank in its socket:* (Mṣb:) or *dried up.* (IḲṭṭ, TA.) Ibn-Aḥmar says,

أَعَارَتْ عَيْنُهُ أَمْ لَمْ تَعَارَا

[*Has his eye become blind or has it not indeed become blind?*] meaning تَعَارَنْ; but, pausing, he makes it to end with ا: in عَوِرَتْ, the و is preserved unaltered because it is so preserved in the original form, which is اِعْوَرَّتْ, on account of the quiescence of the letter immediately preceding: then the augmentatives, the ا and the teshdeed, are suppressed, and thus the verb becomes عَوِرَ: for that اعورّت is the original form is shown by the form of the sister-verbs, اِسْوَدَّ and اِحْمَرَّ; and the analogy of verbs significant of faults and the like, اِعْرَجَّ and اِعْمَىَّ as the original forms of عَرِجَ and عَمِىَ; though these may not have been heard. (Ṣ, O. [See also صَيِدَ.]) — عَارَتِ الرَّكِيَّةُ, aor. تَعُورُ [or تَعْوَرُ or تَعَارُ?], ‡ *The well became filled up.* (TA.) — عَارَهُ, (O, Ḳ,) aor. يَعُورُهُ; (TA;) and ▾ أَعْوَرَهُ, (Ḳ,) inf. n. إِعْوَارٌ; (TA;) and ▾ عوّره, (Ḳ,) inf. n. تَعْوِيرٌ; (TA;) *He rendered him blind of one eye.* (Ḳ.) And عَارَ عَيْنَهُ, (Ṣ, M, IḲṭṭ, O, Mṣb,) aor. يَعُورُهَا, (Ṣ, O, Mṣb,) inf. n. عَوْرٌ: (IḲṭṭ;) and (more commonly, M) ▾ أَعْوَرَهَا; and ▾ عوّرها; (Ṣ, M, IḲṭṭ, Mṣb;) *He put out his eye:* (IḲṭṭ, Mṣb:*) or *made it to sink in its socket.* (Mṣb.) Some say that عُرْتُ عَيْنَهُ and ▾ أَعَارَهَا [sic] are from عَائِرٌ, q. v. (TA.) — عَارَ الرَّكِيَّةَ and ▾ اعارها and ▾ عوّرها, signify the same as ▾ عوّرها, ‡ *He marred*, or *spoiled, the well, so that the water dried up:* (A, TA:) or *he filled it up with earth, so that the springs thereof became stopped up:* and in like manner, ▾ عوّر عُيُونَ المِيَاهِ *he stopped up the sources of the waters:* (Sh, TA:) and ▾ عوّر عَيْنَ الرَّكِيَّةِ *he filled up the source of the well, so that the water dried up.* (Ṣ.) — عَارَهُ, aor. يَعُورُهُ and يَعِيرُهُ, (Ṣ, Ḳ,) or the aor. is not used, or, accord. to IJ, it is scarcely ever used, (TA,) or some say يَعُورُهُ, (Yaḳḳoob,) or يَعِيرُهُ, (Aboo-Shibl,) *He, or it, took, and went away with, him, or it:* (Ṣ, O, Ḳ:) or *destroyed him*, or *it.* (Ḳ, TA.) One says, مَا أَدْرِى أَىُّ الجَرَادِ عَارَهُ *I know not what man went away with him, or it:* (Ṣ, O, TA:) or *took him*, or *it.* (TA.) It is said to be only used in negative phrases: but Lḥ mentions أُرَاكَ عُرْتَهُ, and عِرْتَهُ, *I see thee*, or *hold thee, to have gone away with him*, or *it:* [see also art. عير:] IJ says, It seems that they have scarcely ever used the aor. of this verb because it occurs in a prov. respecting a thing that has passed away. (TA.) — See also 3 in art. عر.

2: see 1, in five places: — and see 3.

3. عاوره الشَّىْءَ *He did with the thing like as he* (the other) *did with it:* (Ṣ:) [or *he did the thing with him by turns;* for] المُعَاوَرَةُ is similar to المُدَاوَلَةُ, with respect to a thing that is between two, or mutual. (TA. [See also 6.]) — See also 4. — عاور المَكَايِيلَ i. q. عَايَرَهَا; [q. v. in art. عير;] (Ṣ, O, Ḳ;) as also ▾ عوّرها. (Ḳ.)

4: see 1, in four places. — اعارهُ الشَّىْءَ, (Az, Mṣb, Ḳ,) inf. n. إِعَارَةٌ and ▾ عَارَةٌ; like as you say أَطَاعَهُ, inf. n. إِطَاعَةٌ and طَاعَةٌ, and أَجَابَهُ, inf. n. إِجَابَةٌ and جَابَةٌ; (Az, Mṣb;) [or rather عَارَةٌ is a quasi-inf. n.; and so is طَاعَةٌ, and جَابَةٌ;] and

اعارهُ مِنْهُ; and ↑ عاورهُ إِيَّاهُ; (Ḳ;) [accord. to the TḲ, all signify *He lent him the thing:* but the second seems rather to signify *he lent him of it:* and respecting the third, see 3 above.] For three exs., see 10. سَيْفٌ أُعِيرَتْهُ المَنِيَّةُ ‡ [*A sword which fate has had lent to it*] is an appellation applied to a man, by En-Nábighah. (TA.) [See also 4 in art. عير.] —— أَعْوَرَ ‡ *It* (a thing) *appeared;* and *was,* or *became, within power,* or *reach.* (IAạr, Ḳ, TA.) One says, أَعْوَرَ لَكَ الصَّيْدُ ‡ *The object of the chase has become within power,* or *reach, to thee;* (Ṣ, O, TA;) and so أَعْوَرَكَ. (TA.) —— † *It* (a thing) *had a place that was a cause of fear,* i. e. what is termed عَوْرَة, *appearing* [*in it*]. (Ḥam p. 34.) ‡ *He* (a horseman) *had, appearing in him, a place open and exposed to striking* (Ṣ, O, TA) *and piercing.* (TA.) ‡ *It* (a place of abode) *had a gap,* or *breach, appearing in it:* (TA:) and [so] a house, or chamber, *by its wall's being in a state of demolition.* (IḲṭṭ, TA.)

5: see 6: see also 10, in two places: and see 5 in art. عير.

6. تعاوروا الشَّىْءَ, and ↑ اعْتَوَرُوهُ, (Ṣ, Mgh, O, Mṣb, Ḳ,) and ↑ تعوّروهُ, (Ṣ, O, Ḳ,) *They took the thing,* or *did it, by turns;* syn. تَدَاوَلُوهُ, (Ṣ, Mgh, O, Mṣb, Ḳ,) فِيمَا بَيْنَهُمْ: (Ṣ, O, TA:) the و is apparent [not changed into ا] in اعتوروا because it signifies the same as تعاوروا. (Ṣ.) Aboo-Kebeer says,

وَإِذَا الكُمَاةُ تَعَاوَرُوا طَعْنَ الكُلَى *

[*And when the men clad in armour interchange the piercing of the kidneys*]. (TA.) And in a trad. it is said, يَتَعَاوَرُونَ عَلَى مِنْبَرِى *They will ascend my pulpit one after another, by turns; whenever one goes, another coming after him.* (TA.) One says also, تعاور القَوْمُ فُلَانًا, meaning *The people aided one another in beating such a one, one after another.* (TA.) And تَعَاوَرْنَا فُلَانًا ضَرْبًا *We beat such a one by turns; I beating him one time, and another another time, and a third another time.* (TA.) And ↑ اعتور القَتِيلَ رَجُلَانِ *Each of the two men* [*in turn*] *struck the slain man.* (Mgh.) And تَعَاوَرَتِ الرِّيَاحُ رَسْمَ الدَّارِ ‡‡ *The winds blew by turns upon,* or *over, the remains that marked the site of the house,* or *dwelling;* (Ṣ, O;*) syn. تَنَاوَبَتْهُ, (Ṣ,) or تَدَاوَلَتْهُ; *one time blowing from the south, and another time from the north, and another time from the east, and another time from the west:* (Az, TA:) or *blew over them perseveringly,* so as to obliterate them; (Lth, TA;) a signification doubly tropical: but Az says that this is a mistake. (TA.) And doubly tropical is the saying الاِسْمُ ↑ تَعْتَوِرُهُ حَرَكَاتُ الإِعْرَابِ ‡‡ [*The noun has the vowels of desinential syntax by turns;* having at one time رَفْع, at another نَصْب, and at another خَفْض]. (TA.) ↑ تَعَاوُرٌ and ↑ اِعْتِوَارٌ denote that this has the place of this, and this the place of this: one says ↑ اِعْتَوَرَاهُ هٰذَا مَرَّةً وَهٰذَا مَرَّةً [*They two took it,* or *did it, by turns; this, one time; and this, one time*]: but you do not say اِعْتَوَرَ زَيْدٌ عَمْرًا. (IAạr.) —— تَعَاوَرْنَا العَوَارِىَّ ‡ *We lent loans, one to another:* (AZ:) and هُمْ يَتَعَاوَرُونَ العَوَارِىَّ ‡ *They lend loans, one to another.* (Ṣ,* Mṣb.) [See also 10.]

8: see 6, in five places.

9: see 1, first quarter, in two places.

10. استعار and ↑ تعوّر (O, Ḳ) *He asked,* or *demanded,* or *sought, what is termed* عَارِيَّة [*a loan*]. (Ḳ.) It is said in the story of the [golden] calf, مِنْ حَلْيٍ تَعَوَّرَهُ ↑ بَنُو إِسْرَائِيلَ i. e. اِسْتَعَارُوهُ [*Of ornaments which the children of Israel had asked to be lent,* or *had borrowed*]. (TA.) —— You say also ↑ اِسْتَعَرْتُ مِنْهُ الشَّىْءَ فَأَعَارَنِيهِ, (Mgh, Mṣb, Ḳ,*) and اِسْتَعَرْتُهُ الشَّىْءَ, (Mgh, TA,) suppressing the preposition, (Mgh,) *I asked of him the* [loan of] *the thing* [*and he lent it to me*]. (Ḳ, TA.) And ↑ اِسْتَعَرْتُ مِنْهُ عَارِيَّةً فَأَعَارَنِيهَا [*I asked of him a loan and he lent it to me*]. (TA.) And اِسْتَعَارَهُ ثَوْبًا فَأَعَارَهُ ↑ إِيَّاهُ [*He asked him to lend to him a garment, or piece of cloth, and he lent it to him*]. (Ṣ, O.) —— استعار سَهْمًا مِنْ كِنَانَتِهِ ‡ *He raised and transferred an arrow from his quiver.* (TA in arts. عور and عير.) —— [Hence, استعار لَفْظًا ‡ *He used a word metaphorically.*]

11: see 1, first quarter, in two places.

عَارٌ: see art. عير.

عَوَرٌ inf. n. of عَوِرَ [q. v.]. (Ṣ, O, Ḳ.) See also عَوْرَة. —— Also *Weakness, faultiness,* or *unsoundness;* and so ↑ عَوْرَة: *badness, foulness,* or *unseemliness,* in a thing: *disgrace,* or *disfigurement.* (TA.) [See also عَوَار.] —— هٰذَا الأَمْرُ بَيْنَنَا عَوَرٌ means *This is a thing,* or *an affair, that we do by turns.* (TA, voce رُوحٌ.)

عَوِرٌ ‡ A thing *having no keeper* or *guardian;* [lit., *having a gap,* or *an opening,* or *a breach,* exposing it to thieves and the like;] as also ↑ مُعْوِرٌ. (TA.) You say ↑ مَكَانٌ مُعْوِرٌ ‡ *A place in which one fears:* (TA:) *a place in which* (فِيهِ) [in one of my copies of the Ṣ (مِنْهُ)] *one fears being cut* [or *pierced* (see 4)]; (Ṣ, TA;) as also ↑ مَكَانٌ عَوْرَةٌ; which is doubly tropical: (TA:) and ↑ طَرِيقٌ مُعْوِرَةٌ ‡ *a road in which is an opening, in which one fears losing his way and being cut off:* and ↑ مُعْوِرٌ signifies *within the power of a person; open, and exposed: appearing;* and *within power,* or *reach:* and a place *feared.* (TA.) I'Ab and some others read, in the Ḳur [xxxiii. 13], إِنَّ بُيُوتَنَا عَوِرَةٌ, meaning, ذَاتُ عَوْرَةٍ; (O, Ḳ;) i. e., ‡ *Verily our houses are* [*open and exposed,*] *not protected, but, on the contrary, within the power of thieves, having no men in them:* (O, TA:) or it means مُعْوِرَة, i. e., *next to the enemy, so that our goods will be stolen from them.* (TA.) See also عَوْرَة, last sentence but one.

عَارَةٌ: see 4: —— and see also عَارِيَّةٌ.

عَوْرَةٌ The *pudendum,* or *pudenda,* (Ṣ, O, Mṣb, Ḳ,) *of a human being,* (Ṣ, O,) *of a man* and *of a woman:* (TA:) so called because it is abominable to uncover, and to look at, what is thus termed: (Mṣb:) said in the B to be from عَارٌ, meaning مَذَمَّةٌ: (TA:) [but see what is said voce عَارِيَّةٌ: the *part,* or *parts, of the person, which it is indecent to expose:*] *in a man, what is between the navel and the knee:* and *so in a woman:* (Jel in xxiv. 31:) or, *in a free woman, all the person, except the face and the hands as far as the wrists; and respecting the hollow of the sole of the foot, there is a difference of opinion: in a female slave, like as in a man; and what appears of her in service, as the head and the neck and the fore arm, are not included in the term* عورة. (TA.) [العَوْرَةُ المُغَلَّظَةُ means *The anterior and posterior pudenda:* العَوْرَةُ المُخَفَّفَةُ, *the other parts included in the term* عورة: so in the law-books.] The covering what is thus termed, in prayer and on other occasions, is obligatory: but respecting the covering the same in a private place, opinions differ. (TA.) The pl. is عَوْرَاتٌ: (Ṣ, O, Mṣb:) for the second letter of the pl. of فَعْلَةٌ as a subst. is movent only when it is not و nor ى: but some read [in the Ḳur xxiv. 31], عَوَرَاتِ النِّسَآءِ, (Ṣ, O,) which is of the dial. of Hudheyl. (Mṣb.) —— *A time in which it is proper for the* عَوْرَة *to appear; each of the following three times; before the prayer of daybreak; at midday; and after nightfall.* (Ḳ.) These three times are mentioned in the Ḳur xxiv. 57. (TA.) —— *Anything that a man veils,* or *conceals, by reason of disdainful pride,* or *of shame* or *pudency:* (Mṣb:) *anything of which one is ashamed* (Ṣ, O, Ḳ, TA) *when it appears.* (TA.) —— See also عَوَرٌ. —— † *A woman:* because one is ashamed at her when she appears, like as one is ashamed at the pudendum (العَوْرَة) when it appears: (L, TA:) or *women.* (Mṣb.) —— *Any place of concealment* (مَكْمَنٌ) [*proper*] *for veiling* or *covering.* (Ḳ.) —— *A gap, an opening,* or *a breach,* (T, Mṣb, Ḳ,) or *any gap, opening,* or *breach,* (Ṣ, O,) *in the frontier of a hostile country,* (T, Ṣ, O, Mṣb, Ḳ,) *&c.,* (Ḳ,) or *in war* or *battle, from which one fears* (T, Ṣ, O, Mṣb) *slaughter.* (T.) —— Sometimes it is applied as an epithet to an indeterminate subst.; and in this case it is applied to a sing. and to a pl., without variation, and to a masc. and a fem., like an inf. n. (TA.) It is said in the Ḳur [xxxiii. 13], إِنَّ بُيُوتَنَا عَوْرَةٌ (O, TA) [*Verily our houses are open and exposed:* or, as expl. by Bḍ and others, *defenceless*]: the epithet being here sing.; and the subst. to which it is applied, pl.: (TA:) but in this instance it may be a contraction of ↑ عَوِرَة; and thus it has been read: (Bḍ:) see عَوِرٌ. —— Also, (Ḳ,) or [the pl.] عَوْرَاتٌ, (Ṣ,) *Clefts,* or *fissures,* of mountains. (Ṣ, Ḳ.)

عَوْرَةٌ a subst. meaning ↑ عَوَرٌ [q. v.]: (O:) [it is mentioned in the Ṣ as a subst., and app., from the context, as signifying عَوَرٌ, i. e. *A blindness of one eye:* (but expl. by Golius as meaning *the succession of a worse after a better:*) after the mention of رَجُلٌ أَعْوَرُ, and the phrase بَدَلٌ أَعْوَرُ and خَلَفٌ أَعْوَرُ, in the Ṣ, it is added, وَالاِسْمُ العَوْرَةُ, or, accord. to one copy, العَوَرَةُ; and then follows, وَقَدْ عَارَتِ العَيْنُ.]

عُورَانٌ a pl. of أَعْوَرُ [q. v.]; as also عِيرَانٌ. —— It is also used as a sing.; رَكِيَّةٌ عُورَانٌ meaning † *A well in a state of demolition.* (O, Ḳ.)

عَارِيَّةٌ (Ṣ, Mgh, O, Mṣb, Ḳ) and sometimes عَارِيَةٌ, without teshdeed, (Mṣb, Ḳ,) when used in poetry, (Mṣb,) and ▼ عَارَةٌ, (Ṣ, O, Ḳ,) *What is taken by persons by turns;* expl. by مَا تَدَاوَلُوهُ بَيْنَهُمْ: (Ḳ:) [generally meaning *a loan:* and the *act of lending;*] the *putting one in possession of the use of a thing without anything given in exchange:* (KT, and Kull p. 262:) the returning of the thing thus termed is obligatory, when the thing itself remains in existence; and if it has perished, then one must be responsible for its value, accord. to Esh-Sháfi'ee, but not accord. to Aboo-Ḥaneefeh: (TA:) pl. [of the first] عَوَارِىُّ, (Ṣ, O, Mṣb, Ḳ,) and [of the second] عَوَارٍ. (Mṣb, Ḳ.) A poet says,

• إِنَّمَا أَنْفُسُنَا عَارِيَّةٌ • وَالْعَوَارِىُّ قُصَارٌ أَنْ تُرَدّْ •

[*Our souls are only a loan: and the end of loans is their being given back:* تُرَدّْ being for تُرَدَّ]. (Ṣ, O.) عَارِيَّةٌ is of the measure فَعْلِيَّةٌ: Az says that it is a rel. n. from عَارَةٌ, which is a subst. from إِعَارَةٌ: (Mgh,* Mṣb:) Lth says that what is thus called is so called because it is a disgrace (عار) to him who demands it; and J says the like; and some say that it is from عَارَ الفَرَسُ, meaning, "the horse went away from his master:" but both these assertions are erroneous; since عَارِيَّةٌ belongs to art. عور, for the Arabs say هُمْ يَتَعَاوَرُونَ العَوَارِىَّ meaning *they lend* [*loans*], *one to another;* and عَارٌ and عَارَ الفَرَسُ belong to art. عير: therefore the correct assertion is that of Az. (Mṣb.)

عَوَارٌ (Ṣ, Mgh, Mṣb, Ḳ) and ▼ عُوَارٌ (AZ, Ṣ, Mṣb, Ḳ) and ▼ عِوَارٌ (Ḳ) *A fault; a defect; an imperfection; a blemish; something amiss;* (Ṣ, Mgh, Mṣb, Ḳ;) in an article of merchandise, (Ṣ, Mgh, Mṣb,) and in a garment, or piece of cloth, (TA,) and in a slave, (Mṣb,) and in a beast: (TA:) or in a garment, or piece of cloth, *a hole,* and *a rent;* (Lth, Mgh, Mṣb, Ḳ, TA;) and so in the like, and in a house or tent and the like; (TA;) and in a garment, or piece of cloth, also *a burn;* and *a rottenness:* (Mgh:) and some say that عَوَارٌ, with fet-ḥ, is only in goods, or commodities, or articles of merchandise. (Mṣb.) You say سِلْعَةٌ ذَاتُ عَوَارٍ, and ▼ عُوَارٍ, accord. to AZ, *An article of merchandise having a fault,* or *the like.* (Ṣ.) [See also عَوَرٌ.]

عُوَارٌ: see عَوَارٌ, in two places.

عِوَارٌ: see عَوَارٌ.

عُوَيْرٌ: see أَعْوَرُ, of which it is the dim.

عُيَيْرَةُ عَيْنَيْنِ: see عَائِرٌ.

عُوَّارٌ: see عَائِرٌ, in four places.

عَائِرٌ *Anything that causes disease in the eye,* (Ḳ, TA,) *and wounds:* so called because the eye becomes closed on account of it, and the person cannot see, the eye being as it were blinded: (TA:) *ophthalmia;* syn. رَمَدٌ; (Ṣ, O, Ḳ;) as also ▼ عُوَّارٌ: (Mṣb:) which latter also signifies *foul, thick, white matter, that collects in the inner corner of the eye; not fluid;* syn. رَمَصٌ: (Mṣb:) or both signify *a fluid matter that makes the eye smart, as though a mote,* or *the like, had fallen into it:* (Lth:) and both signify *a mote,* or *the like,* (Ṣ, O, Ḳ,) *in the eye:* (Ṣ:) or (TA, in the Ḳ "and") عَائِرٌ signifies *pimples,* or *small pustules, in the lower eyelid:* (Ḳ:) a subst., not an inf. n., nor an act. part. n.: (TA:) the pl. of ▼ عُوَّارٌ is عَوَاوِيرُ, and, by poetic license, عَوَاوِرُ. (TA.) One says ▼ بِعَيْنِهِ عُوَّارٌ, meaning, *In his eye is a mote,* or *the like.* (Ṣ.) —— عَيْنٌ عَائِرَةٌ *An eye in which is the fluid matter called* ▼ عُوَّار: but when the eye has this, you do not say of it عَارَتْ. (Lth.) —— عَائِرُ العَيْنِ † *What fills,* or *satisfies, the eye* (مَا يَمْلَؤُهَا), of مَال [meaning camels or the like], *so as almost to put it out;* and in like manner عَائِرَةُ عَيْنَيْنِ. (TA.) One says, عِنْدَهُ مِنَ المَالِ عَائِرَةُ عَيْنٍ, (Ṣ, O,) or عَائِرَةُ عَيْنَيْنِ and ▼ عُيَيْرَةُ عَيْنَيْنِ, (Ḳ, but with عَلَيْهِ in the place of عِنْدَهُ, and in the CḲ عَثَرَةُ is put for عُيَيْرَةُ,) both of these mentioned by Lḥ, (TA,) i. e. † [*He has, of camels* or *the like*], *what fill,* or *satisfy,* (تَمْلَأُ,) *his sight by the multitude thereof;* (Ḳ;) or *that at which the sight is confounded,* or *perplexed, by reason of the multitude thereof, as though it filled,* or *satisfied, the eye, and put it out:* (Ṣ, O:) [and A'Obeyd says the like:] or, accord. to Aṣ, the Arab in the Time of Ignorance used, when his camels amounted to a thousand, to put out an eye of one of them; and hence, by عَائِرَةُ العَيْنِ they meant *a thousand camels, whereof one had an eye put out.* (TA.) ═ عَائِرٌ also signifies An arrow *of which the shooter is not known;* (Ṣ, O, Ḳ;) and in like manner, a stone: (Ṣ, O:) pl. عَوَائِرُ: (TA:) عَوَائِرُ نَبْلٍ means *arrows in a scattered state, of which one knows not whence they have come.* (IB, TA.) [See also art. عير.] And عَوَائِرُ (Ṣ, O, Ḳ) and ▼ عِيرَانٌ (Ḳ) signify *Swarms* of locusts *in a scattered state:* (Ṣ, O, Ḳ: [or] the *first* thereof *going away in a scattered state, and few in number.* (TA.)

أَعْوَرُ *Blind of one eye:* (Ḳ:) *one-eyed; wanting one eye:* or *having one of his eyes sunk in its socket:* (Mṣb:) or *having one of his eyes dried up:* (IKṭṭ:) applied to a man, (Ṣ, Mṣb,) and to a camel, &c.: (TA:) fem. عَوْرَآءُ: (Mṣb:) pl. عُورٌ and عُورَانٌ (O, Ḳ) and عِيرَانٌ. (Ḳ.) The أَعْوَر is considered by the Arabs as of evil omen. (TA.) It is said in a prov., أَعْوَرُ عَيْنَكَ وَالحَجَرَ [*O one-eyed, preserve thine eye* (thine only eye) *from the stone*]. (Meyd, TA.) —— *Squint-eyed;* syn. أَحْوَلُ: (TA:) and عَوْرَآءُ the same, applied to a woman. (Ḳ, TA.) —— *A crow:* (Ṣ, O, Ḳ:) so called as being deemed inauspicious; (Ṣ, O, TA;) or by antiphrasis, (TA,) because of the sharpness of his sight; (Ṣ, O, TA;) or because, when he desires to croak, he closes his eyes; (O, TA;) and ▼ عُوَيْرٌ is the dim., (Ṣ, O,) and signifies the same. (Ḳ.) —— فَلَاةٌ عَوْرَآءُ † *A desert in which is no water.* (Ṣ, O.) —— طَرِيقٌ أَعْوَرُ ‡ *A road in which is no sign of the way.* (Ḳ, TA.) —— عَوْرَآءُ القُرِّ † A night (لَيْلَةٌ), (O, TA,) and a morning (غَدَاةٌ), and a year (سَنَةٌ), (TA,) *in which is no cold.* (Th, O, TA.) —— أَعْوَرُ also signifies † Anything, (O, Ḳ, TA,) and any disposition, temper, or nature, (TA,) *bad, corrupt, abominable,* or *disapproved:* (O, Ḳ, TA:) fem. as above. (TA.) —— بَدَلٌ أَعْوَرُ † [*A bad substitute*]: a prov. applied to a man who is dispraised succeeding one who is praised: and sometimes they said خَلَفٌ أَعْوَرُ: and Aboo-Dhu-eyb uses the expression خِلَافٌ عُورٌ; as though he made خِلَافٌ pl. of خَلَفٌ, like as جِمَالٌ is pl. of جَمَلٌ. (Ṣ, O.) —— عَوْرَآءُ ‡ *A bad, an abominable,* or *a foul, word* or *saying;* (AHeyth, Ṣ, A, O, Ḳ;) opposed to عَيْنَآءُ: (AHeyth, A, TA:) i. q. سَقْطَةٌ; (Ṣ, O;) i. e. *a bad word* or *saying, that swerves from rectitude:* (TA:) or *a word* or *saying that falls inconsistent with reason and rectitude:* (Lth:) or *a word* or *saying which the ear rejects;* and in the pl. sense you say عُورَانُ الكَلَامِ: (AZ:) or *a bad, an abominable,* or *a foul, action:* (Ḳ:) as though the word or saying, or the action, blinded the eye: the attribute which it denotes is transferred to the word or saying, or the action; but properly its author is meant. (TA.) —— مَعَانٍ عُورٌ, in a trad. of 'Omar, † *Obscure, subtile, meanings.* (TA.) —— See also the pl. عِيرَانٌ voce عَائِرٌ, last sentence.

اِسْتِعَارَةٌ [inf. n. of 10. —— And hence, ‡ *A metaphor*].

مُعْوِرٌ: see عَوِرٌ, in four places.

مُسْتَعَارٌ [*Borrowed;* or *asked, demanded,* or *sought, as a loan;*] pass. part. n. of 10 as used in the phrase اِسْتَعَارَهُ ثَوْبًا [q. v.] so in the following verse of Bishr (Ṣ, O) Ibn-Abee-Ḥázim, describing a horse: (O:)

• كَأَنَّ حَفِيفَ مَنْخِرِهِ إِذَا مَا •
• كَتَمْنَ الرَّبْوَ كِيرٌ مُسْتَعَارُ •

[*As though the sound of the wind of his nostril, when they* (i. e. other horses) *suppressed loud breathing, were* the sound of the wind of *a borrowed blacksmith's bellows*]: or, as some say, مستعار here means مُتَعَاوَرٌ i. e. مُتَدَاوَلٌ [app. *worked by turns*]: (Ṣ, O:) he means that his nostril was wide, not suppressing the loud breathing, when other beasts suppressed the breath by reason of the narrowness of the place of exit thereof. (Ṣ in art. كتم.) —— [And hence, ‡ A word, or phrase, *used metaphorically.*]

عوز

1. عَوِزَ, (Ṣ, O, Mṣb, Ḳ,) aor. ـَ, (Mṣb, Ḳ,) inf. n. عَوَزٌ, (Ṣ, O, Mṣb,) *It* (a thing) *was,* or *became, wanting; not found;* or *not existing:* (Ṣ, O, Ḳ:) or *it* (anything) *was wanted, and desired, but not*

attainable: (Lth, O:) or *it was,* or *became, unattainable; not found;* or *not existing.* (Mṣb.) —— The same verb, inf. n. as above, is also said of flesh, or flesh-meat; [app. signifying *It became wasted;* or *it was,* or *became, wanting,* or *not found;*] (A;) or the verb thus used is ▼أَعْوَزَ, inf. n. إِعْوَازٌ. (TA.) —— Also *It* (an affair) *was,* or *became, hard, difficult,* or *strait;* (O, Ḳ,* TA;) and ▼اعوز *it* (a thing) *was,* or *became, difficult.* (IḲṭṭ.) —— And *He* (a man) *was,* or *became, poor, needy,* or *indigent;* (Ṣ, A, O, Ḳ;) as also ▼اعوز, (Ṣ, O, Mṣb, Ḳ,) inf. n. إِعْوَازٌ: (Ṣ, Mṣb:) or the latter signifies *he was,* or *became, poor so as to possess nothing;* (AZ, Mṣb;) or *he became in want, and in an unsound condition;* (A;) as also ▼اعوزّ, (A, TA,) inf. n. اِعْوِزَازٌ; (TA;) or *in an evil condition.* (TA.) ═ عَازَ الشَّىْءَ, aor. يَعُوزُ, [inf. n. عَوْزٌ,] *He wanted, needed,* or *required, the thing, and found it not.* (Mṣb.) [And عَازَهُ الشَّىْءُ, and أَعْوَزَهُ, virtually signify the same.] See 4.

4. اعوز, inf. n. إِعْوَازٌ: see عَوِزَ, in three places. ═ اعوزه الدَّهْرُ *Fortune caused him to become in want,* or *need;* (Ṣ, O, Ḳ;) or *rendered him poor;* (A, Mṣb;) [i. e.,] *poverty befell him.* (TA.) —— اعوزه الشَّىْءُ [lit., *The thing caused him to want;* meaning] *he wanted, needed,* or *required, the thing,* [or *had it not,*] (Ṣ, O, Ḳ,) *and was unable to attain it:* (Ṣ, Ḳ:) and *the thing escaped him, so that he was unable to attain it,* (M, Mgh, Mṣb,) *it being much wanted by him;* (M, TA;) as also ▼عَازَهُ الشَّىْءُ: (M, TA:) or the latter, [virtually, like عَازَ الشَّىْءَ,] *he found not the thing:* (O, Ḳ, TA:) but Az says that this latter phrase is not known. (O, TA.) —— *The thing was little,* or *scarce,* or *scanty, to him,* or *in his estimation, and needful to him.* (Mgh, TA.) —— اعوزه الأَمْرُ *The affair was hard,* or *difficult, to him.* (A, TA.) So in the saying, مَسْأَلَةٌ يَخْتَلِفُ فِيهَا كِبَارُ الصَّحَابَةِ يَعُوزُ فِقْهُهَا [*A question respecting which the great men of the Companions differ;*] *the knowledge whereof is difficult.* (Mgh.) ═ And one says, مَا يَعُوزُ لِفُلَانٍ شَىْءٌ إِلَّا ذَهَبَ بِهِ *A thing does not come within sight of such a one but he takes it away:* (Ibn-Háni, O, Ḳ:) a saying disapproved by Aṣ, but held by AZ to be correct, [thus said by him with ز, (TA,)] and heard from the Arabs. (O.) [See also أَعْوَرَ, with ر.]

9: see 1, latter part.

عَوْزٌ The *berries of the grape-vine* [i. e. *grapes;* العَوْز being expl. as signifying حَبُّ العِنَبِ]: n. un. with ة. (O, Ḳ.) خَرَطْتُ العُنْقُودَ, (O,) or العِنَبَ, (TA,) is expl. by AHeyth as said when one takes, (O,) or strips off, (TA,) the عَوْز (O, TA) that are upon the عنقود [or bunch], (O,) or that are upon the عنب [or grape-vine], (TA,) with all his fingers, (O, TA,) so as to clear it of its عوز, (O,) or so as to clear them from the عود [or stalk] thereof. (TA.)

عَوَزٌ inf. n. of عَوِزَ [q. v.]. (Ṣ, O, Mṣb.) —— [As a simple subst.,] *Want; need; exigency;* (A, O, Ḳ;) in which sense مَعَاوِزُ may be an irreg. pl. thereof similar to مَلَامِحُ and مَشَابِهُ: (Ḥar p. 26:) *destitution:* (TA:) *poverty:* (A:) *evilness of condition:* (TA:) *littleness,* or *scarceness,* or *scantiness, of a thing, to a person,* or *in his estimation, and its needfulness to him:* (Lth,* Mgh, TA:*) *straitness,* or *difficulty, of a thing.* (TA.) You say, أَصَابَهُ عَوَزٌ *Want,* and *poverty, befell him.* (A.) And hence the saying, سَدَادٌ مِنْ عَوَزٍ, (A, Mgh, TA,) a well-known prov., expl. in art. سد. (TA.)

عَوِزٌ *Poor; needy; indigent:* (Ḳ, in this art. and in art. لوز:) and ▼مُعْوِزٌ signifies the same; (Ṣ, TA;) *possessing little;* and *in an evil condition,* as also ▼مُعْوَزٌ, (O, TA,) which latter is anomalous. (TA.) You say, إِنَّهُ لَعَوِزٌ لَوِزٌ *Verily he is poor indeed:* the last word being an imitative sequent, (Ḳ, in this art. and in art. لوز,) and a corroborative. (TA.)

مُعْوَزٌ: see عَوِزٌ. —— هٰذَا شَىْءٌ مُعْوِزٌ *This is a thing that is rare; scarce; hardly to be found:* (TA:) or *not to be found.* (A.)

مِعْوَزٌ: see عَوِزٌ. ═ *An old and worn-out garment* or *piece of cloth, that is worn in service and in labouring;* (Ṣ, O, Ḳ;) as also ▼مِعْوَزَةٌ: (O, Ḳ:) because such is worn by the poor: (O, Ḳ, TA:) wherefore it has the form of an instrumental noun: (TA:) and the latter, *any garment,* or *piece of cloth, with which another is preserved:* or *a new garment* or *piece of cloth,* accord. to AZ: (TA:) but this is [said to be] a mistake ascribed to AZ: (O:) pl. of the former, مَعَاوِزُ; (Ṣ, O, Ḳ; [see also عَوَزٌ;]) and of ▼the latter, مَعَاوِزَةٌ, with ة added to corroborate the fem. character. (TA.) —— Also The *piece of rag which a woman holds when wailing for the dead.* (TA, voce عَذَبٌ.)

مِعْوَزَةٌ: see مِعْوَزٌ, in two places.

عوش

مَعُوشَةٌ i. q. مَعِيشَةٌ, in the dial. of El-Azd. (Ḳ.) See 1 in art. عيش.

عوص

1. عَوِصَ, (Ṣ, O, Mṣb, K,) aor. يَعْوَصُ; (Mṣb, TA;) and عَاصَ, aor. يَعَاصُ; (A, O, Ḳ;) inf. n. (of the former, Mṣb, or of the latter, A) عَوَصٌ (A, O, Mṣb, Ḳ) and عِيَاصٌ; (A, O, Ḳ; [and accord. to the CḲ عَيْصٌ also, but this I do not find elsewhere,]) *It* (a thing [or, accord. to the O, so the former verb, but both as said of language,]) *was,* or *became, difficult;* (Ṣ,* A, O, Mṣb, Ḳ;) syn. اِشْتَدَّ, (A, O, Ḳ,) or صَعُبَ; (Mṣb;) as also ▼اعتاص: (Mṣb:) and *it was,* or *became, impossible; contr. of* أَمْكَنَ. (TA.) You say, ▼اعتاص عَلَيْهِ الأَمْرُ *The thing,* or *affair, was,* or *became, difficult and intricate to him:* (Ṣ, TA:) or *difficult and confused and intricate to him, so that he did not find the right course* (O, Ḳ, TA) *therein.* (O, TA.) —— Also said of language, inf. n. as above, (A, Ḳ,) and عَائِصٌ also, (TA, [see عَوِيصٌ,]) meaning *It was,* or *became, difficult;* syn. صَعُبَ: (A, O,* Ḳ:) and [in like manner] ▼اعتاص, said of language, *it was,* or *became, obscure.* (TA.) —— [The two inf. ns. first mentioned above are also quasi-inf. ns. of أَعْوَصَ, q. v.]

2. عوّص, inf. n. تَعْوِيصٌ, *He put forth,* or *proposed, a verse difficult to be explained,* or *understood.* (O, Ḳ,* TA.) [See also 4.] —— *He did not pursue a right course in saying nor in acting.* (TA.)

3. عاوصهُ *He wrestled with him, each endeavouring to throw down the other.* (Ibn-'Abbád, O, Ḳ.)

4. أَعْوَصَ *He said what was difficult to be understood:* (Mṣb:) *he spoke,* or *made use of, strange language,* or *a strange expression.* (Ṣ, TA.) [See also 2.] You say also, اعوص فِى المَنْطِقِ *He was obscure in speech.* (TA.) And اعوص بِالخَصْمِ, (Ṣ, A, O, Ḳ,) inf. n. [or rather quasi-inf. n.] عَوَصٌ and عِيَاصٌ, (Ḳ, TA, [the latter written in the CḲ عَيَاص,]) *He made the adversary's case,* or *affair, difficult and intricate to him:* (Ṣ, O, Ḳ:) or *he brought upon the adversary that which was difficult and intricate to him:* (A:) or *he brought the adversary into a case which he did not understand.* (TA.) And اعوص عَلَيْهِ, (O, Ḳ, TA,) and بِهِ, (TA,) *He introduced against him, of arguments, what it was difficult for him to evade.* (O, Ḳ, TA.) ═ أَعْوَصَنِى [*It caused me to be in difficulty,* so that I was unable to accomplish it]. (Ibn-'Abbád, in O voce أَعْوَقَ, q. v.)

8: see 1, in three places. —— اعتاصت النَّاقَةُ *The she-camel, being covered, did not conceive,* (Lth, Ṣ, O, Ḳ,) *though there was no disease in her:* (Ṣ, TA:) and in like manner, اعتاصت رَحِمُهَا [*her womb was not impregnated*]: accord. to Yaạkoob, the ص in this verb is substituted for the ط in اعتاطت, which, accord. to Az, is the more common: or, as some say, the former is said particularly of a mare, and the latter of a she-camel. (TA.)

عَوَصٌ [inf. n. of 1]: see عَوِيصٌ.

عَوُوصٌ A ewe, or she-goat, *that does not yield her milk plentifully, though plied hard.* (O, Ḳ.)

عَوِيصٌ A *difficult* thing, or affair: (Mṣb:) and the same, (Ḳ,) or ▼عَوْصَآءُ, (O, TA,) applied to a calamity (دَاهِيَةٌ) *difficult, severe, grievous,* or *distressing:* (O, Ḳ, TA:) IJ holds it to be used [only] as a subst. (M, voce صَوِيبٌ.) —— Also Language *Difficult to be understood:* (Mṣb:) *obscure;* or *not comprehended* or *understood;* as also ▼أَعْوَصُ and ▼عَائِصٌ, which last is [originally] an inf. n., like فَالِجٌ &c.: (TA:) poetry *of which the meaning is difficult to be elicited;* (Ṣ, O, Ḳ;) as also ▼أَعْوَصُ: (O, Ḳ:) also عَوِيصٌ, (Ḳ, TA,) and عَوِيصَةٌ, (TA,) and ▼عَوْصَآءُ, (Ṣ, Mṣb, Ḳ, TA,) applied to a word, or an expression, or a sentence, or the like, (كَلِمَةٌ,) *strange:* (Ṣ, Ḳ:) or *difficult to be understood.* (Mṣb.) —— Also, applied to earth [(تُرَاب)], *Hard:* (Ḳ:) and ↑ عَوْصَآءُ, applied to a piece of sand (رَمْلَة), *difficult to traverse:* (MF:) or, accord. to ISh, the latter is applied as an epithet to what is termed مَيْثَآء, [of which one signification is an even, or a soft, tract of sand,] in the sense of مُخَالِفَة [app. meaning *opposing one's progress*]: and the state, or quality, thereof, is termed ↑ عَوَص. (O, TA.) —— And, applied to a place, *Rugged, high, and difficult.* (Ibn-'Abbád, O, Ḳ.) —— Also, (Ḳ,) or ↑ عَوْصَآءُ, (Ṣ, O, TA,) [as an epithet in which the quality of a subst. predominates,] *A difficult affair:* (Ḳ, TA:) or the *most difficult of affairs.* (Ṣ, O, TA.) You say, ↑ فُلَانٌ يَرْكَبُ العَوْصَآءَ *Such a one embarks in,* or *undertakes, the most difficult of affairs.* (Ṣ, O, TA.) —— Also عَوِيص, (Ḳ,) or ↑ عَوْصَآء, (Ṣ, TA,) *Difficulty,* or *distress:* (Ṣ, Ḳ:) or *difficulty and want.* (TA in art. عيص.) You say, ↑ أَصَابَتْهُمْ عَوْصَآءُ *Difficulty,* or *distress, befell them.* (TA.) And عَيْصَآءُ signifies the same; the ى being interchangeable with the و. (TA.)

عَائِصٌ: see عَوِيص, second sentence. —— Also A ewe, or she-goat, *that has not conceived for some years:* (Ṣ, O, Ḳ:) pl. عُوص, (O, Ḳ,) [and app. عِيص,] made to accord with عُوط and عِيط. (O, TA.)

أَعْوَصُ: fem. عَوْصَآءُ: see عَوِيص, throughout.

نَاقَةٌ مُعْتَاصَةٌ [*An intractable,* or *unmanageable, she-camel*]. (Ḳ in art. أبد; there coupled with وَحْشِيَّة.)

مِعْيَاصٌ: see art. عيص.

عوض

1. عَاضَهُ, (Ṣ, A, O, Mṣb, Ḳ,) first pers. عُضْتُهُ, (A and TA in art. عرض,) aor. يَعُوضُ, (Mṣb,) inf. n. عَوْض (A, O, Mṣb, Ḳ) and عِوَض (O, Ḳ) and عِيَاض, (A, O, Ḳ,) originally عِوَاض, (O, Ḳ,) *He* (God, A, O, Ḳ, or a man, Ṣ, O, Mṣb) *gave him a substitute,* or *something instead* or *in exchange,* or *a compensation,* (Ṣ, A,* O, Mṣb, Ḳ,*) عَنْ كَذَا [*for such a thing*], (Mṣb,) or مِنْهُ [*for it*]; (O, Ḳ;) or عَاضَهُ مَا أُخِذَ مِنْهُ, said of God, [and of a man,] *He gave him a substitute for,* or *replaced to him, what had been taken from him;* (A;) and ↑ عَوَّضَهُ, (Ṣ, A, Mṣb, Ḳ,) inf. n. تَعْوِيض, (TA,) signifies the same; (Ṣ, A, Mṣb, Ḳ;) as also ↑ أَعَاضَهُ; (Ṣ, IJ, Mṣb;) and ↑ عَاوَضَهُ, (Ṣ, O, Ḳ,) inf. n. مُعَاوَضَة. (TA.) —— And عُضْتُهُ *I gave to him.* (IJ.) ═ عِضْتُ, [originally عَوِضْتُ,] aor. أَعَاضُ: see 8.

2 and 3 and 4: see the preceding paragraph.

5: see 8, in two places.

6. تعاوض القَوْمُ, inf. n. تَعَاوُض, *The people,* or *company of men, had their property and their former state restored to them after want.* (TA.)

8. اعتاض *He took,* or *received, a substitute,* or *something instead* or *in exchange,* or *a compensation;* (Ṣ, Mṣb;) as also ↑ تعوّض: (Ṣ, O, Mṣb, Ḳ:) [both of which also signify *he had* a thing *replaced to him:*] and ↑ عِضْتُ, [originally عَوِضْتُ,] (Lth and TA, in this art. and in art. عرض,) aor. أَعَاضُ, (TA in art. عرض,) likewise signifies *I took,* or *received, a substitute,* or *something instead* or *in exchange,* or *a compensation:* (Lth, TA:) but Az says, "I have not heard this on any other authority than that of Lth." (O, TA.) You say also, اِعْتَاضَ خَيْرًا مِمَّا ذَهَبَ مِنْهُ [*He received as a substitute,* or *compensation, what was better than that which had gone from him*]; and [in like manner] ↑ تَعَوَّضَ. (A.) ═ اعتاضهُ *He came to him seeking,* or *demanding, a substitute,* or *something instead* or *in exchange,* or *a compensation;* (O, Ḳ;) and *a free gift,* or *gratuity.* (O, TA.) [See also 10.]

10. استعاض *He sought,* or *demanded,* or *asked for, a substitute,* or *something instead* or *in exchange,* or *a compensation.* (Ṣ, O, Mṣb.) —— It is also trans.: you say, استعاضهُ *He asked him for a substitute,* or *something instead* or *in exchange,* or *a compensation.* (A,* O, Ḳ.) [See also 8, last signification.] —— [استعاضهُ also signifies *He asked,* or *desired, that it should be replaced to him.*] —— And اِسْتَعْوَضَهُ *He took it* (a thing) *as a substitute,* or *in exchange, for another thing;* or *in the place of another thing;* syn. اِسْتَخْلَفَهُ [q. v.]. (TA in art. خلف.)

عَوْضُ and عَوْضَ (Az, Ṣ, O, Mughnee, Ḳ) and عَوْضِ; (Mughnee, Ḳ,) the first accord. to Ks (TA) and the Koofees, and the second accord. to the Baṣrees; (O, TA; [in which latter it is added that the second is the most common; but this I think a mistake; for I have most frequently found the first; and in the Mughnee, عَوْضُ is mentioned first, as in the Ṣ and Ḳ, and عَوْضِ last;]) indecl., (Mughnee, Ḳ,) like قَبْلُ and أَيْنَ and أَمْسِ, (Mughnee,) without tenween; (Ṣ;) [but not always, as will be seen below;] an adv. n., (Mughnee, Ḳ,) denoting future time, (Ṣ, O,) or all future time, (Mughnee, Ḳ,) like as قَطُّ denotes past time; (Ṣ, O;) meaning *Ever;* syn. أَبَدًا; (Ṣ,* O, Ḳ;) but differing from أَبَدًا by being appropriated to negative phrases only: (Mughnee, Ḳ:*) you say لَا أُفَارِقُكَ عَوْضُ, (Ḳ,) or عَوْضُ لَا أُفَارِقُكَ, meaning *I will not separate myself from thee, ever;* like as you say قَطُّ مَا فَارَقْتُكَ; but you may not say عَوْضُ مَا فَارَقْتُكَ, like as you may not say قَطُّ مَا أُفَارِقُكَ: (Ṣ, O:) or it denotes past time also, having the same meaning: for you say, مَا رَأَيْتُ مِثْلَهُ عَوْضُ, (AZ, Ḳ,) meaning *I have not seen the like of him,* or *it, ever:* (AZ:) so in the two books [the O and the TṢ] of Ṣgh: and in like manner a poet says,

* فَلَمْ أَرَ عَامًا عَوْضُ أَكْثَرَ هَالِكًا *

[*And I have not seen a year, ever, more destructive*]. (TA.) But it is decl. when prefixed to another noun; as in the saying, لَا أَفْعَلُهُ عَوْضَ ↑ العَائِضِينَ (Mughnee, Ḳ) *I will not do it, ever;* (TA;) and ↑ لَا آتِيكَ عَوْضَ العَائِضِينَ [*I will not come to thee, ever*]; like as one says, دَهْرَ الدَّاهِرِينَ: (Ṣ, O:) [for in this case you may not say عَوْضُ.] And one also says افعل ذَلِكَ مِنْ ذِى عَوْضٍ, [in which the first word is written in some copies of the Ṣ and Ḳ إِفْعَلْ, and in others أَفْعَلُ,] like as one says, مِنْ ذِى أُنُفٍ, (Ṣ, O, Ḳ,) and مِنْ ذِى قُبُلٍ, (Ṣ, O,) meaning [*Do thou,* or *I will do, that*] *in what is* [*now*] *to be begun* [*of time; meaning, immediately:* see أُنُفٌ]: (Ṣ, O, Ḳ:) [thus making عوض decl., and using it without a negative, which must always accompany it when it is indecl.] [See also عِوَض.] Or عَوْضُ signifies *Time;* syn. الدَّهْرُ (Ḳ) and الزَّمَانُ; (TA;) which is thus called because, as often as a portion thereof passes, it substitutes for it another portion: (Mughnee, Ḳ:) or, as some say, because they assert that it despoils and gives compensation. (Mughnee.) [See an ex. in the Ḥam p. 271, where it occurs in this sense with tenween, in the printed text, though said in the commentary to be indecl., with fet-ḥ or with ḍamm.] Or it is an oath; (Ibn-El-Kelbee, Mughnee, Ḳ,) and is (so in the O and Mughnee, but in the Ḳ "or") the name of *A certain idol, belonging to Bekr Ibn-Wáïl:* (Ṣ, Mughnee, O, Ḳ:) as in a verse cited in art. مور: (O, Mughnee:) but if so, there is no reason for its being used indeclinably in a verse of El-Aạshà cited voce أَسْحَمُ [q. v.]: (Mughnee:) or it is a word used in the manner of an oath; a man saying to his companion, عَوْضُ لَا يَكُونُ ذٰلِكَ أَبَدًا [as though meaning *Nay, that will not,* or *shall not, be, ever*]; for if it were a noun signifying *time,* it would be with tenween; but it is a particle by which is meant an oath, like أَجَلْ and نَعَمْ. (Lth, O.)

عِوَضٌ *A substitute; a thing given,* or *received,* or *put,* or *done, instead of, in place of, in lieu of,* or *in exchange for,* another thing; *a compensation; a thing given,* or *received, by way of replacement;* (O;) syn. بَدَلٌ; (M, Mṣb;) or خَلَفٌ: (A, Ḳ:) pl. أَعْوَاضٌ. (Ṣ, Mṣb.) See also مَعُوضَة. [Hence, عِوَضًا عَنْهُ *As a substitute for it; instead of, in the place of,* or *in exchange for, it; as a compensation for it;* &c.] ═ مِنْ ذِى عِوَضٍ i. q. من ذى عَوْضٍ. (TA in art. قبل.)

العُوَيْضَانِ, in the dim. form, [but whether in the sing. or dual form is not shown,] *The penis of a man:* of the dial. of El-Yemen. (TA.)

عَائِضٌ in the saying of Aboo-Moḥammad El-Faḳ'asee, (Ḳ,) i. e. (TA) in the following saying,

* هَلْ لَكِ وَالعَارِضُ مِنْكِ عَائِضُ *
* فِى هَجْمَةٍ يُغْدِرُ مِنْهَا القَابِضُ *

(Ṣ, O, TA, in this art. and in art. عرض,) is of the measure فَاعِلٌ in the sense of the measure مَفْعُولٌ, like [the epithet in the phrase] عِيشَةٌ رَاضِيَةٌ, (Ṣ, O, Ḳ,) meaning مَرْضِيَّة: (Ṣ, O:) Aṣ says that the poet is addressing a woman whom he is desirous of marrying, saying, *Art thou in want,* (*and the gift appearing from thee shall have an exchange made for it* to thee by me) *of a hundred* camels which I will assign to thee as a dowry, *some whereof the* [*quick*] *driver will abandon*, not being able to collect them together because of their large number? (Ṣ in art. عوض: [and the like is said in the O, as on the authority of Lth: but I have made a transposition in the explanation, directed in the TA, to make it agree with the order of the words of the verse:]) or the meaning is, *and the giver of a thing in exchange for* the enjoyment of *thee receiveth an exchange* from thee by marriage which is equal to that which he giveth in exchange for thee; عائض being from عُضْتُ, not from عِضْتُ: [so that, accord. to this explanation, it is used in the sense of its own proper measure, فَاعِل:] but IB says that the phrase, in his poetry, is وَالعَائِضُ مِنْكِ عَائِضُ, meaning *the thing given in exchange by thee will be* [indeed] *a substitute*, or *a compensation*; like as you say الهِبَةُ مِنْكِ هِبَةٌ: (TA in art. عوض:) the verse is also related differently, with مَائَةٍ in the place of هَجْمَةٍ, and يُسْئِرُ in the place of يُغْدِرُ. (TA.) — See also عَوْض, in two places.

مَعُوضَةٌ, (Ṣ, O, Ḳ,) like مَعُونَةٌ, (O, TA,) a subst. from عَاضَهُ; (Ṣ, O, Ḳ;) [i. e. as expl. in the TḲ, meaning خَلَفٌ and بَدَلٌ;] as also ▼عِوَضٌ. (O, Ḳ.)

عوط

1. عَاطَتْ, aor. تَعُوطُ, (Ṣ, Ḳ,) and تَعِيطُ, (Ḳ,) inf. n. عَوْطٌ (M, TA) and, accord. to some, ▼عُوطَطٌ, which others hold to be a pl. of عَائِطٌ, (A'Obeyd, Ṣ,) but Sb holds it to be a subst. having the sense of an inf. n., (TA,) and عَيْطٌ and عِيَاطٌ, (Ḳ,) *She* (a camel) *did not conceive in the first year after having been covered: nor in the next following year*: (Ṣ:) or *i. q.* ▼ اعتاطت and ▼ تعوّطت and ▼ تعيّطت, (Ḳ,) which (or the first and second of which, IDrd, O) signify *she* (a camel, IDrd, Ṣ, M, A, O, Ḳ, and a woman, A, Ḳ) *did not conceive for several years*, (Lth, IDrd, Ṣ, O, Ḳ,) *without being barren*; (Lth, Ḳ;) and sometimes this is caused by the abundance of her fat: (Lth, Ṣ:) the last three verbs also signify, (the first of them accord. to the Ḳ, and the other two also accord to the TA,) *she* (a camel) *did not conceive, having been covered*; (Ḳ, TA;) or *although her womb had attained to maturity*. (TA. [See also اعتاصت, in art. عوص.]) — [Hence the saying,] هٰذَا زَمَانٌ عَقِمَتْ فِيهِ القَرَائِحُ وَ▼اعْتَاطَتِ الأَذْهَانُ اللَّوَاقِحُ † [*This is a time in which the powers of elicitation have become unproductive, and the pregnant intellectual faculties have become fruitless*]. (A, TA.) [Hence also,] ▼ اعتاط الأَمْرُ † *The affair was*, or *became, difficult*; or *difficult and intricate*; or *impossible*; *i. q.* اعتاص. (Ṣ, O.) — See also art. عيط.

5: see 1: — and see also عَاطَتْ in art. عيط.

8: see 1, in three places.

عُوطَةٌ The *quality denoted by the epithet* عَائِطٌ, in a she-camel; as also ▼ عُوطَطٌ and ▼ عُوطُطٌ and عُيْطَطٌ [perhaps a mistake for عُيطَطٌ]. (TA.)

عُوطَطٌ and عُوطُطٌ: see 1, and عُوطَةٌ, and عَائِطٌ, this last in two places.

عَائِطٌ A she-camel *not conceiving in the first year after having been covered*: (Ks, Az, Ṣ, O:) or a she-camel, (Lth, Ḳ,) and a woman, (Ḳ,) *not conceiving for several years, without being barren*; (Lth, Ḳ;) as also ▼ مُعْتَاطٌ: (Lth, IAth, O,* TA:) and a she-camel *not conceiving when covered*; (Ḳ;) as also ▼ مُعْتَاطٌ, or ▼ مُعْتَاطَةٌ: (accord. to different copies of the Ḳ:) or *not conceiving when her womb has attained to maturity*: (TA:) ▼ مُعْتَاطٌ is also applied to a ewe or she-goat, as meaning *not conceiving, by reason of the abundance of her fat*; (IAth;) and occurs in a trad., so applied, (Ṣ, IAth,) and expl. as signifying الَّتِى لَمْ تَلِدْ وَقَدْ حَانَ وِلَادُهَا; but by this is app. meant *that has not conceived, although the time for her conceiving has come*: (IAth:) the pl. of عَائِطٌ is عُوطٌ, (Ks, Ṣ, M, O, Ḳ,) which is also applied to women, and she-goats, (M,) and عِيطٌ (Ks, Ṣ, O, Ḳ) and عُيْطٌ (M, O, Ḳ) and عَوَائِطُ (TA) and ▼ عُوطَطٌ [which is irregular, like حُوَلَلٌ,] (Ks, Ṣ, O, Ḳ) and عُوطَطٌ (accord. to the CḲ) and عُوطُطٌ, (Ḳ,) but this is a dial. var. of عُوطَطٌ accord. to those who assert it to be an inf. n., (Aṣ, O, TA,) for some assert this last to be an inf. n., not a pl., and in like manner حُوَلَلٌ, (A'Obeyd, Ṣ, O,) but Sb holds it to be a subst. in the sense of an inf. n., originally عُيْطَطٌ. (L, TA.) عَائِطٌ عِيطٌ and عَائِطٌ عُوطٌ and ▼ عَائِطٌ عُوطَطٌ (Ṣ, O, Ḳ) have an intensive signification, (Ḳ,) *Not conceiving in the first year after having been covered, nor in the next following year*; like حَائِلٌ حُولٌ and حَائِلٌ حُوَلَلٌ. (Ṣ, O.) [عِيطٌ is also pl. of أَعْيَطُ, which see in art. عيط.]

مُعْتَاطٌ, and with ة: see عَائِطٌ, in four places.

The author of the Ḳ has confounded the words belonging to this art. with those belonging to art. عيط. (TA.)

عوف

1. عَافَتِ الطَّيْرُ, (Sh, O, Ḳ,) aor. تَعُوفُ, inf. n. عَوْفٌ, (Sh, O,) *The birds circled over a thing*, (Sh, O, Ḳ,) or *over the water*, or *over carcasses* or *corpses*: or *circled over a thing, going to and fro and not going away, desiring to alight*: (Ḳ:) AA says that the medial radical is و; others say that it is ى, as will be shown in art. عيف. (TA.) — And عَافَ *He* (a man, TA) *kept*, or *clave, to the trees*, or *plants, called* عَوْف. (O, Ḳ,* TA.)

5. تعوّف *He* (a lion) *sought*, or *sought for* or *after, the prey*, by night. (TA.) [It is used as intrans. and as trans.:] see عَوْفٌ and عُوَافَةٌ.

عَافٌ *i. q.* سَهْلٌ [*A soft tract*, or *a plain*, &c.]. (O, Ḳ.)

عَوْفٌ *A state, condition*, or *case*. (Ṣ, O, Ḳ.) So in the saying, نَعِمَ عَوْفُكَ [*May thy state*, &c., *be good*, or *pleasant*]. (Ṣ, O.) One says also, أَصْبَحَ فُلَانٌ بِعَوْفِ سَوْءٍ, and بِعَوْفِ خَيْرٍ, meaning [*Such a one entered upon the morning*, or, simply, *became*,] *in an evil state*, and *in a good state*: or, accord. to some of the lexicologists, one should not say بِعَوْفِ خَيْرٍ, but only شَرٍّ [or سَوْءٍ]. (IDrd, O.) — Also *Fortune*; syn. جَدٌّ and حَظٌّ. (O, Ḳ.) And so, accord. to some, in the saying, نَعِمَ عَوْفُكَ [i. e. *May thy fortune be good*]. (O, TA.) — And *i. q.* طَائِرٌ [as meaning *An omen*]. (Ḳ, TA.) And thus it is said to signify in the form of prayer above mentioned: (TA:) [for,] as some say, the meaning is, نَعِمَ طَيْرُكَ [*May thy omen be good*]. (O, TA.) — And The ذَكَر. (O, Ḳ.) One says to a man on the morning after his first going in to his wife, نَعِمَ عَوْفُكَ, meaning thereby the ذَكَر [i. e. *May thy* ذكر *be in a good state*]. (O, TA.) A'Obeyd says, Some men used to explain (يَتَأَوَّلُ [for which يَتَنَاوَلُ is erroneously put in the O]) العَوْف as the فَرْج [meaning the ذَكَر], and I mentioned it to AA, and he disapproved it: (Ṣ, O, TA:) but a verse has been cited in which عَوْفِى [certainly] means ذَكَرِى. (TA.) — And *A guest*. (Lth, O, Ḳ.) And thus it has been expl. as used in the saying, نَعِمَ عَوْفُكَ. (O,* TA.) — And The *cock*. (O, Ḳ.) — And The *lion*: because he seeks his prey (▼يَتَعَوَّفُ) by night. (O, Ḳ.) — And The *wolf*. (O, Ḳ.) — And *One who toils*, or *seeks the means of subsistence, for his household*, or *family*. (IAṭr, O, Ḳ.) — And *A certain idol*. (O, Ḳ.) — And *A species of trees*; (O;) or *a species of plants*, (AḤn, O, Ḳ,) *of the plants of the desert*, (AḤn, O,) *of sweet odour*. (AḤn, O, Ḳ.) — أُمُّ عَوْفٍ *The* جَرَادَة, (Ṣ, O,) [i. e.] the *female of the* جَرَاد [or *locust*]. (Ḳ.) And أَبُو عَوْفٍ *The* جَرَاد [meaning the *male locust*]. (Az, O, Ḳ.) — Also (i. e. عَوْفٌ) *a good manner of tending* or *pasturing* [cattle]: (O, Ḳ:) [or rather, simply,] the *tending* or *pasturing* [cattle]: so in the saying, إِنَّهُ لَحَسَنُ العَوْفِ فِى إِبِلِهِ [*Verily he is one who has a good quality of tending, or pasturing, in respect of his camels*]. (TA.)

عُوَافٌ: see عُوَافَةٌ.

أُمُّ عُوَيْفٍ *A small creeping thing* (دُوَيْبَّة), *other than the* جَرَادَة [which is termed أُمُّ عَوْفٍ]. (TA.) — And, accord. to AHát, أَبُو عَوْفٍ *A species of the* [*beetles called*] جِعْلَان [pl. of جُعَلٌ]: it is a *small creeping thing* (دُوَيْبَّة), *dust-coloured, that excavates with its tail and with its two horns, and* [*then*] *never appears*. (TA.)

عُوَافَةٌ (O, Ḳ) and ▼ عُوَافٌ (Ḳ) The *prey which the lion seeks* (مَا يَتَعَوَّفُهُ ▼ الأَسَدُ) *by night, and which he devours*. (O, Ḳ.) — And (both words, Ḳ) *A thing that becomes*, or *has become, an acquisition of any one* (O, Ḳ, TA) *by night*. (TA.)

عوق

1. عَاقَهُ, aor. يَعُوقُهُ, (Ṣ, O, Mṣb,) inf. n. عَوْقٌ, (Ṣ, O, Mṣb, Ḳ,) with which عَيْقٌ [as inf. n. of

عَاقَهُ having يَعِيقُهُ for its aor.] is syn.; (O and Ḳ in art. عيق;) and ▾ اعتاقهُ, (Ṣ, O,) inf. n. إِعْتِيَاقٌ; (Ḳ;) and ▾ اعاقهُ [if not a mistranscription for اعتاقهُ]; (Mṣb;) and ▾ عوّقهُ, (Mṣb,) inf. n. تَعْوِيقٌ; (Ṣ, O, Ḳ;) and ▾ تعوّقهُ; (IJ, TA;) *He, or it, hindered, prevented, impeded,* or *withheld, him;* (Ṣ, O, Mṣb, Ḳ, TA;) *turned him back* or *away; retarded him;* or *diverted him by occupying him otherwise;* (Ṣ, O, Ḳ, TA;) عَنْ كَذَا [*from such a thing*]; (Ṣ, O, TA;) and عَنِ الوَجْهِ الَّذِى أَرَادَهُ [*from the course that he desired to pursue*]. (TA.) [Accord. to the Ṣ and O and Ḳ, the first is *syn. with* حَبَسَهُ and صَرَفَهُ, and so is the last accord. to IJ and the TA, as is the second accord. to the Ṣ and O, and so app. are this and the fourth accord. to the Ḳ; and accord. to the Ṣ and O and Ḳ and TA, the fourth is *syn. with* ثَبَّطَهُ, as are also the first and second accord. to the Ḳ and TA: accord. to the Mṣb, the first and third and fourth are *syn. with* مَنَعَهُ.] And عَقَاهُ signifies the same as عَاقَهُ and عوّقهُ and اعتاقهُ. (TA.) —— مَا عَاقَتْ عِنْدَ زَوْجِهَا وَلَا لَاقَتْ, (Ṣ,) or مَا عَاقَتْ وَلَا لَاقَتْ عِنْدَ زَوْجِهَا, (O, Ḳ,) means *She did not cleave, or stick, to the heart of her husband;* (Ṣ, O, Ḳ, TA;) to which IḲṭṭ adds, *and did not hinder him from separating himself from her,* or *marrying another:* and some say that it means *she was not happy with her husband; near to his heart; in favour with him,* or *beloved by him:* and some, that عَاقَتْ is an imitative adjunct to لَاقَتْ, because the latter signifies لَصِقَتْ. (TA.)

2: see the first sentence above.

4. اعاقهُ: see 1, first sentence. —— أَعْوَقَ بِىَ الدَّابَّةُ, or الزَّادُ, *The beast,* or *the travelling-provision,* [*by failing me,*] *disabled me from prosecuting my journey;* syn. قَطَعَ. (Ibn-'Abbád, O, Ḳ.) —— And أَعْوَقَ عَنِّى *It caused me to be in difficulty* (أَعْوَصَنِى), *so that I was unable to accomplish it.* (Ibn-'Abbád, O.)

5. تعوّق *He became hindered, prevented, impeded, withheld, turned back* or *away, retarded,* or *diverted by being occupied otherwise;* عَنْ أَمْرٍ [*from an affair;*] syn. تَثَبَّطَ. (Ṣ, O, Ḳ.) —— تعوّقهُ: see 1, first sentence.

8. اعتاقهُ: see 1, first sentence. —— [Accord. to Freytag, اعتاق also signifies *He was detained,* or *retained,* (*retentus fuit,*) with, or at the abode of, any one: and *he was bound.*]

عَاقِ عَاقِ, (thus in copies of the Ḳ,) or [correctly] عَاقٍ عَاقٍ, like غَاقٍ غَاقٍ, (Lḥ, O,) *The cry of the crow;* (Lḥ, O, Ḳ;) an imitation thereof. (Ḳ.)

عَوْقٌ [an inf. n.: and also used as an epithet, signifying] One *who hinders, prevents, impedes,* &c., [see 1,] *people from that which is good;* as also ▾ عَوْقَةٌ [but app. in an intensive sense]. (Ḳ. [See also عُوَّقٌ.]) —— See also عَائِقٌ, in two places. —— And see عُوقٌ. —— Also *A place of bending,* or *inclining, of a valley, to the right* or *left.* (O, Ḳ.) —— And *Time:* so in the saying, لَا يَكُونُ ذٰلِكَ آخِرَ عَوْقٍ [*That will not be to the end of time*]. (Ḳ.)

عُوقٌ A man *in whom,* (O,) or *with whom,* (Ḳ,) *is no good;* (O, Ḳ;) as also ▾ عَوْقٌ; (Ḳ;) occurring in the saying of Ru-beh,

* فِدَاكَ مِنْهُمْ كُلُّ عُوقٍ أَصْلَدُ *

[*May every one of them in whom, or with whom, is no good, who is niggardly, be thy ransom*]: (TA:) pl. أَعْوَاقٌ. (Ḳ.) —— See also عَائِقٌ.

عُوقٌ *Hunger:* (O, Ḳ:) like عُولَقٌ. (O.)

عَوَقٌ: see عُوقٌ: —— and عَائِقٌ. —— Also *Hungry:* [a meaning indicated, but not expressed, in the O and Ḳ:] you say رَجُلٌ عَوَقٌ لَوَقٌ [*A very hungry man*]; (IAạr, O, Ḳ;) لَوَقٌ being an imitative [and corroborative] sequent. (TA in art. لوق.)

عَوِقٌ and ▾ عُوَقَةٌ (Ṣ, O, Ḳ) and ▾ عِوَقٌ, (Ḳ,) which last is from IAạr, and is by some written ▾ عُوَقٌ, (TA,) and ▾ عَيِّقٌ and ▾ عَيَّقٌ, this last with fet-ḥ, (Ḳ,) i. e. with fet-ḥ and teshdeed to the ى, (TA, [but in the CḲ عَيْقٌ,]) A man *having the quality of hindering, preventing, impeding, retarding,* or *diverting by otherwise occupying,* (Ṣ, O, Ḳ, TA,) *men from that which is good, and his companions, because accidents diverting him from his course prevent his attaining the object of his want:* (TA: [see also عَوْقٌ:]) and (O, Ḳ) IDrd says, (O,) ▾ عُوَّقٌ, (O, Ḳ,) thus with teshdeed accord. to El-Arzenee and Aboo-Sahl El-Harawee, applied to a man, (O,) signifies one *who hinders, prevents, impedes,* &c., *men from* [*accomplishing*] *their affairs:* (O, Ḳ:) or it signifies, (Ḳ,) or signifies also, accord. to IDrd, (O,) *a coward,* or *cowardly;* (O, Ḳ;) in this sense peculiar to the dial. of Hudheyl; (O;) and so عُوَّقٌ: and عَوِقٌ is also *syn. with* ▾ عَائِقٌ: (Ḳ:) thus it means accord. to Aboo-Usámeh, as an epithet applied to a man: (O:) and ▾ عُوَّقٌ (O, Ḳ) accord. to him (O) is pl. of ▾ عَائِقٌ: (O, Ḳ:) and عَوِقٌ and ▾ عُوَّقٌ both signify also one *whom affairs cease not to hinder, prevent, impede,* &c., *from* [*accomplishing*] *the object of his want:* and one *who, when he purposes a thing, does it:* (Ḳ:) thus they are expl. by Ibn-'Abbád; as though having two contr. significations. (O.)

عُوَقٌ: see عَوِقٌ, first signification.

عَوْقَةٌ: see عَوْقٌ.

عُوَقَةٌ: see عَوِقٌ, first signification.

عُوَاقٌ *A sound that issues from the belly of a beast,* or *horse* or *the like, when he is going along;* (O, Ḳ;) as also وُعَاقٌ: (O:) and some say, *a sound* of anything. (TA.)

عَوِيقٌ The *sound of the sheath of the penis of the horse;* as also وَعِيقٌ. (TA.)

عَائِقٌ and ▾ عَوْقٌ and ▾ عُوقٌ and ▾ عَوَقٌ all signify the same; (Ḳ, TA;) i. e. [A person, or thing,] *hindering, preventing, impeding, withholding, turning back* or *away, retarding,* or *diverting by occupying otherwise:* (TA:) see also عَوِقٌ, in two places: the pl. of the first is عُوَّقٌ. (O, Ḳ.) One says, عَاقَنِى عَائِقٌ (Ḳ, TA) and عَقَانِى عَاقٍ (TA) [*A hinderer* or *hindrance,* or *an impeder* or *impediment,* &c., *hindered me,* or *impeded me,* &c.,] عَنِ الأَمْرِ الَّذِى أَرَدْتُ [*from the thing that I desired to do*]. (TA.) And عَوَائِقُ الدَّهْرِ signifies *The accidents,* or *casualties, of time* or *fortune, that divert* [or *hinder* or *impede*] *by busying* or *occupying* or *employing:* (Ṣ, O, Ḳ, TA:) the former noun being pl. of عَائِقَةٌ, or anomalously of ▾ عَوْقٌ. (TA.)

عُوَّقٌ: see عَوِقٌ, in three places.

عَيِّقٌ and عَيَّقٌ: see عَوِقٌ, first signification. —— It is also used as an imitative sequent: one says ضَيِّقٌ عَيِّقٌ (Ḳ) or ضَيِّقٌ لَيِّقٌ عَيِّقٌ (IAạr, TA) [app. meaning *Very niggardly*]: or, as some say, عَيِّقٌ signifies as expl. voce عَوِقٌ, and is not an imitative sequent. (TA.)

العَيُّوقُ *A red* [?] *bright star in,* or *on, the right* [?] *edge of the Milky Way, following, not preceding,* الثُّرَيَّا [*the Pleiades*]; *rising before* الجَوْزَآء [by which may be meant either *Orion* or *Gemini*]: (TA:) when it has risen, it is known that الثُّرَيَّا has risen: (O:) [it is the well-known name of the star *Capella,* notwithstanding its being described above as "red," and as in, or on, the "right" of the Milky Way; for Capella, though not now red, has been observed to alter in brightness by astronomers in very recent times; and I think that the word rendered above "right," which is أَيْمَن, is probably a mistranscription for أَيْسَر, i. e. "left:" the description here following plainly indicates Capella:] it is *the bright star* [α] *upon the left shoulder of Auriga:* that upon the left elbow is العَنَزُ: the two on the left wrist together with العَيُّوق are called العِنَازُ: [see عَنْزٌ:] it is also called the رَقِيب [or watcher] of الثُّرَيَّا, because it rises therewith at many places: and the star on the right shoulder [i. e. β] with the two upon the ankle-joints [which may be θ and ι, for the constellation is variously figured,] are called تَوَابِعُ العَيُّوقِ: (Ḳzw:) it is [said to be] called العيّوق because of its [being regarded as] impeding الدَّبَرَان from meeting الثُّرَيَّا: (TA:) عَيُّوقٌ, (Lth, Az, Ṣ, O,) is originally عَيْوُوقٌ, (Ṣ, O,) its medial radical being و; or it may be ى. (Lth, Az, TA.) One says also, هٰذَا عَيُّوقٌ طَالِعًا [meaning *This is* العَيُّوق *rising*]; suppressing the ال, but meaning it to be understood, and therefore leaving the word itself in its former determinate state [without tenween]. (IAạr, TA.)

مُعْوَقٌ One who is *disappointed of attaining his object* [by the failing of his beast or of his travelling-provision: see أَعْوَقَ]; syn. مُنْقَطَعٌ. (Ibn-'Abbád, O, Ḳ.) —— And *Hungry.* (Ibn-'Abbád, O, Ḳ.)

يَعُوقُ *A certain idol which pertained to the*

people of Noah: (Ṣ, O, Ḳ:) or originally *a certain righteous man in his age, of whom and of seven other righteous men after him, by the direction of the Devil, were made images, which in process of time became objects of worship:* (Lth, O, Ḳ:) or *a certain idol which pertained to [the tribe of] Kinánah,* (Zj, TA,) or *to Murád.* (Ksh and Bḍ in lxxi. 23.) [See also وُدّ.]

عول

1. عَالَ عِيَالَهُ, (Ṣ, Mgh, O, Mṣb,* Ḳ, TA,) aor. يَعُولُ, (Ṣ, O, Mṣb,) inf. n. عَوْلٌ (Ṣ, O, Mṣb, Ḳ) and عِيَالَةٌ (Ṣ, O, Ḳ) and عُوُولٌ; (Ḳ;) *He fed, nourished,* or *sustained, his family,* or *household,* (Ṣ, Mgh, O, Mṣb,* Ḳ, [in the Mṣb, اليَتِيمَ, *the orphan,*]) *and expended upon them:* (Ṣ, Mgh, O:) or *he supplied them with what they needed of food and clothing and other things:* (TA:) and ▼أَعَالَهُمْ and ▼عَيَّلَهُمْ signify the same. (Ḳ.) One says, عُلْتُهُ شَهْرًا *I supplied him with his means of subsistence for a month.* (Ṣ, O.) And it is said in a trad., اِبْدَأْ بِمَنْ تَعُولُ i. e. [*Begin thou*] *with those whom thou sustainest, and whose expenses are incumbent on thee;* and if anything remain over and above, let it be for the strangers, or those who are not related to thee. (TA.) ═ And عال, (Ks, Ḳ, TA,) aor. as above, (Ks, TA,) inf. n. عَوْلٌ and عِيَالَةٌ (Ḳ, TA) and عُوُولٌ, (TA,) *He had a numerous family* or *household;* (Ḳ, TA;) [and] so ▼اعال, (Z, Mgh, O, Mṣb,) and ▼أَعْوَلَ, (Z, O, Ḳ,) and ▼أَعْيَلَ, (Mṣb, Ḳ, TA,) this last formed by the change of و into ى, (TA,) [or formed from عِيَالٌ,] and عيل [i. e. ▼عَيَّلَ]: (Mṣb:) ▼اعال is also expl. as meaning [simply] *he had a family,* or *household:* and ▼أَعْوَلَتْ, occurring in a trad., as meaning *she brought forth children,* is said by IAth to be originally أَعْيَلَتْ, signifying *she had a family,* or *household;* but Z says that اعيلت is formed with a regard to the word عِيَالٌ, and is not the original form. (TA.) [See also 4 in art. عيل.] مَا لَهُ عَالَ وَمَالَ is a form of imprecation, meaning [*What ails him?*] *May he have a numerous family* or *household, and may he decline from the right course in his judgment.* (Ḳ. [See another explanation in art. عيل.]) And the saying, in the Ḳur [iv. 3], ذٰلِكَ أَدْنَى أَلَّا تَعُولُوا has been expl. as meaning [*That will be more,* or *most, apt, fit,* or *proper,*] *that ye may not have numerous families* or *households.* (TA.) —— [Hence, probably,] عال, aor. as above, [and يَعِيلُ, (see 1 in art. عيل,)] signifies also *He* (a man) *was,* or *became, poor;* (Ks, TA;) [and] so ▼اعال. (Ḳ.) And Yoo says that لَا يَعُولُ عَلَى القَصْدِ أَحَدٌ signifies لَا يَحْتَاجُ [app. meaning *No one will become poor,* or *in want, while following the right course*]: (TA:) and so لَا يَعِيلُ. (TA in art. عيل.) ═ عال المِيزَانُ, (Ṣ, Mgh, O, Mṣb, Ḳ,) aor. يَعُولُ and يَعِيلُ, (Ḳ, TA,) inf. n. عَوْلٌ and عَيْلٌ, (TA,) *The balance inclined,* or *declined,* (Ṣ, Mgh, O, Mṣb,) *and rose:* (Mgh, Mṣb:) or *one of its extremities rose above the other:* (TA:) or *it was,* or *became, defective, and declined from the right state:* or [in the CḲ "and"] *it was,* or *became, excessive.* (Ḳ, TA.) And [hence,] عال فِي المِيزَانِ † *He was,* or *became, unfaithful;* or *he acted unfaithfully.* (Mṣb.) A poet says,

قَالُوا ٱتَّبَعْنَا رَسُولَ ٱللّٰهِ وَٱطَّرَحُوا

قَوْلَ الرَّسُولِ وَعَالُوا فِى المَوَازِينِ

[*They said, "We have followed the way of the Apostle of God:" but they have rejected the saying of the Apostle,* † *and been false in the balances,* i. e., *unfaithful*]. (Ṣ, O.) —— And عال, (inf. n. عَوْلٌ, Mṣb,) *He* (a judge, Mgh) *deviated from the right course,* or *acted wrongfully,* (Ṣ, Mgh, O, Mṣb, Ḳ,) فِى الحُكْمِ [*in the judgment*]. (Ṣ, O.) Hence, in the Ḳur [iv. 3, mentioned above], أَلَّا تَعُولُوا [*that ye may not deviate from the right course*], (Ṣ, Mgh, O, Mṣb, TA,) accord. to Mujáhid, (Ṣ, O, Mṣb,) and most of the expositors. (TA.) —— And hence, (Ṣ, Mgh, O,) in the opinion of A'Obeyd, (Ṣ, O,) عَالَتِ الفَرِيضَةُ, (Ṣ, Mgh, O, Mṣb, Ḳ,) aor. تَعُولُ, (TA,) inf. n. عَوْلٌ, (Ṣ, Mgh, O, Mṣb,) *The* فَرِيضَة [or *primarily-apportioned inheritance*] *deviated* [*by excess*] *from the limit of the named* [*primary*] *portions* [which are all fractions of four and twenty]; (Bḍ in iv. 3;) [meaning] *it rose* [*above*], (Ṣ, O, Mṣb, Ḳ,) or *exceeded,* (Ḳ,) in the reckoning, (Mṣb, Ḳ,) [*the regular sum of the fixed primary portions,*] i. e., *its* [*fixed primary*] *portions exceeded* [*the regular sum thereof*], *occasioning a diminution to the sharers:* (Ṣ, Mgh, O, Mṣb:) العَوْلُ in this case being *the contr. of* الرَّدّ [which I do not find in any lexicon, but only in dictionaries of conventional terms]. (Mṣb.) As relates, of El-Mufaḍḍal, that, application having been made to him respecting [the shares of inheritance of] two daughters and a father and a mother and a wife, said, "Her [the wife's] eighth has become a ninth:" and A'Obeyd says, he meant that the [primary] portions had exceeded [the regular sum] so that there fell to the wife the ninth, whereas in the original case she would have had the eighth; for if the فريضة had not exceeded [the regular sum], it would have consisted of four and twenty; but when it [so] exceeded, it became of seven and twenty; and there pertained to the two daughters the two thirds [of four and twenty], i. e. sixteen portions; and to the father and the mother the two sixths, i. e. eight portions; and to the wife three reckoned as of seven and twenty, i. e. the ninth, whereas, before the exceeding, it would have been three of four and twenty, i. e. the eighth: and this question is called المَسْأَلَةُ المِنْبَرِيَّةُ, because 'Alee was asked respecting it when he was on the pulpit, and said, without premeditation, "Her eighth has become a ninth." (TA.) Hence the saying, in a trad. of Maryam, [i. e. the Virgin Mary, respecting a story to which allusion is made in the Ḳur iii. 39, (see a note on that verse in Sale's Translation,)] وَعَالَ قَلَمُ زَكَرِيَّآءَ i. e. [*And the divining-arrow of Zacharias*] *rose upon the water.* (TA.) —— And one says also, عال زَيْدٌ الفَرَائِضَ, (Ṣ, Mgh, O,) or الفَرِيضَةَ, (Mṣb,) first pers. عُلْتُهَا, (Ḳ,) meaning *Zeyd made the* فرائض, or فريضة, *to be as described above;* as also ▼أَعَالَهَا; (Ṣ, Mgh, O, Mṣb, Ḳ;*) which latter is the more common. (Mṣb.) —— عال said of an affair, or event, *It was,* or *became, hard to be borne, severe,* or *distressing,* and *great,* or *formidable.* (Ṣ, O, Ḳ.) —— And also, (Ṣ, O, Ḳ,) aor. يَعُولُ, (Ṣ, O,) inf. n. عَوْلٌ, (TA,) *It* (a thing) *overcame* a person; *burdened,* or *oppressed,* him; (Ṣ, O, Ḳ;) *distressed* him; (Fr, O;) and *disquieted* him, or *rendered* him *anxious.* (Ḳ.) [See an ex. in a verse cited voce مَسَافَةٌ, in art. سوف.] One says, عِيلَ مَا هُوَ عَائِلُهُ i. e. غُلِبَ مَا هُوَ غَالِبُهُ [*May he be overcome! Of what is he the overcomer?*]: (Ṣ, Meyd, O, Ḳ:) a prov., (Meyd,) applied to him at whose speech, or some other thing proceeding from him, (Ṣ, Meyd, O, Ḳ,) of a like sort, (Ḳ,) one wonders: (Ṣ, Meyd, O, Ḳ:) it is of the nature of a prayer, (Ṣ, Meyd, O,) for the man; (Meyd;) like the saying, when a thing pleases one, قَاتَلَهُ ٱللّٰهُ, and أَخْزَاهُ ٱللّٰهُ. (TA.) And عِيلَ صَبْرِى *My patience was overcome;* (Ṣ, O, Ḳ;) and so عَالَ صَبْرِى: (Abu-l-Jarráḥ, Lḥ, Ḳ:) or, accord. to Aboo-Ṭálib, the former may mean رُفِعَ [i. e., *was taken away,* lit. *raised;* and if so, the latter may in like manner mean اِرْتَفَعَ]. (TA.) عَالَتِ البَقُورَ, occurring in a verse of Umeiyeh Ibn-Abi-ṣ-Ṣalt, refers to a year of drought, and means *It oppressed the* [*wild*] *oxen,* by occasioning their having سَلَع and عُشَر tied to their tails and set on fire, and being made to ascend upon the mountain; by the doing of which, the Arabs asserted that they obtained rain. (Ṣ, O. [See art. سلع.]) —— عَالَكَ عَالِيًا [in which عَالَكَ app. signifies properly رَفَعَكَ, the agent (ٱللّٰهُ) being understood,] is like the saying لَعًا لَكَ عَالِيًا, (Ḳ, TA, [in the CḲ لَعا لَكَ,]) and is expl. in the T as meaning *Mayest thou rise,* or *be raised, after stumbling,* or *falling.* (TA.) —— عِيلَ عَوْلُهُ [app. signifying lit. *May the wailing for him be raised* (in the CḲ عَوْلَةٌ)] means *may his mother be bereft of him;* as also عَالَ عَوْلُهُ. (Ḳ, TA.)

2. عَيَّلَهُمْ [app. formed from عِيَالٌ, in which the ى is originally و]: see 1, first sentence. —— It signifies also *He made them to become what are termed* عِيَال [i. e. *a family,* or *household*]: or *he neglected them:* (Ḳ:) or تَعْيِيلٌ signifies the *feeding badly.* (Ṣ and O in art. عيل.) ═ عيّل as intrans.: see 1, fourth sentence. ═ عوّل عَلَيْهِ *He acted,* or *behaved, with boldness,* or *presumptuousness, towards him;* or *confided in his love, and therefore acted presumptuously towards him;* and *he put,* or *imposed as a burden, upon him* [some affair]; (AZ, Ṣ, O, Ḳ;) as also ▼أَعْوَلَ عَلَيْهِ, (Ḳ, TA,) part. n. ▼مُعْوِلٌ. (TA.) One says, عَوَّلْتُ عَلَى فُلَانٍ *I put,* or *imposed as a burden, upon such a one, somewhat of my affair:* and عَوِّلْ عَلَىَّ *Put thou,* or *impose thou as a burden, upon me what thou desirest.* (Ḥam p. 125.) —— And *He asked aid of him;* (Ḳ, TA;) as also عوّل بِهِ.

(TA.) One says, عَوِّلْ عَلَىَّ بِمَا شِئْتَ *Ask thou aid of me in what thou wilt*; as though he said, *put thou*, or *impose thou as a burden, upon me, what thou likest.* (Ṣ, O.) — And *He relied upon it*, or *confided in it*; (Mṣb, Ḳ;) namely, a thing; as also عوّل بِهِ; inf. n. تَعْوِيلٌ (Mṣb) and ↓ مُعَوَّلٌ, (Ḳ, TA,) thus on the authority of Th, who thus explains it in the saying, (TA,) of Imra-el-Ḳeys, (O,)

وَإِنَّ شِفَائِى عَبْرَةٌ مُهْرَاقَةٌ •
فَهَلْ عِنْدَ رَسْمٍ دَارِسٍ مِنْ مُعَوَّلِ •

[*When verily my cure is a flow of tears poured forth: but is there reliance*, or *confidence*, to be felt *at the remains of an abode becoming rased*, or *effaced?*]: or ↓ مُعَوَّل is here an inf. n. of عَوَّلْتُ in the sense of أَعْوَلْتُ, i. e. بَكَيْتُ; so that the meaning is, *weeping*: (TA:) or it here means *a place of weeping*: or, as some say, *a seeking of any means of profiting.* (O. [See also EM pp. 6 and 7.]) One says likewise, ↓ عَلَيْهِ المُعَوَّلُ, meaning [*Upon him is placed*] *reliance.* (TA.) — See also 4. — And عوّل, (Ḳ, and Ḥam p. 125,) or عوّل عَالَةً, (Ṣ, O,) inf. n. تَعْوِيلٌ, (Ḳ,) signifies *He* (a pastor, Ḥam) *made*, or *constructed, a shelter from the rain, termed* عالة, (Ṣ, O, Ḳ, and Ḥam* ubi suprà,) *by binding some branches of a tree to some branches of a tree near to the former, and then covering them with small lopped wood such as is used for firewood.* (Ḥam.)

4. أَعَالَهُمْ: see 1, first sentence. — اعال and أَعْوَلَ and أَعْيَلَ as intrans.: see 1, former half, in six places. — اعال الفَرِيضَةَ or اعال الفَرَائِضَ: see 1, latter half. — See also 2, former half. — أَعْوَلَ (Sh, Ṣ, O, Ḳ) and ↓ عوّل (Sh, O, Ḳ) *He wept*; (O;) as also ↓ اِعْتَوَلَ: (O, Ḳ:) or *he wailed*; i. e. *raised his voice with weeping*, (Ṣ, Ḳ,) *and cried out*; (Ḳ;) or *wept, and cried out*; عَلَيْهِ *for him*: (Sh, O, Mṣb:) and an instance occurs, in a verse of 'Obeyd-Allah Ibn-'Abd-Allah Ibn-'Otbeh, cited by Th, of اعول trans. by itself, عَلَى being suppressed. (TA.) — [Hence,] one says also, أَعْوَلَتِ القَوْسُ † *The bow produced a sound*: (Ṣ, M, O, Ḳ, TA:) in some lexicons, as in the L, erroneously, القَوْسَ. (TA.) — And اعال and أَعْوَلَ (AZ, O, Ḳ, and Ṣ in art. عيل) and أَعْيَلَ (Ḳ) signify *He* (a man, Ḳ) *desired vehemently, eagerly, greedily, very greedily*, or *with avidity*; or *did so excessively*, or *culpably*; or *coveted*; (AZ, Ṣ, O, Ḳ;) part. ns. ↓ مُعْوِلٌ and ↓ مُعْيِلٌ. (TA.)

8. اِعْتَوَلَ: see the next preceding paragraph.

عَالٌ a word occurring in the saying مَا لَهُ عَالٌ وَلَا مَالٌ, which means *He has not anything belonging to him.* (Ḳ.)

عَوْلٌ: see عَوِيلٌ. — عَوْلٌ is a word like وَيْبٌ: one says, عَوْلَكَ and عَوْلَ زَيْدٍ [i. e. May God decree *thy woe* and *the woe of Zeyd*, virtually meaning *woe to thee* and *woe to Zeyd*]: (Ṣ, O, Ḳ:) and عَوْلٌ لِزَيْدٍ [lit. meaning *Woe to Zeyd*]: (Ṣ, O:) or, accord. to Sb and others, عَوْلٌ is used only as a sequent to وَيْلٌ; they said وَيْلَهُ وَعَوْلَهُ; in which, Az says, ويل and عول both signify *weeping*, or *lamentation with tears*; and Aboo-Ṭálib says that they are put in the accus. case as expressive of an imprecation and of blame, like as is done in the sayings تُرَابًا لَهُ and وَيْلًا لَهُ. (TA.) — Also *Any affair*, or *event, that renders one anxious*: (Ḳ,* TA:) app. an inf. n. used thus as a subst. (TA.) — And One *whose aid is asked* (Ḳ, TA) *in affairs of difficulty* or *importance.* (TA. [See also مُعَوَّلٌ.]) — And The *food of a family* or *household.* (Ḳ.)

عَوَلٌ: see the next paragraph.

عِوَلٌ is [said to be] a subst. signifying *Reliance*, and *confidence*: (Ṣ,* Ḳ, TA:) and [it is said that] هُوَ عِوَلِى signifies *He is my stay*, or *support*: the word, however, occurs in this form, twice, in a verse of Taäbbaṭa-sharrà, accord. to the relation thereof by Aboo-'Ikrimeh; but accord. to others it is ↓ عَوَلٌ, with fet-ḥ to the ع and و, and is said to be an inf. n.; whereas the former is said to be pl. of ↓ عَوْلَةٌ; [and the two words signify, respectively, *a weeping* and *weepings*; for] by his saying

• لَكِنَّمَا عِوَلِى إِنْ كُنْتُ ذَا عِوَلِ •

the poet means *If I wept* for any one, *I would weep* &c. (TA.) — And عَوَلٌ is also a subst. signifying *An asking for aid.* (Ḳ, TA.)

عَالَةٌ *A* ظُلَّة [or *covering*], (Ḳ,) or *a thing like a* ظُلَّة, (Ṣ, O,) *used as a shelter from the rain*, (Ṣ, O, Ḳ,) *constructed with cuttings of trees* [*in a manner described above*: see 2, last sentence]. (TA.) — And *i. q.* نَعَامَةٌ, (Kr, Ḳ,) either as meaning The *species of animal thus called* [i. e. *an ostrich*], or as meaning *a* ظُلَّة, for thus نَعَامَةٌ also signifies. (TA.) — [As a pl.: see عِيَالٌ.] — See also art. عيل.

عَوْلَةٌ: see the next paragraph, in two places: and see also عِوَلٌ.

عَوِيلٌ *A wailing*; i. e. *a raising of the voice with weeping*; as also ↓ عَوْلٌ and ↓ عَوْلَةٌ: (Ṣ, O, Ḳ:) or *a weeping and crying out*: (Mṣb:) and sometimes it signifies *a cry*, or *voice, from the chest, without weeping*: (O, TA:) and sometimes ↓ عَوْلَةٌ signifies the *burning sensation of grief* and *of love, without a raising of the voice and without weeping.* (TA.) [See also عَوَّالٌ.] — Also *Weak*: — and hence it is used as a name for *One of the ropes of a ship* or boat. (TA.)

عِيَالٌ, belonging to this art. and to art. عيل; (Ḳ, mentioned in the Ṣ and O in the latter art.;) or its ى is substituted for و, for it is from عَالَ, aor. يَعُولُ, in the first of the senses expl. above, and seems to be an inf. n. used in the sense of a pass. part. n.; (IB, TA;) [and if so, it may be used as a sing. (as it is in the Ksh and by Bḍ in xvi. 78 and in the Ṣ and Mgh &c. voce كَلٌّ and in the O and Ḳ voce حَمِيلَةٌ) and also as a pl.; but in general] it signifies *A family*, or *household*; (Mṣb;) [i. e.,] a man's عِيَال are the *persons whom he feeds, nourishes*, or *sustains*; (Ṣ, O, Mṣb, Ḳ;) or the *persons who dwell with him, and whose expenses are incumbent on him, as his young man*, or *slave, his wife, and his young child*: (KT:) and ↓ عَيِّلٌ signifies the same: (Ḳ:) or this latter (which is originally عَيْوِلٌ, TA) is sing. of عِيَالٌ (Ṣ, Mgh, O, Mṣb) and of عَيَائِلُ, (Ṣ, O,) like as جَيِّدٌ is sing. of جِيَادٌ (Ṣ, Mgh, O, Mṣb) and of جَيَائِدُ; (Ṣ, O;) the last being a pl. pl., (Ḳ in art. عيل,) [as also عِيَالَاتٌ, of which see an ex. voce أَزْمَلُ;] but is sometimes used as a pl., for عَشَرَةٌ عَيِّلٌ, accord. to an ex. in a trad., signifies *ten persons fed, nourished*, or *sustained, by a man*: (TA:) or the pl. [of ↓ عَيِّلٌ] is عَالَةٌ, (Kr, Ḳ,) [like as سَادَةٌ is said to be pl. of سَيِّدٌ;] or, accord. to ISd, it is pl. of عَائِلٌ, [q. v. in art. عيل, and in like manner سَادَةٌ is held by him to be pl. of سَائِدٌ, not of سَيِّدٌ,] for [he says that] a word of the measure فَيْعِلٌ never forms a pl. [like عَالَةٌ, which is] of the measure فَعَلَةٌ; (TA;) and [عَيَائِلُ is applied to women, for] one says نِسْوَةٌ عَيَائِلُ. (Ḳ.) — العِيَالُ [as meaning † *The dependants for sustenance*] is also used, metaphorically, in relation to birds, and to predaceous and other beasts. (TA.) And أُمُّ العِيَالِ is a name for † *The cooking-pot.* (T in art. امر.)

عَوَالَةٌ *Want*: and *intrusion at feasts, uninvited.* (TA.)

عَوَّالٌ *A weeping*: an inf. n. [or rather a quasi-inf. n.] of عَوَّلَ: pl. عَوَاوِيلُ, and by poetic license عَوَاوِلُ. (TA.) [See also عَوِيلٌ.]

عَائِلٌ [act. part. n. of عَالَ]. — One says أَمْرٌ عَائِلٌ and عَالٍ, the latter being formed by transposition, meaning [*An affair*, or *event*,] *hard to be borne, severe*, or *distressing*, and *great*, or *formidable.* (TA.) — عَائِلٌ applied to a measure of capacity means *Exceeding others.* (IAạr, TA in art. عيل.)

عَيِّلٌ: see عِيَالٌ, in two places.

أَعْوَلُ *i. q.* أَشَدُّ [*More, and most, hard to be borne*, &c.]: and أَعْلَى, occurring in a verse of Aboo-Dhu-eyb, signifies the same, being formed from أَعْوَلُ by transposition. (TA.)

مَعُولٌ [*Fed, nourished*, or *sustained*: &c. — And] *Overcome*: applied in this sense to patience: (Ḳ:) and to a man, in respect of his opinion, or judgment. (TA.)

مُعَوَّلٌ, followed by عَلَيْهِ, *Wailed for*: thus in the trad., المُعَوَّلُ عَلَيْهِ يُعَذَّبُ, (Ṣ, O,) or, as some relate it, ↓ المُعْوَلُ; i. e. *He* (of the dead) *who is wailed for will be punished.* (O.)

مُعْوِلٌ: see 2: — and see also 4, last sentence.

مِعْوَلٌ [*A pickaxe*, or *stone-cutter's pick*; (so in the present day;)] the *iron implement*, (Ḳ,) *a* large فَأْس, (Ṣ, O, Mṣb,) *with which are pecked,* or *hollowed out,* (Ṣ, O, Ḳ,) *rocks,* or *great masses of stone,* (Ṣ, O,) or *mountains:* (Ḳ:) pl. مَعَاوِلُ. (Ṣ, O.) [See also صَاقُورٌ.]

مُعْيِلٌ A man *having a family,* or *household, whom he has to feed;* [or, accord. to an explanation of its verb, *having a numerous family* or *household;*] as also ▼ مُعَيَّلٌ, like مُحَمَّدٌ [in measure]: (TA: [see also art. عيل:]) or ▼ مُعَوَّلٌ signifies one *whose property is deficient, and whose family,* or *household, have overcome him.* (TA in art. خلع.) ═ See also 4, last sentence.

مُعَوَّلٌ One *of whom aid,* or *succour, is asked:* (Ṣ, O, TA:) and one *upon whom reliance,* or *confidence is placed.* (TA.) One says, مَا لَهُ فِى القَوْمِ مِنْ مُعَوَّلٍ *He has not, among the people,* or *party, any of whom aid is* [*to be*] *asked.* (Ṣ, O.) [See also عَوْلٌ.] ═ It is also an inf. n. of عَوَّلَ. (Th, Ḳ, TA.) See that verb, in three places. ═ Also *A place of weeping* [or *of wailing*]: so, accord. to some, in the verse cited in the second paragraph [q. v.]. (O.) ═ See also مُعْوِلٌ.

مُعَيَّلٌ: see مُعْيِلٌ, in two places.

مُعَوِّلٌ *A constructor of the sort of shelter from the rain called* عَالَةٌ. (Skr, Ṣ, O.)

عوم

1. عَامَ فِى المَآءِ, (Mgh, Mṣb,) aor. يَعُومُ, (Mṣb,) inf. n. عَوْمٌ, (Ṣ, Mṣb, Ḳ,) *He swam in the water;* syn. سَبَحَ: (Mgh:) العَوْمُ signifying السِّبَاحَةُ: (Ṣ, Ḳ:) or, accord. to the author of the "Iḳtiṭáf," the former signifies *the coursing along in water with immersion of oneself;* and the latter, "the coursing along upon water without immersion of oneself:" [but see what follows:] or, as some say, the former is an act of rational beings, and the latter is of irrational; but Bḍ, on the words كُلٌّ فِى فَلَكٍ يَسْبَحُونَ [in the Ḳur xxi. 34], says that السِّبَاحَةُ is the act of rational beings. (MF, TA.) It is said in a trad., عَلِّمُوا صِبْيَانَكُمُ العَوْمَ [*Teach ye your young boys swimming*]. (TA.) And one says, العَوْمُ لَا يُنْسَى [*Swimming once learned will not be forgotten*]. (Ṣ, TA.) — And عَامَتِ السَّفِينَةُ, (TA,) inf. n. as above, (Ṣ, Ḳ,) *The ship coursed along.* (Ṣ, Ḳ, TA.) — And عَامَتِ النُّجُومُ, inf. n. as above, ‡ *The stars coursed along.* (TA.) — And عَامَتِ الإِبِلُ, (TA,) inf. n. as above, (Ṣ, Ḳ,) ‡ *The camels marched along,* or *journeyed,* (Ṣ, Ḳ, TA,) in the desert. (TA.) And يَعُمْنَ فِى لُجِّ السَّرَابِ ‡ [*They course along in the apparently-boundless expanse of the mirage*]. (A, TA.)

2. عَوَّمَ السَّفِينَةَ, inf. n. تَعْوِيمٌ, *He made the ship to swim* [or *float*] in [or upon] the sea. (TA.) ═ [J cites immediately after explaining عَامَةٌ in relation to a turban,]

وَعَامَةٍ عَوَّمَهَا فِى الهَامَةِ

[*Many a turn,* or *twist, of a turban, which he turned,* or *twisted, upon the head*]. (Ṣ.) — And تَعْوِيمٌ also signifies The *putting,* or *placing,* reaped corn *in handfuls.* (Ṣ, Ḳ.) ═ See also the next paragraph, in two places.

3. عَاوَمَهُ, (Lḥ, Ḳ, TA,) inf. n. مُعَاوَمَةٌ and عِوَامٌ, *He hired him,* or *took him as a hired man* or *hireling, for the year:* (Lḥ, TA:) or *he made an engagement,* or *a contract, with him for work* or *the like, by the year:* (Ḳ:) or you say, عَامَلَهُ مُعَاوَمَةً; like as you say, مُشَاهَرَةً; (Ṣ, Mṣb;) the former from العَامُ, and the latter from الشَّهْرُ; &c. (Mṣb.) The مُعَاوَمَة that is forbidden is The *selling the seed-produce of one's year,* (Ṣ, Ḳ, TA,) or *the dates of one's palm-trees,* or *one's trees, for two years,* or *three,* (so in one of my copies of the Ṣ,) or *for what will come forth in the next following year:* or, as in the Nh, the *selling the fruit of one's palm-trees* or *of one's grape-vines* or *of one's* [*other*] *trees for two years,* or *three,* and *more than that:* (TA:) or one's *extending to a man the term of a debt that has become due by him and* his *increasing the amount of the debt:* (Lḥ, TA:) or one's *adding somewhat to a debt and deferring it.* (Ḳ.) — And عَاوَمَتِ النَّخْلَةُ *The palm-tree bore one year and did not bear another year;* (Ṣ, Ḳ;) like سَانَهَتْ; (Aṣ, in Ḳ and TA, art. سنه;) as also ▼ عَوَّمَتْ: (Ḳ:) and ▼ عَوَّمَ الكَرْمُ, inf. n. تَعْوِيمٌ, *The grape-vine bore much one year and little another.* (TA. [See also مُعَوِّمٌ; perhaps a mistranscription for مُعَوِّمٌ.]) — Also (i. e. عاومت النخلة) *The palm-tree completed a year* [*of growth*]. (Z, TA.)

4. أَعَامَتِ الدَّارُ *The house,* or *dwelling, became altered,* or *changed, and years passed over it;* like احالت. (TA in art. حول.)

عَامٌ *A year;* syn. سَنَةٌ; (Ṣ, Ḳ;) or حَوْلٌ; [not سَنَةٌ; for] El-Jawáleeḳee says, the common people do not distinguish between the عام and the سنة, making them both to have the same meaning; but the right state of the case is what I have been told on the authority of Aḥmad Ibn-Yaḥyà [i. e. Th], that the سنة is from any day from which one commences a reckoning to the like thereof, and the عام is only [*a period of*] *a winter and a summer;* and it is also said in the T and in the Bári' that the عام is *a* حَوْل *that makes an end of a winter and a summer;* so that every عام is a سَنَة, but every سنة is not an عام; for when you reckon from a day to the like thereof, that is a سنة, and there may be in it half of the summer, and half of the winter, whereas the عام is only *a winter and a summer, without interruption:* (Mṣb, MF:*) Er-Rághib mentions a difference in the uses of the words عَامٌ and سَنَةٌ [as has been stated in art. سنو and سنى: see سَنَةٌ in that art.]: and Suh says, in the R, that the سنة is longer than the عام; that the former is "a single revolution of the sun;" and that the latter is applied to the [*twelve*] *Arabian months* [*collectively*]: it is said to be called عام because of the sun's عَوْم [or coursing] through all of its zodiacal signs [during the period which it denotes]: (TA:) its pl. is أَعْوَامٌ, (Ṣ, Mṣb, Ḳ,) because the sing. is originally of the measure فَعَلٌ [i. e. عَوَمٌ]: (Mṣb:) it has no other pl. than this. (TA.) — One says, لَقِيتُهُ عَامًا أَوَّلَ [*I met him in a former year;* generally meaning, *the year immediately preceding,* or, as we say, *last year*]; making the last word imperfectly decl. as being an epithet [and of the measure of a verb]: and لَقِيتُهُ عَامًا أَوَّلًا [*I met him in a year before;* generally meaning the same as the phrase preceding]; making the last word perfectly decl. as not being an epithet [but an adv. n.]: (Ṣ and Ḳ in art. وأل:) or the meaning is, [*in a year*] *before this year;* even if it be by a number of years: (Alee El-Ḳári, on the authority of Seer, in a marginal note in my MS. copy of the Ḳ, art. اول:) and one says also, accord. to AZ and IAạr, لَقِيتُهُ عَامَ الأَوَّلِ; (TA in art. وأل;) or this is rarely said; (Ḳ and TA in that art.;) or should not be said; (ISk, Ṣ and TA in that art.;) nor should one say, لَقِيتُهُ عَامَ أَوَّلَ. (ISk, TA in the present art.) And [in like manner] one says, مَا رَأَيْتُهُ مُذْ عَامٌ أَوَّلُ, putting the last word in the nom. case as being an epithet, (Ṣ and Ḳ in art. وأل,) as though he said أَوَّلُ مِنْ عَامِنَا [i. e. *I have not seen him since a year preceding* this our year]; (Ṣ in that art.;) and مُذْ عَامُ أَوَّلَ, putting the last word in the accus. case as an adv. n., (Ṣ and Ḳ* in that art.,) as though he said مُذْ عَامٌ قَبْلَ عَامِنَا [*since a year before* this *our year*]: (Ṣ in that art.:) and مُذْ عَامُ الأَوَّلِ and مُذْ عَامًا أَوَّلَ are also mentioned by different authors. (L in art. منذ.) And [using the dim. form] one says, لَقِيتُهُ ذَاتَ ▼ العُوَيْمِ i. e. [*I met him*] *in the course of some years;* like as one says, لَقِيتُهُ ذَاتَ الزُّمَيْنِ, and ذَاتَ مَرَّةٍ: (Ṣ:) or the meaning is, [*some few years ago;* or] *three years ago* or *more, to ten:* (AZ, Az, TA:) and it is like the saying, لَقِيتُهُ مُنْذُ سُنَيَّاتٍ: the fem. form is used because they mean by it مَرَّةٌ وَاحِدَةٌ. (Az, TA.) — One says also بَازِلُ عَامِهَا and نَاقَةٌ بَازِلُ عَامٍ [*A she-camel that has passed a year,* and *her year, after cutting her tusk*], (TA,) and بَازِلُ عَامَيْنِ *that has passed two years after cutting the tush.* (MF and TA in art. بزل.) ═ See also عَامَةٌ, in two places. ═ It is also said in the Ḳ that العَامُ signifies النَّهَارُ: but this is a mistake and a mistranscription: it is العَيَامُ; and its place is art. عيم; as it is mentioned by Az, on the authority of El-Muärrij. (TA.)

عَامَةٌ *A* [*kind of float, such as is called*] طَوْف [q. v.], *upon which one embarks on the water:* (Ṣ, Ḳ:) accord. to AA, *a small* مِعْبَر [q. v.] *that is upon rivers:* (Az, TA:) in the M, said to be *a thing that is made of the branches of trees,* and *the like, upon which one crosses a river, and which tosses about upon the water:* the pl. is عَامَاتٌ and عوم [app. عُوَمٌ, like نُوَقٌ pl. of نَاقَةٌ,] and [coll. gen. n.] ▼ عَامٌ. (TA.) [See also عَامَةٌ, voce عِمَامَةٌ.] ═ Also The *head of a rider,* or *of a rider upon a camel,* (هَامَةُ رَاكِبٍ,) *when it appears to thee in the* [*desert,* or *plain, called*] صَحْرَاء, (Ḳ, TA,) *as he is journeying:* (TA:) or it is not thus called unless *having upon it a turban*. (K, TA.) —— And *A turn*, or *twist, of a turban*. (S, K.) [See 2, second sentence.] —— And *A quantity* of reaped corn *put*, or *placed, in handfuls*: pl. [or rather coll. gen. n.] ↓ عَامٌ. (S, K.)

عُومَةٌ *A certain insect* (دُوَيْبَّةٌ, S, K) *that swims in the water, resembling a black* فَصّ [or *stone of a ring*], *smooth and round*: (S:) pl. عُوَمٌ. (S, K.) —— And *A species of serpents, in 'Omán*. (TA.)

عَامِىٌّ a rel. n., from عَامٌ; (Msb, TA;) *A year old*. (TA in arts. حول and دول, &c.) And applied to a plant as meaning *A year old, and therefore dry*. (Msb, TA.*) It is also applied to a [vestige, or relic, of a dwelling, such as is termed] رَسْمٌ, or طَلَلٌ, as meaning *Over which a year has passed*. (TA.) And it is applied, in a trad., as an epithet to the حَنْظَل [or colocynth, meaning *That is of service in the year of drought*, or *barrenness*]; because it is procured, or prepared [as an article of food], in the year of drought, or barrenness. (TA.)

عُوَيْمٌ: see عَامٌ [of which it is the dim.], last quarter.

عَوَّامٌ an intensive epithet from عَامَ فِى المَآءِ; (Msb;) A man *skilful in swimming*. (TA.) —— And † A horse *that stretches forth his fore legs well in running* [*like as one does the arms in swimming*]; (S, Z, K, TA;) *fleet*, or *excellent, in his running*. (TA.)

عَائِمٌ [*Swimming*;] part. n. of عَامَ in the phrase عَامَ فِى المَآءِ. (Msb.) —— [Hence,] سُفُنٌ عُوَّمٌ means عَائِمَةٌ [of which عُوَّمٌ is pl.; i. e. *Ships coursing along*]. (TA.) —— One says سِنُونَ عُوَّمٌ, in which the latter word is a corroborative to the former; (S, K;*) [app. meaning *Tedious, because severe, years*;] like as one says شُغْلٌ شَاغِلٌ: as though pl. of عَائِمٌ; but it is not used alone, because it is not a subst., being only a corroborative: (S:) or, as is said in the M, it should by rule be عُوْمٌ; for [it is pl. of ↓ أَعْوَمُ, and] the pl. of أَفْعَل is فُعْل; but they pronounce it as above, as though the sing. were عَائِمٌ: ISd says, عَامٌ ↓ أَعْوَمُ is an intensive expression, and I think that the meaning is, [*A year*] *that seems long to people because of its drought*, or *barrenness*; and similar to it is ↓ عَامٌ مُعِيمٌ, mentioned by Lh. (TA.) —— عَائِمٌ is also [the name of] *A certain idol* (S, K) *of the Arabs*. (S.)

عَامٌ أَعْوَمُ: see the next preceding paragraph, in two places.

عِنَبٌ مُعْوِمٌ [perhaps a mistranscription for ↓ مُعَوِّمٌ, see 2, near the end,] means, as mentioned by Az, on the authority of En-Nadr, [*A grape-vine*] *that bears one year and does not bear another year*. (TA.)

عَامٌ مُعِيمٌ: see عَائِمٌ, last sentence but one. [And see also art. عيم.]

شَجَرٌ مُعَوِّمٌ *Fat of a year after another year*. (TA.) —— See also مُعْوِمٌ.

مُسْتَعَامٌ A ship *upon the sea*. (K.)

عون

1. عَانَتْ, (S, K,) aor. تَعُونُ, inf. n. عَوْنٌ, (S, TA, [but see what follows,]) said of a woman, *She was*, or *became, such as is termed* عَوَانٌ [q. v.]; as also ↓ عَوَّنَتْ, inf. n. تَعْوِينٌ: (S, K:) and in like manner, عانت, aor. as above, inf. n. عُؤُونٌ, [or عَوْنٌ, (Ham p. 630,)] is said of a cow, accord. to AZ. (TA.)

2: see 1: —— and see also 10. —— تَعْوِينٌ signifies also The he-ass's *leaping his she-ass much*, or *often*. (IAar, K.) —— And The *invading* another *in respect of his share*, or *portion*. (K.)

3. عَاوَنَهُ, inf. n. مُعَاوَنَةٌ and عِوَانٌ, (K,) [*He aided, helped*, or *assisted, him, being aided*, &c., *by him*:] see 6: —— and *i. q.* أَعَانَهُ: see the latter, and see also 10.

4. اعانهُ [inf. n. إِعَانَةٌ] and ↓ عَاوَنَهُ signify the same, (S,* MA, K,) i. e. *He aided, helped*, or *assisted, him*. (MA.) رَبِّ أَعِنِّى وَلَا تُعِنْ عَلَىَّ [*O my Lord, aid me, and aid not against me*,] is said in a form of prayer. (S.) [And you say, اعانهُ عَلَى الأَمْرِ lit. *He aided him against*, meaning, *to accomplish*, or *perform, the affair*]. See also 6 and 10, the latter in two places.

5. تَعَيَّنَ, originally تَعَوَّنَ: see 10, last sentence.

6. تَعَاوَنُوا signifies أَعَانَ ↓ بَعْضُهُمْ بَعْضًا, (S, Msb, K,) *They aided, helped*, or *assisted, one another*; (MA;) as also ↓ عَاوَنُوا; (Msb;) and ↓ اِعْتَوَنُوا, (S, K,) in which the و is preserved because it is preserved in تعاونوا with which it is syn.; (Sb, S;) and also ↓ اِعْتَانُوا, accord. to IB, who cites as an ex. a verse in which نَعْتَانُ occurs; but this correctly means تَأْخُذُ العِينَةَ [belonging to art. عين]. (TA.) One says, تعاونوا عَلَى الأَمْرِ, *They aided, helped*, or *assisted, one another* [lit. *against*, meaning, *to accomplish, the affair*]. (MA.)

8. اِعْتَانُوا and اِعْتَوَنُوا: see 6, in two places.

10. استعانهُ and استعان بِهِ *He sought, desired, demanded*, or *begged, of him, aid, help*, or *assistance*. (MA.) You say, اِسْتَعَنْتُهُ, (Mgh,) or اِسْتَعَنْتُ بِهِ, (S, Msb,) or both, (K,) ↓ فَأَعَانَنِى (S, Mgh, Msb,* K) and ↓ عَاوَنَنِى, (S, TA,) for which last, ↓ عَوَّنَنِى is erroneously put in the copies of the K; (TA;) [i. e. *I sought*, &c., *of him, aid*, &c., *and he aided me*.] The alteration of the infirm letter [و into ا] is made in استعان and ↓ اعان in imitation of a general rule [which requires it when that alteration is made in the unaugmented triliteral verb], though عَانَ, aor. يَعُونُ, [as their source of derivation,] is not used. (TA.) ب [i. e. بِ] is called حَرْفُ ٱسْتِعَانَةٍ [*A particle denotative of seeking aid*, &c.,] because when you say كَتَبْتُ بِالقَلَمِ and ضَرَبْتُ بِالسَّيْفِ and بَرَيْتُ بِالمُدْيَةِ, it is as though you said اِسْتَعَنْتُ بِهٰذِهِ الأَدَوَاتِ عَلَى هٰذِهِ الأَفْعَالِ [meaning *I sought aid of these instruments*, or *made use of them as means, against*, i. e. *to perform, these actions* of smiting &c.]. (TA.) [And you say, استعان بِنَفْسِهِ, meaning *He sought self-help*, or *exerted himself*, فِى أَمْرٍ *in an affair*, and عَلَيْهِ *against it*, or *him*.] —— استعان signifies also *He shaved his* عَانَة, or *pubes*; (S, Msb, K;) and so ↓ تَعَيَّنَ, originally تَعَوَّنَ, on the authority of ISd. (TA.)

عَوْنٌ (S, Mgh, K) and ↓ مَعُونَةٌ (S, Mgh, Msb, K) and ↓ مَعْوُنَةٌ, (K, TA,) with damm to the و, agreeably, with analogy, (TA, [in the CK written مَعْوَنَةٌ,]) and ↓ مَعَانَةٌ (S, Msb, K) and ↓ مَعُونٌ, (S, K,) [respecting the second and last of which see what follows,] are simply substs., (Mgh, Msb, K,) and signify *Aid, help*, or *assistance*: (S, Mgh,* Msb,* K:*) عَوْنٌ is one of those quasi-inf. ns. that govern like the inf. n., i. e. like the verb; as in the saying,

* إِذَا صَحَّ عَوْنُ الخَالِقِ المَرْءَ لَمْ يَجِدْ *
* عَسِيرًا مِنَ الآمَالِ إِلَّا مُيَسَّرَا *

[*When the Creator's aiding the man is true, he will not find such as is difficult, of hopes, otherwise than facilitated*]: (I'Ak, § إِعْمَالُ المَصْدَرِ:) or, accord. to AHei, it is an inf. n. [having no verb]: (TA:) ↓ مَعُونَةٌ is of the measure مَفْعُلَةٌ, (Az, Msb, TA,) from العَوْنُ; (Az, TA;) or, as some say, of the measure فَعُولَةٌ, from المَاعُونُ: (Az, Msb, TA:) one says, مَا عِنْدَكَ مَعُونَةٌ and ↓ مَعَانَةٌ and عَوْنٌ [i. e. *There is not with thee any aid*]: (S:) and ↓ مَا أَخْلَانِى فُلَانٌ مِنْ مَعَاوِنِهِ [*Such a one did not make me to be destitute of his aids*]; مَعَاوِنُ being pl. of مَعُونَةٌ: (S, TA:) ↓ مَعُونٌ is said by Ks to be *syn. with* مَعُونَةٌ; (S;) and he says that it is the only masc. of the measure مَفْعُلٌ except مَكْرُمٌ; (TA:) an ex. of it occurs in a verse of Jemeel cited voce أَىُّ: Fr says that it is pl. [virtually, though not in the language of the grammarians,] of مَعُونَةٌ; (S, TA;) and that there is no sing. of the measure مَفْعُلٌ. (S. [On this point, see مَأْلُكٌ, voce أَلُوكٌ.]) —— Also *An aid*, as meaning *an aider, a helper*, or *an assistant*, (S, Msb, K,) to perform, or accomplish, an affair; (S, Msb;) applied to *a single person*, (K, TA,) and also to *two*, (TA,) and to *a pl. number*, (K, TA,) and to *a male*, (TA,) and to *a female*: (K, TA:) and [particularly] *a servant*: (Har p. 95:) [and *an armed attendant, a guard*, or *an officer*, of a king, and of a prefect of the police, and the like:] and ↓ عَوَانِىٌّ is an appellation applied to *an* عَوْنٌ [or *armed attendant*, or *a guard*,] *who accompanies a Sultán, without pay*, or *allowance*: (TA in art. تأر:) أَعْوَانٌ is pl. of عَوْنٌ; (Lth, S, Msb, K;) and ↓ عَوِينٌ is a quasi-pl. n., (K,) said by AA to be syn. with أَعْوَانٌ, and Fr says the like. (TA.) The Arabs say, إِذَا جَآءَتِ السَّنَةُ جَآءَ مَعَهَا أَعْوَانُهَا, meaning *When drought comes*, [*its aiders*] *the locusts and the flies and diseases come with it.* (TA.) And عَوْنٌ signifies *Anything that aids, helps,* or *assists, one:* for instance, [one says,] الصَّوْمُ عَوْنُ العِبَادَةِ [*Fasting is the aider of religious service*]. (Lth, TA.) — See also what next follows.

أُبُو عُونٍ, with damm, *Dates:* and *salt:* (K:) or أَبُو عَوْنٍ ▼ [thus, with fet-h,] has the latter meaning; salt being metonymically thus called because its aid is sought for the eating of food. (Har p. 227.)

عَانَةٌ *A herd of wild asses:* (S, K:) and *a she-ass:* (K:) pl. عُونٌ, (S, K,) and some say عَانَاتٌ. (TA.) — And [hence, app.,] العَانَةُ is the appellation of † *Certain white stars, beneath the* سُعُود [pl. of سَعْدٌ, q. v.]. (K.) = Also The *pubes;* i. e. the *hair of the* رَكَب; (S, Msb, K;) the *hair that grows above the anterior pudendum;* (Mgh;) or, [as some say,] *above that of a woman:* (TA:) or, accord. to Az (Mgh, Msb, TA) and AHeyth, (TA,) the *place of growth of the hair above the anterior pudendum of a man* (Msb, TA) and *of a woman;* (TA;) the hair itself being called the شِعْرَةٌ (Mgh, Msb, TA) and the إِسْب; (Msb, TA;) though it is also called عانة (Mgh, Msb) by an extension of the proper meaning (Mgh) or by an ellipsis: (Msb:) the word is originally عَوَنَةٌ: (Msb:) and the dim. is عُوَيْنَةٌ ▼. (Mgh.) = فُلَانٌ عَلَى عَانَةِ بَكْرِ بْنِ وَائِلٍ is a saying mentioned by Lh as meaning جَمَاعَتِهِمْ وَحُرَمِهِمْ [i. e., app., *Such a one is over the collective body,* or *community, and those who are under the protection,* of the tribe *of Bekr Ibn-Wáïl*]: and it is said to mean, *he is manager, orderer,* or *regulator, of their affairs.* (TA.) = And عَانَةٌ is said to signify in the dial. of 'Abd-El-Keys *A share of water for land.* (TA.)

عَوَانٌ A beast of the bovine kind, or a cow, (AZ, TA,) or anything, (S, TA,) [i. e.] an animal [of any kind], (IAar, TA,) or a woman, and a beast, (Msb,) *Of middle age,* (AZ, IAar, Msb, TA,) *between such as is advanced in age and the youthful,* (AZ, TA,) *neither young nor old;* (IAar, TA:) so in the Kur ii. 63: (S,* TA:) or a cow, and a mare, *that has brought forth after her first-born:* (K, TA: [in the CK, البَكْرُ is erroneously put for البِكْرِ:]) and a woman *who has had a husband;* (K, TA;) in the M, *i. q.* ثَيِّبٌ: (TA:) pl. عُونٌ, (S, Msb, K,) originally عُوُنٌ. (Msb, TA.) لَا تُعَلَّمُ العَوَانُ الخِمْرَةَ is a prov. [expl. in art. خمر]. (S, TA.) And حَرْبٌ عَوَانٌ means † *A war in which fighting has occurred once* [*and is occurring again*]; (S, K;) as though they made the first [fighting] to be a بِكْر [or first-born]. (S.) And ضَرْبَةٌ عَوَانٌ † *A blow inflicted by seizing an opportunity when the object is unaware, and requiring to be repeated:* pl. ضَرَبَاتٌ عُونٌ, occurring in a trad., in which the blows of 'Alee are said to have been not of this kind, but such as are termed مُبْتَكَرَاتٌ. (L. [See بِكْرٌ, last sentence.]) — And Land *watered by rain* (K, TA) *between two portions of land not so watered.* (TA.) — And [the fem. i. e.] with ة, A *tall* palm-tree: (S, K:) of the dial. of 'Omán, (AHn, S, TA,) or of the dial. of Azd: (TA:) or one *standing alone, apart from others.* (IAar, TA.)

عُوَيْنٌ quasi-pl. n. of عَوْنٌ, q. v. (K.)

عَوَانَةٌ [fem. of عَوَانٌ, q. v. = And] *A certain creeping thing* (دَابَّةٌ), *less than the* قُنْفُذ, [or *hedgehog*]: (K:) accord. to As, it is *like the* قُنْفُذ, *found in the midst of an isolated portion of sand, appearing sometimes, and turning round as though it were grinding, then diving* [*into the sand*], *and also called the* طُحَن [q. v.]: (TA:) and, (K, TA,) some say, (TA,) *a certain worm in the sand,* (K, TA,) *that turns round many times.* (TA.)

عُوَيْنَةٌ dim. of عَانَةٌ, q. v. (Mgh.)

عَوَانِىٌّ: see عَوْنٌ.

عَانِيَّةٌ Wine (خَمْر [in the CK erroneously حُمُر]) *of 'Áneh* (عَانَة), a town on the Euphrates. (S, K.) Zuheyr speaks of the wine of 'Aneh (S, TA) in a verse in which he likens to it the saliva of a woman. (TA.) And [عَانِيَّةٌ is used as a subst.:] one says, فُلَانٌ لَا يُحِبُّ إِلَّا العَانِيَّةَ وَلَا يَصْحَبُ إِلَّا الحَانِيَّةَ i. e. [*Such a one does not love* aught *save*] *the wine of 'Áneh, and* [*does not associate save with*] *the vintners.* (A, TA.)

مَعُونٌ } see عَوْنٌ, former half; each in two places.
مَعَانَةٌ }

مَعُونَةٌ and مَعُوْنَةٌ, and the pl. مَعَاوِنُ: see عَوْنٌ, former half, in four places. صَاحِبُ المَعُونَةِ [as used in post-classical times] means *The officer appointed for the rectifying of the affairs of the commonalty;* as though he were the aider of the wronged against the wronger; *i. q.* الوَالِى; or, as Esh-Shereeshee says, وَالِى الجِنَايَاتِ. (Har p. 261.) And دَارُ المَعُونَةِ was the appellation of *The mansion of the* شِحْنَة [q. v.], in Cairo. (Abulf. Ann. vol. iii. p. 632.)

مِعْوَانٌ A man *who aids, helps,* or *assists, people much,* or *often;* (S, K;*) or *well:* (K:) pl. مَعَاوِينُ. (TA.) One says, الكَرِيمُ مِعْوَانٌ [*The generous is one who aids, &c.*]: and هُمْ مَعَاوِينُ فِى الخُطُوبِ [*They are persons who aid, &c., in affairs,* or *great affairs,* or *afflictions*]. (TA.)

مُتَعَاوِنَةٌ A woman *advanced in age,* (S, K,) but not unless *with fleshiness:* (S:) or, accord. to Az, *symmetrical,* or *proportionate, in her make, so that there is no appearance of protrusion,* or *protuberance, of her form:* and accord. to the A, a woman *fat, with symmetry,* or *proportionateness.* (TA.) — And بِرْذَوْنٌ مُتَعَاوِنٌ [*A hackney*] *whose strength and age have reached their full states* [so I render the explanation إِذَا لَحِقَتْ قُوَّتُهُ وَسِنُّهُ, in which I suppose لحقت to mean أَدْرَكَتْ]; as also مُتَلَاحِقٌ [the fem. of which, applied to a she-camel, is expl. as meaning "strong in make"]. (TA.)

عوه

1. عَاهَ المَالُ, (K, TA,) aor. يَعُوهُ, (TA,) and يَعِيهُ, (K, TA,) inf. n. عَاهَةٌ and عَوْهٌ and عُوُوهٌ (TA) and عَيْهٌ, (CK, [the only inf. n. there mentioned, and not in my MS. copy of the K nor in the TA,]) *The* مال [meaning *camels,* or *cattle,*] *became smitten with what is termed* عَاهَة [i. e. *a bane, disease, pest,* or *murrain*]; (K, TA;) as also عِيهَ. (TA.) And in like manner, عاه الزَّرْعُ, aor. يَعُوهُ and يَعِيهُ; (TA;) or عِيهَ, like إِيفَ; (S;) or عَيِهَ, of the class of تَعِبَ; (Msb; [but this I find not elsewhere, and it is app. a mistake for the well-known form عِيهَ;]) *The* زرع [or *seed-produce*] *became smitten with what is termed* عَاهَة [i. e. *a bane, blight, blast, taint, canker,* or *the like*]; (S, Msb, TA;) as also أَعَاهَ ▼. (TA.)

2: see 4. = تَعْوِيهٌ also signifies The *alighting in the last part of the night* (S, K, TA) *for rest;* (so in a copy of the S;) syn. with تَعْرِيسٌ: (S, TA:) or both of these words signify [the *taking*] *a slight sleep on the occasion of the morning-rest.* (Lth, TA.) — And The *confining oneself in a place.* (K.) You say of any one عَوَّهَ meaning *He confined himself in a place:* (S:) or *he remained, stayed,* or *abode.* (Az, TA.) = And The *calling* a young ass *by saying* عَوْهِ عَوْهِ. (K, TA.) You say, عَوَّهَ بِهِ, inf. n. تَعْوِيهٌ, *He called him to come up with him.* (TA.) And عَيَّهَ بِالرَّجُلِ *He called,* or *called out, to the man.* (TA.)

4. أَعَاهُوا and أَعْوَهُوا, (S, Msb, K,) the latter mentioned by El-Umawee, (S,) and عَوَّهُوا ▼, (IAar, K,) *They had their cattle,* (S, Msb, K,) or *their seed-produce,* (K,) or *their fruits,* (TA,) *smitten with what is termed* عَاهَة [i. e. *a bane,* such as *a disease, pest,* or *murrain,* or *a blight, blast, taint, canker,* or *the like*]. (S, Msb, K, TA.) — See also 1.

عَاهٍ; pl. عَاهُونَ: see عَائِهٌ.

عَاهِ عَاهِ *A cry by which camels are chidden in order that they may confine themselves to a spot;* as also عِيهِ عِيهِ; (K, TA;) and عَهْ عَهْ. (TA.)

عَوْهِ عَوْهِ *A cry by which a young ass is called.* (K, TA.)

عَاهَةٌ, in which the ا is substituted for ى accord. to some, and for و accord. to others, (Msb,* TA,) is originally of the measure فَعَلَةٌ, with fet-h to the ع, (Msb,) and is *syn. with* آفَةٌ [signifying *A bane;* such as *a disease, pest,* or *murrain;* and *a blight, blast, taint, canker,* or *the like:* see 1, in two places]. (S, Msb, K, TA.) It is said in a trad., لَا يُورِدَنَّ ذُو عَاهَةٍ عَلَى مُصِحٍّ i. e. *One whose camels are affected with a bane, such as mange &c., shall not bring them to water immediately after one whose camels are in a healthy,* or *sound, state.* (TA. [See also art. صح.]

رَجُلٌ عَائِهٌ and ▼ عَاهٌ are like مَائِلٌ and مَالٌ, and رَجُلٌ عَاهٌ is like كَبْشٌ صَافٌ [so in my original, but correctly عَائِهٌ and صَائِفٌ: both app. mean *A man having some moral bane* or *malady*]: accord. to IAạr, عَاهُونَ [the pl. of عَاهٌ] signifies *persons having in them what occasions suspicion*, and *what is evil*, or *corrupt*. (TA.)

عَائِهَةٌ *A raising of the voice, calling* or *calling out*, or *doing so vehemently*: (Ḳ:) a word from which they form no derivative. (Ṣgh, TA.)

مَعُوهٌ and مَعِيهٌ *Smitten with what is termed* عَاهَة [expl. above]: (Mṣb, TA:) applied to مَال [i. e. camels, or cattle]: (TA:) and to زَرْع [or seed-produce]; (Mṣb, TA;) as also مَعيوه [so in my original, a mistranscription for ▼ مَعْيُوهٌ]: and to a man, as meaning *smitten therewith* فِى نَفْسِهِ [*in himself*] and فِى مَالِهِ [*in his camels*, or *cattle*]: and in like manner مَعُوهٌ applied to طَعَام [or food]: (TA:) and ▼ مَعْيُوهَةٌ applied to a land (أَرْض), (Ṣ, Ḳ,) meaning *having what is termed* عَاهَة. (Ḳ.)

مَعُوهَةٌ [*A cause of what is termed* عَاهَة, q. v.]. طَعَامٌ ذُو مَعُوهَةٍ means *Food that affects him who eats it with what is termed* عَاهَة. (IAạr, TA.)

مَعُوهٌ *A place in which one remains, stays*, or *abides*. (Az, TA.)

مَعْيُوهٌ; and its fem., with ة: see مَعُوهٌ.

عوى

For words mentioned under this head in many of the lexicons, see art. عو.

عى

1. عَىَّ بِأَمْرِهِ, (Ṣ,) or بِالأَمْرِ, (MA, Mṣb, Ḳ,) and عَنِ الأَمْرِ, (MA,) and also, (MA, and Ḥam p. 717,) and عَيِىَ, (Ṣ, Mṣb, Ḳ,) [which is the original form,] but عَىَّ is more common, (Ṣ, TA,) and أَعْيَا بِهِ is not allowable, (TA,) first pers. عَيِيتُ, (Ṣ,) pl. عَيُوا, (Ṣ, TA,) like حَيُوا [from حَىَّ and حَيِىَ], (Ṣ,) and عَيُّوا also, which is used by a poet, (Ṣ, TA,) aor. يَعْيَا, (Mṣb, TA), inf. n. عِىٌّ; (Mṣb, TA;) as also ▼ تعيّا, and ▼ تعايا, and ▼ استعيا; (Ḳ;) *He found not the right way*, or *manner*, (Ṣ, Mṣb, Ḳ, TA,) *that he desired*, (Ḳ, TA,) or *the way*, or *manner*, *of his acting* [i. e. *in which he should act*], (TA,) *to perform*, or *accomplish, his*, or *the, affair*: (Ṣ, Mṣb, Ḳ, TA:) or *he lacked power, strength*, or *ability, for it*; (MA, Mgh,* Ḳ, TA;) and *was unable to perform it*, or *execute it, thoroughly*. (Ḳ, TA.) [Hence,] one says, شِفَآءُ العِىِّ السُّؤَالُ ‡ [*The remedy of inability is the asking information*]. (TA in art. شفى.) —— And in like manner one says, عَىَّ عَنْ حُجَّتِهِ, (Mṣb, TA,) and عَيِىَ, aor. and inf. n. as above, i. e. *He found not the right way*, or *manner*, *of adducing his argument, plea*, or *evidence*. (Mṣb, TA.*) —— And عَىَّ فِى مَنْطِقِهِ, (Ṣ, Mṣb,) and عَيِىَ, (Ṣ, Mṣb, Ḳ,) aor. as above, (Mṣb,) and so the inf. n., (Mṣb, Ḳ,) *He found not the right way*, or *manner, in his expressing of his ideas*: (Mṣb:) or *i. q.* حَصِرَ; (Ḳ;) or [nearly so, i. e.] عَيِىَ [or عَىَّ] signifies *he was*, or *became, unable to express his mind, to say what he would, to find words to express what he would say; he faltered in speech*; like حَصِرَ, except that the latter denotes what is by reason of shame and confusion of mind, or some [other] accidental cause: (TA in art. حصر, from the Expos. of the "Mufaṣṣal" of Z:) العِىُّ is *the contr. of* البَيَانُ [q. v.]: (Ṣ, TA:) or, accord. to Er-Rághib, it is *an inability that ensues to one who has taken upon himself an affair or a speech*. (TA.) One says, جَآءَ بِالعِىِّ وَالشِّىِّ [app. meaning *He exhibited much impotence of expression*]; (Ṣ and Ḳ and TA in art. شوى;) using the latter noun as an imitative sequent to the former [for the purpose of corroboration]. (TA in that art.) —— And عَيِيتُهُ *I was ignorant of it*: (Ḳ, TA:) originally meaning *I was unable to give information respecting it when asked, by reason of ignorance of it*. (TA.) One says, لَا يَعْيَاهُ أَحَدٌ *No one will be ignorant of it*. (TA.)

2: see the next paragraph.

3. مُعَايَاةٌ [inf. n. of عَايَا] signifies The *saying*, or *doing, a thing to* [*the understanding of*] *which the right direction is not to be found*: (Ṣ:) or, as also ▼ تَعْيِيَةٌ [inf. n. of عَيَّا], the *uttering speech to* [*the understanding of*] *which the right direction is not to be found*; (Ḳ, TA;) *making one's speech enigmatical*, or *obscure*; syn. إِلْغَازٌ: or *doing a deed to* [*the understanding of*] *the way*, or *manner, of which the right direction is not to be found*. (TA.) One says, إِيَّاكَ وَمَسَائِلَ المُعَايَاةِ فَإِنَّهَا صَعْبَةُ المُعَانَاةِ [*Avoid thou the questions of enigmatical*, or *obscure, diction; for they are difficult to be endured*]: and عَايَاهُ, [*He addressed to him enigmatical*, or *obscure, speech*, (like حَاجَاهُ, and لَاغَزَهُ,)] inf. n. مُعَايَاةٌ. (TA. [See also أُعْيِيَةٌ.])

4. أَعْيَا [*He was*, or *became, disabled*, or *incapacitated*]: you say, اعيا عَنِ الجِمَاعِ *he was*, or *became, disabled*, or *incapacitated, from copulation*; syn. عَرِسَ. (IḲṭṭ, TA in art. عرس.) —— *He was*, or *became, fatigued, tired*, or *wearied*, (Mgh, Mṣb, Ḳ, TA,) in walking, or going, (Ṣ, Mṣb, Ḳ, TA,) said of a man (Ṣ) [and of a beast]. You say, اعيا بِهِ بَعِيرُهُ and أَذَمَّ, both meaning the same [i. e. *His camel became jaded, and lagged behind with him*], aor. يُعْيِى, and some incorporate [one ى into the other, transferring the kesreh of the former ى to the ع], as is done in a verse of El-Ḥoṭei-ah. (TA.) —— اعياهُ *It made him to be without power*, or *strength*, or *ability; disabled*, or *incapacitated, him*; (Ṣ,* MA, TA;) said of an affair; (Ṣ, MA;) and [app. in like manner] of God. (Ṣ.) It is also said of a disease, meaning *It disabled him*, or *incapacitated him, from curing it*: (Ḳ,* TA:) [or] one says of a difficult disease, for which there is no cure, كَأَنَّهُ أَعْيَا الأَطِبَّآءَ [*It is as though it disabled*, or *incapacitated, the physicians*; or *frustrated their skill*; or *baffled them*]. (Ṣ, TA.) And a poet says, (namely, 'Amr Ibn-Ḥassán, TA)

فَإِنَّ الكُثْرَ أَعْيَانِى قَدِيمًا
وَلَمْ أُقْتِرْ لَدُنْ أَنِّى غُلَامُ

[*And*, or *for, abundance* of wealth *baffled my attempts* to obtain it *of old; but I have not been poor from the time of my being a boy*]: (Ṣ, TA:) he means, I have been in a middling condition; not very poor, nor able to collect much wealth: but some relate the verse otherwise, saying أَعْنَانِى i. e. "rendered me humble, lowly, or submissive." —— Also *He*, (TA,) or *it*, (Mṣb,) or going or journeying, (MA, Ḳ,) *fatigued, tired*, or *wearied, him*; (MA, Mṣb, Ḳ, TA;) namely, a man, (Mṣb,) or a camel. (Ḳ.) —— And you say, of an affair, (Ṣ, TA,) or a thing, (MA,) اعيا عَلَيْهِ, (Ṣ, MA, TA,) and ▼ تعيّا, and ▼ تعايا, (Ṣ, TA,) all meaning the same, (Ṣ, TA, PṢ,) as also ▼ استعيا, (TA,) i. e. *It was*, or *became, difficult*, or *arduous, to him*; (MA, TA;) or [*impracticable*, i. e.] *such that he found not the right way*, or *manner, to perform it*, or *accomplish it*; (TA;) or *veiled*, or *hidden*. (MA.) —— مَا أَعْيَاهُ [*How wanting is he in ability to find the right way*, or *manner, of acting!* or *how impotent is he!* &c.]. (Ṣ and Ḳ in art. شوى: see 4 in that art.)

5. تعيّا: see 1, first sentence. —— تعيّا عَلَيْهِ: see 4, last sentence but one.

6. تعايا: see 1, first sentence. —— تعايا عَلَيْهِ: see 4, last sentence but one.

10. استعيا: see 1, first sentence. —— استعيا عَلَيْهِ: see 4, last sentence but one.

عَىٌّ and ▼ عَيِىٌّ, (Ṣ, Mṣb, Ḳ, TA,) the former of which is the more common, (TA,) are epithets denoting the agent of the verb in the phrases عَىَّ بِالأَمْرِ (Mṣb, Ḳ) and عَىَّ عَنْ حُجَّتِهِ (Mṣb) and عَىَّ فِى مَنْطِقِهِ: [i. e. they signify *Unable to find the right way*, or *manner*, &c., in relation to an affair, and an argument or the like, and in the expression of his ideas; agreeably with the explanations of these phrases in the first paragraph of this art.:] and ▼ عَيَّانُ (Ḳ) and ▼ عَيَايَآءُ (Ṣ, Ḳ) signify the same, (Ṣ, Ḳ,) in relation to an affair and to the expression of one's ideas: (Ṣ:) the pl. [of عَىٌّ] is أَعْيَآءُ and [of عَيِىٌّ] أَعْيِيَآءُ; (Ṣ, Ḳ;) Sb says, Yoo has informed us of this; and he says, we have also heard some of the Arabs say أَعْيِيَآءُ [as above] and أَعْيِيَةٌ. (Ṣ.)

عَيَآءٌ An *incurable* disease; (Ḳ;) a *difficult* disease, *for which there is no cure*; as though it disabled, or baffled, (أَعْيَا,) the physicians. (Ṣ.) [Hence,] one says, الدَّآءُ العَيَآءُ الحُمْقُ [*The disease for which there is no cure is stupidity*]. (TA.) —— See also عَيَايَآءُ.

عَيِىٌّ: see عَىٌّ. —— Also A stallion-camel *that*

will not cover unless his yard be directed into the vulva. (TA in art. عود.) [See also the next paragraph but one.]

عَيَّانٌ : see عَىٌّ :—and see also مُعْىٍ.

عَيَايَآءُ : see عَىٌّ.—Also, (Ṣ, Ḳ,) and ▼ عَيَاءٌ, (Ḳ,) A camel, (Ṣ,) a stallion [camel], (Ḳ,) *that finds not the right way*, or *manner, to cover:* (Ṣ, Ḳ:) or *that has never covered*, (Ḳ, TA,) or *impregnated:* or *that does not cover well:* (TA:) [see also عَيِىٌّ:] and in like manner applied to a man: (Ḳ:) or, accord. to Az, both signify the *coarse*, or *rude*, or the *heavy, dull*, or *stupid, and impotent, who has no need of women:* (TA voce عَيَا, in art. عبى:) pl. أَعْيَآءُ, formed by considering the augmentative letters as rejected, (Ḳ, TA,) if pl. of عَيَايَآءُ; but not if pl. of عَيَآءٌ, as it appears to be from what is said in the M. (TA.)

أَعْيَا مِنْ بَاقِلٍ is a prov. [meaning *More unable to express what he would say than Báḳil*]. (Ṣ, TA. [See Freytag's Arab. Prov. ii. 146.])

أُعْيِيَّةٌ, (Ḳ, TA,) [originally أُعْيُويَةٌ,] like أُحْجِيَّةٌ (TA) [and أُحْجُوَّةٌ, and أُلْغُوزَةٌ], means مَا عَايَيْتَ بِهِ صَاحِبَكَ [*A saying with which thou addressest thy companion enigmatically*, or *obscurely;* i. e. *an enigmatical*, or *obscure, speech*]. (Ḳ,* TA.)

مُعْىٍ, (Ṣ, Mṣb,) for which one should not say ▼ عَيَّانٌ, applied to a man, (Ṣ,) and to a camel, (TA,) and مَعَايَا and مَعَايِى, (Ḳ, TA, [the latter, erroneously, in the CḲ, مَعاىْ,]) both being pls. of مُعْىٍ, (TA,) applied to camels, as also [the fem.] مُعْيِيَةٌ, (Ḳ, TA,) *Fatigued, tired*, or *wearied*, in going, or journeying. (Ṣ, Mṣb, Ḳ, TA.)

عيب

1. عَابَ, (Ṣ, A, O, Mṣb, Ḳ,) aor. يَعِيبُ, (Mṣb,) inf. n. عَيْبٌ, (Mṣb, TA,) and مَعَابٌ and مَعِيبٌ are allowable as inf. ns., (Ṣ, O, TA,) *It* (a thing, A, TA, or an article of merchandise, Ṣ, O, Mṣb) *was*, or *became, faulty, unsound*, or *defective;* or *had a fault, an unsoundness, a defect, an imperfection, a blemish*, or *something amiss.* (Ṣ, A, O, Mṣb,* Ḳ.) [See also 5.] — عَابَهُ, (Ṣ, O, Mṣb, Ḳ,) [aor. as above,] inf. n. عَيْبٌ and عَابٌ; (TA;) and ▼ عَيَّبَهُ, (Ṣ, A, O,) or this has an intensive signification; (Mṣb;) and ▼ تَعَيَّبَهُ; (Ṣ, A, O;) *He made*, or *caused, it* (a thing, TA in relation to the first, and A in relation to the second and third, or an article of merchandise, Ṣ and O in relation to the first,) *to be faulty, unsound*, or *defective;* or *to have a fault, an unsoundness, a defect, an imperfection, a blemish*, or *something amiss.* (Ṣ, A, O, Mṣb,* Ḳ.) أَرَدْتُ أَنْ أَعِيبَهَا, in the Ḳur [xviii. 78], means *I desired to render it faulty*, or *unsound.* (AHeyth, TA.) — [The same verbs are also often used in relation to a human being as the object.] — And one says عَابَهُ, [aor. as above,] inf. n. عَيْبٌ and عَابٌ and مَعِيبٌ and مَعَابٌ; (MA;) and ▼ عَيَّبَهُ; (Ṣ, A, O, Mṣb;) and ▼ تَعَيَّبَهُ; (TA;) meaning *He* [*found fault with him*, or *it; blamed, upbraided*, or *reproached, him;* or] *attributed* or *imputed to him*, or *it*, or *charged him with*, or *accused him of, a vice, fault*, &c. (Ṣ, A, MA,* O, Mṣb, TA.) [The first of these verbs is of very frequent occurrence as meaning thus: one ex. of it occurs in the saying of a poet cited in the Ṣ and O in this art.,

• أَنَا الرَّجُلُ الَّذِى قَدْ عِبْتُمُوهُ •

I am the man whom ye have charged with a vice, or *fault*, &c. And one says, عاب عَلَيْهِ فِعْلَهُ, meaning *He blamed*, or *discommended, to him his deed.*] — عاب السِّقَآءُ *The skin had milk that had become thick in it.* (O, Ḳ, TA.)

2. عَيَّبَهُ : see 1, in two places. — عيّب also signifies *He made*, or *prepared*, or *took for himself, what is called an* عَيْبَة. (O.)

5. تعيّب *It was*, or *became, rendered faulty, unsound*, or *defective;* or *such as to have a fault, an unsoundness, a defect, an imperfection, a blemish*, or *something amiss.* (A.) [See also 1, first sentence.] — تعيّبهُ : see 1, in two places.

6. تعايبوا [*They found fault, one with another; blamed, upbraided*, or *reproached, one another*]. (Ṣ in explanation of تَعَايَرَ القَوْمُ.)

عَابٌ : see the next paragraph.

عَيْبٌ, (Ṣ, A, O, Mṣb, Ḳ,) an inf. n. used as a simple subst., (Mṣb,) and ▼ عَابٌ [which is also originally an inf. n.] (Ṣ, O, Mṣb, Ḳ) and ▼ عَيْبَةٌ (Ṣ, O) and ▼ مَعَابٌ (Ṣ, O, Mṣb, Ḳ) and ▼ مَعِيبٌ and ▼ مَعَابَةٌ, (Ṣ, O, Ḳ,) signify the same, (Ṣ, O, Mṣb, Ḳ,) i. e. [in a man, and in any animal,] *A vice*, [and in the same, and in anything,] *a fault* or *faultiness, an unsoundness, a defect, an imperfection, a blemish*, or *something amiss;* syn. وَصْمَةٌ, (A, Ḳ,) and نَقِيصَةٌ; (TḲ;) in Pers. آهُو: (PṢ:) or ▼ مَعَابٌ and ▼ مَعَابَةٌ signify *a place of* عَيْب [or *vice, fault*, &c.; app. as meaning *a ground for* عَيْب or *finding fault*, &c.], ▼ مَا فِيهِ مَعَابٌ and ▼ مَعَابَةٌ meaning [*There is not in him*, or *it*,] عَيْب, or مَوْضِعُ عَيْبٍ; [and so ▼ مَعِيبٌ, as is shown by what follows; and ▼ مَعِيبَةٌ as expl. in Ḥar p. 475, which last and ▼ مَعَابَةٌ may be expl. agreeably with analogy as signifying *a cause of* عَيْب, i. e. *a thing for which one is to be found fault with, blamed, upbraided*, or *reproached;* like مَذَمَّةٌ;] for [although] مَفْعِل from a triliteral-radical verb such as كَالَ, aor. يَكِيلُ, as the measure of a subst. [or n. of place] is with kesr [to the ع], and as the measure of an inf. n. with fet-ḥ, yet it is allowable to use fet-ḥ or kesr in either case, for the Arabs say مَسَارٌ and مَسِيرٌ, and مَعَاشٌ and مَعِيشٌ, and ▼ مَعَابٌ and ▼ مَعِيبٌ: (Ṣ, O:) the pl. of عَيْبٌ is عُيُوبٌ [a pl. of mult.] (Ṣ, A, O, Mṣb) and أَعْيَابٌ [a pl. of pauc.]; (Th, TA;) and مَعَايِبُ [as pl. of ▼ مَعَابٌ or ▼ مَعِيبٌ or ▼ مَعَابَةٌ, or as an anomalous pl. of عَيْبٌ like as مَشَايِنُ is of شَيْنٌ,] is syn. with عُيُوبٌ. (Ṣ, O.)

عَيْبَةٌ : see the next preceding paragraph. — Also *A receptacle in which clothes are put:* (Ṣ, O, Ḳ:) and *a receptable of skin*, or *leather, in which goods*, or *utensils, are put:* (TA:) and *a* زَبِيل [or *receptacle like a basket*] *of skin*, or *leather*, or *the like*, (Ḳ, TA,) *in which reaped corn is conveyed to the threshing-floor:* (TA:) or *a thing like the* خَرِيطَة [q. v.], *of skin*, or *leather:* (Ḥam p. 362:) [*it has loops with which it is closed and fastened by the insertion of one into another:* (see 4 in art. شرج:)] pl. عَيْبٌ and عِيَابٌ and عَيْبَاتٌ. (Ṣ, O, Ḳ.) — Hence, (A,) ‡ *The depositary of* one's *secret* [or *secrets*]: (A, O, Ḳ:) [and it is used as a sing. and a pl.:] one says, هُوَ عَيْبَةُ فُلَانٍ ‡ *He is the depositary of the secret* [or *secrets*] *of such a one:* (A:) and it is said in a trad., الأَنْصَارُ كَرِشِى وَعَيْبَتِى (Ṣ, O, TA) ‡ *The Anṣár are my intimates, and the depositary of my secret* [or *secrets*]. (TA. [See also other explanations in art. كرش.]) And [in like manner] العِيَابُ is used as meaning ‡ *The breasts*, and *the hearts:* (O, Ḳ:) for, as the Arab deposits in his عَيْبَة the best of his goods, or utensils, and of his clothes, so he conceals in his breast his most particular secrets, which may not be divulged. (O,* TA.) Hence, (TA,) a poet says,

• وَكَادَتْ عِيَابُ الوُدِّ مِنَّا وَمِنْكُمُ •
• وَإِنْ قِيلَ أَبْنَآءُ العُمُومَةِ تَصْفَرُ •

[*And our and your depositories of love, although it be said* that we and you are *the children of paternal uncles, were near to becoming void*]: (O, TA:) by عياب الودّ he means their breasts. (TA.) And بَيْنَنَا وَبَيْنَهُمْ عَيْبَةٌ مَكْفُوفَةٌ, a phrase in the treaty of El-Ḥodeybiyeh, means ‡ *Between us and them*, in respect of this peace, is [determined that there shall be, in each party,] *a breast bound to fulfil the terms of this writing*, [like the عيبة that is closed and fastened by its loops over its contents,] clear of secret enmity, and perfidy, and deceit: (IAṣr, O,* TA:) or, accord. to some, as related by Sh, *evil between us* [*and them*] *shall be* [as it were] *tied up*, like as the عيبة is tied up: or *there shall be mutual reconciliation, and abstaining from war, like that kind of friendship that subsists between sincere friends who confide in each other.* (Az, TA. [See also art. كف.]) — عَلَيْكَ بِعَيْبَتِكَ, said by 'Áïsheh to 'Omar on an occasion of his blaming her, means † *Busy thyself with thine own family*, or *wife*, and let me alone. (TA.)

عَيَّبَةٌ : see عَيَّابٌ.

عِيَابٌ a pl. of عَيْبَةٌ. (Ṣ, O, Ḳ.) — Also The [*wooden implement commonly called*] مِنْدَف [*with which cotton is separated and loosened*]: (O, Ḳ:) so says Lth, the only authority for it known (O, TA) to Az. (TA.)

عَيَّابٌ (Ṣ, A, O, Mṣb, Ḳ) and ▼ عَيَّابَةٌ (A, O, Ḳ [but this has a more intensive signification]) and ▼ عَيَّبَةٌ (A, Ḳ) One [*who finds fault with others*, or] *who attributes* or *imputes to others*, or *charges them with*, or *accuses them of, vices, faults*, &c., *much*, or *often.* (A and Ḳ in explanation of all, and O in explanation of the second.)

عَيَّابَةٌ : see the next preceding paragraph.

عائِبٌ part. n. of the intrans. v. عَابَ ; [i. e. *Being*, or *becoming, faulty*, &c.;] applied to an article of merchandise [&c.]. (Mṣb.) — And also act. part. n. of عَابَهُ. (Mṣb.) = Also, applied to milk, *Thick*, or *becoming thick*. (O, Ḳ.)

مَعَابٌ : see عَيْبٌ, in five places.

مَعِيبٌ : see عَيْبٌ, in four places. — Also, (Ṣ, A, O, Mṣb, Ḳ) and ▼ مَعْيُوبٌ, (Ṣ, O, Ḳ,) agreeably with the original form, (Ṣ, O,) and ▼ مُعَيَّبٌ, [or this has an intensive signification, (see its verb,)] and ▼ مُتَعَيَّبٌ, (TA,) *Made*, or *caused, to be faulty, unsound*, or *defective*; or *to have a fault*, &c. (Ṣ, A, O, Mṣb,* Ḳ, TA. [See the verbs.]) — And [*Found fault with*, &c.; or] *charged with*, or *accused of, a vice, fault*, &c. (TA. [See, again, the verbs.])

مَعَابَةٌ : see عَيْبٌ, in five places.

مَعِيبَةٌ : see عَيْبٌ.

مُعَيَّبٌ : }
مَعْيُوبٌ : } see مَعِيبٌ.
مُتَعَيَّبٌ : }

عيث

1. عَاثَ, aor. يَعِيثُ, inf. n. عَيْثٌ (Ṣ, O, Ḳ) and عُيُوثٌ and عَيَثَانٌ, (TA,) *He acted corruptly*; or *made*, or *did, mischief*; syn. أَفْسَدَ : (Ṣ, O, Ḳ:) or, accord. to Az, *he hastened*, or *was hasty* or *quick, in so acting*: (TA:) accord. to Er-Rághib, عَيْثٌ and عَثْىٌ, or عِثِىٌّ, and عُثُوٌّ are nearly alike; but عَيْثٌ is mostly used in relation to that which is perceived by sense; and عثىّ and عثوّ, in relation to that which is perceived by the [mind or] judgment: some say that عثوّ is the "acting corruptly in the utmost degree:" and some, that it is the "acting wrongfully, injuriously, or unjustly;" and sometimes does not involve the acting corruptly: (MF, TA:) Lḥ says that عَثَىَ is of the dial. of El-Ḥijáz, and is the [more] approved form; and عاث is of the dial. of the Benoo-Temeem, who say, لَا تَعِيثُوا فِى الْأَرْضِ [*Act not ye corruptly*, or *do not ye mischief, in the earth*]. (TA.) Hence one says, عاث الذِّئْبُ فِى الغَنَمِ *The wolf made*, or *did, mischief among the sheep* or *goats*; syn. أَفْسَدَ. (Ṣ, A, O.) And عِيثِى جَعَارِ [*Do mischief, O she-hyena*]: a prov. used in declaring a thing to be vain, or false. (Ḳ in art. جعر.) And عاث فِى مَالِهِ *He dissipated his property*; or *squandered, and wasted*, or *ruined, it*: and *he expended it quickly*. (TA.) — عاث, aor. and inf. ns. as above, also signifies *He took without gentleness*. (L.) — And عاث, inf. n. عَيْثٌ, *He ventured upon an affair not caring what he fell upon*. (AA.)

2. عيّث, (Ṣ, O, Ḳ,) inf. n. تَعْيِيثٌ, (Ṣ, O,) *He searched* [or *groped*] *for a thing with the hand, without his seeing it*: (Ṣ, O, Ḳ:) or, said of a blind man, *he searched* [or *groped*] *for a thing*: and, said of a man possessing sight, *he searched* [or *groped*] *for a thing in the dark*: written by Kr with غ. (L.) [It is said in the TA, in art. غيث, that ISd thought عيّث, with the unpointed ع, to be a mistranscription; but that it is correct.] — And hence, عيّث فِى الكِنَانَةِ *He put his hand into the quiver to search for an arrow*: (TA:) or *he turned about his hand in the quiver to search for the arrow*. (A.) — عيّث يَفْعَلُ كَذَا *He set about, began*, or *commenced, doing such a thing*. (O, Ḳ.) — عَيَّثَتْ طَيْرُهُ [lit.] *His birds* [from which he augured] *became confused to him*; [meaning † *his affairs*, or *case, became confused and perplexing to him*]; syn. اِخْتَلَطَتْ عَلَيْهِ. (O, Ḳ.) [See also غَيَّرَ.] — عيّث فِى السَّنَامِ *He made a mark*, or *an impression, upon the camel's hump* with a knife. (TA.)

5. تعيّثت الإِبِلُ *The camels drank less than what would satisfy their thirst*. (O, Ḳ.)

عَيْثَةٌ *A plain*, or *soft, tract of land*, (O, Ḳ,) *not consisting of sand nor of dust nor of clay*. (O.)

عَيْثَى is like عَجَبًا : (Ḳ, TA: [in the O, like عَجَبَى :]) a word expressive of wonder: one says أَعْجَبُ عَجَبًا لَهُ, meaning عَيْثَى لَهُ, for [*I wonder greatly*, lit. *with wondering, at him*, or *it*]: (TḲ: [but a verse cited in the O indicates that one says عَيْثَى بِهِ :]) in one copy of the Ḳ, عَيْثًا. (TA.)

رَجُلٌ عَيْثَانٌ *A man who acts corruptly*; or *who makes*, or *does, mischief*: [or rather, *who does so much*, or *often*:] fem., applied to a woman, عَيْثَى. (Seer, TA.)

العَيُوثُ : see what next follows.

العَيَّاثُ *The lion*; (A, O, Ḳ;) as also ▼ العَيُوثُ and ▼ العَائِثُ. (O, Ḳ.)

العَائِثُ : see what next precedes.

أَعْيَثُ مِنْ جَعَارِ [*More mischievous than the she-hyena*]: is a prov. (Meyd, and A and TA in art. جعر.)

عيج

1. مَا أَعِيجُ بِهِ, (Lth, O, Ḳ, TA,) inf. n. عَيْجٌ (Lth, O, TA*) and عُيُوجٌ (Lth, O, TA) and عُيُوجٌ [app. عُؤُوجٌ], (TA,) *I do not regard it*; *do not care for it*. (Lth, O, TA.) One says, مَا عَاجَ بِقَوْلِهِ, inf. n. عَيْجٌ and عَيْجُوجَةٌ, *He did not regard his saying*: or *he did not believe it*. (ISd, TA.) And مَا أَعِيجُ مِنْ كَلَامِهِ بِشَىْءٍ *I care not for anything of his speech*, or *of what he says*: (Fr, ISk, Ṣ, O:) and the Benoo-Asad say, مَا أَعُوجُ بِكَلَامِهِ [expl. in art. عوج]; taking it from عُجْتُ النَّاقَةَ. (ISk, Ṣ.) — مَا عِجْتُ بِهِ *I was not pleased, well pleased, content*, or *satisfied, with it*; or *did not approve it*. (IAạr, Ṣ, O, Ḳ.) — مَا عِجْتُ بِخَبَرِ فُلَانٍ *I was not satisfied in my mind by the information of such a one, and did not deem it certain*. (L.) — مَا عِجْتُ بِالْمَآءِ *I did not satisfy my thirst with the water*: (Ṣ, O, Ḳ, TA:) said by one who has drunk salt water: (Ṣ, O, TA:) or *I did not profit by it*: and sometimes the verb is used in this sense in an affirmative phrase. (TA.) And مَا عِجْتُ بِالدَّوَآءِ *I did not profit by the medicine*. (Ṣ, O, Ḳ.) And عاج, aor. يَعِيجُ, [thus used affirmatively,] *He profited* by speech, &c. (TA.) — مَا يَعِيجُ بِقَلْبِى شَىْءٌ مِنْ كَلَامِكَ [app. meaning *Nothing of thy speech remains in my heart*, or *mind*, (compare عُجْتُ بِالْمَكَانِ, in art. عوج,)] is a saying mentioned by IAạr. (TA.) — [And it seems that عاج عَلَى الشَّىْءِ signifies *He took to, set about*, or *commenced, the thing*: for Ṣgh says that] العَيْجُ signifies الإِقْبَالُ عَلَى الشَّىْءِ. (O.)

عَيْجٌ an inf. n. of 1. (Lth, O, &c.) — Also *Profit, advantage*, or *utility*. (TA.) — And [its pl.] أَعْيَاجٌ signifies *Any means of satisfying a man's thirst*: [and ▼ عِيَاجٌ seems to have a similar signification, for it is immediately added,] and one says, اللَّبَنُ عِيَاجٌ [app. meaning *Milk is a thing that satisfies thirst*]. (O.)

عِيَاجٌ : see what next precedes.

Quasi عيد

2. عيّد : see 2 in art. عود.

عِيدٌ : and عِيدِيَّةٌ : and عَيْدَانٌ : and عُيَيْدٌ : see art. عود.

عير

1. عَارَ, aor. يَعِيرُ, *He went*, or *journeyed*. (TA.) — عَارَ فِى الْأَرْضِ, aor. as above, *He went away in*, or *into, the land*, or *country*. (Ṣ.) — And عَارَ, (Ṣ, O, &c.,) aor. as above, (Mṣb, Ḳ,) inf. n. عِيَارٌ, (Mṣb, TA,) or this is a simple subst., (Ḳ,) *He* (a horse, Ṣ, Mgh, O, Mṣb, Ḳ, and a dog, Ḳ) *went away* (O, Ḳ, TA) *hither and thither*, (O, TA,) which action is also termed مُعَايَرَةٌ [inf. n. of ▼ عَايَرَ], (O,) *as though he had made his escape* (Ḳ, TA) *from his master, going to and fro*: (TA:) and the same is said of news: (IḲṭṭ, TA:) or *escaped*, or *got loose, and went away hither and thither, by reason of his exceeding sprightliness*: (Ṣ:) or *escaped*, or *got loose, and went away at random*: (Mṣb:) or *went away hither and thither, by reason of his sprightliness*: or *strayed at random, nothing turning him*: (Mgh:) or *went away at random, far from his master*. (TA.) — And عَارَ, (aor. as above, TA,) *He* (a man) *came and went*, (Ḳ,) *moving to and fro*. (TA.) — عَارَ فِى القَوْمِ يَضْرِبُهُمْ بِالسَّيْفِ, (Ṣ,* TA,) inf. n. عَيَرَانٌ, (TA,) *He* (a man) *went and came among the people*, (TA,) or *did mischief among them*, (Ṣ,) *smiting them with the sword*. (Ṣ,* TA.) — عَارَتِ القَصِيدَةُ † *The ode became current*. (Ḳ.) — عَارَ, (Ḳ,) aor. as above, inf. n. عِيَارٌ and عَيَرَانٌ, (TA,) *He* (a camel) *left his females*

that were seven months gone with young, and went away to others, (IKtt, L, K,) *to cover them.* (IKtt, L.) In [some of] the copies of the K, شَوْلًا is put in the place of شَوْلَهُ, which latter is the reading in the Tahdheeb of IKtt [and in the CK]. (TA.) ═ عَارَهُ, aor. يَعِيرُهُ and يَعُورُهُ, (S and K in art. عور,) or the aor. is not used, or it is scarcely ever used, (TA in the same art.,) *He,* or *it, took, and went away with, him,* or *it:* (S and K in the same art.:) or *destroyed him,* or *it.* (K and TA in the same art.) See art. عور. You say عِرْتُ ثَوْبَهُ, *I took,* or *went away with, his garment.* (TA.) And it is said in a prov., عَيْرٌ عَارَهُ وَتِدُهُ *An ass which his peg* [to which he was tethered] *destroyed* [by preventing his escape from wild beasts that attacked him]. (Meyd, TA. [See Freytag's Arab. Prov., ii. 87.]) ═ عَارَهُ, [aor. as above,] also signifies *He blamed,* or *reproached, him; found fault with him; attributed* or *imputed to him,* or *charged him with,* or *accused him of, a vice,* or *fault,* or *the like.* (S, O, TA.) [See also what next follows.]

2. عَيَّرَهُ كَذَا, (S, O, Msb, K,) and عيّره بِهِ, though the former is the more approved, (El-Marzookee, in his Expos. of the Hamáseh, and Msb, and MF,) or the latter is peculiar to the vulgar, (S, and El-Hareeree in the Durrat el-Ghowwás,) and should not be used, (O, K,) inf. n. تَعْيِيرٌ, (S, O,) *He upbraided him with such a thing; reproached him for it; declared it to be bad, evil, abominable,* or *foul, and charged him with it.* (Msb.) [You also say عَيَّرَهُ عَلَى فِعْلِهِ *He upbraided him,* or *reproached him, for his deed.*] And عَيَّرَ عَلَيْهِ [is an elliptical phrase, signifying the same; فِعْلَهُ or the like being understood: or *He upbraided him; charged him with acting disgracefully*]. (TA, voce تعريب.) [See also 1, last signification.] ═ عَيَّرَ الدَّنَانِيرَ, (K,) inf. n. as above, (TA,) *He weighed the pieces of gold one after another:* (K:) and *he put,* or *threw down, the pieces of gold, one by one, and compared them, one by one.* (TA.) The verb is [said to be] used in relation to measuring and weighing; but, says Az, Lth makes a distinction between عَايَرْتُ and عَيَّرْتُ, making the former to relate to a measure of capacity, and the latter to an instrument for weighing: and [SM adds,] F mentions the former in art. عور, and the latter in the present art. (TA.) See also 3, in five places. ═ And عَيَّرَ المَآءُ *The water became overspread with* [*the green substance termed*] طُحْلُب: (O, K:) but [SM adds,] it is more probably أَغْثَرَ, with ا and غ and ث. (TA.)

3. عَايَرَ المَكَايِيلَ, (S, Mgh, and K in art. عور,) and المَوَازِينَ, (S, Mgh,) inf. n. عِيَارٌ; (S;) and عاورها, (S, K,) and عوّرها; (K;) signify the same, (S, K,) *He measured,* or *compared, the measures of capacity,* (Mgh, K,) and *the instruments for weighing, one by,* or *with, another.* (Mgh.) One should not say ▼ عَيَّرَ. (S.) The saying اِسْتَعَارَ دَرَاهِمَ لِيُعَيِّرَ ▼ بِهَا صَنَجَاتِهِ, meaning, [*He borrowed pieces of money*] *that he might equalize* [*with them the weights of his balance*], should be, correctly, لِيُعَايِرَ. (Mgh.) You say عَايَرْتُ المِكْيَالَ, and المِيزَانَ, inf. n. مُعَايَرَةٌ and عِيَارٌ, meaning *I tried,* or *proved, the measure of capacity,* and *the instrument for weighing,* [or *gauged the former,*] *that I might know its correctness* [or *incorrectness*]: this, says Az, is the correct form: one should not say ▼ عَيَّرْتُ, except from العَارُ, accord. to the leading lexicologists: and ISk says, عَايَرْتُ بَيْنَ المِكْيَالَيْنِ signifies *I tried,* or *proved, the two measures of capacity, that I might know their equality* [or *inequality*]: you should not say ▼ عَيَّرْتُ المِيزَانَيْنِ. (Msb.) [But in the TA, ▼ عيّر المكيال and الميزان is mentioned without any remark of disapproval, with عاورهما and عايرهما.] You also say عَايَرَ بَيْنَهُمَا, inf. n. مُعَايَرَةٌ and عِيَارٌ, *He measured,* or *compared, them two, each by,* or *with, the other, and examined what* [*difference*] *was between them.* (K in art. عور.) — [Hence, عاير app. signifies also *He assayed* gold &c.] ═ See also 1, third sentence.

4. اعار الفَرَسَ, (S, K,) and الكَلْبَ, (K,) *He* (his master) *made the horse,* and *the dog, to go away as though he had escaped,* or *got loose:* (K:) or *made him to escape:* (TA:) or *made him to escape,* or *get loose, and go away hither and thither, by reason of his exceeding sprightliness.* (S.) ═ أَعْيَرَ النَّصْلَ *He made to the iron head* or *blade of an arrow,* or *of a spear,* or *of a sword,* or *of a knife,* or *the like, what is called* عَيْرٌ. (AA, K.) ═ أَعَارَتْ حَافِرًا means *She* (a mare) *raised and shifted a hoof:* — and hence, accord. to Az, إِعَارَةُ الثِّيَابِ [*The lending of garments*] &c. (L, TA. [See 4 in art. عور.]) ═ And اعارهُ is also said to signify *He fattened him;* namely, a horse: — and *He plucked out the hair of his tail;* like أَعْرَاهُ: both of which meanings are mentioned by IKtt and others: — and i. q. ضَمَّرَهُ [*He made him lean,* or *light of flesh,* &c.]; from عَارَ "he went and came." (TA.)

5. هُمْ يَتَعَيَّرُونَ مِنْ جِيرَانِهِمُ الأَمْتِعَةَ is said to mean يَسْتَعِيرُونَ [i. e. *They ask of their neighbours the loan of the household-goods,* &c.]: but Az says that the word used by the Arabs is يَتَعَوَّرُونَ. (TA. [See 10 in art. عور.])

6. تعايروا *They blamed, upbraided,* or *reproached, one another; found fault, one with another;* i. q. تَعَايَبُوا, (S, O, Msb,) or عَيَّرَ بَعْضُهُمْ بَعْضًا: (K:) or *they reviled,* or *vilified, one another;* syn. تَسَابُّوا. (AZ.)

10. اِستعار سَهْمًا مِنْ كِنَانَتِهِ: see art. عور.

عَارٌ *A disgrace; a shame; a thing that occasions one's being reviled; a vice,* or *fault,* or *the like;* (S, O;) *a thing for which one is,* or *is to be, blamed,* or *dispraised;* (B, in TA, art. عور;) *anything that necessarily occasions blame* or *reproach,* (Msb, K,) or *disgrace:* (Msb:) pl. أَعْيَارٌ: (TA:) and ▼ مَعَايِرُ, (S, O, K,) of which the sing. is app. ▼ مَعْيَرَةٌ, (O,) [is syn. with أعيار, for it] signifies *things for which one is,* or *is to be, blamed, upbraided, reproached,* or *found fault with;* syn. مَعَايِبُ. (S, O, K.)

عَيْرٌ *The ass;* (S, O, Msb, K;) both the *wild* and the *domestic;* (S, O, Msb;) its predominant application is to the former: (K:) so called because he goes away hither and thither (يَعِيرُ فَيَتَرَدَّدُ) in the desert: (TA:) fem. with ة: (S, Msb:) pl. [of pauc.] أَعْيَارٌ, (S, O, Msb, K,) and [of mult.] عُيُورٌ and عِيَارٌ (K) and عُيُورَةٌ (S, O, Msb, K) and عِيَرَةٌ (O) and ▼ مَعْيُورَآءُ, (S, O, K,) like مَشْيُوخَآءُ &c., or this is [properly speaking] a quasi-pl. n., (TA,) and ▼ مَعْيُورَى, [also a quasi-pl. n.,] (Az, TA,) and pl. pl. عِيَرَاتٌ (O) and عِيَارَاتٌ. (K.) [Dim. عُيَيْرٌ, q. v. infrà.] — It is said in a prov., relating to contentment with that which is present and forgetting what is absent, إِنْ ذَهَبَ العَيْرُ فَعَيْرٌ فِي الرِّبَاطِ [*If the ass has gone away, there is an ass in the tether*]. (A'Obeyd.) — You say also, of a place in which is no good, هُوَ كَجَوْفِ عَيْرٍ [*It is like the belly of an ass*], (S, TA,) or كجوف العَيْرِ [*like the belly of the ass*]; (TA;) because there is nothing in his belly of which any use is made: (S, TA:) or this originated from the saying هُوَ أَخْلَى مِنْ جَوْفِ حِمَارٍ [*It is more empty than the valley of Himár*]; (S, O,* TA;) for حمار was the name of a certain unbeliever, who possessed a valley, which, for his infidelity, God rendered waste and unproductive; (O,* TA;) and Imra-el-Keys, (O, TA,) as some say, but correctly Taäbbata-sharrà, (O,) quoting the above-mentioned saying, has substituted العير for حمار, for the sake of the metre. (O, TA.) — One says also أَذَلُّ مِنَ العَيْرِ *More vile than the ass.* (TA.) [But this is doubtful: see the same phrase expl. differently later in this paragraph. The wild ass is superior to every other kind of animal that is an object of the chase: (see فَرَأ:) and hence, app., the signification here next following.] — عَيْرٌ also signifies *A lord,* or *chief,* (S, O, K,) of a people: (S, O:) *a king:* (K:) pl. أَعْيَارٌ. (O.) — The saying (S, K) of the people of Syria, used by them proverbially, (TA,) عَيْرٌ بِعَيْرٍ وَزِيَادَةُ عَشَرَةٍ [*A lord for a lord,* or *a lord is succeeded by a lord, and an increase of ten*] is expl. by the fact that, when the Khaleefeh of the sons of Umeiyeh died, and another arose, he increased their stipends by ten dirhems: (S, O, K:) so they said thus on that occasion. (O, TA.) — عَيْرُ السَّرَاةِ is an appellation of *A certain bird,* (S, O, K, TA,) *resembling the pigeon,* (S, O, TA,) *short in the legs, which are covered with feathers, yellow in the legs and bill, having the eye bordered with black, of a clear colour inclining to greenness,* or *dark dust-colour,* (خُضْرَة,) *yellow in the belly and the part beneath its wings and the inner part of its tail; as though it were a variegated* بُرْد: pl. عُيُورُ السَّرَاةِ: السَّرَاةُ being a place in the district of Et-Táif: they assert that this bird eats three hundred figs, from the time of their coming forth from among the leaves, small; and in like manner, grapes. (TA.) ═ Also *The prominence,* or *ridge, in the middle* of the iron head or blade of an arrow or of a spear or of a sword or of a knife or the like. (Ṣ, O.) [See ذُبَابٌ.] —— The *prominent line,* (Ṣ, O, TA,) *like a little wall,* (TA,) *in the middle* of a leaf; its *middle rib.* (Ṣ, O, TA.) —— The *spine,* i. e. the *prominent part, in the middle* of the scapula, or shoulder-blade. (Ṣ, O.) —— The *prominent,* or *projecting, bone in the middle* of the hand: pl. أَعْيَارٌ. (TA.) [In the Ḳ, it is expl. simply by العَظْمُ النَّاتِئُ وَسَطَهَا: but this is a wrong reading, app. occasioned by an omission, which is supplied in the TA, though somewhat awkwardly: it seems that we should read وَمِنَ الكَفِّ العَظْمُ النَّاتِئُ وَسَطَهَا; or, more probably, ومن الكَتِفِ الخ; for I incline to think that الكفّ in the TA is a mistake for الكتف, and that the last signification of عير, given here, is doubtful.] —— The *prominence,* or *protuberance, in the upper,* or *convex, part,* or *back,* of the foot. (Ṣ, O, TA.) —— *Any prominent,* or *protuberant, bone in the body.* (TA.) —— *An edge,* or *a ridge,* of a rock, *naturally prominent.* (TA.) —— *Anything prominent,* or *protuberant, in an even thing,* (Ḳ,) or *in the middle of an even thing* [or *surface*]. (TA.) —— *Each of the two portions of flesh and sinew next the back bone, one on either side thereof:* both together are called عَيْرَانِ. (Ḳ,* TA.) [So called because it forms a kind of ridge.] —— The *prominent,* or *protuberant, part at the pupil* (مُؤْقٌ) *of the eye:* (AA, TA:) or the *lid* of the eye: (Ṣ, O, Ḳ:) or the *inner angle* [for مَأْقِى, in the CḲ, I read مُؤْقٍ, as in other copies of the Ḳ,] of the eye: (Th, Ḳ:) or the *image that is seen in the black of the eye when a thing faces it;* (Aboo-Ṭálib, L, Ḳ;*) also called لُعْبَة: (Aboo-Ṭálib, L:) or the *eye-ball:* (TA:) or a *looking from the outer angle* (لَحْظ [or perhaps this signifies here the *outer angle itself*]) *of the eye.* (Ḳ.) Hence the saying, (Ṣ, O,) فَعَلْتُ ذَاكَ قَبْلَ عَيْرٍ وَمَا جَرَى *I did that before a look from the outer angle of the eye:* (Ṣ, O, Ḳ:*) or *before he winked* [or *could wink*]; عير meaning the "image that is seen in the black of the eye;" and ما جرى, "what moved," i. e., "the eye itself:" (Aboo-Ṭálib:) or *before I looked* [or *could look*] *at thee;* not used with a negative: (Th:) nor do you say أَفْعَلُ ذَاكَ [instead of فعلت ذاك in this phrase]: (AO, Ṣ:) or عير here signifies the *wild ass.* (Lḥ.) You say also أَتَيْتُكَ قَبْلَ عَيْرٍ وَمَا جَرَى, meaning *I came to thee before a sleeper awoke* [or *could awake*]. (AA, TA.) —— The وَتِد [or *tragus*] *which is in the inner part* of the ear: (Ṣ:) [see وَتِدٌ:] or the *part of the interior of the ear which is below the* فَرْع [or *upper portion thereof*], (Ḳ,) in a man and in a horse, *like the* عَيْر [*of the head*] *of an arrow:* (TA:) or the عَيْرَانِ are the مَتْنَانِ [app. meaning the *two backs,* though the word may have some other application in this case,] *of the two ears* of a horse: pl. عِيَارٌ. (TA.) —— *A wooden pin, peg,* or *stake, which is fixed in the ground* or *in a wall.* (Ṣ, O, Ḳ.) Hence, as some say, the prov. فُلَانٌ أَذَلُّ مِنَ العَيْرِ [*Such a one is more vile than the wooden pin,* or *peg, of a tent* &c.]. (TA.) [See another explanation above: and see also مَذَلَّة.] Hence also, accord. to some, (TA,) one says, مَا أَدْرِى أَىُّ مَنْ ضَرَبَ العَيْرَ هُوَ, meaning *I known not what one of mankind is he.* (Yaạḳoob, Ṣ, O, Ḳ, TA.) And hence too, as some say, the saying of El-Ḥárith Ibn-Ḥillizeh, (O, TA,)

* زَعَمُوا أَنَّ كُلَّ مَنْ ضَرَبَ العَيْـ *
* ـرَ مَوَالٍ لَنَا وَأَنَّا الوَلَآءُ *

of which Aboo-'Amr Ibn-El-'Alà said that he had passed away, or died, who knew the meaning of this verse, (Ṣ, O, TA,) and which is differently related, some saying مَوَالٍ لَنَا, and some saying الوَلَآءُ: (TA:) but various meanings are assigned to العير in this instance; and some expl. it as a proper name: (O, TA:) and some, relating this verse, say العَيْر [q. v.]: (TA:) [the following explanation of the verse has been given as preferable to others:] *They* (the Aráḳim, mentioned two verses before,) *have asserted that all who have hunted the wild ass are the sons of our paternal uncles, and that we are the relations* of them; الولآء being for أَصْحَابُ وَلَائِهِمْ: meaning that we are responsible for their crimes, or offences, as though we were their heirs. (EM p. 261.) —— Also *A certain piece of wood which is in the fore part of the* [*vehicle called*] هَوْدَج. (O, Ḳ.) —— And *A drum.* (O, Ḳ.) And so, as some say, in the verse cited above. (O, TA.) —— And *A mountain.* (Ḳ.) And also the name of *A mountain of El-Medeeneh:* (Ḳ, TA:) and, as some say, of *a mountain of Mekkeh.* (TA.) —— And الأَعْيَارُ (of which the sing. is العَيْرُ, TA) is a name of *Certain bright stars in the track of the feet of* سُهَيْل [or *Canopus*]. (O, Ḳ.)

عِيرٌ *A caravan;* syn. قَافِلَةٌ; of the fem. gen.: (Ḳ:) from عَارَ "he journeyed:" (TA:) or *camels that carry provision of corn:* (Ṣ, Mgh, O, Mṣb, Ḳ:) then generally applied to *any caravan:* (Mgh, Mṣb:) or *a caravan of asses;* and then extended to any caravan; as though pl. of عَيْرٌ, being originally and regularly of the measure فُعْلٌ, [i. e. عُيْرٌ,] like سُقْفٌ as pl. of سَقْفٌ; (TA;) but it has no proper sing.: (Ḳ:) or *any beasts upon which provision of corn is brought,* whether *camels* or *asses* or *mules:* (Ḳ:) the عير mentioned in the Ḳur xii. 94 consisted of asses; and the assertion of him who says that عير is applied specially to camels is false: (AHeyth, O, TA:) Nuṣeyr cites the poet Aboo-'Amr El-Asadee as applying this appellation to asses; and says that camels are not so called unless employed for bringing provision of corn: (AHeyth, TA:) IAạr says that it is applied to *camels bearing burdens,* and *not bearing burdens:* (Az:) but camels are not thus called that bring corn for their owners: (TA, voce رِكَابٌ:) pl. عِيَرَاتٌ, (O, Ḳ,) with ا and ت because it is of the fem. gender, and, being a subst., with the ى movent, accord. to the dial. of Hudheyl, for they say جَوَزَاتٌ and بَيَضَاتٌ; (Sb;) and عِيْرَاتٌ (Ṣ, Ḳ) is allowable, (Ṣ,) and is the regular form, and occurs in a trad., meaning *horses* or *the like,* and *camels carrying merchandise.* (TA.)

عَيْرَانٌ applied to a he-camel, (O,) and عَيْرَانَةٌ applied to a she-camel, (Ṣ, O, Ḳ,) *Resembling the* [*wild*] *ass* (العَيْر) *in quickness and briskness:* (Ṣ, O:) or the latter, *swift, with briskness;* (Ḳ, TA;) so termed because of her frequent going round about [or to and fro], rather than as being likened to the [wild] ass: and also *hard,* or *hardy.* (TA.)

عَيْرَانٌ: see عَائِرٌ in art. عور.

عِيَارٌ and ↓ مِعْيَارٌ are syn.; (Ṣ;) both signify [*A standard of measure* or *weight;*] *a thing with which another thing is measured,* or *compared, and equalized;* (Mgh;) [and *with which it is assayed:*] or *a thing with which measures of capacity are measured, compared,* or *equalized:* (Lth:) the عِيَار of a thing is *that which is made,* or *appointed, a standard* thereof, *by which to regulate* or *adjust* it; expl. by مَا جُعِلَ نِظَامًا لَهُ. (Mṣb.) —— The عِيَار of dirhems, and of deenárs, is [The *rate,* or *standard, of fineness;*] the *quantity of pure silver,* and *of pure gold, that is put* into them. (Mgh.) —— [See also 1.]

عِيَارَةٌ *Currency* of a poem. (Ḳ.)

عُيَيْرٌ [dim. of عَيْرٌ]. You say, فُلَانٌ عُيَيْرُ وَحْدِهِ † *Such a one is a person who is pleased with his own opinion;* (Ṣ, O, Ḳ;) an expression of dispraise; (Ṣ;) like as نَسِيجُ وَحْدِهِ is one of praise: (TA:) or *a person who does not consult others, nor mix with them, yet in whom is ignobleness and weakness;* as also جُحَيْشُ وَحْدِهِ [q. v.]: (Az:) or *a person who eats by himself.* (Th, Ḳ.) You may also say عُيَيْرٌ, like شُيَيْخٌ for شُيَيْخٌ; but you should not say عُوَيْرٌ, nor شُوَيْخٌ. (Ṣ, O.)

عَيُّورٌ: see عَائِرٌ.

عَيَّارٌ: see the next paragraph, in five places.

عَائِرٌ *That goes to and fro,* and *round about;* as also ↓ عَيَّارٌ: both are applied [to a man and] also to a dog: (TA:) and ↓ the latter is also expl. as follows: a man (TA) *often coming and going* (Ḳ, TA) *in the land:* (TA:) *often going round about,* (Fr, Ṣ, Mṣb, Ḳ,) *often in motion,* (Fr, Ṣ, Mṣb,) *and sharp,* or *quick, of intellect:* (Ṣ, Ḳ:) it is used as an epithet of praise and as one of dispraise: for instance, applied to a boy, it signifies *brisk in obeying God,* and *brisk in acts of disobedience:* (IAạr:) and ↓ عَيُّورٌ, applied to a horse, signifies *brisk, lively,* or *sprightly:* (IAạr:) and ↓ عَيَّارٌ, so applied, *mischievous;* and *that is brisk, lively,* or *sprightly, so that he goes on one side of the way, and then turns to the other side:* (TA:) and, applied to a man, *that goes to and fro without work:* (Ajnás en-Náṭifee, Mgh:) or *that leaves himself to follow his natural desire, not restraining himself.* (IAmb, Mgh, Mṣb.) It is said in a prov., كَلْبٌ عَائِرٌ خَيْرٌ مِنْ أَسَدٍ رَابِضٍ *A dog going to and fro and round about is better* [as a guard] *than a lion lying down.* (TA.) You say also شَاةٌ عَائِرَةٌ *A sheep that goes to and fro between two flocks, not knowing which of them to follow:* to such is a hypocrite likened. (TA.) And نَاقَةٌ عَائِرَةٌ *A she-camel that goes forth from the other camels in order that the stallion may cover her.* (Ṣ, O, TA.) And جَمَلٌ عَائِرٌ *A he-camel that leaves the females seven months gone with young, and goes to others.* (Ṣ.) And عَيَّارٌ ↓ بِأَوْصَالٍ A horse *that goes away hither and thither, by reason of his sprightliness:* (Ṣ, O:) or a lion *that goes away with the joints,* or *whole bones, of men to his thicket.* (IB.) ↓ العَيَّارُ is an appellation given to *The lion,* (Ṣ, O, Ḳ,) because of his coming and going in search of his prey. (Ṣ, O.) — قَصِيدَةٌ عَائِرَةٌ † *An ode having currency.* (O.) — سَهْمٌ عَائِرٌ *An arrow from an unknown shooter.* (Mṣb. [Mentioned also in art. عور.]) And ثَمْرَةٌ عَائِرَةٌ *A fallen fruit, of which the owner is not known.* (TA.) — عَائِرُ العَيْنِ, and عَائِرَةُ عَيْنٍ or عَيْنَيْنِ, &c.: see art. عور.

مَا قَالَتِ العَرَبُ بَيْتًا أَعْيَرَ مِنْهُ *The Arabs have not uttered a verse more current than it.* (A, O, TA.)

مُعَارٌ A horse, (Ṣ, Ḳ,) and a dog, (Ḳ,) *made to go away as though he had escaped,* or *got loose:* (Ḳ:) or *made to escape:* (TA:) or *made to escape, or get loose, and go away hither and thither, by reason of his exceeding sprightliness.* (Ṣ.) It is also expl. as signifying, applied to a horse, *Fattened:* and *having the hair of his tail plucked out:* these two explanations mentioned by IḲṭṭ and others: and *made lean,* or *light of flesh.* (TA. [See 4, last sentence.]) See also the next paragraph.

مِعَارٌ, (O, Ḳ,) as though originally مِعْيَرٌ, from عَارَ, aor. يَعِيرُ, (Az, O,) A horse *that turns away from the road with his rider.* (O, Ḳ.) Hence the saying of Bishr Ibn-Abee-Ḥázim, (Ḳ,) or Kházim, as written by Ṣgh, (TA,) not Eṭ-Ṭirimmáḥ, J having made a mistake [in ascribing it to him (but in one of my copies of the Ṣ it is ascribed to Bishr Ibn-Abee-Ḥázim and in the other to a poet unnamed)],

* أَحَقُّ الخَيْلِ بِالرَّكْضِ المِعَارُ *

[*The most deserving, of horses, of being urged to run by the striking with the foot is he that turns away from the road with his rider*]. (Ḳ.) Aboo-'Obeyd, (so in my copies of the Ṣ,) or Aboo-'Obeydeh, (so in the Ḳ and TA,) says that the people, in relating this, say ↓ المُعَارُ, [deriving it] from العَارِيَّةُ; which is a mistake: (Ṣ, Ḳ, TA:) the truth being that this is a mistake as to the ḍamm and the derivation; which is the saying of IAạr alone, and is mentioned by IB also: (TA:) or the last word is المُغَارُ. (TA in art. غور, q. v.)

نَصْلٌ مُعَيَّرٌ *An iron head* or *blade, of an arrow* or *of a spear* or *of a sword* or *of a knife* or *the like, having what is termed* عَيْر. (AḤn, from AA.) And كَفٌّ مُعَيَّرَةٌ, and ↓ مُعْيَرَةٌ, [so in the TA, but more probably مُعَيَّرَةٌ and مُعْيَرَةٌ,] *A* كَفٌّ [or *hand*] *having what is so termed.* (TA. [But I think that كَفٌّ is here a mistranscription for كَتِفٌ: see عَيْرٌ.])

ابْنَةُ مِعْيَرٍ *Calamity,* (Ḳ, TA,) and *hardship.* (TA.) And بَنَاتُ مِعْيَرٍ *Calamities,* (Ṣ, O, TA,) and *hardships.* (TA.)

مُعْيَرَةٌ, and the pl. مَعَايِرُ: see عَارٌ.

كَفٌّ مُعْيَرَةٌ [or كَتِفٌ?]: see مُعَيَّرٌ.

مِعْيَارٌ: see عِيَارٌ.

مَعْيُورَآءُ and مَعْيُورَى: see عَيْرٌ, first sentence.

مُسْتَعْيِرٌ *Resembling the* عَيْر [i. e. *ass,* or *wild ass,*] *in make.* (O, Ḳ.)

عيس

5. تَعَيَّسَتِ الإِبِلُ *The camels were,* or *became,* [*of the colour termed* عَيَس: or] *white inclining to black.* (O, Ḳ.)

عَيَسٌ (Ṣ, TA) and ↓ عِيسَةٌ, the latter of the measure فُعْلَةٌ, [originally عُيْسَةٌ,] like صُهْبَةٌ and كُمْتَةٌ, (Lth, O, TA,) *Whiteness in a camel, mixed with somewhat of* [*the red hue termed*] شُقْرَة; (Ṣ, TA;) [i. e., *a reddish whiteness:*] or [*a dingy whiteness;*] *whiteness in which is a mixture of clearness with slight darkness:* (TA:) [or *a yellowish whiteness:* see أَعْيَسُ.]

عِيسَةٌ: see the next preceding paragraph.

أَعْيَسُ A camel *of a white colour mixed with somewhat of* [*the red hue termed*] شُقْرَة; (Ṣ, O, Ḳ;*) [i. e., *reddish white:*] or [*dingy white;*] *white with a slight darkness:* (Mṣb:) or *inclining to yellow;* [i. e., *yellowish white:*] (IAạr:) fem. عَيْسَآءُ: pl. عِيسٌ: (Ṣ, O, Mṣb, Ḳ:) the camels thus termed are said to be of good breed. (Ṣ, O.) Also A gazelle, or an antelope, and a bull, [app. meaning a wild bull,] *in which is* [*a hue such as is termed*] أُدْمَة. (TA.) And you say رَجُلٌ أَعْيَسُ الشَّعَرِ *A man having white hair.* (TA.) And رَسْمٌ أَعْيَسُ *A white mark, trace, relic,* or *remain.* (TA.) — العَيْسَآءُ *The female locust.* (Ṣ, O, Ḳ.)

عيش

1. عَاشَ, (Ṣ, A, O, Mṣb, Ḳ,) aor. يَعِيشُ, inf. n. عَيْشٌ (Ṣ, O, Mṣb, Ḳ) and مَعَاشٌ and مَعِيشٌ (Ṣ, O, Ḳ) and مَعِيشَةٌ and عِيشَةٌ and عَيْشُوشَةٌ (O, Ḳ) and in the dial. of El-Azd مَعُوشَةٌ, (Ḳ in art. عوش, and TA,) *He lived;* (Ṣ, A,* O, Ḳ;) [*he passed life in a particular manner or state:*] *he became possessed of life.* (Mṣb.) You say, عَاشَ فُلَانٌ عِيشَةً رَاضِيَةً *Such a one lived a pleasant* [*life,* (if we regard عِيشَة as a simple inf. n., as it is said to be above,) or] *state* [or *sort*] *of life.* (A.) [See also عِيشَةٌ, below.]

2: see 4.

3. عَايَشَهُ, inf. n. مُعَايَشَةٌ, *He lived with him;* like as you say عَاشَرَهُ. (TA.)

4. أَعَاشَهُ *He* (God, Ṣ, A) *made him to live;* (Ṣ, A, O,* Ḳ;) as also ↓ عَيَّشَهُ, (O,* Ḳ,) inf. n. تَعْيِيشٌ. (TA.) You say, أَعَاشَهُ اللّٰهُ عِيشَةً رَاضِيَةً [*God made him to live a pleasant life,* or *state* or *sort of life*]. (Ṣ.)

5. تعيّش *He constrained himself to obtain the means of life:* (Ṣ:) or *he had what was barely sufficient, of sustenance, nothing remaining over and above it.* (TA.)

6. تعايشوا [*They lived together; one with another*]. You say, تعايشوا بِأُلْفَةٍ وَمَوَدَّةٍ [*They lived together with sociableness and affection*]. (A, TA.)

عَيْشٌ [an inf. n. of 1. — As a subst.,] *Life:* (Ṣ, O, Ḳ:) or particularly *animal life.* (Kull p. 262.) It is said in a prov., أَنْتَ مَرَّةً عَيْشٌ وَمَرَّةً جَيْشٌ, meaning, *Thou art at one time in an easy state of life, and at one time in the state of life of warriors:* (A'Obeyd, as cited in the TA: [but for عَيْشٍ غَزِيٍّ in my original, we should perhaps read عَيْشٍ عَزِيزٍ, i. e. *a difficult state of life:*]) or *thou benefitest at one time, and injurest at another.* (TA.) And a man to whom IAạr said "How is such a one?" answered عَيْشٌ وَجَيْشٌ, meaning *At one time with me, and at one time against me.* (TA.) [See also Freytag's Arab. Prov. i. 70 and ii. 699.] — Also, *I. q.* مَعِيشَةٌ, in senses pointed out below: (Ḳ:) see the latter, in four places. — And [hence,] *Wheat,* or other *food;* syn. طَعَامٌ; (IDrd, A, O, Ḳ;) in the dial. of El-Ḥijáz, (A,) or of El-Yemen: (IDrd, O, TA:) and *seed-produce;* in the dial. of El-Ḥijáz: (A, TA:) and *bread;* (Ḳ;) in the dial. of Egypt. (TA.)

عِيشَةٌ [see 1, in two places. —] *A state,* (A,) or *sort,* (TA,) *of life.* (A, TA.) You say, عَاشَ عِيشَةَ صِدْقٍ, and عِيشَةَ سَوْءٍ, *He lived a good sort of life,* and *an evil sort of life.* (TA.)

عَيَّاشٌ: see the paragraph here following.

عَائِشٌ [*Living:*] *having life:* and in like manner, but in an intensive sense, [app. meaning *having much of the means of life,* or *living well,*] ↓ عَيَّاشٌ: fem. of the former with ة. (Mṣb.) — A man *in a good state* or *condition* [*of life*]. (Lth, A, O, Ḳ.)

مَعَاشٌ and ↓ مَعِيشٌ may be used as substantives as well as inf. ns., like مَعَابٌ and مَعِيبٌ; (Ṣ, O, TA;) and signify, like مَعِيشَةٌ, *That whereby one lives:* or *that* [*place* and *time*] *in which one lives:* (TA:) [or rather, they have both these significations; but معاش has generally the latter; whereas معيشة, q. v., and معيش, are generally used in the former sense, or one similar to it:] مَعَاشٌ also signifies the *place of subsistence;* or the *known,* or *usual, place thereof:* and the *time wherein one seeks sustenance.* (TA.) Thus, (TA,) الأَرْضُ مَعَاشُ الخَلْقِ [*The earth is the place of subsistence of mankind, or of the created beings*]. (A, O, TA.) And النَّهَارُ مَعَاشٌ *The day is the time for seeking sustenance:* as in the Ḳur, lxxviii. 11. (O, TA.) See also مَعِيشَةٌ, in two places.

مَعِيشٌ : see مَعِيشَةٌ, in four places: and مَعَاشٌ.

مَعِيشَةٌ inf. n. of عَاشَ [q. v.]. (Ḳ.) — Also *Victuals, living, sustenance,* or *food and drink by which one lives;* (Lth, A, O, Ḳ;) as also ↑ عَيْشٌ; (A;) whence you say that dates are the عَيْش of such a family: (TA:) *that whereby life subsists;* the *means of life* or *subsistence;* (A, Ḳ;) as also ↑ عَيْشٌ: (A, TA:) *that whereby one lives;* as also ↑ عِيشٌ (A, Ḳ, TA) and ↑ مَعَاشٌ and ↑ مَعِيشٌ; (TA;) or [the *state*] *wherein one lives;* (A, Ḳ, TA;) as also ↑ عَيْشٌ (A) and ↑ مَعَاشٌ and ↑ مَعِيشٌ: (TA:) the *means of obtaining that whereby one lives:* (Aboo-Is-ḥáḳ, TA:) the *gain,* or *earnings, by means of which a man lives;* (Mgh, Mṣb;) as also ↑ مَعِيشٌ: (Mṣb:) the pl. is مَعَايِشُ, (Ṣ, O, Mṣb,) accord. to general opinion, (Mṣb,) without ء, (Ṣ, O, Mṣb,) when formed from the original of the sing., which is مَعْيِشَةٌ, of the measure مَفْعِلَةٌ; (Ṣ, O;) or because it is from عَاشَ, so that the measure of the pl. is مَفَاعِلُ: (Mṣb:) but when it is formed from the secondary form of the sing., it is with ء, [مَعَائِشُ,] مَفْعِلَةٌ being in this case likened to فَعِيلَةٌ, like as مَصَائِبُ is with ء because the ى [in its sing.] is quiescent; but some of the grammarians hold this latter pl. to be incorrect: (Ṣ, O:) all the Baṣree grammarians hold it to be so: (TA:) or, accord. to some, ↑ مَعِيشٌ and مَعِيشَةٌ are from معش; and the pl. in question is therefore of the measure فَعَائِلُ, with ء. (Mṣb.) — مَعِيشَةٌ ضَنْكٌ The *punishment of the grave:* (O, Ḳ:) so, accord. to most of the expositors, in the Ḳur xx. 123: or, as some say, [*strait sustenance*] *in the fire of hell.* (O, TA.)

مُتَعَيِّشٌ One *who constrains himself to obtain the means of life:* (TA:) or *who has what is barely sufficient, of sustenance, nothing remaining over and above it.* (Lth, A, O, Ḳ.)

عيص

عِيصٌ *A dense, or tangled wood; a numerous collection of dense, or tangled, trees:* (Ṣ, O, Ḳ:) or [*lote-trees of the species called*] سِدْر (AḤn, O, TA) *collected together in one place,* (AḤn, O,) *of which the lower parts are dense,* or *tangled:* (AḤn, TA:) or *dense,* or *tangled, trees, some growing in,* or *among, the lower parts of others:* (TA:) pl. [of pauc.] أَعْيَاصٌ and [of mult.] عِيصَانٌ: (O, Ḳ:) also *what are collected together* (AḤn, O, Ḳ, TA) *in a place,* (AḤn, O, TA,) *and are near together, and dense,* or *tangled,* (AḤn, O, Ḳ, TA,) *of* [*trees of the kinds called*] عِضَاه, (O, Ḳ,) or *of* [*the trees called*] سِدْر *and* عَوْسَج *and* نَبْع *and* سَلَم *and all kinds of* عِضَاه: so says 'Omárah, (O, TA,) and AḤn says the like: (TA:) or (Ḳ) *what are dense,* or *tangled, and numerous,* (El-Kilábee, O, TA,) *of thick and tough trees,* (El-Kilábee, O, Ḳ, TA,) *such as the* سَلَم *and* طَلْح *and* سَيَال *and* سِدْر *and* سَمُر *and* عِضَاه *and* عُرْفُط. (El-Kilábee, O, TA.) — Also *A place of growth of the best of trees:* (Lth, A, O, Ḳ:) or, as some say, the *lower parts of trees.* (TA.) — And hence, (A,) *A stock,* or *race.* (Ṣ,* A, Ḳ.*) You say, هُوَ مِنْ عِيصِ بَنِى هَاشِمٍ *He is of the stock,* or *race, of Benoo-Háshim.* (A.) And مَا أَكْرَمَ عِيصَهُ *How generous,* or *noble, are his fathers,* or *ancestors, and paternal and maternal uncles, and the people of his house!* (TA.) And it is said in a prov., عِيصُكَ مِنْكَ وَإِنْ كَانَ أَشِبًا, i. e. *Thy stock is an appertenance of thine though it be thorny and intricate* or *confused:* (AZ, O, TA:) meaning, accord. to A'Obeyd, those who are connected with thee by origin are thy kinsmen, although they follow a different way of life: have patience, therefore, for thou canst not remove them from thee: (Meyd:) [see Freytag's Arab. Prov., ii. 95:] implying dispraise: or, accord. to AHeyth, عِيصٌ أَشِبٌ denotes praise; force of resistance, or inaccessibleness or unapproachableness, and numerousness, being meant thereby. (O, TA.) You say also, هُوَ فِى عِيصِ صِدْقٍ *He is of a good,* or *an excellent, stock.* (Sh, O, TA.) — جِئْ بِهِ مِنْ عِيصِكَ means *Bring thou it from wherever it is.* (TA.)

عَيْصَآءُ : see عَوِيصٌ, (in art. عوص,) last sentence.

مَعِيصٌ *A place of growth* [app., as seems to be implied in the Ṣ, *of trees such as are termed* عِيص]. (Ṣ, O, Ḳ.)

مِعْيَاصٌ *Any one who is hard,* or *difficult, with respect to that which another desires of him:* (O, Ḳ:) app. originally مِعْوَاصٌ: mentioned in the L in art. عوص. (TA.)

عيط

1. عَاطَتْ, aor. تَعِيطُ and تَعُوطُ, (Ḳ,) inf. n. عَيْطٌ [perhaps a mistake for عَيَطٌ, which see below, like غَلَبٌ and طَلَبٌ], (TA,) *She* (a woman, TA) *was,* or *became, long in the neck,* (Ḳ, TA,) *with justness of stature;* (TA;) as also ↑ تعيّطت and تعوّطت. (Ḳ.) — See also art. عوط.

5: see above: — and see also عَاطَتْ in art. عوط.

8: see عَاطَتْ in art. عوط, in three places.

عَيَطٌ *Length of the neck;* (Ṣ, O, Ḳ, TA;) to which some add, *with justness of stature.* (TA.)

عَيْطَطٌ : see عُوطَطٌ and عَائِطٌ, in art. عوط.

عَيَّاطٌ : see أَعْيَطُ.

عَائِطٌ : see art. عوط.

أَعْيَطُ *Long in the neck;* (Ṣ, O, Ḳ;) accord. to some, *with justness of stature;* (TA;) applied to a camel; (Ṣ, O;) as also ↑ عَيَّاطٌ: (TA:) fem. عَيْطَآءُ; (Ṣ, O, Ḳ;) applied to a she-camel; (Ṣ;) and to a woman, in the sense expl. above: (Mgh:) pl. عِيطٌ. (TA.) — *Long in the head and neck;* (Ḳ;) which is ugly. (TA.) — *Tall;* the fem. being applied in this sense to a mare; and the pl. to horses: (TA:) *high; lofty;* (Ṣ, O, Ḳ, TA;) applied to † a mountain; (TA;) and the fem. to † a [mountain such as is termed] قَارَة, (Ṣ, O, TA,) and to ‡ [such as is termed] a هَضْبَة; (TA;) and the masc. also, in this sense, to ‡ a palace, or the like; (Ṣ, O, Ḳ, TA;) and to ‡ عِزّ [or might, or nobility, or the like]. (O, Ḳ, TA.) The pl. also signifies *Excellent,* and *youthful,* camels; (O, Ḳ, TA;) *between the* حِقَّة *and the* رَبَاعِيَة. (O, TA.) — † *Refusing; resisting; withstanding:* (Ḳ, TA:) applied to a man, and to a wild ass. (TA.)

مُعْتَاطٌ, and with ة: see عَائِطٌ in art. عوط, in four places.

عيف

1. عَافَهُ, aor. يَعَافُهُ, (Ṣ, Mgh, O, Mṣb, Ḳ,) and يَعِيفُهُ, (Fr, O, Ḳ,) inf. n. عِيَافٌ, (Ṣ, Mgh, O,) or عِيَافَةٌ, (Mṣb, [but probably a mistranscription for the former,]) or both, or the latter is a simple subst., and the former is an inf. n., also عَيْفٌ and عَيَفَانٌ, (ISd, Ḳ,) *He* (a man, Ṣ, O, Mṣb, [and any animal,]) *disliked it,* or *loathed it,* (Ṣ, Mgh, O, Mṣb, Ḳ,) namely, food, (Ṣ, O, Mṣb, Ḳ,) or water, (Mgh,) or beverage, (Ṣ, O, Mṣb, Ḳ,) *and would not drink it,* (Ṣ, O, Ḳ,) and sometimes it is said in relation to other things, (Ḳ,) but mostly in relation to food: (ISd, TA:) and ↑ اِعْتَافَهُ signifies the same as عَافَهُ. (TA.) A poet says, (namely, Anas Ibn-Mudrik, O, TA, and so in a copy of the Ṣ,)

* إِنِّى وَقَتْلِى سُلَيْكًا ثُمَّ أَعْقِلَهُ *
* كَالثَّوْرِ يُضْرَبُ لَمَّا عَافَتِ البَقَرُ *

[*Verily I, in the case of my slaying Suleyk and then giving the bloodwit for slaying him, am like the bull that is beaten when the cows loathe the water*]: for when the cows hold back from entering into the water and drinking, they are not beaten, because they have milk, but only the bull is beaten, in order that they may be frightened, and therefore drink. (Ṣ, O, TA. [See also the Ḥam, p. 416; where the former hemistich is somewhat differently related.]) And hence the saying, هٰذَا مِمَّا يَعَافُهُ الطَّبْعُ [*This is of the things that the natural disposition dislikes,* or *loathes*]. (Mgh.) — عِفْتُ الطَّيْرَ, aor. أَعِيفُهَا, inf. n. عِيَافَةٌ, *I augured from the birds,* (Ṣ, O, Ḳ, TA,) *good or evil,* (O, Ḳ, TA,) *taking warning, or the like, by considering their names, and their places of alighting* (Ṣ, O, Ḳ, TA) *and of passage,* (TA,) *and their cries:* thus, correctly, as in the T and Ṣ and M and L, i. e. وَأَصْوَاتِهَا; for which the authors of the O and Ḳ have substituted وَأَنْوَائِهَا, deceived by the word مَسَاقِط in what goes before: and the verb is used in like manner in relation to gazelles or other animals passing with the right side, or the left side, turned towards the spectator: (TA:) العِيَافَةُ primarily signifies *the man's throwing a pebble at a bird,* or *crying out at it; and, if it turn its right side towards him in flying, the auguring good from it; and if its left side, evil:* (Ḥar p. 308:) or, accord. to Az, it signifies *the seeing a bird,* (TA,) *or a raven,* or *crow,* (Mṣb, TA,) *or the like,* (Mṣb,) *and auguring evil* [or *good*] *therefrom:* (Mṣb, TA:) and also *the saying* [a thing] *conjecturally,* or *surmising; without seeing anything:* and it is said in a trad. to be مِنَ الجِبْتِ [expl. in art. جبت]: the verb in عِفْتُ الطَّيْرَ, as ISd says, is originally عَيِفْتُ. (TA.) ═ عَافَتِ الطَّيْرُ, aor. تَعِيفُ, inf. n. عَيْفٌ, (Ṣ, O, Ḳ,) is like عافت having for its aor. تَعُوفُ and inf. n. عَوْفٌ, (Ḳ, TA,) i. e. (TA) *The birds circled over the water, or over carcasses or corpses, and went to and fro, not going away, desiring to alight.* (Ṣ, O, TA. [See also art. عوف.])

4. أَعَافُوا [*They became in the condition of finding that*] *their beasts disliked, or loathed, the water, and would not drink it.* (ISk, O, Ḳ.)

[5. تعيّف is probably used as signifying *He practised* عِيَافَة, i. e. *auguration from birds, &c.*: see its part. n., below.]

8: see 1, first sentence. ═ Accord. to Ibn-'Abbád, (O,) اعتاف signifies *He furnished himself with provisions for journeying.* (O, Ḳ.)

عَيْفَةٌ is a term employed in the case when a woman brings forth and her milk is suppressed in her breast, wherefore her fellow-wife, or female neighbour, draws it, by the single sucking and the two suckings: (Nh, O, L, Ḳ,* TA: but in the Ḳ, فَتَرْضِعُهَا is erroneously put for فَتَرْضَعُهُ; and المَرَّةُ and المَرَّتَيْنِ are put for المَزَّةُ and المَزَّتَيْنِ: TA:) thus in the saying of El-Mugheereh, (O, Ḳ, TA,) as expl. by himself, (O, TA,) لَا تُحَرِّمُ العَيْفَةُ [i. e. *The woman's sucking once and twice in drawing the breast of another woman whose milk is suppressed after child-birth will not render unlawful* the marriage of either of them to a relation of the other, nor the marriage of a relation of either to a relation of the other; as the case of regular or continued suckling of a child does]: (O, Ḳ, TA: [but in the O and CḲ, تُحَرَّمُ is erroneously put for تُحَرِّمُ: see a similar saying voce مَزَّةٌ:]) the action is performed in order that the obstructed channels by which the milk issues may become opened: and it is thus termed because the woman loathes it: (Az, O, Ḳ:) A'Obeyd says, We know not العَيْفَة in sucking the breast, but think it to be العَفَّة: his saying thus, however, is disapproved by Az. (O, Ḳ,* TA.) ═ عَيْفَةٌ is also the subst. from عَافَتِ الطَّيْرُ [q. v., app. signifying *A circling of* birds *over the water,* &c.]. (Ṣ, O, Ḳ.)

عِيفَةٌ *A good* thing: (O:) or the *choice,* or *best,* or *excellent,* of camels or cattle or other property: (Ḳ:) like عِيمَةٌ. (O, Ḳ.)

العَيَافُ and الطُّرَيْدَةُ are *Two games* (Sh, O, Ḳ) *of the boys of the Arabs of the desert:* (Sh, O: [see the latter of these words:]) or the former is *what is called* لُعْبَةُ الغُمَيْضَآءِ, or, as in some of the copies of the Ḳ, الغُمَيْضَآءُ. (Ḳ, TA. [But I do not find elsewhere الغُمَيْضَآءُ as the name of a game, nor الغُمَيْضَآءُ in any sense.])

عَيُوفٌ: see عَائِفٌ. Applied to a camel, it means *That smells the water and then leaves it, though thirsty.* (Ṣ, O, Ḳ.)

عَيْفَانٌ: see عَائِفٌ.

عَيِّفَانٌ, like تَيِّهَانٌ, (O, Ḳ,) or عَيْفَانٌ, like تَيْهَانٌ, (so in the CḲ,) One *whose natural disposition,* (O, Ḳ,) *and habit,* or *wont,* (Ḳ,) *it is to dislike,* or *loathe, a thing.* (O, Ḳ.)

عَائِفٌ *Disliking,* or *loathing,* food or beverage: (Ṣ, TA:) and ▼ عَيُوفٌ and ▼ عَيْفَانٌ, applied to a man, signify the same as عَائِفٌ [app. in this sense: see an ex. of the former in a verse of Ibn-Muḳbil cited voce سَوْفٌ, last sentence]. (TA.) ═ *Auguring,* or *divining,* (Ṣ, O, Ḳ,) *from birds* or *other things.* (O, Ḳ.) — كَانَ عَائِفًا, said of Shureyḥ, in a trad. of Ibn-Seereen, means *He was true in conjecture and opinion:* like the saying, of him who is right in his opinion, مَا هُوَ إِلَّا كَاهِنٌ; and of him who is eloquent in his speech, مَا هُوَ إِلَّا سَاحِرٌ. (TA.) ═ طَيْرٌ عَائِفَةٌ *Birds circling over water, or over carcasses or corpses, and going to and fro, not going away, desiring to alight.* (Ṣ, O.) And نُسُورٌ عَوَائِفُ [*Vultures*] *circling over the slain, and going to and fro.* (TA.)

مَعِيفٌ, applied to food [and beverage], *Disliked,* or *loathed.* (Mṣb.)

مُتَعَيِّفٌ One *who practises auguration from birds* [*&c.*]. (Ḥar p. 564.)

عيق

1. عَيْقٌ [as inf. n. of عَاقَ having يَعِيقُ for its aor.] is syn. with عَوْقٌ [as inf. n. of عَاقَ having يَعُوقُ for its aor.], (O, Ḳ, TA,) signifying The act of *hindering, preventing, impeding, withholding,* or *turning back* or *away.* (TA.)

2. عيّق, inf. n. تَعْيِيقٌ, *He raised his voice, called* or *called out, cried* or *cried out,* or *vociferated.* (O, Ḳ.)

عَيْقٌ *A share of water.* (L, Ḳ.)

عِيقِ (in the CḲ عِيقْ) *A cry used in chiding.* (Ibn-'Abbád, O, Ḳ.)

عَيْقَةٌ *The shore,* and *side,* of the sea: (A'Obeyd, Ṣ, O, Ḳ:) pl. عَيْقَاتٌ. (TA.) — And *An open,* or *a wide, space of ground, in front,* or *extending from the sides, of a house:* or *a yard,* or *court.* (TA.)

عَيُّوقٌ: } see art. عوق.
العَيُّوقُ: }

عيل

1. عَالَ, aor. يَعِيلُ, inf. n. عَيْلَةٌ (Ṣ, Mgh, O, Mṣb, Ḳ) [afterwards said in the Ḳ to be the subst. from this verb] and عُيُولٌ (Ṣ, O, Ḳ) and عِيُولٌ (TA) and عَيْلٌ and مَعِيلٌ; (Ḳ;) and عال, aor. يَعُولُ; (Ks, TA in art. عول;) and ▼ اعال; (Ḳ in that art.;) *He was,* or *became, poor,* (Ṣ, Mgh, O, Mṣb, Ḳ,) and *in want.* (Ṣ, O.) So in the saying مَا لَهُ عَالَ وَعَالَ, [of which see another explanation in art. عول,] a form of imprecation. (TA.) It is said in a trad., مَا عَالَ مُقْتَصِدٌ وَلَا يَعِيلُ i. e. [*One following the right course*] *has not become poor* [*nor will he become poor*]. (TA.) And one says, لَا يَعِيلُ أَحَدٌ عَلَى القَصْدِ [and لَا يَعُولُ, expl. in art. عول]. (Yoo, TA.) — See also 4. ═ عَالَنِى, (Ṣ, O, Ḳ,) aor. as above, (Ṣ, O,) inf. n. عَيْلٌ and مَعِيلٌ, *It* (a thing) *was,* or *became, wanted by me, and unattainable to me:* (Ṣ, O, Ḳ:) mentioned by El-Aḥmar. (Ṣ, O.) — And عَالَ الضَّالَّةَ, (Ṣ, O, Ḳ,) aor. as above, inf. n. عَيْلٌ and عَيَلَانٌ, (Ṣ, O,) *He knew not where to seek the stray beast.* (Ṣ, O, Ḳ.) ═ عَالَ, (Ṣ, O,) or عَالَ فِى مَشْيِهِ, (Ḳ,) aor. as above, inf. n. عَيْلٌ, (Ṣ, O,) said of a horse, (Ṣ, O, TA,) and of a man, (Ṣ, TA,) *He inclined from side to side in his gait,* (Ṣ, O, Ḳ,) *and* (when said of a man, Ṣ) *was proud, haughty,* or *self-conceited, therein:* (Ṣ, Ḳ:) the doing so in a horse is commended, as indicative of his generousness: (TA:) and ▼ تَعَيَّلَ signifies the same, (O, Ḳ,) said of a man. (O.) — And عَالَ فِى الأَرْضِ, (O, Ḳ,) aor. as above, (O,) inf. n. عَيْلٌ and عُيُولٌ and عَيُولٌ, thus in the Ḳ, i. e. with ḍamm and fet-ḥ, but in the M عُيُولٌ and عِيُولٌ, i. e.] with ḍamm and kesr, [of the like whereof there are many instances, one of them in the first sentence above,] (TA,) *He* (a man, O) *went,* or *went away,* (O, Ḳ,) *and round about,* (Ḳ, TA, but not in the CḲ,) *in the land;* (O, Ḳ;) or *journeyed therein seeking sustenance,* or *for the purpose of traffic;* syn. ضَرَبَ فِيهَا: so says IAmb. (O.) — عَالَ المِيزَانُ, aor. يَعِيلُ and يَعُولُ, inf. n. عَيْلٌ and عَوْلٌ: see art. عول.

2. عيّل as intrans.: see 4; and see also 1 in art. عول, fourth sentence. ═ عيّل عِيَالَهُ *He neglected his family,* or *household:* (TA, and Ḳ in art. عول:) or تَعْيِيلٌ signifies the *feeding badly.* (Ṣ, O.) See also 2 in art. عول, second sentence. — And see 1 in that art., first sentence. — عيّل فَرَسَهُ *He* (a man) *left his horse alone, or by himself, to pasture where he would, without a pastor, in the desert.* (Ṣ, O.)

4. اعال *He* (a man) *had a family,* or *household;* so accord. to Akh: or *he had a numerous family or household;* (Ṣ, O, TA;) as also أَعْيَلَ, and ▼ عال, and ▼ عيّل. (TA.) [See also 1 in art. عول, fourth sentence.] — And see the first sentence of the present art. — Also, said of a wolf, (O, Ḳ,) and of a lion, and of a leopard, (Ḳ,) *He sought,* or *sought after,* (O, Ḳ,) a thing, (O,) or prey. (Ḳ.) — See also 4 in art. عول, last sentence.

5: see 1, latter half.

عَيْلٌ: see عَيْلَةٌ: ═ and see also عَائِلٌ.

عَيْلٌ *The propounding of one's narration, and talk, to him who does not desire it and whom it does not concern;* (O, Ḳ;) [and so, app., ▼ عِيَالٌ; for it is said that] this is what is meant in the saying of the Prophet, إِنَّ مِنَ القَوْلِ عَيْلًا, or, as some relate it, عِيَالًا: [whence it seems that both readings mean *Verily of what is said is the propounding of one's narration,* &c.:] so says Şaşa'ah. (O.)

عَالَةٌ: see the next paragraph. [— And see عَائِلٌ, of which it is a pl.] — See also art. عول.

عَيْلَةٌ [mentioned above as an inf. n., and also said in the Ḳ to be a subst.,] *Poverty,* (Ṣ, O, Ḳ,) and *want;* thus in the Ḳur ix. 28; as also ▼ عَالَةٌ; (Ṣ, O;) and ▼ عَائِلَةٌ, and thus accord. to one reading in the Ḳur ix. 28; and accord. to IAạr, ▼ عِيلٌ, with kesr, is syn. with عَيْلَةٌ. (TA.) — It is also a pl. [or rather a quasi-pl. n.] of عَائِلٌ q. v. (Ṣ, TA.) — طَالَ عَيْلَتِى إِيَّاكَ means *Long has continued my feeding, nourishing,* or *sustaining, thee.* (O, Ḳ. [But this app. belongs to art. عول: see the first sentence in that art.])

عَيْلَى A woman *that weeps* [or *wails*] *for the dead.* (AA, O. [But this also app. belongs to art. عول.]) — Also a pl. of عَائِلٌ [q. v.]. (Ṣ, O, Ḳ.)

عَيْلَانُ The *male hyena.* (Ṣ, O, Ḳ.)

عِيَالٌ a pl. of which the sing is عَيِّلٌ and of which the pl. is عَيَائِلُ, this last being a pl. pl.: see art. عول. — See also عَيِّلٌ, above.

عِيَالَةٌ The *fodder,* or *provender,* of a بِرْذَوْن [or hackney]; as also ▼ مُعَالَةٌ. (Fr, O, Ḳ.)

عَيَّالٌ *That inclines from side to side in gait, and is proud, haughty,* or *self-conceited, therein:* (Ṣ, O, TA;) as also ▼ عَائِلٌ, of which عَيْلَةٌ is a pl. [or rather a quasi-pl. n.]: (IAạr, TA:) the former applied to a horse, (Ṣ, TA,) and to a lion: (Ṣ, O, TA:) and so with ة applied to a woman. (Ḳ, TA.) Respecting the saying of Ḥokeym Ibn-Mo'eiyeh Er-Raba'ee, cited by Sb,

فِيهَا عَيَايِيلُ أُسُودٌ وَنُمُرْ

Ibn-Es-Seeráfee says, it is as though he said فيها مُتَبَخْتِرَاتٌ &c. [i. e. *In it are such as walk with a proud gait and an inclining from side to side, of lions and of leopards*]; making عيايل to be pl. of عَيَّالٌ; not of ▼ عَيِّلٌ; (O, TA;*) of which latter, as signifying *seeking* [prey, like مُعِيلٌ], it is also [said to be] an anomalous pl.: (TA:) but Aboo-Mohammad Ibn-El-Aạrábee says that Ibn-Es-Seeráfee has miswritten عيايل, and that it is correctly غَيَايِيلُ, with the pointed غ, an anomalous pl. of غِيلٌ [signifying "a thicket," &c.; so that the meaning is, *in it are thickets* the lurking-places *of lions and of leopards*]. (O, TA.)

عَائِلٌ *Poor,* (Ṣ, Mgh, O, Mṣb, Ḳ,) and *needy,* or *in want;* (Ṣ, O;) occurring in the Ḳur xciii. 8; (TA;) as also ▼ عَيِّلٌ, (TA,) and ▼ مُعِيلٌ: (Ibn-El-Kelbee, TA:) pl. of the first عَالَةٌ, (Mgh, O, Mṣb, Ḳ,) [originally] of the measure فَعَلَةٌ, like كَفَرَةٌ pl. of كَافِرٌ, (Mṣb,) and عُيَّلٌ (Ḳ) and عَيْلَى (Ṣ, O, Ḳ) and [quasi-pl. ns.] ▼ عَيْلَةٌ (Ṣ, TA) and ▼ عِيلٌ. (IAạr, TA.) — See also عَيَّالٌ.

عَائِلَةٌ: see عَيْلَةٌ.

عَيِّلٌ, originally of the measure فَيْعِلٌ: (ISd, TA in art. عول:) see عِيَالٌ, in two places, in art. عول. — See also عَائِلٌ. — And see مُعِيلٌ: and عَيَّالٌ.

مُعِيلٌ: see عَائِلٌ. — Also A man *having a family,* or *household;* and so ▼ مُعَيَّلٌ: (TA:) or *having a numerous family* or *household;* and in like manner, with ة, applied to a woman. (Ṣ, O, TA.) [See also art. عول.] — Also, applied to a wolf, a lion, and a leopard, *Seeking,* or *seeking after,* prey; (Ḳ, TA;) and so ▼ عَيِّلٌ. (TA.)

مُعَيَّلٌ: see مُعِيلٌ in this art., and also in art. عول.

مُعَيَّلٌ: see art. عول.

مُعَالَةٌ: see عِيَالَةٌ.

عيم

1. عَامَ, aor. يَعِيمُ and يَعَامُ, inf. n. عَيْمَةٌ (Ṣ, Ḳ) and عَيْمٌ, (thus in copies of the Ḳ,) or عَيَمٌ, thus accord. to Lth, (TA,) *He* (a man, Ṣ) *desired,* or *desired eagerly,* or *longed for, milk:* (Ṣ, Ḳ:) and *he thirsted:* (Ḳ: [like غَامَ:]) [or *thirsted vehemently:* (see عَيْمَةٌ, below:)] or, accord. to ISk, عام إِلَى اللَّبَنِ means *he* (a man) *desired,* or *longed for, milk very immoderately:* (Ṣ:) or *he betook himself to milk,* or *the milk, and desired it eagerly,* or *longed for it;* like اِسْتَشَنَّ إِلَيْهِ. (TA in art. شن.) — And عامَ القَوْمُ *The people,* or *party, became scant in milk; their milk became little in quantity:* or, accord. to Lḥ, عام signifies *he lacked milk;* or *became destitute thereof;* (TA;) [and] thus ▼ اعام signifies: (Ḳ:) and ▼ اعاموا *they became scant in milk,* or *their milk became little in quantity,* (Ḳ, TA,) *their camels having died.* (TA.) مَا لَهُ آمَ وَعَامَ is a form of imprecation, meaning [*What aileth him?*] *May his wife and his cattle die,* (TA,) [*so that he shall have no wife and no milk,* or *and be eagerly desirous of milk.*]

4. اعامهُ اللّٰهُ *God left him* [or *made him to be*] *without milk.* (Ṣ, Ḳ.) And أَعَامَنَا بَنُو فُلَانٍ *The sons of such a one took our milk* [or *our milch cattle*]. (TA.) And أَصَابَتْنَا سَنَةٌ أَعَامَتْنَا [*A year,* or *year of drought, that deprived us of our milk,* or *of our milch cattle, befell us*]. (TA.) — See also 1, in two places.

8. اعتام, (Ṣ, Ḳ,) aor. يَعْتَامُ, inf. n. اِعْتِيَامٌ, (TA,) *He took,* (Ṣ, Ḳ,) or *chose,* (T, TA,) *the* عِيمَة, i. e. *the choice,* or *best,* or *excellent, of the camels* or other *property.* (T, Ṣ, Ḳ, TA.) Ṭarafeh says,

أَرَى المَوْتَ يَعْتَامُ الكِرَامَ وَيَصْطَفِى

عَقِيلَةَ مَالِ الفَاحِشِ المُتَشَدِّدِ

[*I see that death chooses the generous, and selects the most excellent of the property of the tenacious niggard*]. (TA.) [See also اِعْتَمَاهُ, in art. عمى.] — And اعتامهُ signifies also قَصَدَهُ [i. e. *He tended, betook himself,* or *directed himself* or *his course* or *aim, to,* or *towards, him,* or *it;* &c.]; like اِعْتَمَاهُ. (TA.)

عَيْمَةٌ [mentioned above as an inf. n.] *Desire,* or *eager desire,* or *longing, for milk:* (Ṣ, Ḳ:) or *vehemence of desire,* or *of longing, for milk, so that one cannot endure with patience the want of it.* (TA.) It is said in a trad., كَانَ يَتَعَوَّذُ مِنَ العَيْمَةِ وَالغَيْمَةِ وَالأَيْمَةِ i. e. [*He used to pray for protection from*] *vehemence of desire,* or *of longing, for milk, so as not to be able to endure with patience the want of it; and vehemence of thirst; and the remaining long without a wife.* (TA.) — And *Thirst:* (Ḳ:) or, as some say, *vehemence thereof;* and so غَيْمَةٌ, as mentioned above. (TA.)

عِيمَةٌ The *choice,* or *best,* or *excellent,* (Az, Ṣ, Ḳ, TA,) of camels or cattle or other property, (Ṣ, Ḳ, TA,) like عِيفَةٌ, (O and Ḳ in art. عيف,) and عِينَةٌ, (Ṣ in art. عين,) or, accord. to Az, *of anything:* pl. عِيَمٌ. (TA.)

عَيْمَانُ *Desiring,* or *desiring eagerly,* or *longing for, milk:* fem. عَيْمَى: (Ṣ, Ḳ:) the former applied to a man; and the latter, to a woman: (Ṣ:) pl. عِيَامٌ and عَيَامَى, like عِطَاشٌ and عَطَاشَى. (TA.) And [hence] one says رَجُلٌ عَيْمَانُ أَيْمَانُ meaning *A man whose camels have gone* [*so that he is in want of milk*] *and whose wife has died:* (Ṣ, Ḳ:) and AZ mentions, on the authority of Eṭ-Ṭufeyl Ibn-Yezeed, اِمْرَأَةٌ عَيْمَى أَيْمَى *a woman who has no camels, or the like, and whose husband has died.* (TA.) — And *Thirsty:* (Ḳ:) [or *vehemently thirsty.* (See عَيْمَةٌ.)]

عَيَامٌ The *day;* syn. نَهَارٌ: (Ḳ:) mentioned by Az, on the authority of El-Muärrij. (TA.) One says, طَابَ العَيَامُ i. e. النَّهَارُ [*The day became pleasant*]. (TA.) [See عَامٌ, last sentence; in art. عوم.]

عَامٌ مُعِيمٌ *A long* [or *tedious*] *year:* (Ḳ:) or, as some say, *a year of vehement* عَيْمَة [i. e. *desire, or longing, for milk; or thirst*]: mentioned on the authority of Lḥ. (TA.) [See also art. عوم.]

عين

1. عَيْنٌ [app. as inf. n. of عَانَ, agreeably with analogy, (like as أَذْنٌ is of أَذَنَ, and أَنْفٌ of أَنَفَ, &c.,) aor. يَعِينُ,] signifies The *hitting,* or *hurting,* [another] *in the eye.* (Ḳ.) — And The *smiting with the* [*evil*] *eye:* (Ḳ:) which is said in a trad. to be a reality. (TA.) You say, عِنْتُ الرَّجُلَ *I smote the man with my* [*evil*] *eye.* (Ṣ.) And إِنَّكَ لَجَمِيلٌ وَلَا أَعِنْكَ, meaning [*Verily thou art beautiful,*] *and may I not smite thee with the* [*evil*] *eye;* and ولا أَعِينُكَ, meaning *and I will not smite thee* &c. (Lḥ, TA.) And تعيّن ▼ المَالَ *He* (a man) *smote the* مال [i. e. *cattle,* or *camels,* &c.,] *with an* [*evil*] *eye:* (Ṣ:) or تعيّن ▼ الإِبِلَ, and ▼ اعتانها, and ▼ اعانها, *he raised his eyes towards the camels, looking at them, and expanded his hand over his eyebrow like as does he who shades his eyes from the sun,* (Ḳ, TA,) *to smite them*

with an [evil] eye, (Ḳ,* TA,) *and he so smote them.* (TA.) — عَانَ عَلَيْنَا, (Ṣ, TA,) aor. يَعِينُ, (Ṣ,) inf. n. عِيَانَةٌ; (Ṣ, TA; [in one of my copies of the Ṣ, عَيَانَة;]) and ▼ اعتان لَنَا; both signify *He was,* or *became, a spy,* or *scout, for us.* (Ṣ, TA.) [Golius mentions also ▼ عاين, construed with ل, in this sense, as from the Ṣ; in which I do not find it.] And one says, اِذْهَبْ فَاعْتَنْ ▼ لَنَا مَنْزِلًا *Go thou, and look for,* or *seek, a place of alighting for us:* (Ṣ:) and Lḥ says the like, making the verb trans. (TA.) And ▼ بَعَثْنَا عَيْنًا يَعْتَانُنَا, and يَعْتَانُ لَنَا; (Ḳ, TA;) and يَعِينُنَا, (Ḳ, TA, but omitted in the CḲ,) and يَعِينُ لَنَا, (El-Hejeree, TA,) inf. n. عِيَانَةٌ, (Ḳ, TA,) with fet-ḥ; (TA; [in the CḲ عِيانة;]) i. e. [*We sent a spy,* or *scout,*] *to bring us information.* (Ḳ, TA.) [See also عَيْنَانٌ مُعْتَانٌ.] — عان الدَّمْعُ, and المَآءُ, (Ṣ,) inf. n. عَيَنَانٌ (Ṣ, Ḳ) and عَيْنٌ, (Ḳ, TA,) *The tears,* and † *the water, flowed.* (Ṣ, Ḳ.*) And عَانَتِ البِئْرُ, inf. n. عَيْنٌ, *The well had in it much water.* (TA.) — And حَفَرْتُ حَتَّى عِنْتُ † *I dug until I reached the springs,* or *sources:* (Ṣ, TA:) and in like manner one says, ▼ أَعْيَنْتُ المَآءَ [*I reached the water*]: (Ṣ:) or, accord. to the T, one says, حَفَرَ ▼ الحَافِرُ فَأَعْيَنَ and ▼ أَعَانَ, meaning [*The digger dug,*] *and reached the springs,* or *sources.* (TA.) == عَيِنَ, (Ḳ,) inf. n. عَيَنٌ, (Ṣ,* Ḳ, [not, as in the CḲ, with the ى quiescent,]) and عِينَةٌ, (Lḥ,* Ḳ,) [*He was wide in the eye:* or *large and wide therein:* (see أَعْيَنُ:) or] *he was large in the black of the eye, with width* [*of the eye itself*]. (Ḳ.)

2. عَيَّنَ اللُّؤْلُؤَةَ † *He bored, perforated,* or *pierced, the pearl;* (Ṣ, Ḳ, TA;) as though he made to it an eye. (TA.) — عَيَّنَ القِرْبَةَ *He poured water into the skin in order that the stitch-holes might become closed* (Ṣ, Ḳ, TA) *by swelling,* (Ṣ,) *it being new:* and سَرَّبَهَا [q. v.] signifies the same, as mentioned by Aṣ. (TA.) == تَعْيِينُ الشَّىْءِ signifies † *The individuating of a thing,* or *particularizing it;* i. e. *the distinguishing it from the generality,* or *aggregate.* (Ṣ, Mṣb, TA.) [عَيَّنَهُ means † *He individuated it,* &c.: and *he particularized,* or *specified, it by words; mentioned it particularly,* or *specially.* And عَيَّنَ لَهُ كَذَا † *He appointed,* or *prescribed, for him,* or *he assigned to him, particularly, such a thing:* and عَيَّنَ عَلَيْهِ كَذَا *He appointed against him,* or *imposed upon him, particularly, such a thing*]. You say, عَيَّنْتُ المَالَ لِزَيْدٍ † *I assigned the property particularly,* or *specially, to Zeyd.* (Mṣb.) And مَا عَيَّنَنِى بِشَىْءٍ and أَتَيْتُ فُلَانًا فَمَا عَيَّنَ لِى بِشَىْءٍ i. e. † [*I came to such a one,*] *and he did not give me anything:* (Lḥ, TA:) or, as some say, *he did not direct me to anything.* (TA.) And عَيَّنَ عَلَى السَّارِقِ † *He distinguished,* or *singled out, the thief from among the suspected persons:* or, as some say, *he manifested against the thief his theft.* (TA.) And عَيَّنْتُ النِّيَّةَ فِى الصَّوْمِ † *I purposed the performance of a particular fast.* (Mṣb.) — عَيَّنَ فُلَانًا *He told such a one to his face of his vices,* or *faults,* or *the like.* (Lḥ, Ṣ, Ḳ.) == عَيَّنَ الحَرْبَ بَيْنَنَا i. q. أَدَارَهَا [*He, or it, stirred war,* or *conflict,* or *the war* or *conflict, between us,* or *among us*]: so in the Ḳ: in the L, ادرها [perhaps for أَدَرَّهَا, but more probably, I think, for أَدَارَهَا]. (TA.) == عَيَّنَ الشَّجَرُ ‡ *The trees became beautiful and bright, and blossomed.* (Ḳ, TA.) == عَيَّنَ الرَّجُلُ *The man took* [or *bought*] بِالعِينَةِ i. e. السَّلَفَ [meaning *for payment in advance,* accord. to all the explanations that I find of السَّلَف as used in buying and selling; but accord. to the TḲ, *upon credit,* i. e. *for payment at a future period,* agreeably with an explanation of عِينَة in the A and Mgh; see this word in its place, and see also 8]: or *he so gave* [or *sold*]. (Ḳ.) — And (Ḳ) عَيَّنَ التَّاجِرُ, (Mṣb, Ḳ, TA,) accord. to Az, (Mṣb, TA,) *The merchant,* or *trader, sold* (Mṣb, Ḳ, TA) *to a man* (Mṣb, TA) *a commodity for a certain price to be paid at a certain period, and then bought it of him for less than that price* (Mṣb, Ḳ, TA) *with ready money.* (Mṣb.) == عَيَّنَ العَيْنَ, (Ḳ, TA,) inf. n. تَعْيِينٌ, (TA,) *He wrote the letter* ع. (Ḳ, TA.) One says, عَيَّنَ عَيْنًا حَسَنَةً *He made* [or *wrote*] *a beautiful* ع. (Th, TA.)

3. عَايَنَهُ, inf. n. عِيَانٌ, (Ṣ, Mṣb) and مُعَايَنَةٌ, (Mṣb,) *I saw it* [or *him*] *with my eye* [or *eyes, ocularly,* or *before my eyes*]; (Ṣ;) [or *I viewed with my eye, and faced,* or *confronted, him,* or *it;* for] المُعَايَنَةُ signifies *the viewing with the eye, and facing,* or *confronting.* (TA.) [See also 5.] You say, لَقِيَهُ عِيَانًا, thus in copies of the Ḳ; but in some copies ▼ عَيَنَةً, with fet-ḥ to the second and third letters and with kesr to the ع, and thus accord. to Lḥ, (TA,) i. e. [*He met him*] *eye to eye* (مُعَايَنَةً), [or *face to face,*] *not doubting of his seeing him.* (Ḳ, TA.) — See also 1. == مُعَايَنَةٌ signifies also † The *dealing in buying and selling with ready money* [which is termed عَيْنٌ]. (KL.) == See also عَيْنٌ, in the third quarter of the paragraph.

4: see 1, former half: — and last sentence but one, in three places. == مَا أَعْيَنَهُ *How evil-eyed is he!* (Ḳ,* TḲ.)

5. تَعَيَّنَهُ *He saw him,* or *it;* or *he looked,* or *looked at* or *towards,* [or *eyed,*] *trying whether he could see, him,* or *it;* syn. أَبْصَرَهُ. (TA.) *He saw him* (a man) *with certainty.* (Ḳ.) [See also 3.] — تَعَيَّنَ المَالَ, and الإِبِلَ: see 1, former half, in two places. — تَعَيَّنَ, said of a man, also signifies *He was,* or *became, confounded,* or *perplexed, and unable to see his right course, by reason of shame,* (تَشَوَّرَ, for which تَشَوَّهَ is erroneously put in the copies of the Ḳ, TA,) or, accord. to some copies, تَشَوَّسَ [app. as syn. with, or perhaps a mistake for, تَشَاوَسَ, meaning *he contracted his eye to look*], (TḲ,) *and acted leisurely,* or *waited,* or *waited patiently, to smite a thing with his* [*evil*] *eye.* (Ḳ, TA.) — Said of a skin, † *It had thin circles,* or *rings,* or *round places,* [*likened to eyes,*] (Fr, Ṣ, TA,) *rendering it faulty:* (Ṣ:) or, said of a water-skin, *it was,* or *became, thin by reason of oldness:* (TA:) [or *it became lacerated,* or *worn in holes;* as is shown by what here follows.] One says also, تَعَيَّنَتْ أَخْفَافُ الإِبِلِ, meaning † *The feet of the camels became lacerated* [*in the soles*], or *worn in holes,* or *blistered;* like the water-skin of which one says تعيّن. (IAạr, TA.) == تعيّن also signifies † *It was,* or *became, clear,* or *distinct.* (KL.) — And † *It was* or *became, individuated,* or *particularized;* i. e., *distinguished from the generality,* or *aggregate.* (KL.) [Thus signifying, it is quasi-pass. of عَيَّنَهُ. Hence it means † *It had,* or *assumed, the quality of individuality.* And † *It was,* or *became, particularized,* or *specified, by words; mentioned particularly,* or *specially.* And تَعَيَّنَ لَهُ † *It was appointed,* or *prescribed, for him,* or *was assigned to him, particularly* or *peculiarly.* And تَعَيَّنَ عَلَيْهِ † *It was appointed against him,* or *imposed upon him, particularly.* And hence,] one says, تَعَيَّنَ عَلَيْهِ الشَّىْءُ, meaning لَزِمَهُ بِعَيْنِهِ [i. e. † *The thing was,* or *became, incumbent,* or *obligatory, on him in particular*]. (Ṣ, Ḳ.) == See also the next paragraph.

8: see 1, in four places. == اعتان الشَّىْءَ † *He took the* عَيْن *of the thing,* (Ṣ,) *the choice,* or *best, thereof.* (Ṣ, TA. [See also 8 in art. عون.]) == And *He bought the thing upon credit, for payment at a future time:* (Ṣ, Mṣb, KL, TA:) [i. e.] اعتان signifies *he took upon credit, for payment at a future time;* (Mgh; [in which it is expl. by the words أَخَذَ بِالعِينَةِ, and in which عِينَة in a sale is expl. as meaning نَسِيئَة;]) and so ▼ تعيّن; (KL;) [but Mṭr says,] the saying تَعَيَّنَ عَلَىَّ حَرِيرًا as meaning اِشْتَرِهِ بِبَيْعِ العِينَةِ [or اِشْتَرَاهُ] I have not found. (Mgh.) [See also عَيَّنَ الرَّجُلُ expl. as meaning "The man took بِالعِينَةِ."]

عَيْنٌ is a homonym, applying to various things: (Mṣb:) in the Ḳ, forty-seven meanings are assigned to it; but it is said by MF that its meanings exceed a hundred: those occurring in the Ḳur-án are seventeen. (TA.) By that which is app. its primary application, and which is by many affirmed to be so, (TA,) العَيْنُ signifies *The eye; the organ of sight;* (Ṣ, Mgh, Mṣb, Ḳ, TA; [in the Ṣ expl. by حَاسَّةُ الرُّؤْيَةِ, evidently used in this sense; in the Mgh, by المُبْصِرَةُ; in the Mṣb and Ḳ, by البَاصِرَةُ; and in a later place in the Ḳ, by حَاسَّةُ الرُّؤْيَةِ, app. as meaning *the sense of sight;*]) also denoted [emphatically] by the term الجَارِحَةُ [i. e. *the organ*]; (TA;) it is *that with which the looker sees;* (ISk, TA;) and is of a human being and of any other animal: (TA:) it is of the fem. gender: (Ṣ, Ḳ:) and the pl. [of mult.] is عُيُونٌ, (Ṣ, Mgh, Mṣb, Ḳ,) also pronounced عِيُونٌ, (Ḳ, [in which وتُكْسَرُ, immediately following عُيُونٌ, has been erroneously supposed by Golius and Freytag to relate to the sing.,]) and [of pauc.] أَعْيُنٌ and أَعْيَانٌ, (Ṣ, Mgh, Mṣb, Ḳ,) which last is asserted by Lḥ to be sometimes a pl. of mult., as it is in the Ḳur vii. [178 and] 194; (TA;) and pl. pl. أَعْيُنَاتٌ: (Ḳ:) the dim. is ▼ عُيَيْنَةٌ. (Ṣ.)

Hence the saying in a trad. of 'Alee, قَاسَ عَيْنًا بِبَيْضَةٍ جَعَلَ عَلَيْهَا خُطُوطًا [*He measured the reach of an eye by means of an egg upon which he made lines*]. (Mgh.) And [hence also] one says, بِعَيْنٍ مَا أَرَيَنَّكَ [lit. *With some eye I will assuredly see thee*]: it is said to one whom you send, and require to be quick; and means † *pause not for anything, for it is as though I were looking at thee.* (TA. [See also art. رأى.]) And لَقِيتُهُ عَيْنَ عَنَّةٍ [*I met him so that*] *I saw him with* [or *before*] *my eye, he not seeing me.* (Ṣ, TA.) [And رَأَيْتُهُ عَيْنَ عَنَّةٍ, or عَنَّةً, which see in art. عن. And أَعْطَيْتُهُ عَيْنَ عَنَّةٍ and عَنَّةً, which also see in art. عن.] And رَأَيْتُهُ عَرْضَ عَيْنٍ *I saw him, or it, obviously; nearly.* (TA, voce عَرْض, q. v.) And هَا هُوَ عَرْضَ عَيْنٍ [or عَرْضَ عَيْنٍ ?] i. e. [*Lo, he, or it, is*] *near* [*before thee*]: and in like manner, هُوَ مِنِّى عَيْنُ عَنَّةٍ [or عَيْنَ عَنَّةٍ ?] i. e. *He is near before me*]. (Ḳ.) And لَقِيتُهُ أَوَّلَ عَيْنٍ, (Ṣ, Ḳ,) and أَوَّلَ ذِى عَيْنٍ and ▼ عَائِنَةٍ, (TA,) *I met him, or it, the first thing:* (Ṣ, Ḳ, TA:) and *before every* [*other*] *thing*; as also ▼ أَوَّلَ عَائِنَةٍ and أَدْنَى عَائِنَةٍ: (Ṣ:) or this last means *the nearest thing perceived by the eye.* (TA.) And فَعَلْتُ ذَاكَ عَمْدًا عَلَى عَمْدِ عَيْنٍ and عَمْدًا عَلَى عَيْنٍ † *I did that purposely, with seriousness, or earnestness, and certainty:* (Ṣ:) or صَنَعَ ذٰلِكَ عَلَى عَيْنٍ and عَلَى عَيْنَيْنِ, (Ḳ, TA,) and عَمْدَ عَيْنٍ and عَمْدَ عَيْنَيْنِ, (Ḳ,) or عَلَى عَمْدِ عَيْنٍ and عَلَى عَمْدٍ, عَيْنَيْنِ, (TA,) † *He did that purposely,* (Lḥ, Ḳ, TA,) *with seriousness, or earnestness, and certainty.* (Ḳ.) And هُوَ عَبْدُ عَيْنٍ † *He is like the slave to thee as long as thou seest him,* (Ṣ, Ḳ,* TA,) *but not when thou art absent*; and so هُوَ عَبْدُ العَيْنِ: (Ṣ:) or *he is a man who pretends, or feigns, to thee, his doing that which he does not perform:* (TA:) and (Ḳ, TA) in this sense, (TA,) one says also, هُوَ صَدِيقُ عَيْنٍ i. e. † [*He is a friend, or a true friend,*] *as long as thou seest him:* (Ḳ, TA:) and هُوَ أَخُو عَيْنٍ † *He is one who acts as a friend hypocritically with thee.* (TA.) أَنْتَ عَلَى عَيْنِى is said in relation to honouring and protecting: (Ṣ, Ḳ, TA:) [accordingly I would render it ‡ *Thou art* entitled to be honoured and protected by me *above my eye:* for the eye is esteemed the most excellent of the organs, (as is said in this art. in the TA,) and it is that which most needs protection:] أَنْتَ عَلَى رَأْسِى is said in relation to honouring only. (TA.) And the Arabs say, عَلَى عَيْنِى قَصَدْتُ زَيْدًا, meaning thereby the regarding with solicitude mixed with fear [so that I would render it † As one to be regarded with solicitude mixed with fear *above my eye I made Zeyd the object to which my mind was directed*]. (TA.) [See another ex. of عَلَى عَيْنِى (in which it cannot be rendered as above) in a later part of this paragraph.] نَعِمَ اللّٰهُ بِكَ عَيْنًا [in the CK نَعَّمَ, which is wrong,] means the same as أَنْعَمَ. (Ḳ. [See both in art. نعم.]) قُرَّةُ العَيْنِ [signifying مَا قَرَّتْ بِهِ العَيْنُ, as expl. in the M and Ḳ in art. قر, i. e. *That by which, or in consequence of which, the eye becomes cool,* or *refrigerated,* or *refreshed,* &c.,] is a phrase used as meaning † A man's *child* or *offspring.* (TA.) فَقَأَ عَيْنَهُ [properly signifying *He put out his eye,* or *blinded it,* &c.,] means [sometimes] ‡ *he struck him; or struck him vehemently with a broad thing,* or *with anything;* or *slapped him with his hand:* (صَكَّهُ:) or *he was rough, rude,* or *ungentle, to him in speech.* (TA.) الَّذِى فِيهِ عَيْنَاكَ means *Thy head.* (TA. [There mentioned preceded by لا تحرمن: thus dubiously, and perhaps incorrectly, written. What it means, or should be, I know not.]) — عَيْنُ الثَّوْرِ † [*The eye of the Bull;*] *the great red star* [α] *that is upon the southern eye of Taurus, and also* [*more commonly*] *called* الدَّبَرَانُ. (Ḳzw, Descr. of Taurus.) [And عَيْنُ الرَّامِى † *The eye of Sagittarius;* app. *the two stars* ν, *on the eye thereof.*] — عَيْنُ البَقَرِ † [*The buphthalmum,* or *ox-eye;*] *the* [*plant called*] بَهَار [q. v.]. (Ṣ in art. بهر.) And عُيُونُ البَقَرِ ‡ *A sort of grapes,* (Ṣ, Ḳ, TA,) *black,* (Ḳ, TA,) *but not intensely so, large in the berries,* (TA,) *and round,* (Ḳ, TA,) *which are converted into raisins, and are not very sweet:* so says AḤn: thus called as being likened to the eyes of the animals termed بَقَر: (TA:) they are *found in Syria:* (Ṣ:) or *said by some to be peculiar to Syria.* (TA.) And *Certain black* إِجَّاص [or *plums*]: (Ḳ, TA:) thus called for the same reason. (TA.) — عَيْنُ الهِرِّ † [*Cat's-eye;*] *a certain stone, well known, of no utility.* (TA.) — فَتَحَ عَيْنَ النَّارِ means † *He made an opening in the live coals of the fire, that had become compacted; in order that it might burn up well.* (See 1 in art. سخو and سخى.)] — And عَيْنٌ signifies also † The عَيْن [i. e. *eye*] of the needle: such as is narrow is termed عَيْنُ صَفِيَّةَ [in which the latter word is app. a proper name, and, as such and of the fem. gender, imperfectly decl., i. e., in this case, written صَفِيَّةَ]. (TA.) — Also, as being likened to the organ [of sight] in form, or appearance, ‡ *A* [*small round hole* or] *place of perforation* in a [leathern water-bag such as is called] مَزَادَة. (TA.) And ‡ *Thin circles,* or *rings,* or *round places,* in a skin, (Ṣ, Ḳ, TA,) which are a fault therein, (Ṣ, TA,) *like* أَعْيُن [or *eyes;* or *one of such thin circles* &c.]; being likened to the organ [of sight] in form. (TA.) [See 10.] And (Ḳ) ‡ *A fault,* or *defect,* (Ḳ, TA,) *of this description,* in a skin. (TA.) — And ‡ The *small hollow* or *cavity* of the knee; (Ṣ, Ḳ; in [some of] the copies of the latter of which, الرَّكِيَّة is erroneously put for الرُّكْبَة; TA;) likened to the socket of the eye: (TA:) each knee has عَيْنَانِ [i. e. *two small hollows* or *cavities,* the *articular depressions for the condyles of the femur*], *in the fore part thereof, at* [*the joint of*] *the* سَاق. (Ṣ, TA.) — And ‡ The *piece of skin* [or *small leathern receptacle*] *in which are put the* بُنْدُق [or *bullets*] (Ḳ, TA) *that are shot from the* قَوْس [app. meaning the *large kind of cross-bow, called balista,* or *ballista*]: (Ḳ,* TA:) likened to the organ [of sight] in form. (TA.) — [In the B, accord. to the TA, it is also expl. as meaning the سَنَام: but this, I think, is most probably a mistranscription for سَامّ (q. v.) as signifying † *The hollow,* or *cavity, in the ground, thus called, in which water remains,* or *stagnates, and collects.*] And ‡ The *place* [or *aperture*] *whence the water of a* قَنَاة [i. e. *pipe,* or *the like,*] *pours forth:* (Ḳ, TA:) as being likened to the organ [of sight] because of the water that is in it. (TA.) And, (Ḳ, TA,) for the same reason, (TA,) ‡ The *place whence issues the water of a well.* (TA.) And, (Ṣ, Mṣb, Ḳ, &c.,) for the same reason, as is said by Er-Rághib, (TA,) ‡ The عَيْن, (Ṣ, Mṣb,) or *source,* or *spring,* (Ḳ, TA,) *of water,* (Ṣ, Mṣb, Ḳ, TA,) *that wells forth from the earth,* or *ground, and runs:* (TA:) [and accord. to the Mṣb, it app. signifies *a running spring:*] of the fem. gender: (TA:) pl. عُيُونٌ and أَعْيُنٌ, (Mṣb, Ḳ,) and accord. to ISk, sometimes the Arabs said, as a pl. thereof, أَعْيَانٌ, but this is rare. (Mṣb.) Hence a saying, in a trad., cited and expl. voce سَاهِرٌ. (TA.) Also † *Abundance of water* of a well. (TA.) And *A drop of water.* (TA.) عَيْنُ المَآءِ, [originally signifying "the source of water,"] accord. to Th, means † *Life for men;* thus in the following verse:

أُولَائِكَ عَيْنُ المَآءِ فِيهِمْ وَعِنْدَهُمْ
مِنَ الخِيفَةِ المَنْجَاةُ وَالمُتَحَوَّلُ

† [*Those, life for men is among them; and with them are the means of safety, and the place of removal, from fear*]: accord. to the A, عَيْنُ المَآءِ فِيهِمْ means *good,* or *means of attaining good, and provision of corn,* or *abundance of the produce of the earth, are among them.* (TA.) — Also † The عَيْن [meaning *eye,* or *bud,* (thus called in the present day,)] of a tree. (Es-Subkee, TA.) — [And ‡ *Sprouting herbage;* as being likened to the eye or eyes:] one says, نَظَرَتِ البِلَادُ بِعَيْنٍ or بِعَيْنَيْنِ [lit. ‡ *The lands looked with an eye* or *with two eyes*], meaning, *had their herbage come forth:* (Ḳ:) or it is said when their herbage comes forth: or, as in the A, when that which cattle depasture comes forth without [as yet] becoming firm [in the ground, or firmly rooted]: taken from the saying of the Arabs, إِذَا سَقَطَتِ الجَبْهَةُ نَظَرَتِ الأَرْضُ بِإِحْدَى عَيْنَيْهَا فَإِذَا سَقَطَتِ الصَّرْفَةُ نَظَرَتْ بِهِمَا جَمِيعًا † [lit. *When El-Jebheh* (the 10th Mansion of the Moon) *sets aurorally* (i. e. about the 11th of Feb., O.S.), *the land looks with one of its eyes; then, when Eṣ-Ṣarfeh* (the 12th Mansion) *sets aurorally* (about the 9th of March), *it looks with both of them*]. (TA. [See also art. نظر.]) — عَيْنٌ also, (Ṣ, Mṣb, Ḳ, &c.,) as being likened to the organ of sight, (TA,) signifies ‡ *A spy;* and ▼ ذُو العُيَيْنَتَيْنِ [in the CK ذُو العَيْنَتَيْنِ], in like manner, signifies *the spy,* (Ṣ, Ḳ, TA,) and ▼ ذُو العُوَيْنَتَيْنِ likewise, and ذُو العَيْنَيْنِ: (TA:) *he who looks for a people,* or *party:* (M, TA:) *the watcher,* or *observer;* (Ṣ,* Ḳ,* TA;) or *the scout:* (Ṣ,* Mṣb, Ḳ,* TA:) masc. and fem.: (M, TA:) accord. to the opinion of ISd, made by some to accord with a part [i. e. the eye], and

therefore fem.; and by some, to accord with the whole [person], and therefore masc.: (TA:) pl. عُيُونٌ and أَعْيُنٌ, and, accord. to ISk, sometimes أَعْيَانٌ. (Mṣb.) — And *i. q.* مُكَاشِفٌ [app. as meaning † *A discoverer*, or *revealer*, of tidings &c.]. (Es-Subkee, TA.) = [And † *An eye* as meaning *a look*, i. e. *an act of looking*: and hence, *a stroke of an evil eye*: or, simply, *an evil eye*: a meaning of frequent occurrence.] أَصَابَتْ فُلَانًا عَيْنٌ † [*An evil eye smote such a one*] is said of a person when an enemy or an envier has looked at him and produced such an effect upon him that he has fallen sick in consequence thereof. (TA.) [عَيْنُ الكَمَالِ is applied to an eye believed to have the power of killing by its glance: see an ex. voce قَفًا.] — And † *Sight with the eye* [or *before the eyes*; or *ocular view*]: thus in the saying, لَا أَطْلُبُ أَثَرًا بَعْدَ عَيْنٍ † [*I will not seek a trace*, or *vestige*, (or, as we rather say in English, *a shadow*,) *after an ocular view*]: (Ṣ, TA:) or the meaning is, *after* suffering *a reality*, or *substance*, to escape me: (Ḥar pp. 120 and 174: [this latter rendering being agreeable with explanations of عَيْنٌ which will be found in a later part of this paragraph:]) i. e. I will not leave the thing when I see it ocularly, and seek the trace, or vestige, thereof, after its [the thing's] disappearing from me: and the origin of it was the fact that a man saw the slayer of his brother, and when he desired to slay him, he [the latter] said, "I will ransom myself with a hundred she-camels;" whereupon he [the other] said, لَسْتُ أَطْلُبُ أَثَرًا بَعْدَ عَيْنٍ; and slew him: (TA:) it is a prov., thus, or, as some relate it, لَا تَطْلُبْ. (Ḥar p. 120.) — And † *Look*, or *view*. (Ḳ, TA.) It is said in the Ḳur [xx. 40], وَلِتُصْنَعَ عَلَى عَيْنِى, (Ṣ, TA,) and it has been expl. as there having this meaning [i. e. † *And* this I did *that thou mightest be reared and nourished in my view*], as in the B; or, as Th says, *that thou mightest be reared where I should see thee*: (TA:) or the meaning is, † *in my watch*, or *guard*, (Bd,* Jel,) and *my keeping*, or *protection*. (Jel. [It is implied by the context in the Ṣ, that عَلَى عَيْنِى is said in this instance in relation to honouring and protecting, as it is in a phrase mentioned in the first quarter of this paragraph; but my rendering of it there is obviously inapplicable here. See also 1 in art. صنع.]) And in like manner it has been expl. as used in the Ḳur [xi. 39], وَٱصْنَعِ ٱلْفُلْكَ بِأَعْيُنِنَا † [*And make thou the ark in our view*]. (TA.) [In like manner, also,] فَأْتُوا بِهِ عَلَى أَعْيُنِ ٱلنَّاسِ, in the Ḳur [xxi. 62], means عَلَى مَنْظَرِهِمْ † [i. e. *Then bring ye him in the view of the people*; منظر being here evidently an inf. n.]: (B, TA:) or [*bring ye him*] *openly*, or *conspicuously*. (Jel.) = And † The مَنْظَر [as meaning *aspect*, or *outward appearance*], (Ṣ, Ḳ,) and شَاهِد [meaning the same as being an evidence of the intrinsic qualities], (Ṣ,) of a man. (Ṣ, Ḳ.) So in the saying of El-Ḥajjáj to El-Ḥasan [El-Baṣree, when he (the former) had asked مَا أَمَدُكَ "What was the time of thy birth?" and the latter had answered (see أَمَدٌ)], لَعَيْنُكَ أَكْبَرُ مِنْ أَمَدِكَ † [*Verily thy aspect is greater than thy age*], أَمَدُكَ meaning سِنُّكَ. (Ṣ.) And it is said in a prov.,

* إِنَّ الجَوَادَ عَيْنُهُ فُرَارُهُ *

† [*Verily the fleet and excellent horse, his aspect is (equivalent to) the examination of his teeth*]: (Ṣ, TA: [accord. to the latter, عَيْنُهُ meaning شَاهِدُهُ:]) i. e. his external appearance renders it needless for thee to try him and to examine his teeth. (Ṣ and Ḳ in art. فر, q. v.) = Also, [by a synecdoche, as when it means "a spy,"] † *A human being*: (Ḳ:) and *any one*: (Ṣ, Ḳ:) [in which sense, as when it means "a spy," it may be masc. or fem.:] and *human beings*: (Ṣ:) or *a company* [*of people*]; (Ḳ;) as also ▼ عَيَنٌ: (Ṣ, Ḳ:) and the *people of a house* or *dwelling*: (Ḳ:) and so ▼ عَيَنٌ; (Ṣ, Ḳ;) and the *people of a town* or *country*; as also ▼ عَيَنٌ. (Ḳ.) One says, مَا بِهَا عَيْنٌ † *There is not in it any one*; (Ṣ, Ḳ, TA;) [i. e. بِالدَّارِ *in the house*, or *dwelling*;] as also ▼ عَيَنٌ, (TA,) and ▼ عَائِنٌ, (Ṣ, TA,) and ▼ عَائِنَةٌ: (TA:) and مَا بِهَا عَيْنٌ تَطْرِفُ [virtually meaning the same, but lit. *There is not in it an eye twinkling*]. (TA.) And ▼ مَا رَأَيْتُ ثَمَّ عَائِنَةً i. e. † [*I saw not there*] *a human being*. (TA.) And بَلَدٌ قَلِيلُ العَيْنِ † [*A town, or country*,] *having few human beings*, (Ṣ,) or *few people*. (TA.) = And † *A lord, chief*, or *chief personage*: (Ḳ, TA:) in [some of] the copies of the Ḳ, السِّنّ or الشِّقّ is erroneously put for السَّيِّدُ: (TA:) the *great*, or *great and noble, person* of a people or party: (Ḳ, TA:) and the *head, chief*, or *commander*, of an army: (TA:) the pl. is أَعْيَانٌ: (TA:) which signifies [*lords, chiefs*, or *chief personages*: &c.: and] the *eminent*, or *high-born*, or *noble, individuals* (Ṣ, Mgh, Mṣb, TA) of a people, or party, (Ṣ, Mgh,) or of men; (Mṣb;) and the *most excellent persons*. (TA.) — Hence, (Mgh, Mṣb,) as pl. of عَيْنٌ, (Ḳ,) أَعْيَانٌ signifies also † *Brothers from the same father and mother*: (Ṣ, Mgh, Mṣb, Ḳ:) this brotherhood is termed ▼ مُعَايَنَةٌ: (Ṣ, Ḳ:) and أَوْلَادُ الأَعْيَانِ means *the sons of the same father and mother*. (Mṣb in art. عل. [See عَلَّةٌ.]) — Also, the sing., † The *choice*, or *best*, (Ṣ, Mgh, Mṣb, Ḳ,) of a thing, (Ṣ, Ḳ,) or of goods, or household-goods, or furniture and utensils, (Mgh, Mṣb, TA,) and of camels, or cattle, or other property, (TA,) and so ▼ عِينَةٌ, (Ṣ, Ḳ, TA,) of which the pl. is عِيَنٌ, (TA,) like عِيمَةٌ: (Ṣ:) ▼ عِينَةُ الخَيْلِ signifies † *the fleet and excellent of horses*. (Lḥ, TA.) And † *Highly prized, in much request*, or *excellent*. (TA.) And, as applied to a deenár, † *Outweighing, so that the balance inclines with it*. (TA.) — And † *i. q.* مَالٌ, (Ḳ, TA,) [i. e. *Property*, or *such as consists of camels or cattle*,] *when of a choice*, or *of the best, sort*. (TA.) = And † *Such as is ready*, or *at hand*, (Ḳ, TA,) *present*, (TA,) or *within one's power*, or *reach*, (Ṣ, TA,) of property. (Ṣ, Ḳ, TA.) And † Anything *present*, or *ready*, (Ḳ, TA,) *found before one*. (TA.) You say, بِعْتُهُ عَيْنًا بِعَيْنٍ † *I sold it ready* merchandise *for ready* money. (Mṣb.) — [Hence,] † *Ready money; cash*: or simply *money*: syn. نَقْدٌ: (T, Mgh, Mṣb, TA:) *not* عَرْضٌ [q. v.]: (Mgh:) and sometimes, دَرَاهِمُ. (Mṣb.) So in the saying عَيْنٌ غَيْرُ دَيْنٍ † [*Ready money, not debt*]. (TA.) And [hence also] one says, اِشْتَرَيْتَ بِالدَّيْنِ أَوْ بِالعَيْنِ † [*Didst thou buy on credit or with ready money?*]. (Mṣb.) — And † *A present gift*. (Mgh, TA.) So in the saying (Mgh, TA) of a rájiz (TA) satirizing a man, (Mgh,)

* وَعَيْنُهُ كَالكَالِئِ الضِّمَارِ *

[*And his present gift is* a thing not hoped for, *like the unseen debt of which the payment is deferred by the creditor*:] meaning, his present gift is like the absent that is not hoped for. (Mgh, TA.) [And hence, app.,] أَصَابَتْهُ عَيْنٌ مِنْ عُيُونِ ٱللّٰهِ, occurring in a trad., means, خَاصَّةٌ مِنْ خَوَاصِّ ٱللّٰهِ [i. e. † *A particular*, or *special, gift of God betided him*]. (TA.) — Also † *A deenár*: (Ṣ, Ḳ:) or *deenárs*; (Az, TA;) [i.e.] *coined gold*; (Mgh, Mṣb;*) different from وَرِقٌ [which signifies "coined silver" or "dirhems"]. (Mgh.) They said, عَلَيْهِ مِائَةٌ عَيْنًا † [*On him is* incumbent the payment of *a hundred deenars*]: but properly one should say عَيْنٍ, because it is identical with what precedes it. (Sb, TA.) — And The *half of a dánik* [app. *deducted*] *from seven deenars*: (Ḳ, TA:) mentioned by Az. (TA.) — And ‡ *Gold*, (Ḳ, TA,) in a general sense; as being likened to the organ [of sight], in that the former is the most excellent of the metals, like as the latter is the most excellent of the organs. (TA.) = And ‡ The *sun itself*; (A, Ḳ, TA;) as being likened to the organ [of sight], because the former is the most noble of the stars, like as the latter is the most noble of the organs: (TA:) or (Ḳ, TA) the عَيْن *of the sun*; (Ṣ, Mṣb, TA;) i. e. the شُعَاع *thereof*; (Ḳ, TA;) [meaning *its rays*, or *beams*,] *upon which the eye will not remain fixed*: (TA:) or [more commonly] the عَيْن means the قُرْص [q. v., that is *disk*] of the sun. (KL.) [Using it in the first of these senses,] one says, طَلَعَتِ العَيْنُ ‡ [*The sun rose*], and غَابَتِ العَيْنُ [*The sun set*]. (Lḥ, TA.) = And † A thing's نَفْس [i. e. its *self*]; (Ṣ, Mgh, Mṣb, Ḳ, TA;) and its ذَات [which means the same]; (Ḳ, TA;) and its شَخْص, which means nearly, or rather exactly, the same as its ذات; (TA;) [and likewise a man's *person*, as does also ▼ عِيَانٌ, (see exs. in Ḥar pp. 20 and 45,) and the *material substance* of a thing;] and its أَصْل [as meaning its *essence*, or *constituent substance*]: (TA:) pl. أَعْيَانٌ, (Mgh, Mṣb, TA,) not أَعْيُنٌ nor عُيُونٌ. (Mgh, TA.) One says, هُوَ هُوَ عَيْنًا and هُوَ هُوَ بِعَيْنِهِ † [*It is it itself*, or *he is he himself*]: (Ṣ, TA:) ب when prefixed to عَيْن, [thus] used as a corroborative, being redundant. (Mughnee in art. ب.) And لَا آخُذُ إِلَّا دِرْهَمِى بِعَيْنِهِ † [*I will not take* aught *save my dirhem itself*]. (Ṣ.) And أَخَذْتُ مَالِى بِعَيْنِهِ † *I took my property itself*. (Mṣb.) And هٰذِهِ أَعْيَانُ دَرَاهِمِكَ (Lḥ, TA) and دَرَاهِمُكَ بِأَعْيَانِهَا (Lḥ, Mgh,* Mṣb, TA) † *These are thy dirhems* *themselves*]. And هُمْ إِخْوَتُكَ بِأَعْيَانِهِمْ † [*They are thy brothers themselves*]. (Mṣb.) And عَيْنُ الرِّبَا occurs in a trad. as meaning † *Usury itself*. (TA.) [مَوْضِعٌ بِعَيْنِهِ, a phrase very frequently occurring in the L and TA &c., means † *A certain*, or *particular, place*: and in a similar manner بِعَيْنِهِ is used after the mention of a plant &c.] One says also جَآءَ بِالأَمْرِ مِنْ عَيْنٍ صَافِيَةٍ i. e. † [*He brought forth, brought to light*, or *declared, the affair*] *from its very essence*. (TA.) And بِالحَقِّ بِعَيْنِهِ means † *With truth, clearly and manifestly*. (TA.) [In grammar, اِسْمُ عَيْنٍ means † *A real substantive; the name of a real thing;* also termed اِسْمُ ذَاتٍ; and sometimes termed عَيْنٌ alone: opposed to اِسْمُ مَعْنًى i. e. an ideal substantive.] ═ عَيْنٌ ثَاقِبَةٌ means † *Certain*, or *sure, news* or *information*. (A and TA in art. ثقب.) ═ And العَيْنُ [sometimes] signifies † *Knowledge;* [or rather *sure*, or *certain, and manifest, knowledge;*] which is also termed عَيْنُ اليَقِينِ. (TA.) ═ And † *Might* (العِزُّ). (TA.) — And † *Health and safety* (العَافِيَةُ). (TA.) — And † *Thirst;* and so الغَيْنُ. (TA in art. غين.) ═ And † *The* صُورَة [which generally means *form*, or the like: but it has many other significations; one of which is *essence*, before mentioned as a meaning of عَيْنٌ]. (TA.) ═ And it signifies also النَّاحِيَةُ [app. as meaning † *The part*, or *point, towards which one directs himself*]: (Ḳ, TA:) or, accord. to some, particularly *that of the* قِبْلَة [i. e. *that towards which one directs his face in prayer*]: (TA:) [or] it signifies also *the true direction of the* قِبْلَة: (Ḳ, TA:) or *the part that is on the right of the* قِبْلَة *of El-'Irák:* [whence] one says, نَشَأَتِ السَّحَابَةُ مِنْ قِبَلِ العَيْنِ † [*The cloud rose from the part on the right of the* قبلة *of El-'Irák*]: (Ṣ: [see also خَسْفٌ:]) or this means, *from the direction of the* قبلة *of El-'Irák;* and the Arabs say that this scarcely ever, or never, breaks its promise [of giving rain]: when it rises from the direction of the sea, and then goes northward, one says عَيْنٌ غُدَيْقَةٌ; and this is usually most disposed to rain: (TA:) غُدَيْقَةٌ is a dim. of magnification, meaning *abounding with water*. (TA in art. غدق.) Also † *The clouds* (سَحَاب) *that have come from the direction of the* قِبْلَة: (Ḳ,* TA:) or, *from the direction of the* قبلة *of El-'Irák:* or, *from the right thereof:* (Ḳ, TA:) and it is said in the B to signify [simply] السَّحَابُ [*the clouds*]; (TA;) and so الغَيْنُ. (TA in art. غين.) And, accord. to Th, مَطَرُ العَيْنِ signifies † *The rain that is from the direction of the* قِبْلَة: or, *from the direction of the* قبلة *of El-'Irák:* or, *from the right thereof*. (TA.) The saying of the Arabs مُطِرْنَا بِالعَيْنِ † [*We were*, or *have been, rained upon by the* عين] is allowed by some, but disapproved by others. (TA.) — And [hence, app.,] † *The rain that continues during some days*, (Ṣ, Ḳ, TA,) some say *five*, and some say *six*, or *more*, (TA,) *without clearing away*. (Ṣ, Ḳ, TA.) ═ عَيْنٌ signifies also † *Usury;* syn. رِبًا; (Ḳ, TA; [see also عَيْنُ الرِّبَا above;]) and so ▼ عِينَةٌ. (TA.) ═ And † *An inclining* in the balance; (Kh, Mgh, Ḳ, TA;) said to be the *case in which one of the two scales* thereof *outweighs the other:* (TA:) one says, فِى المِيزَانِ عَيْنٌ, meaning † *In the balance is an unevenness;* (Ṣ, TA;) *a little inclining in the tongue thereof:* and the word is fem. (TA.) — And † The *tongue* [or *cock*, itself,] of the balance. (TA.) — And † *A scale* of a balance; i. e. *either of the two scales* thereof. (TA.) ═ Also † *A small* بَيْت [meaning *partition*, or *part divided from the rest*,] *in a chest*. (TA.) — And † *A* مِحَشَّة [app. meaning *a thing in which* حَشِيش, or *dry herbage, is put*]. (TA.) — [And † *Either half*, or *one side, of a* خُرْج, or *pair of saddle-bags*.] ═ And *A certain bird*, (Ḳ, TA,) *yellow in the belly*, أَخْضَر [generally in a case of this kind meaning *of a dingy*, or *dark, ash-colour* or *dust-colour*] *in the back; of the size of the* [*species of collared turtle-dove called*] قُمْرِىّ. (TA.) ═ Also † [The *letter* ع;] *one of the letters of the alphabet*, (Ṣ, Ḳ,) *of those termed* مَجْهُورَة and حَلْقِيَّة. (Ḳ. [See art. ع.]) — And † The *middle* [*radical letter*] *of a word* [*of the triliteral-radical class;* the root of such a word being represented by فعل]. (TA.) — In the calculation by means of the letters ا, ب, ج, د, &c., it denotes *Seventy*. (TA.)

عِينٌ, originally عُيْنٌ, pl. of أَعْيَنُ [q. v.]: (Ṣ, Ḳ:*) ═ and also, (as a contraction of عُيُنٌ, IB, TA,) pl. of عِيَانٌ: (AA, Ṣ, IB:) [and of عَيُونٌ.]

عَيَنٌ The *quality denoted by the epithet* أَعْيَنُ [q. v.; i. e. *width in the eye; &c.*]; (Ṣ;) and so ▼ عِينَةٌ. (Lḥ, TA.) [See also 1, last sentence; where both are mentioned as inf. ns.] ═ See also عَيْنٌ, in the third quarter of the paragraph, in four places. ═ And see the paragraph here following.

عِينَةٌ: see the next preceding paragraph. — Also The *part that surrounds the eye* of a ewe; (Ḳ, TA;) like the مَحْجِر of a human being. (TA.) — And *Goodly appearance:* so in the saying, هٰذَا ثَوْبٌ عِينَةٌ [*This is a garment of goodly appearance*]. (Ṣ, Ḳ) — See also عَيْنٌ, latter half, in three places. — Also *i. q.* سَلَفٌ [in buying and selling; i. e. *Any money*, or *property, paid in advance*, or *beforehand, as the price of a commodity for which the seller has become responsible and which one has bought on description:* or *payment for a commodity to be delivered at a certain future period with something additional to the equivalent of the current price at the time of such payment:* or *a sort of sale in which the price is paid in advance, and the commodity is withheld, on the condition of description, to a certain future period:* but it seems to be in most cases used in one or another of the senses expl. in what here follows]. (Ṣ, Mgh, Mṣb, Ḳ, TA.) And one says, بَاعَهُ بِعِينَةٍ meaning بِنَسِيْئَةٍ [i. e. *He sold it upon credit, for payment at a future time*]: (A, Mgh: [see 3:]) or, as some say, [and more commonly,] العِينَةُ is *the buying what one has sold for less than that for which one has sold it:* and ▼ العَيَنُ signifies the same: (Mgh:) or, accord. to Az, *the selling a commodity for a certain price to be paid at a certain period, and then buying it for less than that price with ready money:* [see 3, last quarter:] this is unlawful when the buyer makes it a condition with the seller that he shall buy it for a certain price; but when there is no condition between them, it is allowable accord. to Esh-Sháfi'ee, though forbidden by some others; and he used to call it the sister of usury: and *the sale of a commodity by the purchaser* [*thereof upon credit*] *to other than the seller of it, on the spot* (lit. *in the sitting-place*), is also termed عِينَةٌ; but is lawful by common consent: (Mṣb:) or it is *the case of a man's coming to another man to ask of him a loan, which the latter does not desire to grant, coveting profit, which is not to be obtained by a loan, wherefore he says, "I will sell to thee this garment for twelve dirhems upon credit, for payment at a certain time, and its value is ten* [*which thou mayest obtain by selling it for ready money*]." (KT: in some copies of which the word thus expl. is [erroneously] written العَيْنِيَّةُ instead of العِينَةُ.) [See also زَرْنَقَةٌ. The word is generally held to be derived from عَيْنٌ as signifying "ready money" or "ready merchandise."] — Also The مَادَّة [meaning *accession to the strength* or *forces*] of war: (Ḳ,* TA:) used in this sense in a verse of Ibn-Muḳbil [in which it is shown to be so used as being likened to the accession, to the quantity of milk, which has collected and become added to that previously left in the udder: see مَادَّة]. (TA.)

لَقِيَهُ عِينَةً: see 3.

عَيْنُونٌ *A certain plant, found in El-Andalus, that attenuates the humours of the body, when cooked with figs*. (TA.)

عِيَانٌ an inf. n. of 3. (Ṣ, Mṣb.) — [And *Clear, evident, manifest, open*, or *public:* thus, by the Pers. word آشْكَار, the KL explains عيان, which, in my copy of that work, is written عَيَان, evidently, I think, a mistranscription for عِيَان, an inf. n. of 3, used in the sense of a pass. part. n., agreeably with a well-known license, lit. meaning *ocularly seen:* see ضِمَار, under which I have rendered its contrary by "unseen; not apparent."] — See also عَيْنٌ, latter half. ═ Also *A certain iron thing among the appertenances of the* فَدَّان, (Ṣ, Ḳ,) or فَدَان [i. e. *plough*], this word (فدان) written in the copies of the Ṣ, [as in the Ḳ,] with teshdeed to the د, but, as IB says, it is without teshdeed when signifying the implement with which ploughing is performed: accord. to AA, the لُؤْمَة, i. e. the سِنَّة [or *share*] *with which the earth is ploughed up*, is called the عِيَان *when it is upon the* فَدَان [or *plough*]: or, accord. to the M, the عِيَان is *a ring at the extremity of the* لُؤْمَة *and the* سَلِيب [app. a mistranscription] *and the*

دُجْرَانِ [*two pieces of wood upon which the share is bound*]: (TA:) pl. [of pauc.] أَعْيِنَةٌ and [of mult.] عُيُنٌ, with two dammehs; (Ḳ;) or عِينٌ, originally of the measure فُعْلٌ [i. e. عُيْنٌ]; (Ṣ;) accord. to AA, عِينٌ, with kesr only; accord. to IB, عُيُنٌ, with two dammehs, and, when the ي is made quiescent, عِينٌ, not عُيْنٌ. (TA.) — ابْنَا عِيَانٍ means *Two birds,* (Ḳ, TA,) *from the flight,* or *alighting-places,* or *cries,* &c., *of which, the Arabs augur:* (TA:) or *two lines which are marked upon the ground* (Ṣ, Ḳ) *by the* عَائِف [or *augurer*], *by means of which one augurs, from the flight,* &c., *of birds;* (Ṣ;) or *which are made for the purpose of auguring;* (TA;) *then the augurer says,* ابْنَى عِيَانٍ أَسْرِعَا البَيَانَ [*O two sons of 'Iyán, hasten ye the manifestation*]: (Ḳ,* TA: [see 1 in art. خط:]) in the copies of the Ḳ, ابْنَا is here erroneously put for ابْنَى: or, as some say ابْنَا عِيَانٍ means *two well-known divining-arrows:* (TA:) and when it is known that the gaming arrow of him who plays therewith wins, one says, جَرَى ابْنَا عِيَانٍ [app. meaning *The two sons of 'Iyán have hastened;* i. e. the two arrows so termed; as seems to be indicated by a verse cited in the L (in which it is followed by the words بِالشِّوَآءِ المُضَهَّبِ *with the roast meat not thoroughly cooked*), and also by what here follows]: (Ṣ, L, Ḳ, TA:) these [arrows] being called ابْنَا عِيَانٍ because by means of them the people [playing at the game called المَيْسِر] see the winning and the food [i. e. the hastily-cooked flesh of the slaughtered camel]. (L, TA.)

رَجُلٌ عَيُونٌ (Ḳ, TA) and ↑ عَيَّانٌ (TA) *A man who smites vehemently with the* [*evil*] *eye;* as also ↑ مِعْيَانٌ: (Ḳ, TA:) pl. [of the first] عِينٌ and عُيُنٌ. (Ḳ.)

عُيَيْنَةٌ: and ذُو العُوَيْنَتَيْنِ and ذُو العُيَيْنَتَيْنِ: see عَيْنٌ, in the former half of the paragraph.

عَيِّنٌ: see the next paragraph, in two places.

رَجُلٌ عَيِّنٌ *A man quick to weep.* (TA.) — And سِقَآءٌ عَيِّنٌ, (Ṣ, Ḳ,) and ↑ عَيْنٌ, (Ḳ,) the latter less common, and said to be the only instance of an epithet of the measure فَيْعَلٌ with an infirm [medial] radical, or it may be of the measure فَعْوَلٌ or فَوْعَلٌ, and in either of these two cases not without a parallel, (TA,) and ↑ مُتَعَيِّنٌ, (Ṣ, Ḳ,) † *A skin, for water,* or *for milk, having thin circles,* or *rings,* or *round places,* [*likened to eyes,*] *rendering it faulty:* (Ṣ:) or *of which the water runs forth:* (Lḥ, Ḳ:) or *new;* (Ḳ;) or thus عَيِّنٌ and ↑ عَيْنٌ, in the dial. of Ṭeiyi; and so قِرْبَةٌ عَيِّنٌ in that dial.: the pl. of عَيِّن applied to a skin is عَيَائِنُ, with hemzeh because the place thereof is near to the end. (TA.)

عَيَّانٌ: see عَيُونٌ.

عَائِنٌ *Smiting with the* [*evil*] *eye.* (Ṣ, TA.) — And † *Flowing water:* (Ṣ:) or so مَآءٌ عَائِنٌ; from عَيْنُ المَآءِ. (TA.) — See also عَيْنٌ, third quarter.

عَائِنَةٌ: see عَيْنٌ, first quarter, in two places: — and again, third quarter, in two places. — One says also, رَأَيْتُ عَائِنَةً مِنْ أَصْحَابِهِ, meaning *I saw a party of his companions who saw me.* (TA.) — And رَأَيْتُهُ بِعَائِنَةِ العِدَا, *I saw him where the eyes of the enemy were seeing him.* (TA.) — And عَائِنَةُ بَنِى فُلَانٍ *The herds,* or *flocks,* or *herds and flocks,* (أَمْوَال,) *and pastors, of the sons of such a one.* (Ṣ.)

أَعْيَنُ A man *wide in the eye:* (Ṣ, Mgh:) or *large and wide therein:* (Lḥ, TA:) or *large in the black of the eye, with width* [*of the eye itself*]: (Ḳ:) fem. عَيْنَآءُ; (Ṣ;) which is applied to a woman as meaning *beautiful and wide in the eyes:* (Mṣb:) pl. عِينٌ, (Ṣ, Mṣb,) originally عُيْنٌ. (Ṣ.) — Hence, (Ṣ,) عِينٌ is an appellation of *Wild oxen;* (Ṣ, Ḳ, TA;) as an epithet in which the quality of a subst. predominates: (TA:) and أَعْيَنُ, of the *wild bull,* (Ṣ, ISd, Ḳ,) which one should not call ثَوْرٌ أَعْيَنُ: (ISd, Ḳ:) and عَيْنَآءُ, of the *wild cow:* (Ṣ:) and women are likened to these wild animals. (TA.) — عَيْنَآءُ also signifies, applied to a sheep or goat (شَاة), *Of which the eyes are black and the rest white;* and some say, or *the converse thereof;* in this sense used as an epithet. (TA.) — And ‡ *A good,* or *beautiful, word* or *saying;* likened to a woman beautiful and wide in the eyes; (Mṣb;) opposed to عَوْرَآءُ. (AHeyth, A and TA in art. عور.) — And, applied to a قَافِيَة, *i. q.* نَافِذَة (Ḳ) [i. e., accord. to the TḲ, which is followed by Freytag, applied to a rhyme as meaning *Having what is termed* نَفَاذ: (see De Sacy's Ar. Gr., sec. ed., ii. 657:) but this explanation may be conjectural; and, if so, the meaning may be † *penetrating,* or *effective,* as applied to a verse or an ode]. — And *i. q.* خَضْرَآءُ (Ḳ) [accord. to the TḲ as an epithet applied to land, and meaning † *Black;* likened to the eye of the buffalo; for سَوَاد was sometimes termed by the Arabs خُضْرَة: but this explanation also may be conjectural; and I rather think that it is so, and that by خَضْرَآءُ is here meant † *a bucket with which water has been drawn long,* so that it has become green or blackish; (see أَخْضَرُ;) agreeably with the following explanation, which is immediately subjoined in the Ḳ]. — And *A water-skin* (قِرْبَة) *ready to become lacerated,* or *rent,* (Ḳ, TA, [see عَيِّنٌ,]) *and worn out.* (TA.)

مَعَانٌ [*A place in which one is seen*]. One says, القَوْمُ مِنْكَ مَعَانٌ [in which the last word is app. a mistranscription, for بِمَعَانٍ, as in Ḥar p. 22,] *The people,* or *party, are* [*in a place*] *where thou seest them with thine eye.* (TA.) — And *A place of alighting* or *abode,* (Ḳ, TA,) and *one in which one is known to be.* (TA.) So in the saying, الكُوفَةُ مَعَانٌ مِنَّا [*El-Koofeh is a place of our alighting* or *abode,* &c.]. (TA.)

مَعِينٌ *Smitten with the* [*evil*] *eye;* as also ↑ مَعْيُونٌ, the complete form: (Ṣ, TA:) or, accord. to Ez-Zejjájee, the former has this meaning, but ↑ المَعْيُونُ means أَلَّذِى فِيهِ عَيْنٌ [in which the last word is probably a mistranscription for عَيْبٌ; so that the meaning is, *in whom is a fault,* or *defect*]. (L, TA.) A poet says, (Ṣ,) namely, 'Abbás, (TA,)

* قَدْ كَانَ قَوْمُكَ يَحْسَبُونَكَ سَيِّدًا *

* وَإِخَالُ أَنَّكَ سَيِّدٌ مَعْيُونُ ↑ *

[*Thy people,* or *party, used to reckon thee a chief; but I think that thou art a chief smitten with the evil eye,* or, perhaps, *in whom is a fault,* or *defect*]. (Ṣ, TA.) — مَآءٌ مَعِينٌ and ↑ مَعْيُونٌ (Ṣ, Ḳ) † *Water of which one has reached the springs,* or *sources, by digging:* (Ṣ:) or *water that is apparent* (ظَاهِرٌ, for which the CḲ has طَاهِرٌ), (Ḳ, TA,) *seen by the eye,* (TA,) *running upon the surface of the earth:* (Ḳ, TA:) Bedr Ibn-'Ámir El-Hudhalee says,

* مَآءٌ يَجِمُّ لِحَافِرٍ مَعْيُونِ ↑ *

[meaning *Water collecting for a digger, of which the springs have been reached by digging*]; the last word, it is said, being put by him in the gen. case because of the proximity [to a word in that case, agreeably with a poetic license of which there are many exs.], for by rule it should be مَعْيُونٌ, as it is an epithet relating to مَآء: but respecting the measure of مَعِينٌ, which IB derives from عَيْنُ المَآءِ, and explains as meaning *having the source apparent,* there are differences of opinion; some say that it is an instance of مَفْعُولٌ, though not having a verb; and some, that it is of the measure فَعِيلٌ, from المَعْنُ signifying "the drawing" of water. (TA.) In the saying, إِنْ كَانَتِ البِئْرُ مَعِينًا لَا تُنْزَحُ, meaning [*If the well be one*] *having a running spring,* [*that will not be entirely exhausted,*] معينا is made masc. to accord with the word [بِئْر, which is masc. in form though fem. by usage]; or it is thus because it is imagined to be of the measure فَعِيل, in the sense of the measure مَفْعُول; or because it is for ذَاتَ مَعِينٍ, i. e. [*having*] *water running upon the surface of the earth.* (Mgh.) In the Ḳur xxxvii. 44, [and in like manner in lvi. 18,] مَعِين is used as meaning † *Wine running upon the surface of the earth, like rivers of water.* (Jel.) — عَيْنٌ ↑ مَعْيُونَةٌ means † *A spring,* or *source, having a continual increase of water.* (Aboo-Sa'eed, TA.)

مُعَيَّنٌ † A garment *figured with eyes:* (Ṣ in art. برج:) or a garment *in the figuring of which are small* تَرَابِيع [app. meaning *quadrangular forms* (in the CḲ تَرْبِيع)] *like the eyes of wild animals.* (Ḳ.) — And † A bull *having a blackness between his eyes:* (Ḳ:) or *a bull;* so called because of the largeness of his eyes: or so called because *having spots of black and white, as though there were eyes upon his skin.* (Ḥam p. 293.) —

And † Locusts (جَرَاد) *which, when stripped of the integument, are seen to be white and red:* mentioned by Az in art. ينع, on the authority of ISh. (TA.) ▬ [Also, as pass. part. n. of 2, † *Individuated,* or *particularized;* i. e. *distinguished from the generality,* or *aggregate:* &c.: see the verb. Hence] نِيَّةٌ مُعَيَّنَةٌ means [*A distinct, particular,* or *special, purpose;* lit.] *a purpose made distinct:* and it is allowable for one to attribute the action to the purpose, tropically; and thus to say ▼ نِيَّةٌ مُعَيِّنَةٌ [*A distinguishing purpose*], using the act. part. n. (Mṣb.)

مُعَيِّنٌ: see an ex. of its fem. in what next precedes.

مُعْيَانٌ: see عَيُونٌ. [And see also مُعْتَانٌ.]

مَعْيُونٌ and its fem.: see مَعِينٌ, in six places.

مُعْتَانٌ *An explorer* of a people or party, *who is sent before to seek for herbage and water and the places where rain has fallen,* (Ḳ, TA, [in the CḲ, المِعْيانُ is erroneously put for المُعْتَانُ,]) *and who searches for news or tidings.* (TA.)

مُتَعَيِّنٌ: see عَيِّنٌ.

عيه

For the verbs (1 and 2) and other words belonging to this art., see art. عوه.

End of the Fifth Part of Book I.